16th Edition

TOYS & PRICES 2009

Tom Bartsch, Contributing Editor

Published by

700 East State Street • Iola, WI 54990-0001
715-445-2214 • 888-457-2873
www.krausebooks.com

Our toll-free number to place an order or obtain a free catalog is (800) 258-0929.

ISSN 1935-6714

ISBN-13: 978-0-89689-666-6
ISBN-10: 978-0-89689-666-8

Designed by Sandi Morrison
Edited by Joe Kertzman

Printed in the United States of America

Contents

On The Cover

Barbie	The All-American Doll, Mattel, 1965, $1,900 (Mint in Box)
Advertising Toys	Mr. Peanut, 1992, 8 ½" yellow and black plastic, $20-$25
G.I. Joe	Man of Action, Hasbro, 1974, $200
Lunch Box	Toppie the Elephant, American Thermos, 1957, $3,850
PEZ	Kermit, Muppets, $1-$2
Vehicles	Hot Wheels 1964 Falcon, '68 Series, $2-$5
Vehicles	Tonka Service Truck, 1959-'60, $350
Vehicles	Tom Corbett Polaris wind-up, Marx, 1952, $600

Introduction

The Pinnacle Price Guide

By Tom Bartsch

Well, you've found it once again—the 16th edition of what is considered to be the pinnacle price guide on post-World War II collectible toys. Yes, *Toy & Prices* has been providing collectors with values on varying conditions of toys since 1993. Inside these pages, you'll find one of the most comprehensive price guides on toys, and photos you won't find grouped together anywhere else.

Collecting toys has gone through some dramatic changes in the last 16 years, but the premise of collecting remains the same—holding onto something from childhood that brings a smile to your face every time you see it. Gone are the investment days of the 1990s. If you collect now, during a challenging economy and high gas prices, you're doing it as a passion and not as a get-rich-quick scheme. And that's what toys are all about, a piece of nostalgia that can grow into a fascination that fills rooms in houses and provides endless stories for relatives and visitors.

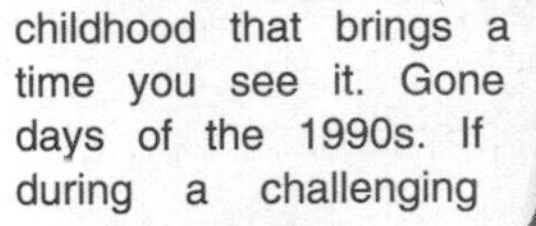

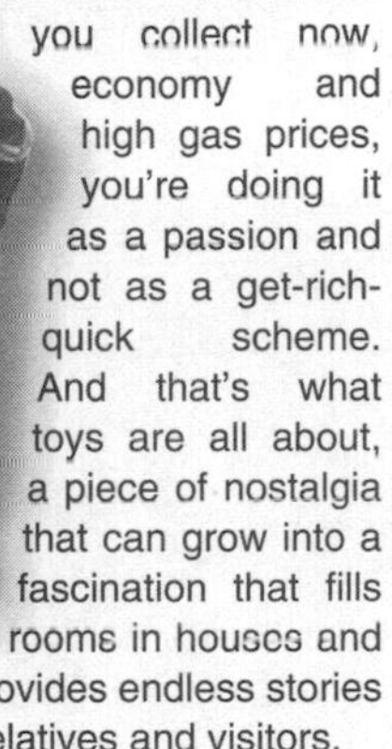

People always ask collectors, "Why do you collect?" The answers vary from "It's a piece of my childhood" to "Because it's fun." And that's what toys are, fun. There are no hidden messages when it comes to toys. They are produced for entertainment, and while they can also be quite valuable, that is not the driving force behind collecting toys (though it doesn't hurt to know how much those toys are worth that are providing so much joy). That's where *Toys & Prices* comes into play.

Many of the questions that *Toys & Prices* receives regarding toys are from people who found a toy and just want to know something about it. Education is power, and *Toys & Prices* can educate. Collecting toys hasn't changed much over time. People collect for the same reasons; they just now have more resources to do so. Condition is still important to collectors.

Everyone remembers that toy when it first came out of the box, and to have the chance to get that toy in that same, new condition again is the goal of many collectors. And those toys are out there! With the Internet and a growing secondary market for collectibles, toys are more available than ever before. And the information about these toys is growing, as well, as more material is unearthed. Sure, toy shows have decreased over time, but the number of collectors hasn't. Sure, people might kick the tire a little more than in the past, but when that one toy comes before them, that same joy explodes once again, and soon that toy has a new home.

Indiana Jones Meets the Incredible Hulk

We've got a lot of new toys that have found a home in *Toys & Prices*, too. As some iconic franchises come out with some new renditions (Indiana Jones, Batman, Incredible Hulk, James Bond and new comic book-related films, to name a few), the toy category continues to grow, too. Hot Wheels, slot cars and model kits are getting new life as collectors stick closer to home and enjoy their hobbies. Action figures constantly fill toy aisles, and the generations that preceded them always find a willing audience.

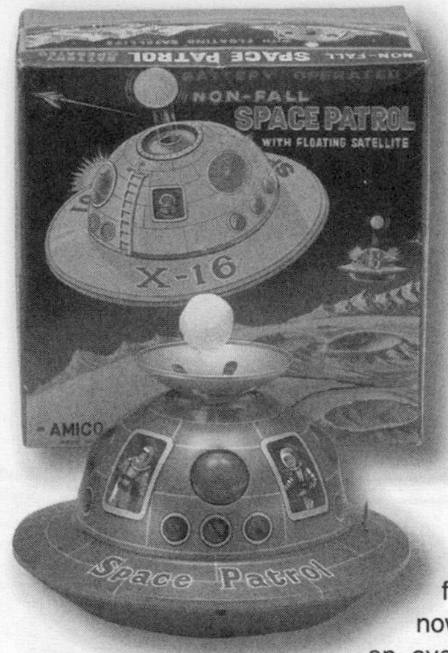

As you page through *Toys & Prices* and contemplate some of the changing values, just remember one thing—as the 1950s and '60s toys continue to age, collectors are looking for examples in the best condition and they will pay for it. Again, going back to availability, everyone has a shot at any toy these days. So once collectors get that first taste, they are now going back to get an even better slice of the pie. Toy collecting is becoming a mature hobby (similar to sports memorabilia collecting), and people know what they want and how they want it.

If you're one of the veterans, see what it's going to cost to take that next step. In the classic categories, such as pressed-steel trucks, lunch boxes and Western toys, the values aren't going to go down. What's out there is what's there. In some of the ever-growing areas, such as action figures and Barbies, you won't see a lot of price growth in the last five years for newer toys in average condition. Again, it's rarity and condition that drive prices now.

But there's still something for every collecting taste at every budget, and that's where *Toys & Prices* shines. Thanks to readers, contributors and friends in the hobby, *Toys & Prices* once again shines in helping collectors identify, describe, educate and price toys of all types. Here's hoping you find something new and exciting—in these pages and out in the field.

Become a Correspondent

Do you want to contribute to the next edition? Communicating with collectors and dealers is the best way to keep the information in these pages current and ensure that it accurately reflects the hobby. Drop us a line and let *Toys & Prices* know the prices you see realized at toy shows, auctions, estate sales, flea markets and anywhere else collectible toys are bought and sold. Any information is welcome, and even if it's just for a single toy, your perspective on the hobby ensures that trends across the nation are represented within these pages.

We're always looking for toy photos for the archives. High-resolution digital images are welcome.

If you have information or can donate photos of toys not pictured in these pages, please contact *Toys & Prices* at the following address:

Toys & Prices
Krause Publications
700 E. State St., Iola, WI 54990
(715) 445-4612
joe.kertzman@fwpubs.com

How To Use This Book

Toys & Prices 2009 is organized alphabetically by chapter (see Contents on p. 3). The quick-reference tabs on the side of the pages indicate the chapter. The headers at the top of each page have the chapter title followed by the section. For example, the header on page 10 reads:

3D Animation from Japan (McFarlane, 2000)

Therefore, page 12 is in the Action Figures chapter. The last section on the page is "Aliens from Kenner, 1992-94."

As a general rule, individual chapters override a character name. If there is a chapter devoted to the type of toy you're looking for, check there first. For example, if you're looking up a Superman lunch box, look first in the Lunch Boxes chapter. Likewise, a Yogi Bear board game will most likely appear in the Games-Postwar chapter rather than the Character Toys chapter.

The Character Toys chapter includes items that do not fit into one of the established sections or are more difficult to classify.

Also be aware that the words "figure" and "doll" are sometimes used interchangeably, although we have tried to remain consistent.

Overlap is the nature of the beast with toy classification, so if you don't find what you're looking for in one place, check a related chapter. For example, space-related action figures are most likely to be listed in the Action Figures chapter, but you may also find some listed in the Sci-Fi and Space Toys chapter. We're working on ways to streamline such listings to make finding items easier for readers. Your input and suggestions are welcomed.

Condition is Everything

When estimating the value of a toy, you must first evaluate its condition. Mint toys in mint packaging command higher prices than well played with toys whose boxes disappeared with the wrapping paper on Christmas Day. Mint is a rare condition indeed as toys were meant to be played with by children—a group not normally disposed to the meticulous maintenance of the toys in their toy boxes, sand boxes, backyards, garages, and strewn across the living room floor.

Realistic evaluation of condition is essential, as grading standards do vary from class to class. Grading a 1960s G.I. Joe is a different task than grading a Mattel Fanner 50 cap pistol.

Ultimately, the market is driven by buyers, and the bottom line final value of a toy is often the last price at which it is sold. Repeated sales of specific items create precedents and establish a standard for asking prices across the market. It is by comparison of such multiple transactions that price guides such as this one are created. In the end, the value of the toy is decided by one person—the buyer.

Common Abbreviations

MIB or MIP (Mint in Box, Mint in Package, C10): Just like new, in the original package, preferably still sealed. Boxes may have been opened, but any packages inside (as with model kits) remain unopened. Blister cards should be intact, undamaged, and unopened. Factory-sealed boxes should be unopened and often command higher prices.

MNP or MNB (Mint no Package, Mint no Box, C10): This describes a toy typically produced in the 1960s or later in Mint condition with all of its pieces, but missing its original package. This may also include a prototype or one-of-a-kind toy. A toy outside its original package is often referred to as "loose."

NM (Near Mint, C9): A toy that is complete and appears like new in overall appearance, but exhibits very minor wear and may or may not have the original box. An exception would be a toy that came in kit form. A kit in Near Mint condition would be expected to have the original box, but the box would display some wear.

EX (Excellent, C8): A toy that is complete and has been played with. Signs of minor wear may be evident, but the toy is very clean and well cared for.

VG (Very Good, C6): A toy that obviously has been played with and shows general overall wear. Paint chipping is readily apparent. In metal toys, some minor rust may be evident. Some minor pieces may be missing.

GD or G (Good, C4): A toy with evidence of heavy play, dents, chips, and possibly moderate rust. The toy may be missing a major replaceable component, such as a battery compartment door, or may be in need of repair. In sets, several pieces may be missing.

How To Use The CD

This DVD is PC and Macintosh® compatible when used with Adobe Acrobat Reader® version 6.0 or later. A step-by-step free download of Adobe Acrobat Reader® 8 is available at www.adobe.com. Adobe Reader® 8 was used in creating the instructions that follow.

To help you successfully navigate through the PDF document, several types of searches are available.

USING BOOKMARKS

Click on the Bookmarks icon to open the Bookmarks window. Use these links to go to specific points of interest. To scroll through pages in each section, use the arrows at the top of the screen (see next page for instructions to find page navigators).

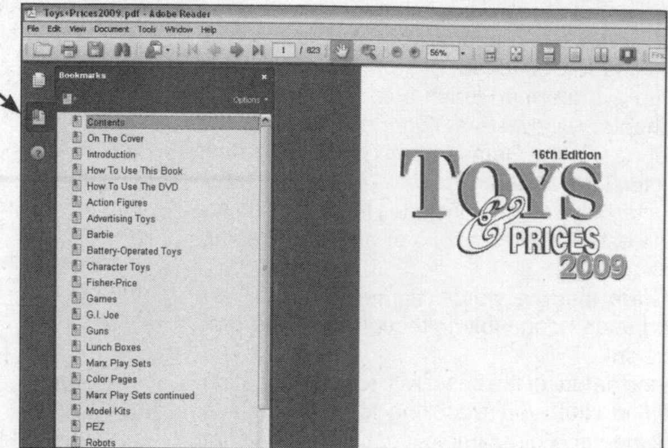

USING THE FIND BOX

Locate the find box in the tool bar and enter the word(s) you are searching for.

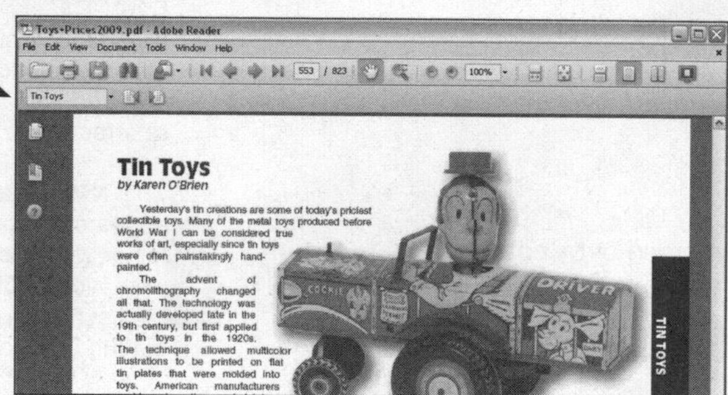

To navigate through the results of your search, use the Find Next icon.

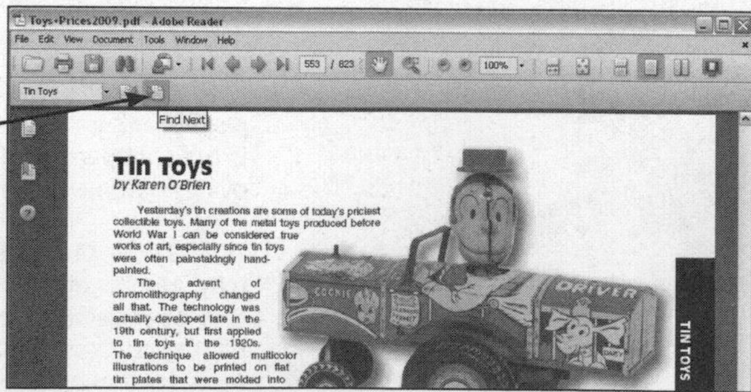

USING THE SEARCH OPTION

Locate the Search button by choosing Customize Toolbars in the Tools pull-down menu. Check Search (binocular icon) to have the Search option available in the toolbar.

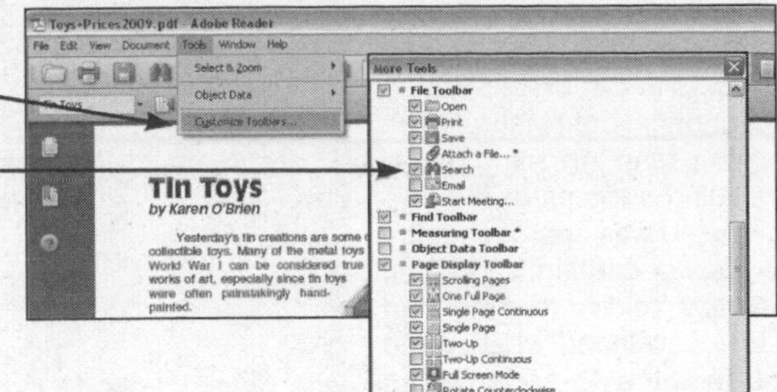

Click on the Search icon to open the Search dialog box.

In the Search dialog box, enter the word(s) you are searching for and click on the Search button.

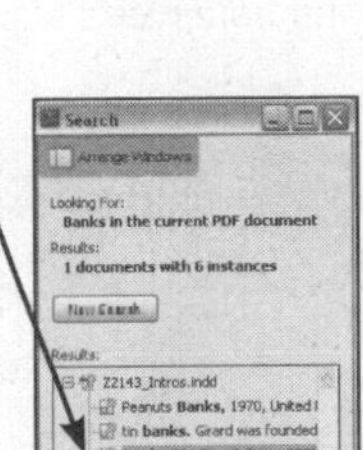

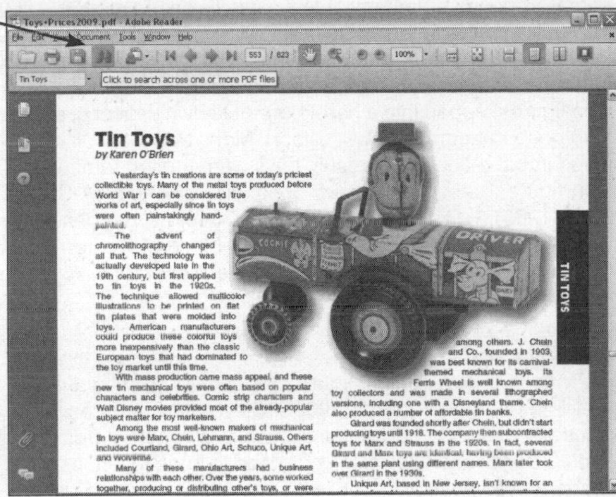

The list of results will appear in the dialog box. Click on the listings to view each page that contains your searched word(s).

To begin a new word search, click on the New Search button.

USING PAGE NAVIGATORS

Activate the Page Navigator Toolbar by choosing Customize Toolbars in the Tools pull-down menu. Check each tool as shown at right. You are now able to page through the PDF document by using the arrows at the top of the screen or by entering a page number you wish to view.

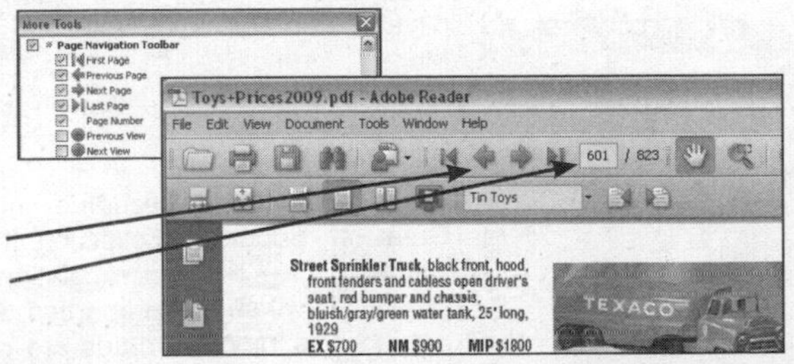

The Table of Contents is on page 3

You may also enlarge the images up to 400% for easy viewing

Action Figures

by Mark Bellomo

The 1960s

The production of action figures in the United States can be traced back to the nascent origins of Hasbro's G.I. Joe, "America's Moveable Fighting Man," in early 1964. Hoping to build on the overwhelming success of Mattel's Barbie doll (launched in 1959), Hasbro was approached by a designer who concocted the idea of crafting a foot-tall, fully articulated, military-themed toy soldier to American boys. Hasbro loved the idea, and developed what would be called the G.I. Joe line, and thus the 11-1/2" toy was born. G.I. Joe was a huge hit for Hasbro, who labeled the toy an "action figure" in order to differentiate and dissociate it from Barbie and other female fashion dolls on the market, knowing full well that young boys would *not* play with dolls.

Due to the success of G.I. Joe, other companies entered into the action figure market. Realizing that poseable male action figures tapped into a heretofore-unknown aspect of a young boy's imagination, A.C. Gilbert, Marx, and Ideal also forayed into the field. As a result, boys were treated to new action figures based on James Bond, Secret Agent (A.C. Gilbert, 1965), D.C. Comics and Marvel Comics super hero costumes for Captain Action (Ideal, 1966-68), and Western heroes and knights in Marx's Best of the West (1965-75) and Noble Knights (1968) lines, respectively.

The 1970s

The '70s saw action figure companies building on the strong foundation of the 1960's. Clever designers and executives realized that licensing popular characters from motion pictures and television could lead to huge revenues. A leader in the push for the use of licensed toy properties is the now defunct but legendary Mego Corporation (1971-1983), a '70s business juggernaut that captured a wealth of different film and TV licenses. An abbreviated list of Mego's licenses reads like a summation of '70s popular culture: *C.H.I.P.S., Planet of the Apes, The Black Hole, Captain & Tennille, The Love Boat, Dukes of Hazzard, Happy Days, Laverne & Shirley, James Bond, KISS,* and a wealth of others. Perhaps Mego's most famous product was the company's Official World's Greatest Super Heroes (1972-1978), which are, to this day considered to be some of the most popular and desirable of all comic book action figures. Expect prices of Mint on Card and Mint in Box Mego figures (particularly the aforementioned super heroes) to be extraordinarily high.

Although Mego's Micronauts (1976-1980) and Comic Action Heroes (1975-1978) were among the very first 3-¾" action figures, Kenner's stellar line of *Star Wars* figures, vehicles, creatures, and playsets took America by storm in 1977. *Star Wars* revolutionized play for a whole generation of American children with this new scale of action figures, and the franchise's success spans three decades.

With the triumph of the *Star Wars* line, toy manufacturers began looking at action figures in a new light, understanding the wealth of possibilities that could be explored in this new 3-¾" format. What once was a shoebox full of 2" tall hard-plastic little green army men in the 1950s, in the 1970s became a colorful carrying case chock full of 4" tall, fully poseable, distinctly different characters with a slew of different weapons and accessories.

The 1980s

Although the 1970s ushered in a new format (and era) of action figure collecting, it wasn't until the 1980's (and Ronald Reagan's deregulation of children's television) that licensed properties *exploded* into children's toy rooms. The 1980s are considered by many collectors to be a renaissance for action figures, as Reagan's deregulation allowed companies to provide children with—in essence—24-minute long animated toy commercials. These animated programs were so popular that they volleyed into syndication, some cable channels showing a block of toy cartoons for hours on end, every day of the week. As a result, the characters from these action figure lines of the '80s permeated the American collective consciousness for an entire generation, and many toy lines that were born in the '80s are still über popular to this day: G.I. Joe: A Real American Hero, Transformers, He-Man and the Masters of the Universe,

Thundercats, Voltron, M.A.S.K., Dungeons & Dragons, The Real Ghostbusters, Indiana Jones, Robotech, She-Ra Princess of Power, the World Wrestling Federation, and those plucky Teenage Mutant Ninja Turtles.

Many casual fans don't recognize what any conscientious collector of 1980s action figures knows: these '80s toys are worth quite a bit of money in good condition, whether the toy is Mint Loose and Complete, or even better, Mint in Package (Mint in Box or Mint on Card). Of course, casual fans are well aware that "big" G.I. Joes (the 11 ½" figures from 1964-1976) are worth a considerable amount of money, and that vintage Star Wars figures will command a good price at auction, but in recent years, even secondary and tertiary toy lines from the 1980s have caught steam (i.e. M.A.S.K., She-Ra Princess of Power, etc.).

The 1990s

With the introduction of many new super hero toy lines from novice toy maker Toy Biz (DC Super Heroes, Marvel Super Heroes, Batman, X-Men and Spider-Man), the 1990s started with a bang. Toy Biz would fizzle for a bit due to criticism of their poor sculpting, terrible action features, and inferior plastics, but the company would come back strong in the new millennium with their stunning Marvel Legends line (2002-present, with the license now owned by Hasbro).

New toy lines sprung up seemingly out of nowhere. Licensed properties were being utilized to the max, from the *Aliens* franchise to *Austin Powers*, from Playmate's *Star Trek: The Next Generation* (among their many other *Star Trek* offerings) to *Tim Burton's Nightmare Before Christmas*.

A few toy lines truly stand out from this decade. Todd MacFarlane's line of expertly crafted *Spawn* (1994-present) action figures based on his No. 1 selling Image comic book, and Playmate's revolutionary *Simpsons* (1999-2004) line of figures and playsets dominated toy shelves. With the vast amount of different product offered, it seemed that collectors couldn't get enough of the wide variety. Unfortunately, the secondary market prices of many of these '90s toys have declined. The action figure market, however, is based on the value of popular lines increasing across the board on the secondary market after eight to fifteen years have passed. Hopefully, by 2010, we'll see some modest price increases.

However, one action figure line from the 1990s that has heated up the secondary market recently is the *(Mighty Morphin) Power Rangers* by Bandai (1993-present). The first few years of Power Ranger toys, vehicles, accessories, and role-play devices have garnered quite a bit of attention from collectors surfing online auction sites and visiting collectible shops. High-grade samples sell very briskly. Keep your eye on *Transformers: Beast Wars* (1996-1999), and Hasbro's and Jakks Pacific's WWF/WWE figures (1990-1994, and 1997-present, respectively), as these have recently piqued collector interest.

The 2000s

The new millennium produced many advances in action figure production: improved articulation (*Star Wars*, G.I. Joe), better paint applications and sculpting (McFarlane Toys), and even "Real Scan Technology" (World Wrestling Entertainment). "Real Scan Technology" (pioneered by Jakks Pacific) allowed an actual human face to be scanned and grafted into the mold of an action figure. Only time will tell which of the many toy lines of the new millennium will be prized as collectibles, determined by supply-and-demand and the desire of passionate aficionados who control the secondary market.

2009 Trends

As always, there will be premiere pieces in the action figure world that attract the most attention by collectors: Mego's Official World's Greatest Super-Heroes' Secret Identity Outfits, Ideal's Super Queens, Captain Action outfits (Spider-Man, the Green Hornet, etc.), and vintage Star Wars figures will always be incredibly valuable, but many toy lines from the 1980s—even secondary or tertiary lines such as She-Ra and M.A.S.K.—are commanding premium prices as collectors finish other more common lines as G.I. Joe and *Star Wars*. Also, watch out for the attention that major motion pictures give action figure lines, notable films such as *G.I. Joe*, *Transformers II: Rise of the Fallen*, *Star Wars: The Clone Wars*, and even the proposed *Voltron* and *He-Man* movies. The premiere pieces in these lines—usually the priciest toys—will consistently increase in value over time.

THE *TOP 10* ACTION FIGURES (In Mint Condition)

1. Captain Action, Spider-Man Costume, Ideal, 1967 .... $10,500
2. Captain Action, Green Hornet Costume, Ideal, 1967 .... $7,500
3. Batgirl, Comic Heroine Posin' Dolls, Ideal, 1967 .... $6,500
4. Supergirl, Comic Heroine Posin' Dolls, Ideal, 1967 .... $5,500
5. Wonder Woman, Comic Heroine Posin' Dolls, Ideal, 1967 ...... $5,500
6. Mera, Comic Heroine Posin' Dolls, Ideal, 1967 .... $5,000
7. Captain Action, Dr. Evil Gift Set, 1967 .... $4,400
8. Captain Action, Action Boy Superboy Costume, 1967 .... $3,800
9. Captain Action, Dr. Evil Sanctuary, 1967 .... $3,700
10. Captain Action, Silver Streak Vehicle, 1967 .... $2,500

3D Animation from Japan (McFarlane, 2000)

AKIRA

Kaneda with Motorcycle, 2000, McFarlane
NM $3 **MIP** $10

Tetsuo, 2000, McFarlane
NM $3 **MIP** $10

TENCHI MUYO!

Ryoko, 2000, McFarlane
NM $3 **MIP** $15

TRIGUN

Vash with Stampede, 2000, McFarlane
NM $3 **MIP** $13

Action Jackson (Mego, 1974)

8" FIGURES

Action Jackson, 1974, 8", Mego, blond, brown, or black hair
NM $15 **MIP** $35

Action Jackson, 1974, 8", Mego, blond, brown, or black beard
NM $15 **MIP** $35

Action Jackson, 1974, 8", Mego, Black version
NM $25 **MIP** $45

ACCESSORIES

Fire Rescue Pack, 1974, Mego
NM $5 **MIP** $15

Parachute Plunge, 1974, Mego
NM $5 **MIP** $15

Strap-On Helicopter, 1974, Mego
NM $5 **MIP** $15

Water Scooter, 1974, Mego
NM $5 **MIP** $15

OUTFITS

Air Force Pilot, 1974, Mego
NM $7 **MIP** $10

Army Outfit, 1974, Mego
NM $7 **MIP** $10

Aussie Marine, 1974, Mego
NM $7 **MIP** $10

Baseball, 1974, Mego
NM $7 **MIP** $10

Fisherman, 1974, Mego
NM $7 **MIP** $10

Football, 1974, Mego
NM $7 **MIP** $10

Frog Man, 1974, Mego
NM $7 **MIP** $10

Hockey, 1974, Mego
NM $7 **MIP** $10

Jungle Safari, 1974, Mego
NM $7 **MIP** $10

Karate, 1974, Mego
NM $7 **MIP** $10

Navy Sailor, 1974, Mego
NM $7 **MIP** $10

Rescue Squad, 1974, Mego
NM $7 **MIP** $10

Scramble Cyclist, 1974, Mego
NM $7 **MIP** $10

Secret Agent, 1974, Mego
NM $7 **MIP** $10

Ski Patrol, 1974, Mego
NM $7 **MIP** $10

Snowmobile Outfit, 1974, Mego
NM $7 **MIP** $10

Surf and Scuba Outfit, 1974, Mego
NM $7 **MIP** $10

Western Cowboy, 1974, Mego
NM $7 **MIP** $10

PLAY SETS

Jungle House, 1974, Mego
NM $100 **MIP** $250

Lost Continent Play Set, 1974, Mego
NM $150 **MIP** $350

VEHICLES

Adventure Set, 1974, Mego
NM $40 **MIP** $100

Campmobile, 1974, Mego
NM $40 **MIP** $90

Dune Buggy, 1974, Mego
NM $30 **MIP** $60

Formula Racer, 1974, Mego
NM $30 **MIP** $75

Mustang, 1974, Mego
NM $30 **MIP** $100

Rescue Helicopter, 1974, Mego
NM $40 **MIP** $90

Safari Jeep, 1974, Mego
NM $40 **MIP** $100

Scramble Cycle, 1974, Mego
NM $20 **MIP** $50

Snowmobile, 1974, Mego
NM $15 **MIP** $40

Addams Family (Playmates, 1992)

FIGURES

Gomez, 1992, Playmates
NM $4 **MIP** $10

Granny, 1992, Playmates
NM $4 **MIP** $10

Lurch, 1992, Playmates
NM $4 **MIP** $10

Morticia, 1992, Playmates
NM $4 **MIP** $10

Pugsley, 1992, Playmates
NM $4 **MIP** $10

Uncle Fester, 1992, Playmates
NM $4 **MIP** $10

Addams Family (Remco, 1964)

FIGURES

Lurch, 1964, Remco
NM $150 **MIP** $450

Morticia, 1964, Remco
NM $160 **MIP** $500

Uncle Fester, 1964, Remco
NM $160 **MIP** $500

Alien (Kenner, 1979)

18" FIGURE

Alien, 1979, Kenner, This is the ultimate figure for Alien collectors, to be complete it must have the plastic headpiece
NM $225 **MIP** $525

Aliens (Kenner, 1992-94)

ACCESSORIES

Evac Fighter, 1992-94, Kenner
NM $7 **MIP** $20

Hovertread, 1992-94, Kenner
NM $5 **MIP** $20

Power Loader, 1992-94, Kenner
NM $5 **MIP** $20

Stinger XT-37, 1992-94, Kenner
NM $5 **MIP** $20

SERIES 1, 1992

Apone, 1992, Kenner
NM $5 **MIP** $8

Bishop, 1992, 4-1/4", Kenner, Gatlin gun, body breaks into two parts
NM $5 **MIP** $8

Bull Alien, 1992, Kenner
NM $7 **MIP** $8

Drake, 1992, Kenner
NM $5 **MIP** $8

Gorilla Alien, 1992, Kenner
NM $8 **MIP** $8

Hicks, 1992, Kenner
NM $5 **MIP** $8

Queen Alien, 1992, Kenner
NM $10 **MIP** $20

Ripley, 1992, Kenner, with Turbo Torch
NM $5 **MIP** $12

Scorpion Alien, 1992, Kenner
NM $5 **MIP** $12

SERIES 2, 1993

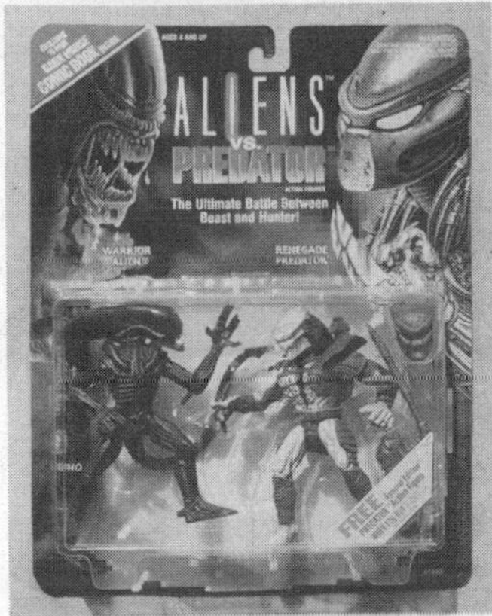

Alien vs. Predator, 1993, Kenner, Billed as the "ultimate battle between beast and hunter."
NM $5 MIP $20

Flying Queen Alien, 1993, Kenner
NM $5 MIP $12

Queen Face Hugger, 1993, Kenner
NM $5 MIP $12

Snake Alien, 1993, Kenner
NM $5 MIP $12

SERIES 3, 1994

Arachnid Alien, 1994, Kenner
NM $4 MIP $15

Atax, 1994, Kenner
NM $4 MIP $15

Clan Leader Predator, 1994, Kenner
NM $4 MIP $15

Cracked Tusk Predator, 1994, Kenner
NM $4 MIP $10

Hudson (foreign release), 1994, Kenner
NM $7 MIP $15

Invisible Predator (mail-in), 1994, Kenner
NM $5 MIP $15

Kill Krab Alien, 1994, Kenner
NM $4 MIP $10

King Alien, 1994, Kenner
NM $8 MIP $15

Lasershot Predator (electronic), 1994, Kenner
NM $5 MIP $12

Lava Predator, 1994, Kenner
NM $4 MIP $10

Mantis Alien, 1994, Kenner
NM $4 MIP $10

Night Cougar Alien, 1994, Kenner
NM $4 MIP $10

Night Storm Predator, 1994, Kenner
NM $4 MIP $10

O'Malley (foreign release), 1994, Kenner
NM $7 MIP $15

Panther Alien, 1994, Kenner
NM $4 MIP $10

Rhino Alien, 1994, Kenner
NM $4 MIP $10

Spiked Tail Predator, 1994, Kenner
NM $3 MIP $10

Stalker Predator, 1994, Kenner
NM $3 MIP $10

Swarm Alien (electronic), 1994, Kenner
NM $5 MIP $10

Vasquez (foreign release), 1994, Kenner
NM $7 MIP $15

Wild Boar Alien, 1994, Kenner
NM $3 MIP $10

Alpha Fight (Toy Biz, 1999)

5" FIGURES

Northstar & Aurora, 1999
NM $3 MIP $12

Sasquatch & Vindicator, 1999
NM $3 MIP $12

Snowbird & Puck, 1999
NM $3 MIP $12

American West (Mego, 1973)

8" FIGURES

Buffalo Bill Cody, 1973, Mego, carded
NM $40 MIP $100

Buffalo Bill Cody, 1973, Mego, boxed, shirt, pants, belt, 2 boots, rifle, hat, gun, holster
NM $40 MIP $75

Cochise, 1973, Mego, carded
NM $40 MIP $100

Cochise, 1973, Mego, boxed
NM $40 MIP $75

Davy Crockett, 1973, Mego, carded
NM $70 MIP $140

Davy Crockett, 1973, Mego, boxed
NM $70 MIP $110

Shadow (horse), 1973, Mego, boxed
NM $70 MIP $140

Sitting Bull, 1973, Mego, carded
NM $45 MIP $125

Sitting Bull, 1973, Mego, boxed
NM $45 MIP $90

Wild Bill Hickok, 1973, Mego, carded
NM $40 MIP $125

Wild Bill Hickok, 1973, Mego, boxed
NM $40 MIP $75

Wyatt Earp, 1973, Mego, carded
NM $40 MIP $125

Wyatt Earp, 1973, Mego, boxed
NM $40 MIP $75

PLAY SETS

Dodge City Play Set, 1973, Mego, vinyl
NM $100 MIP $200

Angel (Moore Action Collectibles, 2002-04)

SERIES 1

Angel, 8", Moore Action Collectibles
NM $6 MIP $25

Cordelia, 8", Moore Action Collectibles, summer show exclusive, red shirt w/short hair
NM $8 MIP $30

Cordelia, 8", Moore Action Collectibles
NM $8 MIP $30

Faith, 8", Moore Action Collectibles, Action Figure Express exclusive, leather jacket
NM $8 MIP $30

Faith, 8", Moore Action Collectibles
NM $8 MIP $30

Slave Cordelia, 8", Moore Action Collectibles, Suncoast exclusive, carded
NM $5 MIP $15

Slave Cordelia, 8", Moore Action Collectibles, ToyFare exclusive, boxed
NM $5 MIP $15

Vampire Angel, 8", Moore Action Collectibles, M.A.C. Collector's Club exclusive, leather jacket
NM $6 MIP $25

Vampire Angel, 8", Moore Action Collectibles, Diamond exclusive
NM $12 MIP $25

SERIES 2

Lorne, 8", Moore Action Collectibles, white jacket
NM $5 MIP $15

Lorne, 8", Moore Action Collectibles, red suit chase figure; "There's No Place Like Glrb"
NM $6 MIP $25

Lorne, 8", Moore Action Collectibles, Vegas: "The House Always Wins;" Time and Space Toys Wizard World Chicago exclusive
NM $6 MIP $25

Wesley, 8", Moore Action Collectibles, unpainted, Wizard World Philadelphia exclusive
NM $10 MIP $30

Wesley, 8", Moore Action Collectibles, "Waiting in the Wings;" Tower Records exclusive
NM $4 MIP $12

Wesley, 8", Moore Action Collectibles, "Season Four"
NM $4 MIP $12

Wesley, 8", Moore Action Collectibles, "Rain of Fire;" Time and Space Toys exclusive
NM $5 MIP $20

Wesley, 8", Moore Action Collectibles, "Parting Gifts;" ToyFare exclusive
NM $5 MIP $20

Wesley, 8", Moore Action Collectibles, "Bad Girls;" Diamond exclusive
NM $4 MIP $12

SERIES 3

Angel, 8", Moore Action Collectibles, "Graduation Day;" Suncoast exclusive
NM $6 MIP $16

Angel, 8", Moore Action Collectibles, "The Ring;" Action Figure Express exclusive
NM $6 MIP $16

Angel, 8", Moore Action Collectibles, "Season Five"
NM $6 MIP $15

Fred, 8", Moore Action Collectibles, "Season Three"
NM $6 MIP $15

Angel (Moore Action Collectibles, 2002-04)

Illyria, 8", Moore Action Collectibles, "Shells"
NM $6 MIP $20

Illyria, 8", Moore Action Collectibles, Diamond exclusive
NM $6 MIP $15

Pylean Demon Angel, 8", Moore Action Collectibles, Time and Space Toys exclusive
NM $6 MIP $15

Vampire Angel w/Baby Connor, 8", Moore Action Collectibles, Tower Records exclusive
NM $6 MIP $16

ANTZ (Playmates, 1998)

FIGURES

Colonel Cutter, 1998, Playmates
NM $2 MIP $4

General Mandible, 1998, Playmates
NM $2 MIP $4

Princess Bala, 1998, Playmates
NM $2 MIP $4

Weaver, 1998, Playmates
NM $2 MIP $4

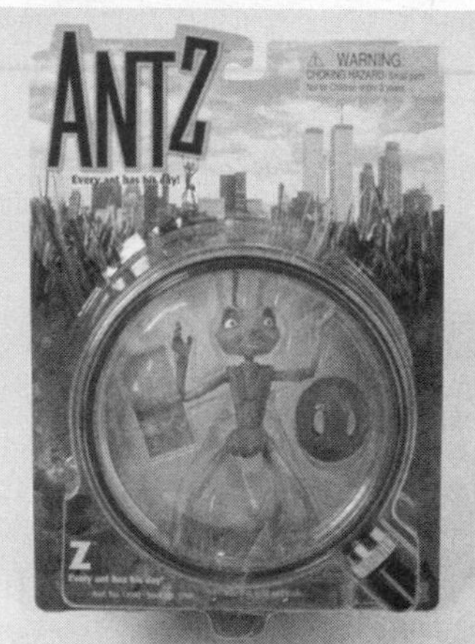

Z, 1998, Playmates, Figure includes map and helmet. Interesting to note the World Trade Center Towers on the packaging
NM $2 MIP $4

Archies (Marx, 1975)

FIGURES

Archie, 1975, Marx, shown with Jughead
NM $15 MIP $70

Betty, 1975, Marx
NM $15 MIP $70

Jughead, 1975, Marx
NM $15 MIP $70

Veronica, 1975, Marx, shown with Betty, Archie, Jughead
NM $15 MIP $70

Armageddon (Mattel, 1998)

FIGURES

A.J. Frost, 1998, Mattel
NM $3 MIP $10

Harry Stamper, 1998, Mattel
NM $3 MIP $10

Army of Darkness (Sideshow Toys, 1998-Present)

12" FIGURES

Bruce Campbell as Ash, 1998, 12", Sideshow Toys, #1301
NM n/a MIP $40

Evil Ash, 1998, 12", Sideshow Toys, #1302
NM n/a MIP $40

Astronauts (Marx, 1969)

FIGURES

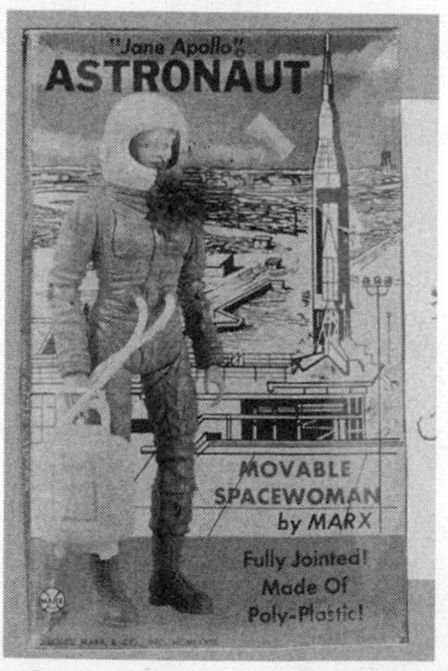

Jane Apollo Astronaut, 1969, Marx, movable, includes helmet and a variety of plastic accessories, much in the style of the "Best of the West" series
NM $65 MIP $125

Johnny Apollo Astronaut, 1969, Marx, movable
NM $125 MIP $200

Kennedy Space Center Astronaut, 1969, Marx, movable
NM $65 MIP $140

A-Team (Galoob, 1984)

12" FIGURES

Mr. T, non-talking, 1984, 12", Galoob
NM $20 MIP $50

Mr. T, talking, 1984, 12", Galoob
NM $25 MIP $60

3-3/4" FIGURES AND ACCESSORIES

Armored Attack Adventure with B.A. Figure, 1984, 3-3/4", Galoob, vehicle with 3-3/4" figure
NM $25 MIP $55

A-Team Four Figure Set, 1984, 3-3/4", Galoob, 3-3/4" figures
NM $40 MIP $65

Bad Guys Figure Set: Viper, Rattler, Cobra, Python, 1984, 3-3/4", Galoob, 3-3/4" figures on card
NM $35 MIP $60

Combat Attack Gyrocopter with Murdock, 1984, 3-3/4", Galoob, vehicle with 3-3/4" figure
NM $30 MIP $60

Combat Headquarters with four A-Team figures, 1984, 3-3/4", Galoob, 3-3/4" figures
NM $25 MIP $60

Corvette with Face Figure, 1984, 3-3/4", Galoob, vehicle and 3-3/4" figure
NM $25 MIP $65

Motorized Patrol Boat, 1984, 3-3/4", Galoob
NM $15 MIP $35

Tactical Van Play Set, 1984, 3-3/4", Galoob
NM $25 MIP $45

6-1/2" FIGURES AND ACCESSORIES

Amy Allen, 1984, 6-1/2", Galoob
NM $30 MIP $58

B.A. Baracus, 1984, 6-1/2", Galoob
NM $15 MIP $40

Cobra, 1984, 6-1/2", Galoob
NM $10 MIP $15

Combat Attack Gyrocopter, 1984, Galoob
NM $15 MIP $35

Face, 1984, 6-1/2", Galoob
NM $15 MIP $35

Hannibal, 1984, 6-1/2", Galoob
NM $15 MIP $40

Murdock, 1984, 6-1/2", Galoob
NM $15 MIP $40

Off Road Attack Cycle, 1984, Galoob
NM $8 MIP $20

Python, 1984, 6-1/2", Galoob
NM $12 MIP $25

Rattler, 1984, 6-1/2", Galoob
NM $12 MIP $25

Viper, 1984, 6-1/2", Galoob
NM $12 MIP $25

Austin Powers (McFarlane, 1999-2000)

9" FIGURES

Austin Powers, 2000, 9", McFarlane
NM $5 MIP $10

Dr. Evil, 2000, 9", McFarlane
NM $5 MIP $10

Fat Bastard, 2000, 9", McFarlane
NM $10 MIP $20

SERIES 1, 6" FIGURES

Austin in Union Jack underwear, 1999, 6", McFarlane
NM $3 MIP $8

Austin in Union Jack Underwear, "dirty version", 1999, 6", McFarlane
NM $5 MIP $10

Austin in velvet suit, 1999, 6", McFarlane
NM $3 MIP $8

Austin in velvet suit, "dirty version", 1999, 6", McFarlane
NM $5 MIP $10

Dr. Evil with Mr. Bigglesworth, 1999, 6", McFarlane
NM $3 MIP $10

Dr. Evil with Mr. Bigglesworth, "dirty version", 1999, 6", McFarlane
NM $5 MIP $15

Fat Bastard, 1999, 6", McFarlane
NM $10 MIP $20

Fat Man, 2000, 6", McFarlane, altered version of Fat Bastard
NM $5 MIP $15

Felicity Shagwell, 1999, 6", McFarlane
NM $3 MIP $8

Felicity Shagwell, "dirty version", 1999, 6", McFarlane
NM $10 MIP $16

Mini-Me, 1999, 6", McFarlane
NM $10 MIP $16

SERIES 2, 6" FIGURES

Austin Powers in striped suit, 2000, 6", McFarlane, Carnaby Street version
NM $3 MIP $8

Austin Powers, "dirty version", 2000, 6", McFarlane
NM $3 MIP $10

Dr. Evil and Mini-Me with Mini-Mobile, 2000, 6", McFarlane
NM $8 MIP $20

Dr. Evil, Moon Mission, 2000, 6", McFarlane
NM $4 MIP $12

Fembot, 2000, 6", McFarlane
NM $3 MIP $8

Mini-Me, Moon Mission, 2000, 6", McFarlane
NM $8 MIP $20

Scott Evil, 2000, 6", McFarlane, says "Get away from me, you lazy-eyed psycho"
NM $3 MIP $8

Scott Evil, 2000, 6", McFarlane, says "A trillion is worth more than a billion, numbnuts"
NM $3 MIP $10

Vanessa Kensington, 2000, 6", McFarlane
NM $4 MIP $12

Austin Powers (Trendmasters, 1999)

9" FIGURES

Austin Powers, 1999, 9", McFarlane
NM $4 MIP $12

Dr. Evil, 1999, 9", McFarlane
NM $4 MIP $12

Fembot, 1999, 9", McFarlane
NM $8 MIP $20

Austin Powers (Mezco, 2002)

FIGURES

'70s Austin Powers, 2002, Mezco, platform shoes, oh my!
NM $2 MIP $6

Canaby Street Austin Powers, 2002, Mezco, dressed in striped suit
NM $2 MIP $6

Fat Bastard, 2002, Mezco, in sumo outfit
NM $2 MIP $6

Goldmember, 2002, Mezco, comes with gold brick
NM $2 MIP $6

Prison Dr. Evil & Mini-Me, 2002, Mezco, dressed in blue prison outfits
NM $2 MIP $6

Avengers (Toy Biz, 1997-2000)

6" FIGURES

Iron Man, 1997, 6", Toy Biz, with "Power Converter"
NM $4 MIP $8

Loki, 1997, 6", Toy Biz
NM $4 MIP $8

Scarlett Witch, 1997, 6", Toy Biz
NM $4 MIP $8

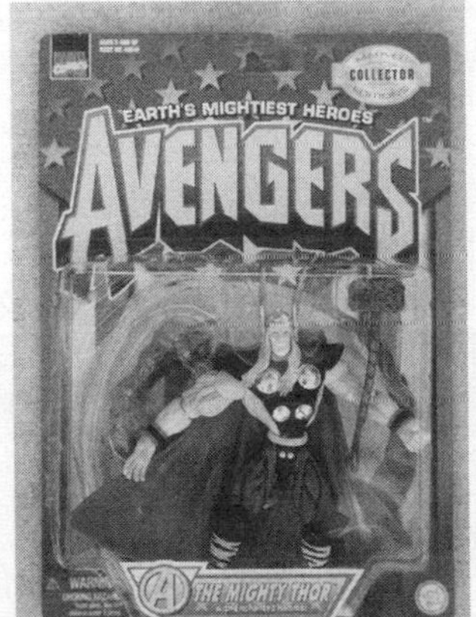

(Lenny Lee)

The Mighty Thor, 1997, 6", Toy Biz, with hammer
NM $4 MIP $8

SERIES I, 5" FIGURES

Ant-Man, 1999, 5", Toy Biz
NM $4 MIP $8

Captain America, 1999, 5", Toy Biz
NM $4 MIP $8

Ultron, 1999, 5", Toy Biz
NM $4 MIP $8

Vision, 1999, 5", Toy Biz
NM $4 MIP $8

Wasp, 1999, 5", Toy Biz
NM $4 MIP $8

Avengers (Toy Biz, 1997-2000)

SERIES II, 5" FIGURES

Falcon, 1999, 5", Toy Biz
NM $4 MIP $8

Hawkeye, 1999, 5", Toy Biz
NM $4 MIP $8

Kang, 1999, 5", Toy Biz
NM $4 MIP $8

Tigra, 1999, 5", Toy Biz
NM $4 MIP $8

Wonder Man, 1999, 5", Toy Biz
NM $4 MIP $8

SERIES III, 5" FIGURES

Ant-Man, 1999, 5", Toy Biz
NM $4 MIP $8

Hawkeye, 1999, 5", Toy Biz
NM $4 MIP $8

Iron Man, 1999, 5", Toy Biz
NM $4 MIP $8

Remnant I, 1999, 5", Toy Biz
NM $4 MIP $8

Thor, 1999, 5", Toy Biz
NM $4 MIP $8

SHAPE SHIFTERS

Ant-Man transforms into Armored Ant, 2000, 5", Toy Biz
NM $4 MIP $8

Captain America transform into American Eagle, 2000, 5", Toy Biz
NM $4 MIP $8

Hawykeye transforms into Armored Hawk, 2000, 5", Toy Biz
NM $4 MIP $8

Thor transforms into Flying Horse, 2000, 5", Toy Biz
NM $4 MIP $8

TEAM GIFT PACK

Hulk, Iron Man, Thor, Ant-Man/Giant Man, The Wasp, 1999, 5", Toy Biz
NM $8 MIP $30

Babylon 5 (Exclusive Toy Products, 1997)

6" FIGURES

Ambassador Delenn, 1997, 6", Exclusive, Series I
NM $3 MIP $10

Ambassador Delenn with Minbari Flyer, Diamond Exclusive, 1997, 6", Exclusive, Series I
NM $5 MIP $15

Ambassador Juphar Trkider, 1997, 6", Exclusive, Series IV
NM $10 MIP $25

Ambassador Kosh, 1997, 6", Exclusive, Series II
NM $3 MIP $10

Ambassador Londo Mollari, 1997, 6", Exclusive, Series I
NM $3 MIP $10

Ambassador She'Lah, 1997, 6", Exclusive, Series IV
NM $12 MIP $25

Ambassador Vlur/Nhur, 1997, 6", Exclusive
NM $3 MIP $10

Captain Elizabeth Lochley, 1997, 6", Exclusive, Series IV
NM $3 MIP $10

Captain John Sheridan, 1997, 6", Exclusive, Series I
NM $3 MIP $10

Chief Garibaldi, 1997, 6", Exclusive, Series III
NM $4 MIP $10

G'Kar, 1997, 6", Exclusive, Series I
NM $3 MIP $10

G'Kar, green outfit, Diamond Exclusive, 1997, 6", Exclusive, Series I
NM $5 MIP $15

Lennier, 1997, 6", Exclusive, Series III
NM $4 MIP $10

Lyta Alexander, 1997, 6", Exclusive, Series III
NM $4 MIP $10

Marcus Cole, 1997, 6", Exclusive, Series II, w/White Star
NM $4 MIP $10

PSI Cop Bester, 1997, 6", Exclusive, Series IV
NM $4 MIP $10

Shadow Sentient, Diamond Exclusive, 1997, 6", Exclusive, Series III
NM $10 MIP $50

Stephen Franklin, 1997, 6", Exclusive, Series III
NM $3 MIP $10

Susan Ivanova, 1997, 6", Exclusive, Series II, w/Starfury
NM $4 MIP $10

Susan Ivanova, White's Collecting Figures Exclusive, 1997, 6", Exclusive, Series II
NM $5 MIP $20

Vir Cotto, 1997, 6", Exclusive, Series II
NM $3 MIP $10

Vorlon Visitor, Diamond Exclusive, 1997, 6", Exclusive, Series II
NM $5 MIP $20

9" FIGURES

Ambassador Delenn, 1997, 9", Exclusive, Series II
NM $5 MIP $20

Ambassador G'Kar, 1997, 9", Exclusive, Series II
NM $5 MIP $20

Ambassador G'Kar, Diamond Exclusive, 1997, 9", Exclusive, Series II
NM $5 MIP $25

Ambassador Londo Mollari, 1997, 9", Exclusive, gray hair, gold outfit
NM $5 MIP $20

Chief Michael Garibaldi, 1997, 9", Exclusive, Series III
NM $5 MIP $25

John Sheridan, 1997, 9", Exclusive, Series II
NM $5 MIP $25

Lennier, Diamond Exclusive, 1997, 9", Exclusive, Series I
NM $5 MIP $25

Londo, 1997, 9", Exclusive, Series III
NM $5 MIP $25

Marcus Cole, 1997, 9", Exclusive, Series I
NM $5 MIP $20

Michael Garibaldi, 1997, 9", Exclusive
NM $5 MIP $20

Susan Ivanova, 1997, 9", Exclusive, Series III
NM $5 MIP $25

Vir Cotto, 1997, 9", Exclusive, Series I
NM $5 MIP $20

Banana Splits (Sutton, 1970)

FIGURES

Bingo the Bear, 1970, Sutton
NM $60 MIP $150

Drooper the Lion, 1970, Sutton
NM $60 MIP $150

Fleagle Beagle, 1970, Sutton
NM $60 MIP $150

Snorky the Elephant, 1970, Sutton
NM $60 MIP $150

Batman (Mattel, 2003-04)

FIGURES

Arctic Shield Batman, 2004, 6", Mattel, w/arctic shield, axe launcher
NM $5 MIP $10

Battle Armor Batman, 2003, 6", Mattel, w/ combat blade and battle armor
NM $5 MIP $10

Battle Board Robin, 2003, 6", Mattel, w/ disc missile and battle board
NM $5 MIP $10

Battle Board Robin - repaint, 2004, 6", Mattel, green vest version
NM $10 MIP $15

Battle Spike Batman, 2004, 6", Mattel, spike gauntlets, battle armor
NM $5 MIP $10

Croc Armor Batman, 2004, 6", Mattel, wing blades, claws, armor
NM $5 MIP $10

Drill Cannon Batman, 2004, 6", Mattel, cannon, 6 missiles, battle wings, claw
NM $7 MIP $12

Electro-Net Batman, 2004, 6", Mattel, 2 disks, launcher, green armor
NM $5 MIP $10

Hydro-Suit Batman, 2003, 6", Mattel, w/ dive pack, breathing mask, missile launcher
NM $5 MIP $10

Ice Cannon Mr. Freeze, 2004, 6", Mattel, w/ice cannon; version w/out goggles doubles value
NM $7 MIP $14

Killer Croc, 2003, 6", Mattel, bendable tail
NM $10 MIP $12

Martial Arts Batman, 2003, 6", Mattel, w/ dual axe staff and hand blade
NM $5 MIP $10

Night Patrol Batman, 2003, 6", Mattel, Deluxe figure w/ shield and batarang launcher
NM $5 MIP $10

Quick Fire Joker, 2003, 6", Mattel, w/ cane and gun
NM $7 MIP $12

Sky Strike Batman, 2004, 6", Mattel, Deluxe, wing pack, net missile
NM $7 MIP $12

Sling Strike Nightwing, 2004, 6", Mattel, green costume
NM $6 MIP $12

Snare Strike Batman, 2004, 6", Mattel, retractable snare rope, missile launcher
NM $7 MIP $12

Stealth Armor Batman, 2003, 6", Mattel, Deluxe, w/ stealth armor, missile launcher, jet boots
NM $5 MIP $10

Tech Armor Batman, 2003, 6", Mattel, Deluxe figure w/ laser cannon, claw arm, disc missile launcher
NM $5 MIP $10

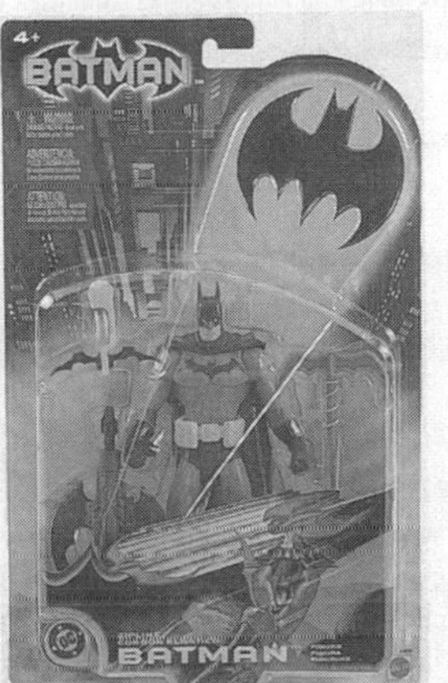

Zipline Batman, 2003, 6", Mattel, w/ zipline and batarang
NM $5 MIP $10

MULTI-PACKS

Attack of the Penguin, 2004, Mattel, Animated, Batman, Penguin, Nightwing, Batgirl
NM $15 MIP $30

Batman and Nightwing, 2003, Mattel, New sculpt
NM $10 MIP $15

Batman and Nightwing, 2003, Mattel, Animated
NM $7 MIP $12

Batman and Robin, 2003, Mattel, Animated
NM $5 MIP $10

Batman and Superman, 2003, Mattel, New sculpt
NM $10 MIP $15

Batman vs. Joker, 2003, Mattel, Animated
NM $7 MIP $12

Battle Armor Batman & Quick Fire Joker, 2004, Mattel, combat blade, cane, quick-fire gun
NM $10 MIP $20

Battle Scars, Batman vs. Catwoman, 2003, Mattel, Animated
NM $7 MIP $12

Gotham City Figures, 2004, Mattel, Batman, Robin, Nightwing, exclusive silver Batgirl
NM $20 MIP $40

Gotham City Figures, Series 2, 2004, Mattel, Batman, Joker, Catwoman, Two-Face
NM $12 MIP $25

Tech Suit Batman vs. Two-Face, 2003, Mattel, Animated
NM $7 MIP $12

Zipline Batman & Battle Board Robin, 2004, Mattel, batarang, zipline, missile, battle board
NM $10 MIP $20

VEHICLES

Batcopter, 2003, Mattel, fixed Batman figure
NM $12 MIP $22

Batcycle, 2003, Mattel, fixed Batman figure
NM $10 MIP $20

Batjet, 2003, Mattel, Batman figure, 2 missiles, retractable wing
NM $10 MIP $20

Batmobile, 2003, 20", Mattel, w/ detachable Robin Cycle, recalled
NM $10 MIP $25

Batplane, 2003, Mattel, Batman figure, 2 missiles
NM $10 MIP $20

Batman & Robin (Kenner, 1997-98)

12" FIGURES

Batgirl, 1997-98, 12", Kenner
NM $15 MIP $35

Batman, 1997-98, 12", Kenner
NM $13 MIP $25

Batman and Poison Ivy, 1997-98, 12", Kenner, 2-pack, cloth outfits
NM $20 MIP $40

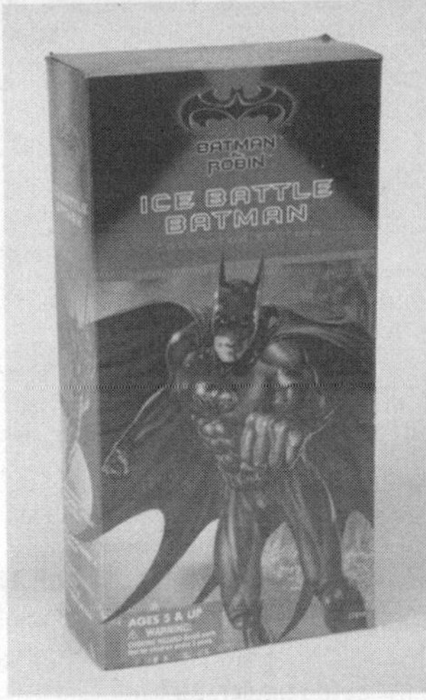

(Kenner)

Ice Battle Batman (WB Exclusive), 1997-98, 12", Kenner, Includes Batarang and Bat Laser
NM $10 MIP $25

Mr. Freeze, 1997-98, 12", Kenner
NM $10 MIP $20

Robin, 1997-98, 12", Kenner
NM $13 MIP $23

Ultimate Batman, 1997-98, 12", Kenner
NM $8 MIP $20

Ultimate Robin, 1997-98, 12", Kenner
NM $8 MIP $20

5" FIGURES

Bane, 1997, 5", Kenner, Series 1, w/double-attack axe and colossial crusher gauntlet
NM $3 MIP $8

Batgirl, 1997, 5", Kenner, w/battle blade blaster and strike scythe
NM $3 MIP $5

Batman, Ambush Attack, 1998, 5", Kenner, Series 2, w/Arsenal Cape and Restraint Rockets
NM $3 MIP $8

Batman, Battle Board with Ring, 1997-98, 5", Kenner
NM $3 MIP $8

Batman, Heat Scan, 1997, 5", Kenner, Series 1, w/opti-scope launcher and laser ray emitters
NM $3 MIP $8

Batman, Hover Attack, 1997, 5", Kenner, Series 1, w/Blasting battle sled and sickle shields
NM $3 MIP $8

Batman, Ice Blade, 1997-98, 5", Kenner
NM $3 MIP $8

Batman, Ice Blade with Ring, 1997-98, 5", Kenner
NM $3 MIP $8

Batman, Laser Cape with Ring, 1997-98, 5", Kenner
NM $3 MIP $8

Batman, Mail Away from Fuji, 1997-98, 5", Kenner
NM $5 MIP $12

Batman & Robin (Kenner, 1997-98)

Batman, Neon Armor, 1997-98, 5", Kenner
NM $3 MIP $8

Batman, Neon Armor with Ring, 1997-98, 5", Kenner
NM $3 MIP $10

Batman, Rotoblade with ring, 1997-98, 5", Kenner
NM $3 MIP $10

Batman, Sky Assault with ring, 1997-98, 5", Kenner
NM $3 MIP $10

Batman, Snow Tracker, 1997-98, 5", Kenner
NM $3 MIP $8

Batman, Thermal Shield with ring, 1998, 5", Kenner, Series 2, w/Heatblast cape and flying disc blaster
NM $3 MIP $10

Batman, Wing Blast, 1997-98, 5", Kenner
NM $3 MIP $8

Batman, Wing Blast with Ring, 1997-98, 5", Kenner
NM $3 MIP $10

Bruce Wayne, Battle Gear, 1997, 5", Kenner, Series 1, w/ice block armor suit and cryo claw shooter
NM $3 MIP $8

Frostbite, 1997-98, 5", Kenner
NM $3 MIP $8

Jungle Venom Poison Ivy, 1997, 5", Kenner, on the left, Batgirl on right; Series 1, w/ toxic spray venom cannon and entanglement vines
NM $3 MIP $5

Mr. Freeze, Ultimate Armor with Ring, 1997, 5", Kenner, Series 2, w/freeze-on missile
NM $5 MIP $10

Robin, Attack Wing with Ring, 1998, 5", Kenner, Series 2, w/vertical assault cape
NM $3 MIP $8

Robin, Blade Blast, 1998, 5", Kenner, Series 2, w/rapid deploy vine slicers and blasting battle spear
NM $3 MIP $8

Robin, Iceboard, 1997-98, 5", Kenner
NM $3 MIP $5

Robin, Razor Skate, 1997, 5", Kenner, Series 1, w/chopping blade launcher and ice battle armor
NM $3 MIP $5

Robin, Talon Strike, 1998, 5", Kenner, Series 2, w/twin capture claws and roto blade
NM $3 MIP $5

Robin, Talon Strike with Ring, 1997-98, 5", Kenner
NM $3 MIP $10

Robin, Triple Strike, 1997-98, 5", Kenner
NM $3 MIP $5

Robin, Triple Strike with Ring, 1997-98, 5", Kenner
NM $3 MIP $13

ACCESSORIES

Batmobile, 1998, 5", Kenner
NM $8 MIP $20

Batmobile, Sonic, 1998, 5", Kenner
NM $8 MIP $15

Cryo Freeze Chamber, 1998, 5", Kenner
NM $3 MIP $8

Ice Fortress, 1998, 5", Kenner
NM $5 MIP $8

Ice Hammer, 1998, 5", Kenner
NM $10 MIP $20

Iceglow Bathammer, 1997, Kenner
NM $15 MIP $30

Jet Blade, 1998, 5", Kenner
NM $8 MIP $20

NightSphere, 1998, 5", Kenner
NM $10 MIP $25

Wayne Manor Batcave, 1998, Kenner
NM $23 MIP $53

DELUXE FIGURES, 1997

Batgirl with Icestrike Cycle, 1997, 5", Kenner, w/snow assault mode and razor wheel launcher
NM $10 MIP $20

Batman, 1998, 5", Kenner
NM $5 MIP $10

Batman, Blast Wing, 1997, 5", Kenner, w/ ice chopper hover pack and freeze-seeker missile
NM $5 MIP $8

Batman, Rooftop Pursuit, 1997, 5", Kenner
NM $5 MIP $8

Mr. Freeze, Ice Terror, 1997, 5", Kenner
NM $5 MIP $8

Robin, 1998, 5", Kenner
NM $5 MIP $10

Robin, Blast Wing, 1997, 5", Kenner
NM $5 MIP $8

Robin, Glacier Battle, 1997, 5", Kenner, Tandem Assault Snow Skiff and Stinger Missile
NM $5 MIP $13

Robin, Redbird Cycle, 1997, 5", Kenner, w/ Night strike missile and ice slice blades
NM $10 MIP $20

FIGURES

Aerial Combat Batman, 1997, Kenner
NM $10 MIP $20

Mr. Freeze, Iceblast, 1997, 5", Kenner, Series 1, w/ Ice ray cannon and rocket thrusters
NM $7 MIP $12

Mr. Freeze, Jet Wing with Ring, 1998, 5", Kenner, Series 2, w/ Glacier assault wing and ice blaster
NM $10 MIP $20

TWO-PACK FIGURES, 1998

A Cold Night At Gotham, 1998, 5", Kenner
NM $5 MIP $10

Batman vs Poison Ivy, 1998, 5", Kenner
NM $20 MIP $40

Brain vs. Brawn, 1998, 5", Kenner, Batman and Bane
NM $5 MIP $10

Challengers Of The Night, 1998, 5", Kenner
NM $10 MIP $15

Guardians Of Gotham, 1998, 5", Kenner, Batman and Robin
NM $5 MIP $10

Night Hunter Robin vs. Evil Entrapment Poison Ivy, 1998, 5", Kenner
NM $5 MIP $8

Batman 100th Edition Figure

FIGURES

Batman, 1996, Hasbro, With diorama display stand
NM n/a MIP $15

Batman 200th Edition Figure

FIGURES

Batman, 2001, Hasbro, Batman Beyond figure w/ cloth wings
NM $10 MIP $20

Batman Beyond (Hasbro, 1999-01)

ACCESSORIES

Street-to-Sky Batmobile, 1999-01, Hasbro
NM $10 MIP $20

FIGURES

Ballistic Blade Batman, 1999-01, 5", Hasbro, w/ Batarang Disc Barrage
NM $5 MIP $10

Bat Hang Batman, 1999-01, 5", Hasbro, w/ covert Cape and Upside-down action
NM $5 MIP $10

Blight, 1999-01, 5", Hasbro, w/ Radiation Blaster and Plasma Missile
NM $15 MIP $25

Covert Batman, 1999-01, 5", Hasbro, w/ Shield Cape and Retriever Missile
NM $5 MIP $10

Energy Strike Batman, 1999-01, 5", Hasbro, w/ Lightning Cape and Neutron Weapons
NM $5 MIP $10

Future Knight Batman, 1999-01, 5", Hasbro, w/ Glide Wings and Electro Swords
NM $5 **MIP** $10

Hydro-Force Batman, 1999-01, 5", Hasbro, w/ Aqua Torpedo and Propulsion Armor
NM $5 **MIP** $10

J's Gang Power Throw, 1999-01, 5", Hasbro, Happy tosses Smirk!
NM $5 **MIP** $10

Laser Batman, 1999-01, 5", Hasbro, w/ Hyper Flight gear and Pulse Missile
NM $5 **MIP** $10

Lightning Storm Batman, 1999-01, 5", Hasbro, w/ Forcefields and Lightning Weapons
NM $5 **MIP** $10

Manta Racer Batman, 1999-01, 5", Hasbro, w/ Surf Sled and Stinger Tail
NM $5 **MIP** $10

Neon Camo Batman, 1999-01, 5", Hasbro, Deluxe figure w/ Pump Action Launcher and combat ready canine
NM $5 **MIP** $10

Power Armor Batman, 1999-01, 5", Hasbro, w/ Anti-Gravity and Strike R.O.B.I.N.
NM $5 **MIP** $10

Power Cape Batman, 1999-01, 5", Hasbro, w/ Jet Thrusters and Sual Batarang
NM $5 **MIP** $10

Sonar Strike Batman, 1999-01, 5", Hasbro, w/ Ramjet Rocket Pack and Dual Wing Blast
NM $5 **MIP** $10

Strato Defense Batman, 1999-01, 5", Hasbro, Deluxe figure w/ Knight hunter patrol jet & Thermal disc blaster
NM $5 **MIP** $10

Strikecycle Batman, 1999-01, 5", Hasbro, Deluxe figure
NM $5 **MIP** $10

Surface-to-Air Batman, 1999-01, 5", Hasbro, w/ Converting mobile assault cape
NM $5 **MIP** $10

The Jokerz, 1999-01, 5", Hasbro, w/ Assault Hover Cycle
NM $15 **MIP** $25

Tomorrow Armor Batman, 1999-01, 5", Hasbro, Deluxe figure
NM $7 **MIP** $12

Batman Beyond: Batlink (Hasbro 2000-01)

ACCESSORIES

Net Escape Playset, 2000-01, Hasbro
NM $10 **MIP** $20

Netrunner Batmobile, 2000-01, Hasbro
NM $10 **MIP** $15

Virtual Bat, 2000-01, Hasbro, vehicle lights up Batlink figures
NM $7 **MIP** $12

FIGURES

Circutry Storm Batman, 2000-01, 5", Hasbro
NM $5 **MIP** $10

Codebuster Batman, 2000-01, 5", Hasbro, w/ Optical Disk Phaser
NM $5 **MIP** $10

Energy Surge Batman, 2000-01, 5", Hasbro, w/ Batlink story on CD-ROM
NM $5 **MIP** $10

Firewall Robin, 2000-01, 5", Hasbro, w/Anti-virus Blaster
NM $5 **MIP** $10

Mainframe Attack Batman, 2000-01, 5", Hasbro
NM $5 **MIP** $10

Particle Burst Batman, 2000-01, 5", Hasbro, w/ Quantimizer Batarang
NM $7 **MIP** $12

Power Grid Batman, 2000-01, 5", Hasbro, w/ 5-finger Booster Shield
NM $5 **MIP** $10

Search Engine Batman, 2000-01, 5", Hasbro, w/ Cyborscope vision
NM $7 **MIP** $12

Virtual Joker, 2000-01, 5", Hasbro, w/ Virus-tech lasers and Byte mouth
NM $5 **MIP** $10

Batman Beyond: Return of the Joker (Hasbro, 2000)

FIGURES

Arkham Assault Joker, 2000, 5", Hasbro, w/ Secret image card launcher
NM $10 **MIP** $15

Golden Armor Batman, 2000, 5", Hasbro
NM $10 **MIP** $15

Gotham Defender Batman, 2000, 5", Hasbro
NM $7 **MIP** $12

Gotham Knight Batman, 2000, 5", Hasbro, w/ Jet-Booster Cape and Ion Swords
NM $10 **MIP** $20

Rapid Switch Bruce Wayne, 2000, 5", Hasbro, w/ Quick change outfit and Disk launcher
NM $7 **MIP** $12

Batman Forever (Kenner, 1995)

ACCESSORIES

Batboat, 1995, Kenner
NM $15 **MIP** $25

Batcave, 1995, Kenner, playset
NM $25 **MIP** $50

Batmobile, 1995, Kenner
NM $20 **MIP** $40

Batwing, 1995, Kenner
NM $10 **MIP** $25

Robin Cycle, 1995, Kenner, vehicle only, no figure
NM $7 **MIP** $12

Triple Action Vehicle Set, 1995, Kenner, Batmobile, Batwing, Batboat
NM $20 **MIP** $40

Wayne Manor, 1995, Kenner, playset
NM $25 **MIP** $50

FIGURES

Attack Wing Batman, 1995, 5", Kenner, Deluxe figure
NM $10 **MIP** $25

Batarang Batman, 1995, 5", Kenner, Series 2
NM $7 **MIP** $12

Blast Cape Batman, 1995, 5", Kenner, Series 1, w/ assault blades and launching attack cape
NM $10 **MIP** $15

Bruce Wayne/Batman, 1996, 5", Kenner, Target Exclusive, w/ snap-on crimefighting armor and side swords
NM $20 **MIP** $40

Fireguard Batman, 1995, 5", Kenner, Series 1, w/ spinning attack cape
NM $10 **MIP** $15

Hydro Claw Robin, 1995, 5", Kenner, Series 1, w/ aqua attack launcher and diving gear
NM $10 **MIP** $15

Ice Blade Batman, 1995, 5", Kenner, Series 2
NM $7 **MIP** $12

Laser Disc Batman, 1995, 5", Kenner, Deluxe figure
NM $10 **MIP** $25

Lightwing Batman, 1995, 5", Kenner, Deluxe figure w/ electra-glow wings and lightning launcher
NM $10 **MIP** $25

Manta Ray Batman, 1995, 5", Kenner, Series 1, w/ firing sea sled and pop-out breathing gear
NM $10 **MIP** $15

Martial Arts Robin, 1995, 5", Kenner, Deluxe figure
NM $10 **MIP** $15

Neon Armor Batman, 1995, 5", Kenner, Series 2
NM $10 **MIP** $15

Night Flight Batman, 1995, 5", Kenner, w/ winged backpack
NM $10 **MIP** $20

Night Hunter Batman, 1995, 5", Kenner, Series 1
NM $10 **MIP** $15

Power Beacon Batman, 1995, 5", Kenner, Series 2
NM $10 **MIP** $15

Recon Hunter Batman, 1995, 5", Kenner, Series 2, w/ missile firing surveillance drone
NM $10 **MIP** $15

Skyboard Robin, 1995, 5", Kenner, Series 2, w/ missile blasting pursuit vehicle
NM $10 **MIP** $15

Solar Shield Batman, 1995, 5", Kenner, Series 2
NM $10 **MIP** $15

Batman Forever (Kenner, 1995)

ACTION FIGURES

Sonar Sensor Batman, 1995, 5", Kenner, Series 1, w/ flying disc blaster and pop-up sonar scope
NM $10 MIP $15

Street Biker Robin, 1995, 5", Kenner, Series 1, w/ launching grappling hooks and battle staff
NM $10 MIP $15

Street Racer Batman, 1995, 5", Kenner, Series 2
NM $10 MIP $15

The Riddler, 1995, 5", Kenner, Target Exclusive, w/ brain drain helmet, green figure w/ silver trim
NM $20 MIP $40

The Riddler w/ Brain Drain, 1995, 5", Kenner, Series 1, w/ brain drain helmet, green figure w/ black trim
NM $3 MIP $10

The Riddler w/ Question Mark Bazooka, 1995, 5", Kenner, Series 2, w/ question mark gun, black figure w/ green trim
NM $4 MIP $12

The Talking Riddler, 1995, 5", Kenner, Deluxe figure, says three movie phrases
NM $10 MIP $20

Tide Racer Robin, 1995, 5", Kenner, Target Exclusive, w/ deep dive gear and sea claw launcher
NM $10 MIP $20

Transforming Bruce Wayne, 1995, 5", Kenner, Series 1, Target Exclusive
NM $10 MIP $15

Transforming Dick Grayson, 1995, 5", Kenner, Series 1, w/ crime fighting suit and sudden reveal mask
NM $10 MIP $15

Triple Strike Robin, 1995, 5", Kenner, Series 2
NM $7 MIP $12

Two-Face, 1995, 5", Kenner, Series 1, w/ coin
NM $10 MIP $15

Wing Blast Batman, 1995, 5", Kenner, Series 2, w/ sudden alert bio wings
NM $10 MIP $15

MULTI-PACKS

Batman v. The Riddler, 1995, 5", Kenner, Batman, Riddler
NM $20 MIP $40

Guardians of Gotham City, 1995, 5", Kenner, Batman and Robin
NM $20 MIP $40

Riddler and Two-Face, 1995, 5", Kenner
NM $20 MIP $40

Batman Movie Collection (Kenner, 1997)

FIGURES

Batman v. Catwoman, 1997, Kenner, Batman Returns, Toys R Us
NM $10 MIP $30

Batman v. Joker, 1997, Kenner, Batman movie, Toys R Us
NM $10 MIP $30

Batman v. Riddler, 1997, Kenner, Batman Forever, Toys R Us
NM $10 MIP $30

Batman Returns (Kenner, 1992-94)

FIGURES

Aerostrike Batman, 1993, 5", Kenner, Series 1
NM $5 MIP $10

Air Attack Batman, 1992, 5", Kenner, Series 1, w/ camouflage artillary gear
NM $4 MIP $10

Arctic Batman, 1992, 5", Kenner, Series 1
NM $4 MIP $10

Batman, 16", 1992-94, 16", Kenner
NM $15 MIP $50

Bola Strike Batman, 1992, 5", Kenner, Toys R Us exclusive boxed figure
NM $4 MIP $15

Bruce Wayne, 1992, 5", Kenner, Series 1, w/ quick change Batman armor
NM $5 MIP $12

Catwoman, 1992, 5", Kenner, Series 1, w/ whipping arm action and taser gun
NM $4 MIP $10

Claw Climber Batman, 1992, 5", Kenner, Toys R Us exclusive boxed figure
NM $4 MIP $10

Crime Attack Batman, 1992, 5", Kenner, Series 1
NM $4 MIP $10

Deep Dive Batman, 1992, 5", Kenner, Series 1, w/ torpedo launching scuba gear
NM $4 MIP $10

Firebolt Batman, 1992, Kenner, Toys R Us exclusive boxed electronic figure
NM $12 MIP $30

Glider Batman, 1992-94, 5", Kenner
NM $4 MIP $10

High Wire Batman, 1992-94, 5", Kenner
NM $4 MIP $10

Hydrocharge Batman, 1994, 5", Kenner, Series 2, w/ water blast missile
NM $4 MIP $10

Jungle Tracker Batman, 1994, 5", Kenner, Series 2, w/ shoulder mount launcher
NM $4 MIP $10

Laser Batman, 1992, 5", Kenner, Series 1
NM $4 MIP $10

Night Climber Batman, 1994, 5", Kenner, Series 2
NM $4 MIP $10

Penguin, 1992, 5", Kenner, Series 1
NM $8 MIP $20

Penguin Commandos, 1992, 5", Kenner, Series 1, w/ mind control gear and missiles
NM $4 MIP $15

Polar Blast Batman, 1992, 5", Kenner, Toys R Us exclusive boxed figure
NM $4 MIP $10

Powerwing Batman, 1992, 5", Kenner, Series 1, wing fires missile
NM $4 MIP $10

Robin, 1992, 5", Kenner, Series 1, On the left, shown here with Catwoman; w/ launching grappling hook
NM $5 MIP $10

Rocket Blast Batman, 1992, Kenner, Toys R Us exclusive boxed electronic figure
NM $12 MIP $20

Shadow Wing Batman, 1992, 5", Kenner, Series 1
NM $4 MIP $10

Sky Winch Batman, 1992, 5", Kenner, Series 1
NM $4 MIP $10

Thunder Strike Batman, 1992-94, 5", Kenner
NM $4 MIP $10

Thunder Whip Batman, 1992, 5", Kenner, Series 1
NM $4 MIP $10

VEHICLES

All-Terrain Batskiboat, 1992, Kenner
NM $20 MIP $40

Bat Cycle, 1992, Kenner
NM $5 MIP $20

Batcave Command Center, 1992, Kenner
NM $22 MIP $60

Batmissle Batmobile, 1992, Kenner, removable sides reveal Batmissile
NM $25 MIP $75

Batmobile, 1992, Kenner
NM $20 MIP $65

Bat-Signal Jet, 1992, Kenner
NM $4 MIP $15

Bruce Wayne Custom Coupe, 1992, Kenner
NM $12 MIP $25

Camo Attack Batmobile, 1994, Kenner
NM $22 MIP $60

Penguin Umbrella Jet, 1992, Kenner, w/2 umbrella bombs
NM $8 MIP $18

Robin Jetfoil, 1992, Kenner
NM $6 MIP $18

Sky Blade, 1992, Kenner
NM $15 MIP $35

Sky Drop, 1992, Kenner, airship w/ hidden compartment
NM $12 MIP $25

Batman: Crime Squad (Kenner, 1995-96)

ACCESSORIES

Batcycle, 1995, Kenner, Series 1 vehicle
NM $10 MIP $20

Triple Attack Jet, 1995, 5", Kenner, Series 1, Batman: The Animated Series card
NM $8 MIP $20

FIGURES

Air Assault Batman, 1995, 5", Kenner, Series 1, Batman: The Animated Series card
NM $5 MIP $10

Bomb Control Batman, 1996, 5", Kenner, Series 2, The Adventures of Batman and Robin card
NM $5 MIP $10

Disaster Control Batman, 1996, 5", Kenner, Series 2, The Adventures of Batman and Robin card
NM $5 MIP $10

Fast Pursuit Batman, 1996, 5", Kenner, Series 2, The Adventures of Batman and Robin card
NM $5 MIP $10

Land Strike Batman, 1995, 5", Kenner, Series 1, Batman: The Animated Series card
NM $5 MIP $10

Piranha Blade Batman, 1995, 5", Kenner, Series 1, Batman: The Animated Series card
NM $5 MIP $10

Sea Claw Batman, 1995, 5", Kenner, Series 1, Batman: The Animated Series card
NM $5 MIP $10

Ski Blast Robin, 1995, 5", Kenner, Series 1, Batman: The Animated Series card
NM $5 MIP $10

Skycopter Batman, 1996, 5", Kenner, Series 2, Deluxe figure, Batman: The Adventures of Batman and Robin
NM $5 MIP $10

Stealthwing Batman, 1995, 5", Kenner, Series 1, Batman: The Animated Series card
NM $5 MIP $10

Supersonic Batman, 1996, 5", Kenner, Series 2, The Adventures of Batman and Robin card
NM $5 MIP $10

Torpedo Batman, 1995, 5", Kenner, Series 1, Batman: The Animated Series card
NM $5 MIP $10

Tri-Wing Batman, 1996, 5", Kenner, Series 2, Deluxe figure, Batman: The Adventures of Batman and Robin, w/ Techno-glide backpack
NM $8 MIP $15

Batman: Knight Force Ninjas (Hasbro, 1998-99)

FIGURES

Arsenal Cape Batman, 1999, 7", Kenner, Series 3
NM $5 MIP $10

Batman Ally Azrael, 1998, 7", Kenner, Series 2
NM $3 MIP $10

Batman vs. The Joker, 1998, 7", Kenner, Series 1
NM $8 MIP $12

Fist Fury Batman, 1998, 7", Kenner, Series 2
NM $3 MIP $10

Hyper Crush Robin, 1999, 7", Kenner, Series 3
NM $7 MIP $12

Karate Chop Batman, 1998, 7", Kenner, Series 1
NM $3 MIP $10

Knight Blade Batman, 1999, 7", Kenner, Series 3
NM $3 MIP $10

Multi-Blast Batman, 1998, 7", Kenner, rare
NM $3 MIP $10

Power Kick Batman, 1998, 7", Kenner, Series 1
NM $3 MIP $10

Side Strike Robin, 1998, 7", Kenner, Series 1
NM $3 MIP $10

Tail Whip Killer Croc, 1998, 7", Kenner, Series 1
NM $3 MIP $10

Thunder Kick Batman, 1998, 7", Kenner, Series 2
NM $3 MIP $10

Tornado Blade Riddler, 1998, 7", Kenner, Series 2
NM $3 MIP $10

VEHICLES

Knight Force Batmobile, 1998, 7", Kenner
NM $8 MIP $18

Batman: Legends of Batman (Kenner 1994-96)

12" FIGURES

Batman vs. Catwoman, 1994-96, 12", Kenner, figures in cloth costumes
NM $20 MIP $40

ACCESSORIES

Batcycle, 1994, Kenner, w/ Batman rider
NM $10 MIP $25

Batmobile, 1994-96, Kenner, w/ missile detonator and quick lift canopy
NM $15 MIP $35

Sky Bat, 1994-96, Kenner, w/ wing mount missile and menacing jaw attack
NM $20 MIP $40

FIGURES

Buccaneer Batman, 1996, 5", Kenner, Series 3, w/ slamming mace actions and pirate sword
NM $3 MIP $10

Catwoman, 1994, 5", Kenner, Series 1, w/ quick climb claw and capture net
NM $3 MIP $10

Crusader Batman, 1994, 5", Kenner, Series 1, w/ punching action
NM $3 MIP $10

Crusader Robin, 1995, 5", Kenner, Series 2, w/ firing crossbow and battle shield
NM $3 MIP $10

Cyborg Batman, 1994, 5", Kenner, Series 1, w/ light-up eye and laser weapon
NM $3 MIP $10

Dark Rider Batman, 1994, 5", Kenner, Series 1, featuring battle stallion
NM $10 MIP $18

Dark Warrior Batman, 1995, 5", Kenner, Series 2, w/ slamming mace attack
NM $3 MIP $10

Desert Knight Batman, 1995, 5", Kenner, Series 2, Deluxe figure w/ whirling scimitar swords and double battle axes
NM $6 MIP $15

First Mate Robin, 1996, 5", Kenner, Series 3, blasting cannon and cutlass sword
NM $3 MIP $10

Flightpak Batman, 1995, 5", Kenner, Series 2, Deluxe figure w/ battle ready jet-wing
NM $6 MIP $15

Future Batman, 1994, 5", Kenner, Series 1, w/ pop-up aero-power wings
NM $3 MIP $10

Gladiator Batman, 1996, 5", Kenner, Series 3, w/ spear launcher
NM $3 MIP $10

Knightquest Batman, 1994, 5", Kenner, Series 1, Azrael w/ Battle wings and blazing missile
NM $3 MIP $10

Knightsend Batman, 1995, 5", Kenner, Series 2, Jean-Paul Valley w/ Arial torpedo launcher
NM $3 MIP $10

Long Bow Batman, 1995, 5", Kenner, Series 2, w/ arrow slinging assault
NM $3 MIP $10

Nightwing, 1994, 5", Kenner, Series 1, w/ super-strike rocket launcher
NM $3 MIP $10

Power Guardian Batman, 1994, 5", Kenner, Series 1, w/ real sword fighting action and shield
NM $3 MIP $10

Samuri Batman, 1995, 5", Kenner, Series 2, w/ slashing sword and banner
NM $3 MIP $10

Silver Knight Batman, 1995, 5", Kenner, Series 2, Deluxe figure w/ smashing battle axe and slashing sword
NM $6 MIP $15

The Joker, 1994, 5", Kenner, Series 1, w/ snapping jaw
NM $3 MIP $10

The Laughing Man Joker, 1996, 5", Kenner, Series 3, w/ gatling gun, pirate outfit
NM $3 MIP $10

The Riddler, 1995, 5", Kenner, Series 2, w/ firing question mark ammo
NM $3 MIP $10

Ultra Armor Batman, 1996, 5", Kenner, Series 3, Azrael w/ blasting battle cannon
NM $5 MIP $12

Viking Batman, 1995, 5", Kenner, Series 2, w/ battle axe and shield
NM $3 MIP $10

Batman: Legends of Batman (Kenner 1994-96)

MULTI-PACKS

Egyptian Batman and Egyptian Catwoman, 1994-96, 5", Kenner
NM $5 MIP $12

Pirate Batman vs. Pirate Two-Face, 1994-96, 5", Kenner
NM $5 MIP $12

Batman: Legends of the Dark Knight (Kenner, 1996-98)

ACCESSORIES

Skywing Street Bike, 1996, Kenner, w/Batman figure
NM $12 MIP $25

FIGURES

Assault Gauntlet Batman, 1996, 6.5", Kenner, w/ Neural pumped power and Spike strike missile gloves
NM $3 MIP $10

Bat Attack Batman, 1997, 6.5", Kenner
NM $3 MIP $10

Batgirl, 1998, 6.5", Kenner, w/ Knightscan wings and Batarang
NM $3 MIP $10

Batman The Dark Knight, 1998, 6.5", Kenner, blue and gray costume
NM $12 MIP $25

Batman The Dark Knight, 1998, 6.5", Kenner, black costume re-issue
NM $6 MIP $12

Clayface, 1996-98, 6.5", Kenner, Internet exclusive
NM $8 MIP $16

Dark Knight Detective Batman, 1996-98, 6.5", Kenner, Internet exclusive
NM $15 MIP $35

Dive Claw Robin, 1996, 6.5", Kenner, w/ Blast Attack Missile and Power Glide Wings
NM $3 MIP $10

Glacier Shield Batman, 1997, 6.5", Kenner
NM $3 MIP $10

Jungle Rage Robin, 1998, 6.5", Kenner, w/ Battle Staff and Utility Gauntlet
NM $3 MIP $10

Laughing Gas Joker, 1997, 6.5", Kenner
NM $5 MIP $10

Lava Fury Batman, 1998, 6.5", Kenner, w/ Solar arrary wings, fire swallower blast shield
NM $3 MIP $10

Lethal Impact Bane, 1996-98, 6.5", Kenner, w/ venom-powered punch and stinger gauntlet
NM $3 MIP $10

Man-Bat, 1998, 6.5", Kenner
NM $3 MIP $10

Neutral Claw Batman, 1996, 6.5", Kenner
NM $3 MIP $10

Panther Prowl Catwoman, 1997, 6.5", Kenner, w/ Battle panther exoskeleton
NM $3 MIP $10

Penguin, 1998, 6.5", Kenner, w/ Spinning Attack Umbrella
NM $3 MIP $10

Shatter Blade Batman, 1996-98, 6.5", Kenner, w/ Assault cape and arm swords
NM $3 MIP $10

Spline Cape Batman, 1996, 6.5", Kenner
NM $3 MIP $10

Twister Strike Scarecrow, 1996, 6.5", Kenner, w/ Scythe Slash attack and Nightmare glow eyes
NM $3 MIP $10

Underwater Assault Batman, 1998, 6.5", Kenner
NM $3 MIP $10

Batman: Mask of the Phantasm (Kenner, 1994)

FIGURES

Decoy Batman, 1994, 5", Kenner
NM $5 MIP $10

Jet Pack Joker (green face), 1994, 5", Kenner
NM $5 MIP $10

Jet Pack Joker (white face), 1994, 5", Kenner
NM $5 MIP $10

Phantasm, 1994, 5", Kenner
NM $12 MIP $20

Rapid Attack Batman, 1994, 5", Kenner, also released on Batman: The Animated Series card
NM $5 MIP $10

Retro Batman, 1994, 5", Kenner
NM $5 MIP $10

Tornado Batman, 1994, 5", Kenner, also released on Batman: The Animated Series card
NM $5 MIP $10

Total Armor Batman, 1994, 5", Kenner
NM $5 MIP $10

Batman: Mission Masters (Hasbro, 1997-2002)

SERIES 1 FIGURES

Anti-Blaze Batman, 1997-2002, 5", Hasbro, Series 1
NM $3 MIP $7

Arctic Blast Robin, 1997-2002, 5", Hasbro, Series 1
NM $3 MIP $7

Cave Climber Batman, 1997-2002, 5", Hasbro, Series 1
NM $3 MIP $7

Desert Attack Batman, 1997-2002, 5", Hasbro, Series 1
NM $3 MIP $7

Glider Strike Batman, 1997-2002, 5", Hasbro, Series 1
NM $3 MIP $7

Insect-Body Mr. Freeze, 1997-2002, 5", Hasbro, Series 1, head detaches from body, attaches to insect legs
NM $3 MIP $7

Jungle Tracker Batman, 1997-2002, 5", Hasbro, Series 1
NM $3 MIP $7

Mr. Freeze, 1997-2002, 5", Hasbro, Series 1
NM $5 MIP $7

Rumble Ready Riddler, 1997-2002, 5", Hasbro, Series 1
NM $6 MIP $15

Slalom Racer Batman, 1997-2002, 5", Hasbro, Series 1
NM $3 MIP $7

Speedboat Batman, 1997-2002, 5", Hasbro, Series 1
NM $3 MIP $7

SERIES 2 FIGURES

Arctic Ambush Robin, 1997-2002, 5", Hasbro, Series 2
NM $3 MIP $7

Desert Attack Batman, 1997-2002, 5", Hasbro, Series 2
NM $3 MIP $7

Hydro Assault Joker, 1997-2002, 5", Hasbro, Series 2
NM $3 MIP $8

Knight Strike Batman, 1997-2002, 5", Hasbro, Series 2
NM $3 MIP $7

Land Strike Batman, 1997-2002, 5", Hasbro, Series 2
NM $3 MIP $7

Radar Batman, 1997-2002, 5", Hasbro, Series 2, Deluxe figure
NM $3 MIP $7

Sea Claw Batman, 1997-2002, 5", Hasbro, Series 2
NM $3 MIP $7

Skychopper Batman, 1997-2002, 5", Hasbro, Series 2, Deluxe figure
NM $3 MIP $7

SERIES 3 FIGURES

Capture Cape Batman, 1997-2002, 5", Hasbro, Series 3
NM $3 MIP $7

Firewing Batman, 1997-2002, 5", Hasbro, Series 3
NM $3 MIP $7

Freestyle Skate Batman, 1997-2002, 5", Hasbro, Series 3
NM $3 MIP $7

Gotham Crusader Batman, 1997-2002, 5", Hasbro, Series 3
NM $3 MIP $7

Ground Pursuit Batman, 1997-2002, 5", Hasbro, Series 3
NM $3 MIP $7

Highwire Zip Line Batman, 1997-2002, 5", Hasbro, Series 3
NM $3 MIP $7

Inferno Extinction Batman, 1997-2002, 5", Hasbro, Series 3
NM $3 MIP $7

Knight Assault Batman, 1997-2002, 5", Hasbro, Series 3
NM $3 MIP $7

Mountain Pursuit Batman, 1997-2002, 5", Hasbro, Series 3
NM $3 MIP $7

Quick Attack Batman, 1997-2002, 5", Hasbro, Series 3
NM $3 MIP $7

Sky Attack Batman, 1997-2002, 5", Hasbro, Series 3
NM $3 MIP $7

Virus Attack Mr. Freeze, 1997-2002, 5", Hasbro, Series 3
NM $3 MIP $7

Virus Delete Batman, 1997-2002, 5", Hasbro, Series 3
NM $3 MIP $7

SERIES 4 ACCESSORIES

B.A.T.V., 1997-2002, 5", Hasbro, Batman all-terrain vehicle and projectile launcher w/ Batman figure
NM $10 MIP $20

Team Batcycle, 1997-2002, 5", Hasbro, w/ Batman and Nightwing
NM $15 MIP $25

SERIES 4 FIGURES

Attack Wing Batman, 1997-2002, 5", Hasbro, Deluxe figure w/ flight mechanized wings
NM $10 MIP $7

Battle Staff Batman, 1997-2002, 5", Hasbro, w/ Hover Jet
NM $3 MIP $7

Jet Wing Batman, 1997-2002, 5", Hasbro, w/ Rocket Strike Blaster
NM $3 MIP $7

Lunar Force Batman, 1997-2002, 5", Hasbro, w/ Night Attack Wing
NM $3 MIP $7

Midnight Hunter Batman, 1997-2002, 5", Hasbro
NM $3 MIP $7

Midnight Pursuit Batman, 1997-2002, 5", Hasbro, w/ Night Assault Jet
NM $3 MIP $7

Midnight Rescue Batman, 1997-2002, 5", Hasbro, w/ Strike Wing
NM $3 MIP $7

Night Assault Batman, 1997-2002, 5", Hasbro, Deluxe figure w/ Land Runner
NM $3 MIP $7

Night Fury Robin, 1997-2002, 5", Hasbro, w/ Triple Bolo Striker
NM $3 MIP $7

Night Shadow Batman, 1997-2002, 5", Hasbro
NM $3 MIP $7

Night Spark Joker, 1997-2002, 5", Hasbro, w/ Wildcard Launcher
NM $3 MIP $8

Photon Armor Batman, 1997-2002, 5", Hasbro, w/ Shadow Blast Cape
NM $3 MIP $7

Rocket Blast Mr. Freeze, 1997-2002, 5", Hasbro, w/ Ice Disk Launcher
NM $4 MIP $9

Shadow Blast Batman, 1997-2002, 5", Hasbro, Deluxe figure w/ Night Charge Hoverpack
NM $3 MIP $7

Shadow Copter Batman, 1997-2002, 5", Hasbro, Deluxe figure w/ Night Sting Missile
NM $3 MIP $7

Tunnel Racer Batman, 1997-2002, 5", Hasbro, w/ Lightning Luge and Homing Batarang
NM $3 MIP $7

Turbo Force Nightwing, 1997-2002, 5", Hasbro, Deluxe figure w/ Dual Mode Action Craft
NM $4 MIP $9

Velocity Storm Batman, 1997-2002, 5", Hasbro, w/ High Speed Glider
NM $3 MIP $7

SERIES 4 MULTI-PACKS

Night Shadow Batman and Night Fury Robin, 1997-2002, 5", Hasbro, w/ Hyper-Speed Stun Rockets and Triple Bolo Striker
NM $10 MIP $20

Batman: Spectrum of the Bat (Hasbro, 2000-01)

FIGURES

Fractal Armor Batman, 2000-01, 5", Hasbro
NM $2 MIP $5

Gamma Blast Batman, 2000-01, 5", Hasbro
NM $2 MIP $5

Infared Armor Batman, 2000-01, 5", Hasbro
NM $2 MIP $5

Signal Hacker Batman, 2000-01, 5", Hasbro
NM $2 MIP $5

Sonic Stun Batgirl, 2000-01, 5", Hasbro
NM $4 MIP $8

Sub-Frequency Armor Batman, 2000-01, 5", Hasbro
NM $2 MIP $5

Sub-Pulse Detonator Robin, 2000-01, 5", Hasbro
NM $2 MIP $5

Technocast Catwoman, 2000-01, 5", Hasbro
NM $4 MIP $8

Technocast Jervis Tetch, 2000-01, 5", Hasbro, a.k.a. the Mad Hatter
NM $4 MIP $8

Terrorcast Joker, 2000-01, 5", Hasbro
NM $2 MIP $6

Ultra-Frequency Armor Batman, 2000-01, 5", Hasbro
NM $2 MIP $5

Ultraviolet Ambush Batman, 2000-01, 5", Hasbro
NM $2 MIP $5

X-Ray Assailant Robin, 2000-01, 5", Hasbro
NM $2 MIP $5

Batman: The Adventures of Batman and Robin (Kenner, 1996-97)

DUO FORCE

Air Strike Robin, 1996, 5", Kenner, Series 1
NM $5 MIP $10

Cycle Thruster Batman, 1997, 5", Kenner, Series 2
NM $5 MIP $10

Hydro Storm Robin, 1997, 5", Kenner, Series 2
NM $5 MIP $10

Mr. Freeze, 1996, 5", Kenner, Series 1
NM $5 MIP $10

The Riddler Roto Chopper, 1997, 5", Kenner, Series 2
NM $5 MIP $10

Turbo Surge Batman, 1996, 5", Kenner, Series 1
NM $5 MIP $10

Vector Wing Batman, 1996, 5", Kenner, Series 1
NM $5 MIP $10

Wind Blitz Batgirl, 1997, 5", Kenner, Series 2 Sky Glider and Wave Racer
NM $5 MIP $10

MULTI-PACKS

Rogues Gallery, 1997, 5", Kenner, Figure 8-pack w/ Catwoman, Killer Croc, Man-Bat, Poison Ivy, Scarecrow, Joker, Phantasm, Clayface
NM $25 MIP $55

SERIES 1

Bane, 1996, 5", Kenner, w/ Body slam arm action and venom tube
NM $5 MIP $10

Hover Jet Batman, 1996, 5", Kenner
NM $5 MIP $10

Paraglide Batman, 1996, 5", Kenner, w/ Dive Bomb Sky Wing
NM $5 MIP $10

Pogo Stick Joker, 1996, 5", Kenner, w/ Power Launcher
NM $5 MIP $10

Ra's Al Ghul, 1996, 5", Kenner, w/ Strike Shooter and Combat Sword
NM $5 MIP $10

Rocketpack Batman, 1996, 5", Kenner
NM $5 MIP $10

SERIES 1 ACCESSORIES

Nightsphere, 1996, Kenner, w/ Batman figure
NM $20 MIP $40

SERIES 2

Bola Trap Robin, 1997, 5", Hasbro, Also released in Batman: The Animated Series figures
NM $5 MIP $10

Harley Quinn, 1997, 5", Kenner, w/ Knockout Punching Glove and Trick Pistol
NM $5 MIP $10

Batman: The Adventures of Batman and Robin (Kenner, 1996-97)

Joker Machine Gun, 1997, 5", Kenner, w/ Machine Gun and Joke-A-Matic Time Bomb
NM $5 **MIP** $10

Batman: The Animated Series (Kenner, 1992-95)

ACCESSORIES

AeroBat, 1992, Kenner
NM $12 **MIP** $25

B.A.T.V. Vehicle, 1992, Kenner
NM $10 **MIP** $20

Batcave, 1993, Kenner, playset
NM $50 **MIP** $125

Batcycle, 1992, Kenner, w/ Batman figure
NM $10 **MIP** $20

Batcycle, 1992, Kenner, with Nightwing
NM $10 **MIP** $20

Batmobile, 1992, Kenner
NM $22 **MIP** $55

Bat-Signal Jet, 1992, Kenner
NM $10 **MIP** $20

Crime Stalker, 1992, Kenner
NM $10 **MIP** $20

Hoverbat Vehicle, 1992, Kenner
NM $5 **MIP** $15

Ice Hammer, 1994, Kenner
NM $10 **MIP** $15

Joker Mobile, 1992, Kenner
NM $12 **MIP** $25

Robin Dragster, 1992, Kenner, very rare
NM $75 **MIP** $225

Street Jet, 1993, Kenner
NM $15 **MIP** $25

Turbo Batplane, 1992, Kenner
NM $6 **MIP** $20

FIGURES

Anti-Freeze Batman, 1994, 5", Kenner, Series 3, w/ Firing Shield and Blaster
NM $4 **MIP** $10

(Lenny Lee)

Bane, 1995, 5", Kenner, Series 4, w/ "Body Slam" action and venom tube
NM $4 **MIP** $10

Battle-Helmet Batman, 1995, Kenner, mail-order figure
NM $12 **MIP** $25

Bola Trap Robin, 1994, 5", Kenner, Series 3
NM $4 **MIP** $10

Bruce Wayne, 1993, 5", Kenner, Series 2
NM $4 **MIP** $10

Catwoman, 1993, 5", Kenner, Series 2, w/ Whipping arm action and Claw Hook
NM $7 **MIP** $25

Clayface, 1994, 5", Kenner, Series 3
NM $5 **MIP** $20

Combat Belt Batman, 1992, 5", Kenner, Series 1
NM $12 **MIP** $30

Cyber Gear Batman, 1995, 5", Kenner, Series 4
NM $4 **MIP** $10

Dick Grayson/Robin, 1994, 5", Kenner, Series 3
NM $5 **MIP** $12

Glider Robin, 1995, 5", Kenner, Series 4, w/ Winged Jet Pack and Firing Claw
NM $4 **MIP** $10

Ground Assault Batman, 1994, 5", Kenner, Deluxe figure w/ Motorized turbo-powered ground jet
NM $4 **MIP** $10

High-Wire Batman, 1994, 5", Kenner, Deluxe figure w/ Quick Escape Cable Wire and Cable-Riding Action
NM $10 **MIP** $30

Infrared Batman, 1993, 5", Kenner, Series 2 w/ Launching Bat-Signal Disks
NM $4 **MIP** $10

Joker, 1993, 5", Kenner, Series 2 w/Laughing gas spray gun
NM $5 **MIP** $15

Killer Croc, 1994, 5", Kenner, Series 3 w/ Power punch arm and pet crocodile
NM $5 **MIP** $12

Knight Star Batman, 1994, 5", Kenner, Series 3 w/ Star Blade Rocket Launcher
NM $4 **MIP** $10

Lightning Strike Batman, 1994, 5", Kenner, Series 3 w/ Transforming Cape Glider
NM $4 **MIP** $10

Manbat, 1993, 5", Kenner, Series 2
NM $7 **MIP** $15

Mech-Wing Batman, 1994, 5", Kenner, Deluxe figure w/ Mechanized Soaring Wings and pop-out wing action
NM $4 **MIP** $10

Mr. Freeze, 1994, 5", Kenner, Series 3 w/ Firing Ice Blaster
NM $7 **MIP** $15

Ninja Robin, 1993, 5", Kenner, Series 2 w/ chopping arm action and ninja weapons
NM $4 **MIP** $10

Penguin, 1992, 5", Kenner, Series 1
NM $20 **MIP** $50

Poison Ivy, 1994, 5", Kenner, Series 3, w/ crossbow and Venus Flytrap weapon
NM $18 **MIP** $25

Power Vision Batman, 1994, 5", Kenner, Deluxe figure w/ electric light up eyes, firing missile
NM $4 **MIP** $10

Radar Scope Batman, 1995, 5", Kenner, Series 4
NM $4 **MIP** $10

Rapid Attack Batman, 1994, 5", Kenner, Series 3 w/ Escape Hook and Utility Belt
NM $4 **MIP** $10

Riddler, 1992, 5", Kenner, Series 1 w/ Question mark launcher
NM $8 **MIP** $20

Robin, 1992, 5", Kenner, Series 1 with Turbo Glider
NM $4 **MIP** $10

Scarecrow, 1993, 5", Kenner, Series 2
NM $7 **MIP** $15

Sky Dive Batman, 1993, 5", Kenner, Series 2 w/ working parachute
NM $4 **MIP** $10

Tornado Batman, 1994, 5", Kenner, Series 3 w/ Whirling Weapon
NM $4 **MIP** $10

Turbojet Batman, 1992, 5", Kenner, Series 1 w/ Firing Wrist Rocket & Pivoting Engines
NM $4 **MIP** $10

Two Face, 1992, 5", Kenner, Series 1
NM $7 **MIP** $20

Ultimate Batman (16"), 1994, 16", Kenner
NM $22 **MIP** $60

MULTI-PACKS

Ninja Batman and Robin, 1994, 5", Kenner, w/ Duo-power Ninja weapons
NM $10 **MIP** $20

Batman: The Dark Knight Collection (Kenner, 1990-91)

ACCESSORIES

Batcycle, 1990-91, Kenner
NM $10 **MIP** $20

Batjet, 1990, Kenner
NM $25 **MIP** $45

Batmobile, 1990-91, Kenner
NM $55 MIP $95

Batwing, 1990-91, Kenner
NM $25 MIP $65

Bola Bullet, 1991, Kenner
NM $20 MIP $35

The Joker Cycle, 1990-91, Kenner
NM $8 MIP $15

FIGURES

Blast Shield Batman, 1990-91, 5", Kenner, Deluxe figure, boxed
NM $12 MIP $25

Bruce Wayne, 1990, 5", Kenner, Series 1, w/ quick change suit
NM $10 MIP $20

Claw Climber Batman, 1990-91, 5", Kenner, Deluxe figure, boxed
NM $12 MIP $25

Crime Attack Batman, 1990, 5", Kenner, Series 1, w/ batarang and claw
NM $10 MIP $20

Iron Winch Batman, 1990, 5", Kenner, Series 1, w/ batarang winch
NM $10 MIP $20

Knockout Joker, 1991, 5", Kenner, Series 2
NM $15 MIP $50

Night Glider Batman, 1990-91, 5", Kenner, Deluxe figure, boxed
NM $20 MIP $35

Power Wing Batman, 1991, 5", Kenner, Series 2
NM $12 MIP $25

Shadow Wing Batman, 1990, 5", Kenner, Series 1, w/ cape spreading pop-up arms and handcuffs
NM $10 MIP $20

Sky Escape Joker, 1990, 5", Kenner, Series 1, w/ whirling copter pack
NM $15 MIP $25

Tec-Shield Batman, 1990, 5", Kenner, Series 1, w/flight pack and gold shield suit
NM $10 MIP $20

Thunder Whip Batman, 1991, 5", Kenner, Series 2
NM $12 MIP $25

Wall Scaler Batman, 1990, 5", Kenner, Series 1, w/ climbing action pack
NM $10 MIP $20

Batman: The New Batman Adventures (Hasbro, 1997-2000)

ACCESSORIES

Batmobile, 1997-2000, Hasbro, fits Batman, Robin or Nightwing figure
NM $25 MIP $40

Joker Toxic Lab, 2000, Hasbro
NM $12 MIP $25

FIGURES

Crime Fighter Robin, 1997, 5", Hasbro
NM $4 MIP $10

Crime Solver Nightwing, 1997, 5", Hasbro
NM $4 MIP $10

Detective Batman, 1997, 5", Hasbro
NM $8 MIP $20

Force Shield Nightwing, 1998, 5", Hasbro
NM $3 MIP $8

Heavy Artillery Batman, 1998, 5", Hasbro
NM $3 MIP $8

Hydrojet Nightwing, 1998, 5", Hasbro, Deluxe figure
NM $10 MIP $15

Knight Glider Batman, 1998, 5", Hasbro
NM $3 MIP $8

Mad Hatter, 1997, 5", Hasbro
NM $5 MIP $10

Shatter Blade Batman, 1998, 5", Hasbro
NM $3 MIP $8

Silver Defender Batman, 1998, 5", Hasbro, Deluxe figure
NM $10 MIP $15

Street Strike Batman, 1998, 5", Hasbro
NM $7 MIP $12

The Creeper, 1998, 5", Hasbro
NM $3 MIP $8

Undercover Bruce Wayne, 1998, 5", Hasbro
NM $3 MIP $10

Wildcard Joker, 1998, 5", Hasbro
NM $5 MIP $15

MULTI-PACKS

Arkham Asylum Escape (4-pack): Batman, Two-Face, Poison Ivy, Harley Quinn, 1997-2000, 5", Hasbro
NM $12 MIP $25

Arkham Asylum Escape: Batman v. Two-Face, 2000, 5", Hasbro
NM $8 MIP $18

Batman and Robin, 2000, 5", Hasbro, Wal-Mart exclusive
NM $8 MIP $18

Batman and Superman, 2000, 5", Hasbro, Wal-Mart exclusive
NM $8 MIP $18

Batman Figure (4-pack): Batman, Robin, Alfred, Clayface, 1997-2000, 5", Hasbro
NM $8 MIP $18

Batman v. Joker, 2000, 5", Hasbro, Wal-Mart exclusive
NM $28 MIP $45

Knight Force (4-pack): Batman, Robin, Nightwing, Batgirl, 1997-2000, 5", Hasbro
NM $8 MIP $18

World's Finest: Batman and Superman, 2001, 5", Hasbro, Wal-Mart exclusive
NM $8 MIP $40

Batman: The New Batman Adventures (Hasbro, 1998-99)

12" FIGURES

Batgirl, 1998-99, Hasbro
NM $12 MIP $30

Batman, 1998-99, Hasbro, The most valuable figure in this series
NM $20 MIP $60

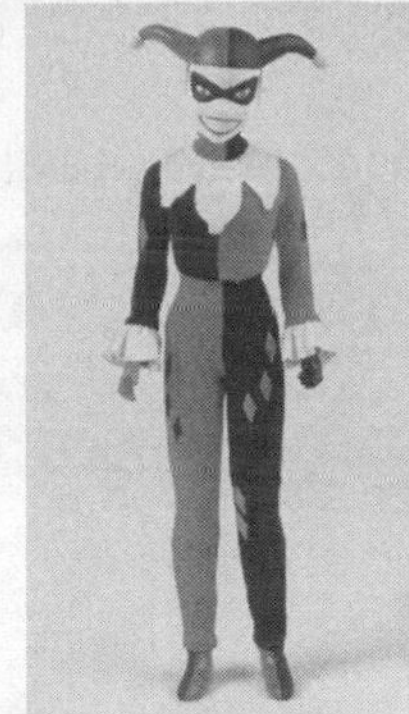

Harley Quinn, 1998-99, Hasbro, Mr. J's favorite henchperson
NM $10 MIP $20

Joker, 1998-99, Hasbro
NM $10 MIP $38

Nightwing, 1998-99, Hasbro
NM $10 MIP $30

Robin, 1998-99, Hasbro
NM $10 MIP $40

Batman: World of Batman (Hasbro, 2001)

FIGURES

Aqua Sled Batman, 2001, 5", Hasbro, w/ sub-marine assault sled and scuba armor
NM $3 MIP $10

Hover Jet Batman, 2001, 5", Hasbro, w/ blasting battle sled
NM $3 MIP $10

Plasma Glow Joker, 2001, 5", Hasbro
NM $3 MIP $10

Quick Change Bruce Wayne, 2001, 5", Hasbro
NM $3 MIP $10

Radar Scope Batman, 2001, 5", Hasbro, w/ pulse-scan blaster
NM $3 MIP $10

Rapid Attack Robin, 2001, 5", Hasbro
NM $3 MIP $10

MULTI-PACKS

Batman 2-Pack, 2001, 5", Hasbro, Gotham City Adventures Batman and Knight Watch Batman
NM $8 MIP $18

Battlestar Galactica (Mattel, 1978-79)

12" FIGURES

Colonial Warrior, 1979, 12", Mattel
NM $30 MIP $85

Battlestar Galactica (Mattel, 1978-79)

Cylon Centurian, 1979, 12", Mattel, Silver armor
NM $30 **MIP** $95

3-3/4" FIGURES, SERIES 1, 1978

Commander Adama, 1978, 3-3/4", Mattel, With cloth robe and laser pistol, shown with Starbuck
NM $15 **MIP** $40

Cylon Centurian, 1978, 3-3/4", Mattel
NM $15 **MIP** $40

Daggit (brown), 1978, 3-3/4", Mattel
NM $15 **MIP** $30

Daggit (tan), 1978, 3-3/4", Mattel, shown with Imperious Leader
NM $15 **MIP** $30

Imperious Leader, 1978, 3-3/4", Mattel, With red-purple cloth robe
NM $15 **MIP** $30

Ovion, 1978, 3-3/4", Mattel
NM $12 **MIP** $35

Starbuck, 1978, 3-3/4", Mattel
NM $15 **MIP** $40

3-3/4" FIGURES, SERIES 2, 1979

Baltar, 1979, 3-3/4", Mattel
NM $30 **MIP** $75

Boray, 1979, 3-3/4", Mattel
NM $30 **MIP** $75

Cylon Commander, 1979, 3-3/4", Mattel
NM $55 **MIP** $110

Lucifer, 1979, 3-3/4", Mattel
NM $55 **MIP** $110

ACCESSORIES

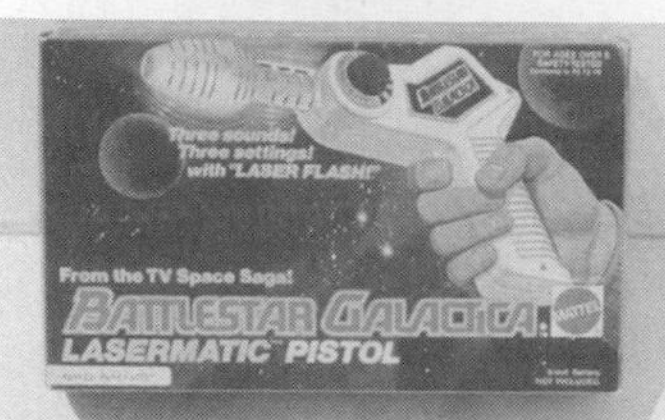

Lasermatic Pistol, 1978, Mattel, Barrel lights up when fired, has three different laser-firing sounds
NM $35 **MIP** $75

VEHICLES

Colonial Scarab, 1978-79, Mattel, 1978 versions came w/ red missiles, 1979 versions didn't
NM $25 **MIP** $75

Colonial Stellar Probe, 1978-79, Mattel, 1978 versions came w/ red missiles, 1979 versions didn't
NM $30 **MIP** $80

Colonial Viper, 1978-79, Mattel, 1978 editions came w/ red missiles, 1979 editions didn't
NM $30 **MIP** $75

Cylon Raider, 1978-79, Mattel, 1978 editions came w/ red missiles, 1979 editions didn't
NM $30 **MIP** $85

Beavis & Butthead (Moore, 1998)

FIGURES

Beavis, 1998, Moore
NM $4 **MIP** $10

Butthead, 1998, Moore
NM $4 **MIP** $10

Cornholio, 1998, Moore
NM $5 **MIP** $12

Beetlejuice (Kenner, 1989-90)

ACCESSORIES

Creepy Cruiser, 1989-90, Kenner
NM $3 **MIP** $13

Gross Out Meter, 1990, Kenner
NM $7 **MIP** $15

Phantom Flyer, 1989-90, Kenner
NM $4 **MIP** $8

Snake Mask, 1989-90, Kenner
NM $4 **MIP** $8

Vanishing Vault, 1989-90, Kenner
NM $5 **MIP** $10

FIGURES

Adam Maitland, 1989-90, Kenner
NM $4 **MIP** $10

(Lenny Lee)

Exploding Beetlejuice, 1989-90, Kenner, Body flies apart to reveal bug. Also includes smaller dragon figure
NM $3 **MIP** $5

Harry the Haunted Hunter, 1989-90, Kenner
NM $4 **MIP** $10

Old Buzzard, 1989-90, Kenner
NM $4 **MIP** $10

Otho the Obnoxious, 1989-90, Kenner
NM $4 **MIP** $10

Shipwreck Beetlejuice, 1989-90, Kenner
NM $3 **MIP** $8

Shish Kabab Beetlejuice, 1989-90, Kenner
NM $3 **MIP** $8

Showtime Beetlejuice, 1989-90, Kenner
NM $3 **MIP** $8

Spinhead Beetlejuice, 1989-90, Kenner
NM $3 **MIP** $8

Street Rat, 1989-90, Kenner
NM $4 **MIP** $10

Talking Beetlejuice, 1989-90, 12", Kenner
NM $18 **MIP** $38

Teacher Creature, 1989-90, Kenner
NM $5 **MIP** $10

Best of the West (Marx, 1965-75)

ACCESSORIES

Buckboard with Horse & Harness, 1967-75, Marx, #4424, with Thunderbolt
NM $105 **MIP** $235

Buckskin Horse, 1967, Marx, #2036, for 12" figures, head nods and neck bends
NM $65 **MIP** $110

Circle X Ranch Playset, 1967, 4', Marx, #5275, 22 pieces, cardboard, rare
NM $210 **MIP** $325

Comanche Horse, 1967, Marx, #1861, for 12" figures, head and leg articulation
NM $65 **MIP** $125

Covered Wagon, 1967-75, 34", Marx, #4434, with horse and harness
NM $120 **MIP** $240

Flame Horse, 1966, Marx, #2081, for 12" figures, legs in trotting pose
NM $65 **MIP** $130

Fort Apache Playset, 1967, Marx, #1875, scaled for 12" figures
NM $210 **MIP** $400

Pancho Pony, 1967, 9", Marx, #1061, for 7-1/2" figures, brown with off-white mane and tail. Includes black plastic saddle and bridle
NM $50 **MIP** $80

Storm Cloud Horse, 1967, Marx, #2071, originally "Pinto," brown w/ white spots
NM $60 **MIP** $125

Thunderbolt Horse, 1965-75, Marx, #2061, most common horse produced, black version rarest
NM $75 **MIP** $135

Thundercolt Horse, 1967-69, Marx, #2031a, for use with ranch and corral sets
NM $30 **MIP** $60

FIGURES

Bill Buck, 1967, 12", Marx, #1868, Fort Apache Fighters Series
NM $325 **MIP** $500

Captain Tom Maddox, 1967, 12", Marx, #1865, Fort Apache Fighters, blue body, brown hair
NM $80 **MIP** $175

Chief Cherokee, 1965, 12", Marx, includes headdress, rifle, spear, Bowie knife, ceremonial mask, pipe and more
NM $150 **MIP** $210

Daniel Boone, 1965, 12", Marx, #2060, limited articulation
NM $155 **MIP** $250

Davy Crockett, 1960s, Marx
NM $180 **MIP** $260

Fighting Eagle, 1967, 12", Marx, #1864, Fully poseable, includes spear, Bowie knife, hatchet, bear claw necklace, pouch and more
NM $175 **MIP** $260

General Custer, 1967, 12", Marx, #1866, blue molded uniform, with yellow and dark blue plastic accessories
NM $110 **MIP** $200

Geronimo, 1967, 12", Marx, #1863, with tan molded buckskin uniform, darker brown, yellow and medium brown plastic accessories, including Bowie knife, headband, mask, spear, rifle and more
NM $100 **MIP** $150

Geronimo and Pinto, 1967-75, 12", Marx, #2087, mail-order set
NM $160 **MIP** $240

Geronimo w/ Storm Cloud, 1967-75, 12", Marx, figure and horse in colored box
NM $100 **MIP** $210

Jamie West, 1967, 7-1/2", Marx, #1062A, body molded in carmel, lt. blue, or black in Canada
NM $65 **MIP** $115

Jane West, 1966, 12", Marx, #2067, includes white plastic clothes and accessories
NM $70 **MIP** $130

Jane West w/Flame, 1967-75, 12", Marx, mail-order figure and horse
NM $115 **MIP** $195

Janice West, 1967, 7-1/2", Marx, #1067b, turquoise body, short black hair
NM $65 **MIP** $120

Jay West, 1967, 7-1/2", Marx, #1062b, carmel body, blonde hair
NM $65 **MIP** $110

Jed Gibson, 1975, 12", Marx, #2057c, African-American cavalry soldier, teal body, rare
NM $500 **MIP** $1000

Best of the West (Marx, 1965-75)

Johnny West, 1965, 12", Marx, #2062, straight hands in 1965, curved hands 1966-75, carmel body, brown hair
NM $80 **MIP** $160

Johnny West w/Thunderbolt, 1967-75, 12", Marx, #2062, mail-order figure and horse
NM $90 **MIP** $175

Johnny West with Comanche, 1967, Marx, fully jointed
NM $95 **MIP** $150

Josie West, 1967, 7-1/2", Marx, #1067a, turquoise body, blonde hair
NM $65 **MIP** $110

Princess Wildflower, 1974, 12", Marx, #2097, includes 22 accessories and gear
NM $110 **MIP** $180

Sam Cobra, 1972, 12", Marx, #2072, black molded-plastic clothing and accessories
NM $125 **MIP** $250

Sam Cobra w/Thunderbolt, 1975, 12", Marx, #4959075, mail-order figure and horse
NM $90 **MIP** $250

Sheriff Garrett, 1973, 12", Marx, #2085, blue-molded clothing with white and blue plastic clothing and accessories included
NM $165 **MIP** $200

Sheriff Garrett w/horse, 1967-75, 12", Marx, mail-order figure and horse, rare
NM $180 **MIP** $310

Zeb Zachary, 1967-69, 12", Marx, #1862, Fort Apache Fighters, blue body, black hair
NM $210 **MIP** $325

Big Jim (Mattel, 1971-77)

ACCESSORIES

Baja Beast, 1973, Mattel
NM $25 **MIP** $90

Boat and Buggy Set, 1973, Mattel
NM $30 **MIP** $75

Camping Tent, 1973, Mattel
NM $12 **MIP** $35

Devil River Trip, 1974, Mattel
NM $20 **MIP** $60

Jungle Truck, 1974, Mattel
NM $25 **MIP** $65

Motorcross Honda, 1973, Mattel
NM $30 **MIP** $60

Olympic Basketball player, 1975, Mattel, Olympic series, #7374
NM $15 **MIP** $25

Olympic Boxer, 1975, Mattel, Olympic series, #7348
NM $15 **MIP** $25

Olympic Karate, 1975, Mattel, Olympic series, #7344
NM $15 **MIP** $25

Olympic Ski Run Playset, 1975, Mattel, Olympic series, #7369
NM $50 **MIP** $100

Olympic Skier, 1975, Mattel, Olympic series, #7350
NM $15 **MIP** $25

Rescue Rig, 1973, Mattel
NM $45 **MIP** $100

Rugged Rider and Cycle Set, 1973, Mattel
NM $30 **MIP** $65

Sky Commander, 1974, Mattel
NM $40 **MIP** $85

Sport Camper, 1973, Mattel
NM $50 **MIP** $125

FIGURES

Big Jack, 1973, Mattel
NM $25 **MIP** $65

Big Jeff, 1973, Mattel
NM $25 **MIP** $65

Big Jim, 1971-77, Mattel, window box
NM $25 **MIP** $85

Big Josh, 1973, Mattel
NM $25 **MIP** $60

Dr. Steel, 1975, Mattel
NM $25 **MIP** $60

Gold Medal Big Jack, 1975, 9-1/2", Mattel, Olympic series
NM $30 **MIP** $80

Gold Medal Big Jim, 1975, 9-1/2", Mattel, Olympic series
NM $60 **MIP** $120

Gold Medal Big Jim Olympic Boxing Match, 1975, 9-1/2", Mattel, Olympic series, #7425
NM $60 **MIP** $200

Big Jim's P.A.C.K. (Mattel, 1974-77)

ACCESSORIES

Beast, 1976-77, Mattel
NM $45 **MIP** $100

BlitzRig, 1976-77, Mattel
NM $60 **MIP** $120

Frogman, 1974-77, Mattel, Double Trouble Disguise
NM $12 **MIP** $40

Hard Hat Gunner, 1974-77, Mattel, Double Trouble Adventure Sets
NM $10 **MIP** $40

Howler, 1976-77, Mattel
NM $30 **MIP** $60

LazerVette, 1976-77, Mattel
NM $45 **MIP** $85

Martial Arts, 1974-77, Mattel, Double Trouble Disguise
NM $7 **MIP** $12

Motocross, 1974-77, Mattel, Double Trouble Disguise
NM $7 **MIP** $12

S.W.A.T., 1974-77, Mattel, Double Trouble Adventure Sets
NM $10 **MIP** $40

Secret Spy, 1974-77, Mattel, Double Trouble Adventure Sets
NM $25 **MIP** $60

Ski Patrol, 1974-77, Mattel, Double Trouble Disguise
NM $7 **MIP** $40

Swamp Patrol, 1974-77, Mattel, Sears exclusive
NM $60 **MIP** $125

The Whip's Dune Buggy, 1974-77, Mattel, dune buggy vehicle
NM $25 **MIP** $50

Underworld Gunner, 1974-77, Mattel, Double Trouble Adventure Sets
NM $10 **MIP** $40

FIGURES

Big Jim, window box, 1974-77, 9-1/2", Mattel, Series 2, #9258, a.k.a. "The Gold Commander," gold pants, black shirt
NM $50 **MIP** $200

Big Jim, window box, 1974-77, 9-1/2", Mattel, Series 1, #9092, a.k.a. "The Blue Commander," white pants, blue shirt
NM $40 **MIP** $125

Double Trouble Commander, 1974-77, 9-1/2", Mattel, Series 2, #9287, Face changes
NM $75 **MIP** $190

Dr. Steel, window box, 1974-77, 9-1/2", Mattel, Series 1, #7367, w/ pipe
NM $30 **MIP** $110

Torpedo Fist, 1974-77, 9-1/2", Mattel, Series 2, #9289, eye patch, hat
NM $40 **MIP** $130

Warpath, window box, 1974-77, 9-1/2", Mattel, Series 1, #9059, w/ bow, quiver, two arrows
NM $35 **MIP** $130

Whip, The, window box, 1974-77, 9-1/2", Mattel, Series 1, #9060, w/ bull whip, bolos, shinai stick, boomerangs
NM $35 **MIP** $130

Zorak, 1974-77, 9-1/2", Mattel, Series 2
NM $50 **MIP** $130

Bill & Ted's Excellent Adventure (Kenner, 1991)

ACCESSORIES

Phone Booth, 1991, Kenner
NM $5 **MIP** $10

Wild Stallyns Speaker and Tape, 1991, Kenner
NM $3 MIP $10

FIGURES

Abe Lincoln, 1991, Kenner
NM $4 MIP $12

Bill, 1991, Kenner
NM $4 MIP $10

Bill & Ted Jam Session, two pack, 1991, Kenner
NM $10 MIP $20

Billy The Kid, 1991, Kenner
NM $4 MIP $12

Genghis Khan, 1991, Kenner
NM $4 MIP $12

Grim Reaper, 1991, Kenner
NM $4 MIP $12

Rufus, 1991, Kenner
NM $4 MIP $12

Ted, 1991, Kenner
NM $4 MIP $10

Bionic Six (LJN, 1986)

ACCESSORIES

Dirt Bike, 1986, LJN
NM $5 MIP $10

Flying Laser Throne, 1986, LJN
NM $5 MIP $10

Laser Aero Chair, 1986, LJN
NM $5 MIP $10

M.U.L.E.S. Van, 1986, LJN
NM $5 MIP $10

Quad Runner, 1986, LJN, 4x4
NM $5 MIP $10

Secret Headquarters, 1986, LJN, Super Hi-Tech Bionic Laboratory
NM $25 MIP $50

FIGURES

Bunji, 1986
NM $4 MIP $10

Chopper, 1986
NM $4 MIP $10

Dr. Scarab, 1986
NM $4 MIP $12

Eric, 1986
NM $4 MIP $10

F.L.U.F.F.I., 1986
NM $8 MIP $20

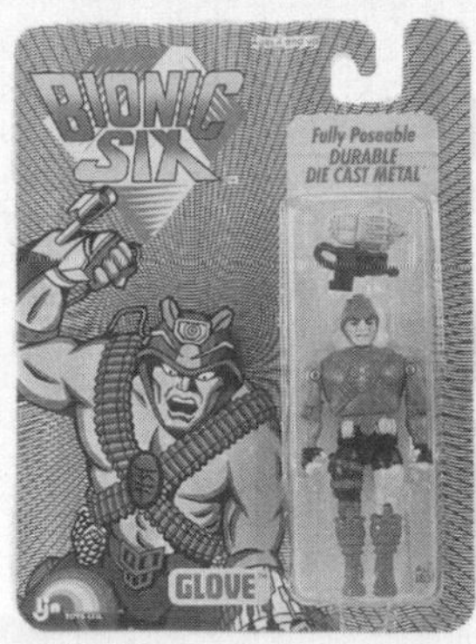

Glove, 1986
NM $4 MIP $10

Helen, 1986
NM $4 MIP $10

J.D., 1986
NM $4 MIP $10

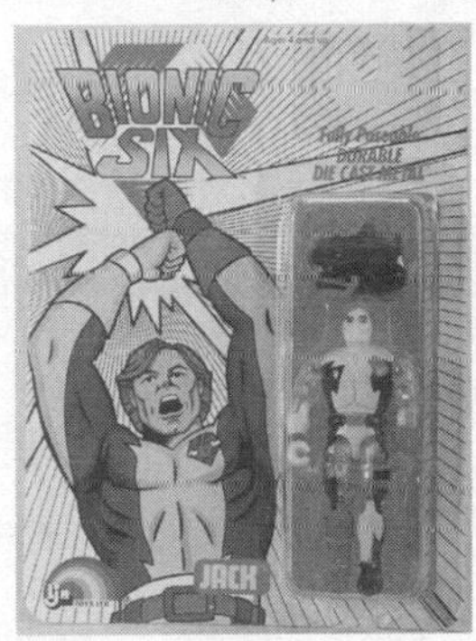

Jack, 1986
NM $4 MIP $10

Klunk, 1986
NM $4 MIP $10

Madame O, 1986
NM $4 MIP $10

Mechanic, 1986
NM $4 MIP $10

Meg, 1986
NM $4 MIP $10

Bionic Woman (Kenner, 1976-77)

12" FIGURES

Fembot, 1977, 12"
NM $65 MIP $235

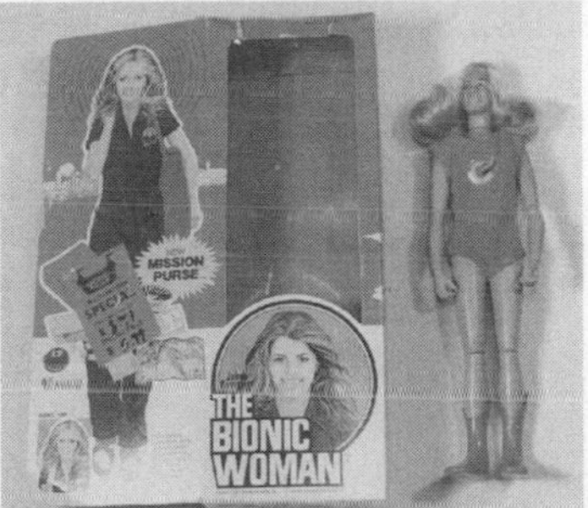

Jamie Sommers, 1976, 12", with purse
NM $50 MIP $185

Jamie Sommers, 1976, 12", in jogging suit, white top, navy pants
NM $40 MIP $160

ACCESSORIES

Beauty Salon, 1976
NM $30 MIP $75

Carriage House, 1977
NM $60 MIP $150

Classroom, 1976-77
NM $100 MIP $210

Dome House, 1976-77
NM $60 MIP $150

Sports Car, 1976
NM $45 MIP $100

FASHIONS

Designer Budget Fashions, 1976, Kenner, Red evening gown w/ red shoes
NM $15 MIP $30

Designer Budget Fashions, 1976, Kenner, Green dress w/ white shoes
NM $15 MIP $30

Designer Collection, 1976, Kenner, Floral party dress w/ platform shoes
NM $12 MIP $25

Designer Collection, 1976, Kenner, "Peach Dream," peach evening dress w/ peach shoes
NM $12 MIP $25

Designer Collection, 1976, Kenner, Light blue two-piece pant outfit w/ white shoes
NM $25 MIP $45

Designer Collection, 1976, Kenner, Calico dress red/yellow w/ apron
NM $12 MIP $25

Black Hole (Mego, 1979-80)

12" FIGURES

Captain Holland, 1979, 12", Mego, Shown with other figures from the Black Hole
NM $40 MIP $75

Dr. Alex Durant, 1979, 12", Mego
NM $40 MIP $75

Dr. Hans Reinhardt, 1979, 12", Mego
NM $40 MIP $75

Harry Booth, 1979, 12", Mego
NM $45 MIP $90

Kate McCrae, 1979, 12", Mego
NM $50 MIP $100

Pizer, 1979, 12", Mego
NM $40 MIP $80

Black Hole (Mego, 1979-80)

3-3/4" FIGURES

Captain Holland, 1979, 3-3/4", Mego, Shown with other figures from the Black Hole
NM $5 **MIP** $25

Dr. Alex Durant, 1979, 3-3/4", Mego
NM $5 **MIP** $25

Dr. Hans Reinhardt, 1979, 3-3/4", Mego
NM $5 **MIP** $25

Harry Booth, 1979, 3-3/4", Mego
NM $5 **MIP** $25

Humanoid, 1980, 3-3/4", Mego
NM $200 **MIP** $775

Kate McCrae, 1979, 3-3/4", Mego
NM $5 **MIP** $25

Maximillian, 1979, 3-3/4", Mego
NM $20 **MIP** $75

Old B.O.B., 1980, 3-3/4", Mego
NM $60 **MIP** $210

Pizer, 1979, 3-3/4", Mego
NM $10 **MIP** $50

S.T.A.R., 1980, 3-3/4", Mego
NM $85 **MIP** $360

Sentry Robot, 1980, 3-3/4", Mego
NM $15 **MIP** $75

V.I.N.cent., 1979, 3-3/4", Mego
NM $15 **MIP** $70

Blackstar (Galoob, 1984)

ACCESSORIES

Ice Castle, 1984
NM $90 **MIP** $175

Triton, 1984
NM $60 **MIP** $150

Warlock Dragon Mount, 1984
NM $60 **MIP** $150

FIGURES

Blackstar, 1984
NM $12 **MIP** $25

Blackstar with Laser Light, 1984
NM $15 **MIP** $40

Devil Knight with Laser Light, 1984
NM $25 **MIP** $50

Gargo, 1984
NM $12 **MIP** $35

Gargo with Laser Light, 1984
NM $12 **MIP** $40

Kadray, 1984
NM $12 **MIP** $40

Kadray with Laser Light, 1984
NM $15 **MIP** $40

Klone with Laser Light, 1984
NM $20 **MIP** $50

Lava Loc with Laser Light, 1984
NM $15 **MIP** $45

Mara, 1984
NM $30 **MIP** $60

Meuton, 1984
NM $12 **MIP** $40

Neptul, 1984
NM $15 **MIP** $55

Overlord, 1984
NM $15 **MIP** $25

Overlord with Laser Light, 1984
NM $15 **MIP** $45

Palace Guard, 1984
NM $15 **MIP** $30

Palace Guard with Laser Light, 1984
NM $12 **MIP** $40

Togo, 1984
NM $12 **MIP** $38

Togo with Laser Light, 1984
NM $12 **MIP** $38

Vizir with Laser Light, 1984
NM $12 **MIP** $40

White Knight, 1984
NM $12 **MIP** $45

Blade (Toy Biz, 1998)

6" FIGURES

Blade, 1998, 6", Toy Biz
NM $10 **MIP** $30

Deacon Frost, 1998, 6", Toy Biz
NM $10 **MIP** $30

Vampire Blade, 1998, 6", Toy Biz
NM $8 **MIP** $20

Whistler, 1998, 6", Toy Biz
NM $8 **MIP** $20

Blade Vampire Hunter (Toy Biz, 1998)

FIGURES

Blade, 1998
NM $5 **MIP** $10

Deacon Frost, 1998
NM $2 **MIP** $8

Vampire Blade, 1998
NM $2 **MIP** $8

Whistker, 1998
NM $2 **MIP** $8

Bob & Doug McKenzie (McFarlane, 2000)

FIGURES

Bob McKenzie with half of Great White North stage set, 2000, McFarlane
NM $5 **MIP** $15

Doug McKenzie with half of Great White North stage set, 2000, McFarlane
NM $5 **MIP** $15

Bonanza (American Character, 1966)

ACCESSORIES

4 in 1 Wagon, 1966
NM $45 **MIP** $110

Ben's Palomino, 1966
NM $40 **MIP** $80

Hoss' Stallion, 1966
NM $40 **MIP** $80

Little Joe's Pinto, 1966
NM $40 **MIP** $80

FIGURES

Ben, 1966
NM $50 **MIP** $160

Ben with Palomino, 1966
NM $80 **MIP** $225

Hoss, 1966
NM $70 **MIP** $160

Hoss with Stallion, 1966
NM $70 **MIP** $210

Little Joe, 1966
NM $50 **MIP** $160

Little Joe with Pinto, 1966
NM $70 **MIP** $210

Outlaw, 1966
NM $50 **MIP** $160

BraveStarr (Mattel, 1986)

FIGURES

BraveStarr and Thirty/Thirty, two-pack, 1986, 5", Mattel
NM $20 **MIP** $50

Col. Borobot, 1986, 5", Mattel
NM $8 **MIP** $25

Deputy Fuzz, 1986, 5", Mattel
NM $8 **MIP** $25

Handle Bar, 1986, 5", Mattel
NM $8 **MIP** $25

Laser-Fire BraveStarr, 1986, 5", Mattel
NM $8 **MIP** $25

Laser-Fire Tex Hex, 1986, 5", Mattel
NM $10 MIP $30

Marshal BraveStarr, 1986, 5", Mattel
NM $10 MIP $30

Outlaw Skuzz, 1986, 5", Mattel
NM $8 MIP $25

Sand Storm, 1986, 5", Mattel
NM $8 MIP $25

Skull Walker, 1986, 5", Mattel
NM $5 MIP $20

Tex Hex, 1986, 5", Mattel
NM $10 MIP $30

Thunder Stick, 1986, 5", Mattel
NM $10 MIP $30

Bruce Lee (Sideshow Toys, 1999)

8" FIGURES

Bruce Lee, bare chested, 1999, With stand, nunchaku and staff
NM $7 MIP $15

Bruce Lee, traditional outfit, 1999
NM $7 MIP $15

Buck Rogers (Mego, 1979)

12" FIGURES

Buck Rogers, 1979, 12", Mego
NM $30 MIP $75

Doctor Huer, 1979, 12", Mego
NM $30 MIP $65

Draco, 1979, 12", Mego
NM $30 MIP $60

Draconian Guard, 1979, 12", Mego, With brown and silver uniform
NM $30 MIP $75

Killer Kane, 1979, 12", Mego
NM $30 MIP $80

Tiger Man, 1979, 12", Mego, With tattooed face and head and tiger-skin vest and clothing
NM $30 MIP $125

Twiki, 1979, 12", Mego
NM $30 MIP $60

3-3/4" FIGURES

Ardella, 1979, 3-3/4", Mego
NM $6 MIP $15

Buck Rogers, 1979, 3-3/4", Mego
NM $25 MIP $60

Doctor Huer, 1979, 3-3/4", Mego
NM $6 MIP $20

Draco, 1979, 3-3/4", Mego
NM $6 MIP $20

Draconian Guard, 1979, 3-3/4", Mego
NM $10 MIP $20

Killer Kane, 1979, 3-3/4", Mego
NM $6 MIP $15

Tiger Man, 1979, 3-3/4", Mego
NM $10 MIP $25

Twiki, 1979, 3-3/4", Mego
NM $20 MIP $40

Wilma Deering, 1979, 3-3/4", Mego
NM $12 MIP $25

3-3/4" PLAY SETS

Star Fighter Command Center, 1979, Mego
NM $50 MIP $110

3-3/4" VEHICLES

Draconian Marauder, 1979, Mego
NM $30 MIP $90

Land Rover, 1979, Mego
NM $25 MIP $45

Laserscope Fighter, 1979, Mego
NM $25 MIP $60

Star Fighter, 1979, Mego
NM $50 MIP $100

Star Searcher, 1979, Mego
NM $40 MIP $80

Buffy the Vampire Slayer (Diamond Select, 1999)

FIGURES

Prophecy Girl Buffy, 1999, Diamond Select
NM $5 MIP $15

Vampiric Angel, 1999, Diamond Select
NM $5 MIP $15

Willow, 1999, Diamond Select
NM $5 MIP $15

Buffy the Vampire Slayer (Moore Action Collectibles, 1999-Present)

SERIES I

Angel, 1999, Moore Action Collectibles
NM $5 MIP $18

Buffy, 1999, Moore Action Collectibles, blue shirt and black pants, crossbow, stakes, dagger, Moore Action Collectibles Exclusive
NM $10 MIP $25

Buffy, 1999, Moore Action Collectibles
NM $5 MIP $18

Master, The, 1999, Moore Action Collectibles
NM $5 MIP $15

Willow, 1999, Moore Action Collectibles
NM $5 MIP $18

SERIES II

3-Pack, 2000, Moore Action Collectibles, Buffy, Giles, Oz
NM $10 MIP $30

Buffy, red leather pants, 2000
NM $3 MIP $15

Exclusive Entertainment Earth Oz, 2000, Moore Action Collectibles
NM $6 MIP $15

Exclusive MAC's Fiesta Giles, 2000, Moore Action Collectibles
NM $6 MIP $15

Exclusive Spike, 2000, Moore Action Collectibles
NM $6 MIP $15

Exclusive Toy Fare Season 2 hair Buffy, 2000, Moore Action Collectibles
NM $6 MIP $15

Exclusive Vampire Spike, 2000, Moore Action Collectibles
NM $6 MIP $15

Buffy the Vampire Slayer (Moore Action Collectibles, 1999-Present)

Exclusive Werewolf Oz, 2000, Moore Action Collectibles
NM $6 MIP $15

Giles, 2000
NM $4 MIP $12

Oz, 2000
NM $4 MIP $12

Spike, 2000, Moore Action Collectibles, In black trenchcoat. Includes gravesite stand
NM $4 MIP $12

SERIES III

3-Pack, 2001, Moore Action Collectibles, Cordelia, Xander, Cheerleader Cordelia
NM $15 MIP $35

Cordelia, 2001, Moore Action Collectibles
NM $5 MIP $15

Exclusive Cheerleader Cordelia, 2001, Moore Action Collectibles
NM $5 MIP $15

Exclusive Cordelia T1, 2001, Moore Action Collectibles, Summer Show Special
NM $5 MIP $15

Exclusive Military Xander, 2001, Moore Action Collectibles
NM $5 MIP $25

Xander, 2001, Moore Action Collectibles
NM $5 MIP $13

SERIES IV

Drusilla, 2002, Moore Action Collectibles
NM $5 MIP $14

Exclusive Bunny Anya, 2002, Moore Action Collectibles
NM $5 MIP $15

Exclusive Vampire Drusilla, 2002, Moore Action Collectibles
NM $5 MIP $15

Geltleman #2, 2002, Moore Action Collectibles, Tilted head
NM $5 MIP $14

Gentleman #1, 2002, Moore Action Collectibles, Straight head
NM $5 MIP $14

Buffy the Vampire Slayer (Sideshow Toys, 1998-Present)

12" FIGURES

Angel, 2004, 12", Sideshow Toys, #2006, "Becoming"
NM n/a MIP $40

Buffy Summers, 1998, 12", Sideshow Toys, #2001, from the television series
NM n/a MIP $30

Buffy Summers, 2004, 12", Sideshow Toys, #2005, "Graduation Day"
NM n/a MIP $40

Buffy/Gentlemen, 1998, 12", Sideshow Toys, #2000, four figures from "Hush" Season 4
NM n/a MIP $120

Gentlemen, 1998, 12", Sideshow Toys, #20002R, three Gentlemen figures from "Hush"
NM n/a MIP $90

Bug's Life, A (Mattel, 1998)

FIGURES

Enemy Hopper, 1998, Mattel
NM $2 MIP $5

Enemy Molt, 1998, Mattel
NM $2 MIP $5

Francis & Slim, 1998, Mattel
NM $2 MIP $5

Hang Glider Flik, 1998, Mattel
NM $2 MIP $5

Inventor Flik, 1998, Mattel
NM $2 MIP $5

Princess Atta, 1998, Mattel
NM $2 MIP $5

Tuck & Roll, 1998, Mattel
NM $2 MIP $5

Warrior Flik, 1998, Mattel
NM $2 MIP $5

Butch and Sundance: The Early Days (Kenner, 1979)

ACCESSORIES AND VEHICLES

Bluff, Butch's horse, 1979, Kenner
NM $20 MIP $55

Mint Wagon, 1979, Kenner
NM $25 MIP $70

Saloon Play Set, 1979, Kenner
NM $45 MIP $120

Spurs, Sundance's horse, 1979, Kenner
NM $20 MIP $55

FIGURES

Butch Cassidy, 1979, Kenner
NM $12 MIP $30

Marshall LeFors, 1979, Kenner
NM $12 MIP $30

O.C. Hanks, 1979, Kenner
NM $12 MIP $30

Sheriff Bledsoe, 1979, Kenner
NM $12 MIP $30

Sundance Kid, 1979, Kenner
NM $12 MIP $30

Cadillacs and Dinosaurs (Tyco, 1994)

FIGURES

Hammer Terhune, 1994, Tyco
NM $2 MIP $5

Hannah Dundee, 1994, Tyco
NM $3 MIP $6

Hermes, 1994, Tyco
NM $2 MIP $5

Jack Cadillac Tenrec, 1994, Tyco
NM $2 MIP $5

Jungle Fighting Jack Tenrec, 1994, Tyco
NM $3 MIP $8

Kentrosaurus, 1994, Tyco
NM $5 MIP $15

Mustapha Cairo, 1994, Tyco
NM $2 MIP $5

Snake Eyes, 1994, Tyco
NM $5 MIP $15

Vice Terhune, 1994, Tyco
NM $3 MIP $8

Zeke, 1994, Tyco
NM $2 MIP $5

Captain & Tennille (Mego, 1970s)

FIGURES

Daryl Dragon (Captain), 1977, Mego, Model No. 7501
NM $55 MIP $125

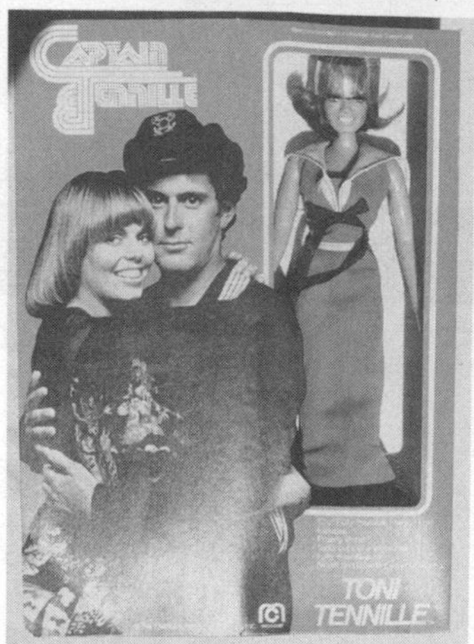

Toni Tennille, 1977, Mego, Features a stand and "fully washable hair...wash and blow dry on cool setting." Interesting choice for an action figure, but after KISS, why not?
NM $55 MIP $125

Captain Action (Ideal, 1966-68)

12" FIGURES

Captain Action, 1966, 12", Ideal, with red-shirted Lone Ranger on box
NM $210 **MIP** $575

Captain Action, 1966, 12", Ideal, with blue-shirted Lone Ranger on box
NM $210 **MIP** $575

Captain Action, 1966, 12", Ideal, photo box
NM $300 **MIP** $925

Captain Action, 1967, 12", Ideal, parachute offer on box
NM $275 **MIP** $725

Dr. Evil, 1967, 12", Ideal, photo box
NM $250 **MIP** $460

Dr. Evil, Lab Set Display Box, 1967, 12", Ideal, all Dr. Evil accessories plus white lab coat, blue/red thought-control helmet, reducer wand w/prism, gun, hypnotic eye (eyelid often missing), Dr. Ling mask
NM $1100 **MIP** $3100

Dr. Evil, Mailer box version of lab set, 1968, 12", Ideal
NM $1100 **MIP** $2600

9" FIGURES

Action Boy, 1967, 9", Ideal
NM $275 **MIP** $925

Action Boy, 1968, 9", Ideal, with space suit
NM $350 **MIP** $1200

ACCESSORIES

Action Cave Carrying Case, 1967, Ideal, vinyl
NM $400 **MIP** $710

Directional Communicator Set, 1966, Ideal
NM $110 **MIP** $320

Dr. Evil Sanctuary, 1967, Ideal
NM $2500 **MIP** $3600

Jet Mortar, 1966, Ideal, two shells
NM $110 **MIP** $310

Parachute Pack, 1966, Ideal, silver boots, orange helmet, working (sometimes) parachute
NM $110 **MIP** $235

Power Pack, 1966, Ideal, Jet pack w/handles; silver helmet, gloves and boots, CA belt w/o slit for sword
NM $125 **MIP** $250

Quick Change Chamber, 1967, Ideal, Sears Exclusive, cardboard
NM $760 **MIP** $910

Silver Streak Amphibian, 1967, Ideal
NM $810 **MIP** $1300

Silver Streak Garage, 1966-68, Ideal, Sears Exclusive, with Silver Streak Vehicle
NM $1600 **MIP** $2100

Survival Kit, 1967, Ideal, twenty pieces; orange vest
NM $130 **MIP** $280

Vinyl Headquarters Carrying Case, 1967, Ideal, Sears Exclusive
NM $210 **MIP** $525

Weapons Arsenal, 1966, Ideal, ten pieces
NM $110 **MIP** $230

ACTION BOY COSTUMES

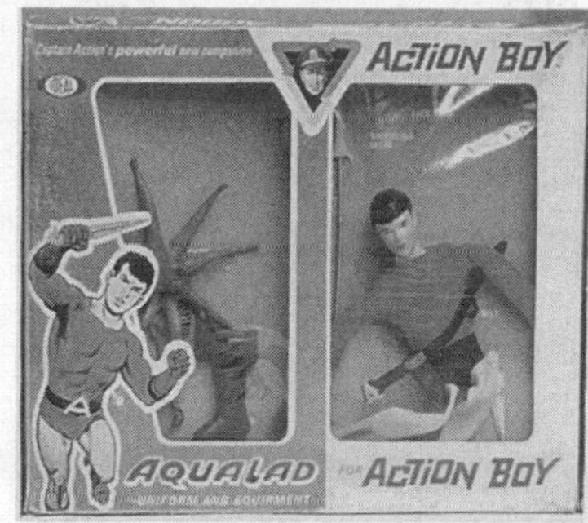

Aqualad, 1967, Ideal
NM $300 **MIP** $950

Robin, 1967, Ideal, included gloves, batarangs, boots, uniform, face mask, suction cups for climbing buildings
NM $325 **MIP** $1300

Superboy, 1967, Ideal
NM $325 **MIP** $1100

CAPTAIN ACTION COSTUMES

Aquaman, 1966, Ideal, costume, mask, yellow flippers, trident, seashell w/strap, yellow belt, lance-like sword, yellow/silver knife; Photo shows Batman, Captain America, Aquaman, and Superman
NM $175 **MIP** $650

Aquaman, 1967, Ideal, with flasher ring, 1966 accessories
NM $200 **MIP** $975

Batman, 1966, Ideal, costume, 2-piece mask, batarang, blue cape, utility belt and boots, blue flashlight w/hook, drill, rope w/reel and hook
NM $225 **MIP** $700

Batman, 1967, Ideal, with flasher ring, 1966 accessories
NM $250 **MIP** $1100

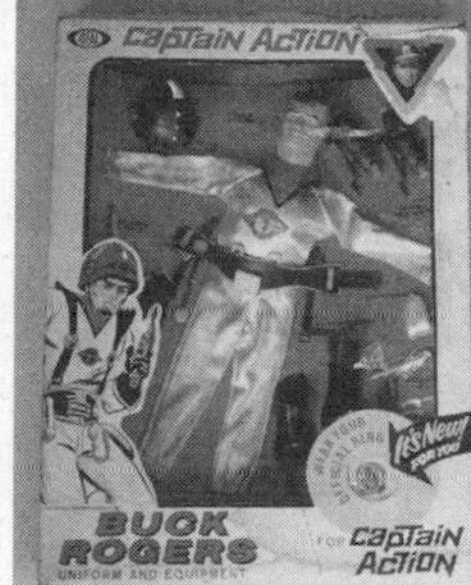

Buck Rogers, 1967, Ideal, with flasher ring, silver suit, mask, black boots and gloves, black belt/shoulder harness, 2 blue rocket packs, blue helmet, canteen, raygun, flashlight
NM $450 **MIP** $2700

Captain America, 1966, Ideal, red, white, blue costume, mask, red boots, white belt w/gun holster, laser pistol, laser rifle, shield (red, white and blue w/star in middle)
NM $220 **MIP** $900

Captain America, 1967, Ideal, with flasher ring, 1966 accessories
NM $225 **MIP** $1200

Flash Gordon, 1966, Ideal, white spacesuit with helmet, silver boots, space pistol, propellant gun, belt and mask
NM $200 **MIP** $600

Flash Gordon, 1967, Ideal, with flasher ring, 1966 accessories
NM $225 **MIP** $800

Green Hornet, 1967, Ideal, with flasher ring, green trench coat, mask, black pants, white scarf, black hat w/green band, yellow gas mask, shoulder holster, pistol, tv w/phone, gold pocket watch, black cane w/removable handle
NM $2000 **MIP** $7500

Lone Ranger, 1966, Ideal, red shirt, black pants, white hat, mask, black belt w/2 holsters, 2 silver pistols, rifle, black boots w/spurs
NM $200 **MIP** $700

Lone Ranger, 1967, Ideal, blue shirt (1967 only), with flasher ring, 1966 accessories
NM $500 **MIP** $1000

Phantom, 1966, Ideal, purple uniform, black boots, knife, rifle, two pistols, double-rig holster, mask, brass knuckles
NM $225 **MIP** $775

Captain Action (Ideal, 1966-68)

Phantom, 1967, Ideal, with flasher ring, 1966 accessories
NM $250 **MIP** $900

Sgt. Fury, 1966, Ideal, camo uniform, bearded mask, moustache mask, clean-shaven mask, black boots, helmet, walkie-talkie, bandolier, machine gun, 3 grenades, .45 pistol
NM $200 **MIP** $800

Spider-Man, 1967, Ideal, with flasher ring, red/blue uniform, spider mask, red boots, yellow spider, web fluid tank w/shoulder strap and hoses, "web" sword, flashlight, grappling hook
NM $550 **MIP** $8000

Steve Canyon, 1966, Ideal, green flight suit, black boots, mask, blue cap, white flight helmet, parachute pack, oxygen mask, green belt/holster, pistol, knife
NM $200 **MIP** $700

Steve Canyon, 1967, Ideal, with flasher ring, 1966 accessories
NM $225 **MIP** $850

Superman, 1966, Ideal, costume, mask, red boots, yellow belt, green Kryptonite, yellow shackles and chain, Krypto, Phantom Zone Projector
NM $210 **MIP** $710

Superman, 1967, Ideal, with flasher ring, 1966 accessories
NM $275 **MIP** $1200

Tonto, 1967, Ideal, with flasher ring, brown costume, headband w/feather, moccasins, brown belt, brown quiver and boe, gun, knife, four arrows (each has different color feather: red, blue, yellow, green), Taka the eagle
NM $375 **MIP** $1100

Captain Action (Playing Mantis, 1998-99)

FIGURES AND COSTUMES

Captain Action, 1998-99, Playing Mantis
NM $15 **MIP** $25

Dr. Evil, 1998-99, Playing Mantis
NM $15 **MIP** $30

Flash Gordon, 1998-99, Playing Mantis
NM $15 **MIP** $25

Green Hornet, 1998-99, Playing Mantis, Kay-Bee exclusive
NM $15 **MIP** $25

Kabai Singh, 1999, Playing Mantis, outfit only, for Dr. Evil
NM $10 **MIP** $25

Kato, 1998-99, Playing Mantis, Kay-Bee exclusive
NM $15 **MIP** $20

(Playing Mantis)

Lone Ranger, 1998-99, Playing Mantis, Photo shows Lone Ranger and Tonto
NM $15 **MIP** $25

Ming the Merciless, 1998-99, Playing Mantis
NM $15 **MIP** $25

The Phantom, 1999, Playing Mantis
NM $10 **MIP** $25

(Playing Mantis)

Tonto, 1998-99, Playing Mantis
NM $15 **MIP** $20

Captain Power and the Soldiers of the Future (Mattel, 1987-88)

ACCESSORIES

Dread Stalker, 1988, Mattel
NM $12 **MIP** $20

Interlocker Throne, 1987, Mattel
NM $15 **MIP** $30

Magna Cycle, 1988, Mattel
NM $12 **MIP** $25

Phantom Striker, 1987, Mattel
NM $12 **MIP** $25

Power Base, 1987, Mattel
NM $25 **MIP** $50

Power Jet XT-7, 1987, Mattel
NM $25 **MIP** $60

Power on Energizer with figure, 1987, Mattel
NM $10 **MIP** $18

Trans-Field Base Station, 1988, Mattel
NM $15 **MIP** $30

Trans-Field Communication Station, 1988, Mattel
NM $10 **MIP** $20

Wind-Up Soaron Beam Deflector, 1988, Mattel
NM $10 **MIP** $20

FIGURES, SERIES I

Blastarr Ground Guardian, 1987, Mattel
NM $10 **MIP** $20

Captain Power, 1987, Mattel
NM $10 **MIP** $22

Lord Dread, 1987, Mattel
NM $8 **MIP** $20

Lt. Tank Ellis, 1987, Mattel
NM $10 **MIP** $20

Major Hawk Masterson, 1987, Mattel
NM $8 **MIP** $20

Soaron Sky Sentry, 1987, Mattel
NM $8 **MIP** $20

FIGURES, SERIES II

Col. Stingray Johnson, 1988, Mattel
NM $12 **MIP** $30

Cpl. Pilot Chase, 1988, Mattel
NM $10 **MIP** $25

Dread Commander, 1988, Mattel
NM $45 **MIP** $110

Dread Trooper, 1988, Mattel
NM $45 **MIP** $110

Sgt. Scout Baker, 1988, Mattel
NM $12 **MIP** $25

Tritor, 1988, Mattel
NM $15 **MIP** $110

Captain Scarlett (Pedigree, 1967)

12" FIGURE

Captain Scarlet, 1967, 12", Pedigree
NM $550 **MIP** $1300

Captain Scarlett (Vivid Imaginations, 1993-94)

12" FIGURES

Captain Black, 1993-94
NM $25 **MIP** $50

Captain Scarlett, 1993-94
NM $25 **MIP** $50

3-3/4" FIGURES

Captain Black, 1993-94
NM $3 **MIP** $8

Captain Blue, 1993-94
NM $3 **MIP** $8

Captain Scarlett, 1993-94
NM $4 **MIP** $10

Colonel White, 1993-94
NM $3 **MIP** $8

Destiny Angel, 1993-94
NM $5 **MIP** $12

Lieutenant Green, 1993-94
NM $3 **MIP** $8

Centurions (Kenner, 1986)

ACCESSORIES

Power Pack, 1986, Kenner, Series 1
NM $5 **MIP** $12

FIGURES

Ace McCloud, 1986, Kenner, Series 1, Air operations expert
NM $15 MIP $30

Dr. Terror, 1986, Kenner, Series 1, Evil genius
NM $15 MIP $30

Hacker, 1986, Kenner, Series 1, Dr. Terror's Henchman
NM $15 MIP $30

Jake Rockwell, 1986, Kenner, Series 1, Land operations expert
NM $15 MIP $30

Max Ray, 1986, Kenner, Series 1, Sea operations expert
NM $15 MIP $30

VEHICLES

Detonator, 1986, Kenner, Series 1
NM $18 MIP $40

Skybolt, 1986, Kenner, Series 1
NM $18 MIP $40

Strafer, 1986, Kenner, Series 1
NM $18 MIP $40

Tidal Blast, 1986, Kenner, Series 1
NM $18 MIP $40

Wild Weasel, 1986, Kenner, Series 1
NM $18 MIP $40

Chaos! (Moore Action Collectibles, 1997-1999)

SERIES I, 12" FIGURES

Lady Death, 1997-99
NM $10 MIP $30

Royal Lady Death, 1997-99
NM $10 MIP $30

SERIES I, FIGURES

Evil Ernie, 1997-99
NM $3 MIP $10

Evil Ernie, glow in the dark, 1997-99
NM $8 MIP $20

Lady Death, 1997-99
NM $3 MIP $10

Lady Death, chrome, 1997-99
NM $10 MIP $20

Lady death, glow in the dark, 1997-99
NM $10 MIP $20

Lady Demon, 1997-99
NM $3 MIP $10

Lady Demon, glow in the dark, 1997-99
NM $10 MIP $20

Purgatori, 1997-99
NM $3 MIP $10

Purgatori, metallic, 1997-99
NM $8 MIP $20

SERIES II, FIGURES

Cremator, 1997-99
NM $6 MIP $15

Cremator, 1997-99
NM $3 MIP $10

Lady Death in Battle Armor, 1997-99
NM $3 MIP $10

Lady Death, Azure, 1997-99
NM $10 MIP $20

Lady Death, bronze, 1997-99
NM $10 MIP $20

Charlie's Angels (Hasbro, 1977)

8-1/2" FIGURES

Jill — Farrah Fawcett, 1977, Hasbro
NM $50 MIP $100

Kelly — Jaclyn Smith, 1977, Hasbro
NM $40 MIP $75

Kris — Cheryl Ladd, 1977, Hasbro
NM $40 MIP $75

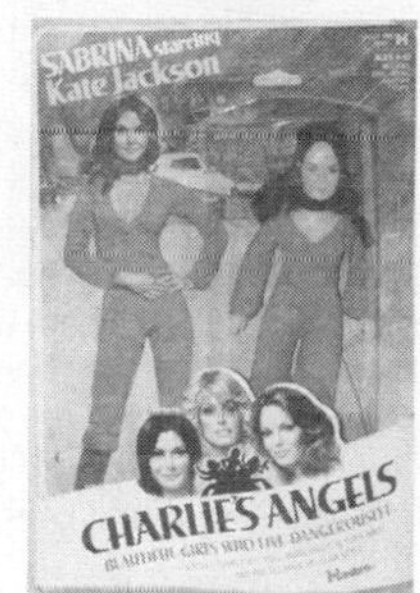

Sabrina — Kate Jackson, 1977, Hasbro
NM $40 MIP $75

Sabrina, Kris, and Kelly Gift Set, 1977, Hasbro
NM $75 MIP $225

ACCESSORIES

Adventure Van, 1977, 16", Hasbro, "Headquarters on Wheels"
NM $25 MIP $75

Charlie's Angels (JAKKS Pacific, 2000)

FIGURES

Alex, 2000, 11-1/2", JAKKS Pacific, Played by Lucy Liu in "Charlie's Angels"
NM $8 MIP $25

Dylan Saunders, 2000, 11-1/2", JAKKS Pacific, Model of Drew Barrymore's character in "Charlie's Angels" movie
NM $8 MIP $25

Natalie, 2000, 11-1/2", JAKKS Pacific, Played by Cameron Diaz in "Charlie's Angels"
NM $8 MIP $25

CHiPs (Mego, 1979)

3-3/4" FIGURES AND ACCESSORIES

Jimmy Squeaks, 1979, 3-3/4", Mego
NM $5 MIP $15

Jon, 1979, 3-3/4", Mego
NM $10 MIP $25

Launcher with Motorcycle, 1979, 3-3/4", Mego
NM $25 MIP $50

Motorcycle, boxed, 1979, 3-3/4", Mego
NM $10 MIP $35

Ponch, 1979, 3-3/4", Mego
NM $8 MIP $25

Sarge, 1979, 3-3/4", Mego
NM $10 MIP $32

Wheels Willie, 1979, 3-3/4", Mego
NM $6 MIP $15

8" FIGURES AND ACCESSORIES

Jon, 1979, 8", Mego
NM $20 MIP $50

Motorcycle, 1979, 8", Mego
NM $30 MIP $85

Ponch, 1979, 8", Mego
NM $15 MIP $40

Sarge, 1979, 8", Mego
NM $25 MIP $50

Chuck Norris Karate Kommandos (Kenner, 1986-87)

6" FIGURES

Chuck Norris Battle Gear, 1986, 6", Kenner
NM $10 MIP $25

Chuck Norris Kung Fu Training, 1986, 6", Kenner
NM $8 MIP $18

Chuck Norris Undercover Agent, 1986, 6", Kenner
NM $10 MIP $20

Kimo, 1986, 6", Kenner
NM $10 MIP $18

Ninja Master, 1986, 6", Kenner
NM $10 MIP $18

Ninja Serpent, 1986, 6", Kenner
NM $10 MIP $18

Ninja Warrior, 1986, 6", Kenner
NM $10 MIP $18

Super Ninja, 1986, 6", Kenner
NM $10 MIP $18

Tabe, 1986, 6", Kenner
NM $10 MIP $18

VEHICLES

Karate Corvette, 1986, Kenner
NM $15 MIP $25

Clash of The Titans (Mattel, 1980)

FIGURES

Calibos, 1980, Mattel, Lord of the Marsh
NM $25 **MIP** $70

Charon, 1980, Mattel, Ferryman of the River Styx
NM $30 **MIP** $75

Kraken, 1980, 15" tall, 22" long, Mattel, Sea Monster
NM $175 **MIP** $350

Pegasus, 1980, Mattel
NM $25 **MIP** $75

Perseus, 1980, Mattel, Hero Son of Zeus
NM $30 **MIP** $65

Perseus and Pegasus, two-pack, 1980, Mattel
NM $75 **MIP** $150

Thallo, 1980, Mattel, Captain of the Guard
NM $18 **MIP** $40

Comic Action Heroes (Mego, 1975-78)

3-3/4" FIGURES

Aquaman, 1975, Mego
NM $30 **MIP** $80

Batman, 1975, Mego
NM $25 **MIP** $80

Captain America, 1975, Mego
NM $20 **MIP** $80

Green Goblin, 1975, Mego
NM $30 **MIP** $125

Hulk, 1975, Mego
NM $20 **MIP** $50

Joker, 1975, Mego
NM $25 **MIP** $80

Penguin, 1975, Mego, Shown here with Robin
NM $25 **MIP** $80

Robin, 1975, Mego, Shown here with The Penguin. Many of the components of Mego action figures were interchangeable, allowing the company to release almost limitless variations of popular figures
NM $20 **MIP** $65

Shazam, 1975, Mego
NM $25 **MIP** $80

Spider-Man, 1975, Mego
NM $20 **MIP** $75

Superman, 1975, Mego
NM $20 **MIP** $70

Wonder Woman, 1975, Mego
NM $25 **MIP** $70

ACCESSORIES

Batcopter, 1975-78, Mego, w/ Batman figure
NM $60 **MIP** $125

Batmobile, 1975-78, Mego, w/ Batman and Robin figures
NM $75 **MIP** $150

Collapsing Tower (with Invisible Plane & Wonder Woman), 1975, Mego
NM $100 **MIP** $225

Exploding Bridge with Batmobile, 1975, Mego
NM $100 **MIP** $200

Fortress of Solitude with Superman, 1975, Mego
NM $100 **MIP** $200

Mangler, 1975, Mego
NM $125 **MIP** $300

Spidercar, 1975-78, Mego, w/ Spider-Man and Green Goblin figures
NM $100 **MIP** $300

Comic Heroine Posin' Dolls (Ideal, 1967)

12" BOXED FIGURES

(KP Photo, Joe Desris collection)

Batgirl, 1967, Ideal, Purple gloves, boots, cape and mask
NM $1600 **MIP** $5500

Mera, 1967, Ideal
NM $1200 **MIP** $5000

Supergirl, 1967, Ideal
NM $1200 **MIP** $5000

Wonder Woman, 1967, Ideal
NM $1200 **MIP** $5000

Commander Power (Mego, 1975)

FIGURE WITH VEHICLE

Commander Power with Lightning Cycle, 1975, 6-1/2", Mego
NM $20 **MIP** $40

Commando (Diamond, 1985)

18" FIGURES

Arnold Schwarzenegger, black box, 1985
NM $70 **MIP** $175

Arnold Schwarzenegger, red box, 1985
NM $70 **MIP** $275

3-3/4" FIGURES

Blaster, 1985
NM $10 **MIP** $25

Chopper, 1985
NM $10 **MIP** $25

Lead Head, 1985
NM $10 **MIP** $25

Matrix, 1985
NM $40 **MIP** $125

Psycho, 1985
NM $10 **MIP** $25

Sawbones, 1985
NM $10 **MIP** $25

Spex, 1985
NM $10 **MIP** $25

Stalker, 1985
NM $10 **MIP** $25

6" FIGURES

Blaster, 1985
NM $10 **MIP** $30

Chopper, 1985
NM $10 **MIP** $30

Lead Head, 1985
NM $10 **MIP** $30

Matrix, 1985
NM $25 **MIP** $65

Pyscho, 1985
NM $10 **MIP** $30

Sawbones, 1985
NM $10 **MIP** $30

Spex, 1985
NM $10 **MIP** $30

Stalker, 1985
NM $10 **MIP** $30

Conan (Hasbro, 1994)

FIGURES, ASST. I

Conan the Adventurer with Star Metal Slash, 1994, Hasbro
NM $2 **MIP** $8

Conan the Warrior with Slashing Battle Action, 1994, Hasbro
NM $2 **MIP** $8

Wrath-Amon with Serpent Slash, 1994, Hasbro
NM $2 **MIP** $8

Zulu with Dart Firing Crossbow, 1994, Hasbro
NM $2 **MIP** $8

FIGURES, ASST. II

Conan the Exlporer with Two-fisted Chopping Action, 1994, Hasbro
NM $2 **MIP** $8

Greywolf with Cyclone Power Punch, 1994, Hasbro
NM $2 **MIP** $8

Ninja Conan with Katana Chop, 1994, Hasbro
NM $2 **MIP** $8

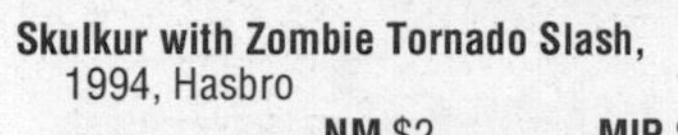

Skulkur with Zombie Tornado Slash, 1994, Hasbro
NM $2 **MIP** $8

Conan (Remco, 1984)

FIGURES

Conan The Warrior, 1984, Remco
NM $18 **MIP** $50

Devourer Of Souls, 1984, Remco
NM $15 **MIP** $50

Jewel Man, 1984, Remco
NM $15 **MIP** $50

Throth Amon, 1984, Remco
NM $15 **MIP** $50

Coneheads (Playmates, 1995)

FIGURES

(Playmates Toys)

Agent Seedling, 1998, Playmates, Shown here with group of figures in the series
NM $2 **MIP** $4

Beldar in flight uniform, 1998, Playmates
NM $2 **MIP** $4

Beldar in street clothes, 1998, Playmates
NM $2 **MIP** $4

Connie, 1998, Playmates
NM $2 **MIP** $4

Prymaat in flight uniform, 1998, Playmates
NM $2 **MIP** $4

Prymaat in street clothes, 1998, Playmates
NM $2 **MIP** $4

Congo (Kenner, 1995)

FIGURES

Amy, 1995, Kenner, Shown here with a group of Congo figures
NM $3 **MIP** $5

Blastface, 1995, Kenner, Shown here with Congo figure group
NM $3 **MIP** $5

Bonecrucher, Deluxe, 1995, Kenner
NM $4 **MIP** $6

Kahega, 1995, Kenner
NM $2 **MIP** $4

Karen Ross, 1995, Kenner
NM $2 **MIP** $4

Mangler, 1995, Kenner
NM $2 **MIP** $4

Monroe, 1995, Kenner
NM $2 **MIP** $4

Monroe, Deluxe, 1995, Kenner
NM $4 **MIP** $8

Peter Elliot, 1995, Kenner
NM $2 **MIP** $4

VEHICLES

Net trap Vehicle, 1995, Kenner
NM $4 **MIP** $8

Trail Hacker Vehicle, 1995, Kenner
NM $4 **MIP** $8

Danger Girl (McFarlane, 1999)

FIGURES

Abbey Chase, 1999, McFarlane
NM $8 **MIP** $20

Major Maxim, 1999, McFarlane
NM $3 **MIP** $8

Natalia Kassle, 1999, McFarlane
NM $8 **MIP** $20

Sydney Savage, 1999, McFarlane
NM $8 **MIP** $20

DC Comics Super Heroes (Toy Biz, 1989)

FIGURES

Aquaman, 1989, 5", Toy Biz
NM $5 **MIP** $12

Batman, 1989, 5", Toy Biz
NM $5 **MIP** $12

Bob The Goon, 1989, 5", Toy Biz
NM $5 **MIP** $10

Flash, 1989, 5", Toy Biz
NM $3 **MIP** $8

Flash II with Turbo Platform, 1989, 5", Toy Biz
NM $5 **MIP** $10

Green Lantern, 1989, 5", Toy Biz
NM $10 **MIP** $22

Hawkman, 1989, 5", Toy Biz
NM $10 **MIP** $22

Joker, no forehead curl, 1989, 5", Toy Biz
NM $3 **MIP** $10

Joker, with forehead curl, 1989, 5", Toy Biz
NM $5 **MIP** $10

Lex Luthor, 1989, 5", Toy Biz
NM $3 **MIP** $10

Mr. Freeze, 1989, 5", Toy Biz
NM $5 **MIP** $12

Penguin, long missile, 1989, 5", Toy Biz
NM $8 **MIP** $20

Penguin, short missile, 1989, 5", Toy Biz
NM $8 **MIP** $30

Penguin, umbrella-firing, 1989, 5", Toy Biz
NM $4 **MIP** $10

DC Comics Super Heroes (Toy Biz, 1989)

Riddler, 1989, 5", Toy Biz
NM $4 **MIP** $10

Superman, 1989, 5", Toy Biz
NM $15 **MIP** $30

Two Face, 1989, 5", Toy Biz
NM $15 **MIP** $20

Wonder Woman, 1989, 5", Toy Biz
NM $8 **MIP** $15

Defenders of the Earth (Galoob, 1985)

FIGURES

Flash Gordon, 1985, 5-1/2", Galoob, Model No. 5100
NM $8 **MIP** $25

Garaz, 1985, 5-1/2", Galoob
NM $8 **MIP** $25

Lothar, 1985, 5-1/2", Galoob
NM $8 **MIP** $25

Mandrake, 1985, 5-1/2", Galoob
NM $8 **MIP** $25

Ming, 1985, 5-1/2", Galoob
NM $8 **MIP** $20

Phantom, The, 1985, 5-1/2", Galoob
NM $10 **MIP** $30

VEHICLES

Claw Copter, 1985, Galoob
NM $8 **MIP** $25

Flash Swordship, 1985, Galoob
NM $8 **MIP** $25

Garax Swordship, 1985, Galoob
NM $8 **MIP** $25

Phantom Skull Copter, 1985, Galoob
NM $10 **MIP** $35

Dick Tracy (Playmates, 1990)

FIGURES, LARGE

Breathless Mahoney, 1990, Playmates, Based on the movie, shown here with the Dick Tracy figure
NM $25 **MIP** $50

Dick Tracy, 1990, Playmates
NM $25 **MIP** $50

FIGURES, SMALL

Al "Big Boy" Caprice, 1990, Playmates, Photo with The Blank, Dick Tracy, Influence, Lips Manlis, and Sam Catchem
NM $3 **MIP** $10

Blank, The, 1990, Playmates
NM $45 **MIP** $100

Brow, The, 1990, Playmates, Photo with Mumbles, Flattop, Shoulders
NM $3 **MIP** $10

Dick Tracy, 1990, Playmates
NM $3 **MIP** $10

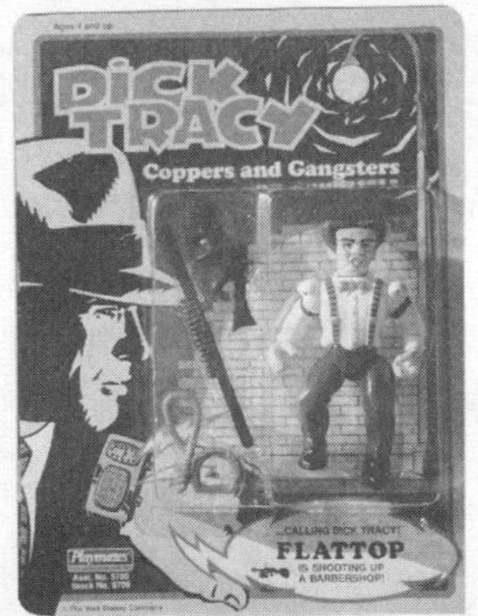

Flattop, 1990, Playmates, Includes Tommy gun and bullwhip
NM $3 **MIP** $10

Influence, 1990, Playmates
NM $3 **MIP** $10

Itchy, 1990, Playmates
NM $3 **MIP** $10

Lips Manlis, 1990, Playmates
NM $3 **MIP** $10

Mumbles, 1990, Playmates
NM $3 **MIP** $10

Pruneface, 1990, Playmates
NM $3 **MIP** $10

Rodent, The, 1990, Playmates
NM $3 **MIP** $10

Sam Catchem, 1990, Playmates
NM $3 **MIP** $10

Shoulders, 1990, Playmates
NM $3 **MIP** $10

Steve the Tramp, 1990, Playmates
NM $3 **MIP** $10

Die-Cast Super Heroes (Mego, 1979)

6" FIGURES

Batman, 1979, 6", Mego
NM $30 **MIP** $125

Hulk, 1979, 6", Mego
NM $25 **MIP** $75

Spider-Man, 1979, 6", Mego
NM $30 **MIP** $125

Superman, 1979, 6", Mego
NM $30 **MIP** $100

Doctor Who (Dapol, 1988-95)

FIGURES

Ace with bat and pack, 1988-95, Dapol
NM $4 **MIP** $10

Cyberman, 1988-95, Dapol
NM $4 **MIP** $10

Dalek, black and gold, with friction drive, 1988-95, Dapol
NM $5 **MIP** $12

Dalek, black and silver, with friction drive, 1988-95, Dapol
NM $5 **MIP** $12

Dalek, gold, with friction drive, 1988-95, Dapol
NM $5 **MIP** $12

Dalek, gray and black, with friction drive, 1988-95, Dapol
NM $5 **MIP** $12

Dalek, gray and black, with friction drive, 1988-95, Dapol
NM $5 **MIP** $12

Dalek, red and black, with friction drive, 1988-95, Dapol
NM $5 **MIP** $12

Dalek, red and gold, with friction drive, 1988-95, Dapol
NM $5 **MIP** $12

Dalek, white and gold, with friction drive, 1988-95, Dapol
NM $5 **MIP** $12

Doctor Who (2nd) Pat Troughton, 1988-95, Dapol
NM $5 **MIP** $12

Doctor Who (3rd), Jon Pertwee, 1988-95, Dapol
NM $5 **MIP** $12

Doctor Who (4th), Tom Baker, 1988-95, Dapol
NM $4 **MIP** $12

Doctor Who (7th) with brown coat, 1988-95, Dapol
NM $5 **MIP** $12

Doctor Who (7th) with gray coat, 1988-95, Dapol
NM $5 **MIP** $12

Early Cybermen, 1988-95, Dapol
NM $4 **MIP** $10

Ice Warrior, 1988-95, Dapol
NM $4 **MIP** $10

K9 with motor action, 1988-95, Dapol
NM $4 **MIP** $10

Master, The, 1988-95, Dapol
NM $4 **MIP** $10

Mel, blue shirt, 1988-95, Dapol
NM $4 **MIP** $10

Mel, pink shirt, 1988-95, Dapol
NM $4 **MIP** $10

Melkur, 1988-95, Dapol
NM $4 **MIP** $10

Sea Devil with cloth outfit, 1988-95, Dapol
NM $4 **MIP** $10

Silurian, 1988-95, Dapol
NM $4 **MIP** $10

Silurian, armored, 1988-95, Dapol
NM $4 **MIP** $10

Sontaran Captain with helmet, 1988-95, Dapol
NM $4 **MIP** $10

Tetrap, 1988-95, Dapol
NM $4 **MIP** $10

Time Lords, brown, 1988-95, Dapol
NM $4 **MIP** $10

Time Lords, burgundy, 1988-95, Dapol
NM $4 **MIP** $10

Time Lords, gray, 1988-95, Dapol
NM $4 **MIP** $10

Time Lords, off-white, 1988-95, Dapol
NM $4 **MIP** $10

PLAYSETS

Anniversary playset, 1988-95, Dapol
NM $30 **MIP** $70

Doctor Who (3rd) Play Set, 1988-95, Dapol
NM $20 **MIP** $60

Doctor Who playset w/ Console, 1988, Dapol
NM $100 **MIP** $200

VEHICLES AND ACCESSORIES

Dalek Play Set, 1988-95, Dapol, 4 figures
NM $20 **MIP** $40

Tardis with flashing light, 1988-95, Dapol
NM $25 **MIP** $50

Doctor Who (Denys Fisher, 1976)

FIGURES

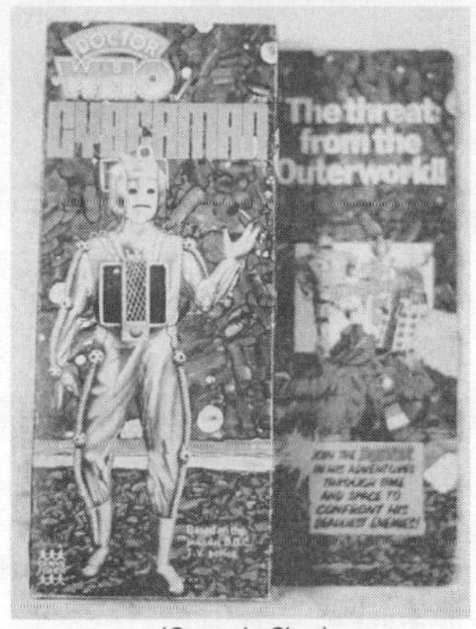

(Corey LeChat)

Cyberman, 1976, Denys Fisher, Very 1930s-looking robotic figure from the BBC-TV series. Called "The Threat from the Outerworld" on the box
NM $250 **MIP** $500

Dalek, 1976, Denys Fisher
NM $250 **MIP** $625

Doctor Who (4th), 1976, Denys Fisher
NM $100 **MIP** $250

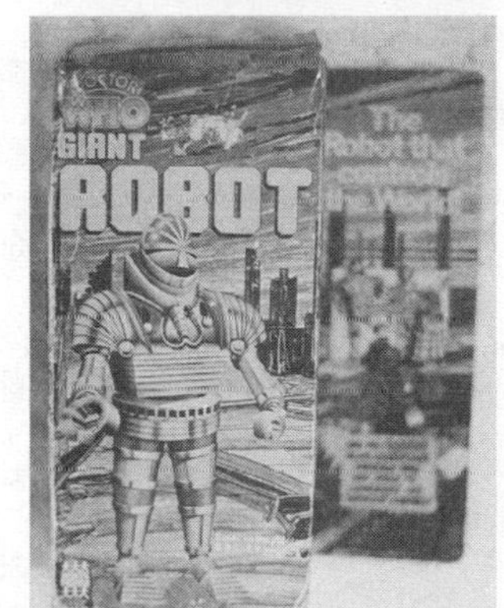

(Corey LeChat)

Giant Robot, 1976, Denys Fisher, Gray plastic robot from the BBC-TV series
NM $175 **MIP** $310

(Corey LeChat)

K-9, 1976, Denys Fisher, Looking much like today's toy robot dogs, this Talking K-9 could say a variety of phrases by pressing the control panel on his back
NM $160 **MIP** $310

Leela, 1976, Denys Fisher
NM $200 **MIP** $310

VEHICLES

(Corey LeChat)

Tardis play set, 1976, Denys Fisher, Plastic model of the time-travelling police call box as seen in the popular BBC-TV series
NM $160 **MIP** $325

Doctor Who (Palitoy, 1976)

FIGURES

(Corey LeChat)

Dalek, Talking, 1976, Palitoy, Shown on the right
NM $110 **MIP** $160

(Corey LeChat)

K-9, Talking, 1976, Palitoy
NM $160 **MIP** $260

Dukes of Hazzard (Mego, 1981-82)

3-3/4" CARDED FIGURES

Bo Duke, 1981-82, Mego
NM $8 **MIP** $20

Boss Hogg, 1981-82, Mego
NM $8 **MIP** $25

Cletus, 1981-82, Mego
NM $15 **MIP** $30

Cooter, 1981-82, Mego
NM $15 **MIP** $30

Coy Duke, 1981-82, Mego
NM $15 **MIP** $30

Dukes of Hazzard (Mego, 1981-82)

Daisy Duke, 1981-82, Mego
NM $12 MIP $25

Luke Duke, 1981-82, Mego
NM $8 MIP $20

Rosco Coltrane, 1981-82, Mego
NM $15 MIP $30

Uncle Jesse, 1981-82, Mego
NM $15 MIP $30

Vance Duke, 1981-82, Mego
NM $15 MIP $30

3-3/4" FIGURES WITH VEHICLES

Boss Hogg's Cadillac, 1981, Mego, w/ Boss Hogg figure
NM $45 MIP $90

Daisy Jeep with Daisy, 1981, boxed, 1981-82, Mego
NM $25 MIP $60

General Lee Car with Bo and Luke, 1981, boxed, 1981-82, Mego
NM $30 MIP $55

Police Car, 1981, Mego, w/ Sheriff Roscoe P. Coltrane
NM $40 MIP $80

8" CARDED FIGURES

Bo Duke, 1981-82, Mego
NM $15 MIP $30

Boss Hogg, 1981-82, Mego
NM $20 MIP $40

Coy Duke (card says Bo), 1981-82, Mego
NM $25 MIP $50

Daisy Duke, 1981-82, Mego
NM $25 MIP $50

(Lenny Lee)

Luke Duke, 1981-82, Mego
NM $15 MIP $30

Vance Duke (card says Luke), 1981-82, Mego
NM $25 MIP $50

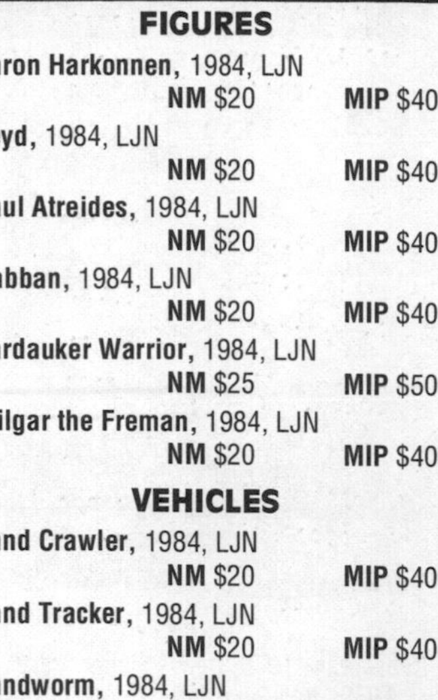

Dune (LJN, 1984)

FIGURES

Baron Harkonnen, 1984, LJN
NM $20 MIP $40

Feyd, 1984, LJN
NM $20 MIP $40

Paul Atreides, 1984, LJN
NM $20 MIP $40

Rabban, 1984, LJN
NM $20 MIP $40

Sardauker Warrior, 1984, LJN
NM $25 MIP $50

Stilgar the Freman, 1984, LJN
NM $20 MIP $40

VEHICLES

Sand Crawler, 1984, LJN
NM $20 MIP $40

Sand Tracker, 1984, LJN
NM $20 MIP $40

Sandworm, 1984, LJN
NM $25 MIP $50

Spice Scout, 1984, LJN
NM $25 MIP $50

Dungeons & Dragons (LJN, 1983-84)

MONSTERS

Dragonne, 1983, LJN
NM $25 MIP $75

Hook Horror, 1983, LJN
NM $20 MIP $45

Tiamat, 1983, LJN
NM $155 MIP $500

MOUNTS

Bronze Dragon, 1983, LJN
NM $20 MIP $60

Destrier, 1983, LJN
NM $15 MIP $45

Nightmare, 1983, LJN
NM $15 MIP $50

PLAY SETS

Fortress of Fangs, 1983, LJN
NM $125 MIP $300

SERIES I, 3-3/4" FIGURES, 1983

Elkhorn, 1983, LJN
NM $15 MIP $30

Kelek, 1983, LJN
NM $15 MIP $30

Melf, 1983, LJN
NM $15 MIP $40

Mercion, 1983, LJN
NM $18 MIP $40

Peralay, 1983, LJN
NM $15 MIP $40

Ringlerun, 1983, LJN
NM $15 MIP $30

Strongheart, 1983, LJN
NM $15 MIP $30

Warduke, 1983, LJN
NM $15 MIP $30

Zarak, 1983, LJN
NM $15 MIP $30

SERIES I, 5" FIGURES, 1983

Northlord, 1983, LJN
NM $20 MIP $50

Ogre King, 1983, LJN
NM $20 MIP $45

Young Male Titan, 1983, LJN
NM $12 MIP $30

SERIES II, 3-3/4" FIGURES, 1984

Bowmarc, 1984, LJN, w/"Battle-Matic Action"
NM $40 MIP $100

Deeth, 1984, LJN, w/"Battle-Matic Action"
NM $75 MIP $160

Drex, 1984, LJN, w/"Battle-Matic Action"
NM $55 MIP $120

Elkhorn, 1984, LJN, w/"Battle-Matic Action"
NM $20 MIP $60

Grimsword, 1984, LJN, w/"Battle-Matic Action"
NM $30 MIP $75

Hawkler, 1984, LJN, w/"Battle-Matic Action"
NM $60 MIP $120

Strongheart, 1984, LJN, w/"Battle-Matic Action"
NM $20 MIP $60

Warduke, 1984, LJN, w/"Battle-Matic Action"
NM $25 MIP $65

Zarak, 1984, LJN, w/"Battle-Matic Action"
NM $25 MIP $60

Zorgar, 1984, LJN, w/"Battle-Matic Action"
NM $60 MIP $135

SERIES II, 5" FIGURES, 1984

Mandoom, 1984, LJN
NM $100 MIP $175

Mettaflame, 1984, LJN
NM $110 MIP $175

Northlord, 1984, LJN
NM $75 MIP $200

Ogre King, 1984, LJN
NM $175 MIP $350

Young Male Titan, 1984, LJN
NM $70 MIP $150

E.T. the Extra-Terrestrial (LJN, 1982-83)

FIGURES

E.T and Elliot with bike, 1982-83, LJN
NM $10 MIP $20

E.T. with dress and hat, 1982-83, LJN
NM $6 MIP $12

E.T. with robe, 1982-83, LJN
NM $6 MIP $12

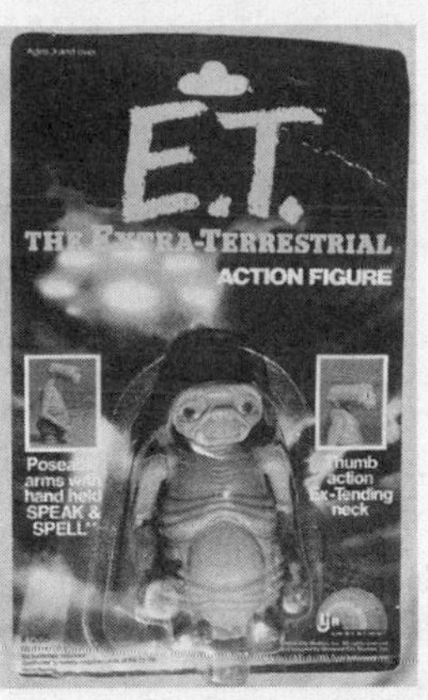

E.T. with Speak and Spell, 1982-83, LJN, Thumb-operated switch on E.T.'s back extends neck
NM $6 **MIP** $12

E.T., talking, 1982-83, LJN
NM $15 **MIP** $35

E.T., walking, 1982-83, LJN
NM $12 **MIP** $25

Earthworm Jim (Playmates, 1995)

FIGURES

Bob, 1995, Playmates
NM $5 **MIP** $12

Earthworm Jim with Battle Damage, 1995, Playmates
NM $5 **MIP** $10

(Playmates Toys)

Earthworm Jim with Pocket Rocket, 1995, Playmates, Figure with small turbo-driven vehicle (looks a bit like a Gee-Bee racer)
NM $5 **MIP** $10

Earthworm Jim with Snott, 1995, Playmates
NM $5 **MIP** $10

Hench Rat with Evil Cat, 1995, Playmates
NM $5 **MIP** $10

Monstrous Peter Puppy, 1995, Playmates
NM $5 **MIP** $10

Peter Puppy, 1995, Playmates
NM $5 **MIP** $10

Princess What's-Her-Name, 1995, Playmates
NM $7 **MIP** $12

Psycrow with Major Mucus, 1995, Playmates
NM $4 **MIP** $10

Emergency (LJN, 1973)

FIGURES

John, 1973, LJN
NM $35 **MIP** $100

Roy, 1973, LJN
NM $35 **MIP** $100

PLAY SETS

Fire House Play Set, 1973, LJN
NM $100 **MIP** $250

VEHICLES

Rescue Truck, 1973, LJN
NM $100 **MIP** $300

Evel Knievel (Ideal, 1973-74)

FIGURES

Evel Knievel, 1973-74, Ideal, red suit
NM $25 **MIP** $50

Robby Knievel, 1973-74, Ideal
NM $30 **MIP** $75

VEHICLES AND ACCESSORIES

Arctic Explorer set, 1973-74, Ideal
NM $35 **MIP** $75

Canyon Stunt Cycle, 1973-74, Ideal
NM $40 **MIP** $80

Chopper, 1973-74, Ideal
NM $35 **MIP** $80

Dragster, 1973-74, Ideal
NM $50 **MIP** $120

Explorer Set, 1973-74, Ideal
NM $20 **MIP** $40

Racing Set, 1973-74, Ideal
NM $20 **MIP** $40

Rescue Set, 1973-74, Ideal
NM $20 **MIP** $40

Road and Trail Set, 1973-74, Ideal
NM $50 **MIP** $125

Scramble Van, 1973-74, Ideal
NM $30 **MIP** $100

Skull Canyon Play Set, 1973-74, Ideal
NM $65 **MIP** $150

Stunt and Crash Car, 1973-74, Ideal
NM $50 **MIP** $120

Stunt Cycle, 1973-74, Ideal
NM $40 **MIP** $110

Stunt Stadium, 1973-74, Ideal
NM $50 **MIP** $110

Tail Bike, 1973-74, Ideal
NM $35 **MIP** $60

ExoSquad (Playmates, 1993-95)

EXOCONVERTING SERIES

J.T. Marsh with Exoconverting E-frame, 1993-94, Playmates
NM $8 **MIP** $15

EXOWALKING SERIES

Marsala with ExoWalking E-frame, 1993-94, Playmates
NM $8 **MIP** $15

GENERAL PURPOSE E-FRAMES WITH FIGURE, ORIGINAL SERIES

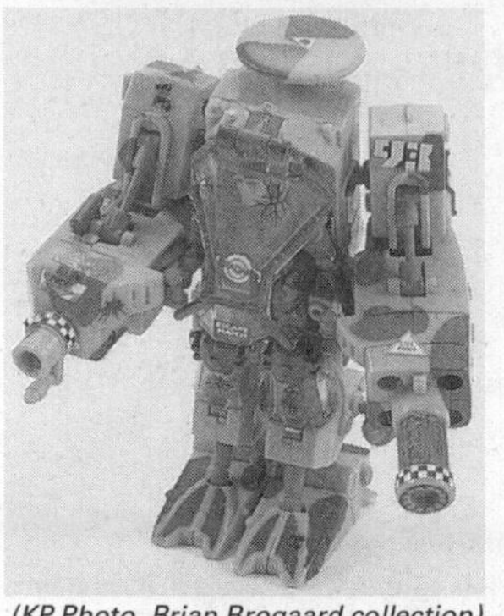
(KP Photo, Brian Brogaard collection)

Alec DeLeon with Field Communications, 1993-95, Playmates
NM $8 **MIP** $15

J.T. Marsh with Aerial Attack E-Frame, 1993-95, Playmates
NM $8 **MIP** $15

Pheaton with Command E-Frame, 1993-95, Playmates
NM $8 **MIP** $15

Typhonus with High Speed Stealth E-Frame, 1993-95, Playmates
NM $8 **MIP** $15

GENERAL PURPOSE E-FRAMES WITH FIGURE, SECONDARY SERIES

Draconis with Interrogator E-frame, 1994, Playmates
NM $8 **MIP** $15

Jinx Madison with Fire Warrior E-frame, 1994, Playmates
NM $8 **MIP** $15

Jonas Simbacca with Pirate Captain E-frame, 1994, Playmates
NM $8 **MIP** $15

Nara Burns with Reconnaissance E-frame, 1994, Playmates
NM $8 **MIP** $15

Peter Tanaka with Samurai E-frame, 1994, Playmates
NM $8 **MIP** $15

(KP Photo, Brian Brogaard collection)

Rita Torres with Field Sergeant E-frame, 1994, Playmates
NM $8 **MIP** $15

Sean Napier with police Enforcer E-frame, 1994, Playmates
NM $8 **MIP** $15

ExoSquad (Playmates, 1993-95)

Wolf Bronski with Ground Assault E-frame, 1994, Playmates
NM $8 MIP $15

GENERAL PURPOSE E-FRAMES WITH FIGURE, THIRD SERIES

(KP Photo, Brian Brogaard collection)

J.T. Marsh with Gridiron Command E-frame, 1995, Playmates
NM $8 MIP $15

Kaz Takagi with Gorilla E-frame, 1995, Playmates
NM $8 MIP $15

Marsala with Sub-Sonic Scout E-frame, 1995, Playmates
NM $8 MIP $15

Wolf Bronski with Medieval Knight E-frames, 1995, Playmates
NM $8 MIP $15

JUMPTROOPS

Captain Avery Butler, 1993-94, Playmates
NM $4 MIP $10

Gunnery Sergeant Ramon Longfeather, 1993-94, Playmates
NM $4 MIP $10

Lance Corporal Vince Pelligrino, 1993-94, Playmates
NM $4 MIP $10

Lieutenant Colleen O'Reilly, 1993-94, Playmates
NM $4 MIP $10

LIGHT ATTACK E-FRAMES

Livanus with Troop Transport E-frame, 1993-94, Playmates
NM $12 MIP $25

Maggie Weston with Field Repair E-frame, 1993-94, Playmates
NM $12 MIP $25

(KP Photo, Brian Brogaard collection)

Marsala with rapid Assault E-frame, 1993-94, Playmates
NM $12 MIP $25

Shiva with Amphibious Assault E-frame, 1993-94, Playmates
NM $50 MIP $110

MINI EXO-COMMAND BATTLE SETS

Alec DeLeon and Phaeton with Vesta Space Port Battleset, 1995, Playmates
NM $4 MIP $10

J.T. Marsh and Typhonus with Resolute II Hangar Battleset, 1995, Playmates
NM $4 MIP $10

Phaeton and J.T. Marsh with Olympus Mons Command Ship Bridge Battleset, 1995, Playmates
NM $4 MIP $10

NEO WARRIORS

Neo Cat, 1993-94, Playmates
NM $4 MIP $10

Neo Lord, 1993-94, Playmates
NM $4 MIP $10

ROBOTECH SERIES, 3" FIGURES

Excaliber, 1995, Playmates
NM $2 MIP $4

Gladiator, 1995, Playmates
NM $2 MIP $4

RaidarX, 1995, Playmates
NM $2 MIP $4

Spartan, 1995, Playmates
NM $2 MIP $4

ROBOTECH SERIES, 7" FIGURES

Excaliber MK VI, 1995, Playmates
NM $5 MIP $10

Gladiator Destroid, 1995, Playmates
NM $5 MIP $10

RaidarX, 1995, Playmates
NM $5 MIP $10

Spartan Destroid, 1995, Playmates
NM $5 MIP $10

Zentraedi Power Armor Botoru Battalion, 1995, Playmates
NM $5 MIP $10

Zentraedi Power Armor Quadrono Battalion, 1995, Playmates
NM $5 MIP $10

ROBOTECH SERIES, VEHICLES

VeriTech Hover Tank, 1995, Playmates
NM $12 MIP $24

VF-IS Veritech Fighter, 1995, Playmates
NM $8 MIP $15

SPACE SERIES

Exocarrier Resolute II, 1993-94, Playmates, with Mini E-frames
NM $12 MIP $25

Kaz Takagi, 1993-94, Playmates, with ExoFighter Space E-frame
NM $12 MIP $25

Thrax, 1993-94, Playmates, with NeoFighter Space E-frame
NM $12 MIP $25

SPECIAL MISSION E-FRAMES

Alec DeLeon, 1993-94, Playmates, with All-Terrain Special Mission E-frame
NM $8 MIP $15

J.T. Marsh, 1993-94, Playmates, with Deep Space Special Mission E-frame
NM $8 MIP $15

Typhonus, 1993-94, Playmates, with Deep Submergence Special Mission E-frame
NM $8 MIP $15

Wolf Ronski, 1993-94, Playmates, with Subterranean Special Mission E-frame
NM $8 MIP $15

Extreme Ghostbusters (Trendmasters, 1997-98)

FIGURES

Eduardo, 1997, Trendmasters
NM $2 MIP $5

Eduardo, Deluxe edition, 1997, Trendmasters
NM $2 MIP $5

Egon, 1997, Trendmasters
NM $2 MIP $5

Egon, Deluxe edition, 1997, Trendmasters
NM $2 MIP $5

House Ghost, 1997, Trendmasters
NM $2 MIP $5

Kylie, 1997, Trendmasters
NM $2 MIP $5

Kylie, Deluxe edition, 1997, Trendmasters
NM $2 MIP $5

Mouth Critter, 1997, Trendmasters
NM $2 MIP $5

Roland, 1997, Trendmasters
NM $2 MIP $5

Roland, Deluxe edition, 1997, Trendmasters
NM $2 MIP $5

Sam Hain, 1997, Trendmasters
NM $2 MIP $5

Slimer, 1997, Trendmasters
NM $2 MIP $5

VEHICLES AND ACCESSORIES

Ecto 1, 1997, Trendmasters
NM $12 MIP $25

Eduardo with Motorcycle, 1998, Trendmasters
NM $5 MIP $10

Roland and Gyro-Copter, 1998, Trendmasters
NM $5 MIP $10

Fantastic Four (Toy Biz, 1995)

10" BOXED FIGURES

Dr. Doom, 1995, Toy Biz
NM $6 MIP $12

Human Torch, 1995, Toy Biz
NM $6 MIP $12

Silver Surfer, 1995, Toy Biz
NM $10 MIP $15

The Thing, 1995, Toy Biz
NM $6 **MIP** $12

5" FIGURES

Annihilus, 1995, Toy Biz
NM $4 **MIP** $12

Attuma, 1995, Toy Biz
NM $4 **MIP** $12

Black Bolt, 1995, Toy Biz
NM $4 **MIP** $15

Blastaar, 1995, Toy Biz
NM $4 **MIP** $12

Dr. Doom, 1995, Toy Biz
NM $4 **MIP** $12

Dragon Man, 1995, Toy Biz
NM $4 **MIP** $12

Firelord, 1995, Toy Biz
NM $4 **MIP** $12

Gorgon, 1995, Toy Biz
NM $4 **MIP** $12

Human Torch, 1995, Toy Biz
NM $4 **MIP** $12

Invisible Woman, 1995, Toy Biz
NM $10 **MIP** $15

Mole Man, 1995, Toy Biz
NM $4 **MIP** $12

Mr. Fantastic, 1995, Toy Biz
NM $4 **MIP** $12

Namor the Sub-Mariner, 1995, Toy Biz
NM $4 **MIP** $12

Silver Surfer, 1995, Toy Biz
NM $4 **MIP** $12

Super Skrull, 1995, Toy Biz
NM $5 **MIP** $12

Terrax, 1995, Toy Biz
NM $4 **MIP** $12

Thanos, 1995, Toy Biz
NM $5 **MIP** $12

Thing, 1995, Toy Biz
NM $4 **MIP** $12

Thing II, 1995, Toy Biz
NM $4 **MIP** $12

Triton, 1995, Toy Biz
NM $4 **MIP** $12

ELECTRONIC 14" FIGURES

Galactus, 1995, Toy Biz
NM $10 **MIP** $40

Talking Thing, 1995, Toy Biz
NM $10 **MIP** $20

VEHICLES

Fantasticar, 1995, Toy Biz
NM $15 **MIP** $35

Mr. Fantastic Sky Shuttle, 1995, Toy Biz
NM $8 **MIP** $20

The Thing's Sky Cycle, 1995, Toy Biz
NM $8 **MIP** $20

Flash Gordon (Mego, 1976)

9" FIGURES

Dale Arden, 1976, 9", Mego
NM $35 **MIP** $85

Dr. Zarkow, 1976, 9", Mego
NM $55 **MIP** $110

Flash Gordon, 1976, 9", Mego
NM $55 **MIP** $110

Ming the Merciless, 1976, 9", Mego
NM $30 **MIP** $85

PLAY SETS

Flash Gordon Play Set, 1976, Mego
NM $55 **MIP** $130

Flash Gordon (Mattel, 1979)

FIGURE SETS

Bad Guys Set, 1979, 4", Mattel, 3 figures: Ming, Lizard Woman, Beastman, JCPenny exclusive
NM $30 **MIP** $75

Sears Set #1, 1979, 4", Mattel, four figures: Dr. Zarkhov, Ming, Vultan, Beastman, #59353, Sears exclusive
NM $30 **MIP** $75

Sears Set #2, 1979, 4", Mattel, four figures: Flash, Thun, Arak, Lizard Woman, #59357, Sears exclusive
NM $30 **MIP** $75

FIGURES

Beastman, 1979, 4", Mattel, Series 2, no accessories
NM $7 **MIP** $15

Captain Arak, 1979, 4", Mattel, Series 3, no accessories
NM $10 **MIP** $18

Dr. Zarkhov, 1979, 4", Mattel, Series 2, no accessories
NM $7 **MIP** $15

Flash Gordon, 1979, 4", Mattel, Series 1, white gun
NM $7 **MIP** $15

Lizard Woman, 1979, 4", Mattel, Series 1, white staff
NM $7 **MIP** $15

Ming the Merciless, 1979, 4", Mattel, Series 1, white gun
NM $7 **MIP** $15

Thun, the Lion Man, 1979, 4", Mattel, Series 1, white staff
NM $7 **MIP** $15

Vultan, 1979, 4", Mattel, Series 3, detachable wings
NM $12 **MIP** $25

VEHICLES

Ming's Shuttle, 1979, Mattel, plastic, scarce, includes blue cannon
NM $40 **MIP** $90

Rocket Ship, 1979, Mattel, plastic inflatable ship, detachable cockpit, orange nose cone cannon
NM $30 **MIP** $65

Flintstones (Mattel, 1994)

FIGURES

Betty and Bamm Bamm, 1994, Mattel
NM $1 **MIP** $2

Big Shot Fred, 1994, Mattel
NM $1 **MIP** $2

Evil Cliff Vandercave, 1994, Mattel
NM $1 **MIP** $2

Filling Station Barney, 1994, Mattel
NM $1 **MIP** $2

Hard Hat Fred, 1994, Mattel
NM $1 **MIP** $2

Lawn Bowling Barney, 1994, Mattel
NM $1 **MIP** $2

Licking Dino, 1994, Mattel
NM $1 **MIP** $2

Wilma and Pebbles, 1994, Mattel
NM $1 **MIP** $2

Gargoyles (Kenner, 1995-96)

ACCESSORIES

Gargoyle Castle, 1995, Kenner, Series 1
NM $20 **MIP** $40

Night Striker, 1995, Kenner
NM $10 **MIP** $20

Rippin' Rider Cycle, 1995, Kenner
NM $7 **MIP** $12

FIGURES

Battle Goliath, 1995, 5", Kenner, Series 2
NM $4 **MIP** $15

Broadway, 1995, 5", Kenner, Series 1, w/Power Slam Arms
NM $4 **MIP** $15

Broadway, 1996, 5", Hasbro, Hard Wired
NM $15 **MIP** $30

Bronx, 1995, 5", Kenner, Series 1
NM $4 **MIP** $15

Brooklyn, 1995, 5", Kenner, Series 1, w/Striking Horns and Snapping Jaw
NM $4 **MIP** $15

Castle Playset, 1995, Hasbro
NM $100 **MIP** $225

Claw Climber Goliath, 1995, 5", Kenner, Series 1
NM $4 **MIP** $15

Coldstone, 1996, 5", Hasbro, Hard Wired
NM $15 **MIP** $30

Demona, 1995, 5", Kenner, Series 1, w/Firing Stungun and Wingflap Attack
NM $4 **MIP** $15

Elisa Maza, 1995, 5", Hasbro, Series 1
NM $15 **MIP** $30

Flamestorm Goliath, 1996, 5", Hasbro
NM $15 **MIP** $30

Goliath, 1996, 5", Hasbro, Hard Wired
NM $15 **MIP** $30

Lexington, 1995, 5", Kenner, Series 1, w/Firing Stinging Crossbow
NM $4 **MIP** $15

Mighty Roar Goliath, 1995, 5", Kenner
NM $4 **MIP** $15

Power Wing Goliath, 1995, 5", Kenner
NM $4 **MIP** $15

Quick Strike Goliath, 1995, 5", Kenner, Series 1, w/Springing Attack Action
NM $4 **MIP** $15

Gargoyles (Kenner, 1995-96)

Steel Clan Robot, 1995, 5", Kenner, Series 1, w/Exploding Body Power
NM $4 MIP $15

Stone Armor Goliath, 1995, 5", Kenner, Series 1, w/Breaking Away Stone Plates and Flapping Wings
NM $4 MIP $15

Stone Camo Broadway, 1996, 5", Hasbro, Series 2
NM $15 MIP $30

Stone Camo Lexington, 1996, 5", Hasbro, Series 2
NM $15 MIP $30

Strike Hammer Macbeth, 1995, 5", Kenner, Series 1
NM $4 MIP $15

Xanatos, 1995, 5", Kenner, Series 1, w/Gargoyles Disguise Armor and Battle Wings
NM $4 MIP $15

Xanatos, 1996, 5", Hasbro, Series 2
NM $15 MIP $30

Generation X (Toy Biz, 1995-96)

FRESHMAN, 5" FIGURES

Chamber, 1995
NM $2 MIP $6

Emplate, 1995, Toy Biz
NM $2 MIP $6

Jubilee, 1995, Toy Biz
NM $2 MIP $6

Penance, 1995, Toy Biz
NM $2 MIP $6

Phalanx, 1995, Toy Biz
NM $2 MIP $6

Skin, 1995, Toy Biz
NM $2 MIP $6

SOPHOMORE, 5" FIGURES

Banshee, 1996, Toy Biz
NM $3 MIP $6

Marrow, 1996, Toy Biz
NM $3 MIP $6

Mondo, 1996, Toy Biz
NM $3 MIP $6

Protector, The, 1996, Toy Biz
NM $3 MIP $6

White Queen, 1996, Toy Biz
NM $4 MIP $8

Ghost Rider (Toy Biz, 1995-96)

10" FIGURES

Blaze, 1995, 10"
NM $5 MIP $12

Ghost Rider, 1995, 10"
NM $6 MIP $15

Vengence, 1995, 10"
NM $5 MIP $12

5" FIGURES

Armored Blaze, 1996, Toy Biz
NM $3 MIP $8

Blackout, 1995, 5"
NM $4 MIP $10

Blaze, 1995, 5"
NM $4 MIP $10

Ghost Rider, 1995, 5"
NM $3 MIP $8

Ghost Rider II, 1996, Toy Biz, w/transforming action
NM $3 MIP $8

Outcast, 1996, Toy Biz
NM $3 MIP $8

Skinner, 1995, 5", w/ Extending Rib action
NM $6 MIP $15

Vengence, 1995, 5"
NM $10 MIP $20

Zarathos, 1995, 5"
NM $8 MIP $18

FLAMIN' STUNT CYCLES WITH MOLDED-ON FIGURES

Blaze, 1995
NM $10 MIP $25

Ghost Rider, 1995
NM $8 MIP $18

Vengeance, 1995
NM $10 MIP $25

PLAY SETS

Ghost Rider Play Set, 1995
NM $8 MIP $18

SPIRIT OF VENGEANCE MOTORCYCLES AND FIGURES

Blaze, 1995, Toy Biz
NM $8 MIP $18

Ghost Rider, 1995, Toy Biz
NM $10 MIP $25

Vengeance, 1995
NM $8 MIP $18

Ghostbusters (Kenner, 1986-91)

1986

Bad to the Bone Ghost, Kenner
NM $5 MIP $15

Banshee Bomber Gooper Ghost with Ecto-Plazm, Kenner
NM $15 MIP $35

Bug-Eye Ghost, Kenner
NM $5 MIP $15

Ecto-1, Kenner
NM $35 MIP $80

Egon Spengler & Gulper Ghost, Kenner, 5-1/4" tall
NM $15 MIP $60

Firehouse Headquarters, Kenner
NM $50 MIP $110

Ghost Popper, Kenner
NM $15 MIP $35

Ghost Zapper, Kenner
NM $7 MIP $18

Gooper Ghost Sludge Bucket, Kenner
NM $15 MIP $35

Gooper Ghost Squisher with Ecto-Plazm, Kenner
NM $15 MIP $35

Green Ghost with Pizza, Kenner
NM $20 MIP $50

H2 Ghost, Kenner
NM $5 MIP $15

Peter Venkman & Grabber Ghost, 5-1/4", Kenner
NM $15 MIP $60

Proton Pack, Kenner
NM $20 MIP $45

Ray Stantz & Wrapper Ghost, 5-1/4", Kenner
NM $15 MIP $60

Slimer Plush Figure, 13", Kenner
NM $20 MIP $35

Stay-Puft Marshmallow Man Plush, 13-3/4", Kenner, plush
NM $45 MIP $75

Winston Zeddmore & Chomper Ghost, 5-1/4", Kenner
NM $15 MIP $60

1988

Brain Blaster Ghost Haunted Human, Kenner
NM $5 MIP $15

Ecto-2 Helicopter, Kenner
NM $14 MIP $25

Fright Feature Egon, Kenner
NM $8 MIP $25

Fright Feature Janine Melnitz, Kenner
NM $8 MIP $25

Fright Feature Peter, Kenner
NM $8 MIP $25

Fright Feature Ray, Kenner
NM $8 MIP $25

Fright Feature Winston, Kenner
NM $8 MIP $25

Granny Gross Haunted Human, Kenner
NM $5 MIP $15

Green Ghost, Kenner
NM $12 MIP $25

Hard Hat Horror Haunted Human, Kenner
NM $5 MIP $15

Highway Haunter, Kenner
NM $12 MIP $25

Mail Fraud Haunted Human, Kenner
NM $5 MIP $15

Mini Ghost Mini-Gooper, Kenner
NM $5 MIP $12

Mini Ghost Mini-Shooter, Kenner
NM $5 MIP $12

Mini Ghost Mini-Trap, Kenner
NM $5 MIP $12

Pull Speed Ahead Ghost, Kenner
NM $5 MIP $15

Terror Trash Haunted Human, Kenner
NM $5 MIP $15

Tombstone Tackle Haunted Human, Kenner
NM $5 MIP $15

X-Cop Haunted Human, Kenner
NM $5 MIP $15

1989

Dracula, Kenner
NM $12 MIP $25

Ecto-3, Kenner
NM $12 MIP $25

Fearsome Flush, Kenner
NM $10 MIP $22

Frankenstein, Kenner
NM $10 MIP $22

Hunchback, Kenner
NM $10 MIP $22

Mummy, Kenner
NM $10 MIP $22

Screaming Hero Egon, Kenner
NM $10 MIP $25

Screaming Hero Janine Melnitz, Kenner
NM $10 MIP $15

Screaming Hero Peter, Kenner
NM $10 MIP $15

Screaming Hero Ray, Kenner
NM $10 MIP $15

Screaming Horo Winston, Kenner
NM $10 MIP $15

Slimer with Proton Pack, red or blue, Kenner, red or blue
NM $15 MIP $35

Super Fright Egon with Slimy Spider, Kenner
NM $10 MIP $25

Super Fright Janine with Boo Fish Ghost, Kenner
NM $10 MIP $25

Super Fright Peter Venkman & Snake Head, Kenner
NM $10 MIP $25

Super Fright Ray, Kenner
NM $10 MIP $25

Super Fright Winston Zeddmore & Meanie Wienie, Kenner
NM $10 MIP $25

Wolfman, Kenner
NM $10 MIP $25

Zombie, Kenner
NM $10 MIP $25

1990

Ecto Bomber with Bomber Ghost, Kenner
NM $10 MIP $25

Ecto-1A with Ambulance Ghost, Kenner
NM $20 MIP $55

Ghost Sweeper, Kenner, vehicle in box
NM $10 MIP $22

Gobblin' Goblin Nasty Neck, Kenner
NM $12 MIP $25

Gobblin' Goblin Terrible Teeth, Kenner, boxed action figure
NM $12 MIP $25

Gobblin' Goblin Terror Tongue, Kenner, boxed action figure
NM $12 MIP $25

Slimed Hero Egon, Kenner
NM $8 MIP $15

Slimed Hero Louis Tully & Four Eyed Ghost, Kenner
NM $8 MIP $15

Slimed Hero Peter Venkman & Tooth Ghost, Kenner
NM $8 MIP $15

Slimed Hero Ray Stantz & Vapor Ghost, Kenner
NM $8 MIP $15

Slimed Hero Winston, Kenner, boxed action figure
NM $8 MIP $15

1991

Ecto-Glow Egon, Kenner
NM $12 MIP $25

Ecto-Glow Louis Tully, Kenner
NM $12 MIP $25

Ecto-Glow Peter, Kenner
NM $12 MIP $25

Ecto-Glow Ray, Kenner
NM $12 MIP $25

Ecto-Glow Winston Zeddmore, Kenner
NM $12 MIP $25

Ghostbusters, Filmation (Schaper, 1986)

FIGURES

Belfry and Brat-A-Rat, 1986, Schaper
NM $10 MIP $15

Bone Troller, 1986, Schaper
NM $10 MIP $15

Eddie, 1986, Schaper
NM $10 MIP $15

Fangster, 1986, Schaper
NM $10 MIP $15

Fib Face, 1986, Schaper
NM $10 MIP $15

Futura, 1986, Schaper
NM $10 MIP $15

Ghost Popper Ghost Buggy, 1986, Schaper
NM $20 MIP $40

Haunter, 1986, Schaper
NM $10 MIP $15

Jake, 1986, Schaper
NM $10 MIP $15

Jessica, 1986, Schaper
NM $10 MIP $15

Mysteria, 1986, Schaper
NM $10 MIP $15

Prime Evil, 1986, Schaper
NM $12 MIP $18

Scare Scooter Vehicle, 1986, Schaper
NM $10 MIP $20

Scared Stiff, 1986, Schaper
NM $6 MIP $15

Tracy, 1986, Schaper
NM $10 MIP $15

VEHICLES

Time Hopper Vehicle, 1986, Schaper
NM $10 MIP $15

Godzilla (Trendmasters, 1998-99)

FIGURES

Baby X Baby Godzilla, 1998-99
NM $3 MIP $8

Capture Net Phillipe, 1998-99
NM $2 MIP $8

Claw Slashing Baby Godzilla, 1998-99
NM $3 MIP $6

Combat Claw Godzilla, 1998-99
NM $8 MIP $12

Double Blast O'Neil, 1998-99
NM $3 MIP $7

Fang Bite Godzilla, 1998-99
NM $3 MIP $7

Grapple Gear Nick, 1998-99
NM $3 MIP $7

Hammer Tail Baby Godzilla Hatchling, 1998-99
NM $3 MIP $7

Living Godzilla, 1998-99
NM $8 MIP $20

Monster Claw Baby Godzilla Hatching, 1998-99
NM $3 MIP $7

Nuclear Strike Godzilla vs. Hornet Jet, 1998-99
NM $3 MIP $7

Power Shield Jean-Luc, 1998-99
NM $3 MIP $7

Razor Bite Godzilla, 1998-99
NM $8 MIP $20

Razor Fang Baby Godzilla, 1998-99
NM $3 MIP $7

Shatter Blast Godzilla vs. Rocket Launcher, 1998-99
NM $3 MIP $7

Shatter Tail Godzilla, 1998-99
NM $7 MIP $15

Spike Jaw Baby Godzilla Hatchling, 1998-99
NM $3 MIP $7

Supreme Godzilla, 1998-99
NM $12 MIP $25

Tail Thrasher Baby Godzilla, 1998-99
NM $3 MIP $7

Thunder Tail Godzilla, 1998-99
NM $7 MIP $15

Ultimate Godzilla, 1998-99
NM $12 MIP $30

Ultra Attack Animal, 1998-99
NM $3 MIP $7

VEHICLES

All-Terrain Vehicle with figure, 1998-99
NM $7 MIP $15

Apache Attack Copter, 1998-99
NM $10 MIP $20

Battle Bike with figure, 1998-99
NM $7 MIP $15

Battle Blaster with figure, 1998-99
NM $7 MIP $15

Godzilla (Trendmasters, 1998-99)

Combat Cannon with figure, 1998-99
NM $7 MIP $15

Thunderblast Tank, 1998-99
NM $7 MIP $15

Godzilla Wars (Trendmasters, 1996)

FIGURES

Battra, 1996
NM $4 MIP $8

Biollante, 1996
NM $4 MIP $8

Gigan, 1996
NM $4 MIP $8

Moguera, 1996
NM $4 MIP $8

Space Godzilla, 1996
NM $4 MIP $8

Supercharged Godzilla, 1996
NM $4 MIP $8

Godzilla: King of the Monsters (Trendmasters, 1995)

10" FIGURES

Ghidorah, 1995
NM $4 MIP $10

Ghidorah, walking, 1995
NM $6 MIP $12

Godzilla, 1995
NM $4 MIP $10

Godzilla, walking, 1995
NM $7 MIP $15

Mecha-Ghidora, 1995
NM $6 MIP $12

Mecha-Godzilla, 1995
NM $6 MIP $12

Mothra, 1995
NM $8 MIP $16

Rodan, 1995
NM $4 MIP $10

4-6" FIGURES

Battra, 1995
NM $4 MIP $8

Biollante, 1995
NM $4 MIP $8

Ghidorah, boxed, 1995, 5-6"
NM $4 MIP $8

Ghidorah, carded, 1995, 4-5"
NM $5 MIP $10

Gigan, 1995
NM $5 MIP $10

Godzilla, boxed, 1995, 5-6"
NM $4 MIP $8

Mecha-Ghidorah, boxed, 1995, 5-6"
NM $4 MIP $8

Mecha-Ghidorah, carded, 1995, 4-5"
NM $3 MIP $6

Mecha-Godzilla, boxed, 1995, 5-6"
NM $4 MIP $8

Mecha-Godzilla, carded, 1995, 4-5"
NM $3 MIP $6

Moguera, 1995
NM $4 MIP $10

Mothra, boxed, 1995, 5-6"
NM $5 MIP $10

Mothra, carded, 1995, 4-5"
NM $4 MIP $8

Rodan, boxed, 1995, 5-6"
NM $4 MIP $8

Rodan, carded, 1995, 4-5"
NM $3 MIP $6

Greatest American Hero, The (Mego, 1981)

VEHICLES

Convertible Bug with Ralph and Bill figures, 1981, Mego
NM $175 MIP $520

Happy Days (Mego, 1978)

FIGURES

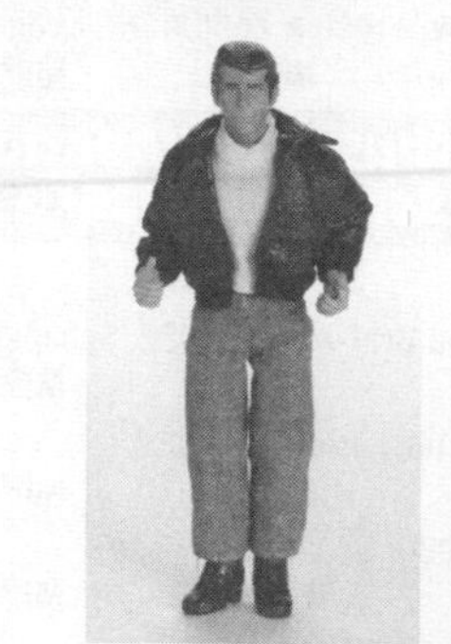

Fonzie, boxed, 1978, 8", Mego
NM $30 MIP $100

Fonzie, carded, 1978, 8", Mego
NM $30 MIP $75

Potsie, carded, 1978, 8", Mego
NM $30 MIP $75

(Lenny Lee)

Ralph, carded, 1978, 8", Mego
NM $30 MIP $75

Richie, carded, 1978, 8", Mego
NM $30 MIP $75

PLAY SETS

Fonzie's Garage Play Set, 1978, Mego
NM $75 MIP $180

VEHICLES

Fonzie's Jalopy, 1978, Mego
NM $45 MIP $85

Fonzie's Motorcycle, 1978, Mego
NM $40 MIP $80

He-Man 2nd Animated Series (Mattel, 1989-1992)

ACCESSORIES

Electronic Terror Punch, 1992, Mattel
NM $4 MIP $10

Electronic Thunder Punch, 1992, Mattel
NM $4 MIP $10

Power Sword, 1989, Mattel
NM $10 MIP $20

Rocket Disk Power Pack, 1989, Mattel
NM $4 MIP $8

Sagitar (Tharkus), 1991, Mattel, creature
NM $10 MIP $20

Skull Staff, 1991, Mattel
NM $10 MIP $20

Turbo Tormentor, 1989, Mattel
NM $4 MIP $8

FIGURES

Artilla (Weaponstronic), 1991, 5", Mattel, Series 3
NM $5 MIP $15

Battle Blade Skeletor, 1992, 5", Mattel, Series 4
NM $5 MIP $12

Battle Punching He-Man, 1990, 5", Mattel, Series 2
NM $5 MIP $15

Butthead, 1991, 5", Mattel, Series 3
NM $5 MIP $15

Disk of Doom Skeletor, 1990, 5", Mattel, Series 2
NM $7 MIP $18

Flipshot (Icarius), 1989, 5", Mattel, Series 1
NM $5 MIP $25

Flogg (Brakk), 1989, 5", Mattel, Series 1
NM $5 MIP $25

He-Man, 1989, Mattel, Series 1
NM $6 MIP $12

He-Man with Flogg, 1989, Mattel, Series 1
NM $7 MIP $18

He-Man with Skeletor, 1989, Mattel, Series 1
NM $12 MIP $30

He-Man with Slush Head, 1989, Mattel, Series 1
NM $12 MIP $30

Hoove, 1990, 5", Mattel, Series 2
NM $5 MIP $15

Hydron, 1989, 5", Mattel, Series 1
NM $5 MIP $25

Kalamarr, 1989, Mattel, Series 1
NM $6 MIP $12

Karatti, 1991, Mattel, Series 3
NM $6 MIP $12

Kayo (Tartarus), 1990, 5", Mattel, Series 2
NM $5 MIP $15

Lizorr, 1990, 5", Mattel, Series 2
NM $5 MIP $15

Missile Armor Flipshot Hook 'em Flogg, 1992, 5", Mattel
NM $12 MIP $30

Nocturna, 1990, 5", Mattel, Series 2
NM $5 MIP $15

Optikk, 1990, 5", Mattel, Seires 2, Model No. 3262
NM $5 MIP $15

Quakke (Earthquake), 1991, 5", Mattel, Series 3
NM $5 MIP $15

Skeletor, 1989, Mattel, Series 1
NM $6 MIP $12

Slush Head (Kalamarr), 1989, 5", Mattel, Series 1
NM $7 MIP $25

Spin-Fist Hydron, 1992, 5", Mattel, Series 4
NM $5 MIP $12

Spinwit (Tornado), 1991, 5", Mattel, Series 3
NM $5 MIP $15

Staghorn, 1991, 5", Mattel, Series 3
NM $5 MIP $15

Thunder Punch He-Man, 1992, 5", Mattel, Series 4
NM $5 MIP $12

Too-Tall Hoove, 1992, 5", Mattel, Series 4
NM $5 MIP $12

Tuskador (Insyzor), 1991, 5", Mattel, Series 3
NM $5 MIP $15

Vizar, 1990, 5", Mattel, Series 2
NM $5 MIP $15

PLAY SETS

Nordor, 1990, Mattel
NM $100 MIP $250

Starship Eternia, 1989, Mattel
NM $100 MIP $250

VEHICLES

Astrosub, 1989, Mattel
NM $10 MIP $20

Battle Bird, 1991, Mattel
NM $10 MIP $20

Bolajet, 1989, Mattel
NM $10 MIP $20

Doomcopter (Skullcopter), 1991, Mattel
NM $10 MIP $20

Dreadwing (Shuttlepod), 1989, Mattel
NM $5 MIP $15

Sagitar, 1989-91, Mattel
NM $6 MIP $14

Terrorclaw (Terrapod), 1989, Mattel
NM $5 MIP $15

Terrortread (Dreadtread), 1991, Mattel
NM $10 MIP $20

He-Man Reissues (Mattel, 2000-01)

ACCESSORIES

He-Man with Battle Cat, 2000, Mattel, Series 1
NM $20 MIP $50

Skeletor with Panthor, 2000, Mattel, Series 1
NM $20 MIP $50

FIGURES

Battle Armor He-Man, 2001, 5", Mattel, Series 2
NM $5 MIP $15

Battle Armor Skeletor, 2001, 5", Mattel, Series 2
NM $5 MIP $15

Beast Man, 2000, 5", Mattel, Series 1
NM $5 MIP $18

Buzz Off, 2001, 5", Mattel, Series 2
NM $5 MIP $15

Clawful, 2001, 5", Mattel, Series 2
NM $5 MIP $15

Evil-Lyn, 2000, 5", Mattel, Series 1
NM $5 MIP $20

Faker, 2000, 5", Mattel, Series 1
NM $10 MIP $22

He-Man, 2000, 5", Mattel, Series 1
NM $10 MIP $22

Man-At-Arms, 2000, 5", Mattel, Series 1
NM $5 MIP $15

Mer-Man, 2000, 5", Mattel, Series 1
NM $5 MIP $15

Skeletor, 2000, 5", Mattel, Series 1
NM $10 MIP $22

Stratos, 2001, 5", Mattel, Series 2
NM $5 MIP $15

Teela, 2000, 5", Mattel, Series 1
NM $5 MIP $15

Trap Jaw, 2000, 5", Mattel, Series 1
NM $5 MIP $15

Tri-Klops, 2000, 5", Mattel, Series 1
NM $5 MIP $15

Zodac, 2001, 5", Mattel, Series 2
NM $5 MIP $15

GIFTSETS

Figure 10-pack, JC Penney exclusive, 2001, 5", Mattel, Series 2
NM $75 MIP $250

Figure 5-pack w/ exclusive Moss Man, 2001, 5", Mattel, Series 2
NM $40 MIP $100

Figure 5-pack w/ exclusive Prince Adam, 2001, 5", Mattel, Series 2
NM $40 MIP $100

Hercules: The Legend Continues (Toy Biz, 1995-97)

DELUXE 10" FIGURES

Hercules and Xena, 1995-97, Toy Biz
NM $20 MIP $40

FIGURES

Ares, Detachable Weapons of War, 1995-97, 5", Toy Biz
NM $3 MIP $5

Centaur, Bug Horse Kick, 1995-97, 5", Toy Biz
NM $3 MIP $5

Hercules I, Iron Spiked Spinning Mace, 1995-97, 5", Toy Biz
NM $3 MIP $5

Hercules II, Archery Combat Set, 1995-97, 5", Toy Biz
NM $3 MIP $5

Hercules III, Herculean Assault Blades, 1995-97, 5", Toy Biz
NM $3 MIP $5

Hercules with Chain Breaking Strength, 1995-97, 5", Toy Biz
NM $3 MIP $5

Hercules, Swash Buckling, 1995-97, 5", Toy Biz
NM $3 MIP $5

Iolaus, Catapult Battle Gear, 1995-97, 5", Toy Biz
NM $3 MIP $5

Minotaur, Immobilizing Sludge Mask, 1995-97, 5", Toy Biz
NM $3 MIP $5

Mole-Man, Exploding Body, 1995-97, 5", Toy Biz
NM $3 MIP $5

She-Demon, Stone Strike Tail, 1995-97, 5", Toy Biz
NM $4 MIP $5

Xena, Warrior Princess Weaponry, 1995-97, 5", Toy Biz
NM $7 MIP $28

MONSTERS

Cerberus, 1995-97, Toy Biz
NM $4 MIP $8

Echidna, 1995-97, Toy Biz
NM $4 MIP $8

Graegus, 1995-97, Toy Biz
NM $4 MIP $8

Hydra, 1995-97, Toy Biz
NM $4 MIP $8

Labyrinth Snake, 1995-97, Toy Biz
NM $4 MIP $8

Stymphalian Bird, 1995-97, Toy Biz
NM $4 MIP $8

PLAY SETS

Hercules Tower of Power Play Set, 1995-97, Toy Biz
NM $4 MIP $10

Hercules: The Legendary Journeys (Toy Biz, 1995-97)

DELUXE 10" FIGURES

Hercules with bladed shield and sword dagger, 1997, Toy Biz
NM $8 MIP $20

Xena with two sets of body armor, 1997, Toy Biz
NM $8 MIP $20

LEGENDARY WARRIOR TWIN PACKS, 5" FIGURES

Hercules and Iolaus, 1997, Toy Biz
NM $8 MIP $20

Hercules and Xena, 1997, Toy Biz
NM $8 MIP $20

Xena and Gabrielle, 1997, Toy Biz
NM $10 MIP $40

Hercules: The Legendary Journeys (Toy Biz, 1995-97)

LEGENDARY WARRIORS, 5" FIGURES

Hercules, Mace Hurling Hercules, 1997, Toy Biz
NM $3 MIP $8

Iolaus, Catapult Back-pack Iolaus, 1997, Toy Biz
NM $4 MIP $10

Nessus, Leg Kicking Centaur, 1997, Toy Biz
NM $3 MIP $8

Xena, Temptress Costume Xena, 1997, Toy Biz
NM $4 MIP $10

MONSTERS, 6" FIGURES

Cerberus, 1997, Toy Biz
NM $3 MIP $10

Graegus, 1997, Toy Biz
NM $3 MIP $10

Hydra, 1997, Toy Biz
NM $3 MIP $10

MT. OLYMPUS GAMES, 5" FIGURES

Atlanta, Spear Shooting Weaponry Rack, 1997, Toy Biz
NM $4 MIP $12

Hercules, Discus Launcher, 1997, Toy Biz
NM $3 MIP $8

Mesomorph, Shield Attack Action, 1997, Toy Biz
NM $3 MIP $8

Salmoneus, Light-up Olympic Torch, 1997, Toy Biz
NM $3 MIP $8

Heroes of the American Revolution (Bonanza, 1970s)

FIGURES

Benjamin Franklin, 7", Bonanza
NM $10 MIP $25

Daniel Boone, 7", Bonanza
NM $10 MIP $25

George Washington, 7", Bonanza
NM $10 MIP $25

John Paul Jones, 7", Bonanza
NM $10 MIP $25

Marquis de Lafayette, 7", Bonanza
NM $10 MIP $25

Nathan Hale, 7", Bonanza
NM $10 MIP $25

Patrick Henry, 7", Bonanza
NM $10 MIP $25

Paul Revere, 7", Bonanza
NM $10 MIP $25

Thomas Jefferson, 7", Bonanza
NM $10 MIP $25

Honey West (Gilbert, 1965)

ACCESSORIES

Formal Outfit, 1965, 1965
NM $55 MIP $110

Honey West Accessory Set, 1965, Gilbert, telephone purse, lipstick, handcuffs and telescope
NM $50 MIP $95

Honey West Accessory Set, 1965, Gilbert, cap-firing pistol, binoculars, shoes and glasses
NM $50 MIP $95

Karate Outfit, 1965, Gilbert
NM $55 MIP $110

Pet Set with Ocelot, 1965, Gilbert
NM $60 MIP $110

Secret Agent Outfit, 1965, Gilbert
NM $55 MIP $100

FIGURES

Honey West Doll, 1965, 12", Gilbert
NM $175 MIP $325

Hook (Mattel, 1991-92)

5" FIGURES

Captain Hook, Multi-blade, 1991-92, Mattel
NM $4 MIP $10

Captain Hook, Swiss Army, 1991-92, Mattel
NM $8 MIP $18

Captain Hook, Tall Terror, 1991-92, Mattel
NM $4 MIP $10

Lost Boy Ace, 1991-92, Mattel
NM $3 MIP $10

Lost Boy Ruffio, 1991-92, Mattel
NM $3 MIP $10

Lost Boy Thud Butt, 1991-92, Mattel
NM $8 MIP $18

Peter Pan, Air Attack, 1991-92, Mattel
NM $4 MIP $10

Peter Pan, Battle Swing, 1991-92, Mattel
NM $5 MIP $15

Peter Pan, Food Fighting, 1991-92, Mattel
NM $5 MIP $15

Peter Pan, Swashbuckling, 1991-92, Mattel
NM $4 MIP $10

Pirate Bill Jukes, 1991-92, Mattel
NM $4 MIP $10

Pirate Smee, 1991-92, Mattel
NM $5 MIP $12

DELUXE FIGURES

Captain Hook, Skull Armor, 1991-92, Mattel
NM $10 MIP $25

Lost Boy Attack Croc, 1991-92, Mattel
NM $8 MIP $18

Pete Pan, Learn to Fly, 1991-92, Mattel
NM $10 MIP $25

VEHICLES

Lost Boy Attack Raft, 1991-92, Mattel
NM $8 MIP $20

Lost Boy Strike Tank, 1991-92, Mattel
NM $8 MIP $20

Incredible Hulk, The (Toy Biz, 1996-97)

6" FIGURES

Abomination, Toxic Blaster, 1996
NM $5 MIP $12

Gray Hulk Battle Damaged, 1996
NM $4 MIP $10

Leader, Anti-Hulk Armor, 1996
NM $4 MIP $10

Savage Hulk, Transforming Action, 1996
NM $4 MIP $10

She Hulk, Gamma Cross Bow, 1996
NM $5 MIP $12

OUTCASTS, 5" FIGURES

Battle Hulk, Mutant Outcast, 1997
NM $4 MIP $10

Chainsaw, Gamma Outcast Bat, 1997
NM $4 MIP $10

Leader-Hulk Metamorphosized, Gargoyle Sidekick, 1997
NM $4 MIP $10

Two-Head, Gamma Outcast Kangaroo-Rat, 1997
NM $4 MIP $10

Wendingo, Gamma Outcast Rattlesnake, 1997
NM $4 MIP $10

PLAY SETS

Gamma Ray Trap, 1997
NM $4 MIP $10

Steel Body Trap, 1997
NM $4 MIP $10

SMASH AND CRASH, 5" FIGURES

Battle-Damaged Hulk with Restraints and Smash Out Action, 1997
NM $4 MIP $10

Doc Samson, Omega with Missile Firing Action, 1997
NM $4 MIP $12

Incredible Hulk, Crash out Action, 1997
NM $4 MIP $10

Leader, Evil Robot Drone with Missile Firing Action, 1997
NM $4 MIP $10

Zzzax with Energy Trap, 1997
NM $3 MIP $8

TRANSFORMATIONS, 6" FIGURES

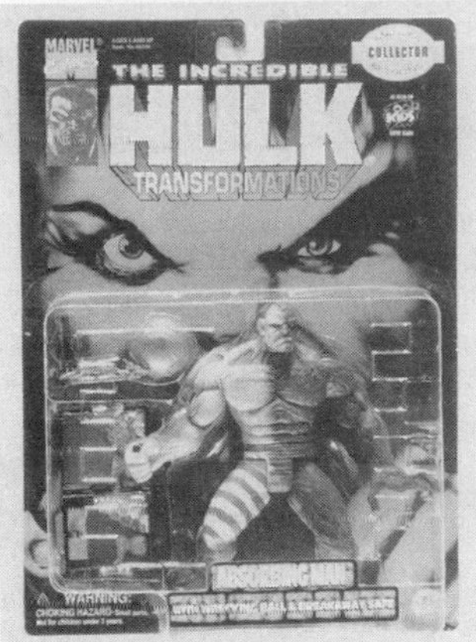

Absorbing Man, Breakaway Safe and Wrecking Ball, 1997, Includes accessories
NM $4 MIP $10

Hulk 2099, Futuristic Clip-on Weapons, 1997
NM $3 MIP $8

Maestro, Fallen Hero Armor, 1997, Includes Captain America's broken shield, and a belt featuring the masks of Iron Man and other Marvel characters
NM $10 MIP $18

Smart Hulk, Gamma Blaster Backpack, 1997
NM $3 MIP $8

Independence Day (Trendmasters, 1996)

FIGURES

Alien Attacker Pilot, 1996, Trendmasters
NM $5 MIP $10

Alien in Bio Chamber, 1996, Trendmasters
NM $8 MIP $12

Alien Science Officer, 1996, Trendmasters
NM $5 MIP $10

Alien Shock Trooper, 1996, Trendmasters
NM $5 MIP $10

Alien Supreme Commander, 1996, Trendmasters
NM $15 MIP $25

David Levinson, 1996, Trendmasters
NM $5 MIP $10

President Thomas Whitmore, 1996, Trendmasters
NM $5 MIP $10

Steve Hiller, 1996, Trendmasters
NM $5 MIP $10

Ultimate Alien Commander, 1996, Trendmasters, FAO Schwarz Exclusive
NM $15 MIP $30

Weapons Expert, 1996, Trendmasters
NM $10 MIP $20

Zero Gravity, 1996, Trendmasters
NM $8 MIP $15

Indiana Jones (Toys McCoy, 1999)

12" FIGURES

Arabian Horse, 1999
NM $150 MIP $450

Indiana Jones, 1999
NM $275 MIP $700

Indiana Jones and The Temple of Doom (LJN, 1984)

FIGURES

Giant Thugee, 1984, LJN, On the right
NM $75 MIP $175

Indiana Jones, 1984, LJN, Shown in the center
NM $125 MIP $300

Mola Ram, 1984, LJN, On the left. These figures didn't enjoy as much popularity at the time, probably reflecting the public's mood about the film
NM $85 MIP $225

Indiana Jones, The Adventures of (Kenner, 1982-1983)

12" FIGURES

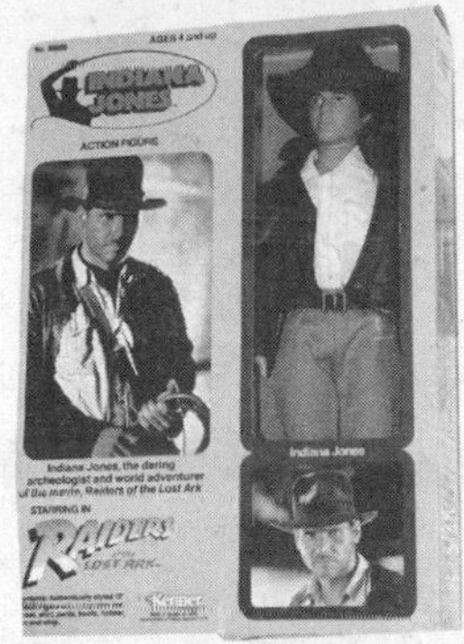

Indiana Jones, 12", 1982-83, Kenner, Includes leather jacket, fedora, bullwhip and pistol, Model No. 46000
NM $100 MIP $250

4" FIGURES

Belloq, 1982-83, Kenner
NM $25 MIP $65

Belloq in Ceremonial Robe Carded, 1982-83, Kenner
NM $20 MIP $800

Belloq in Ceremonial Robe, mail away, 1982-83, Kenner
NM $18 MIP $35

Cairo Swordsman, 1982-83, Kenner
NM $15 MIP $35

German Mechanic, 1982-83, Kenner
NM $25 MIP $65

Indiana Jones in German Uniform, 1982-83, Kenner
NM $20 MIP $80

Indiana Jones with whip, 1982-83, Kenner, Includes fedora, leather jacket and pistol, too, Model No. 46060
NM $100 MIP $250

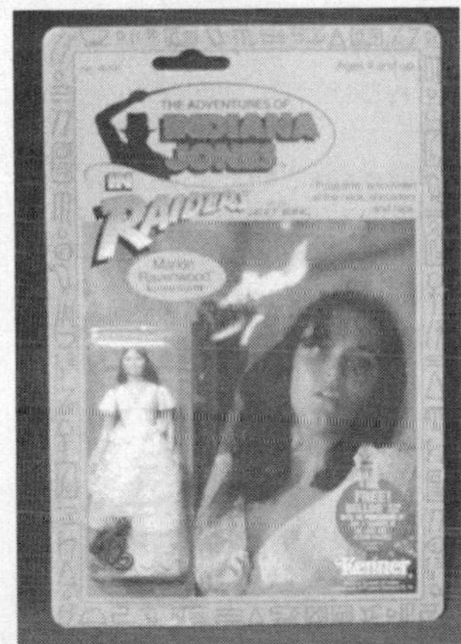

(Lenny Lee)

Marion Ravenwood, 1982-83, Kenner, Includes small monkee
NM $95 MIP $300

Indiana Jones, The Adventures of (Kenner, 1982-1983)

Sallah, 1982-83, Kenner
NM $30 **MIP** $80

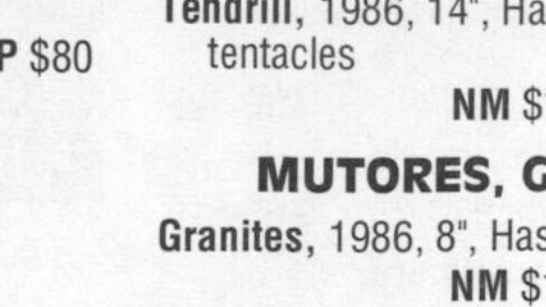

(Lenny Lee)

Toht, 1982-83, Kenner, Fully poseable, black plastic overcoat and hat. Packaging has mail-in offer for ceremonial Beloq figure
NM $15 **MIP** $30

PLAY SETS

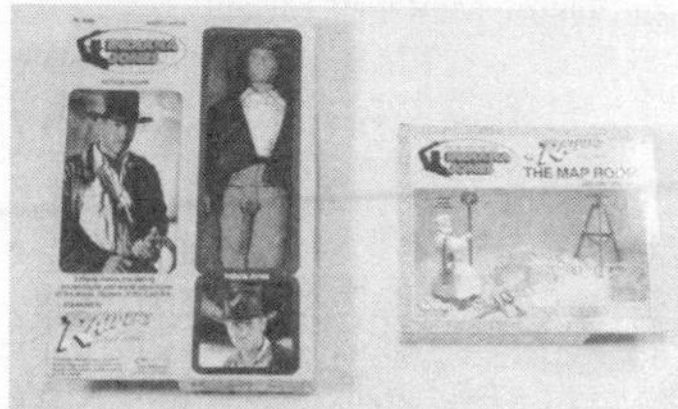

Map Room Play Set, 1982-83, Kenner
NM $75 **MIP** $150

Streets of Cairo Play Set, 1982-83, Kenner
NM $65 **MIP** $125

Well of Souls Play Set, 1982-83, Kenner
NM $80 **MIP** $175

VEHICLES AND ACCESSORIES

Arabian Horse, 1982-83, Kenner
NM $65 **MIP** $150

Convoy Truck, 1982-83, Kenner
NM $75 **MIP** $150

Inhumanoids (Hasbro, 1986)

EARTH CORPS

Auger, 1986, 6-1/2", Hasbro, helmet, drill
NM $12 **MIP** $25

Dr. Derek Bright, 1986, 6-1/2", Hasbro, helmet, movable claws
NM $12 **MIP** $25

Herc Armstrong, 1986, 6-1/2", Hasbro, helmet, grappling hook arm
NM $12 **MIP** $25

Liquidator, 1986, 6-1/2", Hasbro, helmet, water shooting backpack
NM $12 **MIP** $25

INHUMANOIDS

D.Compose, 1986, 14", Hasbro, opening ribcage
NM $15 **MIP** $30

Metlar, 1986, 14", Hasbro, Inhumanoid leader
NM $15 **MIP** $30

Tendrill, 1986, 14", Hasbro, movable tentacles
NM $15 **MIP** $30

MUTORES, GRANITES

Granites, 1986, 8", Hasbro, rock-like, tan
NM $10 **MIP** $18

Granok, 1986, 8", Hasbro, rock-like, gray
NM $10 **MIP** $18

MUTORES, REDWOODS

Redlen, 1986, 8", Hasbro, tree-like, yellow
NM $10 **MIP** $18

Redsun, 1986, 8", Hasbro, tree-like, orange-brown
NM $10 **MIP** $18

The Redwoods, 1986, 8", Hasbro, tree-like, gray
NM $10 **MIP** $18

MUTROES, MAGNOKOR

Magnokor, 1986, 8", Hasbro, splits into Crygen and Pyre
NM $10 **MIP** $30

VEHICLES

Terrascout, 1986, Hasbro, movable gun, scanner
NM $18 **MIP** $35

Trappeur, 1986, Hasbro, movable claw, grapping hook, hovercraft
NM $18 **MIP** $35

Inspector Gadget (Galoob, 1984)

12" FIGURE

Inspector Gadget, 1984, Galoob
NM $80 **MIP** $175

Inspector Gadget (Tiger Toys, 1992)

FIGURES

Dr. Claw, 1992, Tiger Toys
NM $10 **MIP** $25

Inspector Gadget that Falls Apart, 1992, Tiger Toys
NM $5 **MIP** $15

Inspector Gadget that Squirts Water, 1992, Tiger Toys
NM $5 **MIP** $15

Inspector Gadget with Expanding Arms, 1992, Tiger Toys
NM $4 **MIP** $12

Inspector Gadget with Expanding Legs, 1992, Tiger Toys
NM $5 **MIP** $15

Inspector Gadget with Snap Open Hat, 1992, Tiger Toys
NM $5 **MIP** $15

Inspector Gadget with Telescopic Neck, 1992, Tiger Toys
NM $5 **MIP** $15

MAD Agent with Bazooka, 1992, Tiger Toys
NM $8 **MIP** $20

Penny and Brain, 1992, Tiger Toys
NM $8 **MIP** $20

VEHICLES

Gadgetmoile, 1992, Tiger Toys
NM $35 **MIP** $70

Iron Man (Toy Biz, 1995-96)

5" FIGURES, 1995

Blacklash, Nunchaku and Whip-cracking Action, 1995
NM $3 **MIP** $10

Blizzard, Ice-Fist Punch, 1995
NM $4 **MIP** $12

Century, Cape and Battle Staff, 1995
NM $3 **MIP** $10

Dreadknight, Firing Lance Action, 1995
NM $3 **MIP** $10

Grey Gargoyle, Stone Hurling Action, 1995
NM $3 **MIP** $10

Hawkeye, Bow and Arrow, 1995
NM $4 **MIP** $12

Hulkbuster Iron Man, Removable Armor, 1995
NM $3 **MIP** $10

Iron Man Arctic Armor, Removable Armor and Launching Claw Action, 1995
NM $3 **MIP** $10

Iron Man Hologram, 1995, Toy Biz
NM $3 **MIP** $10

Iron Man Space Armor, Power-lift Space Pack, 1995, Toy Biz
NM $3 **MIP** $10

Iron Man Stealth Armor, 1995, Toy Biz
NM $3 **MIP** $10

Iron Man, Hydro Armor, 1995
NM $3 **MIP** $10

Iron Man, Plasma Cannon Missile Launcher, 1995
NM $3 **MIP** $10

Mandarin, Light-up Power Rings, 1995
NM $3 **MIP** $10

Modok, Energy Brain Blasts, 1995, Toy Biz
NM $3 **MIP** $10

Spider-Woman, Psisonic Web Hurling Action, 1995
NM $4 **MIP** $12

Titanium Man, Retractable Blade Action, 1995
NM $4 **MIP** $12

Tony Stark, Armor Carrying Suitcase, 1995
NM $4 **MIP** $12

U.S. Agent, Firing Shield Action, 1995
NM $18 **MIP** $35

War Machine, Shoulder-Mount Cannons, 1995
NM $3 **MIP** $10

Whirlwind, Whirling Battle Action, 1995
NM $4 **MIP** $12

5" FIGURES, 1996

Crimson Dynamo, 1996
NM $4 **MIP** $10

Iron Man Inferno Armor, 1996
NM $3 **MIP** $8

Iron Man Lava Armor, 1996
NM $3 MIP $8

Iron Man Magnetic Armor, 1996
NM $3 MIP $8

Iron Man Radiation Armor, 1996
NM $3 MIP $8

Iron Man Samurai Armor, 1996
NM $3 MIP $8

Iron Man Subterranean Armor, 1996
NM $3 MIP $8

War Machine 2, 1996
NM $4 MIP $10

DELUXE 10" FIGURES

Iron Man, 1995
NM $4 MIP $12

Mandarin, 1995
NM $4 MIP $12

War Machine, 1995
NM $4 MIP $12

DELUXE DRAGONS

Argent, 1995
NM $7 MIP $15

Aureus, 1995
NM $7 MIP $15

FinFang Foom, 1995
NM $7 MIP $15

Island of Misfit Toys (Playmates, 2002)

FIGURES

Abominable Snowman, 2002, Playing Mantis
NM $5 MIP $12

Clarice, 2002, Playing Mantis, Includes two racoons and two rabbits
NM $5 MIP $12

Hermey, 2002, Playing Mantis, With a hat, book, tools and two of Bumble's teeth
NM $5 MIP $12

Rudolph, 2002, Playing Mantis, Features a light-up nose and includes misfit doll
NM $5 MIP $12

Sam, 2002, Playing Mantis, With removeable hat, banjo and umbrella
NM $5 MIP $12

Santa Claus, 2002, Playing Mantis, Features a removeable hat, toy bag and spotted elephant
NM $5 MIP $12

Yukon Cornelius, 2002, Playing Mantis, In familiar bright orange hat, blue jacket and snowshoes. Includes knife, pick and hammer
NM $5 MIP $12

James Bond Secret Agent 007 (Gilbert, 1965)

12" FIGURES

James Bond, 1965, Gilbert, Sean Connery likeness from "Dr. No.," white shirt, swimming trunks, goggles, snorkel, fins, gun
NM $160 MIP $375

Odd Job, 1965, Gilbert, in white judo outfit w/blackbelt and headband, bowler hat
NM $130 MIP $300

4" FIGURES

Domino, 1965, Gilbert, light blue shirt, blue pants
NM $10 MIP $22

Dr. No, 1965, Gilbert, in white lab coat
NM $10 MIP $22

Goldfinger, 1965, Gilbert
NM $10 MIP $27

James Bond #1, 1965, Gilbert, in white tuxedo w/gun
NM $10 MIP $22

James Bond #2, 1965, Gilbert, in black scuba outfit, Model No. 16503
NM $10 MIP $22

James Bond Casual, 1965, Gilbert, in blue shirt, blue pants
NM $10 MIP $22

Largo, 1965, Gilbert
NM $10 MIP $22

M, 1965, Gilbert
NM $10 MIP $22

Moneypenny, 1965, Gilbert
NM $10 MIP $22

Odd Job, 1965, Gilbert, throwing bowler
NM $10 MIP $22

ACCESSORIES

Action Toys Dr. No's Dragon Tank and Largo's Hydrofoil/Yacht, 1965, Gilbert, Model No. 16543
NM $15 MIP $30

Secret Agent Gun Case and Bullet Shield "M"s Desk, 1965, Gilbert, both in one package, Model No. 16543
NM $12 MIP $24

Spy Wrist Watch w/Decoder, 1965, Gilbert, with Secret Sighting lenses & World Time Guide
NM $75 MIP $135

FIGURE SETS

Action Toy Set #5, 1965, Gilbert, includes M, Moneypenny, Bond in tux
NM $25 MIP $50

Movie Characters Set, 1965, Gilbert, 10 characters
NM $300 MIP $600

VEHICLES

Aston Martin DB5, 1965, Gilbert, battery-operated, working ejection seat, 11" long
NM $160 MIP $275

James Bond: Moonraker (Mego, 1979)

12" FIGURES

Drax, 1979, Mego
NM $150 MIP $200

Holly, 1979, Mego
NM $150 MIP $200

James Bond, 1979, Mego
NM $125 MIP $150

James Bond, deluxe version, 1979, Mego
NM $350 MIP $500

James Bond: Moonraker (Mego, 1979)

Jaws, 1979, Mego
NM $300 MIP $500

Johnny Hero (Rosko, 1965-68)

13" FIGURES

Johnny Hero, 1965-68
NM $65 MIP $100

Johnny Hero, Olympic Hero, 1965-68
NM $65 MIP $100

Outfits, 1965-68
NM $40 MIP $75

Jonny Quest (Galoob, 1996)

ACCESSORIES

Cyber Copter, 1996, Galoob
NM $5 MIP $12

Quest Porpoise with Deep Sea Jonny, 1996, Galoob
NM $5 MIP $12

Quest Rover, 1996, Galoob
NM $5 MIP $12

QUEST WORLD FIGURES

Cyber Cycle Jonny Quest, 1996, Galoob
NM $5 MIP $10

Cyber Jet Race, 1996, Galoob
NM $5 MIP $10

Cyber Suit Hadji, 1996, Galoob
NM $5 MIP $10

Cyber Trax Surd, 1996, Galoob
NM $5 MIP $10

REAL WORLD FIGURES

Deep Sea Race Bannon & Hadji, 1996, Galoob
NM $4 MIP $8

Jungle Commando Dr. Quest & Ezekiel Rage, 1996, Galoob
NM $4 MIP $8

Night Stryker Jonny Quest & Jessie, 1996, Galoob
NM $5 MIP $10

Shuttle Pilot Jonny Quest & Race Bannon, 1996, Galoob
NM $4 MIP $8

X-Treme Action Jonny Quest & Hadji, 1996, Galoob
NM $4 MIP $8

KISS (McFarlane, 1997)

6" FIGURES

(McFarlane Toys)

Ace Frehley with album, 1997, 6", McFarlane, Series 1, Shown with his other bandmates
NM $4 MIP $12

Ace Frehley with letter stand, 1997, 6", McFarlane, Series 1
NM $4 MIP $10

Gene Simmons with album, 1997, 6", McFarlane, Series 1
NM $4 MIP $12

Gene Simmons with letter base, 1997, 6", McFarlane, Series 1
NM $4 MIP $10

Paul Stanley with album, 1997, 6", McFarlane, Series 1
NM $4 MIP $12

Paul Stanley with letter stand, 1997, 6", McFarlane, Series 1
NM $4 MIP $10

Peter Criss with album, 1997, 6", McFarlane, Series 1
NM $4 MIP $12

Peter Criss with letter stand, 1997, 6", McFarlane, Series 1
NM $4 MIP $10

KISS (Mego, 1978)

12" BOXED FIGURES

Ace Frehley, 1978, 12", Mego
NM $110 MIP $275

Gene Simmons, 1978, 12", Mego, With accurate face make-up and realistic "wild" hair
NM $125 MIP $275

Paul Stanley, 1978, 12", Mego, Another in Mego's series--they wisely made the boxes interchangeable. The package shown appears to have been autographed. Face make-up is accurate, and figure also features realistic "wild" hair
NM $110 MIP $275

Peter Criss, 1978, 12", Mego, Editor's note: Three cheers for drummers!
NM $110 MIP $275

KISS: Alive (McFarlane, 2000)

FIGURES

Ace, 2000, 6-1/2", McFarlane, Series 4, Figure includes guitar and amp
NM $3 MIP $8

Gene, 2000, 7", McFarlane, Series 4, Includes figure, amp, guitar and candelabra
NM $3 MIP $8

Paul, 2000, 5", McFarlane, Series 4, Includes guitar and amp
NM $3 MIP $8

Peter, 2000, 6", McFarlane, Series 4, Includes drumkit
NM $3 MIP $8

KISS: KISS Creatures (McFarlane, 2002)

FIGURES

Deluxe boxed set, 2002, McFarlane, included full drum kit
NM $20 MIP $45

Space Ace, 2002, 6-7/8", McFarlane
NM $5 MIP $15

The Demon, 2002, 6-1/2", McFarlane
NM $5 MIP $15

The Fox, 2002, 6-7/8", McFarlane
NM $5 MIP $15

The Starchild, 2002, 6-3/4", McFarlane
NM $5 MIP $15

KISS: Psycho Circus (McFarlane, 1998)

FIGURES

(McFarlane Toys)

Ace Frehley with Stiltman, 1998, McFarlane, Series 2, Includes two figures, Stiltman with base and skull-topped stilts
NM $5 MIP $10

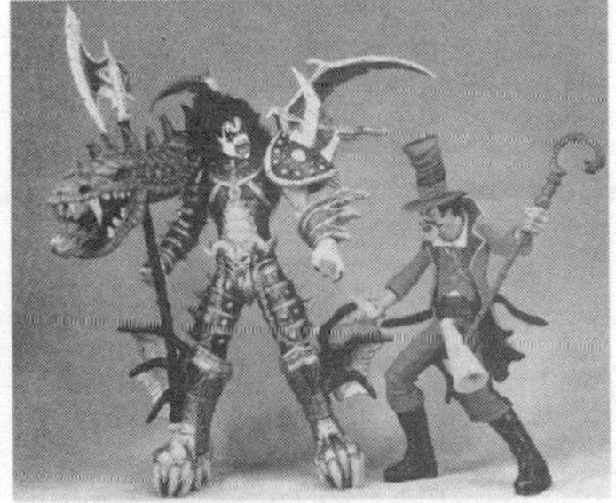

(McFarlane Toys)

Gene Simmons with Ring Master, 1998, McFarlane, Series 2, Each poseable figure includes staff
NM $5 MIP $10

(McFarlane Toys)

Paul Stanley with The Jester, 1998, McFarlane, Series 2
NM $5 MIP $10

(McFarlane Toys)

Peter Criss with Animal Wrangler, 1998, McFarlane, Series 2
NM $5 MIP $10

KISS: Psycho Circus Tour (McFarlane, 1999)

FIGURES

Ace Frehley, 1999, McFarlane, Series 3
NM $4 MIP $8

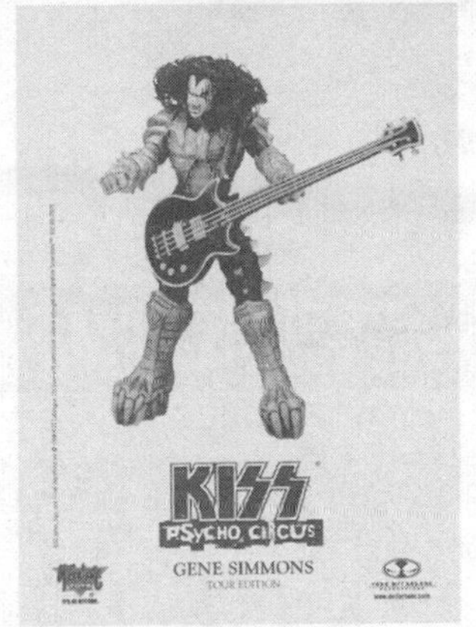

(McFarlane Toys)

Gene Simmons, 1999, McFarlane, Series 3, Fierce-looking Gene with black bass guitar
NM $4 MIP $8

(McFarlane Toys)

Paul Stanley, 1999, McFarlane, Series 3, Paul includes flying-V guitar
NM $4 MIP $8

Peter Criss, 1999, McFarlane, Series 3
NM $4 MIP $8

Lara Croft (Playmates, 1999)

FIGURES

Lara in Area 51 outfit, 1999, Playmates
NM $8 MIP $18

Lara in jungle outfit, 1999, Playmates
NM $8 MIP $18

Lara in wet suit, 1999, Playmates
NM $8 MIP $18

talking Lara, 1999, Playmates
NM $12 MIP $25

Laverne and Shirley (Mego, 1978)

12" BOXED FIGURES

Laverne and Shirley, 1978, Mego
NM $60 MIP $150

Lenny and Squiggy, 1978, Mego
NM $90 MIP $150

Legends of the West (Excel Toy Co., 1974)

FIGURES

Buffalo Bill Cody, 1974, 9", Excel Toy Co., hat, gun, and holster
NM $25 MIP $50

Cochise, 1974, 9", Excel Toy Co., rifle
NM $25 MIP $50

Davy Crockett, 1974, 9", Excel Toy Co.
NM $25 MIP $50

Deadwood Dick, 1974, 9", Excel Toy Co., rarest figure in series
NM $30 MIP $70

Jesse James, 1974, 9", Excel Toy Co.
NM $25 MIP $50

Wild Bill Hickok, 1974, 9", Excel Toy Co., gun, holster
NM $25 MIP $50

Wyatt Earp, 1974, 9", Excel Toy Co., gun, holster
NM $25 MIP $50

Lone Ranger (Hubley, 1973)

FIGURES

Lone Ranger, 1973, 10", Hubley, w/hat, mask, 2-guns and holster rig, scarf, Model No. 23620
NM $30 MIP $65

Silver, 1973, 12", Hubley, w/stand, saddle, halter, bit, reins, martingale, girth, stirrups, poseable and rears up, No. 27625, Model No. 23625
NM $20 MIP $45

Tonto, 1973, 10", Hubley
NM $25 MIP $60

Lone Ranger Rides Again (Gabriel, 1979)

FIGURES

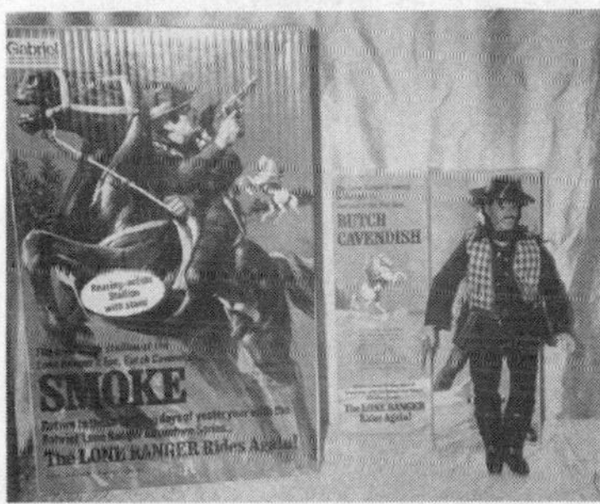

Butch Cavendish, 1979, 9", Gabriel, Figure shown here with Smoke, Butch's horse
NM $45 MIP $80

Lone Ranger Rides Again (Gabriel, 1979)

Dan Reid, 1979, 9", Gabriel
NM $30 **MIP** $70

Little Bear with Hawk, 1979, 9", Gabriel
NM $30 **MIP** $70

Lone Ranger, 1979, 9", Gabriel, Figure includes revolvers, hat, mask, scarf. Shown here with Silver
NM $35 **MIP** $75

Red Sleeves, 1979, 9", Gabriel
NM $30 **MIP** $70

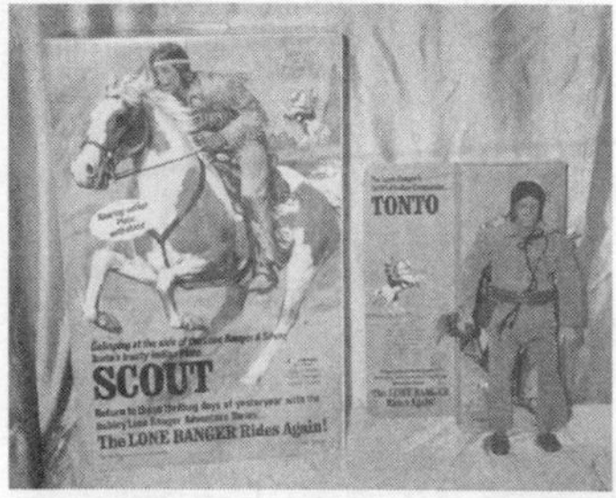

Tonto, 1979, 9", Gabriel, Includes buckskin cloth outfit. Shown here with Scout. The horses in this series were fully poseable and included stands
NM $30 **MIP** $70

Lone Ranger, Legend of (Gabriel, 1982)

FIGURES

Buffalo Bill Cody, 1982, 3-3/4", Gabriel
NM $10 **MIP** $25

Butch Cavendish, 1982, 3-3/4", Gabriel
NM $10 **MIP** $20

General Custer, 1982, 3-3/4", Gabriel
NM $10 **MIP** $20

Lone Ranger, 1982, 3-3/4", Gabriel
NM $15 **MIP** $30

Lone Ranger with Silver, 1982, 3-3/4", Gabriel
NM $25 **MIP** $50

Scout, 1982, 3-3/4", Gabriel
NM $10 **MIP** $20

Silver, 1982, 3-3/4", Gabriel
NM $15 **MIP** $30

Smoke, 1982, 3-3/4", Gabriel
NM $10 **MIP** $25

Tonto, 1982, 3-3/4", Gabriel
NM $7 **MIP** $15

Tonto with Scout, 1982, 3-3/4", Gabriel
NM $25 **MIP** $50

Lord of the Rings (Toy Vault, 1998-99)

FIGURES

Earth Balrog, 6", Toy Vault, sword, fire whip
NM $7 **MIP** $13

Frodo in Lorien, 6", Toy Vault, w/dagger, belt, pack walking stick, and cloak
NM $7 **MIP** $13

Frodo in the Barrow Downs, 6", Toy Vault, In white ceremonial cloak w/ gold highlights
NM $8 **MIP** $18

Frodo the Hobbit, 6", Toy Vault, w/cloak, sword, pack, belt and blanket
NM $8 **MIP** $14

Gandalf the Wizard, 6", Toy Vault, In gray cloth robe w/hat, food pouch, pipeweed pouch, staff, belt, sword, and scabbard
NM $7 **MIP** $13

Gimli in Battle, 6", Toy Vault, w/helmet, shield, battle axe
NM $7 **MIP** $13

Gimli in Lorien, 6", Toy Vault, w/cloth blindfold, cloth Lorien cloak, helmet, pipe
NM $7 **MIP** $13

Gimli of the Fellowship, 6", Toy Vault, w/dragon helmet, battle axe, pipe, hexagonal stand
NM $8 **MIP** $18

Gollum, 6", Toy Vault
NM $7 **MIP** $13

Gollum the Fisherman, 6", Toy Vault
NM $7 **MIP** $13

Ugluk at War, 6", Toy Vault, Fierce Orc w/sword, helmet, dagger and shield
NM $7 **MIP** $13

Ugluk on the Hunt, 6", Toy Vault, w/bow, arrows, quiver, medicine bottle
NM $7 **MIP** $13

Ugluk the Orc, 6", Toy Vault, Figure in gold armor w/medicine bottle, sword, dagger, and helmet
NM $7 **MIP** $13

Lord of the Rings (Knickerbocker, 1979)

CREATURES

Charger of the Ringwraith, 1979, 7-1/2", Knickerbocker
NM $85 **MIP** $175

Frodo's Horse, 1979, 7-1/2", Knickerbocker
NM $75 **MIP** $175

Ringwraith the Black Rider, 1979, 7-1/2", Knickerbocker, sword, axe
NM $150 **MIP** $310

FIGURES

Aragorn, 1979, Knickerbocker, sword
NM $50 **MIP** $125

Frodo, 1979, Knickerbocker, sword
NM $50 **MIP** $125

Gandalf, 1979, Knickerbocker, staff, hat
NM $75 **MIP** $125

Gollum, 1979, Knickerbocker
NM $50 **MIP** $125

Samwise, 1979, Knickerbocker
NM $50 **MIP** $125

Lost (McFarlane, 2006-07)

SERIES 1

Charlie, 2006, 6", McFarlane, hood up, seated on wreckage writing "FATE" on his finger bandages, Drive Shaft ring. Sing it with me: "You all, everybody!"
NM $6 **MIP** $12

Hurley, 2006, 6", McFarlane, "Island Open" base, winning lottery ticket
NM $6 **MIP** $12

Jack, 2006, 6", McFarlane, in suit, plane crash base
NM $6 **MIP** $12

Kate, 2006, 6", McFarlane, toy plane, jungle base w/tall reeds
NM $6 **MIP** $12

Locke, 2006, 6", McFarlane, hunting knife, water bottle, Walkabout brochure, hatch base
NM $6 **MIP** $12

Shannon, 2006, 6", McFarlane, in red bikini sunning herself among the wreckage
NM $6 **MIP** $12

The Hatch Boxed Set, 2006, 6", McFarlane, Locke, Jack, Kate, Hurley at the partially excavated hatch. Lights up from within.
NM $12 **MIP** $25

SERIES 2

Jin, 2007, 6", McFarlane, from Season 2 Episode 2 "Adrift." arms tied behind him, Jin races on the beach to warn Sawyer and Michael "Others." says four phrases
NM $6 **MIP** $12

Mr. Eko, 2007, 6", McFarlane, from Season 2 Episode 10 "The 23rd Psalm." says three phrases
NM $6 **MIP** $12

Sawyer, 2007, 6", McFarlane, from Season 2 Episode 20 "Born to Run." says four phrases
NM $6 **MIP** $12

Sun, 2007, 6", McFarlane, from Season 1 Episode 15 "In Translation." Sun asserts her independence by wearing a bikini on the beach, says four phrases
NM $6 **MIP** $12

Lost In Space (Trendmasters, 1998)

9" CLASSIC FIGURES

Cyclops, 1998, 13", Trendmasters
NM $25 **MIP** $50

Don West, 1998, 9", Trendmasters
NM $10 **MIP** $20

Dr. Smith, 1998, 9", Trendmasters
NM $20 **MIP** $40

Judy Robinson, 1998, 9", Trendmasters
NM $10 **MIP** $20

Robot B9, 1998, 11", Trendmasters
NM $20 **MIP** $45

Tybo the Carrot Man, 1998, 9", Trendmasters
NM $20 **MIP** $40

Will Robinson, 1998, 9", Trendmasters
NM $15 **MIP** $30

FIGURES

(Lenny Lee)

Battle Armor Don West, 1998, Trendmasters, Includes blaster rifle and magnet attack micro-spider
NM $4 **MIP** $8

Cryo Chamber Judy Robinson, 1998, Trendmasters
NM $4 **MIP** $8

(Lenny Lee)

Cryo Chamber Will Robinson, 1998, Trendmasters, With chamber, camera and magnet attack micro-spiders
NM $4 **MIP** $8

(Lenny Lee)

Cryo-Suit Dr. Judy Robinson, 1998, Trendmasters, With accessories and magnet attack micro-spider
NM $4 **MIP** $8

Cyclops, 1998, Trendmasters
NM $25 **MIP** $60

(Lenny Lee)

Dr. Smith, sabotage action, 1998, Trendmasters, Includes rifle, magnet attack micro-spider and accessories
NM $7 **MIP** $15

Future Smith, 1998, Trendmasters
NM $5 **MIP** $10

Judy Robinson, 1998, Trendmasters
NM $7 **MIP** $15

Lost In Space (Trendmasters, 1998)

(Lenny Lee)

Proteus Armor Dr. Smith, 1998, Trendmasters, With rifle, and magnet attack micro-spider
NM $4 **MIP** $8

(Lenny Lee)

Proteus Armor John Robinson, 1998, Trendmasters, Includes micro-spider and accessories
NM $4 **MIP** $8

Will Robinson, 1998, Trendmasters
NM $7 **MIP** $15

PLAY SETS

(Lenny Lee)

Bubble Fighter, 1998, Trendmasters, Fighter ship as seen in the beginning of the movie. Features: swiveling cockpit, missile launchers, ejecting bubble section and breakaway battle damage
NM $20 **MIP** $80

Classic Jupiter 2 play set, 1998, 11", Trendmasters
NM $50 **MIP** $100

(Lenny Lee)

Jupiter 2 play set, 1998, Trendmasters, Ship fits action figure in cockpit and features: pop-out hyperspace struts, missile launchers, "battle damage" and more magnet-attack micro spiders
NM $25 **MIP** $75

Lost World of The Warlord (Remco, 1983)

ACCESSORIES AND TEAMS

Warpult, 1983, Remco
NM $20 **MIP** $45

Warteam with Arak, 1983, Remco
NM $30 **MIP** $80

Warteam with Deimos, 1983, Remco
NM $30 **MIP** $80

Warteam with Manchitse, 1983, Remco
NM $30 **MIP** $80

Warteam with Mikola, 1983, Remco
NM $30 **MIP** $80

FIGURES

Arak, 1983, Remco
NM $15 **MIP** $35

Deimos, 1983, Remco
NM $18 **MIP** $45

Hercules, 1983, Remco
NM $15 **MIP** $35

Manchiste, 1983, Remco
NM $18 **MIP** $45

Mikola, 1983, Remco
NM $18 **MIP** $45

Warlord, 1983, Remco
NM $12 **MIP** $32

Love Boat (Mego, 1982)

4" FIGURES

Captain Stubing, 1982, 4", Mego
NM $10 **MIP** $20

Doc, 1982, 4", Mego
NM $10 **MIP** $20

Gopher, 1982, 4", Mego
NM $10 **MIP** $20

Isaac, 1982, 4", Mego
NM $10 **MIP** $20

Julie, 1982, 4", Mego
NM $10 **MIP** $25

Vicki, 1982, 4", Mego
NM $10 **MIP** $25

ACCESSORIES

Love Boat Playset, 1982, Mego
NM $150 **MIP** $300

M*A*S*H (Durham, 1973)

8" FIGURES

B.J., 1973, Durham, 8"
NM $40 **MIP** $80

Hawkeye, 1973, Durham, 8"
NM $30 **MIP** $65

Hot Lips, 1973, Durham, 8"
NM $30 **MIP** $65

M*A*S*H (Tristar, 1982)

3-3/4" FIGURES AND VEHICLES

B.J., 1982, Tristar, 3-3/4" tall
NM $7 **MIP** $18

Base Playset, 1982, Tristar
NM $65 **MIP** $125

Colonel Potter, 1982, Tristar, 3-3/4" figure on car
NM $7 **MIP** $18

Father Mulcahy, 1982, Tristar, 3-3/4" figure on car
NM $7 **MIP** $18

Hawkeye, 1982, Tristar, 3-3/4" figure on car
NM $7 **MIP** $18

Hawkeye with Ambulance, 1982, Tristar
NM $25 **MIP** $50

Hawkeye with Helicopter, 1982, Tristar
NM $20 **MIP** $50

Hawkeye with Jeep, 1982, Tristar
NM $20 **MIP** $45

Hot Lips, 1982, Tristar, 3-3/4" figure on car
NM $18 **MIP** $25

Klinger, 1982, Tristar, 3-3/4" figure on car
NM $7 **MIP** $18

Klinger in Drag, 1982, Tristar, 3-3/4" figure on car
NM $15 **MIP** $35

M*A*S*H Figures Collectors Set, 1982, Tristar
NM $40 **MIP** $80

Winchester, 1982, Tristar, 3-3/4" tall
NM $7 **MIP** $15

M.A.S.K. (Kenner, 1985-88)

ADVENTURE PACKS

Coast Patrol, 1986
NM $12 **MIP** $25

Jungle Challenge, 1986
NM $12 **MIP** $25

Rescue Mission, 1986
NM $12 **MIP** $25

T-Bob, 1986
NM $12 **MIP** $25

Venom's Revenge, 1986
NM $12 MIP $25

M.A.S.K. VEHICLES

Billboard Blast with Dusty Hayes, 1987, Series 3
NM $15 MIP $40

Bulldog with Boris Bushkin, 1987, Series 3
NM $30 MIP $65

Bullet with Ali Bombay, 1987, Series 3
NM $18 MIP $40

Buzzard with Miles Mayhem and Maximus Mayhem, 1987, Series 3
NM $25 MIP $60

Collector, 1987, Kenner, Series 3
NM $25 MIP $55

(Mark Bellomo collection)

Condor with Brad Turner, 1985, Series 1
NM $18 MIP $40

Firecracker with Hondo Mac Lean, 1985, Series 1
NM $28 MIP $50

Firefly with Julio Lopez, 1986, Series 2
NM $15 MIP $35

Gator with Dirty Hayes, 1985, Series 1
NM $25 MIP $50

Goliath with Matt Tracker, 1987, Series 3
NM $45 MIP $110

Hurricane with Hondo Mac Lean, 1986, Series 2
NM $25 MIP $50

Iguana with Lester Sludge, 1987, Series 3
NM $20 MIP $40

Manta with Vanessa Warfield, 1987, Series 3
NM $25 MIP $55

Meteor with Ace Riker, 1987, Series 3
NM $40 MIP $90

Pit Stop Catapult with Sly Rax, 1987, Series 3
NM $18 MIP $35

Raven with Calhoun Burns, 1986, Series 2
NM $25 MIP $55

Razorback with Brad Turner, 1987, Series 3
NM $20 MIP $45

Rhino with Bruce Sato and Matt Tracker, 1985, Series 1
NM $35 MIP $75

Slingshot with Ace Riker, 1986, Series 2
NM $20 MIP $45

Thunder Hawk with Matt Tracker, 1985, Series 1
NM $30 MIP $125

Volcano with Matt Tracker and Jacques LaFleur, 1986, Series 2
NM $45 MIP $85

Wildcat with Clutch Hawks, 1987, Series 3
NM $10 MIP $35

MYSTERY ADVENTURE PACKS

Arctic Assault, 1988, Kenner
NM $10 MIP $20

Glider Strike, 1988, Kenner
NM $10 MIP $20

Racing Arena, 1988, Kenner
NM $10 MIP $20

Sea Attack, 1988, Kenner
NM $10 MIP $20

PLAY SETS

Boulder Hill Play Set, 1985, Series 1
NM $65 MIP $175

SPLIT SECONDS M.A.S.K. VEHICLES

Afterburner with Dusty Hanes, 1988, Series 4
NM $25 MIP $60

Detonator, 1988, Series 4
NM $20 MIP $50

Dynamo with Bruce Sato, 1988, Series 4
NM $20 MIP $65

Fireforce, 1988, Series 4
NM $20 MIP $45

Jackal with Bruno Shepherd, 1988, Kenner, Series 4
NM $10 MIP $30

Skybolt, 1988, Kenner, Series 4
NM $40 MIP $100

Stiletto, 1988, Kenner, Series 4
NM $15 MIP $35

Wolfbeast with Miles Mayhem, 1988, Kenner, Series 4
NM $25 MIP $50

SPLIT SECONDS V.E.N.O.M. VEHICLES

Barracuda with Bruno Shepherd, 1988, Series 4
NM $30 MIP $75

Vandal with Floyd Malloy, 1988, Series 4
NM $25 MIP $55

V.E.N.O.M. VEHICLES

Jackhammer with Cliffhanger, 1985, Series 1
NM $30 MIP $60

Outlaw with Miles Mayhem and Nash Gorey, 1986, Series 2
NM $50 MIP $100

Piranha with Sly Rax, 1985, Series 1
NM $25 MIP $50

Stinger with Bruno Shepherd, 1986, Series 2
NM $25 MIP $50

Switchblade with Miles Mayhem, 1985, Series 1
NM $60 MIP $100

Vampire with Floyd Malloy, 1986, Series 2
NM $20 MIP $40

Mad Monster Series (Mego, 1974)

8" FIGURES

The Dreadful Dracula, 1974, 8", Mego
NM $80 MIP $200

The Horrible Mummy, 1974, 8", Mego
NM $50 MIP $175

The Human Wolfman, 1974, 8", Mego
NM $75 MIP $175

The Monster Frankenstein, 1974, 8", Mego, With glow-in-the-dark eyes and hands
NM $50 MIP $175

ACCESSORIES

Mad Monster Castle, vinyl, 1974, Mego
NM $300 MIP $600

Major Matt Mason (Mattel, 1967-70)

FIGURES

Callisto, 1967, 6", Mattel, #6331, friend from Jupiter
NM $110 MIP $260

Captain Lazer, 1967, 12", Mattel, #6330,

Major Matt Mason (Mattel, 1967-70)

blue plastic w/ silver trim, friend from Mars
NM $135 **MIP** $325

Doug Davis, 1967, 6", Mattel, yellow figure
NM $110 **MIP** $310

(Corey LeChat)

Jeff Long, 1967, 6", Mattel, blue figure
NM $175 **MIP** $560

Major Matt Mason, 1967, 6", Mattel, white figure
NM $75 **MIP** $225

Scorpio, 1970, 8", Mattel, rare
NM $360 **MIP** $875
(Corey LeChat)

Sergeant Storm, 1967, 6", Mattel, red figure
NM $110 **MIP** $410

Space Mission Team, 1969, Mattel, Four-pack w/MMM, Callisto, Doug Davis, and Sgt. Storm
NM $360 **MIP** $650

VEHICLES AND ACCESSORIES

Astro Trac Missile Convoy Set, 1968, Mattel, #6327, Sears exclusive set
NM $150 **MIP** $325

Astro-Trak, 1967, Mattel, #6302, vehicle
NM $50 **MIP** $150

Doug Davis w/ Cat Trac, 1968, Mattel, #6333, figure w/ red/orange vehicle
NM $80 **MIP** $150

Firebolt Space Cannon, 1968, Mattel, #6340, accessory
NM $45 **MIP** $125

Firebolt Space Cannon Super Action Set, 1968, Mattel, #6341, w/ Major Matt Mason, Sgt. Storm, and Captain Lazer
NM $45 **MIP** $150

Gamma Ray-Gard Pak, 1969, Mattel, #6342, accessory
NM $30 **MIP** $100

Jeff Long w/ Cat Trac, 1968, Mattel, #6332, figure w/ white vehicle
NM $80 **MIP** $150

Lunar Base Command Set, 1969, Mattel, #6353, largest boxed set of the series
NM $250 **MIP** $525

Major Matt Mason w/ Cat Trac, 1968, Mattel, #6318, figure w/ red/orange vehicle
NM $80 **MIP** $160

Major Matt Mason w/ Moonsuit, 1967, Mattel, #6303, w/ jet pack, space sled, moon suit and tools
NM $100 **MIP** $300

Mobile Launch Pad, 1968, Mattel, #6328, Sears exclusive
NM $35 **MIP** $100

Moon Suit Pak, 1967, Mattel, #6301, accessory
NM $35 **MIP** $100

Reconojet Pak, 1968, Mattel, #6320, accessory
NM $25 **MIP** $75

Rocket Launch Pak, 1967, Mattel, #6305, accessory
NM $25 **MIP** $75

Satellite Launch Pak, 1968, Mattel, #6306, accessory
NM $25 **MIP** $75

Satellite Locker, 1968, Mattel, #6322, carry case
NM $30 **MIP** $80

Sgt. Storm w/ Cat Trac, 1968, Mattel, #6319, figure w/ white vehicle
NM $80 **MIP** $150

Space Bubble, 1969, Mattel, #6345, vehicle
NM $80 **MIP** $150

Space Crawler, 1967, Mattel, #6304, vehicle, battery op
NM $80 **MIP** $150

Space Crawler Action Set, 1967, Mattel, #6311, w/ MMM, Space Crawler, jet pack, and space sled
NM n/a **MIP** n/a

Space Discovery Set, 1969, Mattel, #6355, w/ Doug Davis, Callisto, Space Crawler, Space Bubble, Space Power Suit
NM n/a **MIP** n/a

Space Power Suit, 1969, Mattel, #6336, accessory
NM $30 **MIP** $110

Space Power Suit Pak, 1969, Mattel, #6344, accessory
NM n/a **MIP** n/a

Space Probe Pak, 1967, Mattel, #6307, accessory
NM $25 **MIP** $75

Space Shelter Pak, 1968, Mattel, #6321, accessory
NM $25 **MIP** $75

Space Station & Space Crawler Deluxe Action Set, 1967, Mattel, #6310, play set
NM n/a **MIP** n/a

Space Station Set, 1967, Mattel, #6308, play set, three decks
NM $150 **MIP** $350

Space Travel Pak, 1969, Mattel, #6347, w/ Jet propulsion pack, space sled, rifle, chemical tanks
NM n/a **MIP** n/a

Spaceship Carry Case, 1967, Mattel, #6316, accessory
NM $25 **MIP** $50

Star Seeker, 1970, Mattel, #6357, vehicle
NM $85 **MIP** $180

Star Seeker Walk in Space Set, 1970, Mattel, #6386, space walk feature
NM n/a **MIP** n/a

Super Power Set, 1970, Mattel, #6379, MMM figure, Cat Trac, Space Power Suit, Supernaut Power Limbs, rare set
NM n/a **MIP** n/a

Supernaut Power Limbs Pak, 1968, Mattel, #6343, accessory
NM $30 **MIP** $110

Talking Command Console, 1969, Mattel, #5157, accessory, says nine commands
NM $80 **MIP** $150

Talking Flying Major Matt Mason, 1970, Mattel, #6378, figure, talking jet pack, XRG-1 Reentry Glider
NM n/a **MIP** n/a

Talking Major Matt Mason, 1970, Mattel, #6362, figure with talking jet pack
NM n/a **MIP** n/a

Uni-Tred & Space Bubble, 1969, Mattel, #6339, vehicle
NM $95 **MIP** $175

Uni-Tred Space Hauler, 1969, Mattel, #6346, vehicle set
NM n/a **MIP** n/a

XRG-1 Reentry Glider, 1969, Mattel, #6360, vehicle
NM $150 **MIP** $395

XRG-1 Reentry Glider w/ Major Matt Mason, 1969, Mattel, #6361, glider with figure
NM n/a **MIP** n/a

Man from U.N.C.L.E. (Gilbert, 1965)

FIGURES

Illya Kuryakin, 1965, 1965, black sweater, pants and shoes, spring loaded arm
NM $200 **MIP** $400

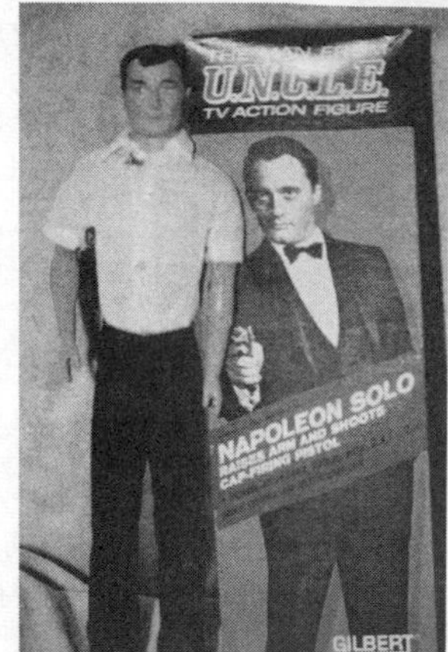

Napoleon Solo, 1965, 1965, plastic, white shirt, black pants and shoes, spring loaded arm to shoot pistol
NM $145 **MIP** $325

Mars Attacks! (Trendmasters, 1997)

FIGURES

Martian Ambassador, 1997, 6", Trendmasters
NM $4 MIP $10

Martian Leader, 1997, 6", Trendmasters
NM $4 MIP $10

Martian Spy Girl, 1997, 6", Trendmasters, talking version
NM $25 MIP $50

Martian Spy Girl, 1997, 6", Trendmasters
NM $32 MIP $60

Martian Trooper, 1997, 6", Trendmasters
NM $8 MIP $15

Marvel Famous Covers (Toy Biz, 1997-98)

8" FIGURES

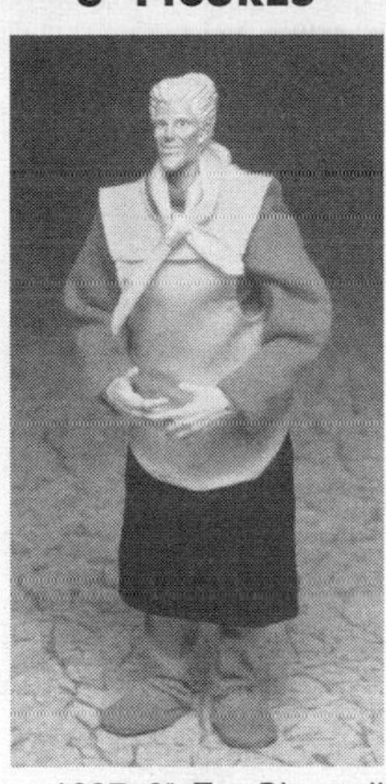

Aunt May, 1997, 8", Toy Biz, mail-away exclusive, with tied bandana around neck
NM $12 MIP $25

Captain America, 1998, 8", Toy Biz
NM $8 MIP $20

Cyclops, 1999, 8", Toy Biz
NM $7 MIP $15

Dark Phoenix, 1998, 8", Toy Biz
NM $7 MIP $15

Dr. Doom, 1998, 8", Toy Biz
NM $7 MIP $15

Green Goblin, 1997, 8", Toy Biz
NM $12 MIP $25

Magneto, 1999, 8", Toy Biz
NM $7 MIP $15

Nightcrawler, 1999, 8", Toy Biz
NM $7 MIP $15

Rogue, 1999, 8", Toy Biz
NM $7 MIP $15

Spider-Man, red and black costume, 1997, 8", Toy Biz
NM $15 MIP $40

Storm, 1997, 8", Toy Biz
NM $12 MIP $25

Thor, 1998, 8", Toy Biz
NM $7 MIP $15

Wolverine, 1997, 8", Toy Biz
NM $8 MIP $25

MARVEL MILESTONE, 8" FIGURES

Black Widow, 1998, 8", Toy Biz
NM $3 MIP $8

Daredevil, 1998, 8", Toy Biz
NM $3 MIP $8

Falcon, 1998, 8", Toy Biz
NM $3 MIP $8

Mr. Sinister, 1998, 8", Toy Biz
NM $3 MIP $8

Marvel Famous Covers Avengers Assemble (Toy Biz, 1999)

8" FIGURES

Hawkeye, 1999, 8", Toy Biz
NM $7 MIP $18

Hulk, 1999, 8", Toy Biz
NM $7 MIP $15

Iron man, 1999, 8", Toy Biz
NM $7 MIP $18

Vision, 1999, 8", Toy Biz
NM $7 MIP $15

Marvel Gold (Toy Biz, 1998)

FIGURES

Black Panther, 1998, Toy Biz
NM $8 MIP $16

Captain Marvel, 1998
NM $8 MIP $16

Iron Fist, 1998
NM $10 MIP $20

Marvel Girl, 1998, Toy Biz
NM $8 MIP $16

Moon Knight, 1998, Toy Biz
NM $8 MIP $16

Power Man, 1998, Toy Biz
NM $8 MIP $16

Vision, 1998, Toy Biz
NM $8 MIP $16

Marvel Shape Shifters (Toy Biz, 1999)

7" FIGURES

Hulk forms into Dino Beast, 1999
NM $3 MIP $7

Rhino forms into Racing Rhino, 1999
NM $3 MIP $7

Sabretooth forms into Sabretooth Tiger, 1999
NM $3 MIP $7

Spider Sense Spider-Man forms into Spider-Dat, 1999
NM $3 MIP $7

Marvel Shape Shifters II (Toy Biz, 1999)

7" FIGURES

Captain America forms into American Eagle, 1999
NM $3 MIP $7

Colossus forms into Cyborg Gorilla, 1999
NM $3 MIP $7

Kraven forms into Mighty Lion, 1999
NM $3 MIP $7

Thor forms into Winged Stallion, 1999
NM $3 MIP $7

Marvel Shape Shifters Weapons (Toy Biz, 1999)

DELUXE FIGURES

Apocalypse forms into Gattling Gun, 1999
NM $3 MIP $7

Iron Man forms into Battle Axe, 1999
NM $3 MIP $7

Punisher forms into Power Pistol, 1999
NM $3 MIP $7

Spider-Man forms into Wrist Blaster, 1999
NM $3 MIP $7

Marvel Special Edition Series (Toy Biz, 1998)

12" FIGURES

Dr. Octopus, 1998
NM $10 MIP $25

Punisher, 1998
NM $10 MIP $25

Spider-Woman, 1998
NM $10 MIP $25

Marvel Super Heroes (Toy Biz, 1990-92)

SERIES 1, 1990

Captain America, Toy Biz
NM $10 MIP $20

Daredevil, Toy Biz
NM $15 MIP $40

Doctor Doom, Toy Biz
NM $10 MIP $25

Doctor Octopus, Toy Biz
NM $8 MIP $20

Hulk, Toy Biz
NM $4 MIP $12

Punisher (cap firing), Toy Biz
NM $4 MIP $12

Silver Surfer, Toy Biz
NM $8 MIP $25

Spider-Man (suction cups), Toy Biz
NM $5 MIP $20

SERIES 2, 1991

Green Goblin (back lever), Toy Biz
NM $12 MIP $30

Green Goblin (no lever), Toy Biz
NM $8 MIP $20

Marvel Super Heroes (Toy Biz, 1990-92)

Iron Man, Toy Biz
NM $8 **MIP** $20

Punisher (machine gun sound), Toy Biz
NM $5 **MIP** $15

Spider-Man (web climbing), Toy Biz
NM $10 **MIP** $30

Spider-Man (web shooting), Toy Biz
NM $8 **MIP** $25

Thor (back lever), Toy Biz
NM $12 **MIP** $30

Thor (no lever), Toy Biz
NM $8 **MIP** $20

Venom, Toy Biz
NM $7 **MIP** $18

SERIES 3, 1992

Annihilus, Toy Biz
NM $5 **MIP** $15

Deathlok, Toy Biz
NM $5 **MIP** $15

Human Torch, Toy Biz
NM $5 **MIP** $15

Invisible Woman, catapult
NM $5 **MIP** $15

Invisible Woman, vanishing, Toy Biz, turns from color uniform to translucent
NM $30 **MIP** $60

Mister Fantastic, Toy Biz
NM $5 **MIP** $15

Silver Surfer (chrome), Toy Biz
NM $5 **MIP** $15

Spider-Man (ball joints), Toy Biz
NM $5 **MIP** $15

Spider-Man (web tracer), Toy Biz
NM $5 **MIP** $15

Thing, Toy Biz
NM $5 **MIP** $15

Venom (tongue flicking), Toy Biz
NM $15 **MIP** $20

TALKING HEROES

Cyclops, 1990-92, Toy Biz
NM $7 **MIP** $15

Hulk, 1990-92, Toy Biz
NM $7 **MIP** $15

Magneto, 1990-92, Toy Biz
NM $7 **MIP** $15

Punisher, 1990-92, Toy Biz
NM $7 **MIP** $15

Spider-Man, 1990-92, Toy Biz
NM $7 **MIP** $15

Venom, 1990-92, Toy Biz
NM $7 **MIP** $15

Wolverine, 1990-92, Toy Biz
NM $7 **MIP** $15

Marvel Super Heroes Cosmic Defenders (Toy Biz, 1992-93)

FIGURES

Annihilus, 1992-93, Toy Biz
NM $4 **MIP** $12

Deathlok, 1992-93, Toy Biz
NM $4 **MIP** $12

Human Torch, 1992-93, Toy Biz
NM $4 **MIP** $12

Invisible Woman, vanishing color action, 1992-93, Toy Biz
NM $30 **MIP** $60

Mr. Fantastic, 1992-93, Toy Biz
NM $4 **MIP** $12

Silver Surfer, 1992-93, Toy Biz
NM $4 **MIP** $12

Spider-Man, enemy tracking tracer, 1992-93, Toy Biz
NM $4 **MIP** $12

Spider-Man, multi-jointed, 1992-93, Toy Biz
NM $4 **MIP** $12

Marvel Super Heroes Secret Wars (Mattel, 1984-85)

4" FIGURES

Baron Zemo, 1984-85, Mattel
NM $12 **MIP** $25

(Lenny Lee)

Captain America, with secret shield, 1984-85, Mattel, includes figure, shield and mini comic book
NM $10 **MIP** $25

Constrictor (foreign release), 1984-85, Mattel
NM $55 **MIP** $125

Daredevil, 1984-85, Mattel
NM $15 **MIP** $35

(Lenny Lee)

Doctor Doom, 1984-85, Mattel, shown at left with Kang
NM $10 **MIP** $20

(Lenny Lee)

Doctor Octopus, 1984-85, Mattel, Spidey's nemesis with mechanical arms and shield
NM $10 **MIP** $20

Electro (foreign release), 1984-85, Mattel
NM $50 **MIP** $115

Falcon, 1984-85, Mattel
NM $22 **MIP** $50

Hobgoblin, 1984-85, Mattel
NM $35 **MIP** $75

Ice Man (foreign release), 1984-85, Mattel
NM $50 **MIP** $130

Iron Man, 1984-85, Mattel
NM $12 **MIP** $25

(Lenny Lee)

Kang, 1984-85, Mattel, shown at right
NM $8 **MIP** $12

Magneto, 1984-85, Mattel
NM $8 **MIP** $12

Spider-Man, black outfit, 1984-85, Mattel
NM $20 **MIP** $45

Spider-Man, red and blue outfit, 1984-85, Mattel
NM $12 **MIP** $30

Three-Figure Set, 1984-85, Mattel, includes DareDevil, Spidey (in black costume) and Captain America
NM $55 MIP $100

Two-Figure Set, 1984-85, Mattel
NM $25 MIP $50

Wolverine, black claws, 1984-85, Mattel
NM $35 MIP $120

Wolverine, silver claws, 1984-85, Mattel
NM $15 MIP $40

ACCESSORIES

Secret Messages Pack, 1984-85, Mattel
NM $3 MIP $6

Tower of Doom, 1984-85, Mattel
NM $25 MIP $50

VEHICLES

Doom Copter, 1984-85, Mattel
NM $20 MIP $55

Doom Copter with Doctor Doom, 1984-85, Mattel
NM $30 MIP $125

Doom Cycle, 1984-85, Mattel
NM $10 MIP $20

Doom Cycle with Doctor Doom, 1984-85, Mattel
NM $16 MIP $35

Doom Roller, 1984-85, Mattel
NM $10 MIP $20

Doom Star Glider with Kang, 1984-85, Mattel
NM $15 MIP $30

Freedom Fighter, 1984-85, Mattel
NM $10 MIP $30

Star Dart with Spider-Man (black outfit), 1984-85, Mattel
NM $35 MIP $65

Turbo Copter, 1984-85, Mattel
NM $10 MIP $40

Turbo Cycle, 1984-85, Mattel
NM $5 MIP $20

Marvel's Most Wanted (Toy Biz, 1998)

6" FIGURES

Blink, 1998
NM $3 MIP $7

Spat and Grovel, 1998
NM $3 MIP $7

X-Man, 1998
NM $3 MIP $7

Masters of The Universe (Mattel, 1981-1988)

12" FIGURES (ITALIAN)

Megator, 1987
NM $300 MIP $1000

Tytus, 1987
NM $400 MIP $1200

ACCESSORIES

Battle Bones Carrying Case, 1984
NM $10 MIP $20

Battle Cat, 1982
NM $15 MIP $50

Battle Cat with Battle Armor He-Man, 1984
NM $50 MIP $125

Battle Cat with He-Man, 1982
NM $50 MIP $150

Beam Blaster and Artillery, 1987
NM $25 MIP $60

Bionatops, 1987, Mattel, creature
NM $25 MIP $45

He-Man and Wind Raider, 1982, Mattel
NM $20 MIP $100

Jet Sled, 1986
NM $5 MIP $15

Mantisaur, 1986
NM $15 MIP $25

Megalaser, 1986, While this weapon didn't fire any projectiles, it had a blast-effect action and fit warriors in the series
NM $5 MIP $15

(Lenny Lee)

Monstroid Creature (The Evil Horde), 1986, Mattel, Creature grabs warriors in pincers and whirls them around--pretty neat!
NM $15 MIP $50

Night Stalker, 1984
NM $12 MIP $30

Night Stalker with Jitsu, 1984
NM $40 MIP $75

Panthor, 1983
NM $15 MIP $45

Panthor with Battle Armor Skeletor, 1984
NM $35 MIP $125

Panthor with Skeletor, 1983
NM $40 MIP $150

Ring of caps for Thunder Punch He-Man, 1985, Mattel
NM $3 MIP $6

Road Ripper w/ Battle Armor He-Man, 1984, Mattel
NM $20 MIP $65

Screech, 1983
NM $15 MIP $40

Screech with Skeletor, 1983
NM $40 MIP $70

Screeech w/ Battle Armor Skeletor, 1984, Mattel
NM $22 MIP $60

Slime Vat, 1986, Mattel
NM $3 MIP $6

Stilt Stalkers, 1986
NM $5 MIP $20

Stridor (Armored Horse), 1984
NM $10 MIP $30

Stridor with Fisto, 1984
NM $30 MIP $75

(Lenny Lee)

ACTION FIGURES

Masters of The Universe (Mattel, 1981-1988)

Weapons Pak, 1984, Included laser guns, body armor, battle axe, shield, sword and more
NM $5 **MIP** $15

Zoar, 1983
NM $15 **MIP** $30

Zoar with Teela, 1983
NM $40 **MIP** $120

FIGURES

Battle Armor He-Man, 1984, 5"
NM $16 **MIP** $60

Battle Armor Skeletor, 1984, 5"
NM $14 **MIP** $45

Beast Man, 1982, 5"
NM $20 **MIP** $100

Blade, 1987, 5"
NM $30 **MIP** $65

Blast-Attak, 1987, 5", Limbs actually fly off the figure during battle
NM $20 **MIP** $55

Buzz-Off, 1984, 5"
NM $12 **MIP** $40

Buzz-Saw Hordak (The Evil Horde), 1987, 5"
NM $20 **MIP** $40

Clamp Champ, 1987, 5"
NM $25 **MIP** $70

Clawful, 1984, 5"
NM $12 **MIP** $40

Dragon Blaster Skeletor, 1985, 5"
NM $15 **MIP** $40

Dragstor (The Evil Horde), 1986, Mattel, Ripcord (like the SST's series) makes this "transforming evil warrior vehicle" pursue the good guys
NM $20 **MIP** $60

Evil-Lyn, 1983
NM $25 **MIP** $120

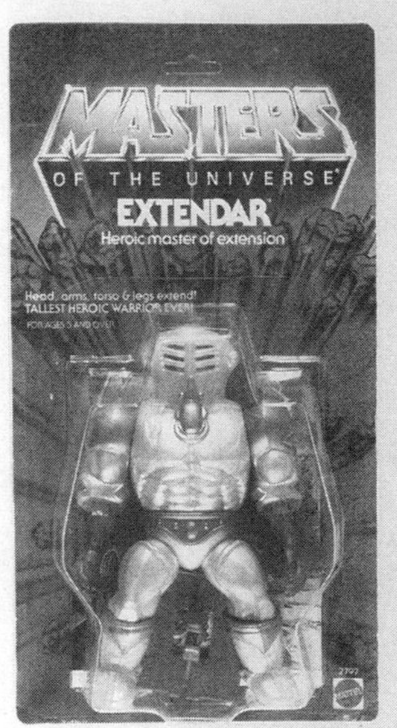

Extendar, 1986, With extending arms, legs, head and torso
NM $18 **MIP** $45

Faker, 1983, Mattel
NM $30 **MIP** $250

Faker (reissue), 1987
NM $20 **MIP** $80

Fisto, 1984
NM $12 **MIP** $40

Flying Fists He-Man, 1986
NM $20 **MIP** $50

Grizzlor (The Evil Horde), 1985
NM $12 **MIP** $40

Grizzlor, black face, 1985
NM $40 **MIP** $125

Gwildor, 1987, figure from Masters of the Universe movie
NM $15 **MIP** $45

He-Man, original, 1982, 1983
NM $22 **MIP** $200

Hordak (The Evil Horde), 1985
NM $20 **MIP** $65

Horde Trooper, 1986
NM $40 **MIP** $140

Hurricane Hordak, 1986
NM $20 **MIP** $60

Jitsu, 1984
NM $12 **MIP** $40

King Hiss (Snake Men), 1986
NM $15 **MIP** $45

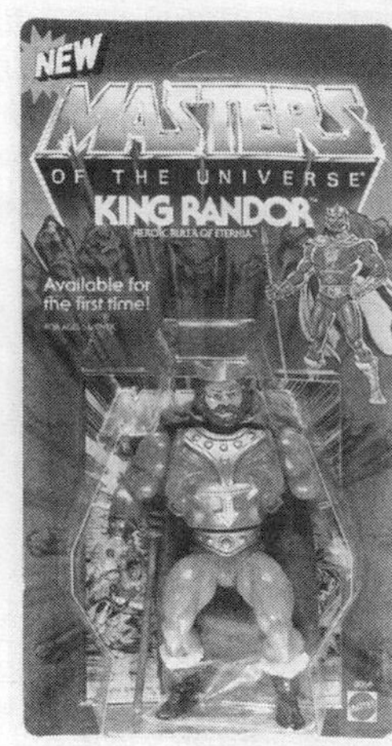

King Randor, 1987, With scepter and mini comic book
NM $40 **MIP** $90

Kobra Kahn (Snake Men), 1984, 1986
NM $15 **MIP** $55

Leech (The Evil Horde), 1985
NM $12 **MIP** $40

Man-At-Arms, 1982, Mattel
NM $15 **MIP** $110

Man-E-Faces, 1983
NM $12 **MIP** $65

Man-E-Faces, five extra weapons, 1983
NM $75 **MIP** $500

Mantenna (The Evil Horde), 1985
NM $12 **MIP** $40

Mekaneck, 1983
NM $10 **MIP** $60

Mer-Man, 1982
NM $20 **MIP** $120

Modulok (The Evil Horde), 1985
NM $15 **MIP** $40

Mosquitor (The Evil Horde), 1987
NM $22 **MIP** $70

Moss Man, 1985
NM $10 **MIP** $40

Multi-Bot (The Evil Horde), 1986
NM $20 **MIP** $40

Ninjor, 1987
NM $30 MIP $85

Orko, 1984
NM $20 MIP $50

Prince Adam, 1984
NM $20 MIP $65

Ram-Man, 1983
NM $12 MIP $60

Rattlor (Snake Men), 1986, With translucent plastic "snake staff" and mini comic book
NM $15 MIP $40

(Lenny Lee)

Rio Blast, 1986, Mattel, An "old West" warrior with hidden weapons. Includes comic book
NM $20 MIP $50

Roboto, 1985
NM $15 MIP $40

Rokkon (Comet Warrior, 1986
NM $12 MIP $35

Rotar (Energy Zoids), 1987
NM $25 MIP $70

Saurod, 1987, figure from Masters of the Universe movie
NM $25 MIP $45

Scare Glow, 1987
NM $40 MIP $125

Skeletor, original, 1982, 1983
NM $22 MIP $210

Snake Face (Snake Men), 1987
NM $22 MIP $70

Snout Spout, 1986
NM $15 MIP $55

Sorceress, 1987
NM $40 MIP $100

Spikor, 1985
NM $12 MIP $40

Sssqueeze (Snake Men), 1987, Mattel, Traps warriors in "slither-hold" grip. Includes serpent
NM $20 MIP $65

Stinkor, 1985
NM $10 MIP $40

Stonedar (Comet Warriors), 1986
NM $15 MIP $35

Stratos, blue wings, 1982, Mattel
NM $12 MIP $120

Stratos, red wings, 1982
NM $12 MIP $120

Sy-klone, 1985
NM $15 MIP $40

Teela, 1982
NM $20 MIP $150

Terror Claws Skeletor, 1986
NM $25 MIP $55

Thunder Punch He-Man, 1985, 5", Mattel
NM $20 MIP $45

Thunder Punch He-Man, 1985
NM $25 MIP $60

Trap Jaw, 1983
NM $20 MIP $70

Tri-Klops, 1983
NM $12 MIP $60

Tung Lashor (Snake Men), 1986
NM $12 MIP $45

Twistoid (Energy Zoids), 1987
NM $40 MIP $80

Two-Bad, 1985
NM $10 MIP $40

Webstor, 1984
NM $12 MIP $40

Whiplash, 1984
NM $10 MIP $35

Zodac, 1982, Mattel
NM $12 MIP $130

GIFT SETS

Battle for Eternia, 1983, 5", Mattel, Skeletor, Panthor, Man-E-Faces
NM $45 MIP $150

Battle for Eternia, 1984, 5", Mattel
NM $50 MIP $150

Evil Horde, 1986, 5", Mattel, Hordak, Leech, Mantenna
NM $60 MIP $150

Evil Warriors, 1983, 5", Mattel, Skeletor, Beast Man, Faker
NM $40 MIP $150

Evil Warriors, 1984, 5", Mattel, Battle Armor Skeletor, Webstor, Mer-Man
NM $45 MIP $175

Evil Warriors, 1985, 5", Mattel, Stinkor, Webstor, Whiplash
NM $60 MIP $150

Flying Fist He-Man and Terror Claws Skeletor, 1986, 5", Mattel
NM $75 MIP $175

Heroic Warriors, 1983, 5", Mattel, He-Man, Teela, Ram-Man
NM $45 MIP $175

Heroic Warriors, 1984, 5", Mattel, Battle Armor He-Man, Man-At-Arms, Man-E-Faces
NM $45 MIP $150

Heroic Warriors, 1985, 5", Mattel, Mekaneck, Buzz-Off, Moss-Man
NM $60 MIP $125

Jet Sled w/ He-Man, 1986, Mattel
NM $45 MIP $85

Mantisaur w/ Hordak, 1986, Mattel
NM $35 MIP $75

GRAYSKULL DINOSAUR SERIES

Bionatops, 1987, Mattel
NM $30 MIP $50

Turbodaltyl, 1987, Mattel
NM $25 MIP $60

Tyrantisaurus Rex, 1987, Mattel
NM $75 MIP $135

LASER FIGURES

Laser Light Skeletor, 1988, Mattel
NM $125 MIP $310

Laser Power He-Man, 1988, Mattel
NM $150 MIP $325

Masters of The Universe (Mattel, 1981-1988)

MAIL AWAY FIGURES

Savage He-Man (Wonder Bread Exclusive), 1982, Mattel
NM $200 **MIP** $500

METEORBS

Astro Lion, 1987, Mattel
NM $25 **MIP** $60

Comet Cat, 1987, Mattel
NM $35 **MIP** $65

Cometroid, 1987, Mattel
NM $15 **MIP** $30

Crocobite, 1987, Mattel
NM $15 **MIP** $30

Dinosorb, 1987, Mattel
NM $15 **MIP** $30

Gore-illa, 1987, Mattel
NM $15 **MIP** $30

Orbear, 1987, Mattel
NM $20 **MIP** $40

Rhinorb, 1987, Mattel
NM $15 **MIP** $30

Tuskor, 1987, Mattel
NM $30 **MIP** $60

Ty-Gyr, 1987, Mattel
NM $20 **MIP** $40

OVERSEAS ACCESSORIES

Cliff Climber, 1987, Mattel
NM $25 **MIP** $60

Scubattack, 1987, Mattel
NM $25 **MIP** $60

Tower Tools, 1987, Mattel
NM $25 **MIP** $60

PLAY SETS

Castle Grayskull, 1982, Mattel
NM $110 **MIP** $250

Eternia, 1986, Mattel
NM $350 **MIP** $700

Fright Zone, 1985, Mattel
NM $60 **MIP** $100

Point Dread and Talon Fighter, 1983, Mattel
NM $20 **MIP** $70

(Lenny Lee)

Slime Pit, 1986, Mattel, Slime oozes from top of pit to trap warriors. The set included real Slime, which actually must have made for a very cool effect on the figures
NM $25 **MIP** $75

Snake Mountain, 1984, Mattel, Snake Pit went quite well with the Slime Pit for play value.
NM $60 **MIP** $125

VEHICLES

Attack Trak, 1983, Mattel
NM $12 **MIP** $35

Bashasaurus, 1985, Mattel
NM $25 **MIP** $50

Battle Ram, 1982, Mattel
NM $15 **MIP** $40

Blaster hawk, 1986, Mattel
NM $25 **MIP** $60

(Lenny Lee)

Dragon Walker, 1984, Mattel, Open-cockpit vehicle that sideways "walks"
NM $12 **MIP** $45

Fright Fighter, 1986, Mattel
NM $15 **MIP** $45

Hordak w/ Grizzlor, 1985, Mattel
NM $10 **MIP** $30

Land Shark, 1985, Mattel
NM $12 **MIP** $25

Land Shark w/ Battle Armor Skeletor, 1985, Mattel
NM $25 **MIP** $48

Laser Bolt, 1986, Mattel
NM $15 **MIP** $40

Point Dread, 1983, Mattel
NM $25 **MIP** $75

Road Ripper, 1983, Mattel, He-Man's motorcycle-type vehicle, ripcord-powered
NM $10 **MIP** $25

Roton, 1984, Mattel
NM $10 **MIP** $25

Spydor, 1985, Mattel
NM $20 **MIP** $45

Wind Raider, 1982, Mattel
NM $12 **MIP** $35

Masters of the Universe (Mattel, 2002-03)

ACCESSORIES

Bat Fight-Pack, 2003, Mattel
NM $4 **MIP** $8

Battle Cat, 2002, Mattel
NM $5 **MIP** $12

Battle Raptor, 2003, Mattel
NM $7 **MIP** $15

Eagle Fight-Pack, 2003, Mattel
NM $4 **MIP** $8

He-Man's Sword, 2002, Mattel
NM $7 **MIP** $12

Panthor, 2002, Mattel
NM $5 **MIP** $12

Samurai Battlecat, 2003, Mattel
NM $10 **MIP** $20

DELUXE FIGURES

Battle Sound He-Man, 2002, 5", Mattel, Series 1
NM $5 **MIP** $12

Battle Sound Skeletor, 2002, 5", Mattel, Series 1
NM $5 **MIP** $12

Samauri Man-At-Arms, 2003, 5", Mattel
NM $7 **MIP** $15

Samurai He-Man, 2003, 5", Mattel
NM $7 **MIP** $15

Samurai Skeletor, 2003, 5", Mattel
NM $7 **MIP** $15

FIGURES

Battle Glove Man-At-Arms, 2003, 5", Mattel, Series 4
NM $5 **MIP** $15

Beast Man, 2002, 5", Mattel, Series 1
NM $5 **MIP** $10

Buzz-Off, 2003, 5", Mattel, Series 4
NM $5 **MIP** $10

Evil-Lyn, 2003, 5", Mattel, Series 3
NM $2 **MIP** $6

Faker, 2003, 5", Mattel, Toy Fare Exclusive
NM $18 **MIP** $35

Fire Armor Skeletor, 2003, 5", Mattel, Series 3
NM $5 **MIP** $10

He-Man, 2002, 5", Mattel, Series 1
NM $5 **MIP** $10

Ice Armor He-Man, 2003, 5", Mattel, Series 4
NM $2 **MIP** $6

Jungle Attack He-Man, 2002, 5", Mattel, Series 2
NM $5 **MIP** $10

Makaneck, 2002, 5", Mattel, Series 2
NM $5 **MIP** $10

Man-At-Arms, 2002, 5", Mattel, Series 1
NM $5 **MIP** $10

Man-E-Faces, 2003, 5", Mattel, Series 4
NM $2 **MIP** $6

Martial Arts He-Man, 2003, 5", Mattel, Series 4
NM $2 **MIP** $6

Mega-Punch He-Man, 2003, 5", Mattel, Series 4
NM $2 **MIP** $6

Mer-Man, 2002, 5", Mattel, Series 1
NM $5 **MIP** $10

Orko, 2003, 5", Mattel, Series 3
NM $5 **MIP** $15

Prince Adam, 2003, 5", Mattel, Series 4
NM $5 **MIP** $15

Ram Man, 2002, 5", Mattel, Series 2
NM $5 **MIP** $10

Skeletor, 2002, 5", Mattel, Series 1
NM $5 **MIP** $10

Smash Blade He-Man, 2003, 5", Mattel, Series 3
NM $2 **MIP** $6

Spin Blade Skeletor, 2003, 5", Mattel, Series 2
NM $2 **MIP** $6

Stratos, 2002, 5", Mattel, Series 1
NM $5 **MIP** $10

Sy-Klone, 2003, 5", Mattel, Series 4
NM $5 **MIP** $15

Teela, 2003, 5", Mattel, Series 3
NM $5 **MIP** $15

Trapjaw, 2003, 5", Mattel, Series 2
NM $5 **MIP** $10

Tri-Klops, 2003, 5", Mattel, Series 2
NM $5 **MIP** $10

Two-Bad, 2003, 5", Mattel, Series 3
NM $5 **MIP** $10

Whiplash, 2003, 5", Mattel, Series 3
NM $5 **MIP** $10

GIFT SETS

Armor Skeletor, 2003, Mattel
NM $10 **MIP** $20

He-Man vs. Skeletor, 2002, Mattel, figure 2-pack
NM $10 **MIP** $20

Wolf Armor He-Man & Snake, 2003, Mattel
NM $10 **MIP** $20

MINI FIGURES

He-Man, 2002, Mattel
NM $2 **MIP** $6

Heroes vs. Villians Giftpack, 2002, Mattel, w/ exclusive Beastman
NM $7 **MIP** $12

Man-At-Arms, 2002, Mattel
NM $2 **MIP** $6

Mekaneck, 2002, Mattel
NM $2 **MIP** $6

Mer-Man, 2002, Mattel
NM $2 **MIP** $6

Skeletor, 2002, Mattel
NM $2 **MIP** $6

Stratos, 2002, Mattel
NM $2 **MIP** $6

PLAY SETS

Castle Grayskull, 2002, Mattel
NM $25 **MIP** $50

VEHICLES

Attack Squid, 2003, Mattel
NM $10 **MIP** $20

Bashin' Beetle, 2002, Mattel
NM $7 **MIP** $15

Battle Hawk, 2002, Mattel
NM $7 **MIP** $15

Battle Ram Chariot, 2002, Mattel
NM $7 **MIP** $15

Battle Tank, 2002, Mattel
NM $10 **MIP** $20

Terrordactyl, 2002, Mattel
NM $7 **MIP** $15

War Whale, 2003, Mattel
NM $10 **MIP** $20

Matrix, The (McFarlane, 2003)

SERIES 1 FIGURES

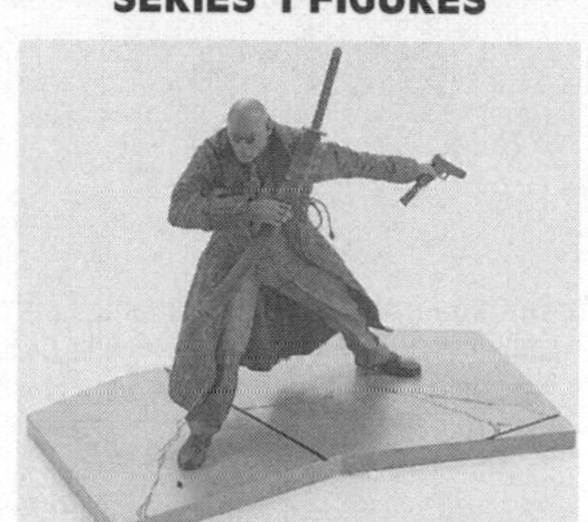

(KP Photo, Brian Brogaard Collection)

Morpheus, 2003, McFarlane, w/gun and sword
NM $5 **MIP** $12

(KP Photo, Brian Brogaard collection)

Neo, 2003, McFarlane
NM $5 **MIP** $10

Neo in Chateau, 2003, McFarlane, Deluxe boxed set
NM $10 **MIP** $17

(KP Photo, Brian Brogaard collection)

Trinity, 2003, McFarlane
NM $5 **MIP** $10

Twin 1, 2003, McFarlane
NM $5 **MIP** $12

Twin 2, 2003, McFarlane
NM $5 **MIP** $12

SERIES 2 FIGURES

A.P.U. Deluxe Boxed Set, 2003, 12", McFarlane, w/Mifune
NM $15 **MIP** $30

Agent Smith, fight scene, 2003, 6-1/2", McFarlane, in suit
NM $5 **MIP** $12

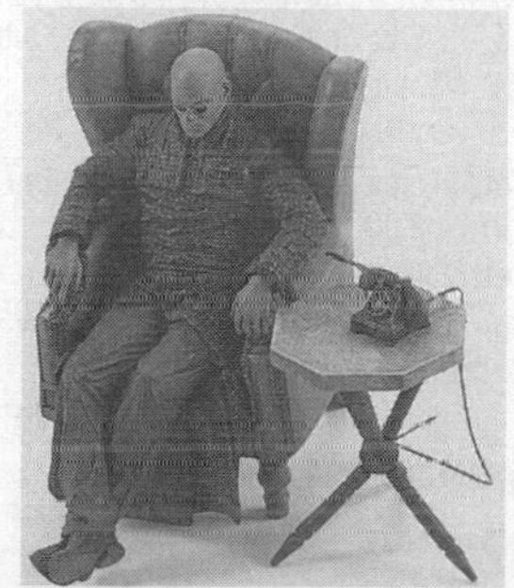

(KP Photo, Brian Brogaard collection)

Matrix, The (McFarlane, 2003)

Morpheus, seated, 2003, 4-1/2", McFarlane, w/red chair, telephone stand and phone
NM $5 **MIP** $12

Neo, fight scene, 2003, 9-1/2", McFarlane, backdrop of Smiths
NM $5 **MIP** $12

(KP Photo, Brian Brogaard collection)

Neo, real world, 2003, 8", McFarlane, w/different heads
NM $5 **MIP** $12

Niobe, 2003, 7", McFarlane
NM $5 **MIP** $12

Sentinel Deluxe Boxed Set, 2003, 27" long, McFarlane, fully articulated tentacles, whew!
NM $20 **MIP** $40

Trinity, 2003, 8-1/2" tall, McFarlane, falling scene
NM $5 **MIP** $12

McFarlane Music (McFarlane, 1999-02)

FIGURES

Alice Cooper, 2000, McFarlane
NM $3 **MIP** $13

Angus Young, 2001, McFarlane, AC/DC guitarist
NM $6 **MIP** $12

Iron Maiden's Eddie: from "Killers", 2002, 6-3/4", McFarlane, based on the album artwork
NM $6 **MIP** $12

Iron Maiden's Eddie: from "Peace of Mind", 2002, 5-5/8", McFarlane, based on the album artwork
NM $6 **MIP** $12

Janis Joplin, 2000
NM $5 **MIP** $15

Jerry Garcia, 2001, McFarlane
NM $6 **MIP** $12

Jim Morrison, 2001, McFarlane
NM $6 **MIP** $12

Metallica: Boxed Set, 2001, McFarlane, pose from "And Justice for All"
NM $17 **MIP** $35

Metallica: James Hetfield, 2001, 6-1/8", McFarlane, pose from "And Justice for All"
NM $6 **MIP** $12

Metallica: Jason Newsted, 2001, 7", McFarlane, pose from "And Justice for All"
NM $6 **MIP** $12

Metallica: Kirk Hammett, 2001, 5-7/8", McFarlane, pose from "And Justice for All"
NM $6 **MIP** $12

Metallica: Lars Ulrich, 2001, 5-1/4, McFarlane, pose from "And Justice for All"
NM $6 **MIP** $12

Ozzie Osbourne, 1999, McFarlane, Fairly buff Ozzy figure holding cross and dead bat with dead bats and doves at his feet. Includes church window diorama backdrop
NM $5 **MIP** $15

Rob Zombie, 2000, Figure with mechanical arms includes "Zombie" base
NM $5 **MIP** $15

Metal Gear Solid (McFarlane, 1998)

FIGURES

(McFarlane Toys)

Liquid Snake, 1998, McFarlane, With pistol and machine gun rifle
NM $4 **MIP** $10

(McFarlane Toys)

Meryl Silverburgh, 1998, McFarlane, With pistol, bayonet, grappling hook and machine gun
NM $4 **MIP** $10

(McFarlane Toys)

Ninja, 1998, McFarlane, Multi-colored figure with sword
NM $4 **MIP** $10

(McFarlane Toys)

Psycho Mantis, 1998, McFarlane, Includes bust, vase, crystal ball and detailed figure
NM $4 **MIP** $10

(McFarlane Toys)

Revolver Ocelot, 1998, McFarlane, Detailed gunslinger figure includes two pistols
NM $4 **MIP** $10

Sniper Wolf, 1998, McFarlane, With rifle and snarling wolf figure
NM $4 **MIP** $10

(McFarlane Toys)

Solid Snake, 1998, McFarlane, Includes a variety of weapons and accessories; rifle, pistol, infra-red goggles and more
NM $4 **MIP** $10

(McFarlane Toys)

Vulcan Raven, 1998, McFarlane, With multi-barreled weapon and barrel-shaped pack
NM $4 **MIP** $10

Micronauts (Mego, 1976-80)

ACCESSORIES

Karrio, 1979, 3-3/4", Mego, carrying case
NM $10 **MIP** $20

ALIEN INVADERS CARDED

Antron, 1979, 3-3/4", Mego
NM $30 **MIP** $150

Centaurus, 1980, 3-3/4", Mego, also a foreign release
NM $65 **MIP** $250

Kronos, 1980, 3-3/4", Mego, also a foreign release
NM $45 **MIP** $250

Lobros, 1980, 3-3/4", Mego, also a foreign release
NM $45 **MIP** $250

Membros, 1979, 3-3/4", Mego
NM $25 **MIP** $125

Repto, 1979, 3-3/4", Mego
NM $25 **MIP** $125

ALIEN INVADERS VEHICLES

Alphatron, 1979, Mego, vehicle w/ figure
NM $5 **MIP** $15

Betatron, 1979, Mego, vehicle w/ figure
NM $5 **MIP** $15

Gammatron, 1979, Mego, vehicle w/ figure
NM $5 **MIP** $15

Hornetroid, 1979, small, Mego, vehicle for Antron
NM $60 **MIP** $100

Hydra, 1976, small, Mego
NM $20 **MIP** $60

Mobile Exploration Lab, 1976, Mego, largest of the vehicles
NM $20 **MIP** $75

Solarion, 1978, Mego, rare
NM $20 **MIP** $65

Star Searcher, 1978, Mego
NM $20 **MIP** $75

Taurion, 1978, Mego
NM $25 **MIP** $70

Terraphant, 1979, small, Mego, vehicle for Membros
NM $25 **MIP** $100

BOXED FIGURES

Andromeda, 1977, 8", Mego
NM $10 **MIP** $25

Baron Karza, 1977, 8", Mego
NM $35 **MIP** $100

Biotron, 1976, 12", Mego
NM $10 **MIP** $25

Force Commander, 1977, 8", Mego
NM $25 **MIP** $75

Giant Acroyear, 1977, 8", Mego
NM $20 **MIP** $70

Megas, 1981, 8", Mego, foreign release
NM $20 **MIP** $75

Microtron, 1976, 8", Mego
NM $20 **MIP** $85

Micronauts (Mego, 1976-80)

Nemesis Robot, 1978, 8", Mego
NM $35 MIP $65

Oberon, 1977, 8", Mego
NM $25 MIP $55

Phobos Robot, 1978, 8", Mego
NM $45 MIP $75

Red Falcon, 1976, Mego
NM $38 MIP $160

CARDED FIGURES

Acroyear, 1976, 3-3/4", Mego, red, blue, orange
NM $30 MIP $70

Acroyear II, 1977, 3-3/4", Mego, red, blue, orange
NM $30 MIP $75

Galactic Defender, 1978, 3-3/4", Mego, white, yellow
NM $15 MIP $45

Galactic Warrior, 1976, 3-3/4", Mego, red, blue, orange
NM $12 MIP $40

Pharoid with Time Chamber, 1977, 3-3/4", Mego, blue, red, gray
NM $25 MIP $55

Space Glider, 1976, 3-3/4", Mego, blue, green, orange
NM $20 MIP $50

Time Traveler, 1976, 3-3/4", Mego, solid plastic, yellow, orange
NM $20 MIP $50

Time Traveler, 1976, 3-3/4", Mego, opaque plastic, yellow, orange
NM $25 MIP $100

MICROPOLIS PLAY SETS

Galactic Command Center, 1978, Mego
NM $45 MIP $110

Interplanetary Headquarters, 1978, Mego
NM $45 MIP $110

Mega City, 1978, Mego, largest of the micro cities, 500+ pieces
NM $45 MIP $110

Microrail City, 1978, Mego
NM $45 MIP $110

PLAY SETS

Astro Station, 1976, Mego
NM $25 MIP $65

Rocket Tubes, 1978, Mego, 2 versions, deluxe and standard
NM $45 MIP $110

Stratstation, 1976, Mego
NM $30 MIP $80

VEHICLES

Aquatron, 1977, small, Mego, two pontoons, detachable motor
NM $15 MIP $50

Battle Cruiser, 1977, large, Mego, Model No. 71054
NM $40 MIP $75

Crater Cruncher with figure, 1976, small, Mego, Time Traveler included
NM $20 MIP $60

Galactic Cruiser, 1976, small, Mego
NM $20 MIP $60

Hydro Copter, 1976, small, Mego
NM $25 MIP $50

Neon Orbiter, 1977, small, Mego
NM $12 MIP $40

Photon Sled, 1976, small, Mego
NM $12 MIP $35

Rhodium Orbiter, 1977, small, Mego
NM $12 MIP $45

Thorium Orbiter, 1977, small, Mego
NM $12 MIP $40

Ultronic Scooter with figure, 1976, small, Mego, Time Traveler included
NM $20 MIP $60

Warp Racer with figure, 1976, small, Mego, Time Traveler included
NM $15 MIP $45

Mighty Morphin Power Rangers (Bandai, 1993-95)

3" FIGURES

Black Ranger, 1995, Bandai
NM $7 MIP $20

Blue Ranger, 1995, Bandai
NM $7 MIP $20

Pink Ranger, 1995, Bandai
NM $7 MIP $20

Red Ranger, 1995, Bandai
NM $7 MIP $20

Yellow Ranger, 1995, Bandai
NM $7 MIP $20

5" FIGURES WITH THUNDER BIKES

Black Ranger, 1995, Bandai
NM $6 MIP $15

Blue Ranger, 1995, Bandai
NM $6 MIP $15

Pink Ranger, 1995, Bandai
NM $6 MIP $15

Red Ranger, 1995, Bandai
NM $6 MIP $15

Yellow Ranger, 1995, Bandai
NM $6 MIP $15

8" ALIENS, 1993

Baboo, 1993, Bandai
NM $8 MIP $20

Bones, 1993, Bandai
NM $8 MIP $20

Finster, 1993, Bandai
NM $8 MIP $20

Goldar, 1993, Bandai
NM $8 MIP $20

King Sphinx, 1993, Bandai
NM $8 MIP $20

Putty Patrol, 1993, Bandai
NM $8 MIP $20

Squatt, 1993, Bandai
NM $8 MIP $20

8" FIGURES, 1993

Black Ranger, 1993, Bandai
NM $7 MIP $20

Blue Ranger, 1993, Bandai
NM $7 MIP $20

Pink Ranger, 1993, Bandai
NM $10 MIP $20

Red Ranger, 1993, Bandai
NM $5 MIP $20

Yellow Ranger, 1993, Bandai
NM $10 MIP $20

8" MOVIE FIGURES, 1995

Black Ranger, 1995, Bandai, metallic
NM $6 MIP $15

Blue Ranger, 1995, Bandai, metallic
NM $6 MIP $15

Pink Ranger, 1995, Bandai, metallic
NM $6 MIP $15

Red Ranger, 1995, Bandai, metallic
NM $6 MIP $15

White Ranger, 1995, Bandai, metallic
NM $6 MIP $15

Yellow Ranger, 1995, Bandai, metallic
NM $6 MIP $15

ACTION FEATURE EVIL SPACE ALIENS, 5-1/2" FIGURES, 1994

Dark Knight, 1994, Bandai
NM $6 MIP $15

Eye Guy, 1994, Bandai
NM $6 MIP $15

Minotar, 1994, Bandai
NM $6 MIP $15

Mutaytus, 1994, Bandai
NM $6 MIP $15

Pudgy Pig, 1994, Bandai
NM $6 MIP $15

Rita Repulsa, 1994, Bandai
NM $6 MIP $15

Snizard Lips, 1994, Bandai
NM $6 MIP $15

Spidertron, 1994, Bandai
NM $6 MIP $15

AUTO-MORPHIN POWER RANGERS, 5-1/2" FIGURES, 1994

Black Ranger, 1994, Bandai
NM $3 MIP $15

Blue Ranger, 1994, Bandai
NM $3 MIP $15

Green Ranger, 1994, Bandai
NM $3 MIP $15

Pink Ranger, 1994, Bandai
NM $3 MIP $15

Red Ranger, 1994, Bandai
NM $2 MIP $15

Yellow Ranger, 1994, Bandai
NM $3 MIP $15

DELUXE EVIL SPACE ALIENS, 8" FIGURES, 1994

Evil Eye, 1994, Bandai
NM $7 MIP $15

Goo Fish, 1994, Bandai
NM $7 MIP $15

Guitardo, 1994, Bandai
NM $7 **MIP** $15

Lord Zedd, 1994, Bandai
NM $8 **MIP** $18

Pirantus Head, 1994, Bandai
NM $7 **MIP** $15

Pudgy Pig, 1994, Bandai
NM $7 **MIP** $15

Putty Patrol, 1994, Bandai
NM $7 **MIP** $15

Rhino Blaster, 1994, Bandai
NM $7 **MIP** $15

Socaddillo, 1994, Bandai
NM $7 **MIP** $15

KARATE ACTION FIGURES, 1994

Black Ranger, 1994, Bandai
NM $6 **MIP** $12

Blue Ranger, 1994, Bandai
NM $6 **MIP** $12

Pink Ranger, 1994, Bandai
NM $8 **MIP** $16

Red Ranger, 1994, Bandai
NM $5 **MIP** $10

Yellow Ranger, 1994, Bandai
NM $8 **MIP** $16

POWER RANGERS FOR GIRLS

Kimberly, 1995, Bandai
NM $10 **MIP** $20

Kimberly/Trini Set, 1995, Bandai
NM $20 **MIP** $40

Trini, 1995, Bandai
NM $10 **MIP** $20

ZORDS, 1993

Dragon Dagger, 1993, Bandai
NM $20 **MIP** $50

Dragon Zord with Green Ranger, 1993, Bandai
NM $25 **MIP** $55

MegaZord, 1993, Bandai
NM $15 **MIP** $30

MegaZord Deluxe, 1993, Bandai
NM $20 **MIP** $40

Titanus the Carrier Zord, 1993, Bandai
NM $35 **MIP** $75

ZORDS, 1994

MegaZord, black/gold, limit. ed., 1994, Bandai
NM $50 **MIP** $100

Power Cannon, 1994, Bandai
NM $15 **MIP** $35

Power Dome Morphin Set, 1994, Bandai
NM $20 **MIP** $50

Red Dragon Thunder Zord, 1994, Bandai
NM $25 **MIP** $45

Saba (White Sword), 1994, Bandai
NM $15 **MIP** $30

Thunder Zord Assault Team, 1994, Bandai
NM $25 **MIP** $45

TOR the Shuttle Zord, 1994, Bandai
NM $30 **MIP** $60

Ultra Thunder Zord, 1994, Bandai
NM $35 **MIP** $70

White Tiger Zord with White Ranger, 1994, Bandai
NM $25 **MIP** $50

Modern Horror Classics (Sideshow Toys, 2003)

12" FIGURES

Freddy Krueger, 2003, Sideshow Toys, #7302
NM n/a **MIP** $40

Furnace Environment, 2003, 15" x 8', Sideshow Toys, #6606
NM n/a **MIP** $40

Furnace/ Freddy Combo Pack, 2003, Sideshow Toys, #6606R, Freddy and the Furnace
NM n/a **MIP** $75

Jason Voorhees, 2003, 12", Sideshow Toys, #7301
NM n/a **MIP** $40

Leatherface - Texas Chainsaw Massacre, 2003, 12", Sideshow Toys, #7303
NM n/a **MIP** $40

Michael Myers - Halloween, 2003, 12", Sideshow Toys, #7304
NM n/a **MIP** $40

Monsters (McFarlane, 1997-2002)

FIGURES

Dracula, 2002, 6", McFarlane
NM $5 **MIP** $20

Frankenstein, 2002, 7", McFarlane
NM $5 **MIP** $20

Mummy, 2002, 7-1/2", McFarlane
NM $5 **MIP** $20

Sea Creature, 2002, 7", McFarlane
NM $5 **MIP** $20

VooDoo Queen, 2002, 6-1/2", McFarlane
NM $5 **MIP** $20

Werewolf, 2002, 6-3/4", McFarlane
NM $5 **MIP** $20

SERIES 1, PLAY SETS WITH 4" FIGURES

(McFarlane Toys)

Dracula and Bat, 1997, McFarlane, Includes Dracula, coffin, masouleum, "bat" figure and accessories
NM $5 **MIP** $20

(McFarlane Toys)

Frankenstein and Igor, 1997, McFarlane, Hunchbacked Igor in lab coat and monster figure on upright table
NM $8 **MIP** $20

(McFarlane Toys)

Hunchback, Quasimodo and Gargoyle, 1997, McFarlane, Includes catapult-topped bell tower and two figures
NM $5 **MIP** $15

Werewolf and Victim, 1997, McFarlane
NM $5 **MIP** $15

SERIES 2, PLAY SETS WITH 4" FIGURES

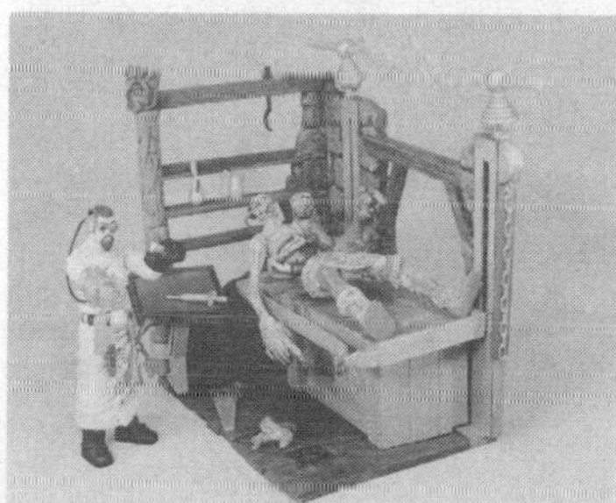

(McFarlane Toys)

Dr. Frankenstein, 1998, McFarlane, Set includes re-animation bed, gruesome Frankenstein monster figure, Dr. F in lab coat. Includes various lab instruments
NM $6 **MIP** $12

Monsters (McFarlane, 1997-2002)

(McFarlane Toys)

The Mummy, 1998, McFarlane, Includes sarcophogus, Anubis figure, jars, and Mummy
NM $6 **MIP** $12

(McFarlane Toys)

The Phantom of the Opera, 1998, McFarlane, Great detail--includes pipe organ, inspector and phantom figures
NM $6 **MIP** $12

(McFarlane Toys)

The Sea Creature, 1998, McFarlane, Set includes diver in old-fashioned dive suit and attacking sea creature
NM $6 **MIP** $12

Mork and Mindy (Mattel, 1980)

FIGURES

Mindy, 1980, 9", Mattel
NM $20 **MIP** $45

Mork from Ork with egg, 1980, 3-3/4", Mattel
NM $10 **MIP** $40

Mork with Talking Spacepack, upside down, 1980, 9", Mattel, Talking Mork says, "Nano, Nano and 7 other crazy things"
NM $25 **MIP** $50

Movie Maniacs (McFarlane, 1998-2004)

18" FIGURES

(KP Photo, Merry Dudley collection)

Ash, 2001, 18", McFarlane, from Army of Darkness
NM $10 **MIP** $25

Edward Scissorhands, 2002, 18", McFarlane
NM $10 **MIP** $25

Freddy Krueger, 2000, 18", McFarlane, from "A Nightmare on Elm Street"
NM $10 **MIP** $25

Leatherface, 2001, 18", McFarlane, from "Texas Chainsaw Massacre"
NM $10 **MIP** $25

Michael Myers, 2000, 18", McFarlane, "Halloween"
NM $10 **MIP** $25

SERIES 1

Eve, "Species II", 1998, McFarlane
NM $4 **MIP** $8

(McFarlane Toys)

Freddy Krueger, "Nightmare on Elm Street", 1998, McFarlane, Classic Freddy with red-striped sweater, fedora and extended claws
NM $5 **MIP** $15

Freddy Krueger, gory, "Nightmare on Elm Street", 1998, McFarlane
NM $5 **MIP** $15

Jason, "Friday the 13th", 1998, McFarlane
NM $4 **MIP** $8

(McFarlane Toys)

Jason, gory, "Friday the 13th", 1998, McFarlane, Detailed figure includes machete
NM $10 **MIP** $30

Leatherface, "The Texas Chainsaw Massacre", 1998, McFarlane
NM $15 **MIP** $25

Leatherface, gory, "The Texas Chainsaw Massacre", 1998, McFarlane
NM $25 **MIP** $45

Patrick, "Species II", 1998, McFarlane
NM $4 **MIP** $8

SERIES 2

Chucky and Tiffany, "Bride of Chucky", 1999, McFarlane
NM $8 **MIP** $20

Chucky, "Child's Play", 1999, McFarlane
NM $5 **MIP** $15

Eric Draven, "The Crow", 1999, McFarlane, With black guitar and crow figure
NM $5 **MIP** $15

Ghostface, "Scream", 1999, McFarlane, Detailed Scream figure with knife and cellphone, movie-poster stand
NM $5 **MIP** $15

Michael Myers, "Halloween", 1999, McFarlane, Michael Myers figure with knife and movie-poster stand
NM $5 **MIP** $15

Norman Bates, "Psycho", 1999, McFarlane, Norman in "mother" outfit and wig with knife, includes movie-poster stand
NM $5 **MIP** $15

Pumkinhead, "Pumpkinhead", 1999, McFarlane, Figure includes movie-poster stand
NM $5 **MIP** $15

SERIES 3

Ash, "Army of Darkness", 2000, McFarlane, Great Bruce Campbell likeness with chainsaw hand, rifle and movie-poster stand
NM $5 **MIP** $15

Blair Monster, "The Thing", 2000, McFarlane, Highly detailed figure with movie stand
NM $5 **MIP** $15

Edward Scissorhands, "Edward Scissorhands", 2000, McFarlane, Very detailed likeness with movie-poster stand
NM $3 **MIP** $12

Fly, The, "The Fly", 2000, McFarlane, Brindle-pattern figure with movie-poster stand
NM $3 **MIP** $10

King Kong, "King Kong", 2000, McFarlane, Deluxe figure
NM $10 **MIP** $25

Norris Creature w/Spider, "The Thing", 2000, McFarlane
NM $5 **MIP** $15

Shaft, "Shaft", 2000, McFarlane, Figures with "The Thing" movie-poster stand
NM $3 **MIP** $10

Snake Plissken, "Escape From L.A.", 2000, McFarlane, Figure with rifle and movie-poster stand
NM $3 **MIP** $10

SERIES 4

Blair Witch, "Blair Witch Project", 2001, McFarlane
NM $5 **MIP** $15

Candyman, 2001, McFarlane
NM $5 **MIP** $15

(KP Photo, Brian Brogaard collection)

Evil Ash, 2001, McFarlane, from "Army of Darkness"
NM $5 **MIP** $15

Freddy Krueger, 2001, McFarlane, from "Nightmare on Elm Street"
NM $5 **MIP** $15

Jaws Deluxe Boxed Set, 2001, McFarlane
NM $15 **MIP** $30

T-1000, 2001, McFarlane, T2
NM $5 **MIP** $15

T-800, 2001, McFarlane, T2
NM $5 **MIP** $15

SERIES 5

Alien and Predator Deluxe Boxed Set, 2002, 8", McFarlane
NM $15 **MIP** $30

Djinn, 2002, 6-3/4", McFarlane, from "Wishmaster"
NM $5 **MIP** $10

Jason X, 2002, 6-7/8", McFarlane
NM $5 **MIP** $10

Lord of Darkness, 2002, 6-7/8", McFarlane, from "Legend"
NM $5 **MIP** $15

Sarah Connor, 2002, 6-3/8", McFarlane
NM $5 **MIP** $15

T-800 Endoskeleton, 2002, 7-1/8", McFarlane
NM $5 **MIP** $15

(KP Photo, Brian Brogaard collection)

Tooth Fairy, 2002, 6-3/4", McFarlane, from "Darkness Falls"
NM $5 **MIP** $10

SERIES 6

(KP Photo, Brian Brogaard collection)

Alien Queen, 2003, McFarlane, large set, w/Ripley
NM $10 **MIP** $30

Dog Alien, 2003, McFarlane
NM $5 **MIP** $15

(KP Photo, Brian Brogaard collection)

Predator, 2003, McFarlane
NM $5 **MIP** $15

(KP Photo, Brian Brogaard collection)

Predator the Hunter, 2003, McFarlane
NM $5 **MIP** $15

(KP Photo, Brian Brogaard collection)

Warrior Alien, 2003, McFarlane
NM $5 **MIP** $15

SERIES 7

12" Leatherface, 2004, 12", McFarlane, from Texas Chainsaw Massacre
NM $10 **MIP** $30

Colonial Marine Corporal Hicks, 2004, 6-3/4", McFarlane, from Aliens
NM $5 **MIP** $15

Erin, 2004, 5-3/4", McFarlane, from Texas Chainsaw Massacre
NM $5 **MIP** $15

Leatherface, 2004, 7-1/2", McFarlane, from Texas Chainsaw Massacre
NM $5 **MIP** $15

Old Monty, 2004, 6", McFarlane, from Texas Chainsaw Massacre
NM $5 **MIP** $15

Robocop, 2004, 7-3/4", McFarlane, from film
NM $5 **MIP** $15

Sherrif Hoyt, 2004, 7-1/4", McFarlane, from Texas Chainsaw Massacre
NM $5 **MIP** $15

Muppets (Palisades, 2002-04)

12" FIGURES

Mega Animal, 2003, 12", Palisades
NM $12 **MIP** $25

Mega Beaker, 2003, 12", Palisades
NM $12 **MIP** $25

Mega Gonzo, 2004, Palisades, in tuxedo
NM $12 **MIP** $25

EXCLUSIVES

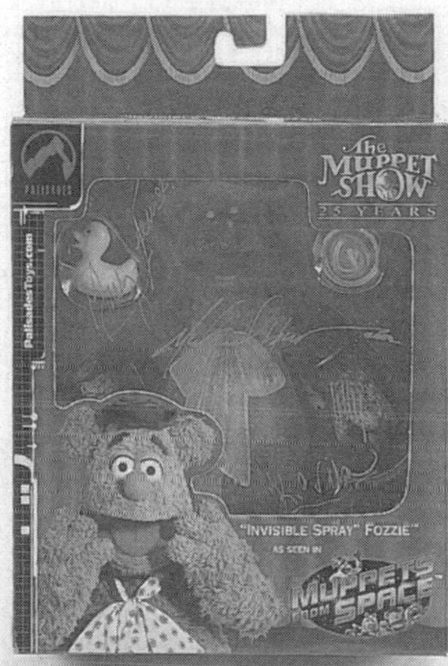

(KP Photo, Merry Dudley collection)

"Invisible Spray" Fozzie, Palisades, exclusive 2002 San Diego Comicon exclusive; from Muppets in Space
NM $7 **MIP** $15

Animal Tour 2003, Palisades, convention special, didn't come w/drumsticks
NM $12 **MIP** $25

PLAY SETS

Electric Mayhem, 2002, Palisades, w/ Animal
NM $18 **MIP** $35

Muppet Labs, 2002, Palisades, w/ Beaker
NM $12 **MIP** $25

Pigs in Space, 2002, Palisades
NM $12 **MIP** $20

Swedish Kitchen, 2002, Palisades, w/ the Swedish Chef
NM $18 **MIP** $40

SERIES 01 FIGURES

Dr. Bunsen Honeydew, 2002, Palisades
NM $6 **MIP** $15

Dr. Teeth, 2002, Palisades
NM $8 **MIP** $18

Kermit the Frog, 2002, Palisades
NM $6 **MIP** $12

Miss Piggy, 2002, Palisades
NM $6 **MIP** $12

SERIES 02 FIGURES

Crazy Harry, 2002, Palisades
NM $5 **MIP** $10

Floyd Pepper, 2002, Palisades
NM $5 **MIP** $12

Fozzie Bear, 2002, Palisades
NM $5 **MIP** $10

Gonzo the Great, 2002, Palisades
NM $5 **MIP** $10

SERIES 03 FIGURES

Lew Zealand, 2002, Palisades
NM $5 **MIP** $9

Rowlf, 2002, Palisades
NM $5 **MIP** $10

Scooter, 2002, Palisades
NM $5 **MIP** $9

Zoot, 2002, Palisades
NM $7 **MIP** $15

SERIES 04 FIGURES

Dr. Strangepork, 2002, Palisades
NM $5 **MIP** $9

Link Hogthrob, 2002, Palisades
NM $5 **MIP** $9

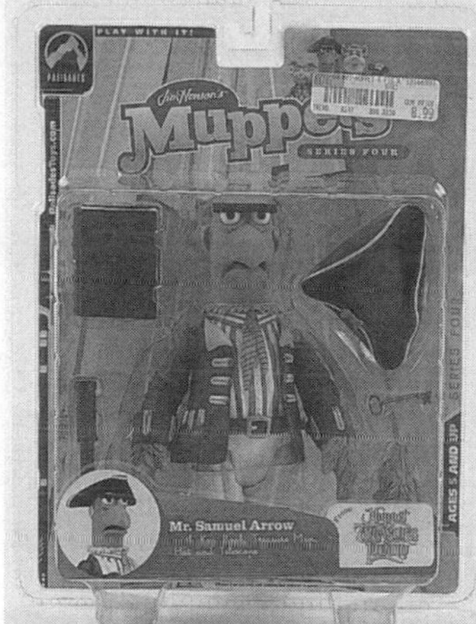

(KP Photo, Merry Dudley collection)

Mr. Samuel Arrow, 2002, Palisades
NM $5 **MIP** $9

Rizzo the Rat, 2002, Palisades
NM $5 **MIP** $9

SERIES 05 FIGURES

Gonzo & Camilla, 2003, Palisades
NM $5 **MIP** $9

Janice, 2003, Palisades
NM $7 **MIP** $12

Muppet Newsman, 2003, Palisades
NM $5 **MIP** $9

Pepe, 2003, Palisades
NM $5 **MIP** $9

SERIES 06 FIGURES

Clifford, 2003, Palisades
NM $4 **MIP** $8

Patrol Bear, 2003, Palisades
NM $4 **MIP** $8

Statler, 2003, Palisades
NM $4 **MIP** $8

Waldorf, 2003, Palisades
NM $4 **MIP** $8

SERIES 07 FIGURES

Beauregard, 2004, Palisades
NM $4 **MIP** $8

Captain Smollet & Polly, 2004, Palisades, Kermit as sea captain
NM $4 **MIP** $8

Frog Scout Robin, 2004, Palisades
NM $4 **MIP** $8

Johnny Fiama, 2004, Palisades, available w/3 different jacket colors, silver, pinstripe, maroon
NM $6 **MIP** $12

SERIES 08 FIGURES

Dr. Phil Van Neuter, 2004, Palisades
NM $4 **MIP** $8

Muppets (Palisades, 2002-04)

Marvin Suggs, 2004, Palisades
NM $4 **MIP** $8

Movie Usher Scooter, 2004, Palisades
NM $4 **MIP** $8

Sam the Eagle, 2004, Palisades
NM $4 **MIP** $8

SERIES 09 FIGURES

Classic Swedish Chef, 2004, Palisades
NM $4 **MIP** $8

Lips, 2004, Palisades
NM $4 **MIP** $8

Pops, 2004, Palisades
NM $4 **MIP** $8

Steppin' Out Fozzie (Tuxedo Fozzie), 2004, Palisades, w/Chucky, the dummy
NM $4 **MIP** $8

Nightmare Before Christmas (Hasbro, 1993)

FIGURES

Behemoth, 1993, Hasbro
NM $35 **MIP** $80

Evil Scientist, 1993, Hasbro
NM $50 **MIP** $150

Jack Skellington, 1993, Hasbro
NM $40 **MIP** $100

Jack Skellington as Santa, 1993, Hasbro
NM $35 **MIP** $80

Lock, Shock and Barrel, 1993, Hasbro
NM $75 **MIP** $250

Mayor, 1993, Hasbro
NM $45 **MIP** $125

Oogie Boogie, 1993, Hasbro
NM $75 **MIP** $250

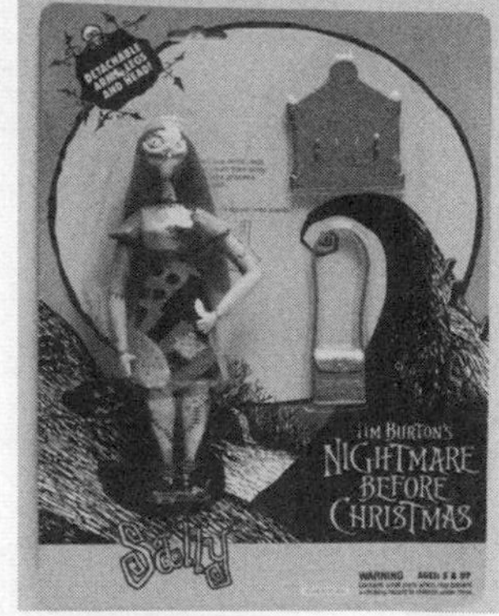

Sally, 1993, Hasbro
NM $40 **MIP** $100

Santa, 1993, Hasbro
NM $75 **MIP** $250

Werewolf, 1993, Hasbro, tombstone, bone
NM $40 **MIP** $100

Noble Knights (Marx, 1968)

FIGURES

Black Knight, Sir Cedric, 1968, 12", Marx, #2082, with removeable helmet, shield and accessories, a UK figure
NM $250 **MIP** $550

Gold Knight, Sir Gordon, 1968, 12", Marx, #5366, like the black knight, this figure had molded-on armor, but included a variety of plastic accessories such as shield, helmet and sword, Sir Percival in UK
NM $75 **MIP** $150

Silver Knight, Sir Stuart, 1968, 12", Marx, #5364, Sir Roland in UK, shown here with most (not all) of his accessories
NM $75 **MIP** $150

HORSES

Bravo Armor Horse, 1968, Marx, #5371, Gold Knight's horse, chestnut color, Victor in UK
NM $75 **MIP** $150

Valiant Armor Horse, 1968, Marx, Black Knight's horse, gray color, UK only
NM $200 **MIP** $400

Valor Armor Horse, 1968, Marx, #5391, Silver Knight's horse, palomino color, Valour in UK, Big Valor on 1970 packaging
NM $75 **MIP** $150

One Million B.C. (Mego, 1976)

FIGURES

Dimetrodon, 1976, Mego, boxed
NM $100 **MIP** $250

Grok, 1976, Mego, carded
NM $25 **MIP** $50

Hairy Rhino, 1976, Mego, boxed
NM $125 **MIP** $300

Mada, 1976, Mego, carded
NM $25 **MIP** $50

Orm, 1976, Mego, carded
NM $25 **MIP** $50

Trag, 1976, Mego, carded
NM $25 **MIP** $50

Tribal Lair, 1976, Mego, boxed
NM $100 **MIP** $200

Tribal Lair Gift Set (five figures), 1976, Mego, boxed
NM $200 **MIP** $400

Tyrannosaur, 1976, Mego, boxed
NM $125 **MIP** $300

Zon, 1976, carded, 1976, Mego, carded
NM $25 **MIP** $50

Outer Space Men (Colorforms, 1968)

FIGURES

Alpha 7 / Man from Mars, 1968, Colorforms
NM $150 **MIP** $450

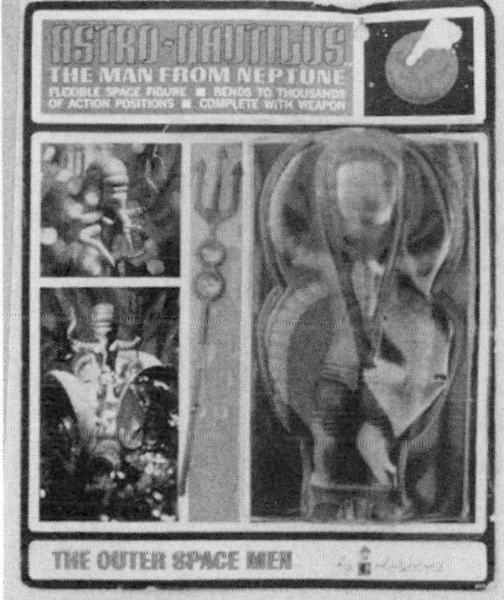

Astro-Nautilus / Man from Neptune, 1968, Colorforms, A freaky-looking dude that is simliar to the work done on today's hit show Futurama.
NM $300 **MIP** $750

Colossus Rex / Man from Jupiter, 1968, Colorforms
NM $300 **MIP** $800

Commander Comet / Man from Venus, 1968, Colorforms
NM $200 **MIP** $500

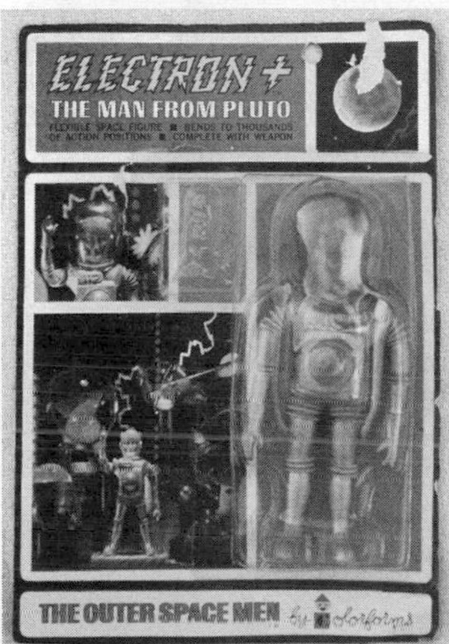

Electron / Man from Pluto, 1968, Colorforms, A flexible figure that packs heat, and by the looks of things, can shoot lightning from his head. Striking!
NM $200 **MIP** $500

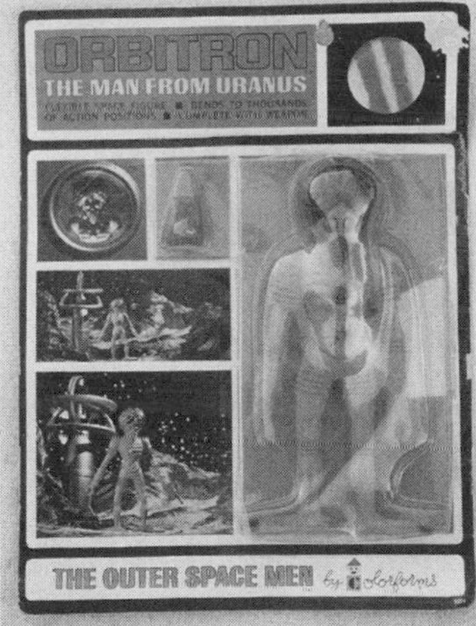

Orbitron / Man from Uranus, 1968, Colorforms, An unfortunately-named, but neat toy nonetheless. Looking very much like the Metaluna Mutant in "This Island Earth," Orbitron was a bendable figure that included a blaster pistol
NM $200 **MIP** $600

Xodiac / Man from Saturn, 1968, Colorforms
NM $200 **MIP** $500

Pee-Wee's Playhouse (Matchbox, 1988)

16" FIGURES

(KP Photo, Kris Manty collection)

Billy Baloney, 1988, Matchbox, his eyes and mouth move
NM $20 **MIP** $50

5" FIGURES

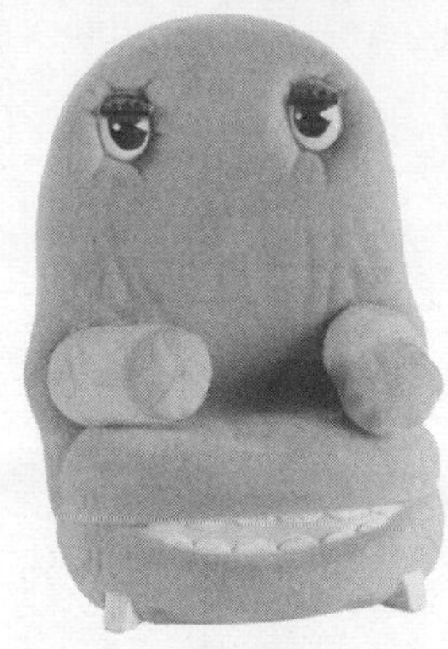

(KP Photo, Kris Manty collection)

Chairry, 1988, 5", Matchbox
NM $10 **MIP** $30

(KP Photo, Kris Manty collection)

Conky, 1988, 5", Matchbox
NM $12 **MIP** $32

Cowboy Curtis, 1988, 5", Matchbox
NM $10 **MIP** $25

(KP Photo, Kris Manty collection)

Globey, 1988, 5", Matchbox, packaged w/Randy
NM $10 **MIP** $25

Jambi and Puppetland Band, 1988, 5", Matchbox
NM $14 **MIP** $35

King of Cartoons, 1988, 5", Matchbox
NM $8 **MIP** $20

Magic Screen, 1988, 5", Matchbox
NM $6 **MIP** $15

Miss Yvonne, 1988, 5", Matchbox
NM $15 **MIP** $30

Pee-Wee's Playhouse (Matchbox, 1988)

(KP Photo, Kris Manty collection)

Pee-Wee Herman, 1988, 5", Matchbox
NM $12 MIP $25

Pee-Wee Herman with Scooter, 1988, 5", Matchbox
NM $18 MIP $40

(KP Photo, Kris Manty collection)

Pterri, 1988, 5", Matchbox
NM $8 MIP $20

(KP Photo, Kris Manty collection)

Randy, 1988, Matchbox, packaged w/Globey
NM $10 MIP $25

Reba, 1988, 5", Matchbox
NM $10 MIP $25

Ricardo, 1988, 5", Matchbox
NM $10 MIP $20

PLAY SETS

Pee-Wee's Playhouse, 1988, 5", Matchbox, w/Scooter, Floory, Clockey, Mr. Window, Dancing Flowers; working front door, fridge, swinging wall; includes platform, island couch, tv console, kitchen table and bench
NM $75 MIP $175

Planet of the Apes (Hasbro, 1998-99)

12" FIGURES

Cornelius, 1999, 12", Hasbro
NM $8 MIP $20

Dr. Zaius, 1999, 12", Hasbro
NM $8 MIP $20

Dr. Zira, 1998, 12", Hasbro
NM $10 MIP $20

General Ursus, 1999, 12", Hasbro
NM $8 MIP $20

Gorilla Sergeant, 1998, 12", Hasbro
NM $10 MIP $20

Gorilla Soldier, 1998, 12", Hasbro, Diamond Previews exclusive
NM $15 MIP $30

Taylor, 1998, 12", Hasbro
NM $10 MIP $20

7" FIGURES

Commander Taylor, 1999, 7", Hasbro
NM $2 MIP $6

Cornelius, 1999, 7", Hasbro
NM $2 MIP $6

Dr. Zaius, 1999, 7", Hasbro
NM $2 MIP $6

Gorilla Sergeant, 1999, 7", Hasbro
NM $2 MIP $6

Gorilla Soldier, 1999, 7", Hasbro
NM $2 MIP $6

Zira, 1999, 7", Hasbro
NM $2 MIP $6

Planet of the Apes (Mego, 1973-75)

8" FIGURES

Astronaut, 1973, 8", Mego, boxed
NM $50 MIP $250

Astronaut, 1975, 8", Mego, carded
NM $50 MIP $100

Astronaut Burke, 1975, 8", Mego, carded
NM $50 MIP $100

Astronaut Burke, 1975, 8", Mego, boxed
NM $50 MIP $250

Astronaut Verdon, 1975, 8", Mego, boxec
NM $50 MIP $250

Astronaut Verdon, 1975, 8", Mego, carded
NM $50 MIP $125

Cornelius, 1973, 8", Mego, boxed
NM $40 MIP $200

Cornelius, 1975, 8", Mego, carded
NM $40 MIP $100

Dr. Zaius, 1973, 8", Mego, boxed
NM $40 MIP $200

Dr. Zaius, 1975, 8", Mego, carded
NM $40 MIP $100

Galen, 1975, 8", Mego, carded
NM $40 MIP $100

Galen, 1975, 8", Mego, boxed
NM $40 MIP $200

General Urko, 1975, 8", Mego, boxed
NM $50 MIP $250

General Urko, 1975, 8", Mego, carded
NM $50 MIP $250

General Ursus, 1975, 8", Mego, boxed
NM $50 MIP $250

General Ursus, 1975, 8", Mego, carded
NM $50 MIP $250

Soldier Ape, 1973, 8", Mego, boxed
NM $50 MIP $250

Soldier Ape, 1975, 8", Mego, carded
NM $50 MIP $200

Zira, 1973, 8", Mego, boxed
NM $30 MIP $200

Zira, 1975, 8", Mego, carded
NM $30 MIP $100

ACCESSORIES

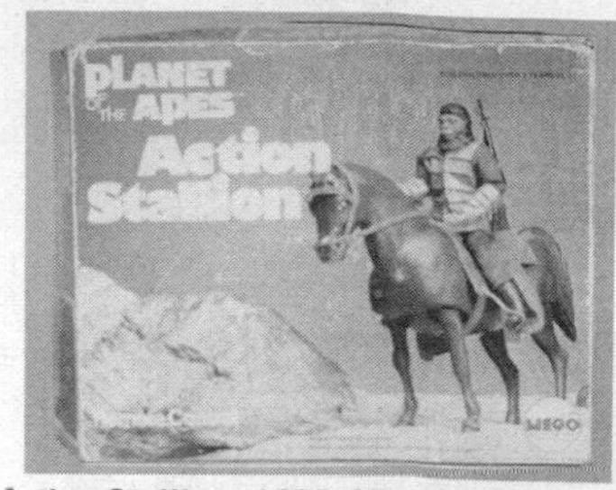

Action Stallion, 1975, Mego, brown, motorized, remote-controlled
NM $50 MIP $100

Battering Ram, 1975, Mego, boxed
NM $20 MIP $40

Dr. Zaius' Throne, 1975, Mego, boxed
NM $20 MIP $40

Jail, 1975, Mego, boxed
NM $20 MIP $40

PLAY SETS

Forbidden Zone Trap, 1975, Mego, boxed
NM $90 MIP $230

Fortress, 1975, Mego, boxed
NM $85 MIP $230

Treehouse, 1975, Mego, boxed
NM $75 MIP $230

Village, 1975, Mego, boxed
NM $85 MIP $230

VEHICLES

Catapult and Wagon, 1975, Mego, boxed
NM $75 MIP $150

Planet of the Apes - Movie (Hasbro 2001)

12" FIGURES

Attar, 2001, 12", Hasbro
NM $5 MIP $15

Leo, 2001, 12", Hasbro
NM $5 MIP $15

FIGURES

Ape Commander, 2001, 6", Hasbro
NM $2 MIP $5

Ari, 2001, 6", Hasbro
NM $2 MIP $5

Attar, 2001, 6", Hasbro
NM $2 MIP $5

Daena, 2001, 6", Hasbro
NM $2 MIP $5

General Thade w/ Horse, 2001, 6", Hasbro
NM $5 MIP $15

Krull, 2001, 6", Hasbro
NM $2 MIP $5

Leo, 2001, 6", Hasbro
NM $2 MIP $5

Limbo, 2001, 6", Hasbro
NM $2 MIP $5

Pericles, 2001, 6", Hasbro
NM $2 MIP $5

Pocket Super Heroes (Mego, 1976-79)

3-3/4" FIGURES

Aquaman, white card, 1976, 3-3/4", Mego
NM $50 MIP $100

Batman, red card, 1976, 3-3/4", Mego
NM $20 MIP $75

Batman, white card, 1976, 3-3/4", Mego
NM $20 MIP $125

Captain America, white card, 1976, 3-3/4", Mego
NM $50 MIP $100

General Zod, red card, 1979, 3-3/4", Mego
NM $5 MIP $25

Green Goblin, white card, 1976, 3-3/4", Mego
NM $50 MIP $150

Hulk, 1976, white card, 1976, 3-3/4", Mego
NM $15 MIP $40

Hulk, 1979, red card, 1979, 3-3/4", Mego, Shown on right with Robin
NM $15 MIP $30

Jor-El (Superman), red card, 1979, 3-3/4", Mego
NM $10 MIP $20

Lex Luthor (Superman), red card, 1979, 3-3/4", Mego
NM $10 MIP $20

Robin, red card, 1979, 3-3/4", Mego, Shown on left with Hulk
NM $20 MIP $60

Robin, white card, 1976, 3-3/4", Mego
NM $20 MIP $100

Spider-Man, red card, 1979, 3-3/4", Mego
NM $15 MIP $50

Spider-Man, white card, 1976, 3-3/4", Mego
NM $15 MIP $100

Superman, white card, 1976, 3-3/4", Mego
NM $15 MIP $75

Superman, red card, 1979, 3-3/4", Mego
NM $15 MIP $40

Wonder Woman, white card, 1979, 3-3/4", Mego
NM $20 MIP $75

ACCESSORIES

Batcave, 1981, Mego
NM $120 MIP $300

VEHICLES

Batmachine, 1979, Mego
NM $40 MIP $100

Batmobile, 1979, Mego, with Batman and Robin
NM $80 MIP $200

Spider-Car, 1979, Mego, with Spider-Man and Hulk
NM $30 MIP $75

Spider-Machine, 1979, Mego
NM $40 MIP $100

Power Rangers in Space (Bandai, 1998)

ACTION ZORDS, 5" FIGURES

Astro Megaship, 1998, Bandai
NM $2 MIP $6

Astro Megazord, 1998, Bandai
NM $2 MIP $6

Delta Megazord, 1998, Bandai
NM $2 MIP $6

Mega Tank, 1998, Bandai
NM $2 MIP $6

Mega Winger, 1998, Bandai
NM $2 MIP $6

ASTRO RANGER, 5" FIGURES

Black Ranger, 1998, Bandai
NM $2 MIP $6

Pink Ranger, 1998, Bandai
NM $2 MIP $6

Red Ranger, 1998, Bandai
NM $2 MIP $6

Red Ranger, 1998, Bandai
NM $2 MIP $6

Silver Ranger, 1998, Bandai
NM $2 MIP $6

Yellow Ranger, 1998, Bandai
NM $2 MIP $6

BATTLIZED POWER RANGERS, 5" FIGURES

Black Ranger, 1998, Bandai
NM $2 MIP $6

Blue Ranger, 1998, Bandai
NM $2 MIP $6

Red Ranger, 1998, Bandai
NM $2 MIP $6

Silver, 1998, Bandai
NM $2 MIP $6

EVIL SPACE ALIENS, 5" FIGURES

Craterite, 1998, Bandai
NM $2 MIP $6

Ecliptor, 1998, Bandai
NM $2 MIP $6

STAR POWER RANGERS IN SPACE, 5" FIGURES

Blue Ranger, 1998, Bandai
NM $2 MIP $6

Green Ranger, 1998, Bandai
NM $2 MIP $6

Pink Ranger, 1998, Bandai
NM $2 MIP $6

Red Ranger, 1998, Bandai
NM $2 MIP $6

Yellow Ranger, 1998, Bandai
NM $2 MIP $6

Power Rangers Turbo (Bandai, 1997)

EVIL SPACE ALIENS, 5" FIGURES

Amphibitor, 1997, Bandai
NM $2 MIP $6

Chromite, 1997, Bandai
NM $2 MIP $6

Divatox, 1997, Bandai
NM $2 MIP $6

Elgar, 1997, Bandai
NM $2 MIP $6

Griller, 1997, Bandai
NM $2 MIP $6

Hammeron, 1997, Bandai
NM $2 MIP $6

Rygog, 1997, Bandai
NM $2 MIP $6

Visceron, 1997, Bandai
NM $2 MIP $6

REPEAT TURBO RANGERS, 5" FIGURES

Blue Ranger, 1997, Bandai
NM $2 MIP $6

Green Ranger, 1997, Bandai
NM $2 MIP $6

Pink Ranger, 1997, Bandai
NM $2 MIP $6

Red Ranger, 1997, Bandai
NM $2 MIP $6

Power Rangers Turbo (Bandai, 1997)

Yellow Ranger, 1997, Bandai
NM $2 MIP $6

TURBO CARTS WITH 4" FIGURE

Cart with Blue Turbo Ranger, 1997, Bandai
NM $3 MIP $8

Cart with Green Turbo Ranger, 1997, Bandai
NM $3 MIP $8

Cart with Pink Turbo Ranger, 1997, Bandai
NM $3 MIP $8

Cart with Red Turbo Ranger, 1997, Bandai
NM $3 MIP $8

Cart with Yellow Turbo Ranger, 1997, Bandai
NM $3 MIP $8

TURBO RANGERS, 5" FIGURES, EACH ACTIVATED WITH KEY

Blue Turbo Ranger, 1997, Bandai
NM $2 MIP $6

Green Turbo Ranger, 1997, Bandai
NM $2 MIP $6

Pink Turbo Ranger, 1997, Bandai
NM $2 MIP $6

Red Turbo Ranger, 1997, Bandai
NM $2 MIP $6

Yellow Turbo Ranger, 1997, Bandai
NM $2 MIP $6

TURBO SHIFTER, 5" FIGURES

Blue Ranger, 1997, Bandai
NM $2 MIP $6

Green Ranger, 1997, Bandai
NM $2 MIP $6

Pink Ranger, 1997, Bandai
NM $2 MIP $6

Red Ranger, 1997, Bandai
NM $2 MIP $6

Yellow Ranger, 1997, Bandai
NM $2 MIP $6

Power Rangers Zeo (Bandai, 1996)

AUTO MORPHIN, 5-1/2" FIGURES

Blue, 1996, Bandai
NM $2 MIP $6

Gold Warrior, 1996, Bandai
NM $2 MIP $6

Green, 1996, Bandai
NM $2 MIP $6

Pink, 1996, Bandai
NM $2 MIP $6

Red, 1996, Bandai
NM $2 MIP $6

Yellow, 1996, Bandai
NM $2 MIP $6

EVIL SPACE ALIENS, 5-1/2" FIGURES

Cogs, 1996, Bandai
NM $2 MIP $6

Drill Master, 1996, Bandai
NM $2 MIP $6

Mechanizer, 1996, Bandai
NM $2 MIP $6

Quadfighter, 1996, Bandai
NM $2 MIP $6

Silo, 1996, Bandai
NM $2 MIP $6

ZEO JET CYCLES WITH FIGURE

Cycle with Blue Zeo Ranger III, 1996, Bandai
NM $2 MIP $6

Cycle with Gold Zeo Ranger, 1996, Bandai
NM $2 MIP $6

Cycle with Green Zeo Ranger IV, 1996, Bandai
NM $2 MIP $6

Cycle with Pink Zeo Ranger I, 1996, Bandai
NM $2 MIP $6

Cycle with Red Zeo Ranger V, 1996, Bandai
NM $2 MIP $6

Cycle with Yellow Zeo Ranger II, 1996, Bandai
NM $2 MIP $6

ZEO POWER ZORDS, 5-1/2" FIGURES

1-2 Punching Action Red Battlezord, 1996, Bandai
NM $2 MIP $6

Auric the Conqueror Zord, 1996, Bandai
NM $2 MIP $6

Power Sword Action Zeo Megazord, 1996, Bandai
NM $2 MIP $6

Pyramidas, 1996, Bandai
NM $2 MIP $6

Super Zeo Megazord, 1996, Bandai
NM $2 MIP $6

Warrior Wheel, 1996, Bandai
NM $2 MIP $6

ZEO RANGERS, 5-1/2" FIGURES

Blue Zeo Ranger III, 1996, Bandai
NM $2 MIP $6

Gold Zeo Ranger, 1996, Bandai
NM $2 MIP $6

Green Zeo Ranger IV, 1996, Bandai
NM $2 MIP $6

Pink Zeo Ranger I, 1996, Bandai
NM $2 MIP $6

Red Zeo Ranger V, 1996, Bandai
NM $2 MIP $6

Yellow Zeo Ranger II, 1996, Bandai
NM $2 MIP $6

ZEO RANGERS, 8" FIGURES

Blue Zeo Ranger III, 1996, Bandai
NM $3 MIP $8

Gold Zeo Ranger, 1996, Bandai
NM $3 MIP $8

Green Zeo Ranger IV, 1996, Bandai
NM $3 MIP $8

Pink Zeo Ranger I, 1996, Bandai
NM $3 MIP $8

Red Zeo Ranger V, 1996, Bandai
NM $3 MIP $8

Yellow Zeo Ranger II, 1996, Bandai
NM $3 MIP $8

Pulsar (Mattel, 1976)

FIGURES

Hypnos, 1976, Mattel, no circulatory system, spinning disk in chest
NM $50 MIP $110

Pulsar the Ultimate Man of Adventure, 1976, 12", Mattel, exposed chest shows veins with "blood" pumping through
NM $25 MIP $45

PLAYSET

Life Systems Center Playset, 1976, Mattel
NM $25 MIP $50

Puppetmaster (Full Moon Toys, 1997-98)

FIGURES

Blade, 1997-98, Full Moon Toys
NM $8 MIP $20

Blade, blood splattered, 1997-98, Full Moon Toys
NM $25 MIP $85

Blade, bullet-eyed (Troll & Joad), 1997-98, Full Moon Toys
NM $15 MIP $40

Blade, gold, 1997-98, Full Moon Toys
NM $8 MIP $20

Blade, red Japanese Exclusive, 1997-98, Full Moon Toys
NM $15 MIP $40

Jester, 1997-98, Full Moon Toys
NM $3 MIP $12

Jester, gold, 1997-98, Full Moon Toys
NM $8 MIP $20

Jester, Japanese Exclusive, Carse of Jester, 1997-98, Full Moon Toys
NM $3 MIP $12

Jester, Previews Exclusive, 1997-98, Full Moon Toys
NM $8 MIP $20

Leech Woman, 1997-98, Full Moon Toys
NM $3 MIP $12

Leech Woman, gold, 1997-98, Full Moon Toys
NM $8 MIP $20

Leech Woman, Japanese Exclusive, Geisha Leech Woman, 1997-98, Full Moon Toys
NM $3 MIP $12

Leech Woman, Previews Exclusive, 1997-98, Full Moon Toys
NM $8 MIP $20

Mephisto, 1997-98, Full Moon Toys
NM $3 MIP $12

Mephisto, clear, 1997-98, Full Moon Toys
NM $5 MIP $15

Mephisto, Japanese Exclusive, death Mephisto, 1997-98, Full Moon Toys
NM $8 MIP $20

Mephisto, Previews Exclusive, 1997-98, Full Moon Toys
NM $8 MIP $20

Pinhead, 1997-98, Full Moon Toys
NM $3 MIP $12

Pinhead, gold, 1997-98, Full Moon Toys
NM $8 MIP $20

Pinhead, Halloween 1999, 1997-98, Full Moon Toys
NM $8 MIP $20

Pinhead, Japanese Exclusive, Pinhead in the Dark, 1997-98, Full Moon Toys
NM $8 MIP $25

Pinhead, Previews Exclusive, 1997-98, Full Moon Toys
NM $8 MIP $20

Sixshooter, 1997-98, Full Moon Toys
NM $8 MIP $20

Sixshooter, gold, 1997-98, Full Moon Toys
NM $8 MIP $20

Sixshooter, Japanese Exclusive, DOA Sixshooter, 1997-98, Full Moon Toys
NM $10 MIP $30

Sixshooter, Troll & Joad edition, 1997-98, Full Moon Toys
NM $10 MIP $30

Torch, 1997-98, Full Moon Toys
NM $3 MIP $12

Torch, gold, 1997-98, Full Moon Toys
NM $8 MIP $20

Torch, Japanese Exclusive, Camouflage Torch, 1997-98, Full Moon Toys
NM $8 MIP $20

Torch, Previews Exclusive, 1997-98, Full Moon Toys
NM $8 MIP $20

Totem, 1997-98, Full Moon Toys
NM $3 MIP $12

Totem, 1998 San Diego Comicon, 1997-98, Full Moon Toys
NM $15 MIP $45

Totem, gold, 1997-98, Full Moon Toys
NM $5 MIP $15

Totem, Japanese Exclusive, Evil Spirit Totem, 1997-98, Full Moon Toys
NM $10 MIP $35

Totem, Preview Exclusive, 1997-98, Full Moon Toys
NM $8 MIP $20

Tunneler, 1997-98, Full Moon Toys
NM $3 MIP $12

Tunneler, Australian Exclusive, 1997-98, Full Moon Toys
NM $15 MIP $45

Tunneler, gold, 1997-98, Full Moon Toys
NM $8 MIP $20

Tunneler, Japanese Exclusive, Cruel Sgt. Tunneler, 1997-98, Full Moon Toys
NM $15 MIP $45

Tunneler, Previews Exclusive, 1997-98, Full Moon Toys
NM $8 MIP $20

Rambo (Coleco, 1985)

FIGURES

Black Dragon, 1985, 5", Coleco, Series 1
NM $4 MIP $10

Chief, 1985, 5", Coleco, Series 2
NM $8 MIP $15

Colonel Troutman, 1985, 5", Coleco, Series 1
NM $4 MIP $8

Dr. Hyde, 1985, 5", Coleco, Series 2
NM $8 MIP $20

General Warhawk, 1985, 5", Coleco, Series 1
NM $4 MIP $10

Gripper, 1985, 5", Coleco, Series 1
NM $4 MIP $10

K.A.T., 1985, 5", Coleco, Series 1
NM $5 MIP $10

Mad Dog, 1985, 5", Coleco, Series 2
NM $4 MIP $10

Nomad, 1985, 5", Coleco, Series 1
NM $8 MIP $13

Rambo, 1985, 5", Coleco, Series 1
NM $5 MIP $13

Rambo with Fire Power, 1985, 5", Coleco, Series 2
NM $5 MIP $13

Sergeant Havoc, 1985, 5", Coleco, Series 1
NM $4 MIP $10

Snakebite, 1985, 5", Coleco, Series 2
NM $10 MIP $20

T.D. Jackson, 1985, 5", Coleco, Series 2
NM $10 MIP $20

Turbo, 1985, 5", Coleco, Series 1
NM $4 MIP $10

White Dragon, 1985, 5", Coleco, Series 1
NM $4 MIP $10

X-Ray, 1985, 5", Coleco, Series 2
NM $10 MIP $20

PLAY SETS

S.A.V.A.G.E. Strike Headquarters, 1985, Coleco, Series 1
NM $32 MIP $65

VEHICLES

Defender 6x6, 1985, Coleco, Series 1
NM $15 MIP $30

S.A.V.A.G.E. Strike Cycle, 1985, Coleco, Series 1
NM $10 MIP $20

Skyfire Assault Copter, 1985, Coleco, Series 1
NM $15 MIP $30

Skywolf Assault Jet, 1985, Coleco, Series 1
NM $15 MIP $25

Swamp Dog, 1985, Coleco, Series 1
NM $10 MIP $20

Resident Evil (Toy Biz, 1998)

5" FIGURES

Chris Redfield and Cerberus, 1998
NM $5 MIP $15

Hunter and Chimera, 1998
NM $3 MIP $8

Jill Valentine and Web Spinner, 1998
NM $3 MIP $8

Maggot Zombie and Forrest Speyer, 1998
NM $3 MIP $8

Tyrant, 1998
NM $3 MIP $8

Resident Evil (Palisades, 2002)

SERIES II

Alexia, 2002, Palisades, Bug-winged figure with "leafy" hair
NM $8 MIP $12

Claire Redfield, 2002, Palisades, Figure includes dagger and pistol
NM $8 MIP $12

Resident Evil (Palisades, 2002)

Mr. X, 2002, Palisades, Black jacket and uniform, dark gray skin, glowing eyes
NM $8 MIP $12

Zombie Cop, 2002, Palisades, Mauled policeman with terrifying ? on a leash...
NM $8 MIP $12

Robin Hood and His Merry Men (Mego, 1974)

FIGURES

Friar Tuck, 1974, 8", Mego
NM $35 MIP $65

Little John, 1974, 8", Mego
NM $70 MIP $165

Robin Hood, 1974, 8", Mego
NM $100 MIP $310

Will Scarlett, 1974, 8", Mego
NM $80 MIP $285

Robin Hood Prince of Thieves (Kenner, 1991)

ACCESSORIES

Battle Wagon, 1991, Kenner
NM $15 MIP $30

Bola Bomber, 1991, Kenner
NM $5 MIP $10

Net Launcher, 1991, Kenner
NM $5 MIP $10

Sherwood Forest Play Set, 1991, Kenner
NM $30 MIP $60

FIGURES

Azeem, 1991, Kenner
NM $5 MIP $12

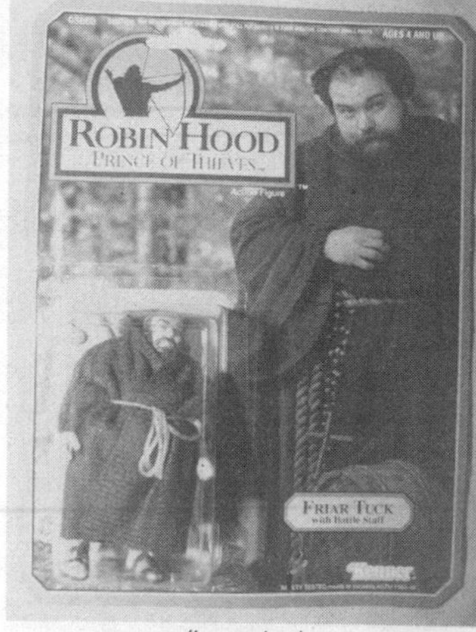

(Lenny Lee)

Friar Tuck, with Battle Staff, 1991, Kenner, with fabric road
NM $10 MIP $20

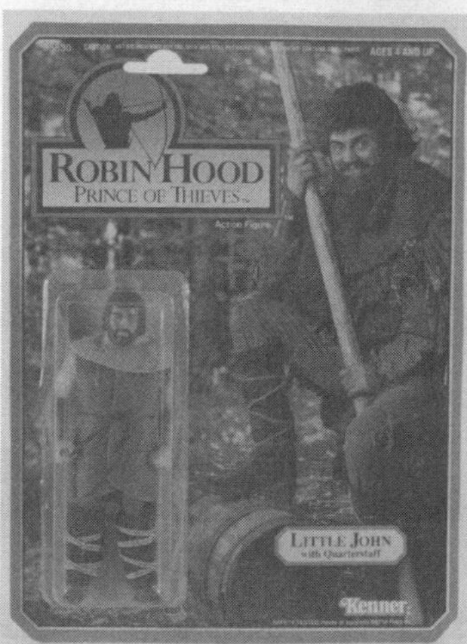

Little John, 1991, Kenner
NM $5 MIP $12

Robin Hood, Crossbow, 1991, Kenner
NM $5 MIP $15

Robin Hood, Crossbow, Costner Head, 1991, Kenner
NM $5 MIP $15

Robin Hood, Long Bow, 1991, Kenner
NM $5 MIP $15

Robin Hood, Long Bow, Costner Head, 1991, Kenner
NM $5 MIP $15

Sheriff of Nottingham, 1991, Kenner
NM $5 MIP $15

The Dark Warrior, 1991, Kenner
NM $8 MIP $18

Will Scarlett, 1991, Kenner
NM $5 MIP $15

RoboCop and the Ultra Police (Kenner, 1989-90)

FIGURES

Ace Jackson, 1989-90, Kenner
NM $5 MIP $15

Anne Lewis, 1989-90, Kenner
NM $5 MIP $15

Birdman Barnes, 1989-90, Kenner
NM $8 MIP $15

Chainsaw, 1989-90, Kenner
NM $5 MIP $15

Claw Callahan, 1989-90, Kenner
NM $7 MIP $15

Dr. McNamara, 1989-90, Kenner
NM $5 MIP $15

Ed-260, 1989-90, Kenner
NM $10 MIP $25

Headhunter, 1989-90, Kenner
NM $5 MIP $15

Nitro, 1989-90, Kenner
NM $5 MIP $15

RoboCop, 1989-90, Kenner
NM $9 MIP $20

RoboCop Night Fighter, 1989-90, Kenner
NM $6 MIP $20

RoboCop, Gatlin' Gun, 1989-90, Kenner
NM $15 MIP $30

Scorcher, 1989-90, Kenner
NM $6 MIP $15

Sgt. Reed, 1989-90, Kenner
NM $6 MIP $15

Toxic Waster, 1989-90, Kenner
NM $10 MIP $20

Wheels Wilson, 1989-90, Kenner
NM $6 MIP $15

VEHICLES

Robo-1, 1989-90, Kenner
NM $10 MIP $25

Robo-Command with figure, 1989-90, Kenner, with figure
NM $10 MIP $30

Robo-Copter, 1989-90, Kenner
NM $15 MIP $35

Robo-Cycle, 1989-90, Kenner
NM $5 MIP $10

Robo-Hawk, 1989-90, Kenner
NM $10 MIP $35

Robo-Jailer, 1989-90, Kenner
NM $15 MIP $40

Robo-Tank, 1989-90, Kenner
NM $10 MIP $35

Skull-Hog, 1989-90, Kenner
NM $5 MIP $10

Vandal-1, 1989-90, Kenner
NM $5 MIP $20

Robotech (Matchbox, 1986)

11-1/2" FIGURES

Dana Sterling, 1986
NM $20 MIP $50

Lisa Hayes, 1986
NM $20 MIP $50

Lynn Minmei, 1986
NM $20 MIP $50

Rick Hunter, 1986
NM $20 MIP $50

3-3/4" FIGURES

Bioroid Terminator, 1986
NM $5 MIP $15

Corg, 1986
NM $8 MIP $20

Dana Sterling, 1986
NM $12 MIP $30

Lisa Hayes, 1986, 3-3/4", Matchbox
NM $7 MIP $12

Lisa Hayes, 1986, Center figure, shown with Roy Fokker and Zor Prime
NM $8 MIP $20

Lunk, 1986
NM $10 MIP $50

Max Sterling, 1986
NM $8 MIP $20

Micronized Zentraedi, 1986, 3-3/4", Matchbox
NM $7 MIP $12

Miriya, black, 1986
NM $25 MIP $65

Miriya, red, 1986
NM $8 MIP $20

Rand, 1986
NM $5 MIP $12

Rick Hunter, 1986
NM $15 MIP $30

Robotech Master, 1986
NM $5 MIP $12

Rook Bartley, 1986
NM $20 MIP $50

Roy Fokker, 1986, At left, shown with Lisa Hayes and Zor Prime
NM $12 MIP $30

Scott Bernard, 1986
NM $20 MIP $45

Zor Prime, 1986, Matchbox, At right, shown with Lisa Hayes and Roy Fokker
NM $8 MIP $15

6" FIGURES

Breetai, 1986
NM $8 MIP $20

Dolza, 1986
NM $5 MIP $15

Exedore, 1986
NM $8 MIP $20

Khryon, 1986
NM $8 MIP $20

Miriya, 1986
NM $8 MIP $20

8" FIGURES

Armoured Zentraedi Warrior, 1986
NM $8 MIP $20

VEHICLES AND ACCESSORIES

Armoured Cyclone, 1986
NM $10 MIP $50

Bioroid Hover Craft, 1986
NM $10 MIP $25

Bioroid Invid Fighter, 1986, Matchbox
NM $20 MIP $40

Dana's Hover Cycle, 1986
NM $12 MIP $35

Excaliber MkVI, 1986, Matchbox
NM $25 MIP $45

Gladiator, 1986, Matchbox
NM $20 MIP $40

Invid Scout Ship, 1986
NM $12 MIP $30

Invid Shock Trooper, 1986, Matchbox
NM $15 MIP $30

Raidar X, 1986, Matchbox
NM $20 MIP $40

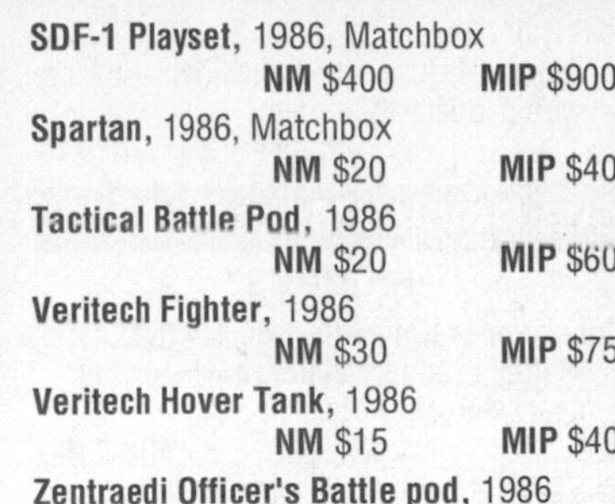

SDF-1 Playset, 1986, Matchbox
NM $400 MIP $900

Spartan, 1986, Matchbox
NM $20 MIP $40

Tactical Battle Pod, 1986
NM $20 MIP $60

Veritech Fighter, 1986
NM $30 MIP $75

Veritech Hover Tank, 1986
NM $15 MIP $40

Zentraedi Officer's Battle pod, 1986
NM $20 MIP $70

Zentraedi Powered Armor, 1986, Matchbox, Botoru or Quadrono Battalion
NM $25 MIP $45

Rocky Horror Picture Show (Vital Toys, 2000)

FIGURES

Columbia, Series 1, 2000, 8", Vital Toys, Gold sequined hat and jacket, silver sequined top
NM $8 MIP $16

Frank N Furter, Series 1, 2000, 8", Vital Toys, Very detailed likeness of Rocky Horror's famous character
NM $8 MIP $16

Rocky Horror Picture Show (Vital Toys, 2000)

Riff Raff, Series 1, 2000, 8", Vital Toys, Detailed figure with yellow hair and face with proper white pallor
NM $8 **MIP** $16

Sea Devils (Mattel, 1970)

FIGURES

Commander Chuck Carter, 1970, 6", Mattel, orange wetsuit, mask, diving gear, sea jet, motor
NM $80 **MIP** $150

Kretar and Zark, 1970, 6", Mattel, sea creature and shark
NM $80 **MIP** $150

Rick Riley, 1970, 6", Mattel, black wetsuit, mask, diving gear, sea jet, motor
NM $80 **MIP** $150

SET

Search and Rescue Set, 1970, Mattel, Commander Carter, Aqualander, Sea Jet, motor, diving gear
NM $100 **MIP** $200

Sectaurs (Coleco, 1984)

FIGURE SETS

Genral Spydrax and Spiderflyer, 1984, Coleco
NM $25 **MIP** $50

Mantor with Rapplor, 1984, 6", Coleco
NM $12 **MIP** $22

Night-Fighting Dargon with Parafly, 1984, 6", Coleco, night-vision trinoculars, gun, knife, double holsters
NM $12 **MIP** $22

Pinsor and Battle Beetle, 1984, Coleco, weapons belt, pistol, sword, axe, shield
NM $25 **MIP** $50

Prince Dargon and Dragonflyer, 1984, Coleco, 2 pistols w/holsters, sword, shield, bag, Slazor
NM $30 **MIP** $65

Skito with Toxcid, 1984, 6", Coleco, gun, sword, holster, shield
NM $10 **MIP** $18

Skulk and Trancula, 1984, Coleco
NM $25 **MIP** $50

Waspax with Wingid, 1984, 6", Coleco
NM $12 **MIP** $22

Zak and Bitaur, 1984, 6", Coleco, gun, Slazor, holster, shield
NM $10 **MIP** $18

PLAYSET

The Hyve, Forbidden Fortress, 1984, Coleco
NM $55 **MIP** $110

She-Ra Princess of Power (Mattel, 1984-86)

CREATURES

Arrow, 1984, Mattel, #9721, Bow's horse, blue
NM $15 **MIP** $40

Clawdeen, 1985, Mattel, #9627, Catra's large cat
NM $15 **MIP** $40

Crystal Moonbeam, 1985, Mattel, #2434
NM $15 **MIP** $45

Crystal Sun Dancer, 1985, Mattel, #2435
NM $15 **MIP** $45

Crystal Swift Wind, 1985, Mattel, #2433
NM $15 **MIP** $45

Enchanta, 1984, Mattel, #9681, She-Ra's swan
NM $15 **MIP** $40

Royal Swift Wind, 1986, Mattel, #3050
NM $15 **MIP** $40

Sea Harp, 1985, Mattel, #2902, She-Ra's Sea Horse
NM $15 **MIP** $40

Silver Storm, 1986, Mattel, #3150
NM $15 **MIP** $40

Storm, 1984, Mattel, #9722, Catra's horse
NM $15 **MIP** $40

Swift Wind, 1984, Mattel, #9191, She-Ra's horse, pink
NM $15 **MIP** $40

FASHIONS

Blue Lightning, 1986, Mattel, #2833
NM $15 **MIP** $50

Colorful Secret, 1986, Mattel, #2837
NM $10 **MIP** $30

Deep Blue Secret, 1984, Mattel, #2836
NM $5 **MIP** $12

Fit To Be Tied, 1984, Mattel, #2825
NM $5 **MIP** $12

Flight of Fancy, 1984, Mattel, #2828
NM $5 **MIP** $12

Flower Power, 1984, Mattel, #2835
NM $5 **MIP** $12

Frosty Fur, 1986, Mattel, #2831
NM $40 **MIP** $100

Heart of Gold, 1986, Mattel, #2838
NM $15 **MIP** $30

Hidden Gold, 1986, Mattel, #2832
NM $15 **MIP** $30

Hold on to Your Hat, 1984, Mattel, #2826
NM $5 **MIP** $12

Ready in Red, 1984, Mattel, #2827
NM $5 **MIP** $12

Reflections in Red, 1986, Mattel, #2834
NM $5 **MIP** $12

Rise and Shine, 1984, Mattel, #2824
NM $5 **MIP** $12

Secret Messanger, 1986, Mattel, #2830
NM $5 **MIP** $12

Veils of Mystery, 1984, Mattel, #2829
NM $5 **MIP** $12

Windy Jumper, 1986, Mattel, #2839
NM $15 **MIP** $50

FIGURE SETS

Bow and Arrow, 1984, Mattel, #9817
NM $25 **MIP** $100

Catra and Clawdeen, 1985, Mattel, #2746
NM $25 **MIP** $100

Catra and Storm, 1984, Mattel, #5047
NM $25 **MIP** $100

Defenders of Good, 1985, Mattel, #1052, She-Ra, Perfuma, and Sweet Bee
NM $45 **MIP** $150

Peekablue and Moonbeam, 1985, Mattel, #2900
NM $25 **MIP** $110

She-Ra and Swift Wind, 1984, Mattel
NM $50 **MIP** $200

Starburst She-Ra and Crystal Swift Wind, 1985, Mattel, #2898
NM $100 **MIP** $400

Sweet Bee and Crystal Sundancer, 1985, Mattel, #2901
NM $100 **MIP** $300

FIGURES

Angella, 1984, 5-1/2", Mattel, #9186
NM $10 **MIP** $40

Bow, 1984, 5-1/2", Mattel, #9183, bow, shield
NM $8 **MIP** $20

Bubble Power She-Ra, 1986, 5-1/2", Mattel, #3023
NM $175 **MIP** $300

Castaspella, 1984, 5-1/2", Mattel, #9187
NM $15 **MIP** $40

Catra, 1984, 5-1/2", Mattel, #9184, tail, mask, shield
NM $25 **MIP** $70

Double Trouble, 1984, 5-1/2", Mattel, #9185
NM $15 **MIP** $50

Entrapta, 1985, 5-1/2", Mattel, #2636
NM $8 **MIP** $15

Flutterina, 1985, 5-1/2", Mattel, #2453
NM $20 **MIP** $65

Frosta, 1984, 5-1/2", Mattel, #9189
NM $12 **MIP** $45

Glimmer, 1984, 5-1/2", Mattel, #9188
NM $12 **MIP** $45

Kowl, 1984, 5-1/2", Mattel, #9190
NM $20 **MIP** $40

Loo-Kee, 1986, 5-1/2", Mattel, #1969
NM $20 **MIP** $40

Mermista, 1985, 5-1/2", Mattel, #2454
NM $8 **MIP** $15

Netossa, 1986, 5-1/2", Mattel, #1835
NM $20 **MIP** $60

Peekablue, 1985, 5-1/2", Mattel, #2452
NM $20 **MIP** $60

Perfuma, 1985, 5-1/2", Mattel, #2455
NM $8 **MIP** $15

Scratchin' Sound Catra, 1985, 5-1/2", Mattel, #2451
NM $20 **MIP** $70

She-Ra, 1984, 5-1/2", Mattel, #9182, helmet, shield, sword
NM $20 **MIP** $50

Shower Power Catra, 1986, 5-1/2", Mattel, #3021
NM $150 **MIP** $300

Spinnerella, 1986, 5-1/2", Mattel, #3053, very rare!
NM $500 **MIP** $1000

Starburst She-Ra, 1985, 5-1/2", Mattel, #2450
NM $20 **MIP** $70

Sweet Bee, 1985, 5-1/2", Mattel, #2635
NM $20 **MIP** $75

PLAYSETS

Crystal Castle, 1984, Mattel, #9193, 30+ pieces
NM $100 **MIP** $200

Crystal Falls, 1985, Mattel, #2456
NM $25 **MIP** $50

Shogun Warriors (Mattel, 1979)

24" FIGURES

Daimos, 1979, 24", Mattel, #2988, shooting fist, calf missile launchers
NM $75 **MIP** $150

Dragun, 1979, 24", Mattel, #9858, fires shurikan and axes
NM $75 **MIP** $150

Gaiking, 1979, 24", Mattel, eye launchers, shooting fist
NM $75 **MIP** $150

Godzilla, 1979, 24", Mattel, fire tongue, shooting fist
NM $100 **MIP** $200

Godzilla (2nd figure), 1979, 24", Mattel, fire tongue, shooting fist
NM $150 **MIP** $200

Great Mazinga, 1979, 24", Mattel, #9860, swords, missile fingers
NM $75 **MIP** $150

Raydeen, 1979, 24", Mattel, #9859, shield, shooting fist, missiles
NM $75 **MIP** $150

Rodan, 1979, 24", 38" wingspan
NM $150 **MIP** $300

2-IN-1 FIGURES

Daimos, 1979, 5-1/2", Mattel, #2992, die-cast, leg cannons, shooting fists
NM $75 **MIP** $150

Danguard, 1979, 5-1/2", Mattel, #2729, die-cast, para-wing, shooting arms and head
NM $75 **MIP** $150

Gaiking, 1979, 5-1/2", Mattel, #2728, die-cast
NM $75 **MIP** $150

Grandizer, 1979, 5-1/2", Mattel, #2994, die-cast, shooting fists, sickles
NM $75 **MIP** $150

Raydeen, 1979, 5-1/2", Mattel, #2727, die-cast
NM $75 **MIP** $150

Voltus V, 1979, 5-1/2", Mattel, #2993, die-cast, changes to battle tank
NM $75 **MIP** $150

3" FIGURES

17, 1979, 3", Mattel, #2997, Series 2
NM $10 **MIP** $25

Combattra, 1979, 3", Mattel, #2512, Series 1
NM $10 **MIP** $25

Dangard, 1979, 3", Mattel, #2995, Series 2
NM $10 **MIP** $25

Dragun, 1979, 3", Mattel, #2515, Series 1
NM $10 **MIP** $25

Gaiking, 1979, 3", Mattel, #2514, Series 1
NM $10 **MIP** $25

Grandizer, 1979, 3", Mattel, #2517, Series 1
NM $10 **MIP** $25

Great Mazinga, 1979, 3", Mattel, #2516, Series 1
NM $10 **MIP** $25

Leopaldon, 1979, 3", Mattel, #2996, Series 2
NM $10 **MIP** $25

Poseidon, 1979, 3", Mattel, #2513, Series 1
NM $10 **MIP** $25

Voltez V, 1979, 3", Mattel, #2994, Series 2
NM $10 **MIP** $25

5" FIGURES

Dragun, 1979, 5", Mattel, #2106, die-cast, w/ 3 axes
NM $75 **MIP** $175

Dragun (2nd figure), 1979, 5", Mattel, #2106, die-cast, w/ 2 axes
NM $75 **MIP** $150

Great Mazinga, 1979, 5", Mattel, #2103, die-cast, knees bend
NM $85 **MIP** $175

Great Mazinga (2nd figure), 1979, 5", Mattel, #2103, die-cast, knees don't bend much
NM $75 **MIP** $150

Poseidon, 1979, 5", Mattel, #2104, die-cast, moveable shins
NM $75 **MIP** $150

Poseidon (second figure), 1979, 5", Mattel, #2104, die-cast, shins don't move
NM $75 **MIP** $125

Poseidon (third figure), 1979, 5", Mattel, #2105, die-cast, four yellow safety missiles
NM $75 **MIP** $125

Raider, 1979, 5", Mattel, #2105, die-cast, knees bend
NM $75 **MIP** $150

Raider (second figure), 1979, 5", Mattel, #2105, die-cast, knees don't bend
NM $75 **MIP** $125

VEHICLES

Bazoler, 1979, Mattel, #2690
NM $30 **MIP** $55

Combatra Vehicle #3 Battle Tank, 1979, Mattel, #2622
NM $70 **MIP** $140

Daimos Truck, 1979, Mattel, #2990
NM $125 **MIP** $275

Dangard Launcher, 1979, Mattel, #2699
NM $30 **MIP** $55

Grand Car, 1979, Mattel, #2696
NM $30 **MIP** $55

Grandizer Saucer, 1979, Mattel, #8998, European release
NM $75 **MIP** $135

Heli-Capter, 1979, Mattel, #2695
NM $35 **MIP** $60

Jetcar, 1979, Mattel, #2698
NM $30 **MIP** $55

Kargosaur, 1979, Mattel, #2694, rare
NM $175 **MIP** $310

Kondar, 1979, Mattel, #2693
NM $30 **MIP** $55

Liabe, 1979, Mattel, #2734
NM $100 **MIP** $200

Nessar, 1979, Mattel, #2691
NM $25 **MIP** $50

Rydoto, 1979, Mattel, #2900
NM $25 **MIP** $55

Schicon Jet, 1979, Mattel, #2732
NM $40 **MIP** $80

Shigcon Tank, 1979, Mattel, #2731
NM $40 **MIP** $85

Sky Arrow, 1979, Mattel, #2733
NM $40 **MIP** $80

Sky Jet, 1979, Mattel, #2697
NM $25 **MIP** $50

Solar Saucer, 1979, Mattel, #2520
NM $50 **MIP** $95

Varitank, 1979, Mattel, #2519
NM $25 **MIP** $50

Vertilift, 1979, Mattel, #2521
NM $25 **MIP** $50

Silver Surfer (Toy Biz, 1997-98)

COSMIC POWER ALIEN FIGHTERS

Adam Warlock with Cosmic Skull Space Racer, 1998
NM $3 **MIP** $8

Cosmic Silver Surfer and Pip the Troll, 1998
NM $3 **MIP** $8

Galactus with Silver Surfer in Cosmic Orb, 8" figure, 1998
NM $3 **MIP** $8

Ivar and Ant Warrior with Alien Annihilator, 1998
NM $3 **MIP** $8

Molten Lava Silver Surfer with Eyeball Alien Space Racer, 1998
NM $3 **MIP** $8

Ronan the Accussor with Tree Root Space Racer, 1998
NM $3 **MIP** $8

Solar Silver Surfer & Draconian Warrior, 1998
NM $3 **MIP** $8

Super Nova with Flaming Bird, 1998
NM $3 **MIP** $8

FIGURES

Beta Ray Bill, Thunder Hammer, 1997
NM $3 **MIP** $10

Classic Silver Surfer with Cosmic Surf Board, 1997
NM $3 **MIP** $10

Meegan Alien, Galactic Weapon Seeker, 1997
NM $3 **MIP** $10

Nova, Poseable Flaming Hair, 1997
NM $3 **MIP** $10

INFINITY GAUNTLET SERIES, 10" FIGURE

Silver Surfer, 1997
NM $5 **MIP** $15

Silverhawks (Kenner, 1987)

ACCESSORIES

Super Attack Bird Sky-Shadow, 1987, Kenner, 20" wingspan
NM $15 MIP $40

Super Attack Bird Stronghold, 1987, Kenner, 20" wingspan
NM $15 MIP $30

Super Attack Bird Tallyhawk, 1987, Kenner, 25" wingspan
NM $15 MIP $30

FIGURES

Bluegrass, 1988, 5", Kenner, w/Hot Licks, guitar transforms, new uniform
NM $8 MIP $20

Condor, 1988, 5", Kenner, w/Jet Stream
NM $10 MIP $20

Copper Kidd, 1988, 5", Kenner, w/Laser Disks
NM $15 MIP $28

Hardware, 1988, 5", Kenner, w/Prowler
NM $10 MIP $20

Mon-Star, 1988, 5", Kenner, w/Laser Lance
NM $22 MIP $42

Moon Stryker, 1988, 5", Kenner, w/Tail-Spin
NM $10 MIP $20

Quicksilver, 1988, 5", Kenner, w/Tallyhawk, black uniform
NM $20 MIP $42

Steelwill, 1988, 5", Kenner, w/Steamer
NM $20 MIP $42

Windhammer, 1988, 5", Kenner, w/Tuning Fork
NM $10 MIP $20

FIGURES, BAD

Buzz Saw, 1987, 5", Kenner, w/Shredator
NM $10 MIP $20

Mo-Lec-U-Lar, 1987, 5", Kenner, w/Volt-Ure
NM $10 MIP $20

Mon-Star, 1987, 5", Kenner, w/Sky Shadow
NM $10 MIP $20

Mumbo-Jumbo, 1987, 5", Kenner, w/Airshock
NM $10 MIP $20

FIGURES, GOOD

Bluegrass, 1987, 5", Kenner, w/Side Man, converts from hawk to guitar
NM $6 MIP $15

Copper Kidd, 1987, 5", Kenner, w/May-Day
NM $6 MIP $15

Flashback, 1987, 5", Kenner, w/Backlash
NM $6 MIP $15

Hotwing, 1987, 5", Kenner, w/Gyro
NM $6 MIP $15

Quicksilver, 1987, 5", Kenner, w/Tallyhawk
NM $12 MIP $23

Stargazer, 1987, 5", Kenner, w/Sly-Bird
NM $6 MIP $15

Steelheart, 1987, 5", Kenner, w/Rayzor
NM $12 MIP $20

Steelwill, 1987, 5", Kenner, w/Stronghold
NM $18 MIP $35

PLAYSETS

Hawkhaven, 1987, Kenner, hawk-shaped fortress on asteroid, not mass produced
NM $125 MIP $250

VEHICLES

Copper Racer, 1988, Kenner, friction motor, for Copper Kidd
NM $12 MIP $22

Maraj, 1987, Kenner, holds five figures
NM $35 MIP $60

Sky-Runner, 1988, Kenner, for Mon-Star
NM $20 MIP $60

Sprinthawk, 1988, Kenner, for Quicksilver
NM $12 MIP $22

Simpsons (Mattel, 1990)

FIGURES

Bart, 1990, Mattel
NM $6 MIP $15

Bartman, 1990, Mattel
NM $6 MIP $15

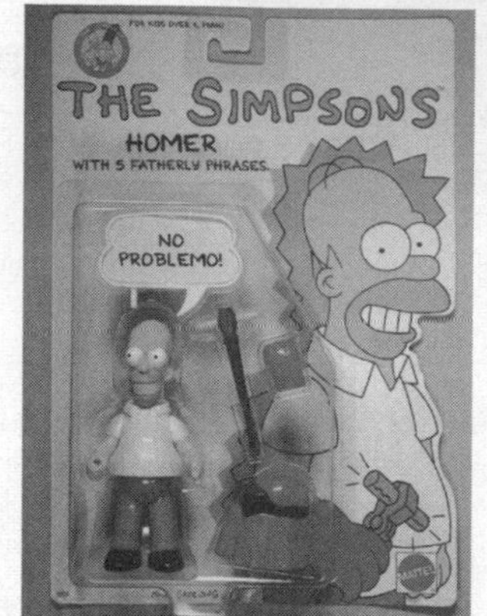

Homer, 1990, Mattel
NM $6 MIP $15

Lisa, 1990, Mattel
NM $12 MIP $35

Maggie, 1990, Mattel
NM $12 MIP $35

Marge, 1990, Mattel
NM $8 MIP $25

Nelson, 1990, Mattel
NM $6 MIP $15

Sofa Set, 1990, Mattel
NM $16 MIP $30

Simpsons (Playmates, 1999-2004)

ALL STAR VOICES

Brad Goodman, 2002, Playmates, by Albert Brooks
NM $4 MIP $8

Fat Tony, 2002, Playmates, by Joe Mantegna
NM $4 MIP $8

Herb Powell, 2002, Playmates, by Danny DeVito
NM $4 MIP $8

Lionel Hutz, 2002, Playmates, by Phil Hartman
NM $4 MIP $8

Troy McClure, 2002, Playmates, by Phil Hartman
NM $4 MIP $8

ENVIRONMENTS

Aztec Theater, 2003, Playmates, w/McBain,
NM $8 MIP $16

Bart's Treehouse, 2003, Playmates, w/ Military Bart
NM $10 MIP $20

Bowl-A-Rama, 2001, Playmates, w/ Pin Pal Apu
NM $10 MIP $20

Burns Manor, 2002, Playmates, w/ P.J. Burns
NM $8 MIP $15

Comic Book Shop, 2001, Playmates, w/Comic Book Guy
NM $10 MIP $20

Court Room, 2002, Playmates, w/ Judge Snyder
NM $8 MIP $15

Doctor's Office, 2002, Playmates, w/ Dr. Nick Riviera
NM $8 MIP $15

First Church of Springfield, 2001, Playmates, w/ Reverend Lovejoy
NM $10 MIP $20

Krusty Burger, 2002, Playmates, w/Pimply Faced Teen
NM $10 MIP $20

Krustylu Studios, 2001, Playmates, w/Sideshow Bob
NM $10 MIP $20

Kwik-E-Mart, 2000, Playmates, w/ Apu
NM $8 MIP $20

Living Room, 2000, Playmates, w/ Marge and Maggie
NM $10 MIP $40

Military Antique Shop, 2003, Playmates, w/Herman
NM $8 MIP $16

Noiseland Arcade, 2001, Playmates, w/Jimbo Jones
NM $10 MIP $20

Nuclear Power Plant, 2000, Playmates, w/Homer
NM $10 MIP $40

Nuclear Power Plant Lunch Room, 2004, Playmates, w/Frank Grimes
NM $8 MIP $16

Police Station, 2002, Playmates, w/Officer Eddie
NM $10 MIP $20

Retirement Castle, 2002, Playmates, w/Jasper
NM $10 MIP $20

Simpson's Family Kitchen, 2002, Playmates, w/ Muumuu Homer
NM $10 MIP $20

Springfield DMV, 2002, Playmates, w/Selma Bouvier
NM $8 MIP $16

Springfield Elementary, 2000, Playmates, w/ Principal Skinner
NM $10 **MIP** $20

Springfield Elementary School Cafeteria, 2002, Playmates, w/ Lunchlady Doris
NM $10 **MIP** $20

Town Hall, 2001, Playmates, w/ Mayor Quimby
NM $10 **MIP** $20

EXCLUSIVES

All-Star Voices 2-Pack #1, 2002, Playmates, Toys R Us, Lurleen Lumpkin, Colonel Homer
NM $10 **MIP** $20

All-Star Voices 2-Pack #2, 2002, Playmates, Toys R Us, Jacques, Bowling Marge
NM $10 **MIP** $20

Barney Gumble, 2002, 9", Playmates, Target, Wave 2
NM $7 **MIP** $12

Be-Sharp Apu, 1999-2004, Playmates, Playmates mail-in
NM $12 **MIP** $20

Be-Sharp Barney, 1999-2004, Playmates, Playmates mail-in
NM $12 **MIP** $20

Be-Sharp Homer, 1999-2004, Playmates, Playmates mail-in
NM $20 **MIP** $40

Be-Sharp Skinner, 1999-2004, Playmates, Playmates mail-in
NM $12 **MIP** $20

Bongo Comics 3-Pack, 1999-2004, Playmates, Homer as Ingestible Bulk, Edna Krabappel as Vampiredna, Apu as Captain Kwik
NM $9 **MIP** $18

Boxing Homer, 2001, Playmates, ToyFare
NM $10 **MIP** $20

Convention Comic Book Guy, 2001, Playmates, ToyFare
NM $15 **MIP** $30

Cooder, 1999-2004, Playmates, Playmates mail-in
NM $12 **MIP** $25

Evil Krusty Doll, 2001, Playmates, Diamond, talks
NM $10 **MIP** $20

Family Christmas, 2001, Playmates, Toys R Us
NM $20 **MIP** $40

Family New Years, 2002, Playmates, Toys R Us
NM $10 **MIP** $20

High School Prom, 2002, Playmates, Diamond, Homer and Marge
NM $10 **MIP** $20

Homer Simpson, 2002, 9", Playmates, Target, Wave 1
NM $7 **MIP** $12

KBBL Radio, 2002, Playmates, Diamond
NM $10 **MIP** $20

Llewellyn Sinclair, 1999-2004, Playmates, Playmates mail-in
NM $12 **MIP** $25

Lunar Base Environment, 2001, Playmates, Diamond
NM $10 **MIP** $20

Mainstreet Environment, 2002, Playmates, Toys R Us
NM $20 **MIP** $40

Moe Szyslak, 2002, 9", Playmates, Target, Wave 2
NM $7 **MIP** $12

Moe's Tavern Environment, 2003, Playmates, Diamond
NM $10 **MIP** $20

Mr. Burns, 2002, 9", Playmates, Target, Wave 1
NM $7 **MIP** $12

Pin Pal Moe, 2001, Playmates, ToyFare
NM $10 **MIP** $20

Pin Pal Mr. Burns, 2001, Playmates, ToyFare
NM $15 **MIP** $30

Radio Active Homer, 2000, Playmates, ToyFare Exclusive, w/radioactive plate of donuts, glow, helmet, glowing tongs
NM $50 **MIP** $200

Radioactive Homer, 2000, Playmates, ToyFare
NM $35 **MIP** $70

Treehouse of Horror I, 2000, Playmates, Toys R Us, Springfield Cemetary
NM $50 **MIP** $100

Treehouse of Horror II, 2001, Playmates, Toys R Us, Alien Ship
NM $50 **MIP** $100

Treehouse of Horror III, 2002, Playmates, Toys R Us, Ironic Punishment
NM $40 **MIP** $80

Treehouse of Horror IV, 2003, Playmates, Toys R Us, Collector's Lair; Bart as Stretch Dude, Lisa as Clobber Girl, Comic Book Guy as The Collector, Lucy Lawless as Xena
NM $15 **MIP** $30

Treehouse of Horrors, 2000, Playmates, Toys R Us Exclusive
NM $25 **MIP** $75

SERIES 01 FIGURES

Bart, 1999, Playmates, Series 1
NM $6 **MIP** $20

Grandpa, 1999, Playmates, Series 1
NM $10 **MIP** $30

Homer, 1999, Playmates, Series 1
NM $8 **MIP** $20

Krusty, 1999, Playmates, Series 1
NM $10 **MIP** $30

Lisa, 1999, Playmates, Series 1
NM $10 **MIP** $30

Mr. Burns, 1999, Playmates, Series 1
NM $10 **MIP** $20

SERIES 02 FIGURES

Barney, 2000, Playmates, Series 2
NM $6 **MIP** $20

Chief Wiggum, 2000, Playmates, Series 2
NM $6 **MIP** $20

Ned Flanders, 2000, Playmates, Series 2
NM $6 **MIP** $20

Pin Pal Homer, 2000, Playmates, Series 2
NM $6 **MIP** $20

Smithers, 2000, Playmates, Series 2
NM $5 **MIP** $15

Sunday Best Bart, 2000, Playmates, Series 2
NM $3 **MIP** $10

SERIES 03 FIGURES

Kamp Krusty Bart, 2000, Playmates, Series 3
NM $5 **MIP** $9

Milhouse, 2000, Playmates, Series 3
NM $5 **MIP** $10

Moe, 2000, Playmates, Series 3
NM $7 **MIP** $15

Nelson, 2000, Playmates, Series 3
NM $5 **MIP** $10

Otto, 2000, Playmates, Series 3
NM $5 **MIP** $10

Sunday Best Homer, 2000, Playmates, Series 3
NM $5 **MIP** $9

SERIES 04 FIGURES

Casual Homer, 2001, Playmates, Series 4
NM $5 **MIP** $10

Groundskeeper Willie, 2001, Playmates, Series 4
NM $5 **MIP** $10

Itchy and Scratchy, 2001, Playmates, Series 4
NM $5 **MIP** $10

Lenny, 2001, Playmates, Series 4
NM $5 **MIP** $10

Patty, 2001, Playmates, Series 4
NM $5 **MIP** $10

Ralph Wiggum, 2001, Playmates, Series 4
NM $5 **MIP** $10

SERIES 05 FIGURES

Bartman, 2001, Playmates, Series 5
NM $5 **MIP** $10

Bumble Bee Man, 2001, Playmates, Series 5
NM $7 **MIP** $12

Captain McCallister, 2001, Playmates, Series 5
NM $5 **MIP** $10

Kent Brockman, 2001, Playmates, Series 5
NM $5 **MIP** $10

Martin, 2001, Playmates, Series 5
NM $5 **MIP** $10

Sideshow Mel, 2001, Playmates, Series 5
NM $5 **MIP** $10

SERIES 06 FIGURES

Bleeding Gums Murphy, 2001, Playmates, Series 6
NM $5 **MIP** $10

Carl, 2001, Playmates, Series 6
NM $4 **MIP** $8

Dr. Hibbert, 2001, Playmates, Series 6
NM $5 **MIP** $10

Isotopes Mascot Homer, 2001, Playmates, Series 6
NM $4 **MIP** $8

Simpsons (Playmates, 1999-2004)

ACTION FIGURES

Professor Frink, 2001, Playmates, Series 6
NM $5 **MIP** $10

Snake, 2001, Playmates, Series 6
NM $5 **MIP** $10

SERIES 07 FIGURES

Cletus, 2001, Playmates, Series 7
NM $5 **MIP** $10

Dolph, 2001, Playmates, Series 7
NM $5 **MIP** $10

Hans Moleman, 2001, Playmates, Series 7
NM $4 **MIP** $8

Mrs. Krabappel, 2001, Playmates, Series 7
NM $4 **MIP** $8

Officer Lou, 2001, Playmates, Series 7
NM $4 **MIP** $8

Officer Marge, 2001, Playmates, Series 7
NM $4 **MIP** $8

SERIES 08 FIGURES

Daredevil Bart, 2002, Playmates, Series 8
NM $4 **MIP** $8

Kearney, 2002, Playmates, Series 8
NM $4 **MIP** $8

Ragin' Willie, 2002, Playmates, Series 8
NM $4 **MIP** $8

Sherri and Terri, 2002, Playmates, Series 8
NM $4 **MIP** $8

Superintendent Chalmers, 2002, Playmates, Series 8
NM $4 **MIP** $8

Uter, 2002, Playmates, Series 8
NM $4 **MIP** $8

SERIES 09 FIGURES

Busted Krusty the Clown, 2002, Playmates, Series 9
NM $4 **MIP** $8

Disco Stu, 2002, Playmates, Series 9
NM $4 **MIP** $8

Prison Sideshow Bob, 2002, Playmates, Series 9
NM $4 **MIP** $8

Rod and Todd Flanders, 2002, Playmates, Series 9
NM $4 **MIP** $8

Sunday Best Grandpa, 2002, Playmates, Series 9
NM $4 **MIP** $8

SERIES 10 FIGURES

Hank Scorpio, 2002, Playmates, Series 10
NM $5 **MIP** $10

Marvin Monroe, 2002, Playmates, Series 10
NM $4 **MIP** $8

Resort Smithers, 2002, Playmates, Series 10
NM $4 **MIP** $8

Scout Leader Flanders, 2002, Playmates, Series 10
NM $4 **MIP** $8

Stonecutter Homer, 2002, Playmates, Series 10
NM $4 **MIP** $8

Sunday Best Marge and Maggie, 2002, Playmates, Series 10
NM $4 **MIP** $8

Wendell, 2002, Playmates, Series 10
NM $4 **MIP** $8

SERIES 11 FIGURES

Blue Haired Lawyer, 2002, Playmates, Series 11
NM $4 **MIP** $8

Gil, 2002, Playmates, Series 11
NM $4 **MIP** $8

Kirk VanHouten, 2002, Playmates, Series 11
NM $4 **MIP** $8

Larry Burns, 2002, Playmates, Series 11
NM $4 **MIP** $8

Plow King Barney, 2002, Playmates, Series 11
NM $4 **MIP** $8

Rainier Wolfcastle, 2002, Playmates, Series 11
NM $4 **MIP** $8

SERIES 12 FIGURES

Database, 2003, Playmates, Series 12
NM $4 **MIP** $8

Don Vittorio, 2003, Playmates, Series 12
NM $4 **MIP** $8

Luann VanHouten, 2003, Playmates, Series 12
NM $4 **MIP** $8

Moe, 2003, Playmates, Series 12, re-release
NM $4 **MIP** $8

Mr. Burns, 2003, Playmates, Series 12, re-release
NM $4 **MIP** $8

Mr. Largo, 2003, Playmates, Series 12
NM $4 **MIP** $8

Mr. Plow Homer, 2003, Playmates, Series 12
NM $4 **MIP** $8

Number 1, 2003, Playmates, Series 12
NM $4 **MIP** $8

SERIES 13 FIGURES

Dr. Stephen Hawking, 2003, Playmates, Series 13
NM $8 **MIP** $12

Freddy Quimby, 2003, Playmates, Series 13
NM $4 **MIP** $8

Helen Lovejoy, 2003, Playmates, Series 13
NM $4 **MIP** $8

Legs, 2003, Playmates, Series 13
NM $4 **MIP** $8

Princess Kashmir, 2003, Playmates, Series 13
NM $4 **MIP** $8

Tuxedo Krusty the Clown, 2003, Playmates, Series 13
NM $4 **MIP** $8

SERIES 14 FIGURES

Groundskeeper Willie in kilt, 2003, Playmates, Series 14
NM $4 **MIP** $8

Louie, 2003, Playmates, Series 14
NM $4 **MIP** $8

Luigi, 2003, Playmates, Series 14
NM $4 **MIP** $8

Miss Botz, 2003, Playmates, Series 14
NM $4 **MIP** $8

Miss Hoover, 2003, Playmates, Series 14
NM $4 **MIP** $8

Sarcastic Man, 2003, Playmates, Series 14
NM $4 **MIP** $8

SERIES 15 FIGURES

Brandine, 2004, Playmates, Series 15
NM $4 **MIP** $8

Comic Book Guy, 2004, Playmates, Series 15, re-release
NM $4 **MIP** $8

Deep Space Homer, 2004, Playmates, Series 15
NM $4 **MIP** $8

Handsome Moe, 2004, Playmates, Series 15, re-release
NM $4 **MIP** $8

Manjula, 2004, Playmates, Series 15
NM $4 **MIP** $8

Octuplets, 2004, Playmates, Series 15
NM $4 **MIP** $8

SERIES 16 FIGURES

Agnes Skinner, 2004, Playmates, Series 16
NM $4 **MIP** $8

Artie Ziff, 2004, Playmates, Series 16
NM $4 **MIP** $8

Benjamin and Gary, 2004, Playmates, Series 16
NM $4 **MIP** $8

Brain Freeze Bart, 2004, Playmates, Series 16
NM $4 **MIP** $8

Doug, 2004, Playmates, Series 16
NM $4 **MIP** $8

Evil Homer, 2004, Playmates, Series 16, also called Devil Homer
NM $7 **MIP** $15

VEHICLES

Elementary School Bus, 2002, Playmates, interactive
NM $7 **MIP** $15

Family Car, 2001, Playmates
NM $7 **MIP** $15

Six Million Dollar Man (Kenner, 1975-78)

ACCESSORIES

Back Pack Radio, 1975-78, Kenner, working crystal radio needs no batteries, white radio, white helmet for Steve and earpiece so you can listen to the radio
NM $15 **MIP** $50

Bionic Cycle, 1975-78, Kenner
NM $10 **MIP** $20

Bionic Mission Vehicle, 1975-78, Kenner
NM $40 **MIP** $100

Bionic Transport, 1975-78, Kenner
NM $30 **MIP** $90

Bionic Video Center, 1975-78, Kenner
NM $40 **MIP** $140

Critical Assignment Arms, 1975-78, Kenner
NM $60 **MIP** $120

Critical Assignment Legs, 1975-78, Kenner
NM $22 **MIP** $70

Dual Launch Drag Set with 4" Steve Austin Bionic Bigfoot figure, 1975-78, Kenner
NM $45 **MIP** $90

Flight Suit, 1975-78, Kenner
NM $15 **MIP** $30

Mission Control Center, 1975-78, Kenner
NM $45 **MIP** $150

Mission to Mars Space Suit, 1975-78, Kenner
NM $15 **MIP** $30

OSI Headquarters, 1975-78, Kenner
NM $60 **MIP** $100

OSI Undercover Blue Denims, 1975-78, Kenner
NM $15 **MIP** $30

Porta-Communicator, 1975-78, Kenner, Steve wears the backpack speaker, you talk into a battery-operated walkie and voice is amplified out of the backpack
NM $20 **MIP** $50

Tower & Cycle Set, 1975-78, Kenner
NM $25 **MIP** $50

Venus Space Probe, 1975-78, Kenner, very rare
NM $180 **MIP** $350

FIGURES

Bionic Bigfoot, 1975-78, Kenner, Must have the chestplate to be complete
NM $75 **MIP** $180

Maskatron, 1975-78, Kenner, 3 faces, 2 arms
NM $80 **MIP** $150

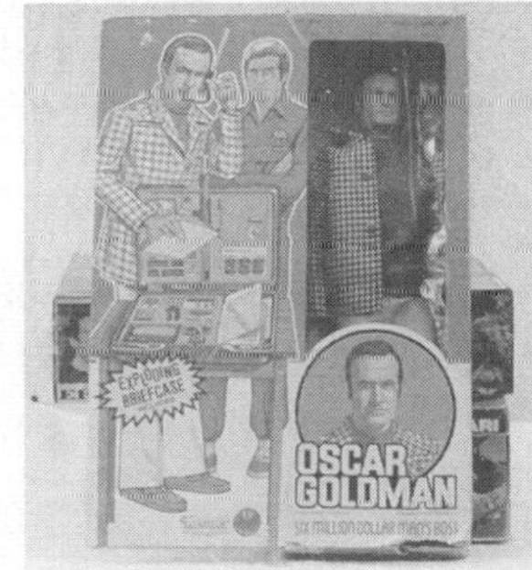

Oscar Goldman, 1975-78, Kenner, Wearing familiar checked jacket and carrying exploding briefcase, should Steve Austin's secrets fall into the wrong hands
NM $60 **MIP** $120

Steve Austin with biosonic arm, 1975-78, Kenner
NM $110 **MIP** $450

Steve Austin with engine block, 1975-78, Kenner
NM $50 **MIP** $150

Steve Austin with girder, 1975-78, Kenner
NM $60 **MIP** $150

Slap Shot (McFarlane, 2000)

FIGURES

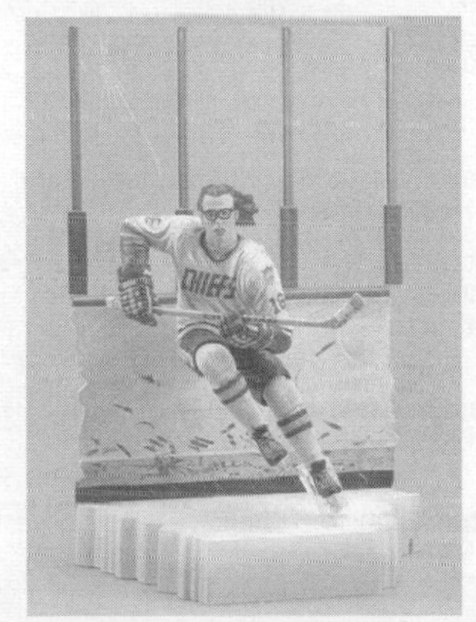

Jack Hanson, 2000, McFarlane Toys, From movie "Slap Shot." Includes detailed figure and rink diorama
NM $5 **MIP** $10

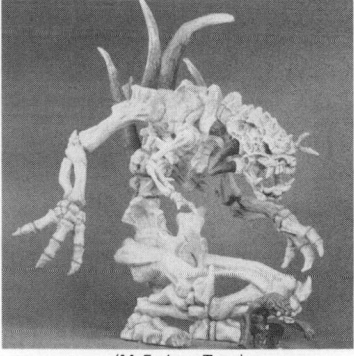

(McFarlane Toys)

Jeff Hanson, 2000, McFarlane Toys, Detailed figure with hockey rink base and background
NM $5 **MIP** $10

Steve Hanson, 2000, McFarlane Toys, Part of the trio of figures from the movie "Slap Shot."
NM $5 **MIP** $10

Sleepy Hollow (McFarlane, 1999)

FIGURES

Crone, 1999, McFarlane Toys
NM $3 **MIP** $10

Headless Horseman, 1999, McFarlane Toys
NM $3 **MIP** $10

Headless Rider and Horse box set, 1999, McFarlane Toys
NM $12 **MIP** $25

Ichabod Crane, 1999, McFarlane Toys
NM $3 **MIP** $10

Space:1999 (Mattel, 1976)

FIGURES

(Corey LeChat)

Commander Koenig, 1976, Mattel, Shown at center with Bergman and Russell
NM $30 **MIP** $65

Dr. Russell, 1976, Mattel
NM $30 **MIP** $65

Professor Bergman, 1976, Mattel
NM $30 **MIP** $65

Zython Alien, 1976, Mattel
NM $100 **MIP** $275

PLAY SETS

Eagle Playset with three 3" figures, 1976, Mattel
NM $160 **MIP** $325

Moonbase Alpha Deluxe Playset with three figures, 1976, Mattel
NM $80 **MIP** $210

Moonbase Alpha Playset, 1976, Mattel
NM $35 **MIP** $85

Space:1999 (Palitoy, 1975)

FIGURES

Alan Carter, 1975, Palitoy
NM $200 **MIP** $425

Captain Koenig, 1975, Palitoy
NM $150 **MIP** $250

Captain Zantor, 1975, Palitoy
NM $75 **MIP** $160

Mysterious Alien, 1975, Palitoy
NM $75 **MIP** $160

Paul Morrow, 1975, Palitoy
NM $175 **MIP** $300

Spawn (McFarlane, 1994-present)

13" FIGURES

Angela, 1996, McFarlane
NM $10 **MIP** $25

Medieval Spawn, Kay Bee Exclusive, 1997, McFarlane
NM $10 **MIP** $25

Spawn, 1996, McFarlane
NM $10 **MIP** $25

ACCESSORIES

Spawn Alley Play Set, 1994-96, McFarlane
NM $15 **MIP** $50

Spawnmobile, 1994-96, McFarlane
NM $12 **MIP** $40

Violator Monster Rig, 1994-96, McFarlane
NM $12 **MIP** $45

MCFARLANE TOYS COLLECTOR'S CLUB EXCLUSIVES

Cogliosto, 1994, McFarlane
NM $5 **MIP** $15

Terry Fitzgerald, 1994, McFarlane
NM $5 **MIP** $15

Todd the Artist, 1994, McFarlane
NM $5 **MIP** $15

Wanda and Cyan, 2000, McFarlane
NM $3 **MIP** $13

SERIES 01, 1994 (TODD TOYS PACKAGING)

Clown, clown head, 1994, McFarlane
NM $6 **MIP** $20

Clown, Kay Bee Exclusive, 1994, McFarlane
NM $3 **MIP** $10

Clown, monster head, 1994, McFarlane
NM $6 **MIP** $10

Medieval Spawn, black armor, 1994, McFarlane
NM $5 **MIP** $20

Medieval Spawn, Kay Bee Exclusive, 1994, McFarlane
NM $5 **MIP** $15

Medieval Spawn, blue armor, 1994, McFarlane
NM $5 **MIP** $20

Overtkill, dark green, 1994, McFarlane
NM $5 **MIP** $15

Overtkill, Kay Bee Exclusive, 1996, McFarlane
NM $3 **MIP** $12

Overtkill, turquoise, 1994, McFarlane
NM $3 **MIP** $12

Spawn, Club Exclusive, blue body, 1997, McFarlane
NM $8 **MIP** $20

Spawn, Club Exclusive, green body, 1997, McFarlane
NM $8 **MIP** $20

Spawn, Diamond Exclusive, 1994, McFarlane
NM $45 **MIP** $120

Spawn, full mask, 1994, McFarlane
NM $5 **MIP** $25

Spawn, Kay Bee Exclusive, 1995, McFarlane
NM $10 **MIP** $30

Spawn, Spawn No. 50 premium (Worm Head), 1996, McFarlane
NM $50 **MIP** $150

Spawn, unmasked (Hamburger Head), first card, 1994, McFarlane
NM $15 **MIP** $40

Tremor, dark green costume, 1994, McFarlane
NM $8 **MIP** $15

Tremor, Kay Bee Exclusive, 1996, McFarlane
NM $3 **MIP** $12

Tremor, orange skin, 1994, McFarlane
NM $5 **MIP** $15

Violator, 1994, McFarlane
NM $5 **MIP** $20

Violator, chrome card, 1994, McFarlane
NM $8 **MIP** $20

Violator, club version, 1997, McFarlane
NM $8 **MIP** $20

Violator, green card, 1994, McFarlane
NM $5 **MIP** $15

Violator, Kay Bee Exclusive, 1996, McFarlane
NM $4 **MIP** $12

Violator, mail-order, 1995, McFarlane
NM $20 **MIP** $75

Violator, red card, 1994, McFarlane
NM $5 **MIP** $15

SERIES 02, 1995

Angela, 1995, McFarlane
NM $5 **MIP** $25

Angela, Club Exclusive, blue, 1997, McFarlane
NM $8 **MIP** $20

Angela, Club Exclusive, pewter, 1997, McFarlane
NM $8 **MIP** $20

Angela, gold headpiece with gold and purple costume, 1995, McFarlane, Includes sword, belt and accessories
NM $20 **MIP** $50

Angela, Kay Bee Exclusive, 1997, McFarlane
NM $3 **MIP** $12

Angela, McFarlane Toy Collector's Club Exclusive, 1996, McFarlane
NM $12 **MIP** $35

Angela, silver headpiece with silver and blue costume, 1995, McFarlane
NM $10 **MIP** $25

(McFarlane Toys)

Badrock, blue, 1995, McFarlane, With firing missiles
NM $10 **MIP** $25

Badrock, red pants, 1995, McFarlane
NM $3 **MIP** $12

(McFarlane Toys)

Chapel, blue/black pants, 1995, McFarlane, Includes gun and jagged-edge sword
NM $6 **MIP** $20

Chapel, green khaki pants, 1995, McFarlane
NM $3 **MIP** $12

(McFarlane Toys)

Commando Spawn, 1995, McFarlane, Black and red uniform, includes weapons and headset
NM $7 **MIP** $20

(McFarlane Toys)

Malebolgia, 1995, McFarlane, Highly-detailed figure
NM $30 **MIP** $60

Pilot Spawn, black costume, 1995, McFarlane, Black uniform with red highlights, includes jet pack and dagger
NM $8 **MIP** $20

Pilot Spawn, Kay Bee Toys, 1997, McFarlane
NM $3 **MIP** $12

Pilot Spawn, white "Astronaut Spawn", 1995, McFarlane
NM $5 **MIP** $15

SERIES 03, 1995

Cosmic Angela, 1995, McFarlane
NM $5 **MIP** $15

Cosmic Angela, McFarlane Collector's Club Exclusive, 1997, McFarlane
NM $5 **MIP** $15

Cosmic Angela, No. 62 Spawn and No. 9 Curse of Spawn, Diamond Exclusive, 1997, McFarlane
NM $18 **MIP** $75

Curse, The, 1995, McFarlane
NM $5 **MIP** $15

Curse, The, McFarlane Collector's Club Exclusive, 1997, McFarlane
NM $5 **MIP** $15

Ninja Spawn, 1995, McFarlane
NM $7 **MIP** $15

Ninja Spawn, McFarlane Collector's Club Exclusive, 1997, McFarlane
NM $5 **MIP** $15

Redeemer, 1995, McFarlane
NM $5 **MIP** $15

Redeemer, McFarlane Collector's Club Exclusive, 1997, McFarlane
NM $5 **MIP** $15

Spawn II, 1995, McFarlane
NM $10 **MIP** $15

Spawn II, McFarlane Collector's Club Exclusive, 1997, McFarlane
NM $5 **MIP** $15

Vertebreaker, 1995, McFarlane
NM $10 **MIP** $25

Vertebreaker, gray or black body, Exclusive available through various store, 1996, McFarlane
NM $5 **MIP** $15

Vertebreaker, McFarlane Collector's Club Exclusive, 1997, McFarlane
NM $5 **MIP** $15

Violator II, 1995, McFarlane
NM $10 **MIP** $20

Violator II, McFarlane Collector's Club Exclusive, 1997, McFarlane
NM $5 **MIP** $15

SERIES 04, 1996

Clown II, black guns, 1996, McFarlane
NM $6 **MIP** $20

Clown II, neon orange guns, 1996, McFarlane
NM $3 **MIP** $12

Cy-Gor, gold trim, 1996, McFarlane
NM $4 **MIP** $15

Cy-Gor, purple trim, 1996, McFarlane
NM $4 **MIP** $15

Cy-Gor, Target Exclusive, 1996, McFarlane
NM $5 **MIP** $15

Exo-Skeleton Spawn, black and gray exo-skeleton, 1996, McFarlane
NM $5 **MIP** $20

Exo-Skeleton Spawn, Target Exclusive, 1997, McFarlane
NM $5 **MIP** $15

Exo-Skeleton Spawn, white and light gray bones and white costume, 1996, McFarlane
NM $8 **MIP** $20

Future Spawn, red trimmed, 1996, McFarlane
NM $10 **MIP** $15

Maxx, The, FAO Schwarz Exclusive, 1996, McFarlane
NM $15 **MIP** $40

Maxx, The, with black Isz, 1996, McFarlane
NM $15 **MIP** $40

Maxx, The, with white Isz, 1996, McFarlane
NM $10 **MIP** $35

Shadowhawk, black with silver trim, 1996, McFarlane
NM $4 **MIP** $15

Shadowhawk, gold with gray trim, 1996, McFarlane
NM $3 **MIP** $10

She-Spawn, black mask, 1996, McFarlane
NM $5 **MIP** $20

She-Spawn, red face mask, 1996, McFarlane
NM $5 **MIP** $20

SERIES 05, 1996

Nuclear Spawn, green skin, 1996, McFarlane
NM $3 **MIP** $10

Nuclear Spawn, orange skin, 1996, McFarlane
NM $4 **MIP** $15

Overtkill II, flesh colored with gray trim, 1996, McFarlane
NM $5 **MIP** $15

Overtkill II, silver with gold trim, 1996, McFarlane
NM $5 **MIP** $15

Tremor II, orange with red blood, 1996, McFarlane
NM $5 **MIP** $15

Tremor II, purple with green blood, 1996, McFarlane
NM $3 **MIP** $10

Vandalizer, FAO Schwarz Exclusive, 1996, McFarlane
NM $10 **MIP** $25

Vandalizer, gray skinned with black trim, 1996, McFarlane
NM $3 **MIP** $10

Vandalizer, tan skinned with brown trim, 1996, McFarlane
NM $3 **MIP** $10

Viking Spawn, 1996, McFarlane
NM $5 **MIP** $25

Widow Maker, black and red with flesh-colored body, 1996, McFarlane
NM $5 **MIP** $15

Spawn (McFarlane, 1994-present)

Widow Maker, purple and rose outfit, gray body, 1996, McFarlane
NM $8 MIP $20

SERIES 06, 1996

Alien Spawn, black with white, 1996, McFarlane
NM $5 MIP $15

Alien Spawn, white with black, 1996, McFarlane
NM $3 MIP $10

Battleclad Spawn, black costume, 1996, McFarlane
NM $5 MIP $20

Battleclad Spawn, tan sections, 1996, McFarlane
NM $4 MIP $12

Chameleon Spawn, 1996, McFarlane
NM $4 MIP $12

Freak, The, purplish flesh with brown and silver weapons, 1996, McFarlane
NM $3 MIP $10

Freak, The, tan flesh, 1995, McFarlane
NM $5 MIP $15

Sansker, black and yellow, 1996, McFarlane
NM $3 MIP $10

Sansker, brown and tan, 1996, McFarlane
NM $5 MIP $15

Superpatriot, metallic blue arms and legs, 1996, McFarlane
NM $3 MIP $10

Superpatriot, silver arms and legs, 1996, McFarlane
NM $3 MIP $10

Tiffany the Amazon, green trim, 1996, McFarlane
NM $5 MIP $15

Tiffany the Amazon, McFarlane Collector's Club Exclusive, 1998, McFarlane
NM $8 MIP $25

Tiffany the Amazon, red trim, 1996, McFarlane
NM $5 MIP $15

SERIES 07, 1997

Crutch, green goatee, 1977, McFarlane
NM $5 MIP $15

Crutch, purple goatee, 1997, McFarlane
NM $3 MIP $10

(McFarlane Toys)

Mangler, The, 1997, McFarlane, Figure includes skull-topped staff
NM $5 MIP $15

(McFarlane Toys)

No-Body, 1997, McFarlane, Detailed robotic figure containing smaller "No-Body" inside
NM $5 MIP $15

(McFarlane Toys)

Sam and Twitch, 1997, McFarlane, Sam with donut and pistol, Twitch with rifle
NM $5 MIP $15

(McFarlane Toys)

Scourge, 1997, McFarlane
NM $5 MIP $15

Spawn III, with owl and bat, 1997, McFarlane
NM $8 MIP $25

Spawn III, with wolf and bat, 1997, McFarlane, Figure also includes "spring up action cape"
NM $8 MIP $25

(McFarlane Toys)

Zombie Spawn, tan skin with red tunic, 1997, McFarlane, Figure includes chainsaw and large machine-gun rifle
NM $3 MIP $10

SERIES 08, 1997

Curse of the Spawn, 1997, McFarlane
NM $5 MIP $15

Gate Keeper, 1997, McFarlane
NM $4 MIP $12

Grave Digger, 1997, McFarlane
NM $4 MIP $12

Renegade, tan flesh, 1997, McFarlane
NM $4 MIP $12

Rotarr, 1997, McFarlane
NM $4 MIP $12

Sabre, 1997, McFarlane
NM $4 MIP $12

SERIES 09, 1997

Goddess, The, 1997, McFarlane
NM $4 MIP $12

Manga Clown, 1997, McFarlane
NM $4 MIP $12

Manga Curse, 1997, McFarlane
NM $4 MIP $12

Manga Ninja Spawn, 1997, McFarlane
NM $4 MIP $12

Manga Spawn, 1997, McFarlane
NM $5 MIP $15

Manga Violator, 1997, McFarlane
NM $4 MIP $12

SERIES 10, MANGA 2, 1998

Cybertooth, 1998, McFarlane
NM $4 MIP $15

Manga Cyber Violator, 1998, McFarlane
NM $4 MIP $8

Manga Dead Spawn, 1998, McFarlane
NM $4 MIP $8

Manga Freak, 1998, McFarlane
NM $4 MIP $8

Manga Overtkill, 1998, McFarlane
NM $4 MIP $8

Manga Samurai Spawn, 1998, McFarlane
NM $4 MIP $8

SERIES 11, DARK AGES, 1998

Horrid, The, 1998, McFarlane, Two figures; one winged human-type (larger) and the other, a small skeletal figure with weapon
NM $3 **MIP** $8

Ogre, The, 1998, McFarlane, Large Ogre figure controlled by smaller figure riding on shoulders. Also includes war club
NM $5 **MIP** $15

Raider, The, 1998, McFarlane, Centaur figure with battle armor, double-edged pike/axe, string of defeated skulls
NM $3 **MIP** $8

Skull Queen, The, 1998, McFarlane, Figure includes battle axes, flying skeletal warrior
NM $4 **MIP** $12

Spawn The Black Knight, 1998, McFarlane
NM $5 **MIP** $15

Spellcaster, The, 1998, McFarlane, Includes battle axe, shield and helmet
NM $4 **MIP** $15

SERIES 12, 1998

BottomLine, 1998, McFarlane
NM $5 **MIP** $15

Creech, The, 1998, McFarlane
NM $5 **MIP** $20

Cy-Gor II, 1998, McFarlane, Deluxe boxed figure
NM $5 **MIP** $25

Heap, The, 1998, McFarlane
NM $5 **MIP** $15

Re-Animated Spawn, 1998, McFarlane
NM $5 **MIP** $15

Spawn IV, 1998, McFarlane
NM $5 **MIP** $15

TopGun, 1998, McFarlane
NM $5 **MIP** $15

SERIES 13, CURSE OF THE SPAWN, 1999

Curse of the Spawn II, 1999, McFarlane
NM $5 **MIP** $10

Desiccator, 1999, McFarlane, Deluxe boxed figure
NM $7 **MIP** $12

Hatchet, 1999, McFarlane
NM $5 **MIP** $10

Medusa, 1999, McFarlane
NM $5 **MIP** $10

Priest and Mr. Obersmith, 1999, McFarlane
NM $5 **MIP** $10

Raenius, 1999, McFarlane
NM $5 **MIP** $10

Zeus, 1999, McFarlane
NM $5 **MIP** $10

SERIES 14, DARK AGES 2, 1999

Iguantus and Tuskadon, 1999, 5" and 2", McFarlane
NM $5 **MIP** $15

(McFarlane Toys)

Mandarin Spawn the Scarlet Edge, 1999, 9", McFarlane, A double-edged sword that is twice the size of the figure. Who wants one? I do.
NM $5 **MIP** $15

Necromancer, 1999, 6-1/8", McFarlane
NM $5 **MIP** $15

Spawn the Black Heart, 1999, 6", McFarlane
NM $5 **MIP** $15

Tormentor, 1999, 7", McFarlane
NM $5 **MIP** $15

Viper King, 1999, 6-1/8", McFarlane
NM $5 **MIP** $15

SERIES 15, TECHNO SPAWN, 1999

Code Red, 1999, 7-1/2", McFarlane
NM $5 **MIP** $15

Cyber Spawn, 1999, 8-1/2", McFarlane
NM $5 **MIP** $15

Gray Thunder, 1999, 7", McFarlane
NM $3 **MIP** $10

Iron Express, 1999, 9-1/2", McFarlane
NM $3 **MIP** $10

Steel Trap, 1999, 7", McFarlane
NM $3 **MIP** $10

Spawn (McFarlane, 1994-present)

Warzone, 1999, 6-1/2", McFarlane
NM $3 **MIP** $10

SERIES 16, NITRO RIDERS, 2000

Spawn: After Burner, 2000, McFarlane, 5-1/4" figure and 9x4-1/4"cycle
NM $3 **MIP** $10

Spawn: Eclipse 5000, 2000, McFarlane, 5-1/2" figure and 9-1/2x5-1/2" cycle
NM $3 **MIP** $10

Spawn: Flash Point, 2000, McFarlane, 5-1/4" figure and 9x4-1/2" cycle
NM $3 **MIP** $10

Spawn: Green Vapor, 2000, McFarlane, 5-1/4" figure and 9-1/2x5-1/2" cycle
NM $3 **MIP** $10

SERIES 17, SPAWN CLASSIC, 2001

Al Simmons, 2001, McFarlane, Includes stand, machine gun, pistol and accessories
NM $3 **MIP** $8

Clown III, 2001, McFarlane, Includes wrapped body and stretcher
NM $3 **MIP** $8

Malebogia II, 2001, McFarlane
NM $3 **MIP** $8

Medieval Spawn II, 2001, McFarlane, Includes chain, sword and accessories
NM $5 **MIP** $15

Spawn V, 2001, McFarlane, With stand
NM $5 **MIP** $15

Tiffany II, 2001, McFarlane, Includes swords, knives, pike, battle staff, accessories and stand
NM $5 **MIP** $15

SERIES 18, INTERLINK 6, 2001

HD-1, 2001, McFarlane
NM $3 **MIP** $10

LA-6, 2001, McFarlane
NM $3 **MIP** $10

LL-4, 2001, McFarlane
NM $3 **MIP** $10

RA-5, 2001, McFarlane
NM $3 **MIP** $10

RL-3, 2001, McFarlane
NM $3 **MIP** $10

TS-2, 2001, McFarlane
NM $3 **MIP** $10

SERIES 19, DARK AGES SPAWN: THE SAMURAI WARS, 2001

Dojo, 2001, 7-1/2", McFarlane
NM $5 **MIP** $10

Jookyl Assassin, 2001, 6-3/4", McFarlane
NM $5 **MIP** $10

Jyaaku the Nightmare, 2001, 11-1/4", McFarlane, Deluxe boxed figure
NM $7 **MIP** $12

Lotus the Angel Warrior, 2001, 6-7/8", McFarlane
NM $5 **MIP** $10

(KP Photo, Brian Brogaard collection)

Samurai Spawn, 2001, 8", McFarlane
NM $5 **MIP** $10

Scorpion Assassin, 2001, 8-1/2", McFarlane
NM $5 **MIP** $10

SERIES 20, SPAWN CLASSIC 2, 2001

Clown IV, 2001, McFarlane
NM $5 **MIP** $10

Domina, 2001, McFarlane
NM $5 **MIP** $10

Medieval Spawn III, 2001, McFarlane
NM $5 **MIP** $10

Overtkill III, 2001, McFarlane
NM $5 **MIP** $10

Spawn VI, 2001, McFarlane
NM $5 **MIP** $10

Violator III, 2001, McFarlane
NM $5 **MIP** $10

SERIES 21, ALTERNATE REALITIES, 2002

Alien Spawn, 2002, 8", McFarlane
NM $7 **MIP** $12

Pirate Spawn, 2002, 6-5/8", McFarlane
NM $7 **MIP** $12

Raven Spawn, 2002, 6-1/2", McFarlane
NM $7 **MIP** $12

She Spawn, 2002, 6-5/8", McFarlane
NM $7 **MIP** $12

Spawn VII, 2002, 9-5/8", McFarlane
NM $7 **MIP** $12

Wings of Redemption Spawn, 2002, 6-1/2", McFarlane
NM $10 **MIP** $20

SERIES 22, DARK AGES SPAWN: THE VIKING AGE, 2002

Berserker the Troll, 2002, 5-5/8", McFarlane
NM $7 **MIP** $12

Bluetooth, 2002, 6-7/8", McFarlane
NM $7 **MIP** $12

Dark Raider, 2002, 7-3/4", McFarlane
NM $7 **MIP** $12

Skullsplitter, 2002, 7-3/4", McFarlane
NM $7 **MIP** $12

Spawn the Bloodaxe, 2002, 7-1/2", McFarlane
NM $7 **MIP** $12

Spawn the Bloodaxe and Thunderhoof, 2002, McFarlane, Deluxe boxed set
NM $10 **MIP** $22

Valkerie, 2002, 6-1/2", McFarlane
NM $7 **MIP** $15

SERIES 23, MUTATIONS, 2003

Al Simmons, 2003, McFarlane
NM $5 **MIP** $10

Kin, 2003, McFarlane
NM $5 **MIP** $10

Malebolgia, 2003, McFarlane
NM $5 **MIP** $10

Spawn, 2003, McFarlane
NM $5 **MIP** $10

Warrior Lilith, 2003, McFarlane
NM $5 **MIP** $10

SERIES 23.5, SPAWN REBORN

Clown IV, 2003, McFarlane, from Series 20
NM $5 **MIP** $10

Curse of the Spawn II, 2003, McFarlane, from Series 13
NM $5 **MIP** $10

Domina, 2003, McFarlane, from Series 20
NM $5 **MIP** $10

(KP Photo, Brian Brogaard collection)

Raven Spawn, 2003, McFarlane, from Series 21
NM $5 **MIP** $10

Redeemer, 2003, McFarlane, from Series 03
NM $5 **MIP** $10

Wings of Redemption Spawn, 2003, McFarlane, from Series 21
NM $5 **MIP** $10

SERIES 24, THE CLASSIC COMIC COVERS, 2003

Hellspawn i.001, 2003, McFarlane
NM $5 **MIP** $10

Spawn i.039, 2003, McFarlane
NM $5 **MIP** $10

Spawn i.043, 2003, McFarlane
NM $5 **MIP** $10

Spawn (McFarlane, 1994-present)

Spawn i.064, 2003, McFarlane
NM $5 MIP $10

Spawn i.088, 2003, McFarlane
NM $5 MIP $10

Spawn i.109, 2003, McFarlane
NM $5 MIP $10

SERIES 25, CLASSIC COMIC COVERS 2

Creech CI.001, 2004, McFarlane
NM $5 MIP $10

Redeemer I.117, 2004, McFarlane
NM $5 MIP $10

Sam and Twitch STI.022, 2004, McFarlane
NM $5 MIP $10

Spawn HSI.005, 2004, McFarlane
NM $5 MIP $10

Spawn HSI.011, 2004, McFarlane
NM $5 MIP $10

Spawn I.095, 2004, McFarlane
NM $5 MIP $10

SERIES 26, ART OF SPAWN

Curse 2, 2004, McFarlane, Spawn Bible art
NM $5 MIP $10

Spawn the Black Knight, 2004, McFarlane, Dark Ages Issue 1 cover art
NM $5 MIP $10

Spawn v. Cy-Gor, 2004, McFarlane, Issue 57 cover art
NM $5 MIP $10

Spawn, Issue 7, 2004, McFarlane
NM $5 MIP $10

Spawn, Issue 8, 2004, McFarlane
NM $5 MIP $10

Tiffany 3, 2004, McFarlane, Issue 45 art
NM $5 MIP $10

Tremor 3, 2004, McFarlane, Spawn Bible art
NM $5 MIP $10

SERIES 27, ART OF SPAWN

Clown 5, 2005, McFarlane, original art
NM $5 MIP $10

Spawn v. Al Simmons, 2005, McFarlane, deluxe boxed setfd
NM $10 MIP $25

Spawn, Issue 119, 2005, McFarlane, interior art
NM $5 MIP $10

Spawn, Issue 131, 2005, McFarlane, cover art
NM $5 MIP $10

Spawn, Issue 85, 2005, McFarlane, cover art
NM $5 MIP $10

Vandalizer 2, 2005, McFarlane, original art
NM $5 MIP $10

Wanda 2, 2005, McFarlane, Issue 65 interior art
NM $5 MIP $10

SERIES 28, REGENERATED

Commando Spawn 2, 2005, McFarlane
NM n/a MIP n/a

Cyber Spawn 2, 2005, McFarlane
NM n/a MIP n/a

Grave Digger 2, 2005, McFarlane
NM n/a MIP n/a

Lotus Warrior Angel 2, 2005, McFarlane
NM n/a MIP n/a

Mandarin Spawn 2, 2005, McFarlane
NM n/a MIP n/a

Spawn v. Urizen, 2005, McFarlane, deluxe boxed set
NM n/a MIP n/a

Zombie Spawn 2, 2005, McFarlane
NM n/a MIP n/a

SERIES 29, EVOLUTIONS, 2006

Disciple, 2006, 6", McFarlane
NM $6 MIP $12

Man of Miracles, 2006, 6", McFarlane
NM $6 MIP $12

Ninja Swawn 2, 2006, 6", McFarlane
NM $6 MIP $12

Spawn 9, 2006, 6", McFarlane
NM $6 MIP $12

Thamuz, 2006, 6", McFarlane
NM $6 MIP $12

Zera, 2006, 6", McFarlane
NM $6 MIP $12

SERIES 30, THE ADVENTURES OF SPAWN, 2006

Codename: Cy-Gor, 2006, 6", McFarlane
NM $6 MIP $12

Omega Spawn, 2006, 6", McFarlane
NM $6 MIP $12

Overtkill The Destroyer, 2006, 6", McFarlane
NM $6 MIP $12

Spawn X, 2006, 6", McFarlane
NM $6 MIP $12

The Redeemer, 2006, 6", McFarlane
NM $6 MIP $12

Tiffany the Amazon, 2006, 6", McFarlane
NM $6 MIP $12

SERIES 31, OTHER WORLDS

Goddess Llyra, 2007, 6", McFarlane
NM $6 MIP $12

Lord Covenant, 2007, 6", McFarlane
NM $6 MIP $12

Necro Cop, 2007, 6", McFarlane
NM $6 MIP $12

Nightmare Spawn, 2007, 6", McFarlane
NM $6 MIP $12

Spawn 11, 2007, 6", McFarlane
NM $6 MIP $12

Spawn the Maurader, 2007, 6", McFarlane
NM $6 MIP $12

SERIES 32, THE ADVENTURES OF SPAWN SERIES 2

Agent 8, 2007, 6", McFarlane
NM $6 MIP $12

Commando Spawn, 2007, 6", McFarlane
NM $6 MIP $12

Creech, 2007, 6", McFarlane
NM $6 MIP $12

Omega Squadron, 2007, 6", McFarlane
NM $6 MIP $12

Raven Spawn, 2007, 6", McFarlane
NM $6 MIP $12

Spawn X (Blue), 2007, 6", McFarlane
NM $6 MIP $12

Tremor, 2007, 6", McFarlane
NM $6 MIP $12

Spawn: The Movie (McFarlane, 1997)

DELUXE FIGURES

Attack Spawn, 1997, McFarlane
NM $10 MIP $30

(McFarlane Toys)

Malebolgia, 1997, McFarlane, Detailed figure includes skull-topped staff
NM $10 MIP $30

(McFarlane Toys)

Violator, 1997, McFarlane, From the Spawn Deluxe Boxed Set, highly-detailed figure
NM $10 **MIP** $30

FIGURES

(McFarlane Toys)

Al Simmons, 1997, McFarlane, With rifle and mobile rocket launcher
NM $4 **MIP** $10

(McFarlane Toys)

Burnt Spawn, 1997, McFarlane, With rifle and femur-bone handled shovel
NM $4 **MIP** $10

(McFarlane Toys)

Clown, 1997, McFarlane, Truly terrifying figure in referee shirt and pale blue face makeup
NM $4 **MIP** $10

(McFarlane Toys)

Jason Wynn, 1997, McFarlane, With rifle, headset and accessories
NM $4 **MIP** $10

(McFarlane Toys)

Jessica Priest, 1997, McFarlane, With rifle and accessories
NM $4 **MIP** $10

PLAY SETS

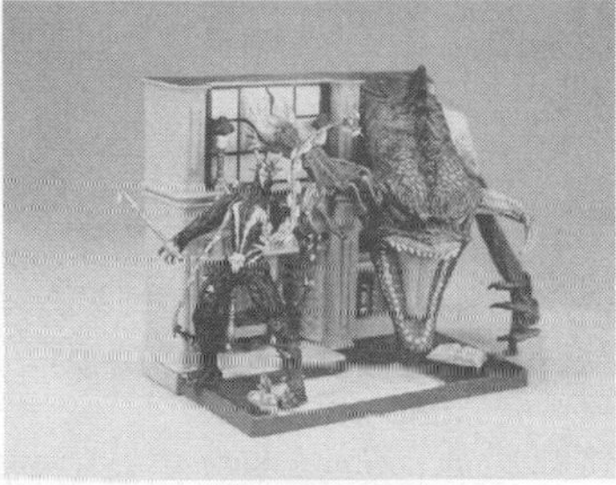

(McFarlane Toys)

Final Battle, 1997, McFarlane, Spawn with creature crashing through house diorama
NM $10 **MIP** $20

(McFarlane Toys)

Graveyard, 1997, McFarlane, Includes two figures and open grave
NM $10 **MIP** $20

(McFarlane Toys)

Spawn Alley, 1997, McFarlane, Set includes Spawn, alley backdrop and creature
NM $10 **MIP** $20

Spider-Man Electro-Spark (Toy Biz, 1997)

5" FIGURES

Captain America, 1997, Toy Biz
NM $5 **MIP** $15

Electro, 1997, Toy Biz
NM $3 **MIP** $8

Electro-Shock Spidey, 1997, Toy Biz
NM $3 **MIP** $8

Electro-Spark Spider-Man, 1997, Toy Biz
NM $3 **MIP** $8

Steel-Shock Spider-Man, 1997, Toy Biz
NM $3 **MIP** $8

Spider-Man Sneak Attack (Toy Biz, 1998)

BUG BUSTERS, 5" FIGURES

Jack O'Lantern and Bug Eye Blaster, 1998, Toy Biz
NM $3 **MIP** $8

Silver Sable and Beetle Basher, 1998, Toy Biz
NM $3 **MIP** $8

Spider-Man and Spider Stinger, 1998, Toy Biz
NM $3 **MIP** $8

Vulture and Jaw Breaker, 1998, Toy Biz
NM $3 **MIP** $8

SHAPE SHIFTERS, 7" FIGURES

Lizard forms into Mutant Alligator, 1998, Toy Biz
NM $2 **MIP** $6

Spider-Man Sneak Attack (Toy Biz, 1998)

Spider-Man forms into Monster Spider, 1998, Toy Biz
NM $2 MIP $6

Venom forms into 3-Headed Serpent, 1998, Toy Biz
NM $2 MIP $6

STREET WARRIORS, 5" FIGURES

Scarecrow with Pitchfork Projectile, 1998, Toy Biz
NM $2 MIP $6

Spider-Sense Peter Parker, 1998, Toy Biz
NM $2 MIP $6

Street War Spider-Man, 1998, Toy Biz
NM $2 MIP $6

Vermin with Rat-firing Fire Hydrant, 1998, Toy Biz
NM $2 MIP $6

WEB FLYERS, 5" FIGURES

Carnage, 1998, Toy Biz
NM $2 MIP $6

Copter Spider-Man, 1998, Toy Biz
NM $2 MIP $6

Hobgoblin, 1998, Toy Biz
NM $2 MIP $6

Spider-Man, 1998, Toy Biz
NM $2 MIP $6

Spider-Man Special Edition Series (Toy Biz, 1998)

12" FIGURES

Black Cat, 1998, Toy Biz
NM $10 MIP $25

Spider-Man, 1998, Toy Biz
NM $8 MIP $25

Venom, 1998, Toy Biz
NM $8 MIP $25

Spider-Man Spider Force (Toy Biz, 1997)

5" FIGURES

Beetle with Transforming Beetle Armor, 1997, Toy Biz
NM $2 MIP $6

Cybersect Spider-Man with Transforming Cyber Spider, 1997, Toy Biz
NM $2 MIP $6

Swarm with Transforming Bee Action, 1997, Toy Biz
NM $2 MIP $6

Tarantula with Transforming Tarantula Armor, 1997, Toy Biz
NM $2 MIP $6

Wasp with Transforming Wasp Armor, 1997, Toy Biz
NM $2 MIP $6

Spider-Man Spider Power (Toy Biz, 1999)

SERIES I, 5" FIGURES

Slime Shaker Venom, 1999, Toy Biz
NM $2 MIP $6

Spider Sense Spider-Man, 1999, Toy Biz
NM $2 MIP $6

Street Warrior Spider-Man, 1999, Toy Biz
NM $2 MIP $6

Triple Threat Spider-Man, 1999, Toy Biz
NM $2 MIP $6

SERIES II, 5" FIGURES

Doctor Octopus, 1999, Toy Biz
NM $2 MIP $6

Flip and Swing Spider-man, 1999, Toy Biz
NM $2 MIP $6

J. Jonah Jameson, 1999, Toy Biz
NM $2 MIP $6

Spider Sense Peter Parker, 1999, Toy Biz
NM $2 MIP $6

Spider-Man Vampire Wars (Toy Biz, 1996)

5" FIGURES

Air-Attack Spider-Man, 1997, Toy Biz
NM $3 MIP $8

Anti-Vampire Spider-Man, 1997, Toy Biz
NM $3 MIP $8

Blade-The Vampire Hunter, 1997, Toy Biz
NM $3 MIP $12

Morbius Unbound, 1997, Toy Biz
NM $3 MIP $10

Vampire Spider-Man, 1997, Toy Biz
NM $3 MIP $8

Spider-Man Venom (Toy Biz, 1996-97)

ALONG CAME A SPIDER, 6" FIGURES

Bride of Venom and Vile the Spider, 1997, Toy Biz
NM $3 MIP $10

Phage and Pincer the Spider, 1997, Toy Biz
NM $3 MIP $8

Spider-Carnage and Spit the Spider, 1997, Toy Biz
NM $3 MIP $8

Venom the Symbiote and Riper the Spider, 1997, Toy Biz
NM $3 MIP $8

PLANET OF THE SYMBIOTES, 6" FIGURES

Hybrid, pincer Wing Action, 1997, Toy Biz
NM $3 MIP $8

Lasher, Tentacle Whipping Action, 1997, Toy Biz
NM $3 MIP $8

Riot, Launching Attack Arms, 1997, Toy Biz
NM $3 MIP $8

Venom the Madness, Surprise Attack Heads, 1997, Toy Biz
NM $3 MIP $8

PLANET OF THE SYMBIOTES, DELUXE 6" FIGURES

Hybrid, Pincer Wing Action, 1996, Toy Biz
NM $3 MIP $8

Lasher, Tentacle Whipping Action, 1996, Toy Biz
NM $3 MIP $8

Riot, Launcing Attack Arms, 1996, Toy Biz
NM $3 MIP $8

Scream, Living Tendril Hair, 1996, Toy Biz
NM $3 MIP $8

Venom the Madness, Surprise Attack Heads, 1996, Toy Biz
NM $3 MIP $8

Spider-Man Web Force (Toy Biz, 1997)

5" FIGURES

Daredevil, Transforming Web Tank Armor, 1997, Toy Biz
NM $2 MIP $6

Lizard, Transforming Swamp Rider, 1997, Toy Biz
NM $2 MIP $6

Vulture, Transforming Vuture-Bot, 1997, Toy Biz
NM $2 MIP $6

Web Commando Spidey, Transforming Web Copter, 1997, Toy Biz
NM $2 MIP $6

Web Swamp Spidey, Transforming Web Swamp Seeker Armor, 1997, Toy Biz
NM $2 MIP $6

Spider-Man Web Traps (Toy Biz, 1997)

5" FIGURES

Future Spider-Man with Snapping Cocoon Trap, 1997, Toy Biz
NM $2 MIP $6

Monster Spider-Man with Grappling Spider Sidekick, 1997, Toy Biz
NM $2 MIP $6

Rhino with Rotating Web Snare, 1997, Toy Biz
NM $2 MIP $6

Scorpion with Whipping Tail Attacker trap, 1997, Toy Biz
NM $3 MIP $8

Spider-Man with Pull-string Web Trap, 1997, Toy Biz
NM $2 MIP $6

Spider-Man: The New Animated Series (Toy Biz, 1994-96)

15" TALKING FIGURES

Spider-Man, 1994-96, 15", Toy Biz
NM $12 MIP $25

Venom, 1994-96, 15", Toy Biz
NM $12 MIP $25

2-1/2" DIE-CAST FIGURES

Spider-Man vs. Carnage, 1994-96, 2-1/2", Toy Biz
NM $2 MIP $4

Spider-Man vs. Dr. Octopus, 1994-96, 2-1/2", Toy Biz
NM $2 MIP $4

Spider-Man vs. Hobgoblin, 1994-96, 2-1/2", Toy Biz
NM $2 **MIP** $4

Spider-Man vs. Venom, 1994-96, 2-1/2", Toy Biz
NM $2 **MIP** $4

5" FIGURES

Alien Spider Slayer, 1994-96, 5", Toy Biz
NM $3 **MIP** $8

Battle-Ravaged Spider-Man, 1994-96, 5", Toy Biz
NM $3 **MIP** $10

Cameleon, 1994-96, 5", Toy Biz
NM $4 **MIP** $12

Carnage, 1994-96, 5", Toy Biz
NM $5 **MIP** $15

Carnage II, 1994-96, 5", Toy Biz
NM $4 **MIP** $12

Carnage II, 1996, Toy Biz, Series 6
NM $5 **MIP** $10

Dr. Octopus, 1994-96, 5", Toy Biz
NM $4 **MIP** $12

(KP Photo, Brian Brogaard collection)

Green Goblin, 1994-96, 5", Toy Biz
NM $5 **MIP** $15

Hobgoblin, 1994-96, 5", Toy Biz
NM $4 **MIP** $12

Kingpin, 1994-96, 5", Toy Biz
NM $5 **MIP** $15

Kraven, 1994-96, 5", Toy Biz
NM $4 **MIP** $12

Lizard, 1994-96, 5", Toy Biz
NM $5 **MIP** $15

Man-Spider, 1996, Toy Biz, Series 6
NM $5 **MIP** $10

Morbius, 1994-96, 5", Toy Biz
NM $4 **MIP** $12

(KP Photo, Brian Brogaard collection)

Mysterio, 1994-96, 5", Toy Biz, Series 4
NM $3 **MIP** $12

Nick Fury, 1994-96, 5", Toy Biz, Series 5
NM $3 **MIP** $12

Peter Parker, 1994-96, 5", Toy Biz
NM $5 **MIP** $15

Prowler, 1994-96, 5", Toy Biz
NM $3 **MIP** $12

Punisher, 1994-96, 5", Toy Biz, The recognizable man in black (and white)
NM $3 **MIP** $12

Rhino, 1994-96, 5", Toy Biz
NM $6 **MIP** $18

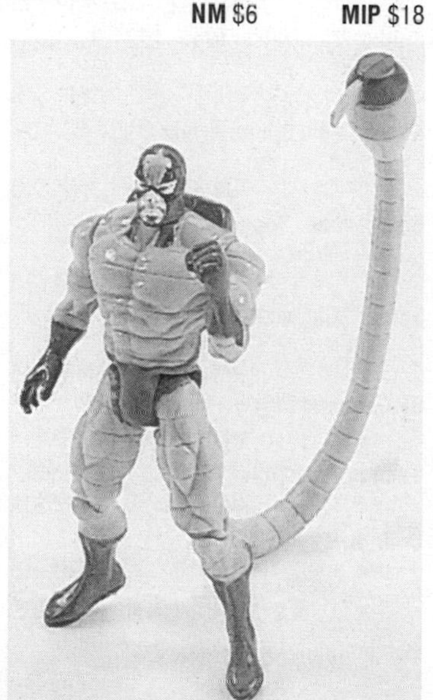
(KP Photo, Brian Brogaard collection)

Scorpion, 1994-96, 5", Toy Biz
NM $5 **MIP** $15

Shocker, 1994-96, 5", Toy Biz
NM $4 **MIP** $15

Smythe, 1994-96, 5", Toy Biz
NM $5 **MIP** $12

(KP Photo, Brian Brogaard collection)

Spider-Man 2099, 1996, Toy Biz, Series 7
NM $6 **MIP** $12

(KP Photo, Brian Brogaard collection)

Spider-Man in Black Costume, 1994-96, 5", Toy Biz
NM $3 **MIP** $12

Spider-Man Octo, 1996, Toy Biz, Series 6
NM $5 **MIP** $10

Spider-Man: The New Animated Series (Toy Biz, 1994-96)

(KP Photo, Brian Brogaard collection)

Spider-Man Six Arm, 1994-96, 5", Toy Biz
NM $3 **MIP** $12

Spider-Man with Parachute Web, 1994-96, 5", Toy Biz
NM $3 **MIP** $12

Spider-Man with Spider Armor, 1994-96, 5", Toy Biz.
NM $3 **MIP** $15

Spider-Man with Web Cannon, 1996, Toy Biz, Series 6
NM $9 **MIP** $18

Spider-Man with Web Racer, 1994-96, 5", Toy Biz
NM $5 **MIP** $15

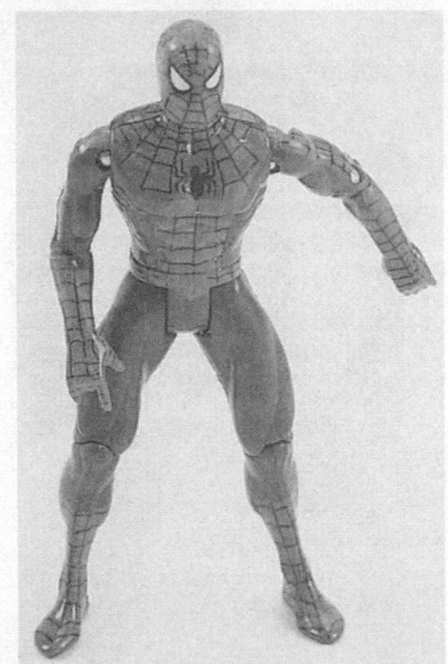
(KP Photo, Brian Brogaard collection)

Spider-Man with Web Shooter, 1994-96, 5", Toy Biz
NM $5 **MIP** $15

Spider-Man, multi-jointed, 1994-96, 5", Toy Biz
NM $3 **MIP** $15

Spider-Sense Spider-Man, 1994-96, 5", Toy Biz
NM $3 **MIP** $12

Symbiotic Venom Attack, 1994-96, 5", Toy Biz
NM $3 **MIP** $12

Tombstone, 1996, Toy Biz, Series 6
NM $5 **MIP** $10

Venom, 1994-96, 5", Toy Biz
NM $4 **MIP** $15

Venom II, 1994-96, 5", Toy Biz
NM $3 **MIP** $12

Vulture, 1994-96, 5", Toy Biz
NM $5 **MIP** $15

ACCESSORIES

Daily Bugle Play Set, 1994-96, 5", Toy Biz
NM $10 **MIP** $15

DELUXE 10" FIGURES

Carnage, 1994-96, 10", Toy Biz
NM $8 **MIP** $20

Dr. Octopus, 1994-96, 10", Toy Biz
NM $7 **MIP** $15

Hobgoblin, 1994-96, 10", Toy Biz
NM $7 **MIP** $15

Kraven, 1994-96, 10", Toy Biz
NM $7 **MIP** $15

Lizard, 1994-96, 10", Toy Biz
NM $7 **MIP** $15

Myserio, 1994-96, 10", ToyBiz
NM $7 **MIP** $15

Punisher, 1994-96, 10", ToyBiz
NM $7 **MIP** $15

Spider-Man Spider Sense, 1994-96, 10", Toy Biz
NM $7 **MIP** $15

Spider-Man with suction cups, 1994-96, 10", Toy Biz
NM $7 **MIP** $15

Spider-Man, Armor, 1994-96, 10", ToyBiz
NM $7 **MIP** $15

Spider-Man, Sensational, 1994-96, 10", ToyBiz
NM $7 **MIP** $15

Spider-Man, Silver Web, 1994-96, 10", ToyBiz
NM $7 **MIP** $15

Spider-Man, Spider Armor, 1994-96, 10", ToyBiz
NM $7 **MIP** $15

Spider-Man, Super Posable, 1994-96, 10", ToyBiz
NM $7 **MIP** $15

Spider-Man, wall hanging, 1994-96, 10", Toy Biz
NM $7 **MIP** $15

Venom, 1994-96, 10", Toy Biz
NM $7 **MIP** $15

Venom, Dark Blue, 1994-96, 10", ToyBiz
NM $7 **MIP** $15

Vulture, 1994-96, 10", Toy Biz
NM $10 **MIP** $15

PROJECTORS

Hobgoblin, 1994-96, Toy Biz
NM $5 **MIP** $15

Lizard, 1994-96, Toy Biz
NM $5 **MIP** $15

Spider-Man, 1994-96, Toy Biz
NM $5 **MIP** $15

Venom, 1994-96, Toy Biz
NM $5 **MIP** $15

VEHICLES

Hobgoblin Wing Bomber, 1994-96, Toy Biz
NM $10 **MIP** $25

Smythe Battle Chair Attack Vehicle, 1994-96, Toy Biz
NM $15 **MIP** $35

Spider-Man Wheelie Cycle, 1994-96, Toy Biz
NM $7 **MIP** $15

Spider-Man's Cycle (radio-controlled), 1994-96, Toy Biz
NM $15 **MIP** $30

Tri-Spider Slayer, 1994-96, Toy Biz
NM $10 **MIP** $25

Star Trek (Mego, 1974-80)

CARDED FIGURES

Andorian, 1976, 8", Mego
NM $300 **MIP** $675

Captain Kirk, 1974, 8", Mego
NM $25 **MIP** $60

Cheron, 1975, 8", Mego, Black and white face and uniform
NM $85 **MIP** $180

(Karen O'Brien collection)

Dr. McCoy, 1974, 8", Mego, Medical tricorder pack
NM $35 **MIP** $80

Gorn, 1975, 8", Mego
NM $80 **MIP** $180

(Corey LeChat)

Klingon, 1974, 8", Mego, Black boots, brown plastic body armor, brown tunic
NM $25 **MIP** $50

Lt. Uhura, 1974, 8", Mego
NM $50 **MIP** $140

(Karen O'Brien collection)

Mr. Spock, 1974, 8", Mego, tricorder, communicator, phaser, belt
NM $25 **MIP** $55

Mugato, 1976, 8", Mego
NM $275 **MIP** $500

Neptunian, 1975, 8", Mego
NM $100 **MIP** $225

Romulan, 1976, 8", Mego
NM $600 **MIP** $1300

Scotty, 1974, 8", Mego
NM $35 **MIP** $80

Talos, 1976, 8", Mego
NM $275 **MIP** $500

The Keeper, 1975, 8", Mego
NM $75 **MIP** $250

PLAY SETS

Mission to Gamma VI, 1974-80, Mego, w/four generic aliens, rare
NM $300 **MIP** $725

U.S.S. Enterprise Bridge, 1974-80, Mego, captain's chair, navigation console, 2 crew seats, 3 double-sided cards for screen,, Model No. 51210
NM $75 **MIP** $200

U.S.S. Enterprise Gift Set, 1975, Mego, bridge set w/5 figures Kirk, Spock, McCoy, Mr. Scott, Klingon, rare
NM $150 **MIP** $350

Star Trek Alien Combat (Playmates, 1999)

FIGURES

Borg Drone, 1999, Playmates
NM $15 **MIP** $25

Klingon Warrior, 1999, Playmates
NM $15 **MIP** $25

Star Trek Collector Assortment (Playmates, 1999)

FIGURES

Andorian Ambassador, 1999, Playmates
NM $5 **MIP** $10

Captain Janeway, 1999, Playmates
NM $5 **MIP** $10

Counselor Troi, 1999, Playmates
NM $5 **MIP** $10

Dr. McCoy, 1999, Playmates
NM $5 **MIP** $10

Ensign Chekov, 1999, Playmates
NM $5 **MIP** $10

Geordi LaForge, 1999, Playmates
NM $5 **MIP** $10

Gorn Captain, 1999, Playmates
NM $5 **MIP** $10

Khan, 1999, Playmates
NM $5 **MIP** $10

Lieutenant Sulu, 1999, Playmates
NM $5 **MIP** $10

Lieutenant Uhura, 1999, Playmates
NM $5 **MIP** $10

Locutus of Borg, 1999, Playmates
NM $5 **MIP** $10

Mr. Spock, 1999, Playmates
NM $5 **MIP** $10

Mugatu, 1999, Playmates
NM $5 **MIP** $10

Q, 1999, Playmates
NM $5 **MIP** $10

Scotty, 1999, Playmates
NM $5 **MIP** $10

Seven of Nine, 1999, Playmates
NM $5 **MIP** $10

Star Trek Collector Series (Playmates, 1994-95)

9-1/2" BOXED FIGURES

Borg, 1995, Playmates, #6069
NM $10 **MIP** $25

Captain Benjamin Sisko, 1995, 9-1/2", Playmates, #16188
NM $10 **MIP** $25

Captain Benjamin Sisko (Command Edition), 1994, Playmates, #6067
NM $10 **MIP** $25

Captain Jean-Luc Picard (Command Edition), 1994, Playmates, #6066
NM $10 **MIP** $25

Captain Jean-Luc Picard (Movie Edition), 1994, Playmates, #6288
NM $10 **MIP** $25

Captain Jean-Luc Picard, Dress Uniform, 1995, 9-1/2", Playmates, #6289
NM $10 **MIP** $25

Captain Kirk (Command Edition), 1994, Playmates, #6068
NM $10 **MIP** $25

Captain Kirk (Movie Edition), 1994, Playmates, #6288
NM $10 **MIP** $25

Captian Christopher Pike, 1995, 9-1/2", Playmates, #16183
NM $10 **MIP** $25

Chief Miles O'Brien, 1995, 9-1/2", Playmates, #16182
NM $10 **MIP** $20

Commander Riker, 1995, Playmates, #6285
NM $10 **MIP** $25

Data (Movie Edition), 1995, Playmates, #6284
NM $10 **MIP** $25

Dr. Beverly Crusher, 1995, Playmates, #6282
NM $10 **MIP** $25

Dr. Leonard McCoy, 1995, 9-1/2", Playmates, #6292
NM $10 **MIP** $25

Ensign Pavel Chekov, 1995, 9-1/2", Playmates, #16185
NM $10 **MIP** $25

Geordi La Forge (Movie Edition), 1994, Playmates, #6287
NM $10 **MIP** $25

Guinan, 1995, 9-1/2", Playmates, #6283
NM $10 **MIP** $25

Lt. Cmdr. Deanna Troi, 1995, 9-1/2", Playmates, #6281
NM $10 **MIP** $25

Lt. Cmdr. Montgomery Scott, 1995, 9-1/2", Playmates, #6293
NM $10 **MIP** $25

Lt. Cmdr. Worf in DS9 uniform, 1995, 9-1/2", Playmates, #6295
NM $10 **MIP** $25

Lt. Hikaur Sulu, 1995, 9-1/2", Playmates, #16184
NM $10 **MIP** $25

Lt. Jadzia Dax, 1995, 9-1/2", Playmates, #16186
NM $10 **MIP** $25

Lt. Uhura, 1995, 9-1/2", Playmates, #6294
NM $10 **MIP** $25

Lt. Worf in Ritual Klingon Attire, 1995, 9-1/2", Playmates, #6286
NM $10 **MIP** $25

Major Kira Nerys, 1995, 9-1/2", Playmates, #16189
NM $10 **MIP** $20

Mr. Spock, 1995, 9-1/2", Playmates, #6291
NM $10 **MIP** $25

Q in Judges Robes, 1995, 9-1/2", Playmates, #16187
NM $10 **MIP** $25

Star Trek Collector Series (Playmates, 1994-95)

Romulan Commander, 1995, 9-1/2", Playmates, #16181
NM $10 **MIP** $20

Star Trek Electronic Display Assortment (Playmates, 1999)

FIGURES

Captain Kirk, 1999, Playmates
NM $20 **MIP** $40

Captain Picard, 1999, Playmates
NM $20 **MIP** $40

Commander Riker, 1999, Playmates
NM $20 **MIP** $40

Lieutenant Commander Data, 1999, Playmates
NM $20 **MIP** $40

Lieutenant Worf, 1999, Playmates
NM $20 **MIP** $40

Mr. Spock, 1999, Playmates
NM $20 **MIP** $40

Star Trek Millennium Collector's Set (Playmates, 1999)

FIGURES

Captain Janeway/Commander Chakotay, 1999, Playmates
NM $15 **MIP** $40

Captain Kirk/Mr. Spock, 1999, Playmates
NM $15 **MIP** $40

Captain Picard/Commander Riker, 1999, Playmates
NM $15 **MIP** $40

Captain Sisko/, 1999, Playmates
NM $15 **MIP** $40

Star Trek V (Galoob, 1989)

BOXED FIGURES

Captain Kirk, 1989, 7", Galoob
NM $10 **MIP** $25

Dr. McCoy, 1989, 7", Galoob
NM $10 **MIP** $25

Klaa, 1989, 7", Galoob
NM $10 **MIP** $25

Mr. Spock, 1989, 7", Galoob
NM $10 **MIP** $25

Sybok, 1989, 7", Galoob
NM $10 **MIP** $25

Star Trek: Classic Movie Figures (Playmates, 1995)

FIGURES

Admiral Kirk, 1995, 5", Playmates, #6451, "ST:TMP"
NM $6 **MIP** $12

Cmdr. Kruge, 1995, 5", Playmates, #6459, "STIII:TSFS"
NM $6 **MIP** $12

Cmdr. Spock, 1995, 5", Playmates, #6452, "ST:TMP"
NM $6 **MIP** $12

Dr. McCoy, 1995, 5", Playmates, #6453, "ST:TMP"
NM $6 **MIP** $12

General Chang, 1995, 5", Playmates, #6458, "STVI:TUC"
NM $7 **MIP** $15

Khan, 1995, 5", Playmates, #6456, "STII:TWOK"
NM $10 **MIP** $25

Lt. Saavik, 1995, 5", Playmates, #6460, "STII:TWOK" Kirstie Alley likeness
NM $7 **MIP** $14

Lt. Sulu, 1995, 5", Playmates, #6454, "ST:TMP"
NM $6 **MIP** $12

Lt. Uhura, 1995, 5", Playmates, #6455, "ST:TMP"
NM $6 **MIP** $12

Martia, 1995, 5", Playmates, #6457, "STVI:TUC"
NM $10 **MIP** $20

Star Trek: Deep Space Nine (Playmates, 1994-95)

SERIES 1

Chief Miles O'Brien, 1994, 5", Playmates, #6204
NM $6 **MIP** $10

Cmdr. Benjamin Sisko, 1994, 5", Playmates, #6201
NM $4 **MIP** $8

Cmdr. Gul Ducat, 1994, 5", Playmates, #6207
NM $8 **MIP** $12

Dr. Julian Bashir, 1994, 5", Playmates, #6208
NM $10 **MIP** $22

Lt. Jadzia Dax, 1994, 5", Playmates, #6205
NM $8 **MIP** $16

Major Kira Nerys, 1994, 5", Playmates, #6206
NM $4 **MIP** $8

Morn, 1994, 5", Playmates, #6210
NM $4 **MIP** $10

Odo, 1994, 5", Playmates, #6202
NM $4 **MIP** $10

Quark, 1994, 5", Playmates, #6203
NM $4 **MIP** $10

SERIES 2

Captain Jean-Luc Picard, 1995, 5", Playmates, #6245, DS9 uniform
NM $4 **MIP** $8

Chief Miles O'Brien, dress uniform, 1995, 5", Playmates, #6226
NM $5 **MIP** $10

Chief Miles O'Brien, duty uniform, 1995, 5", Playmates, #6244
NM $5 **MIP** $10

Cmdr. Benjamin Sisko, dress uniform, 1995, 5", Playmates, #6220
NM $5 **MIP** $10

Dr. Julian Bashir, duty uniform, 1995, 5", Playmates, #6243
NM $5 **MIP** $10

Jake Sisko, 1995, 5", Playmates, #6235
NM $5 **MIP** $10

Lt. Jadzia Dax, duty uniform, 1995, 5", Playmates, #6242
NM $5 **MIP** $10

Lt. Thomas Riker, 1995, 5", Playmates, #6246, DS9 uniform
NM $6 **MIP** $12

Q, 1995, 5", Playmates, #6247, DS9 uniform
NM $6 **MIP** $12

Rom w/ Nog, 1995, 5", Playmates, #6241
NM $7 **MIP** $14

Tosk, 1995, 5", Playmates, #6237
NM $5 **MIP** $10

Vedek Bareil, 1995, 5", Playmates, #6236
NM $8 **MIP** $16

Star Trek: First Contact (Playmates, 1996)

6" FIGURES

Borg, 1996, 5", Playmates, #16108
NM $7 **MIP** $12

Captain Jean-Luc Picard, 1996, 5", Playmates, #16101
NM $5 **MIP** $10

Captain Jean-Luc Picard in space suit, 1996, 5", Playmates, #16115
NM $5 **MIP** $10

Cmdr. Deanna Troi, 1996, 5", Playmates, #16106
NM $5 **MIP** $10

Cmdr. William T. Riker, 1996, 5", Playmates, #16102
NM $5 **MIP** $10

Dr. Beverly Crusher, 1996, 5", Playmates, #16107
NM $5 **MIP** $10

Lily, 1996, 5", Playmates, #16110
NM $8 **MIP** $15

Lt. Cmdr. Data, 1996, 5", Playmates, #16104
NM $5 **MIP** $10

Lt. Cmdr. Geordi LaForge, 1996, 5", Playmates, #16103
NM $5 **MIP** $10

Lt. Cmdr. Worf, 1996, 5", Playmates, #16105
NM $5 **MIP** $10

Zefram Cochrane, 1996, 5", Playmates, #16109
NM $5 **MIP** $10

9" FIGURES

Data, 1996, 9", Playmates, #16133
NM $12 **MIP** $18

Jean-Luc Picard, 1996, 9", Playmates, #16131
NM $12 **MIP** $18

Jean-Luc Picard in 21st century outfit, 1996, 9", Playmates, #16153
NM $15 **MIP** $23

William Riker, 1996, 9", Playmates, #16132
NM $12 **MIP** $18

Zefram Cochrane, 1996, 9", Playmates, #16134
NM $18 **MIP** $25

Star Trek: Generations (Playmates: 1995)

5" FIGURES

Admiral James T. Kirk, 1995, 5", Playmates, #6911
NM $7 **MIP** $14

B'Etor, 1995, 5", Playmates, #6928
NM $7 **MIP** $14

Captain James T. Kirk in spacesuit, 1995, 5", Playmates, #6930
NM $8 **MIP** $15

Captain Jean-Luc Picard, 1995, 5", Playmates, #6918
NM $5 **MIP** $10

Cmdr. Deanna Troi, 1995, 5", Playmates, #6920
NM $5 **MIP** $10

Dr. Beverly Crusher, 1995, 5", Playmates, #6924
NM $7 **MIP** $14

Dr. Soran, 1995, 5", Playmates, #6925
NM $6 **MIP** $12

Guinan, 1995, 5", Playmates, #6927
NM $7 **MIP** $14

Lt. Cmdr. Data, 1995, 5", Playmates, #6921
NM $5 **MIP** $10

Lt. Cmdr. Geordi LaForge, 1995, 5", Playmates, #6923
NM $7 **MIP** $14

Lt. Cmdr. William Riker, 1995, 5", Playmates, #6919 should be a Commander
NM $5 **MIP** $10

Lt. Cmdr. Worf, 1995, 5", Playmates, #6922
NM $5 **MIP** $10

Lt. Cmdr. Worf in 19th Century outfit, 1995, 5", Playmates, #6931
NM $6 **MIP** $12

Lursa, 1995, 5", Playmates, #6929
NM $7 **MIP** $14

Montgomery Scott, 1995, 5", Playmates, #6914
NM $12 **MIP** $25

Pavel A. Chekov, 1995, 5", Playmates, #6916
NM $12 **MIP** $25

9" FIGURES

Captain James T. Kirk, 1995, 9", Playmates, #6142
NM $20 **MIP** $40

Captain Jean-Luc Picard, 1995, 9", Playmates, #6141
NM $10 **MIP** $20

Lt. Cmdr. Data, 1995, 9", Playmates, #6143
NM $10 **MIP** $20

Lt. Cmdr. Geordi LaForge, 1995, 9", Playmates, #6144
NM $10 **MIP** $20

Star Trek: Insurrection (Playmates, 1998)

12" FIGURES

Captain Picard, 1998, 12", Playmates, #65071
NM $7 **MIP** $14

Data, 1998, 12", Playmates, #65074
NM $7 **MIP** $14

Geordi LaForge, 1998, 12", Playmates, #65504
NM $7 **MIP** $14

William Riker, 1998, 12", Playmates, #65072
NM $7 **MIP** $14

Worf, 1998, 12", Playmates, #65073
NM $7 **MIP** $14

9" FIGURES

Anji, 1998, 9", Playmates, #65358
NM $5 **MIP** $10

Counselor Troi, 1998, 9", Playmates, #65355
NM $8 **MIP** $15

Data, 1998, 9", Playmates, #65356
NM $8 **MIP** $15

Geordi LaForge, 1998, 9", Playmates, #65354
NM $8 **MIP** $15

Jean-Luc Picard, 1998, 9", Playmates, #65351
NM $8 **MIP** $15

Ru' Afo, 1998, 9", Playmates, #65357
NM $8 **MIP** $15

William Riker, 1998, 9", Playmates, #65352, clean shaven
NM $5 **MIP** $10

Worf, 1998, 9", Playmates, #65353
NM $8 **MIP** $15

Star Trek: Mixed Sets (Playmates, 1996-97)

SERIES 1

Captain Jean Luc Picard, 1996, 5", Playmates, #6442, "Tapestry," limited to 1701 figures
NM $150 **MIP** $300

Christine Chapel, 1996, 5", Playmates, #6447
NM $5 **MIP** $10

Cmdr. Benjamin Sisko, 1996, 5", Playmates, #6445, "Crossover"
NM $5 **MIP** $10

Grand Negus Zek, 1996, 5", Playmates, #6444
NM $5 **MIP** $10

Janice Rand, 1996, 5", Playmates, #6449
NM $5 **MIP** $10

Star Trek: Mixed Sets (Playmates, 1996-97)

Worf, Governor of H'Atoria, 1996, 5", Playmates, #6437, "All Good Things"
NM $5 **MIP** $10

SERIES 2

Admiral William Riker, 1996, 5", Playmates, #16034, "All Good Things"
NM $4 **MIP** $8

Captain Kirk, casual, 1996, 5", Playmates, #16031
NM $4 **MIP** $8

Jem Haddar, 1996, 5", Playmates, #16032
NM $4 **MIP** $8

Lt. Cmdr. Worf, 1996, 5", Playmates, #16033, DS9 Strategic Operations Officer
NM $4 **MIP** $8

Lt. Natasha Yar, 1996, 5", Playmates, #16043, "Yesterday's Enterprise," limited to 1701 figures
NM $75 **MIP** $160

Security Chief Odo, 1996, 5", Playmates, #6446, "Necessary Evil"
NM $5 **MIP** $10

SERIES 3

Captain Christopher Pike, 1996, 5", Playmates, #6448, "The Cage"
NM $5 **MIP** $10

Elim Garak, 1996, 5", Playmates, #16035, DS9 Tailor
NM $4 **MIP** $8

Lt. Reginald Barclay, 1996, 5", Playmates, #16044, "Projections," limited to 3000 figures
NM $60 **MIP** $100

Mr. Spock, 1996, 5", Playmates, #16038, "The Cage"
NM $5 **MIP** $10

Talosian Keeper, 1996, 5", Playmates, #16039, "The Cage"
NM $5 **MIP** $10

Vina, The Orion Slave Girl, 1996, 5", Playmates, #16040, "The Cage"
NM $20 **MIP** $40

SERIES 4

Captain Benjamin Sisko, 1997, 5", Playmates, #16021, bald head
NM $4 **MIP** $8

Captain Kurn, 1997, 5", Playmates, #16020, "Sons of Mogh"
NM $4 **MIP** $8

Dr. Beverly Crusher, 1997, 5", Playmates, #16047, movie "Generations," limited to 10,000 figures
NM $12 **MIP** $25

Gorn Captain, 1997, 5", Playmates, #16041, "Arena"
NM $7 **MIP** $15

Seska as Cardassian, 1997, 5", Playmates, #16022, ST:Voy "Maneuvers"
NM $4 **MIP** $8

Tom Paris Mutated, 1997, 5", Playmates, #16023, ST:Voy "Threshold"
NM $4 **MIP** $8

SERIES 5

Captain Kirk in Environmental Suit, 1997, 5", Playmates, #16048, "The Tholian Web"
NM $6 **MIP** $12

Dr. McCoy in dress uniform, 1997, 5", Playmates, #16155, "Journey to Babel," limited to 10,000 figures
NM $15 **MIP** $30

Harry Mudd, 1997, 5", Playmates, #16154, "I, Mudd" and "Mudd's Women"
NM $5 **MIP** $10

Professor Data, 1997, 5", Playmates, #16152, "All Good Things"
NM $5 **MIP** $10

The Mugatu, 1997, 5", Playmates, #16042, "A Private Little War"
NM $6 **MIP** $12

Star Trek: Space Talk Series (Playmates, 1995)

SPACE TALK SERIES

Borg, 1995, Playmates
NM $5 **MIP** $20

Picard, 1995, Playmates
NM $5 **MIP** $10

Q, 1995, Playmates
NM $5 **MIP** $20

Riker, 1995, Playmates
NM $5 **MIP** $10

Star Trek: Starfleet Academy (Playmates, 1996)

FIGURES

Cadet Geordi LaForge, 1996, 5", Playmates, #16004, radiation repair suit
NM $8 **MIP** $15

Cadet Jean-Luc Picard, 1996, 5", Playmates, #16001, flight training suit
NM $8 **MIP** $15

Cadet William Riker, 1996, 5", Playmates, #16002, geo-hazard suit
NM $8 **MIP** $15

Cadet Worf, 1996, 5", Playmates, #16005, night reconnaissance suit
NM $8 **MIP** $15

Star Trek: The Motion Picture (Mego, 1979-81)

12" BOXED FIGURES

Arcturian, 1979, 12", Mego
NM $40 **MIP** $125

Captain Kirk, 1979, 12", Mego
NM $40 **MIP** $75

Decker, 1979, 12", Mego
NM $45 **MIP** $115

Ilia, 1979, 12", Mego
NM $40 **MIP** $75

Klingon, 1979, 12", Mego
NM $40 **MIP** $125

Mr. Spock, 1979, 12", Mego
NM $40 **MIP** $75

3-3/4" CARDED FIGURES

Acturian, 1980, 3-3/4", Mego, Series 2, Light tan uniform
NM $75 **MIP** $150

Betelgeusian, 1980, 3-3/4", Mego, Series 2
NM $75 **MIP** $150

Captain Kirk, 1979, 3-3/4", Mego, Series 1
NM $12 **MIP** $35

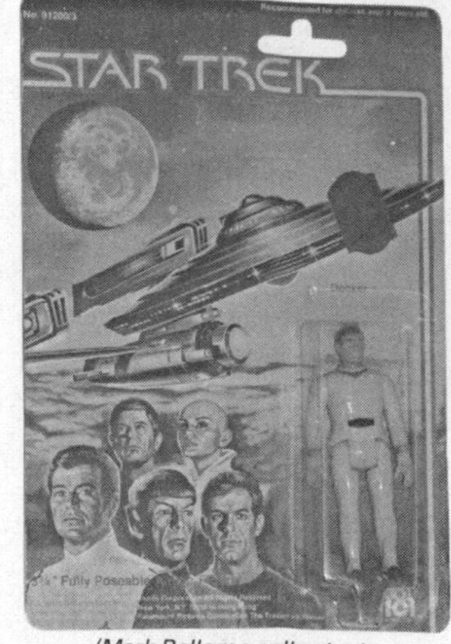

(Mark Bellomo collection)

Decker, 1979, 3-3/4", Mego, Series 1
NM $12 **MIP** $35

Dr. McCoy, 1979, 3-3/4", Mego, Series 1, White shirt, gray pants
NM $12 **MIP** $35

Ilia, 1979, 3-3/4", Mego, Series 1
NM $10 **MIP** $20

Klingon, 1980, 3-3/4", Mego, Series 2
NM $75 **MIP** $150

Megarite, 1980, 3-3/4", Mego, Series 2
NM $75 **MIP** $150

Mr. Spock, 1979, 3-3/4", Mego, Series 1, Dark gray uniform as seen in movie
NM $12 **MIP** $35

Rigellian, 1980, 3-3/4", Mego, Series 2
NM $75 **MIP** $150

Scotty, 1979, 3-3/4", Mego, Series 1
NM $12 **MIP** $35

Zatanite, 1980, 3-3/4", Mego, Series 2
NM $75 **MIP** $150

PLAY SETS

U.S.S. Enterprise Bridge, 1980, Mego
NM $45 **MIP** $105

Star Trek: The Next Generation (Galoob, 1988-89)

ACCESSORIES

Enterprise, 1989, Galoob, die-cast vehicle
NM $10 **MIP** $35

Ferengi Fighter, 1989, Galoob, vehicle
NM $15 **MIP** $50

Galileo Shuttle, 1989, Galoob, vehicle
NM $15 **MIP** $50

Phaser, 1989, Galoob, role playing toy
NM $20 **MIP** $40

SERIES 1 FIGURES

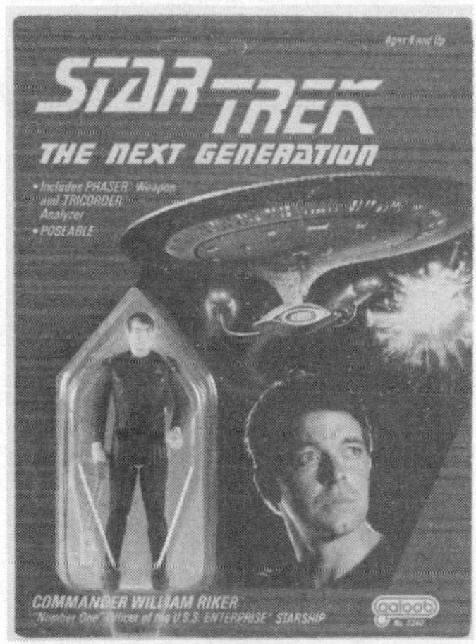

Commander William Riker, 1988, 3-3/4", Galoob, w/phaser and tricorder
NM $5 **MIP** $12

Data, blue face, 1988, 3-3/4", Galoob
NM $20 **MIP** $50

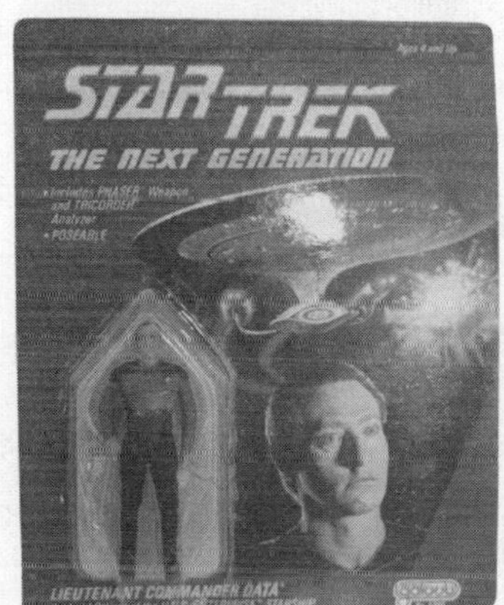

Data, brown face, 1988, 3-3/4", Galoob
NM $15 **MIP** $30

Data, flesh face, 1988, 3-3/4", Galoob
NM $8 **MIP** $20

Data, spotted face, 1988, 3-3/4", Galoob
NM $5 **MIP** $12

Geordi La Forge, 1988, 3-3/4", Galoob
NM $5 **MIP** $12

Jean-Luc Picard, 1988, 3-3/4", Galoob
NM $5 **MIP** $12

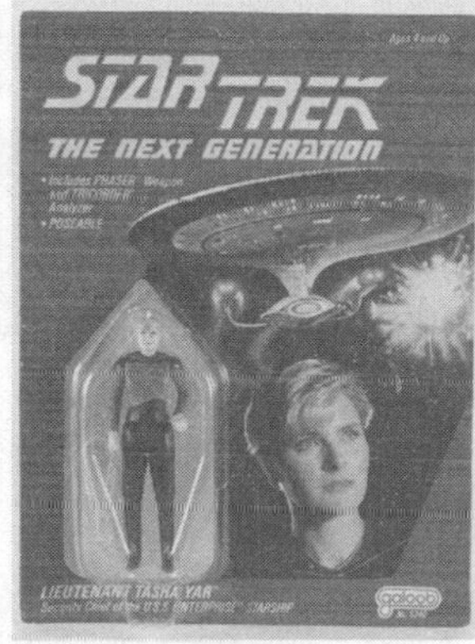

Lt. Tasha Yar, 1988, 3-3/4", Galoob, w/phaser and tricorder
NM $8 **MIP** $20

Lt. Worf, 1988, 3-3/4", Galoob
NM $5 **MIP** $12

SERIES 2 FIGURES

Antican, 1989, 3-3/4", Galoob
NM $25 **MIP** $65

Ferengi, 1989, 3-3/4", Galoob
NM $25 **MIP** $65

Q, 1989, 3-3/4", Galoob
NM $25 **MIP** $65

Selay, 1989, 3-3/4", Galoob
NM $25 **MIP** $65

Star Trek: The Next Generation (Playmates, 1992-97)

SERIES 1

Borg, 1992, 5", Playmates, #6055
NM $8 **MIP** $15

Captain Jean-Luc Picard, 1992, 5", Playmates, #6011
NM $8 **MIP** $15

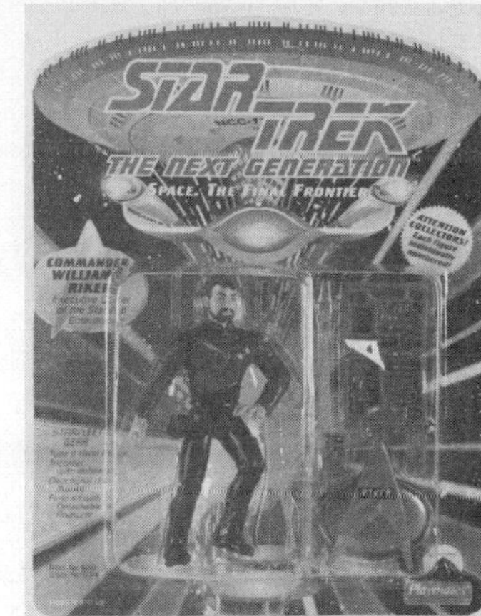

Commander Riker, 1992, 5", Playmates, #6014
NM $8 **MIP** $14

(Lenny Lee)

Counselor Deanna Troi, 1992, 5", Playmates, #6016
NM $8 **MIP** $15

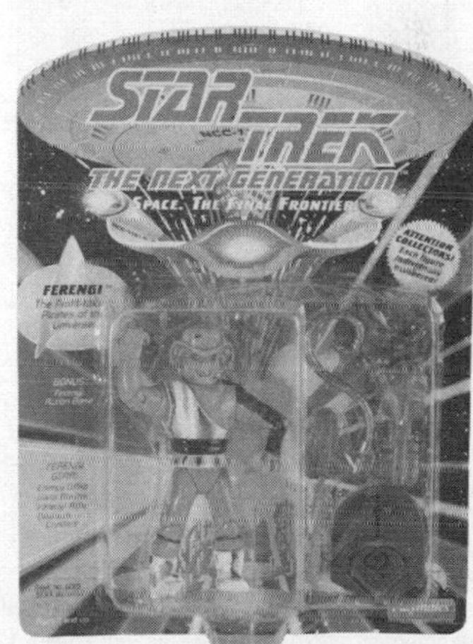

Ferengi, 1992, 5", Playmates, #6052
NM $8 **MIP** $15

Gowron the Klingon, 1992, 5", Playmates, #6053
NM $10 **MIP** $15

Star Trek: The Next Generation (Playmates, 1992-97)

Lt. Commander Data, 1992, 5", Playmates, #6012
NM $8 **MIP** $15

Lt. Commander Geordi LaForge, 1992, 5", Playmates, #6015
NM $8 **MIP** $15

Lt. Worf, 1992, 5", Playmates, #6013
NM $8 **MIP** $15

Romulan, 1992, 5", Playmates, #6051
NM $10 **MIP** $20

SERIES 2

Admiral McCoy, 1993, 5", Playmates, #6028, with card or space cap
NM $5 **MIP** $12

Ambassador Spock, 1993, 5", Playmates, #6027, with card or space cap
NM $5 **MIP** $12

Benzite, 1993, 5", Playmates, #6057, with card or space cap
NM $6 **MIP** $12

Borg, 1993, 5", Playmates, #6077, with card or space cap
NM $5 **MIP** $10

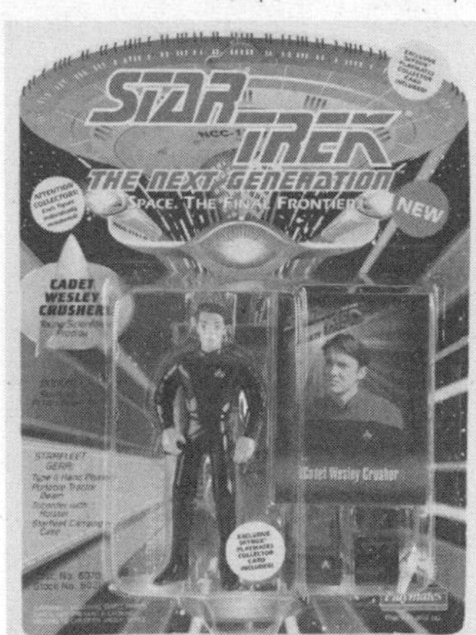

Cadet Wesley Crusher, 1993, 5", Playmates, #6021, with card or space cap
NM $8 **MIP** $15

Captain Jean-Luc Picard, 1993, 5", Playmates, #6071, with card or space cap
NM $6 **MIP** $12

Captain Scott (Scotty), 1993, 5", Playmates, #6029, with card or space cap
NM $5 **MIP** $10

Commander Sela, 1993, 5", Playmates, #6056, with card or space cap
NM $6 **MIP** $12

Commander William Riker, 1993, 5", Playmates, #6074, with card or space cap
NM $6 **MIP** $12

Counselor Deanna Troi, 1993, 5", Playmates, #6076, with card or space cap, second season uniform
NM $6 **MIP** $10

Dathon, 1993, 5", Playmates, #6060, with card or space cap
NM $7 **MIP** $15

Dr. Beverly Crusher, 1993, 5", Playmates, #6019, with card or space cap
NM $6 **MIP** $10

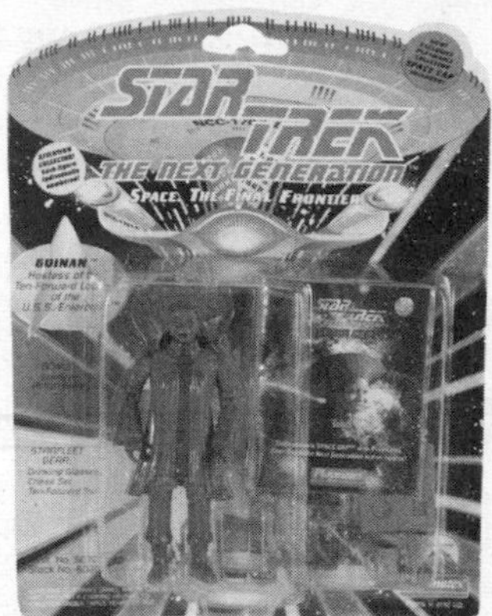

Guinan, 1993, 5", Playmates, #6020, with card or space cap
NM $7 **MIP** $12

K'Ehleyr, 1993, 5", Playmates, #6059, with card or space cap
NM $6 **MIP** $12

Klingon Warrior Worf, 1993, 5", Playmates, #6024, with card or space cap
NM $7 **MIP** $12

Locutus, 1993, 5", Playmates, #6023, with card or space cap
NM $6 **MIP** $10

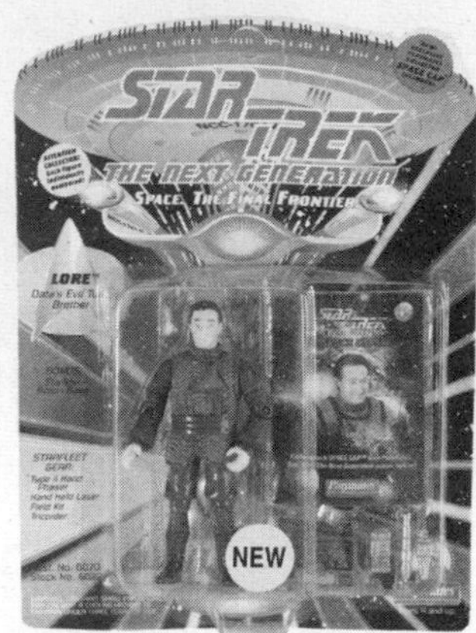

Lore, 1993, 5", Playmates, #6022, with card or space cap
NM $7 **MIP** $12

Lt. Cmdr. Geordi LaForge in Dress Uniform, 1993, 5", Playmates, #6026, with card or space cap
NM $7 **MIP** $15

Lt. Commander Data, 1993, 5", Playmates, #6072, with card or space cap
NM $6 **MIP** $10

Lt. Geordi LaForge, 1993, 5", Playmates, #6075, with card or space cap
NM $7 **MIP** $15

Lt. Worf, 1993, 5", Playmates, #6073, with card or space cap
NM $6 **MIP** $12

Q, red shirt, 1993, 5", Playmates, #6058, with card or space cap
NM $7 **MIP** $15

Vorgon, 1993, 5", Playmates, #6061, with card or space cap
NM $8 **MIP** $15

SERIES 3

Ambassador Sarek, 1994, 5", Playmates, #6042, Canadian release
NM $5 **MIP** $12

Captain Jean-Luc Picard as Dixon Hill, 1994, 5", Playmates, #6050
NM $5 **MIP** $12

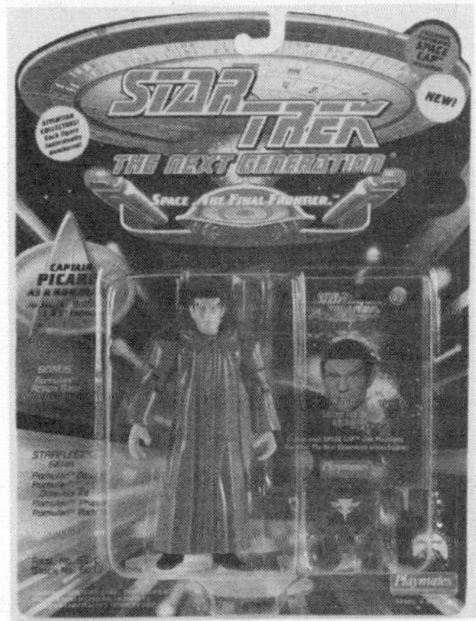

Captain Picard as Romulan, 1994, 5", Playmates, #6032
NM $3 **MIP** $12

Captain Picard, red duty uniform, 1994, 5", Playmates, #6942
NM $3 **MIP** $12

Commander Riker, Malcorian, 1994, 5", Playmates, #6034, 7th season episode
NM $3 **MIP** $12

Dr. Noonian Soong, 1994, 5", Playmates, #6038
NM $5 **MIP** $12

Ensign Ro, 1994, 5", Playmates, #6044
NM $8 **MIP** $15

Ensign Wesley Crusher, 1994, 5", Playmates, #6943
NM $5 **MIP** $12

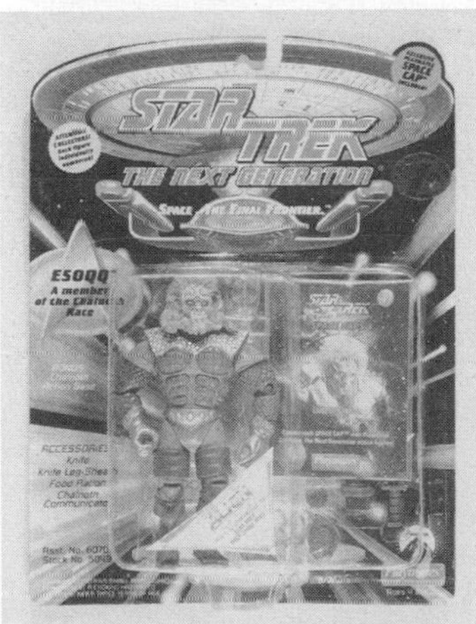

(Lenny Lee)

Esoqq, 1994, 5", Playmates, #6049, Fearsome-looking alien includes; knife, food ration, communicator, collector card
NM $12 **MIP** $30

Gowron in Ritual Klingon attire, 1994, 5", Playmates, #6945
NM $5 **MIP** $12

Hugh Borg, 1994, 5", Playmates, #6037
NM $5 **MIP** $12

Lt. Barclay, 1994, 5", Playmates, #6045
NM $5 **MIP** $12

Lt. Cmdr. Data as Romulan, 1994, 5", Playmates, #6031
NM $5 **MIP** $12

Lt. Cmdr. Data, dress uniform, 1994, 5", Playmates, #6941
NM $5 **MIP** $12

Lt. Cmdr. Data, red "Redemption" outfit, 1994, 5", Playmates, #6947, JC Penney exclusive, rare
NM $30 **MIP** $70

Lt. Cmdr. Deanna Troi, 1994, 5", Playmates, #6035, 6th season uniform, includes a stand, laptop computer, tricorder, PADD and accessories
NM $3 **MIP** $12

Lt. Cmdr. Geordi La Forge as Tarchannen III alien, 1994, 5", Playmates, #6033
NM $5 **MIP** $12

Lt. Thomas Riker, 1994, 5", Playmates, #6946
NM $12 **MIP** $30

Lt. Worf in Starfleet Rescue Outfit, 1994, 5", Playmates, #6036
NM $8 MIP $12

Lwaxana Troi, 1994, 5", Playmates, #6041, Canadian release
NM $3 MIP $12

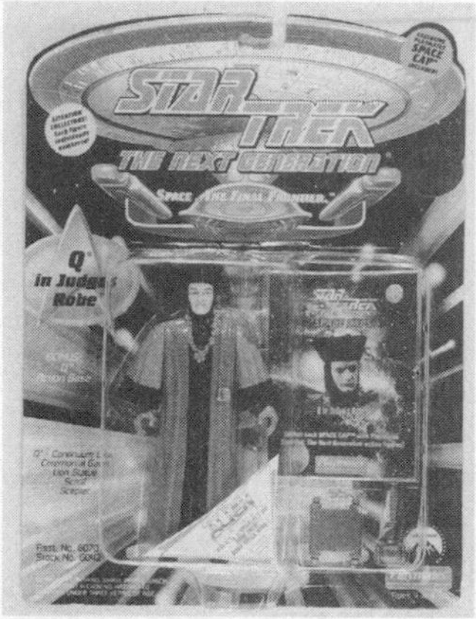

Q in Judge's Robe, 1993, 5", Playmates, #6042, Q as he appears in "Encounter at Farpoint," Next Gen's first episode, and "All Good Things," its last. Includes scroll, scepter, lion statue and gavel
NM $6 MIP $10

SERIES 4

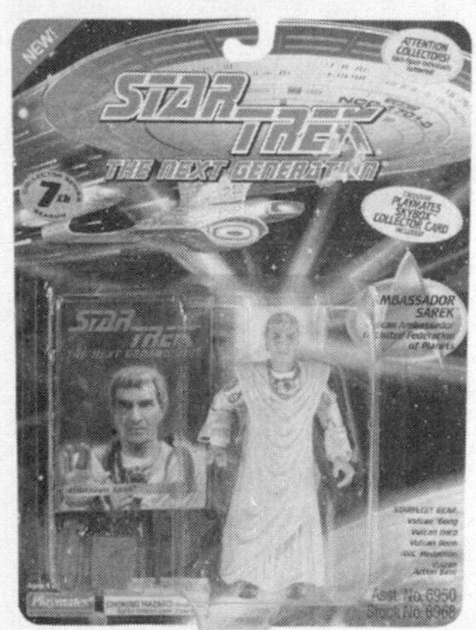

Ambassador Sarek, 1995, 5", Playmates, #6968
NM $5 MIP $10

Captain Jean-Luc Picard as Locutus, 1995, 5", Playmates, #6986, Supernova Series
NM $7 MIP $12

Captain Jean-Luc Picard in "All Good Things", 1995, 5", Playmates, #6974, Picard is older
NM $7 MIP $15

Dr. Beverly Crusher, duty uniform, 1994, 5", Playmates, #6961
NM $5 MIP $15

Dr. Noonian Soong, 1995, 5", Playmates, #6982
NM $5 MIP $10

Ensign Ro Laren, 1995, 5", Playmates, #6981
NM $5 MIP $10

Lt. Cmdr. Data in 1940s attire, 1995, 5", Playmates, #6979, Holodeck Series
NM $7 MIP $15

Lt. Cmdr. Data in movie uniform, 1995, 5", Playmates, #6962
NM $5 MIP $10

Lt. Cmdr. Geordi LaForge in movie uniform, 1995, 5", Playmates, #6960
NM $5 MIP $10

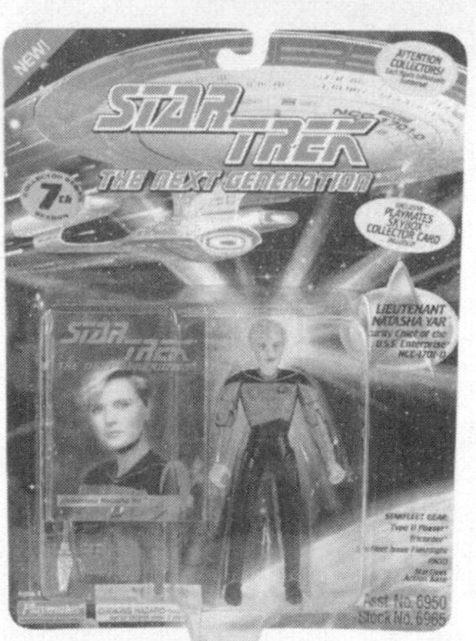

Lt. Natasha Yar, 1994, 5", Playmates, #6965
NM $5 MIP $15

Lt. Worf in Ritual Klingon attire, 1995, 5", Playmates, #6985, Supernova Series
NM $5 MIP $10

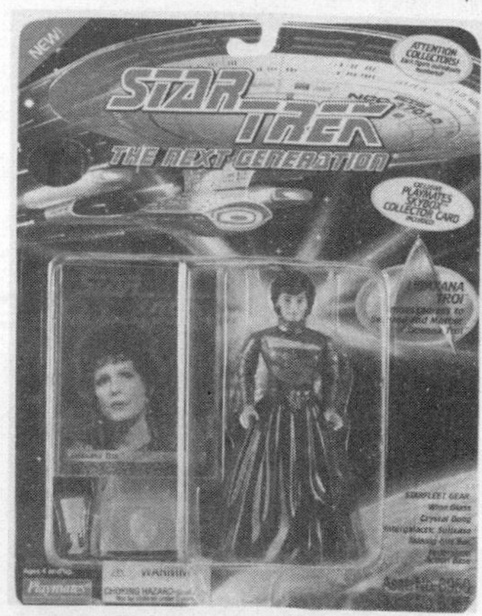

Lwaxana Troi, 1995, 5", Playmates, #6967, 7th Season
NM $5 MIP $10

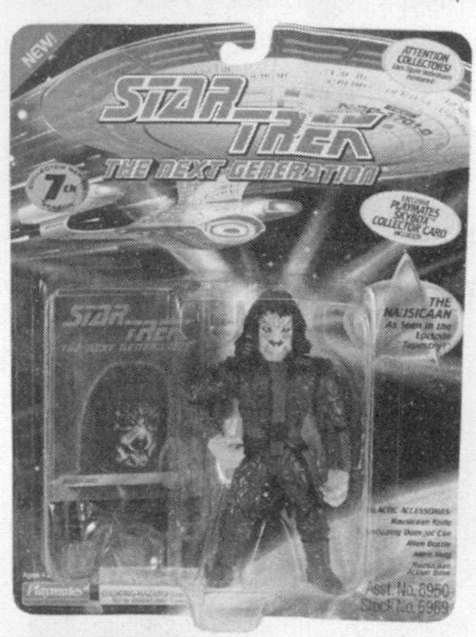

Nausicaan, 1994, 5", Playmates, #6969, "Tapestry"
NM $5 MIP $15

SERIES 5

Borg, 1995, 5", Playmates, #6441, Interstellar Action Series
NM $7 MIP $15

Captain Picard, 1995, 5", Playmates, #6442, "Tapestry" One of the show's finest episodes, Picard discovers what his world would have been like if he had been less reckless in his youth. Only 1701 produced.
NM $200 MIP $350

Commander Benjamin Sisko, 1995, 5", Playmates, #6445, "Crossover"
NM $5 MIP $11

Counselor Troi as Durango, 1995, 5", Playmates, #6438, "A Fist Full of Datas"
NM $5 MIP $10

Dr. Beverly Crusher in 1940s attire, 1995, 5", Playmates, #6435, "The Big Goodbye"
NM $5 MIP $10

Dr. Katherine Pulaski, 1995, 5", Playmates, #6428
NM $5 **MIP** $10

Geordi LaForge, 1995, 5", Playmates, #6433, "All Good Things"
NM $7 **MIP** $12

Governor Worf of H'Atoria, 1995, 5", Playmates, #6437, "All Good Things"
NM $5 **MIP** $10

Grand Nagus Zek, 1995, 5", Playmates, #6444
NM $5 **MIP** $10

Lt. Geordi LaForge, 1995, 5", Playmates, #6443, Interstellar Action Series
NM $7 **MIP** $15

Lt. Jadzia Dax, 1995, 5", Playmates, #6440, "Blood Oath" in ritual Klingon attire
NM $5 **MIP** $10

Picard as Galen, 1995, 5", Playmates, #6432, "The Gambit"
NM $5 **MIP** $10

Sheriff Worf, 1995, 5", Playmates, #6434, "A Fist Full of Datas"
NM $7 **MIP** $12

The Hunter of Tosk, 1995, 5", Playmates, #6439
NM $5 **MIP** $10

The Traveler, 1995, 5", Playmates, #6436
NM $5 **MIP** $10

Vash, 1995, 5", Playmates, #6429
NM $5 **MIP** $10

SERIES 6

Admiral William T. Riker, 1996, 5", Playmates, #16034, "All Good Things"
NM $5 **MIP** $12

Captain Christopher Pike, 1996, 5", Playmates, #6448, "The Cage"
NM $6 **MIP** $12

Captain James T. Kirk, 1996, 5", Playmates, #16031, in casual attire, green shirt
NM $6 **MIP** $12

Elim Garak, 1996, 5", Playmates, #16035
NM $10 **MIP** $20

Jem'Hadar, 1996, 5", Playmates, #16032
NM $6 **MIP** $12

Lt. Commander Worf, 1996, 5", Playmates, #16033, in DS9 uniform
NM $5 **MIP** $10

Lt. Natasha Yar, 1996, 5", Playmates, #16043, "Yesterday's Enterprise" Another great episode. Only 1701 produced.
NM $150 **MIP** $300

Lt. Reginald Barclay, 1996, 5", Playmates, #16044, ST:VOY "Projections" Only 3,000 produced.
NM $5 **MIP** $10

Mr. Spock, 1996, 5", Playmates, #16038, "The Cage"
NM $7 **MIP** $14

Nurse Christine Chapel, 1996, 5", Playmates, #6447
NM $15 **MIP** $25

Security Chief Odo, 1996, 5", Playmates, #6446, "Necessary Evil"
NM $5 **MIP** $10

The Talosian Keeper, 1996, 5", Playmates, #16039, "The Cage"
NM $7 **MIP** $14

Vina the Orion Animal Woman, 1996, 5", Playmates, #16040, "The Cage"
NM $7 **MIP** $14

Yeoman Janice Rand, 1996, 5", Playmates, #6449
NM $6 **MIP** $12

SERIES 7

Beverly Crusher, 1997, 5", Playmates, #16047, as seen in Star Trek:Generations
NM $5 **MIP** $10

Captain Benjamin Sisko, 1997, 5", Playmates, #16021, bald w/goatee
NM $5 **MIP** $10

Captain Kirk in Environmental Suit, 1997, 5", Playmates, #16048, "The Tholian Web"
NM $7 **MIP** $14

Captain Kurn, 1997, 5", Playmates, #16020, ST:DS9 "Sons of Mogh"
NM $5 **MIP** $10

Dr. McCoy in Dress Uniform, 1997, 5", Playmates, #16155, "Journey to Babel"
NM $15 **MIP** $25

Gorn Captain, 1997, 5", Playmates, #16041, "Arena" one of the best opponents Capt. Kirk ever faced
NM $10 **MIP** $20

Harry Mudd, 1997, 5", Playmates, #16154, "Mudd's Women," and "I, Mudd"
NM $5 **MIP** $10

Professor Data, 1997, 5", Playmates, #16152, "All Good Things" Nice hair, Data!
NM $5 **MIP** $10

Seska as a Cardassian, 1997, 5", Playmates, #16022, ST:VOY "Maneuvers"
NM $4 **MIP** $8

The Mugato, 1997, 5", Playmates, #16042, "A Private Little War"
NM $4 **MIP** $8

Tom Paris Mutated, 1997, 5", Playmates, #16023, ST:VOY "Maneuvers"
NM $4 **MIP** $8

ACTION FIGURES

Star Trek: Transporter Series (Playmates, 1997)

EXCLUSIVES

Ensign Pavel Checkov, 1998, 6", Playmates, #65231, Target exclusive
NM $10 MIP $15

Lt. Hikaru Sulu, 1998, 6", Playmates, #65232, Target exclusive
NM $10 MIP $15

Nurse Christine Chapel, 1998, 6", Playmates, #65441, Target exclusive
NM $10 MIP $15

Yeoman Janice Rand, 1998, 6", Playmates, #65442, Target exclusive
NM $10 MIP $15

SERIES 1

Captain James T. Kirk, 1998, 6", Playmates, #65401, yellow shirt
NM $10 MIP $15

Dr. McCoy, 1998, 6", Playmates, #65403
NM $10 MIP $15

Lt. Scott, 1998, 6", Playmates, #65405
NM $10 MIP $15

Lt. Uhura, 1998, 6", Playmates, #65404
NM $10 MIP $15

Mr. Spock, 1998, 6", Playmates, #65402
NM $10 MIP $15

SERIES 2

Captain Jean Luc Picard, 1998, 6", Playmates, #65422
NM $10 MIP $15

Cmdr. William T. Riker, 1998, 6", Playmates, #65432
NM $10 MIP $15

Lt. Cmdr. Data, 1998, 6", Playmates, #65421
NM $10 MIP $15

Lt. Cmdr. Geordi LaForge, 1998, 6", Playmates, #65433
NM $10 MIP $15

Lt. Worf, 1998, 6", Playmates, #65423
NM $10 MIP $15

Star Trek: Voyager (Playmates, 1995-96)

SERIES 1

Captain Kathryn Janeway, 1996, 5", Playmates, #6481
NM $8 MIP $15

Cmdr. Chakotay, 1996, 5", Playmates, #6482
NM $5 MIP $10

Doctor, 1996, 5", Playmates, #6486
NM $8 MIP $15

En. Harry Kim, 1996, 5", Playmates, #6484
NM $8 MIP $15

Kes the Ocampa, 1996, 5", Playmates, #6488
NM $7 MIP $15

Lt. B'Elanna Torres, 1996, 5", Playmates, #6485
NM $7 MIP $15

Lt. Tom Paris, 1996, 5", Playmates, #6483
NM $5 MIP $10

Lt. Tuvok, 1996, 5", Playmates, #6487
NM $5 MIP $10

Neelix the Telaxian, 1996, 5", Playmates, #6489
NM $5 MIP $10

SERIES 2

Chakotay the Maquis, 1996, 5", Playmates, #16466
NM $8 MIP $15

En. Seska, 1996, 5", Playmates, #16460
NM $5 MIP $10

Kazon, 1996, 5", Playmates, #16462
NM $5 MIP $10

Lt. Carey, 1995, 5", Playmates, #16461
NM $7 MIP $15

Torres as Klingon, 1995, 5", Playmates, #16465
NM $7 MIP $15

Vidiian, 1995, 5", Playmates, #16463
NM $7 MIP $15

VEHICLES

U.S.S. Voyager, 1995, Playmates, #6479
NM $15 MIP $30

Star Trek: Warp Factor (Playmates, 1997-98)

COMBAT ACTION SERIES 1

Borg, 1997, 6", Playmates, #16234, spring-firing arm
NM $5 MIP $10

Captain Jean-Luc Picard, 1997, 6", Playmates, #16251, fencing action
NM $5 MIP $10

Cmdr. William T. Riker, 1997, 6", Playmates, #16252, phaser drawing action
NM $5 MIP $10

Lt. Cmdr. Worf, 1997, 6", Playmates, #16253, bat'leth slashing action
NM $5 MIP $10

Q, 1997, 6", Playmates, #16255, fencing action
NM $5 MIP $10

COMBAT ACTION SERIES 2

Captain Benjamin Sisko, 1998, 6", Playmates, #16258
NM $5 MIP $10

Cardassian Soldier, 1998, 6", Playmates, #16256
NM $5 MIP $10

Chief Miles O'Brien, 1998, 6", Playmates, #16266
NM $5 MIP $10

Jem'Hadar Soldier, 1998, 6", Playmates, #16257
NM $5 MIP $10

Lt. Cmdr. Jadzia Dax, 1998, 6", Playmates, #16260
NM $5 MIP $10

SERIES 1

Captain Benjamin Sisko, 1997, 5", Playmates, #65107, DS9 "Trials and Tribbleations"
NM $7 MIP $14

Captain Koloth, 1997, 5", Playmates, #65111, DS9 "Trials and Tribbleations"
NM $5 MIP $10

Chief Miles O'Brien, 1997, 5", Playmates, #65106, DS9 "Trials and Tribbleations," limited to 10,000
NM $12 MIP $25

Constable Odo, 1997, 5", Playmates, #65109, DS9 "Trials and Tribbleations"
NM $5 MIP $10

Dr. Julian Bashir, 1997, 5", Playmates, #65110, DS9 "Trials and Tribbleations"
NM $7 MIP $14

Lt. Cmdr. Jadzia Dax, 1997, 5", Playmates, #65108, DS9 "Trials and Tribbleations"
NM $7 MIP $14

SERIES 2

Captain Beverly Picard, 1997, 5", Playmates, #65112, "All Good Things"
NM $5 MIP $10

Ilia Probe, 1997, 5", Playmates, #65102, ST:TMP
NM $5 MIP $10

Leeta the Dabo Girl, 1997, 5", Playmates, #65102, DS9
NM $5 MIP $10

Sisko as a Klingon, 1997, 5", Playmates, #65101, DS9 "Apocalypse Rising"
NM $4 MIP $8

Swarm Alien, 1997, 5", Playmates, #65104, ST:YOY "The Swarm"
NM $5 MIP $10

SERIES 3

Cadet Beverly Howard Crusher, 1997, 5", Playmates, #65117
NM $4 MIP $8

Cadet Data, 1997, 5", Playmates, #65116
NM $4 MIP $8

Cadet Deanna Troi, 1997, 5", Playmates, #65115
NM $4 MIP $8

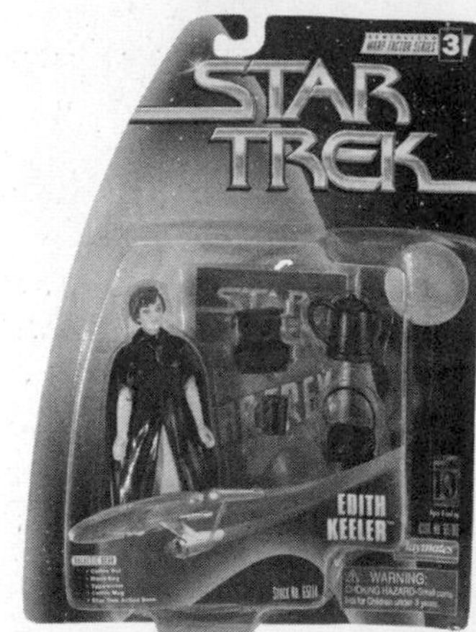

Edith Keeler, 1997, 5", Playmates, #65114, "City on the Edge of Forever"
NM $4 MIP $8

Mr. Spock, 1997, 5", Playmates, #65105, "Mirror, Mirror"
NM $5 MIP $10

SERIES 4

Andorian, 1998, 5", Playmates, #65120, "Whom Gods Destroy"
NM $4 MIP $8

Intendant Kira, 1998, 5", Playmates, #65124, DS9 "Crossover"
NM $4 MIP $8

Kang, 1998, 5", Playmates, #65123, DS9 "Blood Oath"
NM $4 MIP $8

Keiko O'Brien, 1998, 5", Playmates, #65121
NM $4 MIP $8

Trelane, 1998, 5", Playmates, #65122, "The Squire of Gothos"
NM $4 MIP $8

SERIES 5

Borg Queen, 1998, 5", Playmates, #65130, ST:FC
NM $5 MIP $10

James Kirk, 1998, 5", Playmates, #65128, "City on the Edge of Forever"
NM $5 MIP $10

Mr. Spock, 1998, 5", Playmates, #65129, "City on the Edge of Forever"
NM $5 MIP $10

Seven of Nine, 1998, 5", Playmates, #65131, ST:VOY "The Gift"
NM $5 MIP $10

Stargate (Hasbro, 1994)

FIGURES

Anubis, 1998, Hasbro
NM $2 MIP $4

(Lenny Lee)

Col. O'Neil, 1998, Hasbro, Group shot
NM $2 MIP $4

Daniel Jackson, 1994, Hasbro
NM $2 MIP $5

Horus, Attack Pilot, 1998, Hasbro
NM $2 MIP $4

Horus, Palace Guard, 1998, Hasbro
NM $2 MIP $4

Lt. Kawalsky, 1998, Hasbro
NM $2 MIP $4

Ra, 1998, Hasbro
NM $2 MIP $4

Skaara, 1998, Hasbro
NM $2 MIP $4

Starsky and Hutch (Mego, 1976)

FIGURES

Captain Dobey, 1976, 8", Mego
NM $25 MIP $50

Chopper, 1976, 8", Mego, In cable-knit sweater and dark pants
NM $25 MIP $45

Huggy Bear, 1976, 8", Mego
NM $25 MIP $60

Hutch, 1976, 8", Mego
NM $25 MIP $55

Starsky, 1976, 8", Mego
NM $25 MIP $55

VEHICLES

Car, 1976, Mego
NM $85 MIP $195

Strawberry Shortcake (Kenner, 1979-85)

SERIES 1

Apple Dumplin' and Tea Time Turtle, Kenner
NM $20 MIP $40

Apricot and Hopsalot, Kenner
NM $20 MIP $45

Blueberry Muffin, Kenner
NM $20 MIP $40

Huckleberry Pie, Kenner
NM $20 MIP $55

Lemon Meringue, Kenner
NM $20 MIP $40

Orange Blossom, Kenner
NM $20 MIP $40

Purple Pieman and Cackle, Kenner
NM $20 MIP $40

Raspberry Tart, Kenner
NM $20 MIP $40

Strawberry Shortcake, Kenner
NM $20 MIP $70

SERIES 2

Almond Tea and Marza Panda, Kenner
NM $25 MIP $50

Angel Cake and Souffl'e, Kenner
NM $20 MIP $40

Apple Dumplin' and Tea Time Turtle, Kenner
NM $20 MIP $40

Apricot and Hopsalot, Kenner
NM $20 MIP $40

Blueberry Muffin and Cheesecake, Kenner
NM $30 MIP $55

Butter Cookie and Jelly Bear, Kenner
NM $15 MIP $35

Café Ole' and Burrito, Kenner
NM $30 MIP $50

Cherry Cuddler and Gooseberry, Kenner
NM $20 MIP $30

Crepe Suzette and Éclair, Kenner
NM $35 MIP $50

Huckleberry pie and Pupcake, Kenner
NM $25 MIP $45

Lem n' Ada and Sugarwoofer, Kenner
NM $35 MIP $50

Lemon Meringue and Frappe, Kenner
NM $30 MIP $45

Lime Chiffon and Parfait, Kenner
NM $25 MIP $40

Mint Tulip and Marsh Mallard, Kenner
NM $35 MIP $50

Orange Blossom and Marmalade, Kenner
NM $20 MIP $35

Purple Pieman and Cackle, Kenner
NM $20 MIP $40

Raspberry Tart and Rhubarb Doll, Kenner
NM $20 MIP $45

Sour Grapes and Dregs the Snake, Kenner
NM $20 MIP $50

Strawberry Shortcake and Custard, Kenner
NM $25 MIP $40

SERIES 3

Almond Tea and Marza Panda Doll, Kenner, Party Pleasers
NM $65 MIP $100

Angel Cake and Souffl'e, Kenner, Party Pleasers
NM $65 MIP $100

Apple Dumplin' and Tea Time Turtle, Kenner, Party Pleasers
NM $65 MIP $100

Café O'le and Burrito, Kenner, Party Pleasers
NM $50 MIP $90

Cherry Cuddler and Gooseberry, Kenner, Party Pleasers
NM $100 MIP $150

Mint Tulip and Marsh Mallard, Kenner, Party Pleasers
NM $120 MIP $165

Orange Blossom and Marmalade, Kenner, Party Pleasers
NM $65 MIP $100

Peach Blush and Melonie Belle, Kenner, Party Pleasers
NM $110 MIP $150

Plum Puddin' and Elderberry Owl, Kenner, Party Pleasers
NM $135 MIP $210

Strawberry Shortcake and Custard, Kenner, Party Pleasers
NM $50 MIP $85

SERIES 4

Banana Twirl, Kenner, Berrykins
NM $350 MIP $500

Mint Tulip, Kenner, Berrykins
NM $350 MIP $525

Orange Blossom, Kenner, Berrykins
NM $325 MIP $425

Peach Blush, Kenner, Berrykins
NM $375 MIP $500

Plum Puddin', Kenner, Berrykins
NM $300 MIP $425

Strawberry Shortcake, Kenner, Berrykins
NM $300 MIP $400

Street Fighter (Hasbro, 1994)

12" FIGURES

Blanka, 1994, 12", Hasbro
NM $15 **MIP** $25

Colonel Guile, 1994, 12", Hasbro
NM $15 **MIP** $25

General Bison, 1994, 12", Hasbro
NM $15 **MIP** $25

Ryu Hoshi, 1994, 12", Hasbro
NM $15 **MIP** $25

Super Hero Bend 'n Flex (Mego, 1974-75)

5" FIGURES

Aquaman, 1974-75, 5", Mego
NM $30 **MIP** $120

Batgirl, 1974-75, 5", Mego
NM $50 **MIP** $120

Batman, 1974-75, 5", Mego
NM $35 **MIP** $90

Captain America, 1974-75, 5", Mego
NM $35 **MIP** $90

Catwoman, 1974-75, 5", Mego
NM $70 **MIP** $175

Joker, 1974-75, 5", Mego
NM $40 **MIP** $150

Mr. Mxyzptlk, 1974-75, 5", Mego
NM $40 **MIP** $125

Penguin, 1974-75, 5", Mego
NM $40 **MIP** $150

Riddler, 1974-75, 5", Mego
NM $60 **MIP** $150

Robin, 1974-75, 5", Mego
NM $30 **MIP** $75

Shazam, 1974-75, 5", Mego
NM $50 **MIP** $125

Spider-Man, 1974-75, 5", Mego
NM $50 **MIP** $125

Supergirl, 1974-75, 5", Mego
NM $70 **MIP** $175

Superman, 1974-75, 5", Mego
NM $30 **MIP** $75

Tarzan, 1974-75, 5", Mego
NM $25 **MIP** $60

Wonder Woman, 1974-75, 5", Mego
NM $50 **MIP** $100

ACCESSORIES

Carry Case, 1974-75, 5", Mego, red vinyl case w/ red plastic handle, "World's Greatest Super Heroes" logo
NM $40 **MIP** $85

Super Powers (Kenner, 1984-86)

5" FIGURES

Aquaman, 1984, 5", Kenner
NM $10 **MIP** $60

Batman, 1984, 5", Kenner
NM $50 **MIP** $110

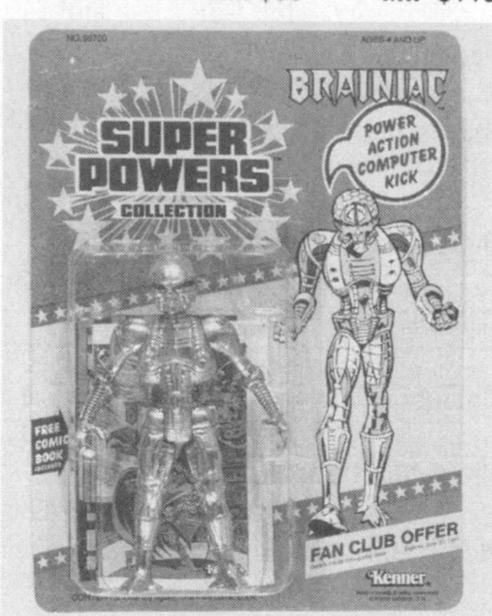

(Lenny Lee)

Braniac, 1984, 5", Kenner, chrome plastic figure, includes free mini comic book
NM $15 **MIP** $32

Clark Kent, mail-in figure, 1986, 5", Kenner
NM $30 **MIP** $55

Cyborg, 1986, 5", Kenner
NM $150 **MIP** $290

Cyclotron, 1986, 5", Kenner
NM $20 **MIP** $50

Darkseid, 1985, 5", Kenner, gray and blue figure with "Power Action Raging Motion"
NM $8 **MIP** $18

Desaad, 1985, 5", Kenner
NM $10 **MIP** $25

Dr. Fate, 1985, 5", Kenner
NM $22 **MIP** $60

Firestorm, 1985, 5", Kenner
NM $12 **MIP** $35

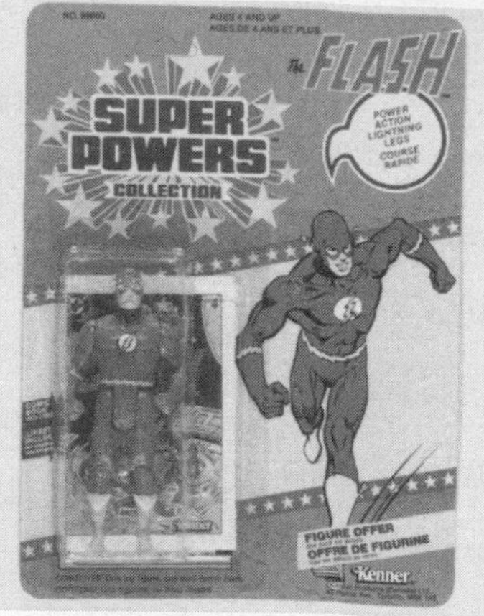

(Lenny Lee)

Flash, 1984, 5", Kenner, figure has power action legs that simulate the Flash's lightning-speed running style
NM $8 **MIP** $20

Golden Pharaoh, 1986, 5", Kenner
NM $35 **MIP** $75

Green Arrow, 1985, 5", Kenner, with bow
NM $40 **MIP** $65

Green Lantern, 1984, 5", Kenner, with lantern
NM $25 **MIP** $60

Hawkman, 1984, 5", Kenner
NM $22 **MIP** $60

Joker, 1984, 5", Kenner
NM $10 **MIP** $25

Kalibak, 1985, 5", Kenner
NM $10 **MIP** $25

(Lenny Lee)

Lex Luthor, 1984, 5", Kenner, has "Power Action Nuclear Punch"
NM $6 **MIP** $15

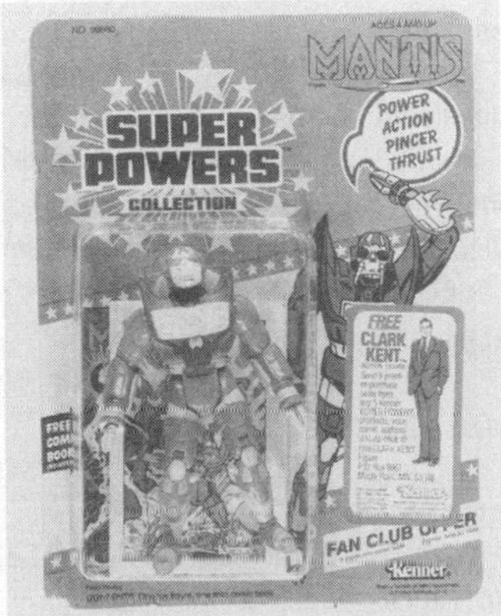

(Lenny Lee)

Mantis, 1985, 5", Kenner, figure has "Power Action Pincer Thrust" and includes a free comic book
NM $10 **MIP** $25

Martian Manhunter, 1985, 5", Kenner
NM $15 **MIP** $45

Mister Miracle, 1986, 5", Kenner
NM $60 **MIP** $130

Mr. Freeze, 1986, 5", Kenner
NM $25 **MIP** $65

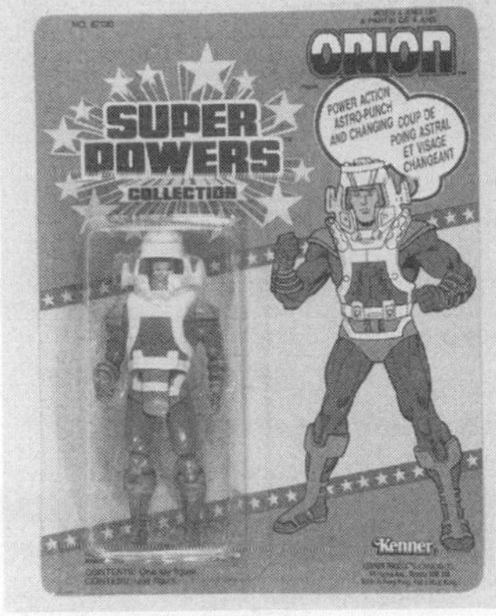

(Lenny Lee)

Orion, 1986, 5", Kenner, with "Power Action Astro Punch"
NM $15 **MIP** $35

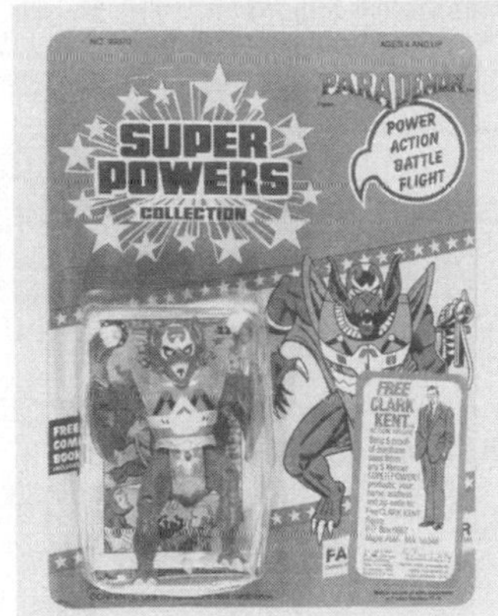

(Lenny Lee)

Parademon, 1985, 5", Kenner, includes mini-comic book
NM $15 **MIP** $28

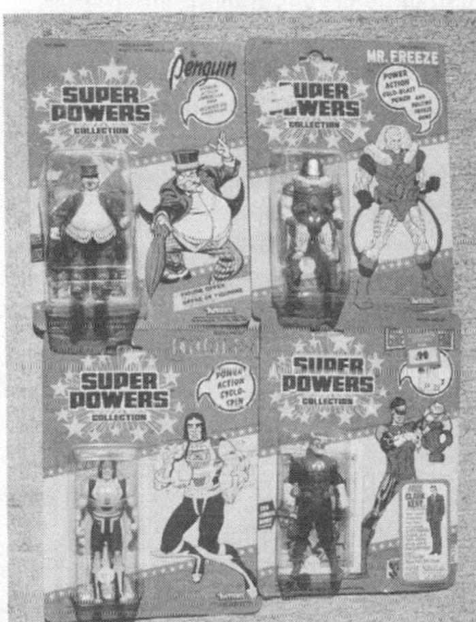

(Lenny Lee)

Penguin, 1984, 5", Kenner
NM $15 **MIP** $50

(Lenny Lee)

Plastic Man, 1986, 5", Kenner
NM $40 **MIP** $100

Red Tornado, 1985, 5", Kenner
NM $25 **MIP** $50

Robin, 1984, 5", Kenner
NM $12 **MIP** $50

Samurai, 1986, 5", Kenner
NM $55 **MIP** $90

Shazam (Captain Marvel), 1986, 5", Kenner, bright-colored figure, very "cartoony" look
NM $55 **MIP** $120

Steppenwolf, in mail-in bag, 1985, 5", Kenner
NM $8 **MIP** $18

Steppenwolf, on card, 1985, 5", Kenner
NM $8 **MIP** $80

Superman, 1984, 5", Kenner
NM $22 **MIP** $50

Tyr, 1986, 5", Kenner, with yellow attached "Power Action Rocket Launcher"
NM $20 **MIP** $50

(Lenny Lee)

Wonder Woman, 1981, 5", Kenner
NM $22 **MIP** $60

ACCESSORIES

Collector's Case, 1984, Kenner, 11-1/4" x 10" x 3-3/4"
NM $20 **MIP** $40

PLAY SETS

Hall of Justice, 1984, Kenner
NM $110 **MIP** $210

VEHICLES

Batcopter, 1986, Kenner
NM $55 **MIP** $150

Super Powers (Kenner, 1984-86)

Batmobile, 1984, Kenner
NM $50 **MIP** $150

Darkseid Destroyer, 1985, Kenner
NM $25 **MIP** $50

Delta Probe One, 1985, Kenner
NM $15 **MIP** $30

Justice Jogger, wind-up, 1986, Kenner
NM $12 **MIP** $30

Kalibak Boulder Bomber, 1985, Kenner
NM $10 **MIP** $25

Lex-Soar 7, 1984, Kenner
NM $10 **MIP** $25

Supermobile, 1984, Kenner
NM $20 **MIP** $45

Superman: Man of Steel (Kenner, 1995-96)

FIGURES

Blast Hammer Steel, 1995, 5", Kenner, Deluxe
NM $5 **MIP** $10

Conduit, 1995, 5", Kenner
NM $4 **MIP** $8

Laser Superman, 1995, 5", Kenner
NM $4 **MIP** $8

Lex Luthor, 1995, 5", Kenner
NM $15 **MIP** $20

Power Flight Superman, 1995, 5", Kenner
NM $4 **MIP** $8

Solar Suit Superman, 1995, 5", Kenner
NM $5 **MIP** $10

Steel, 1995, 5", Kenner
NM $4 **MIP** $8

Street Guardian Superman, 1995, 5", Kenner
NM $4 **MIP** $8

Superboy, 1995, 5", Kenner
NM $5 **MIP** $10

Ultra Heat Vision Superman, 1995, 5", Kenner
NM $5 **MIP** $10

Ultra Shield Superman, 1995, 5", Kenner
NM $4 **MIP** $8

MULTI-PACKS

Cyber-Link Superman & Cyber-Link Batman, 1995, 5", Kenner, Wal-Mart exclusive
NM $10 **MIP** $20

Hunter-Prey Superman v. Doomsday, 1995, 5", Kenner
NM $6 **MIP** $12

Superman v. Massacre, 1995, 5", Kenner
NM $6 **MIP** $12

VEHICLES

Kryptonian Battle Suit, 1995, Kenner
NM $10 **MIP** $20

Superboy VTOL Cycle, 1995, Kenner
NM $7 **MIP** $15

Superman Matrix Conversion Coupe, 1995, Kenner, Silver w/ Clark Kent
NM $10 **MIP** $20

Superman: The Animated Series (Kenner, 1995-96)

FIGURES

Anti-Kryptonite Superman, 1995, 5", Kenner, Series 3
NM $6 **MIP** $12

Brainiac, 1995, 5", Kenner, Series 1
NM $5 **MIP** $10

Capture Claw Superman, 1995, 5", Kenner, Series 2
NM $7 **MIP** $15

Capture Net Superman, 1995, 5", Kenner, Series 1
NM $5 **MIP** $10

City Camo Superman, 1995, 5", Kenner, Deluxe
NM $6 **MIP** $12

Cyber Crunch Superman, 1996, 5", Kenner, European release
NM $10 **MIP** $20

Darkseid, 1995, 5", Kenner, Series 2
NM $15 **MIP** $30

Deep Dive Superman, 1995, 5", Kenner, Series 1
NM $5 **MIP** $10

Electro Energy Superman, 1995, 5", Kenner, Series 2
NM $7 **MIP** $15

Evil Bizzaro, 1995, 5", Kenner, Series 3
NM $15 **MIP** $30

Flying Superman, 1995, 5", Kenner, Deluxe, a glider
NM $6 **MIP** $12

Fortress of Solitude Superman, 1995, 5", Kenner
NM $10 **MIP** $20

Kryptonite Escape Superman, 1995, 5", Kenner, Deluxe
NM $7 **MIP** $15

Lex Luthor, 1995, 5", Kenner, Series 1
NM $6 **MIP** $12

Metallo, 1995, 5", Kenner, Series 3, Diamond
NM $10 **MIP** $20

Mission Masters 3: Quick Change Superman, 1999, 5", Hasbro, Wal-Mart exclusive
NM $7 **MIP** $15

Neutron Star Superman, 1995, 5", Kenner, Series 1
NM $50 **MIP** $10

Power Swing Superman, 1995, 5", Kenner, Series 3
NM $8 **MIP** $16

Quick Change Superman, 1995, 5", Kenner, Series 1
NM $5 **MIP** $10

Strong Arm Superman, 1995, 5", Kenner, Series 3
NM $6 **MIP** $12

Supergirl, 1995, 5", Kenner, Series 3, Diamond
NM $7 **MIP** $14

Tornado Force Superman, 1995, 5", Kenner, Series 3
NM $8 **MIP** $16

Ultra Shield Superman, 1995, 5", Kenner
NM $5 **MIP** $10

Vision Blast Superman, 1995, 5", Kenner, Deluxe
NM $7 **MIP** $15

X-Ray Vision Superman, 1995, 5", Kenner
NM $5 **MIP** $10

MULTI-PACKS

Battle for Metropolis, 1999, 5", Kenner, Toys R Us exclusive, Superman, Lois Lane, Lex Luthor, Brainiac,
NM $12 **MIP** $30

Super Heroes v. Super Villians, 1995, 5", Kenner, Superman, Supergirl, Bizzaro, Metallo
NM $12 **MIP** $25

PLAY SETS

Metropolis Bank, 1995, 5", Kenner, w/ Superman figure, foreign release
NM $25 **MIP** $50

VEHICLES

Superman Conversion Coupe, 1995, Kenner, Red w/ Clark Kent
NM $10 **MIP** $20

Teenage Mutant Ninja Turtles (Playmates, 1988-92)

GIANT TURTLES, 1991

Donatello, 1991, 13", Playmates
NM $20 **MIP** $40

Leonardo, 1991, 13", Playmates
NM $20 **MIP** $40

Michelangelo, 1991, 13", Playmates
NM $20 **MIP** $40

Raphael, 1991, 13", Playmates
NM $20 **MIP** $40

GIANT TURTLES, 1992

Bebop, 1992, 13", Playmates
NM $20 **MIP** $40

Movie Don, 1992, 13", Playmates
NM $20 **MIP** $40

Movie Leo, 1992, 13", Playmates
NM $20 **MIP** $40

Movie Mike, 1992, 13", Playmates
NM $20 **MIP** $40

Movie Raph, 1992, 13", Playmates
NM $20 **MIP** $40

Rocksteady, 1992, 13", Playmates
NM $20 **MIP** $40

SERIES 01, 1988

April O'Neil, no stripe, 1988, 4-1/2", Playmates
NM $50 **MIP** $100

Bebop, 1988, 4-1/2", Playmates
NM $10 **MIP** $20

Donatello, 1988, 4-1/2", Playmates
NM $7 **MIP** $15

Donatello, with fan club form, 1988, 4-1/2", Playmates
NM $12 **MIP** $50

Foot Soldier, 1988, 4-1/2", Playmates
NM $8 **MIP** $20

Leonardo, 1988, 4-1/2", Playmates
NM $7 **MIP** $15

Leonardo, with fan club form, 1988, 4-1/2", Playmates
NM $12 **MIP** $50

Michelangelo, 1988, 4-1/2", Playmates
NM $8 **MIP** $15

Michelangelo, with fan club form, 1988, 4-1/2", Playmates
NM $12 **MIP** $50

Raphael, 1988, 4-1/2", Playmates
NM $7 **MIP** $15

Raphael, with fan club form, 1988, 4-1/2", Playmates
NM $12 **MIP** $50

Rocksteady, 1988, 4-1/2", Playmates
NM $10 **MIP** $20

Shredder, 1988, 4-1/2", Playmates
NM $8 **MIP** $15

Splinter, 1988, 4-1/2", Playmates
NM $10 **MIP** $18

SERIES 02, 1989

Ace Duck, hat off, 1989, 4-1/2", Playmates
NM $6 **MIP** $25

Ace Duck, hat on, 1989, 4-1/2", Playmates
NM $6 **MIP** $12

April O'Neil, blue stripe, 1989, 4-1/2", Playmates
NM $10 **MIP** $20

Baxter Stockman, 1989, 4-1/2", Playmates, A man who had a nasty run-in with a bug.
NM $8 **MIP** $20

Genghis Frog, black belt, 1989, 4-1/2", Playmates
NM $4 **MIP** $12

Genghis Frog, black belt, bagged weapons, 1989, 4-1/2", Playmates
NM $5 **MIP** $30

Genghis Frog, yellow belt, 1989, 4-1/2", Playmates
NM $20 **MIP** $60

Krang, 1989, 4-1/2", Playmates
NM $6 **MIP** $12

SERIES 03, 1989

Casey Jones, 1989, 4-1/2", Playmates
NM $6 **MIP** $12

General Traag, 1989, 4-1/2", Playmates
NM $6 **MIP** $12

Leatherhead, 1989, 4-1/2", Playmates, Way too much sun for this guy.
NM $10 **MIP** $20

Metalhead, 1989, 4-1/2", Playmates, carded
NM $6 **MIP** $12

Rat King, 1989, 4-1/2", Playmates
NM $6 **MIP** $12

Usagi Yojimbo, 1989, 4-1/2", Playmates
NM $6 **MIP** $12

SERIES 04, 1990

Mondo Gecko, 1990, 4-1/2", Playmates
NM $6 **MIP** $15

Muckman and Joe Eyeball, 1990, 4-1/2", Playmates
NM $6 **MIP** $15

Scumbag, 1990, 4-1/2", Playmates
NM $6 **MIP** $12

Wingnut & Screwloose, 1990, 4-1/2", Playmates
NM $6 **MIP** $12

SERIES 05, 1990

Fugitoid, 1990, 4-1/2", Playmates
NM $5 **MIP** $15

Slash, black belt, 1990, 4-1/2", Playmates
NM $3 **MIP** $25

Slash, purple belt, red "S", 1990, 4-1/2", Playmates
NM $25 **MIP** $65

Triceraton, 1990, 4-1/2", Playmates
NM $8 **MIP** $18

SERIES 06, 1990

Mutagen Man, 1990, 4-1/2", Playmates
NM $5 **MIP** $15

Napoleon Bonafrog, 1990, 4-1/2", Playmates
NM $5 **MIP** $12

Panda Khan, 1990, 4-1/2", Playmates
NM $5 **MIP** $12

SERIES 07, 1991

April O'Neil, 1991, 4-1/2", Playmates
NM $25 **MIP** $100

April O'Neil, "Press", 1991, 4-1/2", Playmates
NM $5 **MIP** $15

Pizza Face, 1991, 4-1/2", Playmates
NM $5 **MIP** $10

Ray Fillet, purple body, red "V", 1991, 4-1/2", Playmates, purple torso, red V
NM $10 **MIP** $25

Ray Fillet, red body, maroon "V", 1991, 4-1/2", Playmates, red torso, maroon V
NM $10 **MIP** $30

Ray Fillet, yellow body, blue "V", 1991, 4-1/2", Playmates, yellow torso, blue V
NM $8 **MIP** $12

SERIES 08, 1991

Don The Undercover Turtle, 1991, 4-1/2", Playmates
NM $5 **MIP** $10

Leo the Sewer Samurai, 1991, 4-1/2", Playmates
NM $5 **MIP** $10

Mike the Sewer Surfer, 1991, 4-1/2", Playmates
NM $5 **MIP** $10

Raph the Space Cadet, 1991, 4-1/2", Playmates
NM $5 **MIP** $10

SERIES 09, 1991

Chrome Dome, 1991, 4-1/2", Playmates, carded
NM $5 **MIP** $12

Dirt Bag, 1991, 4-1/2", Playmates, carded
NM $6 **MIP** $15

Ground Chuck, 1991, 4-1/2", Playmates
NM $6 **MIP** $15

Storage Shell Don, 1991, 4-1/2", Playmates
NM $5 **MIP** $10

Storage Shell Leo, 1991, 4-1/2", Playmates
NM $5 **MIP** $10

Storage Shell Michelangelo, 1991, 4-1/2", Playmates
NM $5 **MIP** $10

Storage Shell Raphael, 1991, 4-1/2", Playmates
NM $5 **MIP** $10

SERIES 10, 1991

Grand Slam Raph, 1991, 4-1/2", Playmates
NM $5 **MIP** $10

Hose 'em Down Don, 1991, 4-1/2", Playmates
NM $5 **MIP** $10

Lieutenant Leo, 1991, 4-1/2", Playmates
NM $5 **MIP** $10

Make My Day Leo, 1991, 4-1/2", Playmates
NM $5 **MIP** $10

Midshipman Mike, 1991, 4-1/2", Playmates
NM $5 **MIP** $10

Teenage Mutant Ninja Turtles (Playmates, 1988-92)

Pro Pilot Don, 1991, 4-1/2", Playmates
NM $5 MIP $10

Raph the Green Teen Beret, 1991, 4-1/2", Playmates
NM $5 MIP $10

Slam Dunkin' Don, 1991, 4-1/2", Playmates
NM $5 MIP $10

Slapshot Leo, 1991, 4-1/2", Playmates
NM $5 MIP $10

T.D. Tossin' Leonardo, 1991, 4-1/2", Playmates
NM $5 MIP $10

SERIES 11, 1992

Rahzar, black nose, 1992, 4-1/2", Playmates
NM $5 MIP $12

Rahzar, red nose, 1992, 4-1/2", Playmates
NM $8 MIP $25

Skateboard'n Mike, 1992, 4-1/2", Playmates
NM $5 MIP $10

Super Shredder, 1992, 4-1/2", Playmates
NM $5 MIP $10

Tokka, brown trim, 1992, 4-1/2", Playmates
NM $9 MIP $25

Tokka, gray trim, 1992, 4-1/2", Playmates
NM $6 MIP $15

SERIES 12, 1992

Movie Don, 1992, 4-1/2", Playmates
NM $7 MIP $15

Movie Leo, 1992, 4-1/2", Playmates
NM $7 MIP $15

Movie Mike, 1992, 4-1/2", Playmates
NM $7 MIP $15

Movie Raph, 1992, 4-1/2", Playmates
NM $7 MIP $15

Movie Splinter, no tooth, 1992, 4-1/2", Playmates
NM $7 MIP $15

Movie Splinter, with tooth, 1992, 4-1/2", Playmates
NM $25 MIP $75

VEHICLES AND ACCESSORIES

Flushomatic, 1988-92, Playmates
NM $4 MIP $10

Foot Cruiser, 1988-92, Playmates
NM $14 MIP $35

Foot Ski, 1988-92, Playmates
NM $4 MIP $10

Mega Mutant Killer Bee, 1988-92, Playmates
NM $6 MIP $12

Mega Mutant Needlenose, 1988-92, Playmates
NM $8 MIP $20

Mike's Pizza Chopper Backpack, 1988-92, Playmates
NM $4 MIP $10

Mutant Sewer Cycle with Sidecar, 1988-92, Playmates
NM $4 MIP $10

Ninja Newscycle, 1988-92, Playmates
NM $5 MIP $12

Oozey, 1988-92, Playmates
NM $4 MIP $10

Pizza Powered Sewer Dragster, 1988-92, Playmates
NM $5 MIP $15

Pizza Thrower, 1988-92, Playmates
NM $14 MIP $35

Psycho Cycle, 1988-92, Playmates
NM $10 MIP $25

Raph's Sewer Dragster, 1988-92, Playmates
NM $6 MIP $16

Raph's Sewer Speedboat, 1988-92, Playmates
NM $5 MIP $12

Retrocatapult, 1988-92, Playmates
NM $4 MIP $10

Retromutagen Ooze, 1988-92, Playmates
NM $2 MIP $4

Sewer Seltzer Cannon, 1988-92, Playmates
NM $4 MIP $10

Sludgemobile, 1988-92, Playmates
NM $7 MIP $18

Technodrome, 1988-92, 22", Playmates
NM $24 MIP $60

Toilet Taxi, 1988-92, Playmates
NM $5 MIP $12

Turtle Blimp, green vinyl, 1988-92, 30", Playmates, green vinyl
NM $30 MIP $70

Turtle Party Wagon, 1988-92, Playmates
NM $16 MIP $40

Turtle Trooper Parachute, 1988-92, 22", Playmates
NM $4 MIP $10

Turtlecopter, 1988-92, Playmates
NM $16 MIP $40

WACKY ACTION, 1991

Breakfightin' Raphael, 1988-92, 4-1/2", Playmates
NM $5 MIP $10

Creepy Crawlin' Splinter, 1988-92, 4-1/2", Playmates
NM $5 MIP $10

Headspinnin' Bebop, 1988-92, 4-1/2", Playmates
NM $5 MIP $10

Machine Gunnin' Rocksteady, 1988-92, 4-1/2", Playmates
NM $5 MIP $10

Rock & Roll Michelangelo, 1988-92, 4-1/2", Playmates
NM $5 MIP $10

Sewer Swimmin' Don, 1988-92, 4-1/2", Playmates
NM $5 MIP $10

Slice 'n Dice Shredder, 1988-92, 4-1/2", Playmates
NM $10 MIP $20

Sword Slicin' Leonardo, 1988-92, 4-1/2", Playmates
NM $5 MIP $10

Wacky Walkin' Mouser, 1988-92, 4-1/2", Playmates
NM $8 MIP $18

Terminator 3 (McFarlane, 2003)

FIGURES

12" T-850 Terminator, 2003, 12", McFarlane, w/ sound chip
NM $15 MIP $30

T-850 Terminator, 2003, 7-1/2", McFarlane
NM $7 MIP $15

T-850 Terminator w/ Coffin, 2003, 8-1/2", McFarlane
NM $7 MIP $15

T-850 vs. T-X, 2003, McFarlane, Deluxe Boxed Set
NM $15 MIP $30

T-X Terminatrix, 2003, 7-1/8", McFarlane
NM $7 MIP $15

T-X Terminatrix Endoskeleton, 2003, 7-1/8", McFarlane
NM $7 MIP $15

This is Spinal Tap (Sideshow Toys, 2000)

FIGURES

David St. Hubbins, 2000
NM $10 MIP $25

Derek Smalls, 2000
NM $10 MIP $25

Nigel Tufnel, 2000
NM $10 MIP $25

Thundercats (LJN, 1985-87)

6" FIGURES

Ben-Gali, 1985-87, 6", LJN
NM $75 MIP $300

Capt. Cracker, 1985-87, 6", LJN
NM $35 MIP $90

Capt. Shiner, 1985-87, 6", LJN
NM $15 MIP $40

Cheetara, 1985-87, 6", LJN
NM $32 MIP $150

Cheetara and Wilykit, 1985-87, 6", LJN
NM $28 MIP $175

Grune the Destroyer, 1985-87, 6", LJN
NM $15 MIP $30

Hachiman, 1985-87, 6", LJN
NM $12 MIP $40

Jackalman, 1985-87, 6", LJN
NM $15 MIP $45

Jaga, 1986, 6", LJN, Series 3, w/ Sword of Omens and Helmet, rare
NM $75 MIP $250

Lion-O, 1985-87, 6", LJN
NM $35 MIP $250

Lion-O and Snarf, 1985-87, 6", LJN
NM $35 MIP $210

Lynx-O, 1985-87, 6", LJN
NM $40 MIP $125

Mongor, 1985-87, 6", LJN
NM $45 MIP $100

Monkian, 1985-87, 6", LJN
NM $20 MIP $45

Mumm-ra, 1985-87, 6", LJN
NM $15 MIP $70

Panthro, 1985-87, 6", LJN
NM $30 MIP $105

Pumyra, 1985-87, 6", LJN
NM $45 MIP $90

Ratar-O, 1985-87, 6", LJN
NM $12 MIP $35

Safari Joe, 1985-87, 6", LJN
NM $40 MIP $95

Snowman of Hook Mountain, 1985-87, 6", LJN
NM $15 MIP $45

S-S-Slithe, 1985-87, 6", LJN
NM $12 MIP $40

Tuska Warrior, 1985-87, 6", LJN
NM $12 MIP $35

Tygra, 1985-87, 6", LJN
NM $35 MIP $110

Tygra and Wilykat, 1985-87, 6", LJN
NM $40 MIP $110

Vultureman, 1985-87, 6", LJN
NM $12 MIP $40

ACCESSORIES

Astral Moat Monster, 1986, LJN
NM $100 MIP $250

Laser Sabers Backpacks, 1986, LJN, Evil, red pack w/ black strap
NM $5 MIP $10

Laser Sabers Backpacks, 1986, LJN, Evil, black pack w/ red strap
NM $5 MIP $10

Laser Sabers Backpacks, 1986, LJN, Good, orange pack w/ blue strap
NM $5 MIP $10

Laser Sabers Backpacks, 1986, LJN, Good, blue pack w/ red strap
NM $5 MIP $10

Luna-Lasher, 1986, LJN
NM $7 MIP $15

Stilt Runner, 1986, LJN
NM $7 MIP $15

Sword of Omens, 1986, LJN, role playing toy for kids
NM $100 MIP $250

Thunder Wings, 1986, LJN
NM $25 MIP $75

Tongue-A-Saurus, 1986, LJN
NM $40 MIP $80

BERSERKERS

Cruncher, 1985-87
NM $15 MIP $40

Hammerhead, 1985-87
NM $15 MIP $40

Ram-Bam, 1985-87
NM $15 MIP $40

Top-Spinner, 1985-87
NM $15 MIP $40

COMPANIONS

Berbil Belle, 1985-87
NM $15 MIP $50

Berbil Bert, 1986, LJN
NM $15 MIP $50

Berbil Bill, 1985-87
NM $15 MIP $50

Ma-Mut, 1985-87
NM $10 MIP $45

Snarf, 1985-87
NM $10 MIP $45

Wilykat, 1985-87
NM $15 MIP $60

Wilykit, 1985-87
NM $15 MIP $60

DELUXE FIGURES

Luna-Laser Mumm-Ra, 1986, LJN
NM $110 MIP $500

Thunderwings Lion-O, 1986, LJN
NM $150 MIP $600

PLAY SETS

Cat's Lair, 1986, LJN
NM $150 MIP $300

Mumm-Ra's Tomb Fortress, 1986, LJN, w/ Mumm-Ra
NM $150 MIP $300

RAM-PAGERS

Driller, the, 1985-87
NM $65 MIP $150

Mad Bubbler, The, 1985-87
NM n/a MIP n/a

Stinger, The, 1985-87
NM $60 MIP $125

VEHICLES

Hovercat, 1986, LJN
NM $10 MIP $20

Mutant Fistpounder, 1986, LJN
NM $20 MIP $45

Mutant Nose Diver, 1986, LJN
NM $15 MIP $32

Mutant Skycutter, 1986, LJN
NM $15 MIP $32

Thunderclaw, 1986, LJN
NM $12 MIP $25

Thundertank, 1986, LJN
NM $40 MIP $100

Thundercats: Miniatures (Kid Works, 1986)

ACCESSORIES

Mutant 4-Pack, 1986, LJN, four figures
NM $20 MIP $40

Snowman and Snowmeow, 1986, LJN
NM $10 MIP $20

Thundercats 4-Pack, 1986, LJN, four figures
NM $20 MIP $40

Weapons Pack, 1986, LJN
NM $5 MIP $10

FIGURES

Cheetara, 1986, 2-3", LJN
NM $4 MIP $12

Grune, 1986, 2-3", LJN
NM $3 MIP $10

Hachiman, 1986, 2-3", LJN
NM $2 MIP $8

Jackalman, 1986, 2-3", LJN
NM $2 MIP $8

Lion-O, 1986, 2-3", LJN
NM $4 MIP $10

Monkian, 1986, 2-3", LJN
NM $2 MIP $8

Mumm-Ra, 1986, 2-3", LJN
NM $4 MIP $10

Panthro, 1986, 2-3", LJN
NM $4 MIP $10

Ratar-O, 1986, 2-3", LJN
NM $3 MIP $8

Reptilian, 1986, 2-3", LJN
NM $2 MIP $8

S-S-Slithe, 1986, 2-3", LJN
NM $2 MIP $8

Tuska Warrior, 1986, 2-3", LJN
NM $2 MIP $8

Tygra, 1986, 2-3", LJN
NM $4 MIP $10

Vulturman, 1986, 2-3", LJN
NM $2 MIP $8

PLAY SETS

Cat's Lair, 1986, LJN
NM $20 MIP $50

Eye of Thundera, 1986, LJN
NM $7 MIP $14

Mumm-Ra's Crypt, 1986, LJN
NM $25 MIP $60

Tick, The (Bandai, 1994-95)

ACCESSORIES

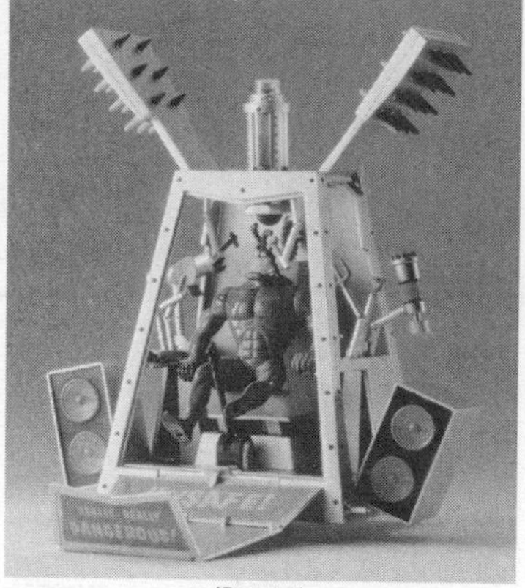

(Bandai)

Steel Box, 1994, Bandai, Figure-sized box with "Really, Really Dangerous!" and "Unsafe" in yellow type
NM $6 **MIP** $20

SERIES I, FIGURES

Bounding Tick, 1994, 6", Bandai
NM $6 **MIP** $10

Death Hug Dean, 1994, 6", Bandai
NM $6 **MIP** $10

Exploding Dyne-Mole, 1994, 6", Bandai
NM $4 **MIP** $10

Fluttering Arthur, 1994, 6", Bandai
NM $6 **MIP** $10

Grasping El Seed, 1994, 6", Bandai
NM $6 **MIP** $10

Growing Dinosaur Neil, 1994, 6", Bandai
NM $6 **MIP** $10

Man Eating Cow, 1994, 6", Bandai, Brown and white cow with moving jaw (and a set of teeth!)
NM $10 **MIP** $25

Pose Striking Die Fledermaus, 1994, 6", Bandai
NM $10 **MIP** $25

Projectile Human Bullet, 1994, 6", Bandai
NM $6 **MIP** $10

Sewer Spray Sewer Urchin, 1994, 6", Bandai
NM $6 **MIP** $10

SERIES II, FIGURES

Color Changing Chameleon, 1995, 6", Bandai
NM $10 **MIP** $25

Hurling Stop Sign Tick, 1995, 6", Bandai
NM $6 **MIP** $10

Propellerized Skippy the Dog, 1995, 6", Bandai
NM $6 **MIP** $10

Sliming Mucus Tick, 1995, 6", Bandai
NM $8 **MIP** $15

Thrakkorzog, 1995, 6", Bandai
NM $8 **MIP** $15

Twist and Chop American Maid, 1995, 6", Bandai
NM $10 **MIP** $22

Tomb Raider (Playmates, 1999)

12" FIGURE

Talking Lara Croft, 1999, Playmates
NM $8 **MIP** $25

9" FIGURES

Lara Croft in Area 51 outfit with hand guns and an M-16, on base, 1999
NM $8 **MIP** $20

Lara Croft in jungle outfit with two guns, on base, 1999
NM $8 **MIP** $20

(Playmates Toys)

Lara Croft in wet suit with harpoon and two pistols, on base, 1999, Detailed figure with stand
NM $8 **MIP** $20

ADVENTURES OF LARA CROFT, 6" FIGURES

Lara Croft escapes a Bengal, on diorama base, 1999
NM $3 **MIP** $10

Lara Croft escapes the yeti, on diorama base, 1999
NM $3 **MIP** $10

Lara Croft faces a Bengal, on diorama base, 1999
NM $3 **MIP** $10

Total Chaos (McFarlane, 1996-97)

SERIES 1, FIGURES

Al Simmons, 1996, McFarlane
NM $5 **MIP** $15

Al Simmons, blue uniform, 1996
NM $3 **MIP** $12

Al Simmons, red uniform with "Spawn" on visor, available through convention, 1997
NM $15 **MIP** $45

Conqueror, 1996
NM $5 **MIP** $15

Dragon Blade vs. Conqueror, Puzzle Zoo Exclusive, 1997
NM $6 **MIP** $18

Dragon Blade, black tunic, 1996
NM $4 **MIP** $12

Dragon Blade, white tunic, 1996, McFarlane
NM $5 **MIP** $15

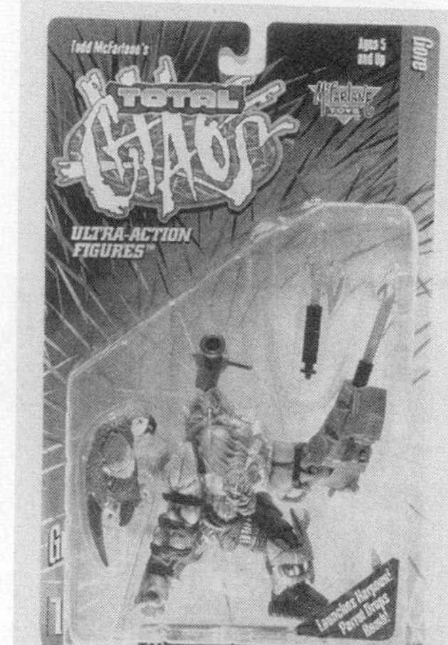

Gore, 1996, McFarlane, With harpoon-launching arm and bomb-dropping parrot figure
NM $5 **MIP** $15

Hoof, black body with khaki armor, 1996
NM $3 **MIP** $12

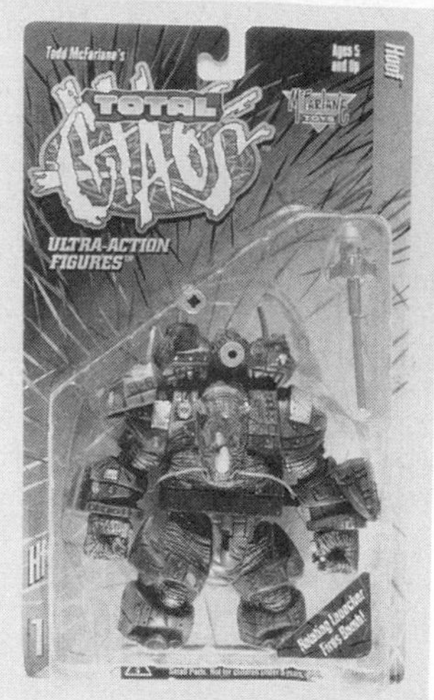

(Lenny Lee)

Hoof, gray body with brown armor, 1996, McFarlane, With rotating and firing missile launcher
NM $5 **MIP** $15

Thorax, black and yellow, 1996
NM $3 MIP $12

Thorax, green and red, 1996, McFarlane
NM $4 MIP $12

Thresher, light blue skin, 1996, McFarlane
NM $5 MIP $15

Thresher, violet skin, 1996
NM $3 MIP $10

SERIES 2, FIGURES

Blitz, 1997
NM $3 MIP $10

Brain Drain, 1997
NM $3 MIP $10

Corn Boy, 1997
NM $3 MIP $10

Poacher, 1997
NM $3 MIP $10

Quartz, 1997
NM $3 MIP $10

Smuggler, 1997
NM $3 MIP $10

Total Justice (Kenner, 1996)

FIGURES

Aquaman, black armor, 1996, 5", Kenner
NM $5 MIP $8

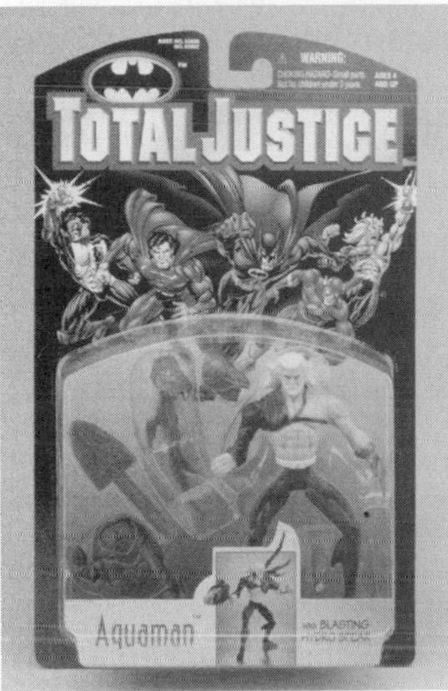

(Kenner)

Aquaman, with Hydro-Blasting Spear, gold armor, 1996, 5", Kenner
NM $7 MIP $8

(Kenner)

Batman, 1996, 5", Kenner, With flight armor and glider cape
NM $5 MIP $15

Batman, Fractal Armor, 1986, 5", Kenner
NM $8 MIP $17

Black Lightning, 1996, 5", Kenner
NM $7 MIP $8

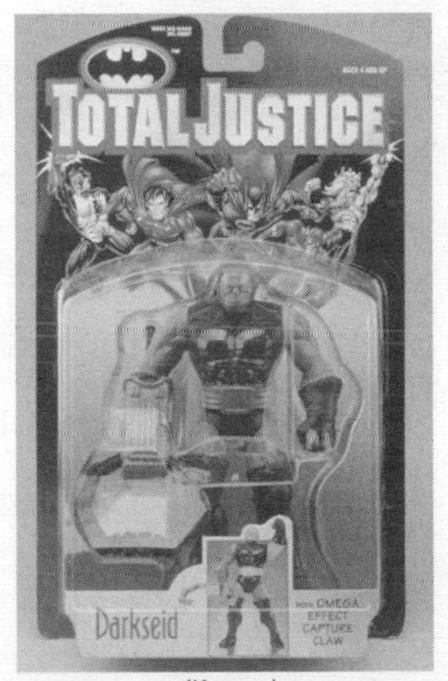

(Kenner)

Darkseid, 1996, 5", Kenner, With omega-effect capture claw
NM $5 MIP $8

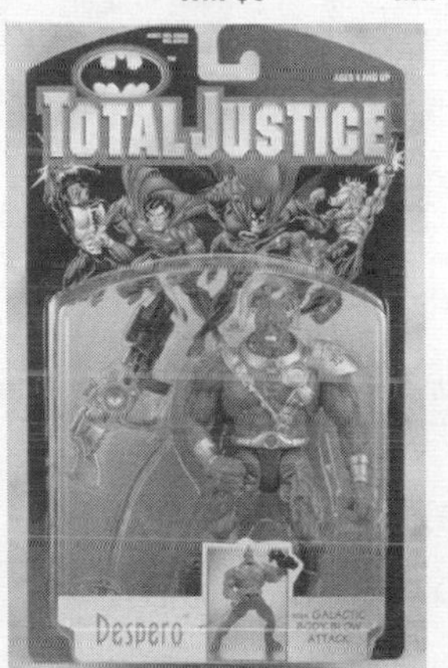

(Kenner)

Despero, 1996, 5", Kenner, With galactic body blow attack
NM $5 MIP $8

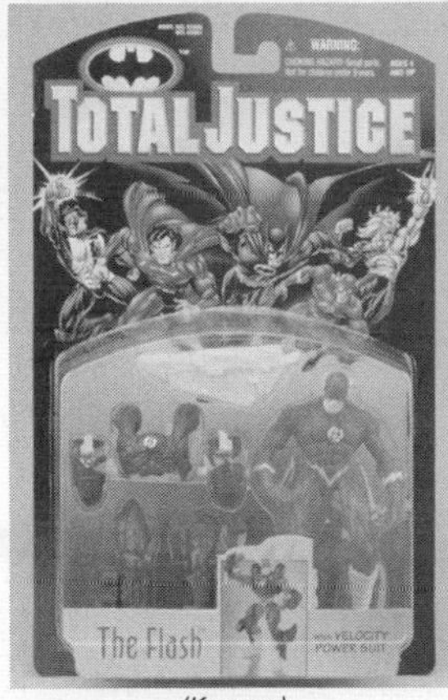

(Kenner)

Flash, The, 1996, 5", Kenner, With velocity power suit
NM $5 MIP $8

Green Arrow, 1996, 5", Kenner
NM $5 MIP $8

(Kenner)

Green Lantern, 1996, 5", Kenner
NM $5 MIP $8

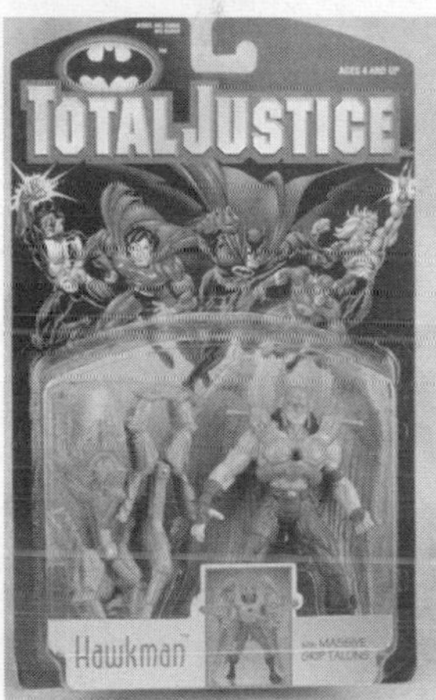

(Kenner)

Hawkman, 1996, 5", Kenner, With talon
NM $5 MIP $8

Huntress, 1996, 5", Kenner
NM $5 MIP $12

Parallax, 1996, 5", Kenner
NM $5 MIP $8

Total Justice (Kenner, 1996)

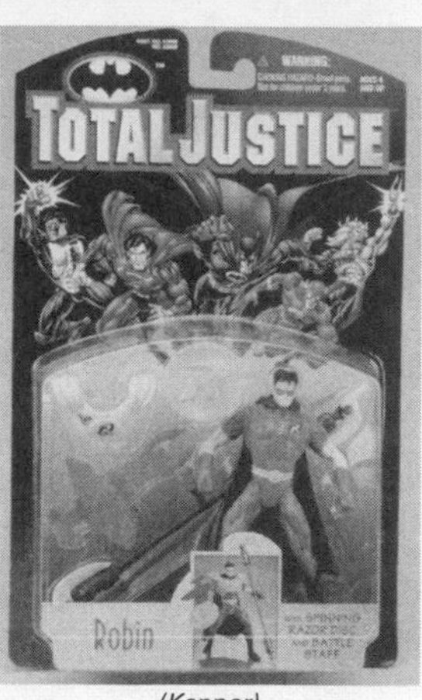

(Kenner)

Robin, 1996, 5", Kenner, With spinning razor disc and battle staff
NM $5 MIP $12

(Kenner)

Superman, 1996, 5", Kenner, With shield and kryptonite ray emitter
NM $5 MIP $8

Toy Story (Thinkway, 1996)

5" FIGURES

Alien, 1996, 5", Thinkway
NM $5 MIP $15

Boxer Buzz, 1996, 5", Thinkway
NM $4 MIP $8

Crawling Baby Face, 1996, 5", Thinkway
NM $3 MIP $9

Fighting Woody, 1996, 5", Thinkway
NM $3 MIP $9

Flying Buzz (Rocket), 1996, 5", Thinkway
NM $4 MIP $8

Hamm, 1996, 5", Thinkway
NM $4 MIP $8

Karate Buzz, 1996, 5", Thinkway
NM $4 MIP $8

Kicking Woody, 1996, 5", Thinkway
NM $4 MIP $8

Quick-Draw Woody, 1996, 5", Thinkway
NM $4 MIP $8

Rex, 1996, 5", Thinkway
NM $4 MIP $8

Super Sonic Buzz, 1996, 5", Thinkway
NM $3 MIP $9

LARGE FIGURES

Talking Buzz Lightyear, 1996, Thinkway
NM $15 MIP $50

Talking Woody, 1996, Thinkway
NM $15 MIP $60

Transformers (Kenner, 1984-1995)

GENERATION 1, SERIES 1, 1984

Bluestreak, silver, 1984, Kenner
NM $70 MIP $350

Brawn, 1984, Kenner
NM $10 MIP $70

Bumblebee, red, 1984, Kenner
NM $25 MIP $100

Bumblebee, yellow, 1984, Kenner
NM $25 MIP $110

Cliffjumper, red, 1984, Kenner
NM $20 MIP $75

Cliffjumper, yellow, 1984, Kenner
NM $15 MIP $75

Gears, 1984, Kenner
NM $20 MIP $70

Hound, 1984, Kenner
NM $55 MIP $275

Huffer, 1984, Kenner
NM $10 MIP $60

Ironhide, 1984, Kenner
NM $45 MIP $155

Jazz, 1984, Kenner
NM $60 MIP $275

(Lenny Lee)

Megatron, 1984, Kenner, Deception Leader turns from handgun to robot
NM $65 MIP $175

Mirage, 1984, Kenner
NM $65 MIP $225

Optimus Prime with gray or blue roller, 1984, Kenner
NM $65 MIP $175

Prowl, 1984, Kenner
NM $65 MIP $300

Ratchet with cross, 1984, Kenner
NM $55 MIP $135

Ratchet without cross, 1984, Kenner
NM $45 MIP $135

Sideswipe, 1984, Kenner
NM $60 MIP $275

Skywarp, 1984, Kenner
NM $55 MIP $135

Soundwave and Buzzsaw, 1984, Kenner
NM $55 MIP $140

Starscream, 1984, Kenner
NM $60 MIP $215

Sunstreaker, 1984, Kenner
NM $65 MIP $300

Thundercracker, 1984, Kenner
NM $55 MIP $125

Trailbreaker, 1984, Kenner
NM $55 MIP $150

Wheeljack, 1984, Kenner
NM $55 MIP $260

Windcharger, 1984, Kenner
NM $10 MIP $65

GENERATION 1, SERIES 2, 1985

Astrotrain, 1985, Kenner, triple changer
NM $35 MIP $95

Barrage, 1985, Kenner
NM $30 MIP $75

Beachcomber, 1985, Kenner
NM $10 MIP $35

Blaster, 1985, Kenner
NM $55 MIP $120

Blitzwing, 1985, Kenner
NM $35 MIP $90

Bombshell, 1985, Kenner
NM $15 MIP $40

Bonecrusher, 1985, Kenner
NM $15 MIP $65

Brawn, 1985, Kenner
NM $12 MIP $70

Brawn with Minispy, 1985, Kenner
NM $23 MIP $110

Bumblebee with Minispy, yellow, 1985, Kenner
NM $28 MIP $110

Bumblebee, red, 1985, Kenner
NM $25 MIP $100

Bumblebee, yellow, 1985, Kenner
NM $25 MIP $100

Chop Shop, 1985, Kenner
NM $30 MIP $65

Cliffjumper with Minispy, red, 1985, Kenner
NM $25 MIP $95

Cliffjumper, red, 1985, Kenner
NM $20 MIP $75

Cliffjumper, yellow, 1985, Kenner
NM $15 MIP $60

Cosmos, 1985, Kenner
NM $8 MIP $32

Dirge, 1985, Kenner
NM $40 MIP $100

Gears, 1985, Kenner
NM $10 MIP $65

Gears with Minispy, 1985, Kenner
NM $20 MIP $75

Grapple, 1985, Kenner
NM $50 MIP $150

Grimlock, 1985, Kenner
NM $35 MIP $180

Hoist, 1985, Kenner
NM $50 MIP $125

Hook, 1985, Kenner
NM $15 MIP $60

Huffer, 1985, Kenner
NM $10 MIP $50

Huffer with Minispy, 1985, Kenner
NM $20 MIP $70

Inferno, 1985, Kenner
NM $45 MIP $135

Jazz, 1985, Kenner
NM $60 MIP $225

(Lenny Lee)

Jetfire, 1985, Kenner, Red and white pieces transform from folding-wing jet bomber to robot
NM $115 MIP $310

Kickback, 1985, Kenner
NM $15 MIP $40

Long Haul, 1985, Kenner
NM $15 MIP $60

Mixmaster, 1985, Kenner
NM $15 MIP $60

Omega Supreme, 1985, Kenner
NM $120 MIP $210

Optimus Prime, 1985, Kenner
NM $75 MIP $250

Perceptor, 1985, Kenner
NM $35 MIP $110

Powerglide, 1985, Kenner
NM $10 MIP $40

Ramjet, 1985, Kenner
NM $50 MIP $110

Ransack, 1985, Kenner
NM $30 MIP $65

Red Alert, 1985, Kenner
NM $45 MIP $145

Roadbuster, 1985, Kenner
NM $75 MIP $165

Scavenger, 1985, Kenner
NM $15 MIP $60

Scrapper, 1985, Kenner
NM $15 MIP $60

Seaspray, 1985, Kenner
NM $8 MIP $35

Shockwave, 1985, Kenner
NM $100 MIP $180

Shrapnel, 1985, Kenner
NM $12 MIP $40

Skids, 1985, Kenner
NM $60 MIP $210

Slag, 1985, Kenner
NM $40 MIP $110

Sludge, 1985, Kenner
NM $40 MIP $140

Smokescreen, 1985, Kenner
NM $50 MIP $185

Snarl, 1985, Kenner
NM $40 MIP $140

Thrust, 1985, Kenner
NM $45 MIP $100

Tracks, 1985, Kenner
NM $60 MIP $200

Ultra Magnus, 1985, Kenner
NM $60 MIP $150

Venom, 1985, Kenner
NM $30 MIP $65

Warpath, 1985, Kenner
NM $8 MIP $50

Whirl, 1985, Kenner
NM $55 MIP $140

Windcharger, 1985, Kenner
NM $10 MIP $60

Windcharger with Minispy, 1985, Kenner
NM $20 MIP $70

GENERATION 1, SERIES 3, 1986

Air Raid, 1986, Kenner
NM $15 MIP $50

Air Raid with patch, 1986, Kenner
NM $18 MIP $60

Beachcomber, 1986, Kenner
NM $10 MIP $30

Beachcomber with patch, 1986, Kenner
NM $12 MIP $35

Blades, 1986, Kenner
NM $13 MIP $50

Blades, plastic chest, 1986, Kenner
NM $10 MIP $45

Blast Off, metal treads, 1986, Kenner
NM $22 MIP $60

Blast Off, plastic chest, 1986, Kenner
NM $10 MIP $55

Blurr, 1986, Kenner
NM $30 MIP $100

Blurr with poster, 1986, Kenner
NM $30 MIP $80

Brawl, metal treads, 1986, Kenner
NM $14 MIP $50

Brawl, plastic treads, 1986, Kenner
NM $12 MIP $45

Breakdown, 1986, Kenner
NM $15 MIP $55

Breakdown with patch, 1986, Kenner
NM $18 MIP $60

Broadside, 1986, Kenner
NM $30 MIP $70

Broadside with poster, 1986, Kenner
NM $32 MIP $75

Bumblebee, 1986, Kenner
NM $25 MIP $70

Bumblebee with patch, 1986, Kenner
NM $25 MIP $75

Cosmos, 1986, Kenner
NM $8 MIP $30

Cosmos with patch, 1986, Kenner
NM $10 MIP $32

Cyclonus, 1986, Kenner
NM $55 MIP $120

Dead End, 1986, Kenner
NM $15 MIP $55

Dead End with patch, 1986, Kenner
NM $18 MIP $60

Divebomb with poster, plastic body, 1986, Kenner
NM $45 MIP $85

Divebomb, metal body, 1986, Kenner
NM $50 MIP $90

Divebomb, plastic body, 1986, Kenner
NM $40 MIP $80

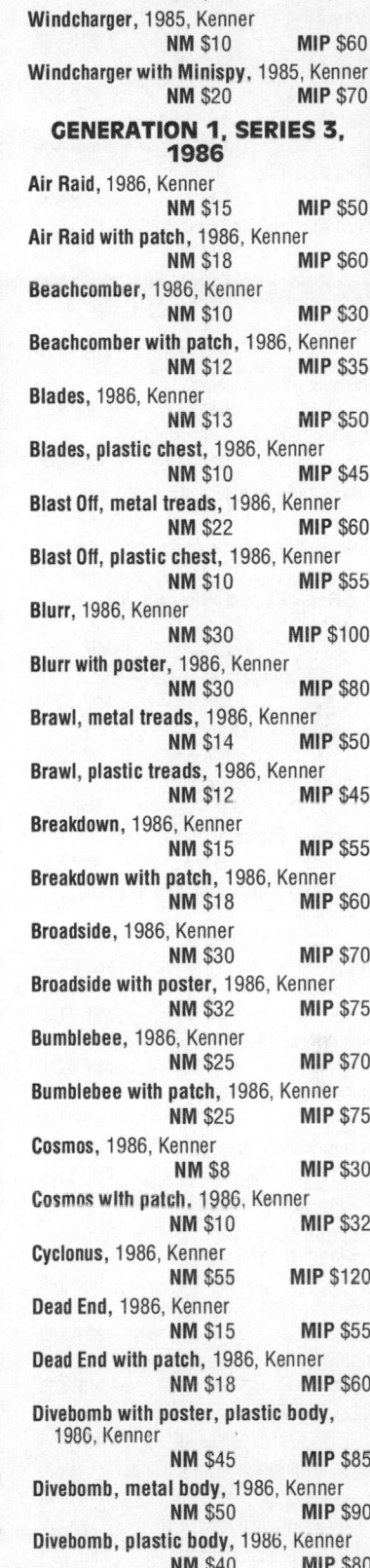

Transformers (Kenner, 1984-1995)

Drag Strip, 1986, Kenner
NM $15 **MIP** $55

Drag Strip with patch, 1986, Kenner
NM $18 **MIP** $60

Fireflight, 1986, Kenner
NM $15 **MIP** $55

Fireflight with patch, 1986, Kenner
NM $18 **MIP** $60

First Aid, 1986, Kenner
NM $15 **MIP** $55

First Aid, plastic chest, 1986, Kenner
NM $10 **MIP** $60

Galvatron, 1986, Kenner, City Commander
NM $60 **MIP** $125

Gnaw, 1986, Kenner
NM $60 **MIP** $110

Groove, 1986, Kenner
NM $15 **MIP** $55

Groove, silver chest, 1986, Kenner
NM $18 **MIP** $60

Headstrong, metal body, 1986, Kenner
NM $40 **MIP** $80

Headstrong, plastic body, 1987, Kenner
NM $38 **MIP** $75

Hot Rod with poster, plastic toes, 1986, Kenner
NM $55 **MIP** $200

Hot Rod, metal toes, 1986, Kenner
NM $55 **MIP** $200

Hot Spot, 1986, Kenner
NM $32 **MIP** $85

Hubcap, 1986, Kenner
NM $6 **MIP** $30

Hubcap with patch, 1986, Kenner
NM $8 **MIP** $32

Kup, plastic tires and wheels, 1986, Kenner
NM $22 **MIP** $110

Kup, rubber tires and metal wheels, 1986, Kenner
NM $25 **MIP** $120

Metroplex, 1986, Kenner
NM $110 **MIP** $210

Motormaster, 1986, Kenner
NM $40 **MIP** $85

Octane, 1986, Kenner
NM $55 **MIP** $100

Octane with poster, 1986, Kenner
NM $60 **MIP** $110

Onslaught, 1986, Kenner
NM $32 **MIP** $75

Outback, 1986, Kenner
NM $10 **MIP** $50

Outback with patch, 1986, Kenner
NM $12 **MIP** $55

Pipes, 1986, Kenner
NM $8 **MIP** $45

Pipes with patch, 1986, Kenner
NM $10 **MIP** $48

Powerglide, 1986, Kenner
NM $8 **MIP** $35

Powerglide with patch, 1986, Kenner
NM $8 **MIP** $40

Rampage, metal body, 1986, Kenner
NM $42 **MIP** $85

Rampage, plastic body, 1986, Kenner
NM $38 **MIP** $85

Razorclaw, metal body, 1986, Kenner
NM $50 **MIP** $90

Razorclaw, plastic body, 1986, Kenner
NM $45 **MIP** $90

Rodimus Prime, metal toes, 1986, Kenner
NM $55 **MIP** $130

Rodimus Prime, plastic toes, 1986, Kenner
NM $55 **MIP** $130

Sandstorm, metal or plastic toes, 1986, Kenner
NM $30 **MIP** $85

Scourge, 1986, Kenner
NM $45 **MIP** $150

Seaspray, 1986, Kenner
NM $6 **MIP** $30

Seaspray with patch, 1986, Kenner
NM $8 **MIP** $35

Silverbolt, 1986, Kenner
NM $38 **MIP** $110

Skydive, 1986, Kenner
NM $15 **MIP** $55

Skydive with patch, 1986, Kenner
NM $18 **MIP** $60

Slingshot, 1986, Kenner
NM $15 **MIP** $55

Slingshot with patch, 1986, Kenner
NM $18 **MIP** $60

Springer, metal or plastic front, 1986, Kenner
NM $60 **MIP** $120

Streetwise, 1986, Kenner
NM $18 **MIP** $50

Swerve, 1986, Kenner
NM $12 **MIP** $45

Swerve with patch, 1986, Kenner
NM $14 **MIP** $50

Swindle, gray plastic chest, 1986, Kenner
NM $12 **MIP** $50

Swindle, metal treads, 1986, Kenner
NM $14 **MIP** $55

Tailgate, 1986, Kenner
NM $12 **MIP** $40

Tailgate with patch, 1986, Kenner
NM $14 **MIP** $45

Tantrum with poster, plastic body, 1986, Kenner
NM $42 **MIP** $80

Tantrum, metal body, 1986, Kenner
NM $45 **MIP** $95

Tantrum, plastic body, 1986, Kenner
NM $40 **MIP** $85

Trypticon, 1986, Kenner, battery-operated, walks
NM $110 **MIP** $180

Vortex, metal treads, 1986, Kenner
NM $25 **MIP** $60

Vortex, plastic chest, 1986, Kenner
NM $22 **MIP** $65

Warpath, 1986, Kenner
NM $8 **MIP** $45

Warpath with patch, 1986, Kenner
NM $10 **MIP** $50

Wheelie, 1986, Kenner
NM $6 **MIP** $25

Wheelie with patch, 1986, Kenner
NM $8 **MIP** $30

Wildrider, 1986, Kenner
NM $15 **MIP** $55

Wildrider with patch, 1986, Kenner
NM $18 **MIP** $60

Wreck-gar, 1986, Kenner
NM $45 **MIP** $90

Wreck-gar with poster, 1986, Kenner
NM $50 **MIP** $100

GENERATION 1, SERIES 4, 1987

Afterburner, 1987, Kenner
NM $20 **MIP** $50

Afterburner with decoy, 1987, Kenner
NM $24 **MIP** $60

Air Raid, 1987, Kenner
NM $15 **MIP** $45

Air Raid with decoy, 1987, Kenner
NM $20 **MIP** $55

Apeface, 1987, Kenner
NM $50 **MIP** $100

Battletrap, 1987, Kenner
NM $15 **MIP** $35

Blades with decoy, plastic chest, 1987, Kenner
NM $13 **MIP** $55

Blades, plastic chest, 1987, Kenner
NM $13 **MIP** $50

Blast Off with decoy, plastic chest, 1987, Kenner
NM $25 **MIP** $60

Blot with decoy, 1987, Kenner
NM $12 **MIP** $45

Blurr, 1987, Kenner
NM $60 **MIP** $175

Brainstorm, 1987, Kenner
NM $50 **MIP** $100

Brawl with decoy, plastic treads, 1987, Kenner
NM $16 **MIP** $50

Breakdown with decoy, 1987, Kenner
NM $20 **MIP** $60

Chase, 1987, Kenner
NM $8 **MIP** $30

Chase with decoy, 1987, Kenner
NM $9 **MIP** $35

Chromedome, 1987, Kenner
NM $45 **MIP** $110

Computron Gift Set, 1987, Kenner, all five Technobots in one boxed set
NM $200 **MIP** $650

Crosshairs, 1987, Kenner
NM $50 **MIP** $125

Cutthroat with decoy, 1987, Kenner
NM $12 **MIP** $45

Cyclonus, 1987, Kenner
NM $90 **MIP** $175

Dead End with decoy, 1987, Kenner
NM $20 **MIP** $60

Doublecross, 1987, Kenner
NM $40 **MIP** $75

Drag Strip with decoy, 1987, Kenner
NM $20 **MIP** $60

Fireflight, 1987, Kenner
NM $15 **MIP** $55

Fireflight with decoy, 1987, Kenner
NM $20 **MIP** $65

First Aid with decoy, plastic chest, 1987, Kenner
NM $22 **MIP** $60

First Aid, plastic chest, 1987, Kenner
NM $15 **MIP** $55

Flywheels, 1987, Kenner
NM $15 **MIP** $35

Fortess Maximus, 1987, Kenner
NM $350 **MIP** $900

Freeway, 1987, Kenner
NM $8 **MIP** $30

Freeway with decoy, 1987, Kenner
NM $10 **MIP** $35

Goldbug, 1987, Kenner
NM $10 **MIP** $55

Goldbug with decoy, 1987, Kenner
NM $14 **MIP** $60

Groove with decoy, silver chest, 1987, Kenner
NM $14 **MIP** $60

Groove, silver chest, 1987, Kenner
NM $15 **MIP** $55

Grotusque, 1987, Kenner
NM $40 **MIP** $75

Hardhead, 1987, Kenner
NM $50 **MIP** $100

Highbrow, 1987, Kenner
NM $55 **MIP** $110

Hot Rod, 1987, Kenner
NM $100 **MIP** $310

Kup, 1987, Kenner
NM $50 **MIP** $175

Lightspeed, 1987, Kenner
NM $20 **MIP** $50

Lightspeed with decoy, 1987, Kenner
NM $24 **MIP** $55

Mindwipe, 1987, Kenner
NM $50 **MIP** $100

Misfire, 1987, Kenner
NM $60 **MIP** $140

Nosecone, 1987, Kenner
NM $12 **MIP** $45

Nosecone with decoy, 1987, Kenner
NM $16 **MIP** $50

Pointblank, 1987, Kenner
NM $50 **MIP** $95

Repugnus, 1987, Kenner
NM $40 **MIP** $80

Rippersnapper with decoy, 1987, Kenner
NM $16 **MIP** $45

Rollbar, 1987, Kenner
NM $8 **MIP** $30

Rollbar with decoy, 1987, Kenner
NM $12 **MIP** $34

Scourge, 1987, Kenner
NM $110 **MIP** $400

Searchlight, 1987, Kenner
NM $8 **MIP** $30

Searchlight with decoy, 1987, Kenner
NM $12 **MIP** $35

Sinnertwin with decoy, 1987, Kenner
NM $12 **MIP** $45

Skullcruncher, 1987, Kenner
NM $50 **MIP** $90

Skydive, 1987, Kenner
NM $15 **MIP** $55

Skydive with decoy, 1987, Kenner
NM $18 **MIP** $60

Slingshot, 1987, Kenner
NM $15 **MIP** $55

Slingshot with decoy, 1987, Kenner
NM $18 **MIP** $60

Slugslinger, 1987, Kenner
NM $60 **MIP** $110

Snapdragon, 1987, Kenner
NM $55 **MIP** $110

Strafe, 1987, Kenner
NM $20 **MIP** $55

Strafe with decoy, 1987, Kenner
NM $24 **MIP** $60

Streetwise, 1987, Kenner
NM $18 **MIP** $50

Streetwise with decoy, 1987, Kenner
NM $22 **MIP** $55

Sureshot, 1987, Kenner
NM $45 **MIP** $100

Swindle with decoy, gray plastic chest, 1987, Kenner
NM $12 **MIP** $50

Triggerhappy, 1987, Kenner
NM $60 **MIP** $120

Vortex with decoy, plastic chest, 1987, Kenner
NM $22 **MIP** $65

Weirdwolf, 1987, Kenner
NM $45 **MIP** $100

Wideload, 1987, Kenner
NM $8 **MIP** $30

Wideload with decoy, 1987, Kenner
NM $12 **MIP** $35

Wildrider with decoy, 1987, Kenner
NM $20 **MIP** $60

GENERATION 1, SERIES 5, 1988

Afterburner, 1988, Kenner
NM $20 **MIP** $50

Backstreet, 1988, Kenner
NM $12 **MIP** $35

Blot, 1988, Kenner
NM $10 **MIP** $40

Bomb-burst, clear insert, 1988, Kenner
NM $40 **MIP** $70

Bugly, 1988, Kenner
NM $35 **MIP** $55

Carnivac, 1988, Kenner
NM $35 **MIP** $75

Catilla, 1988, Kenner
NM $40 **MIP** $70

Chainclaw, 1988, Kenner
NM $40 **MIP** $70

Cindersaur, 1988, Kenner
NM $10 **MIP** $40

Cloudburst, clear insert, 1988, Kenner
NM $40 **MIP** $70

Crankcase, 1988, Kenner
NM $12 **MIP** $35

Cutthroat, 1988, Kenner
NM $10 **MIP** $40

Darkwing, 1988, Kenner
NM $75 **MIP** $150

Dogfight, 1988, Kenner
NM $15 **MIP** $35

Dreadwind, 1988, Kenner
NM $75 **MIP** $150

Fangry, 1988, Kenner
NM $40 **MIP** $90

Finback, 1988, Kenner
NM $40 **MIP** $70

Fizzle, 1988, Kenner
NM $12 **MIP** $35

Flamefeather, 1988, Kenner
NM $10 **MIP** $40

Getaway, 1988, Kenner
NM $35 **MIP** $75

Groundbreaker, 1988, Kenner
NM $100 **MIP** $165

Gunrunner, 1988, Kenner
NM $35 **MIP** $70

Guzzle, 1988, Kenner
NM $12 **MIP** $35

Horri-bull, 1988, Kenner
NM $40 **MIP** $90

Hosehead, 1988, Kenner
NM $40 **MIP** $90

Iguanus, 1988, Kenner
NM $40 **MIP** $75

Joyride, 1988, Kenner
NM $35 **MIP** $75

Landfill, 1988, Kenner
NM $25 MIP $70

Landmine, clear insert, 1988, Kenner
NM $40 MIP $75

Lightspeed, 1988, Kenner
NM $20 MIP $50

Nautilator, 1988, Kenner
NM $30 MIP $65

Needlenose, 1988, Kenner
NM $40 MIP $125

Nightbeat, 1988, Kenner
NM $40 MIP $90

Nosecone, 1988, Kenner
NM $12 MIP $45

Overbite, 1988, Kenner
NM $30 MIP $65

Override, 1988, Kenner
NM $15 MIP $35

Quake, 1988, Kenner
NM $30 MIP $75

Quickmix, 1988, Kenner
NM $30 MIP $75

Rippersnapper, 1988, Kenner
NM $12 MIP $40

Roadgrabber, 1988, Kenner
NM $40 MIP $90

Ruckus, 1988, Kenner
NM $20 MIP $40

Scoop, 1988, Kenner
NM $30 MIP $70

Seawing, 1988, Kenner
NM $30 MIP $60

Sinnertwin, 1988, Kenner
NM $10 MIP $40

Siren, 1988, Kenner
NM $40 MIP $90

Sizzle, 1988, Kenner
NM $10 MIP $40

Skalor, 1988, Kenner
NM $35 MIP $65

Skullgrin, clear insert, 1988, Kenner
NM $40 MIP $70

Sky High, 1988, Kenner
NM $55 MIP $100

Slapdash, 1988, Kenner
NM $50 MIP $80

Snarler, 1988, Kenner
NM $35 MIP $75

Sparkstalker, 1988, Kenner
NM $10 MIP $40

Spinister, 1988, Kenner
NM $35 MIP $90

Splashdown, 1988, Kenner
NM $40 MIP $90

Squeezeplay, 1988, Kenner
NM $40 MIP $90

Strafe, 1988, Kenner
NM $20 MIP $50

Submarauder, clear insert, 1988, Kenner
NM $35 MIP $75

Tentakil, 1988, Kenner
NM $30 MIP $65

Waverider, clear insert, 1988, Kenner
NM $35 MIP $70

Windsweeper, 1988, Kenner
NM $15 MIP $35

GENERATION 1, SERIES 6, 1989

Air Strike Patrol, 1989, Kenner
NM $10 MIP $30

Airwave, 1989, Kenner
NM $15 MIP $35

Battle Patrol, 1989, Kenner
NM $10 MIP $30

Birdbrain, 1989, Kenner
NM $30 MIP $75

Bludgeon, 1989, Kenner
NM $70 MIP $175

Bomb-burst, 1989, Kenner
NM $35 MIP $70

Bristleback, 1989, Kenner
NM $30 MIP $75

Cloudburst, 1989, Kenner
NM $35 MIP $75

Crossblades, 1989, Kenner
NM $75 MIP $125

Doubleheader, 1989, Kenner
NM $40 MIP $90

Erector, 1989, Kenner
NM $15 MIP $30

Flattop, 1989, Kenner
NM $15 MIP $30

Greasepit, 1989, Kenner
NM $15 MIP $35

Groundshaker, 1989, Kenner
NM $30 MIP $65

Hot House, 1989, Kenner
NM $15 MIP $30

Ironworks, 1989, Kenner
NM $15 MIP $30

Landmine, 1989, Kenner
NM $35 MIP $60

Longtooth, 1989, Kenner
NM $40 MIP $90

Octopunch, 1989, Kenner
NM $40 MIP $90

Off Road Patrol, 1989, Kenner
NM $15 MIP $30

Overload, 1989, Kenner
NM $15 MIP $30

Pincher, 1989, Kenner
NM $40 MIP $90

Race Car Patrol, 1989, Kenner
NM $10 MIP $30

Rescue Patrol, 1989, Kenner
NM $10 MIP $30

Roadblock, 1989, Kenner
NM $40 MIP $90

Roughstuff, 1989, Kenner
NM $15 MIP $30

Scowl, 1989, Kenner
NM $30 MIP $75

Skullgrin, 1989, Kenner
NM $35 MIP $70

Skyhammer, 1989, Kenner
NM $35 MIP $75

Skyhopper, 1989, Kenner
NM $30 MIP $60

Slog, 1989, Kenner
NM $30 MIP $75

Sports Car Patrol, 1989, Kenner
NM $10 MIP $30

Stranglehold, 1989, Kenner
NM $30 MIP $80

Submarauder, 1989, Kenner
NM $35 MIP $70

Thunderwing, 1989, Kenner
NM $80 MIP $170

Vroom, 1989, Kenner
NM $80 MIP $160

Waverider, 1989, Kenner
NM $35 MIP $70

Wildfly, 1989, Kenner
NM $30 MIP $70

GENERATION 1, SERIES 7, 1990

Air Patrol, 1990, Kenner
NM $10 MIP $30

Astro Squad, 1990, Kenner
NM $20 MIP $40

Axer, 1990, Kenner
NM $20 MIP $40

Banzai-Tron, 1990, Kenner
NM $12 MIP $25

Battle Squad, 1990, Kenner
NM $15 MIP $40

Blaster, 1990, Kenner
NM $15 MIP $25

Bumblebee, 1990, Kenner
NM $12 MIP $22

Cannon Transport, 1990, Kenner
NM $15 MIP $30

Construction Patrol, 1990, Kenner
NM $10 MIP $25

Constructor Squad, 1990, Kenner
NM $15 MIP $30

Devastator, 1990, Kenner
NM $15 MIP $30

Erector, 1990, Kenner
NM $12 MIP $30

Flattop, 1990, Kenner
NM $15 MIP $30

Grimlock, 1990, Kenner
NM $15 MIP $30

Gutcruncher, 1990, Kenner
NM $60 MIP $100

Hot Rod Patrol, 1990, Kenner
NM $25 MIP $45

Inferno, 1990, Kenner
NM $10 MIP $20

Jackpot, 1990, Kenner
NM $10 MIP $20

Jazz, 1990, Kenner
NM $12 MIP $25

Kick-Off, 1990, Kenner
NM $10 MIP $20

Krok, 1990, Kenner
NM $12 MIP $20

Mainframe, 1990, Kenner
NM $10 MIP $20

Megatron, 1990, Kenner
NM $80 MIP $125

Metro Squad, 1990, Kenner
NM $20 MIP $45

Military Patrol, 1990, Kenner
NM $25 MIP $50

Missile Launcher, 1990, Kenner
NM $45 MIP $70

Monster Trucks Patrol, 1990, Kenner
NM $20 MIP $45

Overload, 1990, Kenner
NM $15 MIP $25

Over-Run, 1990, Kenner
NM $25 MIP $40

Prowl, 1990, Kenner
NM $20 MIP $45

Race Track Patrol, 1990, Kenner
NM $10 MIP $20

Rad, 1990, Kenner
NM $12 MIP $20

Rollout, 1990, Kenner
NM $15 MIP $25

Roughstuff, 1990, Kenner
NM $15 MIP $30

Shockwave, 1990, Kenner
NM $15 MIP $30

Skyfall, 1990, Kenner
NM $12 MIP $25

Snarl, 1990, Kenner
NM $12 MIP $25

Soundwave, 1990, Kenner
NM $15 MIP $30

Sprocket, 1990, Kenner
NM $35 MIP $55

Tanker Truck, 1990, Kenner
NM $35 MIP $65

Treadshot, 1990, Kenner
NM $10 MIP $20

Wheeljack, 1990, Kenner
NM $35 MIP $55

GENERATION 2, SERIES 1, 1993

Afterburner, 1993, Kenner
NM $3 MIP $12

Bonecrusher, orange, 1993, Kenner
NM $5 MIP $17

Bonecrusher, yellow, 1993, Kenner
NM $3 MIP $12

Bumblebee, 1993, Kenner
NM $5 MIP $15

Deluge, changes colors, 1993, Kenner
NM $5 MIP $15

Drench, changes colors, 1993, Kenner
NM $5 MIP $15

Eagle Eye, 1993, Kenner
NM $3 MIP $12

Gobots, changes colors, 1993, Kenner
NM $5 MIP $15

Grimlock, dark blue, 1993, Kenner
NM $20 MIP $45

Grimlock, silver, 1993, Kenner
NM $25 MIP $75

Grimlock, turquoise, 1993, Kenner
NM $40 MIP $120

Hook, orange, 1993, Kenner
NM $5 MIP $15

Hook, yellow, 1993, Kenner
NM $3 MIP $12

Hubcap, 1993, Kenner
NM $5 MIP $15

Inferno, 1993, Kenner
NM $15 MIP $40

Jazz, 1993, Kenner
NM $40 MIP $120

Jetstorm, changes colors, 1993, Kenner
NM $5 MIP $15

Long Haul, orange, 1993, Kenner
NM $5 MIP $15

Long Haul, yellow, 1993, Kenner
NM $3 MIP $12

Mixmaster, orange, 1993, Kenner
NM $5 MIP $15

Mixmaster, yellow, 1993, Kenner
NM $3 MIP $12

Ramjet, missiles grouped, 1993, Kenner
NM $15 MIP $45

Ramjet, missiles separate, 1993, Kenner
NM $20 MIP $55

Rapido, 1993, Kenner
NM $3 MIP $12

Scavenger, orange, 1993, Kenner
NM $5 MIP $15

Scavenger, yellow, 1993, Kenner
NM $3 MIP $12

Scrapper, orange, 1993, Kenner
NM $5 MIP $15

Scrapper, yellow, 1993, Kenner
NM $5 MIP $15

Seaspray, 1993, Kenner
NM $5 MIP $15

Sideswipe, 1993, Kenner
NM $35 MIP $65

Skram, 1993, Kenner
NM $5 MIP $15

Slag, green, 1993, Kenner
NM $20 MIP $60

Slag, red, 1993, Kenner
NM $25 MIP $75

Slag, silver, 1993, Kenner
NM $35 MIP $80

Snarl, green, 1993, Kenner
NM $20 MIP $60

Snarl, red, 1993, Kenner
NM $15 MIP $75

Snarl, silver, 1993, Kenner
NM $20 MIP $80

Starscream, missiles grouped, 1993, Kenner
NM $15 MIP $45

Starscream, missiles separate, 1993, Kenner
NM $20 MIP $55

Terradive, 1993, Kenner
NM $5 MIP $15

Turbofire, 1993, Kenner
NM $5 MIP $15

Windbreaker, 1993, Kenner
NM $5 MIP $15

Windrazor, 1993, Kenner
NM $5 MIP $15

GENERATION 2, SERIES 2, 1994

Air Raid, 1994, Kenner
NM $5 MIP $15

Blast Off, 1994, Kenner
NM $5 MIP $15

Brawl, 1994, Kenner
NM $8 MIP $20

Electro, 1994, Kenner
NM $5 MIP $15

Fireflight, 1994, Kenner
NM $5 MIP $15

Jolt, 1994, Kenner
NM $5 MIP $15

Leadfoot, 1994, Kenner
NM $3 MIP $12

Manta Ray, 1994, Kenner
NM $3 MIP $12

Megatron, purple and black camouflage, 1994, Kenner
NM $30 MIP $55

Onslaught, 1994, Kenner
NM $10 MIP $40

Optimus Prime, red and white, 1994, Kenner
NM $35 MIP $80

Powerdive, black rotors, 1994, Kenner
NM $8 MIP $20

Powerdive, red rotors, 1994, Kenner
NM $3 MIP $12

Ransack, black rotors, 1994, Kenner
NM $8 MIP $20

Ransack, red rotors, 1994, Kenner
NM $3 MIP $12

Silverbolt, 1994, Kenner, blue and red body
NM $15 MIP $40

Sizzle, 1994, Kenner
NM $5 MIP $15

Skydive, 1994, Kenner
NM $5 MIP $15

Slingshot, 1994, Kenner
NM $5 MIP $15

Swindle, 1994, Kenner
NM $5 MIP $15

Volt, 1994, Kenner
NM $5 MIP $15

Vortex, 1994, Kenner
NM $5 MIP $15

GENERATION 2, SERIES 3, 1995

Air Raid, 1995, Kenner
NM $2 MIP $6

Blowout, 1995, Kenner
NM $3 MIP $10

Bumblebee, 1995, Kenner
NM $3 MIP $10

Transformers (Kenner, 1984-1995)

ACTION FIGURES

Dirtbag, 1995, Kenner
NM $3 MIP $12

Double Clutch, 1995, Kenner
NM $3 MIP $10

Firecracker, 1995, Kenner
NM $3 MIP $10

Frenzy, 1995, Kenner
NM $3 MIP $10

Gearhead, clear, 1995, Kenner
NM $3 MIP $10

Gearhead, solid, 1995, Kenner
NM $3 MIP $10

High Beam, 1995, Kenner
NM $3 MIP $10

Hooligan, 1995, Kenner
NM $2 MIP $6

Ironhide, 1995, Kenner
NM $3 MIP $10

Jetfire, 1995, Kenner
NM $2 MIP $6

Megatron, 1995, Kenner
NM $3 MIP $10

Mirage, 1995, Kenner
NM $3 MIP $10

Motormouth, clear, 1995, Kenner
NM $3 MIP $10

Motormouth, solid, 1995, Kenner
NM $3 MIP $10

Optimus Prime, 1995, Kenner
NM $20 MIP $45

Roadblock, 1995, Kenner
NM $3 MIP $12

Sideswipe, 1995, Kenner
NM $3 MIP $10

Skyjack, 1995, Kenner
NM $2 MIP $6

Soundwave, 1995, Kenner
NM $3 MIP $10

Space Case, 1995, Kenner
NM $2 MIP $6

Strafe, 1995, Kenner
NM $2 MIP $6

Transformers: Beast Wars (Kenner, 1996-1999)

BASIC BEAST, 1996

Airazor, 1996, Kenner
NM $10 MIP $30

Armordillo, 1996, Kenner
NM $5 MIP $15

Claw Jaw, 1996, Kenner
NM $8 MIP $25

Drill Bit, 1996, Kenner
NM $8 MIP $25

Iguanus, 1996, Kenner
NM $10 MIP $30

Insecticon, 1996, Kenner
NM $5 MIP $15

Lazorbeak, 1996, Kenner
NM $8 MIP $25

Rattrap, 1996, Kenner
NM $15 MIP $50

Razorbeast, 1996, Kenner
NM $15 MIP $45

Razorclaw, 1996, Kenner
NM $10 MIP $30

Snapper, 1996, Kenner
NM $8 MIP $20

Snarl, 1996, Kenner
NM $8 MIP $25

Terrorsaur, 1996, Kenner
NM $15 MIP $50

BASIC BEAST, 1997

Powerpinch, 1997, Kenner
NM $8 MIP $25

Spittor, 1997, Kenner
NM $8 MIP $25

BASIC FUZORS, 1998

Air Hammer, 1998, Kenner
NM $5 MIP $15

Bantor, 1998, Kenner
NM $3 MIP $8

Buzzclaw, 1998, Kenner
NM $3 MIP $8

Noctorro, 1998, Kenner
NM $3 MIP $8

Quickstrike, 1998, Kenner
NM $5 MIP $15

Terragator, 1998, Kenner
NM $4 MIP $12

BASIC TRANSMETAL 2, 1999

Optimus Minor, 1999, Kenner
NM $8 MIP $25

Scarem, 1999, Kenner
NM $3 MIP $8

Sonar, 1999, Kenner
NM $3 MIP $8

Spittor, 1999, Kenner
NM $3 MIP $10

COMIC 2-PACK, 1996

Megatron, 1996, Kenner
NM $15 MIP $50

Optimus Primal, 1996, Kenner
NM $15 MIP $50

DELUXE BEAST, 1996

Blackarachnia, 1996, Kenner
NM $40 MIP $115

Bonecrusher, 1996, Kenner
NM $15 MIP $50

Buzz Saw, 1996, Kenner
NM $25 MIP $75

Cheetor, blue eyes, 1996, Kenner
NM $50 MIP $150

Cheetor, red eyes, 1996, Kenner
NM $40 MIP $120

Cybershark, 1996, Kenner
NM $30 MIP $90

Dinobot, 1996, Kenner
NM $40 MIP $110

Jetstorm, 1996, Kenner
NM $15 MIP $45

Rhinox, 1996, Kenner
NM $40 MIP $110

Tarantulas, 1996, Kenner
NM $40 MIP $125

Tigatron, 1996, Kenner
NM $30 MIP $100

Waspinator, 1996, Kenner
NM $40 MIP $125

Wolfang, 1996, Kenner
NM $40 MIP $110

DELUXE BEAST, 1997

Grimlock, 1997, Kenner
NM $25 MIP $75

K-9, 1997, Kenner
NM $8 MIP $25

Manterror, 1997, Kenner
NM $15 MIP $50

Retrax, 1997, Kenner
NM $8 MIP $25

DELUXE FUZORS, 1998

Injector, 1998, Kenner
NM $4 MIP $12

Silverbolt, 1998, Kenner
NM $8 MIP $25

Sky Shadow, 1998, Kenner
NM $4 MIP $12

Torca, 1998, Kenner
NM $3 MIP $10

DELUXE TRANSMETAL 2, 1999

Iguanus, 1999, Kenner
NM $3 MIP $10

Jawbreaker, 1999, Kenner
NM $3 MIP $10

Ramulus, 1999, Kenner
NM $5 MIP $15

Scourge, 1999, Kenner
NM $4 MIP $12

DELUXE TRANSMETALS, 1998

Airazor, 1998, Kenner
NM $8 MIP $20

Cheetor, 1998, Kenner
NM $8 MIP $25

Rattrap, 1998, Kenner
NM $10 MIP $30

Rhinox, 1998, Kenner
NM $15 MIP $35

Tarantulas, 1998, Kenner
NM $8 MIP $20

Terrorsaur, 1998, Kenner
NM $5 MIP $15

Waspinator, 1998, Kenner
NM $8 MIP $25

MEGA BEAST, 1996

B'Boom, 1996, Kenner
NM $8 MIP $25

Polar Claw, 1996, Kenner
NM $20 MIP $65

Scorponok, 1996, Kenner
NM $15 MIP $45

MEGA BEAST, 1997

Inferno, 1997, Kenner
NM $15 MIP $45

Transquito, 1997, Kenner
NM $8 MIP $20

MEGA TRANSMETAL 2, 1999

Blackarachnia, 1999, Kenner
NM $15 MIP $45

Cybershark, 1999, Kenner
NM $5 MIP $15

MEGA TRANSMETALS, 1998

Megatron, 1998, Kenner
NM $8 MIP $20

Optimus Primal, 1998, Kenner
NM $8 MIP $25

Scavenger, 1998, Kenner
NM $5 MIP $15

SUPER BEAST, 1998

Optimal Optimus, 1998, Kenner
NM $8 MIP $20

ULTRA BEAST, 1996

Megatron, 1996, Kenner
NM $15 MIP $50

Optimus Primal, 1996, Kenner
NM $20 MIP $60

ULTRA TEAM, 1997

Magnaboss (Maximal Team)—Ironhide, Silverbolt, Prowl, 1997, Kenner
NM $8 MIP $25

Tripredacus (Predacon Team)-Ram Horn, Sea Clamp, Cicadacon, 1997, Kenner
NM $8 MIP $25

ULTRA TRANSMETAL 2, 1999

Megatron, 1999, Kenner
NM $25 MIP $70

Tigerhawk, 1999, Kenner
NM $20 MIP $40

ULTRA TRANSMETALS, 1998

Depth Charge, 1998, Kenner
NM $10 MIP $35

Rampage, 1998, Kenner
NM $8 MIP $20

VIDEO PACK-IN, 1998

Airazor, 1998, Kenner
NM $8 MIP $25

Razorclaw, 1998, Kenner
NM $8 MIP $25

Tron (Tomy, 1981)

FIGURES

Flynn, 1981, 4", Tomy, disk
NM $15 MIP $50

Sark, 1981, 4", Tomy, red figure w/disk
NM $15 MIP $50

Tron, 1981, 4", Tomy, disk
NM $15 MIP $65

Warrior, 1981, 4", Tomy, red figure w/staff
NM $15 MIP $55

VEHICLES

Light Cycle, 1981, 4", Tomy, red or yellow
NM $25 MIP $55

Tuff Talkin' Wrestlers (Toy Biz, 1999)

FIGURES

Goldberg/Kevin Nash, 1999, Toy Biz
NM $20 MIP $40

Sting/Diamond Dallas Page, 1999, Toy Biz
NM $20 MIP $40

Universal Monsters (Remco, 1979)

8" FIGURES

Creature From the Black Lagoon, 1979, 8"
NM $75 MIP $200

Dracula, 1979, 8"
NM $40 MIP $100

Frankenstein, 1979, 8"
NM $20 MIP $40

Mummy, The, 1979, 8"
NM $20 MIP $40

Phantom of the Opera, 1979, 8"
NM $100 MIP $250

Wolfman, The, 1979, 8"
NM $55 MIP $130

Universal Monsters (Sideshow Toys, 1998-Present)

1/4 SCALE

Frankenstein, 2004, 18", Sideshow Toys, #7102, limited to 1,000
NM n/a MIP $225

Vampyre - Count Orlock, 1998, 18", Sideshow Toys, #7101R, limited to 700
NM n/a MIP $150

12" FIGURES

Bela Lugosi as Bela the Gypsy, 1998, 12", Sideshow Toys, #4412
NM n/a MIP $30

Bela Lugosi as Dracula, 1998, 12", Sideshow Toys, #4405
NM n/a MIP $40

Bela Lugosi as Frankenstein, 1998, 12", Sideshow Toys, #4410
NM n/a MIP $30

Bela Lugosi as Murder Legendre, 1998, 12", Sideshow Toys, #7002
NM n/a MIP $40

Boris Karloff as the Monster from Bride of Frankenstein, 1998, 12", Sideshow Toys, #4413
NM n/a MIP $40

Boris Karloff as The Mummy, 1998, 12", Sideshow Toys, #4418R
NM n/a MIP $40

Creature from the Black Lagoon, 2003, 12", Sideshow Toys, #4423
NM n/a MIP $75

Dwight Frye as Fritz, 1998, 12", Sideshow Toys, #4406, from Frankenstein
NM n/a MIP $30

Dwight Frye as Renfield, 1998, 12", Sideshow Toys, #4411
NM n/a MIP $30

Elsa Lanchester as Bride of Frankenstein, 1998, 12", Sideshow Toys, #4414
NM n/a MIP $40

Frankenstein Monster, 1998, 12", Sideshow Toys, #4416R, Son of Frankenstein
NM n/a MIP $40

Glenn Strange as Frankenstein, 1998, 12", Sideshow Toys, #4409
NM n/a MIP $30

Henry Hill as Werewolf of London, 1998, 12", Sideshow Toys, #4421R
NM n/a MIP $40

Lon Chaney as Frankenstein, 1998, 12", Sideshow Toys, #4408
NM n/a MIP $30

Lon Chaney as the Vampire, 1998, 12", Sideshow Toys, #4404, London After Midnight
NM n/a MIP $30

Lon Chaney Jr. as Larry Talbot, 1998, 12", Sideshow Toys, #4407
NM n/a MIP $40

Lon Chaney Sr. as Phantom, 1998, 12", Sideshow Toys, #4403
NM n/a MIP $40

Max Schreck as Vampyre, 1998, 12", Sideshow Toys, #7001
NM n/a MIP $30

Phantom of the Opera Mask of the Red Death, 1998, 12", Sideshow Toys, #4415R
NM n/a MIP $40

The Creature from The Creature Walks Among Us, 1998, 12", Sideshow Toys, #4419R
NM n/a MIP $40

The Mole Man from The Mole People, 1998, 12", Sideshow Toys, #4422R
NM n/a MIP $40

Wolfman, The, 2000, 12", Sideshow Toys
NM $8 MIP $30

SERIES I, 8" FIGURES

Creature from the Black Lagoon, special edition, 2001, Sideshow Toys, Fully poseable translucent figure
NM $10 MIP $15

Universal Monsters (Sideshow Toys, 1998-Present)

Frankenstein, 1998-99, 8", Sideshow Toys
NM $6 **MIP** $15

Mummy, The, 1998-99, 8", Sideshow Toys
NM $8 **MIP** $20

Wolfman, The, 1998-99, 8", Sideshow Toys, With log base and trap. Packaged in movie-poster style box
NM $8 **MIP** $20

SERIES II, 8" FIGURES

Bride of Frankenstein, 1998-99, 8", Sideshow Toys, Detailed figure with stand
NM $8 **MIP** $20

Creature from the Black Lagoon, 1998-99, 8", Sideshow Toys, Realistic-looking gilled Creature with stand (showing abandoned harpoon gun)
NM $8 **MIP** $20

Phantom of the Opera, 1998-99, 8", Sideshow Toys, Highly-detailed figure with stand
NM $8 **MIP** $20

SERIES III, 8" FIGURES

Hunchback of Notre Dame, 1998-99, 8", Sideshow Toys, Detailed figure with purple cloak, scepter and green crown
NM $7 **MIP** $15

Invisible Man, 1998-99, 8", Sideshow Toys
NM $7 **MIP** $15

Metaluna Mutant, 1998-99, 8", Sideshow Toys, Blue-gray detailed alien from "This Island Earth." A neat figure
NM $7 **MIP** $15

SERIES IV, 8" FIGURES

Mole People, The, 2000, 8", Sideshow Toys, Fun-looking figure--even includes mushroom accessories!
NM $5 **MIP** $15

Son of Frankenstein, 2000, 8", Sideshow Toys, Figure with fabric outer garment and replaceable arm
NM $5 **MIP** $15

Werewolf of London, 2000, 8", Sideshow Toys, With cap, scarf and flower
NM $5 **MIP** $15

SILVER SCREEN EDITION

Boris Karloff as Frankenstein, 1998, 12", Sideshow Toys, #44012R
NM n/a **MIP** $40

Frankenstein, 2000, 8", Sideshow Toys, Series 1
NM $5 **MIP** $15

Lon Chaney as Phantom of the Opera, 1998, 12", Sideshow Toys, #44032R
NM n/a **MIP** $40

Lon Chaney in London After Midnight, 1998, 12", Sideshow Toys, #44042R
NM n/a **MIP** $40

Lon Chaney Jr. as The Wolf Man, 1998, 12", Sideshow Toys, #44022R
NM n/a **MIP** $40

Max Schreck as Vampyre, 1998, 12", Sideshow Toys, #70012R
NM n/a **MIP** $40

Mummy, The, 2000, 8", Sideshow Toys, Series 1
NM $5 **MIP** $15

Wolfman, The, 2000, 8", Sideshow Toys, Series 1
NM $5 **MIP** $15

Universal Monsters: Hasbro Signature Series (Hasbro, 1998)

FIGURES

Bride of Frankenstein, The, 1998, 12", Hasbro
NM $10 **MIP** $25

Creature from the Black Lagoon, 1998, 12", Hasbro, Series 2
NM $10 **MIP** $20

Frankenstein, 1998, 12", Hasbro
NM $10 **MIP** $25

Mummy, The, 1998, 12", Hasbro
NM $10 **MIP** $25

Phantom of the Opera, 1998, 12", Hasbro, Series 2
NM $10 **MIP** $20

Son of Dracula, 1998, 12", Hasbro, Series 2
NM $10 **MIP** $20

The Invisible Man, 1998, 12", Hasbro, Series 2
NM $10 **MIP** $20

Wolf Man, The, 1998, 12", Hasbro
NM $10 **MIP** $25

Vault, The (Toy Biz, 1998)

6" FIGURES

Stegron, 1998, 6", Marvel
NM $3 **MIP** $6

Typhoid Mary, 1998, 6", Marvel
NM $3 **MIP** $6

Ultron, 1998, 6", Marvel
NM $3 **MIP** $6

Vikings (Marx, 1960s)

FIGURES

Brave Erik the Viking, 1970-72, 12", Marx, #5430, lime-green outfit, blonde hair, blue eyes - like many Marx figures, this too had a molded-uniform with other plastic accessories and clothing included in the package
NM $125 **MIP** $300

Mighty Viking Horse, 1970-72, Marx, #5381, Palomino for Erik, Brown for Odin, 11-piece vinyl tack set, wheels in hooves, nodding heads
NM $125 **MIP** $300

Odin the Viking Chieftan, 1970-72, 12", Marx, #5440, molded carmel outfit, brown hair, full beard
NM $125 **MIP** $300

Voltron (LJN, 1984)

FIGURES

Battling Black Lion, 1984, LJN
NM $7 **MIP** $30

Black Lion, 1984, LJN, Motorized Lion Force
NM $7 **MIP** $20

Blue Lion & Red Lion, 1984, LJN, Motorized Lion Force
NM $7 **MIP** $20

Green Lion & Yellow Lion, 1984, LJN, Motorized Lion Force
NM $7 **MIP** $20

Lion Force Fortress, 1984, LJN
NM $15 **MIP** $35

Radio-Controlled Voltron, 1984, LJN
NM $10 **MIP** $20

Voltron Assembler - Lion Force, 1984, 6", LJN, disassembles
NM $7 **MIP** $15

Voltron Assembler - Vehicle Team, 1984, 6", LJN, disassembles
NM $7 **MIP** $15

Voltron Assembler Gift Set, 1984, 6", LJN, both Lion Force and Vehicle Team assemblers
NM $10 **MIP** $20

Voltron Motorized, 1984, LJN, w/ Motorized Black, Blue, Red, Green & Yellow Lions
NM $20 **MIP** $40

Voltron (Matchbox, 1985-86)

3-3/4" FIGURES

Doom Commander, 1985-86, 3-3/4", Matchbox
NM $5 **MIP** $15

Haggar the Witch, 1985-86, 3-3/4", Matchbox
NM $5 **MIP** $15

Hunk, 1985-86, 3-3/4", Matchbox
NM $8 **MIP** $20

Keith, 1985-86, 3-3/4", Matchbox
NM $8 **MIP** $20

King Zarkon, 1985-86, 3-3/4", Matchbox
NM $5 **MIP** $15

Lance, 1985-86, 3-3/4", Matchbox
NM $5 **MIP** $15

Pidge, 1985-86, 3-3/4", Matchbox
NM $5 **MIP** $15

Prince Lotor, 1985-86, 3-3/4", Matchbox
NM $8 **MIP** $20

Princess Allura, 1985-86, 3-3/4", Matchbox
NM $8 **MIP** $20

Robeast Mutilor, 1985-86, 3-3/4", Matchbox
NM $4 **MIP** $10

Robeast Scorpious, 1985-86, 3-3/4", Matchbox
NM $4 **MIP** $12

Skull Scavenger, 1985-86, 3-3/4", Matchbox, pilot of the Skull Tank
NM $7 **MIP** $15

Voltron Robot, 1985-86, 3-3/4", Matchbox
NM $10 **MIP** $30

GIFT SETS

Deluxe Gift Set I, 1985-86, Matchbox, Warrior
NM $65 **MIP** $225

Deluxe Gift Set II, 1985-86, Matchbox, Gladiator
NM $55 **MIP** $200

Deluxe Gift Set III, 1985-86, Matchbox, Lion
NM $55 **MIP** $200

MINIATURES

Voltron I, 1985-86, 7", Matchbox, die-cast
NM $15 **MIP** $30

Voltron II, 1985-86, 7", Matchbox, die-cast
NM $15 **MIP** $30

Voltron III, 1985-86, 7", Matchbox, die-cast
NM $15 **MIP** $30

VEHICLES

Castle of Lions, 1985-86, Matchbox
NM $80 **MIP** $160

Voltron (Matchbox, 1985-86)

Coffin of Darkness, 1985-86, Matchbox
NM $8 **MIP** $20

Coffin of Doom, 1985-86, Matchbox
NM $8 **MIP** $20

Doom Blaster, 1985-86, Matchbox
NM $12 **MIP** $25

Skull Tank, 1985-86, Matchbox
NM $12 **MIP** $25

Zarkon Zapper, 1985-86, Matchbox
NM $12 **MIP** $25

Waltons (Mego, 1975)

8" FIGURES

Grandma and Grandpa, 1975, Mego
NM $32 **MIP** $70

John Boy and Ellen, 1975, Mego
NM $32 **MIP** $70

Mom and Pop, 1975, Mego
NM $32 **MIP** $70

ACCESSORIES

Barn, 1975, Mego
NM $55 **MIP** $150

Country Store, 1975, Mego
NM $65 **MIP** $110

Truck, 1975, Mego
NM $40 **MIP** $80

PLAY SETS

Farm House, 1975, Mego
NM $75 **MIP** $150

Farm House with Six Figures, 1975, Mego
NM $200 **MIP** $400

Warrior Beasts, The (Remco, 1983)

FIGURES

Craven, 1983
NM $15 **MIP** $50

Gecko, 1983
NM $15 **MIP** $60

Guana, 1983
NM $15 **MIP** $50

Hydraz, 1983
NM $15 **MIP** $60

Ramar, 1983
NM $15 **MIP** $50

Skullman, 1983
NM $25 **MIP** $90

Snake Man, 1983
NM $25 **MIP** $90

Stegos, 1983
NM $15 **MIP** $50

Wolf Warrior, 1983
NM $30 **MIP** $90

Zardus, 1983
NM $15 **MIP** $50

WCW Bash at the Beach (Toy Biz, 2000)

6" FIGURES

Diamond Dallas Page, 2000, Toy Biz
NM $3 **MIP** $8

Goldberg, 2000, Toy Biz
NM $3 **MIP** $8

Hulk Hogan, 2000, Toy Biz
NM $3 **MIP** $8

Lex Luger, 2000, Toy Biz
NM $3 **MIP** $8

Sting, 2000, Toy Biz
NM $3 **MIP** $8

WCW Collector Series (Toy Biz, 2000)

12" FIGURES

Goldberg, 2000, Toy Biz
NM $5 **MIP** $15

Hulk Hogan, 2000, Toy Biz
NM $5 **MIP** $15

Sting, 2000, Toy Biz
NM $5 **MIP** $15

WCW Cyborg Wrestlers (Toy Biz, 2000)

6" FIGURES

Bret Hart, 2000, Toy Biz
NM $3 **MIP** $8

Goldberg, 2000, Toy Biz
NM $3 **MIP** $8

Kevin Nash, 2000, Toy Biz
NM $3 **MIP** $8

Sid Vicious, 2000, Toy Biz
NM $3 **MIP** $8

Sting, 2000, Toy Biz
NM $3 **MIP** $8

WCW Nitro Active Wrestlers (Toy Biz, 2000)

6" FIGURES

Buff Bagwell, 2000, Toy Biz
NM $3 **MIP** $8

Goldberg, 2000, Toy Biz
NM $3 **MIP** $8

Jeff Jarrett, 2000, Toy Biz
NM $3 **MIP** $8

Sid Vicious, 2000, Toy Biz
NM $3 **MIP** $8

Vampiro, 2000, Toy Biz
NM $3 **MIP** $8

WCW Power Slam Wrestlers I (Toy Biz, 2000)

6" FIGURES

Goldberg, 2000, Toy Biz
NM $3 **MIP** $8

Hak, 2000, Toy Biz
NM $3 **MIP** $8

Hulk Hogan, 2000, Toy Biz
NM $3 **MIP** $8

Rodman, 2000, Toy Biz
NM $3 **MIP** $8

Sid Vicious, 2000, Toy Biz
NM $3 **MIP** $8

WCW Power Slam Wrestlers II (Toy Biz, 2000)

6" FIGURES

Buff Bagwell, 2000, Toy Biz
NM $3 **MIP** $8

Kanyon, 2000, Toy Biz
NM $3 **MIP** $8

Kevin Nash, 2000, Toy Biz
NM $3 **MIP** $8

Roddy Piper, 2000, Toy Biz
NM $3 **MIP** $8

Sting, 2000, Toy Biz
NM $3 **MIP** $8

WCW S.L.A.M. Force (Toy Biz, 2000)

6" FIGURES

Benoit with comic book, 2000, Toy Biz
NM $3 **MIP** $8

Bret Hart with comic book, 2000, Toy Biz
NM $3 **MIP** $8

Goldberg with comic book, 2000, Toy Biz
NM $3 **MIP** $8

Kevin Nash with comic book, 2000, Toy Biz
NM $3 **MIP** $8

Sting with comic book, 2000, Toy Biz
NM $3 **MIP** $8

WCW Thunder Slam Twin Packs (Toy Biz, 2000)

6" FIGURES

Bam Bam Bigelow and Goldberg, 2000, Toy Biz
NM $3 **MIP** $10

Kevin Nash and Scott Hall, 2000, Toy Biz
NM $3 **MIP** $10

Sting and Bret Hart, 2000, Toy Biz
NM $3 **MIP** $10

WCW World Championship Wrestling Ring Fighters (Toy Biz, 1999)

6" FIGURES

Booker T, 1999
NM $3 **MIP** $10

Bret Hart, 1999
NM $3 **MIP** $10

Chris Benoit, 1999
NM $3 **MIP** $10

Scott Steiner, 1999
NM $3 **MIP** $10

WCW World Championship Wrestling Smash 'n Slam (Toy Biz, 1999)

6" FIGURES

Hollywood Hogan, 1999
NM $5 **MIP** $15

Kevin Nash, 1999
NM $5 MIP $15

Macho Man Randy Savage, 1999
NM $4 MIP $12

Scott Hall, 1999
NM $5 MIP $15

WCW World Championship Wrestling Smash 'n Slam II (Toy Biz, 1999)

6" FIGURES

D.D.P., 1999
NM $3 MIP $10

Giant & Rey Mysterio Jr., 1999
NM $3 MIP $10

Goldberg & Masked Wrestler, 1999
NM $3 MIP $10

Lex Luger, 1999
NM $3 MIP $10

Sting, 1999
NM $3 MIP $10

WCW/NWO Ring Masters (Toy Biz, 1998)

6" FIGURES

Bret Hart, 1999
NM $3 MIP $10

Chris Jericho, 1999
NM $3 MIP $10

Goldberg, 1999
NM $3 MIP $10

Lex Luger, 1999
NM $3 MIP $10

WCW/NWO Slam 'n Crunch (Toy Biz, 1998)

6" FIGURES

Buff Bagwell, 1999
NM $3 MIP $10

Goldberg, 1999
NM $3 MIP $10

Konnan, 1999
NM $3 MIP $10

Sting, 1999
NM $3 MIP $10

WCW/NWO Two Packs (Toy Biz, 1999)

BATTLE OF THE GIANTS, 6" FIGURES

Giant vs. Kevin Nash, 1999
NM $3 MIP $10

CLASH OF THE CHAMPIONS, 6" FIGURES

Sting vs. Hollywood Hogan, 1999
NM $5 MIP $15

GRIP 'N FLIP WRESTLERS II, 6" FIGURES

Kevin Nash vs. Bret Hart, 1999
NM $3 MIP $10

Scott Steiner vs. Rick Steiner, 1999
NM $3 MIP $10

Sting vs. Lex Luger, 1999
NM $3 MIP $10

GRIP 'N FLIP WRESTLERS, 6" FIGURES

Chris Jericho vs. Dean Malenko, 1999, Toy Biz
NM $3 MIP $10

Goldberg vs. Hollywood Hogan, 1999, Toy Biz
NM $5 MIP $15

Raven vs. Diamond Dallas Page, 1999
NM $3 MIP $10

POWER AND BEAUTY, 6" FIGURES

Macho Man & Elizabeth, 1999
NM $3 MIP $10

Welcome Back, Kotter (Mattel, 1976)

FIGURES

Barbarino, 1976
NM $40 MIP $80

Epstein, 1976
NM $20 MIP $50

Horshback, 1976
NM $20 MIP $50

Mr. Kotter, 1976
NM $20 MIP $50

Washington, 1976
NM $20 MIP $50

PLAY SETS

Welcome Back Kotter Play Set, Deluxe, 1976
NM $50 MIP $150

Welcome Back, Kotter Play Set, 1976, Classroom shown here w/all five figures
NM $40 MIP $100

Wetworks (McFarlane, 1995-96)

SERIES 1

Dane, 1995
NM $3 MIP $10

Dozer, 1995
NM $3 MIP $10

Grail, 1995
NM $3 MIP $10

Mother-One, 1995
NM $5 MIP $15

Vampire, dark green, 1995
NM $5 MIP $15

Vampire, gray, 1995
NM $5 MIP $15

Werewolf, light blue, 1995
NM $5 MIP $15

Werewolf, reddish brown, 1995
NM $8 MIP $20

SERIES 2

Assasin One, blue, 1996
NM $3 MIP $10

Assasin One, red, 1996
NM $3 MIP $10

Blood Queen, all black, 1996
NM $8 MIP $20

Blood Queen, all black with red trim, 1996
NM $8 MIP $20

Delta Commandor, flesh tones, 1996
NM $3 MIP $10

Delta Commander, gold, 1996
NM $3 MIP $10

Frankenstein, brown, 1996
NM $3 MIP $10

Frankenstein, green, 1996
NM $3 MIP $10

Mendoza, flesh colored, 1996
NM $3 MIP $10

Mendoza, half gold, 1996
NM $3 MIP $10

Pilgrim, flesh tones, 1996
NM $5 MIP $15

Pilgrim, gold, 1996
NM $8 MIP $20

Where the Wild Things Are (McFarlane, 2000)

FIGURES

Aaron, 2000
NM $4 MIP $15

Bernard, 2000
NM $4 MIP $15

Emil, 2000
NM $4 MIP $15

Max and Goatboy, 2000
NM $4 MIP $15

Moishe, 2000
NM $4 MIP $15

Tzippy, 2000
NM $4 MIP $15

Witchblade (Moore Action Collectibles, 1998-present)

SERIES I, FIGURES

Ian Nottingham, 1998-present
NM $3 MIP $12

Kenneth Irons, 1998-present
NM $3 MIP $12

Medieval Witchblade, 1998-present
NM $3 MIP $12

Witchblade (Moore Action Collectibles, 1998-present)

Sara Pezzini/Witchblade, 1998-present
NM $3 **MIP** $12

SERIES II, FIGURES

(Moore Action Collectibles)

Aspen Mathews/Fathom, 1998-present, A ripped dude with a mutant right hand.
NM $3 **MIP** $12

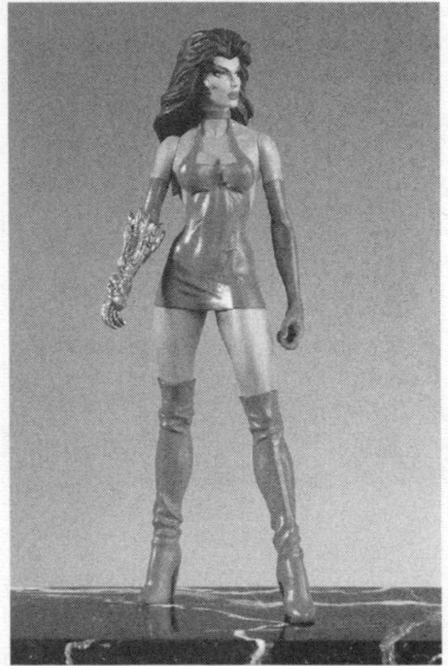

(Moore Action Collectibles)

Sara Pezzini, 1998-present, In red dress, with matching boots.
NM $3 **MIP** $12

Wizard of Oz (Mego, 1974)

4" BOXED FIGURES

Munchkin Dancer, 1974, 4", Mego
NM $75 **MIP** $150

Munchkin Flower Girl, 1974, 4", Mego
NM $75 **MIP** $150

Munchkin General, 1974, 4", Mego
NM $75 **MIP** $150

Munchkin Lollipop Kid, 1974, 4", Mego
NM $75 **MIP** $150

Munchkin Mayor, 1974, 4", Mego
NM $75 **MIP** $150

8" BOXED FIGURES

Cowardly Lion, 1974, 8', Mego
NM $25 **MIP** $60

Dorothy with Toto, 1974, 8', Mego
NM $25 **MIP** $60

Glinda the Good Witch, 1974, 8", Mego
NM $25 **MIP** $60

Scarecrow, 1974, 8", Mego
NM $25 **MIP** $60

Tin Woodsman, 1974, 8", Mego
NM $25 **MIP** $60

Wicked Witch, 1974, 8", Mego
NM $50 **MIP** $100

Wizard of Oz, 1974, 8", Mego
NM $35 **MIP** $250

PLAY SETS

Emerald City, 1974, Mego, Play set with seven 8" figures
NM $125 **MIP** $400

Emerald City with Wizard of Oz, 1974, Mego, Play set with Wizard of Oz
NM $45 **MIP** $100

Munchkin Land, 1974, Mego
NM $150 **MIP** $300

Witch's Castle, Sears Exclusive, 1974, Mego
NM $275 **MIP** $550

Wizard of Oz (Multi-Toys, 1989)

50TH ANNIVERSARY, 12" FIGURES

Cowardly Lion, 1989, Multi-Toys
NM $5 **MIP** $15

Dorothy and Toto, 1989, Multi-Toys
NM $5 **MIP** $15

Glinda, 1989, Multi-Toys
NM $5 **MIP** $15

Scarecrow, 1989, Multi-Toys, Shown with Wicked Witch
NM $5 **MIP** $15

Tin Man, 1989, Multi-Toys
NM $5 **MIP** $15

Wicked Witch, 1989, Multi-Toys
NM $5 **MIP** $15

Wizard, 1989, Multi-Toys
NM $5 **MIP** $15

Wonder Woman Series (Mego, 1977-80)

FIGURES

Major Steve Trevor, 1978, 12", Mego, Left, in white suit
NM $26 **MIP** $100

Nubia, 1978, 12", Mego
NM $50 **MIP** $150

Queen Hippolyte, 1978, 12", Mego
NM $50 **MIP** $125

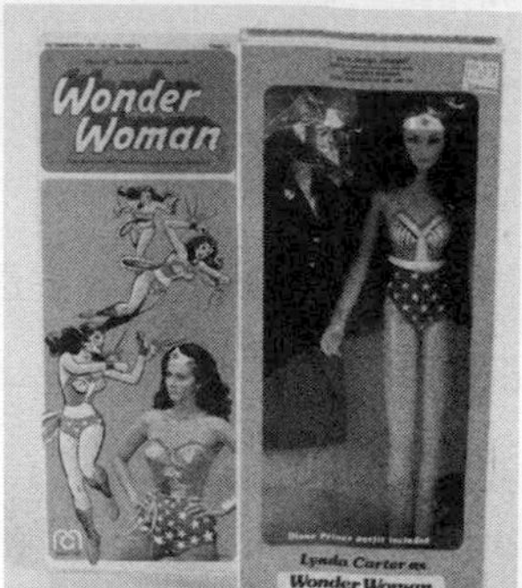

Wonder Woman with Diana Prince Outfit, 1978, 12", Mego
NM $80 **MIP** $250

Wonder Woman with Fly Away Action, 1978, 12", Mego
NM $85 **MIP** $300

World's Greatest Super Knights (Mego, 1975)

8" FIGURES

Black Knight, 1975, 8"
NM $90 **MIP** $355

Ivanhoe, 1975, 8", In full body armor
NM $65 **MIP** $285

King Arthur, 1975, 8"
NM $60 **MIP** $210

Sir Galahad, 1975, 8"
NM $80 **MIP** $300

Sir Lancelot, 1975, 8"
NM $80 **MIP** $300

World's Greatest Super Pirates (Mego, 1974)

FIGURES

Blackbeard, 1974
NM $200 **MIP** $500

Captain Patch, 1974
NM $175 **MIP** $300

Jean Lafitte, 1974
NM $250 **MIP** $550

Long John Silver, 1974
NM $250 **MIP** $550

World's Greatest Super-Heroes (Mego, 1972-78)

12-1/2" FIGURES

Amazing Spider-Man, 1978, 1972-78, 12-1/2", Mego
NM $40 **MIP** $100

Batman, 1978, 1972-78, 12-1/2", Mego, magnetic
NM $100 **MIP** $250

Batman, 1978, 1972-78, 12-1/2", Mego
NM $60 **MIP** $125

Captain America, 1978, 1972-78, 12-1/2", Mego
NM $75 **MIP** $210

Hulk, 1978, 1972-78, 12-1/2", Mego
NM $30 **MIP** $100

Robin, magnetic, 1978, 1972-78, 12-1/2", Mego
NM $125 **MIP** $260

Spider-Man, 1972-78, 12-1/2", Mego, web shooting
NM $75 **MIP** $150

Superman, 1972-78, 12-1/2", Mego
NM $50 **MIP** $135

8" FIGURES

Aquaman, 1972, 8", Mego, carded
NM $50 **MIP** $165

Aquaman, 1972, 8", Mego, Solid box, no window
NM $50 **MIP** $800

Aquaman, 1972, 8", Mego, boxed
NM $50 **MIP** $150

Batgirl, 1973, 8", Mego, boxed
NM $125 **MIP** $325

Batgirl, 1973, 8", Mego, carded
NM $125 **MIP** $300

Batman, 1972, 8", Mego, removable mask, Kresge card only
NM $200 **MIP** $775

Batman, 1972, 8", Mego, painted mask, boxed
NM $60 **MIP** $150

Batman w/ removable cowl, 1972, 8", Mego, Solid box, no window
NM $125 **MIP** $1000

Batman, fist fighting, 1975, 8", Mego, boxed
NM $150 **MIP** $450

Batman, painted mask, 1972, 8", Mego, carded
NM $60 **MIP** $150

Batman, removable mask, 1972, 8", Mego, boxed
NM $200 **MIP** $610

Bruce Wayne, 1974, 8", Mego, boxed, Montgomery Ward Exclusive
NM $1200 **MIP** $2000

Captain America, 1972, 8", Mego, carded
NM $60 **MIP** $160

Captain America, 1972, 8", Mego, boxed
NM $60 **MIP** $250

Catwoman, 1973, 8", Mego, boxed
NM $150 **MIP** $350

Catwoman, 1973, 8", Mego, carded
NM $150 **MIP** $2000

Clark Kent, 1974, 8", Mego, boxed, Montgomery Ward Exclusive
NM $1200 **MIP** $2000

Conan, 1975, 8", Mego, boxed
NM $150 **MIP** $400

Conan, 1975, 8", Mego, carded
NM $150 **MIP** $525

Dick Grayson, 1974, 8", Mego, boxed, Montgomery Ward Exclusive
NM $1200 **MIP** $2000

Falcon, 1974, 8", Mego, boxed
NM $60 **MIP** $150

Falcon, 1974, 8", Mego, carded
NM $60 **MIP** $1500

Green Arrow, 1973, 8", Mego, boxed, with hat, belt and bow and arrow accessories
NM $150 **MIP** $450

Green Arrow, 1973, 8", Mego, carded
NM $150 **MIP** $2000

Green Goblin, 1974, 8", Mego, boxed
NM $90 **MIP** $325

Green Goblin, 1974, 8", Mego, carded
NM $90 **MIP** $2000

Human Torch, Fantastic Four, 1975, 8", Mego, boxed
NM $25 **MIP** $90

Human Torch, Fantastic Four, 1975, 8", Mego, carded
NM $25 **MIP** $55

Incredible Hulk, 1974, 8", Mego, carded
NM $20 **MIP** $55

Incredible Hulk, 1974, 8", Mego, boxed
NM $40 **MIP** $150

World's Greatest Super-Heroes (Mego, 1972-78)

Invisible Girl, Fantastic Four, 1975, 8", Mego, boxed
NM $30 **MIP** $150

Invisible Girl, Fantastic Four, 1975, 8", Mego, carded
NM $30 **MIP** $60

Iron Man, 1974, 8", Mego, boxed
NM $75 **MIP** $125

Iron Man, 1974, 8", Mego, carded
NM $75 **MIP** $475

Isis, 1976, 8", Mego, boxed
NM $75 **MIP** $250

Isis, 1976, 8", Mego, carded
NM $75 **MIP** $125

Joker, 1973, 8", Mego, boxed
NM $60 **MIP** $200

Joker, 1973, 8", Mego, carded
NM $60 **MIP** $150

Joker, fist fighting, 1975, 8", Mego, boxed
NM $150 **MIP** $600

Lizard, 1974, 8", Mego, carded
NM $100 **MIP** $2000

Lizard, 1974, 8", Mego, boxed
NM $75 **MIP** $200

Mr. Fantastic, Fantastic Four, 1975, 8", Mego, boxed
NM $30 **MIP** $140

Mr. Fantastic, Fantastic Four, 1975, 8", Mego, carded
NM $30 **MIP** $60

Mr. Mxyzptlk, open mouth, 1973, 8", Mego, boxed
NM $50 **MIP** $75

Mr. Mxyzptlk, open mouth, 1973, 8", Mego, carded
NM $50 **MIP** $150

Mr. Mxyzptlk, smirk, 1973, 8", Mego, boxed
NM $60 **MIP** $150

Penguin, 1973, 8", Mego, carded
NM $60 **MIP** $125

Penguin, 1973, 8", Mego, boxed
NM $60 **MIP** $150

Peter Parker, 1974, 8", Mego, boxed, Montgomery Ward Exclusive
NM $1200 **MIP** $2000

Riddler, 1973, 8", Mego, carded
NM $100 **MIP** $2000

Riddler, 1973, 8", Mego, boxed
NM $100 **MIP** $250

Riddler, 1975, 8", Mego, fist fighting, boxed
NM $150 **MIP** $600

Robin, 1972, 8", Mego, painted mask, boxed
NM $60 **MIP** $150

Robin, 1972, 8", Mego, painted mask, carded
NM $60 **MIP** $90

Robin, 1972, 8", Mego, removable mask, boxed
NM $250 **MIP** $750

Robin, 1972, 8", removable mask, solid box
NM $250 **MIP** $1500

Robin, 1975, 8", Mego, fist fighting, boxed
NM $125 **MIP** $450

Shazam, 1972, 8", Mego, boxed
NM $75 **MIP** $200

Shazam, 1972, 8", Mego, carded
NM $75 **MIP** $150

Spider-Man, 1972, 8", Mego, boxed
NM $20 **MIP** $100

Spider-Man, 1972, 8", Mego, carded
NM $20 **MIP** $55

Supergirl, 1973, 8", Mego, boxed
NM $300 **MIP** $550

Supergirl, 1973, 8", Mego, carded
NM $300 **MIP** $450

Superman, 1972, 8", Mego, boxed
NM $50 **MIP** $200

Superman, 1972, 8", Mego, carded
NM $50 **MIP** $125

Superman, 1972, 8", Mego, Solid box, no window
NM $50 **MIP** $800

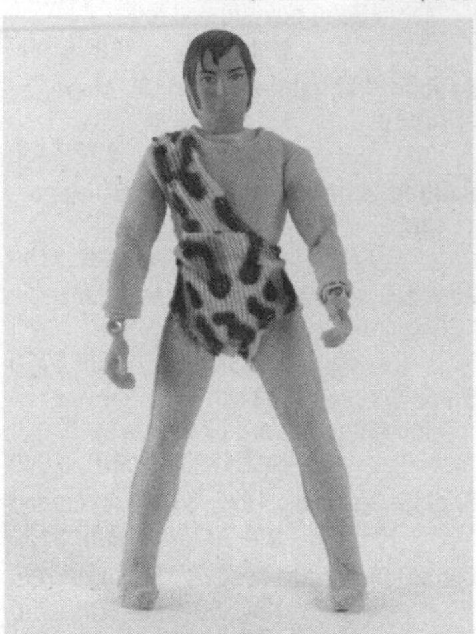

Tarzan, 1972, 8", Mego, boxed
NM $50 **MIP** $150

Tarzan, 1976, 8", Mego, Kresge card only
NM $60 **MIP** $225

Thing, Fantastic Four, 1975, 8", Mego, carded
NM $40 **MIP** $60

Thing, Fantastic Four, 1975, 8", Mego, boxed
NM $40 **MIP** $350

Thor, 1975, 8", Mego, boxed
NM $150 **MIP** $400

Thor, 1975, 8", Mego, carded
NM $150 **MIP** $475

Wonder Woman, 1972-78, 8", Mego, boxed
NM $100 **MIP** $400

Wonder Woman, 1972-78, 8", Mego, Kresge card only
NM $100 **MIP** $475

ACCESSORIES

Super Hero Carry Case, 1973, Mego
NM $40 **MIP** $100

Supervator, 1974, Mego
NM $60 **MIP** $120

PLAY SETS

Aquaman vs. the Great White Shark, 1978, Mego, rare
NM $500 **MIP** $1000

Batcave Play Set, 1974, Mego, vinyl
NM $150 **MIP** $300

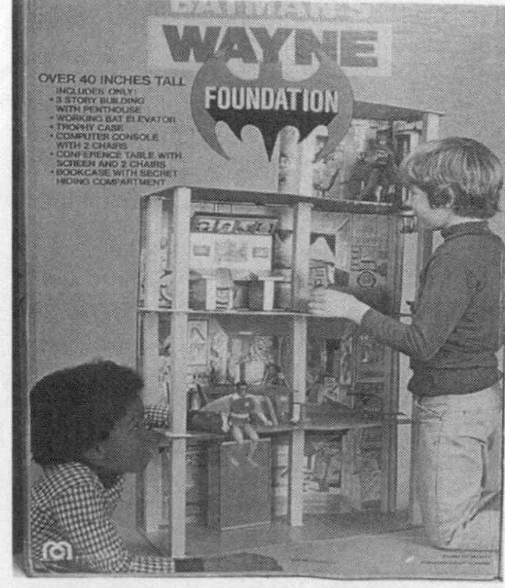

Batman's Wayne Foundation Penthouse, 1977, Mego, fiberboard
NM $600 **MIP** $1000

Hall of Justice, 1976, Mego, vinyl
NM $125 **MIP** $250

SUPERMAN SERIES

General Zod, 1978, 12", Mego
NM $50 **MIP** $100

Jor-El, 1978, 12", Mego
NM $50 **MIP** $100

Lex Luthor, 1978, 12", Mego
NM $50 **MIP** $100

Superman, 1978, 12", Mego, This is easily the best rendition of Superman in an action figure.
NM $55 MIP $135

TEEN TITANS, 6-1/2" FIGURES

Aqualad, 1976, 6-1/2", Mego
NM $175 MIP $350

Kid Flash, 1976, 6-1/2", Mego
NM $175 MIP $450

Speedy, 1976, 6-1/2", Mego
NM $310 MIP $525

Wondergirl, 1976, 6-1/2", Mego
NM $210 MIP $500

VEHICLES

Batcopter, 1974, Mego, on display card
NM $55 MIP $125

Batcopter, 1974, Mego, boxed
NM $75 MIP $160

Batcycle, 1974, Mego, blue, carded
NM $75 MIP $135

Batcycle, 1974, Mego, blue, boxed
NM $75 MIP $170

Batcycle, 1975, Mego, black, carded
NM $60 MIP $150

Batcycle, 1975, Mego, black, boxed
NM $75 MIP $185

Batmobile, 1974, Mego, photo box
NM $75 MIP $400

Batmobile, 1974, Mego, carded
NM $50 MIP $120

Batmobile, 1974, artwork box
NM $75 MIP $325

Batmobile and Batman, 1972-78, Mego
NM $40 MIP $100

Captain Americar, 1976, Mego
NM $125 MIP $275

Green Arrowcar, 1976, Mego
NM $175 MIP $360

Jokermobile, 1976, Mego
NM $150 MIP $410

Mobile Bat Lab, 1975, Mego
NM $125 MIP $410

Spidercar, 1976, 10", Mego
NM $50 MIP $125

WWF (Jakks Pacific, 1997-present)

2-TUFF, SERIES 1

D.O.A., 1997-present
NM $4 MIP $10

Goldust and Marlena, 1997-present
NM $4 MIP $10

HHH and Chyna, 1997-present
NM $4 MIP $10

Truth Commission, 1997-present
NM $4 MIP $10

2-TUFF, SERIES 2

Brian Christopher and Jerry Lawler, 1997-present
NM $4 MIP $12

D-Lo Brown and Kama, 1997-present
NM $4 MIP $12

Kurrgan and Jackyl, 1997-present
NM $4 MIP $12

New Age Outlaws, 1997-present
NM $4 MIP $12

2-TUFF, SERIES 3

Kane and Mankind, 1997-present
NM $4 MIP $12

Legion of Doom 2000, 1997-present
NM $4 MIP $15

Rocky Maivia (The Rock) and Owen Hart, 1997-present
NM $8 MIP $20

Stone Cold Steve Austin/Undertaker, 1997-present
NM $4 MIP $12

2-TUFF, SERIES 4

Billy Gunn and Val Venis, 1997-present
NM $3 MIP $12

Mankind and The Rock, 1997-present
NM $3 MIP $12

Stone Cold Steve Austin and Big Bossman, 1997-present
NM $3 MIP $12

Undertaker and Kane, 1997-present
NM $3 MIP $12

2-TUFF, SERIES 5

Debra and Jarrett, 1997-present
NM $3 MIP $10

Road Dogg and Billy Gunn, 1997-present
NM $3 MIP $10

Stone Cold Steve Austin and The Rock, 1997-present
NM $8 MIP $20

Undertaker and Viscera, 1997-present
NM $3 MIP $10

BEST OF 1997, SERIES 1

Ahmed Johnson, 1997-present
NM $3 MIP $10

Bret Hart, 1997-present
NM $3 MIP $10

British Bulldog, 1997-present
NM $3 MIP $10

Owen Hart, 1997-present
NM $5 MIP $15

Stone Cold Steve Austin, 1997-present
NM $3 MIP $12

Undertaker, 1997-present
NM $3 MIP $10

BEST OF 1997, SERIES 2

Crush, 1997-present
NM $3 MIP $10

Goldust, 1997-present
NM $3 MIP $10

HHH, 1997-present
NM $3 MIP $10

Ken Shamrock, 1997-present
NM $3 MIP $10

Marc Mero, 1997-present
NM $3 MIP $10

Rocky Maivia (The Rock), 1997-present
NM $5 MIP $15

Shawn Michaels, 1997-present
NM $3 MIP $10

Undertaker, 1997-present
NM $3 MIP $10

BEST OF 1998, SERIES 1

8-Ball, 1997-present
NM $3 MIP $8

Blackjack Bradshaw, 1997-present
NM $3 MIP $8

Brian Christopher, 1997-present
NM $3 MIP $8

Chyna, 1997-present
NM $3 MIP $8

Shawn Michaels, 1997-present
NM $3 MIP $8

Skull, 1997-present
NM $3 MIP $8

Stone Cold Steve Austin, 1997-present
NM $4 MIP $10

Vader, 1997-present
NM $3 MIP $8

BEST OF 1998, SERIES 2

Dan Severn, 1997-present
NM $3 MIP $8

Dude Love, 1997-present
NM $3 MIP $8

HHH, 1997-present
NM $3 MIP $8

Jeff Jarrett, 1997-present
NM $3 MIP $8

Ken Shamrock, 1997-present
NM $3 MIP $8

Mark Henry, 1997-present
NM $3 MIP $8

Stone Cold Steve Austin, 1997-present
NM $4 MIP $10

Undertaker, 1997-present
NM $3 MIP $8

BONE CRUNCHIN' BUDDIES, SERIES 1

Dude Love, 1997-present
NM $5 MIP $15

Shawn Michaels, 1997-present
NM $5 MIP $15

Stone Cold Steve Austin, 1997-present
NM $5 MIP $15

Undertaker, 1997-present
NM $5 MIP $15

BONE CRUNCHIN' BUDDIES, SERIES 2

Animal, 1997-present
NM $5 MIP $15

Hawk, 1997-present
NM $5 MIP $15

Rock, The, 1997-present
NM $8 MIP $20

Stone Cold Steve Austin, 1997-present
NM $5 MIP $15

Undertaker, 1997-present
NM $5 MIP $15

BONE CRUNCHIN' BUDDIES, SERIES 3

HHH, 1997-present
NM $5 MIP $15

Kane, 1997-present
NM $5 MIP $15

Rock, The, 1997-present
NM $8 MIP $20

Stone Cold Steve Austin in shirt and pants, 1997-present
NM $5 MIP $15

Stone Cold Steve Austin in tights and vest, 1997-present
NM $5 MIP $15

Undertaker, 1997-present
NM $5 MIP $15

FULLY LOADED, SERIES 1

Al Snow, 1997-present
NM $3 MIP $8

Billy Gunn, 1997-present
NM $3 MIP $8

Hunter Hearst Hemsley, 1997-present
NM $3 MIP $8

Kane, 1997-present
NM $3 MIP $8

Road Dog Jesse James, 1997-present
NM $3 MIP $8

Rocky Maivia (The Rock), 1997-present
NM $5 MIP $15

FULLY LOADED, SERIES 2

Road Dog Jesse James, 1997-present
NM $2 MIP $6

Rock, The, 1997-present
NM $5 MIP $15

Shane McMahon, 1997-present
NM $2 MIP $6

Stone Cold Steve Austin, 1997-present
NM $3 MIP $10

Test, 1997-present
NM $2 MIP $6

X Pac, 1997-present
NM $3 MIP $8

GRUDGE MATCH

Brian Christopher vs. TAKA, 1997-present
NM $5 MIP $15

Dan Severn vs. Ken Shamrock, 1997-present
NM $5 MIP $15

HHH vs. Owen Hart, 1997-present
NM $5 MIP $15

HHHvs HBK, 1997-present
NM $5 MIP $15

Jeff Jarrett vs. X Pac, 1997-present
NM $5 MIP $15

Kane vs. Undertaker, 1997-present
NM $5 MIP $15

Marc Mero vs. Steve Blackman, 1997-present
NM $5 MIP $15

Mark Henry vs. Vader, 1997-present
NM $5 MIP $15

McMahon vs. Stone Cold Steve Austin, 1997-present
NM $5 MIP $15

Road Dog Jesse James vs. Al Snow, 1997-present
NM $5 MIP $15

Sable vs. Luna Vachon, 1997-present
NM $5 MIP $15

Shamrock vs. Billy Gunn, 1997-present
NM $5 MIP $15

Shawn Michaels vs. Stone Cold Steve Austin, 1997-present
NM $8 MIP $20

Stone Cold Steve Austin vs. The Rock, 1997-present
NM $8 MIP $20

LEGENDS, SERIES 1

Andre the Giant, 1997-present
NM $3 MIP $12

Captian Lou Albano, 1997-present
NM $3 MIP $12

Classie Freddie Blassie, 1997-present
NM $3 MIP $12

Jimmy Snuka, 1997-present
NM $3 MIP $12

LIVEWIRE, SERIES 1

Chyna, 1997-present
NM $3 MIP $8

Ken Shamrock, 1997-present
NM $3 MIP $8

Mankind, 1997-present
NM $3 MIP $8

Stone Cold Steve Austin, 1997-present
NM $4 MIP $10

Undertaker, 1997-present
NM $3 MIP $8

Vader, 1997-present
NM $3 MIP $8

LIVEWIRE, SERIES 2

Marc Mero, 1997-present
NM $2 MIP $6

Mark Henry, 1997-present
NM $2 MIP $6

Rock, The, 1997-present
NM $5 MIP $15

Shawn Michaels, 1997-present
NM $2 MIP $6

Val Venis, 1997-present
NM $2 MIP $6

X Pac, 1997-present
NM $2 MIP $6

MANAGER, SERIES 1

Backlund and Sultan, 1997-present
NM $3 MIP $12

Bearer and Mankind, 1997-present
NM $3 MIP $12

Mason and Crush, 1997-present
NM $3 MIP $12

Sable and Mero, 1997-present
NM $3 MIP $12

MAXIMUM SWEAT, SERIES 1

HHH, 1997-present
NM $3 MIP $8

Kane, 1997-present
NM $3 MIP $8

Rock, The, 1997-present
NM $5 MIP $15

Shawn Michaels, 1997-present
NM $3 MIP $8

Stone Cold Steve Austin, 1997-present
NM $3 MIP $10

Undertaker, 1997-present
NM $3 MIP $8

MAXIMUM SWEAT, SERIES 2

Billy Gunn, 1997-present
NM $2 MIP $6

Edge, 1997-present
NM $2 MIP $6

Ken Shamrock, 1997-present
NM $2 MIP $6

Road Dogg Jesse James, 1997-present
NM $2 MIP $6

Stone Cold Steve Austin, 1997-present
NM $3 MIP $10

Undertaker, 1997-present
NM $2 MIP $6

MAXIMUM SWEAT, SERIES 3

Big Bossman, 1997-present
NM $2 MIP $6

Billy Gunn, 1997-present
NM $2 MIP $6

Gangrel, 1997-present
NM $2 MIP $6

Mankind, 1997-present
NM $2 MIP $6

Rock, The, 1997-present
NM $5 MIP $15

Stone Cold Steve Austin, 1997-present
NM $3 MIP $10

RINGSIDE, SERIES 1

Referee, 1997-present
NM $3 MIP $8

Sable, 1997-present
NM $3 MIP $8

Sunny, 1997-present
NM $3 MIP $8

Vince McMahon, 1997-present
NM $3 MIP $8

RINGSIDE, SERIES 2

Honky Tonk Man, 1997-present
NM $2 MIP $6

Jim Cornette, 1997-present
NM $2 MIP $6

Jim Ross, 1997-present
NM $2 MIP $6

Referee, 1997-present
NM $2 MIP $6

Sgt. Slaughter, 1997-present
NM $2 MIP $6

Vince McMahon, 1997-present
NM $2 MIP $6

RIPPED AND RUTHLESS, SERIES 1

Goldust, 1997-present
NM $3 MIP $8

Mankind, 1997-present
NM $3 MIP $8

Stone Cold Steve Austin, 1997-present
NM $4 MIP $10

Undertaker, 1997-present
NM $3 MIP $8

RIPPED AND RUTHLESS, SERIES 2

HHH, 1997-present
NM $3 MIP $10

Kane, 1997-present
NM $5 MIP $15

Sable, 1997-present
NM $5 MIP $15

Shawn Michaels, 1997-present
NM $3 MIP $10

S.T.O.M.P., SERIES 1

Ahmed Johnson, 1997-present
NM $3 MIP $8

Brian Pillman, 1997-present
NM $3 MIP $8

Crush, 1997-present
NM $3 MIP $8

Ken Shamrock, 1997-present
NM $3 MIP $8

Stone Cold Steve Austin, 1997-present
NM $3 MIP $10

Undertaker, 1997-present
NM $3 MIP $8

S.T.O.M.P., SERIES 2

Chyna, 1997-present
NM $3 MIP $8

Mosh, 1997-present
NM $3 MIP $8

Owen Hart, 1997-present
NM $3 MIP $8

Rocky Maivia (The Rock), 1997-present, Jakks Pacific
NM $5 MIP $15

Stone Cold Steve Austin, 1997-present
NM $3 MIP $10

Thrasher, 1997-present
NM $3 MIP $8

S.T.O.M.P., SERIES 3

Animal, 1997-present
NM $3 MIP $8

Hawk, 1997-present
NM $3 MIP $8

Kane, 1997-present
NM $3 MIP $8

Marc Mero, 1997-present
NM $3 MIP $8

Sable, 1997-present
NM $3 MIP $8

Undertaker, 1997-present
NM $3 MIP $8

S.T.O.M.P., SERIES 4

Billy Gunn, 1997-present
NM $2 MIP $6

Chyna, 1997-present
NM $2 MIP $6

HHH, 1997-present
NM $2 MIP $6

Road Dog Jesse James, 1997-present
NM $2 MIP $6

Stone Cold Steve Austin, 1997-present
NM $3 MIP $8

X Pac, 1997-present
NM $2 MIP $6

SHOTGUN SATURDAY NIGHT, SERIES 1

Animal, 1997-present
NM $3 MIP $8

Hawk, 1997-present
NM $3 MIP $8

Henry O. Godwinn, 1997-present
NM $3 MIP $8

Phineas I. Godwinn, 1997-present
NM $3 MIP $8

Rocky Maivia (The Rock), 1997-present
NM $5 MIP $15

Savio Vega, 1997-present
NM $3 MIP $8

Stone Cold Steve Austin, 1997-present
NM $3 MIP $10

Undertaker, 1997-present
NM $3 MIP $8

SHOTGUN SATURDAY NIGHT, SERIES 2

Billy Gunn, 1997-present
NM $2 MIP $6

Jeff Jarrett, 1997-present
NM $2 MIP $6

Kane, 1997-present
NM $2 MIP $6

Road Dog Jesse James, 1997-present
NM $2 MIP $6

Sable, 1997-present
NM $3 MIP $8

Shawn Michaels, 1997-present
NM $2 MIP $6

SIGNATURE, SERIES 1

Animal, 1997-present
NM $3 MIP $8

Goldust, 1997-present
NM $3 MIP $8

Hawk, 1997-present
NM $3 MIP $8

Hunter Hearst Hemsley, 1997-present
NM $3 MIP $8

Mankind, 1997-present
NM $3 MIP $8

Stone Cold Steve Austin, 1997-present
NM $5 MIP $15

SIGNATURE, SERIES 2

Billy Gunn, 1997-present
NM $3 MIP $8

Dude Love, 1997-present
NM $3 MIP $8

Kane, 1997-present
NM $3 MIP $8

Road Dog Jesse James, 1997-present
NM $3 MIP $8

Shawn Michaels, 1997-present
NM $3 MIP $8

Undertaker, 1997-present
NM $3 MIP $8

SIGNATURE, SERIES 3

Edge, 1997-present
NM $3 MIP $8

HHH, 1997-present
NM $2 MIP $6

Jackie, 1997-present
NM $3 MIP $8

Rock, The, 1997-present
NM $5 MIP $15

Stone Cold Steve Austin, 1997-present
NM $5 MIP $15

Undertaker, 1997-present
NM $3 MIP $8

SUNDAY NIGHT HEAT

Billy Gunn, 1997-present
NM $3 MIP $8

Road Dog Jesse James, 1997-present
NM $3 MIP $8

Rock, The, 1997-present
NM $5 MIP $15

Sable, 1997-present
NM $2 MIP $6

Stone Cold Steve Austin, 1997-present
NM $3 MIP $10

Undertaker, 1997-present
NM $3 MIP $8

SUPERSTARS, SERIES 1

Bret Hart, 1997-present
NM $8 MIP $20

Diesel, 1997-present
NM $10 MIP $40

Goldust, 1997-present
NM $8 MIP $20

Razor Ramon, 1997-present
NM $15 MIP $50

Shawn Michaels, 1997-present
NM $5 MIP $15

WWF (Jakks Pacific, 1997-present)

Undertaker, 1997-present
NM $8 MIP $20

SUPERSTARS, SERIES 2

Bret Hart, 1997-present
NM $5 MIP $15

Owen Hart, 1997-present
NM $8 MIP $30

Shawn Michaels, 1997-present
NM $5 MIP $15

Ultimate Warrior, 1997-present
NM $8 MIP $30

Undertaker, 1997-present
NM $10 MIP $30

Vader, 1997-present
NM $5 MIP $15

SUPERSTARS, SERIES 3

Ahmed Johnson, 1997-present
NM $3 MIP $10

Bret Hart, 1997-present
NM $3 MIP $10

British Bulldog, 1997-present
NM $5 MIP $15

Diesel, reissue, 1997-present
NM $5 MIP $15

Goldust, reissue, 1997-present
NM $5 MIP $15

Mankind, 1997-present
NM $3 MIP $10

Shawn Michaels, 1997-present
NM $3 MIP $10

Sycho Sid, 1997-present
NM $3 MIP $10

SUPERSTARS, SERIES 4

Farooq, 1997-present
NM $3 MIP $10

Hunter Hearst Hemsley, 1997-present
NM $3 MIP $10

Jerry The King Lawler, 1997-present
NM $3 MIP $10

Justin Hawk Bradshaw, 1997-present
NM $3 MIP $10

Stone Cold Steve Austin, 1997-present
NM $5 MIP $15

Vader, 1997-present
NM $3 MIP $10

SUPERSTARS, SERIES 5

Flash Funk, 1997-present
NM $3 MIP $10

Ken Shamrock, 1997-present
NM $3 MIP $10

Rocky Maivia, 1997-present
NM $3 MIP $10

Savio Vega, 1997-present
NM $3 MIP $10

Stone Cold Steve Austin, 1997-present
NM $5 MIP $15

Sycho Sid, 1997-present
NM $3 MIP $10

SUPERSTARS, SERIES 6

HHH, 1997-present
NM $3 MIP $10

Jeff Jarrett, 1997-present
NM $2 MIP $6

Marc Mero, 1997-present
NM $2 MIP $6

Mark Henry, 1997-present
NM $2 MIP $6

Owen Hart, 1997-present, Jakks Pacific
NM $5 MIP $15

Steve Blackman, 1997-present
NM $2 MIP $6

SUPERSTARS, SERIES 7

Dr. Death Steve Williams, 1997-present
NM $2 MIP $6

Edge, 1997-present
NM $2 MIP $6

Stone Cold Steve Austin, 1997-present
NM $3 MIP $10

Undertaker, 1997-present
NM $3 MIP $10

Val Venis, 1997-present
NM $2 MIP $6

X Pac, 1997-present
NM $3 MIP $8

SUPERSTARS, SERIES 8

Big Boss Man, 1997-present
NM $2 MIP $6

Ken Shamrock, 1997-present
NM $2 MIP $6

Rock, The, 1997-present
NM $5 MIP $15

Shane McMahon, 1997-present
NM $2 MIP $6

Shawn Michaels, 1997-present
NM $2 MIP $6

SUPERSTARS, SERIES 9

Bob Holly, 1997-present
NM $2 MIP $6

Christian, 1997-present
NM $2 MIP $6

Gangrel, 1997-present
NM $2 MIP $6

Paul Wright, 1997-present
NM $2 MIP $6

Undertaker with robe, 1997-present
NM $2 MIP $6

Vince McMahon, 1997-present
NM $2 MIP $6

TAG TEAM, SERIES 1

Godwinns, 1997-present
NM $4 MIP $15

Headbangers, 1997-present
NM $4 MIP $20

Legion of Doom, 1997-present
NM $4 MIP $25

New Blackjacks, 1997-present
NM $4 MIP $15

TITAN TRON LIVE

Kane, 1997-present
NM $2 MIP $6

Mankind, 1997-present
NM $2 MIP $6

Road Dogg Jesse James, 1997-present
NM $2 MIP $6

Rock, The, 1997-present
NM $5 MIP $15

Stone Cold Steve Austin, 1997-present
NM $3 MIP $10

Undertaker, 1997-present
NM $2 MIP $6

WWF World Wrestling Federation (Hasbro, 1990-94)

FIGURES

1-2-3 Kid, 1994, Hasbro
NM $15 MIP $38

Adam Bomb, 1994, Hasbro
NM $10 MIP $18

Akeem, 1990, Hasbro
NM $15 MIP $38

Andre the Giant, 1990, Hasbro
NM $25 MIP $75

Ax, 1990, Hasbro
NM $5 MIP $15

Bam Bam Bigelow, 1994, Hasbro
NM $6 MIP $15

Bart Gunn, 1994, Hasbro
NM $10 MIP $18

Berzerker, 1993, Hasbro
NM $3 MIP $8

Big Bossman with Jailhouse Jam, 1992, 1992, Hasbro
NM $4 MIP $8

Big Bossman, 1990, 1990, Hasbro
NM $4 MIP $25

Billy Gunn, 1994, Hasbro
NM $10 MIP $18

Bret "Hitman" Hart with Hart Attack, 1992, 1992, Hasbro
NM $5 MIP $13

Bret Hart, 1993 mail-in, 1993, Hasbro
NM $38 MIP n/a

Bret Hart, 1994, 1994, Hasbro
NM $4 MIP $8

British Bulldog with Bulldog Bash, 1992, 1992, Hasbro
NM $4 MIP $8

Brutus "The Barber" Beefcake with Beefcake Flattop, 1992, 1992, Hasbro
NM $6 MIP $13

Brutus the Barber, 1990, 1990, Hasbro
NM $6 MIP $13

Bushwackers, two-pack, 1990-94, Hasbro
NM $5 MIP $25

Butch Miller, 1994, Hasbro
NM $3 MIP $8

Crush, 1993, 1993, Hasbro
NM $6 MIP $13

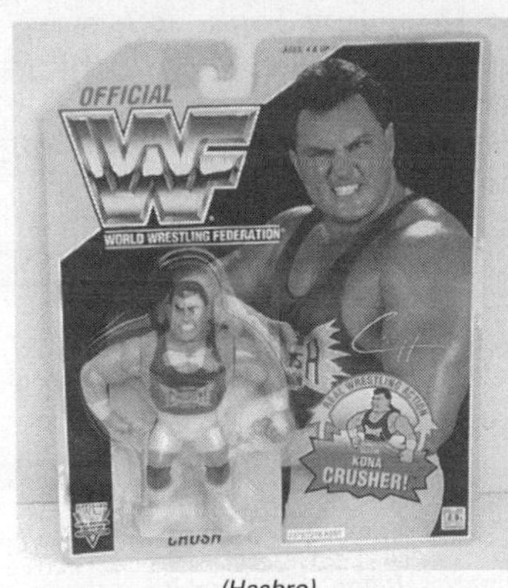

(Hasbro)

Crush, 1994, 1994, Hasbro, Made mincemeat out of his opponents.
NM $3 **MIP** $30

Demolition, two-pack, 1990-94, Hasbro
NM $10 **MIP** $23

Doink the Clown, 1994, Hasbro
NM $4 **MIP** $8

Dusty Rhodes, 1991, Hasbro
NM $63 **MIP** $250

Earthquake, 1991, Hasbro
NM $8 **MIP** $15

Earthquake with Aftershock, 1992, Hasbro
NM $4 **MIP** $13

El Matador, 1993, Hasbro
NM $3 **MIP** $8

Fatu, 1994, Hasbro
NM $3 **MIP** $8

Giant Gonzales, 1994, Hasbro
NM $3 **MIP** $8

Greg "the Hammer" Valentine with Hammer Slammer (1992), 1992, Hasbro
NM $5 **MIP** $15

Hacksaw Jim Duggan, 1991, 1991, Hasbro
NM $3 **MIP** $8

Hacksaw Jim Duggan, 1994, 1994, Hasbro
NM $3 **MIP** $8

Honky Tonk Man, 1991, Hasbro
NM $13 **MIP** $25

Hulk Hogan with Hulkaplex, 1992, 1992, Hasbro
NM $5 **MIP** $10

Hulk Hogan, 1990, 1990, Hasbro
NM $6 **MIP** $13

Hulk Hogan, 1991, 1991, Hasbro
NM $5 **MIP** $10

Hulk Hogan, 1993, mail-in, 1993, Hasbro
NM $38 **MIP** $50

Hulk Hogan, 1993, no shirt, 1993, Hasbro
NM $5 **MIP** $10

I.R.S., 1993, Hasbro
NM $4 **MIP** $8

Jake the Snake Roberts, 1990, Hasbro
NM $5 **MIP** $10

Jim Neidhart, 1993, Hasbro
NM $3 **MIP** $8

Jimmy Superfly Snuka, 1991, Hasbro
NM $6 **MIP** $13

Kamala, 1993, Hasbro
NM $5 **MIP** $13

Koko B. Ware with Bird Man Bounce, 1992, 1992, Hasbro
NM $10 **MIP** $30

Legion of Doom, two-pack, 1990-94, Hasbro
NM $10 **MIP** $20

Lex Luger, 1994, Hasbro
NM $8 **MIP** $15

Ludwig Borga, 1994, Hasbro
NM $20 **MIP** $35

Luke Williams, 1994, Hasbro
NM $5 **MIP** $15

Macho Man Randy Savage with Macho Masher, 1992, 1992, Hasbro
NM $15 **MIP** $35

Macho Man, 1990, 1990, Hasbro
NM $12 **MIP** $25

Macho Man, 1991, 1991, Hasbro
NM $15 **MIP** $35

Macho Man, 1993, 1993, Hasbro
NM $7 **MIP** $15

Marty Jannetty, 1994, Hasbro
NM $5 **MIP** $15

Mountie, 1993, Hasbro
NM $6 **MIP** $15

Mr. Perfect with Perfect Plex, 1992, 1992, Hasbro
NM $8 **MIP** $20

Mr. Perfect with Texas Twister, 1992, 1992, Hasbro
NM $15 **MIP** $35

Mr. Perfect, 1994, 1994, Hasbro
NM $12 **MIP** $25

Nailz, 1993, Hasbro
NM $12 **MIP** $25

Nasty Boys, two-pack, 1990-94, Hasbro
NM $15 **MIP** $80

Owen Hart, 1993, Hasbro
NM $15 **MIP** $45

Papa Shango, 1993, Hasbro
NM $7 **MIP** $25

Razor Ramon, 1993, 1993, Hasbro
NM $15 **MIP** $30

(Hasbro)

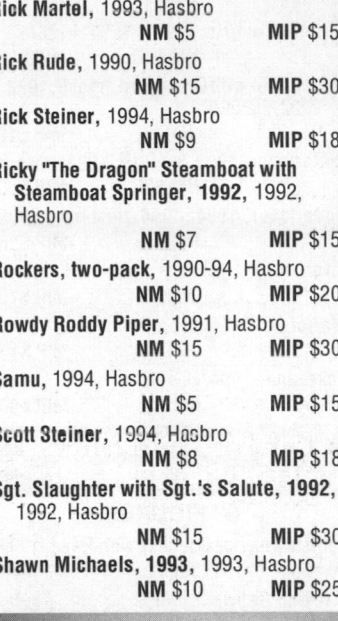

Razor Ramon, 1994, 1994, Hasbro, A bad dude who often sported toothpick in his mouth.
NM $9 **MIP** $18

Repo Man, 1993, Hasbro
NM $7 **MIP** $15

Ric Flair, 1993, Hasbro
NM $7 **MIP** $15

Rick Martel, 1993, Hasbro
NM $5 **MIP** $15

Rick Rude, 1990, Hasbro
NM $15 **MIP** $30

Rick Steiner, 1994, Hasbro
NM $9 **MIP** $18

Ricky "The Dragon" Steamboat with Steamboat Springer, 1992, 1992, Hasbro
NM $7 **MIP** $15

Rockers, two-pack, 1990-94, Hasbro
NM $10 **MIP** $20

Rowdy Roddy Piper, 1991, Hasbro
NM $15 **MIP** $30

Samu, 1994, Hasbro
NM $5 **MIP** $15

Scott Steiner, 1994, Hasbro
NM $8 **MIP** $18

Sgt. Slaughter with Sgt.'s Salute, 1992, 1992, Hasbro
NM $15 **MIP** $30

Shawn Michaels, 1993, 1993, Hasbro
NM $10 **MIP** $25

Shawn Michaels, 1994, 1994, Hasbro, Shown here with group of figures from the series
NM $6 **MIP** $15

Sid Justice, 1993, Hasbro
NM $6 **MIP** $15

Skinner, 1993, Hasbro
NM $6 **MIP** $15

Smash, 1990, Hasbro
NM $12 **MIP** $25

Tatanka, 1993, 1993, Hasbro
NM $7 **MIP** $15

Tatanka, 1994, 1994, Hasbro
NM $7 **MIP** $15

Ted Diabiase, 1990, 1990, Hasbro
NM $10 **MIP** $20

Ted Diabiase, 1991, 1991, Hasbro
NM $7 **MIP** $15

Ted Diabiase, 1994, 1994, Hasbro
NM $7 **MIP** $15

Texas Tornado with Texas Twister, 1992, 1992, Hasbro
NM $10 **MIP** $50

Typhoon with Tidal Wave, 1992, 1992, Hasbro
NM $15 **MIP** $30

WWF World Wrestling Federation (Hasbro, 1990-94)

Ultimate Warrior with Warrior Wham, 1992, 1992, Hasbro
NM $20 MIP $40

Ultimate Warrior, 1990, 1990, Hasbro
NM $12 MIP $25

Ultimate Warrior, 1991, 1991, Hasbro
NM $10 MIP $20

Undertaker with Graveyard Smash, 1992, 1992, Hasbro
NM $9 MIP $18

Undertaker, 1993, mail-in, 1993, Hasbro
NM $25 MIP $50

Undertaker, 1994, 1994, Hasbro
NM $15 MIP $25

Virgil, 1993, Hasbro
NM $7 MIP $15

Warlord, 1993, Hasbro
NM $6 MIP $15

Yokozuna, 1994, Hasbro
NM $15 MIP $30

Xena Warrior Princess (Toy Biz, 1998-99)

6" FIGURES

Callisto Warrior Goddess with Hope, 1999
NM $3 MIP $10

Grieving Gabrielle, 1999
NM $3 MIP $10

Xena Conqueror of Nations, 1999
NM $3 MIP $10

Xena Warrior Huntress, 1999
NM $3 MIP $10

SERIES I, 12" FIGURES

Callisto, 1998
NM $7 MIP $20

Gabrielle, 1998
NM $7 MIP $20

Xena, 1998
NM $7 MIP $20

SERIES II, 12" FIGURES

Ares, 1999
NM $7 MIP $20

Gabrielle Amazon Princess, 1999
NM $7 MIP $20

Roman Xena, 1999
NM $7 MIP $20

Warlord Xena, 1999
NM $7 MIP $20

SERIES III, 12" FIGURES

Empress Gabrielle, 1999
NM $8 MIP $25

Shamaness Xena, 1999
NM $8 MIP $25

Xena the Evil Warrior, 1999
NM $8 MIP $25

X-Files (McFarlane, 1998)

FIGURES

Fireman with Cryolitter, 1998, McFarlane
NM $8 MIP $15

Mulder in Arctic wear, 1998, McFarlane
NM $4 MIP $8

Mulder with docile alien, 1998, McFarlane
NM $4 MIP $8

Mulder with Human Host and Cryopod Chamber, 1998, McFarlane
NM $4 MIP $8

Mulder with victim, 1998, McFarlane
NM $4 MIP $8

Primitive Man with Attack Alien, 1998, McFarlane
NM $4 MIP $8

Scully in Arctic wear, 1998, McFarlane
NM $4 MIP $8

Scully with docile alien, 1998, McFarlane
NM $4 MIP $8

(Lenny Lee)

Scully with Human Host and Cryopod Chamber, 1998, McFarlane, Agent Scully in parka. Bases of human hosts snap together to form a row--just like in the movie
NM $4 MIP $8

Scully with Victim, 1998, McFarlane
NM $4 MIP $8

X-Men (Toy Biz, 1991-96)

FIGURES

Ahab, 1994, Toy Biz
NM $3 MIP $7

Apocalypse I, 1991, Toy Biz
NM $4 MIP $10

Apocalypse I, 1993, Toy Biz
NM $4 MIP $10

Apocolypse, 1996, Toy Biz
NM $3 MIP $8

Archangel, 1991, Toy Biz
NM $3 MIP $8

Archangel, 1996, Toy Biz
NM $3 MIP $8

Archangel II, 1995, Toy Biz
NM $3 MIP $8

Banshee I, 1992, Toy Biz
NM $3 MIP $7

Battle Ravaged Wolverine, 1995, Toy Biz
NM $3 MIP $7

Beast, 1994, Toy Biz
NM $4 MIP $10

Bishop II, 1993, Toy Biz
NM $3 MIP $7

Bishop II, 1996, Toy Biz
NM $3 MIP $7

Blob, 1995, Toy Biz
NM $4 MIP $9

Cable Cyborg, 1995, Toy Biz
NM $3 MIP $5

Caliban, 1995, Toy Biz
NM $3 MIP $7

Cameron Hodge, 1995, Toy Biz
NM $3 MIP $7

Captive Sabretooth, 1995, Toy Biz
NM $4 MIP $10

Colossus, 1991, Toy Biz
NM $3 MIP $7

Colossus, 1993, Toy Biz
NM $4 MIP $10

Colossus, 1996, Toy Biz
NM $33 MIP $7

Corsair, 1995, Toy Biz
NM $3 MIP $7

Cyclops, 1996, Toy Biz
NM $4 MIP $7

Cyclops I, blue, 1991, Toy Biz
NM $4 MIP $8

Cyclops I, stripes, 1991, Toy Biz
NM $4 MIP $8

Cyclops II, 1993, Toy Biz
NM $4 MIP $8

Deadpool, 1995, Toy Biz
NM $3 MIP $12

Domino, 1995, Toy Biz
NM $5 MIP $7

Forge, 1992, Toy Biz
NM $5 MIP $15

Gambit, 1992, Toy Biz
NM $3 MIP $14

Gambit, 1993, Toy Biz
NM $3 MIP $7

Gladiator, 1995, Toy Biz
NM $3 MIP $7

Havok, 1995, Toy Biz
NM $10 MIP $7

Ice Man, 1992, Toy Biz
NM $3 MIP $20

Ice Man II, 1995, Toy Biz
NM $5 MIP $7

Juggernaut, 1991, Toy Biz
NM $4 MIP $10

Juggernaut, 1993, Toy Biz
NM $3 MIP $8

Lady Deathstrike, 1996, Toy Biz
NM $3 MIP $7

Magneto, 1996, Toy Biz
NM $3 MIP $7

Magneto I, 1991, Toy Biz
NM $3 MIP $7

Magneto II, 1992, Toy Biz
NM $3 MIP $7

Morph, 1994, Toy Biz
NM $4 MIP $7

Morph II, Toy Biz, Toyfare mail-away
NM $5 MIP $10

Mr. Sinister, 1992, Toy Biz
NM $4 MIP $8

Nightcrawler, 1993, Toy Biz
NM $3 MIP $10

Nimrod, 1995, Toy Biz
NM $3 MIP $7

Omega Red, 1993, Toy Biz
NM $4 MIP $8

Omega Red II, 1996, Toy Biz
NM $4 MIP $8

Phoenix, 1995, Toy Biz
NM $4 MIP $10

Polaris, 1996, Toy Biz
NM $3 MIP $7

Professor X, 1993, Toy Biz
NM $4 MIP $8

Raza, 1994, Toy Biz
NM $3 MIP $7

Sabretooth, 1996, Toy Biz
NM $3 MIP $8

Sauron, 1992, Toy Biz
NM $3 MIP $7

Savage Land Wolverine, 1996, Toy Biz
NM $3 MIP $7

Spiral, 1995, Toy Biz
NM $4 MIP $10

Storm, 1991, Toy Biz
NM $6 MIP $12

Strong Guy, 1993, Toy Biz
NM $3 MIP $7

Sunfire, 1995, Toy Biz
NM $3 MIP $7

Trevor Fitzroy, 1994, Toy Biz
NM $3 MIP $7

Tusk, 1992, Toy Biz
NM $3 MIP $7

Warstar, 1995, Toy Biz
NM $3 MIP $7

Weapon X, 1996, Toy Biz
NM $3 MIP $7

Wolverine, 1996, Toy Biz
NM $4 MIP $10

Wolverine Fang, 1995, Toy Biz
NM $3 MIP $7

Wolverine I, 1991, Toy Biz
NM $6 MIP $18

Wolverine I, 1993, Toy Biz
NM $4 MIP $12

Wolverine II, 1992, Toy Biz
NM $4 MIP $10

Wolverine III, 1992, Toy Biz
NM $5 MIP $12

Wolverine V, 1993, Toy Biz
NM $4 MIP $10

Wolverine, space armor, 1995, Toy Biz
NM $4 MIP $10

Wolverine, street clothes, 1994, Toy Biz
NM $3 MIP $7

X-Cutioner, 1995, Toy Biz
NM $3 MIP $7

X-Men (Toy Biz, 1996-98)

AGE OF APOCALYPSE, 5" FIGURES, 1996

Apocalypse, Removable Armor and Transforming Limbs, 1996
NM $5 MIP $10

Cyclops, Cybernetic Guardian and Laser Blaster, 1996
NM $2 MIP $6

Gambit, Blast-throwing Action, 1996
NM $2 MIP $6

Magneto, Removable Helmet and Shrapnel, 1996
NM $2 MIP $6

Sabretooth, Wild Child Sidekick Figure, 1996
NM $2 MIP $6

Weapon X, Interchangeable Weaponry, 1996
NM $2 MIP $6

CLASSICS, LIGHT-UP WEAPONS, 5" FIGURES, 1996

Gambit, Light-up Plasma Energy Weapon, 1996
NM $3 MIP $9

Juggernaut, Light-up Jewel Weapon, 1996
NM $3 MIP $12

Nightcrawler, Light-up Sword, 1996
NM $3 MIP $9

Psylock, light-up Psychic Knife, 1996
NM $3 MIP $9

Wolverine Stealth, Light-up Plasma Weapon, 1996
NM $3 MIP $9

MISSLE FLYERS, 5" FIGURES, 1997

Apocalypse, Trap-door Chest, 1997
NM $2 MIP $7

Bishop, Fold-out Armor Wing Blasters, 1997
NM $2 MIP $7

Cable, Attack Wings, 1997
NM $2 MIP $7

Shard, Spring Loaded Firing Wing Extensions, 1997
NM $2 MIP $7

Wolverine, Head Launching Bird of Prey, 1997
NM $2 MIP $7

MONSTER ARMOR, 5" FIGURES, 1997

Cyclops with Snap-on Cyclaw Armor, 1997
NM $2 MIP $6

Mr. Sinister with Snap-on Cyber Tech Armor, 1997
NM $2 MIP $6

Mystique with Snap-on She-Beast Armor, 1997
NM $2 MIP $6

Rogue with Snap-on Leech Bat Armor, 1997
NM $2 MIP $6

Wolverine with Snap-on Fangor Armor, 1997
NM $2 MIP $6

NEW MUTANTS, 5" FIGURES, 1998

Magik, 1998
NM $2 MIP $6

Warlock, 1998
NM $2 MIP $6

Wolfsbane, 1998
NM $2 MIP $6

NINJA FORCE, 5" FIGURES, 1997

Dark Nemesis with Spear Shooting Staff, 1997
NM $2 MIP $7

Ninja Sabretooth with Clip-on Claw Armor, 1997
NM $2 MIP $7

Ninja Wolverine with Warrior Assault Gear, 1997
NM $2 MIP $7

Psylocke with Extending Power Sword, 1997
NM $3 MIP $8

Space Ninja Deathbird with Fold-Out Ninja Wings, 1997
NM $3 MIP $8

ONSLAUGHT, 6" FIGURES, 1997

Apocalypse Rising, Ozymandias, 1997
NM $3 MIP $10

Jean Grey, Psychic Claw, 1997
NM $3 MIP $10

Onslaught, Ultimate Power Armor, 1997
NM $8 MIP $15

Wolverine Unleashed, Franklin Richards, 1997
NM $3 MIP $11

ROBOT FIGHTERS, 5" FIGURES, 1997

Cyclops, Apocalypse Droid with Gattling Gun Arm, 1997
NM $3 MIP $7

Gambit, Attack Robot Droid with Projectile Missile, 1997
NM $3 MIP $7

Jubilee, Grabbing Sentinel Hand with Projectile Finger, 1997
NM $4 MIP $10

Storm, Spinning Weather Station with Lightning Projectile, 1997
NM $4 MIP $10

Wolverine, Slashing Sabretooth Droid with Missile Claw, 1997
NM $3 MIP $7

X-Men (Toy Biz, 1996-98)

SAVAGE LAND, 5" FIGURES, 1997

Angel with Wing Flapping Sauron-Dino, 1997
NM $2 MIP $6

Kazar with Jumping Zabu Tiger, 1997
NM $2 MIP $6

Magneto with Water Spitting Amphibious, 1997
NM $2 MIP $6

Savage Storm with Head Ramming Colossus Dino, 1997
NM $2 MIP $6

Savage Wolverine with Jaw Chomping Crawler-Rex, 1997
NM $2 MIP $6

SECRET WEAPON FORCE BATTLE BASES, 5" FIGURES, 1998

Cyclops with War Tank Blaster, 1998
NM $2 MIP $6

Jean Grey with Catapult Tank Blaster, 1998
NM $2 MIP $6

Magneto Battle Base, 1998
NM $2 MIP $6

Omega with Spinning Rocket Blaster, 1998
NM $2 MIP $6

Wolverine Battle Base, 1998
NM $2 MIP $6

Wolverine with Claw Cannon Blaster, 1998
NM $2 MIP $6

SECRET WEAPON FORCE FLYING FIGHTERS, 5" FIGURES, 1998

Cyclops with High-Flying Hazard Gear, 1998
NM $3 MIP $7

Jean Grey with Fire Bird Flyer, 1998
NM $3 MIP $7

Maggot with Expanding Assault Wings, 1998
NM $3 MIP $7

Mr. Sinister with Bio-Tech Attack Wings, 1998
NM $3 MIP $7

SECRET WEAPON FORCE POWER SLAMMERS, 5" FIGURES, 1998

Gambit with Rapid Fire Card Cannon Slammer, 1998
NM $2 MIP $6

Master Mold with Rapid Fire Sentinels, 1998
NM $2 MIP $6

Rogue with Double Barrel Slammer, 1998
NM $3 MIP $8

Wolverine with Rapid Fire Disk Slammer, 1998
NM $2 MIP $6

SECRET WEAPON FORCE SHAPE SHIFTERS, 7" FIGURES, 1998

Juggernaut forms into Titanic Tank, 1998
NM $2 MIP $6

Morph forms into Mega Missile, 1998
NM $2 MIP $6

Wolverine forms into Mutant Wolf, 1998
NM $2 MIP $6

SECRET WEAPON FORCE SUPER SHOOTER, 5" FIGURES, 1998

Apocalypse, 1998
NM $3 MIP $10

Beast, 1998
NM $3 MIP $8

Colossus, 1998
NM $3 MIP $8

Wolverine, 1998
NM $3 MIP $8

SHATTERSHOT, 5" FIGURES, 1996

Age of Apocalypse Beast, Wind-up Chain Saw, 1996
NM $2 MIP $6

Archangel, Wing-flapping Action, 1996
NM $2 MIP $6

Colossus, Super Punch Gauntlets, 1996
NM $2 MIP $6

Lady Death Strike, Transforming Reaver Armor, 1996
NM $2 MIP $6

Patch Wolverine, Total Assault Arsenal, 1996
NM $2 MIP $6

SPECIAL EDITION SERIES, 12" FIGURES, 1998

Gambit, 1998
NM $8 MIP $25

Storm, 1998
NM $8 MIP $25

Wolverine, 1998
NM $8 MIP $25

X-Men 2099 (Toy Biz, 1996)

5" FIGURES

Bloodhawk, 1996
NM $2 MIP $5

Breakdown, Dominick Sidekick Figure, 1996
NM $2 MIP $5

Brimstone Love, 1996
NM $2 MIP $5

Halloween Jack, 1996
NM $2 MIP $5

Junkpile, Snap-on Battle Armor, 1996
NM $2 MIP $5

La Lunatica, Futuristic Jai-Lai, 1996
NM $2 MIP $5

Meanstreak, 1996
NM $2 MIP $5

Metalhead, 1996
NM $2 MIP $5

Shadow Dancer, 1996
NM $2 MIP $5

Skullfire, Glowing Fire Skeleton, 1996
NM $2 MIP $5

X-Men vs. Street Fighter (Toy Biz, 1998)

5" FIGURES

Apocalypse vs. Dhalism, 1998
NM $6 MIP $15

Cyclops vs. M. Bison, 1998
NM $4 MIP $12

Gambit vs. Cammy, 1998
NM $4 MIP $12

Juggernaut vs. Chun-Li, 1998
NM $6 MIP $15

Magneto vs. Ryu, 1998
NM $5 MIP $12

Rogue vs. Zangief, 1998
NM $4 MIP $12

Sabretooth vs. Ken, 1998
NM $6 MIP $15

Wolverine vs. Akuma, 1998
NM $5 MIP $12

X-Men/X-Force (Toy Biz, 1991-96)

DELUXE 10" FIGURES

Cable, 1995
NM $8 MIP $18

Kane, 1995
NM $8 MIP $18

Shatterstar, 1995
NM $8 MIP $18

FIGURES

Arctic Armor Cable, 1996, Toy Biz
NM $3 MIP $8

Avalanche, 1995, Toy Biz
NM $4 MIP $10

Black Tom, 1994, Toy Biz
NM $5 MIP $15

Black Tom, 1995, Toy Biz
NM $3 MIP $10

Blob, The, 1995, Toy Biz
NM $5 MIP $14

Bonebreaker, 1994, Toy Biz
NM $3 MIP $10

Bridge, 1992, Toy Biz
NM $5 MIP $10

Brood, 1993, Toy Biz
NM $4 MIP $10

Cable Cyborg, 1995, Toy Biz
NM $3 MIP $8

Cable I, 1992, Toy Biz
NM $6 MIP $15

Cable II, 1993, Toy Biz
NM $3 MIP $10

Cable III, 1993, Toy Biz
NM $4 MIP $15

Cable IV, 1994, Toy Biz
NM $3 MIP $12

Cable Stealth, 1996, Toy Biz
NM $3 MIP $7

Cable V, 1994, Toy Biz
NM $4 MIP $15

Cannonball, pink, 1993, Toy Biz
NM $6 MIP $15

Cannonball, purple, 1993, Toy Biz
NM $3 MIP $7

Commando, 1995, Toy Biz
NM $3 MIP $7

Deadpool, 1992, Toy Biz
NM $8 MIP $16

Deadpool, 1995, Toy Biz
NM $3 MIP $10

Domino, 1995, Toy Biz
NM $3 MIP $7

Exodus, 1995, Toy Biz
NM $3 MIP $7

Forearm, 1992, Toy Biz
NM $3 MIP $7

Genesis, 1995, Toy Biz
NM $3 MIP $7

Gideon, 1992, Toy Biz
NM $3 MIP $7

Grizzly, 1993, Toy Biz
NM $3 MIP $7

Kane I, 1992, Toy Biz
NM $4 MIP $10

Kane II, 1993, Toy Biz
NM $4 MIP $10

Killspree, 1994, Toy Biz
NM $3 MIP $7

Killspree II,, 1996, Toy Biz
NM $4 MIP $8

Krule, 1993, Toy Biz
NM $3 MIP $7

Kylun, 1994, Toy Biz
NM $3 MIP $7

Longshot, 1994, Toy Biz
NM $4 MIP $10

Mojo, 1995, Toy Biz
NM $3 MIP $7

Nimrod, 1995, Toy Biz
NM $3 MIP $7

Pyro, 1994, Toy Biz
NM $3 MIP $7

Quark, 1994, Toy Biz
NM $3 MIP $7

Random, 1994, Toy Biz
NM $3 MIP $7

Rictor, 1994, Toy Biz
NM $3 MIP $7

Rogue, 1994, Toy Biz
NM $3 MIP $10

Sabretooth I, 1992, Toy Biz
NM $4 MIP $10

Sabretooth II, 1994, Toy Biz
NM $4 MIP $10

Shatterstar I, 1992, Toy Biz
NM $3 MIP $7

Shatterstar II, 1994, Toy Biz
NM $3 MIP $7

Shatterstar III, 1996, Toy Biz
NM $3 MIP $7

Silver Samurai, 1994, Toy Biz
NM $3 MIP $6

Slayback, 1994, Toy Biz
NM $3 MIP $7

Stryfe, 1992, Toy Biz
NM $3 MIP $7

Sunspot, 1994, Toy Biz
NM $3 MIP $7

Urban Assault, 1995, Toy Biz
NM $3 MIP $7

Warpath I, 1992, Toy Biz
NM $3 MIP $7

Warpath II, 1994, Toy Biz
NM $3 MIP $7

X-Treme, 1994, Toy Biz
NM $3 MIP $7

X-Men: Evolution (Toy Biz, 2001-02)

5" FIGURES

Battle Ravaged Wolverine, 2001-02, 5", Toy Biz, Series 3, w/ Sabretooth
NM $4 MIP $8

Cyclops, 2001-02, 5", Toy Biz, Series 1
NM $4 MIP $8

Juggernaut, 2001-02, 5", Toy Biz, Series 3
NM $4 MIP $8

Logan, 2001-02, 5", Toy Biz, w/ hat and "X" base
NM $4 MIP $8

Magneto, 2001-02, 5", Toy Biz, Series 3
NM $4 MIP $8

Nightcrawler, 2001-02, 5", Toy Biz, Series 1
NM $4 MIP $8

Nightcrawler II, 2001-02, 5", Toy Biz, Series 3
NM $4 MIP $8

Ninja Wolverine, 2001-02, 5", Toy Biz, Series 2
NM $4 MIP $8

Sabretooth, 2001-02, 5", Toy Biz, Series 1
NM $4 MIP $8

Spyke, 2001-02, 5", Toy Biz, Series 2
NM $4 MIP $8

Storm, 2001-02, 5", Toy Biz, Series 2
NM $4 MIP $8

The Blob, 2001-02, 5", Toy Biz, Series 2
NM $4 MIP $8

Toad, 2001-02, 5", Toy Biz, Series 1
NM $4 MIP $8

Wolverine, 2001-02, 5", Toy Biz, Series 1
NM $4 MIP $8

8" FIGURES

Cyclops, 2001-02, 8", Toy Biz
NM $4 MIP $8

Toad, 2001-02, 8", Toy Biz
NM $4 MIP $8

Wolverine, 2001-02, 8", Toy Biz
NM $4 MIP $8

VEHICLES

Logan Battle Cycle, 2001-02, 5-1/2" tall, Toy Biz, w/ Logan
NM $5 MIP $10

Sabretooth Battle Cycle, 2001-02, 5-1/2" tall, Toy Biz, w/ Sabretooth
NM $5 MIP $10

Wolverine Battle Cycle, 2001-02, 5-1/2" tall, Toy Biz, w/ Wolverine
NM $5 MIP $10

X-Men: The Movie (Toy Biz, 2000)

FIGURES

Cyclops, 2000, Toy Biz
NM $3 MIP $8

Jean Grey, 2000, Toy Biz
NM $3 MIP $8

Logan, 2000, Toy Biz
NM $3 MIP $8

Magneto, 2000, Toy Biz
NM $3 MIP $8

Mystique, 2000, Toy Biz
NM $3 MIP $8

Professor X, 2000, Toy Biz
NM $3 MIP $8

Rogue, 2000, Toy Biz
NM $3 MIP $8

Sabretooth, 2000, Toy Biz
NM $3 MIP $8

Storm, 2000, Toy Biz
NM $3 MIP $8

Toad, 2000, Toy Biz
NM $3 MIP $8

Wolverine, 2000, Toy Biz
NM $3 MIP $8

TWO PACKS

Logan and Rogue, 2000, Toy Biz
NM $5 MIP $12

Magneto and Logan, 2000, Toy Biz
NM $5 MIP $12

Wolverine and Sabre, 2000, Toy Biz
NM $5 MIP $12

X-Men: X2, X-Men United (Toy Biz, 2003)

12" FIGURES

Nightcrawler, 2003, 12", Toy Biz
NM $6 MIP $12

Wolverine, 2003, 12", Toy Biz
NM $6 MIP $12

X-Men: X2, X-Men United (Toy Biz, 2003)

5" FIGURES

Cyclops, 2003, 5", Toy Biz, Series 2
NM $4 **MIP** $7

Cyclops, 2003, 5", Toy Biz, Series 1
NM $4 **MIP** $7

Iceman, 2003, 5", Toy Biz, Series 2
NM $4 **MIP** $7

Logan, 2003, 5", Toy Biz, Series 2
NM $4 **MIP** $7

Logan, 2003, 5", Toy Biz, Series 1
NM $4 **MIP** $7

Magneto, 2003, 5", Toy Biz, Series 2
NM $4 **MIP** $7

Nightcrawler, 2003, 5", Toy Biz, Series 1
NM $4 **MIP** $7

Wolverine, 2003, 5", Toy Biz, Series 2
NM $4 **MIP** $7

Wolverine, 2003, 5", Toy Biz, Series 1
NM $4 **MIP** $7

VEHICLES

X-Jet, 2003, Toy Biz, w/ Wolverine figure
NM $8 **MIP** $16

Yellow Submarine (McFarlane, 1999-2004)

SERIES 1, 1999

George with Yellow Submarine, 1999, McFarlane
NM $3 **MIP** $10

John with Jeremy, 1999, McFarlane
NM $3 **MIP** $10

Paul with Captain Fred, 1999, McFarlane
NM $3 **MIP** $10

Paul with Glove and Love base, 1999, McFarlane
NM $4 **MIP** $12

Ringo with Blue Meanie, 1999, McFarlane
NM $3 **MIP** $10

SERIES 2, SGT. PEPPER'S LONELY HEARTS CLUB BAND, 2000

George with Snapping Turk, 2000, McFarlane
NM $3 **MIP** $8

(McFarlane Toys)

John with Bulldog, 2000, McFarlane
NM $3 **MIP** $8

(McFarlane Toys)

Paul with Sucking Monster, 2000, McFarlane
NM $3 **MIP** $9

(McFarlane Toys)

Ringo with Apple Bonker, 2000, McFarlane
NM $3 **MIP** $8

SERIES 3, 2004

George with Blue Meanie, 2004, McFarlane
NM $3 **MIP** $10

John with Love and Glove base, 2004, McFarlane
NM $3 **MIP** $10

Paul with Jeremy, 2004, McFarlane
NM $3 **MIP** $10

Ringo with Yellow Submarine, 2004, McFarlane
NM $3 **MIP** $10

Youngblood (McFarlane, 1995)

FIGURES

Crypt, 1995, McFarlane
NM $4 **MIP** $8

Die Hard, 1995, McFarlane
NM $4 **MIP** $8

Dutch, 1995, McFarlane
NM $4 **MIP** $8

Sentinel, 1995, McFarlane
NM $4 **MIP** $8

Shaft, 1995, McFarlane
NM $4 **MIP** $8

Troll, 1995, McFarlane
NM $5 **MIP** $12

Zorro (Gabriel, 1982)

FIGURES

Amigo, 1982, Gabriel
NM $12 **MIP** $30

Captain Ramon, 1982, Gabriel
NM $12 **MIP** $27

Picaro, 1982, Gabriel, horse
NM $20 **MIP** $55

Sergeant Gonzales, 1982, Gabriel
NM $12 **MIP** $24

Tempest, 1982, Gabriel, horse
NM $20 **MIP** $60

Zorro, 1982, Gabriel
NM $15 **MIP** $35

Zorro (Playmates, 1997)

FIGURES

Barbed Wire Zorro, 1997, Playmates
NM $6 **MIP** $12

Chain Mail Zorro, 1997, Playmates
NM $6 **MIP** $12

Don Diego, 1997, Playmates
NM $6 **MIP** $12

Evil Ramon, 1997, Playmates
NM $6 **MIP** $12

Zorro with Tornado, 1997, Playmates, figure and horse
NM $15 **MIP** $32

Advertising Toys

by Karen O'Brien

Advertising characters are a part of our daily lives. Much the way athletic teams adopt mascots, advertisers create endearing characters to represent everything from cookies to pizza. In addition to product packaging, they appear in television commercials, radio spots, print ads, computer banner ads, and on billboards.

Some of the ad characters of today have been around for more than 100 years. Aunt Jemima, known for her pancake mixes and maple syrups, is a good example. She was first created for advertising pancake flour at the 1893 Columbian Exposition in Chicago, Illinois. Nancy Green, an African-American woman from Chicago, was hired to portray Aunt Jemima and demonstrate the pancake mix at the Fair. She was such a hit that police had to control the crowds. Soon after, a paper doll was released as a promotional item. The character is such a part of Americana, that parent company Quaker Oats once issued a press release to alert the country that Aunt Jemima was receiving a more "modern" hairdo.

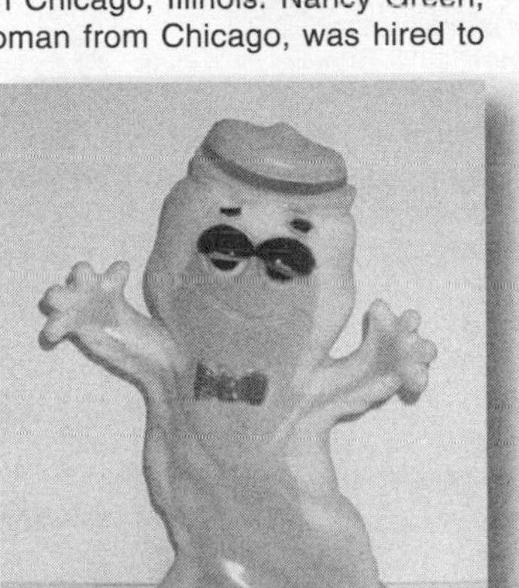

Many companies followed the trend to adopt lovable characters. Kellogg's has long delighted collectors with a wide variety of premiums. A 1920s Kellogg's premium was a set of Goldilocks and the Three Bears dolls where the consumer received a piece of fabric with the image of the doll printed and was to cut, stuff, and sew the doll themselves. Decades before they became cartoons, cereal pixies Snap, Crackle, and Pop were first offered as make-your-own-dolls in the early 1940s.

Food-related characters seem to be the most popular with collectors. Although several popular characters have nothing to do with food, for example, Reddy Kilowatt (Reddy Communications), Bibendum a.k.a. The Michelin Man (Michelin Tires), and Speedy (Alka-Seltzer), food-related characters including, Elsie the Cow (Borden's dairy products), Quisp (Quaker Oats), and Mr. Peanut (Planter's Peanuts), dominate the collecting scene.

THE *TOP 10* ADVERTISING TOYS (In Mint Condition)

1. Quisp Bank, Quaker Oats, 1960s $850
2. Reddy Kilowatt Bobbin' Head, Reddy Communications, 1960s 450
3. Quisp Powered Sugar Space Gun, Quaker Oats...................... 400
4. Esky Store Display, Esquire Magazine, 1940s 375
5. Mr. Peanut Figure, Planters Peanuts, 1930s......................... 375
6. Speedy Figure, Alka-Seltzer, 1963 360
7. Elsie the Cow Cookie Jar, Borden's, 1950s 350
8. Vegetable Man Bank, Kraft, 1970s 280
9. Vegetable Man Display, Kraft, 1980 280
10. Barnum's Animal Crackers Cookie Jar, Nabisco, 1972................ 275

ADVERTISING TOYS

ADVERTISING TOYS

7-Eleven

Big Bite Figures, 1987, 3-1/2" hot dog men holding snacks
EX $10 NM $15 MIP $25

7-Up

Fresh Up Freddie, 1959, 9" tall, vinyl figure, red hair, white shirt, holding bottle of 7-Up
EX $45 NM $100 MIP $150

Spot, 1988, 4" tall, wind up walking figure of the red "spot" w/sunglasses
EX $5 NM $10 MIP $15

Spot Wind-Up, 1990, 3" red circular figure w/sunglasses
EX $8 NM $12 MIP $15

Air India

Air India Man Figure, 1973, 4-1/2" statue of man wearing turban standing on flying carpet
EX $15 NM $25 MIP $40

Alka-Seltzer

Speedy, 2003, Wacky Wobbler, #6012, 8"
EX $3 NM $7 MIP $12

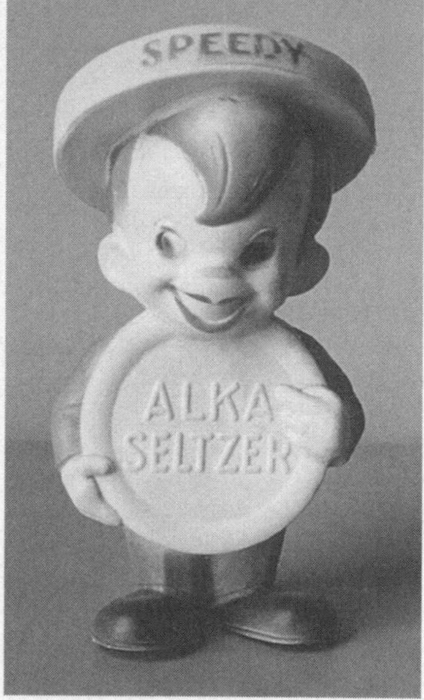

Speedy Figure, 1963, 5-1/2" vinyl boy holding Alka-Seltzer figure
EX $280 NM $310 MIP $360

Alpo

Alpo Winross Semi, 1976, 1:64-scale die-cast truck
EX $8 NM $15 MIP $25

Dan the Dog Cookie Jar, 1980s, 7" ceramic gray and white sheep dog
EX $40 NM $55 MIP $75

Dan the Dog Wind-Up, 1979, 3" wind-up figure of shaggy gray dog walking on his front paws
EX $10 NM $15 MIP $25

American Home Food Products

Marky Maypo Figure, 1960, 9" vinyl figure
EX $45 NM $60 MIP $85

Aunt Jemima Syrup

Aunt Jemima Doll, 1950s, 13" cloth doll wearing red checkered dress
EX $75 NM $90 MIP $110

Salt & Pepper Shakers, Aunt Jemima and Uncle Mose, plastic
EX $35 NM $45 MIP $65

Baskin Robbins

Pinky the Spoon Figure, 1993, 5" bendable figure
EX $6 NM $8 MIP $12

Bazooka

Bazooka Joe, 2003, Wacky Wobbler, #6028, 8"
EX $3 NM $7 MIP $12

Bazooka Joe Doll, 1973, 19" plush boy pirate
EX $30 NM $35 MIP $45

Beatrice Foods

Clark Bar Figure, 1960s, 8-1/2" vinyl boy holding a Clark bar wearing a striped shirt
EX $200 NM $225 MIP $275

Beech-Nut

Fruit Stripe Gum Figure, 1967, 7-1/2" bendable man shaped like a pack of gum riding a motorcycle
EX $150 NM $200 MIP $225

Bob's Big Boy

Big Boy, Wacky Wobbler, 8"
EX $5 NM $10 MIP $15

Big Boy Bank, Bank w/ black or blue shoes, 8"
EX $15 NM $20 MIP $30

Big Boy Cloth Doll, 1970s, 14" tall, smiling Big Boy w/hands holding suspenders
EX $50 NM $100 MIP $150

Big Boy Night Light, 1960s, 6-3/4" tall, vinyl, electric night light
EX $50 NM $100 MIP $150

Dolly Doll, 1978, 14" cloth girl doll w/Dolly nametag
EX $15 NM $25 MIP $30

Nodder, 1960s
EX $15 NM $30 MIP $45

Nugget Doll, 1978, 10" cloth dog doll w/"Nugget" on collar
EX $20 NM $30 MIP $40

Borden's

Elsie the Cow Cookie Jar, 1950s, 12" Elsie w/her head popping out of barrel
EX $275 NM $300 MIP $350

Elsie the Cow Doll, 1950s, 12" plush cow that moos when shaken
EX $55 NM $80 MIP $90

Elsie the Cow Lamp, 1947, electric lamp, ceramic
EX $150 NM $175 MIP $225

Elsie the Cow pull toy, 1944, wooden, "The Cow that Jumped over the Moon"
EX $50 NM $75 MIP $125

Bradford House Restaurants

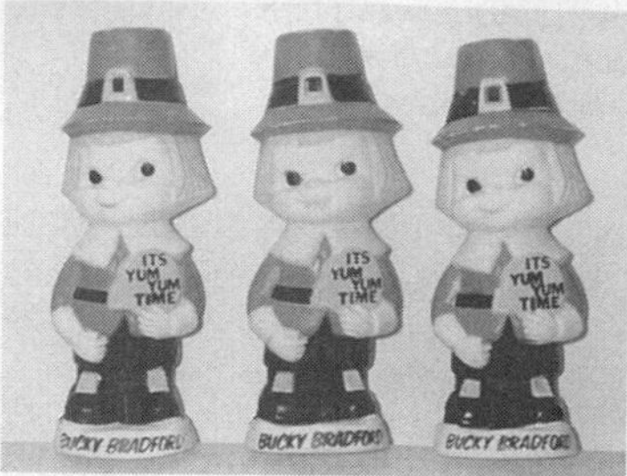

Bucky Bradford Figure, 1960s, 9-1/2" blond pilgrim boy holding dish that reads "It's Yum Yum Time"
EX $35 NM $40 MIP $50

Burger King

Burger King doll, 1980, "Magical Burger King," 20"
EX $10 NM $20 MIP $40

Burger King stuffed toy, 1972, smiling, beardless, 15"
EX $10 NM $18 MIP $35

Burger King stuffed toy, 1977, hands on hips, w/ beard, 13"
EX $15 NM $25 MIP $35

Campbell

Campbell's Kid Doll, 1950s, 9-1/2" vinyl jointed cheerleader wearing a white shirt w/"C" in middle
EX $45 NM $65 MIP $80

Campbell's Kid Doll, 1973, 16" blonde girl w/red hair
EX $35 NM $45 MIP $50

Campbell's Kid Figure, 1950s, 7" boy chef doll w/ "C"on hat and spoon in his hand
EX $50 NM $60 MIP $75

Campbell's Kid Figure, 1970s, 7" vinyl Campbell boy w/blue overalls
EX $35 NM $50 MIP $65

Christmas Ornament, 1989, ball ornament w/picture of Campbell Kid dressed as Santa
EX $5 NM $10 MIP $15

Wizard of O's Figure, 1978, 7-1/2" vinyl wizard w/Spaghetti O's on his hat and bow tie
EX $35 NM $45 MIP $55

Champion Auto Stores

Champ Man Figure, 1991, 6" bendable man; head is a flag
EX $7 NM $10 MIP $15

Chicken Delight International

Chicken Delight Bank, 1960s, 6" yellow and red chicken holding a tray of biscuits
EX $85 NM $125 MIP $150

Chiquita

Chiquita Banana Doll, 1974, 16" plush dancing banana w/fruit on its head
EX $20 NM $25 MIP $30

Coca-Cola

Sprite - Lucky Lymon, 1990, 7-1/2", vinyl, talking doll
EX $25 NM $35 MIP $45

Sprite Boy, 2003, Wacky Wobbler, #5065, 8"
EX $5 NM $10 MIP $15

Cracker Jack

Cracker Jack and Bingo, 1996, 16" doll, 100th anniversary of Cracker Jack
EX $25 NM $30 MIP $45

Cracker Jack and Bingo, 2000, Wacky Wobbler, 8"
EX $3 NM $12 MIP $25

Cracker Jack Doll, 1974, 15" plush sailor holding small box of Cracker Jacks snacks
EX $25 NM $35 MIP $45

Cracker Jack Doll, 1980, vinyl and cloth
EX $7 NM $20 MIP $40

Crest Toothpaste

Sparkle Telephone, 1980s, 11" blue and silver snowman-type character
EX $30 NM $40 MIP $45

Curad

Taped Crusader Figure, 1977, 7-1/2" male cartoon superhero
EX $65 NM $75 MIP $85

Curity

Miss Curity Display, 1950s, 18" plastic store display of a nurse on a base
EX $125 NM $150 MIP $185

Del Monte

Big Top Bonanza Clown Bank, 1985, colorful, smiling clown
EX $6 NM $11 MIP $22

Cobbie Corn, 1984, stuffed ear of corn, Yumkins
EX $8 NM $16 MIP $24

Juicie Pineapple, 1984, 11" stuffed pineapple, Country Yumkin, tan w/green leaves
EX $10 NM $20 MIP $30

Lushy Peach, 1984, stuffed peach, Yumkins
EX $8 NM $16 MIP $24

Precious Pear, 1984, stuffed pear, Yumkins
EX $8 NM $16 MIP $24

Reddie Tomato, 1984, stuffed tomato, Yumkins
EX $8 NM $16 MIP $24

Shoo-Shoo Scarecrow, 1983, 14" stuffed scarecrow, Country Yumkin, white shirt, blue coveralls
EX $10 NM $20 MIP $30

Sweetie Pea, 1984, stuffed pea, Yumkins
EX $8 NM $16 MIP $24

Yumkins Christmas Ornaments, 1984, set of six Yumkins mini characters
EX $6 NM $12 MIP $20

Domino's Pizza

Noid Plush Doll, 1988, 11" plush toy
EX $5 NM $10 MIP $15

Douglas Oil Company

Freddy Fast Figure, 1976, 7" freckled face boy; hat says "Freddy Fast"
EX $90 NM $110 MIP $130

Dow Brands

Scrubbing Bubble Brush, 1980s, 3-1/2" light blue scrub brush
EX $12 NM $15 MIP $18

Scrubbing Bubbles Bank, 1990s, ceramic bubble character bank
EX $5 NM $12 MIP $22

Scrubbing Bubbles Bathroom Shelf, 1992, 6" x 4" x 2-1/2" shelf w/characters
EX $5 NM $10 MIP $15

Scrubbing Bubbles Character, 1989, vinyl bubble character, floats
EX $5 NM $10 MIP $15

Scrubbing Bubbles Shower Radio, 1980s, transistor radio, waterproof, 3-1/2" x 7" w/hook for use in shower
EX $5 NM $10 MIP $15

Esquire Magazine

Esky Store Display, 1940s, 11" old man dressed in a tuxedo standing on an Esquire magazine
EX $300 NM $350 MIP $375

Esso

Esso Tiger Figure, 1960s, 8-1/2" plastic tiger
EX $25 NM $30 MIP $35

Esso Tiger Garbage Can, 1970s, 10" metal garbage can w/picture of the Esso tiger
EX $15 NM $20 MIP $30

Little Oil Drop bank, 1958, plastic, red or white, 6-1/2"
EX $25 NM $50 MIP $100

Tiger mug, 1960s, Fire King/Anchor Hocking, ceramic mug w/Esso Tiger image
EX $3 NM $7 MIP $12

ADVERTISING TOYS

Eveready Batteries

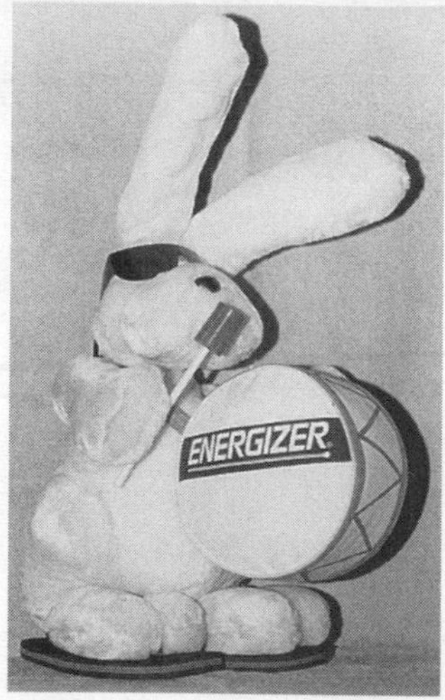

Energizer Bunny Plush, 1996, 22" plush
EX $17 **NM** $42 **MIP** $68

Eveready Cat Bank, 1981, black cat w/Eveready battery on side
EX $10 **NM** $15 **MIP** $20

Facit Adding Machines

Facit Man Figure, 1964, 4" man wearing yellow outfit w/black wizard hat
EX $25 **NM** $35 **MIP** $45

Florida Citrus Department

Florida Orange Bird Hat, 1970s, child's-size hat w/visor, pictures Orange Bird on front and back
EX $10 **NM** $15 **MIP** $20

Florida Orange Bird Nodder, 1970s, 7" plastic
EX $50 **NM** $60 **MIP** $75

Florida Orange Bird Stick Pin, 1980s, metal, depicts the Florida Orange Bird
EX $5 **NM** $10 **MIP** $15

Frito Lay

Chester Cheese, 1998, Cheetos' mascot in a 10" tall plush figure
EX $10 **NM** $20 **MIP** $30

Funny Face Drink

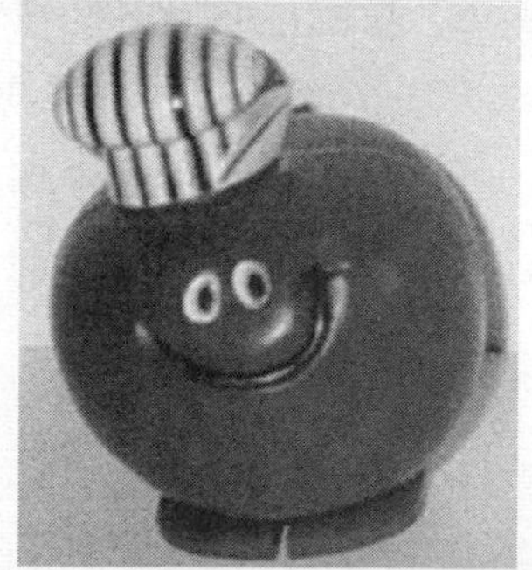

Choo Choo Cherry Ramp Walker, 1971, 3" round, red figure w/conductor's hat
EX $73 **NM** $95 **MIP** $120

Freezer Molds, 1977, mold of each character w/spoon, color variations, value for each
EX $4 **NM** $8 **MIP** $12

Funny Face Mugs, 1969, 3" mugs of Funny Face characters, each
EX $9 **NM** $13 **MIP** $17

Goofy Grape Pitcher, 1973, 10" pitcher of smiling, purple character wearing lime green captain's hat
EX $75 **NM** $95 **MIP** $125

Lefty Lemon Frisbee, 1980s, plastic w/picture of Lefty Lemon
EX $5 **NM** $10 **MIP** $12

Pillows, 1970s, one for each character, sizes from 11" to 15", value for each
EX $20 **NM** $40 **MIP** $60

General Mills

Boo Berry Bank, bank, no moving parts, 8"
EX $3 **NM** $7 **MIP** $15

Boo Berry Figure, 1975, 7-1/2" white and light blue ghost w/hat and bow tie
EX $78 **NM** $97 **MIP** $124

Cereal Card Game, 1981, card game w/different cereal characters
EX $10 **NM** $15 **MIP** $20

Chex Party Mix Snoopy, 1990s, plastic bank, Snoopy on doghouse w/stickers "Chex Pary Mix and Peanuts 40 Years of Tradion"
EX $5 **NM** $10 **MIP** $15

Count Chocula, 2000, Wacky Wobbler, 8"
EX $3 **NM** $7 **MIP** $15

Count Chocula Figure, 1975, 7-1/2" vinyl vampire
EX $70 **NM** $85 **MIP** $110

Count Chocula Plush, 1997, 9" plush figure
EX $5 **NM** $10 **MIP** $15

Franken Berry, 2000, Wacky Wobbler, 8"
EX $3 **NM** $7 **MIP** $15

Frankenberry Figure, 1975, 8" vinyl pink Frankenstein
EX $72 **NM** $100 **MIP** $140

Frankenberry Premium, 1970s, small plastic Frankenberry, cereal premium
EX $2 **NM** $4 **MIP** $8

Frankenberry Toothbrush Holder, 1970s, small plastic for single toothbrush
EX $2 **NM** $4 **MIP** $6

Fruit Brute Figure, 1975, 8" vinyl werewolf w/striped shirt
EX $75 **NM** $90 **MIP** $120

Lucky Charms, 2000, Wacky Wobbler, 8"
EX $3 **NM** $7 **MIP** $15

Lucky Charms Leprechaun Doll, 1978, 17" plush
EX $25 **NM** $35 **MIP** $40

Lucky Charms Plush, 1997, 9" plush figure
EX $5 **NM** $10 **MIP** $15

Monster Cereal Pencil Case, 1980s, 8" x 5", vinyl case featuring Count Chocula, Frankenberry and Boo Berry
EX $10 **NM** $15 **MIP** $20

Monster Cereals Puppets, 1970s, plastic puppets of Count Chocula, Frankenberry, Boo Berry
EX $4 **NM** $8 **MIP** $12

Trix Rabbit, 2000, Wacky Wobbler, 8"
EX $3 **NM** $7 **MIP** $12

Trix Rabbit Figure, 1977, 9" vinyl white rabbit
EX $32 **NM** $44 **MIP** $56

Gerber Products

Gerber Boy figure, 1985, 8" vinyl boy w/baseball cap turned sideways that reads "I'm a Gerber Kid"
EX $25 **NM** $30 **MIP** $35

Good Humor

Good Humor Bar, 1975, 8" vinyl ice cream bar w/a bite out of it
EX $200 **NM** $225 **MIP** $325

Grandma's Cookies

Grandma Bank, 1988, 7-1/2" hard plastic Grandma wearing a blue dress
EX $25 **NM** $30 **MIP** $35

H.P. Hood

Harry Hood Figure, 1981, 7-1/2" delivery man w/ "Hood" inscription on chest
EX $55 **NM** $70 **MIP** $80

Heinz

Aristocrat Tomato, 1939, 6" Aristocrat Tomato bust wearing top hat
EX $150 **NM** $200 **MIP** $225

Hershey's

Hershey's Chocolate Figure, 1987, 4-1/2" bendable candy bar shaped like a man
EX $8 **NM** $12 **MIP** $20

Hostess

Hostess Twinkie Bake Set, 1990s, bake your own Twinkies, non-stick pan, spatula
EX $8 **NM** $15 **MIP** $25

Twinkie Holder, 1990s, plastic Twinkie the Kid holds one Twinkie inside
EX $2 **NM** $5 **MIP** $10

Twinkie the Kid, 2000, Wacky Wobbler, 8"
EX $3 **NM** $7 **MIP** $12

Twinkie the Kid All American Yo-Yo, 1970s, white w/sticker "All American Yo-Yo"
EX $10 **NM** $20 **MIP** $30

Hush Puppies

Hush Puppies Figure, 1970s, 8" tan and brown basset hound
EX $30 **NM** $35 **MIP** $45

ICEE

ICEE Bear Figure, 1970s, 8" vinyl polar bear drinking an ICEE
EX $35 **NM** $45 **MIP** $55

Insty-Prints

Insty-Prints Wizard Figure, 1980s, 9" vinyl figure of wizard dressed in red outfit w/moons and stars
EX $75 **NM** $100 **MIP** $135

Iron Fireman Furnace

Iron Fireman Figure, 1943, 5" metal man shoveling coal
EX $75 **NM** $85 **MIP** $110

Kahn's Wieners

Beefy Frank Figure, 1980, 5-1/2" vinyl figural hot dog mustard dispenser
EX $18 **NM** $20 **MIP** $30

Keebler Company

Ernie the Keebler Elf Figure, 1974, 7" figure of Ernie wearing oange and yellow hat and green jacket
EX $30 **NM** $40 **MIP** $55

Ernie the Keebler Elf Mug, 1972, 3" plastic figural mug
EX $8 **NM** $12 **MIP** $15

Kellogg's

Coppertone, 1998, Coppertone Beach Set: Coppertone girl, black dog, drawstring tote, suntan lotion, towel, radio and umbrella; Madame Alexander, the set
EX $25 **NM** $50 **MIP** $100

Dig 'Em Bendy Figure, 1970, 3-1/2" bendable frog figure w/ "Dig 'Em" on shirt
EX $10 **NM** $15 **MIP** $25

Dig 'Em Doll, 1973, 16" smiling frog w/baseball hat wearing shirt that reads "Dig Em"
EX $15 **NM** $20 **MIP** $30

Dig 'Em Slide Puzzle, 1979, 4" plastic squares that make a scene when put together
EX $8 **NM** $10 **MIP** $15

Milton The Toaster Figure, 1980, 5" white, smiling toaster
EX $50 **NM** $70 **MIP** $90

Newton the Owl License Plate, 1973, 5" x 7" plastic license plate w/Newton the Owl; made in several colors
EX $5 **NM** $8 **MIP** $10

Rice Krispie Dolls, 1998, Snap, Crackle and Pop, the set
EX $100 **NM** $150 **MIP** $200

Rice Krispies Dolls, 1998, 8" Snap, Crackle, Pop; Madame Alexander, each
EX $20 **NM** $40 **MIP** $65

Rice Krispies Towel, 1972, 20" x 38" towel featuring Snap, Crackle and Pop!
EX $10 **NM** $20 **MIP** $25

Snap, Crackle and Pop Figures, 1975, 7-1/2" vinyl, arms at side, each
EX $30 **NM** $40 **MIP** $46

Snap, Crackle and Pop Figures, 1975, 7-1/2" vinyl, arms extended, each
EX $25 **NM** $30 **MIP** $35

Snap, Crackle and Pop Hand Puppets, 1950s, cloth body and vinyl head, each
EX $25 **NM** $35 **MIP** $40

Snap, Crackle and Pop vinyl figures, 1984, 5"
EX $12 **NM** $20 **MIP** $30

Tony the Tiger bank, 1970s, plastic, 8-1/2"
EX $15 **NM** $25 **MIP** $35

Tony the Tiger Cookie Jar, 1968, 7" plastic
EX $70 **NM** $95 **MIP** $125

Tony the Tiger Figure, 1974, 7-1/2" vinyl tiger
EX $45 **NM** $60 **MIP** $75

Tony the Tiger plush toy, 1990, 12" plush toy, orange kerchief,
EX $8 **NM** $17 **MIP** $25

Tony the Tiger stuffed doll, 1973, 14"
EX $10 **NM** $20 **MIP** $30

Tony Tiger, 2003, Wacky Wobbler, #6009, 8"
EX $3 **NM** $7 **MIP** $12

Toucan Sam Backpack, 1983, 12" blue backpack that pictures Toucan Sam sitting on a schoolhouse
EX $15 **NM** $20 **MIP** $25

Toucan Sam Figure, 1984, 3" plastic jointed figure w/blue body and multi-colored beak
EX $12 **NM** $15 **MIP** $20

Toucan Sam Wallet, 1984, plastic w/picture of Toucan Sam
EX $10 **NM** $15 **MIP** $20

Kendall Company

Curad Taped Crusader Figure, 1977, 7-1/2" vinyl figure, green outfit, orange cape and hair
EX $50 **NM** $75 **MIP** $100

Ken-L-Ration

Ken-L-Ration Wall Pockets, 1960s, 3" pair of plastic wall pockets; cat's head and a dog's head
EX $40 **NM** $50 **MIP** $65

Kentucky Fried Chicken

Colonel Sanders, Wacky Wobbler, 8"
EX $3 **NM** $7 **MIP** $15

Colonel Sanders bank, 1965, vinyl, 12-1/2"
EX $35 **NM** $45 **MIP** $65

Colonel Sanders bank, 1977, plastic, red, 8"
EX $10 **NM** $20 **MIP** $30

Colonel Sanders Nodder, 1960s, 7" plastic nodder of Colonel holding bucket of chicken
EX $70 **NM** $85 **MIP** $100

Kiddie City Toy Store

Kaycee Kangaroo Figure, 1980s, vinyl kangaroo w/baby in pouch
EX $40 **NM** $55 **MIP** $65

Kraft

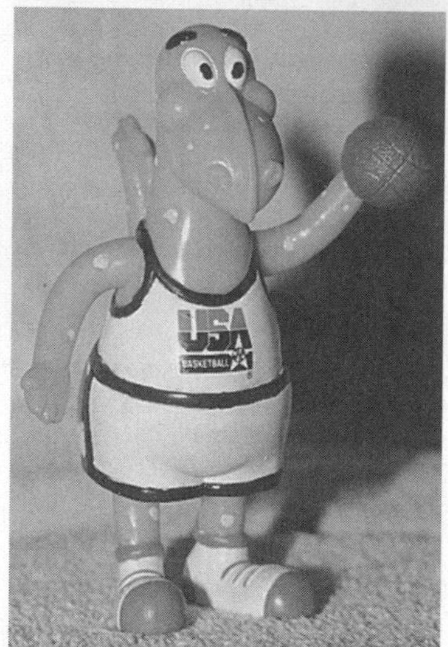

Cheesasaurus Rex Figure, 1990s, 5-1/2" orange dinosaur figures wearing different outfits
EX $4 **NM** $7 **MIP** $10

Mr. Wiggle Hand Puppet, 1966, 6" red rubber
EX $150 **NM** $185 **MIP** $225

Vegetable Man Bank, 1970s, 8" vegetable man w/tomato for a head and a celery body
EX $205 **NM** $260 **MIP** $280

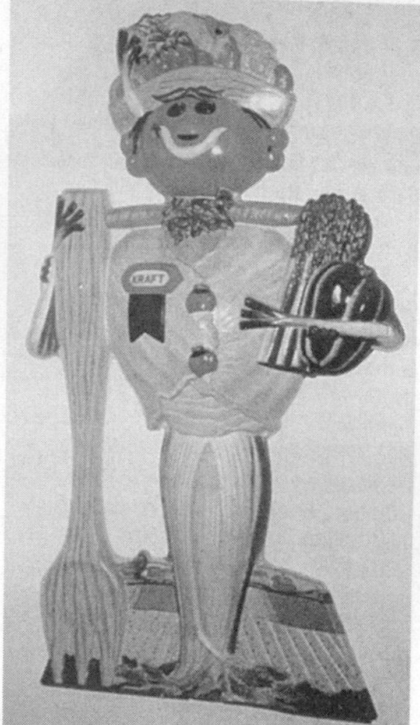

Vegetable Man Display, 1980, 3' plastic vacuuform store display of Vegetable Man
EX $155 **NM** $230 **MIP** $280

Labatt's Brewery

Labatt's Beer Man Figure, 1972, 6" man standing next to wood barrel
EX $35 NM $45 MIP $65

Magic Chef

Magic Chef Figure, 1980s, 7" chef dressed in tuxedo and chef's hat
EX $20 NM $25 MIP $35

McDonald's

Big Mac hand puppet, 1973, 12"
EX $7 NM $14 MIP $25

Big Mac vinyl doll, 1976, 6-1/2"
EX $10 NM $20 MIP $30

Collector Series glasses, 1975-76, 6 in series: Big Mac, Hamburglar, Mayor McCheese, Ronald McDonald, Grimmace, Captain Crook
EX $6 NM $10 MIP $15

Hamburglar stuffed doll, 1971, removable cape, 16"
EX $12 NM $18 MIP $30

Hamburglar stuffed doll, 1972, removable cape, 17"
EX $12 NM $18 MIP $30

Ronald McDonald stuffed doll, 1971, 16"
EX $15 NM $25 MIP $35

Ronald McDonald stuffed doll, 1977, 13"
EX $10 NM $18 MIP $25

Michelin Tires

Mr. Bib Figure, 1980s, 12" plastic figure w/Michelin sash across chest
EX $35 NM $45 MIP $55

Miscellaneous

Nauga, 1960s, 11" tall x 15-1/2" wide, monster, naugahyde promotional piece
EX $30 NM $60 MIP $110

RCA Silverama Repairman Bank, mid-1950s, 5" plastic,
EX $6 NM $14 MIP $27

Mister Softee

Mister Softee, 2000, Wacky Wobbler, vanilla, chocolate, strawberry, 8"
EX $3 NM $7 MIP $15

Mohawk Carpet Company

Mohawk Tommy Doll, 1970, 16" stuffed doll of a little boy marked "Mohawk Tommy" across front
EX $10 NM $15 MIP $20

Nabisco

Barnum's Animal Crackers Cookie Jar, 1972, ceramic, shaped like a box of animal crackers
EX $175 NM $225 MIP $275

Chips Ahoy Girl Figure, 1983, 4-1/2" vinyl figure of girl w/Chips Ahoy cookie on her head and in her hand
EX $15 NM $18 MIP $20

Fig Newton Girl Figure, 1983, 4-1/2" girl w/Fig Newton on her head
EX $17 NM $21 MIP $25

Nabisco Thing, 1996, 5" multi-colored bendable figure w/Nabisco logo for its head
EX $5 NM $10 MIP $15

Oreo Cookie Girl Figure, 1983, 4-1/2" vinyl figure of girl w/Oreo Cookie on head and in her hand
EX $15 NM $18 MIP $20

Nestle's

Milky Bar Kid, 2000s, 8" plush toy, mascot of the U.K. white chocolate "Milky Bar" since the 1960s, plush toy is of recent varitey
EX $5 NM $10 MIP $15

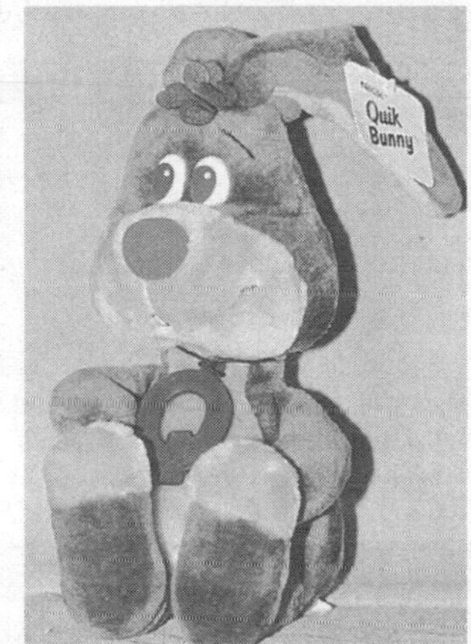

Quik Bunny Doll, 1976, 24" plush rabbit w/letter "Q" on his chest
EX $27 NM $38 MIP $44

Quik Bunny Figure, 1991, 6" bendable brown and tan rabbit w/the letter "Q" hanging from his neck
EX $3 NM $7 MIP $10

Novotel Hotel

Dophi Figure, 1990s, 4-1/2" bendable dolphin figures; set of four produced each year
EX $5 NM $8 MIP $10

Oscar Mayer Foods

Hot Wheels Wienermobile, die-cast Wienermobile
EX $10 NM $12 MIP $15

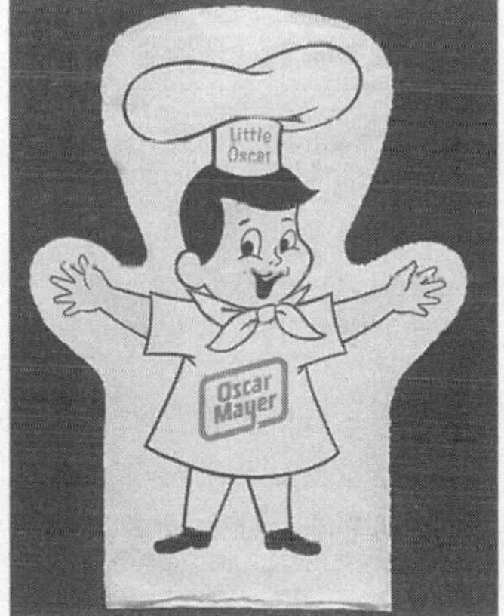

Little Oscar Puppet, thin plastic, theme song on back
EX $5 NM $8 MIP $10

ADVERTISING TOYS

Oscar Mayer Foods

Wienermobile, 1950s, 11" car; Little Oscar pops up when car is rolled
EX $150 **NM** $175 **MIP** $225

Wienermobile Bank, 1984, plastic
EX $15 **NM** $25 **MIP** $45

Wienermobile Beanbag, 1998, 7" plush beanbag
EX $3 **NM** $5 **MIP** $8

Pepperidge Farm

Goldfish Plush, 1970s, 16" plush figure
EX $15 **NM** $20 **MIP** $25

Pillsbury

Biscuit the Cat Puppet, 1974, 2-1/2" vinyl cat finger puppet
EX $18 **NM** $25 **MIP** $30

Grandpopper & Grandmommer Figures, 1974, 5" vinyl pair of figures
EX $85 **NM** $128 **MIP** $155

Green Giant stuffed doll, 1966, 16"
EX $35 **NM** $50 **MIP** $75

Jolly Green Giant Figure, 1970s, 9-1/2" vinyl green man wearing loincloth of leaves
EX $110 **NM** $125 **MIP** $150

Little Sprout Figure, 1970s, 6-1/2" vinyl green figure w/leaves on head and body
EX $10 **NM** $15 **MIP** $25

Little Sprout Inflatable Figure, 1976, 24" vinyl
EX $25 **NM** $30 **MIP** $35

Little Sprout Salt and Pepper Shakers, 1988, 3" ceramic figural shakers
EX $25 **NM** $30 **MIP** $35

Poppie Fresh figure, 1971, vinyl, all white, 5"
EX $10 **NM** $12 **MIP** $15

Poppin' Fresh Doll, 1972, white velour doll w/hat and scarf
EX $20 **NM** $25 **MIP** $30

Poppin' Fresh Figure, 1971, 6-1/2" vinyl white baker w/blue eyes and blue dot on hat
EX $15 **NM** $18 **MIP** $25

Sprout stuffed doll, 1970, small eyes, 10"
EX $7 **NM** $15 **MIP** $25

Sprout vinyl doll, 1996, w/ Pasta Accents sash, 6-1/2"
EX $7 **NM** $12 **MIP** $20

Pizza Hut

Pizza Hut Pete Bank, 1969, 7-1/2" plastic
EX $20 **NM** $35 **MIP** $50

Pizza Time Theatre

Chuck E. Cheese Bank, 1980s, 6-1/2" plastic
EX $12 **NM** $15 **MIP** $18

Planters Peanuts

Mr. Peanut Bank, plastic, rare, orange, hat twists off to get to coins
EX $30 **NM** $70 **MIP** $155

Mr. Peanut Bank, plastic, tan, hat twists off to get to coins
EX $10 **NM** $20 **MIP** $45

Mr. Peanut Bank, 1950s, plastic, pink, 8-1/2" tall, hat twists off to get to coins
EX $15 **NM** $30 **MIP** $50

Mr. Peanut Bank, 1991, 75th Birthday edition; black, yellow, white; base says "Mr. Peanut"
EX $10 **NM** $15 **MIP** $25

Mr. Peanut Doll, 1967, 21" pillow doll
EX $15 **NM** $20 **MIP** $35

Mr. Peanut Figure, 1930s, 8-1/2" painted wood figure w/hat and cane
EX $275 **NM** $300 **MIP** $375

Mr. Peanut Figure, 1992, 8-1/2" yellow and black plastic
EX $20 **NM** $25 **MIP** $35

Mr. Peanut Lamp, 1950s, plastic figure of Mr. Peanut, bulb fits inside
EX $30 **NM** $60 **MIP** $125

Mr. Peanut Pinback Button, celluloid
EX $15 **NM** $30 **MIP** $45

Mr. Peanut Wind-Up, 1984, 3" yellow peanut man w/traditional hat and cane
EX $20 **NM** $25 **MIP** $30

Mr. Peanut Wind-Up Walker, 1950s, black and yellow plastic, 8-1/2" tall, wind-up motor
EX $25 **NM** $75 **MIP** $150

Mr. Peanut Wind-Up Walker, 1950s, red plastic, 8-1/2" tall, wind-up motor
EX $25 **NM** $75 **MIP** $150

Mr. Peanut's Peanut Wagon, 1950s, plastic, 2-1/8" tall, premium, red and yellow
EX $30 **NM** $75 **MIP** $150

Stake Truck, 1950s, plactic, 1-1/2" tall, premium, red, blue and yellow
EX $25 **NM** $65 **MIP** $115

Post Cereal

California Raisins PVC Figure, 1987, 2" male raisin playing drums
EX $10 **NM** $12 **MIP** $18

California Raisins Wind-Up, 1987, 4" female raisin w/tambourine
EX $5 **NM** $7 **MIP** $10

Sugar Bear Doll, 1970s, 12" plush brown bear w/blue "Sugar Bear" shirt
EX $20 **NM** $25 **MIP** $35

Sugar Bear Doll, 1988, 12" plush bear w/blue "Sugar Bear" shirt
EX $15 **NM** $20 **MIP** $25

Proctor & Gamble

24-Hour Flu Bug, 1970s, 7" tall, vinyl bank, spotted green bug
EX $40 **NM** $65 **MIP** $95

Hawaiian Punch Doll, 1983, 15" plush Punchy w/red hair and blue and white striped shirt
EX $20 **NM** $22 **MIP** $25

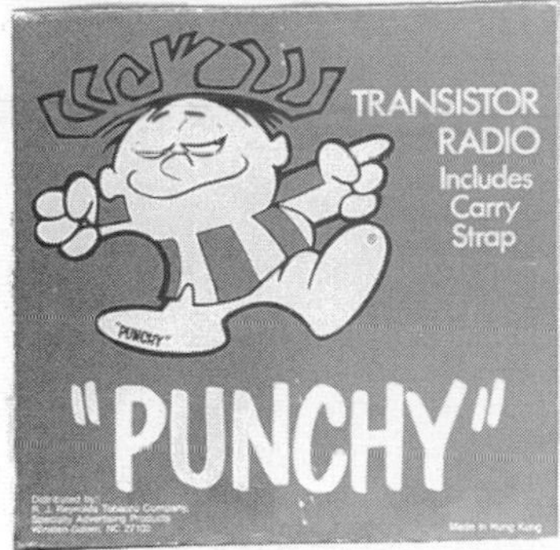

Hawaiian Punch Radio, 1970s, 6" figural radio of Punchy
EX $25 **NM** $35 **MIP** $45

Mr. Clean Figure, 1961, 8" bald man wearing white clothes w/earring; arms are folded
EX $85 **NM** $100 **MIP** $135

Purina Chuck Wagon

Chuck Wagon, 1975, 8" vinyl team of horses and checker board covered wagon
EX $35 **NM** $45 **MIP** $55

Quaker Oats

Cap'n Crunch, Wacky Wobbler, 8"
EX $3 **NM** $7 **MIP** $15

Cap'n Crunch Bank, 1969, 8" vinyl captain wearing blue outfit and sword
EX $45 **NM** $65 **MIP** $85

Cap'n Crunch stuffed doll, 1978, 15"
EX $5 **NM** $10 **MIP** $20

Jean LaFoote Bank, 1975, 8" vinyl pirate wearing green suit and purple hat
EX $60 **NM** $85 **MIP** $125

Quake Cereal Doll, 1965, 9" man w/raised arms and letter "Q" across chest
EX $85 **NM** $95 **MIP** $125

Quaker Oats figure mug, plastic, 4"
EX $25 **NM** $35 **MIP** $45

Quisp, Wacky Wobbler, 8"
EX $3 **NM** $7 **MIP** $15

Quisp Bank, 1960s, 6-1/2" papier-mâché
EX $500 **NM** $750 **MIP** $850

Quisp Cereal Doll, 1965, 10" doll w/pink body, green clothes and letter "Q" across stomach
EX $70 **NM** $85 **MIP** $125

Quisp Powered Sugar Space Gun, 7" long, red, mail away premium
EX $150 **NM** $250 **MIP** $400

R.J. Reynolds

Joe Camel Can Cooler, 1991, 4" vinyl
EX $10 **NM** $15 **MIP** $22

Raid

Raid Bug, 1989, plush green bug
EX $22 **NM** $30 **MIP** $40

Raid Bug Radio, 1980s, Raid bug in standing position w/clock on one side and radio on the other
EX $70 **NM** $200 **MIP** $135

Raid Bug Wind-Up, 1983, 4" yellow and green angry bug
EX $40 **NM** $50 **MIP** $70

Ralston Purina

Meow Mix Cat, 1976, 4-1/2" vinyl yellow cat w/black stripes
EX $20 **NM** $25 **MIP** $30

Reckitt & Colman

Mr. Bubble Figure, 1990, 8" pink vinyl
EX $20 **NM** $30 **MIP** $35

Reddy Communications

Reddy Kilowatt, 2000, Wacky Wobbler, 8"
EX $3 **NM** $7 **MIP** $15

Reddy Kilowatt Bobbin' Head, 1960s, 6-1/2" Reddy wearing cowboy outfit
EX $225 **NM** $275 **MIP** $450

Reddy Kilowatt Figure, 1961, 6" plastic figure w/lightbulb for head and lightning bolts for body
EX $150 **NM** $185 **MIP** $225

Ritalin

Ritalin Man Statue, 1970s, 7" smiling plastic statue w/hat
EX $58 **NM** $67 **MIP** $78

Sea Host

Clem the Clam Push Puppets, 1969, 4" fish push puppets; four different fish were issued
EX $15 **NM** $30 **MIP** $40

Shop Rite

Scrunchy Bear Doll, 1970s, 16" plush bear w/Shop-Rite shirt
EX $20 **NM** $25 **MIP** $30

Smile Orange Drink

Drink Smile Statue, 1930s, 8" plaster statue of character w/orange for head; "Drink Smile" written across base
EX $150 **NM** $200 **MIP** $250

Smith Kline & French Lab

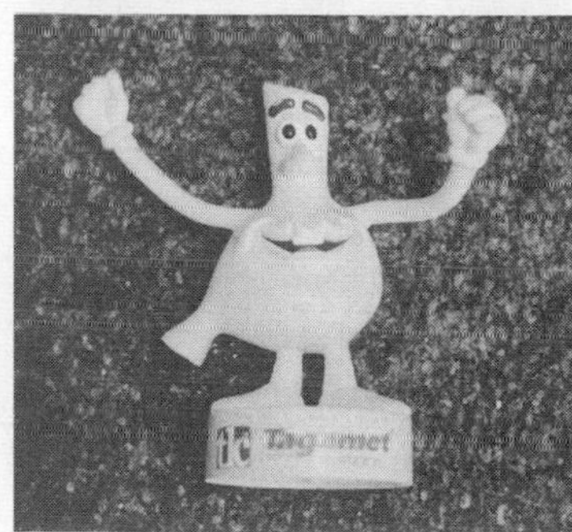

Tagamet Figure, 1989, 2-1/2" bendable pink figure standing on base
EX $15 **NM** $20 **MIP** $25

Sony

Sony Boy Figure, 1960s, 4" vinyl boy wearing yellow "Sony" shirt
EX $150 **NM** $200 **MIP** $225

Squirt Beverage

Squirt Doll, 1961, 17" vinyl boy w/blond hair and removable clothing; "Squirt" written across shirt
EX $100 **NM** $150 **MIP** $175

Starkist

Charlie the Tuna Doll, 1970, 15" pull string talking doll
EX $40 **NM** $50 **MIP** $80

Charlie the Tuna Figure, 1973, 7-1/2" vinyl Charlie; arms pointed down
EX $60 **NM** $75 **MIP** $110

Charlie the Tuna Radio, 1970, 6" radio
EX $50 **NM** $60 **MIP** $90

Charlie the Tuna Scale, 1972, oval shaped bathroom scale w/Charlie the Tuna
EX $50 **NM** $65 **MIP** $80

Charlie Tuna, Wacky Wobbler, 8"
EX $3 **NM** $7 **MIP** $15

Sterling Drug

Diaparene Baby Doll, 1980, 5" baby w/movable arms and legs; baby wears diaper
EX $35 **NM** $40 **MIP** $50

Tastykake

Tastykake Baker Doll, 1974, 13" pillow doll wearing chef outfit
EX $15 **NM** $20 **MIP** $25

Tony's Pizza

Mr. Tony Figure, 1972, 8" vinyl Italian pizza chef
EX $40 **NM** $50 **MIP** $65

Toys 'R Us

Geoffrey Doll, 1967, 2-1/2" plush Geoffrey wearing red and white striped shirt
EX $20 **NM** $25 **MIP** $50

Geoffrey Flashlight, 1989, 8-1/2" plastic figural flashlight of Geoffrey the Giraffe
EX $8 **NM** $10 **MIP** $12

Travelodge

Sleepy Bear Squeeze Toy, 1970s, 5-1/2" bear wearing pajamas
EX $25 **NM** $30 **MIP** $35

Tropicana

Tropic-Ana Doll, 1977, 17" pillow doll of Hawaiian girl
EX $15 **NM** $20 **MIP** $25

U.S. Forestry Department

Smokey the Bear bank, ceramic, 6" tall, Smokey sitting with hand on hat
EX n/a **NM** $10 **MIP** $22

Smokey the Bear bank, 1980s, plastic, 8"
EX $7 **NM** $14 **MIP** $25

Smokey the Bear Bendy, 1967, bendable Smokey
EX n/a **NM** $5 **MIP** $10

Smokey the Bear Boxcar, 60th anniversary boxcar rolling stock, #52334
EX n/a **NM** $55 **MIP** $85

Smokey the Bear Comic book, 1960, "The True Story of Smokey the Bear," first edition 1960
EX n/a **NM** $7 **MIP** $14

Smokey the Bear figure, 1976, plastic, w/ shovel, 8"
EX $40 **NM** $50 **MIP** $65

Smokey the Bear Little Golden Book, 1955, cover reads, "Smokey the Bear"
EX n/a **NM** $10 **MIP** $15

Smokey the Bear nodder, 1960s, 6"
EX $30 **NM** $65 **MIP** $100

Smokey the Bear Pinback Button, 1970s, brown & yellow, reads, "Join Smokey's Campaign, Prevent Forest Fires"
EX n/a **NM** $7 **MIP** $15

Smokey the Bear Puppet, 1960s
EX n/a **NM** $10 **MIP** $20

Smokey the Bear soaky, 1965, 9-1/2"
EX $10 **NM** $20 **MIP** $30

Smokey the Bear stuffed animal, 1960s, 12"
EX $25 **NM** $50 **MIP** $75

Smokey the Bear stuffed animal, 1960s, Smokey in coveralls
EX n/a **NM** $10 **MIP** $20

Smokey the Bear stuffed animal, 1972, 6-3/4" tall; box reads, "The Official Smokey Bear"
EX n/a **NM** $10 **MIP** $20

Smokey the Bear stuffed animal, 1985, 9-1/2" tall, Model No. SB-12-1
EX n/a **NM** $10 **MIP** $25

Woodsy Owl Bank, 1970s, 8-1/2" ceramic figural bank
EX $100 **NM** $125 **MIP** $150

U.S. Postal Service

Mr. ZIP Statue, 1960s, 6-1/2" wood statue w/mailbag and pop-up hat
EX $150 **NM** $180 **MIP** $225

Wonder Bread

Fresh Guy Figure, 1975, 4" smiling loaf of bread w/polka dots, smiling face and "Wonder" on side
EX $100 **NM** $150 **MIP** $175

Barbie

by Sharon Korbeck-Verbeten

The Modest Beginnings of a Teen-Age Model

In 1959, a blond female with a very adult body made a lot of men blush. Of course, she was only 11-1/2 inches tall.

While she initially created shock waves in the mainly male toy industry, that didn't stop the toy world from soon embracing the spirit of what we now fondly just call Barbie.

Mattel's fashion doll icon still captures the essence of little girls' imaginations and dreams—and that's exactly what creator Ruth Handler intended.

Since the doll's introduction, Barbie has seen cosmetic changes (like hairstyle, facial expression, slight changes in body style and even a tattoo!) and more major changes (literally dozens of careers, computer technological advances, etc.). Through it all, however, Barbie has come out ahead of the competitors. Today, Mattel sells roughly $2 billion in Barbie dolls per year.

Barbie's beginnings are well-documented; her birth happened smack in the middle of a strong 1950s postwar economy.

It was then that the Barbie doll came as an inspiration to Mattel co-founder Handler as she watched her young daughter, Barbara, playing with paper dolls.

Barbara and her friends liked to play make-believe with the dolls, imagining them in roles as college students, cheerleaders, and adults with careers.

Handler immediately recognized that playing and pretending about the future was an important part of growing up. In researching the marketplace, she discovered a void and was determined to fill the niche with a three-dimensional fashion doll. Her all-male design staff, however, harbored doubts.

Several designs later, Mattel introduced Barbie, the Teen-Age Fashion Model, to skeptical buyers at New York's annual Toy Fair in 1959. Never before had they seen a doll so completely unlike the baby and toddler dolls popular at the time. A major point of controversy was Barbie's ample bosom. Actually, the contention was that the doll had breasts . . . period.

With fashion and teenage lifestyle trends evolving at a startling rate, the hundreds of people who have worked to keep Barbie current have had their hands full as styles changed from Paris couture to the inspired elegance of the Jacqueline Kennedy years to a more free-flowing, youthful look.

Mattel's design and development staff have remained current by identifying trends that relate to the lives of American teenagers. Barbie has been called an "evergreen" property, an adjective infrequently used in the toy industry. Far too often, toys and the whims of the fickle buying public are fleeting. But unlike decades of toys lost in the attics of memory, Mattel's Barbie has surpassed probably even Handler's expectations.

A Collector's Dream

Barbie's charm as a children's toy may have been immediate, but it wasn't until decades later that collectors started paying more attention. Collectors who had grown up with Barbie wanted to reclaim her. There was, after all, plenty to recapture—the memories of playing with dolls with friends, Barbie's fabulous fancy outfits, dream dates with Ken and, who could forget, Barbie's well-appointed dream house!

Because Barbie dolls were well-loved and played-with, many of the 1959 and early 1960s dolls are found today in less-than-perfect shape. That's why examples of the earliest Barbie dolls regularly command hundreds, even thousands, of dollars each. Having original boxes and clothing increases a doll's value.

Collectors today are interested in both vintage and newer, collector-edition dolls. Collecting is no small hobby. Full-time dealers make their livings off Barbie, and several publications exist solely to cover what's new in Barbie's world.

Nostalgia and investment potential are perhaps the two biggest motivators for Barbie collectors. And investment potential has proven itself over the last decades, especially for 1960s dolls.

Barbie Today: Market Trends

Vintage dolls, particularly early 1960s issues and Ponytails from 1959, remain hard to find in Mint in Box condition. Those with original boxes, accessories, and clothing remain the Holy Grail with collectors.

While it may not be difficult to find a 1960s brunette Bubblecut in Good condition, finding a rare variation (such as one with side-parted hair or with a hard-to-find hair color like brownette) is more challenging . . . and that doll will likely be more valuable than more common ones from the same time period.

The most investment-savvy way to collect Barbie dolls is to focus on early 1960s dolls; they tend to appreciate more in value than newer dolls, especially because supply and condition has diminished over the years. Loose, naked, or damaged vintage Barbie dolls; most of those

THE *TOP* 10 BARBIE (In Mint Condition)

	Item	Value
1.	Ponytail Barbie #2, brunette, Mattel, 1959	$7,000
2.	Ponytail Barbie #1, brunette, Mattel, 1959	5,500
3.	Ponytail Barbie #1, blonde, Mattel, 1959	5,000
4.	Ponytail Barbie #2, blonde, Mattel, 1959	5,000
5.	Roman Holiday, Barbie Vintage Fashions, Mattel, 1959-66	4,800
6.	Gay Parisienne, Barbie Vintage Fashions, Mattel, 1959-66	4,000
7.	Pan Am Stewardess, Barbie Vintage Fashions, Mattel, 1959-66	4,000
8.	Easter Parade, Barbie Vintage Fashions, Mattel, 1959-66	4,000
9.	Barbie's Sport Plane, Barbie vehicles, Mattel, 1964	3,500
10.	Barbie's Airplane, Barbie vehicles, Mattel, 1964	3,500

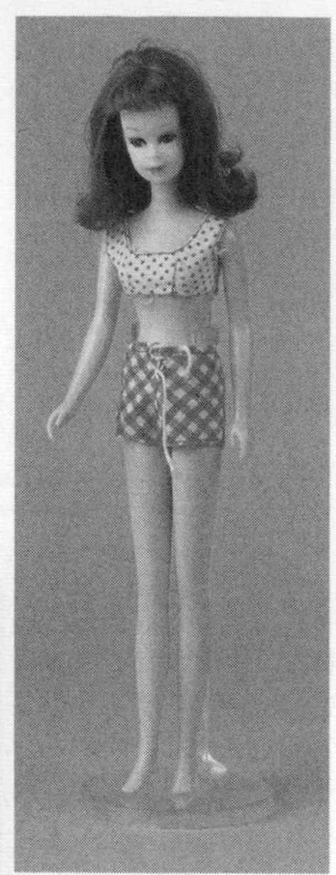

from the 1970s to today will have very little or no collectible value. Some 1960s dolls may have value in any condition because of their rarity.

Recent auction prices for vintage 1959 and 1960s dolls have remained steady, with a few peaks and valleys. In 2003, a pristine Ponytail Barbie #1 sold for more than $25,000 at a California auction, but that's unusual. Other, more realistic, prices noted have included $8,700 (paid in 2000 for a brunette Ponytail #1). A more common price for a Mint in Box example of the first Barbie doll is $3,000 and $4,500. Lesser condition #1 dolls, or those without original boxes, will bring only a fraction (50 percent or less) of those spectacular prices.

Other vintage dolls worthy of picking up include the 1966 Color Magic dolls (with hair that could change colors), Swirl Ponytails (with their swept-back hairstyle still intact) and any early African-American doll (like Black Francie or the first Black Barbie).

Some limited-edition series dolls from the last 10 years are worthy of note since they have shown some appreciation in value. For example, the Harley-Davidson series of Barbie and Ken dolls, begun in the late 1990s, has consistently held its value or increased over the past five years.

In the last five years, however, collector edition Barbie dolls have generated interest at retail, but prices have not soared (or, in some cases, increased at all) on the secondary market.

Generating the most collector attention in the past few years has been the Fashion Model collection, which debuted in 2000. The dolls are made of a revolutionary Silkstone material, a durable material which feels like porcelain but remains unbreakable. The series started off racy with Lingerie #1, with slinky underwear and decidedly retro-looking face. Obviously targeted at a sophisticated adult collector market, the series was a huge success; since then six Lingerie dolls and several other dolls in the series have been made, many selling out at dealers nationwide. In early 2003, however, Mattel announced the end of the Lingerie series, cowering to protests nationwide about the doll's risqué appearance. The cancellation of the series led collectors who got in on the series late to search the secondary market for the earliest Lingerie dolls.

On the retail market, Mattel and Barbie suffered some blows in 2003-04 that continue to impact prices today. Trendy dolls like MGA's Bratz targeted a younger, hipper audience and succeeded in taking market share from Mattel's "pink aisle."

Mattel aimed to recoup its popularity by issuing dolls based on familiar and trendy characters (such as Supergirl or the film property Grease). Mattel's hip and edgy Cali Girl and Mod Circle lines played up a fresh, new look (bare midriff, surf garb, trendy clothes, funky hairstyles)

Collector Alert: Not every doll in a series is a winner in collectors' eyes and not every series will maintain its popularity.

Tips for Collecting

Although many Barbie dolls increase in value, others do not. Here are some tips for smart collecting:

- **Avoid regular issue dolls (also known as pink box dolls or play dolls).** These are the ones that generally retail in toy stores for less than $15. These have limited investment potential. Buy them because you like them, not because you expect them to increase in value.
- **Look for limited-edition exclusives.** Certain dolls are "exclusives" because they are made only for one retail outlet, like Target or FAO Schwarz. Many of these dolls have increased in value; others, however, show less success. Harley-Davidson Barbie, exclusive to Toys R Us, for example, was next to impossible to find in stores. Its secondary market prices immediately soared to $250 or more. Now, the first edition Harley Barbie could bring $800 or more.
- **Look for dolls in the best possible condition.** Dolls in top condition command higher prices than dolls in poor condition. And watch for original boxes, apparel, and even tiny accessories. They can all add value to a doll.
- **Dig carefully through big boxes of loose dolls.** Loose, naked, or damaged vintage Barbie dolls from the 1970s to today, have very little or no collectible value. Dolls from the 1960s in the same condition may be worth something to collectors; for example, even a naked or slightly damaged Color Magic or Miss Barbie doll from the 1960s could bring $100 or more.
- **Don't be fooled by dates!** Barbie dolls have distinct markings on their buttocks, but remember that the date on a doll is likely the date the doll's body style was copyrighted, NOT necessarily the date the doll was made. Therefore, dolls with a 1960s date may actually be made in the 1990s. Plenty of books exist with photos of dolls and markings, making it more accurate to identify your doll.
- **Don't overlook licensed Barbie products.** Mattel licenses the Barbie name to companies which make paper dolls, clothing, cases, watches, lunch boxes, and other collectibles. Anything with the Barbie name is collectible but not necessarily valuable.
- **Buy the less-than-obvious choices.** Lots of collectors are looking for dolls and fashions. Look for the more disposable items bearing the Barbie name: think boxes of bandages or Jell-O or other items meant to be consumed and discarded. The packaging will be a great find years down the road.

To the non-collector, the first Ponytail Barbie dolls all look similar. There are, however, subtle and important differences. Below are characteristics of the first Barbie (1959) known to collectors as Ponytail Barbie #1.

Looking Out for #1

- holes in the bottom of the feet with copper tubes inside the legs
- zebra-stripe one-piece swimsuit
- blond or brunette hair with soft curly bangs
- red fingernails, toenails, and lips
- gold hoop earrings
- white irises and severely pointed black eyebrows

- heavy, black facial paint
- pale, almost white, ivory skin tone
- body markings: Barbie T.M./Pats.Pend./[copyright mark]MCMLVIII/by/Mattel/Inc.

Resources for Collectors

Barbie collectors are never alone. They give a positive and impressive meaning to the word "network" since they find so many ways to communicate with each other. Books, magazines, Web sites, and clubs are plentiful. While not a complete list, here is a look at some of the "best bets" for Barbie collectors today.

Publications

Several publications cater to doll lovers; one is specifically devoted to Barbie doll fans. Check out these fine print resources.

Doll Reader
6405 Flank Dr.
Harrisburg, PA 17112-2753
www.dollreader.com

Auction Houses

Collectors often turn to auction houses to buy and sell Barbie dolls, accessories and collections. Two of the major doll auction venues are

McMasters Harris Doll Auctions
P.O. Box 1755
Cambridge, OH 43725
(800) 842-3526
www.mcmastersauctions.com

Theriault's, The Doll Masters
P.O. Box 151
Annapolis, MD 21401
(301) 224-3655
www.theriaults.com

Clubs

Literally hundreds of clubs, ranging from local and regional to national and international, exist to serve avid collectors. It's unknown if a complete and up-to-date list has ever been compiled, but the other Barbie resources listed on this page are the best bets for locating other collectors and clubs. For more information on Mattel's official Barbie Collector's Club, visit their Web site at www.barbiecollectibles.com or call (800) 491-7503.

Web Sites

This list could be endless, especially with all the dealer, retail, secondary market, and fan sites out there. The best bet for surfing through the sites more successfully is to search the Internet under the keywords "Barbie," "Barbie doll [or dolls]," "Barbie collectibles," "Mattel's Barbie," or other appropriate terms.

Mattel Toys / Barbie Collectibles
www.barbiecollectibles.com

Books

Books on America's favorite fashion doll icon are plentiful as well. A library search or visit to www.bn.com or www.amazon.com will also reveal more complete lists of Barbie books. Here are some favorites.

Warman's Barbie Doll Field Guide
(2009, Kause Publications)

The Best of Barbie
Sharon Korbeck (2001, Krause Publications)

The Ultimate Barbie Doll Book
Marcie Melillo
(revised edition, 2004, Krause Publications)

The Collectible Barbie Doll, Second Edition
Janine Fennick (1999, Running Press/Courage)

Fashion Doll Price Guide 2000-2001
(2000, Portfolio Press)

Collector's Compass Barbie Doll
(2000, Martingale & Company)

The Story of Barbie Doll, Second Edition
Kitturah B. Westenhouser (1999, Collector Books)

The Collectors Encyclopedia of Barbie Dolls and Collectibles
Sibyl DeWein and Joan Ashabraner
(1994 ed., Collector Books)

Contemporary Barbie
Jane Sarasohn-Kahn (1997, Antique Trader Books)

Identifying Barbie Dolls: The New Compact Study Guide and Identifier
Janine Fennick (1998)

The Barbie Doll Years: A Comprehensive Listing and Value Guide of Dolls and Accessories
Patrick C. Olds and Joyce L. Olds
(2000, Collector Books)

Face of the American Dream: Barbie Doll 1959-1971
Christopher Varaste (1999, Hobby House)

Contributors: Sharon Korbeck is the author of *The Best of Barbie* (2001, Krause Publications). Jan Fennick has been an avid doll collector since she was very small. In 1987, an interest in 1960s pop culture and fashion lead her to take her childhood Barbie dolls out of storage and her life hasn't been the same since. She is the author of three books on Barbie doll collecting plus numerous articles and columns for such publications as *Barbie Bazaar, White's Guide to Collecting Figures, Beckett's Hot Toys, Doll Reader, Toy Shop,* and the annual Krause Publications *Toys & Prices* as well as CollectingChannel.com. She's been a member of both the Delaware Valley and Long Island Fashion Doll Collectors Clubs and souvenir program chair person for the 1996 and the 2005 National Barbie Doll Collectors Convention. She's never met a fashion doll she didn't like. She may be reached in care of the editor at Krause Publications, 700 E. State St., Iola, WI 54990.

BARBIE

Accessories

COLORFORMS SETS

Barbie Make-Up Kit, 1989, Colorforms, Barbie make-up face w/stand, 4 easy wipe-off styling crayons, wipe-off cloth, 42 Colorforms Fashion Jewelry accessories
MNP $7 **MIP** $15

Barbie Sport Fashion, 1975, Colorforms
MNP $4 **MIP** $8

Barbie's 3-D Fashion Theatre, 1970, Colorforms
MNP $9 **MIP** $20

Baywatch Barbie, 1995, Colorforms
MNP $7 **MIP** $15

Dress-Up Kit New Living Barbie, 1970, Colorforms
MNP $10 **MIP** $38

Malibu Barbie, 1972, Colorforms
MNP $7 **MIP** $20

Western Barbie, 1982, Colorforms, Barbie and horse
MNP $6 **MIP** $12

MISCELLANEOUS

Barbie & Ken Wipe Away Cloths, 1964
MNP $100 **MIP** $280

Barbie and Ken Hangers, 1960s, SPP, plastic hangers in bag w/cardboard backing
MNP $20 **MIP** $35

Barbie Beauty Kit, 1961, Roclar
MNP $100 **MIP** $200

Barbie Bubble Bath, 1961, Roclar
MNP $45 **MIP** $100

Barbie Carry-All Wallet, 1963, SPP
MNP $145 **MIP** $255

Barbie Disco Record Player, 1976
MNP $85 **MIP** $160

Barbie Dresser Accessories, 1962
MNP $175 **MIP** $300

Barbie Ge-Tar, 1963, Mattel
MNP $200 **MIP** $400

Barbie Hair Fair, 1966, Mattel
MNP $75 **MIP** $145

Barbie Mattel-A-Phone, 1968
MNP $100 **MIP** $175

Barbie Nurse Kit, 1962, Pressman, tin litho box
MNP $100 **MIP** $275

Barbie Powder Mitt, 1961
MNP $75 **MIP** $140

Barbie Pretty Up Time, 1960s, brush/comb/mirror set
MNP $50 **MIP** $125

Barbie Record, 1965, Columbia Records
MNP $70 **MIP** $120

Barbie Store Display, 1980, Mattel
MNP $10 **MIP** $30

Barbie Wig Wardrobe, 1960s, Mattel, doll head w/three wigs
MNP $75 **MIP** $150

Barbie, Ken, Midge Pencil Case, 1964, SPP
MNP $100 **MIP** $260

Barbie's Dog Snowball, 1990s, Arco/Mattel
MNP $10 **MIP** $15

Francie Electric Drawing Table, 1966
MNP $65 **MIP** $130

Jack and Jill magazine advertisements, 1960s
MNP $15 **MIP** $35

Jigsaw Puzzle, 1963-65, Whitman
MNP $30 **MIP** $60

Jumbo Trading Cards, 1962, Dynamic, complete set
MNP $225 **MIP** $365

Record Player, 1961, Emenee
MNP $700 **MIP** $950

Record Tote, 1961, Ponytail, vinyl, several colors
MNP $75 **MIP** $180

Vanity Fair Transistor Radio, 1962, Vanity Fair
MNP $700 **MIP** $1350

Wine Set, 1986
MNP $40 **MIP** $75

PAPER DOLLS

Barbie and Ken Cut-Outs, 1962, Whitman, pink cover, Model No. 1971
MNP $50 **MIP** $135

Barbie and Ken Paper Dolls, 1970, Whitman, Model No. 1986
MNP $25 **MIP** $45

Barbie and Skipper, 1964, Whitman, Model No. 1957
MNP $35 **MIP** $100

Barbie Costume Dolls, 1964, Whitman, Model No. 1976
MNP $60 **MIP** $125

Barbie Cut-Outs, 1962, Model No. 1963
MNP $55 **MIP** $125

Barbie Doll Cut-Outs, 1963, Whitman, Model No. 1962
MNP $45 **MIP** $95

Barbie Dolls and Clothes, 1969, Model No. 1976
MNP $35 **MIP** $50

Barbie Has a New Look Paper Dolls, 1967, Whitman, Model No. 1996
MNP $40 **MIP** $85

Barbie Paper Dolls, boxed, 1967, Whitman, Model No. 4701
MNP $20 **MIP** $50

Barbie, Christie and Stacey, 1968, Whitman, Model No. 1978
MNP $35 **MIP** $65

Barbie, Ken and Midge Paper Dolls, 1963, Whitman, Model No. 1976
MNP $50 **MIP** $75

Barbie, Two Magic Dolls w/stay-on clothes, 1969, Model No. 4763
MNP $30 **MIP** $50

Barbie's Travel Wardrobe, boxed, 1964, Model No. 4616
MNP $50 **MIP** $100

Francie and Casey Paper Dolls, 1967, Whitman, Model No. 1986
MNP $30 **MIP** $50

Francie Paper Dolls, 1967, Whitman, Model No. 1094
MNP $40 **MIP** $70

Malibu Barbie Paper Dolls, 1972, Whitman, Model No. 1994
MNP $20 **MIP** $35

Meet Francie Paper Dolls, 1966, Whitman, Model No. 1980
MNP $35 **MIP** $70

Midge Cut-Outs, 1963, Whitman, Model No. 1962
MNP $45 **MIP** $65

P.J. Cover Girl Paper Dolls, 1971, Whitman, Model No. 1981
MNP $20 **MIP** $40

Skipper Paper Dolls, 1965, Whitman, Model No. 1984
MNP $25 **MIP** $45

Skooter Paper Dolls, 1965, Whitman, Model No. 1985
MNP $35 **MIP** $75

Tutti, boxed, 1967, Model No. 4622
MNP $30 **MIP** $45

Twiggy Paper Dolls, 1967, Whitman, Model No. 1999
MNP $25 **MIP** $40

STRUCTURES

Barbie and Ken Little Theatre, 1964, Mattel, Model No. 4090
MNP $175 **MIP** $250

Barbie Café Today, 1971, Mattel, Model No. 4973
MNP $150 **MIP** $225

Barbie Fashion Stage, 1971, Mattel, Model No. 1148
MNP $50 **MIP** $75

Barbie Goes to College, 1964, Mattel, Model No. 4093
MNP $200 **MIP** $350

Barbie's Dream House, 1962, Mattel, Model No. 816
MNP $50 **MIP** $150

Barbie's Dream Kitchen, 1965, Mattel, Model No. 4095
MNP $300 **MIP** $400

Barbie's New Dream House, 1964, Mattel, Model No. 4092
MNP $75 **MIP** $200

Fashion Shop, 1962, Mattel, Model No. 817
MNP $150 **MIP** $275

Francie and Casey Studio House, 1967, Mattel, Model No. 1026
MNP $50 **MIP** $75

Francie House, 1966, Mattel, Model No. 3302
MNP $40 **MIP** $75

Jamie's Penthouse (Sears), 1971, Mattel, Model No. 31122
MNP $200 **MIP** $425

Quick Curl Boutique, 1973, Mattel, Model No. 8665
MNP $40 **MIP** $80

Skipper's Dream Room, 1965, Mattel, Model No. 4094
MNP $200 **MIP** $350

Skipper's Schoolroom, 1965, Mattel
MNP $250 **MIP** $350

Tutti Ice Cream Stand, 1967, Model No. 3363
MNP $75 **MIP** $175

Tutti's and Todd's Playhouse, 1966
MNP $75 **MIP** $125

TIMEPIECES

Barbie Personal Photo Clock, 1964, Bradley/Elgin
MNP $500 **MIP** $600

Barbie Starbright Boudoir Clock, 1964, Bradley/Elgin
MNP $600 **MIP** $700

Broken Heart Wristwatch, 1964, Bradley/Elgin
MNP $300 **MIP** $400

Brokn' Heart Pendant, 1965, Bradley/Elgin
MNP $400 **MIP** $500

Curly Bangs Pendant, 1963-64, Bradley/Elgin
MNP $150 **MIP** $400

Curly Bangs Wristwatch, 1963-64, Bradley/Elgin
MNP $125 **MIP** $300

Midge Wristwatch, 1964, Bradley/Elgin
MNP $300 **MIP** $450

Skipper Wristwatch, 1964, Bradley/Elgin
MNP $300 **MIP** $450

Swirl Ponytail Wristwatch, 1964, Bradley/Elgin
MNP $150 **MIP** $300

VEHICLES

Allan's Mercedes Roadster, 1964, Irwin, Model No. 5348
MNP $150 **MIP** $575

Barbie and Ken and Midge Convertible, 1964, Irwin
MNP $125 **MIP** $150

Barbie's Airplane, 1964, Irwin
MNP $1000 **MIP** $3500

Barbie's Austin-Healey, 1964, Irwin, lavender, Montgomery Wards exclusive
MNP $800 **MIP** $1000

Barbie's Austin-Healey Convertible, 1962, Irwin, coral
MNP $65 **MIP** $250

Barbie's Speedboat, 1964, Irwin, Shown with Ken at the helm
MNP $100 **MIP** $1800

Barbie's Sport Plane, 1964, Irwin
MNP $1800 **MIP** $3500

Ken's Hot Rod, 1963, Irwin, blue
MNP $125 **MIP** $275

Skipper's Speedboat, 1965, Irwin
MNP $1450 **MIP** $1850

Skipper's Sports Car, 1965, Irwin
MNP $175 **MIP** $400

VINYL CASES

Barbie & Francie Case, 1967, SPP
MNP $20 **MIP** $40

Barbie & Skipper Case, 1964, Mattel, assorted colors - blue or gold most common
MNP $10 **MIP** $25

Barbie & Stacey Sleep & Keep Case, 1969, Sears Exclusive, Model No. 5023
MNP $50 **MIP** $75

Barbie Double Case, 1961, Ponytail, various illustrations/colors
MNP $5 **MIP** $10

Barbie Double Case, 1963, SPP, various illustrations/colors
MNP $5 **MIP** $15

Barbie Goes Travelin' Case, 1965, SPP
MNP $100 **MIP** $325

Barbie Single Case, 1961, Ponytail, various illustrations/colors
MNP $5 **MIP** $15

Barbie Single Case, 1963, SPP, various illustrations/colors
MNP $7 **MIP** $15

Barbie Train Case, 1961, SPP
MNP $45 **MIP** $70

Fashion Queen Case, 1963, SPP
MNP $50 **MIP** $100

Hatbox-Style Cases, 1961, Mattel, assorted styles
MNP $20 **MIP** $50

Ken Cases (U.S. versions), 1961, Ponytail
MNP $5 **MIP** $10

Midge Cases (U.S. versions), 1963
MNP $5 **MIP** $10

Miss Barbie Case, 1964, SPP
MNP $75 **MIP** $125

Skipper Cases (U.S. versions), 1964
MNP $7 **MIP** $15

Dolls

BARBIE & FRIENDS

All American Barbie, 1991, Mattel, Model No. 9423
MNP $4 **MIP** $10

All American Christie, 1991, Mattel, Model No. 9425
MNP $4 **MIP** $10

All American Ken, 1991, Mattel, Model No. 9424
MNP $4 **MIP** $10

All American Kira, 1991, Mattel, Model No. 9427
MNP $4 **MIP** $12

All American Teresa, 1991, Mattel, Model No. 9426
MNP $4 **MIP** $12

All Star Ken, 1981, Mattel, Model No. 3553
MNP $5 **MIP** $10

All Stars Barbie, 1989, Mattel, Model No. 9099
MNP $5 **MIP** $10

All Stars Christie, 1989, Mattel, Model No. 9352
MNP $5 **MIP** $10

All Stars Ken, 1989, Mattel, Model No. 9361
MNP $5 **MIP** $10

All Stars Midge, 1989, Mattel, Model No. 9360
MNP $5 **MIP** $10

All Stars Teresa, 1989, Mattel, Model No. 9353
MNP $5 **MIP** $10

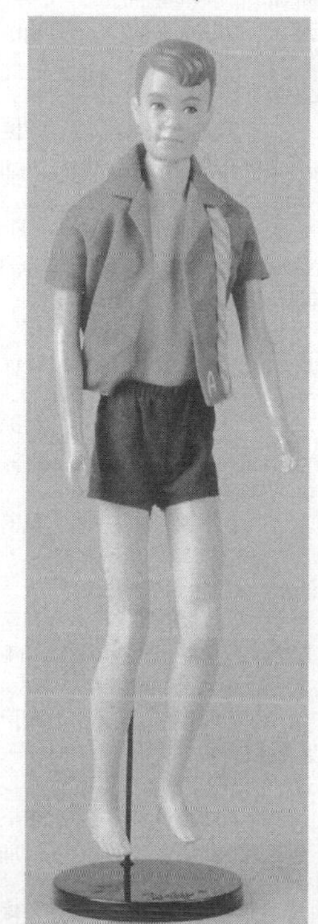

Allan, bendable leg, 1965, Mattel, Model No. 1010
MNP $95 **MIP** $175

Allan, straight leg, 1964, Mattel, Model No. 1000
MNP $20 **MIP** $65

American Beauties Mardi Gras Barbie, 1988, Mattel, Model No. 4930
MNP $10 **MIP** $25

American Beauty Queen, 1991, Mattel, Model No. 3137
MNP $5 **MIP** $10

American Beauty Queen, black, 1991, Mattel, Model No. 3245
MNP $5 **MIP** $10

Angel Face Barbie, 1982, Mattel, Model No. 5640
MNP $8 **MIP** $30

Animal Lovin' Barbie, black, 1989, Mattel, Model No. 4828
MNP $5 **MIP** $10

Animal Lovin' Barbie, white, 1989, Mattel, Model No. 1350
MNP $5 **MIP** $10

Animal Lovin' Ken, 1989, Mattel, Model No. 1351
MNP $5 **MIP** $10

Animal Lovin' Nikki, 1989, Mattel, Model No. 1352
MNP $7 **MIP** $10

Astronaut Barbie, black, 1985, Mattel, Model No. 1207
MNP $15 **MIP** $20

Astronaut Barbie, white, 1985, Mattel, Model No. 2449
MNP $15 **MIP** $25

Babysitter Courtney, 1991, Mattel, Model No. 9434
MNP $4 **MIP** $10

Babysitter Skipper, 1991, Mattel, Model No. 9433
MNP $4 **MIP** $10

Babysitter Skipper, black, 1991, Mattel, Model No. 1599
MNP $4 **MIP** $8

Baggie Casey, blond, 1975, Mattel, (sold in plastic bag), Model No. 9000
MNP $75 **MIP** $200

Ballerina Barbie on Tour, gold, 1st version, 1976, Mattel, Model No. 9613
MNP $45 **MIP** $65

Ballerina Barbie, 1st version, 1976, Mattel, Model No. 9093
MNP $20 **MIP** $40

Ballerina Cara, 1976, Mattel, Model No. 9528
MNP $25 **MIP** $50

Barbie & Her Fashion Fireworks, 1976, Mattel, Model No. 9805
MNP $20 **MIP** $60

Barbie & the Beat, 1990, Mattel, Model No. 3751
MNP $5 **MIP** $10

Barbie & the Beat Christie, 1990, Mattel, Model No. 2752
MNP $5 **MIP** $10

Barbie & the Beat Midge, 1990, Mattel, Model No. 2754
MNP $6 **MIP** $10

Barbie Hair Happenings (department store exclusive, red hair), 1971, Mattel, Model No. 1174
MNP $275 **MIP** $800

Barbie with Growin' Pretty Hair, 1971, Mattel, Model No. 1144
MNP $75 **MIP** $300

Bathtime Fun Barbie, 1991, Mattel, Model No. 9601
MNP $3 **MIP** $10

Bathtime Fun Barbie, black, 1991, Mattel, Model No. 9603
MNP $3 **MIP** $10

Beach Blast Barbie, 1989, Mattel, Model No. 3237
MNP $3 **MIP** $10

Beach Blast Christie, 1989, Mattel, Model No. 3253
MNP $4 **MIP** $10

Beach Blast Ken, 1989, Mattel, Model No. 3238
MNP $4 **MIP** $10

Beach Blast Miko, 1989, Mattel, Model No. 3244
MNP $4 **MIP** $10

Beach Blast Skipper, 1989, Mattel, Model No. 3242
MNP $4 **MIP** $10

Beach Blast Steven, 1989, Mattel, Model No. 3251
MNP $4 **MIP** $10

Beach Blast Teresa, 1989, Mattel, Model No. 3249
MNP $5 **MIP** $10

Beautiful Bride Barbie, 1978, Mattel, Model No. 9907
MNP $40 **MIP** $65

Beauty Secrets Barbie, 1st issue, 1980, Mattel, Model No. 1290
MNP $12 **MIP** $65

Beauty Secrets Christie, 1980, Mattel, Model No. 1295
MNP $12 **MIP** $65

Beauty, Barbie's Dog, 1979, Mattel, Model No. 1018
MNP $12 **MIP** $30

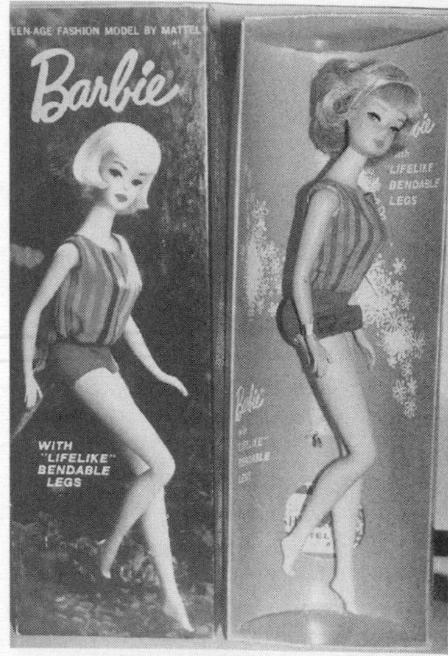

Bendable Leg "American Girl" Barbie, short hair, 1965, Mattel, Model No. 1070
MNP $250 **MIP** $1100

Bendable Leg "American Girl" Barbie, Color Magic Face, 1966, Mattel, Model No. 1070
MNP $700 **MIP** $1500

Bendable Leg "American Girl" Barbie, long hair, 1965, Mattel, Model No. 1070
MNP $700 **MIP** $1500

Bendable Leg "American Girl" Barbie, side-part long hair, 1966, Mattel, Model No. 1070
MNP $1700 **MIP** $2500

Bendable Leg "American Girl" Barbie, Swirl Ponytail or Bubblecut hairstyle, 1965, Mattel, Model No. 1070
MNP $1000 **MIP** $2800

Benetton Barbie, 1991, Mattel, Model No. 9404
MNP $5 **MIP** $15

Benetton Christie, 1991, Mattel, Model No. 9407
MNP $5 **MIP** $15

Benetton Marina, 1991, Mattel, Model No. 9409
MNP $5 **MIP** $15

Black Barbie, 1980, Mattel, Model No. 1293
MNP $20 **MIP** $45

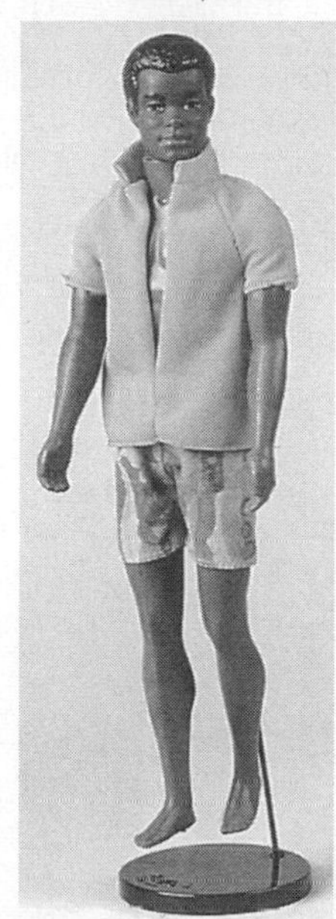

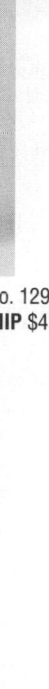

Brad, bendable leg, 1970, Mattel, Model No. 1142
MNP $65 **MIP** $175

Brad, talking, 1970, Mattel, Model No. 1114
MNP $65 **MIP** $200

Bubblecut Barbie Sidepart, all hair colors, 1961, Mattel, Model No. 850
MNP $425 **MIP** $900

Bubblecut Barbie, blond, brunette, titian, 1962, Mattel, Model No. 850
MNP $50 **MIP** $150

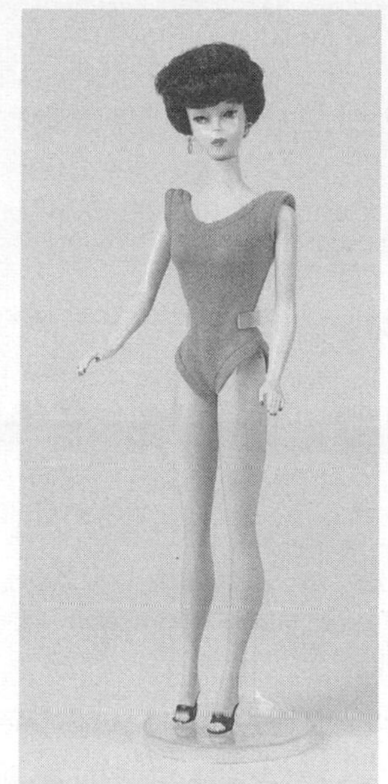

Bubblecut Barbie, brownette, 1961, Mattel, Model No. 850
MNP $500 **MIP** $850

Bubblecut Barbie, white ginger, 1962, Mattel, Model No. 850
MNP $250 **MIP** $600

Busy Barbie, 1971, Mattel, Model No. 3311
MNP $75 **MIP** $175

Busy Francie, 1971, Mattel, Model No. 3313
MNP $125 **MIP** $300

Busy Ken, 1971, Mattel, Model No. 3314
MNP $60 **MIP** $145

Busy Steffie, 1971, Mattel, Model No. 3312
MNP $85 **MIP** $200

Calgary Olympic Skating Barbie, 1987, Mattel, Model No. 4547
MNP $25 **MIP** $45

California Dream Barbie, 1988, Mattel, Model No. 4439
MNP $5 **MIP** $10

California Dream Christie, 1988, Mattel, Model No. 4443
MNP $6 **MIP** $10

California Dream Ken, 1988, Mattel, Model No. 4441
MNP $8 **MIP** $10

California Dream Midge, 1988, Mattel, Model No. 4442
MNP $3 **MIP** $10

California Dream Skipper, 1988, Mattel, Model No. 4440
MNP $13 **MIP** $10

California Dream Teresa, 1988, Mattel, Model No. 4403
MNP $15 **MIP** $10

Carla, European exclusive, 1976, Mattel, Model No. 7377
MNP $65 **MIP** $120

Casey, Twist and Turn, 1967, Mattel, Model No. 1180
MNP $60 **MIP** $250

Chris, titian, blond, brunette (Tutti's friend), 1967, Mattel, Model No. 3570
MNP $50 **MIP** $200

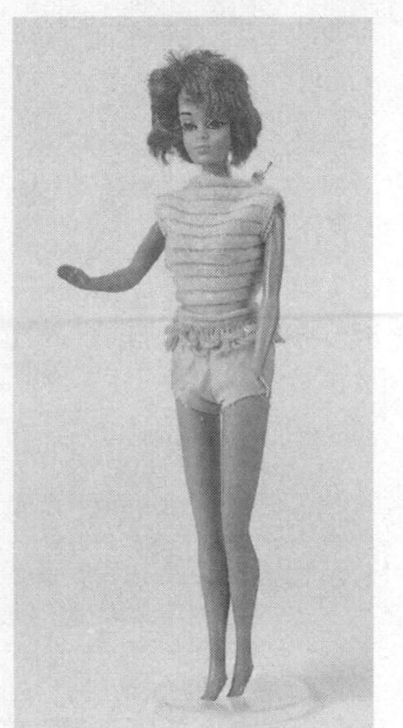

Christie, talking, 1970, Mattel, Model No. 1126
MNP $70 **MIP** $300

Christie, Twist N Turn, 1970, Mattel, Model No. 1119
MNP $70 **MIP** $300

Coach Ken & Tommy, white or black, 2000, Mattel
MNP $7 **MIP** $10

Color Magic Barbie, Golden Blonde, 1966, Mattel, Model No. 1150
MNP $350 **MIP** $1500

Color Magic Barbie, Midnight Black, 1966, Mattel, Model No. 1150
MNP $1100 **MIP** $2500

Cool City Blues: Barbie, Ken, Skipper, 1989, Mattel, Model No. 4893
MNP $5 **MIP** $15

Cool Shavin' Ken, 1996, Mattel, Model No. 15469
MNP $5 **MIP** $10

Cool Times Barbie, 1989, Mattel, Model No. 3022
MNP $5 **MIP** $10

Cool Times Christie, 1989, Mattel, Model No. 3217
MNP $5 **MIP** $10

Cool Times Ken, 1989, Mattel, Model No. 3219
MNP $5 **MIP** $10

Cool Times Midge, 1989, Mattel, Model No. 3216
MNP $7 **MIP** $10

Cool Times Teresa, 1989, Mattel, Model No. 3218
MNP $5 **MIP** $10

Cool Tops Courtney, 1989, Mattel, Model No. 7079
MNP $7 **MIP** $10

Cool Tops Kevin, 1989, Mattel, Model No. 9351
MNP $5 **MIP** $10

Cool Tops Skipper, black, 1989, Mattel, Model No. 5441
MNP $5 **MIP** $10

Cool Tops Skipper, white, 1989, Mattel, Model No. 4989
MNP $7 **MIP** $10

Corduroy Cool Barbie, 2000, Mattel, Model No. 24658
MNP $5 **MIP** $10

Costume Ball Barbie, black, 1991, Mattel, Model No. 7134
MNP $6 **MIP** $10

Costume Ball Barbie, white, 1991, Mattel, Model No. 7123
MNP $6 **MIP** $10

Costume Ball Ken, black, 1991, Mattel, Model No. 7160
MNP $6 **MIP** $10

Costume Ball Ken, white, 1991, Mattel, Model No. 7154
MNP $6 **MIP** $10

Crystal Barbie, black, 1984, Mattel, Model No. 4859
MNP $10 **MIP** $25

Crystal Barbie, white, 1984, Mattel, Model No. 4598
MNP $10 **MIP** $25

Crystal Ken, black, 1983, Mattel, Model No. 9036
MNP $15 **MIP** $25

Crystal Ken, white, 1983, Mattel, Model No. 4898
MNP $8 **MIP** $25

Dance Club Barbie, 1989, Mattel, Model No. 3509
MNP $5 **MIP** $15

Dance Club Devon, 1989, Mattel, Model No. 3513
MNP $5 **MIP** $15

Dance Club Kayla, 1989, Mattel, Model No. 3512
MNP $5 **MIP** $15

Dance Club Ken, 1989, Mattel, Model No. 3511
MNP $5 **MIP** $15

Dance Magic Barbie, 1990, Mattel, Model No. 4836
MNP $7 **MIP** $15

Dance Magic Barbie, black, 1990, Mattel, Model No. 7080
MNP $7 **MIP** $15

Dance Magic Ken, 1990, Mattel, Model No. 7081
MNP $6 **MIP** $10

Dance Magic Ken, black, 1990, Mattel, Model No. 7082
MNP $6 **MIP** $10

Day-to-Night Barbie, black, 1985, Mattel, Model No. 7945
MNP $10 **MIP** $40

Day-to-Night Barbie, Hispanic, 1985, Mattel, Model No. 7944
MNP $17 **MIP** $45

Day-to-Night Barbie, white, 1985, Mattel, Model No. 7929
MNP $10 **MIP** $45

Day-to-Night Ken, black, 1984, Mattel, Model No. 9018
MNP $8 **MIP** $35

Day-to-Night Ken, white, 1984, Mattel, Model No. 9019
MNP $8 **MIP** $35

Dentist Barbie, 1997, Mattel, Model No. 17255
MNP $15 **MIP** $15

Doctor Barbie, 1988, Mattel, Model No. 3850
MNP $8 **MIP** $15

Doctor Ken, 1988, Mattel, Model No. 4118
MNP $5 **MIP** $15

Dolls of the World Princess of Ancient Greece, 2004, Mattel
MNP $10 **MIP** $20

Dolls of the World Princess of Ancient Mexico, 2004, Mattel
MNP $10 **MIP** $20

Dolls of the World Princess of Cambodia, 2004, Mattel
MNP $10 **MIP** $20

(Mattel Photo)

Dolls of the World Princess of China, 2002, Mattel, Model No. 53368
MNP $10 **MIP** $25

Dolls of the World Princess of England (Tudor Rose), 2004, Mattel
MNP $10 **MIP** $20

Dolls of the World Princess of Imperial Russia, 2005, Mattel
MNP $10 **MIP** $20

Dolls of the World Princess of India, 2000, Mattel, Model No. 28374
MNP $8 **MIP** $15

Dolls of the World Princess of Ireland, 2002, Mattel, Model No. 53367
MNP $10 **MIP** $15

(Mattel Photo)

Dolls of the World Princess of South Africa, 2003, Mattel, Model No. 56218
MNP $10 **MIP** $20

Dolls of the World Princess of the Danish Court, 2003, Mattel, Model No. 56216
MNP $10 **MIP** $15

Dolls of the World Princess of the French Court, 2000, Mattel, Model No. 28372
MNP $8 **MIP** $15

Dolls of the World Princess of the Incas, 2000, Mattel, Model No. 28373
MNP $8 **MIP** $15

Dolls of the World Princess of the Korean Court, 2005, Mattel
MNP $10 **MIP** $20

Dolls of the World Princess of the Navajo, 2004, Mattel
MNP $10 **MIP** $50

(Mattel Photo)

Dolls of the World Princess of the Nile, 2002, Mattel, Model No. 53369
MNP $10 **MIP** $15

Dolls of the World Princess of the Portuguese Empire, 2003, Mattel, Model No. 56217
MNP $10 **MIP** $15

Dolls of the World Princess of the Renaissance, 2005, Mattel
MNP $10 **MIP** $20

Dolls of the World/International Arctic, 1997, Mattel, Model No. 16495
MNP $20 **MIP** $25

Dolls of the World/International Australian, two box variations, 1993, Mattel, Model No. 3626
MNP $10 **MIP** $20

Dolls of the World/International Austrian, 1999, Mattel, Model No. 21553
MNP $15 **MIP** $20

Dolls of the World/International Brazillian, 1990, Mattel, Model No. 9094
MNP $15 **MIP** $25

Dolls of the World/International Canadian, 1988, Mattel, Model No. 4928
MNP $15 **MIP** $35

Dolls of the World/International Chilean, 1998, Mattel, Model No. 18559
MNP $10 **MIP** $15

Dolls of the World/International Chinese, 1994, Mattel, Model No. 11180
MNP $10 **MIP** $15

Dolls of the World/International Czechoslovakian, 1991, Mattel, Model No. 7330
MNP $20 **MIP** $30

Dolls of the World/International Dutch, 1994, Mattel, Model No. 11104
MNP $10 **MIP** $20

Dolls of the World/International English, 1992, Mattel, Model No. 4973
MNP $12 **MIP** $25

Dolls of the World/International Eskimo, 1982, Mattel, Model No. 3898
MNP $30 **MIP** $40

Dolls of the World/International Eskimo, 1991, Mattel, Model No. 9844
MNP $8 **MIP** $20

Dolls of the World/International French, 1997, Mattel, Model No. 16499
MNP $10 **MIP** $15

Dolls of the World/International German, 1987, Mattel, Model No. 3188
MNP $25 **MIP** $25

Dolls of the World/International German, 1995, Mattel, Model No. 12598
MNP $10 **MIP** $20

Dolls of the World/International Ghanaian, 1996, Mattel, Model No. 15303
MNP $15 **MIP** $20

Dolls of the World/International Gift Set (Chinese, Dutch, Kenyan), 1994, Mattel, Model No. 12043
MNP $30 **MIP** $70

Dolls of the World/International Gift Set (Irish, German, Polynesian), 1995, Mattel, Model No. 13939
MNP $30 **MIP** $65

Dolls of the World/International Gift Set (Japanese, Indian, Norwegian), 1996, Mattel, Model No. 15283
MNP $30 **MIP** $60

Dolls of the World/International Greek, 1986, Mattel, Model No. 2997
MNP $30 **MIP** $45

Dolls of the World/International Iceland, 1987, Mattel, Model No. 3189
MNP $30 **MIP** $45

Dolls of the World/International Indian, 1982, Mattel, Model No. 3897
MNP $30 **MIP** $45

Dolls of the World/International Indian, 1995, Mattel, Model No. 14451
MNP $12 **MIP** $20

Dolls of the World/International Irish, 1984, Mattel, Model No. 7517
MNP $20 **MIP** $40

Dolls of the World/International Irish, 1995, Mattel, Model No. 12998
MNP $10 **MIP** $20

Dolls of the World/International Italian, 1980, Mattel, Model No. 1601
MNP $65 **MIP** $95

Dolls of the World/International Italian, 1993, Mattel, Model No. 2256
MNP $10 **MIP** $25

Dolls of the World/International Jamaican, silver earrings, 1992, Mattel, Model No. 4647
MNP $12 **MIP** $20

Dolls of the World/International Japanese, 1984, Mattel, Model No. 9481
MNP $25 **MIP** $35

Dolls of the World/International Japanese, 1996, Mattel, Model No. 14163
MNP $10 **MIP** $20

Dolls of the World/International Kenyan, 1994, Mattel, Model No. 11181
MNP $10 **MIP** $20

Dolls of the World/International Korean, 1988, Mattel, Model No. 4929
MNP $15 **MIP** $30

Dolls of the World/International Malaysian, 1991, Mattel, Model No. 7329
MNP $10 **MIP** $25

Dolls of the World/International Mexican, 1989, Mattel, Model No. 1917
MNP $15 **MIP** $20

Dolls of the World/International Mexican, 1995, Mattel, Model No. 14449
MNP $10 **MIP** $15

Dolls of the World/International Moroccan, 1999, Mattel, Model No. 21507
MNP $15 **MIP** $20

Dolls of the World/International Native American #1, two box versions, 1993, Mattel, Model No. 1753
MNP $12 **MIP** $30

Dolls of the World/International Native American #2, 1994, Mattel, Model No. 11609
MNP $10 **MIP** $20

Dolls of the World/International Native American #3, 1995, Mattel, Model No. 12699
MNP $10 **MIP** $15

Dolls of the World/International Nigerian, 1990, Mattel, Model No. 7376
MNP $15 **MIP** $20

Dolls of the World/International Norwegian, pink flowers, limited to 3,000, 1996, Mattel, Model No. 14450
MNP $12 **MIP** $50

Dolls of the World/International NW Coast Native American Barbie, 2000, Mattel, Model No. 24671
MNP $12 **MIP** $15

Dolls of the World/International Oriental, 1981, Mattel, Model No. 3262
MNP $35 **MIP** $50

Dolls of the World/International Parisian, 1980, Mattel, Model No. 1600
MNP $50 **MIP** $45

Dolls of the World/International Parisian, 1991, Mattel, Model No. 9843
MNP $8 **MIP** $25

Dolls of the World/International Peruvian, 1986, Mattel, Model No. 2995
MNP $15 **MIP** $30

Dolls of the World/International Peruvian, 1999, Mattel, Model No. 21506
MNP $10 **MIP** $20

Dolls of the World/International Polish, 1998, Mattel, Model No. 18560
MNP $15 **MIP** $20

Dolls of the World/International Polynesian, 1995, Mattel, Model No. 12700
MNP $10 **MIP** $20

Dolls of the World/International Puerto Rican, 1997, Mattel, Model No. 16754
MNP $15 **MIP** $20

Dolls of the World/International Royal, 1980, Mattel, Model No. 1602
MNP $50 **MIP** $65

Dolls of the World/International Russian, 1989, Mattel, Model No. 1916
MNP $10 **MIP** $20

Dolls of the World/International Russian, 1997, Mattel, Model No. 16500
MNP $10 **MIP** $30

Dolls of the World/International Scottish, 1981, Mattel, Model No. 3263
MNP $50 **MIP** $70

Dolls of the World/International Scottish, 1991, Mattel, Model No. 9845
MNP $8 **MIP** $30

Dolls of the World/International Spanish, 1983, Mattel, Model No. 4031
MNP $40 **MIP** $45

Dolls of the World/International Spanish, 1992, Mattel, Model No. 4963
MNP $12 **MIP** $25

Dolls of the World/International Spanish, 2000, Mattel, Model No. 24670
MNP $12 **MIP** $20

Dolls of the World/International Swedish, 1983, Mattel, Model No. 4032
MNP $25 **MIP** $40

Dolls of the World/International Swedish, 2000, Mattel, Model No. 24672
MNP $12 **MIP** $20

Dolls of the World/International Swiss, 1984, Mattel, Model No. 7451
MNP $30 **MIP** $45

Dolls of the World/International Thai, 1998, Mattel, Model No. 18561
MNP $10 **MIP** $25

Dramatic New Living Barbie, 1970, Mattel, Model No. 1116
MNP $65 **MIP** $175

Dramatic New Living Skipper, 1970, Mattel, Model No. 1117
MNP $40 **MIP** $125

Dream Bride, 1992, Mattel, Model No. 1623
MNP $10 **MIP** $25

Dream Date Barbie, 1983, Mattel, Model No. 5868
MNP $10 **MIP** $20

Dream Date Ken, 1983, Mattel, Model No. 4077
MNP $10 **MIP** $20

Dream Glow Barbie, black, 1986, Mattel, Model No. 2242
MNP $12 **MIP** $30

Dream Glow Barbie, Hispanic, 1986, Mattel, Model No. 1647
MNP $25 **MIP** $50

Dream Glow Barbie, white, 1986, Mattel, Model No. 2248
MNP $12 **MIP** $40

Dream Glow Ken, black, 1986, Mattel, Model No. 2421
MNP $13 **MIP** $20

Dream Glow Ken, white, 1986, Mattel, Model No. 2250
MNP $13 **MIP** $15

Dream Time Barbie, pink, 1985, Mattel, Model No. 9180
MNP $10 **MIP** $20

Earring Magic Barbie, blond, 1993, Mattel, Model No. 7014
MNP $10 **MIP** $15

Earring Magic Ken, 1993, Mattel, Model No. 2290
MNP $10 **MIP** $20

Earring Magic Midge, 1993, Mattel
MNP $10 **MIP** $15

Fabulous Fur Barbie, 1983, Mattel, Model No. 7093
MNP $20 **MIP** $50

Fashion Jeans Barbie, 1981, Mattel, Model No. 5313
MNP $15 **MIP** $50

Fashion Jeans Ken, 1982, Mattel, Model No. 5316
MNP $12 **MIP** $25

Fashion Photo Barbie, two versions, 1978, Mattel, Model No. 2210
MNP $20 **MIP** $60

Fashion Photo Christie, 1978, Mattel, Model No. 2324
MNP $20 **MIP** $60

Fashion Photo P.J., 1978, Mattel, Model No. 2323
MNP $35 **MIP** $70

Fashion Play Barbie, 1983, Mattel, Model No. 7193
MNP $5 **MIP** $15

Fashion Play Barbie, 1987, Mattel, Model No. 4835
MNP $5 **MIP** $15

Fashion Play Barbie, 1990, Mattel, Model No. 9429
MNP $2 **MIP** $15

Fashion Play Barbie, 1991, Mattel, Model No. 9629
MNP $2 **MIP** $15

Fashion Play Barbie, black, 1991, Mattel, Model No. 5953
MNP $2 **MIP** $15

Fashion Play Barbie, Hispanic, 1990, Mattel, Model No. 5954
MNP $2 **MIP** $15

Fashion Queen Barbie, 1963, Mattel, Model No. 870
MNP $65 **MIP** $275

Feelin' Fun Barbie, two versions, white, 1st issue, 1988, Mattel, Model No. 1189
MNP $5 **MIP** $10

Flight Time Barbie, black, 1990, Mattel, Model No. 9916
MNP $5 **MIP** $10

Flight Time Barbie, white, 1990, Mattel, Model No. 9584
MNP $5 **MIP** $15

Flight Time Ken, 1990, Mattel, Model No. 9600
MNP $5 **MIP** $10

Fluff, 1971, Mattel, Model No. 1143
MNP $100 **MIP** $225

Francie with Growin' Pretty Hair, 1971, Mattel, Model No. 1129
MNP $65 **MIP** $175

Francie, bendable leg, blond, brunette, 1966, Mattel, Model No. 1130
MNP $85 **MIP** $350

Francie, Hair Happenins, 1970, Mattel, Model No. 1122
MNP $95 **MIP** $350

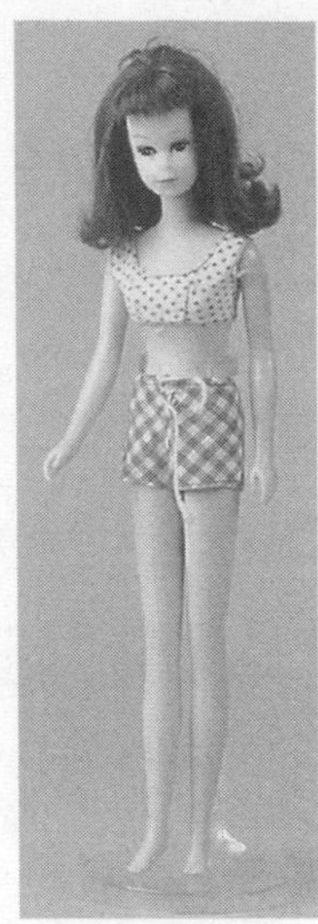

Francie, straight leg, brunette, blond, 1966, Mattel, Model No. 1140
MNP $85 **MIP** $350

Francie, Twist N Turn, "Black Francie" 1st issue, red hair, 1967, Mattel, Model No. 1100
MNP $650 **MIP** $1150

Francie, Twist N Turn, "Black Francie" 2nd issue, black hair, Mattel, Model No. 1100
MNP $650 **MIP** $1500

Francie, Twist N Turn, blond or brunette, "No Bangs", 1967, Mattel, Model No. 1170
MNP $650 **MIP** $1300

Francie, Twist N Turn, blond or brunette, long hair with bangs, 1969, Mattel, Model No. 1170
MNP $75 **MIP** $375

Francie, Twist N Turn, blond or brunette, short hair, 1969, Mattel, Model No. 1170
MNP $75 **MIP** $425

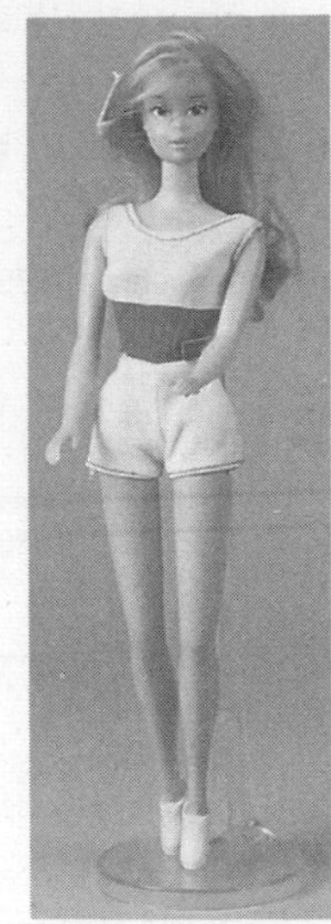

Free Moving Barbie, 1974, Mattel, Model No. 7270
MNP $45 **MIP** $100

Free Moving Cara, 1974, Mattel, Model No. 7283
MNP $50 **MIP** $125

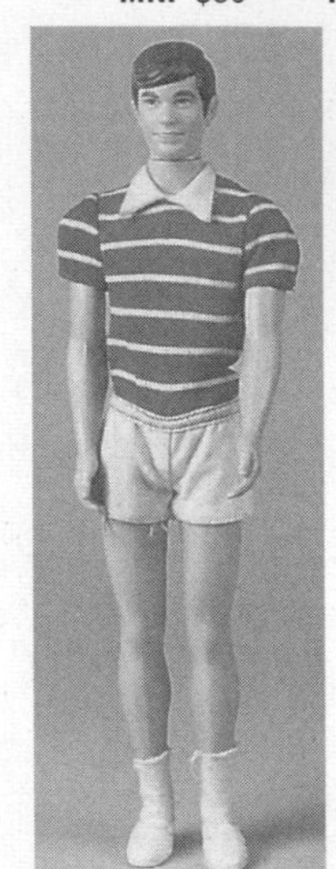

Free Moving Ken, 1974, Mattel, Model No. 7280
MNP $40 **MIP** $75

Free Moving P.J., 1974, Mattel, Model No. 7281
MNP $45 **MIP** $85

Funtime Barbie, black, 1987, Mattel, Model No. 1739
MNP $5 **MIP** $10

Funtime Barbie, white, 1987, Mattel, Model No. 1738
MNP $5 **MIP** $10

Funtime Ken, 1987, Mattel, Model No. 7194
MNP $7 **MIP** $10

Garden Party Barbie, 1989, Mattel, Model No. 1953
MNP $8 **MIP** $15

Gift Giving Barbie, 1986, Mattel, Model No. 1922
MNP $5 **MIP** $15

Gift Giving Barbie, 1989, Mattel, Model No. 1205
MNP $5 **MIP** $15

Gold Medal Olympic Barbie Skater, 1975, Mattel, Model No. 7262
MNP $20 **MIP** $75

Gold Medal Olympic Barbie Skier, 1975, Mattel, Model No. 7264
MNP $20 **MIP** $75

Gold Medal Olympic P.J. Gymnast, 1975, Mattel, Model No. 7263
MNP $20 **MIP** $85

Gold Medal Olympic Skier Ken, 1975, Mattel, Model No. 7261
MNP $20 **MIP** $65

Gold Medal Olympic Skipper, 1975, Mattel, Model No. 7274
MNP $20 **MIP** $65

Golden Dreams Barbie, two versions, 1981, Mattel, Model No. 1974
MNP $15 **MIP** $50

Golden Dreams Christie, 1981, Mattel, Model No. 3249
MNP $15 **MIP** $50

Great Shapes Barbie, black, 1984, Mattel, Model No. 7834
MNP $5 **MIP** $10

Great Shapes Barbie, w/Walkman, 1984, Mattel, Model No. 7025
MNP $12 **MIP** $15

Great Shapes Barbie, white, 1984, Mattel, Model No. 7025
MNP $5 **MIP** $10

Great Shapes Ken, 1984, Mattel, Model No. 7310
MNP $5 **MIP** $10

Great Shapes Skipper, 1984, Mattel, Model No. 7417
MNP $5 **MIP** $10

Groom Todd, 1982, Mattel, Model No. 4253
MNP $15 **MIP** $45

Growin' Pretty Hair Barbie, 1971, Mattel, Model No. 1144
MNP $150 **MIP** $350

Growing Up Ginger, 1977, Mattel, Model No. 9222
MNP $30 **MIP** $125

Growing Up Skipper, 1977, Mattel, Model No. 7259
MNP $30 **MIP** $100

Happy Birthday Barbie, 1981, Mattel, Model No. 1922
MNP $8 MIP $15

Happy Birthday Barbie, 1984, Mattel, Model No. 1922
MNP $8 MIP $20

Happy Birthday Barbie, 1991, Mattel, Model No. 9561
MNP $8 MIP $15

Happy Birthday Barbie, black, 1991, Mattel, Model No. 9561
MNP $8 MIP $10

Hawaiian Barbie, 1975, Mattel, Model No. 7470
MNP $25 MIP $60

Hawaiian Barbie, 1977, Mattel, Model No. 7470
MNP $30 MIP $70

Hawaiian Fun Barbie, 1991, Mattel, Model No. 5040
MNP $3 MIP $10

Hawaiian Fun Christie, 1991, Mattel, Model No. 5044
MNP $3 MIP $10

Hawaiian Fun Jazzie, 1991, Mattel, Model No. 9294
MNP $3 MIP $10

Hawaiian Fun Ken, 1991, Mattel, Model No. 5041
MNP $3 MIP $10

Hawaiian Fun Kira, 1991, Mattel, Model No. 5043
MNP $3 MIP $10

Hawaiian Fun Skipper, 1991, Mattel, Model No. 5042
MNP $3 MIP $10

Hawaiian Fun Steven, 1991, Mattel, Model No. 5045
MNP $3 MIP $10

Hawaiian Ken, 1979, Mattel, Model No. 2960
MNP $13 MIP $50

Hawaiian Ken, 1984, Mattel, Model No. 7495
MNP $7 MIP $30

High School Chelsie, 1989, Mattel, Model No. 3698
MNP $5 MIP $20

High School Dude, Jazzie's boyfriend, 1989, Mattel, Model No. 3600
MNP $5 MIP $20

High School Jazzie, 1989, Mattel, Model No. 3635
MNP $5 MIP $20

High School Stacie, 1989, Mattel, Model No. 3636
MNP $5 MIP $20

Hispanic Barbie, 1980, Mattel, Model No. 1292
MNP $15 MIP $65

Hollywood Nails Barbie, white or black, 1999, Mattel
MNP $7 MIP $10

Hollywood Nails Christie, 1999, Mattel
MNP $7 MIP $10

Hollywood Nails Teresa, white or black, 1999, Mattel
MNP $7 MIP $10

Home Pretty Barbie, 1990, Mattel, Model No. 2249
MNP $8 MIP $15

Homecoming Queen Skipper, black, 1988, Mattel, Model No. 2390
MNP $8 MIP $10

Homecoming Queen Skipper, white, 1988, Mattel, Model No. 1952
MNP $12 MIP $10

Horse Lovin' Barbie, 1983, Mattel, Model No. 1757
MNP $10 MIP $20

Horse Lovin' Ken, 1983, Mattel, Model No. 3600
MNP $8 MIP $15

Horse Lovin' Skipper, 1983, Mattel, Model No. 5029
MNP $8 MIP $15

Hot Stuff Skipper, 1984, Mattel, Model No. 7927
MNP $5 MIP $10

Ice Capades Barbie, 50th Anniversary, black, 1990, Mattel, Model No. 7348
MNP $5 MIP $15

Ice Capades Barbie, 50th Anniversary, white, 1990, Mattel, Model No. 7365
MNP $5 MIP $20

Ice Capades Ken, 1990, Mattel, Model No. 7375
MNP $5 MIP $15

Inline Skating Barbie, 1996, Mattel, Model No. 15473
MNP $5 MIP $15

Inline Skating Ken, 1996, Mattel, Model No. 15474
MNP $5 MIP $15

Inline Skating Midge, 1996, Mattel, Model No. 15475
MNP $5 MIP $15

Island Fun Barbie, 1988, Mattel, Model No. 4061
MNP $3 MIP $10

Island Fun Christie, 1988, Mattel, Model No. 4092
MNP $3 MIP $10

Island Fun Ken, 1988, Mattel, Model No. 4060
MNP $3 MIP $10

Island Fun Skipper, 1988, Mattel, Model No. 4064
MNP $3 MIP $10

Island Fun Steven, 1988, Mattel, Model No. 4093
MNP $3 MIP $10

Island Fun Teresa, 1988, Mattel, Model No. 4117
MNP $3 MIP $10

Jazzie Workout, 1989, Mattel, Model No. 3633
MNP $5 MIP $10

Jewel Girl Barbie, Christie, Teresa (new body style, belly button), 2000, Mattel
MNP $5 MIP $15

Jewel Secrets Barbie, black, two box versions, 1987, Mattel, Model No. 1756
MNP $6 MIP $25

Jewel Secrets Barbie, white, two box versions, 1987, Mattel, Model No. 1737
MNP $6 MIP $25

Jewel Secrets Ken, black, 1987, Mattel, Model No. 3232
MNP $6 MIP $15

Jewel Secrets Ken, rooted hair, 1987, Mattel, Model No. 1719
MNP $6 MIP $15

Jewel Secrets Skipper, 1987, Mattel, Model No. 3133
MNP $6 MIP $15

Jewel Secrets Whitney, 1987, Mattel, Model No. 3179
MNP $8 MIP $20

Julia, talking, first issue with straight hair, 1969, Mattel, Model No. 1128
MNP $75 MIP $250

Julia, talking, second issue, Afro hair, 1969, Mattel, Model No. 1128
MNP $75 MIP $250

Julia, Twist N Turn, one-piece nurse dress, 2nd issue, 1969, Mattel, Model No. 1127
MNP $100 MIP $250

Julia, Twist N Turn, two-piece nurse outfit, 1st issue, 1969, Mattel, Model No. 1127
MNP $125 MIP $300

Ken, bendable leg, brunette, blond, 1965, Mattel, Model No. 750
MNP $125 MIP $275

Ken, flocked hair, brunette, blond, 1961, Mattel, Model No. 750
MNP $45 MIP $85

Ken, painted hair, brunette, blond, 1962, Mattel, Model No. 750
MNP $40 MIP $85

BARBIE

Ken, talking, 1970, Mattel, Model No. 1124
MNP $50 **MIP** $125

Kevin, 1991, Mattel, Model No. 9325
MNP $5 **MIP** $10

Kissing Barbie, 1979, Mattel, Model No. 2597
MNP $8 **MIP** $30

Kissing Christie, 1979, Mattel, Model No. 2955
MNP $10 **MIP** $30

Lights & Lace Barbie, 1991, Mattel, Model No. 9725
MNP $4 **MIP** $10

Lights & Lace Christie, 1991, Mattel, Model No. 9728
MNP $4 **MIP** $10

Lights & Lace Teresa, 1991, Mattel, Model No. 9727
MNP $4 **MIP** $10

Live Action Barbie, 1970, Mattel, Model No. 1155
MNP $60 **MIP** $150

Live Action Barbie Onstage, 1970, Mattel, Model No. 1152
MNP $75 **MIP** $250

Live Action Christie, 1970, Mattel, Model No. 1175
MNP $60 **MIP** $350

Live Action Ken, 1970, Mattel, Model No. 1159
MNP $55 **MIP** $150

Live Action Ken on Stage, 1970, Mattel, Model No. 1172
MNP $40 **MIP** $150

Live Action P.J., 1970, Mattel, Model No. 1156
MNP $65 **MIP** $250

Live Action P.J. on Stage, 1970, Mattel, Model No. 1153
MNP $75 **MIP** $175

Lovin' You Barbie, 1983, Mattel, Model No. 7072
MNP $20 **MIP** $40

Magic Curl Barbie, black, 1982, Mattel, Model No. 3989
MNP $8 **MIP** $15

Magic Curl Barbie, white, 1982, Mattel, Model No. 3856
MNP $10 **MIP** $20

Magic Moves Barbie, black, 1985, Mattel, Model No. 3137
MNP $15 **MIP** $20

Magic Moves Barbie, white, 1985, Mattel, Model No. 2126
MNP $15 **MIP** $20

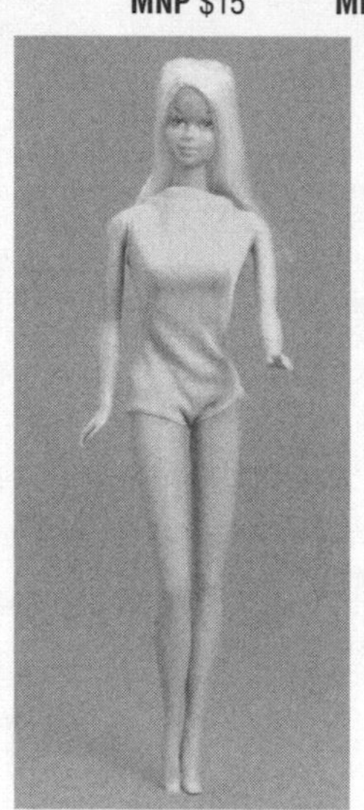

Malibu Barbie, 1971, Mattel, Model No. 1067
MNP $15 **MIP** $50

Malibu Barbie (Sunset), 1975, Mattel, Model No. 1067
MNP $15 **MIP** $30

Malibu Christie, 1975, Mattel, Model No. 7745
MNP $10 **MIP** $50

Malibu Francie, 1971, Mattel, Model No. 1068
MNP $15 **MIP** $50

Malibu Ken, 1976, Mattel, Model No. 1088
MNP $8 **MIP** $25

Malibu P.J., 1975, Mattel, Model No. 1087
MNP $5 **MIP** $50

Malibu Skipper, 1977, Mattel, Model No. 1069
MNP $8 **MIP** $40

Midge, bendable leg, blond, brunette, titian, 1965, Mattel, Model No. 1080
MNP $175 **MIP** $425

Midge, straight leg, blond, brunette, titian, 1963, Mattel, Model No. 860
MNP $35 **MIP** $115

Miss Barbie (sleep eyes), 1964, Mattel, Model No. 1060
MNP $300 **MIP** $1200

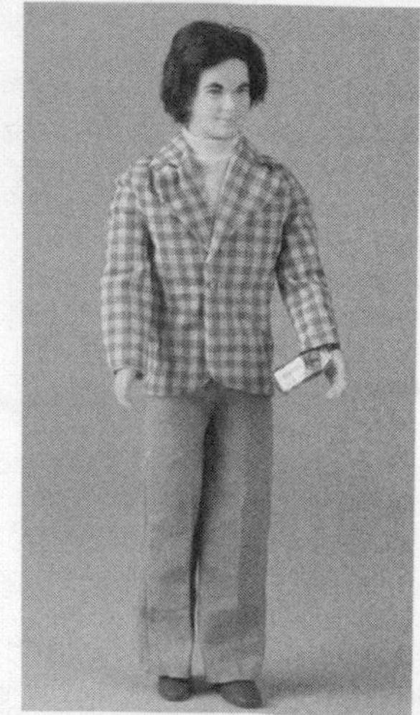

Mod Hair Ken, 1972, Mattel, Model No. 4224
MNP $45 **MIP** $65

Music Lovin' Barbie, 1985, Mattel, Model No. 9988
MNP $10 **MIP** $20

Music Lovin' Ken, 1985, Mattel, Model No. 2388
MNP $10 **MIP** $20

Music Lovin' Skipper, 1985, Mattel, Model No. 2854
MNP $10 **MIP** $20

My First Barbie, 1991, Mattel, Model No. 9942
MNP $5 **MIP** $20

My First Barbie, aqua and yellow dress, 1981, Mattel, Model No. 1875
MNP $5 **MIP** $15

My First Barbie, black, 1990, Mattel, Model No. 9943
MNP $5 **MIP** $15

My First Barbie, Hispanic, 1991, Mattel, Model No. 9944
MNP $3 **MIP** $15

My First Barbie, pink checkered dress, 1983, Mattel, Model No. 1875
MNP $5 **MIP** $15

My First Barbie, pink tutu, black, 1987, Mattel, Model No. 1801
MNP $5 **MIP** $15

My First Barbie, pink tutu, white, 1987, Mattel, Model No. 1788
MNP $5 **MIP** $15

My First Barbie, white, 1990, Mattel, Model No. 9942
MNP $4 **MIP** $15

My First Barbie, white dress, black, 1984, Mattel, Model No. 9858
MNP $7 **MIP** $15

My First Barbie, white dress, white, 1984, Mattel, Model No. 1875
MNP $5 **MIP** $15

My First Barbie, white tutu, black, 1988, Mattel, Model No. 1281
MNP $6 **MIP** $10

My First Barbie, white tutu, Hispanic, 1988, Mattel, Model No. 1282
MNP $6 **MIP** $10

My First Barbie, white tutu, white, 1988, Mattel, Model No. 1280
MNP $5 **MIP** $10

My First Ken, 1st issue, 1989, Mattel, Model No. 1389
MNP $4 **MIP** $15

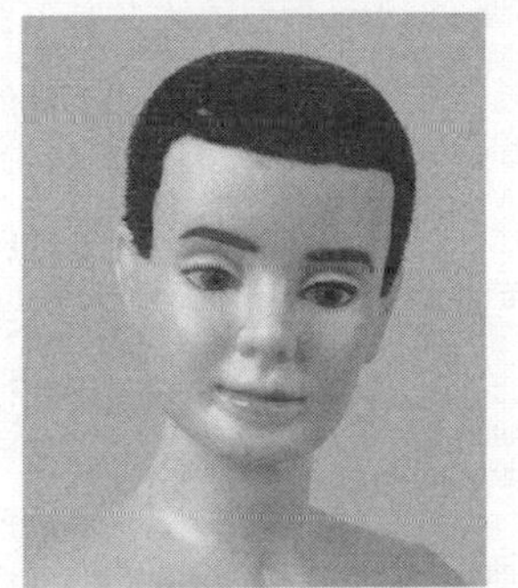

My First Ken, Prince, 1990, Mattel, Model No. 9940
MNP $4 **MIP** $15

New Look Ken, 1976, Mattel, Model No. 9342
MNP $23 **MIP** $65

Newport Barbie, two versions, 1974, Mattel, Model No. 7807
MNP $25 **MIP** $125

Nurse Whitney, 1987, Mattel, Model No. 4405
MNP $15 **MIP** $30

Ocean Friends Barbie, 1996, Mattel, Model No. 15430
MNP $5 **MIP** $10

Ocean Friends Ken, 1996, Mattel, Model No. 15430
MNP $5 **MIP** $10

Ocean Friends Kira, 1996, Mattel, Model No. 15431
MNP $5 **MIP** $10

Olympic Gymnast, blond, 1996, Mattel, Model No. 15123
MNP $7 **MIP** $15

P.J., talking, 1970, Mattel, Model No. 1113
MNP $65 **MIP** $250

P.J., Twist N Turn, 1970, Mattel, Model No. 1118
MNP $65 **MIP** $275

Party Treats Barbie, 1989, Mattel, Model No. 4885
MNP $8 **MIP** $20

Peaches n' Cream Barbie, black, 1984, Mattel, Model No. 9516
MNP $8 **MIP** $30

Peaches n' Cream Barbie, white, 1984, Mattel, Model No. 7926
MNP $8 **MIP** $30

Perfume Giving Ken, black, 1989, Mattel, Model No. 4555
MNP $6 **MIP** $15

Perfume Giving Ken, white, 1989, Mattel, Model No. 4554
MNP $6 **MIP** $15

Perfume Pretty Barbie, black, 1989, Mattel, Model No. 4552
MNP $8 **MIP** $15

Perfume Pretty Barbie, white, 1989, Mattel, Model No. 4551
MNP $8 **MIP** $15

Perfume Pretty Whitney, 1987, Mattel, Model No. 4557
MNP $8 **MIP** $15

Pink 'n Pretty Barbie, 1982, Mattel, Model No. 3551
MNP $12 **MIP** $45

Pink 'n Pretty Christie, 1982, Mattel, Model No. 3554
MNP $10 **MIP** $40

Playtime Barbie, 1984, Mattel, Model No. 5336
MNP $5 **MIP** $10

Ponytail Barbie #1, blond, 1959, Mattel, Model No. 850
MNP $2000 **MIP** $5000

Ponytail Barbie #1, brunette, 1959, Mattel, Model No. 850
MNP $2500 **MIP** $5500

Ponytail Barbie #2, blond, 1959, Mattel, Model No. 850
MNP $2500 **MIP** $5000

Ponytail Barbie #2, brunette, 1959, Mattel, Model No. 850
MNP $3000 **MIP** $7000

Ponytail Barbie #3, blond, 1960, Mattel, Model No. 850
MNP $325 **MIP** $850

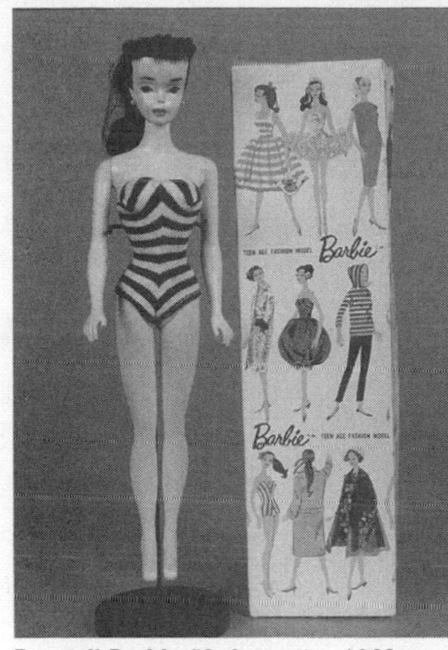

Ponytail Barbie #3, brunette, 1960, Mattel, Model No. 850
MNP $375 **MIP** $900

Ponytail Barbie #4, blond, 1960, Mattel, Model No. 850
MNP $175 **MIP** $400

Ponytail Barbie #4, brunette, 1960, Mattel, Model No. 850
MNP $275 **MIP** $450

Ponytail Barbie #5, blond, 1961, Mattel, Model No. 850
MNP $125 **MIP** $350

Ponytail Barbie #5, brunette, 1961, Mattel, Model No. 850
MNP $200 **MIP** $400

Ponytail Barbie #5, titian, 1961, Mattel, Model No. 850
MNP $225 **MIP** $500

Ponytail Barbie #6, blond, 1962, Mattel, Model No. 850
MNP $125 **MIP** $350

BARBIE

Ponytail Barbie #6, brunette, 1962, Mattel, Model No. 850
MNP $125 **MIP** $350

Ponytail Barbie #6, titian, 1962, Mattel, Model No. 850
MNP $125 **MIP** $350

Ponytail Swirl Style Barbie, blond, 1964, Mattel, Model No. 850
MNP $275 **MIP** $600

Ponytail Swirl Style Barbie, brunette, 1964, Mattel, Model No. 850
MNP $275 **MIP** $600

Ponytail Swirl Style Barbie, platinum, 1964, Mattel, Model No. 850
MNP $500 **MIP** $1200

Ponytail Swirl Style Barbie, titian, 1964, Mattel, Model No. 850
MNP $275 **MIP** $600

Pose 'n Play Skipper (baggie), 1973, Mattel, Model No. 1117
MNP $20 **MIP** $55

Pretty Changes Barbie, 1978, Mattel, Model No. 2598
MNP $8 **MIP** $30

Pretty Party Barbie, 1983, Mattel, Model No. 7194
MNP $12 **MIP** $25

Quick Curl Barbie, 1972, Mattel, Model No. 4220
MNP $20 **MIP** $65

Quick Curl Cara, 1974, Mattel, Model No. 7291
MNP $20 **MIP** $60

Quick Curl Deluxe Barbie, 1976, Mattel, Model No. 9217
MNP $20 **MIP** $65

Quick Curl Deluxe Cara, 1976, Mattel, Model No. 9219
MNP $20 **MIP** $60

Quick Curl Deluxe P.J., 1976, Mattel, Model No. 9218
MNP $20 **MIP** $50

Quick Curl Deluxe Skipper, 1976, Mattel, Model No. 9428
MNP $20 **MIP** $50

Quick Curl Francie, 1972, Mattel, Model No. 4222
MNP $20 **MIP** $55

Quick Curl Kelley, 1972, Mattel, Model No. 4221
MNP $20 **MIP** $75

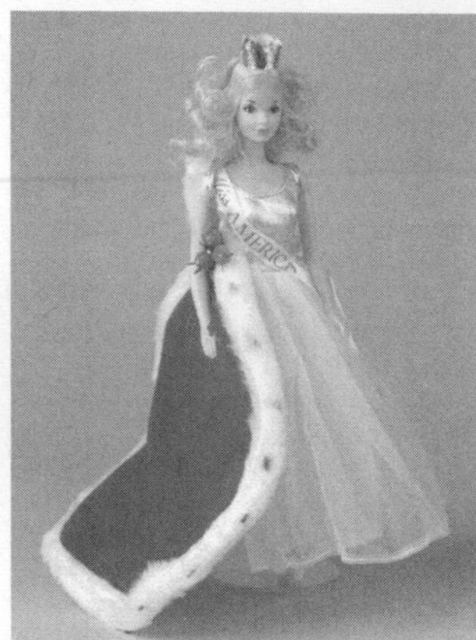

Quick Curl Miss America, blond, 1974, Mattel, Model No. 8697
MNP $35 **MIP** $75

Quick Curl Miss America, brunette, 1973, Mattel, Model No. 8697
MNP $45 **MIP** $125

Quick Curl Skipper, 1974, Mattel, Model No. 4223
MNP $20 **MIP** $50

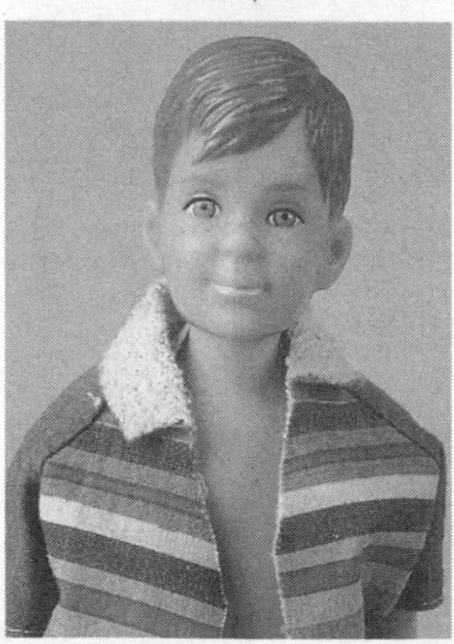

Ricky, 1965, Mattel, Model No. 1090
MNP $55 **MIP** $125

Rocker Barbie, 1st issue, 1986, Mattel, Model No. 1140
MNP $7 **MIP** $25

Rocker Barbie, 2nd issue, 1987, Mattel, Model No. 3055
MNP $7 **MIP** $20

Rocker Dana, 1st issue, 1986, Mattel, Model No. 1196
MNP $7 **MIP** $25

Rocker Dana, 2nd issue, 1987, Mattel, Model No. 3158
MNP $7 **MIP** $15

Rocker Dee-Dee, 1st issue, 1986, Mattel, Model No. 1141
MNP $7 **MIP** $25

Rocker Dee-Dee, 2nd issue, 1987, Mattel, Model No. 3160
MNP $7 **MIP** $15

Rocker Derek, 1st issue, 1986, Mattel, Model No. 2428
MNP $7 **MIP** $25

Rocker Derek, 2nd issue, 1987, Mattel, Model No. 3173
MNP $7 **MIP** $15

Rocker Diva, 1st issue, 1986, Mattel, Model No. 2427
MNP $7 **MIP** $25

Rocker Diva, 2nd issue, 1987, Mattel, Model No. 3159
MNP $7 **MIP** $15

Rocker Ken, 1st issue, 1986, Mattel, Model No. 3131
MNP $7 **MIP** $25

Roller Skating Barbie, 1980, Mattel, Model No. 1880
MNP $8 **MIP** $35

Roller Skating Ken, 1980, Mattel, red shirt, blue shorts, jacket, skates, Model No. 1881
MNP $8 **MIP** $30

Safari Barbie, 1983, Mattel, Model No. 4973
MNP $8 **MIP** $15

Scott, 1979, Mattel, Model No. 1019
MNP $15 **MIP** $60

Sea Lovin' Barbie, 1984, Mattel, Model No. 9109
MNP $8 **MIP** $15

Sea Lovin' Ken, 1984, Mattel, Model No. 9110
MNP $8 **MIP** $15

Secret Messages Barbie, white or black, 2000, Model No. 26422
MNP $7 MIP $10

Sensations Barbie, 1987, Mattel, Model No. 4931
MNP $5 MIP $10

Sensations Becky, 1987, Mattel, Model No. 4977
MNP $5 MIP $10

Sensations Belinda, 1987, Mattel, Model No. 4976
MNP $5 MIP $10

Sensations Bobsy, 1987, Mattel, Model No. 4967
MNP $5 MIP $10

Sit 'n Style Barbie, 2000, Mattel, Model No. 23421
MNP $7 MIP $10

Ski Fun Barbie, 1991, Mattel, Model No. 7511
MNP $6 MIP $15

Ski Fun Ken, 1991, Mattel, Model No. 7512
MNP $6 MIP $15

Ski Fun Midge, 1991, Mattel, Model No. 7513
MNP $6 MIP $25

Skipper, bendable leg, brunette, blond, titian, 1965, Mattel, Model No. 1030
MNP $60 MIP $150

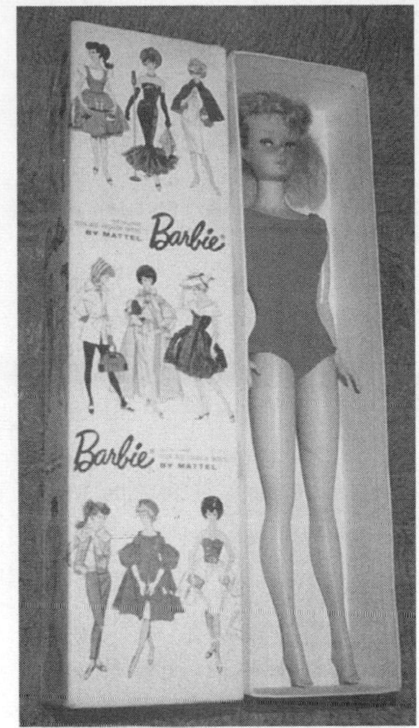

Skipper, straight leg, brunette, blond, titian, 1964, Mattel, Model No. 950
MNP $30 MIP $125

Skipper, straight leg, reissues, brunette, blond, titian, 1971, Mattel, Model No. 950
MNP $125 MIP $350

Skipper, Twist N Turn, blonde or brunette, curl pigtails, 1969, Mattel, Model No. 1105
MNP $75 MIP $225

Skipper, Twist N Turn, blonde, brunette, red hair, long straight hair, 1968, Mattel, Model No. 1105
MNP $75 MIP $200

Skooter, bendable leg, brunette, blond, titian, 1966, Mattel, Model No. 1120
MNP $75 MIP $275

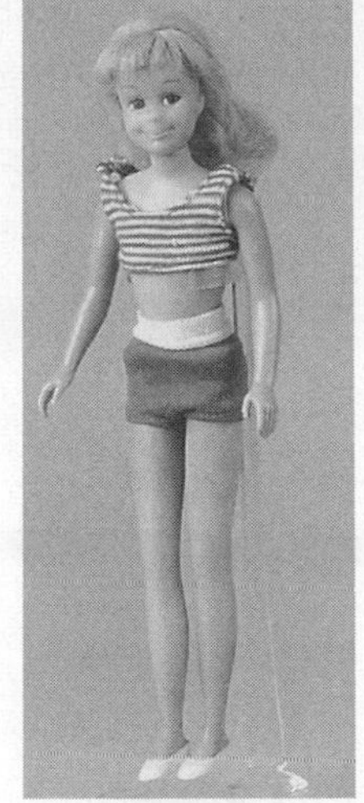

Skooter, straight leg, brunette, blond, titian, 1965, Mattel, Model No. 1040
MNP $30 MIP $125

Snowboard Barbie, 1996, Mattel, Model No. 15408
MNP $10 MIP $15

Sparkle Barbie, 1996, Mattel, Model No. 15419
MNP $10 MIP $15

Sport 'n Shave Ken, 1980, Mattel, Model No. 1294
MNP $8 MIP $30

Stacey, talking, blonde or red hair, side ponytail, 1968, Mattel, Model No. 1125
MNP $175 MIP $400

Stacey, Twist N Turn, blonde or red hair, long ponytail with spit curls, 1968, Mattel, Model No. 1165
MNP $125 MIP $400

Stacey, Twist N Turn, blonde or red hair, short rolled flip, 1969, Mattel, Model No. 1165
MNP $125 MIP $400

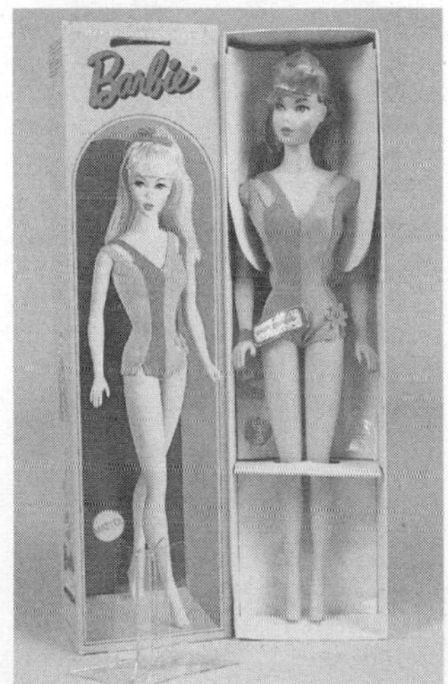

Standard Barbie, blond, brunette, long straight hair with bangs, 1967, Mattel, Model No. 1190
MNP $150 MIP $425

Standard Barbie, centered eyes, 1971, Mattel, Model No. 1190
MNP $300 **MIP** $475

Standard Barbie, titian, long straight hair with bangs, 1967, Mattel, Model No. 1190
MNP $225 **MIP** $450

Stars & Stripes Air Force Barbie, 1990, Mattel, Model No. 3360
MNP $5 **MIP** $10

Stars & Stripes Army Barbie, white or black, 1993, Mattel, Model No. 1234/5618
MNP $10 **MIP** $20

Stars & Stripes Marine Corps Barbie, white or black, 1992, Mattel, Model No. 7549/7594
MNP $10 **MIP** $20

Stars & Stripes Navy Barbie, white or black, 1991, Mattel, Model No. 9693/9694
MNP $10 **MIP** $20

Stars 'n Stripes Air Force Ken, white or black, 1994, Mattel, Model No. 11554/11555
MNP $15 **MIP** $20

Stars 'n Stripes Air Force Thunderbirds Barbie, white or black, 1994, Mattel, Model No. 11552/11553
MNP $15 **MIP** $20

Stars 'n Stripes Army Ken, white or black, 1993, Mattel, Model No. 1237/5619
MNP $15 **MIP** $20

Stars 'n Stripes Marine Corps Ken, black or white, 1992, Mattel, Model No. 5352/7574
MNP $20 **MIP** $20

Style Magic Barbie, 1989, Mattel, Model No. 1283
MNP $5 **MIP** $20

Style Magic Christie, 1989, Mattel, Model No. 1288
MNP $5 **MIP** $10

Style Magic Skipper, 1989, Mattel, Model No. 1915
MNP $5 **MIP** $10

Style Magic Whitney, 1989, Mattel, Model No. 1290
MNP $5 **MIP** $10

Summit Barbie, Asian, 1990, Mattel, Model No. 7029
MNP $10 **MIP** $15

Summit Barbie, black, 1990, Mattel, Model No. 7028
MNP $12 **MIP** $15

Summit Barbie, Hispanic, 1990, Mattel, Model No. 7030
MNP $10 **MIP** $15

Summit Barbie, white, 1990, Mattel, Model No. 7027
MNP $8 **MIP** $15

Sun Gold Malibu Barbie, black, 1983, Mattel, Model No. 7745
MNP $5 **MIP** $15

Sun Gold Malibu Barbie, Hispanic, 1985, Mattel, Model No. 4970
MNP $3 **MIP** $20

Sun Gold Malibu Barbie, white, 1983, Mattel, Model No. 1067
MNP $5 **MIP** $15

Sun Gold Malibu Ken, black, 1983, Mattel, Model No. 3849
MNP $3 **MIP** $15

Sun Gold Malibu Ken, Hispanic, 1985, Mattel, Model No. 4971
MNP $3 **MIP** $20

Sun Gold Malibu Ken, white, 1983, Mattel, Model No. 1088
MNP $3 **MIP** $15

Sun Gold Malibu P.J., 1983, Mattel, Model No. 1187
MNP $5 **MIP** $15

Sun Gold Malibu Skipper, 1983, Mattel, Model No. 1069
MNP $5 **MIP** $15

Sun Lovin' Malibu Barbie, 1978, Mattel, Model No. 1067
MNP $5 **MIP** $20

Sun Lovin' Malibu Ken, 1978, Mattel, Model No. 1088
MNP $5 **MIP** $20

Sun Lovin' Malibu P.J., 1978, Mattel, Model No. 1187
MNP $5 **MIP** $20

Sun Lovin' Malibu Skipper, 1978, Mattel, Model No. 1069
MNP $5 **MIP** $20

Sun Valley Barbie, 1974, Mattel, Model No. 7806
MNP $20 **MIP** $115

Sun Valley Ken, 1974, Mattel, Model No. 7809
MNP $20 **MIP** $95

Sunsational Malibu Barbie, 1982, Mattel, Model No. 1067
MNP $6 **MIP** $25

Sunsational Malibu Barbie, Hispanic, 1982, Mattel, Model No. 4970
MNP $8 **MIP** $25

Sunsational Malibu Christie, 1982, Mattel, Model No. 7745
MNP $6 **MIP** $20

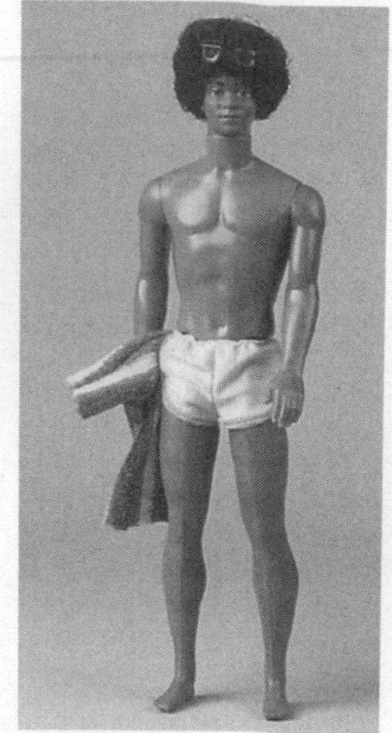

Sunsational Malibu Ken, black, 1981, Mattel, Model No. 3849
MNP $15 **MIP** $35

Sunsational Malibu P.J., 1982, Mattel, Model No. 1187
MNP $6 **MIP** $30

Sunsational Malibu Skipper, 1982, Mattel, Model No. 1069
MNP $5 **MIP** $35

Sunset Malibu Christie, 1973, Mattel, Model No. 7745
MNP $20 **MIP** $65

Sunset Malibu Francie, 1971, Mattel, Model No. 1068
MNP $25 **MIP** $65

Sunset Malibu Ken, 1972, Mattel, Model No. 1088
MNP $15 **MIP** $50

Sunset Malibu P.J., 1971, Mattel, Model No. 1187
MNP $10 **MIP** $50

Sunset Malibu Skipper, 1971, Mattel, Model No. 1069
MNP $20 **MIP** $50

Super Hair Barbie, black, 1987, Mattel, Model No. 3296
MNP $8 **MIP** $15

Super Hair Barbie, white, 1987, Mattel, Model No. 3101
MNP $8 **MIP** $15

Super Sport Ken, 1982, Mattel, Model No. 5839
MNP $8 **MIP** $15

Super Talk Barbie, 1994, Mattel, Model No. 12290
MNP $10 **MIP** $15

Super Teen Skipper, 1978, Mattel, Model No. 2756
MNP $7 **MIP** $15

Supersize Barbie, 1977, Mattel, Model No. 9828
MNP $45 **MIP** $125

Supersize Bride Barbie, 1977, Mattel, Model No. 9975
MNP $100 **MIP** $250

Supersize Christie, 1977, Mattel, Model No. 9839
MNP $75 **MIP** $225

Supersize Super Hair Barbie, 1979, Mattel, Model No. 2844
MNP $85 **MIP** $125

Superstar Ballerina Barbie, 1976, Mattel, Model No. 4983
MNP $20 **MIP** $50

Superstar Barbie, 1977, Mattel, Model No. 9720
MNP $15 **MIP** $60

Superstar Barbie, 1988, Mattel, Model No. 1604
MNP $45 **MIP** $95

Superstar Barbie 30th Anniversary, black, 1989, Mattel, Model No. 1605
MNP $6 **MIP** $25

Superstar Barbie 30th Anniversary, white, 1989, Mattel, Model No. 1604
MNP $8 **MIP** $20

Superstar Christie, 1977, Mattel, Model No. 9950
MNP $20 **MIP** $50

Superstar Ken, 1978, Mattel, Model No. 2211
MNP $17 **MIP** $50

Superstar Ken, black, 1989, Mattel, Model No. 1550
MNP $5 **MIP** $25

Superstar Ken, white, 1989, Mattel, Model No. 1535
MNP $7 **MIP** $40

Superstar Malibu Barbie, 1977, Mattel, Model No. 1067
MNP $10 **MIP** $35

Sweet 16 Barbie, 1974, Mattel, Model No. 7796
MNP $25 **MIP** $100

Sweet Roses P.J., 1983, Mattel, Model No. 7455
MNP $15 **MIP** $40

Swimming Champion Barbie, 2000, Mattel, Model No. 24590
MNP $7 **MIP** $15

Talk With Me Barbie, 1997, Mattel, with software, Model No. 17350
MNP $15 **MIP** $30

Talking Barbie, chignon with nape curls, blonde, brunette, titian, 1970, Mattel, Model No. 1115
MNP $150 **MIP** $500

Talking Barbie, side ponytail with spit curls, blonde or brunette, 1968, Mattel, Model No. 1115
MNP $100 **MIP** $400

Talking Busy Barbie, 1972, Mattel, Model No. 1195
MNP $100 **MIP** $300

Talking Busy Ken, 1972, Mattel, Model No. 1196
MNP $70 **MIP** $140

BARBIE

Talking Busy Steffie, 1972, Mattel, Model No. 1186
MNP $150 **MIP** $350

Talking Ken, 1969, Mattel, Model No. 1111
MNP $60 **MIP** $150

Teacher Barbie, painted on panties, black, 1996, Mattel, Model No. 13915
MNP $10 **MIP** $15

Teacher Barbie, painted on panties, white, 1996, Mattel, Model No. 13914
MNP $10 **MIP** $15

Teen Dance Jazzie, 1989, Mattel, Model No. 3634
MNP $7 **MIP** $20

Teen Fun Skipper Cheerleader, 1987, Mattel, Model No. 5893
MNP $5 **MIP** $10

Teen Fun Skipper Party Teen, 1987, Mattel, Model No. 5899
MNP $5 **MIP** $10

Teen Fun Skipper Workout, 1987, Mattel, Model No. 5889
MNP $5 **MIP** $10

Teen Jazzie (Teen Dance), 1989, Mattel, Model No. 3634
MNP $4 **MIP** $35

Teen Looks Jazzie Cheerleader, 1989, Mattel, Model No. 3631
MNP $4 **MIP** $20

Teen Looks Jazzie Workout, 1989, Mattel, Model No. 3633
MNP $4 **MIP** $20

Teen Scene Jazzie, two box versions, 1991, Mattel, Model No. 5507
MNP $5 **MIP** $35

Teen Sweetheart Skipper, 1988, Mattel, Model No. 4855
MNP $5 **MIP** $10

Teen Talk Barbie, 1992, Mattel, Model No. 5745
MNP $10 **MIP** $20

Teen Talk Barbie, "Math is Tough" variation, 1992, Mattel, Model No. 5745
MNP $50 **MIP** $275

Teen Time Courtney, 1988, Mattel, Model No. 1950
MNP $5 **MIP** $10

Teen Time Skipper, 1988, Mattel, Model No. 1951
MNP $5 **MIP** $10

Tennis Barbie, 1986, Mattel, Model No. 1760
MNP $5 **MIP** $15

Tennis Ken, 1986, Mattel, Model No. 1761
MNP $5 **MIP** $15

Todd, 1967, Mattel, Model No. 3590
MNP $70 **MIP** $200

Tracy Bride, 1983, Mattel, Model No. 4103
MNP $8 **MIP** $45

Tropical Barbie, black, 1986, Mattel, Model No. 1022
MNP $3 **MIP** $10

Tropical Barbie, white, 1986, Mattel, Model No. 1017
MNP $3 **MIP** $10

Tropical Ken, black, 1986, Mattel, Model No. 1023
MNP $3 **MIP** $10

Tropical Ken, white, 1986, Mattel, Model No. 4060
MNP $3 **MIP** $10

Tropical Miko, 1986, Mattel, Model No. 2056
MNP $3 **MIP** $10

Tropical Skipper, 1986, Mattel, Model No. 4064
MNP $3 **MIP** $10

Truly Scrumptious, standard, 1969, Mattel, Model No. 1107
MNP $175 **MIP** $400

Truly Scrumptious, talking, 1969, Mattel, Model No. 1108
MNP $175 **MIP** $450

Tutti, all hair colors, floral dress w/yellow ribbon, 1967, Mattel, Model No. 3580
MNP $45 **MIP** $150

Tutti, all hair colors, pink, white gingham suit, hat, 1966, Mattel, Model No. 3550
MNP $50 **MIP** $170

Tutti, Germany, 1978, Mattel, Model No. 8128
MNP $40 **MIP** $125

Twiggy, 1967, Mattel, Model No. 1185
MNP $95 **MIP** $300

Twirley Curls Barbie, black, 1983, Mattel, Model No. 5723
MNP $10 **MIP** $20

Twirley Curls Barbie, Hispanic, 1982, Mattel, Model No. 5724
MNP $10 **MIP** $20

Twirley Curls Barbie, white, 1982, Mattel, Model No. 5579
MNP $10 **MIP** $20

Twist N Turn Barbie, blonde, brunette, red hair with centered eyes, 1971, Mattel, Model No. 1160
MNP $175 **MIP** $575

Twist N Turn Barbie, flip hair, blonde or brunette, 1969, Mattel, Model No. 1160
MNP $95 **MIP** $450

Twist N Turn Barbie, light blonde, blonde, light brown, brunette, 1967, Mattel, Model No. 1160
MNP $90 **MIP** $450

Twist N Turn Barbie, long straight hair with bangs, red hair, 1967, Mattel, Model No. 1160
MNP $175 **MIP** $550

UNICEF Barbie, Asian, 1989, Mattel, Model No. 4774
MNP $5 **MIP** $10

UNICEF Barbie, black, 1989, Mattel, Model No. 4770
MNP $5 **MIP** $10

UNICEF Barbie, Hispanic, 1989, Mattel, Model No. 4782
MNP $5 **MIP** $10

UNICEF Barbie, white, 1989, Mattel, Model No. 1920
MNP $5 **MIP** $10

University Barbie, 1997, Mattel, many schools offered
MNP $8 **MIP** $15

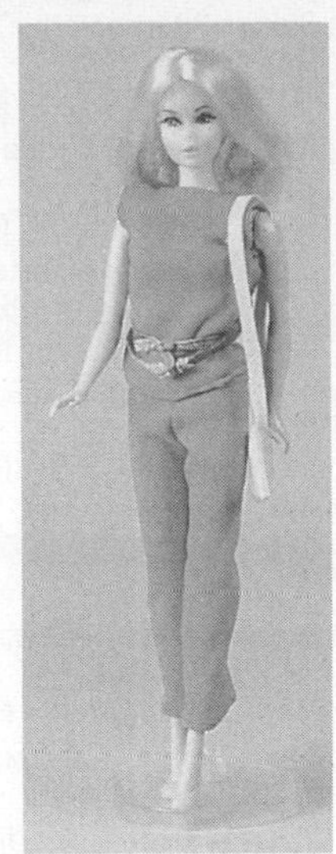

Walk Lively Barbie, 1971, Mattel, Model No. 1182
MNP $75 **MIP** $200

Walk Lively Ken, 1971, Mattel, Model No. 1184
MNP $40 **MIP** $150

Walk Lively Miss America Barbie, brunette, 1971, Mattel, Model No. 3200
MNP $95 **MIP** $200

Walk Lively Steffie, 1971, Mattel, Model No. 1183
MNP $75 **MIP** $300

Walking Jamie, 1970, Mattel, Model No. 1132
MNP $175 **MIP** $400

Wedding Fantasy Barbie, black, 1989, Mattel, Model No. 7011
MNP $7 **MIP** $20

Wedding Fantasy Barbie, white, 1989, Mattel, Model No. 2125
MNP $7 **MIP** $20

Wedding Party Allan, 1991, Mattel, Model No. 9607
MNP $7 **MIP** $20

Wedding Party Barbie, 1991, Mattel, Model No. 9608
MNP $7 **MIP** $20

Wedding Party Kelly & Todd, 1991, Mattel, Model No. 9852
MNP $15 **MIP** $25

Wedding Party Ken, 1991, Mattel, Model No. 9609
MNP $7 **MIP** $20

Wedding Party Midge, 1991, Mattel, Model No. 9606
MNP $7 **MIP** $15

Western Barbie, 1980, Mattel, Model No. 1757
MNP $8 **MIP** $25

Western Fun Barbie, black, 1989, Mattel, Model No. 2930
MNP $5 **MIP** $15

Western Fun Barbie, white, 1989, Mattel, Model No. 9932
MNP $5 **MIP** $15

Western Fun Ken, 1989, Mattel, Model No. 9934
MNP $5 **MIP** $15

Western Fun Nia, 1989, Mattel, Model No. 9933
MNP $5 **MIP** $15

Western Ken, 1981, Mattel, Model No. 3600
MNP $7 **MIP** $25

Western Skipper, 1982, Mattel, Model No. 5029
MNP $8 **MIP** $20

Wet 'n Wild Barbie, 1990, Mattel, Model No. 4103
MNP $8 **MIP** $15

Wet 'n Wild Christie, 1989, Mattel, Model No. 4121
MNP $3 **MIP** $10

Wet 'n Wild Ken, 1989, Mattel, Model No. 4104
MNP $3 **MIP** $10

Wet 'n Wild Kira, 1989, Mattel, Model No. 4120
MNP $3 **MIP** $10

Wet 'n Wild Skipper, 1989, Mattel, Model No. 4138
MNP $3 **MIP** $10

Wet 'n Wild Steven, 1989, Mattel, Model No. 4137
MNP $3 **MIP** $10

Wet 'n Wild Teresa, 1989, Mattel, Model No. 4136
MNP $3 **MIP** $10

Wig Wardrobe Midge, 1965, Mattel, Model No. 1009
MNP $200 **MIP** $500

Working Woman Barbie, black or white, 1999, Mattel
MNP $7 MIP $10

COLLECTORS' EDITIONS, STORE EXCLUSIVES, GIFT SETS

1 Modern Circle Barbie, 2003, Mattel
MNP $15 MIP $20

1 Modern Circle Barbie (Evening Wear), 2004, Mattel
MNP $15 MIP $20

1 Modern Circle Ken, 2003, Mattel
MNP $15 MIP $20

1 Modern Circle Ken (Evening Wear), 2004, Mattel
MNP $15 MIP $20

1 Modern Circle Melody, 2003, Mattel
MNP $15 MIP $20

1 Modern Circle Melody (Evening Wear), 2004, Mattel
MNP $15 MIP $20

1 Modern Circle Simone, 2003, Mattel
MNP $15 MIP $20

1 Modern Circle Simone (Evening Wear), 2004, Mattel
MNP $15 MIP $20

40th Anniversary Barbie, white or black, 1999, Mattel, Model No. 21384/22336
MNP $25 MIP $40

40th Anniversary Gala, 1999, Mattel, "bumblebee"
MNP $30 MIP $90

40th Anniversary Ken, black, 2001, Mattel, Model No. 52967
MNP $15 MIP $35

40th Anniversary Ken, white, 2001, Mattel, Model No. 50722
MNP $15 MIP $35

Alice in Wonderland, Alice, 2007, Mattel
MNP n/a MIP $30

Alice in Wonderland, Mad Hatter, 2007, Mattel
MNP n/a MIP $30

Alice in Wonderland, Queen of Hearts, 2007, Mattel
MNP n/a MIP $30

All American Barbie & Starstepper, 1991, Mattel, Model No. 3712
MNP $12 MIP $35

American Stories #1 American Indian, 1996, Mattel, Model No. 14612
MNP $7 MIP $10

American Stories #2 American Indian, 1997, Mattel, Model No. 17313
MNP $7 MIP $10

American Stories Civil War Nurse, 1996, Mattel, Model No. 14612
MNP $7 MIP $10

American Stories Colonial Barbie, 1995, Mattel, Model No. 12578
MNP $7 MIP $10

American Stories Patriot Barbie, 1997, Mattel, Model No. 17312
MNP $7 MIP $10

American Stories Pilgrim Barbie, 1995, Mattel, Model No. 12577
MNP $7 MIP $10

American Stories Pioneer Barbie, 1995, Mattel, Model No. 12680
MNP $7 MIP $10

American Stories Pioneer Shopkeeper, 1996, Mattel, Model No. 14756
MNP $7 MIP $10

Ames Country Looks Barbie, 1993, Mattel, Model No. 5854
MNP $8 MIP $15

Ames Denim 'N Lace Barbie, 1992, Mattel, Model No. 2452
MNP $5 MIP $20

Ames Hot Looks Barbie, 1992, Mattel, Model No. 5756
MNP $5 MIP $15

Ames Ice Cream Barbie, 1998, Mattel, Model No. 19280
MNP $8 MIP $15

Ames Lady Bug Fun Barbie, 1997, Mattel, Model No. 17695
MNP $5 MIP $15

Ames Party in Pink, 1991, Mattel, Model No. 2909
MNP $5 MIP $15

Ames Strawberry Party Barbie, 1999, Mattel, Model No. 22895
MNP $8 MIP $10

Angel Lights Barbie, 1993, Mattel
MNP $40 MIP $65

Angels of Music Harpist Angel, black or white, 1998, Mattel
MNP $35 MIP $50

Angels of Music Heartstring Angel, black or white, 1999, Mattel
MNP $40 MIP $50

Anna Sui Boho Barbie, 2006, Mattel
MNP n/a MIP $130

Anne Klein Barbie, 1997, Mattel, Model No. 17603
MNP $25 MIP $50

Applause Barbie Holiday, 1991, Mattel, Model No. 3406
MNP $20 MIP $20

Applause Style Barbie, 1990, Mattel, Model No. 5313
MNP $10 MIP $20

Armani Barbie, 2003, Mattel
MNP $75 MIP $150

Artist Series, Reflections of Light Barbie, Renoir, 1999, Mattel, Model No. 23884
MNP $40 MIP $60

Artist Series, Sunflower Barbie, Van Gogh, 1998, Mattel, Model No. 19366
MNP $40 MIP $60

Artist Series, Water Lily Barbie, Monet, 1997, Mattel, Model No. 17783
MNP $50 MIP $60

Avon Blushing Bride Barbie, white or black, 2000, Mattel
MNP $10 MIP $20

Avon Exotic Intrigue, 2004, Mattel, Blonde, Hispanic, African American
MNP $10 MIP $20

Avon Fruit Fantasy Barbie, blonde, 1999, Mattel
MNP $10 MIP $20

Avon Fruit Fantasy Barbie, brunette, 1999, Mattel
MNP $15 MIP $20

Avon Lemon-Lime Barbie, 1999, Mattel, Model No. 20318
MNP $10 MIP $20

Avon Mrs. P.F.E. Albee, 1997, Mattel, Model No. 17690
MNP $15 MIP $35

Avon Mrs. P.F.E. Albee #2, 1998, Mattel, Model No. 20330
MNP $15 MIP $30

Avon Representative Barbie, black, white, Hispanic, 1999, Mattel
MNP $20 MIP $50

Avon Snow Sensation, black or white, 1999, Mattel
MNP $10 MIP $25

Avon Spring Blossom, black, 1996, Mattel, Model No. 15202
MNP $5 MIP $10

Avon Spring Blossom, white, 1996, Mattel, Model No. 15201
MNP $5 MIP $10

Avon Spring Petals Barbie, black, 1997, Mattel, Model No. 16871
MNP $5 MIP $10

Avon Spring Petals Barbie, blond or brunette, 1997, Mattel, Model No. 10746/16872
MNP $5 MIP $10

Avon Spring Tea Party Barbie, black, Mattel
MNP $10 MIP $20

Avon Spring Tea Party Barbie, blond or brunette, Mattel, Model No. 18658
MNP $10 MIP $20

Avon Strawberry Sorbet Barbie, 1999, Mattel, Model No. 20317
MNP $5 MIP $15

Avon Timeless Silhouette Barbie, white or black, 2001, Mattel
MNP $10 MIP $20

Avon Victorian Skater Barbie, white or black, 2000, Mattel
MNP $10 MIP $30

Avon Winter Rhapsody Barbie, black, Mattel, Model No. 16354
MNP $15 MIP $30

Avon Winter Rhapsody Barbie, blond or brunette, Mattel, Model No. 16353/16873
MNP $15 MIP $30

Avon Winter Splendor Barbie, black, 1998, Mattel, Model No. 19358
MNP $20 MIP $40

Avon Winter Splendor Barbie, white, 1998, Mattel, Model No. 19357
MNP $15 MIP $35

Avon Winter Velvet, black, 1996, Mattel, Model No. 15587
MNP $10 MIP $25

Avon Winter Velvet, white, 1996, Mattel, Model No. 15571
MNP $10 MIP $25

B Mine Barbie, 1993, Mattel, Model No. 11182
MNP $7 **MIP** $10

Back To School, 1993, Mattel, Model No. 3208
MNP $15 **MIP** $35

Back to School, 1997, Mattel
MNP $5 **MIP** $10

Badgley Mischka Barbie, 2006, Mattel
MNP $40 **MIP** $90

Badgley Mischka Bride, 2004, Mattel
MNP $40 **MIP** $95

Ballerina Barbie as Juliet, 2004, Mattel
MNP $20 **MIP** $45

Ballerina Barbie as Titania, 2004, Mattel
MNP $20 **MIP** $45

Ballerina Barbie Peppermint Candy Cane, 2003, Mattel
MNP $10 **MIP** $20

Ballerina Dreams Barbie, 2000, Mattel, Model No. 20676
MNP $5 **MIP** $12

Ballerina on Tour Gift Set, 1976, Mattel, Model No. 9613
MNP $25 **MIP** $125

Ballet Lessons Barbie, black or white, 2000, Mattel
MNP $5 **MIP** $12

Ballroom Beauties, Midnight Waltz, 1996, Mattel, Model No. 15685
MNP $25 **MIP** $40

Ballroom Beauties, Moonlight Waltz Barbie, 1997, Mattel, Model No. 17763
MNP $25 **MIP** $40

Ballroom Beauties, Starlight Waltz Barbie, 1995, Mattel, Model No. 14070
MNP $25 **MIP** $40

Barbie 2000, white or black, 2000, Mattel, Model No. 27409/27410
MNP $5 **MIP** $15

Barbie 2001, black or white, 2001, Mattel, Model No. 50842/50841
MNP $5 **MIP** $15

Barbie 2002, (white or black), 2002, Mattel, Model No. 53975/53976
MNP $5 **MIP** $15

Barbie 2003, White or African American, 2003, Mattel
MNP $5 **MIP** $15

Barbie and Friends: Ken, Barbie, P.J., 1983, Mattel, Model No. 4431
MNP $25 **MIP** $75

Barbie and Ken as Arwen & Aragorn in Lord of the Rings: Return of the King, 2004, Mattel
MNP $40 **MIP** $125

Barbie and Ken Camping Out, 1983, Mattel
MNP $25 **MIP** $65

Barbie and Ken Tennis Gift Set, 1962, Mattel, Model No. 892
MNP $400 **MIP** $900

Barbie and Krissy Magical Mermaids, black or white, 2000, Mattel
MNP $15 **MIP** $30

Barbie as DC Comics Bat Girl, 2004, Mattel
MNP $10 **MIP** $20

Barbie as DC Comics Catwoman, 2004, Mattel, comic book store exclusive
MNP $20 **MIP** $110

Barbie as DC Comics Catwoman, 2004, Mattel
MNP $10 **MIP** $20

Barbie as DC Comics Super Girl, 2004, Mattel
MNP $10 **MIP** $20

Barbie as Elle Woods from Legally Blonde 2, 2003, Mattel
MNP $15 **MIP** $24

Barbie as Galadriel in Lord of the Rings: Fellowship of the Ring, 2004, Mattel
MNP $10 **MIP** $25

Barbie as Mary Jane Watson from Spider-Man, 2006, Mattel
MNP n/a **MIP** $15

Barbie as Sue Storm, Invisible Woman from Fantastic Four, 2006, Mattel
MNP n/a **MIP** $15

Barbie Beautiful Blues Gift Set, 1967, Mattel, Model No. 3303
MNP $1600 **MIP** $3000

Barbie Collector's Club Café Society, 1998, Mattel, Model No. 18892
MNP $50 **MIP** $125

Barbie Collector's Club Club Couture, 2000, Mattel, Model No. 26068
MNP $25 **MIP** $65

Barbie Collector's Club Embassy Waltz, 1999, Mattel, Model No. 23386
MNP $45 **MIP** $100

Barbie Collector's Club French Quarter Barbie Fashion, 2003, Mattel
MNP $15 **MIP** $25

Barbie Collector's Club Grand Premiere, 1997, Mattel, Model No. 16498
MNP $100 **MIP** $200

Barbie Collector's Club Holiday Treasures 1999, 1999, Mattel
MNP $75 **MIP** $125

Barbie Collector's Club Holiday Treasures 2000, 2000, Mattel, Model No. 27673
MNP $35 **MIP** $75

Barbie Collectors Club Hollywood Divine Blonde, 2004, Mattel, LE 3000 pcs
MNP $10 **MIP** $50

Barbie Collectors Club Hollywood Divine Brunette, 2004, Mattel, LE 4000 pcs
MNP $10 **MIP** $65

Barbie Collectors Club Melrose Morning Fashion, 2004, Mattel
MNP $10 **MIP** $25

Barbie Collector's Club Midnight Tuxedo, white or black, 2001, Mattel
MNP $25 **MIP** $65

Barbie Collectors Club Nod for Mod, 2004, Mattel
MNP $10 **MIP** $40

Barbie Collector's Club Noir et Blanc Barbie, African American, 2003, Mattel
MNP $40 **MIP** $60

Barbie Collector's Club Noir et Blanc Barbie, White, 2003, Mattel
MNP $40 **MIP** $60

Barbie Fan Club 2006 Rhapsody in New York, 2006, Mattel
MNP n/a **MIP** $50

Barbie Millicent Roberts Matinee Today, 1996, Mattel, Model No. 16079
MNP $22 **MIP** $60

Barbie Millicent Roberts Perfectly Suited, 1997, Mattel, Model No. 17567
MNP $30 **MIP** $45

Barbie Millicent Roberts Pinstripe Power Barbie, 1998, Mattel, Model No. 19791
MNP $30 **MIP** $50

Barbie's Round the Clock Gift Set, Bubblecut, 1964, Mattel, Model No. 1013
MNP $1000 **MIP** $2500

Barbie's Sparkling Pink Gift Set, Bubblecut, 1964, Mattel, Model No. 1011
MNP $1000 **MIP** $2400

Barbie's Wedding Party Gift Set, 1964, Mattel, Model No. 1017
MNP $1000 **MIP** $2400

Beauty Secrets Barbie Pretty Reflections Gift Set, 1979, Mattel, Model No. 1702
MNP $40 **MIP** $100

Best Buy Detective Barbie, 2000, Mattel, Model No. 24189
MNP $8 **MIP** $17

Best Models on Location Milan, African American, 2006, Mattel
MNP n/a **MIP** $35

Best Models on Location Monte Carlo, brunette, 2006, Mattel
MNP n/a **MIP** $35

Best Models on Location South Beach, blonde, 2006, Mattel
MNP n/a **MIP** $35

Bill Blass Barbie, 1997, Mattel, Model No. 17040
MNP $20 **MIP** $40

Billions of Dreams Barbie, 1997, Mattel, Model No. 17641
MNP $150 **MIP** $275

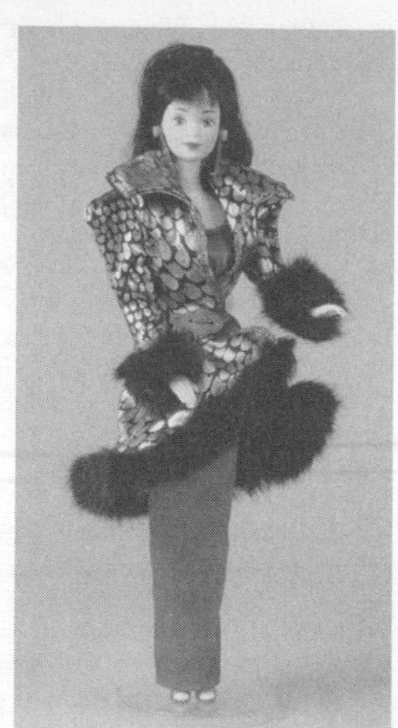

Billy Boy Feelin' Groovy Barbie, 1986, Mattel, Model No. 3421
MNP $75 **MIP** $125

Billy Boy Le Nouveau Theatre de la Mode Barbie, 1985, Mattel, Model No. 6279
MNP $100 **MIP** $200

Birds of Beauty #1 Peacock Barbie, 1998, Mattel, Model No. 19365
MNP $32 **MIP** $50

Birds of Beauty #2 Flamingo Barbie, 1999, Mattel, Model No. 22957
MNP $40 **MIP** $50

Birds of Beauty #3 Swan Barbie, 2000, Mattel, Model No. 27682
MNP $40 **MIP** $50

Birthday Fun at McDonald's Gift Set, 1994, Mattel, Model No. 11589
MNP $15 **MIP** $35

Birthday Wishes #1, black or white, 1999, Mattel, Model No. 21128/21509
MNP $15 **MIP** $35

Birthday Wishes #2, black or white, 2000, Mattel, Model No. 24667/24668
MNP $20 **MIP** $40

Birthday Wishes #3, black or white, 2001, Mattel
MNP $10 **MIP** $35

Birthday Wishes 2005, 2005, Mattel, peach or blue dress
MNP $10 **MIP** $30

Birthday Wishes Barbie African American, 2004, Mattel
MNP $10 **MIP** $30

Birthday Wishes Barbie Blonde, 2004, Mattel
MNP $10 **MIP** $30

Birthday Wishes Barbie Brunette, 2004, Mattel
MNP $10 **MIP** $30

Birthday Wishes Barbie Redhead, 2004, Mattel
MNP $10 **MIP** $30

Birthstone Beauty Collection (Jan-Dec), 2007, Mattel
MNP n/a **MIP** $25

Birthstone Beauty Collection (Jan-Dec), African-American, 2007, Mattel
MNP n/a **MIP** $25

BJ's Fantastica Barbie, 1993, Mattel, Model No. 3196
MNP $10 **MIP** $25

BJ's Festiva, 1993, Mattel
MNP $10 **MIP** $25

BJ's Golden Waltz, blonde or red, 1999, Mattel
MNP $10 **MIP** $25

BJ's Rose Bride Barbie, 1996, Mattel, Model No. 15987
MNP $15 **MIP** $20

BJ's Sparkle Beauty, 1997, Mattel
MNP $15 **MIP** $20

Bloomingdale's Barbie at Bloomingdale's, 1996, Mattel, Model No. 16290
MNP $15 **MIP** $35

Bloomingdale's Calvin Klein Barbie, 1996, Mattel
MNP $20 **MIP** $35

Bloomingdale's Donna Karan, blond, 1995, Mattel, Model No. 14452
MNP $25 **MIP** $45

Bloomingdale's Donna Karan, brunette, 1996, Mattel, Model No. 14452
MNP $25 **MIP** $45

Bloomingdale's Oscar de la Renta, 1998, Mattel, Model No. 20376
MNP $20 **MIP** $45

Bloomingdale's Ralph Lauren, 1997, Mattel, Model No. 15950
MNP $30 **MIP** $45

Bloomingdale's Savvy Shopper, Nicole Miller, 1994, Mattel, Model No. 12152
MNP $25 **MIP** $35

Bob Mackie 45th Anniversary Barbie, 2004, Mattel, White or African American
MNP $15 **MIP** $60

Bob Mackie 45th Anniversary Barbie, 2004, Mattel, White, black hair, LE 1000 pcs
MNP $25 **MIP** $100

Bob Mackie Couture Confection Bride, 2007, Mattel
MNP n/a **MIP** $100

Bob Mackie Couture Confection Bride Barbie, 2006, Mattel
MNP n/a **MIP** $125

Bob Mackie Designer Gold, 1990, Mattel, Model No. 5405
MNP $100 **MIP** $250

Bob Mackie Empress Bride, 1992, Mattel, Model No. 4247
MNP $250 **MIP** $450

Bob Mackie Fantasy Goddess of Africa, 1999, Mattel, Model No. 22044
MNP $100 **MIP** $175

Bob Mackie Fantasy Goddess of Asia, 1998, Mattel, Model No. SA415
MNP $70 **MIP** $95

Bob Mackie Fantasy Goddess of the Americas, 2000, Mattel, Model No. 25859
MNP $70 **MIP** $95

Bob Mackie Fantasy Goddess of the Arctic, 2001, Mattel, Model No. 50840
MNP $70 **MIP** $95

Bob Mackie Goddess of the Moon, 1996, Mattel, Model No. 14105
MNP $30 **MIP** $65

Bob Mackie Goddess of the Sun, 1995, Mattel, Model No. 14056
MNP $30 MIP $65

Bob Mackie Jewel Essence Amethyst Aura, 1997, Mattel, Model No. 15522
MNP $40 MIP $100

Bob Mackie Jewel Essence Diamond Dazzle, 1997, Mattel, Model No. 15519
MNP $40 MIP $100

Bob Mackie Jewel Essence Emerald Embers, 1997, Mattel, Model No. 15521
MNP $40 MIP $100

Bob Mackie Jewel Essence Ruby Radiance, 1997, Mattel, Model No. 15520
MNP $40 MIP $100

Bob Mackie Jewel Essence Sapphire Splendor, 1997, Mattel, Model No. 15523
MNP $40 MIP $100

Bob Mackie Madame du Barbie, 1997, Mattel, Model No. 17934
MNP $100 MIP $200

Bob Mackie Masquerade Ball, 1993, Mattel, Model No. 10803
MNP $125 MIP $250

Bob Mackie Neptune Fantasy, 1992, Mattel, Model No. 4248
MNP $250 MIP $500

Bob Mackie Platinum, 1991, Mattel, Model No. 2703
MNP $175 MIP $300

Bob Mackie Queen of Hearts, 1994, Mattel, Model No. 12046
MNP $70 MIP $150

Bob Mackie Red Carpet, Brunette Brilliance, 2003, Mattel, Model No. B0585
MNP $50 MIP $125

Bob Mackie Red Carpet, Radiant Redhead, 2002, Mattel, Model No. 55501
MNP $100 MIP $125

Bob Mackie Starlight Splendor, 1991, Mattel, Model No. 2704
MNP $150 MIP $250

Bowling Champ Barbie, 2000, Mattel, Model No. 25871
MNP $15 MIP $30

Bridal Collection Millennium Wedding, white, black or Hispanic, 2000, Mattel, Model No. 27674
MNP $25 MIP $50

Burberry Barbie, 2001, Mattel, Model No. 29421
MNP $25 MIP $40

Byron Lars Chapeaux Collection Sugar, 2006, Mattel
MNP n/a MIP $100

Byron Lars Chapeaux Collection, Coco, 2007, Mattel
MNP n/a MIP $100

Byron Lars Cinnabar Sensation, black or white, 1999, Mattel, Model No. 19848
MNP $35 MIP $95

Byron Lars In the Limelight, 1997, Mattel, Model No. 17031
MNP $40 MIP $300

Byron Lars Indigo Obsession, 2000, Mattel, Model No. 26935
MNP $25 MIP $65

Byron Lars Moja Barbie, 2001, Mattel, Model No. 50826
MNP $40 MIP $175

Byron Lars Nne, 2004, Mattel
MNP $10 MIP $80

Byron Lars Plum Royale, 1998, Mattel, Model No. 23478
MNP $40 MIP $95

Byron Lars Tatu, 2003, Mattel
MNP $50 MIP $80

Caroling Fun Barbie, 1995, Mattel, Model No. 13966
MNP $8 MIP $10

Casey Goes Casual Gift Set, 1967, Mattel, Model No. 3304
MNP $800 MIP $1650

Celebration Barbie 2000, white or black, 2000, Mattel
MNP $15 MIP $25

Celebrity Lucy L.A. at Last, 2003, Mattel
MNP $25 MIP $40

Celestial Collection #1 Evening Star, 2000, Mattel, Model No. 27690
MNP $10 MIP $25

Celestial Collection #2 Morning Sun, 2000, Mattel, Model No. 27688
MNP $10 MIP $25

Celestial Collection #3 Midnight Moon Princess, 2000, Mattel, Model No. 27689
MNP $10 MIP $25

Cher 1970s, 2007, Mattel
MNP n/a MIP $35

Cher 1980s, 2007, Mattel
MNP n/a MIP $35

Cher 1990s, Platinum Edition, 2007, Mattel
MNP n/a MIP $200

Children's Collector Series Belle (Beauty and the Beast), 2000, Mattel, Model No. 24673
MNP $15 MIP $30

Children's Collector Series Cinderella, 1997, Mattel, Model No. 16900
MNP $15 MIP $25

Children's Collector Series Little Bo Peep, 1995, Mattel, Model No. 14960
MNP $30 MIP $50

Children's Collector Series Rapunzel, 1995, Mattel, Model No. 13016
MNP $15 MIP $25

Children's Collector Series Sleeping Beauty, 1998, Mattel
MNP $15 MIP $25

Children's Collector Series Snow White, 1999, Mattel, Model No. 21130
MNP $15 MIP $25

Chocolate Obsession Barbie, 2005, Mattel
MNP $15 MIP $40

Christian Dior 50th Anniversary, 1997, Mattel, The New Look, Model No. 16013
MNP $35 MIP $125

Christian Dior Barbie, 1995, Mattel, Model No. 13168
MNP $25 MIP $50

Chuck E. Cheese Barbie, 1996, Mattel, Model No. 14615
MNP $15 MIP $30

Citrus Obsession Barbie, Platinum Pink Grapefruit Edition, 2006, Mattel
MNP n/a MIP $200

Citrus Obsession Barbie, Regular Edition, 2006, Mattel
MNP n/a **MIP** $35

City Seasons Autumn in London, 1999, Mattel, Model No. 22257
MNP $18 **MIP** $25

City Seasons Autumn in Paris, 1998, Mattel, Model No. 19367
MNP $18 **MIP** $25

City Seasons Spring in Tokyo, 1999, Mattel, Model No. 19430
MNP $18 **MIP** $25

City Seasons Spring in Tokyo, Internet Exclusive, 1999, Mattel, Model No. 23499
MNP $18 **MIP** $30

City Seasons Summer in Rome, 1999, Mattel, Model No. 19431
MNP $18 **MIP** $25

City Seasons Winter in Montreal, 1999, Mattel, Model No. 22258
MNP $18 **MIP** $25

City Seasons Winter in New York, 1998, Mattel, Model No. 19429
MNP $18 **MIP** $25

Classic Ballet Flower Ballerina, 2001, Mattel, Model No. 28375
MNP $10 **MIP** $25

Classic Ballet Marzipan, 1999, Mattel, Model No. 20581
MNP $15 **MIP** $25

(Mattel Photo)

Classic Ballet Peppermint Candy Cane, 2003, Mattel, Model No. 57578
MNP $10 **MIP** $25

Classic Ballet Snowflake, 2000, Mattel, Model No. 25642
MNP $15 **MIP** $25

Classic Ballet Sugar Plum Fairy, 1997, Mattel, Model No. 17056
MNP $15 **MIP** $30

Classic Ballet Swan Ballerina, 2002, Mattel, Model No. 53867
MNP $10 **MIP** $25

Classic Ballet Swan Lake, black or white, 1998, Mattel, Model No. 18509/18510
MNP $15 **MIP** $25

Classique Benefit Ball Barbie, 1992, Mattel, Model No. 1521
MNP $40 **MIP** $70

Classique City Style Barbie, 1993, Mattel, Model No. 10149
MNP $25 **MIP** $40

Classique Evening Extravaganza, 1994, Mattel, Model No. 11622
MNP $20 **MIP** $40

Classique Evening Extravaganza, black, 1994, Mattel, Model No. 11638
MNP $20 **MIP** $45

Classique Evening Sophisticate, 1998, Mattel, Model No. 19361
MNP $18 **MIP** $35

Classique Midnight Gala, 1995, Mattel, Model No. 12999
MNP $25 **MIP** $40

Classique Opening Night Barbie, 1993, Mattel, Model No. 10148
MNP $30 **MIP** $45

Classique Romantic Interlude Barbie, 1997, Mattel, Model No. 17136
MNP $15 **MIP** $30

Classique Romantic Interlude Barbie, black, 1997, Mattel, Model No. 17137
MNP $15 **MIP** $30

Classique Starlight Dance, 1996, Mattel, Model No. 15461
MNP $20 **MIP** $35

Classique Starlight Dance, black, 1996, Mattel, Model No. 15819
MNP $20 **MIP** $35

Classique Uptown Chic Barbie, 1994, Mattel, Model No. 11623
MNP $25 **MIP** $40

Coca-Cola #5 (majorette), 2002, Mattel, Model No. 53974
MNP $20 **MIP** $40

Coca-Cola Barbie #1, carhop, 1999, Mattel, Model No. 22831
MNP $20 **MIP** $65

Coca-Cola Barbie #2, 2000, Mattel, Model No. 24637
MNP $25 MIP $59

Coca-Cola Barbie #3, Cheerleader, 2001, Mattel
MNP $15 MIP $50

Coca-Cola Fashion Classic #1, Soda Fountain Sweetheart, 1996, Mattel
MNP $50 MIP $125

Coca-Cola Fashion Classic #2, After the Walk, 1997, Mattel, Model No. 17341
MNP $46 MIP $60

Coca-Cola Fashion Classic #3, Summer Daydreams, 1998, Mattel, Model No. 19739
MNP $30 MIP $60

Coca-Cola Ken, 2000, Mattel, Model No. 25678
MNP $100 MIP $175

Coca-Cola Party, 1999, Mattel, Model No. 22964
MNP $5 MIP $15

Coca-Cola Picnic, 1998, Mattel, Model No. 19626
MNP $5 MIP $15

Coca-Cola Splash, 2000, Mattel, Model No. 22590
MNP $5 MIP $15

Coca-Cola, Disney Teddy & Doll Convention, brunette, limited to 1,500, Mattel
MNP $45 MIP $95

Collectors Request All That Jazz Vintage Repro Barbie, Regular Edition, 2006, Mattel
MNP n/a MIP $50

Collectors Request All That Jazz Vintage Repro Barbie, Sanai Japanese, 2006, Mattel, brunette
MNP n/a MIP $200

Collectors' Request Color Magic Barbie Giftset, 2004, Mattel
MNP $10 MIP $25

Collectors' Request Commuter Set, 1999, Mattel, Model No. 21510
MNP $25 MIP $65

Collector's Request Evening Splendour Barbie, 2005, Mattel
MNP $15 MIP $40

Collectors' Request Gay Parisienne, 2003, Mattel, Model No. 57610
MNP $25 MIP $40

Collectors' Request Gold 'N Glamour, 2002, Mattel, Model No. 54185
MNP $20 MIP $50

Collectors Request Made for Each Other Vintage Repro Barbie, 2006, Mattel
MNP n/a MIP $50

Collector's Request Open Road Barbie, 2004, Mattel
MNP $20 MIP $65

Collector's Request Plantation Barbie, 2004, Mattel
MNP $15 MIP $65

Collectors' Request Sophisticated Lady, 1999, Mattel, Model No. 24930
MNP $25 MIP $60

Collectors' Request Suburban Shopper, 2000, Mattel
MNP $15 MIP $45

Collectors' Request Twist N Turn Smasheroo, brunette, 1998, Mattel, Model No. 18941
MNP $25 MIP $40

Collectors' Request Twist N' Turn Smasheroo, red hair, 1998, Mattel, Model No. 23258
MNP $25 MIP $50

Cool Collecting Barbie, 2000, Mattel, Nostalgic Toys, Model No. 25525
MNP $25 MIP $40

Couture Collection Portrait in Taffeta Barbie, 1996, Mattel, Model No. 15528
MNP $50 MIP $75

Couture Collection Serenade in Satin Barbie, 1997, Mattel, Model No. 17572
MNP $50 MIP $75

Couture Collection Symphony in Chiffon, 1998, Mattel, Model No. 21295
MNP $50 MIP $75

Cracker Barrel Country Charm Barbie, 2001, Mattel
MNP $5 MIP $15

Cynthia Rowley Barbie, 2005, Mattel
MNP $15 MIP $60

Dance Club Barbie Gift Set, 1989, Mattel, Model No. 4917
MNP $25 MIP $60

Dance Magic Gift Set Barbie & Ken, 1990, Mattel, Model No. 5409
MNP $15 MIP $35

Dance Sensation Barbie Gift Set, 1984, Mattel, Model No. 9058
MNP $15 MIP $40

David's Bridal Romance Barbie, African-American, 2007, Mattel
MNP n/a MIP $45

David's Bridal Romance Barbie, Blonde, 2007, Mattel
MNP n/a MIP $45

David's Bridal Romance Barbie, Brunette, 2007, Mattel
MNP n/a MIP $45

David's Bridal Unforgettable Barbie, 2004, Mattel, Blonde, Hispanic, African American
MNP $15 MIP $45

Democratic National Convention Delegate Barbie, 2000, Mattel
MNP $25 MIP $150

Designer Spotlight by Heather Fonesca, 2004, Mattel
MNP $20 MIP $40

Designer Spotlight, Katiana Jimenez, 2003, Mattel, Model No. B0836
MNP $20 MIP $35

Diane Von Furstenburg Barbie, 2006, Mattel
MNP n/a MIP $100

Diva Collection, All that Glitters, 2002, Mattel, Model No. 55426
MNP $20 MIP $40

Diva Collection, Gone Platinum (white or black), 2002, Mattel, Model No. 52739/53868
MNP $20 MIP $40

(Mattel Photo)

Diva Collection, Red Hot (white or black), 2003, Mattel, Model No. 56707/56708
MNP $20 MIP $40

Doone & Bourke #2, 2007, Mattel
MNP n/a MIP $35

Dooney & Bourke Barbie, 2006, Mattel
MNP n/a MIP $35

Dream Seasons I Dream of Autumn, 2006, Mattel, Toys R Us Exclusive
MNP n/a MIP $30

Dream Seasons I Dream of Spring, 2006, Mattel, Toys R Us Exclusive
MNP n/a MIP $30

Dream Seasons I Dream of Summer, 2006, Mattel, Toys R Us Exclusive
MNP n/a MIP $30

Dream Seasons I Dream of Winter, 2006, Mattel, Toys R Us Exclusive
MNP n/a MIP $30

Drug/Grocery Store Halloween Hip Barbie, 2006, Mattel
MNP n/a MIP $20

Drugstore/Grocery Halloween Charm Barbie, African-American, 2007, Mattel
MNP n/a MIP $15

Drugstore/Grocery Halloween Charm Barbie, Blonde, 2007, Mattel
MNP n/a MIP $15

Duchess Emma Barbie, 2004, Mattel
MNP $10 MIP $80

Easter Magic Barbie, 2003, Mattel
MNP $8 MIP $15

Empress Sissy, Barbie as, 1996, Mattel, Model No. 15846
MNP $35 MIP $60

Enchanted Mermaid, 2002, Mattel, Model No. 53978
MNP $100 MIP $250

Enchanted Seasons #1 Snow Princess, 1994, Mattel, Model No. 11875
MNP $30 MIP $75

Enchanted Seasons #2 Spring Bouquet, 1995, Mattel, Model No. 12989
MNP $30 MIP $50

Enchanted Seasons #3 Autumn Glory, 1996, Mattel, Model No. 15204
MNP $30 MIP $50

Enchanted Seasons #4 Summer Splendor, 1997, Mattel, Model No. 15683
MNP $30 **MIP** $50

Enchanted World of Fairies, Fairy of the Forest, 2000, Mattel, Model No. 25639
MNP $25 **MIP** $45

Enchanted World of Fairies, Fairy of the Garden, 2001, Mattel
MNP $15 **MIP** $40

Escada Barbie, 1996, Mattel, Model No. 15948
MNP $40 **MIP** $65

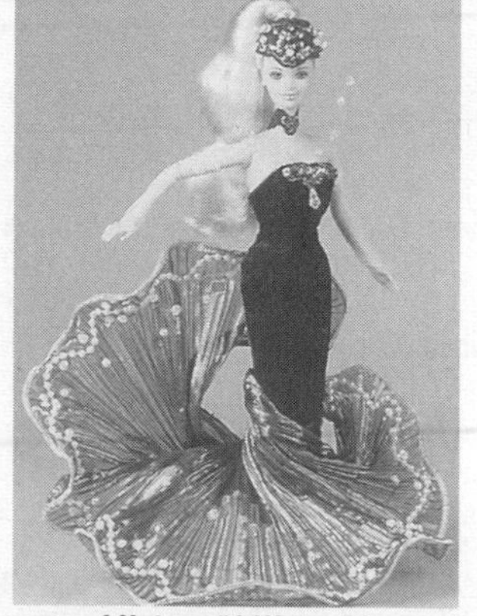

Essence of Nature #1 Water Rhapsody, 1998, Mattel, Model No. 19847
MNP $40 **MIP** $90

Essence of Nature #2 Whispering Wind, 1999, Mattel, Model No. 22834
MNP $40 **MIP** $80

Essence of Nature #3 Dancing Fire, 2000, Mattel, Model No. 26327
MNP $35 **MIP** $80

Ethereal Princess Barbie, 2006, Mattel
MNP n/a **MIP** $40

Fairytopia Elina Barbie, 2006, Mattel, FAO Schwarz Exclusive
MNP n/a **MIPMNP** n/a

(Mattel Photo)

FAO Schwarz American Beauty, Barbie as George Washington, 1996, Mattel, Model No. 17557
MNP $35 **MIP** $65

(Mattel Photo)

FAO Schwarz American Beauty, Statue of Liberty, 1996, Mattel, Model No. 14684
MNP $40 **MIP** $65

FAO Schwarz Barbie & Ken Tango Gift Set, 2002, Mattel
MNP $40 **MIP** $85

FAO Schwarz Barbie Fashion Model Collection Chantaine, 2003, Mattel, LE 600 pcs
MNP $400 **MIP** $600

FAO Schwarz Bob Mackie Lady Liberty, 2000, Mattel, limited to 15,000
MNP $75 **MIP** $125

FAO Schwarz Bob Mackie Le Papillon, 1999, Mattel, Model No. 23276
MNP $70 **MIP** $175

FAO Schwarz Circus Star Barbie, 1995, Mattel, Model No. 13257
MNP $35 **MIP** $70

FAO Schwarz City Seasons Summer in San Francisco, blond, 1998, Mattel, Model No. 19363
MNP $40 **MIP** $95

FAO Schwarz City Seasons Summer in San Francisco, red hair, Mattel
MNP $200 **MIP** $750

FAO Schwarz Exclusive Joyeux Barbie, 2004, Mattel, LE redheaded
MNP $200 **MIP** $300

FAO Schwarz Fashion Model Fashion Designer Barbie, 2002, Mattel
MNP $50 **MIP** $85

FAO Schwarz Fashion Model Fashion Editor, 2000, Mattel
MNP $50 **MIP** $90

FAO Schwarz Floral Signature #1 Antique Rose, 1996, Mattel, limited to 10,000, Model No. 15814
MNP $50 **MIP** $150

FAO Schwarz Floral Signature #2 Lily Barbie, 1997, Mattel, limited to 10,000, Model No. 17556
MNP $50 **MIP** $145

FAO Schwarz Golden Greetings Barbie, 1989, Mattel, Model No. 7734
MNP $50 **MIP** $95

FAO Schwarz Golden Hollywood Barbie, white or black, 1999, Mattel
MNP $35 **MIP** $60

FAO Schwarz Jeweled Splendor (125th Anniversary), 1995, Mattel, Model No. 14061
MNP $75 **MIP** $125

FAO Schwarz Madison Ave. Barbie, 1992, Mattel, Model No. 1539
MNP $75 **MIP** $100

FAO Schwarz Mann's Chinese Theatre Barbie, white or black, 2000, Mattel, Model No. 24636/24998
MNP $35 **MIP** $50

FAO Schwarz Night Sensation, 1991, Mattel, Model No. 2921
MNP $25 **MIP** $50

FAO Schwarz Phantom of the Opera Gift Set, 1998, Mattel, Model No. 20377
MNP $50 **MIP** $85

FAO Schwarz Rockettes Barbie, 1993, Mattel, Model No. 2017
MNP $50 **MIP** $85

FAO Schwarz Shopping Spree, 1994, Mattel, Model No. 12749
MNP $5 **MIP** $15

FAO Schwarz Silver Screen Barbie, 1994, Mattel, Model No. 11652
MNP $65 **MIP** $100

FAO Schwarz Winter Fantasy, 1990, Mattel, Model No. 5946
MNP $45 **MIP** $70

FAO Schwarz, Barbie at FAO, 1997, Mattel, Model No. 17298
MNP $12 **MIP** $25

Fashion Model 45th Anniversary Barbie & Ken Giftset, 2004, Mattel
MNP $40 **MIP** $95

Fashion Model A Model Life Gift Set, 2003, Mattel
MNP $50 **MIP** $85

Fashion Model Capucine Barbie, 2003, Mattel
MNP $50 **MIP** $95

Fashion Model Chinoiserie Red Midnight, Fan Club Exclusive, 2004, Mattel
MNP $10 **MIP** $225

Fashion Model Chinoiserie Red Moon, 2004, Mattel
MNP $10 **MIP** $25

Fashion Model Collection 45th Anniversary Barbie, African American, 2004, Mattel
MNP $10 MIP $50

Fashion Model Collection 45th Anniversary Barbie, Blonde, 2004, Mattel
MNP $10 MIP $50

Fashion Model Collection A Day at the Races Barbie, 2006, Mattel
MNP n/a MIP $60

Fashion Model Collection Capucine, 2003, Mattel, Model No. B0146
MNP $75 MIP $150

Fashion Model Collection Chinoiserie Red Sunset, Barbie Bazaar Exclusive, 2004, Mattel
MNP $10 MIP $150

Fashion Model Collection Continental Holiday Gift Set, 2002, Mattel, Model No. 55497
MNP $50 MIP $100

Fashion Model Collection Dahlia, 2006, Mattel, U.S. Dealers Exclusive
MNP n/a MIP $500

Fashion Model Collection Delphine Barbie, 2000, Mattel, Model No. 26929
MNP $35 MIP $65

Fashion Model Collection Dusk to Dawn, 2001, Mattel, Model No. 29654
MNP $50 MIP $125

Fashion Model Collection High Stepping Fashion, 2006, Mattel
MNP n/a MIP $40

Fashion Model Collection High Tea and Savories Barbie Giftset, 2006, Mattel
MNP n/a MIP $90

Fashion Model Collection Highland Fling, 2006, Mattel
MNP n/a MIP $40

Fashion Model Collection In The Pink, 2001, Mattel, Model No. 27683
MNP $75 MIP $200

Fashion Model Collection Ken Fashion Insider Gift Set, 2003, Mattel
MNP $50 MIP $95

Fashion Model Collection Lady of the Manor Barbie, 2006, Mattel
MNP n/a MIP $150

Fashion Model Collection Lingerie #1, blond, 2000, Mattel, Model No. 26930
MNP $60 MIP $175

Fashion Model Collection Lingerie #2, brunette, 2000, Mattel, Model No. 26931
MNP $60 MIP $175

Fashion Model Collection Lingerie #3, black hair, 2001, Mattel, Model No. 29651
MNP $40 MIP $150

Fashion Model Collection Lingerie #4, 2002, Mattel, Model No. 55498
MNP $20 MIP $50

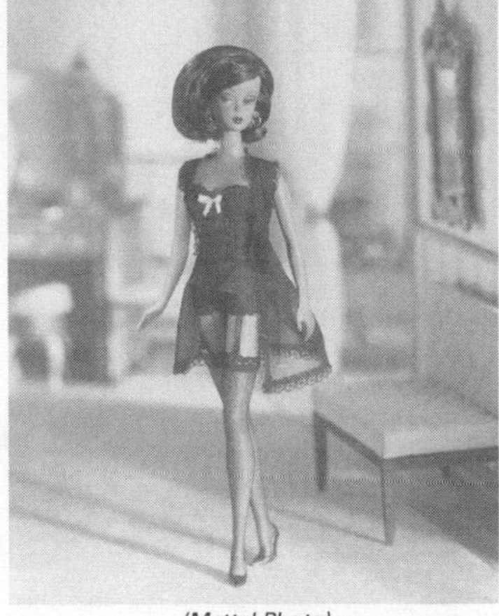

(Mattel Photo)

Fashion Model Collection Lingerie #5 (black), 2002, Mattel, Model No. 56120
MNP $20 MIP $50

Fashion Model Collection Lingerie #6, redhead, 2003, Mattel, Model No. 56948
MNP $25 MIP $50

Fashion Model Collection Lisette, 2001, Mattel, Model No. 29650
MNP $45 MIP $70

Fashion Model Collection Maria Therese (bride), 2002, Mattel, Model No. 55496
MNP $50 MIP $125

Fashion Model Collection Midnight Mischief Fashion, 2003, Mattel
MNP $15 MIP $50

Fashion Model Collection New England Escape Giftset, 2004, Mattel, fashion
MNP $10 MIP $60

Fashion Model Collection Pajama #2 Suite Retreat, 2005, Mattel
MNP $15 MIP $40

Fashion Model Collection Pretty Pleats Barbie, 2006, Mattel
MNP n/a MIP $80

Fashion Model Collection Provencale, 2002, Mattel, Model No. 50829
MNP $50 MIP $120

Fashion Model Collection Sunday Best Barbie, African American, 2003, Mattel
MNP $30 MIP $60

Fashion Model Collection The French Maid, 2006, Mattel, Canadian Exclusive
MNP n/a MIP $75

Fashion Model Collection The Nurse Barbie, 2006, Mattel, European/Australian Exclusive
MNP n/a MIP $200

Fashion Model Collection The Nurse Barbie, African-American, 2006, Mattel, Fan Club Exclusive
MNP n/a MIP $250

Fashion Model Collection The Spa Getaway Gift Set, 2004, Mattel
MNP $10 MIP $125

Fashion Model Collection The Stewardess, 2006, Mattel, Japanese Exclusive
MNP n/a MIP $175

Fashion Model Collection The Teacher, 2006, Mattel, Singapore Exclusive
MNP n/a MIP $90

Fashion Model Collection The Waitress, 2006, Mattel, U.S. Exclusive
MNP n/a MIP $60

Fashion Model Collection Trend Setter Barbie, 2004, Mattel
MNP $10 MIP $65

Fashion Model Collection True Brit Accessories, 2006, Mattel
MNP n/a MIP $40

Fashion Model Collection Tweed Indeed Barbie, 2006, Mattel
MNP n/a MIP $60

Fashion Model Collection Violette, 2006, Mattel, U.S. Dealers Exclusive
MNP n/a MIP $500

Fashion Model Collection, Hollywood Bound, 2007, Mattel, Barbie Fan Club exclusive
MNP n/a MIP $70

Fashion Model Collection, Hollywood Hostess, 2007, Mattel
MNP n/a MIP $100

Fashion Model Collection, Honey in Hollywood Accessory Pack, 2007, Mattel
MNP n/a MIP $45

Fashion Model Collection, Movie Mixer, 2007, Mattel
MNP n/a MIP $70

Fashion Model Collection, Red Hot Reviews, 2007, Mattel
MNP n/a MIP $60

Fashion Model Collection, The Ingenue, 2007, Mattel
MNP n/a MIP $40

Fashion Model Collection, The Interview, 2007, Mattel
MNP n/a MIP $70

Fashion Model Collection, The Secretary, 2007, Mattel, International exclusive
MNP n/a MIP $70

Fashion Model Collection, The Siren, 2007, Mattel
MNP n/a MIP $90

Fashion Model Collection, The Soiree, 2007, Mattel
MNP n/a MIP $140

Fashion Model Collection, The Usherette, 2007, Mattel, Dealer's exclusive
MNP n/a MIP $70

Fashion Queen Barbie & Her Friends, 1964, Mattel, Model No. 863
MNP $1000 MIP $2400

Fashion Queen Barbie & Ken Trousseau Gift Set, 1964, Mattel, Model No. 864
MNP $1200 MIP $2800

Fashion Savvy #1 Tangerine Twist, 1997, Mattel, Model No. 17860
MNP $14 MIP $45

Fashion Savvy #2 Uptown Chic, 1998, Mattel, Model No. 19632
MNP $20 MIP $45

Ferrari Barbie #1, Scuderia, racing outfit, 2001, Mattel, Model No. 25636
MNP $30 MIP $65

Ferrari Barbie #2, red dress, 2001, Mattel, Model No. 29608
MNP $15 MIP $45

Festivals of the World Carnaval Barbie, 2006, Mattel
MNP n/a MIP $20

Festivals of the World Chinese New Year Barbie, 2006, Mattel
MNP n/a MIP $20

Festivals of the World Diwali Barbie, 2006, Mattel
MNP n/a MIP $40

Festivals of the World Kwanzaa Barbie, 2006, Mattel
MNP n/a MIP $20

Festivals of the World Oktoberfest Barbie, 2006, Mattel
MNP n/a MIP $20

Festivals of the World, Cinco de Mayo, 2007, Mattel
MNP n/a MIP $25

Festivals of the World, Irish Dance, 2007, Mattel
MNP n/a MIP $25

Festive Season, 1998, Mattel
MNP $5 MIP $15

Fire and Ice (white or black), 2002, Mattel, Model No. 53511/53863
MNP $20 MIP $40

Flowers in Fashion Orchid Barbie, 2001, Mattel, Model No. 50319
MNP $25 MIP $65

Flowers in Fashion Rose Barbie, 2001, Mattel
MNP $25 MIP $65

Francie Rise n' Shine Gift Set, 1971, Mattel, Model No. 1194
MNP $600 MIP $1200

Francie Swingin' Separates Gift Set, 1966, Mattel, Model No. 1042
MNP $700 MIP $1500

Fun to Dress Barbie Gift Set, 1993, Mattel, Model No. 3826
MNP $5 MIP $10

Gap Barbie and Kelly Gift Set, 1997, Mattel, Model No. 18547
MNP $15 MIP $40

Gap Barbie and Kelly Gift Set, black, 1997, Mattel, Model No. 18548
MNP $15 MIP $40

Gap Barbie, black, 1996, Mattel, Model No. 16450
MNP $20 MIP $50

Gap Barbie, white, 1996, Mattel, Model No. 16449
MNP $30 MIP $50

Garden of Flowers Rose Barbie, 1999, Mattel, Model No. 22237
MNP $25 MIP $50

General Mills Winter Dazzle, black, 1997, Mattel
MNP $5 MIP $20

General Mills Winter Dazzle, white, 1997, Mattel, Model No. 18456
MNP $5 MIP $20

Givenchy Barbie, 2000, Mattel, Model No. 24635
MNP $40 MIP $80

Go For Red American Heart Association, 2007, Mattel
MNP n/a MIP $25

Go For Red American Heart Association, African-American, 2007, Mattel
MNP n/a MIP $25

Goddess of Beauty Barbie, 2000, Mattel, Model No. 27286
MNP $25 MIP $65

Goddess of Spring Barbie, 2000, Mattel, Model No. 28112
MNP $25 MIP $65

Goddess of Wisdom Barbie, 2001, Mattel
MNP $25 MIP $65

Golden Angel Barbie, 2006, Mattel
MNP n/a MIP $40

Graduation Barbie Class of 1996, 1996, Mattel
MNP $5 MIP $15

Graduation Barbie Class of 1997, 1997, Mattel
MNP $5 MIP $10

Graduation Barbie Class of 1998, white or black, 1998, Mattel
MNP $5 MIP $10

Graduation Barbie Class of 2000, black box, 2000, Mattel
MNP $5 MIP $15

Graduation Barbie Class of 2000, blue box, 2000, Mattel
MNP $5 MIP $15

Grand Entrance Barbie (white or black), 2002, Mattel, Model No. 53841/53842
MNP $20 MIP $50

Grand Entrance Barbie, white or black, 2001, Mattel
MNP $25 MIP $65

Grand Ole Opry #1 Country Rose Barbie, 1997, Mattel, Model No. 17782
MNP $40 MIP $80

Grand Ole Opry #2 Rising Star Barbie, 1998, Mattel, Model No. 17864
MNP $50 MIP $100

Grand Ole Opry Barbie and Kenny Country Duet, 1999, Mattel, Model No. 23498
MNP $55 MIP $75

Grease Barbie 2 as Sandy Olsson, 2004, Mattel
MNP $10 MIP $30

Grease Barbie as Sandy Olsson, 2003, Mattel
MNP $20 MIP $40

Great Eras #01, Gibson Girl, 1993, Mattel, Model No. 3702
MNP $25 MIP $75

Great Eras #02, Flapper, 1993, Mattel, Model No. 4063
MNP $25 MIP $60

(Mattel Photo)

Great Eras #03, Egyptian Queen, 1994, Mattel, Model No. 11397
MNP $20 MIP $55

Great Eras #04, Southern Belle, 1994, Mattel, Model No. 11478
MNP $20 MIP $55

Great Eras #05, Medieval Lady, 1995, Mattel, Model No. 12791
MNP $25 MIP $50

Great Eras #06, Elizabethan Queen, 1995, Mattel, Model No. 12792
MNP $25 MIP $50

Great Eras #07, Grecian Goddess, 1996, Mattel, Model No. 15005
MNP $35 MIP $50

Great Eras #08, Victorian Lady, 1996, Mattel, Model No. 14900
MNP $35 MIP $50

Great Eras #09, French Lady, 1997, Mattel, Model No. 16707
MNP $35 MIP $50

Great Eras #10, Chinese Empress, 1997, Mattel, Model No. 16708
MNP $35 MIP $50

Great Fashions of the 20th Century #1, Promenade in the Park, 1998, Mattel, 1910s, Model No. 18630
MNP $20 MIP $50

Great Fashions of the 20th Century #2, Dance 'til Dawn, 1998, Mattel, 1920s, Model No. 19631
MNP $30 MIP $40

Great Fashions of the 20th Century #3, Steppin Out Barbie, 1999, Mattel, 1930s, Model No. 21531
MNP $30 MIP $40

Great Fashions of the 20th Century #4, Fabulous Forties, 2000, Mattel, 1940s, Model No. 22162
MNP $25 MIP $40

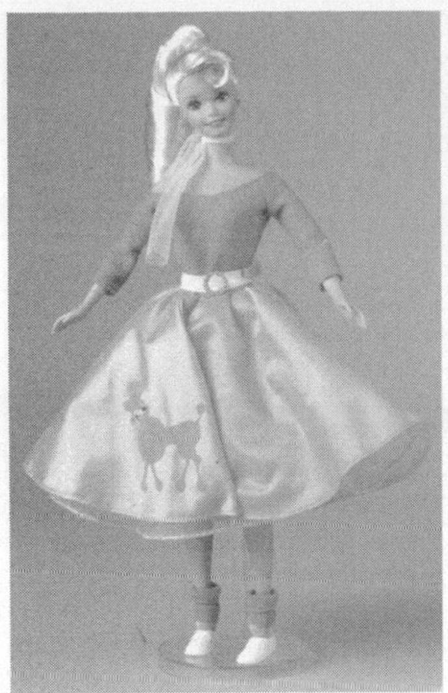

Great Fashions of the 20th Century #5, Nifty Fifties, 2000, Mattel, 1950s, Model No. 27675
MNP $25 **MIP** $50

Great Fashions of the 20th Century #6, Groovy Sixties, 2000, Mattel, 1960s, Model No. 27676
MNP $25 **MIP** $50

Great Fashions of the 20th Century #7, Peace & Love 70s Barbie, 2000, Mattel, 1970s, Model No. 27677
MNP $15 **MIP** $40

Groliers Book Club The Front Window Barbie, 2000, Mattel, Model No. 27968
MNP $10 **MIP** $35

Hallmark Fair Valentine Barbie, 1998, Mattel
MNP $20 **MIP** $40

Hallmark Holiday Memories Barbie, 1995, Mattel, Model No. 14108
MNP $15 **MIP** $20

Hallmark Holiday Sensation Barbie, 1999, Mattel, Model No. 19792
MNP $15 **MIP** $20

Hallmark Holiday Traditions Barbie, 1997, Mattel, Model No. 17094
MNP $15 **MIP** $20

Hallmark Holiday Voyage Barbie, 1998, Mattel
MNP $15 **MIP** $20

Hallmark Sentimental Valentine Barbie, 1997, Mattel
MNP $15 **MIP** $20

Hallmark Sweet Valentine Barbie, 1996, Mattel, Model No. 14880
MNP $15 **MIP** $20

Hallmark Victorian Elegance Barbie, 1994, Mattel, Model No. 12579
MNP $20 **MIP** $40

Hallmark Yuletide Romance Barbie, 1996, Mattel, Model No. 15621
MNP $15 **MIP** $20

Halloween Enchantress Barbie, 2004, Mattel
MNP $10 **MIP** $20

Halloween Glow Barbie, White or African American, 2002, Mattel
MNP $10 **MIP** $25

Halloween Maskerade Barbie, 2004, Mattel
MNP $10 **MIP** $20

Hanae Mori Barbie, 2000, Mattel
MNP $50 **MIP** $75

Happy Birthday Barbie Gift Set, 1985, Mattel
MNP $20 **MIP** $40

Happy Holiday 2005 Barbie, 2005, Mattel
MNP n/a **MIP** $40

Happy Holiday 2005 Barbie, African-American, 2005, Mattel
MNP n/a **MIP** $40

Happy Holiday 2006 Barbie, 2006, Mattel
MNP n/a **MIP** $40

Happy Holiday 2006 Barbie, African-American, 2006, Mattel
MNP n/a **MIP** $40

Happy Holidays 1988, 1988, Mattel, Model No. 1703
MNP $75 **MIP** $350

Happy Holidays 1989, 1989, Mattel, Model No. 3253
MNP $50 **MIP** $125

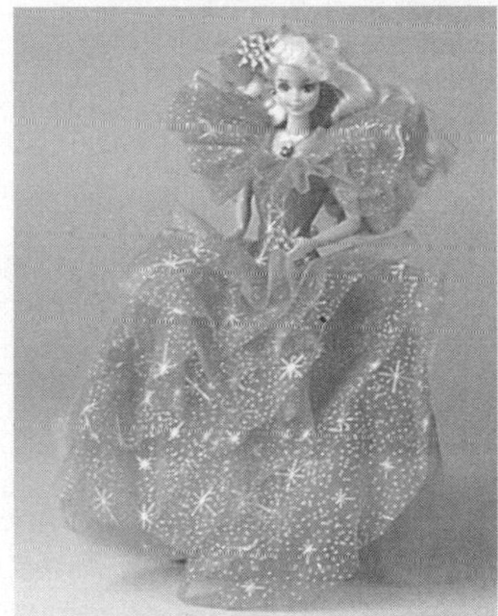

Happy Holidays 1990, 1990, Mattel, Model No. 4098
MNP $25 **MIP** $70

Happy Holidays 1990, black, 1990, Mattel, Model No. 4543
MNP $20 **MIP** $55

Happy Holidays 1991, 1991, Mattel, Model No. 1871
MNP $40 **MIP** $70

Happy Holidays 1991, black, 1991, Mattel, Model No. 2696
MNP $40 **MIP** $60

Happy Holidays 1992, 1992, Mattel, Model No. 1429
MNP $30 **MIP** $50

Happy Holidays 1992, black, 1992, Mattel, Model No. 2396
MNP $30 **MIP** $50

Happy Holidays 1993, 1993, Mattel, Model No. 10824
MNP $30 **MIP** $60

Happy Holidays 1993, black, 1993, Mattel, Model No. 10911
MNP $30 **MIP** $40

Happy Holidays 1994, 1994, Mattel, Model No. 12155
MNP $30 **MIP** $65

Happy Holidays 1994, black, 1994, Mattel, Model No. 12156
MNP $30 **MIP** $45

Happy Holidays 1995, 1995, Mattel, Model No. 14123
MNP $20 **MIP** $40

Happy Holidays 1995, black, 1995, Mattel, Model No. 14124
MNP $15 **MIP** $30

Happy Holidays 1996, white or black, 1996, Mattel, Model No. 15646
MNP $15 **MIP** $30

Happy Holidays 1997, 1997, Mattel, Model No. 17832
MNP $5 **MIP** $25

Happy Holidays 1997, black, 1997, Mattel, Model No. 17833
MNP $5 **MIP** $20

Happy Holidays 1998, white or black, 1998, Mattel, Model No. 20200/20201
MNP $10 **MIP** $15

Hard Rock Café #4, Blonde, 2007, Mattel
MNP n/a **MIP** $35

Hard Rock Café #4, Brunette, 2007, Mattel, Hard Rock exclusive
MNP n/a **MIP** $50

Hard Rock Café Barbie, 2003, Mattel
MNP $25 **MIP** $125

Hard Rock Café Barbie #3, 2006, Mattel
MNP n/a **MIP** $75

Hard Rock Café Barbie 2, 2004, Mattel
MNP $25 **MIP** $75

Harrods/Hamleys West End Barbie, 1996, Mattel, Model No. 17590
MNP $20 **MIP** $40

Harvey Nichols Special Edition (limited to 250), 1995, Mattel, Model No. 0175
MNP $500 **MIP** $700

Hello Kitty Barbie, 2007, Mattel
MNP n/a **MIP** $35

Hills Blue Elegance Barbie, 1992, Mattel, Model No. 1879
MNP $12 **MIP** $25

Hills Evening Sparkle, 1990, Mattel, Model No. 3274
MNP $10 **MIP** $20

Hills Moonlight Rose, 1991, Mattel, Model No. 3549
MNP $7 **MIP** $20

Hills Party Lace Barbie, 1989, Mattel, Model No. 4843
MNP $15 **MIP** $20

Hills Polly Pocket Barbie, 1994, Mattel, Model No. 12412
MNP $12 **MIP** $20

Hills Sea Pearl Mermaid Barbie, 1995, Mattel, Model No. 13940
MNP $8 **MIP** $20

Hills Sidewalk Chalk Barbie, 1998, Mattel, Model No. 19784
MNP $10 **MIP** $20

Hills Teddy Fun Barbie, 1996, Mattel, Model No. 15684
MNP $10 **MIP** $20

Holiday Angel #1, black, 2000, Mattel, Model No. 28080
MNP $20 **MIP** $50

Holiday Angel #1, white, 2000, Mattel, Model No. 26914
MNP $20 **MIP** $50

Holiday Angel #2, black, 2001, Mattel, Model No. 29770
MNP $15 **MIP** $45

Holiday Angel #2, white, 2001, Mattel, Model No. 29769
MNP $15 **MIP** $45

Holiday Barbie 2007, 2007, Mattel
MNP n/a **MIP** $50

Holiday Barbie 2007, African-American, 2007, Mattel
MNP n/a **MIP** $50

Holiday Celebration Barbie 2002, 2002, Mattel
MNP $30 **MIP** $50

Holiday Celebration Barbie 2004, 2004, Mattel, Blonde or African American
MNP $10 **MIP** $40

Holiday Dreams Barbie, 1994, Mattel, Model No. 12192
MNP $10 **MIP** $20

Holiday Hostess Barbie, 1993, Mattel, Model No. 10280
MNP $20 **MIP** $30

Holiday Season, 1996, Mattel, Model No. 15581
MNP $5 **MIP** $10

Holiday Singing Sisters Gift Set, 2000, Mattel
MNP $15 **MIP** $40

Holiday Surprise Barbie, white or black, 2000, Mattel
MNP $5 **MIP** $10

Holiday Treats Barbie, 1997, Mattel
MNP $5 **MIP** $10

Hollywood Hair Deluxe Gift Set, 1993, Mattel, Model No. 10928
MNP $15 **MIP** $35

Hollywood Legends Dorothy (Wizard of Oz), 1995, Mattel, Model No. 12701
MNP $20 **MIP** $60

Hollywood Legends Eliza Doolittle (My Fair Lady), green coat, 1996, Mattel, Model No. 15498
MNP $30 **MIP** $25

Hollywood Legends Eliza Doolittle (My Fair Lady), lace ball gown, 1996, Mattel, Model No. 15500
MNP $30 **MIP** $65

Hollywood Legends Eliza Doolittle (My Fair Lady), pink, 1996, Mattel, Model No. 15501
MNP $30 **MIP** $50

Hollywood Legends Eliza Doolittle (My Fair Lady), white lace gown w/parasol, 1996, Mattel, Model No. 15497
MNP $30 **MIP** $75

Hollywood Legends Glinda (Wizard of Oz), 1996, Mattel, Model No. 14901
MNP $35 **MIP** $50

Hollywood Legends Ken as Cowardly Lion (Wizard of Oz), 1996, Mattel, Model No. 16573
MNP $35 **MIP** $45

Hollywood Legends Ken as Henry Higgins (My Fair Lady), 1996, Mattel, Model No. 15499
MNP $25 **MIP** $30

Hollywood Legends Ken as Rhett Butler, 1994, Mattel, Gone With the Wind, Model No. 12741
MNP $25 **MIP** $30

Hollywood Legends Ken as Scarecrow (Wizard of Oz), 1996, Mattel, Model No. 16497
MNP $35 **MIP** $40

Hollywood Legends Ken as Tin Man (Wizard of Oz), 1996, Mattel, Model No. 14902
MNP $15 **MIP** $25

Hollywood Legends Maria (Sound of Music), 1995, Mattel, Model No. 13676
MNP $20 **MIP** $50

Hollywood Legends Marilyn Monroe, pink, 1997, Mattel, Gentlemen Prefer Blondes, Model No. 17451
MNP $20 **MIP** $45

Hollywood Legends Marilyn Monroe, red, 1997, Mattel, Gentlemen Prefer Blondes, Model No. 17452
MNP $20 **MIP** $45

Hollywood Legends Marilyn Monroe, white, 1997, Mattel, Seven Year Itch, Model No. 17155
MNP $20 **MIP** $45

Hollywood Legends Scarlett O'Hara, black/white dress, 1993, Mattel, Gone With the Wind, Model No. 13254
MNP $25 **MIP** $35

Hollywood Legends Scarlett O'Hara, green velvet curtain, 1994, Mattel, Gone With the Wind, Model No. 12045
MNP $25 **MIP** $50

Hollywood Legends Scarlett O'Hara, green/white silk dress, 1995, Mattel, Gone With the Wind, Model No. 12997
MNP $25 **MIP** $30

Hollywood Legends Scarlett O'Hara, red velvet dress, 1994, Mattel, Gone With the Wind, Model No. 12815
MNP $25 **MIP** $35

Hollywood Movie Star, Between Takes, 2000, Mattel, Model No. 27684
MNP $15 **MIP** $25

Hollywood Movie Star, By the Pool, 2000, Mattel, Model No. 27684
MNP $15 **MIP** $25

Hollywood Movie Star, Day in the Sun, 2000, Mattel, Model No. 2000
MNP $15 **MIP** $25

Hollywood Movie Star, Hollywood Cast Party, 2001, Mattel, Model No. 50825
MNP $15 **MIP** $25

Hollywood Movie Star, Hollywood Premiere, 2000, Mattel, Model No. 26914
MNP $15 **MIP** $25

Hollywood Movie Star, Publicity Tour, 2001, Mattel
MNP $15 **MIP** $25

Home Shopping Club Evening Flame, 1991, Mattel, Model No. 1865
MNP $70 **MIP** $125

Home Shopping Club Golden Allure Barbie, 1999, Mattel
MNP $5 **MIP** $30

Home Shopping Club Premiere Night, 1999, Mattel
MNP $5 **MIP** $30

I Dream of Jeannie Barbie, 2001, Mattel
MNP $15 **MIP** $45

I Love Lucy Sales Resistance, 2004, Mattel
MNP $10 **MIP** $35

Japanese Living Eli, 1970, Mattel, Foreign
MNP $700 **MIP** $1400

JCPenney Enchanted Evening, 1991, Mattel, Model No. 2702
MNP $20 **MIP** $40

JCPenney Evening Elegance, 1990, Mattel, Model No. 7057
MNP $20 **MIP** $40

JCPenney Evening Enchantment, 1998, Mattel, Model No. 19783
MNP $25 **MIP** $40

JCPenney Evening Majesty, 1997, Mattel, Model No. 17235
MNP $10 **MIP** $25

JCPenney Evening Sensation, 1992, Mattel, Model No. 1278
MNP $12 MIP $35

JCPenney Golden Winter, 1993, Mattel, Model No. 10684
MNP $12 MIP $35

JCPenney Night Dazzle, 1994, Mattel, Model No. 12191
MNP $15 MIP $35

JCPenney Original Arizona Jean Co. Barbie #1, 1996, Mattel, Model No. 15441
MNP $12 MIP $25

JCPenney Original Arizona Jean Co. Barbie #2, 1997, Mattel, Model No. 18020
MNP $12 MIP $25

JCPenney Original Arizona Jean Co. Barbie #3, 1998, Mattel, Model No. 19873
MNP $12 MIP $25

JCPenney Royal Enchantment, 1995, Mattel, Model No. 14010
MNP $25 MIP $35

JCPenney Winter Renaissance, 1996, Mattel, Model No. 15570
MNP $10 MIP $25

JCPenney/Sears Evening Recital Barbie, Stacie, Kelly and Tommy, 2000, Mattel, Model No. 27954
MNP $15 MIP $42

Jubilee Series, Crystal Jubilee, limited to 20,000, 1999, Mattel, Model No. 21923
MNP $150 MIP $275

Jubilee Series, Gold Jubilee, limited to 5,000, 1994, Mattel, Model No. 12009
MNP $300 MIP $500

Jubilee Series, Pink Jubilee, limited to 1,200, 1989, Mattel, Model No. 3756
MNP $800 MIP $2000

Jude Deveraux, The Raider, Barbie and Ken Gift Set, 2003, Mattel
MNP $40 MIP $80

Juicy Couture Giftset, 2004, Mattel
MNP $20 MIP $60

Julia Simply Wow Gift Set, 1969, Mattel
MNP $400 MIP $1500

Just for You Barbie, 2003, Mattel, Model No. B0151
MNP $10 MIP $35

Kate Spade Barbie, 2004, Mattel
MNP $20 MIP $80

K-B Fantasy Ball Barbie, 1997, Mattel, Model No. 18594
MNP $10 MIP $20

K-B Fashion Avenue Barbie, 1998, Mattel, Model No. 20782
MNP $8 MIP $15

K-B Glamour Barbie, black, 1997, Mattel
MNP $10 MIP $20

K-B Starlight Carousel Barbie, 1998, Mattel, Model No. 19708
MNP $10 MIP $20

Keepsake Treasures, Barbie and Curious George, 2001, Mattel
MNP $15 MIP $30

Keepsake Treasures, Barbie and the Tale of Peter Rabbit, 1998, Mattel, Model No. 19360
MNP $15 MIP $40

Keepsake Treasures, Peter Rabbit 100th Anniversary Barbie, 2002, Mattel, Model No. 53872
MNP $20 MIP $40

Kelly & Tommy as Alice and the Mad Hatter, 2003, Mattel
MNP $10 MIP $20

Kelly and Friends Wizard of Oz Gift Set, 2003, Mattel
MNP $15 MIP $30

Kelly as the Witches from Wizard of Oz, 2004, Mattel
MNP $10 MIP $30

Kelly Nostalgic Favorites Gift Set, 2003, Mattel
MNP $15 MIP $30

Kelly Princess of the World Collction, Dutch, Scottish, Spanish, 2005, Mattel
MNP $10 MIP $20

Ken as Legolas in the Lord of the Rings: Fellowship of the Ring, 2004, Mattel
MNP $10 MIP $25

Kimora Lee Simmons, 2007, Mattel, (Baby Phat)
MNP n/a MIP $60

Kissing Barbie Gift Set, 1978, Mattel, Model No. 2977
MNP $25 MIP $65

Kmart March of Dimes Walk America Barbie & Kelly Gift Set, 1999, Mattel, Model No. 20843
MNP $15 MIP $25

Kmart March of Dimes Walk America Barbie, black or white, 1998, Mattel, Model No. 18506/18507
MNP $10 MIP $24

Kmart Peach Pretty Barbie, 1989, Mattel, Model No. 4870
MNP $10 MIP $30

Kmart Pretty in Purple, black, 1992, Mattel, Model No. 3121
MNP $12 MIP $25

Kmart Pretty in Purple, white, 1992, Mattel, Model No. 3117
MNP $12 MIP $25

Kmart Route 66 Barbecue Bash, 2000, Mattel
MNP $8 MIP $25

Kmart Very Berry Barbie, white or black, 2000, Mattel
MNP $5 MIP $10

Kool-Aid Barbie, 1996, Mattel
MNP $15 MIP $40

Kool-Aid Wacky Warehouse Barbie I, 1993, Mattel, Model No. 10309
MNP $25 MIP $60

Kool-Aid Wacky Warehouse Barbie II, 1994, Mattel, Model No. 11763
MNP $25 MIP $50

Kraft Treasures Barbie, 1992, Mattel
MNP $30 MIP $55

L.E. Festival Holiday Barbie (540 made), 1994, Mattel
MNP $500 MIP $900

Lady Camille Barbie, 2003, Mattel
MNP $45 MIP $80

Life Ball Barbie #1, Vivienne Westwood, 1998, Mattel
MNP $200 MIP $400

Life Ball Barbie #2, Christian LaCroix, 1999, Mattel
MNP $200 MIP $400

Little Debbie #1, 1993, Mattel, Model No. 10123
MNP $25 MIP $40

Little Debbie #2, 1996, Mattel, Model No. 14616
MNP $15 MIP $25

Little Debbie #3, 1998, Mattel, Model No. 16352
MNP $15 MIP $20

Little Debbie #4, 1999, Mattel, Model No. 24977
MNP $10 MIP $20

Living Barbie Action Accents Gift Set, 1970, Mattel, Model No. 1585
MNP $500 MIP $1500

Lounge Kitty, 2004, Mattel, Black or White
MNP $10 MIP $40

Lounge Kitty, Latina, 2004, Mattel
MNP $10 MIP $60

Loving You Barbie Gift Set, 1983, Mattel, Model No. 7583
MNP $45 MIP $100

M.A.C. Barbie, 2007, Mattel, M.A.C. Cosmetics exclusive
MNP n/a MIP $100

Macy's Anne Klein Barbie, 1997, Mattel, Model No. 17603
MNP $25 MIP $35

Macy's City Shopper, Nicole Miller, 1996, Mattel, Model No. 16289
MNP $25 MIP $30

Mademoiselle Isabelle Barbie, 2002, Mattel
MNP $45 MIP $80

Magic & Mystery, Morgan LeFay and Merlin, 2000, Mattel, Model No. 27287
MNP $50 MIP $75

Magic & Mystery, Tales of the Arabian Nights, 2001, Mattel, Model No. 50827
MNP $40 MIP $65

Maiko Barbie, 2006, Mattel
MNP n/a MIP $150

Major League Baseball Chicago Cubs, 1999, Mattel, Model No. 23883
MNP $20 MIP $35

Major League Baseball Los Angeles Dodgers, 1999, Mattel, Model No. 23882
MNP $20 MIP $11

Major League Baseball New York Yankees, 1999, Mattel, Model No. 23881
MNP $20 MIP $11

Make-A-Valentine Barbie, white or black, 1999, Mattel
MNP $5 MIP $15

Malibu Barbie "The Beach Party," w/case, 1979, Mattel, Model No. 1703
MNP $17 MIP $35

Malibu Ken Surf's Up Gift Set, 1971, Mattel, Model No. 1248
MNP $75 **MIP** $200

Marie Antoinette Barbie, 2003, Mattel
MNP $125 **MIP** $200

Masquerade Gala #1, Illusion, 1997, Mattel, Model No. 18667
MNP $50 **MIP** $100

Masquerade Gala #2, Rendezvous, 1998, Mattel, Model No. 20647
MNP $40 **MIP** $60

Masquerade Gala #3, Venetian Opulence, 2000, Mattel, Model No. 24501
MNP $30 **MIP** $50

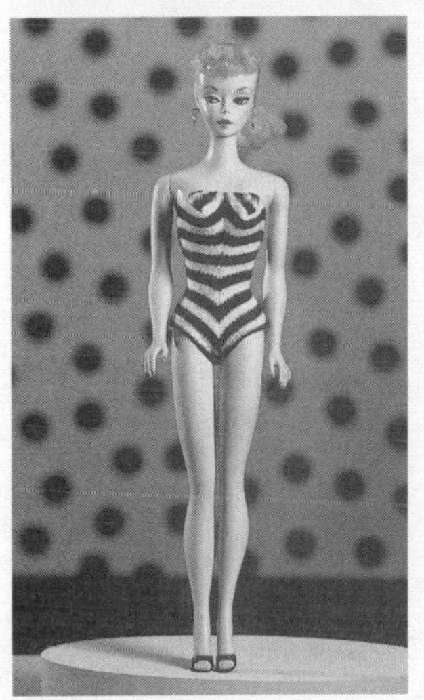

(Mattel Photo)

Mattel Festival 35th Anniversary (3,500 made), 1994, Mattel
MNP $50 **MIP** $150

Mattel Festival 35th Anniversary Gift Set (975 made), 1994, Mattel, Model No. 11591
MNP $70 **MIP** $100

Mattel Festival Banquet, blond, 1994, Mattel
MNP $75 **MIP** $125

Mattel Festival Banquet, brunette, 1994, Mattel
MNP $75 **MIP** $125

Mattel Festival Banquet, red hair, 1994, Mattel
MNP $75 **MIP** $125

Mattel Festival Doctor, brunette (1,500 made), 1994, Mattel, Model No. 11160
MNP $35 **MIP** $60

Mattel Festival Gymnast (1,500 made), 1994, Mattel, Model No. 11921
MNP $35 **MIP** $60

Mattel Festival Happy Holiday, 1994, Mattel, Model No. 12155
MNP $200 **MIP** $450

Mattel Festival Haute Couture, rainbow (500 made), 1994, Mattel
MNP $75 **MIP** $200

Mattel Festival Haute Couture, red velvet (480 made), 1994, Mattel
MNP $75 **MIP** $200

Mattel Festival Night Dazzle, brunette (420 made), 1994, Mattel, Model No. 12191
MNP $100 **MIP** $300

Mattel Festival Snow Princess, brunette (285 made), 1994, Mattel, Model No. 12905
MNP $500 **MIP** $1000

Meijers Hula Hoop, 1997, Mattel, Model No. 18167
MNP $10 **MIP** $20

Meijers Ice Cream, 1998, Mattel, Model No. 19820
MNP $10 **MIP** $20

Meijers Ladybug Fun, 1997, Mattel, Model No. 17695
MNP $10 **MIP** $20

Meijers Shopping Fun, 1993, Mattel, Model No. 10051
MNP $10 **MIP** $20

Meijers Something Extra, 1992, Mattel, Model No. 0863
MNP $10 **MIP** $20

Mervyns Ballerina Barbie, 1983, Mattel, Model No. 4983
MNP $30 **MIP** $75

Mervyns Fabulous Fur, 1986, Mattel, Model No. 7093
MNP $25 **MIP** $65

Midge's Ensemble Gift Set, 1964, Mattel, Model No. 1012
MNP $1200 **MIP** $3150

Millennium Bride, limited to 10,000, 1999, Mattel, Model No. 24505
MNP $150 **MIP** $300

Mix n' Match Gift Set, 1962, Mattel, Model No. 857
MNP $800 **MIP** $1850

Model of the Moment Daria Celebutante, 2004, Mattel, Blonde
MNP $10 **MIP** $50

Model of the Moment Marisa Pretty Young Thing, 2004, Mattel, Latina
MNP $10 **MIP** $50

Model of the Moment Nichelle Urban Hipster, 2004, Mattel, African American
MNP $10 **MIP** $50

Monique Lhuillier Bride Barbie, 2006, Mattel
MNP n/a **MIP** $110

Monique Lhuillier Bride Barbie, Platinum Edition, blond, 2006, Mattel
MNP n/a **MIP** $140

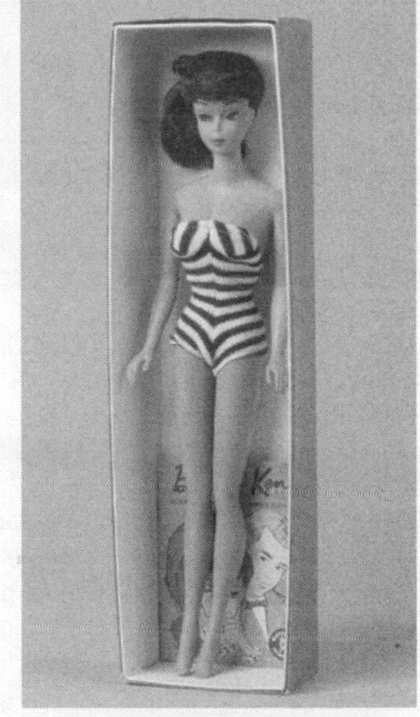

Montgomery Wards (mail order box), 1972, Mattel, Model No. 3210
MNP $30 **MIP** $500

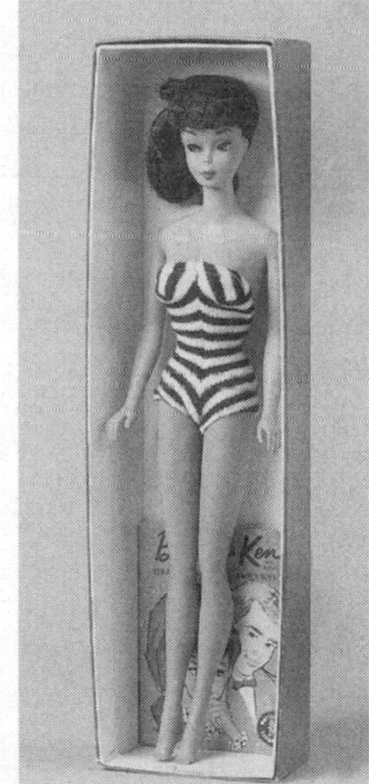

Montgomery Wards Barbie (pink box), 1972, Mattel, Model No. 3210
MNP $350 **MIP** $650

My First Barbie Gift Set, 1991, Mattel, Model No. 2483
MNP $8 **MIP** $20

My First Barbie Gift Set, pink tutu, 1986, Mattel, Model No. 1979
MNP $15 **MIP** $35

My First Barbie Gift Set, pink tutu, 1987, Mattel, Model No. 5386
MNP $18 **MIP** $40

My First Barbie, pink tutu, Zayre's Hispanic, 1987, Mattel, Model No. 1875
MNP $8 **MIP** $45

NASCAR Barbie #1, Kyle Petty #44, 1998, Mattel, Model No. 20442
MNP $5 **MIP** $15

NASCAR Barbie #2, Bill Elliott #94, 1999, Mattel, Model No. 22954
MNP $5 **MIP** $20

NASCAR Dale Earnhardt Jr. Barbie, 2007, Mattel
MNP n/a MIP $35

NASCAR Jeff Gordon Barbie, 2007, Mattel
MNP n/a MIP $35

National Convention A Date with Barbie Doll in Atlanta, 1998, Mattel
MNP $100 MIP $350

National Convention Barbie in the Old West, 2000, Mattel
MNP $85 MIP $225

National Convention We Girls Can Do Anything Right Barbie, 1999, Mattel
MNP $85 MIP $225

National Convention, Barbie and the Bandstand, 1996, Mattel, Pennsylvania
MNP $225 MIP $450

National Convention, Barbie Around the World Festival, 1985, Mattel, Michigan
MNP $125 MIP $300

National Convention, Barbie Convention 1980, 1980, Mattel, New York
MNP $125 MIP $350

National Convention, Barbie Forever Young, 1989, Mattel, California
MNP $125 MIP $300

National Convention, Barbie Loves a Fairytale, 1991, Mattel, Nebraska
MNP $150 MIP $250

National Convention, Barbie Loves New York, 1984, Mattel, New York
MNP $125 MIP $275

National Convention, Barbie Ole, 1995, Mattel, New Mexico
MNP $225 MIP $400

National Convention, Barbie Wedding Dreams, 1992, Mattel, New York
MNP $50 MIP $200

National Convention, Barbie's Pow Wow, 1983, Mattel, Arizona
MNP $125 MIP $350

National Convention, Barbie's Reunion, 1986, Mattel, Arizona
MNP $125 MIP $275

National Convention, Beach Blanket Barbie, 1997, Mattel, California
MNP $225 MIP $375

National Convention, Christmas With Barbie, 1987, Mattel, Oklahoma
MNP $125 MIP $300

National Convention, Come Rain or Shine, 1988, Mattel, Washington
MNP $125 MIP $250

National Convention, Deep in the Heart of Texas, 1990, Mattel, Texas
MNP $125 MIP $250

National Convention, Michigan Entertains Barbie, 1982, Mattel, Michigan
MNP $125 MIP $275

National Convention, The Magic of Barbie, 1994, Mattel, Alabama
MNP $175 MIP $375

National Convention, We Are Family, 2004, 2004, Mattel
MNP $10 MIP $200

National Convention, You've Come a Long Way, 1993, Mattel, Maryland
MNP $225 MIP $450

New Lifestyles of the West Western Plains, 1999, Mattel, Model No. 23205
MNP $40 MIP $80

Nolan Miller #1, Sheer Illusion, 1998, Mattel, Model No. 20662
MNP $45 MIP $60

Nolan Miller #2, Evening Illusion, 1999, Mattel, Model No. 23495
MNP $55 MIP $70

Nostalgic 35th Anniversary Gift Set, 1994, Mattel, Model No. 11591
MNP $50 MIP $75

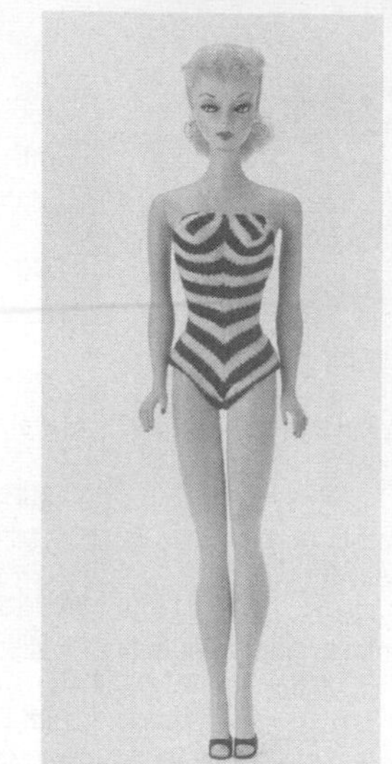

Nostalgic 35th Anniversary, blond, 1994, Mattel, Model No. 11590
MNP $25 MIP $40

Nostalgic 35th Anniversary, brunette, 1994, Mattel, Model No. 11782
MNP $20 MIP $45

Nostalgic Reproductions, Busy Gal Barbie, 1995, Mattel, Model No. 13675
MNP $15 MIP $30

Nostalgic Reproductions, Enchanted Evening Barbie, blond, 1996, Mattel, Model No. 14992
MNP $10 MIP $20

Nostalgic Reproductions, Enchanted Evening, brunette, 1996, Mattel, Model No. 15407
MNP $10 MIP $20

Nostalgic Reproductions, Fashion Luncheon, 1997, Mattel, Model No. 17382
MNP $25 MIP $40

Nostalgic Reproductions, Francie Wild Bunch, 1997, Mattel, Model No. 17601
MNP $20 MIP $50

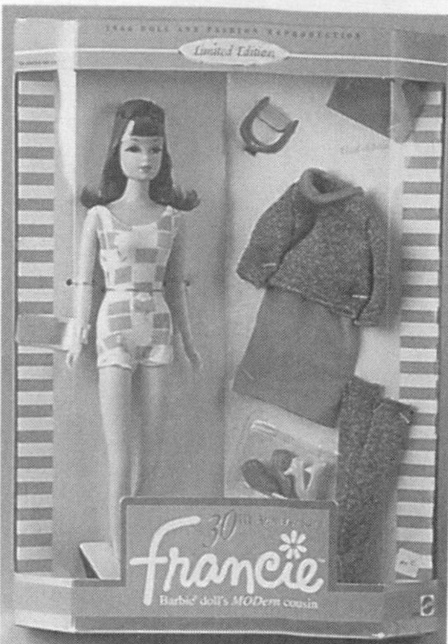

Nostalgic Reproductions, Francie, 30th Anniversary, 1996, Mattel, Model No. 14808
MNP $20 MIP $35

Nostalgic Reproductions, Silken Flame, blond or brunette, 1998, Mattel
MNP $15 MIP $25

Nostalgic Reproductions, Solo in the Spotlight, blond or brunette, 1995, Mattel, Model No. 13534/13820
MNP $12 **MIP** $20

Nostalgic Reproductions, Wedding Day, blond, 1997, Mattel
MNP $10 **MIP** $20

Nursery Rhymes, Barbie Had a Little Lamb, 1999, Mattel, Model No. 21740
MNP $20 **MIP** $40

Nutcracker Barbie, 1992, Mattel, Model No. 5472
MNP $85 **MIP** $225

Ocean Friends Gift Set, 1996, Mattel, Model No. 16442
MNP $20 **MIP** $45

Olympic Barbie Gift Set, 1996, Mattel, Model No. 16443
MNP $15 **MIP** $30

On Location: Barcelona, 2007, Mattel, Target exclusive
MNP n/a **MIP** $25

On Parade Gift Set, Barbie, Ken, Midge, 1964, Mattel, Model No. 1014
MNP $800 **MIP** $2300

Osco Picnic Pretty, 1993, Mattel, Model No. 3803
MNP $15 **MIP** $25

Oshagatsu Barbie, 1995, Mattel, Model No. 14024
MNP $20 **MIP** $50

P.J.'s Swinging Silver Gift Set, 1970, Mattel, Model No. 1588
MNP $700 **MIP** $1500

Pace Party Sensations Barbie, 1990, Mattel
MNP $15 **MIP** $50

Pace Very Violet Barbie, 1992, Mattel
MNP $15 **MIP** $50

Paint 'N Dazzle Deluxe Gift Set, 1993, Mattel, Model No. 10926
MNP $17 **MIP** $35

Paul Frank Barbie, blue pajamas, 2004, Mattel
MNP $10 **MIP** $60

(Mattel Photo)

Peanuts, Barbie and Snoopy, 2002, Mattel, Model No. 55558
MNP $15 **MIP** $25

Peppermint Obsession Barbie, 2006, Mattel
MNP n/a **MIP** $35

Peppermint Princess Barbie, Winter Princess Collection, 1995, Mattel, Model No. 13598
MNP $35 **MIP** $50

Picture Pockets Barbie, Christie, Kira or Teresa, 2000, Mattel
MNP $5 **MIP** $11

Pink & Pretty Barbie Gift Set, 1982, Mattel, Model No. 5239
MNP $35 **MIP** $90

Pink Hope, 2007, Mattel, International Heart Association
MNP n/a **MIP** $26

Pink Ribbion Barbie, African-American, 2006, Mattel
MNP n/a **MIP** $25

Pink Ribbon Barbie, 2006, Mattel
MNP n/a **MIP** $25

Pink Splendor, 1995, Mattel, Model No. 16091
MNP $150 **MIP** $200

Pin-Up Girls Hula Honey, 2006, Mattel
MNP n/a **MIP** $40

Pin-Up Girls Lady Luck, 2006, Mattel
MNP n/a **MIP** $40

Pin-Up Girls Way Out West, 2006, Mattel, regular edition
MNP n/a **MIP** $40

Pin-Up Girls Way Out West, 2006, Mattel, FAO Schwarz Exclusive, blond
MNP n/a **MIP** $75

Pivotal Body Jazz Baby, Blonde, 2007, Mattel
MNP n/a **MIP** $50

Pivotal Body Jazz Baby, Brunette, 2007, Mattel
MNP n/a **MIP** $50

Pivotal Body Jazz Baby, Redhead, 2007, Mattel
MNP n/a **MIP** $50

Pivotal Body Mistress of Ceremonies, 2007, Mattel, Dealer's exclusive
MNP n/a **MIP** $50

Poodle Parade, 1996, Mattel, Model No. 15280
MNP $25 **MIP** $40

Pop Culture Barbie as That Girl, 2003, Mattel
MNP $20 **MIP** $40

Pop Culture James Bond 007 Barbie & Ken Gift Set, 2003, Mattel
MNP $40 **MIP** $75

Pop Culture, Barbie & Ken as Morticia & Gomez Addams, 2000, Mattel, Model No. 27276
MNP $40 **MIP** $65

Pop Culture, Barbie and Ken as Lily and Herman Munster, 2001, Mattel, Model No. 50544
MNP $25 **MIP** $175

(Mattel Photo)

Pop Culture, Barbie as Samantha from Bewitched, 2002, Mattel, Model No. 53510
MNP $20 **MIP** $30

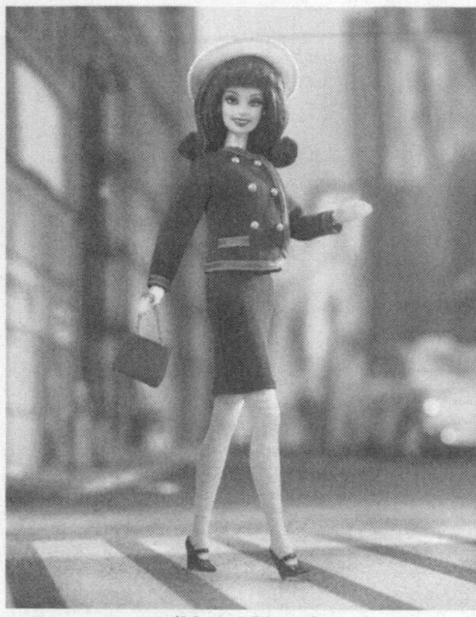

(Mattel Photo)

Pop Culture, Barbie as That Girl, 2003, Mattel, Model No. 56705
MNP $20 **MIP** $30

Pop Culture, Barbie as Wonder Woman, 2000, Mattel, Model No. 24638
MNP $25 **MIP** $40

Pop Culture, Barbie Loves Elvis Gift Set, 1997, Mattel, Model No. 17450
MNP $30 **MIP** $50

Pop Culture, Barbie Loves Frankie Sinatra Gift Set, 1999, Mattel, Model No. 22953
MNP $30 **MIP** $45

(Mattel Photo)

Pop Culture, James Bond 007 Ken and Barbie, 2003, Mattel, Model No. B0150
MNP $30 **MIP** $50

(Mattel Photo)

Pop Culture, Malibu Barbie, 2002, Mattel, Model No. 56061
MNP $10 **MIP** $20

Pop Culture, Star Trek Barbie and Ken, 1996, Mattel, Model No. 15006
MNP $15 **MIP** $25

(Mattel Photo)

Pop Culture, Starring Barbie in King Kong, 2003, Mattel, Model No. 56737
MNP $20 **MIP** $40

Pop Culture, X-Files Barbie and Ken, 1998, Mattel
MNP $20 **MIP** $50

Pretty Changes Barbie Gift Set, 1978, Mattel, Model No. 2598
MNP $35 **MIP** $75

Pretty Hearts Barbie, 1992, Mattel, Model No. 2901
MNP $7 **MIP** $15

Pretty Pairs Angie N' Tangie, 1970, Mattel, Foreign, Model No. 1135
MNP $125 **MIP** $250

Pretty Pairs Lori N' Rori, 1970, Mattel, Foreign, Model No. 1133
MNP $125 **MIP** $250

Pretty Pairs Nan N' Fran, 1970, Mattel, Foreign, Model No. 1134
MNP $125 **MIP** $250

Princess and the Pea Barbie, 2001, Mattel, Model No. 28800
MNP $15 **MIP** $35

Princess Series, Rapunzel, 2002, Mattel, Model No. 53973
MNP $20 **MIP** $40

Queen Elizabeth I Barbie, 2004, Mattel
MNP $10 **MIP** $200

Radio Shack Earring Magic, 1991, Mattel, came with software package, Model No. 25192
MNP $20 **MIP** $40

Red Romance Barbie, 1993, Mattel, Model No. 3161
MNP $7 **MIP** $15

Reem Acra Bride, 2007, Mattel
MNP n/a **MIP** $180

Republican National Convention Delegate Barbie, 2000, Mattel
MNP $25 **MIP** $150

Romantic Bride Barbie, black, 2001, Mattel, Model No. 29439
MNP $15 **MIP** $45

Romantic Bride Barbie, blond, 2001, Mattel, Model No. 29438
MNP $15 **MIP** $45

Royal Jewels Countess of Rubies, 2001, Mattel
MNP $40 **MIP** $100

Royal Jewels Duchess of Diamonds, 2001, Mattel
MNP $40 **MIP** $100

Royal Jewels Empress of Emeralds, 2000, Mattel, Model No. 25680
MNP $50 **MIP** $100

Royal Jewels Queen of Sapphires, 2000, Mattel, Model No. 24924
MNP $50 **MIP** $100

Russell Stover Easter, 1996, Mattel, Model No. 14956
MNP $10 **MIP** $25

Russell Stover Easter, 1997, Mattel, Model No. 17091
MNP $5 **MIP** $15

Russell Stover Easter (w/Easter basket), 1996, Mattel, Model No. 14617
MNP $10 **MIP** $25

Sam's Club 50s Fun Barbie, 1996, Mattel, Model No. 15820
MNP $10 **MIP** $30

Sam's Club 60s Fun Barbie, blond, 1997, Mattel, Model No. 17252
MNP $10 **MIP** $20

Sam's Club 60s Fun Barbie, red hair, 1997, Mattel, Model No. 17693
MNP $10 **MIP** $20

Sam's Club 70s Fun Barbie, blond, 1998, Mattel, Model No. 19928
MNP $10 **MIP** $20

Sam's Club 70s Fun Barbie, brunette, 1998, Mattel, Model No. 19929
MNP $10 **MIP** $20

Sam's Club Barbie Sisters' Celebration, Barbie and Krissy, 2000, Mattel
MNP $10 **MIP** $25

Sam's Club Bronze Sensation Barbie, 1998, Mattel, Model No. 20022
MNP $25 **MIP** $40

Sam's Club Dinner Date Barbie, blond, 1998, Mattel, Model No. 19016
MNP $8 **MIP** $15

Sam's Club Dinner Date Barbie, red hair, 1998, Mattel, Model No. 19037
MNP $9 **MIP** $15

Sam's Club Jewel Jubilee Barbie, 1991, Mattel, Model No. 2366
MNP $20 **MIP** $40

Sam's Club Party Sensation Barbie, 1990, Mattel, Model No. 9025
MNP $20 **MIP** $40

Sam's Club Peach Blossom Barbie, 1992, Mattel, Model No. 7009
MNP $20 **MIP** $30

Sam's Club Season's Greetings Barbie, 1994, Mattel, Model No. 12384
MNP $25 **MIP** $40

Sam's Club Sweet Moments Barbie, 1997, Mattel, Model No. 17642
MNP $12 **MIP** $20

Sam's Club Wedding Fantasy Barbie Gift Set, 1993, Mattel, Model No. 10924
MNP $30 **MIP** $70

Sam's Club Winter Fantasy Barbie, blond or brunette, 1997, Mattel, Model No. 17249/17666
MNP $10 **MIP** $20

Sam's Club Winter's Eve Barbie, 1995, Mattel, Model No. 13613
MNP $12 **MIP** $25

School Spirit Barbie, 1996, Mattel
MNP $5 **MIP** $10

Schooltime Barbie 1995, 1995, Mattel
MNP $5 **MIP** $10

Schooltime Barbie 1998, 1998, Mattel
MNP $5 **MIP** $10

Sears 100th Celebration Barbie, 1986, Mattel, Model No. 2998
MNP $20 **MIP** $45

Sears Barbie Twinkle Town Set, 1969, Mattel, Model No. 1866
MNP $800 **MIP** $1600

Sears Blossom Beautiful Barbie, 1992, Mattel, Model No. 3817
MNP $100 **MIP** $275

Sears Blue Starlight, 1997, Mattel, Model No. 17125
MNP $10 **MIP** $20

Sears Dream Princess, 1992, Mattel, Model No. 2306
MNP $10 **MIP** $20

Sears Enchanted Princess, 1993, Mattel, Model No. 10292
MNP $10 **MIP** $20

Sears Evening Enchantment, 1989, Mattel, Model No. 3596
MNP $10 **MIP** $20

Sears Evening Flame, 1996, Mattel, Model No. 15533
MNP $10 **MIP** $20

Sears Holiday Celebration Barbie 2004 (red dress), 2004, Mattel, Blonde or African American
MNP $10 **MIP** $40

Sears Lavender Surprise, 1990, Mattel, Model No. 9049
MNP $8 **MIP** $20

Sears Lavender Surprise, black, 1990, Mattel, Model No. 5588
MNP $8 **MIP** $20

Sears Lilac and Lovely Barbie, 1988, Mattel, Model No. 7669
MNP $10 **MIP** $20

Sears Perfectly Plaid Gift Set, 1971, Mattel, Model No. 1193
MNP $800 **MIP** $1500

Sears Pink Reflections, 1998, Mattel, Model No. 19130
MNP $10 **MIP** $20

Sears Ribbons and Roses Barbie, 1995, Mattel, Model No. 13011
MNP $10 **MIP** $20

Sears Silver Sweetheart Barbie, 1994, Mattel, Model No. 12410
MNP $17 **MIP** $20

Sears Skooter Cut n' Button Gift Set, 1967, Mattel, Model No. 1036
MNP $150 **MIP** $650

Sears Southern Belle, 1991, Mattel, Model No. 2586
MNP $10 **MIP** $20

Sears Star Dream Barbie, 1987, Mattel, Model No. 4550
MNP $10 **MIP** $20

Sears Winter Sports, 1975, Mattel, Model No. 9042
MNP $65 **MIP** $115

Seasons Sparkle Barbie, 2003, Mattel
MNP $8 **MIP** $15

Secret Hearts Gift Set, 1993, Mattel, Model No. 10929
MNP $17 **MIP** $35

See's Candy Barbie, white or black, 2000, Mattel
MNP $15 **MIP** $45

Service Merchandise Blue Rhapsody, 1991, Mattel, Model No. 1364
MNP $10 **MIP** $30

Service Merchandise City Sophisticate, 1994, Mattel, Model No. 12005
MNP $10 **MIP** $30

Service Merchandise Definitely Diamonds, 1998, Mattel, Model No. 20204
MNP $10 **MIP** $40

Service Merchandise Dream Bride, black or white, 1997, Mattel, Model No. 17933/17153
MNP $10 **MIP** $25

Service Merchandise Evening Symphony, 1998, Mattel, Model No. 19777
MNP $10 **MIP** $25

Service Merchandise Ruby Romance, 1995, Mattel, Model No. 13612
MNP $15 **MIP** $35

Service Merchandise Satin Nights, two earring versions, 1992, Mattel, Model No. 1886
MNP $20 **MIP** $50

Service Merchandise Sea Princess, 1996, Mattel, Model No. 15531
MNP $10 **MIP** $20

Service Merchandise Sparkling Splendor, 1993, Mattel, Model No. 10994
MNP $10 **MIP** $20

Sharin Sisters Gift Set, 1992, Mattel, Model No. 5716
MNP $12 **MIP** $25

Sharin Sisters Gift Set, 1993, Mattel, Model No. 10143
MNP $12 **MIP** $25

Shopko/Venture Blossom Beauty, 1991, Mattel, Model No. 3142
MNP $10 **MIP** $20

Shopko/Venture Party Perfect, 1992, Mattel, Model No. 1876
MNP $12 **MIP** $20

Skipper Party Time Gift Set, 1964, Mattel, Model No. 1021
MNP $100 **MIP** $550

Skipper Swing 'a' Rounder Gym Gift Set, 1972, Mattel, Model No. 1172
MNP $100 **MIP** $400

Snap 'N Play Gift Set (Snap 'N Play Deluxe), 1992, Mattel, Model No. 2262
MNP $12 MIP $35

Society Hound Barbie, 2001, Mattel
MNP $20 MIP $40

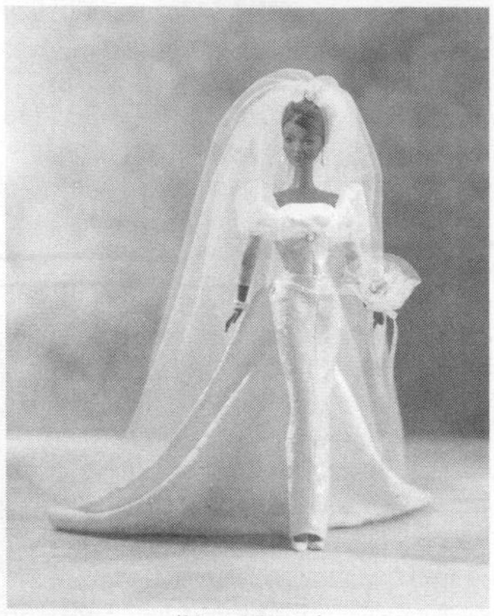
(Mattel Photo)

Sophisticated Wedding (white or black), 2002, Mattel, Model No. 53370/53371
MNP $20 MIP $50

Spiegel Golden Qi-Pao Barbie, 1998, Mattel, Model No. 20866
MNP $30 MIP $65

Spiegel Regal Reflections, 1992, Mattel, Model No. 4116
MNP $20 MIP $75

Spiegel Royal Invitation, 1993, Mattel, Model No. 10969
MNP $15 MIP $50

Spiegel Shopping Chic, 1995, Mattel, Model No. 14009
MNP $15 MIP $40

Spiegel Sterling Wishes, 1991, Mattel, Model No. 3347
MNP $30 MIP $75

Spiegel Summer Sophisticate, 1996, Mattel, Model No. 15591
MNP $10 MIP $25

Spiegel Theatre Elegance, 1994, Mattel, Model No. 12077
MNP $30 MIP $50

Spiegel Winner's Circle, 1997, Mattel, Model No. 17441
MNP $15 MIP $25

Splash 'N Color Barbie Gift Set, 1997, Mattel
MNP $10 MIP $20

Spring Bouquet Barbie, 1993, Mattel, Model No. 3477
MNP $10 MIP $20

Spring Parade Barbie, 1992, Mattel, Model No. 7008
MNP $15 MIP $25

Spring Parade Barbie, black, 1992, Mattel, Model No. 2257
MNP $15 MIP $25

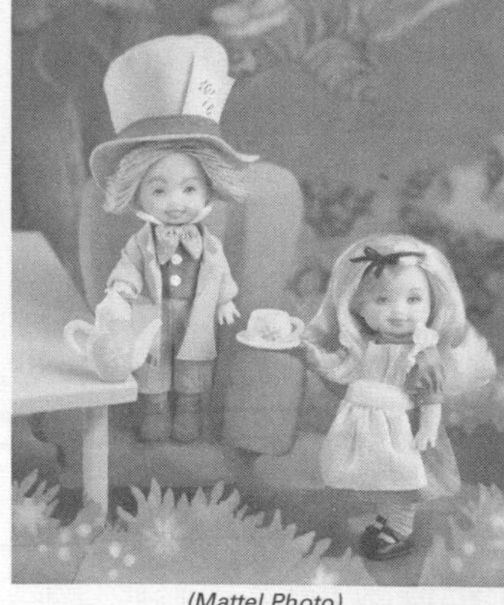
(Mattel Photo)

Storybook Favorites, Alice and Mad Hatter (Kelly and Tommy), 2003, Mattel, Model No. 57577
MNP $10 MIP $30

Storybook Favorites, Goldilocks and the Three Bears (Kelly), 2001, Mattel, Model No. 29605
MNP $8 MIP $25

Storybook Favorites, Hansel & Gretel (Kelly and Tommy), 2000, Mattel, Model No. 28535
MNP $5 MIP $25

(Mattel Photo)

Storybook Favorites, Little Red Riding Hood (Kelly and Tommy), 2002, Mattel, Model No. 52899
MNP $10 MIP $20

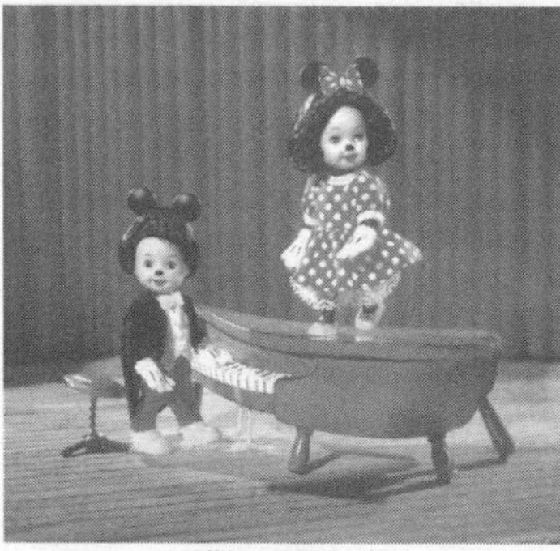
(Mattel Photo)

Storybook Favorites, Mickey and Minnie Mouse (Kelly and Tommy), 2002, Mattel, Model No. 55502
MNP $10 MIP $25

Storybook Favorites, Raggedy Ann and Andy (Kelly and Tommy), 2000, Mattel, Model No. 24639
MNP $5 MIP $25

Style Set Bohemian Glamour Barbie, 2003, Mattel
MNP $25 MIP $40

Style Set Exotic Beauty Barbie, 2002, Mattel
MNP $25 MIP $40

Style Set Exotic Beauty Barbie Limited Edition, 2002, Mattel, w/ Treasure Hunt jewelry
MNP $35 MIP $65

Style Set, Society Girl (white or black), 2002, Mattel, Model No. 56203/56204
MNP $20 MIP $50

Superman Returns Barbie as Lois Lane, 2006, Mattel
MNP n/a MIP $14

Superman Returns Ken as Superman, 2006, Mattel
MNP n/a MIP $14

Sweet Spring Barbie, 1992, Mattel, Model No. 3208
MNP $10 MIP $20

Sydney 2000 Olympic Pin Collector, black or white, 2000, Mattel, Model No. 25644/26302
MNP $20 MIP $30

Target 35th Anniversary Barbie, black, 1997, Mattel, Model No. 176608
MNP $10 MIP $24

Target 35th Anniversary Barbie, white, 1997, Mattel, Model No. 16485
MNP $10 MIP $20

Target Baseball Date Barbie, 1993, Mattel, Model No. 4583
MNP $10 MIP $30

Target City Style #1, 1996, Mattel, Model No. 15612
MNP $8 MIP $15

Target City Style #2, 1997, Mattel, Model No. 17237
MNP $10 MIP $20

Target Club Wedd Barbie, black, 1998, Mattel, Model No. 20423
MNP $10 MIP $20

Target Club Wedd Barbie, blond or brunette, 1998, Mattel, Model No. 19717/19718
MNP $10 MIP $20

Target Cute'n Cool, 1991, Mattel, Model No. 2954
MNP $8 MIP $30

Target Dazzlin' Date Barbie, 1992, Mattel, Model No. 3203
MNP $10 MIP $25

Target Easter Bunny Fun Barbie & Kelly, 1999, Mattel, Model No. 21720
MNP $15 MIP $25

Target Easter Bunny Gia, 2007, Mattel, yellow suit
MNP n/a MIP $15

Target Easter Bunny Kelly, 2007, Mattel, pink suit
MNP n/a MIP $15

Target Easter Bunny Tori, 2007, Mattel, purple suit
MNP n/a MIP $15

Target Easter Egg Hunt, 1998, Mattel, Model No. 19014
MNP $15 MIP $25

Target Easter Egg Party, white or black, 2000, Mattel
MNP $15 MIP $25

Target Easter Garden Hunt Barbie and Kelly, 2001, Mattel
MNP $10 MIP $25

Target Easter Garden Kelly as Bunny, 2003, Mattel
MNP $8 MIP $15

Target Easter Garden Melody as Flower, 2003, Mattel
MNP $8 MIP $15

Target Easter Garden Melody as Lamb, 2003, Mattel
MNP $8 MIP $15

Target Easter Garden Nikki as Chick, 2003, Mattel
MNP $8 MIP $15

Target Easter Garden Tamika as Chick, 2003, Mattel
MNP $8 MIP $15

Target Gold and Lace Barbie, 1989, Mattel, Model No. 7476
MNP $10 MIP $30

Target Golden Evening, 1991, Mattel, Model No. 2587
MNP $6 MIP $45

Target Golf Date Barbie, 1993, Mattel, Model No. 10202
MNP $10 MIP $25

Target Halloween 2006 Kelly as Pumpkin, 2006, Mattel
MNP n/a MIP $15

Target Halloween 2006 Kelly as Spider, 2006, Mattel
MNP n/a MIP $15

Target Halloween 2006 Kelly as Witch, 2006, Mattel
MNP n/a MIP $15

Target Halloween 2006 Kelly as Witch, African-American, 2006, Mattel
MNP n/a MIP $15

Target Halloween 2006 Tommy as Mummy, 2006, Mattel
MNP n/a MIP $15

Target Halloween Fortune Barbie, 2003, Mattel
MNP $10 MIP $25

Target Halloween Fun Barbie & Kelly, white or black, 1999, Mattel, Model No. 23460
MNP $15 MIP $25

Target Halloween Fun Li'l Friends of Kelly, 1999, Mattel, Model No. 23796
MNP $15 MIP $25

Target Halloween Goo-tiful Barbie, 2004, Mattel
MNP $10 MIP $20

Target Halloween Kelly as Pumpkin, 2006, Mattel
MNP n/a MIP $10

Target Halloween Kelly as Spider, 2006, Mattel
MNP n/a MIP $10

Target Halloween Kelly as Witch, 2006, Mattel
MNP n/a MIP $10

Target Halloween Kelly as Witch, African-American, 2006, Mattel
MNP n/a MIP $10

Target Halloween Party Barbie & Ken, pirates, 1998, Mattel, Model No. 19874
MNP $20 MIP $40

Target Halloween Party Belinda as Black Cat, 2003, Mattel
MNP $8 MIP $20

Target Halloween Party Deidre (Pumpkin), 2000, Mattel, Model No. 28310
MNP $5 MIP $15

Target Halloween Party Deirdre as Pumpkin, 2002, Mattel
MNP $8 MIP $15

Target Halloween Party Deirdre as Pumpkin, 2003, Mattel
MNP $8 MIP $15

Target Halloween Party Jenny (Pumpkin), 2000, Mattel, Model No. 28308
MNP $5 MIP $15

Target Halloween Party Jenny as Genie, 2002, Mattel
MNP $8 MIP $20

Target Halloween Party Jenny as Witch, 2003, Mattel
MNP $8 MIP $20

Target Halloween Party Kayla (Ghost), 2000, Mattel, Model No. 28307
MNP $5 MIP $15

Target Halloween Party Kelly (Alien), 2000, Mattel, Model No. 28306
MNP $5 MIP $15

Target Halloween Party Kelly as Pumpkin, 2002, Mattel
MNP $8 MIP $20

Target Halloween Party Kelly as Spider, 2003, Mattel
MNP $8 MIP $20

Target Halloween Party Kelly as Witch, 2004, Mattel, White or African American
MNP $10 MIP $10

Target Halloween Party Kerstie as Pumpkin, 2004, Mattel
MNP $10 MIP $10

Target Halloween Party Lorena as Witch, 2002, Mattel
MNP $8 MIP $20

Target Halloween Party Melody as Tiger, 2004, Mattel
MNP $10 MIP $10

Target Halloween Party Nikki as Pumpkin, 2003, Mattel
MNP $8 MIP $20

Target Halloween Party Nikkie as Ghost, 2004, Mattel
MNP $10 MIP $10

Target Halloween Party Tommy (Cowboy), 2000, Mattel, Model No. 28309
MNP $5 MIP $15

Target Halloween Party Tommy as Dragon, 2003, Mattel
MNP $8 MIP $20

Target Halloween Party Tommy as Scarecrow, 2002, Mattel
MNP $8 MIP $20

Target Halloween Party Tommy as Vampire, 2004, Mattel
MNP $10 MIP $10

Target Halloween Tommy as Mummy, 2006, Mattel
MNP n/a MIP $10

Target Halloween Trick or Chic Barbie, 2006, Mattel
MNP n/a MIP $15

Target Happy Halloween Barbie & Kelly, 1997, Mattel, Model No. 17238
MNP $30 MIP $60

Target Party Pretty Barbie, 1990, Mattel, Model No. 5955
MNP $6 MIP $25

Target Pet Doctor Barbie, brunette, 1996, Mattel, Model No. 16458
MNP $15 MIP $30

Target Pretty in Plaid Barbie, 1992, Mattel, Model No. 5413
MNP $15 MIP $30

Target Purrfectly Halloween Barbie, 2002, Mattel
MNP $10 MIP $25

Target Soccer Kelly & Tommy, 1999, Mattel
MNP $8 MIP $20

Target Steppin' Out Barbie, 1995, Mattel, Model No. 14110
MNP $8 MIP $20

Target Valentine Barbie, 1996, Mattel, Model No. 15172
MNP $8 MIP $20

Target Valentine Date Barbie, 1998, Mattel, Model No. 18306
MNP $8 MIP $20

Target Valentine Kelly and Friend, 2001, Mattel
MNP $5 MIP $15

Target Valentine Lil Heart Kelly, Jenny or Balinda, 2003, Mattel
MNP $8 MIP $15

Target Valentine Romance Barbie, 1997, Mattel, Model No. 16059
MNP $8 **MIP** $20

Target Valentine Style Barbie, black, 1999, Mattel, Model No. 22150
MNP $8 **MIP** $18

Target Valentine Style Barbie, white, 1999, Mattel, Model No. 20465
MNP $8 **MIP** $15

Target Wild Style Barbie, 1992, Mattel, Model No. 0411
MNP $10 **MIP** $24

Target With Love Barbie, 2000, Mattel
MNP $8 **MIP** $15

Target Xhilaration Barbie, white or black, 1999, Mattel
MNP $15 **MIP** $35

Tennis Star Barbie & Ken, 1988, Mattel, Model No. 7801
MNP $18 **MIP** $40

The Waltz Barbie & Ken Gift Set, 2003, Mattel
MNP $40 **MIP** $75

Tiff Pose N' Play, 1972, Mattel, Foreign, Model No. 1199
MNP $125 **MIP** $350

Timeless Sentiments Angel of Hope, 1999, Mattel, Model No. 22955
MNP $25 **MIP** $50

Timeless Sentiments Angel of Joy, white or black, 1998, Mattel, Model No. 19633/20929
MNP $25 **MIP** $50

Timeless Sentiments Angel of Peace, 1999, Mattel, Model No. 24240
MNP $25 **MIP** $50

Timeless Sentiments Angel of Peace, black, 1999, Mattel, Model No. 24241
MNP $25 **MIP** $50

Titanic Rose, 2007, Mattel
MNP n/a **MIP** $35

Todd Oldham (Designer), 1999, Mattel
MNP $35 **MIP** $70

Together Forever, Romeo & Juliet, 1998, Mattel, Model No. 19364
MNP $50 **MIP** $100

Together Forever, King Arthur and Queen Guinevere, 1999, Mattel, Model No. 23880
MNP $50 **MIP** $100

Tommy as Elvis, 2004, Mattel
MNP $10 **MIP** $25

Tooth Fairy Barbie, 2007, Mattel
MNP n/a **MIP** $35

Top Model Barbie, 2007, Mattel
MNP n/a **MIP** $25

Top Model Summer, Redhead, 2007, Mattel
MNP n/a **MIP** $25

Top Model Teresa, Brunette, 2007, Mattel
MNP n/a **MIP** $25

Toys R Us 101 Dalmatians Barbie, black, 1999, Mattel, Model No. 17601
MNP $12 **MIP** $20

Toys R Us 101 Dalmatians Barbie, white, 1997, Mattel, Model No. 17248
MNP $15 **MIP** $28

Toys R Us 35th Anniversary Midge, Senior Prom, 1998, Mattel, Model No. 18976
MNP $25 **MIP** $40

Toys R Us Astronaut Barbie, black, 1994, Mattel, Model No. 12150
MNP $10 **MIP** $20

Toys R Us Astronaut Barbie, white, 1994, Mattel, Model No. 12149
MNP $10 **MIP** $20

Toys R Us Barbie as DC Comics Bat Girl w/Batcycle, 2004, Mattel
MNP $10 **MIP** $30

Toys R Us Barbie for President, 1992, Mattel, Model No. 3722
MNP $17 **MIP** $45

Toys R Us Barbie for President, 2000, Mattel, Model No. 3940
MNP $5 **MIP** $18

Toys R Us Barbie Renaissance Rose Gift Set, 2000, Mattel, Model No. 28633
MNP $15 **MIP** $35

Toys R Us Bath Time Skipper, 1992, Mattel, Model No. 7970
MNP $12 **MIP** $25

Toys R Us Beauty Pagent Skipper, 1991, Mattel, Model No. 9342
MNP $10 **MIP** $25

Toys R Us Bicyclin' Barbie, black or white, 1995, Mattel
MNP $15 **MIP** $25

Toys R Us Birthday Fun Kelly Gift Set, 1996, Mattel
MNP $15 **MIP** $28

Toys R Us Cool 'N Sassy, black, 1992, Mattel, Model No. 4110
MNP $10 **MIP** $20

Toys R Us Cool 'N Sassy, white, 1992, Mattel, Model No. 1490
MNP $10 **MIP** $20

Toys R Us Crystal Splendor, black, 1996, Mattel, Model No. 15137
MNP $10 **MIP** $25

Toys R Us Crystal Splendor, white, 1996, Mattel, Model No. 15136
MNP $12 **MIP** $25

Toys R Us Dream Date Barbie, 1982, Mattel, Model No. 9180
MNP $7 **MIP** $30

Toys R Us Dream Date Ken, 1982, Mattel, Model No. 4077
MNP $5 **MIP** $30

Toys R Us Dream Date P.J., 1982, Mattel, Model No. 5869
MNP $8 **MIP** $40

Toys R Us Dream Date Skipper, 1990, Mattel, Model No. 1075
MNP $10 **MIP** $25

Toys R Us Dream Time Barbie, 1988, Mattel, Model No. 9180
MNP $10 **MIP** $30

Toys R Us Dream Wedding Gift Set, black, 1993, Mattel, Model No. 10713
MNP $22 **MIP** $45

Toys R Us Dream Wedding Gift Set, white, 1993, Mattel, Model No. 10712
MNP $20 **MIP** $45

Toys R Us Faerie Queen of Ireland, 2004, Mattel
MNP $10 **MIP** $30

Toys R Us Fashion Brights Barbie, white or black, 1992, Mattel, Model No. 1882/4112
MNP $10 **MIP** $20

Toys R Us Fashion Fun Barbie Gift Set, 1999, Mattel
MNP $15 **MIP** $25

Toys R Us Firefighter Barbie, white or black, 1995, Mattel, With yellow uniform and hat and dalmatian puppy, Model No. 13553/13472
MNP $10 **MIP** $25

Toys R Us Gardening Fun Barbie & Kelly Gift Set, 1997, Mattel, Model No. 17242
MNP $12 **MIP** $23

Toys R Us Got Milk? Barbie, white or black, 1996, Mattel, Model No. 15721/15122
MNP $8 **MIP** $20

Toys R Us Gran Gala Toresa, 1997, Mattel, Model No. 17239
MNP $8 **MIP** $15

Toys R Us Harley-Davidson Barbie #1, 1997, Mattel, Model No. 17692
MNP $150 **MIP** $325

Toys R Us Harley-Davidson Barbie #2, 1998, Mattel, Model No. 20441
MNP $75 **MIP** $150

Toys R Us Harley-Davidson Barbie #3, 1999, Mattel, Model No. 22256
MNP $25 **MIP** $60

Toys R Us Harley-Davidson Barbie #4, 2000, Mattel, Model No. 25637
MNP $25 **MIP** $45

Toys R Us Harley-Davidson Barbie #5, black, 2001, Mattel, Model No. 29208
MNP $25 **MIP** $60

Toys R Us Harley-Davidson Barbie #5, white, 2001, Mattel, Model No. 29207
MNP $25 **MIP** $45

Toys R Us Harley-Davidson Ken #1, 1999, Mattel, Model No. 22255
MNP $25 **MIP** $60

Toys R Us Harley-Davidson Ken #2, 2000, Mattel, Model No. 25638
MNP $15 **MIP** $40

Toys R Us I'm A Toys R Us Kid Barbie, white or black, 1998, Mattel, Model No. 18895/21040
MNP $15 **MIP** $30

Toys R Us International Pen Friend Barbie, 1995, Mattel, Model No. 13558
MNP $7 **MIP** $16

Toys R Us Love to Read Barbie, 1993, Mattel, Model No. 10507
MNP $12 **MIP** $40

Toys R Us Malt Shop Barbie, 1993, Mattel, Model No. 4581
MNP $10 **MIP** $25

Toys R Us Moonlight Magic Barbie, black, 1993, Mattel, Model No. 10609
MNP $15 **MIP** $55

Toys R Us Moonlight Magic Barbie, white, 1993, Mattel, Model No. 10608
MNP $15 **MIP** $65

Toys R Us My Size Bride Barbie, red hair, 1995, Mattel, Model No. 15649
MNP $60 **MIP** $135

Toys R Us Native Spirit Barbie Spirit of the Sky, 2003, Mattel
MNP $20 **MIP** $50

Toys R Us Native Spirit Barbie Spirit of the Water, 2002, Mattel
MNP $25 **MIP** $50

Toys R Us Olympic Gymnast Barbie, red hair, box w/o special edition marking, 1996, Mattel, Model No. 15725
MNP $15 **MIP** $30

Toys R Us Oreo Fun Barbie, 1997, Mattel, Model No. 18511
MNP $8 **MIP** $18

Toys R Us Paleontologist Barbie, white or black, 1997, Mattel, Model No. 17240/17241
MNP $12 **MIP** $24

Toys R Us Party Time Barbie, white or black, 1994, Mattel, Model No. 12243
MNP $10 **MIP** $20

Toys R Us Pepsi Spirit Barbie, 1989, Mattel, Model No. 4869
MNP $18 **MIP** $70

Toys R Us Pepsi Spirit Skipper, 1989, Mattel, Model No. 4867
MNP $15 **MIP** $65

Toys R Us POG Barbie, 1995, Mattel, Model No. 13239
MNP $7 **MIP** $15

Toys R Us Police Officer Barbie, black, 1993, Mattel, Model No. 10689
MNP $15 **MIP** $65

Toys R Us Police Officer Barbie, white, 1993, Mattel, Model No. 10688
MNP $15 **MIP** $70

Toys R Us Purple Passion, black, 1995, Mattel, Model No. 13554
MNP $10 **MIP** $30

Toys R Us Purple Passion, white, 1995, Mattel, Model No. 13555
MNP $10 **MIP** $30

Toys R Us Radiant in Red Barbie, black, 1992, Mattel, Model No. 4113
MNP $12 **MIP** $55

Toys R Us Radiant in Red Barbie, white, 1992, Mattel, Model No. 1276
MNP $12 **MIP** $55

Toys R Us Sapphire Sophisticate, 1997, Mattel, Model No. 16692
MNP $12 **MIP** $25

Toys R Us School Fun, 1991, Mattel, Model No. 2721
MNP $6 **MIP** $40

Toys R Us School Spirit Barbie, black, 1993, Mattel, Model No. 10683
MNP $10 **MIP** $30

Toys R Us School Spirit Barbie, white, 1993, Mattel, Model No. 10682
MNP $10 **MIP** $25

Toys R Us Share A Smile Barbie, 1997, Mattel, Model No. 17247
MNP $7 **MIP** $15

Toys R Us Share A Smile Becky, 1997, Mattel, Model No. 15761
MNP $15 **MIP** $28

Toys R Us Share A Smile Christie, 1997, Mattel, Model No. 17372
MNP $7 **MIP** $15

Toys R Us Show and Ride Barbie, 1988, Mattel, Model No. 7799
MNP $10 **MIP** $35

Toys R Us Sign Language Barbie, white or black, 2000, Mattel
MNP $8 **MIP** $20

Toys R Us Society Style Emerald Elegance, 1994, Mattel, Model No. 12322
MNP $15 **MIP** $40

Toys R Us Society Style Emerald Enchantment, 1997, Mattel, Model No. 17443
MNP $25 **MIP** $50

Toys R Us Society Style Sapphire Dream, 1995, Mattel, Model No. 13256
MNP $50 **MIP** $70

Toys R Us Space Camp Barbie, white or black, 1999, Mattel, Model No. 22435/22246
MNP $12 **MIP** $28

Toys R Us Spellbound Lover (Iseult), 2005, Mattel
MNP $15 **MIP** $30

Toys R Us Spirit of the Earth Barbie, 2001, Mattel
MNP $25 **MIP** $75

Toys R Us Spots 'N Dots Barbie, 1993, Mattel, Model No. 10491
MNP $12 **MIP** $35

Toys R Us Spots 'N Dots Teresa, 1993, Mattel, Model No. 10885
MNP $12 **MIP** $40

Toys R Us Spring Parade Barbie, white or black, 1992, Mattel, Model No. 7008/2257
MNP $15 **MIP** $30

Toys R Us Sunflower Barbie, 1995, Mattel, Model No. 13488
MNP $9 **MIP** $20

Toys R Us Sunflower Teresa, 1995, Mattel, Model No. 13489
MNP $9 **MIP** $20

Toys R Us Sweet Romance, 1991, Mattel, Model No. 2917
MNP $8 **MIP** $30

Toys R Us Sweet Roses, 1989, Mattel, Model No. 7635
MNP $7 **MIP** $25

Toys R Us The Bard, 2004, Mattel
MNP $10 **MNP** n/a

Toys R Us Totally Hair Courtney, 1992, Mattel, Model No. 1433
MNP $10 **MIP** $25

Toys R Us Totally Hair Skipper, 1992, Mattel, Model No. 1430
MNP $10 **MIP** $25

Toys R Us Totally Hair Whitney, 1992, Mattel, Model No. 7735
MNP $20 **MIP** $40

Toys R Us Travelin' Sisters Gift Set, 1995, Mattel, Model No. 14073
MNP $30 **MIP** $65

Toys R Us Vacation Sensation Barbie, blue, 1986, Mattel, Model No. 1675
MNP $10 **MIP** $40

Toys R Us Vacation Sensation Barbie, pink, 1989, Mattel, Model No. 1675
MNP $12 **MIP** $48

Toys R Us Wedding Fantasy Barbie & Ken Gift Set, 1997, Mattel, Model No. 17243
MNP $20 **MIP** $45

Toys R Us Winter Fun Barbie, 1990, Mattel, Model No. 5949
MNP $10 **MIP** $40

Toys R Us/FAO Schwarz Sea Holiday Barbie #1, with lip gloss, 1993, Mattel
MNP $15 **MIP** $30

Toys R Us/FAO Schwarz Sea Holiday Barbie #2, with lip gloss, 1993, Mattel
MNP $15 **MIP** $24

Toys R Us/FAO/JCPenney, Winter Sports Barbie, 1995, Mattel
MNP $15 **MIP** $30

Toys R Us/FAO/JCPenney, Winter Sports Ken, 1995, Mattel
MNP $15 **MIP** $30

Trail Blazin' Barbie, 1991, Mattel, Model No. 2783
MNP $10 **MIP** $25

Tree Trimming Barbie, white or black, 1999, Mattel
MNP $5 **MIP** $15

Trend Forecaster Barbie, 1999, Mattel, Model No. 22833
MNP $20 **MIP** $45

Tropical Barbie Deluxe Gift Set, 1985, Mattel, Model No. 2996
MNP $20 **MIP** $45

Tutti and Todd Sundae Treat Set, 1966, Mattel, Model No. 3556
MNP $150 **MIP** $350

Tutti Me n' My Dog, 1966, Mattel, Model No. 3554
MNP $150 **MIP** $350

Tutti Nighty Night Sleep Tight, 1965, Mattel, Model No. 3553
MNP $100 **MIP** $300

Twirley Curls Barbie Gift Set, 1982, Mattel, Model No. 4097
MNP $30 **MIP** $85

Twist and Turn Far Out Barbie, 1999, Mattel, Model No. 21911
MNP $20 **MIP** $40

Vera Wang #1, bride, 1998, Mattel, Model No. 19788
MNP $75 **MIP** $150

Vera Wang #2, lavender dress, 1999, Mattel, Model No. 23027
MNP $55 **MIP** $140

Versace Barbie, 2004, Mattel
MNP $50 **MIP** $75

Versus by Versace Barbie, 2004, Mattel
MNP $25 **MIP** $80

Very Violet Barbie, 1992, Mattel, Model No. 1859
MNP $10 **MIP** $20

Victorian Barbie with Cedric Bear, 2000, Mattel
MNP $25 **MIP** $59

Victorian Holiday Barbie, 2006, Mattel
MNP n/a **MNP** n/a

Vintage Reproduction 45th Anniversary Ken, 2006, Mattel
MNP n/a **MIP** $25

Vintage Reproduction Barbie Learns to Cook, Blonde, 2007, Mattel
MNP n/a **MIP** $50

Vintage Reproduction Barbie Learns to Cook, Brunette, 2007, Mattel, limited edition, 999 piecesf
MNP n/a **MIP** $200

Vintage Reproduction Career Girl, 2007, Mattel
MNP n/a **MIP** $50

Vintage Reproduction Evening Gala, 2007, Mattel
MNP n/a **MIP** $50

Vintage Reproduction Friday Night Dream Date Barbie & Ken Giftset, 2006, Mattel
MNP n/a **MIP** $100

Vintage Reproduction Knitting Pretty Barbie & Skipper Gift Set, 2007, Mattel
MNP n/a **MIP** $100

Vintage Reproduction Picnic Set Barbie, 2006, Mattel
MNP n/a **MIP** $50

Vintage Reproduction Red, White & Warm, Brunette, 2007, Mattel
MNP n/a **MIP** $50

Vintage Reproduction Red, White & Warm, Christie, 2007, Mattel, Platinum edition
MNP n/a **MIP** $200

Vintage Reproduction Sleepytime Gal, 2007, Mattel
MNP n/a **MIP** $80

Vintage Reproduction Stacey Night Lightning, 2006, Mattel, Barbie Convention Exclusive, blond
MNP n/a **MIP** $150

Vintage Reproduction Stacey Nite Lightning, 2006, Mattel
MNP n/a **MIP** $60

Walking Jamie Strollin' in Style Gift Set, 1972, Mattel, Model No. 1247
MNP $300 **MIP** $600

Wal-Mart 25th Year Pink Jubilee Barbie, 1987, Mattel, Model No. 4589
MNP $20 **MIP** $50

Wal-Mart 35th Anniversary Barbie, black or white, Mattel, Model No. 17616/17245
MNP $10 **MIP** $24

Wal-Mart 35th Anniversary Teresa, 1997, Mattel, Model No. 17617
MNP $12 **MIP** $25

Wal-Mart Anniversary Star Barbie, 1992, Mattel, Model No. 2282
MNP $15 **MIP** $30

Wal-Mart Ballroom Beauty, 1991, Mattel, Model No. 3678
MNP $8 **MIP** $30

Wal-Mart Bathtime Fun Barbie, 1991, Mattel, Model No. 9601
MNP $5 **MIP** $25

Wal-Mart Country Bride, 1995, Mattel, Model No. 13014
MNP $8 **MIP** $15

Wal-Mart Country Bride, black, 1995, Mattel, Model No. 13015
MNP $8 **MIP** $15

Wal-Mart Country Bride, Hispanic, 1995, Mattel, Model No. 13016
MNP $8 **MIP** $15

Wal-Mart Country Western Star Barbie, black or Hispanic, 1994, Mattel, Model No. 12096
MNP $12 **MIP** $30

Wal-Mart Country Western Star Barbie, white, 1994, Mattel, Model No. 12097
MNP $10 **MIP** $25

Wal-Mart Dream Fantasy, 1990, Mattel, Model No. 7335
MNP $8 **MIP** $35

Wal-Mart Exclusive Barbie 2007, African-American, 2007, Mattel
MNP n/a **MIP** $35

Wal-Mart Exclusive Barbie 2007, Blonde, 2007, Mattel
MNP n/a **MIP** $35

Wal-Mart Exclusive Zodiac Barbie, 2004, Mattel, Aries, Taurus, Gemini, Cancer, Leo, Virgo
MNP $8 **MIP** $20

Wal-Mart Frills and Fantasy Barbie, 1988, Mattel, Model No. 1374
MNP $7 **MIP** $45

Wal-Mart Jewel Skating Barbie, 1999, Mattel, Model No. 23239
MNP $6 **MIP** $12

Wal-Mart Lavender Look Barbie, 1989, Mattel, Model No. 3963
MNP $7 **MIP** $30

Wal-Mart Portrait in Blue Barbie, black, 1998, Mattel, Model No. 19356
MNP $10 **MIP** $20

Wal-Mart Portrait in Blue Barbie, white, 1998, Mattel, Model No. 19355
MNP $8 **MIP** $18

Wal-Mart Pretty Choices Barbie, black, 1997, Mattel, Model No. 18018
MNP $8 **MIP** $18

Wal-Mart Pretty Choices Barbie, blond or brunette, 1997, Mattel, Model No. 17971/18019
MNP $8 **MIP** $18

Wal-Mart Puzzle Craze Barbie, white or black, 1998, Mattel, Model No. 20164/20165
MNP $6 **MIP** $14

Wal-Mart Puzzle Craze Teresa, 1998, Mattel, Model No. 20166
MNP $6 **MIP** $14

Wal-Mart Shopping Time Barbie, black or white, 1997, Mattel, Model No. 18231/18230
MNP $7 **MIP** $15

Wal-Mart Shopping Time Teresa, 1997, Mattel, Model No. 18232
MNP $7 **MIP** $15

Wal-Mart Skating Star Barbie, 1996, Mattel, Model No. 15510
MNP $10 **MIP** $15

Wal-Mart Star Skater Barbie, white or black, 2000, Mattel
MNP $5 **MIP** $15

Wal-Mart Superstar Barbie, black, 1993, Mattel, Model No. 10711
MNP $15 **MIP** $40

Wal-Mart Superstar Barbie, white, 1993, Mattel, Model No. 10592
MNP $15 **MIP** $30

Wal-Mart Sweet Magnolia Barbie, black, white or Hispanic, 1996, Mattel, Model No. 15653/15652/15654
MNP $9 **MIP** $15

Wal-Mart the Birthstone Collection, 2003, Mattel, 12 different dolls
MNP $10 **MIP** $25

Wal-Mart Tooth Fairy #1, 1994, Mattel, Model No. 11645
MNP $7 **MIP** $20

Wal-Mart Tooth Fairy #2, 1995, Mattel, Model No. 11645
MNP $5 **MIP** $20

Wal-Mart Tooth Fairy #3, 1998, Mattel, Model No. 17246
MNP $6 **MIP** $14

Walt Disney World Animal Kingdom Barbie, white or black, 1998, Mattel, Model No. 20363/20989
MNP $15 **MIP** $30

Walt Disney World Barbie 25th Anniversary, 1996, Mattel, Model No. 16525
MNP $15 **MIP** $30

Walt Disney World Disney Fun 1994, 1994, Mattel, Model No. 11650
MNP $15 **MIP** $50

Walt Disney World Disney Fun 1995, 1995, Mattel, Model No. 13533
MNP $15 **MIP** $40

Walt Disney World Disney Fun 1997, 1997, Mattel, Model No. 17058
MNP $8 **MIP** $20

Walt Disney World Millennium Barbie, white or black, 2000, Mattel
MNP $5 **MIP** $15

Walt Disney World Resort Vacation Barbie, Ken, Tommy, Kelly, 1998, Mattel, Model No. 20315
MNP $35 **MIP** $80

Walt Disney World Toontown Stacie, 1994, Mattel, Model No. 11587
MNP $15 **MIP** $30

Warner Bros. Barbie Loves Tweety, 1999, Mattel, Model No. 21632
MNP $8 **MIP** $22

Warner Bros. Scooby-Doo Barbie, 2001, Mattel, Model No. 27966
MNP $5 **MIP** $15

Wedding Fantasy Gift Set, 1993, Mattel, Model No. 10924
MNP $50 **MIP** $125

Wedding Flower Blushing Orchid Bride, 1997, Mattel
MNP $100 **MIP** $200

Wedding Flower Romantic Rose Bride, 1996, Mattel
MNP $100 **MIP** $220

Wedding Party Gift Set, six dolls, 1991, Mattel, Model No. 9852
MNP $45 **MIP** $125

Wedgwood Barbie #1, blue dress, 2000, Mattel, Model No. 25641
MNP $40 **MIP** $80

Wedgwood Barbie #2, pink dress, black, 2001, Mattel, Model No. 50824
MNP $30 **MIP** $85

Wedgwood Barbie #2, pink dress, white, 2001, Mattel, Model No. 50823
MNP $30 **MIP** $85

Wessco Carnival Cruise Barbie, 1997, Mattel, Model No. 15186
MNP $25 **MIP** $40

Wessco International Traveler #1, 1995, Mattel, Model No. 13912
MNP $35 **MIP** $60

Wessco International Traveler #2, 1996, Mattel, Model No. 16158
MNP $25 **MIP** $50

Western Chic Barbie, 2002, Mattel, Model No. 55487
MNP $20 **MIP** $50

Western Fun Gift Set Barbie & Ken, 1989, Mattel, Model No. 5408
MNP $12 **MIP** $30

Western Fun Gift Set Barbie & Ken, 1990, Mattel, Model No. 5408
MNP $12 **MIP** $30

Western Plains Barbie, 2000, Mattel
MNP $40 **MIP** $95

Wind Rider Barbie, 2006, Mattel
MNP n/a **MIP** $150

Winn-Dixie Party Pink Barbie, 1989, Mattel, Model No. 7637
MNP $7 **MIP** $25

Winn-Dixie Pink Sensation, 1990, Mattel, Model No. 5410
MNP $6 **MIP** $20

Winn-Dixie Southern Beauty, 1991, Mattel, Model No. 3284
MNP $10 **MIP** $25

Winter Concert Barbie, 2002, Mattel
MNP $40 **MIP** $80

Winter Princess #1 Winter Princess, 1993, Mattel, Model No. 10655
MNP $35 **MIP** $175

Winter Princess #2 Evergreen Princess, 1994, Mattel, Model No. 12123
MNP $35 **MIP** $100

Winter Princess #3 Peppermint Princess, 1995, Mattel, Model No. 13598
MNP $35 **MIP** $175

Winter Princess #4 Jewel Princess, 1996, Mattel, Model No. 15826
MNP $35 **MIP** $175

BARBIE

Winter Princess #5 Midnight Princess, 1997, Mattel, Model No. 17780
MNP $35 **MIP** $175

Wizard of Oz, Cowardly Lion 2007, 2007, Mattel
MNP n/a **MIP** $25

Wizard of Oz, Dorothy 2007, 2007, Mattel
MNP n/a **MIP** $25

Wizard of Oz, Glinda 2007, 2007, Mattel
MNP n/a **MIP** $25

Wizard of Oz, Munchkins 3-pak 2007, 2007, Mattel
MNP n/a **MIP** $25

Wizard of Oz, Scarecrow 2007, 2007, Mattel
MNP n/a **MIP** $25

Wizard of Oz, Tinman 2007, 2007, Mattel
MNP n/a **MIP** $25

Wizard of Oz, Wicked Witch of the West, 2007, Mattel
MNP n/a **MIP** $25

Wizard of Oz, Winkie Guard, 2007, Mattel, w/Flying Monkey, Toys R Us exclusive
MNP n/a **MIP** $40

Woolworth's Special Expressions, black, blue dress, 1991, Mattel, Model No. 2583
MNP $4 **MIP** $10

Woolworth's Special Expressions, black, peach dress, 1992, Mattel, Model No. 3200
MNP $5 **MIP** $30

Woolworth's Special Expressions, black, pink dress, 1990, Mattel, Model No. 5505
MNP $4 **MIP** $10

Woolworth's Special Expressions, black, white dress, 1989, Mattel, Model No. 7326
MNP $5 **MIP** $20

Woolworth's Special Expressions, blue dress, pastel print, 1993, Mattel, Model No. 10048
MNP $5 **MIP** $15

Woolworth's Special Expressions, pink dress, 1990, Mattel, Model No. 5504
MNP $3 **MIP** $20

Woolworth's Special Expressions, white, 1989, Mattel, Model No. 4842
MNP $5 **MIP** $20

Woolworth's Special Expressions, white, blue dress, 1991, Mattel, Model No. 2582
MNP $4 **MIP** $15

Woolworth's Special Expressions, white, peach dress, 1992, Mattel, Model No. 3197
MNP $5 **MIP** $20

Woolworth's Sweet Lavender Barbie, black or white, 1992, Mattel, Model No. 2523/2522
MNP $12 **MIP** $28

Workin' Out Barbie Gift Set, 1997, Mattel
MNP $10 **MIP** $25

XO Valentine Barbie, 2003, Mattel
MNP $8 **MIP** $15

XXXOOO Barbie Doll, 2000, Mattel
MNP $8 **MIP** $20

Zac Posen Barbie/Ken Gift set, 2007, Mattel, FAO Schwarz and Dealer's exclusive
MNP n/a **MIP** $175

MATTEL DOLLS, NON-BARBIE

Audrey Hepburn, Breakfast At Tiffany's, black dress, 1998, Mattel
MNP $30 **MIP** $50

Audrey Hepburn, Pink Princess, 1998, Mattel
MNP $25 **MIP** $40

Betty Boop #1 Glamour Girl, 2001, Mattel, Model No. 29733
MNP $15 **MIP** $25

Bob Mackie Cher, 2001, Mattel, Model No. 29049
MNP $15 **MIP** $40

Buffy and Mrs. Beasley, 1968, Mattel, Model No. 3577
MNP $125 **MIP** $275

Chatty Cathy, 1999 reissue, 1999, Mattel, Model No. 23782
MNP $50 **MIP** $100

Chatty Cathy, Holiday, 1999, Mattel, Model No. 23783
MNP $50 **MIP** $125

(Mattel Photo)

Clark Gable as Rhett Butler, 2002, Mattel, Model No. 53854
MNP $30 **MIP** $70

Coca-Cola Holiday Series, Santa Claus, 1999, Mattel, Model No. 23288
MNP $25 **MIP** $60

Daytime Drama, Erica Kane #1, 1998, Mattel
MNP $20 **MIP** $50

Daytime Drama, Erica Kane #2, 1999, Mattel
MNP $20 **MIP** $45

Daytime Drama, Marlena Evans, 1999, Mattel
MNP $20 **MIP** $45

Elizabeth Taylor as Cleopatra, 1999, Mattel
MNP $35 **MIP** $60

Elizabeth Taylor in Father of the Bride, 2000, Mattel, Model No. 26836
MNP $30 **MIP** $70

Elvis Presley #1, 1998, Mattel, Model No. 20544
MNP $20 **MIP** $50

Elvis Presley #2 The Army Years, 1999, Mattel, Model No. 21912
MNP $20 **MIP** $50

(Mattel Photo)

Elvis Presley #4 King of Rock 'N Roll, 2002, Mattel, Model No. 53869
MNP $20 **MIP** $40

Flapper Minnie Mouse, 2001, Mattel, Model No. 29734
MNP $30 **MIP** $60

Frank Sinatra The Recording Years, 2001, Mattel
MNP $15 **MIP** $35

Great Villains, Captain Hook (Peter Pan), 1999, Mattel
MNP $30 **MIP** $75

Great Villains, Cruella DeVil, Power in Pinstripes, 1996, Mattel, Model No. 16295
MNP $35 **MIP** $75

Great Villains, Cruella DeVil, Ruthless in Red, 1997, Mattel
MNP $35 **MIP** $75

Great Villains, Evil Queen (Snow White), 1998, Mattel, Model No. 18626
MNP $30 **MIP** $75

Great Villains, Maleficent (Sleeping Beauty), 1999, Mattel
MNP $25 **MIP** $75

Great Villains, Ursula (Little Mermaid), 1997, Mattel, Model No. 17575
MNP $30 **MIP** $75

I Love Lucy, Be a Pal, 2002, Mattel, Model No. 52737
MNP $20 **MIP** $40

I Love Lucy, Job Switching, 1999, Mattel, Model No. 21268
MNP $20 **MIP** $35

I Love Lucy, Lucy and Ricky 50th Anniversary Dolls, 2000, Mattel
MNP $25 **MIP** $75

(Mattel Photo)

I Love Lucy, Lucy Gets a Paris Gown, 2003, Mattel, Model No. B0313
MNP $20 **MIP** $40

I Love Lucy, Lucy's Italian Movie, 2000, Mattel, Model No. 25527
MNP $20 **MIP** $40

I Love Lucy, Vitameatavegemin, 1998, Mattel
MNP $25 **MIP** $45

Jolly Holiday Mary Poppins, 2000, Mattel
MNP $20 **MIP** $40

Marilyn Monroe, 2002, Mattel, Model No. 53873
MNP $20 **MIP** $35

Rosie O'Donnell, 1999, Mattel
MNP $10 **MIP** $25

Tinker Bell, 2001, Mattel, Model No. 29735
MNP $20 **MIP** $40

Vivien Leigh Scarlett O'Hara #1 Barbecue at Twelve Oaks, 2001, Mattel, Model No. 29910
MNP $25 **MIP** $45

Vivien Leigh Scarlett O'Hara #2 Peachtree St. Drapery Dress, 2001, Mattel, Model No. 29771
MNP $25 **MIP** $45

PORCELAIN BARBIES

30th Anniversary Ken, 1991, Mattel, Model No. 1110
MNP $40 **MIP** $65

30th Anniversary Midge, 1993, Mattel, Model No. 7957
MNP $40 **MIP** $65

30th Anniversary Skipper, 1994, Mattel, Model No. 11396
MNP $50 **MIP** $100

Benefit Performance Barbie, 1988, Mattel, Model No. 5475
MNP $150 **MIP** $350

Blue Rhapsody, first porcelain Barbie, 1986, Mattel, Model No. 1708
MNP $200 **MIP** $450

Blushing Orchid Bride Barbie, 1997, Mattel, Model No. 16962
MNP $75 **MIP** $175

Bob Mackie Celebration of Dance Charleston, 2001, Mattel
MNP $100 **MIP** $300

Bob Mackie Celebration of Dance Tango, 1999, Mattel, Model No. 23451
MNP $150 **MIP** $200

Crystal Rhapsody, blond, Presidential Porcelain Barbie collection, 1992, Mattel, Model No. 1553
MNP $100 **MIP** $300

Crystal Rhapsody, brunette, Presidential Porcelain Barbie collection, 1993, Mattel, Model No. 10201
MNP $100 **MIP** $600

Enchanted Evening Barbie, 1987, Mattel, Model No. 3415
MNP $125 **MIP** $200

Faberge Imperial Elegance Barbie, limited to 15,000, 1999, Mattel, Model No. 19816
MNP $150 **MIP** $250

Gay Parisienne, blond, 1991, Mattel, Model No. 9973
MNP $225 **MIP** $400

Gay Parisienne, brunette, 1991, Mattel, Model No. 9973
MNP $75 **MIP** $125

Gay Parisienne, red hair, 1991, Mattel, Model No. 9973
MNP $225 **MIP** $400

Gold Sensation, Gold and Silver Porcelain Barbie Set, 1993, Mattel, Model No. 10246
MNP $175 **MIP** $350

Holiday Porcelain #1, Holiday Jewel, 1995, Mattel, Model No. 14311
MNP $55 **MIP** $125

Holiday Porcelain #2, Holiday Caroler, 1996, Mattel, Model No. 15760
MNP $60 **MIP** $100

Holiday Porcelain #3, Holiday Ball, 1997, Mattel, Model No. 18326
MNP $50 **MIP** $100

Holiday Porcelain #4, Holiday Gift, 1998, Mattel, Model No. 20128
MNP $50 **MIP** $100

Mattel's 50th Anniversary Barbie, 1995, Mattel, Model No. 14479
MNP $75 **MIP** $150

Mint Memories, Victorian Tea Porcelain Collection, 1999, Mattel
MNP $100 **MIP** $215

Plantation Belle, blond, Porcelain Treasures Collection, 1992, Mattel, Model No. 7526
MNP $100 **MIP** $300

Plantation Belle, red, Porcelain Treasures Collection, 1992, Mattel, Model No. 5351
MNP $50 **MIP** $125

Presidential Porcelain Evening Pearl Barbie, 1996, Mattel
MNP $95 **MIP** $225

Romantic Rose Bride, 1995, Mattel, Model No. 14541
MNP $75 **MIP** $175

Royal Splendor, Presidential Porcelain Collection, 1993, Mattel, Model No. 10950
MNP $100 **MIP** $250

Silken Flame Barbie, brunette, Porcelain Treasures Collection, 1993, Mattel, Model No. 1249
MNP $50 **MIP** $75

Silken Flame, blond, 1993, Mattel, Model No. 11099
MNP $150 **MIP** $250

Silver Starlight, Gold and Silver Porcelain Barbie Set, 1994, Mattel, Model No. 11875
MNP $175 **MIP** $350

Solo in the Spotlight, 1990, Mattel, Model No. 7613
MNP $50 **MIP** $75

Sophisticated Lady, 1990, Mattel, Model No. 5313
MNP $75 **MIP** $125

Star Lily Bride Barbie, Wedding Flower Collection, 1995, Mattel, Model No. 12953
MNP $125 **MIP** $250

Victorian Tea Orange Pekoe Barbie, 2000, Mattel, Model No. 25507
MNP $110 **MIP** $220

Wedding Day Barbie, 1989, Mattel, Model No. 2641
MNP $150 **MIP** $250

(Mattel Photo)

Wizard of Oz Cowardly Lion, 2002, Mattel, Model No. 54180
MNP $50 **MIP** $150

Wizard of Oz Dorothy, 2000, Mattel, Model No. 26834
MNP $70 **MIP** $150

Wizard of Oz Scarecrow, 2001, Mattel, Model No. 29190
MNP $50 **MIP** $150

Wizard of Oz Tin Man, 2001, Mattel, Model No. 29676
MNP $50 **MIP** $150

Wizard of Oz Wicked Witch, 2000, Mattel, Model No. 26835
MNP $70 **MIP** $150

Wizard of Oz Winged Monkey, 2001, Mattel, Model No. 29476
MNP $50 **MIP** $150

Fashions

BARBIE VINTAGE FASHIONS 1959-1966

Aboard Ship, Mattel, Model No. 1631
MNP $95 **MIP** $200

After Five, Mattel, Model No. 934
MNP $40 **MIP** $75

American Airlines Stewardess, Mattel, Model No. 984
MNP $30 **MIP** $175

Apple Print Sheath, Mattel, Model No. 917
MNP $15 **MIP** $100

Ballerina, Mattel, Model No. 989
MNP $30 **MIP** $150

Barbie Arabian Nights, Mattel, Model No. 0874
MNP $75 **MIP** $275

Barbie Baby-Sits, 1963, Mattel, Model No. 953
MNP $65 **MIP** $250

Barbie in Hawaii, Mattel, Model No. 1605
MNP $65 **MIP** $225

Barbie in Holland, Mattel, Model No. 0823
MNP $50 **MIP** $175

Barbie in Japan, Mattel, Model No. 0821
MNP $100 **MIP** $400

Barbie in Mexico, Mattel, Model No. 0820
MNP $95 **MIP** $200

Barbie in Switzerland, Mattel, Model No. 0822
MNP $75 **MIP** $225

Barbie Learns to Cook, Mattel, Model No. 1634
MNP $150 **MIP** $500

Barbie Skin Diver, Mattel, Model No. 1608
MNP $15 **MIP** $100

Barbie-Q Outfit, Mattel, Model No. 962
MNP $50 **MIP** $140

Beau Time, Mattel, Model No. 1651
MNP $175 **MIP** $500

Beautiful Bride, Mattel, Model No. 1698
MNP $400 **MIP** $2100

Benefit Performance, Mattel, Model No. 1667
MNP $450 **MIP** $1375

Black Magic, Mattel, Model No. 1609
MNP $60 **MIP** $250

Bride's Dream, Mattel, Model No. 947
MNP $50 **MIP** $200

Brunch Time, Mattel, Model No. 1628
MNP $110 **MIP** $350

Busy Gal, Mattel, Model No. 981
MNP $95 **MIP** $250

Busy Morning, Mattel, Model No. 956
MNP $125 **MIP** $275

Campus Sweetheart, Mattel, Model No. 1616
MNP $400 **MIP** $1600

Candy Striper Volunteer, Mattel, Model No. 0889
MNP $175 **MIP** $365

Career Girl, Mattel, Model No. 954
MNP $60 **MIP** $225

Caribbean Cruise, Mattel, Model No. 1687
MNP $65 **MIP** $200

Cheerleader, Mattel, Model No. 0876
MNP $50 **MIP** $170

Cinderella, Mattel, Model No. 0872
MNP $100 **MIP** $425

Club Meeting, Mattel, Model No. 1672
MNP $75 **MIP** $375

Coffee's On, Mattel, Model No. 1670
MNP $70 **MIP** $150

Commuter Set, Mattel, Model No. 916
MNP $500 **MIP** $1500

Country Club Dance, Mattel, Model No. 1627
MNP $115 **MIP** $400

Country Fair, Mattel, Model No. 1603
MNP $45 **MIP** $165

Crisp 'n Cool, Mattel, Model No. 1604
MNP $30 **MIP** $150

Cruise Stripes, Mattel, Model No. 918
MNP $35 **MIP** $165

Dancing Doll, Mattel, Model No. 1626
MNP $175 **MIP** $450

Debutante Ball, Mattel, Model No. 1666
MNP $375 **MIP** $1200

Dinner At Eight, Mattel, Model No. 946
MNP $60 **MIP** $225

Disc Date, Mattel, Model No. 1633
MNP $125 **MIP** $295

Dog n' Duds, Mattel, Model No. 1613
MNP $125 **MIP** $325

Dreamland, Mattel, Model No. 1669
MNP $110 **MIP** $200

Drum Majorette, Mattel, Model No. 0875
MNP $50 **MIP** $200

Easter Parade, Mattel, Shown on a Ponytail #3 doll, Model No. 971
MNP $950 **MIP** $4000

Enchanted Evening, Mattel, Seen here on a Bubblecut Barbie, Model No. 983
MNP $65 **MIP** $300

Evening Enchantment, Mattel, Model No. 1695
MNP $250 **MIP** $500

Evening Gala, Mattel, Model No. 1660
MNP $110 **MIP** $350

Evening Splendor, Mattel, Model No. 961
MNP $60 **MIP** $300

Fabulous Fashion, Mattel, Model No. 1676
MNP $250 MIP $525

Fancy Free, Mattel, Model No. 943
MNP $15 MIP $65

Fashion Editor, Mattel, Model No. 1635
MNP $225 MIP $650

Fashion Luncheon, Mattel, Model No. 1656
MNP $450 MIP $1200

Fashion Shiner, Mattel, Model No. 1691
MNP $90 MIP $220

Floating Gardens, Mattel, Model No. 1696
MNP $175 MIP $500

Floral Petticoat, Mattel, Model No. 921
MNP $20 MIP $50

Formal Occasion, Mattel, Model No. 1697
MNP $150 MIP $500

Fraternity Dance, Mattel, Model No. 1638
MNP $175 MIP $575

Friday Night Date, Mattel, Model No. 979
MNP $50 MIP $225

Fun At The Fair, Mattel, Model No. 1624
MNP $95 MIP $285

Fun n' Games, Mattel, Model No. 1619
MNP $110 MIP $300

Garden Party, Mattel, Model No. 931
MNP $47 MIP $150

Garden Tea Party, Mattel, Model No. 1606
MNP $50 MIP $175

Garden Wedding, Mattel, Model No. 1658
MNP $195 MIP $650

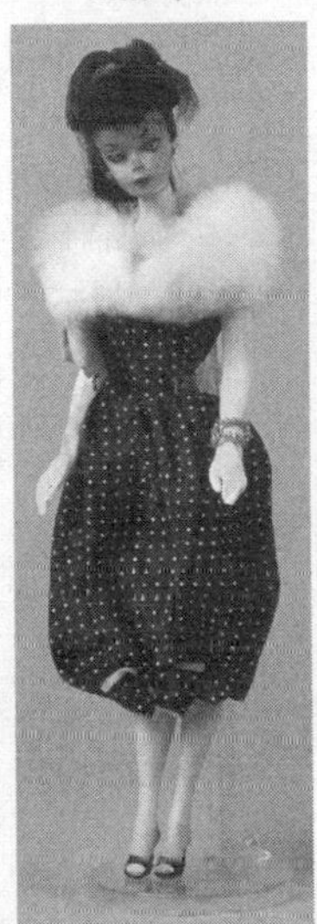

Gay Parisienne, Mattel, Shown here on a Ponytail #1, Model No. 964
MNP $1100 MIP $4000

Gold 'n Glamour, Mattel, Model No. 1647
MNP $600 MIP $1600

Golden Elegance, Mattel, Model No. 992
MNP $150 MIP $350

Golden Evening, Mattel, Model No. 1610
MNP $95 MIP $250

Golden Girl, Mattel, Model No. 911
MNP $65 MIP $150

Golden Glory, Mattel, Model No. 1645
MNP $175 MIP $425

Graduation, Mattel, Model No. 945
MNP $45 MIP $95

Guinevere, Mattel, Model No. 0873
MNP $100 MIP $300

Here Comes The Bride, Mattel, Model No. 1665
MNP $400 MIP $995

Holiday Dance, Mattel, Model No. 1639
MNP $250 MIP $595

Icebreaker, Mattel, Model No. 942
MNP $35 MIP $100

International Fair, Mattel, Model No. 1653
MNP $250 MIP $500

Invitation To Tea, Mattel, Model No. 1632
MNP $265 MIP $525

It's Cold Outside, brown, Mattel, Model No. 0819
MNP $25 MIP $110

It's Cold Outside, red, Mattel, Model No. 0819
MNP $30 MIP $165

Junior Designer, Mattel, Model No. 1620
MNP $150 MIP $350

Junior Prom, Mattel, Model No. 1614
MNP $275 MIP $600

Knit Hit, Mattel, Model No. 1621
MNP $125 MIP $225

Knit Separates, Mattel, Model No. 1602
MNP $70 MIP $160

Knitting Pretty, blue, Mattel, Model No. 957
MNP $65 MIP $150

Knitting Pretty, pink, Mattel, Model No. 957
MNP $75 MIP $300

Let's Dance, Mattel, Model No. 978
MNP $40 MIP $175

Little Red Riding Hood & The Wolf, Mattel, Model No. 0880
MNP $150 MIP $450

London Tour, Mattel, Model No. 1661
MNP $125 MIP $400

Lunch Date, Mattel, Model No. 1600
MNP $45 MIP $125

Lunch On The Terrace, Mattel, Model No. 1649
MNP $175 MIP $325

Lunchtime, Mattel, Model No. 1673
MNP $150 MIP $285

Magnificence, Mattel, Model No. 1646
MNP $350 MIP $595

Masquerade, Mattel, Model No. 944
MNP $40 MIP $175

Matinee Fashion, Mattel, Model No. 1640
MNP $320 MIP $525

Midnight Blue, Mattel, Model No. 1617
MNP $375 MIP $800

Miss Astronaut, Mattel, Shown here with re-constructed helmet, Model No. 1641
MNP $395 MIP $650

Modern Art, Mattel, Model No. 1625
MNP $300 MIP $550

Mood For Music, Mattel, Model No. 940
MNP $70 MIP $150

Movie Date, Mattel, Model No. 933
MNP $30 MIP $50

Music Center Matinee, Mattel, Model No. 1633
MNP $325 MIP $600

Nighty Negligee, Mattel, Model No. 965
MNP $30 MIP $75

On The Avenue, Mattel, Model No. 1644
MNP $200 MIP $525

Open Road, Mattel, The Mattel Road Map included with this outfit is especially hard to find, Model No. 985
MNP $125 MIP $350

Orange Blossom, 1961, Mattel, Model No. 987
MNP $30 MIP $150

Fashions

Outdoor Art Show, Mattel, Model No. 1650
MNP $195 **MIP** $500

Outdoor Life, Mattel, Model No. 1637
MNP $75 **MIP** $275

Pajama Party, Mattel, Model No. 1601
MNP $10 **MIP** $50

Pan Am Stewardess, Mattel, Very rare fashion shown on American Girl doll, Model No. 1678
MNP $1500 **MIP** $4000

Party Date, Mattel, Model No. 958
MNP $85 **MIP** $175

Patio Party, Mattel, Model No. 1692
MNP $100 **MIP** $325

Peachy Fleecy, Mattel, Model No. 915
MNP $35 **MIP** $100

Photo Fashion, Mattel, Model No. 1648
MNP $125 **MIP** $375

Picnic Set, Mattel, Model No. 967
MNP $125 **MIP** $410

Pink Moonbeams, Mattel, Model No. 1694
MNP $85 **MIP** $300

Plantation Belle, Mattel, Model No. 966
MNP $150 **MIP** $350

Poodle Parade, Mattel, Model No. 1643
MNP $400 **MIP** $950

Pretty As A Picture, Mattel, Model No. 1652
MNP $175 **MIP** $450

Print Aplenty, Mattel, Model No. 1686
MNP $75 **MIP** $275

Rain Coat, Mattel, Model No. 949
MNP $20 **MIP** $75

Reception Line, Mattel, Model No. 1654
MNP $350 **MIP** $500

Red Flare, Mattel, Model No. 939
MNP $30 **MIP** $150

Registered Nurse, Mattel, Seen here on Midge, Model No. 991
MNP $55 **MIP** $175

Resort Set, Mattel, Model No. 963
MNP $50 **MIP** $175

Riding In The Park, Mattel, Model No. 1668
MNP $175 **MIP** $595

Roman Holiday, Mattel, Shown on Ponytail #4 Barbie doll, Model No. 968
MNP $750 **MIP** $4800

Satin n' Rose, Mattel, Model No. 1611
MNP $190 **MIP** $375

Saturday Matinee, Mattel, Model No. 1615
MNP $525 **MIP** $900

Senior Prom, Mattel, Model No. 951
MNP $50 **MIP** $200

Sheath Sensation, Mattel, Model No. 986
MNP $80 **MIP** $150

Shimmering Magic, Mattel, Model No. 1664
MNP $350 **MIP** $1600

Silken Flame, Mattel, Model No. 977
MNP $40 **MIP** $125

Singing In The Shower, Mattel, Model No. 988
MNP $65 **MIP** $130

Skater's Waltz, Mattel, Model No. 1629
MNP $125 **MIP** $395

Ski Queen, Mattel, Model No. 948
MNP $50 **MIP** $150

Sleeping Pretty, Mattel, Model No. 1636
MNP $85 **MIP** $350

Sleepytime Gal, Mattel, Model No. 1674
MNP $95 **MIP** $220

Slumber Party, Mattel, Model No. 1642
MNP $95 **MIP** $260

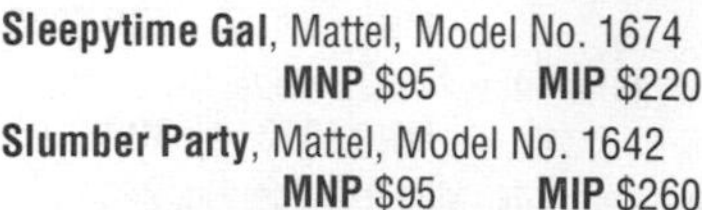

Solo In The Spotlight, Mattel, Seen here on a Ponytail #4 doll, Model No. 982
MNP $75 **MIP** $300

Sophisticated Lady, Mattel, Model No. 993
MNP $125 **MIP** $300

Sorority Meeting, Mattel, Model No. 937
MNP $60 **MIP** $180

Sporting Casuals, Mattel, Model No. 1671
MNP $60 **MIP** $165

Stormy Weather, Mattel, Model No. 0949
MNP $50 **MIP** $95

Student Teacher, Mattel, Model No. 1622
MNP $235 **MIP** $400

Studio Tour, Mattel, Model No. 1690
MNP $110 **MIP** $250

Suburban Shopper, Mattel, Model No. 969
MNP $75 **MIP** $300

Sunday Visit, Mattel, Model No. 1675
MNP $175 **MIP** $450

Sunflower, Mattel, Model No. 1683
MNP $75 **MIP** $245

Sweater Girl, Mattel, Model No. 976
MNP $75 **MIP** $175

Sweet Dreams, pink, Mattel, Model No. 973
MNP $200 **MIP** $425

Sweet Dreams, yellow, Mattel, Model No. 973
MNP $25 **MIP** $125

Swingin' Easy, Mattel, Model No. 955
MNP $95 **MIP** $245

Tennis Anyone, Mattel, Model No. 941
MNP $35 MIP $150

Theatre Date (1963), 1963, Mattel, Model No. 1612
MNP $75 MIP $175

Theatre Date (1964), 1964, Mattel, Model No. 959
MNP $75 MIP $200

Travel Togethers, Mattel, Model No. 1688
MNP $75 MIP $240

Under Fashions, Mattel, Model No. 1655
MNP $175 MIP $500

Undergarments, Mattel, Model No. 919
MNP $25 MIP $65

Underprints, Mattel, Model No. 1685
MNP $55 MIP $225

Vacation Time, Mattel, Model No. 1623
MNP $95 MIP $240

Wedding Day Set, Mattel, Model No. 972
MNP $150 MIP $350

White Magic, Mattel, Model No. 1607
MNP $95 MIP $275

Winter Holiday, Mattel, Model No. 975
MNP $82 MIP $165

FRANCIE VINTAGE FASHIONS 1966

Checkmates, Mattel, Model No. 1259
MNP $65 MIP $140

Clam Diggers, Mattel, Model No. 1258
MNP $100 MIP $250

Concert In The Park, Mattel, Model No. 1256
MNP $75 MIP $250

Dance Party, Mattel, Model No. 1257
MNP $150 MIP $250

First Formal, Mattel, Model No. 1260
MNP $80 MIP $175

First Things First, Mattel, Model No. 1252
MNP $55 MIP $100

Fresh As A Daisy, Mattel, Model No. 1254
MNP $65 MIP $140

Fur Out, 1966, Mattel, Model No. 1262
MNP $195 MIP $400

Gad-About, Mattel, Model No. 1250
MNP $75 MIP $220

Go Granny Go, 1966, Mattel, Model No. 1267
MNP $85 MIP $200

Hip Knits, 1966, Mattel, Model No. 1265
MNP $100 MIP $200

It's A Date, Mattel, Model No. 1251
MNP $70 MIP $125

Leather Limelight, 1966, Mattel, Model No. 1269
MNP $125 MIP $255

Orange Cozy, 1966, Mattel, Model No. 1263
MNP $170 MIP $235

Polka Dots N' Raindrops, Mattel, Model No. 1255
MNP $35 MIP $100

Quick Shift, 1966, Mattel, Model No. 1266
MNP $90 MIP $180

Shoppin' Spree, Mattel, Model No. 1261
MNP $75 MIP $140

Style Setters, 1966, Mattel, Model No. 1268
MNP $95 MIP $260

Swingin' Skimmy, 1966, Mattel, Model No. 1264
MNP $95 MIP $245

Tuckered Out, Mattel, Model No. 1253
MNP $55 MIP $125

KEN VINTAGE FASHIONS 1961-1966

American Airlines Captain #1, Mattel, Model No. 0779
MNP $175 MIP $300

Army and Air Force, Mattel, Model No. 797
MNP $120 MIP $245

Best Man, Mattel, Seen on Allan doll, Model No. 1425
MNP $700 MIP $1100

Business Appointment, Mattel, Model No. 1424
MNP $800 MIP $1150

Campus Corduroys, Mattel, Model No. 1410
MNP $20 MIP $65

Campus Hero, Mattel, Model No. 770
MNP $25 MIP $95

Casuals, striped shirt, Mattel, Model No. 0782
MNP $70 MIP $100

Casuals, yellow shirt, Mattel, Model No. 782
MNP $25 MIP $65

College Student, Mattel, Model No. 1416
MNP $190 MIP $400

Country Clubbin', Mattel, Model No. 1400
MNP $40 MIP $85

Dr. Ken, Mattel, Model No. 793
MNP $55 MIP $130

Dreamboat, Mattel, Model No. 785
MNP $40 MIP $95

Drum Major, Mattel, Model No. 0775
MNP $75 MIP $175

Fountain Boy, Mattel, Model No. 1407
MNP $230 MIP $325

Fraternity Meeting, Mattel, Model No. 1408
MNP $25 MIP $55

Fun On Ice, Mattel, Model No. 791
MNP $55 MIP $105

Going Bowling, Mattel, Model No. 1403
MNP $20 MIP $35

Going Huntin', Mattel, Model No. 1409
MNP $50 MIP $100

Graduation, Mattel, Model No. 795
MNP $35 MIP $65

Here Comes The Groom, Mattel, Model No. 1426
MNP $1000 MIP $1400

Hiking Holiday, Mattel, Model No. 1412
MNP $100 MIP $210

Holiday, Mattel, Model No. 1414
MNP $48 MIP $100

In Training, Mattel, Model No. 780
MNP $30 MIP $50

Jazz Concert, Mattel, Model No. 1420
MNP $135 MIP $250

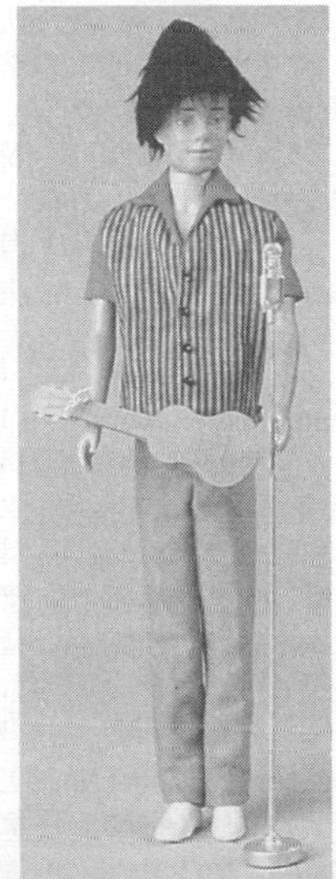

Ken A Go Go, Mattel, This outfit even included a mod-hair wig to make the rather staid Ken look hip, Model No. 1423
MNP $500 MIP $700

Ken Arabian Nights, Mattel, Model No. 0774
MNP $100 MIP $200

Ken In Hawaii, Mattel, Model No. 1404
MNP $100 MIP $195

Fashions

Ken In Holland, Mattel, Model No. 0777
MNP $155 **MIP** $250

Ken In Mexico, Mattel, Model No. 0778
MNP $150 **MIP** $250

Ken In Switzerland, Mattel, Model No. 0776
MNP $150 **MIP** $200

Ken Skin Diver, Mattel, Model No. 1406
MNP $30 **MIP** $50

King Arthur, Mattel, Model No. 0773
MNP $225 **MIP** $375

Masquerade (Ken), Mattel, Model No. 794
MNP $60 **MIP** $145

Mountain Hike, Mattel, Model No. 1427
MNP $150 **MIP** $300

Mr. Astronaut, Mattel, Model No. 1415
MNP $395 **MIP** $650

Off To Bed, Mattel, Model No. 1413
MNP $82 **MIP** $150

Play Ball, Mattel, Model No. 792
MNP $55 **MIP** $110

Rally Day, Mattel, Model No. 788
MNP $66 **MIP** $130

Roller Skate Date, w/hat, Mattel, Model No. 1405
MNP $40 **MIP** $125

Roller Skate Date, w/slacks, Mattel, Model No. 1405
MNP $40 **MIP** $150

Rovin' Reporter, Mattel, Model No. 1417
MNP $175 **MIP** $295

Sailor, Mattel, Model No. 796
MNP $65 **MIP** $120

Saturday Date, Mattel, Model No. 786
MNP $40 **MIP** $105

Seein' The Sights, Mattel, Model No. 1421
MNP $195 **MIP** $455

Ski Champion, Mattel, Model No. 798
MNP $85 **MIP** $155

Sleeper Set, blue, Mattel, Model No. 0781
MNP $60 **MIP** $120

Sleeper Set, brown, Mattel, Model No. 781
MNP $25 **MIP** $70

Special Date, Mattel, Model No. 1401
MNP $70 **MIP** $145

Sport Shorts, Mattel, Model No. 783
MNP $20 **MIP** $55

Summer Job, Mattel, Model No. 1422
MNP $290 **MIP** $475

Terry Togs, Mattel, Model No. 784
MNP $60 **MIP** $90

The Prince, Mattel, Model No. 0772
MNP $285 **MIP** $375

The Yachtsman, no hat, Mattel, Model No. 789
MNP $45 **MIP** $90

The Yachtsman, w/hat, Mattel, Model No. 0789
MNP $235 **MIP** $475

Time For Tennis, Mattel, Model No. 790
MNP $45 **MIP** $140

Time To Turn In, Mattel, Model No. 1418
MNP $80 **MIP** $175

Touchdown, Mattel, Model No. 799
MNP $55 **MIP** $125

Tuxedo, Mattel, Model No. 787
MNP $95 **MIP** $245

TV's Good Tonight, Mattel, Model No. 1419
MNP $110 **MIP** $250

Victory Dance, Mattel, Model No. 1411
MNP $60 **MIP** $135

RICKY FASHIONS 1965-1966

Let's Explore, Mattel, Model No. 1506
MNP $35 **MIP** $85

Lights Out, Mattel, Model No. 1501
MNP $55 **MIP** $100

Little Leaguer, Mattel, Model No. 1504
MNP $65 **MIP** $95

Saturday Show, Mattel, Model No. 1502
MNP $45 **MIP** $70

Skateboard Set, Mattel, Model No. 1505
MNP $55 **MIP** $100

Sunday Suit, Mattel, Model No. 1503
MNP $45 **MIP** $65

SKIPPER VINTAGE FASHIONS 1964-1966

Ballet Class, Mattel, Model No. 1905
MNP $60 **MIP** $135

Can You Play?, Mattel, Model No. 1923
MNP $60 **MIP** $125

Chill Chasers, Mattel, Model No. 1926
MNP $55 **MIP** $100

Cookie Time, Mattel, Model No. 1912
MNP $85 **MIP** $150

Country Picnic, Mattel, Model No. 1933
MNP $300 **MIP** $450

Day At The Fair, Mattel, Model No. 1911
MNP $120 **MIP** $200

Dog Show, Mattel, Model No. 1929
MNP $190 **MIP** $300

Dreamtime, Mattel, Model No. 1909
MNP $60 **MIP** $125

Dress Coat, Mattel, Model No. 1906
MNP $60 **MIP** $80

Flower Girl, Mattel, Model No. 1904
MNP $80 **MIP** $150

Fun Time, Mattel, Model No. 1920
MNP $100 **MIP** $200

Happy Birthday, Mattel, Model No. 1919
MNP $355 **MIP** $500

Junior Bridesmaid, Mattel, Model No. 1934
MNP $285 **MIP** $475

Land & Sea, Mattel, Model No. 1917
MNP $90 **MIP** $155

Learning To Ride, Mattel, Model No. 1935
MNP $185 **MIP** $275

Let's Play House, Mattel, Model No. 1932
MNP $125 **MIP** $250

Loungin' Lovelies, Mattel, Model No. 1930
MNP $55 **MIP** $125

Masquerade (Skipper), Mattel, Model No. 1903
MNP $80 **MIP** $155

Me N' My Doll, Mattel, Model No. 1913
MNP $150 **MIP** $260

Outdoor Casuals, Mattel, Model No. 1915
MNP $85 **MIP** $135

Platter Party, Mattel, Model No. 1914
MNP $75 **MIP** $125

Rain Or Shine, Mattel, Model No. 1916
MNP $50 **MIP** $90

Rainy Day Checkers, Mattel, Model No. 1928
MNP $155 **MIP** $300

Red Sensation, Mattel, Model No. 1901
MNP $65 **MIP** $125

School Days, Mattel, Model No. 1907
MNP $60 **MIP** $130

School Girl, Mattel, Model No. 1921
MNP $200 **MIP** $295

Ship Ahoy, Mattel, Model No. 1918
MNP $155 **MIP** $275

Silk N' Fancy, Mattel, Model No. 1902
MNP $60 **MIP** $125

Skating Fun, Mattel, Model No. 1908
MNP $48 **MIP** $110

Sledding Fun, Mattel, Model No. 1936
MNP $155 **MIP** $275

Sunny Pastels, Mattel, Model No. 1910
MNP $60 **MIP** $125

Tea Party, Mattel, Model No. 1924
MNP $185 **MIP** $300

Town Togs, Mattel, Model No. 1922
MNP $95 **MIP** $170

Under-Pretties, Mattel, Model No. 1900
MNP $25 **MIP** $50

What's New At The Zoo?, Mattel, Model No. 1925
MNP $50 **MIP** $120

TUTTI FASHIONS 1966

Puddle Jumpers, Mattel, Model No. 3601
MNP $20 **MIP** $45

Sand Castles, Mattel, Model No. 3603
MNP $55 **MIP** $98

Ship Shape, Mattel, Model No. 3602
MNP $55 **MIP** $90

Skippin' Rope, Mattel, Model No. 3604
MNP $55 **MIP** $95

Battery-Operated Toys

by Karen O'Brien

Battery-operated toys are the distant cousins of late 19th century automatons. Combining motion with bright tin lithography, quality craftsmanship, and prices the masses could afford, the battery-powered toys produced following World War II brought a new type of toy into American households—toys that moved under their own power.

Japanese companies that perfected tin lithography techniques prior to the war, began replacing wind-up and friction motors with the more reliable battery power source as postwar manufacturing resumed. The results were toys capable of complex and compound motions such as walking, lifting, drumming, and even dancing. The innovative designs and ingenuity employed in their creation make battery-operated toys valuable today for their motion, design, humorous outlook, and nostalgia.

Identifying the manufacturer of a particular toy without the box can be difficult. Many companies used only initials to mark toys, and others didn't mark them at all. Major manufacturers from the 1940s through the 1960s include, Marx, Linemar (Marx's Japanese subsidiary), Alps, Marusan, Yonezawa, Bandai, Ashai Toy, Toy Nomura, and Modern Toy. Marx is identified by a circle with an "X" containing the company name; Alps shows a mountain top with the name "Alps" underneath; Marusan used the initials "SAN"; Yonezawa used the initial "Y" in a leaf; Bandai used the initial "B" in a diamond; and Toy Nomura used the initials "TN."

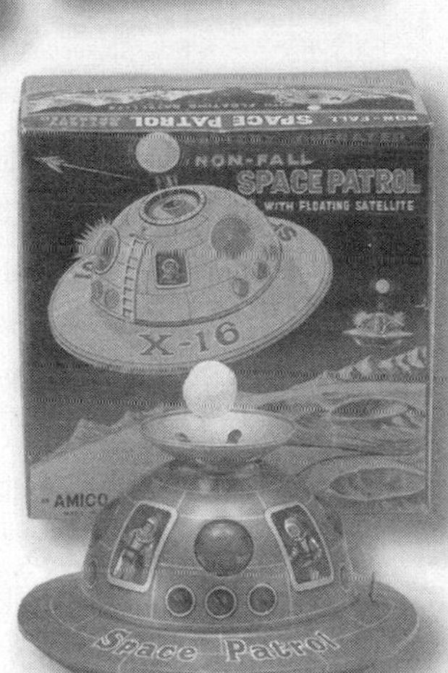

Contributor: Leo Rishty is a long-time collector of battery-ops. Don Hultzman is the author of the Collector's Guide to Battery Toys (Collector Books, 2002). Both contributors may be contacted in care of the editor at: Krause Publications, 700 E. State St., Iola, WI 54990.

THE TOP 10 BATTERY-OPERATED (In Mint Condition)

1. Smoking Popeye, Linemar, 1950s . . . $3,775
2. Bubble Blowing Popeye, Linemar, 1950s . . . 3,100
3. Mickey the Magician, Linemar, 1960s . . . 2,775
4. Gypsy Fortune Teller, Ichida, 1950s . . . 2,360
5. Smoking Spaceman, Linemar, 1950s . . . 2,250
6. Drumming Mickey Mouse, Linemar, 1950s . . . 1,900
7. Main Street, Linemar, 1950s . . . 1,575
8. Nutty Nibs, Linemar, 1950s . . . 1,500
9. Kooky-Spooky Whistling Tree, Marx, 1950s . . . 1,475
9. Climbing Donald Duck on Friction Fire, Linemar, 1950s . . . 1,350

ABC Fairy Train, 1950s, MT, 14-1/2" long
EX $95 **NM** $135 **MIP** $190

Accordion Bear, 1950s, Alps, 11" tall, 5 actions
EX $250 **NM** $450 **MIP** $650

Accordion Player Bunny, 1950s, Alps, 12" tall, 9" long
EX $300 **NM** $450 **MIP** $600

Accordion Playing Hobo w/Chimp, 1950s, Alps, 10" tall, 6 actions, plays cymbals
EX $280 **NM** $500 **MIP** $700

Air Cargo Prop-Jet Airplane, 1960s, Marx, Seaboard World Airlines, 12" long, 14-1/2" wingspan
EX $220 **NM** $350 **MIP** $465

Air Control Tower, 1960s, Bandai, 11" tall, 37" span, 4 actions
EX $265 **NM** $385 **MIP** $535

Air Defense Truck w/Pom-Pom Gun, 1950s, Linemar, 14" long
EX $170 **NM** $255 **MIP** $340

Air Mail Helicopter, 1960s, K-O, 10" long, 7 actions
EX $100 **NM** $200 **MIP** $300

Aircraft Carrier, 1950s, Marx, 20" long, 6 actions
EX $325 **NM** $475 **MIP** $625

Alley, the Exciting New Roaring Stalking Alligator, 1960s, Marx, 17-1/2" long
EX $175 **NM** $265 **MIP** $345

American Airlines DC-7, 1960s, Linemar, 17-1/2" long, 19" wingspan
EX $215 **NM** $330 **MIP** $435

American Airlines Electra, 1950s, Linemar, 18" long, 19-1/2" wingspan
EX $215 **NM** $350 **MIP** $440

American Airlines Flagship Caroline, 1950s, Linemar, 18" long,
EX $215 **NM** $350 **MIP** $440

Anti-Aircraft Unit No. 1, 1950s, Linemar, 12-1/2" long
EX $150 **NM** $235 **MIP** $310

Antique Gooney Car, 1960s, Alps, 9" long, 4 actions
EX $50 **NM** $95 **MIP** $135

Armored Knights Contest Set, 1950s, Bandai, 8" high, 6 actions,
EX $125 **NM** $250 **MIP** $375

Army Radio Jeep—J1490, 1950s, Linemar, 7-1/4" long
EX $105 **NM** $155 **MIP** $210

Arthur A-Go-Go, 1960s, Alps, 10" tall, drum lights up, cymbals detach, 6 actions
EX $215 **NM** $335 **MIP** $430

Atomic Rocket X-1800, 1960s, MT, 9" long, 3 actions
EX $180 **NM** $275 **MIP** $370

B-58 Hustler Jet, 1950s, Marx, 21" long, 12" wingspan
EX $350 **NM** $525 **MIP** $700

Ball Blowing Clown, 1950s, TN, w/2 balls and "mystery action"
EX $150 **NM** $200 **MIP** $270

Ball Playing Dog, 1950s, Linemar, 9"
EX $115 **NM** $175 **MIP** $230

Barber Bear, 1950s, Linemar, 9-1/2" tall
EX $325 **NM** $430 **MIP** $600

Barking Boxer Dog, 1950s, Marx, 7" long
EX $55 **NM** $80 **MIP** $120

Barney Bear Drummer, 1950s, Alps, 11" tall
EX $135 **NM** $205 **MIP** $265

Barnyard Rooster, 1950s, Marx, 10" tall
EX $100 **NM** $150 **MIP** $210

Bartender, 1960s, TN, 6 actions - shakes Martini, drinks, face turns red, puckers lips, smoke shoots out ears, 11-1/2" tall
EX $75 **NM** $100 **MIP** $145

Bear the Cashier, 1950s, MT, 7-1/2" tall
EX $210 **NM** $315 **MIP** $420

Bengali—The Exciting New Growling, Prowling Tiger, 1961, Linemar, 18-1/2" long
EX $175 **NM** $245 **MIP** $350

Big John, 1960s, Alps, 12" tall
EX $75 **NM** $110 **MIP** $150

Big John the Indian Chief, 1960s, TN, 12-1/2" tall
EX $100 **NM** $150 **MIP** $200

Big Max & Conveyor, 1958, Remco, 7" tall
EX $135 **NM** $190 **MIP** $275

Bimbo the Clown, 1950s, Alps, 9-1/4" tall
EX $225 **NM** $340 **MIP** $460

Blushing Gunfighter, 1960s, Y Co., 11" tall
EX $100 **NM** $160 **MIP** $200

Blushing Willie, 1960s, Y Co., 4 actions - pours real water, drinks, eyes spin, hair stands up, 10" tall
EX $75 **NM** $110 **MIP** $150

Bobby the Drumming Bear, 1950s, Alps, 10" tall
EX $225 **NM** $350 **MIP** $475

Bongo Player, 1960s, Alps, 10" tall
EX $80 **NM** $120 **MIP** $165

Bongo the Drumming Monkey, 1960s, Alps, 9-1/2" tall
EX $80 **NM** $125 **MIP** $170

Brave Eagle, 1950s, TN, 11" tall
EX $100 **NM** $150 **MIP** $215

Brewster the Rooster, 1950s, Marx, 9-1/2" tall
EX $120 **NM** $175 **MIP** $250

Bubble Blowing Bear, 1950s, MT, 9-1/2" tall
EX $175 **NM** $255 **MIP** $345

Bubble Blowing Boy, 1950s, Y Co., 7" tall
EX $150 **NM** $225 **MIP** $300

Bubble Blowing Monkey, 1950s, Alps, 5 actions, 10" tall
EX $150 **NM** $200 **MIP** $300

Bubble Blowing Popeye, 1950s, Linemar, 11-3/4" tall
EX $1550 **NM** $2325 **MIP** $3100

Bubbling Bull, 1950s, Linemar, 8" tall
EX $100 **NM** $165 **MIP** $215

Bunny the Magician, 1950s, Alps, 14-1/2" tall
EX $275 **NM** $435 **MIP** $550

Burger Chef Dog, 1950s, Y Co., 9" tall, dog cooking w/frying pan
EX $170 **NM** $250 **MIP** $340

Busy Housekeeper, 1950s, Alps, 8-1/2" tall
EX $225 **NM** $345 **MIP** $385

Busy Secretary, 1950s, Linemar, 7-1/2" tall
EX $235 **NM** $340 **MIP** $450

Busy Shoe Shining Bear, 1950s, Alps, 10" tall
EX $155 **NM** $230 **MIP** $295

Cabin Cruiser with Outboard Motor, 1950s, Linemar, 12" long
EX $135 **NM** $210 **MIP** $275

Calypso Joe, 1950s, Linemar, 11" tall
EX $300 **NM** $450 **MIP** $600

Camera Shooting Bear, 1950s, Linemar, 11" tall
EX $500 **NM** $750 **MIP** $1000

Cappy the Baggage Porter Dog, 1960s, Alps, 12" tall
EX $150 **NM** $225 **MIP** $300

Caterpillar, 1950s, Alps, 16" long
EX $60 **NM** $95 **MIP** $135

Central Choo Choo, 1960s, MT, 15" long
EX $50 **NM** $75 **MIP** $100

Charlie the Drumming Clown, 1950s, Alps, 9-1/2" tall
EX $155 **NM** $235 **MIP** $315

Charlie Weaver, 1962, TN, 12"
EX $85 **NM** $120 **MIP** $175

Charm the Cobra, 1960s, Alps, 6" tall
EX $130 **NM** $200 **MIP** $280

Chee Chee Chihuahua, 1960s, Mego, 8" tall
EX $45 **NM** $65 **MIP** $90

Chef Cook, 1960s, Y Co., 11-1/2" tall
EX $155 **NM** $245 **MIP** $325

Chippy the Chipmunk, 1950s, Alps, 12" long
EX $75 **NM** $125 **MIP** $165

Circus Elephant, 1950s, TN, w/ball and umbrella
EX $65 **NM** $110 **MIP** $155

Circus Fire Engine, 1960s, MT, 11" long
EX $125 **NM** $205 **MIP** $265

Clancy the Great, 1960s, Ideal, 19-1/2" tall
EX $110 **NM** $175 **MIP** $235

Climbing Donald Duck on Friction Fire Engine, 1950s, Linemar, 12" long
EX $675 **NM** $950 **MIP** $1350

Clown Circus Car, 1960s, MT, 8-1/2" long
EX $125 **NM** $200 **MIP** $260

Clown on Unicycle, 1960s, MT, 10-1/2" tall
EX $230 **NM** $365 **MIP** $475

Coney Island Penny Machine, 1950s, Remco, 13" tall
EX $125 **NM** $140 **MIP** $275

Coney Island Rocket Ride, 1950s, Alps, 13-1/2" tall
EX $460 **NM** $710 **MIP** $925

Cragstan 2-Gun Sheriff, 1950s, Cragstan, remote control, two guns
EX $65 **NM** $110 **MIP** $155

Cragstan Beep Beep Greyhound Bus, 1950s, Cragstan, 20" long
EX $155 **NM** $230 **MIP** $285

Cragstan Crapshooter, 1950s, Y Co., 9-1/2" tall
EX $140 **NM** $200 **MIP** $250

Cragstan Crapshooting Monkey, 1950s, Alps, 9" tall
EX $140 **NM** $200 **MIP** $250

Cragstan Mother Goose, 1960s, Y Co., 8-1/4" tall
EX $110 **NM** $165 **MIP** $220

Cragstan Playboy, 1960s, Cragstan, 13" tall
EX $95 **NM** $155 **MIP** $200

Cragstan Roulette, A Gambling Man, 1960s, Y Co., 9" tall
EX $200 **NM** $275 **MIP** $345

Crawling Baby, 1940s, Linemar, 11" long
EX $40 **NM** $60 **MIP** $80

Daisy, the Jolly Drumming Duck, 1950s, Alps, 9" tall
EX $175 **NM** $260 **MIP** $350

Dancing Merry Chimp, 1960s, Kuramochi, 11" tall
EX $105 **NM** $155 **MIP** $225

Dandy, the Happy Drumming Pup, 1950s, Alps, 8-1/2" tall
EX $110 **NM** $165 **MIP** $230

Dennis the Menace, 1950s, Rosko, 9" tall, with xylophone
EX $185 **NM** $265 **MIP** $345

Disney Acrobats, 1950s, Linemar, 9" tall; Mickey, Donald, and Pluto
EX $585 **NM** $890 **MIP** $1200

Disney Fire Engine, 1950s, Linemar, 11" long
EX $575 **NM** $830 **MIP** $1130

Disneyland Fire Engine, 1950s, Linemar, 18" long
EX $500 **NM** $750 **MIP** $1000

Dolly Dressmaker, 1950s, TN, 7-1/2" tall
EX $250 **NM** $350 **MIP** $510

Donald Duck, 1960s, Linemar, 8" tall
EX $275 **NM** $385 **MIP** $525

Doxie the Dog, 1950s, Linemar, 9" long
EX $35 **NM** $50 **MIP** $65

Drinking Captain, 1960s, S & E, 12" tall
EX $110 **NM** $165 **MIP** $220

Drummer Bear, 1950s, Alps, 10" tall
EX $150 **NM** $225 **MIP** $300

Drumming Mickey Mouse, 1950s, Linemar, 10" tall
EX $950 **NM** $1425 **MIP** $1900

Drumming Polar Bear, 1960s, Alps, 12"
EX $85 **NM** $125 **MIP** $170

Ducky Duckling, 1960s, Alps, 8"
EX $50 **NM** $80 **MIP** $110

El Toro, Cragstan Bullfighter, 1950s, TN, 9-1/2" long
EX $120 **NM** $190 **MIP** $270

Feeding Bird Watcher, 1950s, Linemar, 9" tall
EX $300 NM $465 MIP $625

Fido the Xylophone Player, 1950s, Alps, 8-3/4" tall
EX $150 NM $230 MIP $300

Flintstone Yacht, 1961, Remco, 17" long
EX $110 NM $165 MIP $225

Frankenstein Monster, 1960s, TN, 14" tall
EX $165 NM $250 MIP $330

Frankie the Rollerskating Monkey, 1950s, Alps, 12"
EX $150 NM $225 MIP $300

Fred Flintstone Bedrock Band, 1962, Alps, 9-1/2" tall
EX $400 NM $595 MIP $760

Fred Flintstone Flivver, 1960s, Marx, 7" long
EX $430 NM $670 MIP $850

Fred Flintstone on Dino, 1961, Marx, 22"
EX $550 NM $775 MIP $1000

Friendly Jocko, My Favorite Pet, 1950s, Alps, 8" tall
EX $115 NM $175 MIP $240

Gino, Neapolitan Balloon Blower, 1960s, Tomiyama, 10" tall
EX $150 NM $225 MIP $275

Girl with Baby Carriage, 1960s, TN, 8" tall
EX $110 NM $165 MIP $215

Godzilla Monster, 1970s, Marusan, 11-1/2" tall
EX $190 NM $285 MIP $375

Good Time Charlie, 1960s, MT, 12" tall
EX $130 NM $185 MIP $225

Grandpa Panda Bear, 1950s, MT, 9" tall
EX $130 NM $205 MIP $275

Great Garloo, 1960s, Marx, 23" tall green monster
EX $385 NM $550 MIP $765

Green Caterpillar, 1950s, Daiya, 19-1/2" long
EX $125 NM $185 MIP $250

Gypsy Fortune Teller, 1950s, Ichida, 12" tall, twenty cards
EX $1200 NM $1775 MIP $2360

Happy & Sad Face Cymbal Clown, 1960s, Y Co., 10" tall
EX $175 NM $260 MIP $340

Happy Fiddler Clown, 1950s, Alps, 9-1/2" tall
EX $285 NM $410 MIP $530

Happy Naughty Chimp, 1960s, Daishin, 9-1/2" tall
EX $75 NM $110 MIP $155

Happy Santa One-Man Band, 1950s, Alps, 9" tall
EX $130 NM $205 MIP $275

Hippo Chef, 1960s, Y Co., 10" tall
EX $145 NM $230 MIP $315

Hobo Clown with Accordion, 1950s, Alps, 10-1/2" tall
EX $300 NM $425 MIP $600

Hong Kong Rickshaw, 1960s, PMC Co., all plastic, made in Hong Kong
EX $55 NM $85 MIP $125

Hoop Zing Girl, 1950s, Linemar, 11-1/2" tall
EX $145 NM $225 MIP $300

Hoopy the Fishing Duck, 1950s, Alps, 10" tall
EX $275 NM $410 MIP $555

Hooty the Happy Owl, 1960s, Alps, 9" tall
EX $85 NM $125 MIP $170

Hungry Baby Bear, 1950s, Y Co., 9-1/2" tall
EX $215 NM $315 MIP $415

Hungry Cat, 1960s, Linemar, 9" tall
EX $340 NM $485 MIP $730

Hungry Hound Dog, 1950s, Y Co., 9-1/2" tall
EX $205 NM $310 MIP $405

Hy-Que, the "Speak no Evil, See No Evil, Hear No Evil" Monkey, 1960s, TN, 6 actions, shake his hand and he raises arms, 17" tall
EX $200 NM $285 MIP $430

Ice Cream Baby Bear, Vanilla, 1950s, MT, 9-1/2"
EX $225 NM $340 MIP $435

Indian Joe, 1960s, Alps, 12" tall
EX $95 NM $140 MIP $190

Jocko the Drinking Monkey, 1950s, Linemar, 11" tall
EX $125 NM $175 MIP $240

Jo-Jo the Flipping Monkey, 1970s, TN, 10" tall
EX $45 NM $70 MIP $100

Jolly Bambino, 1950s, Alps, 9" tall
EX $275 NM $410 MIP $540

Jolly Bear Peanut Vendor, 1950s, TN, 8" tall
EX $260 NM $375 MIP $510

Jolly Daddy, 1950s, Marusan, 8-3/4" tall
EX $165 NM $245 MIP $325

Jolly Drummer Chimpy, 1950s, Alps, 9" tall
EX $75 NM $115 MIP $150

Jolly Pianist, 1950s, Marusan, 8" tall
EX $110 NM $175 MIP $230

Jolly Santa on Snow, 1950s, Alps, 12-1/2" tall
EX $170 NM $265 MIP $350

Josie the Walking Cow, 1950s, Daiya, 14" long
EX $175 NM $235 MIP $355

Jumbo the Bubble Blowing Elephant, 1950s, Y Co., 7-1/4" tall
EX $90 NM $135 MIP $230

Jungle Jumbo [Elephant], 1950s, B-C Toy Co., walks & bellows, remote control
EX $85 NM $145 MIP $195

Jungle Trio, 1950s, Linemar, 8" tall
EX $485 NM $740 MIP $990

King Zor, 1962, Ideal, blue plastic dinosaur, 30" long
EX $325 NM $510 MIP $725

Kissing Couple, 1950s, Ichida, 10-3/4" long
EX $170 NM $225 MIP $340

Knitting Grandma, 1950s, TN, 8-1/2" tall
EX $185 NM $275 MIP $365

Kooky-Spooky Whistling Tree, 1950s, Marx, 14-1/4" tall
EX $775 NM $1135 MIP $1475

Lambo Elephant, 1950s, Alps, 16" long with trailer
EX $230 NM $350 MIP $470

Linemar Music Hall, 1950s, Linemar, 8" tall
EX $125 NM $175 MIP $235

Lion, 1950s, Linemar, 9" long
EX $75 NM $110 MIP $155

Loop the Loop Clown, 1960s, TN, 10" tall
EX $70 NM $120 MIP $170

Mac the Turtle, 1960s, Y Co., 8" tall
EX $130 NM $195 MIP $265

Magic Man Clown, 1950s, Marusan, 11" tall
EX $225 NM $325 MIP $450

Magic Snowman, 1950s, MT, 11-1/4" tall
EX $135 **NM** $195 **MIP** $270

Main Street, 1950s, Linemar, 19-1/2" long
EX $775 **NM** $1175 **MIP** $1575

Major Tooty, 1960s, Alps, 14" tall
EX $110 **NM** $155 **MIP** $210

Mambo the Jolly Drumming Elephant, 1950s, Alps, 9-1/2" tall
EX $155 **NM** $230 **MIP** $315

Marching Bear, 1960s, Alps, 10" tall
EX $110 **NM** $165 **MIP** $225

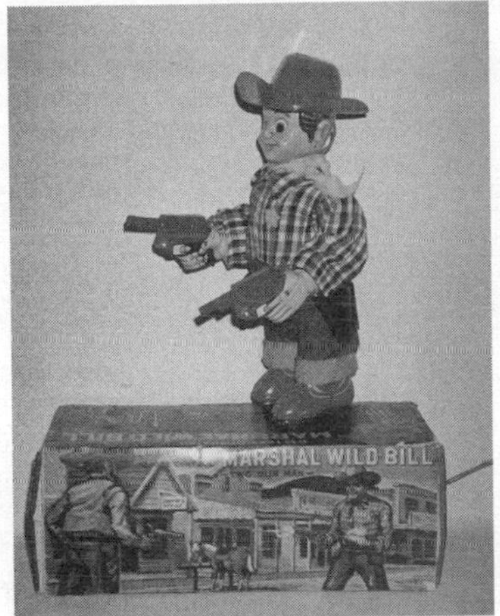

(Don Hultzman)

Marshal Wild Bill, 1950s, Y Co., 10-1/2" tall
EX $185 **NM** $285 **MIP** $380

Marvelous Mike, 1950s, Saunders, 17" long
EX $170 **NM** $260 **MIP** $350

Maxwell Coffee-Loving Bear, 1960s, TN, 10" tall
EX $150 **NM** $225 **MIP** $350

McGregor, 1960s, Rosko, 12" tall
EX $155 **NM** $220 **MIP** $315

Mew-Mew Walking Cat, 1950s, MT, three actions, remote control
EX $70 **NM** $125 **MIP** $150

Mickey the Magician, 1960s, Linemar, 10" tall
EX $1375 **NM** $2050 **MIP** $2775

Mighty Kong, 1950s, Marx, 11" tall
EX $295 **NM** $430 **MIP** $575

Mischievous Monkey, 1950s, MT, 18" tall
EX $210 **NM** $315 **MIP** $430

Miss Friday the Typist, 1950s, TN, 6 actions, 8" tall
EX $240 **NM** $350 **MIP** $440

Motorcycle Cop, 1950s, Daiya, 10-1/2" long, 8-1/4" tall
EX $475 **NM** $695 **MIP** $920

Mr. MacPooch, 1950s, Marusan, 8" tall
EX $155 **NM** $225 **MIP** $300

Mr. Traffic Policeman, 1950s, A-I, 14" tall
EX $235 **NM** $350 **MIP** $475

Mumbo Jumbo, 1960s, Alps, 9-3/4" tall
EX $130 **NM** $195 **MIP** $250

Musical Bear, 1950s, Linemar, 10" tall
EX $285 **NM** $425 **MIP** $575

Musical Jackal, 1950s, Linemar, 10" tall
EX $175 **NM** $315 **MIP** $700

(Don Hultzman)

Musical Jolly Chimp, 1960s, Daishin, 10-1/2" tall, plays cymbals, glares w/ eyes, shows teeth and chatters
EX $50 **NM** $75 **MIP** $110

Musical Marching Bear, 1950s, Alps, 11" tall
EX $250 **NM** $385 **MIP** $550

NASA Space Capsule, 1950s, four actions
EX $200 **NM** $315 **MIP** $430

Nutty Mad Indian, 1960s, Marx, 12" tall
EX $125 **NM** $185 **MIP** $240

Nutty Nibs, 1950s, Linemar, 11-1/2" tall
EX $750 **NM** $1125 **MIP** $1500

Odd Ogg, 1962, Ideal, large plastic turtle-frog creature
EX $145 **NM** $225 **MIP** $365

Ol' Sleepy Head RIP, 1950s, Y Co., 9" tall
EX $190 **NM** $300 **MIP** $400

Panda Bear, 1970s, MT, 10" long
EX $55 **NM** $80 **MIP** $110

Pat the Roaring Elephant, 1950s, Y Co., 9" long
EX $155 **NM** $225 **MIP** $310

Peppermint Twist Doll, 1950s, Haji, 12" tall
EX $185 **NM** $285 **MIP** $375

Peppy Puppy, 1950s, Y Co., 8" long
EX $65 **NM** $95 **MIP** $120

Pet Turtle, 1960s, Alps, 7" long
EX $85 **NM** $130 **MIP** $175

Pete the Space Man, 1960s, Bandai, 5" tall
EX $75 **NM** $110 **MIP** $155

Peter the Drumming Rabbit, 1950s, Alps, 13" tall
EX $170 **NM** $250 **MIP** $335

Phantom Raider, 1963, Ideal, 33", freighter turned warship
EX $80 **NM** $135 **MIP** $200

Picnic Bear, 1950s, Alps, 5 actions - pours real water, 10" tall
EX $150 **NM** $200 **MIP** $265

Picnic Bunny, 1950s, Alps, 10" tall
EX $150 **NM** $185 **MIP** $240

Picnic Monkey, 1950s, Alps, 10" tall
EX $125 **NM** $185 **MIP** $240

Picnic Poodle, 1950s, STS, 7" long
EX $45 **NM** $70 **MIP** $95

Pierrot Monkey Cycle, 1950s, MT, 8" tall
EX $255 **NM** $370 **MIP** $500

Piggy Cook, 1950s, Y Co., 9-1/2" tall
EX $160 **NM** $240 **MIP** $325

Pinkee the Farmer, 1950s, MT, 9-1/2" long
EX $125 **NM** $190 **MIP** $250

Pipie the Whale, 1950s, Alps, 12" long
EX $175 **NM** $260 **MIP** $365

Pistol Pete, 1950s, Marusan, 10-1/4" tall
EX $275 **NM** $460 **MIP** $550

Playful Puppy w/Caterpillar, 1950s, MT, 5" tall
EX $115 **NM** $170 **MIP** $230

Polar Bear, 1970s, Alps, 8" long
EX $75 **NM** $110 **MIP** $150

Popcorn Eating Bear, 1950s, MT, 9" tall
EX $135 **NM** $200 **MIP** $265

Rambling Ladybug, 1960s, MT, 8" long
EX $70 **NM** $100 **MIP** $135

Reading Bear, 1950s, Alps, 9" tall
EX $165 **NM** $245 **MIP** $330

Rembrandt the Monkey Artist, 1950s, Alps, 8" tall
EX $215 **NM** $315 **MIP** $430

Ricki the Begging Poodle, 1950s, Rock Valley, 9" long
EX $40 **NM** $55 **MIP** $70

Roarin' Jungle Lion, 1950s, Marx, 16" long
EX $170 **NM** $240 **MIP** $320

Rock 'N Roll Monkey, 1950s, Rosko, 13" tall
EX $200 **NM** $290 **MIP** $385

Rocking Chair Bear, 1950s, MT, 10" tall
EX $135 **NM** $200 **MIP** $265

Roller Skater, 1950s, Alps, 12" tall
EX $175 **NM** $260 **MIP** $355

Root Beer Counter, 1960s, K Co., 8" tall
EX $155 **NM** $230 **MIP** $310

Sam the Shaving Man, 1960s, Plaything Toy, 11-1/2" tall
EX $155 NM $230 MIP $310

Sammy Wong the Tea Totaler, 1950s, TN, 10" tall
EX $155 NM $230 MIP $310

Santa Claus on Handcar, 1960s, MT, 10" tall
EX $140 NM $220 MIP $290

Santa Claus on Reindeer Sleigh, 1950s, MT, 17" long
EX $425 NM $640 MIP $850

Santa Claus on Scooter, 1960s, MT, 10" tall
EX $150 NM $225 MIP $300

Santa Copter, 1960s, MT, 8-1/2" high
EX $115 NM $170 MIP $225

Saxophone Playing Monkey, 1950s, Alps, 9-1/2" tall
EX $250 NM $385 MIP $510

Serpent Charmer, 1950s, Linemar, 7" tall
EX $345 NM $485 MIP $700

Shaggy the Friendly Pup, 1960s, Alps, 8" long
EX $30 NM $50 MIP $70

Shoe Maker Bear, 1960s, TN, 8-1/2" tall
EX $165 NM $245 MIP $325

Shoe Shine Bear, 1950s, TN, 9" tall
EX $175 NM $250 MIP $350

Shoe Shine Joe, 1950s, Alps, 11" tall, monkey w/pipe polishing a shoe
EX $175 NM $235 MIP $325

Shoe Shine Monkey, 1950s, TN, 9" tall
EX $175 NM $235 MIP $325

Shooting Gorilla, 1950s, MT, 12" tall
EX $210 NM $300 MIP $420

Shutterbug Photographer, 1950s, TN, 9" tall
EX $600 NM $850 MIP $1025

Skating Circus Clown, 1950s, TPS, 6" tall
EX $600 NM $850 MIP $1025

Skiing Santa, 1960s, MT, 12" tall
EX $175 NM $260 MIP $345

Skipping Monkey, 1960s, TN, 9-1/2" tall
EX $45 NM $65 MIP $90

Slalom Game, 1960s, TN, 15-1/4" long
EX $115 NM $175 MIP $235

Sleeping Baby Bear, 1950s, Linemar, 9" long
EX $275 NM $420 MIP $550

Sleepy Pup, 1960s, Alps, 9" long
EX $45 NM $75 MIP $100

Slurpy Pup, 1960s, TN, 6-1/2" long
EX $55 NM $80 MIP $110

Smoking Bunny, 1950s, Marusan, 10-1/2" tall
EX $125 NM $190 MIP $260

Smoking Elephant, 1950s, Marusan, 8-3/4" tall
EX $135 NM $200 MIP $250

Smoking Grandpa in Rocker, 1950s, Marusan, 8" tall, 4 actions
EX $190 NM $300 MIP $390

Smoking Popeye, 1950s, Linemar, 9" tall
EX $1875 NM $2625 MIP $3775

Smoking Spaceman, 1950s, Linemar, 12" tall
EX $1125 NM $1675 MIP $2250

Smoky Bear, 1950s, Marusan, 9" tall
EX $250 NM $335 MIP $500

Sneezing Bear, 1950s, Linemar, 9" tall
EX $190 NM $270 MIP $380

Snoopy Sniffer, 1960s, MT, 8" long
EX $45 NM $70 MIP $90

Spanking Bear, 1950s, Linemar, 9" tall
EX $190 NM $300 MIP $385

Struttin' Sam, 1950s, Haji, 10-1/2" tall
EX $215 NM $370 MIP $430

Sunday Driver, 1950s, MT, 10" long
EX $75 NM $115 MIP $155

Super Susie, 1950s, Linemar, 9" tall
EX $575 NM $860 MIP $1175

Suzette the Eating Monkey, 1950s, Linemar, 8-3/4" tall
EX $425 NM $585 MIP $800

Switchboard Operator, 1950s, Linemar, 7-1/2" tall
EX $475 NM $725 MIP $950

Tarzan, 1966, Marusan, 13" tall
EX $625 NM $935 MIP $1250

Teddy Bear Swing, 1950s, TN, 17" tall
EX $325 NM $425 MIP $650

Teddy the Artist, 1950s, Y Co., 8-1/2" tall
EX $375 NM $560 MIP $800

Teddy the Boxing Bear, 1950s, Y Co., 9" tall
EX $150 NM $225 MIP $300

Teddy the Rhythmical Drummer, 1960s, Alps, 11" tall
EX $110 NM $170 MIP $230

Teddy-Go-Kart, 1960s, Alps, 10-1/2" long
EX $120 NM $180 MIP $225

Telephone Bear, 1950s, Linemar, 7-1/2" tall
EX $225 NM $315 MIP $425

Telephone Bear with Rocking Chair, 1950s, MT, 10" tall
EX $250 NM $350 MIP $450

Television Spaceman, 1960s, Alps, 14-1/2" tall
EX $475 NM $700 MIP $975

Tinkling Trolley, 1950s, MT, 10-1/2" long
EX $150 NM $225 MIP $300

Tom and Jerry Choo Choo, 1960s, MT, 10-1/4" long
EX $175 NM $250 MIP $325

Tom and Jerry Handcar, 1960s, MT, 7-3/4" long
EX $160 NM $270 MIP $350

Tom-Tom Indian, 1961, Y Co., 10-1/2" tall
EX $100 NM $150 MIP $185

Topo Gigio Playing the Xylophone, 1960s, TN
EX $350 NM $550 MIP $725

Traveler Bear, 1950s, Linemar, 8" tall
EX $150 NM $225 MIP $300

Trumpet Playing Bunny, 1950s, Alps, 10" tall
EX $200 NM $300 MIP $400

Trumpet Playing Monkey, 1950s, Alps, 9" tall
EX $200 NM $300 MIP $400

Tubby the Turtle, 1950s, Y Co., 7" long
EX $70 NM $110 MIP $140

Tumbles the Bear, 1960s, Yanoman, 8-1/2" tall
EX $95 NM $140 MIP $190

Twirly Whirly, 1950s, Alps, 13-1/2" tall
EX $400 NM $600 MIP $800

Walking Bear with Xylophone, 1950s, Linemar, 10" tall
EX $270 NM $420 MIP $540

Walking Elephant, 1950s, Linemar, 8-1/2" tall
EX $100 NM $150 MIP $225

Walking Esso Tiger, 1950s, Marx, 11-1/2" tall
EX $190 NM $285 MIP $380

Walking Itchy Dog, 1950s, Alps, 9" long
EX $55 NM $85 MIP $110

Western Locomotive, 1950s, MT, 10-1/2" long
EX $45 NM $35 MIP $90

Windy the Elephant, 1950s, TN, 9-3/4" tall
EX $150 NM $220 MIP $310

Yeti the Abominable Snowman, 1960s, Marx, 12" tall
EX $425 NM $625 MIP $850

Yo-Yo Clown, 1960s, Alps, 9" tall
EX $190 NM $275 MIP $390

Yo-Yo Monkey, 1960s, Alps, 9" tall
EX $135 NM $200 MIP $265

Yo-Yo Monkey, 1960s, YM, 12" tall
EX $125 NM $200 MIP $270

Yummy Yum Kitty, 1950s, Alps, 9-1/2" tall
EX $275 NM $425 MIP $550

Zero Fighter Plane, 1950s, Bandai, 15" wingspan
EX $185 NM $270 MIP $375

Character Toys

By Tom Bartsch

Welcome to perhaps the most widely collected category in toys. That's simply because you could place almost any toy related to characters (movies, television, comic books, etc.) into this category and no one would blink an eye. Character toys hold a timeless appeal that can date back to comic characters in the mid-1800s. The appeal of the character can lead collectors to acquire anything associated to that character, from drinking glasses, coloring books and backpacks to dolls, Halloween costumes and membership rings.

While the category is huge, most collectors simplify their collections to certain characters, and even then the shelves can fill up pretty quickly. In fact, that's the best advice you can give when it comes to character toys—narrow down your search in the character or characters, and the type of collectibles you want related to that character or characters. Trying to collect everything, even with just one character, will leave your wallet empty and your house empty of free space.

With character toys, licenses were handed out like candy. Many manufacturers produced character toys because they were good sellers. However, that also leads to many similar toys on the market. It's up to what you want, whether a modern version that costs less, or the original real deal that will cost you more money. For example, let's say you're looking for a Popeye Bubble Pipe. Ja-Ru produced one in the mid-1980s that can be found for well under $10. However, if you want one from KFS produced in the 1960s, it will cost you three times as much. And that is for a relatively low-rent collectible. Do your research when collecting. Seek out the manufacturers you are looking for and pay attention to markings on the collectibles. Not every seller knows what he or she is talking about when describing something they are selling.

The beauty of character toys is that you'll always have plenty of products for the venerable characters, such as Superman, James Bond and Mickey Mouse. But you can also find items for the latest characters, such as characters from Family Guy and even Hanna Montana.

When it comes to trends of character toys, you can't really say prices are up or down. You have to do it by time period, condition and character involved. For instance, you're not going to get a lot of money for a Mighty Mouse-related piece. The character doesn't have the demand of a higher-profile superhero, he isn't that old relative to other characters and manufacturers didn't produce anything that special related to him.

To break it down in the simplest terms, the older the toy is, the better condition it is in, and the popularity of said character ultimately determines the value. Pieces produced on an exclusive basis, dating more than 50 years ago and still in excellent shape will command top dollar, and there are plenty of collectors going after them. Popeye was on a roll in the secondary market of late, with many fine pieces striking it rich on the auction block. Now you're seeing TV characters from the 1950s scoring big. The baby boomers are collecting, and they're collecting characters.

The areas where you're going to see a lot of movement in this category are for those items in top condition. A lot of character collectors start small and advance their collections through time. The beauty of it, however, is that there is something for every character at every price level. It all depends on what you want to pay.

THE TOP 10 CHARACTER TOYS (In Mint Condition)

1. Superman Club Member Ring, 1940 .... $70,000
2. Superman Trading Cards, Gum Inc., set of 72, 1940 .... $33,300
3. Superman Milk Defense Club Ring, 1941 .... $25,000
4. Little Orphan Annie Altascope Ring, Quaker, 1942 .... $22,000
5. Mickey Mouse Lionel Circus Train, Lionel, 1935 .... $17,000
6. Batman Play Set, Ideal, 1966 .... $10,000
7. Superman Bubblegum Badge, Fo-Lee Gum Co., 1948 .... $10,000
8. Donald Duck Bicycle, Shelby, 1949 .... $8,000
9. Doc Savage Medal of Honor Award, 1930s $6,200
10. Mickey Mouse Radio, Emerson, 1934 .... $6,000

101 Dalmatians

ACCESSORIES

101 Dalmatians Snow Dome, 1961, Marx, 3" x 5" x 3-1/2" tall
EX $35 **NM** $65 **MIP** $110

FIGURES

Dalmatian Pups Figures, 1960s, Enesco, 4-1/2" tall, set of three
EX $25 **NM** $50 **MIP** $160

Lucky Figure, 1960s, Enesco, 4" tall
EX $35 **NM** $65 **MIP** $100

TOY

101 Dalmatians Wind-Up, 1959, Linemar
EX $125 **NM** $250 **MIP** $500

Lucky Squeeze Toy, Dell, 7" tall, squeakers in the bottom
EX $10 **NM** $20 **MIP** $50

Alice in Wonderland

ACCESSORIES

Clock Radio, 1970s, General Electric, features characters on face
EX $20 **NM** $40 **MIP** $85

Film Viewer, 1950s, Tru-Vue, viewer and filmstrip
EX $30 **NM** $60 **MIP** $100

Handbag, 1950s, ACME Briefcase, child's red leather shoulder bag
EX $30 **NM** $80 **MIP** $120

Handbag, 1950s, Salient, child's pink vinyl shoulder bag, Alice w/rocking fly
EX $30 **NM** $80 **MIP** $120

Hatbox, 1950s, Neevel, Caterpillar or Tea Party graphics
EX $55 **NM** $100 **MIP** $150

Picture Frame, 1970s, Dexter-Mahnke, cloth picture frame, featuring Mad Tea Party
EX $20 **NM** $35 **MIP** $60

Record Player, 1951, RCA Victor, 45 rpm
EX $75 **NM** $225 **MIP** $400

School Bag, 1950s, ACME Briefcase, fabric and leather
EX $30 **NM** $100 **MIP** $150

Soap Set, 1951
EX $40 **NM** $120 **MIP** $250

Wall Decor, 1951, Dolly Toy, #260 contains Alice, Mad Hatter, March Hare and a lamp
EX $50 **NM** $100 **MIP** $200

Wall Plaque, 1974, Leisuramics, bisque, oval shape, featuring TweedleDee and TweedleDum
EX $20 **NM** $40 **MIP** $60

Wall Plaque, 1974, Leisuramics, bisque, oval shape, featuring Mad Hatter
EX $20 **NM** $40 **MIP** $75

BANK

Alice Bank, 1950s, Leeds, figural
EX $100 **NM** $200 **MIP** $275

BOOK

Alice in Wonderland and Cinderella Book, 1950s, Collins, Great Britain version
EX $25 **NM** $60 **MIP** $120

Alice in Wonderland Book, 1950s, Whitman, #2074 Cozy Corner Book, green endpapers
EX $30 **NM** $60 **MIP** $100

Alice in Wonderland Book, 1950s, Whitman, #10426, without gold backing
EX $30 **NM** $70 **MIP** $150

Alice in Wonderland Book, 1950s, Whitman, #10426, Big Golden Book, gold foil backing
EX $50 **NM** $100 **MIP** $175

Alice in Wonderland Book, 1951, Whitman, Sandpiper Book w/dust jacket
EX $50 **NM** $100 **MIP** $200

Alice in Wonderland Book, 1951, Dell Publishing, #331
EX $35 **NM** $75 **MIP** $175

Alice in Wonderland Book, 1951, Whitman, #426, Big Golden Book
EX $50 **NM** $100 **MIP** $175

Alice in Wonderland Classic Series with Disney Book, 1950s, Whitman, #2140 Lewis Carroll text w/Disney dust jacket
EX $50 **NM** $100 **MIP** $200

Alice in Wonderland Paint Book, 1951, Whitman, #2167
EX $55 **NM** $110 **MIP** $225

Alice in Wonderland Punch-Out Book, 1951, Whitman, #2164
EX $80 **NM** $200 **MIP** $350

Alice in Wonderland Sticker Fun, 1950s, Whitman, #2193 stencil and coloring book
EX $30 **NM** $60 **MIP** $100

Alice Meets the White Rabbit Book, 1951, Whitman, #D-19, Little Golden Book
EX $15 **NM** $45 **MIP** $80

Mad Hatter's Tea Party Book, 1951, Whitman, #D-23 Little Golden Book
EX $15 **NM** $45 **MIP** $60

Unbirthday Party Book, The, 1974, Whitman, #22, Walt Disney Showcase
EX $8 **NM** $15 **MIP** $30

CANDY TIN

Candy Tin, 1950s, Edward Sharp and Sons, Great Britain English Toffee Tin
EX $125 **NM** $250 **MIP** $325

COLLECTIBLE

Alice Snow Dome, 1961, Marx, 3" tall featuring Alice and the White Rabbit in front of tree
EX $15 **NM** $35 **MIP** $100

Caterpillar Figure, 1956, Hagen-Renaker
EX $200 **NM** $400 **MIP** $600

Mad Hatter Snow Dome, 1980s, New England Collectors Society, crystal, Mad Hatter, St. Patrick's Day
EX $15 **NM** $25 **MIP** $50

Mad Hatter Teapot, 1950s, Regal
EX $500 **NM** $1000 **MIP** $1600

Pitcher, 1950s, Regal, King of Hearts
EX $200 **NM** $375 **MIP** $650

Plaque, 1970s, Disneyland, wooden, w/Alice and live flowers
EX $15 **NM** $25 **MIP** $50

Salt and Pepper Shakers, 1950s, Regal, featuring TweedleDee and TweedleDum
EX $150 **NM** $300 **MIP** $525

Salt and Pepper Shakers, 1950s, Regal, blue or white featuring Alice
EX $150 **NM** $300 **MIP** $500

Tea Cake Box, 1980s, TDL, w/a Mad Tea Party lid
EX $10 **NM** $15 **MIP** $30

Tea Cup and Saucer, 1986, TDL, ceramic, Mad Tea Party
EX $60 **NM** $120 **MIP** $200

Thimble, 1980s, New England Collectors Society, Mad Hatter and Alice
EX $5 **NM** $15 **MIP** $25

Vase, 1960s, Enesco, featuring Alice's head
EX $75 **NM** $150 **MIP** $250

White Rabbit Creamer, 1950s, Regal
EX $175 **NM** $350 **MIP** $500

White Rabbit Sugar Bowl, 1950s, Regal
EX $200 NM $400 MIP $600

COLORING BOOK

Alice in Wonderland Big Coloring Book, 1951, Whitman, #301 Big Golden, Model No. 301
EX $75 NM $150 MIP $225

Alice in Wonderland Coloring Book, 1974, Whitman, #1049
EX $5 NM $20 MIP $40

COOKIE JAR

Alice Cookie Jar, Regal, 13-1/2" tall
EX $375 NM $1000 MIP $1650

Alice Cookie Jar, 1950s, Leeds, printed in relief
EX $150 NM $300 MIP $425

Looking Glass Cookie Jar, Fred Roberts, raised characters on the body of the jar w/a mirror lid
EX $200 NM $450 MIP $725

COSTUMES

Alice Costume, 1950s, Ben Cooper, costume made until 1970s
EX $50 NM $100 MIP $200

Mad Hatter Costume, 1950s, Ben Cooper, costume made until 1970s
EX $30 NM $60 MIP $120

March Hare Costume, 1950s, Ben Cooper, costume made until 1970s
EX $30 NM $60 MIP $120

DOLLS

Alice Doll, 1950s, Gund, flat vinyl, stuffed
EX $50 NM $125 MIP $200

Alice Doll, 1951, Duchess, 12-1/2" tall
EX $100 NM $225 MIP $350

Alice Doll, 1951, Duchess, #739, 7-1/2" tall
EX $80 NM $200 MIP $300

Alice Doll, 1970s, Horsman, Alice has a castle on her apron
EX $20 NM $45 MIP $90

Alice Doll, 1970s, Pedigree, Great Britain
EX $20 NM $40 MIP $75

Alice Doll, 1970s, Horsman, #1071, Walt Disney Classics
EX $20 NM $35 MIP $75

Cheshire Cat Doll, 1970s, Disneyland, plush
EX $10 NM $25 MIP $60

Dormouse Doll, 1950s, Lars/Italy, stuffed
EX $160 NM $330 MIP $550

Mad Hatter Doll, 1950s, Gund, flat vinyl, stuffed
EX $40 NM $90 MIP $150

Mad Hatter Doll, 1950s, Gund, plush
EX $125 NM $275 MIP $425

March Hare Doll, 1950s, Gund, plush
EX $175 NM $350 MIP $600

March Hare Doll, 1950s, Gund, flat vinyl, stuffed
EX $50 NM $60 MIP $135

Queen of Hearts Doll, 1950s, Gund, flat vinyl, stuffed
EX $40 NM $80 MIP $150

TweedleDee and TweedleDum Dolls, 1950s, Gund, flat vinyl, stuffed, each
EX $75 NM $150 MIP $225

TweedleDee and TweedleDum Dolls, 1980s, TDL, plush, each
EX $15 NM $30 MIP $60

Walrus Doll, 1950s, Lars/Italy, stuffed
EX $200 NM $500 MIP $675

White Rabbit Doll, 1950s, Gund, flat vinyl, stuffed
EX $50 NM $125 MIP $175

White Rabbit Doll, 1950s, Gund
EX $110 NM $300 MIP $450

White Rabbit Doll, 1970s, Sears, plush w/ waistcoat and umbrella
EX $12 NM $25 MIP $50

White Rabbit Doll, 1970s, Disneyland, large, plush w/ yellow spectacles
EX $12 NM $25 MIP $50

White Rabbit Doll, 1970s, Disneyland, small w/ black spectacles
EX $10 NM $20 MIP $40

White Rabbit Doll, 1974, Buena Vista/Disney, plush
EX $50 NM $100 MIP $150

White Rabbit Doll, 1980s, TDL, plush
EX $10 NM $25 MIP $50

FIGURES

Alice Figure, 1950s, Marx, painted w/"Holland" stamped on the bottom
EX $40 NM $75 MIP $120

Alice Figure, 1950s, Aldon Industries, plastic, cut-out standup
EX $50 NM $110 MIP $150

Alice Figure, 1951, Shaw
EX $120 NM $300 MIP $725

Alice Figure, 1956, Hagen-Renaker
EX $200 NM $400 MIP $600

Alice Figure, 1980s, Sears, Magic Kingdom Collection, bone china
EX $15 NM $25 MIP $35

Alice Figure, 1984, Bully, Germany, PVC, wearing a blue or red dress, each
EX $10 NM $15 MIP $20

Disneyland Figures Set, 1960s, United China, large set, each piece
EX $15 NM $30 MIP $60

Disneyland Figures Set, 1970s, United China, small figures, each piece
EX $10 NM $15 MIP $30

Dormouse Figure, 1951, Shaw
EX $130 NM $225 MIP $400

Mad Hatter Figure, 1950s, Marx, painted w/ "Holland" stamped on the bottom
EX $20 NM $35 MIP $75

Mad Hatter Figure, 1950s, Sydney Pottery, large size, sold only in Australia
EX $250 NM $425 MIP $600

Mad Hatter Figure, 1951, Shaw
EX $65 NM $200 MIP $350

Mad Hatter Figure, 1956, Hagen-Renaker
EX $150 NM $300 MIP $425

Mad Hatter Figure, 1980s, Schmid, playing xylophone
EX $20 NM $40 MIP $75

Mad Hatter/March Hare Figure, 1980s, TDL, Mad Hatter, March Hare w/saxophone
EX $20 NM $40 MIP $60

March Hare Figure, 1950s, Sydney Pottery, large size, sold only in Australia
EX $200 NM $400 MIP $600

March Hare Figure, 1950s, Marx, painted w/ "Holland" stamped on the bottom
EX $15 NM $30 MIP $60

March Hare Figure, 1951, Shaw
EX $170 NM $320 MIP $500

March Hare Figure, 1956, Hagen-Renaker
EX $110 NM $275 MIP $450

Queen of Hearts Figure, 1950s, Marx, painted w/ "Holland" stamped on the bottom
EX $12 NM $25 MIP $50

Queen of Hearts Figure, 1980s, Sears, Magic Kingdom Collection, bone china
EX $15 NM $25 MIP $35

TweedleDee Figure, 1950s, Sydney Pottery, large size, sold only in Australia
EX $200 NM $400 MIP $575

TweedleDee Figure, 1951, Shaw
EX $70 NM $150 MIP $235

TweedleDum Figure, 1950s, Sydney Pottery, large size, sold only in Australia
EX $200 NM $400 MIP $575

TweedleDum Figure, 1951, Shaw
EX $70 NM $150 MIP $235

Walrus Figure, 1950s, Sydney Pottery, large size, sold only in Australia
EX $160 NM $375 MIP $550

Walrus Figure, 1951, Shaw
EX $110 NM $250 MIP $425

White Rabbit Figure, Italy, 5-1/2" tall, ceramic
EX $15 NM $35 MIP $60

White Rabbit Figure, 1950s, Marx, painted w/ "Holland" stamped on the bottom
EX $12 NM $25 MIP $50

White Rabbit Figure, 1951, Shaw
EX $65 NM $140 MIP $250

White Rabbit Figure, 1980s, Sears, Magic Kingdom Collection, bone china
EX $12 NM $25 MIP $50

GAMES

Adventures in Costumeland Game, 1980s, Walt Disney World, created for Disney costume division members, game board and pieces in a small vinyl garment bag
EX $75 NM $150 MIP $200

Alice in Wonderland Card Game, 1980s, Thos. De LaRue
EX $10 NM $20 MIP $35

Bridge Card Game, 1950s, Whitman, two decks of cards
EX $35 NM $75 MIP $175

Canasta Card Game, 1950s, Whitman, two Canasta decks of White Rabbit cards
EX $50 NM $100 MIP $150

Alice in Wonderland

Queen of Hearts Card Game, 1975, Edu-Cards
EX $20 NM $35 MIP $65

GLASSWARE

Alice and White Rabbit Mug, 1991, TDL/Daiichi Seimei, promo piece
EX $25 NM $40 MIP $65

Alice Mug, 1970s, Disney
EX $12 NM $20 MIP $40

Glass, 1970s, Pepsi Cola, featuring Alice, part of Wonderful World of Disney set
EX $10 NM $20 MIP $35

Glasses, 1951, Libbey, eight styles released for film opening, each
EX $40 NM $60 MIP $120

Mad Tea Party/Cheshire Cat Mug, 1988, Applause, Cheshire Cat handle w/Tea Party on the mug
EX $12 NM $18 MIP $30

MUSIC BOX

Music Box, 1980s, Disneyland, Wooden box features Alice and White Rabbit "I'm Late"
EX $30 NM $60 MIP $100

Music Box, 1980s, TDL, plastic, tea cup rotates
EX $45 NM $80 MIP $150

Music Box, 1980s, TDL, ceramic teacup
EX $45 NM $80 MIP $150

PAPER DOLLS

Alice Paper Dolls, 1972, Whitman, #4712
EX $25 NM $50 MIP $80

Alice Paper Dolls, 1976, Whitman, #1948
EX $20 NM $40 MIP $75

PAPER GOODS

Alice Stationery and Notepad, 1970s, Pak-Well, #77065 w/a fan card cover
EX $10 NM $20 MIP $35

Cheshire Cat Costume Pattern, 1951, McCall's
EX $25 NM $40 MIP $75

Fan Card, 1951, Walt Disney, premium sent to fans who wrote letters to studio
EX $30 NM $50 MIP $75

Fan Card, 1951, Walt Disney, original release w/1973 invitation to studio screening
EX $40 NM $60 MIP $80

Mad Hatter Costume Pattern, 1951, McCall's
EX $20 NM $35 MIP $55

March Hare Costume Pattern, 1951, McCall's
EX $20 NM $35 MIP $60

Poster, 1958, Disneyland, Alice attraction
EX $400 NM $700 MIP $1000

Poster, 1980s, Walt Disney World, costume division poster featuring Cheshire Cat
EX $20 NM $40 MIP $65

Ticket, 1970s, Disneyland, employee screening ticket featuring Cheshire Cat
EX $10 NM $15 MIP $25

PREMIUMS

Bread Labels, 1950s, NBC, 12 different styles, each
EX $25 NM $40 MIP $80

Bread Seal Poster, 1950s, NBC
EX $40 NM $60 MIP $100

Bread Stickers, 1974, Continental Baking/Wonder, five styles, each
EX $5 NM $10 MIP $15

Cards, 1951, Royal Desserts, 16 different cards on the back of dessert packages, each
EX $20 NM $35 MIP $70

Cereal Box with Record, 1956, General Mills, Wheaties
EX $400 NM $500 MIP $600

Magic Picture Kit Set, 1974, Jiffy Pop, set of four
EX $12 NM $25 MIP $50

Poster, 1980, Kraft, Disneyland 25th Anniversary Family Reunion
EX $15 NM $30 MIP $65

RECORD

Record/Little Nipper Giant Storybook, 1951, RCA Victor, LY-437, 33, 45, or 78 rpm, each
EX $80 NM $120 MIP $160

TOY

Alice Disneykin, 1950s, Marx, unpainted, soft plastic
EX $10 NM $20 MIP $40

Alice Disneykin, 1950s, Marx, hard plastic
EX $10 NM $25 MIP $50

Alice Marionette, 1950s, Peter Puppet, comes in two different boxes, one "Alice in Wonderland" the other Peter Puppet Disney
EX $70 NM $225 MIP $425

Balloons, 1951, Oak Rubber, four different designs
EX $12 NM $20 MIP $50

Balloons, 1951, Eagle Rubber
EX $12 NM $20 MIP $50

Blocks, 1950s, Chad Valley, five cylindrical tin blocks w/color graphics
EX $75 NM $150 MIP $300

Child's Vanity, 1950s, Neevel, illustrated w/film scenes
EX $70 NM $120 MIP $200

Disneykin Play Set, 1950s, Marx
EX $200 NM $400 MIP $650

Jingle Ball, 1951, Vanguard
EX $12 NM $25 MIP $50

Mad Hatter Disneykin, 1950s, Marx, unpainted, soft plastic
EX $10 NM $16 MIP $30

Mad Hatter Disneykin, 1950s, Marx
EX $25 NM $45 MIP $85

Mad Hatter Hand Puppet, 1960s, hand puppet w/cloth body
EX $40 NM $75 MIP $100

Mad Hatter Marionette, 1950s, Peter Puppet
EX $100 NM $150 MIP $275

Mad Hatter Nodder, 1950s, Marx
EX $100 NM $250 MIP $375

Mad Hatter Snap Eeze, 1950s, Marx
EX $15 NM $30 MIP $50

Make-Up Kit, 1951, Hasbro
EX $25 NM $55 MIP $100

March Hare Disneykin, 1950s, Marx, unpainted and soft plastic
EX $12 NM $18 MIP $35

March Hare Marionette, 1950s, Peter Puppet
EX $100 NM $150 MIP $250

March Hare Snap Eeze, 1950s, Marx
EX $15 NM $20 MIP $50

March Hare Twistoy, 1950s, Marx
EX $15 NM $20 MIP $50

Molding Set, 1951, Model Craft
EX $50 NM $100 MIP $200

Molding Set, 1952, Great Britain, similar to Model Craft set
EX $60 NM $120 MIP $210

Puppet Theatre, 1950s, Peter Puppet
EX $125 NM $200 MIP $300

Puzzle, 1951, Jaymar, Alice and Rabbit
EX $50 NM $90 MIP $150

Puzzle, 1951, Jaymar, Alice under a tree
EX $50 NM $90 MIP $150

Puzzle, 1951, Jaymar, Croquet cast scene
EX $50 NM $90 MIP $150

Puzzle, 1951, Jaymar, Tea Party scene
EX $50 NM $90 MIP $150

Puzzle, 1979, Stafford/England, wooden, Great Britain Tea Party
EX $10 NM $25 MIP $40

Puzzle, 1980s, TDL, #18, Mad Tea Party and Cast
EX $5 NM $10 MIP $25

Queen of Hearts Disneykin, 1950s, Marx
EX $30 NM $55 MIP $85

Queen of Hearts Disneykin, 1950s, Marx, unpainted, soft plastic
EX $15 NM $20 MIP $35

Ramp Walker, 1950s, Marx, Mad Hatter and White Rabbit
EX $40 NM $80 MIP $100

Rubber Stamp Set, 1970s, Multiprint, Italy, #177
EX $20 NM $30 MIP $55

Rubber Stamp Set, 1989, All Night Media
EX $10 NM $15 MIP $25

Sewing Cards, 1951, Whitman
EX $40 NM $75 MIP $125

Sewing Kit, 1951, Hasbro, 7" sewing machine and 5" doll, all plastic
EX $50 NM $100 MIP $150

TV Scene, White Rabbit and March Hare, 1950s, Marx
EX $30 NM $65 MIP $100

CHARACTER TOYS

View-Master Set, 1970s, GAF, three reels, Disney
EX $12 NM $25 MIP $40

Wallet, 1950s, Salient, vinyl, featuring Mad Tea Party
EX $30 NM $60 MIP $100

Wallet, 1950s, Salient, vinyl, featuring White Rabbit
EX $30 NM $60 MIP $100

White Rabbit Disneykin, 1950s, Marx
EX $30 NM $60 MIP $85

White Rabbit Disneykin, 1950s, Marx, unpainted and soft plastic
EX $10 NM $20 MIP $35

White Rabbit Ears, 1980s, TDL
EX $10 NM $20 MIP $35

White Rabbit Rolykin, 1950s, Marx
EX $20 NM $40 MIP $70

WATCH

Alice Wristwatch, 1950s, U.S. Time, Alice peeking through pink flowers and a plastic statue
EX $400 NM $750 MIP $1000

Alice Wristwatch, 1950s, U.S. Time, came w/ ceramic statue
EX $400 NM $750 MIP $1000

Alice Wristwatch, 1990s, Alba, Japan, gold tone face
EX $15 NM $30 MIP $60

Tea Cup Wristwatch, 1950s, U.S. Time, picture of Mad Hatter w/ an overlay
EX $450 NM $850 MIP $1100

Amos and Andy

ACCESSORIES

Amos and Andy Card Party, 1930, A.M. Davis, 6" x 8", score pads and tallies
EX $50 NM $100 MIP $200

Contest Winner Check, 1936, Pepsodent, $2.00 winner's check for contest
EX $1500 NM $1650 MIP $2000

Stock Certificate, 1930s, Bogus Taxi Company, premium
EX $300 NM $400 MIP $450

TOY

Puzzle, 1932, Pepsodent, 8-1/2" x 10", pictured Amos, Andy and other characters
EX $100 NM $200 MIP $300

Andy Gump

ACCESSORIES

Andy Gump Dummy Punchout, 1938, Malt-O-Meal, premium, paper ventriloquist dummy, 11"x20"
EX $175 NM $350 MIP $550

Brush and Mirror, 4" diameter, red on ivory colored surface of brush
EX $65 NM $125 MIP $200

TOY

Andy Gump Figure, 1930s, wood jointed figure
EX $50 NM $100 MIP $150

Chester Gump Playstone Funnies Mold Set, 1940s
EX $100 NM $150 MIP $200

Chester Gump/Herby Nodders, 1930s, ceramic 2-1/4" string nodders, each
EX $125 NM $250 MIP $375

Archies

ACCESSORIES

Archie Halloween Costume, 1969, Ben Cooper
EX $50 NM $75 MIP $100

TOY

Archies Paper Dolls, 1969, Whitman
EX $25 NM $50 MIP $100

Jalopy, 1975, Marx, 12", plastic
EX $80 NM $150 MIP $275

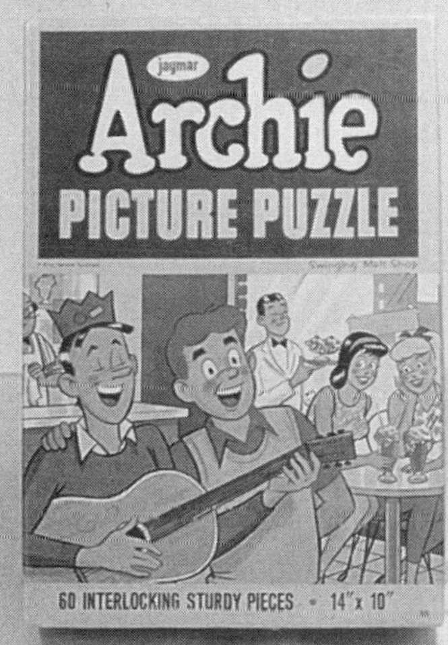

Puzzle, 1960s, Jaymar, "Swinging Malt Shop"
EX $40 NM $60 MIP $100

Atom Ant and Friends

TOY

Atom Ant Kite, 1960s, Roalex
EX $40 NM $80 MIP $150

Atom Ant Punch-Out Set, 1966, Whitman
EX $100 NM $175 MIP $325

Atom Ant Push Puppet, 1960s, Kohner
EX $40 NM $65 MIP $90

Atom Ant Puzzle, 1966, Whitman
EX $40 NM $80 MIP $100

Atom Ant Soaky, 1966, Purex
EX $35 NM $70 MIP $100

Morocco Mole Bubble Club Soaky, 1960s, Purex, 7" hard plastic
EX $35 NM $70 MIP $100

Squiddly Diddly Bubble Club Soaky, 1960s, Purex, 10-1/2" hard plastic
EX $35 NM $70 MIP $100

Winsome Witch Bubble Club Soaky, 1960s, Purex, 10-1/2" hard plastic
EX $35 NM $70 MIP $100

Babes in Toyland

DOLL

Cadet Doll, Gund, 15-1/2" tall, fabric
EX $35 NM $80 MIP $150

TOY

Babes in Toyland Go Mobile Friction Car, 1961, Linemar, 4" x 5" x 6"
EX $150 NM $300 MIP $450

Babes in Toyland Hand Puppets, Gund, Silly Dilly Clown, Soldier, or Gorgonzo, each
EX $50 NM $100 MIP $150

Babes in Toyland Twist 'N Bend Toy, 1963, Marx, 4" tall flexible toy w/Private Valiant holding a baton
EX $10 NM $25 MIP $55

Babes in Toyland Wind-Up Toy, 1950s, Linemar, tin
EX $200 NM $400 MIP $525

Puzzle, 1961, Jaymar
EX $20 NM $45 MIP $65

Bambi

ACCESSORIES

Bambi Prints, 1947, New York Graphic Society, 11" x 14" framed
EX $25 NM $50 MIP $100

Lamp, Bambi and Thumper
EX $150 NM $275 MIP $400

Throw Rug, 1960s, 21" x 39", Bambi and Thumper
EX $30 NM $60 MIP $100

Thumper Ashtray, 1950s, Goebel, 4" tall
EX $75 NM $150 MIP $200

Wristwatch, 1949, US Time
EX $150 NM $275 MIP $425

BANK

Flower Bank, 1940s, 5" x 5"x 7" tall, plaster
EX $75 NM $125 MIP $250

Thumper Bank, 1950s, Leeds, ceramic, figural
EX $75 NM $100 MIP $185

BOOK

Bambi Book, 1942, Grosset and Dunlap, black and white illustrations
EX $40 NM $70 MIP $100

Big Little Book, 1942, #1469
EX $50 NM $125 MIP $175

Thumper Book, 1942, Grosset and Dunlap, color and black/white illustrations
EX $40 NM $80 MIP $125

DOLL

Thumper Doll, 16" tall, plush
EX $15 NM $30 MIP $75

TOY

Bambi Soaky, Colgate-Palmolive
EX $20 NM $40 MIP $80

Thumper Pull Toy, 1942, Fisher-Price, #533, 7-1/2" x 12", wood and metal, Thumper's tail rings the bell
EX $100 NM $250 MIP $400

Bambi

Thumper Soaky, 1960s, Colgate-Palmolive
EX $25 **NM** $60 **MIP** $100

Barney Google

DOLL

Barney Google Doll, 1922, Schoenhut, 8-1/2" tall, wood and wood composition
EX $500 **NM** $1000 **MIP** $1250

Spark Plug Doll, 1922, Schoenhut, 9" long x 6-1/2" tall, jointed wood construction w/fabric
EX $500 **NM** $1000 **MIP** $1250

FIGURE

Barney Google and Spark Plug Figurines, 3" x 3", bisque, on white bisque pedestal
EX $200 **NM** $350 **MIP** $475

TOY

Barney Google and Spark Plug, 1920s, Nifty, 7-1/2" tall, wind-up
EX $750 **NM** $1500 **MIP** $2200

Spark Plug in Bathtub, 1930, 5" long die-cast, white
EX $200 **NM** $350 **MIP** $525

Spark Plug Pull Toy, 10" x 8" tall, wood
EX $150 **NM** $250 **MIP** $400

Spark Plug Squeaker Toy, 1923, 5" long, rubber w/squeaker in mouth
EX $100 **NM** $200 **MIP** $300

Spark Plug Toy, 1920s, 5" tall, wood, on wheels
EX $125 **NM** $250 **MIP** $350

Batman

ACCESSORIES

Batcoin Lot, 1966, Space Magic Limited, Four 1-1/2" diameter metal coins, each depicting a scene featuring Batman and Robin battling villains
EX $30 **NM** $75 **MIP** $100

Batman and Robin Society Membership Button, 1966, Button World, full color litho metal button featuring Batman and Robin and the words "Charter Member-Batman and Robin Society"
EX $15 **NM** $25 **MIP** $35

Batman Candy Box, 1966, Phoenix Candy, 2-1/2" x 3-1/2" x 1", several color scenes
EX $100 **NM** $150 **MIP** $250

Batman Cereal Box, 1966, Kellogg's, w/Yogi Bear on front
EX $1000 **NM** $1750 **MIP** $2500

Batman Crazy Foam, 1974
EX $20 **NM** $40 **MIP** $100

Batman Dinner Set, 1966, ceramic; three pieces
EX $40 **NM** $70 **MIP** $175

Batman Fork, 1966, Imperial, 6" stainless steel w/embossed figure of Batman, w/"Batman" engraved towards the bottom
EX $15 **NM** $30 **MIP** $60

Batman Halloween Costume, 1965, Ben Cooper, plastic Halloween mask and purple and yellow cape, several versions, some feature logo on chest
EX $40 **NM** $75 **MIP** $150

Batman Helmet and Cape Set, 1966, Ideal, blue hard plastic cowl shaped helmet and soft blue vinyl cape w/drawstring
EX $250 **NM** $450 **MIP** $650

Batman Lamp, Vanity Fair, Made in Taiwan
EX $50 **NM** $100 **MIP** $220

Batman Pencil Box, 1966, Empire Pencil, gun-shaped pencil box w/set of Batman pencils
EX $30 **NM** $55 **MIP** $125

Batman Pillow, 1966, 10" x 12" w/1940s logo
EX $20 **NM** $40 **MIP** $75

Batman Wastepaper Basket, 1966, 10" tall, color tin litho
EX $30 **NM** $60 **MIP** $125

Batmobile AM Radio, 1970s, Bandai
EX $50 **NM** $100 **MIP** $225

Beach Towel, 1966, 34" x 58" white, Batman hitting a crook
EX $40 **NM** $95 **MIP** $180

Cake Decoration, 1960s, 2" hard plastic figure of Robin or Batman, each
EX $8 **NM** $15 **MIP** $30

Cake Decorations, 1966, Space Magic Limited, 4" plastic one dimensional figures of Batman, Robin and old 1940s Batman logo
EX $20 **NM** $40 **MIP** $70

Catwoman Iron-On Patch, 1966, Catwoman w/the words "Batkids Fan Club"
EX $20 **NM** $50 **MIP** $80

Charm Bracelet, 1966, on card
EX $50 **NM** $85 **MIP** $150

Child's Dinner Plate, 1966, Boontonware, 7" plastic w/image of Batman and Robin
EX $15 **NM** $30 **MIP** $60

Christmas Ornament, 1989, Presents
EX $5 **NM** $10 **MIP** $20

Coins, 1966, Transogram, plastic, set
EX $50 **NM** $75 **MIP** $120

Costume Patterns, 1960s, McCalls, patterns for making Batman, Robin, and Superman costumes, paper envelope, each
EX $15 **NM** $35 **MIP** $85

Inflatable TV Chair, 1982
EX $10 **NM** $20 **MIP** $35

Joker Cereal Bowl, 1966, Sun Valley, 5" hard plastic
EX $15 **NM** $30 **MIP** $55

Lapel Pin, 1966, Mamsell, 2" bat-shaped metal, black w/yellow eyes
EX $20 **NM** $35 **MIP** $60

Mug, 1966, 5" clear plastic; color wrap around sheet
EX $30 **NM** $60 **MIP** $100

Paper Mask, 1943, newspaper premium, announced first newspaper comic
EX $1500 **NM** $2200 **MIP** $3000

Pennant, 1966, 11 x 29" white felt, illustration of the Dynamic Duo swinging on ropes w/the Bat-signal in the background
EX $80 **NM** $150 **MIP** $250

Robin Character Sponge, 1966, Epic, 5"
EX $10 **NM** $30 **MIP** $80

Robin Iron-on Patch, 1966, 2-1/2" diameter patch, Batkids Fan Club
EX $12 **NM** $35 **MIP** $60

Robin Ornament, 1989, Presents
EX $5 **NM** $13 **MIP** $20

Robin Placemat, 1966, 13" x 18" vinyl
EX $35 **NM** $80 **MIP** $110

Sip-A-Drink Cup, 1966, British, 6" tall, white plastic
EX $50 **NM** $100 **MIP** $200

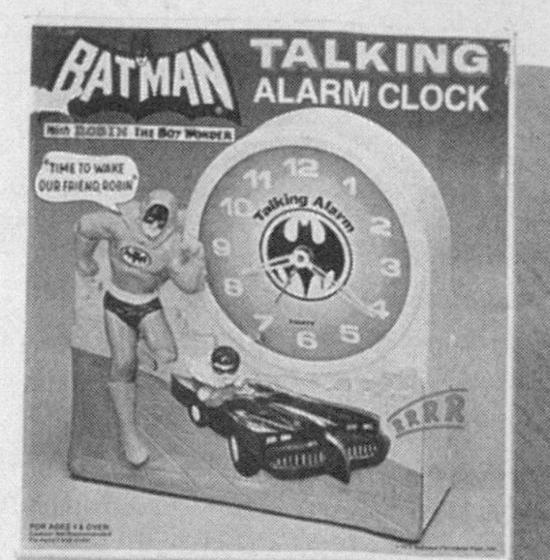

Talking Alarm Clock, 1975, Janex, plastic clock w/Bat logo on face
EX $75 **NM** $100 **MIP** $180

CHARACTER TOYS

ACTION FIGURES

Batman Bendy Figure, 1960s, Diener, on card
EX $35 **NM** $65 **MIP** $90

Batman Figure, 1966, Ideal, 3" yellow plastic, detachable gray plastic cape
EX $12 **NM** $25 **MIP** $50

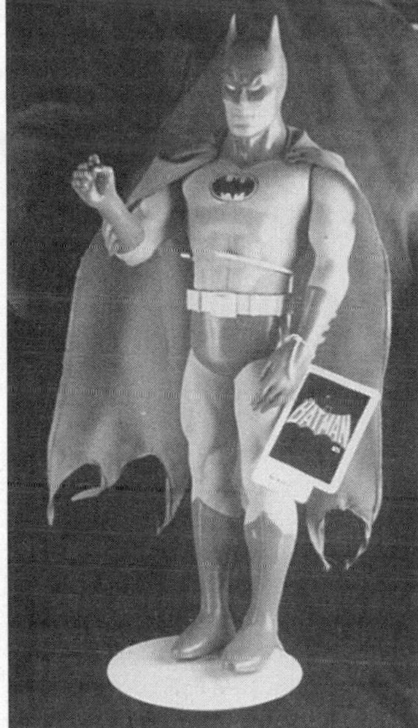

Batman Figure, 1988, Applause, 15" tall w/stand
EX $15 **NM** $25 **MIP** $45

Batman Figure, 1989, Billiken, 8" on card
EX $8 **NM** $15 **MIP** $30

Batman Figure, 1989, Bully, 7" bendy
EX $8 **NM** $15 **MIP** $25

Batman Figure, 1989, Presents, 15-1/2" tall vinyl and cloth figure on base, 1970s logo, metal stand
EX $20 **NM** $40 **MIP** $75

Batman Figure, 1989, Takara/Japan
EX $40 **NM** $80 **MIP** $150

Batman Figure and Parachute, 1966, CDC, 11" x 9" card, metallic blue figure of Batman and working parachute
EX $40 **NM** $75 **MIP** $150

Batman Flying Figure on String, 1973, Ben Cooper, 6" rubber figure of Batman w/rubber cape
EX $12 **NM** $25 **MIP** $55

Batman Inflated Gliding Figure, 1966, Ideal, 16" soft plastic inflatable Batman w/free flowing cape and hard plastic cable rail
EX $40 **NM** $60 **MIP** $125

Batman on a String Figure, 1966, Fun Things, 4" rubber, flexible arms, legs and removable cape
EX $20 **NM** $30 **MIP** $60

Joker Figure, Presents, 15" vinyl figure
EX $10 **NM** $20 **MIP** $40

Joker Figure, 1966, Ideal, 3" blue plastic
EX $20 **NM** $30 **MIP** $50

Joker Figure, 1988, Applause, vinyl w/stand
EX $10 **NM** $20 **MIP** $40

Robin Figure, Presents, cloth and vinyl, on base
EX $10 **NM** $20 **MIP** $35

Robin Figure, 1966, Ideal, 3" plastic, detachable yellow plastic cape
EX $15 **NM** $30 **MIP** $50

Robin Figure, 1970s, Palitoy, 8" figure on card
EX $20 **NM** $40 **MIP** $80

Robin Figure, 1988, Applause, vinyl w/stand
EX $10 **NM** $20 **MIP** $35

Robin on a String Figure, Ben Cooper, 4" tall, rubber
EX $10 **NM** $25 **MIP** $50

BANK

Batman Bank, 1966, 7" tall glazed china figural bank depicts Batman w/hands on hip
EX $90 **NM** $120 **MIP** $160

Batman Bank, 1989, figural bank given away w/Batman Cereal
EX $6 **NM** $12 **MIP** $25

Joker Bank, 1974, Mego, plastic
EX $30 **NM** $60 **MIP** $125

Robin Bank, 1966, ceramic bank depicts Robin removing mask, 7" tall
EX $80 **NM** $110 **MIP** $150

BOOK

Batman 3-D Comic Book, 1966, DC Comics, 9" x 11" comic w/3-D pages and glasses
EX $200 **NM** $500 **MIP** $1000

Batman Annual, 1965-66, 8" x 10" hardback annual contains reprinted stories from 1950s Batman and Detective Comics
EX $25 **NM** $50 **MIP** $85

Batman Comic Book and Record Set, 1966, Golden Records, 33-1/3 rpm record, full size Batman comic book, official Batman membership card w/secret Batman code on back
EX $60 **NM** $125 **MIP** $175

Batman vs. the Joker Book, 1966, Signet, 160-page paperback
EX $10 **NM** $20 **MIP** $30

Dot-To-Dot and Coloring Book, 1967, Vasquez Brothers, Batman w/Robin the Boy Wonder, printed in the Phillipines, 20 pages
EX $30 **NM** $50 **MIP** $100

From Alfred to Zowie! Book, 1966, Golden Press
EX $10 **NM** $20 **MIP** $35

Paint-By-Number Book, 1966, Whitman
EX $20 **NM** $40 **MIP** $85

Sticker Fun with Batman Book, 1966, Watkins-Strathmore, 8" x 11" softbound w/stickers
EX $15 **NM** $50 **MIP** $110

Three Villains of Doom Book, 1966, Signet, 160 pages
EX $10 **NM** $40 **MIP** $85

CLOTHING

Child's Belt, 1960s, elastic w/bronze logo buckle
EX $22 **NM** $40 **MIP** $90

Child's Mittens, 1973, children's blue plastic vinyl, raised illustration of Batman and logo
EX $12 **NM** $25 **MIP** $50

Child's Pajamas, 1966, Wormser, light blue, two piece pajamas, full color Batman logo on chest
EX $200 **NM** $450 **MIP** $900

FOOD PRODUCTS

Batman "Punch-O" Drink Mix, 1966, small paper packet
EX $25 **NM** $40 **MIP** $75

Batman Cereal Box, 1989, Ralston
EX $20 **NM** $30 **MIP** $60

Batman Crusader Sundae Fudgesicle, 1966, Popsicle, 7" white and brown paper wrapper
EX $10 **NM** $20 **MIP** $30

Bread Wrapper, 1966, New Century Bread, plastic
EX $25 **NM** $45 **MIP** $85

Candy Cigarettes, 1960s, made in England
EX $30 **NM** $60 **MIP** $90

Chocolate Milk Carton, 1966, Reiter and Hart, one-quart carton in yellow, red and brown, features front and back panels of Batman in action poses
EX $100 **NM** $200 **MIP** $400

Jelly Jar, 1966, W.H. Marvin, 5"-6" glass jar w/color label, "Bat" Pure Apple Jelly
EX $200 **NM** $400 **MIP** $600

Slam Bang Ice Cream Carton, 1966, Cabarrus Creamery, features Batman and Robin on side panels
EX $20 **NM** $45 **MIP** $65

GAMES

Batman Arcade Game, 1989, Bluebox, electronic
EX $75 **NM** $120 **MIP** $165

Batman Pinball Game, 1960s, Marx, tin litho w/plastic casing
EX $35 **NM** $90 **MIP** $175

Batman Target Game, 1966, Hasbro, tin litho target w/plastic revolver and rubber-tipped darts
EX $75 **NM** $100 **MIP** $200

GLASSWARE

Batman Drinking Glass, 1976, Pepsi, 7" tall glass tumbler, all Batman characters, each
EX $10 **NM** $20 **MIP** $30

Coffee Mug, 1966, Anchor-Hocking, milk glass, action pose of Batman on one side and the Bat logo on the opposite side
EX $15 **NM** $30 **MIP** $50

Drinking Glass, 1989, 5", made in France
EX $10 **NM** $25 **MIP** $40

MAGAZINE

Life Magazine, 1966, March 11, 1966 issue, Adam West as Batman on cover
EX $50 **NM** $70 **MIP** $125

TV Guide, 1966, TV Guide, March 26-April 1 issue, photo cover of Adam West as Batman
EX $120 **NM** $250 **MIP** $385

MODEL KIT

Catwoman Returns, 1990s, Horizon, vinyl model kit
EX $10 **NM** $20 **MIP** $40

Penguin Returns Model Kit, Horizon
EX $10 **NM** $20 **MIP** $40

PAINT SET

Batman Cast and Paint Set, 1960s, plaster casting mold and paint set
EX $50 **NM** $100 **MIP** $200

Batman Paint by Number Set, 1965, Hasbro, five pre-numbered sketches, ten oil paint vials and brush
EX $50 **NM** $100 **MIP** $200

Batman Super Powers Stain and Paint Set, 1984
EX $15 **NM** $30 **MIP** $70

Sparkle Paint Set, 1966, Kenner, paint and six pre-numbered sketches of Batman
EX $50 **NM** $100 **MIP** $175

PAPER GOODS

Batman and Robin Valentine, 1966
EX $10 **NM** $30 **MIP** $60

Batman Lobby Display, 1989, Warner Bros., Michael Keaton cardboard stand up
EX $125 **NM** $200 **MIP** $250

Batman Lucky Charm Display Card, 1966, 4" x 4" paper display card used in bubble gum machines, card shows Bat logo and red "Be protected—Get your Batman lucky charm now"
EX $12 **NM** $35 **MIP** $70

Batman Postcards, 1966, Dexter Press, set of eight postcards w/Carmine Infantino artwork
EX $40 **NM** $100 **MIP** $160

Batman Postcards, 1966, Dexter Press, three full-color postcards, each taken from a comic panel from Batman comics, each
EX $8 **NM** $15 **MIP** $30

Batman Returns Display, 1992, Warner Bros.
EX $50 **NM** $90 **MIP** $160

Batman Returns Lobby Display, 1992, Warner Bros., Michael Keaton life-size cardboard stand up
EX $125 **NM** $200 **MIP** $325

Batmobile Display Sign, 1969, Burry's, 34" x 48" die-cut 3-D plastic story display, raised images of Batman, Robin, and Batmobile, bright orange w/yellow lettering
EX $600 **NM** $1000 **MIP** $1500

Button Display Card, 1966, full color display card used in bubble gum machines which offered Batman buttons
EX $30 **NM** $60 **MIP** $100

Costume Store Poster, 1966, Ben Cooper, 12" x 24", yellow
EX $80 **NM** $160 **MIP** $220

Flicker Pictures Display Card, 1966, bubble gum machine display card
EX $10 **NM** $25 **MIP** $50

Glow-in-the Dark Poster, 1966, Ciro Art, 18" x 14" poster of Batman and Robin swinging across Gotham City
EX $50 **NM** $100 **MIP** $150

Official Bat-Signal Stickers, 1966, Alan-Whitney
EX $10 **NM** $20 **MIP** $35

Party Hat, 1972, Amscan/Canadian, 7" child's cardboard hat depicts Batman and Robin
EX $8 **NM** $15 **MIP** $30

PLAYSET

Batcave Play Set, 1974, Mego, vinyl
EX $200 **NM** $400 **MIP** $600

Batman and Robin playset, 1973, Ideal, "Fantastic Batcave, Gotham Museum, Wayne Manor," vinyl fold-over w/cardboard figures
EX $15 **NM** $30 **MIP** $55

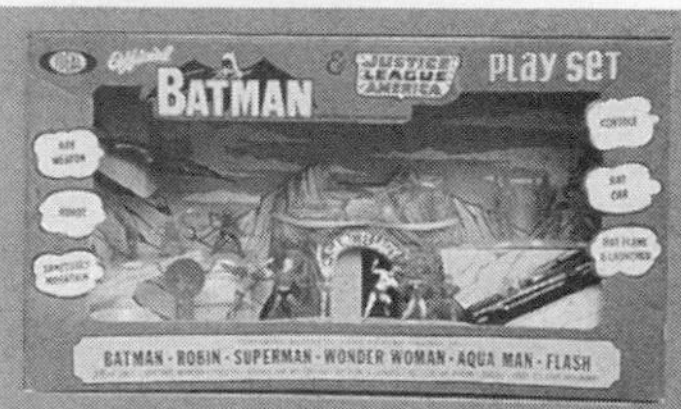

Batman Play Set, 1966, Ideal, eleven pieces including characters and vehicles
EX $3000 **NM** $8000 **MIP** $12000

Batman Shaker Maker Playset, 1974, Ideal, Batman, Robin and Joker: bodies included, head molds, shaker cup, molding compound, paints
EX $20 **NM** $40 **MIP** $60

Batman Switch and Go Play Set, 1966, Mattel, 9" plastic Batmobile, forty feet of track, figures, etc.
EX $175 **NM** $450 **MIP** $750

Magic Magnetic Gotham City Play Set, 1966, Remco, cardboard city, character figures
EX $300 **NM** $700 **MIP** $1000

PUPPET

Batman and Robin Hand Puppets, 1966, Ideal, 12" soft vinyl head, plastic body, each
EX $100 **NM** $200 **MIP** $300

Batman Push Puppet, 1966, Kohner, 3" plastic w/push button on bottom
EX $25 **NM** $50 **MIP** $100

Batman String Puppet, 1977, Madison
EX $35 **NM** $75 **MIP** $160

Robin Push Puppet, 1966, Kohner, 3" plastic, push button on bottom
EX $40 **NM** $85 **MIP** $150

PUZZLE

Frame Tray Puzzle, 1966, Whitman, 11" x 14", Batman and Robin thwarting the Joker
EX $20 **NM** $40 **MIP** $80

RECORD

Batman and Superman Record Album, 1969-71, Wonderland, 45 rpm record Batman theme song from the 1966 television show and "The Superman Song"
EX $20 **NM** $75 **MIP** $100

Batman Record, 1966, SPC, 45 rpm, sleeve shaped like Batman's head; also available in Robin, Joker, Penguin, Riddler and Batmobile versions
EX $15 **NM** $50 **MIP** $100

Batman Soundtrack Record, 1966, 20th Century Fox, mono and stereo versions, each
EX $60 **NM** $150 **MIP** $275

Catwoman's Revenge Record, 1975, Power Records, 33-1/3 rpm story record
EX $10 NM $25 MIP $60

Joker Record, 1966, SPC, 45 rpm, sleeve shaped like Joker's head
EX $20 NM $50 MIP $90

RINGS

Bat Ring, 1966, yellow plastic, originally for a gumball machine
EX $20 NM $40 MIP $65

Batman/Robin Flicker-Flasher Ring, 1966, Vari-Vue, silver plastic base
EX $10 NM $20 MIP $25

Riddler/Batman Punching Riddler Flicker-Flasher Ring, 1966, Vari-Vue, silver plastic base
EX $10 NM $25 MIP $45

Robin/Dick Grayson Flicker-Flasher Ring, 1966, Vari-Vue, silver plastic base
EX $10 NM $25 MIP $45

TOY

Bat Bomb, 1966, Mattel
EX $75 NM $100 MIP $210

Batman Batarang Bagatelle, 1966, Marx, throw at targets
EX $15 NM $35 MIP $65

Batman Cartoon Kit, 1966, Colorforms
EX $25 NM $55 MIP $85

Batman Kite, 1982, Hiflyer
EX $8 NM $15 MIP $35

Batman Radio Belt and Buckle, 1966
EX $60 NM $125 MIP $200

Batman Superfriends Lite Brite Refill Pack, 1980, Hasbro
EX $5 NM $15 MIP $25

Batman Superhero Stamp Set, 1970s
EX $10 NM $25 MIP $60

Batman Trace-a-Graph, 1966, Emenee
EX $50 NM $100 MIP $200

Batman Utility Belt, 1960s, Ideal
EX $1500 NM $3500 MIP $5750

Batman Wind-Up, 1989, 9", Billiken, Tin litho
EX $25 NM $50 MIP $100

Batman Yo-Yo, 1989, SpectraStar
EX $10 NM $20 MIP $35

Batphone, 1966, Marx
EX $100 NM $175 MIP $350

Batscope Dart Launcher, 1966, Tarco
EX $25 NM $45 MIP $100

Bat-Troll Doll, 1966, Wish-Nik, vinyl, dressed in a blue felt Batman outfit w/cowl and cape
EX $125 NM $200 MIP $350

Cave Tun-L, 1966, New York Toy, 26" x 26" x 2" tunnel
EX $700 NM $1500 MIP $2350

Escape Gun, 1966, Lincoln, red plastic spring-loaded pistol w/Batman decal, two separate firing barrels
EX $75 NM $150 MIP $225

Give-A-Show Projector Cards, 1960s, Kenner, four slide cards in box
EX $10 NM $30 MIP $60

Gotham City Stunt Set, 1989, Tonka
EX $15 NM $55 MIP $85

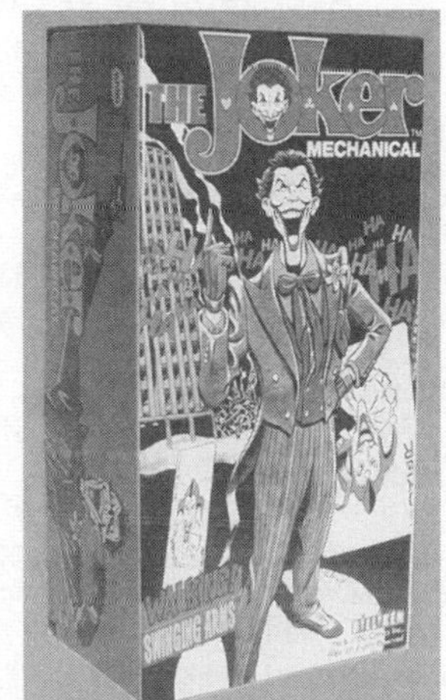

Joker Wind-up, 1989, 6", Billiken, Tin litho
EX $50 NM $100 MIP $185

Joker Yo-Yo, 1989, SpectraStar
EX $10 NM $20 MIP $45

Projector Gun, 1989, Toy Biz
EX $15 NM $30 MIP $70

Puppet Theater Stage, 1966, Ideal, marketed by Sears, 19" x 11" x 20" cardboard stage w/hand puppets
EX $200 NM $400 MIP $675

Ray Gun, 1960s, 7" long blue and black futuristic space gun w/bat sights and bats on handgrip
EX $125 NM $350 MIP $450

Rubber Stamp Set, 1966, Kellogg's, 2" x 5" hard black plastic case, set of six plastic stamps plus ink pad: Batman, Robin, Batmobile, Joker, Riddler and Penguin
EX $60 NM $100 MIP $160

Shooting Arcade, 1970s, AHI, graphics of Joker, Catwoman and Penguin
EX $35 NM $100 MIP $175

VEHICLES

Bat Cycle, 1989, Toy Biz
EX $10 NM $30 MIP $60

Bat Machine, 1979, Mego
EX $30 NM $75 MIP $120

Batboat, 1987, Duncan
EX $10 NM $30 MIP $70

Batboat Pullstring Toy, Eidai, made in Japan
EX $60 NM $140 MIP $200

Batman Flying Copter, 1966, Remco, 12" plastic w/guide-wire control
EX $50 NM $120 MIP $210

Batman Road Race Set, 1960s, slot car racing set
EX $150 NM $300 MIP $550

Batman Slot Car, 1966, Magicar (England), 5" long Batmobile being driven by Batman and Robin in illustrated display window box
EX $150 NM $325 MIP $550

Batmobile, Apollo (Japan), radio-controlled
EX $60 NM $125 MIP $260

Batmobile, Matsushiro, radio-controlled
EX $60 NM $125 MIP $260

Batman

Batmobile, 1960s, Simms, plastic car on card
EX $25 NM $60 MIP $125

Batmobile, 1972, AHI, 11" long tin litho battery-operated mystery action car w/blinking light and jet engine noise
EX $75 NM $150 MIP $300

Batmobile, 1974, Azrak-Hamway, battery operated
EX $50 NM $100 MIP $210

Batmobile, 1977, Duncan, 12" x 8" on card
EX $25 NM $50 MIP $100

Batmobile, 1980s, Aoshinu (Japan), motorized
EX $30 NM $60 MIP $150

Batmobile, 1980s, Bandai, pullback vehicle w/machine guns
EX $25 NM $60 MIP $135

Batmobile, 1989, Toy Biz, remote control
EX $12 NM $30 MIP $65

Batmobile, 1989, Rich Man's Toys, remote control
EX $85 NM $160 MIP $350

Batmobile Motorized Kit, 1980s, Aoshinu (Japan), smaller snap kit
EX $20 NM $35 MIP $75

Batwing, 1980s, Toy Biz
EX $15 NM $30 MIP $60

Joker Van, 1989, Ertl, die-cast vehicle on card
EX $5 NM $20 MIP $40

Robin Shuttle, 1979, Mego, sized for British-made Mego figures, in box
EX $20 NM $40 MIP $90

Super Accelerator Batmobile, 1970s, AHI, on card
EX $25 NM $60 MIP $120

Turbine-Sound Batmobile, 1989, Toy Biz
EX $10 NM $15 MIP $25

WATCH

Batman Returns Watch, 1989, Consort, gray or yellow Bat logo
EX $20 NM $40 MIP $80

Batman Wristwatch, 1991, Quintel, digital
EX $10 NM $15 MIP $35

Catwoman Watch, 1991, Quintel, digital
EX $10 NM $20 MIP $50

Catwoman Watch, 1991, Consort, Batman Returns
EX $10 NM $20 MIP $60

Joker Wristwatch, 1980s, Fossil
EX $25 NM $65 MIP $120

Joker Wristwatch, 1989, Quintell, digital
EX $10 NM $20 MIP $60

Video Game Watch, 1989, Tiger, w/alarm
EX $8 NM $20 MIP $40

Betty Boop

DOLL

Betty Boop Doll, 1930s, Cameo products, wood w/composition head
EX $400 NM $800 MIP $1200

Betty Boop Doll, 1986, M-Toy, 12" vinyl jointed
EX $20 NM $30 MIP $70

Betty Boop Doll Clothing, 1986, M-Toy, outfits for 12" dolls high fashion boutique, each
EX $7 NM $15 MIP $30

FIGURE

Betty Boop Figure, 1980s, 3" PVC figure, eight different poses and outfits, each
EX $5 NM $10 MIP $20

Betty Boop Figure, 1988, NJ Croce, 9" bendy
EX $7 NM $20 MIP $30

TOY

Betty Boop Delivery Truck, 1990, Schylling, tin litho
EX $15 NM $30 MIP $60

Betty Boop Wacky Wobbler, 2000, Funko, nodder
EX $6 NM $12 MIP $25

Blondie and Dagwood

ACCESSORIES

Blondie Paint Set, 1946, American Crayon
EX $75 NM $150 MIP $275

Blondie's Peg Board Set, 1934, King Features, 9" x 15-1/2", multi-colored pegs, hammer, cut-outs of Dagwood, Blondie, etc.
EX $100 NM $200 MIP $375

Blondie's Presto Slate, 1944, Presto, 10" x 13" illustration of Blondie and Dagwood and other characters
EX $50 NM $80 MIP $110

Dagwood Marionette, 1945, 14"
EX $100 NM $225 MIP $375

Dagwood's Solo Flight Airplane, 1935, Marx, 12" wingspan, plane 9" in length
EX $750 NM $1200 MIP $1550

Lucky Safety Card, 1953, 2" x 4" cards, Dagwood offers safety tips
EX $10 NM $55 MIP $80

BOOK

Blondie Paint Book, 1947, Whitman
EX $60 NM $150 MIP $250

DOLL

Blondie, 1985, Presents, released by Presents, a division of Tomy. Plastic head and hands, red dress
EX $10 NM $20 MIP $30

Blondie Paper Dolls, 1944, Whitman
EX $100 NM $225 MIP $400

Blondie Paper Dolls, 1955, Whitman
EX $40 NM $125 MIP $225

Dagwood, 1985, Presents, released by Presents, a division of Tomy. Plastic head and hands, black pants, white shirt, red tie
EX $10 NM $20 MIP $30

FIGURE

Blondie Figure, 1940s, 2-1/2" tall, lead
EX $30 NM $75 MIP $150

Dagwood and Kids Figures, 1944, King Features, Dagwood, Alexander, and Cookie, each
EX $50 NM $85 MIP $150

PUZZLE

Puzzle, 1930s, Featured Funnies
EX $75 NM $125 MIP $175

Bugs Bunny

ACCESSORIES

Bugs Bunny Charm Bracelet, 1950s, brass charms of Bugs Bunny, Tweety, Sniffles, Fudd, etc.
EX $40 NM $80 MIP $125

Bugs Bunny Chatter Chum, 1982, Mattel
EX $10 NM $25 MIP $50

Bugs Bunny Clock, 1972, Litech, 12" x 14"
EX $35 NM $100 MIP $185

Bugs Bunny Mini Snow Dome, 1980s, Applause
EX $5 NM $15 MIP $35

Bugs Bunny Musical Ge-Tar, 1977, Mattel
EX $30 NM $70 MIP $110

Bugs Bunny Night Light, 1980s, Applause
EX $5 NM $10 MIP $15

Bugs Bunny Talking Alarm Clock, 1974, Janex, battery-operated
EX $50 NM $100 MIP $175

Bugs Bunny Wristwatch, 1978, Lafayette
EX $50 NM $120 MIP $180

BANK

Bugs Bunny Bank, 1940s, 5-3/4" x 5-1/2", pot metal, figure on base
EX $70 NM $140 MIP $260

Bugs Bunny Bank, 1971, Dakin, on a basket of carrots
EX $15 NM $30 MIP $60

COSTUME

Bugs Bunny Costume, 1960s, Collegeville, mask and costume
EX $25 NM $50 MIP $85

DOLL

Bugs Bunny Talking Doll, 1971, Mattel
EX $50 NM $110 MIP $180

FIGURE

Bugs Bunny Bendy, 1980s, Applause, 4" tall
EX $5 NM $15 MIP $30

Bugs Bunny Figure, 1971, Dakin, 10" tall
EX $10 NM $35 MIP $75

Bugs Bunny Figure, 1975, Warner Bros., 5-1/2" tall, ceramic, holding carrot
EX $30 **NM** $70 **MIP** $120

Bugs Bunny Figure, 1975, Warner Bros., 2-3/4" tall, ceramic
EX $15 **NM** $30 **MIP** $75

Bugs Bunny Figure, 1976, Dakin, yellow globes in "Cartoon Theater" box
EX $15 **NM** $35 **MIP** $75

Bugs Bunny in Uncle Sam Outfit, 1976, Dakin, distributed through Great America Theme Park, Illinois
EX $25 **NM** $70 **MIP** $110

TOY

Bugs Bunny Colorforms Set, 1958, Colorforms
EX $15 **NM** $50 **MIP** $100

Bugs Bunny Soaky, soft rubber
EX $10 **NM** $30 **MIP** $65

California Raisins

ACCESSORIES

California Raisins Chalkboard, 1988, Rose Art
EX $7 **NM** $15 **MIP** $40

California Raisins Clay Factory, 1988, Rose Art
EX $15 **NM** $45 **MIP** $75

California Raisins Crayon By Number, 1988, Rose Art
EX $15 **NM** $35 **MIP** $70

TOY

California Raisins Colorforms Play Set, 1987, Colorforms
EX $10 **NM** $30 **MIP** $65

California Raisins Wind-Up Walkers, 1987, Rasta
EX $6 **NM** $15 **MIP** $35

Captain America

ACCESSORIES

Captain America Club Kit, 1941, includes two badges (copper and bronze), card, envelope
EX $1500 **NM** $2500 **MIP** $3500

FIGURE

Captain America Bendy Figure, 1966, Lakeside, 6", rubber
EX $50 **NM** $85 **MIP** $150

Powerized Captain America, 1980, Remco, plastic figure, wind up shield spins
EX $10 **NM** $20 **MIP** $30

TOY

Captain America Rocket Racer, 1984, Buddy L, Secret Wars remote controlled battery operated car
EX $75 **NM** $150 **MIP** $200

Captain America Scooter, 1967, Marx, 4", yellow plastic friction toy w/figure
EX $200 **NM** $350 **MIP** $450

Captain America Shooting Gallery, 1976, Larami, red dart gun, 2 darts, 3 duck targets, carded, Model No. 7068-0
EX $5 **NM** $10 **MIP** $14

Hand Puppet, 1960s, Ideal, box reads, "Super Hero TV Favorites"
EX $15 **NM** $30 **MIP** $65

Propeller toy, 1968, Ohio Art, rubber band driven, fragile
EX $10 **NM** $20 **MIP** $30

Captain Marvel

ACCESSORIES

Adventures of Captain Marvel Ink Blotter/Ruler, 1940s, Republic/Fawcett, 6" blotter w/ruler advertises the 12-part serial, theatre premium
EX $200 **NM** $625 **MIP** $825

Captain Marvel Booklet, 1940s, Fawcett
EX $50 **NM** $100 **MIP** $350

Captain Marvel Button, 1940s, celluloid, pinback
EX $30 **NM** $95 **MIP** $150

Captain Marvel Club Button, 1941, tin litho, showing Captain Marvel in bust 3/4 view, w/"Shazam" in lightning bolts at bottom
EX $30 **NM** $95 **MIP** $150

Captain Marvel Club Felt Shoulder Patches, 1940s, Fawcett, Captain Marvel diving towards Earth, yellow
EX $200 **NM** $475 **MIP** $675

Captain Marvel Club Felt Shoulder Patches, 1940s, Fawcett, Captain Marvel diving towards Earth, blue
EX $50 **NM** $100 **MIP** $200

Captain Marvel Club Membership Card, 1940s, Fawcett
EX $50 **NM** $75 **MIP** $120

Captain Marvel Code Finder, 1943
EX $225 **NM** $475 **MIP** $675

Captain Marvel Felt Pennant, 1940s, Fawcett, yellow, shows Captain Marvel flying
EX $100 **NM** $190 **MIP** $300

Captain Marvel Felt Pennant, 1940s, Fawcett, blue, shows Captain Marvel flying
EX $100 **NM** $135 **MIP** $200

Captain Marvel Film Viewer Gun, 1940s, gun-shaped movie viewer w/film strips from Paramount series
EX $125 **NM** $250 **MIP** $425

Captain Marvel Flannel Patch, 1940s, Fawcett
EX $50 **NM** $80 **MIP** $175

Captain Marvel Glow Pictures, 1940s, Fawcett, set of four
EX $350 **NM** $750 **MIP** $1000

Captain Marvel Iron-Ons, 1950s, Fawcett, sheet
EX $30 **NM** $60 **MIP** $100

Captain Marvel Jr. Wristwatch, 1940s, blue band, round dial w/blue costumed Jr., no box issued
EX $400 **NM** $850 **MIP** $1200

Captain Marvel Key Chain, 1940s, Fawcett
EX $60 **NM** $125 **MIP** $175

Captain Marvel Magic Dime Register Bank, 1948, Fawcett, available in three colors
EX $200 **NM** $425 **MIP** $650

Captain Marvel Magic Flute, 1940s, on die-cut card, shows Captain Marvel on side
EX $60 **NM** $100 **MIP** $160

Captain Marvel Magic Lightning Box, 1940s, Fawcett
EX $50 **NM** $100 **MIP** $175

Captain Marvel Magic Membership Card, 1940s, Fawcett
EX $40 **NM** $60 **MIP** $100

Captain Marvel Magic Picture, 1940s, Reed and Associates, paper, shows Billy Batson "transforming" into Captain Marvel
EX $50 **NM** $80 **MIP** $160

Captain Marvel Magic Whistle, 1948, Fawcett, seed company premium, picture of Captain Marvel on both sides, on card
EX $60 **NM** $120 **MIP** $175

Captain Marvel Neck Tie, 1940s, Fawcett
EX $60 **NM** $150 **MIP** $250

Captain Marvel Overseas Cap, 1940s, rare
EX $400 **NM** $800 **MIP** $1000

Captain Marvel Paint Set, 1940s, paint set w/five chalk figurines
EX $500 **NM** $1100 **MIP** $1600

Captain Marvel Paper Horn, 1940s, Fawcett
EX $20 **NM** $40 **MIP** $75

Captain Marvel Patch, 1940s, Fawcett
EX $30 **NM** $75 **MIP** $150

Captain Marvel

Captain Marvel Pinback Pattern, 1940s, Fawcett, pattern for original pinback
EX $15 **NM** $30 **MIP** $100

Captain Marvel Portrait, 1940s, Whiz Comics/Fawcett
EX $75 **NM** $125 **MIP** $250

Captain Marvel Portrait, 1940s, Republic, different version than Whiz Comics portrait
EX $75 **NM** $150 **MIP** $250

Captain Marvel Power Siren, 1940s, Fawcett
EX $60 **NM** $125 **MIP** $185

Captain Marvel Secret Code Sheet, 1940s, Fawcett
EX $15 **NM** $30 **MIP** $75

Captain Marvel Skull Cap, 1940s
EX $125 **NM** $500 **MIP** $700

Captain Marvel Soap, 1947, Fawcett, three illustrated bars in box
EX $300 **NM** $600 **MIP** $800

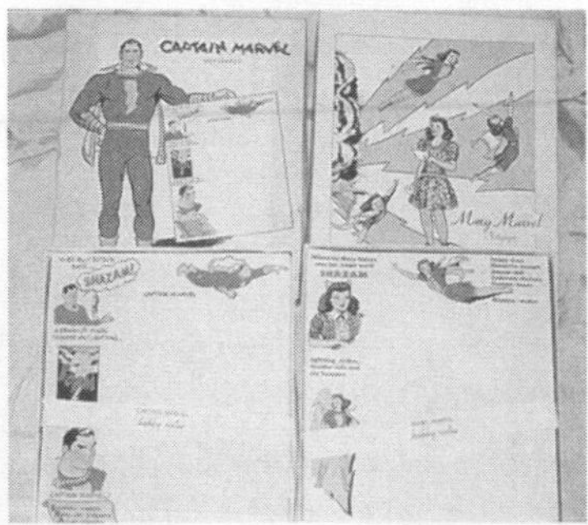

Captain Marvel Stationary, 1940s, Fawcett, paper and envelopes in box
EX $150 **NM** $250 **MIP** $400

Captain Marvel Suspenders, 1940s, Fawcett
EX $50 **NM** $125 **MIP** $185

Captain Marvel Sweater, 1940s, white or off-white, red Captain Marvel logo
EX $60 **NM** $300 **MIP** $400

Captain Marvel Tattoo Transfers, 1940s, Fawcett
EX $30 **NM** $110 **MIP** $200

Captain Marvel Tie Bar, 1940s, on card
EX $40 **NM** $65 **MIP** $150

Captain Marvel Wristwatch, 1948, in box, shows Captain Marvel holding an airplane
EX $400 **NM** $900 **MIP** $1350

Captain Marvel, Jr. Booklet, 1940s, Fawcett
EX $25 **NM** $50 **MIP** $100

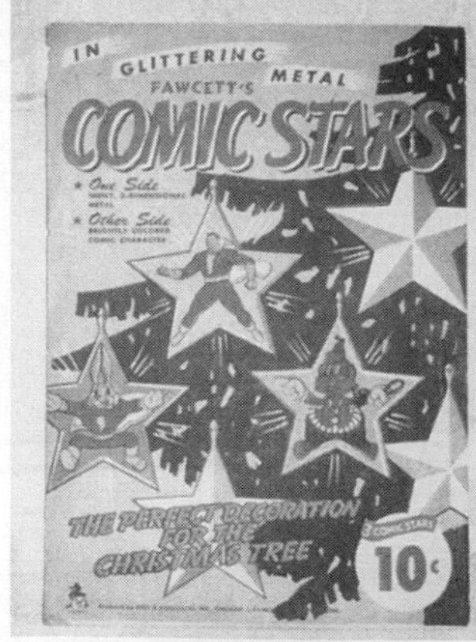

Fawcett's Comic Stars Christmas Tree Ornaments, 1940s, Fawcett, metal star-shaped ornaments w/art of Captain Marvel and Hoppy
EX $25 **NM** $45 **MIP** $100

Mary Marvel Illustrated Soap, 1947, Fawcett, three soap bars in box
EX $300 **NM** $500 **MIP** $700

Mary Marvel Patch, 1940s, Fawcett
EX $150 **NM** $300 **MIP** $450

Mary Marvel Pin, 1940s, Fawcett, fiberboard
EX $50 **NM** $150 **MIP** $250

Mary Marvel Stationery, 1940s, Fawcett, boxed
EX $100 **NM** $200 **MIP** $400

Mary Marvel Wristwatch, 1948, in box
EX $400 **NM** $900 **MIP** $1300

Membership Secret Code Card, 1940s, Fawcett
EX $150 **NM** $250 **MIP** $400

Rocket Raider, 1940s, Fawcett, paper airplane in envelope
EX $20 **NM** $40 **MIP** $70

COMIC

Boy Who Never Heard of Captain Marvel Mini Comic, 1940s, Bond Bread
EX $40 **NM** $100 **MIP** $210

Captain Marvel and Billy's Big Game Mini Comic, 1940s
EX $90 **NM** $250 **MIP** $410

Captain Marvel Meets the Weatherman Mini Comic, 1940s, Bond Bread, Bond Bread premium
EX $50 **NM** $110 **MIP** $185

Giveaway Comics #1, Captain Marvel and the Lt. of Safety, 1950, Danger Flies a Kite
EX $400 **NM** $800 **MIP** $1300

Giveaway Comics #2, Captain Marvel and the Lt. of Safety, 1950, Danger Takes to Climbing
EX $400 **NM** $800 **MIP** $1300

Giveaway Comics #3, Captain Marvel and the Lt. of Safety, 1951, Danger Smashes Street Lights
EX $400 **NM** $800 **MIP** $1300

FIGURE

Captain Marvel Comic Hero Punch-Outs, 1942, Lowe, cardboard figures
EX $75 **NM** $200 **MIP** $375

Captain Marvel Sirocco Figurine, 1940s, Fawcett
EX $1500 **NM** $3000 **MIP** $4000

Mary Marvel Figurine, 5"
EX $500 **NM** $1250 **MIP** $2000

PUZZLE

Captain Marvel Puzzle, 1940s, Reed and Associates, in envelope
EX $50 **NM** $350 **MIP** $425

Captain Marvel Puzzle, 1941, Fawcett, in box
EX $40 **NM** $200 **MIP** $375

TOY

Captain Marvel Beanbags, 1940s, Captain Marvel, Mary Marvel or Hoppy, each
EX $75 **NM** $175 **MIP** $325

Captain Marvel Beanie, 1940s, cap shows image of Captain Marvel flying toward word "Shazam," blue
EX $175 **NM** $350 **MIP** $600

Captain Marvel Beanie, 1940s, girls' cap shows image of Captain Marvel flying toward word "Shazam," pink, rare
EX $750 **NM** $1500 **MIP** $2000

Captain Marvel Buzz Bomb, 1950s, Fawcett, paper airplane in envelope
EX $25 **NM** $85 **MIP** $150

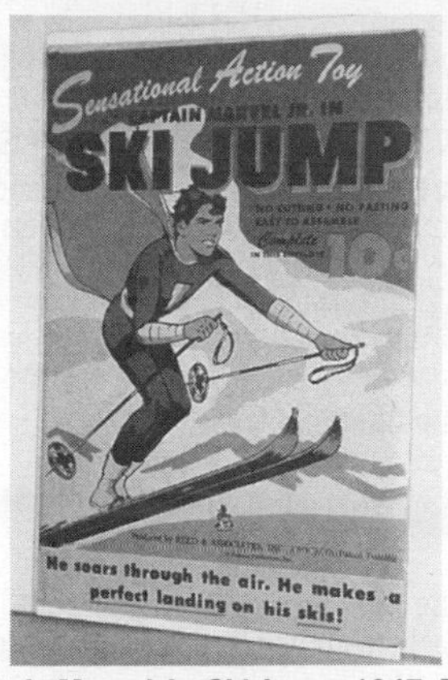

Captain Marvel Jr. Ski Jump, 1947, Reed and Associates, paper, in envelope
EX $10 **NM** $20 **MIP** $65

Captain Marvel Jr. Statuette, 1940s, Fawcett, hand-painted plastic
EX $500 **NM** $1500 **MIP** $2500

Captain Marvel Lightning Race Cars, 1940s, Automatic Toy Co., set of four cars w/ wind-up keys; green, yellow, orange or blue; rare
EX $2000 **NM** $3000 **MIP** $4000

Captain Marvel Statuette, 1940s, Fawcett, hand-painted plastic, shows Captain Marvel standing w/arms crossed, on base w/name engraved
EX $1000 **NM** $2500 **MIP** $4000

Mary Marvel Statuette, 1940s, Fawcett, hand-painted plastic
EX $500 **NM** $1750 **MIP** $3000

Captain Midnight

ACCESSORIES

Captain Midnight Badge Brass, 1930s, gold, wings and words "Flight Commander," fying cross
EX $90 **NM** $210 **MIP** $400

Captain Midnight Cup, plastic, 4" tall, "Ovaltine-The Heart of a Hearty Breakfast"
EX $30 **NM** $70 **MIP** $150

Captain Midnight Map, 1940, Skelly Oil, 11" x 17"
EX $450 **NM** $750 **MIP** $1200

Captain Midnight Membership Manual, 1930s, Secret Squadron official code and manual guide
EX $55 **NM** $125 **MIP** $275

Captain Midnight Secret Society Decoder, 1949, w/key
EX $85 **NM** $180 **MIP** $375

Captain Midnight's Spy Scope, 1950s, Ovaltine, plastic telescope
EX $20 **NM** $40 **MIP** $60

Decoder, 1948, radio premium, copper disc w/ signal mirror
EX $15 **NM** $30 **MIP** $75

Medal of Membership, 1940, Flight Patrol Spinner coin
EX $20 **NM** $40 **MIP** $70

Mug w/ handle, 1952, 3", Ovaltine, sticker says "Ovaltine-The Heart of a Hearty Breakfast"
EX $15 **NM** $30 **MIP** $60

Photo-matic Code-O-Graph, 1942, radio show premium, brass badge
EX $20 **NM** $40 **MIP** $70

Premium Ring, 1957, Ovaltine, Ovaltine premium, adjustable ring
EX $150 **NM** $300 **MIP** $500

Whistle, 1947, 1-5/8"x1-1/4", Code-A-Graph Decoder, radio premium
EX $15 **NM** $30 **MIP** $65

BOOK

Better Little Book, 1941, Whitman, "Captain Midnight and the Secret Squadron";
EX $30 **NM** $80 **MIP** $120

Better Little Book, 1942, Chicago Sun Syndicate, "Captain Midnight and the Moon Woman," #1452
EX $30 **NM** $80 **MIP** $120

Better Little Book, 1944, Whitman, "Captain Midnight and Sheik Jomk Khan," #1402
EX $30 **NM** $80 **MIP** $120

Cartoon/Comic Characters

ACCESSORIES

Beetle Bailey Comic Strip Stamper Set, 1981, Ja-Ru, 7 stampers, book, crayon
EX $8 **NM** $25 **MIP** $60

Beetle Bailey Gun Set, 1981, Ja-Ru, cord gun and target
EX $10 **NM** $40 **MIP** $90

Daffy Dog Poster, 10" x 13", The Morning After
EX $10 **NM** $17 **MIP** $30

Dan Dunn Pinback Button, 1930s, 1-1/4"
EX $50 **NM** $200 **MIP** $375

Doggie Daddy Metal Trivet, 1960s, says "You have to work like a dog to live like one"
EX $15 **NM** $35 **MIP** $70

Dudley Do-Right Jigsaw Puzzle, 1975, Whitman, Dudley and Snidley
EX $15 **NM** $35 **MIP** $75

Easy Show Movie Projector Films, 1965, Kenner, numerous cartoon characters, each film
EX $8 **NM** $15 **MIP** $30

Favorite Funnies Printing Set, 1930s, #4004, Orphan Annie, Herby, and Dick Tracy, six stamps, pad, paper and instructions
EX $75 **NM** $175 **MIP** $275

Geoffrey Jack-In-the-Box, 1970s, Toys R Us, jack-in-the-box
EX $20 **NM** $40 **MIP** $80

Hair Bear Bunch Mug, 1978, Square Bear figural mug
EX $5 **NM** $13 **MIP** $20

Hair Bear Bunch Wristwatch, 1972, medium gold tone case, base metal back, articulated hands, red leather snap down band
EX $30 **NM** $70 **MIP** $150

Harold Teen Playstone Funnies Mold Set, 1940s
EX $40 **NM** $100 **MIP** $200

Herman and Katnip Punch Out Kite, 1960s, Saalfield, folds into a kite
EX $12 **NM** $30 **MIP** $75

Josie and the Pussycats Paper Doll Book, 1971, Whitman, Model No. 1982
EX $25 **NM** $50 **MIP** $110

Little Audrey Dress Designer Kit, 1962, Saalfield, die cut doll and accessories in illustrated box
EX $60 **NM** $125 **MIP** $185

Little Audrey Shoulder Bag Leathercraft Kit, 1961, Jewel
EX $75 **NM** $150 **MIP** $200

Little Lulu Dish, 1940s, 5-1/2" hand painted ceramic, pictures of Lulu, Tubby and her friends
EX $100 **NM** $200 **MIP** $350

Nancy Music Box, 1968, United Feature, ceramic
EX $80 **NM** $150 **MIP** $225

Supercar Molding Color Kit, 1960s, Sculptorcraft, set of rubber plaster casting models of vehicle and show characters, including Mike Mercury, Beaker and Popkiss, Jimmy and Mitch, Masterspy
EX $150 **NM** $300 **MIP** $445

Winnie Winkle Playstone Funnies Mold Set, 1940s
EX $30 **NM** $75 **MIP** $150

BANK

Andy Panda Bank, 1977, Walter Lantz, 7" tall, hard plastic
EX $15 **NM** $50 **MIP** $85

Little Lulu Bank, 8" tall hard plastic w/black fire hydrant
EX $60 **NM** $125 **MIP** $185

Scrappy Bank, 3" x 3-1/2" metal, embossed illustration of Scrappy and his dog
EX $150 **NM** $300 **MIP** $425

BOOK

Little Lulu Paint Book, 1944, Whitman
EX $100 **NM** $200 **MIP** $300

DOLL

Bloom County Opus Doll, 1986, 10" tall, plush, penguin Opus wearing a Santa Claus cap
EX $10 **NM** $30 **MIP** $75

Chilly Willy Doll, 1982, Walter Lantz, plush
EX $7 NM $25 MIP $60

Dudley Do-Right Doll, 1972, Wham-O, bendy
EX $20 NM $40 MIP $80

Hagar the Horrible Doll, 1983, 12" tall
EX $12 NM $22 MIP $70

King Leonardo Doll, 1960s, Holiday Fair, cloth plush dressed in royal robe
EX $75 NM $100 MIP $200

FIGURE

Alfred E. Neuman Figurine, 1960s, base says "What Me Worry?"
EX $70 NM $140 MIP $225

Cadbury the Butler Figure, 1981, DFC, 3-1/2" figure from Richie Rich
EX $7 NM $20 MIP $35

Wonder Woman Figure, Presents, 14" tall cloth and vinyl figure on base
EX $9 NM $25 MIP $50

PUZZLE

Katzenjammer Kids Jigsaw Puzzle, 1930s, 9-1/2" x 14", Featured Funnies
EX $100 NM $200 MIP $325

Little Lulu Puzzles, 1973, Whitman, four frame tray puzzles
EX $30 NM $60 MIP $100

Rosie's Beau Puzzle, 1930s, 9-1/2" x 14", Featured Funnies
EX $50 NM $85 MIP $150

Smilin' Jack Puzzle, 1930s, 9-1/2" x 14", Featured Funnies
EX $100 NM $150 MIP $200

TOY

Breezley Soaky, 1967, Purex, 9" tall, plastic
EX $25 NM $60 MIP $110

Henry on Trapeze Toy, G. Borgfeldt, 6" x 9", celluloid, wind-up, jointed Henry suspended from trapeze
EX $400 NM $700 MIP $1250

Mush Mouse Pull Toy, 1960s, Ideal, pull toy w/vinyl figure
EX $40 NM $100 MIP $180

Peter Potamus Soaky, 11" tall
EX $20 NM $40 MIP $90

Touche Turtle Soaky, 1960s, lying down
EX $15 NM $40 MIP $75

Touche Turtle Soaky, 1960s, standing
EX $25 NM $60 MIP $110

Yipee Pull Toy, 1960s, Ideal, w/vinyl figures of Yipee, Yapee and Yahoee
EX $40 NM $80 MIP $150

Casper the Friendly Ghost

ACCESSORIES

Casper Figure Lamp, 1950, Archlamp, 17" tall
EX $75 NM $175 MIP $275

Casper Light Shade, 1960s
EX $70 NM $100 MIP $175

Casper Night Light, 1975, Duncan, 6-1/2" tall
EX $15 NM $40 MIP $75

COSTUME

Casper Costume, Collegeville, "Ghostland" costume, #216
EX $45 NM $70 MIP $110

Casper Halloween Costume, 1960s, Collegeville, mask and costume
EX $20 NM $40 MIP $90

DOLL

Casper Doll, 7-3/4" tall squeeze doll holds black spotted puppy
EX $30 NM $65 MIP $125

Casper Doll, 1960s, 15" cloth
EX $30 NM $60 MIP $125

Casper Doll, 1972, Sutton and Sons, rubber squeeze doll w/logo
EX $20 NM $30 MIP $60

Casper the Friendly Ghost Talking Doll, 1961, Mattel, 15" tall, terry cloth, plastic head w/a pull string voice box
EX $75 NM $175 MIP $250

PUZZLE

Casper Jigsaw Puzzle, 1988, Ja-Ru
EX $4 NM $10 MIP $20

TOY

Casper Hand Puppet, 1960s, Commonwealth Toys, all fuzzy, ribbon says "Casper the Friendly Ghost"
EX $15 NM $30 MIP $60

Casper Hand Puppet, 1960s, 8" tall, cloth and plastic head
EX $20 NM $40 MIP $100

Casper Pull Toy, 1950s, 9" l x 10" h, red wheels, paper litho of cartoon Casper on wood, arms play xylophone when pulled
EX $50 NM $125 MIP $250

Casper Soaky, 1960s, Colgate-Palmolive, 10" tall
EX $20 NM $55 MIP $90

Casper Spinning Top, 1960s, blue top w/figure of Casper inside
EX $25 NM $60 MIP $90

Casper Wind-Up Toy, 1950s, Linemar, tin
EX $300 NM $500 MIP $850

Wacky Wobbler, 2001, Funko, nodder
EX $5 NM $10 MIP $25

Wendy the Good Witch Soaky, 1960s, Colgate-Palmolive
EX $20 NM $55 MIP $90

Charlie Chaplin

ACCESSORIES

Charlie Chaplin Pencil Case, 8" long
EX $50 NM $100 MIP $200

Charlie Chaplin Wristwatch, 1972, Bubbles/Cadeaux, Swiss, large chrome case, black and white dial, articulated sweep cane second hand, black leather band
EX $45 NM $100 MIP $225

Charlie Chaplin Wristwatch, 1985, Bradley, oldies series, quartz, large black plastic case and band, sweep seconds, shows Chaplin as Little Tramp
EX $20 NM $50 MIP $100

DOLL

Charlie Chaplin Cloth Doll, patterned fabric
EX $225 NM $375 MIP $475

Charlie Chaplin Doll, 11-1/2" tall, wind-up
EX $500 NM $1000 MIP $1500

FIGURE

Charlie Chaplin Figure, 2-1/2" tall, lead
EX $60 NM $175 MIP $325

Charlie Chaplin Figure, 8-1/2" tall, tin w/cast iron feet, wind-up
EX $600 NM $1100 MIP $1800

TOY

Charlie Chaplin Toy, 4" tall, spring mechanism tips his hat when string is pulled
EX $100 NM $175 MIP $300

Chipmunks

ACCESSORIES

Chipmunks Toothbrush, 1984, battery-operated
EX $10 NM $25 MIP $50

Chipmunks Wallet, 1959, vinyl
EX $40 NM $80 MIP $120

DOLL

Alvin Doll, 1963, Knickerbocker, 14" tall plush w/vinyl head
EX $30 NM $70 MIP $120

TOY

Chipmunks Bean Bags, 1998, three in set, talking
EX $20 NM $40 MIP $60

Chipmunks Soaky, 1960s, 10" tall, Alvin, Simon, or Theodore, each
EX $10 NM $40 MIP $80

Cinderella

ACCESSORIES

Cinderella Alarm Clock, Westclox, 2-1/2" x 4-1/2" x 4" tall
EX $70 NM $125 MIP $275

Cinderella Bank, 1950s, ceramic, Cinderella holding magic wand
EX $40 NM $75 MIP $150

Cinderella Charm Bracelet, 1950, golden brass link w/five charms, Cinderella, Fairy Godmother, slipper, pumpkin coach and Prince
EX $40 NM $80 MIP $150

Cinderella Molding Set, 1950s, Model Craft, set of character molds in illustrated box
EX $40 NM $100 MIP $200

Cinderella Musical Jewelry Box, mahogany music box plays "So This Is Love"
EX $20 NM $40 MIP $85

Cinderella Wristwatch, 1950, US Time
EX $225 NM $450 MIP $750

Cinderella Wristwatch, 1958, Timex, Cinderella and castle, pink leather band
EX $150 NM $350 MIP $650

Fairy Godmother Pitcher, 7" tall figural pitcher
EX $22 **NM** $50 **MIP** $100

Gus/Jaq Serving Set, 1960s, Westman, creamer, pitcher and sugar bowl
EX $50 **NM** $100 **MIP** $200

DOLL

Cinderella Doll, 11" tall, blue stain ballgown w/white bridal gown, glass slippers, holding Little Little Golden Book
EX $20 **NM** $40 **MIP** $120

Cinderella Doll, Horsman, 8" tall in illustrated box
EX $30 **NM** $75 **MIP** $175

Cinderella Paper Dolls, 1965, Whitman
EX $50 **NM** $100 **MIP** $185

Gus Doll, 1950s, Gund, 13" tall, gray doll w/dark red shirt and green felt hat
EX $75 **NM** $150 **MIP** $250

FIGURE

Cinderella Figurine, 5" tall, plastic
EX $10 **NM** $20 **MIP** $50

Cinderella Figurine, 5" tall, ceramic
EX $20 **NM** $40 **MIP** $100

PUZZLE

Cinderella Puzzle, 1960s, Jaymar
EX $15 **NM** $30 **MIP** $60

TOY

Cinderella Soaky, 1960s, 11" tall, blue
EX $15 **NM** $40 **MIP** $80

Cinderella Wind-Up Toy, 1950, Irwin, 5" tall, Cinderella and Prince dancing
EX $75 **NM** $225 **MIP** $350

Prince Charming Hand Puppet, 1959, Gund, 10" tall
EX $25 **NM** $50 **MIP** $100

Crusader Rabbit

ACCESSORIES

Crusader Rabbit Paint Set, 1960s, 13" x 19"
EX $90 **NM** $135 **MIP** $200

BOOK

Crusader Rabbit Book, 1958, Wonder Book
EX $30 **NM** $60 **MIP** $100

Crusader Rabbit in Bubble Trouble Book, 1960, Whitman
EX $30 **NM** $60 **MIP** $95

Crusader Rabbit Trace and Color Book, 1959, Whitman
EX $55 **NM** $110 **MIP** $175

TOY

Crusader Rabbit Soaky, 1960s, Purex
EX $50 **NM** $100 **MIP** $150

Danger Mouse

ACCESSORIES

Danger Mouse ID Set, 1985, Gordy
EX $10 **NM** $15 **MIP** $50

Danger Mouse Pendant Necklace, 1986, Gordy
EX $10 **NM** $15 **MIP** $50

DOLL

Danger Mouse Doll, 1988, Russ, 15" tall
EX $40 **NM** $60 **MIP** $100

TOY

Danger Mouse Bendy, 1986, Cosgrove, 5" tall, bendable
EX $7 **NM** $14 **MIP** $25

Dennis the Menace

ACCESSORIES

Giant Mischief Kit, 1950s, Hasbro
EX $60 **NM** $110 **MIP** $210

Paint Set, 1954, Pressman, paints, crayons, brush and trays
EX $40 **NM** $100 **MIP** $185

BOOK

Dennis the Menace and Ruff Book, 1959, Whitman, Little Golden Book
EX $10 **NM** $18 **MIP** $40

Dennis the Menace and Ruff Book Ends, 1974, ceramic
EX $30 **NM** $65 **MIP** $125

PUZZLE

TV Show Puzzle, 1960, Whitman
EX $20 **NM** $40 **MIP** $60

TOY

Colorforms Set, 1961, Colorforms
EX $15 **NM** $45 **MIP** $100

Doll, 1959, blue and white stripped shirt w/red overalls, 13" tall
EX $25 **NM** $50 **MIP** $70

Hand Puppet, 1950s, plastic head, cloth body
EX $10 **NM** $20 **MIP** $35

Plastic Figure, 1954, press his cowlick and he raises his right arm holding a gun
EX $10 **NM** $20 **MIP** $30

Tiddley Winks, 1961, Whitman
EX $25 **NM** $45 **MIP** $90

Deputy Dawg

DOLL

Deputy Dawg Doll, 1960s, Ideal, 14" tall, cloth w/plush arms and vinyl head
EX $75 **NM** $135 **MIP** $195

FIGURE

Deputy Dawg Figure, 1977, Dakin, 6" tall, plastic body w/vinyl head
EX $30 **NM** $55 **MIP** $100

TOY

Deputy Dawg Soaky, 1966, 9-1/2" tall, plastic
EX $15 **NM** $45 **MIP** $80

Dick Tracy

ACCESSORIES

Air Detective Bracelet, 1938
EX $500 **NM** $625 **MIP** $825

Air Detective Cap, 1938, Quaker
EX $200 **NM** $400 **MIP** $600

Bonny Braids Store Contest Card, 1951, 5-1/2" x 5-1/2"
EX $25 **NM** $65 **MIP** $125

Candy Box, 1940s, Novel Package, box w/cartoons and story on back; comic strips on bottom
EX $150 **NM** $275 **MIP** $385

Christmas Tree Light Bulb, 1930s, early painted figure of Dick Tracy
EX $40 **NM** $90 **MIP** $100

Detective Club Pin, 1942, yellow, tab back
EX $25 **NM** $50 **MIP** $90

Dick Tracy Jr. Detective Agency Tie Clasp, 1930s, silver or brass, each
EX $75 **NM** $125 **MIP** $200

Dick Tracy Lamp, 1950s, painted ceramic bust of Tracy in black coat, yellow hat and red tie
EX $1500 **NM** $2000 **MIP** $3500

Dick Tracy Mask, 1933, Philadelphia Inquirer, paper
EX $200 **NM** $350 **MIP** $450

Dick Tracy Picture, 1940s, Pillsbury, part of set of eight, each 7" x 10" in mat, shows Tracy and Junior
EX $60 **NM** $130 **MIP** $250

Dinnerware Set, 1950s, Homer Laughlin, bowl, dinner plate, and mug
EX $70 **NM** $150 **MIP** $300

Dinnerware Set, 1980s, Zak Designs, plate, cup, bowl
EX $10 **NM** $15 **MIP** $30

Hat, 1940s, Miller Bros. Hat, wool fedora, blue/gray
EX $50 **NM** $100 **MIP** $175

Secret Service Patrol Bracelet, 1938, Quaker, chain bracelet w/small head of Dick Tracy and Junior and four leaf clover
EX $100 **NM** $150 **MIP** $250

Sparkle Plenty Christmas Tree Lights, 1940s, Mutual Equipment, seven-light set
EX $30 **NM** $65 **MIP** $125

Sparkle Plenty Christmas Tree Lights, 1940s, Mutual Equipment, 15-light set
EX $40 **NM** $90 **MIP** $175

Super 8 Color Film, 1965, Republic, b/w cartoon "Trick or Treat"
EX $10 **NM** $25 **MIP** $55

Dick Tracy

Wall Clock, 1990s, 16" x 20" battery power quartz, face shows Disney movie Tracy talking into wrist radio
EX $15 **NM** $20 **MIP** $40

Wallpaper Section, 1950s, shows comic strip scenes of Tracy and seven other characters
EX $15 **NM** $40 **MIP** $75

BADGE

Air Detective Member Badge, 1938, Quaker, brass, wing shape
EX $90 **NM** $125 **MIP** $175

Detective Club Crime Stoppers Badge, 1940s, Guild
EX $30 **NM** $60 **MIP** $100

Dick Tracy Crime Stopper Badge, 1960s, star shape giveaway badge from WGN "9 Official Dick Tracy Crimestopper" TV Badge
EX $30 **NM** $65 **MIP** $125

Dick Tracy Detective Club Belt Badge with belt, premium
EX $35 **NM** $150 **MIP** $350

Secret Service Patrol Badge, 1938, Quaker, Sergeant
EX $40 **NM** $100 **MIP** $225

Secret Service Patrol Badge, 1938, Quaker, 2nd year chevron
EX $10 **NM** $30 **MIP** $60

Secret Service Patrol Badge, 1938, Quaker, Lieutenant
EX $50 **NM** $185 **MIP** $350

Secret Service Patrol Badge, 1938, Quaker, Inspector General, brass, 2-1/2"
EX $350 **NM** $650 **MIP** $950

Secret Service Patrol Badge, 1938, Quaker, brass girl's division badge
EX $20 **NM** $50 **MIP** $100

Secret Service Patrol Badge, 1938, Quaker, brass Captain badge
EX $75 **NM** $185 **MIP** $375

BANK

Sparkle Plenty Bank, 1940s, Jayess, 12" tall, base features a medallion of Dick Tracy as Godfather
EX $150 **NM** $300 **MIP** $525

BOOK

Ace Detective Book, 1943, Whitman
EX $30 **NM** $60 **MIP** $150

Adventures of Dick Tracy and Dick Tracy Jr. Book, 1933, Whitman, 320 pages, hardcover Big Little Book
EX $500 **NM** $1000 **MIP** $1500

Adventures of Dick Tracy the Detective Book, 1933, Whitman, first of Big Little Book series, hardcover
EX $850 **NM** $1400 **MIP** $2200

Booklet, 1934, Big Thrill Chewing Gum, five different premium books, eight pages, each
EX $75 **NM** $100 **MIP** $130

Capture of Boris Arson Book, The, 1935, Pleasure Books, pop-up book
EX $200 **NM** $400 **MIP** $750

Detective Dick Tracy and the Spider Gang Book, 1937, Whitman, 240 pages, Big Little Book
EX $75 **NM** $150 **MIP** $200

Dick Tracy and His G-Men Book, 1941, Whitman, 432 pages, Big Little Book, hardcover w/flip pictures
EX $75 **NM** $150 **MIP** $200

Dick Tracy and the Bicycle Gang Book, 1948, Whitman, 288 pages, Big Little Book, hardcover
EX $60 **NM** $120 **MIP** $180

Dick Tracy and the Boris Arson Gang Book, 1935, Whitman, 432 pages, Big Little Book, hardcover
EX $75 **NM** $150 **MIP** $200

Dick Tracy and the Hotel Murders Book, 1937, Whitman, 432 pages, hardcover Big Little Book
EX $60 **NM** $125 **MIP** $180

Dick Tracy and the Invisible Man Book, 1939, Whitman, Quaker premium, 132 pages, softcover Big Little Book
EX $100 **NM** $250 **MIP** $350

Dick Tracy and the Mad Killer Book, 1947, Whitman, 288 pages, hardcover Big Little Book
EX $40 **NM** $90 **MIP** $150

Dick Tracy and the Mystery of the Purple Cross Book, 1938, Whitman, 320 pages, Big Big Book, hardcover
EX $200 **NM** $400 **MIP** $800

Dick Tracy and the Phantom Ship Book, 1940, Whitman, 432 pages, hardcover Big Little Book
EX $45 **NM** $90 **MIP** $170

Dick Tracy and the Racketeer Gang Book, 1936, Whitman, 432 pages, hardcover Big Little Book
EX $60 **NM** $125 **MIP** $180

Dick Tracy and the Stolen Bonds Book, 1934, Whitman, 320 pages, hardcover, Big Little Book
EX $60 **NM** $125 **MIP** $180

Dick Tracy and the Tiger Lilly Gang Book, 1949, Whitman, 288 pages, hardcover Big Little Book
EX $35 **NM** $80 **MIP** $140

Dick Tracy and the Wreath Kidnapping Case Book, 1945, Whitman, 432 pages, hardcover Big Little Book
EX $40 **NM** $90 **MIP** $150

Dick Tracy and Yogee Yamma Book, 1946, Whitman, 352 pages, hardcover Big Little Book
EX $35 **NM** $80 **MIP** $135

Dick Tracy Encounters Facey Book, 1967, Whitman, 260 pages, hardcover Big Little Book, cover price 39 cents
EX $10 **NM** $15 **MIP** $30

Dick Tracy From Colorado to Nova Scotia Book, 1933, Whitman, 320 pages, hardcover Big Little Book
EX $50 **NM** $100 **MIP** $175

Dick Tracy in Chains of Crime Book, 1936, Whitman, 432 pages, hardcover, Big Little Book
EX $50 **NM** $100 **MIP** $180

Dick Tracy Junior Detective Kit Book, 1962, Golden Press, punchout book of Tracy tools, including badges, revolver, wrist radio
EX $25 **NM** $50 **MIP** $100

Dick Tracy Little Golden Book, 1962, Golden Press, features characters from the TV show
EX $20 **NM** $30 **MIP** $60

Dick Tracy Meets a New Gang Book, 1939, Whitman, Quaker premium, 132 pages, softcover Big Little Book
EX $100 **NM** $200 **MIP** $375

Dick Tracy on the High Seas Book, 1939, Whitman, 432 pages, hardcover Big Little Book
EX $50 **NM** $100 **MIP** $180

Dick Tracy on the Trail of Larceny Lu Book, 1935, Whitman, 432 pages, hardcover Big Little Book
EX $50 **NM** $100 **MIP** $175

Dick Tracy on Voodoo Island Book, 1944, Whitman, 352 pages, hardcover Big Little Book
EX $40 **NM** $75 **MIP** $150

Dick Tracy Out West Book, 1933, Whitman, 300 pages, hardcover, Big Little Book
EX $50 **NM** $100 **MIP** $180

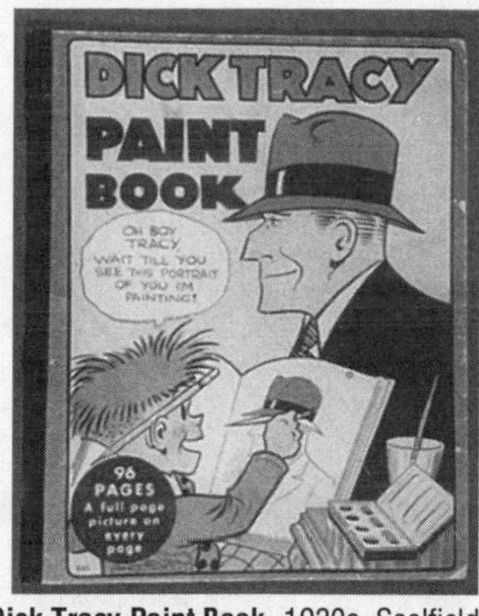

Dick Tracy Paint Book, 1930s, Saalfield, 96 pages
EX $100 NM $200 MIP $400

Dick Tracy Returns Book, 1939, Whitman, 432 pages, hardcover Big Little Book, Republic movie serial tie-in
EX $50 NM $100 MIP $180

Dick Tracy Solves the Penfield Mystery Book, 1934, Whitman, 320 pages, hardcover, Big Little Book
EX $50 NM $100 MIP $180

Dick Tracy Special FBI Operative Book, 1943, Whitman, 432 pages, hardcover, Big Little Book
EX $40 NM $75 MIP $150

Dick Tracy Super Detective Book, 1941, Whitman
EX $35 NM $65 MIP $135

Dick Tracy the Man with No Face Book, 1938, Whitman, 432 pages, hardcover, Big Little Book
EX $50 NM $100 MIP $175

Dick Tracy the Super Detective Book, 1939, Whitman, 432 pages, hardcover Big Little Book
EX $50 NM $100 MIP $180

Dick Tracy vs. Crooks in Disguise Book, 1939, Whitman, 352 pages, hardcover, Big Little Book w/flip pictures
EX $50 NM $100 MIP $180

Dick Tracy's Ghost Ship Book, 1939, Whitman, Quaker premium, 132 pages, softcover Big Little Book
EX $100 NM $200 MIP $375

Secret Code Book, 1938, Quaker, premium
EX $50 NM $100 MIP $175

Secret Detective Methods and Magic Tricks Book, 1939, Quaker, cereal premium
EX $75 NM $175 MIP $250

BUTTON

Detective Button, 1930s, celluloid pinback w/portrait, newspaper premium
EX $25 NM $50 MIP $90

Dick Tracy and Little Orphan Annie Button, Genung Promo
EX $1000 NM $2400 MIP $3000

Pep Flintheart Pin, 1945, Kellogg's, tin litho button
EX $10 NM $20 MIP $45

Secret Service Patrol Member Button, 1938, Quaker, 1-1/4" blue and silver, pinback
EX $20 NM $45 MIP $90

COMIC BOOK

Dick Tracy Comic Book, 1947, Popped Wheat Cereal, premium
EX $6 NM $10 MIP $20

Dick Tracy in 3-D Comic Book, 1986, Blackthorne, Ocean Death Trap
EX $4 NM $8 MIP $15

Motorola Presents Dick Tracy Comic Book, 1953, Motorola, premium comic book w/paper mask and vest
EX $50 NM $100 MIP $175

DOLL

Bonny Braids Doll, 1950s, 6" tall, plastic, walking wobble doll
EX $30 NM $75 MIP $150

Bonny Braids Doll, 1951, Ideal, 14" tall w/toothbrush
EX $90 NM $180 MIP $375

Bonny Braids Doll, 1952, Ideal, 8" tall, crawls when wound
EX $80 NM $170 MIP $325

Dick Tracy Doll, 1930s, 13" tall, composition, grey trench coat w/moveable head and mouth that operates w/back pull string, gray or yellow coat
EX $200 NM $450 MIP $700

Little Honey Moon Doll, 1965, Ideal, 16" space baby, bubble helmet and outfit w/white pigtails, doll sitting on half a moon w/stars in the background
EX $200 NM $350 MIP $500

Sparkle Plenty Doll, 1947, Ideal, 12" tall
EX $125 NM $250 MIP $450

FIGURES

B.O. Plenty Figure, 1950s, Marx, Famous Comic Figures series, waxy cream, pink, 60mm tall
EX $20 NM $40 MIP $65

Blank Figure, The, 1990, Playmates, figure w/gun and hat w/featureless face attached
EX $60 NM $100 MIP $150

Breathless Mahoney Figure, 1990, Applause, 14" tall
EX $5 NM $10 MIP $20

Dick Tracy Figure, 1940s, Professional Art, 7" unpainted, detailed white chalk figure or painted
EX $80 NM $200 MIP $375

Dick Tracy Figures, 1950s, Marx, Famous Comic Figures series, several characters, each
EX $40 NM $75 MIP $150

Dick Tracy Nodder, 1960s, 6-1/2" tall, ceramic nodding head bust
EX $350 NM $800 MIP $1200

Gravel Gertie Figure, 1950s, Marx, Famous Comic Figures series
EX $12 NM $20 MIP $40

Sparkle Plenty Figure, 1950s, Marx, Famous Comic Figures series
EX $10 NM $15 MIP $50

Steve the Tramp Figure, 1990, Playmates, discontinued
EX $10 NM $20 MIP $40

GAME

Dick Tracy Bingo, Lock Them Up in Jail and Harmonize with Tracy Game, 1940s, object of each is to roll BBs into different holes on the face of a glass framed game card for points
EX $45 NM $90 MIP $160

Dick Tracy Crime Stopper Game, 1963, Ideal, workstation contains crime indicator dial, decoder knobs, criminal buttons, clue cards and holders and clue windows
EX $40 NM $90 MIP $180

Dick Tracy Pinball Game, 1967, Marx, 14 x 24", shows characters from TV show pilot
EX $40 NM $90 MIP $175

Dick Tracy Pop-Pop Game, 1980s, Ja-Ru, Diet Smith and Flattop are targets
EX $10 NM $15 MIP $25

GUN

.45 Special Water Handgun, 1950s, Tops Plastics, plastic
EX $50 NM $100 MIP $160

Automatic Target Range Gun, 1967, Marx, BB gun mounted in an enclosed plastic shooting gallery
EX $60 NM $125 MIP $300

Dick Tracy Jr. Click Pistol #78, 1930s, Marx, aluminum
EX $75 NM $175 MIP $350

Luger Water Gun, 1971, Larami
EX $15 NM $35 MIP $90

Pop Gun, 1944, Tip Top Bread, 7-1/2" x 4-1/2" paper pop gun, premium
EX $50 NM $100 MIP $195

Power Jet Squad Gun, 1962, Mattel, 29" long cap and water rifle
EX $60 NM $120 MIP $220

Rapid Fire Tommy Gun, 1940s, Parker Johns, 20" long tommy gun w/Tracy on stock
EX $250 NM $400 MIP $600

Siren Pistol, 1930s, Marx, pressed steel, 8-1/2" long
EX $150 NM $425 MIP $675

Sub-Machine Gun, 1950s, Tops Plastics, 12" long, red, green or blue, water gun "holds over 500 shots on one filling," Dick Tracy decal on magazine
EX $100 NM $200 MIP $350

PIN

Bonny Braids Pin, 1951, Charmore, 1-1/4" figure plastic pin on full color card
EX $20 NM $60 MIP $100

Pep B.O. Plenty Pin, 1945, Kellogg's, tin litho button
EX $20 NM $30 MIP $50

Pep Chief Brandon Pin, 1945, Kellogg's, tin litho button
EX $10 **NM** $15 **MIP** $30

Pep Dick Tracy Pin, 1945, Kellogg's, tin litho button
EX $25 **NM** $45 **MIP** $80

Pep Flattop Pin, 1945, Kellogg's, tin litho button
EX $20 **NM** $35 **MIP** $60

Pep Gravel Gertie Pin, 1945, Kellogg's, tin litho button
EX $20 **NM** $35 **MIP** $50

Pep Junior Tracy Pin, 1945, Kellogg's, tin litho button
EX $10 **NM** $20 **MIP** $40

Pep Pat Patten Pin, 1945, Kellogg's, tin litho button
EX $10 **NM** $20 **MIP** $35

Pep Tess Trueheart Pin, 1945, Kellogg's, tin litho button
EX $12 **NM** $20 **MIP** $35

Secret Service Patrol Leader Pin, 1938, Quaker, litho bar pin, Patrol Leader, rare
EX $600 **NM** $1000 **MIP** $1200

RECORD

Dick Tracy Original Radio Broadcast Album, 1972, Coca-Cola, presents the cast from "The Case of the Firebug Murders" radio show
EX $20 **NM** $60 **MIP** $80

Flattop Story Double Record Set, 1947, Mercury Records, record, book, comics
EX $65 **NM** $125 **MIP** $225

RING

Dick Tracy Monogram Ring, 1938, Quaker, ring shows initials only, no Tracy name or picture
EX $175 **NM** $400 **MIP** $600

Dick Tracy Ring, 1940s, Miller Bros. Hat, enameled portrait
EX $60 **NM** $100 **MIP** $200

Dick Tracy Service Patrol Ring, 1966, premium
EX $20 **NM** $40 **MIP** $60

Secret Compartment Ring, 1938, Quaker, removable cover picturing Tracy and good luck symbols
EX $100 **NM** $200 **MIP** $300

TOY

Auto Magic Picture Gun, 1950s, 6-1/2" x 9" metal picture gun and filmstrip
EX $30 **NM** $100 **MIP** $175

Automatic Police Station, 1950s, Marx, tin litho police station and car
EX $500 **NM** $800 **MIP** $1500

B.O. Plenty Walker, 1940s, 8-1/2" tall, Marx, holds Sparkle Plenty
EX $175 **NM** $300 **MIP** $500

B.O. Plenty Wind-Up, 1940s, Marx, 8-1/2" tall holding baby Sparkle, litho tin, walks, hat tips up and down when key is wound
EX $150 **NM** $300 **MIP** $700

Baby Sparkle Plenty Paper Dolls, 1948, Saalfield, #1510, on cover, Baby Sparkle is standing by a clothes line
EX $22 **NM** $75 **MIP** $150

Baking Set, 1937, Pillsbury, cookie cutter, six press-out sheets w/pictures of Dick Tracy and his pals
EX $75 **NM** $150 **MIP** $245

Big Boy Figure, 1990, Playmates
EX $6 **NM** $12 **MIP** $25

Black Light Magic Kit, 1952, Stroward, ultra-violet bulb, cloth, invisible pen, brushes and fluorescent dyes
EX $75 **NM** $125 **MIP** $250

Bonny Braids Paper Dolls, 1951, Saalfield, #1559, Dick Tracy's new daughter and Tess
EX $50 **NM** $100 **MIP** $200

Bonny Braids Stroll Toy, 1951, Charmore, tin litho, Bonny doll in carriage
EX $35 **NM** $80 **MIP** $175

Camera Dart Gun, 1971, Larami, 8mm camera-shaped toy w/dart-shooting viewer
EX $30 **NM** $70 **MIP** $150

Coloring Set, 1967, Hasbro, six pre-sketched, numbered pictures to color, w/pencils
EX $30 **NM** $70 **MIP** $140

Crimestopper Club Kit, 1961, Chicago Tribune, premium kit containing badge, whistle, decoder, magnifying glass, fingerprinting kit, ID card, crimestopper textbook
EX $35 **NM** $60 **MIP** $100

Crimestopper Play Set, 1970s, Hubley, Dick Tracy cap gun, holster, handcuffs, wallet, flashlight, badge and magnifying glass
EX $35 **NM** $70 **MIP** $50

Crimestoppers Set, 1973, Larami, handcuffs, nightstick and badge
EX $12 **NM** $25 **MIP** $50

Decoder Card, Post Cereal, cereal premium, red or green
EX $30 **NM** $50 **MIP** $100

Detective Club Belt, 1937, leather w/secret pouch
EX $75 **NM** $225 **MIP** $400

Detective Kit, 1944, Dick Tracy Junior Detective Manual, Secret Decoder, ruler, Certificate of Membership and badge
EX $175 **NM** $400 **MIP** $700

Dick Tracy Braces, 1940s, Deluxe, Chicago Tribune premium, suspenders on colorful card
EX $50 **NM** $100 **MIP** $185

Dick Tracy Braces for Smart Boys and Girls, 1950s, Deluxe, Police badge, metal handcuffs, whistle, suspenders w/a Dick Tracy badge as a holder and magnifying glass
EX $50 **NM** $100 **MIP** $175

Dick Tracy Candid Camera, 1950s, Seymour Sales, w/50mm lens, plastic carrying case and 127 film
EX $60 **NM** $125 **MIP** $200

Dick Tracy Cartoon Kit, 1962, Colorforms
EX $20 **NM** $45 **MIP** $90

Dick Tracy Crime Lab, 1980s, Ja-Ru, click pistol, fingerprint pad, badge and magnifying glass, available in orange and bright yellow
EX $8 **NM** $15 **MIP** $30

Dick Tracy Crime Stoppers Laboratory, 1955, Porter Chemical, 60 power microscope, fingerprint pack, glass slides and magnifying glass and textbook
EX $150 **NM** $250 **MIP** $450

Dick Tracy Detective Club Wrist Radios, 1945, Gaylord
EX $85 **NM** $180 **MIP** $375

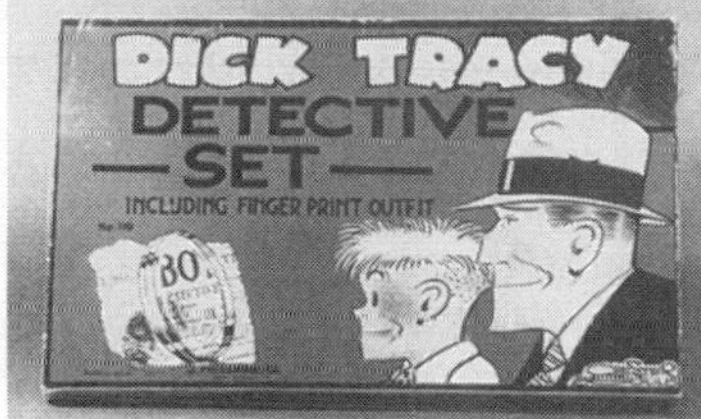

Dick Tracy Detective Set, 1930s, Pressman, color graphics of Junior and Dick Tracy, ink roller, glass plate, and Dick Tracy fingerprint record paper
EX $150 **NM** $225 **MIP** $400

Dick Tracy Figure, Lakeside, bendy
EX $15 **NM** $30 **MIP** $50

Dick Tracy Hand Puppet, 1961, Ideal, 10-1/2", fabric and vinyl, w/record
EX $35 **NM** $80 **MIP** $150

Dick Tracy Jr. Bombsight, 1940s, Miller Bros. Hat, cardboard
EX $50 **NM** $80 **MIP** $175

Dick Tracy Play Set, 1973, Ideal, contains 18 cardboard figures that measure 3 1/2" to 5" tall, w/carrying case
EX $50 **NM** $120 **MIP** $225

Dick Tracy Play Set, 1982, Placo, plastic dart gun, targets of different villians and a set of handcuffs
EX $10 **NM** $30 **MIP** $50

Dick Tracy Puzzle, 1952, 11" x 14" frame tray
EX $25 **NM** $85 **MIP** $150

Dick Tracy Soaky, 1965, Colgate-Palmolive, 10" tall
EX $25 **NM** $60 **MIP** $100

Dick Tracy Sparkle Paints, 1963, Kenner, paints, brushes and six pictures to paint
EX $25 **NM** $50 **MIP** $100

Dick Tracy Target, 1941, Marx, 10" square tin litho w/"Recovery" and "Rescuing" points on front and bullseye target on back
EX $75 **NM** $200 **MIP** $325

Dick Tracy Target Game, 1940s, Marx, 17" circular cardboard target, w/dart gun and box
EX $150 **NM** $350 **MIP** $525

Dick Tracy Target Set, 1969, Larami, red, green or blue; shoots rubber bands
EX $15 **NM** $35 **MIP** $75

Dick Tracy's Two-in-One Mystery Puzzle, 1958, Jaymar, one puzzle shows the crime and the other the solution
EX $30 **NM** $60 **MIP** $120

Famous Funnies Deluxe Printing Set, 1930s, 14 stamps, paper and stamp pad, in illustrated box
EX $80 **NM** $125 **MIP** $225

Favorite Funnies Printing Set, 1935, Stampercraft, features Tracy and other cartoon characters
EX $80 **NM** $110 **MIP** $180

Film Strip Viewer, 1948, Acme, viewer and two films in colorful illustrated box
EX $100 **NM** $175 **MIP** $225

Film Strip Viewer, 1964, Acme, viewer w/two boxes of film, on card, jumbo movie style
EX $20 **NM** $45 **MIP** $90

Film Viewer, 1973, Larami, mini color televiewer w/two paper filmstrips
EX $10 **NM** $20 **MIP** $50

Fingerprint Set, 1933, Pressman, microscope, fingerprint pad, magnifying glass and badge
EX $150 **NM** $300 **MIP** $475

Flashlight, 1939, Quaker, red, green, and black; bullet shaped w/shield tag, pocket size
EX $60 **NM** $175 **MIP** $300

Flashlight, 1939, Quaker, 3" pen light, black
EX $50 **NM** $120 **MIP** $250

Flashlight, 1961, Bantam Lite, metal wrist light
EX $25 **NM** $55 **MIP** $150

Handcuffs, 1946, John Henry, metal toy handcuffs on display header card
EX $25 **NM** $55 **MIP** $110

Hemlock Holmes Hand Puppet, 1961, Ideal, includes record
EX $40 **NM** $90 **MIP** $175

Hingees "Dick Tracy and his Friends to Life" Punch-outs, 1944, Reed and Associates, 6-1/2" tall figures, Tess Trueheart, Chief Brandon, Junior, Pat Patton and Tracy
EX $25 **NM** $75 **MIP** $125

Joe Jitsu Hand Puppet, 1961, Ideal, 10-1/2", fabric and vinyl, includes record
EX $45 **NM** $150 **MIP** $250

Junior Detective Kit, 1944, Sweets Company, certificate, secret code dial, wall chart, file cards and tape measure
EX $70 **NM** $250 **MIP** $425

Junior Dick Tracy Crime Detection Folio, 1942, radio premium, contained detective's notebook, decoder w/three mystery sheets, and puzzle
EX $70 **NM** $200 **MIP** $425

Mobile Commander, 1973, Larami, toy telephone w/plastic connecting tube, plastic gun and badge
EX $20 **NM** $40 **MIP** $100

Offical Holster Outfit, 1940s, Classy Products, leather holster w/painted Tracy profile
EX $150 **NM** $300 **MIP** $450

Playstone Funnies Kasting Kit, 1930s, Allied, molds for casting figures of Tracy and other characters
EX $40 **NM** $80 **MIP** $150

Police Whistle No. 64, Marx, tin
EX $20 **NM** $40 **MIP** $80

Puzzle, "Dick Tracy's New Daughter", 1951, Saalfield, tray puzzle of Bonny Braids
EX $22 **NM** $65 **MIP** $125

Puzzle, "The Bank Holdup", 1960s, Jaymar, triple-thick interlocking pieces featuring the TV cartoon
EX $20 **NM** $65 **MIP** $110

Puzzles, Dick Tracy Big Little Book Picture Puzzles, 1938, Whitman, 8" x 10" x 2" contains two puzzles of BLB scenes
EX $250 **NM** $350 **MIP** $550

Secret Code Writer and Pencil, 1939
EX $100 **NM** $150 **MIP** $275

Secret Detector Kit, 1938, Quaker, Secret Formula Q-11 and negatives
EX $200 **NM** $400 **MIP** $600

Secret Service Phones, 1938, Quaker, cardboard phones, walkie talkie type
EX $100 **NM** $200 **MIP** $340

Shoulder Holster Set, 1950s, J. Hapern, leather holster w/Dick Tracy's profile
EX $45 **NM** $90 **MIP** $185

Sparkle Plenty Islander Ukette, 1950, Styron, musical instrument, junior size, w/instruction book
EX $60 **NM** $130 **MIP** $300

Sparkle Plenty Washing Machine, 1940s, Kalon Radio, 12" tall tin litho, pictured outside on tub is Gravel Gertie doing the wash as B.O. Plenty holds baby Sparkle
EX $125 **NM** $200 **MIP** $400

Dick Tracy

Talking Phone, 1967, Marx, green w/ivory handle, battery-operated w/10 different phrases
EX $35 **NM** $75 **MIP** $125

Transistor Radio Receivers, 1961, American Doll and Toy, shoulder holster and secret ear plug w/two transistor radio receivers
EX $40 **NM** $80 **MIP** $160

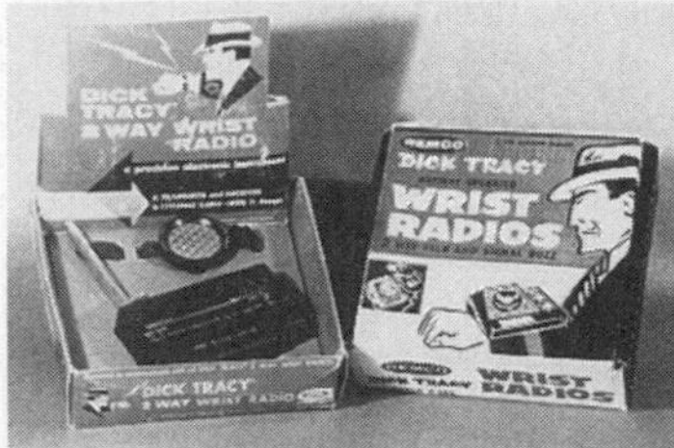

Two-Way Electronic Wrist Radios, 1950s, Remco, 2-1/2" x 9 1/2" x 13-1/2", plastic battery-operated wrist radios
EX $80 **NM** $150 **MIP** $250

Two-Way Wrist Radios, 1960s, American Doll and Toy, plastic w/power pack, battery-operated
EX $50 **NM** $100 **MIP** $185

Two-Way Wrist Radios, 1990, Ertl, battery-operated
EX $15 **NM** $20 **MIP** $30

Wrist Band AM Radio, 1976, Creative Creations, w/earphone and two mercury batteries; box shows Tracy and Flattop
EX $30 **NM** $65 **MIP** $150

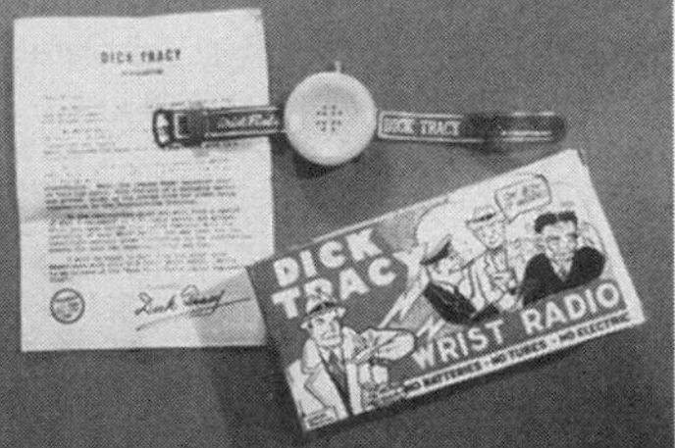

Wrist Radio, 1947, Da-Myco Products, crystal set w/receiver on a leather band, 30" wires and connectors for aerial and ground, no batteries, no tubes and no electric
EX $350 **NM** $500 **MIP** $750

Wrist TV, 1980s, Ja-Ru, paper roll of cartoon strips are threaded through the TV viewer
EX $10 **NM** $20 **MIP** $40

VEHICLE

Convertible Squad Car, 1948, Marx, 20", friction power w/flashing lights
EX $300 **NM** $450 **MIP** $800

Copmobile, 1963, Ideal, 24" long, white and blue plastic, battery-operated w/a microphone w/amplified speaker on top
EX $100 **NM** $200 **MIP** $400

Dick Tracy Car, 1950s, Marx, 6-1/2" long, light blue w/machine gun pointing out of the front window
EX $125 **NM** $275 **MIP** $475

Get Away Car, 1990, Playmates
EX $15 **NM** $25 **MIP** $50

Space Coupe, 1968, Aurora, assembly required, all plastic
EX $150 **NM** $350 **MIP** $600

WATCH

Dick Tracy Two-Way Wristwatch, 1990, Playmates, watch w/no radio function
EX $4 **NM** $7 **MIP** $20

Dick Tracy Wristwatch, 1937, New Haven, oblong, round, or square face, in box
EX $300 **NM** $600 **MIP** $1000

Dick Tracy Wristwatch, 1959, Bradley
EX $50 **NM** $100 **MIP** $210

Dick Tracy Wristwatch, 1981, Omni, digital; police car box
EX $15 **NM** $40 **MIP** $90

Dick Tracy Wristwatch with Animated Gun, 1951, New Haven
EX $200 **NM** $450 **MIP** $750

Disney

ACCESSORIES

Disney Figure Golf Balls, set of twelve
EX $12 **NM** $23 **MIP** $35

Disney Filmstrips, 1940s, Craftman's Guild, 13 color filmstrips
EX $95 **NM** $180 **MIP** $275

Disney Tin Tray, Ohio Art, 8" x 10", pictures Mickey and Minnie Mouse, Goofy, Horace, Pluto, Donald Duck and Clarabelle
EX $25 **NM** $50 **MIP** $85

Disney World Globe, 1950s, Rand McNally, 6-1/2" metal base, 8" diameter w/Disney characters
EX $60 **NM** $125 **MIP** $200

Disneyland Ashtray, 1950s, 5" diameter, china, w/Tinker Bell and castle
EX $20 **NM** $65 **MIP** $150

Disneyland Electric Light, 1950s, Econlite, picture of Disney characters leaving a bus on a drum base
EX $45 **NM** $80 **MIP** $235

Disneyland Felt Banner, 1960s, Disney, "The Magic Kingdom," 24-1/2" red/white/blue coat of arms
EX $25 **NM** $60 **MIP** $90

Disneyland Give-A-Show Projector Color Slides, 1960s, 112 color slides
EX $85 **NM** $140 **MIP** $250

Disneyland Metal Craft Tapping Set, 1950s, Pressman
EX $25 **NM** $40 **MIP** $100

Disneyland Miniature License Plates, 1966, Marx, 2" x 4" plates w/Mickey, Minnie and Pluto, or Snow White, Donald and Goofy, each
EX $12 **NM** $23 **MIP** $35

Disneyland Pen, 1960s, 6" long w/a picture of a floating riverboat
EX $15 **NM** $25 **MIP** $40

Duck Tales Travel Tote, 1980s, travel agency premium
EX $5 **NM** $20 **MIP** $35

Fantasia Bowl, 1940, Vernon Kilns, 12" diameter and 2-1/2" tall, pink bowl w/a winged nymph from Fantasia
EX $150 **NM** $300 **MIP** $475

Fantasia Cup and Saucer Set, 1940, Vernon Kilns, 6-1/4" diameter saucer and 2" tall cup
EX $70 **NM** $160 **MIP** $235

Fantasia Musical Jewelry Box, 1990, Schmid Bros., box features Mickey and plays "The Sorcerer's Apprentice"
EX $30 **NM** $55 **MIP** $90

Figural Light Switch Plates, Monogram, hand-painted switch plates: Goofy, Donald, Mickey, on card, each
EX $6 **NM** $12 **MIP** $25

Happy Birthday/Pepsi Placemats, 1978, Pepsi, set of four mats
EX $15 **NM** $35 **MIP** $60

Lap Trays, 1960s, Hasko, set of four: Donald, Goofy and Pluto, Peter Pan, and the Seven Dwarfs
EX $35 **NM** $65 **MIP** $150

Silly Symphony Lights, Noma, set of eight
EX $100 **NM** $150 **MIP** $375

BANK

Color Television Bank, 1950s, Linemar, 4" x 4-1/2", tin, Mickey or Donald on side panels, litho screen rotates
EX $200 **NM** $400 **MIP** $600

Disneyland Haunted House Bank, 1960s, Japanese
EX $35 **NM** $65 **MIP** $225

Second National Duck Bank, Chein, 3-1/2" tall x 7" long
EX $100 **NM** $200 **MIP** $375

BOOK

Robin Hood of the Range Better Little Book, 1942, Whitman
EX $20 **NM** $50 **MIP** $100

CHARACTER TOYS

Toby Tyler Circus Playbook, 1959, Whitman, punch-out character activity book
EX $25 **NM** $50 **MIP** $100

Walt Disney's Clock Cleaners Book, 1938, Whitman, linen-like illustrated book
EX $85 **NM** $175 **MIP** $250

FIGURES

Aristocats Thomas O'Malley Figure, 1967, Enesco, 8" tall ceramic
EX $30 **NM** $65 **MIP** $125

Fantasia Figure, Vernon Kilns, half-woman, half-zebra centaur
EX $85 **NM** $180 **MIP** $400

Fantasia Unicorn Figure, 1940s, Vernon Kilns, ceramic black-winged unicorn
EX $75 **NM** $110 **MIP** $250

Johnny Tremain Figure and Horse, 1957, Marx, plastic, 9-1/2" tall horse and 5-1/2" tall Johnny
EX $80 **NM** $120 **MIP** $225

Jose Carioca Figure, Marx, 2" tall, plastic
EX $30 **NM** $55 **MIP** $80

Jose Carioca Figure, 1960s, Marx, 5-1/2" tall plastic, wire arms and legs
EX $50 **NM** $110 **MIP** $200

GAME

Disneyland Bagatelle, 1970s, Wolverine, large game w/Disneyland graphics
EX $15 **NM** $25 **MIP** $100

Walt Disney's Game/Parade/Academy Award Winners, American Toy Works, 15 games for all ages
EX $60 **NM** $120 **MIP** $185

PUZZLE

Black Hole Puzzle, 1979, Whitman, jigsaw puzzle, V.I.N.C.E.N.T. or Cygnus
EX $15 **NM** $30 **MIP** $85

Disney "Sea Scouts" Puzzle, 1930s, Williams Ellis
EX $100 **NM** $175 **MIP** $225

Disneyland Puzzle, 1956, Whitman, frame tray
EX $20 **NM** $50 **MIP** $100

TOY

Carousel, Linemar, 7" tall w/3" figures, wind-up
EX $200 **NM** $350 **MIP** $500

Casey Jr. Disneyland Express Train, 1950s, Marx, 12" long, tin, wind-up
EX $200 **NM** $300 **MIP** $550

Character Molding and Coloring Set, 1950s, red rubber molds of Bambi, Thumper, Dumbo, Goofy, Flower and Jose Carioca to make plaster figures
EX $35 **NM** $75 **MIP** $150

Disney Rattle, 1930s, Noma, 4" tall w/Mickey and Minnie, Donald and Pluto carrying a Christmas tree
EX $100 **NM** $150 **MIP** $300

Disney Shooting Gallery, 1950s, Wolso Toys, 8" x 12" x 1-1/2" tin target w/molded figures of Mickey, Donald, Goofy and Pluto
EX $75 **NM** $150 **MIP** $300

Disney Treasure Chest Set, 1940s, Craftman's Guild, red plastic film viewer and filmstrips in blue box designed like a chest
EX $70 **NM** $145 **MIP** $210

Disneyland Auto Magic Picture Gun and Theater, 1950s, battery-operated metal gun w/oval filmstrip
EX $50 **NM** $90 **MIP** $150

Disneyland F.D. Fire Truck, Linemar, 18" long, battery-operated, moveable, Donald Duck fireman climbs the ladder
EX $250 **NM** $400 **MIP** $600

Early Settlers Log Set, 1960s, Halsam, log building set based on Disneyland's Tom Sawyer's Island
EX $40 **NM** $75 **MIP** $150

Horace Horsecollar Hand Puppet, 1950s, Gund
EX $30 **NM** $75 **MIP** $150

Jose Carioca Wind-Up Toy, 1940s, France, 3-1/2" x 5" x 7-1/2" tall
EX $100 **NM** $300 **MIP** $450

Nautilus Expanding Periscope, 1954, Pressman, inspired by 20,000 Leagues Under the Sea, 19" long
EX $75 **NM** $160 **MIP** $250

Nautilus Wind-Up Submarine, 1950s, Sutcliffe/England
EX $150 **NM** $250 **MIP** $475

Official Santa Fe and Disneyland R.R. Scale Model Train, 1966, Tyco, HO scale, electric
EX $200 **NM** $350 **MIP** $600

Pecos Bill Wind-Up Toy, 1950s, Marx, 10" tall, riding his horse Widowmaker and holding a metal lasso
EX $75 **NM** $200 **MIP** $400

Sand Pail and Shovel, 1930s, Ohio Art, features pie-eyed Mickey selling cold drinks to Pluto, Minnie and Clarabelle
EX $35 **NM** $110 **MIP** $275

Walt Disney Movie Viewer and Cartridge, 1972, Action Films, #9312 w/the cartridge "Lonesome Ghosts"
EX $10 **NM** $16 **MIP** $35

Walt Disney's Character Scramble, 1940s, Plane Facts, 10 cardboard figures, 6" tall
EX $30 **NM** $70 **MIP** $175

Walt Disney's Realistic Noah's Ark, 1940s, W.H. Greene, 6" x 7" x 18" Ark, 101 2" animals, and 4" human figures on cardboard
EX $150 **NM** $350 **MIP** $700

Walt Disney's Silly Symphony Bells, Noma, Christmas tree bells
EX $60 **NM** $125 **MIP** $275

Walt Disney's Snap-Eeze Set, 1963, Marx, 12-1/2" x 15" x 1" box w/12 flat plastic figures
EX $60 **NM** $115 **MIP** $275

Walt Disney's Television Car, Marx, 8" long, friction toy lights up a picture on the roof when motor turns
EX $500 **NM** $750 **MIP** $1500

Doc Savage

ACCESSORIES

Club Card, 1930s
EX $150 **NM** $200 **MIP** $300

Club Kit, 1975, comics premium; includes card, button and mailer
EX $40 **NM** $75 **MIP** $150

Club Mailer for Pin, 1930s
EX $250 **NM** $300 **MIP** $400

Club Pin, 1930s, Pulp premium, brass
EX $100 **NM** $225 **MIP** $375

Medal of Honor Award, 1930s, brass
EX $2000 **NM** $3600 **MIP** $6000

Donald Duck

ACCESSORIES

Donald Duck Alarm Clock, 1950s, Glen Clock/Scotland, 5-1/2" x 5-1/2" x 2", Donald pictured w/blue bird on his hand
EX $150 **NM** $300 **MIP** $675

Donald Duck Alarm Clock, 1960s, Bayard, 2" x 4-1/2" x 5"
EX $125 **NM** $275 **MIP** $600

Donald Duck Lamp, 1940s, 9" tall, china, Donald holding an axe standing next to a tree trunk
EX $150 **NM** $275 **MIP** $425

Donald Duck Lamp, 1970s, Dolly Toy, Donald on a tug boat
EX $75 **NM** $150 **MIP** $250

Donald Duck Light Switch Cover, 1976, Dolly Toy, plastic, Donald on a boat
EX $5 **NM** $10 **MIP** $25

Donald Duck Music Box, 1971, Anri, Donald w/guitar, plays "My Way"
EX $75 **NM** $100 **MIP** $200

Donald Duck Pinback, 1930s, Wanna Fight movie premium
EX $250 **NM** $650 **MIP** $875

Donald Duck Pinback, 1935, Jackets premium, cello
EX $250 **NM** $650 **MIP** $875

Donald Duck Soap, Disney, figural castile soap
EX $40 **NM** $70 **MIP** $140

Donald Duck Toothbrush Holder, 1930s, bisque, figural
EX $200 **NM** $450 **MIP** $725

Donald Duck Umbrella Holder, 1930s, 3-1/4" tall
EX $100 **NM** $200 **MIP** $350

Donald Duck

Donald Duck WWI Pencil Box, Dixon, 5" x 8-1/2" x 1-1/4" deep, Donald flying a plane, holding a tomahawk
EX $50 **NM** $125 **MIP** $250

Ludwig Von Drake Wonderful World of Color Pencil Box, 1961, Hasbro, box shows Ludwig and the nephews
EX $25 **NM** $55 **MIP** $85

Uncle Scrooge Wallet, 1970s, 3" x 4", Uncle Scrooge tossing coins
EX $20 **NM** $40 **MIP** $85

BANK

Donald Duck Bank, 1938, Crown Toy, 6" tall, composition, movable head
EX $150 **NM** $400 **MIP** $600

Donald Duck Bank, 1940s, 5-1/2" x 6" x 7-1/2" tall, china, Donald seated holding a coin in one hand
EX $75 **NM** $200 **MIP** $325

Donald Duck Bank, 1940s, 4-1/2" x 4-1/2" x 6-1/2" tall, ceramic, Donald holding a rope w/a large brown fish by his side
EX $50 **NM** $100 **MIP** $250

Donald Duck Telephone Bank, 1938, N.N. Hill Brass, 5" tall w/cardboard figure
EX $85 **NM** $225 **MIP** $375

DOLL

Donald Duck Doll, 1938, Knickerbocker, 17" tall, red jacket, black plush hat, Donald as drum major
EX $550 **NM** $1250 **MIP** $1700

Donald Duck Doll, 1976, Mattel, talking doll
EX $75 **NM** $250 **MIP** $425

Huey, Dewey and Louie Dolls, 1950s, Gund, set of three 8" tall dolls
EX $65 **NM** $125 **MIP** $350

Louie Doll, 1940s, Gund, 8" tall, white/light green plush
EX $40 **NM** $70 **MIP** $115

FIGURES

Donald Duck Figure, Seiberling, 6" tall, hollow rubber w/squeaker in the base
EX $175 **NM** $260 **MIP** $500

Donald Duck Figure, Seiberling, 6" tall, solid rubber w/movable head
EX $175 **NM** $260 **MIP** $500

Donald Duck Figure, Seiberling, 5" tall, rubber
EX $175 **NM** $260 **MIP** $500

Donald Duck Figure, 1930s, Japanese, celluloid, long-billed Donald
EX $100 **NM** $350 **MIP** $650

Donald Duck Figure, 1950s, Dell, 7" tall, rubber
EX $75 **NM** $150 **MIP** $250

Donald Duck Fun-E-Flex Figure, 1930s, Fun-E-Flex, wooden Donald on red sled w/rope
EX $100 **NM** $200 **MIP** $500

Donald Duck Nodder, 1960s, 5-1/2" tall on green base
EX $50 **NM** $150 **MIP** $200

Ludwig Von Drake Figure, 1961, Marx, 3" tall, from the "Snap-Eeze" collection
EX $10 **NM** $20 **MIP** $40

TOY

Carpet Sweeper, 1930s, Ohio Art, 3" w/wooden handle, Donald Duck and Minnie Mouse
EX $50 **NM** $125 **MIP** $250

Crayon Box, 1946, Transogram, tin, pictures Donald and Mickey
EX $30 **NM** $55 **MIP** $150

Donald and Donna Duck, 1937, Fisher-Price, 14" long, wooden, rare, Donald plays xylophone, Donna glides back and forth w/rubber wings, Donna became Daisy hence its rarity
EX $2000 **NM** $3500 **MIP** $5000

Donald Duck and Pluto Car, Sun Rubber, 6-1/2" long, hard rubber, blue
EX $50 **NM** $125 **MIP** $375

Donald Duck Bicycle, 1949, Shelby
EX $2500 **NM** $4500 **MIP** $8000

Donald Duck Camera, 1950s, Herbert-George, 3" x 4" x 3"
EX $60 **NM** $150 **MIP** $300

Donald Duck Car, 1950s, Sun Rubber, 2-1/2" x 3-1/2" x 6-1/2", rubber
EX $40 **NM** $110 **MIP** $375

Donald Duck Driving Pluto Toy, 9" long, wind-up, celluloid
EX $500 **NM** $800 **MIP** $1600

Donald Duck Dump Truck, 1950s, Linemar
EX $150 **NM** $275 **MIP** $525

Donald Duck Funnee Movie Set, 1940, Transogram, box features Donald, Mickey, and the nephews
EX $75 **NM** $200 **MIP** $300

Donald Duck Funnee Movie Set, 1949, Irwin, hand-crank viewer and four films in box
EX $85 **NM** $150 **MIP** $250

Donald Duck Marionette, 1950s, Peter Puppet, 6-1/2" tall
EX $50 **NM** $150 **MIP** $250

Donald Duck Paint Box, 1938, Transogram
EX $40 **NM** $120 **MIP** $275

Donald Duck Projector, 1950s, Stephens, projector w/four films
EX $55 **NM** $125 **MIP** $250

Donald Duck Puppet, 1960s, Pelham Puppets, 10" tall, hollow composition
EX $40 **NM** $75 **MIP** $200

Donald Duck Push Puppet, 1950s, Kohner, sailor Donald
EX $30 **NM** $100 **MIP** $160

Donald Duck Push Toy, 1950s, Gong Bell
EX $35 **NM** $60 **MIP** $100

Donald Duck Puzzle, 1940s, Jaymar, frame tray
EX $50 **NM** $100 **MIP** $175

Donald Duck Ramp Walker, 1950s, Marx, 1-1/4" x 3-1/2" x 3" tall, Donald is pulling red wagon w/his nephews
EX $110 **NM** $175 **MIP** $325

Donald Duck Sand Pail, 1939, Ohio Art, 4-1/2" tall, tin, Donald at beach playing tug-of-war w/his two nephews
EX $60 **NM** $120 **MIP** $300

Donald Duck Sand Pail, 1950s, Ohio Art, 3-1/2" tall, tin, Donald in life preserver fighting off seagulls
EX $65 **NM** $175 **MIP** $300

Donald Duck Scooter, 1960s, Marx, tin wind-up, 4" x 4" x 2"
EX $150 **NM** $250 **MIP** $350

Donald Duck Skating Rink Toy, 1950s, Mettoy, 4" diameter, Donald is skating while other Disney characters circle the rink
EX $40 **NM** $70 **MIP** $160

Donald Duck Sled, 1935, S.L. Allen, 36" long wooden slat and metal runner sled w/character decals, Donald and nephews
EX $400 **NM** $650 **MIP** $1200

Donald Duck Snow Shovel, Ohio Art, wood, tin, litho
EX $60 **NM** $130 **MIP** $250

Donald Duck Soaky, 1950s, 7" tall
EX $15 **NM** $50 **MIP** $100

Donald Duck Squeeze Toy, 1960s, Dell, 8" tall, rubber
EX $15 **NM** $40 **MIP** $80

Donald Duck Tea Set, Ohio Art, 7-1/2" tray, 2-1/4" diameter cups, saucers
EX $100 **NM** $175 **MIP** $250

Donald Duck the Drummer, 1940s, Marx, 5" x" 7 x 10" tall, Donald beats on a metal drum
EX $300 **NM** $500 **MIP** $725

Donald Duck Toy, Schuco, 5-1/2" tall, wind-up w/a bellows, quacking sound
EX $350 **NM** $700 **MIP** $1000

Donald Duck Toy Raft, 1950s, Ideal, 2" tall, blue plastic raft w/yellow sail w/Donald looking through a telescope
EX $400 **NM** $75 **MIP** $110

Donald Duck Trapeze Toy, Linemar, 5" tall, celluloid, wind-up
EX $60 **NM** $200 **MIP** $600

Donald Duck Watering Can, 1938, Ohio Art, 6" tall, tin litho
EX $25 **NM** $75 **MIP** $175

Donald Duck Wind-Up, 1972, Durham Plastic, 6-1/2" tall, hard plastic
EX $15 **NM** $40 **MIP** $85

Donald Tricycle Toy, 1950s, Linemar, tin
EX $500 **NM** $800 **MIP** $1200

Ludwig Von Drake in Go Cart, 1960s, Linemar, tin and plastic
EX $115 **NM** $250 **MIP** $500

Ludwig Von Drake Mug, 1961, 3-1/2" white china
EX $15 **NM** $20 **MIP** $50

Ludwig Von Drake Squeeze Toy, 1961, Dell, 8" tall, rubber
EX $10 **NM** $20 **MIP** $50

Ludwig Von Drake Tiddly Winks, 1961, Whitman
EX $10 **NM** $20 **MIP** $60

WATCH

Daisy Duck Wristwatch, 1948, US Time
EX $275 NM $550 MIP $875

Donald Duck Wristwatch, 1940s, US Time
EX $275 NM $550 MIP $950

Dr. Doolittle

FIGURES

Dr. Doolittle Figure, 1967, Mattel, 5" tall w/parrot
EX $15 NM $30 MIP $50

Dr. Doolittle Figure, 1967, Mattel, 7" tall
EX $15 NM $35 MIP $75

TOY

Dr. Doolittle Giraffe-in-the-Box, jack-in-the-box
EX $50 NM $100 MIP $200

Dr. Seuss

ACCESSORIES

Mattel-O-Phone, 1970, Mattel
EX $40 NM $75 MIP $225

DOLL

Cat in the Hat Doll, 1983, Coleco, plush
EX $10 NM $40 MIP $90

Grinch Doll, 1983, Coleco
EX $55 NM $110 MIP $300

Horton the Elephant Doll, 1983, Coleco
EX $25 NM $65 MIP $135

Lorax Doll, 1983, Coleco
EX $25 NM $65 MIP $135

Star-Bellied Sneetch Doll, 1983, Coleco
EX $40 NM $70 MIP $140

Talking Cat in the Hat Doll, 1970, Mattel
EX $60 NM $175 MIP $300

Talking Hedwig Doll, 1970, Mattel
EX $50 NM $125 MIP $250

Talking Horton Doll, 1970, Mattel
EX $60 NM $175 MIP $350

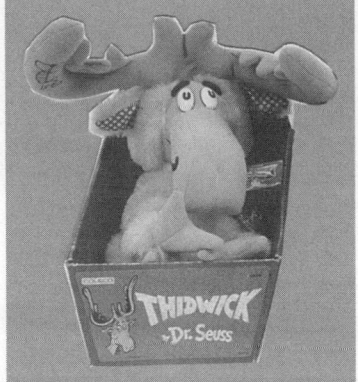

Thidwick the Moose Doll, 1983, Coleco
EX $15 NM $40 MIP $90

Yertle the Turtle Doll, 1983, Coleco, 12" plush
EX $15 NM $45 MIP $100

TOY

Cat in the Hat Ge-Tar, 1970, Mattel
EX $40 NM $110 MIP $220

Cat in the Hat Jack-in-the-Box, 1969, Mattel
EX $100 NM $180 MIP $310

Cat in the Hat Riding Toy, 1983, Coleco
EX $25 NM $50 MIP $135

Cat in the Hat Rocking Toy, 1983, Coleco
EX $25 NM $50 MIP $135

Cat in the Hat Talking Puppet, 1970, Mattel, vinyl head
EX $75 NM $125 MIP $300

Dumbo

ACCESSORIES

Dumbo Christmas Ornament, 2" porcelain bisque, 50th anniversary
EX $8 NM $15 MIP $35

Dumbo Milk Pitcher, 1940s, 6" tall
EX $65 NM $110 MIP $250

DOLL

Dumbo Doll, 12" plush
EX $10 NM $20 MIP $50

FIGURES

Dumbo Figure, Dakin
EX $12 NM $25 MIP $50

TOY

Dumbo Roll Over Wind-Up Toy, 1941, Marx, 4" tall, tin w/tumbling action
EX $175 NM $350 MIP $675

Dumbo Squeeze Toy, 1950s, Dell, 5" tall
EX $15 NM $30 MIP $75

Elmer Fudd

ACCESSORIES

Elmer Fudd Mini Snow Dome, 1980s, Applause
EX $10 NM $20 MIP $35

Elmer Fudd Mug, 1980s, Applause, figural
EX $5 NM $10 MIP $20

FIGURES

Elmer Fudd Figure, 1950s, metal 5", on green base w/his name embossed, Elmer in hunting outfit
EX $55 NM $125 MIP $275

Elmer Fudd Figure, 1968, Dakin, 8" tall
EX $20 NM $60 MIP $100

Elmer Fudd Figure, 1971, Dakin, in a red hunting outfit
EX $30 NM $70 MIP $125

Elmer Fudd Figure, 1977, Dakin, Fun Farm
EX $18 NM $33 MIP $65

TOY

Elmer Fudd Pull Toy, 1940s, Brice Toys, 9", wooden, Elmer in fire chief's car
EX $100 NM $225 MIP $400

Felix the Cat

ACCESSORIES

Felix Cartoon Lamp Shade, 6" tall
EX $75 NM $150 MIP $250

Felix Flashlight, 1960s, contains whistle
EX $50 NM $200 MIP $325

Felix Pencil Case, 1950s
EX $25 NM $75 MIP $120

Felix Sip-a-Drink Cup, 5" tall
EX $15 NM $25 MIP $60

DOLL

Felix Doll, 1920s, 8" tall, wood, fully jointed
EX $200 NM $350 MIP $750

Felix Doll, 1920s, 13" tall, jointed arms
EX $200 NM $350 MIP $750

FIGURES

Felix Figure, 1920s, Schoenhut, 4" tall, wood, leather ears, stands on a white wood base
EX $200 NM $400 MIP $675

GAME

Felix Manual Dexterity Game, 1920s, German, 2", round, metal
EX $100 NM $175 MIP $325

TOY

Felix on a Scooter, 1924, Nifty, tin wind-up
EX $500 NM $800 MIP $1000

Felix Punching Bag, 1960s, 11" tall inflatable bobber
EX $25 NM $60 MIP $110

Felix Soaky, 1960s, 10" tall, blue plastic
EX $20 NM $60 MIP $100

Felix Soaky, 1960s, 10" tall, red plastic
EX $20 NM $60 MIP $100

Felix Soaky, 1960s, 10" tall, black plastic
EX $15 NM $50 MIP $90

Felix Squeak Toy, 1930s, 6" tall, soft rubber
EX $35 NM $110 MIP $185

Felix the Cat Pull Toy, 1920s, Nifty, 5-1/2" tall, 8" long, tin, cat is chasing two red mice on the front of the cart, litho pictures of Felix on side
EX $400 NM $750 MIP $1000

WATCH

Felix Wristwatch, 1960s
EX $65 NM $150 MIP $275

Ferdinand the Bull

BANK

Ferdinand Savings Bank, Crown Toy, 5" tall, wood composition w/silk flower w/metal trap door
EX $50 NM $100 MIP $250

BOOK

Ferdinand the Bull Book, 1938, Whitman, linen picture book
EX $75 NM $125 MIP $225

DOLL

Ferdinand Doll, 1938, Knickerbocker, 5" x 9" x 8-1/2" tall, joint composition w/cloth tail and flower stapled in his mouth
EX $100 NM $210 MIP $375

FIGURES

Ferdinand Figure, 9" tall, plastic
EX $20 NM $35 MIP $150

Ferdinand Figure, 3-1/2" bisque
EX $15 NM $40 MIP $110

Ferdinand Figure, 1930s, Seiberling, 3" x 5-1/2" x 4" tall, rubber
EX $75 NM $110 MIP $225

Ferdinand Figure, 1938, Delco, 4-1/2" tall, ceramic, bull seated w/a purple garland around his neck
EX $75 NM $110 MIP $225

Ferdinand Figure, 1940s, Disney, composition
EX $125 NM $200 MIP $350

TOY

Ferdinand Hand Puppet, 1938, Crown Toy, 9-1/2" tall
EX $75 NM $110 MIP $230

Ferdinand Toy, 1940, Knickerbocker, wood composition w/jointed head and legs w/flower in his mouth
EX $125 NM $175 MIP $325

Flipper

TOY

Flipper Halloween Costume, 1964, Collegeville
EX $20 NM $40 MIP $125

Flipper Magic Slate, 1960s, Lowe
EX $12 NM $24 MIP $75

Flipper Model Kit, 1965, Revell
EX $17 NM $35 MIP $100

Flipper Puzzle, 1960s, Whitman, several variations, each
EX $12 NM $22 MIP $50

Flipper Ukelele, 1968, Mattel
EX $12 NM $22 MIP $60

Foghorn Leghorn

FIGURES

Foghorn Leghorn Figure, 1970, Dakin, 6-1/4" tall
EX $22 NM $45 MIP $100

Foghorn Leghorn Figure, 1980s, Applause, PVC
EX $3 NM $50 MIP $75

TOY

Foghorn Leghorn Hand Puppet, 1960s, 9", fabric w/vinyl head
EX $20 NM $75 MIP $150

Fontaine Fox

TOY

Powerful Katrinka Toy, 1923, 5-1/2" tall, wind-up, pushing Jimmy in a wheelbarrow
EX $1200 NM $1500 MIP $2000

Toonerville Trolley, Nifty, miniature, 2" tall
EX $250 NM $350 MIP $525

Toonerville Trolley, 3" tall
EX $200 NM $350 MIP $450

Toonerville Trolley, 4" tall, red pot metal
EX $500 NM $800 MIP $1450

Toonerville Trolley, 1922, 7-1/2" tall, wind-up
EX $750 NM $1000 MIP $1500

Garfield

BANK

Garfield Chair Bank, 1981, Enesco
EX $12 NM $25 MIP $80

Garfield Figure Bank, 1981, Enesco, 4-3/4"
EX $12 NM $24 MIP $70

FIGURES

Garfield Easter Figure, 1978, Enesco
EX $7 NM $20 MIP $50

Garfield Figure, 1978, Enesco, Garfield as graduate
EX $6 NM $12 MIP $40

MUSIC BOX

Garfield Music Box, 1981, Enesco, Garfield dancing
EX $50 NM $75 MIP $150

Gasoline Alley

ACCESSORIES

Skeezix Stationery, 1926, 6" x 8-1/2"
EX $50 NM $75 MIP $125

Uncle Walt and Skeezix Pencil Holder, F.A.S., 5" tall, bisque
EX $125 NM $200 MIP $325

FIGURES

Skeezix Comic Figure, 1930s, 6" chalk statue
EX $30 NM $50 MIP $100

Uncle Walt and Skeezix Figure Set, bisque, Uncle Walt, Skeezix, Herby and Smitty
EX $125 NM $250 MIP $400

Goofy

ACCESSORIES

Goofy Night Light, 1973, Horsman, green, figural
EX $16 NM $30 MIP $45

Goofy Toothbrush, 1970s, Pepsodent
EX $5 NM $10 MIP $40

DOLL

Goofy Doll, 1970s, 5" x 6" x 13" tall, fabric and vinyl, laughing doll
EX $50 NM $100 MIP $200

FIGURES

Goofy Figure, Marx, Snap-Eeze figure
EX $15 NM $35 MIP $50

Goofy Figure, Arco, bendy
EX $10 NM $15 MIP $25

Goofy Lil' Headbobber, Marx
EX $50 NM $100 MIP $160

Goofy Rolykin, Marx
EX $25 NM $50 MIP $75

Goofy Twist 'n Bend Figure, 1963, Marx, 4" tall
EX $11 NM $20 MIP $30

TOY

Goofy Car, Spain, vinyl head Goofy drives tin litho car
EX $50 NM $100 MIP $150

Goofy Safety Scissors, 1973, Monogram, on card
EX $5 NM $10 MIP $20

Goofy with Bump 'n Go Action Lawn Mower, 1980s, Illfelder, 3-1/2" x 10" x

11", plastic figure pushing lawn mower w/silver handle
EX $40 **NM** $70 **MIP** $125

WATCH

Backwards Goofy Wristwatch, Pedre, silver case 2nd edition
EX $40 **NM** $75 **MIP** $225

Backwards Goofy Wristwatch, 1972, Helbros
EX $325 **NM** $650 **MIP** $1000

Gumby

ACCESSORIES

Gumby Adventure Costume, 1960s, Lakeside, fireman, cowboy, knight and actronaut, each
EX $25 **NM** $50 **MIP** $90

FIGURES

Gumby Figure, 1980s, large, foam rubber
EX $20 **NM** $40 **MIP** $100

Gumby Figure, 1980s, Applause, 12" tall, poseable
EX $10 **NM** $20 **MIP** $40

Gumby Figure, 1980s, Applause, 5-1/2" bendy, three styles
EX $5 **NM** $10 **MIP** $30

Pokey Figure, 1960s, Lakeside
EX $20 **NM** $40 **MIP** $95

TOY

Adventures of Gumby Electric Drawing Set, 1966, Lakeside
EX $22 **NM** $50 **MIP** $125

Gumby Colorforms Set, 1988, Colorforms
EX $8 **NM** $12 **MIP** $50

Gumby Hand Puppet, 1965, Lakeside, 9" tall w/vinyl head
EX $15 **NM** $40 **MIP** $90

Gumby Modeling Dough, 1960s, Chemtoy
EX $25 **NM** $50 **MIP** $90

Gumby's Jeep, 1960s, Lakeside, yellow tin litho, Gumby and Pokey's names are printed on seat
EX $150 **NM** $250 **MIP** $400

Pokey Modeling Dough, 1960s, Chemtoy
EX $25 **NM** $50 **MIP** $90

Happy Hooligan

ACCESSORIES

Happy Hooligan Songsheet, 1905, newspaper premium
EX $100 **NM** $150 **MIP** $250

TOY

Happy Hooligan Nesting Toys, Anri, 4" tall, wooden set of four nesting pieces
EX $100 **NM** $150 **MIP** $350

Happy Hooligan Toy, 1932, Chein, 6" tall, wind-up, walking figure
EX $350 **NM** $450 **MIP** $750

Heckle and Jeckle

BOOK

Heckle and Jeckle Story Book, 1957, Wonder Book
EX $30 **NM** $50 **MIP** $75

FIGURES

Heckle and Jeckle Figures, 7" soft foam figures
EX $25 **NM** $70 **MIP** $135

Little Roquefort Figure, 1959, 8-1/2" tall, wood
EX $20 **NM** $40 **MIP** $80

TOY

Heckle and Jeckle Skooz-It Game, 1963, Ideal, cylindrical container
EX $40 **NM** $80 **MIP** $125

Huckleberry Hound

BANK

Huckleberry Hound Bank, 1960, Knickerbocker, 10" tall, hard plastic figural
EX $30 **NM** $60 **MIP** $100

Huckleberry Hound Bank, 1980, Dakin, 5" tall figural bank of Huck sitting
EX $20 **NM** $40 **MIP** $80

DOLL

Huckleberry Hound Doll, 1959, Knickerbocker, 18" plush, vinyl hands and face
EX $60 **NM** $125 **MIP** $175

Mr. Jinks Doll, 1959, Knickerbocker, 13" tall, plush, vinyl face
EX $50 **NM** $110 **MIP** $230

Pixie and Dixie Dolls, 1960, Knickerbocker, 12" tall, each
EX $25 **NM** $45 **MIP** $100

FIGURES

Hokey Wolf Figure, 1961, Marx, TV-Tinykin
EX $15 **NM** $40 **MIP** $85

Hokey Wolf Figure, 1970, Dakin
EX $30 **NM** $75 **MIP** $150

Huckleberry Hound Figure, Dakin, 8" tall
EX $25 **NM** $50 **MIP** $90

Huckleberry Hound Figure, 1960s, 6" tall, glazed china
EX $20 **NM** $40 **MIP** $100

Huckleberry Hound Figure, 1961, Marx, TV-Tinykins
EX $15 **NM** $25 **MIP** $60

Huckleberry Hound Figure Set, 1961, Marx, TV-Tinykins
EX $50 **NM** $80 **MIP** $125

TOY

Huckleberry Hound Go-Cart, 1960s, Linemar, 6-1/2" tall, friction
EX $100 **NM** $200 **MIP** $375

Huckleberry Hound Wind-Up Toy, 1962, Linemar, 4" tall, tin
EX $175 **NM** $350 **MIP** $500

Mr. Jinks Soaky, 1960s, Purex, 10" tall, Pixie and Dixie, hard plastic
EX $15 **NM** $35 **MIP** $75

Pixie and Dixie Magic Slate, 1959
EX $30 **NM** $50 **MIP** $80

WATCH

Huckleberry Hound Wristwatch, 1965, Bradley, chrome case, wind-up mechanism, gray leather band, face shows Huck in full view
EX $100 **NM** $150 **MIP** $300

Humpty Dumpty

ACCESSORIES

Humpty Dumpty Bubble Bath, 1960s, Avon, figural plastic container
EX $7 **NM** $30 **MIP** $85

Humpty Dumpty Figural Soap, 1990s, Avon
EX $3 **NM** $6 **MIP** $20

Humpty Dumpty Magazine, 1960s
EX $3 **NM** $7 **MIP** $25

Humpty Dumpty Potato Chip Tin, 1990s, large blue and gold tin
EX $7 **NM** $15 **MIP** $40

FIGURE

Humpty Dumpty Figure, 1950s, Marx, Fairy Tale series, plastic
EX $5 **NM** $10 **MIP** $40

Humpty Dumpty Game, 1981, Orchard Toys, British matching game
EX $8 **NM** $15 **MIP** $50

PUZZLE

Humpty Dumpty Puzzle, 1970s, wood frame tray puzzles, several varieties
EX $5 **NM** $15 **MIP** $40

TOY

Humpty Dumpty Crib Toy, 1980s, Mattel, plastic, sits on crib rail
EX $4 **NM** $8 **MIP** $25

Humpty Dumpty Musical Toy, 1960s, Alladin Plastics, plastic, record inside toy
EX $15 **NM** $30 **MIP** $70

Humpty Dumpty Pull Toy, 1970s, Fisher-Price, plastic, several color variations
EX $5 **NM** $10 **MIP** $30

Indiana Jones

ACCESSORIES

Indiana Jones Backpack, Pepsi
EX $20 **NM** $45 **MIP** $90

Indiana Jones The Legend Mug
EX $5 **NM** $10 **MIP** $15

Last Crusade Button, Pepsi, retailer button
EX $5 **NM** $15 **MIP** $30

Patch, 1990
EX $10 **NM** $20 **MIP** $40

Temple of Doom Calendar
EX $5 **NM** $10 **MIP** $30

Temple of Doom Storybook, hardbound
EX $7 **NM** $20 **MIP** $30

TOY

Indiana Jones 3-D View-Master Gift Set, View-Master
EX $20 NM $35 MIP $75

James Bond

ACCESSORIES

007 Flicker Rings, 1967, set of 11
EX $75 NM $110 MIP $220

007 Video Disc Promo Kit, 1980s, RCA, disc, poster, pamphlet
EX $15 NM $30 MIP $60

Bond Golf Tees, 1987, British, six tees and pencil in leather pouch
EX $8 NM $15 MIP $30

James Bond Alarm Clock, painting of Roger Moore in center
EX $20 NM $40 MIP $100

James Bond B.A.R.K. Attache Case With Box, 1965, Multiple Toys, 007 luger, missiles, hideaway pistol and rocket launching device, case and gun bears 007 logo
EX $1000 NM $1500 MIP $3000

James Bond Jr. Bath Towel
EX $10 NM $20 MIP $20

James Bond Parachute Set, 1984, Imperial, orange and green parachutist figures
EX $12 NM $35 MIP $80

James Bond Ring, 1964, glass oval w/photo of Sean Connery
EX $10 NM $25 MIP $40

James Bond Wall Clock, 1981, large clock w/painting of Roger Moore in action
EX $25 NM $45 MIP $100

View to a Kill Michelin Button, Bond on large size pinback w/Midas man
EX $5 NM $12 MIP $25

ACTION FIGURES

James Bond Jr. Action Ninja figure, Hasbro
EX $8 NM $15 MIP $80

James Bond Jr. Buddy Mitchell figure, Hasbro
EX $5 NM $10 MIP $30

James Bond Jr. Capt. Walker D. Plank figure, Hasbro
EX $3 NM $6 MIP $20

James Bond Jr. Dr. Derange figure, Hasbro
EX $3 NM $6 MIP $25

James Bond Jr. Dr. No. figure, Hasbro
EX $3 NM $6 MIP $25

James Bond Jr. figure, Hasbro, w/pistol
EX $3 NM $8 MIP $35

James Bond Jr. figure, Hasbro, w/scuba gear
EX $3 NM $8 MIP $35

James Bond Jr. Gordo Leiter figure, Hasbro
EX $4 NM $10 MIP $40

James Bond Jr. I.Q. figure, Hasbro, w/weapon device
EX $3 NM $6 MIP $25

James Bond Jr. Jaws figure, Hasbro
EX $5 NM $12 MIP $40

James Bond Jr. Odd Job figure, Hasbro
EX $6 NM $15 MIP $50

BOOK

Bond Pocket Diary, 1988, British leather bound
EX $5 NM $15 MIP $40

James Bond Jr. Sticker Book
EX $3 NM $6 MIP $20

COSTUME

James Bond Costume, 1966, Ben Cooper, tuxedo
EX $50 NM $100 MIP $200

Moonraker Halloween Costume, 1979, mask of Roger Moore and space suit costume
EX $30 NM $75 MIP $150

DOLL

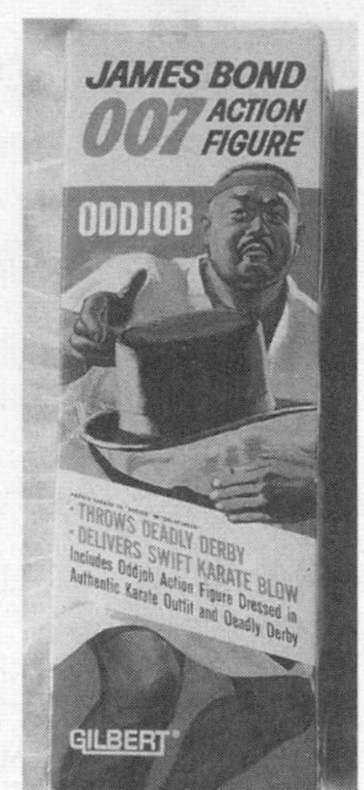

Odd Job Action figure, 1965, Gilbert, 12" doll in karate outfit, w/derby
EX $300 NM $550 MIP $750

FIGURES

Jaws figure, 1979, Mego
EX $135 NM $300 MIP $600

GAME

Goldfinger II Role Playing Game
EX $6 NM $15 MIP $40

James Bond Computer Game "The Stealth Affair", 1990, based on Licence to Kill
EX $15 NM $30 MIP $70

James Bond Jr. Karate Punch Target Game, gun w/boxing glove and targets of villain
EX $8 NM $15 MIP $45

James Bond Secret Service Game, 1965, Spears
EX $150 NM $275 MIP $625

James Bond Tarot Game, 1973
EX $15 NM $30 MIP $70

James Bond Video Game, 1983, Coleco
EX $15 NM $25 MIP $60

Moonraker Spanish Card Game, 33 cards w/different color stills
EX $15 NM $30 MIP $70

The James Bond Box, 1965, rare game played w/dice
EX $50 NM $100 MIP $200

Thunderball Balloon Target Game, 1965
EX $40 NM $95 MIP $200

GUN

007 Dart Gun, 1984, Imperial, photo of Roger Moore
EX $15 NM $35 MIP $100

007 Submachine Gun, 1984, Imperial, photo of Roger Moore
EX $10 NM $30 MIP $100

007 Toy Pistol, Edgemark
EX $5 NM $15 MIP $50

James Bond Harpoon Gun (Thunderball), 1960s, Lone Star, box illustrated w/undersea fight scene graphics
EX $125 NM $250 MIP $400

James Bond Hideaway Pistol, 1985, Coibel
EX $40 NM $90 MIP $170

James Bond Sting Pistol, Coibel, 8-shot cap pistol and booklet from On Her Majesty's Secret Service
EX $20 NM $40 MIP $120

Living Daylights German Pistol, 1980s, Wicke, 25-shot cap gun
EX $12 NM $30 MIP $90

May Day Pistol, 1985
EX $12 NM $30 MIP $75

PUPPETS

Odd Job Puppet, Gilbert, plastic hand puppet
EX $250 NM $500 MIP $750

PUZZLE

Goldfinger Puzzle, 1965, Milton Bradley, Bond and Golden Girl
EX $25 NM $55 MIP $120

Goldfinger Puzzle, 1965, Milton Bradley, Bond's Bullets Blaze
EX $20 NM $40 MIP $95

Spy Who Loved Me Puzzle, Milton Bradley, several scenes, each
EX $20 NM $40 MIP $90

STICKERS

007 Bullet Hole Stickers, 1987, simulated bullet holes, magnetic license holder
EX $6 NM $15 MIP $40

TOY

007 Exploding Cigarette Lighter, Coibel
EX $12 NM $30 MIP $100

007 Exploding Coin, Coibel, on blister pack
EX $6 NM $20 MIP $50

007 Exploding Pen, Coibel, on blister pack
EX $6 NM $20 MIP $50

007 Exploding Spoon, Coibel, on blister pack
EX $6 NM $20 MIP $50

007 Radio Trap, 1966, Multiple Toys, radio w/secret business cards
EX $50 NM $105 MIP $220

Electric Drawing Set, 1965, Lakeside, plastic tracing board, pencils, sharpener, adventure sheets
EX $55 NM $110 MIP $250

James Bond Disguise Kit, 1965, Gilbert
EX $40 NM $85 MIP $200

James Bond Disguise Kit #2, 1965, Gilbert
EX $40 NM $85 MIP $200

James Bond Hand Puppet, 1965, Gilbert
EX $45 NM $100 MIP $175

James Bond Jr. CD Player/Weapons Kit, Hasbro
EX $10 NM $20 MIP $60

James Bond Jr. Crime Fighter Set, includes handcuffs, watch and walkie-talkie
EX $5 NM $15 MIP $50

James Bond Jr. Ninja Play Set, throw stars, nunchukas and badge
EX $8 NM $15 MIP $60

James Bond Jr. Ninja Wrist Weapon Set
EX $5 NM $10 MIP $50

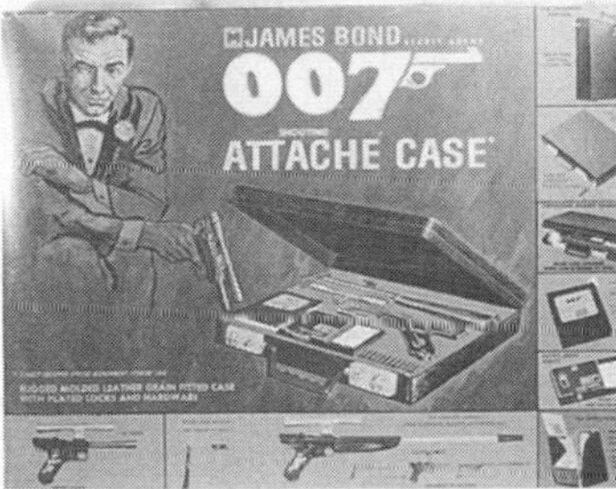

James Bond Secret Attache Case, 1965, MPC, box is rare
EX $1000 NM $1500 MIP $3000

Spy Who Loved Me Jr. Set, Corgi, Lotus and Copter
EX $15 NM $40 MIP $95

Thunderball Puzzle, 1965, Milton Bradley, several pictures, each
EX $20 NM $45 MIP $95

Thunderball Set, 1965, Gilbert
EX $40 NM $105 MIP $220

Tuxedo Outfit, 1965, Gilbert
EX $50 NM $110 MIP $230

VEHICLES

James Bond Aston Martin, 1965, Gilbert, 12", battery operated
EX $150 NM $300 MIP $575

James Bond Aston Martin Slot Car, 1965, Gilbert
EX $75 NM $150 MIP $325

James Bond Jr. Corvette, Hasbro
EX $15 NM $35 MIP $90

James Bond Jr. Scum Shark Mobile, Hasbro
EX $10 NM $15 MIP $40

James Bond Jr. Sub Cycle, Hasbro
EX $10 NM $15 MIP $40

James Bond Jr. Vehicles, Ertl, S.C.U.M. Helicopter, Bond's car and van; set of three
EX $20 NM $65 MIP $150

James Bond Roadrace Set, 1965, Gilbert, scenery tracks, Aston Martin and other cars
EX $350 NM $600 MIP $1000

Licence to Kill Car Set, Matchbox, jeep, seaplane, oil tanker, and copter
EX $25 NM $50 MIP $125

Living Daylights Record Mobile, 1980s
EX $5 NM $20 MIP $50

Moonraker Drax Copter, Corgi
EX $15 NM $40 MIP $85

Moonraker Jr. Set, Corgi, Aston Martin and Lotus
EX $25 NM $60 MIP $175

Moonraker Jr. Shuttle, Corgi
EX $15 NM $35 MIP $80

Moonraker Shuttle and Drax Copter Jr.'s, Corgi, set of two
EX $15 NM $35 MIP $80

Moonraker Space Shuttle, Corgi
EX $25 NM $50 MIP $150

Multi-Action Aston Martin, 1960s, friction operated car for Agent 711
EX $90 NM $200 MIP $400

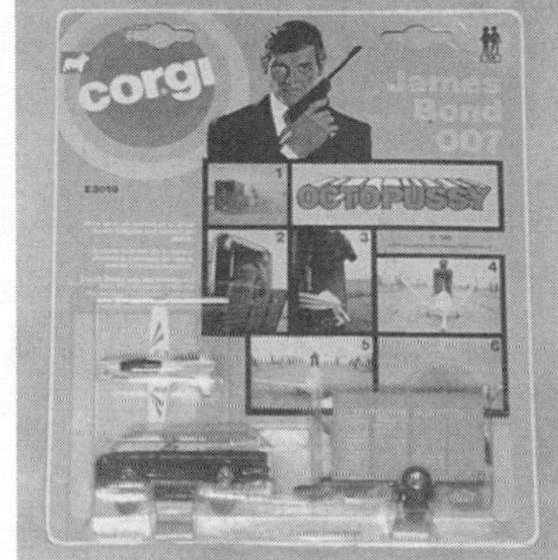

Octopussy Gift Set, Corgi, plane, truck and horse trailer
EX $35 NM $100 MIP $200

Spy Who Loved Me Helicopter Jr., Corgi
EX $10 NM $25 MIP $60

Stromberg Helicopter, Corgi
EX $25 NM $60 MIP $100

WATCHES

James Bond Pocket Watch, 1981, Roger Moore on face
EX $40 NM $80 MIP $175

CHARACTER TOYS

Jungle Book

ACCESSORIES

Jungle Book Dinner Set, vinyl placemat, bowl, plate and cup
EX $10 NM $20 MIP $70

Jungle Book Utensils, fork and spoon w/melamine handles
EX $5 NM $12 MIP $50

DOLL

Baloo Doll, 12" tall, plush
EX $10 NM $50 MIP $120

FIGURES

Mowgli Figure, 1967, Holland Hill, 8", vinyl
EX $20 NM $40 MIP $90

Shere Kahn Figure, 1965, Enesco, 5" tall, ceramic
EX $20 NM $40 MIP $85

TOY

Jungle Book Carrying Case, 1966, Ideal, 5" x 14" x 8"
EX $25 NM $60 MIP $150

Jungle Book Fun-L Tun-L, 1966, New York Toy, 108" x 24"
EX $40 NM $70 MIP $150

Jungle Book Magic Slate, 1967, Watkins-Strathmore
EX $10 NM $25 MIP $75

Jungle Book Sand Pail and Shovel, 1966, Chein, tin litho, illustrated w/Jungle Book characters
EX $25 NM $60 MIP $120

Jungle Book Tea Set, 1966, Chein, tin litho, plates, saucers, tea cups and serving tray
EX $35 NM $75 MIP $140

Mowgli's Hut Mobile and Figures, 1968, Multiple Toymakers, 2" x 3" x 3" mobile w/Baloo and King Louis figures
EX $35 NM $100 MIP $150

WATCH

Mowgli/Baloo Wristwatch, digital, clear plastic band
EX $5 NM $10 MIP $30

Lady and the Tramp

DOLL

Lady Doll, 1955, Woolikin, 5" x 8" x 8-1/2", light tank w/burnt orange accents on face, ears, stomach and tail, plastic eyes, nose and a white silk ribbon around neck
EX $75 NM $150 MIP $300

Perri Doll, 1950s, Steiff, 6" tall, plush
EX $40 NM $85 MIP $175

Tramp Doll, 1955, Schuco, 8" tall, brown w/a white underside and face, hard plastic eyes and nose
EX $100 NM $175 MIP $375

FIGURES

Lady and Tramp Figures, 1955, Marx, Lady is 1-1/2" tall and white, Tramp is 2" tall and tan
EX $30 NM $75 MIP $150

TOY

Modeling Clay, 1955, Pressman
EX $30 NM $120 MIP $185

Puzzle, 1954, Whitman, 11" x 15", frame tray
EX $20 NM $35 MIP $75

Toy Bus, 1966, Modern Toys/Japan, 3-1/2" x 4" x 14" long
EX $20 NM $40 MIP $90

Laurel and Hardy

BANK

Oliver Hardy Bank, 1974, Play Pal, 13-1/2" tall, plastic
EX $15 NM $30 MIP $85

Stan Laurel Bank, 1972, 15" tall, vinyl figural bank
EX $22 NM $50 MIP $95

Stan Laurel Bank, 1974, Play Pal, 13-1/2" tall, plastic
EX $15 NM $30 MIP $85

FIGURES

Oliver Hardy Figure, 1974, Dakin, 7-1/2" tall
EX $60 NM $120 MIP $175

Stan Laurel Figure, 1974, Dakin, 8" tall
EX $60 NM $120 MIP $130

TOY

Laurel and Hardy Die-Cut Puppets, 1970s, Larry Harmon, moveable, each
EX $25 NM $125 MIP $275

Laurel and Hardy Die-Cut Puppets, 1982, Dell, soft vinyl, each
EX $20 NM $75 MIP $175

Laurel and Hardy TV Set, 1976, w/paper filmstrips
EX $25 NM $50 MIP $125

Oliver Hardy Doll, Dakin, 5" tall wind-up dancing/shaking vinyl doll
EX $35 NM $50 MIP $125

Little Mermaid

ACCESSORIES

Ariel Jewelry Box, 5-3/4" x 4-1/2", musical
EX $10 NM $16 MIP $40

Ariel Toothbrush, battery operated w/holder
EX $10 NM $16 MIP $35

Flounder and Ariel Faucet Cover, plastic
EX $6 NM $10 MIP $30

Flounder Pillow, 14" x 24" shaped like Flounder
EX $8 NM $13 MIP $35

Little Mermaid Purse, 6" diameter, vinyl, canteen style purse
EX $6 NM $12 MIP $30

Little Mermaid Snow Globe, 4" water globe
EX $10 NM $16 MIP $40

Under the Sea Jewelry Box, 4" mahogany, musical
EX $20 NM $35 MIP $75

DOLL

Eric Doll, 9-1/2" tall in full dress uniform
EX $10 NM $16 MIP $35

Flounder Doll, 15" plush fish
EX $10 NM $16 MIP $35

Scuttle Doll, 15" seagull, plush
EX $12 NM $20 MIP $40

Sebastian Doll, 16" crab, plush
EX $10 NM $16 MIP $35

FIGURES

Little Mermaid Figures, Applause, several PVC characters, each
EX $2 NM $5 MIP $12

Little Orphan Annie

ACCESSORIES

Beetleware Mug, 1933, Ovaltine
EX $25 NM $70 MIP $120

Beetleware Mug, 1935, Ovaltine
EX $35 NM $80 MIP $150

ID Bracelet, 1934, Ovaltine
EX $25 NM $60 MIP $150

Little Orphan Annie Altascope Ring, 1942, Quaker, premium, only eight known to exist
EX $8500 NM $12000 MIP $22000

Little Orphan Annie and Sandy Ashtray, 1930s, 3" tall, ceramic
EX $100 NM $200 MIP $400

Little Orphan Annie and Sandy Toothbrush Holder, 1930s, bisque
EX $100 NM $160 MIP $350

Little Orphan Annie Clothespins, 1938, Gold Medal, clothesline and pulley
EX $20 NM $40 MIP $80

Little Orphan Annie Glassips, 1936, drinking straws
EX $500 NM $600 MIP $750

Little Orphan Annie Mug, 1930, Ovaltine, Uncle Wiggily
EX $40 NM $100 MIP $200

Little Orphan Annie Music Box, 1970, N.Y. News, figural
EX $25 NM $60 MIP $100

Little Orphan Annie Periscope, 1942, Quaker, offered in handbook
EX $400 NM $600 MIP $750

Little Orphan Annie Stamper, 1941, Quaker, premium, w/wood handle; secret guard
EX $600 NM $1000 MIP $1200

CHARACTER TOYS

Round Decoder Pin, 1936, Ovaltine
EX $30 **NM** $130 **MIP** $220

Secret Compartment Decoder Pin, 1936, Ovaltine
EX $20 **NM** $150 **MIP** $325

Shake-Up Mug, 1931, Ovaltine
EX $30 **NM** $75 **MIP** $140

Sunburst Decoder Pin, 1937, Ovaltine
EX $30 **NM** $75 **MIP** $180

BOOK

Little Orphan Annie and Chizzler Book, 1930s, Big Little Book
EX $25 **NM** $75 **MIP** $160

Little Orphan Annie and the Gooneyville Mystery Book, 1947, Whitman
EX $20 **NM** $100 **MIP** $180

Little Orphan Annie and the Haunted House Comic Book, 1928, Cupples and Leon
EX $60 **NM** $150 **MIP** $300

Little Orphan Annie Bucking the World Comic Book, 1929, Cupples and Leon, hardcover
EX $60 **NM** $150 **MIP** $310

Little Orphan Annie in the Circus Comic Book, 1927, Cupples and Leon, 9" x 7", 86 pages
EX $60 **NM** $150 **MIP** $310

Little Orphan Annie Shipwrecked Comic Book, 1931, Cupples and Leon, 9" x 7", 86 pages
EX $60 **NM** $120 **MIP** $310

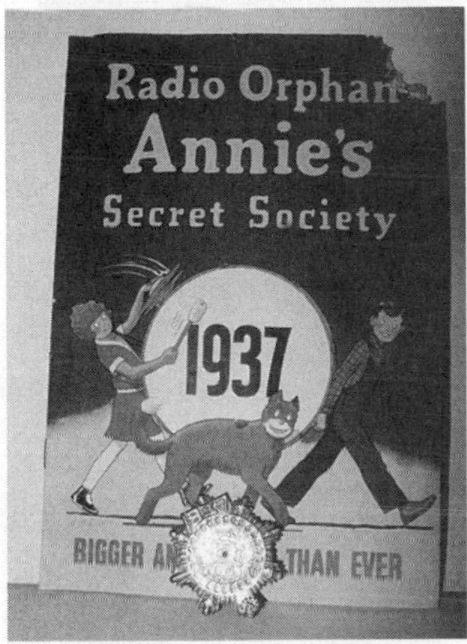

Radio Annie's Secret Society Booklet, 1936, 6" x 9"
EX $40 **NM** $65 **MIP** $160

Radio Annie's Secret Society Manual, 1938, 6" x 9", 12 pages
EX $60 **NM** $100 **MIP** $185

DOLL

Annie Doll, 1982, Knickerbocker, 10" doll without locket
EX $2 **NM** $7 **MIP** $20

Annie Doll, 1982, Knickerbocker, 10" tall, w/two dresses and removable heart locket
EX $5 **NM** $12 **MIP** $30

Daddy Warbucks Doll, 1982, Knickerbocker
EX $10 **NM** $50 **MIP** $90

Little Orphan Annie and Sandy Dolls, 1930, Famous Artists Syndicate, 9-3/4" tall, each
EX $90 **NM** $150 **MIP** $300

Little Orphan Annie Doll, 1973, Well Toy, 7" tall
EX $15 **NM** $20 **MIP** $60

Miss Hannigan Doll, 1982, Knickerbocker
EX $5 **NM** $10 **MIP** $30

Molly Doll, 1982, Knickerbocker
EX $5 **NM** $10 **MIP** $30

Punjab Doll, 1982, Knickerbocker
EX $5 **NM** $15 **MIP** $50

Snow White Paper Dolls, 1938, rare red cover version; Ovaltine Annie premium
EX $800 **NM** $1200 **MIP** $2000

FIGURES

Annie Figures, 1982, Knickerbocker, six figures, 2" tall, each
EX $2 **NM** $5 **MIP** $10

Little Orphan Annie Figure, 1940s, 1-1/2" tall, lead
EX $20 **NM** $40 **MIP** $80

Sandy Figure, 1940s, 3/4" tall, lead
EX $20 **NM** $55 **MIP** $120

GAME

Little Orphan Annie Light Up the Candles Game, Ovaltine, 3-1/2" x 5", premium
EX $125 **NM** $175 **MIP** $350

Little Orphan Annie Rummy Cards, 1937, Whitman, 5" x 6", colored silhouettes of Annie on the back
EX $60 **NM** $90 **MIP** $175

TOY

Little Orphan Annie Colorforms Set, 1970s, Colorforms
EX $10 **NM** $20 **MIP** $50

Little Orphan Annie Costume, 1930s, mask and slip-over paper dress w/belt
EX $300 **NM** $450 **MIP** $525

Little Orphan Annie Cut-Outs, 1960s, Miller Toys, Sandy, Grunts the Pig, Pee Wee the Elephant
EX $50 **NM** $100 **MIP** $200

Little Orphan Annie Punch-Outs, 1944, King, Larson, McMahon, 3-D punch-outs of Annie, Sandy, Punjab and Daddy Warbucks
EX $75 **NM** $125 **MIP** $175

Little Orphan Annie Stove, 1930s, electric version, 8" x 9", gold metal, litho plates, functional oven doors and back burner
EX $150 **NM** $250 **MIP** $375

Little Orphan Annie Stove, 1930s, non-electric model, gold-brass lithographed labels of Annie and Sandy, oven doors functional
EX $150 **NM** $250 **MIP** $375

Pastry Set, 1950s, Transogram, Model No. 3993
EX $20 **NM** $40 **MIP** $75

Puzzle, Novelty Dist., Famous Comics
EX $35 **NM** $100 **MIP** $210

Looney Tunes

BANK

Daffy Duck Bank, 1980s, Applause, figural
EX $10 **NM** $20 **MIP** $50

Sylvester and Tweety Bank, 1972, vinyl
EX $15 **NM** $25 **MIP** $90

Tasmanian Devil Bank, 1980s, Applause
EX $10 **NM** $20 **MIP** $70

DOLL

Tasmanian Devil Doll, 1971, Mighty Star, 13" tall, plush
EX $20 **NM** $40 **MIP** $100

Tweety Doll, 1969, Dakin, 6", moveable head and feet
EX $10 **NM** $25 **MIP** $80

FIGURE

Daffy Duck Figure, 1968, Dakin, 8-1/2" tall
EX $15 **NM** $25 **MIP** $80

Daffy Duck Figure, 1970s, Dakin
EX $15 **NM** $30 **MIP** $90

Daffy Duck Figure, 1980s, Applause, 4" bendy
EX $10 **NM** $20 **MIP** $60

Sylvester Figure, 1971, Dakin, Sylvester on a fish crate
EX $15 **NM** $25 **MIP** $80

Sylvester Figure, 1976, Dakin, Cartoon Theater
EX $11 **NM** $22 **MIP** $60

FIGURES

Pepe Le Pew Figure, 1971, Dakin, 8" tall
EX $25 **NM** $50 **MIP** $100

Speedy Gonzales Figure, Dakin, 5", vinyl
EX $10 **NM** $20 **MIP** $60

Speedy Gonzales Figure, 1970, Dakin, 7-1/2" tall, vinyl
EX $15 **NM** $25 **MIP** $65

Sylvester and Tweety Figures, 1975, Warner Bros., 6" tall
EX $10 **NM** $16 **MIP** $50

Sylvester Figure, 1950, Oak Rubber, 6", rubber
EX $40 NM $80 MIP $135

Sylvester Figure, 1969, Dakin
EX $15 NM $25 MIP $70

Tasmanian Devil Figure, 1989, Superior, 7", plastic, on base
EX $5 NM $15 MIP $50

Tweety Figure, 1971, Dakin, on bird cage
EX $14 NM $25 MIP $70

Tweety Figure, 1971, Dakin, Goofy Gram, holding red heart
EX $15 NM $25 MIP $70

Tweety Figure, 1976, Dakin, Cartoon Theater
EX $15 NM $25 MIP $70

TOY

Bugs Bunny Hand Puppet, 1940s, Zany, rubber head
EX $60 NM $125 MIP $200

Elmer Fudd Hand Puppet, 1940s, Zany, rubber head
EX $30 NM $70 MIP $150

Foghorn Leghorn Hand Puppet, 1940s, Zany, rubber head
EX $45 NM $85 MIP $175

Pepe Le Pew Goofy Gram, 1971, Dakin
EX $25 NM $50 MIP $100

Sylvester Hand Puppet, 1940s, Zany, rubber head
EX $60 NM $125 MIP $200

Sylvester Soaky, Colgate
EX $10 NM $30 MIP $70

Tweety Hand Puppet, 1940s, Zany, rubber head
EX $60 NM $125 MIP $200

Tweety Soaky, 1960s, Colgate, 8-1/2", plastic
EX $10 NM $30 MIP $70

Magilla Gorilla

ACCESSORIES

Magilla Gorilla Cereal Bowl, MB Inc.
EX $10 NM $35 MIP $90

Magilla Gorilla Plate, 1960s, 8" diameter, plastic
EX $7 NM $20 MIP $50

BOOK

Magilla Gorilla Book, 1964, Golden, Big Golden Book
EX $12 NM $30 MIP $70

DOLL

Magilla Gorilla Doll, 1960s, 11" tall, cloth body, hard arms and legs, hard plastic head
EX $125 NM $225 MIP $400

Magilla Gorilla Doll, 1966, Ideal, 18-1/2" plush w/vinyl head
EX $135 NM $250 MIP $450

TOY

Droop-A-Long Coyote Soaky, 1960s, Purex, 12", plastic
EX $20 NM $45 MIP $90

Droop-A-Long Hand Puppet, Ideal, vinyl head
EX $25 NM $60 MIP $135

Magilla Gorilla Cannon, 1964, Ideal
EX $60 NM $90 MIP $200

Magilla Gorilla Pull Toy, 1960s, Ideal, w/vinyl figure
EX $75 NM $150 MIP $250

Magilla Gorilla Puppet, Ideal
EX $40 NM $110 MIP $210

Magilla Gorilla Push Puppet, 1960s, Kohner, brown plastic figure in pink shorts and shoes, yellow base
EX $25 NM $55 MIP $110

Punkin' Puss Soaky, 1960s, Purex, 11-1/2" tall, plastic
EX $20 NM $50 MIP $85

Ricochet Rabbit Hand Puppet, 1960s, Ideal, 11", vinyl head
EX $35 NM $65 MIP $125

Ricochet Rabbit Soaky, 1960s, Purex, 10-1/2" tall, plastic
EX $30 NM $70 MIP $140

Mary Poppins

ACCESSORIES

Mary Poppins Pencil Case, 1964, vinyl w/zipper top
EX $10 NM $22 MIP $60

DOLL

Mary Poppins Doll, 1964, Gund, 11-1/2" tall, bendable
EX $75 NM $150 MIP $300

FIGURES

Mary Poppins Figure, 8" tall, ceramic
EX $20 NM $40 MIP $90

PUZZLE

Mary Poppins Puzzle, 1964, Jaymar, frame tray
EX $8 NM $20 MIP $50

TOY

Mary Poppins Manicure Set, 1964, Tre-Jur
EX $20 NM $45 MIP $95

Mary Poppins Paper Dolls, 1973, Whitman, w/magic tote bag, Model No. 1977
EX $40 NM $75 MIP $120

Mary Poppins Tea Set, 1964, Chein, tin, creamer, plates, place settings, cups, serving tray
EX $60 NM $110 MIP $200

Mickey and Minnie Mouse

ACCESSORIES

Mickey and Donald Alarm Clock, 1960s, Jerger/Germany, 2-1/2" x 5" x 7"; metal case, dark brass finish, 3-D plastic figures of Mickey and Donald on either side
EX $70 NM $140 MIP $210

Mickey and Minnie and Donald Throw Rug, 26" x 41", Mickey and Minnie in an airplane w/Donald parachuting
EX $60 NM $120 MIP $210

Mickey and Minnie Carpet, 27" x 41", Peg Leg Pete is lassoed by Mickey; all characters in western outfits
EX $130 NM $225 MIP $360

Mickey and Minnie Snow Dome, 1970s, Monogram, 3" x 4" x 3" tall, Mickey and Minnie w/a pot of gold at the end of the rainbow
EX $12 NM $25 MIP $50

Mickey and Minnie Toothbrush Holder, 4-1/2" tall, bisque, toothbrush holes are located behind their heads
EX $120 NM $200 MIP $400

Mickey and Minnie Toothbrush Holder, 2-1/2" x 4" x 3-1/2", Mickey and Minnie on sofa w/Pluto at their feet
EX $130 NM $210 MIP $425

Mickey and Minnie Trash Can, 1970s, Chein, 13" tall tin litho, Mickey and Minnie fixing a flat tire on one side, other side shows Mickey feeding Minnie soup
EX $25 NM $80 MIP $160

Mickey and Pluto Ashtray, 3" x 4" x 3" tall, ceramic, Mickey and Pluto playing banjos while sitting on the edge of the ashtray
EX $250 NM $400 MIP $625

Mickey Mouse Alarm Clock, 1960s, Bayard, 2" x 4-1/2" x 4-1/2" tall, 1930s style Mickey w/movable head that ticks off the seconds
EX $100 NM $200 MIP $350

Mickey Mouse Alarm Clock, 1975, Bradley, travel alarm, large red cube case, shut off button on top, separate alarm wind, in sleeve box
EX $30 NM $55 MIP $100

Mickey Mouse Alarm Clock, 1988, House Martin, 5" x 7" x 2"
EX $11 NM $20 MIP $50

Mickey Mouse Ashtray, 3-1/2" tall, wood composition figure of Mickey
EX $75 NM $150 MIP $310

Mickey Mouse Beanie, 1950s, blue/yellow felt hat w/Mickey on front
EX $200 NM $350 MIP $500

Mickey Mouse Christmas Lights, 1930s, Noma, eight lamps w/holiday decals of characters
EX $125 NM $225 MIP $375

Mickey Mouse Clock, 1970s, Elgin, 10" x 15" x 3", electric wall clock
EX $12 NM $25 MIP $50

Mickey Mouse Club Coffee Tin, 1950s, illustrated lid promotes the club, tin included MM badge
EX $50 NM $100 MIP $200

Mickey Mouse Club Mousketeer Handbag, Connecticut Leather, leather/vinyl crafting set
EX $45 NM $60 MIP $125

Mickey Mouse Club Plastic Plate, 1960s, Arrowhead, 9" diameter, clubhouse w/Goofy, Pluto and Donald wearing mouse ears and sweaters w/club emblems
EX $16 NM $30 MIP $45

Mickey Mouse Club Toothbrush, 1970s, Pepsodent
EX $4 NM $7 MIP $30

Mickey Mouse Cup, 1950s, Cavalier, 3" tall, silver-plated cup w/a 2-1/2" opening
EX $25 NM $50 MIP $100

Mickey Mouse Electric Table Radio, 1960s, General Electric, 4-1/2" x 10-1/2" x 6" tall
EX $50 NM $150 MIP $225

Mickey Mouse Lamp, 1935, Soreng-Manegold, 10-1/2" tall
EX $200 NM $350 MIP $600

Mickey Mouse Map of the United States, 1930s, Dixon, 9-1/4" x 14"
EX $100 NM $250 MIP $425

Mickey Mouse Night Light, 1938, Disney, 4" tall, tin
EX $100 NM $200 MIP $300

Mickey Mouse Pencil Box, 1930s, Dixon, 5-1/2" x 10-1/2" x 1-1/4", Mickey in a gymnasium
EX $60 NM $125 MIP $275

Mickey Mouse Pencil Box, 1930s, Dixon, Mickey ready to hitch Horace to a carriage in which Minnie is sitting
EX $100 NM $150 MIP $300

Mickey Mouse Pencil Box, 1937, Dixon, 5-1/2" x 9" x 3/4", Mickey, Goofy and Pluto riding a rocket
EX $100 NM $150 MIP $300

Mickey Mouse Pencil Box, 1937, Dixon, 5" x 8-1/2" x 1-1/4", Mickey is a circus ringmaster and Donald riding a seal
EX $100 NM $150 MIP $300

Mickey Mouse Pencil Holder, 1930s, Dixon, 4-1/2" tall
EX $100 NM $150 MIP $300

Mickey Mouse Pencil Sharpener, 3" tall, celluloid, sharpener located on base
EX $65 NM $125 MIP $250

Mickey Mouse Pencil Sharpener, 1960s, Hasbro, shape of Mickey's head, pencil goes into mouth
EX $12 NM $25 MIP $50

Mickey Mouse Pitcher, 1930s, Germany, 2" x 3" diameter, china, white w/green shading around the base, Mickey on each side
EX $75 NM $150 MIP $325

Mickey Mouse Radio, 1934, Emerson, wood composition cabinet w/designs of Mickey playing musical instruments
EX $2000 NM $3200 MIP $6000

Mickey Mouse Radio, 1970s, Philgee
EX $20 NM $40 MIP $80

Mickey Mouse Record Player, 1970s, General Electric, playing arm is the design of Mickey's arm
EX $60 NM $125 MIP $175

Mickey Mouse Throw Rug, 1935, Alex. Smith Carpet, 26" x 42"
EX $130 NM $250 MIP $400

Mickey Mouse Transistor Radio, 1950s, Gabriel, 6-1/2" x 7" x 1-1/2"
EX $40 NM $80 MIP $160

Mickey Mouse Wall Clock, 1978, Elgin, 9" diameter dial, 15" long, shaped like oversize watchband, "50 Happy Years" logo on dial
EX $30 NM $60 MIP $90

Minnie Mouse Alarm Clock, 1970s, Bradley, pink metal electric two-bell clock w/articulated hands
EX $25 NM $50 MIP $85

Minnie Mouse Clock, 1970s, Phinney-Walker, 8" diameter by 1-1/2" deep, plastic, "Behind Every Great Man, There is a Woman!"
EX $40 NM $70 MIP $125

BANK

Mickey Mouse Band Leader Bank, Knickerbocker, 7-1/2" tall, plastic
EX $10 NM $25 MIP $50

Mickey Mouse Bank, 1930s, 2" x 3" x 2-1/4", tin, shaped like a treasure chest w/Mickey and Minnie on the "Isle of the Thrift"
EX $200 NM $300 MIP $520

Mickey Mouse Bank, 1930s, 2-1/2" x 6", shaped like a mailbox w/Mickey holding an envelope
EX $150 NM $250 MIP $425

Mickey Mouse Bank, 1934, German, 2-1/2" x 3", tin, bright yellow bank shaped like a beehive, Mickey approaching door holding a honey jar in one arm and key to open the door in the other
EX $400 NM $750 MIP $1000

Mickey Mouse Bank, 1938, Crown Toy, 6" tall, composition, key locked trap door on base, w/figure standing next to treasure chest and head is movable
EX $175 NM $250 MIP $500

Mickey Mouse Bank, 1950s, 5" x 5-1/2" x 6", china, shaped like Mickey's head w/slot between his ears
EX $30 NM $70 MIP $160

Mickey Mouse Bank, 1960s, Wolverine, 1-1/2" x 5-1/2" x 1" tall, plastic
EX $50 NM $60 MIP $125

Mickey Mouse Bank, 1970s, Transogram, 5" x 7-1/2" x 19" tall, plastic w/Mickey standing on a white chest
EX $15 NM $25 MIP $40

Mickey Mouse Bank, 1978, Fricke and Nacke, 3" x 5" x 7" tall, embossed image of Mickey in front, side panels have Minnie, Goofy, Donald and Pluto
EX $15 NM $25 MIP $175

Mickey Mouse Club Bank, 1970s, Play Pal Plastics, 4-1/2" x 6" x 11-1/2" tall, vinyl
EX $16 NM $30 MIP $60

Mickey Mouse Gumball Bank, 1968, Hasbro
EX $15 NM $40 MIP $90

Mickey Mouse Telephone Bank, 1938, N.N. Hill Brass, 5" tall w/cardboard figure of Mickey
EX $130 NM $275 MIP $450

BOOK

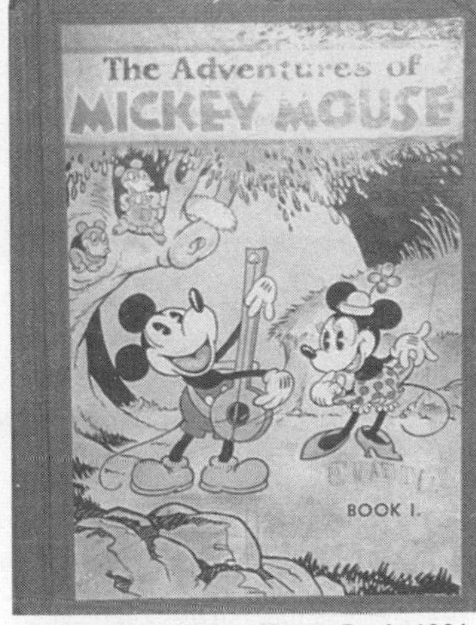

Adventures of Mickey Mouse Book, 1931, David McKay, full color illustrations, softcover
EX $100 NM $275 MIP $525

Mickey Mouse Activity Book, 1936, Whitman, 40 pages
EX $100 NM $150 MIP $325

Mickey Mouse Club Fun Box, 1957, Whitman, box includes stamp book, club scrapbook, six coloring books and four small gameboards
EX $45 NM $85 MIP $175

Mickey Mouse Has a Busy Day Book, 1937, Whitman, 16 pages
EX $50 NM $100 MIP $210

Mickey Mouse in Giantland Book, 1934, David McKay, 45 pages, hardcover
EX $75 NM $150 MIP $300

Mickey Mouse Presents a Silly Symphony Book, 1934, Whitman, Big Little Book
EX $100 NM $175 MIP $350

DOLL

Mickey and Minnie Dolls, 1940s, Gund, 13" tall, each
EX $300 NM $500 MIP $1000

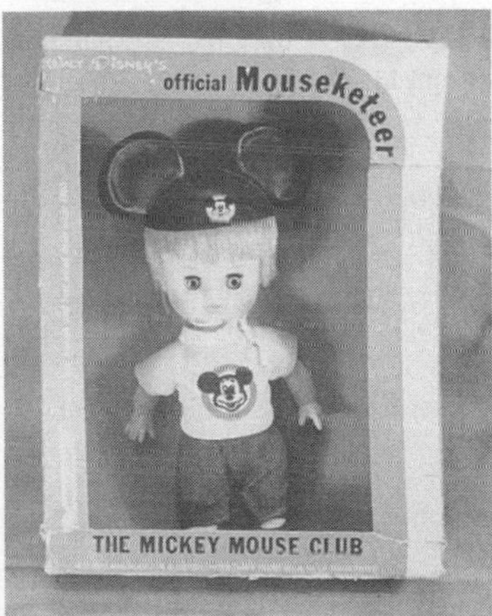

Mickey Mouse Club Mouseketeer Doll, 1960s, Horsman, 8" tall, denim outfit
EX $35 NM $75 MIP $200

Mickey and Minnie Mouse

Mickey Mouse Doll, Knickerbocker, 5" x 7" x 12" tall, fabric, Mickey in checkered shorts and green jacket w/white felt flower stapled to it
EX $400 **NM** $650 **MIP** $1000

Mickey Mouse Doll, 1930s, 4" x 7" x 10-1/2" tall, movable arms and legs, swivel head, black velveteen body and red felt pants
EX $750 **NM** $1200 **MIP** $2000

Mickey Mouse Doll, 1935, Knickerbocker, 11" tall, stuffed w/removable shoes and jointed head, red shorts
EX $200 **NM** $350 **MIP** $600

Mickey Mouse Doll, 1950s, Schuco, 10" tall
EX $110 **NM** $225 **MIP** $400

Mickey Mouse Doll, 1960s, Gund, 12", Mickey as fireman
EX $30 **NM** $55 **MIP** $90

Mickey Mouse Doll, 1970s, Hasbro, 4" x 5-1/2" x 7-1/2" tall, talks
EX $20 **NM** $40 **MIP** $60

Mickey Mouse Doll, 1972, Horsman, 3" x 10" x 12" tall, talking doll, says five different phrases
EX $20 **NM** $40 **MIP** $70

Minnie Mouse Doll, 1935, Knickerbocker, 14" tall, stuffed, cloth, polka-dot skirt and lace pantaloons
EX $400 **NM** $750 **MIP** $1000

Minnie Mouse Doll, 1940s, Petz, 10" tall
EX $135 **NM** $260 **MIP** $500

FIGURES

Mickey Mouse Figure, 4" tall, bisque, dressed in a green nightshirt
EX $40 **NM** $80 **MIP** $140

Mickey Mouse Figure, composition, part of the Lionel Circus Train Set
EX $150 **NM** $200 **MIP** $375

Mickey Mouse Figure, 1930s, Seiberling, 6-1/2" tall, rubber
EX $100 **NM** $200 **MIP** $375

Mickey Mouse Figure, 1930s, Goebel, 3-1/2" tall, in a hunting outfit reading a book
EX $45 **NM** $100 **MIP** $185

Mickey Mouse Figure, 1930s, Seiberling, 3-1/2" tall, black hard rubber
EX $60 **NM** $112 **MIP** $275

Mickey Mouse Figure, 1930s, 3" tall, bisque, holding a parade flag and sword
EX $60 **NM** $125 **MIP** $210

Mickey Mouse Figure, 1930s, 3" tall, bisque, plays saxophone
EX $60 **NM** $125 **MIP** $210

Mickey Mouse Figure, 1930s, Seiberling, 3-1/2" tall, latex
EX $100 **NM** $175 **MIP** $300

Mickey Mouse Figure, 1970, Marx, 6" tall, vinyl
EX $10 **NM** $20 **MIP** $40

Mickey Mouse Fun-E-Flex Figure, 1930s, Fun-E-Flex, 7", bendy
EX $350 **NM** $475 **MIP** $750

Minnie Mouse Figure, 1958, Ingersoll, 5-1/2" tall, plastic
EX $35 **NM** $60 **MIP** $125

Minnie Mouse Fun-E-Flex Figure, 1930s, Fun-E-Flex, 5", bendy
EX $130 **NM** $250 **MIP** $375

GAME

Mickey Mouse Bean Bag Game, 1930s, Marks Bros.
EX $100 **NM** $130 **MIP** $240

Mickey Mouse Club Magic Divider, 1950s, Jacmar, arithmetic game
EX $30 **NM** $55 **MIP** $100

Mickey Mouse Club Magic Subtractor, 1950s, Jacmar, arithmetic game
EX $11 **NM** $20 **MIP** $60

MUSIC BOX

Mickey Mouse Music Box, 4-1/2" x 5" x 7", plays "It's a Small World," Mickey in conductor's uniform standing on cake
EX $20 **NM** $35 **MIP** $100

Mickey Mouse Music Box, Schmid, 3" x 6" x 7-1/2" tall, bisque, Spirit of '76, plays "Yankee Doodle;" Mickey, Goofy and Donald are dressed as Revolutionary War Minutemen
EX $60 **NM** $120 **MIP** $220

Mickey Mouse Music Box, 1970s, Schmid, 3-1/2" x 5-1/2", plays "Mickey Mouse Club March," ceramic, Mickey in western clothes standing next to a cactus
EX $35 **NM** $60 **MIP** $125

Mickey Mouse Music Box, 1970s, Japan, 4" x 6" tall, china, plays "Side by Side," Mickey is brushing a kitten in a washtub
EX $15 **NM** $25 **MIP** $90

Mickey Mouse Music Box, 1971, Anri, 5" x 3-1/2", plays "If I Were Rich Man"
EX $50 **NM** $90 **MIP** $180

Minnie Mouse Music Box, 1970s, Schmid, 3-1/2" diameter, plays "Love Story"
EX $25 **NM** $40 **MIP** $150

TOY

Crayons, 1946, Transogram
EX $30 **NM** $60 **MIP** $100

Mickey and Donald Jack-in-the-Box, 1966, Lakeside, Donald pops out
EX $100 **NM** $175 **MIP** $300

Mickey and Minnie Flashlight, 1930s, Usalite Co., 6" long, Mickey leading Minnie through the darkness guided by flashlight and Pluto
EX $50 **NM** $85 **MIP** $150

Mickey and Minnie Sand Pail, Ohio Art, 5" x 5", tin, Mickey, Minnie, Pluto and Donald in boat looking across water at castle, w/swivel handle
EX $100 **NM** $160 **MIP** $340

Mickey and Minnie Sled, 1935, S.L. Allen, 32" long, wooden slat sled, metal runners, "Mickey Mouse" decal on steering bar
EX $400 **NM** $550 **MIP** $800

Mickey and Minnie Tea Set, 1930s, Ohio Art, 5" x 8", pitcher pictures Mickey at piano and cups picture Mickey, Pluto and Minnie
EX $125 **NM** $200 **MIP** $350

Mickey and Minnie Tray, 1930s, Ohio Art, 5-1/2" x 7-1/4", tin, Mickey and Minnie in rowboat
EX $75 **NM** $125 **MIP** $225

Mickey and Three Pigs Spinning Top, Lackawanna, 9" diameter, tin
EX $50 **NM** $100 **MIP** $200

Mickey Mouse Baby Gift Set, 1930s, silver-plated cup, fork, spoon, cup and napkin holder
EX $100 **NM** $200 **MIP** $350

Mickey Mouse Band Drum, 1936, 7" x 14" diameter, cloth mesh and paper drum heads
EX $250 **NM** $350 **MIP** $500

Mickey Mouse Band Sand Pail, 1938, Ohio Art, 6" tall, tin, pictures of Mickey Mouse, Minnie, Horace, Pluto, and Clarabelle the cow parading down street
EX $125 **NM** $225 **MIP** $350

Mickey Mouse Band Spinning Top, 9" diameter
EX $40 **NM** $80 **MIP** $175

Mickey Mouse Boxed Lantern Slides, 1930s, Ensign, 5" x 6" x 2", cartoons: Traffic Troubles, Gorilla Mystery, Cactus Kid, Castaway, Delivery Boy, Fishin' Around, Firefighters, Moose Hunt and Mickey Steps Out
EX $160 **NM** $325 **MIP** $500

Mickey Mouse Bubble Buster Gun, 1936, Kilgore, 8" long, cork gun
EX $75 **NM** $150 **MIP** $250

Mickey Mouse Bump-N-Go Spaceship, 1980s, Matsudaya, battery operated tin litho w/clear dome, has six flashing lights, rotating antenna
EX $35 **NM** $65 **MIP** $150

Mickey Mouse Camera, 1960s, Ettelson, 3" x 3" x 5"
EX $18 **NM** $40 **MIP** $100

Mickey Mouse Camera, 1970s, Child Guidance, 4" x 7" x 7"
EX $12 **NM** $25 **MIP** $100

Mickey Mouse Camera, 1970s, Helm Toy, 2" x 5" x 4-1/2", Mickey in engineer's uniform riding on top of the train
EX $13 **NM** $25 **MIP** $85

Mickey Mouse Car, 1970s, Polistil, 2" x 4" x 1-1/2" tall plastic car w/rubber figure, Mickey in driver's seat
EX $30 **NM** $55 **MIP** $125

Mickey Mouse Cardboard House, 1930s, O.B. Andrews, 14" x 12" x 13" tall
EX $200 **NM** $350 **MIP** $500

Mickey Mouse Chatty Chums, 1979, Mattel
EX $8 **NM** $15 **MIP** $40

Mickey Mouse Club Magic Kit, 1950s, Mars Candy, two 8" x 20" punch-out sheets
EX $75 **NM** $100 **MIP** $160

Mickey Mouse Club Marionette, 1950s, 3" x 6-1/2" x 13-1/2" tall, composition

figure of a girl w/black felt hat and mouse ears
EX $300 **NM** $425 **MIP** $600

Mickey Mouse Club Mousketeer Ears, Kohner, 7" x 12-1/2"
EX $11 **NM** $20 **MIP** $40

Mickey Mouse Club Newsreel with Sound, 1950s, Mattel, 4" x 4-1/2" x 9" tall, orange box, plastic projector w/two short filmstrips, record, cardboard screen, cartoons "Touchdown Mickey" and "No Sail"
EX $100 **NM** $170 **MIP** $300

Mickey Mouse Club Rhythm Makers Set, Emenee
EX $100 **NM** $200 **MIP** $350

Mickey Mouse Colorforms Set, 1976, Colorforms, 8" x 12-1/2" x 1", Spirit of '76
EX $10 **NM** $30 **MIP** $75

Mickey Mouse Dart Gun Target, 1930s, Marks Brothers, 10" target, dart gun and suction darts
EX $125 **NM** $250 **MIP** $400

Mickey Mouse Dinner Set, 1930s, Empresa Electro, china, 2" creamer, 3-4-1/2" plates and 3-5" plates, 7" long dish, two oval platters
EX $350 **NM** $500 **MIP** $750

Mickey Mouse Dominoes, Halsam, Mickey and Pluto on dominoes
EX $80 **NM** $100 **MIP** $180

Mickey Mouse Drum, 1930s, Ohio Art, 6" diameter
EX $200 **NM** $350 **MIP** $500

Mickey Mouse Electric Casting Set, 1930s, Home Foundary, 9-1/2" x 16" x 2"
EX $125 **NM** $200 **MIP** $400

Mickey Mouse Fire Engine, Sun Rubber, 7" long, rubber, push toy
EX $75 **NM** $150 **MIP** $275

Mickey Mouse Fire Truck with Figure, Sun Rubber, 2-1/2" x 6-1/2" x 4", Mickey driving and mold-in image of Donald standing on the back holding onto his helmet
EX $75 **NM** $150 **MIP** $275

Mickey Mouse Jack-In-the-Box, 1970s, 5-1/2" square tin litho box shows Mickey, Pluto, Donald and Goofy, Mickey pops out
EX $25 **NM** $50 **MIP** $100

Mickey Mouse Lionel Circus Train, 1935, Lionel, five cars w/Mickey, 30" train, 84 inches of track, circus tent, Sunoco station, truck, tickets, Mickey composition statue
EX $5000 **NM** $7500 **MIP** $10000

Mickey Mouse Lionel Circus Train Handcar, Lionel, metal, 9" long w/6" tall composition/rubber figures of Mickey and Minnie
EX $600 **NM** $1000 **MIP** $1500

Mickey Mouse Magic Slate, 1950s, Watkins-Strathmore, 8-1/2" x 14" tall
EX $15 **NM** $30 **MIP** $90

Mickey Mouse Marbles, Monarch, marbles and Mickey bag, on card
EX $10 **NM** $20 **MIP** $60

Mickey Mouse Mechanical Pencil, 1930s, head of Mickey on one end and decal of Mickey walking on other side of pencil
EX $100 **NM** $175 **MIP** $300

Mickey Mouse Mechanical Robot, Gabriel
EX $70 **NM** $125 **MIP** $150

Mickey Mouse Mousegetar, 1960s, 10" x 30" x 2-1/2" black plastic
EX $40 **NM** $85 **MIP** $175

Mickey Mouse Movie Projector, 1934, Keystone, 5-1/2" x 11-1/2" x 11" tall for 8mm movies
EX $275 **NM** $500 **MIP** $800

Mickey Mouse Movie-Fun Shows, 1940s, Mastercraft, 7-1/2" square by 4" deep, animated action movies
EX $106 **NM** $212 **MIP** $325

Mickey Mouse Musical Money Box, 1970s, 3" x 6", tin box w/Mickey, Pluto, Donald and Goofy
EX $30 **NM** $55 **MIP** $90

Mickey Mouse Old Timers Fire Engine, 1980s, Matsudaya, red, tin and plastic fire truck w/Mickey at the wheel
EX $40 **NM** $70 **MIP** $125

Mickey Mouse Picture Gun, 1950s, Stephens, 6-1/2" x 9-1/2" x 3", metal, lights to show filmstrips
EX $65 **NM** $125 **MIP** $250

Mickey Mouse Play Tiles, 1964, Halsam, 336 tiles
EX $15 **NM** $25 **MIP** $50

Mickey Mouse Print Shop Set, 1930s, Fulton Specialty, 6-1/2" x 6-1/2", ink pad, stamper, metal tweezers, wooden tray
EX $125 **NM** $250 **MIP** $350

Mickey Mouse Pull Toy, Toy Kraft, 7" x 22" x 8" tall, horse cart drawn by wooden horses
EX $450 **NM** $600 **MIP** $1100

Mickey Mouse Pull Toy, 1935, N.N. Hill Brass, 14" tall, wood and metal
EX $250 **NM** $400 **MIP** $650

Mickey Mouse Puppet Forms, 1960s, Colorforms
EX $10 **NM** $25 **MIP** $60

Mickey Mouse Riding Toy, 1930s, Mengel, 6" x 17" x 16" tall
EX $800 **NM** $1200 **MIP** $1750

Mickey Mouse Rodeo Rider, 1980s, Matsudaya, plastic wind-up, cowboy Mickey rides a bucking bronco
EX $25 **NM** $45 **MIP** $75

Mickey Mouse Rolykin, Marx, 1-1/2" tall, ball bearing action
EX $12 **NM** $20 **MIP** $70

Mickey Mouse Rub 'N Play Magic Transfer Set, 1978, Colorforms
EX $15 **NM** $30 **MIP** $80

Mickey Mouse Safety Blocks, 1930s, Halsam, nine blocks
EX $175 **NM** $300 **MIP** $450

Mickey Mouse Sand Pail, 1938, Ohio Art, 6" tall, tin, Mickey, Donald and Goofy playing golf
EX $125 **NM** $225 **MIP** $400

Mickey Mouse Sand Pail, 1938, Ohio Art, 3" tall, tin
EX $80 **NM** $150 **MIP** $300

Mickey Mouse Sand Shovel, Ohio Art, 10" long, tin
EX $35 **NM** $70 **MIP** $175

Mickey Mouse Saxophone, 1930s, 16" tall
EX $150 **NM** $250 **MIP** $400

Mickey Mouse Scissors, Disney, 3" long, child's scissors w/Mickey figure
EX $20 **NM** $35 **MIP** $100

Mickey Mouse Serving Tray, 1960s, 11" diameter, tin
EX $11 **NM** $35 **MIP** $70

Mickey Mouse Sewing Cards, 1978, Colorforms, 7-1/2" x 12" cut-out card designs of Mickey, Minnie, Pluto, Clarabelle, Donald Duck and Horace
EX $10 **NM** $20 **MIP** $85

Mickey Mouse Sled, 1930s, Flexible Flyer, 18" x 30" x 6" tall, wood
EX $800 **NM** $1200 **MIP** $2000

Mickey Mouse Squeeze Toy, 1950s, Dell, rubber, Mickey as hitchhiking hobo
EX $35 **NM** $75 **MIP** $160

Mickey Mouse Squeeze Toy, 1950s, Sun Rubber, 10" tall, rubber
EX $25 **NM** $50 **MIP** $110

Mickey Mouse Squeeze Toy, 1960s, Dell, 8" tall
EX $15 **NM** $30 **MIP** $70

Mickey Mouse Stamp Pad, 1930s, 3" long
EX $75 **NM** $150 **MIP** $250

Mickey Mouse Steamboat, 1988, Matsudaya, wind-up plastic steamboat w/Mickey as Steamboat Willie, runs on floor as smokestacks go up and down, box says "60 Years w/You"
EX $30 **NM** $60 **MIP** $135

Mickey Mouse Tea Set, Wolverine, plastic
EX $50 **NM** $175 **MIP** $175

Mickey Mouse Tea Set, 1930s, 3" saucer, 2" pitcher, 2-1/2" sugar bowl each piece shows Mickey and Minnie in a rowboat
EX $125 **NM** $250 **MIP** $350

Mickey and Minnie Mouse

Mickey Mouse Tractor, Sun Rubber, 5" long, rubber
EX $85 **NM** $200 **MIP** $400

Mickey Mouse Tricycle Toy, 1932, Steiff, 8-1/2" x 7", wood and metal frame, action movement
EX $1500 **NM** $3300 **MIP** $5000

Mickey Mouse Twirling Tail Toy, 1950s, Marx, 3" x 5-1/2" x 5-1/2" tall, w/a built-in key, metal tail spins around as the toy vibrates
EX $120 **NM** $225 **MIP** $400

Mickey Mouse Utensils, 1947, Wm. Rogers and Son, 6" fork and 5-1/2" spoon
EX $75 **NM** $100 **MIP** $185

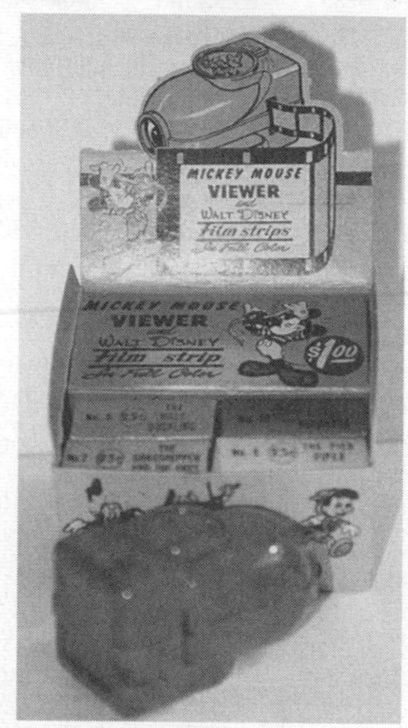

Mickey Mouse Viewer, 1940s, Craftsmen's Guild, film viewer w/12 films
EX $85 **NM** $150 **MIP** $300

Mickey Mouse Wash Machine, Ohio Art, 8" tin litho w/Mickey and Minnie Mouse pictured doing their wash
EX $150 **NM** $350 **MIP** $550

Mickey Mouse Water Globes, 1970s, 3" x 4-1/2" x 5" tall, three dimensional plastic figures of Mickey seated w/a plastic water globe between his legs
EX $25 **NM** $50 **MIP** $150

Mickey Mouse Watering Can, 1938, Ohio Art, 6" tin litho
EX $100 **NM** $175 **MIP** $325

Mickey Mouse Wind-Up Musical Toy, 1970s, Illco, 6" tall, plays "Lullaby and Goodnight," 3-D figure of Mickey in red pants and yellow shirt
EX $25 **NM** $35 **MIP** $75

Mickey Mouse Wind-Up Toy, 1978, Gabriel, plastic transparent figure of Mickey w/visible metal gears
EX $10 **NM** $20 **MIP** $60

Mickey Mouse Wind-Up Trike, 1960s, Korean, tin litho trike w/plastic Mickey w/flag and balloon on handle, bell on back
EX $100 **NM** $175 **MIP** $300

Mickey Mouse Yarn Sewing Kit, 1930s, Marks Bros., seven cards, yarn, needle
EX $40 **NM** $165 **MIP** $300

Mickey's Air Mail Plane, 1940s, Sun Rubber, 3-1/2" x 6" long, 5" wingspan, rubber
EX $150 **NM** $300 **MIP** $500

Minnie Mouse Car, 1979, Matchbox
EX $5 **NM** $15 **MIP** $45

Minnie Mouse Choo-Choo Train Pull Toy, 1940s, Linemar, 3" x 8-1/2" x 7" tall, green metal base and green wooden wheels
EX $125 **NM** $250 **MIP** $450

Minnie Mouse Hand Puppet, 1940s, 11" tall, white on red polka-dot, fabric hard cover and a pair of black and white felt hands
EX $55 **NM** $135 **MIP** $225

Minnie Mouse Rocker, 1950s, Marx, tin wind-up, rocker moves back and forth w/gravity motion of her head and ears
EX $250 **NM** $480 **MIP** $720

Minnie with Bump-n-Go Action Shopping Cart, 1980s, Illfelder, 4" x 9-1/2" x 11-1/2" tall, plastic, battery operated Minnie pushing cart
EX $30 **NM** $55 **MIP** $80

Mouseketeer Cut-Outs, 1957, Whitman, figures and accessories
EX $60 **NM** $125 **MIP** $200

Mouseketeer Fan Club Typewriter, 1950s, lithographed tin
EX $75 **NM** $125 **MIP** $225

Puzzle, 1930s, Marks Brothers, 10" x 12", Mickey polishing the boiler on his "Mickey Mouse R.R." train engine and Minnie waving from the cab
EX $55 **NM** $110 **MIP** $250

Puzzle, 1957, Whitman, Adventureland, 11" x 15" frame tray; Mickey, Minnie, Donald and his nephew in boat surrounded by jungle beasts
EX $15 **NM** $40 **MIP** $80

Puzzle, 1960s, Jaymar, Pluto's Wash and Scrub Service
EX $15 **NM** $40 **MIP** $80

Spinning Top, 1930s, Fritz Bueschel, 7" diameter, 7" tall, Mickey, Minnie, a nephew, Donald and Horace playing a musical instrument
EX $100 **NM** $175 **MIP** $350

Spinning Top, 1950s, Chein, tin litho, features Mickey in cowboy outfit and other characters
EX $60 **NM** $140 **MIP** $280

WATCH

50 Years with Mickey Wristwatch, 1983, Bradley, small round chrome case, inscription and serial number on back
EX $45 **NM** $85 **MIP** $200

Mickey and Pluto Wristwatch, 1980, Bradley, LCD quartz, black vinyl band
EX $20 **NM** $45 **MIP** $110

Mickey Mouse Pocket Watch, 1930s, Ingersoll, 2" diameter
EX $1200 **NM** $2000 **MIP** $3500

Mickey Mouse Pocket Watch, 1970s, Bradley
EX $50 **NM** $100 **MIP** $250

Mickey Mouse Pocket Watch, 1976, Bradley, 3-1/2" x 4-1/2" x 3/4", Mickey in his Bicentennial outfit
EX $75 **NM** $175 **MIP** $300

Mickey Mouse Pocket Watch, 1988, Lorus, #2202, quartz, small gold bezel, gold chain and clip fob, articulated hands
EX $25 **NM** $50 **MIP** $100

Mickey Mouse Wristwatch, two-gun Mickey, saddle tan western style band
EX $25 **NM** $45 **MIP** $90

Mickey Mouse Wristwatch, 1939, Ingersoll, rectangular w/standard second hand between Mickey's legs
EX $225 **NM** $425 **MIP** $900

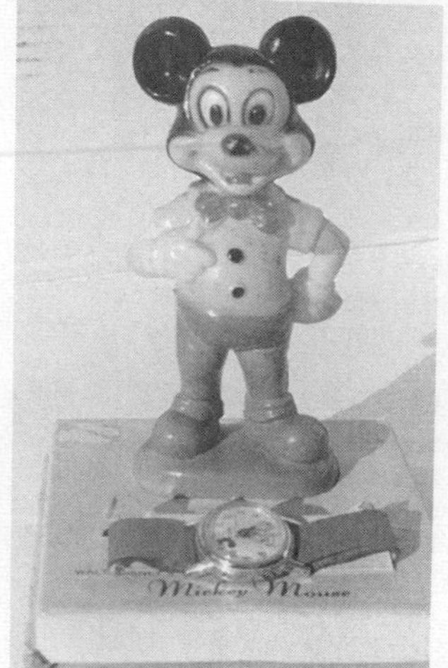

Mickey Mouse Wristwatch, 1958, Timex, electric
EX $140 **NM** $300 **MIP** $550

Mickey Mouse Wristwatch, 1960s, Timex, large round case, stainless back, articulated hands, red vinyl band
EX $50 **NM** $80 **MIP** $160

Mickey Mouse Wristwatch, 1970s, Bradley, white plastic case, watch on pendant, bubble crystal, articulated hands, gold chain
EX $25 **NM** $60 **MIP** $135

Mickey Mouse Wristwatch, 1970s, Bradley, 2-1/2" x 6" x 2-1/2", plastic case, white dial w/Mickey playing tennis, the second hand has a tennis ball on the end of it
EX $35 **NM** $75 **MIP** $175

Mickey Mouse Wristwatch, 1978, Bradley, commemorative edition
EX $65 **NM** $130 **MIP** $300

Mickey Mouse Wristwatch, 1983, Bradley, medium black octagonal case, articulated hands, no numbers on face, in plastic window box
EX $25 **NM** $260 **MIP** $400

Mickey Mouse Wristwatch, 1984, Bradley, medium white case, articulated hands, black face, sweep seconds, white vinyl band, in plastic window box
EX $20 **NM** $40 **MIP** $80

Minnie Mouse Wristwatch, 1958, Timex, small round chrome case, stainless back, articulated hands, yellow vinyl band
EX $75 NM $150 MIP $275

Minnie Mouse Wristwatch, 1978, Bradley, gold case, sweep seconds, red vinyl band, articulated hands
EX $16 NM $35 MIP $70

Mighty Mouse

ACCESSORIES

Charm Bracelet, 1950s, brass charms of Gandy Goose, Terry Bear, Mighty Mouse and other Terrytoon characters
EX $75 NM $125 MIP $200

Mighty Mouse Sneakers, 1960s, Randy Co., children's, graphics on box, picture on sneakers
EX $75 NM $125 MIP $200

DOLL

Mighty Mouse Doll, 1942, rubber head, yellow suit w/red cape
EX $750 NM $1000 MIP $1350

Mighty Mouse Doll, 1942, rubber head, wearing red suit
EX $750 NM $1100 MIP $1500

Mighty Mouse Doll, 1950s, Ideal, 14" tall, stuffed, cloth
EX $50 NM $100 MIP $250

FIGURES

Mighty Mouse Figure, 1950s, 9-1/2" rubber, squeaks
EX $20 NM $60 MIP $150

Mighty Mouse Figure, 1977, Dakin, hard and soft vinyl figure
EX $30 NM $60 MIP $125

Mighty Mouse Figure, 1978, Dakin, Fun Farm
EX $35 NM $70 MIP $135

GAME

Mighty Mouse Ball Game, 1981, Ja-Ru
EX $5 NM $12 MIP $50

TOY

Mighty Mouse Cinema Viewer, 1979, Fleetwood, w/four strips
EX $10 NM $30 MIP $75

Mighty Mouse Dynamite Dasher, 1981, Takara
EX $50 NM $110 MIP $275

Mighty Mouse Flashlight, 1979, Dyno, 3-1/2" figural light
EX $50 NM $80 MIP $120

Mighty Mouse Hit the Claw Target Set, Parks
EX $100 NM $150 MIP $275

Mighty Mouse Make-a-Face Sheet, 1958, Towne, w/dials to change face parts
EX $40 NM $80 MIP $160

Mighty Mouse Mighty Money, 1979, Fleetwood
EX $20 NM $55 MIP $85

Mighty Mouse Money Press, 1981, Ja-Ru, stampers, pads and money
EX $8 NM $15 MIP $30

Mighty Mouse Movie Viewer, 1980, Chemtoy
EX $10 NM $15 MIP $50

Mighty Mouse Picture Play Lite, 1983, Janex
EX $8 NM $15 MIP $40

Mighty Mouse Wallet, 1978, Larami
EX $15 NM $35 MIP $80

Puzzle, tray puzzle; Mighty Mouse and his TV Pals
EX $20 NM $35 MIP $80

Puzzle, 1979, Fleetwood, Mighty Mouse/Heckle and Jeckle
EX $45 NM $90 MIP $140

WATCH

Mighty Mouse Wristwatch, 1979, Bradley, chrome case
EX $40 NM $60 MIP $100

Miscellaneous Characters

ACCESSORIES

Amy Carter Paper Dolls, 1970s, Toy Factory, 14" cardboard doll w/accessories
EX $15 NM $30 MIP $60

Holly Hobbie Wristwatch, 1982, Bradley, small gold tone case, base metal back, yellow plastic band
EX $5 NM $10 MIP $50

Jimmy Carter Radio, peanut-shaped transistor radio
EX $20 NM $45 MIP $125

Kennedy Kards, 1960s, red, white, and blue playing cards w/cartoon artwork
EX $10 NM $20 MIP $50

Little King Lucky Safety Card, 1953, New York Journal, 2" x 4" cards, Little King warns of safety
EX $15 NM $30 MIP $75

Mr. Potato Head Ice Pops, 1950s, Hasbro, plastic molds for freezing treats, in box
EX $16 NM $35 MIP $80

Sandra Dee Paper Dolls, 1959, Saalfield, two cardboard dolls w/outfits
EX $30 NM $75 MIP $150

Tuesday Weld Paper Dolls, 1960, Saalfield, two cardboard dolls w/outfits
EX $30 NM $60 MIP $135

Uncle Don's "Puzzy and Sizzy" Membership Card, 1950s
EX $20 NM $50 MIP $75

Willie Whopper Pencil Case, 1930s, green w/illustrations of Willie, Pirate and his gal
EX $80 NM $125 MIP $200

BANK

Sir Reginald Play-N-Save Bank, 1960s, 7" tall plastic lion and hunter, on a 15" green plastic base, the hunter fires the coin into the lion's mouth
EX $45 NM $125 MIP $180

DOLL

Hardy Boys Dolls, 1979, Kenner, 12" tall Joe Hardy (Shaun Cassidy) or Frank Hardy (Parker Stevenson)
EX $20 NM $40 MIP $90

FIGURES

Bruce Lee Figure, 1986, Largo, 8" w/weapon
EX $20 NM $40 MIP $100

Diamond Jim Figure, 1930s, 5-1/2" tall
EX $30 NM $80 MIP $160

George Bush Figure, 7" tall
EX $8 NM $20 MIP $40

Lyndon Johnson Figure, 1960s, Remco
EX $17 NM $35 MIP $60

Patton Figure, Excel Toy, poseable doll w/clothing and accessories
EX $20 NM $40 MIP $80

Prince Charles of Wales Figure, 1982, Goldberger, 13" tall, dressed in palace guard uniform
EX $18 NM $35 MIP $70

Sylvester Stallone Rambo Figure, 1986, 18" tall, poseable figure
EX $10 NM $20 MIP $40

TOY

Bonzo Scooter Toy, 7" scooter w/6" Bonzo, wind-up
EX $185 NM $400 MIP $600

Daktari Puzzle, 1967, Whitman, 100 pieces
EX $10 NM $30 MIP $100

Evel Knievel Stunt Stadium, 1974, Ideal, large vinyl case w/accessories
EX $50 NM $100 MIP $200

Jimmy Carter Wind-Up Walking Peanut, 5" tall
EX $10 NM $22 MIP $50

Joan Palooka Stringless Marionette, 1952, Nat'l Mask and Puppet, 12-1/2" tall "daughter of Joe Palooka" doll comes w/pink blanket and birth certificate
EX $75 NM $110 MIP $235

Komic Kamera Film Viewer Set, 1950s, 5" long, Dick Tracy, Little Orphan Annie, Terry and the Pirates and The Lone Ranger
EX $40 NM $100 MIP $175

Mr. and Mrs. Potato Head Set, 1960s, Hasbro, cars, boats, shopping trailer, etc.
EX $25 NM $55 MIP $110

Mr. Potato Head Frankie Frank, 1966, Hasbro, companion to Mr. Potato Head, w/accessories
EX $20 NM $40 MIP $90

Miscellaneous Characters

Mr. Potato Head Frenchy Fry, 1966, Hasbro, companion to Mr. Potato Head, w/accessories
EX $20 **NM** $40 **MIP** $90

Red Ranger Ride 'Em Cowboy, 1930s, Wyandotte, tin wind-up rocker
EX $350 **NM** $500 **MIP** $750

Ringling Bros. and Barnum and Bailey Circus Play Set, 1970s, vinyl, w/animals, trapeze personnel, clowns and assorted circus equipment
EX $25 **NM** $50 **MIP** $125

Rin-Tin-Tin Magic Erasable Pictures, 1955, Transogram
EX $75 **NM** $135 **MIP** $260

Space Ghost Puzzle, 1967, Whitman
EX $20 **NM** $55 **MIP** $110

Moon Mullins

ACCESSORIES

Moon Mullins and Kayo Toothbrush Holder, 4" tall, bisque
EX $100 **NM** $150 **MIP** $250

Moon Mullins Playstone Funnies Mold Set, 1940s
EX $40 **NM** $80 **MIP** $160

FIGURE

Moon Mullins Figure Set, bisque, Uncle Willie, Kayo, Moon Mullins and Emmy, 2-1/4" to 3-1/2"
EX $150 **NM** $300 **MIP** $550

TOY

Moon Mullins and Kayo Railroad Handcar Toy, 1930s, Marx, 6" long, wind-up, both figures bendable arms and legs
EX $475 **NM** $750 **MIP** $1300

Puzzle, 1930s, 9-1/2" x 14", Featured Funnies
EX $20 **NM** $60 **MIP** $140

Mr. Magoo

ACCESSORIES

Mr. Magoo Drinking Glass, 1962, 5-1/2" tall
EX $10 **NM** $25 **MIP** $50

DOLL

Mr. Magoo Doll, 1962, Ideal, 5" tall, vinyl head w/cloth body
EX $75 **NM** $125 **MIP** $250

Mr. Magoo Doll, 1970, Ideal, 12" tall
EX $50 **NM** $75 **MIP** $120

FIGURES

Mr. Magoo Figure, Dakin, 7" tall
EX $40 **NM** $90 **MIP** $180

TOY

Mr. Magoo Car, 1961, Hubley, 7-1/2" x 9" long, metal, battery-operated
EX $350 **NM** $450 **MIP** $700

Mr. Magoo Hand Puppet, 1960s, vinyl head, cloth body
EX $35 **NM** $80 **MIP** $145

Mr. Magoo Puzzle, 1978, Warren, frame tray
EX $10 **NM** $20 **MIP** $50

Mr. Magoo Soaky, 1960s, Palmolive, 10" tall, vinyl and plastic
EX $20 **NM** $50 **MIP** $90

Mutt and Jeff

BANK

Mutt and Jeff Bank, 5" tall, cast iron, two piece construction held together by screw in the back
EX $150 **NM** $200 **MIP** $325

BOOK

Big Little Book, Whitman, Mutt and Jeff, #1113
EX $35 **NM** $75 **MIP** $140

Mutt and Jeff Cartoon Book, 1910, Ball Publications, 68 pages
EX $300 **NM** $500 **MIP** $900

DOLL

Mutt and Jeff Dolls, 1920s, 8" x 6-1/2" tall, composition hands and heads w/heavy cast iron feet, movable arms and legs, fabric clothing; pair
EX $225 **NM** $400 **MIP** $750

FIGURES

Mutt and Jeff Figures, 1911, A. Steinhardt and Bros, ceramic, w/a coin inserted into base; pair
EX $120 **NM** $225 **MIP** $425

Nightmare Before Christmas

ACCESSORIES

Beach Towel, Fashion Victim
EX $22 **NM** $29 **MIP** $40

Brass Keychain, Disney, Jack Skellington's Tombstone
EX $3 **NM** $8 **MIP** $20

Buttons, set of 12 featuring logo, characters, etc.
EX $15 **NM** $20 **MIP** $75

Comforter, Wamsutta, twin size featuring Lock, Shock and Barrel
EX $45 **NM** $55 **MIP** $100

Drawstring Bag, Jack Skellington on front
EX $10 **NM** $15 **MIP** $25

Jack Soaky, glow head
EX $20 **NM** $35 **MIP** $75

Mug, Selandia, 16 oz. acrylic mug w/floating snowflakes and glitter
EX $5 **NM** $10 **MIP** $30

Mug, Selandia, 10 oz. acrylic mug w/floating snowflakes and glitter
EX $5 **NM** $10 **MIP** $30

Mylar Balloons, Anagram, five variations, each
EX $10 **NM** $15 **MIP** $35

Pencil, Whirly Sally or Whirly Jack
EX $4 **NM** $10 **MIP** $25

Purse, multi-compartment w/mirror
EX $10 **NM** $25 **MIP** $75

PVC Figure on Drinking Straws, Jack or Sally
EX $3 **NM** $7 **MIP** $10

Sunglasses, Jet Vision Limited
EX $12 **NM** $15 **MIP** $30

Tumbler, Selandia, 7 oz., acrylic
EX $10 **NM** $13 **MIP** $20

BOOK

Pop-Up Book
EX $20 **NM** $45 **MIP** $90

CLOTHING

Bandanna, Fashion Victim, two styles: Jack or Lock, Shock and Barrel
EX $5 **NM** $15 **MIP** $45

Baseball Caps, Fashion Victim, three styles: Fishbone w/metal keychain; Lock, Shock and Barrel; or Jack "Bone Daddy"
EX $8 **NM** $10 **MIP** $20

Boxer Shorts, Stanley DeSantis, Lock, Shock and Barrel or Jack styles; cotton
EX $6 **NM** $8 **MIP** $12

Silk Necktie, many styles/patterns
EX $15 **NM** $22 **MIP** $45

Vest, Fashion Victim, Lock, Shock and Barrel or Jack styles
EX $12 **NM** $15 **MIP** $40

DOLL

Lock, Shock, and Barrel Dolls, Applause, set of three; 6" cloth and vinyl dolls
EX $25 **NM** $60 **MIP** $120

Oogie Boogie Doll, Applause, 16"; makes farting noise when squeezed
EX $15 **NM** $40 **MIP** $90

Sally Doll, Hasbro, removable limbs
EX $100 **NM** $250 **MIP** $425

Santa Claus Doll, Applause, 10" plush
EX $10 **NM** $30 **MIP** $60

Santa Puppet Doll, Hasbro
EX $25 **NM** $50 **MIP** $85

Talking Jack Doll, Hasbro
EX $50 **NM** $130 **MIP** $360

FIGURES

Glow Oogie Boogie Figure, Applause, PVC figure
EX $7 **NM** $25 **MIP** $45

Jack Figure, Hasbro, bendy on card
EX $6 **NM** $20 **MIP** $40

Jack in Coffin Figure, Applause, 12"
EX $30 **NM** $100 **MIP** $325

Lock, Shock and Barrel Figures, Applause, set of three, 3" PVC figures
EX $10 **NM** $30 **MIP** $60

CHARACTER TOYS

Magic Action Figures, Applause, set of three; 4" figures has its own action when rolled
EX $20 NM $30 MIP $60

Mayor Figure, Hasbro, bendy on card
EX $10 NM $30 MIP $60

Sally Figure, Hasbro, bendy on card
EX $15 NM $40 MIP $80

Sally in Coffin Figure, Applause, 12"
EX $125 NM $250 MIP $500

Santa Jack Figure, Hasbro, bendy on card
EX $6 NM $12 MIP $25

MISCELLANEOUS

Cardboard Store Display, Applause, over 6" wide
EX $150 NM $200 MIP $300

Cookie Jar, Treasure Craft, ceramic; Jack on Tombstone
EX $100 NM $250 MIP $400

Handheld Video Game, Tiger
EX $25 NM $35 MIP $80

Kaleidoscope, C. Bennett Scopes
EX $20 NM $35 MIP $90

Mayor Wind-Up Music Box, Schmid, head spins while music plays "What's This?"
EX $60 NM $125 MIP $225

Pin, Oopsa Daisy, several character styles, pewter
EX $10 NM $18 MIP $30

Rhinestone Pin, Oopsa Daisy, red stones featuring Jack Skellington
EX $40 NM $65 MIP $100

Rhinestone Pin, white stones featuring Jack Skellington
EX $30 NM $55 MIP $85

Sky Floater Kite, Spectra Star
EX $5 NM $15 MIP $50

Temporary Tattoos, US Kids
EX $2 NM $4 MIP $10

Wooden Ornaments, Kurt S. Adler, set of 10; 4" to 6" tall; individually packaged
EX $20 NM $65 MIP $80

Wristwatch, Timex, six styles available, each
EX $10 NM $40 MIP $90

Yo-Yo, Spectra Star
EX $10 NM $25 MIP $45

PAPER GOODS

Bionic Airwalker Balloon, Anagram, featuring Jack Skellington; over 7" tall
EX $15 NM $20 MIP $50

Bookmarks, OSP Publishing, set of eight styles including wallet cards
EX $10 NM $15 MIP $30

Gift Bags, Cleo, five styles available
EX $6 NM $10 MIP $20

Greeting Cards, set of six featuring various characters
EX $15 NM $35 MIP $85

Notepad, Beach, 75-sheet pad featuring Lock, Shock and Barrel
EX $3 NM $5 MIP $20

Partyware, Beach, 65 pieces
EX $14 NM $16 MIP $35

Postcard Book, 30 full-color postcards
EX $5 NM $20 MIP $60

Stickers, Gibson, featuring movie characters
EX $2 NM $6 MIP $15

Video Release Poster, Touchstone, 24" x 36"
EX $15 NM $50 MIP $75

Peanuts

ACCESSORIES

Lucy Candlestick Holder, Hallmark, 7-1/4" figural composition
EX $15 NM $21 MIP $60

Snoopy Snippers Scissors, 1975, Mattel, plastic, Model No. 7410
EX $30 NM $45 MIP $70

Snoopy Toothbrush, 1972, Kenner, Snoopy on doghouse holder, Model No. 30301
EX $15 NM $30 MIP $50

Vaporizer/Humidifier, Milton Bradley, plastic, 13" x 16", Snoopy on doghouse
EX $45 NM $75 MIP $110

BANK

Peanuts Banks, 1970, United Features, set of five
EX $60 NM $100 MIP $200

Snoopy Bank, 1968, United Feature, 7" figural bank
EX $15 NM $35 MIP $90

BOOKS

Peanuts Projects, 1963, Determined, activity book
EX $30 NM $45 MIP $75

Peanuts Trace and Color, 1960s, Saalfield, five book set, Model No. 6122
EX $35 NM $50 MIP $125

Peanuts: A Book to Color, Saalfield, cover features Snoopy and Charlie Brown on skateboard, Model No. 4629
EX $25 NM $75 MIP $150

Speak Up, Charlie Brown Talking Storybook, 1971, Mattel, cardboard w/vinyl pages, Model No. 4812
EX $75 NM $150 MIP $200

COSTUMES

Charlie Brown Costume, Collegeville, w/mask
EX $15 NM $30 MIP $100

Snoopy as Flying Ace Costume, Collegeville, w/mask
EX $15 NM $30 MIP $100

Snoopy Costume, Collegeville, w/mask
EX $12 NM $25 MIP $100

Woodstock Costume, Collegeville, w/mask
EX $12 NM $25 MIP $75

DOLL

Peppermint Patty Doll, 14" tall, cloth
EX $10 NM $20 MIP $60

Tub Time Snoopy Doll, 1980s, Knickerbocker, rubber, Model No. 0539
EX $15 NM $35 MIP $70

DOLLS

Charlie Brown Doll, 1958, Hungerford Plastics, 8-1/2" plastic
EX $60 NM $125 MIP $250

Charlie Brown Doll, 1970s, Determined, plastic; wearing baseball gear
EX $60 NM $100 MIP $200

Charlie Brown Doll, 1976, Ideal, removable clothing, Model No. 1412-6
EX $30 NM $70 MIP $140

Charlie Brown Pocket Doll, 1968, Boucher, 7", Model No. 800
EX $20 NM $32 MIP $100

Dolls, 1960s, Simon Simple, 7-1/2", Charlie Brown, Lucy, or Linus
EX $20 NM $50 MIP $100

Dress Me Belle Doll, 1983, Knickerbocker, Belle wearing pink dress w/blue dots, Model No. 1581
EX $15 NM $40 MIP $70

Dress Me Snoopy Doll, 1983, Knickerbocker, Snoopy wearing blue jeans and red/yellow shirt, Model No. 1580
EX $15 NM $40 MIP $70

Linus Doll, 1958, Hungerford Plastics, 8-1/2" plastic
EX $50 NM $100 MIP $225

Linus Doll, 1976, Ideal, removable clothing, Model No. 1414-2
EX $55 NM $100 MIP $215

Linus Pocket Doll, 1968, Boucher, 7", Model No. 801
EX $15 NM $25 MIP $60

Lucy Doll, 1958, Hungerford Plastics, 8-1/2" plastic
EX $50 NM $90 MIP $175

Lucy Doll, 1976, Ideal, removable clothing, Model No. 1411-8
EX $30 NM $60 MIP $125

Lucy Pocket Doll, 1968, Boucher, 7" open mouth, Model No. 802
EX $15 NM $25 MIP $50

Lucy Pocket Doll, 1968, Boucher, 7" smiling, Model No. 802
EX $15 NM $30 MIP $60

Peppermint Patty Doll, 1976, Ideal, removable clothing, Model No. 1413-4
EX $30 NM $45 MIP $70

Pigpen Doll, 1958, Hungerford Plastics, 8-1/2" plastic
EX $65 NM $100 MIP $175

Playmate Snoopy Doll, 1971, Determined, 6" plush, Model No. 819
EX $10 NM $20 MIP $70

Sally Doll, 1958, Hungerford Plastics, 6-1/2" plastic
EX $65 NM $100 MIP $175

Schroeder and Piano Doll, 1958, Hungerford Plastics, 7" plastic
EX $175 NM $275 MIP $450

Snoopy as Astronaut Doll, Knickerbocker, 5" vinyl
EX $75 NM $150 MIP $225

Snoopy as Astronaut Doll, 1969, Determined, 9", rubber head, plastic body, Model No. 808
EX $75 **NM** $150 **MIP** $225

Snoopy as Astronaut Doll, 1977, Ideal, 14" plush w/helmet and space suit, Model No. 1441-5
EX $200 **NM** $300 **MIP** $400

Snoopy as Magician Doll, 1977, Ideal, 14" plush w/cape, hat, and mustache, Model No. 1448-0
EX $110 **NM** $180 **MIP** $250

Snoopy as Rock Star Doll, 1977, Ideal, 14" plush w/wig, shoes and microphone, Model No. 1446-4
EX $115 **NM** $200 **MIP** $280

Snoopy Autograph Doll, 1971, Determined, 10-1/2", Model No. 838
EX $20 **NM** $25 **MIP** $60

Snoopy Doll, Ideal, 7" rag doll
EX $8 **NM** $20 **MIP** $60

Snoopy Doll, 1958, Hungerford Plastics, 7" plastic
EX $60 **NM** $100 **MIP** $225

Snoopy Doll, 1970s, Determined, plastic jointed
EX $25 **NM** $40 **MIP** $90

Snoopy Doll, 1971, Determined, 15" plush, felt eyes, eyebrows, and nose; red tag around neck
EX $25 **NM** $45 **MIP** $95

Snoopy Paper Dolls, 1976, Determined, w/10 outfits
EX $20 **NM** $40 **MIP** $75

Snoopy Pocket Doll, 1968, Boucher, 7" w/Flying Ace outfit, Model No. 803
EX $20 **NM** $35 **MIP** $80

GAME

Lucy Tea Party Game, 1972, Milton Bradley, Model No. 4129
EX $25 **NM** $50 **MIP** $100

Snoopy Snack Attack Game, 1980, Gabriel, Model No. 70345
EX $25 **NM** $40 **MIP** $75

Snoopy's Pound-A-Ball Game, 1980, Gabriel/Child Guidance, Model No. 51702
EX $35 **NM** $65 **MIP** $90

Table Top Snoopy Game, 1980s, Nintendo, Model No. SM-73
EX $65 **NM** $125 **MIP** $160

Tabletop Hockey, 1972, Munro Games
EX $65 **NM** $125 **MIP** $160

Tell Us a Riddle, Snoopy Game, 1974, Colorforms, Model No. 2397
EX $20 **NM** $55 **MIP** $100

MUSIC BOX

Linus Music Box, Anri, wood, Linus in pumpkin patch on cover, plays "Who Can I Turn To?"
EX $100 **NM** $150 **MIP** $200

Lucy and Charlie Brown Music Box, 1971, Anri, 4", each character beside large mushroom, plays "Rose Garden", Model No. 81973
EX $100 **NM** $175 **MIP** $250

Lucy Music Box, 1969, Anri, 6-1/2", Lucy behind psychiatrist booth, plays "Try to Remember", Model No. 819400
EX $100 **NM** $250 **MIP** $325

Lucy Music Box, 1971, Anri, 5", Lucy w/mushrooms on ground, plays "Love Story", Model No. 81981
EX $100 **NM** $250 **MIP** $325

Peanuts Music Box, 1972, Schmid, 8" wooden ferris wheel box/bank, plays "Spinning Wheel", Model No. 277408
EX $175 **NM** $600 **MIP** $375

Peanuts Music Box, 1984, Schmid, 8", ceramic, characters revolve around Christmas tree, plays "Joy to the World", Model No. 253724
EX $100 **NM** $200 **MIP** $325

Peanuts Music Box, 1985, Schmid, ceramic, characters piled on car, "Clown Capers," plays "Be a Clown", Model No. 289052
EX $85 **NM** $120 **MIP** $200

Schroeder Music Box, 1971, Anri, 5", Schroeder at the piano, plays "Beethoven's Emperor's Waltz", Model No. 819030
EX $110 **NM** $150 **MIP** $275

Snoopy as Astronaut Music Box, 1970s, Schmid
EX $25 **NM** $40 **MIP** $100

Snoopy Music Box, 1974, Aviva, 6", Snoopy w/hobo pack w/Woodstock, plays "Born Free"
EX $30 **NM** $45 **MIP** $100

Snoopy Music Box, 1979, Aviva, 8", Snoopy on doghouse shaped box, roof is removable lid, plays "Candy Man", Model No. 214
EX $50 **NM** $90 **MIP** $150

Snoopy Music Box, 1982, Aviva, ceramic heart-shaped base w/Snoopy and Woodstock hugging on top, plays "Love Makes the World Go Round", Model No. 215
EX $30 **NM** $60 **MIP** $100

Snoopy Music Box, 1984, Schmid, 7" ceramic, Snoopy and Woodstock on seesaw, plays "Playmates", Model No. 253709
EX $100 **NM** $125 **MIP** $175

Snoopy Music Box, 1984, Quantasia, ceramic Snoopy and musical note on base, plays "Fur Elise", Model No. 141017
EX $50 **NM** $65 **MIP** $85

Snoopy Music Box, 1985, Quantasia, plastic, Snoopy in boat inside waterglobe, plays "Blue Hawaii", Model No. 141020
EX $20 **NM** $40 **MIP** $75

Snoopy Music Box, 1986, Schmid, 6" ceramic, Snoopy as Lion Tamer, plays "Pussycat, Pussycat", Model No. 289053
EX $60 **NM** $85 **MIP** $150

Snoopy Music Box, 1986, Schmid, 7-1/2" ceramic, Snoopy next to Christmas tree, plays "O, Tannenbaum", Model No. 159101
EX $125 **NM** $175 **MIP** $250

PUZZLES

Puzzle, 1971, Determined, eight-panel cartoon strip, 1,000 pieces, Model No. 711-2
EX $15 **NM** $25 **MIP** $60

Puzzle, 1971, Determined, four "Love Is" scenes, 1,000 pieces, Model No. 711-4
EX $25 **NM** $40 **MIP** $80

Puzzle, 1973, Milton Bradley, Schroeder, Charlie Brown, Snoopy, and Lucy on baseball mound, Model No. 4383-3
EX $10 **NM** $22 **MIP** $60

Puzzle, 1979, Playskool, six pieces, Snoopy leaning on bat, Model No. 230-27
EX $5 **NM** $10 **MIP** $40

RADIOS

Snoopy and Woodstock Radio, 1970s, Determined, plastic, two-dimensional doghouse, Model No. 354
EX $30 **NM** $50 **MIP** $100

Snoopy Bank Radio, 1978, Concept 2000, plastic, Snoopy dancing, Model No. 4442
EX $65 **NM** $100 **MIP** $150

Snoopy Doghouse Radio, 1970s, Determined, plastic
EX $60 **NM** $85 **MIP** $140

Snoopy Hi-Fi Radio, 1977, Determined, three-dimensional Snoopy wearing headphones, plastic, Model No. 405
EX $60 **NM** $125 **MIP** $200

Snoopy Radio, 1970s, Determined, figural radio, Snoopy on green grass, plastic
EX $20 **NM** $40 **MIP** $85

Snoopy Radio, 1975, Determined, plastic two-dimensional, Model No. 351
EX $30 **NM** $65 **MIP** $150

Snoopy Radio, 1977, Determined, plastic square radio w/Snoopy pointing to dial
EX $30 **NM** $65 **MIP** $150

Snoopy, Woodstock, and Charlie Brown Radio, 1970s, Concept 2000, two-dimensional plastic, Model No. 4443
EX $20 **NM** $35 **MIP** $80

Snoopy's Spaceship AM Radio, 1978, Concept 2000, plastic, Model No. 4443
EX $75 **NM** $125 **MIP** $250

TOY

Batter-Up Snoopy Colorforms, 1979, Colorforms
EX $10 **NM** $35 **MIP** $60

Big Quart-O-Snoopy Bubbles, 1970s, Chemtoy
EX $9 **NM** $13 **MIP** $20

Camp Kamp Play Set, 1970s, Child Guidance, rubber camp building w/characters, Model No. 1683
EX $75 **NM** $100 **MIP** $150

Charlie Brown Deluxe View-Master Gift Pak, 1970s, GAF/View-Master, cylindrical container holds seven reels and viewer, Model No. 2380
EX $40 **NM** $75 **MIP** $100

Charlie Brown Nodder, 1960s, Japanese, 5-1/2" tall, bobbing head
EX $125 **NM** $200 **MIP** $350

Charlie Brown Punching Bag, 1970s, Determined
EX $15 **NM** $30 **MIP** $60

Charlie Brown Push Puppet, 1977, Ideal
EX $20 **NM** $45 **MIP** $85

Charlie Brown's All-Star Dugout Play Set, 1970s, Child Guidance, Model No. 1636
EX $20 **NM** $40 **MIP** $75

Charlie Brown's Backyard Play Set, 1970s, Child Guidance
EX $20 **NM** $40 **MIP** $80

Chirping Woodstock, 1977, Aviva, plastic w/electronic sound, Model No. 477
EX $18 **NM** $25 **MIP** $80

Electronic Snoopy Playmate, 1980, Romper Room/Hasbro, Model No. 830
EX $80 **NM** $125 **MIP** $200

Express Station Set, 1977, Aviva, Snoopy riding locomotive, Model No. 988
EX $40 **NM** $60 **MIP** $100

Joe Cool Punching Bag, 1976, Ideal, Model No. 5530-1
EX $20 **NM** $30 **MIP** $60

Joe Cool Push Puppet, 1977, Ideal
EX $20 **NM** $40 **MIP** $100

Kaleidorama, 1979, Determined, Model No. 4961
EX $20 **NM** $35 **MIP** $65

Lucy Nurse Push Puppet, 1977, Ideal
EX $20 **NM** $35 **MIP** $75

Lucy's Winter Carnival Colorforms, 1973, Colorforms, Model No. 7400
EX $20 **NM** $40 **MIP** $70

Official Peanuts Baseball, 1969, Wilson, illustrated w/characters
EX $40 **NM** $100 **MIP** $150

Parade Drum, 1969, Chein, large tin drum features characters in director's chairs, Model No. 1798
EX $100 **NM** $165 **MIP** $250

Peanuts Deluxe Play Set, 1975, Determined, includes Lucy's psychiatrist booth and three action figures, Model No. 575
EX $100 **NM** $200 **MIP** $300

Peanuts Drum, 1974, Chein, tin, features characters w/instruments, Model No. 1713
EX $85 **NM** $120 **MIP** $200

Peanuts Kindergarten Rhythm Set, 1972, Chein, four percussion instruments, Model No. 327
EX $100 **NM** $160 **MIP** $240

Peanuts Magic Catch Puppets, 1978, Synergistics, four characters w/Velcro balls
EX $10 **NM** $20 **MIP** $60

Peanuts Pelham Puppets, 1979, Pelham/Tiderider, 7"-8" Charlie Brown, Snoopy or Woodstock
EX $45 **NM** $90 **MIP** $180

Peanuts Puppets Display, 1979, Pelham/Tiderider, display theater
EX $350 **NM** $550 **MIP** $800

Peanuts Show Time Finger Puppets, 1977, Ideal, several rubber character puppets, Model No. 5379-3
EX $25 **NM** $35 **MIP** $70

Peanuts Skediddler Clubhouse Set, 1970, Mattel, three rubber skediddlers, Snoopy, Lucy, Charlie Brown, Model No. 3803
EX $125 **NM** $185 **MIP** $275

Peanuts Stackables, 1979, Determined, four hard rubber figures, Model No. 8642
EX $18 **NM** $25 **MIP** $35

Peanuts Tea Set, 1961, one tray, two plates, two cups, four small plates
EX $40 **NM** $60 **MIP** $100

Piano, 1960s, Ely, wood w/characters on top
EX $165 **NM** $275 **MIP** $425

Picture Maker, 1971, Mattel, plastic character stencils, Model No. 4153
EX $45 **NM** $65 **MIP** $90

Push and Play with the Peanuts Gang, 1970s, Child Guidance, plastic w/rubber characters, Model No. 1700
EX $30 **NM** $50 **MIP** $100

Push 'N' Fly Snoopy, 1980, Romper Room/Hasbro, pull toy featuring Snoopy the Flying Ace, Model No. 824
EX $12 **NM** $20 **MIP** $60

Rowing Snoopy, 1981, Mattel, Model No. 3478
EX $20 **NM** $40 **MIP** $90

Schroeder's Piano, 1970s, Child Guidance, Model No. 1701
EX $75 **NM** $150 **MIP** $300

See 'N' Say Snoopy Says, 1969, Mattel, Model No. 4864
EX $40 **NM** $80 **MIP** $125

Snoopy Action Toys, 1977, Aviva, wind-up Snoopy as drummer or boxer
EX $25 **NM** $45 **MIP** $70

Snoopy and Charlie Brown Copter, 1979, Aviva/Hasbro, plastic, Model No. 600
EX $15 **NM** $25 **MIP** $50

Snoopy and his Flyin' Doghouse, 1974, Mattel, Model No. 8263
EX $60 **NM** $100 **MIP** $175

Snoopy Color 'N' Recolor, 1980, Avalon, Model No. 742
EX $30 **NM** $50 **MIP** $80

Snoopy Copter Pull Toy, 1980, Romper Room, sound and action toy, Model No. 822
EX $6 **NM** $10 **MIP** $25

Snoopy Deep Diver Submarine, 1980s, Knickerbocker, plastic, Model No. 0553
EX $35 **NM** $55 **MIP** $70

Snoopy Drive-In Movie Theater, 1975, Kenner, Model No. 39570
EX $95 **NM** $160 **MIP** $300

Snoopy Express, 1977, Aviva, mechanical wind-up train, wood, includes track, tunnel, and signs, Model No. 922
EX $20 **NM** $55 **MIP** $90

Snoopy Express, 1982, Aviva, mechanical wind-up train, plastic, Model No. 70911
EX $20 **NM** $35 **MIP** $50

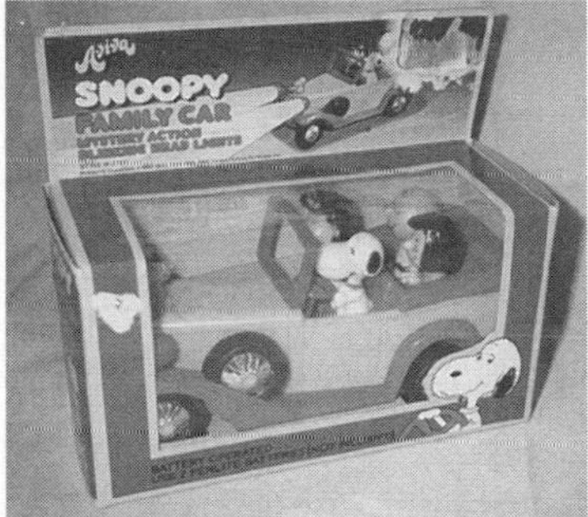

Snoopy Family Car, 1978, Aviva, Model No. 2700
EX $40 **NM** $70 **MIP** $90

Snoopy Gravity Raceway, 1977, Aviva, Model No. 990
EX $40 **NM** $70 **MIP** $120

Snoopy Gyro Cycle, 1982, Aviva/Hasbro, plastic friction toy, Model No. 70440
EX $20 **NM** $50 **MIP** $100

Snoopy High Wire Act, 1973, Monogram/Mattel, Model No. 6661
EX $25 **NM** $45 **MIP** $70

Snoopy in the Music Box, 1969, Mattel, metal jack-in-the-box, Model No. 4747
EX $15 **NM** $30 **MIP** $100

Snoopy is Joe Cool Model Kit, 1971, Monogram/Mattel, Snoopy rides surfboard, Model No. 7502
EX $40 **NM** $80 **MIP** $140

Snoopy Jack-in-the-Box, 1980, Romper Room/Hasbro, plastic doghouse jack-in-the-box, Model No. 818
EX $8 **NM** $15 **MIP** $40

Snoopy Magician Push Puppet, 1977, Ideal
EX $15 **NM** $35 **MIP** $80

Snoopy Marionette, 1979, Pelham/Tiderider, 27", Pelham Puppets, Model No. DP10
EX $300 **NM** $475 **MIP** $700

Snoopy Movie Viewer, 1975, Kenner, Model No. 35900
EX $15 **NM** $25 **MIP** $60

Snoopy Musical Ge-tar, 1969, Mattel, crank handle, Model No. 4715
EX $30 **NM** $60 **MIP** $120

Snoopy Musical Guitar, 1980, Aviva, plastic, crank handle, Model No. 444
EX $15 **NM** $35 **MIP** $70

Snoopy Nodder, 1960s, Japanese, 5-1/2" tall, bobbing head
EX $45 **NM** $100 **MIP** $225

Snoopy Paint-by-Number Set, 1980s, Craft House, 12" x 16"
EX $10 **NM** $20 **MIP** $50

Snoopy Phonograph, 1979, Vanity Fair, features picture of dancing Snoopy, Model No. 66
EX $100 **NM** $130 **MIP** $175

Snoopy Playhouse, 1977, Determined, plastic doghouse w/furniture, Snoopy, and Woodstock, Model No. 120
EX $50 **NM** $80 **MIP** $150

Snoopy Playland, 1978, Aviva, Snoopy in bus and six other characters, Model No. 888
EX $60 **NM** $80 **MIP** $125

Snoopy Radio-Controlled Doghouse, 1980, Aviva, Model No. 988
EX $35 **NM** $60 **MIP** $125

Snoopy Radio-Controlled Fire Engine, 1980, Aviva, w/Woodstock transmitter, Model No. 988
EX $50 **NM** $75 **MIP** $120

Snoopy Sheriff Push Puppet, 1977, Ideal
EX $20 **NM** $30 **MIP** $80

Snoopy Sign Mobile, 1970s, Avalon, Model No. 262
EX $50 **NM** $80 **MIP** $160

Snoopy Skediddler and His Sopwith Camel, 1969, Mattel, w/carrying case, Model No. 4954
EX $250 **NM** $400 **MIP** $500

Snoopy Slugger, 1979, Playskool, ball, bat and cap, Model No. 411
EX $20 **NM** $40 **MIP** $85

Snoopy Soaper, 1975, Kenner, gold soap dispenser w/Snoopy on top, Model No. 30700
EX $30 **NM** $50 **MIP** $85

Snoopy Tea Set, 1970, Chein, metal, features tray, plate, cups, and saucers, Model No. 276
EX $100 **NM** $175 **MIP** $250

Snoopy the Critic, 1977, Aviva, Snoopy and Woodstock on doghouse w/microphone, Model No. 222
EX $120 **NM** $250 **MIP** $300

Snoopy the Flying Ace Push Puppet, 1977, Ideal
EX $20 **NM** $30 **MIP** $90

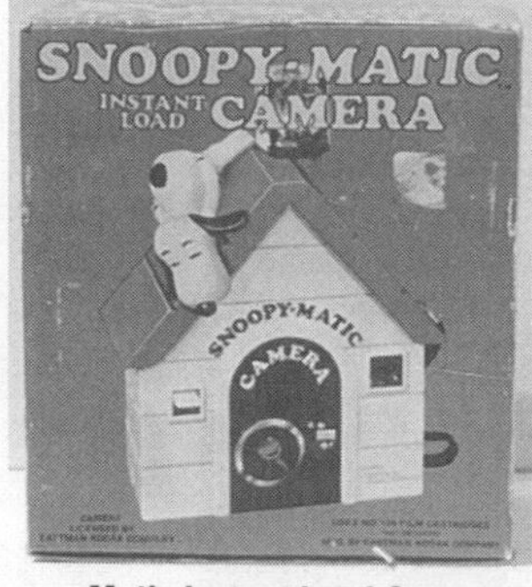

Snoopy-Matic Instant Load Camera, 1970s, Helm Toy, uses 110 film, Model No. 975
EX $95 **NM** $150 **MIP** $225

Snoopy's Beagle Bugle, 1970s, Child Guidance, plastic, Model No. 1730
EX $55 **NM** $80 **MIP** $120

Snoopy's Bubble Blowing Bubble Tub, 1970s, Chemtoy
EX $20 **NM** $45 **MIP** $60

Snoopy's Dog House, 1978, Romper Room/Hasbro, Snoopy walks on roof, Model No. 815
EX $20 **NM** $45 **MIP** $90

Snoopy's Dream Machine, 1979, DCS, w/blinking lights
EX $95 **NM** $155 **MIP** $220

Snoopy's Dream Machine, 1980, DCS, small version, no blinking lights, laminated cardboard, Model No. 417-M
EX $55 **NM** $80 **MIP** $120

Snoopy's Fantastic Automatic Bubble Pipe, 1970s, Chemtoy, Model No. 126
EX $5 **NM** $12 **MIP** $30

Snoopy's Good Grief Glider, 1970s, Child Guidance, spring load launcher, Model No. 1775
EX $50 **NM** $75 **MIP** $120

Snoopy's 'Lectric Comb and Brush, 1975, Kenner, Model No. 30900
EX $35 **NM** $50 **MIP** $70

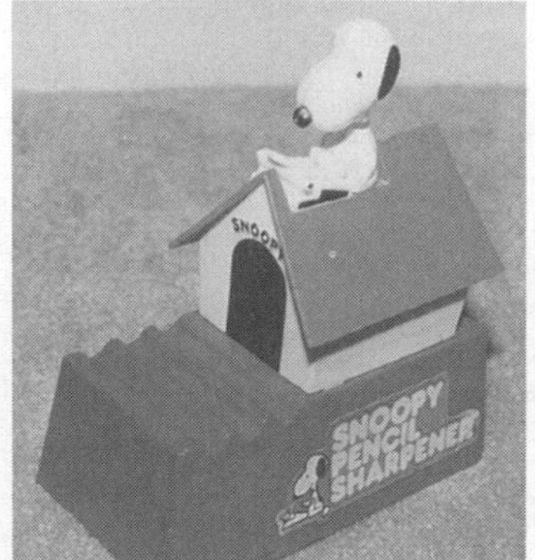

Snoopy's Pencil Sharpener, 1974, Kenner, Model No. 3550
EX $25 **NM** $50 **MIP** $100

Snoopy's Shape Register, 1980, Gabriel/Child Guidance, plastic cash register, Model No. 51740
EX $30 **NM** $60 **MIP** $90

Snoopy's Soft House, 1980, Knickerbocker, soft cloth house, Model No. 0573
EX $25 **NM** $40 **MIP** $75

Snoopy's Stunt Spectacular, 1978, Child Guidance, Snoopy on motorcycle, Model No. 1750
EX $35 **NM** $50 **MIP** $90

Snoopy's Swim and Sail Club, 1970s, Child Guidance, characters and water vehicles, Model No. 1710
EX $45 **NM** $75 **MIP** $120

Snoopy's Take-a-Part Doghouse, 1980, Gabriel/Child Guidance, Model No. 51705
EX $15 **NM** $30 **MIP** $60

Spinning Top, Ohio Art, 5", Snoopy and the Gang
EX $10 **NM** $30 **MIP** $80

Spinning Top, 1960s, Chein, faces of Snoopy, Charlie Brown, Lucy, and Linus, Model No. 263
EX $40 **NM** $75 **MIP** $150

Stack-Up Snoopy, 1980, Romper Room/Hasbro, Model No. 818
EX $10 **NM** $13 **MIP** $25

Super Cartoon Maker, 1970, Mattel, molds to make character figures, Model No. 4696
EX $80 **NM** $130 **MIP** $180

Swimming Snoopy, 1970s, Concept 2000, Model No. 106
EX $15 **NM** $40 **MIP** $80

Talking Peanuts Bus, 1967, Chein, metal, chracters seen in windows, Model No. 261
EX $300 **NM** $500 **MIP** $800

Tell Time Clock, 1980s, Concept 2000, three styles: Snoopy, Woodstock or Charlie Brown
EX $15 **NM** $25 **MIP** $60

Woodstock Climbing String Action, 1977, Aviva/Hasbro, plastic, Model No. 667
EX $15 **NM** $28 **MIP** $60

Yankee Doodle Snoopy, 1975, Colorforms, Model No. 756
EX $20 **NM** $35 **MIP** $70

VEHICLES

Formula-1 Racing Car, 1978, Aviva, 11-1/2" plastic w/Woodstock or Snoopy, Model No. 950
EX $80 **NM** $125 **MIP** $185

Schroeder's Piano, Aviva
EX $30 **NM** $60 **MIP** $100

Snoopy and Woodstock in Wagon, Aviva, green die-cast w/white wheels, Model No. 72060
EX $10 **NM** $15 **MIP** $25

Snoopy and Woodstock on Skateboard, Aviva
EX $10 **NM** $15 **MIP** $25

Snoopy as Beagle Scout in Bus, 1983, Hasbro, die-cast
EX $4 NM $10 MIP $25

Snoopy as Flying Ace in Wagon, Aviva, yellow die-cast w/red wheels, Model No. 72057
EX $10 NM $20 MIP $45

Snoopy as Joe Cool in Wagon, Aviva, purple die-cast w/orange wheels, Model No. 72055
EX $10 NM $15 MIP $30

Snoopy Biplane, 1977, Aviva, die-cast, Snoopy as Flying Ace, Model No. 2024
EX $30 NM $50 MIP $90

Snoopy Emergency Set, Hasbro, Snoopy in three vehicles
EX $20 NM $50 MIP $90

Snoopy Family Car, 1977, Aviva, die-cast convertible, 2-1/4", Model No. 2028
EX $35 NM $55 MIP $90

Snoopy Handfuls, Hasbro, twin pack; characters in die-cast racers
EX $15 NM $35 MIP $60

Snoopy in Tow Truck, 1983, Hasbro, die-cast
EX $5 NM $10 MIP $30

Snoopy Racing Car Stickshifter, 1978, Aviva, Model No. 975
EX $90 NM $150 MIP $210

Snoopy Slot Car Racing Set, 1977, Aviva, Model No. XL500
EX $75 NM $120 MIP $220

Woodstock in Ice Cream Truck, Aviva, friction vehicle
EX $6 NM $9 MIP $15

WATCHES

Charlie Brown Wristwatch, 1970s, Determined, Charlie Brown in baseball gear, yellow face, black band
EX $65 NM $200 MIP $325

Lucy Wristwatch, 1970s, Timex, small chrome case, articulated arms, sweep seconds, white vinyl band
EX $35 NM $100 MIP $200

Lucy's Watch Wardrobe, 1970s, Determined, white face, comes w/blue, white, and pink bands
EX $60 NM $100 MIP $175

Snoopy Hero Time Watch, 1970s, Determined, Snoopy in dancing pose, red band
EX $75 NM $150 MIP $300

Snoopy Wristwatch, 1969, Determined, Snoopy in dancing pose, silver or gold case, various colors
EX $70 NM $140 MIP $275

Snoopy Wristwatch, 1970s, Lafayette Watch, Snoopy dancing, Woodstock is the second hand, silver case w/red face and black band
EX $70 NM $140 MIP $275

Snoopy Wristwatch, 1970s, Timex, gold bezel, tennis ball circles Snoopy on clear disk, articulated hands holding racket, denim background and band
EX $60 NM $90 MIP $175

Peter Pan

ACCESSORIES

Peter Pan Charm Bracelet, 1974
EX $30 NM $50 MIP $100

Peter Pan Map of Neverland, 1953, 18" x 24", collectors issue for users of Peter Pan Beauty Bar
EX $250 NM $400 MIP $600

Tinker Bell Pincushion, 1960s, w/1-1/2" tall Tinker Bell figure, in clear plastic display can
EX $25 NM $40 MIP $125

DOLL

Peter Pan Doll, 1953, Ideal, 18" tall
EX $100 NM $200 MIP $500

Peter Pan Doll, 1953, Duchess Doll, 11-1/2" tall, brown trim fabric shoes, green mesh stockings w/flocked outfit, hat w/a large red feather, shiny silver white metal dagger in belt, eyes, arms and head move
EX $175 NM $350 MIP $700

Tinker Bell Doll, 1953, Duchess Doll, 8" tall, flocked green outfit w/a pair of large white fabric wings w/gold trim, eyes open and close, jointed arms and head moves
EX $150 NM $300 MIP $600

Wendy Doll, 1953, Duchess Doll, 8" tall, full purple length skirt w/purple bow in back of dress, eyes open and close, jointed arms and head moves
EX $150 NM $275 MIP $525

FIGURES

Captain Hook Figure, 8" tall, plastic
EX $10 NM $20 MIP $50

Peter Pan Baby Figure, 1950s, Sun Rubber
EX $70 NM $125 MIP $250

Peter Pan Paper Dolls, 1952, Whitman, 11 die-cut cardboard figures
EX $100 NM $175 MIP $300

Tinker Bell Figure, 1960s, Sutton, 7" tall, plastic and rubber figure
EX $25 NM $50 MIP $100

TOY

Captain Hook Hand Puppet, 1950s, Gund, 9" tall
EX $35 NM $70 MIP $175

Peter Pan Hand Puppet, 1953, Oak Rubber, rubber
EX $30 NM $70 MIP $160

Peter Pan Nodder, 1950s, 6" tall
EX $125 NM $250 MIP $400

Peter Pan Push Puppet, 1950s, Kohner, 6" tall, green and flesh colored beads, plastic head, light green plastic hat
EX $25 NM $50 MIP $110

Peter Pan Sewing Cards, 1952, Whitman
EX $15 NM $30 MIP $70

Puzzle, 1950s, Jaymar, frame tray puzzle shows Peter, Wendy, John and Michael flying over Neverland
EX $20 NM $42 MIP $90

Phantom

ACCESSORIES

Oil Paint by Numbers Set, 1967, Hasbro
EX $225 NM $320 MIP $550

Phantom 2040 Rubber Ball, 1995, Unice
EX $12 NM $17 MIP $30

Phantom Binoculars, 1976, Larami
EX $120 NM $155 MIP $225

Phantom Candy Jar, 1996, KFS, plastic w/figural lid
EX $12 NM $22 MIP $70

Phantom Club Rubber Stamper Skull Ring, 1950s
EX $500 NM $800 MIP $1200

Phantom Costume, 1950s, Ben Cooper
EX $175 NM $225 MIP $350

Phantom Costume, 1970s, Collegeville
EX $70 NM $90 MIP $150

Phantom Puffy Magnet, 1975, Hanna-Barbera
EX $40 NM $50 MIP $70

Phantom Squirt Camera, 1976, Larami
EX $100 NM $120 MIP $225

Playing Cards, 1990, Bulls Dist., Swedish
EX $16 NM $25 MIP $60

Playing Cards, 1990, John Sands
EX $16 NM $25 MIP $60

Rub-On Transfer Set, 1967, Hasbro
EX $100 NM $120 MIP $200

BOOK

Phantom Giant Games Book, 1968, World Distributors
EX $80 NM $125 MIP $200

COSTUME

Phantom Costume, 1989, Character Costumes
EX $40 NM $55 MIP $80

FIGURE

Phantom Figure, 1980s, 6" dark blue PVC figure
EX $25 NM $35 MIP $60

Phantom Figure, 1990s, 6" purple PVC figure
EX $12 NM $30 MIP $60

Phantom Figure, 1996, Street Players, 4" action figure w/skull throne or horse
EX $10 NM $20 MIP $40

Phantom Figures, 1990, Spain, 3-1/2", two pieces, purple PVC
EX $10 NM $20 MIP $40

Syrocco Figure, 1944, Pillsbury Mills, brown
EX $700 NM $1000 MIP $1600

Syrocco Figure, 1944, Pillsbury Mills, purple
EX $500 NM $900 MIP $1400

TOY

Phantom 2040 Carded Toys, 1995, Ja-Ru, sword, crossbow, gun or whistle light
EX $8 NM $12 MIP $30

Phantom Archery Set, 1976, Larami, bow, arrows, animals
EX $100 **NM** $125 **MIP** $220

Phantom Dagger Set, 1976, Larami, knife and sheath
EX $100 **NM** $120 **MIP** $250

Phantom Desert Survival Kit, 1976, Larami, canteen and Thermos bottle
EX $80 **NM** $120 **MIP** $200

Phantom Jungle Play Set, 1976, Larami, figure, palm trees, animals
EX $110 **NM** $160 **MIP** $325

Phantom Pathfinder Set, 1976, Larami, compass, canteen, binoculars, case
EX $80 **NM** $120 **MIP** $185

Phantom Pinback, 1940s, club member cello, Australia
EX $300 **NM** $750 **MIP** $1000

Phantom Safari Set, 1976, Larami, figure, truck, trailer, animals
EX $130 **NM** $180 **MIP** $275

Phantom Water Pistol, 1974, Nasta, w/holster
EX $70 **NM** $90 **MIP** $160

Phantom Water Pistol, 1974, Nasta
EX $80 **NM** $120 **MIP** $175

Pink Panther

ACCESSORIES

Pink Panther Memo Board, write on/wipe off memo board
EX $5 **NM** $10 **MIP** $25

BOOK

Pink Panther and The Fancy Party Book, Golden
EX $5 **NM** $10 **MIP** $30

Pink Panther and The Haunted House Book, Golden
EX $5 **NM** $10 **MIP** $35

Pink Panther at Castle Kreep Book, Whitman
EX $5 **NM** $10 **MIP** $35

Pink Panther at The Circus Sticker Book, 1963, Golden
EX $10 **NM** $20 **MIP** $50

Pink Panther Coloring Book, 1976, Whitman, cover shows Pink Panther roasting hot dogs
EX $10 **NM** $20 **MIP** $50

FIGURES

Pink Panther Figure, 1971, Dakin, 8" tall, w/legs open
EX $25 **NM** $50 **MIP** $100

Pink Panther Figure, 1971, Dakin, 8" tall, w/legs closed
EX $25 **NM** $50 **MIP** $100

GAME

Pink Panther Pool Game, 1980s, Ja-Ru
EX $10 **NM** $20 **MIP** $40

MUSIC BOX

Pink Panther Music Box, 1982, Royal Orleans, Christmas limited edition
EX $60 **NM** $80 **MIP** $150

Pink Panther Music Box, 1983, Royal Orleans, Christmas limited edition
EX $60 **NM** $80 **MIP** $150

Pink Panther Music Box, 1984, Royal Orleans, Christmas limited edition
EX $60 **NM** $80 **MIP** $150

TOY

Pink Panther Motorcycle, 2-1/2" plastic
EX $7 **NM** $15 **MIP** $50

Pink Panther One-Man Band, 1980, Illco, 10" tall, battery-operated, plush body w/vinyl head
EX $35 **NM** $70 **MIP** $100

Pink Panther Putty, 1970s, Ja-Ru
EX $4 **NM** $7 **MIP** $10

Pink Panther Wind-Up, 3" tall, plastic, walking wind-up w/trench coat and glasses
EX $20 **NM** $40 **MIP** $60

Puzzle, 1960s, Whitman, 100 pieces, several pictures available, each
EX $20 **NM** $35 **MIP** $60

Pinocchio and Jiminy Cricket

ACCESSORIES

Jiminy Cricket Toothbrush Set, 1950s, Dupont, plastic wall hanging Jiminy holds a toothbrush
EX $30 **NM** $55 **MIP** $90

Pinocchio Paperweight and Thermometer, 1940, Plastic Novelties
EX $30 **NM** $60 **MIP** $100

Pinocchio Plastic Cup, 1939, Safetyware, 2-3/4" tall, plastic
EX $35 **NM** $70 **MIP** $110

Pinocchio Snow Dome, 1970s, Disney, 3" x 4-1/2" x 5" tall, Pinocchio holds plastic dome between hands and feet
EX $20 **NM** $50 **MIP** $100

BANK

Pinocchio Bank, 1939, Crown Toy, 5" tall, wood composition w/metal trap door on back
EX $150 **NM** $300 **MIP** $450

Pinocchio Bank, 1960s, Play Pal Plastics, 11-1/2" tall, plastic
EX $15 **NM** $25 **MIP** $50

Pinocchio Bank, 1970s, Play Pal Plastics, 7" x 7" x 10" tall, vinyl, 3-D molded head of Pinocchio
EX $10 **NM** $20 **MIP** $50

BOOK

Pinocchio Book, 1939, Whitman, 96 pages
EX $40 **NM** $80 **MIP** $135

Pinocchio Book, 1939, Grosset and Dunlap, 9-1/2" x 13", laminated cover
EX $60 **NM** $125 **MIP** $200

Pinocchio Book, 1940, Big Little Book
EX $50 **NM** $100 **MIP** $200

Pinocchio Book Set, 1940, Whitman, 8-1/2" x 11-1/2", set of six books, 24 pages each
EX $200 **NM** $400 **MIP** $600

Pinocchio Cut-Out Book, 1940, Whitman
EX $125 **NM** $250 **MIP** $400

Pinocchio Paint Book, 1939, Disney, 11" x 15", heavy paper cover
EX $75 **NM** $150 **MIP** $300

Walt Disney Tells the Story of Pinocchio Book, 1939, Whitman, 4-1/4" x 6-1/2" paperback, 144 pages
EX $50 **NM** $80 **MIP** $140

Walt Disney's Pinocchio Book, 1939, Random House, 8-1/2" x 11-1/2", hardcover
EX $50 **NM** $100 **MIP** $180

DOLL

Jiminy Cricket Doll, 1940, Ideal, wooden jointed
EX $200 **NM** $400 **MIP** $750

Pinocchio and Jiminy Cricket Dolls, 1962, Knickerbocker, 6" tall, vinyl, titled "Knixies," each
EX $40 **NM** $60 **MIP** $110

Pinocchio Doll, 1939, Ideal, 12" tall w/wire mesh arms and legs
EX $225 **NM** $450 **MIP** $775

Pinocchio Doll, 1940, Ideal, 8" tall, wood composition head, others are jointed wood
EX $110 **NM** $250 **MIP** $550

Pinocchio Doll, 1940, Ideal, 10" tall, wood composition head, jointed arms and legs attached to body
EX $120 **NM** $300 **MIP** $600

Pinocchio Doll, 1940, Ideal, 19-1/2" tall, composition
EX $600 **NM** $950 **MIP** $1200

Pinocchio Doll, 1940, Knickerbocker, 3-1/2" x 4" x 9-1/2" tall, jointed composition doll w/movable arms and head
EX $600 **NM** $950 **MIP** $1200

FIGURES

Figaro Figure, 1940, Multi-Wood Products, 3" tall, wood composition
EX $65 **NM** $110 **MIP** $240

Figaro Figure, 1940s, Knickerbocker, composition, movable limbs and head
EX $120 **NM** $200 **MIP** $350

Gepetto Figure, 1940, Multi-Wood Products, 5-1/2" tall, wood composition
EX $55 **NM** $100 **MIP** $180

Gideon Figure, Multi-Wood Products, 5" tall
EX $40 **NM** $70 **MIP** $200

Honest John Figure, Multi-Wood Products, 2-1/2" x 3" base w/a 7" tall figure
EX $300 **NM** $400 **MIP** $500

Jiminy Cricket Figure, Marx, 3-1/2" x 4-3/4" tall, Snap-Eeze, white plastic base w/movable arms and legs
EX $30 **NM** $55 **MIP** $95

Jiminy Cricket Figure, 1940s, Ideal, wood jointed, hand painted
EX $200 **NM** $300 **MIP** $500

CHARACTER TOYS

Lampwick Figure, 1940, Multi-Wood Products, 5-1/2" tall, wood composition
EX $80 **NM** $120 **MIP** $240

Pinocchio Figure, Crown Toy, 9-1/2" tall, jointed arms
EX $60 **NM** $110 **MIP** $275

Pinocchio Figure, 1940, Multi-Wood Products, 5" tall, wood composition
EX $80 **NM** $125 **MIP** $240

GAME

Pin the Nose on Pinocchio Game, 1939, Parker Brothers, 15-1/2" x 20"
EX $60 **NM** $120 **MIP** $210

MUSIC BOX

Pinocchio Music Box, plays "Puppet on a String"
EX $18 **NM** $35 **MIP** $85

TOY

Jiminy Cricket Hand Puppet, 1950s, Gund, 11" tall
EX $30 **NM** $60 **MIP** $140

Jiminy Cricket Marionette, 1950s, Pelham Puppets, 3" x 6" x 10" tall, dark green head with, large eyes, gray felt hat
EX $75 **NM** $160 **MIP** $350

Jiminy Cricket Ramp Walker, 1960s, Marx, 1" x 3" x 3" tall, pushing a bass fiddle
EX $80 **NM** $140 **MIP** $270

Jiminy Cricket Soaky, 7" tall bottle
EX $15 **NM** $50 **MIP** $80

Pinocchio and Jiminy Push Puppet, 1960s, Marx, 2-1/2" x 5" x 4" tall, double puppet
EX $30 **NM** $45 **MIP** $100

Pinocchio Color Box, Transogram, also known as paint box
EX $18 **NM** $35 **MIP** $80

Pinocchio Crayon Box, 1940s, Transogram, 4-1/2" x 5-1/2" x 1/2" deep, tin
EX $18 **NM** $35 **MIP** $85

Pinocchio Hand Puppet, Crown Toy, 9" tall, composition
EX $25 **NM** $45 **MIP** $70

Pinocchio Hand Puppet, 1950s, Gund, 10" tall, w/squeaker
EX $40 **NM** $75 **MIP** $150

Pinocchio Hand Puppet, 1962, Knickerbocker
EX $25 **NM** $50 **MIP** $85

Pinocchio Push Puppet, 1960s, Kohner, 5" tall
EX $15 **NM** $25 **MIP** $75

Pinocchio Soaky
EX $20 **NM** $40 **MIP** $85

Pinocchio Tea Set, 1939, Ohio Art, tin tray, plates, saucers, serving platter, cups, bowls and smaller plates
EX $175 **NM** $250 **MIP** $400

Pinocchio Walker, 1939, Marx, 9" tall, tin, animated eyes, rocking action
EX $375 **NM** $750 **MIP** $1000

Pinocchio Wind-Up Toy, Linemar, 6" tall, tin wind-up, arms and legs move
EX $200 **NM** $300 **MIP** $500

Puzzle, 1960s, Jaymar, 5" x 7", "Pinocchio's Expedition"
EX $12 **NM** $22 **MIP** $50

WATCH

Jiminy Cricket Wristwatch, 1948, US Time, Birthday Series
EX $250 **NM** $450 **MIP** $750

Pluto

ACCESSORIES

Pluto Alarm Clock, 1955, Allied, 4" x 5-1/2" x 10" tall, eyes and hands shaped like dog bones, glow in the dark
EX $100 **NM** $200 **MIP** $325

Pluto Purse, 1940s, Gund, 9" x 14" x 2"
EX $25 **NM** $55 **MIP** $100

BANK

Pluto Bank, 1940s, Disney, 4" x 4-1/2" x 6-1/2", ceramic
EX $60 **NM** $100 **MIP** $200

Pluto Bank, 1970s, Animal Toys Plus, 9" tall vinyl, Pluto standing in front of a doghouse
EX $20 **NM** $35 **MIP** $85

FIGURES

Pluto Figure, 1930s, Seiberling, 7" tall, rubber
EX $90 **NM** $120 **MIP** $200

Pluto Figure, 1930s, Seiberling, 3-1/2" long, rubber
EX $90 **NM** $120 **MIP** $200

Pluto Fun-E-Flex Figure, 1930s, Fun-E-Flex, wood
EX $50 **NM** $85 **MIP** $160

Pluto Pop-Up Critter Figure, 1936, Fisher-Price, wooden, Pluto standing on base 10-1/2" long
EX $100 **NM** $160 **MIP** $225

TOY

Pluto Hand Puppet, 1950s, Gund, 9" tall
EX $15 **NM** $35 **MIP** $80

Pluto Lantern Toy, 1950s, Linemar
EX $250 **NM** $350 **MIP** $500

Pluto Pop-A-Part Toy, 1965, Multiple Toymakers, 9" long, plastic
EX $20 **NM** $35 **MIP** $50

Pluto Push Toy, 1936, Fisher-Price, 8" long, wood
EX $150 **NM** $200 **MIP** $320

Pluto Rolykin, Marx, 1" x 1" x 1-1/2" tall, ball bearing action
EX $15 **NM** $35 **MIP** $70

Pluto Sports Car, Empire, 2" long
EX $10 **NM** $20 **MIP** $50

Pluto the Acrobat Trapeze Toy, Linemar, 10" tall, metal, celluloid, wind-up
EX $120 **NM** $250 **MIP** $350

Pluto the Drum Major, 1950s, Marx/Linemar, tin, mechanical
EX $300 **NM** $450 **MIP** $750

Popeye

ACCESSORIES

60th Anniversary Candle Box, 1989, Presents, metal, heart shaped, #P5979
EX $5 **NM** $12 **MIP** $30

Bell, 1980, Vandor, Popeye on top, ceramic
EX $15 **NM** $20 **MIP** $35

Belt Buckle, U.S. Spinach Growers, Strength thru Spinach
EX $8 **NM** $20 **MIP** $40

Belt Buckle, 1973, Pyramid Belt, Popeye w/sailor hat
EX $10 **NM** $20 **MIP** $50

Belt Buckle, 1980, Lee, Popeye w/spinach
EX $8 **NM** $15 **MIP** $35

Blinky Cup, Beacon Plastics
EX $8 **NM** $15 **MIP** $25

Bookends, 1980, Vandor, ceramic, Popeye and Brutus
EX $20 **NM** $45 **MIP** $100

Bowl, 1971, Deka, oval, plastic
EX $10 **NM** $20 **MIP** $50

Bowl, 1979, National Home Products, plastic
EX $6 **NM** $12 **MIP** $25

Bowl, 1980, Vandor, ceramic, 1 of 3
EX $8 **NM** $18 **MIP** $40

Cabinet, mirrored
EX $75 **NM** $100 **MIP** $175

Candy, 1980, Alberts, bonbons
EX $6 **NM** $10 **MIP** $15

Candy Box, 1960, Phoenix Candy, Popeye and his pals
EX $20 **NM** $50 **MIP** $100

Candy Cigarettes, 1959, Primrose Confectionery - England
EX $15 **NM** $35 **MIP** $100

Candy Sticks, 1989, Hearst, red box
EX $6 **NM** $15 **MIP** $30

Candy Sticks, 1990, World Candies, 48 count
EX $6 **NM** $15 **MIP** $25

Cereal Bowl, 1979, National Home Products
EX $8 **NM** $20 **MIP** $45

Cereal Box, 1987, Cocoa-Puffs, w/gum
EX $25 **NM** $50 **MIP** $75

Charm Bracelet, 1990, Peter Brams, silver or gold
EX $10 **NM** $20 **MIP** $40

Chocolate Mold, 1940s, metal, Popeye
EX $35 **NM** $90 **MIP** $150

Chocolate Mold, 1991, Turmic Plastics, plastic, Popeye
EX $3 **NM** $6 **MIP** $10

Christmas Lamp Shades, 1930s, General Electric, set of ten
EX $150 **NM** $250 **MIP** $450

Christmas Light Covers, 1929, General Electric Textolite, "Cheers"
EX $125 **NM** $250 **MIP** $450

Popeye

Christmas Ornament, 1981, Bully, Bluto
EX $8 NM $15 MIP $40

Christmas Ornament, 1981, Bully, Dufus
EX $8 NM $15 MIP $40

Christmas Ornament, 1987, Presents, Alice the Goon, Swee'Pea, Wimpy, Popeye, Olive Oyl or Brutus, each
EX $8 NM $15 MIP $40

Christmas Ornament, 1989, Presents, Season's Greetings
EX $8 NM $15 MIP $40

Christmas Tree Lamp Set, 1935, General Electric
EX $100 NM $300 MIP $500

Circus Man Film, 1950s, Brumberger, 8mm
EX $20 NM $30 MIP $60

Clothes Brush, 1929, KFS, wooden, black or brown
EX $30 NM $100 MIP $250

Color Markers, 1990, Sanrio, six
EX $2 NM $5 MIP $10

Comb and Brush, 1979, KFS
EX $8 NM $25 MIP $60

Cookie Jar, 1965, McCoy, ceramic white-suited Popeye
EX $200 NM $310 MIP $475

Cook's Catch-All, 1980, KFS, ceramic, Wimpy
EX $10 NM $20 MIP $50

Cup, 1940s, New Zealand, Popeye on skis, ceramic
EX $18 NM $40 MIP $80

Dice, 1990, w/Popeye head
EX $2 NM $5 MIP $15

Dish, 1940s, New Zealand, ceramic, Popeye and Olive Oyl
EX $30 NM $50 MIP $100

Dish Set, 1964, Boontonware, three piece plastic
EX $30 NM $45 MIP $90

Egg Cup, 1940s, Japan, Popeye sitting at table w/spinach
EX $30 NM $65 MIP $125

Egg Cup and Mug, 1989, Magna, Great Britain
EX $15 NM $40 MIP $75

Film Card, 1959, Tru-Vue, T-28
EX $8 NM $20 MIP $60

Freezicles, 1980, Imperial
EX $5 NM $15 MIP $20

Indian Fighter Film, Atlas Films, 8mm
EX $5 NM $10 MIP $20

Jackknife, 1940s, Imperial, green Popeye on pearl handle
EX $150 NM $250 MIP $350

Jeep Wall Plaque, ceramic
EX $6 NM $12 MIP $50

King of the Jungle Film, 1960s, Atlas Films, 8mm
EX $5 NM $10 MIP $30

Knapsack, 1979, Fabil
EX $10 NM $15 MIP $30

Kooky Straw, 1980, Imperial
EX $4 NM $10 MIP $20

Lamp, 1940s, boat w/Popeye light bulb
EX $500 NM $1000 MIP $1500

Life Raft, 1979, KFS, large, blue
EX $10 NM $20 MIP $40

Magic Eyes Film Card, 1962, Tru-Vue, set of three
EX $15 NM $25 MIP $60

Mini Hurricane Lamp, 1989, Presents, P5981-1993, 60th year
EX $4 NM $10 MIP $30

Mini Memo Board, 1980, Freelance
EX $5 NM $10 MIP $15

Mirror, 1978, Freelance, Popeye lifting weights
EX $7 NM $15 MIP $35

Mirror, 1979, Freelance, Olive w/mirror
EX $7 NM $15 MIP $35

Mirror Rattle, 1979, Cribmates
EX $8 NM $13 MIP $30

Mug, 1950s, Schmid, ceramic
EX $10 NM $20 MIP $40

Music Lovers Film, 1960s, Atlas Films, 8mm
EX $8 NM $15 MIP $20

Musical Mug, 1982, KFS, ceramic
EX $10 NM $20 MIP $35

Musical Rattle, 1979, Cribmates
EX $8 NM $15 MIP $30

Olive Oyl and Swee'Pea Hot Water Bottle, 1970, Duarry
EX $75 NM $100 MIP $200

Olive Oyl and Swee'Pea Snow Globe, 1989, Presents, several styles
EX $7 NM $15 MIP $40

Olive Oyl and Swee'Pea Telephone Shoulder Rest, 1982, Comvu
EX $6 NM $15 MIP $40

Olive Oyl and Swee'Pea Thermometer, 1981, KFS
EX $8 NM $13 MIP $20

Olive Oyl Cup, 1977, Coke, Coke Kollect-A-Set
EX $4 NM $10 MIP $30

Olive Oyl Hairbrush, 1979, Cribmates, musical
EX $8 NM $20 MIP $60

Olive Oyl Mug, 1950s, Schmid, musical ceramic
EX $15 NM $40 MIP $80

Olive Oyl Mug, 1980, Vandor, ceramic
EX $8 NM $15 MIP $25

Olive Oyl Wall Plaque, ceramic
EX $3 NM $7 MIP $20

Paper Party Blowouts, 1988, Gala/James River
EX $2 NM $4 MIP $10

Paperweight, 1937, "Popeye Eats Del Monte Spinach"
EX $100 NM $175 MIP $250

Pencil Case, 1936, Eagle, beige, #9027
EX $75 NM $125 MIP $250

Pencil Case, 1950s, Hassenfeld Bros., red
EX $35 NM $75 MIP $150

Pencil Case, 1990, Sanrio
EX $5 NM $10 MIP $20

Pencil Sharpener, 1929, KFS, orange celluloid
EX $40 NM $75 MIP $125

Pig for a Friend Mug, 1980, Vandor, ceramic
EX $6 NM $12 MIP $50

Playing Cards, 1988, Presents, metal box, #P5998, two decks, 60th year
EX $4 NM $10 MIP $25

Popeye Alarm Clock, 1967, Smiths, British
EX $100 NM $180 MIP $320

Popeye and Betty Boop Film, 1935, Exclusive Films, 8mm film
EX $15 NM $25 MIP $50

Popeye and Cast Cigar Box
EX $25 NM $45 MIP $90

Popeye and Olive Oyl Suspenders, 1979, KFS, blue
EX $6 NM $12 MIP $25

Popeye and Swee'Pea Snow Globe, 1989, Presents, several varieties
EX $5 NM $10 MIP $25

Popeye Apron, 1990, Chester
EX $4 NM $8 MIP $15

Popeye Beach Set, 1950s, Peer Products/KFS, plastic rowboat, accessories
EX $25 NM $50 MIP $100

Popeye Charm, silver w/ dangly parts
EX $20 NM $30 MIP $60

Popeye Charm, solid gold
EX $100 NM $150 MIP $200

Popeye Charm, 1930s, celluloid
EX $40 NM $60 MIP $100

Popeye Cup, 1979, Deca Plastics, plastic
EX $5 NM $10 MIP $25

Popeye Cup, 1989, Popeye Picnic, plastic
EX $1 NM $2 MIP $5

Popeye Cup and Saucer, 1930s, Japan
EX $40 NM $85 MIP $185

Popeye Glass, 1977, Coke, Coke Kollect-A-Set
EX $4 NM $10 MIP $25

Popeye Hot Water Bottle, 1970, Duarry
EX $40 NM $90 MIP $175

CHARACTER TOYS

Popeye Lamp, 1940s, telescope w/Popeye at base
EX $225 **NM** $350 **MIP** $575

Popeye Lamp, 1959, Alan Jay, Popeye w/legs folded holding spinach
EX $75 **NM** $100 **MIP** $210

Popeye Mechanical Pencil, 1929, Eagle, 10-1/2" long illustrated pencil w/box
EX $50 **NM** $75 **MIP** $150

Popeye Night Light, Arrow Plastic
EX $8 **NM** $13 **MIP** $20

Popeye Picture, KFS-Sears, silver foil
EX $10 **NM** $20 **MIP** $40

Popeye Pin, Popeye at steering wheel, stick pin
EX $5 **NM** $12 **MIP** $35

Popeye Popcorn, 1949, Purity Mills, in can
EX $65 **NM** $100 **MIP** $150

Popeye Snow Globe, 1960s, KFS, Popeye holds globe between legs
EX $25 **NM** $45 **MIP** $100

Popeye Thimble, 1990
EX $4 **NM** $7 **MIP** $10

Popeye Toothbrush Holder, Vandor, 5" tall, figural
EX $10 **NM** $15 **MIP** $30

Popeye Toothbrush Set, 1980s, Nasta, holds two toothbrushes
EX $6 **NM** $15 **MIP** $25

Popeye Utensils, 1970s, Arrow Plastic, spoon and fork
EX $8 **NM** $15 **MIP** $30

Popeye Wall Hanging, 1979, Amscan, 42", jointed
EX $8 **NM** $13 **MIP** $20

Popeye Writing Tablet, 1929, KFS, Popeye w/spinach hypo
EX $75 **NM** $100 **MIP** $185

Popeye/Olive Oyl/Swee'Pea Lamp Shade, 1950s
EX $50 **NM** $75 **MIP** $185

Popeye/Olive Oyl/Wimpy Decals, 1935, IGS Stores
EX $25 **NM** $40 **MIP** $85

Punching Bag Film, 1950s, Brumberger, 8mm
EX $8 **NM** $15 **MIP** $30

Rain Boots, 1950s, KFS, spinach power
EX $15 **NM** $30 **MIP** $60

Record Player, 1960s, Emerson, Dynamite Music Machine
EX $50 **NM** $100 **MIP** $170

Secret Message Pen, 1981, Gordy
EX $6 **NM** $12 **MIP** $30

Sketchbook, 1960, Japan
EX $15 **NM** $25 **MIP** $60

Sleeping Bag, 1979, KFS
EX $15 **NM** $35 **MIP** $65

Soap Dispenser, 1970s, Woolfoam
EX $15 **NM** $25 **MIP** $35

Soap on a Rope, KFS, white, shaped like Popeye's head
EX $15 **NM** $25 **MIP** $60

Soap Set, 1930s, Kerk Guild, Olive Oyl, Swee'Pea, and Popeye soap figures
EX $200 **NM** $400 **MIP** $600

Stationery, 1989, Presents, metal box, heart-shaped note paper, #P5976
EX $6 **NM** $10 **MIP** $20

Storage Box, 1990, Sanrio, smoke colored
EX $6 **NM** $10 **MIP** $15

Sunday Funnies Soda Can, 1970s, Flavor Valley
EX $8 **NM** $15 **MIP** $25

Suspenders, 1970s, red, white and blue w/plastic emblems
EX $10 **NM** $20 **MIP** $35

Swee'Pea Cup, 1977, Coke, Coke Kollect-A-Cup
EX $4 **NM** $7 **MIP** $12

Swee'Pea Egg Cup, 1980, Vandor, ceramic
EX $10 **NM** $20 **MIP** $35

Swee'Pea Night Light, 1978, Presents, bone china
EX $20 **NM** $30 **MIP** $60

Swee'Pea Snow Globe, 1989, Presents, several styles
EX $10 **NM** $15 **MIP** $30

Swee'Pea Wall Plaque, 1950s, ceramic
EX $12 **NM** $35 **MIP** $70

Swee'Pea's Lemonade Stand Television Film, 1950s, Zaboly
EX $12 **NM** $25 **MIP** $60

Training Cup, 1971, Deka
EX $8 **NM** $13 **MIP** $30

Transistor Radio, 1960s, Philgee
EX $35 **NM** $60 **MIP** $100

Trash Can, 1980s, KFS
EX $10 **NM** $30 **MIP** $50

Trinket Box, 1980, Vandor, Popeye's head in preserver, ceramic
EX $10 **NM** $18 **MIP** $35

Trinket Box, 1980, Vandor, Popeye laying on top, ceramic
EX $10 **NM** $16 **MIP** $30

TV Tray, 1979, KFS
EX $8 **NM** $15 **MIP** $30

Umbrella, 1979, KFS, blue and white
EX $20 **NM** $35 **MIP** $80

Wagon Works Film, 1960s, Atlas Films, 8mm
EX $6 **NM** $10 **MIP** $25

Wallet, 1978, Larami
EX $8 **NM** $20 **MIP** $50

Wallet, 1990, Sanrio
EX $6 **NM** $10 **MIP** $20

Wallet, 1991, Presents, P-5432, tri-fold
EX $6 **NM** $10 **MIP** $20

Whistle Candy, 1989, Alberts
EX $6 **NM** $10 **MIP** $20

Wimpy Cup, 1977, Coke, Coke Kollect-A-Set
EX $4 **NM** $7 **MIP** $10

Wimpy Magnet
EX $6 **NM** $10 **MIP** $15

Wimpy Thermometer, 1981, KFS
EX $10 **NM** $15 **MIP** $25

Write on/Wipe Off Board, 1979, Freelance
EX $10 **NM** $20 **MIP** $40

BADGE

Popeye and Swee'Pea Flicker Badge, 1960s, Varivue
EX $10 **NM** $20 **MIP** $50

Popeye and Wimpy Flicker Badge, 1960s, Varivue
EX $10 **NM** $20 **MIP** $50

BANK

60th Anniversary Bank, 1988, Presents, metal, P5988
EX $15 **NM** $30 **MIP** $60

Brutus Mini Bank, 1979, KFS
EX $10 **NM** $20 **MIP** $50

Daily Dime Bank, 1956, KFS
EX $60 **NM** $150 **MIP** $260

Daily Quarter Bank, 1950s, Kalon, 4-1/2" tall, metal
EX $150 **NM** $300 **MIP** $500

Dime Register Bank, 1929, KFS, square, window shows total deposits
EX $175 **NM** $300 **MIP** $525

Knockout Bank, 1935, Straits
EX $500 **NM** $800 **MIP** $1300

Olive Oyl Bank, 1940s, cast iron
EX $200 **NM** $300 **MIP** $500

Olive Oyl Mini Bank, 1979, KFS
EX $15 **NM** $30 **MIP** $60

Popeye Bank, ceramic, Popeye in light blue cap
EX $5 **NM** $10 **MIP** $30

Popeye Bank, 1940s, Popeye w/life preserver
EX $100 **NM** $150 **MIP** $300

Popeye Bank, 1940s, 9" cast iron
EX $175 **NM** $250 **MIP** $375

Popeye Bank, 1970s, Play Pal, plastic, Popeye sitting on rope
EX $10 **NM** $30 **MIP** $55

Popeye Bank, 1972, Play Pal, shape of Popeye's head, plastic
EX $15 **NM** $30 **MIP** $65

Popeye Bank, 1979, Renz, beige bust
EX $12 **NM** $25 **MIP** $60

Popeye Bank, 1980, Leonard, silver, Popeye sitting
EX $15 **NM** $30 **MIP** $60

Popeye Bank, 1980, Vandor, ceramic, Popeye sitting on rope
EX $12 **NM** $25 **MIP** $50

Popeye Bank, 1980, Vandor, ceramic
EX $130 **NM** $260 **MIP** $525

Popeye Bank, 1990, Sanrio, w/padlock
EX $5 **NM** $10 **MIP** $25

Popeye Bank, 1990, Mexico, ceramic bust
EX $20 **NM** $35 **MIP** $50

Popeye Bank, 1991, Presents, vinyl, Popeye w/removable pipe
EX $6 **NM** $12 **MIP** $25

Popeye Mini Bank, 1979, KFS
EX $10 **NM** $20 **MIP** $40

Spinach Can Bank, 1975, KFS, blue can w/raised characters
EX $20 **NM** $40 **MIP** $80

Swee'Pea Bank, 1980, Vandor, 6-1/2" figural
EX $80 **NM** $125 **MIP** $200

Swee'Pea Mini Bank, 1979, KFS
EX $20 **NM** $40 **MIP** $90

BOOK

60th Anniversary Collection Book, 1990, Hawk Books
EX $20 **NM** $40 **MIP** $60

Adventures of Popeye Book, 1934, Saalfield
EX $75 **NM** $175 **MIP** $400

Big Surprise Book, 1976, Wonder Books
EX $5 **NM** $15 **MIP** $40

Captain George Presents Popeye Book, 1970, Memory Lane
EX $10 **NM** $25 **MIP** $55

Danger Ahoy! Book, 1969, Whitman, Big Little Book
EX $5 **NM** $15 **MIP** $35

Deep Sea Danger Book, 1980, Whitman, Big Little Book
EX $2 **NM** $6 **MIP** $20

Fun Booklets, 1980, Spot-O-Gold, set of 10
EX $20 **NM** $40 **MIP** $80

Ghost Ship to Treasure Island Book, 1967, Whitman, Big Little Book
EX $8 **NM** $15 **MIP** $45

Giant 24 Big Picture Coloring Book, 1981, Merrigold Press
EX $6 **NM** $12 **MIP** $50

Giant Paint Book, 1937, Whitman, blue or red
EX $100 **NM** $175 **MIP** $300

Great Big Popeye Paint and Crayon Book, 1937, McLoughlin Bros.
EX $125 **NM** $250 **MIP** $400

Hag of the Seven Seas Pop-Up Book, 1935, Blue Ribbon Books
EX $200 **NM** $350 **MIP** $600

House that Popeye Built Book, 1960, Wonder Books
EX $8 **NM** $25 **MIP** $55

In a Sock for Susan's Sake Book, 1940, Whitman, Big Little Book
EX $30 **NM** $75 **MIP** $180

In Quest of Poopdeck Pappy Book, 1937, Whitman, Big Little Book
EX $30 **NM** $75 **MIP** $180

Jiffy Pop Fun 'N Games Booklet, 1980, Spot-O-Gold
EX $6 **NM** $12 **MIP** $30

Little Pops the Ghost Book, 1981, Random House
EX $5 **NM** $10 **MIP** $30

Little Pops the Magic Flute Book, 1981, Random House
EX $5 **NM** $10 **MIP** $30

Little Pops the Spinach Burgers Book, 1981, Random House
EX $5 **NM** $10 **MIP** $30

Little Pops the Treasure Hunt Book, 1981, Random House
EX $5 **NM** $10 **MIP** $30

Mix or Match Storybook, 1981, Random House
EX $8 **NM** $15 **MIP** $30

Olive Oyl and Swee'Pea Wash Up Book, 1980, Tuffy Books
EX $4 **NM** $10 **MIP** $25

Paint with Water Book, 1981, Whitman
EX $3 **NM** $6 **MIP** $20

Painting and Crayon Book, 1960, England
EX $15 **NM** $25 **MIP** $80

Popeye Activity Pad, 1982, Merrigold Press
EX $3 **NM** $7 **MIP** $15

Popeye All Picture Comic Book, 1942, Whitman, Big Little Book
EX $50 **NM** $100 **MIP** $200

Popeye and his Jungle Pet Book, 1937, Whitman
EX $50 **NM** $100 **MIP** $200

Popeye and Swee'Pea Coloring Book, 1970, Whitman, 1056-31
EX $7 **NM** $15 **MIP** $50

Popeye and the Deep Sea Mystery Big Little Book, 1939, Whitman
EX $50 **NM** $100 **MIP** $200

Popeye and the Jeep Book, 1937, Whitman, Big Little Book
EX $50 **NM** $100 **MIP** $200

Popeye and the Pet Book, 1987, Peter Haddock, book three of four
EX $3 **NM** $5 **MIP** $25

Popeye and the Time Machine Book, 1990, Quaker, mini comic
EX $3 **NM** $5 **MIP** $25

Popeye Book, 1980, Random House, hardcover, based on movie
EX $4 **NM** $8 **MIP** $20

Popeye Calls on Olive Oyl Book, 1937, Whitman, 8-1/2" x 9-1/2"
EX $50 **NM** $80 **MIP** $180

Popeye Climbs a Mountain Book, 1983, Wonder Books
EX $3 **NM** $7 **MIP** $20

Popeye Color and Recolor Book, 1957, Jack Built, color, wipe and color again
EX $25 **NM** $50 **MIP** $120

Popeye How to Draw Cartoons Book, 1939, Joe Musial/D. McKay
EX $100 **NM** $150 **MIP** $300

Popeye in Puddleburg Book, 1934, Saalfield, Big Little Book
EX $50 **NM** $100 **MIP** $200

Popeye Learn and Play Activity Book, 1985, Allen Canning
EX $2 **NM** $5 **MIP** $10

Popeye Meets his Rival Book, 1937, Whitman, 8-1/2" x 11-1/2"
EX $50 **NM** $100 **MIP** $200

Popeye on Rocket Coloring Book, 1980, Whitman - France
EX $8 **NM** $15 **MIP** $40

Popeye on Safari Book, 1990, Quaker, mini comic
EX $2 NM $4 MIP $8

Popeye Paint Book, 1932, McLoughlin Bros., blue
EX $100 NM $150 MIP $325

Popeye Paint Coloring Book, 1951, Whitman
EX $25 NM $60 MIP $140

Popeye Pop-Up Book, 1981, Random House
EX $6 NM $12 MIP $40

Popeye Punch-Out Play Book, 1961, Whitman
EX $12 NM $22 MIP $45

Popeye Puppet Show Book, 1936, Pleasure Books
EX $75 NM $125 MIP $200

Popeye Sees the Sea Book, 1936, Whitman, Big Little Book
EX $50 NM $100 MIP $200

Popeye Song Folio Book, 1936, Famous Music, Z
EX $50 NM $90 MIP $160

Popeye Stay in Shape Book, 1980, Tuffy Books
EX $6 NM $10 MIP $20

Popeye Surprise Present Book, 1987, Peter Haddock
EX $6 NM $10 MIP $20

Popeye the Movie Book, 1980, Avon Printing
EX $6 NM $10 MIP $25

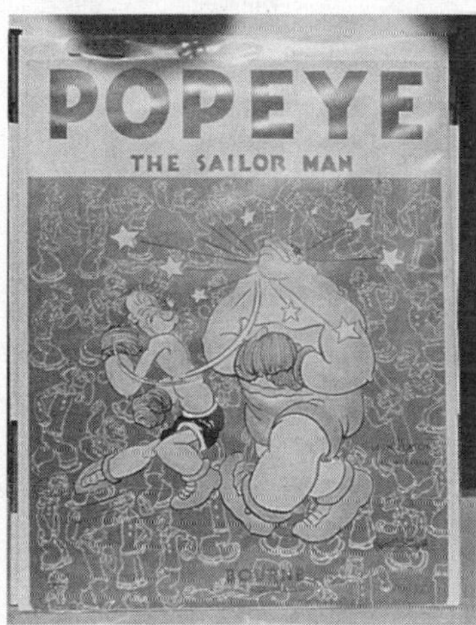

Popeye the Sailor Man Book, 1942, Whitman, Big Little Book
EX $40 NM $90 MIP $180

Popeye vs. Bluto the Bad Book, 1990, Quaker, mini comic
EX $2 NM $4 MIP $10

Popeye with his Friends Book, 1937, Whitman
EX $50 NM $100 MIP $200

Popeye's Adventure Book, 1958, Purnell, England
EX $15 NM $30 MIP $80

Popeye's Ark Book, 1936, Saalfield, Big Little Book
EX $50 NM $100 MIP $200

Puzzle Party Book, 1979, Cinnamon House
EX $6 NM $12 MIP $25

Quest for the Rainbird Book, 1943, Whitman, Big Little Book
EX $40 NM $75 MIP $120

Race to Pearl Peak Book, 1982, Golden
EX $6 NM $10 MIP $20

S.S. Funboat Coloring Book, 1981, Merrigold Press
EX $5 NM $10 MIP $40

Sailor and the Spinach Stalk Coloring Book, 1982, Whitman, 1150-1
EX $6 NM $15 MIP $30

Scott Fun 'N Games Booklet, 1980, Spot-O-Gold, set of five
EX $10 NM $20 MIP $40

The Outer Space Zoo Book, 1980, Golden
EX $6 NM $12 MIP $30

Thimble Theatre Book, 1935, Whitman, Big Big Book
EX $200 NM $350 MIP $650

What! No Spinach? Book, 1981, Golden
EX $6 NM $10 MIP $25

Wimpy in Back to his First Love Book, eight pages
EX $6 NM $10 MIP $15

Wimpy the Hamburger Eater Book, 1938, Whitman, Big Little Book
EX $50 NM $100 MIP $200

Wimpy Tricks Popeye and Roughhouse Book, 1937, Whitman
EX $50 NM $100 MIP $200

Wimpy Tricks Popeye Book, 1937, Whitman
EX $50 NM $90 MIP $180

Wimpy What's Good to Eat? Book, 1980, Tuffy Books
EX $6 NM $12 MIP $30

BUTTON

Bluto Button, 1979, Lisa Frank, 2", Bluto getting socked
EX $2 NM $7 MIP $15

Brutus Button, 1980, Factors, 3", movie
EX $2 NM $5 MIP $10

Brutus Button, 1983, Mini Media, 1", "I'm Mean"
EX $2 NM $5 MIP $10

Brutus Button, 1985, Strand, 3", "Gonna Eat You for Breakfast"
EX $3 NM $6 MIP $12

Brutus Button, 1985, Strand, 3", "Ya Little Runt"
EX $2 NM $5 MIP $10

Button, 1930s, Offset Gravure, 1", New York Evening Journal
EX $50 NM $80 MIP $135

Button, 1983, Mini Media, 1", "No Wimps"
EX $3 NM $7 MIP $15

Olive Oyl Button, 1946, Pep
EX $8 NM $25 MIP $45

Olive Oyl Button, 1980, Factors, 3"
EX $2 NM $4 MIP $8

Olive Oyl Button, 1983, Mini Media, 1", "More than just a pretty face"
EX $2 NM $4 MIP $8

Popeye and Olive Oyl Button, 1970s, 1-1/2", "I Love You"
EX $5 NM $10 MIP $22

Popeye and Olive Oyl Button, 1980, Lisa Frank, 1", cowboy Popeye and Indian Olive
EX $5 NM $10 MIP $20

Popeye Button, 1946, Pep
EX $15 NM $35 MIP $65

Popeye Button, 1950s, KFS, 1", Famous Studios
EX $20 NM $40 MIP $100

Popeye Button, 1959, Lowe, sew-on card
EX $12 NM $20 MIP $60

Popeye Button, 1960s, KMOX TV, 1", S.S. Popeye
EX $5 NM $15 MIP $65

Popeye Button, 1980, Factors, 3", movie
EX $2 NM $4 MIP $10

Popeye Button, 1985, Strand, 3", several styles
EX $3 NM $6 MIP $20

Popeye Button, 1989, KFS, 3", marine conservation
EX $2 NM $4 MIP $10

Popeye Button, 1990, S. Cruz, 2", Santa Cruz boardwalk
EX $2 NM $4 MIP $10

Swee'Pea Button, 1980, Lisa Frank, 1", Swee'Pea w/Jeep
EX $2 NM $5 MIP $12

Wimpy Button, 1946, Pep
EX $10 NM $20 MIP $50

Wimpy Button, 1979, Lisa Frank, 2"
EX $3 NM $8 MIP $15

Wimpy Button, 1985, Strand, 3", "Must Go Home and Water the Ducks"
EX $3 NM $8 MIP $15

DOLL

Brutus Doll, 1985, Presents, large with tag
EX $20 NM $50 MIP $120

Brutus Doll, 1985, Presents, small
EX $12 NM $25 MIP $75

Chimes Doll, 1950s, J. Swedlin, gray plush body, chimes
EX $20 NM $50 MIP $100

Jeep Doll, 1985, Presents, two sizes
EX $10 NM $25 MIP $80

Olive Oyl Doll, 9" vinyl sqeeze doll, Olive w/ Swee'Pea
EX $15 NM $40 MIP $100

Olive Oyl Doll, 1950s, Rempel, small
EX $25 NM $50 MIP $120

Olive Oyl Doll, 1960s, Dakin, 8" tall
EX $25 **NM** $50 **MIP** $120

Olive Oyl Doll, 1970s, Dakin, Cartoon Theatre, in box
EX $25 **NM** $50 **MIP** $120

Olive Oyl Doll, 1970s, Dakin, hard plastic w/ removable clothes
EX $20 **NM** $40 **MIP** $100

Olive Oyl Doll, 1979, Uneeda, removable clothing
EX $15 **NM** $30 **MIP** $80

Olive Oyl Doll, 1985, Presents, Christmas, large
EX $14 **NM** $30 **MIP** $65

Olive Oyl Doll, 1985, Presents, small
EX $10 **NM** $18 **MIP** $45

Olive Oyl Doll, 1990, Presents, small molded plastic, musical # P5948
EX $10 **NM** $20 **MIP** $40

Olive Oyl Doll, 1990, Toy Toons
EX $4 **NM** $9 **MIP** $20

Olive Oyl Doll, 1991, Presents, small molded plastic, # P5966
EX $4 **NM** $8 **MIP** $25

Olive Oyl Doll, 1991, Presents, Christmas, small
EX $8 **NM** $13 **MIP** $30

Poopdeck Pappy Doll, 1985, Presents, with tag
EX $35 **NM** $75 **MIP** $200

Popeye Doll, 23" china
EX $200 **NM** $350 **MIP** $500

Popeye Doll, 1935, Cameo
EX $250 **NM** $500 **MIP** $800

Popeye Doll, 1936, Stack, 12" tall, wood jointed, w/ pipe
EX $225 **NM** $475 **MIP** $775

Popeye Doll, 1950s, Chicago Herald American
EX $30 **NM** $85 **MIP** $250

Popeye Doll, 1950s, Rempel, small
EX $20 **NM** $45 **MIP** $120

Popeye Doll, 1950s, Woolikin, white plush
EX $30 **NM** $65 **MIP** $180

Popeye Doll, 1950s, Chad Valley, 7" tall, squeaks
EX $20 **NM** $55 **MIP** $140

Popeye Doll, 1957, Sears/Cameo, 13" in box
EX $300 **NM** $600 **MIP** $1000

Popeye Doll, 1958, Gund, 20" tall
EX $55 **NM** $110 **MIP** $250

Popeye Doll, 1960s, Quaker, 12" cloth
EX $20 **NM** $40 **MIP** $100

Popeye Doll, 1960s, 9" vinyl squeeze doll, Popeye w/Swee'Pea
EX $15 **NM** $30 **MIP** $100

Popeye Doll, 1968, Lakeside, 12" tall, sponge rubber
EX $15 **NM** $30 **MIP** $100

Popeye Doll, 1970s, Dakin, Cartoon Theatre, in box
EX $30 **NM** $60 **MIP** $150

Popeye Doll, 1970s, Dakin, hard plastic w/removable clothes
EX $20 **NM** $60 **MIP** $150

Popeye Doll, 1974, Dakin, squeaks
EX $15 **NM** $30 **MIP** $85

Popeye Doll, 1979, Uneeda
EX $20 **NM** $40 **MIP** $90

Popeye Doll, 1979, Uneeda, 16" tall
EX $22 **NM** $45 **MIP** $100

Popeye Doll, 1983, Etone, 8" plush
EX $7 **NM** $15 **MIP** $40

Popeye Doll, 1985, Presents, small
EX $8 **NM** $13 **MIP** $40

Popeye Doll, 1985, Presents, small doll w/pipe molded into hand
EX $10 **NM** $15 **MIP** $45

Popeye Doll, 1990, Presents, small molded plastic, musical #P5949
EX $10 **NM** $15 **MIP** $35

Popeye Doll, 1990, Toy Toons
EX $7 **NM** $15 **MIP** $40

Sea Hag Doll, 1985, Presents
EX $30 **NM** $75 **MIP** $225

Swee'Pea Doll, 1979, Uneeda
EX $10 **NM** $20 **MIP** $70

Swee'Pea Doll, 1985, Presents, large
EX $15 **NM** $30 **MIP** $80

Swee'Pea Doll, 1985, Presents, small
EX $12 **NM** $25 **MIP** $60

Swee'Pea Doll, 1991, Presents, small molded plastic, # P5968
EX $10 **NM** $15 **MIP** $40

Swee'Pea Doll, 1991, Presents, Christmas, small
EX $10 **NM** $20 **MIP** $60

Wimpy Doll, 1950s, KFS, rubber
EX $40 **NM** $75 **MIP** $135

Wimpy Doll, 1985, Presents, holding a hamburger
EX $50 **NM** $100 **MIP** $200

FIGURES

Bluto Figure, Cristallerie Antonio, Italian crystal
EX $15 **NM** $35 **MIP** $85

Brutus Figure, 1962, Japan Olympics, wood, Brutus in barrel
EX $75 **NM** $180 **MIP** $350

Brutus Figure, 1981, Bully, pink shirt
EX $7 **NM** $15 **MIP** $30

Brutus Figure, 1984, Comic-Spain, Brutus w/club
EX $4 **NM** $7 **MIP** $15

Brutus Figure, 1990, Presents, PVC
EX $2 **NM** $3 **MIP** $10

Brutus Figure, 1991, KFS-Hearst, wood
EX $4 **NM** $7 **MIP** $12

Character Figures, 1980, Spoontiques, two 1" figures: Jeep lifting tail, Swee'Pea w/feet showing, each
EX $10 **NM** $25 **MIP** $50

Character Figures, 1980, Spoontiques, 2" figures: Popeye w/barbell, Popeye w/parrot, Olive walking, Popeye flexing muscles, Popeye w/spinach, each
EX $10 **NM** $20 **MIP** $40

Character Figures, 1981, Spoontiques, pewter, three 1" figures: Olive w/hands clasped, Popeye w/muscles, Jeep standing, each
EX $10 **NM** $25 **MIP** $50

Character Figures, 1991, Popeye's Chicken, blue plastic, several characters available
EX $2 **NM** $5 **MIP** $10

Dufus Figure, 1981, Bully, w/hand on stomach
EX $8 **NM** $15 **MIP** $28

Jeep Figure, 1991, KFS-Hearst, wood
EX $7 **NM** $20 **MIP** $50

Olive Oyl Figure, Cristallerie Antonio, Italian crystal
EX $10 **NM** $15 **MIP** $50

Olive Oyl Figure, 1940, KFS, 8" tall
EX $70 **NM** $140 **MIP** $350

Olive Oyl Figure, 1940s, lead
EX $15 **NM** $30 **MIP** $100

Olive Oyl Figure, 1940s, 5" wooden jointed
EX $75 **NM** $165 **MIP** $400

Olive Oyl Figure, 1950s, Multiple Toymakers, 2" tall
EX $15 **NM** $40 **MIP** $75

Olive Oyl Figure, 1974, Ben Cooper, rubber
EX $20 **NM** $40 **MIP** $85

Olive Oyl Figure, 1980, KFS, arms clamped together, hanging figure
EX $5 **NM** $10 **MIP** $30

Olive Oyl Figure, 1980, Amscan, large bendy
EX $6 **NM** $12 **MIP** $30

Olive Oyl Figure, 1981, Bully, w/hands clasp
EX $8 **NM** $15 **MIP** $30

Olive Oyl Figure, 1981, Bully, holding flower
EX $8 **NM** $15 **MIP** $30

Olive Oyl Figure, 1984, Comics Spain, PVC, Olive w/flower
EX $6 **NM** $10 **MIP** $20

Olive Oyl Figure, 1986, Comics Spain, 6" bendy
EX $6 **NM** $10 **MIP** $20

Olive Oyl Figure, 1988, Jesco, small bendy
EX $2 **NM** $4 **MIP** $12

Olive Oyl Figure, 1988, Jesco, large bendy
EX $3 **NM** $6 **MIP** $18

Olive Oyl Figure, 1990, Presents, 3" tall, plastic
EX $2 **NM** $5 **MIP** $10

Olive Oyl Figure, 1990, Presents, PVC
EX $2 **NM** $5 **MIP** $10

Olive Oyl Figure, 1990, Chester, 10", Olive w/rolling pin
EX $10 **NM** $25 **MIP** $50

Olive Oyl Figure, 1990, Mexico, ceramic
EX $10 **NM** $25 **MIP** $50

Olive Oyl Figure, 1991, KFS-Hearst, wood
EX $5 **NM** $10 **MIP** $20

Popeye Figure, Cristallerie Antonio Imperatore, Italian crystal
EX $20 **NM** $30 **MIP** $60

Popeye Figure, Dakin, 8" tall w/ spinach can
EX $22 **NM** $45 **MIP** $100

Popeye Figure, 1930s, 12" tall, chalk, w/ pipe and hat, ashtray base
EX $100 **NM** $250 **MIP** $350

Popeye Figure, 1930s, 5" tall, wood jointed, held together w/string
EX $100 **NM** $200 **MIP** $400

Popeye Figure, 1940s, celluloid w/ wooden feet
EX $75 **NM** $125 **MIP** $225

Popeye Figure, 1940s, lead
EX $25 **NM** $50 **MIP** $100

Popeye Figure, 1944, Sirocco-KFS, 5", wood
EX $70 **NM** $120 **MIP** $220

Popeye Figure, 1950s, England, 7", bendy, yellow pants
EX $30 **NM** $60 **MIP** $170

Popeye Figure, 1950s, plastic, Popeye on four wheels w/telescope
EX $25 **NM** $50 **MIP** $130

Popeye Figure, 1950s, Japan, celluloid
EX $40 **NM** $75 **MIP** $150

Popeye Figure, 1960s, Combex, rubber, Popey w/ a can of spinach
EX $20 **NM** $40 **MIP** $90

Popeye Figure, 1962, Japan Olympics, wood, Popeye at bat
EX $150 **NM** $325 **MIP** $550

Popeye Figure, 1968, Lakeside, miniflex
EX $10 **NM** $25 **MIP** $70

Popeye Figure, 1969, Lakeside, superflex
EX $10 **NM** $25 **MIP** $60

Popeye Figure, 1970, Duncan, 8" tall
EX $20 **NM** $40 **MIP** $70

Popeye Figure, 1970s, ceramic, removeable head Popeye
EX $30 **NM** $60 **MIP** $100

Popeye Figure, 1974, Ben Cooper, rubber
EX $8 **NM** $15 **MIP** $40

Popeye Figure, 1978, Bronco, bendy
EX $6 **NM** $10 **MIP** $25

Popeye Figure, 1979, Imperial
EX $6 **NM** $10 **MIP** $20

Popeye Figure, 1980, Amscan, small bendy
EX $4 **NM** $7 **MIP** $14

Popeye Figure, 1980, Amscan, large bendy
EX $8 **NM** $12 **MIP** $20

Popeye Figure, 1981, Bully, several variations
EX $9 **NM** $18 **MIP** $30

Popeye Figure, 1984, Comics Spain, PVC, Popeye w/ spinach
EX $5 **NM** $10 **MIP** $20

Popeye Figure, 1986, Comics Spain, 6" bendy, white pants
EX $3 **NM** $6 **MIP** $20

Popeye Figure, 1988, Jesco, bendy
EX $6 **NM** $10 **MIP** $25

Popeye Figure, 1988, Jesco, small bendy
EX $2 **NM** $5 **MIP** $15

Popeye Figure, 1990, Mexico, ceramic
EX $7 **NM** $15 **MIP** $35

Popeye Figure, 1990, Presents, PVC
EX $1 **NM** $4 **MIP** $8

Popeye Figure, 1990, Presents, 3" tall, plastic
EX $2 **NM** $3 **MIP** $6

Popeye Figure, 1990, Chester, 10", ceramic, Popeye w/spinach
EX $6 **NM** $10 **MIP** $30

Popeye Figure, 1991, KFS-Hearst, wood
EX $8 **NM** $12 **MIP** $25

Popeye Galley Steward Figure, 1980, KFS, ceramic
EX $10 **NM** $22 **MIP** $50

Swee'Pea Figure, ceramic, one of five
EX $5 **NM** $15 **MIP** $45

Swee'Pea Figure, Cristallerie Antionio Imperatore, Italian crystal
EX $15 **NM** $30 **MIP** $50

Swee'Pea Figure, 1984, Comics Spain, PVC, Swee'Pea w/cake
EX $4 **NM** $8 **MIP** $20

Swee'Pea Figure, 1984, Presents, PVC
EX $2 **NM** $4 **MIP** $10

Swee'Pea Figure, 1990, Presents, 3" tall, plastic
EX $5 **NM** $10 **MIP** $20

Wimpy Figure, Cristallerie Antionio Imperatore, Italian crystal
EX $25 **NM** $40 **MIP** $75

Wimpy Figure, 1940s, lead
EX $15 **NM** $30 **MIP** $80

Wimpy Figure, 1944, Sirocco-KFS, 5", wood
EX $60 **NM** $90 **MIP** $200

Wimpy Figure, 1950s, Buitoni, premium
EX $40 **NM** $70 **MIP** $150

Wimpy Figure, 1981, Bully, yellow hat
EX $6 **NM** $12 **MIP** $25

Wimpy Figure, 1984, Comics Spain, Wimpy w/hamburger
EX $7 **NM** $15 **MIP** $30

Wimpy Figure, 1990, Presents, PVC
EX $2 **NM** $5 **MIP** $10

GAME

Adventures of Popeye Game, 1957, Transogram
EX $50 **NM** $80 **MIP** $160

Boxing Game, 1981, Harmony
EX $7 **NM** $15 **MIP** $40

Jumbo Card Game, 1978, House of Games
EX $10 **NM** $20 **MIP** $35

Jumbo Trading Card Game, 1960s, Dynamic Toy
EX $15 **NM** $30 **MIP** $60

Magic Play Around Game, 1960s, Amsco
EX $20 **NM** $45 **MIP** $100

Pocket Pin Ball, 1983, Nintendo/Ja-Ru, holes
EX $5 **NM** $10 **MIP** $20

Pocket Pin Ball, 1983, Nintendo/Ja-Ru, cups
EX $5 **NM** $10 **MIP** $20

Popeye Arcade Game, 1980, Parker Bros., card game
EX $5 **NM** $10 **MIP** $25

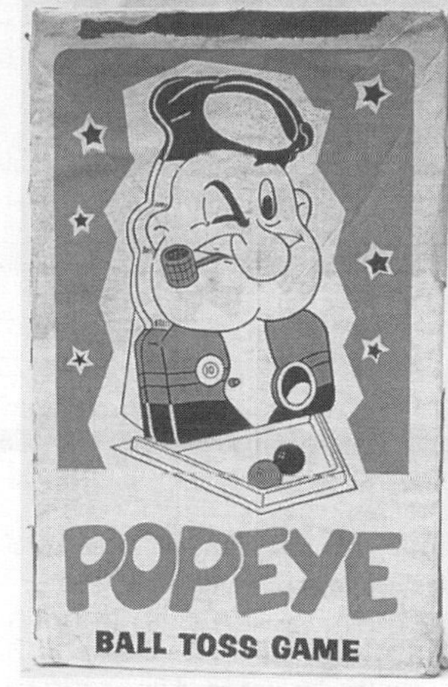

Popeye Ball Toss Game, 1950s, KFS
EX $50 **NM** $75 **MIP** $160

Popeye Bingo, 1929, Bar Zim
EX $75 **NM** $100 **MIP** $200

Popeye Break-A-Plate Game, 1963, Combex
EX $30 **NM** $80 **MIP** $150

Popeye Fishing Game, 1962, Transogram, magnetic
EX $15 **NM** $30 **MIP** $80

Popeye Fishing Game, 1980, Fleetwood
EX $5 **NM** $10 **MIP** $25

Popeye Games, 1960s, Ed-U-Card, set of four games
EX $15 **NM** $30 **MIP** $60

Popeye Hammer Game, 1960s, Holgate
EX $70 **NM** $140 **MIP** $280

Popeye Menu Pinball Game, 1935, Durable Toy and Novelty
EX $100 **NM** $175 **MIP** $275

Popeye Mini Tennis Game, 1970s, Nordic
EX $10 **NM** $15 **MIP** $30

Popeye Nail-On Game, 1963, Colorforms
EX $20 **NM** $45 **MIP** $100

Popeye Party Game, 1937, Whitman, posters, paper pipes, game box
EX $50 **NM** $85 **MIP** $170

Popeye Pinball Game, 1983, Ja-Ru
EX $6 **NM** $10 **MIP** $25

Popeye Pipe Toss Game, 1935, Rosebud Art, small version w/wooden pipe
EX $50 **NM** $120 **MIP** $210

Popeye

Popeye Playing Card Game, 1934, Whitman, 5" x 7", green box
EX $50 **NM** $85 **MIP** $160

Popeye Playing Card Game, 1938, Whitman, blue box
EX $40 **NM** $70 **MIP** $150

Popeye Playing Card Game, 1983, Parker Bros.
EX $6 **NM** $10 **MIP** $30

Popeye Ring Toss Game, 1957, Transogram
EX $32 **NM** $65 **MIP** $135

Popeye Ring Toss Game, 1980, Fleetwood
EX $6 **NM** $10 **MIP** $25

Popeye Shipwreck Game, 1933, Einson-Freeman
EX $75 **NM** $125 **MIP** $250

Popeye Spinach Target Game, 1960s, Gardner
EX $40 **NM** $75 **MIP** $120

Popeye the Juggler Bead Game, 1929, Bar-Zim, 3-1/2" x 5", covered w/glass
EX $40 **NM** $60 **MIP** $120

Popeye Video Game, 1983, Nintendo
EX $12 **NM** $20 **MIP** $30

Popeye/Olive Oyl/Wimpy Skill Games, 1965, Lido
EX $10 **NM** $16 **MIP** $40

Popeye's Gang Pinball Game, 1970s, MSS
EX $13 **NM** $25 **MIP** $50

Popeye's Lucky Jeep Game, 1936, Northwestern Products
EX $100 **NM** $175 **MIP** $300

Popeye's Peg Board Game, 1934, Bar Zim
EX $100 **NM** $200 **MIP** $375

Popeye's Sliding Boards and Ladders, 1958, Warren Built-Rite
EX $12 **NM** $25 **MIP** $80

Popeye's Spinach Hunt Game, 1976, Whitman
EX $11 **NM** $22 **MIP** $50

Popeye's Three Game Set, 1956, Built-Rite
EX $20 **NM** $40 **MIP** $90

Popeye's Tiddly Winks, 1948, Parker Bros.
EX $20 **NM** $40 **MIP** $100

Popeye's Treasure Map Game, 1977, Whitman
EX $12 **NM** $25 **MIP** $50

Popeye's Where's Me Pipe Game
EX $30 **NM** $50 **MIP** $90

Puzzle Game, 1978, Waddington's House of Games
EX $10 **NM** $20 **MIP** $40

Ring the Bell with Hammer Game, 1960s, Harett-Gilmar
EX $25 **NM** $42 **MIP** $70

Ring Toss Stand-Up Game, 1958, Transogram
EX $15 **NM** $30 **MIP** $70

Roly Poly and Cork Gun Game, 1958, Knickbocker
EX $60 **NM** $120 **MIP** $210

Rub 'N Win Party Game, 1980, Spot-O-Gold
EX $5 **NM** $10 **MIP** $25

Skeet Shoot Game, 1950, Irwin
EX $75 **NM** $125 **MIP** $185

Skoozit Pick-A-Puzzle Game, 1966, Ideal
EX $15 **NM** $35 **MIP** $70

Water Ball Game, 1983, Nintendo, one basket
EX $6 **NM** $10 **MIP** $25

LUNCH BOX

Mini Lunch Box, 1990, Sanrio, plastic
EX $4 **NM** $10 **MIP** $25

MUSIC BOX

Brutus Music Box, 1980, KFS, Brutus dancing
EX $10 **NM** $15 **MIP** $40

Brutus Music Box, 1989, Presents, #P5984
EX $8 **NM** $17 **MIP** $45

Music Box, 1980, Vandor, revolving Popeye spanks Swee'Pea, ceramic
EX $20 **NM** $45 **MIP** $100

Music Box, 1980, Vandor, revolving Olive w/Popeye dancing, ceramic
EX $20 **NM** $45 **MIP** $100

Music Box, 1980, Vandor, Wimpy on top of hamburger, ceramic
EX $20 **NM** $45 **MIP** $100

Olive Oyl Music Box, 1980, KFS, Olive dancing
EX $8 **NM** $20 **MIP** $50

Olive Oyl Music Box, 1989, Presents, #P5983
EX $8 **NM** $20 **MIP** $50

Popeye and Olive Oyl Music Box, Schmid, 8-1/4" figural box
EX $50 **NM** $100 **MIP** $180

Swee'Pea Music Box, 1980, KFS, Swee'Pea dancing
EX $8 **NM** $15 **MIP** $50

Swee'Pea Music Box, 1989, Presents, #P5986
EX $8 **NM** $15 **MIP** $50

Wimpy Music Box, 1989, Presents, #P5985
EX $8 **NM** $15 **MIP** $40

PIN

Pin, 1935, JCPenney, Back to School Days w/Popeye
EX $20 **NM** $40 **MIP** $90

RECORD

Fleas A Crowd Record, 1962, Peter Pan, 78 rpm
EX $10 **NM** $25 **MIP** $50

Olive Oyl on Troubled Waters Record, 1976, Peter Pan, 45 rpm
EX $7 **NM** $20 **MIP** $40

Original Radio Broadcasts Record, 1977, Golden Age, 33 rpm
EX $7 **NM** $25 **MIP** $60

Picture Disc Record, 1948, Record of America, 78 rpm
EX $25 **NM** $50 **MIP** $100

Picture Disc Record, 1982, Peter Pan, 33 rpm
EX $6 **NM** $10 **MIP** $25

Pollution Solution Record, 1970s, Peter Pan, 45 rpm
EX $5 **NM** $10 **MIP** $35

Popeye and Friends Record, 1981, Merry Records, 33 rpm
EX $3 **NM** $10 **MIP** $25

Popeye French Record, 1981, Polygram, 45 rpm
EX $7 **NM** $15 **MIP** $35

Popeye in the Movies Record, Peter Pan, 33 rpm w/book
EX $6 **NM** $15 **MIP** $35

Popeye Launches His New Song Hits Record, 1958, Peter Pan, 45 rpm
EX $15 **NM** $30 **MIP** $80

Popeye on Parade/Strike Me Pink Record, 1950s, Cricket, 45 rpm
EX $12 **NM** $25 **MIP** $60

Popeye Record, 1977, Peter Pan, 33 rpm, four stories, #1114
EX $6 **NM** $15 **MIP** $30

Popeye the Ladies Man Record, 33 rpm
EX $8 **NM** $15 **MIP** $35

Popeye the Movie Soundtrack Record, 1980, Paramount
EX $6 **NM** $15 **MIP** $30

Popeye the Sailor Man and His Friends Record, 1960s, Golden, 33 rpm
EX $8 **NM** $15 **MIP** $30

Popeye the Sailor Man Record, 1959, Golden, 45 rpm
EX $7 **NM** $15 **MIP** $30

Popeye the Sailor Man Record, 1960, Diplomat Records, 33 rpm
EX $7 **NM** $15 **MIP** $35

Popeye the Sailor Man Record, 1976, Peter Pan, 33 rpm
EX $7 **NM** $15 **MIP** $35

Popeye's Favorite Sea Shanties Record, 1960, RCA Camden
EX $10 **NM** $25 **MIP** $50

Popeye's Favorite Sea Songs Record, 1959, Peter Pan, 45 rpm
EX $10 **NM** $25 **MIP** $60

Popeye's Favorite Stories Record, 1960, RCA Camden, 33 rpm
EX $10 **NM** $20 **MIP** $40

Popeye's Songs About...... Record, 1961, Golden, 33 rpm
EX $8 **NM** $18 **MIP** $35

Six Popeye Songs Record, 1950s, Wonderland Records, 45 rpm
EX $8 **NM** $30 **MIP** $70

Song and Story Skin Diver Record, 1964, KFS
EX $10 **NM** $20 **MIP** $40

Songs of Health Record, 1960s, Golden, 45 rpm
EX $6 **NM** $10 **MIP** $25

Songs of Safety Record, 1960s, Golden, 45 rpm
EX $6 **NM** $10 **MIP** $25

Whale of a Tale Record, 1981, Peter Pan, 45 rpm
EX $6 NM $10 MIP $20

RING

Candy Rings, 1989, Alberts
EX $6 NM $15 MIP $25

Popeye and Oscar Flicker Ring, blue
EX $8 NM $20 MIP $35

Popeye and Swee'Pea Flicker Ring, blue
EX $8 NM $15 MIP $35

Popeye and Wimpy Flicker Ring, blue
EX $8 NM $15 MIP $35

TOY

Apprentice Printer, 1970s, MSS
EX $6 NM $20 MIP $40

Ball and Jacks Set, MSS
EX $6 NM $12 MIP $3035

Ball and Paddle, BC
EX $6 NM $15 MIP $35

Balloon Pump, 1957, inflato pump
EX $40 NM $60 MIP $120

Barber Shop, 1970s, Larami
EX $5 NM $15 MIP $30

Baseball, 1983, Ja-Ru
EX $10 NM $20 MIP $40

Beach Boat, 1980, H.G. Industries, red or yellow
EX $5 NM $10 MIP $35

Biffbat-Fly Back Paddle, 1935
EX $75 NM $100 MIP $175

Billion Bubbles, 1984, Larami
EX $4 NM $8 MIP $15

Blackboard, 1962, Bar Zim
EX $20 NM $40 MIP $85

Bluto's Road Roller, 1980, Lesney/Matchbox, CS-14, 2-3/4" x 2-7/8"
EX $8 NM $18 MIP $50

Bop Bag, 1981, Miner Industries
EX $8 NM $15 MIP $30

Boxing Gloves, 1960s, Everlast
EX $35 NM $60 MIP $150

Brutus Dog Toy, 1986, Petex
EX $6 NM $12 MIP $25

Brutus Figure Painting Kit, 1980, Avalon
EX $8 NM $15 MIP $35

Brutus Hand Puppet, 1960s, Gund
EX $25 NM $60 MIP $120

Brutus Hi-Pop Ball, 1981, Ja-Ru
EX $6 NM $10 MIP $20

Brutus Hookies, 1977, Tiger
EX $5 NM $18 MIP $50

Brutus Horse and Cart, 1938, Marx, celluloid, w/Brutus, horse, and cart
EX $500 NM $825 MIP $1050

Brutus In Jeep, 1950s, tiny plastic car
EX $15 NM $35 MIP $80

Brutus Jump-Up, 1970s, Imperial
EX $8 NM $20 MIP $40

Brutus Painting Kit, 1980, Avalon
EX $8 NM $15 MIP $25

Brutus Soaky, 1960s, Colgate-Palmolive
EX $15 NM $35 MIP $80

Brutus Sports Car, 1950s, tiny plastic car
EX $15 NM $35 MIP $75

Brutus Wind-Up Toy, 1980, Durham
EX $5 NM $10 MIP $25

Bubble Blower, 1958, Transogram
EX $15 NM $35 MIP $90

Bubble Blower Boat, 1984, Larami
EX $7 NM $15 MIP $40

Bubble Blowing Popeye, 1950s, Linemar
EX $550 NM $1000 MIP $1650

Bubble Blowing Train, 1970s, Hong Kong, pink
EX $10 NM $20 MIP $60

Bubble 'N Clean, 1960s, Woolfoam
EX $20 NM $45 MIP $75

Bubble Pipe, 1960s, KFS, yellow w/red end
EX $15 NM $30 MIP $80

Bubble Pipe, 1985, Ja-Ru
EX $5 NM $12 MIP $35

Bubble Set, 1936, Transogram, two wooden pipes, tray, soap in 5" x 7-1/2" box
EX $100 NM $200 MIP $300

Bubble Shooter, 1980s, Ja-Ru, orange or yellow body
EX $5 NM $10 MIP $30

Bubbleblaster, 1980, Carlin Playthings
EX $10 NM $15 MIP $30

Bubbles Blaster, 1984, Larami
EX $5 NM $10 MIP $20

Bubbles with Dip Pow Bubbles, 1986, MSS
EX $5 NM $10 MIP $20

Cap Gun, 1981, Ja-Ru
EX $10 NM $25 MIP $60

Chain Bubbles Maker, 1984, Larami, red Popeye
EX $6 NM $10 MIP $20

Chalk, 1936, American Crayon, white, 18 pieces
EX $50 NM $90 MIP $125

Change Purse, 1990, Sanrio
EX $5 NM $10 MIP $20

Checker Board, 1959, Ideal
EX $20 NM $35 MIP $90

Chinese Jump Rope, MSS
EX $4 NM $12 MIP $25

Colorforms Birthday Party Set, 1961, Colorforms
EX $25 NM $70 MIP $110

Colorforms Movie Version, 1980, Colorforms
EX $7 NM $15 MIP $30

Color-Me Stickers, 1983, Diamond Toymakers
EX $5 NM $12 MIP $25

Color-Vue Pencil-by-Numbers, 1979, Hasbro
EX $10 NM $20 MIP $35

Construction Trucks, 1981, Larami
EX $6 NM $15 MIP $30

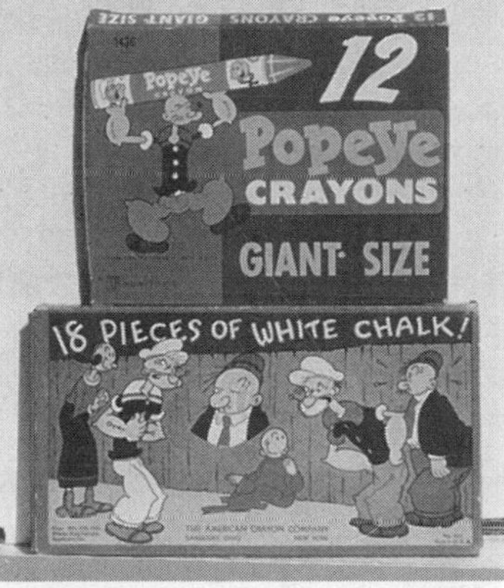

Crayons, 1933, American Crayon, 12 giant crayons
EX $50 NM $75 MIP $150

Crayons, 1950s, American Crayon
EX $20 NM $35 MIP $80

Crayons, 1958, Dixon, 12 giant crayons
EX $20 NM $35 MIP $80

Dockside Presto Magix, 1980, APC
EX $3 NM $6 MIP $12

Double Action Water Gun Set, MSS
EX $10 NM $20 MIP $40

Drawing Board, 1978, KFS, slate w/rope attached
EX $8 NM $16 MIP $40

Drawing Desk, 1980, Carlin Playthings
EX $10 NM $25 MIP $60

Duck Shoot, 1980s, Ja-Ru
EX $5 NM $15 MIP $30

Erase-O-Board and Magic Screen Set, 1957, Hassenfeld Bros.
EX $50 NM $90 MIP $180

Film Projector, Cinexin-Spain, 8mm w/13 movies
EX $85 NM $140 MIP $250

Finger Puppet Family, 1960s, Denmark Plastics
EX $25 NM $50 MIP $100

Flashlight, 1960s, Bantam-Lite, three color, wrist light
EX $10 NM $20 MIP $40

Flashlight, 1983, Larami, blue, yellow, or red
EX $7 NM $15 MIP $30

Foto-Fun Printing Kit, 1958, Fun Bilt
EX $32 NM $65 MIP $130

Funny Color Foam, 1983, Creative Aerosol
EX $5 NM $15 MIP $60

Funny Face Maker, 1962, Jaymar
EX $15 NM $30 MIP $70

Funny Films Viewer, 1940s, Acme
EX $50 NM $75 MIP $120

Funny Fire Fighters, 1930s, Marx, celluloid figures, Popeye on ladder and Bluto drives fire truck--both figures wear boxing gloves
EX $1250 NM $2500 MIP $3500

Give-A-Show Projector, Kenner, projector w/slides
EX $75 NM $100 MIP $180

Gumball Dispenser, 1983, Superior Toys, pocket pack
EX $10 NM $20 MIP $40

Gumball Machine, 1968, Hasbro, 6", shape of Popeye's head
EX $30 NM $50 MIP $100

Gumball Machine, 1983, Superior Toys, Popeye gives Olive flowers
EX $10 NM $20 MIP $45

Gumball Machine, 1983, Superior Toys, Popeye eating spinach
EX $10 NM $20 MIP $45

Halloween Bucket, 1979, Renz, shaped like Popeye's head, red, yellow or blue
EX $10 NM $20 MIP $40

Harmonica, 1973, Larami
EX $15 NM $40 MIP $90

Hat and Pipe, 1950s, Empire Plastics
EX $40 NM $60 MIP $110

Holster Set, 1960s, Halco
EX $90 NM $150 MIP $250

Horseshoe Magnets, 1984, Larami
EX $5 NM $15 MIP $30

Hunting Knife, 1973, Larami
EX $20 NM $50 MIP $85

ID Set, 1982, Gordy
EX $5 NM $15 MIP $40

Jack-in-the-Box, 1961, Mattel
EX $60 NM $120 MIP $210

Jack-in-the-Box, 1979, Nasta
EX $25 NM $50 MIP $100

Jack-in-the-Box, 1983, Nasta
EX $20 NM $40 MIP $85

Jeep Lucky Spinner, 1936, KFS, on card
EX $250 NM $400 MIP $600

Kaleidoscope, 1979, Larami
EX $10 NM $25 MIP $85

Kazoo and Harmonica, 1979, Larami
EX $8 NM $20 MIP $35

Kazoo Pipe, 1934, Northwestern Products
EX $75 NM $125 MIP $200

Kazoo Pipe, 1960s, Peerless Playthings, yellow
EX $15 NM $30 MIP $60

Kite, 1980, Sky-Way, regular
EX $4 NM $8 MIP $25

Kite, 1980, Sky-Way, inflatable
EX $6 NM $12 MIP $25

Lantern, 1950s, Linemar, 7-1/2" tall, battery operated, light in belly
EX $130 NM $275 MIP $525

Magic Glow Putty, FC Famous Toys
EX $6 NM $10 MIP $15

Magic Slate, 1959, Lowe
EX $20 NM $40 MIP $90

Magic Slate Paper Saver, 1981, Whitman
EX $4 NM $8 MIP $25

Make-A-Picture Premium, 1934, Quaker
EX $100 NM $175 MIP $250

Marble, 1940s
EX $8 NM $20 MIP $50

Marble Set, 1935, Akro Agate, #116
EX $1000 NM $1500 MIP $2200

Marble Set, 1980, Imperial
EX $12 NM $25 MIP $70

Marble Shooter, 1940s, milk glass container
EX $35 NM $50 MIP $100

Metal Tapping Set, 1950s, Carlton Dank
EX $25 NM $50 MIP $120

Metal Target Set, 1983, Ja-Ru
EX $8 NM $18 MIP $60

Metal Whistle, 1981, Ja-Ru
EX $5 NM $12 MIP $35

Micro-Movie, 1990, Fascinations, Popeye-Ali Baba
EX $4 NM $8 MIP $15

Miniature Train Set, 1980, Larami
EX $8 NM $15 MIP $60

Model Kit, 1970s, Carto, Popeye and Olive Oyl
EX $25 NM $60 MIP $120

Modeling Clay, 1936, American Crayon
EX $75 NM $125 MIP $200

Motor Friend, 1976, Nasta
EX $10 NM $20 MIP $50

Muscle Builder Bluto, 1980, Carlin Playthings
EX $6 NM $12 MIP $25

Muscle Builder Popeye, 1980, Carlin Playthings
EX $6 NM $12 MIP $30

My Popeye Coloring Kit, 1957, American Crayon
EX $50 NM $100 MIP $175

Official Popeye Pipe, 1958, 5" stem w/2" bowl, battery operated, "It lites, it toots"
EX $45 NM $100 MIP $200

Old Time Wild West Train, 1984, Larami
EX $5 NM $20 MIP $70

Olive Oyl Bike Bobbers, 1960s, KFS
EX $15 NM $25 MIP $60

Olive Oyl Costume, 1950s, Collegeville
EX $40 NM $75 MIP $120

Olive Oyl Costume, 1976, Ben Cooper
EX $10 NM $20 MIP $70

Olive Oyl Figure Painting Kit, 1980, Avalon
EX $6 NM $12 MIP $20

Olive Oyl Foam Toy, 1979, Cribmates
EX $8 NM $15 MIP $35

Olive Oyl Hand Puppet, 1960s, Gund, comic strip body
EX $30 NM $75 MIP $150

Olive Oyl Hi-Pop Ball, 1981, Ja-Ru
EX $5 NM $10 MIP $40

Olive Oyl Hookies, 1977, Tiger
EX $4 NM $10 MIP $30

Olive Oyl in Airplane, 1970s, Corgi
EX $12 NM $30 MIP $70

Olive Oyl Jump-Up, Imperial
EX $5 NM $10 MIP $20

Olive Oyl Marionette, 1950s, Gund, 11-1/2" tall
EX $70 NM $120 MIP $210

Olive Oyl Painting Kit, 1980, Avalon
EX $5 NM $10 MIP $25

Olive Oyl Push Puppet, 1960s, Kohner, 4" tall, plastic
EX $15 NM $35 MIP $75

Olive Oyl Sports Car, 1950s, tiny plastic car
EX $15 NM $35 MIP $80

Olive Oyl Squeak Toy, 1979, Cribmates, on a stick
EX $5 NM $13 MIP $30

Olive Oyl Squeeze Toy, 1950s, Rempel, vinyl
EX $30 NM $60 MIP $120

Olive Oyl Swim Ring, 1979, Wet Set-Zee Toys
EX $5 NM $10 MIP $25

Olive Oyl Tiles, 1970s, Italy, 3" x 5" w/stand
EX $12 **NM** $25 **MIP** $50

Olive Oyl Toboggan, 1979, KFS
EX $6 **NM** $15 **MIP** $35

Olive Oyl's Convertible, 1980, Lesney/Matchbox, CS-15, 2-3/4" x 2-7/8"
EX $12 **NM** $30 **MIP** $75

Paint 'N Puff Set, 1979, Art Award, two versions
EX $6 **NM** $12 **MIP** $35

Pick-Up Sticks, 1957, Lido
EX $20 **NM** $40 **MIP** $80

Pirate Island Presto Magix, 1980, American Pub.
EX $10 **NM** $20 **MIP** $25

Plane and Parachute, 1980, Fleetwood
EX $8 **NM** $15 **MIP** $35

Play Money, 1930s, color bucks-framed
EX $12 **NM** $35 **MIP** $80

Play Money, 1970, The Toy House
EX $5 **NM** $10 **MIP** $30

Pool Table, 1984, Larami
EX $5 **NM** $10 **MIP** $25

Pop Maker and Son, 1987, Ja-Ru
EX $2 **NM** $4 **MIP** $15

Pop Pistol, 1984, Larami
EX $4 **NM** $10 **MIP** $40

Popeye Air Mattress, 1979, Zee Toys
EX $8 **NM** $20 **MIP** $25

Popeye and Brutus Punch Me Bop Bag, 1960s, Dartmore
EX $15 **NM** $30 **MIP** $60

Popeye and Olive Oyl Sand Set, 1950s, Peer Products, bucket, shovel
EX $20 **NM** $50 **MIP** $125

Popeye and Olive Oyl Toy Watch, 1970s, Unknown, flicker
EX $6 **NM** $12 **MIP** $30

Popeye and Shark Swim Ring, 1960s, Laurel Star-Japan
EX $10 **NM** $25 **MIP** $35

Popeye and Wimpy Walk-A-Way Toy, 1964, Marx
EX $25 **NM** $50 **MIP** $120

Popeye Arcade, 1980, Fleetwood
EX $6 **NM** $12 **MIP** $25

Popeye at the Wheel, 1950s, Woolnough, musical
EX $150 **NM** $300 **MIP** $625

Popeye Ball, rubber kick ball
EX $7 **NM** $13 **MIP** $30

Popeye Bathtub Toy, 1960s, Stahlwood, floating boat
EX $20 **NM** $40 **MIP** $90

Popeye Bend-I-Face, 1967, Lakeside
EX $15 **NM** $35 **MIP** $65

Popeye Bingo, 1980, Nasta
EX $6 **NM** $10 **MIP** $20

Popeye Blow Me Down Airport, 1935, Marx
EX $1600 **NM** $2300 **MIP** $3000

Popeye Bubble Liquid, 1970s, M. Shimmel Sons, shaped like Popeye w/necktie similar to a sailor's knot
EX $8 **NM** $15 **MIP** $25

Popeye Car, 1980, Vandor, Popeye and Olive in blue or pink car
EX $20 **NM** $45 **MIP** $100

Popeye Carnival, 1965, Toymaster
EX $75 **NM** $100 **MIP** $250

Popeye Coloring Set, 1960s, Hasbro, numbered, w/pencils
EX $12 **NM** $30 **MIP** $70

Popeye Costume, 1950s, Collegeville
EX $40 **NM** $75 **MIP** $120

Popeye Costume, 1980s, Collegeville
EX $9 **NM** $18 **MIP** $40

Popeye Costume, 1984, Ben Cooper
EX $7 **NM** $15 **MIP** $35

Popeye Dog Toy, 1986, Petex
EX $3 **NM** $6 **MIP** $10

Popeye Figure Painting Kit, 1980, Avalon
EX $4 **NM** $8 **MIP** $20

Popeye Finger Rings, 1949, Post Toasties
EX $20 **NM** $50 **MIP** $125

Popeye Flicker Badge, 1960s, Varivue, Popeye eating spinach
EX $8 **NM** $15 **MIP** $35

Popeye Flickers, 1960s, Sonwell
EX $8 **NM** $15 **MIP** $35

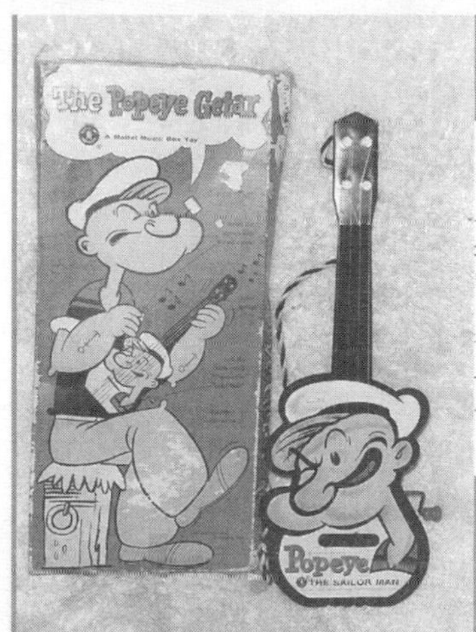

Popeye Ge-tar, 1960s, Mattel, 14" long, shaped like Popeye's face, plays "I'm Popeye the Sailor Man"
EX $30 **NM** $60 **MIP** $125

Popeye Glow Putty, 1984, Larami
EX $3 **NM** $6 **MIP** $10

Popeye Goes Swimming Colorforms, 1963, Colorforms
EX $15 **NM** $35 **MIP** $75

Popeye Goes to School Television, 1950s, Zaboly
EX $30 **NM** $50 **MIP** $100

Popeye Hand Puppet, 1950s, Gund, plush
EX $15 **NM** $40 **MIP** $100

Popeye Hand Puppet, 1960s, Gund, Popeye's head on cloth body
EX $20 **NM** $50 **MIP** $120

Popeye Hi-Pop Ball, 1981, Ja-Ru
EX $4 **NM** $8 **MIP** $25

Popeye in Boat, 1970s, Corgi
EX $10 **NM** $20 **MIP** $60

Popeye Jump-Up, 1970s, Imperial
EX $8 **NM** $20 **MIP** $50

Popeye Magic Play Around, 1950s, Amsco, characters w/magnetic bases that slide across play set
EX $35 **NM** $70 **MIP** $150

Popeye Marionette, Create-Japan, wood
EX $100 **NM** $200 **MIP** $425

Popeye Marionette, 1950s, Gund, 11-1/2" tall
EX $75 **NM** $150 **MIP** $325

Popeye Mini Winder, 1980, Durham
EX $4 **NM** $10 **MIP** $30

Popeye Model Kit, 1964, Tokyo Plamo, #808
EX $60 **NM** $120 **MIP** $250

Popeye on Tricycle, Linemar, 4-1/2", tin wind-up w/celluloid arms and legs, bell rings behind Popeye
EX $350 **NM** $750 **MIP** $1000

Popeye One Man Band, 1980s, Larami
EX $6 **NM** $10 **MIP** $30

Popeye Paddle Ball, 1984, Larami, w/color photo of Popeye
EX $7 **NM** $15 **MIP** $40

Popeye Paint and Crayon Set, 1934, Milton Bradley
EX $75 **NM** $150 **MIP** $300

Popeye Paint By Numbers, 1960s, Hasbro
EX $12 **NM** $25 **MIP** $75

Popeye Paint Set, 1933, American Crayon, 6", tin
EX $75 **NM** $150 **MIP** $300

Popeye Paint-By-Numbers, 1981, Hasbro
EX $8 **NM** $13 **MIP** $30

Popeye Painting Kit, 1980, Avalon
EX $6 **NM** $10 **MIP** $25

Popeye Pencil-By-Numbers, 1979, Hasbro
EX $10 **NM** $25 **MIP** $60

Popeye Peppy Puppet, 1970, Kohner
EX $12 **NM** $25 **MIP** $50

Popeye Pipe, 1940s, red wooden
EX $20 **NM** $40 **MIP** $100

Popeye Pipe, 1958, Micro-Lite-KFS
EX $12 **NM** $30 **MIP** $100

Popeye Pipe, 1970, Edmonton Pipe, figural head
EX $15 **NM** $25 **MIP** $60

Popeye Pipe, 1970s, MSS, plastic, white
EX $8 **NM** $20 **MIP** $50

Popeye Pipe, 1970s, KFS, plastic kazoo, red and blue
EX $6 **NM** $20 **MIP** $50

Popeye Pipe, 1980, Harmony
EX $6 **NM** $10 **MIP** $20

Popeye Pistol, Delcast, Super mini cap w/24 caps No. 807-BB
EX $15 **NM** $30 **MIP** $80

Popeye Pistol, 1935, Marx
EX $400 NM $800 MIP $1300

Popeye Play Set, 1979, Cribmates, Popeye, Olive Oyl, and Swee' Pea squeak toys, mirror, rattle and pillow
EX $15 NM $30 MIP $60

Popeye Presto Paints, 1961, Kenner
EX $15 NM $50 MIP $70

Popeye Pull Toy, 1950s, Metal Masters, 10-1/2" x 11-1/2", xylophone, wood w/paper litho labels, metal wheels
EX $150 NM $225 MIP $500

Popeye Puppet, Kohner, pull string, Popeye jumps
EX $10 NM $15 MIP $30

Popeye Push Puppet, 1960, Kohner, 4" tall
EX $20 NM $45 MIP $90

Popeye Sailboat, 1976, KFS
EX $9 NM $15 MIP $60

Popeye Service Station, 1979, Larami
EX $8 NM $25 MIP $70

Popeye Soaky, 1960s, Colgate-Palmolive
EX $15 NM $40 MIP $75

Popeye Soaky, 1987, KFS, British
EX $12 NM $20 MIP $45

Popeye Sparkler, 1959, Chein
EX $90 NM $125 MIP $200

Popeye Speed Boat, 1981, Harmony
EX $10 NM $16 MIP $40

Popeye Speedboard Pull Toy, 1960s
EX $175 NM $375 MIP $700

Popeye Sports Car, 1950s, Linemar
EX $225 NM $425 MIP $800

Popeye Squeeze Toy, 1950s, Rempel, 8" tall, vinyl
EX $25 NM $50 MIP $120

Popeye Squeeze Toy, 1979, Cribmates, Popeye on a stick
EX $8 NM $15 MIP $40

Popeye Supergyro, 1980s, Larami
EX $6 NM $10 MIP $25

Popeye the Pilot, 1940s, Chein, tin wind-up airplane, 8" long, 8" wingspan
EX $750 NM $1200 MIP $1600

Popeye the Weatherman Colorforms, 1959, Colorforms
EX $20 NM $50 MIP $120

Popeye Tiles, 1970s, Italy, 3" x 5" w/stand
EX $15 NM $35 MIP $70

Popeye Toboggan, 1979, KFS
EX $6 NM $10 MIP $30

Popeye Train Pull Toy, Larami
EX $150 NM $250 MIP $450

Popeye Train Set, 1973, Larami
EX $6 NM $15 MIP $50

Popeye Transit Company Moving Van, 1950, Linemar, tin
EX $550 NM $900 MIP $1300

Popeye Tricky Trapeze, 1970, Kohner
EX $15 NM $35 MIP $80

Popeye Tricky Walker, 1960s, Jaymar, plastic
EX $10 NM $25 MIP $60

Popeye Tricycling, 1950s, Linemar
EX $400 NM $650 MIP $1000

Popeye Tug and Dingy Pull Toy, 1950s, Fisher-Price, wood
EX $135 NM $225 MIP $375

Popeye Tugboat, 1961, Ideal, inflatable
EX $15 NM $35 MIP $70

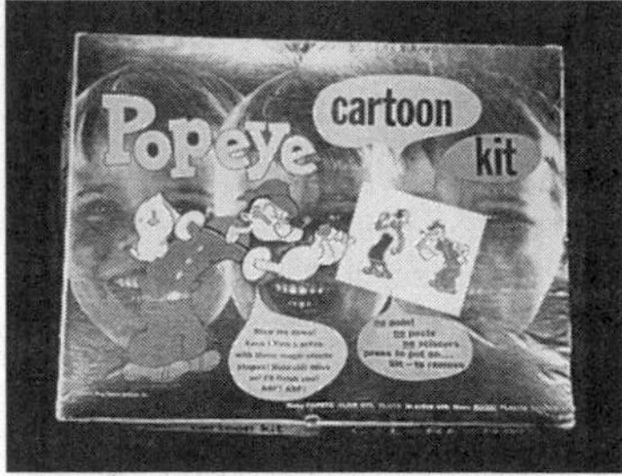

Popeye TV Cartoon Kit, 1966, Colorforms
EX $20 NM $40 MIP $80

Popeye TV Magic Putty, 1970s, MSS
EX $6 NM $10 MIP $15

Popeye Water Colors, 1933, American Crayon
EX $25 NM $60 MIP $110

Popeye Water Sprinkler, 1960s, KFS, w/rubbber head
EX $15 NM $25 MIP $40

Popeye's Official Wallet, 1959, KFS
EX $10 NM $30 MIP $70

Popeye's Spinach Wagon, 1980, Lesney/Matchbox, CS-13, 2-3/4" x 2-7/8"
EX $8 NM $15 MIP $40

Popeye's Submarine, 1973, Larami
EX $10 NM $30 MIP $60

Popsicle Harmonica, 1929, Czech
EX $100 NM $200 MIP $375

Punch Ball, 1970s, National Latex
EX $10 NM $20 MIP $50

Punch'Em Talking Rattle Toy, 1950s, Sanitoy
EX $15 NM $35 MIP $85

Punching Bag, 1960s, Dartmore
EX $15 NM $30 MIP $60

Puppetforms, 1950s, Colorforms
EX $25 NM $40 MIP $80

Puzzle, 1932, Saalfield, Popeye in Four
EX $50 NM $100 MIP $250

Puzzle, 1945, Jaymar, 22" x 13-1/2", Popeye
EX $40 NM $100 MIP $200

Puzzle, 1959, England, 120 pieces, "What a Catch"
EX $25 NM $55 MIP $80

Puzzle, 1960s, Roalex, tile
EX $20 NM $35 MIP $50

Puzzle, 1962, Tower Press, wood, Popeye
EX $10 NM $16 MIP $30

Puzzle, 1973, Larami, magnetic
EX $6 NM $15 MIP $40

Puzzle, 1976, American Pub. Corp., 5-1/2" round can
EX $10 NM $20 MIP $35

Puzzle, 1977, Opera Mundi, tile, "Popeye's Riddle"
EX $11 NM $18 MIP $30

Puzzle, 1978, Waddington's House of Games, 27" x 18" floor puzzle
EX $8 NM $15 MIP $35

Puzzle, 1981, Ja-Ru, comic
EX $6 NM $12 MIP $30

Puzzle, 1987, Illco, 11 pieces, Olive 3-D
EX $6 NM $10 MIP $20

Puzzle, 1987, Illco, 11 pieces, Popeye 3-D
EX $6 NM $10 MIP $20

Puzzle, 1987, Ja-Ru, Popeye and Son TV show
EX $5 NM $10 MIP $20

Puzzle, 1989, Ja-Ru, "Birthday Cake and Ice Cream"
EX $6 NM $10 MIP $20

Puzzle, 1989, Ja-Ru, boating and dancing
EX $6 NM $10 MIP $20

Puzzle, 1991, Jaymar, 63 pieces, jumbo, Popeye's boat
EX $6 NM $12 MIP $25

Puzzle, 1991, Jaymar, 63 pieces, jumbo, Popeye rescues Olive
EX $6 NM $10 MIP $20

Puzzle, 1991, Jaymar, 63 pieces, Popeye blowing candles
EX $6 NM $10 MIP $20

Puzzle, 1991, Jaymar, 63 pieces, jumbo, Popeye and Olive surfing
EX $6 **NM** $10 **MIP** $20

Puzzle, 1991, Jaymar, Christmas scene, inlaid, 12 pieces
EX $6 **NM** $10 **MIP** $20

Puzzle, 1991, Jaymar, 12 pieces, Popeye holding turkey
EX $6 **NM** $10 **MIP** $20

Puzzle, 1991, Jaymar, 12 pieces, Popeye gang swimming
EX $6 **NM** $10 **MIP** $20

Race Set, 1989, Ja-Ru
EX $6 **NM** $12 **MIP** $35

Road Building Set, 1979, Larami
EX $6 **NM** $12 **MIP** $35

Roller Skating Popeye, 1950s, Linemar
EX $150 **NM** $225 **MIP** $350

Roly Poly Popeye, 1940s, w/beaded arms and celluloid
EX $100 **NM** $175 **MIP** $300

Sailboats, 1981, Larami
EX $6 **NM** $10 **MIP** $25

Sailor's Knife, 1981, Ja-Ru
EX $10 **NM** $20 **MIP** $45

Screen-A Show Projector, 1973, Denys Fisher
EX $35 **NM** $90 **MIP** $160

Sea Hag Hand Puppet, 1987, Presents
EX $15 **NM** $35 **MIP** $110

Shaving Kit, 1979, Larami
EX $6 **NM** $10 **MIP** $35

Sling Darts, KFS
EX $20 **NM** $35 **MIP** $70

Soapy Popeye Boat, 1950s, Kerk Guild
EX $200 **NM** $300 **MIP** $500

Squirt Face, 1981, Ja-Ru
EX $6 **NM** $10 **MIP** $20

Stitch-A-Story, KFS
EX $12 **NM** $20 **MIP** $35

Sun-Eze Pictures, 1962, Tillman Toy
EX $10 **NM** $25 **MIP** $60

Sunglasses, 1980s, Larami, red, yellow, or blue
EX $6 **NM** $10 **MIP** $20

Super Race with Launcher, 1980, Fleetwood
EX $6 **NM** $12 **MIP** $25

Surf Rider, 1979, Wet Set-Zee Toys
EX $10 **NM** $25 **MIP** $65

Swee'Pea Bean Bag, 1974, Dakin
EX $10 **NM** $25 **MIP** $65

Swee'Pea Hand Puppet, 1960s, Gund, bonnet on head, cloth body decorated w/baby lambs
EX $15 **NM** $40 **MIP** $100

Swee'Pea Hand Puppet, 1987, Presents
EX $8 **NM** $25 **MIP** $70

Swee'Pea Hi-Pop Ball, 1981, Ja-Ru
EX $6 **NM** $12 **MIP** $30

Swee'Pea Squeak Toy, 1970s, frowning or smiling
EX $12 **NM** $25 **MIP** $75

Swirler Flying Barrel Toy, 1980, Imperial
EX $8 **NM** $15 **MIP** $30

Talking View-Master Set, 1962, GAF, old type
EX $12 **NM** $25 **MIP** $70

Tambourine, 1980s, Larami
EX $6 **NM** $10 **MIP** $20

Tambourine, 1990, Santa Cruz
EX $6 **NM** $10 **MIP** $20

Target Ball, 1981, Ja-Ru
EX $6 **NM** $10 **MIP** $20

Telephone, 1982, Comvu
EX $15 **NM** $30 **MIP** $70

Telescope, 1973, Larami
EX $10 **NM** $25 **MIP** $60

Thimble Theatre Cut-Outs, 1950s, Aldon
EX $50 **NM** $85 **MIP** $140

Toy Watch, 1987, Sekonda-Japan, comic strip band
EX $30 **NM** $50 **MIP** $100

Trace and Color, 1980, Fleetwood
EX $6 **NM** $10 **MIP** $20

Trumpet Bubble Blower, 1984, Larami, pink or yellow pan
EX $6 **NM** $12 **MIP** $25

Tube-A-Loonies, 1973, Larami, five small tubes on card
EX $6 **NM** $15 **MIP** $35

Turn-A-Scope, 1979, Larami
EX $6 **NM** $20 **MIP** $50

TV Set with Three Film Scrolls, 1957
EX $12 **NM** $20 **MIP** $50

View-Master Set, 1959, Sawyers, three reels
EX $15 **NM** $30 **MIP** $80

View-Master Set, 1959, GAF, "The Fish Story"
EX $8 **NM** $15 **MIP** $40

View-Master Set, 1959, GAF, "The Hunting Bird"
EX $8 **NM** $15 **MIP** $40

View-Master Set, 1962, GAF, three pack
EX $8 **NM** $15 **MIP** $50

Whistling Flashlights, 1960s, Bantam-Lite, six w/display
EX $300 **NM** $500 **MIP** $800

Whistling Wing Ding, 1950s, Mego
EX $20 **NM** $40 **MIP** $80

Wimpy Dog Toy, 1986, Petex
EX $8 **NM** $13 **MIP** $25

Wimpy Hand Puppet, 1950s, Gund, fabric hand cover, vinyl squeaker head and voice
EX $15 **NM** $50 **MIP** $120

Wimpy Hand Puppet, 1960s, Gund, cloth body
EX $15 **NM** $40 **MIP** $80

Wimpy Hand Puppet, 1987, Presents
EX $8 **NM** $13 **MIP** $90

Wimpy Ring, 1949, Post Toasties
EX $12 **NM** $45 **MIP** $110

Wimpy Squeeze Toy, 1950s, Rempel, vinyl
EX $20 **NM** $40 **MIP** $80

Wimpy Squeeze Toy, 1979, Cribmates
EX $12 **NM** $20 **MIP** $40

Wimpy Tugboat, 1961, Ideal, inflatable
EX $20 **NM** $40 **MIP** $60

Wood Slate, 1983, Ja-Ru
EX $6 **NM** $15 **MIP** $40

WATCH

Popeye Wristwatch, 1938, New Haven
EX $1500 **NM** $2500 **MIP** $4000

Popeye Wristwatch, 1964, Bradley, #308, green case
EX $115 **NM** $210 **MIP** $375

Popeye Wristwatch, 1979, Bradley
EX $60 **NM** $110 **MIP** $170

Popeye Wristwatch, 1987, Unique, Popeye's head pops open, digital
EX $12 **NM** $30 **MIP** $80

Popeye Wristwatch, 1990, KFS-Japan, Popeye in ship's wheel
EX $40 **NM** $80 **MIP** $130

Popeye Wristwatch, 1991, Armitron
EX $20 **NM** $35 **MIP** $80

Porky Pig

BANK

Porky Pig Bank, 1930s, bisque, orange, blue, and yellow
EX $60 **NM** $120 **MIP** $225

DOLL

Porky Pig Doll, 1950, Gund, 14" tall
EX $60 **NM** $120 **MIP** $225

Porky Pig Doll, 1960s, Mattel, 17", cloth, vinyl head
EX $15 **NM** $35 **MIP** $85

Porky Pig Doll, 1968, Dakin, 7-3/4" tall in black velvet jacket
EX $15 **NM** $35 **MIP** $85

FIGURES

Porky and Petunia Figures, 1975, Warner Bros., 4-1/2" tall
EX $9 **NM** $16 **MIP** $50

TOY

Porky Pig Soaky
EX $15 **NM** $35 **MIP** $75

Porky Pig Umbrella, 1940s, hard plastic 3" figure on end, Porky and Bugs printed in red cloth
EX $100 **NM** $150 **MIP** $200

Quick Draw McGraw

ACCESSORIES

Cereal Box, 1960, Kellogg's
EX $250 **NM** $400 **MIP** $600

BANK

Baba Looey Bank, 1960s, Knickerbocker, 9" tall, vinyl, plastic head
EX $16 **NM** $32 **MIP** $80

Quick Draw McGraw Bank, 1960, 9-1/2", plastic, orange, white, and blue
EX $40 **NM** $75 **MIP** $150

BOOK

Quick Draw McGraw Book, 1960, Whitman
EX $30 **NM** $45 **MIP** $90

Quick Draw McGraw

DOLL

Auggie Doggie Doll, 1959, Knickerbocker, 10" tall, plush w/vinyl face
EX $40 **NM** $85 **MIP** $150

Baba Looey Doll, 1959, Knickerbocker, 20" tall, plush w/vinyl donkey ears and sombrero
EX $75 **NM** $125 **MIP** $250

Blabber Doll, 1959, Knickerbocker, 15" tall, plush w/vinyl face
EX $50 **NM** $100 **MIP** $180

Quick Draw McGraw Doll, 1959, Knickerbocker, 16", plush w/vinyl face, cowboy hat
EX $150 **NM** $300 **MIP** $450

Scooper Doll, 1959, Knickerbocker, 20", plush w/vinyl face
EX $75 **NM** $100 **MIP** $175

TOY

Auggie Doggie Soaky, 1960s, Purex, 10" tall, plastic
EX $15 **NM** $45 **MIP** $90

Blabber Soaky, 1960s, Purex, 10-1/2" tall, plastic
EX $18 **NM** $45 **MIP** $100

Quick Draw McGraw Moving Target Game, 1960s, Knickerbocker
EX $125 **NM** $175 **MIP** $300

Quick Draw Mold and Model Cast Set, 1960
EX $75 **NM** $100 **MIP** $150

Raggedy Ann and Andy

ACCESSORIES

Raggedy Ann/Andy Wastebasket, 1972, tin
EX $8 **NM** $20 **MIP** $60

BANK

Raggedy Andy Bank, Play Pal, 11"
EX $15 **NM** $20 **MIP** $50

Raggedy Ann Bank, 1974, Play Pal, 11"
EX $15 **NM** $20 **MIP** $50

BOOK

Camel with the Wrinkled Knees Book, 1924
EX $125 **NM** $200 **MIP** $350

Raggedy Ann Coloring Book, 1968
EX $6 **NM** $12 **MIP** $50

Raggedy Ann/Andy Paper Doll Book, 1974, Whitman, #1962
EX $15 **NM** $25 **MIP** $75

FIGURES

Raggedy Andy Figure, 1970s, rubber/wire, 4" tall
EX $5 **NM** $10 **MIP** $35

TOY

Raggedy Andy Puppet, 1975, Dakin, cloth
EX $20 **NM** $35 **MIP** $70

Raggedy Ann Puppet, 1975, Dakin, cloth
EX $20 **NM** $35 **MIP** $70

Raggedy Ann/Andy Record Player, square, cardboard
EX $45 **NM** $100 **MIP** $175

Raggedy Ann/Andy Record Player, 1950s, plastic, heart shaped
EX $100 **NM** $150 **MIP** $275

Road Runner and Wile E. Coyote

ACCESSORIES

Road Runner and Coyote Lamp, 1977, 12-1/2", figures standing on base
EX $40 **NM** $100 **MIP** $250

Road Runner Costume, 1960s, Collegeville
EX $30 **NM** $50 **MIP** $100

Wile E. Coyote Night Light, 1980s, Applause
EX $20 **NM** $45 **MIP** $90

BANK

Road Runner Bank, standing on base
EX $8 **NM** $15 **MIP** $50

DOLL

Road Runner Doll, 1971, Mighty Star, 13" tall
EX $12 **NM** $30 **MIP** $90

Wile E. Coyote Doll, 1970, Dakin, on explosive box
EX $40 **NM** $75 **MIP** $150

Wile E. Coyote Doll, 1971, Mighty Star, 18" tall, plush
EX $40 **NM** $75 **MIP** $150

FIGURES

Road Runner Figure, Dakin, plastic, Cartoon Theater
EX $18 **NM** $50 **MIP** $125

Road Runner Figure, 1968, Dakin, 8-3/4" tall
EX $18 **NM** $50 **MIP** $125

Road Runner Figure, 1971, Dakin, Goofy Gram
EX $15 **NM** $50 **MIP** $125

Wile E. Coyote and Road Runner Figures, 1979, Royal Crown, 7" tall, each
EX $15 **NM** $30 **MIP** $85

Wile E. Coyote Figure, 1968, Dakin, 10" tall
EX $30 **NM** $75 **MIP** $180

Wile E. Coyote Figure, 1971, Dakin, Goofy Gram, fused bomb in right hand
EX $20 **NM** $50 **MIP** $125

Wile E. Coyote Figure, 1976, Dakin, Cartoon Theater
EX $18 **NM** $32 **MIP** $100

TOY

Road Runner Hand Puppet, 1970s, Japanese, 10", vinyl head
EX $8 **NM** $20 **MIP** $60

Wile E. Coyote Hand Puppet, 1970s, Japanese, 10" vinyl head
EX $10 **NM** $20 **MIP** $60

Rocky

DOLL

Apollo Creed Doll, 1983, Phoenix Toys, 8" tall
EX $5 **NM** $10 **MIP** $25

Clubber Lang Doll, 1983, Phoenix Toys, 8" tall
EX $6 **NM** $12 **MIP** $35

Rocky Balboa Doll, 1983, Phoenix Toys, 8" tall
EX $7 **NM** $15 **MIP** $35

Roger Rabbit

ACCESSORIES

Baby Herman and Roger Rabbit Mug, Applause
EX $5 **NM** $8 **MIP** $15

Jessica Zipper Pull
EX $5 **NM** $10 **MIP** $15

BOOK

Paint with Water Book, Golden, #1702
EX $6 **NM** $12 **MIP** $30

Trace and Color Book, Golden, #2355
EX $5 **NM** $10 **MIP** $30

DOLL

Benny the Cab Doll, 1988, Applause, 6" long
EX $6 **NM** $12 **MIP** $30

Roger Rabbit Doll, Applause, 8-1/2" tall
EX $7 **NM** $15 **MIP** $60

Roger Rabbit Doll, Applause, 17" tall
EX $10 **NM** $30 **MIP** $125

FIGURES

Baby Herman Figure, 1987, LJN, 6" figure on card
EX $9 **NM** $20 **MIP** $35

Baby Herman Figure, 1988, LJN, ceramic
EX $9 **NM** $15 **MIP** $35

Boss Weasel Figure, 1988, LJN, 4" bendable
EX $4 **NM** $10 **MIP** $20

Eddie Valiant Figure, 1988, LJN, 4", flexible
EX $5 **NM** $10 **MIP** $20

Judge Doom Figure, 1988, LJN, 4" bendable
EX $4 **NM** $8 **MIP** $24

Roger Rabbit Figure, 1988, LJN, 4" bendable
EX $4 **NM** $10 **MIP** $30

Smart Guy Figure, 1988, LJN, flexible
EX $4 **NM** $8 **MIP** $15

GAME

Dip Flip Game, LJN
EX $8 **NM** $15 **MIP** $30

Who Framed Roger Rabbit Game, 1988, Milton Bradley low production run
EX $75 **NM** $125 **MIP** $200

TOY

Animates, 1988, Doom, Roger, Eddie and Smart Guy, each
EX $5 **NM** $8 **MIP** $15

Benny the Cab, LJN
EX $20 **NM** $40 **MIP** $75

Eddie Valiant Animate, 1988, LJN, 6" tall, bendable
EX $4 **NM** $8 **MIP** $15

Jessica License Plate
EX $6 NM $12 MIP $20

Judge Doom Animate, 1988, LJN, 6" tall poseable
EX $6 NM $12 MIP $25

Paint-A-Cel Set, Benny the Cab and Roger pictures
EX $8 NM $15 MIP $60

Roger Rabbit Animate, 1988, LJN, 6" poseable
EX $4 NM $10 MIP $20

Roger Rabbit Blow-Up Buddy, 36" tall
EX $6 NM $12 MIP $30

Roger Wacky Head Puppets, Applause, hand puppets
EX $6 NM $12 MIP $50

Roger Wind-Up, 1988, Matsudaya
EX $18 NM $35 MIP $100

Talking Roger in Benny the Cab, 17" tall
EX $12 NM $35 MIP $100

WATCH

Roger Rabbit Bullet Hole Wristwatch, 1987, Shiraka, white case and leather band, in plastic display box
EX $40 NM $85 MIP $160

Roger Rabbit Silhouette Wristwatch, 1987, Shiraka, large gold case, black band
EX $35 NM $80 MIP $160

Rootie Kazootie

BOOK

Cut-Out Coloring Book, 1952, Western Publishing, Funtime Books, Rootie Kazootie, red cover - kids drawing, baseball bat and glove
EX $10 NM $20 MIP $30

Cut-Out Coloring Book, 1954, Western Publishing, Funtime Books, Rootie Kazootie and his Wonderful Games, green cover - pin the tail on the donkey
EX $10 NM $20 MIP $30

Little Golden Book, 1953, Simon & Schuster, Rootie Kazootie Detective
EX $10 NM $20 MIP $60

Little Golden Book, 1954, Simon & Schuster, Rootie Kazootie Baseball Star, #190
EX $10 NM $30 MIP $60

Little Golden Book, 1955, Simon & Schuster, Rootie Kazootie Joins the Circus
EX $10 NM $20 MIP $60

BUTTON

Rootie Kazootie Club Button, 1950s, 1" tin litho
EX $18 NM $42 MIP $80

TOY

Rootie Kazootie Doll, 1950s, 19", Effanbee, cloth body, vinyl head and hands, baseball outfit
EX $75 NM $125 MIP $200

Rootie Kazootie Drum, 1950s, 8" diameter drum, Rootie on the drum head
EX $40 NM $75 MIP $150

Rootie Kazootie Fishing Tackle Box, 1950s, RK Inc., tin litho, bright graphics
EX $15 NM $30 MIP $70

Ruff and Reddy

BOOK

Ruff and Reddy Go To A Party Tell-A-Tale Book, 1958, Whitman
EX $15 NM $35 MIP $70

TOY

Ruff and Reddy Draw Cartoon Set Color, Wonder Art
EX $50 NM $85 MIP $175

Ruff and Reddy Magic Rub-Off Picture Set, 1958, Transogram
EX $45 NM $80 MIP $175

Secret Squirrel

TOY

Secret Squirrel Bubble Club Soaky, 1960s, Purex
EX $20 NM $35 MIP $90

Secret Squirrel Push Puppet, 1960s, Kohner, plastic figure in white coat, blue hat holding binoculars
EX $20 NM $40 MIP $80

Secret Squirrel Puzzle, 1967, frame tray
EX $15 NM $30 MIP $65

Secret Squirrel Ray Gun
EX $25 NM $50 MIP $100

Shirley Temple

ACCESSORIES

Doll Buggy, 1935, F.A. Whitney Carriage, wicker, hubcaps are labeled Shirley Temple
EX $300 NM $400 MIP $625

Doll Trunk, 18" tall w/"Our Little Girl" decal on the side, photo of Shirley
EX $100 NM $200 MIP $375

Doll Wardrobe Trunk, 20" heavy cardboard/wood steamer trunk for 18" doll, leather strap, metal latch w/lock and key, two drawers, and four cardboard hangers
EX $120 NM $200 MIP $375

Hair Ribbon and Band, 1934, Ribbon Mills, Several colors/styles
EX $15 NM $30 MIP $80

Hanger, cardboard; picture of Shirley Temple, came w/all outfits
EX $15 NM $25 MIP $60

Pen and Pencil Set, 1930s, David Kahn
EX $90 NM $140 MIP $250

Pin, Reliable, "The World's Darling/Genuine Shirley Temple, A Reliable Doll"
EX $65 NM $80 MIP $100

Purse, 1950s, red, white, and black w/Shirley Temple lettering
EX $30 NM $40 MIP $80

Stand Up and Cheer Doll Trunk, 1934
EX $125 NM $200 MIP $400

Texas Ranger/Cowgirl Gun, Came w/Texas Ranger outfit
EX $35 NM $70 MIP $200

BOOK

Composition Book, 1935, Western
EX $25 NM $50 MIP $100

My Life and Times by Shirley Temple Book, 1936, Saalfield, Big Little Book #116, Model No. 116
EX $30 NM $85 MIP $180

Scrap Book, 1935, Saalfield, #1714, Model No. 1714
EX $60 NM $85 MIP $185

Shirley Temple at Play Book, 1935, Saalfield, #1712, Model No. 1712
EX $40 NM $50 MIP $140

Shirley Temple Five Books About Me, 1936, Saalfield, Just a Little Girl, Twinkletoes, On the Movie Lot, In Starring Roles, and Little Playmate, #1730, Model No. 1730
EX $90 NM $150 MIP $250

Shirley Temple in The Littlest Rebel, 1935, Saalfield, Big Little Book, #1595, Model No. 1595
EX $20 NM $60 MIP $140

Shirley Temple My Book to Color, 1937, Saalfield, #1768, Model No. 1768
EX $35 NM $50 MIP $120

Shirley Temple Pastime Box, 1937, Saalfield, Four activity books: Favorite Puzzles, Favorite Games, Favorite Sewing Cards, and Favorite Coloring Book, #1732, Model No. 1732
EX $55 NM $125 MIP $220

Shirley Temple Scrap Book, 1936, Saalfield, #1722, Model No. 1722
EX $65 NM $85 MIP $200

Shirley Temple Scrap Book, 1937, Saalfield, #1763, Model No. 1763
EX $50 NM $85 MIP $200

Shirley Temple Story Book, 1935, Saalfield, #1726, Model No. 1726
EX $25 NM $40 MIP $120

Shirley Temple Treasury Book, 1959, Random House
EX $20 NM $30 MIP $75

Shirley Temple with Lionel Barrymore in The Little Colonel, 1935, Saalfield, Big Little Book, #1095, Model No. 1095
EX $20 NM $60 MIP $140

Shirley Temple's Blue Bird Coloring Book, 1939, Saalfield
EX $35 NM $65 MIP $150

Shirley Temple's Busy Book, 1958, Saalfield, Activity book, #5326, Model No. 5326
EX $40 NM $50 MIP $80

Shirley Temple's Favorite Poems, 1936, Saalfield, #1720, Model No. 1720
EX $20 NM $60 MIP $90

The Story of Shirley Temple Book, 1934, Saalfield, Big Little Book, #1089, Model No. 1089
EX $20 NM $35 MIP $140

Shirley Temple

DOLL

Blue Bird Doll, 1939, 18", felt skirt and vest, organdy blouse and apron w/blue bird appliques
EX $910 **NM** $1025 **MIP** $1600

Blue Bird Doll, 1939, 20" composition
EX $800 **NM** $1000 **MIP** $1600

Bright Eyes Doll, 1936, 13" composition, plaid dress, leather shoes
EX $610 **NM** $700 **MIP** $1100

Captain January Doll, Ideal, 22", dark blue sailor suit w/white trim
EX $700 **NM** $910 **MIP** $1500

Captain January Doll, 1936, 16", green pique w/silk ribbons
EX $650 **NM** $750 **MIP** $1300

Captain January Doll, 1936, 13", white sailor suit, red bow tie, white hat, original pin
EX $600 **NM** $700 **MIP** $1300

Captain January Doll, 1936, 18", cotton sailor suit w/anchor applique and red silk tie
EX $650 **NM** $750 **MIP** $1400

Captain January Doll, 1936, Ideal, 20", blue floral print, cotton school dress w/ruffled collar
EX $725 **NM** $800 **MIP** $1450

Captain January Doll, 1957, Ideal, 12", vinyl head, dark blonde hair, plastic body, arms and legs
EX $175 **NM** $225 **MIP** $400

Curly Top Doll, 1935, Ideal, 11", pink organdy dress
EX $875 **NM** $1050 **MIP** $1500

Curly Top Doll, 1935, 11", dotted swiss dress, blue silk ribbons
EX $600 **NM** $685 **MIP** $1200

Curly Top Doll, 1935, 16" composition; different versions available
EX $675 **NM** $750 **MIP** $1200

Curly Top Doll, 1935, 18" composition, mohair hair, hazel eyes
EX $600 **NM** $685 **MIP** $1100

Curly Top Doll, 1935, 18", pleated dotted swiss w/blue silk ribbons, red or lavender
EX $600 **NM** $700 **MIP** $1200

Heidi Doll, 1937, 18", striped cotton skirt, black velveteen top w/red braid, apron, mohair pigtails w/red ribbons
EX $950 **NM** $1075 **MIP** $1650

Heidi Doll, 1957, Ideal, 12", vinyl head, dark blonde hair and plastic body, arms and legs
EX $200 **NM** $285 **MIP** $400

Heidi Doll, 1960-61, 17"
EX $250 **NM** $325 **MIP** $450

Little Colonel Doll, Alexander, 13", pink hat w/ruffle, pink dress and bloomers
EX $475 **NM** $575 **MIP** $1600

Little Colonel Doll, 13", variations in pantaloons, bonnets and shoes
EX $775 **NM** $900 **MIP** $2000

Little Colonel Doll, 13", taffeta outfit, variations in the collar, ruffles and pantaloons
EX $775 **NM** $900 **MIP** $2000

Little Colonel Doll, 20", blue organdy, bonnet w/pink feather
EX $925 **NM** $1100 **MIP** $2200

Little Colonel Doll, 1934, 18", pink organdy dress, bonnet, white pantaloons
EX $775 **NM** $900 **MIP** $2000

Little Colonel Doll, 1934, Ideal, 13", smiling, pink hat w/feather and dress and bloomers
EX $775 **NM** $900 **MIP** $2000

Little Colonel Doll, 1934, 13", light blue dress w/bonnet, pantaloons and shoes w/buckles
EX $775 **NM** $900 **MIP** $2000

Littlest Rebel Doll, 1935, 13", yellow/brown dress, white ruffled collar, yellow shoes
EX $775 **NM** $900 **MIP** $2000

Littlest Rebel Doll, 1935, 16", polka dot outfit, pantaloons, gray felt hat
EX $625 **NM** $700 **MIP** $1500

Littlest Rebel Doll, 1935, 18", cotton and organdy outfit
EX $675 **NM** $725 **MIP** $1500

Littlest Rebel Doll, 1935, 22", red/white cotton dress w/organdy collar
EX $775 **NM** $900 **MIP** $2000

Poor Little Rich Girl Doll, 1936, 13", blue silk pajamas
EX $325 **NM** $750 **MIP** $1500

Poor Little Rich Girl Doll, 1936, 13", sailor dress w/white trim and matching tam
EX $275 **NM** $375 **MIP** $1200

Poor Little Rich Girl Doll, 1936, 18", pique sunsuit w/matching tam
EX $325 **NM** $750 **MIP** $1500

Rebecca of Sunnybrook Farm Doll, 1957, Ideal, 12", vinyl head, dark blonde hair, plastic body, arms and legs
EX $175 **NM** $230 **MIP** $400

Rebecca of Sunnybrook Farm Doll, 1957, 12" vinyl, blue bib overalls w/plaid blouse, black low shoes
EX $125 **NM** $185 **MIP** $300

Rebecca of Sunnybrook Farm Doll, 1957, 12" vinyl, red felt jumper and plastic purse
EX $175 **NM** $230 **MIP** $400

Rebecca of Sunnybrook Farm Doll, 1957, 12" vinyl, blue bib overalls, blue polka dot blouse, straw hat
EX $125 **NM** $230 **MIP** $400

Shirley Temple Baby, Ideal, 18", painted hair, chubby toddler body w/dimpled cheeks, flirty eyes, dressed in pink organdy w/silk ribbons
EX $600 **NM** $925 **MIP** $1850

Shirley Temple Baby, 20", composition head, arms and legs, cloth body
EX $700 **NM** $975 **MIP** $2300

Shirley Temple Baby, 16", mohair wig, flirty eyes
EX $525 **NM** $800 **MIP** $2100

Shirley Temple Doll, Made in Japan, 8" composition w/pink silk undies
EX $175 **NM** $210 **MIP** $400

Shirley Temple Doll, Ideal, 22" jointed, composition body, blonde mohair, hazel glass eyes, open mouth, red/white polka dot dress
EX $225 **NM** $500 **MIP** $1350

Shirley Temple Doll, Reliable (Ideal/Canada), 13", yellow organdy dress, silk ribbon
EX $460 **NM** $760 **MIP** $1500

Shirley Temple Doll, 13", pleated pique w/ white applique
EX $275 **NM** $550 **MIP** $1350

Shirley Temple Doll, 16" composition
EX $375 **NM** $675 **MIP** $1350

Shirley Temple Doll, 16", light blue organdy w/pink hemstitching and silk ribbons
EX $275 **NM** $575 **MIP** $1400

Shirley Temple Doll, 16", black velveteen coat and hat
EX $180 **NM** $350 **MIP** $1400

Shirley Temple Doll, 20" composition w/facial molding
EX $500 **NM** $750 **MIP** $1500

Shirley Temple Doll, Ideal, 19" vinyl, twinkle eyes, dressed in pink nylon, black purse
EX $180 **NM** $340 **MIP** $600

Shirley Temple Doll, 27" composition w/pink taffeta, bonnet and pantaloons
EX $850 **NM** $1250 **MIP** $2600

Shirley Temple Doll, 18" composition w/facial molding
EX $525 **NM** $700 **MIP** $1400

Shirley Temple Doll, 22" composition w/facial molding
EX $600 **NM** $800 **MIP** $1500

Shirley Temple Doll, 1934, Ideal, 18", pleated pale green, pink, or blue dress, embroidered collar and pink silk ribbon
EX $520 **NM** $675 **MIP** $1200

Shirley Temple Doll, 1934, Ideal, 18", light pink organdy
EX $475 **NM** $650 **MIP** $1500

Shirley Temple Doll, 1935, 18" facial molding doll w/mohair wig (parted in the center), light complexion, outfit from "Curly Top"
EX $260 **NM** $525 **MIP** $1500

Shirley Temple Doll, 1957, 12" vinyl, pink/blue nylon dress w/daisy appliques, hat, purse
EX $125 **NM** $250 **MIP** $500

Shirley Temple Doll, 1957, 12" vinyl, molded hands and feet, synthetic rooted wig, two piece slip/undies
EX $110 **NM** $225 **MIP** $475

Shirley Temple Doll, 1957, 12", vinyl, molded hands and feet, synthetic rooted wig, pink slip trimmed w/lace
EX $125 **NM** $225 **MIP** $500

Shirley Temple Doll, 1958, 15" vinyl, red nylon dress w/floral detailing at collar, hair ribbon, purse
EX $110 **NM** $210 **MIP** $375

Shirley Temple Doll, 1958, Ideal, 15" vinyl, yellow nylon dress trimmed w/lace and ribbon around skirt
EX $175 **NM** $320 **MIP** $550

Shirley Temple Doll, 1958-59, Ideal, 17" vinyl, brown twinkle eyes, pink/blue dress
EX $210 **NM** $320 **MIP** $700

Shirley Temple Doll, 1960, 15" vinyl, blue jumper w/red/white gingham blouse and pocket facing
EX $100 **NM** $200 **MIP** $375

Shirley Temple Doll, 1960s, 17", yellow party dress, white purse w/Shirley Temple lettering
EX $225 **NM** $325 **MIP** $700

Shirley Temple Doll, 1960s, Ideal, 17", yellow nylon dress and Twinkle Eyes wrist tag
EX $210 **NM** $320 **MIP** $700

Shirley Temple Doll, 1972, Ideal/Hong Kong, 16", vinyl, red polka dot dress, Stand Up and Cheer
EX $155 **NM** $185 **MIP** $300

Shirley Temple Doll, 1972, Ideal/Hong Kong, 15" vinyl manufactured for Montgomery Ward's
EX $175 **NM** $210 **MIP** $375

Stand Up and Cheer Doll, 11" composition, short rayon dress w/blue polka dots
EX $675 **NM** $925 **MIP** $1600

Stand Up and Cheer Doll, 1934, 13" composition, dotted organdy green dress
EX $150 **NM** $200 **MIP** $600

Stand Up and Cheer Doll, 1934, 11", dotted red, blue, or green organdy dress w/silk ribbon
EX $450 **NM** $675 **MIP** $1500

Stowaway Doll, 1936, 25", pink taffeta, mohair hair
EX $700 **NM** $950 **MIP** $2100

Stowaway Doll, 1936, 20", two-piece linen w/brass buttons
EX $650 **NM** $825 **MIP** $2000

Texas Ranger Doll, 20", plaid shirt, leather vest w/trim, chaps, holster, and metal gun
EX $700 **NM** $950 **MIP** $2000

Texas Ranger Doll, 17", plaid shirt, leather vest w/trim
EX $550 **NM** $700 **MIP** $1500

Texas Ranger/Cowgirl Doll, 11", plaid cotton shirt, leather vest, chaps, holster, metal gun, felt 10 gallon hat w/"Ride 'Em Cowboy" printed band
EX $450 **NM** $750 **MIP** $2000

Wee Willie Winkie Doll, 1937, 18", long sleeve cotton jacket, two pockets and six brass buttons, plaid wool skirt, tan belt w/brass buckle
EX $700 **NM** $1050 **MIP** $2100

Wee Willie Winkie Doll, 1957, Ideal, 12", vinyl head, dark blonde hair, plastic body, arms and legs
EX $190 **NM** $250 **MIP** $475

DOLL CLOTHING

Baby Take A Bow Dress, 1934, red cotton, red polka dots on collar and reverse on the bottom w/silk ribbons, fits 16" doll
EX $85 **NM** $95 **MIP** $150

Ballerina Outfit, 1957-58, blue/green nylon and tulle, flower hair piece; fits 12" vinyl doll
EX $80 **NM** $85 **MIP** $120

Bright Eyes Dress, 1934, fits 16" dolls, several colors variations
EX $85 **NM** $90 **MIP** $140

Bright Eyes Outfit, white corduroy coat and hat w/original pin, fits 16" doll
EX $100 **NM** $150 **MIP** $240

Captain January Outfit, 1936, red or green pleated pique, silk ribbons; fits a 16" doll
EX $85 **NM** $95 **MIP** $160

Coat and Hat, velveteen coat and hat w/red buttons; fits 16" doll
EX $80 **NM** $90 **MIP** $130

Coat and Hat, 1958, Ideal, red corduroy coat and hat, fits 12" doll
EX $60 **NM** $70 **MIP** $95

Curly Top Dress, 1935, striped cotton dress, fits 20" doll
EX $85 **NM** $95 **MIP** $160

Dimples Outfit, 1936, heavy felt jacket w/red trim; fits 16" doll
EX $85 **NM** $95 **MIP** $160

Dress, light blue organdy; fits 16" doll
EX $85 **NM** $95 **MIP** $160

Dress, 1958, Ideal, nylon w/loop details; fits 12" doll
EX $65 **NM** $80 **MIP** $110

Dress, Jacket, and Purse, 1959, nylon
EX $65 **NM** $75 **MIP** $100

Jumper and Blouse, 1959, Ideal, blue velveteen jumper w/floral applique, cotton blouse
EX $60 **NM** $70 **MIP** $100

Jumpsuit, red w/white flowers
EX $80 **NM** $85 **MIP** $120

Jumpsuit, red/white checkered
EX $35 **NM** $40 **MIP** $70

Littlest Rebel Dress, 1935, yellow/brown, fits an 18" doll
EX $150 **NM** $185 **MIP** $500

Littlest Rebel Outfit, checkered dress, rick rack ribbon on sleeves, lace collar and apron
EX $85 **NM** $110 **MIP** $450

Nightcoat and Cap, 1958-59, Ideal, flannel; fits 12" doll
EX $60 **NM** $70 **MIP** $100

Our Little Girl Outfit, 1935, blue or white pique, white dog appliques, fits 16" doll
EX $85 **NM** $100 **MIP** $220

Our Little Girl Outfit, 1935, red or blue dress w/music appliques, matching hat, fits 16" doll
EX $85 **NM** $100 **MIP** $220

Polka Dot Dancing Dress, 1935, blue organdy w/matching hat and sunsuit
EX $85 **NM** $90 **MIP** $150

Poor Little Rich Girl Outfit, 1935, blue sailor dress, fits 16" doll
EX $90 **NM** $100 **MIP** $160

Poor Little Rich Girl Outfit, 1935, pique and organdy dress, fits 16" doll
EX $90 **NM** $100 **MIP** $160

Poor Little Rich Girl Outfit, 1936, pleated red plaid w/white collar, fits 16" doll
EX $90 **NM** $100 **MIP** $160

Rain Cape and Umbrella, plaid red or blue rain cape w/hood and matching umbrella; fits 18" doll
EX $80 **NM** $100 **MIP** $185

Stowaway Outfit, 1936, red or blue pique, fits 16" doll
EX $90 **NM** $125 **MIP** $275

Wee Willie Winkie Outfit, 1937, pique outfit and tam, slip/undies; fits 16" doll
EX $125 **NM** $160 **MIP** $285

Wool Coat, fits 18" dolls, from Little Miss Marker
EX $60 **NM** $90 **MIP** $190

PAPER DOLLS

Paper Doll Book, 1976, Whitman, #1986, Model No. 1986
EX $8 **NM** $15 **MIP** $50

Paper Dolls, 1934, Saalfield, four 8" dolls and 30 outfits; first licensed set, #2112, Model No. 2112
EX $175 **NM** $350 **MIP** $600

Paper Dolls, 1958, Saalfield, #4435, Model No. 4435
EX $35 **NM** $50 **MIP** $170

Paper Dolls, 1959, Saalfield, 18" folding doll w/easel, costumes, and accessories, #5110, Model No. 5110
EX $10 **NM** $40 **MIP** $120

Shirley Standing Doll, 1935, Saalfield, cardboard doll on platform and different outfits, #1719, Model No. 1719
EX $150 **NM** $250 **MIP** $475

Shirley Temple Dolls and Dresses, 1960, Saalfield, Two dolls w/different outfits, #1789, Model No. 1789
EX $12 **NM** $20 **MIP** $50

PHOTOGRAPH

Promo Photo, 8" x 10" photo of Shirley w/facsimile autograph, came w/all composition dolls and outfits
EX $30 **NM** $45 **MIP** $75

PLAYING CARDS

Bridge Cards, 1934, U.S. Playing Card
EX $40 **NM** $60 **MIP** $90

Sleeping Beauty

ACCESSORIES

Sleeping Beauty Alarm Clock, 1950s, Phinney-Walker, 2-1/2" x 4" x 4-1/2" tall, Sleeping Beauty surrounded by three birds and petting a rabbit
EX $75 **NM** $125 **MIP** $250

Sleeping Beauty

Sleeping Beauty Doll Crib Mattress, 1960s, 9" x 17", Sleeping Beauty and the fairies
EX $15 **NM** $25 **MIP** $50

BOOK

Sleeping Beauty Sticker Fun Book, 1959, Whitman
EX $15 **NM** $30 **MIP** $75

TOY

Fairy Godmother Hand Puppets, 1958, set of three: 10-1/2" tall, Flora, Merryweather, and Fauna, each
EX $75 **NM** $125 **MIP** $250

King Huber/King Stefan Hand Puppets, 1956, Gund, 10" tall, molded rubber heads w/fabric hand cover
EX $30 **NM** $75 **MIP** $150

Puzzle, 1958, Whitman, 11-1/2" x 14-1/2", Three Good Fairies circling around a baby in a crib
EX $15 **NM** $35 **MIP** $80

Puzzle, 1958, Whitman, 11-1/2" x 14-1/2", Sleeping Beauty w/Prince Phillip and Three Good Fairies circling
EX $15 **NM** $35 **MIP** $80

Puzzle, 1958, Whitman, 11-1/2" x 14-1/2", Sleeping Beauty w/forest animals
EX $15 **NM** $35 **MIP** $80

Sleeping Beauty Jack-In-The-Box, 1980s, Enesco, Princess Aurora, wooden box, plays "Once Upon A Dream"
EX $65 **NM** $125 **MIP** $250

Sleeping Beauty Magic Paint Set, Whitman
EX $25 **NM** $50 **MIP** $90

Sleeping Beauty Squeeze Toy, 1959, Dell, 4" x 4" x 5" tall, rubber, Sleeping Beauty w/rabbit
EX $30 **NM** $60 **MIP** $90

Smokey Bear

BANK

Smokey Bank, 6" tall, china
EX $50 **NM** $100 **MIP** $175

BOOK

Smokey Bear and the Campers Book, 1961, Golden
EX $10 **NM** $20 **MIP** $50

Smokey Bear Coloring Book, 1958, Whitman
EX $25 **NM** $40 **MIP** $75

DOLL

Smokey Doll, 1950s, Ideal, 15" plush, vinyl face
EX $100 **NM** $175 **MIP** $350

FIGURES

Smokey Bobbing Head Figure, 1960s, 6-1/4" tall
EX $100 **NM** $250 **MIP** $450

Smokey Figure, 1971, Dakin, figure on a tree stump
EX $30 **NM** $75 **MIP** $185

TOY

Smokey Bear Record, Peter Pan, 45 rpm
EX $5 **NM** $15 **MIP** $35

Smokey Soaky, 1960s, 9" tall, plastic
EX $10 **NM** $25 **MIP** $60

WATCH

Smokey Wristwatch, 1960s, Hawthorne
EX $75 **NM** $150 **MIP** $300

Snow White and the Seven Dwarfs

ACCESSORIES

Doc Lamp, 1938, LaMode Studios, 8" tall, plaster
EX $150 **NM** $300 **MIP** $500

Dopey Lamp, 1940s, 9" tall, ceramic base w/Dopey
EX $125 **NM** $275 **MIP** $475

Pencil Box, Venus Pencil, 3" x 8" x 1"
EX $75 **NM** $125 **MIP** $200

Radio, 1938, Emerson, 8" x 8" w/characters on cabinet
EX $1400 **NM** $3000 **MIP** $4500

Snow White Lamp, 1938, LaMode Studios, 8-1/2" tall
EX $200 **NM** $350 **MIP** $600

Snow White Mirror, 1940s, 9-1/2", plastic handle
EX $30 **NM** $100 **MIP** $200

Snow White Table Quoits, 1930s, Chad Valley, 9-1/2" x 21" x 1-1/4" deep
EX $125 **NM** $225 **MIP** $375

BANK

Dime Register Bank, 1938, Disney, holds up to five dollars
EX $150 **NM** $350 **MIP** $500

Dopey Bank, 1938, Crown Toy, 7-1/2" tall, wood composition
EX $100 **NM** $200 **MIP** $375

Dopey Dime Register Bank, 1938, Disney, holds up to $5
EX $200 **NM** $350 **MIP** $550

BOOK

Snow White and the Seven Dwarfs Book, 1938, Whitman, Big Little Book
EX $25 **NM** $80 **MIP** $200

Snow White Paper Dolls, 1938, Whitman, 10" x 15" x 1-1/2", blue
EX $200 **NM** $450 **MIP** $850

DOLL

Bashful Doll, 1930s, Ideal
EX $100 **NM** $200 **MIP** $450

Doc Doll, 1930s, Ideal
EX $100 **NM** $200 **MIP** $450

Dopey Doll, Krueger, 14" tall
EX $100 **NM** $220 **MIP** $450

Dopey Doll, 1930s, Ideal
EX $90 **NM** $200 **MIP** $425

Dopey Doll, 1938, Knickerbocker, 11" tall composition
EX $150 **NM** $350 **MIP** $800

Dopey Doll, 1938, Chad Valley, cloth body
EX $55 **NM** $150 **MIP** $350

Dopey Ventriloquist Doll, 1938, Ideal, 18" tall
EX $160 **NM** $325 **MIP** $775

Grumpy Doll, 1938, Knickerbocker, 11" tall, composition
EX $100 **NM** $350 **MIP** $750

Happy Doll, 1930s, 5-1/2" tall, composition, holding a silver pick w/a black handle
EX $50 **NM** $175 **MIP** $400

Sneezy Doll, Krueger, 14" tall
EX $125 **NM** $250 **MIP** $600

Snow White and the Seven Dwarfs Dolls, 1940s, Deluxe, 22" Snow White and 7" dwarfs
EX $1000 **NM** $1500 **MIP** $2500

Snow White Doll, Horsman, 8", in illustrated box
EX $25 **NM** $50 **MIP** $125

Snow White Doll, 1938, Ideal, 3-1/2" x 6-1/2" x 16" tall, fabric face and arms, red/white dress w/dwarf and forest animal design
EX $500 **NM** $1000 **MIP** $1500

Snow White Doll, 1939, Knickerbocker, 3" x 7" x 3-1/2", composition w/movable arms and legs
EX $275 **NM** $550 **MIP** $1100

Snow White Doll, 1940, Knickerbocker, 12" tall, composition
EX $250 **NM** $500 **MIP** $1000

FIGURES

Dopey Figure, 1960s, ceramic figure and barrel
EX $15 **NM** $30 **MIP** $100

Seven Dwarfs Figures, 1938, Seiberling, 5-1/2", rubber
EX $450 **NM** $600 **MIP** $850

GAME

Seven Dwarfs Target Game, 1930s, Chad Valley, 6-1/2" x 11-1/2" target, spring locked gun
EX $250 **NM** $300 **MIP** $500

TOY

Baby Rattle, 1938, Krueger, Snow White at piano, Dwarfs playing instruments
EX $150 **NM** $250 **MIP** $400

Dopey Rolykin, Marx, 2"
EX $35 **NM** $75 **MIP** $125

Dopey Soaky, 1960s, 10" tall
EX $11 **NM** $30 **MIP** $80

Dopey Walker, 1938, Marx, 9" tall, tin, rocking walker
EX $300 **NM** $650 **MIP** $1000

Happy Toy, YS Toys (Taiwan), battery operated, Happy fries eggs
EX $50 **NM** $120 **MIP** $300

Ironing Board, Wolverine, tin board and cover
EX $15 **NM** $30 **MIP** $80

Puzzle, 1960s, Jaymar, 11" x 14"
EX $20 **NM** $35 **MIP** $65

Puzzles, 1938, Whitman, set of two
EX $100 **NM** $200 **MIP** $400

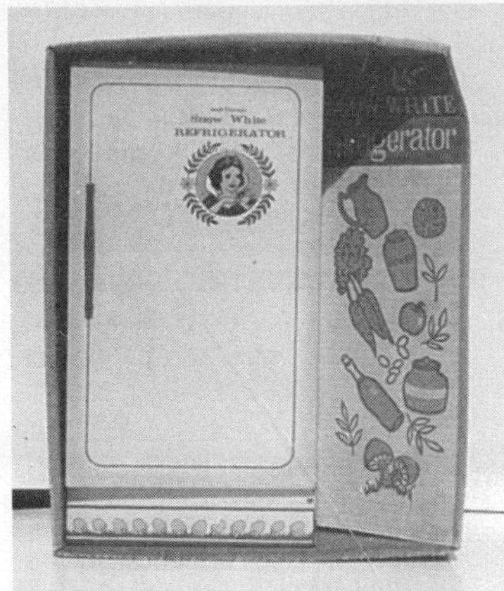

Refrigerator, 1970s, Wolverine, 15", tin, single door, white and yellow depicting Snow White
EX $25 NM $60 MIP $150

Safety Blocks, 1938, Halsam, 7-1/2" x 14-1/2"
EX $50 NM $150 MIP $350

Sand Pail, 1938, Ohio Art, 8", tin, Snow White plays hide-n-seek w/the dwarfs
EX $100 NM $200 MIP $400

Sled, 1938, S. L. Allen, 40" long wood slat and metal runner sled w/character decals
EX $250 NM $600 MIP $1000

Snow White Marionette, 1930s, Tony Sarg/Alexander, 12-1/2" tall
EX $100 NM $300 MIP $600

Snow White Model Making Set, 1930s, Sculptorcraft
EX $100 NM $250 MIP $525

Snow White Sewing Set, 1940s, Ontex
EX $30 NM $100 MIP $200

Snow White Sink, 1960s, Wolverine, tin
EX $15 NM $30 MIP $75

Snow White Soaky
EX $15 NM $40 MIP $80

Tea Set, 1930s, Wadeheath, white china, teapot, cups, saucers, and creamer
EX $175 NM $350 MIP $600

Tea Set, 1937, Ohio Art, plates, cups, tray, saucers
EX $175 NM $350 MIP $500

Tea Set, 1960s, Marx, teapot, five saucers, large plates and tea cups
EX $40 NM $70 MIP $175

Spider-Man

ACCESSORIES

Button, 1966, Button World, 3", "Superhero Club"
EX $15 NM $35 MIP $75

Crazy Foam, 1974, American Aerosol
EX $10 NM $30 MIP $50

BOOKS

Big Little Book, 1976, Whitman, Spider-Man Zaps Mr. Zodiak
EX $5 NM $10 MIP $15

Coloring Book, 1983, Marvel Books, oversized, "The Arms of Doctor Octopus"
EX $10 NM $20 MIP $50

TOY

Costume, 1972, Ben Cooper, plastic costume w/mask
EX $15 NM $30 MIP $45

Fisher-Price Cartoon Viewer, 1985, Fisher-Price, Spider-Man and His Amazing Friends, cartridge for viewer
EX $5 NM $10 MIP $15

Hand Puppet, 1976, Imperial, 9", vinyl head, plastic body
EX $15 NM $35 MIP $90

Mechanical Marvel Super Heroes Spider-Man, 1968, Marx, plastic, wind-up, made in Japan, Model No. 6257
EX $25 NM $60 MIP $100

Radio-Controlled Spider-Man Car, 1977, Marvel, battery-operated red racer w/Spidey driving, Model No. 6852
EX $25 NM $50 MIP $75

Super 8 Film, 1976, Marvel, Spider-Man in King Pinned
EX $7 NM $14 MIP $25

Talking View-Master set, 1970s, GAF, talking View-Master, 6 reels w/Spider-Man, Captain America, and Thor
EX $15 NM $30 MIP $50

The Amazing Energized Green Goblin, 1978, 13", Remco, with Motorized action, web cutter, Goblin Ray gun
EX $50 NM $100 MIP $150

The Amazing Energized Spider-Man, 1978, 13", Remco, with Motorized Web Climber, plastic bodied Spidey w/raised left hand, no articulation, battery-operated, flashlight, net, clamp
EX $50 NM $100 MIP $150

The Amazing Energized Spider-Man Accessory Pack, 1978, Remco, for Energized Spider-Man, spider trap, spider ray gun, rocket camera, all attach to figure's belt
EX $15 NM $35 MIP $60

The Amazing Energized Spider-Man Copter, 1978, Remco, helicopter-like vehicle
EX $50 NM $125 MIP $175

TOYS

Spider-Man Friction Vehicle, 1968, Marx, tin litho w/Spider-Man figure at wheel
EX $150 NM $300 MIP $500

Sports

DOLL

Dorothy Hamill Doll, 1975, Ideal, 11-1/4" tall
EX $30 NM $55 MIP $100

Evel Knievel Doll, Ideal, 6" tall
EX $20 NM $35 MIP $100

Julius Erving (Dr. J) Doll, 1974
EX $20 NM $40 MIP $100

Wayne Gretzky Doll, Mattel, 12" tall
EX $25 NM $50 MIP $80

WATCH

Muhammed Ali Wristwatch, 1980, Bradley, chrome case, sweep seconds, brown leather band, face shows Ali in trunks and gloves, w/signature beneath
EX $100 NM $175 MIP $300

Steve Canyon

BOOK

Steve Canyon's Interceptor Station Punch Out, 1950s, Golden
EX $75 NM $100 MIP $160

TOY

Jet Helmet, 1959, Ideal, U.S. Air Force helmet w/sun visor and speaker mask
EX $40 NM $80 MIP $120

Steve Canyon Costume, 1959, Halco
EX $25 NM $60 MIP $185

Steve Canyon's Membership Card and Badge, 1/2" x 4" Milton Caniff membership card for the Airagers, Morse code on back, 3" tin litho color badge w/gold feathers w/Steve's face centered
EX $100 NM $150 MIP $220

Superheroes

ACCESSORIES

Aquaman Halloween Costume, 1967, Ben Cooper
EX $35 NM $55 MIP $100

Captain America Halloween Costume, 1967, Ben Cooper
EX $100 NM $200 MIP $375

Comic Book Tattoos, 1967, Topps, Aquaman, Wonder Woman, Superman, or Batman
EX $20 NM $30 MIP $80

Flash Glass, 1978, Pepsi
EX $20 NM $40 MIP $70

Green Lantern Halloween Costume, 1967, Ben Cooper
EX $100 NM $175 MIP $300

Hawkman Button, 1966, Button World, 3", "Hawkman Superhero Club"
EX $20 NM $30 MIP $60

Justice League of America Display Card, 1970, Fleer, cardboard display from inside gumball machine
EX $30 NM $45 MIP $85

Mr. Bubble Superfriends Box, 1984, bubble bath box features Superman, Wonder Woman, Batman, and Robin
EX $20 NM $30 MIP $85

Wonder Woman Glass, 1978, Pepsi, 6"
EX $10 NM $25 MIP $45

Wonder Woman Record, 1977, Peter Pan Records, 33-1/3" rpm record w/comic book
EX $10 NM $30 MIP $50

BOOKS

Aquaman Scourge of the Sea Book, 1968, Whitman, Big Little Book
EX $15 NM $30 MIP $65

GAMES

Marvel Superheroes Card Game, 1978, Milton Bradley
EX $20 **NM** $30 **MIP** $90

TOY

Aquaman Jigsaw Puzzle, 1968, Whitman, 100 pieces; Aquaman and Mera
EX $20 **NM** $40 **MIP** $70

Marvel Superheroes Colorforms Set, 1983, Colorforms
EX $10 **NM** $20 **MIP** $60

Marvel Superheroes Easy Show Projector, 1967, Kenner, projector and three cartridges
EX $150 **NM** $300 **MIP** $450

Marvel Superheroes Puzzle, 1967, Milton Bradley, 100 pieces
EX $40 **NM** $80 **MIP** $175

Marvel Superheroes Sparkle Paint Set, 1967, Kenner
EX $40 **NM** $80 **MIP** $175

Marvel World Adventure Play Set, 1975, Amsco, w/stand-up scenes and figures
EX $100 **NM** $200 **MIP** $350

Mechanical Marvel Super Heroes Captain America, 1968, Marx, plastic, wind-up, made in Japan
EX $25 **NM** $60 **MIP** $100

Mechanical Marvel Super Heroes Thor, 1968, Marx, plastic, wind-up, made in Japan
EX $25 **NM** $60 **MIP** $100

Thor Flashlight, 1976, Marvel, yellow plastic, image of Thor on side, battery-operated
EX $10 **NM** $20 **MIP** $30

Superman

ACCESSORIES

Children's Dish Set, 1966, Boontonware, 7" plate, 5-1/2" bowl, 3-1/2" cup, all white plastic w/Superman image
EX $50 **NM** $100 **MIP** $150

Fan Card, 1942, 7" x 10", shows full color Superman in hands on hips pose, reads, "Best wishes from your friend Superman"
EX $400 **NM** $700 **MIP** $1000

Fan Card, 1950s, National Comics, 5" x 7" promo b/w post card w/signature "Best Wishes, George Reeves"
EX $75 **NM** $150 **MIP** $200

Hair Brush, 1940, Monarch, wood, full length decal of Superman, brush came in handle and no-handle styles w/box
EX $100 **NM** $175 **MIP** $350

Hair Brush, 1976, Avon, Superman handle, illustrated box
EX $15 **NM** $25 **MIP** $50

Junior Defense League of America Membership Certificate, 1940s, Superman, Inc., Superman Bread premium, red/blue print and Superman bust and logo on paper, "signed" by Clark Kent
EX $600 **NM** $1000 **MIP** $1250

Membership Certificate, 1965, last year of club
EX $175 **NM** $350 **MIP** $500

Original Radio Broadcasts Record, 1977, Nostalgia Lane, old Superman radio teleplays, in illustrated sleeve showing chain breaking pose in color and b/w strip panels
EX $10 **NM** $25 **MIP** $50

Patch, 1939, 5-1/2" diameter fabric premium patch, shows 3/4 profile of Superman breaking chains off chest, Supermen of America -- Action Comics
EX $1000 **NM** $4000 **MIP** $6000

Patch, 1940s, 3-1/2" round patch shows chain breaking pose
EX $750 **NM** $2000 **MIP** $5000

Patch, 1942, Superman Bread, cardboard shield
EX $1000 **NM** $1500 **MIP** $2500

Patch, 1970s, cloth diamond-shaped patch of "S" logo in gold/red, several sizes, each
EX $5 **NM** $10 **MIP** $20

Patch, 1970s, triangular orange cloth patch w/red border shows Superman flying over desert scene
EX $5 **NM** $10 **MIP** $20

Patch, 1970s, rectangular white patch w/green border shows full color Superboy running toward viewer
EX $20 **NM** $40 **MIP** $70

Patch, 1970s, rectangular white cloth patch w/green border shows full color Supergirl flying
EX $5 **NM** $10 **MIP** $20

Patch, 1973, diamond-shaped cloth patch shows Superman standing against vertical red/white stripes, wide yellow border has stars and reads "Superman Junior Olympics"
EX $5 **NM** $10 **MIP** $20

Pen, 1947, Jaffe, red/blue pen on illustrated card
EX $300 **NM** $450 **MIP** $750

Pencil Box, 1966, Mattel
EX $25 **NM** $50 **MIP** $75

Pencil Holder, 1940s, Superman, Inc., hollow holder in shape of large pencil, illustrated on shaft w/red and blue on white images and Superman-Tim Club logos
EX $500 **NM** $850 **MIP** $1250

Pennant, 1940s, yellow pennant w/Superman image and raised logo
EX $500 **NM** $800 **MIP** $1500

Pennant, 1973, 35th anniversary item, felt pennant has Amazing World of Superman logo and reads "Metropolis, Illinois, Home of Superman", came in two sizes, each
EX $12 **NM** $25 **MIP** $85

Pillow, 1960s, 12" square felt pillow w/color art of flying Superman
EX $35 **NM** $65 **MIP** $100

Pin, 1940s, Kellogg's, 7/8" round pin w/black/red/blue bust of Superman, most common pin in Pep Cereal series of late 1940s
EX $12 **NM** $25 **MIP** $60

Record and Club Membership Kit, 1966, 33-1/3 rpm record of the original comic, Superman Club card, shoulder patch and 1" tin litho club button, in 12" square illustrated box
EX $100 **NM** $150 **MIP** $200

Super Candy and Toy, 1967, Phoenix Candy, boxed candy w/a small toy inside each box
EX $50 **NM** $75 **MIP** $135

Superman 3-D Cut-Out Picture, 1950s, Kellogg's, 4-1/2 x 6-1/2" premium framed cut-out of Superman from the back of cereal box, reads "Best Wishes From Your Friend Superman"
EX $60 **NM** $80 **MIP** $100

Superman Candy, 1940, Leader Novelty Candy, boxed candy w/punch-out trading cards on box back and coupons redeemable for Superman items, red box, front shows chain-breaking pose
EX $750 **NM** $1000 **MIP** $1500

Superman Christmas Card, 1940s, 4" x 5", Superman Brings You Christmas Greetings, shows him flying w/small tree in hands
EX $50 **NM** $150 **MIP** $300

Superman Cigarette Lighter, 1940s, Dunhill, battery-operated table-top lighter has chrome finish figure standing on black base
EX $750 **NM** $1000 **MIP** $1500

Superman Crazy Foam, 1970s, American Aerosol, spray bath soap in full color illustrated can
EX $25 **NM** $50 **MIP** $75

Superman Cup, 1984, Burger King, one of four in set w/figural handles, others are Batman, Wonder Woman and Darkseid
EX $5 **NM** $7 **MIP** $10

Superman Figurine, 1966, Ideal, 3" tall hard plastic painted or unpainted figure on base, removable cape, part of Justice League series
EX $35 **NM** $65 **MIP** $85

Superman Figurine, 1984, Craft Master, solid figurine and paint set, on illustrated card
EX $25 **NM** $50 **MIP** $80

Superman Hood Ornament, 1940s, Lee, chrome finish, shows Superman in stylized running pose w/box
EX $500 **NM** $2000 **MIP** $3000

Superman Junior Defense League Pin, 1940s, die cut pin in shape of flying Superman holding banner aloft, gold finish pin w/red/white/blue detailing
EX $75 **NM** $150 **MIP** $250

Superman Krypto-Raygun Filmstrips, 1940s, Daisy, extra boxed films for Krypto-Raygun, each
EX $25 **NM** $50 **MIP** $100

Superman Mug, 1950s, left handed mug, shows Superman on front and name

across cape in back, handle has arrow and star
EX $75 **NM** $150 **MIP** $250

Superman Mug, 1966, white glass, red and blue logo w/Superman image, reverse picture is Superman breaking chain
EX $20 **NM** $40 **MIP** $65

Superman of Metropolis Award Certificate, 1973, premium given out during Metropolis, Illinois' 1973 35th anniversary of Superman celebration
EX $20 **NM** $40 **MIP** $75

Superman Phone Booth Radio, 1978, Vanity Fair, battery operated AM radio of green British-style booth has color bas-relief Superman exiting
EX $35 **NM** $75 **MIP** $175

Superman Planter, 1970s, 3" diameter painted ceramic
EX $5 **NM** $10 **MIP** $25

Superman Radio, 1973, transistor radio made in punch-out shape of Superman from waist up
EX $50 **NM** $75 **MIP** $200

Superman Record Player, 1978, latching box briefcase type record player illustrated on all sides in full color, also features b/w origin strip on back
EX $55 **NM** $100 **MIP** $200

Superman School Bag, 1950s, Acme, red/blue fold-over clasp vinyl bag, screened full color Superman figure, black plastic handle and shoulder strap
EX $100 **NM** $200 **MIP** $450

Superman Soaky, 1965, Colgate Palmolive, 10" soap bottle, shows him standing w/hands at sides
EX $20 **NM** $40 **MIP** $100

Superman Soaky, 1978, Avon, 9-1/2" bubble bath bottle, Superman stands atop building
EX $30 **NM** $40 **MIP** $65

Superman Song Record, 1950s, A.A. Records, 6" two-song, 45 rpm record in sleeve, other song is "Tarzan Song", Model No. 723
EX $25 **NM** $50 **MIP** $100

Superman Statue, 1940s, 15" tall, crude painted plaster carnival prize
EX $300 **NM** $450 **MIP** $600

Superman Statue, 1942, Syracuse Ornament, 5-1/2" tall composition statue of Superman in hands on hips pose, finished in brown patina w/red/black highlights
EX $1000 **NM** $2000 **MIP** $3500

Superman Telephone, 1979, ATE, plastic phone w/large figure of Superman in hands on hips pose standing over key pad, receiver hangs up into back of his cape, illustrated box
EX $150 **NM** $600 **MIP** $1000

Superman Toothbrush, 1970s, Janex, figural, battery operated
EX $20 **NM** $35 **MIP** $65

Superman Towels, 1970s, G.H. Wood, children's sponge towels, illustrated
EX $14 **NM** $30 **MIP** $65

Superman Wall Clock, 1978, New Haven, plastic and cardboard battery operated framed wall clock showing Superman fighting alien spaceship
EX $30 **NM** $60 **MIP** $150

Superman Wallet, 1950s, Croyden, brown, color embossed flying Superman and logo
EX $100 **NM** $175 **MIP** $375

Superman Wallet, 1960s, brown leather
EX $25 **NM** $40 **MIP** $70

Superman's Christmas Adventure Record, 1940s, Decca, set of three 78 rpm records in illustrated sleeves
EX $150 **NM** $500 **MIP** $900

Superman-Tim Club Membership Card, 1940s, Superman, Inc., blue/red or red/black card
EX $150 **NM** $200 **MIP** $325

Superman-Tim Club Press Card, 1940s, blue/red card for identifying self as an Official Reporter for club
EX $150 **NM** $225 **MIP** $350

Superman-Tim Club Redbacks, 1940s, Superman, Inc., red on white imprinted coupons styled to look like money, denominations of $1, $5 and $10 "redbacks", each
EX $10 **NM** $20 **MIP** $35

Superman-Tim Magazine, 1940s, 5" x 7" monthly store premium, each
EX $50 **NM** $75 **MIP** $160

Supermen of America Membership Certificate, 1948, 8-1/2" x 11", signed by "Clark Kent"
EX $75 **NM** $150 **MIP** $350

Utensil Set, 1966, Imperial Knife, stainless steel spoon and fork set w/Superman on the handles, on 4-1/2 x 10" illustrated card
EX $50 **NM** $100 **MIP** $200

Wall Banner, 1966, 16" x 25" w/hanging rod at top, shows large central picture of Superman in front of city skyline and two lower panels of him smashing rocks and flying through space
EX $40 **NM** $85 **MIP** $175

ACTION FIGURES

Energized Superman Figure, 1979, Remco, 12" tall battery operated hard body figure, in box
EX $35 **NM** $65 **MIP** $190

Flying Superman, 1950s, Kellogg's, plastic premium, 5" x 6-1/2", toy only
EX $50 **NM** $100 **MIP** $200

Flying Superman, 1950s, Kellogg's, premium, 5" x 6-1/2", rubber band propelled, w/instruction sheet and mailer
EX $150 **NM** $200 **MIP** $350

Flying Superman, 1955, Transogram, 12-1/2" tall molded plastic figure propelled by "super flight launcher," a rubber band attached to a pistol grip holder, on illustrated card
EX $75 **NM** $125 **MIP** $250

Superman Figure, Chemtoy, rubber, three different poses, on card, each
EX $25 **NM** $40 **MIP** $55

Superman Figure, Fun Things, 6" rubber figure on card
EX $9 **NM** $16 **MIP** $35

Superman Figure, Palitoy, 8" figure on card
EX $35 **NM** $65 **MIP** $120

Superman Figure, 1979, Japan, plastic body w/soft vinyl head, movable arms and head, in illustrated window box
EX $40 **NM** $60 **MIP** $90

BANK

Superman Bank, 1949, 9-1/2" painted ceramic shows youthful looking Superman standing on a cloud
EX $300 **NM** $500 **MIP** $800

Superman Bank, 1974, bust of Superman
EX $50 **NM** $75 **MIP** $125

Superman Dime Register Bank, 1940s, 1/2" x 2-1/2" x 2-1/2" yellow tin, front shows full color Superman breaking chains off chest, held $5 in dimes
EX $200 **NM** $300 **MIP** $525

BOOKS

Adventures of Superman Book, 1942, Random House, 4" x 5-1/2" armed services edition
EX $150 **NM** $225 **MIP** $500

Adventures of Superman Book, 1942, Random House, 6-1/2" x 9" hardcover by George Lowther, no dust jacket
EX $100 **NM** $200 **MIP** $350

Adventures of Superman Book, 1942, Random House, 6-1/2" x 9" hardcover, 220 pages, author George Lowther, full color dust jacket
EX $500 **NM** $800 **MIP** $1250

Book and Record Set, 1947, Musette Records, The Magic Ring
EX $100 **NM** $150 **MIP** $200

Book and Record Set, 1947, Musette Records, The Flying Train
EX $40 **NM** $100 **MIP** $200

Book, With Superman at the Gilbert Hall of Science, 1948, Gilbert, 32-page promo catalog for Gilbert's Erector Sets and other toys, illustrated w/Superman
EX $75 **NM** $100 **MIP** $175

Superman Book and Record Set, 1970s, Peter Pan, two stories w/record
EX $5 **NM** $10 **MIP** $18

Superman Cut-Outs, 1940, Saalfield, red cover, lighter paper than blue book, non-perforated cut-outs
EX $1500 **NM** $3000 **MIP** $4500

Superman Cut-Outs, 1940, Saalfield, perforated figures, heavy stock paper, blue cover
EX $1500 **NM** $3000 **MIP** $4500

Superman Paint-by-Number Book, 1966, Whitman, 11"x 13-1/2", 40 pictures plus coloring guide on back cover
EX $15 **NM** $50 **MIP** $100

Superman Pop-Up Book, 1979, Random House, hardcover, full color
EX $15 **NM** $30 **MIP** $60

Superman Press-Out Book, 1966, Whitman, punch out, assemble and hang scenes and characters
EX $20 **NM** $35 **MIP** $85

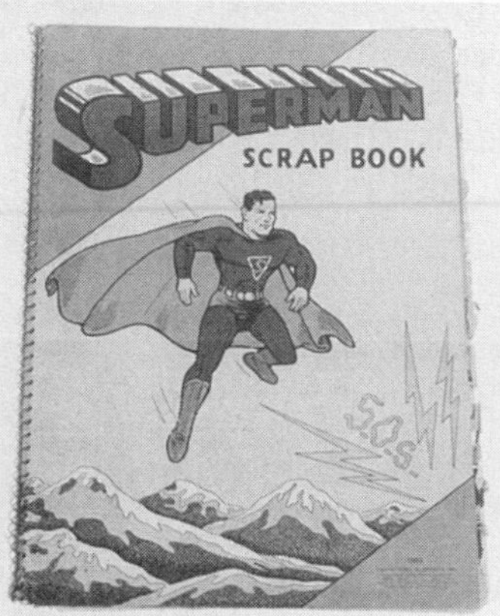

Superman Scrap Book, 1940, Saalfield, cover shows Superman flying over mountains toward stylized S.O.S. transmission
EX $75 **NM** $150 **MIP** $450

Superman To The Rescue Coloring Book, 1964, Whitman, cover shows Superman rescuing woman, Model No. 1001
EX $25 **NM** $50 **MIP** $100

Superman Workbook, 1940s, DC Comics, English grammar workbook
EX $200 **NM** $500 **MIP** $825

BUTTONS

Superman Button, 1966, WABC Radio, radio premium button for "It's a Bird, It's a Plane..." production, shows faceless Superman w/"WABC 77" across chest
EX $100 **NM** $150 **MIP** $300

Superman Club Button, 1966, 3-1/2" celluloid button, shows 3/4 profile thigh-up view of Superman in hands on hips pose, reads, "Official Member Superman Club"
EX $10 **NM** $20 **MIP** $30

Superman Muscle Building Club Button, 1954, Peter Puppets Playthings, part of Golden Muscle Building set, full color bust in sunburst circle in white button, reads "Superman Muscle Building Club"
EX $50 **NM** $150 **MIP** $250

Superman-Tim Club Button, 1940s, Superman, Inc., two different, both say Superman-Tim Club and have red/blue lettering and images on white background
EX $50 **NM** $75 **MIP** $120

CLOTHING

Superman Beanie, 1940s, hat w/two-color Superman embossed images on brim
EX $750 **NM** $900 **MIP** $1650

Superman Belt, 1940s, Pioneer, clear plastic w/color images and round brass buckle in box
EX $300 **NM** $500 **MIP** $700

Superman Belt, 1940s, Pioneer, brown leather w/Superman images and rectangular buckle, in box
EX $300 **NM** $500 **MIP** $750

Superman Belt, 1950s, Kellogg's, 28" long red plastic, aluminum "S" symbol buckle in red/yellow
EX $100 **NM** $250 **MIP** $450

Superman Belt Buckle, 1940s, square metal buckle shows red/blue chain breaking pose
EX $100 **NM** $150 **MIP** $425

Superman Moccasins, 1940s, Penobscot Shoe, leather moccasins w/Superman chain breaking pose on toe upper
EX $350 **NM** $750 **MIP** $2000

Superman Necktie, 1940s
EX $100 **NM** $200 **MIP** $350

Superman Necktie Set, 1940s, boxed set of two ties, small tie shows Superman standing w/arms crosses, larger tie shows Superman landing
EX $500 **NM** $1000 **MIP** $1500

Superman Suspenders, 1948, Pioneer, elastic, illustrated box
EX $350 **NM** $500 **MIP** $900

COMIC BOOKS

3-D Adventures of Superman Comic Book, 1950s, DC Comics, w/3-D goggles
EX $150 **NM** $250 **MIP** $850

Action Comics #1, 1938, DC Comics Top 9.2, first appearance of Superman
EX $125000**NM** $350000**MIP** $500000

Mini Comic Book, 1955, Kellogg's, cereal premium, #1, The Superman Time Capsule
EX $75 **NM** $100 **MIP** $225

Mini Comic Book, 1955, Kellogg's, cereal premium, #1-A, Duel in Space
EX $75 **NM** $100 **MIP** $210

Mini Comic Book, 1955, Kellogg's, cereal premium, #1-B, Supershow of Metropolis
EX $75 **NM** $100 **MIP** $200

Superman's Christmas Adventure Comic Book, 1940, Macy's, 1940 Macy's holiday premium
EX $1500 **NM** $2500 **MIP** $4000

Superman's Christmas Play Book, 1944, department store premium
EX $400 **NM** $600 **MIP** $1250

DOLLS

Super Babe Doll, 1947, Imperial Crown Toy, 15" tall, rubber skin, movable arms and legs, sleep eyes, composition head
EX $1000 **NM** $1500 **MIP** $2500

Superman Doll, Knickerbocker, 20" tall plush in box
EX $12 **NM** $25 **MIP** $40

Superman Doll, 1940, Ideal, 13-1/2" tall, wood jointed body w/composition head, movable head, arms and legs, ball knob hands
EX $750 **NM** $1000 **MIP** $2000

Superman Doll, 1977, Toy Works, 25-1/2" tall, cloth, w/cape
EX $12 **NM** $25 **MIP** $40

GAMES

Superman Action Game, 1940s, American Toy Works, wood and cardboard wartime game, Superman holds tottering bridge and kids shoot darts at tanks on bridge, Model No. 530
EX $1000 **NM** $1500 **MIP** $2500

Superman City Game, 1966, Remco, board game w/magnetic figures and buildings
EX $500 **NM** $750 **MIP** $1500

Superman Electronic Question and Answer Quiz Machine, 1966, Lisbeth Whiting Co., battery operated quiz game in full color illustrated box
EX $50 **NM** $100 **MIP** $225

Superman Official Eight-Piece Junior Quoit Set, 1940s, game in illustrated box includes wood and rubber game pieces, instruction booklet and membership card for "Superman Official Sports Club"
EX $75 **NM** $100 **MIP** $150

Superman Pinball Game, 1978, Bally, full-sized arcade game
EX $500 **NM** $750 **MIP** $1000

Superman Tilt Track, 1966, Kohner, marble skill game, in illustrated window box
EX $65 **NM** $95 **MIP** $175

PUZZLES

Puzzle, 1940, Saalfield, 300 pieces, 12 x 16", Superman w/Muscles Like Steel
EX $375 **NM** $500 **MIP** $750

Puzzle, 1940, Saalfield, 300 pieces, 12 x 16", Superman the Man of Tomorrow
EX $375 **NM** $500 **MIP** $750

Puzzle, 1940, Saalfield, 500 pieces, 16 x 20", Superman Stands Alone
EX $375 **NM** $500 **MIP** $850

Puzzle, 1940, Saalfield, 300 pieces, 12 x 16", Superman Shows his Super Strength
EX $375 **NM** $500 **MIP** $750

Puzzle, 1940, Saalfield, 300 pieces, 12 x 16", Superman Saves the Streamliner
EX $375 **NM** $500 **MIP** $750

Puzzle, 1940, Saalfield, 500 pieces, 16 x 20", Superman Saves a Life
EX $375 **NM** $500 **MIP** $850

Puzzle, 1966, Whitman, 150 pieces, 14" X 18", Superman
EX $12 **NM** $25 **MIP** $50

Puzzle, 1966, Whitman, two frame tray puzzles: one shows Superman fighting space robot, other shows him flying past manned rocket ship in outer space, each
EX $25 **NM** $50 **MIP** $85

Puzzle, 1973, APC
EX $10 **NM** $15 **MIP** $25

Puzzles, 1940, Saalfield, set of six small puzzles w/ 42 pieces each
EX $800 **NM** $1300 **MIP** $2000

Puzzles, 1940, set of three Superman puzzles
EX $750 **NM** $1000 **MIP** $1500

RINGS

Superman Crusader Ring, 1940s, brass or silver finish ring shows forward facing bust of Superman
EX $75 **NM** $120 **MIP** $250

Superman Member Ring, 1940, red paint on top of gold finish
EX $25000 **NM** $40000 **MIP** $75000

Superman Milk Defense Club Ring, 1941, gold finish hidden compartment ring, face is embossed milk companies initial, different initials known, lightning bolt and eyeball symbol, compartment shows Superman decal image
EX $5000 **NM** $15000 **MIP** $25000

Superman Milk Defense Club Ring, 1941, Different Milk Companies Sponsors, gold finish hidden compartment ring, face is embossed w/"S," lightning bolt and Superman bust, compartment shows Superman image, b/c of restrike none are found in MIP condition
EX $5000 **NM** $20000 **MIP** n/a

Superman Ring, 1978, Nestle's, premium ring, gold finish w/white circle center and yellow/red diamond "S" logo in middle
EX $20 **NM** $40 **MIP** $70

Superman-Tim Club Ring, 1940s, bronze finish metal ring w/embossed image of Superman in flight, w/initials S and T near his feet
EX $1500 **NM** $3000 **MIP** $4000

TOY

Bicycle Siren, 1970s, Empire
EX $10 **NM** $20 **MIP** $50

Bubble Gum Badge, 1948, Fo-Lee Gum Corp., shield-shaped brass finish badge shows a variant of the chain breaking pose inside a sun burst pattern ringed w/stars
EX $4000 **NM** $7000 **MIP** $10000

Cinematic Picture Pistol, 1940, Daisy, non-electric, film is viewed through view in back of gun, metal gun w/one pre-loaded 28 scene Superman film, Model No. 96
EX $300 **NM** $900 **MIP** $1800

Crayon-by-Numbers Set, 1954, Transogram, 16 crayons and 44 action scenes
EX $100 **NM** $200 **MIP** $400

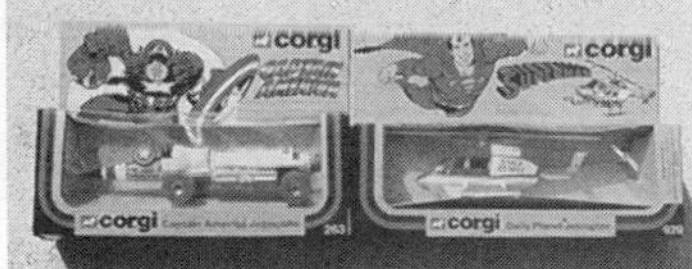

Daily Planet Jetcopter, 1979, Corgi, Model No. 929
EX $20 **NM** $40 **MIP** $75

Dangle Dandies Mobile, 1955, Kellogg's, set of eight cut outs on boxes of Rice Krispies and Corn Flakes
EX $75 **NM** $100 **MIP** $200

Film Viewer, 1947, 1-1/2"x4"x6-1/2" wide boxed set of hand-held viewer and six films
EX $350 **NM** $550 **MIP** $800

Film Viewer, 1947, Acme, 1-1/2" x 6-1/2" wide boxed set of hand-held viewer and two films
EX $200 **NM** $500 **MIP** $700

Film Viewer, 1965, plastic hand viewer w/two boxes of film, on illustrated card
EX $25 **NM** $40 **MIP** $85

Flying Noise Balloon, 1966, Van Dam, oversized balloon makes noise in flight, Superman illustration on balloon and card
EX $12 **NM** $23 **MIP** $50

Jumbo Movie Viewer, 1950s, Acme, blue/yellow plastic viewer w/35 mm "theatre size" film, on illustrated card, w/one filmstrip
EX $125 **NM** $200 **MIP** $350

Kryptonite Rock, 1970s, glow-in-the-dark rocks sold as kryptonite chunks, in illustrated box
EX $10 **NM** $15 **MIP** $25

Krypto-Raygun Film Viewer, 1940, Daisy, battery-operated metal projector gun, seven Superman filmstrips, illustrated box, No. 94
EX $1000 **NM** $1600 **MIP** $3000

Movie Viewer, 1940, Acme Plastics, tortoise shell plastic, and three individually boxed Superman films, in large full color die-cut box
EX $450 **NM** $850 **MIP** $1200

Movie Viewer, 1947, Acme Plastics, black plastic viewer, white knob and two individually boxed Superman films, in red/blue die-cut box
EX $175 **NM** $450 **MIP** $675

Movie Viewer, 1948, Acme Plastics, red plastic viewer and three individually boxed Superman films, in small full color die-cut box
EX $150 **NM** $400 **MIP** $600

Movie Viewer, 1950s, Acme, black/red plastic viewer w/two individually boxed Superman films
EX $90 **NM** $150 **MIP** $300

Official Magic Kit, 1956, Bar-Zim, magic balls, disappearing cards, multiplying corks, vanishing trick, shell game, balancing belt and directions, in illustrated box
EX $350 **NM** $750 **MIP** $1500

Official Superman Costume, 1954, Ben Cooper, blue/red suit w/red/yellow monogram and belt, in box
EX $140 **NM** $260 **MIP** $425

Official Superman Krypto-Raygun Film Viewer, 1940, Daisy, includes raygun, battery, bulb, lens and one film strip, in illustrated box
EX $800 **NM** $1400 **MIP** $2000

Official Superman Playsuit, 1954, Funtime Playwear, rayon outfit, red cap w/screened Superman image, navy and red suit w/5" gold monogram and belt
EX $200 **NM** $400 **MIP** $625

Official Superman Playsuit, 1970, Ben Cooper, cloth suit in illustrated box
EX $20 **NM** $40 **MIP** $70

Official Superman Two-Piece Kiddie Swim Set, 1950s, set of rubber swim fins and goggles w/Superman's image or "S" symbol, in box
EX $50 **NM** $150 **MIP** $250

Paint-by-Numbers Watercolor Set, 1954, Transogram, 16 watercolors and 44 action scenes
EX $75 **NM** $200 **MIP** $375

Super Heroes String Puppets, 1978, Madison, string controlled cloth and vinyl marionette
EX $25 **NM** $75 **MIP** $150

Superman and Supergirl Push Puppets, 1968, Kohner, set of two: 5-1/4" on bases, in window box
EX $350 **NM** $600 **MIP** $1000

Superman Back-a-Wack, 1966, Dell, blue plastic paddle w/gold imprinted "S" logo and name, elastic string and red ball, on illustrated card, Model No. 1194
EX $50 **NM** $100 **MIP** $150

Superman Balloon, 1966, small balloon w/centered image
EX $5 **NM** $15 **MIP** $35

Superman

Superman Costume, 1950s, red pants and tie-on cape, blue shirt w/red, blue and yellow "S" emblem on chest, yellow belt
EX $100 **NM** $300 **MIP** $425

Superman Figure, Presents, 15" vinyl/cloth figure on base
EX $25 **NM** $40 **MIP** $60

Superman Golden Muscle Building Set, 1954, Peter Puppets Playthings, handles, springs, hand grippers, jump rope, wall hooks, measuring tape, progress chart, membership certificate and button, illustrated box
EX $700 **NM** $1000 **MIP** $1600

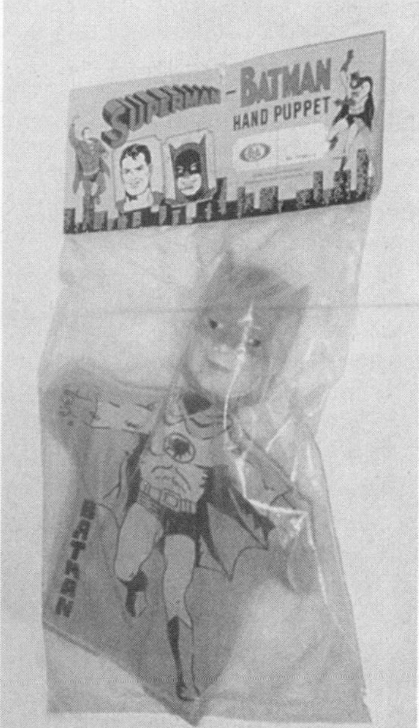

Superman Hand Puppet, 1966, Ideal, 11", cloth body, vinyl head
EX $50 **NM** $75 **MIP** $120

Superman II View-Master Set, three reels, based on film, Model No. L46
EX $5 **NM** $10 **MIP** $35

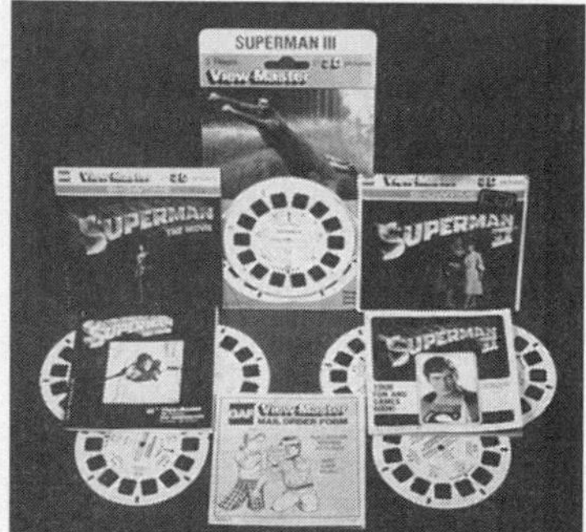

Superman III View-Master Set, three reels, based on film, Model No. 4044
EX $5 **NM** $10 **MIP** $30

Superman Junior Horseshoe Set, 1950s, Super Swim, four rubber horseshoes, two rubber bases and two wood pegs and Official Sports Club card and rules for sportsmanship
EX $75 **NM** $150 **MIP** $300

Superman Junior Swim Goggles, 1950s, Super Swim, plastic lenses, rubber goggles w/red strap, "S" logo and membership card for Superman Safety Swim Club
EX $50 **NM** $125 **MIP** $225

Superman Kite, 1966, Pressman
EX $50 **NM** $75 **MIP** $135

Superman Kite, 1982, Hiflyer
EX $5 **NM** $10 **MIP** $35

Superman Krypton Rocket, 1954, Kellogg's, 2" x 9" x 9-1/2" water powered rocket w/"Krypton generating pump," in mailer box
EX $150 **NM** $325 **MIP** $425

Superman Krypton Rocket, 1956, Park Plastics, 2" x 9" x 9-1/2" water powered rocket w/Krypton generating pump, reserve fuel tank and Krypton Rocket, in illustrated box, same as Kellogg's rocket but in mass market packaging w/added fuel tank
EX $150 **NM** $325 **MIP** $425

Superman Paint Set, 1940, American Toy Works, three brushes, small palette, water cup, 14 different paints and four b/w cartoon panels, in 11" x 14-1/2" color illustrated box
EX $400 **NM** $800 **MIP** $1250

Superman Paint Set, 1940s, American Toy Works, box shows Superman flying up toward upper right corner of box, w/pallet and brushes at lower right, "Paint Set" inside pallet
EX $400 **NM** $800 **MIP** $1250

Superman Paint Set, 1940s, American Toy Works, larger version, shows Superman in front of pallet background
EX $400 **NM** $800 **MIP** $1250

Superman Play Set, 1973, Ideal, self-contained vinyl covered full color snap-close case opens to three backdrops, Fortress of Solitude, Daily Planet and villain's hideout, for staging action scenes w/supplied color punch-outs
EX $50 **NM** $75 **MIP** $175

Superman Playsuit, 1940, Fishback, red and blue imprinted blue smock shirt and pants w/tie-on red cape
EX $200 **NM** $500 **MIP** $1250

Superman Pogo Stick, 1977, 48" w/a vinyl bust on top
EX $50 **NM** $100 **MIP** $225

Superman Push Puppet, 1966, Kohner, 5-1/4" on base, in window box
EX $50 **NM** $75 **MIP** $110

Superman Roller Skates, 1975, Larami, plastic w/color bust of Superman shaped around front of each skate, in illustrated window box
EX $20 **NM** $50 **MIP** $100

Superman Rub-Ons, 1966, Hasbro, magic picture transfers in box illustrated w/picture of Superman flying
EX $50 **NM** $100 **MIP** $150

Superman Senior Rubber Horseshoe Set, 1950s, in box
EX $75 **NM** $125 **MIP** $200

Superman Senior Swim Goggles, 1950s, Super Swim, plastic lenses, rubber goggles w/red strap, "S" logo on bridge, membership card for Superman Safety Swim Club
EX $40 **NM** $80 **MIP** $175

Superman Sky Hero, 1977, Marx, rubber band glider w/color Superman image, on card, Model No. 9310
EX $25 **NM** $40 **MIP** $85

Superman Space Satellite Launcher Set, 1950s, Kellogg's, premium set of generic plastic gun w/firing "satellite wheel" and illustrated instruction sheet, in mailer box
EX $300 **NM** $600 **MIP** $1000

Superman Stamp Set, 1965, set of six wood-backed character stamps
EX $25 **NM** $50 **MIP** $200

Superman Super Watch, 1967, Toy House, plastic toy watch w/moveable hands, watch "case" is large "S" chest symbol, on illustrated card
EX $25 **NM** $50 **MIP** $150

Superman Tank, 1958, Linemar, large battery operated tin, 3-D Superman w/a cloth cape, in illustrated box
EX $1200 **NM** $2500 **MIP** $3500

Superman the Movie View-Master Set, 1979, three reels, based on film, Model No. J78
EX $5 **NM** $10 **MIP** $30

Superman Utility Belt, 1979, Remco, illustrated window box, decoder glasses, kryptonite detector, nonworking watch, handcuffs, ring, decoder map, press card and secret message
EX $50 **NM** $150 **MIP** $275

Superman Water Gun, 1967, Multiple Toymakers, 6" plastic, Model No. 484
EX $50 **NM** $100 **MIP** $200

Toy Wristwatch, 1950s, Germany, non-working toy watch, blue plastic band, rectangular case w/full color full standing pose on white dial
EX $35 **NM** $65 **MIP** $200

Trick Picture Sun Camera, 1950s, Made in Japan, when left in the sun for two minutes, the camera "develops" a picture of Superman fighting a space monster
EX $75 **NM** $150 **MIP** $250

TRADING CARDS

Superman II Trading Cards, 1981, Costa Rican, set of 88 cards, complete set
EX $18 **NM** $35 **MIP** $50

Superman II Trading Cards, 1981, Topps, set of 88 cards, complete set
EX $20 **NM** $30 **MIP** $40

Superman III Trading Cards, 1983, Topps, set of 99 cards, complete set
EX $5 **NM** $10 **MIP** $15

Superman the Movie Trading Cards, 1978, Topps, set of 77 cards, first issue
EX $20 **NM** $40 **MIP** $65

Superman the Movie Trading Cards, 1979, Topps, set of 88 cards, second issue
EX $12 **NM** $25 **MIP** $35

Superman the Movie Trading Cards, 1979, French, set of 180 cards
EX $18 **NM** $35 **MIP** $50

Superman the Movie Trading Cards, 1979, OPC, set of 132 cards
EX $12 **NM** $25 **MIP** $35

Superman Trading Cards, 1940, Gum Inc., 2-1/2" x 3-1/4" cards, set of 72
EX $7500 **NM** $15000 **MIP** $20000

Superman Trading Cards, 1940, Gum Inc., 2-1/2" x 3-1/4" cards, each
EX $75 **NM** $125 **MIP** $275

Superman Trading Cards, 1966, Topps, set of 66 cards, George Reeves TV series scenes
EX $90 **NM** $165 **MIP** $400

Superman Trading Cards, 1966, Topps, set of 66 cards, shows George Reeves TV series scenes, price per each card
EX $5 **NM** $10 **MIP** $15

Superman Trading Cards Display Box, 1966, Topps, 2" x 4" x 8" display box of 24 unopened packs, box shows George Reeves bust
EX $500 **NM** $750 **MIP** $1350

Superman Trading Cards Wrapper, 1940, Gum Inc., 4-1/2" x 6" waxed paper
EX $500 **NM** $650 **MIP** $900

WATCHES

Superman Supertime Wristwatch, 1950s, National Comics, gray band, stamped red "S" logo, silver western style buckle, full color hands on hips pose inside chrome finish case, second hand, even-hour numbers around face, in full color box
EX $750 **NM** $1250 **MIP** $2500

Superman Wristwatch, 1939, New Haven Clock Boxed, flattened oval face, shows color image of standing Superman from knees up, leather band
EX $2000 **NM** $3500 **MIP** $5000

Superman Wristwatch, 1940s, New Haven Clock, squared-oval faced watch, leather band, dial shows Superman standing, hands on hips, in illustrated box
EX $2000 **NM** $3500 **MIP** $5000

Superman Wristwatch, 1959, Bradley, dial shows Superman flying over city, second hand, chrome finish case
EX $750 **NM** $1000 **MIP** $1750

Superman Wristwatch, 1977, gold bezel, stainless back, blue leather band, face shows Superman flying upward from below
EX $35 **NM** $65 **MIP** $200

Superman Wristwatch, 1986, Una-Donna, plastic case and band, several color and face illustrations, each
EX $10 **NM** $20 **MIP** $75

Tarzan

ACCESSORIES

Bracelet, 1934, drink more milk radio premium
EX $1500 **NM** $3500 **MIP** $5000

Jungle Map, 1933, radio premium
EX $500 **NM** $1000 **MIP** $1500

Poster, 1933, Paper Mills, three masks; premium
EX $500 **NM** $800 **MIP** $1200

Tarzan Flasher Ring, 1960s, Vari-Vue
EX $10 **NM** $20 **MIP** $50

Tarzan Party Set, 1977, Amscan
EX $10 **NM** $25 **MIP** $60

FIGURES

Figure, 1950s, 2-1/2" tall, celluloid, French
EX $750 **NM** $1000 **MIP** $1550

Kala Ape Figure, 1984, Dakin, 3" tall
EX $10 **NM** $15 **MIP** $30

Young Tarzan Figure, 1984, Dakin, 4", bendable
EX $10 **NM** $15 **MIP** $30

Three Little Pigs

ACCESSORIES

Three Little Pigs Cuff Bracelet, 1930s, 1/2" x 2-1/4", wolf blowing down a house w/pig running away
EX $350 **NM** $500 **MIP** $750

GAME

Who's Afraid of the Big Bad Wolf Game, 1930s, Parker Brothers
EX $200 **NM** $350 **MIP** $600

TOY

Puzzle, 1940s, Jaymar, 7" x 10" x 2"
EX $100 **NM** $200 **MIP** $300

Three Little Pigs Sand Pail, 1930s, Ohio Art, 4-1/2", tin
EX $100 **NM** $200 **MIP** $450

Three Little Pigs Soaky Set, 1960s, Drew Chemical, 8" tall each: Three Little Pigs and the Big Bad Wolf
EX $70 **NM** $125 **MIP** $275

WATCH

Big Bad Wolf Pocket Watch Box, 1934, Ingersoll
EX $2000 **NM** $3300 **MIP** $5000

Tom and Jerry

BANK

Tom and Jerry Bank, 1980, Gorham, 6" tall
EX $20 **NM** $35 **MIP** $80

FIGURES

Jerry Figure, 1973, Marx, 4" tall
EX $15 **NM** $25 **MIP** $70

Tom and Jerry Figure Set, 1975, walking, Tom, Jerry, and Droopy
EX $25 **NM** $50 **MIP** $125

Tom Figure, 1973, Marx, 6" tall
EX $15 **NM** $30 **MIP** $70

TOY

Puzzles, Whitman, four frame tray puzzles
EX $20 **NM** $35 **MIP** $90

Tom and Jerry Go Kart, 1973, Marx, plastic, friction drive
EX $50 **NM** $75 **MIP** $150

Tom and Jerry on Scooter, 1971, Marx, plastic friction drive
EX $30 **NM** $50 **MIP** $100

WATCH

Tom and Jerry Wristwatch, 1985, Bradley, quartz, oldies series, small white plastic case and band, sweep seconds, face shows Tom squirting Jerry w/hose
EX $15 **NM** $35 **MIP** $90

Tony the Tiger

ACCESSORIES

Cookie Jar, 1960s, Kellogg's, plastic, figural
EX $25 **NM** $70 **MIP** $120

Radio, 1980s, plastic, figural
EX $20 **NM** $45 **MIP** $80

BANK

Figural Bank, 1967, Kellogg's
EX $30 **NM** $45 **MIP** $90

FIGURES

Inflatable Tiger, 1950s, Kellogg's
EX $7 **NM** $20 **MIP** $35

Plush Tiger, 1970s, Kellogg's
EX $10 **NM** $25 **MIP** $75

Top Cat

FIGURES

Top Cat Figure, 1961, Marx, TV-Tinykins, plastic
EX $20 **NM** $35 **MIP** $70

TOY

Top Cat Soaky, 1960s, 10" tall, vinyl
EX $25 **NM** $45 **MIP** $90

Viewmarx Micro-Viewer, 1963, Marx, plastic
EX $40 **NM** $60 **MIP** $120

Winnie the Pooh

ACCESSORIES

Lamp, 1964, Dolly Toy, 7" tall
EX $35 **NM** $90 **MIP** $200

Radio, 1970s, Thilgee, 5" x 6" x 1-1/2" tall
EX $45 **NM** $90 **MIP** $135

Winnie the Pooh Button, 1960s, 3-1/2" celluloid
EX $10 **NM** $25 **MIP** $60

Winnie the Pooh Snow Globe, 5-1/2", musical
EX $15 **NM** $35 **MIP** $80

DOLL

Winnie the Pooh and Christopher Robin Dolls, 1964, Horsman, Winnie the Pooh 3-1/2" tall and Christopher 11" tall, set
EX $100 **NM** $175 **MIP** $350

Winnie the Pooh Doll, 1960s, 12" tall
EX $40 **NM** $60 **MIP** $120

TOY

Jack-In-The-Box, 1960s, Carnival Toys
EX $40 **NM** $60 **MIP** $120

Kanga and Roo Squeak Toy, 1966, Holland Hill, vinyl
EX $20 **NM** $40 **MIP** $80

Winnie the Pooh

Magic Slate, 1965, Western Publishing, 8-1/2" x 13-1/2"
EX $30 NM $50 MIP $120

Puzzle, 1964, Whitman, frame tray
EX $10 NM $30 MIP $70

Wizard of Oz

ACCESSORIES

Christmas Ornaments, 1977, Bradford Novelty, 4-1/2" tall, Dorothy, Scarecrow, Tin Man, Cowardly Lion, each
EX $5 NM $10 MIP $30

Christmas Ornaments, 1989, Presents, cloth and vinyl: Dorothy, Scarecrow, Tin Man, Cowardly Lion, Glinda and Wicked Witch, each
EX $8 NM $10 MIP $20

Cookie Jar, 1990, Clay Art, white w/relief figures of characters
EX $50 NM $100 MIP $175

Crayon Box, 1975, Cheinco, rectangular, metal
EX $5 NM $10 MIP $30

Erasers, 1989, Applause, set of six: figural, Scarecrow, Cowardly Lion, Dorothy, Wicked Witch, Tin Man, Glinda, set
EX $15 NM $20 MIP $40

Give-A-Show Projector Slides, 1968, Kenner, 35 color slides, five different shows
EX $20 NM $40 MIP $100

Magnets, 1987, Grynnen Barrett, six character magnets in box
EX $6 NM $10 MIP $15

Magnets, 1989, Vanderbilt Products, several characters available, each
EX $2 NM $3 MIP $5

Pails, 1950s, Swift and Company, Oz Peanut Butter, red and yellow and red, yellow and white tin
EX $25 NM $40 MIP $100

Scarecrow Night Light, 1989, Hamilton Gifts, 7", unpainted bone china
EX $10 NM $15 MIP $25

Snack 'N Sip Pals, 1989, Multi Toys, 12 red and white striped straws w/detachable character figures
EX $4 NM $7 MIP $25

Stationery, 1939, Whitman, 10 sheets and envelopes, w/character illustations
EX $175 NM $300 MIP $500

Tin, 1989, Multi Toys, 8" x 10" x 2", illustrated w/Emerald City and characters
EX $8 NM $15 MIP $35

Trash Can, 1975, Chein, oval metal
EX $20 NM $35 MIP $70

Wall Decorations, 1967, Shepard Press, 20 punch-out decorations
EX $20 NM $35 MIP $65

BANK

Cowardly Lion Bank, 1960s, ceramic, red nose
EX $30 NM $75 MIP $160

Dorothy Bank, 1960s, ceramic, blue dress w/brown wicker basket
EX $30 NM $60 MIP $160

Scarecrow Bank, 1960s, ceramic
EX $30 NM $50 MIP $135

Tin Man Bank, 1960s, ceramic, silver
EX $30 NM $70 MIP $150

BOOK

Cut and Make Masks, 1982, Dover, eight cut-out color masks
EX $5 NM $10 MIP $30

Dorothy and Friends Visit Oz Book, 1967, Curtis Candy, candy premium
EX $8 NM $20 MIP $45

Dorothy Meets the Wizard Book, 1967, Curtis Candy, candy premium
EX $15 NM $30 MIP $65

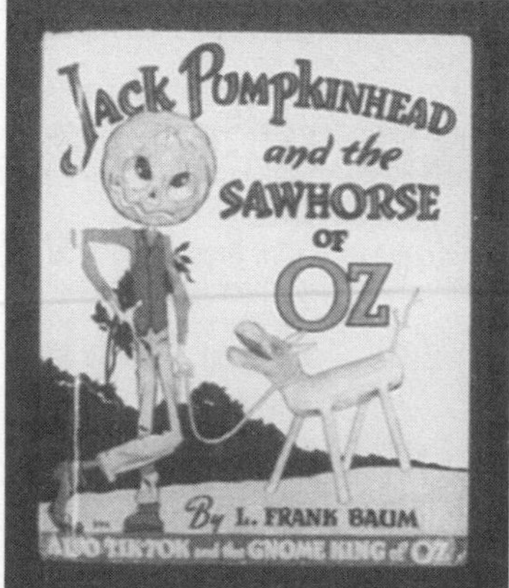

Jack Pumpkinhead and the Sawhorse of Oz Book, 1939, Rand McNally, hardcover, also contains "Tik Tok and the Gnome King of Oz"
EX $100 NM $200 MIP $400

Little Dorothy and Toto of Oz Book, 1939, Rand McNally, hardcover, also contains "The Cowardly Lion and the Hungry Tiger"
EX $110 NM $250 MIP $500

Little Golden Book Series, 1951, The Road to Oz, The Emerald City of Oz, and The Tin Woodman of Oz, each
EX $8 NM $20 MIP $70

Mask Book, 1990, Watermill Press, four paper masks
EX $3 NM $10 MIP $30

Return To Oz Little Golden Books, 1985, Western, Dorothy Returns to Oz, Escape from the Witch's Castle, Dorothy in the Ornament Room, Dorothy Saves the Emerald City, each
EX $2 NM $5 MIP $10

Scarecrow and the Tin Man Book, 1904, G. W. Dillingham
EX $300 NM $600 MIP $850

Scarecrow and the Tin Man Book, 1946, Perks Publishing, black and yellow pictures
EX $30 NM $60 MIP $120

Tales of the Wizard of Oz Coloring Book, 1962, Whitman, art from animated TV show
EX $15 NM $20 MIP $70

The Tin Woodsman and Dorothy Book, 1967, Curtis Candy, candy premium
EX $12 NM $40 MIP $80

The Wonderful Cut-Outs of Oz Book, 1985, Crown, 35 figures to cut out
EX $7 NM $15 MIP $50

Wizard of Oz Book, 1975, Western, #310-32, Little Golden Book
EX $5 NM $10 MIP $40

Wizard of Oz Christmas Book, 1968, Gimbel's, New York department store premium
EX $20 NM $50 MIP $100

Wizard of Oz Color-By-Number Book, 1962, Karas Publishing, #A-116, Twinkle Books series
EX $10 NM $30 MIP $70

Wizard of Oz Paint Book, 1939, Whitman
EX $200 NM $400 MIP $600

Wizard of Oz Paper Dolls, 1976, Whitman
EX $7 NM $15 MIP $50

Wizard of Oz Sticker Fun Book, 1976, Whitman
EX $6 NM $12 MIP $35

COMIC BOOK

Tales of the Wizard of Oz Comic Book, 1962, Dell, #1306
EX $10 NM $15 MIP $50

Wizard of Oz Comic Book, 1956, Dell, Dell Junior Treasury, #5
EX $12 NM $40 MIP $100

Wizard of Oz Comic Book, 1957, Dell, Classic Illustrated Jr., #535
EX $6 NM $20 MIP $60

DOLL

Cowardly Lion Doll, 1971, M-D Tissue, cloth, light brown body w/white snout
EX $10 NM $20 MIP $40

Cowardly Lion Doll, 1984, Ideal, 9", Character Dolls series
EX $20 NM $40 MIP $90

Cowardly Lion Doll, 1988, Presents, vinyl
EX $20 NM $40 MIP $90

Cowardly Lion Doll, 1989, Largo Toys, rag doll
EX $8 NM $18 MIP $50

Dandy Lion Doll, 1962, Artistic, 14" tall, cloth and vinyl
EX $35 NM $85 MIP $175

Doodle Dolls, 1979, Whiting, three dolls: cardboard parts, yarn, Styrofoam balls, fabric
EX $8 NM $20 MIP $40

Dorothy and Toto Doll, 1984, Ideal, 9", Character Dolls series
EX $20 NM $40 MIP $80

Dorothy Doll, 1939, Sears, 15-1/2", Judy Garland, red or blue checked jumper w/black pin curls
EX $800 NM $1500 MIP $2500

Dorothy Doll, 1939, Ideal, 13", Judy Garland, blue checked jumper, open and close brown eyes
EX $600 NM $900 MIP $1350

Dorothy Doll, 1939, Ideal, 15-1/2", Judy Garland, blue checked jumper, open and close brown eyes
EX $700 **NM** $1300 **MIP** $2200

Dorothy Doll, 1939, Ideal, 18", Judy Garland, blue checked jumper, open and close brown eyes
EX $1000 **NM** $1750 **MIP** $3000

Dorothy Doll, 1971, M-D Tissue, cloth, stuffed, yellow hair, orange jumper
EX $10 **NM** $20 **MIP** $60

Dorothy Doll, 1984, Effanbee, 14-1/2" tall, vinyl, Judy Garland, blue dress and hair ribbons, ruby slippers, Legend Series
EX $45 **NM** $100 **MIP** $150

Dorothy Doll, 1988, Presents, vinyl, blue checkered jumper, white blouse, red slippers, yellow brick road base
EX $20 **NM** $35 **MIP** $80

Dorothy Doll, 1989, Largo Toys, Judy Garland
EX $8 **NM** $20 **MIP** $60

Dorothy Doll, 1991, Madame Alexander, 8", blue checked jumper w/white blouse, basket w/Toto and red shoes, Storyland Dolls series
EX $20 **NM** $40 **MIP** $80

Glinda Doll, 1989, Presents, vinyl, pink dress w/pink crown and wand, yellow brick road base
EX $20 **NM** $40 **MIP** $90

Jack Pumpkinhead Doll, 1924, Oz Doll and Toy, 13"
EX $750 **NM** $1300 **MIP** $2000

Lollipop Guild Boy Doll, 1989, Presents, vinyl, plaid shirt, green shorts and striped socks, on a yellow brick road base
EX $20 **NM** $40 **MIP** $80

Lullabye League Girl Doll, 1989, Presents, vinyl, pink ballerina dress and slippers w/hat on a yellow brick road base
EX $20 **NM** $40 **MIP** $80

Mayor of Munchkinland Doll, 1989, Presents, vinyl, black suit and shoes on a yellow brick road base
EX $20 **NM** $40 **MIP** $80

Patchwork Girl Doll, 1924, Oz Doll and Toy, 13"
EX $150 **NM** $300 **MIP** $600

Rusty the Tin Man Doll, 1962, Artistic Toy Company, 14" tall, cloth and vinyl
EX $35 **NM** $60 **MIP** $150

Scarecrow Doll, 1924, Oz Doll and Toy, 13"
EX $800 **NM** $1400 **MIP** $2200

Scarecrow Doll, 1971, M-D Tissue, cloth, stuffed, frowning, blue pants and red and white plaid jacket
EX $10 **NM** $15 **MIP** $45

Scarecrow Doll, 1984, Ideal, 9", Character Dolls series
EX $25 **NM** $40 **MIP** $75

Scarecrow Doll, 1988, Presents, vinyl, brown pants, green shirt, and black hat and shoes, on a yellow brick road base
EX $25 **NM** $40 **MIP** $85

Scarecrow Doll, 1989, Largo Toys, rag doll
EX $9 **NM** $15 **MIP** $60

Scarecrow Talkin' Patter Pillow Doll, 1968, Mattel, cloth, pull-string, says 10 phrases, dark blue pants and sleeves, white gloves, black boots
EX $50 **NM** $100 **MIP** $200

Socrates the Scarecrow Doll, 1962, Artistic, 14" tall, cloth and vinyl
EX $30 **NM** $70 **MIP** $160

Strawman Doll, 1939, Ideal, 17", Ray Bolger, tan or pink pants, black or navy jacket
EX $600 **NM** $1000 **MIP** $1800

Tin Man Doll, 1924, Oz Doll and Toy, 13"
EX $800 **NM** $1200 **MIP** $2000

Tin Man Doll, 1971, M-D Tissue, cloth, stuffed, gray body, blue eyes, red heart
EX $8 **NM** $20 **MIP** $50

Tin Man Doll, 1984, Ideal, 9", Character Dolls series
EX $20 **NM** $35 **MIP** $75

Tin Man Doll, 1988, Presents, vinyl, silver body w/a heart clock on chaint, on a yellow brick road base
EX $20 **NM** $35 **MIP** $75

Tin Man Doll, 1989, Largo Toys, rag doll
EX $10 **NM** $15 **MIP** $40

Toto Doll, 1988, Presents, 5-1/2" plush
EX $15 **NM** $30 **MIP** $75

Wicked Witch Doll, 1989, Presents, vinyl, black dress and hat, green face and hands holding broom on a yellow brick road base
EX $25 **NM** $40 **MIP** $100

Wizard of Oz Dolls, 1985, Effanbee, 11-1/2", Dorothy, Scarecrow, Tin Man, Cowardly Lion, each
EX $15 **NM** $22 **MIP** $70

Wizard of Oz Live! Dolls, Applause, cloth, three different sizes, each
EX $8 **NM** $15 **MIP** $40

FIGURES

Jack Pumpkinhead Figure, 1985, Heart and Heart, Return to Oz, 3"-4" tall, plastic jointed
EX $35 **NM** $55 **MIP** $100

Munchkins Figures, 1988, Presents, PVC, 1-3/4" to 2-3/4": Mayor, Lollipop Guild Boy, Sleepyhead Girl, Lady, Soldier and Ballerina, each
EX $5 **NM** $10 **MIP** $35

Oz-Kins Figures, 1967, Aurora, plastic Burry Biscuit premium: set of 10
EX $50 **NM** $100 **MIP** $220

Scarecrow Figure, 1939, Artisans Studio, 4", wood composition
EX $100 **NM** $250 **MIP** $550

Scarecrow Figure, 1968, 15", ceramic, painted or unpainted
EX $20 **NM** $50 **MIP** $110

Scarecrow Figure, 1984, Dalen Products, 6' inflatable
EX $12 **NM** $20 **MIP** $60

Scarecrow Figure, 1985, Heart and Heart, Return to Oz, 3"-4" tall, plastic jointed
EX $30 **NM** $45 **MIP** $100

Tik Tok Figure, 1985, Heart and Heart, Return to Oz, 3"-4" tall, plastic jointed
EX $35 **NM** $55 **MIP** $105

Tin Man Figure, 1939, Artisans Studio, 4", wood composition
EX $100 **NM** $250 **MIP** $500

Tin Man Figure, 1968, 15", ceramic, painted or unpainted
EX $20 **NM** $30 **MIP** $80

Tin Man Figure, 1985, Return to Oz, 3"-4" tall, plastic jointed
EX $20 **NM** $35 **MIP** $100

Wizard of Oz Figures, 1967, Multiple Toymakers, 6" tall, bendy, several characters, on card
EX $16 **NM** $30 **MIP** $75

Wizard of Oz Figures, 1988, Presents, 3-3/4": Dorothy, Scarecrow, Tin Man, Cowardly Lion, Wicked Witch, Glinda, each
EX $4 **NM** $6 **MIP** $15

Wizard of Oz Figures, 1989, Multi Toys, 4" poseable figures, set of six
EX $15 **NM** $25 **MIP** $50

Wizard of Oz Figures, 1989, Presents, six figures on musical bases, each
EX $10 **NM** $12 **MIP** $25

Wizard of Oz Figures, 1989, Just Toys, several characters, bendy, each
EX $4 **NM** $6 **MIP** $15

Wizard of Oz Squeak Toy, 1939, Burnstein, 7" tall, hollow rubber, several characters
EX $200 **NM** $300 **MIP** $500

GAME

Game of The Wizard of Oz, 1939, Whitman
EX $300 **NM** $400 **MIP** $700

Return to Oz Game, 1985, Golden Press
EX $8 **NM** $13 **MIP** $30

Wizard of Oz Dart Game, 1939, Dart Board Equipment, board illustrated w/yellow brick road and circular targets of Oz characters, w/three darts
EX $500 **NM** $800 **MIP** $1200

MUSIC BOX

Cowardly Lion Music Box, 1983, Schmid
EX $20 **NM** $35 **MIP** $60

Dorothy Music Box, 1983, Schmid, plays "Over the Rainbow"
EX $25 **NM** $40 **MIP** $65

Scarecrow Music Box, 1983, Schmid
EX $20 **NM** $35 **MIP** $60

Tin Man Music Box, 1983, Schmid
EX $20 **NM** $35 **MIP** $60

TOY

Carpet Sweeper, 1939, Bissell, child-sized
EX $150 **NM** $225 **MIP** $375

Cast 'N Paint Set, 1975, makes six 6" figures
EX $15 **NM** $25 **MIP** $75

Chalkboard, 1975, Roth American, wood frame, steel stand w/chalk, chalk holder and eraser
EX $16 **NM** $27 **MIP** $75

Cowardly Lion Costume, 1975, Ben Cooper, costume and mask
EX $15 **NM** $25 **MIP** $60

Cowardly Lion Costume, 1989, Collegeville, plastic mask and vinyl bodysuit
EX $10 **NM** $15 **MIP** $30

Cowardly Lion Costume, 1989, Collegeville, deluxe
EX $20 **NM** $40 **MIP** $75

Cowardly Lion Mask, 1939, Newark Mask Company, linen, hand painted
EX $60 **NM** $90 **MIP** $160

Cowardly Lion Mask, 1983, Don Post Studios, rubber
EX $35 **NM** $55 **MIP** $90

Cowardly Lion Wind-Up, 1975, Durham Industries, on illustrated card
EX $20 **NM** $30 **MIP** $60

Decoupage Kit, 1975, two wooden plaques, scenes based on film
EX $15 **NM** $25 **MIP** $60

Dorothy Costume, 1975, Ben Cooper, costume and mask
EX $15 **NM** $25 **MIP** $70

Dorothy Costume, 1989, Collegeville, plastic mask and vinyl bodysuit
EX $8 **NM** $15 **MIP** $40

Dorothy Costume, 1989, Collegeville, deluxe, includes red metallic glitter chips for shoes
EX $20 **NM** $40 **MIP** $85

Dorothy Squeak Toy, 1939, Burnstein, 7", hollow rubber
EX $150 **NM** $300 **MIP** $550

Fun Shades, 1989, Multi Toys, children's sunglasses w/character images
EX $5 **NM** $8 **MIP** $20

Glinda Squeak Toy, 1939, Burnstein, 7", hollow rubber
EX $150 **NM** $300 **MIP** $450

Glinda's Magic Wand, 1989, Multi Toys, battery operated wand w/red glitter star on end, lights up, on illustrated card
EX $5 **NM** $10 **MIP** $30

Magic Picture Kit, 1968, Jiffy Pop Popcorn
EX $5 **NM** $25 **MIP** $70

Magic Slate, 1961, Lowe, art based on animated TV show
EX $12 **NM** $30 **MIP** $80

Magic Slate, 1976, Whitman
EX $6 **NM** $18 **MIP** $40

Magic Slate, 1985, Western, Return to Oz
EX $4 **NM** $10 **MIP** $35

Magic Slate, 1989, Western
EX $3 **NM** $6 **MIP** $30

Magic Story Cloth, 1978, Raco, 38" x 44" plastic sheet, eight crayons and sponge
EX $6 **NM** $12 **MIP** $35

Off to See the Wizard Colorforms, 1967, Colorforms
EX $25 **NM** $50 **MIP** $100

Off to See the Wizard Dancing Toys, 1967, Marx, mechanical, dancing Tin Man, the Cowardly Lion and the Scarecrow, Montgomery Ward's Exclusive, each
EX $100 **NM** $150 **MIP** $250

Off to See the Wizard Flasher Rings, 1967, Vari-Vue, gumball machine prizes, silver painted resin, gold painted, dark or light blue plastic, each
EX $10 **NM** $20 **MIP** $30

Off to See the Wizard Hand Puppet, 1968, Mattel, talking, four vinyl heads on finger tips, Toto and Cowardly Lion on thumb pad, ten phrases
EX $30 **NM** $45 **MIP** $100

Paint by Number 'N Frame Set, 1969, Hasbro, 16" x 18", two plastic frames, 18 watercolors, brush and eight pictures to paint
EX $20 **NM** $30 **MIP** $90

Paint by Number Set, 1968, Craft Master, six paints, brush, picture of Tin Man, Cowardly Lion, or the Scarecrow
EX $20 **NM** $35 **MIP** $95

Paint by Number Set, 1973, Hasbro, six oil paint vials and brush
EX $6 **NM** $20 **MIP** $50

Paint by Number Set, 1979, Craft House, two 10" x 14" panels, 15 colors, brush and instructions
EX $10 **NM** $25 **MIP** $50

Paint by Number Set, 1989, Art Award, three different versions
EX $6 **NM** $10 **MIP** $20

Paint with Crayons Set, 1989, Art Award, four pictures based on MGM film characters, in illustrated box
EX $5 **NM** $10 **MIP** $20

Paper Dolls, 1975, The Toy Factory, Dorothy, Tin Man, Scarecrow, Cowardly Lion and Toto, clothes and accessories
EX $10 **NM** $20 **MIP** $60

Playing Cards, 1988, Presents, tin holds two decks
EX $5 **NM** $10 **MIP** $40

Puppet Theatre, 1965, Proctor and Gamble, cardboard theater designed for P and G puppets
EX $100 **NM** $175 **MIP** $300

Puzzle, 1960s, Haret-Gilmar, 10" x 14" puzzle in canister
EX $15 **NM** $30 **MIP** $70

Puzzle, 1976, American Puzzle Company, 200 piece puzzle in canister
EX $15 **NM** $30 **MIP** $50

Puzzle, 1976, Whitman, frame tray
EX $4 **NM** $8 **MIP** $35

Puzzle, 1984, Effanbee, in canister
EX $8 **NM** $15 **MIP** $40

Puzzle, 1985, Crisco Oil, Return to Oz, mail away premium, 200 piece puzzle
EX $30 **NM** $50 **MIP** $80

Puzzle, 1989, Western, frame tray, 100 pieces, Glinda and Dorothy in Munchkinland
EX $5 **NM** $10 **MIP** $35

Puzzle, 1990, Milton Bradley, 1000 piece jigsaw featuring the 1989 Norman James Company poster
EX $6 **NM** $15 **MIP** $30

Puzzles, 1932, Reilly and Lee, set #2, two softcover editions of Tik-Tok and Jack Pumpkinhead and the Sawhorse, plus 25 piece puzzles
EX $250 **NM** $500 **MIP** $850

Puzzles, 1932, Reilly and Lee, #1, two softcover editions of the Scarecrow and the Tin Man, Ozma and the Little Wizard, plus two puzzles, in box
EX $225 **NM** $475 **MIP** $800

Puzzles, 1960s, Jaymar, frame tray
EX $10 **NM** $20 **MIP** $65

Puzzles, 1960s, Jaymar, set of four, 100 pieces each, each
EX $15 **NM** $30 **MIP** $90

Puzzles, 1967, Whitman, set of three: Peter Pan, Alice in Wonderland and The Wizard of Oz, in box
EX $12 **NM** $18 **MIP** $60

Puzzles, 1977, Doug Smith, 17" x 22" each, frame tray
EX $10 **NM** $20 **MIP** $50

Puzzles, 1985, Golden Press, frame tray, Return to Oz characters
EX $3 **NM** $5 **MIP** $15

Return to Oz Hand Puppets, 1985, Welch's Jelly, Scarecrow, Gump, or Tik-Tok, Return to Oz promotion
EX $20 **NM** $40 **MIP** $60

Rubber Stamps, 1989, set of 11 characters in plastic case
EX $10 **NM** $15 **MIP** $30

Rubber Stamps, 1989, Multi Toys, 12 figural stampers
EX $4 **NM** $6 **MIP** $15

Rubber Stamps, 1989, 18 chracter stamps
EX $12 **NM** $20 **MIP** $35

Scarecrow Costume, 1967, Ben Cooper
EX $30 **NM** $40 **MIP** $75

Scarecrow Costume, 1968, Ben Cooper, battery-operated light-up mask
EX $30 **NM** $40 **MIP** $75

Scarecrow Costume, 1989, Collegeville, plastic mask and vinyl bodysuit
EX $6 **NM** $12 **MIP** $30

Scarecrow Costume, 1989, Collegeville, deluxe, includes straw
EX $20 **NM** $35 **MIP** $50

Scarecrow Mask, 1939, Newark Mask, linen, hand painted
EX $100 **NM** $150 **MIP** $250

Scarecrow Mask, 1983, Don Post Studios, rubber
EX $40 **NM** $60 **MIP** $90

Scarecrow Wind-Up, 1975, Durham Industries, on illustrated card
EX $20 **NM** $30 **MIP** $75

Scarecrow-in-the-Box, 1967, Mattel, jack-in-the-box
EX $40 **NM** $60 **MIP** $120

Showboat Play Set, 1962, Remco, pink plastic showboat w/oversized central stage area, four different plays, scenery, players and scripts
EX $75 **NM** $100 **MIP** $175

Stand-Up Rub-Ons, 1968, Hasbro, three full color transfer sheets, character outline sheets of 10 characters
EX $20 **NM** $30 **MIP** $75

Stitch a Story Set, 1973, Hasbro, two framed pictures, thread and embroidery needle
EX $10 **NM** $15 **MIP** $35

Tea Set, 1970s, Ohio Art, 30-piece set, red and yellow plastic
EX $40 **NM** $60 **MIP** $120

Tin Man Costume, 1961, Halco, costume and mask
EX $20 **NM** $35 **MIP** $90

Tin Man Costume, 1968, Ben Cooper
EX $20 **NM** $30 **MIP** $65

Tin Man Costume, 1975, Ben Cooper, costume and mask
EX $15 **NM** $25 **MIP** $55

Tin Man Costume, 1989, Collegeville, plastic mask and vinyl bodysuit
EX $6 **NM** $10 **MIP** $25

Tin Man Costume, 1989, Collegeville, deluxe
EX $20 **NM** $35 **MIP** $70

Tin Man Mask, 1939, Newark Mask, linen, hand painted
EX $100 **NM** $150 **MIP** $250

Tin Man Mask, 1983, Don Post Studios, rubber
EX $35 **NM** $55 **MIP** $85

Tin Man Robot, 1969, Remco, 21-1/2" tall, battery operated, lifts legs and swings arms as he walks
EX $125 **NM** $200 **MIP** $325

Tin Man Wind-Up, 1975, Durham Industries
EX $25 **NM** $50 **MIP** $100

Toy Watch, 1940s, tin, Scarecrow and the Tin Man on either side of non-working dial
EX $75 **NM** $125 **MIP** $175

Vinyl Stick-On Play Set, 1989, Multi Toys, 10 vinyl stickers w/Emerald City background, on header card
EX $4 **NM** $6 **MIP** $10

Water Guns, 1976, Durham, heads of Scarecrow, Tin Man, or Cowardly Lion, water squirts out of nose, each
EX $15 **NM** $30 **MIP** $70

Wicked Witch Mask, 1975, Ben Cooper
EX $6 **NM** $12 **MIP** $25

Wicked Witch Squeak Toy, 1939, Burnstein, 7", hollow rubber
EX $250 **NM** $400 **MIP** $600

Wizard of Oz Costume, 1961, Halco, costume and mask
EX $20 **NM** $35 **MIP** $75

Wizard of Oz Hand Puppets, 1965, Proctor and Gamble, plastic
EX $8 **NM** $20 **MIP** $40

Wizard of Oz Hand Puppets, 1989, Multi Toys, set of six on blister cards, each
EX $6 **NM** $20 **MIP** $50

Wizard of Oz Hand Puppets, 1989, Presents, several characters available, each
EX $8 **NM** $15 **MIP** $35

Wizard of Oz Wind-Ups, 1989, Multi Toys, 50th anniversary editions, several characters, each
EX $4 **NM** $12 **MIP** $25

Wizard Squeak Toy, 1939, Burnstein, 7", hollow rubber
EX $175 **NM** $300 **MIP** $500

WATCH

Oz Time Wristwatch, 1989, Macy's, 50th anniversary premium, round face w/Emerald City, black plastic band
EX $30 **NM** $50 **MIP** $100

Wizard of Oz Pocket Watch, 1980s, Westclock, silver finish case, four characters on dial
EX $20 **NM** $35 **MIP** $85

Wizard of Oz Wristwatch, 1989, EKO, child's LCD, red face in round yellow case, plastic band shows yellow brick road and Emerald City
EX $15 **NM** $25 **MIP** $60

Wizard of Oz Wristwatch, 1989, EKO, quartz, illustrated face showing Emerald City, black plastic band
EX $15 **NM** $25 **MIP** $60

Woody Woodpecker

ACCESSORIES

Alarm Clock, 1959, Columbia Time, Woody's Cafe
EX $100 **NM** $200 **MIP** $400

Lamp, 1971, 20" tall
EX $30 **NM** $60 **MIP** $135

Wrist Watch, 1940s, in box
EX $750 **NM** $1000 **MIP** $1500

BOOK

Woody Woodpecker's Fun-o-Rama Punch-Out Book, 1972
EX $20 **NM** $30 **MIP** $60

TOY

Paper Dolls, 1968, Saalfield, Woody Woodpecker and Andy Panda
EX $30 **NM** $50 **MIP** $90

Playing Cards, 1950s, two decks in a carrying case
EX $40 **NM** $65 **MIP** $100

Woody Woodpecker Hand Puppet, 1963, Mattel, pull-string voice box
EX $50 **NM** $90 **MIP** $135

Woody Woodpecker Nodder, 1950s
EX $75 **NM** $125 **MIP** $200

Yogi Bear

ACCESSORIES

Coat Rack, 1979, Wolverine, 48", red wood, Yogi and Boo Boo cut out in front, growth chart on back
EX $40 **NM** $70 **MIP** $100

Hot Water Bottle, 1966
EX $25 **NM** $50 **MIP** $75

Safety Scissors, 1973, Monogram, on card
EX $4 **NM** $7 **MIP** $15

BANK

Yogi Bear Bank, 1960s, Knickerbocker, 22", figural
EX $40 **NM** $75 **MIP** $150

Yogi Bear Bank, 1980, Dakin, 7", figural
EX $6 **NM** $15 **MIP** $50

BOOK

Snagglepuss Sticker Fun Book, 1963, Whitman
EX $15 **NM** $35 **MIP** $80

Yogi vs. Magilla for President Coloring Book, 1964, Whitman, Model No. 1144
EX $35 **NM** $70 **MIP** $125

DOLL

Boo Boo Doll, 1960s, Knickerbocker, 9-1/2" tall, plush
EX $30 **NM** $60 **MIP** $120

Yogi Bear

Cindy Bear Doll, 1959, Knickerbocker, 16", plush w/vinyl face
EX $40 **NM** $70 **MIP** $140

Yogi Bear Doll, 1959, Knickerbocker, 16" plush w/vinyl face
EX $75 **NM** $150 **MIP** $300

Yogi Bear Doll, 1959, Knickerbocker, 10" tall
EX $125 **NM** $250 **MIP** $400

Yogi Bear Doll, 1960s, Knickerbocker, 19" plush
EX $75 **NM** $150 **MIP** $300

Yogi Bear Doll, 1962, 6", soft vinyl w/movable arms and head
EX $75 **NM** $125 **MIP** $200

Yogi Bear Stuff and Lace Doll, 1959, Knickerbocker, items to make a 13" x 5" doll
EX $30 **NM** $60 **MIP** $125

Yogi Squeeze Doll, 1979, Sanitoy, 12", vinyl
EX $10 **NM** $35 **MIP** $75

FIGURES

Character Figures, 1960, 12" tall, Yogi, Boo Boo, and Ranger Smith, each
EX $30 **NM** $60 **MIP** $90

Snagglepuss Figure, 1970, Dakin
EX $30 **NM** $75 **MIP** $140

Yogi Bear Figure, 1960s, Knickerbocker, 9" tall, plastic
EX $25 **NM** $50 **MIP** $120

Yogi Bear Figure, 1961, Marx, TV-Tinykins
EX $20 **NM** $35 **MIP** $80

Yogi Bear Figure, 1970, Dakin, 7-3/4" tall
EX $20 **NM** $35 **MIP** $80

GAME

Yogi Bear and Pixie and Dixie Game Car, Whitman, 7-1/2" pile on game in car
EX $30 **NM** $60 **MIP** $120

Yogi Score-A-Matic Ball Toss Game, 1960, Transogram
EX $50 **NM** $100 **MIP** $150

TOY

Bubble Pipe, 1963, Transogram, Yogi Bear figural pipe
EX $20 **NM** $35 **MIP** $50

Magic Slate, 1963
EX $20 **NM** $40 **MIP** $75

Snagglepuss Soaky, 1960s, Purex, 9" tall, vinyl/plastic
EX $20 **NM** $40 **MIP** $90

Yogi Bear and Cindy Push Puppet Set, 1960s, Kohner, boxed set of two
EX $60 **NM** $125 **MIP** $250

Yogi Bear Cartoonist Stamp Set, 1961, Lido
EX $30 **NM** $70 **MIP** $100

Yogi Bear Friction Toy, 1960s, Yogi in yellow tie and green hat, illustrated red box
EX $100 **NM** $175 **MIP** $300

Yogi Bear Ge-Tar, 1960s, Mattel
EX $55 **NM** $100 **MIP** $160

Yogi Bear Hand Puppet, Knickerbocker
EX $20 **NM** $35 **MIP** $75

Yogi Bear Paint 'em Pals, 1978, Craft Master, paint-by-number set
EX $15 **NM** $30 **MIP** $75

Yogi Bear Push Puppet, 1960s, Kohner
EX $35 **NM** $45 **MIP** $90

WATCH

Yogi Bear Wristwatch, 1963
EX $80 **NM** $125 **MIP** $250

Yogi Wristwatch, 1967, Bradley, medium base metal case, shows Yogi w/hobo sack on stick, black vinyl band
EX $80 **NM** $120 **MIP** $250

Yosemite Sam

ACCESSORIES

Mini Snow Dome, 1980s, Applause
EX $9 **NM** $16 **MIP** $25

Musical Snow Dome, 1980s, Applause
EX $15 **NM** $30 **MIP** $50

FIGURES

Yosemite Sam Figure, 1968, Dakin, 7" tall
EX $20 **NM** $40 **MIP** $80

Yosemite Sam Figure, 1971, Dakin, on treasure chest
EX $20 **NM** $40 **MIP** $80

Yosemite Sam Figure, 1978, Dakin, Fun Farm
EX $15 **NM** $25 **MIP** $60

TOY

Yosemite Sam Nodder, 1960s, 6-1/4", bobbing head and spring mounted head
EX $125 **NM** $175 **MIP** $350

Fisher-Price

With their colorful paper lithography attached to sturdy wooden toys, Fisher-Price toys conjure nostalgic images of youth among today's collectors. More than seventy-five years after the production of their first toys, Fisher-Price is still the first choice of parents seeking safe, well-made toys for their children.

Founded by Herman Fisher, Irving Price, and Helen Schelle, in 1930 in East Aurora, New York, the company was determined to bring toys with a matchless charm and inherent quality to children. Sixteen toys were introduced in 1931 including Granny Doodle and Doctor Doodle, a pair of charming ducks that initiated the use of animal characters as a staple in the Fisher-Price line.

Most collectors are familiar with the look of vintage Fisher-Price toys with their crisp, colorful paper lithography on wooden toys. Fisher-Price quickly realized the value of licensing, and in 1935 the company issued the Walt Disney Mickey Mouse Band, featuring Mickey and Pluto. That piece alone can command more than $2,000 in MIB condition. Other Disney characters and Popeye also became favorites and are very desirable in today's market. Musical toys, especially items featuring bells or xylophones, became perennial favorites.

The Fisher-Price Play Family Little People appeared as early as 1959 in a yellow wooden Safety School Bus. With bodies made of wood, the Play Family could be removed from their vehicles. Their body styles and compositions have changed through the years, and today, the Little People are about three times the size of the originals and are made of plastic.

Fisher-Price is currently a subsidiary of Mattel. The company continues to produce Little People play sets in a variety of themes, and has expanded its line to include outdoor playground and riding toys, apparel, and books. Its wildly popular Rescue Heroes line is a hit with today's kids—and is surely a future collectible.

The Fisher-Price Collector's Club is an excellent resource for collectors. Their Web site is: www.fpclub.org

Note: Many Fisher-Price toys had several variations, which often means several different values. The date on the toy may only be a copyright date, which may be earlier than the actual date of manufacture. For more information on Fisher-Price toys see *Fisher-Price: Historical, Rarity, and Value Guide 1931-Present 3rd Edition* by Bruce R. Fox and John J. Murray, (Krause Publications, 2002).

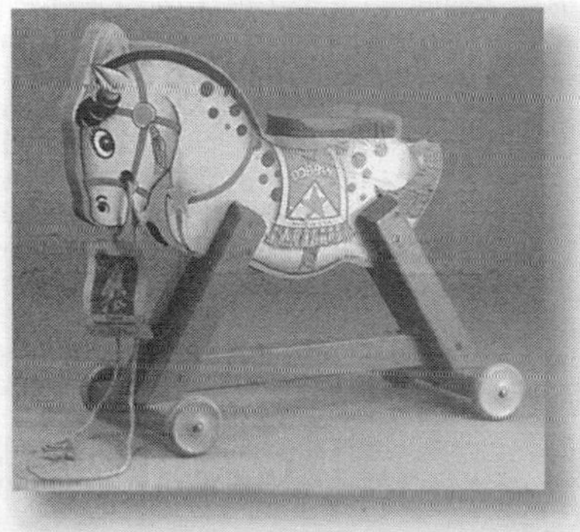

THE ***TOP* 10** **FISHER-PRICE** (In Mint Condition)

1. Raggedy Ann & Andy, 1941 .... $3,875
2. Skipper Sam, 1934 3,800
3. Mickey Mouse Band, 1935 2,800
4. Doc & Dopey Dwarfs, 1938 2,600
5. Dogcart Donald, 1936 2,500
6. Popeye, 1935 2,500
7. Woodsy-Wee Circus, 1931 2,500
8. Streamline Express, 1935 2,400
9. Walt Disney's Easter Parade, 1936 2,400
10. Walt Disney's Carnival, 1936 2,400

Plastic

ADVENTURE PEOPLE SETS

Aero-Marine Search Team, 1979, Model No. 323
EX $25 **NM** $45 **MIP** $80

Alpha Probe, 1980, Model No. 325
EX $40 **NM** $50 **MIP** $135

Alpha Star, 1983, Model No. 326
EX $30 **NM** $50 **MIP** $95

Construction Workers, 1976, Model No. 352
EX $10 **NM** $20 **MIP** $30

Cycle Racing Team, 1977, Model No. 356
EX $10 **NM** $20 **MIP** $30

Daredevil Skydiver, 1976, Model No. 354
EX $7 **NM** $14 **MIP** $20

Daredevil Sport Van, 1978, Model No. 318
EX $40 **NM** $75 **MIP** $100

Deep Sea Diver, 1980, Model No. 358
EX $10 **NM** $20 **MIP** $30

Dune Buster, 1979, Model No. 322
EX $25 **NM** $50 **MIP** $75

Farm Fun, green tractor w/yellow wheels, farmer, hay, dog, chicken, yellow trailer, Model No. 2448
EX n/a **NM** $10 **MIP** $20

Firestar 1, 1980, Model No. 357
EX $10 **NM** $20 **MIP** $30

Motocross Team, 1983, Model No. 335
EX $15 **NM** $30 **MIP** $45

Mountain Climbers, 1976, Model No. 351
EX $15 **NM** $30 **MIP** $45

Northwoods Trailblazer, 1977, Model No. 312
EX $25 **NM** $65 **MIP** $110

Rescue Copter, 1975, Model No. 305
EX $20 **NM** $45 **MIP** $70

Rescue Team, 1976, Model No. 350
EX $10 **NM** $20 **MIP** $30

Rescue Truck, 1975, Model No. 303
EX $20 **NM** $45 **MIP** $70

Safari, 1975, Model No. 304
EX $60 **NM** $85 **MIP** $115

Scuba Divers, 1976, Model No. 353
EX $10 **NM** $20 **MIP** $30

Sea Explorer, 1976, Model No. 310
EX $20 **NM** $40 **MIP** $60

Sea Shark, 1981, Model No. 334
EX $20 **NM** $45 **MIP** $70

Sport Plane, 1975, Model No. 306
EX $20 **NM** $45 **MIP** $70

Super Speed Racer, 1976, Model No. 308
EX $15 **NM** $30 **MIP** $50

T.V. Action Team, 1977, Model No. 309
EX $60 **NM** $75 **MIP** $140

Wheelie Dragster, 1981, with driver, Model No. 333
EX $15 **NM** $20 **MIP** $35

White Water Kayak, 1977, Model No. 355
EX $10 **NM** $20 **MIP** $30

Wilderness Patrol, 1976, Model No. 307
EX $50 **NM** $75 **MIP** $105

HUSKY PLAY SETS

Dozer Loader, 1980, Model No. 329
EX $15 **NM** $30 **MIP** $50

Farm Set, 1981, Model No. 331
EX $15 **NM** $30 **MIP** $55

Fire Pumper, 1983, Model No. 336
EX $20 **NM** $40 **MIP** $65

Firefighters, 1979, Model No. 321
EX $15 **NM** $30 **MIP** $50

Highway Dump Truck, 1980, Model No. 328
EX $15 **NM** $30 **MIP** $50

Hook & Ladder, 1979, Model No. 319
EX $15 **NM** $30 **MIP** $50

Load Master Dump, 1984, Model No. 327
EX $15 **NM** $30 **MIP** $45

Police Patrol Squad, 1981, Model No. 332
EX $20 **NM** $40 **MIP** $65

Power & Light Service Rig, 1983, Model No. 339
EX $20 **NM** $40 **MIP** $65

Power Tow Truck, 1982, Model No. 338
EX $20 **NM** $40 **MIP** $65

Race Car Rig, 1979, Model No. 320
EX $15 **NM** $30 **MIP** $50

Rescue Rig, 1981, Model No. 337
EX $20 **NM** $40 **MIP** $65

Rodeo Rig, 1980, with figure and horses, Model No. 330
EX $15 **NM** $30 **MIP** $50

LITTLE PEOPLE

3-Car Circus Train, 1979, three-car train, engine w/silver imprinted headlight, green or blue cage car w/lion litho, red caboose, light blue engineer, short ringmaster, and a red clown w/pointed yellow hat, Model No. 991
EX $25 **NM** $40 **MIP** $65

4-Car Circus Train, 1973, four-car train, engine w/paper headlight litho, blue or green car w/giraffe litho, blue or green flat car w/lion litho, red caboose, elephant, monkey, lion, giraffe, tan bear, short, light blue engineer, red clown w/pointed yellow hat, and a short ringmaster, Model No. 991
EX $25 **NM** $40 **MIP** $60

A-Frame, 1974, A-frame house w/removable door and sidewalk, three-rung white ladder, two sets of yellow bunk beds, two yellow lounge chairs, grill, two white picnic benches, white table w/steak litho, two yellow captain chairs, four-seat jeep, dad, mom, boy, girl and Lucky the dog, Model No. 990
EX $35 **NM** $50 **MIP** $80

Airport, 1972, large fold out airport base, white/turquoise jet, orange/yellow helicopter, four-car tram front car, two luggage cars, fuel car, two white/green two seat cars w/luggage rack, two green hat boxes, two yellow pieces of luggage, cardboard hanger parts box, dad, mom, boy, girl, stewardess, African-American pilot w/turquoise base, Model No. 996
EX $35 **NM** $65 **MIP** $110

Airport, 1986, airport building, blue and yellow copter, large blue and yellow plane, four captain chairs, two orange coffee tables, green and white two-seat car w/luggage rack, one brown and one blue suitcase, three-car tram, tan bald man, short light blue blond stewardess, short pilot, mom, boy and girl, Model No. 2502
EX $25 **NM** $50 **MIP** $85

Airport Crew, 1983, green pilot, black pilot w/blue body, and a tall light blue stewardess, Model No. 678
EX $4 **NM** $7 **MIP** $15

Amusement Park, 1963, large vinyl mat, tunnel/bridge, four-chair swing ride, single-seat swing ride, merry-go-round, four-piece train, two small single-seat cars (no holes for gas), two small single-seat boats, two small boats, straight-sided Little People including two blue boys, two mauve girls, two green boys and a black dog w/yellow or white ears, Model No. 932
EX $175 **NM** $250 **MIP** $500

Bath and Utility Sets, 1971, toilet, sink, tub, captains chair, sewing machine, washer, dryer, all wooded family consisting of a dad, mom, boy and a girl; many color variations exist, Model No. 725
EX $12 **NM** $35 **MIP** $60

Beauty Salon, 1990, small beauty salon connects w/No. 2454 and No. 2455; set comes w/one pink and white car w/a luggage rack and a girl, Model No. 2453
EX $7 **NM** $12 **MIP** $25

Boat Rig, 1981, blue and white truck and trailer w/snap on gray boat holder, blue and white speedboat, one man w/white body and blue ca and one dark blue worker, Model No. 345
EX $5 **NM** $12 **MIP** $25

Brown Roof House, 1980, fold-open house w/a garage, green and white car, one double bed, two twin beds, four captain chairs, one round table, two lounge chairs, one coffee table, dad, mom, boy, girl, and Lucky the dog, Model No. 952
EX $25 **NM** $35 **MIP** $45

Car and Camper, 1980, 15-pieces, white and red four-seat SUV, white and red pop-up camper w/yellow canvas tent inside, yellow clam carrier w/litho on top, green and yellow boat that sits on top of jeep, two green lounge chairs, grill, green table w/steak litho, motorcycle, dad, mom, boy and girl, Model No. 992
EX $25 **NM** $45 **MIP** $75

Castle, 1974, 21-pieces, castle w/attached flag, pink dragon, oone brown and one black horse, white or yellow horse armor, white or yellow scalloped horse harness, castle coach, two short red or yellow thrones, two tall red or yellow thrones, two red or yellow twin beds w/crown headboard, one red or yellow double bed w/crwon headboard, one red or yellow round table w/medievil-style litho, plastic knight, woodsman, king, queen, prince, princess and a cardboard parts box; reissued in 1987 w/no flag and all plastic people, Model No. 993
EX $60 **NM** $125 **MIP** $200

FISHER-PRICE

Change-a-Tune Carousel, 1981, three records labeled A-B-C, two boys and a girl, Model No. 170
EX $25 **NM** $50 **MIP** $70

Choo-Choo Train, 1963, small wood and plastic train engine w/three, three straight-sided Little People and a Lucky the dog, Model No. 719
EX $25 **NM** $35 **MIP** $50

Circus Clowns, 1983, three different clowns, on card, Model No. 675
EX $4 **NM** $7 **MIP** $15

Crazy Clown Brigade, 1983, large clown car, two white crooked hoses, two white crooked ladders, white hose reel, and small green bathtub w/wheels, clown feet, tall blue clown w/white or yellow tie, and a short black clown w/a red fireman hat, Model No. 657
EX $35 **NM** $50 **MIP** $70

Cruise Boat, 1988, S.S. Tadpole, small ship, one-piece chair w/fishing pole, one yellow life preserver, short blue sea captain w/white beard, blond boy w/green base boy, Model No. 2524
EX $15 **NM** $25 **MIP** $40

Decorator Set, 1970, double bed, two twin beds, T.V., checkerboard litho round table, two stuffed chairs, coffee table, all wooden family consisting of a dad, mom, boy and a girl; many color variations exist, Model No. 728
EX $13 **NM** $35 **MIP** $60

Drive In Movie, 1990, small drive in movie building w/movie screen connects w/No. 2453 and No. 2455; set comes w/one white and yellow car w/a luggage rack and a boy, Model No. 2454
EX $7 **NM** $12 **MIP** $25

Dump Truckers, 1965, dumping station w/three slots for trucks, three trucks of different shape and color, three balls in wood or plastic, three light or dark blue straight-sided boys (one smiling, one frowning, and one w/freckles), Model No. 979
EX $45 **NM** $70 **MIP** $120

Express Train, 1987, three-car train, flat car, caboose, solid yellow one-seat car w/luggage rack, one yellow and one blue suitcase, dad, mom, light blue engineer and Lucky the dog, Model No. 2581
EX $10 **NM** $17 **MIP** $35

Farm, 1986, barn base w/mooing door, silo, four pieces of fence, tractor, cart, white harness, white trough, red chicken, white chicken, horse, cow, pig, jointed dog, sheep, dad w/cowboy hat, mom, boy w/cowboy hat and a girl, Model No. 2501
EX $20 **NM** $50 **MIP** $80

Farm family on card, 1983, dark red woman w/blond hair, tall green dad w/white hat and yellow scarf, and a blue girl w/blond hair, Model No. 677
EX $4 **NM** $7 **MIP** $15

Ferris Wheel, 1966, ferris wheel base winds up plays music, three Little People and Lucky the dog; first year versions come w/straight-sided Little People, Model No. 969
EX $35 **NM** $75 **MIP** $110

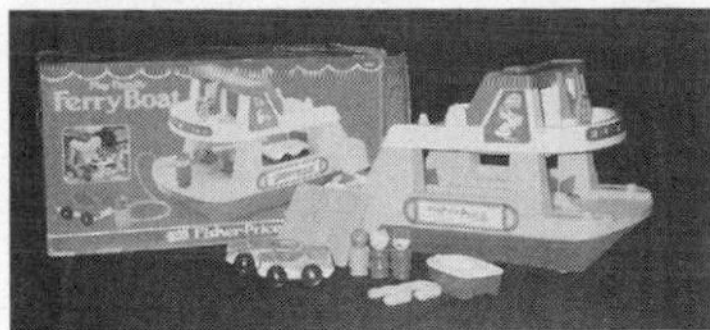

(Sean and Debbie Craig)

Ferry Boat, 1979, w/pull string and wheels, white and blue speed boat, two yellow life preservers, two two-seat cars, orange and black man w/o mustache, blue mom w/blond hair, tall blue captain, Model No. 932
EX $25 **NM** $45 **MIP** $70

Fire Engine, 1969, wooden truck and a fireman, Model No. 720
EX $12 **NM** $24 **MIP** $40

Fire Pumper, 1983, long red fire engine w/two yellow braces, w/two firemen, Model No. 336
EX $15 **NM** $35 **MIP** $65

Fire Station, 1980, fire house building, gray fire training tower, two yellow connecting ladders, two barricades, ambulance, fire truck w/ladder, fire chief car, two yellow truck braces, two black connecting fire hoses, two black rubber hoses, two yellow truck braces, three fireman and one dalmatian dog, Model No. 928
EX $45 **NM** $60 **MIP** $80

Fire Truck, 1989, large red and white truck w/cherry picker and attached yellow hose, red fire hydrant, two firemen and one dalmatian, Model No. 2361
EX $7 **NM** $12 **MIP** $25

Floating Marina, 1987, floating marina building w/two boats slips, orange seaplane, one yellow life preserver, detachable clear lighthouse dome, orange boat, red and white boat w/steering wheel, short blue captain w/white beard, boy and girl, Model No. 2582
EX $10 **NM** $17 **MIP** $35

Fun Jet, 1970, plane w/red wings and tail, one green and one yellow suitcase, w/dad, mom, boy and a girl, Model No. 183
EX $25 **NM** $45 **MIP** $75

Garage, 1970, two-story building, elevator and car ramps, car grease rack, four single-seat cars in red, blue, green, yellow, and three little boys and one little girl, Model No. 930
EX $25 **NM** $60 **MIP** $90

Garage, 1986, two-story building, elevator and car ramps, fire hydrant, pay phone, gas pump, three single-seat cars, and three little boys and one little girl, Model No. 2504
EX $25 **NM** $50 **MIP** $80

Garage Squad, 1983, three workers, Model No. 679
EX $4 **NM** $7 **MIP** $15

Gas Station, 1990, small gas station building connects w/No. 2453 and No. 2454; set comes w/one red and white car w/a luggage rack and a boy, Model No. 2455
EX $7 **NM** $12 **MIP** $25

Goldilocks and the Three Bears, 1967, playhouse w/yellow key attached, w/mama bear, papa bear, baby bear, and blue girl w/blond braids, Model No. 151
EX $35 **NM** $75 **MIP** $125

Happy Hoppers, 1969, push toy playset w/three Little People that pop up and down as toy is pushed; value may fluctuate depending on version of Little People, Model No. 121
EX $15 **NM** $25 **MIP** $45

Helicopter Rig, 1981, green and white truck and trailer w/gray snap-on compass, gold one-seat helicopter, one tall blue pilot and one worker w/tan base, Model No. 344
EX $5 **NM** $12 **MIP** $25

Hospital, Children's, 1976, building w/fold down door and elevator and white ambulance, turquoise plastic pieces include stretcher, x-ray, scale, two chairs, two beds, large sink, baby cradle; white plastic pieces include wheelchair, operating table, privacy screen; white baby without bib, white nurse w/white mask, doctor, African-American doctor, dad, mom and girl, Model No. 931
EX $65 **NM** $85 **MIP** $110

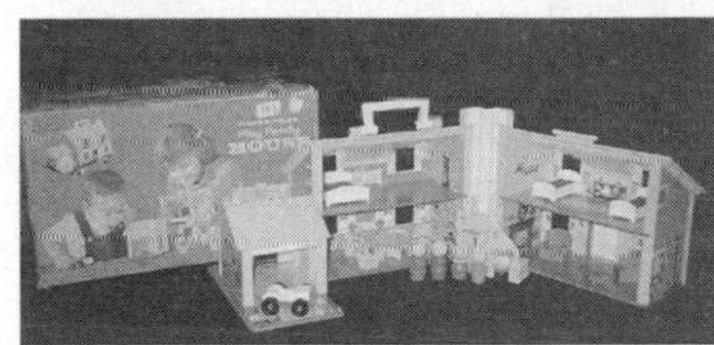
(Sean and Debbie Craig)

House, 1969, fold-open house w/yellow roof and attached garage, car w/hook, one double bed, two twin beds, four captain chairs, one round table, two lounge chairs, one coffee table, yellow stairs w/closet and litho, blue cardboard moving van parts box, dad, mom, boy, girl and Lucky the dog; complete w/moving van add $100-200 to total value, Model No. 952
EX $25 **NM** $55 **MIP** $90

Houseboat, 1972, blue base boat w/wheels and fold open lid, two yellow lounge chairs, two yellow life preservers, two red captain chairs, red lobster litho table, yellow grill, white/blue speedboat, white-bodied dad w/blue hat, mom, boy, girl and Lucky the dog, Model No. 985
EX $25 **NM** $40 **MIP** $75

Indy Race Rig, 1983, yellow and white truck w/trailer, red Indy-type racecar, w/dad engineer and a driver w/a black body and helmet, Model No. 347
EX $5 **NM** $12 **MIP** $25

Jetliner, 1981, green/white yellow plane, one brown and one blue suitcase, w/dad, mom, boy, and a girl, Model No. 182
EX $15 **NM** $30 **MIP** $50

Jetliner, 1986, large yellow and blue plane, one blue and one brown suitcase, dad, mom, boy and girl, Model No. 2360
EX $15 **NM** $30 **MIP** $55

Jetport, 1981, 22-pieces, airport building, blue and yellow copter, large blue and yellow plane, four captain chairs, two orange coffee tables, green and white two-seat car w/luggage rack, one brown and one blue suitcase, three-car tram, tan bald man, light blue short stewardess w/blond hair, short pilot, mom, boy and girl, Model No. 933
EX $25 **NM** $35 **MIP** $50

Kitchen Set, 1970, 12-pieces, stove, sink, fridge, litho table, four captain chairs, all wooden family consisting of a dad, mom, boy and a girl; many color variations exist, Model No. 729
EX $12 **NM** $35 **MIP** $50

Lacing Shoe, 1970, shoe w/mostly brown litho and wheels, special lace, mom wearing glasses w/regular shaped body, two yellow triangle-shaped girls w/different faces, two square red boys w/different faces, and a dog w/marshmallow-shaped base, Model No. 146
EX $35 **NM** $45 **MIP** $80

Lift & Load Depot, 1977, building, green and yellow dump truck, fork lift, scoop loader, yellow sling, four brown pallets, two brown crates, two gray crates, two black barrels, orange scoop bucket attached to building, and one African-American and two white workers w/light blue bodies and orange hardhats, Model No. 942
EX $20 **NM** $40 **MIP** $60

Lift & Load Lumber Yard, 1979, small lumber yard building w/yellow ramp, green and yellow lift truck, truck and trailer, six pieces of wood lumber (two square, two long rectangular, two short rectangular), four brown pallets, one white and one African-American worker w/light blue bodies and orange hardhats, Model No. 944
EX $15 **NM** $30 **MIP** $45

Lift & Load Railroad, 1978, train depot building w/track section, seven-piece track (makes a oval), two-piece train (engine winds up), orange sling, two gray crates, two black barrels, four brown pallets, orange ramp, green/yellow lift truck, one white and one Afrrican-American worker w/light blue body and orange hardhats, tall light blue train engineer w/mustache, Model No. 943
EX $35 **NM** $50 **MIP** $80

Little Mart, 1987, small shopping mart building, red tow truck w/orange hook, orange shopping cart, brown bag of groceries, two-seat car w/solid greenback, yellow pay phone, dad, mom, policewoman and Lucky the dog, Model No. 2580
EX $10 **NM** $25 **MIP** $50

Little People Construction Set, 1985, orange and yellow dump truck, scoop loader, bulldozer, two black barrels, one gold-cone barricade, one brown crate, two yellow w/black stripes road barricades, two white and one African-American construction workers, Model No. 2352
EX $7 **NM** $12 **MIP** $25

Little Riders, 1976, plane, rocking horse, tricycle, wagon, train, w/boy and girl, Model No. 656
EX $10 **NM** $25 **MIP** $50

Little Trucks, 1981, orange and yellow scoop loader, bulldozer, dump truck, lift truck, one brown pallet, one gray crate, w/two light blue construction workers and two green construction workers, Model No. 397
EX $12 **NM** $17 **MIP** $35

Main Street, 1986, large building of main street w/a pull up background, two blue ramps, yellow two-seat taxi, blue mailbox, parking meter, pay phone, red fire hydrant, red stop sign, yellow turning stop light, yellow-and-black striped road diverter, mail truck, seven plastic letters, small one-seat fire truck, shopkeeper, fireman, mom, mailman, and a little girl, Model No. 2500
EX $17 **NM** $45 **MIP** $80

McDonald's, 1990, McDonald's restaurant w/pull-out playground, one blue and white two-seat car, one brown trash can, one McDonald's sign, french fry cart, Ronald McDonald, Hamburglar, mom, yellow boy w/black molded hair and girl, Model No. 2552
EX $27 **NM** $85 **MIP** $150

Merry-Go-Round, 1972, merry-go-round playset base, w/mom, two boys and a girl, Model No. 111
EX $35 **NM** $60 **MIP** $110

Mini Boat Set, 1969, car w/hook, boat w/two holes in bottom, V-shaped trailer, straight yellow body boy w/cap, and a straight-sided Lucky, Model No. 685
EX $50 **NM** $80 **MIP** $120

Mini Camper Set, 1969, car and trailer same as mini boat, wood camper marked "Fisher Price," straight yellow body boy w/cap, and a straight-sided Lucky the dog, Model No. 686
EX $50 **NM** $75 **MIP** $120

Mini Snowmobile, 1971, snowmobile w/detachable sled, turquoise boy red cap, turquoise girl w/red hair and Lucky the dog, Model No. 705
EX $20 **NM** $40 **MIP** $60

Mini Van, 1969, w/five Little People-dad, mom, girl, boy, and a dog, Model No. 141
EX $5 **NM** $10 **MIP** $25

More Sesame Street Characters, 1977, Boxed set showing Sesame Street scenes comes w/Roosevelt Franklin, Grover, Sherlock Hemlock, Prairie Dawn, The Count, Harry Monster, and Snuffleupagus, Model No. 940
EX $35 **NM** $80 **MIP** $135

Musical Lacing Shoe, 1964, wind-up musical shoe w/wheels and special lace, and three straight-sided people w/red bases, all w/different facial imprints (girl, two different boys), Model No. 991
EX $45 **NM** $65 **MIP** $110

Neighborhood, 1989, pull apart two-piece building connected by tree, attached basketball hoop w/ball, yellow five-rung ladder, two twin beds w/teddy bear imprint, one bed w/quilt imprint, one lounge chair, modular kitchen insert, modular bathroom insert, two-seat car, turquoise pool, one round table, two captain chairs, dad, mom, boy, girl and Lucky the dog, Model No. 2551
EX $17 **NM** $25 **MIP** $40

New School, 1988, school house building w/pull-out playground, red stop sign, small school bus, yellow skateboard, white flag, chalk, orange and blue jump rope, white drum, red-bodied woman teacher w/glasses, boy, African-American girl, Asian-American boy, and orange-bodied girl w/glasses, Model No. 2550
EX $17 **NM** $35 **MIP** $70

(John Murray, Photo by Ross MacKearnin)

Nifty Station Wagon, 1960, wooden car w/wood top and two plastic braces on top, w/four large straight wooden figures, blue dad, green mom, yellow cone-shaped boy, and a black dog w/white ears and a ribbed body. The people from this set are similar in design to the people from the No. 990-984 Safety School Bus, Model No. 234
EX $175 **NM** $325 **MIP** $675

(Sean and Debbie Craig)

Nursery School, 1978, flat base w/dividing rooms and plastic edges, cardboard roof/play area, gold bus w/apple, double sink, stove, toilet, bathroom sink, slide, merry-go-round, blue easel, teeter totter, four captain chairs, round arts-and-craft table, dad, mom, African-American boy and two girls, Model No. 929
EX $20 **NM** $45 **MIP** $70

Nursery Sets, 1972, changing table, highchair, cradle, rocking horse, playpen, stroller, dad, mom, girl and a baby; many color variations exist, Model No. 761
EX $8 **NM** $13 **MIP** $20

Off-Shore Cargo Base, 1979, one large rectangular and square black floats, crane, tan cargo hold, helicopter landing pad, cargo hold cover, tug boat, helicopter, white and blue barge, two gold feed bags, two sections of pipe, two crates, mesh cargo net, two black tow chains, red diver, tall blue captain, and

one white and one African-American worker w/light green bodies and yellow hardhats, Model No. 945
EX $20 **NM** $40 **MIP** $60

Pampers Promotional, 1988 only, yellow mini van w/family, green body boy and red cap exclusive to the set
EX $5 **NM** $10 **MIP** $25

Patio Set, 1970, flowered umbrella table, pool w/imprint, four captain chairs, BBQ grill, all wooden family consisting of a dad, mom, boy and a girl; many color variations exist, Model No. 726
EX $13 **NM** $35 **MIP** $55

Play Family Animal Circus, 1974, two yellow ladders, red hoop, yellow trapeze, blue tub (base w/clown on cardboard litho), yellow elephant stand, w/bear, monkey, lion, blue elephant, giraffe, short ringmaster and red clown, Model No. 135
EX $17 **NM** $35 **MIP** $50

Play Family Camper, 1972, green flatbed truck, white removable camper, green boat w/litho inside, boat sits on top of camper, yellow/red umbrella table, four red captain chairs, grill, yellow motorcycle, red table w/hot dog litho, toilet, sink, red ladder, dad, mom, boy, girl and Lucky the dog, Model No. 994
EX $25 **NM** $45 **MIP** $85

(KP Photo, Brent Frankenhoff collection)

Play Family Farm, 1968, barn base w/mooing door, silo, four pieces of fence, tractor, cart, white harness, white trough, red chicken, white chicken, horse, cow, pig, jointed dog, sheep, dad w/cowboy hat, mom, boy w/cowboy hat, and a girl; many variations exist, Model No. 915
EX $25 **NM** $40 **MIP** $75

Play Family Lacing Shoe, 1965, shoe w/mostly black litho and blue base, special lace, w/large all-wood mom wearing glasses, two yellow triangle-shaped girls w/different faces, two square red boys w/different faces, and a dog w/marshmallow-shaped base, Model No. 136
EX $35 **NM** $75 **MIP** $120

Play Family Tow Truck and Car, 1969, tow truck, car w/hook, and a straight body yellow boy w/cap, Model No. 718
EX $20 **NM** $35 **MIP** $55

Playground, 1986, green base playground w/spring rides and a slide, orange and yellow swing, orange and yellow merry-go-round, blue climbing cube, boy and girl, Model No. 2525
EX $10 **NM** $20 **MIP** $30

Rooms—Sears Exclusive, 1971, flat base w/divided rooms, yellow fridge, yellow double sink, yellow stove w/litho, green table w/formal setting, four green captain chairs, white tub, scale, toilet, sink, red or blue couch, two red or blue twin beds, red or blue T.V. w/litho puppet, red or blue coffeetable, red and blue stuffed chair, turquoise umbrella table, two yellow captain chairs, turquoise or yellow grill, white cotton drawstring bag, all wooden family consisting of a green bald man, blue mom w/blond hair, orange bald boy, red girl w/blond hair and Lucky the dog, Model No. 909
EX $180 **NM** $250 **MIP** $350

Safety School Bus, 1959, First version-yellow school bus w/stop sign on the drivers side and a flat nose, wooden top piece reads "Fisher Price," six removable people w/litho on wooden bodies; Second version-four removable people and two that are fixed in the back, as the bus moves the fixed people bounce up and down, Model No. 983
EX $150 **NM** $400 **MIP** $675

Safety School Bus, 1961, yellow school bus w/stop sign on the drivers side and a flat nose, five tall wooden people, the people from this bus are similar in design to the people from the No. 990 Safety School Bus and the No. 234 Nifty Station wagon, Model No. 984
EX $150 **NM** $2755 **MIP** $475

Safety School Bus, 1962, yellow school bus w/stop sign on the drivers side and a flat nose, five tall wooden people; the people from this bus and similar in design to the people from the No. 984 Safety School Bus and the No. 234 Nifty Station wagon, Model No. 990
EX $75 **NM** $560 **MIP** $300

School, 1971, schoolhouse building w/bell and pull down sidewall w/chalkboard, four green or yellow student desks, one green or yellow teachers desk w/chair, green and yellow swing, merry-go-round, green or yellow slide, numbers tray, letter tray w/letters A-Z and extra P, S, T, N, R, I, and E letters, chalk box, eraser, blue teacher w/blond hair, two boys and two girls, Model No. 923
EX $25 **NM** $50 **MIP** $90

School Bus, 1965, five Little People kids, and one dog. There have been many variations of the School bus over the years years; all brown dog from first issue is worth $30-50 in Excellent condition, Model No. 192
EX $55 **NM** $125 **MIP** $175

Sesame Street Characters, 1976, boxed set showing Sesame Street scenes comes w/Ernie, Bert, Cookie Monster, Susan, Gordon, Mr. Hooper, Big Bird and Oscar in his can, Model No. 939
EX $35 **NM** $80 **MIP** $135

Sesame Street Clubhouse, 1977, clubhouse w/bird nest and shaker board and attached tire swing, yellow slide, three barrels (red, blue, yellow), yellow cable drum, black and red jump rope, two-seat wagon, Big Bird, Roosevelt Franklin, Grover, The Count, Bert, and Ernie, Model No. 937
EX $45 **NM** $110 **MIP** $195

Sesame Street House, 1975, brownstone fold-out building, Sesame Street lamppost, mailbox w/litho, garbage truck, five-rung white ladder, newsstand, fire hydrant on gray triangle, soda fountain stand, T.V. showing Grover, sofa, table w/pork chop litho, two captain chairs, two twin beds marked "B" and "E," chalk box, eraser, Big Bird's nest, coffeetable, Bert, Ernie, Mr. Hooper, Big Bird, Cookie Monster, Susan, Gordon, and Oscar in his can, Model No. 938
EX $60 **NM** $125 **MIP** $195

Snorkey Fire Engine, 1960, fire truck w/white base and blue wheels and yellow boom, w/four firemen w/green bases, red arms and hats, and a black dog exclusive to this set, Model No. 168
EX $150 **NM** $225 **MIP** $425

Snorkey Fire Engine, 1961, fire truck w/red base, black wheels and a yellow boom, w/four firemen w/white bases, red arms and hats, Model No. 169
EX $150 **NM** $225 **MIP** $400

Swimming Pool, 1986, swimming pool base, black stand-up grill, diving board, slide, lifeguard stand w/white life preserver, two lounge chairs (one orange and one yellow), umbrella table w/base shaped to fit in hole, boy, and a girl, Model No. 2526
EX $10 **NM** $20 **MIP** $30

Village, 1973, large fold out village base, connecting bridge and traffic light, six letters, one yellow single bed, small fire engine, red and blue police car, mail truck, four yellow captain chairs, umbrella table, green and white one-seat car w/luggage rack, white and green back-to-back two-seat car, phone booth, yellow grill, dentist chair, barber chair, yellow couch and coffeetable, African-American doctor, white doctor, fireman, mailman w/gray base, policewoman, mom, boy, girl and Lucky the dog, Model No. 997
EX $35 **NM** $55 **MIP** $80

Western Town, 1982, building w/shaker board, tan or green buckboard, tan or green stagecoach w/removable red top, one brown and one black horse, two brown harnesses, brown saddle, gray crate, green hatbox luggage, four pieces fence, blue sheriff w/star badge on chest, red sod-buster man w/black hat and mustache, Native American w/chest markings on front, yellow lady w/green hat, Model No. 934
EX $25 **NM** $55 **MIP** $90

Westerners, 1983, tall ringmaster, Native American w/headdress, and a green cowboy w/ten-gallon hat, on card, Model No. 676
EX $4 **NM** $7 **MIP** $15

Zoo, 1984, zoo base, tree, orange and yellow parrots, vulture, black and yellow parrots, vulture, black and

orange monkeys, orange cabaña, black seal, blue elephant, yellow lion cub, hippo, gorilla, mountain goat, four food trays, two green benches, one green table, three car tram, dad, mom, girl, boy, and a zookeeper w/safari-style hat, Model No. 916
EX $35 **NM** $70 **MIP** $110

Wooden

Allie Gator, 1960, w/ plastic flippers on wooden wheels, Model No. 653
EX $45 **NM** $140 **MIP** $175

Amusement Park, 1963, 20-pieces, chair ride, musical merry-go-round, play swing, choo-choo, play people and more, Model No. 932
EX $125 **NM** $310 **MIP** $585

Baby Chick Tandem Cart, 1953, Easter only, Model No. 50
EX $50 **NM** $75 **MIP** $110

Barky Buddy, 1934, blue and yellow military uniform, red hat, red wheels, Model No. 150
EX $450 **NM** $1100 **MIP** $2000

Barky Dog, 1958, black and white w/ red wheels, Model No. 462
EX $110 **NM** $145 **MIP** $220

Barky Puppy, 1931, blue wheels, oilcloth ears, pipecleaner and wooden ball tail, Model No. 103
EX $550 **NM** $1000 **MIP** $2000

Big Bill Pelican, 1961, opening bill, cardboard fish the first three years of release (add $25 if present), light blue feet, Model No. 794
EX $95 **NM** $135 **MIP** $195

Big Performing Circus, 1932, included nine figures, original retail price was $2.75, Model No. 250
EX $450 **NM** $900 **MIP** $1800

Blackie Drummer, 1939, bear in parade uniform strikes bass drum w/ right arm and cymbal w/ left arm, Model No. 785
EX $550 **NM** $800 **MIP** $1300

Bonny Bunny Wagon, 1959, Easter release, bunny pulling wagon, light blue wheels, Model No. 318
EX $30 **NM** $55 **MIP** $90

(John Murray, Photo by Ross MacKearnin)

Boom Boom Popeye, 1937, Popeye and Sweatpea, two mallets hit litho drum, unpainted wheels, Model No. 491
EX $600 **NM** $1100 **MIP** $1600

Bossy Bell, 1959, bell, light blue wheels, yellow tail and horns, Model No. 656
EX $50 **NM** $80 **MIP** $110

Bouncing Bunny Wheelbarrow, 1939, bell on head, Model No. 727
EX $450 **NM** $750 **MIP** $1300

Bouncy Racer, 1960, driver w/ helmet bounces and arms move as pulled, large red plastic wheels, Model No. 8
EX $40 **NM** $75 **MIP** $125

Bruno Bak-Up, 1932, pushes wheelbarrow, Model No. 375
EX $500 **NM** $1000 **MIP** $1500

(John Murray. Photo by Russ MacKearnin)

Bucky Burro, 1955, yellow burro that bucks, spring tail, driver w/ sombrero, Model No. 166
EX $225 **NM** $375 **MIP** $495

Buddy Bronc, 1938, cowboy bounces on horse, Model No. 430
EX $275 **NM** $450 **MIP** $975

Buddy Bullfrog, 1959, offered w/ checkered pants in last year, croaking noise, jumping action, top hat, Model No. 728
EX $85 **NM** $120 **MIP** $185

Bunny Basket Cart, 1957, woven basket, Model No. 301
EX $30 **NM** $45 **MIP** $80

Bunny Basket Cart, 1960, plastic basket, Model No. 303
EX $30 **NM** $55 **MIP** $85

Bunny Bell Cart, 1941, two mallets strike bell, yellow wheels, cart in front of bunny, Model No. 520
EX $125 **NM** $250 **MIP** $550

Bunny Bell Cart, 1954, two mallets strike bell, light blue wheels, cart behind bunny, Model No. 604
EX $45 **NM** $80 **MIP** $160

Bunny Cart, 1948, white bunny pulls cylindrical cart w/ metal rim, Model No. 5
EX $75 **NM** $100 **MIP** $165

Bunny Drummer, 1942, two mallets hit painted wood disk or metal bell, yellow wagon in front of bunny, red wheels, Model No. 512
EX $150 **NM** $225 **MIP** $550

Bunny Drummer, 1946, two mallets hit metal bell, yellow cart in front of bunny, red wheels, Model No. 505
EX $150 **NM** $225 **MIP** $550

Bunny Egg Cart, 1949, new for 1949, forerunner of the No. 406 Bunny Cart, Model No. 404
EX $40 **NM** $95 **MIP** $155

Bunny Egg Cart, 1950, bunny pulling cart-sides are colorful eggs, dark blue/purple wheels, Model No. 28
EX $100 **NM** $160 **MIP** $225

Bunny Engine, 1954, train w/ bell and bunny engineer, blue w/ yellow wheels, Model No. 703
EX $45 **NM** $85 **MIP** $160

Bunny Push Cart, 1957, bunny pushes cart, six light blue wheels, Model No. 303
EX $40 **NM** $80 **MIP** $120

Bunny Racer, 1942, yellow and blue "racecar" w/ red wood wheels, wooden axles during WWII, Model No. 474
EX $125 **NM** $235 **MIP** $475

BunnyScoot, 1931, yellow wheels, oilcloth ears, Model No. 105
EX $1000 **NM** $2000 **MIP** $3000

Busy Bunny Cart, 1936, bunny pulls 7" cart, Easter release, Model No. 719
EX $300 **NM** $600 **MIP** $1000

Butch the Pup, 1951, yellow wheels, tail wags, felt ears, Model No. 333
EX $50 **NM** $70 **MIP** $110

Buzzy Bee, 1950, first use of acetate (form of plastic) in a Fisher-Price toy, two spring antennae, Model No. 325
EX $25 **NM** $45 **MIP** $70

Campbell Kids Farm Truck, 1954, swayed back and forth, paper vegetable cut-outs, Model No. 845
EX $145 **NM** $300 **MIP** $750

Cash Register, 1960, three numbered coins, plastic keys pop up characters, Model No. 972
EX $55 **NM** $115 **MIP** $195

Chatter Monk, 1957, monkey w/ jumping action, wooden hat, vinyl tail, chatter sound, Model No. 798
EX $85 **NM** $125 **MIP** $175

Chatter Telephone, 1962, same as the Talk-Back Telephone of 1961, red plastic handle, blue wheels, wooden wheels through 1966, Model No. 747
EX $30 **NM** $45 **MIP** $65

Choo-Choo Local, 1936, push toy, 18" stick, six wheels, steel bell, Model No. 517
EX $350 **NM** $850 **MIP** $1800

Chubby Chief, 1932, elephant on bicycle w/ steel bell, retailed for $1, Model No. 110
EX $450 **NM** $950 **MIP** $2000

Chuggy Pop-Up, 1955, red train, yellow wheels, pop-up engineer, metal boiler, realistic sound, Model No. 616
EX $85 **NM** $125 **MIP** $170

(John Murray. Photo by Russ MacKearnin)

Circus Wagon, 1942, Ringmaster's arms move up and down and pipes play, blue wheels, Model No. 156
EX $525 **NM** $750 **MIP** $1100

Concrete Mixer Truck, 1959, mixing drum rotates and pops, plastic grille, lithographed sides, Model No. 926
EX $150 **NM** $300 **MIP** $485

Corn Popper, 1957, red and blue push toy, Model No. 785
EX $35 **NM** $95 **MIP** $175

Corn Popper, 1963, push toy, variations of this toy endured through 1990, Model No. 788
EX $15 **NM** $30 **MIP** $50

Cotton Tail Cart, 1940, upright bunny pulls red cart, legs rotate, clicking sound, yellow wheels, Model No. 525
EX $150 **NM** $400 **MIP** $675

Cowboy Chime, 1951, New version of old Dandy Dobbin, western pony head and litho saddle graphics attached to stick. Metal musical hush chime base had cowboy and indian graphics, Model No. 700
EX $110 **NM** $285 **MIP** $475

(John Murray. Photo by Russ MacKearnin)

Dandy Dobbin, 1941, 14-1/2" long, 12-1/4" high, riding horse w/ red seat, green or yellow wheels, braided cord bridle, Model No. 765
EX $285 **NM** $375 **MIP** $565

Dapper Donald Duck, 1936, Model No. 460
EX $175 **NM** $425 **MIP** $650

Dashing Dobbin, 1938, riding horse, blue or red versions, braided cord bridle, 150lb capacity, Model No. 742
EX $450 **NM** $650 **MIP** $900

Ding Dong Duckey, 1940, Easter release, duck's head turned side to side and concealed wires played a tune as pulled, Model No. 724
EX $175 **NM** $225 **MIP** $425

Dinkey Engine, 1959, "chug-chug" sound, pistons moved, plastic cowcatcher and cab, Model No. 642
EX $35 **NM** $50 **MIP** $95

Dizzy Dino, 1931, Pop-Up Kritters, dinosaur on banjo paddle, pulley system used 50lb test fish line, retailed for $1, Model No. 407
EX $250 **NM** $400 **MIP** $800

(John Murray. Photo by Russ MacKearnin)

Dizzy Donkey, 1939, Pop-Up Kritters, donkey on blue paddle, black ears, Model No. 433
EX $85 **NM** $130 **MIP** $175

(John Murray, Photo by Ross MacKearnin)

Doc & Dopey Dwarfs, 1938, each has hammer that hits stump, red wheels, Model No. 770
EX $875 **NM** $1750 **MIP** $2600

Doctor Doodle, 1931, styled by Margaret Evans Price, blue wheels, black topcoat and hat, orange bill, Model No. 100
EX $600 **NM** $950 **MIP** $1500

Doctor Doodle, 1940, green wheels, waddle, lower bill moves with clicker as quacking sound, Model No. 477
EX $300 **NM** $450 **MIP** $675

Dogcart Donald, 1936, Pluto pulls Donald in cart, Model No. 149
EX $600 **NM** $1400 **MIP** $2500

Doggy Racer, 1942, black wheels, arms "turned" the steering wheel, Model No. 7
EX $150 **NM** $300 **MIP** $525

(John Murray, Photo by Ross MacKearnin)

Donald Duck & Nephews, 1941, w/ two nephews Huey and Louie, red wheels, Model No. 479
EX $425 **NM** $575 **MIP** $875

(John Murray, Photo by Ross MacKearnin)

Donald Duck Cart, 1937, unpainted wheels, red cart behind Donald, Easter release, Model No. 500
EX $350 **NM** $675 **MIP** $1200

Donald Duck Cart, 1940, red wheels, blue base, Easter release, chick can behind Donald, Model No. 469
EX $200 **NM** $450 **MIP** $775

(John Murray. Photo by Russ MacKearnin)

Donald Duck Cart, 1942, swinging arms, concealed voice, blue cart behind Donald in red outfit, red wheels, Model No. 544
EX $275 **NM** $350 **MIP** $485

Donald Duck Cart, 1954, orange flip-flop feet, quack-quack sound, flowers litho on blue and yellow cart behind Donald, Model No. 605
EX $125 **NM** $250 **MIP** $425

Donald Duck Choo-Choo, 1940, yellow wheels, blue base, red engineer's hat, steel bell, 9-1/2" long in 1940, 8-1/2" long in 1941, Model No. 450
EX $300 **NM** $400 **MIP** $675

(John Murray, Photo by Ross MacKearnin)

Donald Duck Choo-Choo, 1942, yellow wheels, red base, blue engineer's hat, steel bell, Model No. 450
EX $95 **NM** $200 **MIP** $325

Donald Duck Delivery, 1936, long-billed Donald in front of pink cart w/ blue wheels, Model No. 715
EX $350 **NM** $750 **MIP** $1100

Wooden

Donald Duck Drum Major, 1940, red wheels, green base, Donald holding green baton, Model No. 550/463
EX $150 **NM** $350 **MIP** $725

Donald Duck Drum Major, 1948, blue wheels, red base, Donald holding yellow baton, Model No. 432/532
EX $85 **NM** $175 **MIP** $325

Donald Duck Drummer, 1949, two mallets, arms move to strike red drum, red wheels, blue base, Model No. 454
EX $285 **NM** $325 **MIP** $475

Donald Duck Pop-Up, 1938, red paddle, rubber bill, oilcloth wings, Model No. 425
EX $325 **NM** $650 **MIP** $1100

Donald Duck Xylophone, 1938, red wheels, blue base, blue hat, two arms hold mallets to strike xylophone when pulled, Model No. 185
EX $475 **NM** $700 **MIP** $925

(John Murray, Photo by Ross MacKearnin)

Donald Duck Xylophone, 1946, red wheels, green base, blue hat (different from No. 185), two arms hold mallets that strike xylophone when pulled, Model No. 177
EX $350 **NM** $450 **MIP** $675

Dopey Dwarf, 1939, blue wheels, red base, two mallets move hit drum when pulled, Model No. 770
EX $350 **NM** $650 **MIP** $1375

Doughboy Donald, 1942, 13-3/4" long, soldier outfit, two mortars, Pluto pulling green base w/ red wheels, Model No. 744
EX $550 **NM** $1000 **MIP** $2375

Drummer Bear, 1931, yellow wheels, blue base, black hat, Model No. 102
EX $550 **NM** $1000 **MIP** $2000

Drummer Bear, 1932, yellow wheels, Model No. 102
EX $500 **NM** $1000 **MIP** $1500

Ducky Cart, 1948, duck pulls cylinder-shaped cart w/ red wheels, Model No. 6
EX $45 **NM** $85 **MIP** $165

Ducky Cart, 1950, litho yellow duck w/ blue background, red wheels, Model No. 51
EX $45 **NM** $85 **MIP** $125

Ducky Daddles, 1941, yellow duck w/ blue wheels, exclusive for F.W. Woolworth Company, Model No. 14
EX $35 **NM** $90 **MIP** $165

Ducky Daddles, 1942, predecessor of Snap Quack, waddle, movable feet, head turns side to side, quacks, Model No. 148
EX $175 **NM** $300 **MIP** $625

Dumbo Circus Racer, 1941, rubber arms turned steering wheel, 10-3/4" long,, Model No. 738
EX $450 **NM** $1000 **MIP** $2000

Easter Bunny, 1936, pink and white, Model No. 490
EX $125 **NM** $350 **MIP** $600

(John Murray, Photo by Ross MacKearnin)

Elsie's Dairy Truck, 1948, F-P's second advertising toy, based on Borden's Elsie the Cow, truck driven by her son Beauregard, movable arms struck nickel bell on grille, came with two glass square bottles (add $50 for each bottle), Model No. 745
EX $525 **NM** $725 **MIP** $975

Farmer in Dell Music Box, 1962, formerly #764, red crank/handle on side, Model No. 763
EX $30 **NM** $65 **MIP** $130

Farmer in the Dell Music Box Barn, 1960, crank, strap, Swiss music box, Model No. 764
EX $25 **NM** $65 **MIP** $135

Farmer in the Dell TV Radio, 1963, spring anetnnae, white handle, Model No. 166
EX $25 **NM** $35 **MIP** $60

Fido Zilo, 1955, movable arms w/ mallets to strike four nickel keys, red wheels, Model No. 707
EX $90 **NM** $130 **MIP** $165

Fire Truck, 1959, red truck w/ yellow grille & ladder, driver bounces and turns when pulled, Model No. 630
EX $35 **NM** $55 **MIP** $110

Fred Flintstone Zilo, 1962, Sears exclusive, Model No. 712
EX $250 **NM** $500 **MIP** $800

(John Murray. Photo by Russ MacKearnin)

Fuzzy Fido, 1941, spring wire tail, offset green wheels caused waddling, Model No. 444
EX $225 **NM** $325 **MIP** $450

Gabby Duck, 1952, blue wheels, yellow duck, orange bill opens, waddling motion, quacks, Model No. 767
EX $55 **NM** $80 **MIP** $225

Gabby Goofies, 1956, first version, red Daddy Goofy w/ three ducklings, twirling acetate wings, Model No. 775
EX $40 **NM** $60 **MIP** $80

Gabby Goofies, 1963, final version, blue Mama Goofy w/ three ducklings, Model No. 777
EX $20 **NM** $30 **MIP** $45

Gabby Goose, 1936, red wheels, sailor suit, concealed voice, Model No. 120
EX $400 **NM** $750 **MIP** $1100

Galloping Horse & Wagon, 1948, horse pulling red wagon w/ yellow wheels, Model No. 737
EX $150 **NM** $325 **MIP** $475

(John Murray. Photo by Russ MacKearnin)

Gold Star Stagecoach, 1954, two horses pull stagecoach, driver sways side to side, two mail pouches, Model No. 175
EX $285 **NM** $390 **MIP** $625

Golden Gulch Express, 1961, red and green train, spring mounted indian on the tender, Model No. 191
EX $110 **NM** $145 **MIP** $225

Go'N Back Bruno, 1931, Model No. 355
EX $750 **NM** $1500 **MIP** $2200

Go'N Back Jumbo, 1931, Walky-Balky Back-Up Toys, wind up w/ removable key, oilcloth ears, pipecleaner tail, styled by Evans Price, designed by Edward Savage, Model No. 360
EX $450 **NM** $900 **MIP** $1200

Go'N Back Mule, 1931, Model No. 350
EX $400 **NM** $800 **MIP** $1200

Granny Doodle, 1931, felt bonnet, orange wheels, orange bill, Model No. 101
EX $600 **NM** $1000 **MIP** $1500

Granny Doodle & Family, 1933, duck followed by two baby ducks, green wheels, Model No. 101
EX $650 **NM** $1500 **MIP** $2000

Happy Helicopter, 1953, litho teddy bear pilot, yellow wheels and propellers, Model No. 498
EX $150 **NM** $200 **MIP** $300

Happy Hippo, 1962, vinyl ears, spring tail, storage inside for other toys, Model No. 151
EX $115 **NM** $170 **MIP** $230

Horse & Wagon, 1933, Model No. 605
EX $500 **NM** $1000 **MIP** $1500

FISHER-PRICE

Horse and Wagon, 1934, w/2 wooden blocks, Model No. 610
EX $600 **NM** $1100 **MIP** $1600

Hot Diggety, 1934, wind up, hat, painted face, heavy metal dancing feet, Model No. 800
EX $600 **NM** $1200 **MIP** $1800

Howdy Bunny, 1939, orange "running" legs, green base, red wheels, Model No. 757
EX $300 **NM** $650 **MIP** $975

Huckleberry Hound Zilo, 1961, Sears exclusive, Model No. 711
EX $175 **NM** $475 **MIP** $800

Huffy Puffy Train, 1958, engine, coal car, cattle car, caboose, yellow wheels, "chug-chug" sound, Model No. 999
EX $110 **NM** $150 **MIP** $225

Humpty Dump Truck, 1963, big yellow wheels, two characters, Model No. 145
EX $40 **NM** $90 **MIP** $160

Humpty Dumpty, 1957, smiling face one side, crying face on the other, bells for hands, could roll along on arms or feet, Model No. 757
EX $265 **NM** $350 **MIP** $425

Husky Dump Truck, 1961, big orange tires, two characters, Model No. 145
EX $30 **NM** $85 **MIP** $140

Jack-n-Jill TV Radio, 1959, Swiss music box, winding knob, spring aerial, Model No. 148
EX $25 **NM** $65 **MIP** $110

Jingle Giraffe, 1956, blue wheels, spring tail, nickeled bell, Model No. 472
EX $150 **NM** $275 **MIP** $385

Johnny Jumbo, 1933, circus elephant, bell, yellow wheels, Model No. 712
EX $500 **NM** $1000 **MIP** $1500

Jolly Jumper, 1954, red wheels w/ green feet, googly eyes, Model No. 450
EX $35 **NM** $60 **MIP** $100

Jolly Jumper, 1963, green frog, big yellow wheels, mouth opens "croak" sound, Model No. 793
EX $25 **NM** $50 **MIP** $80

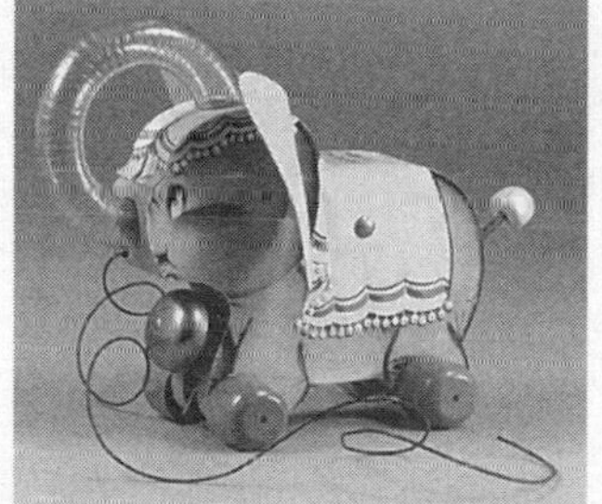
(John Murray, Photo by Ross MacKearnin)

Juggling Jumbo, 1958, crank pops five colored wooden balls through circular acetate trunk, spring tail, vinyl ears, Model No. 735
EX $235 **NM** $300 **MIP** $425

Jumbo Jitterbug, 1940, Pop-Up Kritter, movable trunk & legs, oilcloth ears, blue paddle, Model No. 422
EX $65 **NM** $150 **MIP** $375

Jumbo Rolo, 1951, blue elephant pedals tricycle, six colored balls rattle in cage behind tricycle, Model No. 755
EX $235 **NM** $300 **MIP** $425

Junior Circus, 1963, 22-pieces in reusable container, Model No. 902
EX $75 **NM** $350 **MIP** $395

(John Murray. Photo by Russ MacKearnin)

Katy Kackler, 1954, wings and feet move up and down, "cluck-cluck-squawk" sound, red wheels, first of three versions, Model No. 140
EX $80 **NM** $120 **MIP** $175

Kicking Donkey, 1937, large rubber ears, red wheels, rope tail, Model No. 175
EX $400 **NM** $850 **MIP** $1300

(John Murray, Photo by Ross MacKearnin)

Kitty Bell, 1950, cat's arms rotate ball that strikes bell, blue base, yellow wheels, Model No. 499
EX $125 **NM** $170 **MIP** $285

Lady Bug, 1961, two spring antennae, red shell, "twirp-twirp" sound, Model No. 658
EX $35 **NM** $70 **MIP** $100

Leo the Drummer, 1952, red base, yellow wheels, two spring "sticks" to strike drum, Model No. 480
EX $235 **NM** $285 **MIP** $390

Lofty Lizzy, 1931, giraffe on paddle, Model No. 405
EX $200 **NM** $400 **MIP** $600

Lookee Monk, 1931, hat w/tassel, Model No. 104
EX $500 **NM** $1000 **MIP** $1500

(John Murray, Photo by Ross MacKearnin)

Looky Chug-Chug, 1949, engine and coal car, red wheels, nickel bell, moving pistons, Model No. 161
EX $125 **NM** $225 **MIP** $375

(John Murray, Photo by Ross MacKearnin)

Looky Fire Truck, 1950, three firemen, moving eyes, nickel bell, red truck w/ yellow wheels, Model No. 7
EX $125 **NM** $160 **MIP** $240

(John Murray. Photo by Russ MacKearnin)

Lop-Ear Looie, 1934, Pop-Up Kritter, mouse, retailed for 25 cents; paddle in red, blue, yellow or green, Model No. 415
EX $225 **NM** $335 **MIP** $450

Lucky Monk, 1932, monkey in orange cart w/ blue wheels, felt hat, sound, retailed for $1, Model No. 109
EX $350 **NM** $850 **MIP** $1700

Merry Mousewife, 1962, red wheels, sweeps broom, yellow tail and hat, Model No. 662
EX $60 **NM** $90 **MIP** $125

Merry Mutt, 1949, red base, blue wheels, two nicleled 3" xylophone keys, two spring mallets, Model No. 473
EX $85 **NM** $125 **MIP** $155

Mickey Mouse Band, 1935, first Disney-themed release, blue base, yellow wheels, Mickey and Pluto, push toy w/ 18" stick, Model No. 530
EX $750 **NM** $1500 **MIP** $2800

Mickey Mouse Choo-Choo, 1938, blue base, yellow wheels, Mickey w/ long-billed red hat, nickel bell, Model No. 432
EX $750 **NM** $1125 **MIP** $1500

Mickey Mouse Drummer, 1941, red base, blue wheels, Mickey's arms move and mallets hit metal-topped drum, Model No. 476
EX $257 **NM** $350 **MIP** $475

Mickey Mouse Puddle Jumper, 1953, yellow wheels, car sways, Mickey bounces side to side, Model No. 310
EX $125 **NM** $200 **MIP** $275

(John Murray, Photo by Ross MacKearnin)

Mickey Mouse Safety Patrol, 1956, Mickey the motorcycle cop pulls cart, yellow wheels, hands swing reading "STOP" and "GO", Model No. 733
EX $265 **NM** $400 **MIP** $575

Mickey Mouse Xylophone, 1939, band outfit, blue base, yellow wheels, 5-key xylophone, arms hold mallets, Model No. 798
EX $575 **NM** $800 **MIP** $1250

Mickey Mouse Xylophone, 1942, w/out band outfit, Model No. 798
EX $275 **NM** $500 **MIP** $925

Mickey Mouse Zilo, 1963, last Sears exclusive xylophone, last Disney pull-toy, Mickey in band outfit, 3 xylophone keys, Model No. 714
EX $165 **NM** $350 **MIP** $675

Molly Moo-Moo, 1956, red wheels, head "moo"ves up and down, spring tail, Model No. 190
EX $65 **NM** $225 **MIP** $400

Moo-oo Cow, 1958, black and white cow, vinyl ears, pink wheels, spring tail, Model No. 155
EX $125 **NM** $170 **MIP** $230

Mother Goose, 1964, orange plastic wheels, blue scarf on head, Model No. 164
EX $20 **NM** $40 **MIP** $75

Mother Goose Music Cart, 1955, yellow goose pulls red cart, feet flip flop as pulled, Model No. 784
EX $35 **NM** $70 **MIP** $145

Music Box Sweeper, 1961, final version, Swiss music box, steel yoke, Model No. 131
EX $40 **NM** $65 **MIP** $120

(John Murray, Photo by Ross MacKearnin)

Musical Elephant, 1948, Model No. 145
EX $165 **NM** $325 **MIP** $700

Musical Mutt, 1935, large wheels w/bell inbetween, Model No. 725
EX $400 **NM** $800 **MIP** $1200

Musical Push Chime, 1950, Model No. 722
EX $35 **NM** $50 **MIP** $125

Musical Sweeper, 1950, Model No. 100
EX $65 **NM** $135 **MIP** $235

Musical Sweeper, 1953, Model No. 225
EX $40 **NM** $65 **MIP** $160

Musical Tick Tock Clock, 1962, Model No. 997
EX $25 **NM** $45 **MIP** $90

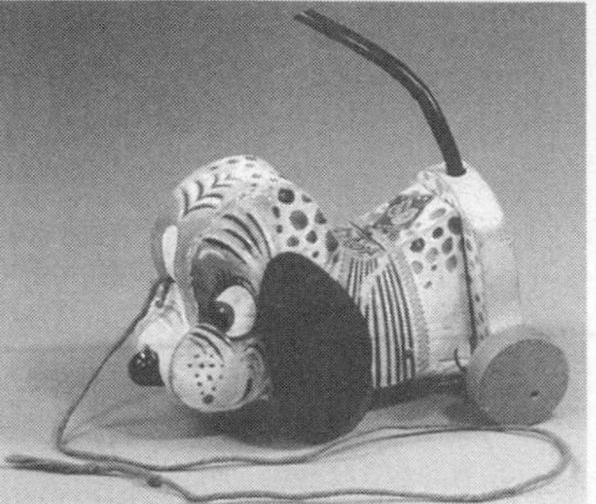

(John Murray. Photo by Russ MacKearnin)

Nosey Pup, 1956, Model No. 445
EX $25 **NM** $60 **MIP** $95

Patch Pony, 1963, Model No. 616
EX $20 **NM** $35 **MIP** $50

Perky Pot, 1958, Model No. 686
EX $85 **NM** $110 **MIP** $155

(John Murray, Photo by Ross MacKearnin)

Peter Bunny Cart, 1939, Model No. 472
EX $100 **NM** $235 **MIP** $425

Peter Bunny Engine, 1941, Model No. 715
EX $85 **NM** $225 **MIP** $475

Peter Bunny Engine, 1949, Model No. 721
EX $150 **NM** $275 **MIP** $425

Peter Pig, 1959, Model No. 479
EX $35 **NM** $50 **MIP** $90

Pinky Pig, 1956, first version, wooden eyes, Model No. 695
EX $40 **NM** $70 **MIP** $110

Pinky Pig, 1958, Model No. 695
EX $35 **NM** $90 **MIP** $140

Pinocchio Express, 1939, Model No. 720
EX $650 **NM** $850 **MIP** $1300

Playful Puppy, 1961, Model No. 625
EX $55 **NM** $70 **MIP** $100

Playland Express, 1962, Model No. 192
EX $105 **NM** $140 **MIP** $195

(John Murray, Photo by Ross MacKearnin)

Plucky Pinocchio, 1939, Model No. 494
EX $450 **NM** $725 **MIP** $1100

Pluto Pop-Up, 1936, Model No. 440
EX $70 **NM** $135 **MIP** $185

Pony Chime, 1962, Model No. 137
EX $40 **NM** $70 **MIP** $95

Pony Express, 1941, Model No. 733
EX $110 **NM** $250 **MIP** $585

Poodle Zilo, 1962, Model No. 739
EX $50 **NM** $110 **MIP** $185

Pop 'N Ring, 1959, Model No. 809
EX $40 **NM** $65 **MIP** $135

Popeye, 1935, red base, yellow wheels, Model No. 700
EX $700 **NM** $1750 **MIP** $2500

Popeye Cowboy, 1937, Model No. 705
EX $700 **NM** $1650 **MIP** $2300

Popeye Spinach Eater, 1939, Model No. 488
EX $650 **NM** $1300 **MIP** $1600

(John Murray. Photo by Russ MacKearnin)

Popeye the Sailor, 1936, unpainted wheels, arms strike bell attached to steering wheel, green boat-shaped base, Model No. 703
EX $850 **NM** $1475 **MIP** $2100

Prancing Horses, 1937, Model No. 766
EX $400 **NM** $975 **MIP** $1800

Pudgy Pig, 1962, Model No. 478
EX $40 **NM** $60 **MIP** $85

Puffy Engine, 1951, Model No. 444
EX $50 **NM** $70 **MIP** $110

Pull-A-Tune Xylophone, 1957, Model No. 870
EX $45 NM $80 MIP $110

Puppy Bak-Up, 1932, oilcloth ears, Model No. 365
EX $300 NM $600 MIP $900

Pushy Bruno, 1933, Model No. 777
EX $400 NM $800 MIP $1200

Pushy Doddle, 1933, Model No. 507
EX $550 NM $1350 MIP $2000

Pushy Drummer, 1934, Model No. 520
EX $500 NM $1350 MIP $2100

Pushy Elephant, 1934, Model No. 525
EX $450 NM $975 MIP $1800

Pushy Pat, 1933, dog rings bell, Model No. 515
EX $400 NM $800 MIP $1200

Pushy Piggy, 1932, first push toy, Model No. 500
EX $700 NM $1500 MIP $2300

Quacko Duck, 1939, Model No. 300
EX $60 NM $110 MIP $175

Quacky Family, 1946, Model No. 799
EX $75 NM $130 MIP $185

(John Murray. Photo by Russ MacKearnin)

Queen Buzzy Bee, 1962, Model No. 444
EX $25 NM $45 MIP $70

Rabbit Cart, 1950, Model No. 52
EX $35 NM $70 MIP $125

Racing Bunny Cart, 1938, Model No. 723
EX $150 NM $295 MIP $425

Racing Ponies, 1936, Model No. 760
EX $450 NM $850 MIP $1300

Racing Pony, 1933, Model No. 705
EX $500 NM $1000 MIP $1500

(John Murray, Photo by Ross MacKearnin)

Racing Rowboat, 1952, Model No. 730
EX $235 NM $280 MIP $390

Raggedy Ann & Andy, 1941, 12" long, green base, red wheels, arms attached to mallet that hits drum between them, Model No. 711
EX $1000 NM $2300 MIP $3875

Rattle Ball, 1959, Model No. 682
EX $20 NM $30 MIP $40

Riding Horse, 1940, Model No. 254
EX $400 NM $625 MIP $975

Road Roller, 1934, Model No. 152
EX $500 NM $1350 MIP $2100

Rock-A-Bye Bunny Cart, 1940, Model No. 788
EX $175 NM $425 MIP $775

Rock-A-Stack, 1960, Model No. 627
EX $15 NM $40 MIP $70

Roller Chime, 1953, Model No. 123
EX $85 NM $120 MIP $155

Rolling Bunny Basket, 1961, Model No. 310
EX $35 NM $65 MIP $110

Rooster Cart, 1938, Model No. 469
EX $110 NM $325 MIP $675

Safety School Bus, 1959, first appearance of "Play Family" figures, Model No. 983
EX $300 NM $450 MIP $700

Safety School Bus, 1962, Model No. 990
EX $80 NM $175 MIP $295

Scotty Dog, 1933, Model No. 710
EX $350 NM $850 MIP $1500

Shaggy Zilo, 1960, Model No. 738
EX $90 NM $120 MIP $180

Skipper Sam, 1934, Model No. 155
EX $850 NM $2100 MIP $3800

Sleepy Sue (Turtle), 1962, Model No. 495
EX $55 NM $75 MIP $90

Smokie Engine, 1960, Model No. 642
EX $45 NM $70 MIP $90

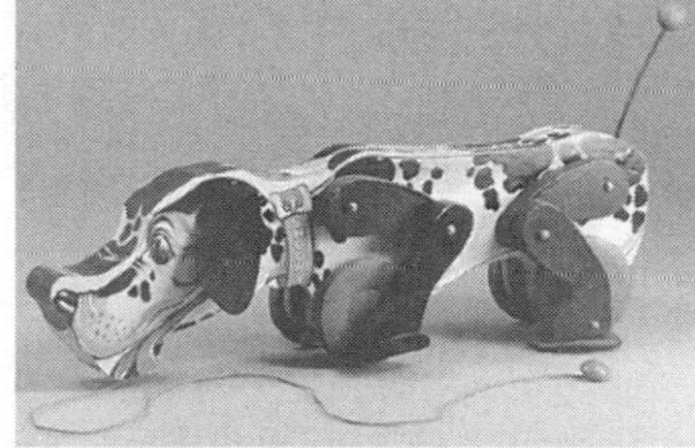

(John Murray, Photo by Ross MacKearnin)

Snoopy Sniffer, 1938, Model No. 180
EX $130 NM $290 MIP $475

Snoopy Sniffer, 1958, Model No. 180
EX $50 NM $115 MIP $235

Snorky Fire Engine, 1960, four fireman figures included, Model No. 168
EX $185 NM $300 MIP $425

Sonny Duck Cart, 1941, Model No. 410
EX $75 NM $200 MIP $425

Space Blazer, 1953, Model No. 750
EX $375 NM $525 MIP $725

(John Murray. Photo by Russ MacKearnin)

Squeaky the Clown, 1958, Model No. 777
EX $250 NM $325 MIP $475

Stake Truck, 1960, Model No. 649
EX $40 NM $80 MIP $160

Stoopy Storky, 1931, stork on paddle, Model No. 410
EX $200 NM $400 MIP $600

Streamline Express, 1935, Model No. 215
EX $900 NM $1700 MIP $2400

Strutter Donald Duck, 1941, Model No. 510
EX $125 NM $275 MIP $485

Struttin' Donald Duck, 1939, Model No. 900
EX $450 NM $975 MIP $1500

Sunny Fish, 1955, Model No. 420
EX $100 NM $200 MIP $395

Suzie Seal, 1961, Model No. 460
EX $25 NM $40 MIP $85

Tabby Ding Dong, 1939, Model No. 730
EX $350 NM $925 MIP $1450

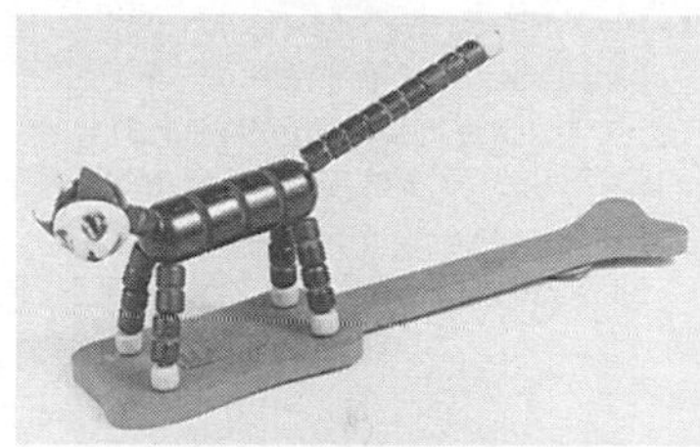

(David W Mapes Inc)

Tailspin Tabby, 1931, Model No. 400
EX $225 NM $610 MIP $1000

Tailspin Tabby Pop-Up, 1947, Model No. 600
EX $145 NM $170 MIP $225

Talk-Back Telephone, 1961, Model No. 747
EX $75 NM $165 MIP $225

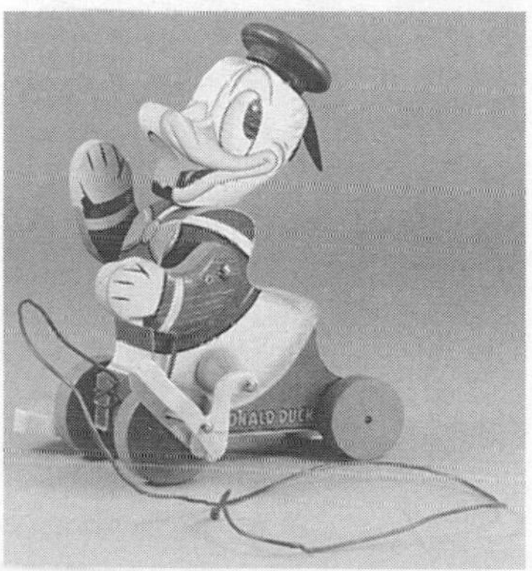

(John Murray, Photo by Ross MacKearnin)

Wooden

Talking Donald Duck, 1955, Model No. 765
EX $100 **NM** $140 **MIP** $195

(John Murray, Photo by Ross MacKearnin)

Talky Parrot, 1963, Model No. 698
EX $145 **NM** $180 **MIP** $260

Tawny Tiger, 1962, Model No. 654
EX $115 **NM** $130 **MIP** $180

Teddy Bear Parade, 1938, Model No. 195
EX $850 **NM** $1400 **MIP** $1750

Teddy Choo-Choo, 1937, Model No. 465
EX $200 **NM** $475 **MIP** $825

Teddy Drummer, 1936, Model No. 775
EX $300 **NM** $695 **MIP** $1400

Teddy Station Wagon, 1942, Model No. 480
EX $150 **NM** $300 **MIP** $475

Teddy Tooter, 1940, Model No. 150
EX $200 **NM** $475 **MIP** $985

Teddy Tooter, 1957, Model No. 712
EX $225 **NM** $275 **MIP** $395

Teddy Trucker, 1949, Model No. 711
EX $100 **NM** $225 **MIP** $395

Teddy Xylophone, 1948, Model No. 752
EX $250 **NM** $300 **MIP** $425

(John Murray. Photo by Russ MacKearnin)

Teddy Zilo, 1950, Model No. 777
EX $60 **NM** $130 **MIP** $225

Ten Little Indians TV Radio, 1961, Model No. 159
EX $25 **NM** $45 **MIP** $60

This Little Pig, 1963, Model No. 910
EX $20 **NM** $35 **MIP** $50

Thumper Bunny, 1942, Model No. 533
EX $225 **NM** $575 **MIP** $800

Timber Toter, 1957, Model No. 810
EX $50 **NM** $100 **MIP** $150

Timmy Turtle, 1953, Model No. 150
EX $85 **NM** $135 **MIP** $180

Tiny Teddy, 1955, Model No. 634
EX $40 **NM** $75 **MIP** $110

Tiny Tim, 1957, Model No. 496
EX $35 **NM** $70 **MIP** $120

Tip-Toe Turtle, 1962, Model No. 773
EX $30 **NM** $45 **MIP** $80

Toot Toot Engine, 1962, Model No. 641
EX $30 **NM** $45 **MIP** $85

Tow Truck, 1960, Model No. 615
EX $45 **NM** $70 **MIP** $160

Toy Wagon, 1951, Model No. 131
EX $240 **NM** $325 **MIP** $450

Trotting Donald Duck, 1937, Model No. 741
EX $550 **NM** $825 **MIP** $1800

Tuggy Turtle, 1959, Model No. 139
EX $95 **NM** $130 **MIP** $185

(John Murray, Photo by Ross MacKearnin)

Uncle Timmy Turtle, 1956, Model No. 125
EX $50 **NM** $120 **MIP** $150

Waggy Woofy, 1942, Model No. 437
EX $100 **NM** $185 **MIP** $300

Walt Disney's Carnival, 1936, Model No. 483
EX $325 **NM** $850 **MIP** $2400

Walt Disney's Easter Parade, 1936, Model No. 475
EX $450 **NM** $1250 **MIP** $2400

Walt Disney's Mickey Mouse, 1936, Model No. 209
EX $250 **NM** $400 **MIP** $800

Walt Disney's Pluto-the-Pup, 1936, Model No. 210
EX $225 **NM** $450 **MIP** $800

Wheel Horse, 1934, red wheels, Model No. 200
EX $600 **NM** $1100 **MIP** $1600

Whistling Engine, 1957, Model No. 617
EX $75 **NM** $115 **MIP** $185

Wiggily Woofer, 1957, Model No. 640
EX $85 **NM** $120 **MIP** $185

Winky Blinky Fire Truck, 1954, Model No. 200
EX $55 **NM** $110 **MIP** $185

Woodsy Carts, 1932, easter theme, Model No. 600
EX $300 **NM** $600 **MIP** $900

Woodsy Circus Wagon, 1933, clown, giraffe, lion, elephant, camel, pony, ticket booth, Model No. 202
EX $500 **NM** $1000 **MIP** $1400

Woodsy-Wee Circus, 1931, Model No. 201
EX $500 **NM** $1400 **MIP** $2500

Woodsy-Wee Dog Show, 1932, Model No. 209
EX $300 **NM** $1300 **MIP** $180

Woofy Wagger, 1947, Model No. 447
EX $45 **NM** $140 **MIP** $265

Woofy Wowser, 1940, Model No. 700
EX $100 **NM** $325 **MIP** $475

Ziggy Zilo, 1958, Model No. 737
EX $50 **NM** $100 **MIP** $185

Games

Board games are a peculiar bunch when it comes to collectible toys. If you had to hazard a guess as to which category of toys were most often played with in the entire toy category, board games would rank among the highest, if not the highest. Think about it—what kid didn't play some sort of board game growing up?

However, as much as nostalgia drives the toy market, you don't see the proportionate numbers of board game players become board game collectors, thus keeping values for games relatively low and easily affordable for everyone. This is due to a number of reasons. Most modern games were produced in massive numbers, thus taking scarcity out of the equation. Also, keeping all of the pieces together for games—one of the main drawing points in collecting—is a challenge. Collectors want Mint games, and that means not only having all of the pieces, but also having those pieces in good shape. Those chewed up by the family pet are not welcome here.

The games section is divided up into Prewar and Postwar games. Prewar games, or Victorian games, are generally thought of as those produced before World War II. These are where you are going to find the real valuable games. The beautiful box art, rarity and subject matter help inflate these games to, at times, astronomical levels. If you're looking for a manufacturer to target, look no further than McLoughlin Bros. This was the premier game maker of the era. If you're looking for a theme, go with baseball. Games that depict players from the turn of the century, such as Honus Wagner and Cy Young will command attention on the secondary market.

Postwar games is where you're going to find the majority of product, and games based on television shows dominate the category. You'll find a lot more collectors acquiring postwar games, usually because of their association with characters and licensed properties. For instance, even those who collect James Bond toys will have a James Bond Message From M Game. Manufacturers to keep in mind in this era include Ideal, Hasbro and Milton Bradley. There is no shortage of these games, though again, condition is the key factor. However, there is a growing number of collectors acquiring just the boards themselves and hanging them on the wall as art in themed rooms.

Trends

What people are looking for now, with the baby boomers having more time to collect and admire, are games from the 1950s and '60s in Excellent condition. Anyone can get nicely used games at any show or online venue. Most people already have that. Condition is key and collectors will pay to upgrade their collections.

Prewar games will still do well, with the right audience and subject matter, but these are getting increasingly harder to find and aren't driving the market like postwar games. As we approach the 50-year mark on many of these games, values will start to climb even more.

For more information

Association of Games and Puzzle Collectors www.agpc.org

Games and Puzzles www.gamesandpuzzles.com

THE TOP 10 PREWAR GAMES (In Mint Condition)

1. Zimmer's Base Ball Game, McLoughlin Bros., 1893 .... $30,000
2. Bulls and Bears, McLoughlin Bros., 1896 .... $15,000
3. Egerton R. Williams Popular Indoor Baseball Game, Hatch, 1886 ..... $8,000
4. New Parlor Game of Baseball, Sumner, 1869 .... $7,000
5. Darrow Monopoly, Charles Darrow, 1934 .... $7,000
6. The Champion Baseball Game, Schultz, 1889 .... $6,800
7. Major League Indoor Base Ball Game, Philadelphia Game Co., 1912 ... $6,000
8. Teddy's Ride from Oyster Bay to Albany, Jesse Crandall, 1899 .... $5,500
9. Little Fireman Game, McLoughlin Bros., 1897 .... $5,000
10. Golf, Schoenhut, 1900 .... $5,000

THE TOP 10 POSTWAR GAMES (In Mint Condition)

1. Elvis Presley Game, Teen Age Games, 1957 .... $4,000
2. Challenge the Yankees, Hasbro, 1964 .... $1,800
3. Red Barber's Big League Baseball Game, G&R Anthony, 1950s $1,700
4. Munsters Masquerade Game, Hasbro, 1965 .... $1,300
5. Munsters Drag Race Game, Hasbro, 1965 .... $1,000
6. Munster Picnic Game, Hasbro, 1965 .... $1,000
7. Willie Mays "Say Hey," Toy Development, 1954 .... $700
8. Creature From the Black Lagoon, Hasbro, 1963 .... $600
9. Mickey Mouse Haunted Bagatelle, 1950s $550
10. Man From U.N.C.L.E. Target Game, 1966 .... $550

Prewar Games

BOARD GAMES

21st Century Football, 1930s, Kerger
EX $55 NM $90

400 Game, The, 1890s, J.H. Singer
EX $100 NM $150

A&P Relay Boat Race Coast-to-Coast, 1930s, A&P
EX $30 NM $40

ABC Baseball Game, 1910s
EX $430 NM $715

ABC, Game of, 1914
EX $60 NM $100

Abcdarian, The, 1899, Chaffee & Selchow
EX $40 NM $100

Across the Channel, 1926, Wolverine
EX $50 NM $85

Across the Continent, 1892, Parker Brothers
EX $100 NM $175

Across the Continent, 1922, Parker Brothers
EX $300 NM $500

Across the Sea Game, 1930, Gabriel
EX $50 NM $80

Across the Yalu, 1905, Milton Bradley
EX $95 NM $125

Add-Too, 1940, All-Fair
EX $5 NM $10

Admiral Byrd's South Pole Game Little America, 1930s, Parker Brothers
EX $350 NM $600

Admirals, The Naval War Game, 1939, Merchandisers
EX $75 NM $120

ADT Delivery Boy, 1890, Milton Bradley
EX $120 NM $200

ADT Messenger Boy (Small Version), 1915, Milton Bradley
EX $30 NM $60

Advance And Retreat, Game of, 1900s, Milton Bradley
EX $95 NM $125

Aero-Chute, 1940, American Toy Works
EX $75 NM $125

Aeroplane Race, 1922, Wolverine
EX $60 NM $75

After Dinner, 1937, Frederick H. Beach (Beachcraft)
EX $5 NM $15

Air Base Checkers, 1942, Einson-Freeman
EX $20 NM $30

Air Mail, The, 1930, Archer Toy
EX $75 NM $125

Air Mail, The Game of, 1927, Milton Bradley
EX $30 NM $60

Air Ship Game, The, 1904, McLoughlin Bros.
EX $300 NM $600

Air Ship Game, The, 1912, McLoughlin Bros.
EX $300 NM $600

Airplane Speedway Game, 1941, Lowe
EX $20 NM $30

Akins Real Baseball, 1915, Akins
EX $450 NM $750

Aldjemma, 1944, Corey Games
EX $25 NM $40

Alee-Oop, 1937, Royal Toy
EX $15 NM $25

Alexander's Baseball, 1940s
EX $245 NM $400

Alice in Wonderland, 1930s, Parker Brothers
EX $75 NM $150

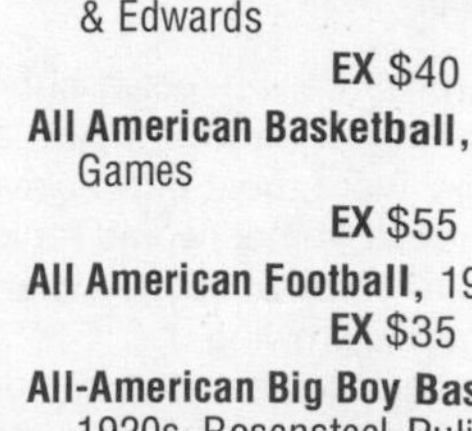

Alice In Wonderland, Game of, 1923, Stoll & Edwards
EX $40 NM $60

All American Basketball, 1941, Corey Games
EX $55 NM $65

All American Football, 1935
EX $35 NM $55

All-American Big Boy Baseball Game, 1920s, Rosensteel-Pulich
EX $200 NM $500

All-American Football, 1925, Parker Brothers
EX $100 NM $165

All-Star Baseball Game, 1935, Whitman
EX $100 NM $150

Alpha Baseball Game, 1930s, Redlich
EX $100 NM $150

Alpha Football Game, 1940s, Replica
EX $70 NM $115

Amateur Golf, 1928, Parker Brothers
EX $145 NM $245

Ambuscade, Constellations And Bounce, 1877, McLoughlin Bros.
EX $75 NM $150

American Boys, 1920s, Milton Bradley
EX $85 NM $125

American Derby, 1931, Henschel
EX $55 NM $90

American Football Game, 1930, Ace Leather Goods
EX $70 NM $115

American Revolution, The New Game of The, 1844, Lorenzo Burge
EX $960 NM $1600

American Sports, 1880s
EX $110 NM $180

America's Football, 1939, Trojan Games
EX $55 NM $90

America's Yacht Race, 1904, McLoughlin Bros.
EX $500 NM $850

Amusing Game of Innocence Abroad, The, 1888, Parker Brothers
EX $75 NM $175

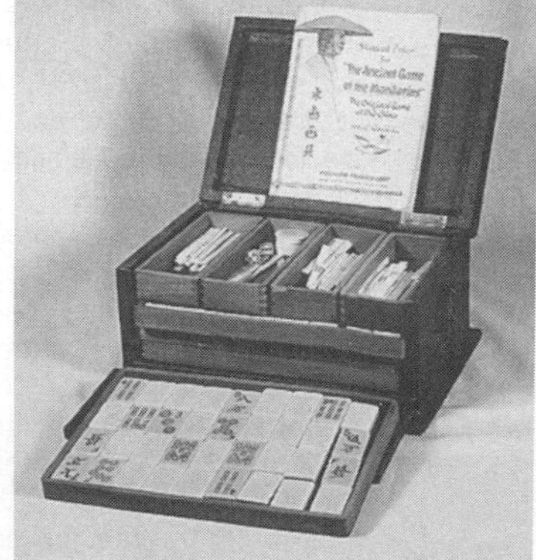

Ancient Game of the Mandarins, The, 1923, Parker Brothers
EX $45 NM $75

Andy Gump, His Game, 1924, Milton Bradley
EX $45 NM $75

Anex-A-Gram, 1938, Embossing
EX $20 NM $40

Animal & Bird Lotto, 1926, All-Fair
EX $15 NM $20

Arena, 1896, Bliss
EX $200 NM $300

Athletic Sports, 1900, Parker Brothers
EX $300 NM $500

Attack, Game of, 1889, Bliss
EX $800 NM $1200

Authors, 1861, Whipple & Smith
EX $150 NM $250

Authors, 1890s, J.H. Singer
EX $25 NM $50

Auto Game, The, 1906, Milton Bradley
EX $150 NM $275

Auto Race Electro Game, 1929, Knapp Electric & Novelty
EX $150 NM $300

Auto Race Game, 1925, Milton Bradley
EX $200 NM $300

Auto Race Jr., 1925, All-Fair
EX $75 NM $125

Auto Race, Army, Navy, Game Hunt (four game set), 1920s, Wilder
EX $50 NM $90

Auto Race, Game Of, 1920s, Orotech
EX $40 NM $75

Automobile Race, Game of the, 1904, McLoughlin Bros.
EX $650 NM $1200

Auto-Play Baseball Game, 1911, Auto-Play
EX $425 NM $700

Aydelott's Parlor Baseball, 1910
EX $225 NM $375

Babe Ruth National Game of Baseball, 1929, Keiser-Fry
EX $550 NM $910

Babe Ruth's Baseball Game, 1926, Milton Bradley
EX $300 NM $500

Babe Ruth's Official Baseball Game, 1940s, Toytown
EX $300 NM $500

Baby Barn Yard, 1940s, B.L. Fry Products
EX $15 NM $25

Bagatelle, Game of, 1898, McLoughlin Bros.
EX $300 NM $550

Bagdad, The Game of The East, 1940, Clover Games
EX $25 NM $40

Bambino (Baseball, Chicago World's Fair), 1933, Johnson Store Equipment
EX $295 NM $490

Bambino Baseball Game, 1940, Mansfield-Zesiger
EX $145 NM $250

Bamboozle, or The Enchanted Isle, 1876, Milton Bradley
EX $75 NM $150

Bang, Game of, 1903, McLoughlin Bros.
EX $100 NM $200

Banner Lye Checkerboard, 1930s, Geo E. Schweig & Son
EX $15 NM $20

Barage, 1941, Corey Games
EX $50 NM $100

Bargain Day, A Game, Parker Brothers, "by the famous inventor Elizabeth Magie Phillips"
EX $25 NM $50

Barney Google and Spark Plug Game, 1923, Milton Bradley
EX $50 NM $100

Baron Munchausen Game, The, 1933, Parker Brothers
EX $20 NM $40

Base Hit, 1944, Games
EX $75 NM $100

Baseball, 1942, Lowe
EX $15 NM $25

Baseball & Checkers, 1925, Milton Bradley
EX $75 NM $150

Baseball Dominoes, 1910, Evans
EX $250 NM $400

Baseball Game, 1930, All-Fair
EX $125 NM $200

Baseball Game & G-Man Target Game, 1940, Marks Brothers
EX $150 NM $225

Baseball Game, New, 1885, Clark & Martin
EX $165 NM $275

Baseball Wizard Game, 1916, Morehouse
EX $265 NM $450

Baseball, Game of, 1886, J.H. Singer
EX $600 NM $900

Base-Ball, Game of, 1886, McLoughlin Bros.
EX n/a NM n/a

Basilinda, 1890, Horsman
EX $105 NM $175

Basketball, 1942, Lowe
EX $15 NM $25

Basketball Game, Official, 1940, Toy Creations
EX $45 NM $75

Battle Checkers, 1925, Pen Man
EX $15 NM $50

Battle Game, The, 1890s, Parker Brothers
EX $120 NM $200

Battle of Ballots, 1931, All-Fair
EX $85 NM $125

Battle of Manila, 1899, Parker Brothers
EX $600 NM $1000

Bear Hunt, Game of, 1923, Milton Bradley
EX $45 NM $60

Beauty And The Beast, Game of, 1905, Milton Bradley
EX $45 NM $75

Bee Gee Baseball Dart Target, 1935s, Bee Gee
EX $70 NM $115

Bell Boy Game, The, 1898, Chaffee & Selchow
EX $425 NM $600

Belmont Park, 1930, Marks Brothers
EX $60 NM $90

Bengalee, 1940s, Advance Games
EX $20 NM $35

Benny Goodman Swings, 1930s, Toy Creations
EX $40 NM $80

Benson Football Game, The, 1930s, Benson
EX $85 NM $140

Bible Boys, 1901, Zondervan
EX $10 NM $15

Bible Characters, 1890s, Decker & Decker
EX $10 NM $25

Bible Lotto, 1933, Goodenough and Woglom
EX $10 NM $15

Bible Quotto, 1932, Goodenough and Woglom
EX $6 NM $10

Bible Rhymes, 1933, Goodenough and Woglom
EX $10 NM $15

Bicycle Game, 1896, Donaldson Brothers
EX $205 NM $350

Bicycle Game, The New, 1894, Parker Brothers
EX $200 NM $400

GAMES

Bicycle Race, 1910, Milton Bradley
EX $125 NM $250

Bicycle Race Game, The, 1898, Chaffee & Selchow
EX $430 NM $600

Bicycle Race, A Game for the Wheelmen, 1891, McLoughlin Bros.
EX $450 NM $800

Bicycling, The Merry Game of, 1900, Parker Brothers150
EX $200 NM $275

Big Apple, 1938, Rosebud Art
EX $20 NM $40

Big Bad Wolf Game, 1930s, Parker Brothers
EX $50 NM $90

Big Business, 1936, Parker Brothers
EX $10 NM $25

Big Business, 1937, Transogram
EX $20 NM $40

Big League Basketball, 1920s, Baumgarten
EX $145 NM $300

Big Six: Christy Mathewson Indoor Baseball Game, 1922, Piroxloid
EX $500 NM $800

Big Ten Football Game, 1936, Wheaties
EX $55 NM $90

Bike Race Game, The, 1930s, Master Toy
EX $15 NM $30

Bild-A-Word, 1929, Educational Card & Game
EX $5 NM $10

Billy Whiskers, 1923, Saalfield
EX $20 NM $40

Billy Whiskers, 1924, Russell
EX $45 NM $75

Bilt-Rite Miniature Bowling Alley, 1930s, Atwood Momanus
EX $70 NM $115

Bing Miller Base Ball Game, 1932, Ryan
EX $750 NM $2000

Bingo, 1925, Rosebud Art
EX $15 NM $20

Bingo or Beano, 1940s, Parker Brothers
EX $5 NM $10

Bird Lotto, 1940s, Gabriel
EX $10 NM $20

Black Beauty, 1921, Stoll & Edwards
EX $40 NM $65

Black Falcon of The Flying G-Men, The, 1939, Ruckelshaus
EX $300 NM $500

Black Sambo, Game of, 1939, Gabriel
EX $75 NM $125

Blackout, 1939, Milton Bradley
EX $30 NM $60

Blockade, 1941, Corey Games
EX $40 NM $75

Blondie Goes To Leisureland, 1935, Westinghouse
EX $20 NM $35

Blow Football Game, 1912
EX $30 NM $50

Blox-O, 1923, Lubbers & Bell
EX $10 NM $20

Bluff, 1944, Games of Fame
EX $15 NM $25

Bo Bang & Hong Kong, 1890, Parker Brothers
EX $275 NM $450

Bo McMillan's Indoor Football, 1939, Indiana Game
EX $60 NM $125

Bo Peep, The Game of, 1890, J.H. Singer
EX $200 NM $300

Boake Carter's Star Reporter, 1937, Parker Brother75s
EX $50 NM $75

Bomb The Navy, 1940s, Pressman
EX $10 NM $30

Bombardment, Game of, 1898, McLoughlin Bros.
EX $150 NM $250

Bombs Away, 1944, Toy Creations
EX $75 NM $125

Bookie, 1931, Bookie Games
EX $55 NM $90

Boston Baseball Game, 1906, Boston Game
EX $495 NM $825

Boston Globe Bicycle Game of Circulation, 1895, Boston Globe
EX $55 NM $90

Boston-New York Motor Tour, 1920s, American Toy
EX $60 NM $100

Bottle-Quoits, 1897, Parker Brothers
EX $50 NM $85

Bottoms Up, 1934, Embossing
EX $20 NM $30

Bowl 'em, 1930s, Parker Brothers
EX $20 NM $35

Bowling Board Game, 1896, Parker Brothers
EX $350 NM $575

Box Hockey, 1941, Milton Bradley45
EX $35 NM $60

Boxing Game, The, 1928, Stoll & Edwards
EX $85 NM $140

Boy Scouts, 1910s, McLoughlin Bros.
EX $125 NM $250

Boy Scouts in Camp, McLoughlin Bros.
EX $175 NM $300

Boy Scouts Progress Game, 1924, Parker Brothers
EX $225 NM $350

Boys Own Football Game, 1900s, McLoughlin Bros.
EX $600 NM $1000

Bradley's Circus Game, 1882, Milton Bradley
EX $60 NM $150

Bradley's Telegraph Game, 1900s, Milton Bradley
EX $85 NM $125

Bradley's Toy Town Post Office, 1910s, Milton Bradley
EX $90 NM $150

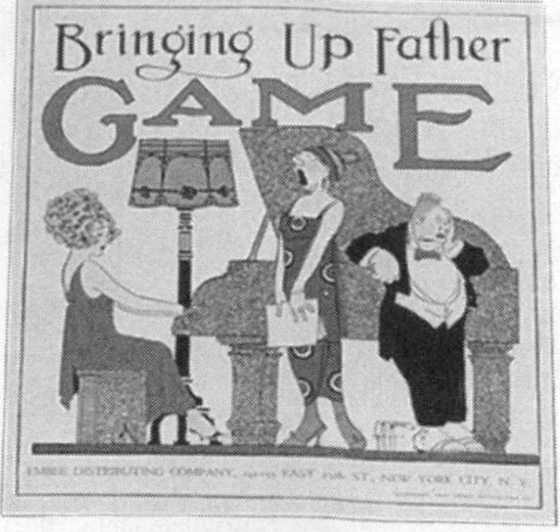

Bringing Up Father Game, 1920, Embee Distributing
EX $75 NM $100

Broadway, 1917, Parker Brothers
EX $75 NM $125

Brownie Auto Race, 1920s, Jeanette Toy & Novelty
EX $60 NM $125

Brownie Horseshoe Game, 1900s, M.H. Miller
EX $30 NM $50

Brownie Ring Toss, 1920s, M.H. Miller
EX $30 NM $50

Buck Rogers and His Cosmic Rocket Wars Game, 1934, Lutz & Scheinkman, Inc.
EX $400 NM $550

Buck Rogers Game of the 25th Century, 1934, Lutz & Sheinkman, Inc., 13 x 18" board
EX $400 NM $550

Buck Rogers Siege of Gigantica Game, 1934, Lutz & Scheinkman, Inc., 3 boards, 40 cards, 12 wooden pegs
EX $750 NM $1000

Bucking Bronco, 1930s, Transogram
EX $30 NM $50

Buffalo Bill, The Game of, 1898, Parker Brothers
EX $300 NM $500

Buffalo Hunt, 1898, Parker Brothers
EX $175 NM $250

Bugville Games, 1915, Animate Toy
EX $75 NM $100

Bulls and Bears, 1896, McLoughlin Bros.
EX $7000 NM $13000

Bulls and Bears, 1936, Parker Brothers
EX $75 NM $150

Bunker Golf, 1932
EX $115 NM $195

Bunny Rabbit, or Cottontail & Peter, The Game of, 1928, Parker Brothers
EX $85 NM $145

Buried Treasure, The Game of, 1930s, Russell
EX $35 NM $60

Buster Brown at Coney Island, 1890s, J. Ottmann Lith.
EX $225 NM $500

Buster Brown Hurdle Race, 1890s, J. Ottmann Lith.
EX $300 NM $500

Buying and Selling Game, 1903, Milton Bradley
EX $100 NM $200

Cabby, 1940, Selchow & Righter
EX $30 NM $60

Cabin Boy, 1910, Milton Bradley
EX $50 NM $100

Cadet Game, The, 1905, Milton Bradley
EX $100 NM $200

Cake Walk Game, The, 1900s, Parker Brothers
EX $750 NM $1700

Cake Walk, The, 1900s, Anglo American
EX $750 NM $2000

Calling All Cars, 1938, Parker Brothers
EX $25 NM $30

Camelot, 1950s, Parker Brothers
EX $20 NM $25

Canoe Race, 1910, Milton Bradley
EX $35 NM $60

Capital Cities Air Derby, The, 1929, All-Fair
EX $200 NM $350

Captain and the (Katzenjammer) Kids, 1940s, Milton Bradley
EX $40 NM $75

Captain Hop Across Junior, 1928, All-Fair
EX $100 NM $250

Captain Kidd and His Treasure, 1896, Parker Brothers
EX $200 NM $350

Captain Kidd Junior, 1926, Parker Brothers
EX $50 NM $75

Captive Princess, 1880, McLoughlin Bros.
EX $135 NM $225

Captive Princess, 1899, McLoughlin Bros.
EX $65 NM $150

Captive Princess, Tournament And Pathfinders, Games of, 1888, McLoughlin Bros.
EX $75 NM $200

Capture The Fort, 1914, Valley Novelty Works
EX $45 NM $75

Car Race and Game Hunt, 1920s, Wilder
EX $75 NM $165

Cargo For Victory, 1943, All-Fair
EX $75 NM $125

Cargoes, 1934, Selchow & Righter
EX $40 NM $60

Carl Hubbell Mechanical Baseball, Gotham
EX $75 NM $200

Carnival, The Show Business Game, 1937, Milton Bradley
EX $50 NM $100

Casey on the Mound, 1940s, Kamm Games
EX $150 NM $300

Cat, 1915, Carl F. Doerr
EX $15 NM $25

Cat, Game of, 1900, Chaffee & Selchow
EX $150 NM $300

Catching Mice, Game of, 1888, McLoughlin Bros.
EX $150 NM $250

Cats And Dogs, 1929, Parker Brothers
EX $100 NM $225

Cavalcade, 1930s, Selchow & Righter
EX $40 NM $60

Century Ride, 1900, Milton Bradley
EX $150 NM $250

Century Run Bicycle Game, The, 1897, Parker Brothers
EX $210 NM $300

Champion Baseball Game, The, 1889, Schultz
EX $4100 NM $6800

Champion Game of Baseball, The, 1910s, Proctor Amusement
EX $75 NM $100

Champion Road Race, 1934, Champion Spark Plugs
EX $20 NM $30

Championship Baseball Parlor Game, 1914, Grebnelle Novelty
EX $225 NM $500

Championship Fight Game, 1940s, Frankie Goodman
EX $20 NM $50

Champs, The Land of Brawno, 1940, Selchow & Righter
EX $30 NM $50

Charge, The, 1898, E.O. Clark
EX $300 NM $500

Charlie Chan, The Great Charlie Chan Detective Game, 1937, Milton Bradley
EX $300 NM $550

Charlie McCarthy Game of Topper, 1938, Whitman
EX $20 NM $45

Charlie McCarthy Put and Take Bingo Game, 1938, Whitman
EX $30 NM $45

Charlie McCarthy's Flying Hats, 1938, Whitman
EX $25 NM $40

Chasing Villa, 1920, Smith, Kline & French
EX $65 NM $125

Checkered Game of Life, 1860, Milton Bradley
EX $250 NM $400

Checkered Game of Life, 1866, Milton Bradley
EX $150 NM $300

Checkered Game of Life, 1911, Milton Bradley
EX $75 NM $125

Checkers & Avion, 1925, American Toy Works
EX $30 NM $50

GAMES

Chee Chow, 1939, Gabriel
EX $15 NM $25

Cheerios Bird Hunt, 1930s, General Mills
EX $15 NM $25

Cheerios Hook The Fish, 1930s, General Mills
EX $15 NM $25

Chessindia, 1895, Clark & Sowdon
EX $40 NM $80

Chester Gump Game, 1938, Milton Bradley
EX $65 NM $100

Chester Gump Hops over the Pole, 1930s, Milton Bradley
EX $75 NM $100

Chevy Chase, 1890, Hamilton-Myers
EX $75 NM $125

Chicago Game Series Baseball, 1890s, Doan
EX $1175 NM $1950

China, 1905, Wilkens Thompson
EX $50 NM $85

Chin-Chow and Sum Flu, 1925, Novitas Sales
EX $6 NM $10

Ching Gong, 1937, Gabriel
EX $20 NM $25

Chiromagica, or The Hand of Fate, 1901, McLoughlin Bros.
EX $250 NM $450

Chivalry, 1925, Parker Brothers
EX $75 NM $125

Chocolate Splash, 1916, Willis G. Young
EX $40 NM $60

Christmas Goose, 1890, McLoughlin Bros.
EX $750 NM $1200

Christmas Jewel, Game of the, 1899, McLoughlin Bros.
EX $400 NM $600

Christmas Mail, 1890s, J. Ottmann Lith.
EX $390 NM $550

Chutes And Ladders, 1943, Milton Bradley
EX $10 NM $20

Cinderella, 1923, Stoll & Edwards
EX $40 NM $95

Circus Game, 1914
EX $75 NM $125

Citadel, 1940, Parker Brothers
EX $20 NM $40

Cities, 1932, All-Fair
EX $15 NM $20

City of Gold, 1926, Zulu Toy
EX $150 NM $250

Classic Derby, 1930s, Doremus Schoen
EX $30 NM $50

Clipper Race, 1930, Gabriel
EX $20 NM $50

Clown Tenpins Game, 1912
EX $60 NM $100

Coast to Coast, 1940s, Master Toy
EX $15 NM $25

Cock-A-Doodle-Doo Game, 1914
EX $60 NM $100

Cocked Hat, Game of, 1892, J.H. Singer
EX $75 NM $150

College Baseball Game, 1890s, Parker Brothers
EX $450 NM $800

College Boat Race, Game of, 1896, McLoughlin Bros.
EX $600 NM $900

Colors, Game of, 1888, McLoughlin Bros.
EX $150 NM $225

Columbus, 1892, Milton Bradley
EX $775 NM $1300

Combination Board Games, 1922, Wilder
EX $40 NM $50

Comical Animals Ten Pins, 1910, Parker Brothers
EX $185 NM $310

Coney Island Playland Park, 1940, Vitaplay Toy
EX $54 NM $90

Conflict, 1942, Parker Brothers
EX $30 NM $50

Construction Game, 1925, Wilder
EX $500 NM $1500

Coon Hunt Game, The, 1903, Parker Brothers
EX $450 NM $1000

Corn & Beans, 1875, E.G. Selchow
EX $20 NM $40

Corner The Market, 1938, Whitman
EX $25 NM $40

Cortella, 1915, Atkins
EX $20 NM $30

Cottontail and Peter, The Game of, 1922, Parker Brothers
EX $75 NM $150

Country Club Golf, 1920s, Hustler Toy
EX $75 NM $125

Country Store, The, 1890s, J.H. Singer
EX $100 NM $250

Covered Wagon, 1927, Zulu Toy
EX $55 NM $85

Cowboy Game, The, 1898, Chaffee & Selchow
EX $400 NM $600

Crash, The New Airplane Game, 1928, Nucraft Toys
EX $30 NM $60

Crazy Traveller, 1908, Parker Brothers
EX $20 NM $40

Crime & Mystery, 1940s, Frederick H. Beach (Beachcraft)
EX $15 NM $25

Criss Cross Words, 1938, Alfred Butts
EX $90 NM $150

Crooked Man Game, 1914
EX $45 NM $75

Cross Country, 1941, Lowe
EX $10 NM $15

Cross Country Marathon, 1920s, Milton Bradley
EX $75 NM $125

Cross Country Marathon Game, 1930s, Rosebud Art
EX $100 NM $200

Cross Country Racer, 1940, Automatic Toy
EX $45 NM $75

Cross Country Racer (w/wind-up cars), 1940s
EX $75 NM $130

Crossing the Ocean, 1893, Parker Brothers
EX $75 NM $150

Crow Hunt, 1904, Parker Brothers
EX $30 NM $50

Crusade, 1930s, Gabriel
EX $27 NM $45

Crusaders, Game of the, 1888, McLoughlin Bros.
EX $150 NM $300

Cuckoo, A Society Game, 1891, J.H. Singer
EX $75 NM $125

Curly Locks Game, 1910, United Game
EX $50 NM $75

Cycling, Game of, 1910, Parker Brothers
EX $150 NM $300

Daisy Clown Ring Game, 1927, Schacht Rubber
EX $9 NM $15

Daisy Horseshoe Game, 1927, Schacht Rubber
EX $9 NM $15

Danny McFayden's Stove League Baseball Game, 1920s, National Game
EX $295 NM $490

Darrow Monopoly, 1933, Charles Darrow, white box
EX $4000 NM $7000

Day at the Circus, Game of, 1898, McLoughlin Bros.
EX $300 NM $400

Deck Derby, 1920s, Wolverine
EX $36 NM $60

Decoy, 1940, Selchow & Righter
EX $35 NM $50

Defenders of The Flag Game, 1920s
EX $24 NM $40

Democracy, 1940, Toy Creations
EX $50 NM $75

Department Store, Game of Playing, 1898, McLoughlin Bros.
EX $600 NM $1200

Derby Day, 1930, Parker Brothers
EX $45 NM $60

Derby Steeple Chase, 1888, McLoughlin Bros.
EX $150 NM $300

Detective, The Game of, 1889, Bliss
EX $1000 NM $1600

Dewey's Victory, 1900s, Parker Brothers
EX $120 NM $200

Diamond Game of Baseball, The, 1894, McLoughlin Bros.
EX $1275 NM $2150

Diamond Heart, 1902, McLoughlin Bros.
EX $150 NM $225

Diceball, 1938, Ray-Fair
EX $90 NM $145

Dicex Baseball Game, The, 1925, Chester S. Howland
EX $195 NM $325

Dick Tracy Detective Game, 1933, Einson-Freeman
EX $75 NM $150

Dick Tracy Detective Game, 1937, Whitman
EX $40 NM $100

Discretion, 1942, Volume Sprayer
EX $30 NM $45

District Messenger Boy, Game of, 1886, McLoughlin Bros.
EX $300 NM $500

District Messenger Boy, Game of, 1904, McLoughlin Bros.
EX $80 NM $200

Dog Race, 1937, Transogram
EX $20 NM $30

Dog Show, 1890s, J.H. Singer
EX $125 NM $300

Dog Sweepstakes, 1935, Stoll & Einson
EX $40 NM $60

Donald Duck's Own Party Game, 1938, Parker Brothers
EX $40 NM $80

Double Game Board (Baseball), 1925, Parker Brothers
EX $30 NM $50

Double Header Baseball, 1935, Redlich
EX $145 NM $250

Dreamland Wonder Resort Game, 1914, Parker Brothers
EX $500 NM $800

Drive 'n Putt, 1940s, Carrom Industries
EX $50 NM $90

Drummer Boy Game, The, 1890s, Parker Brothers
EX $250 NM $500

Dubble Up, 1940s, Gabriel
EX $15 NM $25

Dudes, Game of the, 1890, Bliss
EX $225 NM $400

Durgin's New Baseball Game, 1885, Durgin & Palmer
EX $425 NM $700

Eagle Bombsight, 1940s, Toy Creations
EX $75 NM $125

East is East and West is West, 1920s, Parker Brothers
EX $100 NM $175

Easy Money, 1936, Milton Bradley
EX $35 NM $45

Ed Wynn The Fire Chief, 1937, Selchow & Righter
EX $40 NM $60

Eddie Cantor's Tell It To The Judge, 1930s, Parker Brothers
EX $15 NM $30

E-E-YAH Base Ball Game, 1900s, National Games
EX $600 NM $1800

Electric Baseball, 1935, Einson-Freeman
EX $35 NM $60

Electric Football, 1930s, Electric Football
EX $20 NM $30

Electric Magnetic Baseball, 1900
EX $175 NM $295

Electric Questioner, 1920, Knapp Electric & Novelty
EX $15 NM $30

Electric Speed Classic, 1930, Pressman
EX $390 NM $650

Electro Gameset, 1930, Knapp Electric & Novelty
EX $30 NM $45

Elementaire Musical Game, 1896, Theodore Presser
EX $20 NM $35

Ella Cinders, 1944, Milton Bradley
EX $20 NM $40

Elmer Layden's Scientific Football Game, 1936, Cadaco
EX $20 NM $50

Elsie the Cow Game, The, 1941, Selchow & Righter
EX $30 NM $60

Enchanted Forest Game, 1914
EX $120 NM $200

Endurance Run, 1930, Milton Bradley
EX $75 NM $125

Errand Boy, The, 1891, McLoughlin Bros.
EX $150 NM $250

Ethan Allen's All-Star Baseball Game, 1942, Cadaco-Ellis
EX $150 NM $350

Evening Parties, Game of, 1910s, Parker Brothers
EX $180 NM $300

Fairyland Game, 1880s, Milton Bradley
EX $60 NM $95

Fan-i-Tis, 1913, C.W. Marsh
EX $110 NM $180

Fan-Tel, 1937, Schoenhut
EX $20 NM $30

Farmer Jones' Pigs, 1890, McLoughlin Bros.
EX $165 NM $200

Fashionable English Sorry Game, The, 1934, Parker Brothers
EX $20 NM $40

Fast Mail Game, 1910, Milton Bradley
EX $125 NM $175

Fast Mail Railroad Game, 1930s, Milton Bradley
EX $75 NM $125

Favorite Steeple Chase, 1895, J.H. Singer
EX $200 NM $350

GAMES

Ferdinand The Bull Chinese Checkers Game, 1930s
EX $60 NM $100

Fibber McGee, 1936, Milton Bradley
EX $20 NM $30

Fibber McGee and The Wistful Vista Mystery, 1940, Milton Bradley
EX $20 NM $40

Fig Mill, 1916, Willis G. Young
EX $40 NM $60

Finance, 1937, Parker Brothers
EX $25 NM $35

Finance And Fortune, 1936, Parker Brothers
EX $20 NM $35

Fire Alarm Game, 1899, Parker Brothers
EX $1300 NM $2000

Fire Department, 1930s, Milton Bradley
EX $125 NM $250

Fire Fighters Game, 1909, Milton Bradley
EX $120 NM $150

Flag Travelette, 1895, Archarena
EX $45 NM $100

Flapper Fortunes, 1929, Embossing
EX $25 NM $40

Flight To Paris, 1927, Milton Bradley
EX $100 NM $200

Fling-A-Ring, 1930s, Wolverine
EX $20 NM $35

Flip It, 1925, American Toy Works
EX $40 NM $60

Flip It, 1940, Deluxe Game
EX $20 NM $30

Flip It, Auto Race & Transcontinental Tour, 1920s, Deluxe Game
EX $35 NM $90

Flivver, 1927, Milton Bradley
EX $125 NM $200

Flowers, Game of, 1899, Cincinnati Game
EX $10 NM $20

Flying Aces, 1940s, Selchow & Righter
EX $50 NM $100

Flying the Beam, 1941, Parker Brothers
EX $30 NM $60

Flying the United States Airmail, 1929, Parker Brothers
EX $200 NM $400

Fobaga (football), 1942, American Football
EX $50 NM $80

Follow the Stars, 1922, Watts
EX $225 NM $375

Foot Race, The, 1900s, Parker Brothers
EX $50 NM $75

Football, 1930s, Wilder
EX $50 NM $80

Football Game, 1898, Parker Brothers
EX $295 NM $495

Football Knapp Electro Game Set, 1929, Knapp Electric & Novelty
EX $125 NM $205

Football, The Game of, 1895, George A. Childs
EX $75 NM $125

Football-As-You-Like-It, 1940, Wayne W. Light
EX $85 NM $145

Fore Country Club Game of Golf, 1929, Wilder
EX $100 NM $175

Fortune, 1938, Parker Brothers
EX $25 NM $40

Fortune Teller, The, 1905, Milton Bradley
EX $35 NM $65

Fortune Telling & Baseball Game, 1889
EX $85 NM $140

Fortune Telling Game, 1934, Whitman
EX $50 NM $100

Forty-Niners Gold Mining Game, 1930s, National Games
EX $25 NM $40

Foto World, 1935, Cadaco
EX $90 NM $150

Foto-Electric Football, 1930s, Cadaco
EX $35 NM $50

Foto-Finish Horse Race, 1940s, Pressman
EX $30 NM $45

Fox and Geese, 1903, McLoughlin Bros.
EX $75 NM $125

Fox and Hounds, 1900, Parker Brothers
EX $60 NM $100

Fox Hunt, 1905, Milton Bradley
EX $30 NM $40

Fox Hunt, 1930s, Lowe
EX $20 NM $30

Foxy Grandpa Hat Party, 1906, Selchow & Righter
EX $60 NM $85

Frisko, 1937, Embossing
EX $20 NM $30

Frog He Would a Wooing Go, The, 1898, McLoughlin Bros.
EX $1200 NM $1600

Frog School Game, 1914
EX $75 NM $150

Frog Who Would a Wooing Go, The, 1920s, United Game
EX $60 NM $125

Fun at the Circus, 1897, McLoughlin Bros.
EX $400 NM $600

Fun at the Zoo, A Game, 1902, Parker Brothers
EX $150 NM $200

Fun Kit, 1939, Frederick H. Beach (Beachcraft)
EX $15 NM $20

Fut-Ball, 1940s, Fut-Bal
EX $35 NM $60

Game of Baseball, 1886, McLoughlin Bros.
EX $1500 NM $2000

Game of Friendly Fun, 1939, Milton Bradley
EX $50 NM $145

Games You Like To Play, 1920s, Parker Brothers
EX $40 NM $75

Gang Busters Game, 1938, Lynco
EX $150 NM $250

Gang Busters Game, 1939, Whitman
EX $50 NM $100

General Headquarters, 1940s, All-Fair
EX $60 NM $85

Geographical Lotto Game, 1921
EX $20 NM $30

Geography Game, 1910s, A. Flanagan
EX $15 NM $25

Ges It Game, 1936, Knapp Electric & Novelty
EX $20 NM $25

Get The Balls Baseball Game, 1930
EX $20 NM $30

Glydor, 1931, All-Fair
EX $125 NM $225

G-Men Clue Games, 1935, Whitman
EX $60 NM $125

Go Bang, 1898, Milton Bradley
EX $60 NM $100

Go to the Head of the Class, 1938, Milton Bradley
EX $15 NM $20

Going To The Fire Game, 1914, Milton Bradley
EX $90 NM $125

Gold Hunters, The, 1900s, Parker Brothers
EX $85 NM $150

Goldenlocks & The Three Bears, 1890, McLoughlin Bros.
EX $500 NM $800

Golf Tokalon Series, The Game of, 1890s, E.O. Clark
EX $350 NM $600

Golf, A Game of, 1930, Milton Bradley
EX $145 NM $245

Golf, Game of, 1896, McLoughlin Bros.
EX $500 NM $715

Golf, The Game of, 1898, J.H. Singer
EX $400 NM $600

Golf, The Game of, 1905, Clark & Sowdon
EX $325 NM $550

Gonfalon Scientific Baseball, 1930, Pioneer Game
EX $110 NM $180

Good Old Aunt, The, 1892, McLoughlin Bros.
EX $75 NM $150

Good Old Game of Innocence Abroad, The, 1888, Parker Brothers
EX $125 NM $225

Good Things To Eat Lotto, 1940s, Gabriel
EX $15 NM $25

Goose Goslin Scientific Baseball, 1935, Wheeler Toy
EX $600 NM $1000

Goose, The Jolly Game of, 1851, J.P. Beach
EX $750 NM $1000

Goosey Gander, Or Who Finds the Golden Egg, Game of, 1890, J.H. Singer
EX $675 NM $900

Goosy Goosy Gander, 1896, McLoughlin Bros.
EX $300 NM $500

Graham McNamee World Series Scoreboard Baseball Game, 1930, Radio Sports
EX $225 NM $400

Grand National Sweepstakes, 1937, Whitman
EX $20 NM $50

Grande Auto Race, 1920s, Atkins
EX $50 NM $75

Graphic Baseball, 1930s, Northwestern Products
EX $165 NM $275

Great American Baseball Game, The, 1906, William Dapping
EX $145 NM $250

Great American Flag Game, The, 1940, Parker Brothers
EX $40 NM $60

Great American Game, 1910, Neddy Pocket Game
EX $145 NM $250

Great American Game of Baseball, The, 1907, Pittsburgh Brewing
EX $145 NM $250

Great American Game, Baseball, The, 1923, Hustler Toy
EX $150 NM $225

Great American Game, The, 1925, Frantz
EX $110 NM $225

Great American War Game, 1899, J.H. Hunter
EX $600 NM $1000

Great Family Amusement Game, The, 1889, Einson-Freeman
EX $20 NM $35

Great Horse Race Game, The, 1925, Selchow & Righter
EX $70 NM $115

Gregg Football Game, 1924, Albert A. Gregg
EX $175 NM $285

Greyhound Racing Game, 1938, Rex Manufacturing
EX $15 NM $25

Gumps at the Seashore, The, 1930s, Milton Bradley
EX $75 NM $123

Gym Horseshoes, 1930, Wolverine
EX $30 NM $45

Gypsy Fortune Telling Game, The, 1895, Milton Bradley
EX $50 NM $125

Halma, 1885, Horsman
EX $20 NM $30

Halma, 1885, Milton Bradley
EX $20 NM $30

Hand of Fate, 1901, McLoughlin Bros.
EX $1000 NM $2000

Happy Family, The, 1910, Milton Bradley
EX $15 NM $25

Happy Hooligan Bowling Type Game, 1925, Milton Bradley
EX $150 NM $275

Hardwood Ten Pins Wooden Game, 1889
EX $60 NM $100

Hare & Hound, 1895, Parker Brothers
EX $150 NM $300

Hare and Hounds, 1890, McLoughlin Bros.
EX $200 NM $325

Harlequin, The Game of The, 1895, McLoughlin Bros.
EX $150 NM $300

Harold Teen Game, 1930s, Milton Bradley
EX $75 NM $100

Heedless Tommy, 1893, McLoughlin Bros.
EX $350 NM $700

Hel-Lo Telephone Game, 1898, J.H. Singer
EX $200 NM $400

Helps to History, 1885, A. Flanagan
EX $20 NM $35

Hen that Laid the Golden Egg, The, 1900, Parker Brothers
EX $105 NM $175

Hendrik Van Loon's Wide World Game, 1935, Parker Brothers
EX $30 NM $40

Hening's In-Door Game of Professional Baseball, 1889, Inventor's
EX $525 NM $875

Heroes of America, 1920, Educational Card & Game
EX $20 NM $35

Hialeah Horse Racing Game, 1940s, Milton Bradley
EX $20 NM $35

Hickety Pickety, 1924, Parker Brothers
EX $20 NM $30

Hide and Seek, Game of, 1895, McLoughlin Bros.
EX $1200 NM $1700

Hippodrome Circus Game, 1895, Milton Bradley
EX $175 NM $250

Hippodrome, The, 1900s, E.O. Clark
EX $150 NM $200

EXHit and Run Baseball Game, 1930s, Wilder
EX $150 NM $350

Hit That Line, 1930s, LaRue Sales
EX $100 NM $165

Hi-Way Henry, 1928, All-Fair
EX $600 NM $1000

Hockey, Official, 1940, Toy Creations
EX $40 NM $75

Hold The Fort, 1895, Parker Brothers
EX $150 NM $250

Hold Your Horses, 1930s, Klauber Novelty
EX $10 NM $20

Home Baseball Game, 1897, McLoughlin Bros.
EX $900 NM $1700

Home Defenders, 1941, Saalfield
EX $15 NM $25

Home Diamond, The Great Baseball Game, 1925, Phillips
EX $175 NM $250

Home Games, 1900s, Martin
EX $105 NM $175

Home Run King, 1930s, Selrite
EX $275 NM $450

Home Run with Bases Loaded, 1935, T.V. Morrison
EX $205 NM $350

Honey Bee Game, 1913, Milton Bradley
EX $50 NM $90

Hood's Spelling School, 1897, C.I. Hood
EX $20 NM $35

Hoop-O-Loop, 1930, Wolverine
EX $20 NM $30

Hornet, 1941, Lowe
EX $30 NM $45

Horse Race, 1943, Lowe
EX $10 NM $20

Horse Racing, 1935, Milton Bradley
EX $35 NM $50

Horses, 1927, Modern Makers
EX $45 NM $75

Hounds & Hares, 1894, J.W. Keller
EX $35 NM $60

How Good Are You?, 1937, Whitman
EX $10 NM $15

Howard H. Jones Collegiate Football, 1932, Municipal Service
EX $65 NM $100

Huddle All-American Football Game, 1931
EX $100 NM $165

Hunting Hare, Game of, 1891, McLoughlin Bros.
EX $205 NM $350

Hunting the Rabbit, 1895, Clark & Sowdon
EX $70 NM $115

Hunting, The New Game of, 1904, McLoughlin Bros.
EX $500 NM $800

Hurdle Race, 1905, Milton Bradley
EX $100 NM $175

Hymn Quartets, 1933, Goodenough and Woglom
EX $10 NM $15

Ice Hockey, 1942, Milton Bradley
EX $60 NM $85

Improved Geographical Game, The, 1890s, Parker Brothers
EX $20 NM $45

In and Out the Window, 1940s, Gabriel
EX $20 NM $35

India, 1940, Parker Brothers
EX $15 NM $20

India Bombay, 1910s, Cutler & Saleeby
EX $15 NM $25

India, An Oriental Game, 1890s, McLoughlin Bros.
EX $65 NM $100

India, Game of, 1910s, Milton Bradley
EX $15 NM $40

Indianapolis 500 Mile Race Game, 1938, Shaw
EX $350 NM $575

Indians and Cowboys, 1940s, Gabriel
EX $40 NM $50

In-Door Baseball, 1926, E. Bommer Foundation
EX $100 NM $180

Indoor Football, 1919, Underwood
EX $145 NM $250

Indoor Horse Racing, 1924, Man-O-War
EX $70 NM $115

Inside Baseball Game, 1911, Popular Games
EX $300 NM $500

Intercollegiate Football, 1923, Hustler Toy
EX $175 NM $245

International Automobile Race, 1903, Parker Brothers
EX $600 NM $900

International Spy, Game of, 1943, All-Fair
EX $40 NM $60

Jack and Jill, 1890s, Parker Brothers
EX $55 NM $125

Jack and Jill, 1909, Milton Bradley
EX $50 NM $75

Jack and the Bean Stalk, 1895, Parker Brothers
EX $110 NM $175

Jack and the Bean Stalk, The Game of, 1898, McLoughlin Bros.
EX $500 NM $800

Jack Spratt Game, 1914
EX $45 NM $75

Jack-Be-Nimble, 1940s, Embossing
EX $20 NM $35

Jackie Robinson Baseball Game, 1940s, Gotham
EX $425 NM $900

Jackpot, 1943, B.L. Fry Products
EX $15 NM $25

Japan, The Game of, 1903, J. Ottmann Lith.
EX $180 NM $300

Japanese Games of Cash and Akambo, 1881, McLoughlin Bros.
EX $150 NM $250

Jeep Board, The, 1944, Lowe
EX $10 NM $15

Jeffries Championship Playing Cards, 1904
EX $35 NM $55

Jig Chase, 1930s, Game Makers
EX $10 NM $25

Jig Race, 1930s, Game Makers
EX $20 NM $25

Jockey, 1920s, Carrom Industries
EX $35 NM $60

John Gilpin, Rainbow Backgammon and Bewildered Travelers, 1875, McLoughlin Bros.
EX $150 NM $200

Johnny Get Your Gun, 1928, Parker Brothers
EX $60 NM $90

Jolly Pirates, 1938, Russell
EX $20 NM $35

Journey to Bethlehem, The, 1923, Parker Brothers
EX $95 NM $160

Jumpy Tinker, 1920s, Tinker Toys
EX $20 NM $30

Jungle Hunt, 1940s, Rosebud Art
EX $30 NM $50

Junior Baseball Game, 1915, Benjamin Seller
EX $100 NM $165

Junior Basketball Game, 1930s, Rosebud Art
EX $55 NM $125

Junior Bicycle Game, The, 1897, Parker Brothers
EX $200 NM $300

Junior Combination Board, 1905, McLoughlin Bros.
EX $15 NM $25

Junior Football, 1944, Deluxe Game
EX $30 NM $45

Junior Motor Race, 1925, Wolverine
EX $40 NM $70

Kan-Oo-Win-It, 1893, McLoughlin Bros.
EX $345 NM $575

Kate Smith's Own Game America, 1940s, Toy Creations
EX $30 NM $50

Keeping Up with the Jones', 1921, Parker Brothers
EX $50 NM $85

Keeping Up with the Jones', The Game of, 1921, Phillips
EX $75 NM $100

Kellogg's Baseball Game, 1936, Kellogg's
EX $25 NM $35

Kellogg's Boxing Game, 1936, Kellogg's
EX $35 NM $55

Kellogg's Football Game, 1936, Kellogg's
EX $25 NM $40

Kellogg's Golf Game, 1936, Kellogg's
EX $25 NM $40

Kentucky Derby Racing Game, 1938, Whitman
EX $20 NM $40

Kilkenny Cats, The Amusing Game of, 1890, Parker Brothers
EX $250 NM $650

Kings, 1931, Akro Agate
EX $55 NM $95

King's Quoits, New Game of, 1893, McLoughlin Bros.
EX $300 NM $450

Kitty Kat Cup Ball, 1930s, Rosebud Art
EX $50 NM $75

Klondike Game, 1890s, Parker Brothers
EX $400 NM $725

Knockout, 1937, Scarne Games, Electronic Boxing Game
EX $40 NM $75

Knute Rockne Football Game, Official, 1930, Radio Sports
EX $200 NM $400

Ko-Ko the Clown, 1940, All-Fair
EX $10 NM $20

Kriegspiel Junior, 1915, Parker Brothers
EX $50 NM $80

La Haza, 1923, Supply Sales
EX $10 NM $20

Lame Duck, The, 1928, Parker Brothers
EX $60 NM $100

Land and Sea War Games, 1941, Lowe
EX $40 NM $65

Lasso the Jumping Ring, 1912
EX $60 NM $100

Le Choc, 1919, Milton Bradley
EX $50 NM $85

League Parlor Base Ball, 1889, Bliss
EX $600 NM $1000

Leap Frog Game, 1900, McLoughlin Bros.
EX $150 NM $200

Leap Frog, Game of, 1910, McLoughlin Bros.
EX $100 NM $150

Lee at Havana, 1899, Chaffee & Selchow
EX $100 NM $200

Leslie's Baseball Game, 1909, Perfection Novelty
EX $145 NM $250

Let's go to College, 1944, Einson-Freeman
EX $30 NM $45

Let's Play Games, Golf, 1939, American Toy Works
EX $50 NM $80

Let's Play Polo, 1940, American Toy Works
EX $45 NM $75

Letter Carrier, The, 1890, McLoughlin Bros.
EX $150 NM $300

Letters, 1878, Horsman
EX $20 NM $35

Letters or Anagrams, 1890s, Parker Brothers
EX $15 NM $30

Lew Fonseca Baseball Game, The, 1920s, Carrom Industries
EX $525 NM $875

Library of Games, 1938, American Toy Works
EX $15 NM $20

Life in the Wild West, 1894, Bliss
EX $300 NM $500

Life of the Party, 1940s, Rosebud Art
EX $15 NM $30

Life's Mishaps & Bobbing 'Round the Circle, 1891, McLoughlin Bros.
EX $150 NM $200

Light Horse H. Cooper Golf Game, 1943, Trojan Games
EX $175 NM $295

Limited Mail & Express Game, The, 1894, Parker Brothers
EX $150 NM $225

Lindy Hop-Off, 1927, Parker Brothers
EX $250 NM $350

Literature Game, 1897, L.J. Colby
EX $15 NM $25

Little Black Sambo, Game of, 1934, Einson-Freeman
EX $75 NM $125

Little Bo-Beep Game, 1914
EX $60 NM $100

Little Boy Blue, 1910s, Milton Bradley
EX $50 NM $85

Little Colonel, 1936, Selchow & Righter
EX $50 NM $90

Little Cowboy Game, The, 1895, Parker Brothers
EX $200 NM $600

Little Fireman Game, 1897, McLoughlin Bros.
EX $3000 NM $5000

Little Jack Horner Golf Course, 1920s
EX $145 NM $250

Little Jack Horner, A Game, 1910s, Milton Bradley
EX $45 NM $75

Little Nemo Game, 1914
EX $500 NM $1000

Little Orphan Annie Game, 1927, Milton Bradley
EX $125 NM $200

Little Red Riding Hood, 1900, McLoughlin Bros.
EX $300 NM $500

Little Shoppers, 1915, Gibson Game
EX $125 NM $250

Little Soldier, The, 1900s, United Game
EX $75 NM $125

London Bridge, 1899, J.H. Singer
EX $100 NM $150

London Game, The, 1898, Parker Brothers
EX $165 NM $275

Lone Ranger Game, The, 1938, Parker Brothers
EX $40 NM $60

Looping the Loop, 1940s, Advance Games
EX $25 NM $40

Los Angeles Rams Football Game, 1930s, Zondine
EX $175 NM $295

Lost Diamond, Game of, 1896, McLoughlin
EX $200 NM $250

Lost in the Woods, 1895, McLoughlin Bros.
EX $660 NM $850

Lotto, 1932, Milton Bradley
EX $6 NM $15

Lou Gehrig's Official Playball, 1930s, Christy Walsh
EX $525 NM $875

Lowell Thomas' World Cruise, 1937, Parker Brothers
EX $75 NM $175

Luck, The Game of, 1892, Parker Brothers
EX $60 NM $100

Lucky 7th Baseball Game, 1937, All-American
EX $100 NM $250

Mac Baseball Game, 1930s, Mc Dowell
EX $145 NM $250

Macy's Pirate Treasure Hunt, 1942, Einson-Freeman
EX $20 NM $35

Madrap, The New Game of, 1914
EX $45 NM $75

Magic Race, 1942, Habob
EX $55 NM $90

Magnetic Jack Straws, 1891, Horsman
EX $20 NM $30

Magnetic Treasure Hunt, 1930s, American Toy Works
EX $15 NM $25

Mail, Express or Accommodation, Game of, 1895, McLoughlin Bros.
EX $700 NM $1100

Mail, Express or Accommodation, Game of, 1920s, Milton Bradley
EX $100 NM $175

Major League Ball, 1921, National Game Makers
EX $325 NM $550

Major League Base Ball Game, 1912, Philadelphia Game, w/photo
EX $650 NM $1000

Man Hunt, 1937, Parker Brothers
EX $200 NM $350

Man in the Moon, 1901, McLoughlin Bros.
EX $2000 NM $3500

Mansion of Happiness, 1843, Ives
EX $200 NM $300

Mansion of Happiness, 1864, Ives
EX $75 NM $150

Mansion of Happiness, The, 1895, McLoughlin Bros.
EX $400 NM $600

Marathon Game, The, 1930s, Rosebud Art
EX $85 NM $125

Marriage, The Game of, 1899, J.H. Singer
EX $200 NM $300

Match 'em, 1926, All-Fair
EX $10 NM $15

Mathers Parlor Baseball Game, 1909, McClurg
EX $50 NM $100

Meet the Missus, 1937, Fitzpatrick Brothers
EX $45 NM $75

Mental Whoopee, 1936, Simon & Schuster
EX $10 NM $15

Merry Hunt, The, Singer
EX $250 NM $400

Merry Steeple Chase, 1890s, J. Ottmann Lith.
EX $45 NM $100

Merry-Go-Round, 1898, Chaffee & Selchow
EX $1400 NM $1800

Messenger Boy Game, 1910, J.H. Singer
EX $100 NM $200

Messenger, The, 1890, McLoughlin Bros.
EX $175 NM $300

Mexican Pete - I Got It, 1940s, Parker Brothers
EX $25 NM $40

Mickey Mouse Baseball, 1936, Post Cereal
EX $55 NM $90

Mickey Mouse Big Box of Games & Things To Color, 1930s
EX $45 NM $75

Mickey Mouse Circus Game, 1930s, Marks Brothers
EX $180 NM $300

Mickey Mouse Coming Home Game, 1930s, Marks Brothers
EX $125 NM $200

Mickey Mouse Roll'em Game, 1930s, Marks Brothers
EX $90 NM $150

Midget Auto Race, 1930s, Cracker Jack
EX $10 NM $15

Midget Speedway, Game of, 1942, Whitman
EX $55 NM $90

Miles at Porto Rico, 1899, Chaffee & Selchow
EX $150 NM $250

Miniature Golf, 1930s, Miniature Golf
EX $35 NM $60

Miss Muffet Game, 1914
EX $60 NM $100

Mistress Mary, Quite Contrary, 1905, Parker Brothers
EX $60 NM $105

Modern Game Assortment, 1930s, Pressman
EX $25 NM $40

Moneta: "Money Makes Money," Game of, 1889, F.A. Wright
EX $90 NM $150

Monkey Shines, 1940, All-Fair
EX $10 NM $20

Monopolist, Mariner's Compass And Ten Up, 1878, McLoughlin Bros.
EX $200 NM $400

Monopoly, 1935, Parker Brothers
EX $35 NM $75

Monopoly Jr. Edition, 1936, Parker Brothers
EX $20 NM $30

Moon Mullins Automobile Race, 1927, Milton Bradley
EX $125 NM $175

Mother Goose Bowling Game, 1884, Charles M. Crandall
EX $510 NM $850

Mother Goose, Game of, 1921, Stoll & Edwards
EX $30 NM $50

Mother Hubbard Game, 1914
EX $50 NM $80

Motor Boat Race, An Exciting, 1930, American Toy Works
EX $150 NM $300

Motor Cycle Game, 1905, Milton Bradley
EX $350 NM $600

Motor Race, 1922, Wolverine
EX $90 NM $150

Movie Inn, 1917, Willis G. Young
EX $45 NM $75

Movie Millions, 1938, Transogram
EX $100 NM $175

Movie-Land Lotto, 1920s, Milton Bradley
EX $45 NM $75

GAMES

Moving Picture Game, The, 1920s, Milton Bradley
EX $70 NM $100

Mr. Ree, 1937, Selchow & Righter
EX $40 NM $85

Mutuels, 1938, Mutuels
EX $85 NM $150

My Word, Horse Race, 1938, American Toy Works
EX $60 NM $100

Mythology, Game of, 1884, Peter G. Thompson
EX $40 NM $60

Napoleon, Game of, 1895, Parker Brothers
EX $400 NM $600

National Derby Horse Race, 1938, Whitman
EX $20 NM $35

National Game of Baseball, The, 1900s
EX $500 NM $875

National Game of the American Eagle, The, 1844, Ives
EX $1500 NM $1800

National Game, The, 1889, National Game
EX $875 NM $1450

National League Ball Game, 1890, Yankee Novelty
EX $350 NM $575

Naval Maneuvers, 1920, McLoughlin Bros.
EX $700 NM $900

Navigator, 1938, Whitman
EX $45 NM $75

Navigator Boat Race, 1890s, McLoughlin Bros.
EX $115 NM $195

Nebbs on the Air, A Radio Game, 1930s, Milton Bradley
EX $75 NM $125

Nebbs, Game of the, 1930s, Milton Bradley
EX $40 NM $75

Neck and Neck, 1929, Embossing
EX $25 NM $40

Neck and Neck, 1930, Wolverine
EX $60 NM $90

Nellie Bly, 1898, J.H. Singer
EX $200 NM $300

New Baseball Game, 1885, Clark & Martin
EX $165 NM $275

New Parlor Game of Baseball, 1896, Sumner
EX $5000 NM $10000

New York Recorder Newspaper Supplement Baseball Game, 1896
EX $430 NM $715

Newsboy, Game of the, 1890, Bliss
EX $1200 NM $2000

NFL Strategy, 1935, Tudor
EX $45 NM $70

Nine Men Morris, 1930s, Milton Bradley
EX $10 NM $15

Ninteenth Hole Golf Game, 1930s, Einson-Freeman
EX $85 NM $140

Nip & Tuck Hockey, 1928, Parker Brothers
EX $115 NM $195

No-Joke, 1941, Volume Sprayer
EX $12 NM $20

Nok-Out Baseball Game, 1930, Dizzy & Daffy Dean
EX $350 NM $575

North Pole Game, The, 1907, Milton Bradley
EX $200 NM $400

Object Lotto, 1940s, Gabriel
EX $15 NM $25

Obstacle Race, 1930s, Wilder
EX $70 NM $115

Ocean to Ocean Flight Game, 1927, Wilder
EX $30 NM $50

Office Boy, The, 1889, Parker Brothers
EX $200 NM $300

Official Radio Baseball Game, 1930s, Toy Creations
EX $35 NM $60

Official Radio Basketball Game, 1939, Toy Creations
EX $25 NM $50

Official Radio Football Game, 1940, Toy Creations
EX $25 NM $50

Old Hunter & His Game, 1870
EX $175 NM $295

Old Maid, 1898, Chaffee & Selchow
EX $50 NM $90

Old Maid & Old Bachelor, The Merry Game of, 1898, McLoughlin Bros.
EX $300 NM $500

Old Maid or Matrimony, Game of, 1890, McLoughlin Bros.
EX $300 NM $500

Old Mother Goose, 1898, Chaffee & Selchow
EX $105 NM $175

Old Mother Hubbard, Game of, 1890s, Milton Bradley
EX $40 NM $60

Old Mrs. Goose, Game of, 1910, Milton Bradley
EX $50 NM $85

Oldtimers, 1940, Frederick H. Beach (Beachcraft)
EX $15 NM $20

Ollo, 1944, Games Of Fame
EX $15 NM $25

Olympic Runners, 1930, Wolverine
EX $125 NM $150

On the Mid-Way, 1925, Milton Bradley
EX $70 NM $125

One Two Button Your Shoe, 1940s, Master Toy
EX $15 NM $25

Open Championship Golf Game, 1930s, Beacon Hudson
EX $45 NM $75

Opportunity Hour, 1940, American Toy Works
EX $20 NM $35

Ot-O-Win Football, 1920s, Ot-O-Win Toys & Games, W. Planchette
EX $55 NM $90

Ouija, plywood, 1920, William Fuld
EX $60 NM $175

Our Defenders, 1944, Master Toy
EX $20 NM $30

Our National Ball Game, 1887, McGill & DeLany
EX $500 NM $750

Our No. 7 Baseball Game Puzzle, 1910, Satisfactory
EX $110 NM $180

Our Union, 1896, Fireside Game
EX $25 NM $40

Outboard Motor Race, The, 1930s, Milton Bradley
EX $75 NM $100

Overland Limited, The, 1920s, Milton Bradley
EX $100 NM $150

Owl and the Pussy Cat, The, 1900s, E.O. Clark
EX $210 NM $350

Pana Kanal, The Great Panama Canal Game, 1913, Chaffee & Selchow
EX $65 NM $110

Panama Canal Game, 1910, Parker Brothers
EX $200 NM $400

Pan-Cake Tiddly Winks, 1920s, Russell
EX $55 NM $90

Par Golf Card Game, 1920, National Golf Services
EX $115 NM $195

Par, The New Golf Game, 1926, Russell
EX $115 NM $195

Parcheesi, 1880s, H.B. Chaffee
EX $50 NM $75

Parker Brothers Post Office Game, 1910s, Parker Brothers
EX $105 NM $175

Parlor Base Ball, Game of, 1892, McLoughlin
EX $1400 NM $2200

Parlor Baseball Game, 1908, Mathers
EX $200 NM $325

Parlor Croquet, 1940, Pressman
EX $10 NM $20

Parlor Football Game, 1890s, McLoughlin Bros.
EX $700 NM $1500

Parlor Golf, 1897, Chaffee & Selchow
EX $55 NM $90

Pat Moran's Own Baseball Game, 1919, Smith, Kline & French
EX $325 NM $400

Patent Parlor Bowling Alley, 1899, Thomas Kochka
EX $70 NM $115

Pedestrianism, 1879
EX $350 NM $700

Peg at my Heart, 1914, Willis G. Young
EX $20 NM $45

Peg Baseball, 1915, Parker Brothers
EX $75 NM $125

Peg Baseball, 1924, Parker Brothers
EX $30 NM $50

Peggy, 1923, Parker Brothers
EX $35 NM $55

Peg'ity, 1925, Parker Brothers
EX $10 NM $25

Pegpin, Game of, 1929, Stoll & Edwards
EX $25 NM $45

Pe-Ling, 1923, Cookson & Sullivan
EX $25 NM $45

Pennant Puzzle, 1909, L.W. Hardy
EX $250 NM $400

Pennant Winner, 1930s, Wolverine
EX $175 NM $225

Penny Post, 1892, Parker Brothers
EX $150 NM $350

Peter Pan, 1927, Selchow & Righter
EX $75 NM $125

Peter Peter Pumpkin Eater, 1914, Parker Brothers
EX $60 NM $80

Peter Rabbit Game, 1910, Milton Bradley
EX $55 NM $95

Peter Rabbit Game, 1940s, Gabriel
EX $45 NM $75

Philadelphia Inquirer Baseball Game, The, 1896
EX $145 NM $250

Philo Vance, 1937, Parker Brothers
EX $75 NM $125

Phoebe Snow, Game of, 1899, McLoughlin Bros.
EX $125 NM $275

Piggies, The New Game, 1894, Selchow & Righter
EX $330 NM $550

Pigskin, 1940, Parker Brothers
EX $20 NM $40

Pigskin, Tom Hamilton's Football Game, 1934, Parker Brothers
EX $20 NM $40

Pilgrim's Progress, Going To Sunday School, Tower of Babel, 1875, McLoughlin Bros.
EX $100 NM $200

Pinafore, 1879, Fuller Upham
EX $45 NM $125

Pinch Hitter, 1930s
EX $110 NM $180

Pines, The, 1896, Fireside Game
EX $15 NM $25

Pinocchio Pitfalls Marble Game, 1940
EX $30 NM $50

Pinocchio Ring The Nose Game, 1940
EX $20 NM $30

Pioneers of the Santa Fe Trail, 1935, Einson-Freeman
EX $25 NM $40

Pirate & Traveller, 1936, Milton Bradley
EX $15 NM $35

Pirate Ship, 1940, Lowe
EX $15 NM $25

Pla-Golf Board Game, 1938, Pla-Golf
EX $775 NM $1300

Play Ball, 1920, National Game
EX $145 NM $250

Play Football, 1934, Whitman
EX $55 NM $90

Play Hockey Fun with Popeye & Wimpy, 1935, Barnum
EX $205 NM $350

Pocket Baseball, 1940, Toy Creations
EX $15 NM $25

Pocket Edition Major League Baseball Game, 1943, Anderson
EX $85 NM $140

Pocket Football, 1940, Toy Creations
EX $25 NM $40

Polar Ball Baseball, 1940, Bowline Game
EX $90 NM $145

Pool, Game of, 1898
EX $700 NM $1175

Posting, A Merry Game of, 1890s, J.H. Singer
EX $180 NM $300

Pro Baseball, 1940
EX $70 NM $115

Professional Game of Base Ball, 1896, Parker Bros.
EX $500 NM $1500

Psychic Baseball Game, 1935, Parker Brothers
EX $75 NM $150

Quarterback, 1914, Littlefield
EX $100 NM $165

Rabbit Hunt, Game of, 1870, McLoughlin Bros.
EX $150 NM $250

Race for the Cup, 1910s, Milton Bradley
EX $225 NM $350

Race, The Game of the, 1860s
EX $425 NM $715

Races, The Game of the, 1844, William Crosby
EX $850 NM $1400

Racing Stable, Game of, 1936, D & H Games
EX $115 NM $195

Radio Game, 1926, Milton Bradley
EX $50 NM $90

Raggedy Ann's Magic Pebble Game, 1941, Milton Bradley
EX $30 NM $70

Rainy Day Golf, 1920, Selchow & Righter
EX $75 NM $100

Rambles, 1881, American
EX $100 NM $200

Razz-O-Dazz-O Six Man Football, 1938, Gruhn & Melton
EX $60 NM $100

Realistic Baseball, 1925, Realistic Game & Toy
EX $205 NM $350

Realistic Golf, 1898, Parker Brothers
EX $875 NM $1450

Red Riding Hood, Game of, 1898, Chaffee & Selchow
EX $200 NM $350

Red Ryder Target Game, 1939, Whitman
EX $100 NM $150

Rex and the Kilkenny Cats Game, 1892, Parker Brothers
EX $100 NM $200

Ring-A-Peg, 1885, Horsman
EX $25 NM $45

Rip Van Winkle, 1890s, Clark & Sowdon
EX $175 NM $225

Rival Policemen, 1896, McLoughlin Bros.
EX $1500 NM $2500

Road Race, Air Race (Two-game set), 1928, Wilder
EX $75 NM $125

Robinson Crusoe, Game of, 1909, Milton Bradley
EX $30 NM $75

Roll-O Football, 1923, Supply Sales
EX $35 NM $60

Roll-O Golf, 1923, Supply Sales
EX $35 NM $60

Roll-O Junior Baseball Game, 1922, Roll-O
EX $325 NM $550

Roll-O-Motor Speedway, 1922, Supply Sales
EX $65 NM $110

Roly Poly Game, 1910
EX $30 NM $50

Rose Bowl Championship Football Game, 1940s, Lowe
EX $40 NM $80

Rough Riders, The Game of, 1898, Clark & Sowdon
EX $225 NM $350

Roulette Baseball Game, 1929, W. Barthonomae
EX $115 NM $195

Round the World Game, 1914, Milton Bradley
EX $75 NM $125

Round the World with Nellie Bly, 1890, McLoughlin Bros.
EX $210 NM $300

Royal Game of Kings and Queens, 1892, McLoughlin Bros.
EX $375 NM $500

Rube Bressler's Baseball Game, 1936, Bressler
EX $130 NM $215

Rube Walker & Harry Davis Baseball Game, 1905
EX $875 NM $1450

Rummy Football, 1944, Milton Bradley
EX $35 NM $60

Runaway Sheep, 1892, Bliss
EX $165 NM $275

Saratoga Horse Racing Game, 1920, Milton Bradley
EX $20 NM $45

Saratoga Steeple Chase, 1900, J.H. Singer
EX $250 NM $350

Scout, The, 1900s, E.O. Clark
EX $105 NM $175

Scouting, Game of, 1930s, Milton Bradley
EX $200 NM $250

Scrambles, 1941, Frederick H. Beach (Beachcraft)
EX $15 NM $20

Shadow Game, The, 1940s, Toy Creations
EX $1000 NM $1500

Shopping, Game of, 1891, Bliss
EX $1500 NM $2000

Shufflebug, Game of, 1921
EX $20 NM $30

Siege of Havana, The, 1898, Parker Brothers
EX $180 NM $250

Sippa Fish, 1936, Frederick H. Beach (Beachcraft)
EX $5 NM $10

Skating Race Game, The, 1900, Chaffee & Selchow
EX $600 NM $800

Skeezix and the Air Mail, 1930s, Milton Bradley
EX $50 NM $75

Skeezix Visits Nina, 1930s, Milton Bradley
EX $65 NM $125

Ski-Hi New York to Paris, 1927, Cutler & Saleeby
EX $50 NM $80

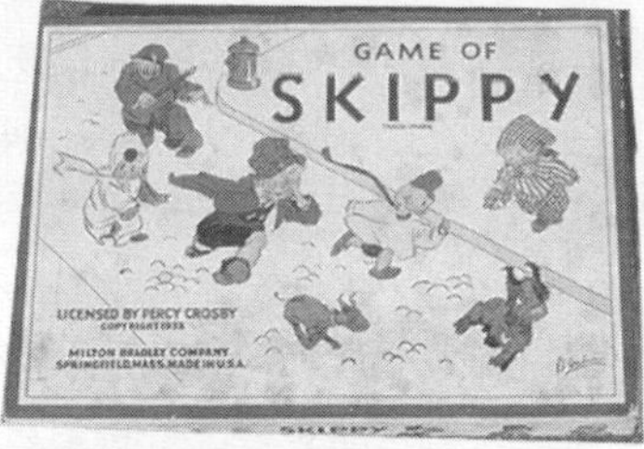

Skippy, Game of, 1932, Milton Bradley
EX $75 NM $100

Skirmish at Harper's Ferry, 1891, McLoughlin Bros.
EX $450 NM $1200

Skor-It Bagatelle, 1930s, Northwestern Products
EX $145 NM $250

Sky Hawks, 1931, All-Fair
EX $120 NM $200

Skyscraper, 1937, Parker Brothers
EX $250 NM $500

Slide Kelly! Baseball Game, 1936, B.E. Ruth
EX $70 NM $115

Slugger Baseball Game, 1930, Marks Brothers
EX $110 NM $180

Smitty Game, 1930s, Milton Bradley
EX $200 NM $300

Smitty Speed Boat Race Game, 1930s, Milton Bradley
EX $50 NM $100

Snake Game, 1890s, McLoughlin Bros.
EX $1500 NM $2500

Snap Dragon, 1903, H.B. Chaffee
EX $135 NM $225

Sniff, 1940s, The Embossing Co.
EX $20 NM $30

Snow White and the Seven Dwarfs, 1938, Parker Brothers
EX $150 NM $300

Snow White and the Seven Dwarfs, 1938, Milton Bradley
EX $75 NM $150

Snug Harbor, 1930s, Milton Bradley
EX $50 NM $85

Socko the Monk, The Game of, 1935, Einson-Freeman
EX $15 NM $25

Soldier Boy Game, 1914, United Game
EX $80 NM $150

Soldier's Cavalry, McLouglin Bros.
EX $150 NM $300

Soldiers on Guard
EX $300 NM $500

Speculation, 1885, Parker Brothers
EX $40 NM $65

Speed Boat, 1920s, Parker Brothers
EX $75 NM $150

Speed Boat Race, 1926, Wolverine
EX $70 NM $115

Speed King, Game Of, 1922, Russell
EX $100 NM $125

Speedem Junior Auto Race Game, 1929, All-Fair
EX $70 NM $125

Speedway Motor Race, 1920s, Smith, Kline & French
EX $145 NM $250

Spider's Web, Game of, 1898, McLoughlin Bros.
EX $75 NM $125

Squails, 1870s, Adams
EX $100 NM $150

Squails, 1877, Milton Bradley
EX $50 NM $75

Stanley in Africa, 1891, Bliss
EX $1500 NM $3000

Star Basketball, 1926, Star Paper Products
EX $125 NM $205

Star Ride, 1934, Einson-Freeman
EX $200 NM $250

Stars on Stripes Football Game, 1941, Stars & Stripes Games
EX $45 NM $55

Steeple Chase, 1890, J.H. Singer
EX $200 NM $300

Steeple Chase & Checkers, 1910, Milton Bradley
EX $50 NM $75

Steeple Chase, Game of, 1900s, E.O. Clark
EX $100 NM $200

Steeple Chase, Game of, 1910s, Milton Bradley
EX $40 NM $65

Steeple Chase, Improved Game of, 1890s, McLoughlin Bros.
EX $195 NM $325

Steps to Health Coke Game, 1938, CDN
EX $40 NM $70

Sto-Auto Race, 1920s, Stough
EX $65 NM $110

Stock Exchange, 1936, Parker Brothers, Monopoly add on
EX $100 NM $200

Stock Exchange, The Game of, 1940s, Stox
EX $40 NM $65

Stop & Go, 1936, Einson-Freeman
EX $25 NM $50

Stop and Go, 1928, All-Fair
EX $75 NM $100

Stop and Shop, 1930, All-Fair
EX $65 NM $80

Stop, Look, and Listen, Game of, 1926, Milton Bradley
EX $40 NM $75

Sto-Quoit, 1920s, Stough
EX $10 NM $15

Strat: The Great War Game, 1915, Strat Game
EX $25 NM $45

Strategy, Game of, 1891, McLoughlin Bros.
EX $240 NM $400

Strategy, Game of Armies, 1938, Corey Games
EX $55 NM $80

Stratosphere, 1930s, Parker Brothers
EX $75 NM $100

Stratosphere, 1936, Whitman
EX $100 NM $150

Street Car Game, The, 1890s, Parker Brothers
EX $175 NM $225

Strike Out, 1920s, All-Fair
EX $175 NM $295

Strike-Like, 1940s, Saxon Toy
EX $55 NM $90

Stubborn Pig, Game of the, Milton Bradley
EX $100 NM $200

Stunt Box, 1941, Frederick H. Beach (Beachcraft)
EX $12 NM $20

Submarine Drag, 1917, Willis G. Young
EX $50 NM $75

Substitute Golf, 1906, John Wanamaker
EX $400 NM $700

Suffolk Downs, 1930s, Corey Game
EX $65 NM $100

Susceptibles, The, 1891, McLoughlin Bros.
EX $400 NM $700

Sweep, 1929, Selchow & Righter
EX $25 NM $60

Sweeps, 1930s, E.E. Fairchild
EX $25 NM $60

Sweepstakes, 1930s, Haras
EX $55 NM $90

Swing A Peg, 1890s, Milton Bradley
EX $30 NM $45

T.G.O. Klondyke, 1899, J.H. Singer
EX $150 NM $250

Table Golf, 1909, McClurg
EX $15 NM $25

Tackle, 1933, Tackle Game
EX $70 NM $115

Tait's Table Golf, 1914, John Tait
EX $350 NM $575

Take It And Double, 1943, Frederick H. Beach (Beachcraft)
EX $20 NM $35

Take It or Leave It, 1942, Zondine Game
EX $15 NM $25

Tak-Tiks, Basketball, 1939, Midwest Products
EX $15 NM $25

Teddy's Bear Hunt, 1907, Bowers & Hard
EX $700 NM $900

Teddy's Ride from Oyster Bay to Albany, 1899, Jesse Crandall
EX $3000 NM $5500

Tee Off, 1935, Donogof
EX $115 NM $195

Telegrams, 1941, Whitman
EX $30 NM $50

Telegraph Boy, Game of the, 1888, McLoughlin Bros.
EX $350 NM $500

Telepathy, 1939, Cadaco-Ellis
EX $65 NM $110

Tell Bell, The, 1928, Knapp Electric & Novelty
EX $75 NM $100

Ten Pins, 1920, Mason & Parker
EX $35 NM $60

Tennis & Baseball, 1930, All Fair
EX $100 NM $150

Terry and the Pirates, 1930s, Whitman
EX $75 NM $100

Tete-A-Tete, 1892, Clark & Sowdon
EX $40 NM $100

They're Off, Race Horse Game, 1930s, Parker Brothers
EX $15 NM $30

Thorobred, 1940s, Lowe
EX $55 NM $90

Thorton W. Burgess Animal Game, 1925, Saalfield
EX $400 NM $600

Three Bears, 1910s, Milton Bradley
EX $20 NM $50

Three Blind Mice, Game of, 1930s, Milton Bradley
EX $25 NM $45

Three Little Kittens, 1910s, Milton Bradley
EX $60 NM $100

Three Little Pigs Game, 1933, Einson-Freeman
EX $55 NM $75

Three Little Pigs, The Game of the, 1933, Kenilworth Press
EX $100 NM $165

Three Men in a Tub, 1935, Milton Bradley
EX $40 NM $65

Three Men on a Horse, 1936, Milton Bradley
EX $20 NM $30

Three Point Landing, 1942, Advance Games
EX $25 NM $40

Thrilling Indoor Football Game, 1933, Cronston
EX $70 NM $115

Through The Clouds, 1931, Milton Bradley
EX $75 NM $125

Through the Locks to the Golden Gate, 1905, Milton Bradley
EX $100 NM $200

Ticker, 1929, Glow Products
EX $50 NM $75

Tiddley Golf Game, 1928, Milton Bradley
EX $125 NM $200

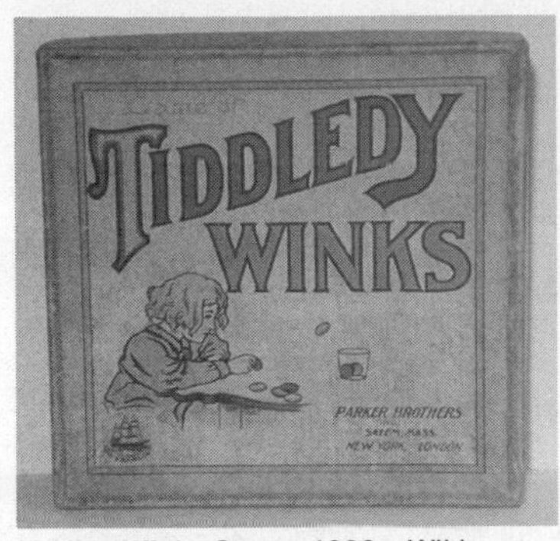

Tiddley Winks Game, 1920s, Wilder
EX $15 NM $25

Tiger Hunt, Game of, 1899, Chaffee & Selchow
EX $270 NM $450

Tiger Tom, Game of, 1920s, Milton Bradley
EX $30 NM $75

Ting-A-Ling, The Game of, 1920, Stoll & Edwards
EX $25 NM $45

Tinkerpins, 1916, Toy Creations
EX $55 NM $80

Tipit, 1929, Wolverine
EX $15 NM $20

Tip-Top Boxing, 1922, LaVelle
EX $200 NM $300

Tit for Tat Indoor Hockey, 1920s, Lemper Novelty
EX $45 NM $75

Tit-Tat-Toe, 1929, The Embossing
EX $15 NM $25

Tit-Tat-Toe, Three in a Row, 1896, Austin & Craw
EX $45 NM $75

To the Aid of your Party, 1942, Leister Game
EX $15 NM $25

Tobagganing at Christmas, Game of, 1899, McLoughlin Bros.
EX $1000 NM $1500

Toboggan Slide, 1890s, J.H. Singer
EX $200 NM $325

Toboggan Slide, 1890s, Hamilton-Myers
EX $225 NM $385

Toll Gate, Game of, 1890s, McLoughlin Bros.
EX $280 NM $400

Tom Hamilton's Pigskin, 1935, Parker Brothers
EX $40 NM $50

Tom Sawyer and Huck Finn, Adventures of, 1925, Stoll & Edwards
EX $70 NM $125

Tom Sawyer on the Mississippi, 1935, Einson-Freeman
EX $100 NM $200

Tom Sawyer, The Game of, 1937, Milton Bradley
EX $75 NM $100

Toonerville Trolley Game, 1927, Milton Bradley
EX $100 NM $200

Toonin Radio Game, 1925, All-Fair
EX $125 NM $225

Top-Ography, 1941, Cadaco
EX $20 NM $35

Topsy Turvey, Game of, 1899, McLoughlin Bros.
EX $150 NM $250

Tortoise and the Hare, 1922, Russell
EX $40 NM $50

Toto, The New Game, 1925, Baseball Toto Sales
EX $55 NM $90

Touchdown, 1937, Cadaco
EX $65 NM $110

Touchdown Football Game, 1920s, Wilder
EX $100 NM $165

Touchdown or Parlor Football, Game of, 1897, Union Mutual Life
EX $85 NM $140

Touchdown, The New Game, 1920, Hartford
EX $70 NM $115

Tourist, A Railroad Game, 1900s, Milton Bradley
EX $150 NM $325

Tournament, 1858, Mayhew & Baker
EX $180 NM $300

Town Hall, 1939, Milton Bradley
EX $20 NM $30

Toy Town Bank, 1910, Milton Bradley
EX $90 NM $150

Toy Town Conductors Game, 1910, Milton Bradley
EX $105 NM $175

Toy Town Telegraph Office, 1910s, Parker Brothers
EX $100 NM $150

Trackle-Lite, 1940s, Saxon Toy
EX $55 NM $90

Traffic Hazards, 1939, Trojan Games
EX $30 NM $50

Trailer Trails, 1937, Offset Gravure
EX $35 NM $60

Train for Boston, 1900, Parker Brothers
EX $500 NM $700

Transatlantic Flight, Game of the, 1925, Milton Bradley
EX $175 NM $250

Transport Pilot, 1938, Cadaco
EX $30 NM $50

Trap-A-Tank, 1920s, Wolverine
EX $75 NM $125

Traps & Bunkers, 1926?, Milton Bradley
EX $75 NM $125

Travel, The Game of, 1894, Parker Brothers
EX $150 NM $200

Treasure Hunt, 1940, All-Fair
EX $20 NM $50

Treasure Island, 1923, Stoll & Edwards
EX $75 NM $125

Treasure Island, 1934, Stoll & Einson
EX $60 NM $80

Treasure Island, Game of, 1923, Gem
EX $40 NM $65

Triangular Dominoes, 1885, Frank H. Richards
EX $35 NM $60

Trilby, 1894, E.I. Horsman
EX $270 NM $450

Trip Around the World, A, 1920s, Parker Brothers
EX $30 NM $75

Trip Round the World, Game of, 1897, McLoughlin Bros.
EX $300 NM $600

Trip to Washington, 1884, Milton Bradley
EX $100 NM $175

Triple Play, 1930s, National Games
EX $12 NM $20

Trolley Ride, The Game of the, 1890s, Hamilton-Myers
EX $175 NM $250

Trunk Box Lotto Game, 1890s, McLoughlin Bros.
EX $15 NM $25

Tumblin Five Acrobats, 1925, Doremus Schoen
EX $12 NM $20

Turn Over, 1908, Milton Bradley
EX $40 NM $75

Turnover, 1898, Chaffee & Selchow
EX $50 NM $85

Tutoom, Journey to the Treasures of Pharoah, 1923, All-Fair
EX $75 NM $150

Twentieth Century Limited, 1900s, Parker Brothers
EX $125 NM $175

Ty Cobb's Own Game of Baseball, 1920s, National Novelty
EX $350 NM $650

U.S. Postman Game, 1914
EX $60 NM $100

U-Bat-It, 1920s, Schultz Star
EX $70 NM $115

Uncle Jim's Question Bee, 1938, Kress
EX $10 NM $20

Uncle Sam at War with Spain, Great Game of, 1898, Rhode Island Game
EX $300 NM $400

Uncle Sam's Baseball Game, 1890, J.C. Bell
EX $525 NM $875

Uncle Sam's Mail, Game of, 1893, McLoughlin Bros.
EX $250 NM $400

GAMES

Uncle Wiggily's New Airplane Game, 1920s, Milton Bradley
EX $75 NM $175

Van Loon Story of Mankind Game, The, 1931, Kerk Guild
EX $50 NM $85

Vanderbilt Cup Race, 1906, Bowers & Hard
EX $2000 NM $2500

Varsity Football Game, 1942, Cadaco-Ellis
EX $45 NM $75

Varsity Race, 1899, Parker Brothers
EX $425 NM $725

Vassar Boat Race, The, 1899, Chaffee & Selchow
EX $700 NM $900

Vest Pocket Checker Set, 1929, Embossing
EX $15 NM $25

Vest Pocket Quoits, 1944, Colorful Creations
EX $25 NM $45

Victo, 1943, Spare Time
EX $20 NM $25

Victory, 1920s, Klak New Haven
EX $105 NM $175

Vignette Author, 1874, E.G. Selchow
EX $30 NM $50

Visit of Santa Claus, Game of the, 1899, McLoughlin Bros.
EX $800 NM $1500

Visit to the Farm, 1893, Bliss
EX $300 NM $500

Vox-Pop, 1938, Milton Bradley
EX $10 NM $20

Voyage Around the World, Game of, 1930s, Milton Bradley, Zepplin
EX $150 NM $175

Wachter's Parlor Base Ball (bagatelle), 1925, Wachter
EX $145 NM $250

Walk the Plank, 1925, Milton Bradley
EX $100 NM $150

Walking the Tightrope, 1897, McLoughlin Bros.
EX $125 NM $250

Walking the Tightrope, 1920, Milton Bradley
EX $50 NM $100

Walt Disney's Game Parade, 1930s
EX $30 NM $50

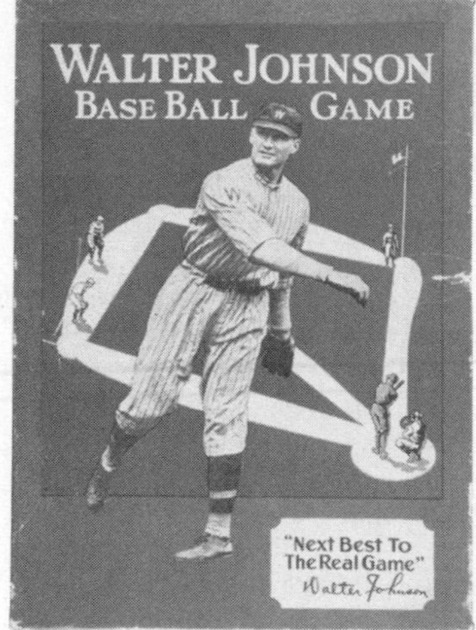

Walter Johnson Baseball Game, 1930s
EX $195 NM $325

Waner's Baseball Game, 1930s, Waner's Baseball Game
EX $250 NM $300

War of Nations, 1915, Milton Bradley
EX $75 NM $200

Ward Cuff's Football Game, 1938, Continental Sales
EX $125 NM $200

Watch on De Rind, 1931, All-Fair
EX $400 NM $650

Waterloo, 1895, Parker Brothers
EX $325 NM $550

Watermelon Frolic, 1900, Horsman
EX $135 NM $225

Watermelon Patch, 1940s, Craig Hopkins
EX $25 NM $45

Way to the White House, The, 1927, All-Fair
EX $150 NM $200

We, The Magnetic Flying Game, 1928, Parker Brothers
EX $100 NM $200

West Point, 1902, Ottoman
EX $125 NM $300

What's My Name?, 1920s, Jaymar
EX $15 NM $25

Whippet Race, 1940s, Pressman
EX $20 NM $35

Whirlpool Game, 1890s, McLoughlin Bros.
EX $85 NM $150

White Wings, 1930s, Glevum Games
EX $45 NM $70

Wide Awake, Game of, 1899, McLoughlin Bros.
EX $150 NM $300

Wide World and a Journey Round It, 1896, Parker Brothers
EX $165 NM $275

Wild West Cardboard Game, 1914
EX $90 NM $150

Wild West, Game of the, 1889, Bliss
EX $1000 NM $1700

Wilder's Football Game, 1930s, Wilder
EX $100 NM $175

Win, Place & Show, 1940s, 3M
EX $25 NM $40

Winko Baseball, 1940, Milton Bradley
EX $45 NM $60

Winnie Winkle Glider Race Game, 1930s, Milton Bradley
EX $100 NM $175

Winnie-The-Pooh Game, 1933, Parker Brothers
EX $75 NM $100

Winnie-The-Pooh Game, A. A. Milne's, 1931, Kerk Guild
EX $50 NM $85

Witzi-Wits, 1926, All-Fair
EX $150 NM $250

Wizard, The, 1921, Fulton Specialty
EX $15 NM $25

Wonderful Game of Oz (pewter pieces), 1921, Parker Brothers
EX $800 NM $1200

Wonderful Game of Oz (wooden pieces), 1921, Parker Brothers
EX $300 NM $500

Wordy, 1938, Pressman
EX $25 NM $45

World Flyers, Game of the, 1926, All-Fair
EX $200 NM $350

World Series Baseball Game, 1940s, Radio Sports
EX $205 NM $350

World Series Parlor Baseball, 1916, Clifton E. Hooper
EX $150 NM $250

World's Championship Baseball, 1910, Champion Amusement
EX $175 NM $295

World's Championship Golf Game, 1930s, Beacon Hudson
EX $145 NM $250

World's Columbian Exposition, Game of the, 1893, Bliss
EX $600 NM $1000

World's Educator Game, 1889, Reed
EX $250 NM $350

World's Fair Game, 1939, Milton Bradley
EX $90 NM $150

World's Fair Game, The, 1892, Parker Brothers
EX $800 NM $1400

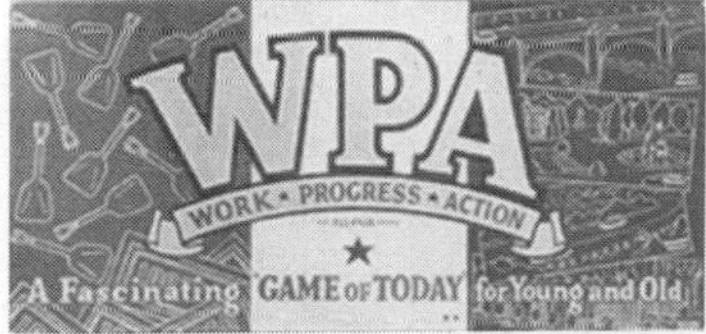

WPA, Work, Progress, Action, 1935, All-Fair
EX $100 NM $200

Wyntre Golf, 1920s, All-Fair
EX $175 NM $300

X-Plor-US, 1922, All-Fair
EX $100 NM $150

Yacht Race, 1890s, Clark & Sowdon
EX $200 NM $350

Yacht Race, 1930s, Pressman
EX $100 NM $150

Yachting, 1890, J.H. Singer
EX $125 NM $175

Yale Harvard Football Game, 1922, LaVelle
EX $200 NM $300

Yale Harvard Game, 1890, McLoughlin Bros.
EX $2000 NM $3000

Yale-Princeton Football Game, 1895, McLoughlin Bros.
EX $1500 NM $3000

Ya-Lo Football Card Game, 1930s
EX $85 NM $140

Yankee Doodle!, 1940, Cadaco-Ellis
EX $10 NM $20

Yankee Doodle, A Game of American History, 1895, Parker Brothers
EX $250 NM $300

Yankee Trader, 1941, Corey Games
EX $45 NM $75

Young Athlete, The, 1898, Chaffee & Selchow
EX $425 NM $700

You're Out! Baseball Game, 1941, Corey Games
EX $35 NM $65

Yuneek Game, 1889, McLoughlin Bros.
EX $300 NM $600

Zimmer Baseball Game, 1885, McLoughlin Bros.
EX $20000 NM $28000

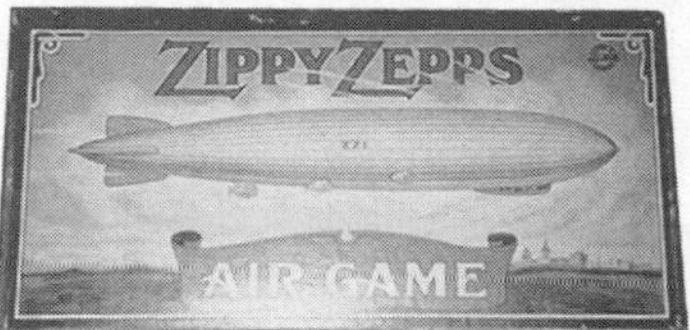

Zippy Zepps, 1930s, All-Fair
EX $500 NM $800

Zip-Top, 1940, Deluxe Game
EX $35 NM $45

Zoo Hoo, 1924, Lubbers & Bell
EX $125 NM $150

Zoom, Original Game of, 1940s, All-Fair
EX $40 NM $50

Zulu Blowing Game, 1927, Zulu Toy
EX $50 NM $100

CARD GAMES

ABC, 1900s, Parker Brothers
EX $25 NM $40

Airship Game, The, 1916, Parker Brothers
EX $30 NM $50

Allegrando, 1884, Theodore Presser
EX $20 NM $25

Allie-Patriot Game, 1917, McDowell And Mellor
EX $30 NM $50

American History, The Game of, 1890s, Parker Brothers
EX $40 NM $75

American League Fan Craze Card Game, 1904, Fan Craze
EX $1950 NM $3250

American National Game Baseball, 1909, American National Game Co.
EX $75 NM $200

Amusing Game of Conundrums, 1853, John McLoughlin
EX $750 NM $1300

Amusing Game of the Corner Grocery, 1890s
EX $75 NM $125

Anagrams, 1885, Peter G. Thompson
EX $10 NM $30

Apple Pie, 1895, Parker Brothers
EX $40 NM $60

Armstead's Play Ball, 1910s, Austin
EX $200 NM $500

Astronomy, 1905, Cincinnati Game
EX $20 NM $30

Auction Letters, 1900, Parker Brothers
EX $30 NM $50

Authors Illustrated, 1893, Clark & Sowdon
EX $30 NM $50

Authors, Game of Standard, 1890s, McLoughlin Bros.
EX $25 NM $50

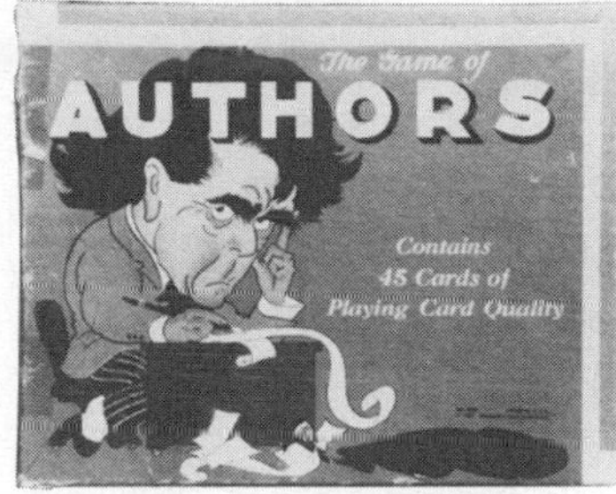

Authors, The Game of, 1890s, Parker Brothers
EX $15 NM $35

Avilude, 1873, West & Lee
EX $30 NM $60

Balance The Budget, 1938, Elten Game
EX $45 NM $75

Bally Hoo, 1931, Gabriel
EX $30 NM $50

Baseballitis Card Game, 1909, Baseballitis Card
EX $125 NM $205

Basketball Card Game, 1940s, Warren/Built-Rite
EX $20 NM $35

Batter Up, Game of, 1908, Fenner Game
EX $150 NM $200

Betty Boop Coed Bridge, 1930s
EX $50 NM $75

Bible ABCs and Promises, 1940s, Judson Press
EX $15 NM $25

Bible Authors, 1895, Evangelical Pub.
EX $20 NM $35

Bible Cities, 1920s, Nellie T. Magee
EX $15 NM $25

Bicycle Cards, 1898, Parker Brothers
EX $100 NM $150

Big League Baseball Card Game, 1940s, State College Game Lab
EX $35 NM $60

Billy Bump's Visit To Boston, 1888, Parker Brothers
EX $25 NM $40

Bird Center Etiquette, 1904, Home Game
EX $25 NM $50

Birds, Game of, 1899, Cincinnati Game
EX $25 NM $40

Black Cat Fortune Telling Game, The, 1897, Parker Brothers
EX $95 NM $150

Block, 1905, Parker Brothers
EX $25 NM $40

Blondie Playing Card Game, 1941, Whitman
EX $20 NM $35

Bo Peep Game, 1895, McLoughlin Bros.
EX $40 NM $65

Botany, 1900s, G.H. Dunston
EX $50 NM $100

Bourse, or Stock Exchange, 1903, Flinch Card
EX $35 NM $75

Boy Scouts, The Game of, 1912, Parker Brothers
EX $75 NM $125

Boy Scouts, The Game of, 1926, Parker Brothers
EX $200 NM $350

Buck Rogers in the 25th Century, 1936, All-Fair, 35 full-color cards plus instruction card
EX $300 NM $500

Bugle Horn or Robin Hood, 1850s, McLoughlin Bros.
EX $300 NM $500

Bugle Horn or Robin Hood, Game of, 1895, McLoughlin Bros.
EX $250 NM $500

Bunco, 1904, Home Game
EX $10 NM $30

Buster Brown at the Circus, 1900s, Selchow & Righter
EX $100 NM $250

Camouflage, The Game of, 1918, Parker Brothers
EX $20 NM $40

Captain Jinks, 1900s, Parker Brothers
EX $30 NM $50

Characteristics, 1845, Ives
EX $180 NM $300

Characters, A Game of, 1889, Decker & Decker
EX $10 NM $15

Charlie Chan Game, 1939, Whitman
EX $30 NM $60

Charlie McCarthy Question and Answer Game, 1938, Whitman
EX $20 NM $40

Charlie McCarthy Rummy Game, 1938, Whitman
EX $15 NM $30

Chestnut Burrs, 1896, Fireside Game
EX $35 NM $65

Cinderella, 1895, Parker Brothers
EX $30 NM $60

Cinderella, 1905, Milton Bradley
EX $25 NM $40

Cinderella, 1921, Milton Bradley
EX $15 NM $25

Cinderella or Hunt the Slipper, 1887, McLoughlin Bros.
EX $50 NM $75

City Life, or The Boys of New York, The Game of, 1889, McLoughlin Bros.
EX $150 NM $250

Cock Robin, 1895, Parker Brothers
EX $20 NM $40

Cock Robin and His Tragical Death, Game of, 1885, McLoughlin Bros.
EX $30 NM $60

Columbia's Presidents and Our Country, Game of, 1886, McLoughlin Bros.
EX $150 NM $250

Comic Conversation Cards, 1890, J. Ottmann Lith.
EX $100 NM $200

Comic Leaves of Fortune-The Sibyl's Prophecy, 1850s, Charles Magnus
EX $500 NM $900

Comical Game of "Who," The, 1910s, Parker Brothers
EX $20 NM $25

Comical Game of Whip, The, 1920s, Russell
EX $15 NM $30

Comical History of America, 1924, Parker Brothers
EX $30 NM $50

Comical Snap, Game of, 1903, McLoughlin Bros.
EX $30 NM $50

Commanders of Our Forces, The, 1863, E.C. Eastman
EX $150 NM $225

Commerce, 1900s, J. Ottmann Lith.
EX $40 NM $80

Competition, or Department Store, 1904, Flinch Card
EX $100 NM $150

Conquest of Nations, or Old Games With New Faces, The, 1853, Willis P. Hazard
EX $100 NM $175

Costumes and Fashions, Game of, 1881, Milton Bradley
EX $80 NM $225

County Fair, The, 1891, Parker Brothers
EX $45 NM $75

Cousin Peter's Trip to New York, Game of, 1898, McLoughlin Bros.
EX $30 NM $50

Crow Cards, 1910, Milton Bradley
EX $9 NM $15

Defenders of the Flag, 1922, Stoll & Edwards
EX $35 NM $65

Derby Day, 1900s, Parker Brothers
EX $30 NM $50

Dewey at Manila, 1899, Chaffee & Selchow
EX $150 NM $225

Dick Tracy Playing Card Game, 1934, Whitman
EX $30 NM $50

Dick Tracy Super Detective Mystery Card Game, 1937, Whitman
EX $65 NM $90

Din, 1905, Horsman
EX $25 NM $45

Dixie Land, Game of, 1897, Fireside
EX $30 NM $40

Doctor Quack, Game of, 1922, Russell
EX $15 NM $25

Doctors and the Quack, 1890s, Parker Brothers
EX $75 NM $125

Donald Duck Game, 1930s, Whitman
EX $15 NM $30

Donald Duck Playing Card Game, 1941, Whitman, 35 cards, box image of Donald storming away
EX $25 NM $40

Double Eagle Anagrams, 1890, McLoughlin Bros.
EX $35 NM $60

Double Flag Game, The, 1904, McLoughlin Bros.
EX $60 NM $90

Down the Pike with Mrs. Wiggs at the St. Louis Exposition, 1904, Milton Bradley
EX $50 NM $65

Dr. Busby, 1890s, J.H. Singer
EX $60 NM $75

Dr. Busby, Game of, 1890s, McLoughlin Bros.
EX $125 NM $200

Dr. Busby, 1900s, J. Ottmann Lith.
EX $60 NM $75

Dr. Busby, 1937, Milton Bradley
EX $20 NM $50

Dr. Busby, Game of, 1910
EX $25 NM $45

Egerton R. Williams Popular Indoor Baseball Game, 1886, Hatch
EX $2500 NM $5000

Election, 1896, Fireside
EX $20 NM $30

Elite Conversation Cards, 1887, McLoughlin Bros.
EX $35 NM $70

Excursion to Coney Island, 1880s, Milton Bradley
EX $100 NM $200

Excuse Me!, 1923, Parker Brothers
EX $15 NM $25

Famous Authors, 1910, Parker Brothers
EX $15 NM $30

Famous Authors, 1943, Parker Brothers
EX $10 NM $15

Fan Craze Card Game, Generic, 1904, Fan Craze
EX $100 NM $150

Fan Craze Card Game, Name Players, 1904, Fan Craze
EX $1500 NM $2000

Favorite Art, Game of, 1897, Parker Brothers
EX $30 NM $40

Ferdinand Card Game, 1938, Whitman
EX $25 NM $65

Five Hundred, Game of, 1900s, Home Game
EX $20 NM $35

Flags, 1899, Cincinnati Game
EX $20 NM $35

Flinch, 1902, Flinch Card
EX $10 NM $15

Foolish Questions, 1920s, Wallie Dorr, color cover
EX $30 NM $60

Fortune Telling, 1920s, All-Fair
EX $20 NM $30

Fortune Telling Game, 1930s, Stoll & Edwards
EX $35 NM $55

Fortune Telling Game, The, 1890s, Parker Brothers
EX $40 NM $50

Fortunes, Game of, 1902, Cincinnati Game
EX $30 NM $60

Fox and Geese, The New, 1888, McLoughlin Bros.
EX $45 NM $75

Foxy Grandpa at the World's Fair, 1904, J. Ottmann Lith.
EX $75 NM $125

Fractions, 1902, Cincinnati Game
EX $20 NM $25

Frank Buck's Bring 'em Back Alive Game, 1937, All-Fair
EX $30 NM $45

Gamevelope, 1944, Morris Systems
EX $20 NM $35

Gavitt's Stock Exchange, 1903, W.W. Gavitt
EX $35 NM $65

Geographical Cards, 1883, Peter G. Thompson
EX $25 NM $40

Geography up to Date, 1890s, Parker Brothers
EX $20 NM $35

George Washington's Dream, 1900s, Parker Brothers
EX $25 NM $40

G-Men, 1936, Milton Bradley
EX $35 NM $50

Goat, Game of, 1916, Milton Bradley
EX $15 NM $35

Gold Rush, The, 1930s, Cracker Jack
EX $20 NM $50

Golden Egg, 1850s, McLoughlin Bros.
EX $350 NM $500

Golden Egg, The, 1845, R.H. Pease
EX $165 NM $275

Golliwogg, 1907, Milton Bradley
EX $200 NM $250

Good Old Game of Corner Grocery, The, 1900s, Parker Brothers
EX $40 NM $75

Good Old Game of Dr. Busby, 1900s, Parker Brothers
EX $55 NM $75

Good Old Game of Dr. Busby, 1920s, United Game
EX $25 NM $50

Grandmama's Improved Arithmetical Game, 1887, McLoughlin Bros.
EX $50 NM $60

Grandmama's Improved Geographical Game, 1887, McLoughlin Bros.
EX $55 NM $65

Grandmama's Sunday Game: Bible Questions, Old Testament, 1887, McLoughlin Bros.
EX $35 NM $60

Grandma's Game of Useful Knowledge, 1910s, Milton Bradley
EX $20 NM $45

Great Battlefields, 1886, Parker Brothers
EX $150 NM $250

Great Composer, The, 1901, Theodore Presser
EX $35 NM $45

Great Mails Baseball Game, 1919, Walter Mails Baseball Game
EX $2475 NM $4100

Guess Again, The Game of, 1890s, McLoughlin Bros.
EX $75 NM $120

Gypsy Fortune Telling Game, 1909, McLoughlin Bros.
EX $100 NM $175

H.M.S. Pinafore, 1880, McLoughlin Bros.
EX $300 NM $500

Have-U It?, 1924, Selchow & Righter
EX $15 NM $25

Heads and Tails, 1900s, Parker Brothers
EX $30 NM $50

Hens and Chickens, Game of, 1875, McLoughlin Bros.
EX $75 NM $150

Hey What?, 1907, Parker Brothers
EX $20 NM $35

Hidden Titles, 1908, Parker Brothers
EX $20 NM $30

Historical Cards, 1884, Peter G. Thompson
EX $25 NM $50

History up to Date, 1900s, Parker Brothers
EX $20 NM $45

Hokum, 1927, Parker Brothers
EX $10 NM $20

Hollywood Movie Bingo, 1937, Whitman
EX $20 NM $40

Home Diamond, 1913, Phillips
EX $150 NM $225

Home History Game, 1910s, Milton Bradley
EX $20 NM $35

Hood's War Game, 1899, C.I. Hood
EX $40 NM $65

Hoot, 1926, Saalfield
EX $75 NM $150

House that Jack Built, 1900s, Parker Brothers
EX $35 NM $50

House that Jack Built, The, 1887, McLoughlin Bros.
EX $40 NM $80

Household Words, Game of, 1916, Household Words Game
EX $50 NM $85

How Silas Popped the Question, 1915, Parker Brothers
EX $20 NM $25

I Doubt It, 1910, Parker Brothers
EX $20 NM $30

Illustrated Mythology, 1896, Cincinnati Game
EX $15 NM $30

Improved Historical Cards, 1900, McLoughlin Bros.
EX $35 NM $55

Industries, Game of, 1897, A.W. Mumford
EX $15 NM $25

Ivanhoe, 1886, Parker Brothers
EX $55 NM $75

Japanese Oracle, Game of, 1875, McLoughlin Bros.
EX $100 NM $200

Joe "Ducky" Medwick's Big Leaguer Baseball Game, 1930s, Johnson-Breier
EX $125 NM $200

Johnny's Historical Game, 1890s, Parker Brothers
EX $40 NM $50

Jumping Frog, Game of, 1890, J.H. Singer
EX $50 NM $125

Just Like Me, Game of, 1899, McLoughlin Bros.
EX $50 NM $75

Kings, The Game of, 1845, Josiah Adams
EX $150 NM $250

Komical Konversation Kards, 1893, Parker Brothers
EX $20 NM $35

Lawson's Baseball Card Game, 1910
EX $100 NM $175

Lawson's Patent Game of Baseball, 1884, Lawson's Card
EX $500 NM $1000

Letters Improved for the Logomachist, 1878, Noyes & Snow
EX $50 NM $100

Library of Games, 1939, Russell
EX $55 NM $60

Lindy Flying Game, 1927, Parker Brothers
EX $30 NM $40

Lindy Flying Game, The New, 1927, Nucraft Toys
EX $25 NM $50

Lion & the Eagle, or the Days of '76, 1883, E.H. Snow
EX $75 NM $125

Little Orphan Annie Rummy Cards, 1937, Whitman
EX $25 NM $40

Lost Heir, Game of the, 1910, Milton Bradley
EX $15 NM $30

Lost Heir, The Game of, 1893, McLoughlin Bros.
EX $25 NM $45

Major League Baseball Game, 1900s, Parker Brothers
EX $50 NM $150

Make A Million, 1934, Rook Card
EX $35 NM $50

Mayflower, The, 1897, Fireside Game
EX $15 NM $30

Mickey Mouse Bridge Game, 1935, Whitman
EX $35 NM $55

Mickey Mouse Old Maid Game, 1930s, Whitman
EX $35 NM $50

Mother Hubbard, 1875, McLoughlin Bros.
EX $45 NM $75

Movie-Land Keeno, 1929, Wilder
EX $45 NM $80

Musical Lotto, 1936, Tudor Metal Products
EX $20 NM $40

Mythology, 1900, Cincinnati Game
EX $30 NM $45

Napoleon LaJoie Baseball Game, 1913, Parker Brothers
EX $150 NM $500

National American Baseball Game, 1910, Parker Brothers
EX $130 NM $200

National Baseball Game, The, 1913, National Baseball Playing Card
EX $700 NM $1200

Nations or Quaker Whist, Game of, 1898, McLoughlin Bros.
EX $75 NM $110

Nations, Game of, 1908, Milton Bradley
EX $30 NM $65

Naughty Molly, 1905, McLoughlin Bros.
EX $75 NM $100

Nosey, The Game of, 1905, McLoughlin Bros.
EX $250 NM $450

Oh, Blondie!, 1940s
EX $15 NM $30

Old Curiosity Shop, 1869, Novelty Game
EX $200 NM $300

Old Maid, 1890s, J.H. Singer
EX $75 NM $100

Old Maid Card Game, 1889
EX $20 NM $50

Old Maid Fun Full Thrift Game, 1940s, Russell
EX $30 NM $40

Old Maid, Game of, 1870, McLoughlin Bros.
EX $50 NM $100

Old Maid, with Characters from Famous Nursery Rhymes, 1920s, All-Fair
EX $30 NM $50

Oliver Twist, The Good Old Game of, 1888, Parker Brothers
EX $150 NM $225

Our Bird Friends, 1901, Sarah H. Dudley
EX $20 NM $30

Our National Life, 1903, Cincinnati Game
EX $20 NM $40

Patch Word, 1938, All-Fair
EX $10 NM $15

Paws & Claws, 1895, Clark & Sowdon
EX $60 NM $90

Pepper, 1906, Parker Brothers
EX $20 NM $35

Peter Coddle and his Trip to New York, 1890s, J.H. Singer
EX $35 NM $50

Peter Coddle tells of his Trip to Chicago, 1890, Parker Brothers
EX $30 NM $40

Peter Coddle, Improved Game of, 1900, McLoughlin Bros.
EX $35 NM $45

Peter Coddles, 1890s, J. Ottmann Lith.
EX $25 NM $45

Peter Coddle's Trip to New York, 1925, Milton Bradley
EX $20 NM $30

Peter Coddle's Trip to New York, The Game of, 1888, Parker Brothers
EX $25 NM $40

Peter Coddle's Trip to the World's Fair, 1939, Parker Brothers
EX $50 NM $85

Pinocchio Playing Card Game, 1939, Whitman
EX $45 NM $60

Psychic Baseball, 1927, Psychic Baseball
EX $75 NM $125

Real Baseball Card Game, 1900, National Baseball
EX $180 NM $275

Red Riding Hood and the Wolf, The New Game, 1887, McLoughlin Bros.
EX $75 NM $120

Rex, 1920s, J. Ottmann Lith.
EX $20 NM $35

Robinson Crusoe for Little Folks, Game of, 1900s, E.O. Clark
EX $35 NM $65

Roodles, 1912, Flinch Card
EX $15 NM $30

Rook, 1906, Rook Card Co.
EX $10 NM $30

Roosevelt at San Juan, 1899, Chaffee & Selchow
EX $150 NM $350

Sabotage, 1943, Games Of Fame
EX $15 NM $35

Skippy, A Card Game, 1936, All-Fair
EX $30 NM $50

Skit Scat, 1905, McLoughlin Bros.
EX $50 NM $85

Snap, 1883, Horsman
EX $45 NM $65

Snap, Game of, 1892, McLoughlin Bros.
EX $40 NM $85

Snap, Game of, 1910s, Milton Bradley
EX $20 NM $25

Snap, The Game of, 1905s, Parker Brothers
EX $25 NM $40

Stage, 1904, C.M. Clark
EX $50 NM $75

Star Baseball Game, 1941, W.P. Ulrich
EX $70 NM $115

Take-Off, 1930s, Russell
EX $25 NM $45

Three Bears, The, 1922, Stoll & Edwards
EX $30 NM $50

Three Merry Men, 1865, Amsdan
EX $75 NM $100

Tom Barker Card Game, 1913
EX $1400 NM $2300

Toot, 1905, Parker Brothers
EX $65 NM $85

Totem, 1873, West & Lee
EX $45 NM $60

Touring, 1906, Wallie Dorr
EX $50 NM $60

Touring, 1926, Parker Brothers
EX $20 NM $30

Traits, The Game of, 1933, Goodenough and Woglom
EX $20 NM $35

Trip through our National Parks: Game of Yellowstone, A, 1910s, Cincinnati Game
EX $20 NM $45

Trips of Japhet Jenkens & Sam Slick, 1871, Milton Bradley
EX $20 NM $35

Trolley, 1904, Snyder Brothers
EX $40 NM $60

Trolley Came Off, The, 1900s, Parker Brothers
EX $40 NM $75

Twenty Five, Game of, 1925, Milton Bradley
EX $10 NM $15

United States History, The Game of, 1903, Parker Brothers
EX $50 NM $65

Venetian Fortune Teller, Game of, 1898, Parker Brothers
EX $75 NM $85

Verborum, 1883, Peter G. Thompson
EX $35 NM $50

Walt and Skeezix Gasoline Alley Game, 1927, Milton Bradley
EX $50 NM $75

Wang, Game of, 1892, Clark & Sowdon
EX $45 NM $65

War and Diplomacy, 1899, Chaffee & Selchow
EX $85 NM $125

War of Words, 1910, McLoughlin Bros.
EX $35 NM $60

What Would You Do?, 1933, Geo E. Schweig & Son
EX $15 NM $25

When My Ship Comes In, 1888, Parker Brothers
EX $40 NM $50

Where do you Live?, 1890s, J.H. Singer
EX $40 NM $50

Where's Johnny?, 1885, McLoughlin Bros.
EX $100 NM $175

Which is It? Speak Quick or Pay, 1889, McLoughlin Bros.
EX $50 NM $100

Whip, The Comical Game of, 1930, Russell
EX $20 NM $30

Who is the Thief?, 1937, Whitman
EX $35 NM $40

Wogglebug Game of Conundrums, The, 1905, Parker Brothers
EX $300 NM $600

Worth While, 1907, Doan
EX $25 NM $40

Wyhoo!, 1906, Milton Bradley
EX $30 NM $50

Yankee Pedlar, Or What Do You Buy, 1850s, John McLoughlin
EX $725 NM $1200

Yellowstone, Game of, 1895, Fireside Game
EX $65 NM $80

Young Folks Historical Game, 1890s, McLoughlin Bros.
EX $30 NM $50

Young Peddlers, Game of the, 1859, Mayhew & Baker
EX $125 NM $175

Young People's Geographical Game, 1900s, Parker Brothers
EX $30 NM $45

Zoom, 1941, Whitman
EX $10 NM $20

DEXTERITY

Golf, 1900, Schoenhut
EX $2700 NM $5000

SKILL/ACTION GAMES

400, Aristocrat of Games, The, 1933, Morris Systems
EX $15 NM $25

Aero Ball, 1940s, Game Makers
EX $30 NM $75

Animal Bingo, Baldwin Manufacturing
EX $40 NM $75

Bag of Fun, 1932, Rosebud Art
EX $5 NM $10

Balloonio, 1937, Frederick H. Beach
EX $10 NM $15

Bambino, 1934, Bambino Products
EX $100 NM $125

Bang Bird, 1924, Doremus Schoen
EX $20 NM $30

Barber Pole, 1908, Parker Brothers
EX $50 NM $75

Barn Yard Tiddledy Winks, 1910s, Parker Brothers
EX $30 NM $45

Bases Full, 1930
EX $45 NM $70

Basket Ball, 1929, Russell
EX $150 NM $200

Battles, or Fun For Boys, Game of, 1889, McLoughlin Bros.
EX $750 NM $1200

Bean-Em, 1931, All-Fair
EX $500 NM $800

Bingo, 1929, All-Fair
EX $10 NM $15

Bobb, Game of, 1898, McLoughlin Bros.
EX $250 NM $500

Bomber Ball, 1940s, Game Makers
EX $50 NM $75

Bottle Imps, Game of, 1907, Milton Bradley
EX $75 NM $100

Bowling Alley, 1921, N.D. Cass
EX $20 NM $35

Bow-O-Winks, 1932, All-Fair
EX $75 NM $125

Boy Hunter, The, 1925, Parker Brothers
EX $60 NM $100

Brownie Character Ten Pins Game, 1890s
EX $1000 NM $2000

Brownie Kick-In Top, 1910s, M.H. Miller
EX $35 NM $50

Bula, 1943, Games Of Fame
EX $30 NM $45

Bull in the China Shop, 1937, Milton Bradley
EX $20 NM $35

Busto, 1931, All-Fair
EX $100 NM $150

Buzzing Around, 1924, Parker Brothers
EX $40 NM $65

Cat and Witch, 1940s, Whitman
EX $25 NM $65

Cavalcade Derby Game, 1930s, Wyandotte
EX $50 NM $85

Chinaman Party, 1896, Selchow & Righter
EX $75 NM $130

Click, 1930s, Akro Agate
EX $50 NM $85

Prewar Games

Clown Winks, 1930s, Gabriel
EX $15 **NM** $25

Combination Tiddledy Winks, 1910, Milton Bradley
EX $10 **NM** $20

Cones & Corns, 1924, Parker Brothers
EX $30 **NM** $50

Conette, 1890, Milton Bradley
EX $25 **NM** $40

Cows In Corn, 1889, Stirn & Lyon
EX $150 **NM** $250

Crazy Traveller, 1920s, Parker Brothers
EX $25 **NM** $40

Crickets In The Grass, 1920s, Madmar Quality
EX $35 **NM** $45

Crow Hunt, 1930, Parker Brothers
EX $30 **NM** $50

Crows in the Corn, 1930, Parker Brothers
EX $45 **NM** $75

Deck Ring Toss Game, 1910
EX $15 **NM** $30

Dig, 1940, Parker Brothers
EX $2 **NM** $5

Dim Those Lights, 1932, All-Fair
EX $400 **NM** $600

Disk, 1900s, Madmar Quality
EX $35 **NM** $55

Diving Fish, 1920s, C.E. Bradley
EX $20 **NM** $30

Dodging Donkey, The, 1920s, Parker Brothers
EX $45 **NM** $60

Donkey Party, 1887, McLoughlin Bros.
EX $75 **NM** $100

Down and Out, 1928, Milton Bradley
EX $30 **NM** $50

Faba Baga or Parlor Quiots, 1883, Morton E. Converse
EX $40 **NM** $65

Fairies' Cauldron Tiddledy Winks Game, The, 1925, Parker Brothers
EX $35 **NM** $50

Fascination, 1890, Selchow & Righter
EX $35 **NM** $50

Fiddlestix, 1937, Plaza
EX $10 **NM** $15

Fish Pond, 1890, E.O. Clark
EX $50 **NM** $100

Fish Pond, 1920s, Wilder
EX $25 **NM** $50

Fish Pond Game, Magnetic, 1891, McLoughlin Bros.
EX $150 **NM** $300

Fish Pond, Game of, 1910s, Wescott Brothers
EX $30 **NM** $50

Fish Pond, New and Improved, 1890s, McLoughlin Bros.
EX $110 **NM** $200

Fish Pond, The Game of, 1890, McLoughlin Bros.
EX $100 **NM** $175

Fishing Game, 1899, Martin
EX $30 **NM** $65

Five Little Pigs, 1890s, J.H. Singer
EX $50 **NM** $75

Five Wise Birds, The, 1923, Parker Brothers
EX $25 **NM** $40

Flap Jacks, 1931, All-Fair
EX $100 **NM** $175

Flash, 1940s, Pressman
EX $20 **NM** $35

Flitters, 1899, Martin
EX $45 **NM** $75

Floor Croquet Game, 1912
EX $40 **NM** $60

Four and Twenty Blackbirds, 1890s, McLoughlin Bros.
EX $750 **NM** $1500

Four Dare Devils, The, 1933, Marx, Hess & Lee
EX $40 **NM** $65

Gee-Wiz Horse Race, 1928, Wolverine
EX $50 **NM** $85

Genuine Steamer Quoits, 1924, Milton Bradley
EX $15 **NM** $25

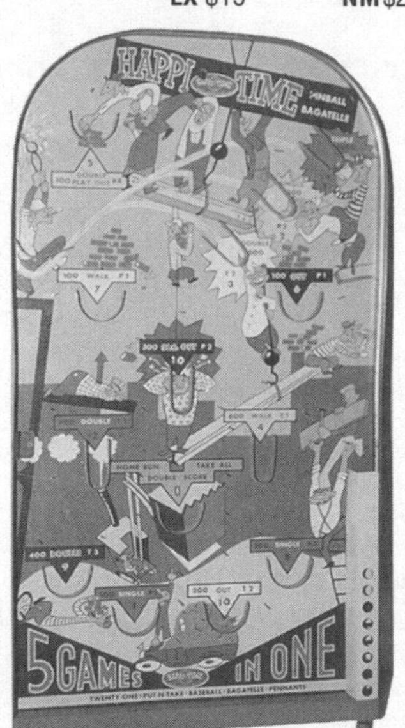

Happitime Bagatelle, 1933, Northwestern Products
EX $30 **NM** $45

Happy Landing, 1938, Transogram
EX $30 **NM** $45

Hop-Over Puzzle, 1930s, Pressman
EX $10 **NM** $20

Hungry Willie, 1930s, Transogram
EX $20 **NM** $40

Hunting in the Jungle, 1920s, A. Gropper
EX $30 **NM** $45

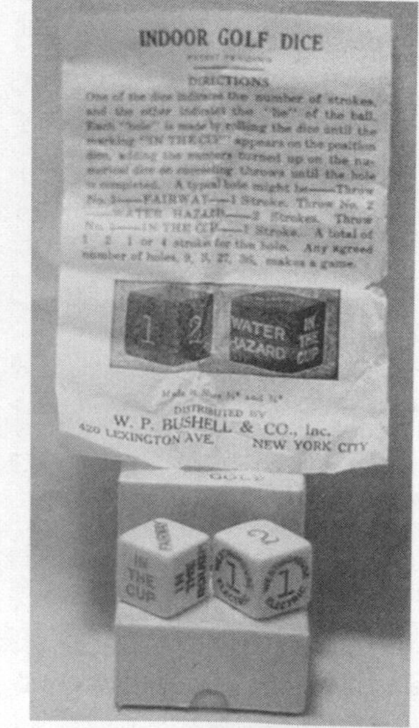

Indoor Golf Dice, 1920s, W.P. Bushell
EX $20 **NM** $35

Jack Straws, The Game of, 1901, Parker Brothers
EX $20 **NM** $30

Jamboree, 1937, Selchow & Righter
EX $40 **NM** $60

Japanese Ball Game, 1930s, Girard
EX $35 **NM** $65

Japanola, 1928, Parker Brothers
EX $35 **NM** $60

Jaunty Butler, 1932, All-Fair
EX $100 **NM** $150

Jav-Lin, 1931, All-Fair
EX $100 **NM** $200

Jolly Clown Spinette, 1932, Milton Bradley
EX $15 **NM** $30

Jolly Robbers, 1929, Wilder
EX $50 **NM** $75

Jumping Jupiter, 1940s, Gabriel
EX $30 **NM** $50

Jungle Hunt, 1940, Gotham Pressed Steel
EX $30 **NM** $45

Jungle Jump-Up Game, 1940s, Judson Press
EX $30 **NM** $45

Katzenjammer Kids Hockey, 1940s, Jaymar
EX $40 **NM** $65

Katzy Party, 1900s, Selchow & Righter
EX $70 **NM** $120

Kindergarten Lotto, 1904, Strauss
EX $30 **NM** $50

GAMES

Knockout Andy, 1926, Parker Brothers
EX $35 NM $75

Kuti-Kuts, 1922, Regensteiner
EX $20 NM $30

Leaping Lena, 1920s, Parker Brothers
EX $100 NM $200

Lid's Off, The, 1937, American Toy Works
EX $45 NM $95

Little Orphan Annie Bead Game, 1930s
EX $20 NM $35

Little Orphan Annie Shooting Game, 1930s, Milton Bradley
EX $200 NM $400

Lone Ranger Hi-Yo Silver!! Target Game, 1939, Marx
EX $75 NM $125

Mammoth Conette, 1898, Milton Bradley
EX $90 NM $150

Marble Muggins, 1920s, American Toy
EX $125 NM $200

Mar-Juck, 1923, Regensteiner
EX $20 NM $30

Meteor Game, 1916, A.C. Gilbert
EX $25 NM $45

Mickey Mouse Miniature Pinball Game, 1930s, Marks Brothers
EX $20 NM $35

Mickey Mouse Shooting Game, 1930s, Marks Brothers
EX $120 NM $200

Mickey Mouse Skittle Ball Game, 1930s, Marks Brothers
EX $60 NM $100

Mickey Mouse Soldier Target Set, 1930s, Marks Brothers
EX $60 NM $100

Mumbly Peg, 1920s
EX $15 NM $20

Old Time Shooting Gallery, 1940, Warren-Built-Rite
EX $15 NM $25

Our Gang Tipple Topple Game, 1930, All-Fair
EX $200 NM $350

Peeza, 1935, Toy Creations
EX $25 NM $45

Pike's Peak or Bust, 1890s, Parker Brothers
EX $100 NM $150

Ping Pong, 1902, Parker Brothers
EX $75 NM $150

Pinocchio Target Game, 1938, American Toy Works
EX $90 NM $150

Pinocchio the Merry Puppet Game, 1939, Milton Bradley
EX $55 NM $95

Pitch Em, The Game of Indoor Horse Shoes, 1929, Wolverine
EX $20 NM $30

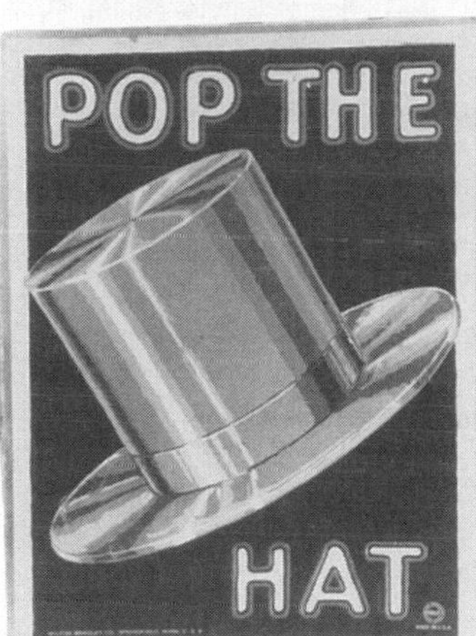

Pop the Hat, 1930s, Milton Bradley
EX $35 NM $50

Ranger Commandos, 1942, Parker Brothers
EX $25 NM $40

Red Ryder "Whirli-Crow" Target Game, 1940s, Daisy
EX $150 NM $250

Ride 'em Cowboy, 1939, Gotham Pressed Steel
EX $25 NM $45

Ring My Nose, 1926, Milton Bradley
EX $75 NM $100

Ring Scaling, 1900, Martin
EX $25 NM $45

Shuffle-Board, The New Game of, 1920, Gabriel
EX $50 NM $85

Simba, 1932, All-Fair
EX $100 NM $150

Smitty Target Game, 1930s, Milton Bradley
EX $30 NM $60

Snap-Jacks, 1940s, Gabriel
EX $15 NM $25

Snow White and the Seven Dwarfs, 1938, American Toy Works
EX $125 NM $200

Spin 'em Target Game, 1930s, All Metal Product
EX $25 NM $40

Spin It, 1910s, Milton Bradley
EX $20 NM $30

Stak, International Game of, 1937, Marks Brothers
EX $15 NM $30

Stax, 1930s, Marks Brothers
EX $12 NM $20

Superman Action Game, 1940, American Toy Works
EX $60 NM $100

Table Croquet, 1890s, Milton Bradley
EX $25 NM $40

Tactics, 1940, Northwestern Products
EX $25 NM $45

Tiddlody Wink Tennis, 1890, E.I. Horsman
EX $45 NM $60

Tiddledy Winks and Bowling, Game of, 1910s, Parker Brothers
EX $25 NM $50

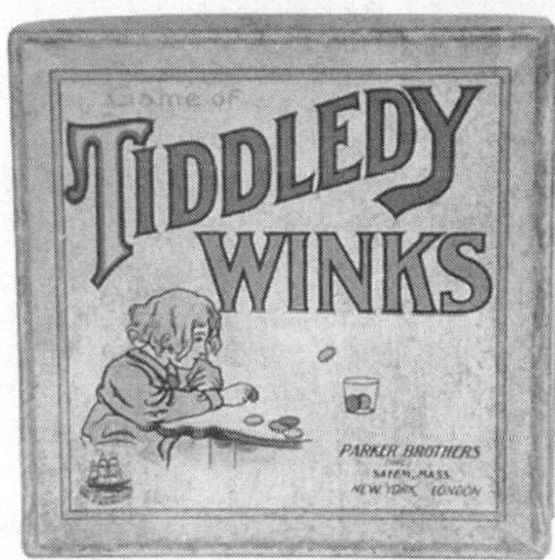

Tiddledy Winks, Game of, 1910s, Parker Brothers
EX $10 NM $20

Tiddledy Winks, The Popular Game of, 1897, Parker Brothers, Salem Edition
EX $30 NM $75

Tinker Toss, 1920s, Toy Creations
EX $25 NM $40

Tip the Bellboy, 1929, All-Fair
EX $150 NM $300

Tip Top Fish Pond, 1930s, Milton Bradley
EX $15 NM $30

Toss-O, 1924, Lubbers & Bell
EX $10 NM $20

Touchdown, 1930s, Milton Bradley
EX $150 NM $250

Toy Town Target with Repeating Pistol, 1911, Milton Bradley
EX $55 NM $95

Traps and Bunkers, A Game of Golf, 1930s, Milton Bradley
EX $25 NM $60

Wa-Hoo Pick-Em Up Sticks, 1936, Doremus Schoen
EX $15 NM $25

Prewar Games

Walt Disney's Ski Jump Target Game, 1930s, American Toy Works
EX $175 **NM** $295

Walt Disney's Uncle Remus Game, 1930s, Parker Brothers
EX $60 **NM** $125

Washington's Birthday Party, 1911, Russell
EX $55 **NM** $95

Watermelon Patch Game, 1896, McLoughlin Bros.
EX $1000 **NM** $2000

Wonder Tiddley Winks, 1899, Martin
EX $20 **NM** $45

Tabletop Games

AUTO RACING

No. 300 Electric Auto Racing, 1948-49, Tudor
EX $50 **NM** $100

No. 530 Tru-Action Electric Sports Car Race, 1959-65, Tudor
EX $25 **NM** $55

No. 590 Mickey Mouse Electric Treasure Hunt Game, 1963-64, Tudor
EX $40 **NM** $85

BASEBALL

No. 550 Tru-Action Electric Baseball, 1950-58, Tudor
EX $30 **NM** $75

No. 550 Tru-Action Electric Baseball, 1958-63, Tudor
EX $25 **NM** $60

No. 555 Tru-Action Electric Baseball, 1964-88, Tudor, square field
EX $22 **NM** $50

BASKETBALL

Gotham Pass 'N Shoot Basketball, 1968, Gotham Pressed Steel Co.
EX $20 **NM** $55

Gotham Pro Basketball, 1950s, Gotham Pressed Steel Co.
EX $15 **NM** $45

No. 475 Magnetic Baseball, 1964-67, Tudor
EX $20 **NM** $45

No. 480 NBPA Game, 1968-70, Tudor
EX $30 **NM** $75

No. 480 NBPA Game, 1971, Tudor
EX $15 **NM** $40

No. 575 Tru-Action Electric Basketball, 1957-58, Tudor
EX $30 **NM** $70

No. 575 Tru-Action Electric Basketball, 1959-63, Tudor
EX $25 **NM** $55

No. G-660 Gotham All Star Basketball, 1947, Gotham Pressed Steel Co.
EX $20 **NM** $50

FOOTBALL

G-890 Dick Butkus, 1972, Gotham
EX $30 **NM** $75

No. G-1400, 1965-67, Gotham
EX $30 **NM** $60

No. G-1440, 1962-64, Gotham
EX $35 **NM** $70

No. G-1503, 1968, Gotham
EX $33 **NM** $70

No. G-1503-S NFL Big Bowl, 1965-67, Gotham
EX $50 **NM** $125

No. G-1506 NFL Players Association, Gotham
EX $25 **NM** $60

No. G-1512 Super Dome, 1969-71, Gotham
EX $45 **NM** $110

No. G-1550 Yankee Stadium Grandstand, 1962-64, Gotham
EX $40 **NM** $80

No. G-812 Joe Namath, 1969-71, Gotham
EX $35 **NM** $75

No. G-812 Joe Namath, 1972, Gotham
EX $35 **NM** $85

No. G-818 Roman Gabriel Model, 1969-71, Gotham
EX $25 **NM** $65

No. G-818 Roman Gabriel Model, 1972, Gotham
EX $25 **NM** $55

No. G-880 Gotham All-Star Electric Football, 1956-58, Gotham
EX $30 **NM** $70

No. G-880 Gotham All-Star Electric Football, 1959-61, Gotham
EX $25 **NM** $50

No. G-882, 1965-67, Gotham
EX $18 **NM** $50

No. G-883, 1968, Gotham
EX $15 **NM** $40

No. G-883, 1972, Gotham
EX $10 **NM** $20

No. G-890 Gotham Official NFL Electric Football, 1962-64, Gotham
EX $20 **NM** $45

No. G-895 NFL Players Association, 1969-71, Gotham
EX $22 **NM** $50

No. G-940 Gotham Electro Magnetic Football, 1954-55, Gotham
EX $38 **NM** $80

Tudor Electronic Football, 1965, Tudor
EX $15 **NM** $35

Tudor Tru-Action Electric Football, 1949, Tudor
EX $25 **NM** $40

HOCKEY

Bobby Hull, 1960s, Munro
EX $125 **NM** $275

Bobby Hull, 1970s, Munro
EX $75 **NM** $155

Bobby Orr, late 1960s-early 1970s, Munro
EX $125 **NM** $265

Canadian, late 1960s, Eagle
EX $75 **NM** $145

Canadian Hockey Master, 1963, Munro, #976
EX $100 **NM** $225

City Series, early 1970s, Coleco
EX $100 **NM** $210

Foster Hewitt, 1950s, Reliable
EX $125 **NM** $235

Hockey games, 1940s-50s, Cresta, various games
EX $200 **NM** $500

Hot Shot, late 1960s, Munro
EX $60 **NM** $125

Hot Shot, mid 1960s, Munro
EX $75 **NM** $160

National, early 1960s, Eagle
EX $125 **NM** $200

NHL All-Pro Hockey, 1969, Tudor
EX $25 **NM** $60

NHPLA, 1969, Tudor
EX $75 **NM** $135

No. 5100 Pro Stars, mid 1960s-early 1970s, Coleco
EX $65 **NM** $125

No. 5160-80 Pro Stars, late 1960s-early 1970s, Coleco
EX $75 **NM** $165

No. 730 NHL All-Star Hockey, 1968, Tudor
EX $25 **NM** $50

No. G1200, 1950s-1960s, Gotham
EX $75 **NM** $155

No. G-200, 1930s-1950s, Gotham
EX $125 **NM** $350

Official Hockey Night, early 1960s, Eagle
EX $150 **NM** $325

Official NHL, 1969-71, Coleco
EX $150 **NM** $500

Olympic, 1964, Eagle
EX $200 **NM** $500

Pee Wee, late 1950s, Eagle
EX $150 **NM** $260

Playmaker, early 1960s, Eagle
EX $150 **NM** $250

Playoff, early 1960s, Eagle
EX $125 **NM** $225

Power Play, early 1960s, Eagle
EX $125 **NM** $200

Power Play, late 1950s, Eagle
EX $125 **NM** $230

Power Play, late 1960s, Coleco
EX $100 **NM** $185

Pro Series, mid 1950s-early 1960s, Eagle
EX $125 **NM** $225

Stanley Cup, mid 1960s, Eagle
EX $150 **NM** $275

Stanley Cup, Beliveau, late 1960s, Coleco
EX $125 **NM** $235

HORSE RACING

Horse and Harness Race Game, 1963-64, Tudor, combined game
EX $20 **NM** $50

No. 525 Horse Race Game, 1950-58, Tudor
EX $25 **NM** $65

No. 525 Horse Race Game, 1959-61, Tudor, grooved plastic track
EX $22 **NM** $55

No. 525 Tru-Action Electric Horse Race Game, 1962, Tudor, plastic track, no grooves
EX $20 NM $40

No. 526 Harness Race Game, 1962, Tudor
EX $20 NM $45

Tru-Action Races Game, 1965-67, Tudor
EX $35 NM $75

TRACK AND FIELD

No. 528 Track and Field Meet, 1963-64, Tudor
EX $35 NM $85

No. 528 Tru-Action Races, 1965-67, Tudor
EX $35 NM $90

No. 528 Tudor Track, 1962, Tudor, plastic track
EX $15 NM $45

Postwar Games

BOARD GAMES

$10,000 Pyramid Game, The, 1974, Milton Bradley
EX $8 NM $15 MIP $20

$20,000 Pyramid Game, The, 1975, Milton Bradley
EX $8 NM $15 MIP $20

$25,000 Pyramid, 1980s, Cardinal Industries
EX $10 NM $15 MIP $25

$64,000 Question Quiz Game, 1955, Lowell
EX $12 NM $25 MIP $30

1-2-3 Game Hot Spot!, 1961, Parker Brothers
EX $6 NM $15 MIP $20

1863, Civil War Game, 1961, Parker Brothers
EX $10 NM $20 MIP $40

2 For The Money, 1955, Lowell
EX $10 NM $15 MIP $20

20,000 Leagues Under the Sea, 1950s, Gardner
EX $30 NM $55 MIP $50

221 B Baker Street, 1978, John Hansen
EX $2 NM $6 MIP $10

25 Ghosts, 1969, Lakeside
EX $15 NM $25 MIP $40

3 Up, 1972, Lakeside
EX $3 NM $7 MIP $12

300 Mile Race, 1955, Warren
EX $15 NM $20 MIP $40

36 Fits, 1966, Watkins-Strathmore
EX $12 NM $30 MIP $40

4 Alarm Game, 1963, Milton Bradley
EX $18 NM $40 MIP $65

4000 A.D. Interstellar Conflict Game, 1972, House of Games
EX $8 NM $20 MIP $35

77 Sunset Strip, 1960, Lowell
EX $30 NM $40 MIP $50

99, The Game of, 1969, Broman-Percepta Corp.
EX $8 NM $17 MIP $25

Abbott & Costello Who's On First?, 1978, Selchow & Righter
EX $5 NM $10 MIP $15

ABC Monday Night Football Roger Staubach Edition, 1973, Aurora
EX $15 NM $25 MIP $35

ABC Sports Winter Olympics, 1987, Mindscape
EX $10 NM $15 MIP $25

Acquire (plastic tiles), 1968, 3M
EX $12 NM $30 MIP $45

Acquire (wood tiles), 1963, 3M
EX $35 NM $75 MIP $100

Across the Board Horse Racing Game, 1975, MPH
EX $8 NM $20 MIP $35

Across the Continent (cars), 1960, Parker Brothers
EX $20 NM $30 MIP $40

Across the Continent (trains), 1952, Parker Brothers
EX $20 NM $30 MIP $40

Action Baseball, 1965, Pressman
EX $20 NM $30 MIP $40

Addams Family, 1965, Ideal
EX $65 NM $90 MIP $125

Addams Family, 1973, Milton Bradley
EX $15 NM $25 MIP $30

Admirals, 1973, Parker Brothers (U.K.)
EX $10 NM $25 MIP $35

Advance To Boardwalk, 1985, Parker Brothers
EX $5 NM $15 MIP $20

Adventure in Science, An, 1950, Jacmar
EX $20 NM $30 MIP $50

Agent Zero-M Spy Detector, 1964, Mattel
EX $30 NM $65 MIP $80

Aggravation, 1970, Lakeside
EX $5 NM $10 MIP $15

Air Assault on Crete, 1977, Avalon Hill
EX $3 NM $10 MIP $15

Air Charter, 1970, Waddington
EX $10 NM $25 MIP $35

Air Empire, 1961, Avalon Hill
EX $100 NM $200 MIP $250

Air Race Around the World, 1950s, Lido
EX $12 NM $30 MIP $50

Air Traffic Controller, 1974, Schaper
EX $12 NM $30 MIP $40

Airline, 1985, Mulgara Products
EX $4 NM $10 MIP $15

Airline: The Jet Age Game, 1977, MPH Games
EX $6 NM $16 MIP $25

Alfred Hitchcock "Why?", 1965, Milton Bradley
EX $10 NM $20 MIP $30

Alfred Hitchcock Presents Mystery Game "Why", 1958, Milton Bradley
EX $20 NM $35 MIP $55

Alien, 1979, Kenner
EX $15 NM $30 MIP $40

All American Football, 1969, Cadaco
EX $5 NM $10 MIP $20

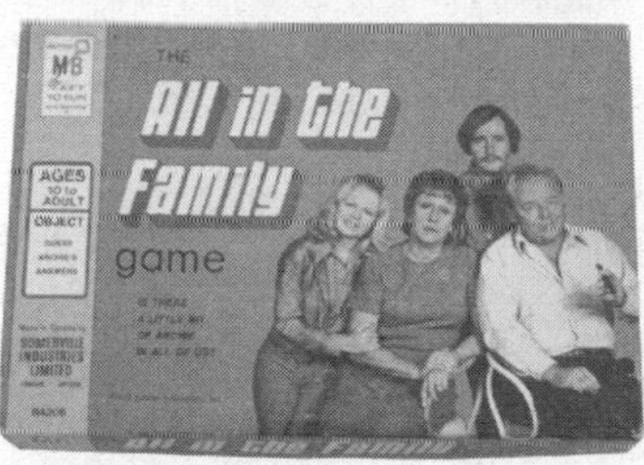

All In The Family, 1972, Milton Bradley
EX $10 NM $20 MIP $30

All My Children, 1985, TSR
EX $5 NM $10 MIP $20

All Pro Baseball, 1969, Ideal
EX $20 NM $35 MIP $55

All Pro Basketball, 1969, Ideal
EX $10 NM $25 MIP $35

All Pro Football, 1967, Ideal
EX $10 NM $30 MIP $30

All Star Baseball, 1960s, Cadaco-Ellis
EX $30 NM $65 MIP $125

All Star Baseball, 1970s, Cadaco-Ellis
EX $10 NM $25 MIP $45

All Star Baseball, 1989, Cadaco
EX $5 NM $12 MIP $20

All Star Baseball Fame, 1962, Cadaco-Ellis
EX $15 NM $25 MIP $40

All Star Basketball, 1950s, Gardner
EX $55 NM $90 MIP $135

All Star Electric Baseball & Football, 1955, Harett-Gilmar
EX $35 NM $65 MIP $90

All Star Football, 1950, Gardner
EX $20 NM $45 MIP $65

All The King's Men, 1979, Parker Brothers
EX $6 NM $10 MIP $15

All Time Greats Baseball Game, 1971, Midwest Research
EX $15 NM $35 MIP $50

Alumni Fun, 1964, Milton Bradley
EX $8 NM $20 MIP $30

Amazing Dunninger Mind Reading Game, 1967, Hasbro
EX $12 NM $20 MIP $25

American Derby, The, 1951, Cadaco-Ellis
EX $15 NM $20 MIP $30

American Dream, The, 1979, Milton Bradley
EX $10 NM $25 MIP $35

Animal Crackers, 1970s, Milton Bradley
EX $4 NM $7 MIP $11

Annette's Secret Passage, 1958, Parker Brothers
EX $10 NM $20 MIP $30

Annie Oakley (larger), 1955, Milton Bradley
EX $20 NM $40 MIP $60

Annie Oakley (smaller game), 1950s, Milton Bradley
EX $12 NM $30 MIP $40

Annie, The Movie Game, 1981, Parker Brothers
EX $4 NM $6 MIP $10

Anti-Monopoly, 1973, Anti-Monopoly
EX $8 NM $20 MIP $30

APBA "Pro" League Football, 1980s, APBA
EX $12 NM $20 MIP $30

APBA Baseball Master Game, 1975, APBA
EX $20 NM $75 MIP $100

APBA Pro League Football, 1964, APBA
EX $25 NM $60 MIP $85

APBA Saddle Racing Game, 1970s, APBA
EX $15 NM $25 MIP $40

Apollo: A Voyage to the Moon, 1969, Tracianne
EX $12 NM $30 MIP $40

Apple's Way, 1974, Milton Bradley
EX $12 NM $20 MIP $30

Archies, The, 1969, Whitman
EX $15 NM $20 MIP $40

Arena, 1962, Lakeside
EX $6 NM $15 MIP $25

Arnold Palmer's Inside Golf, 1961, D.B. Remson
EX $30 NM $45 MIP $75

Around the World, 1962, Milton Bradley
EX $10 NM $25 MIP $35

Around The World in 80 Days, 1957, Transogram
EX $10 NM $20 MIP $30

Art Lewis Football Game, 1955, Morgantown Game
EX $70 NM $115 MIP $175

Art Linkletter's House Party, 1968, Whitman
EX $8 NM $20 MIP $30

As The World Turns, 1966, Parker Brothers
EX $12 NM $20 MIP $30

ASG Baseball, 1989, 3W (World Wide Wargames)
EX $15 NM $35 MIP $50

ASG Major League Baseball, 1973, Gerney Games
EX $35 NM $75 MIP $125

Assembly Line, 1953, Selchow & Righter
EX $18 NM $27 MIP $50

Astro Launch, 1963, Ohio Art
EX $18 NM $40 MIP $60

Astron, 1955, Parker Prothers
EX $25 NM $35 MIP $60

A-Team, 1984, Parker Brothers
EX $5 NM $15 MIP $15

Atom Ant Game, 1966, Transogram
EX $25 NM $60 MIP $90

Aurora Pursuit! Game, 1973, Aurora
EX $8 NM $25 MIP $40

Auto Dome, 1967, Transogram
EX $18 NM $40 MIP $60

Autograph Baseball Game, 1948, Philadelphia Inquirer
EX $110 NM $180 MIP $275

B.T.O. (Big Time Operator), 1956, Bettye-B
EX $20 NM $30 MIP $40

B-17 Queen of The Skies, 1983, Avalon Hill
EX $6 NM $10 MIP $15

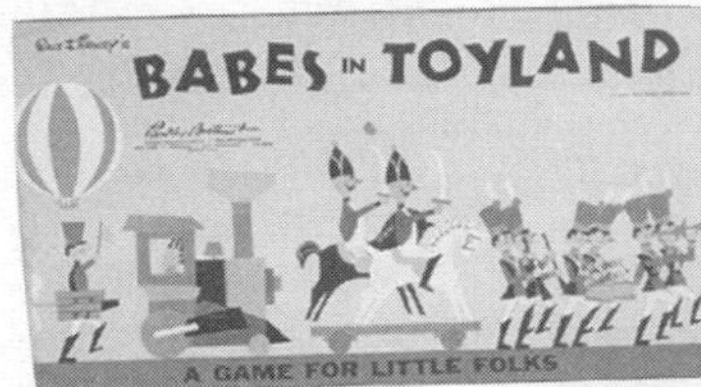

Babes in Toyland, 1961, Whitman
EX $15 NM $27 MIP $35

Ballplayer's Baseball Game, 1955, Jon Weber
EX $30 NM $50 MIP $75

Bamboozle, 1962, Milton Bradley
EX $15 NM $20 MIP $30

Banana Tree, 1977, Marx
EX $10 NM $15 MIP $25

Bang, A Game of the Old West, 1956, Selchow & Righter
EX $35 NM $75 MIP $100

Bantu, 1955, Parker Brothers
EX $15 NM $22 MIP $30

Barbapapa Takes A Trip, 1977, Selchow & Righter
EX $3 NM $5 MIP $8

Barbie, Queen of The Prom, 1960, Mattel
EX $30 NM $60 MIP $85

Barbie's Little Sister Skipper Game, 1964, Mattel
EX $15 NM $40 MIP $60

Baretta, 1976, Milton Bradley
EX $30 NM $50 MIP $75

Bargain Hunter, 1981, Milton Bradley
EX $6 NM $15 MIP $25

Barnabas Collins Game, 1969, Milton Bradley
EX $20 NM $50 MIP $70

Barney Miller, 1977, Parker Brothers
EX $10 NM $15 MIP $25

Barnstormer, 1970s, Marx
EX $20 NM $35 MIP $55

Bart Starr Quarterback Game, 1960s
EX $175 NM $300 MIP $450

Bar-Teen Ranch Game, 1950s, Warren Built-Rite
EX $10 NM $25 MIP $35

Baseball Challenge, 1980, Tri-Valley Games
EX $15 NM $35 MIP $50

Baseball Game, Official, 1969, Milton Bradley
EX $50 NM $77 MIP $100

Baseball Game, The, 1988, Horatio
EX $12 NM $20 MIP $30

Baseball Strategy, 1973, Avalon Hill
EX $6 NM $15 MIP $25

Baseball, A Sports Illustrated Game, 1971-73, Time
EX $60 NM $150 MIP $200

Baseball, Football & Checkers, 1957, Parker Brothers
EX $20 NM $30 MIP $50

Basketball Strategy, 1974, Avalon Hill
EX $10 NM $15 MIP $25

Bat Masterson, 1958, Lowell
EX $20 NM $45 MIP $75

Batman, 1978, Hasbro
EX $15 **NM** $30 **MIP** $50

Batman and Robin Game, 1965, Hasbro
EX $30 **NM** $75 **MIP** $95

Batman Game, 1966, Milton Bradley
EX $25 **NM** $65 **MIP** $90

Batter Up, 1946, M. Hopper
EX $30 **NM** $50 **MIP** $75

Batter-Rou Baseball Game (Dizzy Dean), 1950s, Memphis Plastic
EX $100 **NM** $165 **MIP** $250

Battle Cry, 1962, Milton Bradley
EX $25 **NM** $40 **MIP** $85

Battle Line, 1964, Ideal
EX $25 **NM** $40 **MIP** $75

Battle Masters, 1992, Milton Bradley
EX $15 **NM** $40 **MIP** $60

Battle of the Planets, 1970s, Milton Bradley
EX $15 **NM** $25 **MIP** $35

Battleboard, 1972, Ideal
EX $10 **NM** $25 **MIP** $35

Battleship, 1965, Milton Bradley
EX $10 **NM** $15 **MIP** $20

Battlestar Galactica, 1978, Parker Brothers
EX $10 **NM** $22 **MIP** $25

Battling Tops Game, 1968, Ideal
EX $30 **NM** $50 **MIP** $80

Bazaar, 1967, 3M
EX $12 **NM** $30 **MIP** $40

Bazaar, 1987, Discovery Toys
EX $8 **NM** $20 **MIP** $30

Beany & Cecil Match It, 1960s, Mattel
EX $30 **NM** $55 **MIP** $80

Beat Inflation, 1975, Avalon Hill
EX $8 **NM** $20 **MIP** $30

Beat the 8 Ball, 1975, Ideal
EX $10 **NM** $15 **MIP** $25

Beat The Buzz, 1958, Kenner
EX $10 **NM** $17 **MIP** $25

Beat The Clock, 1954, Lowell
EX $15 **NM** $35 **MIP** $50

Beat The Clock, 1960s, Milton Bradley
EX $6 **NM** $10 **MIP** $16

Beatles Flip Your Wig Game, 1964, Milton Bradley
EX $100 **NM** $150 **MIP** $275

Beetle Bailey, The Old Army Game, 1963, Milton Bradley
EX $20 **NM** $40 **MIP** $65

Behind the 8 Ball Game, 1969, Selchow & Righter
EX $8 **NM** $15 **MIP** $20

Ben Casey MD Game, 1961, Transogram
EX $15 **NM** $20 **MIP** $35

Bermuda Triangle, 1976, Milton Bradley
EX $10 **NM** $15 **MIP** $20

Betsy Ross and the Flag, 1950s, Transogram
EX $18 **NM** $45 **MIP** $70

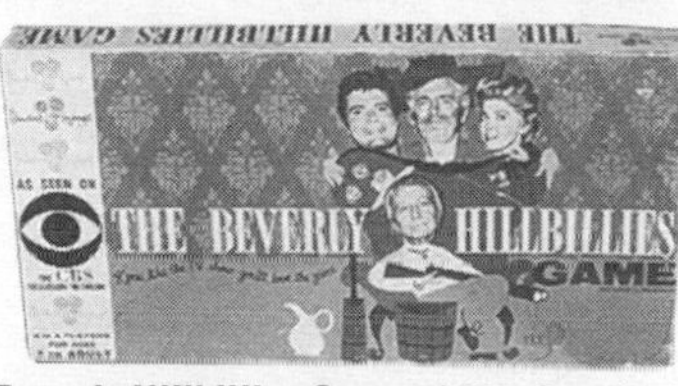

Beverly Hillbillies Game, 1963, Standard Toykraft, "If you like the T.V. show... you'll love the game..."
EX $25 **NM** $40 **MIP** $50

Bewitched, 1965
EX $50 **NM** $75 **MIP** $100

Beyond the Stars, 1964, Game Partners
EX $20 **NM** $45 **MIP** $65

Bible Baseball, 1950s, Standard
EX $50 **NM** $75 **MIP** $150

Big Boggle, 1979, Parker Brothers
EX $10 **NM** $15 **MIP** $20

Big Foot, 1977, Milton Bradley
EX $5 **NM** $12 **MIP** $20

Big League Baseball, 1959, Saalfield
EX $20 **NM** $45 **MIP** $65

Big League Baseball Game, 1966, 3M
EX $15 **NM** $25 **MIP** $40

Big League Manager Football, 1965, BLM
EX $30 **NM** $75 **MIP** $100

Big Payoff, 1984, Payoff Enterprises
EX $6 **NM** $10 **MIP** $15

Big Six Sports Game, 1950s, Gardner
EX $125 **NM** $275 **MIP** $450

Big Time Colorado Football, 1983, B.J. Tall
EX $6 **NM** $10 **MIP** $15

Big Town, 1954, Lowell
EX $10 **NM** $20 **MIP** $40

Billionaire, 1973, Parker Brothers
EX $5 **NM** $10 **MIP** $15

Bing Crosby's Game, Call Me Lucky, 1954, Parker Brothers
EX $15 **NM** $35 **MIP** $50

Bingo-Matic, 1954, Transogram
EX $5 **NM** $10 **MIP** $15

Bionic Crisis, 1975, Parker Brothers
EX $6 **NM** $15 **MIP** $22

Bionic Woman, 1976, Parker Brothers
EX $6 **NM** $15 **MIP** $22

Bird Brain, 1966, Milton Bradley
EX $10 **NM** $25 **MIP** $40

Bird Watcher, 1958, Parker Brothers
EX $15 **NM** $35 **MIP** $50

Birdie Golf, 1964, Barris
EX $15 **NM** $35 **MIP** $50

Black Ball Express, 1957, Schaper
EX $8 **NM** $25 **MIP** $40

Black Beauty, 1957, Transogram
EX $15 **NM** $25 **MIP** $25

Black Box, 1978, Parker Brothers
EX $5 **NM** $10 **MIP** $15

Blade Runner, 1982
EX $25 **NM** $60 **MIP** $85

Blast Off, 1953, Selchow & Righter
EX $50 **NM** $100 **MIP** $125

Blast, The Game of, 1973, Ideal
EX $8 **NM** $20 **MIP** $35

Blitzkrieg, 1965, Avalon Hill
EX $4 **NM** $10 **MIP** $16

Blockhead, 1954, Russell
EX $5 **NM** $10 **MIP** $25

Blondie, 1970s, Parker Brothers
EX $6 **NM** $10 **MIP** $17

Postwar Games

Blondie and Dagwood's Race for the Office, 1950, Jaymar
EX $20 **NM** $35 **MIP** $70

Blue Line Hockey, 1968, 3M
EX $10 **NM** $25 **MIP** $40

Bluff, 1964, Saalfield
EX $10 **NM** $25 **MIP** $40

BMX Cross Challenge Action Game, 1988, Cross Challenge
EX $6 **NM** $10 **MIP** $15

Bob Feller's Big League Baseball, 1949, Saalfield
EX $75 **NM** $100 **MIP** $150

Bobbsey Twins, 1957, Milton Bradley
EX $8 **NM** $15 **MIP** $20

Bobby Shantz Baseball Game, 1955, Realistic Games
EX $80 **NM** $150 **MIP** $235

Body Language, 1975, Milton Bradley
EX $2 **NM** $5 **MIP** $10

Boggle, 1976, Parker Brothers
EX $3 **NM** $8 **MIP** $12

Bonanza Michigan Rummy Game, 1964, Parker Brothers
EX $20 **NM** $35 **MIP** $40

Bonkers!, This Game is, 1978, Parker Brothers
EX $3 **NM** $10 **MIP** $15

Boom or Bust, 1951, Parker Brothers
EX $75 **NM** $150 **MIP** $200

Booth's Pro Conference Football, 1977, Sher-Co
EX $10 **NM** $15 **MIP** $25

Boots and Saddles, 1960, Chad Valley
EX $35 **NM** $65 **MIP** $100

Boris Karloff's Monster Game, 1965, Gems
EX $100 **NM** $150 **MIP** $250

Boston Marathon Game, Official, 1978, Perl Products
EX $15 **NM** $25 **MIP** $35

Bottoms Up, 1970s
EX $3 **NM** $5 **MIP** $8

Boundary, 1970, Mattel
EX $8 **NM** $20 **MIP** $30

Bowl & Score, 1974, Lowe
EX $6 **NM** $8 **MIP** $10

Bowl And Score, 1962, Lowe
EX $6 **NM** $10 **MIP** $15

Bowl Bound!, 1973, Sports Illustrated
EX $15 **NM** $25 **MIP** $40

Brain Waves, 1977, Milton Bradley
EX $6 **NM** $15 **MIP** $25

Branded, 1966, Milton Bradley
EX $25 **NM** $45 **MIP** $60

Brass Monkey Game, The, 1973, U.S. Game Systems
EX $2 **NM** $5 **MIP** $10

Break Par Golf Game, 1950s, Warren/Built-Rite
EX $8 **NM** $20 **MIP** $30

Break The Bank, 1955, Bettye-B
EX $12 **NM** $25 **MIP** $40

Breaker 1-9, 1976, Milton Bradley
EX $5 **NM** $10 **MIP** $15

Breakthru, 1965, 3M
EX $8 **NM** $20 **MIP** $35

Brett Ball, 1981, 9th Inning
EX $15 **NM** $20 **MIP** $30

Bride Bingo, 1957, Leister Game
EX $2 **NM** $5 **MIP** $8

Bride Game, The, 1971, Selchow & Righter
EX $12 **NM** $25 **MIP** $50

Broadside, 1962, Milton Bradley
EX $35 **NM** $75 **MIP** $100

Broadsides & Board Gameing Parties, 1984, Milton Bradley
EX $50 **NM** $125 **MIP** $175

Bruce Jenner Decathlon Game, 1979, Parker Brothers
EX $4 **NM** $7 **MIP** $11

Buck Fever, 1984, L & D Robton
EX $12 **NM** $20 **MIP** $30

Buck Rogers Game, 1979, Milton Bradley
EX $10 **NM** $25 **MIP** $40

Buck Rogers: Battle for the 25th Century, 1988, TSR
EX $18 **NM** $45 **MIP** $65

Buckaroo, 1947, Milton Bradley
EX $20 **NM** $35 **MIP** $45

Bucket Ball, 1972, Marx
EX $10 **NM** $15 **MIP** $25

Bug-A-Boo, 1968, Whitman
EX $6 **NM** $15 **MIP** $20

Bugaloos, 1971, Milton Bradley
EX $15 **NM** $35 **MIP** $50

Bugs Bunny Under the Cawit Game, 1972, Whitman
EX $15 **NM** $25 **MIP** $40

Building Boom, 1950s, Kohner
EX $10 **NM** $20 **MIP** $35

Built-Rite Swish Basketball Game, 1950s, Warren/Built-Rite
EX $10 **NM** $20 **MIP** $40

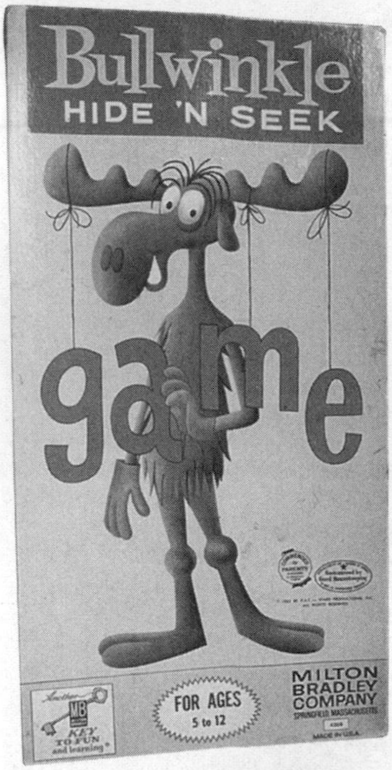

Bullwinkle Hide & Seek Game, 1961, Milton Bradley
EX $20 **NM** $45 **MIP** $90

Bullwinkle's Super Market Game, 1970s, Whitman
EX $15 **NM** $50 **MIP** $75

Buster Brown Game and Play Box, 1950s, Buster Brown Shoes
EX $40 **NM** $75 **MIP** $125

Buy and Sell, 1953, Whitman
EX $8 **NM** $15 **MIP** $20

Buy or Sell, 1967, KMS Industries
EX $5 **NM** $12 **MIP** $18

C&O/B&O, 1969, Avalon Hill
EX $20 **NM** $50 **MIP** $95

Cabbage Patch Kids, 1984, Parker Brothers
EX $5 **NM** $10 **MIP** $15

California Raisins Board Game, 1987, Decipher
EX $4 **NM** $16 **MIP** $25

Call it Golf, 1966, Strauss
EX $15 **NM** $25 **MIP** $40

Call My Bluff, 1965, Milton Bradley
EX $15 **NM** $20 **MIP** $30

Calling All Cars, 1930s-40s, Parker Brothers
EX $40 **NM** $50 **MIP** $75

Calling All Cars, 1950s, Parker Brothers
EX $10 **NM** $20 **MIP** $30

Calling Superman, 1955, Transogram
EX $45 **NM** $85 **MIP** $140

Calvin & The Colonel High Spirits, 1962, Milton Bradley
EX $12 **NM** $25 **MIP** $35

Camelot, 1955, Parker Brothers
EX $15 **NM** $20 **MIP** $25

Camouflage, 1961, Milton Bradley
EX $5 **NM** $20 **MIP** $35

Camp Granada Game, Allan Sherman's, 1965, Milton Bradley
EX $40 **NM** $70 **MIP** $100

Camp Runamuck, 1965, Ideal
EX $25 **NM** $45 **MIP** $55

Campaign, 1966, Campaign Game
EX $8 **NM** $25 **MIP** $40

Campaign, 1971, Waddington
EX $10 **NM** $30 **MIP** $45

Campaign: The American "Go" Game, 1961, Saalfield
EX $15 **NM** $45 **MIP** $65

Can You Catch It Charlie Brown?, 1976, Ideal
EX $10 **NM** $25 **MIP** $35

Candid Camera Game, 1963, Lowell
EX $15 **NM** $25 **MIP** $35

Candyland, 1949, Milton Bradley
EX $25 **NM** $50 **MIP** $75

Candyland, 1955, Milton Bradley
EX $20 **NM** $35 **MIP** $50

Cannonball Run, The, 1981, Cadaco
EX $4 **NM** $16 **MIP** $25

Can't Stop, 1980, Parker Brothers
EX $5 **NM** $12 **MIP** $20

Caper, 1970, Parker Brothers
EX $30 **NM** $70 **MIP** $100

Capital Punishment, 1981, Hammerhead
EX $20 **NM** $35 **MIP** $60

Captain America, 1966, Milton Bradley
EX $25 **NM** $50 **MIP** $75

Captain America, 1977, Milton Bradley
EX $10 **NM** $15 **MIP** $25

Captain Caveman and the Teen Angels, 1981, Milton Bradley
EX $8 **NM** $20 **MIP** $30

Captain Gallant Desert Fort Game, 1956, Transogram
EX $20 **NM** $40 **MIP** $65

Captain Kangaroo, 1956, Milton Bradley
EX $35 **NM** $45 **MIP** $100

Captain Video Game, 1952, Milton Bradley
EX $50 **NM** $75 **MIP** $125

Car Travel Game, 1958, Milton Bradley
EX $5 **NM** $10 **MIP** $15

Carapace, 1970, Plan B Corp.
EX $5 **NM** $16 **MIP** $25

Cardino, 1970, Milton Bradley
EX $10 **NM** $15 **MIP** $25

Careers, 1957, Parker Brothers
EX $8 **NM** $20 **MIP** $30

Careers, 1965, Parker Brothers
EX $15 **NM** $20 **MIP** $33

Cargoes, 1958, Selchow & Righter
EX $10 **NM** $25 **MIP** $50

Carl Hubbell Mechanical Baseball, 1950, Gotham
EX $65 **NM** $100 **MIP** $125

Carl Yastrzemski's Action Baseball, 1968, Pressman
EX $50 **NM** $75 **MIP** $125

Carrier Strike, 1977, Milton Bradley
EX $15 **NM** $25 **MIP** $35

Cars 'n Trucks Build-A-Game, 1961, Ideal
EX $15 **NM** $45 **MIP** $80

Cartel, 1974, Gamut of Games
EX $18 **NM** $45 **MIP** $65

Case of the Elusive Assassin, The, 1967, Ideal
EX $20 **NM** $30 **MIP** $50

Casey Jones, 1959, Saalfield
EX $20 **NM** $45 **MIP** $65

Casper the Friendly Ghost Game, 1959, Milton Bradley
EX $5 **NM** $10 **MIP** $15

Casper the Friendly Ghost Game, 1974, Schaper
EX $8 **NM** $18 **MIP** $30

Castle Risk, 1986, Parker Brothers
EX $15 **NM** $35 **MIP** $50

Cat & Mouse, 1964, Parker Brothers
EX $7 **NM** $15 **MIP** $20

Catchword, 1954, Whitman
EX $3 **NM** $5 **MIP** $10

Catfish Bend Storybook Game, 1978, Selchow & Righter
EX $15 **NM** $20 **MIP** $35

Cathedral, 1986, Mattel
EX $10 **NM** $25 **MIP** $35

Cattlemen, The, 1977, Selchow & Righter
EX $10 **NM** $15 **MIP** $25

Cavalcade, 1953, Selchow & Righter
EX $15 **NM** $25 **MIP** $35

Caveat Emptor, 1971, Plan B
EX $5 **NM** $16 **MIP** $25

Centipede, 1983, Milton Bradley
EX $6 **NM** $10 **MIP** $15

Century of Great Fights, 1969, Research Games
EX $40 **NM** $75 **MIP** $110

Challenge Golf at Pebble Beach, 1972, 3M
EX $6 **NM** $15 **MIP** $25

Challenge the Yankees, 1960s, Hasbro
EX $500 **NM** $1000 **MIP** $1800

Challenge Yahtzee, 1974, Milton Bradley
EX $7 **NM** $15 **MIP** $20

Championship Baseball, 1966, Championship Games
EX $8 **NM** $20 **MIP** $30

Championship Basketball, 1966, Championship Games
EX $8 **NM** $20 **MIP** $30

Championship Golf, 1966, Championship Games
EX $8 **NM** $20 **MIP** $30

Changeover: The Metric Game, 1976, John Ladell
EX $8 **NM** $20 **MIP** $30

Changing Society, 1981, Phil Carter
EX $5 **NM** $16 **MIP** $25

Chaos, 1965, Amsco Toys
EX $5 **NM** $16 **MIP** $25

Chaos, 1971, Lakeside
EX $8 **NM** $20 **MIP** $30

Charlie Brown's All Star Baseball Game, 1965, Parker Brothers
EX $18 **NM** $23 **MIP** $50

Charlie's Angels, 1977, Milton Bradley
EX $6 **NM** $10 **MIP** $20

Charlie's Angels (Farrah Fawcett box), 1977, Milton Bradley, Notice the price difference between this version and the non-Farrah edition? Star power really brings up the price on this game
EX $10 **NM** $20 **MIP** $35

GAMES

Charlotte's Web Game, 1974, Hasbro
EX $10 **NM** $25 **MIP** $35

Chase, The, 1966, Cadaco
EX $12 **NM** $30 **MIP** $35

Chaseback, 1962, Milton Bradley
EX $5 **NM** $16 **MIP** $25

Checkpoint: Danger!, 1978, Ideal
EX $5 **NM** $16 **MIP** $25

Cherry Ames' Nursing Game, 1959, Parker Brothers
EX $50 **NM** $90 **MIP** $115

Chess, 1977, Milton Bradley
EX $3 **NM** $5 **MIP** $8

Chevyland Sweepstakes, 1968, Milton Bradley
EX $25 **NM** $50 **MIP** $100

Chex Ches Football, 1971, Chex Ches Games
EX $15 **NM** $25 **MIP** $40

Cheyenne, 1958, Milton Bradley
EX $25 **NM** $45 **MIP** $60

Chicago Sports Trivia Game, 1984, Sports Trivia
EX $6 **NM** $10 **MIP** $15

Chicken In Every Pot, A, 1980s, Animal Town Game
EX $20 **NM** $30 **MIP** $50

Children's Hour, The, 1946, Parker Brothers
EX $5 **NM** $10 **MIP** $15

CHiPs, 1981, Ideal
EX $7 **NM** $10 **MIP** $20

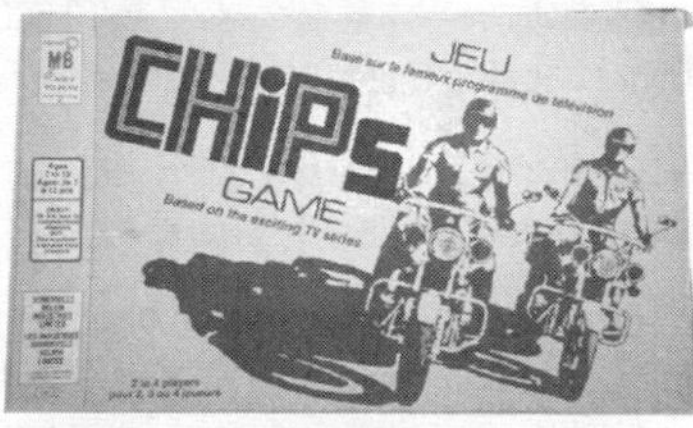

CHiPs Game, 1977, Milton Bradley
EX $4 **NM** $7 **MIP** $10

Chit Chat Game, 1963, Milton Bradley
EX $6 **NM** $10 **MIP** $15

Chopper Strike, 1976, Milton Bradley
EX $10 **NM** $15 **MIP** $20

Chug-A-Lug, 1969, Dynamic
EX $5 **NM** $16 **MIP** $25

Chute-5, 1973, Lowe
EX $5 **NM** $12 **MIP** $20

Chutes & Ladders, 1956, Milton Bradley
EX $10 **NM** $15 **MIP** $20

Chutzpah, 1967, Cadaco
EX $10 **NM** $20 **MIP** $30

Chutzpah, 1967, Middle Earth
EX $15 **NM** $20 **MIP** $40

Cimarron Strip, 1967, Ideal
EX $35 **NM** $75 **MIP** $90

Circle Racer Board Game, 1988, Sport Games USA
EX $6 **NM** $10 **MIP** $15

Cities Game, The, 1970, Psychology Today
EX $5 **NM** $16 **MIP** $25

Civil War, 1961, Avalon Hill
EX $15 **NM** $45 **MIP** $65

Civilization, 1982, Avalon Hill
EX $10 **NM** $17 **MIP** $28

Clash of the Titans, 1981, Whitman
EX $10 **NM** $25 **MIP** $45

Class Struggle, 1978, Bernard Ollman
EX $15 **NM** $25 **MIP** $50

Clean Sweep, 1960s, Schaper
EX $15 **NM** $20 **MIP** $35

Clean Water, 1972, Urban Systems
EX $8 **NM** $25 **MIP** $40

Cloak & Dagger, 1984, Ideal
EX $8 **NM** $25 **MIP** $40

Close Encounters of the Third Kind, 1977, Parker Brothers
EX $7 **NM** $15 **MIP** $20

Clue, 1949, Parker Brothers
EX $35 **NM** $50 **MIP** $75

Clue, 1972, Parker Brothers
EX $4 **NM** $7 **MIP** $11

Clue Master Detective, 1988, Parker Brothers
EX $20 **NM** $15 **MIP** $65

Clue: The Great Museum Caper, 1991, Parker Brothers
EX $8 **NM** $20 **MIP** $30

Code Name: Sector, 1977, Parker Brothers
EX $10 **NM** $30 **MIP** $45

Collector, The, 1977, Avalon Hill
EX $5 **NM** $16 **MIP** $25

College Basketball, 1954, Cadaco-Ellis
EX $10 **NM** $25 **MIP** $35

Columbo, 1973, Milton Bradley
EX $6 **NM** $10 **MIP** $15

Combat, 1963, Ideal
EX $25 **NM** $45 **MIP** $60

Comin' Round The Mountain, 1954, Einson-Freeman
EX $30 **NM** $50 **MIP** $80

Computer Baseball, 1966, Epoch Playtime
EX $25 **NM** $40 **MIP** $65

Computer Basketball, 1969, Electric Data
EX $10 **NM** $25 **MIP** $35

Computerized Pro Football, 1971, Data Prog.
EX $15 **NM** $25 **MIP** $40

Concentration (25th Anniversary Ed.), 1982, Milton Bradley
EX $6 **NM** $10 **MIP** $16

Concentration (3rd Ed.), 1960, Milton Bradley
EX $12 **NM** $15 **MIP** $20

Conestoga, 1964, Washburne Research
EX $25 **NM** $65 **MIP** $95

Coney Island, The Game of, 1956, Selchow & Righter
EX $20 **NM** $35 **MIP** $45

Conflict, 1960, Parker Brothers
EX $25 **NM** $35 **MIP** $50

Confucius Say, 1960s, Pressman
EX $10 **NM** $15 **MIP** $20

Conquer, 1979, Whitman
EX $8 **NM** $17 **MIP** $25

Conquest of the Empire, 1984, Milton Bradley
EX $50 **NM** $105 **MIP** $150

Consetta and Her Wheel of Fate, 1946, Selchow & Righter
EX $20 **NM** $50 **MIP** $65

Conspiracy, 1982, Milton Bradley
EX $4 **NM** $9 **MIP** $11

Containment, 1979, Shamus Gamus
EX $10 **NM** $25 **MIP** $35

Contigo, 1974, 3M
EX $7 **NM** $20 **MIP** $35

Cootie, 1949, Schaper
EX $10 **NM** $20 **MIP** $30

Count Coup, 1979, Marcian Chronicles
EX $10 **NM** $30 **MIP** $45

Count Down Space Game, 1960, Transogram
EX $15 **NM** $25 **MIP** $43

Countdown, 1967, Lowe
EX $15 **NM** $40 **MIP** $60

Counter Point, 1976, Hallmark
EX $10 **NM** $15 **MIP** $25

Cowboy Roundup, 1952, Parker Brothers
EX $10 **NM** $20 **MIP** $30

Cracker Jack Game, 1976, Milton Bradley
EX $5 **NM** $16 **MIP** $25

Creature Castle, 1975, Whitman
EX $12 **NM** $30 **MIP** $40

Creature Features, 1975, Athol
EX $20 **NM** $50 **MIP** $75

Creature From the Black Lagoon, 1963, Hasbro
EX $150 **NM** $410 **MIP** $600

Cribb Golf, 1980s, J.K. Games, Inc.
EX $10 **NM** $22 **MIP** $40

Crosby Derby, The, 1947, Fishlove
EX $25 **NM** $75 **MIP** $100

Cross Up, 1974, Milton Bradley
EX $2 **NM** $5 **MIP** $10

Crosswords, 1954, National Games
EX $12 **NM** $20 **MIP** $32

Crusader Rabbit TV Game, 1960s, Tryne
EX $50 **NM** $100 **MIP** $175

Cub Scouting, The Game of, 1987, Cadaco
EX $5 **NM** $16 **MIP** $25

Curious George Game, 1977, Parker Brothers
EX $4 **NM** $6 **MIP** $10

Curse of the Cobras Game, 1982, Ideal
EX $10 **NM** $25 **MIP** $35

Cut Up Shopping Spree Game, 1968, Milton Bradley
EX $8 **NM** $15 **MIP** $20

Dallas, 1980, Yaquinto
EX $10 **NM** $15 **MIP** $22

Dallas, 1985, Maruca Industries
EX $17 **NM** $35 **MIP** $55

Dallas (TV Role Playing), 1980, SPI
EX $4 **NM** $7 **MIP** $11

Danger Pass, 1964, Game Partners
EX $15 **NM** $45 **MIP** $65

Daniel Boone Trail Blazer, 1964, Milton Bradley
EX $20 **NM** $50 **MIP** $65

Dark Crystal Game, The, 1982, Milton Bradley
EX $7 **NM** $20 **MIP** $35

Dark Shadows Game, 1968, Whitman
EX $20 **NM** $40 **MIP** $60

Dark Tower, 1981, Milton Bradley
EX $125 **NM** $175 **MIP** $350

Dark World, 1992, Mattel
EX $12 **NM** $25 **MIP** $35

Dastardly and Muttley, 1969, Milton Bradley
EX $15 **NM** $25 **MIP** $40

Dating Game, The, 1967, Hasbro
EX $10 **NM** $20 **MIP** $25

Davy Crockett Adventure Game, 1956, Gardner
EX $45 **NM** $75 **MIP** $90

Davy Crockett Frontierland Game, 1955, Parker Brothers
EX $20 **NM** $50 **MIP** $65

Davy Crockett Radar Action Game, 1955, Ewing Mfg. & Sales
EX $40 **NM** $100 **MIP** $150

Davy Crockett Rescue Race Game, 1950s, Gabriel
EX $20 **NM** $50 **MIP** $60

Dawn of the Dead, 1978, SPI
EX $45 **NM** $95 **MIP** $135

Daytona 500 Race Game, 1989, Milton Bradley
EX $10 **NM** $25 **MIP** $35

Dead Pan, 1956, Selchow & Righter
EX $8 **NM** $10 **MIP** $15

Deadlock, 1972, American Greetings
EX $8 **NM** $20 **MIP** $30

Dealer's Choice, 1972, Parker Brothers
EX $10 **NM** $20 **MIP** $35

Dealer's Choice, 1974, Gamut of Games
EX $18 **NM** $45 **MIP** $65

Dear Abby, 1972, Ideal
EX $7 **NM** $20 **MIP** $35

Decathalon, 1972, Sports Illustrated
EX $10 **NM** $25 **MIP** $35

Decoy, 1956, Selchow & Righter
EX $12 **NM** $25 **MIP** $40

Deduction, 1976, Ideal
EX $5 **NM** $9 **MIP** $12

Deluxe Wheel of Fortune, 1986, Pressman
EX $5 **NM** $8 **MIP** $13

Dennis The Menace Baseball Game, 1960
EX $22 **NM** $50 **MIP** $70

Denny McLain Magnetik Baseball Game, 1968, Gotham
EX $115 **NM** $195 **MIP** $295

Deputy Dawg TV Lotto, 1961, Ideal
EX $15 **NM** $35 **MIP** $60

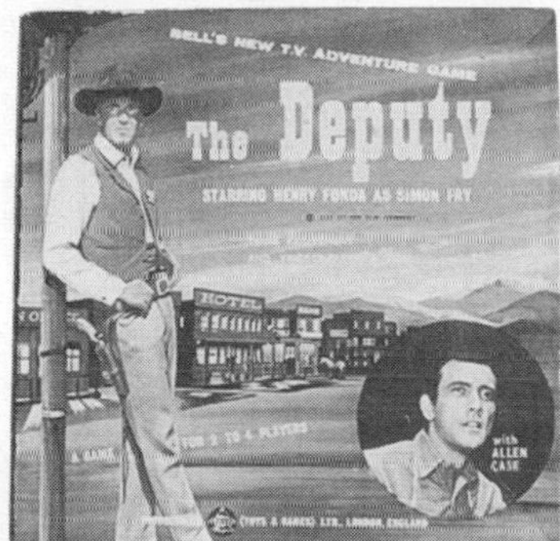

Deputy Game, The, 1960, Bell, "Starring Henry Fonda as Simon Fry"
EX $20 **NM** $50 **MIP** $75

Derby Day, 1959, Parker Brothers
EX $18 **NM** $35 **MIP** $50

Derby Downs, 1973, Great Games
EX $10 **NM** $30 **MIP** $45

Detectives Game, The, 1961, Transogram
EX $15 **NM** $30 **MIP** $40

Dick Tracy Crime Stopper, 1963, Ideal
EX $20 **NM** $30 **MIP** $40

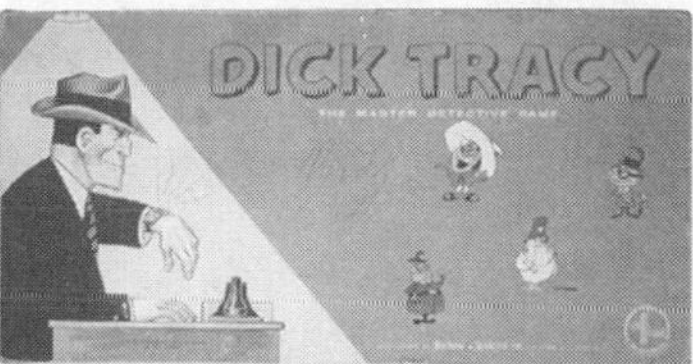

Dick Tracy The Master Detective Game, 1961, Selchow & Righter
EX $25 **NM** $60 **MIP** $75

Dick Van Dyke Board Game, 1964, Standard Toykraft
EX $75 **NM** $150 **MIP** $200

Diet, 1972, Dynamic
EX $5 **NM** $16 **MIP** $25

Diner's Club Credit Card Game, The, 1961, Ideal
EX $15 **NM** $20 **MIP** $30

Dinosaur Island, 1980, Parker Brothers
EX $5 **NM** $16 **MIP** $25

Diplomacy, 1961, Games Research
EX $15 **NM** $25 **MIP** $40

Diplomacy, 1976, Avalon Hill
EX $15 **NM** $25 **MIP** $40

Direct Hit, 1950s, Northwestern Products
EX $40 **NM** $70 **MIP** $110

Dirty Water—The Water Pollution Game, 1970, Urban Systems
EX $8 **NM** $20 **MIP** $30

Disney Mouseketeer, 1964, Parker Brothers
EX $40 **NM** $65 **MIP** $100

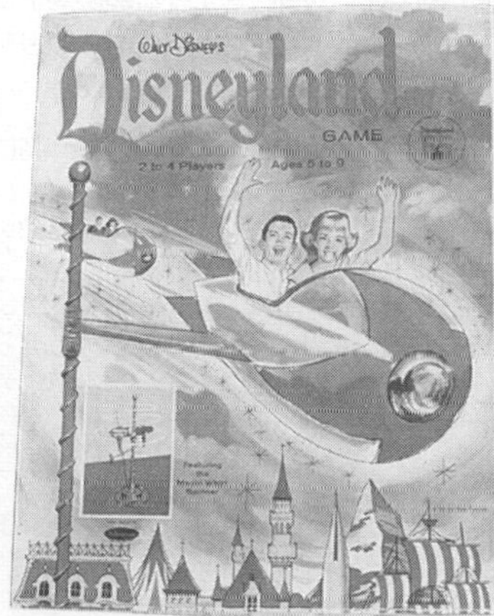

Disneyland Game, 1965, Transogram
EX $25 **NM** $60 **MIP** $100

GAMES

Dispatcher, 1958, Avalon Hill
EX $45 NM $70 MIP $125

Dobbin Derby, 1950, Cadaco-Ellis
EX $8 NM $25 MIP $40

Doctor Who, 1980s, Denys Fisher
EX $35 NM $75 MIP $125

Doctor, Doctor! Game, 1978, Ideal
EX $8 NM $20 MIP $30

Dogfight, 1962, Milton Bradley
EX $35 NM $45 MIP $65

Dollar A Second, 1955, Lowell
EX $12 NM $20 MIP $25

Dollars & Sense, 1946, Sidney Rogers
EX $100 NM $150 MIP $200

Domain, 1983, Parker Brothers
EX $2 NM $3 MIP $5

Domination, 1982, Milton Bradley
EX $8 NM $20 MIP $30

Don Carter's Strike Bowling Game, 1964, Saalfield
EX $20 NM $55 MIP $75

Donald Duck Big Game Box, 1979, Whitman
EX $10 NM $15 MIP $20

Donald Duck Pins & Bowling Game, 1955s, Pressman
EX $35 NM $50 MIP $70

Donald Duck Tiddley Winks Game, 1950s
EX $6 NM $10 MIP $15

Donald Duck's Party Game, 1950s, Parker Brothers
EX $10 NM $35 MIP $50

Dondi Potato Race Game, 1950s, Hasbro
EX $10 NM $20 MIP $35

Donkey Party Game, 1950, Saalfield
EX $4 NM $10 MIP $15

Donny & Marie Osmond TV Show Game, 1977, Mattel
EX $8 NM $25 MIP $40

Don't Miss the Boat, 1965, Parker Brothers
EX $12 NM $30 MIP $40

Doorways to Adventure VCR Game, 1986, Pressman
EX $6 NM $15 MIP $25

Doorways to Horror VCR Game, 1986, Pressman
EX $10 NM $25 MIP $35

Double Cross, 1974, Lakeside
EX $5 NM $16 MIP $25

Double Crossing, 1988, Lionel Games
EX $10 NM $25 MIP $35

Double Trouble, 1987, Milton Bradley
EX $3 NM $5 MIP $8

Doubletrack, 1981, Milton Bradley
EX $2 NM $7 MIP $12

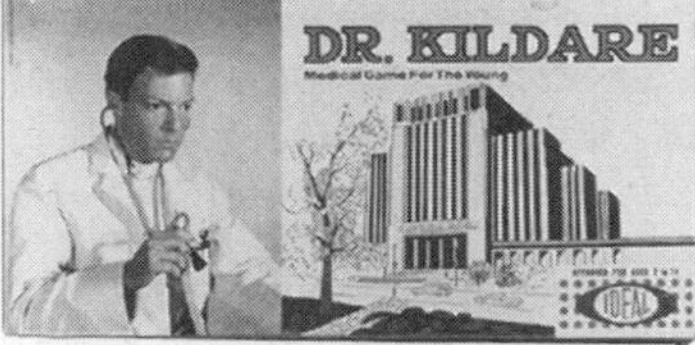

Dr. Kildare, 1962, Ideal
EX $20 NM $25 MIP $35

Dracula Mystery Game, 1960s, Hasbro
EX $80 NM $160 MIP $250

Dracula's "I Vant To Bite Your Finger" Game, 1981, Hasbro
EX $10 NM $20 MIP $30

Dragnet, 1955, Transogram
EX $20 NM $40 MIP $80

Dragonlance, 1988, TSR
EX $15 NM $35 MIP $50

Dragon's Lair, 1983, Milton Bradley
EX $7 NM $10 MIP $20

Dream House, 1968, Milton Bradley
EX $15 NM $35 MIP $50

Driver Ed, 1973, Cadaco
EX $6 NM $10 MIP $20

Duell, 1976, Lakeside
EX $5 NM $16 MIP $25

Dukes of Hazzard, 1981, Ideal
EX $6 NM $15 MIP $25

Dunce, 1955, Schaper
EX $7 NM $20 MIP $35

Dune, 1984, Parker Brothers
EX $10 NM $20 MIP $35

Dune, Frank Herbert's, 1979, Avalon Hill
EX $20 NM $50 MIP $75

Dungeon Dice, 1977, Parker Brothers
EX $5 NM $8 MIP $15

Dungeon!, 1981, TSR
EX $10 NM $25 MIP $35

Dungeons & Dragons, Electronic, 1980, Mattel
EX $12 NM $30 MIP $40

Duplicate Ad-Lib, 1976, Lowe
EX $5 NM $10 MIP $15

Duran Duran Game, 1985, Milton Bradley
EX $45 NM $80 MIP $125

Dynomutt, 1977, Milton Bradley
EX $10 NM $15 MIP $25

E.T. The Extra-Terrestrial, 1982, Parker Brothers
EX $8 NM $12 MIP $20

Earl Gillespie Baseball Game, 1961, Wei-Gill
EX $25 NM $30 MIP $40

Earth Satellite Game, 1956, Gabriel
EX $30 NM $70 MIP $100

Easy Money, 1956, Milton Bradley
EX $10 NM $15 MIP $20

Ecology, 1970, Urban Systems
EX $7 NM $20 MIP $35

Egg and I, The, 1947, Capex
EX $30 NM $50 MIP $80

El Dorado, 1977, Invicta
EX $7 NM $20 MIP $35

Electra Woman and Dyna Girl, 1977, Ideal
EX $10 NM $25 MIP $50

Electric Sports Car Race, 1959, Tudor
EX $35 NM $60 MIP $90

Electronic Detective Game, 1970s, Ideal
EX $12 NM $30 MIP $40

Electronic Lightfight, 1981, Milton Bradley
EX $8 NM $20 MIP $30

Electronic Radar Search, 1967, Ideal
EX $10 NM $15 MIP $25

Eliot Ness and the Untouchables, 1961, Transogram
EX $30 NM $50 MIP $75

Ellsworth Elephant Game, 1960, Selchow & Righter
EX $30 NM $45 MIP $70

Elmer Wheeler's Fat Boys Game, 1951, Parker Brothers
EX $18 NM $25 MIP $30

GAMES

Elvis Presley Game, 1957, Teen Age Games
EX $1000 **NM** $2000 **MIP** $4000

Emenee Chocolate Factory, 1966
EX $6 **NM** $10 **MIP** $15

Emergoncy, 1974, Milton Bradley
EX $15 **NM** $25 **MIP** $40

Emily Post Popularity Game, 1970, Selchow & Righter
EX $10 **NM** $25 **MIP** $40

Emperor of China, 1972, Dynamic
EX $10 **NM** $25 **MIP** $40

Empire Auto Races, 1950s, Empire Plastics
EX $20 **NM** $30 **MIP** $50

Empire Builder (1st edition), 1982, Mayfair Games
EX $20 **NM** $50 **MIP** $75

Empire Strikes Back, Hoth Ice World, 1977, Kenner
EX $10 **NM** $20 **MIP** $30

Encore, 1989, Parker Brothers
EX $8 **NM** $20 **MIP** $30

Enemy Agent, 1976, Milton Bradley
EX $8 **NM** $20 **MIP** $30

Energy Quest, 1977, Weldon
EX $5 **NM** $16 **MIP** $25

Engineer, 1957, Selchow & Righter
EX $8 **NM** $25 **MIP** $40

Entertainment Trivia Game, 1984, Lakeside
EX $5 **NM** $10 **MIP** $15

Entre's Fun & Games In Accounting, 1988, Entrepreneurial Games
EX $4 **NM** $7 **MIP** $12

Ergo, 1977, Invlcta
EX $5 **NM** $16 **MIP** $25

Escape From New York, 1980, TSR
EX $12 **NM** $20 **MIP** $30

Escape from the Casbah, 1975, Selchow & Righter
EX $7 **NM** $20 **MIP** $35

Escape From the Death Star, 1977, Kenner
EX $10 **NM** $20 **MIP** $30

Escort: Game of Guys and Gals, 1955, Parker Brothers
EX $15 **NM** $20 **MIP** $25

Espionage, 1973, MPH
EX $6 **NM** $18 **MIP** $30

Events, 1974, 3M
EX $6 **NM** $15 **MIP** $25

Everybody's Talking!, 1967, Watkins-Strathmore
EX $8 **NM** $25 **MIP** $40

Executive Decision, 1971, 3M
EX $5 **NM** $16 **MIP** $25

Exit, 1983, Milton Bradley
EX $2 **NM** $6 **MIP** $10

Expanse, 1949, Milton Bradley
EX $15 **NM** $20 **MIP** $30

Extra Innings, 1975, J. Kavanaugh
EX $30 **NM** $50 **MIP** $75

Eye Guess, 1960s, Milton Bradley
EX $15 **NM** $20 **MIP** $35

F.B.I., 1958, Transogram
EX $35 **NM** $55 **MIP** $70

F.B.I. Crime Resistance Game, 1975, Milton Bradley
EX $12 **NM** $30 **MIP** $40

F/11 Armchair Quarterback, 1964, James R. Hock
EX $15 **NM** $25 **MIP** $40

Fact Finder Fun, 1963, Milton Bradley
EX $10 **NM** $15 **MIP** $25

Fall Guy, The, 1981, Milton Bradley
EX $10 **NM** $15 **MIP** $25

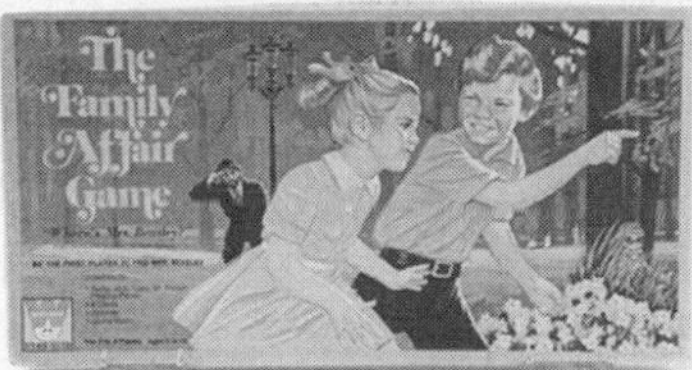

Family Affair, 1967, Whitman
EX $25 **NM** $40 **MIP** $65

Family Feud, 1977, Milton Bradley
EX $4 **NM** $12 **MIP** $20

Family Ties Game, The, 1986, Apple Street
EX $10 **NM** $15 **MIP** $20

Famous 500 Mile Race, 1988
EX $8 **NM** $13 **MIP** $20

Fang Bang, 1966, Milton Bradley
EX $12 **NM** $25 **MIP** $35

Fangface, 1979, Parker Brothers
EX $5 **NM** $8 **MIP** $13

Fantastic Voyage Game, 1968, Milton Bradley
EX $15 **NM** $25 **MIP** $40

Fantasy Island Game, 1978, Ideal
EX $7 **NM** $20 **MIP** $35

Farming Game, The, 1979, Weekend Farmer Co.
EX $8 **NM** $20 **MIP** $30

Fast 111s, 1981, Parker Brothers
EX $5 **NM** $16 **MIP** $25

Fastest Gun, The, 1974, Milton Bradley
EX $10 **NM** $25 **MIP** $40

Fat Albert, 1973, Milton Bradley
EX $15 **NM** $25 **MIP** $40

Fearless Fireman, 1957, Hasbro
EX $45 **NM** $70 **MIP** $150

Felix the Cat Dandy Candy Game, 1957, Warren/Built-Rite
EX $10 **NM** $20 **MIP** $45

Fellx the Cat Game, 1960, Milton Bradley
EX $15 **NM** $25 **MIP** $45

Felix the Cat Game, 1968, Milton Bradley
EX $8 **NM** $20 **MIP** $30

Feudal, 1967, 3M
EX $8 **NM** $20 **MIP** $30

Fighter Bomber, 1977, Cadaco
EX $15 **NM** $25 **MIP** $40

Finance, 1962, Parker Brothers
EX $10 **NM** $15 **MIP** $20

Finger Dinger Man, 1969, Mattel
EX $10 **NM** $25 **MIP** $35

Fingers Harry, 1967, Topper Toys
EX $20 **NM** $50 **MIP** $75

Fire Chief, 1957, Selchow & Righter
EX $10 **NM** $20 **MIP** $30

Fire Fighters!, 1957, Russell
EX $15 **NM** $25 **MIP** $40

Fire House Mouse Game, 1967, Transogram
EX $10 **NM** $35 **MIP** $50

Fireball XL-5, 1963, Milton Bradley
EX $40 **NM** $75 **MIP** $100

First Class Farmer, 1965, F+W Publishing
EX $7 **NM** $20 **MIP** $35

First Down, 1970, TGP Games
EX $50 **NM** $80 **MIP** $125

Fish Bait, 1965, Ideal
EX $20 **NM** $30 **MIP** $50

Fish Pond, 1950s, National Games
EX $10 **NM** $15 **MIP** $20

Flagship Airfreight: The Airplane Cargo Game, 1946, Milton Bradley
EX $30 **NM** $55 **MIP** $80

Flash Gordon, 1977, Waddington/House Of Games
EX $10 **NM** $25 **MIP** $35

Flash: The Press Photographer Game, 1956, Selchow & Righter
EX $35 **NM** $60 **MIP** $100

Flight Captain, 1972, Lowe
EX $5 **NM** $16 **MIP** $25

Flintstones, 1971, Milton Bradley
EX $6 **NM** $15 **MIP** $25

Flintstones, 1980, Milton Bradley
EX $15 **NM** $20 **MIP** $35

Flintstones Dino The Dinosaur Game, 1961, Transogram
EX $45 **NM** $75 **MIP** $100

Flintstones Hoppy The Hopperoo Game, 1964, Transogram
EX $45 **NM** $75 **MIP** $120

Flintstones Mitt-Full Game, 1962, Whitman
EX $25 **NM** $50 **MIP** $75

Flintstones Stone Age Game, 1961, Transogram
EX $20 **NM** $45 **MIP** $65

Flip Flop Go, 1962, Mattel
EX $6 **NM** $10 **MIP** $15

Flip 'N Skip, 1971, Little Kennys
EX $5 **NM** $10 **MIP** $15

Flipper Flips, 1960s, Mattel
EX $30 **NM** $50 **MIP** $70

Flying Nun Game, The, 1968, Milton Bradley
EX $15 **NM** $20 **MIP** $30

Fonz Game, The, 1976, Milton Bradley
EX $15 **NM** $20 **MIP** $30

Fooba-Roo Football Game, 1955, Memphis Plastic
EX $15 **NM** $35 **MIP** $50

Football Fever, 1985, Hansen
EX $20 **NM** $35 **MIP** $50

Football Strategy, 1962, Avalon Hill
EX $8 **NM** $25 **MIP** $40

Football Strategy, 1972, Avalon Hill
EX $3 **NM** $10 **MIP** $15

Football, Baseball, & Checkers, 1948, Parker Brothers
EX $15 **NM** $25 **MIP** $40

Fore, 1954, Artcraft Paper
EX $20 **NM** $35 **MIP** $50

Forest Friends, 1956, Milton Bradley
EX $5 **NM** $12 **MIP** $18

Formula One Car Race Game, 1968, Parker Brothers
EX $25 **NM** $40 **MIP** $50

Fortress America, 1986, Milton Bradley, Part of a series of intricate strategy games developed by Milton Bradley in the 1980s. Two others in the series were "Axis & Allies" and "Conquest of the Empire"
EX $35 **NM** $75 **MIP** $100

Fortune 500, 1979, Pressman
EX $5 **NM** $16 **MIP** $25

Foto-Electric Baseball, 1951, Cadaco-Ellis
EX $15 **NM** $25 **MIP** $40

Foto-Electric Football, 1965, Cadaco-Ellis
EX $10 **NM** $15 **MIP** $20

Four Lane Road Racing, 1963, Transogram
EX $15 **NM** $45 **MIP** $65

Fox & Hounds, Game of, 1948, Parker Brothers
EX $10 **NM** $20 **MIP** $25

Frank Cavanaugh's American Football, 1955, F. Cavanaugh
EX $25 **NM** $60 **MIP** $90

Frankenstein Game, 1962, Hasbro
EX $80 **NM** $160 **MIP** $250

Frantic Frogs, 1965, Milton Bradley
EX $10 **NM** $20 **MIP** $30

Frisky Flippers Slide Bar Game, 1950s, Warren/Built-Rite
EX $5 **NM** $10 **MIP** $15

Frontier Fort Rescue Game, 1956, Gabriel
EX $10 **NM** $35 **MIP** $50

Frontier-6, 1980, Rimbold
EX $8 **NM** $25 **MIP** $40

F-Troop, 1965, Ideal
EX $50 **NM** $100 **MIP** $125

Fu Manchu's Hidden Hoard, 1967, Ideal
EX $23 **NM** $50 **MIP** $75

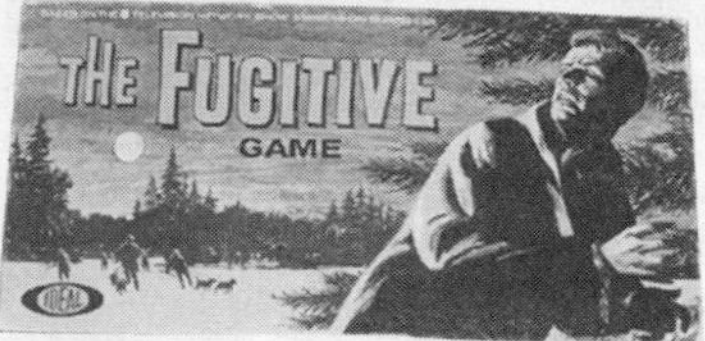

Fugitive, 1966, Ideal
EX $30 **NM** $60 **MIP** $100

Fun City, 1987, Parker Brothers
EX $8 **NM** $20 **MIP** $30

Funky Phantom Game, 1971, Milton Bradley
EX $10 **NM** $15 **MIP** $25

G.I. Joe, 1982, International Games
EX $15 **NM** $25 **MIP** $40

G.I. Joe Adventure, 1982, Hasbro
EX $20 **NM** $30 **MIP** $50

G.I. Joe Card Game, 1965, Whitman
EX $10 **NM** $15 **MIP** $25

G.I. Joe Marine Paratrooper, 1965, Hasbro
EX $20 **NM** $30 **MIP** $50

G.I. Joe Navy Frogman, 1965, Hasbro
EX $25 **NM** $60 **MIP** $75

Gambler, 1977, Parker Brothers
EX $6 **NM** $15 **MIP** $20

Gambler's Golf, 1975, Gammon Games
EX $4 **NM** $10 **MIP** $15

Games People Play Game, The, 1967, Alpsco
EX $7 **NM** $20 **MIP** $35

Gammonball, 1980, Fun-Time Products
EX $10 **NM** $16 **MIP** $25

Gang Way For Fun, 1964, Transogram
EX $25 **NM** $40 **MIP** $65

Gardner's Championship Golf, 1950s, Gardner
EX $10 **NM** $35 **MIP** $50

Garfield, 1981, Parker Brothers
EX $4 **NM** $6 **MIP** $10

Garrison's Gorillas, 1967, Ideal
EX $45 **NM** $75 **MIP** $120

Gay Puree, 1962
EX $25 **NM** $40 **MIP** $65

Gene Autry's Dude Ranch Game, 1950s, Warren/Built-Rite
EX $20 **NM** $25 **MIP** $50

General Hospital, 1974, Parker Brothers
EX $7 **NM** $15 **MIP** $20

General Hospital, 1980s, Cardinal
EX $15 **NM** $20 **MIP** $30

Generals, The, 1980, Ideal
EX $7 **NM** $20 **MIP** $35

Gentle Ben Animal Hunt Game, 1967, Mattel
EX $30 **NM** $70 **MIP** $100

Geo-Graphy, 1954, Cadaco-Ellis
EX $5 **NM** $15 **MIP** $20

George of the Jungle Game, 1968, Parker Brothers
EX $40 **NM** $80 **MIP** $100

Get Beep Beep: The Road Runner Game, 1975, Whitman
EX $15 **NM** $25 **MIP** $35

Get in That Tub, 1969, Hasbro
EX $15 **NM** $35 **MIP** $50

Get Smart Game, 1966, Ideal
EX $20 **NM** $30 **MIP** $50

Get That License, 1955, Selchow & Righter
EX $10 **NM** $15 **MIP** $25

Get the Message, 1964, Milton Bradley
EX $5 **NM** $15 **MIP** $25

Get the Picture, 1987, Worlds Of Wonder
EX $6 **NM** $10 **MIP** $15

Gettysburg, 1960, Avalon Hill
EX $5 **NM** $16 **MIP** $25

Ghosts, 1985, Milton Bradley
EX $8 **NM** $20 **MIP** $35

Giant Wheel Thrills 'n Spills Horse Race, 1958, Remco
EX $15 **NM** $20 **MIP** $30

Gil Hodges' Pennant Fever, 1970, Research Games
EX $35 **NM** $75 **MIP** $90

Gilligan, The New Adventures of, 1974, Milton Bradley
EX $15 **NM** $20 **MIP** $25

Gilligan's Island, 1965, Game Gems
EX $125 **NM** $250 **MIP** $400

Gingerbread Man, 1964, Selchow & Righter
EX $10 **NM** $35 **MIP** $50

Globetrotter Basketball, Official, 1950s, Meljak
EX $60 **NM** $100 **MIP** $150

Globe-Trotters, 1950, Selchow & Righter
EX $8 **NM** $25 **MIP** $35

Go For Broke, 1965, Selchow & Righter
EX $5 **NM** $7 **MIP** $10

Go for the Green, 1973, Sports Illustrated
EX $10 **NM** $25 **MIP** $40

Goal Line Stand, 1980, Game Shop
EX $12 **NM** $20 **MIP** $30

Godfather Game, The (violin case box), 1971, Family Games
EX $35 **NM** $50 **MIP** $75

Godfather, The (white box), 1971, Family Games
EX $8 **NM** $20 **MIP** $30

Godzilla, 1960s, Ideal
EX $100 **NM** $200 **MIP** $300

Godzilla, 1978, Mattel
EX $30 **NM** $50 **MIP** $80

Going to Jerusalem, 1955, Parker Brothers
EX $15 **NM** $20 **MIP** $25

Going, Going, Gone!, 1975, Milton Bradley
EX $6 **NM** $15 **MIP** $25

Gold!, 1981, Avalon Hill
EX $5 **NM** $16 **MIP** $25

Golden Trivia Game, 1984, Western
EX $6 **NM** $10 **MIP** $15

Goldilocks, 1955, Cadaco-Ellis
EX $8 **NM** $25 **MIP** $35

Goldilocks and the Three Bears, 1973, Cadaco
EX $2 **NM** $6 **MIP** $10

Gomer Pyle Game, 1960s, Transogram
EX $15 **NM** $20 **MIP** $30

Gong Show Game, 1975, Milton Bradley
EX $15 **NM** $25 **MIP** $40

Gong Show Game, 1977, American Publishing
EX $15 **NM** $25 **MIP** $40

Good Guys 'N Bad Guys, 1973, Cadaco
EX $5 **NM** $16 **MIP** $25

Good Ol' Charlie Brown Game, 1971, Milton Bradley
EX $8 **NM** $20 **MIP** $30

Goodbye Mr. Chips Game, 1969, Parker Brothers
EX $8 **NM** $20 **MIP** $25

Goofy's Mad Maze, 1970s, Whitman
EX $6 **NM** $10 **MIP** $15

Goonies, 1980s, Milton Bradley
EX $12 **NM** $30 **MIP** $40

Gooses Wild, 1966, CO-5
EX $2 **NM** $7 **MIP** $12

Gotham Professional Basketball, 1950s, Gotham
EX $35 **NM** $50 **MIP** $70

Grand Master of Martial Arts, 1986, Hoyle
EX $6 **NM** $10 **MIP** $15

Gray Ghost, The, 1958, Transogram
EX $30 **NM** $50 **MIP** $80

Great Escape, The, 1967, Ideal
EX $8 **NM** $25 **MIP** $40

Great Grape Ape Game, The, 1975, Milton Bradley
EX $15 **NM** $25 **MIP** $40

Green Acres Game, The, 1960s, Standard Toykraft
EX $73 **NM** $100 **MIP** $200

Green Ghost Game, 1965, Transogram
EX $50 **NM** $90 **MIP** $125

Green Ghost Game (re-issue), 1997, Marx
EX $15 **NM** $35 **MIP** $50

Green Hornet Quick Switch Game, 1966, Milton Bradley
EX $90 **NM** $225 **MIP** $300

Gremlins, 1984, International Games
EX $10 **NM** $15 **MIP** $25

Greyhound Pursuit, 1985, N/N Games
EX $8 **NM** $13 **MIP** $20

Grizzly Adams, 1978, Waddington's House of Games
EX $15 **NM** $25 **MIP** $40

GAMES

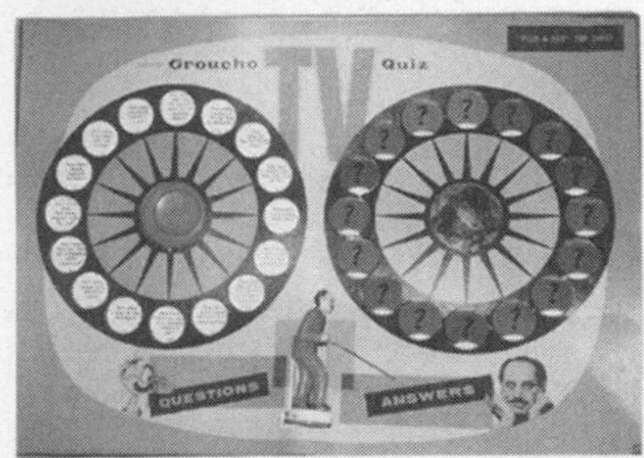

Groucho's TV Quiz Game, 1954, Pressman
EX $40 NM $50 MIP $75

Groucho's You Bet Your Life, 1955, Lowell
EX $25 NM $35 MIP $45

Group Therapy, 1969, Group Therapy Assn.
EX $3 NM $12 MIP $20

Guinness Book of World Records Game, The, 1979, Parker Brothers
EX $5 NM $9 MIP $15

Gulf Strike, 1983, Victory Games
EX $5 NM $16 MIP $25

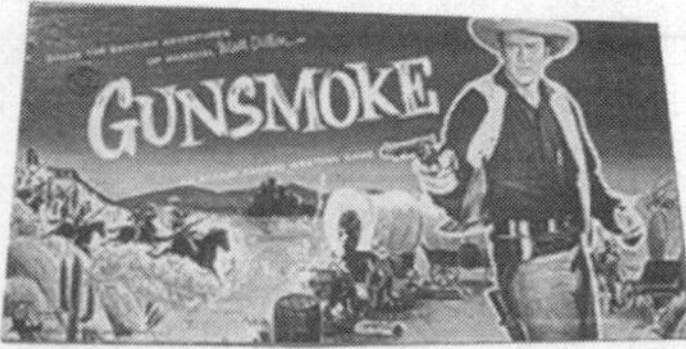

Gunsmoke Game, 1950s, Lowell
EX $40 NM $65 MIP $90

Gusher, 1946, Carrom Industries
EX $50 NM $75 MIP $125

Half-Time Football, 1979, Lakeside
EX $5 NM $9 MIP $15

Handicap Harness Racing, 1978, Hall of Fame Games
EX $15 NM $25 MIP $35

Hang On Harvey, 1969, Ideal
EX $15 NM $20 MIP $30

Hangman, 1976, Milton Bradley
EX $5 NM $8 MIP $15

Hank Aaron Baseball Game, 1970s, Ideal
EX $50 NM $80 MIP $125

Hank Aaron Bases Loaded, 1976, Twentieth Century Enterprises
EX $45 NM $70 MIP $100

Hank Bauer's "Be a Manager", 1960s, Barco Games
EX $75 NM $125 MIP $170

Happiness, 1972, Milton Bradley
EX $12 NM $20 MIP $25

Happy Days, 1976, Parker Brothers
EX $8 NM $15 MIP $25

Happy Little Train Game, The, 1957, Milton Bradley
EX $3 NM $12 MIP $20

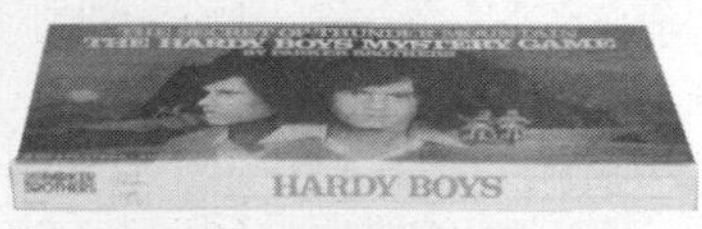

Hardy Boys Mystery Game, Secret of Thunder Mountain, 1978, Parker Brothers
EX $7 NM $15 MIP $20

Hardy Boys Mystery Game, The, 1968, Milton Bradley
EX $6 NM $15 MIP $25

Hardy Boys Treasure, 1960, Parker Brothers
EX $25 NM $35 MIP $50

Harlem Globetrotters Game, 1971, Milton Bradley
EX $12 NM $30 MIP $40

Harlem Globetrotters Official Edition Basketball, 1970s, Cadaco-Ellis
EX $45 NM $75 MIP $105

Harpoon, 1955, Gabriel
EX $20 NM $35 MIP $50

Harry Lorayne Memory Game, The, 1976, Reiss
EX $7 NM $20 MIP $35

Hashimoto San, 1963, Transogram
EX $20 NM $30 MIP $60

Haul the Freight, 1962, Bar-Zim
EX $25 NM $50 MIP $60

Haunted House Game, 1963, Ideal
EX $120 NM $250 MIP $400

Haunted Mansion, 1970s, Lakeside
EX $60 NM $150 MIP $200

Have Gun Will Travel Game, 1959, Parker Brothers
EX $45 NM $65 MIP $85

Hawaii Five-O, 1960s, Remco
EX $30 NM $90 MIP $120

Hawaiian Eye, 1960, Transogram
EX $50 NM $120 MIP $200

Hawaiian Punch Game, 1978, Mattel
EX $5 NM $10 MIP $15

Hector Heathcote, 1963, Transogram
EX $35 NM $45 MIP $60

Hex: The Zig-Zag Game, 1950, Parker Brothers
EX $10 NM $35 MIP $50

Hey Fatso, 1969, Hasbro
EX $15 NM $35 MIP $50

Hey Pa, There's a Goat on the Roof!, 1965, Parker Brothers
EX $40 NM $60 MIP $75

Hide 'N' Thief, 1965, Whitman
EX $7 NM $20 MIP $35

Hide-N-Seek, 1967, Ideal
EX $20 NM $50 MIP $75

High-Bid, 1965, 3M
EX $7 NM $20 MIP $35

Highway Traffic Game, 1957, John H Allison Jr.
EX $15 NM $35 MIP $50

Hi-Ho! Cherry-O, 1960, Whitman
EX $6 NM $10 MIP $15

Hijacked, 1973, Valley Games
EX $12 NM $30 MIP $40

Hip Flip, 1968, Parker Brothers
EX $6 NM $15 MIP $25

Hippety Hop, 1947, Corey Game
EX $20 NM $30 MIP $40

Hippopotamus, 1961, Remco
EX $8 NM $25 MIP $40

Hispaniola, The Game of, 1957, Schaper
EX $30 NM $70 MIP $100

Hit The Beach, 1965, Milton Bradley
EX $45 NM $50 MIP $60

Hobbit Game, The, 1978, Milton Bradley
EX $30 NM $60 MIP $85

Hock Shop, 1975, Whitman
EX $3 NM $12 MIP $20

Hocus Pocus, 1960s, Transogram
EX $40 NM $50 MIP $75

Hog Tied, 1981, Selchow & Righter
EX $3 NM $12 MIP $20

Hogan's Heroes Game, 1966, Transogram
EX $45 NM $85 MIP $120

Holiday, 1958, Replogle Globes
EX $40 NM $65 MIP $100

Holiday, 1973, RGI-Athol
EX $18 NM $40 MIP $60

Hollywood Awards Game, 1976, Milton Bradley
EX $8 NM $25 MIP $40

Hollywood Go, 1954, Parker Brothers
EX $10 NM $25 MIP $35

Hollywood Squares, 1974, Ideal
EX $6 NM $10 MIP $15

Hollywood Squares, 1980, Milton Bradley
EX $4 NM $6 MIP $10

Hollywood Stars, The Game of, 1955, Whitman
EX $8 NM $20 MIP $30

Home Court Basketball, 1954
EX $145 NM $250 MIP $380

Home Game, 1960s, Pressman
EX $30 NM $50 MIP $60

Home Stretch Harness Racing, 1967, Lowe
EX $15 NM $35 MIP $50

Home Team Baseball Game, 1957, Selchow & Righter
EX $18 NM $30 MIP $40

Honey West, 1965, Ideal
EX $35 NM $50 MIP $75

Honeymooners Game, The, 1986, TSR
EX $7 NM $12 MIP $20

Hoodoo, 1950, Tryne
EX $4 NM $10 MIP $15

Hookey Go Fishin', 1974, Cadaco
EX $8 NM $16 MIP $25

Hopalong Cassidy Chinese Checkers Game, 1950s
EX $20 NM $50 MIP $75

Hopalong Cassidy Game, 1950s, Milton Bradley
EX $50 NM $85 MIP $125

Horse Play, 1962, Schaper
EX $10 NM $35 MIP $50

GAMES

Horseshoe Derby Game, 1950s, Built-Rite
EX $8 NM $20 MIP $30

Hot Property!, 1980s, Take One Games
EX $8 NM $25 MIP $40

Hot Rod, 1953, Harett-Gilmar
EX $15 NM $35 MIP $50

Hot Wheels Game, 1982, Whitman
EX $8 NM $13 MIP $20

Hot Wheels Wipe-Out Game, 1968, Mattel
EX $15 NM $35 MIP $60

Hotels, 1987, Milton Bradley
EX $20 NM $35 MIP $50

Houndcats Game, 1970s, Milton Bradley
EX $8 NM $15 MIP $25

House Party, 1968, Whitman
EX $10 NM $25 MIP $35

Houston Astros Baseball Challenge Game, 1980, Croque
EX $15 NM $25 MIP $35

How To Succeed In Business Without Really Trying, 1963, Milton Bradley
EX $6 NM $10 MIP $15

Howard Hughes Game, The, 1972, Family Games
EX $10 NM $35 MIP $50

Howdy Doody Adventure Game, 1950s, Milton Bradley
EX $35 NM $50 MIP $60

Howdy Doody Quiz Show, 1950s, Multiple Products
EX $20 NM $40 MIP $50

Howdy Doody's Electric Carnival Game, Harrett-Gilmar
EX $20 NM $30 MIP $50

Howdy Doody's Own Game, 1949, Parker Brothers
EX $50 NM $60 MIP $75

Howdy Doody's Three Ring Circus, 1950, Harett-Gilmar
EX $35 NM $50 MIP $60

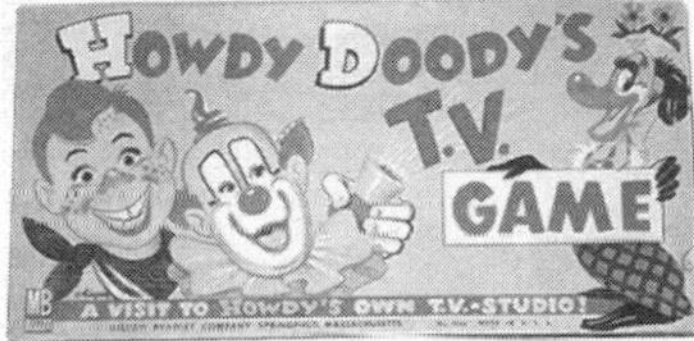

Howdy Doody's TV Game, 1950s, Milton Bradley
EX $50 NM $50 MIP $75

Huckleberry Hound, 1981, Milton Bradley
EX $10 NM $20 MIP $35

Huckleberry Hound Bumps, 1960, Transogram
EX $20 NM $50 MIP $75

Huckleberry Hound Spin-O-Game, 1959
EX $45 NM $75 MIP $120

Huckleberry Hound Tiddly Winks, 1959, Milton Bradley
EX $15 NM $30 MIP $60

Huckleberry Hound Western Game, 1959, Milton Bradley
EX $25 NM $35 MIP $50

Huff 'N Puff Game, 1968, Schaper
EX $6 NM $15 MIP $25

Huggermugger, 1989, Huggermugger Co.
EX $8 NM $20 MIP $30

Hullabaloo, 1965, Remco
EX $25 NM $65 MIP $75

Humor Rumor, 1969, Whitman
EX $10 NM $20 MIP $30

Humpty Dumpty Game, 1950s, Lowell
EX $25 NM $40 MIP $50

Hunch, 1956, Happy Hour
EX $7 NM $20 MIP $35

Hungry Ant, The, 1978, Milton Bradley
EX $5 NM $16 MIP $25

Hunt For Red October, 1988, TSR
EX $5 NM $15 MIP $25

Hurry Up, 1971, Parker Brothers
EX $5 NM $16 MIP $25

Hurry Waiter! Game, 1969, Ideal
EX $8 NM $20 MIP $30

Husker Du, 1970, Regina Products
EX $10 NM $25 MIP $40

I Dream of Jeannie Game, 1965, Milton Bradley
EX $35 NM $50 MIP $75

I Spy, 1965, Ideal
EX $35 NM $75 MIP $95

I Vant to Bite Your Finger, 1981, Hasbro
EX $12 NM $20 MIP $25

I Wanna Be President, 1983, J.R. Mackey
EX $5 NM $16 MIP $25

Ice Cube Game, The, 1972, Milton Bradley
EX $50 NM $125 MIP $175

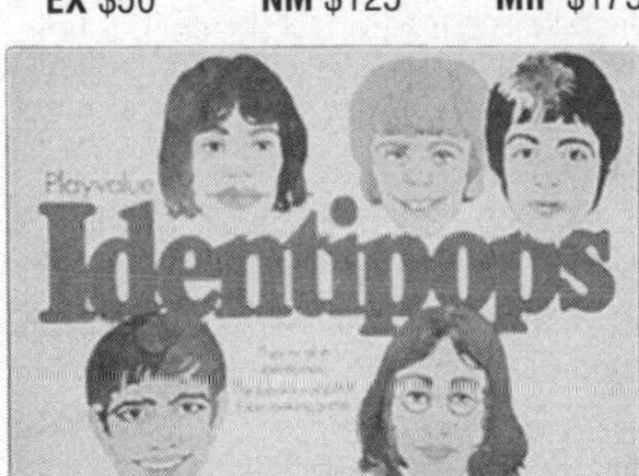

Identipops, 1969, Playvalue
EX $75 NM $175 MIP $250

I'm George Gobel, And Here's The Game, 1955, Schaper
EX $12 NM $20 MIP $32

Image, 1972, 3M
EX $3 NM $12 MIP $20

Incredible Hulk, 1978, Milton Bradley
EX $6 NM $10 MIP $15

Indiana Jones: Raiders of The Lost Ark, 1981, Kenner
EX $15 NM $20 MIP $30

Indianapolis 500 75th Running Race Game, 1991, International Games
EX $8 NM $13 MIP $20

Input, 1984, Milton Bradley
EX $4 NM $7 MIP $15

Inside Moves, 1985, Parker Brothers
EX $3 NM $12 MIP $20

Inspector Gadget, 1983, Milton Bradley
EX $15 NM $25 MIP $40

Instant Replay, 1987, Parker Brothers
EX $8 NM $13 MIP $20

Intercept, 1978, Lakeside
EX $7 NM $20 MIP $35

International Airport Game, 1964, Magic Wand
EX $8 NM $20 MIP $30

International Grand Prix, 1975, Cadaco
EX $8 NM $20 MIP $30

Interpretation of Dreams, 1969, Hasbro
EX $7 NM $15 MIP $25

Interstate Highway, 1963, Selchow & Righter
EX $15 NM $30 MIP $40

Intrigue, 1954, Milton Bradley
EX $12 NM $30 MIP $40

Inventors, The, 1974, Parker Brothers
EX $10 NM $20 MIP $30

Ipcress File, 1966, Milton Bradley
EX $15 NM $25 MIP $35

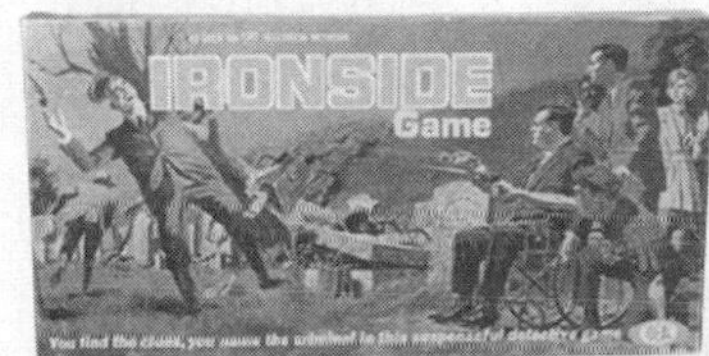

Ironside, 1976, Ideal
EX $55 NM $75 MIP $100

Is the Pope Catholic?!, 1986, Crowley Connections
EX $10 NM $25 MIP $40

Isolation, 1978, Lakeside
EX $2 NM $7 MIP $12

It Takes Two, 1970, NBC-Hasbro
EX $5 NM $12 MIP $18

Itinerary, 1980, Xanadu Leisure
EX $3 **NM** $12 **MIP** $20

Jace Pearson's Tales of The Texas Rangers, 1955, E.E. Fairchild
EX $40 **NM** $60 **MIP** $75

Jack and The Beanstalk, 1946, National Games
EX $25 **NM** $45 **MIP** $50

Jack and The Beanstalk Adventure Game, 1957, Transogram
EX $25 **NM** $30 **MIP** $40

Jack Barry's Twenty One, 1956, Lowell
EX $20 **NM** $30 **MIP** $50

Jackie Gleason's and AW-A-A-A-Y We Go!, 1956, Transogram
EX $50 **NM** $75 **MIP** $125

Jackie Gleason's Story Stage Game, 1955, Utopia Enterprises
EX $50 **NM** $75 **MIP** $125

Jackpot, 1975, Milton Bradley
EX $7 **NM** $11 **MIP** $20

Jacmar Big League Electric Baseball, 1950s, Jacmar
EX $100 **NM** $175 **MIP** $250

James Bond 007 Goldfinger Game, 1966, Milton Bradley
EX $35 **NM** $60 **MIP** $75

James Bond 007 Thunderball Game, 1965, Milton Bradley
EX $35 **NM** $50 **MIP** $75

James Bond Message From M Game, 1966, Ideal
EX $1125 **NM** $250 **MIP** $400

James Bond Secret Agent 007 Game, 1964, Milton Bradley
EX $15 **NM** $30 **MIP** $45

James Bond You Only Live Twice, 1984, Victory Games, box shows helicopter chase
EX $5 **NM** $12 **MIP** $25

James Clavell's Noble House, 1987, FASA
EX $6 **NM** $15 **MIP** $25

James Clavell's Shogun, 1983, FASA
EX $6 **NM** $15 **MIP** $25

James Clavell's Tai-Pan, 1987, FASA
EX $6 **NM** $15 **MIP** $25

James Clavell's Whirlwind, 1986, FASA
EX $6 **NM** $15 **MIP** $25

Jan Murray's Charge Account, 1961, Lowell
EX $10 **NM** $15 **MIP** $20

Jan Murray's Treasure Hunt, 1950s, Gardner
EX $10 **NM** $25 **MIP** $35

JDK Baseball, 1982, JDK Baseball
EX $20 **NM** $45 **MIP** $65

Jeanne Dixon's Game of Destiny, 1968, Milton Bradley
EX $7 **NM** $10 **MIP** $15

Jeopardy, 1964, Milton Bradley
EX $10 **NM** $15 **MIP** $25

Jerry Kramer's Instant Replay, 1970, EMD Enterprises
EX $15 **NM** $25 **MIP** $40

Jet World, 1975, Milton Bradley
EX $5 **NM** $16 **MIP** $25

Jetsons Fun Pad Game, 1963, Milton Bradley
EX $40 **NM** $70 **MIP** $80

Jetsons Game, 1985, Milton Bradley
EX $5 **NM** $10 **MIP** $15

Jetsons Out of this World Game, 1963, Transogram
EX $40 **NM** $75 **MIP** $125

Jimmy the Greek Oddsmaker Football, 1974, Aurora
EX $10 **NM** $25 **MIP** $35

Jockette, 1950s, Jockette
EX $25 **NM** $40 **MIP** $60

Jockey, 1976, Hallmark Games
EX $10 **NM** $25 **MIP** $35

Joe Palooka Boxing Game, 1950s, Lowell
EX $75 **NM** $125 **MIP** $200

John Drake Secret Agent, 1966, Milton Bradley
EX $15 **NM** $20 **MIP** $30

Johnny Ringo, 1959, Transogram
EX $40 **NM** $90 **MIP** $110

Johnny Unitas Football Game, 1970, Pro Mentor
EX $15 **NM** $35 **MIP** $50

Joker's Wild, 1973, Milton Bradley
EX $5 **NM** $10 **MIP** $15

Jonathan Livingston Seagull, 1973, Mattel
EX $8 **NM** $20 **MIP** $30

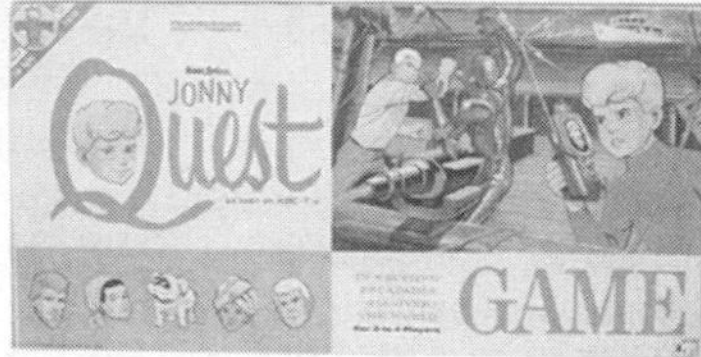

Jonny Quest Game, 1964, Transogram
EX $200 **NM** $350 **MIP** $500

Jose Canseco's Perfect Baseball Game, 1991, Perfect Game
EX $8 **NM** $13 **MIP** $20

Jubilee, 1954, Cadaco-Ellis
EX $10 **NM** $25 **MIP** $35

Jumbo Jet, 1963, Jumbo
EX $18 **NM** $45 **MIP** $65

Jumpin', 1964, 3M
EX $7 **NM** $20 **MIP** $35

Jumping DJ, 1962, Mattel
EX $15 **NM** $50 **MIP** $75

Junior Bingo-Matic, 1968, Transogram
EX $6 **NM** $10 **MIP** $15

Junior Executive, 1963, Whitman
EX $7 **NM** $15 **MIP** $25

Junior Quarterback Football, 1950s, Warren/Built-Rite
EX $7 **NM** $20 **MIP** $35

Junk Yard Game, 1975, Ideal
EX $8 **NM** $20 **MIP** $30

Jurisprudence, 1974, James Vail
EX $8 **NM** $20 **MIP** $30

Justice, 1954, Lowell
EX $25 **NM** $55 **MIP** $75

Justice League of America, 1967, Hasbro
EX $70 **NM** $150 **MIP** $200

Ka Bala, 1965, Transogram
EX $40 **NM** $75 **MIP** $100

Karate, The Game of, 1964, Selchow & Righter
EX $7 **NM** $20 **MIP** $35

Karter Peanut Shell Game, 1978, Morey & Neely
EX $7 **NM** $20 **MIP** $35

Kar-Zoom, 1964, Whitman
EX $15 **NM** $20 **MIP** $35

Kennedys, The, 1962, Transogram
EX $35 **NM** $60 **MIP** $75

Kentucky Derby, 1960, Whitman
EX $25 **NM** $35 **MIP** $50

Kentucky Jones, 1964, T. Cohn
EX $20 **NM** $35 **MIP** $50

Keyword, 1954, Parker Brothers
EX $3 **NM** $6 **MIP** $10

Kick-Off Soccer, 1978, Camden Products
EX $7 **NM** $20 **MIP** $35

King Kong Game, 1963, Ideal
EX $100 **NM** $200 **MIP** $325

King Kong Game, 1966, Milton Bradley
EX $8 **NM** $20 **MIP** $30

King Kong Game, 1976, Ideal
EX $8 **NM** $30 **MIP** $45

King Leonardo and His Subjects Game, 1960, Milton Bradley
EX $18 **NM** $45 **MIP** $65

King of the Hill, 1965, Schaper
EX $35 **NM** $50 **MIP** $70

King of the Sea, 1975, Ideal
EX $8 **NM** $25 **MIP** $40

King Oil, 1974, Milton Bradley
EX $25 **NM** $55 **MIP** $70

King Tut's Game, 1978, Cadaco
EX $5 **NM** $16 **MIP** $25

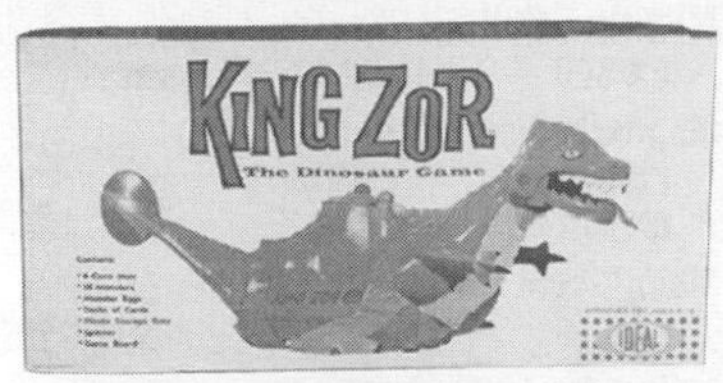

King Zor, The Dinosaur Game, 1964, Ideal
EX $55 **NM** $85 **MIP** $120

Kismet, 1971, Lakeside
EX $6 **NM** $15 **MIP** $25

KISS On Tour Game, 1978, Aucoin
EX $25 **NM** $60 **MIP** $100

Klondike, 1975, Gamma Two
EX $12 **NM** $30 **MIP** $40

Knight Rider, 1983, Parker Brothers
EX $7 **NM** $12 **MIP** $20

Kojak, 1975, Milton Bradley
EX $7 **NM** $12 **MIP** $35

Kommisar, 1960s, Selchow & Righter
EX $12 **NM** $20 **MIP** $30

Koo Koo Choo Choo, 1960s, Ohio Art
EX $12 **NM** $30 **MIP** $40

Kooky Carnival, 1969, Milton Bradley
EX $10 **NM** $35 **MIP** $50

Korg 70,000 BC, 1974, Milton Bradley
EX $7 **NM** $15 **MIP** $25

Kreskin's ESP, 1966, Milton Bradley
EX $4 **NM** $10 **MIP** $15

Krull, 1983, Parker Brothers
EX $6 **NM** $10 **MIP** $15

KSP Baseball, 1983, Koch Sports Products
EX $25 **NM** $60 **MIP** $85

Kukla & Ollie, 1962, Parker Brothers
EX $15 **NM** $25 **MIP** $50

Labyrinth (movie game), 1986, Golden
EX $25 **NM** $60 **MIP** $85

Lancer, 1968, Remco
EX $40 **NM** $90 **MIP** $135

Land of The Giants, 1968, Ideal
EX $75 **NM** $100 **MIP** $175

Land of The Lost, 1975, Milton Bradley
EX $10 **NM** $25 **MIP** $35

Landmarks, The Game of, 1962, Selchow & Righter
EX $6 **NM** $15 **MIP** $25

Landslide, 1971, Parker Brothers
EX $5 **NM** $16 **MIP** $20

Laramie, 1960, Lowell
EX $50 **NM** $100 **MIP** $150

Las Vegas Baseball, 1987, Samar Enterprises
EX $8 **NM** $13 **MIP** $20

Laser Attack Game, 1978, Milton Bradley
EX $7 **NM** $20 **MIP** $35

Lassie Game, 1965, Game Gems
EX $20 **NM** $35 **MIP** $75

Last Straw, 1966, Schaper
EX $5 **NM** $10 **MIP** $15

Laugh-In's Squeeze Your Bippy Game, 1968, Hasbro
EX $35 **NM** $75 **MIP** $100

Laurel & Hardy Game, 1962, Transogram
EX $20 **NM** $30 **MIP** $40

Laverne & Shirley Game, 1977, Parker Brothers
EX $9 **NM** $15 **MIP** $25

Leave It To Beaver Ambush Game, 1959, Hasbro
EX $20 **NM** $35 **MIP** $60

Leave It To Beaver Money Maker, 1959, Hasbro
EX $20 **NM** $35 **MIP** $60

Leave It To Beaver Rocket To The Moon, 1959, Hasbro
EX $20 **NM** $353 **MIP** $60

Lee vs Meade: Battle of Gettysburg, 1974, Gamut of Games
EX $7 **NM** $15 **MIP** $25

Legend of Jesse James Game, The, 1965, Milton Bradley
EX $30 **NM** $50 **MIP** $75

LeMans, 1961, Avalon Hill
EX $25 **NM** $60 **MIP** $85

Let's Bowl a Game, 1960, DMR
EX $5 **NM** $12 **MIP** $20

Let's Drive, 1969, Milton Bradley
EX $8 **NM** $20 **MIP** $30

Let's Go to the Races, 1987, Parker Brothers
EX $7 **NM** $20 **MIP** $35

Let's Make a Deal, 1964, Milton Bradley
EX $12 **NM** $30 **MIP** $40

Let's Make A Deal, 1970s, Ideal
EX $10 **NM** $15 **MIP** $25

Let's Play Golf "The Hawaiian Open", 1968, Burlu
EX $8 **NM** $20 **MIP** $30

Let's Play Safe Traffic Game, 1960s, X-Acto
EX $25 **NM** $50 **MIP** $90

Let's Play Tag, 1958, Milton Bradley
EX $5 **NM** $16 **MIP** $25

Let's Take a Trip, 1962, Milton Bradley
EX $8 **NM** $15 **MIP** $20

Leverage, 1982, Milton Bradley
EX $4 **NM** $6 **MIP** $10

LF Baseball, 1980, Len Feder
EX $18 **NM** $45 **MIP** $65

Lie Detector Game, 1961, Mattel
EX $20 **NM** $40 **MIP** $85

Lie Detector Game, 1987, Pressman
EX $8 **NM** $20 **MIP** $30

Lieutenant, The, 1963, Transogram
EX $20 **NM** $35 **MIP** $60

Life, The Game of, 1960, Milton Bradley
EX $8 **NM** $20 **MIP** $30

Limit Up, 1980, Willem
EX $6 **NM** $18 **MIP** $30

Line Drive, 1953, Lord & Freber
EX $18 **NM** $45 **MIP** $65

Linebacker Football, 1990, Linebacker
EX $12 **NM** $20 **MIP** $30

Linkup, 1972, American Greetings
EX $5 **NM** $16 **MIP** $25

Linus the Lionhearted Uproarious Game, 1965, Transogram
EX $50 **NM** $85 **MIP** $135

Linx, 1972, American Greetings
EX $6 **NM** $15 **MIP** $25

Lion and the White Witch, The, 1983, David Cook
EX $5 **NM** $16 **MIP** $25

Lippy the Lion Game, 1963, Transogram
EX $30 **NM** $45 **MIP** $70

Little Black Sambo, 1952, Cadaco-Ellis
EX $45 **NM** $90 **MIP** $175

Little Boy Blue, 1955, Cadaco-Ellis
EX $6 **NM** $18 **MIP** $30

Little Creepies Monster Game, 1974, Toy Factory
EX $6 **NM** $10 **MIP** $15

Little House On The Prairie, 1978, Parker Brothers
EX $12 **NM** $30 **MIP** $40

Little League Baseball Game, 1950s, Standard Toykraft
EX $20 **NM** $35 **MIP** $60

Little Orphan Annie, 1981, Parker Brothers
EX $10 **NM** $15 **MIP** $20

Little Red Schoolhouse, 1952, Parker Brothers
EX $10 **NM** $20 **MIP** $35

Lobby, 1949, Milton Bradley
EX $8 **NM** $20 **MIP** $30

Long Shot, 1962, Parker Brothers
EX $45 **NM** $75 **MIP** $125

Longball, 1975, Ashburn Industries
EX $35 **NM** $75 **MIP** $100

Look All-Star Baseball Game, 1960, Progressive Research
EX $35 **NM** $60 **MIP** $90

Looney Tunes Game, 1968, Milton Bradley
EX $20 **NM** $40 **MIP** $50

Lord of the Rings, The, 1979, Milton Bradley
EX $40 **NM** $85 **MIP** $125

Los Angeles Dodgers Baseball Game, 1964, Ed-U-Cards
EX $10 **NM** $25 **MIP** $35

Lost Gold, 1975, Parker Brothers
EX $7 **NM** $20 **MIP** $35

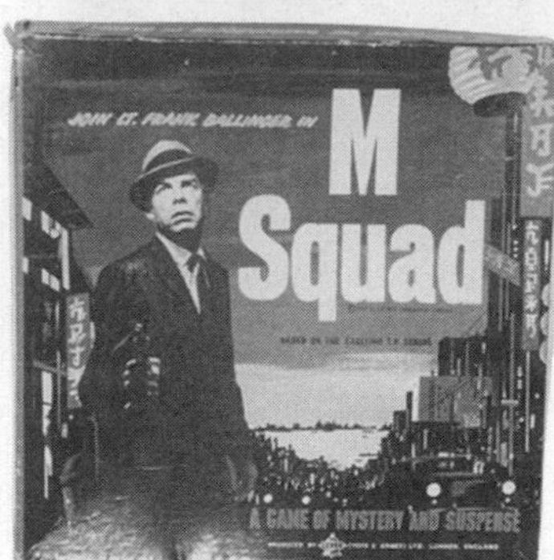

Lost In Space Game, 1965, Milton Bradley
EX $35 **NM** $60 **MIP** $100

Lost Treasure, 1982, Parker Brothers
EX $7 **NM** $20 **MIP** $35

Lottery Game, 1972, Selchow & Righter
EX $6 **NM** $18 **MIP** $30

Louie the Electrician, ca. 1960, Hasbro
EX $20 **NM** $50 **MIP** $70

Love Boat World Cruise, 1980, Ungame
EX $5 **NM** $15 **MIP** $20

Loving Game, The, 1987, R.J.E. Enterprises
EX $4 **NM** $6 **MIP** $10

Lucan, The Wolf Boy, 1977, Milton Bradley
EX $5 **NM** $10 **MIP** $15

Lucky Break, 1975, Gabriel
EX $10 **NM** $20 **MIP** $30

Lucky Strike, 1972, International Toy
EX $5 **NM** $10 **MIP** $15

Lucky Town, 1946, Milton Bradley
EX $15 **NM** $40 **MIP** $50

Lucy Show Game, The, 1962, Transogram
EX $60 **NM** $90 **MIP** $150

Lucy's Tea Party Game, 1971, Milton Bradley
EX $15 **NM** $25 **MIP** $50

Ludwig Von Drake Ball Toss Game, 1960
EX $6 **NM** $10 **MIP** $15

Luftwaffe, 1971, Avalon Hill
EX $3 **NM** $8 **MIP** $15

M Squad, 1958, Bell Toys
EX $35 **NM** $75 **MIP** $125

M*A*S*H* Game, 1981, Milton Bradley
EX $15 **NM** $20 **MIP** $35

MacDonald's Farm, 1948, Selchow & Righter
EX $12 **NM** $20 **MIP** $30

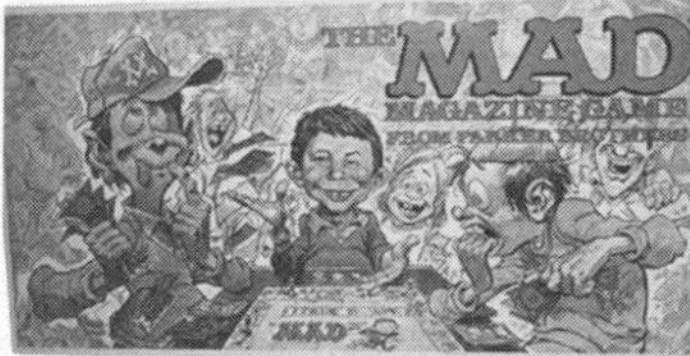

MAD Magazine Game, The, 1979, Parker Brothers
EX $4 **NM** $12 **MIP** $20

MAD, What Me Worry?, 1987, Milton Bradley
EX $6 **NM** $10 **MIP** $15

Madame Planchette Horoscope Game, 1967, Selchow & Righter
EX $6 **NM** $18 **MIP** $30

Magic Miles, 1956, Hasbro
EX $10 **NM** $15 **MIP** $20

Magilla Gorilla, 1964, Ideal
EX $40 **NM** $65 **MIP** $100

Magnetic Flying Saucers, 1950s, Pressman
EX $21 **NM** $35 **MIP** $55

Magnificent Race, 1975, Parker Brothers
EX $10 **NM** $20 **MIP** $30

Mail Run, 1960, Quality Games
EX $35 **NM** $75 **MIP** $100

Main Street Baseball, 1989, Main St. Toy
EX $20 **NM** $35 **MIP** $55

Major League Baseball, 1965, Cadaco
EX $10 **NM** $20 **MIP** $30

Major League Baseball Magnetic Dart Game, 1958, Pressman
EX $20 **NM** $45 **MIP** $65

Man from U.N.C.L.E. Napoleon Solo Game, 1965, Ideal
EX $25 **NM** $45 **MIP** $60

Man from U.N.C.L.E. THRUSH Ray Gun Affair Game, 1966, Ideal
EX $50 **NM** $85 **MIP** $135

Manage Your Own Team, 1950s, Warren
EX $10 **NM** $30 **MIP** $40

Management, 1960, Avalon Hill
EX $10 **NM** $25 **MIP** $40

Mandinka, 1978, Lowe
EX $3 **NM** $12 **MIP** $20

Manhunt, 1972, Milton Bradley
EX $5 **NM** $16 **MIP** $20

Maniac, 1979, Ideal
EX $7 **NM** $15 **MIP** $20

Margie, The Game of Whoopie, 1961, Milton Bradley
EX $12 **NM** $20 **MIP** $30

Marlin Perkins' Zoo Parade, 1965, Cadaco-Ellis
EX $12 **NM** $30 **MIP** $40

Martin Luther King Jr., 1980, Cadaco
EX $6 **NM** $10 **MIP** $15

Mary Hartman, Mary Hartman, 1976, Reiss Games
EX $10 **NM** $25 **MIP** $35

Mary Poppins Carousel Game, 1964, Parker Brothers
EX $12 **NM** $20 **MIP** $30

Masquerade Party, 1955, Bettye-B
EX $25 **NM** $35 **MIP** $75

GAMES

Mastermind, 1970s, Invicta
EX $5 NM $10 MIP $15

Masterpiece, The Art Auction Game, 1971, Parker Brothers
EX $8 NM $15 MIP $30

Match Game (3rd Ed.), The, 1963, Milton Bradley
EX $10 NM $20 MIP $60

Matchbox Traffic Game, 1960s, Bronner
EX $25 NM $45 MIP $70

McDonald's Game, The, 1975, Milton Bradley
EX $12 NM $30 MIP $40

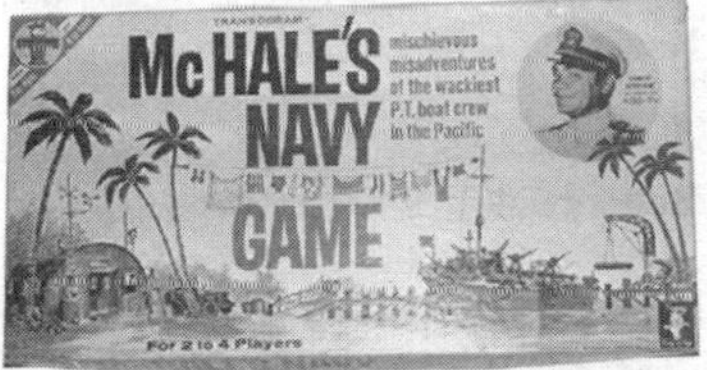

McHale's Navy Game, 1962, Transogram
EX $20 NM $30 MIP $50

McMurtle Turtle, 1965, Cadaco-Ellis
EX $8 NM $25 MIP $40

Mechanic Mac, 1961, Selchow & Richter
EX $15 NM $35 MIP $50

Meet The Presidents, 1953, Selchow & Righter
EX $8 NM $15 MIP $20

Megiddo, 1985, Global Games
EX $8 NM $20 MIP $30

Melvin The Moon Man, 1960s, Remco
EX $30 NM $70 MIP $100

Men Into Space, 1960, Milton Bradley
EX $25 NM $60 MIP $90

Merger, 1965, Universal Games
EX $12 NM $30 MIP $40

Merry Milkman, 1955, Hasbro
EX $50 NM $85 MIP $125

Merv Griffin's Word For Word, 1963, Mattel
EX $5 NM $16 MIP $25

Miami Vice: The Game, 1984, Pepperlane
EX $10 NM $25 MIP $35

Mickey Mantle's Action Baseball, 1960, Pressman
EX $75 NM $125 MIP $200

Mickey Mantle's Big League Baseball, 1958, Gardner
EX $150 NM $225 MIP $325

Mickey Mouse, 1950, Jacmar
EX $35 NM $55 MIP $90

Mickey Mouse, 1976, Parker Brothers
EX $6 NM $10 MIP $15

Mickey Mouse Basketball, 1950s, Gardner
EX $55 NM $90 MIP $135

Mickey Mouse Lotto Game, 1950s, Jaymar
EX $10 NM $15 MIP $25

Mickey Mouse Pop Up Game, 1970s, Whitman
EX $7 NM $15 MIP $20

Mickey Mouse Slugaroo, 1950s
EX $20 NM $30 MIP $50

Mid Life Crisis, 1982, Gameworks
EX $5 NM $10 MIP $20

Mighty Comics Super Heroes Game, 1966, Transogram
EX $30 NM $70 MIP $100

Mighty Hercules Game, 1963, Hasbro
EX $125 NM $300 MIP $500

Mighty Heroes on the Scene Game, 1960s, Transogram
EX $35 NM $75 MIP $100

Mighty Mouse, 1978, Milton Bradley
EX $15 NM $20 MIP $30

Mighty Mouse Rescue Game, 1960s, Harett-Gilmar
EX $25 NM $50 MIP $75

Milton The Monster, 1966, Milton Bradley
EX $10 NM $20 MIP $30

Mind Over Matter, 1968, Transogram
EX $10 NM $15 MIP $25

Miss America Pageant Game, 1974, Parker Brothers
EX $10 NM $20 MIP $30

Miss Popularity Game, 1961, Transogram
EX $10 NM $20 MIP $50

Missing Links, 1964, Milton Bradley
EX $6 NM $18 MIP $35

Mission: Impossible, 1967, Ideal
EX $40 NM $80 MIP $135

Mission: Impossible, 1975, Berwick
EX $10 NM $15 MIP $25

Mister Ed Game, 1962, Parker Brothers
EX $20 NM $40 MIP $75

Mister Football, 1951, Alkay
EX $30 NM $75 MIP $100

Mob Strategy, 1969, NBC-Hasbro
EX $4 NM $10 MIP $15

Mod Squad game, 1960s, Remco
EX $45 NM $85 MIP $125

Monday Morning Quarterback, 1963, Zbinden
EX $8 NM $25 MIP $35

Money Card: Amer. Express Travel Game, 1972, Schaper
EX $8 NM $20 MIP $30

Money! Money! Money!, 1957, Whitman
EX $5 NM $15 MIP $25

Monkees Game, 1968, Transogram
EX $65 NM $100 MIP $150

Monkeys and Coconuts, 1965, Schaper
EX $6 NM $15 MIP $20

Monopoly (large maroon box), 1964, Parker Brothers
EX $15 NM $25 MIP $50

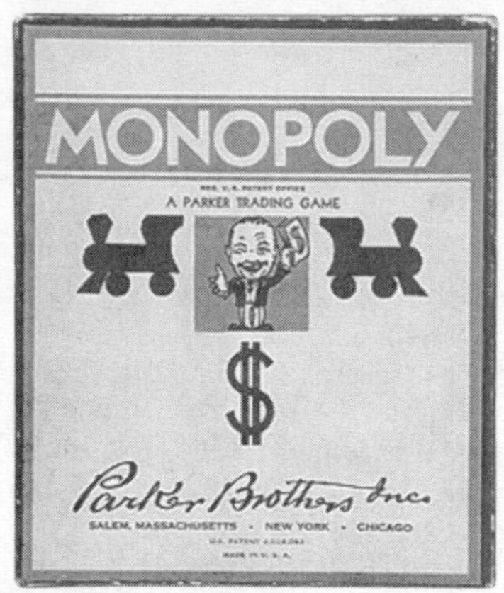

Monopoly (train cover), 1958, Parker Brothers
EX $50 NM $75 MIP $125

Monster Game, 1977, Ideal
EX $25 NM $60 MIP $85

Monster Game, The, 1965, Milton Bradley
EX $15 NM $25 MIP $40

Monster Mansion, 1981, Milton Bradley
EX $20 NM $50 MIP $75

Monster Squad, 1977, Milton Bradley
EX $10 NM $20 MIP $35

Monsters of the Deep, 1976, Whitman
EX $5 NM $16 MIP $25

Moon Blast-Off, 1970, Schaper
EX $12 NM $20 MIP $30

Moon Shot, 1960s, Cadaco
EX $15 NM $35 MIP $60

Moon Tag, Game of, 1957, Parker Brothers
EX $40 NM $60 MIP $100

Mork and Mindy, 1978, Milton Bradley
EX $6 NM $15 MIP $25

Mostly Ghostly, 1975, Cadaco
EX $8 NM $20 MIP $30

Movie Moguls, 1970, RGI
EX $15 NM $35 MIP $50

Movie Studio Mogul, 1981, International Mktg.
EX $8 NM $25 MIP $40

Mr. Bug Goes To Town, 1955, Milton Bradley
EX $10 NM $15 MIP $25

Mr. Doodle's Dog, 1940s, Selchow & Righter
EX $15 NM $25 MIP $40

Mr. Machine Game, 1961, Ideal
EX $60 NM $90 MIP $150

Mr. Magoo Maddening Misadventures Game, The, 1970, Transogram
EX $45 NM $75 MIP $120

Mr. Magoo Visits The Zoo, 1961, Lowell
EX $25 NM $45 MIP $70

Mr. President, 1967, 3M
EX $8 NM $25 MIP $40

Mr. Ree, 1957, Selchow & Righter
EX $15 NM $25 MIP $50

Mt. Everest, 1955, Gabriel
EX $18 NM $25 MIP $50

Mug Shots, 1975, Cadaco
EX $7 NM $12 MIP $20

Munsters Drag Race Game, 1965, Hasbro
EX $250 NM $600 MIP $1000

Munsters Masquerade Game, 1965, Hasbro
EX $250 NM $600 MIP $1000

Munsters Picnic Game, 1965, Hasbro
EX $200 NM $500 MIP $1000

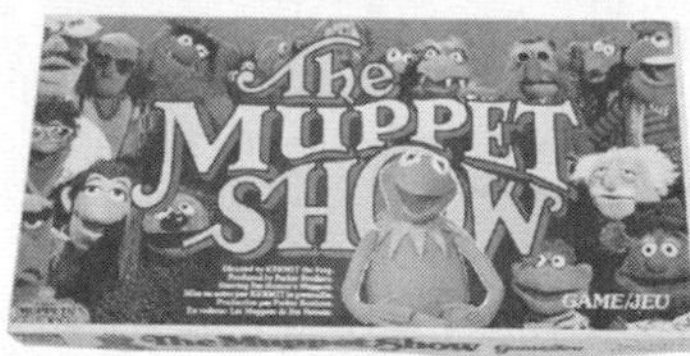

Muppet Show, 1977, Parker Brothers
EX $6 NM $15 MIP $20

Murder on the Orient Express, 1967, Ideal
EX $20 NM $50 MIP $75

Murder She Wrote, 1985, Warren
EX $4 NM $6 MIP $10

Mushmouse & Punkin Puss, 1964, Ideal
EX $45 NM $75 MIP $120

MVP Baseball, The Sports Card Game, 1989, Ideal
EX $8 NM $13 MIP $20

My Fair Lady, 1960s, Standard Toykraft
EX $5 NM $10 MIP $20

My Favorite Martian, 1963, Transogram
EX $40 NM $50 MIP $75

My First (Walt Disney Character) Game, 1963, Gabriel
EX $20 NM $35 MIP $60

Mystery Checkers, 1950s, Creative Designs
EX $15 NM $20 MIP $30

Mystery Date, 1965, Milton Bradley
EX $75 NM $125 MIP $300

Mystery Date Game, 1972, Milton Bradley
EX $50 NM $70 MIP $125

Mystery Mansion, 1984, Milton Bradley
EX $10 NM $25 MIP $35

Mystic Skull The Game of Voodoo, 1965, Ideal
EX $15 NM $30 MIP $50

Mystic Wheel of Knowledge, 1950s, Novel Toy
EX $15 NM $20 MIP $30

Name That Tune, 1959, Milton Bradley
EX $12 NM $20 MIP $30

Names and Faces, 1960, Pressman
EX $6 NM $15 MIP $25

Nancy Drew Mystery Game, 1957, Parker Brothers
EX $35 NM $90 MIP $150

NASCAR Daytona 500, 1990, Milton Bradley
EX $10 NM $25 MIP $35

National Football League Quarterback, Official, 1965, Standard Toykraft
EX $12 NM $30 MIP $40

National Inquirer, 1991, Tyco
EX $10 NM $15 MIP $20

National Lampoon's Sellout, 1970s, Cardinal
EX $6 NM $15 MIP $25

National Pro Football Hall of Fame Game, 1965, Cadaco
EX $15 NM $25 MIP $40

National Pro Hockey, 1985, Sports Action
EX $15 NM $25 MIP $40

National Velvet Game, 1950s, Transogram
EX $15 NM $25 MIP $40

Naval Battle, 1954, Coronet Products
EX $25 NM $60 MIP $85

NBA Basketball Game, Official, 1970s, Gerney Games
EX $35 NM $75 MIP $100

NBC Game of the Week, 1969, Hasbro
EX $10 NM $25 MIP $35

NBC Peacock, 1966, Selchow & Righter
EX $20 NM $50 MIP $75

NBC Pro Playoff, 1969, Hasbro
EX $10 NM $25 MIP $35

NBC TV News, 1960, Dadan
EX $15 NM $35 MIP $50

Nebula, 1976, Nebula
EX $4 NM $6 MIP $10

Neck & Neck, 1981, Yaquinto
EX $8 NM $13 MIP $20

Negamco Basketball, 1975, Nemadji Game
EX $10 NM $16 MIP $25

New Avengers Shooting Game, 1976, Denys Fisher
EX $165 NM $275 MIP $440

New Frontier, 1962, Colorful Products
EX $30 NM $50 MIP $80

New York World's Fair, 1964, Milton Bradley
EX $15 NM $25 MIP $50

Newlywed Game (1st Ed.), 1967, Hasbro
EX $10 NM $15 MIP $20

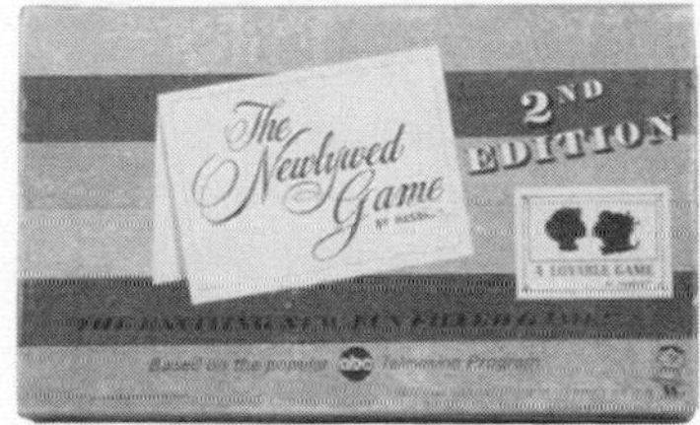

Newlywed Game (2nd Ed.), 1967, Hasbro
EX $8 NM $15 MIP $20

Newtown, 1972, Harwell Associates
EX $15 NM $35 MIP $50

Next President, The, 1971, Reiss
EX $15 NM $35 MIP $50

NFL Armchair Quarterback, 1986, Trade Wind
EX $8 NM $13 MIP $20

NFL Franchise, 1982, Rohrwood
EX $10 NM $16 MIP $25

NFL Game Plan, 1980, Tudor
EX $6 NM $10 MIP $15

NFL Quarterback, 1977, Tudor
EX $8 NM $20 MIP $30

NFL Strategy, 1970, Tudor
EX $10 NM $20

NFL Strategy, 1976, Tudor
EX $15 NM $25 MIP $50

NHL All-Pro Hockey, 1969, Ideal
EX $12 NM $30 MIP $40

NHL Strategy, 1976, Tudor
EX $10 NM $35 MIP $50

Nieuchess, 1961, Avalon Hill
EX $12 NM $40 MIP $60

Nightmare, 1991, Chieftain Products
EX $8 NM $20 MIP $30

Nightmare II, III, IV (add-ons, each), mid-1990s, Chieftain Products
EX $15 NM $35 MIP $50

Nightmare On Elm Street, 1989, Cardinal
EX $20 NM $30 MIP $45

Nile, 1967, Lowe
EX $6 NM $18 MIP $30

Nirtz, The Game is, 1961, Ideal
EX $8 NM $20 MIP $30

No Respect, The Rodney Dangerfield Game, 1985, Milton Bradley
EX $2 NM $6 MIP $8

No Time for Sergeants Game, 1964, Ideal
EX $12 NM $20 MIP $30

Noah's Ark, 1953, Cadaco-Ellis
EX $8 NM $25 MIP $40

Nok-Hockey, 1947, Carrom
EX $20 NM $35 MIP $55

Noma Party Quiz, 1947, Noma Electric
EX $10 NM $15 MIP $25

Northwest Passage, 1969, Impact
EX $5 NM $10 MIP $20

Number Please TV Quiz, 1961, Parker Brothers
EX $10 NM $15 MIP $20

Numble, 1968, Selchow & Righter
EX $4 NM $10 MIP $15

Numeralogic, 1973, American Greetings
EX $6 NM $18 MIP $30

Nurses, The, 1963, Ideal
EX $15 NM $50 MIP $60

Nuts to You, 1969, Hasbro
EX $15 NM $35 MIP $50

O.J. Simpson See-Action Football, 1974, Kenner
EX $50 NM $125 MIP $175

Obsession, 1978, Mego
EX $5 NM $10 MIP $15

Obstruction, 1979, Whitman
EX $4 NM $10 MIP $15

Octopus, 1954, Norton Games
EX $12 NM $40 MIP $60

Off To See The Wizard, 1968, Cadaco
EX $10 NM $15 MIP $25

Oh Magoo Game, 1960s, Warren
EX $10 NM $20 MIP $30

Oh What a Mountain, 1980, Milton Bradley
EX $5 NM $16 MIP $25

Oh, Nuts! Game, 1968, Ideal
EX $10 NM $25 MIP $35

Oh-Wah-Ree, 1966, 3M
EX $8 NM $20 MIP $30

Oil Power, 1980s, Antfamco
EX $20 NM $45 MIP $65

Old Shell Game, The, 1974, Selchow & Righter
EX $7 NM $20 MIP $35

Oldies But Goodies, 1987, Orig. Sound Record
EX $6 NM $18 MIP $30

On Guard, 1967, Parker Brothers
EX $6 NM $10 MIP $15

Oodles, 1992, Milton Bradley
EX $8 NM $20 MIP $30

Operation, 1965, Milton Bradley
EX $5 NM $15 MIP $25

Opinion, 1970, Selchow & Righter
EX $6 NM $15 MIP $25

Option, 1983, Parker Brothers
EX $2 NM $7 MIP $12

Orbit, 1959, Parker Brothers
EX $10 NM $20 MIP $30

Organized Crime, 1974, Koplow Games
EX $6 NM $18 MIP $30

Orient Express, 1985, Just Games
EX $5 NM $16 MIP $25

Original Home Jai-Alai Game, The, 1984, Design Origin
EX $15 NM $25 MIP $35

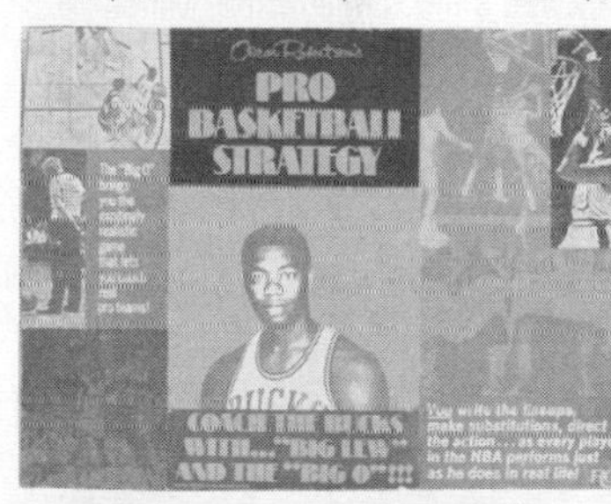

Oscar Robertson's Pro Basketball Strategy, 1964, Research Games
EX $50 NM $72 MIP $150

Our Gang Bingo, 1958
EX $30 NM $50 MIP $75

Outdoor Survival, 1972, Avalon Hill
EX $2 NM $6 MIP $10

Outer Limits, 1964, Milton Bradley
EX $80 NM $180 MIP $225

Outlaw & Posse, 1978, Milton Bradley
EX $8 NM $20 MIP $30

Outlaw Trail, 1972, Dynamic
EX $6 NM $18 MIP $30

Outwit, 1978, Parker Brothers
EX $5 NM $10 MIP $15

Over the Rainbow See-Saw, 1949, Milton Bradley
EX $12 NM $20 MIP $30

Overboard, 1978, Lakeside
EX $3 NM $12 MIP $18

Overland Trail Board Game, 1960, Transogram
EX $45 NM $65 MIP $80

Ozark Ike's Complete 3 Game Set, 1956, Warren Built-Rite
EX $45 NM $80 MIP $110

P.T. Boat 109 Game, 1963, Ideal
EX $25 NM $35 MIP $50

Pac-Man, 1980, Milton Bradley
EX $5 NM $15 MIP $20

Pan American World Jet Flight Game, 1960, Hasbro
EX $10 NM $20 MIP $35

Panic Button, 1978, Mego
EX $7 NM $15 MIP $20

Panzer Blitz, 1970, Avalon Hill
EX $6 NM $12 MIP $20

Panzer Leader, 1974, Avalon Hill
EX $8 NM $15 MIP $25

Par '73, 1961, Big Top Games
EX $15 NM $25 MIP $40

Par Golf, 1950s, National Games
EX $35 NM $40 MIP $60

Parcheesi (Gold Seal Ed.), 1964, Selchow & Righter
EX $7 NM $10 MIP $15

Pari Horse Race Card Game, 1959, Pari Sales
EX $20 NM $35 MIP $50

Paris Metro, 1981, Infinity Games
EX $10 NM $16 MIP $25

Park and Shop, 1952, Traffic Game
EX $35 NM $50 MIP $75

Park and Shop Game, 1960, Milton Bradley
EX $75 NM $100 MIP $175

Parker Brothers Baseball Game, 1955, Parker Brothers
EX $25 NM $50 MIP $75

Parollette, 1946, Selchow & Righter
EX $18 NM $40 MIP $60

Partridge Family, 1974, Milton Bradley
EX $20 NM $25 MIP $50

Pass It On, 1978, Selchow & Righter
EX $3 NM $12 MIP $20

Pass the Buck, 1964, Transco Adult Games
EX $12 NM $30 MIP $40

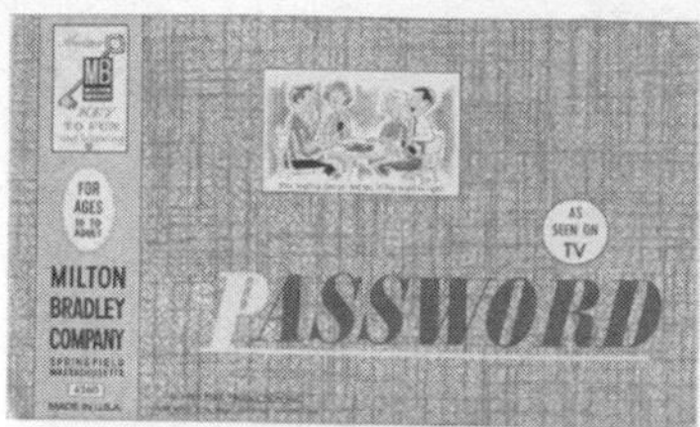

Password, 1963, Milton Bradley
EX $6 NM $15 MIP $20

Pathfinder, 1977, Milton Bradley
EX $5 NM $15 MIP $20

Patty Duke Game, 1963, Milton Bradley
EX $18 NM $25 MIP $50

Paul Brown's Football Game, 1947, Trikilis
EX $110 NM $180 MIP $275

Payday, 1975, Parker Brothers
EX $5 NM $10 MIP $15

Payday: The People's Game, 1975, Payday Game Co/Barker
EX $12 NM $30 MIP $40

Paydirt, 1979, Avalon Hill
EX $12 NM $30 MIP $40

Paydirt!, 1973, Time, Inc., (Sports Illustrated)
EX $10 NM $25 MIP $35

Payoff Machine Game, 1978, Ideal
EX $5 NM $16 MIP $25

Pazaz, 1978, E.S.Lowe
EX $4 NM $10 MIP $15

Peanut Butter & Jelly Game, 1971, Parker Brothers
EX $12 NM $30 MIP $40

Peanuts: The Game of Charlie Brown And His Pals, 1959, Selchow & Righter
EX $20 NM $30 MIP $50

Pebbles Flintstone Game, 1962, Transogram
EX $20 NM $35 MIP $55

Pee Wee Reese Marble Game, 1956, Pee Wee Enterprises
EX $175 NM $295 MIP $450

Penetration, 1968, Crea-Tek
EX $8 NM $20 MIP $30

Pennant Chasers Baseball Game, 1946, Craig Hopkins
EX $25 NM $45 MIP $70

Pennant Drive, 1980, Accu-Stat Game
EX $8 NM $13 MIP $20

People Trivia Game, 1984, Parker Brothers
EX $7 NM $11 MIP $20

People's Court, The, 1986, Pressman
EX $4 NM $10 MIP $15

Per Plexus, 1976, Aladdin
EX $10 NM $25 MIP $35

Perils of Pauline, 1964, Marx
EX $40 NM $90 MIP $135

Perquackey, 1970, Lakeside
EX $4 NM $9 MIP $12

Perry Mason Case of The Missing Suspect Game, 1959, Transogram
EX $20 NM $30 MIP $45

Personalysis, 1957, Lowell
EX $15 NM $25 MIP $40

Pete the Plumber, c. 1960, Hasbro
EX $20 NM $50 MIP $75

Peter Gunn Detective Game, 1960, Lowell
EX $25 NM $35 MIP $50

Peter Pan, 1953, Transogram
EX $10 NM $15 MIP $20

Peter Potamus Game, 1964, Ideal
EX $30 NM $50 MIP $80

Peter Principle Game, 1973, Skor-Mor
EX $6 NM $18 MIP $30

Peter Principle Game, 1981, Avalon Hill
EX $5 NM $16 MIP $25

Petropolis, 1976, Pressman
EX $10 NM $25 MIP $40

Petticoat Junction, 1963, Standard Toykraft
EX $30 NM $50 MIP $85

Phalanx, 1964, Whitman
EX $10 NM $30 MIP $45

Phantom Game, The, 1965, Transogram
EX $50 NM $100 MIP $200

Phantom's Complete Three Game Set, The, 1955, Built-Rite
EX $30 NM $75 MIP $125

Phil Silvers' You'll Never Get Rich Game, 1955, Gardner
EX $25 NM $40 MIP $60

Philip Marlowe, 1960, Transogram
EX $10 NM $20 MIP $50

Phlounder, 1962, 3M
EX $6 NM $18 MIP $30

Pig in the Garden, 1960, Schaper
EX $20 NM $30 MIP $50

Pigskin Vegas, 1980, Jokari/US
EX $6 NM $10 MIP $15

Pilgrimage, 1984, Whitehall Games
EX $8 NM $20 MIP $30

Pinbo Sport-o-Rama, 1950s
EX $35 NM $60 MIP $90

Pinhead, 1959, Remco
EX $10 NM $35 MIP $50

Pink Panther Game, 1977, Warren
EX $8 NM $15 MIP $30

Pink Panther Game, 1981, Cadaco
EX $4 NM $7 MIP $12

Pinky Lee and the Runaway Frankfurters, 1950s, Lisbeth Whiting
EX $30 NM $40 MIP $60

Pinocchio, 1977, Parker Brothers
EX $5 NM $8 MIP $15

Pinocchio Board Game, Disney's, 1960, Parker Brothers
EX $10 NM $15 MIP $25

Pinocchio, The New Adventures of, 1961, Lowell
EX $25 NM $45 MIP $70

Pirate and Traveller, 1953, Milton Bradley
EX $10 NM $25 MIP $40

Pirate Raid, 1956, Cadaco-Ellis
EX $8 NM $25 MIP $40

Pirate's Cove, 1956, Gabriel
EX $15 NM $35 MIP $65

Pizza Pie Game, 1974, Milton Bradley
EX $5 NM $16 MIP $25

Plane Parade, 1950s, Harett-Gilmar Inc.
EX $25 NM $60 MIP $85

Planet of the Apes, 1974, Milton Bradley
EX $20 NM $45 MIP $65

Play Ball! A Baseball Game of Skill, 1940s, Rosebud Art
EX $50 NM $75 MIP $150

Play Basketball with Bob Cousy, 1950s, National Games
EX $50 NM $100 MIP $150

Play Your Hunch, 1960, Transogram
EX $8 NM $25 MIP $40

Playoff Football, 1970s, Crestline
EX $20 NM $35 MIP $50

Plaza, 1947, Parker Brothers
EX $7 NM $20 MIP $35

Plot!, 1968, Cadaco
EX $10 NM $25 MIP $35

Ploy, 1970, 3M
EX $5 NM $16 MIP $25

Plus One, 1980, Milton Bradley
EX $6 NM $18 MIP $30

Pocket Size Bowling Card Game, 1950s, Warren/Built-Rite
EX $15 NM $25 MIP $40

Pocket Whoozit, 1985, Trivia
EX $4 NM $7 MIP $10

Point of Law, 1972, 3M
EX $4 NM $14 MIP $20

Pole Position, 1983, Parker Brothers
EX $8 NM $13 MIP $20

Police Patrol, 1955, Hasbro
EX $50 NM $80 MIP $125

Police State, 1974, Gameophiles Unltd.
EX $25 NM $60 MIP $85

Politics, Game of, 1952, Parker Brothers
EX $10 NM $25 MIP $50

Ponents, 1974, Dynamic
EX $6 NM $15 MIP $25

Pony Express, Game of, 1947, Polygon
EX $12 NM $40 MIP $60

Pooch, 1956, Hasbro
EX $10 NM $20 MIP $30

Pop Yer Top!, 1968, Milton Bradley
EX $15 NM $35 MIP $50

Popeye Spinach Flip, 1969, Whitman
EX $10 NM $25 MIP $35

Popeye, Adventures of, 1957, Transogram
EX $35 NM $60 MIP $100

Poppin Hoppies, 1968, Ideal
EX $10 NM $25 MIP $35

Population, 1970, Urban Systems
EX $6 NM $18 MIP $30

Pop-Up Store Game, 1950s, Milton Bradley
EX $25 NM $40 MIP $75

Post Office, 1968, Hasbro
EX $8 NM $20 MIP $30

Postman, 1957, Selchow & Righter
EX $8 NM $15 MIP $30

Pothole Game, The, 1979, Cadaco
EX $10 NM $25 MIP $40

Pow, The Frontier Game, 1955, Selchow & Righter
EX $12 NM $40 MIP $60

Power 4 Car Racing Game, 1960s, Manning
EX $15 NM $50 MIP $75

Power Play Hockey, 1970, Romac
EX $12 NM $35 MIP $50

Power: The Game, 1981, Power Games
EX $10 NM $25 MIP $35

Prediction Rod, 1970, Parker Brothers
EX $5 NM $16 MIP $25

Presidential Campaign, 1979, John Hansen
EX $6 NM $18 MIP $30

Prince Caspian, 1983, David Cook
EX $5 NM $16 MIP $25

Prince Valiant (Harold Foster's), 1950s, Transogram
EX $20 NM $30 MIP $75

Prize Property, 1974, Milton Bradley
EX $8 NM $15 MIP $30

Pro Draft, 1974, Parker Brothers
EX $15 NM $35 MIP $45

Pro Football, 1980s, Strat-O-Matic
EX $10 NM $20 MIP $30

Pro Foto-Football, 1977, Cadaco
EX $6 NM $15 MIP $25

Pro Franchise Football, 1987, Rohrwood
EX $10 NM $16 MIP $25

Pro Golf, 1982, Avalon Hill
EX $7 NM $11 MIP $17

Pro Quarterback, 1964, Tod Lansing
EX $20 NM $30 MIP $50

Pro Soccer, 1968, Milton Bradley
EX $12 NM $30 MIP $40

Probe, 1964, Parker Brothers
EX $2 NM $7 MIP $12

Products and Resources, Game of, 1962, Selchow & Righter
EX $6 NM $18 MIP $30

Profit Farming, 1979, Foster Enterprises
EX $6 NM $18 MIP $30

Prospecting, 1953, Selchow & Righter
EX $20 NM $30 MIP $50

Prospector, The, 1980, McJay Game Co.
EX $8 NM $20 MIP $30

Public Assistance, 1980, Hammerhead
EX $20 NM $30 MIP $50

Pug-i-Lo, 1960, Pug-i-Lo Games
EX $55 NM $90 MIP $135

Pure Greed, 1971, Crea-Tek
EX $12 NM $30 MIP $40

Pursue the Pennant, 1984, Pursue the Pennant
EX $30 NM $70 MIP $100

Pursuit!, 1973, Aurora
EX $8 NM $25 MIP $40

Push Over, 1981, Parker Brothers
EX $3 NM $12 MIP $18

Put and Take, 1956, Schaper
EX $5 NM $16 MIP $20

Puzzling Pyramid, 1960, Schaper
EX $6 NM $18 MIP $30

Pyramid, 1978, Hasbro
EX $6 NM $15 MIP $25

Pyramid Power, 1978, Castle Toy
EX $8 NM $20 MIP $30

Q*Bert, 1983, Parker Brothers
EX $4 NM $10 MIP $15

Quad-Ominos, 1978, Pressman
EX $2 NM $6 MIP $10

Quarterback Football Game, 1969, Transogram
EX $25 NM $40 MIP $65

Qubic, 1965, Parker Brothers
EX $3 NM $10 MIP $15

Quest, 1962, Lakeside
EX $12 NM $30 MIP $40

Quest, 1978, Gametime/Heritage Models
EX $10 NM $25 MIP $35

Quick Draw McGraw Game, 1981, Milton Bradley
EX $5 **NM** $12 **MIP** $18

Quick Draw McGraw Private Eye Game, 1960
EX $15 **NM** $25 **MIP** $35

Quinto, 1964, 3M
EX $6 **NM** $18 **MIP** $30

Quiz Panel, 1954, Cadaco-Ellis
EX $6 **NM** $18 **MIP** $30

Race-A-Plane, 1947, Phon-O-Game
EX $12 **NM** $40 **MIP** $60

Race-O-Rama, 1960, Warren/Built-Rite
EX $10 **NM** $20 **MIP** $30

Raceway, 1950s, B & B Toy
EX $30 **NM** $50 **MIP** $75

Radaronics, 1946, ARC
EX $15 **NM** $30 **MIP** $40

Raggedy Ann, 1956, Milton Bradley
EX $10 **NM** $20 **MIP** $35

Raiders of the Lost Ark, 1981, Kenner
EX $8 **NM** $20 **MIP** $30

Rainy Day Golf, 1980, Bryad
EX $6 **NM** $18 **MIP** $30

Raise the Titanic, 1987, Hoyle
EX $12 **NM** $30 **MIP** $40

Rat Patrol Game, 1966, Transogram
EX $40 **NM** $70 **MIP** $100

Rawhide, 1959, Lowell
EX $125 **NM** $250 **MIP** $350

Raymar of The Jungle, 1952, Dexter Wayne
EX $30 **NM** $40 **MIP** $50

Razzle, 1981, Parker Brothers
EX $2 **NM** $6 **MIP** $10

Razzle Dazzle Football Game, 1954, Texantics Unlimited
EX $50 **NM** $80 **MIP** $125

React-Or, 1979
EX $15 **NM** $25 **MIP** $40

Real Action Baseball Game, 1966, Real-Action Games
EX $20 **NM** $35 **MIP** $50

Real Baseball Card Game, 1990, National Baseball
EX $110 **NM** $180 **MIP** $275

Real Ghostbusters, The, 1986, Milton Bradley
EX $6 **NM** $18 **MIP** $30

Real Life Basketball, 1974, Gamecraft
EX $20 **NM** $50 **MIP** $75

Realistic Football, 1976, Match Play
EX $15 **NM** $25 **MIP** $35

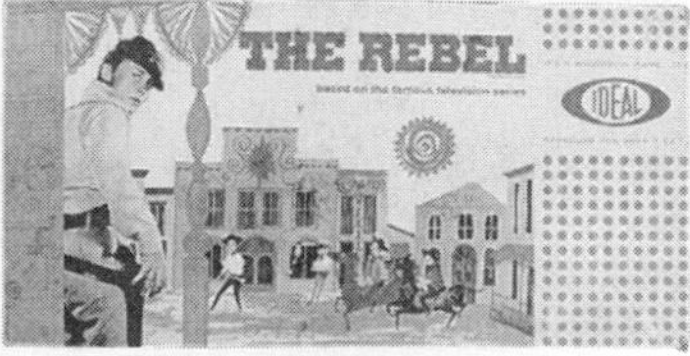

Rebel, The, 1961, Ideal
EX $50 **NM** $75 **MIP** $100

Rebound, 1971, Ideal
EX $5 **NM** $16 **MIP** $25

Record Game, The, 1984, The Record Game
EX $8 **NM** $25 **MIP** $40

Red Barber's Big League Baseball Game, 1950s, G & R Anthony
EX $450 **NM** $1200 **MIP** $1700

Red Herring, 1945, Cadaco-Ellis
EX $12 **NM** $40 **MIP** $60

Red Rover Game, The, 1963, Cadaco-Ellis
EX $5 **NM** $16 **MIP** $25

Reddy Clown 3-Ring Circus Game, 1952, Parker Brothers
EX $15 **NM** $30 **MIP** $45

Reese's Pieces Game, 1983, Ideal
EX $5 **NM** $8 **MIP** $15

Reflex, 1966, Lakeside
EX $5 **NM** $16 **MIP** $25

Regatta, 1946
EX $40 **NM** $70 **MIP** $110

Regatta, 1968, 3M
EX $10 **NM** $15 **MIP** $25

Replay Series Baseball, 1983, Bond Sports
EX $6 **NM** $10 **MIP** $15

Restless Gun, 1950s, Milton Bradley
EX $18 **NM** $35 **MIP** $50

Return To Oz Game, 1985, Western
EX $10 **NM** $15 **MIP** $25

Reward, 1958, Happy Hour
EX $10 **NM** $35 **MIP** $50

Rhyme Time, 1969, NBC-Hasbro
EX $6 **NM** $15 **MIP** $25

Rich Farmer, Poor Farmer, 1978, McJay Game
EX $5 **NM** $16 **MIP** $25

Rich Uncle The Stock Market Game, 1955, Parker Brothers
EX $10 **NM** $20 **MIP** $30

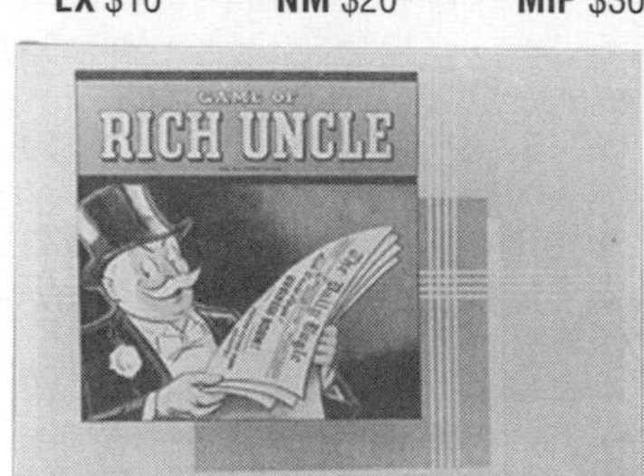

Rich Uncle, Game of, 1946, Parker Brothers
EX $20 **NM** $40 **MIP** $50

Richie Rich, 1982, Milton Bradley
EX $3 **NM** $5 **MIP** $10

Rickenbacker Ace Game, 1946, Milton Bradley
EX $50 **NM** $75 **MIP** $100

Ricochet Rabbit Game, 1965, Ideal
EX $45 **NM** $75 **MIP** $120

Rifleman Game, 1959, Milton Bradley
EX $30 **NM** $50 **MIP** $75

Rin Tin Tin Game, 1950s, Transogram
EX $30 **NM** $50 **MIP** $65

Ringmaster Circus Game, 1947, Cadaco-Ellis
EX $10 **NM** $15 **MIP** $20

Rio, The Game of, 1956, Parker Brothers
EX $10 **NM** $20 **MIP** $30

Ripley's Believe It Or Not, 1979, Whitman
EX $6 **NM** $10 **MIP** $15

Risk, 1959, Parker Brothers
EX $15 **NM** $30 **MIP** $60

Riverboat Game, 1950s, Parker Brothers/Disney
EX $20 **NM** $35 **MIP** $55

Road Runner Game, 1968, Milton Bradley
EX $10 **NM** $25 **MIP** $35

Road Runner Pop Up Game, 1982, Whitman
EX $20 **NM** $30 **MIP** $50

Robert Schuller's Possibility Thinkers Game, 1977, Selchow & Righter
EX $3 **NM** $5 **MIP** $10

Robin Hood, 1955, Harett-Gilmar
EX $30 **NM** $40 **MIP** $55

Robin Hood Game, 1970s, Parker Brothers
EX $7 **NM** $15 **MIP** $30

Robin Hood, Adventures of, 1956, Bettye-B
EX $30 **NM** $40 **MIP** $50

Robin Roberts Sports Club Baseball Game, 1960, Dexter Wayne
EX $100 **NM** $165 **MIP** $250

Robocop VCR Game, 1988, Spinnaker
EX $7 **NM** $20 **MIP** $35

Robot Sam the Answer Man, 1950, Jacmar
EX $15 **NM** $25 **MIP** $30

Rock 'N' Roll Replay, 1984, Baron-Scott
EX $7 **NM** $20 **MIP** $35

Rock the Boat Game, 1978, Milton Bradley
EX $6 **NM** $18 **MIP** $30

Rock Trivia, 1984, Pressman
EX $5 **NM** $10 **MIP** $15

Rocket Race, 1958, Stone Craft
EX $30 **NM** $70 **MIP** $95

Rocket Race To Saturn, 1950s, Lido
EX $15 **NM** $20 **MIP** $30

Rodeo, The Wild West Game, 1957, Whitman
EX $12 **NM** $40 **MIP** $60

GAMES

Roger Maris' Action Baseball, 1962, Pressman
EX $50 **NM** $80 **MIP** $100

Rol-A-Lite, 1947, Durable Toy & Novelty
EX $45 **NM** $75 **MIP** $120

Rol-It, 1954, Parker Brothers
EX $4 **NM** $12 **MIP** $20

Roll And Score Poker, 1977, Lowe
EX $3 **NM** $7 **MIP** $12

Roll-A-Par, 1964, Lowe
EX $8 **NM** $20 **MIP** $30

Roller Derby, 1974, Milton Bradley
EX $70 **NM** $150 **MIP** $225

Roman X, 1964, Selchow & Righter
EX $7 **NM** $20 **MIP** $35

Roscoe Turner Air Race Game, 1960, Southern Games
EX $40 **NM** $90 **MIP** $135

Rose Bowl, 1949, Keck Enterprises
EX $15 **NM** $35 **MIP** $50

Rose Bowl, 1966, E.S.Lowe
EX $15 **NM** $20 **MIP** $25

Roundup, 1952, Wales Game Systems
EX $10 **NM** $20 **MIP** $30

Route 66 Game, 1960, Transogram
EX $70 **NM** $100 **MIP** $160

Roy Rogers Game, 1950s
EX $20 **NM** $35 **MIP** $55

Rribit, Battle of the Frogs, 1982, Genesis Enterprises
EX $6 **NM** $18 **MIP** $30

Ruffhouse, 1980, Parker Brothers
EX $3 **NM** $10 **MIP** $15

Rules of the Road, 1977, Cadaco
EX $5 **NM** $16 **MIP** $25

Run to Win, 1980, Cabela
EX $6 **NM** $18 **MIP** $30

Russian Campaign, The, 1976, Avalon Hill
EX $3 **NM** $5 **MIP** $10

S.O.S., 1947, Durable Toy & Novelty
EX $65 **NM** $85 **MIP** $110

S.W.A.T, 1976, Milton Bradley
EX $5 **NM** $10 **MIP** $15

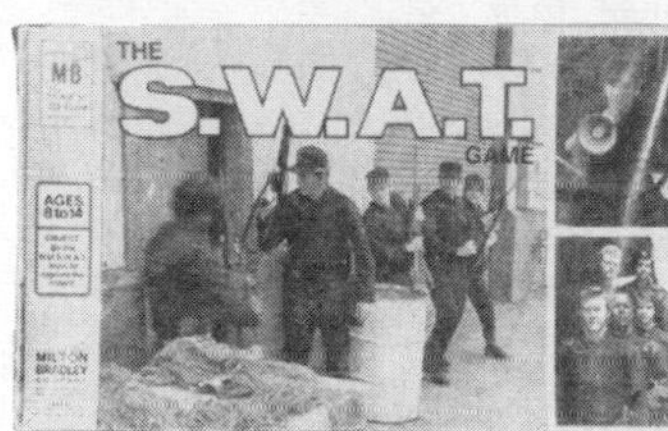

S.W.A.T. Game, 1970s, Milton Bradley
EX $10 **NM** $15 **MIP** $25

Sabotage, 1985, Lakeside
EX $2 **NM** $6 **MIP** $10

Saddle Racing Game, 1974, APBA
EX $20 **NM** $50 **MIP** $75

Safari, 1950, Selchow & Righter
EX $12 **NM** $25 **MIP** $40

Safecrack, 1982, Selchow & Righter
EX $4 **NM** $15 **MIP** $20

Sail Away, 1962, Howard Mullen
EX $12 **NM** $30 **MIP** $40

Salvo, 1961, Ideal
EX $15 **NM** $25 **MIP** $30

Samsonite Basketball, 1969, Samsonite
EX $15 **NM** $30 **MIP** $40

Samsonite Football, 1969, Samsonite
EX $12 **NM** $20 **MIP** $35

Sandlot Slugger, 1960s, Milton Bradley
EX $35 **NM** $60 **MIP** $75

Save the President, 1984, Jack Jaffe
EX $8 **NM** $20 **MIP** $30

Say When!, 1961, Parker Brothers
EX $6 **NM** $15 **MIP** $20

Scarne's Challenge, 1947, John Scarne Games
EX $10 **NM** $15 **MIP** $20

Scavenger Hunt, 1983, Milton Bradley
EX $3 **NM** $5 **MIP** $10

Scooby Doo and Scrappy Doo, 1983, Milton Bradley
EX $3 **NM** $8 **MIP** $16

Scooby-Doo, Where are You?, 1973, Milton Bradley
EX $20 **NM** $30 **MIP** $40

Scoop, 1956, Parker Brothers
EX $20 **NM** $35 **MIP** $45

Scoop: The Newspaper Game, 1976, Western Publishing
EX $18 **NM** $40 **MIP** $55

Score Four, 1968, Funtastic
EX $3 **NM** $10 **MIP** $15

Scotland Yard, 1985, Milton Bradley
EX $3 **NM** $10 **MIP** $15

Scrabble, 1953, Selchow & Righter
EX $5 **NM** $12 **MIP** $20

Scrabble for Juniors, 1968, Selchow & Righter
EX $2 **NM** $5 **MIP** $8

Scrabble RPM, 1971, Selchow & Righter
EX $8 **NM** $20 **MIP** $30

Screaming Eagles, 1987, Milton Bradley
EX $4 **NM** $15 **MIP** $20

Screwball The Mad Mad Mad Game, 1960, Transogram
EX $30 **NM** $40 **MIP** $60

Scribbage, 1963, Lowe
EX $3 **NM** $10 **MIP** $15

Scrimmage, 1973, SPI
EX $5 **NM** $15 **MIP** $25

Scruples, 1986, Milton Bradley
EX $5 **NM** $10 **MIP** $15

Scrutineyes, 1992, Hersch & Co/Mattel
EX $12 **NM** $30 **MIP** $40

Sea World Treasure Key, 1983, International Games
EX $4 **NM** $15 **MIP** $20

Sealab 2020 Game, 1973, Milton Bradley
EX $6 **NM** $10 **MIP** $15

Seance, 1972, Milton Bradley
EX $75 **NM** $100 **MIP** $225

Secrecy, 1965, Universal Games
EX $12 **NM** $30 **MIP** $40

Secret Agent Man, 1966, Milton Bradley
EX $25 **NM** $40 **MIP** $60

Secret of NIMH, 1982, Whitman
EX $15 **NM** $20 **MIP** $30

Secret Weapon, 1984, Selchow & Righter
EX $5 **NM** $16 **MIP** $25

Seduction, 1966, Createk
EX $10 **NM** $25 **MIP** $35

See New York 'Round the Town, 1964, Transogram
EX $50 **NM** $70 **MIP** $90

Sergeant Preston Game, 1950s, Milton Bradley
EX $15 **NM** $30 **MIP** $40

Set Point, 1971, XV Productions
EX $8 **NM** $20 **MIP** $30

Seven Keys, 1961, Ideal
EX $12 **NM** $20 **MIP** $30

GAMES

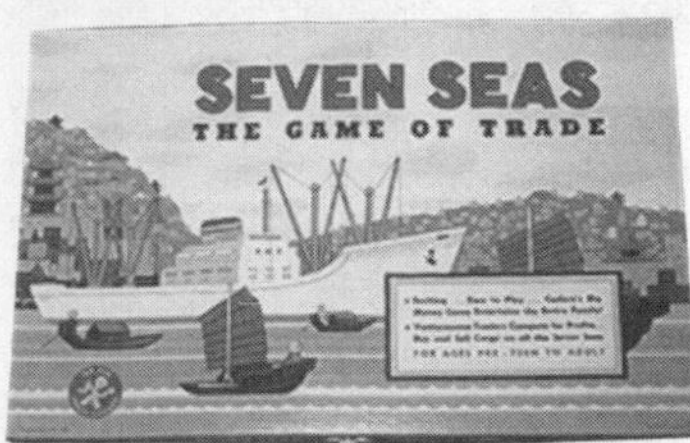

Seven Seas, 1960, Cadaco-Ellis
EX $15 **NM** $25 **MIP** $40

Seven Up, 1960s, Transogram
EX $7 **NM** $12 **MIP** $20

Shadowlord!, 1983, Parker Brothers
EX $3 **NM** $10 **MIP** $15

Sha-ee, the Game of Destiny, 1963, Ideal
EX $20 **NM** $65 **MIP** $90

Shazam, Captian Marvel's Own Game, 1950s, Reed & Associates
EX $30 **NM** $60 **MIP** $95

Shenanigans, 1964, Milton Bradley
EX $15 **NM** $40 **MIP** $50

Sheriff of Dodge City, 1966, Parker Brothers
EX $8 **NM** $25 **MIP** $40

Sherlock Holmes, 1950s, National Games
EX $25 **NM** $50 **MIP** $65

Sherlock Holmes, 1980, Whitman
EX $5 **NM** $16 **MIP** $25

Sherlock Holmes Game, The, 1974, Cadaco
EX $6 **NM** $18 **MIP** $30

Shifty Checkers, 1973, Aurora
EX $8 **NM** $25 **MIP** $40

Shifty Gear Game, 1962, Schaper
EX $5 **NM** $16 **MIP** $25

Shindig, 1965, Remco
EX $30 **NM** $45 **MIP** $60

Shmo, 1960s, Remco
EX $10 **NM** $25 **MIP** $35

Shogun, 1976, Epoch Playthings
EX $6 **NM** $15 **MIP** $25

Shogun, 1986, Milton Bradley
EX $18 **NM** $45 **MIP** $75

Shopping, 1973, John Ladell
EX $5 **NM** $16 **MIP** $25

Shotgun Slade, 1960, Milton Bradley
EX $20 **NM** $45 **MIP** $65

Show-Biz, 1950s, Lowell
EX $15 **NM** $50 **MIP** $75

SI: The Sporting Word Game, 1961, Time
EX $10 **NM** $16 **MIP** $25

Siege Game, 1966, Milton Bradley
EX $20 **NM** $50 **MIP** $60

Silly Carnival, 1969, Whitman
EX $7 **NM** $12 **MIP** $20

Silly Safari, 1966, Topper
EX $30 **NM** $60 **MIP** $90

Silly Sidney, 1963, Transogram
EX $12 **NM** $30 **MIP** $40

Simpsons Mystery of Life, The, 1990, Cardinal
EX $5 **NM** $7 **MIP** $10

Sinbad, 1978, Cadaco
EX $20 **NM** $30 **MIP** $50

Sinking of The Titanic, The, 1976, Ideal
EX $15 **NM** $25 **MIP** $40

Sir Lancelot, Adventures of, 1960s, Lisbeth Whiting
EX $40 **NM** $70 **MIP** $110

Situation 4, 1968, Parker Brothers
EX $5 **NM** $16 **MIP** $20

Situation 7, 1969, Parker Brothers
EX $8 **NM** $25 **MIP** $40

Six Million Dollar Man, 1975, Parker Brothers
EX $10 **NM** $15 **MIP** $25

Skatebirds Game, 1978, Milton Bradley
EX $7 **NM** $20 **MIP** $35

Skatterbug, Game of, 1951, Parker Brothers
EX $30 **NM** $40 **MIP** $50

Skedaddle, 1965, Cadaco-Ellis
EX $8 **NM** $25 **MIP** $40

Ski Gammon, 1962, American Publishing
EX $8 **NM** $20 **MIP** $30

Skill-Drive, 1950s, Sidney Tarrson
EX $10 **NM** $35 **MIP** $40

Skins Golf Game, Official, 1985, O'Connor Hall
EX $12 **NM** $20 **MIP** $30

Skip-A-Cross, 1953, Cadaco
EX $3 **NM** $7 **MIP** $10

Skipper Race Sailing Game, 1949, Cadaco-Ellis
EX $25 **NM** $60 **MIP** $90

Skirmish, 1975, Milton Bradley
EX $30 **NM** $50 **MIP** $60

Skirrid, 1979, Kenner
EX $4 **NM** $15 **MIP** $20

Skudo, 1949, Parker Brothers
EX $8 **NM** $25 **MIP** $40

Skully, 1961, Ideal
EX $3 **NM** $5 **MIP** $10

Skunk, 1950s, Schaper
EX $7 **NM** $12 **MIP** $20

Sky Lanes, 1958, Parker Brothers
EX $15 **NM** $30 **MIP** $50

Sky's The Limit, The, 1955, Kohner
EX $15 **NM** $25 **MIP** $40

Sla-lom Ski Race Game, 1957, Cadaco-Ellis
EX $20 **NM** $50 **MIP** $75

Slap Trap, 1967, Ideal
EX $8 **NM** $25 **MIP** $40

Slapshot, 1982, Avalon Hill
EX $10 **NM** $25 **MIP** $35

Slip Disc, 1980, Milton Bradley
EX $5 **NM** $16 **MIP** $25

Smess, The Ninny's Chess, 1970, Parker Brothers
EX $30 **NM** $40 **MIP** $50

Smog, 1970, Urban Systems
EX $8 **NM** $20 **MIP** $30

Smokey: The Forest Fire Prevention Bear, 1961, Ideal
EX $30 **NM** $65 **MIP** $105

Smurf Game, 1984, Milton Bradley
EX $4 **NM** $7 **MIP** $12

Snafu, 1969, Gamescience
EX $7 **NM** $20 **MIP** $35

Snagglepuss Fun at the Picnic Game, 1961, Transogram
EX $40 **NM** $50 **MIP** $60

Snake Eyes, 1957, Selchow & Righter
EX $15 **NM** $20 **MIP** $30

Snakes & Ladders, 1974, Summmerville/Canada
EX $4 **NM** $7 **MIP** $10

Snake's Alive, Game of, 1967, Ideal
EX $12 **NM** $30 **MIP** $40

Snakes In The Grass, 1960s, Kohner
EX $10 **NM** $15 **MIP** $25

Snappet Catch Game with Harmon Killebrew, 1960, Killebrew
EX $55 **NM** $90 **MIP** $135

Sniggle!, 1980, Amway
EX $4 **NM** $10 **MIP** $15

Snob, A Fantasy Shopping Spree, 1983, Helene Fox
EX $7 **NM** $20 **MIP** $35

Snoopy & The Red Baron, 1970, Milton Bradley
EX $15 NM $35 MIP $45

Snoopy Come Home Game, 1973, Milton Bradley
EX $10 NM $16 MIP $25

Snoopy Game, 1960, Selchow & Righter
EX $25 NM $35 MIP $50

Snoopy's Doghouse Game, 1977, Milton Bradley
EX $5 NM $16 MIP $25

Snow White and the Seven Dwarfs, 1970s, Cadaco
EX $6 NM $10 MIP $15

Snuffy Smith Game, 1970s, Milton Bradley
EX $15 NM $20 MIP $25

Society Scandals, 1978, E.S.Lowe
EX $6 NM $15 MIP $25

Sod Buster, 1980, Santee
EX $10 NM $16 MIP $25

Solar Conquest, 1966, Atech Enterprises
EX $15 NM $35 MIP $50

Solarquest, 1986, Western
EX $6 NM $10 MIP $15

Solid Gold Music Trivia, 1984, Ideal
EX $6 NM $10 MIP $15

Solitaire (Lucille Ball), 1973, Milton Bradley
EX $2 NM $5 MIP $10

Sons of Hercules Game, The, 1966, Milton Bradley
EX $30 NM $45 MIP $60

Soupy Sales Sez Go-Go-Go Game, 1960s, Milton Bradley
EX $35 NM $50 MIP $70

Southern Fast Freight Game, 1970, American Publishing
EX $8 NM $25 MIP $40

Space Angel Game, 1966, Transogram
EX $25 NM $65 MIP $85

Space Chase, 1967, United Nations Constructors
EX $15 NM $35 MIP $50

Space Game, 1953, Parker Brothers
EX $25 NM $65 MIP $85

Space Pilot, 1951, Cadaco-Ellis
EX $20 NM $45 MIP $60

Space Shuttle 101, 1978, Media-Ungame
EX $8 NM $20 MIP $30

Space Shuttle, The, 1981, Ungame
EX $8 NM $20 MIP $30

Space: 1999 Game, 1975, Milton Bradley
EX $10 NM $15 MIP $25

Special Agent, 1966, Parker Brothers
EX $10 NM $25 MIP $40

Special Detective/Speedway, 1959, Saalfield
EX $15 NM $40 MIP $60

Speedorama, 1950s, Jacmar
EX $30 NM $50 MIP $80

Speedway, Big Bopper Game, 1961, Ideal
EX $18 NM $40 MIP $60

Spider and the Fly, 1981, Marx
EX $12 NM $20 MIP $30

Spider-Man Game, The Amazing, 1967, Milton Bradley
EX $20 NM $45 MIP $85

Spider-Man with The Fantastic Four, 1977, Milton Bradley
EX $10 NM $20 MIP $35

Spider's Web Game, The, 1969, Multiple Plastics
EX $7 NM $12 MIP $20

Spin Cycle Baseball, 1965, Pressman
EX $25 NM $40 MIP $65

Spin The Bottle, 1968, Hasbro
EX $8 NM $20 MIP $30

Spin Welder, 1960s, Mattel
EX $7 NM $12 MIP $20

Spiro T. Agnew American History Challenge Game, 1971, Gabriel
EX $20 NM $35 MIP $55

Splat!, 1990, Milton Bradley
EX $8 NM $20 MIP $30

Sporting News: Baseroll, 1986, Mundo Games
EX $8 NM $13 MIP $20

Sports Arena No. 1, 1954, Rennoc Games & Toys
EX $35 NM $60 MIP $90

Sports Illustrated All Time All Star Baseball, 1973, Sports Illustrated
EX $75 NM $175 MIP $250

Sports Illustrated Baseball, 1972, Time, Inc. (Sports Illustrated)
EX $60 NM $120 MIP $175

Sports Illustrated College Football, 1971, Sports Illustrated
EX $8 NM $25 MIP $40

Sports Illustrated Decathlon, 1972, Time
EX $8 NM $25 MIP $40

Sports Illustrated Handicap Golf, 1971, Sports Illustrated
EX $10 NM $25 MIP $35

Sports Illustrated Pro Football, 1970, Time
EX $15 NM $25 MIP $40

Sports Trivia Game, 1984, Hoyle
EX $6 NM $10 MIP $15

Sports Yesteryear, 1977, Skor-Mor
EX $15 NM $25 MIP $35

Spot Cash, 1959, Milton Bradley
EX $7 NM $15 MIP $20

Spy vs. Spy, 1986, Milton Bradley
EX $10 NM $15 MIP $25

Square Mile, 1962, Milton Bradley
EX $15 NM $25 MIP $30

Square Off, 1972, Parker Brothers
EX $8 NM $20 MIP $30

Square-It, 1961, Hasbro
EX $5 NM $16 MIP $25

Squares, 1950s, Schaper
EX $4 NM $15 MIP $20

Squatter: The Australian Wool Game, 1960s, John Sands/Australia
EX $15 NM $25 MIP $45

St. Louis Cardinals Baseball Card Game, 1964, Ed-U-Cards
EX $10 NM $25 MIP $35

Stadium Checkers, 1954, Schaper
EX $7 NM $12 MIP $20

Stagecoach West Game, 1961, Transogram
EX $35 NM $45 MIP $60

Stampede, 1952, Wales Game Systems
EX $15 NM $35 MIP $40

Stampede, 1956, Gabriel
EX $8 NM $25 MIP $30

Star Reporter, 1950s, Parker Brothers
EX $85 NM $125 MIP $175

Star Team Battling Spaceships, 1977, Ideal
EX $8 NM $20 MIP $30

Star Trek, 1979, Milton Bradley
EX $18 NM $30 MIP $40

Star Trek Adventure Game, 1985, West End Games
EX $8 NM $20 MIP $30

GAMES

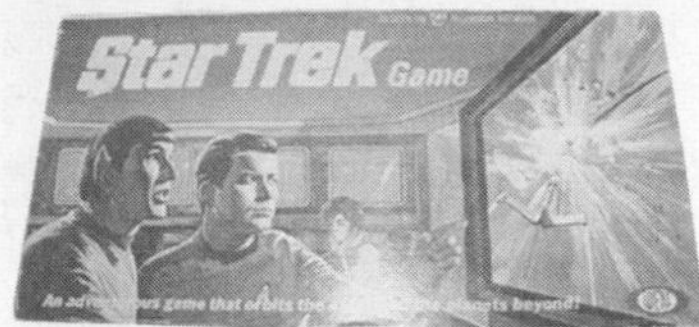

Star Trek Game, 1960s, Ideal
EX $35 NM $70 MIP $85

Star Trek: The Next Generation, 1993, Classic Games
EX $15 NM $25 MIP $50

Star Wars Adventures of R2D2 Game, 1977, Kenner
EX $12 NM $20 MIP $30

Star Wars Battle at Sarlacc's Pit, 1983, Parker Brothers
EX $10 NM $15 MIP $25

Star Wars Escape from Death Star, 1977, Kenner
EX $10 NM $15 MIP $25

Star Wars Monopoly, 1997, Parker Brothers
EX $15 NM $20 MIP $35

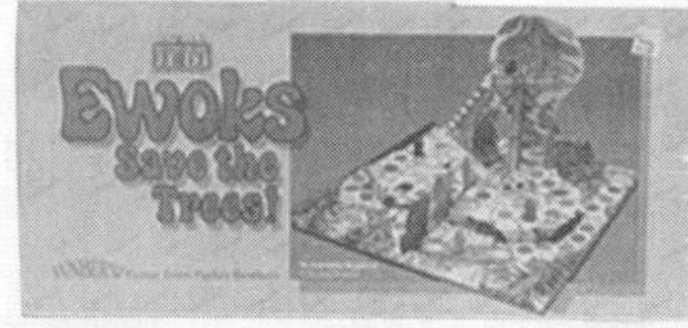

Star Wars ROTJ Ewoks Save The Trees, 1984, Parker Brothers
EX $10 NM $15 MIP $25

Star Wars Wicket the Ewok, 1983, Parker Brothers
EX $7 NM $12 MIP $20

Star Wars X-Wing Aces Target Game, 1978
EX $20 NM $30 MIP $50

Starship Troopers, 1976, Avalon Hill
EX $5 NM $16 MIP $25

Starsky & Hutch, 1977, Milton Bradley
EX $10 NM $16 MIP $25

State Capitals, Game of, 1952, Parker Brothers
EX $4 NM $8 MIP $10

States, Game of the, 1975, Milton Bradley
EX $4 NM $6 MIP $10

Statis Pro Football, 1970s, Statis-Pro
EX $25 NM $40 MIP $65

Stay Alive, 1971, Milton Bradley
EX $6 NM $15 MIP $25

Steps of Toyland, 1954, Parker Brothers
EX $20 NM $35 MIP $55

Steve Allen's Qubila, 1955, Lord & Freber
EX $8 NM $25 MIP $40

Steve Canyon, 1959, Lowell
EX $20 NM $40 MIP $60

Steve Scott Space Scout Game, 1952, Transogram
EX $30 NM $40 MIP $60

Stick the IRS!, 1981, Courtland Playthings
EX $8 NM $12 MIP $15

Sting, The, 1976, Ideal
EX $10 NM $20 MIP $25

Stock Car Race, 1950s, Gardner
EX $25 NM $50 MIP $75

Stock Car Racing Game, 1956, Whitman
EX $12 NM $25 MIP $35

Stock Car Racing Game (w/Petty/Yarborough), 1981, Ribbit Toy
EX $17 NM $30 MIP $45

Stock Car Speedway, Game of, 1965, Johnstone
EX $55 NM $90 MIP $135

Stock Market Game, 1955, Gabriel
EX $20 NM $30 MIP $40

Stock Market Game, 1963, 1968, Whitman
EX $25 NM $45 MIP $60

Stock Market Game, 1970, Avalon Hill
EX $7 NM $12 MIP $20

Stock Market Specialist, 1983, John Hansen
EX $6 NM $18 MIP $30

Stoney Burk, 1963, Transogram
EX $30 NM $60 MIP $80

Stop Thief, 1979, Parker Brothers
EX $15 NM $35 MIP $50

Straight Arrow, 1950, Selchow & Righter
EX $25 NM $35 MIP $55

Straightaway, 1961, Selchow & Righter
EX $45 NM $60 MIP $90

Strata 5, 1984, Milton Bradley
EX $5 NM $16 MIP $25

Strategic Command, 1950s, Transogram
EX $15 NM $30 MIP $40

Stratego (plastic pieces), 1962-on, Milton Bradley
EX $6 NM $10 MIP $15

Stratego (wood pieces), 1961, Milton Bradley
EX $50 NM $75 MIP $90

Strategy Manager Baseball, 1967, McGuffin-Ramsey
EX $2 NM $6 MIP $12

Strato Tac-tics, 1972, Strato-Various
EX $8 NM $25 MIP $40

Strat-O-Matic Baseball, 1961, Strat-O-Matic
EX $125 NM $165 MIP $300

Strat-O-Matic College Football, 1976, Strat-O-Matic
EX $25 NM $55 MIP $75

Strat-O-Matic Hockey, 1978, Strat-O-Matic
EX $12 NM $30 MIP $50

Strat-O-Matic Sports "Know-How", 1984, Strat-O-Matic
EX $6 NM $10 MIP $15

Strato-O-Matic Baseball, 1970, Strat-O-Matic
EX $25 NM $50 MIP $70

Strato-O-Matic Baseball, 1980, Strat-O-Matic
EX $20 NM $35 MIP $50

Strato-O-Matic Baseball (varies by season of cards), 1960s, Strat-O-Matic
EX $80 NM $150 MIP $225

Strato-O-Matic Football (varies by season of cards), 1967-74, Strat-O-Matic
EX $50 NM $125 MIP $175

Strato-O-Matic Football (varies by season of cards), 1975-85, Strat-O-Matic
EX $25 NM $60 MIP $85

Strato-O-Matic Football (varies by season of cards), 1986-90s, Strat-O-Matic
EX $12 NM $30 MIP $40

Stretch Call, 1986, Sevedeo A. Vigil
EX $12 NM $20 MIP $30

Strike Three (Carl Hubbell's), 1948, Tone Products
EX $75 NM $150 MIP $200

Stuff Yer Face, 1982, Milton Bradley
EX $6 NM $20 MIP $35

Stump the Stars, 1962, Ideal
EX $8 NM $25 MIP $40

Sub Attack Game, 1965, Milton Bradley
EX $7 NM $20 MIP $35

Sub Search, 1973, Milton Bradley
EX $8 NM $45 MIP $50

Sub Search, 1977, Milton Bradley
EX $6 NM $18 MIP $30

Sudden Death!, 1978, Gabriel
EX $5 NM $16 MIP $25

Suffolk Downs Racing Game, 1947, Corey Game
EX $40 NM $90 MIP $135

Sugar Bowl, 1950s, Transogram
EX $20 NM $30 MIP $40

Summit, 1961, Milton Bradley
EX $15 NM $20 MIP $30

Sunken Treasure, 1948, Parker Brothers
EX $15 NM $20 MIP $30

Sunken Treasure, 1976, Milton Bradley
EX $7 NM $12 MIP $20

Super Coach TV Football, 1974, Coleco
EX $5 NM $12 MIP $20

Super Market, 1953, Selchow & Righter
EX $10 NM $20 MIP $35

Super Powers, 1984, Parker Brothers
EX $15 NM $25 MIP $40

Super Spy, 1971, Milton Bradley
EX $15 NM $25 MIP $40

Superboy Game, 1960s, Hasbro
EX $45 NM $75 MIP $135

Supercar Road Race, 1962, Standard Toykraft
EX $45 NM $100 MIP $140

GAMES

Supercar to the Rescue Game, 1962, Milton Bradley
EX $25 **NM** $50 **MIP** $75

Superman & Superboy, 1967, Milton Bradley
EX $40 **NM** $65 **MIP** $105

Superman Game, 1965, Hasbro
EX $45 **NM** $75 **MIP** $120

Superman Game, 1966, Merry Manufacturing
EX $35 **NM** $55 **MIP** $90

Superman II, 1981, Milton Bradley
EX $10 **NM** $20 **MIP** $30

Superman III, 1982, Parker Brothers
EX $4 **NM** $12 **MIP** $20

Superman, Adventures of, 1940s, Milton Bradley
EX $125 **NM** $250 **MIP** $450

Superstar Baseball, 1966, Sports Illustrated
EX $30 **NM** $50 **MIP** $75

Superstar Pro Wrestling Game, 1984, Super Star Game
EX $8 **NM** $13 **MIP** $20

Superstar TV Sports, 1980, ARC
EX $6 **NM** $10 **MIP** $15

Superstition, 1977, Milton Bradley
EX $12 **NM** $20 **MIP** $30

Sure Shot Hockey, 1970, Ideal
EX $15 **NM** $25 **MIP** $40

Surfside 6, 1961, Lowell
EX $30 **NM** $50 **MIP** $75

Surprise Package, Your, 1961, Ideal
EX $25 **NM** $60 **MIP** $85

Survive!, 1982, Parker Brothers
EX $12 **NM** $30 **MIP** $40

Swahili Game, 1968, Milton Bradley
EX $8 **NM** $10 **MIP** $20

Swap, the Wheeler-Dealer Game, 1965, Ideal
EX $7 **NM** $20 **MIP** $35

Swat Baseball, 1948, Milton Bradley
EX $20 **NM** $35 **MIP** $50

Swayze, 1954, Milton Bradley
EX $10 **NM** $15 **MIP** $20

Swish, 1948, Jim Hawkers Games
EX $45 **NM** $75 **MIP** $115

Swoop, 1969, Whitman
EX $7 **NM** $12 **MIP** $20

Sword In The Stone Game, 1960s, Parker Brothers
EX $18 **NM** $40 **MIP** $60

Swords and Shields, 1970, Milton Bradley
EX $10 **NM** $35 **MIP** $50

Syncron-8, 1963, Transogram
EX $18 **NM** $40 **MIP** $60

T.V. Bingo, 1970, Selchow & Richter
EX $3 **NM** $5 **MIP** $10

Tabit, 1954, John Norton
EX $25 **NM** $35 **MIP** $75

Tactics II, 1984, Avalon Hill
EX $6 **NM** $10 **MIP** $15

Taffy's Party Game, 1960s, Transogram
EX $10 **NM** $15 **MIP** $25

Taffy's Shopping Spree Game, 1964, Transogram
EX $10 **NM** $25 **MIP** $35

Tagalong Joe, 1950, Wales Game Systems
EX $5 **NM** $10 **MIP** $15

Tales of Wells Fargo, 1959, Milton Bradley
EX $40 **NM** $65 **MIP** $105

Talking Baseball, 1971, Mattel
EX $35 **NM** $60 **MIP** $85

Talking Football, 1971, Mattel
EX $35 **NM** $50 **MIP** $75

Talking Monday Night Football, 1977, Mattel
EX $25 **NM** $30 **MIP** $50

Tally Ho!, 1950s, Whitman
EX $8 **NM** $20 **MIP** $30

Tangle, 1964, Selchow & Righter
EX $6 **NM** $18 **MIP** $30

Tank Battle, 1975, Milton Bradley
EX $15 **NM** $30 **MIP** $40

Tank Command, 1975, Ideal
EX $7 **NM** $20 **MIP** $35

Tantalizer, 1958, Northern Signal
EX $10 **NM** $20 **MIP** $30

Tarzan, 1984, Milton Bradley
EX $5 **NM** $10 **MIP** $15

Tarzan To The Rescue, 1976, Milton Bradley
EX $10 **NM** $15 **MIP** $25

Taxi!, 1960, Selchow & Righter
EX $20 **NM** $30 **MIP** $40

Tee Off by Sam Snead, 1973, Glenn Industries
EX $18 **NM** $40 **MIP** $60

Teed Off!, 1966, Cadaco
EX $6 **NM** $15 **MIP** $25

Teeko, 1948, John Scarne Games
EX $10 **NM** $15 **MIP** $20

Teen Time, 1960s, Warren-Built Rite
EX $6 **NM** $15 **MIP** $25

Telephone Game, The, 1982, Cadaco
EX $7 **NM** $20 **MIP** $35

Television, 1953, National Novelty
EX $35 **NM** $75 **MIP** $100

Tell It To The Judge, 1959, Parker Brothers
EX $20 **NM** $35 **MIP** $50

Temple of Fu Manchu Game, The, 1967, Pressman
EX $20 **NM** $30 **MIP** $50

Ten-Four, Good Buddy, 1976, Parker Brothers
EX $5 **NM** $7 **MIP** $12

Tennessee Tuxedo, 1963, Transogram
EX $75 **NM** $125 **MIP** $200

Tennis, 1975, Parker Brothers
EX $10 **NM** $16 **MIP** $25

Tension, 1970, Kohner
EX $7 **NM** $12 **MIP** $20

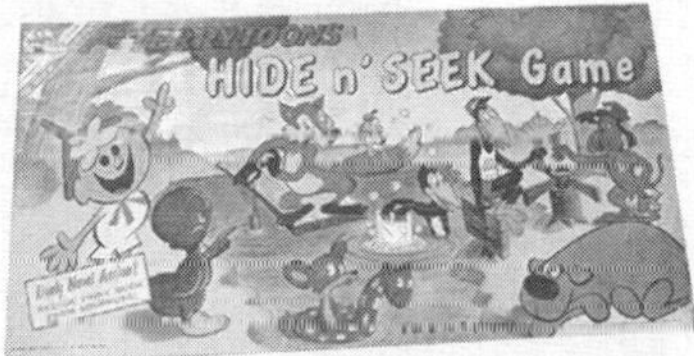

Terrytoons Hide N' Seek Game, 1960, Transogram
EX $30 **NM** $45 **MIP** $60

Test Driver Game, The, 1956, Milton Bradley
EX $45 **NM** $60 **MIP** $75

Texas Millionaire, 1955, Texantics
EX $25 **NM** $55 **MIP** $75

Texas Rangers, Game of, 1950s, All-Fair
EX $25 **NM** $50 **MIP** $75

That's Truckin', 1976, Showker
EX $7 **NM** $20 **MIP** $35

They're at the Post, 1976, MAAS Marketing
EX $12 **NM** $30 **MIP** $40

Thing Ding Robot Game, 1961, Schaper
EX $35 **NM** $75 **MIP** $100

Think Twice, 1974, Dynamic
EX $4 **NM** $15 **MIP** $20

Thinking Man's Football, 1969, 3M
EX $6 **NM** $15 **MIP** $25

Thinking Man's Golf, 1966, 3M
EX $5 **NM** $15 **MIP** $25

Think-Thunk, 1973, Milton Bradley
EX $6 **NM** $18 **MIP** $30

Third Man, 1969, Saalfield
EX $6 **NM** $15 **MIP** $25

Third Reich, 1974, Avalon Hill
EX $3 **NM** $8 **MIP** $15

Thirteen, 1955, Cadaco-Ellis
EX $3 **NM** $7 **MIP** $10

This Is Your Life, 1954, Lowell
EX $20 **NM** $30 **MIP** $35

Three Little Pigs, 1959, Selchow & Righter
EX $7 **NM** $20 **MIP** $35

Three Musketeers, 1958, Milton Bradley
EX $35 **NM** $50 **MIP** $70

Three On a Match, 1972, Milton Bradley
EX $10 **NM** $25 **MIP** $35

Three Stooges Fun House Game, 1950s, Lowell
EX $125 **NM** $275 **MIP** $400

Thunder Road, 1986, Milton Bradley
EX $10 **NM** $16 **MIP** $25

Thunderbirds Game, 1965, Waddington/England
EX $45 **NM** $75 **MIP** $100

Tic-Tac Dough, 1957, Transogram
EX $12 **NM** $20 **MIP** $25

Tiddle Flip Baseball, 1949, Modern Craft
EX $20 **NM** $35 **MIP** $50

Tiddle-Tac-Toe, 1955, Schaper
EX $3 **NM** $10 **MIP** $15

Tilt Score, 1964, Schaper
EX $4 **NM** $15 **MIP** $20

Time Machine, 1961, American Toy
EX $100 **NM** $150 **MIP** $200

Time Tunnel Game, The, 1966, Ideal
EX $90 **NM** $150 **MIP** $240

Time: The Game, 1983, Time/John Hansen
EX $2 **NM** $5 **MIP** $8

Tiny Tim Game of Beautiful Things, The, 1970, Parker Brothers
EX $20 **NM** $30 **MIP** $40

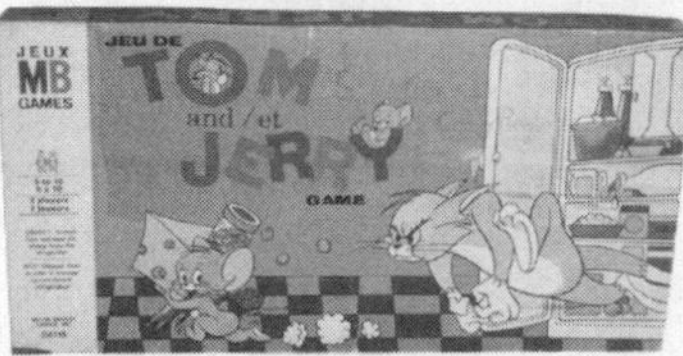

Tom & Jerry, 1977, Milton Bradley
EX $5 **NM** $15 **MIP** $20

Tom & Jerry Adventure In Blunderland, 1965, Transogram
EX $25 **NM** $45 **MIP** $70

Tom Seaver Game Action Baseball, 1969, Pressman
EX $50 **NM** $125 **MIP** $175

Tomorrowland Rocket To Moon, 1956, Parker Brothers
EX $20 **NM** $50 **MIP** $65

Toot! Toot!, 1964, Selchow & Righter
EX $8 **NM** $25 **MIP** $40

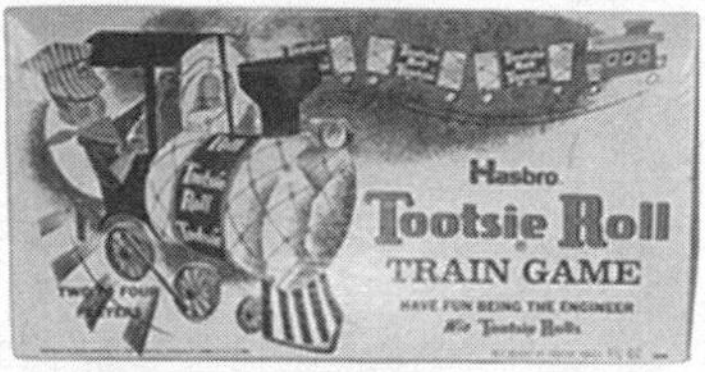

Tootsie Roll Train Game, 1969, Hasbro
EX $20 **NM** $30 **MIP** $50

Top Cat Game, 1962, Transogram
EX $50 **NM** $100 **MIP** $125

Top Cop, 1961, Cadaco-Ellis
EX $25 **NM** $40 **MIP** $55

Top Pro Basketball Quiz Game, 1970, Ed-U-Cards
EX $6 **NM** $15 **MIP** $25

Top Pro Football Quiz Game, 1970, Ed-U-Cards
EX $6 **NM** $15 **MIP** $25

Top Scholar, 1957, Cadaco-Ellis
EX $5 **NM** $16 **MIP** $25

Top Ten College Basketball, 1980, Top Ten Game
EX $30 **NM** $70 **MIP** $100

Top-ography, 1951, Cadaco-Ellis
EX $10 **NM** $15 **MIP** $20

Topper, 1962, Lakeside
EX $15 **NM** $35 **MIP** $50

Topple, 1979, Kenner
EX $4 **NM** $15 **MIP** $20

Tornado Bowl, 1971, Ideal
EX $5 **NM** $16 **MIP** $25

Tornado Rex, 1991, Parker Brothers
EX $10 **NM** $25 **MIP** $35

Total Depth, 1984, Orc Productions
EX $12 **NM** $30 **MIP** $40

Touche Turtle Game, 1964, Ideal
EX $45 **NM** $100 **MIP** $175

Town & Country Traffic Game, 1950s, Ranger Steel
EX $50 **NM** $90 **MIP** $125

Track Meet, 1972, Sports Illustrated
EX $10 **NM** $25 **MIP** $35

Trade Winds: The Caribbean Sea Pirate Treasure Hunt, 1960, Parker Brothers
EX $65 **NM** $100 **MIP** $150

Traffic Game, 1968, Matchbox
EX $35 **NM** $55 **MIP** $90

Traffic Jam, 1954, Harett-Gilmar
EX $15 **NM** $30 **MIP** $45

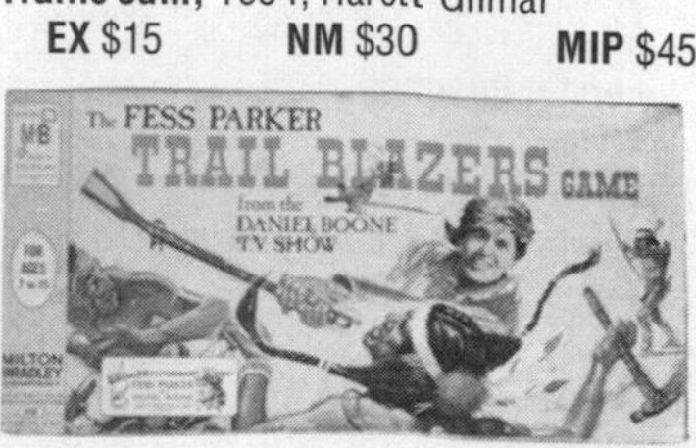

Trail Blazers Game, 1964, Milton Bradley
EX $20 **NM** $35 **MIP** $50

Trails to Tremble By, 1971, Whitman
EX $6 **NM** $18 **MIP** $30

Trap Door, 1982, Milton Bradley
EX $3 **NM** $10 **MIP** $15

Trap-em!, 1957, Selchow & Righter
EX $8 **NM** $25 **MIP** $40

Trapped (Ellery Queen's), 1956, Bettye-B
EX $30 **NM** $50 **MIP** $75

Traps, The Game of, 1950s, Traps
EX $75 **NM** $100 **MIP** $125

Travel America, 1950, Jacmar
EX $15 **NM** $25 **MIP** $40

Travel-Lite, 1946, Saxon Toy
EX $45 **NM** $75 **MIP** $120

Treasure Island, 1954, Harett-Gilmar
EX $15 **NM** $40 **MIP** $60

Tribulation, The Game of, 1981, Whitman
EX $3 **NM** $10 **MIP** $15

Tri-Ominoes, Deluxe, 1978, Pressman
EX $3 **NM** $5 **MIP** $10

Triple Play, 1978, Milton Bradley
EX $5 **NM** $10 **MIP** $15

Triple Yahtzee, 1972, Lowe
EX $4 **NM** $6 **MIP** $10

Tripoley Junior, 1962, Cadaco-Ellis
EX $5 **NM** $16 **MIP** $25

Trivial Pursuit, 1981, Selchow & Righter
EX $10 NM $15 MIP $20

Troke (Castle Checkers), 1961, Selchow & Righter
EX $6 NM $18 MIP $25

Tru-Action Electric Baseball Game, 1955, Tudor
EX $12 NM $30 MIP $50

Tru-Action Electric Sports Car Race, 1959, Tudor
EX $20 NM $50 MIP $75

True Colors, 1990, Milton Bradley
EX $20 NM $50 MIP $70

Trump, the Game, 1989, Milton Bradley
EX $5 NM $10 MIP $15

Trust Me, 1981, Parker Brothers
EX $5 NM $8 MIP $13

Truth or Consequences, 1955, Gabriel
EX $12 NM $40 MIP $60

Truth or Consequences, 1962, Lowell
EX $10 NM $35 MIP $50

TSG I: Pro Football, 1971, TSG
EX $35 NM $55 MIP $85

Tumble Bug, 1950s, Schaper
EX $6 NM $18 MIP $30

Turbo, 1981, Milton Bradley
EX $4 NM $15 MIP $20

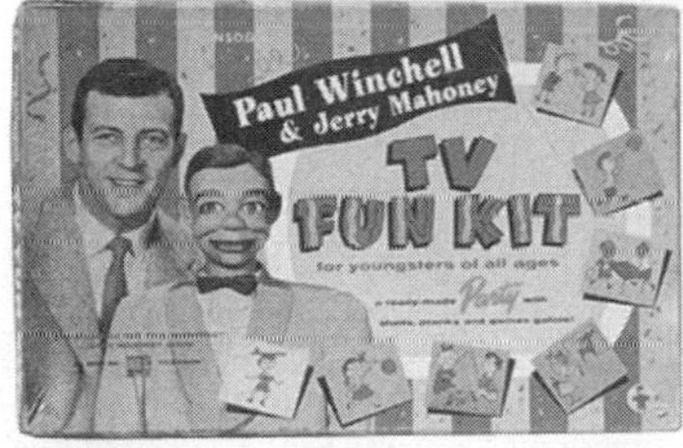

TV Fun Kit, 1950s, Paul Winchell & Jerry Mahoney
EX $10 NM $20 MIP $30

TV Guide Game, 1984, Trivia
EX $8 NM $13 MIP $15

Twelve O'Clock High, 1965, Ideal
EX $35 NM $60 MIP $85

Twiggy, Game of, 1967, Milton Bradley
EX $30 NM $50 MIP $80

Twilight Zone Game, 1960s, Ideal
EX $75 NM $100 MIP $200

Twinkles Trip to the Star Factory, 1960, Milton Bradley
EX $45 NM $75 MIP $120

Twister, 1966, Milton Bradley
EX $15 NM $20 MIP $30

Twixt, 1962, 3M
EX $5 NM $16 MIP $25

Two For The Money, 1950s, Lowell
EX $10 NM $20 MIP $35

Tycoon, 1966, Parker Brothers
EX $12 NM $30 MIP $40

Tycoon, 1981, Wattson Games
EX $4 NM $10 MIP $15

Tycoon: The Real Estate Game, 1986, Ram Innovations
EX $6 NM $15 MIP $20

U.N. Game of Flags, 1961, Parker Brothers
EX $12 NM $20 MIP $25

U.S. Air Force, Game of, 1950s, Transogram
EX $25 NM $45 MIP $60

Ubi, 1986, Selchow & Righter
EX $6 NM $18 MIP $30

Ultimate Golf, 1985, Ultimate Golf
EX $6 NM $18 MIP $25

Uncle Milton's Ant Farm Game, 1969, Uncle Milton Industries
EX $20 NM $35 MIP $50

Uncle Wiggly, 1979, Parker Brothers
EX $8 NM $15 MIP $20

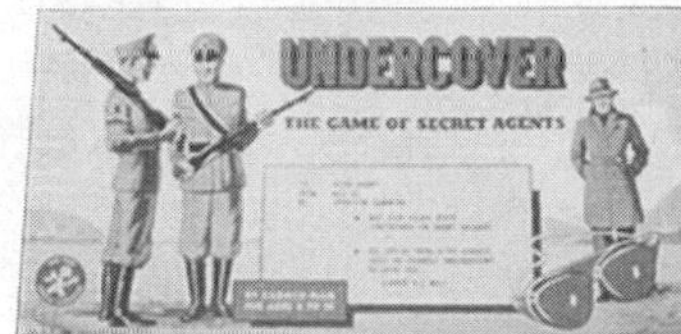

Undercover: The Game of Secret Agents, 1960, Cadaco-Ellis
EX $20 NM $30 MIP $40

Underdog, 1964, Milton Bradley
EX $20 NM $50 MIP $75

Underdog Save Sweet Polly, 1972, Whitman
EX $25 NM $45 MIP $70

Undersea World of Jacques Cousteau, 1968, Parker Brothers
EX $20 NM $35 MIP $50

Ungame, 1975, Ungame
EX $4 NM $6 MIP $10

United Nations, A Game about the, 1961, Payton Products
EX $12 NM $30 MIP $40

Universe, 1966, Parker Brothers
EX $6 NM $18 MIP $30

Up for Grabs, 1978, Mattel
EX $6 NM $15 MIP $20

Up! Against Time, 1977, Ideal
EX $4 NM $10 MIP $15

Ur, Royal Game of Sumer, 1977, Selchow & Righter
EX $3 NM $10 MIP $15

Uranium, 1950s, Saalfield
EX $18 NM $40 MIP $60

Uranium Rush, 1955, Gardner
EX $45 NM $60 MIP $80

USAC Auto Racing, 1980, Avalon Hill
EX $18 NM $45 MIP $65

Vagabondo, 1979, Invicta
EX $5 NM $16 MIP $25

Vallco Pro Drag Racing Game, 1975, Zyla
EX $15 NM $25 MIP $35

Valvigi Downs, 1985, Valvigi
EX $6 NM $18 MIP $30

Vaquero, 1952, Wales Game Systems
EX $15 NM $20 MIP $25

Varsity, 1955, Cadaco-Ellis
EX $12 NM $30 MIP $50

VCR Basketball Game, 1987, Interactive VCR Games
EX $6 NM $10 MIP $15

VCR Quarterback Game, 1986, Interactive VCR Games
EX $8 NM $13 MIP $20

Veda, The Magic Answer Man, 1960s, Pressman
EX $15 NM $20 MIP $25

Vegas, 1969, NBC-Hasbro
EX $6 NM $15 MIP $20

Vegas, 1974, Milton Bradley
EX $4 NM $15 MIP $20

Venture, 1970, 3M
EX $8 NM $20 MIP $30

Verbatim, 1985, Lakeside
EX $3 NM $10 MIP $15

Verdict, 1959, Avalon Hill
EX $15 NM $50 MIP $75

Verdict II, 1961, Avalon Hill
EX $12 NM $40 MIP $60

Verne Gagne World Champion Wrestling, 1950, Gardner
EX $40 NM $90 MIP $135

Vice Versa, 1976, Hallmark Games
EX $5 NM $16 MIP $25

Video Village, 1960, Milton Bradley
EX $15 NM $25 MIP $35

Vietnam, 1984, Victory Games
EX $10 NM $15 MIP $25

Vince Lombardi's Game, 1970, Research Games
EX $35 **NM** $65 **MIP** $85

Virginian, The, 1962, Transogram
EX $45 **NM** $75 **MIP** $90

Visit To Walt Disney World Game, 1970, Milton Bradley
EX $15 **NM** $20 **MIP** $35

Voice of The Mummy, 1960s, Milton Bradley
EX $75 **NM** $125 **MIP** $300

Voodoo Doll Game, 1967, Schaper
EX $12 **NM** $30 **MIP** $40

Voyage of the Dawn Treader, 1983, David Cook
EX $5 **NM** $16 **MIP** $25

Voyage to Cipangu, 1979, Heise-Cipangu
EX $25 **NM** $55 **MIP** $75

Voyage to the Bottom of the Sea, 1964, Milton Bradley, 8 blue & 8 red subs
EX $10 **NM** $20 **MIP** $30

Wackiest Ship In The Army, 1964, Ideal
EX $18 **NM** $25 **MIP** $35

Wacky Races Game, 1970s, Milton Bradley
EX $15 **NM** $25 **MIP** $40

Wagon Train, 1960, Milton Bradley
EX $25 **NM** $40 **MIP** $50

Wahoo, 1947, Zondine
EX $15 **NM** $20 **MIP** $30

Wally Gator Game, 1963, Transogram
EX $65 **NM** $85 **MIP** $130

Walt Disney's 101 Dalmatians, 1960, Whitman
EX $20 **NM** $35 **MIP** $55

Walt Disney's 20,000 Leagues Under The Sea, 1954, Jacmar
EX $45 **NM** $75 **MIP** $120

Walt Disney's Jungle Book, 1967, Parker Brothers
EX $15 **NM** $25 **MIP** $45

Walt Disney's Official Frontierland, 1950s, Parker Brothers
EX $15 **NM** $35 **MIP** $50

Walt Disney's Sleeping Beauty Game, 1958, Whitman
EX $30 **NM** $50 **MIP** $80

Walt Disney's Swamp Fox Game, 1960, Parker Brothers
EX $30 **NM** $40 **MIP** $60

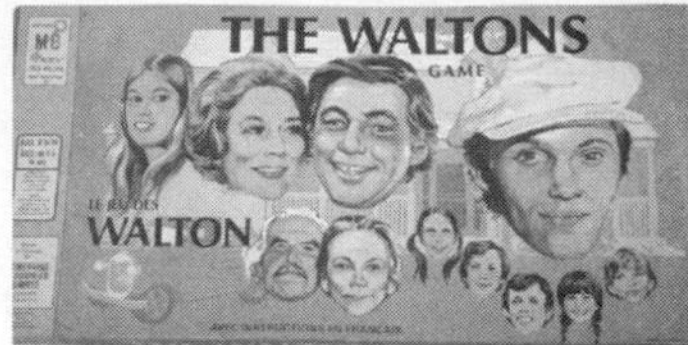

Waltons, 1974, Milton Bradley
EX $15 **NM** $20 **MIP** $30

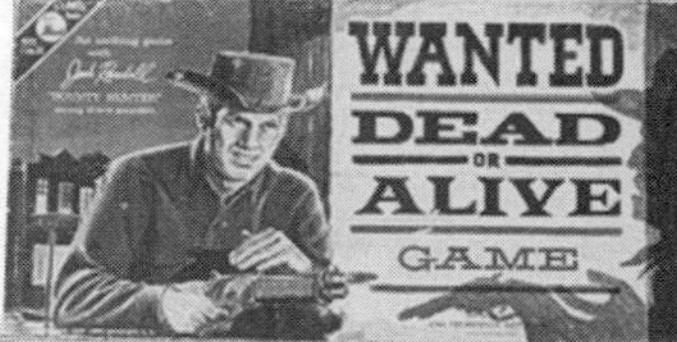

Wanted Dead or Alive, 1959, Lowell
EX $50 **NM** $75 **MIP** $125

War At Sea, 1976, Avalon Hill
EX $10 **NM** $20 **MIP** $30

War of the Networks, 1979, Hasbro
EX $6 **NM** $18 **MIP** $30

Watergate Scandal, The, 1973, American Symbolic
EX $8 **NM** $20 **MIP** $30

Waterloo, 1962, Avalon Hill
EX $10 **NM** $20 **MIP** $45

Weird-Ohs Game, The, 1964, Ideal
EX $85 **NM** $145 **MIP** $230

Welcome Back, Kotter, 1977, Ideal
EX $10 **NM** $20 **MIP** $25

Welfare, 1978, Jedco
EX $12 **NM** $40 **MIP** $60

Wendy, The Good Little Witch, 1966, Milton Bradley
EX $50 **NM** $75 **MIP** $100

West Point Story, The, 1950s, Transogram
EX $25 **NM** $40 **MIP** $60

What Shall I Be?, 1966, Selchow & Righter
EX $15 **NM** $35 **MIP** $45

What Shall I Wear?, 1969, Selchow & Righter
EX $15 **NM** $35 **MIP** $45

What's My Line Game, 1950s, Lowell
EX $20 **NM** $30 **MIP** $40

What's Up, Doc?, 1978, Milton Bradley
EX $6 **NM** $15 **MIP** $20

Whatzit?, 1987, Milton Bradley
EX $5 **NM** $16 **MIP** $25

Wheel of Fortune, 1985, Pressman
EX $5 **NM** $8 **MIP** $13

Where's The Beef?, 1984, Milton Bradley
EX $6 **NM** $10 **MIP** $15

Which Witch?, 1970, Milton Bradley
EX $45 **NM** $75 **MIP** $100

Whirl Out Game, 1971, Milton Bradley
EX $6 **NM** $18 **MIP** $30

Whirl-A-Ball, 1978, Pressman
EX $10 **NM** $15 **MIP** $25

Whirligig, 1963, Milton Bradley
EX $8 **NM** $20 **MIP** $30

Whirly Bird Play Catch, 1960s, Innovation Industries
EX $20 **NM** $35 **MIP** $50

White Shadow Basketball Game, The, 1980, Cadaco
EX $20 **NM** $25 **MIP** $35

Who Can Beat Nixon?, 1971, Dynamic
EX $10 **NM** $35 **MIP** $40

Who Framed Roger Rabbit?, 1987, Milton Bradley
EX $20 **NM** $35 **MIP** $55

Who What Or Where?, 1970, Milton Bradley
EX $5 **NM** $8 **MIP** $13

Who, Game of, 1951, Parker Brothers
EX $20 **NM** $30 **MIP** $40

Whodunit, 1972, Selchow & Righter
EX $10 **NM** $15 **MIP** $25

Whodunit?, 1959, Cadaco-Ellis
EX $8 **NM** $25 **MIP** $40

Whosit?, 1976, Parker Brothers
EX $6 **NM** $10 **MIP** $15

Wide World, 1957, 1962, Parker Brothers
EX $10 **NM** $15 **MIP** $20

Wide World of Sports Auto Racing, 1975, Milton Bradley
EX $12 **NM** $30 **MIP** $45

Wide World of Sports Golf, 1975, Milton Bradley
EX $12 **NM** $30 **MIP** $45

Wide World of Sports Tennis, 1975, Milton Bradley
EX $12 **NM** $30 **MIP** $45

Wide World Travel, 1957, Parker Brothers
EX $15 **NM** $35 **MIP** $50

Wil-Croft Baseball, 1971, Wil-Croft
EX $10 **NM** $16 **MIP** $25

Wild Bill Hickok, 1955, Built-Rite
EX $15 NM $25 MIP $35

Wild Kingdom Game, 1977, Teaching Concepts
EX $20 NM $35 MIP $50

Wild, Wild West, The, 1966, Transogram
EX $125 NM $350 MIP $500

Wildcatter, 1981, Kessler
EX $12 NM $30 MIP $40

Wildlife, 1971, Lowe
EX $15 NM $35 MIP $50

Willie Mays "Say Hey", 1954, Toy Development
EX $200 NM $350 MIP $700

Willie Mays "Say Hey" Baseball, 1958, Centennial Games
EX $190 NM $295 MIP $450

Willie Mays Push Button Baseball, 1965, Eldon
EX $175 NM $295 MIP $450

Willow, 1988, Parker Brothers
EX $10 NM $25 MIP $35

Win, Place & Show, 1966, 3M
EX $6 NM $20 MIP $30

Wine Cellar, 1971, Dynamic
EX $5 NM $16 MIP $25

Winko Baseball, 1940s, Milton Bradley
EX $25 NM $40 MIP $60

Winky Dink Official TV Game Kit, 1950s
EX $50 NM $100 MIP $125

Winnie The Pooh Game, 1959, Parker Brothers
EX $20 NM $30 MIP $40

Winnie The Pooh Game, 1979, Parker Brothers
EX $5 NM $8 MIP $13

Winning Ticket, The, 1977, Ideal
EX $6 NM $20 MIP $30

Wiry Dan's Electric Baseball Game, 1953, Harett-Gilmar
EX $8 NM $25 MIP $35

Wiry Dan's Electric Football Game, 1953, Harett-Gilmar
EX $8 NM $25 MIP $35

Wise Old Owl, 1950s, Novel Toy
EX $20 NM $30 MIP $40

Witch Pitch Game, 1970, Parker Brothers
EX $15 NM $25 MIP $40

Wit's End, Game of, 1948, Parker Brothers
EX $15 NM $35 MIP $50

Wizard of Oz Game, 1962, Lowe
EX $20 NM $30 MIP $50

Wizard of Oz Game, 1974, Cadaco
EX $15 NM $20 MIP $25

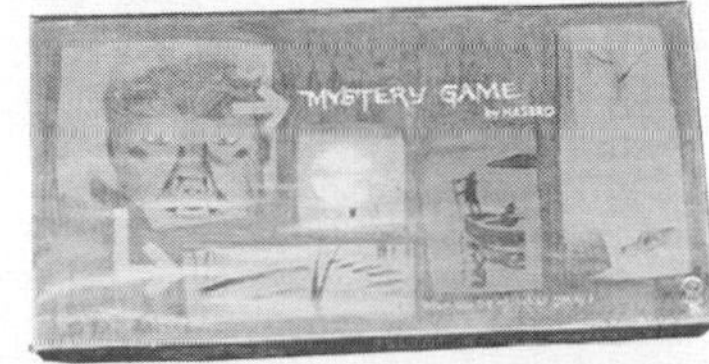

Wolfman Mystery Game, 1963, Hasbro
EX $80 NM $160 MIP $225

Woman & Man, 1971, Psychology Today
EX $4 NM $15 MIP $20

Women's Lib, 1970, Urban Systems
EX $12 NM $30 MIP $40

Wonder Woman Game, 1967, Hasbro
EX $20 NM $35 MIP $50

Wonderbug Game, 1977, Ideal
EX $8 NM $25 MIP $35

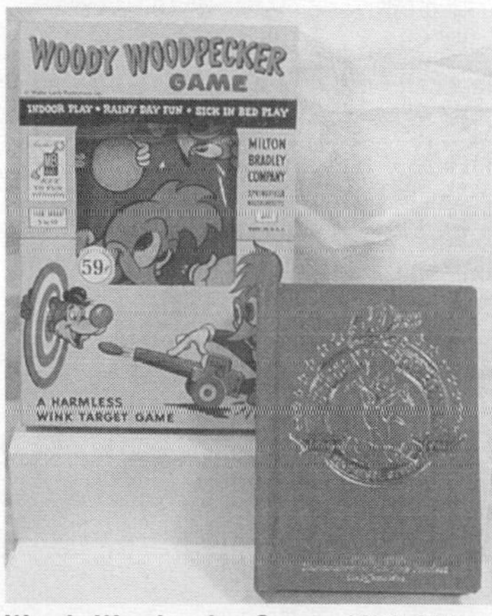

Woody Woodpecker Game, 1959, Milton Bradley
EX $15 NM $25 MIP $35

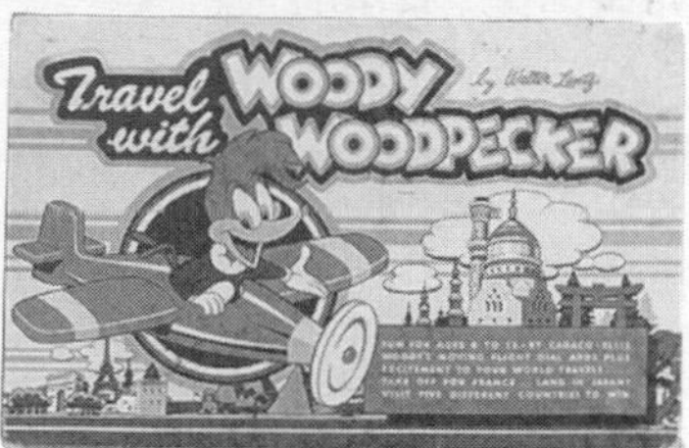

Woody Woodpecker, Travel With, 1950s, Cadaco-Ellis
EX $35 NM $60 MIP $80

Woody Woodpecker's Crazy Mixed Up Color Factory, 1972, Whitman
EX $12 NM $20 MIP $30

Woody Woodpecker's Moon Dash Game, 1976, Whitman
EX $12 NM $20 MIP $30

Word War, 1978, Mattel
EX $6 NM $15 MIP $20

World Bowling Tour, 1979, World Bowling Tour
EX $7 NM $20 MIP $35

World Champion Wrestling Official Slam O' Rama, 1990, International Games
EX $5 NM $8 MIP $12

World of Micronauts, 1978, Milton Bradley
EX $10 NM $15 MIP $25

World of Wall Street, 1969, NBC-Hasbro
EX $4 NM $10 MIP $15

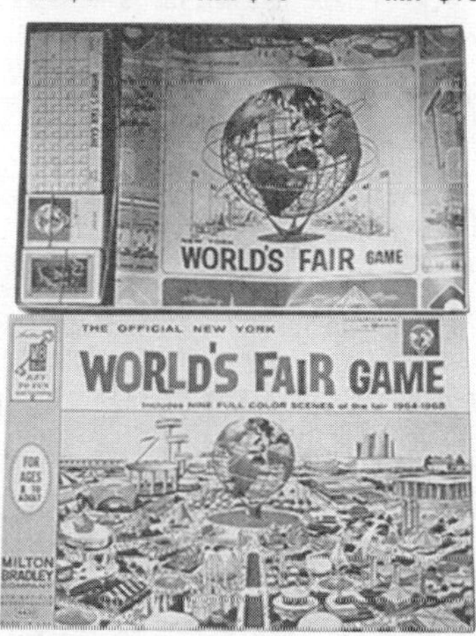

World's Fair Game, 1964, Milton Bradley
EX $10 NM $20 MIP $35

World's Greatest Baseball Game, 1977, J. Woodlock
EX $35 NM $75 MIP $100

Wrestling Superstars, 1985, Milton Bradley
EX $8 NM $13 MIP $20

WWF Wrestling Game, 1991, Colorforms
EX $5 NM $8 MIP $12

Wyatt Earp Game, 1958, Transogram
EX $35 NM $60 MIP $75

Xaviera's Game, 1974, Dynamic
EX $7 NM $20 MIP $35

X-Men Alert! Adventure Game, 1992, Pressman
EX $5 NM $16 MIP $25

Yacht Race, 1961, Parker Brothers
EX $45 **NM** $65 **MIP** $80

Yahtzee, 1956, Lowe
EX $6 **NM** $10 **MIP** $15

Yertle, The Game of, 1960, Revell
EX $30 **NM** $55 **MIP** $75

Yogi Bear Break A Plate Game, 1960s, Transogram
EX $25 **NM** $40 **MIP** $60

Yogi Bear Cartoon Game, 1980, Milton Bradley
EX $3 **NM** $5 **MIP** $10

Yogi Bear Game, 1971, Milton Bradley
EX $8 **NM** $20 **MIP** $30

Yogi Bear Go Fly A Kite Game, 1961, Transogram
EX $25 **NM** $40 **MIP** $60

Your America, 1970, Cadaco
EX $2 **NM** $7 **MIP** $12

Yours For a Song, 1962, Lowell
EX $20 **NM** $35 **MIP** $55

Zaxxon, 1982, Milton Bradley
EX $6 **NM** $10 **MIP** $15

Zig Zag Zoom, 1970, Ideal
EX $10 **NM** $20 **MIP** $30

Ziggy Game, A Day With, 1977, Milton Bradley
EX $4 **NM** $10 **MIP** $15

Zingo, 1950s, Empire Plastics
EX $15 **NM** $20 **MIP** $30

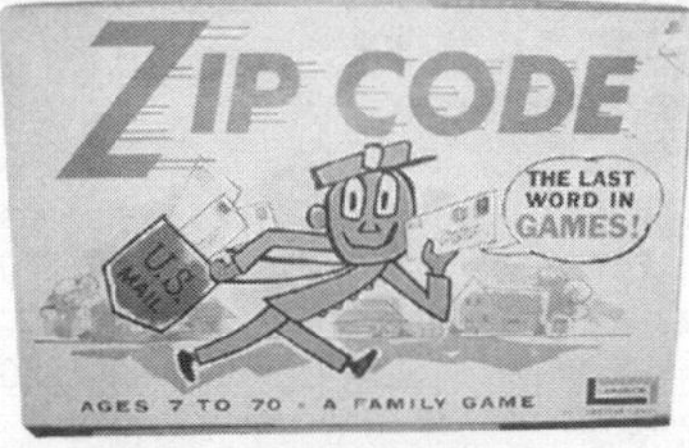

Zip Code Game, 1964, Lakeside
EX $40 **NM** $60 **MIP** $80

Zomax, 1988, Zomax
EX $8 **NM** $25 **MIP** $40

Zoography, 1972, Amway
EX $5 **NM** $16 **MIP** $25

Zorro Game, Walt Disney's, 1966, Parker Brothers
EX $25 **NM** $40 **MIP** $65

Zorro Target Game with Dart Gun, 1950s, Knickerbocker
EX $20 **NM** $30 **MIP** $50

CARD GAMES

Addams Family, 1965, Milton Bradley
EX $20 **NM** $30 **MIP** $60

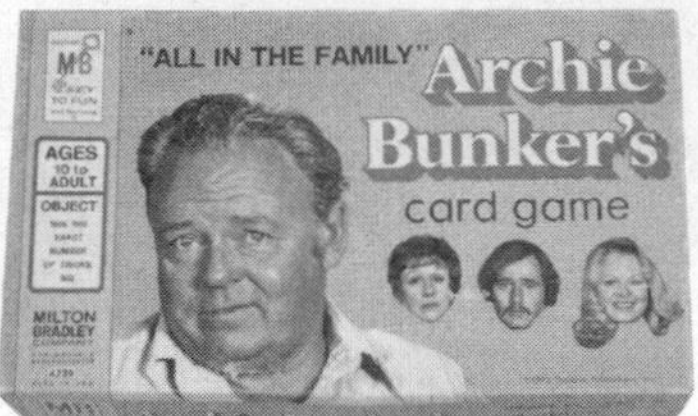

Archie Bunker's Card Game, 1972, Milton Bradley
EX $6 **NM** $10 **MIP** $15

Art Linkletter's People are Funny Party Game, 1954, Whitman
EX $5 **NM** $16 **MIP** $20

Bali, 1954, I-S Unlimited
EX $8 **NM** $20 **MIP** $30

Baseball Card All Star Game, 1987, Captoys
EX $5 **NM** $12 **MIP** $15

Baseball Card Game, 1950s, Ed-U-Cards
EX $8 **NM** $20 **MIP** $30

Baseball Card Game, Official, 1965, Milton Bradley
EX $20 **NM** $40 **MIP** $50

Batman Card Game, 1966, Ideal
EX $35 **NM** $75 **MIP** $95

Batter Up Card Game, 1949, Ed-U-Cards
EX $8 **NM** $20 **MIP** $30

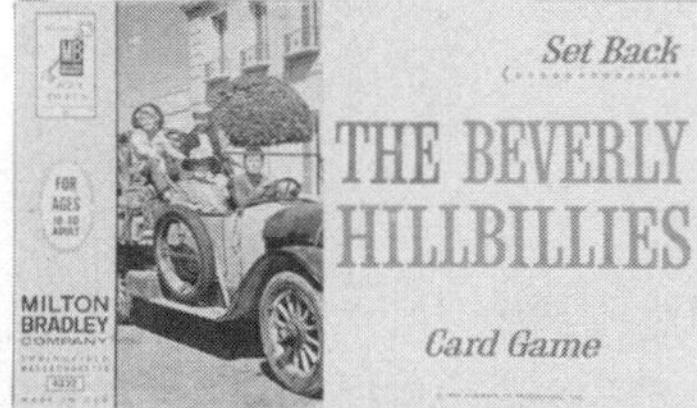

Beverly Hillbillies Game, "Set Back", 1963, Milton Bradley
EX $10 **NM** $15 **MIP** $20

Bewitched Stymie Game, 1960s, Milton Bradley
EX $20 **NM** $50 **MIP** $60

Bible Quiz Lotto, 1949, Jack Levitz
EX $5 **NM** $12 **MIP** $20

Boston Red Sox Game, 1964, Ed-U-Cards
EX $15 **NM** $35 **MIP** $55

Bullwinkle Card Game, 1962, Ed-U-Cards
EX $10 **NM** $30 **MIP** $40

Charge It!, 1972, Whitman
EX $5 **NM** $15 **MIP** $25

Combat, 1964, Milton Bradley
EX $10 **NM** $15 **MIP** $20

Cowboys & Indians, 1949, Ed-U-Cards
EX $8 **NM** $20 **MIP** $35

Dallas Game, 1980, Mego
EX $3 **NM** $10 **MIP** $15

Daniel Boone Wilderness Trail, 1964, Transogram
EX $10 **NM** $40 **MIP** $65

Dick Tracy Playing Card Game, 1934, Whitman
EX $30 **NM** $45 **MIP** $60

Dick Tracy Playing Card Game, 1937, Whitman
EX $20 **NM** $45 **MIP** $60

Dick Tracy Playing Card Game, 1939, Esquire Novelty
EX $20 **NM** $45 **MIP** $60

Dragonmaster, 1981, Lowe
EX $8 **NM** $40 **MIP** $50

Fast Golf, 1977, Whitman
EX $8 **NM** $13 **MIP** $20

Flintstones Animal Rummy, 1960, Ed-U-Cards
EX $7 **NM** $18 **MIP** $25

Flintstones Cut-Ups Game, 1963, Whitman
EX $15 **NM** $45 **MIP** $60

Funny Bones Game, 1968, Parker Brothers
EX $5 **NM** $7 **MIP** $11

Gidget, 1966, Milton Bradley
EX $15 **NM** $35 **MIP** $50

Go Go Go, 1950s, Arco Playing Card
EX $6 **NM** $20 **MIP** $35

Gong Hee Fot Choy, 1948, Zondine Game
EX $20 **NM** $35 **MIP** $55

Grabitz, 1979, International Games
EX $2 **NM** $5 **MIP** $7

Harry's Glam Slam, 1962, Harry Obst
EX $35 **NM** $60 **MIP** $90

Howdy Doody Card Game, 1954, Russell
EX $5 **NM** $10 **MIP** $20

I Survived New York!, 1981, City Enterprises
EX $4 NM $7 MIP $12

James Bond Live and Let Die Tarot Game, 1973, US Games Systems
EX $25 NM $55 MIP $85

Kardball, 1946, Ajak
EX $20 NM $30 MIP $40

Know Your States, 1955, Garrard Press
EX $10 NM $25 MIP $45

Let's Play Basketball, 1965, D.M.R.
EX $12 NM $20 MIP $35

Li'l Abner's Spoof Game, 1950, Milton Bradley
EX $65 NM $95 MIP $135

Man from U.N.C.L.E. Illya Kuryakin Card Game, 1966, Milton Bradley
EX $15 NM $25 MIP $30

Match, 1953, Garrard Press
EX $10 NM $15 MIP $25

Mickey Mouse Canasta Jr., 1950, Russell
EX $20 NM $30 MIP $40

Mickey Mouse Jr. Royal Rummy, 1970s, Whitman
EX $5 NM $15 MIP $30

Mickey Mouse Library of Games, 1946, Russell
EX $30 NM $50 MIP $100

Mille Bornes, 1962, Parker Brothers
EX $10 NM $15 MIP $20

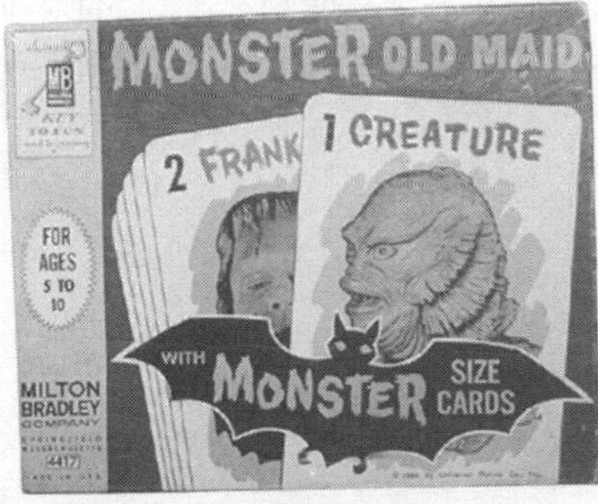

Monster Old Maid, 1964, Milton Bradley
EX $15 NM $40 MIP $55

Mr. T Game, 1983, Milton Bradley
EX $5 NM $15 MIP $25

Munsters Card Game, 1966, Milton Bradley
EX $20 NM $40 MIP $55

New York World's Fair Children's Game, 1964, Ed-U-Cards
EX $15 NM $35 MIP $55

Nuclear War, 1965, Douglas Malewicki
EX $25 NM $40 MIP $75

NY Mets Baseball Card Game, Official, 1961, Ed-U-Cards
EX $20 NM $45 MIP $65

Pro Baseball Card Game, 1980s, Just Games
EX $6 NM $10 MIP $15

Scan, 1970, Parker Brothers
EX $3 NM $10 MIP $15

Scott's Baseball Card Game, 1989, Scott's Baseball Cards
EX $12 NM $20 MIP $30

Skeeter, 1950s, Arco Playing Card
EX $6 NM $20 MIP $35

Strategy Poker Fine Edition, 1967, Milton Bradley
EX $5 NM $12 MIP $18

Superheroes Card Game, 1978, Milton Bradley
EX $15 NM $30 MIP $55

Superman Game, 1966, Whitman
EX $35 NM $75 MIP $110

Syllable, 1948, Garrard Press
EX $10 NM $15 MIP $25

Touch, 1970, Parker Brothers
EX $5 NM $16 MIP $25

Trail Drive, 1950s, Arco Playing Card
EX $15 NM $35 MIP $65

Twelve O'Clock High, 1966, Milton Bradley
EX $15 NM $25 MIP $35

Voyage to the Bottom of the Sea, 1964, Milton Bradley
EX $8 NM $15 MIP $25

Waterworks, 1972, Parker Brothers
EX $5 NM $12 MIP $20

Welcome Back, Kotter, 1976, Milton Bradley
EX $5 NM $16 MIP $25

SKILL GAMES

Call It!, 1978, Ideal
EX $5 NM $12 MIP $20

Chicken Lotto, 1965, Ideal
EX $8 NM $25 MIP $40

Chutes Away!, 1978, Gabriel
EX $15 NM $60 MIP $85

Clickety-Clak, 1950s, Milton Bradley
EX $10 NM $15 MIP $20

Clunk-A-Glunk, 1968, Whitman
EX $8 NM $25 MIP $40

Don't Break the Ice, 1960s, Schaper
EX $5 NM $16 MIP $25

Don't Spill the Beans, 1967, Schaper
EX $10 NM $16 MIP $25

Feed the Elephant!, 1952, Cadaco-Ellis
EX $10 NM $35 MIP $50

Gnip Gnop, 1971, Parker Brothers
EX $5 NM $10 MIP $15

Hoc-Key, 1958, Cadaco-Ellis
EX $10 NM $35 MIP $50

Hungry Henry, 1969, Ideal
EX $7 NM $15 MIP $25

Jack & Jill Target Game, 1948, Cadaco-Ellis
EX $7 NM $20 MIP $35

Jaws, The Game of, 1975, Ideal
EX $10 NM $16 MIP $20

Kick Back, 1965, Schaper
EX $5 NM $16 MIP $25

Leapin' Letters, 1969, Parker Brothers
EX $5 NM $16 MIP $25

Marblehead, 1969, Ideal
EX $5 NM $16 MIP $25

Mark "Three", 1972, Ideal
EX $6 NM $18 MIP $30

Mentor, 1960s, Hasbro
EX $18 NM $40 MIP $60

Mind Maze Game, 1970, Parker Brothers
EX $5 NM $16 MIP $25

Mr. Mad Game, 1970, Ideal
EX $12 NM $40 MIP $60

Nibbles 'N Bites, 1964, Schaper
EX $5 NM $16 MIP $25

On Target, 1973, Milton Bradley
EX $12 NM $40 MIP $60

Pitchin' Pal, 1952, Cadaco-Ellis
EX $7 NM $20 MIP $35

Poosh-em-up Slugger Bagatelle, 1946, Northwestern Products
EX $30 NM $50 MIP $75

Quick Shoot, 1970, Ideal
EX $6 NM $18 MIP $30

Sharpshooter, 1962, Cadaco-Ellis
EX $12 NM $20 MIP $25

Skip Bowl, 1955, Transogram
EX $6 NM $18 MIP $30

Slap Stick, 1967, Milton Bradley
EX $7 NM $20 MIP $35

Smack-A-Roo, 1964, Mattel
EX $6 NM $18 MIP $30

Tight Squeeze, 1967, Mattel
EX $7 NM $20 MIP $35

Tip-It, 1965, Ideal
EX $5 NM $16 MIP $20

Topple Chairs, 1962, Eberhard Faber
EX $6 **NM** $18 **MIP** $30

Wing-Ding, 1951, Cadaco-Ellis
EX $8 **NM** $25 **MIP** $40

SKILL/ACTION GAMES

Airways, 1950s, Lindstrom Tool & Toy
EX $25 **NM** $40 **MIP** $60

Angry Donald Duck Game, 1970s, Mexico
EX $40 **NM** $65 **MIP** $100

Bandu, 1991, Milton Bradley
EX $12 **NM** $30 **MIP** $40

Baseball, 1960s, Tudor
EX $20 **NM** $30 **MIP** $50

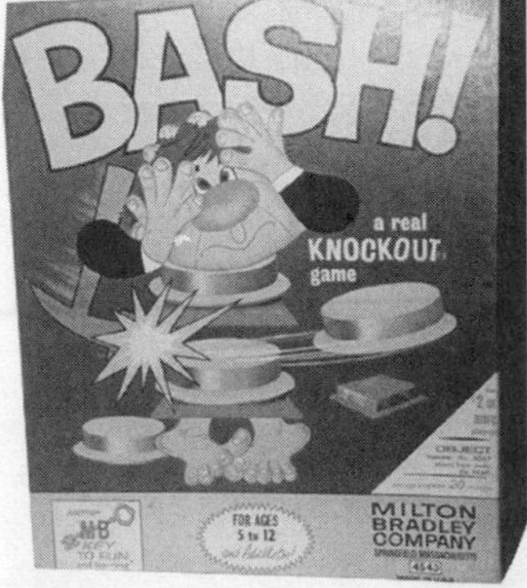

Bash!, 1967, Milton Bradley
EX $10 **NM** $15 **MIP** $25

Batman Batarang Toss, 1966, Pressman
EX $150 **NM** $250 **MIP** $400

Batman Pin Ball, 1966, Marx
EX $55 **NM** $95 **MIP** $150

Bats in the Belfry, 1964, Mattel
EX $35 **NM** $75 **MIP** $100

Big 5 Poosh-M Up, 1950s, Knickerbocker
EX $35 **NM** $40 **MIP** $50

Big Game Hunt, The, 1947, Carrom Industries
EX $15 **NM** $25 **MIP** $30

Big Sneeze Game, The, 1968, Ideal
EX $10 **NM** $25 **MIP** $40

Boob Tube Race, 1962, Milton Bradley
EX $2 **NM** $10 **MIP** $15

Booby Trap, 1965, Parker Brothers
EX $10 **NM** $10 **MIP** $15

Bop Bop 'N Rebop, 1979, Hasbro
EX $12 **NM** $30 **MIP** $40

Bop The Beetle, 1963, Ideal
EX $10 **NM** $20 **MIP** $30

Bowl-A-Matic, 1963, Eldon
EX $100 **NM** $250 **MIP** $350

Bugs Bunny Game (Bagatelle), 1975, Ideal
EX $15 **NM** $25 **MIP** $40

Candid Camera Target Shot, 1950s, Lindstrom Tool & Toy
EX $35 **NM** $50 **MIP** $65

Careful: The Toppling Tower, 1967, Ideal
EX $8 **NM** $20 **MIP** $30

Coney Island Penny Pitch, 1950s, Novel Toy
EX $33 **NM** $55 **MIP** $88

Crazy Clock Game, 1964, Ideal
EX $30 **NM** $40 **MIP** $50

Crazy Maze, 1966, 1975, Lakeside
EX $8 **NM** $20 **MIP** $30

Deputy Dawg Hoss Toss, 1973
EX $15 **NM** $25 **MIP** $40

Disney Dodgem Bagatelle, 1960s, Marx
EX $30 **NM** $65 **MIP** $90

Don't Dump the Daisy, 1970, Ideal
EX $10 **NM** $25 **MIP** $35

Dynamite Shack Game, 1968, Milton Bradley
EX $10 **NM** $25 **MIP** $30

Facts In Five, 1967, 3M
EX $3 **NM** $8 **MIP** $12

Fascination, 1962, Remco
EX $15 **NM** $20 **MIP** $30

Fascination Pool, 1962, Remco
EX $8 **NM** $20 **MIP** $30

Feeley Meeley Game, 1967, Milton Bradley
EX $20 **NM** $50 **MIP** $75

Fireball XL-5 Magnetic Dart Game, 1963, Magic Wand
EX $75 **NM** $125 **MIP** $200

Flea Circus Magnetic Action Game, 1968, Mattel
EX $15 **NM** $25 **MIP** $40

Flintstones Brake Ball, 1962, Whitman
EX $45 **NM** $60 **MIP** $75

Flintstones Mechanical Shooting Gallery, 1962, Marx
EX $75 **NM** $125 **MIP** $200

Flying Nun Marble Maze Game, The, 1967, Hasbro
EX $20 **NM** $30 **MIP** $50

G.I. Joe Bagatelle Gun Action Game, 1970s, Hasbro
EX $7 **NM** $12 **MIP** $15

Gotham's Ice Hockey, 1960s, Gotham
EX $35 **NM** $60 **MIP** $85

Grab A Loop, 1968, Milton Bradley
EX $7 **NM** $12 **MIP** $15

Grand Slam Game, 1969, Ideal
EX $8 **NM** $20 **MIP** $30

Hands Down, 1965, Ideal
EX $10 **NM** $15 **MIP** $20

Hi Pop, 1946, Advance Games
EX $20 **NM** $35 **MIP** $55

Hopalong Cassidy Bean Bag Toss Game, 1950s
EX $20 **NM** $40 **MIP** $60

Hoppity Hooper Pin Ball Game, 1965, Lido
EX $40 **NM** $75 **MIP** $115

Howdy Doody Dominoes Game, 1950s, Ed-U-Cards
EX $50 **NM** $75 **MIP** $100

Huckleberry Hound's Huckle Chuck Target Game, 1961, Transogram
EX $25 **NM** $50 **MIP** $100

Huggin' The Rail, 1948, Selchow & Righter
EX $40 **NM** $50 **MIP** $60

I-Qubes, 1948, Capex
EX $10 **NM** $15 **MIP** $25

Johnny Apollo Moon Landing Bagatelle, 1969, Marx
EX $20 **NM** $35 **MIP** $55

KaBoom!, 1965, Ideal
EX $10 **NM** $15 **MIP** $25

Ker-Plunk, 1967, Ideal
EX $5 **NM** $10 **MIP** $15

Kimbo, 1950s, Parker Brothers
EX $10 **NM** $25 **MIP** $70

King Arthur, 1950s, Northwestern Products
EX $25 **NM** $40 **MIP** $65

King Pin Deluxe Bowling Alley, 1947, Baldwin Mfg.
EX $10 **NM** $20 **MIP** $30

Knockout, Electronic Boxing Game, 1950s, Northwestern Products
EX $75 **NM** $125 **MIP** $175

Krokay, 1955, Transogram
EX $4 **NM** $10 **MIP** $15

Land of The Lost Pinball, 1975, Larami
EX $10 **NM** $20 **MIP** $30

Lone Ranger and Tonto Spin Game, The, 1967, Pressman
EX $15 **NM** $25 **MIP** $40

Loopin' Louie, 1992, Milton Bradley
EX $10 **NM** $25 **MIP** $35

Magnetic Fish Pond, 1948, Milton Bradley
EX $10 **NM** $20 **MIP** $30

Man from U.N.C.L.E. Pinball Game, 1966
EX $80 **NM** $135 **MIP** $215

Man from U.N.C.L.E. Target Game, 1966, Marx
EX $130 **NM** $275 **MIP** $550

Marathon Game, 1978, Sports Games
EX $10 **NM** $20 **MIP** $35

Marx-O-Matic All Star Basketball, 1950s, Marx
EX $150 **NM** $250 **MIP** $400

Mechanical Shooting Gallery, 1950s, Wyandotte
EX $95 **NM** $135 **MIP** $195

Mickey Mouse Haunted House Bagatelle, 1950s
EX $210 **NM** $350 **MIP** $550

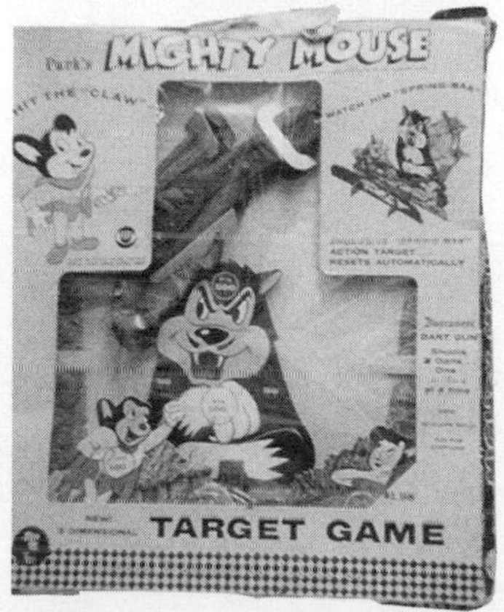

Mighty Mouse Target Game, 1960s, Parks
EX $30 **NM** $60 **MIP** $90

Monster Lab, 1964, Ideal
EX $225 **NM** $275 **MIP** $500

Mouse Trap, 1963, Ideal
EX $20 **NM** $30 **MIP** $50

NFL Football Game, Official, 1968, Ideal
EX $12 **NM** $30 **MIP** $40

Nixon Ring Toss, 1970s
EX $20 **NM** $30 **MIP** $50

Nutty Mads Bagatelle, 1963, Marx
EX $25 **NM** $45 **MIP** $85

Nutty Mads Target Game, 1960s, Marx
EX $35 **NM** $70 **MIP** $125

Par-A-Shoot Game, 1947, Baldwin
EX $15 **NM** $25 **MIP** $40

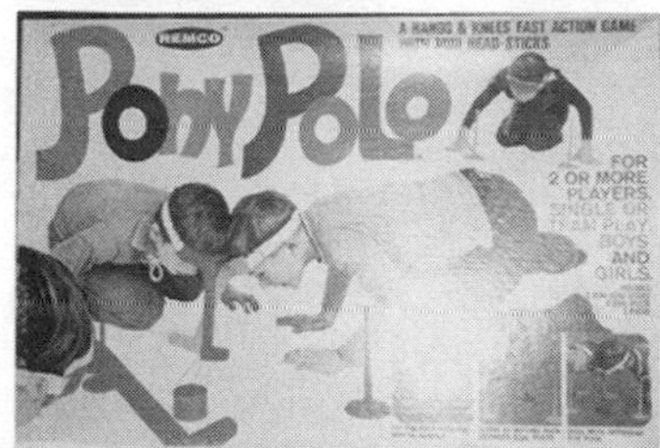

Pony Polo, 1960s, Remco
EX $10 **NM** $20 **MIP** $35

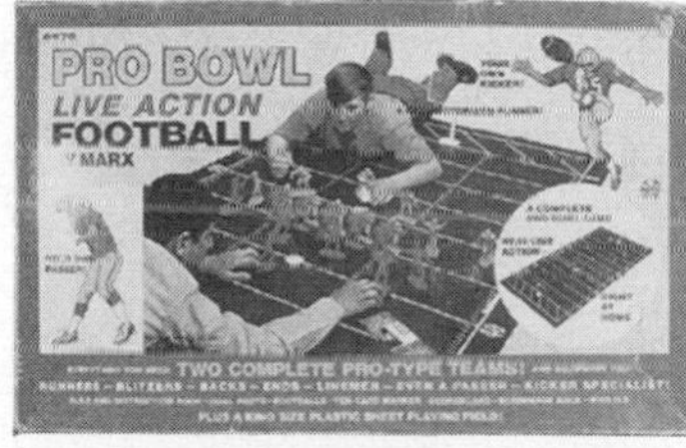

Pro Bowl Live Action Football, 1960s, Marx
EX $35 **NM** $65 **MIP** $95

Rat Patrol Spin Game, 1967, Pressman
EX $30 **NM** $65 **MIP** $85

GAMES

Rocket Patrol Magnetic Target Game, 1950s, American Toy Products
EX $35 **NM** $65 **MIP** $100

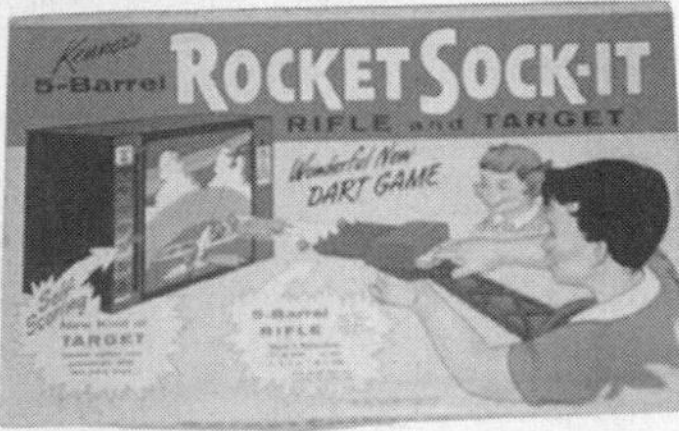

Rocket Sock-It Rifle and Target Game, 1960s, Kenner
EX $20 **NM** $35 **MIP** $75

Saratoga: 1777, 1974, Gamut of Games
EX $10 **NM** $25 **MIP** $50

Simon, 1978, Milton Bradley
EX $6 **NM** $15 **MIP** $20

Space Strike, 1980, Ideal
EX $12 **NM** $30 **MIP** $40

Speed Circuit, 1971, 3M
EX $15 **NM** $30 **MIP** $45

Superman Spin Game, 1967, Pressman
EX $40 **NM** $65 **MIP** $105

Suspense, 1950s, Northwestern Products
EX $15 **NM** $20 **MIP** $30

Tickle Bee, 1956, Schaper
EX $10 **NM** $15 **MIP** $20

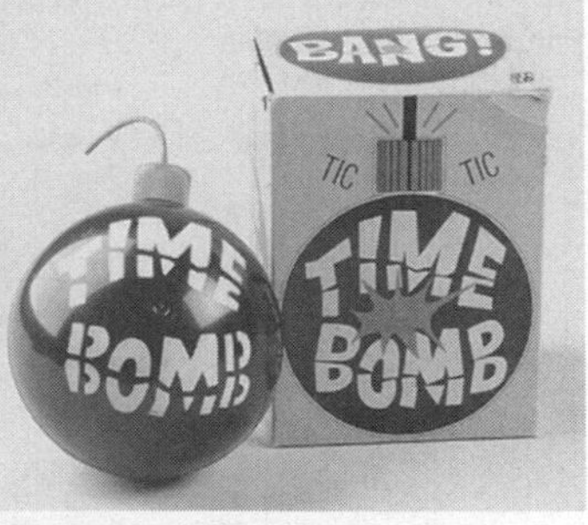

Time Bomb, 1965, Milton Bradley
EX $30 **NM** $60 **MIP** $80

Time Tunnel Spin-to-Win Game, 1967, Pressman
EX $60 **NM** $100 **MIP** $160

Tipp Kick, 1970s, Top Set
EX $15 **NM** $25 **MIP** $40

Tournament Labyrinth, 1980s, Pressman
EX $10 **NM** $15 **MIP** $25

Tru-Action Electric Basketball, 1965, Tudor
EX $25 **NM** $50 **MIP** $75

Tru-Action Electric Harness Race Game, 1950s, Tudor
EX $15 **NM** $40 **MIP** $65

Try-It Maze Puzzle Game, 1965, Milton Bradley
EX $7 **NM** $12 **MIP** $20

Tug Boat, 1974, Parker Brothers
EX $10 **NM** $30 **MIP** $40

Untouchables, The, 1950s, Marx
EX $95 **NM** $160 **MIP** $250

Whiplash, 1966, Lakeside
EX $10 **NM** $25 **MIP** $35

Wow! Pillow Fight For Girls Game, 1964, Milton Bradley
EX $12 **NM** $30 **MIP** $40

Yogi Berra Pitch Kit, 1963, Ross Products
EX $35 **NM** $50 **MIP** $100

Zowie Horseshoe Game, 1947, James L. Decker
EX $20 **NM** $35 **MIP** $55

G.I. Joe

Mark Bellomo

The 1960s

The landscape of the world of boys' toys would be changed forever when designer Stan Weston concocted the idea of marketing a military themed, Barbie-inspired toy line to red-blooded American boys. After pitching the concept to Hasbro, Inc. (a conglomeration of the words "Hassenfeld Brothers" [Has+Bro]), Don Levine, the company's creative director, approved the idea wholeheartedly. The G.I. Joe line was developed in a short amount of time, and presented to toy buyers and the media on February 9, 1964. Released with a WWII theme, this 11-½" G.I. Joe "action figure" line received an overwhelmingly positive response when test-marketed in New York City. Hasbro coined the term "action figures" (instead of *dolls*) to be associated with the G.I. Joe line, because they suspected young boys would not identify G.I. Joes as dolls, for what boy would play with a doll?

We can speculate the myriad reasons why the G.I. Joe line was a roaring success: the figures were wonderfully poseable, with 21 points of articulation ("Move G.I. Joe into action positions," the box touted); the figures' accessories and uniforms were expertly crafted and admirably authentic; the military theme of the line appealed not only to testosterone-filled boys, but to their fathers and grandfathers who were veterans of WWI, WWII, and Korea; and further, these action figures may have built on the memory of moviegoers who popularized the critically praised film *The Story of G.I. Joe* (1945) starring Burgess Meredith and Robert Mitchum.

Regardless of conjecturing into the figures' appeal, it should be noted that each of the four initial action figures were generic soldiers assembled with enough difference to make them interesting and collectible. Hasbro accomplished this feat by constructing G.I. Joe figures to mimic the four branches of the U.S. Armed Forces: Action Soldier (Army); Action Sailor (Navy); Action Pilot (Air Force); and Action Marine (Marine Corps). Each G.I. Joe (where the "G.I." is suggested to mean "General Issue") was boxed individually with a basic, branch-specific uniform, a metal dog tag, and a molded plastic hat and boots. Extra uniforms and accessory sets were also available.

Due to the scarcity of these 1964-1969 items in Mint condition, early pristine pieces command supremely high prices on today's secondary market: sometimes two or three times the value that price guides suggest.

The initial military-themed run of G.I. Joe ended in 1968 with the escalation of the Vietnam War, as many parents refused to purchase a toy soldier for their child. Anti-war activists protested the G.I. Joe line as public sentiment turned against Hasbro's ingenious marketing scheme. In 1969 G.I. Joe toys—known for their military bent—were re-created as civilian men of action. Among Joe's new appellations were Adventurer (and Black Adventurer), Aquanaut, and Talking Astronaut. In 1969, Hasbro re-released accessories from the 1964-1968 run with many recycled pieces and concocted all-new exciting sets. "Danger of the Depths," "Fight for Survival," "Mouth of Doom," "Mysterious Explosion," and the popular "Secret Mission to Spy Island," were among those toys released under the new "Adventures of G.I. Joe" banner.

The 1970s

The "G.I. Joe Adventure Team" rose to prominence from 1970-1976. Among the new innovations to the 11-½" figure line was the addition of Joe's "Life-Like" beard and hair thanks to the discovery of a flocking process by Hasbro's British licensee, Palitoy (the distributor of the British version of G.I. Joe: Action Man). Rounding out the basic figure assortment of the Adventure Team was: Land Adventurer, Sea Adventurer, Air Adventurer, the Man of Action, and the Black Adventurer. Replete with an "AT" dog tag (as the Adventure Team is referred to in collector's circles), shoulder holster and revolver, boots, and either a jumpsuit or combination of shirt and pants, these basic figure assortments were just what Hasbro needed to appeal to cautious shoppers.

All-new accessory and equipment sets were also released in conjunction with the G.I. Joe Adventure Team, and none of these were military inspired. Some of the Adventure Team accessory sets would be the most fondly remembered in the duration of the 11-½" line, such as Danger of the Depths, White Tiger Hunt, Capture of the Pygmy Gorilla, Fantastic Freefall, and Hidden Missile Discovery. G.I. Joe even received a wide range of vehicles in the 1970s (there was a dearth of Joe vehicles in the 1960s) such as the Mobile Support Vehicle, the Secret of the Mummy's Tomb vehicle, the Big Trapper, the Action Sea Sled, and Fate of the Troubleshooter to name a few.

1974 saw the invention and addition of one of the most famous action features in toy history: G.I. Joe with "Kung Fu Grip." Although primitive by modern standards (no buttons were pushed, no bells and whistles went off), the addition of the Kung Fu Grip capitalized on the 1970s martial arts fad, and Joe's hard-plastic hands, with him since 1964, were replaced by soft, pliable fingers that allowed the action figure to better hold weapons and accessories.

In 1975, Hasbro introduced their very first "named" G.I. Joe character: Mike Power: Atomic Man. The production of Mike Power allowed Hasbro to compete with Kenner's hugely

G.I. JOE

popular Six Million Dollar Man toy line. With an atomic "flashing" right eye, atomic right arm with additional dial-spinning feature, atomic left leg (since Hasbro could not use the term "bionic" in their description), Mike Power's transparent limbs added an element of science-fiction to the G.I. Joe Adventure Team.

A new "Life-Like" body was created for G.I. Joe in 1975-76 due to the OPEC oil embargo, as the cost of plastic was at a premium. Now G.I. Joe figures had a mere 15 points of articulation compared to the original 21. Yet another change was introduced during the same time: a new "Eagle Eye" feature. Available with three different figures, the Black Commando, Land Commander, and Man of Action, the "Eagle Eye" action feature allowed the action figures to move their eyes from side-to-side with the movement of a lever.

In 1976, another curious addition to the Adventure Team was Bulletman: The Human Bullet. With a chromed removable helmet, chromed arms, colorful tunic, belt, boots, and zip-line, Bulletman seemed to mimic the current action figure industry push to produce comic book superheroes (see Mego's The Official World's greatest Super-Heroes, 1972-1983), rather than continuing with the Adventure Team feel of G.I. Joe. Bulletman's advertising lauded him as being "faster than the speed of light, more powerful than a dynamo...capable of crashing through a brick wall with his steel arms."

The Intruders ("Strongmen from Another World") were also introduced in 1976, to provide the Adventure Team with adversaries from outer space. With the outward appearance of armored cavemen, the Intruder figures had an action button on their backs that allowed them to grab Joes with their "Crusher Grip" arms.

The final 11-½" G.I. Joe figures produced were The Defenders, a set of plastic-molded mannequins that simply couldn't replace the more sophisticated, more articulated G.I. Joe figures in collector's hearts.

From 1977-78, G.I. Joe figures were scaled down to a more manageable 8" size when Hasbro introduced the Super Joe Adventure Team, and the company went "cosmic" with their toy line. Now G.I. Joe battled intergalactic villains such as Gor, Luminos, and Terron for the fate of the universe with all new equipment sets and a newly constructed command center. The line only lasted two years. The G.I. Joe line ceased production in 1978.

The 1980s

While watching the overwhelming success of Kenner's *Star Wars* line of action figures (1977-1984), Hasbro decided to reintroduce G.I. Joe to the American toy marketplace in the early 1980s. Deciding to make G.I. Joe a *group* of specialists rather than an individual fighting soldier, the G.I. Joe team was launched in 1982, and nobody could have imagined the success this new incarnation would have on the toy market. Shrunk to 3-¾" tall and originally pitched as an action vehicle line, the G.I. Joe team took the world by storm because of the toys' excellent design (the most articulation introduced at such a small scale [along with Mego's Micronauts]), interchangeable "snap on, stay on" accessories, beautiful packaging artwork, and expert characterization by Marvel comic book writer and toy biography author Larry Hama.

As an added bonus, on the back of each figure package was a cut-out "Combat Command File Card" that helped to suspend children's beliefs—collectible biographies that made them consider that the toy they bought was truly a three-dimensional character that might exist as part of the real world. These file cards outlined a G.I. Joe team member's personality (or Cobra villain's persona), the character's military specialty, their personal and military background, and their special code name, which was also provided. These file card dossiers were an important contribution to the process by which toys are marketed – and continues to be an industry standard today.

Originally consisting of 13 G.I. Joe team members and a mere three Cobra villains in 1982, over the course of the next 12 years, Hasbro produced more than 500 different 3-¾" action figures and nearly 300 vehicles and accessories. The success and endurance of the G.I. Joe line was maintained by a Marvel comic book tie-in (155 total issues), a syndicated cartoon program (first produced by Marvel/Sunbow, then by DIC), and television commercials that leapt form the small screen into children's living rooms. The characters introduced in the 1980s incarnation of G.I. Joe still endure: Snake Eyes, Storm Shadow, Duke, Cobra Commander, Scarlett, the Baroness, Shipwreck, Hawk, Destro, and many, many others.

The 1990s

The success of the 3-¾" G.I. Joe line waned in the early '90s as neon action figure colors and poorly designed vehicles dominated the retail shelves. Collectors lost interest in the toy line: it was cancelled in 1994. It wasn't until 1997 and 1998 that these fans would receive new 3-¾" offerings in the form of a few select Toys 'R Us Exclusives that were simple repaints of the original figures and vehicles. These figures sold fairly well, and allowed Hasbro to reintroduce the 3-¾" G.I. Joe line in a larger format in 2000.

The 11-½" G.I. Joe line experienced a renaissance in the 1990s, first with the introduction of 1991's Duke: Master Sergeant exclusive that sold quite briskly. Hasbro capitalized on Duke's success by introducing a "Hall of Fame" line of 11-½" figures based on the characters from the '80s G.I. Joe team.

Although 1994 would mark the final year of production for the original run of 3-¾" Joes, Hasbro still celebrated the 30th Anniversary of the G.I. Joe (1964-1994) line by showing a series of "Commemorative Collection" figures at the 1994 International Toy Fair that were met with thunderous applause. Created in both the 11-½" and 3-¾" scales, collectors were once again treated to the four original Joes from within their respective service branches.

Hasbro still felt that a smaller scale of action figures would be successful, yet 1995 saw the Sgt. Savage and his Screaming Eagles line fail, while 1996's G.I. Joe Extreme fell flat as well, lasting only two years.

1996 gave 11-½" collectors the Classic Collection of "original" Joes, a line that built on the success of the original 1964-1968 run. The Classic Collection grew to incorporate many different figures that represented every branch of military service, and nearly every U.S. military conflict. In 1998, Hasbro released a Timeless Collection (1998-2003) of 11-½" figures. These Target retail exclusives reproduced Joe figures from the 1960's with an assortment of expertly crafted equipment.

In 1999, the G.I. Joe line turned 35, and fans were happy to welcome many celebrity 11-½" figures: Teddy Roosevelt, Ted Williams, John F. Kennedy, and even astronaut Buzz Aldrin. In 2000, Hasbro concocted the Adventures of G.I. Joe, where new action sets were introduced to the marketplace: Save the Tiger, Challenge at Hawk River, and Peril of the Raging Inferno thrilled longtime fans. By 2000, the 11-½" Joe line was still chugging along.

The 2000s

The G.I. Joe Real American Hero Collection (2000-2002) gave Hasbro an opportunity to see how much demand there was for the "little Joes," and since it was modestly popular, the G.I. Joe vs. Cobra line was born in 2002 (sub lines: Spy Troops, Valor vs. Venom). Featuring all new sculpts and accessories, the 3-¾" line met a great deal of success until 2005, when the 3-¾:" line went Direct to Consumer as an Internet exclusive.

In 2007, Hasbro returned to its roots with the 3-¾" line, producing a 25th Anniversary collection of action figures and vehicles, utilizing all-new figure sculpts, fully painted card and packaging artwork, and an eye for detail. These 25th Anniversary figures and vehicles command excellent prices on the secondary market. Although the 25th Anniversary label was dropped from packages, the line of 3-¾" G.I. Joes continues to this day, fueled by the popular new live-action film.

2009 Trends

If you can obtain them, early high-grade samples of 1964-1969 G.I. Joes are always an excellent investment, but don't be caught unaware when the 2009 summer blockbuster *G.I. Joe* hits theaters. Expect figures based on the iconic 1980s characters utilized in the movie to become very desirable. Furthermore, because of their low cost in relationship to the military-themed Joes of the 1960s, 1970 Adventure Team figures are getting more and more attention. Pick them up now before their prices are too prohibitive.

THE TOP 10 G.I.JOE (In Mint Condition)

1. G.I. Nurse, Hasbro, 1967 .... $5,300
2. Action Soldiers of the World Talking Adventure Pack, Hasbro, 1968 .... $5,200
3. Canadian Mountie Set, Sears Exclusive, Hasbro, 1967 .... $4,200
4. Flying Space Adventure Set, Hasbro, 1970 .... $3,750
5. Army Adventure Pack, Bivouac Equipment Set, Hasbro, 1968 .... $3,600
6. Crash Crew Fire Truck Set, Hasbro, 1967 .... $3,600
7. Talking Shore Patrol Set, Hasbro, 1968 .... $3,500
8. Dress Parade Adventure Pack, Hasbro, 1968 .... $3,500
9. Talking Landing Signal Officer Set, 1968 .... $3,500
10. Shore Patrol Equipment Set, Hasbro, 1967 .... $3,500

Original Series and Adventure Team (1964-78)

ACTION GIRL SERIES
Figure Sets

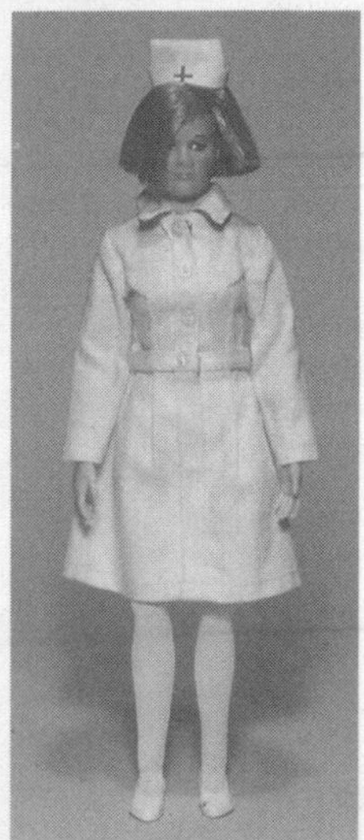

G.I. Nurse, 1967, Hasbro, Red Cross hat and arm band, white dress, stockings, shoes, crutches, medic bag, stethoscope, plasma bottle, bandages and splints, Model No. 8060
EX $1750 **NM** $2000 **MIP** $5000

ACTION MARINE SERIES
Figure Sets

Action Marine, 1964, Hasbro, fatigues, green cap, boots, dog tags, insignias and manual, Model No. 7700
EX $125 **NM** $145 **MIP** $450

Marine Medic Series, 1967, Hasbro, Red Cross helmet, flag and arm bands, crutch, bandages, splints, first aid pouch, stethoscope, plasma bottle, stretcher, medic bag, belt with ammo pouches, Model No. 90711
EX $325 **NM** $425 **MIP** $1550

Talking Action Marine, 1967, Hasbro, Model No. 7790
EX $175 **NM** $200 **MIP** $850

Talking Adventure Pack, 1968, Hasbro, with Field Pack Equipment, Model No. 90712
EX $275 **NM** $325 **MIP** $1550

Talking Adventure Pack and Tent Set, 1968, Hasbro, Model No. 90711
EX $275 **NM** $325 **MIP** $1550

Uniform/Equipment Sets

Beachhead Assault Field Pack Set, 1964, Hasbro, M-1 rifle, bayonet, entrenching shovel and cover, canteen with cover, belt, mess kit with cover, field pack, flamethrower, first aid pouch, tent, pegs and poles, tent camo and camo, Model No. 7713
EX $100 **NM** $175 **MIP** $325

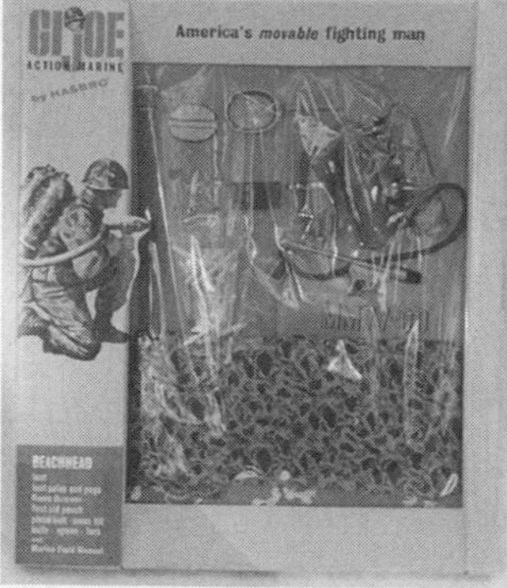

Beachhead Assault Tent Set, 1964, Hasbro, tent, flamethrower, pistol belt, first-aid pouch, mess kit with utensils and manual, Model No. 7711
EX $100 **NM** $200 **MIP** $425

Beachhead Fatigue Pants, 1964, Hasbro, Model No. 7715
EX $15 **NM** $30 **MIP** $200

Beachhead Fatigue Shirt, 1964, Hasbro, Model No. 7714
EX $20 **NM** $30 **MIP** $225

Beachhead Field Pack, 1964, Hasbro, cartridge belt, rifle, grenades, field pack, entrenching tool, canteen and manual, Model No. 7712
EX $40 **NM** $65 **MIP** $150

Beachhead Flamethrower Set, 1964, Hasbro, Model No. 7718
EX $15 **NM** $30 **MIP** $125

Beachhead Flamethrower Set, 1967, Hasbro, reissue, Model No. 7718
EX $15 **NM** $30 **MIP** $225

Beachhead Mess Kit Set, 1964, Hasbro, Model No. 7716
EX $25 **NM** $40 **MIP** $275

Beachhead Rifle Set, 1964, Hasbro, bayonet, cartridge belt, hand grenades and M-1 rifle, Model No. 7717
EX $30 **NM** $50 **MIP** $150

Beachhead Rifle Set, 1967, Hasbro, reissue, Model No. 7717
EX $30 **NM** $50 **MIP** $225

Communications Field Radio/Telephone Set, 1967, Hasbro, reissue, Model No. 7703
EX $35 **NM** $60 **MIP** $275

Communications Field Set, 1964, Hasbro, Model No. 7703
EX $35 **NM** $50 **MIP** $175

Communications Flag Set, 1964, Hasbro, flags for Army, Navy, Air Corps, Marines and United States, Model No. 7704
EX $200 **NM** $250 **MIP** $475

Communications Poncho, 1964, Hasbro, Model No. 7702
EX $35 **NM** $50 **MIP** $250

Communications Post and Poncho Set, 1964, Hasbro, field radio and telephone, wire roll, carbine, binoculars, map, case, manual, poncho, Model No. 7701
EX $125 **NM** $175 **MIP** $475

Dress Parade Set, 1964, Hasbro, Marine jacket, trousers, pistol belt, shoes, hat, M-1 rifle and manual, Model No. 7710
EX $125 **NM** $225 **MIP** $450

Dress Parade Set, 1968, Hasbro, reissue, Model No. 7710
EX $125 **NM** $225 **MIP** $750

Jungle Fighter Set, 1967, Hasbro, bush hat, jacket with emblems, pants, flamethrower, field telephone, knife and sheath, pistol belt, pistol, holster, canteen with cover and knuckle knife, Model No. 7732
EX $450 **NM** $700 **MIP** $1350

Jungle Fighter Set, 1968, Hasbro, reissue, Model No. 7732
EX $450 **NM** $700 **MIP** $1050

Marine Automatic M-60 Machine Gun Set, 1967, Hasbro, Model No. 7726
EX $35 **NM** $75 **MIP** $325

Marine Basics Set, 1966, Hasbro, Model No. 7722
EX $55 **NM** $85 **MIP** $275

Marine Bunk Bed Set, 1966, Hasbro, Model No. 7723
EX $55 **NM** $80 **MIP** $375

Marine Bunk Bed Set, 1967, Hasbro, reissue, Model No. 7723
EX $55 **NM** $175 **MIP** $350

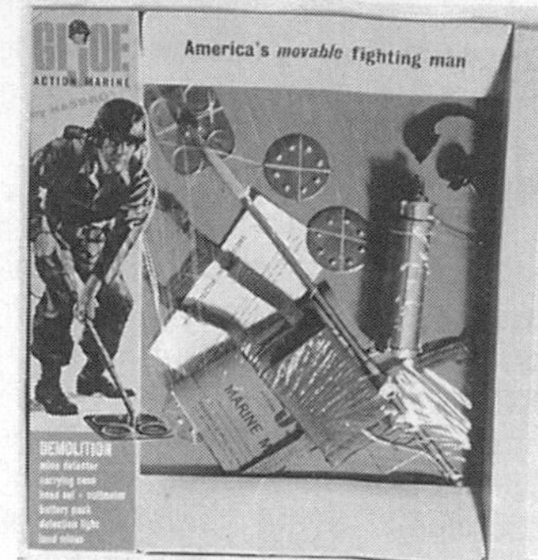

Marine Demolition Set, 1966, Hasbro, mine detector and harness, land mine, Model No. 7730
EX $50 **NM** $100 **MIP** $350

Marine Demolition Set, 1968, Hasbro, reissue, Model No. 7730
EX $50 **NM** $145 **MIP** $400

Marine First Aid Set, 1964, Hasbro, first-aid pouch, arm band and helmet, Model No. 7721
EX $45 **NM** $85 **MIP** $125

Marine First Aid Set, 1967, Hasbro, reissue, Model No. 7721
EX $45 **NM** $85 **MIP** $225

Marine Medic Set, 1965, Hasbro, with crutch, etc., Model No. 7720
EX $25 **NM** $40 **MIP** $125

Marine Medic Set, 1967, Hasbro, reissue, Model No. 7720
EX $25 **NM** $40 **MIP** $225

Marine Medic Set with stretcher, 1964, Hasbro, first-aid shoulder pouch, stretcher, bandages, arm bands, plasma bottle, stethoscope, Red Cross flag, and manual, Model No. 7719
EX $175 **NM** $300 **MIP** $850

Marine Mortar Set, 1967, Hasbro, Model No. 7725
EX $60 NM $80 MIP $350

Marine Weapons Rack Set, 1967, Hasbro, Model No. 7727
EX $75 NM $145 MIP $625

Paratrooper Camouflage Set, 1964, Hasbro, netting and foliage, Model No. 7708
EX $20 NM $35 MIP $65

Paratrooper Helmet Set, 1964, Hasbro, Model No. 7707
EX $20 NM $40 MIP $85

Paratrooper Parachute Pack, 1964, Hasbro, Model No. 7709
EX $30 NM $80 MIP $125

Paratrooper Small Arms Set, 1967, Hasbro, reissue, Model No. 7706
EX $30 NM $75 MIP $225

Tank Commander Set, 1967, Hasbro, includes faux leather jacket, helmet and visor, insignia, radio with tripod, machine gun, ammo box, Model No. 7731
EX $325 NM $500 MIP $1350

Tank Commander Set, 1968, Hasbro, reissue, Model No. 7731
EX $325 NM $500 MIP $1200

ACTION PILOT SERIES

Figure Sets

Action Pilot, 1964, Hasbro, orange jumpsuit, blue cap, black boots, dog tags, insignias, manual, catalog and club application, Model No. 7800
EX $135 NM $165 MIP $600

Talking Action Pilot, 1967, Hasbro, Model No. 7890
EX $190 NM $245 MIP $1500

Uniform/Equipment Sets

Air Academy Cadet Set, 1967, Hasbro, deluxe set with figure, dress jacket, shoes, and pants, garrison cap, saber and scabbard, white M-1 rifle, chest sash and belt sash, Model No. 7822
EX $225 NM $450 MIP $1100

Air Academy Cadet Set, 1968, Hasbro, reissue, Model No. 7822
EX $225 NM $450 MIP $950

Air Force Basics Set, 1966, Hasbro, Model No. 7814
EX $30 NM $55 MIP $200

Air Force Basics Set, 1967, Hasbro, reissue, Model No. 7814
EX $30 NM $55 MIP $275

Air Force Mae West Air Vest & Equipment Set, 1967, Hasbro, Model No. 7816
EX $85 NM $125 MIP $325

Air Force Police Set, 1965, Hasbro, Model No. 7813
EX $70 NM $150 MIP $250

Air Force Police Set, 1967, Hasbro, reissue, Model No. 7813
EX $70 NM $150 MIP $325

Air Force Security Set, 1967, Hasbro, Air Security radio and helmet, cartridge belt, pistol and holster, Model No. 7815
EX $275 NM $350 MIP $590

Air/Sea Rescue Set, 1967, Hasbro, includes black air tanks, rescue ring, buoy, depth gauge, face mask, fins, orange scuba outfit, Model No. 7825
EX $325 NM $550 MIP $1600

Air/Sea Rescue Set, 1968, Hasbro, reissue, Model No. 7825
EX $325 NM $550 MIP $1600

Astronaut Set, 1967, Hasbro, helmet with visor, foil space suit, booties, gloves, space camera, propellant gun, tether cord, oxygen chest pack, silver boots, white jumpsuit and cloth cap, Model No. 7824
EX $100 NM $200 MIP $3000

Astronaut Set, 1968, Hasbro, reissue, Model No. 7824
EX $100 NM $250 MIP $850

Communications Set, 1964, Hasbro, Model No. 7812
EX $55 NM $100 MIP $225

Crash Crew Set, 1966, Hasbro, fire proof jacket, hood, pants and gloves, silver boots, belt, flashlight, axe, pliers, fire extinguisher, stretcher, strap cutter, Model No. 7820
EX $125 NM $250 MIP $450

Dress Uniform Jacket Set, 1964, Hasbro, Model No. 7804
EX $40 NM $65 MIP $250

Dress Uniform Pants, 1964, Hasbro, Model No. 7805
EX $20 NM $35 MIP $200

Dress Uniform Set, 1964, Hasbro, Air Force jacket, trousers, shirt, tie, cap and manual, Model No. 7803
EX $225 NM $550 MIP $1650

Dress Uniform Shirt & Equipment Set, 1964, Hasbro, Model No. 7806
EX $25 NM $40 MIP $200

Fighter Pilot Set, 1967, Hasbro, working parachute and pack, gold helmet, Mae West vest, green pants, flash light, orange jump suit, black boots, Model No. 7823
EX $400 NM $650 MIP $1550

Fighter Pilot Set, 1968, Hasbro, reissue, Model No. 7823
EX $400 NM $650 MIP $1600

Scramble Communications Set, 1965, Hasbro, poncho, field telephone and radio, map with case, binoculars and wire roll, Model No. 7812
EX $35 NM $75 MIP $175

Scramble Communications Set, 1967, Hasbro, reissue, Model No. 7812
EX $35 NM $75 MIP $250

Scramble Crash Helmet, 1964, Hasbro, helmet, face mask, hose, tinted visor, Model No. 7810
EX $65 NM $90 MIP $125

Scramble Crash Helmet, 1967, Hasbro, reissue, Model No. 7810
EX $65 NM $90 MIP $225

Scramble Flight Suit, 1964, Hasbro, gray flight suit, Model No. 7808
EX $50 NM $300 MIP $225

Scramble Flight Suit, 1967, Hasbro, Model No. 7808
EX $50 NM $75 MIP $400

Scramble Parachute Set, 1964, Hasbro, Model No. 7811
EX $20 NM $40 MIP $150

Scramble Parachute Set, 1967, Hasbro, reissue, Model No. 7809
EX $20 NM $40 MIP $250

Scramble Set, 1964, Hasbro, deluxe set, gray flight suit, orange air vest, white crash helmet, pistol belt with .45 pistol, holster, clipboard, flare gun and parachute with insert, Model No. 7807
EX $125 NM $225 MIP $950

Survival Life Raft Set, 1964, Hasbro, raft with oar, flare gun, knife, air vest, first-aid kit, sea anchor and manual, Model No. 7801
EX $75 NM $125 MIP $550

Survival Life Raft Set, 1964, Hasbro, raft with oar and sea anchor, Model No. 7802
EX $45 NM $90 MIP $325

Vehicle Sets

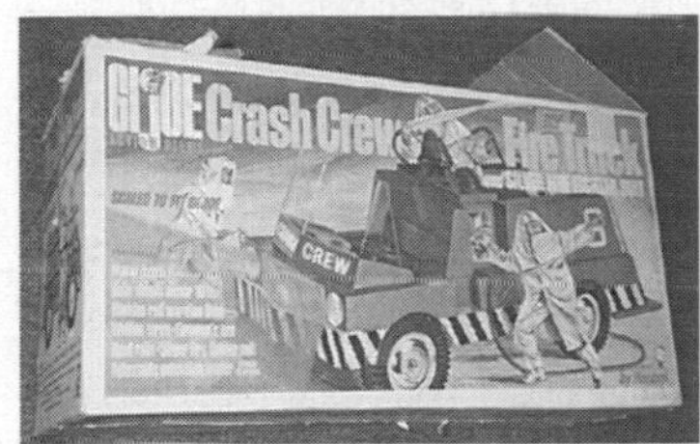

Crash Crew Fire Truck Set, 1967, Hasbro, Includes blue truck and fireproof silver suit. Truck has working firehose, Model No. 8040
EX $950 NM $1700 MIP $3500

Official Space Capsule Set, 1966, Hasbro, space capsule, record, space suit, cloth space boots, space gloves, helmet with visor, Model No. 8020
EX $175 NM $225 MIP $350

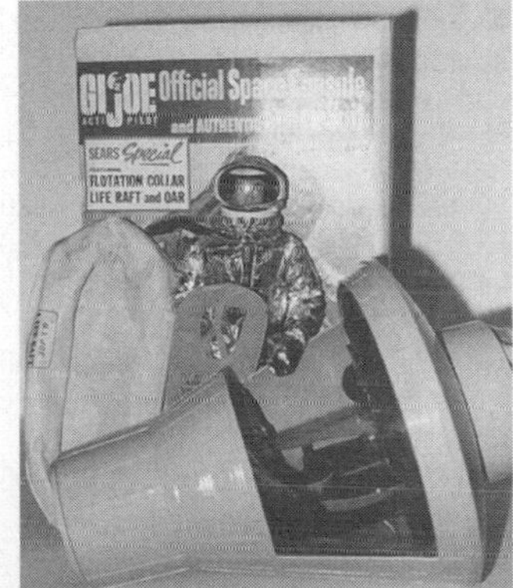

Official Space Capsule Set with flotation, 1966, Hasbro, Sears Exclusive with collar, life raft and oars, Model No. 5979
EX $200 NM $325 MIP $700

Spacewalk Mystery, 1969, Hasbro, Model No. 7981
EX $120 NM $265 MIP $450

ACTION SAILOR SERIES

Figure Sets

Action Sailor, 1964, Hasbro, white cap, denim shirt and pants, boots, dog tags, navy manual and insignias, Model No. 7600
EX $125 **NM** $225 **MIP** $450

Navy Scuba Set, 1968, Hasbro, Adventure Pack, Model No. 7643-83
EX $300 **NM** $450 **MIP** $3250

Talking Action Sailor, 1967, Hasbro, Model No. 7690
EX $200 **NM** $330 **MIP** $1250

Talking Landing Signal Officer Set, 1968, Hasbro, Talking Adventure Pack, Model No. 90621
EX $325 **NM** $350 **MIP** $3500

Talking Shore Patrol Set, 1968, Hasbro, Talking Adventure Pack, Model No. 90612
EX $200 **NM** $450 **MIP** $3500

Uniform/Equipment Sets

Annapolis Cadet, 1967, Hasbro, garrison cap, dress jacket, pants, shoes, sword, scabbard, belt and white M-1 rifle, Model No. 7624
EX $275 **NM** $375 **MIP** $1350

Annapolis Cadet, 1968, Hasbro, reissue, Model No. 7624
EX $275 **NM** $375 **MIP** $1350

Breeches Buoy, 1967, Hasbro, yellow jacket and pants, chair and pulley, flare gun, blinker light, Model No. 7625
EX $325 **NM** $425 **MIP** $1500

Breeches Buoy, 1968, Hasbro, reissue, Model No. 7625
EX $325 **NM** $425 **MIP** $1450

Deep Freeze, 1967, Hasbro, white boots, fur parka, pants, snow shoes, ice axe, snow sled with rope and flare gun, Model No. 7623
EX $250 **NM** $375 **MIP** $1600

Deep Freeze, 1968, Hasbro, reissue, Model No. 7623
EX $250 **NM** $375 **MIP** $1500

Deep Sea Diver Set, 1965, Hasbro, underwater uniform, helmet, upper and lower plate, sledge hammer, buoy with rope, gloves, compass, hoses, lead boots and weight belt, Model No. 7620
EX $325 **NM** $425 **MIP** $1850

Deep Sea Diver Set, 1968, Hasbro, reissue, Model No. 7620
EX $325 **NM** $425 **MIP** $1850

Frogman Scuba Bottoms, 1964, Hasbro, Model No. 7604
EX $20 **NM** $35 **MIP** $100

Frogman Scuba Tank Set, 1964, Hasbro, Model No. 7606
EX $25 **NM** $40 **MIP** $100

Frogman Scuba Top Set, 1964, Hasbro, Model No. 7603
EX $25 **NM** $45 **MIP** $125

Frogman Underwater Demolition Set, 1964, Hasbro, headpiece, face mask, swim fins, rubber suit, scuba tank, depth gauge, knife, dynamite and manual, Model No. 7602
EX $175 **NM** $250 **MIP** $1500

Landing Signal Officer, 1966, Hasbro, jumpsuit, signal paddles, goggles, cloth head gear, headphones, clipboard (complete), binoculars and flare gun, Model No. 7621
EX $225 **NM** $350 **MIP** $575

Navy Attack Helmet Set, 1964, shirt and pants, boots, yellow life vest, blue helmet, flare gun binoculars, signal flags, Model No. 7610
EX $35 **NM** $75 **MIP** $150

Navy Attack Life Jacket, 1964, Hasbro, Model No. 7611
EX $20 **NM** $45 **MIP** $120

Navy Attack Set, 1964, Hasbro, life jacket, field glasses, blinker light, signal flags, manual, Model No. 7607
EX $60 **NM** $125 **MIP** $425

Navy Attack Work Pants Set, 1964, Hasbro, Model No. 7609
EX $25 **NM** $40 **MIP** $150

Navy Attack Work Shirt Set, 1964, Hasbro, Model No. 7608
EX $25 **NM** $40 **MIP** $175

Navy Basics Set, 1966, Hasbro, Model No. 7628
EX $25 **NM** $55 **MIP** $125

Navy Dress Parade Rifle Set, 1965, Hasbro, Model No. 7619
EX $35 **NM** $65 **MIP** $125

Navy Dress Parade Set, 1964, Hasbro, billy club, cartridge belt, bayonet and white dress rifle, Model No. 7619
EX $45 **NM** $80 **MIP** $175

Navy L.S.O. Equipment Set, 1966, Hasbro, helmet, headphones, signal paddles, flare gun, Model No. 7626
EX $40 **NM** $80 **MIP** $150

Navy Life Ring Set, 1966, Hasbro, U.S.N. life ring, helmet sticker, Model No. 7627
EX $25 **NM** $45 **MIP** $150

Navy Machine Gun Set, 1965, Hasbro, MG and ammo box, Model No. 7618
EX $40 **NM** $80 **MIP** $175

Sea Rescue Set, 1964, Hasbro, life raft, oar, anchor, flare gun, first-aid kit, knife, scabbard, manual, Model No. 7601
EX $95 **NM** $135 **MIP** $500

Sea Rescue Set, 1966, Hasbro, reissued with life preserver, Model No. 7622
EX $95 **NM** $135 **MIP** $500

Shore Patrol, 1964, Hasbro, dress shirt, tie and pants, helmet, white belt, .45 and holster, billy club, boots, arm band, sea bag, Model No. 7612
EX $500 **NM** $1000 **MIP** $2000

Shore Patrol, 1967, Hasbro, reissued with radio and helmet and shoes, Model No. 7612
EX $1000 **NM** $2000 **MIP** $3500

Shore Patrol Dress Jumper Set, 1964, Hasbro, Model No. 7613
EX $75 **NM** $125 **MIP** $225

Shore Patrol Dress Pant Set, 1964, Hasbro, Model No. 7614
EX $40 **NM** $75 **MIP** $175

Shore Patrol Helmet and Small Arms Set, 1964, Hasbro, white belt, billy stick, white helmet, .45 pistol, Model No. 7616
EX $40 **NM** $75 **MIP** $150

Shore Patrol Sea Bag Set, 1964, Hasbro, Model No. 7615
EX $25 **NM** $50 **MIP** $125

Vehicle Sets

Official Sea Sled and Frogman Set, 1966, Hasbro, without cave, Model No. 8050
EX $150 **NM** $300 **MIP** $550

Official Sea Sled and Frogman Set, 1966, Hasbro, Sears, with figure and underwater cave, orange scuba suit, fins, mask, tanks, sea sled in orange and black, Model No. 5979
EX $175 **NM** $325 **MIP** $650

ACTION SOLDIER

Figure Sets

Green Beret Machine Gun Outpost Set, 1966, Hasbro, Sears Exclusive, 2 figures, 2 uniform shirts, 2 uniform pants, 2 cartridge belts, 2 green berets, 2 dog tags, 2 pair boots, M-16 rifle, tripod, field radio, bazooka, 6 bazooka shells, foliage, 6 tent poles, 6 grenades, machine gun, ammo box, netting, tent stakes, 6 plugs, 8 rope loops, Model No. 5978
EX $300 **NM** $600 **MIP** $3200

ACTION SOLDIER SERIES
Figure Sets

Action Soldier, 1964, Hasbro, fatigue cap, shirt, pants, boots, dog tags, army manual and insignias, M-1 rifle, Model No. 7500
EX $100 **NM** $175 **MIP** $450

Black Action Soldier, 1965, Hasbro, fatigue cap, shirt, pants, boots, dog tags, army manual and insignias, M-1 rifle, Model No. 7900
EX $450 **NM** $800 **MIP** $2200

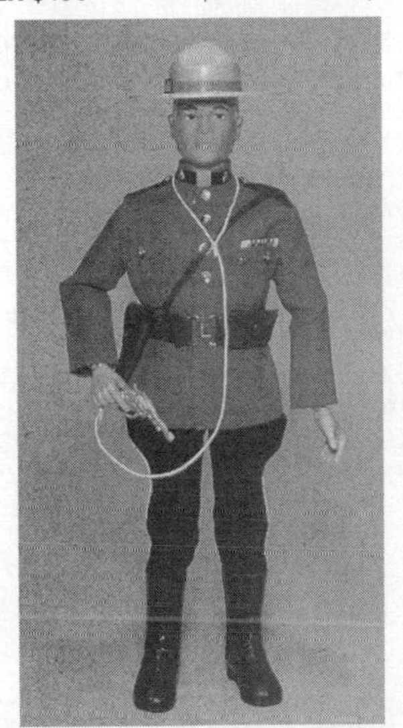

Canadian Mountie Set, 1967, Hasbro, Sears Exclusive, Model No. 5904
EX $850 **NM** $1500 **MIP** $4000

Desert Patrol Attack Jeep Set, 1967, Hasbro, Desert Fighter figure, jeep with steering wheel, spare tire, tan tripod, gun and gun mount and ring, black antenna, tan jacket and shorts, socks, goggles, Model No. 8030
EX $400 **NM** $1250 **MIP** $2000

Forward Observer Set, 1966, Hasbro, Sears Exclusive, 51 pieces, Model No. 5969
EX $200 **NM** $375 **MIP** $750

Green Beret, 1966, Hasbro, field radio, green beret, jacket, pants, M-16 rifle, 6 grenades, camo scarf, belt pistol and holster, Model No. 7536
EX $275 **NM** $550 **MIP** $2800

Machine Gun Emplacement Set, 1965, Hasbro, Sears Exclusive, 27 pieces, Model No. 5931
EX $150 **NM** $275 **MIP** $1250

Talking Action Soldier, 1967, Hasbro, Model No. 7590
EX $85 **NM** $135 **MIP** $825

Talking Adventure Pack, Bivouac Equipment, 1967, Hasbro, Model No. 90513
EX $275 **NM** $325 **MIP** $3000

Talking Adventure Pack, Command Post Equip., 1968, Hasbro, Model No. 90517
EX $275 **NM** $375 **MIP** $2750

Talking Adventure Pack, Mountain Troop Series, 1967, Hasbro, Model No. 7557-83
EX $375 **NM** $650 **MIP** $3150

Talking Adventure Pack, Special Forces Equip., 1968, Hasbro, Model No. 90532
EX $275 **NM** $500 **MIP** $3150

Uniform/Equipment Sets

Adventure Pack with fourteen pieces, 1968, Hasbro, Adventure Pack Footlocker, Model No. 8008.83
EX $75 **NM** $125 **MIP** $600

Adventure Pack with sixteen items, 1968, Hasbro, Adventure Pack Footlocker, Model No. 8007.83
EX $75 **NM** $125 **MIP** $600

Adventure Pack with twelve items, 1968, Hasbro, Adventure Pack Footlocker, Model No. 8005.83
EX $75 **NM** $125 **MIP** $600

Adventure Pack with twelve items, 1968, Hasbro, Adventure Pack Footlocker, Model No. 8006.83
EX $75 **NM** $125 **MIP** $600

Adventure Pack, Army Bivouac Series, 1967, Hasbro, Model No. 7549-83
EX $225 **NM** $450 **MIP** $3500

Air Police Equipment, 1964, Hasbro, gray field phone, carbine, white helmet and bayonet, Model No. 7813
EX $40 **NM** $95 **MIP** $200

Basic Footlocker, 1964, Hasbro, wood tray with cardboard wrapper, Model No. 8000
EX $35 **NM** $75 **MIP** $125

Bivouac Deluxe Pup Tent Set, 1964, Hasbro, M-1 rifle and bayonet, shovel and cover, canteen and cover, mess kit, cartridge belt, machine gun, tent, pegs, poles, camouflage, sleeping bag, netting, ammo box, Model No. 7513
EX $115 **NM** $225 **MIP** $450

Bivouac Machine Gun Set, 1964, Hasbro, machine gun set and ammo box, Model No. 7514
EX $25 **NM** $40 **MIP** $125

Bivouac Machine Gun Set, 1967, Hasbro, reissue, Model No. 7514
EX $25 **NM** $40 **MIP** $225

Bivouac Sleeping Bag, 1964, Hasbro, zippered bag, Model No. 7515
EX $20 **NM** $30 **MIP** $125

Bivouac Sleeping Bag Set, 1964, Hasbro, mess kit, canteen, bayonet, cartridge belt, M-1 rifle, manual, Model No. 7512
EX $25 **NM** $30 **MIP** $150

Combat Camouflaged Netting Set, 1964, Hasbro, foliage and posts, Model No. 7511
EX $25 **NM** $40 **MIP** $85

Combat Construction Set, 1967, Hasbro, orange safety helmet, work gloves, jack hammer, Model No. 7572
EX $325 **NM** $400 **MIP** $575

Combat Demolition Set, 1967, Hasbro, Model No. 7573
EX $65 **NM** $100 **MIP** $525

Combat Engineer Set, 1967, Hasbro, pick, shovel, detonator, dynamite, tripod and transit with grease gun, Model No. 7571
EX $125 **NM** $175 **MIP** $625

Combat Fatigue Pants Set, 1964, Hasbro, Model No. 7504
EX $15 NM $25 MIP $110

Combat Fatigue Shirt Set, 1964, Hasbro, Model No. 7503
EX $20 NM $30 MIP $125

Combat Field Jacket, 1964, Hasbro, Model No. 7505
EX $45 NM $65 MIP $325

Combat Field Jacket Set, 1964, Hasbro, jacket, bayonet, cartridge belt, hand grenades, M-1 rifle and manual, Model No. 7501
EX $65 NM $100 MIP $525

Combat Field Pack & Entrenching Tool, 1964, Hasbro, Model No. 7506
EX $25 NM $45 MIP $125

Combat Field Pack Deluxe Set, 1964, Hasbro, field jacket, pack, entrenching shovel with cover, mess kit, first-aid pouch, canteen with cover, Model No. 7502
EX $75 NM $125 MIP $325

Combat Helmet Set, 1964, Hasbro, with netting and foliage leaves, Model No. 7507
EX $20 NM $35 MIP $75

Combat Mess Kit, 1964, Hasbro, plate, fork, knife, spoon, canteen, etc., Model No. 7509
EX $20 NM $45 MIP $85

Combat Rifle Set, 1967, Hasbro, bayonet, M-1 rifle, belt and grenades, Model No. 7510
EX $55 NM $100 MIP $325

Combat Sandbags Set, 1964, Hasbro, three bags per set, Model No. 7508
EX $10 NM $40 MIP $85

Command Post Field Radio and Telephone Set, 1964, Hasbro, field radio, telephone with wire roll and map, Model No. 7520
EX $35 NM $70 MIP $135

Command Post Field Radio and Telephone Set, 1967, Hasbro, reissue, Model No. 7520
EX $35 NM $70 MIP $400

Command Post Poncho, 1964, Hasbro, on card, Model No. 7519
EX $30 NM $45 MIP $225

Command Post Poncho Set, 1964, Hasbro, poncho, field radio and telephone, wire roll, pistol, belt and holster, map and case and manual, Model No. 7517
EX $85 NM $125 MIP $400

Command Post Small Arms Set, 1964, Hasbro, holster and .45 pistol, belt, grenades, Model No. 7518
EX $30 NM $60 MIP $100

Dress Parade Adventure Pack, 1968, Hasbro, Adventure Pack with thirty-seven pieces, Model No. 8009.83
EX $750 NM $1250 MIP $3500

Green Beret and Small Arms Set, 1966, Hasbro, Model No. 7533
EX $85 NM $110 MIP $300

Green Beret and Small Arms Set, 1967, Hasbro, reissue, Model No. 7533
EX $85 NM $100 MIP $425

Green Beret Machine Gun Outpost Set, 1966, Hasbro, Sears Exclusive with two figures and equipment, Model No. 5978
EX $225 NM $450 MIP $1500

Heavy Weapons Set, 1967, Hasbro, mortar launcher and shells, M-60 machine gun, grenades, flak jacket, shirt and pants, Model No. 7538
EX $175 NM $325 MIP $1750

Heavy Weapons Set, 1968, Hasbro, reissue, Model No. 7538
EX $175 NM $325 MIP $1500

Military Police Duffle Bag Set, 1964, Hasbro, Model No. 7523
EX $25 NM $40 MIP $85

Military Police Helmet and Small Arms Set, 1964, Hasbro, Model No. 7526
EX $35 NM $75 MIP $125

Military Police Helmet and Small Arms Set, 1967, Hasbro, reissue, Model No. 7526
EX $35 NM $75 MIP $250

Military Police Ike Jacket, 1964, Hasbro, jacket with red scarf and arm band, Model No. 7524
EX $40 NM $60 MIP $125

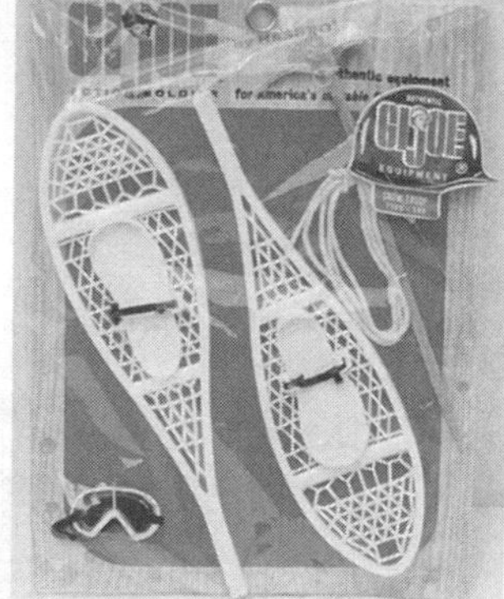

Military Police Ike Pants, 1964, Hasbro, matches Ike jacket, Model No. 7525
EX $20 NM $30 MIP $100

Military Police Uniform Set, 1964, Hasbro, includes Ike jacket and pants, scarf, boots, helmet, belt with ammo pouches, .45 pistol and holster, billy club, armband, duffle bag, Model No. 7521
EX $450 NM $1650 MIP $3000

Military Police Uniform Set, 1967, Hasbro, includes green or tan uniform, black and gold MP Helmet, billy club, belt, pistol and holster, MP armband and red tunic, Model No. 7539
EX $450 NM $1650 MIP $3500

Military Police Uniform Set, 1968, Hasbro, reissue, Model No. 7539
EX $450 NM $900 MIP $3000

Mountain Troops Set, 1964, Hasbro, snow shoes, ice axe, ropes, grenades, camoflage pack, web belt, manual, Model No. 7530
EX $90 NM $175 MIP $350

Sabotage Set, 1967, Hasbro, dingy and oar, blinker light, detonator with strap, TNT, wool stocking cap, gas mask, binoculars, green radio and .45 pistol and holster, Model No. 7516
EX $125 NM $250 MIP $2000

Sabotage Set, 1968, Hasbro, reissued in photo box, Model No. 7516
EX $125 NM $250 MIP $1700

Ski Patrol Deluxe Set, 1964, Hasbro, White parka, boots, goggles, mittens, skis, poles and manual, Model No. 7531
EX $170 NM $350 MIP $1250

Ski Patrol Helmet and Small Arms Set, 1965, Hasbro, Model No. 7527
EX $35 NM $75 MIP $135

Ski Patrol Helmet and Small Arms Set, 1967, Hasbro, reissue, Model No. 7527
EX $75 NM $125 MIP $250

Snow Troop Set, 1966, Hasbro, snow shoes, goggles and ice pick, Model No. 7529
EX $20 NM $45 MIP $150

Snow Troop Set, 1967, Hasbro, reissue, Model No. 7529
EX $20 NM $45 MIP $225

Special Forces Bazooka Set, 1966, Hasbro, Model No. 7528
EX $35 NM $45 MIP $225

Special Forces Bazooka Set, 1967, Hasbro, reissue, Model No. 7528
EX $35 NM $45 MIP $325

Special Forces Uniform Set, 1966, Hasbro, Model No. 7532
EX $200 NM $375 MIP $1000

West Point Cadet Uniform Set, 1967, Hasbro, dress jacket, pants, shoes, chest and belt sash, parade hat with plume, saber, scabbard and white M-1 rifle, Model No. 7537
EX $250 NM $475 MIP $1500

West Point Cadet Uniform Set, 1968, Hasbro, reissue, Model No. 7537
EX $250 NM $375 MIP $1200

Vehicle Sets

Amphibious Duck, 1967, Irwin, 26" long, Model No. 5693
EX $175 NM $375 MIP $700

Armored Car, 1967, Irwin, friction powered, 20" long, Model No. 5397
EX $150 NM $300 MIP $500

Helicopter, 1967, Hasbro, Irwin, friction powered, 28" long, Model No. 5395
EX $150 NM $300 MIP $500

Jet Fighter Plane, 1967, Irwin, friction powered, 30" long, Model No. 5396
EX $225 NM $475 MIP $800

Military Staff Car, 1967, Irwin, friction powered, 24" long, Model No. 5652
EX $200 NM $400 MIP $750

Motorcycle and Sidecar, 1967, Irwin, 14" long, khaki, with decals, Model No. 5651
EX $75 NM $150 MIP $325

Official Combat Jeep Set, 1965, trailer, steering wheel, spare tire, windshield, cannon, search light, shell, flag, guard rails, tripod, tailgate and hood, without Moto-Rev Sound, Model No. 7000
EX $200 NM $375 MIP $550

Official Jeep Combat Set, 1965, With Moto-Rev sound, Model No. 7000
EX $225 NM $400 MIP $650

Personnel Carrier/Mine Sweeper, 1967, Irwin, 26" long, Model No. 5694
EX $300 NM $350 MIP $700

ACTION SOLDIERS OF THE WORLD

Figure Sets

Australian Jungle Fighter, 1966, Hasbro, action figure with jacket, shorts, socks, boots, bush hat, belt, "Victoria Cross" medal, knuckle knife, flamethrower, entrenching tool, bush knife and sheath, Model No. 8105
EX $250 NM $400 MIP $2500

Australian Jungle Fighter, 1966, standard set with action figure uniform, no equipment, Model No. 8205
EX $150 NM $275 MIP $1200

British Commando, 1966, Hasbro, deluxe set with action figure, helmet, night raid green jacket, pants, boots, canteen and cover, gas mask and cover, belt, Sten sub machine gun, gun clip and "Victoria Cross" medal, Model No. 8104
EX $300 NM $425 MIP $2500

British Commando, 1966, Hasbro, standard set with no equipment, Model No. 8204
EX $150 NM $275 MIP $1750

Foreign Soldiers of the World, 1968, Hasbro, Talking Adventure Pack, Model No. 8111-83
EX $750 NM $825 MIP $5000

French Resistance Fighter, 1966, Hasbro, Standard set with action figure and equipment, Model No. 8203
EX $125 NM $225 MIP $1250

French Resistance Fighter, 1966, Hasbro, deluxe set with figure, beret, short black boots, black sweater, denim pants, "Croix de Guerre" medal, knife, shoulder holster, pistol, radio, submachine gun and grenades, Model No. 8103
EX $200 NM $250 MIP $2250

German Storm Trooper, 1966, Hasbro, deluxe set with figure, helmet, jacket, pants, boots, Luger pistol, holster, cartridge belt, cartridges, "Iron Cross" medal, stick grenades, 9mm Schmeisser, field pack, Model No. 8100
EX $275 NM $425 MIP $2500

German Storm Trooper, 1966, Hasbro, standard set with no equipment, Model No. 8200
EX $275 NM $325 MIP $1300

Japanese Imperial Soldier, 1966, Hasbro, deluxe set with figure, Arisaka rifle, belt, cartridges, field pack, Nambu pistol, holster, bayonet, "Order of the Kite" medal, helmet, jacket, pants, short brown boots, Model No. 8101
EX $425 NM $675 MIP $2700

Japanese Imperial Soldier, 1966, Hasbro, Standard set with equipment, Model No. 8201
EX $300 NM $325 MIP $1425

Russian Infantry Man, 1966, Hasbro, standard set with no equipment, Model No. 8202
EX $315 NM $400 MIP $1250

Russian Infantry Man, 1966, Hasbro, deluxe set with action figure, fur cap, tunic, pants, boots, ammo box, ammo rounds, anti-tank grenades, belt, bipod, DP light machine gun, "Order of Lenin" medal, field glasses and case, Model No. 8102
EX $275 NM $400 MIP $2250

Uniforms of Six Nations, 1967, Hasbro, Model No. 5038
EX $750 NM $950 MIP $2500

Uniform/Equipment Sets

Australian Jungle Fighter Set, 1966, Hasbro, basic set with flamethrower, machete, grenades, Victoria Cross medal, shovel, bayonet, Model No. 8305
EX $25 NM $50 MIP $250

British Commando Set, 1966, Hasbro, Sten submachine gun, gas mask and carrier, canteen and cover, cartridge belt, rifle, "Victoria Cross" medal, manual, Model No. 8304
EX $125 NM $200 MIP $325

French Resistance Fighter Set, 1966, Hasbro, shoulder holster, Lebel pistol, knife, grenades, radio, 7.65 submachine gun, "Croix de Guerra" medal, counter-intelligence manual, Model No. 8303
EX $25 NM $50 MIP $275

German Storm Trooper, 1966, Hasbro, Model No. 8300
EX $125 NM $175 MIP $325

Japanese Imperial Soldier Set, 1966, Hasbro, field pack, Nambu pistol and holster, Arisaka rifle with bayonet, cartridge belt, "Order of the Kite" medal, counter-intelligence manual, Model No. 8301
EX $175 NM $275 MIP $625

Russian Infantry Man Set, 1966, Hasbro, DP light machine gun, bipod, field glasses and case, anti-tank grenades, ammo box, "Order of Lenin" medal, counter-intelligence medal, Model No. 8302
EX $175 NM $220 MIP $325

ADVENTURE TEAM

Figure Sets

Air Adventurer, 1970, Hasbro, orange flight suit, short black boots, insignia,

dog tags, revolver, shoulder holster, boots, warranty, club insert, Model No. 7403
EX $120 **NM** $375 **MIP** $400

Air Adventurer, 1974, Hasbro, Kung Fu grip, rifle, orange flight suit w/AT insignia, short black boots, AT Club flyer, boot removal instructions, Model No. 7282
EX $95 **NM** $160 **MIP** $325

Air Adventurer, 1976, Hasbro, life-like body figure, short pants, orange flight suit w/AT insignia, rifle, short black boots, came carded not boxed, w/Kung Fu grip, Model No. 7272 and 7282
EX $75 **NM** $100 **MIP** $200

Black Adventurer, 1970, Hasbro, tan shirt with AT insignia, tan pants, short black boots, dog tags, shoulder holster w/revolver, AT Club flyer, boot removal instructions, boxed, Model No. 7404
EX $125 **NM** $150 **MIP** $375

Black Adventurer, 1974, Hasbro, Kung Fu grip, tan shirt w/AT insignia, tan pants, short black boots, rifle, paperwork, boxed, Model No. 7283
EX $75 **NM** $165 **MIP** $250

Black Adventurer, 1976, Hasbro, life-like body, Kung Fu grip, tan shirt w/AT insignia, tan pants, short black boots, rifle, paperwork, Model No. 7273
EX $85 **NM** $125 **MIP** $225

Bulletman, 1976, Hasbro, black painted hair, silver eyes, silver helmet, red body suit w/bullet insignia, black elastic belt, red boots, handle, flight line, Model No. 8026
EX $60 **NM** $100 **MIP** $175

Eagle Eye Black Commando, 1976, Hasbro, Model No. 7278
EX $85 **NM** $125 **MIP** $250

Eagle Eye Land Commander, 1976, Hasbro, either green shirt and pants or camoflaged shirt and pants, AT insignia, short black boots, rifle, eyes move via lever, paperwork, carded, Model No. 7276
EX $65 **NM** $80 **MIP** $150

Eagle Eye Man of Action, 1976, Hasbro, green shirt and pants, AT insignia, rifle, short black boots, eyes move via lever, paperwork, carded, Model No. 7277
EX $65 **NM** $80 **MIP** $165

Intruder Commander, 1976, Hasbro, gold body armor, Model No. 8050
EX $50 **NM** $60 **MIP** $135

Intruder Warrior, 1976, Hasbro, silver body armor, Model No. 8051
EX $50 **NM** $60 **MIP** $175

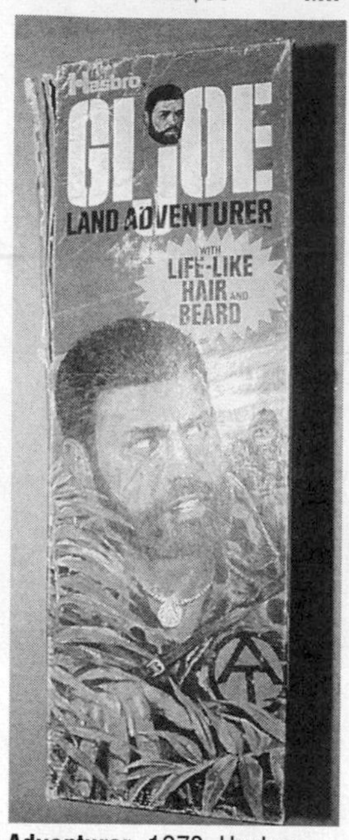

Land Adventurer, 1970, Hasbro, camoflaged shirt and pants, AT insignia, short black boots, shoulder holster w/revolver, dog tags, paperwork, Model No. 7401
EX $45 **NM** $90 **MIP** $160

Land Adventurer, 1974, Hasbro, Kung Fu grip, camoflaged shirt w/AT insignia, camoflaged pants, short black boots, rifle, paperwork, Model No. 7280
EX $50 **NM** $65 **MIP** $200

Land Adventurer, 1976, Hasbro, life-like body, Kung Fu grip, "New," camoflaged shirt and pants, AT insignia, short black boots, rifle, carded, Model No. 7280
EX $35 **NM** $50 **MIP** $150

Land Adventurer, 1976, Hasbro, life-like body, Kung Fu grip, camoflaged shirt and pants, AT insignia, short black boots, rifle, carded, Model No. 7270
EX $20 **NM** $50 **MIP** $180

Man of Action, 1970, Hasbro, green shirt and pants, AT insignia, short black boots, dog tags, hat, team inserts, boxed, Model No. 7500
EX $50 **NM** $75 **MIP** $225

Man of Action, 1974, Hasbro, Kung Fu grip, green shirt w/AT insignia, green pants, short black boots, rifle, paperwork, boxed, Model No. 7284
EX $45 **NM** $75 **MIP** $200

Man of Action, 1976, Hasbro, life-like body, Kung Fu grip, green shirt w/AT insignia, green pants, short black boots, rifle, paperwork, carded, Model No. 7274 and 7284
EX $25 **NM** $45 **MIP** $175

Mike Powers/Atomic Man, 1975, Hasbro, figure with "atomic" flashing eye, arm that spins hand-held helicopter, Model No. 8025
EX $20 **NM** $45 **MIP** $125

Sea Adventurer, 1970, Hasbro, light blue denim shirt w/AT insignia, dark blue dungarees, short black boots, shoulder holster w/revolver, dog tags, paperwork, Model No. 7402
EX $45 **NM** $95 **MIP** $250

Sea Adventurer, 1974, Hasbro, Kung Fu grip, light blue denim shirt w/AT insignia, dark blue dungarees, short black boots, rifle, paperwork, Model No. 7281
EX $55 **NM** $85 **MIP** $200

Sea Adventurer, 1976, Hasbro, life-like body, Kung Fu grip, light blue denim shirt w/AT insignia, dark blue dungarees, short black boots, rifle, carded, Model No. 7271
EX $40 **NM** $75 **MIP** $250

Sea Adventurer, 1976, Hasbro, life-like body, Kung Fu grip, light blue denim shirt w/AT insignia, dark blue

dungarees, short black boots, rifle, "New," carded, Model No. 7281
EX $55 **NM** $135 **MIP** $295

Talking Adventure Team Black Commander, 1973, Hasbro, green shirt w/AT insignia, green pants, short black boots, dog tag, shoulder holster w/revolver, paperwork, boxed, Model No. 7406
EX $150 **NM** $475 **MIP** $825

Talking Adventure Team Black Commander, 1974, Hasbro, Kung Fu grip, green shirt w/AT insignia, green pants, dog tag, rifle, short black boots, paperwork, boxed, Model No. 7291
EX $85 **NM** $350 **MIP** $750

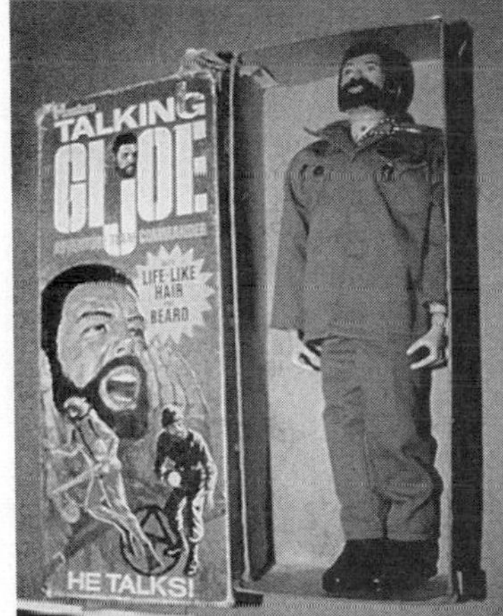

Talking Adventure Team Commander, 1970, Hasbro, two-pocket green shirt w/AT insignia, green pants, short black boots, instructions, dog tag, shoulder holster w/revolver. With life-like hair and beard, Model No. 7400
EX $65 **NM** $140 **MIP** $400

Talking Adventure Team Commander, 1974, Hasbro, Kung Fu grip, green fatigue shirt w/AT insignia, green pants, dog tag, short black boots, rifle, paperwork, boxed, Model No. 7290
EX $75 **NM** $200 **MIP** $500

Talking Astronaut, 1970, Hasbro, white jumpsuit w/AT insignia, dog tag, white boots, Model No. 7405
EX $90 **NM** $175 **MIP** $430

Talking Black Commander, 1976, Hasbro, life-like body, Kung Fu grip, green shirt w/AT insignia, green pants, dog tag, short black boots, rifle, paperwork, Model No. 7291
EX $125 **NM** $300 **MIP** $600

Talking Commander, 1976, Hasbro, life-like body, Kung Fu grip, green shrit w/AT insignia, green pants, dog tag, short black boots, rifle, paperwork, Model No. 7290
EX $75 **NM** $115 **MIP** $500

Talking Man of Action, 1970, Hasbro, green shirt, green pants, short black boots, hat, dog tags, instructions, Model No. 7590
EX $75 **NM** $125 **MIP** $350

Talking Man of Action, 1974, Hasbro, Kung Fu grip, green shirt, green pants, rifle, dog tags, short black boots, paperwork, Model No. 7292
EX $75 **NM** $200 **MIP** $650

Talking Man of Action, 1976, Hasbro, life-like body, Kung Fu grip, green shirt w/AT insignia, green pants, dog tag, short black boots, rifle, paperwork, Model No. 7292
EX $75 **NM** $120 **MIP** $525

Uniform/Equipment Sets

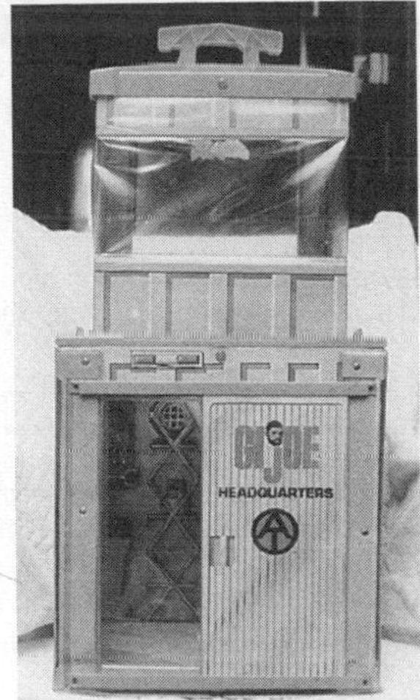

Adventure Team Headquarters Set, 1972, Hasbro, Adventure Team playset, Model No. 7490
EX $50 **NM** $125 **MIP** $300

Adventure Team Training Center Set, 1973, Hasbro, rifle rack, logs, barrel, barbed wire, rope ladder, three tires, two targets, escape slide, tent and poles, first aid kit, respirator and mask, snake, instructions, Model No. 7495
EX $75 **NM** $125 **MIP** $225

Aerial Reconnaissance Set, 1971, Hasbro, jumpsuit, helmet, aerial recon vehicle with built-in camera, Model No. 7345
EX $75 **NM** $125 **MIP** $242

Attack at Vulture Falls, 1975, Hasbro, super deluxe set, Model No. 7420
EX $75 **NM** $150 **MIP** $275

Black Widow Rendezvous, 1975, Hasbro, super deluxe set, Model No. 7414
EX $125 **NM** $200 **MIP** $350

Buried Bounty, 1975, Hasbro, deluxe set, Model No. 7328-5
EX $10 **NM** $25 **MIP** $85

Capture of the Pygmy Gorilla Set, 1970, Hasbro, Model No. 7437
EX $100 **NM** $175 **MIP** $485

Challenge of Savage River, 1975, Hasbro, deluxe set, Model No. 8032
EX $100 **NM** $175 **MIP** $350

Chest Winch Set, 1972, Hasbro, Model No. 7313
EX $10 **NM** $15 **MIP** $65

Chest Winch Set, 1974, Hasbro, reissue, Model No. 7313
EX $10 **NM** $15 **MIP** $75

Command Para Drop, 1975, Hasbro, deluxe set, Model No. 8033
EX $175 **NM** $250 **MIP** $550

Copter Rescue Set, 1973, Hasbro, blue jumpsuit, red binoculars, Model No. 7308-6
EX $15 **NM** $20 **MIP** $30

Danger of the Depths Set, 1970, Hasbro, Model No. 7412
EX $100 **NM** $175 **MIP** $325

Danger Ray Detection, 1975, Hasbro, magnetic ray detector, solar communicator with headphones, two-piece uniform, instructions and comic, Model No. 7338-1
EX $45 **NM** $90 **MIP** $225

Dangerous Climb Set, 1973, Hasbro, Model No. 7309-2
EX $20 **NM** $35 **MIP** $75

Dangerous Mission Set, 1973, Hasbro, green shirt, pants, hunting rifle, Model No. 7308-2
EX $20 **NM** $35 **MIP** $75

Demolition Set, 1971, Hasbro, armored suit, face shield, bomb, bomb disposal box, extension grips, Model No. 7370
EX $20 **NM** $45 **MIP** $125

Desert Explorer Set, 1973, Hasbro, Model No. 7309-5
EX $20 **NM** $40 **MIP** $80

Desert Survival Set, 1973, Hasbro, Model No. 7308-1
EX $20 **NM** $40 **MIP** $80

Dive to Danger, 1975, Hasbro, Mike Powers set, orange scuba suit, fins, mask, spear gun, shark, buoy, knife and scabbard, mini sled, air tanks, comic, Model No. 8031
EX $150 **NM** $250 **MIP** $450

Diver's Distress, 1975, Hasbro, Model No. 7328-6
EX $35 **NM** $70 **MIP** $125

Drag Bike Set, 1971, Hasbro, three-wheel motorcycle brakes down to backpack size, Model No. 7364
EX $25 **NM** $65 **MIP** $125

Eight Ropes of Danger Set, 1970, Hasbro, Model No. 7422
EX $125 **NM** $225 **MIP** $375

Emergency Rescue Set, 1971, Hasbro, shirt, pants, rope ladder and hook, walkie talkie, safety belt, flashlight, oxygen tank, axe, first aid kit, Model No. 7374
EX $45 **NM** $75 **MIP** $145

Equipment Tester Set, 1972, Hasbro, Model No. 7319-5
EX $15 **NM** $75 **MIP** $40

Escape Car Set, 1971, Hasbro, Model No. 7360
EX $30 **NM** $60 **MIP** $85

Escape Slide Set, 1972, Hasbro, Model No. 7319-1
EX $15 **NM** $25 **MIP** $40

Original Series and Adventure Team (1964-78)

Fangs of the Cobra, 1975, Hasbro, deluxe set, Model No. 8028-2
EX $125 **NM** $175 **MIP** $235

Fantastic Freefall Set, 1970, Hasbro, Model No. 7423
EX $125 **NM** $200 **MIP** $345

Fight For Survival Set, 1970, Hasbro, with blue parka, Model No. 7431
EX $300 **NM** $550 **MIP** $2500

Fight for Survival Set, 1973, Hasbro, brown shirt and pants, machete, Model No. 7308-3
EX $20 **NM** $30 **MIP** $70

Fight for Survival Set with Polar Explorer, 1969, Hasbro, Model No. 7982
EX $250 **NM** $450 **MIP** $850

Fire Fighter Set, 1971, Hasbro, Model No. 7351
EX $20 **NM** $30 **MIP** $55

Flying Rescue Set, 1971, Hasbro, Model No. 7361
EX $35 **NM** $60 **MIP** $85

Flying Space Adventure Set, 1970, Hasbro, Model No. 7425
EX $400 **NM** $600 **MIP** $3700

Footlocker, 1974, Hasbro, green plastic with cardboard wrapper, Model No. 8000
EX $35 **NM** $45 **MIP** $200

Green Danger, 1975, Hasbro, Model No. 7328-4
EX $30 **NM** $75 **MIP** $60

Hidden Missile Discovery Set, 1970, Hasbro, Model No. 7415
EX $100 **NM** $225 **MIP** $1750

Hidden Treasure Set, 1973, Hasbro, shirt, pants, pick axe, shovel, Model No. 7308-5
EX $15 **NM** $25 **MIP** $40

High Voltage Escape Set, 1971, Hasbro, net, jumpsuit, hat, wrist meter, wire cutters, wire, warning sign, Model No. 7342
EX $40 **NM** $75 **MIP** $110

Hurricane Spotter Set, 1971, Hasbro, slicker suit, rain measure, portable radar, map and case, binoculars, Model No. 7343
EX $55 **NM** $110 **MIP** $220

Infiltration, 1971, Hasbro, replaced Karate set, black pants, black hooded top, revilver, machine gun, map, knife and scabbard, radio, shoulder holster, map case, Model No. 7372
EX $45 **NM** $90 **MIP** $135

Jaws of Death, 1975, Hasbro, super deluxe set, Model No. 7421
EX $325 **NM** $500 **MIP** $650

Jettison to Safety, 1975, Hasbro, infrared terrain scanner, mobile rocket pack, two-piece flight suit, instructions and comic, Model No. 7339-2
EX $85 **NM** $200 **MIP** $275

Jungle Ordeal Set, 1973, Hasbro, Model No. 7309-3
EX $15 **NM** $25 **MIP** $66

Jungle Survival Set, 1971, Hasbro, Model No. 7323
EX $15 **NM** $60 **MIP** $180

Karate Set, 1971, Hasbro, Model No. 7372
EX $35 **NM** $70 **MIP** $210

Laser Rescue Set, 1972, Hasbro, hand-held laser with backpack generator, Model No. 7311
EX $20 **NM** $35 **MIP** $45

Laser Rescue Set, 1974, Hasbro, reissue, Model No. 7311
EX $20 **NM** $35 **MIP** $100

Life-Line Catapult Set, 1971, Hasbro, Model No. 7352
EX $15 **NM** $25 **MIP** $85

Long Range Recon, 1975, Hasbro, deluxe set, Model No. 7328-3
EX $10 **NM** $20 **MIP** $35

Magnetic Flaw Detector Set, 1972, Hasbro, Model No. 7319-2
EX $10 **NM** $20 **MIP** $56

Mine Shaft Breakout, 1975, Hasbro, sonic rock blaster, chest winch, two-piece uniform, netting, instructions, comic, Model No. 7339-3
EX $70 **NM** $125 **MIP** $250

Missile Recovery Set, 1971, Hasbro, Model No. 7340
EX $100 **NM** $200 **MIP** $325

Mystery of the Boiling Lagoon, 1973, Hasbro, Sears, pontoon boat, diver's suit, diver's helmet, weighted belt and boots, depth gauge, air hose, buoy, nose cone, pincer arm, instructions
EX $150 **NM** $200 **MIP** $295

Night Surveillance, 1975, Hasbro, deluxe set, Model No. 7338-2
EX $65 **NM** $160 **MIP** $165

Peril of the Raging Inferno, 1975, Hasbro, fireproof suit, hood and boots, breathing apparatus, camera, fire extinguisher, detection meter, gaskets, Model No. 7416
EX $85 **NM** $150 **MIP** $275

Photo Reconnaissance Set, 1973, Hasbro, Model No. 7309-4
EX $20 **NM** $30 **MIP** $65

Race for Recovery, 1975, Hasbro, Model No. 8028-1
EX $20 **NM** $35 **MIP** $140

Radiation Detection Set, 1971, Hasbro, jumpsuit with belt, "uranium ore", goggles, container, pincer arm, Model No. 7341
EX $30 **NM** $50 **MIP** $160

Raging River Dam Up, 1975, Hasbro, Model No. 7339-1
EX $100 **NM** $225 **MIP** $450

Rescue Raft Set, 1971, Hasbro, Model No. 7350
EX $15 **NM** $45 **MIP** $65

Revenge of the Spy Shark, 1975, Hasbro, super deluxe set, Model No. 7413
EX $50 **NM** $175 **MIP** $400

Rock Blaster, 1972, Hasbro, sonic blaster with tripod, backpack generator, face shield, Model No. 7312
EX $10 **NM** $20 **MIP** $35

Rocket Pack Set, 1972, Hasbro, Model No. 7315
EX $10 **NM** $20 **MIP** $75

Rocket Pack Set, 1974, Hasbro, reissue, Model No. 7315
EX $10 **NM** $20 **MIP** $50

Sample Analyzer Set, 1972, Hasbro, Model No. 7319-3
EX $45 **NM** $145 **MIP** $255

Search for the Abominable Snowman Set, 1973, Hasbro, Sears, white suit, belt, goggles, gloves, rifle, skis and poles, show shoes, sled, rope, net, supply chest, binoculars, Abominable Snowman, comic book, Model No. 7439.16
EX $110 **NM** $175 **MIP** $290

Secret Agent Set, 1971, Hasbro, Model No. 7375
EX $30 **NM** $55 **MIP** $190

Secret Courier, 1975, Hasbro, Model No. 7328-1
EX $45 **NM** $80 **MIP** $135

Secret Mission Set, 1973, Hasbro, Model No. 7309-1
EX $45 **NM** $65 **MIP** $135

Secret Mission Set, 1975, Hasbro, deluxe set, Model No. 8030
EX $65 **NM** $95 **MIP** $200

Secret Mission to Spy Island Set, 1970, Hasbro, comic, inflatable raft with oar, binoculars, signal light, flare gun, TNT and detonator, wire roll, boots, pants, sweater, black cap, camera, radio with earphones, .45 submachine gun, Model No. 7411
EX $75 **NM** $125 **MIP** $400

Secret Mountain Outpost, 1975, Hasbro, Model No. 8040
EX $50 **NM** $85 **MIP** $200

Secret Rendezvous Set, 1973, Hasbro, parka, pants, flare gun, Model No. 7308-4
EX $10 **NM** $20 **MIP** $35

Seismograph Set, 1972, Hasbro, Model No. 7319-6
EX $10 **NM** $20 **MIP** $35

Shocking Escape, 1975, Hasbro, escape slide, chest pack climber, jumpsuit with gloves and belt, high voltage sign, instructions and comic, Model No. 7338-3
EX $125 **NM** $240 **MIP** $525

Signal Flasher Set, 1971, Hasbro, large back pack type signal flash unit, Model No. 7362
EX $20 **NM** $30 **MIP** $66

Sky Dive to Danger, 1975, Hasbro, super deluxe set, Model No. 7440
EX $90 **NM** $150 **MIP** $350

Smoke Jumper Set, 1971, Hasbro, yellow jumpsuit, yellow helmet, chain saw, cutters, flashlight, black tool belt, red fire extinguisher, pliers, ax, Model No. 7371
EX $75 **NM** $100 **MIP** $250

Solar Communicator Set, 1972, Hasbro, Model No. 7314
EX $10 **NM** $20 **MIP** $35

Solar Communicator Set, 1974, Hasbro, reissue, Model No. 7314
EX $10 **NM** $20 **MIP** $95

Sonic Rock Blaster Set, 1972, Hasbro, Model No. 7312
EX $10 **NM** $20 **MIP** $35

Sonic Rock Blaster Set, 1974, Hasbro, reissue, Model No. 7312
EX $10 **NM** $20 **MIP** $35

Special Assignment, 1975, Hasbro, deluxe set, Model No. 8028-3
EX $30 **NM** $55 **MIP** $135

Thermal Terrain Scanner Set, 1972, Hasbro, Model No. 7319-4
EX $25 **NM** $35 **MIP** $50

Three-in-One Super Adventure Set, 1971, Hasbro, Danger of the Depths, Secret Mission to Spy Island and Flying Space Adventure Packs, Model No. 7480
EX $550 **NM** $975 **MIP** $1250

Three-in-One Super Adventure Set, 1971, Hasbro, cold of the Arctic, Heat of the Desert and Danger of the Jungle, Model No. 7480
EX $250 **NM** $400 **MIP** $750

Thrust into Danger, 1975, Hasbro, deluxe set, Model No. 7328-2
EX $45 **NM** $55 **MIP** $175

Trouble at Vulture Pass, 1975, Hasbro, Sears Exclusive, super deluxe set, Model No. 59289
EX $75 **NM** $175 **MIP** $325

Turbo Copter Set, 1971, Hasbro, strap-on one man helicopter, Model No. 7363
EX $15 **NM** $35 **MIP** $65

Undercover Agent Set, 1973, Hasbro, trenchcoat and belt, walkie-talkie, Model No. 7309-6
EX $15 **NM** $30 **MIP** $45

Underwater Demolition Set, 1972, Hasbro, hand-held propulsion device, breathing apparatus, dynamite, Model No. 7310
EX $15 **NM** $20 **MIP** $40

Underwater Demolition Set, 1974, Hasbro, reissue, Model No. 7310
EX $10 **NM** $20 **MIP** $75

Underwater Explorer Set, 1971, Hasbro, self propelled underwater device, Model No. 7354
EX $15 **NM** $30 **MIP** $60

Volcano Jumper Set, 1971, Hasbro, jumpsuit with hood, belt, nylon rope, chest pack, TNT pack, Model No. 7344
EX $45 **NM** $80 **MIP** $250

White Tiger Hunt Set, 1970, Hasbro, hunter's jacket and pants, hat, rifle, tent, cage, chain, campfire, white tiger, comic, Model No. 7436
EX $80 **NM** $180 **MIP** $340

Windboat Set, 1971, Hasbro, back pack, sled with wheels, sail, Model No. 7353
EX $10 **NM** $25 **MIP** $65

Winter Rescue Set, 1973, Hasbro, Replaced by Photo Reconnaissance Set, Model No. 7309-4
EX $40 **NM** $75 **MIP** $150

Vehicle Sets

Action Sea Sled, 1973, Hasbro, J.C. Penney, 13", Adventure Pack
EX $25 **NM** $40 **MIP** $85

Adventure Team Vehicle Set, 1970, Hasbro, Model No. 7005
EX $50 **NM** $75 **MIP** $225

All Terrain Vehicle, 1973, Hasbro, 14" vehicle, Model No. 23528
EX $50 **NM** $75 **MIP** $125

Amphicat, 1973, Hasbro, Irwin, scaled to fit two figures, Model No. 59158
EX $35 **NM** $55 **MIP** $125

Avenger Pursuit Craft, 1976, Hasbro, Sears Exclusive
EX $100 **NM** $175 **MIP** $275

Big Trapper, 1976, Hasbro, without action figure, Model No. 7498
EX $75 **NM** $245 **MIP** $600

Big Trapper Adventure with Intruder, 1976, Hasbro, with action figure, Model No. 7494
EX $100 **NM** $150 **MIP** $425

Capture Copter, 1976, Hasbro, without action figure, Model No. 7480
EX $80 **NM** $175 **MIP** $325

Capture Copter Adventure with Intruder, 1976, Hasbro, with action figure, Model No. 7481
EX $110 **NM** $200 **MIP** $350

Chopper Cycle, 1973, Hasbro, 15" vehicle, J.C. Penney's, Model No. 59114
EX $30 **NM** $50 **MIP** $100

Combat Action Jeep, 1973, Hasbro, 18" vehicle, J.C. Penney's, Model No. 59751
EX $50 **NM** $65 **MIP** $125

Combat Jeep and Trailer, 1976, Hasbro, Model No. 7000
EX $80 **NM** $135 **MIP** $550

Devil of the Deep, 1974, Hasbro, Model No. 7439
EX $80 **NM** $135 **MIP** $325

Fantastic Sea Wolf Submarine, 1975, Hasbro, Model No. 7460
EX $60 **NM** $100 **MIP** $175

Fate of the Troubleshooter, 1974, Hasbro, Includes vehicle, vulture, instructions and comic book, Model No. 7450
EX $85 **NM** $210 **MIP** $310

Giant Air-Sea Helicopter, 1973, Hasbro, 28" vehicle, J.C. Penney's, Model No. 59189
EX $50 **NM** $125 **MIP** $225

Helicopter, 1973, Hasbro, 14", yellow, with working winch, Model No. 7380
EX $50 **NM** $90 **MIP** $150

Helicopter, 1976, Hasbro, Model No. 7380
EX $50 **NM** $90 **MIP** $300

Mobile Support Vehicle Set, 1972, Hasbro, Model No. 7499
EX $125 **NM** $200 **MIP** $425

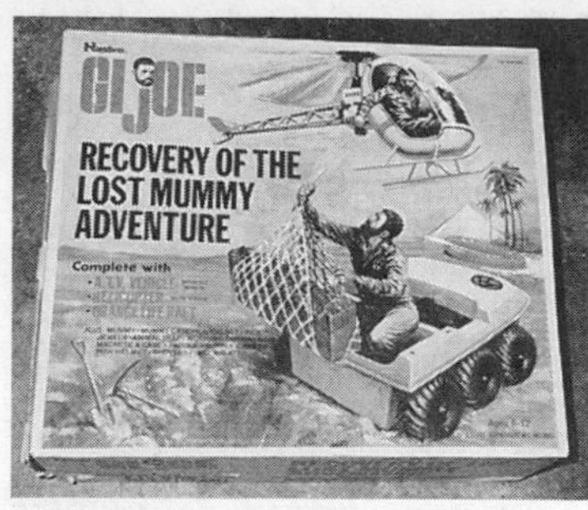

Recovery of the Lost Mummy Adventure Set, 1971, Hasbro, Sears Exclusive
EX $125 **NM** $250 **MIP** $575

Sandstorm Survival Adventure, 1974, Hasbro, Model No. 7493
EX $125 **NM** $200 **MIP** $335

Search for the Stolen Idol Set, 1971, Hasbro, Model No. 7418
EX $120 **NM** $225 **MIP** $400

Secret of the Mummy's Tomb Set, 1970, Hasbro, with Land Adventurer figure, shirt, pants, boots, insignia, pith helmet, pick, shovel, Mummy's tomb, net, gems, vehicle with winch, comic, Model No. 7441
EX $250 **NM** $600 **MIP** $1500

Sharks Surprise Set with Sea Adventurer, 1970, Hasbro, Model No. 7442
EX $250 **NM** $375 **MIP** $550

Signal All Terrain Vehicle, 1973, Hasbro, J.C. Penney's, 12" vehicle
EX $30 **NM** $65 **MIP** $125

Sky Hawk, 1975, Hasbro, 5-3/4-foot wingspan, Model No. 7470
EX $65 **NM** $100 **MIP** $175

Spacewalk Mystery Set with Astronaut, 1970, Hasbro, Model No. 7445
EX $225 **NM** $300 **MIP** $550

Trapped in the Coils of Doom, 1974, Hasbro, J.C. Penney's Exclusive, Model No. 79-59301
EX $250 **NM** $300 **MIP** $550

ADVENTURES OF G.I. JOE

Figure Sets

Aquanaut, 1969, Hasbro, Model No. 7910
EX $175 **NM** $550 **MIP** $3000

Negro Adventurer, 1969, Hasbro, Sears Exclusive, includes painted hair figure, blue jeans, pullover sweater, shoulder holster and pistol, plus product letter from Sears, Model No. 7905
EX $450 **NM** $750 **MIP** $2750

Sharks Surprise Set with Frogman, 1969, Hasbro, with figure, orange scuba suit, blue sea sled, air tanks, harpoon, face mask, treasure chest, shark, instructions and comic, Model No. 7980
EX $125 **NM** $300 **MIP** $750

Talking Astronaut, 1969, Hasbro, hard-hand figure with white coveralls with insignias, white boots, dog tags, Model No. 7615
EX $85 **NM** $275 **MIP** $1000

Uniform/Equipment Sets

Adventure Locker, 1969, Hasbro, Footlocker, Model No. 7940
EX $165 **NM** $400 **MIP** $450

Aqua Locker, 1969, Hasbro, Footlocker, Model No. 7941
EX $110 **NM** $180 **MIP** $325

Astro Locker, 1969, Hasbro, Footlocker, Model No. 7942
EX $90 **NM** $225 **MIP** $375

Danger of the Depths Underwater Diver Set, 1969, Hasbro, Model No. 7920
EX $140 **NM** $275 **MIP** $500

Eight Ropes of Danger Set, 1969, Hasbro, diving suit, treasure chest, octopus, Model No. 7950
EX $110 **NM** $225 **MIP** $525

Fantastic Freefall Set, 1969, Hasbro, includes figure with parachute and pack, blinker light, air vest, flash light, crash helmet with visor and oxygen mask, dog tags, orange jump suit, black boots, Model No. 7951
EX $150 **NM** $325 **MIP** $675

Flight for Survival Set with Polar Explorer, 1969, Hasbro, reissue, Model No. 7982.83
EX $150 **NM** $300 **MIP** $500

Hidden Missile Discovery Set, 1969, Hasbro, Model No. 7952
EX $70 **NM** $135 **MIP** $400

Mouth of Doom Set, 1969, Hasbro, Model No. 7953
EX $125 **NM** $250 **MIP** $550

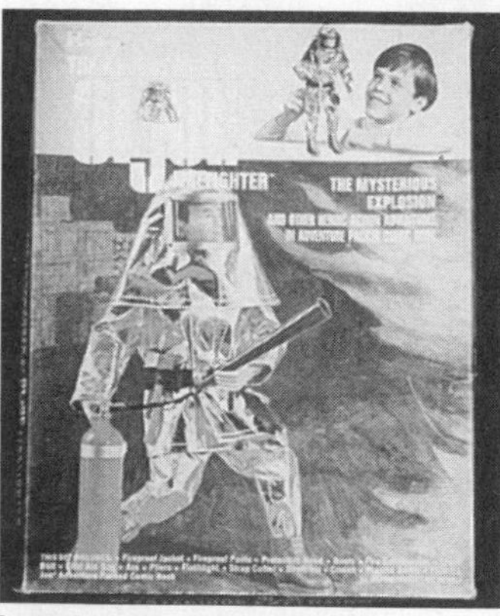

Mysterious Explosion Set, 1969, Hasbro, basic, Model No. 7921
EX $60 **NM** $180 **MIP** $425

Perilous Rescue Set, 1969, Hasbro, basic, Model No. 7923
EX $150 **NM** $300 **MIP** $500

Secret Mission to Spy Island Set, 1969, Hasbro, basic, Model No. 7922
EX $110 **NM** $225 **MIP** $545

Vehicle Sets

Sharks Surprise Set with Frogman, 1969, Hasbro, Model No. 7980
EX $175 **NM** $325 **MIP** $650

Sharks Surprise Set without Frogman, 1969, Hasbro, Model No. 7980.83
EX $150 **NM** $300 **MIP** $550

Spacewalk Mystery Set with Spaceman, 1969, Hasbro, Model No. 7981
EX $150 **NM** $375 **MIP** $650

Spacewalk Mystery Set without Spaceman, 1969, Hasbro, reissue, Model No. 7981.83
EX $125 **NM** $275 **MIP** $550

GI JOE ACTION SERIES, ARMY, NAVY, MARINE AND AIR FORCE

Uniform/Equipment Sets

Basic Footlocker, 1965, Hasbro, Model No. 8000
EX $50 **NM** $75 **MIP** $175

Footlocker Adventure Pack, 1968, Hasbro, 22 pieces, Model No. 8002.83
EX $70 **NM** $145 **MIP** $450

Footlocker Adventure Pack, 1968, Hasbro, 15 pieces, Model No. 8001.83
EX $65 **NM** $135 **MIP** $450

Footlocker Adventure Pack, 1968, Hasbro, 16 pieces, Model No. 8000.83
EX $65 **NM** $135 **MIP** $450

Footlocker Adventure Pack, 1968, Hasbro, 15 pieces, Model No. 8002.83
EX $65 **NM** $135 **MIP** $450

SUPER JOE

Figure Sets

Gor, 1977, Hasbro, Model No. 7510
EX $40 **NM** $70 **MIP** $130

Luminos, 1977, Hasbro, Model No. 7506
EX $45 **NM** $70 **MIP** $130

Super Joe, 1977, Hasbro, Model No. 7503
EX $25 **NM** $50 **MIP** $85

Super Joe (Black), 1977, Hasbro, Model No. 7504
EX $35 **NM** $65 **MIP** $125

Super Joe Commander, 1977, Hasbro, Model No. 7501
EX $25 **NM** $45 **MIP** $75

The Shield, 1977, Hasbro, Model No. 7505
EX $40 **NM** $65 **MIP** $125

Uniform/Equipment Sets

Aqua Laser, 1977, Hasbro, Model No. 7528-1
EX $10 **NM** $20 **MIP** $30

Edge of Adventure, 1977, Hasbro, Model No. 7518-2
EX $10 **NM** $20 **MIP** $35

Emergency Rescue, 1977, Hasbro, Model No. 7518-3
EX $10 **NM** $20 **MIP** $30

Fusion Bazooka, 1977, Hasbro, Model No. 7528-3
EX $10 **NM** $20 **MIP** $30

Helipak, 1977, Hasbro, Model No. 7538-2
EX $10 **NM** $20 **MIP** $30

Invisible Danger, 1977, Hasbro, Model No. 7518-1
EX $10 **NM** $20 **MIP** $35

Magna Tools, 1977, Hasbro, With uniform and rock-cutting drill and saw, Model No. 7538-1
EX $10 **NM** $20 **MIP** $30

Path of Danger, 1977, Hasbro, Model No. 7518-4
EX $10 **NM** $20 **MIP** $30

Sonic Scanner, 1977, Hasbro, Model No. 7538-3
EX $10 **NM** $20 **MIP** $30

Treacherous Dive, 1977, Hasbro, Model No. 7528-2
EX $10 **NM** $20 **MIP** $30

Vehicle Sets

Rocket Command Center, 1977, Hasbro, Super Adventure Set including Gor, Model No. 7571
EX $60 **NM** $115 **MIP** $225

Rocket Command Center, 1977, Hasbro, Model No. 7570
EX $50 **NM** $100 **MIP** $200

3-3/4" Figures

SERIES 01, COBRA Figure Sets

Cobra, 1982, Hasbro, Infantry Soldier, Model No. 6423
EX $25 **NM** $55 **MIP** $225

Cobra Commander, 1982, Hasbro, mail order, Commanding Leader
EX $25 **NM** $55 **MIP** $175

Cobra Officer, 1982, Hasbro, Infantry Officer, Model No. 6424
EX $25 **NM** $55 **MIP** $225

Major Bludd, 1982, Hasbro, mail order; Mercenary with card, Model No. 6426
EX $18 **NM** $30 **MIP** $150

Uniform/Equipment Sets

Headquarters Missile-Command Center, 1982, Hasbro, w/ three figures: Cobra Commander, Officer, Troope, Sears Exclusive offered in 1982 Sears Christmas catalog, Model No. 6200
EX $65 **NM** $125 **MIP** $250

SERIES 01, GI JOE Figure Sets

Breaker, 1982, Hasbro, Communications Officer, Model No. 6403
EX $20 **NM** $35 **MIP** $100

Flash, 1982, Hasbro, Laser Rifle Trooper, Model No. 6406
EX $20 **NM** $35 **MIP** $125

Grunt, 1982, Hasbro, Infantry Trooper, Model No. 6409
EX $20 **NM** $35 **MIP** $100

(Karen O'Brien collection)

Rock 'n Roll, 1982, Hasbro, Machine Gunner, Model No. 6408
EX $30 **NM** $50 **MIP** $150

Scarlett, 1982, Hasbro, Counter Intelligence, Model No. 6407
EX $40 **NM** $85 **MIP** $250

Short-Fuze, 1982, Hasbro, Mortar Soldier, Model No. 6402
EX $20 **NM** $35 **MIP** $125

Snake Eyes, 1982, Hasbro, Commando, Model No. 6404
EX $45 **NM** $85 **MIP** $350

Stalker, 1982, Hasbro, Ranger, Model No. 6401
EX $25 **NM** $40 **MIP** $150

Zap, 1982, Hasbro, Bazooka Soldier, Model No. 6405
EX $20 **NM** $40 **MIP** $160

Uniform/Equipment Sets

F.L.A.K., 1982, Hasbro, Attack Cannon, Model No. 6075
EX $20 **NM** $45 **MIP** $75

H.A.L., 1982, Hasbro, Heavy Artillery Laser with Grand Slam, Model No. 6052
EX $30 **NM** $55 **MIP** $150

J.U.M.P., 1982, Hasbro, Jet Pack with Platform, Model No. 6071
EX $20 **NM** $45 **MIP** $80

M.M.S., 1982, Hasbro, Mobile Missile System with Hawk, Model No. 6054
EX $20 **NM** $45 **MIP** $125

Vehicle Sets

M.O.B.A.T., 1982, Hasbro, Motorized Battle Tank with Steeler, Model No. 6000
EX $40 **NM** $75 **MIP** $150

R.A.M., 1982, Hasbro, Rapid Fire Motorcycle, Model No. 6073
EX $15 **NM** $35 **MIP** $75

V.A.M.P., 1982, Hasbro, Multi-Purpose Attack Vehicle with Clutch, Model No. 6050
EX $30 **NM** $65 **MIP** $125

SERIES 02, COBRA Figure Sets

Cobra, 1983, Hasbro, Reissue, Model No. 6423
EX $25 **NM** $55 **MIP** $225

Cobra Commander, 1983, Hasbro, Reissue, Model No. 6425
EX $25 **NM** $50 **MIP** $300

Cobra Officer, 1983, Hasbro, Reissue, Model No. 6424
EX $25 **NM** $50 **MIP** $225

Destro, 1983, Hasbro, Enemy Weapons Supplier, Model No. 6427
EX $25 **NM** $50 **MIP** $175

Major Bludd, 1983, Hasbro, Model No. 6426
EX $20 **NM** $45 **MIP** $150

3-3/4" Figures

Uniform/Equipment Sets

S.N.A.K.E., 1983, Hasbro, One-Man Battle Armor (white), Model No. 6083
EX $10 **NM** $40 **MIP** $85

Vehicle Sets

Cobra Viper Glider, 1983, Hasbro, Attack Glider with Viper, Model No. 6097
EX $50 **NM** $125 **MIP** $225

F.A.N.G., 1983, Hasbro, Fully Armed Negator Gyro Copter, Model No. 6077
EX $18 **NM** $40 **MIP** $85

H.I.S.S., 1983, Hasbro, High Speed Sentry Tank with H.I.S.S., Model No. 6051
EX $35 **NM** $70 **MIP** $150

SERIES 02, GI JOE Figure Sets

Airborne, 1983, Hasbro, Helicopter Assault Trooper, Model No. 6411
EX $15 **NM** $35 **MIP** $125

Breaker, 1983, Hasbro, Reissue, Model No. 6403
EX $15 **NM** $30 **MIP** $100

Doc, 1983, Hasbro, Medic, Model No. 6415
EX $20 **NM** $40 **MIP** $125

Duke, 1983, Hasbro, mail order; Master Sergeant
EX $20 **NM** $55 **MIP** $100

Flash, 1983, Hasbro, Reissue, Model No. 6406
EX $20 **NM** $45 **MIP** $125

Grunt, 1983, Hasbro, Reissue, Model No. 6409
EX $20 **NM** $40 **MIP** $100

Gung-Ho, 1983, Hasbro, Marine, Model No. 6414
EX $20 **NM** $40 **MIP** $150

Rock 'n Roll, 1983, Hasbro, Reissue, Model No. 6408
EX $30 **NM** $55 **MIP** $150

Scarlett, 1983, Hasbro, Reissue, Model No. 6407
EX $40 **NM** $85 **MIP** $250

Short-Fuze, 1983, Hasbro, Reissue, Model No. 6402
EX $20 **NM** $45 **MIP** $125

Snake Eyes, 1983, Hasbro, Reissue, Model No. 6404
EX $40 **NM** $100 **MIP** $350

Snow Job, 1983, Hasbro, Arctic Trooper, Model No. 6412
EX $15 **NM** $40 **MIP** $125

Stalker, 1983, Hasbro, Reissue, Model No. 6401
EX $25 **NM** $45 **MIP** $150

Torpedo, 1983, Hasbro, Navy S.E.A.L., Model No. 6413
EX $25 **NM** $50 **MIP** $125

Tripwire, 1983, Hasbro, Mine Detector, Model No. 6410
EX $15 **NM** $40 **MIP** $110

Zap, 1983, Hasbro, Reissue, Model No. 6405
EX $25 **NM** $40 **MIP** $160

Uniform/Equipment Sets

Battle Gear Accessory Pack #1, 1983, Hasbro, Model No. 6088
EX $10 **NM** $20 **MIP** $35

Headquarters Command Center, 1983, Hasbro, Model No. 6020
EX $60 **NM** $95 **MIP** $185

Jump, 1983, Hasbro, Jet Pack and Platform with Grand Slam, Model No. 6065
EX $25 **NM** $50 **MIP** $115

Pac/Rats Flamethrower, 1983, Hasbro, Remote Control Weapon, Model No. 6086-1
EX $10 **NM** $22 **MIP** $35

Pac/Rats Machine Gun, 1983, Hasbro, Remote Control Weapon, Model No. 6086-2
EX $10 **NM** $22 **MIP** $35

Pac/Rats Missile Launcher, 1983, Hasbro, Remote Control Weapon, Model No. 6086-3
EX $10 **NM** $22 **MIP** $35

Whirlwind, 1983, Hasbro, Twin Battle Gun, Model No. 6074
EX $15 **NM** $35 **MIP** $60

Vehicle Sets

A.P.C., 1983, Hasbro, Amphibious Personnel Carrier, Model No. 6093
EX $25 **NM** $65 **MIP** $110

Dragon Fly XH-1, 1983, Hasbro, Assault Copter with Wild Bill, Model No. 4025
EX $25 **NM** $65 **MIP** $125

Falcon, 1983, Hasbro, Attack Glider with Grunt, Model No. 6097
EX $30 **NM** $75 **MIP** $150

Polar Battle Bear, 1983, Hasbro, Skimobile, Model No. 6072
EX $15 **NM** $30 **MIP** $60

Sky Striker XP-14F, 1983, Hasbro, F-14 Jet and Parachute with Ace, Model No. 6010
EX $35 **NM** $75 **MIP** $150

Wolverine, 1983, Hasbro, Armored Missile Vehicle with Cover Girl, 12 missiles, plastic tow cable, Model No. 6048
EX $25 **NM** $50 **MIP** $125

SERIES 03, COBRA Figure Sets

Baroness, 1984, Hasbro, Intelligence Officer, Model No. 6428
EX $50 **NM** $85 **MIP** $195

Cobra Commander, 1984, Hasbro, mail order; Enemy Leader with Hood, Model No. 6425
EX $10 **NM** $20 **MIP** $40

Firefly, 1984, Hasbro, Saboteur, Model No. 6432
EX $45 **NM** $85 **MIP** $225

Scrap Iron, 1984, Hasbro, Anti-Armor Specialist, Model No. 6431
EX $17 **NM** $35 **MIP** $85

Storm Shadow, 1984, Hasbro, Ninja, Model No. 6429
EX $40 **NM** $95 **MIP** $225

Uniform/Equipment Sets

A.S.P., 1984, Hasbro, Assault System Pod, Model No. 6070
EX $15 **NM** $30 **MIP** $45

C.L.A.W., 1984, Hasbro, Cobra Covert Light Aerial Weapons, Model No. 6081-1
EX $15 **NM** $30 **MIP** $45

Vehicle Sets

Rattler, 1984, Hasbro, Ground Attack Jet with Wild Weasel, Model No. 6027
EX $25 **NM** $65 **MIP** $120

Stinger, 1984, Hasbro, Night Attack Jeep with Cobra Officer, Model No. 6055
EX $20 **NM** $40 **MIP** $100

Swamp Skier, 1984, Hasbro, Chameleon Vehicle with Zartan, Model No. 6064
EX $55 **NM** $95 **MIP** $185

Water Moccasin, 1984, Hasbro, Swamp Boat with Copperhead, Model No. 6058
EX $35 **NM** $65 **MIP** $100

SERIES 03, GI JOE Figure Sets

Blow Torch, 1984, Hasbro, Flamethrower, Model No. 6421
EX $10 **NM** $20 **MIP** $75

Duke, 1984, Hasbro, First Sergeant, Model No. 6422
EX $20 **NM** $45 **MIP** $130

Mutt, 1984, Hasbro, Dog Handler with Dog, Model No. 6416
EX $15 **NM** $30 **MIP** $85

Recondo, 1984, Hasbro, Jungle Trooper, Model No. 6420
EX $15 **NM** $30 **MIP** $85

Rip Cord, 1984, Hasbro, H.A.L.O. Jumper, Model No. 6418
EX $15 **NM** $30 **MIP** $75

Roadblock, 1984, Hasbro, Heavy Machine Gunner, Model No. 6419
EX $25 **NM** $45 **MIP** $110

Spirit, 1984, Hasbro, Tracker with Eagle, Model No. 6417
EX $20 **NM** $45 **MIP** $110

Uniform/Equipment Sets

Battle Gear Accessory Pack #2, 1984, Hasbro, Model No. 6092
EX $10 **NM** $20 **MIP** $40

Bivouac, 1984, Hasbro, Battle Station, Model No. 6125-1
EX $10 NM $25 MIP $35

M.A.N.T.A., 1984, Hasbro, mail order; Marine Assault Nautical Air Driven Transport
EX $10 NM $20 MIP $35

Machine Gun Defense Unit, 1984, Hasbro, Battlefield Accessories, Model No. 6129-2
EX $10 NM $20 MIP $40

Missile Defense Unit, 1984, Hasbro, Battlefield Accessories, Model No. 6129-1
EX $10 NM $15 MIP $25

Mortar Defense Unit, 1984, Hasbro, Battlefield Accessories, Model No. 6129-3
EX $10 NM $15 MIP $25

Mountain Howitzer, 1984, Hasbro, Battle Station, Model No. 6125-3
EX $10 NM $15 MIP $25

Watchtower, 1984, Hasbro, Battle Station, Model No. 6125-2
EX $10 NM $15 MIP $30

Vehicle Sets

Killer W.H.A.L.E. Hovercraft, 1984, Hasbro, Armored Hovercraft with Cutter driver, Model No. 6005
EX $40 NM $75 MIP $140

RAM, HAL & VAMP, 1984, Hasbro, three-piece, die-cast set, Model No. 74450
EX $10 NM $20 MIP $40

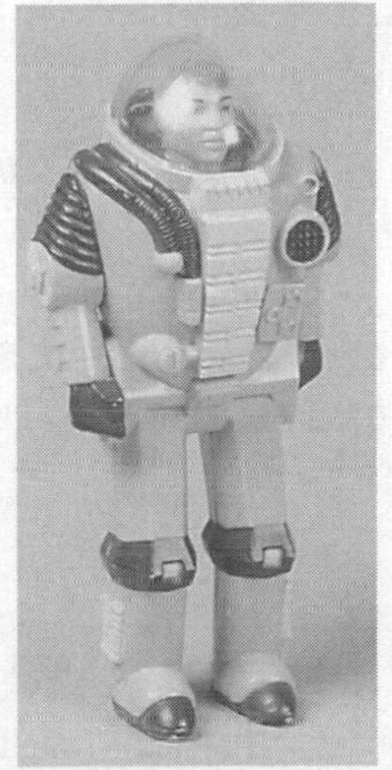

S.H.A.R.C., 1984, Hasbro, Submersible High-Speed Attack & Recon Craft with Deep Six figure (shown), Model No. 6049
EX $25 NM $55 MIP $110

Sky Hawk, 1984, Hasbro, V.T.O.L. Jet, Model No. 6079
EX $15 NM $30 MIP $50

Slugger, 1984, Hasbro, Self-Propelled Cannon with Thunder, Model No. 6056
EX $15 NM $35 MIP $70

V.A.M.P. and H.A.L., 1984, Hasbro, Sears exclusive, no figures, Model No. 7444-2
EX $10 NM $15 MIP $45

V.A.M.P. Mark II, 1984, Hasbro, w/Clutch (tan version) driver, Model No. 7444-1
EX $25 NM $45 MIP $100

SERIES 04, COBRA

Figure Sets

Buzzer, 1985, Hasbro, Dreadnok Mercenary, Model No. 6433
EX $15 NM $30 MIP $75

Crimson Guard, 1985, Hasbro, Elite Trooper, Model No. 6450
EX $25 NM $65 MIP $135

Eel, 1985, Hasbro, Frogman, Model No. 6448
EX $18 NM $35 MIP $75

Ripper, 1985, Hasbro, Mercenary, Model No. 6434
EX $15 NM $30 MIP $65

Snow Serpent, 1985, Hasbro, Polar Assault Trooper, Model No. 6449
EX $20 NM $40 MIP $75

Tele-Viper, 1985, Hasbro, Communications Trooper, Model No. 6447
EX $15 NM $30 MIP $65

Tomax and Xamot, 1985, Hasbro, Crimson Guard Commanders, two blasters, one pulley w/string, Model No. 6063
EX $45 NM $75 MIP $165

Torch, 1985, Hasbro, Mercenary, Model No. 6435
EX $15 NM $30 MIP $65

Uniform/Equipment Sets

Cobra Bunker, 1985, Hasbro, Battle Station, Model No. 6125
EX $5 NM $15 MIP $25

Cobra Rifle Range Unit, 1985, Hasbro, Battlefield Accessories, Model No. 6129
EX $5 NM $15 MIP $25

Flight Pod, 1985, Hasbro, Trouble-Bubble, One-Man Bubble Pod, Model No. 6081
EX $12 NM $25 MIP $50

Night Landing, 1985, Hasbro, small boat, 2 oars, 12mm submachine gun, knife, shovel, radio, .45-cal machine gun, engine, Model No. 6085
EX $5 NM $15 MIP $35

S.N.A.K.E., 1985, Hasbro, One-Man Armored Suit (dark blue), Model No. 6081-2
EX $10 NM $30 MIP $75

Vehicle Sets

C.A.T., 1985, Hasbro, Motorized Crimson Attack Tank, Sears exclusive
EX $40 NM $75 MIP $125

Ferret, 1985, Hasbro, All-Terrain Vehicle, Model No. 6069
EX $10 NM $20 MIP $45

Moray, 1985, Hasbro, Cobra Hydrofoil with Lamprey, Model No. 6024
EX $25 NM $50 MIP $95

Sentry and Missile System, S.M.S., 1985, Hasbro, Sears exclusive, with H.I.S.S. Tank, Model No. 6686
EX $75 NM $140 MIP $225

SERIES 04, GI JOE

Figure Sets

Airtight, 1985, Hasbro, Hostile Environment Trooper, Model No. 6439
EX $20 NM $40 MIP $60

Alpine, 1985, Hasbro, Mountain Trooper, Model No. 6443
EX $15 NM $25 MIP $60

Barbecue, 1985, Hasbro, Fire Fighter, Model No. 6445
EX $20 NM $35 MIP $80

Bazooka, 1985, Hasbro, Missile Specialist, Model No. 6438
EX $20 NM $40 MIP $75

Dusty, 1985, Hasbro, Desert Trooper, Model No. 6442
EX $15 NM $30 MIP $65

Flint, 1985, Hasbro, Warrant Officer, Model No. 6436
EX $22 NM $35 MIP $70

Footloose, 1985, Hasbro, Infantry Trooper, Model No. 6444
EX $15 NM $30 MIP $60

Lady Jaye, 1985, Hasbro, Covert Operations Officer, Model No. 6440
EX $30 NM $55 MIP $95

Quick Kick, 1985, Hasbro, Silent Weapons Martial Artist, Model No. 6441
EX $20 NM $40 MIP $85

Shipwreck, 1985, Hasbro, Sailor and Parrot, Model No. 6446
EX $22 NM $45 MIP $90

3-3/4" Figures

Snake Eyes, 1985, Hasbro, Commando and Wolf, Model No. 6437
EX $50 **NM** $100 **MIP** $265

Tripwire, 1985, Hasbro, Mine Detector, Model No. 6102
EX $20 **NM** $35 **MIP** $70

Uniform/Equipment Sets

Air Defense, 1985, Hasbro, Battle Station, Model No. 6125-2
EX $10 **NM** $15 **MIP** $25

Ammo Dump, 1985, Hasbro, Battlefield Accessories, Model No. 6129-1
EX $10 **NM** $15 **MIP** $25

Battle Gear Accessory Pack #3, 1985, Hasbro, Model No. 6092
EX $5 **NM** $10 **MIP** $20

Bomb Disposal, 1985, Hasbro, small vehicle, Model No. 6085-2
EX $10 **NM** $15 **MIP** $25

Check Point Alpha, 1985, Hasbro, Battle Station, Model No. 6125-1
EX $10 **NM** $15 **MIP** $30

Forward Observer Unit, 1985, Hasbro, Battlefield Accessories, Model No. 6129-2
EX $10 **NM** $15 **MIP** $25

Parachute Pack, 1985, Hasbro, mail order; HALO parachute pack with working parachute, available from 1985-89
EX $5 **NM** $10 **MIP** $25

Transportable Tactical Battle Platform, 1985, Hasbro, with crane, heli-pad, swivel guns and missile launcher, Model No. 6021
EX $25 **NM** $60 **MIP** $100

Weapon Transport, 1985, Hasbro, small vehicle, Model No. 6085-1
EX $10 **NM** $17 **MIP** $25

Vehicle Sets

A.W.E. Striker, 1985, Hasbro, All-Weather Environment Jeep with Crankcase driver, Model No. 6053
EX $25 **NM** $55 **MIP** $90

Armadillo Mini Tank, 1985, Hasbro, holds up to three figures, Model No. 6078
EX $15 **NM** $25 **MIP** $35

Bridge Layer Toss 'n Cross, 1985, Hasbro, Bridge Laying Trank with Toll Booth, Model No. 6023
EX $25 **NM** $55 **MIP** $100

Mauler M.B.T. Tank, 1985, Hasbro, Motorized Battle Tank w/ Heavy Metal driver, Model No. 6015
EX $50 **NM** $90 **MIP** $160

Silver Mirage, 1985, Hasbro, Motorcycle with Sidecar, Model No. 6076
EX $18 **NM** $30 **MIP** $50

Snow Cat, 1985, Hasbro, Snow Half-Track Vehicle with Frost-Bite, Model No. 6057
EX $25 **NM** $50 **MIP** $85

U.S.S. Flagg, 1985, Hasbro, Aircraft Carrier with Admiral Keel Haul, Model No. 6001
EX $200 **NM** $425 **MIP** $700

SERIES 05, COBRA

Figure Sets

B.A.T., 1986, Hasbro, Battle Android Trooper, Model No. 6456
EX $15 **NM** $30 **MIP** $65

Dr. Mindbender, 1986, Hasbro, Master of Mind Control, Model No. 6461
EX $10 **NM** $20 **MIP** $40

Monkeywrench, 1986, Hasbro, Mercenary, Model No. 6460
EX $10 **NM** $20 **MIP** $35

Viper, 1986, Hasbro, Infantry Trooper, Model No. 6473
EX $10 **NM** $25 **MIP** $50

Zandar, 1986, Hasbro, Zartan's Brother, Mercenary, Model No. 6457
EX $10 **NM** $20 **MIP** $35

Zarana, 1986, Hasbro, Zartan's Sister, Mercenary, without earrings, Model No. 6472
EX $10 **NM** $15 **MIP** $35

Zarana, 1986, Hasbro, Reissue with earrings, Model No. 6472
EX $30 **NM** $65 **MIP** $115

Uniform/Equipment Sets

Battle Gear Accessory Pack #4, 1986, Hasbro, Model No. 6096
EX $5 **NM** $10 **MIP** $20

Surveillance Port, 1986, Hasbro, Battle Station, Model No. 6130
EX $7 **NM** $14 **MIP** $25

Terrordrome, 1986, Hasbro, Armored Headquarters with Firebat Jet and A.V.A.C. pilot, Model No. 6003
EX $100 **NM** $195 **MIP** $325

Vehicle Sets

Air Chariot, 1986, Hasbro, w/ Serpentor "Cobra Emperor", Model No. 6062
EX $15 **NM** $25 **MIP** $60

Cobra Hydro Sled, 1986, Hasbro, small vehicle, Model No. 6099-2
EX $10 **NM** $15 **MIP** $25

Dreadnok Air Assault, 1986, Hasbro, Sears Exclusive, VTOL and Gyrocopter
EX $40 **NM** $80 **MIP** $110

Dreadnok Ground Assault, 1986, Hasbro, Sears Exclusive, motorcycle and 4WD vehicle
EX $40 **NM** $85 **MIP** $125

Dreadnok Swampfire, 1986, Hasbro, Air/Swamp Transforming Vehicle with Color-Change, Model No. 6068
EX $10 **NM** $20 **MIP** $30

Dreadnok Thunder Machine, 1986, Hasbro, Compilation vehicle of spare car and truck parts, designed by Destro, w/ Thrasher driver, Model No. 6042
EX $15 **NM** $30 **MIP** $45

Night Raven S-3P, 1986, Hasbro, Surveillance Jet with Drone Pod and Strato Viper pilot, Model No. 6014
EX $25 **NM** $45 **MIP** $85

Stun, 1986, Hasbro, Split Attack Vehicle with Motor Viper driver, Model No. 6041
EX $10 **NM** $25 **MIP** $55

SERIES 05, GI JOE

Figure Sets

Beach Head, 1986, Hasbro, Ranger, Model No. 6463
EX $15 **NM** $35 **MIP** $75

Dial-Tone, 1986, Hasbro, Communications Expert, Model No. 6471
EX $15 **NM** $25 **MIP** $50

Hawk, 1986, Hasbro, Commander, Model No. 6468
EX $15 **NM** $25 **MIP** $50

Iceberg, 1986, Hasbro, Snow Trooper, Model No. 6466
EX $15 **NM** $22 **MIP** $40

Leatherneck, 1986, Hasbro, Marine Gunner, Model No. 6458
EX $15 **NM** $25 **MIP** $50

Lifeline, 1986, Hasbro, Rescue Trooper, Model No. 6465
EX $15 **NM** $30 **MIP** $60

Low-Light, 1986, Hasbro, Night Spotter, Model No. 6459
EX $20 **NM** $40 **MIP** $75

Mainframe, 1986, Hasbro, Computer Specialist, Model No. 6462
EX $15 **NM** $25 **MIP** $50

Roadblock, 1986, Hasbro, Heavy Machine Gunner, Model No. 6467
EX $15 **NM** $25 **MIP** $50

Sci-Fi, 1986, Hasbro, Laser Trooper, Model No. 6469
EX $10 **NM** $20 **MIP** $45

Special Missions: Brazil, 1986, Hasbro, Toys R Us set with five figures: Dial-Tone, Mainframe, Wet-Suit, Leatherneck, and Claymore (this figure's only appearance)
EX $75 **NM** $150 **MIP** $300

The Fridge, 1986, Hasbro, Mail order, Physical Training Instructor
EX $10 **NM** $15 **MIP** $30

Wet-Suit, 1986, Hasbro, Navy S.E.A.L., Model No. 6470
EX $15 **NM** $30 **MIP** $60

Uniform/Equipment Sets

Outpost Defender, 1986, Hasbro, Battle Station, Model No. 6130
EX $7 **NM** $14 **MIP** $25

Vehicle Sets

Conquest X-30, 1986, Hasbro, Super-Sonic Jet with Slip-Stream pilot, Model No. 6031
EX $30 **NM** $65 **MIP** $115

Devilfish, 1986, Hasbro, High-Speed Attack Boat, Model No. 6066
EX $10 **NM** $20 **MIP** $30

G.I. JOE

H.A.V.O.C., 1986, Hasbro, Heavy Artillery Vehicle Ordinance Carrier with Cross-Country driver, Model No. 6030
EX $20 **NM** $40 **MIP** $75

L.V.C. Recon Sled, 1986, Hasbro, Low-Crawl Vehicle Cycle, Model No. 6067
EX $10 **NM** $15 **MIP** $25

Tomahawk, 1986, Hasbro, Troop Transit Helicopter with Lift-Ticket, Model No. 6022
EX $40 **NM** $80 **MIP** $120

(Karen O'Brien collection)

Triple T (Tag Team Terminator), 1986, Hasbro, One-man tank with Sgt. Slaughter driver, Model No. 6061
EX $10 **NM** $25 **MIP** $50

SERIES 06, COBRA Figure Sets

Big Boa, 1987, Hasbro, Troop Trainer, Model No. 6484
EX $8 **NM** $14 **MIP** $25

Cobra Commander, 1987, Hasbro, Cobra Leader with Battle Armor, Model No. 6474
EX $10 **NM** $15 **MIP** $35

Cobra-La Team, 1987, Hasbro, Three-figure set: Nemesis Enforcer, Royal Guard, Golobulus, Model No. 6154
EX $20 **NM** $40 **MIP** $75

Croc Master, 1987, Hasbro, Reptile Trainer, Model No. 6487
EX $10 **NM** $15 **MIP** $25

Crystal Ball, 1987, Hasbro, Hypnotist, Model No. 6479
EX $8 **NM** $14 **MIP** $20

Raptor, 1987, Hasbro, Falconer, Model No. 6485
EX $8 **NM** $14 **MIP** $20

Techno-Viper, 1987, Hasbro, Battlefield Technician, Model No. 6490
EX $8 **NM** $14 **MIP** $25

Uniform/Equipment Sets

Cobra Jet Pack, 1987, Hasbro, accessory for figures
EX $8 **NM** $14 **MIP** $20

Earth Borer, 1987, Hasbro, Motorized Action Packs, Model No. 6133-3
EX $8 **NM** $10 **MIP** $15

Mountain Climber, 1987, Hasbro, Motorized Action Packs, Model No. 6133-7
EX $8 **NM** $10 **MIP** $15

Pom-Pom Gun Pack, 1987, Hasbro, Motorized Action Packs, Model No. 6133-8
EX $8 **NM** $10 **MIP** $15

Rope Crosser, 1987, Hasbro, Motorized Action Packs, Model No. 6133-5
EX $8 **NM** $10 **MIP** $15

Vehicle Sets

Buzz Boar, 1987, Hasbro, Underground Attack Vehicle, Model No. 6087-3
EX $8 **NM** $14 **MIP** $25

Dreadnok Air Skiff, 1987, Hasbro, Mini-set with Zanzibar, Model No. 6070
EX $10 **NM** $20 **MIP** $30

Dreadnok Cycle, 1987, Hasbro, Compilation Cycle with Gunner Station, Model No. 6171
EX $8 **NM** $14 **MIP** $25

Maggot, 1987, Hasbro, three-in-one tank vehicle with W.O.R.M.S. driver, Model No. 6029
EX $15 **NM** $30 **MIP** $65

Mamba, 1987, Hasbro, Attack Copter with removable pods with Gyro-Viper, Model No. 6026
EX $15 **NM** $30 **MIP** $65

Pogo, 1987, Hasbro, Ballistic Battle Ball, Model No. 6170
EX $10 **NM** $20 **MIP** $30

Sea Ray, 1987, Hasbro, Combination Submarine/Jet with Sea Slug, Model No. 6040
EX $15 **NM** $30 **MIP** $55

Wolf, 1987, Hasbro, Arctic Terrain Vehicle with Ice Viper, Model No. 6039
EX $15 **NM** $30 **MIP** $65

SERIES 06, GI JOE Figure Sets

Battleforce 2000 Avalanche, 1987, Hasbro, Dominator Snow Vehicle Driver
EX $10 **NM** $20 **MIP** $30

Battleforce 2000 Blaster, 1987, Hasbro, Vindicator Hovercraft pilot
EX $10 **NM** $20 **MIP** $30

Battleforce 2000 Blocker, 1987, Hasbro, 4-wheeled driver
EX $10 **NM** $20 **MIP** $30

Battleforce 2000 Dodger, 1987, Hasbro, Marauder Half-Track driver
EX $10 **NM** $20 **MIP** $30

Battleforce 2000 Knockdown, 1987, Hasbro, Sky Sweeper Anti-Aircraft operator
EX $10 **NM** $20 **MIP** $30

Battleforce 2000 Maverick, 1987, Hasbro, Jet Fighter Pilot
EX $10 **NM** $20 **MIP** $30

Chuckles, 1987, Hasbro, Undercover M.P., Model No. 6482
EX $10 **NM** $20 **MIP** $30

Crazy Legs, 1987, Hasbro, Air Assault Trooper, Model No. 6475
EX $10 **NM** $17 **MIP** $30

Falcon, 1987, Hasbro, Green Beret, Model No. 6476
EX $10 **NM** $25 **MIP** $50

Fast Draw, 1987, Hasbro, Mobile Missile Specialist, Model No. 6488
EX $10 **NM** $17 **MIP** $30

Gung-Ho, 1987, Hasbro, Marine in Dress Blues, Model No. 6486
EX $10 **NM** $20 **MIP** $30

Jinx, 1987, Hasbro, Ninja Intelligence Officer, Model No. 6480
EX $10 **NM** $22 **MIP** $45

Law & Order, 1987, Hasbro, M.P. with Dog, Model No. 6478
EX $10 **NM** $22 **MIP** $45

Outback, 1987, Hasbro, Survivalist, Model No. 6483
EX $10 **NM** $25 **MIP** $50

Psyche-Out, 1987, Hasbro, Deceptive Warfare Trooper, Model No. 6477
EX $10 **NM** $15 **MIP** $25

Sgt. Slaughter's Renegades, 1987, Hasbro, Three-figure set: Red Dog, Mercer, Taurus, Model No. 6153
EX $20 **NM** $40 **MIP** $65

Sneak Peek, 1987, Hasbro, Advanced Recon Trooper, Model No. 6491
EX $10 **NM** $15 **MIP** $28

Starduster, 1987, Hasbro, Jet Pack Trooper, mail-in figure through 1991
EX $10 **NM** $25 **MIP** $50

Steel Brigade, 1987, Hasbro, Special Forces trooper, mail-in figure through 1994, five versions were produced
EX $10 **NM** $25 **MIP** $40

Tunnel Rat, 1987, Hasbro, Underground Explosive Expert, Model No. 6481
EX $10 **NM** $25 **MIP** $45

Uniform/Equipment Sets

Battle Gear Accessory Pack #5, 1987, Hasbro, Model No. 6677
EX $5 **NM** $10 **MIP** $15

Mobile Command Center, 1987, Hasbro, w/ Steam-Roller driver, large crane play set, Model No. 6006
EX $30 **NM** $60 **MIP** $110

Vehicle Gear Accessory Pack #1, 1987, Hasbro, Model No. 6098
EX $5 **NM** $10 **MIP** $15

Vehicle Sets

Anti-Aircraft Gun, 1987, Hasbro, Motorized Action Pack, Model No. 6133-1
EX $5 **NM** $10 **MIP** $15

Coastal Defender, 1987, Hasbro, Mini-Vehicle with accessories, Model No. 6087-2
EX $7 **NM** $13 **MIP** $20

Crossfire-Alfa, 1987, Hasbro, Radio Control Vehicle with Rumbler, Model No. 6004-1
EX $25 **NM** $60 **MIP** $100

Crossfire-Delta, 1987, Hasbro, Radio Control Vehicle with Rumbler, Model No. 6004-2
EX $25 **NM** $60 **MIP** $100

Defiant Space Shuttle Complex, 1987, Hasbro, Space shuttle, space station, crawler, Model No. 6002
EX $100 **NM** $350 **MIP** $600

Dominator Snow Tank, 1988, Hasbro, Battleforce 2000
EX $10 **NM** $14 **MIP** $25

Eliminator 4WD, 1988, Hasbro, Battleforce 2000
EX $10 NM $14 MIP $25

Helicopter, 1987, Hasbro, Motorized Action Pack, Model No. 6133-2
EX $5 NM $10 MIP $15

Marauder Motorcycle-Tank, 1988, Hasbro, Battleforce 2000
EX $10 NM $14 MIP $25

Persuader, 1987, Hasbro, Laser Tank with Backstop, Model No. 6038
EX $10 NM $20 MIP $35

Radar Station, 1987, Hasbro, Motorized Action Pack, Model No. 6133-3
EX $5 NM $10 MIP $15

Road Toad, 1987, Hasbro, Tow Vehicle with accessories, Model No. 6087-1
EX $10 NM $15 MIP $25

Rope Walker, 1987, Hasbro, Motorized Action Pack, Model No. 6133-4
EX $5 NM $10 MIP $15

S.L.A.M., 1987, Hasbro, Strategic Long-Range Artillery Machine, Model No. 6172
EX $10 NM $20 MIP $30

Sky Sweeper Anti-Aircraft Tank, 1988, Hasbro, Battleforce 2000
EX $7 NM $14 MIP $25

Vector Jet, 1988, Hasbro, Battleforce 2000
EX $7 NM $14 MIP $25

Vindicator Hovercraft, 1988, Hasbro, Battleforce 2000
EX $7 NM $14 MIP $25

SERIES 07, COBRA

Figure Sets

Astro-Viper, 1988, Hasbro, Cobranaut
EX $10 NM $20 MIP $30

Hydro-Viper, 1988, Hasbro, Underwater Elite Trooper
EX $10 NM $20 MIP $30

Iron Grenadier, 1988, Hasbro, Destro's Elite Troops
EX $7 NM $14 MIP $25

Road Pig, 1988, Hasbro, Dreadnok
EX $7 NM $14 MIP $25

Toxo-Viper, 1988, Hasbro, Hostile Environment
EX $7 NM $14 MIP $25

Voltar, 1988, Hasbro, Destro's General
EX $5 NM $12 MIP $20

Uniform/Equipment Sets

Battle Gear Accessory Pack #6, 1988, Hasbro
EX $5 NM $10 MIP $15

Dreadnok Battle Axe, 1988, Hasbro, Motorized Action Packs
EX $4 NM $8 MIP $12

Machine Gun Nest, 1988, Hasbro, Motorized Action Packs
EX $4 NM $8 MIP $12

Twin Missile Launcher, 1988, Hasbro, Motorized Action Packs
EX $4 NM $8 MIP $12

Vehicle Sets

Cobra Adder, 1988, Hasbro, Twin Missile Launcher
EX $5 NM $12 MIP $20

Cobra B.U.G.G, 1988, Hasbro, w/ Secto-Viper driver
EX $30 NM $70 MIP $110

Cobra Battle Barge, 1988, Hasbro, clear labels on retail version, white labels on mail-away version
EX $5 NM $12 MIP $20

Cobra IMP, 1988, Hasbro, w/3 two-part missiles & 24 mines (8 mines per missile)
EX $5 NM $12 MIP $20

Cobra Stellar Stiletto, 1988, Hasbro, w/ Star-Viper
EX $20 NM $40 MIP $65

Gyrocoptor, 1988, Hasbro, Motorized Vehicle Packs
EX $4 NM $8 MIP $12

Iron Grenadiers A.G.P. (Anti-Gravity Pods), 1988, Hasbro, w/ Nullifier pilot
EX $10 NM $20 MIP $30

Iron Grenadiers D.E.M.O.N., 1988, Hasbro, w/ Ferret the driver
EX $15 NM $30 MIP $45

Iron Grenadiers Destro's Despoiler, 1988, Hasbro, w/ Destro, gold helmet, black outfit, gold sword
EX $15 NM $25 MIP $40

Rocket Sled, 1988, Hasbro, Motorized Vehicle Packs
EX $4 NM $8 MIP $12

SERIES 07, GI JOE

Figure Sets

Blizzard, 1988, Hasbro, Artic Attack
EX $7 NM $14 MIP $25

Budo, 1988, Hasbro, Samuri Warrior
EX $7 NM $14 MIP $25

Charbroil, 1988, Hasbro, Flamethrower
EX $7 NM $14 MIP $25

Hardball, 1988, Hasbro, Multi-Shot Grenadier
EX $7 NM $14 MIP $25

Hit & Run, 1988, Hasbro, Light Infantryman
EX $7 NM $14 MIP $25

Lightfoot, 1988, Hasbro, Explosives Expert
EX $7 NM $14 MIP $25

Muskrat, 1988, Hasbro, Swamp Fighter
EX $7 NM $14 MIP $25

Night Force (Toys R Us exclusive), 1988, Hasbro, 2-figure pack: Psyche-Out and Tunnel Rat
EX $30 NM $55 MIP $90

Night Force (Toys R Us exclusive), 1988, Hasbro, 2-figure pack: Outback and Crazylegs
EX $30 NM $55 MIP $90

Night Force (Toys R Us exclusive), 1988, Hasbro, 2-figure pack: Lt. Falcon and Sneak Peek
EX $30 NM $55 MIP $90

Repeater, 1988, Hasbro, Stedi-Cam Machine Gunner
EX $7 NM $14 MIP $25

Shockwave, 1988, Hasbro, S.W.A.T.
EX $7 NM $14 MIP $25

Spearhead & Max, 1988, Hasbro, Point Man & Bobcat
EX $7 NM $14 MIP $25

Storm Shadow, 1988, Hasbro, Ninja
EX $20 NM $40 MIP $75

Super Trooper, 1988, Hasbro, mail-in
EX $10 NM $20 MIP $30

Tiger Force Bazooka, 1988, Hasbro, Missile Specialist
EX $15 NM $25 MIP $45

Tiger Force Duke, 1988, Hasbro, First Sergeant
EX $15 NM $25 MIP $45

Tiger Force Dusty, 1988, Hasbro, Desert Trooper
EX $15 NM $25 MIP $45

Tiger Force Flint, 1988, Hasbro, Warrant Officer
EX $15 NM $25 MIP $45

Tiger Force Lifeline, 1988, Hasbro, Medic
EX $15 NM $25 MIP $45

Tiger Force Roadblock, 1988, Hasbro, Heavy Machine Gunner
EX $15 NM $25 MIP $45

Tiger Force Tripwire, 1988, Hasbro, Mine Detector
EX $15 NM $25 MIP $45

Uniform/Equipment Sets

Double Machine Gun, 1988, Hasbro, Motorized Action Packs
EX $4 NM $8 MIP $12

Mine Sweeper, 1988, Hasbro, Motorized Action Packs
EX $4 NM $8 MIP $12

Mortar Launcher, 1988, Hasbro, Motorized Action Packs
EX $4 NM $8 MIP $12

Vehicle Sets

A.T.V., 1988, Hasbro, Motorized Vehicle Packs
EX $4 NM $8 MIP $12

Desert Fox 6-Wheel Drive, 1988, Hasbro, w/ Skidmark driver
EX $15 NM $30 MIP $50

Mean Dog, 1988, Hasbro, w/ Wildcard driver
EX $20 NM $40 MIP $60

Night Blaster, 1988, Hasbro, Night Force, based on 1987 Cobra Maggot
EX $30 NM $60 MIP $90

Night Raider, 1988, Hasbro, Night Force, based on 1986 Triple T
EX $15 NM $30 MIP $45

Night Shade, 1988, Hasbro, Night Force, based on 1983 S.H.A.R.C.
EX $15 NM $30 MIP $45

Night Storm, 1988, Hasbro, Night Force, based on 1987 Persuader
EX $15 NM $35 MIP $60

Night Striker, 1988, Hasbro, Night Force, based on 1984 W.H.A.L.E.
EX $50 NM $125 MIP $200

Phantom X-19 Stealth Fighter, 1988, Hasbro, w/ Ghostrider pilot
EX $30 NM $60 MIP $100

R.P.V., 1988, Hasbro, Remot Piloted Vehicle
EX $7 **NM** $14 **MIP** $25

Rolling Thunder, 1988, Hasbro, w/ Armadillo driver
EX $35 **NM** $75 **MIP** $115

Scuba Pack, 1988, Hasbro, Motorized Vehicle Packs
EX $4 **NM** $8 **MIP** $12

Skystorm X-Wing Chopper, 1988, Hasbro, w/ Windmill pilot
EX $15 **NM** $30 **MIP** $45

Swampmasher, 1988, Hasbro
EX $5 **NM** $12 **MIP** $20

Tank Car, 1988, Hasbro, Motorized Vehicle Packs
EX $5 **NM** $10 **MIP** $15

Tiger Cat, 1988, Hasbro, Tiger Force snow vehicle w/ Frostbite driver
EX $15 **NM** $30 **MIP** $55

Tiger Fly, 1988, Hasbro, Tiger Force Helicopter w/ Recondo
EX $35 **NM** $65 **MIP** $95

Tiger Paw, 1988, Hasbro, Tiger Force 4WD vehicle
EX $10 **NM** $18 **MIP** $30

Tiger Rat, 1988, Hasbro, Tiger Force Airplane w/ Skystriker pilot
EX $40 **NM** $75 **MIP** $110

Tiger Shark, 1988, Hasbro, Tiger Force (Water Mocassin) boat
EX $10 **NM** $18 **MIP** $30

Warthog A.I.F.V, 1988, Hasbro, Amphibious Infantry Fighting Vehicle w/ Sgt. Slaughter driver
EX $15 **NM** $30 **MIP** $50

SERIES 08, COBRA
Figure Sets

Alley Viper, 1989, Hasbro, Cobra Urban Assault
EX $7 **NM** $14 **MIP** $25

Frag-Viper, 1989, Hasbro, Cobra Grenade Thrower
EX $7 **NM** $14 **MIP** $25

Gnawgahyde, 1989, Hasbro, Dreadnok Poacher
EX $5 **NM** $12 **MIP** $20

H.E.A.T. Viper, 1989, Hasbro, Cobra Bazooka Man
EX $5 **NM** $12 **MIP** $20

Iron Grenadiers Annihilator, 1989, Hasbro, Destro's Elite Trooper
EX $5 **NM** $12 **MIP** $20

Iron Grenadiers T.A.R.G.A.T., 1989, Hasbro, Trans Atmospheric Rapid Global Assault Trooper
EX $5 **NM** $12 **MIP** $20

Night-Viper, 1989, Hasbro, Night Fighter
EX $7 **NM** $14 **MIP** $25

Python Patrol Copperhead, 1989, Hasbro, Swamp Fighter
EX $10 **NM** $18 **MIP** $25

Python Patrol Crimson Guard, 1989, Hasbro, Elite Trooper
EX $10 **NM** $18 **MIP** $25

Python Patrol Officer, 1989, Hasbro
EX $12 **NM** $20 **MIP** $30

Python Patrol Tele-Viper, 1989, Hasbro, Communications
EX $10 **NM** $18 **MIP** $25

Python Patrol Trooper, 1989, Hasbro, Infantry
EX $10 **NM** $18 **MIP** $25

Python Patrol Viper, 1989, Hasbro, Assault Trooper
EX $12 **NM** $20 **MIP** $30

Vehicle Sets

Condor Z25, 1989, Hasbro, w/ Aero-Viper pilot
EX $20 **NM** $45 **MIP** $75

Devastator, 1989, Hasbro, Battlefield Robot
EX $5 **NM** $10 **MIP** $15

F.A.N.G. II, 1989, Hasbro
EX $10 **NM** $20 **MIP** $30

H.I.S.S. II, 1989, Hasbro, Cobra tank w/ Track Viper
EX $30 **NM** $60 **MIP** $85

Hovercraft, 1989, Hasbro, Battlefield Robot
EX $5 **NM** $10 **MIP** $15

Iron Grenadiers Darklon's Evader, 1989, Hasbro, w/ Darklon
EX $10 **NM** $20 **MIP** $30

Iron Grenadiers Destro's Razorback, 1989, Hasbro, w/ Wild Boar
EX $15 **NM** $25 **MIP** $45

Python Patrol ASP, 1989, Hasbro, cannon
EX $10 **NM** $25 **MIP** $40

Python Patrol Conquest, 1989, Hasbro, plane
EX $15 **NM** $25 **MIP** $45

Python Patrol STUN, 1989, Hasbro, tri-wheel vehicle
EX $10 **NM** $20 **MIP** $35

SERIES 08, GI JOE
Figure Sets

Backblast, 1989, Hasbro, Anti-Aircraft Soldier
EX $5 **NM** $10 **MIP** $15

Battleforce 2000 Dee Jay, 1989, Hasbro, Comm-Tech Trooper
EX $5 **NM** $10 **MIP** $15

Countdown, 1989, Hasbro, Astronaut
EX $5 **NM** $12 **MIP** $20

Deep Six, 1989, Hasbro, Deep Sea Diver
EX $5 **NM** $12 **MIP** $20

Downtown, 1989, Hasbro, Mortar Man
EX $5 **NM** $12 **MIP** $20

Night Force (Toys R Us exclusive), 1989, Hasbro, 2-figure pack: Muskrat and Spearhead & Max
EX $30 **NM** $50 **MIP** $85

Night Force (Toys R Us exclusive), 1989, Hasbro, 2-figure pack: Charbroil and Repeater
EX $30 **NM** $50 **MIP** $85

Night Force (Toys R Us exclusive), 1989, Hasbro, 2-figure pack: Lightfoot and Shockwave
EX $30 **NM** $50 **MIP** $85

Recoil, 1989, Hasbro, Long Range Recon Patrol
EX $5 **NM** $10 **MIP** $15

Rock 'N Roll, 1989, Hasbro, Gatling Gunner
EX $5 **NM** $10 **MIP** $15

Scoop, 1989, Hasbro, Information Specialist
EX $5 **NM** $10 **MIP** $15

Slaughler's Marauders Barbecue, 1989, Hasbro, Firefighter
EX $7 **NM** $14 **MIP** $25

Slaughter's Marauders Footloose, 1989, Hasbro, Infantry Trooper
EX $7 **NM** $14 **MIP** $25

Slaughter's Marauders Low Light, 1989, Hasbro, Night Spotter
EX $7 **NM** $14 **MIP** $25

Slaughter's Marauders Mutt & Junkyard, 1989, Hasbro, Animal Control
EX $7 **NM** $14 **MIP** $25

Slaughter's Marauders Sgt. Slaughter, 1989, Hasbro, Commander
EX $7 **NM** $14 **MIP** $25

Slaughter's Marauders Spirit & Freedom, 1989, Hasbro, Tracker
EX $7 **NM** $14 **MIP** $25

Snake Eyes, 1989, Hasbro, Commando
EX $15 **NM** $30 **MIP** $50

Stalker, 1989, Hasbro, Tundra Ranger
EX $7 **NM** $14 **MIP** $25

Vehicle Sets

Battleforce 2000 Pulverizer, 1989, Hasbro, mini-tank
EX $5 **NM** $10 **MIP** $17

Crusader Space Shuttle, 1989, Hasbro, w/ Avenger aircraft and Payload the pilot
EX $40 **NM** $75 **MIP** $100

Mudfighter, 1989, Hasbro, w/ Dogfight driver
EX $10 **NM** $20 **MIP** $35

Night Boomer, 1989, Hasbro, Night Force, based on 1983 Skystriker
EX $75 **NM** $150 **MIP** $250

Night Ray, 1989, Hasbro, Night Force, based on 1985 Cobra Hydrofoil
EX $50 **NM** $125 **MIP** $200

Night Scrambler, 1989, Hasbro, Night Force, based on 1983 APC
EX $30 **NM** $60 **MIP** $100

Radar Rat, 1989, Hasbro, Battlefield Robot
EX $5 **NM** $10 **MIP** $15

Raider, 1989, Hasbro, w/ Hot Seat
EX $20 **NM** $40 **MIP** $60

Slaughter's Marauders Armadillo, 1989, Hasbro, tank w/ rocket launchers
EX $10 **NM** $20 **MIP** $30

Slaughter's Marauders Equalizer, 1989, Hasbro, tank w/ rocket launchers and two laser cannons
EX $10 **NM** $25 **MIP** $45

Slaughter's Marauders Lynx, 1989, Hasbro, tank w/ large cannon
EX $10 **NM** $20 **MIP** $35

Thunderclap, 1989, Hasbro, w/ Long Range driver
EX $40 **NM** $75 **MIP** $100

Tiger Fish, 1989, Hasbro, Tiger Force (Devil Fish) boat
EX $10 **NM** $20 **MIP** $30

Tiger Sting, 1989, Hasbro, Tiger Force (Vamp Mark II) jeep vehicle
EX $10 **NM** $20 **MIP** $30

Tri-Blaster, 1989, Hasbro, Battlefield Robot
EX $5 **NM** $10 **MIP** $15

SERIES 09, COBRA Figure Sets

Iron Grenadiers Metal-Head, 1990, Hasbro, Destro's Anti-Tank Specialist and one crazy guy!
EX $5 **NM** $11 **MIP** $18

Iron Grenadiers Undertow, 1990, Hasbro, Destro's Frogman
EX $7 **NM** $14 **MIP** $25

Laser-Viper, 1990, Hasbro, Laser Trooper
EX $7 **NM** $14 **MIP** $25

Night Creeper, 1990, Hasbro, Ninja
EX $10 **NM** $20 **MIP** $30

Range-Viper, 1990, Hasbro, Wilderness Trooper
EX $7 **NM** $14 **MIP** $25

Rock-Viper, 1990, Hasbro, Mountain Trooper
EX $7 **NM** $14 **MIP** $25

S.A.W.-Viper, 1990, Hasbro, Heavy Machine Gunner
EX $7 **NM** $14 **MIP** $25

Sonic Fighters Lampreys, 1990, Hasbro, Amphibious Assault
EX $7 **NM** $14 **MIP** $25

Sonic Fighters Viper, 1990, Hasbro, Infantry
EX $7 **NM** $14 **MIP** $25

Vehicle Sets

Cobra Piranha, 1990, Hasbro, Depth Charge Firing Sea Marauder
EX $7 **NM** $14 **MIP** $25

Cobra Rage, 1990, Hasbro
EX $12 **NM** $25 **MIP** $35

Hammerhead, 1990, Hasbro, Submersible Sea Tank, 6 vehicles in one, w/ Decimator driver
EX $15 **NM** $30 **MIP** $50

Hurricane VTOL, 1990, Hasbro, Vertical Take-off and Landing plane w/ Vapor pilot
EX $25 **NM** $50 **MIP** $80

Iron Grenadiers Destro's Dominator, 1990, Hasbro, Tank converts to helicopter
EX $15 **NM** $30 **MIP** $45

Overlord's Dictator, 1990, Hasbro, w/ Overlord driver
EX $10 **NM** $20 **MIP** $30

SERIES 09, GI JOE Figure Sets

Ambush, 1990, Hasbro, Concealment Specialist
EX $5 **NM** $10 **MIP** $15

Bullhorn, 1990, Hasbro, Intervention Specialist
EX $5 **NM** $10 **MIP** $15

Captain Grid Iron, 1990, Hasbro, Hand-to-Hand Combat
EX $5 **NM** $10 **MIP** $15

Freefall, 1990, Hasbro, Paratrooper
EX $5 **NM** $10 **MIP** $15

Pathfinder, 1990, Hasbro, Jungle Assault
EX $5 **NM** $10 **MIP** $15

Rampart, 1990, Hasbro, Shoreline Defender
EX $5 **NM** $10 **MIP** $15

Salvo, 1990, Hasbro, Anti-Armor Trooper
EX $5 **NM** $10 **MIP** $15

Sky Patrol Airborne, 1990, Hasbro, Parachute Assembler
EX $7 **NM** $14 **MIP** $25

Sky Patrol Airwave, 1990, Hasbro, Audible Frequency Specialist
EX $7 **NM** $14 **MIP** $25

Sky Patrol Altitude, 1990, Hasbro, Recon Scout
EX $7 **NM** $14 **MIP** $25

Sky Patrol Drop Zone, 1990, Hasbro, Weapons Specialist
EX $7 **NM** $14 **MIP** $25

Sky Patrol Sky Dive, 1990, Hasbro, Leader
EX $7 **NM** $14 **MIP** $25

Sky Patrol Static Line, 1990, Hasbro, Demolitions Expert
EX $7 **NM** $14 **MIP** $25

Sonic Fighters Dial-Tone, 1990, Hasbro, Communications w/ sonic backpack
EX $5 **NM** $12 **MIP** $20

Sonic Fighters Dodger, 1990, Hasbro, Heavy Ordinance Operator w/ sonic backpack
EX $5 **NM** $12 **MIP** $20

Sonic Fighters Law, 1990, Hasbro, M.P. w/ sonic backpack
EX $5 **NM** $12 **MIP** $20

Sonic Fighters Tunnel Rat, 1990, Hasbro, E.O.D. w/ sonic backpack
EX $5 **NM** $12 **MIP** $20

Stretcher, 1990, Hasbro, Medical Specialist
EX $5 **NM** $10 **MIP** $15

Sub-Zero, 1990, Hasbro, Winter Operations
EX $5 **NM** $10 **MIP** $15

Topside, 1990, Hasbro, Navy Assault Seaman
EX $5 **NM** $10 **MIP** $15

Vehicle Sets

Avalanche, 1990, Hasbro, w/ Cold Front driver
EX $10 **NM** $25 **MIP** $50

General, 1990, Hasbro, Mobile Strike Headquarters and Launch Pad w/ Major Storm driver
EX $20 **NM** $40 **MIP** $70

Hammer, 1990, Hasbro, High-Tech Attack Jeep
EX $10 **NM** $20 **MIP** $30

Locust, 1990, Hasbro, Bomb Dropping Assault Copter
EX $7 **NM** $14 **MIP** $25

Mobile Battle Bunker, 1990, Hasbro
EX $7 **NM** $14 **MIP** $25

Retaliator, 1990, Hasbro, Helicopter w/ Updraft the pilot
EX $15 **NM** $30 **MIP** $45

Sky Patrol Sky HAVOC, 1990, Hasbro, Heavy Armored Transport vehicle w/ hidden scout ship
EX $14 **NM** $28 **MIP** $45

Sky Patrol Sky Hawk, 1990, Hasbro, VTOL craft
EX $15 **NM** $25 **MIP** $40

Sky Patrol Sky Raven, 1990, Hasbro
EX $25 **NM** $55 **MIP** $80

Sky Patrol Sky SHARC, 1990, Hasbro
EX $15 **NM** $25 **MIP** $45

SERIES 10, COBRA Figure Sets

B.A.T., 1991, Hasbro, Battle Android Trooper
EX $7 **NM** $14 **MIP** $25

Cobra Commander w/ eyebrows, 1991, Hasbro, Leader
EX $20 **NM** $40 **MIP** $60

Cobra Commander w/out eyebrows, 1991, Hasbro, Leader
EX $7 **NM** $14 **MIP** $25

Crimson Guard Immortal, 1991, Hasbro, Elite Trooper
EX $20 **NM** $40 **MIP** $60

Desert Scorpion, 1991, Hasbro, Desert Fighter
EX $7 **NM** $14 **MIP** $25

Eco Warriors Cesspool, 1991, Hasbro, Chief Environmental Operative
EX $4 **NM** $8 **MIP** $12

Eco Warriors Sludge-Viper, 1991, Hasbro, Hazardous Waste
EX $4 **NM** $8 **MIP** $12

Eco Warriors Toxo-Viper, 1991, Hasbro, Hostile Environment
EX $4 **NM** $8 **MIP** $12

Incinerators, 1991, Hasbro, Flamethrowers
EX $5 **NM** $10 **MIP** $15

Snow Serpent, 1991, Hasbro, Snow Trooper
EX $5 **NM** $10 **MIP** $15

Super Sonic Fighters Major Bludd, 1991, Hasbro, Mercenary
EX $5 **NM** $10 **MIP** $15

Super Sonic Fighters Road Pig, 1991, Hasbro, Dreadnok
EX $5 **NM** $10 **MIP** $15

Talking Battle Commanders Cobra Commander, 1991, Hasbro, Cobra Leader
EX $5 NM $10 MIP $15

Talking Battle Commanders Overkill, 1991, Hasbro, B.A.T. Leader
EX $5 NM $10 MIP $15

Vehicle Sets

Air Commandos w/ Night Vulture, 1991, Hasbro, Air Recon Trooper
EX $10 NM $20 MIP $30

Air Commandos w/ Sky Creeper, 1991, Hasbro, Air Recon Leader
EX $10 NM $20 MIP $30

Battle Copter, 1991, Hasbro, w/ Interrogator pilot
EX $10 NM $15 MIP $25

Eco Warriors Septic Tank, 1991, Hasbro
EX $10 NM $15 MIP $25

Ice Sabre, 1991, Hasbro
EX $5 NM $12 MIP $20

Paralyzer, 1991, Hasbro
EX $5 NM $12 MIP $20

SERIES 10, GI JOE

Figure Sets

Big Ben, 1991, Hasbro, S.A.S
EX $5 NM $12 MIP $20

Dusty & Sandstorm, 1991, Hasbro, Desert Trooper
EX $5 NM $12 MIP $20

Eco Warriors Clean-Sweep, 1991, Hasbro, Anit-Tox Trooper
EX $4 NM $8 MIP $15

Eco Warriors Flint, 1991, Hasbro, Commander
EX $4 NM $8 MIP $15

Eco Warriors Ozone, 1991, Hasbro, Ozone Replenisher
EX $4 NM $8 MIP $15

General Hawk, 1991, Hasbro, Commander
EX $7 NM $14 MIP $20

Grunt, 1991, Hasbro, Infantry Squad Leader
EX $6 NM $12 MIP $18

Heavy Duty, 1991, Hasbro, Heavy Ordinance Trooper
EX $5 NM $10 MIP $16

Lifeline, 1991, Hasbro, Kellogg's mail in, no guns
EX $7 NM $14 MIP $25

Low-Light, 1991, Hasbro, Night Fighter
EX $6 NM $12 MIP $18

Mercer, 1991, Hasbro, Mercenary
EX $7 NM $14 MIP $20

Red Star, 1991, Hasbro, Oktober Guard
EX $7 NM $14 MIP $22

Sci-Fi, 1991, Hasbro, Directed Energy Expert
EX $6 NM $12 MIP $18

Snake Eyes, 1991, Hasbro, Commando
EX $7 NM $14 MIP $25

Super Sonic Fighters Lt. Falcon, 1991, Hasbro, Green Beret
EX $5 NM $12 MIP $20

Super Sonic Fighters Psyche-Out, 1991, Hasbro, Deceptive Warfare
EX $5 NM $12 MIP $20

Super Sonic Fighters Rock 'N Roll, 1991, Hasbro, Machine Gunner
EX $5 NM $12 MIP $20

Super Sonic Fighters Zap, 1991, Hasbro, Ground Artillery Soldier
EX $5 NM $12 MIP $20

Talking Battle Commanders General Hawk, 1991, Hasbro, Commander
EX $5 NM $12 MIP $20

Talking Battle Commanders Stalker, 1991, Hasbro, Ranger
EX $5 NM $12 MIP $20

Tracker, 1991, Hasbro, S.E.A.L.
EX $6 NM $12 MIP $20

Vehicle Sets

Air Commandos w/ Cloudburst, 1991, Hasbro, Glider Trooper
EX $10 NM $20 MIP $30

Air Commandos w/ Skymate, 1991, Hasbro, Glider Trooper, Australian S.A.S.
EX $10 NM $20 MIP $30

Attack Cruiser, 1991, Hasbro, Mobile Attack Vehicle w/ Flying Glider Bomb
EX $10 NM $15 MIP $24

Badger, 1991, Hasbro, Attack Jeep
EX $5 NM $12 MIP $20

Battle Copter, 1991, Hasbro, w/ Major Altitude pilot
EX $10 NM $15 MIP $25

Brawler, 1991, Hasbro
EX $10 NM $20 MIP $30

Motorized Battle Wagon, 1991, Hasbro
EX $10 NM $20 MIP $30

SERIES 11, COBRA

Figure Sets

Cobra Ninja Viper, 1992, Hasbro, mail-in
EX $10 NM $20 MIP $30

Destro, 1992, Hasbro, Weapons Supplier
EX $4 NM $8 MIP $12

Eel, 1992, Hasbro, Underwater Demolitions
EX $4 NM $8 MIP $12

Evil Headhunters Headman, 1992, Hasbro, Drug Kingpin
EX $4 NM $8 MIP $12

Evil Headhunters, Headhunters, 1992, Hasbro, Narcotics Guards
EX $4 NM $8 MIP $12

Firefly, 1992, Hasbro, Saboteur
EX $4 NM $8 MIP $12

Flak-Viper, 1992, Hasbro, Anti-Aircraft Trooper
EX $4 NM $8 MIP $12

Ninja Force Dice, 1992, Hasbro, Cobra Ninja Bo Staff
EX $5 NM $10 MIP $15

Ninja Force Slice, 1992, Hasbro, Cobra Ninja Swordsman
EX $5 NM $10 MIP $15

Toxo-Zombie, 1992, Hasbro, Toxic Disaster Trooper
EX $4 NM $8 MIP $12

Uniform/Equipment Sets

Eco Warriors Toxo-Lab, 1992, Hasbro, Play set for Eco Warriors
EX $10 NM $25 MIP $40

Vehicle Sets

Air Commandos w/ Cobra Air Devil, 1992, Hasbro, Aerobatic Arial Assault Trooper
EX $10 NM $20 MIP $30

Cobra Battle Copter, 1992, Hasbro, w/ Heli-Viper
EX $7 NM $13 MIP $20

Cobra Earthquake, 1992, Hasbro, Bulldozer
EX $10 NM $20 MIP $30

Cobra Liquidator A.T.F., 1992, Hasbro, Advanced Tactical Fighter
EX $7 NM $14 MIP $25

Cobra Parasite, 1992, Hasbro, Armored Personnel Carrier w/ Catapult launcher
EX $7 NM $14 MIP $25

Cobra Rat, 1992, Hasbro, High-Speed Attack Hovercraft
EX $7 NM $14 MIP $25

SERIES 11, GI JOE

Figure Sets

Barricade, 1992, Hasbro, Bunker Buster
EX $4 NM $8 MIP $12

Big Bear, 1992, Hasbro, Oktober Guard Anti-Armor Specialist
EX $4 NM $8 MIP $12

D.E.F. Bullet-Proof, 1992, Hasbro, Drug Elimination Force Leader
EX $4 NM $8 MIP $12

D.E.F. Cutter, 1992, Hasbro, Vehicle Operations Specialist
EX $4 NM $8 MIP $12

D.E.F. Mutt & Junkyard, 1992, Hasbro, K-9
EX $4 NM $8 MIP $12

D.E.F. Shockwave, 1992, Hasbro, S.W.A.T.
EX $4 NM $8 MIP $12

Duke, 1992, Hasbro, Master Sergeant
EX $4 NM $8 MIP $12

Eco-Warriors Barbecue, 1992, Hasbro, Firefighter
EX $4 NM $8 MIP $12

Eco-Warriors Deep Six, 1992, Hasbro, Deep Water Specialist
EX $4 NM $8 MIP $12

General Flagg, 1992, Hasbro, General
EX $4 NM $8 MIP $12

Gung-Ho, 1992, Hasbro, Marine
EX $3 NM $6 MIP $10

Ninja Force Dojo, 1992, Hasbro, Silent Weapons
EX $7 NM $14 MIP $25

Ninja Force Nunchuk, 1992, Hasbro, Nunchaku Ninja
EX $7 NM $14 MIP $25

3-3/4" Figures

Ninja Force Storm Shadow, 1992, Hasbro, Leader
EX $7 NM $14 MIP $25

Ninja Force T'Jbang, 1992, Hasbro, Ninja Swordsman
EX $7 NM $14 MIP $25

Roadblock, 1992, Hasbro, Heavy Machine Gunner, recalled by Hasbro
EX $15 NM $30 MIP $45

Wet-Suit, 1992, Hasbro, S.E.A.L.
EX $4 NM $8 MIP $12

Wild Bill, 1992, Hasbro, Air Cavalry Scout
EX $4 NM $8 MIP $12

Uniform/Equipment Sets

G.I. Joe Headquarters, 1992, Hasbro, Play set w/ electronic battle sounds
EX $20 NM $40 MIP $65

Vehicle Sets

AH-74 Desert Apache, 1992, Hasbro, Sonic Fighters
EX $15 NM $30 MIP $45

Air Commandos w/ Spirit, 1992, Hasbro, Air Commandos Leader
EX $7 NM $14 MIP $25

Barracuda, 1992, Hasbro, One-Man Attack Sub w/ Real Diving Action
EX $5 NM $10 MIP $15

Battle Copter, 1992, Hasbro, w/ Ace
EX $7 NM $13 MIP $20

Eco-Warriors Eco Striker, 1992, Hasbro, All-Terrain Environmental Assault Vehicle
EX $7 NM $14 MIP $25

Fort America, 1992, Hasbro, Sonic Fighters, Fortress turns into tank
EX $10 NM $20 MIP $30

Patriot, 1992, Hasbro, Armored Missile Launcher Transport
EX $7 NM $14 MIP $25

Storm Eagle A.T.F., 1992, Hasbro, Advanced Tactical Fighter
EX $7 NM $14 MIP $25

SERIES 12, COBRA Battle Corps Figure Sets

Alley Viper, #6, 1993, Hasbro, Urban Assault Trooper
EX $4 NM $8 MIP $12

Cobra Commander, #24, 1993, Hasbro, Supreme Leader
EX $5 NM $9 MIP $13

Cobra Eel, #27, 1993, Hasbro, Underwater Demolitions
EX $4 NM $8 MIP $12

Crimson Guard Commander, #23, 1993, Hasbro, Elite Trooper
EX $5 NM $9 MIP $13

Dr. Mindbender, #15, 1993, Hasbro, Master of Mind Control
EX $4 NM $8 MIP $12

Firefly, #18, 1993, Hasbro, Saboteur
EX $5 NM $9 MIP $13

Flak-Viper, #9, 1993, Hasbro, Anti-Aircraft Trooper
EX $5 NM $9 MIP $13

Gristle, #32, 1993, Hasbro, Urban Crime Commander
EX $5 NM $10 MIP $15

H.E.A.T. Viper, #5, 1993, Hasbro, Hi Explosive Anti-Tank Trooper
EX $5 NM $9 MIP $13

Headhunter Stormtrooper, #33, 1993, Hasbro, Elite Urban Crime Guard
EX $5 NM $9 MIP $13

Headhunters, #35, 1993, Hasbro, Cobra Street Troopers
EX $4 NM $8 MIP $12

Night Creeper Leader, #14, 1993, Hasbro, Ninja Supreme Master
EX $4 NM $8 MIP $12

Figure Sets

Ninja Force Night Creeper, 1993, Hasbro, Cobra Ninja
EX $4 NM $8 MIP $12

Ninja Force Slice, 1993, Hasbro, Cobra Ninja Swordsman
EX $4 NM $8 MIP $12

Ninja Force Zartan, 1993, Hasbro, Master of Disguise
EX $4 NM $8 MIP $15

Mail-In Figures

Name Your Own Cobra, 1993, Hasbro, "Create A Cobra" mail-away exclusive
EX $10 NM $20 MIP $30

Mega Marines/Mega Monsters

Bio-Viper, 1993, Hasbro, Genetically Enhanced Undersea Monster
EX $5 NM $10 MIP $15

Cyber-Viper, 1993, Hasbro, Cybernetic Officer
EX $5 NM $10 MIP $15

Mega-Viper, 1993, Hasbro, Mega-Monster Trainer
EX $5 NM $10 MIP $15

Monstro-Viper, 1993, Hasbro, Mega Monster
EX $5 NM $10 MIP $15

Star Brigade Figure Sets

Astro-Viper, #11, 1993, Hasbro, Cobranaut
EX $4 NM $8 MIP $12

B.A.A.T., #6, 1993, Hasbro, Battle Armored Android Trooper
EX $5 NM $10 MIP $15

Destro, #5, 1993, Hasbro, Cobra-Tech Commander
EX $4 NM $8 MIP $12

T.A.R.G.A.T., 1993, Hasbro, Trans Asmospheric Rapid Global Assault Trooper
EX $4 NM $8 MIP $12

Vehicle Sets

Battle Corps Cobra Detonator, 1993, Hasbro, w/ Nitro-Viper
EX $15 NM $25 MIP $40

Battle Corps Ice Snake, 1993, Hasbro
EX $5 NM $10 MIP $15

Ninja Force Battle Ax, 1993, Hasbro, w/ Red Ninja driver
EX $5 NM $10 MIP $15

Star Brigade Cobra Invader, 1993, Hasbro
EX $5 NM $10 MIP $15

SERIES 12, GI JOE Battle Corps Figure Sets

Backblast, #22, 1993, Hasbro, Anti-Aircraft Soldier
EX $5 NM $10 MIP $15

Barricade, #17, 1993, Hasbro, Bunker Buster
EX $5 NM $10 MIP $15

Bazooka, #1, 1993, Hasbro, Missile Specialist
EX $5 NM $10 MIP $15

Beach-Head, #4, 1993, Hasbro, Ranger
EX $5 NM $10 MIP $15

Bulletproof, #34, 1993, Hasbro, Urban Commander
EX $5 NM $10 MIP $15

Colonel Courage, #10, 1993, Hasbro, Strategic Commander
EX $5 NM $10 MIP $15

Cross-Country, #2, 1993, Hasbro, Transport Expert
EX $5 NM $10 MIP $15

Duke, #19, 1993, Hasbro, Battle Commander
EX $5 NM $10 MIP $15

Frostbite, #20, 1993, Hasbro, Arctic Commander
EX $5 NM $10 MIP $15

General Flagg, #26, 1993, Hasbro, General
EX $5 NM $10 MIP $15

Gung-Ho, #16, 1993, Hasbro, Marine
EX $5 NM $10 MIP $15

Iceberg, #3, 1993, Hasbro, Arctic Assault Trooper
EX $5 NM $10 MIP $15

Keel-Haul, #21, 1993, Hasbro, Admiral, most have large logo on back, small logo is rare
EX $5 NM $10 MIP $15

Law, #28, 1993, Hasbro, M.P.
EX $5 NM $10 MIP $15

Leatherneck, #11, 1993, Hasbro, Infantry Training Specialist
EX $5 NM $10 MIP $15

Long Arm, #31, 1993, Hasbro, Fire Strike Specialist
EX $5 NM $10 MIP $15

Mace, #29, 1993, Hasbro, Undercover Operative
EX $5 NM $10 MIP $15

Muskrat, #30, 1993, Hasbro, Heavy Fire Specialist
EX $5 NM $10 MIP $15

Mutt & Junkyard, #36, 1993, Hasbro, K-9
EX $5 NM $10 MIP $15

Outback, #13a, 1993, Hasbro, Survival Specialist, Eco Warriors version released as Battle Corps instead
EX $4 NM $8 MIP $12

Outback, #13b, 1993, Hasbro, Survival Specialist, tan pants, green shirt
EX $4 NM $8 MIP $12

Road Block, #7a, 1993, Hasbro, Heavy Machine Gunner, yellow shirt
EX $4 NM $8 MIP $12

Road Block, #7b, 1993, Hasbro, Heavy Machine Gunner, blue shirt
EX $4 NM $8 MIP $12

Snow Storm, #12a, 1993, Hasbro, High-Tech Snow Trooper, white body w/ orange accents
EX $4 NM $8 MIP $12

Snow Storm, #12b, 1993, Hasbro, High-Tech Snow Trooper, white body w/ blue accents
EX $4 NM $8 MIP $12

Wet-Suit, #8, 1993, Hasbro, S.E.A.L.
EX $5 NM $9 MIP $13

Wild Bill, #25, 1993, Hasbro, Aero Scout
EX $4 NM $8 MIP $12

Figure Sets

Ninja Force Banzai, 1993, Hasbro, Rising Sun Ninja
EX $4 NM $8 MIP $12

Ninja Force Bushido, 1993, Hasbro, Snow Ninja
EX $4 NM $8 MIP $12

Ninja Force Scarlett, 1993, Hasbro, Counter Intelligence
EX $7 NM $14 MIP $25

Ninja Force Snake Eyes, 1993, Hasbro, Covert Mission Specialist
EX $7 NM $14 MIP $25

Mail-In Figures

Arctic Commandos, 1993, Hasbro, 4-figure pack: Dee-Jay, Snow Serpent, Stalker, Sub-Zero
EX $10 NM $20 MIP $30

Copter Pilots, 1993, Hasbro, 2-figure pack: Interrogator and Major Altitude
EX $8 NM $13 MIP $20

Deep Six, 1993, Hasbro, Deep Sea Diver
EX $3 NM $5 MIP $8

General Hawk, 1993, Hasbro, Commander
EX $3 NM $5 MIP $8

International Action Force, 1993, Hasbro, 4-figure pack: Big Bear, Big Ben, Budo, and Spirit
EX $10 NM $20 MIP $30

Rapid Deployment Force, 1993, Hasbro, 3-figure pack: Fast Draw, Night Force Repeater, Night Force Shockwave
EX $12 NM $25 MIP $40

Mega Marines/Mega Monsters

Blast-Off, 1993, Hasbro, Flame Thrower
EX $4 NM $8 MIP $12

Clutch, 1993, Hasbro, Monster Blaster A.P.C.
EX $4 NM $8 MIP $12

Gung-Ho, 1993, Hasbro, Commander
EX $4 NM $8 MIP $12

Mirage, 1993, Hasbro, Bio-Artillery Expert
EX $4 NM $8 MIP $12

Star Brigade Figure Sets

Countdown, #8, 1993, Hasbro, Combat Astronaut
EX $4 NM $8 MIP $12

Duke, #2, 1993, Hasbro, Commander
EX $4 NM $8 MIP $12

Heavy Duty, #4, 1993, Hasbro, Heavy Ordinance Specialist
EX $4 NM $8 MIP $12

Ozone, #10a, 1993, Hasbro, Astro Infantry Trooper, tan suit
EX $4 NM $8 MIP $12

Ozone, #10b, 1993, Hasbro, Astro Infantry Trooper, gray suit
EX $4 NM $8 MIP $12

Payload, #7a, 1993, Hasbro, Astro Pilot, black suit, green and silver accents
EX $4 NM $8 MIP $12

Payload, #7b, 1993, Hasbro, Astro Pilot, black suit, blue and gold accents
EX $4 NM $8 MIP $12

Roadblock, #9, 1993, Hasbro, Space Gunner
EX $4 NM $8 MIP $12

Robo-JOE, #1, 1993, Hasbro, Jet Tech Ops Expert
EX $4 NM $8 MIP $12

Rock 'N Roll, #3, 1993, Hasbro, Robo-Gunner
EX $4 NM $8 MIP $12

Street Fighter Figure Sets

Balrog, #11, 1993, Hasbro, Heavyweight Boxer
EX $3 NM $5 MIP $8

Blanka, #5, 1993, Hasbro, Jungle Fighter
EX $3 NM $5 MIP $8

Chun-Li, #4, 1993, Hasbro, Kung-Fu Fighter
EX $3 NM $5 MIP $8

Dhalsim, #8, 1993, Hasbro, Yoga Fighter
EX $3 NM $5 MIP $8

Edmond Honda, #7, 1993, Hasbro, Sumo Wrestler
EX $3 NM $5 MIP $8

Guile, #3, 1993, Hasbro, Special Forces Fighter
EX $3 NM $5 MIP $8

Ken Masters, #2, 1993, Hasbro, Shotokan Karate Fighter
EX $3 NM $5 MIP $8

M. Bison, #6, 1993, Hasbro, Grand Master
EX $3 NM $5 MIP $8

Ryu, #1, 1993, Hasbro, Kung-Fu Fighter
EX $3 NM $5 MIP $8

Sagat, #12, 1993, Hasbro, Thai Fighter
EX $3 NM $5 MIP $8

Vega, #10, 1993, Hasbro, Spanish Ninja
EX $3 NM $5 MIP $8

Zangeif, #9, 1993, Hasbro, Russian Bear Wrestler
EX $3 NM $5 MIP $8

Street Fighters Vehicle Sets

Beast Blaster, 1993, Hasbro, w/ Blanka and Chun-Li
EX $5 NM $12 MIP $20

Crimson Cruiser, 1993, Hasbro, w/ M. Bison
EX $4 NM $8 MIP $12

Dragon Fortress, 1993, Hasbro, w/ Ken Masters and Ryu
EX $10 NM $20 MIP $30

Sonic Boom, 1993, Hasbro, w/ Guile
EX $4 NM $8 MIP $12

Vehicle Sets

Battle Corps Ghoststriker X-16, 1993, Hasbro, w/ Ace pilot
EX $15 NM $25 MIP $40

Battle Corps Mudbuster, 1993, Hasbro, All-terrain, 4x4 truck
EX $4 NM $8 MIP $12

Battle Corps Shark 9000, 1993, Hasbro, w/ Cutter driver
EX $10 NM $20 MIP $30

Dino-Hunter Mission Playset, 1993, Hasbro, w/ Low-Light and Ambush, Toys R Us exclusive
EX $20 NM $40 MIP $65

Mega Marines Monster Blaster, 1993, Hasbro, APC
EX $6 NM $12 MIP $20

Ninja Force Ninja Lightning, 1993, Hasbro, Fast Attack Ninja Cycle w/ Detachable Sidecar
EX $4 NM $8 MIP $12

Ninja Force Pile Driver, 1993, Hasbro, w/ T'Gin-Zu driver
EX $5 NM $10 MIP $15

Star Brigade Armor-Bot, 1993, Hasbro, w/ Armor-Tech General Hawk
EX $10 NM $20 MIP $30

Star Brigade Starfighter, 1993, Hasbro, w/ Sci-Fi
EX $5 NM $10 MIP $15

SERIES 13, COBRA

Battle Corps Figure Sets

Alley Viper, #7, 1994, Hasbro, Urban Assault Trooper
EX $5 NM $10 MIP $15

Major Bludd, #11, 1994, Hasbro, Mercenary
EX $5 NM $10 MIP $15

Metal-Head, #4, 1994, Hasbro, Anti-Tank Trooper
EX $5 NM $10 MIP $15

Night Creeper Leader, #13, 1994, Hasbro, Cobra Ninja Supreme Leader
EX $5 NM $10 MIP $15

Viper, #5, 1994, Hasbro, Cobra Infantry Trooper
EX $5 NM $10 MIP $15

Shadow Ninjas Figure Sets

Night Creeper, #42, 1994, Hasbro, Cobra Ninja
EX $5 NM $10 MIP $15

Slice, #40, 1994, Hasbro, Cobra Ninja Swordsman
EX $5 NM $10 MIP $15

3-3/4" Figures

Star Brigade Figure Sets

Carcass, #52, 1994, Hasbro, Alien Destroyer
EX $4 **NM** $8 **MIP** $12

Cobra Blackstar, #25, 1994, Hasbro, Cobra Elite Space Pilot
EX $4 **NM** $8 **MIP** $12

Cobra Commander, #24, 1994, Hasbro, Cobra Supreme Leader
EX $5 **NM** $10 **MIP** $15

Lobotomax, #50, 1994, Hasbro, Stellar Explorer
EX $4 **NM** $8 **MIP** $12

Predacon, #51, 1994, Hasbro, Alien Bounty Hunter
EX $4 **NM** $8 **MIP** $12

Vehicle Sets

Battle Corps Scorpion, 1994, Hasbro, 4WD vehicle
EX $5 **NM** $10 **MIP** $15

Star Brigade Cobra Power Fighter, 1994, Hasbro, w/ Techno-Viper driver
EX $7 **NM** $14 **MIP** $25

SERIES 13, GI JOE 30th Anniversary

Action Marine, 1994, Hasbro, #81047, Marine Corps Commando
EX $5 **NM** $10 **MIP** $15

Action Pilot, 1994, Hasbro, #81046, Air Force Fighter Pilot
EX $5 **NM** $10 **MIP** $15

Action Pilot Astronaut, 1994, Hasbro, Astronaut was available in the boxed gift set
EX $7 **NM** $13 **MIP** $20

Action Sailor, 1994, Hasbro, #81048, Navy Frogman
EX $5 **NM** $10 **MIP** $15

Action Soldier, 1994, Hasbro, #81045, U.S. Army Infantryman
EX $5 **NM** $10 **MIP** $15

Battle Corps Figure Sets

Beach-Head, #6, 1994, Hasbro, Ranger
EX $5 **NM** $10 **MIP** $15

Dial-Tone, #2, 1994, Hasbro, Communications Expert
EX $5 **NM** $10 **MIP** $15

Flint, #1, 1994, Hasbro, Desert Paratrooper
EX $5 **NM** $10 **MIP** $15

Ice Cream Soldier, #10, 1994, Hasbro, Flamethrower Commando
EX $6 **NM** $12 **MIP** $17

Lifeline, #8, 1994, Hasbro, Rescue Trooper
EX $5 **NM** $10 **MIP** $15

Shipwreck, #3, 1994, Hasbro, Navy S.E.A.L.
EX $5 **NM** $10 **MIP** $15

Snow Storm, #12, 1994, Hasbro, High Tech Snow Trooper
EX $5 **NM** $10 **MIP** $15

Stalker, #9, 1994, Hasbro, Ranger
EX $5 **NM** $10 **MIP** $15

Windchill, #62, 1994, Hasbro, Blockbuster Driver
EX $5 **NM** $10 **MIP** $15

Mail-In Figures

Lt. Joseph Colton, G.I. Joe, 1994, Hasbro
EX $7 **NM** $14 **MIP** $25

Shadow Ninjas Figure Sets

Bushido, #39, 1994, Hasbro, Shadow Ninja
EX $5 **NM** $10 **MIP** $15

Nunchuk, #41, 1994, Hasbro, Nunchuku Ninja
EX $5 **NM** $10 **MIP** $15

Snake Eyes, #37, 1994, Hasbro, Covert Mission Specialist
EX $7 **NM** $14 **MIP** $25

Storm Shadow, #38, 1994, Hasbro, Shadow Ninja Leader
EX $5 **NM** $10 **MIP** $15

Star Brigade Figure Sets

Countdown, #53, 1994, Hasbro, Combat Astronaut
EX $4 **NM** $8 **MIP** $12

Duke, #21, 1994, Hasbro, Star Brigade Commander
EX $5 **NM** $10 **MIP** $15

Effects, #49, 1994, Hasbro, Explosives Expert
EX $4 **NM** $8 **MIP** $12

Ozone, #54, 1994, Hasbro, Astro-Infantry Trooper
EX $4 **NM** $8 **MIP** $12

Payload, #26a, 1994, Hasbro, Astro Pilot, black suit, blue and gold accents
EX $4 **NM** $8 **MIP** $12

Payload, #26b, 1994, Hasbro, Astro Pilot, white suit, red and silver accents
EX $4 **NM** $8 **MIP** $12

Roadblock, #27, 1994, Hasbro, Space Gunner
EX $4 **NM** $8 **MIP** $12

Sci-Fi, #22, 1994, Hasbro, Star Brigade Pilot
EX $4 **NM** $8 **MIP** $12

Space Shot, #23, 1994, Hasbro, Combat Freighter Pilot
EX $4 **NM** $8 **MIP** $12

Vehicle Sets

Battle Corps Blockbuster, 1994, Hasbro, w/ Windmill driver
EX $7 **NM** $14 **MIP** $25

Battle Corps Manta Ray, 1994, Hasbro, wind up propeller
EX $5 **NM** $10 **MIP** $15

Battle Corps Razor-Blade, 1994, Hasbro, one-man copter
EX $5 **NM** $10 **MIP** $17

Star Brigade Power Fighter, 1994, Hasbro, w/ Gears driver
EX $5 **NM** $10 **MIP** $15

Collector Editions (1990s to Present)

12" HALL OF FAME Figure Sets

Ace, Fighter Pilot, 1993, Hasbro, Model No. 6837
EX $10 **NM** $15 **MIP** $25

Cobra Commander, Cobra Leader, 1992, Hasbro, Model No. 6827
EX $15 **NM** $20 **MIP** $35

Destro, Weapons Manufacturer, 1993, Hasbro, Model No. 6839
EX $10 **NM** $15 **MIP** $25

Duke, Combat Camo, 1994, Hasbro, Model No. 6044
EX $10 **NM** $12 **MIP** $15

Duke, Master Sergeant, 1991, Hasbro, Target exclusive, Model No. 6019
EX $15 **NM** $30 **MIP** $45

Duke, Master Sergeant, 1992, Hasbro, Model No. 6826
EX $15 **NM** $25 **MIP** $35

Flint, Green Beret, 1994, Hasbro, Model No. 6127
EX $10 **NM** $12 **MIP** $30

Grunt, Infantry Squad Leader, 1993, Hasbro, Model No. 6111
EX $10 **NM** $20 **MIP** $25

Gung-Ho, Dress Marine, 1993, Hasbro, Model No. 6849
EX $10 **NM** $20 **MIP** $25

Heavy Duty, Heavy Ordinance Specialist, 1993, Hasbro, Model No. 6114
EX $10 **NM** $20 **MIP** $35

Major Budd, Battle-Pack, 1994, Hasbro, Model No. 6159
EX $10 **NM** $15 **MIP** $30

Martial Arts Specialist, 1995, Hasbro, Kay Bee Exclusive
EX $10 **NM** $20 **MIP** $30

Rapid Fire, Commando, 1993, Hasbro, Model No. 6924
EX $20 **NM** $50 **MIP** $60

Red Beret Commando, 1995, Hasbro, Kay Bee Exclusive
EX $15 **NM** $30 **MIP** $45

Roadblock, Combat Camo, 1994, Hasbro, Model No. 6049
EX $10 **NM** $12 **MIP** $20

Rock n Roll, Gatlin' Blastin', 1994, Hasbro, Model No. 6128
EX $10 **NM** $25 **MIP** $30

Rock 'n Roll, Heavy Weapons Gunner, 1993, Hasbro, Model No. 6128
EX $10 **NM** $20 **MIP** $25

Snake Eyes, Commando, 1992, Hasbro, Model No. 6828
EX $15 **NM** $30 **MIP** $35

Snake-Eyes, Karate Choppin', 1994, Hasbro, Model No. 6089
EX $10 **NM** $25 **MIP** $30

Stalker, Ranger, 1992, Hasbro, Model No. 6829
EX $15 **NM** $30 **MIP** $35

Storm Shadow, Ninja, 1993, Hasbro, Model No. 6848
EX $10 **NM** $20 **MIP** $25

Surveillance Specialist, 1995, Hasbro, Kay Bee Exclusive
EX $10 **NM** $20 **MIP** $30

Talking Duke, Talking Battle Commander, 1993, Hasbro, Model No. 6117
EX $20 NM $40 MIP $60

Uniform/Equipment Sets

Air Force Flyer Gear, 1993, Hasbro
EX $4 NM $8 MIP $12

Arctic Assault Mission Gear, 1993, Hasbro
EX $4 NM $8 MIP $12

Army Boot Camp Gear, 1993, Hasbro
EX $4 NM $8 MIP $12

Backpack Missile Blaster, 1993, Hasbro
EX $3 NM $6 MIP $10

Cobra Helicopter Attack, 1993, Hasbro, Deluxe Mission Gear
EX $5 NM $10 MIP $15

Cobra Infantry Uniform, 1993, Hasbro, mail-in
EX $4 NM $8 MIP $12

Deep Water Salvage Mission Gear, 1995, Hasbro
EX $4 NM $8 MIP $12

Desert Camo Mission Gear, 1993, Hasbro
EX $4 NM $8 MIP $12

Footlocker, 1993, Hasbro, storage for Hall of Fame equipment
EX $4 NM $8 MIP $12

GI Joe Infantry Uniform, 1993, Hasbro, mail-in
EX $4 NM $8 MIP $12

Green Beret Weapons Arsenal, 1993, Hasbro
EX $4 NM $8 MIP $12

High Caliber Weapons Arsenal, 1994, Hasbro, weapons pack
EX $3 NM $6 MIP $10

Jungle Patrol Mission Gear, 1993, Hasbro
EX $4 NM $8 MIP $12

Light Infantry Mission Gear, 1993, Hasbro
EX $4 NM $8 MIP $12

Marine Paris Island Gear, 1993, Hasbro
EX $4 NM $8 MIP $12

Mobile Artillery Assault Set, 1993, Hasbro
EX $5 NM $10 MIP $15

Mountain Assault Mission Gear, 1993, Hasbro
EX $4 NM $8 MIP $12

Navy SEAL Commando, 1993, Hasbro, Deluxe Mission Gear
EX $5 NM $10 MIP $15

Navy Shore Patrol Gear, 1993, Hasbro
EX $4 NM $8 MIP $12

Ocean Enforcer Mission Gear, 1994, Hasbro
EX $4 NM $8 MIP $12

Red Beret Weapons Arsenal, 1993, Hasbro
EX $4 NM $8 MIP $12

Red Ninja Mission Gear, 1993, Hasbro
EX $4 NM $8 MIP $12

S.W.A.T. Assault Mission Gear, 1993, Hasbro
EX $4 NM $8 MIP $12

Smart Gun Blaster, 1993, Hasbro
EX $3 NM $6 MIP $10

Star Brigade Astronaut Mission Gear, 1994, Hasbro
EX $4 NM $8 MIP $12

Swamp Fighter Mission Gear, 1994, Hasbro
EX $4 NM $8 MIP $12

The Ultimate Arsenal, 1993, Hasbro, more than 25 pieces
EX $7 NM $14 MIP $20

Underwater Attack Mission Gear, 1993, Hasbro
EX $4 NM $8 MIP $12

Urban S.W.A.T., 1994, Hasbro, weapons pack
EX $3 NM $6 MIP $10

Vehicle

Jet Pack, 1994, Hasbro
EX $4 NM $8 MIP $12

Strike Cycle, 1994, Hasbro
EX $4 NM $8 MIP $12

Vehicles

Rhino G.P.V., 1993, Hasbro, General Purpose Vehicle, 4WD
EX $8 NM $16 MIP $24

30TH SALUTE SERIES

30th Salute Black Action Soldier, 1994, Hasbro, Model No. 81271
EX $55 NM $100 MIP $150

35th Anniversary Gift Set, 1999, Hasbro, Then and Now, 1964 figure, 1999 figure, set of two, 1999
EX $25 NM $50 MIP $75

Action Marine, 1994, Hasbro, Model No. 81047
EX $45 NM $60 MIP $80

Action Pilot, 1994, Hasbro, Model No. 81046
EX $50 NM $75 MIP $125

Action Sailor, 1994, Hasbro, Model No. 81048
EX $60 NM $80 MIP $100

Action Soldier, 1994, Hasbro, Model No. 81045
EX $25 NM $50 MIP $95

Green Beret Lt. Joseph Colton, 1994, Hasbro, mail order
EX $75 NM $125 MIP $175

ACTION ASSORTMENT

Adventures of G.I. Joe: Peril of the Raging River, 1999, Hasbro
EX $7 NM $12 MIP $25

Delta Force, 1999, Hasbro
EX $7 NM $12 MIP $25

Salute to the Millennium Marine, 1999, Hasbro
EX $7 NM $12 MIP $25

ALPHA ASSORTMENT

Battle of the Bulge, 2000, Hasbro
EX n/a NM n/a MIP n/a

Demolitions Expert, 2000, Hasbro
EX n/a NM n/a MIP n/a

Navy Seal, 2000, Hasbro
EX $7 NM $12 MIP $25

WWII Pacific Marine, 2000, Hasbro
EX n/a NM n/a MIP n/a

ARMED FORCES ASSORTMENT

Army National Guard, 1998, Hasbro
EX $10 NM $12 MIP $25

U.S. Air Force Crew Chief, 1998, Hasbro
EX $10 NM $12 MIP $25

U.S. Marine Corps Korean Soldier, 1998, Hasbro
EX $10 NM $12 MIP $25

U.S. Marine Corps Recruit, 1998, Hasbro
EX $10 NM $12 MIP $25

U.S. Navy Serviceman, 1998, Hasbro
EX $10 NM $12 MIP $25

ARMED FORCES SERVICE COLLECTION

Police Officer, 1999, Hasbro
EX $5 NM $8 MIP $25

U.S. Army Infantry Desert Soldier, 1999, Hasbro
EX $5 NM $8 MIP $25

U.S. Army Pacific Forces, 1999, Hasbro
EX $5 NM $8 MIP $25

U.S. Army Vietnam Soldiers, 1998, Hasbro
EX $5 NM $8 MIP $20

U.S. Navy SEAL, 1999, Hasbro
EX $5 NM $8 MIP $20

USAF Fighter Pilot: Korean War, 1999, Hasbro
EX $5 NM $8 MIP $20

Vietnam Marine, 1999, Hasbro
EX $5 NM $10 MIP $15

ASTRONAUT ASSORTMENT

(Hasbro Photo)

Mercury Astronaut, 1997, Hasbro, In spacesuit and helmet
EX $15 NM $12 MIP $25

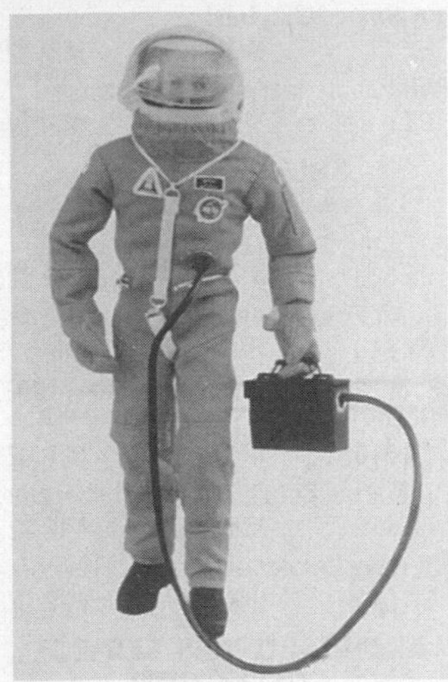
(Hasbro Photo)

Space Shuttle Astronaut, 1997, Hasbro, In orange spacesuit
EX $15 NM $12 MIP $25

BRAVO ASSORTMENT

Vietnam Combat Engineer, 2000, Hasbro
EX n/a NM n/a MIP n/a

Vietnam Jungle Recon Soldier, 2000, Hasbro
EX $5 NM $10 MIP $20

CORE FIGURE ASSORTMENT

Adventures of G.I. Joe: Save the Tiger, 1999, Hasbro
EX $5 NM $10 MIP $15

G.I. Joe: Challenge at Hawk River, 1999, Hasbro
EX $5 NM $10 MIP $15

U.S. Army Nurse: Vietnam, 1999, Hasbro
EX $5 NM $10 MIP $20

U.S. Coast Guard Boarding Party, 1999, Hasbro
EX $5 NM $10 MIP $20

DELTA ASSORTMENT

Navajo Code Talker, 2000, Hasbro
EX $7 NM $15 MIP $30

U.S. Marine Dog Unit, 2000, Hasbro
EX $7 NM $12 MIP $25

ECHO ASSORTMENT

John F. Kennedy, 2000, Hasbro
EX $8 NM $15 MIP $25

Vietnam Wall, 2000, Hasbro
EX n/a NM n/a MIP n/a

WWI Doughboy, 2000, Hasbro
EX $7 NM $12 MIP $20

WWII U.S. Army Airborne Normandy, 2000, Hasbro
EX $7 NM $15 MIP $30

FOREIGN ASSORTMENT

Japanese Zero Pilot, 2000, Hasbro
EX n/a NM n/a MIP n/a

Red Infantry Pilot, 2000, Hasbro
EX n/a NM n/a MIP n/a

FOURTH OF JULY EDITION

(Hasbro Photo)

D-Day Salute, 1997, Hasbro, With M-1 rifle, pack and camo-net helmet
EX $7 NM $12 MIP $20

GREATEST HEROES

Buzz Aldrin, 1999, Hasbro
EX $10 NM $20 MIP $40

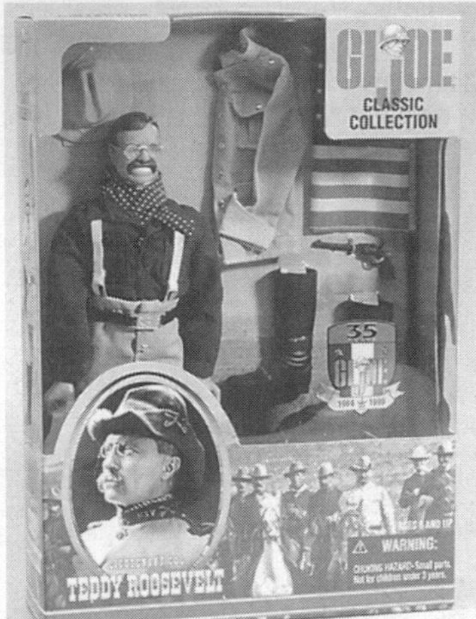

Lt. Colonel Theodore Roosevelt, 1999, Hasbro, In Spanish-American War uniform, dark blue shirt, tan coat and pants. Includes American flag, pistol and other accessories
EX $10 NM $20 MIP $30

Ted Williams, 1999, Hasbro
EX $10 NM $20 MIP $35

WWII Flame Thrower Soldier, 1999, Hasbro
EX $7 NM $12 MIP $25

HISTORICAL COMMANDERS ASSORTMENT

Colin Powell, 1998, Hasbro
EX $10 NM $20 MIP $45

Dwight Eisenhower, 1997, Hasbro
EX $7 NM $12 MIP $20

General Patton, 1997, Hasbro
EX $7 NM $12 MIP $20

Omar Bradley, 1998, Hasbro
EX $7 NM $12 MIP $20

HOLIDAY SALUTE

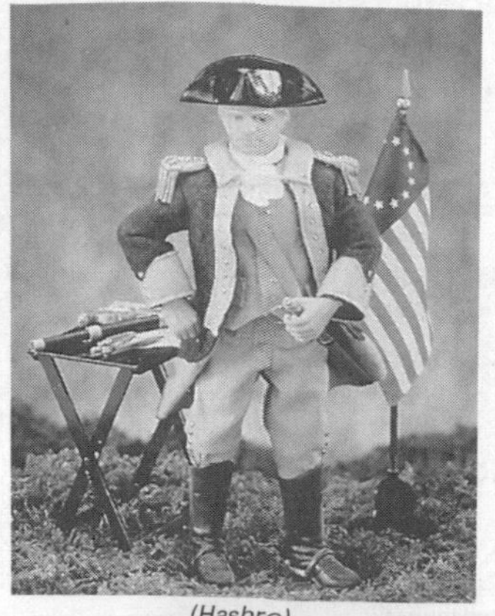
(Hasbro)

George Washington, 1998, Hasbro
EX $7 NM $12 MIP $20

HOLLYWOOD HEROES

Bob Hope, 1998, Hasbro
EX $15 NM $25 MIP $40

MILITARY SPORTS ASSORTMENT

Army Football, 1998, Hasbro
EX $5 NM $8 MIP $15

Navy Football, 1998, Hasbro
EX $5 NM $8 MIP $15

MODERN FORCES ASSORTMENT

82nd Airborne Division, female, 1998, Hasbro
EX $5 NM $8 MIP $15

Australian O.D.F., 1996, Hasbro
EX $5 NM $8 MIP $15

Battle of the Bulge, Toys R Us Exclusive, 1996, Hasbro
EX $8 NM $12 MIP $20

Belgium Para Commando, 1997, Hasbro
EX $8 NM $12 MIP $20

(Hasbro Photo)

British SAS, 1996, Hasbro, Limited edition, with rifle, helmet and goggles
EX $8 NM $15 MIP $25

Dress Marine, Toys R Us Exclusive, 1996, Hasbro
EX $8 NM $15 MIP $25

French Foreign Legion Legionnaire, 1997, Hasbro
EX $8 NM $12 MIP $20

U.S. Airborne Ranger HALO Parachutist, 1996, Hasbro
EX $7 NM $15 MIP $25

U.S. Army Coldweather Soldier, 1998, Hasbro
EX $8 NM $12 MIP $20

U.S. Army Drill Sergeant, 1997, Hasbro
EX $5 NM $10 MIP $15

U.S. Army Helicopter Pilot, female, 1997, Hasbro
EX $10 NM $20 MIP $30

(Hasbro Photo)

U.S. Army Infantry Soldier, 1996, Hasbro, Limited edition, with goggles, machine gun, and desert-pattern uniform
EX $8 NM $12 MIP $20

U.S. Army M-1 Tank Commander, 1997, Hasbro
EX $8 NM $12 MIP $20

U.S. Marine Corp Force Recon, 1998, Hasbro
EX $7 NM $10 MIP $15

(Hasbro Photo)

U.S. Marine Corps Sniper, 1996, Hasbro, Camouflaged rifle with scope, camo netting
EX $10 NM $20 MIP $40

U.S. Navy Blue Angel, 1998, Hasbro
EX $8 NM $12 MIP $20

U.S. Navy Flight Deck Fuel Handler, 1997, Hasbro
EX $7 NM $12 MIP $20

Pearl Harbor Collection

Army Defense Diorama Set, 2000, Hasbro
EX n/a NM n/a MIP n/a

Battleship Row Defender, 2000, Hasbro
EX n/a NM n/a MIP n/a

Diamond Head Lookout Invasion Alert, 2000, Hasbro
EX n/a NM n/a MIP n/a

Hickam Field Army Defender, 2000, Hasbro
EX n/a NM n/a MIP n/a

Vicker's Machine Gun, 2000, Hasbro
EX n/a NM n/a MIP n/a

Wheeler Field Army Air Corp, 2000, Hasbro
EX n/a NM n/a MIP n/a

WWII COMMEMORATIVE FIGURES, TARGET EXCLUSIVE

(Hasbro)

Action Marine, 1995, Hasbro, In camo uniform with cap, rifle, canteen, grenades and pack
EX $8 NM $15 MIP $25

(Hasbro)

Action Pilot, 1995, Hasbro, Khaki uniform, leather jacket and helmet, goggles, bayonet, .45 pistol, dog tags
EX $5 NM $10 MIP $15

(Hasbro)

Action Sailor, 1995, Hasbro, Blue uniform, Shore Patrol armband, M-1 rifle, duffle bag
EX $8 NM $15 MIP $20

Action Soldier, 1995, Hasbro
EX $8 NM $10 MIP $15

WWII FORCES ASSORTMENT

442nd Americans of Japanese Descent Combat Soldiers, 1998, Hasbro
EX $8 NM $15 MIP $25

Congressional Medal of Honor, Platoon Sgt. Mitchell Paige, 1998, Hasbro
EX $8 NM $12 MIP $20

Congressional Medal of Honor, Sgt. Francis S. Currey, 1997, Hasbro
EX $10 NM $20 MIP $40

Tuskegee B-25 Bomber Pilot, African American, 1997, Hasbro
EX $8 NM $10 MIP $15

Tuskegee Fighter Pilot, African American, 1997, Hasbro
EX $8 NM $10 MIP $15

U.S. Air Force B-17 Bomber Crewman, 1998, Hasbro
EX $8 NM $10 MIP $15

U.S. Navy PT-Boat Commander, 1998, Hasbro
EX $8 NM $10 MIP $20

Guns

by Karen O'Brien

I remember the toy guns I had as a kid. Considering the increasing popularity of toy guns at toy shows and auctions, it seems that plenty of other collectors have equally fond memories of backyard bad guys and the good guys who chased them. My plastic double holster rig came with six plastic, silver-colored bullets and six molded places just for them. Mom always made me take the bullets out of the holster when I played outside—didn't want to lose 'em after all. The silver twin cap pistols with white plastic handles never had caps in them, but they made a great sound when I pulled the triggers anyway. I bet you can describe your rig too.

The first cap gun patent dates back to 1860. Until World War II, the preferred material for cap guns was cast iron. Most early cap guns, exploders, and figural guns were made of cast iron, though variations of plastic, tin, and stamped metal also appear. Metal toy gun production ceased around 1940. The companies that survived after 1946 experimented with a variety of materials and methods of production, the most successful of which was die-casting. This involved injecting an alloy mixture into a mold, which resulted in fine detail, lower costs, and a much lighter gun.

Die-cast guns dominated the 1950s and '60s marketplace. Television brought little buckaroos daily installments of the thrilling adventures of cowboy heroes such as Roy Rogers, Gene Autry, and Hopalong Cassidy. Manufacturers such as the George Schmidt Company, Classy Products, Marx, Hubley, Nichols, Kilgore, and Wyandotte all scrambled to arm these cowpokes. The introduction of plastics changed the market as manufacturers lowered production costs.

While cap guns sold in the American market were largely produced by American manufacturers in both the prewar and postwar periods, other toy guns came from overseas producers. Tin lithography became an art form in postwar Japan. The same Japanese companies that produced the robots and tin cars so widely sought by today's collectors also produced space ray guns, cowboy, G-men, and military-style tin litho guns for the American market.

Collecting

Collectors of toy guns vary in scope and focus. While some prefer the guns of a favorite manufacturer, others collect those of a particular type. Space guns in particular, have gained in popularity the last few years.

Condition is a prime consideration. Mint guns in their mint packaging are worth more than well-loved guns that have exploded countless caps. It must be noted that the acidic nature of the paper used to make boxes for toy guns has damaged the pristine finish of many toy guns. Mattel's Fanner 50s have been prone to this problem.

Manufacturers often produced the same gun for several years with only minor changes, thus creating variations the collector should be aware of when valuing toy guns. Repaired or restored guns should always be represented as such to buyers.

THE ***TOP 10*** GUNS (In Mint Condition)

1. Hopalong Cassidy Double Holster Set, Wyandotte, 1940s $4,000
2. Man From U.N.C.L.E. THRUSH Rifle, Ideal, 1966 3,250
3. Hopalong Cassidy Holster/Gun Set, Schmidt, 1950s 3,000
4. Man From U.N.C.L.E. Attache Case, Ideal, 1965 1,650
5. Roy Rogers Double Gun & Holster Set, two 8-1/2" pistols, Classy, 1950s . . $1,600
6. Roy Rogers Double Holster Set, two 9" pistols, Classy, 1950s 1,550
7. Roy Rogers Double Holster Set, two 10" pistols, Classy, 1950s 1,500
8. Dale Evans D-26 cap pistol, Schmidt, 1950s 1,250
9. Maverick Two-Gun Holster Set, 1958 1,200
10. Popeye Pirate Click Pistol, tin litho, Marx, 1930s 1,000

Detective/Spy

Agent Zero M Pocket-Shot, 1965-66, Mattel, cap gun and "knife"
EX $15 **NM** $25 **MIP** $45

Agent Zero M Potshot, 1965, Mattel, 3" die-cast potshot derringer, gold finish, has brown vinyl armband holster holds two Shootin' Shell cartridges, gold buckle w/Agent Zero W logo
EX $40 **NM** $85 **MIP** $125

Agent Zero M Radio Rifle, 1964, Mattel, 8-1/2" closed, 22-1/2" open, looks like portable radio
EX $50 **NM** $100 **MIP** $150

Agent Zero M Snap-Shot Camera Pistol, 1964, Mattel, 7-1/2" extended, camera turns into pistol at press of a button
EX $35 **NM** $60 **MIP** $85

Detective Shell Firing Pistol, 1950s, Nichols, 5-1/2" snub-nose pistol chambers and fires six three-piece cap cartridges, cut-out badge, bullet cartridges, extra red plastic bullet heads
EX $100 **NM** $175 **MIP** $275

Dick Cap Pistol, 1930, Hubley, 4-1/8" cast iron automatic style, side loading, nickel finish, Dick oval in red paint
EX $75 **NM** $150 **MIP** $275

Dick Cap Pistol, 1950s, Hubley, die-cast, 4-1/4" automatic style, side loading w/nickel finish, Model 210A, eagles on grips
EX $25 **NM** $65 **MIP** $120

Dick Cap Pistol, 1950s, Benton Harbor Novelty, 4-3/4", automatic, side loading, black finish
EX $20 **NM** $40 **MIP** $85

Dragnet Badge 714 Detective Special Repeating Revolver, 1955, Knickerbocker, no. 639, plastic cap pistol, 6-3/4", black plastic w/gold "Dragnet" and "714" badge on grip
EX $45 **NM** $110 **MIP** $200

Dragnet Badge 714 Triple Fire Comb. Game, 1955, Knickerbocker, tin litho stand-up target has four plastic spinners, includes two 6" black plastic guns, one fires darts, the other cork gun, includes four plastic darts and three corks
EX $90 **NM** $150 **MIP** $275

Dragnet Snub Nose Cap Pistol, 1960s, Knickerbocker, plastic/die-cast works, 6-3/4", black plastic w/gold "Dragnet" and "714" badge on grip, on card
EX $45 **NM** $110 **MIP** $200

Dragnet Water Gun, 1960s, Knickerbocker, 6" black plastic, .38 Special-style w/gold "714" shield on grip
EX $25 **NM** $65 **MIP** $200

Girl From U.N.C.L.E. Garter Holster, 1966, Lone Star, "gang buster" metal gun fires plastic bullets from metal shells, checker design vinyl holster and bullet pouch, on card
EX $80 **NM** $145 **MIP** $225

G-Man Gun Wind-Up Machine Gun, 1948, Marx, 23" tin-litho, red, black, orange and gray litho, round drum magazine, wind-up mechanism makes sparks from muzzle, uses cigarette flint, wooden stock
EX $145 **NM** $285 **MIP** $450

Man From U.N.C.L.E. Attache Case, 1965, Ideal, 15" x 10" x 2-1/2", comes w/cap firing pistol and clip, ID card, wallet, cap grenade, badge, passport and secret message sender
EX $525 **NM** $1050 **MIP** $1650

Man From U.N.C.L.E. Attache Case, 1966, Lone Star, small cardboard briefcase, contains die-cast Mauser and parts to assemble U.N.C.L.E. Special
EX $140 **NM** $280 **MIP** $450

Man From U.N.C.L.E. Attache Case, 1966, Lone Star, vinyl covered cardboard, 9mm automatic Luger, shoulder stock, sight, silencer, belt, holster, secret wrist holster and pistol, grenade, wallet, passport, money
EX $300 **NM** $600 **MIP** $800

Man From U.N.C.L.E. Attache Case, 1966, Lone Star, vinyl case w/pistol, holster, walkie talkie, cigarette box gun, badge, passport, invisible cartridge pen, handcuffs
EX $265 **NM** $530 **MIP** $775

Man From U.N.C.L.E. Illya K. Special Lighter Gun, 1966, Ideal, cigarette lighter gun shoots caps, has radio compartment concealed behind fake cigs, in window box
EX $125 **NM** $225 **MIP** $350

Man From U.N.C.L.E. Illya Kuryakin Gun Set, 1966, Ideal, includes clip loading, cap firing plastic pistol, badge, wallet, ID card, in window box
EX $210 **NM** $420 **MIP** $650

Man From U.N.C.L.E. Napoleon Solo Gun Set, 1965, Ideal, clip loading, cap firing plastic pistol w/rifle attachments, badge, ID card, in window box
EX $280 **NM** $560 **MIP** $875

Man From U.N.C.L.E. Pistol and Holster, 1965, Ideal, 7" long pistol and plastic holster, both w/orange ID sticker
EX $45 **NM** $90 **MIP** $135

Man From U.N.C.L.E. Pistol Cane, 1966, Marx, 25" long, cap firing, bullet shooting aluminum cane w/eight bullets and one metal shell, on card
EX $175 **NM** $350 **MIP** $550

Man From U.N.C.L.E. Secret Service Pop Gun, 1960s, Unknown, bagged Luger pop gun on header card w/unlicensed art of Napoleon and Illya
EX $4 **NM** $12 **MIP** $30

Man From U.N.C.L.E. Stash Away Guns, 1966, Ideal, three cap firing guns, holsters, two straps, ID card and badge, in window box
EX $210 **NM** $420 **MIP** $650

Man From U.N.C.L.E. THRUSH Rifle, 1966, Ideal, 36" long
EX $875 **NM** $1750 **MIP** $3250

Official Detective Shootin' Shell Snub-Nose .38, 1959, Mattel, .38 die-cast chrome w/brown plastic grips, black vinyl shoulder holster, wallet, badge, ID card, Pistol Range Target and bullets
EX $95 **NM** $175 **MIP** $250

Official Detective Shootin' Shell Snub-Nose .38, 1960, Mattel, .38 die-cast 7" chrome finish, gold cylinder, brown plastic grips, Private Detective badge and Shootin' Shell bullets
EX $60 **NM** $100 **MIP** $165

Official Dick Tracy Shootin' Shell Snub-Nose .38, 1961, Mattel, die-cast chrome .38 w/brown plastic grips, chrome finish w/Shootin' Shell bullets and Stick-m caps
EX $75 **NM** $150 **MIP** $250

Sharkmatic Cap Gun, 1980s, Edison, 6" automatic, style pistol, fires "Supermatic System" strip caps
EX $10 **NM** $15 **MIP** $20

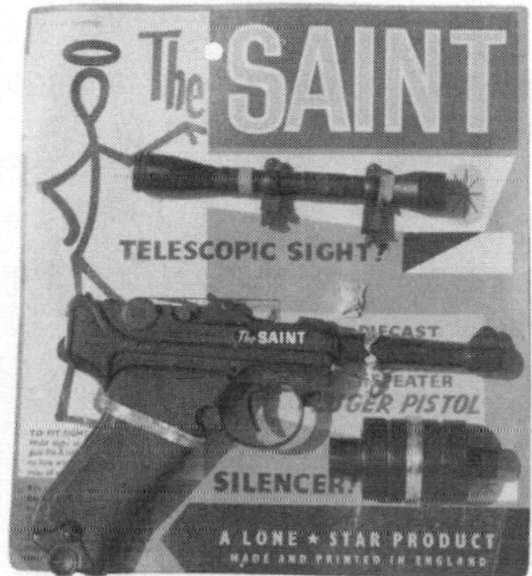

The Saint Ruger, 1960s, Lone Star, die-cast w/telescopic sight and silencer
EX $50 **NM** $100 **MIP** $150

Military/Automatics

7580 UZI Automatic, 1986, Esquire Novelty, 10-1/2", battery-operated, black plastic uses 250-shot roll caps, shoulder strap
EX $20 **NM** $45 **MIP** $60

9mm Z-Matic Uzi Cap Gun, 1984, Larami, 8" replica, removeable cap storage magazine, black finish, small orange plug in barrel
EX $5 **NM** $10 **MIP** $15

Anti Aircraft Gun, Marx, mechanical, sparks, tin litho, 16-1/2" long, 1941
EX $50 **NM** $135 **MIP** $275

Army .45 Cap Pistol, 1950s, Hubley, 6-1/2" automatic, dark gray finish, white plastic grips, pop-up cap
EX $50 **NM** $150 **MIP** $300

Army 45 Automatic, 1959, Nichols, 4-1/4" all metal, side loading automatic, olive
EX $15 **NM** $25 **MIP** $50

Army Automatic Pistol, 1950s, Marx, 2-1/2" automatic, (ACP style), black w/white grips, small leather holster w/flaps (Marx Miniature)
EX $10 **NM** $20 **MIP** $40

Army Pistol with Revolving Cylinder, Marx, tin litho
EX $35 **NM** $60 **MIP** $125

Army Sparking Pop Gun, Marx, 1940-50
EX $45 **NM** $75 **MIP** $150

Automatic Cap Pistol, 1925, National, 4-1/4" automatic style, grip swivels to load, black finish
EX $45 **NM** $100 **MIP** $200

Automatic Cap Pistol, 1950s, National, 6-1/2" silver finish w/simulated walnut grip
EX $35 **NM** $65 **MIP** $90

Automatic Cap Pistol No. 290, Hubley, die-cast, 6-1/2", nickel finish, brown checkered grips, magazine pops up when slider is pulled back
EX $85 **NM** $170 **MIP** $310

Burp Gun, 1960s, Marx, 20" battery-operated, green and black plastic
EX $20 **NM** $35 **MIP** $75

Desert Patrol Machine Pistol, Marx, plastic, 11" long
EX $30 **NM** $45 **MIP** $75

Falcon Service Automatic, 1950s, Kilgore, Colt .45 cap pistol
EX $8 **NM** $16 **MIP** $25

Green Beret Tommy Gun, 1960s, Marx, sparkles, trigger action, on card
EX $35 **NM** $55 **MIP** $95

Johnny Seven One Man Army-OMA, 1964, Topper/Deluxe, 36" multi-purpose seven guns in one, removeable pistol fires caps, rifle fires white plastic bullets, bolt spring fired machine gun "tommy gun" sound, rear launcher fires grenades, forward diff. shell
EX $125 **NM** $225 **MIP** $350

M-1 Kadet Training Rifle, 1960s, Parris, 32" wood/metal M-1 carbine, clicker action, metal barrel, trigger guard, bolt
EX $20 **NM** $35 **MIP** $50

Matic 45 Cap Gun, 1980s, Edison, 24", plastic gun w/stock, fires "Supermatic System" strip caps
EX $10 **NM** $15 **MIP** $20

Mattel-O-Matic Air Cooled Machine Gun, 1955, Mattel, 16" machine gun fires perforated roll caps by cranking handle, plastic w/die-cast, tripod-mounted, plastic/die-cast works, red and black plastic, box
EX $45 **NM** $85 **MIP** $125

Mini-M.A.G. Combat Gun, Marx, cap pistol, miniature scale, die-cast
EX $20 **NM** $30 **MIP** $40

MM Automatic Carbine, 1960s, Unknown, 24" recoil red slide in muzzle and flashing light, brown and black plastic
EX $15 **NM** $30 **MIP** $45

Model 12 SoftAir Gun, 1990, Daisy, machine gun style, loads "SoftAir" pellets in plastic cartridge, ten rounds, spring fired, can be cocked by barrel grip or bolt
EX $35 **NM** $50 **MIP** $75

Molotov Cocktail Tank Buster Cap Bomb, 1964, Maco, 6" plastic and die-cast, insert caps in head and throw
EX $10 **NM** $15 **MIP** $25

MP Holster Set, 1950s, Maco, plastic pistol has removeable magazine, loads and ejects bullets, white leather belt and holster
EX $65 **NM** $120 **MIP** $175

Mustang Toy Machine Gun, 1950s, Main Machine, 25" long chrome and hard plastic paper firing gun
EX $75 **NM** $125 **MIP** $175

Official James Bond 007 Thunderball Pistol, 1985, Coibel, 4-1/2" Walther PPK style, single shot fires plastic caps, Secret Agent ID
EX $15 **NM** $30 **MIP** $65

Paratrooper Carbine, 1950s, Maco, 24" carbine, removeable magazine, fires plastic bullets, bayonet and target
EX $75 **NM** $115 **MIP** $165

Revolver Mauser Cap Pistol, 1960s, Redondo, 6-1/4", Mauser style automatic pop-up magazine, silver finish, brown plastic grips
EX $4 **NM** $15 **MIP** $30

SA Automatic Burp Gun, 1970s, Daisy, 10" w/stock, black plastic, burp-gun style, removeable clip, loads and fires white plastic bullets
EX $20 **NM** $35 **MIP** $50

Siren Sparkling Airplane Pistol, Marx, heavy-gauge enamel steel, 9-1/2" wingspan, 7" long
EX $50 **NM** $75 **MIP** $100

Sparkling Siren Machine Gun, 1949, Marx, 26" long
EX $45 **NM** $90 **MIP** $175

Special Mission Tommy Gun, Marx
EX $20 **NM** $35 **MIP** $45

Spitfire Automatic Cap Pistol, 1940, Stevens, 4-5/8" cast iron, side loading, silver finish, "flying airplanes" white plastic grips
EX $65 **NM** $150 **MIP** $300

Spitfire Cap Firing Machine Gun, 1950, Buddy L, biped stand attached to muzzle, black plastic stock and grip w/cap or clicker firing
EX $80 **NM** $140 **MIP** $200

Tommy Burp Gun, 1957, Mattel, 17" plastic w/die-cast works, perforated roll caps fired by cranking the handle
EX $100 **NM** $200 **MIP** $350

Tommy Gun, 1939, Marx, sparks and makes noise
EX $65 **NM** $130 **MIP** $225

USA Machine Gun, 1950s, Maco, 12" tripod-mounted gun fires plastic bullets, red and yellow plastic
EX $65 **NM** $130 **MIP** $200

Wind-Up Burp Gun, 1955, Mattel, plastic/pressed steel, 24", "Grease Gun," fires perforated roll caps, fold-over wire stock, cap storage in magazine, boxed
EX $50 **NM** $90 **MIP** $150

Miscellaneous

25 Jr. Cap Pistol, 1930, Stevens, 4-1/8" automatic, side loading, silver finish
EX $25 **NM** $75 **MIP** $150

6 Shot Cap Pistol, Stevens, 6-3/4", six separate triggers revolve to deliver caps to hammer, metal finish
EX $85 **NM** $150 **MIP** $300

Airplane Clicker Pistol, 1950s, Palmer Plastics, 4-1/2" yellow and black plane, red pilot and guns
EX $25 **NM** $45 **MIP** $65

Atomee Water Pistol, 1960s, Park Plastics, 4-1/4" black plastic
EX $10 **NM** $20 **MIP** $35

Automatic Repeater Paper Pop Pistol, Marx, 7-3/4" long
EX $35 **NM** $65 **MIP** $125

Automatic Sparkling Pistol, 1960s, EMU Rififi, 6-1/2", plastic/metal, uses cigarette lighter flints to make sparks, available in green-red, yellow-green, red or white colors
EX $15 **NM** $30 **MIP** $45

Blastaway Cap Gun, Marx, 50 shooter repeater
EX $25 **NM** $35 **MIP** $75

Buzz Barton Special, No. 195, 1930s, Daisy, blue metal finish, wood stock w/ring sight
EX $85 **NM** $125 **MIP** $200

Click Pistol, Marx, pressed steel, 7-3/4" long
EX $20 **NM** $50 **MIP** $100

Click Pistol, Marx, tin litho
EX $20 **NM** $50 **MIP** $100

Clip 50 Cap Pistol, 1940, Kilgore, 4-1/4", unusual automatic style, black Bakelite plastic frame, removeable cap magazine clip
EX $75 **NM** $110 **MIP** $200

Crack Shot Dart Pistol, 1950s, Wyandotte, black plastic, shoots darts at target
EX $10 **NM** $25 **MIP** $45

Double Holster Set, 1950s, Unknown, black leather, large size, steer head conches, lots of red jewels, fringe, holsters only, no guns
EX $75 **NM** $125 **MIP** $250

Dynamic Automatic Repeating Bubble Gun, Atomic Industries, 8" black plastic pistol projects bubbles
EX $25 **NM** $40 **MIP** $65

Famous Firearms Deluxe Edition Collectors Album, 1959, Marx, set of four rifles, five pistols and four holsters miniature series, includes: Mare's Laig, Thompson machine gun, Sharps rifle, Winchester saddle rifle, Derringer, .38 snub-nose, Civil War pistol, six shooter/Flint
EX $50 **NM** $100 **MIP** $200

Hideaway Derringer, 1950s, Esquire Novelty, 3-1/2" single shot, loads solid metal bullet, grip is removeable to store two more bullets, gold finish, white plastic grips
EX $65 **NM** $90 **MIP** $110

Jack Armstrong Shooting Propeller Plane Gun, 1933, Daisy, 5-1/2" gun, shoots flying disk, pressed tin, in box
EX $100 **NM** $200 **MIP** $350

Johnny Tremain Flintlock Pistol, 1950s, Swansea Industries, cap gun based on Walt Disney character
EX $35 **NM** $70 **MIP** $110

Long Tom Dart Gun, 1950s, Midwest, 11" pressed steel
EX $35 **NM** $50 **MIP** $100

M240 Machine Pistol, 1970s, Marx, black plastic, no caps, pull trigger produces sound
EX $5 **NM** $12 **MIP** $20

Marx Miniatures Famous Gun Sets, 1958, Marx, set of four guns, features tommy gun, Civil War revolver, "Mare's Laig" and western saddle rifle
EX $25 **NM** $50 **MIP** $100

Marxman Target Pistol, Marx, plastic, 5-1/2" long
EX $35 **NM** $50 **MIP** $100

Midget Cap Pistol, 1950s, Hubley, 5-1/2" long, die-cast, all metal flintlock w/silver finish
EX $20 **NM** $35 **MIP** $50

Model 25-50, 1930, Stevens, 4-1/2" nickel finish
EX $35 **NM** $90 **MIP** $175

Model No. 25 Pump Action BB Gun, 1960s, Daisy, plastic stock
EX $35 **NM** $65 **MIP** $125

Mountie Automatic Cap Pistol, Kilgore, 6", double action, automatic style w/pop-up magazine, unusual nickel finish, black plastic grips
EX $20 **NM** $30 **MIP** $60

Nu-Matic Paper Popper Gun, 1940s, Langson, pressed steel, 7" squeeze grip trigger, mechanism pops roll of paper (reel at top of gun) to make loud noise, black finish
EX $30 **NM** $50 **MIP** $75

P-38 Clicker Pistol, 1950s, Meldon, 7-1/2" black finish, automatic style
EX $35 **NM** $50 **MIP** $100

Paper Cracker Rifle, 1940s, Buddy L, 26" steel and machined aluminum mechanism, barrel, trigger and operating lever, uses 1000 shot paper roll, brown plastic stock
EX $95 **NM** $190 **MIP** $250

Pirate Cap Pistol, 1940s, Hubley, 9-1/2" side-by-side flintlock style w/die-cast frame and cast double hammers and trigger, chrome finish, white plastic grips feature Pirate in red oval
EX $70 **NM** $250 **MIP** $500

Pluck Cap Pistol, 1930, Stevens, 3-1/2" cast iron, single shot single action
EX $30 **NM** $80 **MIP** $125

Popeye Pirate Click Pistol, Marx, tin litho, 10" long, 1930s, with box
EX $225 **NM** $600 **MIP** $1000

Potato Gun, 1991, Hong Kong, Spud Gun, plastic, pneumatic action fires potato pellet from muzzle
EX $3 **NM** $7 **MIP** $10

Presto Cap Pistol, 1940, Kilgore, 5-1/8", pop up cap magazine nickel finish brown plastic grips
EX $65 **NM** $120 **MIP** $225

Repeating Cap Pistol, Marx, aluminum
EX $20 **NM** $30 **MIP** $50

Revolver Aquila Pop Pistol, 1960s, Rosvi, 10" green finish, pop gun breaks to cock, fires cork from barrel, sparks from mechanism under barrel
EX $15 **NM** $30 **MIP** $60

Rex Automatic Cap Pistol, 1939, Kilgore, 3-7/8", blue metal finish cast iron, small size automatic style, side loading, white pearlized grips
EX $45 **NM** $100 **MIP** $200

Sparkling Machine Gun "Sure-Shot", 1950s, T. Cohn, tin litho in red, yellow and blue, turn handle and barrel sparks
EX $30 **NM** $60 **MIP** $110

Sparkling Pop Gun, Marx
EX $25 **NM** $50 **MIP** $100

Spud Gun, 1950s, Ambrit Industries, case aluminum, pneumatic all-metal gun shoots pellets
EX $15 **NM** $35 **MIP** $50

Spud Gun (Tira Papas), 1960s, Welco, 6" all-metal gun
EX $10 **NM** $20 **MIP** $35

Streamline Siren Sparkling Pistol, Marx, tin litho
EX $25 **NM** $50 **MIP** $100

Targeteer No. 18 Target Air Pistol, 1949, Daisy, 10" gun metal finish, push barrel to cock, Daisy BB tin w/special BBs, spinner target
EX $50 **NM** $90 **MIP** $135

Tiger Cap Pistol, 1935, Hubley, 6 7/8", single action, mammoth caps, metal finish
EX $35 **NM** $100 **MIP** $200

Trooper Cap Pistol, 1950, Hubley, 6-1/2" all metal, pop up cap magazine, nickel finish, black grips
EX $30 **NM** $85 **MIP** $175

Water Pistol No. 17, 1940, Daisy, 5-1/4" tin
EX $25 **NM** $50 **MIP** $75

Water Pistol No. 8, 1930s, Daisy, 5-1/4" tin
EX $30 **NM** $60 **MIP** $85

Winner Cap Pistol, 1940, Hubley, 4-3/8" automatic style, pop-up magazine release in front of trigger guard, nickel finish
EX $45 **NM** $100 **MIP** $200

Police

.38 Cap Pistol, Marx, w/caps, miniature scale, die-cast
EX $35 **NM** $75 **MIP** $125

Detective Snub-Nose Special, 1950s, Marx, die-cast, 5-3/4" top release break, unusual revolving cylinder, fires Kilgore style disc caps, chrome finish w/black plastic grips
EX $65 **NM** $100 **MIP** $150

Dick Tracy Click Pistol, Marx
EX $50 **NM** $125 **MIP** $200

Dick Tracy Jr. Click Pistol, 1930s, Marx, aluminum
EX $75 **NM** $150 **MIP** $275

Dick Tracy Siren Pistol, 1935, Marx, pressed steel, 8-1/2" long
EX $85 **NM** $150 **MIP** $350

Dick Tracy Sparkling Pop Pistol, Marx, tin litho
EX $50 **NM** $125 **MIP** $200

Gang Buster Crusade Against Crime Sub-Machine Gun, 1938, Marx, litho, metal w/wooden stock, 23" long
EX $110 **NM** $225 **MIP** $450

G-Boy Pistol, 1950s, Acme Novelty, 7" automatic (ACP) style entire left rear side of gun swings down to load
EX $15 **NM** $35 **MIP** $65

GUNS

G-Man Automatic Silent Arm Pistol, Marx, tin
EX $35 NM $55 MIP $100

G-Man Automatic Sparkling Pistol, 1930s, Marx, pressed steel, 4" long
EX $45 NM $85 MIP $175

G-Man Machine Gun, 1940s, Marx, tin miniature, wind-up, wood stock, red and yellow litho
EX $25 NM $35 MIP $65

G-Man Sparkling Sub-Machine Gun, Marx
EX $50 NM $75 MIP $150

G-Man Tommy Gun, 1936, Marx, sparkles when wound
EX $65 NM $110 MIP $225

Machine Gun Cap Pistol, 1938, Kilgore, 5-1/8", long cast iron crank-fired gun
EX $125 NM $225 MIP $350

Marx Miniatures Detective Set, 1950s, Marx, miniature cap firing brown and gray tommy gun, chrome pistol and holster on card w/wood grain frame border
EX $25 NM $45 MIP $75

Mountie Automatic Cap Pistol, 1960s, Hubley, die-cast, 7-1/4" automatic style, pop up lever-release magazine, blue finish
EX $20 NM $35 MIP $65

Official Dick Tracy Tommy Burst Machine Gun, 1960s, Mattel, 25" Thompson style machine gun fire perforated roll caps, single shot or in full burst when bolt is pulled back, brown plastic stock and black plastic body, lift up rear sight, Dick Tracy decal on stock
EX $130 NM $275 MIP $450

Peter Gunn Private Eye Revolver & Holster Set, 1959, Pilgrim Leather, 36" die-cast Remington w/six two-piece bullets, badge and wallet, Peter Gunn business cards, black leather shoulder holster
EX $200 NM $325 MIP $450

Sheriff Signal Pistol, 1950, Marx, plastic, 5-1/2" long
EX $20 NM $30 MIP $60

Siren Sparkling Pistol, Marx, tin litho
EX $20 NM $30 MIP $60

Sparkling "Sure-Shot" Machine Gun, 1950s, T. Cohn, long body tin multicolored red/yellow/blue tin noise making gun, great box graphics show boy shooting sparks as pigtailed blond girl looks
EX $50 NM $75 MIP $150

Western

2 Guns in 1 Cap Pistol, 1950s, Hubley, die-cast, 8" w/long barrel, twist-off barrels to change from long to short, side loading, white plastic grips
EX $75 NM $125 MIP $200

45 Smoker, 1950s, Product Engineering, 10" single cap, shoots talcum-like powder by use of bellows when trigger is pulled, aluminum finish
EX $50 NM $100 MIP $175

49er Cap Pistol, 1940, Stevens, cast iron, 9", unusual internal hammer w/revolving steel cylinder, nickel finish, white plastic figural grips
EX $125 NM $350 MIP $600

760 Rapid Fire Shotgun Air Rifle, 1960s, Daisy, 31" pump shotgun, gray metal one piece frame, brown plastic stock and slider grip, fires blast of air
EX $65 NM $95 MIP $150

Authentic Derringer, 1960, Esquire Novelty, die-cast, 2" cap firing, copper finish, twin swivel barrel
EX $15 NM $25 MIP $60

Authentic Derringer, 1960, Esquire Novelty, classic miniature Series #10, 2" cap firing, copper finish, twin swivel barrel
EX $15 NM $25 MIP $60

Big Horn Cap Pistol, 1950s, Kilgore, 7" all metal revolving cylinder, break-to-front, disk caps, silver finish
EX $100 NM $175 MIP $300

Billy The Kid Cap Pistol, Stevens, 8" long, cap pistol
EX $55 NM $110 MIP $225

Bobcat Saddle Gun, 1960s, USA, 5-1/2" black finish, imprinted w/"Official Wanted Dead or Alive" Mare's Laig logo, brown plastic stock, Model No. 57-G1025
EX $10 NM $25 MIP $50

Bonanza Guns Outfit, 1960s, Marx, 25" cap firing saddle rifle, magazine pulls down to load, 9-1/2" Western pistol fires two-piece Marx shooting bullets, wood plastic stocks and gun metal gray plastic body, tan vinyl holster
EX $75 NM $145 MIP $300

Bronco Cap Pistol, 1950s, Kilgore, 8-1/2", revolving swing-out cylinder fires Kilgore disc caps, silver finish, black plastic "Bronco" grips
EX $65 NM $125 MIP $250

Buck'n Bronc Marshal Cap Pistol, 1950s, Schmidt, 10" long barrel revolver style, lever release, break-to-front, plain silver finish, copper color metal grips
EX $125 NM $250 MIP $400

Buck'n Bronc Shoot'n Iron, 1950s, Schmidt, cap gun, 50-shot repeater
EX $100 NM $175 MIP $250

Buffalo, Marx, 50 shooter repeater
EX $70 NM $100 MIP $140

Buffalo Bill Cap Pistol, 1940, Stevens, 7-3/4", silver nickel finish, side loading magazine door, white "tenite" plastic horse and cowboy grips, red jewels
EX $65 NM $125 MIP $250

Cap Gun Store Display, 1950s, Nichols, 24" x 14" wood board, derringer and two strips of Nichols bullets
EX $300 NM $600 MIP $950

Centennial Rifle, Marx, w/big sound
EX $25 NM $35 MIP $65

Champion Quick Draw Timer Cap Pistol, 1959, Kilgore, silver finish, side loading, wind up mechanism in grip records elapsed time of draw, black plastic grips
EX $100 NM $200 MIP $375

Cheyenne Cap Pistol, 1974, Kilgore, 9-3/4" side loading, "Sure-K" plastic stag grips, silver finish
EX $10 NM $25 MIP $50

Cody Colt Paper Buster Gun, 1950s, Langson, 7-3/4", paper popper, nickel finish, white plastic steer grips fires Cody Colt ammunition
EX $40 NM $80 MIP $125

Colt .38 Detective Special, 1959, Hubley, 4-1/2" Colt .38 pistol single shot caps and loads six play bullets w/suspenders chest holster
EX $35 NM $75 MIP $150

Colt .45 Cap Pistol, 1959, Hubley, die-cast, 13", revolving cylinder produced w/open or closed chamber ends, loads six two-piece cap-firing bullets, white plastic grips, red felt box
EX $110 NM $225 MIP $425

Colt Cap Pistol, 1935, Stevens, 6-1/2", revolver-style double action
EX $20 NM $55 MIP $110

Cork-Shooting Rifle, Marx
EX $25 NM $40 MIP $60

Cowboy Cap Pistol, 1935, Stevens, 3-1/2" cast iron, single shot single action, sold loose
EX $20 NM $55 MIP $110

Cowboy Cap Pistol, 1940, Hubley, 8" friction break-to-front nickel finish cast iron, rose swirl plastic grips w/Colt logo
EX $110 NM $225 MIP $350

Cowboy Cap Pistol, 1950s, Hubley, die-cast, 12" swing out revolving cyclinder, release on barrel, nickel or aluminum finish, white plastic steer grips w/black steer head
EX $115 NM $235 MIP $375

Cowboy Cap Pistol, 1950s, Hubley, 12", die-cast, swing-out revolving cylinder, release on barrel, nickel finish, black plastic steer grips
EX $125 NM $250 MIP $400

Cowboy Jr. Cap Pistol No. 225, 1950s, Hubley, 9" die-cast, revolving cylinder, side loading, release on barrel, silver finish, white plastic cow grips, lanyard ring and cord
EX $65 NM $130 MIP $275

Cowboy King Cap Pistol, 1940, Stevens, 9" break-to-front release, gold finish cast iron, black plastic grips, yellow jewels
EX $110 NM $275 MIP $450

Dagger Derringer, 1958, Hubley, 7", unusual over and under pistol has hidden red plastic dagger that slides out from between barrels, rotating barrels load and fire two-piece bullets
EX $55 NM $100 MIP $145

Dale Evans D-26, 1950s, Schmidt, initials in butterfly symbol
EX $450 NM $900 MIP $1250

Dale Evans Holster Set, Classy, brown and yellow leather, white fringe on holsters, stylized blue butterflies are also "DE" logo, if buckled in front, holsters are backwards; holsters only, no guns
EX $100 NM $200 MIP $375

Davy Crockett Buffalo Rifle, 1950s, Hubley, 25" die-cast and plastic, unusual flintlock style, fires single cap under pan cover, brown plastic stock, ammo storage door in stock
EX $75 **NM** $145 **MIP** $225

Davy Crockett Frontier Fighter Cork Gun, 1950s, Unknown, 21" pop gun shoots cork on string and has cigarette flint mechanism at muzzle that makes sparks when fired, wood stock, leather sling
EX $75 **NM** $150 **MIP** $250

Deputy Cap Pistol, 1950s, Hubley, 10" die-cast, front breaking, release on barrel, ornate scroll work, nickel finish
EX $50 **NM** $100 **MIP** $200

Double Holster Set, 1950s, Classy, imitation alligator-texture brown leather, steer-head conches on holsters, lots of studs, yellow felt backing, holsters only, no guns
EX $150 **NM** $300 **MIP** $500

Double Holster Set, 1960, Marx, 10" two pistols similar to 1860s Remington, fires roll caps by use of a lanyard that is pulled from the bottom of the grip, internal hammer, white plastic horse and steer grips, silver, brown vinyl holster
EX $70 **NM** $120 **MIP** $300

Double-Barrel Pop Gun Rifle, 1935, Marx, 28" long
EX $50 **NM** $100 **MIP** $200

Double-Barrel Pop Gun Rifle, 1935, Marx, 22" long
EX $45 **NM** $85 **MIP** $175

Dyna-Mite Derringer, 1955, Nichols, 3-1/4" die-cast, loads single cap cartridge, silver finish, white plastic grips
EX $15 **NM** $30 **MIP** $45

Dyna-Mite Derringer in Clip, Nichols, 3-1/2" die-cast, fires single cap in Nichols cartridge, nickel finish, white plastic grips w/small leather holster
EX $25 **NM** $45 **MIP** $65

Fanner 50 "Swivelshot Trick Holster" Set, 1958, Mattel, die-cast bullet loading Fanner 50, leather swivel style holster, attaches to any belt, gun fires in holster when swiveled, string included for last ditch draw
EX $110 **NM** $225 **MIP** $375

Fanner 50 Cap Pistol, 1960s, Mattel, later version 11" fires perforated roll caps, black finish, white plastic antelope grips
EX $45 **NM** $90 **MIP** $175

Fanner 50 Cap Pistol, 1960s, Mattel, 11" fanner non-revolving cylinder, stag plastic grips, nickel finish, black vinyl "Durahyde" holster
EX $55 **NM** $110 **MIP** $225

Fanner 50 Smoking Cap Pistol, 1957, Mattel, 10-1/2" w/revolving cylinder, first version w/grapefruit cylinder does not chamber bullets
EX $100 **NM** $200 **MIP** $400

Fanner 50 Smoking Cap Pistol, 1958, Mattel, 10-1/2" w/revolving cylinder, chambers six metal play bullets, die-cast
EX $90 **NM** $180 **MIP** $400

Fastest Gun Electronic Draw Game, 1958, Kilgore, die-cast, wire plug into "Rangers" gun grips, gun that shoots first lights eye of plastic battery-operated steer head, red and blue plastic holsters w/matching cowboy gun grips, plastic belts
EX $90 **NM** $175 **MIP** $300

Flintlock Jr. Cap Pistol, 1955, Hubley, 7-1/2" single shot, double action, brown swirl plastic stock
EX $20 **NM** $45 **MIP** $85

Flintlock Pistol, 1954, Hubley, 9-1/4", two shot cap shooting single action double barrel, over and under style, brown swirl plastic stock, nickel finish
EX $50 **NM** $110 **MIP** $175

Frontier Repeating Cap Rifle, 1950s, Hubley, 35-1/4" rifle nickel finish w/brown plastic stock and forestock, blue metal barrel, red plastic choke and front sight, pop down magazine, released by catch in front of trigger, scroll work
EX $75 **NM** $165 **MIP** $210

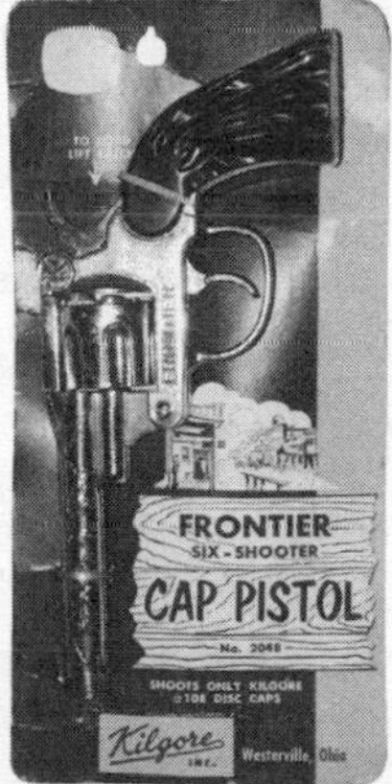

Frontier Six-Shooter Cap Pistol, 1950s, Kilgore, black handle, Model No. 2048
EX $65 **NM** $110 **MIP** $155

Frontier Smoker, Product Engineering, 9-1/2" cap pistol, die-cast, pop up magazine shoots white powder from internal bellows, all metal, black grips, silver finish, gold magazine, hammer and trigger
EX $85 **NM** $150 **MIP** $225

Gene Autry 44 Cap Pistol, 1950s, Leslie-Henry, 11" lever release, side loading, long barrel, loads solid metal bullets, nickel finish, brown translucent plastic horse-head grips
EX $175 **NM** $500 **MIP** $800

Gene Autry 44 Cap Pistol, 1950s, Leslie-Henry, 11" lever release, side loading, long barrel, nickel finish, white plastic horse-head grips
EX $125 **NM** $300 **MIP** $550

Gene Autry Cap Pistol, 1939, Kenton, 8-3/8" cast iron, long barrel, dark gray gunmetal finish w/white plastic grips w/signature, (Best/Logan G3.1.1), Model No. 36-G1067
EX $200 **NM** $275 **MIP** $500

Gene Autry Cap Pistol, 1940, Kenton, 6-1/2" cast iron, nickel finish, red plastic grips w/etched signature (Best/Logan G3.2.1), Model No. 37-G1111
EX $125 **NM** $225 **MIP** $450

Gene Autry Cap Pistol, 1950s, Leslie-Henry, 7-3/4" die-cast, small size, lever release, break-to-front, nickel finish w/extension scroll work, black plastic horse-head grips
EX $115 **NM** $275 **MIP** $500

Gene Autry Cap Pistol, 1950s, Leslie-Henry, 9" break-to-front lever release, copper finish, white plastic horse-head grips
EX $115 **NM** $275 **MIP** $500

Gene Autry Cap Pistol, 1950s, Leslie-Henry, 9" break-to-front, lever release, nickel finish, black plastic horse-head grips
EX $115 **NM** $275 **MIP** $500

Gene Autry Cap Pistol, 1950s, Leslie-Henry, 9", break-to-front lever release, nickel finish, white plastic horse-head grips
EX $115 **NM** $275 **MIP** $500

Gene Autry Champion Single Holster Set, 1940s, Unknown, leather and cardboard, red, yellow and green "jewels," four white wooden bullets, silver buckle
EX $125 **NM** $250 **MIP** $400

Gene Autry Dummy Cap Pistol, 1939, Kenton, cast iron, 8-3/8", long barrel, dark gray, gunmetal finish, white plastic grips
EX $125 **NM** $225 **MIP** $450

Grizzly Cap Pistol, 1950s, Kilgore, 10" revolving cylinder fires disc caps, swing out cylinder, black plastic grips w/grizzly bear
EX $100 **NM** $200 **MIP** $375

Gunfighter Holster Set, 1960s, Lone Star, 9" Frontier Ace, lever release, break-to-front, silver finish, brown plastic grips, white and red leather "Laramie" single holster w/separate belt
EX $60 **NM** $125 **MIP** $250

Gunsmoke Double Holster Set, Leslie-Henry, w/copper clad grips
EX $250 **NM** $520 **MIP** $750

Hawkeye Cap Pistol, 1950s, Kilgore, 4-1/4" all metal, automatic style, side loading, silver finish
EX $20 **NM** $40 **MIP** $75

Historic Guns Derringer, 1974, Marx, Marx Historic Guns series, derringer w/plastic presentation case, 4-1/2" long, on card
EX $15 **NM** $25 **MIP** $30

Hi-Yo Silver Lone Ranger Pistol, Marx, tin gun
EX $60 **NM** $200 **MIP** $350

Hopalong Cassidy Cap Pistol, 1950, Schmidt, 9" pull hammer to release, scroll work, nickel finish w/black plastic grips w/white bust of Hopalong Cassidy, Model No. 80-G1140
EX $175 **NM** $400 **MIP** $750

Hopalong Cassidy Double Holster Set, 1940s, Wyandotte, w/two guns; gold guns w/black grips; holster has silver studs w/Hoppy's name in belt
EX $1250 **NM** $2500 **MIP** $4000

Hopalong Cassidy Holster/Gun Set, 1950s, Schmidt, black holster; black grips on gun w/bust of Hoppy
EX $1000 **NM** $2000 **MIP** $3000

How the West Was Won Gun Rifle, Marx, deep gray Winchester model w/tan stock, in box
EX $55 **NM** $85 **MIP** $145

Johnny Eagle Red River Bullet Firing, 1965, Topper/Deluxe, over 12" double action revolving cylinder pistol, die-cast hammer, trigger, blue plastic overall w/wood plastic grips w/gold horse, side loading, shell ejector, fires two-piece plastic bullets
EX $65 **NM** $95 **MIP** $175

Johnny Ringo Gun & Holster Set, 1960, Marx, die-cast gun, white plastic head grips, vinyl quick draw holster has rawhide tie, gun is fired by lanyard which passes through grip butt and attaches to belt, when pulled lanyard trips internal hammer
EX $100 **NM** $200 **MIP** $375

Johnny Ringo, Adventure of, Gun & Holster, 1960, Esquire Novelty, 10-3/4" long barrel Actoy, friction break, black/gold plastic stag grips, black leather two-gun holster, felt backing, loops hold four to six bullets, silver buckle
EX $250 **NM** $500 **MIP** $750

Johnty West Cowboy Rifled, 1950s, Marx, repeater cap action, winchester-style,
EX $35 **NM** $80 **MIP** $155

Johnty West, The Cowboy Rifle, 1960s, Marx, repeater cap action
EX $25 **NM** $50 **MIP** $85

Lawmaker Cap Pistol, 1941, Kenton, 8-3/8", break-to-front friction break, unusual dark gray gunmetal finish, white plastic raised grips
EX $125 **NM** $225 **MIP** $450

Lone Ranger 45 Flasher Flashlight Pistol, Marx, in box
EX $60 **NM** $125 **MIP** $200

Lone Ranger Cap Pistol, 1938, Kilgore, 8-1/4" cast iron, small hammer, nickel finish, friction break, purple plastic "Hi-Yo Silver" grips
EX $125 **NM** $300 **MIP** $500

Lone Ranger Cap Pistol, 1940, Kilgore, 8-1/2" cast iron, large hammer, nickel finish, spring release on side for break, red-brown, Hi-Yo Silver grips
EX $110 **NM** $275 **MIP** $450

Lone Ranger Carbine, 1950s, Marx, 26" gray plastic repeater-style rifle has pull down cap magazine, western trim and Lone Ranger signature on stock
EX $65 **NM** $100 **MIP** $165

Lone Ranger Clicker Pistol, 1938, Marx, 8", nickel finish, red jewels, inlaid white plastic grip w/the Lone Ranger, Hi-Yo Silver and LR head embossed, brown leather holster
EX $100 **NM** $300 **MIP** $400

Lone Ranger Double Target Set, 1939, Marx, 9-1/2" square stand up target, tin litho, wire frame holds target upright, backed w/bulls-eye target, 8" metal dart gun fires wooden shaft dart
EX $150 **NM** $325 **MIP** $450

Lone Ranger Holster, Unknown, 9", leather/pressboard, Hi-Yo Silver and Lone Ranger printed, red jewel, belt loop
EX $50 **NM** $100 **MIP** $200

Lone Ranger Rifle, 1973, Hubley, 29" long
EX $55 **NM** $100 **MIP** $150

Lone Rider Cap Pistol, 1950s, Buzz-Henry, 8" die-cast, white plastic inset rearing horse grips
EX $40 **NM** $100 **MIP** $175

Long Boy Cap Gun, Kilgore, 11-1/2" long, cast iron
EX $75 **NM** $1335 **MIP** $275

Longhorn Cap Pistol, 1950s, Leslie-Henry, 10" die-cast, release in front of trigger guard, scroll work, white plastic horse head grips, unusual pop-up cap magazine, Model No. 38-G927
EX $85 **NM** $125 **MIP** $225

Mare's Laig Rifle Pistol, Marx, 13-1/2" brown plastic, black plastic body, pull down magazine
EX $60 **NM** $95 **MIP** $135

Marshal Cap Pistol, 1950s, Leslie-Henry, 10" revolving cylinder chambers, Nichols-style bullets, white plastic grips w/star ovals
EX $35 **NM** $75 **MIP** $150

Marshal Cap Pistol, 1960, Hubley, 9-3/4" die-cast, side loading, nickel finish w/scrollwork, w/brown and white plastic stag grips w/a clip on left grip, Model No. 24-G1142
EX $35 **NM** $75 **MIP** $150

Marshal Matt Dillon "Gunsmoke" Cap Pistol, 1950s, Leslie-Henry, 10" pop-up cap magazine, release in front of trigger guard, scroll work, bronze steer-head grips
EX $60 **NM** $125 **MIP** $275

Matt Dillon Marshal Set, John Henry Products, gun and holster set w/jail keys, handcuffs and badge
EX $55 **NM** $100 **MIP** $200

Maverick Cap Pistol, 1960, Carnell, 9" break-to-front, lever release, nickel finish, Maverick on sides, cream and brown swirl colored grips features notch bar w/extra set of black plastic grips
EX $60 **NM** $175 **MIP** $300

Maverick Derringer, 1958, Leslie-Henry, 3-1/4" w/removeable cap-shooting bullets, tan vinyl holster w/two bullets
EX $35 **NM** $55 **MIP** $85

Maverick Two Gun Holster Set, 1958, Leslie-Henry, 11x14" box picutres James Garner as Maverick, two six-shooters w/individual bullets
EX $400 **NM** $800 **MIP** $1200

Maverick Two Gun Holster Set, 1960, Carnell, 9" break-to-front, lever release, nickel finish, Maverick on sides, cream/brown swirl grips features notch bar, black leather dbl. holster set w/silver plates, studs and white trim, six loops, buckle
EX $225 **NM** $450 **MIP** $750

Model 1860 Cal .44 Cap Pistol, 1959, Hubley, 13", revolving cylinder w/closed chamber ends, six two-piece bullets, flat aluminum finish, white plastic grips, complete w/wooden display plaque
EX $130 **NM** $275 **MIP** $450

Model 95 Shell Firing Rifle, 1961, Nichols, 35-1/2" rifle uses shell firing cartridges, holds five in removeable magazine and one chamber, lever action ejects cartridges, open frame box holds six bullets and twelve additional red bullet heads
EX $200 **NM** $350 **MIP** $550

Mustang Cap Pistol, 1960s, Kilgore, 9-1/2" chrome finish w/"stag" plastic grips
EX $20 **NM** $35 **MIP** $75

Official Wanted Dead or Alive Mare's Laig Rifle, Marx, 19" bullet loading, cap firing saddle rifle-pistol ejects plastic bullets, w/holster
EX $110 **NM** $225 **MIP** $350

Official Wyatt Earp Buntline Clicker Pistol, Young Premiums, 18-1/2" plastic
EX $50 **NM** $125 **MIP** $200

Panther Pistol, 1958, Hubley, die-cast, 4" derringer style pistol snaps out from secret spring-loaded wrist holster
EX $85 **NM** $130 **MIP** $185

Pecos Kid Cap Pistol, 1970s, Lone Star, 9" silver chrome finish, brown plastic grips, lever release
EX $10 **NM** $15 **MIP** $50

Pepperbox Derringer Cap Pistol, 1960, Lone Star, die-cast, 6-1/4" rotating barrel holds four cap loads, silver finish w/black plastic grips
EX $75 **NM** $110 **MIP** $185

Pinto Cap Pistol, 1950s, Nichols, 3-1/2", chrome finish, black plastic grips, flip out cylinder, white plastic "Pinto" holster in leather holster clip
EX $20 **NM** $35 **MIP** $75

Pony Boy Double Holster Set, 1950s, Esquire Novelty, brown leather double holster w/bucking broncs and studs, cuffs, spurs and spur leathers, guns are Actoy "Spitfires", die-cast 8-1/2" copper finish, white plastic grips
EX $200 **NM** $400 **MIP** $600

Pony Cap Pistol, 1950s, Actoy, single shot, all-metal, nickel finish w/eagle on grip
EX $25 **NM** $45 **MIP** $100

Ranch Rifle, Marx, plastic, repeater
EX $30 **NM** $45 **MIP** $60

Ranger Cap Pistol, 1950s, Leslie-Henry, 7-3/4" derringer w/removeable cap, shooting bullets, tan vinyl holster w/two bullets
EX $85 **NM** $110 **MIP** $150

Ranger Cap Pistol, 1950s, Kilgore, 8-1/2" nickel finish, brown swirl plastic grips, spring release on right side, break-to-front
EX $110 **NM** $145 **MIP** $275

Real Texan Outfit with Nichols Stallion .22, 1950s, Smart Style, brown/white leather double holsters have silver conches w/red reflectors, silver horses at top of holster, belt w/three bullet loops, guns are a pair of double action .22s
EX $125 **NM** $250 **MIP** $500

Rebel Holster & Pistol, 1960s, Classy, 12" die-cast long barrel pistol, brown plastic grips, black leather single holster left side, Rebel insignia on holster flap,
EX $225 **NM** $450 **MIP** $800

Red Ranger Jr. Cap Pistol, 1950s, Wyandotte, 7-1/2" lever release, break-to-front, silver finish, white plastic horse grips
EX $65 **NM** $100 **MIP** $165

Red Ryder BB Rifle, 1980, Daisy, carved wooden stock
EX $35 **NM** $75 **MIP** $125

Remington .36 Cap Pistol, 1950s, Hubley, 8" long, nickel finish, black plastic grips, revolving cylinder chambers two-piece bullets
EX $80 **NM** $160 **MIP** $275

Rex Trailer Two Gun & Holster Set, 1960, Hubley, 9-1/2" side loading, nickel finish, stag plastic grips, brown textured tooled leather w/white holsters and trim, six bullet loops w/plastic silver bullets, plain buckle
EX $110 **NM** $225 **MIP** $450

Ric-O-Shay .45 Cap Pistol, 1959, Hubley, 13" die-cast, nickel chrome finish, large frame, revolving cylinder, fires rolled caps, chambers brass bullets and fires caps, black plastic grips, makes a twang sound when fired, Model No. 28-G938
EX $85 **NM** $150 **MIP** $300

Ric-O-Shay .45 Cap Pistol Holster Set, Hubley, 13", die-cast, revolving cylinder swings out to chamber six brass bullets, six loaded in gun and 12 on holster, 1" flake in nickel finish at heel, holster black leather w/separate belt, horse-head emblem, rawhide tiedown, Model No. 26-G1141
EX $250 **NM** $500 **MIP** $875

Rifleman Flip Special Cap Rifle, 1959, Hubley, 3' long rifle, resembles classic Winchester w/ring lever, brown plastic stock, pop down cap magazine
EX $160 **NM** $350 **MIP** $500

Rodeo Cap Pistol, 1950s, Hubley, 7-1/2" single shot, white plastic steer grips
EX $20 **NM** $50 **MIP** $100

Roy Rogers Cap Pistol, 1950s, Kilgore, 10" revolving cylinder swings out to load, fires disc caps, white plastic horse-head grips w/"RR" logo
EX $150 **NM** $300 **MIP** $550

Roy Rogers Carbine, 1950s, Marx, 26" gray plastic repeater-style rifle has pull down cap magazine, western trim and Roy Rogers signature on stock
EX $80 **NM** $150 **MIP** $300

Roy Rogers Double Gun & Holster Set, 1950s, Classy, die-cast two 8-1/2" nickel finish pistols w/copper figural grips, holster is brown and black leather w/raised detail, plastic play bullets and leather tie-downs
EX $550 **NM** $1100 **MIP** $1600

Roy Rogers Double Holster Set, Classy, 10" guns w/plain nickel finish and copper grips, lever release, brown and cream leather set, silver studs, gold fleck jewels and four wooden bullets
EX $500 **NM** $1000 **MIP** $1500

Roy Rogers Double Holster Set, 1950s, Classy, black and white leather set, silver studs and conches, 9" Roy Rogers pistols w/plain nickel finish and copper figural grips, friction release
EX $525 **NM** $1050 **MIP** $1550

Roy Rogers Tiny Tots Double Holster Set, Hubley
EX $55 **NM** $100 **MIP** $165

Ruff Rider Western Holster Set, Pilgrim Leather, brown leather double holster, variety of studs and red jewels, twelve plastic silver bullets, tie-downs
EX $110 **NM** $275 **MIP** $450

Sheriff's Derringer Pocket Pistol, 1960s, Ohio Art, 3-1/4" silver finish derringer chambers two-piece, Nichols-style cartridge, red plastic grips w/an "A" logo, on card
EX $10 **NM** $20 **MIP** $25

Shootin' Shell .45 Fanner Cap Pistol, 1959, Mattel, 11" revolving cylinder pistol shoots Mattel Shootin' Shell cartridges, shell ejector
EX $250 **NM** $400 **MIP** $675

Shootin' Shell Buckle Gun, 1958, Mattel, cap and bullet shooting copy of Remington Derringer pops out from belt buckle, two brass cartridges and six bullets
EX $45 **NM** $80 **MIP** $125

Shootin' Shell Fanner, 1958, Mattel, 9" die-cast chrome finish, revolving cylinder chambers six Shootin' Shell bullets
EX $100 **NM** $200 **MIP** $375

Shootin' Shell Fanner & Derringer Set, 1958, Mattel, small size Shooting Shell Fanner w/chrome finish, revolving cylinder, chambers six Shootin' Shell bullets, brown leather holster
EX $100 **NM** $200 **MIP** $375

Shootin' Shell Fanner Single Holster, 1959, Mattel, cowhide holster takes small size Shootin' Shell Fanner w/six brass play bullets and tie-downs
EX $105 **NM** $210 **MIP** $375

Shootin' Shell Indian Scout Rifle, 1958, Mattel, 29-1/2" plastic/metal Sharps rolling block rifle, chambers two-piece Shootin' Shell bullets, secret compartment in stock for ammo storage, plastic stock and metal barrel
EX $100 **NM** $175 **MIP** $300

Shootin' Shell Potshot Remington Derringer, 1959, Mattel, 3" derringer, on card
EX $35 **NM** $60 **MIP** $90

Shootin' Shell Winchester Rifle, Mattel, 26" long
EX $100 **NM** $165 **MIP** $225

Showdown Set with Three Shootin' Shell Guns, 1958, Mattel, 30" single shot rifle w/metal barrel, die-cast w/plastic stock, Shootin' Shell Fanner sm. size, revolving cylinder, chrome finish and imitation stag plastic grips, tan holster w/bullet loops
EX $300 **NM** $600 **MIP** $950

Side-By Double Barrel Pop Gun Rifle, Marx, 9" long
EX $20 **NM** $35 **MIP** $45

Western

GUNS

Silver Pony Cap Pistol, 1950s, Nichols, 7-1/2" single shot, silver metal grip and one replacement black plastic grip, silver finish
EX $30 **NM** $45 **MIP** $100

Spitfire Hip Gun No. 100, 1950s, Nichols, 9" cap cartridge loading mini rifle, chrome finish, tan plastic stock
EX $15 **NM** $20 **MIP** $35

Spitfire with Clip, 1950s, Nichols, 9" mini rifle, chrome finish, plastic stock, plastic holders w/two extra cartridges
EX $12 **NM** $25 **MIP** $35

Spittin Image Peacemaker BB Pistol, Daisy, 10-1/2" die-cast, spring fired, single action, BBs load into spring fed magazine under barrel
EX $25 **NM** $60 **MIP** $120

Stagecoach Pistol, 1950s, Marx, 5" pistol with plastic box marked "Stagecoach Pistol"
EX $40 **NM** $65 **MIP** $90

Stallion .22 Cap Pistol, 1950s, Nichols, 7" revolving cylinder chambers five two-piece cartridges, single action, black plastic stag grips, never came in box
EX $30 **NM** $75 **MIP** $150

Stallion .22 Double Action Cap Pistol, 1950s, Nichols, 7" double action, pull trigger to fire, white plastic grips, nickel finish, cylinder revolves
EX $50 **NM** $150 **MIP** $300

Stallion .38 Cap Pistol, 1955, Nichols, 9-1/2", chambers six two-piece cap cartridges, nickel finish, white plastic grips
EX $85 **NM** $175 **MIP** $375

Stallion .45 MK I Cap Pistol, 1950, Nichols, die-cast, 12" chrome finish, revolving cylinder, chambers six two-piece bullets, shell ejector, white "pearlescent" plastic grips w/rearing stallion, red jewels and 6 bullets and Stallion caps
EX $1550 **NM** $300 **MIP** $500

Stallion .45 MK II Cap Pistol, 1956, Nichols, 12" pistol, chrome finish, revolving cylinder, chambers six two-piece, bullets, shell ejector, extra set of white grips to replace black grips on gun and box of Stallion caps
EX $100 **NM** $185 **MIP** $375

Stallion 32 Six Shooter, 1955, Nichols, 8" revolving cylinder chambers six two-piece cartridges, nickel finish, black plastic grips
EX $75 **NM** $150 **MIP** $300

Stallion 41-40 Cap Pistol, 1950s, Nichols, 10-1/2" revolving cylinder chrome finish pistol, swing out cylinder that chambers six two-piece cap cartridges, shell ejector, scroll work on frame, cream-purple swirl colored plastic grips
EX $160 **NM** $375 **MIP** $500

Susanna 90 12 Shot Cap Pistol, 1980s, Edison, 9" uses ring caps, wind out cylinder, black finish, plastic wood grips
EX $10 **NM** $15 **MIP** $25

Tales of Wells Fargo Double Barrel Shotgun, 1950s, Marx, 26" long double barrel shotgun, two toy shotgun shells, decal on the butt of the gun, Model No. 44
EX $100 **NM** $210 **MIP** $350

Texan .38 Cap Pistol, 1950s, Hubley, 10" long, revolving cylinder gun chambers six solid brass bullets (caps go into cylinder first), top release front break automatically ejects shells, plastic steer grips
EX $100 **NM** $200 **MIP** $350

Texan Cap Pistol, 1940, Hubley, 9-1/4" cast iron revolving cylinder lever release, white plastic steer grips, nickel finish, Colt rearing horse logo on grips
EX $110 **NM** $225 **MIP** $400

Texan Cap Pistol, 1950s, Hubley, die-cast, nickel finish, white plastic steer grips, star logo on grips
EX $75 **NM** $150 **MIP** $300

Texan Cap Pistol No. 285, 1940, Hubley, 9-1/4", cast iron, revolving cylinder, lever release, white plastic steer grips, nickel finish w/star logo in grip
EX $120 **NM** $250 **MIP** $425

Texan Dummy Cap Pistol, 1940, Hubley, 9-1/4" revolving cylinder, lever release, white plastic steer grips, nickel finish, Colt rearing horse logo
EX $85 **NM** $150 **MIP** $300

Texan Dummy Cap Pistol, 1950s, Hubley, 9-1/4", revolving cylinder, lever release, white plastic steer grips, nickel finish, star logo on grip
EX $90 **NM** $165 **MIP** $350

Texan Jr. Cap Pistol, 1950s, Hubley, 10", spring button release on side of cylinder, break-to-front, nickel finish white plastic grips w/black steers
EX $85 **NM** $125 **MIP** $250

Texan Jr. Cap Pistol, 1954, Hubley, die-cast, release under cylinder, nickel finish, white plastic Longhorn grips
EX $65 **NM** $110 **MIP** $225

Texan Jr. Gold Plated Cap Pistol, 1950s, Hubley, 9", gold finish w/black longhorn steer grips, break-to-front release from cylinder
EX $95 **NM** $175 **MIP** $350

Texas Cap Pistol, 1950s, Long Island Die Casting, die-cast, 8-1/2" friction break, Circle "T" logo, scroll work on barrel
EX $50 **NM** $100 **MIP** $200

Texas Ranger Cap Pistol, Leslie-Henry, 8-1/4" die-cast, lever release break to front, nickel finish, scroll work, vasoline colored plastic grips
EX $85 **NM** $150 **MIP** $350

The Plainsman Cap Pistol, 1950s, National Metal & Plastic Toy, 10-1/2" revolving cylinder loads Kilgore-style disk caps, lever holds cylinder forward for loading, scroll work, white plastic grips, Model No. 62-G1101
EX $125 **NM** $225 **MIP** $350

Thundergun Cap Pistol, 1950s, Marx, 12-1/2" single action,"Thundercaps" perforated roll cap system, silver finish, brown plastic grips
EX $100 **NM** $200 **MIP** $300

Tom Mix Wooden Gun, 1930s, Ralston-Purina, three all-wood versions w/leather holster, came in mailer, each
EX $125 **NM** $275 **MIP** $400

Tophand 250 Cap Pistol, 1960, Nichols, 9-1/2" break-to-front, lever release, black finish, brown plastic grips w/a roll of "Tophand 250" caps
EX $45 **NM** $90 **MIP** $180

Wagon Train Complete Western Cowboy Outfit, 1960, Leslie-Henry, plastic flip ring lever rifle and wagon train pistol (late model L-H pistol) and leather holster
EX $110 **NM** $225 **MIP** $450

Wagon Train Gun & Holster Set, 1950s, Unknown, two 5" plastic guns, vinyl holster w/plastic bullets and metal badge, Model No. 45
EX $25 **NM** $50 **MIP** $100

Wanted Dead or Alive Miniature Mare's Laig, 1959, Marx, Marx Miniatures series miniature cap rifle on "wood frame" card
EX $20 **NM** $40 **MIP** $65

Wells Fargo Buntline Cap Pistol, 1950s, Actoy, 11" long barrel, break-to-front, cream plastic stag grips
EX $85 **NM** $160 **MIP** $350

Western Buntline Pistol, 1963, Haig, 13", pistol fires single caps and/or BBs, BBs are propelled down barrel sleeve by cap explosion
EX $75 **NM** $130 **MIP** $175

Western Cap Pistol, 1950s, Hubley, 9" die-cast, friction break, nickel finish w/white plastic steer grips w/black steer, Model No. 33-G1100
EX $40 **NM** $75 **MIP** $150

Wild Bill Hickok 44 Cap Pistol Set, 1950s, Leslie-Henry, 11" nickel finish, swing-out side loading action, revolving cylinder chambers six metal bullets, amber plastic horse-head grips, single

holster black and brown leather w/silver studs, diamond conches
EX $200 **NM** $400 **MIP** $650

Wild Bill Hickok Cap Pistol, 1950s, Leslie-Henry, 10" pop-up cap magazine, release in front of trigger guard, scroll work, translucent brown plastic grips w/oval star inserts
EX $100 **NM** $200 **MIP** $375

Wild Bill Hickok Gun & Holster, Leslie-Henry, single gun and holster set
EX $150 **NM** $300 **MIP** $500

Wild West Rifle, Marx, 30" long w/sight, cap rifle
EX $40 **NM** $75 **MIP** $125

Winchester Saddle Gun Rifle, 1959, Mattel, 33" die-cast and plastic, perforated roll caps and chambers eight play bullets loaded through side door
EX $50 **NM** $125 **MIP** $375

Wyatt Earp Buntline Special, 1950s, Actoy, 11" barrel, die-cast, friction break-to-front, white plastic grips, nickel finish
EX $100 **NM** $250 **MIP** $425

Wyatt Earp Double Holster Set, 1950s, Unknown, med. size, reflectors, black leather w/brown rawhide fringe, holsters only
EX $50 **NM** $80 **MIP** $125

Wyatt Earp Double Holster Set, 1950s, Hubley, black and white leather holster w/silk screened "Marshal Wyatt Earp" logo, two No. 247 Hubley Wyatt Earp Buntline Specials, 10-3/4" nickel finish, purple swirl grips
EX $250 **NM** $500 **MIP** $850

Yo Gun, 1960s, Ideal, 7-1/4" red plastic gun releases yellow plastic ball which snaps back when trigger is pulled, functions like a yo-yo
EX $30 **NM** $45 **MIP** $60

Young Buffalo Bill Cowboy Outfit, Leslie-Henry, black and white leather holster set w/pistol, white grip, holster bands read Texas Ranger
EX $100 **NM** $200 **MIP** $350

Zorro Flintock Pistol, Marx
EX $45 **NM** $80 **MIP** $140

Zorro Rifle, Marx
EX $60 **NM** $125 **MIP** $175

Zorro Rifle, 1958, Daisy, pressed steel barrel w/wood stock. Zorro logo, 25" long
EX $100 **NM** $200 **MIP** $300

Lunch Boxes

by Karen o'Brien

Lunch kits have been manufactured since the 1920s, but the boxes that are most collectible today are those bearing illustrations of popular licensed characters.

It took the power of television to launch the lunch box industry out of the domed steel domain of workmen and into the colorful art boxes generations of children carried to school each day.

As World War II ended, Aladdin Industries returned to providing millions of workmen with sturdy, if uninspired, lunch kits designed to take the beating of the workplace. Great change occurred in 1950 when Aladdin released a pair of rectangular steel boxes, one red and one blue, sporting scalloped color decals of the television Western hero of the day, Hopalong Cassidy. Soon thereafter, 600,000 Hoppy boxes were carried to school by proud young owners. Once discovered, the youth market would never be ignored again.

The envious classmates of those first Hoppy boxers would not be denied. American Thermos, Aladdin's chief competitor, went one up on Aladdin by introducing the 1953 Roy Rogers box in full-color lithography. Aladdin responded by issuing a new 1954 Hoppy box in full color litho, and the lunch box era officially began.

Throughout the later 1950s, the box wars were fought in earnest between Aladdin and American Thermos, with occasional challenges by Adco Liberty, Ohio Art, and Okay Industries.

The smaller firms produced some classic boxes, notably Mickey Mouse and Donald Duck (1954), Howdy Doody (1954), and Davy Crockett (1955) from Adco Liberty; and Captain Astro (1966), Bon XX (1967), Snow White (1980), and Pit Stop (1968) from Ohio Art. Okay Industries weighed in briefly later on with the now highly prized Wake Up America (1973) and Underdog (1974) boxes, but from the beginning it had always been a two-horse race.

The popular boxes of each year mirrored the stars, heroes, and interests of the times. From the Westerns and space explorations of the late 1950s through the 1960s, Americans enjoyed a golden age of cartoon and film heroes such as the Flintstones (1962), Dudley Do-Right (1962), Bullwinkle and Rocky (1962), and Mary Poppins (1965). As the decade progressed, America grew more aggressive, turning toward such violent heroes as the Man from U.N.C.L.E. (1966) and G.I. Joe (1967) before Vietnam changed the national consciousness.

The early 1970s brought us such innocuous role models as H.R. Pufnstuf (1970), The Partridge Family (1971), and Bobby Sherman (1972). By decade's end, we were greeting both the promise and the threat from beyond in *Close Encounters of the Third Kind* (1978) and (1978).

The metal box reigned supreme through the mid-1980s when parental groups began calling for a ban on metal boxes as "deadly weapons." The industry capitulated, and by 1986, both Aladdin and American Thermos were producing all of their boxes in plastic.

The switch to plastic was not nearly as abrupt as might be expected. Aladdin and Thermos had been making plastic and vinyl boxes since the late 1950s. These included many character boxes that had no counterparts in metal, which is presently their major saving grace in the collector market.

Vinyl boxes were made of lower-cost materials consisting basically of cardboard sheathed in thin vinyl. They were not as popular as metal boxes, and their poor construction combined with lower unit sales have resulted in a field with higher rarity factors than the metal box arena. Additionally, vinyl was more affordable to small companies that produced numerous limited-run boxes for sale or use as premiums.

Vinyl box collecting is an emerging field with few firmly established prices compared to the relative maturity of the metal box market, so any price guide such as this will be more open to debate. As the field matures, the pricing precedents of sales and time will build into a stronger body of knowledge. In this book, for ease of searching, boxes are listed alphabetically by box composition—plastic, steel, and vinyl.

Contributor: Joe Soucy of Seaside Toys specializes in pristine-condition lunch boxes. He can be reached at the Seaside Toy Center, 179 Main St., Westerly, RI, 02891.

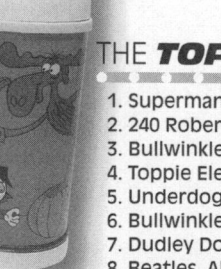

THE *TOP 10* LUNCH BOXES (In Mint Condition)

1. Superman, Universal, 1954 .... $16,750
2. 240 Robert, Aladdin, 1978 5,500
3. Bullwinkle, vinyl, King Seeley Thermos, 1963 4,500
4. Toppie Elephant, American Thermos, 1957 3,850
5. Underdog, Okay Industries, 1974 3,500
6. Bullwinkle & Rocky, Universal, 1962, ... 3,500
7. Dudley Do-Right, Universal, 1962 3,450
8. Beatles, Aladdin, 1966 2,800
9. Jetsons Dome, Aladdin, 1963 2,650
10. Star Trek Dome, Aladdin, 1968 2,350

Plastic

101 Dalmatians, 1990, Aladdin
BOX $25 **BOTTLE** $8

18 Wheeler, 1978, Aladdin
BOX $40 **BOTTLE** $10

ALF, 1987, Thermos, red plastic
BOX $35 **BOTTLE** n/a

Animalympics Dome, 1979, Thermos
BOX $40 **BOTTLE** $10

Astronauts, 1986, Thermos
BOX $35 **BOTTLE** $15

Atari Missile Command Dome, 1983, Aladdin
BOX $55 **BOTTLE** $10

Back to School, 1980, Aladdin
BOX $75 **BOTTLE** $20

Back to the Future, 1989, Thermos
BOX $45 **BOTTLE** $15

Bang Bang, 1982, Thermos
BOX $50 **BOTTLE** n/a

Barbie with Hologram Mirror, 1990, Thermos
BOX $30 **BOTTLE** $8

Batman (dark blue), 1989, Thermos
BOX $30 **BOTTLE** $10

Batman (light blue), 1989, Thermos
BOX $55 **BOTTLE** $10

Batman Returns, 1991, Thermos
BOX $30 **BOTTLE** $5

Beach Bronto, 1984, Aladdin, no bottle
BOX $45 **BOTTLE** n/a

Beach Party (blue/pink), 1988, Deka, with generic plastic bottle
BOX $20 **BOTTLE** $5

Bear with Heart (3-D), 1987, Servo
BOX $20 **BOTTLE** n/a

Beauty & the Beast, 1991, Aladdin
BOX $30 **BOTTLE** $7

Bee Gees, 1978, Thermos
BOX $45 **BOTTLE** $20

Beetlejuice, 1980, Thermos
BOX $20 **BOTTLE** $10

Big Jim, 1976, Thermos
BOX $100 **BOTTLE** $30

Bozostuffs, 1988, Deka
BOX $30 **BOTTLE** $10

C.B. Bears, 1977, Thermos
BOX $30 **BOTTLE** n/a

Care Bears, 1986, Aladdin
BOX $20 **BOTTLE** $5

Centurions, 1986, Thermos
BOX $25 **BOTTLE** $8

Chiclets, 1987, Thermos, no bottle
BOX $45 **BOTTLE** n/a

Chipmunks, Alvin and The, 1983, Thermos
BOX $25 **BOTTLE** $10

CHiPs, 1977, Thermos
BOX $65 **BOTTLE** $20

Cinderella, 1992, Aladdin
BOX $30 **BOTTLE** $10

Civil War, The, 1961, Universal, generic "Thermax" bottle
BOX $200 **BOTTLE** $25

Colonial Bread Van, 1984, Moldmark Industries
BOX $65 **BOTTLE** $20

Crestman Tubular!, 1980, Taiwan
BOX $55 **BOTTLE** $20

Days of Thunder, 1988, Thermos
BOX $35 **BOTTLE** $10

Deka 4 x 4, 1988, Deka, generic plastic bottle
BOX $35 **BOTTLE** $5

Dick Tracy, 1989, Aladdin
BOX $30 **BOTTLE** $10

Dino Riders, 1988, Aladdin
BOX $25 **BOTTLE** $10

Dinobeasties, 1988, Thermos
BOX $25 **BOTTLE** n/a

Dinorocker with Radio & Headset, 1986, Fundes
BOX $55 **BOTTLE** n/a

Disney on Parade, 1970, Aladdin, plastic bottle, glass liner
BOX $50 **BOTTLE** $15

Disney's Little Mermaid, 1989, Thermos, w/generic plastic bottle
BOX $35 **BOTTLE** $5

Duck Tales (4 X 4/Game), 1986, Aladdin
BOX $25 **BOTTLE** $5

Dukes of Hazzard, 1981, Aladdin
BOX $50 **BOTTLE** $10

Dukes of Hazzard Dome, 1981, Aladdin
BOX $75 **BOTTLE** $10

Dune, 1984, Aladdin
BOX $60 **BOTTLE** $20

Dunkin Munchkins, 1972, Thermos
BOX $30 **BOTTLE** $15

Ecology Dome, 1980, Thermos
BOX $45 **BOTTLE** $20

Ed Grimley, 1988, Aladdin
BOX $30 **BOTTLE** $5

Entenmann's, 1989, Thermos
BOX $20 **BOTTLE** n/a

Ewoks, 1983, Thermos, red box
BOX $45 **BOTTLE** $15

Fame, 1972, Thermos
BOX $50 **BOTTLE** $15

Fievel Goes West, 1991, Aladdin
BOX $20 **BOTTLE** $4

Fire Engine Co. 7, 1985, D.A.S., w/generic plastic bottle
BOX $30 **BOTTLE** $5

Fisher-Price Mini Lunch Box, 1962, Fisher-Price, red w/barnyard scenes, matching bottle
BOX $25 **BOTTLE** $5

Flash Gordon Dome, 1979, Aladdin
BOX $75 **BOTTLE** $20

Flintstones, unknown, premium, Denny's Restaurants
BOX $35 **BOTTLE** n/a

Flintstones Kids, 1987, Thermos
BOX $45 **BOTTLE** $10

Food Fighters, 1988, Aladdin
BOX $25 **BOTTLE** $10

Fraggle Rock, 1987, Thermos
BOX $35 **BOTTLE** $7

Frito Lay's, 1982, Thermos, no bottle
BOX $60 **BOTTLE** n/a

G.I. Joe (Space Mission), 1989, Aladdin
BOX $35 **BOTTLE** $10

G.I. Joe, Live the Adventure, 1986, Aladdin
BOX $30 **BOTTLE** $10

Garfield (food fight), 1979, Thermos
BOX $25 **BOTTLE** $10

Garfield (lunch), 1977, Thermos
BOX $25 **BOTTLE** $10

Geoffrey, 1981, Aladdin
BOX $35 **BOTTLE** $10

Get Along Gang, 1983, Aladdin
BOX $15 **BOTTLE** $5

Ghostbusters, 1986, Deka
BOX $40 **BOTTLE** $11

Go Bots, 1984, Thermos
BOX $30 **BOTTLE** $5

Golden Girls, 1984, Thermos
BOX $20 **BOTTLE** $5

Goonies, 1985, Aladdin
BOX $35 **BOTTLE** $10

Gumby, 1986, Thermos
BOX $65 **BOTTLE** $20

Hot Wheels, 1984, Thermos
BOX $55 **BOTTLE** $20

Howdy Doody Dome, 1977, Thermos
BOX $90 **BOTTLE** $35

Incredible Hulk Dome, 1980, Aladdin
BOX $35 **BOTTLE** $10

Incredible Hulk, The, 1978, Aladdin, plastic bottle
BOX $40 **BOTTLE** $10

Inspector Gadget, 1983, Thermos
BOX $30 **BOTTLE** $8

It's Not Just the Bus - Greyhound, 1980, Aladdin
BOX $60 **BOTTLE** $20

Jabber Jaw, 1977, Thermos
BOX $60 **BOTTLE** $20

Jetsons (3-D), 1987, Servo
BOX $75 **BOTTLE** $30

Jetsons (paper picture), 1987, Servo
BOX $125 **BOTTLE** $30

Jetsons, The Movie, 1990, Aladdin
BOX $30 **BOTTLE** $15

Kermit the Frog, Lunch With, 1988, Thermos
BOX $25 **BOTTLE** $5

Kermit's Frog Scout Van, 1989, Superseal, no bottle
BOX $15 **BOTTLE** n/a

Kool-Aid Man, 1986, Thermos
BOX $20 **BOTTLE** $10

Lisa Frank, 1980, Thermos
BOX $20 **BOTTLE** $5

Little Orphan Annie, 1973, Thermos
BOX $70 **BOTTLE** $20

Looney Tunes Birthday Party, 1989, Thermos, blue or red
BOX $25 **BOTTLE** $10

Looney Tunes Dancing, 1977, Thermos
BOX $20 **BOTTLE** $10

Looney Tunes Playing Drums, 1978, Thermos
BOX $35 **BOTTLE** $10

Looney Tunes Tasmanian Devil, 1988, Thermos, w/generic plastic bottle
BOX $20 **BOTTLE** $10

Los Angeles Olympics, 1984, Aladdin
BOX $55 **BOTTLE** $5

Lucy's Luncheonette, 1981, Thermos, Peanuts characters
BOX $25 **BOTTLE** $5

Lunch Man with Radio, 1986, Fun Design, w/built-in radio, no bottle
BOX $40 **BOTTLE** n/a

Lunch 'N Tunes Safari, 1986, Fun Design, w/built-in radio, no bottle
BOX $35 **BOTTLE** n/a

Lunch 'N Tunes Singing Sandwich, 1986, Fun Design, w/built-in radio, no bottle
BOX $40 **BOTTLE** n/a

Lunch Time with Snoopy Dome, 1981, Thermos
BOX $30 **BOTTLE** $5

Mad Balls, 1986, Aladdin
BOX $30 **BOTTLE** $10

Marvel Super Heroes, 1990, Thermos
BOX $35 **BOTTLE** $10

Max Headroom (Coca-Cola), 1985, Aladdin
BOX $55 **BOTTLE** $25

McDonald's Happy Meal, 1986, Fisher-Price
BOX $25 **BOTTLE** n/a

Menudo, 1984, Thermos
BOX $15 **BOTTLE** $5

Mickey & Minnie Mouse in Pink Car, 1988, Aladdin
BOX $20 **BOTTLE** $5

Mickey Mouse & Donald Duck, 1984, Aladdin, Dome-style lunchbox with image of Mickey, Minnie, Donald and Daisy having a picnic
BOX $25 **BOTTLE** $5

Mickey Mouse & Donald Duck See-Saw, 1986, Aladdin
BOX $15 **BOTTLE** $5

Mickey Mouse at City Zoo, 1985, Aladdin
BOX $10 **BOTTLE** $5

Mickey Mouse Head, 1989, Aladdin
BOX $25 **BOTTLE** $5

Mickey on Swinging Bridge, 1987, Aladdin
BOX $15 **BOTTLE** $5

Mickey Skateboarding, 1980, Aladdin
BOX $25 **BOTTLE** $5

Mighty Mouse, 1979, Thermos, light blue, Viacom Int'l
BOX $50 **BOTTLE** $15

Miss Piggy's Safari Van, 1989, Superseal, no bottle
BOX $18 **BOTTLE** n/a

Monster in My Pocket, 1990, Aladdin
BOX $30 **BOTTLE** $5

Movie Monsters, 1979, Universal
BOX $35 **BOTTLE** $12

Mr. T, 1984, Aladdin
BOX $35 **BOTTLE** $10

Munchie Tunes Bear with Radio, 1986, Fun Design, w/built-in radio
BOX $35 **BOTTLE** $5

Munchie Tunes Punchie Pup w/Radio, 1986, Fun Design, w/built-in radio
BOX $40 **BOTTLE** $5

Munchie Tunes Robot with Radio, 1986, Fun Design, w/built-in radio
BOX $35 **BOTTLE** $5

Muppets, 1982, Thermos, blue
BOX $35 **BOTTLE** $5

Muppets Dome, 1981, Thermos, plastic red box w/matching bottle
BOX $20 **BOTTLE** $5

New Kids on the Block, 1990, Thermos, pink/orange
BOX $20 **BOTTLE** $5

Nosy Bears, 1988, Aladdin
BOX $15 **BOTTLE** $5

Official Lunch Football, 1974, unknown, football shaped box, red or brown
BOX $100 **BOTTLE** n/a

Peanuts, Wienie Roast, 1985, Thermos
BOX $15 **BOTTLE** $4

Pee Wee's Playhouse, 1987, Thermos, w/generic plastic bottle
BOX $35 **BOTTLE** $10

Peter Pan Peanut Butter, 1984, Taiwan
BOX $90 **BOTTLE** $20

Pickle, 1972, Fesco, no bottle
BOX $140 **BOTTLE** n/a

Popeye & Son, 1987, Servo, plastic red box, flat paper label, w/matching bottle
BOX $65 **BOTTLE** $12

Popeye & Son (3-D), 1987, Servo, plastic box, red or yellow, w/matching bottle
BOX $50 **BOTTLE** $12

Popeye Dome, 1979, Aladdin, blue
BOX $50 **BOTTLE** $15

Popeye, Truant Officer, 1964, King Seeley Thermos, plastic red box, matching metal bottle (Canada)
BOX $150 **BOTTLE** $35

Punky Brewster, 1984, Deka
BOX $25 **BOTTLE** $10

Q-Bert, 1983, Thermos, bright yellow
BOX $20 **BOTTLE** $12

Race Cars, 1987, Servo
BOX $25 **BOTTLE** n/a

Raggedy Ann & Andy, 1988, Aladdin
BOX $45 BOTTLE $20

Rainbow Bread Van, 1984, Moldmark Industries
BOX $60 BOTTLE $20

Rainbow Brite, 1983, Thermos
BOX $35 BOTTLE $8

Robot Man and Friends, 1984, Thermos
BOX $25 BOTTLE $10

Rocketeer, 1990, Aladdin
BOX $20 BOTTLE $5

Rocky Roughneck, 1977, Thermos
BOX $25 BOTTLE $10

Roller Games, 1989, Thermos
BOX $30 BOTTLE $10

S.W.A.T. Dome, 1975, Thermos
BOX $70 BOTTLE $15

Scooby Doo, 1973, Thermos
BOX $40 BOTTLE $20

Scooby Doo, 1984, Aladdin
BOX $40 BOTTLE $20

Scooby-Doo, A Pup Named, 1988, Aladdin
BOX $25 BOTTLE $10

Sesame Street, 1985, Aladdin/Canada
BOX $15 BOTTLE $5

Shirt Tales, 1981, Thermos
BOX $18 BOTTLE $5

Sky Commanders, 1987, Thermos, generic plastic bottle
BOX $20 BOTTLE $5

Smurfette, 1984, Thermos
BOX $15 BOTTLE $7

Smurfs, 1984, Thermos
BOX $35 BOTTLE $15

Smurfs Dome, 1981, Thermos
BOX $35 BOTTLE $15

Smurfs Fishing, 1984, Thermos
BOX $20 BOTTLE $5

Snak Shot Camera, 1987, Hummer, camera-shaped box, blue or green, w/generic plastic bottle
BOX $30 BOTTLE $2

Snoopy Dome, 1978, Thermos
BOX $25 BOTTLE $5

Snorks, 1984, Thermos
BOX $12 BOTTLE $5

Snow White, 1980, Aladdin
BOX $45 BOTTLE $15

Spare Parts, 1982, Aladdin, w/generic plastic bottle
BOX $35 BOTTLE $10

Sport Billy, 1982, Thermos
BOX $20 BOTTLE $10

Sport Goofy, 1986, Aladdin
BOX $30 BOTTLE $10

Star Com. U.S. Space Force, 1987, Thermos
BOX $20 BOTTLE $10

Star Trek Next Generation, 1988, Thermos, blue box, group picture, matching bottle
BOX $75 BOTTLE $25

Star Trek Next Generation, 1989, Thermos, red box, Picard, Data, Wesley, matching bottle
BOX $90 BOTTLE $20

Star Wars, Droids, 1985, Thermos
BOX $65 BOTTLE $25

Strawberry Shortcake, 1980, Aladdin
BOX $10 BOTTLE $5

Superman II Dome, 1986, Aladdin
BOX $75 BOTTLE $25

Superman, This is a Job For, 1980, Aladdin, no bottle
BOX $25 BOTTLE n/a

Tail Spin, 1986, Aladdin
BOX $25 BOTTLE $10

Tang Trio, 1988, Thermos, red or yellow box w/generic plastic bottle
BOX $35 BOTTLE $5

Teenage Mutant Ninja Turtles, 1990, Thermos, w/generic plastic bottle
BOX $35 BOTTLE $5

Thundarr the Barbarian Dome, 1981, Aladdin, plastic dome box w/matching bottle
BOX $25 BOTTLE $10

Timeless Tales, 1989, Aladdin
BOX $10 BOTTLE $5

Tiny Toon Adventures, 1990, Thermos
BOX $10 BOTTLE $5

Tom & Jerry, 1989, Aladdin
BOX $30 BOTTLE $10

Transformers, 1985, Aladdin
BOX $75 BOTTLE $25

Transformers Dome, 1986, Aladdin/Canada, dome box, generic plastic bottle
BOX $85 BOTTLE $20

Tweety & Sylvester, 1986, Thermos
BOX $45 BOTTLE $20

Wayne Gretzky, 1980, Aladdin
BOX $100 BOTTLE $30

Wayne Gretzky Dome, 1980, Aladdin
BOX $120 BOTTLE $30

Where's Waldo, 1990, Thermos
BOX $10 BOTTLE $5

Who Framed Roger Rabbit, 1987, Thermos, red or yellow, w/matching bottle
BOX $25 BOTTLE $10

Wild Fire, 1986, Aladdin
BOX $15 BOTTLE $8

Wizard of Oz, 50th Anniversary, 1989, Aladdin
BOX $60 BOTTLE $20

Woody Woodpecker, 1972, Aladdin, yellow box, red bottle
BOX $50 BOTTLE $40

World Wrestling Federation, 1986, Thermos
BOX $30 BOTTLE $10

Wrinkles, 1984, Thermos
BOX $10 BOTTLE $5

Wuzzles, 1985, Aladdin
BOX $10 BOTTLE $5

Yogi's Treasure Hunt, 1987, Servo, flat paper label, w/matching bottle
BOX $25 BOTTLE $30

Yogi's Treasure Hunt (3-D), 1987, Servo, 3-D box, green or pink, w/matching bottle
BOX $65 BOTTLE $30

Steel

240 Robert, 1978, Aladdin
BOX $5500 BOTTLE n/a

Action Jackson, 1973, Okay Industries, matching steel bottle
BOX $1500 BOTTLE $650

Adam-12, 1973, Aladdin, matching plastic bottle
BOX $375 BOTTLE $100

Addams Family, 1974, King Seeley Thermos, matching plastic bottle
BOX $350 BOTTLE $75

Airline, 1969, Ohio Art, no bottle
BOX $175 BOTTLE n/a

All American, 1954, Universal, steel/glass bottle
BOX $525 BOTTLE $125

America on Parade, 1976, Aladdin, matching plastic bottle
BOX $95 BOTTLE $40

Americana, 1958, King Seeley Thermos, steel/glass bottle
BOX $425 BOTTLE $165

Animal Friends, 1978, Ohio Art, yellow or red background behind name
BOX $100 BOTTLE n/a

Annie Oakley & Tagg, 1955, Aladdin, matching steel bottle
BOX $725 BOTTLE $175

Annie, The Movie, 1982, Aladdin, plastic bottle, shown with Dukes of Hazzard & Magic Kindon lunch boxes
BOX $95 BOTTLE $25

Apple's Way, 1975, King Seeley Thermos, plastic bottle
BOX $175 **BOTTLE** $40

Archies, 1969, Aladdin, matching plastic bottle
BOX $325 **BOTTLE** $75

Astronaut Dome, 1960, King Seeley Thermos, steel/glass bottle
BOX $350 **BOTTLE** $75

Astronauts, 1969, Aladdin, matching plastic bottle
BOX $300 **BOTTLE** $95

A-Team, 1985, King Seeley Thermos, plastic bottle
BOX $100 **BOTTLE** $35

Atom Ant/Secret Squirrel, 1966, King Seeley Thermos, matching steel bottle
BOX $360 **BOTTLE** $120

Auto Race, 1967, King Seeley Thermos, matching steel bottle
BOX $280 **BOTTLE** $75

Back in '76, 1975, Aladdin, plastic bottle
BOX $110 **BOTTLE** $40

Barbie Lunch Kit, 1962, King Seeley Thermos, steel/glass bottle
BOX $300 **BOTTLE** $90

Basketweave, 1968, Ohio Art, no bottle
BOX $75 **BOTTLE** n/a

Batman and Robin, 1966, Aladdin, matching steel bottle
BOX $625 **BOTTLE** $175

Battle Kit, 1965, King Seeley Thermos, matching steel bottle
BOX $350 **BOTTLE** $75

Battle of the Planets, 1979, King Seeley Thermos, matching plastic bottle, shown with Chan Clan, The & Hot Wheels lunch boxes
BOX $175 **BOTTLE** $50

Battlestar Galactica, 1978, Aladdin, matching plastic bottle
BOX $275 **BOTTLE** $45

Beatles, 1966, Aladdin, blue, matching bottle
BOX $2800 **BOTTLE** $500

Bedknobs & Broomsticks, 1972, Aladdin, plastic bottle
BOX $225 **BOTTLE** $45

Bee Gees, 1978, King Seeley Thermos, Maurice on back, matching plastic bottle
BOX $200 **BOTTLE** $45

Bee Gees, 1978, King Seeley Thermos, Barry on back, matching plastic bottle
BOX $250 **BOTTLE** $45

Bee Gees, 1978, King Seeley Thermos, Robin on back, matching plastic bottle
BOX $200 **BOTTLE** $45

Berenstain Bears, 1983, American Thermos, matching plastic bottle
BOX $125 **BOTTLE** $40

Beverly Hillbillies, 1963, Aladdin, matching steel bottle
BOX $375 **BOTTLE** $95

Bionic Woman, with Car, 1977, Aladdin, plastic bottle
BOX $250 **BOTTLE** $50

Bionic Woman, with Dog, 1978, Aladdin, matching plastic bottle
BOX $275 **BOTTLE** $50

Black Hole, 1979, Aladdin, matching plastic bottle
BOX $125 **BOTTLE** $40

Blondie, 1969, King Seeley Thermos, matching steel bottle
BOX $350 **BOTTLE** $75

Boating, 1959, American Thermos, matching steel bottle
BOX $450 **BOTTLE** $125

Bobby Sherman, 1972, King Seeley Thermos, matching steel bottle
BOX $300 **BOTTLE** $75

Bonanza, 1963, Aladdin, green rim box, steel bottle
BOX $400 **BOTTLE** $110

Bonanza, 1965, Aladdin, brown rim box, steel bottle
BOX $300 **BOTTLE** $75

Bonanza, 1968, Aladdin, black rim box, steel bottle
BOX $475 **BOTTLE** $120

Bond XX, 1967, Ohio Art, no bottle
BOX $200 **BOTTLE** n/a

Boston Bruins, 1973, Okay Industries, steel/glass bottle
BOX $525 **BOTTLE** $250

(Joe Soucy collection)

Bozo the Clown Dome, 1963, Aladdin, steel bottle
BOX $375 **BOTTLE** $120

Brady Bunch, 1970, King Seeley Thermos, matching steel bottle
BOX $575 **BOTTLE** $150

Brave Eagle, 1957, American Thermos, red, blue, gray or green band, matching steel bottle
BOX $375 **BOTTLE** $150

Bread Box Dome, 1968, Aladdin, Campbell's Soup bottle
BOX $450 **BOTTLE** $125

Buccaneer Dome, 1957, Aladdin, matching bottle, shown with Julia lunch box
BOX $425 **BOTTLE** $125

Buck Rogers, 1979, Aladdin, matching plastic bottle
BOX $120 **BOTTLE** $35

Bugaloos, 1971, Aladdin, matching plastic bottle
BOX $360 **BOTTLE** $75

Bullwinkle & Rocky, 1962, Universal, blue box, steel bottle
BOX $3500 **BOTTLE** $1500

Cabbage Patch Kids, 1984, King Seeley Thermos, matching plastic bottle
BOX $75 **BOTTLE** $20

Cable Car Dome, 1962, Aladdin, steel/glass bottle
BOX $600 **BOTTLE** $125

Campbell's Kids, 1973, Okay, matching steel bottle
BOX $285 **BOTTLE** $150

Campus Queen, 1967, King Seeley Thermos, matching steel bottle
BOX $250 **BOTTLE** $65

Canadian Pacific Railroad, 1970, Ohio Art, no bottle
BOX $65 **BOTTLE** n/a

Captain Astro, 1966, Ohio Art, no bottle
BOX $525 **BOTTLE** n/a

Care Bear Cousins, 1985, Aladdin, matching plastic bottle
BOX $75 **BOTTLE** $20

Care Bears, 1984, Aladdin, plastic bottle
BOX $95 **BOTTLE** $20

Carnival, 1959, Universal, matching steel bottle
BOX $750 **BOTTLE** $250

Cartoon Zoo Lunch Chest, 1962, Universal, steel/glass bottle
BOX $525 **BOTTLE** $125

Casey Jones, 1960, Universal, steel dome box, steel/glass bottle
BOX $650 **BOTTLE** $125

Chan Clan, The, 1973, King Seeley Thermos, plastic bottle, shown with Battle of the Planets & Hot Wheels lunch boxes
BOX $225 **BOTTLE** $40

Charlie's Angels, 1978, Aladdin, matching plastic bottle
BOX $250 **BOTTLE** $50

Chavo, 1979, Aladdin, matching plastic bottle
BOX $285 **BOTTLE** $50

Children, blue, 1974, Okay Industries, plastic bottle
BOX $175 **BOTTLE** $40

Children, yellow, 1974, Okay Industries, plastic bottle
BOX $250 **BOTTLE** $40

Children's, 1984, Ohio Art, no bottle
BOX $75 **BOTTLE** n/a

Chitty Chitty Bang Bang, 1969, King Seeley Thermos, matching steel bottle
BOX $400 **BOTTLE** $75

Chuck Wagon Dome, 1958, Aladdin, matching bottle
BOX $375 **BOTTLE** $90

Circus Wagon Dome, 1958, King Seeley Thermos, steel/glass bottle
BOX $350 **BOTTLE** $150

(Joe Soucy collection)

Clash of the Titans, 1981, King Seeley Thermos, matching plastic bottle
BOX $175 **BOTTLE** $40

Close Encounters of the Third Kind, 1978, King Seeley Thermos, plastic bottle
BOX $150 **BOTTLE** $40

Color Me Happy, 1984, Ohio Art, no bottle
BOX $300 **BOTTLE** n/a

Corsage, 1958, American Thermos, matching steel bottle
BOX $115 **BOTTLE** $60

Cowboy in Africa, Chuck Connors, 1968, King Seeley Thermos, matching steel bottle
BOX $350 **BOTTLE** $75

Cracker Jack, 1969, Aladdin, matching plastic bottle
BOX $150 **BOTTLE** $50

Curiosity Shop, 1972, King Seeley Thermos, matching steel bottle
BOX $150 **BOTTLE** $60

Cyclist Dirt Bike, 1979, Aladdin, plastic bottle
BOX $125 **BOTTLE** $45

Daniel Boone, 1955, Aladdin, matching steel bottle
BOX $575 **BOTTLE** $110

Daniel Boone, 1965, Aladdin, matching steel bottle
BOX $400 **BOTTLE** $90

Dark Crystal, 1982, King Seeley Thermos, matching plastic bottle
BOX $95 **BOTTLE** $25

(Joe Soucy)

Davey Crocket at the Alamo, 1955, Adco
BOX $1800 **BOTTLE** $3500

Davy Crockett, 1955, Kruger, no bottle
BOX $900 **BOTTLE** n/a

Davy Crockett, 1955, Holtemp, matching steel bottle (shown)
BOX $375 **BOTTLE** $75

Davy Crockett/Kit Carson, 1955, Adco Liberty
BOX $350 **BOTTLE** n/a

Debutante, 1958, Aladdin, matching steel bottle
BOX $110 **BOTTLE** $75

Denim Diner Dome, 1975, Aladdin, matching plastic bottle
BOX $95 **BOTTLE** $30

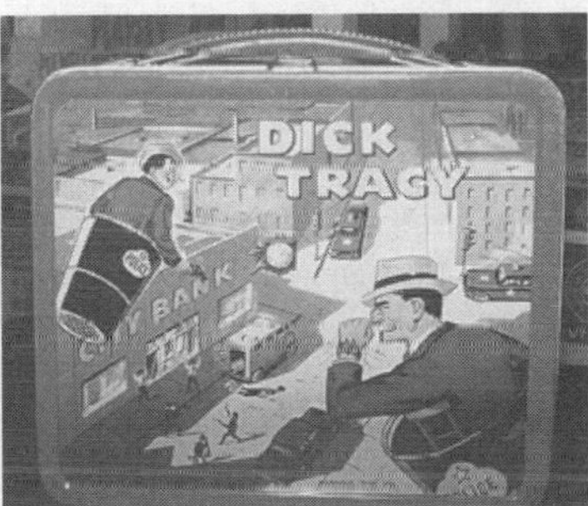

Dick Tracy, 1967, Aladdin, matching steel bottle
BOX $450 **BOTTLE** $125

Disco, 1979, Aladdin, matching plastic bottle
BOX $120 **BOTTLE** $45

Disco Fever, 1980, Aladdin, matching plastic bottle
BOX $130 **BOTTLE** $45

Disney Express, 1979, Aladdin, matching plastic bottle, shown with Disney, Wonderful World & Mickey Mouse Club lunch boxes
BOX $95 **BOTTLE** $25

Disney Fire Fighters Dome, 1974, Aladdin, matching plastic bottle
BOX $225 **BOTTLE** $60

Disney School Bus Dome, 1968, Aladdin, steel/glass bottle
BOX $150 **BOTTLE** $40

Disney World, 1972, Aladdin, matching plastic bottle
BOX $95 **BOTTLE** $40

Disney, Wonderful World of Ice, 1982, Aladdin, plastic bottle, shown with Mickey Mouse Club & Disney Express lunch boxes
BOX $125 **BOTTLE** $30

Disneyland (Castle), 1957, Aladdin, matching steel bottle
BOX $550 **BOTTLE** $125

Disneyland (Monorail), 1968, Aladdin, matching steel bottle
BOX $600 **BOTTLE** $125

Disney's Magic Kingdom, 1980, Aladdin, plastic bottle
BOX $95 **BOTTLE** $40

Disney's Rescuers, The, 1977, Aladdin, plastic bottle
BOX $125 **BOTTLE** $35

Disney's Robin Hood, 1974, Aladdin, plastic bottle
BOX $100 **BOTTLE** $30

Donald Duck, 1980, Cheinco, no bottle
BOX $75 **BOTTLE** n/a

Double Decker, 1970, Aladdin, matching plastic bottle
BOX $225 **BOTTLE** $50

Dr. Dolittle, 1968, Aladdin, steel/glass bottle
BOX $350 **BOTTLE** $90

Dr. Seuss, 1970, Aladdin, matching plastic bottle
BOX $525 **BOTTLE** $75

Drag Strip, 1975, Aladdin, matching plastic bottle
BOX $200 **BOTTLE** $45

Dragon's Lair, 1983, Aladdin, matching plastic bottle
BOX $75 **BOTTLE** $25

Duchess, 1960, Aladdin, steel/glass bottle
BOX $125 **BOTTLE** $40

(Joe Soucy collection)

Dudley Do-Right, 1962, Universal, matching steel bottle
BOX $3450 **BOTTLE** $1450

Dukes of Hazzard, 1983, Aladdin, matching plastic bottle, shown with Annie & Magic Kingdom lunch boxes
BOX $225 **BOTTLE** $50

Dutch Cottage Dome, 1958, King Seeley Thermos, steel/glass bottle
BOX $450 **BOTTLE** $150

Dyno Mutt, 1977, King Seeley Thermos, plastic bottle
BOX $150 **BOTTLE** $40

E.T., The Extra-Terrestrial, 1982, Aladdin, matching plastic bottle
BOX $125 **BOTTLE** $25

Early West Indian Territory, 1982, Ohio Art, no bottle
BOX $120 **BOTTLE** n/a

Early West Oregon Trail, 1982, Ohio Art, no bottle
BOX $120 **BOTTLE** n/a

Early West Pony Express, 1982, Ohio Art, no bottle
BOX $120 **BOTTLE** n/a

Emergency!, 1973, Aladdin, plastic bottle
BOX $350 **BOTTLE** $50

Emergency! Dome, 1977, Aladdin, plastic bottle
BOX $400 **BOTTLE** $50

(Joe Soucy collection)

Evel Knievel, 1974, Aladdin, plastic bottle
BOX $225 **BOTTLE** $45

Exciting World of Metrics, The, 1976, King Seeley Thermos, plastic bottle
BOX $80 **BOTTLE** $30

Fall Guy, 1981, Aladdin, matching plastic bottle
BOX $85 **BOTTLE** $30

Family Affair, 1969, King Seeley Thermos, matching steel bottle
BOX $375 **BOTTLE** $90

Fat Albert and the Cosby Kids, 1973, King Seeley Thermos, plastic bottle
BOX $120 **BOTTLE** $30

Fess Parker, 1965, King Seeley Thermos, matching steel bottle
BOX $325 **BOTTLE** $90

Fireball XL5, 1964, King Seeley Thermos, steel/glass bottle
BOX $400 **BOTTLE** $85

Firehouse Dome, 1959, American Thermos, steel/glass bottle
BOX $475 **BOTTLE** $150

Flag-O-Rama, 1954, Universal, steel/glass bottle
BOX $475 **BOTTLE** $110

Flintstones, 1962, Aladdin, orange, 1st issue, matching bottle
BOX $600 **BOTTLE** $110

Flintstones, 1964, Aladdin, yellow, 2nd issue, matching bottle
BOX $675 **BOTTLE** $110

Flintstones, 1973, Aladdin, matching plastic bottle
BOX $350 **BOTTLE** $50

Flipper, 1966, King Seeley Thermos, matching steel bottle
BOX $350 **BOTTLE** $75

Floral, 1970, Ohio Art, no bottle
BOX $40 **BOTTLE** n/a

Flying Nun, 1968, Aladdin, matching steel bottle
BOX $475 **BOTTLE** $95

Fonz, The, 1978, King Seeley Thermos, plastic bottle
BOX $250 **BOTTLE** $40

Fox and the Hound, 1981, Aladdin, plastic bottle
BOX $85 **BOTTLE** $30

Fraggle Rock, 1984, King Seeley Thermos, matching plastic bottle
BOX $110 **BOTTLE** $30

Fritos, 1975, King Seeley Thermos, generic bottle
BOX $300 **BOTTLE** n/a

Frontier Days, 1957, Ohio Art, no bottle
BOX $350 **BOTTLE** n/a

Frost Flowers, 1962, Ohio Art, no bottle
BOX $70 **BOTTLE** n/a

Fruit Basket, 1975, Ohio Art, no bottle
BOX $45 **BOTTLE** n/a

Funtastic World of Hanna-Barbera, 1977, King Seeley Thermos, Huck Hound, plastic bottle
BOX $350 **BOTTLE** $45

Funtastic World of Hanna-Barbera, 1978, King Seeley Thermos, Flintstones & Yogi, plastic bottle
BOX $375 **BOTTLE** $45

G.I. Joe, 1967, King Seeley Thermos, steel/glass bottle
BOX $425 **BOTTLE** $90

G.I. Joe, 1982, King Seeley Thermos, plastic bottle
BOX $125 **BOTTLE** $25

Gene Autry, 1954, Universal, steel/glass bottle
BOX $1050 **BOTTLE** $225

Gentle Ben, 1968, Aladdin, plastic bottle, glass liner, shown here with Lance Link lunch box
BOX $225 **BOTTLE** $75

Get Smart, 1966, King Seeley Thermos, steel/glass bottle
BOX $650 **BOTTLE** $95

Ghostland, 1977, Ohio Art, spinner game, no bottle
BOX $80 **BOTTLE** n/a

Globe-Trotter Dome, 1959, Aladdin, steel dome box, matching steel/glass bottle
BOX $300 **BOTTLE** $120

Gomer Pyle USMC, 1966, Aladdin, matching steel bottle
BOX $450 **BOTTLE** $110

Goober and the Ghostchasers / Inch High, 1974, King Seeley Thermos, matching plastic bottle
BOX $120 **BOTTLE** $25

Great Wild West, 1959, Universal, matching steel bottle
BOX $625 **BOTTLE** $225

Green Hornet, 1967, King Seeley Thermos, matching steel bottle
BOX $750 **BOTTLE** $175

Gremlins, 1984, Aladdin, matching plastic bottle
BOX $95 **BOTTLE** $35

Grizzly Adams Dome, 1977, Aladdin, plastic bottle
BOX $250 **BOTTLE** $40

Guns of Will Sonnett, The, 1968, King Seeley Thermos, steel/glass bottle
BOX $300 **BOTTLE** $90

Gunsmoke, 1959, Aladdin, plastic bottle
BOX $375 **BOTTLE** $95

Gunsmoke, 1972, Aladdin, mule splashing box w/matching bottle
BOX $300 **BOTTLE** $75

Gunsmoke, 1973, Aladdin, stagecoach box, matching bottle
BOX $325 **BOTTLE** $75

Gunsmoke, Double L Version, 1959, Aladdin, double L error version, matching bottle
BOX $1350 **BOTTLE** $150

Gunsmoke, Marshal Matt Dillon, 1962, Aladdin, matching steel bottle
BOX $450 **BOTTLE** $95

H.R. Pufnstuf, 1970, Aladdin, matching plastic bottle
BOX $850 **BOTTLE** $110

Hair Bear Bunch, The, 1972, King Seeley Thermos, plastic bottle
BOX $150 **BOTTLE** $35

Hansel and Gretel, 1982, Ohio Art, no bottle
BOX $100 **BOTTLE** n/a

Happy Days, 1977, American Thermos, matching plastic bottle
BOX $300 **BOTTLE** $40

Hardy Boys Mysteries, 1977, King Seeley Thermos, matching plastic bottle
BOX $200 **BOTTLE** $45

Harlem Globetrotters, 1971, King Seeley Thermos, steel bottle, blue or purple uniforms
BOX $225 **BOTTLE** $65

Have Gun, Will Travel, 1960, Aladdin, matching bottle, Paladin
BOX $600 **BOTTLE** $150

Heathcliff, 1982, Aladdin, matching plastic bottle
BOX $85 **BOTTLE** $20

Hector Heathcote, 1964, Aladdin, matching steel bottle
BOX $325 **BOTTLE** $90

Hee Haw, 1971, King Seeley Thermos, matching steel bottle
BOX $300 **BOTTLE** $75

He-Man & Masters of the Universe, 1984, Aladdin, matching plastic bottle
BOX $95 **BOTTLE** $30

Highway Signs, 1972, Ohio Art, no bottle
BOX $70 **BOTTLE** n/a

Hogan's Heroes Dome, 1966, Aladdin, steel/glass bottle
BOX $650 **BOTTLE** $200

Holly Hobbie, 1968, Aladdin, red rim, matching plastic bottle
BOX $85 **BOTTLE** $20

Holly Hobbie, 1973, Aladdin, matching plastic bottle
BOX $85 **BOTTLE** $20

Holly Hobbie, 1979, Aladdin, matching plastic bottle
BOX $85 **BOTTLE** $20

Home Town Airport Dome, 1960, King Seeley Thermos, steel/glass bottle
BOX $1200 **BOTTLE** $275

Hong Kong Phooey, 1975, King Seeley Thermos, steel/glass bottle
BOX $275 **BOTTLE** $50

Hopalong Cassidy, 1950, Aladdin, red or blue, steel/glass bottle
BOX $400 **BOTTLE** $90

Hopalong Cassidy, 1952, Aladdin, steel bottle
BOX $400 **BOTTLE** $90

Hopalong Cassidy, 1954, Aladdin, black rim, steel/glass bottle, full litho
BOX $525 **BOTTLE** $150

Hot Wheels, 1969, King Seeley Thermos, matching steel bottle
BOX $325 **BOTTLE** $75

How the West Was Won, 1979, King Seeley Thermos, matching plastic bottle
BOX $125 **BOTTLE** $40

Howdy Doody, 1954, Adco Liberty
BOX $1100 **BOTTLE** n/a

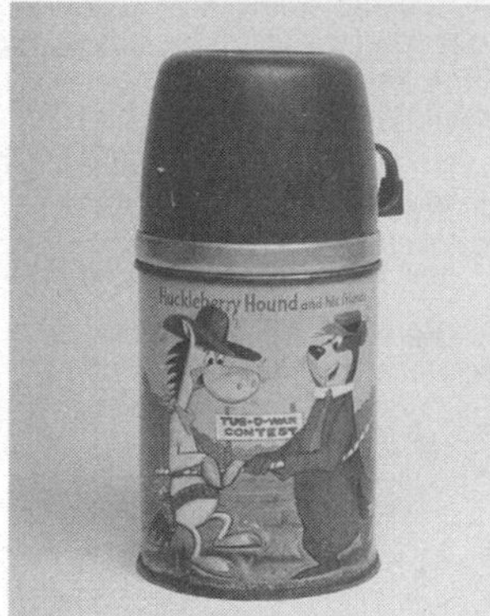

Huckleberry Hound, 1961, Aladdin, steel/glass bottle
BOX $350 **BOTTLE** $90

Indiana Jones, 1984, King Seeley Thermos, matching plastic bottle
BOX $150 **BOTTLE** $30

Indiana Jones Temple of Doom, 1984, King Seeley Thermos, matching plastic bottle
BOX $150 **BOTTLE** $30

It's About Time Dome, 1967, Aladdin, matching bottle
BOX $425 **BOTTLE** $125

Jack and Jill, 1982, Ohio Art
BOX $400 **BOTTLE** n/a

(Joe Soucy collection)

James Bond 007, 1966, Aladdin, matching steel bottle
BOX $775 **BOTTLE** $150

Jet Patrol, 1957, Aladdin, matching steel bottle
BOX $400 **BOTTLE** $150

Jetsons Dome, 1963, Aladdin, matching bottle
BOX $2650 **BOTTLE** $450

Joe Palooka, 1949, Continental Can, no bottle
BOX $125 **BOTTLE** n/a

Johnny Lightning, 1970, Aladdin, plastic bottle
BOX $250 **BOTTLE** $60

Jonathan Livingston Seagull, 1973, Aladdin, matching plastic bottle
BOX $150 **BOTTLE** $50

Julia, 1969, King Seeley Thermos, matching steel bottle, shown with Buccaneer Dome lunch box
BOX $250 **BOTTLE** $75

Jungle Book, 1968, Aladdin, matching steel bottle
BOX $275 **BOTTLE** $75

Junior Miss, 1978, Aladdin, matching plastic bottle
BOX $110 **BOTTLE** $40

Kellogg's, 1969, Aladdin, plastic bottle
BOX $325 **BOTTLE** $75

King Kong, 1977, King Seeley Thermos, plastic bottle
BOX $250 **BOTTLE** $40

(Joe Soucy collection)

KISS, 1977, King Seeley Thermos, plastic bottle
BOX $350 **BOTTLE** $50

Knight in Armor, 1959, Universal, matching steel bottle
BOX $1250 **BOTTLE** $300

Knight Rider, 1984, King Seeley Thermos, matching plastic bottle
BOX $95 **BOTTLE** $25

Korg, 1975, King Seeley Thermos, matching plastic bottle
BOX $150 **BOTTLE** $45

Krofft Supershow, 1976, Aladdin, matching plastic bottle
BOX $300 **BOTTLE** $50

Kung Fu, 1974, King Seeley Thermos, matching plastic bottle
BOX $250 **BOTTLE** $40

Lance Link, Secret Chimp, 1971, King Seeley Thermos, matching steel bottle, shown here with Gentle Ben lunch box
BOX $300 **BOTTLE** $75

Land of the Giants, 1968, Aladdin, plastic bottle
BOX $325 **BOTTLE** $85

Land of the Lost, 1975, Aladdin, matching plastic bottle
BOX $350 **BOTTLE** $50

Laugh-In (Helmet), 1969, Aladdin, helmet on back, matching plastic bottle
BOX $325 **BOTTLE** $65

Laugh-In (Tricycle), 1969, Aladdin, trike on back, matching plastic bottle
BOX $325 **BOTTLE** $65

Lawman, 1961, King Seeley Thermos, generic bottle
BOX $300 **BOTTLE** $85

Legend of the Lone Ranger, 1980, Aladdin, plastic bottle
BOX $175 **BOTTLE** $45

Lidsville, 1971, Aladdin, matching plastic bottle
BOX $375 **BOTTLE** $65

Little Dutch Miss, 1959, Universal, matching steel bottle
BOX $225 **BOTTLE** $75

Little Friends, 1982, Aladdin, matching plastic bottle
BOX $850 **BOTTLE** $260

Little House on the Prairie, 1978, King Seeley Thermos, matching plastic bottle
BOX $350 **BOTTLE** $45

Little Red Riding Hood, 1982, Ohio Art, no bottle
BOX $75 **BOTTLE** n/a

Lone Ranger, 1955, Adco Liberty, blue band, no bottle
BOX $1150 **BOTTLE** n/a

Lone Ranger, 1955, Adco Liberty, red rim, no bottle
BOX $900 **BOTTLE** n/a

Looney Tunes TV Set, 1959, King Seeley Thermos, steel/glass bottle
BOX $350 **BOTTLE** $95

(Joe Soucy collection)

Lost in Space Dome, 1967, King Seeley Thermos, steel/glass bottle
BOX $1350 **BOTTLE** $100

Ludwig Von Drake, 1962, Aladdin, steel/glass bottle
BOX $350 **BOTTLE** $90

Luggage Plaid, 1955, Adco Liberty, no bottle
BOX $75 **BOTTLE** n/a

Luggage Plaid, 1957, Ohio Art, no bottle
BOX $75 **BOTTLE** n/a

Magic of Lassie, 1978, King Seeley Thermos, matching plastic bottle
BOX $250 **BOTTLE** $40

Major League Baseball, 1968, King Seeley Thermos, matching bottle
BOX $275 **BOTTLE** $55

Man from U.N.C.L.E., 1966, King Seeley Thermos, matching steel bottle
BOX $850 **BOTTLE** $90

(Joe Soucy collection)

Marvel Super Heroes, 1976, Aladdin, black rim, matching plastic bottle
BOX $200 **BOTTLE** $45

Mary Poppins, 1965, Aladdin, steel/glass bottle
BOX $250 **BOTTLE** $75

Masters of the Universe, 1983, Aladdin, matching plastic bottle
BOX $75 **BOTTLE** $25

Mickey Mouse & Donald Duck, 1954, Adco Liberty, matching steel bottle
BOX $900 **BOTTLE** $1650

Mickey Mouse Club, 1963, Aladdin, yellow, steel/glass bottle, shown with Disney, Wonderful World & Mickey Mouse Club lunch boxes
BOX $375 **BOTTLE** $60

Mickey Mouse Club, 1976, Aladdin, white, matching steel bottle
BOX $450 **BOTTLE** $90

Mickey Mouse Club, 1977, Aladdin, red rim, sky boat, matching bottle
BOX $150 **BOTTLE** $40

(Joe Soucy collection)

Mickey Mouse School Days, plastic bottle, Mickey as school teacher
BOX $80 **BOTTLE** $15

Miss America, 1972, Aladdin, matching plastic bottle
BOX $325 **BOTTLE** $50

Mod Floral Dome, 1975, Okay Industries, matching steel bottle
BOX $400 **BOTTLE** n/a

Monroes, 1967, Aladdin, matching steel bottle
BOX $550 **BOTTLE** $110

Mork & Mindy, 1979, American Thermos, matching plastic bottle
BOX $175 **BOTTLE** $45

Mr. Merlin, 1982, King Seeley Thermos, matching plastic bottle
BOX $100 **BOTTLE** $35

Munsters, 1965, King Seeley Thermos, matching steel bottle
BOX $900 **BOTTLE** $150

Muppet Babies, 1985, King Seeley Thermos, matching plastic bottle
BOX $75 **BOTTLE** $20

Muppet Movie, 1979, King Seeley Thermos, plastic bottle
BOX $225 **BOTTLE** $40

Muppet Show, 1978, King Seeley Thermos, plastic bottle
BOX $150 **BOTTLE** $30

Muppets, 1979, King Seeley Thermos, back shows Animal, Fozzie or Kermit, matching plastic bottle
BOX $125 **BOTTLE** $30

My Lunch, 1976, Ohio Art, no bottle
BOX $65 **BOTTLE** n/a

Nancy Drew, 1978, King Seeley Thermos, plastic bottle
BOX $250 **BOTTLE** $30

NFL, 1962, Okay, black rim, steel/glass bottle
BOX $350 **BOTTLE** $130

NFL, 1975, King Seeley Thermos, yellow rim, plastic bottle
BOX $225 **BOTTLE** $40

NFL, 1976, King Seeley Thermos, red rim, matching plastic bottle
BOX $225 **BOTTLE** $40

NFL, 1978, King Seeley Thermos, blue rim, matching plastic bottle
BOX $150 **BOTTLE** $40

NFL Quarterback, 1964, Aladdin, matching steel bottle
BOX $450 **BOTTLE** $95

NHL, 1970, Okay Industries, plastic bottle
BOX $600 **BOTTLE** $250

Orbit, 1963, King Seeley Thermos, matching steel bottle
BOX $500 **BOTTLE** $90

(Joe Soucy collection)

Osmonds, The, 1973, Aladdin, matching plastic bottle
BOX $300 **BOTTLE** $45

Our Friends, 1982, Aladdin, matching plastic bottle
BOX $900 **BOTTLE** $350

Pac-Man, 1980, Aladdin, matching plastic bottle
BOX $125 **BOTTLE** $25

Para-Medic, 1978, Ohio Art, no bottle
BOX $75 **BOTTLE** n/a

Partridge Family, 1971, King Seeley Thermos, plastic or steel bottle
BOX $275 **BOTTLE** $60

Pathfinder, 1959, Universal, matching steel bottle
BOX $750 **BOTTLE** $225

Patriotic, 1974, Ohio Art, no bottle
BOX $75 **BOTTLE** n/a

Peanuts, 1966, King Seeley Thermos, orange rim, matching steel bottle (shown)
BOX $325 **BOTTLE** $50

Peanuts, 1973, King Seeley Thermos, red rim psychiatric box, plastic bottle
BOX $125 **BOTTLE** $30

Peanuts, 1976, King Seeley Thermos, red pitching box, plastic bottle
BOX $150 **BOTTLE** $35

Peanuts, 1980, King Seeley Thermos, pitching box, yellow face, green band, matching bottle
BOX $125 **BOTTLE** $35

Pebbles & Bamm-Bamm, 1971, Aladdin, matching plastic bottle
BOX $300 **BOTTLE** $60

Pele, 1975, King Seeley Thermos, matching plastic bottle
BOX $250 **BOTTLE** $45

Pennant, 1950, Ohio Art, basket type box, no bottle
BOX $50 **BOTTLE** n/a

Peter Pan, 1969, Aladdin, matching plastic bottle, Disney
BOX $285 **BOTTLE** $50

Pete's Dragon, 1978, Aladdin, matching plastic bottle
BOX $150 **BOTTLE** $35

Pets 'n Pals, 1961, King Seeley Thermos, matching steel bottle
BOX $250 **BOTTLE** $65

Pigs In Space, 1977, King Seeley Thermos, matching plastic bottle
BOX $75 **BOTTLE** $30

Pink Gingham, 1976, King Seeley Thermos, matching plastic bottle
BOX $60 **BOTTLE** $20

Pink Panther & Sons, 1984, King Seeley Thermos, matching plastic bottle
BOX $100 **BOTTLE** $30

Pinocchio, 1938, unknown, steel round tin w/handle
BOX $250 **BOTTLE** n/a

Pinocchio, 1938, unknown, square
BOX $200 **BOTTLE** n/a

Pinocchio, 1971, Aladdin, plastic bottle
BOX $250 **BOTTLE** $50

(Joe Soucy collection)

Pit Stop, 1968, Ohio Art
BOX $450 **BOTTLE** n/a

Planet of the Apes, 1974, Aladdin, matching plastic bottle
BOX $475 **BOTTLE** $80

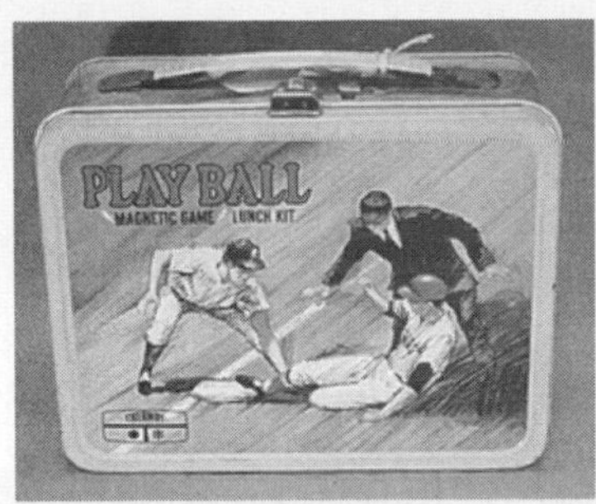

Play Ball, 1969, King Seeley Thermos, game on back, steel bottle
BOX $250 **BOTTLE** $55

Police Patrol, 1978, Aladdin, plastic bottle
BOX $300 **BOTTLE** $45

Polly Pal, 1975, King Seeley Thermos, matching plastic bottle
BOX $60 **BOTTLE** $20

Pony Express, 1982, Ohio Art
BOX $110 **BOTTLE** n/a

(Joe Soucy collection)

Popeye, 1962, Universal, "Popeye socks Bluto" box, matching bottle
BOX $900 **BOTTLE** $450

Popeye, 1964, King Seeley Thermos, "Popeye in boat" box w/matching steel bottle
BOX $450 **BOTTLE** $80

Popeye, 1980, Aladdin, "arm wrestling" box, plastic bottle
BOX $200 **BOTTLE** $45

Popples, 1986, Aladdin, plastic bottle
BOX $95 **BOTTLE** $20

Porky's Lunch Wagon Dome, 1959, King Seeley Thermos, steel/glass bottle
BOX $625 **BOTTLE** $95

Pro Sports, 1974, Ohio Art, no bottle
BOX $95 **BOTTLE** n/a

Psychedelic Dome, 1969, Aladdin, plastic bottle
BOX $350 **BOTTLE** $85

Racing Wheels, 1977, King Seeley Thermos, plastic bottle
BOX $150 **BOTTLE** $25

Raggedy Ann & Andy, 1973, Aladdin, plastic bottle
BOX $175 **BOTTLE** $40

Rambo, 1985, King Seeley Thermos, matching plastic bottle
BOX $95 **BOTTLE** $20

Rat Patrol, 1967, Aladdin, steel/glass bottle
BOX $400 **BOTTLE** $90

Red Barn Dome, 1957, King Seeley Thermos, closed door version, plain Holtemp bottle
BOX $225 **BOTTLE** $30

Red Barn Dome, 1958, King Seeley Thermos, open door version, matching steel bottle
BOX $175 **BOTTLE** $50

Red Barn Dome, 1972, Thermos, matching steel/glass bottle
BOX $175 **BOTTLE** $50

Rifleman, The, 1961, Aladdin, steel/glass bottle
BOX $625 **BOTTLE** $175

Road Runner, 1970, King Seeley Thermos, lavender or purple rim, steel or plastic bottle
BOX $275 **BOTTLE** $75

Robin Hood, 1956, Aladdin, matching bottle
BOX $425 **BOTTLE** $120

Ronald McDonald, Sheriff, 1982, Aladdin, plastic bottle
BOX $125 **BOTTLE** $20

Rose Petal Place, 1983, Aladdin, plastic bottle
BOX $75 **BOTTLE** $20

Rough Rider, 1973, Aladdin, plastic bottle
BOX $125 **BOTTLE** $40

Roy Rogers & Dale Double R Bar Ranch, 1953, King Seeley Thermos, steel/glass bottle
BOX $425 **BOTTLE** $75

Roy Rogers & Dale Double R Bar Ranch, 1954, American Thermos, blue or red band, woodgrain tall bottle
BOX $350 **BOTTLE** $95

Roy Rogers & Dale Double R Bar Ranch, 1955, American Thermos, eight-scene box, red or blue band, matching bottle
BOX $375 **BOTTLE** $95

Roy Rogers & Dale Double R Bar Ranch, 1955, American Thermos, cowhide back box, red or blue band, matching bottle
BOX $350 **BOTTLE** $95

Roy Rogers & Dale on Rail, 1957, American Thermos, red or blue band, matching bottle
BOX $450 **BOTTLE** $95

Roy Rogers Chow Wagon Dome, 1958, King Seeley Thermos, steel/glass bottle
BOX $525 **BOTTLE** $95

Saddlebag, 1977, King Seeley Thermos, generic plastic bottle
BOX $195 **BOTTLE** $40

Steel

Satellite, 1958, American Thermos, matching bottle, narrow band
BOX $400 **BOTTLE** $60

Satellite, 1960, King Seeley Thermos, steel bottle
BOX $350 **BOTTLE** $60

Scooby Doo, 1973, King Seeley Thermos, orange rim, plastic bottle
BOX $800 **BOTTLE** $40

Scooby Doo, 1973, King Seeley Thermos, yellow rim, plastic bottle
BOX $750 **BOTTLE** $40

Secret Agent T, 1968, King Seeley Thermos, matching bottle
BOX $325 **BOTTLE** $75

Secret of NIMH, 1982, Aladdin, plastic bottle
BOX $75 **BOTTLE** $30

Secret Wars, 1984, Aladdin, plastic bottle
BOX $195 **BOTTLE** $40

See America, 1972, Ohio Art, no bottle
BOX $95 **BOTTLE** n/a

Sesame Street, 1983, Aladdin, yellow or green rim, plastic bottle
BOX $125 **BOTTLE** $30

Sigmund and the Sea Monsters, 1974, Aladdin, plastic bottle
BOX $475 **BOTTLE** $75

Six Million Dollar Man, 1974, Aladdin, plastic bottle
BOX $200 **BOTTLE** $40

(Joe Soucy collection)

Six Million Dollar Man, 1978, Aladdin, plastic bottle
BOX $225 **BOTTLE** $40

Skateboarder, 1977, Aladdin, plastic bottle
BOX $175 **BOTTLE** $40

Sleeping Beauty, 1960, General Steel Ware/Canada, generic steel bottle
BOX $450 **BOTTLE** $55

Smokey Bear, 1975, Okay Industries, plastic bottle
BOX $550 **BOTTLE** $350

Smurfs, 1983, King Seeley Thermos, blue box, plastic bottle
BOX $225 **BOTTLE** $30

Snoopy Dome, 1968, King Seeley Thermos, yellow, "Have Lunch w/Snoopy," matching bottle
BOX $225 **BOTTLE** $50

Snow White, Disney, 1975, Aladdin, orange rim, plastic bottle
BOX $110 **BOTTLE** $30

Snow White, with Game, 1980, Ohio Art, no bottle
BOX $95 **BOTTLE** n/a

Space Explorer Ed McCauley, 1960, Aladdin, matching steel bottle
BOX $475 **BOTTLE** $150

Space Ship, 1950, unknown, Decoware, dark blue square
BOX $250 **BOTTLE** n/a

Space Shuttle Orbiter Enterprise, 1977, King Seeley Thermos, plastic bottle
BOX $250 **BOTTLE** $45

Space: 1999, 1976, King Seeley Thermos, plastic bottle
BOX $300 **BOTTLE** $40

Speed Buggy, 1974, King Seeley Thermos, red rim, plastic bottle
BOX $225 **BOTTLE** $25

Spider-Man & Hulk, 1980, Aladdin, Captain America on back, plastic bottle
BOX $200 **BOTTLE** $30

Sport Goofy, 1983, Aladdin, yellow rim, plastic bottle
BOX $95 **BOTTLE** $25

Sport Skwirts, 1982, Ohio Art, several variations
BOX $95 **BOTTLE** n/a

Sports Afield, 1957, Ohio Art, no bottle
BOX $275 **BOTTLE** n/a

Star Trek Dome, 1968, Aladdin, matching bottle
BOX $2350 **BOTTLE** $450

Star Trek, The Motion Picture, 1980, King Seeley Thermos, matching bottle
BOX $300 **BOTTLE** $60

Star Wars, 1978, King Seeley Thermos, cast or stars on band, matching plastic bottle
BOX $300 **BOTTLE** $40

Star Wars, Empire Strikes Back, 1980, King Seeley Thermos, swamp scene, plastic bottle
BOX $250 **BOTTLE** $40

Star Wars, Empire Strikes Back, 1980, King Seeley Thermos, ship scene, plastic bottle
BOX $250 **BOTTLE** $30

Star Wars, Return of the Jedi, 1983, King Seeley Thermos, plastic bottle
BOX $150 **BOTTLE** $30

Stars and Stripes Dome, 1970, King Seeley Thermos, matching plastic bottle
BOX $150 **BOTTLE** $40

Steve Canyon, 1959, Aladdin, steel/glass bottle
BOX $450 **BOTTLE** $150

Strawberry Land, 1985, Aladdin, no bottle
BOX $150 **BOTTLE** n/a

Strawberry Shortcake, 1980, Aladdin, plastic bottle
BOX $100 **BOTTLE** $15

Strawberry Shortcake, 1981, Aladdin, plastic bottle
BOX $100 **BOTTLE** $15

Street Hawk, 1985, Aladdin, plastic bottle
BOX $300 **BOTTLE** $90

Submarine, 1960, King Seeley Thermos, steel/glass bottle
BOX $325 **BOTTLE** $80

Super Friends, 1976, Aladdin, matching plastic bottle
BOX $150 **BOTTLE** $40

Super Powers, 1983, Aladdin, plastic bottle
BOX $150 **BOTTLE** $40

Supercar, 1962, Universal, steel/glass bottle
BOX $400 **BOTTLE** $150

Superman, 1954, Universal, blue rim
BOX $16500**BOTTLE** $250

Superman, 1967, King Seeley Thermos, red rim, "under fire" art on back, matching steel/glass bottle
BOX $1200 **BOTTLE** $125

Superman, 1978, Aladdin, red rim, Daily Planet Office on back, matching bottle
BOX $250 **BOTTLE** $50

Tapestry, 1963, Ohio Art, no bottle
BOX $60 **BOTTLE** n/a

Tarzan, 1966, Aladdin, steel/glass bottle
BOX $325 **BOTTLE** $65

Teenager, 1957, King Seeley Thermos, generic bottle
BOX $225 **BOTTLE** $35

Teenager Dome, 1957, King Seeley Thermos, generic bottle
BOX $225 **BOTTLE** $35

Three Little Pigs, 1982, Ohio Art, red rim, generic/plastic bottle
BOX $95 **BOTTLE** n/a

Thundercats, 1985, Aladdin, plastic bottle
BOX $175 **BOTTLE** $25

Tom Corbett Space Cadet, 1952, Aladdin, blue or red paper decal box, steel/glass bottle
BOX $375 **BOTTLE** $95

(Joe Soucy collection)

Tom Corbett Space Cadet, 1954, Aladdin, full litho, matching bottle
BOX $625 **BOTTLE** $110

Toppie Elephant, 1957, American Thermos, yellow, matching bottle
BOX $3850 **BOTTLE** $800

Track King, 1975, Okay Industries, matching steel bottle
BOX $350 **BOTTLE** $650

Train, 1971, Ohio Art, no bottle
BOX $45 **BOTTLE** n/a

Transformers, 1986, Aladdin, red box, matching plastic bottle
BOX $95 **BOTTLE** $15

Traveler, 1962, Ohio Art, no bottle
BOX $85 **BOTTLE** n/a

Trigger, 1956, King Seeley Thermos, no bottle
BOX $700 **BOTTLE** n/a

U.S. Mail Dome, 1969, Aladdin, plastic bottle
BOX $175 **BOTTLE** $45

U.S. Space Corps, 1961, Universal, plastic rocket bottle
BOX $525 **BOTTLE** $150

UFO, 1973, King Seeley Thermos, plastic bottle
BOX $225 **BOTTLE** $40

(Joe Soucy collection)

Underdog, 1974, Okay Industries, plastic bottle
BOX $3500 **BOTTLE** $1250

Universal's Movie Monsters, 1980, Aladdin, plastic bottle
BOX $400 **BOTTLE** $50

Voyage to the Bottom of the Sea, 1967, Aladdin, steel/glass bottle
BOX $750 **BOTTLE** $175

VW Bus Dome, 1960, Omni, plastic bottle
BOX $850 **BOTTLE** $220

Wagon Train, 1964, King Seeley Thermos, matching steel bottle
BOX $325 **BOTTLE** $75

Wags 'n Whiskers, 1978, King Seeley Thermos, matching plastic bottle
BOX $125 **BOTTLE** $25

Wake Up America, 1973, Okay Industries, matching steel bottle
BOX $700 **BOTTLE** $250

Waltons, The, 1973, Aladdin, plastic bottle
BOX $325 **BOTTLE** $40

Washington Redskins, 1970, Okay Industries, steel bottle
BOX $375 **BOTTLE** $140

Wee Pals Kid Power, 1974, American Thermos, matching plastic bottle
BOX $150 **BOTTLE** $35

Welcome Back Kotter, 1977, Aladdin, flat or embossed face, red rim, matching plastic bottle
BOX $275 **BOTTLE** $50

Western, 1963, King Seeley Thermos, gear band, steel/glass bottle
BOX $225 **BOTTLE** $75

Western, 1963, King Seeley Thermos, tan band, steel/glass bottle
BOX $275 **BOTTLE** $75

Wild Bill Hickok, 1955, Aladdin, steel/glass bottle
BOX $400 **BOTTLE** $110

Wild Frontier, 1977, Ohio Art, spinner game on back, no bottle
BOX $125 **BOTTLE** n/a

Wild, Wild West, 1969, Aladdin, plastic bottle
BOX $700 **BOTTLE** $120

Winnie the Pooh, 1976, Aladdin, blue rim, plastic bottle
BOX $325 **BOTTLE** $80

Yankee Doodles, 1975, King Seeley Thermos, plastic bottle
BOX $95 **BOTTLE** $25

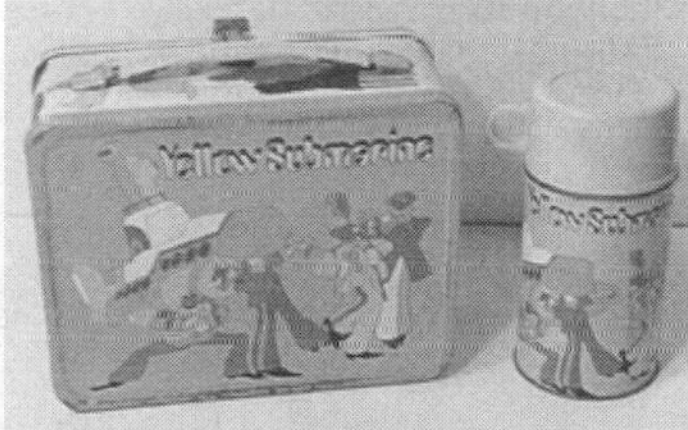

Yellow Submarine, 1968, King Seeley Thermos, steel/glass bottle
BOX $1300 **BOTTLE** $350

Yogi Bear, 1974, Aladdin
BOX $325 **BOTTLE** $60

LUNCH BOXES

Steel

Yogi Bear & Friends, 1961, Aladdin, black rim, matching steel bottle
BOX $350 **BOTTLE** $80

Zorro, 1958, Aladdin, black band, steel/glass bottle
BOX $450 **BOTTLE** $120

Zorro, 1966, Aladdin, red band, steel/glass bottle
BOX $650 **BOTTLE** $180

Vinyl

Alice in Wonderland, 1972, Aladdin, matching plastic bottle
BOX $225 **BOTTLE** $45

All American, 1976, Bayville, Styrofoam bottle
BOX $160 **BOTTLE** $20

All Dressed Up, 1970s, Bayville, Styrofoam bottle
BOX $90 **BOTTLE** $20

All Star, 1960, Aladdin
BOX $475 **BOTTLE** $95

Alvin and the Chipmunks, 1963, King Seeley Thermos, matching plastic bottle
BOX $425 **BOTTLE** $140

Annie 1, 1981, Aladdin, matching plastic bottle
BOX $75 **BOTTLE** $20

Bach's Lunch, 1975, Volkwein Bros., red Styrofoam bottle
BOX $130 **BOTTLE** $20

Ballerina, 1960s, Universal, black, Thermax bottle
BOX $800 **BOTTLE** $150

Ballerina, 1962, Aladdin, pink, steel/glass bottle
BOX $200 **BOTTLE** $60

Ballet, 1961, Universal, red, plastic generic bottle
BOX $500 **BOTTLE** $20

Banana Splits, 1969, King Seeley Thermos, matching steel/glass bottle
BOX $500 **BOTTLE** $150

Barbarino Brunch Bag, 1977, Aladdin, zippered bag, plastic bottle
BOX $300 **BOTTLE** $60

Barbie & Francie, 1965, King Seeley Thermos, black, matching steel/glass bottle
BOX $150 **BOTTLE** $65

Barbie & Midge, 1963, King Seeley Thermos, black, matching steel/glass bottle
BOX $150 **BOTTLE** $65

Barbie & Midge Dome, 1964, King Seeley Thermos, matching glass/steel bottle
BOX $530 **BOTTLE** $65

Barbie Softy, 1988, King Seeley Thermos, generic plastic bottle
BOX $45 **BOTTLE** $15

Barbie, World of, 1971, King Seeley Thermos, pink box, matching steel/glass bottle
BOX $130 **BOTTLE** $40

Barbie, World of, 1971, King Seeley Thermos, blue box, matching steel/glass bottle
BOX $100 **BOTTLE** $25

Barnum's Animals, 1978, Adco Liberty, no bottle
BOX $75 **BOTTLE** n/a

Beany & Cecil, 1963, King Seeley Thermos, steel/glass bottle
BOX $850 **BOTTLE** $150

Beatles, 1965, Air Flite, no bottle
BOX $1000 **BOTTLE** n/a

Beatles Brunch Bag, 1966, Aladdin, zippered bag, matching bottle
BOX $775 **BOTTLE** $300

Beatles Kaboodles Kit, 1965, Standard Plastic Products, no bottle
BOX $950 **BOTTLE** n/a

Betsey Clark, 1977, King Seeley Thermos, yellow box, matching plastic bottle
BOX $110 **BOTTLE** $15

Betsey Clark Munchies Bag, 1977, King Seeley Thermos, zippered bag, plastic bottle
BOX $90 **BOTTLE** $10

Blue Gingham Brunch Bag, 1975, Aladdin, zippered box and plastic bottle
BOX $50 **BOTTLE** $30

Bobby Soxer, 1959, Aladdin
BOX $575 **BOTTLE** n/a

Boston Red Sox, 1960s, Universal
BOX $90 **BOTTLE** $20

Boy on the Swing, Abeama Industries
BOX $80 **BOTTLE** $20

Buick 1910, 1974, Bayville, Styrofoam bottle
BOX $90 **BOTTLE** $20

Bullwinkle, 1963, King Seeley Thermos, yellow, generic steel bottle
BOX $575 **BOTTLE** $60

Bullwinkle, 1963, King Seeley Thermos, white, steel/glass bottle
BOX $4500 **BOTTLE** $250

Bullwinkle, 1963, King Seeley Thermos, blue, steel/glass bottle
BOX $900 **BOTTLE** $250

Calico Brunch Bag, 1980, Aladdin, zippered bag, plastic bottle
BOX $70 **BOTTLE** $30

Captain Kangaroo, 1964, King Seeley Thermos, steel/glass bottle
BOX $550 **BOTTLE** $150

Captain Marvel Brunch Bag, 1947, red rectangular vinyl w/strap handle
BOX $425 **BOTTLE** $200

Carousel, 1962, Aladdin, matching steel/glass bottle
BOX $425 **BOTTLE** $130

Cars, 1960, Universal
BOX $175 **BOTTLE** n/a

(Joe Soucy collection)

Casper the Friendly Ghost, 1966, King Seeley Thermos, blue box, orange steel bottle
BOX $600 **BOTTLE** $150

Challenger, Space Shuttle, 1986, Babcock, puffy box, no bottle
BOX $300 **BOTTLE** n/a

Charlie's Angels Brunch Bag, 1978, Aladdin, zippered bag, plastic bottle
BOX $300 **BOTTLE** $50

Coca-Cola, 1947, Aladdin, Styrofoam bottle
BOX $175 **BOTTLE** $20

Coco the Clown, 1970s, Gary, Styrofoam bottle
BOX $90 **BOTTLE** $20

Combo Brunch Bag, 1967, Aladdin, zippered bag, steel/glass bottle
BOX $300 **BOTTLE** $80

Corsage, 1970, King Seeley Thermos, steel/glass bottle
BOX $90 **BOTTLE** $30

Cottage, 1974, King Seeley Thermos
BOX $95 **BOTTLE** n/a

Cowboy, 1960, Universal, plain plastic bottle
BOX $170 **BOTTLE** $20

Dateline Lunch Kit, 1960, Hasbro, blue/pink, no bottle
BOX $250 **BOTTLE** n/a

Dawn, 1971, Aladdin, matching plastic bottle
BOX $140 **BOTTLE** $35

Dawn, 1972, Aladdin, matching plastic bottle
BOX $140 **BOTTLE** $35

Dawn Brunch Bag, 1971, Aladdin, zippered bag, plastic bottle
BOX $180 **BOTTLE** $35

Denim Brunch Bag, 1980, Aladdin, zippered bag, plastic bottle
BOX $80 **BOTTLE** $15

Deputy Dawg, King Seeley Thermos, steel/glass bottle
BOX $600 **BOTTLE** $50

Deputy Dawg, 1964, Thermos, no bottle
BOX $550 **BOTTLE** n/a

Donny & Marie, 1977, Aladdin, long hair version, matching plastic bottle
BOX $135 **BOTTLE** $40

Donny & Marie, 1978, Aladdin, short hair version, matching plastic bottle
BOX $140 **BOTTLE** $40

Donny & Marie Brunch Bag, 1977, Aladdin, zippered bag, plastic bottle
BOX $150 **BOTTLE** $40

Dr. Seuss, 1970, Aladdin, plastic bottle
BOX $575 **BOTTLE** $95

Dream Boat, 1960, Feldco, dark brown, Styrofoam bottle
BOX $350 **BOTTLE** $20

Dream Boat, 1960, Feldco, white, Styrofoam bottle
BOX $500 **BOTTLE** $20

Dream Boat, 1960, Feldco, blue, Styrofoam bottle
BOX $700 **BOTTLE** $20

Eats 'n Treats, King Seeley Thermos, blue or pink steel/glass bottle
BOX $200 **BOTTLE** $40

Fess Parker Kaboodle Kit, 1960s, Aladdin, matching steel bottle
BOX $425 **BOTTLE** n/a

Fishing, 1970, Universal, Styrofoam bottle
BOX $90 **BOTTLE** $20

Frog Flutist, 1975, Aladdin, matching plastic bottle
BOX $75 **BOTTLE** $20

Fun to See'n Keep Tiger, 1960, unknown, no bottle
BOX $350 **BOTTLE** n/a

G.I. Joe, 1960s, Hasbro, styrofoam thermos, Hasbro license
BOX $350 **BOTTLE** $20

G.I. Joe, 1989, King Seeley Thermos, generic plastic bottle
BOX $55 **BOTTLE** $10

Gigi, 1962, Aladdin, matching steel/glass bottle
BOX $280 **BOTTLE** $80

Girl & Poodle, 1960, Universal, Styrofoam bottle
BOX $140 **BOTTLE** $20

Glamour Gal, 1960, Aladdin, steel/glass bottle
BOX $100 **BOTTLE** $35

Goat Butt Mountain, 1960, Universal, Styrofoam bottle
BOX $90 **BOTTLE** $20

Go-Go Brunch Bag, 1966, Aladdin, plastic bottle
BOX $245 **BOTTLE** $60

Happy Powwow, 1970s, Bayville, red, blue or yellow, w/Styrofoam bottle
BOX $90 **BOTTLE** $20

Highway Signs Snap Pack, 1988, Avon
BOX $50 **BOTTLE** n/a

Holly Hobbie, 1972, Aladdin, white bag, matching plastic bottle
BOX $110 **BOTTLE** $30

I Love a Parade, 1970, Universal, Styrofoam bottle
BOX $130 **BOTTLE** $20

Ice Cream Cone, 1975, Aladdin, matching plastic bottle
BOX $55 **BOTTLE** $20

It's a Small World, 1968, Aladdin, matching steel/glass bottle
BOX $250 **BOTTLE** $110

Jonathan Livingston Seagull, 1974, Aladdin, matching plastic bottle
BOX $175 **BOTTLE** $50

Junior Deb, 1960, Aladdin, steel/glass bottle
BOX $175 **BOTTLE** $50

Junior Miss Safari, 1962, Prepac, no bottle
BOX $150 **BOTTLE** n/a

Junior Nurse, 1963, King Seeley Thermos, steel/glass bottle
BOX $320 **BOTTLE** $90

Kaboodle Kit, 1960s, Aladdin, pink or white, no bottle
BOX $220 **BOTTLE** n/a

Kewtie Pie, Aladdin, steel/glass bottle
BOX $200 **BOTTLE** $60

Kodak Gold, 1970s, Aladdin
BOX $85 **BOTTLE** $20

Kodak II, 1970s, Aladdin
BOX $85 **BOTTLE** $20

Lassie, 1960s, Universal, Styrofoam bottle
BOX $150 **BOTTLE** $20

Laugh-In, 1960s, "Sock it to Me" brunch bag
BOX $225 **BOTTLE** $65

L'il Jodie (Puffy), 1985, Babcock
BOX $90 **BOTTLE** n/a

Linus the Lion-Hearted, 1965, Aladdin, steel/glass bottle
BOX $600 **BOTTLE** $125

Little Ballerina, 1975, Bayville, Styrofoam bottle
BOX $75 **BOTTLE** $20

Little Old Schoolhouse, 1974, Dart
BOX $80 **BOTTLE** n/a

Love-Peace, 1972, Aladdin, matching plastic bottle
BOX $160 **BOTTLE** $45

Lunch 'n Munch, 1959, American Thermos, boys on raft, tan, boating bottle
BOX $400 **BOTTLE** $125

Lunch 'n Munch, 1959, King Seeley Thermos, space theme, red, satellite bottle
BOX $450 **BOTTLE** $60

Lunch 'n Munch, 1959, American Thermos, boys on raft, red, boating bottle
BOX $450 **BOTTLE** $125

Lunch 'n Munch, 1959, King Seeley Thermos, space theme, tan, satellite bottle
BOX $450 **BOTTLE** $60

M.A.S.H., 1981, 20th Century Fox, beige w/red cross and "M.A.S.H." symbols
BOX $100 **BOTTLE** n/a

Mam'zelle, 1971, Aladdin, light blue, plastic bottle
BOX $180 **BOTTLE** $60

Mardi-Grass, 1971, Aladdin, matching plastic bottle
BOX $110 **BOTTLE** $25

Mary Ann, 1960, Aladdin, matching steel/glass bottle
BOX $75 **BOTTLE** $25

Mary Ann Lunch 'N Bag, 1960, Universal, no bottle
BOX $110 **BOTTLE** n/a

Mary Poppins, 1973, Aladdin, matching plastic bottle
BOX $275 **BOTTLE** $65

Mary Poppins Brunch Bag, 1966, Aladdin, steel/glass bottle
BOX $225 **BOTTLE** $50

Mod Miss Brunch Bag, 1969, Aladdin, plastic bottle
BOX $80 **BOTTLE** $30

Monkees, 1967, King Seeley Thermos, matching steel/glass bottle
BOX $650 **BOTTLE** $125

Moon Landing, 1960, Universal, Styrofoam bottle
BOX $250 **BOTTLE** $20

Mr. Peanut Snap Pack, 1979, Dart, snap close bag, no bottle
BOX $110 **BOTTLE** n/a

Mushrooms, 1972, Aladdin, matching plastic bottle
BOX $95 **BOTTLE** $45

New Zoo Revue, 1975, Aladdin, plastic bottle
BOX $275 **BOTTLE** $60

Pac-Man (Puffy), 1985, Aladdin
BOX $65 **BOTTLE** n/a

Peanuts, 1967, King Seeley Thermos, red "kite" box, steel/glass bottle
BOX $175 **BOTTLE** $50

Peanuts, 1969, King Seeley Thermos, red "baseball" box, steel bottle
BOX $150 **BOTTLE** $50

Peanuts, 1971, King Seeley Thermos, green "baseball" box, steel bottle
BOX $200 **BOTTLE** $50

Peanuts, 1973, King Seeley Thermos, white "piano" box, steel bottle
BOX $150 **BOTTLE** $50

Pebbles & Bamm-Bamm, 1973, Aladdin, matching plastic bottle
BOX $275 **BOTTLE** $55

Penelope & Penny, 1970s, Gary, yellow box w/Styrofoam bottle
BOX $80 **BOTTLE** $20

Peter Pan, 1969, Aladdin, white box, matching plastic bottle
BOX $250 **BOTTLE** $65

Pink Panther, 1980, Aladdin, matching plastic bottle
BOX $225 **BOTTLE** $50

Pony Tail, 1960s, Thermos, white box, original art w/gray border added, no bottle
BOX $200 **BOTTLE** n/a

Pony Tail, 1965, King Seeley Thermos, white box, fold over lid, steel/glass bottle
BOX $200 **BOTTLE** $40

Pony Tail Tid-Bit-Kit, 1962, King Seeley Thermos, steel/glass satellite bottle
BOX $200 **BOTTLE** $40

Ponytails Poodle Kit, 1960, King Seeley Thermos, steel/glass bottle
BOX $150 **BOTTLE** $20

Princess, 1963, Aladdin, steel/glass bottle
BOX $190 **BOTTLE** $55

Psychedelic, 1969, Aladdin, yellow, matching steel/glass bottle
BOX $150 **BOTTLE** $30

Pussycats, The, 1968, Aladdin, plastic bottle
BOX $225 **BOTTLE** $80

Ringling Bros. Circus, 1970, King Seeley Thermos, orange box w/matching steel/glass bottle
BOX $425 **BOTTLE** $140

Ringling Bros. Circus, 1971, King Seeley Thermos, puffy blue box, steel/glass bottle
BOX $250 **BOTTLE** $40

Robo Warriors, 1970, unknown, no bottle
BOX $35 **BOTTLE** n/a

Roy Rogers Saddlebag, 1960, King Seeley Thermos, cream, steel/glass bottle
BOX $650 **BOTTLE** $95

Roy Rogers Saddlebag, 1960, King Seeley Thermos, brown, steel/glass bottle
BOX $400 **BOTTLE** $95

Sabrina, 1972, Aladdin, yellow box w/matching plastic bottle
BOX $230 **BOTTLE** $85

Sesame Street, 1979, Aladdin, orange, matching plastic bottle
BOX $120 **BOTTLE** $30

Sesame Street, 1981, Aladdin, yellow, matching plastic bottle
BOX $150 **BOTTLE** $30

Shari Lewis, 1963, Aladdin, matching steel/glass bottle
BOX $475 **BOTTLE** $120

Sizzlers, Hot Wheels, 1971, King Seeley Thermos, matching steel/glass bottle
BOX $375 **BOTTLE** $60

Skipper, 1965, King Seeley Thermos, steel/glass bottle
BOX $220 **BOTTLE** $60

Sleeping Beauty, Disney, 1970, Aladdin, white box, matching plastic bottle
BOX $240 **BOTTLE** $80

Smokey the Bear, 1965, King Seeley Thermos, steel/glass bottle
BOX $450 **BOTTLE** $110

Snoopy Munchies Bag, 1977, King Seeley Thermos, plastic bottle
BOX $75 **BOTTLE** $20

Snoopy Softy, 1988, King Seeley Thermos, matching plastic bottle
BOX $45 **BOTTLE** $20

Snow White, 1975, Aladdin, white box w/matching plastic bottle
BOX $290 **BOTTLE** $45

Snow White, Disney, 1967, unknown, fold-over lid, tapered box, no bottle
BOX $400 **BOTTLE** n/a

Soupy Sales, 1966, King Seeley Thermos, blue box, no bottle
BOX $600 **BOTTLE** n/a

Spirit of '76, unknown, red
BOX $110 **BOTTLE** n/a

Sports Kit, 1960, Universal
BOX $350 **BOTTLE** $40

Stewardess, 1962, Aladdin, steel/glass bottle
BOX $650 **BOTTLE** $110

Strawberry Shortcake, 1980, Aladdin, matching plastic bottle
BOX $65 **BOTTLE** $15

Tammy, 1964, Aladdin, matching steel/glass bottle
BOX $250 **BOTTLE** $85

Tammy & Pepper, 1965, Aladdin, matching steel/glass bottle
BOX $240 **BOTTLE** $85

Tinker Bell, Disney, 1969, Aladdin, plastic bottle
BOX $260 **BOTTLE** $90

Twiggy, 1967, King Seeley Thermos, steel/glass bottle
BOX $225 **BOTTLE** $80

Twiggy, 1967, Aladdin, matching steel/glass bottle
BOX $225 **BOTTLE** $80

U.S. Mail Brunch Bag, 1971, Aladdin, zippered bag, plastic bottle
BOX $160 **BOTTLE** $80

Winnie the Pooh, Aladdin, steel/glass bottle
BOX $450 **BOTTLE** $110

Wonder Woman (blue), 1977, Aladdin, matching plastic bottle
BOX $350 **BOTTLE** $50

Wonder Woman (yellow), 1978, Aladdin, matching plastic bottle
BOX $350 **BOTTLE** $50

Wrangler, 1982, Aladdin, steel/glass bottle
BOX $325 **BOTTLE** $95

Yogi Bear, 1960s, Aladdin, white, Yogi taking photo
BOX $150 **BOTTLE** n/a

Yosemite Sam, 1971, King Seeley Thermos, matching steel/glass bottle
BOX $560 **BOTTLE** $140

Ziggy, 1980, Aladdin, orange brunch bag, plastic bottle
BOX $85 **BOTTLE** $15

Ziggy's Munch Box, 1979, Aladdin, plastic bottle
BOX $140 **BOTTLE** $40

Marx Play Sets

by Karen O'Brien

For all practical purposes, play sets could have been invented by Louis Marx...at least as far as boys growing up in the 1950s and 1960s were concerned. The words "Marx" and "play set" just went together. And they still go together today for many dedicated collectors.

A typical Marx play set included buildings, figures, and lots of realistic accessories that helped bring the miniature world to life. The Fort Apache Stockade, for example, came with a hard plastic log fort, a colorful lithographed tin cabin, and, of course, pioneers and Indians locked in combat. It was no wonder millions of kids had a burning desire for these toys. The play scenarios were almost endless.

This modern version of an age-old toy was a tribute to the marketing and manufacturing talents and whimsical genius of Louis Marx, the modern-day king of toys.

Not only was he responsible for developing the play set, but he also popularized the yo-yo and produced some of the most innovative tin wind-ups, guns, dolls, trains, trikes, trucks, and other toys that were commercially feasible. In 1955, Marx sold more than $30 million worth of toys, easily making it the largest toy manufacturer in the world.

What makes Marx's domination even more impressive was the fact that he rose from humble beginnings. He was born in Brooklyn in 1896 and didn't learn to speak English until he started school. At age 16, Marx went to work for Ferdinand Strauss, a toy manufacturer who produced items for Abraham & Strauss department stores. By the age of 20, Marx was managing the company's New Jersey factory.

After being fired by Strauss, Marx contracted with manufacturers to produce toys he designed. By the mid-1920s, Marx had three plants in the United States. By 1955, there were more than 5,000 items in the Marx toy line with plants worldwide.

Mass production and mass marketing through stores such as Sears and Montgomery Ward allowed Marx to keep prices low and quality high. Marx was also a master at producing new toys from the same basic components. Existing elements could be modified slightly, and new lithography would produce a new building from standard stock.

Part of Marx's repackaging genius included using popular television or movie tie-ins to breathe new life into existing products. The Rifleman Rage, Roy Rogers' Ranch, Wyatt Earp, and Wagon Train play sets were examples of repackaging existing toys and parts to capture the fad of the day.

Marx sold his company to the Quaker Oats Company in 1972 for $31 million. Quaker Oats sold the company four years after for $15 million after losing money every year of its ownership.

The Marx Toy Company is in existence once again and making favorite Marx toys from original molds.

With the passing of a few short decades, once affordable children's toys have become highly prized collectibles. Play sets are among the price leaders in today's market for childhood treasures. And the figures that accompanied the play sets are also highly desired for their craftsmanship and detail.

A play set listed as MIB (Mint in Box) should be untouched and unassembled in the original box. Excellent condition means a complete set, but the buildings are assembled and the box may be worn or damaged. Good condition means the play set shows wear and may be missing a few minor pieces.

THE ***TOP 10*** MARX PLAY SETS (In Mint Condition)

1. Johnny Ringo Western Frontier, 1959 .... $5,200
2. Johnny Tremain Revolutionary War, 1957 2,750
3. Gunsmoke Dodge City, 1960 2,200
4. Fire House, 1960s 2,000
5. Ben Hur, Series 5000, 1959 1,900
6. Sears Store, 1961 1,850
7. Civil War Centennial, 1961 1,800
8. Custer's Last Stand, 1963 1,800
9. Wagon Train, 1959 1,800
10. Untouchables, 1961 1,550

Miniature Play Sets

101 Dalmatians, 1961, "The Barn Scene"
EX $75 **NM** $300 **MIP** $450

101 Dalmatians, 1961, "The Wedding Scene"
EX $75 **NM** $300 **MIP** $450

20 Minutes to Berlin, 1964, 174 handpainted pieces
EX $110 **NM** $320 **MIP** $520

Alice in Wonderland, 1961, New series
EX $100 **NM** $225 **MIP** $350

Attack on Fort Apache, stable, cowboys, Indians, Model No. HK-8078
EX $85 **NM** $225 **MIP** $500

Babes In Toyland, six different scenes, each
EX $25 **NM** $65 **MIP** $125

Battleground, 1963, 170 pieces, Model No. HK-6111
EX $20 **NM** $60 **MIP** $200

Blue and Gray, 1960s, 101 individual pieces, "Featured on T.V.", Model No. HK-6109
EX $95 **NM** $180 **MIP** $350

Border Battle, Mexican-American War set with plastic Alamo, Mexican and Texan troops, horses and accessories
EX $150 **NM** $365 **MIP** $725

Charge of the Bengal Lancers, British/Turks
EX $125 **NM** $325 **MIP** $500

Charge of the Light Brigade, Sears, 216 pieces, Lancers/Cossacks
EX $175 **NM** $325 **MIP** $400

Charge of the Light Brigade, 2nd version, photo box art, Lancers/Turks
EX $110 **NM** $300 **MIP** $400

Charge of the Light Brigade, smaller version, Lancers/Russians
EX $75 **NM** $225 **MIP** $325

Cinderella, New series
EX $100 **NM** $225 **MIP** $350

Covered Wagon Attack
EX $95 **NM** $200 **MIP** $400

Custer's Last Stand, 1964, 181 pieces
EX $125 **NM** $325 **MIP** $600

Disney 3-in-1 Set, original series
EX $100 **NM** $225 **MIP** $365

Disney Circus Parade, Super Circus performers, Disneykins
EX $85 **NM** $225 **MIP** $350

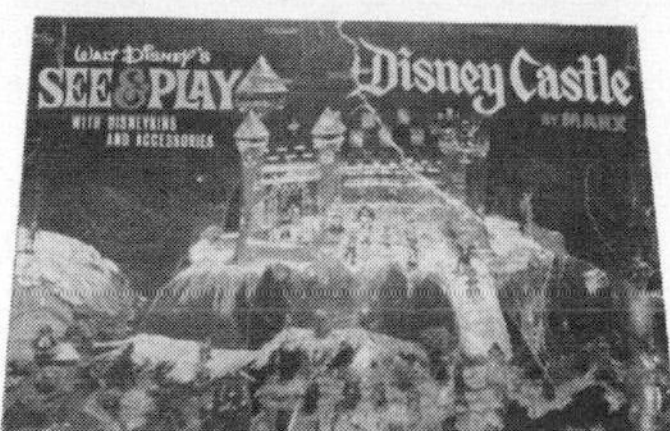

Disney See and Play Castle, 1st and 2nd series Disneykins, Model No. 48-24388
EX $155 **NM** $360 **MIP** $465

Disney See and Play Doll House, 1st series Disneykins
EX $100 **NM** $265 **MIP** $350

Donald Duck, original series; Donald, Daisy, Louie, Goofy
EX $45 **NM** $100 **MIP** $150

Dumbo's Circus, original series
EX $50 **NM** $100 **MIP** $165

Fairykin, six different, each
EX $30 **NM** $80 **MIP** $125

Fairykin TV Scenes, 12 different, each
EX $8 **NM** $20 **MIP** $30

Fairykin TV Scenes Gift Set, two different, each w/six scenes, each
EX $65 **NM** $165 **MIP** $250

Fairykins 3-in-1 Diorama Set
EX $100 **NM** $265 **MIP** $400

Fairykins Gift Set, 34 in window box
EX $40 **NM** $175 **MIP** $250

Fairykins TV Scenes Boxed Set of Eight
EX $45 **NM** $200 **MIP** $250

Fort Apache, large set, HQ bldg., cavalry/cowboys/Indians
EX $115 **NM** $295 **MIP** $375

Fort Apache, 1963, 90 pieces, Indians, Model No. HK-7526
EX $55 **NM** $80 **MIP** $185

Guerrilla Warfare, 1960s, Viet Cong
EX $275 **NM** $350 **MIP** $450

Huckleberry Hound Presents, two different, each
EX $75 **NM** $115 **MIP** $175

Invasion Day, 1964, 304 pieces, miniature D-Day Invasion set
EX $70 **NM** $205 **MIP** $450

Jungle, smaller than Jungle Safari
EX $50 **NM** $85 **MIP** $175

Jungle Safari, 260 pieces, hunters/natives
EX $55 **NM** $100 **MIP** $225

Knights and Castle, 1963, 132 pieces, Model No. HK-7563
EX $130 **NM** $200 **MIP** $315

Knights and Castle, 1964, 64 pieces, Model No. HK-7562
EX $95 **NM** $175 **MIP** $275

Knights and Vikings, 1964, 143 pieces
EX $145 **NM** $275 **MIP** $425

Lady and the Tramp, 1961, New series
EX $100 **NM** $225 **MIP** $350

Lost Boys, New series
EX $100 **NM** $225 **MIP** $350

Lost Boys, 1961, second series
EX $40 **NM** $120 **MIP** $200

Ludwig Von Drake, RCA premium set
EX $65 **NM** $130 **MIP** $200

Ludwig Von Drake, 1962, "The Professor Misses"
EX $50 **NM** $100 **MIP** $150

Ludwig Von Drake, 1962, "The Nearsighted Professor"
EX $50 **NM** $115 **MIP** $165

Mickey Mouse and Friends, original series, display box
EX $50 **NM** $100 **MIP** $150

Munchville, vegetable characters
EX $65 **NM** $165 **MIP** $265

Noah's Ark, Ward's version, soft plastic figures
EX $20 **NM** $50 **MIP** $85

Noah's Ark, 1968, 100 pieces
EX $28 **NM** $70 **MIP** $110

MARX PLAY SETS

Miniature Play Sets

Over The Top, WWI, Germans/Doughboys
EX $200 **NM** $600 **MIP** $950

Panchito Western, original series, display box
EX $50 **NM** $100 **MIP** $150

Pinocchio, six different sets, each original series, display box
EX $65 **NM** $165 **MIP** $280

Pinocchio 3-in-1 Set
EX $115 **NM** $295 **MIP** $450

Quick Draw McGraw, two different, each
EX $75 **NM** $115 **MIP** $200

Revolutionary War, British/Colonials
EX $95 **NM** $250 **MIP** $475

Sands of Iwo Jima, 1963, 205 pieces
EX $115 **NM** $210 **MIP** $325

Sands of Iwo Jima, 1963, 88 pieces
EX $75 **NM** $145 **MIP** $225

Sands of Iwo Jima, 1964, 296 pieces
EX $150 **NM** $295 **MIP** $425

See and Play Dollhouse, American Beauties/Campus Cuties
EX $75 **NM** $175 **MIP** $350

Sleeping Beauty, 1961, new series
EX $75 **NM** $175 **MIP** $275

Snow White and the Seven Dwarfs, original series, display box
EX $50 **NM** $100 **MIP** $185

Sunshine Farm Set, farmers and animals
EX $45 **NM** $115 **MIP** $175

Sword in the Stone, British only Disney release
EX $310 **NM** $1050 **MIP** $1560

Ten Commandments, Montgomery Ward
EX $150 **NM** $395 **MIP** $600

Three Little Pigs, new series
EX $100 **NM** $225 **MIP** $350

Tiger Town, 1960s, ENCO-like tigers
EX $75 **NM** $175 **MIP** $300

Top Cat, three different, each
EX $75 **NM** $115 **MIP** $200

Troll Village, Includes hillside, troll figures, ox cart, trees, fence sections and accessories
EX $85 **NM** $220 **MIP** $360

TV-Tinykins Gift Set, set of 34 figures
EX $115 **NM** $350 **MIP** $550

TV-Tinykins TV Scenes, 12 different, each
EX $12 **NM** $35 **MIP** $50

Western Town, over 170 pieces, hand painted buildings, stagecoach, fence sections, figures and accessories, Model No. 48-24398
EX $55 **NM** $160 **MIP** $265

Wooden Horse of Troy, British only issue
EX $175 **NM** $600 **MIP** $850

Zorro, 1958, painted figures
EX $40 **NM** $80 **MIP** $125

Play Sets

Adventures of Robin Hood, 1956, Richard Greene TV series, Model No. 4722
EX $300 **NM** $750 **MIP** $1250

Alamo, 1957, only two cannons, w/ metal Alamo, Model No. 3546
EX $100 **NM** $300 **MIP** $500

Alamo, 1960, for 54mm figures, four cannons, Model No. 3534
EX $140 **NM** $250 **MIP** $400

Alamo, 1960, Sears exclusive, Model No. 3543
EX $50 **NM** $140 **MIP** $265

Alaska, 1959, 100 pieces including: igloos, polar bears, kayak, dog sled team, litho storefront, prospectors. Just in time for Alaskan statehood, this is a neat set, Model No. 3707-8
EX $300 **NM** $650 **MIP** $1000

Alaska, 1960, Model No. 2755-6
EX $250 **NM** $550 **MIP** $800

American Airlines Astro Jet Port, 1961, Model No. 4821-2
EX $150 **NM** $250 **MIP** $450

American Airlines International Jet Port, 1960, 98 pieces, Model No. 4810
EX $150 **NM** $250 **MIP** $450

Arctic Explorer, 1958, Series 2000, Model No. 3702
EX $250 **NM** $475 **MIP** $725

Army Combat Set, 1963, Sears exclusive, 411 pieces, Model No. 4158
EX $100 **NM** $300 **MIP** $475

Army Combat Training Center, 1958, Model No. 4153
EX $40 **NM** $60 **MIP** $95

Army Combat Training Center, 1959, Model No. 2654
EX $35 **NM** $55 **MIP** $90

Babyland Nursery, 1955, Model No. 3379-80
EX $125 **NM** $225 **MIP** $375

Bar-M Ranch, 1957, Model No. 3956
EX $65 **NM** $125 **MIP** $200

Battle of Iwo Jima, 1964, 247 pieces, U.S. and Japanese, Model No. 4147
EX $125 **NM** $250 **MIP** $425

Battle of Iwo Jima, 1964, 128 pieces, Sears exclusive, Model No. 4154
EX $50 **NM** $110 **MIP** $185

Battle of Little Big Horn, 1972, includes cavalrymen, Indians, horses, wagons, totem pole (?), and tepees, Model No. 4679MO
EX $140 **NM** $265 **MIP** $425

Battle of the Blue & Gray, Series 2000, large set, Model No. 4658
EX $250 **NM** $700 **MIP** $1250

Battle of the Blue & Gray, 1959, Series 2000, 54mm, Model No. 4745-6
EX $175 **NM** $375 **MIP** $625

Battle of the Blue & Gray, 1960, Series 1000, small set, no house, Model No. 2645-6
EX $80 **NM** $240 **MIP** $425

Battle of the Blue & Gray, 1963, Centennial edition, Model No. 4744
EX $200 **NM** $700 **MIP** $1250

Battlefield, 1958, Series 5000, Model No. 4756
EX $25 **NM** $95 **MIP** $175

Battleground, 1958, largest of military sets, Model No. 4749-50
EX $155 **NM** $395 **MIP** $660

Battleground, 1959, 180 pieces, Model No. 4751
EX $40 **NM** $110 **MIP** $190

Battleground, 1960s, U.S. and Nazi troops, Model No. 4756
EX $45 **NM** $100 **MIP** $165

Battleground, 1962, 200 pieces, Model No. 4754
EX $40 **NM** $110 **MIP** $195

Battleground, 1965, Montgomery Ward, Model No. 4139
EX $80 **NM** $240 **MIP** $425

Battleground, 1965, Sears, 160 pieces, Model No. 4150
EX $70 **NM** $210 **MIP** $350

Major Matt Mason, **Sgt. Storm**, Mattel, 1967-79, 6", $410

Spawn, McFarlane Toys, 1994, 5-1/4" , $25

Comic Heroine Posin' Dolls, **Supergirl**, **Batgirl**, **Mera** and **Wonder Woman**, Ideal, 1967, 12", $5,000 each

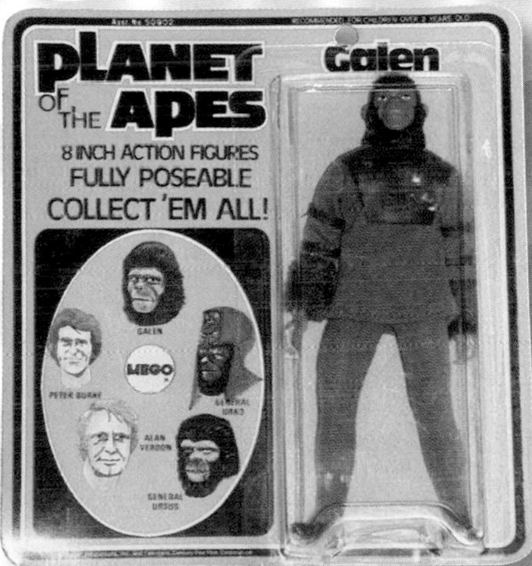

Planet of the Apes, **Galen**, Mego, 1973-75, 8", $100

A-Team Combat Headquarters Set, Galoob, 1984, four 3-3/4" figures, $60

Lone Ranger Rides Again, **Lone Ranger** and **Tonto**, Gabriel, 1979, 9", $75 each

Yellow Submarine, **Series 2**, **Sgt Pepper's Lonely Heart Club Band**, **Ringo with Apple Bonker**, McFarlane Toys, 2000, $8

Marvel Super Heroes Secret Wars, **HobGoblin**, Mattel, 1984-85, 4", $76

Bob and Doug McKenzie, **Doug McKenzie**, McFarlane Toys, 2000, $15

X-Men: The Movie, **Storm**, Toy Biz, 2000, $8

The Simpsons, **Homer**, Mattel, 1990, $15

Six Million Dollar Man, **Maskatron**, Kenner, 1975-78, $150

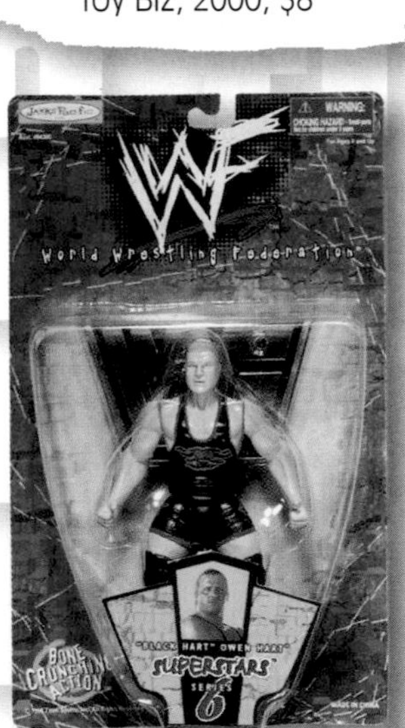

WF, **Superstars Series 6**, **"Black Hart" Owen Hart**, Jakks Pacific, 1997, $15

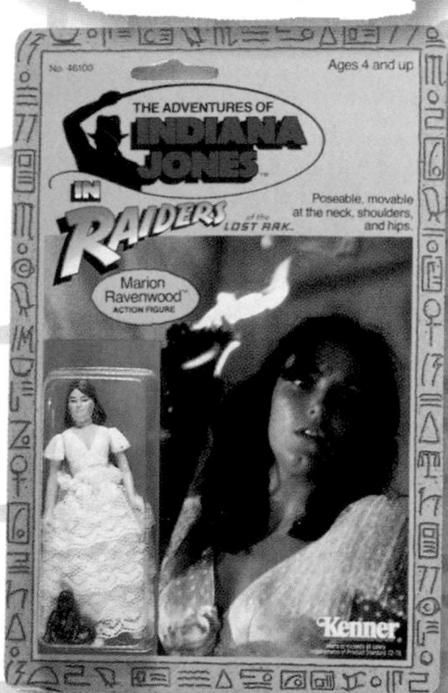

The Adventures of Indiana Jones, **Marion Ravenwood**, Kenner, 1982-83, $300

Snap, Crackle, Pop Vinyl Figures, 1984, 5", $30

Labatt's Beer Man Figures, Labatt's Brewery, 1972, 6", $65

Bucky Bradford Figure, Bradford House Restaurants, 1960s, 9-1/2", $50

Ernie the Keebler Elf, 1974, 7", $55

Fig Newton Girl, Nabisco, 1983, 4-1/2", $25

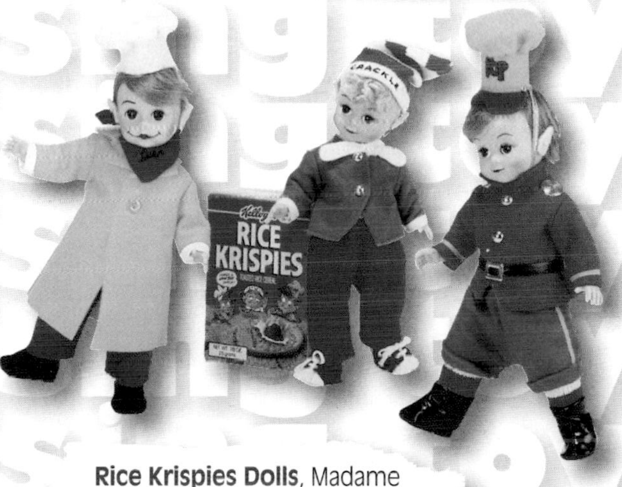

Rice Krispies Dolls, Madame Alexander, 1998, 8", $65 each

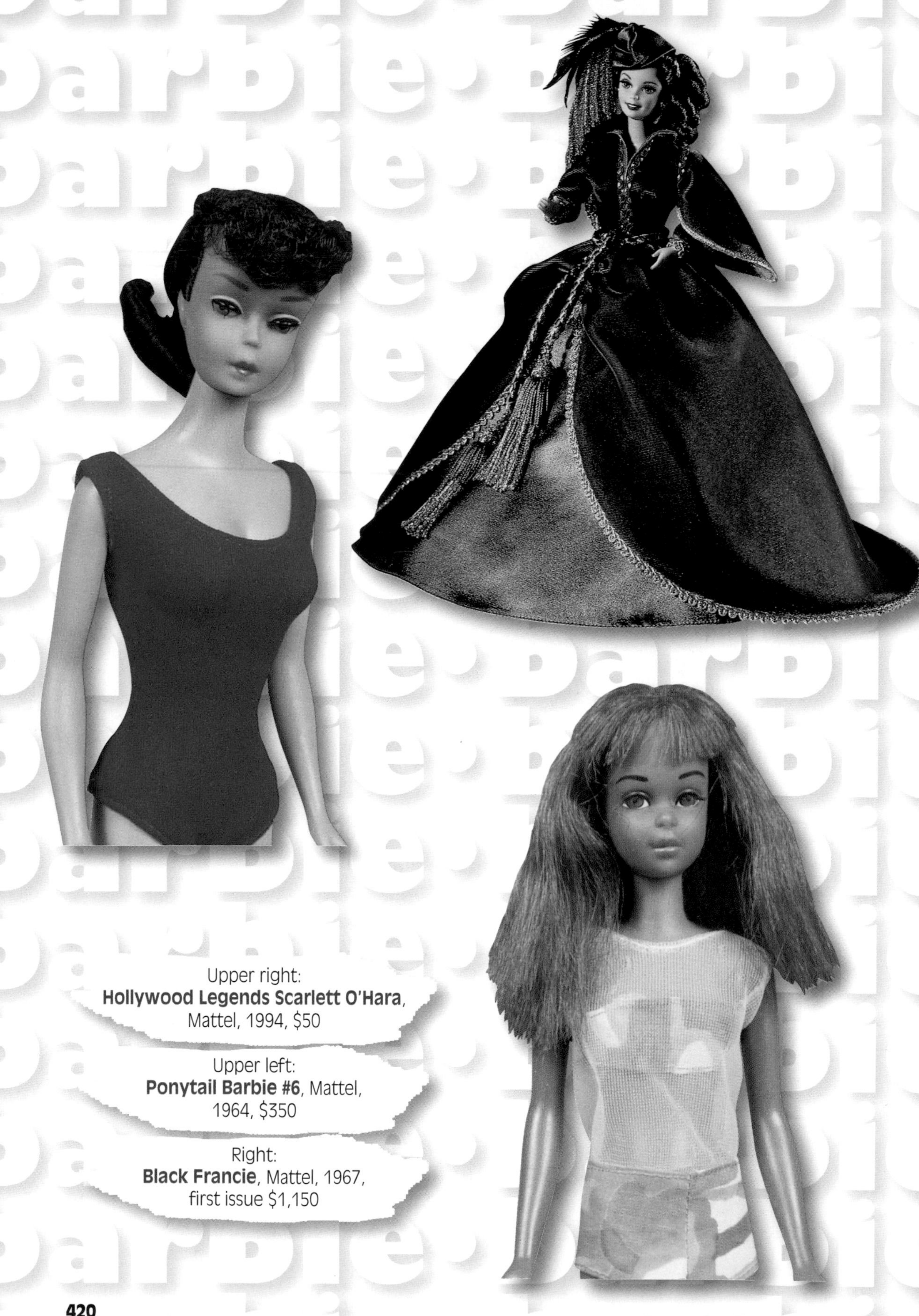

Upper right:
Hollywood Legends Scarlett O'Hara, Mattel, 1994, $50

Upper left:
Ponytail Barbie #6, Mattel, 1964, $350

Right:
Black Francie, Mattel, 1967, first issue $1,150

Mighty Mouse Sneakers, Randy Co., 1960s, $200

Dick Tracy Target Game, Marx, 1940s, $525

Planet of the Apes Fortress play set, Mego, 1975, $230

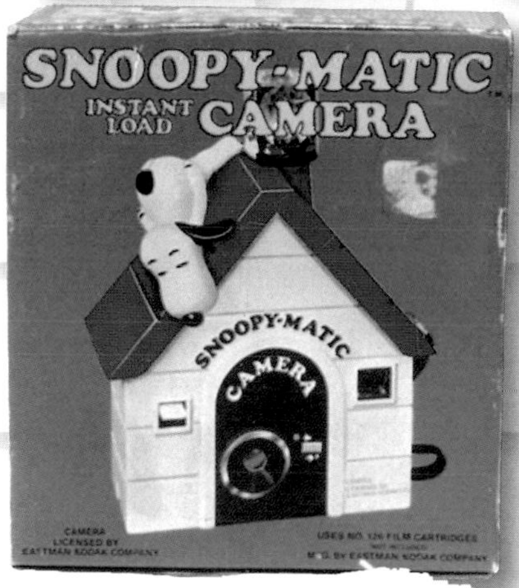

Peanuts, Snoopy-Matic Instant Load Camera, Helm Toy, 1970s, $225

Dr. Seuss, Thidwick ($90), **The Lorax** ($135) and **Yertle the Turtle** ($100) dolls, Coleco, 1983

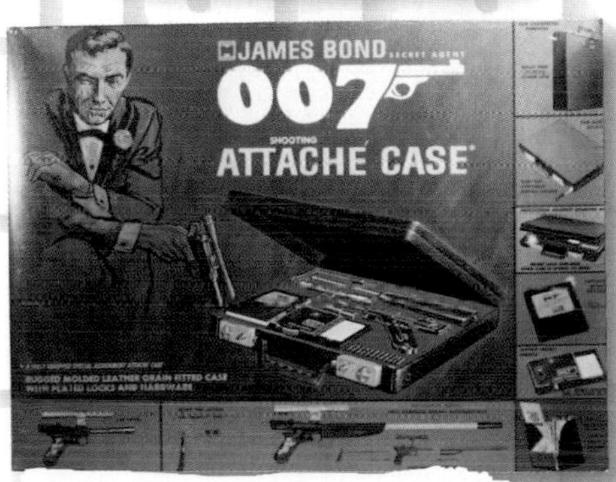

James Bond 007 Secret Agent Attache Case, MPC, 1965, $3,000

Hall of Justice play set, Mego, 1976 $250

Toss N' Cross
(Bridge Layer), 1985 $60

Baroness,
1982, 3-3/4 " $275

Cobra Commander,
1982, 3-3/4",
Mail Away exclusive $50

G. I. Joe Action Soldier,
Hasbro, 1964, 12" $450

G.I. Joe Attack Glider Falcon, 1983, $150

Cobra Missile Command Headquarters, Sears Exclusive,
1982 $500

Green Beret Machine Gun Outpost Set, G.I. Joe, Hasbro,
1966, $1,500

Disney School Bus Dome, Aladdin, 1968, $150 (steel box), $40 (bottle)

Roy Rogers Chow Wagon Dome, King Seeley Thermos, 1958, $525 (box)

Howdy Doody Dome (plastic), Thermos, 1977, $90 (box), $35 (bottle)

Gentle Ben, Aladdin, 1968, $225 (metal box), $75 (bottle)

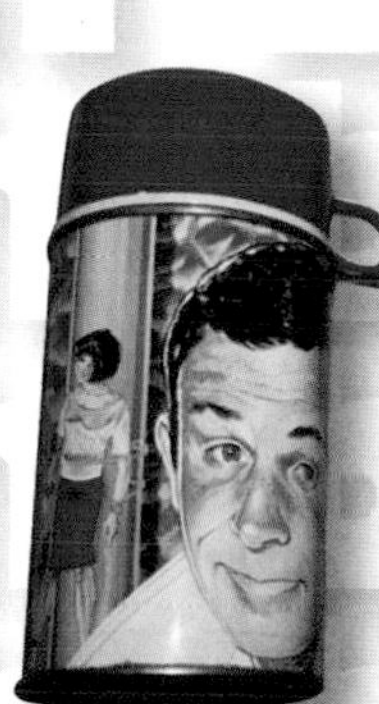

Get Smart!, King Seeley Thermos, 1966, $650 (steel box), $95 (bottle)

Play Ball, King Seeley Thermos, 1969, $250 (steel box)

Shari Lewis, Aladdin, 1963, vinyl, $475 (box)

Battle of the Blue and Gray, 1959-63 $425-$1,250

Prince Valiant Castle Fort, 1954-55, $475-$550

Noah's Ark Miniature play set, 1968, $110

Fighting Knights Carry-All, 1966-68 $200

Roy Rogers Rodeo Ranch, 1952-58, $235-$1,250

Tales of Wells Fargo, 1959, $750-$800

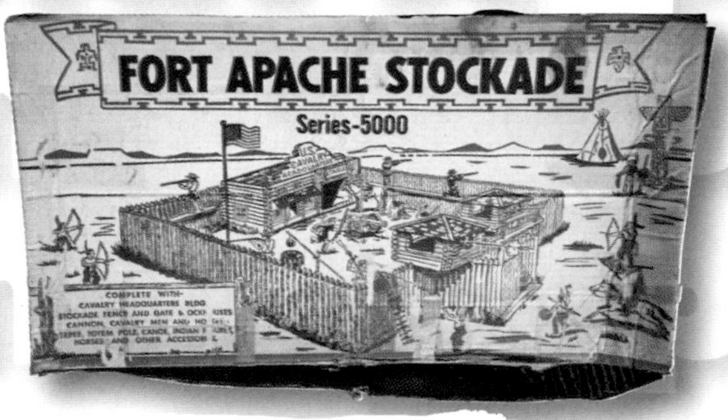

Fort Apache Stockade, 1951-61, $285-$400

Cape Canaveral Missle Center, 1958-61, $265-$400

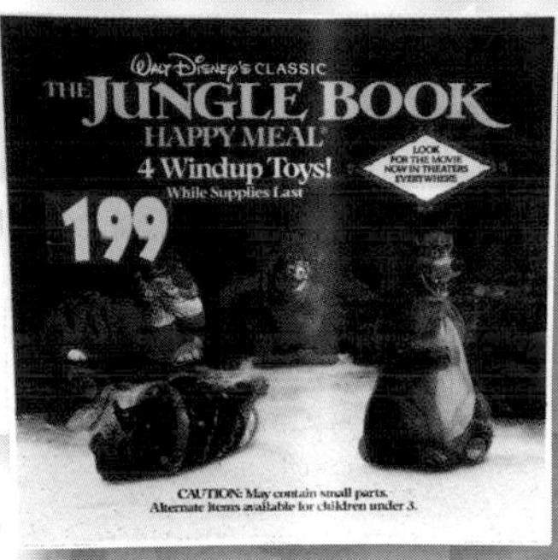

Jungle Book, McDonald's, 1990, (set of 4 wind-ups), $3 each

Angelica's Princess Castle Ride, Rugrats in Paris, Burger King, 2000 (set of 8), $3 each

Extreme Ghostbusters, KFC, 1997 (set of six), $3 each

Machine Man, Masudaya, 1950s, 15", $45,000 (Robert Lesser Collection)

Cragstan Robot, Cragstan, 1962, 12", $1,800 (Robert Lesser Collection)

Tom Corbett Push-Outs Book, Saalfield, 1952, $100

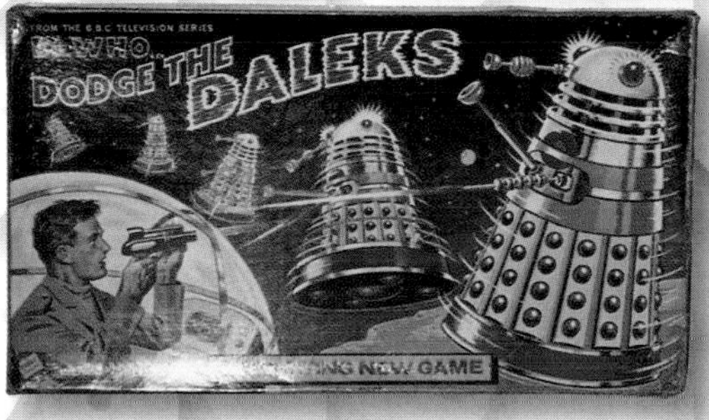

Doctor Who Dodge the Daleks Board Game, 1965, $280

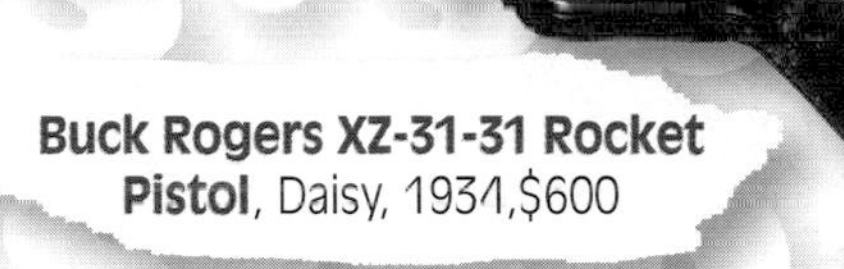

Buck Rogers XZ-31-31 Rocket Pistol, Daisy, 1934,$600

Lost In Space Robot, Remco, 1966, $700

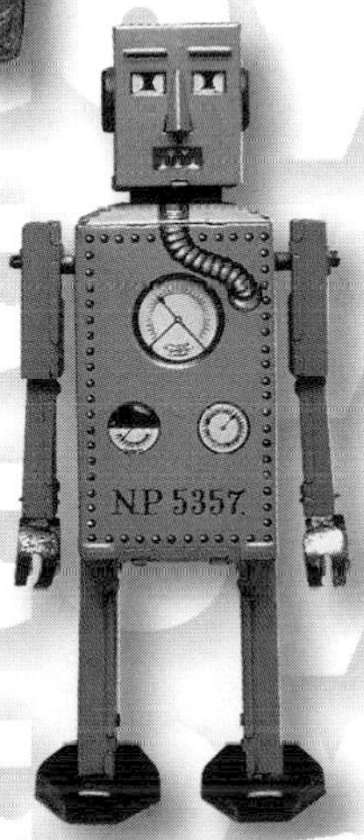

Robot Lilliput, KTA, 1939, 6", $10,000 (Robert Lesser Collection)

Princess Leia Combat Poncho, The Power of the Force, Kenner, 1985, reissue, $100

Return of the Jedi Scout Walker Vehicle, Kenner, 1983, $55

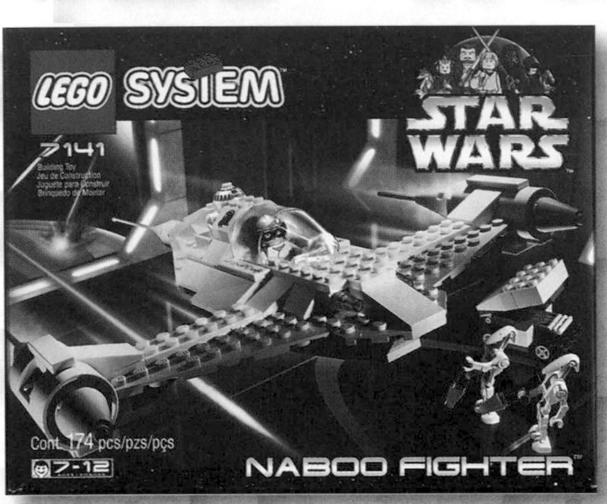

Naboo Fighter, LEGO, 1999, $25

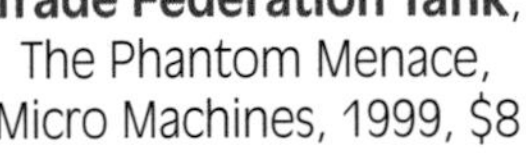

Trade Federation Tank, The Phantom Menace, Micro Machines, 1999, $8

The Empire Strikes Back Carry Case, Kenner, 1980, $50

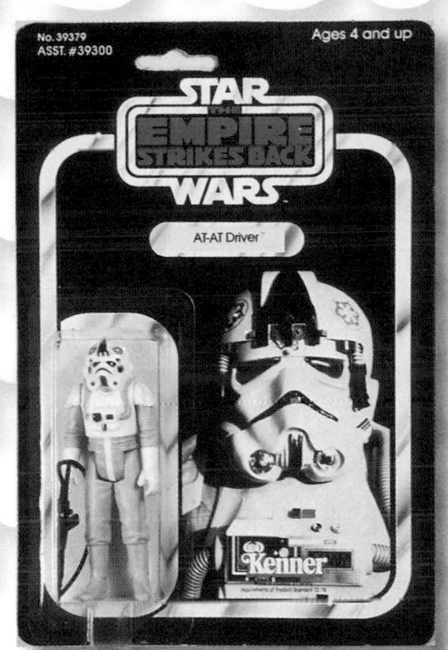

AT-AT Driver, The Empire Strikes Back, Kenner 1981, 3-3/4", $90

Chewbacca, Star Wars first series, 12-back cards, 1978-79, 3-3/4", $300

Boba Fett Doll, 13", Kenner, 1979-80, $200 loose

Mickey Mouse Lionel Circus Train Hand Car, 9" long, $1,500

Popeye Heavy Hitter, Chein, $6,400

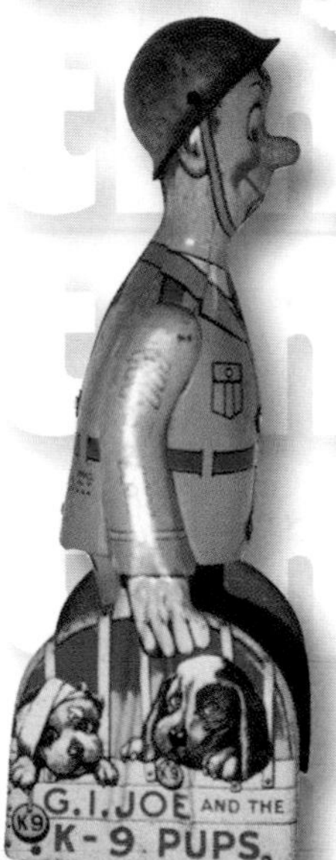

Lil' Abner and His Dogpatch Band, Unqiue Art, $950

G.I. J0E and His K-9 Pups, Unique Art, 1940s, $250

G.I. Joe and His Jouncing Jeep, Unique Art, 1940s, 7", $275

Charlie McCarthy, Marx, 1930s, $700

Mystic Motorcycle Cop, Marx, 1930s, 9", $400

Flipper Jack in the Box, Mattel, 1967, $135

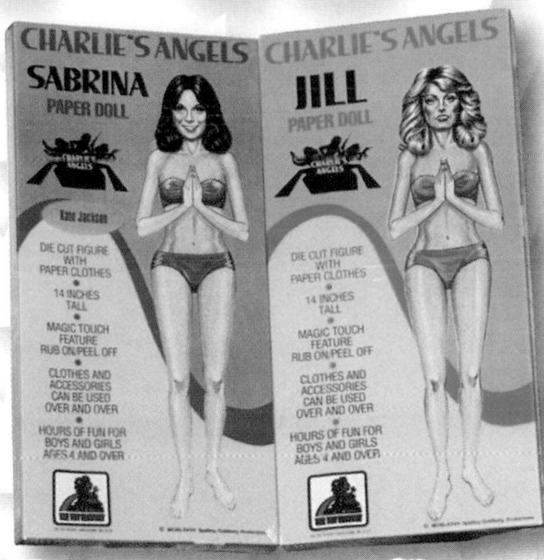

Charlie's Angels Paper Dolls, Toy Factory, 1977, Jill and Sabrina, $90 each

The Munsters Dolls, Remco, 1964: Grandpa ($610), Herman ($720) and Lilly ($625)

Honey West, TV Private Eye-Full, Gilbert 1965, 12", $325

Flintstones, Barney Wind-Up, Marx, 1960s, 3-1/2", $375

Dukes of Hazzard, Daisy's Jeep, Mego, 1981, $60

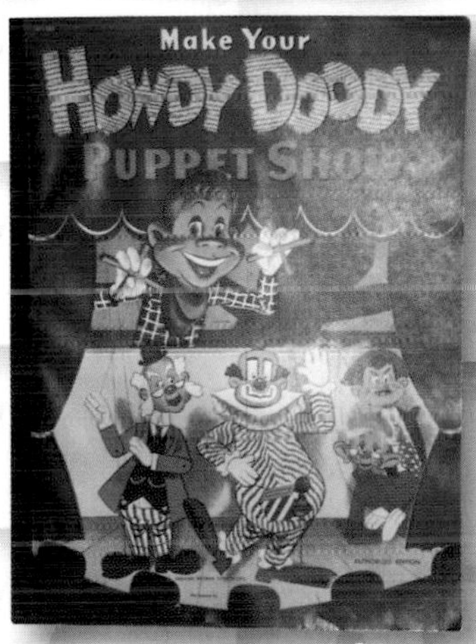

Howdy Doody Puppet Show Set, 1950s, $325

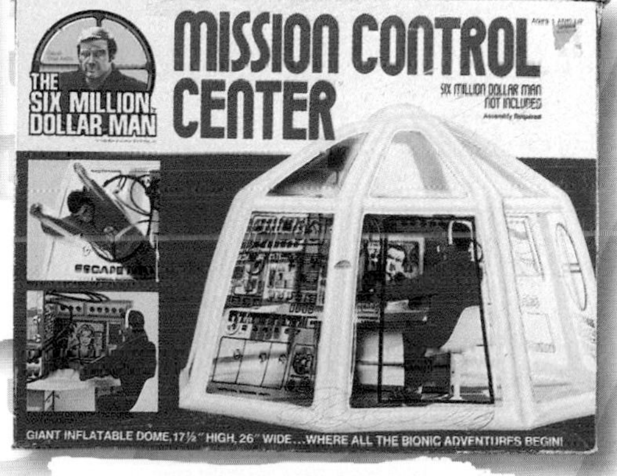

Six Million Dollar Man Mission Control Center, Kenner, 1975-78, $150

Topper Johnny Lightning '32 Roadster, 1969, $150

Topper Johnny Lightning Custom Spoiler, 1970, $160

Topper Johnny Lightning Custom Turbine, 1969, $125

Corgi Rover 2000 Ralley, 1965-66, $265

Hot Wheels Demon, Redline, Mattel, 1970, $110

Hot Wheels Cockney Cab, Redline, Mattel, 1971, $210

Hot Wheels Double Header, Redline, Mattel, 1973, $500

Hot Wheels Noodle Head, Redline, Mattel, 1971, $200

Jaguar XK-120, Doepke, 18" long, 1955-56, $650

Structo Wrecker Truck, #822, $450

Corgi Volkswagen Military Personnel Carrier, 1964-66, $180

Magnetic Crane and Truck, Mark, 1950, $275

GMC Bank of America Truck, Smith-Miller, 1949, $600

Carnation Milk Step Van, Tonka, 11-3/4", 1954, $600

Nylint Payloader No. 1600, 1951-55, $350

Carousel Truck, Marx, 7-1/2 " long, 1967-68, $45

Roy Rogers and Dale Evans Western Dinner Set, Ideal, 1950s, $100

Lucas McCain, The Rifleman, Hartland statue, $300

Johnny Ringo Gun and Holster Set, Marx, 1960, $375

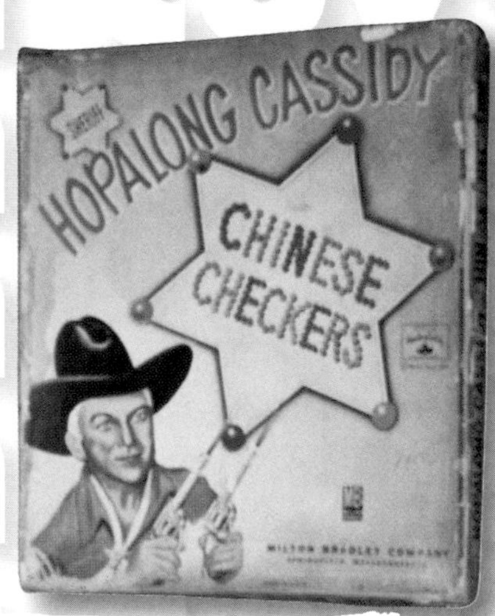

Hopalong Cassidy Chinese Checkers, Milton Bradley, 1950, $225

Roy Rogers Cap Pistols, Kilgore, 1950s, 10", $550

Battleground, 1971, Montgomery Ward Exclusive, Model No. 4752
EX $100 **NM** $285 **MIP** $465

Battleground Convoy, 1962, Model No. 3745-6
EX $40 **NM** $125 **MIP** $275

Beach Head Landing Set, U.S. and Nazi Troops, Model No. 4939
EX $25 **NM** $65 **MIP** $110

Ben Hur, blister card, Model No. 2648
EX $25 **NM** $95 **MIP** $150

Ben Hur, 1959, Series 5000, large set, Model No. 4701
EX $475 **NM** $1100 **MIP** $1900

Ben Hur, 1959, Series 2000, medium set, Model No. 4702
EX $255 **NM** $770 **MIP** $1450

Ben Hur, 1959, 132 pieces, Model No. 4696
EX $185 **NM** $275 **MIP** $525

Big Inch Pipeline, 1963, 200 pieces, Model No. 6008
EX $85 **NM** $250 **MIP** $400

Big Top Circus, 1952, Model No. 4310
EX $125 **NM** $325 **MIP** $550

Boot Camp, Carry-All, tin box set, with tank, half-track, jeep, artillery, figures and tents, Model No. 4645
EX $35 **NM** $135 **MIP** $215

Boy Scout
EX $115 **NM** $600 **MIP** $925

Boys Camp, 1956, Model No. 4103
EX $130 **NM** $395 **MIP** $650

Cape Canaveral, 1959, Sears set, Model No. 5963
EX $90 **NM** $325 **MIP** $510

Cape Canaveral, 1960, Series 2000, Model No. 4524
EX $95 **NM** $195 **MIP** $325

Cape Canaveral Missile Center, 1959, includes four-stage rocket, missile and launcher, flying saucer and launcher, scientists, and other accessories, Model No. 2656
EX $75 **NM** $160 **MIP** $265

Cape Canaveral Missile Center, 1959, Model No. 4528
EX $90 **NM** $240 **MIP** $400

Cape Canaveral Missile Center, 1961, Model No. 4525
EX $65 **NM** $195 **MIP** $310

Cape Canaveral Missile Set, 1958, Model No. 4526
EX $65 **NM** $225 **MIP** $350

Cape Kennedy Carry All, 1968, tin box set, Model No. 4625
EX $45 **NM** $65 **MIP** $110

Captain Gallant of the Foreign Legion, 1956, includes foreign legion soldiers, sheiks, horses, camel and "Cuffy." A hard-to-find set, Model No. 4729/4730
EX $210 **NM** $620 **MIP** $1200

Captain Space Solar Academy, 1953, Model No. 7026
EX $100 **NM** $325 **MIP** $500

Captain Space Solar Port, 1954, Model No. 7018
EX $75 **NM** $250 **MIP** $425

Castle and Moat Set, Sears Exclusive, Model No. 4734
EX $65 **NM** $260 **MIP** $400

Cattle Drive, 1972-73, Model No. 3983
EX $70 **NM** $250 **MIP** $385

Civil War Centennial, 1961, Model No. 5929
EX $400 **NM** $1200 **MIP** $1800

Comanche Pass, 1976, Model No. 3416
EX $30 **NM** $130 **MIP** $225

Complete Happitime Dairy Farm, Sears, Model No. 5957
EX $85 **NM** $325 **MIP** $510

Complete U.S. Army Training Center, 1954, Model No. 4145
EX $80 **NM** $210 **MIP** $350

Construction Camp, 1954, includes trucks, figures, buildings and accessories, Model No. 4439
EX $100 **NM** $290 **MIP** $475

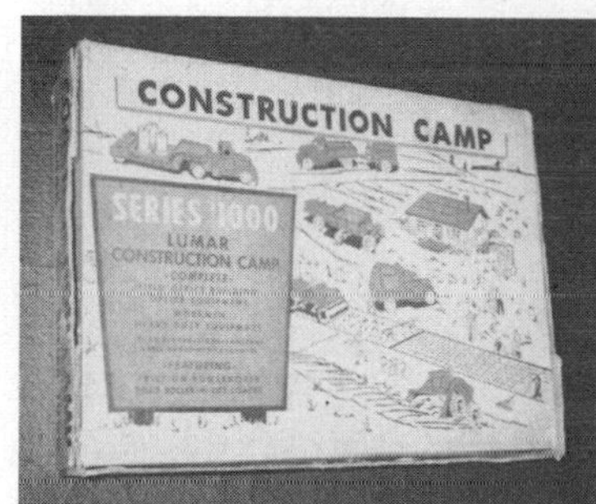

Construction Camp, 1956, 54mm, Series 1000, includes: field office building, workmen, heavy duty equipment (friction-power dozer, road roller, high-lift loader), Model No. 4442
EX $120 **NM** $330 **MIP** $600

Cowboy And Indian Camp, 1953, Model No. 3950
EX $100 **NM** $275 **MIP** $450

Custer's Last Stand, 1956, Series 500, Model No. 4779
EX $110 **NM** $325 **MIP** $575

Custer's Last Stand, 1963, Sears, 187 pieces, Model No. 4670
EX $195 **NM** $1200 **MIP** $1800

D.E.W. Defense Line Arctic Satellite Base, Model No. 4802
EX $125 **NM** $300 **MIP** $500

Daktari, Model No. 3718
EX $100 **NM** $325 **MIP** $500

Daktari, 1967, 110 pieces, Model No. 3717
EX $100 **NM** $300 **MIP** $525

Daktari, 1967, 140 pieces, Model No. 3720
EX $145 **NM** $395 **MIP** $660

Daniel Boone Frontier, 1958, includes covered wagon and horses with driver, Indians, Frontiersman, other accessories, Model No. 1393
EX $85 **NM** $235 **MIP** $375

Daniel Boone Wilderness Scout, 1964, Model No. 0670
EX $90 **NM** $225 **MIP** $385

Daniel Boone Wilderness Scout, 1964, Model No. 0631
EX $85 **NM** $225 **MIP** $425

Daniel Boone Wilderness Scout, 1964, Model No. 2640
EX $120 **NM** $360 **MIP** $650

Davy Crockett at the Alamo, Model No. 3442
EX $150 **NM** $360 **MIP** $650

Davy Crockett at the Alamo, 1955, official Walt Disney, biggest set, Model No. 3544
EX $160 **NM** $500 **MIP** $825

Davy Crockett at the Alamo, 1955, official Walt Disney, 100 pieces, first set, Model No. 3530
EX $80 **NM** $275 **MIP** $450

D-Day Army Set, U.S. and Nazi troops, Model No. 6027
EX $125 **NM** $300 **MIP** $575

Desert Fox, 1966, 244 pieces, Model No. 4177
EX $105 **NM** $275 **MIP** $475

Desert Patrol, 1967, U.S. and Nazi troops, Model No. 4174
EX $85 **NM** $185 **MIP** $325

Farm Set, Model No. 6006
EX $50 **NM** $195 **MIP** $300

Farm Set, Model No. 6050
EX $50 **NM** $180 **MIP** $275

Farm Set, 1958, 100 pieces, Series 2000, Model No. 3948
EX $80 **NM** $250 **MIP** $400

Farm Set, 1965, 1968-73, w/ 20" steel barn, 14 farm animals, 5 sections of fence, 4 rows of crops, plastic tractor w/ 7 attachments, farm tools, feed boxes, Model No. 5942
EX $45 **NM** $160 **MIP** $250

Farm Set, 1969, deluxe, Model No. 3953
EX $75 **NM** $225 **MIP** $375

Fighting Knights Carry All, 1966-68, includes litho walls, plastic towers, metallic and solid color knights, catapults and horses, Model No. 4635
EX $55 **NM** $140 **MIP** $200

Fire House, Model No. 4819
EX $225 **NM** $700 **MIP** $1100

Fire House, w/two friction vehicles, Model No. 4820
EX $500 **NM** $1500 **MIP** $2000

Flintstones, The, 1960s, Bedrock, stone fences, buildings, palm trees, play mat, vehicles, figures, dinosaurs, Model No. 4672
EX $175 **NM** $250 **MIP** $575

Fort Apache, Model No. 3616
EX $45 **NM** $90 **MIP** $150

Fort Apache, Model No. 6068
EX $40 **NM** $100 **MIP** $165

Fort Apache, Sears, Model No. 6059
EX $20 **NM** $35 **MIP** $75

Fort Apache, giant set, Model No. 3685
EX $140 **NM** $425 **MIP** $700

Fort Apache, Model No. 3681A
EX $35 **NM** $90 **MIP** $150

Fort Apache, Model No. 3682
EX $15 **NM** $50 **MIP** $85

Fort Apache, 1965, Sears, 335 pieces, Model No. 6063
EX $125 **NM** $315 **MIP** $550

Fort Apache, 1965, Sears, 147 pieces
EX $45 **NM** $120 **MIP** $225

Fort Apache, 1967, Model No. 3681
EX $55 **NM** $135 **MIP** $225

Fort Apache, 1970s, Model No. 4202
EX $25 **NM** $50 **MIP** $80

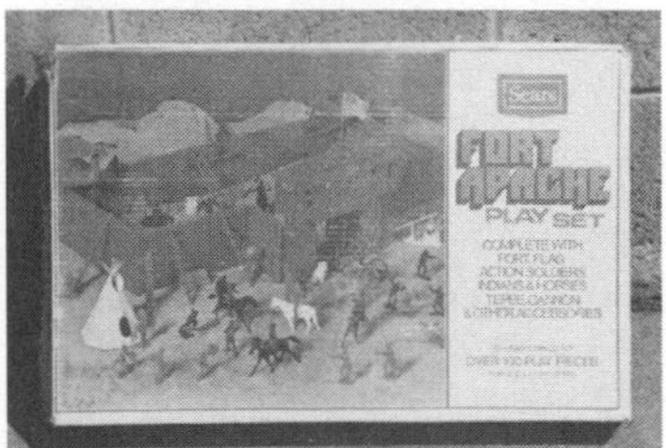

Fort Apache, 1972, Sears, over 100 pieces including: plastic fort, U.S. flag, Indians, tepee, horses, soldiers, cannon and accessories, Model No. 59093C
EX $45 **NM** $95 **MIP** $160

Fort Apache, 1976, Model No. 3681
EX $50 **NM** $120 **MIP** $210

Fort Apache Carry All, 1967, with plastic block houses, cowboys, horses and Indians, Model No. 4685
EX $35 **NM** $55 **MIP** $100

Fort Apache Rin Tin Tin, 1956, early, 60mm, Model No. 3627
EX $125 **NM** $300 **MIP** $475

Fort Apache Rin Tin Tin, 1957, 54mm, Model No. 3658
EX $100 **NM** $250 **MIP** $375

Fort Apache Rin Tin Tin, 1958, mixed scale set, Model No. 3957
EX $90 **NM** $275 **MIP** $350

Fort Apache Stockade, 1951, Model No. 3610
EX $70 **NM** $210 **MIP** $350

Fort Apache Stockade, 1953, includes stockade, block house, ladders, cowboys and Indians, Model No. 3612
EX $55 **NM** $160 **MIP** $260

Fort Apache Stockade, 1960, Series 2000, 60mm figures, Model No. 3660
EX $85 **NM** $225 **MIP** $400

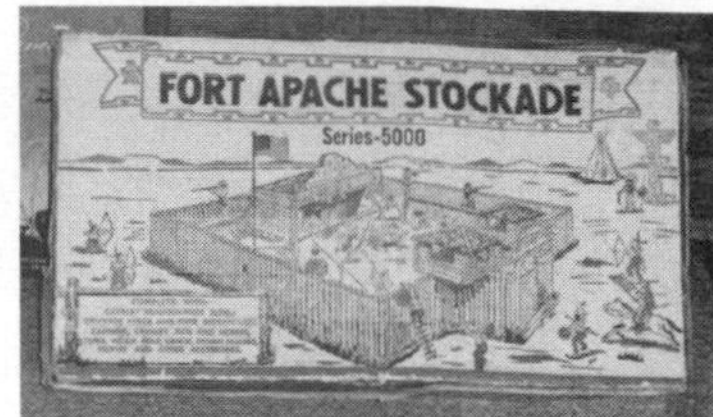

Fort Apache Stockade, 1961, Series 5000 includes: cavalry HQ building, stockade fence and gate blockhouses, cannon, cavalry men and horses, tepee, Indian figures, totem pole, canoe, horses and other accessories
EX $60 **NM** $170 **MIP** $285

Fort Apache with Famous Americans, Model No. 3636
EX $55 **NM** $165 **MIP** $270

Fort Dearborn, w/plastic walls, Model No. 3688
EX $80 **NM** $240 **MIP** $400

Fort Dearborn, larger set, Model No. 3514
EX $20 **NM** $60 **MIP** $100

Fort Dearborn, 1952, w/metal walls, Model No. 3510
EX $100 **NM** $255 **MIP** $375

Fort Mohawk, 1958, British, Colonials, Indians, 54mm, Model No. 3751-2
EX $100 **NM** $325 **MIP** $550

Fort Pitt, 1959, Series 1000, 54mm, Model No. 3742
EX $100 **NM** $300 **MIP** $475

Fort Pitt, 1959, Series 750, 54mm, Model No. 3741
EX $65 **NM** $260 **MIP** $400

Four-Level Allstate Service Station, 1962, Model No. 3499
EX $80 **NM** $325 **MIP** $500

Four-Level Parking Garage, Model No. 3511
EX $40 **NM** $200 **MIP** $300

Four-Level Parking Garage, Model No. 3502
EX $40 **NM** $120 **MIP** $200

Freight Trucking Terminal, 1950, plastic trucks, Model No. 5220
EX $30 **NM** $90 **MIP** $150

Freight Trucking Terminal, 1950, friction trucks, Model No. 5422
EX $30 **NM** $90 **MIP** $150

Galaxy Command, 1976, Model No. 4206
EX $25 **NM** $55 **MIP** $90

Gallant Men, official set from TV series, Model No. 4634
EX $70 **NM** $290 **MIP** $450

Gallant Men Army, 1963, U.S. troops, Model No. 4632
EX $65 **NM** $260 **MIP** $400

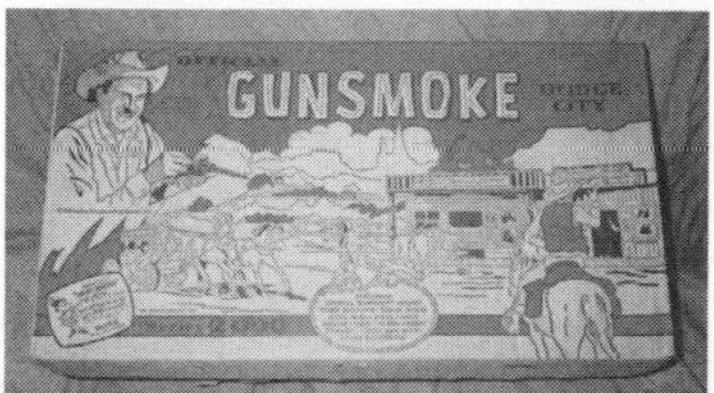

Gunsmoke Dodge City, 1960, official, Series 2000, 80 pieces including: Gunsmoke characters, town building, ranch house, gold mine, stagecoach, wagon, oxen, horses, cowboys, trees, steers and other accessories, Model No. 4268
EX $375 **NM** $1300 **MIP** $2200

Happi-time Army and Air Force Training Center, 1954, Sears, 147 pieces, Model No. 4159
EX $50 **NM** $150 **MIP** $250

Happi-time Civil War Centennial, 1962, Sears, Model No. 5929
EX $115 **NM** $455 **MIP** $700

Happi-Time Deluxe Farm Set, 1958, Sears, Series 2000, tin litho barn and silo, Model No. 3949
EX $50 **NM** $150 **MIP** $250

Happi-time Farm Set, Sears, Model No. 3480
EX $35 **NM** $95 **MIP** $150

Happi-Time Farm Set, 1953, Sears, barn, silo, no figures, 60mm animals and implements, Model No. 3940
EX $65 **NM** $150 **MIP** $275

Happi-Time Farm Set, 1958, Sears, Series 2000, 100 pieces, chicken shed, Model No. 3943
EX $65 **NM** $150 **MIP** $260

Happi-Time Farm Set, 1959-60, Sears, Deluxe Platform Farm, barn and 2 silos on raised platform, 2-wheel cart pictured on box never included, Model No. 5931
EX $100 **NM** $225 **MIP** $375

Happi-time Roy Rogers Rodeo Ranch, 1953, Sears, Model No. 3990
EX $90 **NM** $185 **MIP** $350

Heritage Battle of the Alamo, 1972, Heritage Series, Model No. 59091
EX $80 **NM** $240 **MIP** $400

History in the Pacific, 1972-73, Model No. 4164
EX $100 **NM** $285 **MIP** $450

Holiday Turnpike, battery-operated w/HO scale vehicles, Model No. 5230
EX $10 **NM** $30 **MIP** $45

I.G.Y. Arctic Satellite Base, 1959, Series 1000, with quonset hut, missiles, launchers, explorer figures, eskimo figures, igloos, sleds, animals, weather station, skis, etc. A true "cold war" play set, for sure, Model No. 4800
EX $250 **NM** $750 **MIP** $1250

Indian Warfare, Series 2000, Model No. 4778
EX $65 **NM** $260 **MIP** $400

International Airport, 1973, terminal, planes, cars, trucks, people, accessories, Model No. 4814
EX $35 **NM** $75 **MIP** $150

Irrigated Farm Set, working pump, Model No. 6021
EX $7 **NM** $20 **MIP** $35

Johnny Apollo Moon Launch Center, 1970, Model No. 4630
EX $75 **NM** $150 **MIP** $275

Johnny Ringo Western Frontier Set, 1959, Series 2000, Model No. 4784
EX $1400 **NM** $2750 **MIP** $5200

Johnny Tremain Revolutionary War, 1957, official Walt Disney, Series 1000, Model No. 3401-2
EX $635 **NM** $1400 **MIP** $2750

Jungle, metal trading post, Series 500, Model No. 3705
EX $110 **NM** $325 **MIP** $550

Jungle, 1960, 48 pieces, Sears, large animals, Model No. 3716
EX $25 **NM** $95 **MIP** $150

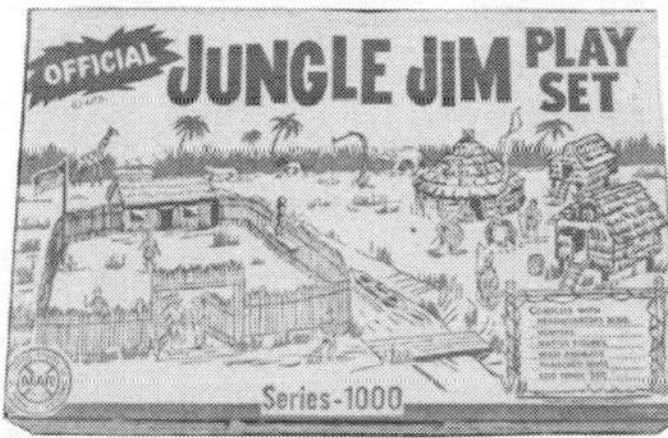

Jungle Jim, 1957, official, Series 1000, includes: HQ building, hunters, natives, wild animals, thatched huts, log fence and accessories, Model No. 3705-6
EX $290 **NM** $875 **MIP** $1450

King Arthur's Castle Medieval Play Set, 1960s, w/ 22 knights on horses, benches, working drawbridge, accessories, Model No. 4800
EX $100 **NM** $200 **MIP** $325

Knights and Vikings, Model No. 4773
EX $50 **NM** $90 **MIP** $150

Knights and Vikings, 1972, Model No. 4743
EX $60 **NM** $150 **MIP** $275

Knights and Vikings, 1973, includes plastic castle and mat with metallic silver knights fighting Vikings, Model No. 4733
EX $65 **NM** $175 **MIP** $285

Lazy Day Farm, 1951, Wards, barn, 60mm people, no silos, animals, Model No. 3931
EX $60 **NM** $150 **MIP** $250

Lazy Day Farm Set, 1958, Wards, Series 1000, no silo, 54mm people and animals, Model No. 3942
EX $50 **NM** $150 **MIP** $250

MARX PLAY SETS

Lazy Day Farm Set, 1960, Wards, 100 pieces, Model No. 3945
EX $60 **NM** $165 **MIP** $275

Little Red School House, 1956, Model No. 3381-2
EX $90 **NM** $270 **MIP** $450

Lone Ranger Ranch, 1957, Series 500, includes: Lone Ranger, Tonto, cabin, gateway, cowboys, horses, saddles, Indians and accessories, Model No. 3969
EX $125 **NM** $260 **MIP** $475

Lone Ranger Rodeo Set, 1952-53, Model No. 3696
EX $65 **NM** $130 **MIP** $210

Medieval Castle, Sears, w/knights and Vikings, Model No. 4734
EX $100 **NM** $290 **MIP** $465

Medieval Castle, w/knights and Vikings, Model No. 4733
EX $60 **NM** $130 **MIP** $210

Medieval Castle, w/knights and Vikings, Model No. 4707
EX $45 **NM** $110 **MIP** $195

Medieval Castle, 1954, Model No. 4709
EX $35 **NM** $95 **MIP** $150

Medieval Castle, 1959, Sears, Series 2000, Model No. 4708
EX $125 **NM** $350 **MIP** $600

Medieval Castle, 1960, metallic knights, castle, horses, tree and catapult, Model No. 4700
EX $80 **NM** $295 **MIP** $460

Medieval Castle, 1964, gold knights, moat, Model No. 4704
EX $40 **NM** $90 **MIP** $150

Medieval Castle Fort, 1953, included: fortress, figures, horses, cannons and accessories, Model No. 4709-10
EX $65 **NM** $150 **MIP** $260

Midtown Service Station, 1960, electric elevator, pumps with canopy, attendants, cars and accessories, Model No. 3420
EX $52 **NM** $155 **MIP** $255

Midtown Shopping Center, Model No. 2644
EX $30 **NM** $90 **MIP** $150

Military Academy, 1954, w/ six generals, Model No. 4718
EX $100 **NM** $350 **MIP** $500

Modern Farm Set, 1951, 54mm, Model No. 3931
EX $50 **NM** $150 **MIP** $250

Modern Farm Set, 1967, Model No. 3932
EX $65 **NM** $185 **MIP** $310

Modern Farm Set, c.1951, metal barn, fence, tractor, animals, Model No. 3925
EX $50 **NM** $150 **MIP** $250

Modern Service Center, 1962, Model No. 3471
EX $70 **NM** $210 **MIP** $350

Modern Service Station, 1966, plastic building with gray metal base, plastic vehicles, gas pumps, mechanics and attendants, Model No. 6044
EX $45 **NM** $115 **MIP** $190

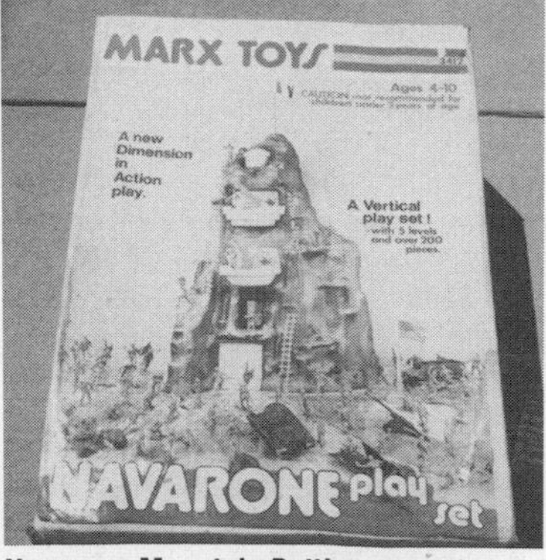

Navarone Mountain Battleground Set, 1976, included 5-level plastic mountain with two gun emplacements, German troops, ladders, communication and radio benches, tank, landing craft, halftrack, jeep, American soldiers, over 200 pieces, Model No. 3412
EX $45 **NM** $120 **MIP** $200

New Car Sales and Service, With battery powered light, Model No. 3466, 3465
EX $80 **NM** $295 **MIP** $460

One Million, B.C., 1970s
EX $50 **NM** $115 **MIP** $225

Operation Moon Base, 1962, includes vehicles, moon base structure, space man, moon ship and accessories, Model No. 4653-4
EX $95 **NM** $275 **MIP** $465

Pet Shop, Model No. 4209
EX $60 **NM** $230 **MIP** $350

Pet Shop, 1953, includes Shop building, fence, tree, cages, crates, dogs, monkees, rabbits, birds, aquarium and accessories, Model No. 4209-10
EX $65 **NM** $240 **MIP** $365

Prehistoric, 1969, Model No. 3398
EX $35 **NM** $105 **MIP** $175

Prehistoric Dinosaur, 1978, Model No. 4208
EX $35 **NM** $105 **MIP** $175

Prehistoric Times, Series 500, plain box that reads, "Prehistoric Play Set Complete with Animals in Natural Setting", Model No. 3389
EX $50 **NM** $120 **MIP** $195

Prehistoric Times, Model No. 2650
EX $35 **NM** $130 **MIP** $200

Prehistoric Times, Model No. 3388
EX $30 **NM** $75 **MIP** $150

Prehistoric Times, Model No. 3391
EX $20 **NM** $55 **MIP** $95

Prehistoric Times, 1957, Series 1000, big set, includes: molded terrain base, cavemen, prehistoric animals, palm trees, ferns, tree stumps and accessories, Model No. 3390
EX $85 **NM** $230 **MIP** $400

Prince Valiant Castle, 1954, has figures, Model No. 4706
EX $110 **NM** $320 **MIP** $550

Prince Valiant Castle, 1955, Model No. 4705
EX $100 **NM** $270 **MIP** $475

Project Apollo Cape Kennedy, Model No. 4523
EX $45 **NM** $75 **MIP** $125

Project Apollo Moon Landing, Model No. 4646
EX $55 **NM** $150 **MIP** $250

Project Mercury Cape Canaveral, 1959, Model No. 4524
EX $100 **NM** $270 **MIP** $450

Raytheon Missile Test Center, 1961, Model No. 603-A
EX $70 **NM** $180 **MIP** $325

Real Life Western Wagon, Model No. 4998
EX $15 **NM** $45 **MIP** $75

Red River Gang, 1970s, mini set w/cowboys, Model No. 4104
EX $35 **NM** $105 **MIP** $175

Revolutionary War, 1950s, Series 1000, includes British Redcoats, stone wall section, shooting cannon, trees, litho building, Revolutionary troops and more, Model No. 3404
EX $125 **NM** $500 **MIP** $850

Revolutionary War, 1957, Series 500, Model No. 3401
EX $225 **NM** $550 **MIP** $1150

Revolutionary War, 1959, No. 3408, 80 pieces, Sears, Model No. 3408
EX $100 **NM** $390 **MIP** $650

Rex Mars Planet Patrol, Model No. 7040
EX $125 **NM** $310 **MIP** $575

Rex Mars Space Drome, 1954, Model No. 7016
EX $150 **NM** $395 **MIP** $700

Rifleman Ranch, The, 1959, Model No. 3997-8
EX $130 **NM** $455 **MIP** $750

Rin Tin Tin at Fort Apache, 1956, Series 5000, Model No. 3686R
EX $250 **NM** $725 **MIP** $1250

Rin Tin Tin at Fort Apache, 1956, Series 500, 60mm, Model No. 3628
EX $160 **NM** $475 **MIP** $800

Robin Hood Castle, 1956, 60mm, Model No. 4717
EX $175 **NM** $375 **MIP** $660

Robin Hood Castle, 1958, 54mm, Model No. 4718
EX $125 **NM** $325 **MIP** $500

Robin Hood Castle Set, 1950s, Series 1000, 54mm, Model No. 4724
EX $100 **NM** $225 **MIP** $400

Roy Rogers Double R Bar Ranch, 1962, Model No. 3982
EX $100 **NM** $300 **MIP** $525

Roy Rogers Mineral City, 1958, 95 pieces, Model No. 4227
EX $110 **NM** $300 **MIP** $500

Roy Rogers Ranch, 1950s, w/ranch kids, Model No. 3980
EX $200 **NM** $300 **MIP** $525

Roy Rogers Rodeo, 1952, w/fence pieces, Model No. 3689-90
EX $60 **NM** $80 **MIP** $150

Roy Rogers Rodeo Ranch, 54mm, Model No. 3988
EX $90 **NM** $195 **MIP** $345

Roy Rogers Rodeo Ranch, Series 2000, Model No. 3996
EX $130 **NM** $395 **MIP** $650

Roy Rogers Rodeo Ranch, 1952, Model No. 3979
EX $55 **NM** $165 **MIP** $275

Roy Rogers Rodeo Ranch, 1952, 60mm, includes: bunk house, rodeo chute, cowboys, horses, steers, saddles, bridles, fence and accessories, Model No. 3985
EX $75 **NM** $140 **MIP** $235

Roy Rogers Rodeo Ranch, 1958, Model No. 3986R
EX $250 **NM** $750 **MIP** $1250

Roy Rogers Western Town, official, Series 5000, Model No. 4259
EX $95 **NM** $235 **MIP** $450

Roy Rogers Western Town, Model No. 4216
EX $80 **NM** $240 **MIP** $400

Roy Rogers Western Town, 1952, large set, Mineral City, Model No. 4257-8
EX $160 **NM** $475 **MIP** $800

Sears Store, 1961, Allstate box, Model No. 5490
EX $350 **NM** $1200 **MIP** $1850

Service Station, Model No. 5459
EX $25 **NM** $60 **MIP** $125

Service Station, with parking garage, includes: service station, cars, attendants, high-level parking garage, Model No. 3485
EX $115 **NM** $325 **MIP** $540

Service Station, w/elevator, Model No. 3495
EX $30 **NM** $90 **MIP** $150

Service Station, deluxe, Model No. 3501
EX $50 **NM** $150 **MIP** $250

Shopping Center, 1962, Model No. 3755-6
EX $40 **NM** $120 **MIP** $200

Silver City Frontier Town, 1555, Model No. 4219-20
EX $50 **NM** $150 **MIP** $250

Silver City Western Town, 1956, has Custer, Boone, Carson, Buffalo Bill, Sitting Bull, Model No. 4220
EX $50 **NM** $150 **MIP** $250

Silver City Western Town (Ward's), 1954, Montgomery Wards exclusive, Model No. 4256
EX $65 **NM** $150 **MIP** $275

Skyscraper, 1957, working elevator, Model No. 5449-50
EX $155 **NM** $800 **MIP** $1200

Skyscraper (Ward's), 1957, Montgomery Ward's exclusive, working elevator and light, Model No. 5450
EX $155 **NM** $800 **MIP** $1250

Sons of Liberty, 1972, Sears Exclusive set includes: litho building, plastic figures and accessories, flag and stand, historic booklet, Model No. 4170
EX $55 **NM** $155 **MIP** $260

Star Station Seven, 1978, 32 pieces
EX $10 **NM** $30 **MIP** $50

Strategic Air Command, Model No. 6013
EX $130 **NM** $520 **MIP** $800

Super Circus, 1952, w/character figures, Model No. 4320
EX $75 **NM** $290 **MIP** $450

Super Circus, 1952, over 70 pieces, including big top, Model No. 4319
EX $95 **NM** $245 **MIP** $435

Tactical Air Command, 1970s, Model No. 4106
EX $25 **NM** $50 **MIP** $85

Tales of Wells Fargo, Model No. 4263
EX $80 **NM** $240 **MIP** $450

Tales of Wells Fargo, Series 1000, play set includes Wells Fargo office, western town building, stagecoach, horses and cowboys, Indians and accessories, Model No. 4264
EX $155 **NM** $465 **MIP** $760

Tales of Wells Fargo, Model No. 4262
EX $150 **NM** $450 **MIP** $750

Tales of Wells Fargo Train Set, 1959, w/electric train, Model No. 54752
EX $240 **NM** $600 **MIP** $800

Tank Battle, 1964, Sears, U.S., Nazi troops, Model No. 6056
EX $40 **NM** $120 **MIP** $200

Tank Battle, 1964, U.S., Nazi troops, Model No. 6060
EX $60 **NM** $120 **MIP** $225

Tom Corbett Space Academy, 1952, No. 7099, 9 wall sections and gate,
EX $150 **NM** $375 **MIP** $710

Treasure Cove Pirate Set, 1962, Model No. 4597-8
EX $50 **NM** $125 **MIP** $210

Turnpike Service Center, 1961, Model No. 3459-60
EX $100 **NM** $300 **MIP** $500

U.S. Air Force, 1963, Model No. 4807
EX $30 **NM** $90 **MIP** $160

U.S. Armed Forces, Model No. 4151
EX $70 **NM** $210 **MIP** $350

U.S. Armed Forces Training Center, Model No. 4150
EX $50 **NM** $150 **MIP** $265

U.S. Armed Forces Training Center, Marines, soldiers, sailors, airmen, tin litho building, Model No. 4144
EX $40 **NM** $160 **MIP** $250

U.S. Armed Forces Training Center, 1955, Series 500, "Featuring Guided Missiles," and including: HQ building, flag, fence, jet plane, compass, helicopter, Air Force, Navy, Army and Marines figures, Model No. 4149-50
EX $90 **NM** $265 **MIP** $430

U.S. Armed Forces Training Center, 1956, includes barracks, tents, planes, soldiers, Marines, sailors, Air Force personnel, guns and accessories, Model No. 4158
EX $115 **NM** $340 **MIP** $600

U.S. Army Mobile Set, 1956, flat figures, includes vehicles, Model No. 3655
EX $25 **NM** $75 **MIP** $125

U.S. Army Training Center, Model No. 4153
EX $20 **NM** $60 **MIP** $100

U.S. Army Training Center, Model No. 4122
EX $25 **NM** $60 **MIP** $100

U.S. Army Training Center, Model No. 3378
EX $30 **NM** $65 **MIP** $110

U.S. Army Training Center, Model No. 3146
EX $30 **NM** $55 **MIP** $95

U.S. Army Training Center, 1954, 45mm, includes: HQ building, vehicle, soldiers and accessories, Model No. 4123
EX $30 **NM** $80 **MIP** $130

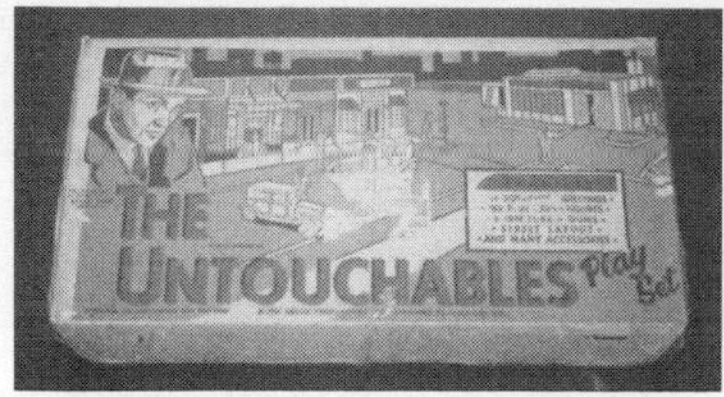

Untouchables, 1961, 90 pieces including: buildings, figures, guns, street layout, furniture and accessories, Model No. 4676
EX $325 **NM** $985 **MIP** $1550

Vikings and Knights, Model No. 6053
EX $60 **NM** $180 **MIP** $300

Wagon Train, 1959, official, Series 2000, Model No. 4788
EX $120 **NM** $360 **MIP** $600

Wagon Train, 1959, official, Series 5000, Model No. 4888
EX $275 **NM** $975 **MIP** $1800

Wagon Train, 1960, Series 1000, X Team, Model No. 4805
EX $160 **NM** $480 **MIP** $800

Walt Disney Television Playhouse, 1953, Model No. 4352
EX $120 **NM** $360 **MIP** $600

Walt Disney Television Playhouse, 1953, Peter Pan figures, Model No. 4352
EX $105 **NM** $420 **MIP** $750

Walt Disney Television Playhouse, 1953, Model No. 4350
EX $100 **NM** $300 **MIP** $475

Walt Disney's Zorro, 1958, official, Series 1000, includes buildings, horses, figures and accessories, Model No. 3754
EX $275 **NM** $780 **MIP** $1400

Walt Disney's Zorro, 1958, official, Model No. 3758
EX $250 **NM** $725 **MIP** $1150

Walt Disney's Zorro, 1958, official, Series 500, Model No. 3753
EX $230 **NM** $695 **MIP** $1100

Walt Disney's Zorro, 1972, official, Series 1000, Model No. 3758
EX $160 **NM** $500 **MIP** $800

Ward's Service Station, 1959, included service station with elevator, water-filled gasoline pump, cars and attendants, Model No. 3488
EX $82 **NM** $245 **MIP** $410

Western Frontier Set
EX $90 **NM** $275 **MIP** $450

Western Mining Town, 1950s, 1950s, Model No. 4266
EX $135 **NM** $405 **MIP** $675

Western Mining Town, 1950s, 1950s, Model No. 4265
EX $135 **NM** $400 **MIP** $675

Western Ranch Set, Model No. 3954
EX $50 **NM** $105 **MIP** $175

Western Ranch Set, Model No. 3980
EX $50 **NM** $105 **MIP** $175

Western Stagecoach, 1965, Model No. 1395
EX $45 **NM** $60 **MIP** $110

Western Town, single level, Model No. 2652
EX $60 **NM** $180 **MIP** $400

Western Town, 1952, bi-level town, Model No. 4229
EX $120 **NM** $490 **MIP** $650

Westgate Auto Center, 1968, nice-looking litho building and base, plastic accessories and "New, Fast Rolling Cars!"
EX $45 **NM** $125 **MIP** $205

White House, house w/eight figures
EX $20 **NM** $45 **MIP** $125

White House & Presidents, house & figures, Model No. 3921
EX $35 **NM** $55 **MIP** $125

White House & Presidents, house & figures, 1/48 scale presidents, Model No. 3920
EX $35 **NM** $55 **MIP** $150

Wild Animal Jungle, large animals, Model No. 3716
EX $25 **NM** $50 **MIP** $85

WORLD WAR II BATTLEGROUND!

World War II Battleground, 1966, with U.S. and German troops, halftrack, landing craft, barbed wire, barricades, gun emplacements, tank and jeep, Model No. 4204
EX $35 **NM** $95 **MIP** $175

World War II European Theatre, rare big set, Model No. 5949
EX $255 **NM** $1200 **MIP** $1500

World War II European Theatre, 1966, Sears, Model No. 5939
EX $165 **NM** $470 **MIP** $780

World War II Set, U.S., Nazi troops, Model No. 5938
EX $50 **NM** $80 **MIP** $150

Wyatt Earp Dodge City Western Town, 1957, Series 1000, Model No. 4228
EX $175 **NM** $465 **MIP** $825

Yogi Bear at Jellystone National Park, 1962, w/ Ranger station, jeep, well, benches, Yogi and friends, Model No. 4363-4
EX $125 **NM** $285 **MIP** $500

Zorro, 1958, Series 500
EX $100 **NM** $200 **MIP** $310

Zorro, 1958, Series 1000, Model No. 3754
EX $125 **NM** $250 **MIP** $500

Model Kits

by Karen O'Brien

Building model kits has been a popular hobby since the 1960s, and in recent years, unbuilt model kits have found a loyal following among collectors seeking to recapture a part of their youth. Plastic model kits were first produced shortly before World War II, but it wasn't until after the war that plastic kit building really began to take off as a hobby. Automobiles, aircraft, and ships all became the subject matter for miniature replicas popularized by companies including Aurora, Revell, Monogram, and Lindberg.

Each type of model kit has its own enthusiastic following, but probably the most collectible kits today are the figure and character kits produced in the 1960s. These kits continue to increase in value despite the up and down fluctuations of the model kit market over the last twelve years.

The Aurora Company is responsible for popularizing figure model kits, with its early 1960s representations of the Universal Pictures monsters. Aurora went into business in August of 1950 and ventured into the hobby business in 1952 with two plastic model airplanes. Aurora expanded its line through the 1950s to include ships, modern and historic aircraft, and trucks before issuing its first figure kits, the knights, starting with the Silver Knight in 1956.

The vision and tenacity of Aurora employee Bill Silverstein in 1961 would change Aurora forever. The remarkable popularity of the 1930s Universal monster films at Saturday matinees and on television prompted the idea of producing a Frankenstein model. Repeated rejections by the Aurora staff almost killed the project, but Silverstein won enough support for the model pattern to be displayed at the January, 1962, HIAA show. No distributors placed orders and on the last day of the convention, two boys accompanying a wholesaler came to the table, ignored the popular Model Motoring layout and headed straight for Frankenstein. Orders trickled in, then poured in, and the rest is history. Frankenstein production began in earnest in 1962, followed by Dracula and the Wolfman. The Creature from the Black Lagoon, The Phantom of the Opera, and The Mummy were released in 1963. The Hunchback of Notre Dame, Godzilla, and King Kong followed in 1964, and Dr. Jekyll and Mr. Hyde joined the lineup in 1965. The Universal monster kits propelled Aurora to the top of the hobby and remain some of the most desired kits by collectors today.

During the 1960s, Aurora also produced kits of more general monstrosities, such as its famous working guillotine kit. These toys offended the sensibilities of some groups, who brought about the political pressure that spelled the end of these kits. Aurora also produced kits based on popular television shows, comic book characters, and sports celebrities. Monogram and Revell reissued some of the popular Aurora kits, and resin copies of the harder-to-find Aurora kits are still being produced and sold today by independent "garage kit" makers. Recently, Polar Lights (a division of the Playing Mantis company) has enjoyed tremendous success with its award-winning reissues of old Aurora favorites, as well as new releases of television and movie favorites.

Other popular monster kits continued the fad of the 1960s. These kits weren't of traditional movie monsters, rather, they were an assortment of strange characters that often came in wild hot rods. Among the most popular were the Revell kits based on Ed "Big Daddy" Roth's Rat Fink concept. (The modern reissues of those classic kits are certain to be collectibles of the future.) Other companies, notably Hawk, also produced kits with this monstrous hot rod theme. Hawk's Weird-Ohs kits are still popular with collectors today. Even popular celebrities became model kit subjects. Airfix produced a series of historical figures, and Revell issued figure kits for each of the four Beatles.

After a slow period in the late 1970s, (the OPEC oil shortage sent plastic costs soaring, which had a ripple-effect throughout the toy and hobby industry) figure kits enjoyed a renewed popularity in the 1980s as new large-scale kits of rather limited production runs were offered in vinyl and resin. Billiken, a Japanese company, produced vinyl kits of the classic movie monsters, some of which have become highly collectible. Screamin' and Horizon are two leaders in the burgeoning "garage kit" field of large-scale vinyl and resin kits of movie, monster, and comic book characters. This area continues to command collector's attention, as the limited runs of these "garage kits" will likely translate into future desirability.

The prices listed provide a general guideline as to the amount these kits would sell for today. MIB refers to a kit that is Mint in Box, in original condition in the original Mint condition box with instructions. The box may not be in the original factory seal, but if the kit pieces are contained within bags inside the box, those original bags have not been opened. Kits that remain in pristine condition and are still in their factory seals may command a slight premium over the MIB price. Near Mint (NM) refers to a kit that is like new, complete, and unassembled. The box may show some shelf wear and the interior bags may have been opened. B/U refers to a kit that has been assembled, or built up and assumes a neatly built, cleanly painted, complete kit.

THE *TOP* 10 MODEL KITS (In Mint Condition)

1. Godzilla's Go-Cart, Aurora, 1966 .... $3,750
2. Lost in Space large kit w/Chariot, Aurora, 1966 1,600
3. Munsters Living Room, Aurora, 1964 1,450
4. Frankenstein Gigantic 1:5 scale, Aurora, 1964 1,430
5. King Kong's Thronester, Aurora, 1966 1,375
6. Lost in Space small kit, Aurora, 1966 1,100
7. Lost in Space Robot, Aurora, 1966 895
8. Addams Family Haunted House, Aurora, 1964 880
9. Bride of Frankenstein, Aurora, 1965 825
10. The Penguin, Aurora, 1967 625

Addar

Caesar, Planet of the Apes, 1974, Model No. 106
EX $15 NM $42 MIP $55

Cornelius, Planet of the Apes, 1974, Planet of the Apes, Model No. 101
EX $12 NM $33 MIP $55

Cornfield Roundup, Planet of the Apes, 1975, Planet of the Apes, Model No. 216
EX $15 NM $42 MIP $55

Dr. Zaius, Planet of the Apes, 1974, Planet of the Apes, Model No. 102
EX $10 NM $28 MIP $44

Dr. Zira, Planet of the Apes, 1974, Planet of the Apes, Model No. 105
EX $10 NM $28 MIP $44

Evil Knievel, 1974, w/cycle, Model No. 152
EX $12 NM $28 MIP $55

Evil Knievel's Sky Cycle, 1974, Model No. 154
EX $12 NM $28 MIP $85

Gen. Aldo, Planet of the Apes, 1974, Planet of the Apes, Model No. 104
EX $10 NM $28 MIP $55

Gen. Ursus, Planet of the Apes, 1974, Planet of the Apes, Model No. 103
EX $12 NM $34 MIP $50

Jail Wagon, Planet of the Apes, 1975, Planet of the Apes, Model No. 217
EX $15 NM $42 MIP $52

Jaws, 1975, Model No. 270
EX $35 NM $60 MIP $110

Jaws in a Bottle, 1975, Jaws, Model No. 270
EX $20 NM $55 MIP $75

Spirit in a Bottle, 1975, Model No. 227
EX $10 NM $21 MIP $55

Stallion & Soldier, Planet of the Apes, 1974, Model No. 107
EX $25 NM $75 MIP $125

Tree House, Planet of the Apes, 1975, Model No. 215
EX $15 NM $42 MIP $55

Airfix

10th British Hussar 1915, 1976, 1:32, Model No. 2551
EX $10 NM $18 MIP $28

2001: A Space Odyssey Orion, 1970, Model No. 701
EX $60 NM $80 MIP $110

2001: A Space Odyssey Orion, 1980, Model No. 5175
EX $10 NM $20 MIP $40

Anne Boleyn, 1974, Model No. 3542
EX $7 NM $16 MIP $25

Anne Boleyn, 1976, 1:32, Model No. 3542
EX $10 NM $18 MIP $30

Black Prince, 1973, Model No. 2502
EX $10 NM $26 MIP $35

Boy Scout, 1965, Model No. 212
EX $7 NM $16 MIP $25

Charles I, 1965, Model No. 211
EX $10 NM $21 MIP $40

Empire Strikes Back, Slave I, 1982
EX $35 NM $45 MIP $60

English Musketeer 1642, 1976, Model No. 1560
EX $12 NM $18 MIP $30

English Pikeman 1642, 1976, Model No. 1559
EX $12 NM $18 MIP $30

Flying Saucer, 1981, Model No. 7171
EX $12 NM $18 MIP $30

George Washington, 1980, 1:32, Model No. 2554
EX $12 NM $18 MIP $30

Henry VIII, 1973, Model No. 2501
EX $10 NM $15 MIP $20

James Bond and Odd Job, 1966, Model No. M401F
EX $65 NM $135 MIP $225

James Bond Autogyro, 1996, 1:24, Model No. 4401
EX $10 NM $18 MIP $50

James Bond's Aston Martin DB-5, 1965, Model No. 823
EX $100 NM $185 MIP $275

Julius Caesar, 1973, Model No. 2504
EX $10 NM $26 MIP $35

Napoleon, 1978, Model No. 2508
EX $10 NM $15 MIP $20

Queen Elizabeth I, 1980, Model No. 3546
EX $12 NM $22 MIP $35

Queen Victoria, 1976, Model No. 3544
EX $12 NM $22 MIP $35

Richard I, 1965, Model No. 203
EX $10 NM $27 MIP $33

Space: 1999 Eagle Transporter, 1979, 1:72, Model No. 6174
EX $25 NM $45 MIP $60

Space: 1999 Hawk Spaceship, 1977, 1:72, Model No. 5173
EX $80 NM $95 MIP $110

Yeoman of the Guard, 1978, Model No. 2507
EX $4 NM $9 MIP $11

Amazing Figure Modeler

London After Midnight, 1998, London After Midnight
EX $30 NM $60 MIP $90

AMT

B.J. and the Bear "Big Rig" set, 1980, 1:32, Model No. 7705
EX $30 NM $40 MIP $55

B.J. and the Bear Kenworth cap, 1980, Snap-together, 1:32, Model No. 5025
EX $17 NM $25 MIP $35

Bigfoot, 1978, Model No. 7701
EX $20 NM $63 MIP $83

Brute Farce, 1960s, Model No. 611
EX $5 NM $11 MIP $25

Cliff Hanger, 1960s, Model No. 610
EX $5 NM $11 MIP $25

Drag-U-La, Munsters, 1965, Munsters, Model No. 905
EX $40 NM $185 MIP $275

Farrah's Foxy Vette, 1977, 1:25, Model No. 3101
EX $40 NM $50 MIP $70

Fireball 500 Plymouth by George Barris, 1967, Model No. 911
EX $50 NM $65 MIP $80

Flintstones Rock Crusher, 1974, Flintstones, Model No. 497
EX $20 NM $53 MIP $75

Flintstones Sports Car, 1974, Model No. 495
EX $20 NM $58 MIP $73

Get Smart Sunbeam, 1967, 1:25, Model No. 925
EX $50 NM $65 MIP $85

Girl From U.N.C.L.E. Car, 1974, Model No. 913
EX $75 NM $265 MIP $375

Graveyard Ghoul Duo (Munsters cars), 1970, Graveyard Ghoul Duo, Model No. 309
EX $50 NM $105 MIP $175

Hero, 1966 Chrysler Imperial, 1966, 1:25, Model No. 914
EX $75 NM $105 MIP $145

KISS Custom Chevy Van, 1977, KISS, Model No. 2501
EX $20 NM $53 MIP $125

Laurel & Hardy '27 T Roadster, 1976, Model No. 462
EX $20 NM $55 MIP $66

Laurel & Hardy '27 T Touring Car, 1976, Model No. 461
EX $20 NM $60 MIP $75

Man From U.N.C.L.E. Car, 1966, Model No. 912
EX $75 NM $185 MIP $250

Matilda Custom Ford Van, 1978, 1:25, Model No. 2504
EX $25 NM $35 MIP $45

Mr. Spock, large box, 1973, Model No. 956
EX $15 NM $79 MIP $225

Mr. Spock, small box, 1973
EX $20 **NM** $105 **MIP** $175

Munster Koach, 1964, Munsters, Model No. 901
EX $80 **NM** $145 **MIP** $235

My Mother The Car, 1965, Model No. 904
EX $15 **NM** $30 **MIP** $45

Sonny & Cher Mustang, 1960s, Sonny & Cher, Model No. 907
EX $75 **NM** $265 **MIP** $350

Star Trek the Motion Picture, Klingon Cruiser, 1979, Model No. 971
EX $19 **NM** $28 **MIP** $40

Star Trek the Motion Picture, Mr. Spock, 1979, Model No. 973
EX $25 **NM** $38 **MIP** $55

Star Trek the Motion Picture, U.S.S. Enterprise, 1979, Model No. 970
EX $50 **NM** $85 **MIP** $150

Star Trek the Motion Picture, Vulcan Shuttle, 1979, Model No. 972
EX $25 **NM** $35 **MIP** $50

Star Trek, Command Bridge Model Kit, 1975, Model No. S950-601
EX $40 **NM** $50 **MIP** $85

Star Trek, Galileo Shuttle Model Kit, 1974, #S959-602, Model No. 959
EX $80 **NM** $95 **MIP** $175

Star Trek, K-7 Space Station, 1976, Model No. 955
EX $19 **NM** $60 **MIP** $160

Star Trek, Klingon Cruiser Model Kit, Model No. PK-5111
EX $45 **NM** $60 **MIP** $100

Star Trek, Klingon Cruiser Model Kit, 1968, Model No. S952-802
EX $135 **NM** $180 **MIP** $250

Star Trek, Romulan Bird of Prey Model Kit, 1975, Model No. S957-601
EX $100 **NM** $120 **MIP** $130

Star Trek, Space Ship Set, 1976, Snap-together, Model No. 953
EX $50 **NM** $65 **MIP** $85

T.h.e. Cat, 1967 Custom Corvette, 1967, 1:25, Model No. 915
EX $50 **NM** $60 **MIP** $75

Threw'd Dude, 1960s, Model No. 612
EX $10 **NM** $15 **MIP** $20

Touchdown?, 1960s, Model No. 614
EX $10 **NM** $18 **MIP** $25

UFO Mystery Ship, UFO
EX $15 **NM** $63 **MIP** $85

USS Enterprise Bridge, Star Trek, 1975, Model No. 950
EX $10 **NM** $27 **MIP** $55

USS Enterprise w/lights, Star Trek, 1967, Model No. 921-200
EX $40 **NM** $210 **MIP** $275

USS Enterprise, Star Trek, 1966, Model No. 951-250
EX $40 **NM** $132 **MIP** $165

Vega$, 1957 Thunderbird, 1979, 1:25, Model No. 3105
EX $35 **NM** $45 **MIP** $60

Aurora

Addams Family Haunted House, 1964, Addams Family, Model No. 805
EX $300 **NM** $630 **MIP** $880

Alfred E. Neuman (MAD), 1965, Model No. 802
EX $150 **NM** $175 **MIP** $200

American Astronaut, 1967, Astronaut, Model No. 409
EX $25 **NM** $71 **MIP** $90

American Buffalo, 1964, Model No. 402
EX $19 **NM** $37 **MIP** $52

American Buffalo, reissue, 1972, Model No. 402
EX $10 **NM** $20 **MIP** $30

Apache Warrior on Horse, 1960, Model No. 401
EX $180 **NM** $320 **MIP** $500

Aramis, Three Musketeers, 1958, Three Musketeers, Model No. K-10
EX $25 **NM** $85 **MIP** $115

Archie's Car, 1969, Model No. 582
EX $25 **NM** $90 **MIP** $110

Aston Martin Super Spy Car, 1965, Model No. 819
EX $40 **NM** $158 **MIP** $220

Athos, Three Musketeers, 1958, Three Musketeers, Model No. K-8
EX $20 **NM** $80 **MIP** $115

Banana Splits Banana Buggy, 1969, Banana Splits, Model No. 832
EX $150 **NM** $420 **MIP** $550

Batboat, 1968, Batman, Model No. 811
EX $150 **NM** $315 **MIP** $500

Batcycle, 1967, Batman, Model No. 810
EX $125 **NM** $265 **MIP** $450

Batman, 1964, Batman, Model No. 467
EX $20 **NM** $80 **MIP** $275

Batman, Comic Scenes, 1974, Batman, Model No. 187
EX $20 **NM** $42 **MIP** $90

Batmobile, 1966, Batman, Model No. 486
EX $100 **NM** $225 **MIP** $475

Batplane, 1967, Batman, Model No. 487
EX $50 **NM** $105 **MIP** $285

Black Bear and Cubs, 1962, Model No. 407
EX $15 **NM** $30 **MIP** $44

Black Bear and Cubs, reissue, 1969, Model No. 407
EX $17 **NM** $25 **MIP** $35

Black Fury, 1958, Black Fury, Model No. 400
EX $10 **NM** $26 **MIP** $33

Black Fury, reissue, 1969, Black Fury, Model No. 400
EX $12 **NM** $13 **MIP** $17

Black Knight, 1956, Black Knight, Model No. K-3
EX $12 **NM** $55 **MIP** $85

Black Knight, reissue, 1963, Black Knight, Model No. 473
EX $12 **NM** $30 **MIP** $45

Blackbeard, 1965, Blackbeard, Model No. 463
EX $75 **NM** $210 **MIP** $248

Blue Knight, 1956, Blue Knight, Model No. K-2
EX $15 **NM** $35 **MIP** $55

Blue Knight, reissue, 1963, Model No. 472
EX $15 **NM** $25 **MIP** $35

Bond, James, 1966, James Bond, Model No. 414
EX $250 **NM** $315 **MIP** $525

Bride of Frankenstein, 1965, Bride of Frankenstein, Model No. 482
EX $300 **NM** $525 **MIP** $825

Brown, Jimmy, 1965, Brown, Jimmy, Model No. 863
EX $75 **NM** $155 **MIP** $200

Canyon, Steve, 1958, Canyon, Steve, Model No. 409
EX $75 **NM** $180 **MIP** $275

Captain Action, 1966, Captain Action, Model No. 480
EX $100 **NM** $290 **MIP** $330

Captain America, 1966, Captain America, Model No. 476
EX $85 **NM** $200 **MIP** $330

Captain America, Comic Scenes, 1974, Captain America, Model No. 192
EX $30 **NM** $84 **MIP** $145

Captain Kidd, 1965, Captain Kidd, Model No. 464
EX $25 **NM** $100 **MIP** $150

Cave Bear, 1971, Cave Bear, Model No. 738
EX $15 **NM** $30 **MIP** $45

Chinese Girl, 1957, Chinese Girl, Model No. 416
EX $15 **NM** $27 **MIP** $50

Chinese Junk, 1962, Model No. 430
EX $100 **NM** $125 **MIP** $150

Chinese Mandarin, 1957, Chinese Mandarin, Model No. 415
EX $12 **NM** $25 **MIP** $50

Chinese Mandarin & Girl, 1957, Model No. 213
EX $75 **NM** $105 **MIP** $330

Chitty Chitty Bang Bang, 1968, Chitty Chitty Bang Bang, Model No. 828
EX $45 **NM** $90 **MIP** $175

Confederate Raider, 1959, Model No. 402
EX $150 **NM** $210 **MIP** $385

Creature From the Black Lagoon, 1963, Creature, Model No. 426
EX $125 **NM** $325 **MIP** $475

Creature From The Black Lagoon, Glow Kit, 1969, Creature, Model No. 483
EX $65 **NM** $105 **MIP** $250

Creature From The Black Lagoon, Glow Kit, 1972, Creature, Model No. 483
EX $85 **NM** $130 **MIP** $240

Creature, Monsters of Movies, 1975, Creature, Model No. 653
EX $100 **NM** $145 **MIP** $265

Cro-Magnon Man, 1971, Model No. 730
EX $10 **NM** $32 **MIP** $50

Cro-Magnon Woman, 1971, Model No. 731
EX $7 **NM** $26 **MIP** $39

Crusader, 1959, Model No. K-7
EX $75 **NM** $160 **MIP** $220

D'Artagnan, Three Musketeers, 1966, Three Musketeers, Model No. 410
EX $50 **NM** $160 **MIP** $200

Dempsey vs Firpo, 1965, Dempsey, Model No. 861
EX $40 **NM** $100 **MIP** $125

Dick Tracy in Action Model Kit, 1968, plastic, Model No. 818
EX $85 **NM** $175 **MIP** $350

Dr. Deadly, 1971, Dr. Deadly, Model No. 631
EX $25 **NM** $70 **MIP** $85

Dr. Deadly's Daughter, 1971, Dr. Deadly's Daughter, Model No. 632
EX $25 **NM** $70 **MIP** $85

Dr. Jekyll as Mr. Hyde, 1964, Dr. Jekyll, Model No. 460
EX $45 **NM** $250 **MIP** $385

Dr. Jekyll, Glow Kit, 1969, Dr. Jekyll, Model No. 482
EX $45 **NM** $105 **MIP** $195

Dr. Jekyll, Glow Kit, 1972, Dr. Jekyll, Model No. 482
EX $45 **NM** $65 **MIP** $85

Dr. Jekyll, Monster Scenes, 1971, Dr. Jekyll, Model No. 462
EX $40 **NM** $90 **MIP** $125

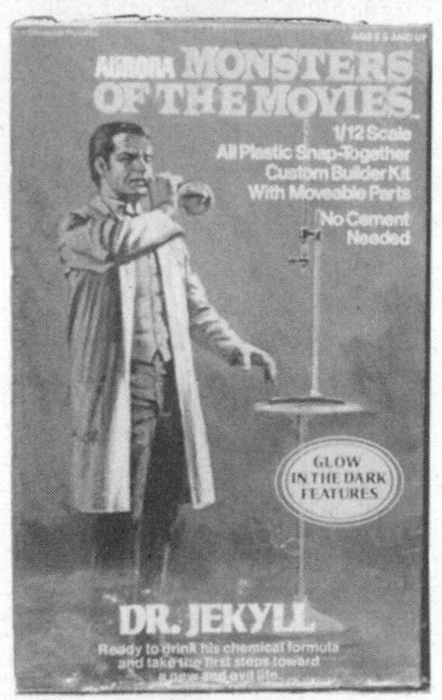

Dr. Jekyll, Monsters of Movies, 1975, Dr. Jekyll, Model No. 654
EX $25 **NM** $50 **MIP** $77

Dracula, 1962, Dracula, Model No. 424
EX $25 **NM** $225 **MIP** $330

Dracula, Frightning Lightning, 1969, Dracula, Model No. 454
EX $30 **NM** $315 **MIP** $550

Dracula, Glow Kit, 1969, Dracula, Model No. 454
EX $20 **NM** $80 **MIP** $165

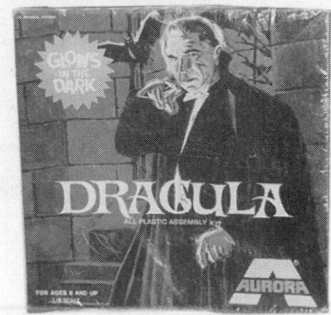

Dracula, Glow Kit, 1972, Dracula, Model No. 454
EX $20 **NM** $63 **MIP** $83

Dracula, Monster Scenes, 1971, Dracula, Model No. 641
EX $75 **NM** $105 **MIP** $220

Dracula, Monsters of Movies, 1975, Dracula, Model No. 656
EX $75 **NM** $105 **MIP** $275

Dracula's Dragster, 1966, Dracula, Model No. 466
EX $125 **NM** $315 **MIP** $450

Dutch Boy, 1957, Dutch Boy, Model No. 413
EX $20 **NM** $45 **MIP** $80

Dutch Boy & Girl, 1957, Model No. 209
EX $75 **NM** $210 **MIP** $330

Dutch Girl, 1957, Dutch Girl, Model No. 414
EX $20 **NM** $40 **MIP** $60

Flying Sub, 1968, Model No. 817
EX $35 **NM** $175 **MIP** $220

Flying Sub, reissue, 1975, Model No. 254
EX $35 **NM** $85 **MIP** $110

Forgotten Prisoner, 1966, Forgotten Prisoner, Model No. 422
EX $65 **NM** $325 **MIP** $440

Forgotten Prisoner, Frightning Lightning, 1969, Forgotten Prisoner, Model No. 453
EX $65 **NM** $320 **MIP** $500

Forgotten Prisoner, Glow Kit, 1969, Forgotten Prisoner, Model No. 453
EX $65 **NM** $180 **MIP** $220

Forgotten Prisoner, Glow Kit, 1972, Forgotten Prisoner, Model No. 453
EX $65 **NM** $155 **MIP** $193

Frankenstein, 1961, Frankenstein, Model No. 423
EX $30 **NM** $210 **MIP** $345

Frankenstein, Frightning Lightning, 1969, Frankenstein, Model No. 449
EX $30 **NM** $315 **MIP** $440

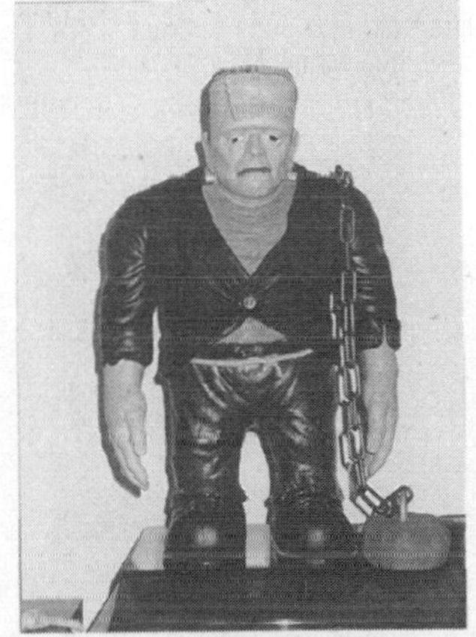

Frankenstein, Gigantic 1:5 scale, 1964, Frankenstein, Model No. 470
EX $300 **NM** $945 **MIP** $1430

Frankenstein, Glow Kit, 1969, Frankenstein, Model No. 449
EX $20 **NM** $70 **MIP** $165

Frankenstein, Glow Kit, 1972, Frankenstein, Model No. 449
EX $20 **NM** $50 **MIP** $90

Frankenstein, Monster Scenes, 1971, Frankenstein, Model No. 633
EX $50 **NM** $80 **MIP** $120

Frankenstein, Monsters of Movies, 1975, Frankenstein, Model No. 651
EX $100 **NM** $210 **MIP** $350

Frankie's Flivver, 1964, Frankenstein, Model No. 465
EX $150 **NM** $375 **MIP** $500

Frog, Castle Creatures, 1966, Frog, Model No. 451
EX $75 **NM** $210 **MIP** $275

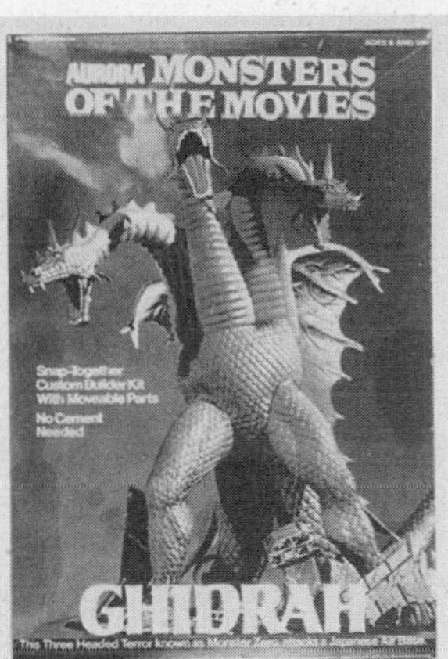

Ghidrah, 1975, Model No. 658
EX $95 **NM** $275 **MIP** $345

Giant Insect, Monster Scene, 1971, Model No. 643
EX $95 **NM** $365 **MIP** $450

Gladiator, The, w/ trident, Model No. 406
EX $50 **NM** $110 **MIP** $185

Godzilla, 1964, Godzilla, Model No. 469
EX $85 **NM** $425 **MIP** $575

Godzilla, Glow Kit, 1969, Godzilla, Model No. 466
EX $75 **NM** $225 **MIP** $360

Godzilla, Glow Kit, 1972, Godzilla, Model No. 466
EX $75 **NM** $150 **MIP** $200

Godzilla's Go-Cart, 1966, Godzilla, Model No. 485
EX $850 **NM** $2500 **MIP** $3750

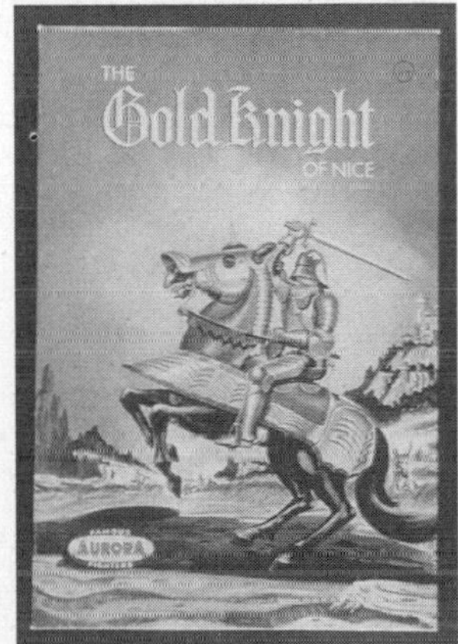

Gold Knight of Nice, 1957, Gold Knight, Model No. 475
EX $145 **NM** $280 **MIP** $350

Gold Knight of Nice, 1965, Gold Knight, Model No. 475
EX $125 **NM** $260 **MIP** $310

Green Beret, 1966, Green Beret, Model No. 413
EX $75 **NM** $160 **MIP** $200

Green Hornet Black Beauty, 1966, Green Hornet, Model No. 489
EX $125 **NM** $365 **MIP** $550

Gruesome Goodies, 1971, Model No. 634
EX $45 **NM** $85 **MIP** $115

Guillotine, 1964, Guillotine, Model No. 800
EX $125 **NM** $350 **MIP** $440

Hanging Cage, 1971, Model No. 637
EX $30 **NM** $80 **MIP** $110

Hercules, 1965, Hercules, Model No. 481
EX $125 **NM** $235 **MIP** $375

Hulk, Comic Scenes, 1974, Hulk, Model No. 184
EX $25 **NM** $75 **MIP** $110

Hulk, Original, 1966, Hulk, Model No. 421
EX $75 **NM** $260 **MIP** $325

Hunchback of Notre Dame, 1964, Hunchback, Model No. 460
EX $45 **NM** $210 **MIP** $330

Hunchback of Notre Dame, Glow Kit, 1969, Hunchback, Model No. 481
EX $45 **NM** $95 **MIP** $165

Hunchback of Notre Dame, Glow Kit, 1972, Hunchback, Model No. 481
EX $45 **NM** $85 **MIP** $125

Indian Chief, 1957, Model No. 417
EX $35 **NM** $85 **MIP** $100

Indian Chief & Squaw, 1957, Model No. 212
EX $60 **NM** $125 **MIP** $165

Indian Squaw, 1957, Model No. 418
EX $15 **NM** $40 **MIP** $65

Infantryman, 1957, Infantryman, Model No. 411
EX $20 **NM** $75 **MIP** $110

Invaders UFO, 1968, Model No. 813
EX $35 **NM** $85 **MIP** $110

Invaders UFO, 1975, Model No. 256
EX $30 **NM** $55 **MIP** $85

Iwo Jima, 1966, Model No. 853
EX $75 **NM** $185 **MIP** $220

Jesse James, 1966, Jesse James, Model No. 408
EX $60 **NM** $105 **MIP** $210

Kennedy, John F., 1965, Kennedy, John F., Model No. 851
EX $50 **NM** $75 **MIP** $175

King Arthur, 1973, Model No. 885
EX $65 **NM** $105 **MIP** $220

King Arthur of Camelot, 1967, King Arthur, Model No. 825
EX $30 **NM** $70 **MIP** $85

King Kong, 1964, King Kong, Model No. 468
EX $75 **NM** $315 **MIP** $495

King Kong, Glow Kit, 1969, King Kong, Model No. 468
EX $75 **NM** $185 **MIP** $275

King Kong, Glow Kit, 1972, King Kong, Model No. 468
EX $75 **NM** $132 **MIP** $195

King Kong's Thronester, 1966, King Kong, Model No. 484
EX $370 **NM** $840 **MIP** $1375

Land of the Giants Space Ship, 1968, Land of Giants, Model No. 830
EX $150 **NM** $308 **MIP** $440

Land of the Giants, Diorama, 1968, Land of the Giants, Model No. 816
EX $150 **NM** $368 **MIP** $500

Lone Ranger, 1967, Lone Ranger, Model No. 808
EX $75 **NM** $105 **MIP** $196

Lone Ranger, Comic Scenes, 1974, Lone Ranger, Model No. 188
EX $20 **NM** $42 **MIP** $65

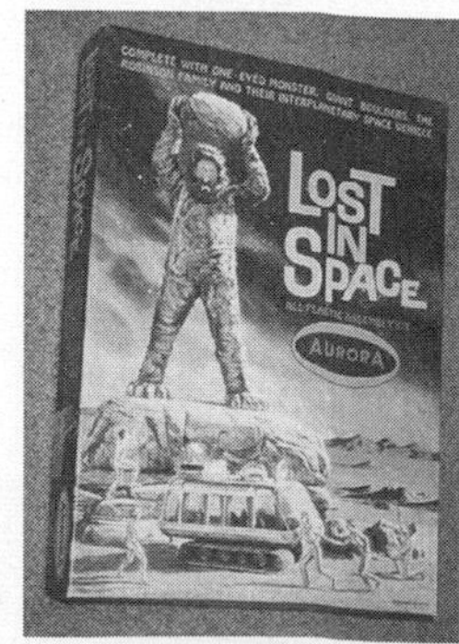

Lost In Space, Large kit w/chariot, 1966, Lost in Space, Model No. 420
EX $450 **NM** $1100 **MIP** $1600

Lost In Space, Small kit, 1966, Lost in Space, Model No. 419
EX $300 **NM** $735 **MIP** $1100

Lost In Space, The Robot, 1968, Robot B-9, Model No. 418
EX $250 **NM** $630 **MIP** $895

Mad Barber, 1972, Mad Barber, Model No. 455
EX $50 **NM** $105 **MIP** $165

Mad Dentist, 1972, Model No. 457
EX $50 **NM** $105 **MIP** $165

Mad Doctor, 1972, Model No. 456
EX $50 **NM** $105 **MIP** $165

Man From U.N.C.L.E., Illya Kuryakin, 1966, Man From U.N.C.L.E., Model No. 412
EX $75 **NM** $105 **MIP** $300

Man From U.N.C.L.E., Napoleon Solo, 1966, Man From U.N.C.L.E., Model No. 411
EX $75 **NM** $165 **MIP** $350

Marine, 1959, Marine, Model No. 412
EX $45 **NM** $100 **MIP** $160

Mays, Willie, 1965, Model No. 860
EX $100 **NM** $210 **MIP** $330

Mexican Caballero, 1957, Model No. 421
EX $95 **NM** $100 **MIP** $175

Mexican Senorita, 1957, Mexican Senorita, Model No. 422
EX $50 **NM** $96 **MIP** $170

Mod Squad Wagon, 1970, Model No. 583
EX $50 **NM** $132 **MIP** $192

Monster Customizing Kit #1, 1964, Model No. 463
EX $35 **NM** $117 **MIP** $140

Monster Customizing Kit #2, 1964, Model No. 464
EX $65 **NM** $160 **MIP** $195

Moon Bus from 2001, 1968, Model No. 828
EX $100 **NM** $250 **MIP** $330

Mr. Hyde, Monsters of the Movies, 1975, Mr. Hyde, Model No. 655
EX $40 **NM** $110 **MIP** $150

Mr. Spock, 1972, Star Trek, Model No. 922
EX $40 **NM** $125 **MIP** $185

Mummy, 1963, Mummy, Model No. 427
EX $60 **NM** $175 **MIP** $400

Mummy, Frightning Lightning, 1969, Mummy, Model No. 452
EX $30 **NM** $210 **MIP** $440

Mummy, Glow Kit, 1969, Mummy, Model No. 452
EX $20 **NM** $80 **MIP** $190

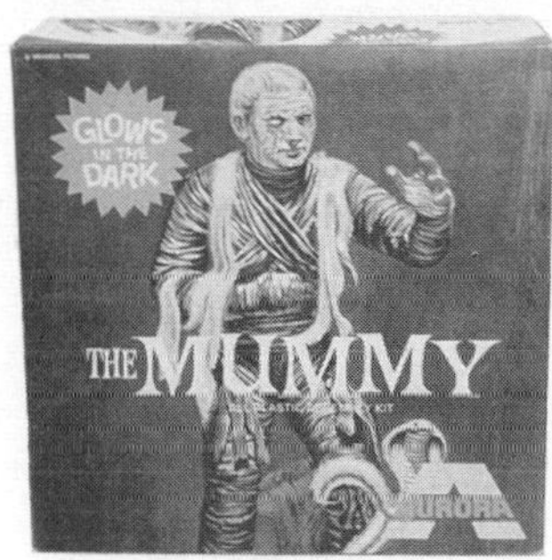

Mummy, Glow Kit, 1972, Mummy, Model No. 452
EX $20 **NM** $42 **MIP** $75

Mummy's Chariot, 1965, Mummy, Model No. 459
EX $200 **NM** $350 **MIP** $600

Munsters, Living Room, 1964, Munsters, Model No. 804
EX $400 **NM** $945 **MIP** $1450

Neanderthal Man, 1971, Neanderthal Man, Model No. 729
EX $15 **NM** $42 **MIP** $75

Neuman, Alfred E., 1965, Alfred E. Neuman, Model No. 802
EX $100 **NM** $289 **MIP** $440

Nutty Nose Nipper, 1965, Nutty Nose Nipper, Model No. 806
EX $45 **NM** $185 **MIP** $220

Odd Job, 1966, Odd Job, Model No. 415
EX $200 **NM** $360 **MIP** $495

Pain Parlor, 1971, Model No. 635
EX $25 **NM** $105 **MIP** $140

Pendulum, 1971, Model No. 636
EX $25 **NM** $55 **MIP** $90

Penguin, 1967, Penguin, Model No. 416
EX $200 **NM** $420 **MIP** $625

Phantom of the Opera, 1963, Phantom of the Opera, Model No. 428
EX $85 **NM** $250 **MIP** $350

Phantom of the Opera, Frightning Lightning, 1969, Phantom of the Opera, Model No. 451
EX $65 **NM** $250 **MIP** $385

Phantom of the Opera, Glow Kit, 1969, Phantom of the Opera, Model No. 451
EX $20 **NM** $75 **MIP** $165

Phantom of the Opera, Glow Kit, 1972, Phantom of the Opera, Model No. 451
EX $20 **NM** $63 **MIP** $88

Pilot USAF, 1957, Model No. 409
EX $75 **NM** $145 **MIP** $200

Porthos, Three Musketeers, 1958, Three Musketeers, Model No. K-9
EX $25 **NM** $75 **MIP** $110

Pushmi-Pullyu, Dr. Dolittle, 1968, Model No. 814
EX $60 **NM** $110 **MIP** $160

Rat Patrol, 1967, Rat Patrol, Model No. 340
EX $45 **NM** $85 **MIP** $135

Red Knight, 1957, Red Knight, Model No. K-4
EX $40 **NM** $70 **MIP** $125

Red Knight, 1963, Red Knight, Model No. 474
EX $25 **NM** $85 **MIP** $150

Robin, 1966, Robin, Model No. 488
EX $60 **NM** $85 **MIP** $165

Robin, Comic Scenes, 1974, Robin, Model No. 193
EX $40 **NM** $70 **MIP** $120

Rodan, 1975, Rodan, Model No. 657
EX $125 **NM** $210 **MIP** $450

Roman Gladiator with sword, 1959, Model No. 405
EX $75 **NM** $130 **MIP** $200

Roman Gladiator with Trident, 1964, Gladiator, Model No. 406
EX $75 **NM** $140 **MIP** $200

Roman Gladiators, 1959, Model No. 216
EX $100 **NM** $210 **MIP** $275

Ruth, Babe, 1965, Ruth, Babe, Model No. 862
EX $100 **NM** $240 **MIP** $360

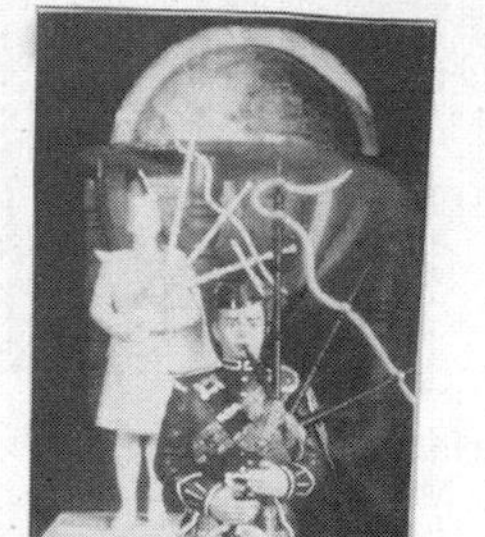

Scotch Lad, 1957, Scoth Lad, Model No. 419
EX $25 **NM** $45 **MIP** $75

Scotch Lad & Lassie, 1957, Model No. 214
EX $60 **NM** $95 **MIP** $110

Scotch Lassie, 1957, Scotch Lassie, Model No. 420
EX $25 **NM** $45 **MIP** $75

Seaview, Voyage to the Bottom of Sea, 1966, Voyage to the Bottom, Model No. 707
EX $100 **NM** $225 **MIP** $330

Seaview, Voyage to the Bottom of Sea, 1975, Model No. 253
EX $100 **NM** $168 **MIP** $209

Silver Knight, 1956, Silver Knight, Model No. K-1
EX $15 **NM** $42 **MIP** $60

Silver Knight, 1963, Silver Knight, Model No. 471
EX $15 **NM** $21 **MIP** $40

Sir Galahad, 1973, Model No. 881
EX $15 **NM** $42 **MIP** $70

Sir Galahad of Camelot, 1967, Galahad, Model No. 826
EX $25 **NM** $95 **MIP** $195

Sir Kay, 1973, Model No. 882
EX $20 **NM** $42 **MIP** $55

Sir Lancelot, 1973, Model No. 883
EX $20 **NM** $42 **MIP** $55

Sir Lancelot of Camelot, 1967, Lancelot, Model No. 827
EX $25 **NM** $95 **MIP** $140

Sir Percival, 1973, Model No. 884
EX $20 **NM** $30 **MIP** $75

Spartacus (Gladiator/sword reissue), 1964, Spartacus, Model No. 405
EX $85 **NM** $150 **MIP** $275

Spider-Man, 1966, Spider-Man, Model No. 477
EX $110 **NM** $235 **MIP** $425

Spider-Man, Comic Scenes, 1974, Spider-Man, Model No. 182
EX $75 **NM** $100 **MIP** $150

Star Trek, Klingon Cruiser, 1972, Model No. 923
EX $20 **NM** $50 **MIP** $90

Star Trek, U.S.S. Enterprise, 1972, Model No. 921
EX $20 **NM** $65 **MIP** $130

Superboy, 1964, Superboy, Model No. 478
EX $75 **NM** $210 **MIP** $275

Superboy, Comic Scenes, 1974, Superboy, Model No. 186
EX $45 **NM** $80 **MIP** $125

Superman, 1963, Superman, Model No. 462
EX $100 **NM** $100 **MIP** $425

Superman, Comic Scenes, 1974, Superman, Model No. 185
EX $20 **NM** $42 **MIP** $66

Tarpit, 1972, Model No. 735
EX $65 **NM** $110 **MIP** $150

Tarzan, 1967, Tarzan, Model No. 820
EX $40 **NM** $105 **MIP** $220

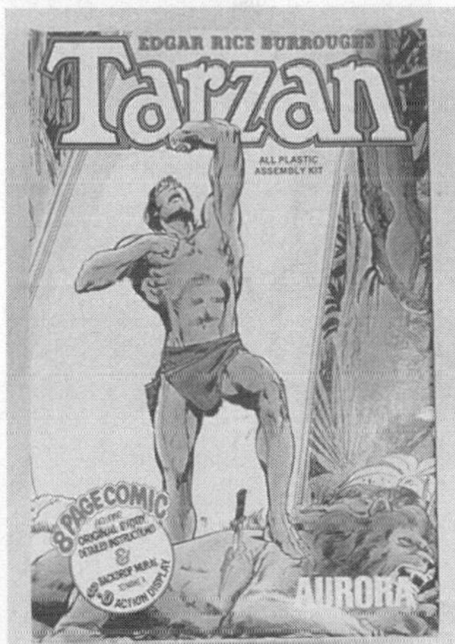

Tarzan, Comic Scenes, 1974, Tarzan, Model No. 181
EX $25 **NM** $50 **MIP** $75

Three Knights Set, 1959, Model No. 207
EX $50 **NM** $105 **MIP** $190

MODEL KITS

Aurora

Three Musketeers Set, 1958, Model No. 398
EX $95 **NM** $210 **MIP** $385

Tonto, 1967, Tonto, Model No. 809
EX $25 **NM** $150 **MIP** $220

Tonto, Comic Scenes, 1974, Tonto, Model No. 183
EX $30 **NM** $60 **MIP** $90

Tracy, Dick, 1968, Tracy, Dick, Model No. 818
EX $60 **NM** $105 **MIP** $275

Tracy, Dick, Space Coupe, 1968, Tracy, Dick, Model No. 819
EX $50 **NM** $105 **MIP** $165

U.S. Marshal, 1958, Model No. 408
EX $55 **NM** $78 **MIP** $115

Unitas, Johnny, 1965, Unitas, Johnny, Model No. 864
EX $75 **NM** $132 **MIP** $195

United States Sailor, 1957, Sailor, Model No. 410
EX $40 **NM** $80 **MIP** $120

Vampire, Castle Creatures, 1966, Model No. 452
EX $60 **NM** $185 **MIP** $275

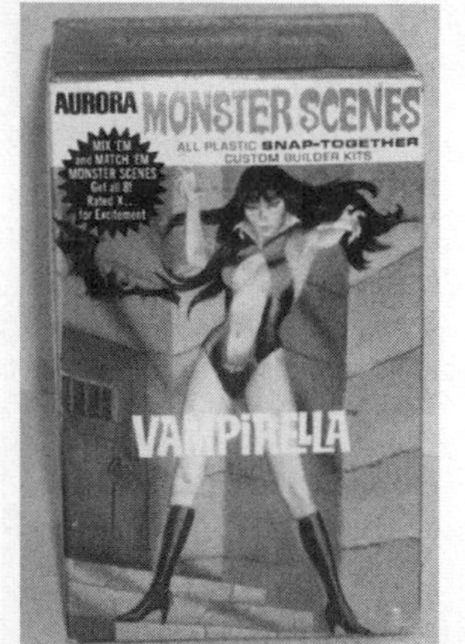

Vampirella, 1971, Vampirella, Model No. 638
EX $75 **NM** $132 **MIP** $225

Victim, 1971, Model No. 632
EX $20 **NM** $70 **MIP** $85

Viking, 1959, Viking, Model No. K-6
EX $65 **NM** $105 **MIP** $275

Voyager, Fantastic Voyage, 1969, Model No. 831
EX $125 **NM** $235 **MIP** $525

Wacky Back-Whacker, 1965, Model No. 807
EX $50 **NM** $105 **MIP** $275

Washington, George, 1965, Great American Presidents, Model No. 852
EX $25 **NM** $60 **MIP** $110

West, Jerry, 1965, West, Jerry, Model No. 865
EX $50 **NM** $105 **MIP** $165

White Stallion, 1964, Model No. 401
EX $12 **NM** $25 **MIP** $35

White Stallion, reissue, 1969, Model No. 401
EX $12 **NM** $25 **MIP** $35

White-tailed Deer, 1962, Model No. 403
EX $12 **NM** $25 **MIP** $35

White-tailed Deer, reissue, 1969, Model No. 403
EX $12 **NM** $18 **MIP** $25

Whoozis, Alfalfa, 1966, Whoozis, Model No. 204
EX $25 **NM** $50 **MIP** $85

Whoozis, Denty, 1966, Whoozis, Model No. 203
EX $25 **NM** $50 **MIP** $85

Whoozis, Esmerelda, 1966, Whoozis, Model No. 202
EX $25 **NM** $50 **MIP** $85

Whoozis, Kitty, 1966, Whoozis, Model No. 205
EX $25 **NM** $50 **MIP** $85

Whoozis, Snuffy, 1966, Whoozis, Model No. 206
EX $25 **NM** $50 **MIP** $85

Whoozis, Susie, 1966, Whoozis, Model No. 201
EX $25 **NM** $50 **MIP** $85

Witch, 1965, Witch, Model No. 483
EX $100 **NM** $210 **MIP** $330

Witch, Glow Kit, 1969, Witch, Model No. 470
EX $55 **NM** $105 **MIP** $220

Witch, Glow Kit, 1972, Witch, Model No. 470
EX $75 **NM** $105 **MIP** $138

Wolfman, 1962, Wolfman, Model No. 425
EX $95 **NM** $210 **MIP** $330

Wolfman, Frightning Lightning, 1969, Wolfman, Model No. 450
EX $75 **NM** $315 **MIP** $440

Wolfman, Glow Kit, 1969, Wolfman, Model No. 450
EX $35 **NM** $75 **MIP** $165

Wolfman, Glow Kit, 1972, Wolfman, Model No. 450
EX $35 **NM** $65 **MIP** $100

Wolfman, Monsters of the Movies, 1975, Wolfman, Model No. 652
EX $100 **NM** $210 **MIP** $275

Wolfman's Wagon, 1965, Wolfman, Model No. 458
EX $175 **NM** $315 **MIP** $468

Wonder Woman, 1965, Wonder Woman, Model No. 479
EX $150 **NM** $315 **MIP** $575

Zorro, 1965, Zorro, Model No. 801
EX $125 **NM** $210 **MIP** $340

Billiken

Batman, type A, 1989, Batman
EX $35 **NM** $90 **MIP** $110

Batman, type B, 1989, Batman
EX $35 **NM** $95 **MIP** $140

Bride of Frankenstein, 1984, Bride of Frankenstein
EX $75 **NM** $105 **MIP** $250

Colossal Beast, 1986, Colossal Beast
EX $20 NM $32 MIP $44

Creature From the Black Lagoon, 1991, Creature
EX $70 NM $100 MIP $160

Cyclops, 1984
EX $75 NM $105 MIP $220

Dracula, 1989, Dracula
EX $60 NM $105 MIP $165

Frankenstein, 1988, Frankenstein
EX $60 NM $125 MIP $180

Joker, 1989
EX $40 NM $95 MIP $165

Mummy, 1990, Mummy
EX $60 NM $125 MIP $180

Phantom of the Opera, 1980s, Phantom of the Opera
EX $100 NM $210 MIP $305

Predator, 1991, Predator
EX $25 NM $53 MIP $75

Saucer Man, Saucer Man
EX $20 NM $32 MIP $44

She-Creature, 1989, She-Creature
EX $25 NM $42 MIP $55

Syngenor, 1984, Syngenor
EX $100 NM $160 MIP $275

The Thing, 1984, The Thing
EX $150 NM $210 MIP $330

Ultraman, 1987, Ultraman
EX $25 NM $35 MIP $50

Bowen Designs

Kongzilla, 1998, Kongzilla
EX $15 NM $30 MIP $50

Geometric Designs

Alien, Ripley, 1998
EX $35 NM $45 MIP $60

Aliens, Alien Warrior, 1996
EX $50 NM $65 MIP $80

Creature From the Black Lagoon, vinyl kit, figure from original film, sculpted by Jim Gorman, 1:8
EX $20 NM $40 MIP $60

Hunchback of Notre Dame, The, vinyl kit, figure of Charles Laughton as the Hunchback, 1:8
EX $20 NM $40 MIP $60

King Kong, vinyl kit, figure from original King Kong film, 1:35
EX $25 NM $50 MIP $100

Masters of the Universe, Talon Fighter, 1984, Model No. 6015
EX $20 NM $30 MIP $40

Mummy, The, vinyl kit, figure of Boris Karloff from original Mummy film, 1:8
EX $20 NM $40 MIP $60

Predator, vinyl kit, figure from original Predator film, 1:8
EX $20 NM $40 MIP $60

Shogun Warriors, Raider, 1978, Model No. 6023
EX $12 NM $18 MIP $25

Son of Frankenstein, 1998, Frankenstein monster from Son of Frankenstein, sculpted by William Paquet, 1:8
EX $10 NM $20 MIP $35

Wolfman, The, 1998, vinyl kit, depicting Lon Chaney, Jr., sculpted by Mike Hill, 1:8
EX $20 NM $40 MIP $60

Hawk

Beach Bunny Catchin' Rays, 1964, Silly Surfer, Model No. 542
EX $35 NM $65 MIP $150

Daddy the Way-Out Suburbanite, 1963, Weird-Ohs, Model No. 532
EX $40 NM $70 MIP $125

Davey the Way-Out Cyclist, 1963, Weird-Ohs, Model No. 531
EX $40 NM $70 MIP $125

Digger and Dragster, 1963, Weird-Ohs, Model No. 530
EX $40 NM $70 MIP $125

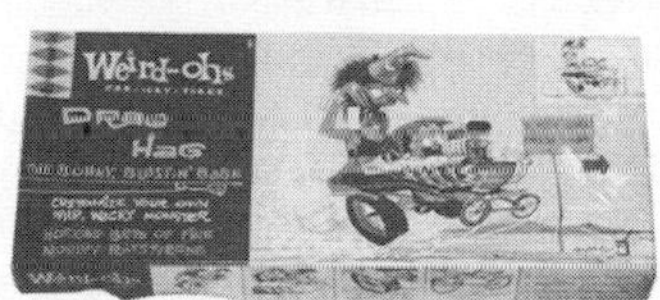

Drag Hag, 1963, Weird-Ohs, Model No. 536
EX $40 NM $70 MIP $125

Endsville Eddie, 1963, The Short Stop Stupe, Weird-Ohs, Model No. 537
EX $30 NM $50 MIP $110

Francis The Foul, 1963, basketball player, Weird-Ohs, Model No. 535
EX $30 NM $50 MIP $95

Frantic Banana, 1965, Frantics, Model No. 548
EX $30 NM $84 MIP $175

Frantic Cats, 1965, Frantics dancing, Model No. 550
EX $30 NM $75 MIP $135

Freddy Flameout, 1963, The Way-Out Jet Jockey, Weird-Ohs, Model No. 533
EX $30 NM $70 MIP $125

Hidad Silly Surfer, 1964, Hidad Silly Surfer, Model No. 543
EX $30 NM $70 MIP $125

Hot Dogger Hangin' Ten, 1964, Silly Surfer, Model No. 541
EX $30 NM $65 MIP $125

Huey's Hut Rod, 1963, Weird-Ohs, Model No. 538
EX $30 NM $50 MIP $90

Killer McBash, 1963, football player, Weird-Ohs
EX $70 NM $125 MIP $185

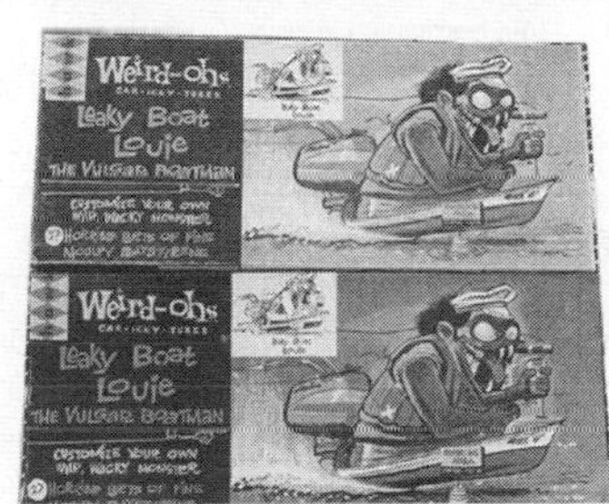

Leaky Boat Louie, 1963, Weird-Ohs, Model No. 534
EX $35 NM $84 MIP $135

Ridin' Tandem, Silly Surfer
EX $35 NM $65 MIP $100

Sling Rave Curvette, 1964, The Way-Out Specatator, Weird-Ohs, Model No. 637
EX $30 NM $50 MIP $95

Steel Pluckers, 1965, Frantics, Model No. 547
EX $30 NM $65 MIP $125

Totally Fab, 1965, Frantics, Model No. 550
EX $35 NM $75 MIP $135

Wade A. Minut, 1963, The Wild Starter, Weird-Ohs, Model No. 636
EX $55 NM $90 MIP $145

Weird-Ohs Customizing Kit, 1964, Weird-Ohs
EX $125 NM $250 MIP $375

MODEL KITS

Hawk

Weirdsville Customizing Kit, 1964, plastic kit featuring multiple characters
EX $125 **NM** $200 **MIP** $325

Wild Woodie Car, Wild Woodie, Model No. 545
EX $30 **NM** $55 **MIP** $85

Woodie on a Surfari, 1964, Silly Surfer, Model No. 540
EX $55 **NM** $90 **MIP** $125

Horizon

Bride of Frankenstein, 1990s, vinyl kit, 1:6
EX $20 **NM** $40 **MIP** $75

Creature From the Black Lagoon, 1990s, vinyl kit, rare, 1:6
EX $35 **NM** $75 **MIP** $110

Dracula, 1990s, vinyl kit, 1:6, Model No. HM004
EX $25 **NM** $50 **MIP** $85

Frankenstein, 1990s, vinyl kit, 1:6
EX $25 **NM** $50 **MIP** $85

Invisible Man, The, 1990s, vinyl kit, 1:6
EX $20 **NM** $40 **MIP** $70

Mole People, The, 1990s, vinyl kit, 1:6
EX $20 **NM** $40 **MIP** $70

Mummy, The, 1990s, vinyl kit, 1:6
EX $20 **NM** $40 **MIP** $70

Phantom of the Opera, 1990s, vinyl kit, 1:6
EX $20 **NM** $40 **MIP** $70

Wolfman, The, 1990s, vinyl kit, 1:6
EX $20 **NM** $40 **MIP** $65

Lindberg

Baywatch Pickup, 1995, Model No. 72598
EX $5 **NM** $10 **MIP** $15

Bert's Bucket, 1971, Model No. 6422
EX $30 **NM** $84 **MIP** $110

Big Wheeler, 1965, Lindberg Loony, Model No. 277
EX $30 **NM** $84 **MIP** $110

Blurp, 1964, Lindy Loony Repulsive, Model No. 280
EX $10 **NM** $21 **MIP** $50

Captain Kidd Pirate Ship, 1990, 14"
EX $10 **NM** $15 **MIP** $45

Creeping Crusher, 1965, Model No. 273
EX $20 **NM** $42 **MIP** $60

Fat Max, 1971, Model No. 6420
EX $30 **NM** $84 **MIP** $99

Flintstones, Flintmobile, 1994, Model No. 72411
EX $10 **NM** $15 **MIP** $20

Flintstones, Le Sabertooth 5000, 1994, Model No. 72412
EX $5 **NM** $10 **MIP** $15

Giant American Bullfrog, 1973
EX $15 **NM** $30 **MIP** $50

Glob, 1964, Lindy Loony Repulsive, Model No. 281
EX $10 **NM** $21 **MIP** $55

Godzilla, 1995, Model No. 71344
EX $15 **NM** $22 **MIP** $40

Green Ghoul, 1965, Model No. 274
EX $20 **NM** $35 **MIP** $55

Independence Day, Alien Exskeleton, 1996, Model No. 77312
EX $5 **NM** $10 **MIP** $15

Independence Day, Capt. Hiller's F/A-18 Hornet, 1996, Model No. 77313
EX $20 **NM** $30 **MIP** $40

Independence Day, Captured Alien Attacker, 1996, Model No. 77311
EX $20 **NM** $30 **MIP** $40

Independence Day, Russell Casse's PT-17 Bi-Plane, 1996, Model No. 77314
EX $20 **NM** $30 **MIP** $40

Jurassic Park, Vilociraptor, 1993, 15"
EX $10 **NM** $15 **MIP** $25

Krimson Terror, 1965, Model No. 272
EX $20 **NM** $42 **MIP** $65

Mad Mangler, 1965, Model No. 275
EX $20 **NM** $42 **MIP** $65

Road Hog, 1964, Lindberg Loony, Model No. 276
EX $30 **NM** $84 **MIP** $100

Satan's Crate, 1964, Lindberg Loony
EX $75 **NM** $130 **MIP** $165

Scuttle Bucket, 1964, Lindberg Loony, Model No. 278
EX $30 **NM** $84 **MIP** $100

Shrieker, Glo-Monster, 1971, Model No. 290
EX $35 **NM** $45 **MIP** $75

Sick Cycle, 1971, Model No. 6421
EX $30 **NM** $84 **MIP** $100

UFO, 1976, Model No. 1152
EX $35 **NM** $45 **MIP** $60

Voop, 1964, Lindy Loony Repulsive, Model No. 283
EX $10 **NM** $21 **MIP** $60

Zopp, 1964, Lindy Loony Repulsive, Model No. 282
EX $35 **NM** $65 **MIP** $110

Monogram

Battlestar Galactica, 1979, Model No. 6028
EX $20 **NM** $35 **MIP** $60

Battlestar Galactica, Colonial Viper, 1979, Model No. 6027
EX $20 **NM** $35 **MIP** $65

Battlestar Galactica, Cylon Base Star Model Kit, 1979, Model No. 6029
EX $20 **NM** $40 **MIP** $55

Battlestar Galactica, Cylon Raider, 1979, Model No. 6026
EX $20 **NM** $35 **MIP** $55

Buck Rogers, Marauder, 1979, Model No. 6031
EX $30 **NM** $50 **MIP** $75

Dracula, 1983, Dracula, 1:8, Model No. 6008
EX $20 **NM** $30 **MIP** $40

Elvira Macabre Mobile, 1988, Model No. 2783
EX $10 **NM** $20 **MIP** $30

Flip Out, 1965, Fred Flypogger, Model No. 105
EX $50 **NM** $150 **MIP** $220

Flying Sub, Voyage to the Bottom of the Sea, 1979, Model No. 6011
EX $25 **NM** $45 **MIP** $55

Frankenstein, 1983, Frankenstein, 1:8, Model No. 6007
EX $20 **NM** $30 **MIP** $40

Godzilla, 1978, Model No. 6300
EX $40 **NM** $65 **MIP** $100

Masters of the Universe, Roton Assault Vehicle, 1984, Model No. 6016
EX $5 **NM** $10 **MIP** $15

Mummy, 1983, Mummy, 1:8, Model No. 6010
EX $20 **NM** $30 **MIP** $40

Skull, Lizard & Rat, 1998, Model No. 5020
EX $10 **NM** $15 **MIP** $30

Sleepy Hollow, Headless Horseman, 1999, Model No. 5022
EX $15 **NM** $20 **MIP** $35

Snoopy & Motorcycle, 1971, snap-tite, Model No. 5902
EX $30 **NM** $65 **MIP** $110

Snoopy & Sopwith Camel, 1971, Model No. 6779
EX $20 **NM** $35 **MIP** $75

Snoopy as Joe Cool, 1971, Model No. 7502
EX $25 **NM** $55 **MIP** $110

Speed Racer Mach 5, 2000, Model No. 6700
EX $10 **NM** $15 **MIP** $35

Speed Shift, 1965, Fred Flypogger, Model No. MM106
EX $70 **NM** $105 **MIP** $220

Super Fuzz, 1965, Fred Flypogger
EX $80 **NM** $105 **MIP** $250

Superman, 1978, Superman, Model No. 6301
EX $25 **NM** $35 **MIP** $50

Three Stooges, Curly, 1999, Model No. 5063
EX $10 **NM** $20 **MIP** $30

Three Stooges, Larry, 1999, Model No. 5061
EX $10 **NM** $15 **MIP** $20

Three Stooges, Moe, 1999, Model No. 5062
EX $10 **NM** $15 **MIP** $20

UFO, The Invaders, 1979, UFO, Model No. 6012
EX $15 **NM** $32 **MIP** $45

Undertaker Dragster, 1997, Model No. 5014
EX $10 **NM** $15 **MIP** $20

Vulture, Customizing Monster kit, 1998, Model No. 5021
EX $10 **NM** $15 **MIP** $20

Witch, 2000, Model No. 5092
EX $15 **NM** $20 **MIP** $25

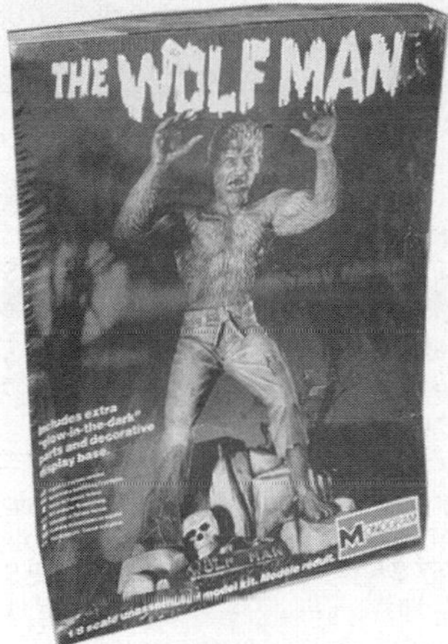

Wolfman, 1983, Wolfman, 1:8, Model No. 6009
EX $20 **NM** $30 **MIP** $40

Wolfman's Wagon, 1997, Model No. 5015
EX $10 **NM** $15 **MIP** $20

MPC

Alien, 1979, Alien, Model No. 1-1961
EX $25 **NM** $76 **MIP** $110

Ape Man Haunted Glow Head, 1975, Ape Man, Model No. 0303
EX $17 **NM** $38 **MIP** $60

AT-AT, Empire Strikes Back, 1980, Model No. 190218
EX $15 **NM** $35 **MIP** $60

Barnabas Vampire Van, 1969, Dark Shadows, Model No. 626
EX $75 **NM** $105 **MIP** $300

Barnabas, Dark Shadows, 1968, Dark Shadows, Model No. 1550
EX $100 **NM** $325 **MIP** $450

Batman, 1984, Super Powers, Model No. 1702
EX $20 **NM** $35 **MIP** $75

Beverly Hillbillies Truck, 1968, Beverly Hillbillies, Model No. 612
EX $60 **NM** $105 **MIP** $225

Bionic Bustout, Six Million Dollar Man, 1975, Model No. 0609
EX $15 **NM** $35 **MIP** $75

Bionic Repair, Bionic Woman, 1976, Bionic Woman, Model No. 0610
EX $15 **NM** $35 **MIP** $75

Black Hole, Cygnus, 1979, Model No. 1983
EX $75 **NM** $150 **MIP** $200

Black Hole, Maximillian, 1979, Model No. 1982
EX $65 **NM** $85 **MIP** $115

Black Hole, V.I.N.CENT., 1979, Model No. 1915
EX $65 **NM** $85 **MIP** $110

Bloody Mama, Ma Barker Getaway Special, 1970, Model No. 625
EX $30 **NM** $45 **MIP** $65

C-3PO, Structors Action Walker, 1984, Model No. 1901
EX $5 **NM** $10 **MIP** $15

Cannonball Run, "Hawaiian Tropic" Malibu, 1981, Model No. 681
EX $25 **NM** $38 **MIP** $65

Cannonball Run, Emergency Van, 1981, Model No. 447
EX $11 **NM** $16 **MIP** $30

Cannonball Run, Lamborghini Countach, 1981, Model No. 682
EX $18 **NM** $25 **MIP** $35

CB Freak, 1975, Model No. 778
EX $10 **NM** $17 **MIP** $30

Condemned to Chains Forever, 1974, Model No. 5003
EX $20 **NM** $42 **MIP** $65

Creepy T, 1970, Model No. 631
EX $20 **NM** $35 **MIP** $50

Curl's Gurl, 1960s, Model No. 103
EX $25 **NM** $65 **MIP** $100

Darth Vader Bust, 1977, Model No. 1921
EX $20 **NM** $42 **MIP** $60

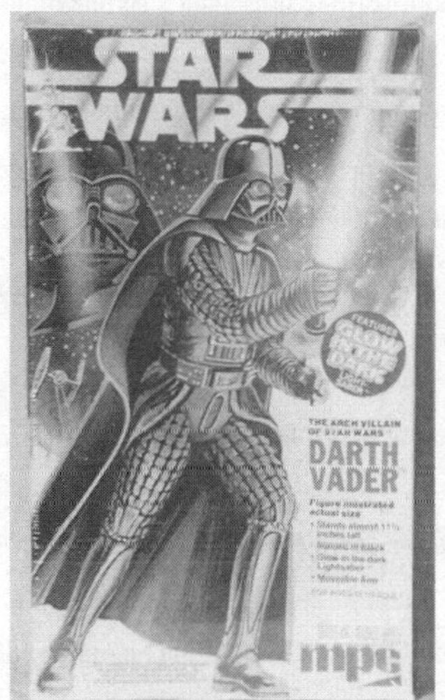

Darth Vader with Light Saber, 1979, Model No. 1916
EX $15 **NM** $30 **MIP** $44

Dead Man's Raft, 1974, Model No. 5005
EX $20 **NM** $84 **MIP** $110

Dead Men Tell No Tales, 1972, Model No. 5001
EX $60 **NM** $100 **MIP** $125

Dukes of Hazzard, Cooter's Cruiser, 1980, Snap-together, Model No. 3220
EX $12 **NM** $17 **MIP** $25

Dukes of Hazzard, Cooter's Tow Truck, 1981, Model No. 441
EX $15 **NM** $20 **MIP** $25

Dukes of Hazzard, Daisy's Jeep CJ, 1980, Model No. 662
EX $17 **NM** $25 **MIP** $35

Dukes of Hazzard, Duke's Digger, 1980, Snap-together, Model No. 3219
EX $15 **NM** $20 **MIP** $25

Dukes of Hazzard, General Lee, 1979, 1:25, Model No. 661
EX $40 **NM** $65 **MIP** $90

Dukes of Hazzard, General Lee, 1981, 1:16, Model No. 3058
EX $20 **NM** $45 **MIP** $50

Dukes of Hazzard, Sheriff Rosco's Police Car, 1982, Model No. 663
EX $10 **NM** $17 **MIP** $25

Empire Strikes Back, Battle on Ice Planet Hoth, 1981, Snap-together, Model No. 1922
EX $10 **NM** $15 **MIP** $20

Empire Strikes Back, Luke Skywalker Snowspeeder, 1980, Model No. 1917
EX $20 **NM** $30 **MIP** $40

Empire Strikes Back, Rebel Base, 1981, Model No. 1924
EX $10 **NM** $15 **MIP** $20

Empire Strikes Back, Slave I, 1982, Model No. 1919
EX $20 **NM** $45 **MIP** $80

Empire Strikes Back, Snow Speeder, 1980
EX $10 **NM** $20 **MIP** $35

Empire Strikes Back, Star Destroyer, 1980, Model No. 1926
EX $20 **NM** $35 **MIP** $75

Encounter With Yoda Diorama, 1981, Model No. 1983
EX $20 **NM** $40 **MIP** $60

Escape From the Crypt, 1974, Disney's Haunted Mansion series, Model No. 5053
EX $60 **NM** $100 **MIP** $125

Evil Rider, Six Million Dollar Man, 1975, Model No. 604
EX $15 **NM** $21 **MIP** $44

Fate of the Mutineers, 1974, Model No. 5004
EX $20 **NM** $42 **MIP** $55

Fight for Survival, Six Million Dollar Man, 1975, Model No. 602
EX $15 **NM** $21 **MIP** $50

Fonzie & Dream Rod, 1976, Fonzie, Model No. 0635
EX $20 **NM** $35 **MIP** $50

Fonzie & Motorcycle, 1976, Fonzie, Model No. 0634
EX $20 **NM** $28 **MIP** $45

Freed in the Nick of Time, 1972, Model No. 5007
EX $20 **NM** $63 **MIP** $85

Ghost of America, Hot Rodder's, 1960s, Model No. 104
EX $50 **NM** $65 **MIP** $80

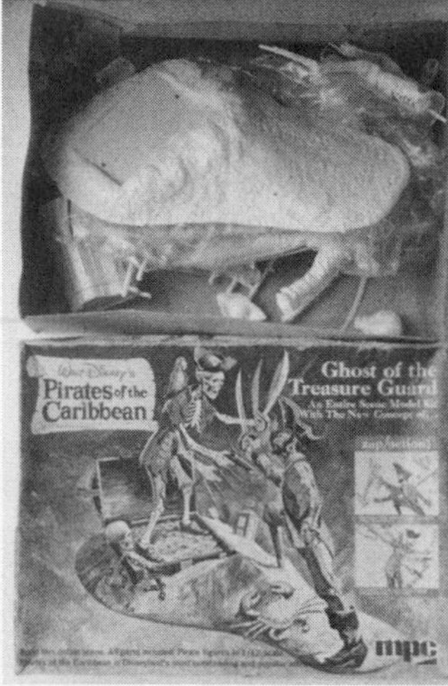

Ghost of the Treasure Guard, 1974, Disney's Pirates of the Caribbean, Model No. 5006
EX $45 **NM** $75 **MIP** $95

Grave Robber's Reward, 1974, Model No. 5051
EX $20 **NM** $42 **MIP** $55

Hardcastle & McCormick, GMC Truck, 1984, Model No. 450
EX $20 **NM** $32 **MIP** $45

Hogan's Heroes Jeep, 1968, Hogan's Heroes, Model No. 402
EX $30 **NM** $80 **MIP** $140

Hoist High the Jolly Roger, 1974, Disney's Pirates of the Caribbean, Model No. 5002
EX $35 **NM** $55 **MIP** $70

Hot Curl, 1960s, Hot Curl, Model No. 101
EX $20 **NM** $42 **MIP** $55

Hot Shot, Hot Shot
EX $20 **NM** $42 **MIP** $55

Hulk, 1978, Hulk, Model No. 1932
EX $20 **NM** $32 **MIP** $44

Jaws of Doom, Six Million Dollar Man, 1975, Model No. 603
EX $15 **NM** $21 **MIP** $44

Knight Rider, Knight 2000 "KITT", 1982, Model No. 675
EX $15 **NM** $22 **MIP** $30

Mannix Roadster, 1968, Model No. 609
EX $35 **NM** $45 **MIP** $60

Monkeemobile, 1967, Monkees, Model No. 605
EX $75 **NM** $165 **MIP** $250

Muldowney, Shirley, 1970s, Shirley "Cha Cha" Muldowney Funny Car Plymouth Hemi, Model No. 1-0702
EX $20 **NM** $45 **MIP** $65

Mummy Haunted Glow Head, 1975, Model No. 304
EX $20 **NM** $32 **MIP** $55

Mummy, Strange Changing, 1974, Model No. 902
EX $50 **NM** $75 **MIP** $100

Night Crawler Wolfman Car, 1971
EX $45 **NM** $80 **MIP** $140

Paul Revere & The Raiders Coach, 1970, Model No. 622
EX $55 **NM** $95 **MIP** $150

Play It Again Sam, 1974, Model No. 5052
EX $35 **NM** $84 **MIP** $110

Raiders of the Lost Ark Chase Scene, 1982, Model No. 1906
EX $15 **NM** $32 **MIP** $60

Raiders of the Lost Ark, Desert Chase, 1982, Snap-together, Model No. 1906
EX $15 **NM** $25 **MIP** $35

Return of the Jedi, AT-ST, 1984, Snap-together, Model No. 1903
EX $10 **NM** $15 **MIP** $22

Return of the Jedi, B-Wing Fighter, 1984, Snap-together, Model No. 1974
EX $15 **NM** $25 **MIP** $35

Return of the Jedi, C-3PO, 1983, Model No. 1935
EX $10 **NM** $20 **MIP** $50

Return of the Jedi, Jabba's Throne Room, 1983, Model No. 1928
EX $20 **NM** $32 **MIP** $50

Return of the Jedi, Millennium Falcon, 1983, Model No. 1933
EX $50 **NM** $65 **MIP** $90

Return of the Jedi, R2-D2, 1983, Model No. 1934
EX $15 **NM** $25 **MIP** $35

Return of the Jedi, Shuttle Tyridium, 1983, Model No. 1920
EX $15 **NM** $25 **MIP** $55

Return of the Jedi, Speeder Bike, 1983, Model No. 1927
EX $12 **NM** $17 **MIP** $25

Return of the Jedi, TIE Interceptor, 1983, Model No. 1972
EX $15 **NM** $25 **MIP** $35

Return of the Jedi, X-Wing Fighter, 1983, Snap-together, Model No. 1971
EX $11 **NM** $18 **MIP** $25

Return of the Jedi, X-Wing Fighter, 1983, Model No. 1930
EX $15 **NM** $22 **MIP** $30

Return of the Jedi, Y-Wing Fighter, 1983, Snap-together, Model No. 1975
EX $11 **NM** $18 **MIP** $25

Road Runner Beep Beep, Road Runner
EX $20 **NM** $50 **MIP** $85

Space: 1999 Hawk Spaceship, 1977, Model No. 1904
EX $30 **NM** $50 **MIP** $65

Space: 1999, Eagle One Model Kit, 1976
EX $50 **NM** $90 **MIP** $125

Space: 1999, Moon Base Alpha Model Kit, 1976
EX $20 **NM** $35 **MIP** $70

Space: 1999, The Alien vehicle, 1976, Model No. 1902
EX $30 **NM** $50 **MIP** $65

Spider-Man, 1978, Snap-together, clings to wall, Model No. 1931
EX $20 **NM** $30 **MIP** $40

Spider-Van, 1977, snap kit
EX $10 **NM** $17 **MIP** $22

Star Wars, C-3PO, 1978, Model No. 1913
EX $17 **NM** $30 **MIP** $45

Star Wars, Darth Vader TIE Fighter, 1978, Model No. 1915
EX $12 **NM** $20 **MIP** $30

Star Wars, Darth Vader Van, 1979, Snap-together, Model No. 3209
EX $10 **NM** $15 **MIP** $20

Star Wars, Luke Skywalker Van, 1977, Snap-together, Model No. 3210
EX $10 **NM** $15 **MIP** $20

Star Wars, Luke Skywalker's X-Wing Fighter, 1978, Model No. 1914
EX $15 **NM** $25 **MIP** $35

Star Wars, Millennium Falcon with Light, 1977, Model No. 1925
EX $35 **NM** $85 **MIP** $150

Star Wars, R2-D2, 1977, Model No. 1912
EX $20 **NM** $30 **MIP** $40

Star Wars, R2-D2 Van, 1977, Snap-together, Model No. 3211
EX $15 **NM** $25 **MIP** $35

Strange Changing Mummy, 1974, Model No. 0902
EX $15 **NM** $32 **MIP** $44

Strange Changing Time Machine, 1974, Model No. 0903
EX $20 **NM** $42 **MIP** $55

Strange Changing Vampire, 1974, Model No. 0901
EX $20 **NM** $42 **MIP** $55

Stroker McGurk & Surf Rod, 1960s, Stroker McGurk, Model No. 100
EX $30 **NM** $84 **MIP** $140

Stroker McGurk Tall T, 1964, Stroker McGurk, Model No. 102
EX $30 **NM** $84 **MIP** $140

Superman, 1984, Super Powers, Model No. 1701
EX $20 **NM** $35 **MIP** $55

Sweathog Dream Machine, 1976, Model No. 641
EX $15 **NM** $25 **MIP** $40

T.J. Hooker, Police Car, 1982, Model No. 676
EX $10 **NM** $20 **MIP** $30

The Fall Guy, GMC Pickup, 1982, Model No. 673
EX $15 **NM** $20 **MIP** $25

Time Machine, Strange Changing, 1974, Model No. 903
EX $50 **NM** $75 **MIP** $100

Vampire Haunted Glow Head, 1975, Model No. 301
EX $15 **NM** $21 **MIP** $50

Vampire, Strange Changin, 1974, Model No. 901
EX $50 **NM** $75 **MIP** $100

Vampire's Midnight Madness, 1974, Model No. 5050
EX $20 **NM** $45 **MIP** $55

Wacky Races, Compact Pussycat w/Penelope, 1969, Model No. 901
EX $125 **NM** $160 **MIP** $225

Wacky Races, Mean Machine, 1969, Model No. 900
EX $100 **NM** $145 **MIP** $175

Werewolf Haunted Glow Head, 1975, Model No. 302
EX $20 **NM** $35 **MIP** $50

Werewolf, Dark Shadows, 1969, Dark Shadows, Model No. 1552
EX $75 **NM** $200 **MIP** $325

Wile E. Coyote, Wile E. Coyote, Model No. 2651
EX $20 **NM** $50 **MIP** $75

Yellow Submarine, 1968, Beatles, Model No. 617
EX $75 **NM** $190 **MIP** $400

Multiple Toymakers

Automatic Baby Feeder, 1965, Rube Goldberg, Model No. 955
EX $25 **NM** $63 **MIP** $85

Back Scrubber, 1965, Rube Goldberg, Model No. 958
EX $25 **NM** $63 **MIP** $85

Iron Maiden, 1966, Model No. 981
EX $35 **NM** $105 **MIP** $165

Painless Tooth Extractor, 1965, Rube Goldberg, Model No. 956
EX $25 **NM** $63 **MIP** $85

Signal for Shipwrecked Sailors, 1965, Rube Goldberg, Model No. 957
EX $25 **NM** $63 **MIP** $85

Torture Chair, 1966, Model No. 980
EX $35 **NM** $95 **MIP** $165

Torture Wheel, 1966, Model No. 979
EX $35 **NM** $95 **MIP** $165

Park

Castro, Born Losers, 1965, Castro, Model No. 803
EX $35 **NM** $70 **MIP** $140

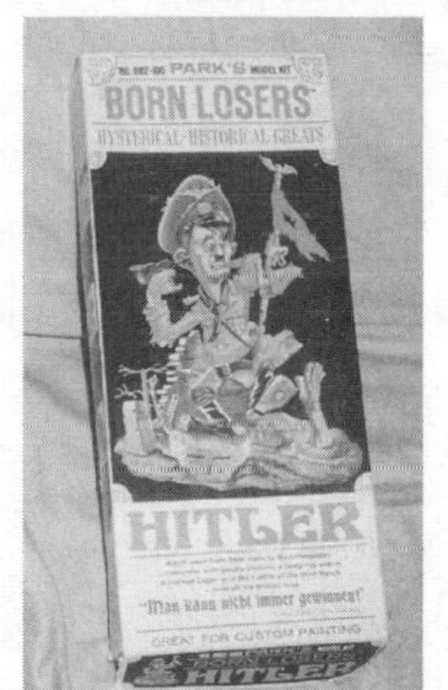

Hitler, Born Losers, 1965, Hitler, Model No. 802
EX $35 **NM** $70 **MIP** $200

Napoleon, Born Losers, 1965, Napoleon, Model No. 801
EX $35 **NM** $70 **MIP** $145

Playing Mantis/Polar Lights

Addams Family Haunted House, 1995, Model No. 5002
EX $15 **NM** $30 **MIP** $40

Back to the Future Delorean, 2002, movie version
EX $5 **NM** $10 **MIP** $15

Batcycle, 2002, DC Comic Book 1960s version, Model No. 6902
EX $5 **NM** $10 **MIP** $15

(Playing Mantis)

Bates Mansion from Psycho, 1998, Model No. 5028
EX $10 **NM** $20 **MIP** $30

Batplane, 2002, DC Comic Book 1960s version, Model No. 6905
EX $5 **NM** $10 **MIP** $15

Beatles Yellow Submarine, George, 1999, Model No. 5071
EX $10 **NM** $15 **MIP** $20

Beatles Yellow Submarine, John, 2000, Model No. 5074
EX $10 **NM** $15 **MIP** $20

Beatles Yellow Submarine, Paul, 2000, Model No. 5073
EX $10 **NM** $15 **MIP** $20

Beatles Yellow Submarine, Ringo, 1999, Model No. 5072
EX $10 **NM** $15 **MIP** $20

Bellringer of Notre Dame, 2000, Model No. 5090
EX $10 **NM** $20 **MIP** $30

Boris Karloff, The Mummy, 1998
EX $35 **NM** $45 **MIP** $60

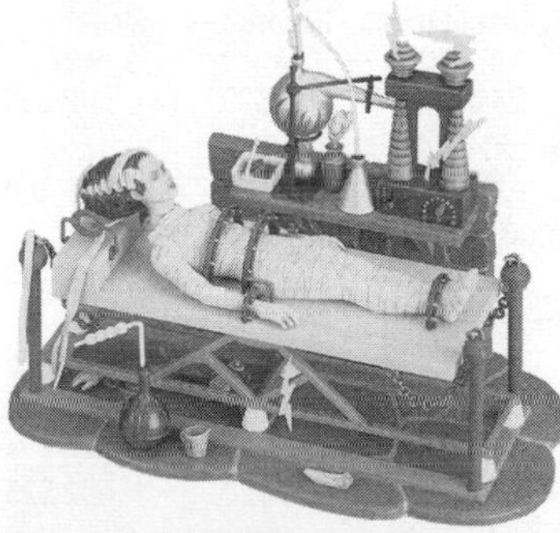

(Playing Mantis)

Bride of Frankenstein, 1997, Model No. 5005
EX $10 **NM** $20 **MIP** $30

Cats, Bats, n' Rats, 1998
EX $10 **NM** $20 **MIP** $30

Chamber of Horrors, Guillotine, 2000, Model No. 5091
EX $15 **NM** $20 **MIP** $25

Playing Mantis/Polar Lights

Clash of the Titans, Medusa, 1994
EX $50 **NM** $65 **MIP** $80

Crash Bandicoot on Jet Board, 1999, Model No. 6026
EX $10 **NM** $15 **MIP** $20

Creature From the Black Lagoon, 1998, The Creature
EX $10 **NM** $20 **MIP** $35

Creature from the Black Lagoon, 1999
EX $35 **NM** $45 **MIP** $60

Creepy Critters, 1998
EX $10 **NM** $20 **MIP** $30

Cyclops, The 7th Voyage of Sinbad, 1990
EX $34 **NM** $45 **MIP** $60

Demolition Man, Sandra Bullock, 1990s
EX $25 **NM** $35 **MIP** $50

Dick Tracy, 2000, on fire escape, Model No. 5093
EX $4 **NM** $8 **MIP** $12

(Playing Mantis)

Dick Tracy, Space Coupe, 2000, Model No. 5097
EX $10 **NM** $15 **MIP** $20

Dracula, Aurora box reissue, 1999, Model No. 424
EX $20 **NM** $30 **MIP** $40

Dracula's Dragster, 1999, Model No. 5025
EX $10 **NM** $20 **MIP** $30

Forgotten Prisoner of Castel-Mare', 1999, Model No. 7509
EX $10 **NM** $20 **MIP** $30

Frankenstein, 1999, Model No. 423
EX $30 **NM** $45 **MIP** $60

Frankenstein's Flivver, 1997, Model No. 5006
EX $10 **NM** $20 **MIP** $30

Fright Night, Amy, 1990
EX $35 **NM** $45 **MIP** $60

Ghost of Frankenstein, bust, 1997
EX $35 **NM** $45 **MIP** $60

Ghostbusters ECTO 1, 2002, movie version, Model No. 6812
EX $4 **NM** $8 **MIP** $12

Godzilla, 2000, Model No. 7502
EX $15 **NM** $20 **MIP** $25

Godzilla's Go-Cart, 1999, Model No. 5029
EX $25 **NM** $35 **MIP** $60

Green Hornet Black Beauty, 1999, Model No. 5017
EX $10 **NM** $20 **MIP** $30

H.P. Lovecraft's The UnNamable II, 1999
EX $50 **NM** $60 **MIP** $70

(Playing Mantis)

James Bond 007, 1999, Model No. 5035
EX $10 **NM** $15 **MIP** $20

King Ghidorah, 2000, Model No. 6802
EX $10 **NM** $15 **MIP** $20

King Kong, 1990s
EX $50 **NM** $65 **MIP** $80

King Kong, 2000, Model No. 7507
EX $10 **NM** $15 **MIP** $20

King Kong's Thronester, 1998, Model No. 5016
EX $10 **NM** $15 **MIP** $20

KISS, Ace Frehley, 1998, Ace Frehley
EX $10 **NM** $20 **MIP** $30

KISS, Gene Simmons, 1998, Gene Simmons, Model No. 5058
EX $10 **NM** $20 **MIP** $30

KISS, Paul Stanley, 1998, Paul Stanley, Model No. 5055
EX $10 **NM** $20 **MIP** $30

KISS, Peter Criss, 1998, Peter Criss, Model No. 5056
EX $10 **NM** $20 **MIP** $30

Land of the Giants Diorama, 2002, Diorama w/ snake & crew, Model No. 7512
EX $7 **NM** $14 **MIP** $20

Land of the Giants, Spaceship Spindrift, 2000, Model No. 7513
EX $7 **NM** $14 **MIP** $20

Lon Chaney, The Wolfman, 1999
EX $35 **NM** $45 **MIP** $60

Lost in Space Cyclops w/Chariot, 1998, Lost in Space Cyclops
EX $10 **NM** $20 **MIP** $30

(Playing Mantis)

Lost In Space, Cyclops, 1997, Model No. 5031
EX $10 **NM** $15 **MIP** $20

Lost In Space, Cyclops w/ diorama and vehicle, 1998, Model No. 5032
EX $10 **NM** $20 **MIP** $30

Lost In Space, Dr. Smith and Robot B-9, 1999, Model No. 5019
EX $10 **NM** $20 **MIP** $30

Lost In Space, Jupiter 2, 1998, Model No. 5033
EX $10 **NM** $20 **MIP** $30

Lost In Space, Jupiter 2 new box, 2000, Model No. 5033
EX $15 **NM** $25 **MIP** $35

Lost In Space, Robot, 1997, Model No. 5030
EX $10 **NM** $15 **MIP** $20

Michael Myers, Halloween, 2000, Model No. 5095
EX $10 **NM** $20 **MIP** $30

Mummy, 1999, Model No. 427
EX $30 **NM** $45 **MIP** $60

Mummy, 1999 movie version, 1999, Model No. 5023
EX $15 **NM** $20 **MIP** $30

Mummy's Chariot, 1995, Model No. 5003
EX $10 **NM** $15 **MIP** $20

Munsters Living Room diorama, 1997, Model No. 5013
EX $10 **NM** $15 **MIP** $25

(Playing Mantis)

Mystery Machine, 2000, Model No. 6808
EX $10 NM $15 MIP $20

Nosferatu, 1998
EX $35 NM $45 MIP $60

Odd Job, 1999, Model No. 5036
EX $10 NM $15 MIP $20

Phantom of the Opera, 2000, Model No. 5027
EX $30 NM $45 MIP $60

Phantom of the Opera, bust, 1997
EX $35 NM $45 MIP $60

Planet of the Apes, Cornelius, reissue, 2000, Model No. 6803
EX $10 NM $15 MIP $20

Planet of the Apes, Dr. Zaius, 2000, Model No. 6805
EX $10 NM $15 MIP $20

Planet of the Apes, Dr. Zira, 2000, Model No. 6804
EX $10 NM $15 MIP $20

Planet of the Apes, General Ursus, 2000, Model No. 6806
EX $10 NM $15 MIP $20

Predator, 1997
EX $35 NM $45 MIP $60

Pumpkinhead the Metamorphosis, 1994
EX $35 NM $45 MIP $60

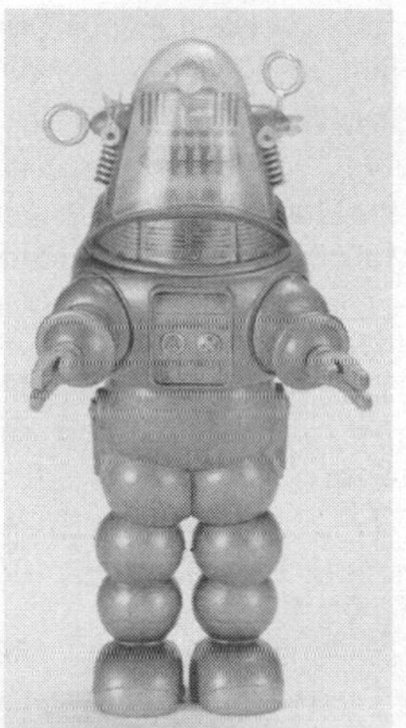
(Playing Mantis)

Robby the Robot, Forbidden Planet, 1999, Model No. 5025
EX $10 NM $20 MIP $30

Rodan, Aurora reissue, 2000, Model No. 6801
EX $10 NM $15 MIP $20

Sleepy Hollow, Headless Horseman, 1999, movie version, Model No. 5022
EX $5 NM $10 MIP $15

Son of Frankenstein, 1998
EX $35 NM $45 MIP $60

Star Trek the Next Generation, Ambassador Spock, 1996
EX $50 NM $65 MIP $75

Star Trek the Next Generation, Capt. Picard, 1992
EX $25 NM $35 MIP $50

Star Trek the Next Generation, Commander Riker, 1993
EX $25 NM $35 MIP $50

Star Trek the Next Generation, Counselor Troi, 1993
EX $25 NM $35 MIP $50

Star Trek the Next Generation, Ferengi, 1995
EX $25 NM $35 MIP $50

Star Trek the Next Generation, Geordi La Forge, 1993
EX $25 NM $35 MIP $50

Star Trek the Next Generation, Gowron the Klingon, 1995
EX $25 NM $35 MIP $50

Star Trek the Next Generation, Lieutenant Worf, 1992
EX $25 NM $35 MIP $50

Star Trek the Next Generation, Locutus of Borg, 1994
EX $25 NM $35 MIP $50

Star Trek the Next Generation, Lt. Comdr. Data, 1993
EX $25 NM $35 MIP $50

Star Trek the Next Generation, Romulan, 1994
EX $25 NM $35 MIP $50

The Wolf Man, 1998, cold-cast resin, Model No. 5018
EX $50 NM $100 MIP $200

Titan A.E., Drej Alien, 2000, Model No. 5094
EX $10 NM $15 MIP $20

Tremors, 1999
EX $35 NM $45 MIP $60

Voyage to the Bottom of the Sea, Seaview Submarine, 2001, Model No. 5099
EX $5 NM $10 MIP $15

Ymir, 20 Million Miles to Earth, 1990s
EX $50 NM $60 MIP $70

Precision

Cap'n Kidd the Pirate, 1959, Captain Kidd, Model No. 402
EX $25 NM $63 MIP $125

Crucifix, Jesus Christ, Model No. 501
EX $20 NM $42 MIP $75

Fighting Blue Marlin, 1958, Model No. 101
EX $10 NM $20 MIP $35

Pyro

Der-Baron, 1958, Model No. 166
EX $50 NM $80 MIP $125

Gladiator Show Cycle, Gladiator, Model No. 175
EX $20 NM $42 MIP $75

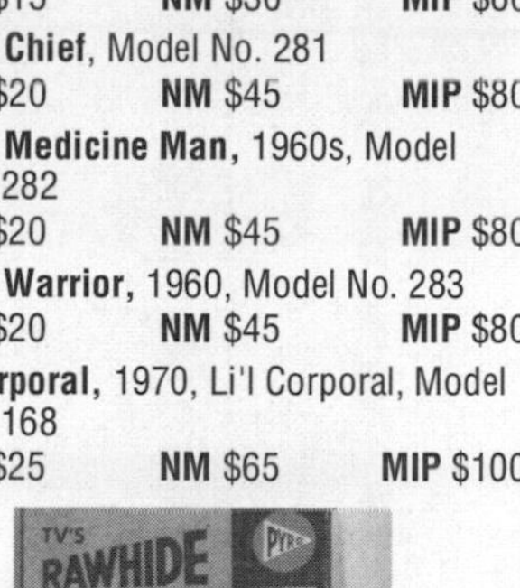

Human Eye
EX $15 NM $30 MIP $60

Indian Chief, Model No. 281
EX $20 NM $45 MIP $80

Indian Medicine Man, 1960s, Model No. 282
EX $20 NM $45 MIP $80

Indian Warrior, 1960, Model No. 283
EX $20 NM $45 MIP $80

Li'l Corporal, 1970, Li'l Corporal, Model No. 168
EX $25 NM $65 MIP $100

Rawhide, Gil Favor, 1958, Rawhide, Model No. 276
EX $25 NM $53 MIP $100

Restless Gun Deputy, 1959, Restless Gun, Model No. 277
EX $20 NM $45 MIP $66

Surf's Up, 1970, Surf's Up, Model No. 176
EX $15 NM $32 MIP $44

The Curler: Super Surf Tri-Cycle, 1970, tricycle w/surfboard, 1:8, Model No. M177-300
EX $10 NM $20 MIP $30

U.S. Marshal, Model No. 286
EX $40 NM $60 MIP $80

Wyatt Earp, 1958, Hugh O'Brian, Model No. 278
EX $30 **NM** $75 **MIP** $110

Remco

Flintstones Motorized Paddy Wagon, 1961, Model No. 452
EX $30 **NM** $105 **MIP** $220

Flintstones Motorized Sports Car & Trailer, 1961, Model No. 450
EX $30 **NM** $105 **MIP** $225

Flintstones Motorized Yacht, 1961, Model No. 451
EX $30 **NM** $105 **MIP** $220

Revell

Angel Fink, 1965, Big Daddy Roth, 1:25, Model No. 1307
EX $40 **NM** $105 **MIP** $175

Apollo Astronaut on the Moon, 1970, Model No. 1860
EX $115 **NM** $130 **MIP** $155

Apollo II Columbia and Eagle, 1969, Model No. 1862
EX $115 **NM** $130 **MIP** $165

Apollo II Tranquility Base, 1975, Model No. 714
EX $75 **NM** $100 **MIP** $125

Beatles, George Harrison, 1965, Beatles, Model No. 1353
EX $75 **NM** $150 **MIP** $275

Beatles, John Lennon, 1965, Beatles, Model No. 1352
EX $75 **NM** $150 **MIP** $275

Beatles, Paul McCartney, 1965, Beatles, Model No. 1350
EX $75 **NM** $150 **MIP** $250

Beatles, Ringo Starr, 1965, Beatles, Model No. 1351
EX $75 **NM** $150 **MIP** $250

Beatnik Bandit, 1963, Big Daddy Roth, 1:25, Model No. 1279
EX $125 **NM** $190 **MIP** $250

Billy Carter's Pickup, 1978, Model No. 1385
EX $35 **NM** $50 **MIP** $65

Birthday Bird, 1959, Dr. Seuss
EX $40 **NM** $150 **MIP** $275

Bonanza, 1965, Bonanza, Model No. 1931
EX $50 **NM** $105 **MIP** $165

Brother Rat Fink, 1963, Big Daddy Roth, 1:25, Model No. 1304
EX $35 **NM** $75 **MIP** $125

Busby the Tasselated Afghan Spaniel Yak, 1960, Dr. Seuss
EX $50 **NM** $125 **MIP** $275

Cat in the Hat, 1960, Dr. Seuss, Model No. 2000
EX $45 **NM** $105 **MIP** $165

Cat in the Hat with Thing 1 and Thing 2, 1960s, Model No. 2050
EX $45 **NM** $120 **MIP** $250

Charlie's Angels Mobile Unit Van, 1977, 1:25, Model No. 1397
EX $30 **NM** $40 **MIP** $75

CHiPs Helicopter, 1980, Model No. 6102
EX $20 **NM** $30 **MIP** $40

CHiPs Kawasaki Motorcycle, 1980, Model No. 7800
EX $20 **NM** $30 **MIP** $40

CHiPs Z-28 Chase Car, 1980, Model No. 6228
EX $10 **NM** $20 **MIP** $30

Dallas Cowboys Cheerleaders Van, 1979, Snap-together, Model No. 6405
EX $10 **NM** $20 **MIP** $30

Dr. Seuss Zoo Kit #1, 1959, three kits: Gowdy, Tingo, Norval
EX $50 **NM** $240 **MIP** $440

Dr. Seuss Zoo Kit #2, 1960, three kits: Roscoe, Grickily, Busby
EX $50 **NM** $350 **MIP** $550

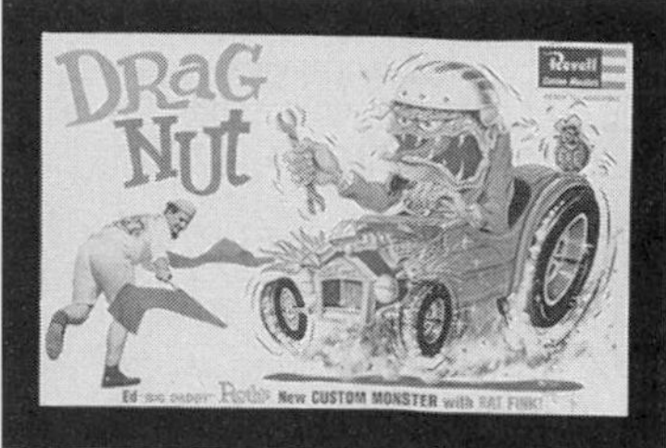

Drag Nut, 1963, Big Daddy Roth, 1:25, Model No. 1303
EX $50 **NM** $95 **MIP** $160

Fink-Eliminator, 1965, Big Daddy Roth, 1:25, Model No. 1310
EX $50 **NM** $105 **MIP** $225

Flash Gordon & Martian, 1965, Flash Gordon, Model No. 1450
EX $60 **NM** $105 **MIP** $165

Flipper, 1965, Flipper, Model No. 1930
EX $75 **NM** $105 **MIP** $165

G.I. Joe Attack Vehicle, 1982, Model No. 8901
EX $10 **NM** $20 **MIP** $30

G.I. Joe Rapid Fire Motorcycle, 1982, Model No. 8900
EX $10 **NM** $20 **MIP** $30

Gowdy the Dowdy Grackle, 1959, Dr. Seuss
EX $40 **NM** $85 **MIP** $190

Grickily the Gractus, 1960, Dr. Seuss
EX $50 **NM** $135 **MIP** $275

Hardy Boys Van, 1977, Model No. 1398
EX $10 **NM** $20 **MIP** $50

Horton the Elephant, 1960, Dr. Seuss
EX $150 **NM** $210 **MIP** $440

Jacques Cousteau Calypso, 1976, Model No. 575
EX $30 **NM** $45 **MIP** $60

Magnum P.I., 308 Ferrari GTS, 1981, Model No. 7378
EX $25 **NM** $35 **MIP** $50

Magnum P.I., T.C.'s Chopper, 1981, Model No. 4416
EX $25 **NM** $35 **MIP** $50

McHale's Navy PT-73, 1965, McHale's Navy, Model No. 323
EX $25 **NM** $63 **MIP** $83

Model Racer, Mr. Gasser, 1964, Big Daddy Roth, 1:25
EX $50 **NM** $100 **MIP** $175

Model Racer, Rat Fink, 1964, Big Daddy Roth, 1:25
EX $50 **NM** $100 **MIP** $175

Moonraker Space Shuttle, 1979, Model No. 4306
EX $10 **NM** $20 **MIP** $30

Mother's Worry, 1963, Big Daddy Roth, 1:25, Model No. 1302
EX $50 NM $100 MIP $175

Mr. Gasser, 1963, Big Daddy Roth, 1:25, Model No. 1301
EX $50 NM $100 MIP $175

Mr. Gasser BMR Racer, 1964, Big Daddy Roth, 1:25, Model No. 3181
EX $50 NM $100 MIP $175

Mysterion, 1964, Big Daddy Roth, 1:25
EX $55 NM $110 MIP $185

Norval the Bashful Blinket, 1959, Dr. Seuss
EX $40 NM $85 MIP $193

Outlaw, 1962, Big Daddy Roth, 1:25
EX $50 NM $100 MIP $175

Outlaw w/ Robin Hood Fink, 1960s, Big Daddy Roth, 1:25
EX $50 NM $125 MIP $200

Peter Pan Pirate Ship, 1960, Model No. 377
EX $75 NM $85 MIP $110

Peter Pan, Pirate Ship, 1969, Model No. 364
EX $25 NM $60 MIP $100

Phantom & Voodoo Witch Doctor, 1965, Phantom, Model No. 1451
EX $50 NM $105 MIP $220

Rat Fink, 1963, Big Daddy Roth, 1:25, Model No. 1305
EX $125 NM $200 MIP $250

Rat Fink Lotus Racer, 1964, Big Daddy Roth, 1:25
EX $75 NM $125 MIP $175

Red October Submarine, 1990, Model No. 4006
EX $45 NM $60 MIP $75

Road Agent, 1960s, Big Daddy Roth, 1:25
EX $50 NM $100 MIP $175

Robbin' Hood Fink, 1965, Big Daddy Roth, 1:25
EX $200 NM $325 MIP $475

Robotech Defenders Aqualo, 1984, Model No. 1148
EX $10 NM $15 MIP $20

Robotech Defenders Robot Revovery Unit, 1984, Model No. 1194
EX $25 NM $40 MIP $50

Robotech Defenders Thoren, 1984, Model No. 1150
EX $10 NM $20 MIP $30

Robotech Defenders Zoltek, 1984, Model No. 1151
EX $20 NM $30 MIP $50

Robotech Nebo, 1984, Model No. 1400
EX $10 NM $20 MIP $30

Robotech SDF1, 1985, Model No. 1143
EX $45 NM $80 MIP $125

Robotech Trigon, 1985, Model No. 1405
EX $10 NM $20 MIP $30

Robotech VF-1A Fighter, 1985, Model No. 1409
EX $30 NM $40 MIP $50

Robotech VF-1D Fighter, 1985, Model No. 1408
EX $30 NM $40 MIP $50

Robotech VF-1J Fighter, 1985, Model No. 1406
EX $30 NM $40 MIP $50

Robotech, Condar, 1984, Model No. 1152
EX $20 NM $30 MIP $45

Robotech, Decimax, 1985, Model No. 1148
EX $20 NM $30 MIP $50

Robotech, Recon Team 2 In 1, 1984, Model No. 1135
EX $20 NM $35 MIP $50

Robotech, Tactical Unit 2 in 1, 1984, Model No. 1136
EX $10 NM $15 MIP $20

Roscoe the Many-Footed Lion, 1960s, Dr. Seuss, Model No. 2004
EX $30 NM $85 MIP $190

Saint's Jaguar XJS, 1979, Model No. 6402
EX $25 NM $50 MIP $75

Scuz-Fink with Dingbat, 1965, Big Daddy Roth, 1:25, Model No. 1309
EX $275 NM $350 MIP $500

Superfink, 1964, Big Daddy Roth, 1:25
EX $150 NM $275 MIP $400

Surfink, 1965, Big Daddy Roth, 1:25, Model No. 1306
EX $50 NM $100 MIP $175

Surfite w/ Tiki Hut, 1960s, Big Daddy Roth, 1:25
EX $50 NM $100 MIP $175

Tingo the Noodle-Topped Stroodle, 1960s, Dr. Seuss
EX $50 NM $75 MIP $185

Tweedy Pie with Boss-Fink, 1965, Big Daddy Roth, 1:25, Model No. 1271
EX $200 NM $335 MIP $465

Toy Biz

Ghost Rider, 1996, Model No. 48660
EX $7 NM $17 MIP $30

Hulk, 1996, Model No. 48656
EX $5 NM $12 MIP $22

Onslaught, 1997, Model No. 48640
EX $7 NM $12 MIP $28

Silver Surfer, 1996, Model No. 48653
EX $5 NM $12 MIP $22

Spider-Man, 1996, Model No. 48651
EX $5 NM $12 MIP $22

Spider-Man, with wall, 1996, Model No. 48658
EX $5 NM $12 MIP $22

Storm, 1996, Model No. 48659
EX $5 NM $12 MIP $22

Thing, 1996, Model No. 48652
EX $5 NM $12 MIP $22

Venom, 1996, Model No. 48654
EX $5 NM $12 MIP $22

Wolverine, 1996, Model No. 48657
EX $5 NM $12 MIP $22

ToyBiz

Beast, 1998, Marvel Comics, Model No. 47782
EX $5 NM $10 MIP $15

Captain America, 1998, Marvel Comics, Model No. 48622
EX $5 NM $10 MIP $15

Rhino, 1998, Marvel Comics, Model No. 48886
EX $5 NM $10 MIP $15

Thor, 1998, Marvel Comics, Model No. 48621
EX $5 NM $10 MIP $15

PEZ

2009 Trends

Collecting PEZ is still gaining popularity. It seems more people than ever are interested in these cute character pieces. Even with the higher costs of food, fuel, etc. attendance throughout the year at national PEZ conventions has been strong.

The items that seem to sell the best and have the most interest are the contemporary pieces. Prices and demand for recent additions have held steady while mid-range vintage pieces have softened to a degree. The mid-range pieces, priced from $50 to $200 may have come down in price as much as 10 to 20 percent in some cases. High-end dispensers and related material continue to have strong interest and selling prices reflect the fact.

Current sales show, without a doubt, it's a buyers market. If you have been collecting the new releases for a while and have been reluctant to move to the next price plateau, now is a great time to pick up some good deals.

Word of caution: When purchasing vintage PEZ, know what you are buying and, when possible, buy from a reputable dealer. Several fake dispensers have recently been released to unknowing buyers via online auction sites. Dispensers such as Indian Chiefs, One Eye Monsters and Mimic the Monkey, to name a few, have been completely remade and sold as originals. Many of these sales have come from overseas sellers and the buyer has little recourse once they realize they have been taken. If the deal seems too good to be true, it probably is. Take the time to read up and understand what the subtle characteristics of a certain dispenser should be. When possible, attend a PEZ convention. There is no substitute for actually seeing a rare old dispenser in person, holding it, and giving it a thorough inspection before making a purchase.

It also helps to meet the dealers. Most are well known throughout the hobby and if there is a problem, they will stand behind what they are selling. A bargain purchased online is no bargain if there is a problem with the dispenser.

PEZ the company continues to stay on top of the latest trends and licenses the hottest properties. New dispensers are added regularly and other lines are retired almost as quickly. Given the short retail lifespan of some of these offerings, speculation would say prices for these short runs will increase in the short term.

A set such as the unmasked Incredibles (European edition) is very difficult to find. This set was released in 2004 and now sells in the $25 to $35 range – if you can find them. The best advice I can give anyone is to not to buy as an investment. Buy only what you like, enjoy your purchase, and have *FUN*!

Contributor Shawn Peterson is the author of ***Collectors Guide to PEZ: Identification and Price Guide, 3rd edition*** (Krause Publications 2008). Shawn is available for book signings and PEZ speaking engagements in your area. He is always interested in adding to his collection or talking to former PEZ Candy employees for continuing book research.

You may contact him by writing to: P.O. Box 571 Blue Springs, Missouri 64013, or emailing PEZbook@comcast.net.

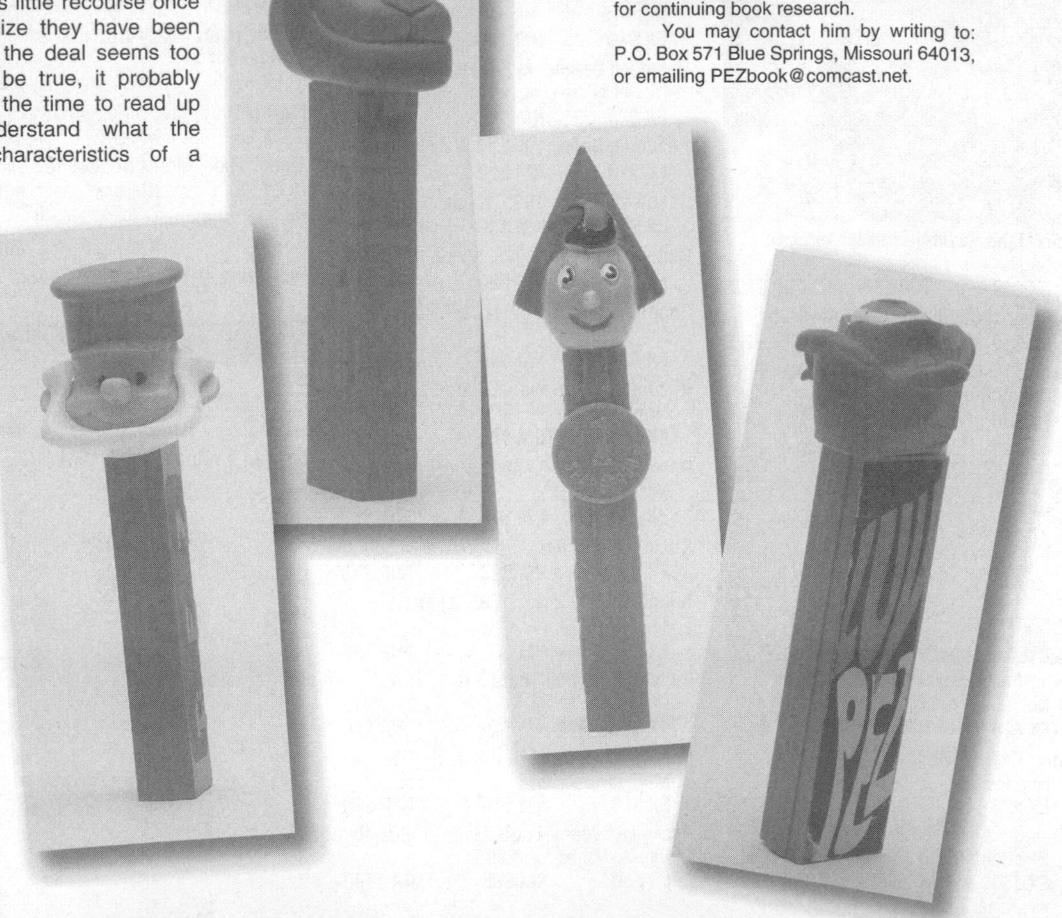

Bicentennial

Betsy Ross, 1970s, no feet, dark hair and white hat, Bicentennial issue
NM $130 **MIP** $175

Captain (Paul Revere), 1970s, no feet, blue hat, Bicentennial issue
NM $125 **MIP** $150

Daniel Boone, 1970s, no feet, light brown hair under dark brown hat, Bicentennial issue
NM $150 **MIP** $215

(Barry Koester)

Indian Brave, early 1970s, no feet, small human head, Indian headband w/one feather, Bicentennial issue. Shown here with Indian Chief, Indian Woman, and Pilgrim.
NM $150 **MIP** $200

Indian Chief, 1975, no feet, war bonnet, swirled colors
NM $100 **MIP** $125

Indian Maiden, 1975, no feet, black hair in braids w/headband
NM $95 **MIP** $175

Uncle Sam, 1975, no feet, stars and stripes on hat band, white hair and beard, Bicentennial issue
NM $150 **MIP** $200

Wounded Soldier, 1970s, no feet, white bandage, brown hair, Bicentennial issue
NM $135 **MIP** $170

Christmas

Angel, 1970s, w/feet, yellow hair and halo
NM $50 **MIP** $75

Angel, 1970s, no feet, yellow hair and halo
NM $85 **MIP** $100

Elf, 2002, w/feet, green hat, pointy ears
NM $1 **MIP** $2

Icee Bear, 1999, w/feet, re-released w/Christmas assortment
NM $1 **MIP** $3

Polar Bear (Icee Bear), 2002, w/feet, red hat
NM $1 **MIP** $2

Reindeer, 2002, w/feet, black nose
NM $1 **MIP** $2

Rudolph, 1970s, no feet, brown deer head, red nose
NM $35 **MIP** $60

Santa (Full Bodied), 1950s, full body stem w/painted Santa suit and hat
NM $135 **MIP** $200

Santa A, 1950s, no feet, ivory head w/painted hat
NM $80 **MIP** $125

Santa B, 1960s, no feet, small head w/flesh painted face, black eyes, red hat
NM $85 **MIP** $150

Santa C, 1970s, w/feet, removable red hat, white beard
NM $2 **MIP** $4

Santa C, 1970s, no feet or w/feet, large head w/white beard, flesh face, red open mouth and hat
NM $7 **MIP** $12

Santa D, 1990s, w/feet, painted blue eyes
NM $2 **MIP** $4

(KP Photo, Sharon Bartsch collection)

Santa E, 2000s, w/feet, current version
NM $1 **MIP** $2

Snowman, 1970s, no feet, black hat, white face
NM $10 **MIP** $15

Snowman, 2002, w/feet, new scarf and hat
NM $1 **MIP** $2

Circus

Big Top Elephant, 1970s, no feet, gray-green head, red flat hat
NM $90 **MIP** $125

Big Top Elephant, 1970s, no feet, orange head w/blue pointed hat
NM $80 **MIP** $120

Big Top Elephant With Hair, 1970s, no feet, yellow head and red hair
NM $125 **MIP** $250

Clown with Chin, 1970s, no feet, long chin, hat and hair
NM $80 **MIP** $100

Clown with Collar, 1960s, no feet, yellow collar, red hair, green hat
NM $60 **MIP** $80

Giraffe, 1970s, no feet, orange head w/horns, black eyes
NM $125 **MIP** $200

Gorilla, 1970s, no feet, black head w/red eyes and white teeth
NM $85 **MIP** $120

Li'l Lion, 1960s, no feet, yellow head w/brown mane
NM $65 **MIP** $80

Lion with Crown, 1970s, no feet, black mane, green head w/yellow cheeks and red crown
NM $95 **MIP** $150

Mimic the Monkey, 1970s, no feet, wearing baseball cap, white eyes
NM $35 **MIP** $45

Monkey Sailor, 1960s, no feet, cream face, brown hair, white sailor cap, whistlehead
NM $40 **MIP** $50

Pony-Go-Round, 1970s, no feet, orange head, white harness, blue hair
NM $60 **MIP** $85

Crazy Fruits

Orange, 1970s, no feet, orange (fruit) head w/face and leaves on top
NM $200 **MIP** $250

(Barry Koester)

Pear, 1970s, no feet, yellow pear face, green visor
NM $800 **MIP** $1000

Pineapple, 1970s, no feet, pineapple head w/greenery and sunglasses
NM $3000 **MIP** $3500

Die-Cuts

Bozo the Clown, 1960s, no feet, die-cut Bozo and Butch on stem, no feet, white face, red hair and nose
NM $150 **MIP** $185

Casper the Friendly Ghost, 1950s, no feet, die-cut
NM $165 **MIP** $225

Donald Duck Die-Cut, 1960s, no feet, die-cut
NM $150 **MIP** $200

Easter Bunny, 1950s, no feet, die-cut
NM $350 **MIP** $400

Mickey Mouse Die-Cut, 1960s, no feet, die-cut stem w/Minnie, painted face
NM $200 **MIP** $350

Mickey Mouse Die-Cut, 1960s, no feet, die-cut stem w/Minnie, die-cut face mask
NM $150 **MIP** $200

Disney

Baloo, 1960s, no feet, Jungle Book
NM $20 **MIP** $40

Baloo, 1960s, w/feet, Jungle Book
NM $12 **MIP** $25

Bambi, 1970s, w/feet
NM $30 **MIP** $50

Best of Pixar, The, 2006, w/feet, Buzz Lightyear (Toy Story), Nemo (Finding Nemo), Mike Wazowski (Monsters, Inc.), Sulley (Monsters Inc.)
NM $1 **MIP** $2

Bouncer Beagle, 1990s, w/feet, Ducktails
NM $5 **MIP** $6

Captain Hook, 1960s, no feet, black hair, flesh face winking w/right eye open
NM $75 **MIP** $100

Cars, 2006, w/feet, Lightning McQueen, Mater the Tow Truck, Sally the Porsche, Doc Hudson
NM $1 **MIP** $2

Chip, 1970s, w/feet
NM $40 **MIP** $75

Chip, 1970s, no feet, black top hat, tan head w/white sideburns, brown nose, foreign issue
NM $80 **MIP** $100

Dalmatian Pup, 1970s, w/feet, white head w/left ear cocked, foreign issue
NM $35 **MIP** $55

Dewey, 1970s, (Donald Duck's nephew) no feet, blue hat, white head, yellow beak, small black eyes
NM $20 **MIP** $35

Disney Princesses, 2005, w/feet, Jasmine (Aladdin), Cinderella, Belle (Beauty and the Beast)
NM $2 **MIP** $4

Disney Princesses, 2006, w/feet, Ariel (Little Mermaid), Aurora (Sleeping Beauty)
NM $2 **MIP** $4

Disney Princesses, 2007, w/feet, Snow White
NM $1 **MIP** $2

Donald Duck A, 1960s, no feet, blue hat, one-piece head and bill, open mouth
NM $12 **MIP** $25

Donald Duck B, 1960s, w/feet, blue hat, white head and hair w/large eyes, removable beak
NM $1 **MIP** $3

Dopey, 1960s, no feet, flesh colored die-cut face w/wide ears, orange cap
NM $150 **MIP** $175

Duck Nephews, 1980s, w/feet, (Huey, Dewey or Louie Duck) red, blue, or green stem and matching cap, white head and orange beak
NM $5 **MIP** $10

Dumbo, 1970s, no feet, gray head w/large ears, red hat
NM $40 **MIP** $60

Dumbo, 1970s, w/feet, blue head w/large ears, yellow hat
NM $30 **MIP** $40

Extreme Disney, 2003, w/feet, Mickey Mouse w/ski hat and goggles, Minnie Mouse w/new sunglasses, Daisy Duck w/headphones, Goofy w/headphones, Donald Duck good and mad, Pluto w/bone
NM $2 **MIP** $4

Goofy A, 1970s, no feet, removable nose, ears, and teeth
NM $30 **MIP** $50

Goofy B, 1970s, no feet, red hat, painted nose, removable white teeth
NM $35 **MIP** $50

Goofy C, 1970s, same as version B except teeth are part of head
NM $15 **MIP** $25

Goofy D, 1980s, w/feet, beige snout, green hat
NM $1 **MIP** $3

Goofy E, 1990s, w/feet, current
NM $2 **MIP** $4

Gyro Gearloose, 1990s, w/feet, Ducktails
NM $5 **MIP** $8

Huey, 1970s, (Donald Duck's nephew) no feet, red hat, white head, yellow beak, small black eyes
NM $20 **MIP** $35

Incredibles, The, 2004, w/feet, Mr. Incredible, Elastigirl, Dash, Jack Jack. No Violet? C'mon guys, half visible, half "invisible" w/ crystal would look great!
NM $2 **MIP** $4

Jiminy Cricket, 1970s, no feet, green hatband and collar, flesh face, black top hat
NM $180 **MIP** $225

(KP Photo, Sharon Bartsch collection)

Jungle Book 2, 2003, w/feet, Mowgli, Bagherra, Kaa, Shir Kahn, Baloo
NM $1 **MIP** $3

(KP Photo, Sharon Bartsch collection)

King Louie, 1960s, w/feet, brown hair and "sideburns" over light brown head
NM $20 **MIP** $30

Li'l Bad Wolf, 1960s, w/feet, black ears, white face, red tongue
NM $12 **MIP** $20

Li'l Bad Wolf, 1960s, no feet, black ears, white face, red tongue
NM $15 **MIP** $25

Lion King, 2004, w/feet, Mufasa, Nala, Simba, Pumbaa, Timon
NM $2 **MIP** $4

Louie, 1970s, (Donald Duck's nephew) no feet, green hat, white head, yellow beak, small black eyes
NM $10 **MIP** $30

Mary Poppins, 1970s, no feet, flesh face, reddish hair, lavender hat
NM $800 **MIP** $1100

Meet the Robinsons, 2007, w/feet, Lewis, Wilber Robinson, Carl the Robot, Bowler Hat Guy
NM $1 **MIP** $2

Mickey Mouse A, 1970s, no feet, black head and ears, pink face, mask w/cut out eyes and mouth, nose pokes through mask
NM $85 **MIP** $125

Mickey Mouse B, 1980s, no feet, painted face, non-painted black eyes and mouth
NM $125 **MIP** $175

Mickey Mouse C, 1990s, no feet, flesh face, removable nose, painted eyes
NM $10 **MIP** $15

Mickey Mouse D, 1990s, no feet, flesh face, mask embossed white and black eyes
NM $5 **MIP** $10

Mickey Mouse E, 1990s, w/feet, flesh face, bulging black and white eyes, oval nose
NM $1 **MIP** $3

Mowgli, 1960s, no feet, black hair over brown head, Jungle Book
NM $20 **MIP** $35

PEZ

Mowgli, 1960s, w/feet, black hair over brown head, Jungle Book
NM $5 **MIP** $20

Peter Pan, 1960s, no feet, green hat, flesh face, orange hair
NM $100 **MIP** $175

Pinocchio A, 1960s, no feet, red or yellow cap, pink face, black painted hair
NM $145 **MIP** $180

Pinocchio B, 1970s, no feet, black hair, red hat
NM $110 **MIP** $175

Pluto A, 1960s, no feet, yellow head, long black ears, small painted eyes
NM $10 **MIP** $20

Pluto B, 1970s, w/feet, flat head, movable ears
NM $10 **MIP** $17

Pluto C, 1980s, w/feet, yellow head, long painted black ears, large white and black decal eyes
NM $2 **MIP** $5

Pluto D, 1990s, w/feet, large eyes, current
NM $2 **MIP** $4

Practical Pig A, 1960s, no feet, rounded blue hat, round snout
NM $45 **MIP** $65

Practical Pig B, 1960s, no feet, crooked blue hat
NM $40 **MIP** $60

Ratatouille, 2007, w/feet, Remy, Emile, Skinner, Linguini
NM $1 **MIP** $2

Scrooge McDuck A, 1970s, no feet, white head, yellow beak, black top hat and glasses, white sideburns
NM $15 **MIP** $30

Scrooge McDuck B, 1970s, w/feet, white head, removable yellow beak, tall black top hat and glasses, large eyes
NM $5 **MIP** $10

Snow White, 1960s, no feet, flesh face, black hair w/ribbon and matching collar
NM $170 **MIP** $220

Thumper, 1970s, w/feet, no Disney logo
NM $30 **MIP** $50

Thumper, 1970s, no feet, orange face, w/logo
NM $200 **MIP** $300

Tinkerbell, 1960s, no feet, pale pink stem, white hair, flesh face w/blue and white eyes
NM $180 **MIP** $230

Webagail or Webby, 1990s, w/feet, Ducktails
NM $2 **MIP** $4

Winnie the Pooh, 1970s, w/feet, yellow head
NM $65 **MIP** $85

Winnie the Pooh, 1970s, no feet, European release
NM $75 **MIP** $110

(KP Photo, Sharon Bartsch collection)

Winnie the Pooh, 2001, w/feet, remakes of originals, Tigger, Piglet, Eeyore, Pooh
NM $1 **MIP** $2

Winnie the Pooh, 2005, w/feet, Roo, Heffalump
NM $1 **MIP** $3

Zorro, 1960s, no feet, w/Disney logo
NM $100 **MIP** $130

Zorro, 1960s, no feet, black mask and hat, no Disney logo
NM $75 **MIP** $100

Zorro with Logo, 1960s, no feet, black mask and hat, says "Zorro" on stem
NM $95 **MIP** $125

Easter

Bunny, 1999
NM $1 **MIP** $3

Bunny 1990, 1990, w/feet, long ears, white face
NM $1 **MIP** $3

Bunny A, 1950s, no feet, narrow head and tall ears
NM $225 **MIP** $275

Bunny B, 1950s, no feet, tall ears and full face, smiling buck teeth
NM $275 **MIP** $375

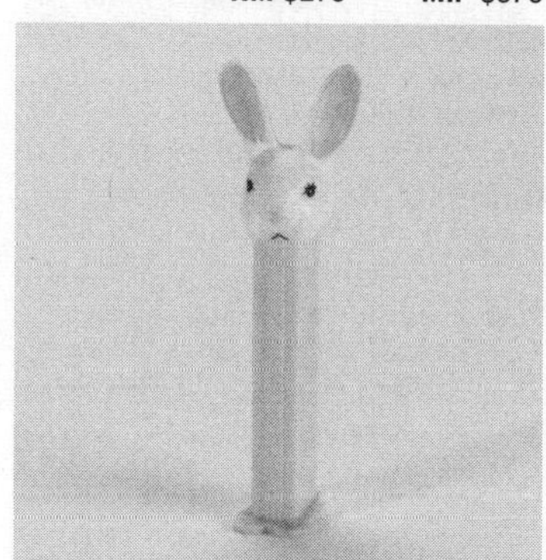

(KP Photo, Sharon Bartsch collection)

Bunny D, 1990s, w/feet
NM $2 **MIP** $4

Bunny E, 2000s, w/feet, painted face, current
NM $1 **MIP** $3

Bunny with Fat Ears, 1960s, no feet, wide ear version, assorted colors
NM $25 **MIP** $40

Bunny with Fat Ears, 1970s, w/feet, wide ear version
NM $10 **MIP** $20

Chick in Egg, 1970s, no feet, yellow chick in egg shell, no hat
NM $80 **MIP** $125

Chick In Egg A, 1970s, no feet, yellow chick in egg shell, red hat
NM $15 **MIP** $25

Chick in Egg B, 1970s, no feet, red hat, shell thin and flexible
NM $15 **MIP** $25

Chick in Egg C, 1980s, no feet, red hat, thicker shell
NM $9 **MIP** $15

(KP Photo, Sharon Bartsch collection)

Chick in Egg C, 1980s, w/feet, red hat
NM $5 **MIP** $11

Chick in Egg D, 1990s, w/feet, red hat, rounded shell design
NM $2 **MIP** $4

Chick in Egg E, 2000s, w/feet, red hat, current
NM $1 **MIP** $2

Duck with Flower, 1970s, no feet, flower, duck head w/beak, many color combinations
NM $75 **MIP** $125

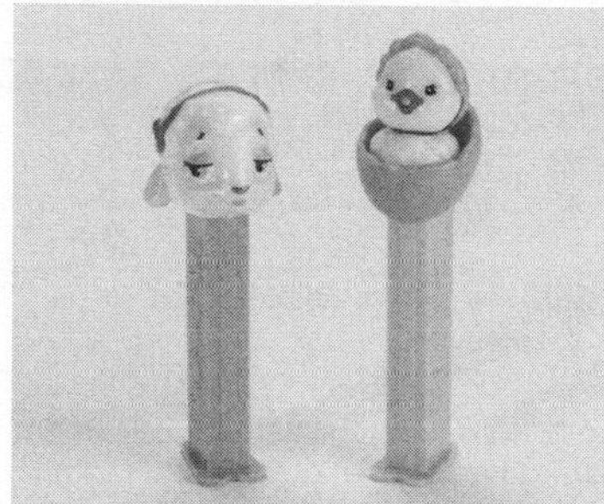

Easter 2004, 2004, w/feet, new sculpts, Chick in Egg, Lamb, Bunny (pink), baby-faced Egg
NM $1 **MIP** $2

Lamb, 1970s, no feet, white head w/pink bow
NM $10 **MIP** $15

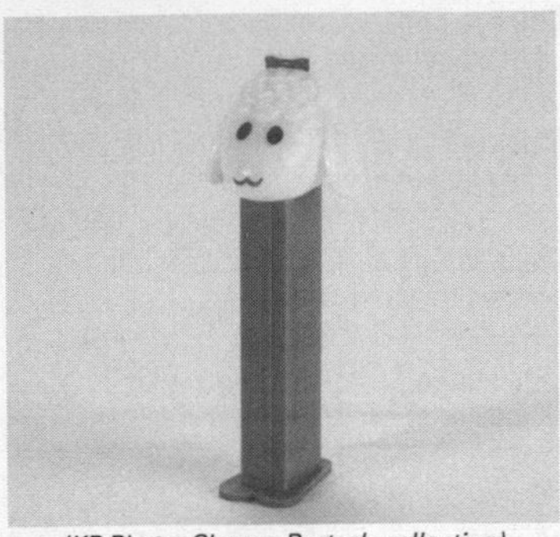

(KP Photo, Sharon Bartsch collection)

Lamb, 1970s-80s, w/feet
NM $2 **MIP** $4

Rooster, 1970s, no feet, yellow head, comb and wattle
NM $75 **MIP** $125

Eerie Spectres

Air Spirit, 1970s, no feet, reddish triangular fish face
NM $200 **MIP** $250

Diabolic, 1970s, no feet, soft orange monster head
NM $200 **MIP** $250

Scarewolf, 1970s, no feet, soft head w/orange hair and ears
NM $200 **MIP** $250

Spook, 1970s, no feet, blue head w/horns, soft head
NM $200 **MIP** $250

Vamp, 1970s, no feet, light gray head on black collar, green hair and face, red teeth
NM $225 **MIP** $280

Zombie, 1970s, no feet, burgundy and black soft head
NM $175 **MIP** $250

Halloween

Black Cat, 2006, w/feet, glow-in-the-dark stem, red collar w/pumpkin
NM $1 **MIP** $2

Halloween Crystal Series, 1999, w/feet, mail-in series, Happy Henry, Naughty Neil, Slimy Sid, and Polly Pumpkin
NM $2 **MIP** $4

Halloween Ghosts, 1999, w/feet, non-glowing, Happy Henry, Naughty Neil, Slimy Sid
NM $2 **MIP** $4

Halloween Glowing Ghosts, 2002, w/feet, glow-in-the-dark, Happy Henry, Naughty Neil, Slimy Sid, Polly Pumpkin
NM $2 **MIP** $4

Jack-O-Lantern A, 1980s, no feet, green stem, carved face
NM $10 **MIP** $15

Jack-O-Lantern B, 1980s, black facial features
NM $1 **MIP** $3

Mr. Ugly, 1970s, no feet, black hair, many color variations
NM $60 **MIP** $85

Mr. Ugly, 1970s, w/feet
NM $40 **MIP** $70

Octopus, 1970s, no feet; black; orange or black head
NM $45 **MIP** $75

One-Eyed Monster, 1970s, w/feet
NM $55 **MIP** $80

One-Eyed Monster, 1970s, no feet, gorilla head w/one eye missing
NM $75 **MIP** $95

Skull A, 1970s, w/feet, small white head, black body
NM $10 **MIP** $16

Skull A, 1970s, no feet, small white head, black dispenser body
NM $15 **MIP** $25

Skull B, 1970s, no feet, black collar, larger head
NM $10 **MIP** $15

Skull B, 1980s, w/feet, glow-in-dark version
NM $2 **MIP** $4

Skull Misfit, 1998, w/feet, mail-in, black head, yellow body
NM $6 **MIP** $10

Witch 1 Piece, 1950s, no feet, black stem w/witch embossed on stem, orange one-piece head
NM $200 **MIP** $250

Witch 3-Piece A, 1970s, no feet, chartreuse face, black hair, orange hat
NM $70 **MIP** $120

Witch 3-Piece B, 1980s, w/feet, red head and hair, green mask, black hat
NM $3 **MIP** $7

Witch C, 1990s, w/feet, glow-in-the-dark, current
NM $2 **MIP** $4

Humans

Astronaut A, early 1960s, no feet, helmet, yellow visor, small head
NM $600 **MIP** $700

Astronaut B, 1970s, no feet, green stem, white helmet, yellow visor, large head
NM $100 **MIP** $150

Cowboy, 1970s, no feet, human head, brown hat
NM $225 **MIP** $275

Emergency Heroes, 2003, w/feet, Army Soldier, Policeman, Scuba Diver, Construction Worker, Police K-9, Policewoman, Nurse, Fireman, Jet Pilot. Fireman and Construction Worker have African-American variations ($3-5 each)
NM $1 **MIP** $2

Football Player, 1960s, no feet, white stem, red helmet w/white stripe
NM $100 **MIP** $150

Orange County Chopper Set, 2006, w/feet, special edition tin w/Paul Sr., Paul Jr., Mikey
NM $10 **MIP** $20

Pilgrim, 1975, no feet, pilgrim hat, blond hair, hat band
NM $125 **MIP** $160

Pilot, 1970s, no feet, blue hat, gray headphones
NM $150 **MIP** $225

Spaceman, 1950s, no feet, clear helmet over flesh-color head
NM $90 **MIP** $150

Stewardess, 1970s, no feet, light blue flight cap, blond hair
NM $150 **MIP** $225

Kooky Zoo

Cockatoo, 1970s, no feet, yellow beak and green head, red head feathers
NM $60 **MIP** $85

Cow A, 1970s, no feet, cow head, separate nose
NM $75 **MIP** $95

Cow B, 1970s, no feet, blue head, separate snout, horns, ears and eyes
NM $85 **MIP** $120

Crocodile, 1970s, no feet, dark green head w/red eyes
NM $75 **MIP** $120

Kooky Zoo Crystal Series, 1999, w/feet, "crystal" versions of Blinky Bill, Lion, Gator, Hippo, Elephant
NM $3 **MIP** $6

(KP Photo, Sharon Bartsch collection)

Kooky Zoo Series, late 1990s, w/feet, Blinky Bill the koala (shown), Lion, Gator (shown), Hippo, Elephant
NM $2 **MIP** $5

Panda A, 1970s, no feet, white head w/black eyes and ears
NM $20 **MIP** $28

Panda A, 1970s, no feet, yellow head w/black eyes and ears
NM $350 **MIP** $450

(KP Photo, Sharon Bartsch collection)

Panda B, 1990s, w/feet, white head w/black eyes and ears
NM $1 **MIP** $3

Panther, 1970s, no feet, blue head w/pink nose
NM $100 **MIP** $200

Puzzy Cat, 1970s, no feet, cat head w/hat
NM $65 **MIP** $95

Raven, 1970s, no feet, black head, short or long beak, glasses
NM $60 **MIP** $85

Yappy Dog, 1970s, no feet, black floppy ears and nose, green or orange head
NM $75 **MIP** $90

Licensed Characters

Arlene, early 1990s, w/feet, 1st series, pink head, Garfield's girlfriend
NM $2 **MIP** $5

Asterix, 1970s, no feet, blue hat w/wings, yellow mustache, European
NM $1500 **MIP** $2000

Asterix (1998 foreign issue), 1998, head different than old
NM $3 **MIP** $5

(KP Photo, Sharon Bartsch collection)

Barney Rubble, 1990s, w/feet, Flintstones, shown w/Pebbles, Dino and Fred
NM $1 **MIP** $2

Bart Simpson, 2000, w/feet
NM $1 **MIP** $2

(KP Photo, Sharon Bartsch collection)

Bob the Builder, 2002, w/feet, four characters:Wendy, Bob, Pilchard, and Spud
NM $1 **MIP** $2

Brainy Smurf, 1990s, w/feet, second series
NM $2 **MIP** $4

Bratz, 2005, w/feet, Yasmine, Chloe, Sasha, Jade
NM $2 **MIP** $4

Brutus, 1960s, no feet, black beard and hair
NM $175 **MIP** $250

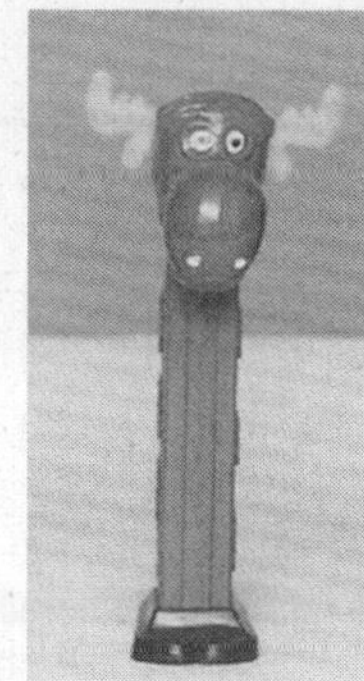

Bullwinkle, 1960s, no feet, brown head, yellow antlers, yellow or brown stem
NM $200 **MIP** $275

Casper the Friendly Ghost, 1950s, no feet, white face
NM $125 **MIP** $200

Chicken Little, 2005, w/feet, Chicken Little, Fish out of Water, Ugly Duckling
NM $1 **MIP** $2

Dino the Dinosaur, 1990s, w/feet, Flintstones
NM $1 **MIP** $2

E.T., 2002, w/feet, w/ or w/out red hood
NM $2 **MIP** $4

Fozzie Bear, 1990s, w/feet, brown head, bow tie, small brown hat
NM $1 **MIP** $2

Fred Flintstone, 1990s, w/feet, Flintstones
NM $1 **MIP** $2

(KP Photo, Sharon Bartsch collection)

Garfield, early 1990s, w/feet, 1st series, orange head, smirk, eyes half shut, shown w/other Series 1 releases
NM $1 **MIP** $2

(KP Photo, Sharon Bartsch collection)

Garfield, late 1990s, w/feet, 2nd series, smiling, eyes wide open
NM $1 **MIP** $2

Garfield Aviator, late 1990s, w/feet, 2nd series, hat and goggles
NM $1 **MIP** $2

Garfield Chef, late 1990s, w/feet, 2nd series, chef's hat, smiling
NM $1 **MIP** $2

Garfield Sleepy, late 1990s, w/feet, 2nd series, night cap
NM $1 **MIP** $2

Garfield w/teeth, early 1990s, w/feet, 1st series, orange head, wide painted toothy grin
NM $1 **MIP** $2

Garfield w/visor, early 1990s, w/feet, 1st series, orange face, green visor
NM $1 **MIP** $2

Gargamel, 1990s, w/feet, second series
NM $2 **MIP** $4

Gonzo, 1990s, w/feet, blue head, yellow eyelids, bow tie
NM $1 **MIP** $2

Green Hornet, 1960s, no feet, green mask and hat; two hat styles exist
NM $175 **MIP** $255

Gundam, 2005, w/feet, individually boxed; Gundam RX-78-2, Char's Zaku MS-06S, Zaku II MS-06F, Z'Gock MSM-07
NM $5 **MIP** $10

Hello Kitty, 2005, w/feet, Aloha Kitty, Hello Kitty w/Rabbit, Hello Kitty, My Melodie
NM $1 **MIP** $2

Hello Kitty, Crystal, 2005, w/feet, crystal versions: Kuririn, Hello Kitty w/Rabbit, Hello Kitty, My Melodie
NM $3 **MIP** $5

Hello Kitty, tin box set, 2006, w/feet, crystal versions in tin box
NM $12 **MIP** $22

(KP Photo, Sharon Bartsch collection)

Homer Simpson, 2000, w/feet, shown w/Maggie, Bart, Lisa, Marge
NM $1 **MIP** $2

Ice Age 2, 2006, w/feet, Manny the mastadon, Diego the saber toothed tiger, Sid the sloth, Scrat the squirrel
NM $1 **MIP** $2

Jack-In-The-Box, 1999, w/feet, restaurant premium, three stem colors - yellow, red, blue
NM $4 **MIP** $10

(KP Photo, Sharon Bartsch collection)

Kermit the Frog, 1990s, w/feet, green head, shown with Miss Piggy, Gonzo, Fozzie
NM $1 **MIP** $2

Lisa Simpson, 2000, w/feet
NM $1 **MIP** $2

Little Orphan Annie, 1982, no feet, light brown hair, flesh face w/black painted features
NM $100 **MIP** $160

Madagascar, 2005, w/feet, Alex the lion, Marty the zebra, Gloria the hippo
NM $1 **MIP** $2

Maggie Simpson, 2000, w/feet
NM $1 **MIP** $2

Marge Simpson, 2000, w/feet
NM $1 **MIP** $2

Miss Piggy, 1990s, w/feet, pink face, yellow hair
NM $1 **MIP** $2

Miss Piggy, 1990s, w/eyelashes
NM $10 **MIP** $15

Miss Piggy B, 1999, w/feet, current version larger ears
NM $1 **MIP** $3

(KP Photo, Sharon Bartsch collection)

Mr. Bean, 2005, w/feet, European release, Mr. Bean, Irma Gobb, Mini Cooper, Teddy
NM $3 **MIP** $6

Mueslix, 1970s, no feet, white beard, moustache and eyebrows, European
NM $2000 **MIP** $2500

Nermal, early 1990s, w/feet, 1st series, gray stem and head
NM $3 **MIP** $5

Nintendo, Diddy Dong, 1990s, w/feet, yellow stem, red cap
NM $4 **MIP** $6

Nintendo, Koopa Trooper, 1990s, w/feet, green stem, orange head
NM $4 **MIP** $6

Nintendo, Mario, 1990s, w/feet, blue stem, red cap
NM $4 **MIP** $6

Nintendo, Yoshi, 1990s, w/feet, red stem, green head
NM $4 **MIP** $6

Obelix, 1970s, no feet, red mustache and hair, blue hat, European
NM $1500 **MIP** $2000

Obelix (1998 foreign issue), 1998, head different than old
NM $3 **MIP** $5

Odie, late 1990s, w/feet, 2nd series, tongue wagging
NM $1 **MIP** $2

Olive Oyl, 1960s, no feet, black hair and flesh painted face
NM $175 **MIP** $250

Open Season, 2006, w/feet, Boog the bear, Elliot the mule deer, McSquizzy the owl, Mr. Weenie the dog
NM $1 **MIP** $3

Over the Hedge, 2006, w/feet, RJ the racoon, Verne the turtle, Stella the skunk, Hammy the squirrel
NM $1 **MIP** $2

Papa Smurf, 1980s, original, no feet, white beard, red hat
NM $10 **MIP** $20

Papa Smurf, 1980s, w/feet, red hat, white beard, blue face
NM $3 **MIP** $6

Papa Smurf, 1990s, w/feet, second series
NM $2 **MIP** $4

Pebbles Flintstone, 1990s, w/feet, Flintstones
NM $1 **MIP** $2

Peter PEZ, 1970s, no feet, blue top hat that says "PEZ," white face, yellow hair
NM $50 **MIP** $65

(KP Photo, Sharon Bartsch collection)

Peter PEZ, 1993-2001, w/feet, remake
NM $1 **MIP** $2

(KP Photo, Sharon Bartsch collection)

Pink Panther, 1990s, w/feet, Pink Panther, Inspector Clouseau (shown here), Ant, Aardvark; value for each
NM $2 **MIP** $4

Pokemon, 2001, w/feet, Pikachu, Meowth, Mew, Psyduck and Kofing; value for each
NM $1 **MIP** $4

Popeye A, 1950s, no feet, yellow face, painted hat
NM $125 **MIP** $150

Popeye B, 1960s, no feet, removable white sailor cap
NM $65 **MIP** $100

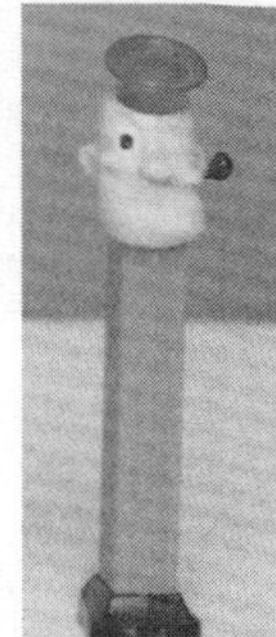

Popeye C, 1970s, no feet, one eye painted, removeable pipe and red cap. Shown here in stand.
NM $85 **MIP** $125

(KP Photo, Sharon Bartsch collection)

Sesame Street, 2004, w/feet, Bert (shown), Ernie (shown), Zoe, Elmo, Cookie Monster (shown), Big Bird
NM $1 **MIP** $2

Sesame Street, 35th Anniversary, 2004, w/feet, crystal versions of Cookie Monster, Big Bird and Elmo. Each came in own commemorative box
NM $15 **MIP** $25

Shrek 2, 2004, w/feet, European release, Shrek, Fiona, Donkey, Puss 'n Boots
NM $1 **MIP** $2

Shrek the Third, 2007, w/feet, Shrek, Fiona, Donkey, Puss 'n Boots
NM $1 **MIP** $2

Smurf, 1980s, original, no feet, blue face, white hat
NM $10 **MIP** $20

Smurf, 1980s, w/feet, blue face, white hat
NM $3 **MIP** $6

Smurf, 1990s, w/feet, second series
NM $2 **MIP** $4

Smurfette, 1980s, original, no feet, blue face, white hat
NM $10 **MIP** $20

Smurfette, 1980s, w/feet, blue face, yellow hair, white hat
NM $3 **MIP** $8

Smurfette, 1990s, w/feet, second series
NM $2 **MIP** $4

Sponge Bob Squarepants, 2004, w/feet, Sponge Bob, Patrick, Squidward
NM $1 **MIP** $3

(KP Photo, Sharon Bartsch collection)

Teenage Mutant Ninja Turtles, 1990s, four different characters, 1st series, shown w/one new series on left
NM $2 **MIP** $3

Teenage Mutant Ninja Turtles, 2005, w/feet, new series, angry faces, Michaelangelo, Raphael, Donatello, Leonardo
NM $1 **MIP** $2

Tweenies, 2002, w/feet, 5 characters, Jake, Fuzz, Milo, Bella, and Doodles
NM $2 **MIP** $4

Merry Music Makers

Camel, 1980s, w/feet, brown face w/red fez hat
NM $35 **MIP** $50

(KP Photo, Sharon Bartsch collection)

Clown, 1980s, w/feet, green hat, foreign issue (Merry Music Makers)
NM $5 **MIP** $10

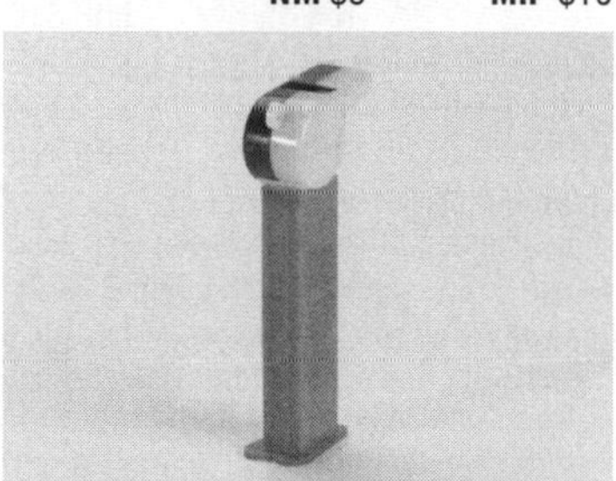
(KP Photo, Sharon Bartsch collection)

Coach's Whistle, 1980s, no feet and w/feet, police whistles on top
NM $25 **MIP** $40

Dog, 1980s, no feet and w/feet
NM $20 **MIP** $40

Donkey, 1980s, w/feet, gray head w/pink nose, whistlehead
NM $5 **MIP** $10

Duck, 1980s, no feet, brown head w/yellow beak, whistlehead
NM $30 **MIP** $55

Duck, 1980s, w/feet, brown head w/yellow beak, whistlehead
NM $25 **MIP** $50

Frog, 1980s, no feet, yellow and green head w/black eyes, foreign issue
NM $40 **MIP** $50

Frog, 1980s, w/feet, yellow and green head w/black eyes, foreign issue
NM $35 **MIP** $45

Indian, 1980s, w/feet, black hair and green headband w/feather, foreign issue (Merry Music Makers)
NM $15 **MIP** $25

Koala, 1980s, w/feet, brown head w/a black nose, foreign issue, whistlehead
NM $3 **MIP** $5

Lamb, 1980s, no feet, pink stem, white head, whistle
NM $10 **MIP** $25

Monkey, 1980s, w/feet, whistle head, tan monkey face in brown head, foreign issue
NM $12 **MIP** $25

Parrot, 1980s, w/feet, red hair, yellow beak and green eyes, whistle head
NM $5 **MIP** $10

Penguin, 1980s, w/feet, penguin head w/yellow beak and red hat, foreign issue, whistle head
NM $5 **MIP** $10

(KP Photo, Sharon Bartsch collection)

Pig Whistle, 1980s, w/feet, pink head, whistlehead
NM $25 **MIP** $50

Rhino, 1980s, w/feet, green head, red horn, foreign issue, whistle head
NM $5 **MIP** $10

Rooster, 1980s, no feet, white head, comb
NM $40 **MIP** $65

Tiger, 1980s, w/feet, tiger head w/white snout, whistle head
NM $5 **MIP** $10

MGM

Barney Bear, 1980s, w/feet, brown head, white cheeks and snout, black nose
NM $15 **MIP** $30

Barney Bear, 1980s, no feet, brown head, white cheeks and snout, black nose
NM $30 **MIP** $45

Droopy Dog A, 1980s, w/feet, white face, flesh snout, black movable ears and red hair
NM $10 **MIP** $25

Droopy Dog B, 1992, w/feet, painted ears
NM $5 **MIP** $6

Jerry (Tom & Jerry), 1980s, w/feet, brown face, multiple piece head
NM $8 **MIP** $10

Jerry (Tom & Jerry), 1980s, no feet, rare variation w/brown face, pink lining in ears is removable
NM $75 **MIP** $125

Spike, 1980s, w/feet, brown face, pink snout
NM $5 **MIP** $6

MGM

Tom A (Tom & Jerry), 1980s, no feet, gray cat head w/painted black features
NM $25 **MIP** $35

Tom B (Tom & Jerry), 1980s, w/feet, gray cat head w/removable facial features
NM $10 **MIP** $15

Tuffy, 1990s, w/feet, non-U.S. release, similar to Jerry but has gray face rather than Jerry's brown
NM $3 **MIP** $6

Tyke, 1990s, w/feet, brown head
NM $10 **MIP** $25

Miscellaneous

Advertising Regular, 1950s, no feet, no head, advertising printed on side MUST be complete
NM $1500 **MIP** n/a

Arithmetic Regular, 1960s, no feet, headless dispenser w/white top, side of body has openings w/columns of numbers
NM $500 **MIP** $700

Barky Brown, 2005, w/feet, special edition for Australia's Animal Welfare League
NM $10 **MIP** $18

Baseball, 2002, w/feet, Arizona Diamondbacks, LSU (2004), Philadelphia Phillies
NM $25 **MIP** $35

Baseball Dispenser Set, 1960s, no feet, baseball glove w/ball, bat, white home plate marked "PEZ"
NM $500 **MIP** $800

Baseball Glove only, 1960s, no feet, brown baseball glove w/white ball
NM $125 **MIP** $150

Basketball, 2002-2005, w/feet, Seattle Sonics, Washington Mystics, Connecticut Suns
NM $20 **MIP** $40

(KP Photo, Sharon Bartsch collection)

Bubbleman, 1996, w/feet, Neon, Crystal, and Glowing varieties
NM $5 **MIP** $9

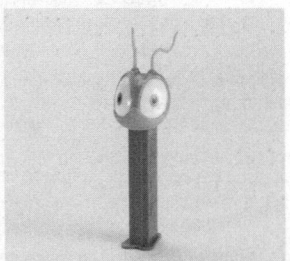

(KP Photo, Sharon Bartsch collection)

Bugz, 2000, w/feet, Jumpin' Jack (grasshopper), Sam Snuffle (fly), Florence Flutterfly (butterfly, shown here), Super Bee (bee), Sweet Ladybird, Clumsy Worm, Baby Bee, Centipede
NM $1 **MIP** $2

Bugz, Crystal, 2002, w/feet, crystal series of all Bugz characters
NM $2 **MIP** $5

Candy Shooter, 1960s, black gun w/PEZ logo on stock
NM $85 **MIP** $135

Candy Shooter, 1960s, red body, white grip, w/German license and double PEZ candy
NM $65 **MIP** $85

Cat with Derby (Puzzy Cat), 1970s, no feet, blue hat most valuable
NM $80 **MIP** $125

Crazy Animals, 1999, w/feet, not sold in U.S., Frog, Shark, Octopus, Camel
NM $2 **MIP** $4

Crystal Ball, 2002, w/base, mail-in premium, silver or blue stars
NM $10 **MIP** $16

eBay, 2000, crystal head dispensers, set of 4
NM $40 **MIP** $60

eBay Crystal Hearts, 2000, w/feet, yellow, blue, red or green crystal hearts w/eBay logo
NM $5 **MIP** $10

eBay Employee Heart, 2000, w/feet, black stem, white heart, eBay logo
NM $45 **MIP** $75

Elephant, early 1960s, aka Political Elephant, gold or black, one-piece head
NM $3000 **MIP** $10000

Funky Faces, 2003, w/feet, round heads w/13 different expressions: Open Smile, Cool Sunglasses Smile, Nerdy Egghead, Smiley Face, Winking Smiley Face, Kissy Face, Smiling w/Eyelashes, Baby Face, Crying Face, Smiley w/Tongue, Embarassed Face, Angry Face, Toothy Smile
NM $1 **MIP** $2

Katrina PEZ, 2005, w/feet, issued to raise funds for hurricane victims, red stem, white ball w/"Katrina August 29, 2005 10:30 am"
NM $50 **MIP** $75

Make-A-Face, 1970s, no card, feet, oversized head w/18 facial parts
NM $2000 **MIP** $2500

Make-A-Face, 1970s, German "Super Spiel" card
NM $2500 **MIP** $3000

Make-A-Face, 1970s, American card
NM $2400 **MIP** $3400

NASCAR Helmets, 2005, w/feet, helmets of drivers: Richard Petty, Rusty Wallace, Kasey Kane, Bobby LaBonte, Tony Stewart, Matt Kenseth, Jeff Gordon
NM $2 **MIP** $4

NCAA Footballs, 2006, w/feet, football w/team logos: Penn State, Georgia, Texas, Florida, Florida St., Michigan, Alabama
NM $1 **MIP** $2

NCAA Footballs, 2007, w/feet, Ohio State, Notre Dame, Univ. of Louisville
NM $1 **MIP** $2

Octopus, 1970s, no feet, red head
NM $70 **MIP** $90

Personalized Regular, 1960s, no feet, no head, paper label for monogramming
NM $175 **MIP** $250

(KP Photo, Sharon Bartsch collection)

Pez-A-Saurs (Dinosaurs), 1993, four different dinosaurs, Hesaur, Shesaur, Flysaur, Isaur
NM $2 **MIP** $5

Pez-A-Saurs (Dinosaurs), Crystal, 1999, w/feet, mail-in premium
NM $2 **MIP** $4

Phone, not sold in the U.S.
NM $2 **MIP** $5

Psychedelic Flower, 1960s, no feet, stem w/decal on side, many color variations
NM $225 **MIP** $400

Psychedelic Flower, 1998, reproduction
NM $10 **MIP** $20

Psychedelic Hand, 1960s, no feet, decal design on stem, beige or black hands; many color variations, shown with Psychedelic Flower
NM $200 **MIP** $350

Psychedelic Hand, 1998, 1998 limited edition, has 1967 copyright date
NM $10 **MIP** $20

Regular, 1950s, no feet, no head, stem w/top only
NM $80 **MIP** $160

Regular, 1990s, no feet, no head, stem w/top only; assorted colors; reissues
NM $2 **MIP** $3

Roman Soldier (1998 foreign issue), 1998, w/feet, Asterix series featured this dispenser and reissues of the 1970s releases
NM $4 **MIP** $6

Smiley, 2000s, w/feet, Wal-Mart character exclusive
NM $1 **MIP** $3

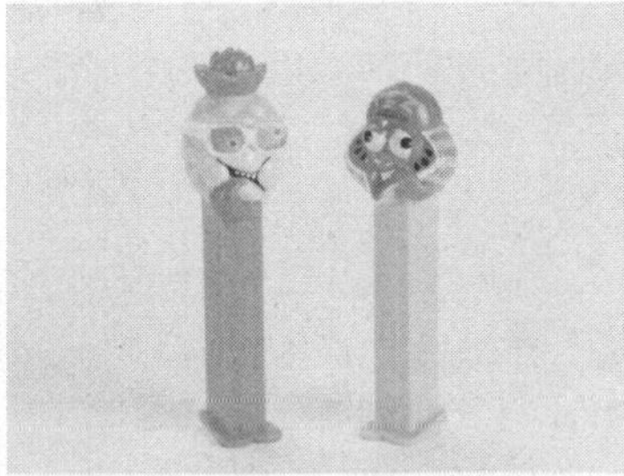

(KP Photo, Sharon Bartsch collection)

Sourz, 2002, w/feet, Pineapple (shown), Blue Raspberry, Watermelon (shown), Green Apple
NM $1 **MIP** $2

Space Gun 1950s, 1950s, various colors
NM $275 **MIP** $500

Space Gun 1980s, 1980s, red or silver, on blister pack
NM $150 **MIP** $200

Space Gun 1980s, 1980s, red, loose
NM $55 **MIP** $85

Space Gun 1980s, 1980s, silver
NM $100 **MIP** $125

Space Trooper, 1950s, full bodied robot, gold, "PEZ" on back
NM $1400 **MIP** $2000

Space Trooper, 1950s, full bodied robot w/backpack; blue, red, or yellow
NM $250 **MIP** $375

Sports teams, 2000-present, w/feet, professional baseball, basketball, soccer teams
NM $20 **MIP** $30

USA Hearts, 2002, w/feet, mail in offer, 6 different hearts that say "USA"
NM $1 **MIP** $2

Zielpunkt, 1999, w/feet, from Austrian grocery chain
NM $10 **MIP** $15

Olympics

Alpine Man, 1972, 1972 Munich Olympics, no feet, green hat w/beige plume, black mustache
NM $2000 **MIP** $2500

Vucko Wolf, 1984, 1984 Sarajevo Olympics issue, w/feet, gray or brown face
NM $200 **MIP** $350

Vucko Wolf, 1984, 1984 Sarajevo Olympics issue, w/feet, gray or brown face w/ski hat
NM $300 **MIP** $500

(Barry Koester)

Vucko Wolf, 1984, 1984 Sarajevo Olympics issue, w/feet, gray or brown face w/bobsled helmet
NM $300 **MIP** $500

Winter Olympics Snowman, 1976, 1976 Innsbruck, red nose and hat, white head w/arms extended, black eyes, blue smile
NM $375 **MIP** $425

Peanuts

Charlie Brown, 1990s, w/feet, blue cap, eyes closed
NM $45 **MIP** $75

Charlie Brown, 1990s, w/feet, blue cap, smile w/red tongue at corner
NM $15 **MIP** $20

(KP Photo, Sharon Bartsch collection)

Charlie Brown, 1990s, w/feet, crooked smile, blue cap, shown w/Woodstock, Snoopy, Lucy
NM $1 **MIP** $2

Charlie Brown Cubs, 2001, w/feet, first PEZ Cubs promotion
NM $5 **MIP** $15

Charlie Brown Yankees, 2003, w/feet, Yankees cap
NM $20 **MIP** $30

Lucy, 1990s, w/feet, black hair
NM $1 **MIP** $2

(KP Photo, Sharon Bartsch collection)

Peppermint Patty, 2000, w/foot, green stem, smiling. Shown w/Snoopy as Joe Cool and Charlie Brown
NM $1 **MIP** $2

Snoopy, 1990s, w/feet, w/white head and black ears
NM $1 **MIP** $2

Snoopy as Joe Cool, 2000, w/feet, black stem, sunglasses
NM $1 **MIP** $2

Woodstock, 1990s, w/painted feathers
NM $5 **MIP** $10

Woodstock, 1990s, w/feet, yellow head
NM $1 **MIP** $2

PEZ Pals

Boy, 1960s, no feet, brown hair
NM $20 **MIP** $35

Boy with Cap, 1960s, no feet, white hair, blue cap
NM $85 **MIP** $100

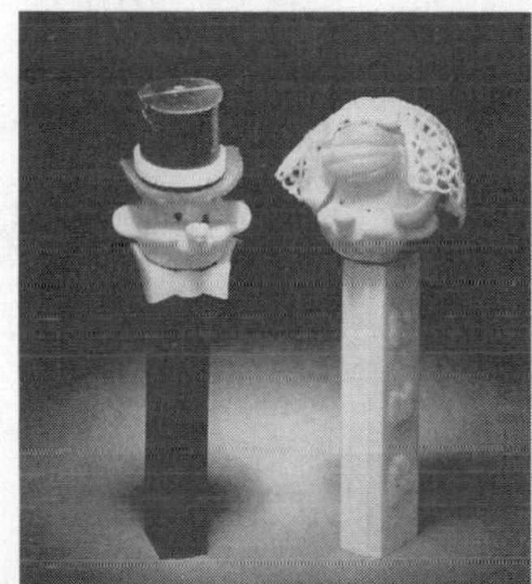

Bride, 1970s, no feet, white veil, light brown, blond or red hair. Shown here with Groom
NM $1500 **MIP** $2000

Bride, limited edition, 2000s, w/feet, mail-order
NM $10 **MIP** $20

Doctor, 1970s, no feet, white hair and mustache, gray reflector on white band, black stethoscope
NM $175 **MIP** $225

PEZ Pals

Engineer, 1970s, no feet, blue hat
NM $100 **MIP** $175

Fireman, 1970s, no feet, red hat w/gray #1 insignia
NM $75 **MIP** $95

Girl, 1970s, no feet, blond pigtails
NM $25 **MIP** $35

Girl, 1970s, w/feet, pigtails
NM $4 **MIP** $8

Groom, 1970s, no feet, black top hat, white bow tie
NM $500 **MIP** $775

Groom, limited edition, 2000s, w/feet, mail-order
NM $15 **MIP** $25

Knight, 1970s, no feet, gray helmet w/plume
NM $400 **MIP** $600

Maharajah, 1970s, no feet, green turban w/red inset
NM $60 **MIP** $85

Mexican, 1960s, no feet, yellow sombrero, black beard and mustache, two earrings
NM $140 **MIP** $185

Nurse, 1970s, no feet, hair color variations, white nurse's cap
NM $150 **MIP** $220

Pirate, 1970s, no feet, red cap, patch over right eye
NM $50 **MIP** $60

Policeman, 1970s, no feet, blue hat w/gray badge
NM $60 **MIP** $75

Ringmaster, 1970s, no feet, white bow tie, white hat w/red hatband, and black handlebar moustache
NM $200 **MIP** $325

Sailor, 1960s, no feet, blue hat, white beard
NM $150 **MIP** $200

Sheik, 1970s, no feet, white head drape, headband
NM $75 **MIP** $95

Sheriff, 1970s, no feet, brown hat w/badge
NM $125 **MIP** $175

Premiums

Cocoa Marsh Spaceman, 1950s, no feet, clear helmet on small male head, w/Cocoa Marsh embossed on side
NM $175 **MIP** $225

Donkey Kong Jr., 1980s, no feet, blond monkey face, dark hair, white cap w/"J" on it, w/box
NM $250 **MIP** $500

Golden Glow, 1950s, no feet, no head, gold stem and top
NM $80 **MIP** $150

Hippo, 1970s, no feet, green stem w/"Hippo" printed on side, foreign issue
NM $650 **MIP** $900

Lion's Club Lion, 1962, no feet, stem imprinted "1962 Lion's Club Inter'l Convention," yellow roaring lion head
NM $2000 **MIP** $3000

Sparefroh (foreign issue), 1970s, no feet, green stem, red triangle hat, coin glued on stem
NM $575 **MIP** $850

Stand By Me, 1986, dispenser packed w/mini film poster and candy
NM $150 **MIP** $200

Regulars

Witch Regular, 1950s, no feet, orange stem w/black witch graphics, no head
NM $2000 **MIP** $3500

Sport Toons

Bugs Bunny, 1999
NM $1 **MIP** $3

Daffy Duck, 1999
NM $1 **MIP** $3

Sylvester, 1999
NM $1 **MIP** $3

(KP Photo, Sharon Bartsch collection)

Taz, 1999
NM $1 **MIP** $3

Tweety, 1999, w/feet, baseball cap
NM $1 **MIP** $3

Star Wars

Boba Fett, 1999, with feet, 2nd series
NM $1 **MIP** $4

C-3PO, 1990s, with feet, 1st series
NM $1 **MIP** $4

(KP Photo, Sharon Bartsch collection)

Chewbacca, 1990s, with feet, 1st series, shown w/other 1st Series releases
NM $1 **MIP** $4

Clone Trooper, 2002, with feet, 3rd series
NM $1 **MIP** $3

Darth Vader, 1990s, with feet, 1st series. Shown here with other 1st series releases.
NM $1 **MIP** $4

Darth Vader, 2000s, current
NM $1 **MIP** $2

Death Star, 2005, with feet, 4th series
NM $1 **MIP** $2

Emperor Palpatine, 2005, with feet, 4th series, red cloak
NM $1 **MIP** $2

Ewok, 1999, with feet, 2nd series
NM $1 **MIP** $4

General Grievous, 2005, with feet, 4th series
NM $1 **MIP** $2

Jango Fett, 2002, with feet, 3rd series
NM $1 **MIP** $3

Luke Skywalker, 1999, with feet, 2nd series, pilot
NM $1 **MIP** $4

(KP Photo, Sharon Bartsch collection)

Princess Leia, 1999, with feet, 2nd series, shown w/Boba Fett and Ewok
NM $1 **MIP** $4

R2-D2, 2002, with feet, 3rd series
NM $1 **MIP** $3

Stormtrooper, 1990s, with feet, 1st series
NM $1 **MIP** $4

Wookie Warrior, 2005, with feet, 4th series
NM $1 **MIP** $2

Yoda, 1990s, with feet, 1st series
NM $1 **MIP** $4

Superheroes

Batgirl, 1970s, Soft Head Superhero, no feet, blue mask, black hair
NM $120 **MIP** $150

Batman, 1960s, no feet, blue cape, mask and hat
NM $100 **MIP** $125

Batman, 1970s, Soft Head Superhero, no feet, blue mask
NM $150 **MIP** $225

Batman, 1970s, w/feet, blue
NM $3 **MIP** $6

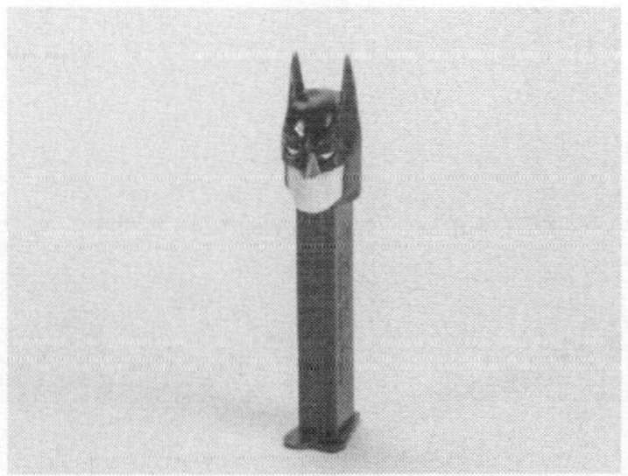

(KP Photo, Sharon Bartsch collection)

Batman, 1990s, w/feet, large ears, dark blue, current
NM $1 **MIP** $2

Captain America, 1970s, blue mask
NM $125 **MIP** $150

Captain America, 1970s, no feet, blue cowl, black mask w/white letter A
NM $150 **MIP** $175

Hulk A, 1970s, no feet, dark green head, black hair
NM $30 **MIP** $60

Hulk B, 1970s, no feet, light green head, dark green hair
NM $25 **MIP** $30

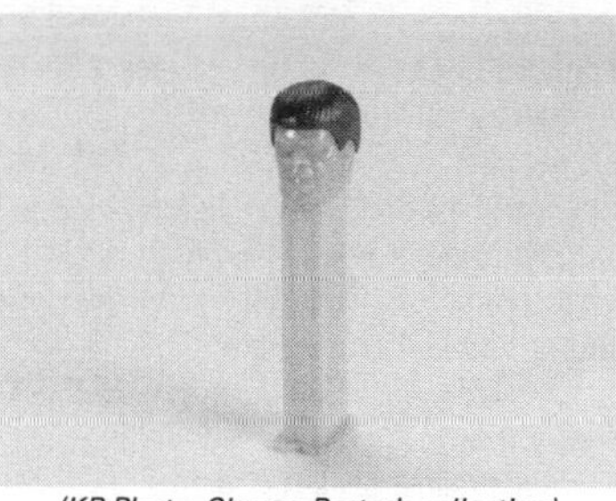

(KP Photo, Sharon Bartsch collection)

Hulk B, 1970s, w/feet, light green head, tall dark green hair
NM $3 **MIP** $6

Hulk C, 1999, w/teeth
NM $1 **MIP** $2

Joker, 1970s, Soft Head Superhero, no feet, green painted hair
NM $150 **MIP** $200

Penguin (Batman villain), 1970s, Soft Head Superhero, no feet, yellow top hat, black painted monocle, whistlehead
NM $130 **MIP** $175

Spider-Man A, 1970s, no feet, small head w/black eyes
NM $10 **MIP** $15

(KP Photo, Sharon Bartsch collection)

Spider-Man B, 1980s, w/feet, bigger head
NM $1 **MIP** $2

Spider-Man C, 1990s, w/feet, larger head
NM $1 **MIP** $2

Thor, 1970s, no feet, yellow hair, gray winged helmet
NM $225 **MIP** $325

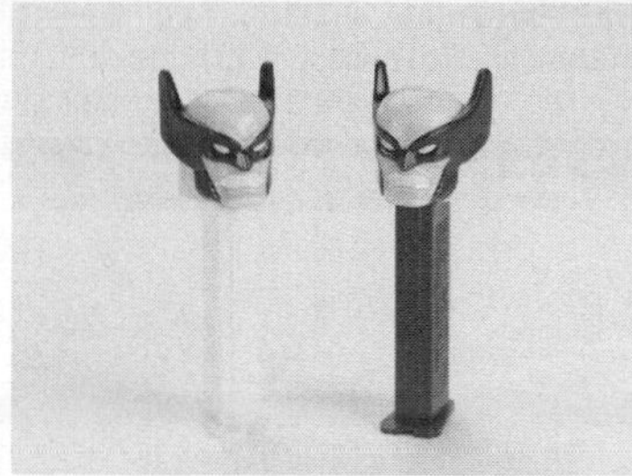

(KP Photo, Sharon Bartsch collection)

Wolverine, 1999, w/feet
NM $1 **MIP** $2

Wonder Woman, 1970s, Soft Head Superhero, no feet, black hair and yellow band w/raised red star
NM $100 **MIP** $165

Wonder Woman, 1970s, no feet, black hair and yellow band w/red star
NM $5 **MIP** $10

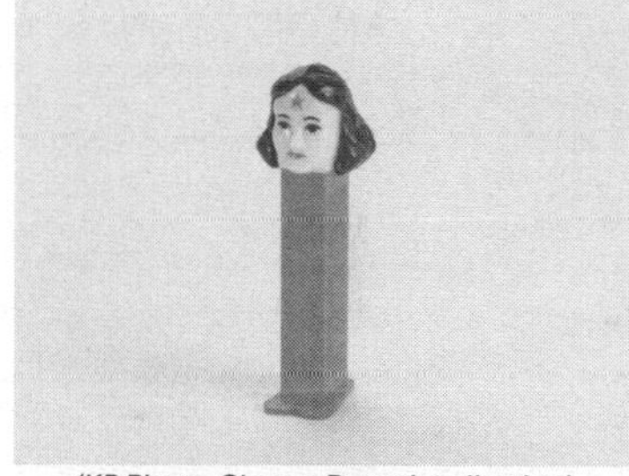

(KP Photo, Sharon Bartsch collection)

Wonder Woman, 1990s, w/feet, red stem
NM $1 **MIP** $3

Trucks

Truck A, 1970s, cab, stem body, single rear axle
NM $50 **MIP** $90

Truck B, 1970s, cab, stem body, dual rear axle and dual arch fenders
NM $40 **MIP** $65

(KP Photo, Sharon Bartsch collection)

Truck C, 1980s, cab, stem body, dual rear wheels w/single arch fender, movable wheels
NM $15 **MIP** $20

Truck D, 1990s, cab, stem body, dual rear wheels, single arch fender, nonmovable wheels
NM $1 **MIP** $2

Trucks 2005, 2005, darker cabs and trailers, four different styles
NM $1 **MIP** $2

Trucks

Walgreens Trucks, 2005, set of 2, Walgreens logos
NM $2 **MIP** $4

Wal-Mart Trucks, 2006-07, four different cab styles to collect, white trucks
NM $1 **MIP** $2

Universal Monsters

Creature From the Black Lagoon, 1960s, no feet, green head and matching stem, w/copyright
NM $225 **MIP** $275

Frankenstein, 1960s, no feet, black hair, gray head
NM $180 **MIP** $300

(Barry Koester)

Wolf Man, 1960s, no feet, black stem, gray head
NM $200 **MIP** $275

Valentine's Day

Boy and Girl PEZ Pals, 1970s, no feet, value for each
NM $125 **MIP** $185

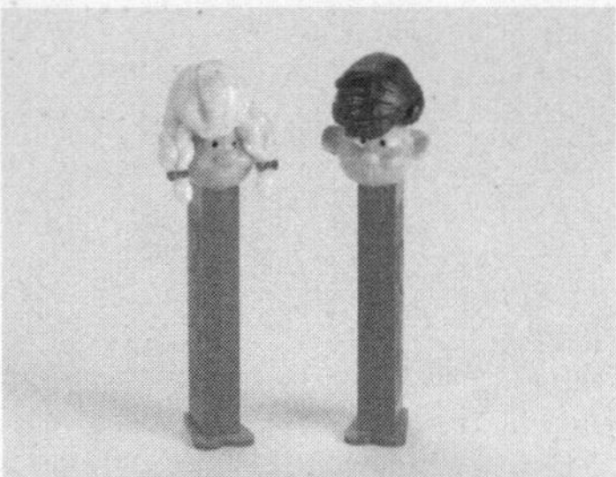

(KP Photo, Sharon Bartsch collection)

Boy and Girl PEZ Pals, 1980s/1990s, w/feet
NM $15 **MIP** $22

Valentine Heart, 1990s, no feet, red stem
NM $1 **MIP** $2

Warner Brothers

Bugs Bunny, w/feet, gray head w/white cheeks
NM $2 **MIP** $4

Bugs Bunny, 1970s, no feet, gray head w/white cheeks
NM $15 **MIP** $22

Cool Cat, 1980, w/feet, orange head, blue snout, black ears
NM $50 **MIP** $75

Daffy Duck A, 1970s, no feet, black head, yellow beak, removable white eyes
NM $10 **MIP** $15

Daffy Duck B, w/feet, black head, yellow beak
NM $3 **MIP** $5

Foghorn Leghorn, 1980s, no feet, brown head, yellow beak, red wattle
NM $75 **MIP** $95

Foghorn Leghorn, 1980s, w/feet, brown head, yellow beak, red wattle
NM $60 **MIP** $85

Henry Hawk, 1980s, w/feet
NM $55 **MIP** $80

Henry Hawk, 1980s, no feet, light brown head, yellow beak
NM $60 **MIP** $95

Looney Tunes Back in Action, 2003, w/feet, European release, Taz, Daffy, Tweety, Bugs, Yosemite Sam
NM $4 **MIP** $8

Merlin Mouse, 1980s, no feet, gray head w/flesh cheeks, green hat
NM $20 **MIP** $30

Merlin Mouse, 1980s, w/feet, gray head w/flesh cheeks, green hat
NM $10 **MIP** $15

Petunia Pig, 1980s, w/or without feet, black hair in pigtails
NM $25 **MIP** $35

Road Runner A, 1980s, no feet, purple head, yellow beak
NM $25 **MIP** $35

Road Runner B, 1980s, w/feet, purple head, yellow beak
NM $15 **MIP** $20

(KP Photo, Sharon Bartsch collection)

Speedy Gonzales, w/feet, brown head, yellow sombrero
NM $12 **MIP** $20

Speedy Gonzales, 1970s, no feet, brown head, yellow sombrero
NM $30 **MIP** $45

Sylvester, w/feet, black head, white whiskers, red nose
NM $1 **MIP** $2

Sylvester, 1970s, no feet, black head, white whiskers, red nose
NM $10 **MIP** $15

Tweety Bird, with feet, painted eyes
NM $3 **MIP** $5

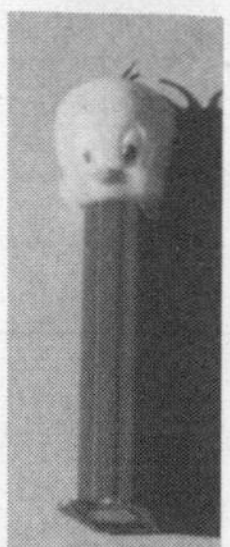

Tweety Bird, 1970s, no feet, painted eyes
NM $14 **MIP** $20

Tweety Bird, 1970s, no feet, removable eyes
NM $17 **MIP** $25

Wile E. Coyote, 1980s, no feet, brown head
NM $60 **MIP** $75

Wile E. Coyote, 1980s, w/feet, brown head
NM $30 **MIP** $40

(KP Photo, Sharon Bartsch collection)

Yosemite Sam, 1990s, w/feet
NM $2 **MIP** $4

Robots

by Karen O'Brien

The word "robot" is derived from the Czech world "robota" meaning forced labor or drudgery. The word quickly gained usage in English after 1920.

The style, look, composition, and purpose of robots has changed quite a bit throughout the past sixty years, since the time when the earliest toy robots were made. But collectors have remained enamored of the artistry, design, and function of these otherworldly pieces of pop culture.

Think of a toy robot, and it's likely you'll think of Japan. As early as the 1940s, Japan was making somewhat crude walking robots. Among the earliest is Atomic Robot Man, made in occupied Japan in the late 1940s. The small robot, a mere five inches tall, featured clunky red feet, a blank facial expression, and oversized gauges. Its value, like many early robots, can soar to four figures or more in Mint-in-Box condition.

The 1950s was the true golden age of robots and space toys. Science fiction exploded into the pop culture sensibilities with television shows and movies catering to space themes. The lithographed tin toymakers in Japan responded accordingly, setting the world awash in a sea of spacemen robots. One of the world's major Japanese makers of robots at the time was Alps.

Notable entries to the robot field in the 1950s included Ideal's Robert the Robot, unusual because it was made of plastic, unlike Japan's tin-litho giants. Louis Marx's Japanese subsidiary, Linemar, also brought many Japanese-made robots to the United States.

Easily the most popular robots ever made are known as the Gang of Five—a series of five skirted robots made in the mid-1950s by Masudaya of Japan. These stunningly colorful robots (the most familiar is the Lavender Robot) have easily commanded five to six figures when sold at top-of-the-line space auctions.

According to Jim Bunte's book, *Vintage Toys* (Krause Publications, 1999), "Japan had dominated the 1950s robot and space toy category with innovation, creativity, and perhaps most important, low price points.

"Yet their success was also their undoing, because as the Japanese saw their standard of living grow, the costs associated with their successful industries also rose, reducing their marketplace competitiveness...Most Japanese toymakers fought this losing battle well into the decade, but by the end of the 1960s, most had either vanished or constricted precipitously. In fact, as the 1970s dawned, it was becoming difficult to find playthings on American toy shelves marked 'Made in Japan.'"

By the mid-1970s, interest in robots and space toys had waned. Japan's reign in the space toys arena had fallen. Items made in Hong Kong and Taiwan were more readily available.

By the late 1970s, however, the space toy world would turn its focus from robots and space men to Star Wars and other licensed realms.

The exciting historic and artistic world of robot toys would be gone, but those toys remain valuable vintage icons.

THE *TOP 10* ROBOTS (In Mint Condition)

1. Machine Man, Masudaya, 1950s	$45,000
2. Robby Space Patrol, Nomura/TN, 1957	37,000
3. Musical Drummer Robot R-57, Nomura/TN, 1950s	20,000
4. Giant Sonic Robot (Train Robot), Masudaya, 1959	16,000
5. Deep-Sea Robot, Naito Shoten, 1956	16,000
6. Mr Atomic, Cragstan, 1962	15,000
7. Eightman, Yonezawa, 1966	10,000
8. Robot Lilliput, KTA-Japan, 1939	10,000
9. Thunder Robot, Asakusa-Japan, 1950s	9,000
10. Radar Robot, ASC-Japan, 1950s	7,000

Advance Toys

Mr. Atom, 1960s, 18", red and silver plastic, battery-operated. "The Electronic Walking Robot... Completely Harmless," according to the box
EX $125 **NM** $300 **MIP** $650

AHI

Lost in Space Robot, 1977, battery-operated, different in design than the Robinson family's companion but desirable, 12"
EX $150 **NM** $300 **MIP** $500

Alps

Cragstan Great Astronaut, 1960s, 11", red tin, battery-operated, w/video scene, key in head
EX $500 **NM** $1250 **MIP** $2000

Door Robot, 1958, 9 1/2", tin, battery-operated, remote cont, revolving head
EX $725 **NM** $1700 **MIP** $3500

Mechanical Television Spaceman, 1965, wind-up, w/chest scene and antenna, 7"
EX $95 **NM** $185 **MIP** $500

Mr. Robot the Mechanical Brain, 1954, tin wind-up
EX $500 **NM** $1000 **MIP** $1500

Television Space Man, 1959, battery-operated, chest video, key in head operates as antenna, 11"
EX $175 **NM** $350 **MIP** $800

AN-Japan

Astronaut Robot, 1950s, wind-up, tanks on back, gun in hand, 8"
EX $500 **NM** $1250 **MIP** $2000

Arco

Ro-Gun "It's A Robot", 1984, robot changes into a rifle
EX $11 **NM** $16 **MIP** $25

Asak

Space Guard Pilot, 1975, 8"
EX $20 **NM** $30 **MIP** $45

Asakusa-Japan

Thunder Robot, 1950s, battery-operated, w/antenna and guns in palms of hands, 11"
EX $1500 **NM** $5000 **MIP** $9000

ASC Japan

Radar Robot, 1950s, wind-up, orange body, rotating antenna, chest sparks, 11"
EX $1500 **NM** $4000 **MIP** $7000

Bandai

Batman, 1960s, battery-operated, juvenille apperance, vinyl and tin, symbol lights in chest, rare, 10"
EX n/a **NM** n/a **MIP** n/a

Moon Explorer, 1958, battery-operated, chest-mounted clock, antenna on head, 14"
EX $600 **NM** $1300 **MIP** $2000

CDI

Star Robot, 1978, battery-operated, knock-off Storm Trooper helmet, chest cannons behind a door, made in Hong Kong, 11"
EX $50 **NM** $150 **MIP** $225

Cragstan

Astronaut, 1961, battery-operated, head-mounted antenna spins, jackhammer gun, barrel chest, 11"
EX $300 **NM** $650 **MIP** $1200

Astronaut, 1962, battery-operated, round chest, laster rifle in right hand, "Cragstan Astronaut" written on waist, 15"
EX $275 **NM** $550 **MIP** $900

Countdown-Y, 1960s, 9"
EX $125 **NM** $175 **MIP** $275

Cragstan Robot, 1962, battery-operated, bump-and-go action, silver body, skirted legs, plastic domed head, 12"
EX $500 **NM** $1100 **MIP** $1800

Cragstan's Mr. Robot, 1960s, battery-operated, red or white body, clear dome head, 10-1/2"
EX $325 **NM** $525 **MIP** $925

Magnor, 1975, 9", plastic, 9"
EX $23 **NM** $35 **MIP** $50

Mr. Atomic, 1962, rare, battery-operated, bump-and-go action, built by Yonezawa, 16 lights under plastic dome, 9"
EX $5000 **NM** $10000 **MIP** $15000

Mr. LEM Astronaut Robot, 1970, battery-operated, rotates, 13"
EX $150 **NM** $310 **MIP** $475

Mr. Robot, 1960, battery-operated, skirted legs, "Cragstan Mr. Robot" on chest, red body (white body variation worth 25% more), black wrench arms,, 12"
EX $600 **NM** $1200 **MIP** $1700

Space Robot Patrol, 1959, friction motor, robot driving red Mercedes convertible, 11" long
EX $500 **NM** $1000 **MIP** $1500

Talking Robot, 1963, battery-operated voice, friction-motor robot, three functions, says four messages, "Cragstan Talking Robot" on chest, 12"
EX $375 **NM** $650 **MIP** $1300

Daiya

Astro Captain, 1970s, wind-up, red/white/blue sparker, NASA on helmet, 6"
EX $35 **NM** $65 **MIP** $125

Diaya

Astronaut, 1963, battery-operated, identical to Cragstan Astronaut, different litho design, laser rifle, 15"
EX $600 **NM** $1300 **MIP** $2200

Durham

Robot 2500, 1970s, battery-operated, "cyclops", 10"
EX $25 **NM** $45 **MIP** $65

Dux

Astroman, 1962, battery-operated w/ corded remote, green plastic allows view of inner workings, antenna on head, 12"
EX $500 **NM** $1100 **MIP** $1750

Haji

Space Trooper, 1955, wind-up, human face in helmet, holding rifle across left arm, blue barrel chest, yellow arms and legs
EX $500 **NM** $1000 **MIP** $1750

Hong Kong

Action Robot, 1970s, battery-operated, yellow/blue, multiple functions, 10"
EX $15 **NM** $35 **MIP** $55

Radar Hunter, 1970s, wind-up, red/silver or orange, 5"
EX $15 **NM** $35 **MIP** $55

Robbie Robot, 1970s, battery-operated, blue/red/yellow, blinks, 9"
EX $25 **NM** $45 **MIP** $85

See-Thru Robot, 1970s, battery-operated, clear head and chest w/gears, 10"
EX $125 **NM** $325 **MIP** $600

Sounding Robot, 1970s, battery-operated, three push buttons on head, 8"
EX $25 **NM** $50 **MIP** $75

Sparking Robot, 1970s, wind-up, black body, 6"
EX $20 **NM** $35 **MIP** $50

Star Robot, 1970s, battery-operated, Star Wars Storm Trooper head, 10"
EX $25 **NM** $45 **MIP** $70

Horikawa/SH

Astronaut, 1963, battery-operated, human face, opening chest doors w/firing guns, 11"
EX $200 **NM** $400 **MIP** $700

Attack Robot, 1962, battery-operated, block head w/mesh eyes, chest doors open and guns fire, 11"
EX $250 **NM** $450 **MIP** $650

Attacking Martian, 1964, battery-operated, guns in chest, red mesh eyes, black body, 11"
EX $100 **NM** $250 **MIP** $425

Battle Robot, 1962, battery-operated, silver body, round eyes, red lights on head, 11"
EX $200 **NM** $350 **MIP** $575

Cosmic Fighter Robot, 1970s, head opens to reveal gunner inside while body spins, 11-1/2"
EX $50 **NM** $85 **MIP** $130

Dino Robot, 1960s, battery-operated, head opens to reveal dinosaur, 11"
EX $450 **NM** $950 **MIP** $1600

Engine Robot, 1968, battery-operated, square chest w/four rotating chest gears, 9"
EX $150 **NM** $300 **MIP** $500

Engine Robot, 1970s, battery-operated, 10"
EX $75 **NM** $150 **MIP** $350

Excavator Robot, 1960s, battery-operated, w/drill type hands, 10"
EX $275 **NM** $550 **MIP** $875

Excavator Robot, 1970s, battery-operated, w/drill-type hands, 10"
EX $60 **NM** $125 **MIP** $250

Fighting Martian, 1960s, battery-operated, single gun in chest, moving antennas in shoulders, sounds,
EX $150 **NM** $350 **MIP** $750

Fighting Robot, 1960s, battery-operated, single chest gun, flashing light on head. "Sounding and lighted rapid fire gun" on box, 11"
EX $150 **NM** $350 **MIP** $600

Fighting Space Man, 1962, battery-operated, same toy as Fighting Robot but head has a human face, 11"
EX $200 **NM** $400 **MIP** $650

Gear Robot, 1960s, battery-operated, plastic gears in chest, antennae on shoulders, 11-1/2"
EX $225 **NM** $500 **MIP** $850

Gear Robot, 1960s, wind-up, visible gears, 9"
EX $125 **NM** $275 **MIP** $450

Giant Robot, 1960s, battery-operated, yellow legs, red feet and head, 17"
EX $150 **NM** $300 **MIP** $450

Golden Gear Robot, 1960s, gold, battery-operated, w/chest gears and lit dome, 9"
EX $225 **NM** $500 **MIP** $850

Launching Robot, 1975, 10"
EX $25 **NM** $35 **MIP** $75

Mr. Zerox, 1968, battery-operated, w/blinking chest guns, uses parts from other SH robots, 9-1/2"
EX $100 **NM** $210 **MIP** $350

Piston Robot, 1972, battery-operated, lighted pistons in square head, black body, 11"
EX $200 **NM** $450 **MIP** $750

Radar Robot, 1970s, wind up, red body, yellow arms, radar rotates, 6-1/2"
EX $25 **NM** $50 **MIP** $75

Radar Scope Space Scout, 1964, battery-operated, TV screen w/noise, 10"
EX $85 **NM** $200 **MIP** $375

Robot, 1958, battery-operated, early models tin, late models tin and plastic, square chest opens to reveal guns, mesh eyes
EX $250 **NM** $500 **MIP** $800

Silver Ray Secret Weapon Space Scout, 1962, battery-operated, chrome silver body, chest doors open to expose spy camera that transforms to cannons, 9"
EX $275 **NM** $550 **MIP** $825

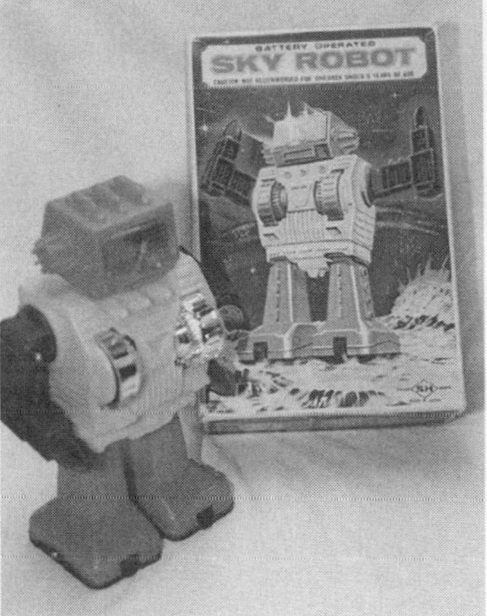

Sky Robot, 1970s, battery-operated, yellow and red, 8"
EX $20 **NM** $45 **MIP** $65

Smoking Engine Robot, 1970s, battery-operated, piston action, w/sound and smoke, 10"
EX $45 **NM** $85 **MIP** $135

Space Astronaut, 1969, battery-operated, human face, doors open to show chest cannons
EX $85 **NM** $200 **MIP** $350

Space Capsule, 1963, battery-operated, blinking nosecone on top, opening panels and spacewalking astronaut, rolling action
EX $220 **NM** $375 **MIP** $600

Space Commander Robot, 1960s, tank type base, bump-and-go motion, w/guns, 10"
EX $500 **NM** $1200 **MIP** $2000

Space Explorer Robot, 1960s, battery-operated, drop down chest cover reveals video, 11"
EX $100 **NM** $225 **MIP** $350

Space Fighter, 1960s, battery-operated, w/chest doors and guns, 9"
EX $100 **NM** $225 **MIP** $350

Space Station, 1959, battery-operated, circular station w/5 animated bays, large satalite dish in center
EX $700 **NM** $1400 **MIP** $2250

Super Giant (Rotate-a-Matic) Robot, 1970s, battery-operated, w/chest guns, 16"
EX $85 **NM** $150 **MIP** $250

Super Moon Explorer, 1969, battery-operated, torso swivels, plastic arms and feet
EX $100 **NM** $200 **MIP** $300

Super Robot Tank, 1950s, friction powered w/two guns, 9" long
EX $80 **NM** $175 **MIP** $400

Super Space Commander, 1970s, battery-operated, blue body, chest video, 10"
EX $20 **NM** $40 **MIP** $60

Swivel-O-Matic Astronaut, 1960s, battery-operated, black body, 12"
EX $75 **NM** $150 **MIP** $350

Video Robot, 1969, battery-operated, blue body, red feet, simple motion, w/chest video, 9"
EX $75 **NM** $175 **MIP** $350

Ideal

Maxx Steele Robot, 1984, programmable servant, w/charger, 30"
EX $100 **NM** $250 **MIP** $425

Mighty Zogg the Leader Zeroid, 1967, battery-operated, w/Motorific motors, 6"
EX $60 **NM** $100 **MIP** $175

Mr. Machine, 1961, wind-up, w/bell and key, disassembles, 18"
EX $100 **NM** $325 **MIP** $600

Mr. Machine, 1977, wind-up, whistles, does not disassemble, 18"
EX $20 **NM** $40 **MIP** $75

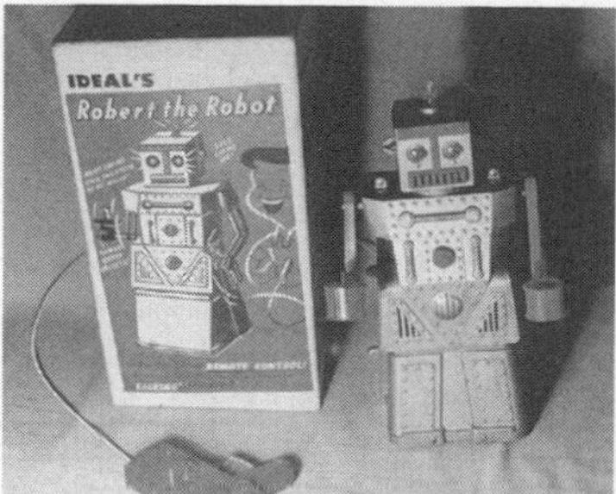

Robert the Robot, 1954, battery-operated, remote "laser gun" styled control attached to toy, 14"
EX $100 **NM** $250 **MIP** $550

(Edwin Price, Jr.)

Robot Commando, 1961, battery-operated, blue/red, remote control, fires rockets and balls, 19"
EX $150 **NM** $450 **MIP** $800

Zerak the Blue Destroyer Zeroid, 1968, battery-operated, w/Motorific motors, 6"
EX $75 **NM** $100 **MIP** $175

Zeroid Alien, 1970, battery-operated, 12"
EX $75 **NM** $100 **MIP** $250

Zintar the Silver Explorer Zeroid, 1967, battery-operated, w/Motorific motors, 6"
EX $75 **NM** $100 **MIP** $175

Zobor the Bronze Transporter Zeroid, 1967, battery-operated, w/Motorific motors, 6"
EX $50 **NM** $100 **MIP** $175

Zogg, Zeroid Commander-in-Chief, 1970, battery-operated, 6"
EX $50 **NM** $100 **MIP** $175

Irwin

Man From Mars, 1950s, wind-up, red w/yellow body, shooting "space boy", 11"
EX $275 **NM** $750 **MIP** $1500

Man from Mars, 1950s, wind-up, red body, "space boy", 11"
EX $125 **NM** $275 **MIP** $500

Japan

Answer Game Machine, 1960s, battery-operated, performs math tricks, 14"
EX $350 **NM** $675 **MIP** $950

Apollo 2000 Robot, 1960s, battery-operated, red and blue, w/chest guns, 12"
EX $95 **NM** $175 **MIP** $300

Apollo 2000X, 1970s, wind-up, blue and red, w/spark, 6"
EX $45 **NM** $95 **MIP** $165

Atomic Robot Man, 1948, wind-up, 6"
EX $325 **NM** $900 **MIP** $1700

Blink-A-Gear Robot, 1960s, battery-operated, black body, clear plastic front w/gears, 14"
EX $250 **NM** $600 **MIP** $1150

Construction Robot, 1960s, battery-operated, yellow body with forklift, 12"
EX $450 **NM** $1000 **MIP** $1650

High-Wheel Robot, 1950s, battery-operated, blue body, remote control, 9"
EX $325 **NM** $750 **MIP** $1250

High-Wheel Ronot, 1950s, wind-up, black body w/chest gears, 9"
EX $175 **NM** $425 **MIP** $700

Machine Robot, 1960s, battery-operated, w/shoulder antennae, 11"
EX $145 **NM** $325 **MIP** $600

Mars Explorer, 1950s, battery-operated, red body, w/wheels, face doors open, 9-1/2"
EX $450 **NM** $1000 **MIP** $1750

Mars King, 1960s, battery-operated, w/video, siren and treads, 9"
EX $125 **NM** $350 **MIP** $650

Mr. Chief, 1960s, battery-operated, smoking action, 11-1/2"
EX $475 **NM** $1000 **MIP** $1950

Mr. Patrol, 1960s, battery-operated, meter in chest, 11"
EX $150 **NM** $350 **MIP** $575

New Astronaut Robot, 1970s, battery-operated, w/three firing chest guns, 9"
EX $45 **NM** $85 **MIP** $135

Piston Robot, 1970s, 10", tin and plastic, battery-operated, lighted chest pistons, 10"
EX $60 **NM** $110 **MIP** $225

Piston Robot, 1980s, battery-operated, lighted chest pistons, 10"
EX $35 **NM** $65 **MIP** $125

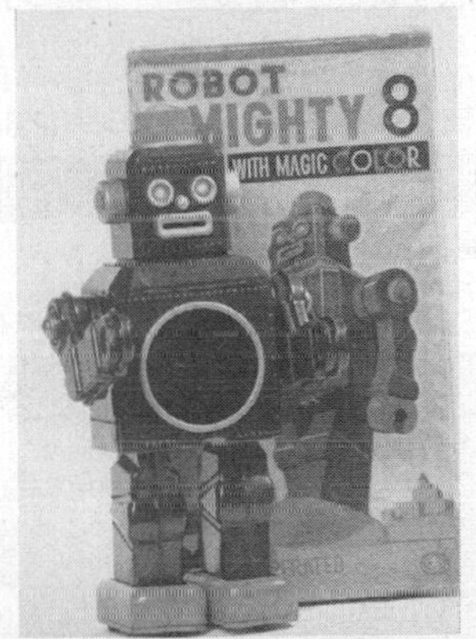

Robot Mighty 8, 1960s, Dark blue metal body, red feet, electric color display on chest
EX $100 **NM** $225 **MIP** $450

Robot Tank - Mini, battery-operated, w/two guns, 5 1/2"
EX $85 **NM** $160 **MIP** $275

Roto-Robot, 1960s, battery-operated, w/chest guns, rotates 360 degrees, 9"
EX $95 **NM** $185 **MIP** $325

RX-008 Robot, 1960s, wind-up, w/sparking chest, 5"
EX $150 **NM** $400 **MIP** $700

Singing Robot, 1970s, battery-operated, missiles in head, 10"
EX $35 **NM** $75 **MIP** $100

Space Explorer Robot, 1950s, wind-up, w/O2 gauge on chest, 9"
EX $450 **NM** $1000 **MIP** $1650

Space Explorer Robot, 1960s, battery-operated, rotating shoulder antenna, 12"
EX $450 **NM** $1000 **MIP** $1650

Space Ranger, 1970s, battery-operated, R/C, fires balls from chest, 10"
EX $50 **NM** $110 **MIP** $165

Space Robot X-70, 1960s, battery-operated, lights, noise, and "Tulip Head", 12"
EX $450 **NM** $1000 **MIP** $1650

Sparky Robot, 1960s, wind-up, green cylindrical body, 7"
EX $45 **NM** $65 **MIP** $150

Super Astronaut, 1960s, battery-operated, man's face, w/chest guns, 10"
EX $100 **NM** $200 **MIP** $300

Zoomer Robot, 1950s, battery-operated, blue or silver w/red, w/wrench, 7"
EX $295 **NM** $525 **MIP** $900

KTA-Japan

Robot Lilliput, 1939, wind-up, one of the oldest, square "block" head w/yellow litho, "N.P. 5257" on chest, 6"
EX $1500 **NM** $5000 **MIP** $10000

Linemar

Golden Robot, 1958, battery-operated w/corded remote, gold color, smiling, "ROBOT" lights up in chest, 6-1/2"
EX $600 **NM** $1300 **MIP** $2000

Lantern Robot, 1955, battery-operated w/corded remote, holds illuminated lantern, blows smoke from mouth, 8"
EX $500 **NM** $1000 **MIP** $1500

Mechanical Walking Sparking Robot, 1950s, batttery-operated, 6"
EX $250 **NM** $550 **MIP** $1000

Spaceman, 1958, battery-operated, small face within helmet, lights up, has gun, 8"
EX $1000 **NM** $2000 **MIP** $3000

Marx

Big Loo, 1963, battery-operated, water squirter, w/rockets and tools, 36"
EX $450 **NM** $1300 **MIP** $2600

Colonel Hap Hazard, 1968, rotating antenna on head, 11"
EX $250 **NM** $575 **MIP** $1200

Electric Robot, 1950s, battery-operated, blk and red, w/morse code, 15"
EX $125 **NM** $250 **MIP** $550

Frankenstein, 1960s, wind-up walker, 6"
EX $100 **NM** $250 **MIP** $450

Frankenstein Robot, 1968, battery-operated, wired remote control, 14"
EX $575 **NM** $1250 **MIP** $2000

Great Garloo, The, 1962, battery-operated, remote control, monster features, 7 movements, popular, 23"
EX $100 **NM** $300 **MIP** $600

Hi-Bouncer Moon Scout, 1968, battery-operated w/corded remote, human face, 11-1/2"
EX $550 **NM** $1200 **MIP** $2000

Moon Creature, 1968, Bug-eyed, mechanical, wind-up, 5-1/2"
EX $95 **NM** $165 **MIP** $275

Moon Scout, 1968, shoots balls from chest, 11"
EX $500 **NM** $1050 **MIP** $2200

Marx

Mr. Mercury, 1962-64, battery-operated w/corded remote, bending action, "Mr. Mercury" on chest, 14"
EX $275 **NM** $650 **MIP** $1200

Mr. Smash, 1970s, wind-up, red body, Martian Mashed Potato promo, 6"
EX $50 **NM** $95 **MIP** $150

Robot and Son, 1956, battery-operated, similar to Marx Robot toy but comes with small plastic son holding a bar overhead used by Robot to lift him, 15"
EX $125 **NM** $250 **MIP** $450

Rock 'Em, Sock 'Em Robots, 1966-1976, Two plastic robots in boxing ring controlled by handles, when one is punched just right his head flies upward on a sping. Just plain goofy fun
EX $60 **NM** $120 **MIP** $200

Son of Garloo, 1960s, wind-up, green body, monster walker, 6"
EX $100 **NM** $225 **MIP** $450

Masudaya

Forbidden Planet Robby, 1985, wind-up, 5"
EX $15 **NM** $25 **MIP** $40

Forbidden Planet Robby, 1985, battery-operated, talks, 16"
EX $65 **NM** $125 **MIP** $200

Giant Sonic Robot (Train Robot), 1959, battery-operated, red body, black arms and head, robot makes "trainlike" sound as it rolls along. Very hard to find, one of the "Gang of Five", 15"
EX $4000 **NM** $7300 **MIP** $16000

(Sotheby's Photo)

Machine Man, 1950s, battery-operated, the rarest robot from Masudaya's "Gang of Five" series, this robot sold for $42,550 at the Sotheby's auction of the Tin Toy Robot Collection of Matt Wyse in 1996, 15"
EX n/a **NM** n/a **MIP** $45000

Non-Stop (Lavender) Robot, 1956, battery-operated, part of the skirted "Gang of Five"
EX $2000 **NM** $3500 **MIP** $6000

R-35 Robot, 1962, battery-operated, remote control - battery box is red, eyes light up, 8"
EX $175 **NM** $400 **MIP** $650

Robot YM-3, 1985, wind-up, "Lost in Space B9" type, 5"
EX $10 **NM** $20 **MIP** $35

Space Commando, 1958, battery-operated w/corded remote, one of a few astronauts produced by Masudaya, poseable head, 7-1/2"
EX $600 **NM** $1300 **MIP** $2000

Target Robot, 1958, battery-operated, blue skirted robot w/red target disk in chest, one of the "Gang of Five", 15"
EX $2000 **NM** $4000 **MIP** $6000

The Gang of Five, 1997, five mini-robots, Mini Sonic Robot, Mini Target Robot, Mini Machine Man, Mini Non-Stop Lavender Robot, Mini Radicon Robot, 5"
EX $50 **NM** $75 **MIP** $110

Mego

Gigantor Robot, 1960s, battery-operated, silver w/ white "hands" and red feet, 17"
EX $50 **NM** $100 **MIP** $200

Mego-Japan

Krome-Dome Robot, 1960s, plastic, battery-operated, disk-type head opes w/sound, 11"
EX $125 **NM** $295 **MIP** $525

Mikes Toy House

Mr. Atomic, 1990s, Limited reproduction
EX $95 **NM** $200 **MIP** $350

Miscellaneous

Lightning Robot, 1980s, battery-operated, looks like R2D2 w/ flashing lights
EX $20 **NM** $40 **MIP** $80

Lunar Spaceman, 1978, battery operated, 12"
EX $20 **NM** $30 **MIP** $45

Mechanical Interplanetary Explorer, 1950s, wind-up, 8"
EX $180 **NM** $260 **MIP** $400

Mechanized Robot, 1950s, battery-operated, black body, "Robby the Robot" type, 13"
EX $500 **NM** $1200 **MIP** $2100

Myrobo, 1970s, battery operated, 9"
EX $25 **NM** $35 **MIP** $55

Raid "Bug" Robot, Large, battery-operated, remote control, ad promo, Korea
EX $75 **NM** $150 **MIP** $250

Ranger Robot, battery-operated, clear body, w/smoke and sound, Japan, 11"
EX $500 **NM** $1200 **MIP** $2250

Space Scout, 1950s, Rare, wind-up, w/radiation meter in chest, 10"
EX $1000 **NM** $2250 **MIP** $5000

Zero of Space, 1970s, battery-operated, red and yellow w/visor, w/lights, 14"
EX $100 **NM** $225 **MIP** $350

MTU-Korea

Captain the Robot, 1970s, gray wind-up, sparking, 6"
EX $15 **NM** $35 **MIP** $50

Naito Shoten

Deep-Sea Robot, 1956, very rare, 8"
EX $4000 **NM** $9000 **MIP** $16000

N-Japan

Mighty Robot, 1969, wind-up, paddle-feet rotate to move robot forward, sparks in chest
EX $50 **NM** $100 **MIP** $150

Robot-7, 1966, wind-up, paddle-feet forward motion
EX $65 **NM** $125 **MIP** $225

Wind-Up Walking Robot, 1960s, wind-up sparker, plastic antenna on head, 7"
EX $100 **NM** $225 **MIP** $350

Nomura/TN

Batman, 1966, battery-operated, walks forward, head lights up, cloth cape w/yellow "Batman" logo stenciled, 12"
EX n/a **NM** n/a **MIP** n/a

Earth Man, 1957, battery-operated w/corded remote, walks and fires his gun, 9"
EX $600 **NM** $1450 **MIP** $2500

Mechanized Robot, 1957, battery-operated; the icon of the hobby, this is based on Robby the Robot from the 1956 film "The Forbidden Planet", 14"
EX $1500 **NM** $3000 **MIP** $4500

Moon Space Ship, 1958, battery-operated, cousin of the cancelled Robby Space Patrol, this ship features blue litho and bump-and-go action
EX $600 **NM** $1300 **MIP** $2000

Musical Drummer Robot R 57, 1950s, From the Matt Wyse collection, this robot sold for $17,250 at a Sotheby's auction in 1996
EX n/a **NM** n/a **MIP** $20000

Piston Action Robot, 1958, battery-operated w/corded remote, Robby-like w/pistons moving in clear dome, 11"
EX $500 **NM** $1200 **MIP** $2000

Radar Robot, 1955-58, battery-operated w/corded remote, wrench in right hand, webbed radar dish from back, several color variations, 9"
EX $600 **NM** $1250 **MIP** $1900

Ratchet Robot, 1957, wind-up, based on Zoomer design, sparks from chest, coiled antenna across head, 7-1/2"
EX $600 **NM** $1250 **MIP** $1900

Robby Space Patrol, 1957, battery-operated, bump-and-go motion. This is one of the most famous space toys, representing (in an unlicensed way) the robot and his transport vehicle from the 1956 film, "The Forbidden Planet."
EX $7000 **NM** $17500 **MIP** $37000

Robot Tank-Z, 1960s, battery-operated, bump-and-go motion, 10"
EX $200 **NM** $425 **MIP** $700

Space Command Robot, 1950s, wind-up, w/gun in hand, 7-1/2"
EX $375 **NM** $1000 **MIP** $1650

Space Commando, 1956, battery-operated, plastic helmet only part of face visible, laser rifle, 11"
EX $500 **NM** $1000 **MIP** $1550

Tetsujin T-28, 1960s, a sereis of battery-operated robots based on the popular Japanese character known as "Gigantor" in the U.S. These are rare and very desirable
EX n/a **NM** n/a **MIP** n/a

Walking Mechanical Astroman with Sparks, 1960s, battery-operated, distinctive red litho w/horizontal lines, body similar to Tetsujin T-28, plastic helmet, human face
EX n/a **NM** n/a **MIP** n/a

Zoomer the Robot, 1954, battery-operated, holding wrench in right hand, eyes glow red, antenna spins, many color variations
EX $250 **NM** $500 **MIP** $750

Orikawa

Mr. Hustler, 1960s, battery-operated, center chest light, 11-1/2"
EX $100 **NM** $225 **MIP** $400

Playing Mantis

Robot B-9, Lost In Space, 1990s, rolling wheels under base, sold individually, part of a series of four Lost-In-Space toys made by Playing Mantis Johnny Lightning, 3"
EX $4 **NM** $8 **MIP** $15

R.M.

Astronaut, 1960s, wind up, arms move back and forth, red body, human face, 7"
EX $50 **NM** $85 **MIP** $125

Remco

Big Max & His Electronic Conveyor, 1958, battery-operated, w/truck and coins, 8" x 7"
EX $100 **NM** $185 **MIP** $300

Lost in Space Motorized Robot, 1966, battery-operated, black and red body, lights up, arms move, 14"
EX $125 **NM** $250 **MIP** $450

Mr. Brain, 1970, battery-operated, programmable memory, 13"
EX $75 **NM** $150 **MIP** $250

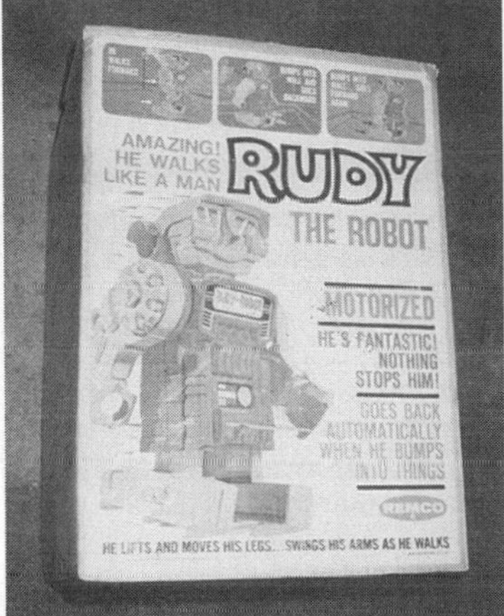

Rudy the Robot, 1967, orange, battery-operated, "He Walks Like a Man!", 16"
EX $75 **NM** $165 **MIP** $375

Rosko

Astronaut, 1962, battery-operated, blue or red litho, uses legs and torso of Nomura Robby series, human face
EX $550 **NM** $1300 **MIP** $2000

Space Conqueror, 1961, battery-operated, blue and yellow litho, copy of Cragstan Astronaut, human face
EX $550 **NM** $1300 **MIP** $2000

S.J.M.

Super Astronaut, 1981, battery-operated, man's face, w/chest guns, 10"
EX $12 **NM** $20 **MIP** $30

Saunders

Marvelous Mike, 1955, battery-operated, plastic robot on yellow tin Caterpillar bulldozer, rubber treads, 14" long
EX $110 **NM** $225 **MIP** $395

Schaper

Tobor, 1978, black, battery-operated, radio control, 7"
EX $15 **NM** $30 **MIP** $50

SNK

Flashy Jim, 1955, battery-operated, square head, "R7" on chest, walks forward, eyes light up, 7-1/2"
EX $250 **NM** $500 **MIP** $800

Robbie the Roving Robot, 1956, wind-up, antenna,, 7"
EX $450 **NM** $1000 **MIP** $1800

Sparkling Mike Robot, 1957, wind-up, red diamonds in knees, hole in chest shoots sparks, antenna, 7"
EX $150 **NM** $300 **MIP** $550

Sonsco

Space Man, 1958, battery-operated, rifle in right hand, flashlight in left hand, antenna
EX $1000 **NM** $2000 **MIP** $3000

Straco-Japan

Hysterical Robot, 1970s, battery-operated, black body, bump-and-go and laughing actions, 13"
EX $100 **NM** $250 **MIP** $400

SY Japan

Fireman Robot, 1960s, wind-up, "Fire Man" on chest, flapping feet, with or without hat
EX $100 **NM** $200 **MIP** $300

Mechanical Sparking Robot, 1965, keywound, silver w/litho, "W" in chest, flapping feet, 7"
EX $125 **NM** $275 **MIP** $450

Mechanical Walking Space Man, 1962, wind-up, black body, w/floppy arms and forward walking motion, 7-1/2"
EX $150 **NM** $400 **MIP** $700

Mechanical Walking Space Man w/Spark, 1970s, wind-up, silver litho, this variation sparks from chest, 7"
EX $100 **NM** $175 **MIP** $275

The Mego Man, 1960s, wind-up, top hat w/"Mego Man" in hat band, inspiried by Mr. Machine, red laughing face, silver bell in chest
EX $100 **NM** $225 **MIP** $350

Taiyo

Wheel-A-Gear Robot, 1950s, battery-operated, black body, w/mutli-chest gears and pullies, 15"
EX $425 **NM** $1000 **MIP** $1850

Tomy

Chatbot, 1970s, battery-operated, tape recorder in head, serving tray, speaks, remote control, 8"
EX $30 **NM** $65 **MIP** $110

Omnibot 2000, 1980s, battery-operated, remote control, programmable servant, 24"
EX $175 **NM** $400 **MIP** $675

Verbot, 1984, battery-operated, radio control, programmable, 8"
EX $15 **NM** $35 **MIP** $60

Topper

Boxer Ding-A-Ling, 1970s, battery-operated, orange and blue body
EX $20 **NM** $40 **MIP** $60

Chef Ding-A-Ling, 1970s, battery-operated, red, white and blue body
EX $20 **NM** $40 **MIP** $60

King-Ding Robot, 1970, battery-operated, separate brain robot goes in head, 12"
EX $110 **NM** $275 **MIP** $500

Waco-Japan

Laughing Robot, 1960s, battery-operated, mouth opens, laughs loudly, 13"
EX $125 **NM** $275 **MIP** $500

Yanoman

Rendezvous 7.8, 15"
EX $170 **NM** $245 **MIP** $375

Yonezawa

Conehead Robot, 1962, wind-up, Robby body and legs, cone-shaped head w/large eyes, 8-1/2"
EX $650 **NM** $1400 **MIP** $2300

Directional Robot, 1963, battery-operated, blue body, head rotates, bump-and-go action, 10"
EX $225 **NM** $650 **MIP** $1500

Eightman, 1966, battery-operated, based on the anime superhero cyborg, rare, 14"
EX $2500 **NM** $5500 **MIP** $10000

Lunar Robot, 1960s, wind-up, sparks, companion to Thunder Robot, 7"
EX $225 **NM** $550 **MIP** $800

Mechanic Robot, 1969, battery-operated, phone dial in chest
EX $65 **NM** $135 **MIP** $250

Mechanical Mighty Robot, 1967, a.k.a. "Athlete Robot" due to its flexing arm motion, wind-up, red tin body, grey plastic head, Model No. 811
EX n/a **NM** n/a **MIP** n/a

Modern Robot, 1962, battery-operated, copy of Cragstan Robot w/new litho, "Modern Robot" written on chest
EX $650 **NM** $1400 **MIP** $2000

Mr. Mercury, 1961, battery-operated, believed to be the first model in the series, "Mr. Mercury" across chest, 13"
EX $650 **NM** $1500 **MIP** $2100

Robby Robot, 1958, wind-up, wrenches for arms, 8"
EX $600 **NM** $1500 **MIP** $2400

Robot Captain, 1968, wind-up, wrenches for arms,, 5-1/2"
EX $50 **NM** $100 **MIP** $150

Roby Robot, 1960, wind-up, wrenches for arms, black body w/red feet, 8"
EX $800 **NM** $1750 **MIP** $2600

Scare Mighty Robot, 1960s, wind-up, red and white, sparking action, 10"
EX $175 **NM** $550 **MIP** $1000

Smoking Spaceman, 1960, battery-operated, dark gray metal body, smoke puffs from mouth as robot walks, 12"
EX $1250 **NM** $1900 **MIP** $3750

Space Explorer, 1959, wind-up, astronaut face, oxygen meter in chest, swings arms, 9-1/2"
EX $350 **NM** $700 **MIP** $1450

Space Explorer, 1959, battery-operated, tv screen in chest, robot transforms into a tv
EX $350 **NM** $700 **MIP** $1300

Swinging Baby Robot, 1958, wind-up, clockwork swings the square-head baby, counterweight often missing
EX $350 **NM** $700 **MIP** $1300

X-27 Explorer, 1958, wind-up, barrel-chest, human face in helmet, two antennae
EX $600 **NM** $1350 **MIP** $2500

Yoshiya/KO

Action Planet Robot, 1958, wind-up, Robby look-alike, forward walking, grate over face, black body w/red feet, 8"
EX $175 **NM** $400 **MIP** $700

Atom Robot, mid-1960s, wind-up, small skirted robot, bump-and-go action
EX n/a **NM** n/a **MIP** n/a

Chief Robotman, 1959, battery-operated, bump-and-go motion, two spinning antennae, swinging arms, flashing lights, turning head, skirted robot, 12"
EX $450 **NM** $900 **MIP** $1550

Chief Smokey/Mr. Chief, 1959, battery-operated, skirted robot, smokes from head, 12"
EX $450 **NM** $900 **MIP** $1500

Jupiter Robot, 1969, wind-up, red body, w/two antennae, sparks, 7"
EX $85 **NM** $175 **MIP** $350

Mechanical Space Man Robot, 1950s, wind-up, silver litho, full face showing in helmet, antenna moves as he walks, 6"
EX $100 **NM** $200 **MIP** $500

Mighty Robot, 1959, battery-operated, bump-and-go motion, skirted robot, grey-blue tin body, red plastic arms, clear plastic head, 12"
EX $450 **NM** $900 **MIP** $1500

Moon Explorer, 1959, wind-up, fixed legs, human-faced astronaut in dome helmet, 7-1/2"
EX $550 **NM** $1200 **MIP** $2000

Moon Explorer, 1960s, battery-operated, w/clock in chest, 12"
EX $475 **NM** $1000 **MIP** $1850

Planet Robot, 1958, battery-operated w/corded remote, just like Action Planet Robot, blue and other color variations, 8"
EX $250 **NM** $600 **MIP** $1000

Robby, 1958, wind-up, fixed-legs, red body, plastic dome head, 7"
EX $200 **NM** $500 **MIP** $850

Robot Dog, 1956, wind-up, 7" long
EX $250 **NM** $600 **MIP** $1000

Space Whale, 1957, wind-up, vehicle moves forward when antenna is raised, white and blue litho, google eyes,, 7" long
EX $175 **NM** $285 **MIP** $600

Sparky Robot, 1954-59, wind-up, silver and red, w/head spring antenna; earliest version all silver from 1954, 7"
EX $275 **NM** $650 **MIP** $1000

Venus Robot, 1960s, battery-operated, blue/red, remote control, 8"
EX $95 **NM** $200 **MIP** $325

Rock and Roll

by Karen O'Brien

The beginnings of rock and roll took root with the rhythm and blues music popularized after World War II. In the 1950s, Elvis Presley revolutionized the rock sound. Elvis memorabilia and licensed products are highly sought by fans of the King. And nothing is more certain to cause a stir in the auction world than an Elvis memorabilia auction. The popularity of the King wasn't rivaled until Liverpool's four young men swept America in the early 1960s. In fact, the impact of the Beatles and Elvis was so strong that it resonated not only in the music world but also in the merchandising and collectibles arena.

It's not surprising that images of the Beatles were used to endorse products. What's surprising is that so many toys were made to help kids re-create the frenzy at home. Toy guitars, drums, and dolls brought the Beatles to life to a younger audience. Today, collectors are thrilled to find such remnants of rock and roll history. And while Beatles collectibles aren't particularly difficult to find, those in the best condition are treasured.

After the success of marketing Beatles toys, rock and roll continued to be a booming business for merchandisers. Although their musical talent was scrutinized, both the Monkees and the Partridge Family enjoyed added exposure on television. That exposure created much interest in related memorabilia, especially for young fans.

In the 1970s, KISS stormed onto the rock scene in wild face makeup and costumes unlike anything previously seen. Armies of KISS fans rocked and rolled all night long, and in 1979, Mego made 12-inch dolls of band members Paul Stanley, Gene Simmons, Ace Frehley, and Peter Criss. Dozens of KISS toys followed to the delight of eager fans. McFarlane Toys continues the KISS craze today with their action figures. (See the Action Figure chapter for values.)

But KISS was one of the last rock and roll groups featured on numerous toys and memorabilia. While 1980s and 1990s icons like Michael Jackson and Madonna have been the subjects of some toys and collectibles, the trend died for a few years. Then with the teen pop craze phenomenon in the early part of the twenty-first century, toys related to stars again found an avid audience. At this point, however, the trend of pop-music figures seems to be waning again.

McFarlane Toys continues to enjoy success with new KISS figures marketed toward an older collector. The company has also released figures of heavy metal rockers like Ozzy Osbourne, Metallica, and Rob Zombie along with figures of classic crooners such as Janis Joplin and Jim Morrison. And even Art Asylum joined the ranks with figures of iconic rap group Run DMC.

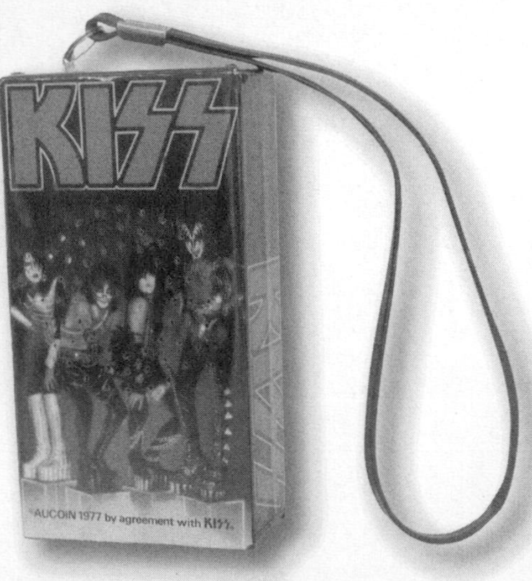

THE *TOP* 10 ROCK AND ROLL (In Mint Condition)

1. Beatles Banjo, Mastro, 1964 .... $800
2. Beatles Bobbin' Head Dolls, set of four, 1960s 750
3. Beatles Guitar, Selcol, 1960s 600
4. Beatles Cartoon Kit, Colorforms, 1966 525
5. Beatles Magic Slate, Merit, 1960s 500
6. Beatles Costume, Ben Cooper, 1960s 425
7. Beatles Jr. Guitar, Mastro, 1960s 425
8. Paint Your Own Beatle Kit, Artistic Creations, 1960s 400
9. Yellow Submarine Costume, Collegeville, 1960s 375
10. Paul McCartney Doll, Remco, 1964 275

Beatles

Beatles Banjo, 1964, Mastro
EX $200 NM $400 MIP $800

Beatles Cartoon Kit, 1966, Colorforms
EX $150 NM $300 MIP $525

Beatles Costume, 1960s, Ben Cooper, child's costume and mask; John, Paul, George, or Ringo, each
EX $100 NM $200 MIP $425

Beatles Forever Cloth Dolls, 1987, Applause, 22" tall, each
EX $55 NM $75 MIP $100

Beatles Guitar, 1960s, Selcol, 23", plastic
EX $200 NM $300 MIP $600

Beatles in Pepperland Puzzles, Jaymar, many variations and sizes, each
EX $35 NM $60 MIP $100

Beatles Jr. Guitar, 1960s, Mastro, 14" red/pink plastic guitar w/Beatles graphics
EX $100 NM $225 MIP $425

Beatles Magic Slate, Merit, British
EX $150 NM $300 MIP $500

Beatles Notebook Binder, 1960s, binder from Beatles Fan Club
EX $50 NM $75 MIP $135

Beatles Toy Watches, 1960s, four, tin w/plastic bands, on card
EX $30 NM $75 MIP $150

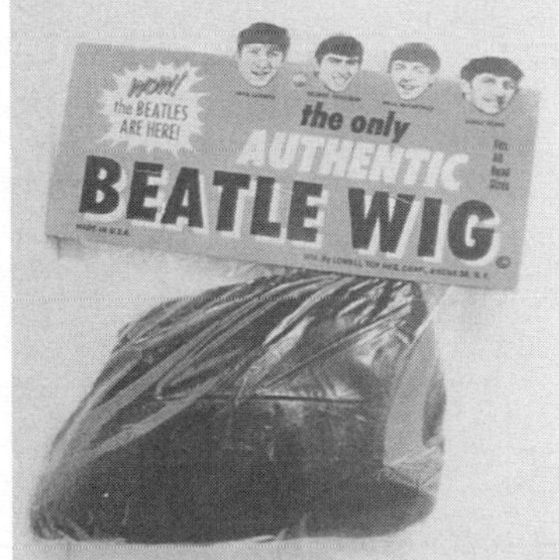

Beatles Wig, Lowell Toy
EX $65 NM $90 MIP $150

Bobbin' Head Dolls, 1960s, 8" tall, ceramic, four in set
EX $300 NM $500 MIP $750

Disk Go Case, 1966, Charter, 45 rpm carrying case; several colors
EX $100 NM $150 MIP $250

George Harrison Doll, 1964, Remco
EX $50 NM $100 MIP $275

Harmonica, Hohner, in Beatles box
EX $35 NM $50 MIP $85

Inflatable Dolls, 1966, Lux promotional; 13" tall; each
EX $25 NM $35 MIP $50

John Lennon Doll, 1964, Remco
EX $50 NM $100 MIP $275

Paint Your Own Beatle Kit, 1960s, Artistic Creations, oil painting kit; John, Paul, George, or Ringo, each
EX $150 NM $300 MIP $400

Paul McCartney Doll, 1964, Remco
EX $50 NM $100 MIP $275

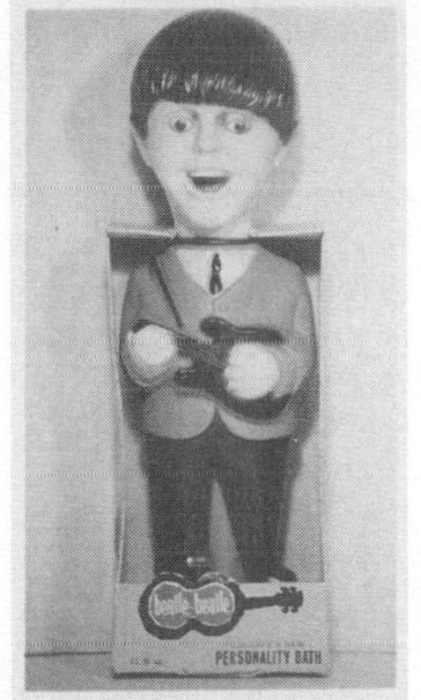

Paul McCartney Soaky, 1965, Colgate, red plastic
EX $70 NM $125 MIP $250

Ringo Starr Doll, 1964, Remco
EX $50 NM $100 MIP $275

Ringo Starr Soaky, 1965, Colgate, blue plastic
EX $70 NM $125 MIP $275

Yellow Submarine Halloween Costume, 1960s, Collegeville, Blue Meanie costume and mask
EX $100 NM $200 MIP $375

Yellow Submarine Water Color Set, 1960s, Craft Master, pictures and paints
EX $40 NM $80 MIP $145

Elvis Presley

Elvis Presley Doll, 1984, World Dolls, 21" tall
EX $50 NM $100 MIP $200

Elvis Presley Doll, 1984, Eugene, 12" tall
EX $20 NM $40 MIP $80

Elvis Presley Wristwatch, 1983, Bradley, white plastic case, quartz, stainless back, face shows a young Elvis, white vinyl band
EX $25 NM $45 MIP $85

Jigsaw Puzzle, 1992, Milton Bradley, Elvis postage stamp
EX $5 NM $10 MIP $20

KISS

Jigsaw Puzzles, 1970s, Milton Bradley
EX $10 NM $20 MIP $35

KISS Rub n' Play Magic Transfer Set, 1979, Colorforms
EX $20 NM $40 MIP $80

KISS Van Model Kit, 1977, AMT
EX $35 NM $70 MIP $140

KISS Your Face Make-Up Kit, 1978, Remco
EX $30 NM $65 MIP $115

Trading Cards Set, 1978, Donruss, set of 132 cards
EX $25 NM $35 MIP $70

View-Master Set, 1978, GAF
EX $10 NM $20 MIP $35

Wastebasket, 1978, metal, cylindrical
EX $20 NM $45 MIP $70

Michael Jackson

Michael Jackson AM Radio, 1984, Ertl
EX $12 NM $25 MIP $45

Michael Jackson Doll, 1984, LJN, several styles
EX $12 NM $25 MIP $50

Michael Jackson Dress-Up Set, 1984, Colorforms
EX $10 NM $15 MIP $25

Michael Jackson Microphone, 1984, LJN, cordless, electronic
EX $10 NM $20 MIP $35

Michael's [Jackson] Pets, 1987, Ideal, plush animals, 10 kinds, each
EX $7 NM $15 MIP $25

Miscellaneous

Andy Gibb Doll, 1979, Ideal, 7" tall
EX $15 NM $30 MIP $60

Boy George Doll, 1980s, LJN, 15", polka dot shirt
EX $20 NM $40 MIP $75

Boy George Doll, 1980s, LJN, 12", poseable in alphabet shirt
EX $30 NM $60 MIP $120

Cher Doll, 1976, Mego, 12", w/growing hair
EX $55 NM $125 MIP $175

Cher Doll, 1976, Mego, 12"
EX $50 NM $100 MIP $150

Debby Boone Doll, Mattel, 10" tall
EX $20 NM $40 MIP $80

Dolly Parton Doll, 1970s, Goldberger, 12" tall
EX $20 NM $40 MIP $80

Pat Boone Paper Dolls, 1959, Whitman, two cardboard dolls plus clothes
EX $20 NM $45 MIP $75

Miscellaneous

Pinky Lee Costume, 1950s, hat, pants, and shirt
EX $35 **NM** $75 **MIP** $145

Pinky Lee Xylophone, Emenee
EX $35 **NM** $70 **MIP** $120

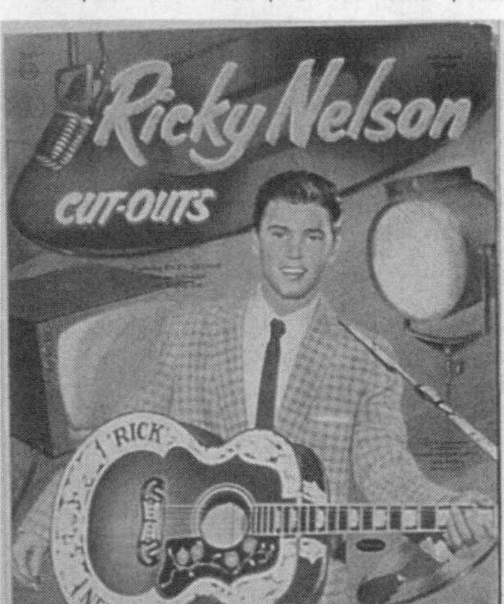

Rick Nelson Paper Dolls, 1959, Whitman
EX $20 **NM** $45 **MIP** $80

Sonny & Cher Play Set, 1976, Mego
EX $25 **NM** $50 **MIP** $85

Toni Tennile Doll, 12" tall
EX $8 **NM** $15 **MIP** $30

Osmonds

Donny & Marie TV Show Play Set, 1976, Mattel
EX $15 **NM** $35 **MIP** $55

Donny Osmond Doll, 1976, Mattel, 12" tall
EX $15 **NM** $25 **MIP** $45

Donny Osmond String Puppet, 1978, Madison
EX $20 **NM** $35 **MIP** $60

Marie Osmond Doll, 1976, Mattel, 12" tall
EX $10 **NM** $25 **MIP** $40

Marie Osmond Modeling Doll, 1976, Mattel, 30" tall
EX $20 **NM** $40 **MIP** $80

Marie Osmond String Puppet, 1978, Madison
EX $25 **NM** $35 **MIP** $65

Osmonds Colorforms Dress-Up Set, 1976, Colorforms
EX $10 **NM** $25 **MIP** $50

Sci-Fi and Space Toys

by Karen O'Brien

Some would trace the modern age of science fiction to 1956 and *Forbidden Planet*. Undoubtedly, the toy world would be poorer for the lack of the movie's Robby the Robot. But through one medium or another, science fiction has enthralled millions for many years, right back to Jonathan Swift's *Gulliver's Travels*.

The first universally acclaimed work of science fiction was Mary Shelley's *Frankenstein or The Modern Prometheus*, and her vision made way for Verne, Wells, Burroughs, Lovecraft, Heinlein, Asimov, Clarke, and a host of others whose collective imaginations led us up to today and through tomorrow.

Even with its classical pedigree, science fiction is almost exclusively a product of the twentieth century as the hard foundation of science had to exist before fiction writers could extrapolate upon it. In particular, science fiction is a phenomenon of the atomic age. World War II, more than any other event this century, opened our eyes to the wondrous and horrific potential of applied science.

Just as science fiction has captivated readers of all ages, so have toys. Buck Rogers made his first appearance in 1928. But in 1929, Buck Rogers went from pulp to newsprint, becoming the first science fiction comic strip. Flash Gordon followed Buck Rogers into print in 1934 and was an immediate success. Within two years, Flash was on the silver screen, portrayed by Buster Crabbe. Buck Rogers finally made it to the screen in 1939, also played by Crabbe.

During this period, Marx produced numerous toys in support of each character, including two ships that have become classics in the space toy field. Opinions vary as to which wind-up is better executed—Buck Rogers' 25th Century Rocket Ship or Flash Gordon's Rocket fighter. Both are considered superb examples of tin character space toys.

From Ray Guns to Star Wars

No discussion of space toys would be complete without mention of ray guns. Here again Marx is a major player, producing numerous generic and character space guns. Daisy, Hubley, and Wyandotte, among others, all made memorable contributions as well.

Space toys have been made continuously for most of the twentieth century. The 1930s and 1940s saw Buck Rogers and Flash Gordon. The 1950s saw fiction become reality with the growth of television. *Captain Video* was the first space series on television, appearing in the summer of 1949. Buzz Correy and his Space Patrol and Tom Corbett, Space Cadet would feed the appetite for adventure until 1956 when the heavens took on a visual scale and grandeur never see before—in the panoramic wonder of *Forbidden Planet*.

In 1966, when the low-budget *Star Trek* went on the air, few dreamed that for millions of people, life would never be the same. Even though the original show ran only three seasons, its impact and legacy are undeniable. The phenomenon of *Star Trek* has grown far beyond cult status, and the extraordinary success of *Star Trek: The Next Generation* has only broadened its reach.

Star Trek may be big. But the king of space toys has to be *Star Wars*. The array of books, models, figures, play sets, and other items released since its debut in 1977 continued unabated until 1988. The license gained a new lease in 1987 with the opening of Star Tours at Disneyland and Disney World, generating still more new merchandise.

Today, store shelves are again featuring new *Star Wars* toys thanks to the phenomenal success of the Prequel trilogy that recently concluded with 2005's *Episode III: Revenge of the Sith*. *Star Wars*' longevity and international name recognition are excellent assurances of the continuing popularity of its toys. (See the Star Wars chapter for values.)

Editor's Note: Several abbreviations are used in this section to denote *Star Trek* properties. Key is as follows: ST:TMP – *Star Trek: The Motion Picture*. ST:TNG – *Star Trek: The Next Generation*.

Contributor: Justin Pinchot is an avid collector of toy space guns and he provided pricing updates for this chapter. He may be reached through his Web site: www.toyraygun.com

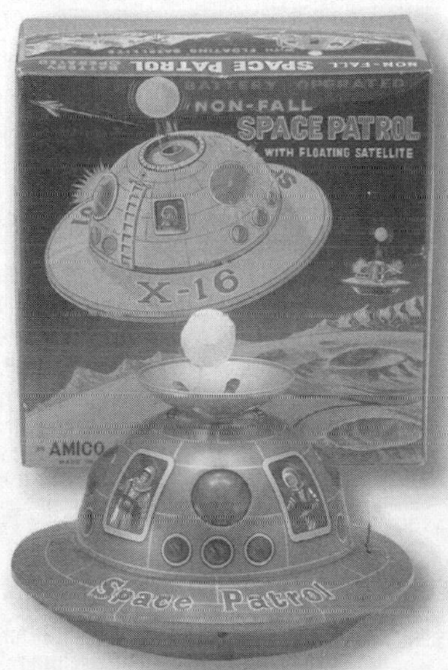

THE *TOP 10* SCI-FI & SPACE TOYS (In Mint Condition)

1. Buck Rogers Solar Scouts Patch, Cream of Wheat, 1936 .... $7,200
2. Lost in Space Doll Set, Marusan, 1960s 7,000
3. Buck Rogers Cut-Out Adventure Book, Cocomalt, 1933 6,500
4. Space Patrol Monorail Set, Toys of Tomorrow, 1950s 4,200
5. Buck Rogers Pocket Watch, Ingraham, 1935 3,750
6. Space Patrol Lunar Fleet Base, 1950s 3,200
7. Lost in Space Roto-Jet Gun Set, Mattel, 1966 2,600
8. Space Patrol, Emergency Kit, 1950s 2,500
9. Buck Rogers Repeller Ray Ring, 1936 2,500
10. Space Patrol, Emergency Kit, 1950s, ... 2,500

Alien/Aliens

Alien Blaster Target Game, 1979, H.G. Toys, set features large free standing cardboard Alien target and plastic dart shooting rifle, gun has large block letters "Alien" on side, based on the movie
EX $65 **NM** $135 **MIP** $225

Alien Blaster Target Set, HG Toys, larger set
EX $110 **NM** $220 **MIP** $325

Alien Chase Target Set, HG Toys, dart pistol, cardboard target
EX $80 **NM** $190 **MIP** $250

Alien Costume, Ben Cooper, black/white
EX $50 **NM** $65 **MIP** $110

Alien Model Kit, 1980s, Tsukuda, vinyl, 1/6 scale
EX $60 **NM** $225 **MIP** $350

Alien Warrior Model Kit, Halcyon, base and egg
EX $30 **NM** $40 **MIP** $60

Aliens Colorforms Set, Colorforms
EX $10 **NM** $20 **MIP** $45

Aliens Computer Game, 1985, Commodore
EX $5 **NM** $15 **MIP** $30

Glow Putty, Laramie, unlicensed art, carded
EX $10 **NM** $15 **MIP** $25

Movie Viewer, Kenner, "Alien Terror" film clip
EX $40 **NM** $75 **MIP** $125

Battlestar Galactica

Colorforms Adventure Set, 1978, Colorforms
EX $12 **NM** $25 **MIP** $35

Cylon Helmet Radio, 1979, Vanity Fair
EX $25 **NM** $50 **MIP** $85

Cylon Warrior Costume, 1978, boxed
EX $10 **NM** $15 **MIP** $35

Galactic Cruiser, 1978, Larami, die-cast
EX $5 **NM** $10 **MIP** $25

Game of Starfighter Combat, 1978, FASA, role playing game
EX $10 **NM** $17 **MIP** $30

L.E.M. Lander, 1978, Larami, die-cast
EX $5 **NM** $10 **MIP** $15

Lasermatic Pistol, 1978, Mattel
EX $15 **NM** $35 **MIP** $60

Lasermatic Rifle, 1978, Mattel
EX $25 **NM** $50 **MIP** $75

Muffit the Daggit Halloween Costume, 1978, Collegeville
EX $10 **NM** $17 **MIP** $35

Poster Art Set, 1978, Craft Master
EX $10 **NM** $15 **MIP** $25

Puzzles, 1978, Parker Brothers, The Rag-Tag Fleet, Starbuck, Interstellar Battle, price for each
EX $10 **NM** $15 **MIP** $25

Space Alert Game, 1978, Mattel, hand-held electronic game
EX $10 **NM** $25 **MIP** $50

Viper Vertibird, 1979, Mattel
EX $60 **NM** $120 **MIP** $220

Buck Rogers

25th Century Police Patrol Rocket, 1939, Marx, tin wind-up, 12" long
EX $325 **NM** $600 **MIP** $1200

25th Century Scientific Laboratory, 1934, Porter Chemical, w/three manuals
EX $800 **NM** $1300 **MIP** $2200

Adventures of Buck Rogers Book, 1934, Whitman, All Pictures Comics edition, Big Big Book
EX $25 **NM** $100 **MIP** $200

Battle Cruiser Rocket, 1937, Tootsietoy, two grooved wheels to run on string
EX $75 **NM** $225 **MIP** $350

Buck and Wilma Masks, 1933, Einson-Freeman, paper litho, each
EX $120 **NM** $220 **MIP** $375

Buck Rogers 25th Century Rocket, 1934, Marx, Buck and Wilma in window, 12" long, tin wind-up
EX $250 **NM** $650 **MIP** $1200

Buck Rogers and the Children of Hopetown Book, 1979, Golden Press, Little Golden Book
EX $4 **NM** $7 **MIP** $15

Buck Rogers and the Depth Men of Jupiter Book, 1935, Whitman, Big Little Book
EX $50 **NM** $100 **MIP** $160

Buck Rogers and the Doom Comet Book, 1935, Whitman, Big Little Book
EX $50 **NM** $100 **MIP** $160

Buck Rogers and the Overturned World Book, 1941, Whitman, Big Little Book
EX $50 **NM** $85 **MIP** $130

Buck Rogers and the Planetoid Plot Book, 1936, Whitman, Big Little Book
EX $50 **NM** $100 **MIP** $160

Buck Rogers and the Super Dwarf of Space Book, 1943, Whitman, Big Little Book
EX $50 **NM** $85 **MIP** $130

Buck Rogers Battlecruiser, 1937, Tootsietoy, with wheels that run on string to simulate flying
EX $75 **NM** $110 **MIP** $200

Buck Rogers Figure, 1937, Tootsietoy, 1-3/4" tall, cast, gray
EX $100 **NM** $150 **MIP** $275

Buck Rogers Films, 1936, Irwin, set of six
EX $110 **NM** $190 **MIP** $285

Buck Rogers Flash Blast Attack Cruiser, 1937, Tootsietoy
EX $50 **NM** $90 **MIP** $165

Buck Rogers Holster for U-238 Atomic Pistol, 1946, Daisy, leather holster only
EX $40 **NM** $150 **MIP** $300

Buck Rogers Holster for XZ-35 Pop Gun, 1935, Daisy, embossed leather, attached to belt by two short riveted straps
EX $50 **NM** $175 **MIP** $350

Buck Rogers in the 25th Century Book, 1933, Whitman, Big Little Book, Cocomalt premium
EX $50 **NM** $90 **MIP** $160

Buck Rogers in the 25th Century Book, 1933, Whitman, Big Little Book
EX $75 **NM** $130 **MIP** $210

Buck Rogers in the 25th Century Button, 1935, pinback, color Buck bust profile on blue background, w/small ray gun and rocket ship at his shoulders
EX $30 **NM** $75 **MIP** $150

Buck Rogers in the 25th Century Pistol Set, 1934, Daisy, XA-32, holster is red, yellow and blue suede cloth, gun is 9-1/2" pressed steel pop gun
EX $210 **NM** $425 **MIP** $750

Buck Rogers in the 25th Century Star Fighter, 1979, Mego, vehicle for 3-3/4" figures
EX $20 **NM** $35 **MIP** $60

Buck Rogers in the 25th Century XZ-31 Rocket Pistol, 1934, Daisy, holster is red, yellow and blue leather, gun is 9-1/2" pressed steel Rocket Pistol w/single cooling fin at barrel base
EX $180 **NM** $400 **MIP** $725

Buck Rogers in the City Below the Sea Book, 1934, Whitman, Big Little Book
EX $75 **NM** $160 **MIP** $275

Buck Rogers in the City of Floating Globes Book, 1935, Whitman, Cocomalt premium, paperback Big Little Book
EX $125 **NM** $250 **MIP** $500

Buck Rogers in the War With the Planet Venus Book, 1938, Whitman, Big Little Book
EX $45 **NM** $80 **MIP** $130

Buck Rogers on the Moons of Saturn Book, 1934, Whitman, premium, paperback Big Little Book
EX $75 **NM** $160 **MIP** $260

Buck Rogers Rubber Band Gun, 1930s, Unknown, cut-out paper gun, on card, advertising premium item
EX $30 **NM** $75 **MIP** $150

Buck Rogers Sonic Ray Flashlight Gun, 1955, Norton-Honer, 7-1/4" black, green and yellow plastic w/code signal screw
EX $80 **NM** $150 **MIP** $325

Buck Rogers Starfighter, 1980, Corgi, white body w/yellow plastic wings, amber windows, blue jets, color decal, Buck and Wilma figures, 6-1/2", Model No. 647-A
EX $32 **NM** $48 **MIP** $100

Buck Rogers U-235 Atomic Pistol, 1945, Daisy, 9-1/2" long, pressed steel, makes pop noise and flash in window when trigger is pulled
EX $125 **NM** $325 **MIP** $900

Buck Rogers vs. The Fiend of Space Book, 1940, Whitman, Big Little Book
EX $45 **NM** $80 **MIP** $130

Buck Rogers Wristwatch, 1935, E. Ingraham
EX $400 **NM** $750 **MIP** $1500

Buck Rogers Wristwatch, 1971, Huckleberry Time
EX $50 **NM** $125 **MIP** $250

Buck Rogers XXVc Role Playing Game, 1990, TSR, numerous game modules, paperback books, comics and a board game sprang from this concept
EX $10 **NM** $20 **MIP** $30

Buck Rogers XZ-35 Space Gun, 1934, Daisy, 7-1/2" long, heavy blued metal ray gun, the grip pumps the action and the gun pops when trigger is pulled, single cooling fin at barrel base, also called "Wilma Gun"
EX $125 **NM** $275 **MIP** $695

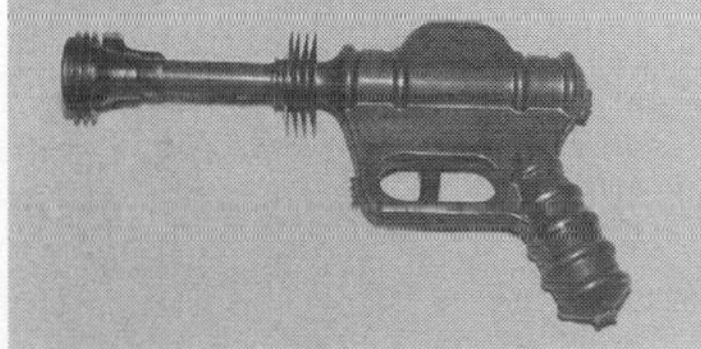

Buck Rogers XZ-38 Disintegrator Pistol, 1935, Daisy, 10-1/2" long, polished copper finish, four flutes on barrel, spark is produced in the window on top of the gun when the trigger is pulled
EX $115 **NM** $400 **MIP** $1295

Buck Rogers XZ-44 Liquid Helium Water Gun, 1936, Daisy, 7-1/4" long, red and yellow lightning bolt design stamped metal body w/a leather bladder to hold water; a later version was available in copper finish
EX $200 **NM** $550 **MIP** $950

Century of Progess Key Fob, 1934, metal, coin style, reverse shows Buck silhouette profile
EX $135 **NM** $275 **MIP** $500

Century of Progress Button, 1934, pinback, I Saw Buck Rogers 25th Century Show, color litho
EX $135 **NM** $250 **MIP** $500

Chemistry Set, 1937, Gropper, advanced
EX $350 **NM** $800 **MIP** $1600

Chemistry Set, 1937, Gropper, beginners
EX $325 **NM** $775 **MIP** $1350

Chief Explorer Badge, 1936, gold
EX $150 **NM** $350 **MIP** $750

Chief Explorer Badge, 1936, red enamel
EX $90 **NM** $215 **MIP** $385

Chief Explorer Folder, 1936
EX $70 **NM** $125 **MIP** $250

Clock, 1990s, Ingraham, wall clock
EX $15 **NM** $30 **MIP** $45

Colorforms Set, 1979, Colorforms
EX $10 **NM** $15 **MIP** $40

Comet Socker Paddle Ball, 1935, Lee-Tex
EX $35 **NM** $100 **MIP** $200

Communicator Set, 1979, w/silver Twiki figure
EX $10 **NM** $20 **MIP** $45

Costume, 1934, Sackman Bros.
EX $850 **NM** $1400 **MIP** $2500

Cut-Out Adventure Book, 1933, Cocomalt premium
EX $1250 **NM** $3500 **MIP** $6500

Electric Caster Rocket, 1934, Marx
EX $125 **NM** $210 **MIP** $350

Flash Blast Attack Ship Rocket, 1937, Tootsietoy, Flash Blast Attack Ship 4-1/2", Venus Duo-Destroyer w/two grooved wheels to run on string
EX $90 **NM** $150 **MIP** $250

Galactic Play Set, 1980s, HG Toys
EX $17 **NM** $30 **MIP** $55

Helmet and Rocket Pistol Set, 1933, Einson-Freeman, set of paper partial-face "helmet" mask and paper pop gun, in envelope
EX $115 **NM** $275 **MIP** $550

Helmet XZ-34, 1935, Daisy, leather
EX $285 **NM** $500 **MIP** $750

Interplanetary Games Set, 1934, three game boards in box: Cosmic Rocket Wars, Secrets of Atlantis, Siege of Gigantica, set
EX $235 **NM** $425 **MIP** $700

Interplanetary Space Fleet Model Kit, 1935, six different kits, including instructions and poster, in box, each
EX $100 **NM** $200 **MIP** $350

Lite-Blaster Flashlight, 1936
EX $155 **NM** $285 **MIP** $500

Martian Wars Game, 1990s, TSR, role playing game expansion set for the Buck Rogers XXVc game
EX $10 **NM** $20 **MIP** $35

Midget Caster, 1934, Rapaport Bros., mold and metal to cast lead figures
EX $150 **NM** $300 **MIP** $450

Official Utility Belt, 1979, Remco, in window box, w/decoder glasses, wristwatch, disk-shooting ray gun, intruder detection badge, city decoder map, secret message
EX $20 **NM** $40 **MIP** $85

Paint By Number Set, 1980s, Transogram
EX $15 **NM** $25 **MIP** $40

Pencil Box, 1930s, American Pencil
EX $75 **NM** $150 **MIP** $275

Pendant Watch, 1971, Huckleberry Time
EX $115 **NM** $200 **MIP** $300

Pocket Knife, 1935, Adolph Kastor, red, green, blue
EX $450 **NM** $900 **MIP** $2000

Pocket Watch, 1935, E. Ingraham, round, face shows Buck and Wilma, lightning bolt hands
EX $500 **NM** $1800 **MIP** $3750

Pocket Watch, 1971, Huckleberry Time
EX $90 **NM** $175 **MIP** $275

Punching Bag, 1942, Morton Salt, balloon w/characters
EX $50 **NM** $75 **MIP** $150

Puzzle, 1945, Puzzle Craft, Buck Rogers and His Atomic Bomber, three different each
EX $75 **NM** $150 **MIP** $300

Puzzle, 1979, Milton Bradley, four versions showing TV scenes, each
EX $6 **NM** $15 **MIP** $30

Puzzle with sleeve, 1952, Milton Bradley, space station scene, 14" x 10"
EX $75 **NM** $150 **MIP** $200

Repeller Ray Ring, 1936, brass w/inset green stone
EX $400 **NM** $1250 **MIP** $2500

Rocket Rangers Iron-On Transfers, 1944, set of three
EX $30 **NM** $50 **MIP** $100

Rocket Rangers Membership Card, 1939
EX $45 **NM** $75 **MIP** $150

Rocket Skates, 1935, Marx, roller skates w/leather straps, red jeweled reflector on back, 11-1/2"
EX $600 **NM** $1000 **MIP** $2200

Satellite Pioneers Button, 1958, green or blue
EX $20 NM $50 MIP $125

Satellite Pioneers Map of Solar System, 1958
EX $20 NM $40 MIP $85

Satellite Pioneers Membership Card, 1958
EX $30 NM $60 MIP $110

Satellite Pioneers Starfinder, 1958, paper
EX $20 NM $50 MIP $75

Saturn Ring, 1946, Post Corn Toasties, red stone, glow-in-the-dark white plastic on crocodile base
EX $150 NM $300 MIP $650

School Bag, 1935, suede cloth
EX $100 NM $400 MIP $850

Solar Scouts Member Badge, 1936, gold color
EX $60 NM $100 MIP $160

Solar Scouts Patch, 1936, Cream of Wheat, three colors
EX $1500 NM $5000 MIP $7200

Solar Scouts Radio Club Manual, 1936
EX $125 NM $275 MIP $550

Space Glasses, 1955, Norton-Honer, No. 1440
EX $40 NM $75 MIP $200

Space Ranger Halolight Ring, 1953, Sylvania
EX $300 NM $750 MIP $1000

Space Ranger Kit, 1952, Sylvania, 11" x 15" premium, envelope w/six punch-out sheets
EX $50 NM $100 MIP $200

Spaceship Commander, 1936, stationery
EX $50 NM $100 MIP $200

Spaceship Commander Banner, 1936
EX $350 NM $1000 MIP $2000

Spaceship Commander Whistling Badge, 1936
EX $50 NM $110 MIP $225

Strange Adventures in the Spider Ship Pop-Up Book, 1935
EX $110 NM $250 MIP $400

Strato-Kite, 1946, Aero-Kite
EX $20 NM $35 MIP $75

Super Foto Camera, 1955, Norton-Honer
EX $40 NM $70 MIP $150

Super Scope Telescope, 1955, Norton-Honer, No. 1430, 9" plastic telescope
EX $40 NM $70 MIP $150

Super Sonic Ray Gun, 1950, Norton-Honer, No. 1432, 6-1/4", black w/ red and green knobs on the side
EX $75 NM $150 MIP $225

Superdreadnought SD51X Model Kit, 1936, 6-1/2" long, balsa wood, one of Interplanetary Space Fleet kit set
EX $100 NM $200 MIP $350

Toy Watch, 1978, GLJ Toys
EX $15 NM $30 MIP $60

Two-Way Transceiver, 1948, DA Myco
EX $80 NM $130 MIP $200

View-Master Set, 1979, View-Master, three-reel set, in envelope or on blister card
EX $5 NM $7 MIP $10

Walkie Talkies, 1950s, Remco
EX $60 NM $150 MIP $200

Wilma Deering Figure, 1937, Tootsietoy, 1-3/4" tall, cast, gold color
EX $70 NM $125 MIP $230

Captain Midnight

Air Heroes Stamp Album, 1930s, twelve stamps
EX $35 NM $75 MIP $150

Captain Midnight Medal, 1930s, gold medal pin w/centered wings and words "Flight Commander"; Capt. is embossed on top w/medal dangling beneath
EX $65 NM $150 MIP $200

Cup, Ovaltine, plastic, 4" tall, "Ovaltine-The Heart of a Hearty Breakfast"
EX $15 NM $35 MIP $65

Key-O-Matic Code-O-Graph w/key, 1949, Secret Squadron brass decoder sets number and letter combinations
EX $80 NM $185 MIP $325

Membership Manual, 1930s, Secret Squadron official code and manual guide
EX $40 NM $60 MIP $110

Captain Video

Captain Video and Ranger Photo, 1950s, premium
EX $25 NM $50 MIP $90

Captain Video Game, 1952, Milton Bradley
EX $75 NM $150 MIP $250

Captain Video Rite-O-Lite Flashlight Gun, 1950s, Power House Candy, 3" long, red plastic gun w/bulb, space map, paper, directions and order form, in mailing envelope
EX $40 NM $95 MIP $200

Captain Video Rocket Launcher, 1952, Lido
EX $65 NM $185 MIP $360

Comic Book, Captain Video No. 1, 1951, Fawcett
EX $100 NM $375 MIP $1000

Flying Saucer Ring, 1950s, w/two saucers and papers
EX $500 NM $1000 MIP $1500

Galaxy Spaceship Riding Toy, 1950s
EX $250 NM $425 MIP $725

Interplantary Space Men Figures, 1950s, in die-cut box
EX $55 NM $110 MIP $185

Kukla, Fran and Ollie Puppet Show, 1962, Milton Bradley, cardboard stage, puppets, props
EX $50 NM $200 MIP $375

Mysto-Coder, 1950s, w/photo
EX $65 NM $200 MIP $400

Rocket Tank, 1952, Lido
EX $55 NM $95 MIP $175

Secret Seal Ring, 1950s, w/initials CV, gold or copper
EX $250 NM $400 MIP $600

Space Port Play Set, 1950s, Superior, All tin set, including rocket (not shown)
EX $250 NM $430 MIP $660

Troop Transport Ship, 1950s, Lido, in box
EX $55 NM $95 MIP $155

Defenders of the Earth

Gripjaw Vehicle, 1985, Galoob
EX $11 NM $16 MIP $25

Mongor Figure, 1985, Galoob
EX $16 NM $23 MIP $35

Puzzle, 1985, frame tray
EX $9 NM $15 MIP $25

Doctor Who

Cyberman Robot Doll, 1970s, Denys Fisher, 10"
EX $250 NM $350 MIP $550

Dalek Bagatelle, 1976, Denys Fisher
EX $70 NM $110 MIP $175

Dalek Shooting Game, 1965, Marx, 8" x 20", four-color tin litho stand up target and generic cork rifle
EX $225 NM $325 MIP $525

Dalek's Oracle Question & Answer Board Game, 1965, magnetized Dalek that spins
EX $115 NM $165 MIP $250

Davros Figure, 1986, Dapol, villain w/left arm
EX $11 NM $16 MIP $45

Doctor Who Card Set, 1970s, 12 octagon cards
EX $14 NM $20 MIP $35

Doctor Who Card Set, 1976, Denys Fisher, 24 cards
EX $18 NM $26 MIP $45

Doctor Who Trump Card Game, 1970s
EX $9 NM $13 MIP $20

Doctor Who...Dodge the Daleks Board Game, 1965
EX $120 NM $175 MIP $280

Flash Gordon

Adventure on the Moons of Mongo Game, 1977, House of Games
EX $15 NM $25 MIP $40

Arak Figure, 1979, Mattel, 3-3/4", carded
EX $17 NM $30 MIP $50

Battle Rocket with Space Probing Action, 1976
EX $6 NM $10 MIP $20

Beastman Figure, 1979, Mattel, 3-3/4", carded
EX $15 NM $25 MIP $45

Book Bag, 1950s, 12" wide, three-color art on flap
EX $17 NM $35 MIP $75

Candy Box, 1970s, eight illustrated boxes, each
EX $4 NM $10 MIP $20

Dr. Zarkov Figure, 1979, Mattel, 3-3/4" figure, on card
EX $15 NM $35 MIP $50

Flash and Ming Button, 1970s, shows Flash and Ming crossing swords
EX $4 NM $10 MIP $20

Flash Gordon Air Ray Gun, 1950s, Budson, 10" unusual air blaster, handle on top cocks mechanism, pressed steel
EX $150 NM $225 MIP $450

Flash Gordon and Martian, 1965, Revell, #1450
EX $60 NM $125 MIP $175

Flash Gordon and the Ape Men of Mor Book, 1942, Dell, 196 pages, Fast Action Story
EX $75 NM $150 MIP $250

Flash Gordon and the Fiery Desert of Mongo Book, 1948, Whitman, Big Little Book
EX $30 NM $60 MIP $90

Flash Gordon and the Monsters of Mongo Book, 1935, Whitman, hardback Big Little Book
EX $50 NM $90 MIP $135

Flash Gordon and the Perils of Mongo Book, 1940, Whitman, Big Little Book
EX $35 NM $70 MIP $100

Flash Gordon and the Power Men of Mongo Book, 1943, Whitman, Big Little Book
EX $35 NM $65 MIP $95

Flash Gordon and the Red Sword Invaders Book, 1945, Whitman, Big Little Book
EX $30 NM $60 MIP $90

Flash Gordon and the Tournaments of Mongo Book, 1935, Whitman, paperback Big Little Book
EX $45 NM $80 MIP $120

Flash Gordon and the Tyrant of Mongo Book, 1941, Whitman, Big Little Book, w/flip pictures
EX $35 NM $70 MIP $105

Flash Gordon and the Witch Queen of Mongo Book, 1936, Whitman, Big Little Book
EX $45 NM $80 MIP $120

Flash Gordon Arresting Ray Gun, 1939, Marx, picture of Flash on handle, 12" long
EX $200 NM $350 MIP $950

Flash Gordon Costume, 1951, Esquire Novelty
EX $90 NM $145 MIP $250

Flash Gordon Figure, 1944, wood composition, 5" tall
EX $115 NM $195 MIP $300

Flash Gordon Game, 1970s, House of Games
EX $15 NM $30 MIP $40

Flash Gordon Hand Puppet, 1950s, rubber head
EX $90 NM $145 MIP $250

Flash Gordon in the Forest Kingdom of Mongo Book, 1938, Whitman, Big Little Book
EX $40 NM $75 MIP $110

Flash Gordon in the Ice World of Mongo Book, 1942, Whitman, Big Little Book, w/flip pictures
EX $35 NM $70 MIP $100

Flash Gordon in the Jungles of Mongo Book, 1947, Whitman, Big Little Book
EX $35 NM $65 MIP $95

Flash Gordon in the Water World of Mongo Book, 1937, Whitman, Big Little Book
EX $35 NM $70 MIP $105

Flash Gordon Kite, 1950s, 21" x 17", paper
EX $55 NM $90 MIP $135

Flash Gordon on the Planet Mongo Book, 1934, Whitman, Big Little Book
EX $55 NM $105 MIP $155

Flash Gordon Paint Book, 1930s
EX $60 NM $125 MIP $200

Flash Gordon Radio Repeater Clicker Pistol, Marx, 10" long, 1930s
EX $250 NM $350 MIP $950

Flash Gordon Signal Pistol, 1930s, Marx, 7", siren sounds when trigger is pulled, tin/pressed steel, green w/red trim
EX $250 NM $600 MIP $1200

Flash Gordon Space Water Gun, 1976, Nasta, water ray gun on illustrated card
EX $10 NM $25 MIP $50

Flash Gordon Three Color Ray Gun, 1976, Nasta, battery-operated
EX $8 NM $35 MIP $80

Flash Gordon vs. the Emperor of Mongo Book, 1936, Dell, 244 pages, Fast Action Story
EX $70 NM $140 MIP $225

Flash Gordon Water Pistol, 1940s, Marx, plastic w/whistle in handle, 7-1/2" long
EX $80 NM $250 MIP $500

Flash Gordon Wristwatch, 1979, Bradley, medium chrome case, back and sweep seconds, Flash in foreground w/city behind
EX $70 NM $115 MIP $175

Flash Gordon, The Movie Buttons, 1980, set of five, each
EX $2 NM $4 MIP $8

Home Foundry Casting Set, 1935, lead casting set w/molds of Flash and other characters
EX $575 NM $975 MIP $1500

Lizard Woman Figure, 1979, Mattel, 3-3/4", carded
EX $15 NM $25 MIP $40

Medals and Insignia, 1978, Larami, set of five on blister card
EX $10 NM $25 MIP $50

Ming Figure, 1979, Mattel, 3-3/4", carded
EX $12 NM $20 MIP $35

Ming's Space Shuttle, Mattel
EX $15 NM $25 MIP $50

Pencil Box, 1951
EX $75 NM $150 MIP $225

Puzzle, 1930s, Featured Funnies
EX $55 NM $110 MIP $160

Puzzle, 1951, Milton Bradley, frame tray
EX $45 NM $80 MIP $125

Puzzles, 1951, Milton Bradley, set of three
EX $105 NM $200 MIP $300

Rocket Fighter, 1939, Marx, tin wind-up, 12" long
EX $175 NM $350 MIP $600

Rocket Ship, 1975, 3" die-cast metal
EX $10 NM $20 MIP $35

Rocket Ship, 1979, Mattel, inflatable, 3' long, w/plastic nose, rocket and gondola attachments
EX $20 NM $40 MIP $60

Solar Commando Set, 1950s, Premier Products
EX $65 NM $115 MIP $175

Space Compass, 1950s, ornately housed compass on illustrated watchband
EX $25 NM $40 MIP $75

Space Water Gun, 1976, Nasta, water ray gun on illustrated card
EX $6 NM $15 MIP $30

Sunglasses, 1981, Ja-Ru, plastic w/emblem on bridge, carded
EX $3 NM $5 MIP $10

Three-Color Ray Gun, 1976, Nasta
EX $8 NM $15 MIP $30

Thun, Lion Man Figure, 1979, Mattel, 3-3/4", carded
EX $15 NM $25 MIP $45

Two-Way Telephone, 1940s, Marx
EX $60 NM $110 MIP $185

View-Master Set, 1963, View-Master, three reels in envelope
EX $20 NM $35 MIP $60

Flash Gordon

View-Master Set, 1976, View-Master, three reels, In the Planet Mongo
EX $6 **NM** $10 **MIP** $20

Vultan Figure, 1979, Mattel, 3-3/4", carded
EX $15 **NM** $30 **MIP** $50

Wallet, 1949, w/zipper
EX $70 **NM** $115 **MIP** $175

Water Pistol, 1950s, Marx, 7-1/2" plastic
EX $155 **NM** $275 **MIP** $500

Land of the Giants

Annual Book, 1969, World Dist./UK, two volumes, set
EX $30 **NM** $50 **MIP** $75

Colorforms Set, 1968, Colorforms
EX $30 **NM** $50 **MIP** $75

Costumes, 1968, Ben Cooper, Steve Burton, Giant Witch, or Scientist, each
EX $35 **NM** $60 **MIP** $150

Deluxe Numbered Pencil Coloring Set, 1969, Hasbro
EX $60 **NM** $100 **MIP** $150

Double Action Bagatelle Game, 1969, Hasbro, pinball game, cardboard back
EX $35 **NM** $75 **MIP** $160

Flight of Fear Book, Whitman, hardcover
EX $8 **NM** $15 **MIP** $35

Flying Saucer, 1968, Remco, flying disk
EX $60 **NM** $100 **MIP** $150

Land of the Giants Book, Pyramid, paperback by Murray Leinster
EX $8 **NM** $13 **MIP** $25

Land of the Giants Comic Book #1, 1968, Gold Key
EX $10 **NM** $15 **MIP** $30

Land of the Giants Comic Books #2-#5, 1968, Gold Key, each
EX $8 **NM** $13 **MIP** $25

Motorized Flying Rocket, 1968, Remco, plastic airplane w/motor, LOTG logo on wings
EX $80 **NM** $130 **MIP** $200

Movie Viewer, 1968, Acme, film strip viewer, on card
EX $25 **NM** $45 **MIP** $65

Painting Set, 1969, Hasbro
EX $40 **NM** $65 **MIP** $100

Puzzle, 1968, Whitman, round floor puzzle w/cartoon illustration
EX $35 **NM** $55 **MIP** $85

Rub-Ons, 1969, Hasbro
EX $30 **NM** $50 **MIP** $75

Shoot & Stick Target Rifle Set, 1968, Remco, western rifle w/logo decals
EX $90 **NM** $145 **MIP** $225

Signal Ray Space Gun, 1968, Remco, ray gun w/logo decals
EX $70 **NM** $115 **MIP** $175

Space Sled, 1968, Remco, Supercar refitted w/LOTG decals—Mike Mercury still sits behind the wheel
EX $200 **NM** $350 **MIP** $525

Spaceship Control Panel, 1968, Remco, Firebird 99 dashboard w/a cardboard cut-out of logo on top
EX $200 **NM** $300 **MIP** $525

Spindrift Interior Model Kit, 1989, Lunar Models, #Sf029, interior for 16" model shell
EX $35 **NM** $55 **MIP** $85

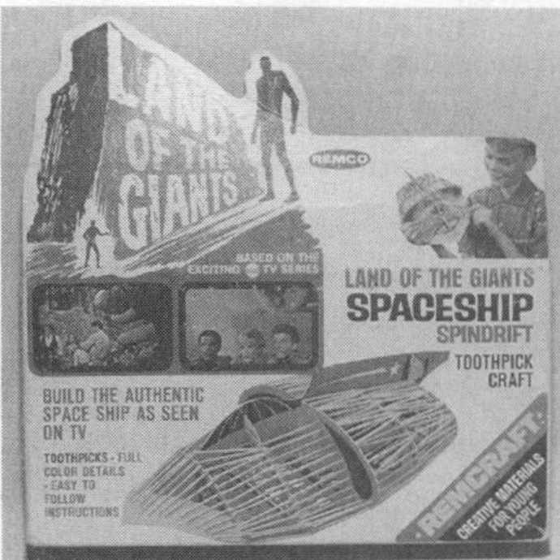

Spindrift Toothpick Kit, 1968, Remco, box of toothpicks w/a few cardboard pieces to build ship
EX $35 **NM** $60 **MIP** $85

Target Set, 1969, Hasbro, small guns w/darts
EX $60 **NM** $100 **MIP** $160

The Hot Spot Book, Pyramid, paperback, #2 in series, by Leinster
EX $12 **NM** $20 **MIP** $35

Trading Card Wrapper, 1968, Topps/A & BC
EX $60 **NM** $100 **MIP** $160

Trading Cards, 1968, A & BC/England, 55 cards
EX $275 **NM** $450 **MIP** $710

Trading Cards, 1968, Topps USA, 55 cards
EX $275 **NM** $450 **MIP** $710

Trading Cards Box, 1968, Topps/A & BC, display box only
EX $395 **NM** $650 **MIP** $1000

Unknown Danger Book, Pyramid, paperback #3 by Leinster
EX $12 **NM** $20 **MIP** $35

View-Master Set, 1968, GAF, three reels, first episode
EX $20 **NM** $35 **MIP** $50

Walkie Talkies, 1968, Remco, generic walkie talkies w/LOTG decals added
EX $80 **NM** $130 **MIP** $210

Wrist Flashlight, 1968, Bantam Lite
EX $30 **NM** $50 **MIP** $80

Lost in Space

Chariot Model Kit, Marusan/Japanese, figures and motor
EX $625 **NM** $975 **MIP** $1500

Chariot Model Kit, 1987, Lunar Models, #SF009, 1:35 scale, w/clear vacuform canopy and dome, plastic body, treads, roof rack
EX $35 **NM** $50 **MIP** $80

Costume, 1965, Ben Cooper, silver spacesuit w/logo
EX $85 **NM** $150 **MIP** $225

Doll Set, Marusan/Japanese, dressed in spacesuits w/their own freezing tubes w/a cardboard insert w/color photos and description
EX $2900 **NM** $4500 **MIP** $7000

Fan Cards, 1960s, promo cards mailed to fans; color photo
EX $20 **NM** $35 **MIP** $60

Fan Cards, 1960s, promo cards mailed to fans; black/white photo
EX $15 **NM** $25 **MIP** $50

Helmet and Gun Set, 1967, Remco, child size helmet w/blue flashing light and logo decals, blue and red molded gun
EX $300 **NM** $530 **MIP** $880

Jupiter Model Kit, 1966, Marusan/Japanese, large version
EX $425 **NM** $650 **MIP** $1000

Jupiter-2 Model Kit, Comet/England, 2" diameter, solid metal
EX $8 **NM** $13 **MIP** $35

Jupiter-2 Model Kit, 1966, Marusan/Japanese, 6" molded in green plastic w/wheels and wind-up motor
EX $425 **NM** $650 **MIP** $1000

Laser Water Pistol, Unknown, 5" long, first season pistol style
EX $30 **NM** $50 **MIP** $80

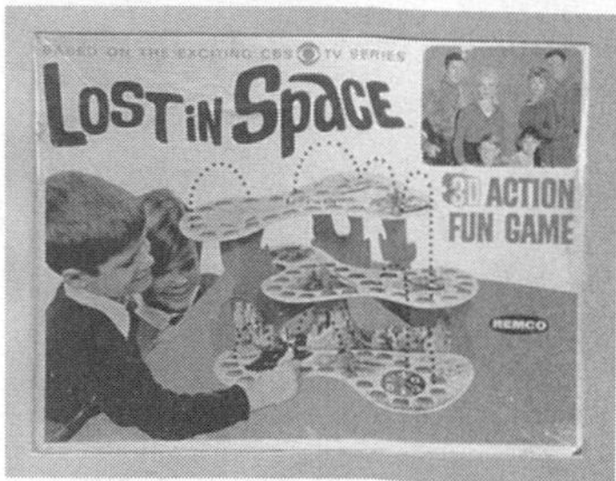

Lost In Space 3-D Action Fun Game, 1966, Remco, three levels w/small cardboard figures
EX $530 **NM** $785 **MIP** $1250

Note Pad, June Lockhart on front
EX $25 **NM** $40 **MIP** $65

Puzzles, 1966, Milton Bradley, frame tray; three poses w/Cyclops, 10 x 14"
EX $40 **NM** $65 **MIP** $100

Robot, 1966, Remco, 12" high, motorized w/blinking lights
EX $180 **NM** $365 **MIP** $700

Robot, 1968, Aurora, 6" high w/base
EX $150 **NM** $400 **MIP** $1100

Robot, 1977, K-mart/Ahi, 10", plastic w/green dome, battery-operated
EX $85 **NM** $200 **MIP** $325

Robot YM-3, 1985, Masudaya, 4" high, wind-up
EX $20 **NM** $30 **MIP** $50

Robot YM-3, 1986, Masudaya, 16" high, speaks English and Japanese
EX $85 **NM** $150 **MIP** $250

Roto-Jet Gun Set, 1966, Mattel, TV tie-in, modular gun can be reconfigured into different variations, shoots discs
EX $775 **NM** $1300 **MIP** $2600

Saucer Gun, 1977, Ahi, disk shooting gun
EX $30 **NM** $60 **MIP** $150

Space Family Robinson Comic Book, 1960s, Gold Key
EX $15 **NM** $25 **MIP** $45

Switch-and-Go Set, 1966, Mattel, figures, Jupiter and chariot that ran around track
EX $975 **NM** $1500 **MIP** $2400

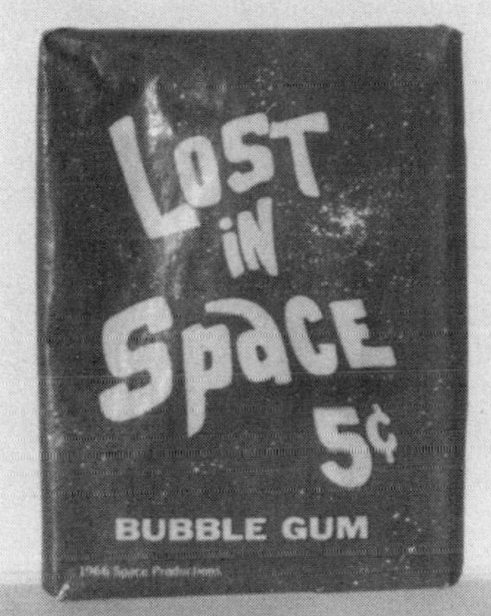

Trading Cards, 1966, Topps, 55 black and white cards, no wrappers or box
EX $175 **NM** $300 **MIP** $525

Tru-Vue Magic Eyes Set, 1967, GAF, rectangular reels
EX $30 **NM** $50 **MIP** $80

View-Master Set, 1967, GAF, Condemned of Space
EX $25 **NM** $40 **MIP** $65

Walkie Talkies, 1977, AHI, small card
EX $30 **NM** $50 **MIP** $85

Miscellaneous

Astro Base, 1960, Ideal, 22" tall, red/white astronaut base, control panel opens lock door, extends crane and lowers astronaut in scout car
EX $225 **NM** $325 **MIP** $525

Astro Boy Mask/Glasses, 1960s, blue glasses w/Astro boy hair on top
EX $25 **NM** $50 **MIP** $75

Astronaut Costume, 1960, Collegeville
EX $18 **NM** $25 **MIP** $50

Astronaut Costume, 1962, Ben Cooper
EX $18 **NM** $25 **MIP** $50

Astronaut Space Commander Play Suit, 1950s, Yankeeboy, green outfit and cap (military style) w/gold piping on collar and pants
EX $35 **NM** $50 **MIP** $85

Fireball XL-5 Space City Play Set, 1963, MPC, includes ship, base and figures
EX $550 **NM** $1100 **MIP** $2200

Fireball XL-5 Spaceship, 1963, MPC, plastic, 20" ship w/figures
EX $200 **NM** $500 **MIP** $1300

Martian Bobbing Head, 1960s, 7" tall, blue vinyl martian w/bobbing eyes and exposed brain
EX $23 **NM** $35 **MIP** $60

Men into Space Astronaut Space Helmet, 1960s, Ideal, plastic helmet w/visor
EX $35 **NM** $50 **MIP** $80

Puzzle, 1970, Selchow & Righter, 10" x 14", picture of the moon's surface
EX $14 **NM** $20 **MIP** $35

Rex Mars Atomix Pistol Flashlight, 1950s, Marx, plastic
EX $50 **NM** $80 **MIP** $175

Space Safari Planetary Play Set, 1969, four battery operated space vehicles, 3" tall astronaut figures in silver plastic, 2" hard plastic aliens
EX $45 **NM** $65 **MIP** $100

TV Space Riders Coloring Book, 1952, Abbott, 14" X 15"
EX $7 **NM** $12 **MIP** $25

V-Enemy Visitor Doll, 1984, LJN, 12"
EX $16 **NM** $30 **MIP** $60

Voyage to the Bottom of the Sea Scout Play Set, 1964, Remco, includes mini-sub, sea crawler and divers
EX $250 **NM** $650 **MIP** $1300

Voyage to the Bottom of the Sea Seaview Play Set, 1964, Remco, includes plastic sub, sea monster and divers
EX $320 **NM** $675 **MIP** $1625

Monsters

Creature From the Black Lagoon Aquarium Figure, 1950s, Japan, 3 1/2" Lead figure
EX $85 **NM** $150 **MIP** n/a

Creature from the Black Lagoon Aquarium Figure, 1971, Penn-Plax, 6" Moving Figure
EX $150 **NM** $250 **MIP** $450

Creature From the Black Lagoon Figure, 1963, Marx, 5", hard plastic blue or orange
EX $10 **NM** $20 **MIP** $40

Creature From the Black Lagoon Figure, 1973, 74, AHI, 5", hard rubber like bendy
EX $40 **NM** $65 **MIP** $100

Creature From the Black Lagoon Figure, 1974, AHI, 8", plastic, bendable joints
EX $295 **NM** $425 **MIP** $700

Creature From the Black Lagoon Halloween Costume, 1973, Ben Cooper, Child's Mask and Costume
EX $35 **NM** $80 **MIP** $120

Creature From the Black Lagoon Motionette, 1992, Telco, 24", Electric, w/sound
EX $100 **NM** $200 **MIP** $350

Creature From the Black Lagoon Motionette, 1992, Telco, 17", Batt op, w/sound
EX $10 **NM** $15 **MIP** $30

Creature From the Black Lagoon Robot, 1991, Robot House, 9", tin/plastic, wind-up
EX $35 **NM** $65 **MIP** $110

Creature From the Black Lagoon Soaky, 1963, Colgate-Palmolive, 10", plastic, bubble bath bottle
EX $35 **NM** $75 **MIP** $110

Creature From the Black Lagoon Sparky, 1970s, Hong Kong, 3 1/2", plastic, wind-up
EX $10 **NM** $20 **MIP** $35

Creature From the Black Lagoon Wiggle Ick Figure, 1960s, Japan, 7", rubbery plastic, bobbin' head
EX $50 **NM** $85 **MIP** $150

Deadly Grell Figure, 1983, LJN, bendable
EX $5 **NM** $7 **MIP** $10

Dracula Action Figure, AHI, w/Aurora head
EX $65 **NM** $125 **MIP** $200

Dracula Glow-in-the-Dark Mini Monsters, Remco
EX $23 **NM** $30 **MIP** $45

Dwarves of the Mountain Human/Monster Figure, 1983, LJN
EX $5 **NM** $7 **MIP** $10

Evil Monster Figure Bugbear & Goblin, 1983, LJN, Orcs of the Broken Bone
EX $5 **NM** $7 **MIP** $10

Frankenstein Figure, AHI, w/Aurora head
EX $65 **NM** $125 **MIP** $200

Frankenstein Figure, 1978, Remco, poseable, glow-in-the-dark features and removable cloth costumes
EX $23 **NM** $35 **MIP** $50

Godzilla Combat Joe Set, 1984, vinyl, w/12" tall Combat Joe figure, poseable
EX $450 **NM** $650 **MIP** $1000

Godzilla Figure, 1977, Mattel, 19" tall
EX $20 **NM** $30 **MIP** $60

Godzilla Figure, 1985, Imperial, 6-1/2" tall, arms, legs and tail movable
EX $5 **NM** $10 **MIP** $20

Godzilla Figure, 1985, Imperial, 13" tall, arms, legs and tail movable
EX $15 **NM** $23 **MIP** $40

Moon McDare

Action Communication Set, 1966, Gilbert
EX $25 **NM** $35 **MIP** $60

Moon Explorer Set, 1966, Gilbert
EX $35 **NM** $50 **MIP** $85

Moon McDare Figure, 1966, Gilbert, 12" tall astronaut w/blue jumpsuit
EX $55 **NM** $80 **MIP** $150

Moon McDare Space Gun Set, 1966, Gilbert
EX $25 **NM** $50 **MIP** $130

Space Accessory Pack, 1966, Gilbert
EX $25 **NM** $35 **MIP** $75

Space Gun Set, 1966, Gilbert
EX $40 **NM** $80 **MIP** $125

Space Mutt Set, 1966, Gilbert
EX $30 **NM** $45 **MIP** $75

Other Worlds, The

Castle Zendo, 1983, Arco
EX $20 **NM** $30 **MIP** $50

Fighting Glowgons Figure Set, 1983, Arco
EX $18 **NM** $25 **MIP** $40

Fighting Terrans Figure Set, 1983, Arco
EX $20 **NM** $30 **MIP** $50

Kamaro Figure, 1983, Arco
EX $8 **NM** $12 **MIP** $18

Sharkoss Figure, 1983, Arco
EX $8 **NM** $12 **MIP** $18

Planet of the Apes

Cap Pistol, 1974, Mattel, Fanner 50
EX $30 **NM** $65 **MIP** $95

Color-Vue Set, 1970s, Hasbro, eight pencils and nine 12" x 13" pictures to color
EX $30 **NM** $45 **MIP** $70

Dr. Zaius Bank, 1967, Play Pal, figural, vinyl, 11"
EX $20 **NM** $30 **MIP** $60

Fun-Doh Modeling Molds, 1974, Chemtoy, molds of Zira, Cornelius, Zaius, and Aldo
EX $20 **NM** $30 **MIP** $50

Galen Bank, 1960s, Play Pal
EX $25 **NM** $35 **MIP** $60

Machine Gun, 1974, Mattel, "Planet of the Apes" sticker on stock, sub-machine gun
EX $40 **NM** $85 **MIP** $125

Planet of the Apes Activity Book, 1974, Saalfield, #C3031
EX $15 **NM** $30 **MIP** $45

Puzzle, 1974, Whitman, #7512, 224 pieces, 18-1/2 x 13",
EX $5 **NM** $10 **MIP** $15

Puzzle, Battle on Planet of the Apes, 1967, H.G. Toy Co., #486-01, 500 pieces, 16 x 20"
EX $7 **NM** $14 **MIP** $20

Puzzle, General Aldo, 1967, H.G. Toy Co., #485-05, 96 pieces, 10 x 14"
EX $5 **NM** $10 **MIP** $15

Puzzle, On Patrol, 1967, H.G. Toy Co., #486-06, 96 pieces, 10 x 14"
EX $5 **NM** $10 **MIP** $15

Puzzle, The Chase, 1967, H.G. Toy Co., #486-02, 500 pieces, 16 x 20"
EX $7 **NM** $14 **MIP** $20

Puzzles, H.G. Toys, 96-piece canister puzzles, each
EX $7 **NM** $12 **MIP** $25

Rapid Fire Rifle, 1974, Mattel, "Planet of the Apes" sticker on stock, Winchester mechanism
EX $40 **NM** $85 **MIP** $125

Wagon, AHI, friction powered prison wagon
EX $20 **NM** $45 **MIP** $70

Wastebasket, 1967, Chein, oval, tin
EX $25 **NM** $35 **MIP** $60

Zaius, Zera, or Cornelius Walkers, 1970s, Hong Kong, 3 1/2" plastic, wind-up
EX $20 **NM** $40 **MIP** $80

Rocky Jones, Space Ranger

Pin, Silvercup Bread, 1950s, 1-1/2", photo, "Rocky Jones Space Ranger Silvercup Bread"
EX $10 **NM** $20 **MIP** $35

Rocky Jones, Space Ranger Coloring Book, 1951, Whitman, 14" x 16"
EX $25 **NM** $50 **MIP** $80

Space Ranger Button, 1954
EX $17 **NM** $35 **MIP** $75

Space Ranger Wings Pin, 1954, gold wings say "Space Ranger" silver ring w/spaceship around it
EX $17 **NM** $40 **MIP** $85

Wristwatch, 1954, in illustrated box
EX $80 **NM** $150 **MIP** $300

Space Guns

4-Barrel Waist Space Dart Gun Belt, 1950s, Knickerbocker, 11" wide gun system on belt, designed to be worn on waist or chest and aimed w/periscope sight, red plastic belt
EX $30 **NM** $50 **MIP** $85

888 Space Gun, 1955, Japan, 3" long, tin, shoots caps, painted blue body and grip w/stars, planets and spaceship, red barrel w/"888" above grip
EX $30 **NM** $60 **MIP** $120

Astro Ray Gun, 1960s, Shudo/Japan, 5-7/8" long, silver finish body w/red, yellow and black detailing, friction sparkling action, single large spark window near muzzle, prominent "Astro Ray Gun" in center of body
EX $15 **NM** $30 **MIP** $60

Astro Ray Gun, 1968, Shudo/Japan, 9" long, friction spark action, tin litho body w/clear red plastic barrel, red on yellow "ASTRO RAY GUN" lettering
EX $25 **NM** $40 **MIP** $75

Astro Ray Laser Lite Beam Dart Gun, 1960s, Ohio Art, 10" red and white plastic flashlight lights target w/four darts
EX $70 **NM** $95 **MIP** $200

Astroray Gun, 1960s, MTU, 10", tin litho, blue w/ red and silver accents, red transparent plastic barrel, Korea, unusual triangular box
EX $20 **NM** $40 **MIP** $65

Astro-Ray Space Gun, 10"
EX $20 **NM** $30 **MIP** $50

Atom Bubble Gun, 1940s, Unknown, red tubular barrel w/handle attached, two sets of silver finish fins--at barrel base and muzzle, wire loop projects from muzzle for bubble blowing, handle embossed "Atom Trade Mark"
EX $95 **NM** $175 **MIP** $200

Atom Buster Mystery Gun, 1950s, Webb Electric, 11" long yellow plastic gun w/inner bladder, fires blast of air at tissue paper atomic mushroom target, w/instructions, atomic explosion cover art on box
EX $105 **NM** $200 **MIP** $300

Atom Ray Gun, 1949, Hiller, 5-1/2" long, sleek red body gun of aluminum and brass w/bulbous water reservoir on top of gun, reads "Atom Ray Gun" between two lightning bolts on reservoir
EX $135 **NM** $300 **MIP** $650

Atomee Water Pistol, 1960s, Park Plastics, 4-1/4" black plastic
EX $15 **NM** $25 **MIP** $40

Atomic Disintegrator Ray Gun, 1954, Hubley, 8" long, die-cast metal w/red handles, ornately embellished w/dials and other equipment outcroppings, shoots caps
EX $175 **NM** $300 **MIP** $750

Atomic Flash Gun, 1955, Chein, 7-1/2" long, tin, sparkling action seen through tinted elongated oval plastic muzzle, w/yellow and red on turquoise body w/red lettered "Atomic Flash" over trigger
EX $40 **NM** $80 **MIP** $195

Atomic Gun, 1960s, Japan, 5" long, gold, blue, white and red tin litho, friction sparkling action, "Atomic Gun" on body sides
EX $20 **NM** $40 **MIP** $75

Atomic Gun, 1969, Haji, 9" long, red, gray and yellow tin litho gun w/plastic muzzle, friction sparkling action, large hollow letter "ATOMIC GUN" on body
EX $15 **NM** $35 **MIP** $70

Atomic Jet Gun, 1954, Stevens, 8-1/2" long, gold chromed die-cast metal, cap

shooting, "Atomic Jet" and large circular "S" logo on grip
EX $100 **NM** $200 **MIP** $350

Atomic Ray Gun, 1957, Marx, 30" long,"Captain Space Solar Scout," blue plastic w/oversized telescope sight flashlight and "electric buzzer" sound
EX $75 **NM** $175 **MIP** $300

Baby Space Gun, 1950s, Daiya/Japan, 6" friction siren and spark action
EX $35 **NM** $60 **MIP** $135

Batman Ray Gun, 1960s, Unknown, cap pistol w/bat symbol for the sight
EX $35 **NM** $65 **MIP** $140

Battlestar Galactica Lasermatic Pistol, 1978, Mattel
EX $15 **NM** $30 **MIP** $60

Battlestar Galactica Lasermatic Rifle, 1978, Mattel
EX $25 **NM** $40 **MIP** $80

Bee-Vo Bell Gun, 1950s, Beaver Toys, #204, 6-1/2" long, red plastic, fires trapped marble at bell in muzzle, in box
EX $25 **NM** $40 **MIP** $80

Bicycle Water Cannon Ray Gun, 1950s, Unknown, 10", red plastic, swivel mount attached to bicycle handles, fired by lever
EX $30 **NM** $75 **MIP** $125

Cherilea Space Gun, Marx, miniature scale, die-cast
EX $27 **NM** $40 **MIP** $65

Clicker Ray Gun, 1950s, Unknown, 5" red, blue or gray hard plastic, no boxes, sold loose
EX $15 **NM** $25 **MIP** $50

Clicker Ray Gun, 1960, Irwin, 9" long, red plastic w/deep blue cooling fins on barrel base
EX $30 **NM** $45 **MIP** $75

Clicker Whistle Ray Gun, 1950s, Unknown, 5" plastic, blue/green or olive/green swirl plastic, imprinted spacemen and rocket ships, back of gun is a whistle
EX $15 **NM** $25 **MIP** $50

Daisy Rocket Dart Pistol, 1954, Daisy, 7" long, red, blue and yellow sheet metal gun w/blue body, blue grips w/yellow trim, blue and yellow barrel stripes, same body as Zooka Pop Pistol but w/connecting rod from gun to barrel
EX $80 **NM** $175 **MIP** $350

Daisy Zooka Pop Pistol, 1954, Daisy, 7" long, colorful red, blue and yellow sheet metal gun w/blue body, red grips w/yellow trim and litho star reading "It's a Daisy Play Gun," yellow barrel w/red stripes, and wide red muzzle, handle cock
EX $80 **NM** $175 **MIP** $350

Dan Dare & the Aliens Ray Gun, 1950s, 21", tin litho gun
EX $105 **NM** $175 **MIP** $300

Dune Fremen Tarpel Gun, 1984, LJN, 8" long, battery-operated w/internal light, light beam and chirping sound, plastic
EX $25 **NM** $40 **MIP** $70

Dune Sardaukar Laser Gun, 1984, LJN, 7" black plastic w/flashing lights, battery-operated
EX $20 **NM** $35 **MIP** $55

Flash-O-Matic, The Safe Gun, 1950s, Royal Plastics, 7" long red and yellow plastic battery-operated light beam gun
EX $60 **NM** $100 **MIP** $160

Flashy Ray Gun, 1960s, TN, battery-operated, tin litho, machine gun by Nomura of Japan
EX $70 **NM** $140 **MIP** $200

Floating Satellite Target Game, 1958, S. Horikawa/Japan, 6-1/2" x 9", battery-operated, includes a pistol and three rubber tipped darts, a blower supports the styrofoam ball on a column of air and the players shoot darts to knock it down
EX $95 **NM** $150 **MIP** $300

Ideal Flash Gun, 1957, Ideal, 9" long, plastic three-color flashlight gun w/red or blue body and bulbous contrasting-color blue or red rimmed flash unit, trigger switch and tail battery compartment cover, w/color switch at top of flash unit
EX $45 **NM** $95 **MIP** $220

Jack Dan Space Gun, 1959, Metamol/Spain, 7-1/2" long, in black, red or blue painted die-cast metal cap gun w/"Jack Dan" over trigger
EX $105 **NM** $200 **MIP** $300

Jet Gun, 1957, Japan, 6" long, tin, sparkling action, red body w/three small red tinted spark windows near muzzle, grip shows silver-suited astronaut in modern helmet and wording "JET GUN" at top of grip near trigger
EX $35 **NM** $60 **MIP** $130

Jet Jr. Cap Gun, 1950s, Stevens, 6-1/2" long, fires roll caps, side loading door, silver finish, rear jet "Blast Off Fins"
EX $85 **NM** $175 **MIP** $300

Jet Plane Missile Gun, 1968, Hasbro, jet shaped handgun shoots darts, targets supplied on box back
EX $35 **NM** $60 **MIP** $100

Jupiter 4 Color Signal Gun, 1950s, Remco, 9" long black, red and yellow plastic gun that lights up in four colors, red telescoping sight
EX $35 **NM** $55 **MIP** $90

Over and Under Ray Gun, 1960s, Haji, 8-1/2" long, red, yellow, white and black tin litho gun w/two over and under reciprocating plastic muzzles, friction sparkling action
EX $30 **NM** $50 **MIP** $80

Planet Clicker Bubble Gun, 1953, Mercury Toys, 8" long, plastic, red body w/yellow accents, dip the barrel in bubble solution and pull trigger to make bubbles and produce click sound, in illustrated box
EX $40 **NM** $65 **MIP** $110

Planet Patrol Saucer Gun, 1950s, Unknown, w/spaceman motif
EX $40 **NM** $70 **MIP** $120

Pop Gun, 1967, Chemtoy, 4-1/2" long red hard plastic gun w/space designs on handle
EX $25 **NM** $35 **MIP** $80

Pop Ray Gun, 1930s, Wyandotte, red pressed steel body w/five widely spaced vertical round fins, unpainted trigger and muzzle w/large gunsight, rod connects body to pop mechanism in muzzle
EX $70 **NM** $125 **MIP** $200

Radar Gun, 1956, Unknown, 5-1/2" long, mauve or silver/gray swirl plastic body w/green or yellow spaceman sight and trigger, Saturn and star embossed above grip and "Radar Gun" embossed above that
EX $20 **NM** $35 **MIP** $60

Ranger Gun, 1960s, KO-Japan, 15", No. 2057, Double barreled, friction powered, tin litho, camo pattern, white barrels, spark action
EX $50 **NM** $100 **MIP** $150

Ratchet Sound Space Gun, 1950s, Ideal, 7" long, red plastic w/silver trim, flywheel ratchet on top of gun
EX $30 **NM** $50 **MIP** $80

Ratchet Water Pistol Ray Gun, 1960s, Hong Kong, 6-1/2" unusual pull back mechanism loads pistol, ratchet forces water out when trigger is pulled
EX $25 **NM** $40 **MIP** $70

Space Guns

Ray Dart Gun, 1968, Tarrson, 9-1/2" long, blue plastic body w/yellow muzzle, w/three darts, storage compartment in red handle base
EX $15 **NM** $27 **MIP** $55

Ray Gun, 1936, Wyandotte, 7" stamped metal pop gun that uses a captive cork to make the pop, red body, unpainted muzzle, w/connecting rod from body to barrel tip
EX $50 **NM** $100 **MIP** $175

Ray Gun, 1957, Japan, 6-1/2" long, tin, sparkling action w/two red tinted plastic tapered rectangle windows at muzzle, "Ray Gun" in red at top of body w/rocket exhaust encircling green/blue planet against deep blue star studded background
EX $32 **NM** $65 **MIP** $130

Ray Gun Water Pistol, 1950s, Palmer Plastics, 5-1/2" many color variations: green, orange, translucent blue, royal blue, black, yellow and red
EX $10 **NM** $15 **MIP** $30

Razer Ray Gun, 1972, H.Y. Mfg./Hong Kong, plastic bronze finish body w/five large cooling fins near red plastic barrel, friction sparkling action, chrome finish muzzle tip, "Razer Ray Gun" embossed on rear of barrel
EX $10 **NM** $15 **MIP** $30

Rex Mars Planet Patrol 45 Caliber Machine Gun, 1950s, Marx, 22" long, tin and plastic, wind-up
EX $60 **NM** $150 **MIP** $300

Rex Mars Planet Patrol Space Pistol Arresting Ray, 1950, Marx, tin w/ red and yellow litho
EX $100 **NM** $200 **MIP** $300

Rex Mars Planet Patrol Super Beam Signal Ray Gun, 1950s, Marx, flashlight gun, red plastic, name in grip, clear plastic cap at end of barrel reveals battery compartment, blue trigger
EX $35 **NM** $125 **MIP** $350

Robot Raiders Space Signal Gun, 1980s, TNT/Hong Kong, 6" long flashlight gun w/interchangeable lenses and click sound
EX $6 **NM** $10 **MIP** $20

Robotech Water Pistol, 1985, Matchbox
EX $6 **NM** $10 **MIP** $20

Rocket Gun, 1958, Jak-Pak, 7" hard yellow/green plastic w/spring loaded plunger that shoots corks up to 50 feet
EX $10 **NM** $15 **MIP** $30

Rocket Jet Water Pistol, 1957, U.S. Plastics, 5" long, red, orange or yellow clear plastic body, fill plug at top of gun, large integral gunsight fin at rear, small sight fin at front
EX $12 **NM** $30 **MIP** $60

Rocket Pop Gun, 1955, Unknown, wood, green and red horizontal striped body w/black tri-fin pump base, cork and string stopper in nose, pump fins into body to make it pop
EX $25 **NM** $40 **MIP** $75

Rocket Signal Pistol, 1930s, Marx, same bulbous teardrop metal body as Flash Gordon Signal Pistol and Siren sparkling Airplane Pistol but without siren hole or wings; same rear fin, red w/litho of three horizontally stacked finned orange/yellow bombs
EX $135 **NM** $275 **MIP** $525

Ro-Gun "It's A Robot", 1984, Arco, Shogun-type robot transforms into a rifle, in window box
EX $8 **NM** $13 **MIP** $25

S-58 Space Gun, 1957, Japan, 12" long, tin litho, deep metallic blue body w/friction sparkling action, "S-58" on muzzle, w/ringed planet graphic on front sight
EX $35 **NM** $70 **MIP** $135

Satellite & Rocket Pistol, 1960s, Hong Kong, 5" long, green plastic gun fires either yellow plastic darts or saucers, on card
EX $12 **NM** $20 **MIP** $60

Secret Squirrel Ray Gun, 1960s, Unknown
EX $25 **NM** $50 **MIP** $100

Signal Flash Gun, 1957, Unknown, 6" long, plastic flashlight, black body w/translucent white plastic light housing at muzzle and pearl finish plastic grip plates, modern missile type sight on top of barrel, large "SIGNAL FLASH" above trigger
EX $20 **NM** $40 **MIP** $75

Smoke Ring Gun, 1950s, Nu-Age Products, large, sleek gray finished breakfront pistol w/red barrel and muzzle ring, used rocket shaped matches to produce smoke, trigger fired smoke rings, small engraved "Smoke Ring Gun" logo on gunsight fin
EX $175 **NM** $295 **MIP** $450

Space Atomic Gun, 1955, Japan, 5-1/2" long, tin, sparkling action seen through red tinted plastic window, two-tone blue body w/red/white atomic symbol on grip, "Space Atomic Gun" letters around oval spaceship-and-stars logo above trigger
EX $32 **NM** $65 **MIP** $130

Space Atomic Gun, 1960, T/Japan, 4" long, tin litho, friction sparkling action, silver gray finish w/yellow and red trim, w/"SPACE" on body in white small all caps and large yellow lower caps "atomic gun," small "T/Made in JAPAN" logo above trigger
EX $25 **NM** $40 **MIP** $70

Space Atomic Gun, 1960s, Unknown, 4" silver, orange/red tin litho, sparking action
EX $25 **NM** $40 **MIP** $70

Space Control Ray Gun, 1956, Unknown, 5-1/2" long, red plastic w/yellow trigger, clicks
EX $25 **NM** $42 **MIP** $85

Space Control Space Gun, 1954, Nomura/Japan, 3" long, tin sparkling gun w/green body, red sights, decorated all over w/stars and planets, red and yellow "Space Control" letters over trigger and spacemen firing gun and rocket flying overhead on grips
EX $30 **NM** $40 **MIP** $65

Space Dart Gun, 1950s, Arliss, 4" solid color plastic gun, shoots standard rubber tipped darts
EX $12 **NM** $35 **MIP** $70

Space Dart Gun, 1950s, Unknown, 6" long, gun has one white side and one black side, both w/star and lightning motif, eight thin cooling fins on barrel
EX $30 **NM** $50 **MIP** $90

Space Gun, 1955, San/Japan, 3-1/4" long, tin, sparkling action, aqua blue body w/red and yellow highlights and "Space" in script lettering over grip, grip shows rocket shooting toward planets, circular San/Japan logo behind trigger
EX $30 **NM** $85 **MIP** $250

Space Gun, 1957, Daiya/Japan, 6" long, tin, sparkling action, metallic teal finish w/red grooves and muzzle, green spaceship on body above "Space Gun," small Daiya logo inside red/yellow burst on grip w/"577001" at bottom of grip
EX $35 **NM** $75 **MIP** $150

Space Gun, 1957, Japan, 9" long, friction sparkling action w/three red tinted plastic spark windows and clear red plastic barrel, body in metallic blue w/large red "SPACE GUN" letters on yellow background
EX $35 **NM** $65 **MIP** $140

Space Gun, 1957, Yoshiya/Japan, 7" long, tin w/sparkling action, shows a realistic white rocket blasting off over lunar terrain on side of body and atomic symbol on grip center w/diamond-shaped "SY" logo and "Made in Japan" at bottom of grip
EX $40 **NM** $65 **MIP** $120

Space Gun, 1960, Hero Toy/Japan, 7" long, tin litho, friction sparkling action, yellow body w/blue and red trim, small Hero Toy logo by trigger
EX $35 **NM** $60 **MIP** $95

Space Gun, 1960s, TN/Japan, 8" long, battery-operated, reciprocating barrel shaft has red and blue lenses that flash when fired, makes rat-a-tat noise, large circular "8" over handgrip, winged eagle over trigger, large block letter "SPACE GUN" on barrel
EX $70 **NM** $115 **MIP** $185

Space Gun, 1967, Shudo/Japan, 4" tin litho, friction sparkling action, red body w/blue inset and grips, yellow block letter "SPACE GUN," large yellow and white vertical painted fins, six red tinted plastic sparkling windows, oval Shudo logo by grip
EX $20 **NM** $35 **MIP** $70

Space Jet Gun, 1957, KO/Japan, 9" long, tin, sparkling action w/black body, orange "Space Jet" on body w/orange and red atomic symbol on grip, clear green plastic finned barrel base, clear blue plastic finned muzzle
EX $35 **NM** $60 **MIP** $120

SCI-FI AND SPACE TOYS

Space Jet Water Pistol, 1957, Knickerbocker, 4" long, black plastic w/white "Space Jet" lettering and spaceship line art on sides, fill plug in gunsight
EX $15 **NM** $30 **MIP** $65

Space Navigator Gun, 1953, Asahitoy/Japan, 3-1/2" long, tin, looks like sawed off military .45, colorfully trimmed blue body w/smiling spaceman, blasting winged rocketship and "Space Navigator" logo on grips, planets and star on body
EX $35 **NM** $60 **MIP** $135

Space Outlaw Ray Gun, 1965, B.C.M., 10" long, chrome plated, die-cast metal, recoiling barrel action, "Cosmic," "Sonic," or "Gamma" power levels, large red clear plastic teardrop shaped window
EX $115 **NM** $200 **MIP** $275

Space Pilot Junior Jet Ray Gun, 1960s, Taiyo-Japan, friction powered, gold plastic w/silver and green accents
EX $45 **NM** $90 **MIP** $135

Space Pilot Super-Sonic Gun, 1953, J&C Randall Ltd., gun flashes red, white, and green light, battery-operated
EX $30 **NM** $60 **MIP** $95

Space Rocket Gun, 1950s, M & L Toy, 9" gray plastic, modern police-style pistol grip and shell chamber body w/oversized barrel and muzzle sights, spring loaded, shoots rocket projectiles, in box w/two "rockets"
EX $55 **NM** $95 **MIP** $185

Space Scout Spud Gun, 1960s, Mil Jo, 7" black and white plastic
EX $15 **NM** $30 **MIP** $50

Space Ship Flashlight Gun, 1950s, Irwin, 7-1/4", blue plastic ray gun has cockpit w/orange spaceman, nose unscrews for AAA batteries, pulling trigger lights nose and moves guns and spaceman
EX $60 **NM** $150 **MIP** $250

Space Target Game, 1952, T. Cohn, 24" tall, metal target w/rubber tipped darts and dartgun to shoot down all the jet rockets and missiles
EX $40 **NM** $80 **MIP** $175

Space Water Gun, 1957, Palmer Plastics, 5-1/2" long, clear red plastic body w/embossed Ringed planet and star, four cooling fins at barrel base, hollow telescope sight, yellow plastic trigger, white plastic stopper attached by loop to red knob at gun back
EX $15 **NM** $30 **MIP** $50

Space Water Gun, 1960, Park Plastics, 6" long, red transparent plastic, stopper at rear of gun, finned trigger guard, zeppelin-shaped reservoir w/single embossed lightning bolt running its length, tiny "Park Plastics" imprinted along lateral reservoir fin
EX $15 **NM** $25 **MIP** $40

Space Water Pistol, 1976, Nasta
EX $7 **NM** $10 **MIP** $20

Space X-Ray Gun, 1970s, Lido, #46598, 8-1/2" long, plastic, friction sparkling action, same body as Razer Ray Gun but w/more futuristic handgrip and noisemaker at rear, sold in bag w/header card
EX $15 **NM** $25 **MIP** $40

Sparking Atom Buster Pistol, Marx, aluminum
EX $30 **NM** $50 **MIP** $85

Sparking Space Gun Rifle, Marx
EX $50 **NM** $100 **MIP** $175

Sparkling Machine Gun "Sure-Shot", 1950s, T. Cohn, tin litho machine gun sends sparks out of barrel
EX $30 **NM** $65 **MIP** $120

Sparkling Ray Gun, 1976, Nasta
EX $6 **NM** $10 **MIP** $20

Star Team Ionization Nebulizer, 1969, Ideal, 9" water gun fires water mist, red, white, blue and black plastic, Star Team decal
EX $30 **NM** $50 **MIP** $85

Strato Gun, 1950s, Futuristic Products, 9" long, gray finish die-cast, cap firing, internal hammer, top of gun lifts to load
EX $70 **NM** $250 **MIP** $500

Strato Gun, 1950s, Futuristic Products, 9" long, chrome finish die-cast, red cooling fins, cap firing, internal hammer, top of gun lifts to load
EX $100 **NM** $175 **MIP** $325

Super Sonic Gun, 1957, Endoh/Japan, 9" long, tin, sparkling action w/three red plastic spark windows and clear red plastic barrel, blue body w/red lightning bolt beneath yellow "Super Sonic" on rounded gun body, small ENDOH logo printed above grips
EX $40 **NM** $80 **MIP** $160

Super Sonic Space Gun, 1957, Daiya/Japan, 7-1/2" long, tin litho, metallic gray body w/red gunsight fin, friction siren and sparkling action, large oval center art w/outstanding lunar scene of rockets, mountains and Earth in sky, red helmeted spaceman on grip
EX $40 **NM** $80 **MIP** $160

Super Space Gun, 1960, Japan, 6" long, tin litho, friction sparkling action, blue on blue body w/white/yellow/red highlights, large red on white "SUPER SPACE" lettering on side
EX $25 **NM** $50 **MIP** $100

Superior Rocket Gun, 1956, Unknown, 8" long, dark gray plastic, embossed "Superior Rocket Gun" on grip
EX $30 **NM** $50 **MIP** $85

Tom Corbett Space Cated Atomic Pistol, 1950s, Marx, Flashlight, battery-operated, "Space Cadet" on handle
EX $100 **NM** $200 **MIP** $450

Tomi Space Gun, 1950s, Shawnee, solid red plastic w/yellow barrel plug, modelled after modern .45 caliber pistol w/rounded reservoir lined w/two horizontal fins over grip; embossed logo and circular Shawnee logos on grip
EX $50 **NM** $90 **MIP** $135

Universe Gun, 1960s, T/Japan, 4" long, blue, yellow and red tin litho gun w/friction sparkling action, large all caps italic "Universe" on body side, sold in bag w/header card
EX $15 **NM** $25 **MIP** $40

Visible Sparkling Ray Gun, Hong Kong, 8-1/2" long, plastic, mechanism visible, bagged w/header card
EX $15 **NM** $32 **MIP** $65

Wham-O Air Blaster, 1960s, Wham-O, 10" long plastic gun uses rubber diaphragm to shoot air; styling is reminiscent of Budson Flash Gordon Air Ray Gun
EX $70 **NM** $120 **MIP** $185

X100 Mystery Dart Gun, 1956, Arliss, 3-3/4" long, yellow or gray plastic gun on cardboard display card, w/two yellow and blue talcum impregnated darts which create a smoke effect when striking any target
EX $25 **NM** $45 **MIP** $125

X-Ray Gun, 1950s, Daiya, Japan, red see-through plastic, friction toy, sparks
EX $50 **NM** $85 **MIP** $125

Space Patrol

Atomic Pistol Flashlight Gun, 1950s, Marx, plastic
EX $85 **NM** $220 **MIP** $450

Cosmic Cap, 1950s
EX $125 **NM** $200 **MIP** $400

Cosmic Gun, 1970, Nomura/Japan, 12" long, plastic, battery-operated w/a small electric motor that runs reciprocating light in clear red plastic barrel, dark blue body, red and orange lettered "COSMIC GUN" decal
EX $35 **NM** $55 **MIP** $90

Cosmic Ray Gun, 1954, Ranger Steel Products, 9" long, tin body w/plastic barrel, boldly painted in blue, yellow and red lightning bolts
EX $50 **NM** $90 **MIP** $150

Cosmic Ray Gun #249, 1953, Ranger Steel Products, 8" long, plastic, blue body, yellow barrel, red tip, in box showing two space kids in bubble helmets and backpacks shooting at spaceships
EX $40 **NM** $75 **MIP** $135

Cosmic Rocket Launcher Set, 1950s
EX $300 **NM** $525 **MIP** $850

Cosmic Smoke Gun, 1950s, green
EX $120 **NM** $325 **MIP** $675

Cosmic Smoke Gun, 1950s, red
EX $110 **NM** $170 **MIP** $325

Drink Mixer, 1950s, boxed
EX $60 **NM** $100 **MIP** $200

Emergency Kit, 1950s, w/rations, plastic w/yellow insert
EX $600 **NM** $1350 **MIP** $2500

Space Patrol

Handbook, 1950s
EX $55 NM $125 MIP $200

Interplanetary Space Patrol Credits Coins, different denominations and colors: Terra, Moon and Saturn, each
EX $10 NM $16 MIP $35

Jet Glow Code Belt, 1950s, gold-finish metal, spaceship-shaped buckle, decoder ring behind buckle
EX $120 NM $200 MIP $375

Lunar Fleet Base, 1950s, premium punch-outs in mailing envelope
EX $500 NM $1700 MIP $3200

Man From Mars Totem Head Mask, 1950s, paper, several styles
EX $65 NM $150 MIP $350

Monorail Set, 1950s, Toys of Tomorrow
EX $1650 NM $3000 MIP $4200

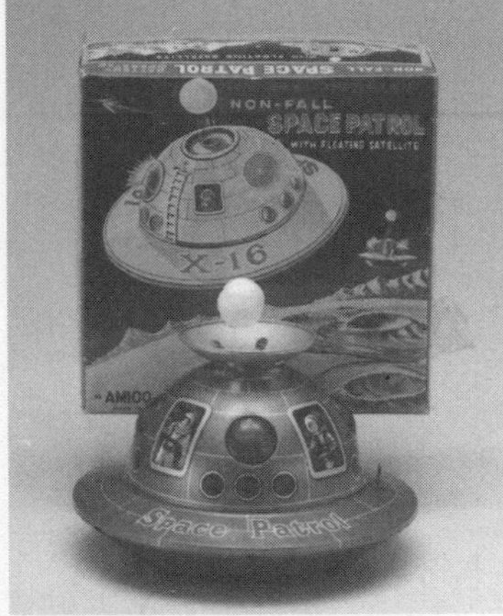

Non-Fall Space Patrol X-16, 1950s, Masudaya
EX $50 NM $150 MIP $300

Outer Space Helmet Mask, 1950s, paper helmet w/plastic one-way visor
EX $110 NM $170 MIP $300

Project-O-Scope, 1950s, rocket-shaped film viewer w/filmstrips
EX $175 NM $350 MIP $800

Puzzle, 1950s, Milton Bradley, frame tray w/sleeve
EX $40 NM $75 MIP $175

Rocket Gun and Holster Set, 1950s, w/darts
EX $200 NM $300 MIP $525

Rocket Gun Set, 1950s, w/darts, without holster
EX $110 NM $185 MIP $360

Rocket Lite Flashlight, 1950s, Rayovac, in box
EX $140 NM $250 MIP $375

Rocket Port Set, 1950s, Marx
EX $125 NM $200 MIP $375

Rocket-Shaped Pen, 1950s
EX $120 NM $185 MIP $350

Space Binoculars, 1950s, Ralston Purina, black plastic, logo on sides
EX $80 NM $125 MIP $200

Space Binoculars, 1950s, Ralston Purina, green plastic, large logo on top, premium
EX $120 NM $190 MIP $300

Space Holster with oval badge, 1950, w/unmarked blue gun
EX $200 NM $500 MIP $800

Space Patrol Atomic Flashlight Pistol, 1950s, Marx, gold/bronze finish pistol w/seven large cooling fins on barrel and three smaller ones at back of gun, large clear plastic diffuser on muzzle, white "Official Space Patrol" on handgrip
EX $135 NM $225 MIP $525

Space Patrol Badge, 1950s, plastic, w/ship and crest
EX $75 NM $150 MIP $300

Space Patrol Badge, 1950s, metal oval on card
EX $125 NM $400 MIP $800

Space Patrol Cadet Membership Card, 1950s
EX $25 NM $75 MIP $175

Space Patrol Cereal Box, 1953, Wheat Chex Magic Picture Offer
EX $125 NM $275 MIP $450

Space Patrol Commander Helmet, 1950s, plastic, in box
EX $140 NM $275 MIP $425

Space Patrol Cosmic Glow Ring, 1950s, red and blue
EX $450 NM $900 MIP $1800

Space Patrol Cosmic Smoke Gun, 1950s, Unknown, solid color red or green plastic w/"Space Patrol" on body above grip, TV show tie-in, shoots baking powder, on card
EX $135 NM $375 MIP $750

Space Patrol Hydrogen Ray Gun Ring, 1950s, Unknown, glow-in-the-dark ring
EX $80 NM $125 MIP $275

Space Patrol Mobile Store Display, Wheat Chex, 1953
EX $400 NM $1200 MIP $1600

Space Patrol Periscope, 1950s, paper w/mirrors
EX $75 NM $200 MIP $400

Space Patrol Printing Ring, 1950s
EX $200 NM $400 MIP $800

Space Patrol Wristwatch, 1950s, illustrated box w/"Terra" compass
EX $275 NM $500 MIP $750

Space-A-Phones, 1950s
EX $175 NM $500 MIP $750

Space:1999

Adventure Play Set, 1976, Amsco/Milton Bradley, Paper color and cut-out construction, included two Eagle Spacecraft, Moonbase Alpha with moving antenna, six-wheeled moon buggy, complete cast
EX $40 NM $55 MIP $85

Astro Popper Gun, 1976, Mattel, on card
EX $6 NM $10 MIP $20

Astro Popper Gun, 1976, Larami, on card
EX $10 NM $15 MIP $45

Colorforms Adventure Set, 1975, Colorforms
EX $10 NM $16 MIP $25

Cut and Color Book, 1975, Saalfield
EX $6 NM $12 MIP $25

Dr. Russell Figure, 1976, Mattel
EX $17 NM $30 MIP $45

Eagle Freighter, 1975, Dinky, No. 360, die-cast
EX $25 NM $80 MIP $160

Eagle One Spaceship, 1976, Mattel
EX $125 NM $325 MIP $525

Eagle Transport, 1975, Dinky, No. 359, die-cast
EX $25 NM $55 MIP $110

Eagle Transporter Model Kit, 1976, Airfix
EX $12 **NM** $20 **MIP** $80

Film Viewer TV Set, 1976, Larami
EX $8 **NM** $20 **MIP** $55

Galaxy Time Meter, 1976, Larami
EX $6 **NM** $10 **MIP** $20

Puzzle, 1976, HG Toys
EX $8 **NM** $15 **MIP** $30

Space Expedition Dart Set, 1976, Larami, carded
EX $6 **NM** $10 **MIP** $20

Stamping Set, 1976, Larami
EX $8 **NM** $13 **MIP** $25

Superscope, 1976, Larami
EX $6 **NM** $10 **MIP** $18

Utility Belt Set, 1976, Remco
EX $12 **NM** $40 **MIP** $110

Utility Belt Set, 1976, Remco, w/disc shooting stun gun, watch and compass
EX $12 **NM** $30 **MIP** $60

Walking Spaceman, 1975, Azrak Hamway
EX $50 **NM** $175 **MIP** $425

Zython Figure, 1976, Mattel
EX $40 **NM** $80 **MIP** $100

Spaceships

Eagle Lunar Module, 1960s, 9"
EX $80 **NM** $115 **MIP** $185

Friendship 7, 9-1/2", friction
EX $35 **NM** $50 **MIP** $80

Inter-Planet Toy Rocketank Patrol, 1950, Macrey, 10"
EX $30 **NM** $45 **MIP** $75

Jupiter Space Station, 1960s, TN/Japan, 8"
EX $90 **NM** $135 **MIP** $225

Moon-Rider Spaceship, 1930s, Marx, tin wind-up
EX $125 **NM** $200 **MIP** $275

Mystery Action Satellite, 1950s, Cragstan, battery-operated, puts astronaut in "orbit"
EX n/a **NM** $600 **MIP** $1350

Mystery Spaceship, 1960s, Marx, 35mm astronauts and moonmen, rockets, launchers
EX $80 **NM** $165 **MIP** $260

Rocket Fighter, 1950s, Marx, w/tail fin and sparking action, tin wind-up
EX $250 **NM** $375 **MIP** $525

Rocket Fighter Spaceship, 1930s, Marx, celluloid window, tin wind-up, 12" long
EX $125 **NM** $225 **MIP** $300

Satellite X-107, 1965, Cragstan, 9"
EX $90 **NM** $130 **MIP** $200

Sky Patrol Jet, 1960s, TN/Japan, 5" x 13" x 5", battery operated, working taillights
EX $295 **NM** $425 **MIP** $650

Solar-X Space Rocket, TN/Japan, 15"
EX $45 **NM** $65 **MIP** $100

Space Bus, tin helicopter, battery operated w/wired remote
EX $350 **NM** $500 **MIP** $750

Space Pacer, 1978, 7", battery operated
EX $20 **NM** $29 **MIP** $50

Space Survey X-09, battery operated, tin and plastic flying saucer w/clear bubble
EX $175 **NM** $375 **MIP** $550

Space Train, 1950s, 9" long, engine and three metallic cars
EX $18 **NM** $26 **MIP** $50

Spaceship, Marx, bronze plastic
EX $40 **NM** $60 **MIP** $100

Super Space Capsule, 1960s, 9-1/2"
EX $70 **NM** $100 **MIP** $160

X-3 Rocket Gyro, 1950s
EX $25 **NM** $35 **MIP** $60

Star Trek

Action Toy Book, 1976, Random House
EX $7 **NM** $10 **MIP** $20

Astro-Buzz-Ray Gun, 1967, Remco, blue gun w/large yellow barrel and yellow sights, buzzer signal, 3 color flashing light beam, battery operated, revolving turret, Spock pictured on box
EX $50 **NM** $100 **MIP** $150

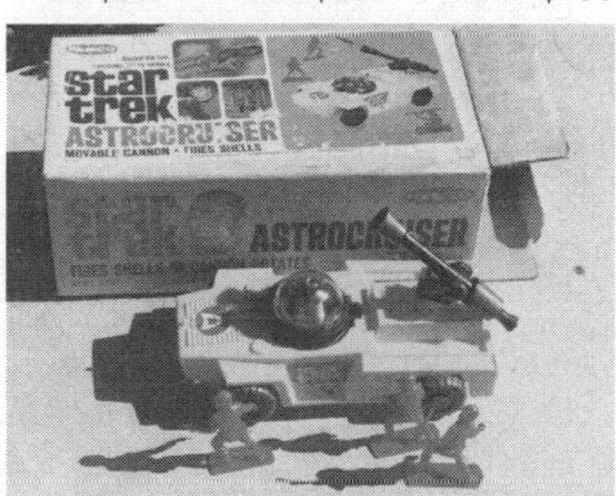

Astrocruiser, 1967, Remco, movable cannon, fires shells, 3 military figures, rare
EX $100 **NM** $200 **MIP** $325

Beanbag Chair, ST:TMP
EX $25 **NM** $35 **MIP** $55

Bowl, ST:TMP, 1979, Deka, plastic
EX $3 **NM** $7 **MIP** $15

Bridge Punch-Out Book, ST:TMP, 1979, Wanderer
EX $7 **NM** $10 **MIP** $25

Bulletin Board, ST:TMP, 1979, Milton Bradley, w/four pens
EX $6 **NM** $8 **MIP** $15

Clock, 1986, white wall clock, red 20th anniversary logo on face, Official Star Trek Fan Club
EX $14 **NM** $20 **MIP** $40

Clock, 1989, Enterprise orbiting planet, rectangular
EX $23 **NM** $33 **MIP** $60

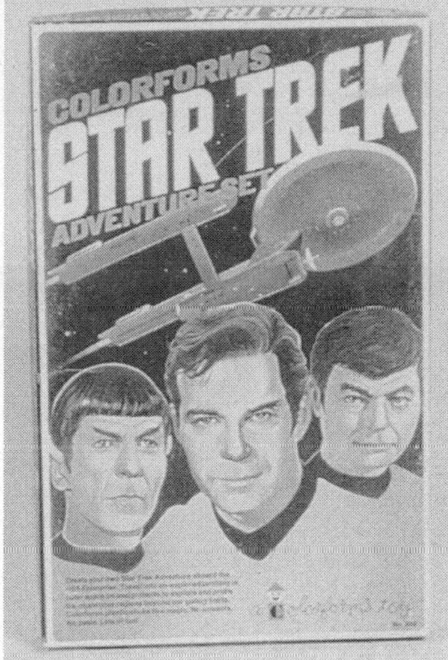

Colorforms Set, 1975, Colorforms
EX $15 **NM** $20 **MIP** $50

Comb & Brush Set, 1977, 6" x 3", blue, oval brush
EX $14 **NM** $20 **MIP** $35

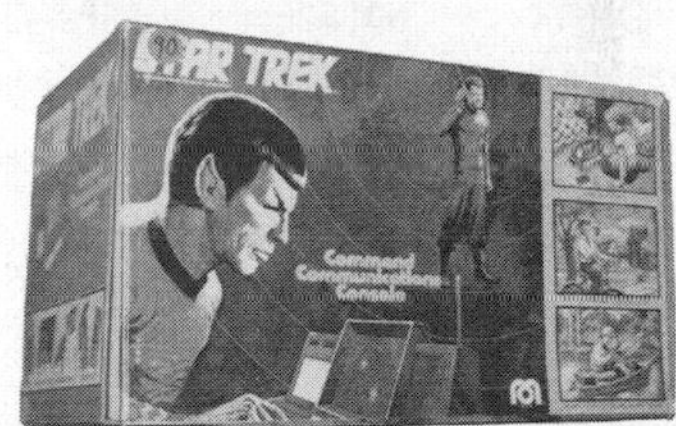

Command Communications Console, 1976, Mego, coordinates w/Mego's communicators, lights up
EX $45 **NM** $100 **MIP** $155

Communicators, 1976, Mego, blue plastic walkie talkies
EX $70 **NM** $125 **MIP** $200

Communicators, 1989, McNerney, black plastic walkie talkies
EX $35 **NM** $50 **MIP** $85

Communicators, ST:TMP, 1980, Mego, plastic wristband walkie talkies belt pack, battery operated
EX $90 **NM** $150 **MIP** $250

Controlled Space Flight, 1976, Remco, plastic Enterprise, battery operated
EX $80 **NM** $125 **MIP** $225

Costume, 1979, Collegeville, one-piece outfit, Spock, Kirk, Ilia or Klingon, each
EX $11 **NM** $16 **MIP** $25

Digital Travel Alarm, Lincoln Enterprises
EX $15 **NM** $20 **MIP** $35

Dinnerware Set, ST:TMP, 1979, Deka, plate, bowl, glass and cup
EX $15 **NM** $25 **MIP** $40

Enterprise Make-A-Model, ST:TNG, 1990, Chatham River Press
EX $4 **NM** $5 **MIP** $10

Enterprise Model Kit, 1980, Mego/Grand Toys, #91232/B, Canadian issue, ST:TMP
EX $90 **NM** $100 **MIP** $150

Enterprise Punch-Out Book, ST:TMP, 1979, Wanderer
EX $9 **NM** $15 **MIP** $30

Enterprise Wristwatch, ST:TMP, Bradley
EX $20 **NM** $30 **MIP** $50

Enterprise Wristwatch, ST:TMP, 1989, Rarities Mint, gold-plated silver
EX $55 **NM** $80 **MIP** $125

Enterprise, ST:III, 1984, Ertl, 4" long, die-cast w/black plastic stand
EX $10 **NM** $15 **MIP** $30

Enterprise, ST:IV, 1986, Sterling, 24", silver plastic, inflatable
EX $20 **NM** $30 **MIP** $45

Enterprise, ST:TMP, 1979, South Bend, 20" long, white plastic, battery powered lights and sound w/stand
EX $80 **NM** $120 **MIP** $185

Excelsior, ST:III, 1984, Ertl, 4" long, die-cast w/black plastic stand
EX $7 **NM** $10 **MIP** $40

Ferengi Costume, ST:TNG, 1988, Ben Cooper
EX $7 **NM** $10 **MIP** $25

Figurine Paint Set, 1979, Milton Bradley
EX $14 **NM** $25 **MIP** $40

Flashlight, 1976, battery operated, small phaser shape
EX $6 **NM** $10 **MIP** $15

Flashlight, ST:TMP, 1979, Larami
EX $6 **NM** $10 **MIP** $15

Giant in the Universe Pop-Up Book, 1977, Random House
EX $14 **NM** $20 **MIP** $35

Golden Trivia Game, 1985, Western
EX $20 **NM** $30 **MIP** $50

Helmet, 1976, Remco, plastic, w/sound and red lights
EX $55 **NM** $80 **MIP** $130

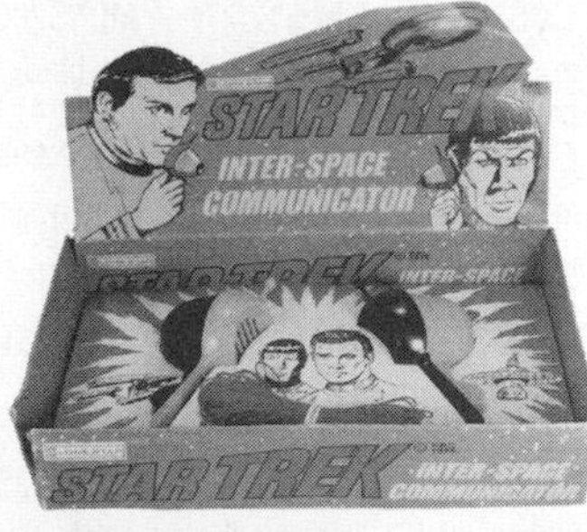

Inter-Space Communicator, 1974, Lone Star, 6 x 9" box, 2 yellow and black hand-held devices connected by wire
EX $25 **NM** $55 **MIP** $90

Kirk & Spock Wristwatch, ST:TMP, Bradley, LCD rectangular face display, Enterprise on blue face w/Kirk and Spock
EX $25 **NM** $35 **MIP** $60

Kirk Bank, 1975, Play Pal, 12" plastic
EX $25 **NM** $35 **MIP** $60

Kirk Costume, 1975, Ben Cooper, plastic mask, one-piece jumpsuit
EX $9 **NM** $13 **MIP** $25

Kirk Doll, ST:TMP, shown here w/Spock, 1979, Knickerbocker, 13" tall, soft body w/plastic head
EX $16 **NM** $23 **MIP** $50

Kirk or Spock Costumes, 1967, Ben Cooper, tie-on jumpsuit, mask
EX $11 **NM** $16 **MIP** $30

Kirk Puzzle, ST:TMP, 1979, Larami, fifteen-piece sliding puzzle
EX $5 **NM** $7 **MIP** $12

Kite, 1975, Hi-Flyer, TV Enterprise or Spock
EX $14 **NM** $20 **MIP** $35

Kite, ST:III, 1984, Lever Bros., pictures Enterprise
EX $14 **NM** $20 **MIP** $35

Kite, ST:TMP, 1976, Aviva, picture of Spock
EX $17 **NM** $22 **MIP** $38

Klingon Bird of Prey, ST:III, 1984, Ertl, 3-1/2", die-cast w/black plastic stand
EX $7 **NM** $10 **MIP** $30

Klingon Costume, 1975, Ben Cooper, plastic mask, one piece jumpsuit
EX $9 **NM** $13 **MIP** $30

Klingon Costume, ST:TNG, 1988, Ben Cooper
EX $7 **NM** $10 **MIP** $20

Light Switch Cover, 1985, American Tack & Hardware, ST:TMP
EX $6 **NM** $8 **MIP** $15

Magic Slates, 1979, Whitman, four designs: Spock, Kirk, Kirk and Spock
EX $7 **NM** $10 **MIP** $20

Make-a-Game Book, 1979, Wanderer
EX $7 **NM** $10 **MIP** $20

Metal Detector, 1976, Jetco, U.S.S. Enterprise decal
EX $100 **NM** $145 **MIP** $225

Mirror, 1966, 2" x 3" metal, w/black and white photo of crew
EX $2 **NM** $5 **MIP** $10

Mix 'N Mold, 1975, Kirk, Spock or McCoy, molding compound, paint and brush
EX $35 **NM** $50 **MIP** $75

Movie Viewer, 1967, Chemtoy, 3" red and black plastic
EX $10 **NM** $16 **MIP** $35

Needlepoint Kit, 1980, Arista, 14" x 18", "Live Long and Prosper"
EX $16 **NM** $23 **MIP** $35

Needlepoint Kit, 1980, Arista, Kirk
EX $16 **NM** $23 **MIP** $35

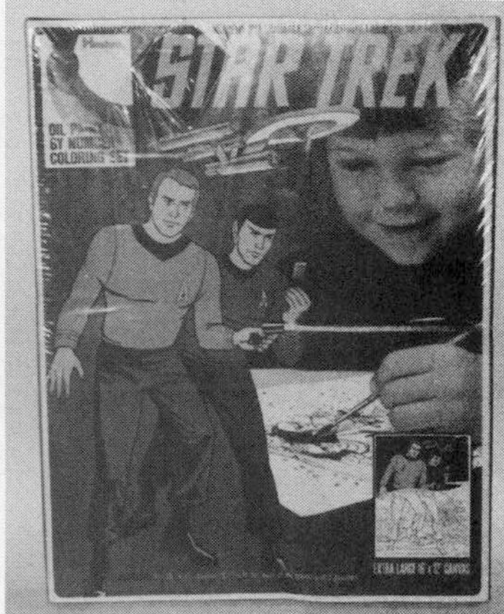

Paint-By-Numbers Set, 1972, Hasbro, small
EX $20 **NM** $35 **MIP** $55

Paint-By-Numbers Set, 1972, Hasbro, large
EX $35 **NM** $50 **MIP** $80

Pen & Poster Kit, 1976, Open Door, four versions; each
EX $11 **NM** $16 **MIP** $30

Pen & Poster Kit, ST:III, 1984, Placo, 3-D poster "Search for Spock" w/overlay, 3-D glasses and four felt tip pens
EX $10 **NM** $20 **MIP** $40

Pennant, 1982, Image Products, 12" x 30" triangular, black, yellow and red on white w/"Spock Lives"
EX $6 **NM** $10 **MIP** $15

Pennant, 1982, Image Products, 12" x 30" triangle, The Wrath of Khan
EX $6 **NM** $10 **MIP** $15

Pennant, 1988, Universal Studios, Paramount Pictures Adventure
EX $6 **NM** $10 **MIP** $15

Phaser, 1975, Remco, black plastic, shaped like pistol, electronic sound, flashlight projects target
EX $35 **NM** $100 **MIP** $200

Phaser Battle Game, 1976, Mego, black plastic, 13" high battery operated electronic target game, LED scoring lights, sound effects and adjustable controls
EX $195 **NM** $275 **MIP** $450

Phaser Gun, 1967, Remco, Astro Buzz-Ray Gun w/three-color flash beam
EX $80 **NM** $150 **MIP** $250

Phaser Gun, ST:III, 1984, Daisy, white and blue plastic gun w/light and sound effects
EX $35 **NM** $60 **MIP** $100

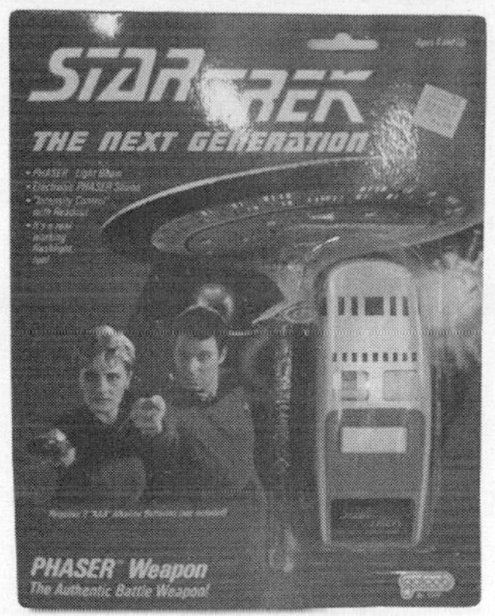

Phaser Gun, ST:TNG, 1988, Galoob, gray plastic light and sound hand phaser
EX $14 **NM** $20 **MIP** $40

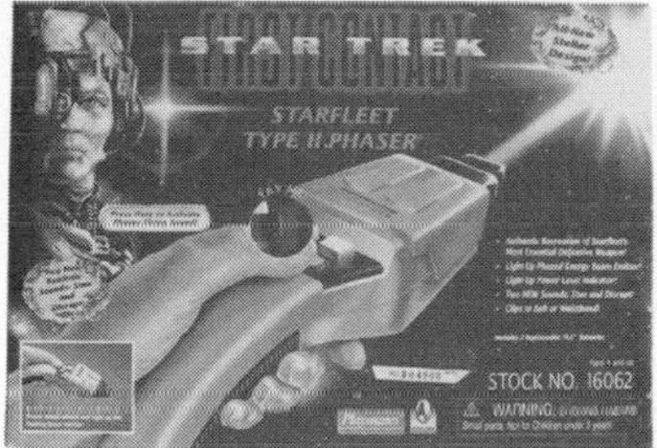

Phaser, ST:FC, 1996, Playmates, #16062, Starfleet Type II Phaser from film, First Contact
EX $8 **NM** $16 **MIP** $25

Pinball Game, ST:TMP, Azrak-Hamway, 12", plastic, Kirk or Spock
EX $23 **NM** $35 **MIP** $80

Pinball Game, ST:TMP, 1979, Bally, electronic
EX $200 **NM** $350 **MIP** $650

Pocket Flix, 1978, Ideal, battery operated movie viewer and film cartridge
EX $18 **NM** $25 **MIP** $50

Pop-Up Book, ST:TMP, 1980, Wanderer
EX $10 **NM** $20 **MIP** $40

Puzzle, 1974, H.G. Toys, 150 pieces, Battle on the Planet Romulon
EX $5 **NM** $10 **MIP** $15

Puzzle, 1974, H.G. Toys, 150 pieces, Battle on the Planet Klingon
EX $3 **NM** $7 **MIP** $12

Puzzle, 1974, H.G. Toys, 150 pieces, Kirk and officers beaming down
EX $3 **NM** $7 **MIP** $12

Puzzle, 1974, H.G. Toys, 150 pieces, Attempted Hijacking of U.S.S. Enterprise
EX $4 **NM** $8 **MIP** $15

Puzzle, 1976, H.G. Toys, 150 pieces; Kirk, Spock, and McCoy
EX $4 **NM** $8 **MIP** $12

Puzzle, 1976, H.G. Toys, 150 pieces, "Force Field Capture"
EX $4 **NM** $8 **MIP** $15

Puzzle, 1978, Whitman, 8-1/2" x 11" tray, Spock in spacesuit
EX $2 **NM** $5 **MIP** $10

Puzzle, 1979, Aviva, 551 pieces
EX $8 **NM** $15 **MIP** $25

Puzzle, 1979, Milton Bradley, ST:TMP, 50 pieces
EX $3 **NM** $7 **MIP** $12

Puzzle, 1979, Larami, ST:TMP, 15-piece sliding puzzle
EX $3 **NM** $7 **MIP** $12

Puzzle, 1986, Mind's Eye Press, 551 pieces, ST:IV, "The Voyage Home"
EX $10 **NM** $20 **MIP** $30

Role Playing Game, 2001 Deluxe Edition, FASA, Star Trek Basic Set and the Star Trek III Combat Game
EX $20 **NM** $30 **MIP** $50

Role Playing Game, 2004 Basic Set, FASA, three books outlining Star Trek Universe
EX $7 **NM** $10 **MIP** $20

Role Playing Game, Second Deluxe Edition, FASA
EX $14 **NM** $20 **MIP** $35

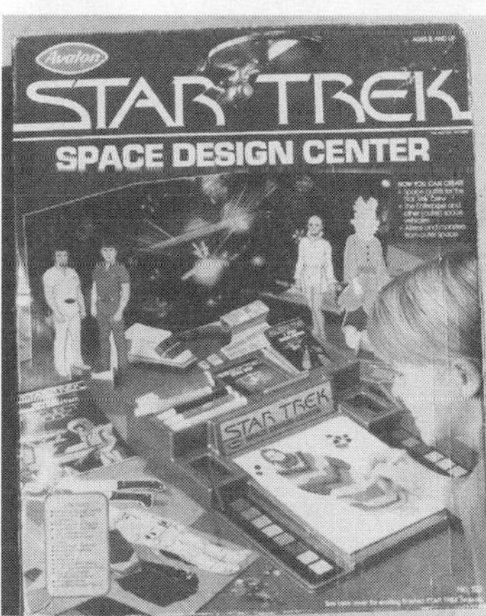

Space Design Center, ST:TMP, 1979, Avalon, blue plastic tray, paints, pens, crayons, project book and crew member cut-outs
EX $70 **NM** $110 **MIP** $175

Spock & Enterprise Wristwatch, ST:TMP, 1986, Lewco, 20th anniversary, digital
EX $9 **NM** $20 **MIP** $40

Spock Bank, 1975, Play Pal, 12" plastic
EX $25 **NM** $35 **MIP** $60

Spock Bop Bag, 1975, plastic, inflatable
EX $55 **NM** $80 **MIP** $125

Spock Chair, ST:TMP, 1979, inflatable
EX $16 **NM** $23 **MIP** $40

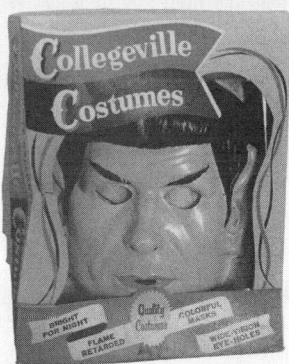

Spock Costume, 1970s, Collegeville
EX $30 **NM** $65 **MIP** $150

Spock Costume, 1973, Ben Cooper, plastic mask, one-piece jumpsuit
EX $11 **NM** $16 **MIP** $30

Spock Doll, ST:TMP, 1979, Knickerbocker, 13" tall, soft body, plastic head
EX $16 **NM** $25 **MIP** $50

Spock Ears, ST:TMP, 1979, Aviva
EX $7 **NM** $10 **MIP** $20

Spock Tray, 1979, Aviva, 17-1/2" metal lap tray
EX $9 **NM** $13 **MIP** $20

Spock Wristwatch, Bradley, ST:TMP
EX $20 **NM** $30 **MIP** $50

Star Trek Cartoon Puzzle, 1978, Whitman
EX $4 **NM** $5 **MIP** $10

Star Trek II U.S.S. Enterprise Ship, 1982, Corgi, 3" die-cast
EX $9 **NM** $13 **MIP** $25

Star Trekulator, 1970s, Mego, working calculator, blue plastic, image of Kirk in green v-neck shirt on screen
EX $25 **NM** $50 **MIP** $75

Super Phaser II Target Game, 1976, Mego, way before Laser Tag you could shoot Klingon ships or each other with phasers
EX $35 **NM** $80 **MIP** $125

Telescreen Console Playset, 1976, Mego, plastic, battery operated target game w/light and sound effects
EX $70 **NM** $100 **MIP** $160

Tracer Gun, 1966, Rayline, plastic pistol w/colored plastic discs
EX $45 **NM** $65 **MIP** $135

Tracer Gun, 1966, Rayline, 6-1/2" plastic firing tracer gun
EX $40 **NM** $65 **MIP** $125

Tracer Scope, 1968, Rayline, rifle w/disks
EX $50 **NM** $80 **MIP** $150

Transporter Room, 1975, Palitoy, playset for Mego figures, made in England
EX $75 **NM** $150 **MIP** $280

Tricorder, 1976, Mego, blue plastic tape recorder, battery operated w/shoulder strap, 30-minute tape played "The Menagerie" on one side and space sounds on the other
EX $70 **NM** $110 **MIP** $175

Star Trek

Trillions of Trilligs Pop-Up Book, 1977, Random House
EX $16 **NM** $25 **MIP** $40

Utility Belt, 1975, Remco, black plastic phaser miniature, tricorder, communicator and belt w/Star Trek buckle
EX $45 **NM** $85 **MIP** $155

Vulcan Shuttle Model Kit, 1980, Mego/Grand Toy, #91231, ST:TMP
EX $100 **NM** $120 **MIP** $145

Vulcan Shuttle Model Kit, 1984, Ertl, #6679, ST:TMP
EX $18 **NM** $20 **MIP** $35

Vulcan Shuttle Model Kit, 1984, Ertl, #6679, ST:III
EX $20 **NM** $25 **MIP** $50

Wastebasket, 1977, Chein, black metal
EX $35 **NM** $50 **MIP** $80

Wastebasket, ST:TMP, 1979, Chein, 13" high, metal rainbow painting w/photograph of Enterprise surrounded by smaller pictures
EX $11 **NM** $16 **MIP** $35

Water Pistol, 1976, Azrak-Hamway, white plastic, shaped like U.S.S. Enterprise
EX $20 **NM** $30 **MIP** $50

Water Pistol, 1976, Azrak-Hamway, white plastic, shaped like U.S.S. Enterprise
EX $15 **NM** $30 **MIP** $60

Water Pistol, ST:TMP, 1979, Aviva, gray plastic, early phaser
EX $11 **NM** $16 **MIP** $30

Water Pistol, Star Trek:TMP, 1979, Aviva, gray plastic, early pistol-grip phaser design
EX $10 **NM** $20 **MIP** $60

Writing Tablet, 1967, 8" x 10"
EX $11 **NM** $16 **MIP** $30

Yo-Yo, 1979, Aviva, ST:TMP, blue sparkle plastic
EX $10 **NM** $20 **MIP** $40

Tom Corbett

Atomic Flashlight Pistol, 1950s, Marx, identical to Space Patrol Atomic Flashlight Pistol except for body colors and "Tom Corbett Space Cadet" printed upside down on handgrip
EX $135 **NM** $300 **MIP** $650

Binoculars
EX $60 **NM** $100 **MIP** $150

Coloring Book, 1950s, Saalfield, two versions, each
EX $25 **NM** $40 **MIP** $80

Flash X-1, 1967, Shudo/Japan, 4" long, tin litho, friction sparkling action, red body w/blue and yellow inset and grips, large white "Flash X-1" on body, four red tinted plastic sparkling windows
EX $15 **NM** $25 **MIP** $75

Flash X-1 Space Gun, 5" long
EX $55 **NM** $110 **MIP** $160

Model Craft Molding and Coloring Set, 1950s, Kay Standley, various characters
EX $150 **NM** $350 **MIP** $500

Official Space Cadet Gun, 1950s, Marx, poorly designed composite rifle w/modern military plastic stock and front grip at ends of long tin litho gun body w/litho bombs and "Ray Adjuster" scale
EX $135 **NM** $300 **MIP** $500

Official Sparking Space Gun, Marx, 21" long, w/numerous apparatus on body
EX $80 **NM** $150 **MIP** $250

Polaris Wind-Up Spaceship, 1952, Marx, 12" long, blue litho w/yellow, Tom, Astro and Roger visible in the litho cockpit
EX $200 **NM** $375 **MIP** $600

Portrait Ring, 1950s, premium
EX $20 **NM** $35 **MIP** $60

Push-Outs Book, 1952, Saalfield
EX $35 **NM** $65 **MIP** $100

Puzzles, 1950s, Saalfield, frame tray, three versions, each
EX $17 **NM** $30 **MIP** $50

Rocket Scout Ring, 1950s
EX $10 **NM** $20 **MIP** $35

School Bag, 1950s, 15" long, 10" wide, plastic vinyl w/ Tom's picture and rocketships on front
EX $25 **NM** $55 **MIP** $85

Signal Siren Flashlight, 1950s, Usalite
EX $70 **NM** $115 **MIP** $200

Space Academy Play Set, 1950s, Marx, #7020
EX $195 **NM** $550 **MIP** $600

Space Academy Play Set, 1952, Marx, #7010, 45mm figures
EX $205 **NM** $360 **MIP** $515

Space Cadet Belt, 1950s
EX $65 **NM** $105 **MIP** $175

Space Cadet Gun, 1952, Marx, 10-1/2" long, sheet metal clicker based on Flash Gordon Radio repeater molds, red body, blue barrel reads "Space Cadet," handgrips show bust of Tom in front of planet w/rocket ship symbol above
EX $150 **NM** $550 **MIP** $850

Space Gun, 1950s, 9-1/2" long light blue and black sparking
EX $70 **NM** $130 **MIP** $250

Space Suit Ring, 1950s
EX $10 **NM** $16 **MIP** $35

Wristwatch, 1950s, Ingraham, round dial, embossed band w/ship and planets, on illustrated rocket shaped card
EX $195 **NM** $250 **MIP** $600

Star Wars

by Mark Bellomo

The foundation of global popular culture was shaken to its core in 1977 when George Lucas released one of the most important films in modern American history: the science fiction space opera, *Star Wars: A New Hope*. Over the past 30+ years, eager fans have popularized Star Wars terms that have been indelibly stamped onto our collective consciousness and even introduced into the American lexicon: words like "light saber," "Jedi Knight," and "droids"; expressions such as "May The Force Be With You," and the moral/psychic concept of "the dark side of the Force."

Little did 20th Century Fox realize the impact that the film would have on children and adult collectors everywhere, and in a brilliant stroke of prescience, Lucas may have subconsciously realized the potential of the *Star Wars* franchise. Lucas alone contracted to retail all sequel and merchandising rights for the film(s).

Kenner toys obtained the rights to produce 3-¾" action figures, playsets, creatures and vehicles based on important scenes from *Star Wars*. The smaller 3 ¾" scale was utilized in direct response to the OPEC oil shortages of the 1970s, shortages that increased the cost of plastic production which was affecting many major toy companies such as Hasbro and Mego. Little would Kenner realize the overwhelming response that their more portable Star Wars figures would attract at retail. Soon after their release, the 3-¾" action figure format would become the standard in the field: at this smaller size (as opposed to Hasbro's enormous G.I. Joe figures' 11-½" or Mego's interchangeable 8" body), characters were easier to produce, simpler to manufacture, could sell higher numbers in order to allow consumers to purchase many more units ("collect them all"), ultimately refreshing sold-out retail pegs much more quickly.

Star Wars figures became a sensation—a phenomenon—in the late 1970s/early 1980s, and the items sold briskly throughout the release of the original trilogy, producing a bevy of toys for each of the three films: *A New Hope (Episode IV)*, *The Empire Strikes Back (Episode V)*, and *The Return of the Jedi (Episode VI)*. A total of 96 figures were available in the original "vintage" line (1977-1985), not including myriad figure variations (telescoping light sabers, vinyl-caped jawas, etc.), or the Sy Snootles and the Rebo band three-pack set. The most popular and valuable of these carded figures are the earliest *Star Wars* releases, those figures found on original "12-back cards"—those card backs that showed only the first 12 Star Wars action figures in 1977. Other pricey figures can be found within the final run of the line, 1984/85's "Power of the Force" collection, where figures (both new sculpts and previously released characters) were carded along with a collector's coin. A few of these carded samples are worth thousands of dollars in Mint condition.

Along with the standard 3-¾" figures was a collection of deluxe 12" figures based on more popular characters from the films. Apart from releasing 96 Star Wars action figures, Kenner crafted five creatures, 31 vehicles (including store exclusives), 13 playsets (again, including exclusives), a few accessories, and seven action figure storage cases. Also adding to the collecting fun were proof-of-purchase mail-aways that children desired: Collector's Action Stands, Survival Kits, Display Arenas, Power of the Force coins, posters, and special bagged figures before their official retail carded release. These special offers added an air of anticipation to the hobby of collecting, and most kids couldn't wait for these packages to arrive in the mail.

Regardless of promotion, mail-away premiums, and large discounts at retail, the vintage Star Wars line was cancelled in 1985 due to poor sales and a shrinking sci-fi marketplace. Sadly, it would be ten very long years before Star Wars collectors would be treated to any new toys.

To much fanfare, Kenner released a new series of Star Wars action figures in 1995, and the "Power of the Force" line (or, as fans dubbed it, the "POTF II" line) was born. Although initially criticized for their bulky statures and poor facial sculpts, the POTF II action figure line lasted five years and yielded many excellent new figures, a slew of unproduced characters, and even improved paint applications, sculpting, and articulation. From 1995-present, Hasbro (the most recent owner of the Star Wars action figure license) has produced many different lines under the Star Wars brand: Shadows of the Empire (1996); Episode I (1999-2002); Power of the Jedi (2000-2002); Star Wars Saga (2002-2004); Clone Wars (2004-2005); Original Trilogy Collection (2004); Revenge of the Sith (2005); The Saga Collection (2006); The 30th Anniversary Collection (2006-2008); The Clone Wars (2008-current); and The Legacy Collection (2008-current).

Star Wars toys are some of the most desirable action figures on the secondary market, and the people who collect them are often the most devoted in the hobby. Vintage figures and vehicles still sealed in their packages command outrageous prices on online auction sites such as eBay and in collectible stores.

2009 Trends

As always, Star Wars toys will retain their value, but key pieces in each of the respective lines will keep climbing. Besides picking up Mint on Card and Mint in Box vintage items, even some of the rarer loose pieces from modern Star Wars lines have caught steam lately. Also, with the creation of the all-new CGI animated *Star Wars: The Clone Wars* film and accompanying CGI television show, be on the lookout for price increases on the original Clone Wars (2004-2005) toys; they should experience a quite a renaissance in 2009.

Furthermore, as many longtime vintage and modern Star Wars collectors finish their respective collections to their satisfaction, look for "trooper" action figures (i.e. Stormtrooper, Sandtrooper, Clone Trooper, etc.) to increase in value, as these collectors/completionists will start to "army build" these figures: amassing large amounts of these characters in order to create a their own private army.

Editor's Note: Some common Star Wars action figure abbreviations include: SW for Star Wars, ESB for Empire Strikes Back, RotJ for Return of the Jedi, POTF for Power of the Force, POTF 2 (or II) for Power of the Force second series, EpI: TPM for Episode I: The Phantom Menace, EpII: AotC for Episode II: Attack of the Clones, and EpIII: RotS for Episode III: Revenge of the Sith.

THE TOP 10 STAR WARS (In Mint Condition)

1. Anakin Skywalker, POTF card, Kenner, 1985 .... $2,800
2. Jawa, plastic cape, SW card, Kenner, 1978 .... $2,500
3. Yak Face, POTF card, Kenner, 1985 .... $1,650
4. Boba Fett, Droids card, Kenner, 1985 .... $1,300
5. IG-88, 12" figure, ESB box, Kenner, 1982 .... $1,100
6. AT-AT Driver, POTF card, Kenner, 1985 .... $1,000
7. Boba Fett, 12" figure, ESB box, Kenner, 1982 .... $975
8. Han Solo (large head), SW card, Kenner, 1978 .... $900
9. Star Wars Early Bird Kit, (four figures), mail-away, Kenner, 1978 .. $850
10. Nitko, POTF card, Kenner, 1985 .... $800

Action Figures, 03-3/4"

STAR WARS
Series 1

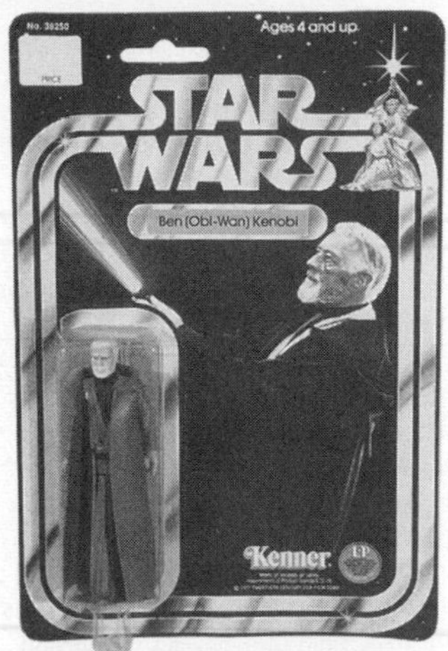

Ben (Obi-Wan) Kenobi, 1977-78
MNP $21 **MIP $425**

Boba Fett, 1979
MNP $19 **MIP $650**

C-3PO, 1977-78
MNP $20 **MIP $250**

Chewbacca, 1977-78, Everyone's favorite Wookie!
MNP $13 **MIP $250**

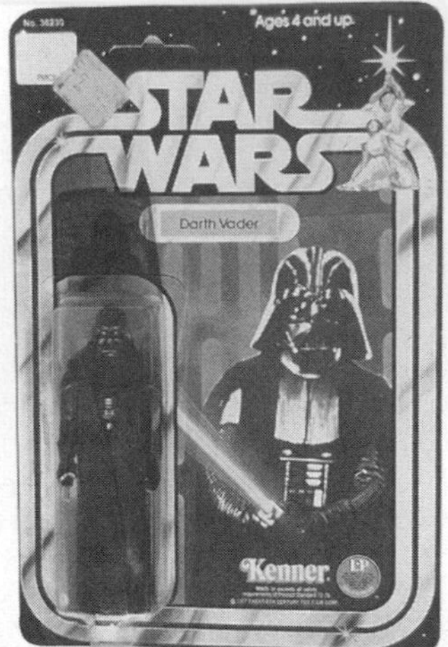

Darth Vader, 1977-78
MNP $15 **MIP $550**

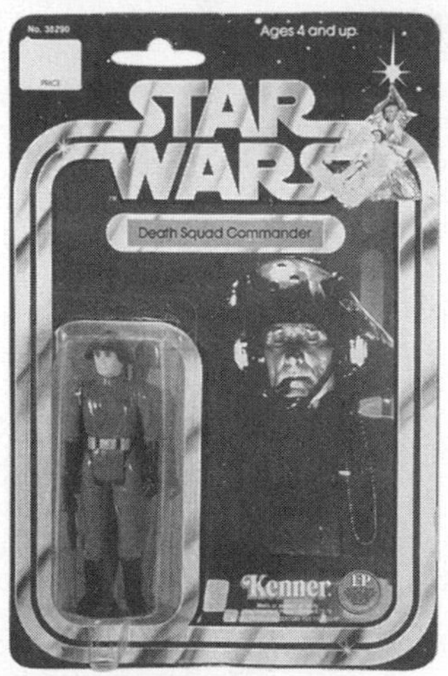

Death Squad Commander, 1977-78
MNP $12 **MIP $200**

Death Star Droid, 1979
MNP $30 **MIP $190**

Early Bird Figures — Luke, Leia, R2-D2, Chewbacca, 1977-78
MNP $195 **MIP $425**

Greedo, 1979
MNP $18 **MIP $220**

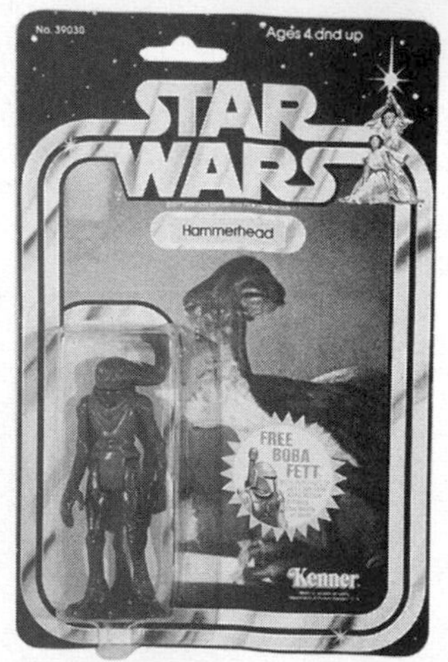

Hammerhead, 1979
MNP $15 **MIP $190**

Han Solo, Large Head, 1977-78
MNP $22 MIP $575

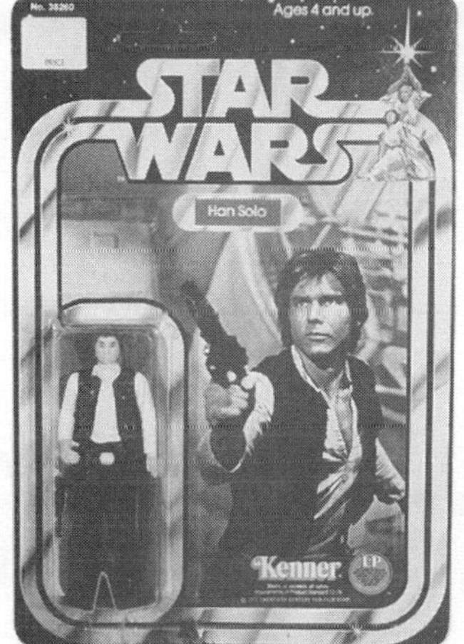

Han Solo, Small Head, 1977-78
MNP $32 MIP $525

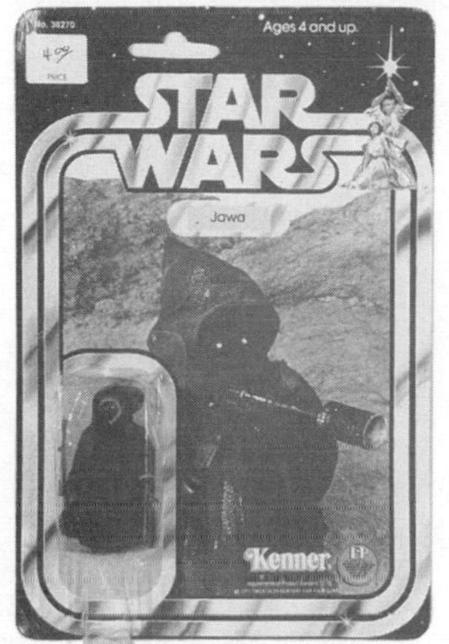

Jawa, Cloth Cape, 1977-78
MNP $20 MIP $210

Jawa, Vinyl Cape, 1977-78
MNP $250 MIP $3000

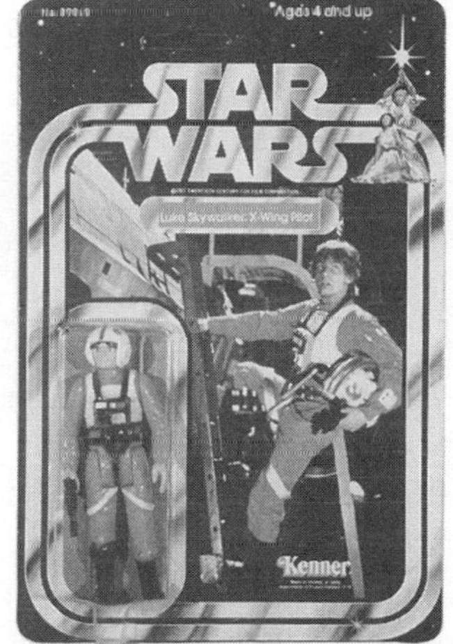

Luke as X-Wing Pilot, 1979
MNP $15 MIP $225

Luke Skywalker, 1977-78
MNP $45 MIP $575

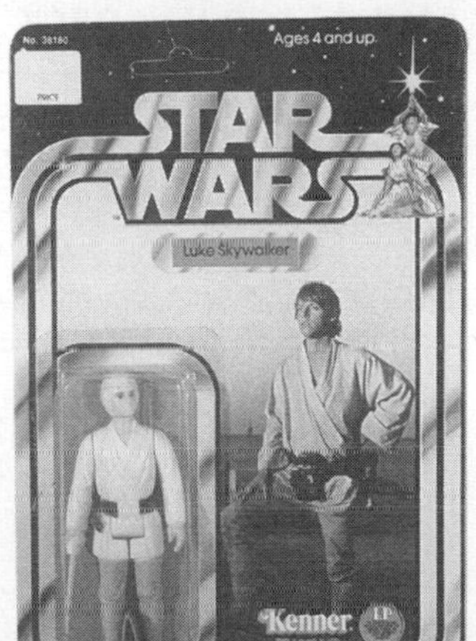

Luke w/Telescoping Saber, 1977-78
MNP $185 MIP $3500

Power Droid, 1979, Dark blue body with stocky legs. These robots are also called "Gonk" droids, based on the sound they make as seen in Star Wars Episode IV, "A New Hope." Very reminiscent of the robots in the movie "Silent Running"
MNP $11 MIP $140

Princess Leia Organa, 1977-78
MNP $28 MIP $525

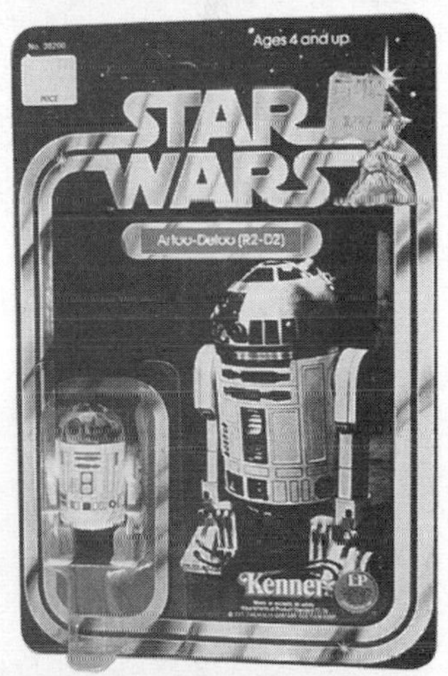

R2-D2, 1977-78
MNP $26 MIP $250

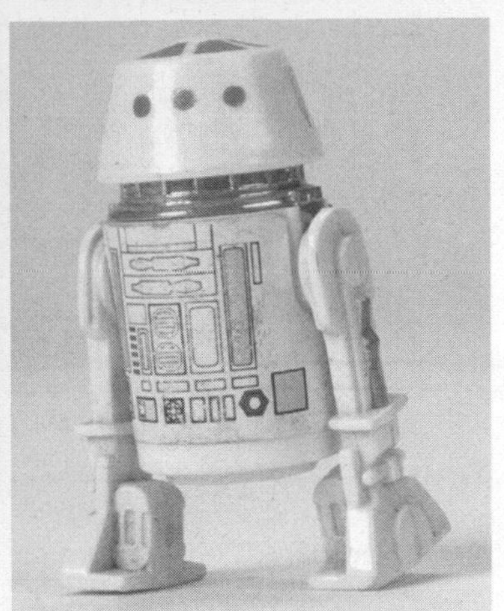

R5-D4, 1979
MNP $17 **MIP $225**

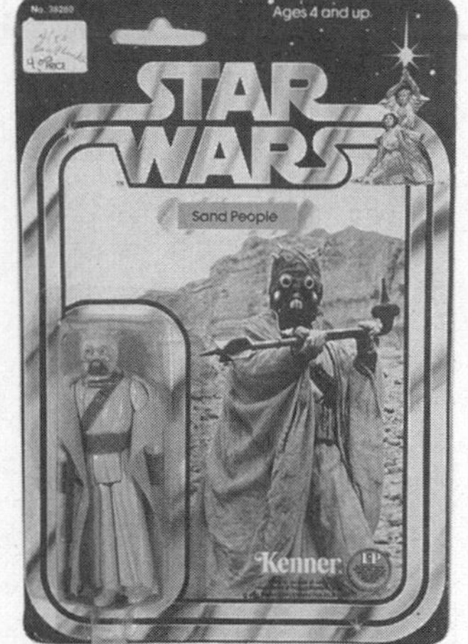

Sand People (Tusken Raider), 1977-78
MNP $17 **MIP $250**

Snaggletooth, Blue Body, Sears exclusive, 1979, price is for sealed in baggie condition
MNP $300 **MIP** n/a

Snaggletooth, Red Body, 1979
MNP $10 **MIP $170**

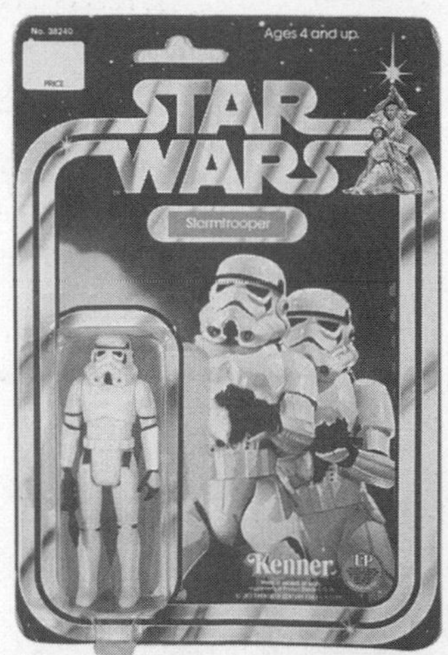

Stormtrooper, 1977-78
MNP $30 **MIP $270**

Walrus Man, 1979
MNP $15 **MIP $150**

EMPIRE STRIKES BACK
Series 2

2-1B, 1981, The medical droid who assists Luke's recovery after his duel with Vader. In the movie, you actually never see his legs
MNP $9 **MIP $95**

4-LOM, 1982, Tan plastic cloak with brown belt worn over the top, unique blaster rifle
MNP $13 **MIP $155**

AT-AT Commander, 1982, Available with Sears Exclusive Hoth Rebel base set, or individually. Includes blaster pistol
MNP $8 **MIP $95**

AT-AT Driver, 1981, White and gray uniform, includes blaster rifle
MNP $7 **MIP $85**

Bespin Security Guard, black, 1980, Includes blaster pistol
MNP $15 **MIP $55**

Bespin Security Guard, white, 1980, With blaster pistol
MNP $11 **MIP $60**

Bossk, 1980, Includes blaster rifle with forward grip so rifle body rests against arm
MNP $10 **MIP $85**

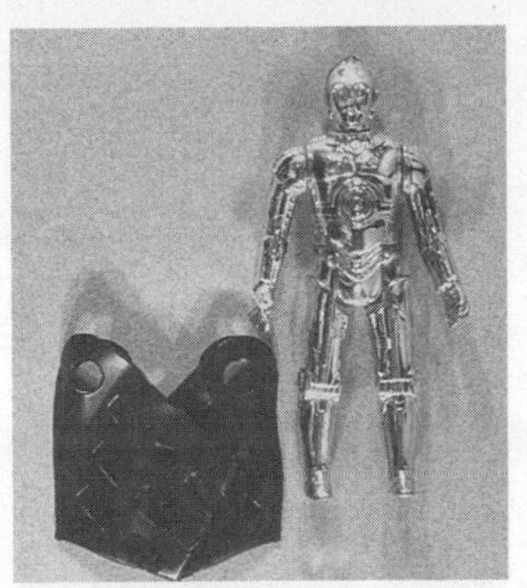

C-3PO w/Removable Limbs, 1982, Included pouch for Chewbacca to carry the disassembled 3PO
MNP $10 MIP $60

Cloud Car Pilot, 1982, White uniform, orange and yellow helmet. Style of figure reminiscent of rebel troops
MNP $18 MIP $80

Dengar, 1980, One of the bounty hunters hired by Vader ("we don't need their scum..."). This figure originally came with a long rifle
MNP $9 MIP $90

FX-7, 1980, Also called the "medical droid," this model had a series of spindly arms that pivoted up from the cylindrical body
MNP $8 MIP $55

Han in Bespin Outfit, 1981, Includes blaster pistol
MNP $10 MIP $95

Han in Hoth Gear, 1980, In dark blue parka, khaki pants, includes small blaster pistol
MNP $10 MIP $95

Hoth Rebel Soldier, 1980, Light brown and off-white uniform, small blaster pistol looking a bit like a Star Trek phaser
MNP $8 MIP $55

IG-88, 1980, One of the most highly-collected ESB figures, very classic robot look. According to Star Wars lore, IG88's head was one of the props behind the bar in the Cantina scene from the first movie. Includes two blasters
MNP $25 MIP $150

Imperial Commander, 1981, The packaging showed General Veers in a green uniform, but the figure was an anonymous black-uniformed officer. Some variation in hair color paint exists. Included standard-issue Stormtrooper blaster
MNP $8 MIP $65

Imperial TIE Fighter Pilot, 1982, Black uniform, gray gloves and boots, included gray blaster pistol
MNP $13 MIP $85

Lando Calrissian, 1980, Two-tone blue clothing with gray plastic cloak and blaster pistol
MNP $12 MIP $75

Leia in Bespin Gown, 1980, Brown outfit with printed plastic cloak. Included blaster pistol
MNP $30 MIP $145

Leia in Hoth Gear, 1981, White uniform with light tan vest and brown boots, included small blaster pistol
MNP $22 MIP $110

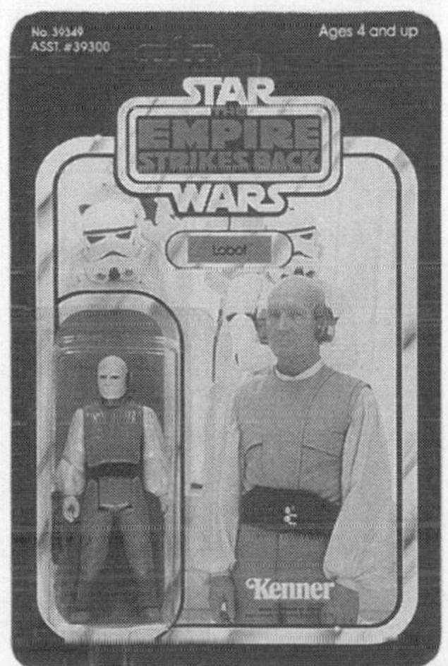

Lobot, 1981, Includes blaster pistol
MNP $8 MIP $80

Luke in Bespin Fatigues, 1980, Included blaster pistol and stand-alone lightsaber (not part of the figure)
MNP $20 MIP $175

Luke in Hoth Gear, 1982, White uniform with brown vest and gray boots. Included blaster rifle
MNP $10 MIP $115

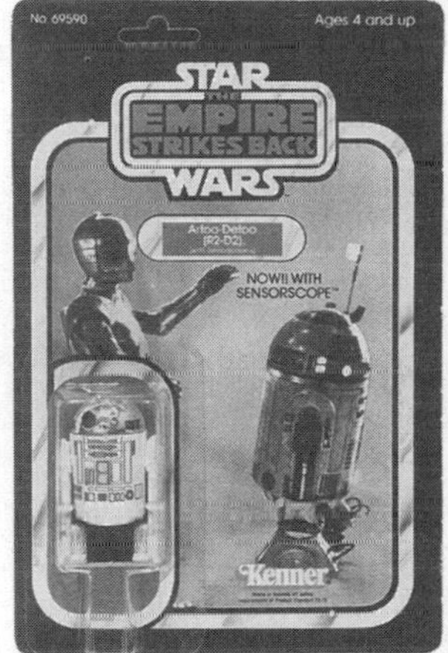

R2-D2 with Sensorscope, 1982, Available first with Sears Exclusive Hoth Rebel Base play set, or individually. Essentially the same as the standard R2, but with a blue plastic sensorscope that could be raised or lowered from his head
MNP $21 MIP $90

Rebel Commander, 1981, Off-white uniform, brown boots, blaster rifle
MNP $9 MIP $85

Snowtrooper, 1980, Plastic cloak along belt, included heavy laser rifle
MNP $16 MIP $125

Ugnaught, 1981, With blue cloth apron and white toolkit
MNP $9 MIP $75

Yoda, 1981, With cloth cloak, plastic belt, snake and walking stick. The plastic accessories were produced in varying colors
MNP $40 MIP $225

Zuckuss, 1982, Includes long blaster rifle
MNP $10 MIP $95

RETURN OF THE JEDI
Series 3

8D8, 1984
MNP $7 MIP $55

Admiral Ackbar, 1983
MNP $7 MIP $35

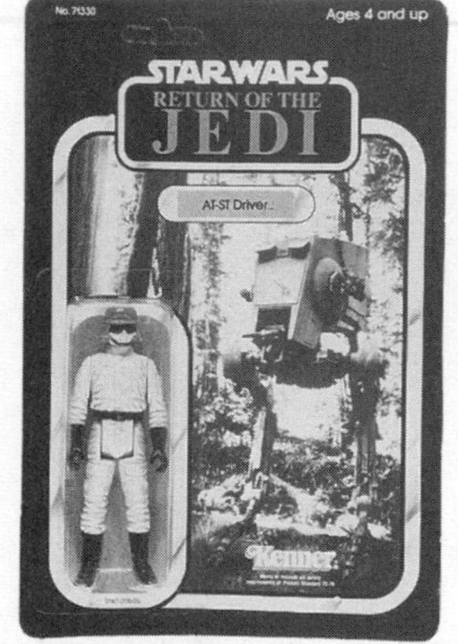

AT-ST Driver, 1984
MNP $10 MIP $55

Bib Fortuna, 1983, "Pay Jabba no bother…" This figure is the original sculpt of Jabba's major domo who apparently, was weak-minded enough to allow Luke's Jedi mind trick to work on him
MNP $8 MIP $38

Biker Scout, 1983, short laser pistol
MNP $25 MIP $100

B-Wing Pilot, 1984
MNP $9 MIP $35

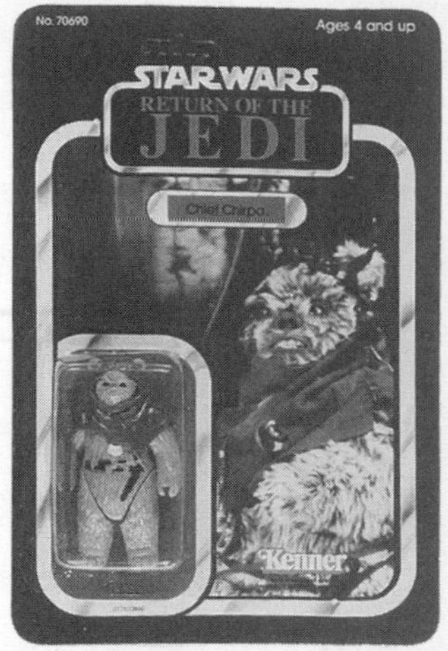

Chief Chirpa, 1983
MNP $8 MIP $49

Emperor Palpatine, 1984
MNP $10 MIP $75

Emperor's Royal Guard, 1983
MNP $10 MIP $55

Gamorrean Guard, 1983
MNP $6 MIP $27

General Madine, 1983
MNP $10 MIP $50

Han in Trenchcoat, 1984
MNP $12 MIP $45

Klaatu, 1984
MNP $9 MIP $38

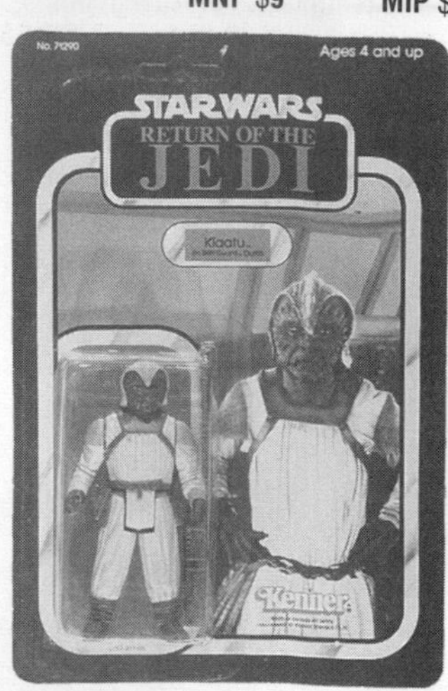

Klaatu in Skiff Guard Outfit, 1983
MNP $8 MIP $35

Lando Calrissian, Skiff Guard Outfit, 1983
MNP $8 MIP $47

Leia in Battle Poncho, 1984, Green camo pattern cloth poncho, removeable helmet, ammo belt and blaster pistol
MNP $20 MIP $55

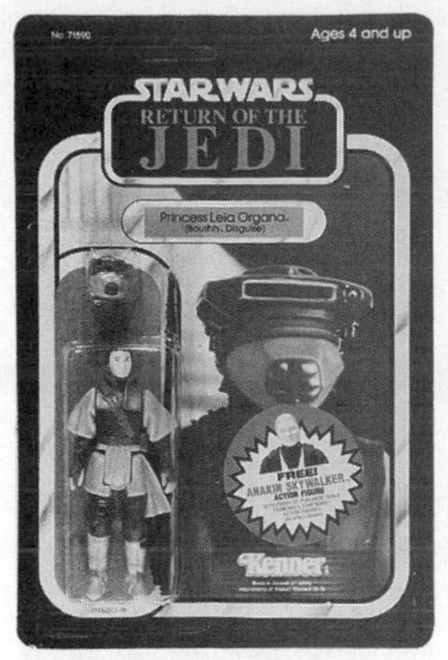

Leia in Boushh Disguise, 1983, w/removable helmet and tall gun
MNP $20 MIP $50

Logray, 1983
MNP $10 MIP $50

Luke as Jedi Knight, Blue Saber, 1983
MNP $45 MIP $145

Luke as Jedi Knight, Green Saber, 1983
MNP $30 MIP $75

Lumat, 1984
MNP $29 MIP $55

Nien Nunb, 1983
MNP $8 MIP $55

Nikto, 1984
MNP $7 MIP $30

Paploo, 1984
MNP $29 MIP $48

Prune Face, 1984
MNP $8 MIP $43

Rancor Keeper, 1984
MNP $7 MIP $39

Rebel Commando, 1983
MNP $8 MIP $45

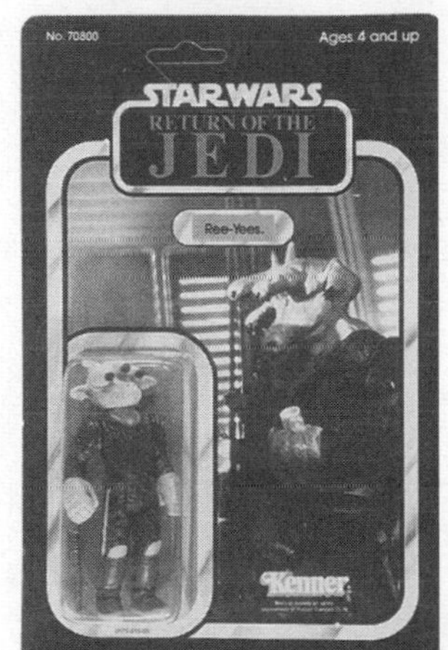

Ree-Yees, 1983
MNP $7 MIP $35

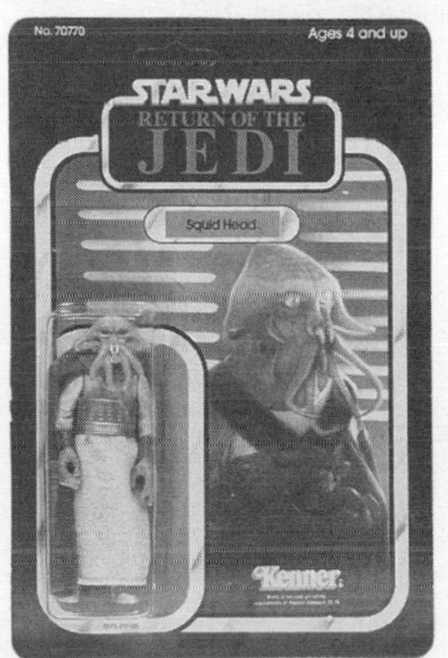

Squid Head, 1983
MNP $8 MIP $55

Sy Snootles and the Rebo Band, 1984, 3 figures: Sy Snootles, Droopy McCool, Max Rebo
MNP $65 MIP $140

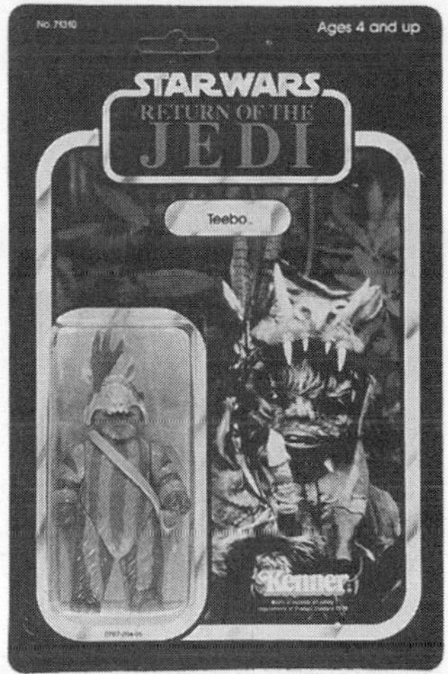

Teebo, 1984
MNP $13 MIP $40

Weequay, 1984
MNP $7 MIP $49

Wicket W. Warrick, 1984, w/long staff
MNP $14 MIP $60

POTF

Amanaman, 1984 85, w/coin
MNP $90 MIP $170

Anakin Skywalker, 1984-85, w/coin
MNP $23 MIP $1625

Artoo-Detoo (R2-D2) with pop-up Lightsaber, 1984-85, w/coin
MNP $85 MIP $140

AT-AT Driver, 1984-85, w/coin
MNP $9 MIP $575

AT-ST Driver, 1984-85, w/coin
MNP $9 **MIP $70**

A-Wing Pilot, 1984-85, w/coin
MNP $48 **MIP $125**

Barada, 1984-85, w/coin
MNP $40 **MIP $90**

Ben (Obi-Wan) Kenobi, 1984-85, w/coin
MNP $13 **MIP $135**

Biker Scout, 1984-85, w/coin
MNP $12 **MIP $150**

B-Wing Pilot, 1984-85, w/coin
MNP $9 **MIP $65**

Chewbacca, 1984-85, w/coin
MNP $9 **MIP $85**

Darth Vader, 1984-85, w/coin
MNP $12 **MIP $150**

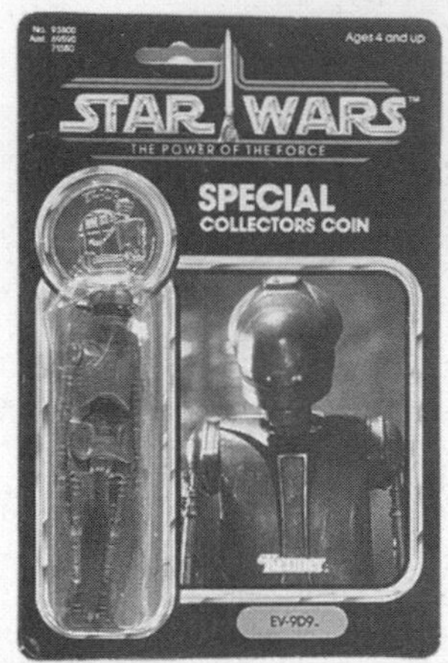

EV-9D9, 1984-85, w/coin
MNP $65 **MIP $130**

Gamorrean Guard, 1984-85, w/coin
MNP $5 **MIP $250**

Han Solo in Carbonite Chamber, 1984-85, w/coin
MNP $75 **MIP $225**

Han Solo in Trench Coat, 1984-85, w/coin
MNP $50 **MIP $350**

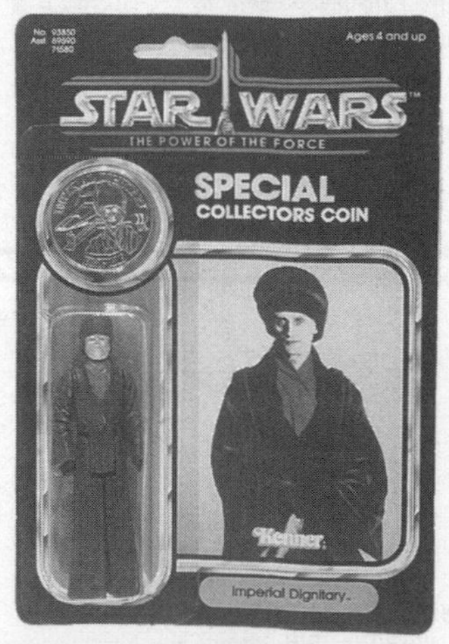

Imperial Dignitary, 1984-85, w/coin
MNP $45 **MIP $105**

Imperial Gunner, 1984-85, w/coin
MNP $48 **MIP $110**

Imperial Stormtrooper, 1984-85, w/coin
MNP $35 **MIP $140**

Jawa, 1984-85, w/coin
MNP $11 **MIP $110**

Lando Calrissian (General Pilot), 1984-85, w/coin
MNP $55 **MIP $95**

Luke Skywalker (Imperial Stormtrooper Outfit), 1984-85, w/coin,
MNP $80 MIP $260

Luke Skywalker (in Battle Poncho), 1984-85, w/coin
MNP $60 MIP $115

Luke Skywalker (Jedi Knight Outfit), 1984-85, w/coin, green lightsaber
MNP $30 MIP $165

Luke Skywalker (X-Wing Fighter Pilot), 1984-85, w/coin
MNP $12 MIP $85

Lumat, 1984-85, w/coin
MNP $18 MIP $65

Nikto, 1984-85, w/coin
MNP $10 MIP $725

Paploo, 1984-85, w/coin
MNP $16 MIP $60

Princess Leia Organa (in Combat Poncho), 1984-85, w/coin
MNP $16 MIP $75

Romba, 1984-85, w/coin
MNP $35 MIP $70

See-Threepio C-3PO (Removable Limbs), 1984-85, w/coin
MNP $6 MIP $80

Teebo, 1984-85, w/coin
MNP $13 MIP $85

The Emperor, 1984-85, w/coin, cane
MNP $6 MIP $110

Warok, 1984-85, w/coin
MNP $45 MIP $75

Wicket W. Warrick, 1984-85, w/coin
MNP $10 MIP $105

Yak Face, 1984-85, w/coin
MNP $175 MIP $1150

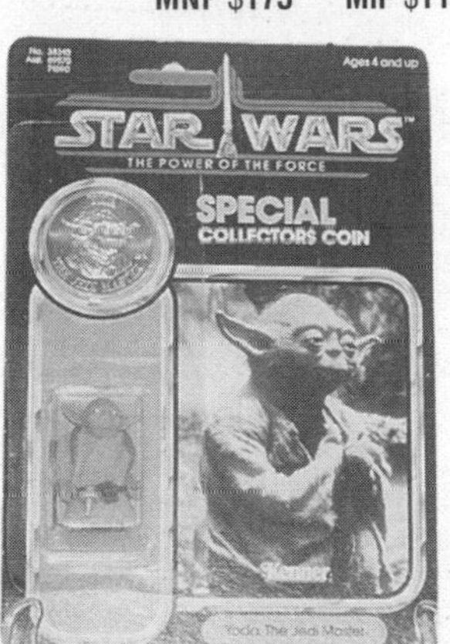

Yoda, The Jedi Master, 1984-85, w/coin
MNP $25 MIP $350

DROIDS

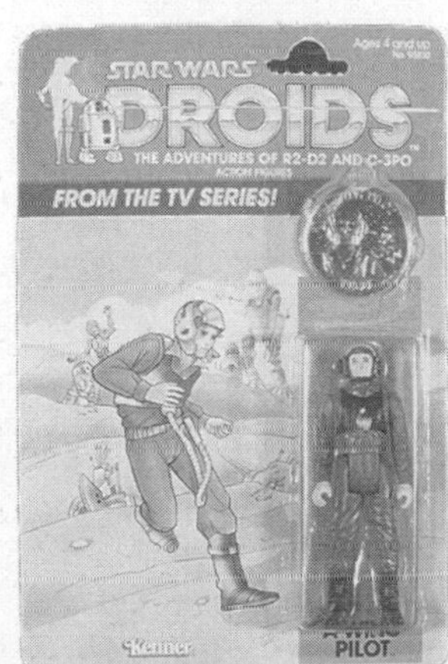

A-Wing Pilot, 1985
MNP $40 MIP $90

Boba Fett, 1985
MNP $35 MIP $650

C-3PO, 1985, Solid, multicolored plastic body (not gold chromed) with painted eyes
MNP $85 MIP $175

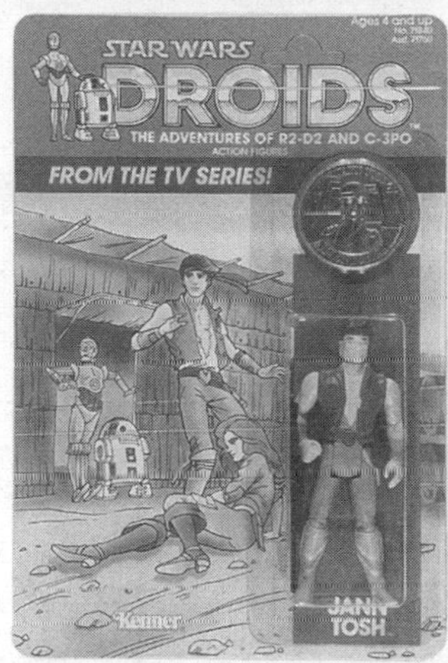

Jann Tosh, 1985
MNP $18 MIP $50

Jord Dusat, 1985
MNP $17 MIP $40

Kea Moll, 1985, Light tan and darker brown clothing, includes blaster pistol
MNP $18 MIP $36

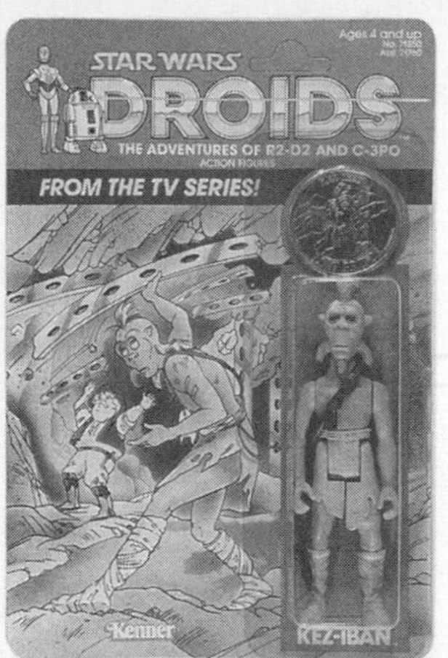

Kez-Iban, 1985, Purple body, tan clothing, standard-issue blaster (same as early Stormtroopers)

MNP $17 **MIP $39**

R2-D2, 1985, Simplified body markings and head--same sculpt and legs as regular (vintage) R2, though

MNP $55 **MIP $125**

Sise Fromm, 1985, Large-headed, green skinned figure with purple cloth robe

MNP $55 **MIP $250**

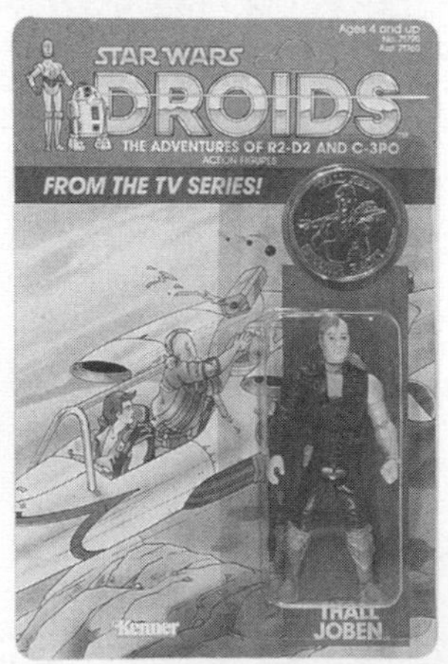

Thall Joben, 1985

MNP $15 **MIP $40**

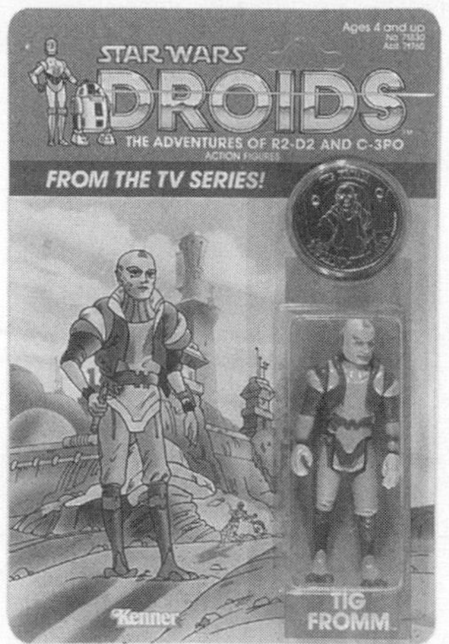

Tig Fromm, 1985, Blue and gray figure

MNP $50 **MIP $115**

Uncle Gundy, 1985, Short, portly figure with white hair and mustache. Includes blaster pistol

MNP $18 **MIP $32**

EWOKS
Series 5

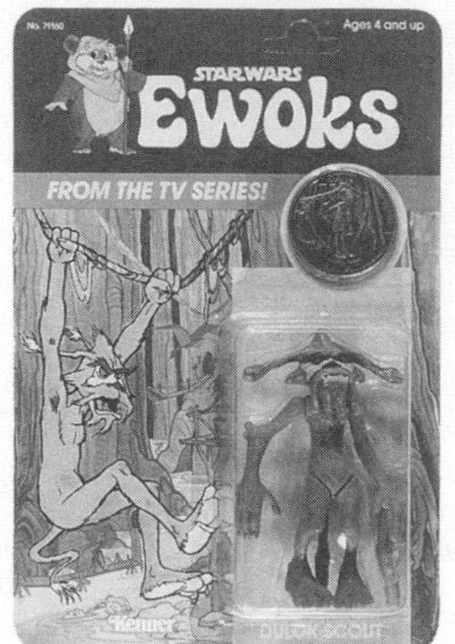

Dulok Scout, 1985, Medium-green figure with club

MNP $14 **MIP $28**

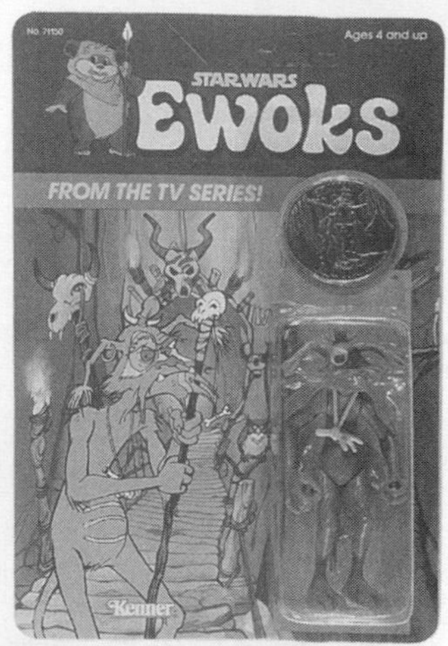

Dulok Shaman, 1985, Bright green figure with skull-topped staff

MNP $12 **MIP $29**

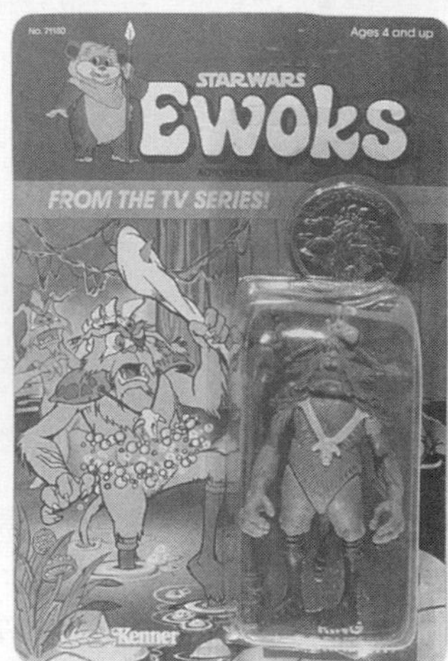

King Gorneesh, 1985, Fearsome bright green figure with staff

MNP $12 **MIP $27**

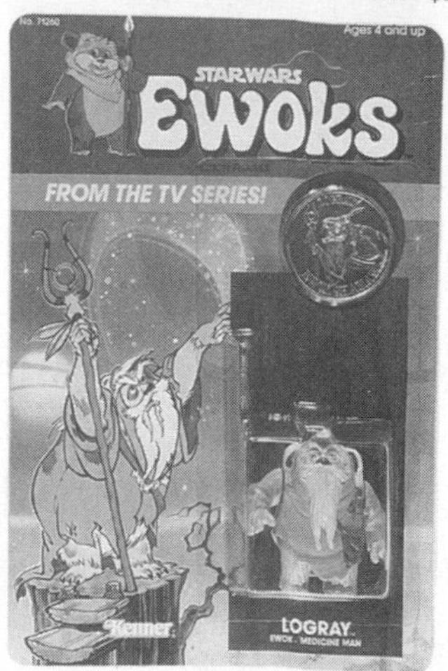

Logray, 1985, With bright blue plastic robe and staff

MNP $11 **MIP $38**

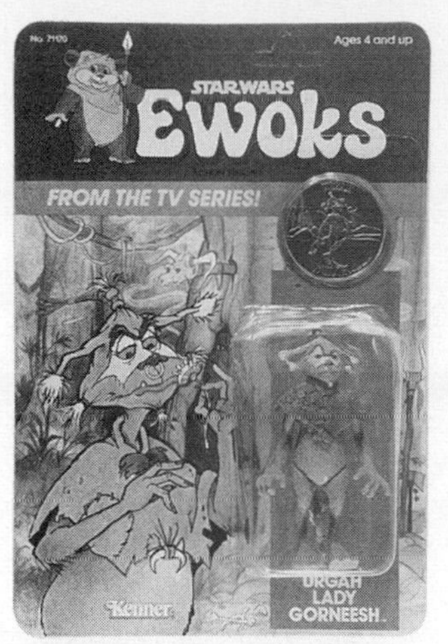

Urgah Lady Gorneesh, 1985, Green figure with red-brown poncho, blue highlights on head and face
MNP $10 MIP $26

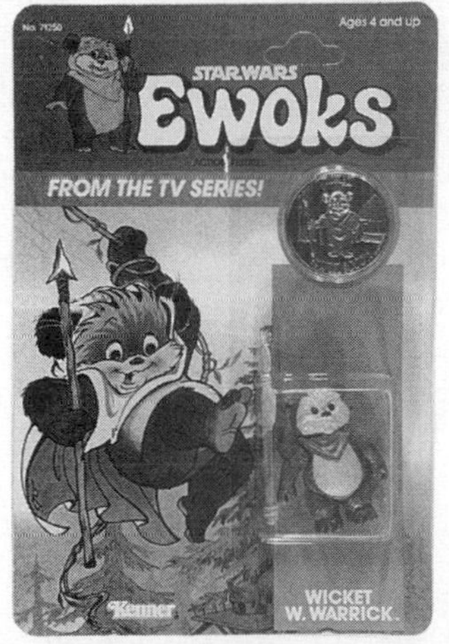

Wicket, 1985, Fittingly, a more "cartoony" simplified version of the Wicket from ROTJ. Included spear
MNP $14 MIP $45

POTF2-1

(Hasbro Photo)

2-1B Medic Droid, 1997, Series 5
MNP $2 MIP $10

4-LOM, 1997, Series 7
MNP $3 MIP $12

8-D8 Droid, 1998, Series 14
MNP $3 MIP $10

Admiral Ackbar, 1997, Series 7
MNP $3 MIP $10

Admiral Motti, 1999, Series 20
MNP $5 MIP $20

Anakin Skywalker, 1999, Series 17
MNP $3 MIP $12

ASP-7 Droid, 1997, Series 7
MNP $3 MIP $10

AT-ST Driver, 1997, Series 5
MNP $3 MIP $12

Aunt Beru, 1999, Series 17
MNP $3 MIP $12

Bib Fortuna, 1997, Series 6
MNP $3 MIP $10

(Hasbro Photo)

Biggs Darklighter, 1998, Series 11
MNP $3 MIP $20

Boba Fett, 1996, Series 2, Variation: half circle one hand, full circle on other hand, scarce $350
MNP $4 MIP $50

(Hasbro Photo)

Bossk, 1997, Series 5
MNP $3 MIP $12

C-3PO, 1995, Series 1
MNP $3 MIP $10

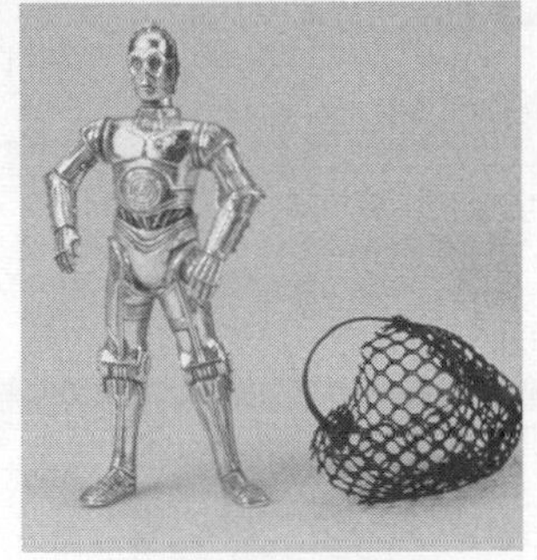

(Hasbro Photo)

C-3PO w/Removable Limbs and Backpack, 1998, Series 13
MNP $3 MIP $15

C-3PO, Shop Worn, 1999, Series 17
MNP $3 MIP $10

Cantina Greedo, 1999, Series 18
MNP $3 MIP $8

Cantina Han Solo, 1999, Series 18
MNP $3 MIP $8

Captain Piett, 1998, Series 12
MNP $5 MIP $30

Chewbacca, 1995, Series 1
MNP $3 MIP $15

Chewbacca (Hoth), 1998, Series 16, with painted "snow" on face
MNP $3 MIP $10

Chewbacca as Boushh's Bounty, 1998, Series 15
MNP $3 MIP $15

Darth Vader, 1995, Series 1, long lightsaber
MNP $4 MIP $25

Darth Vader, 1998, Series 16, removable cape
MNP $3 MIP $20

Darth Vader w/Interrogation Droid, 1999, Series 19, Commtech chip version
MNP $5 MIP $12

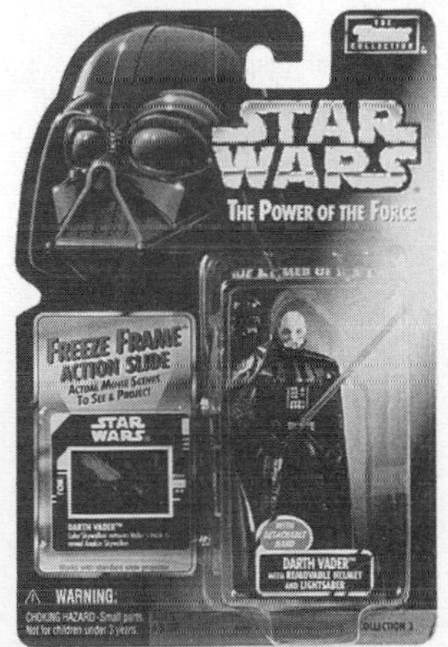

Darth Vader w/Removable Helmet, 1998, Series 12
MNP $4 MIP $40

(Hasbro Photo)

Death Star Gunner, 1996, Series 3
MNP $3 **MIP $25**

Death Star Trooper, 1998, Series 15
MNP $3 **MIP $25**

Dengar, 1997, Series 7
MNP $3 **MIP $12**

Emperor Palpatine, 1997, Series 6, Collection 1
MNP $3 **MIP $12**

Emperor Palpatine, 1998, Series 16
MNP $3 **MIP $10**

Emperor's Royal Guard, 1997, Series 8
MNP $3 **MIP $10**

(Hasbro Photo)

Endor Rebel Soldier, 1998, Series 10
MNP $3 **MIP $10**

(Hasbro Photo)

EV-9D9, 1997, Series 9
MNP $3 **MIP $12**

(Hasbro Photo)

Gamorrean Guard, 1997, Series 9
MNP $3 **MIP $10**

Garindan (Long Snoot), 1997, Series 7
MNP $3 **MIP $7**

Grand Moff Tarkin, 1997, Series 7, Collection 2, surprisingly not produced until the re-release of the first three movies
MNP $3 **MIP $40**

Greedo, 1996, Series 3, Collection 1
MNP $3 **MIP $25**

Han in Bespin Outfit, 1997, Series 8
MNP $3 **MIP $7**

Han in Endor Gear, 1997, Series 6, blue pants
MNP $3 **MIP $12**

Han in Hoth Gear, 1996, Series 2
MNP $3 **MIP $15**

Han Solo, 1995, Series 1
MNP $3 **MIP $15**

Han Solo in Carbonite, 1996, Han in Bespin outfit, frozen in carbonite, blaster
MNP $3 **MIP $6**

Hoth Rebel Soldier, 1997, Series 5
MNP $3 **MIP $10**

(Hasbro Photo)

Ishi Tib, 1998, Series 12
MNP $3 **MIP $20**

Jawa & Gonk Droid, 1999, Series 18, Droid also known as "power droid," a walking generator. Called "Gonk" because of the noise it makes when walking around on the Jawas' Sandcrawer in Episode IV
MNP $3 **MIP $8**

(Hasbro Photo)

Jawas, 1996, Series 4
MNP $3 **MIP $25**

(Hasbro Photo)

Lak Sivrak, 1998, Series 11
MNP $3 **MIP $20**

(Hasbro Photo)

Lando as General, 1998, Series 10
MNP $3 **MIP $20**

Lando as Skiff Guard, 1997, Series 6
MNP $3 **MIP $10**

(Hasbro Photo)

Lando Calrissian, 1996, Series 2
MNP $3 **MIP $10**

Leia as Jabba's Prisoner, 1997, Series 8
MNP $3 **MIP $8**

(Hasbro Photo)

Leia in Ewok Celebration Outfit, 1998, Series 10
MNP $3 **MIP $20**

Leia w/All-New Likeness, 1998, Series 13, a much better sculpt than the first re-release
MNP $3 **MIP $10**

Lobot, 1998, Series 15
MNP $3 **MIP $15**

(Hasbro Photo)

Luke as X-Wing Pilot, 1996, Series 2, short lightsaber
MNP $3 **MIP $15**

Luke in Bespin Outfit, 1998, Series 10, detachable hand
MNP $3 **MIP $10**

Luke in Ceremonial Garb, 1997, Series 10, Collection 1
MNP $3 **MIP $8**

Luke in Dagobah Fatigues, 1996, Series 3, short lightsaber
MNP $3 **MIP $20**

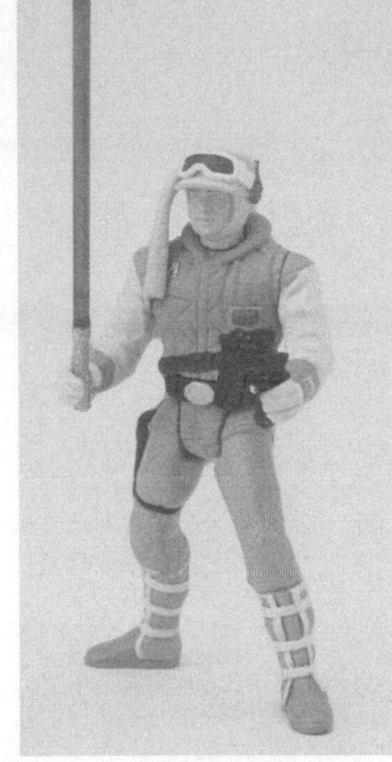

(Hasbro Photo)

Luke in Hoth Gear, 1997, Series 5, Collection 1
MNP $3 **MIP $10**

Luke in Stormtrooper Disguise, 1996, Series 4
MNP $4 **MIP $35**

Luke Skywalker, 1995, Series 1, short lightsaber
MNP $4 **MIP $15**

Luke Skywalker, 1998, Series 16, Flashback photo
MNP $3 **MIP $10**

Luke Skywalker w/T16, 1999, Series 18
MNP $3 **MIP $8**

Luke w/Blast Shield Helmet, 1998, Series 13
MNP $3 **MIP $15**

(Hasbro Photo)

Malakili (Rancor Keeper), 1997, Series 9
MNP $3 MIP $10

(Hasbro Photo)

Momaw Nadon (Hammerhead), 1996, Series 4, Collection 2
MNP $2 MIP $35

Mon Mothma, 1998, Series 15
MNP $3 MIP $20

(Hasbro Photo)

Nien Nunb, 1997, Series 9
MNP $3 MIP $10

Obi-Wan Kenobi, 1995, Series 1, short lightsaber
MNP $4 MIP $15

Obi-Wan Kenobi, 1998, Series 16
MNP $3 MIP $20

Orrimaarko (Prune Face), 1998, Series 15, with brown plastic cloak
MNP $3 MIP $15

Ponda Baba, 1997, Series 7, Collection 3, Collection 2 issue $40
MNP $3 MIP $7

Princess Leia, 1995, Series 1
MNP $3 MIP $20

Princess Leia, 1998, Series 16
MNP $3 MIP $10

Princess Leia Organa, 1997, Series 9
MNP $5 MIP $10

R2-D2, 1995, Series 1
MNP $3 MIP $15

R2-D2, 1998, Series 16
MNP $3 MIP $10

R2-D2 w/Datalink and Sensorscope, 1998, Series 13
MNP $3 MIP $15

R2-D2 w/Holographic Princess Leia, 1999, Series 20
MNP $12 MIP $45

(Hasbro Photo)

R5-D4, 1996, Series 4
MNP $3 MIP $25

Rebel Fleet Trooper, 1997, Series 7, Collection 1
MNP $3 MIP $10

Ree-Yees, 1998, Series 15
MNP $3 MIP $25

(Hasbro Photo)

Saelt-Marae (Yak Face), 1997, Series 9
MNP $3 MIP $12

Sandtrooper, 1996, Series 3, with blaster rifle and backpack
MNP $3 MIP $15

Snowtrooper, 1997, Series 8, nicely detailed sculpt
MNP $3 MIP $8

Stormtrooper, 1995, Series 1
MNP $3 MIP $12

Stormtrooper, 1999, Series 19, Commtech Chip
MNP $5 MIP $15

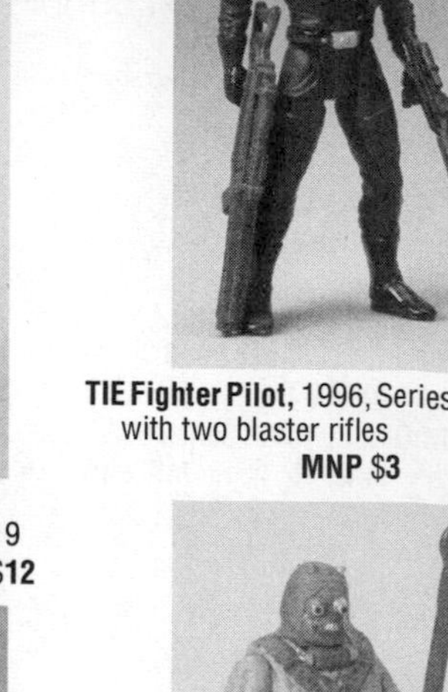

TIE Fighter Pilot, 1996, Series 2, equipped with two blaster rifles
MNP $3 MIP $6

Tusken Raider, 1996, Series 4
MNP $3 MIP $25

Ugnaught, 1998, Series 13
MNP $3 MIP $12

Weequay Skiff Guard, 1997, Series 7, Collection 3
MNP $3 MIP $7

(Hasbro Photo)

Wicket and Logray, 1998, Series 11
MNP $3 MIP $18

Yoda, 1996, Series 2
MNP $3 MIP $12

Yoda, 1998, Series 16
MNP $3 MIP $12

Zuckuss, 1998, Series 12
MNP $3 MIP $30

POTF2-2
Cinema Scene 3-Packs

Cantina Aliens, 1999, Labria, Nabrun Leids, Takeel
MNP $10 MIP $18

(Hasbro Photo)

Cantina Showdown, 1997, Obi-Wan Kenobi, Ponda Baba, Dr. Evazan
MNP $10 MIP $20

(Karen O'Brien)

Death Star Escape, 1997, Luke and Han in Stormtrooper Disguise, Chewbacca
MNP $10 MIP $45

Final Jedi Duel, 1998, Darth Vader, Luke, Emperor Palpatine
MNP $10 MIP $28

Jabba the Hutt's Dancers, 1998, Rystall, Greeata, Lyn Me
MNP $10 MIP $15

Jabba's Skiff Guards, 1999, Klaatu, Barada, Nikto. Keeping them in-pack, the box doubles as a diorama background
MNP $10 MIP $35

Jedi Spirits, 1999, Anakin Skywalker, Yoda, Obi-Wan Kenobi
MNP $10 MIP $18

Mynock Hunt, 1998, Han, Leia, Chewbacca
MNP $10 MIP $50

Purchase of the Droids, 1998, Luke, C-3PO, Uncle Owen
MNP $10 MIP $20

Rebel Pilots, 1999, Wedge Antilles, B-Wing Pilot (Ten Nunb), Y-Wing Pilot
MNP $10 MIP $15

POTF2-3
Complete Galaxy

Dagobah w/Yoda, 1998
MNP $10 MIP $12

Death Star w/Darth Vader, 1998
MNP $10 MIP $12

Endor w/Wicket, 1998
MNP $10 MIP $22

Tatooine w/Luke Skywalker, 1998
MNP $10 MIP $25

POTF2-4
Dark Empire

Clone Emperor, 1998
MNP $3 MIP $18

Imperial Sentinel, 1998
MNP $3 MIP $18

Kyle Katarn, 1998
MNP $3 MIP $35

Luke Skywalker (Dark Empire), 1998
MNP $3 MIP $18

Princess Leia Organa Solo, 1998
MNP $3 MIP $18

POTF2-4
Dark Forces

Darktrooper, 1998
MNP $3 MIP $30

POTF2-5
Deluxe

Boba Fett, 1997
MNP $5 MIP $12

Crowd Control Stormtrooper, 1996
MNP $5 MIP $7

Han Solo w/Smuggler's Flight Pack, 1996
MNP $5 MIP $10

Hoth Rebel Soldier w/Anti-Vehicle Laser Canon, 1996
MNP $5 MIP $12

Imperial Probe Droid, 1997
MNP $5 MIP $10

Luke Skywalker's Desert Sport Skiff, 1996
MNP $5 MIP $10

Snowtrooper (Deluxe), 1997, With tripod laser cannon
MNP $5 MIP $10

POTF2-6
Deluxe 2-Packs

Boba Fett vs. IG-88, 1996, Packaged with comic book
MNP $6 MIP $30

Droopy McCool and Barquin D'an, 1998
MNP $6 MIP $35

Leia and Han, 1998
MNP $6 MIP $10

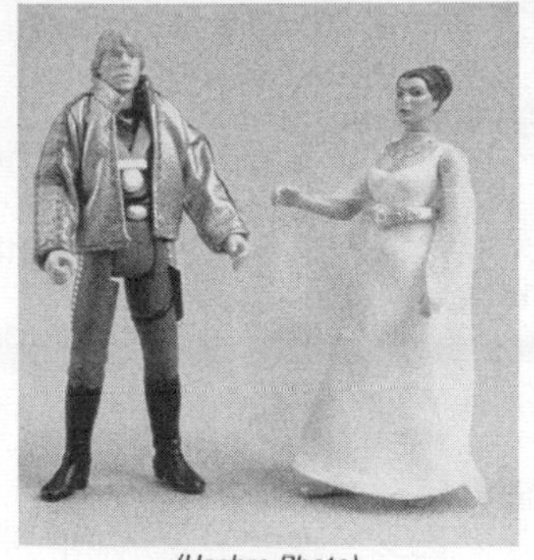

(Hasbro Photo)

Leia and Luke, 1998
MNP $6 MIP $10

Leia and R2-D2, 1998
MNP $6 MIP $10

(Hasbro Photo)

Leia and Wicket the Ewok, 1998
MNP $6 MIP $10

Max Rebo and Doda Bodonawieedo, 1998
MNP $6 MIP $38

Prince Xizor vs. Darth Vader, 1996
MNP $6 MIP $25

Sy Snootles and Joh Yowza, 1998
MNP $6 MIP $35

POTF2-7
Electronic Power F/X

Ben (Obi-Wan) Kenobi, 1997
MNP $5 MIP $10

Darth Vader, 1997
MNP $5 MIP $10

Emporer Palpatine, 1997
MNP $5 MIP $10

Jedi Knight Luke Skywalker, 1997
MNP $5 MIP $10

R2-D2, 1997
MNP $5 MIP $10

POTF2-8
Fan Club Four

AT-AT Driver, 1998
MNP $3 MIP $20

Death Star Droid w/Mouse Droid, 1998
MNP $3 MIP $20

Leia in Hoth Gear, 1998
MNP $3 MIP $22

Pote Snitkin, 1998
MNP $3 MIP $20

POTF2-9 Gunner Stations

Falcon w/Han Solo, 1998
MNP $6 MIP $10

Falcon w/Luke Skywalker, 1998
MNP $6 MIP $10

Tie Fighter w/Darth Vader, 1998
MNP $6 MIP $30

POTF2-10 Heir to the Empire

Grand Admiral Thrawn, 1998
MNP $3 MIP $20

Mara Jade, 1998
MNP $3 MIP $35

Spacetrooper, 1998
MNP $3 MIP $25

POTF2-11 Millennium Minted Coin

C-3PO, 1998, w/Millennium Minted Coin
MNP $5 MIP $12

Chewbacca, 1998, w/Millennium Minted Coin
MNP $5 MIP $12

Emperor Palpatine, 1998, w/Millennium Minted Coin
MNP $5 MIP $12

Han in Bespin Outfit, 1998, w/Millennium Minted Coin
MNP $5 MIP $12

Leia in Endor Gear, 1998, w/Millennium Minted Coin
MNP $5 MIP $12

Luke in Battle Poncho, 1998, w/Millennium Minted Coin
MNP $5 MIP $12

Snowtrooper, 1998, w/Millennium Minted Coin
MNP $5 MIP $12

POTF2-12 Promotional 3" Figures

B'omarr Monk, 1997, Internet exclusive offer. Moving spider-like legs and brain encased in plastic bubble
MNP $10 MIP $15

Figrin D'an (Cantina Band Member), 1997, Star Wars Insider magazine exclusive
MNP $10 MIP $15

Han Solo in Stormtrooper Disguise, 1995-96, Kellogg's Fruit Loops exclusive from Aug. 1995 through Dec. 1996
MNP $10 MIP $20

Mace Windu Episode I Sneak Preview, 1998, Hasbro mail-in exclusive
MNP $5 MIP $10

Muftak and Kabe, 1997, Internet exclusive
MNP $10 MIP $16

Obi-Wan Kenobi Spirit, 1997, Figure was a mail-in offer from Frito Lay. Made of translucent blue plastic
MNP $10 MIP $10

Oola and Salacious Crumb, 1998, fan club exclusive
MNP $10 MIP $14

STAP and Battle Droid Episode I Sneak Preview, 1998, Hasbro mail-in exclusive
MNP $10 MIP $12

Theater Edition Jedi Knight Luke Skywalker, 1997, RotJ-SE opening day exclusive 3/7/97
MNP $10 MIP $65

POTF2-13 Shadows of the Empire

Chewbacca in Bounty Hunter Disguise, 1996
MNP $3 MIP $10

Dash Rendar, 1996
MNP $3 MIP $20

Han in Carbonite, 1996
MNP $3 MIP $10

Leia in Boushh Disguise, 1996
MNP $3 MIP $10

Luke in Imperial Guard Disguise, 1996
MNP $3 MIP $20

Prince Xizor, 1996
MNP $3 MIP $10

POTJ Collection 1

Anakin Skywalker, Mechanic, 2000, young Anakin, droid, wrench
MNP $4 MIP $8

Aurra Sing, Bounty Hunter, 2001
MNP $5 MIP $15

Battle Droid, Boomer Damage, 2000, blaster, power pack
MNP $4 MIP $8

Ben (Obi-Wan) Kenobi, Jedi Knight, 2000, older Ben (ANH), lightsaber
MNP $4 MIP $8

Chewbacca, Millennium Falcon Mechanic, 2001, welder, goggles
MNP $4 MIP $10

Coruscant Guard, 2001, large blaster rifle
MNP $3 MIP $14

Darth Maul, Final Duel, 2000, lightsaber, body breaks into 2 pieces
MNP $7 MIP $22

Darth Maul, Sith Apprentice, 2001, lightsaber, tan training attire
MNP $3 MIP $25

Darth Vader, Dagobah, 2000, lightsaber, removable cape, detachable head, removable faceplate reveals Luke's face
MNP $4 MIP $16

Darth Vader, Emperor's Wrath, 2001, suffering from Jedi lightning 'cause he won't kill Luke
MNP $4 MIP $12

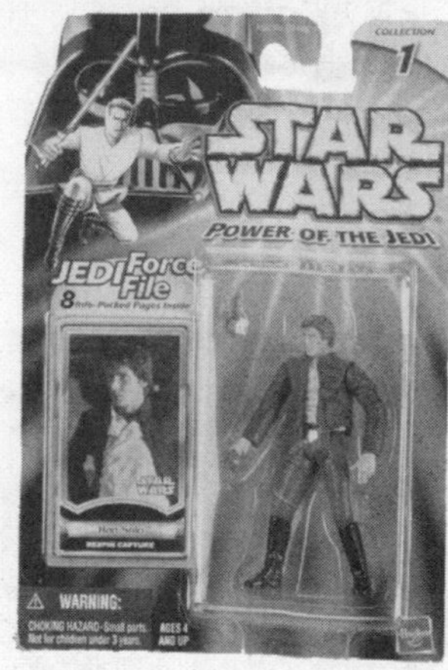

Han Solo, Bespin Capture, 2002, blaster pistol, cuffs and 8-page "Jedi Force File"
MNP $5 MIP $20

Han Solo, Death Star Escape, 2001, blaster, ready to chase the Stormtroopers
MNP $4 MIP $8

Leia Organa, Bespin Escape, 2001, blaster
MNP $4 MIP $8

Leia Organa, General, 2000, 2 blasters
MNP $4 MIP $8

Luke Skywalker, X-Wing Pilot, 2000, lightsaber
MNP $4 MIP $8

Obi-Wan Kenobi, Cold Weather Gear, 2001, lightsaber, backpack, face mask
MNP $3 MIP $9

Obi-Wan Kenobi, Jedi, 2000, lightsaber, removable cloak, young Obi-Wan at the end of Episode I
MNP $4 MIP $8

Qui-Gon Jinn, Jedi Training Gear, 2001, lightsaber
MNP $3 MIP $9

Qui-Gon Jinn, Mos Espa Disguise, 2000, gray cloth poncho, lightsaber
MNP $5 MIP $10

R2-D2, Naboo Escape, 2000
MNP $3 MIP $10

Sandtrooper, Tatooine Patrol, 2001, binoculars, backpack, pistol
MNP $5 MIP $8

POTJ Collection 2

Battle Droid, Security, 2000, blaster
MNP $4 MIP $8

Bespin Guard, Cloud City Security, 2000
MNP $4 MIP $8

BoShek, 2002, pilot's outfit, removable helmet
MNP $3 MIP $9

Boss Nass, Gungan Sacred Place, 2000
MNP $3 MIP $13

Chewbacca, Dejarik Champion, 2000
MNP $3 MIP $15

Eeth Koth, Jedi Master, 2001, lightsaber
MNP $3 MIP $8

Ellorrs Madak, Duros, 2001, Fan Choice Figure #1
MNP $3 MIP $8

Fode and Beed, Podrace Announcers, 2000
MNP $4 MIP $8

FX-7, Medical Droid, 2001
MNP $3 MIP $9

Gungan Warrior, 2000, shield, energy weapon
MNP $3 MIP $10

IG-88, Bounty Hunter, 2000
MNP $4 MIP $10

Imperial Officer, 2001, pistol
MNP $3 MIP $9

Jar Jar Binks, Tatooine, 2000
MNP $3 MIP $8

Jek Porkins, Rebel Pilot, 2000, the original "Red Six" himself, removable helmet, "Stay on target!"
MNP $4 MIP $9

K-3PO, Echo Base Protocol Droid, 2000, pouch
MNP $4 MIP $9

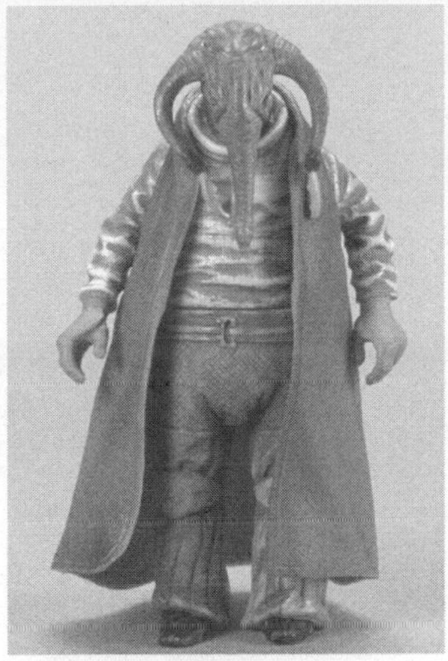

Ketwol, 2001
MNP $3 MIP $11

Lando Calrissian, Bespin Escape, 2000, pistol
MNP $4 MIP $9

Mas Amedda, 2000
MNP $3 MIP $10

Mon Calamari Officer, 2000
MNP $4 MIP $8

Obi-Wan Kenobi, Jedi Training Gear, 2001, lightsaber, helmet
MNP $3 MIP $12

Plo Koon, Jedi Master, 2000, lightsaber
MNP $3 MIP $9

Queen Amidala, Royal Decoy, 2001, black outfit
MNP $3 MIP $8

Queen Amidala, Theed Invasion, 2001, red outfit
MNP $3 MIP $8

R2-Q5, Imperial Astromech Droid, 2001
MNP $3 MIP $8

R4-M9, 2001, w/small black droid
MNP $3 MIP $9

Rebel Trooper, Tantive IV Defender, 2001, pistol, removable helmet
MNP $3 MIP $9

Sabe, Queen's Decoy, 2001, blaster pistol
MNP $3 MIP $9

Saesee Tiin, Jedi Master, 2000, lightsaber
MNP $3 MIP $10

Scout Trooper, Imperial Patrol, 2000, biker scout in clean or dirty armor variations, pistol
MNP $4 MIP $12

Sebulba, 2000, removeable helmet, wrench
MNP $3 MIP $9

Shmi Skywalker, 2001
MNP $3 MIP $8

Teebo, 2001, staff
MNP $3 MIP $9

Tessek, 2001, blaster pistol
MNP $3 MIP $9

Tusken Raider, Desert Sniper, 2001, long rifle
MNP $3 MIP $10

Zutton, Snaggletooth, 2001, rifle
MNP $3 MIP $10

POTJ Deluxe

Amanaman w/Salacious Crumb, 2001
MNP $4 MIP $12

Darth Maul w/Sith Attack Droid
MNP $3 MIP $15

Luke Skywalker in Echo Base Bacta Tank, 2001
MNP $4 MIP $12

Princess Leia w/Sail Barge Cannon, 2001
MNP $4 MIP $12

POTJ Mega Action

Darth Maul, 2000, Lightsaber Action Moves
MNP $5 MIP $15

Destroyer Droid, Battle Damaged, 2000
MNP $5 MIP $15

Obi-Wan Kenobi, 2000, Lightsaber Battle Moves
MNP $5 MIP $15

POTJ Multi-Packs

Darth Maul and Darth Vader, 2000, Masters of the Dark Side, lightsabers, base
MNP $7 MIP $16

POTJ Silver Anniv.

Han Solo and Chewbacca, 2001, Death Star Escape
MNP $5 MIP $10

Luke Skywalker and Princess Leia Organa, 2001, Swing to Freedom
MNP $5 MIP $10

Obi-Wan Kenobi and Darth Vader, 2001, Final Duel
MNP $5 MIP $10

POTJ Special Edition

Boba Fett, 2000, 300th figure
MNP $5 MIP $14

THE PHANTOM MENACE Cinema Scene 3-Packs

Mos Espa Encounter, 1999, Sebulba, Jar Jar, Anakin
MNP $5 MIP $18

Tatooine Showdown, 1999, Darth Maul, Qui-Gon, Anakin
MNP $5 MIP $18

Watto's Box, 2000, Watto, Graxol Kelvyyn, Shakka
MNP $5 MIP $25

Action Figures, 03-3/4"

THE PHANTOM MENACE
Deluxe

Darth Maul, 1999
MNP $5 **MIP $9**

Obi-Wan Kenobi, 1999
MNP $5 **MIP $9**

Qui-Gon Jinn, 1999
MNP $5 **MIP $9**

THE PHANTOM MENACE

Adi Gallia, 1999, With removeable cloak and lightsaber
MNP $3 **MIP $10**

Anakin Skywalker, Mechanic, 2000, Includes pit droid figure
MNP $3 **MIP $7**

Anakin Skywalker, Naboo, 1999, With removable plastic cloak
MNP $3 **MIP $7**

Anakin Skywalker, Naboo Pilot, 2000, Includes helmet and ship controls
MNP $3 **MIP $12**

Anakin Skywalker, Tatooine, 1999, With backpack and blaster pistol
MNP $3 **MIP $12**

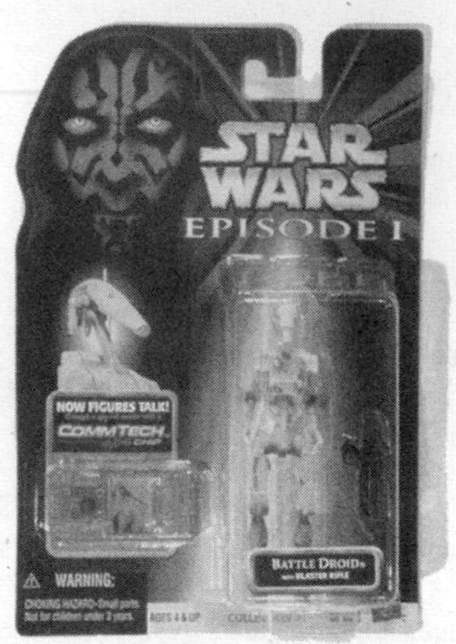

Battle Droid w/Federation Issue Blaster, 1999, These droids came in variety of paint finishes--some pristine, others with battle damage
MNP $3 **MIP $7**

Battle Droid, Battle Damage, 1999, Variations on this model include: "star" blast point on chest, silver lines on body, and lighter and darker sand marks
MNP $3 **MIP $10**

Battle Droid, Security, 2000, Fairly plain light tan with dark brown. Includes blaster rifle
MNP $3 **MIP $8**

Boss Nass, 1999, With staff
MNP $3 **MIP $8**

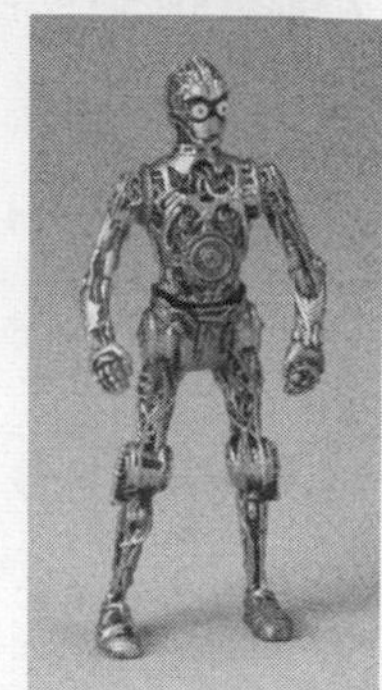

C-3PO, 1999, Skeletal-looking version of 3PO before he had metal "skin"
MNP $3 **MIP $10**

Captain Panaka, 2000, With blaster rifle
MNP $3 **MIP $10**

Captain Tarpals, 1999, With "electropole" staff
MNP $3 **MIP $12**

Chancellor Valorum, 1999, Includes staff
MNP $3 **MIP $12**

Darth Maul, Jedi Duel, 1999, The first release of a 3-3/4" Darth Maul figure
MNP $5 **MIP $20**

Darth Maul, Sith Lord, 2000, With double-edged lightsaber, second stand-alone release of figure
MNP $3 **MIP $12**

Darth Maul, Tatooine, 1999, With black cloth cloak--the cloak and other weapons were also available in an accessory set
MNP $3 **MIP $7**

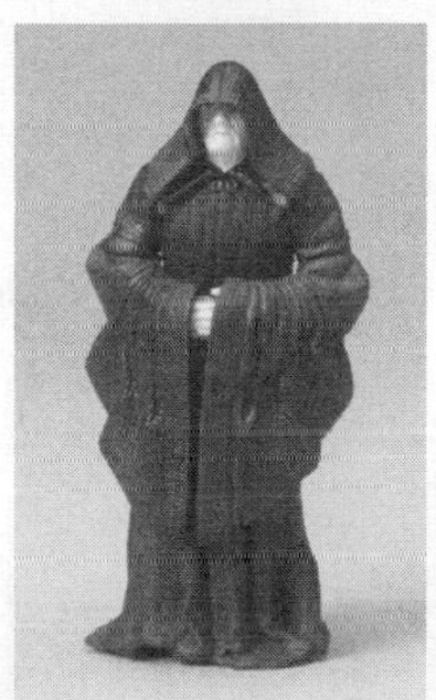

Darth Sidious, 1999, Black-robed figure with Commtech chip
MNP $3 **MIP $12**

Darth Sidious, Holograph, 2000, Translucent purple figure with Commtech chip
MNP $3 **MIP $30**

Destroyer Droid, 1999, Includes Commtech chip
MNP $3 **MIP $7**

Gasgano, w/pit droid, 1999, Mult-armed figure packaged with pit droid and Commtech chip
MNP $3 **MIP $10**

Jar Jar Binks, 1999, Figure included Gungan Battle Staff and comtech chip stand
MNP $3 **MIP $20**

Jar Jar Binks, Naboo Swamp, 2000, Specially made to be posed in swimming motion, includes fish
MNP $3 **MIP $18**

Ki-Adi-Mundi, 1999, With lightsaber
MNP $3 **MIP $10**

Mace Windu, 1999, With lightsaber and removeable plastic cloak
MNP $3 **MIP $12**

Mace Windu, Sneak Preview, 1998, Includes different cloak and has a more stoic, less active pose and expression than the regular-issue Mace Windu
MNP $3 **MIP $30**

Naboo Royal Guard, 2000, Includes removeable helmet and blaster pistol
MNP $3 **MIP $20**

Naboo Royal Security, 2000, Included two blaster rifles
MNP $3 **MIP $7**

Nute Gunray, 1999, A good likeness--includes Commtech chip
MNP $3 **MIP $6**

Obi-Wan Kenobi, Jedi Duel, 1999, Includes lightsaber
MNP $3 MIP $10

Obi-Wan Kenobi, Jedi Knight, 2000, In plain white robe, much like the Jedi Duel figure, but includes extra belt and gear, along with lightsaber
MNP $3 MIP $20

Obi-Wan Kenobi, Naboo, 1999, In dark robe--has two lightsabers, one activated, the other not
MNP $3 MIP $7

Ody Mandrell w/Pit Droid, 1999, Another two-figure pack with Commtech chip
MNP $3 MIP $7

OOM-9, 1999, Yellow markings on head and body. This figure includes binoculars and blaster rifle
MNP $3 MIP $7

Padme Naberrie, 1999, Figure included viewscreen to watch the pod race
MNP $3 MIP $12

Pit Droids, 2000, Highly-detailed sculpts of the ubiquitous droids seen in Episode 1
MNP $3 MIP $25

Queen Amidala, Battle, 2000, In dark robe, includes blaster pistol and grappling hook crossbow
MNP $3 MIP $30

Queen Amidala, Coruscant, 1999, In full royal outfit and makeup
MNP $3 MIP $15

Queen Amidala, Naboo w/Blaster Pistols, 1999, Figure included two sleek blaster pistols and comtech chip stand
MNP $3 MIP $12

Qui-Gon Jinn, Jedi Duel, 1999, In plain-colored robe. Includes lightsaber
MNP $3 MIP $10

Qui-Gon Jinn, Jedi Master, 2000, With lightsaber and Commtech chip
MNP $3 MIP $20

Qui-Gon Jinn, Naboo, 1999, Includes two lightsabers: one activated, the other not
MNP $3 MIP $7

R2-B1 Astromech Droid, 2000, Dark blue with light green body, includes harness pod
MNP $3 MIP $25

R2-D2, 1999, With retractable middle "foot"
MNP $3 MIP $7

Ric Olie, 1999, Removeable helmet and two blaster pistols
MNP $3 MIP $8

Rune Haako, 1999, Includes Commtech chip
MNP $3 MIP $6

Senator Palpatine, 1999, With cam droid and Commtech chip
MNP $3 MIP $12

Sio Bibble, 2000, Includes blaster pistol and Commtech chip
MNP $3 MIP $45

TC-14, 2000, Silver-plated, includes serving tray and Commtech chip. Somewhat harder to find, almost exlusively available from dealers
MNP $3 MIP $35

Watto, 1999, Highly-detailed figure
MNP $3 MIP $10

Yoda, w/Jedi Council Chair, 1999, Includes blue chair and Commtech chip
MNP $3 MIP $8

SAGA
Basic

Aayla Secura, Jedi Knight, 2003, platform, blue lightsaber
MNP $3 MIP $7

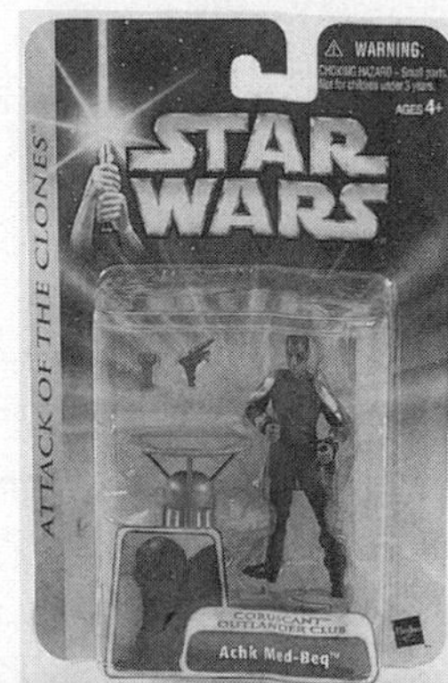

Achk Med-Beq, Courscant Outlander Club, 2003
MNP $3 MIP $7

Admiral Ozzel, 2004, Star Destroyer
MNP $3 **MIP** $7

Anakin Skywalker, Hangar Duel, 2002, Includes two lightsabers, has fighting action
MNP n/a **MIP** $13

Anakin Skywalker, Outland Peasant Disguise, 2002, Includes cloak, lightsaber, and cargo
MNP n/a **MIP** $6

Anakin Skywalker, Secret Ceremony, 2003, flowing robes, mechanical hand
MNP $3 **MIP** $7

Anakin Skywalker, Tatooine Attack, 2002, mad Anakin, blue lightsaber, Tusken stand
MNP $3 **MIP** $7

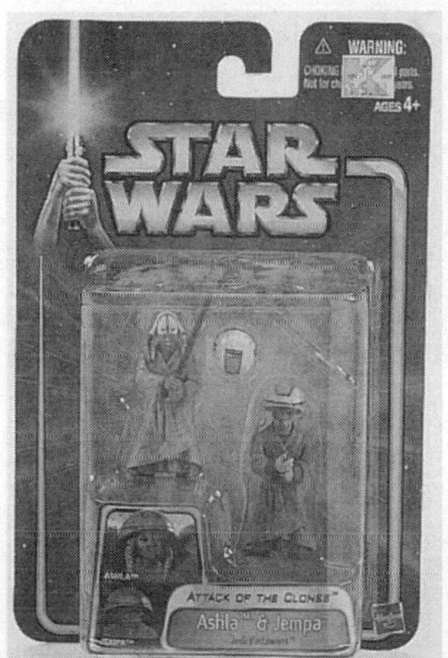

Ashla & Jempa, Younglings, 2003, 2-pack, helmet and blue lightsaber for Ashla and helmet, green lightsaber for Jempa
MNP $3 **MIP** $7

Ayy Vida, Outlander Nightclub Patron, 2003, barstool and drink
MNP $5 **MIP** $10

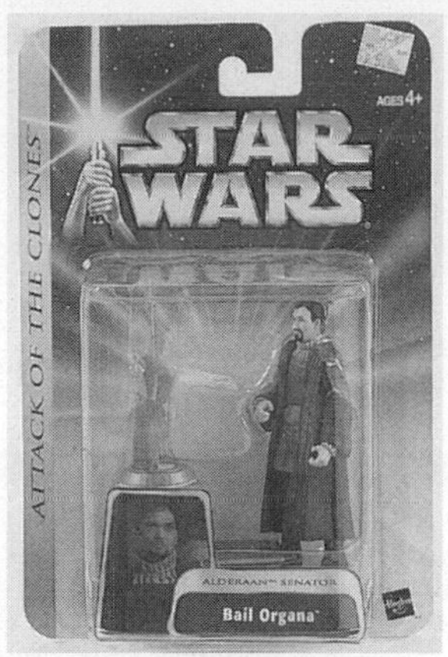

Bail Organa, Alderaan Senator, 2003, holographic Jedi and projector
MNP $5 **MIP** $10

Barriss Offee, Luminara Unduli's Padawan, 2003, flowing robes, green lightsaber
MNP $3 **MIP** $7

Battle Droid, Arena Battle, 2002, With orange laser blast
MNP n/a **MIP** $6

Boba Fett, Kamino Escape, 2002, Two blaster pistols, flame effect, missile pack
MNP n/a **MIP** $12

Boba Fett, The Pit of Carkoon, 2003, molded engine flames and energy blast, laser rifle
MNP $5 **MIP** $10

Bossk, Executor Meeting, 2004
MNP $3 **MIP** $7

C-3PO, Hoth Evacuation, 2004
MNP $3 **MIP** $7

C-3PO, Protocol Droid, 2002, Comes with removeable outer plating and box for storage
MNP n/a **MIP** $6

C-3PO, Tatooine Ambush, 2003, removable arm, serving tray
MNP $3 **MIP** $7

Captain Antilles, Tantive IV Invasion, Fan's Choice Figure #5, 2004
MNP $3 **MIP** $7

Captain Typho, 2002, With removeable helmet, blaster with blast effect
MNP n/a **MIP** $18

Chewbacca, Cloud City, 2002, w/net and C3PO in pieces
MNP $3 **MIP** $7

Chewbacca, Mynock Hunt, 2003, crossbow, red bolt, Mynock
MNP $3 **MIP** $7

Clone Trooper, 2002, With rifle and tripod-style gun. This figure also lacks the painted-on sand and grime that the preview model features
MNP n/a **MIP** $9

Clone Trooper, Republic Gunship Pilot, 2002, white figure w/yellow stripe on helmet, gun turret attaches to Republic Gunship
MNP $3 **MIP** $7

Coleman Trebor, Battle of Geonosis, 2003, Jedi knight, green lightsaber
MNP $3 **MIP** $7

Count Dooku, 2002, Includes lightsaber and smaller Darth Sidious hologram figure
MNP n/a **MIP $18**

Darth Maul, Sith Training, 2002, flowing black robes w/red accents, double-sided retractable lightsaber, training droid
MNP $3 **MIP $7**

Darth Maul, Theed Hangar Duel, 2003, two-ended red lightsaber
MNP $5 **MIP $10**

Darth Tyranus, Geonosian Escape, 2003, flowing robes, red lightsaber, jedi lightning
MNP $3 **MIP $7**

Darth Vader, Bespin Duel, 2002, "Luke, I am your father..."
MNP $3 **MIP $7**

Darth Vader, Death Star Clash, 2003, cloth robe, red lightsaber
MNP $5 **MIP $10**

Darth Vader, Throne Room Duel, 2003, removable helmet, red lightsaber
MNP $5 **MIP $10**

Dengar, Executor Meeting, 2004
MNP $3 **MIP $7**

Destroyer Droid, Arena Battle, 2002, w/two energy beams
MNP $3 **MIP $7**

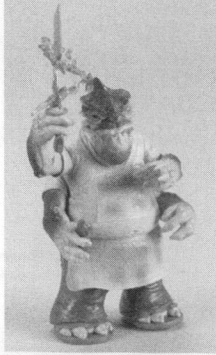

Dexter Jetster, 2002, Detailed sculpt with four moving arms. Includes cutlery
MNP n/a **MIP $9**

Djas Puhr, Alien Bounty Hunter, 2002, A New Hope, w/ two long pistols
MNP $3 **MIP $7**

Dutch Vander: Gold Leader, Battle of Yavin, 2004
MNP $3 **MIP $7**

Eeth Koth, Jedi Master, 2002, green lightsaber
MNP $3 **MIP $7**

Elan Sleazebaggano, Outlander Nightclub Encounter, 2003, "I do not want to sell you death sticks," bar, death sticks, drink
MNP $3 **MIP $7**

Emperor, Throne Room, 2003, cane, Jedi lightning
MNP $3 **MIP $7**

Endor Rebel Soldier, 2002, Bearded or non-bearded versions
MNP $3 **MIP $7**

Ephant Mon, Fan's Choice Figure #3, 2002, w/cane and axe head
MNP $7 **MIP $17**

General Jan Dodonna, Battle of Yavin, 2004
MNP $3 **MIP $7**

General Madine, Imperial Shuttle Capture, 2004
MNP $3 **MIP $7**

Geonosian Warrior, 2002, Poseable wings
MNP n/a **MIP $9**

Han Solo, Endor Raid, 2002, w/two detonators and pistol
MNP $3 **MIP $7**

Han Solo, Endor Strike, 2004, dressed as AT-ST driver
MNP $3 **MIP $7**

Han Solo, Flight to Alderan, 2003, pistol
MNP $3 **MIP $7**

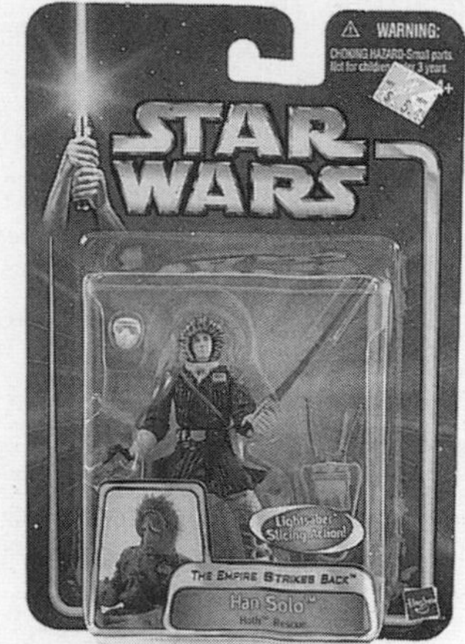

Han Solo, Hoth Rescue, 2003, two versions-blue or brown coat, snow mask, pistol, radio, blue lightsaber
MNP $3 **MIP $7**

Holographic Luke Skywalker, Jabba's Palace, 2004
MNP $3 **MIP $7**

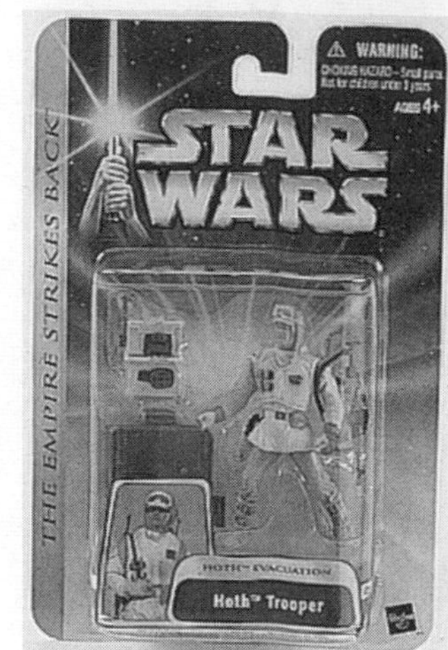

Hoth Trooper, Hoth Evacuation, 2004
MNP $3 **MIP $7**

Imperial Dignitary Janus Greejatus, Death Star Procession, 2003
MNP $3 **MIP $7**

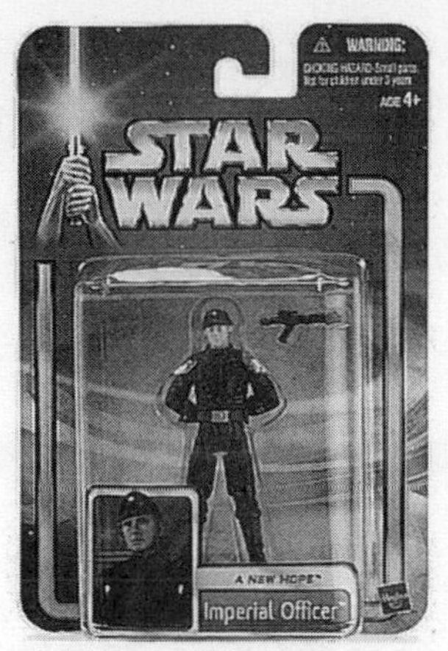

Imperial Officer, 2002, Blonde or Brown hair version, w/laser rifle
MNP $3 **MIP** $7

Jango Fett, Final Battle, 2002, Includes pack, two blasters, and plastic "flame"
MNP n/a **MIP** $18

Jango Fett, Kamino Escape, 2002, With two pistols, grappling hook, and firing missile pack
MNP n/a **MIP** $12

Jango Fett, Kamino Escape, 2003, removable helmet, two pistols, string from wrist w/hook, backpack missile
MNP $3 **MIP** $7

Jango Fett, Slave 1 Pilot, 2002, two silver pistols, can see his face
MNP $3 **MIP** $7

Jar Jar Binks, Gungan Senator, 2002, With staff and blue energy bolts
MNP n/a **MIP** $6

J'Quille, Jabba's Sail Barge, 2004
MNP $3 **MIP** $7

Ki-Adi Mundi, Jedi Master, 2002, blue lightsaber, deflected energy beam
MNP $3 **MIP** $7

Kit Fisto, Jedi Master, 2002, With "laser blast" attachment for lightsaber
MNP n/a **MIP** $9

Klen Blista-Vanee, Imperial Dignitary, 2003
MNP $3 **MIP** $7

Lama Su with Clone Youth, 2003, 2-pack
MNP $3 **MIP** $7

Lando Calrissian, Death Star Attack, 2004
MNP $3 **MIP** $7

Lando Calrissian, Jabba's Sail Barge, 2004
MNP $3 **MIP** $7

Lott Dod, Neimoidian Senator, 2002, w/tall hat and small holographic Darth Sidious
MNP $3 **MIP** $7

Lt. Danni Faytonni, Coruscant Outlander Club, 2003, table, drink, pistol
MNP $3 **MIP** $7

Luke Skywalker, Bespin Duel, 2002, "Bloody Luke," right hand removable, comes with antenna
MNP $3 **MIP** $7

Luke Skywalker, Hoth Attack, 2004
MNP $3 **MIP** $7

Luke Skywalker, Jabba's Palace, 2004
MNP $3 **MIP** $7

Luke Skywalker, Tatooine Encounter, 2003, blue lightsaber
MNP $3 **MIP** $7

Luke Skywalker, Throne Room Duel, 2003, green lightsaber, slashing action, causeway breaks - error version has black glove on left hand rather than right
MNP $5 **MIP** $10

Luminara Unduli, Jedi Master, 2002, Extremely detailed sculpt. Figure includes lightsaber with blaster deflect attachement
MNP n/a **MIP** $14

Mace Windu, Arena Confrontation, 2003, purple lightsaber, flowing robes
MNP $3 **MIP** $7

Mace Windu, Geonosian Rescue, 2002, Pushing a button on Mace's back moves arm with lightsaber in a "slashing attack." These newest Star Wars figures probably have the most detail and moving parts of any series yet--and this is just one example
MNP n/a **MIP** $18

Massiff w/ Geonosian Warrior, 2002
MNP $3 **MIP** $7

Massiff with Geonosian Warrior, 2002, Includes Geonosian warrior with Massiff on chain leash
MNP n/a **MIP** $14

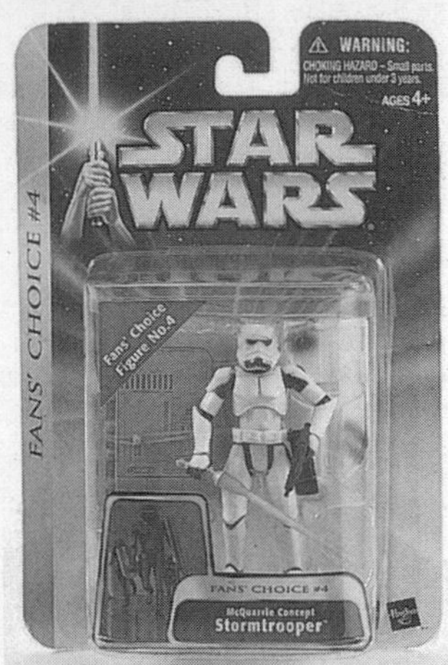

McQuarrie Concept Stormtrooper, Fan Choice Figure #4, 2003, shield, blaster, lightsaber
MNP $5 **MIP** $10

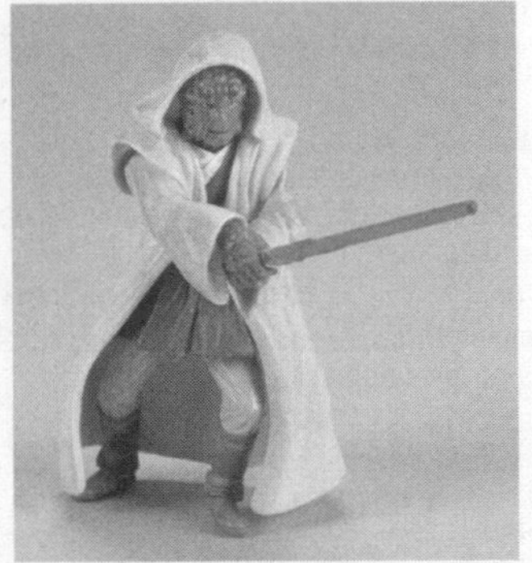

Nikto, Jedi Knight, 2002, With lightsaber and "force blast effect"
MNP n/a **MIP** $7

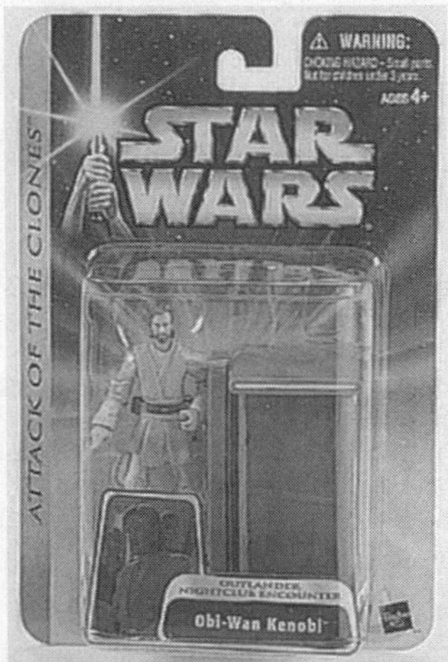

Obi Wan Kenobi, Outlander Nightclub Encounter, 2003, bar and drink
MNP $3 **MIP** $7

Obi-Wan Kenobi, Acklay Battle, 2003, w/break-away column, handcuffs, spear, blue lightsaber
MNP $3 **MIP** $7

Obi-Wan Kenobi, Coruscant Chase, 2002, With flying droid that magnetically attaches to Obi-Wan's hand
MNP n/a **MIP** $8

Obi-Wan Kenobi, Jedi Starfighter Pilot, 2002
MNP $3 **MIP** $7

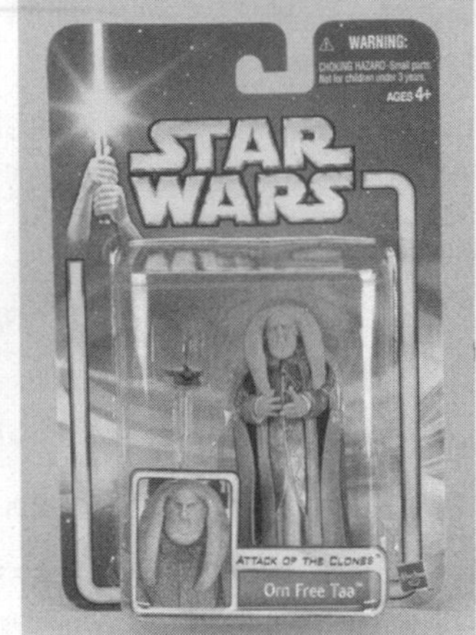

Orn Free Taa, 2002, With floating camera droid
MNP n/a **MIP** $14

Padme Amidala, Arena Escape, 2002, Swinging arm with blaster pistol and column
MNP n/a **MIP** $8

Padme Amidala, Coruscant Arrival, 2002, pilot outfit w/ helmet
MNP $3 **MIP** $7

Padme Amidala, Droid Factory Chase, 2003, platform, white cape, pistol
MNP $3 **MIP** $7

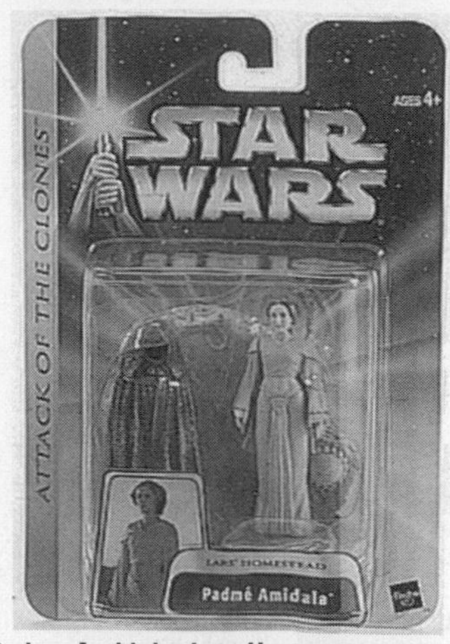

Padme Amidala, Lars Homestead, 2003, cloak and platform
MNP $3 **MIP** $7

Padme Amidala, Secret Ceremony, 2003, in wedding dress, ornate railing and flowers
MNP $3 **MIP** $7

Plo Koon, Arena Battle, 2002, With lightsaber
MNP n/a **MIP** $13

Princess Leia, Imperial Captive, 2003, pistol and laser rifle
MNP $3 **MIP** $7

Qui-Gon Jinn, Jedi Master, 2002, better robes
MNP $3 **MIP** $7

R1-G4, Tatooine Transaction, 2004
MNP $3 **MIP** $7

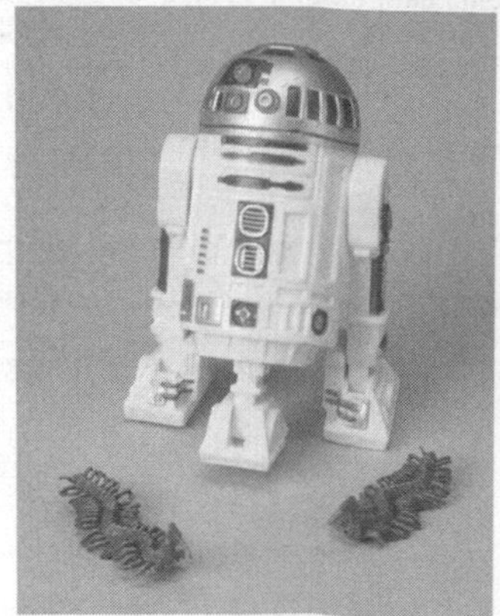

R2-D2, Coruscant Sentry, 2002, With two plastic assassin bugs. Probably the best R2 sculpt yet, with lights and sound, to boot
MNP n/a **MIP** $8

R2-D2, Droid Factory Flight, 2003, molded energy bolts, string, retractable side rockets
MNP $5 **MIP** $10

R2-D2, Jabba's Sail Barge, 2004, w/drink tray
MNP $3 **MIP** $7

Rappertunie, Jabba's Palace, 2004
MNP $3 **MIP** $7

Rebel Fleet Trooper, 2002, Red or Black hair version, w/pistol
MNP $3 **MIP** $7

Royal Guard, Coruscant Security, 2002, Red figure with staff and blue "energy bolts." Definitely the prototype for the Imperial Guard after the fall of the Republic
MNP n/a **MIP** $14

Saesee Tiin, Jedi Master, 2002, With lightsaber and force-repelled blast effect
MNP n/a **MIP** $8

Shaak Ti, Jedi Master, 2002, With "blast effect" lightsaber. Very well-detailed figure
MNP n/a **MIP** $12

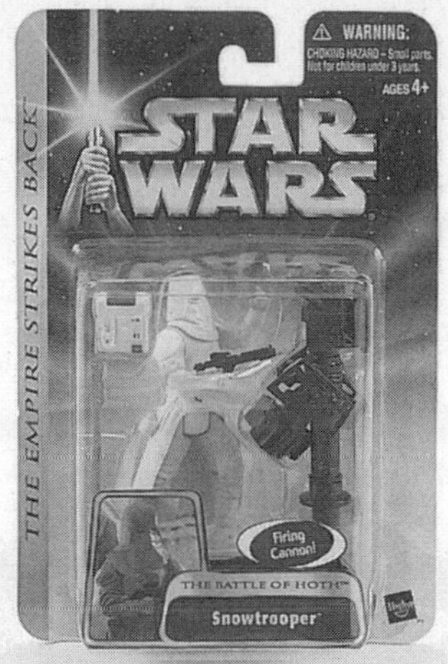

Snowtrooper, The Battle of Hoth, 2003, backpack, laser pistol, cannon w/missile
MNP $5 **MIP** $10

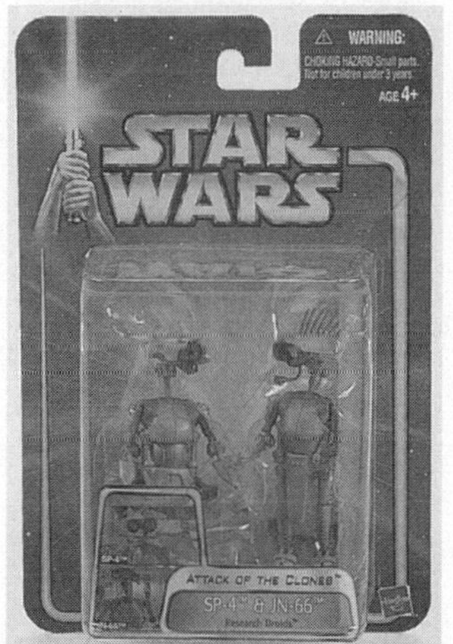

SP-4 and JN-66, Research Droids, 2003, SP-4 has spiked head, JN-66 has flat head
MNP $3 **MIP** $7

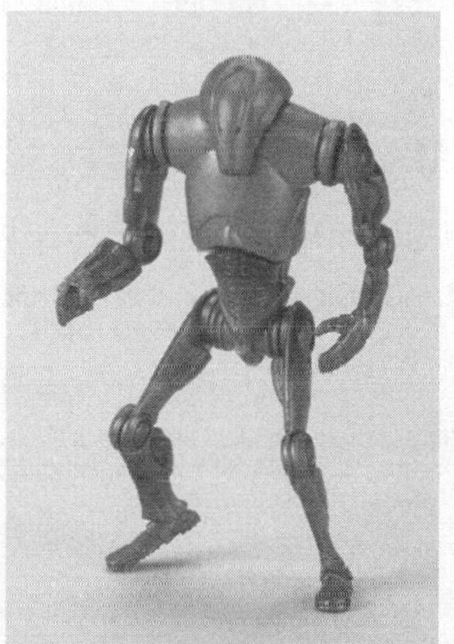

Super Battle Droid, 2002, With laser blast battle damage and attachments
MNP n/a **MIP** $6

Supreme Chancellor Palpatine, 2002
MNP $3 **MIP** $7

Tanus Spijek, Jabba's Sail Barge, 2004
MNP $3 **MIP** $7

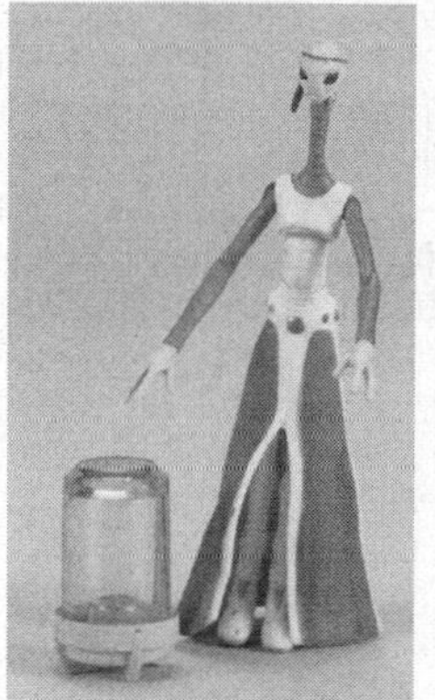

Taun We, Kamino Cloner, 2002, With cloning pod
MNP n/a **MIP** $14

Teebo, Ewok, 2002, w/horn
MNP $3 **MIP** $7

Teemto Pagalies, Pod Racer, 2002, arms in the air, w/droid and engine part
MNP $3 **MIP** $7

TIE Fighter Pilot, Battle of Yavin, 2004
MNP $3 **MIP** $7

Tusken Raider w/Massiff, 2002
MNP $3 **MIP** $7

Tusken Raider, Female w/Tusken Child, 2002, Child figure can be freestanding or fit in pack
MNP n/a **MIP** $11

Tusken Raider, Tatooine Camp Ambush, 2003, gaffi stick, platform
MNP $3 **MIP** $7

WA-7, Dexter's Diner, 2003, waitress w/ platform and tray
MNP $3 **MIP** $7

Wat Tambor, Geonosis War Room, 2003, mechanical console
MNP $3 **MIP** $7

Watto, Mos Espa Junk Dealer, 2002, wearing hat
MNP $3 **MIP** $7

Yoda & Chian, 2003, 2-pack, hoverchair, cane, green lightsaber for Yoda and helmet, blue lightsaber for Chian
MNP $3 MIP $7

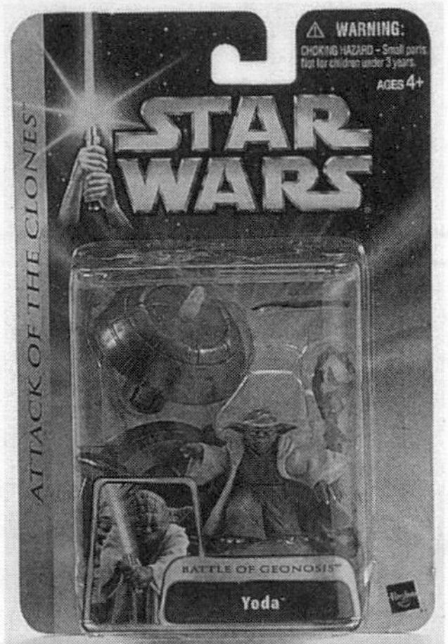

Yoda, Battle of Geonosis, 2004, Hall of Fame assortment
MNP $3 MIP $6

Yoda, Jedi High Council, 2002, w/elevated chair
MNP $5 MIP $12

Yoda, Jedi Master, 2002, Includes lightsaber, walking stick, and base
MNP $5 MIP $17

Zam Wessell, Bounty Hunter, 2002, Shorter blaster than preview edition, removable changeling face
MNP $5 MIP $11

SAGA
Deluxe

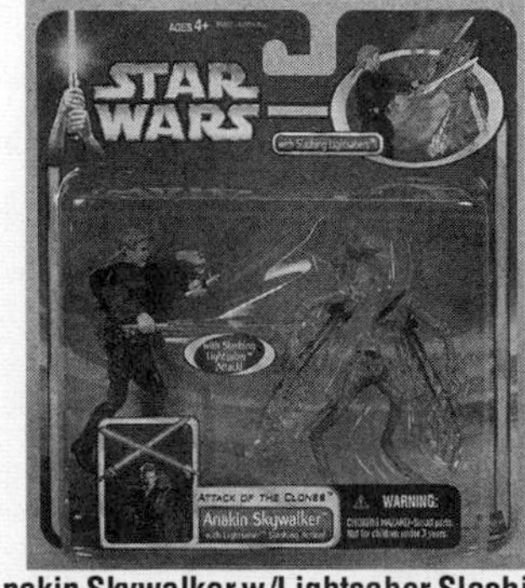

Anakin Skywalker w/Lightsaber Slashing Action, 2002, Includes two lightsabers and an easily-sliced Geonosian warrior
MNP $5 MIP $19

Anakin Skywalker, Flipping, 2002, Force Flipping action, lands on his feet
MNP $5 MIP $10

C-3PO and Battle Droid, 2002, interchangable heads
MNP $5 MIP $10

Clone Trooper w/Speeder Bike, 2002, blaster, grenade, removable armor and helmet
MNP $7 MIP $14

Darth Tyranus w/Force Flipping Attack, 2002, Like the Obi-Wan version, pushing a button on the launch pad makes Tyranus leap, flip and land on his feet
MNP $5 MIP $11

Geonosian Warrior, 2002, w/ insect pod and energy weapon
MNP $5 MIP $10

Jango Fett, Kamino Showdown, 2003, 2 pistols, jet pack w/ missile, column w/ flipping base
MNP $5 MIP $10

Jango Fett, w/Electronic Attack and Snap-On Armor, 2002, Another incredibly detailed Jango figure
MNP $5 MIP $11

Mace Windu w/Blast-Apart Battle Droid, 2002, Battle droid breaks apart as Mace stikes with saber
MNP $5 MIP $11

Nexu w/Snapping Jaw and Attack Roar, 2002, Well detailed with snapping jaw and roaring sound
MNP $5 MIP $19

Obi-Wan Kenobi w/Force Flipping Attack, 2002, Includes platform and launcher that makes Obi-Wan figure flip over and then land on his feet (after a few tries, usually). A neat idea that easily lends itself to "I betcha can't make him land this time" games
MNP $5 MIP $9

Obi-Wan, Kamino Showdown, 2003, flowing robes, blue lightsaber, terrace pieces
MNP $5 MIP $10

Spider Droid, 2003, creepy
MNP $5 MIP $10

Super Battle Droid Builder, 2003, factory to "finish" the SBD
MNP $5 MIP $10

Yoda and Super Battle Droid, 2002, w/Force powers
MNP $5 MIP $10

SAGA
Multi-Packs

Battle of Hoth, 2003, Chewbacca, Princess Leia, Luke Skywalker, R3-A2, Taun Taun, TRU exclusive
MNP $7 MIP $15

Imperial Forces, 2003, AT-ST Driver, Darth Vader, R4-19, Stormtrooper, accessories, TRU exclusive
MNP $7 MIP $15

Ultimate Bounty, 2003, Aurra Sing, Boba Fett, Bossk, IG-88, Swoop Bike, TRU exclusive
MNP $7 MIP $15

SAGA
Screen Scenes

Geonosian War Room No. 1, 2003, Poggle the Lesser, Count Dooku, San Hill
MNP $7 MIP $15

Geonosian War Room No. 2, 2003, Nute Gunray, Passel Argente, Shu Mai
MNP $7 MIP $15

Jedi High Council No. 1, 2003, Mace Windu, Oppo Rancisis, Even Piell
MNP $7 MIP $15

Jedi High Council No. 2, 2003, Yarael Poof, Depa Billaba, Yaddle
MNP $7 MIP $15

Trash Compactor No. 1, 2003, Han and Luke
MNP $7 MIP $15

Trash Compactor No. 2, 2003, Leia and Chewbacca
MNP $7 MIP $15

SAGA

Sneak Preview

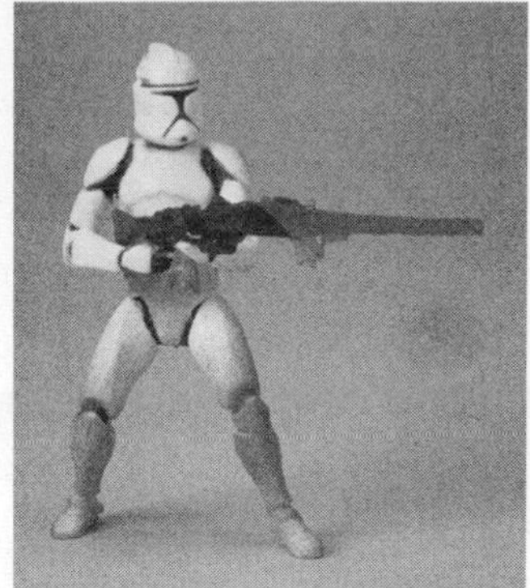

Clone Trooper, 2002, With laser rifle and blue "blast" attachment. This model shows painted-on battlefield "dirt" detail
MNP n/a **MIP** $11

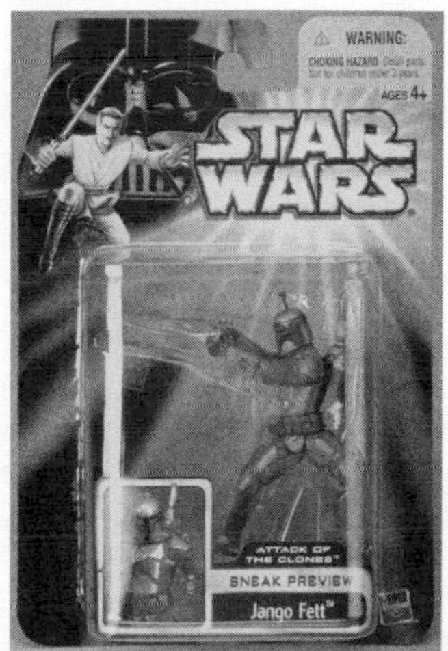

Jango Fett, 2002
MNP n/a **MIP** $14

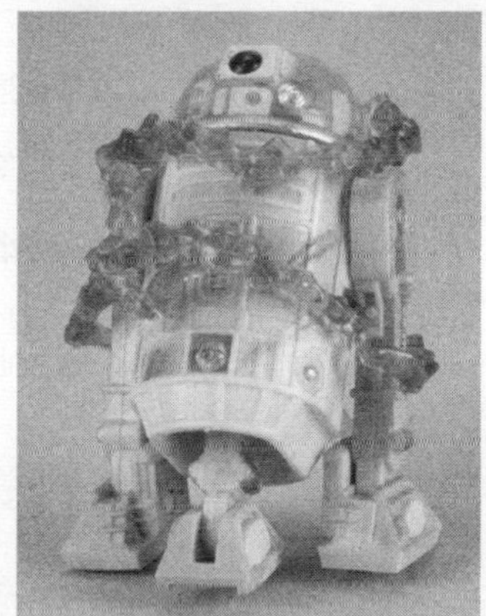

R3-T7, 2002, Detailed astromech droid with blue engergy bolts that wrap around body
MNP n/a **MIP** $11

Zam Wessell, 2002, With long gun, human face partially covered by scarf
MNP n/a **MIP** $11

CLONE WARS

Basic

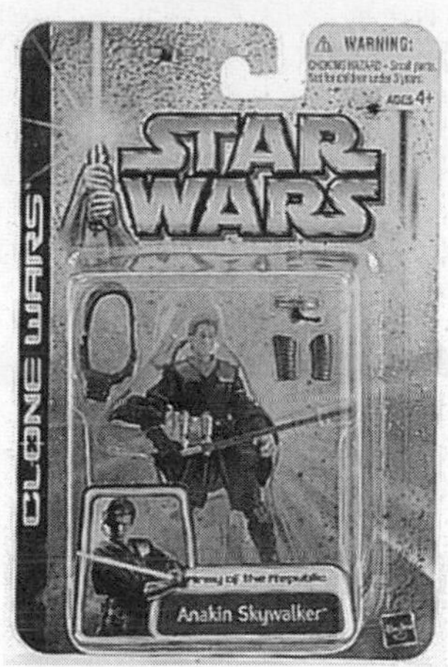

Anakin Skywalker, Army of the Republic, 2003, 2 armor pieces, headgear, belt, blue lightsaber
MNP $3 **MIP** $7

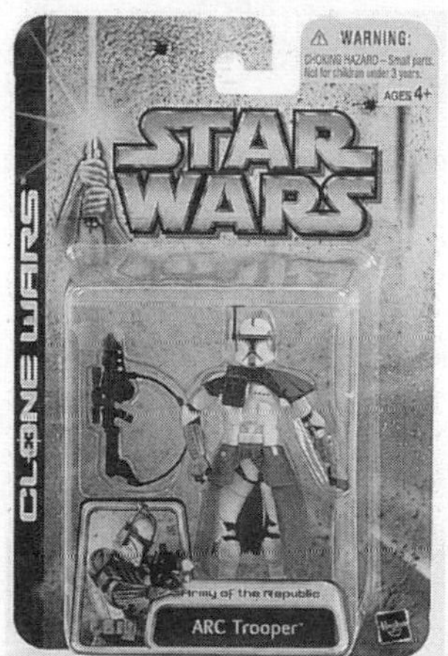

ARC Trooper, Army of the Republic, 2003, laser rifle
MNP $3 **MIP** $7

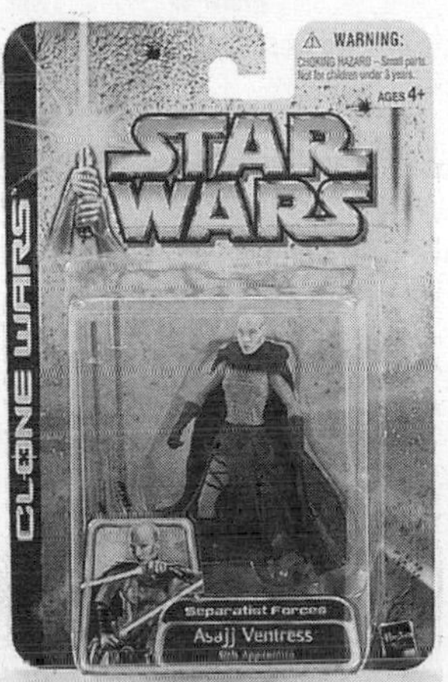

Asajj Ventress, Sith Apprentice, 2003, 2 curved-handled red lightsabers, flowing black robes
MNP $3 **MIP** $7

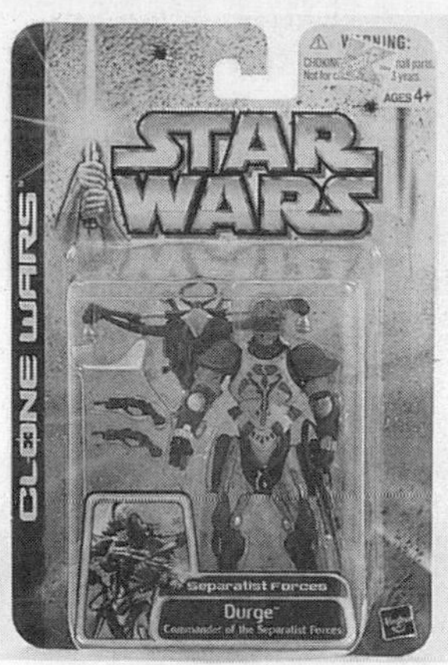

Durge, Commander of the Separatist Forces, 2003, laser rifle, pistol, rocket backpack, mace
MNP $3 **MIP** $7

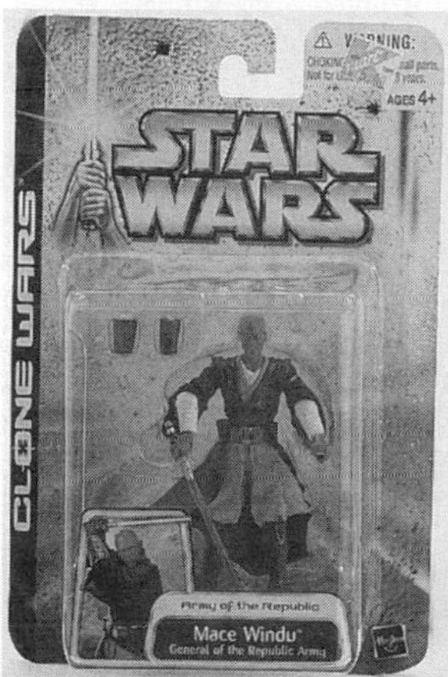

Mace Windu, General of the Republic Army, 2003, 2 armor pieces, purple lightsaber
MNP $3 **MIP** $7

Obi-Wan Kenobi, General of the Republic Army, 2003, belt, backpack, blue lightsaber
MNP $3 **MIP** $7

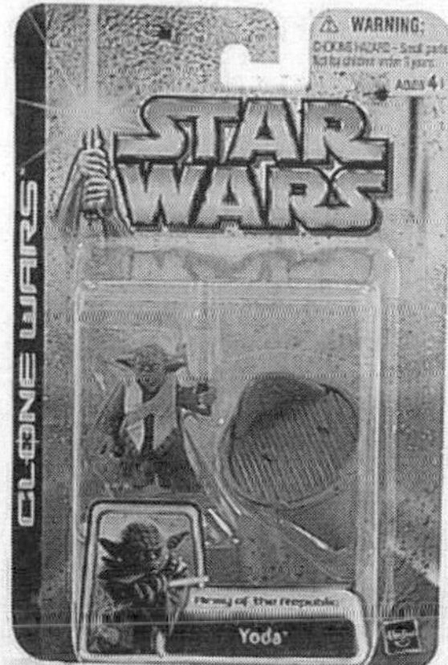

Yoda w/Hoverchair, 2003, green lightsaber
MNP $3 **MIP** $7

CLONE WARS
Deluxe

Clone Trooper w/Speeder Bike, 2003
MNP $5 MIP $10

Destroyer Droid w/Battle Launcher, 2003
MNP $7 MIP $10

Durge w/Swoop Bike, 2003
MNP $7 MIP $10

CLONE WARS
Multi-Packs

Clone Trooper Army (White), 2003, Kneeling Trooper, Prone Trooper, Standing Trooper
MNP $9 MIP $15

Clone Trooper Army w/Clone Captain (Red), 2003, Prone Clone Captain (Red), Standing Clone Trooper (White), Kneeling Clone Trooper (White)
MNP $9 MIP $15

Clone Trooper Army w/Clone Commander, 2003, Standing Clone Trooper w/Binoculars (Yellow), Standing Clone Trooper (White), Kneeling Clone Trooper (White)
MNP $9 MIP $15

Clone Trooper Army w/Clone Lieutenant (Blue), 2003, Kneeling Trooper, Prone Trooper, Standing Lieutenant (Blue)
MNP $9 MIP $15

Clone Trooper Army w/Clone Sergeant (Green), 2003, Standing Clone Trooper (White), Kneeling Clone Sergeant (Green), Standing Clone Trooper w/Binoculars (White)
MNP $9 MIP $15

Droid Army, 2003, Battle Droid, Super Battle Droid, Destroyer Droid
MNP $9 MIP $15

Jedi Knight Army, 2003, Human Jedi, Rodian Jedi, Twi'lek Jedi
MNP $9 MIP $15

ORIGINAL TRILOGY COLLECTION
Multipacks

Empire Strikes Back, 2004, Wal-Mart exclusive; Chewbacca, Princess Leia, Han Solo
MNP $7 MIP $15

Endor Ambush, 2004, TRU exclusive; Han Solo, Endor Rebel Soldier, Wicket, Logray, Biker Scout, Imperial Speeder Bike, Model No. 34515
MNP $10 MIP $22

Naboo Final Combat, 2005, TRU exclusive; Naboo Palace Guard, Battle Droid, Captain Tarpals, Gungan Soldier, Kaadu
MNP $10 MIP $22

Return of the Jedi, 2004, Wal-Mart exclusive; Darth Vader, Emperor Palpatine, Stormtrooper
MNP $7 MIP $15

Star Wars, 2004, Wal-Mart exclusive; Luke Skywalker, Obi-Wan Kenobi, C-3PO, R2-D2
MNP $7 MIP $15

ORIGINAL TRILOGY COLLECTION

Bib Fortuna, 2004, #31, RotJ, w/blaster
MNP $2 MIP $7

Biker Scout, 2004, #11, RotJ, w/blaster
MNP $2 MIP $7

Boba Fett, 2004, #14, RotJ, quick draw
MNP $2 MIP $7

Bossk, 2004, #28, ESB, w/rifle, shoulder strap
MNP $2 MIP $7

C-3PO, 2004, #13, SW, clean
MNP $2 MIP $7

Chewbacca, 2004, #8, ESB, w/welding goggles
MNP $2 MIP $7

Cloud Car Pilot, 2004, #19, ESB, w/blaster, comlink
MNP $2 MIP $7

Darth Vader, 2004, #10, RotJ, w/lightsaber, throws it
MNP $2 MIP $7

Darth Vader, 2004, #34, SW, w/lightsaber
MNP $2 MIP $7

Darth Vader, Hoth, 2004, #29, ESB, w/lightsaber
MNP $2 MIP $7

Gamorrean Guard, 2004, #30, RotJ, w/axe
MNP $2 MIP $7

General Lando Calrissian, 2004, #37, RotJ
MNP $2 MIP $7

General Madine, 2004, #36, RotJ, Battle of Endor, w/baton
MNP $2 MIP $7

Greedo, 2004, #22, SW, w/blaster
MNP $2 MIP $7

Han Solo, 2004, #7, SW, w/blaster
MNP $2 MIP $7

Han Solo AT-ST Driver, 2004, #35, RotJ, Battle of Endor
MNP $2 MIP $7

IG-88, 2004, #27, ESB, w/rifle
MNP $2 MIP $7

Imperial Trooper, 2004, #38, SW, Scanning Crew
MNP $2 MIP $7

Jawa, 2004, #24, SW
MNP $2 MIP $7

Lando Skiff Guard Disguise, 2004, #32, RotJ, w/helmet, blaster pistol, staff
MNP $2 MIP $7

Lobot, 2004, #20, ESB, w/datapad, comlink
MNP $2 MIP $7

Luke Skywalker, 2004, #1, ESB, on Dagobah, w/extra arms
MNP $2 MIP $7

Luke Skywalker Bespin, 2004, #26, ESB, on Bespin
MNP $2 MIP $7

Luke Skywalker Jedi, 2004, #6, RotJ, w/lightsaber
MNP $2 MIP $7

Luke Skywalker X-Wing Pilot, 2004, #5, SW, w/helmet
MNP $2 MIP $7

Obi-Wan Kenobi, 2004, #15, SW, lightsaber, light robes
MNP $2 MIP $7

Obi-Wan Spirit, 2004, #3, ESB, on Dagobah
MNP $2 MIP $7

Princess Leia, 2004, #9, SW, white outfit, w/2 blasters
MNP $2 MIP $7

Princess Leia Bespin Gown, 2004, #18, ESB, w/blaster rifle
MNP $2 MIP $7

R2-D2, 2004, #12, SW, clean
MNP $2 MIP $7

R2-D2, 2004, #4, ESB, on Dagobah, dirty, w/sounds
MNP $2 MIP $7

Slave Leia, 2004, #33, RotJ, w/staff
MNP $2 MIP $7

Snowtrooper, 2004, #25, ESB, w/blaster
MNP $2 MIP $7

Stormtrooper, 2004, #16, SW, w/blaster rifle
MNP $2 MIP $7

TIE Fighter Pilot, 2004, #21, SW, w/blaster
MNP $2 MIP $7

Tusken Raider, 2004, #23, SW, w/rifle
MNP $2 MIP $7

Wicket, 2004, #17, RotJ, w/staff
MNP $2 MIP $7

Yoda, 2004, #2, ESB, on Dagobah
MNP $2 MIP $7

ORIGINAL TRILOGY COLLECTION
Transition

Dannik Jerriko, 2005, #1, Cantina Encounter
MNP $4 MIP $8

Feltipern Trevagg, 2005, #6, Cantina Encounter
MNP $4 MIP $8

Myo, 2005, #7, Cantina Encounter
MNP $4 MIP $8

Pablo-Jill, 2005, #1, Geonosis Arena
MNP $4 MIP $8

Queen Amidala, 2005, #4, Celebration Ceremony
MNP $4 MIP $8

Rabe, 2005, #5, Queen's Chambers, w/pistol, TPM
MNP $4 MIP $8

Sly Moore, 2005, #3, Coruscant Senate, AotC
MNP $4 MIP $8

Yarua, 2005, #2, Coruscant Senate, AotC, This is one mad Wookie!
MNP $4 MIP $8

ORIGINAL TRILOGY COLLECTION

Vintage

Ben (Obi-Wan) Kenobi, 2004, SW card, sealed case
MNP $9 MIP $16

Boba Fett, 2004, RotJ card, sealed case
MNP $9 MIP $16

Chewbacca, 2004, RotJ card, sealed case
MNP $9 MIP $16

Darth Vader, 2004, ESB card, sealed case
MNP $9 MIP $16

Han Solo, 2004, SW card, sealed case
MNP $9 MIP $16

Lando Calrissian, 2004, ESB card, sealed case
MNP $9 MIP $16

Luke Skywalker, 2004, SW card, sealed case
MNP $9 MIP $16

Princess Leia Organa, 2004, SW card, sealed case
MNP $9 MIP $16

See-Threepio (C-3PO), 2004, ESB card, sealed case
MNP $9 MIP $16

Stormtrooper, 2004, RotJ card, sealed case
MNP $9 MIP $16

Yoda, 2004, ESB card, sealed case
MNP $9 MIP $19

REVENGE OF THE SITH

Basic 1

Anakin Skywalker, Battle Damage, 2005, #50, interchangable body parts, cloak, lightsaber
MNP $5 MIP $10

Anakin Skywalker, Lightsaber Attack, 2005, #2, many variations, w/blue lightsaber and Count Dooku's lightsaber
MNP $4 MIP $8

Anakin Skywalker, Slashing Attack, 2005, #28, fallen to the dark side, cloak, lightsaber
MNP $4 MIP $8

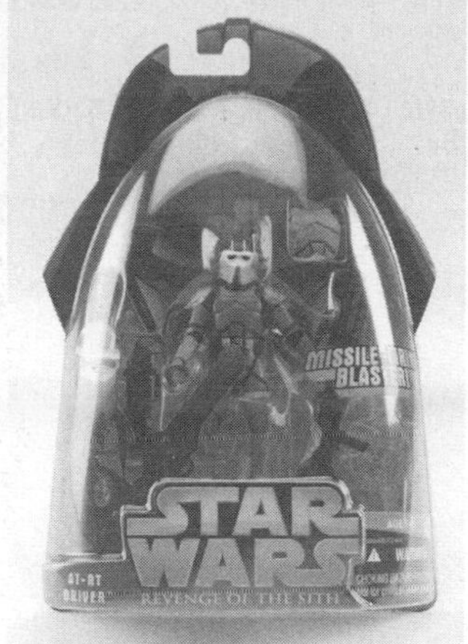

AT-RT Driver, 2005, #54, w/Missile-Firing Blaster, missile, blaster rifle
MNP $4 MIP $8

Cat Miin, Separatist, 2005, #62, base
MNP $4 MIP $8

Chewbacca, Wookie Rage, 2005, #5, bowcaster
MNP $4 MIP $8

Clone Commander, Battle Gear, 2005, #33, green or red gear variations
MNP $5 MIP $10

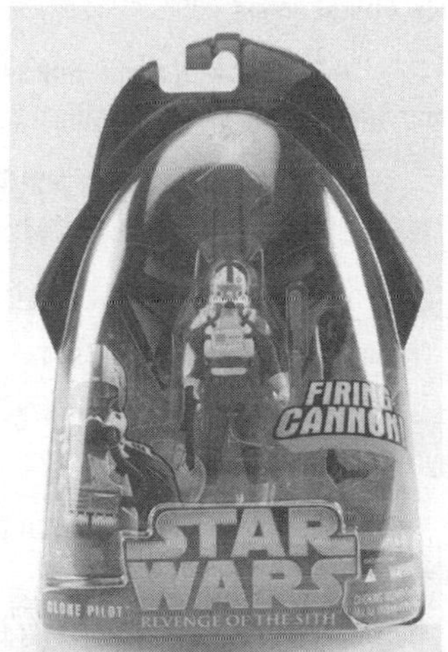

Clone Pilot, Firing Cannon, 2005, #34, white and grey uniform
MNP $4 MIP $8

Clone Trooper, Quick-Draw Attack, 2005, #6, blaster
MNP $4 MIP $8

Clone Trooper, Super Articulation, 2005, #41, blaster, antenna
MNP $5 MIP $10

Commander Bacara, Quick-Draw Attack, 2005, #49, blaster, rifle, fought w/Ki-Adi-Mundi on Mygeeto
MNP $5 MIP $10

Commander Bly, Battle Gear, 2005, #57, rifle, 2 blasters, fought w/Aayla Secura on Felucia
MNP $5 MIP $10

Commander Gree, Battle Gear, 2005, #59, missile-firing cannon, missile, blaster, fought w/Yoda on Kashyyyk and lost his head!
MNP $5 MIP $10

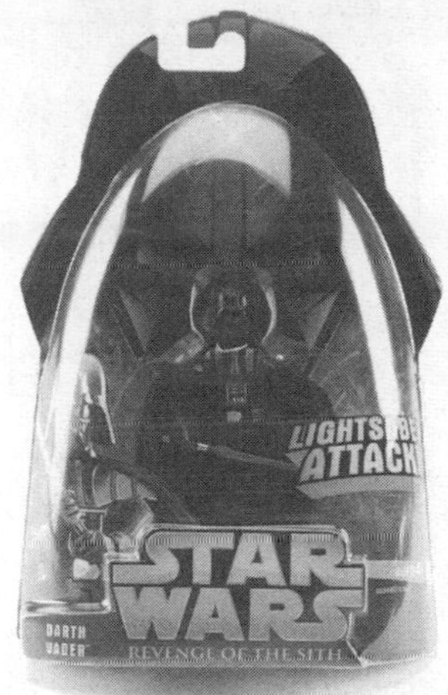

Darth Vader, Lightsaber Attack, 2005, #11, lightsaber, "Lord Vader...rise!"
MNP $4 MIP $8

Destroyer Droid, Firing Arm-Blaster, 2005, #44, 2 missiles
MNP $4 MIP $8

Emperor Palpatine, Firing Force Lightning, 2005, #12, lightsaber, lightning
MNP $4 MIP $8

General Grievous, Exploding Body, 2005, #36, lightsaber, cloak, blaster
MNP $4 MIP $8

General Grievous, Four Lightsaber Attack, 2005, #9, 4 lightsabers
MNP $4 MIP $8

Grievous' Bodyguard, Battle Attack, 2005, #60, electrostaff, cloak
MNP $4 MIP $8

Mace Windu, Force Combat, 2005, #10, force lightning, cool purple lightsaber
MNP $5 MIP $10

Mustafar Sentry, Spinning Energy Bolt, 2005, #56, rifle, energy bolt, base
MNP $4 MIP $8

Neimoidian Commander, Separatist Bodyguard, 2005, #63, staff, helmet
MNP $4 MIP $8

Neimoidian Warrior, Neimoidian Weapon Attack, 2005, #42, rifle, helmet
MNP $4 MIP $8

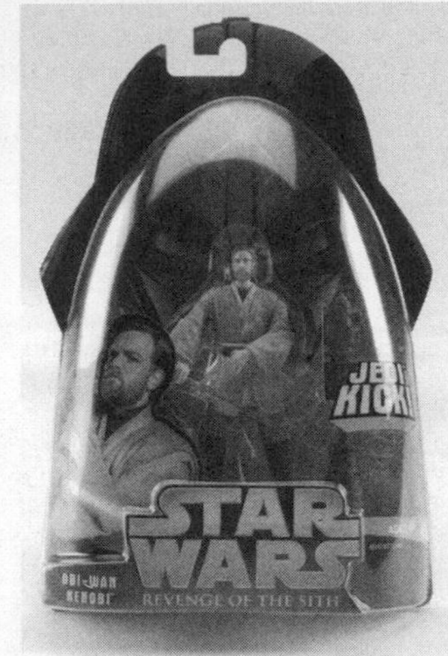

Obi-Wan Kenobi, Jedi Kick, 2005, #27, lightsaber
MNP $4 MIP $8

Obi-Wan Kenobi, Slashing Attack, 2005, #1, lightsaber
MNP $4 MIP $8

Obi-Wan Kenobi, With Pilot Gear, 2005, #55, lightsaber, headgear, cloak
MNP $4 MIP $8

Palpatine, Lightsaber Attack, 2005, #35, base, red lightsaber (blue variations), 2 heads, 2 sets of hands
MNP $4 MIP $8

Passel Argente, Separatist Leader, 2005, #61, base
MNP $4 MIP $8

R2-D2, Droid Attack, 2005, #7, w/tools, base
MNP $4 MIP $8

R2-D2, Try Me, 2005, Electronic Light and Sounds, #48
MNP $5 MIP $10

Super Battle Droid, Firing Arm-Blaster, 2005, #4, blaster mounts to right arm
MNP $4 MIP $8

Tarfful, Firing Bowcaster, 2005, #25, bowcaster
MNP $5 MIP $10

Wookie Commando, Kashyyyk Battle Bash, 2005, #58, cannon, missile, bandolier
MNP $4 MIP $8

Wookie Warrior, Wookie Battle Bash, 2005, #43, shield, blaster, bowcaster, bandolier, missile
MNP $5 MIP $10

Yoda, Firing Cannon, 2005, #3, lightsaber, cannon
MNP $5 MIP $10

Yoda, Spinning Attack, 2005, #26, lightsaber
MNP $4 MIP $8

REVENGE OF THE SITH
Basic 2

Aayla Secura, Jedi Hologram Transmission, 2005, #67, all blue plastic
MNP $5 MIP $10

Aayla Secura, Jedi Knight, 2005, #32, w/lightsaber, base
MNP $4 MIP $8

Agen Kolar, Jedi Master, 2005, #20, w/lightsaber, base
MNP $4 MIP $8

Ask Aak, Senator, 2005, #46, blaster rifle, base
MNP $4 MIP $8

AT-TE Tank Gunner, 2005, #38, blaster pistol, sniper pistol
MNP $4 MIP $8

Bail Organa, Republic Senator, 2005, #15, pistol, base
MNP $4 MIP $8

Battle Droid, Separatist Army, 2005, #17, blaster, base
MNP $4 MIP $8

C-3PO, Protocol Droid, 2005, #18, base, C-3PO finally has his gold coverings
MNP $4 MIP $8

Captain Antilles, Senate Security, 2005, #51, pistol, base
MNP $4 MIP $8

Chancellor Palpatine, Supreme Chancellor, 2005, #14, base, handcuffs
MNP $4 MIP $8

Count Dooku, Sith Lord, 2005, #13, lightsaber (pink or red variations), cloth cape, removable hands, base
MNP $4 MIP $8

Ki-Adi-Mundi, Jedi Master, 2005, #29, lightsaber
MNP $5 MIP $10

Kit Fisto, Jedi Master, 2005, #22, lightsaber, base, removable head (courtesy of Palpatine)
MNP $5 MIP $10

Luminara Unduli, Jedi Master, 2005, #31, lightsaber, base, in Kashyyyk attire
MNP $5 MIP $10

Mas Amedda, Republic Senator, 2005, #40, staff, base, removable tongue
MNP $4 MIP $8

Meena Tills, Senator, 2005, #47, blaster, base
MNP $4 MIP $8

Mon Mothma, Republic Senator, 2005, #24, baton, helmet, base
MNP $4 MIP $8

Padme, Republic Senator, 2005, #19, pistol, base
MNP $4 MIP $8

Plo Koon, Jedi Hologram Transmission, 2005, #66, clear blue plastic, lightsaber, base
MNP $4 MIP $8

Plo Koon, Jedi Master, 2005, #16, lightsaber, base
MNP $4 MIP $8

Polis Massan, Medic, 2005, #39, pistol, headset, base
MNP $4 MIP $8

R4-P17, Rolling Action, 2005, #64, base
MNP $4 MIP $8

Royal Guard, Senate Security, 2005, #23, rifle, pistol, base, cloth cloak
MNP $4 MIP $8

Saesee Tiin, Jedi Master, 2005, #30, lightsaber, base
MNP $4 MIP $8

Shaak Ti, Jedi Master, 2005, #21, lightsaber, datapad, base
MNP $4 MIP $8

Tactical Ops Trooper, Vader's Legion, 2005, #65, blue highlights, blaster, base, removable helmet
MNP $5 MIP $10

Tarkin, Governor, 2005, #45, blaster, base
MNP $4 MIP $8

Utapaun Warrior, Utapaun Security, 2005, #53, shield, staff, base
MNP $4 MIP $8

Vader's Medical Droid, Chopper Droid, 2005, #37, base
MNP $4 MIP $8

Wookie Heavy Gunner, Blast Attack, 2005, #68
MNP $5 MIP $10

Zett Jukassa, Jedi Padawan, 2005, #52, lightsaber, base, played in the film by Jett Lucas, George's son
MNP $4 MIP $8

REVENGE OF THE SITH
Battle Arena

Senate Chamber, 2005, Palpatine v. Mace Windu
MNP $10 MIP $20

Trade Federation Cruiser, 2005, Count Dooku v. Anakin Skywalker
MNP $10 MIP $20

Utapau Landing Platform, 2005, Obi-Wan Kenobi v. Grievous' Guard
MNP $10 MIP $20

REVENGE OF THE SITH
Deluxe

Anakin Skywalker, 2005, Changes to Darth Vader; interchangable limbs and outfits
MNP $8 MIP $16

Clone Trooper, 2005, Firing Jet Backpack; missiles, laser rifle
MNP $7 MIP $14

Clone Troopers, 2005, 3 per pack; variations with 2 white and 1 red, green, or blue trooper
MNP $7 MIP $14

Crab Droid, 2005, Moving Legs and Missile Launcher; missile, used on Utapau
MNP $7 MIP $14

Darth Vader, 2005, Rebuild Darth Vader, limbs, helmet, swivel table, chest box, lightsaber
MNP $8 MIP $16

Darth Vader, 2005, Special Edition 500th Figure; Vader's ESB chamber w/removable helmet
MNP $8 MIP $16

Emperor Palpatine, 2005, Changes to Darth Sideous; jedi lightning, hand w/lightsaber, left hand, heads
MNP $7 MIP $14

General Grievous, 2005, Secret Lightsaber Attack; 4 lightsabers, cloak, grappling hook
MNP $8 MIP $16

Obi-Wan Kenobi, 2005, Force Jump Attack; lightsaber, Super Battle Droid that breaks apart
MNP $7 MIP $14

Spider Droid, 2005, Firing Laser Action; missile, wind-up walking action
MNP $7 MIP $14

Stass Allie w/BARC Speeder, 2005, Exploding Action; Jedi Master Stass Allie, BARC Speeder
MNP $7 MIP $14

Vulture Droid, 2005, Firing Missile Launcher; Buzz Droid, movable wings
MNP $8 MIP $16

Yoda, 2005, Fly Into Battle; lightsaber, flying Can-Cell native to Kashyyyk
MNP $8 MIP $16

REVENGE OF THE SITH
Evolutions

Anakin Skywalker to Darth Vader, 2005, AotC Anakin, RotS Anakin, Darth Vader
MNP $20 MIP $30

Clone Trooper to Stormtrooper, 2005, Clone Trooper (the Clone Wars), Clone Trooper (Fall of the Republic), Sandtrooper (the Rebellion)
MNP $20 MIP $30

The Sith, 2005, Darth Maul, Count Dooku, Emperor Palpatine
MNP $20 MIP $30

REVENGE OF THE SITH
Multipacks

Clone Troopers, 2005, Wal-Mart exclusive; 3 Clone Troopers w/unique paint design, DVD Collection
MNP $10 MIP $20

Jedi Knights, 2005, Wal-Mart exclusive; Anakin Skywalker, Mace Windu, Obi-Wan Kenobi, DVD Collection
MNP $10 MIP $20

Sith Lords, 2005, Wal-Mart exclusive; Emperor Palpatine, Count Dooku, Darth Vader, DVD Collection
MNP $10 MIP $20

REVENGE OF THE SITH
Sneak Peek

General Grievous, 2005, #1, lightsaber, blaster, cape
MNP $5 MIP $10

R4-G9, 2005, #4, planet hologram
MNP $5 MIP $10

Tion Medon, 2005, #2, staff, rifle
MNP $5 MIP $10

Wookie Warrior, 2005, #3, helmet, shin guards, rifle, bandolier
MNP $5 MIP $10

SAGA 2006
Basic

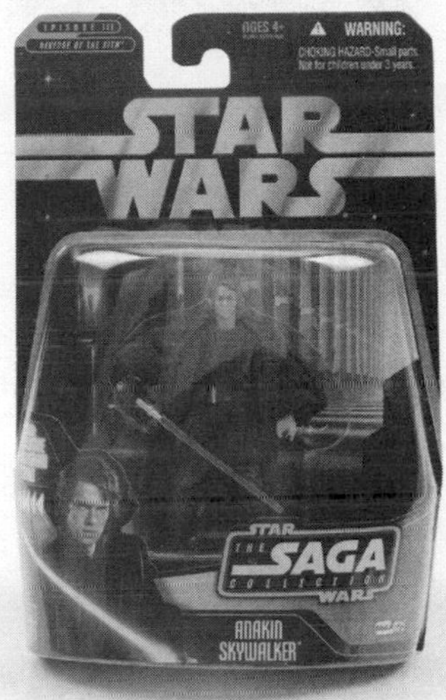

Anakin Skywalker, 2006, #25, Battle of Coruscant, lightsaber, cloak
MNP $4 MIP $8

AT-AT Driver, 2006, #9, Battle of Hoth, blaster pistol, base, hologram figure
MNP $4 MIP $8

Aurra Sing, 2006, #70, Wal-Mart exclusive, long rifle, pistol, lightsaber
MNP $3 MIP $7

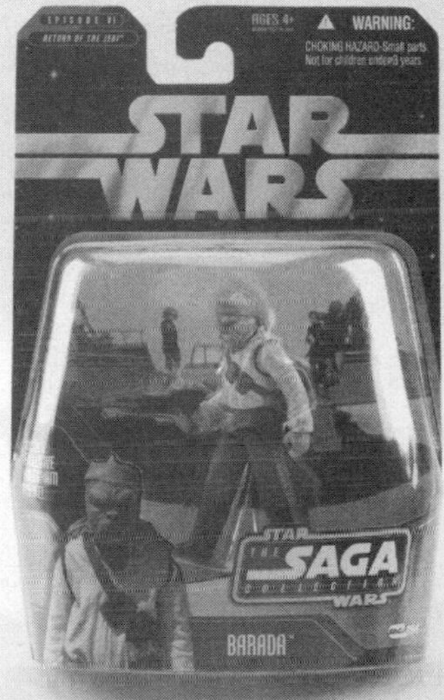

Barada, 2006, #4, Battle of Carkoon, blaster, base, hologram figure
MNP $4 MIP $8

Battle Droids, 2006, #62, two battle droids
MNP $3 MIP $6

Bib Fortuna, 2006, #3, Battle of Carkoon, base
MNP $4 MIP $8

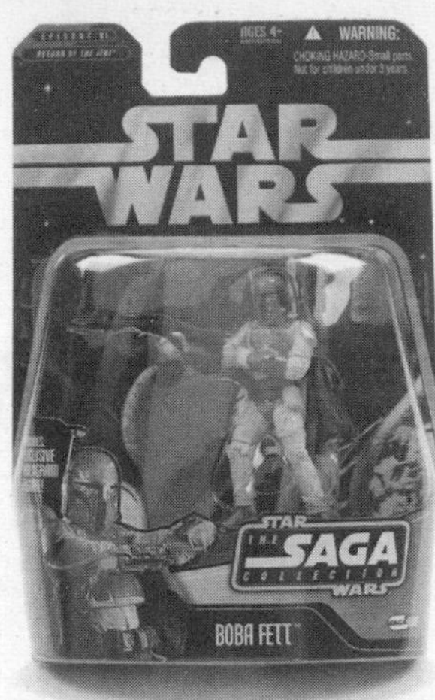

Boba Fett, 2006, #6, Battle of Carkoon, flame exhaust base, blaster, hologram figure
MNP $4 MIP $8

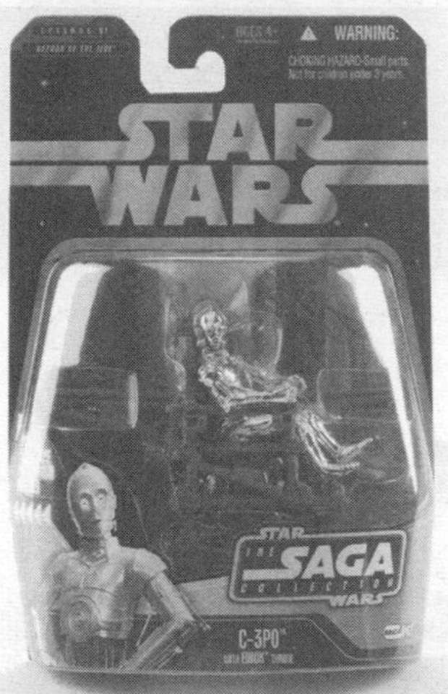

C-3PO Ewok Throne, 2006, #42, Battle of Endor, hologram figure
MNP $4 MIP $8

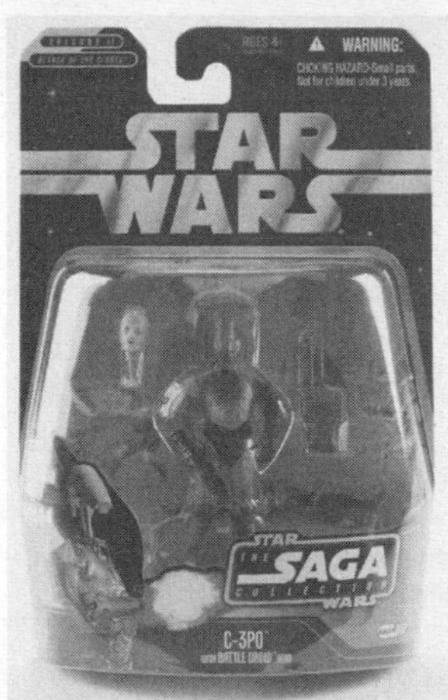

C-3PO with Battle Droid Head, 2006, #17, Battle of Geonosis, base, blaster, "regular" head, hologram figure
MNP $4 MIP $8

Chewbacca w/Electronic C-3PO, 2006, #54, ESB, C-3PO has gone all to pieces
MNP $3 MIP $6

Chewbacca, Boushh Prisoner, 2006, #5, Battle of Carkoon, chain, base, hologram figure
MNP $4 MIP $8

Chief Chirpa, 2006, #39, Battle of Endor, staff, base, hologram figure
MNP $4 MIP $8

Clone Commander Cody, 2006, #24, Battle of Utapau, blaster, helmet, rifle, base, hologram figure
MNP $4 MIP $8

Clone Trooper, 2006, #26, Battle of Utapau, blaster, communications backpack, base, hologram figure
MNP $4 MIP $8

Clone Trooper 442nd Siege Battalion, 2006, #57, blaster, antenna on back
MNP $3 MIP $6

Clone Trooper 5th Fleet Security, 2006, #59, blue stripes, blaster, antenna on back
MNP $3 MIP $6

Clone Trooper Sergeant, 2006, #60, Battle of Geonosis, blaster, base, hologram figure
MNP $4 MIP $8

Clone Trooper Sergeant, 2006, #60, green accents
MNP $3 MIP $6

Clone Trooper, 442nd Siege Battallion, 2006, #57, Battle of Coruscant, blaster, base, hologram figure
MNP $5 MIP $10

Combat Engineer Trooper, 2006, #68, removable helmet, black striping on helmet
MNP $3 MIP $6

Commander Appo, 2006, #64, blue shoulder pads
MNP $3 MIP $6

Darth Maul, Holographic, 2006, #48, clear blue plastic, lightsaber, base
MNP $5 MIP $10

Darth Maul, Sith Training, 2006, #53, Battle of Naboo, lightsaber, base, hologram figure
MNP $5 MIP $10

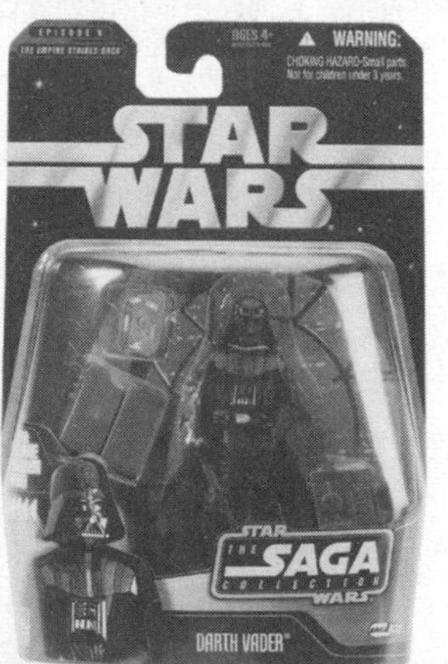

Darth Vader, 2006, #38, Bespin Confession
MNP $3 MIP $6

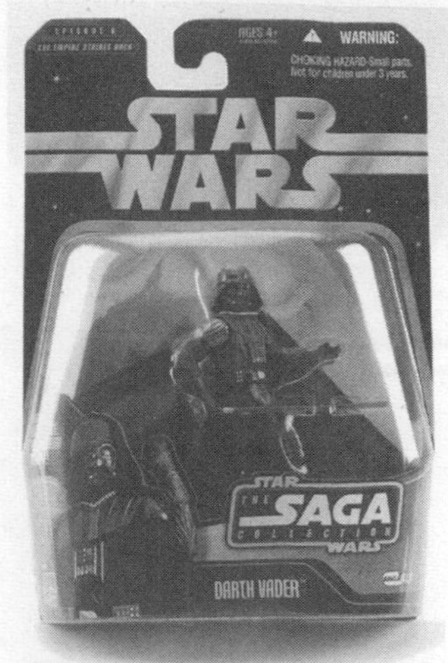

Darth Vader, 2006, #13, Battle of Hoth, helmet, lightsaber, base, hologram figure
MNP $4 MIP $8

Darth Vader, 2006, #45, Endor Confrontation, lightsaber, base, hologram figure
MNP $4 MIP $8

Death Star Gunner, 2006, #37, Battle of Endor, base, hologram figure
MNP $4 MIP $8

Death Star Trooper, 2006, Battle of Yavin, hologram figure
MNP $4 MIP $8

Dud Bolt and Mars Guo, 2006, #51, Podracer Pilots, Mos Espa, bases, hologram figure
MNP $4 MIP $8

Elite Corps Clone Trooper, 2006, #65, Biker Scout armor in camo pattern
MNP $3 MIP $6

Emperor Palpatine, 2006, #43, Battle of Endor, hologram figure
MNP $4 MIP $8

Firespeeder Pilot, 2006, #22, Battle of Coruscant, helmet, fire supression gear, hologram figure
MNP $4 MIP $8

Foul Moudama, 2006, #29, Clone Wars Battle of Coruscant, character was featured in the animated series, lightsaber, hologram figure
MNP $4 MIP $8

Garindan, 2006, #34, Battle of Tatooine, base, hologram figure
MNP $5 MIP $10

General Grievous, 2006, #30, Battle of Coruscant, lightsaber, electrostaff, base, hologram figure
MNP $4 MIP $8

General Rieekan, 2006, #12, Battle of Hoth, pistol, base, hologram figure
MNP $4 MIP $8

General Veers, 2006, #10, Battle of Hoth, pistol, base, hologram figure
MNP $4 MIP $8

Gragra, 2006, #52, Battle of Naboo
MNP $3 MIP $6

Han Solo, 2006, #35, Battle of Tatooine, blaster, base, hologram figure
MNP $4 MIP $8

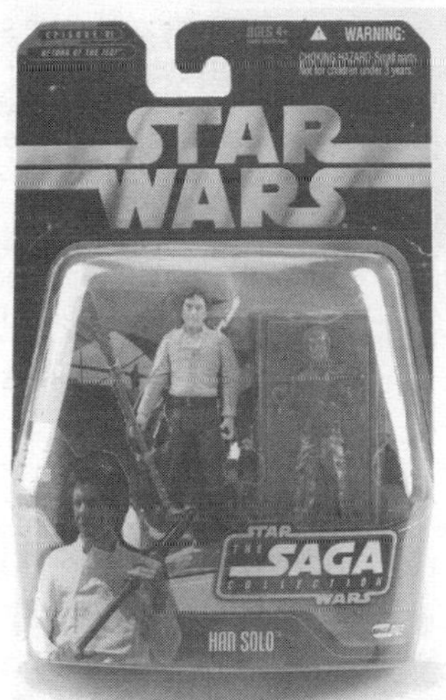

Han Solo w/Carbonite, 2006, #2, Battle of Carkoon, base, force pike, Han in carbonite block, hologram figure
MNP $4 MIP $8

Hem Dazon, 2006, #33, Battle of Tatooine, base, hologram figure
MNP $4 MIP $8

Holographic Clone Commnader Cody, 2006, #56, helmet removable, blaster
MNP $3 MIP $6

Holographio Ki Adi-Mundi, 2006, #27, Battle of Coruscant, clear blue plastic, lightsaber, base, hologram figure
MNP $4 MIP $8

Holographic Obi-Wan Kenobi, 2006, #63, removable robe, lightsaber
MNP $3 MIP $6

Jango Fett, 2006, #20, Battle of Geonosis, 2 blasters, jetpack, grappling hook, removable helmet, `base, hologram figure
MNP $4 MIP $8

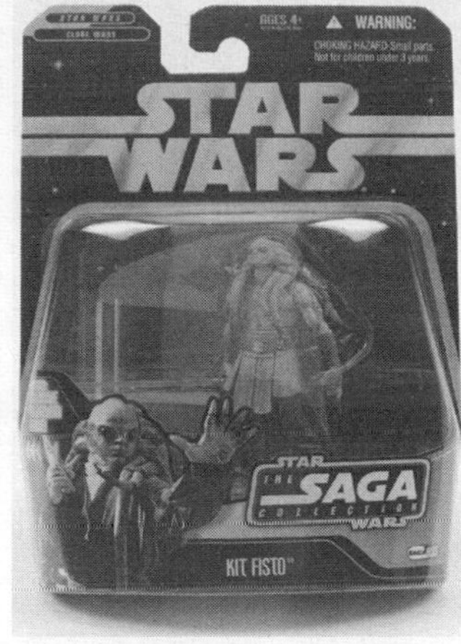

Kit Fisto, 2006, #55, bare chested
MNP $3 MIP $6

Kitik Keed'kak, 2006, #71, Wal-Mart exclusive
MNP $3 MIP $6

Labria, 2006, #73, Wal-Mart exclusive, Cantina alien
MNP $3 MIP $6

Luke Skywalker, 2006, #36, Battle of Tatooine, desert poncho, desert hat, goggles, base, hologram figure
MNP $4 MIP $8

Luke Skywalker, 2006, #44, Battle of Endor, cammo poncho, helmet, lightsaber, base, hologram figure
MNP $4 MIP $8

Lushros Dofine, 2006, #23, Battle of Coruscant, datapad, console, base, hologram figure
MNP $4 MIP $8

Major Bren Derlin, 2006, #8, Battle of Hoth, pistol, base, hologram figure
MNP $4 MIP $8

Moff Jerjerrod, 2006, #40, Battle of Endor, pistol, base, hologram figure
MNP $4 MIP $8

Momaw Nadon, 2006, #30, Battle of Tatooine, staff, bar table, drink, base, hologram figure
MNP $4 MIP $8

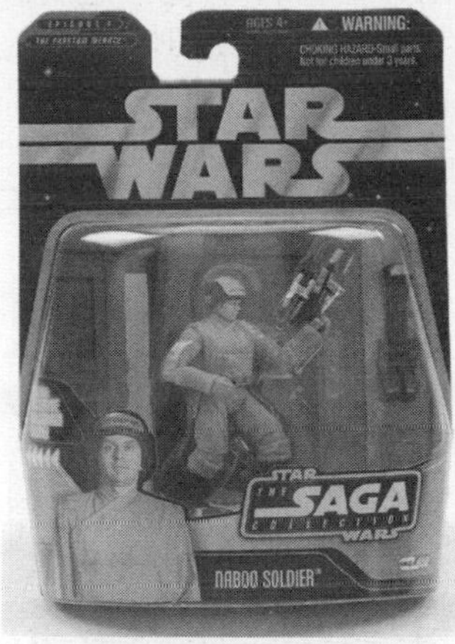

Naboo Soldier, 2006, #50, Battle of Naboo, rifle, base, hologram figure
MNP $4 MIP $8

Nabrun Leids & Kabe, 2006, #72, Wal-Mart exclusive
MNP $3 MIP $6

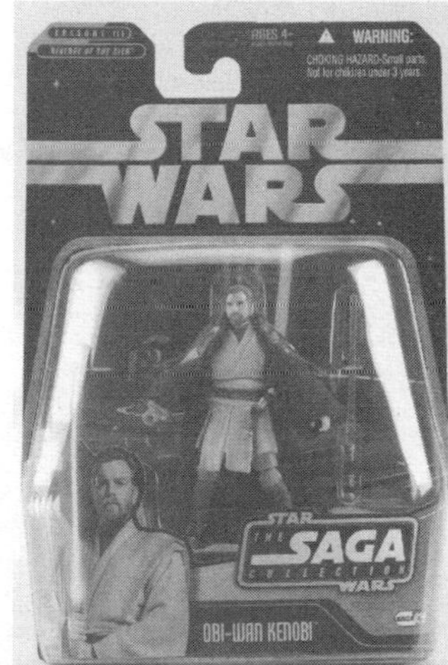

Obi-Wan Kenobi, 2006, #28, Battle of Coruscant, cloth robe, lightsaber, base, hologram figure
MNP $4 MIP $8

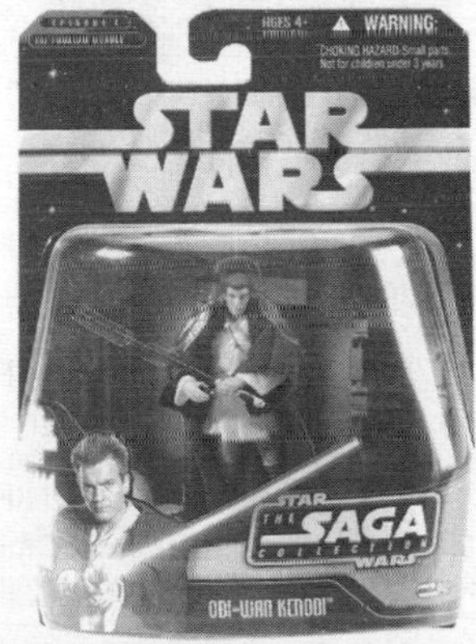

Obi-Wan Kenobi, 2006, #47, Battle of Naboo, cloth robe, lightsaber, base, hologram figure
MNP $4 MIP $8

Action Figures, 03-3/4"

Padme Amidala, 2006, #67, Geonosian Arena
MNP $3 MIP $6

Poggle the Lesser, 2006, #18, Battle of Geonosis, walking stick, base, hologram figure
MNP $4 MIP $8

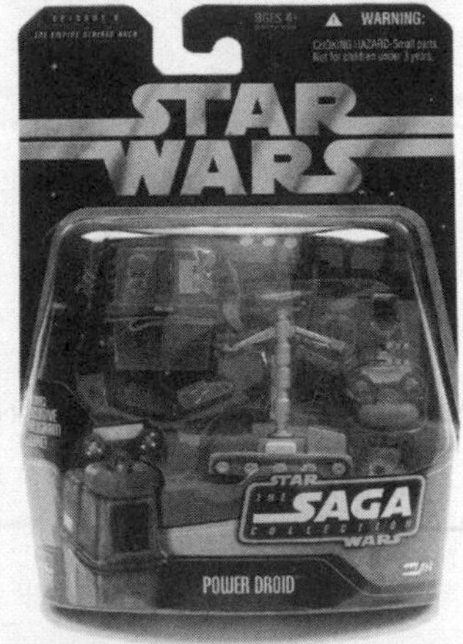

Power Droid, 2006, #14, Battle of Hoth, Gonk and Treadwell droids, base, hologram figure
MNP $4 MIP $8

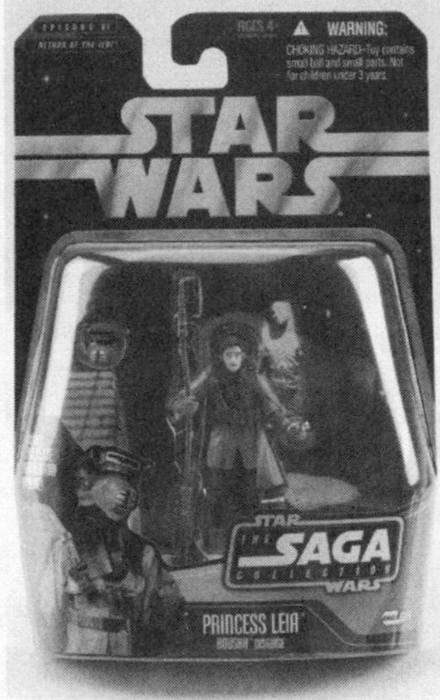

Princess Leia, Boushh Disguise, 2006, #1, Battle of Carkoon, thermal detonator, removable helmet, staff, base, hologram figure
MNP $4 MIP $8

R2-D2, 2006, #10, Battle of Hoth, rations kit, lantern, base, hologram figure
MNP $4 MIP $8

R4-K5 (Darth Vader's Astromech Droid), 2006, #66, looks like R2's evil twin
MNP $3 MIP $6

R4-M6 (Mace Windu's Astromech Droid), 2006, #74, Wal-Mart exclusive. Yep, he's purple!
MNP $3 MIP $6

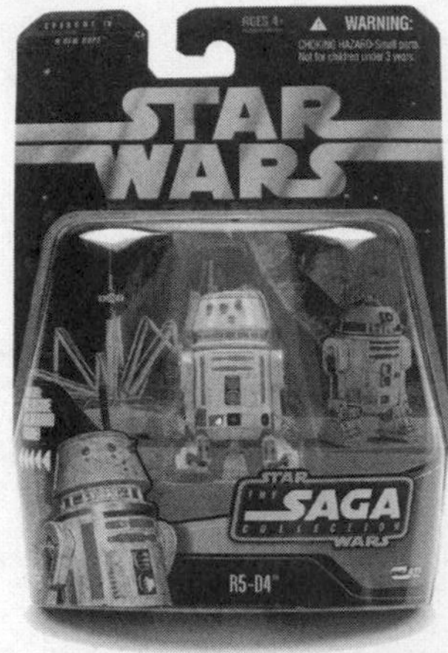

R5-D4, 2006, #32, Tatooine, base, hologram figure
MNP $4 MIP $8

R5-J2, 2006, #58
MNP $3 MIP $6

Rebel Trooper, 2006, #46, Battle of Endor, hologram figure
MNP $4 MIP $8

Rep Been, 2006, #49, Battle of Naboo, Gungan record keeper, staff, base, hologram figure
MNP $4 MIP $8

Sandtrooper, 2006, #37, Battle of Tatooine, staff, blaster, base, hologram figure
MNP $4 MIP $8

Scorch Republic Commando, 2006, #21, Expanded Universe, base, hologram figure
MNP $4 MIP $8

Sith Training Darth Maul, 2006, #53, dual-sided lightsaber, training droid
MNP $3 MIP $6

Snowtrooper, 2006, #11, Battle of Hoth, backpack, blaster, base, hologram figure
MNP $4 MIP $8

Sora Bulq, 2006, #15, Battle of Geonosis, lightsaber, base, hologram figure
MNP $4 MIP $8

Sun Fac, 2006, #16, Battle of Geonosis, Geonosian staff and blaster, base, hologram figure
MNP $4 MIP $8

Super Battle Droid, 2006, #61, Battle of Geonosis
MNP $3 MIP $6

Yarael Poof, 2006, #69, Jedi High Council
MNP $3 MIP $6

Yoda, 2006, #19, Battle of Geonosis, lightsaber, cloak, base, hologram figure
MNP $4 MIP $8

SAGA 2006 Exclusive

501st Stormtrooper, 2006, Comic-Con Int'l 2006 exclusive
MNP $10 MIP $20

Astromech Droid Pack Series 1, 2006, R3-T6, R2-C4, R4-A22, R2-Q2, R3-T2, Entertainment Earth exclusive
MNP $10 MIP $25

Astromech Droid Pack Series 2, 2006, R3-Y2, R2-X2, R4-E1, R2-A6, R2-M5, Entertainment Earth exclusive
MNP $10 MIP $25

General Grievous, Demise of Grievous, 2006, Target exclusive, electrostaff, flames from eyes are removable
MNP $6 MIP $12

Infant Leia Organa w/Bail Organa, 2005, Separation of the Twins, Wal-Mart exclusive
MNP $6 MIP $12

Infant Luke Skywalker w/Obi-Wan Kenobi, 2005, Separation of the Twins, Wal-Mart exclusive
MNP $6 MIP $12

Lucas Collector's Set, 2006, George Lucas as Baron Papanoida, Katie Lucas as Chi Eekway, Amanda Lucas as Terr Taneel, and Jett Lucas as Zett Jukassa, StarWarsShop.com exclusive
MNP $20 MIP $40

Shadow Stormtrooper, 2006, Expanded Universe, blaster, StarWarsShop.com exclusive
MNP $6 MIP $12

SAGA 2006 Greatest Battles

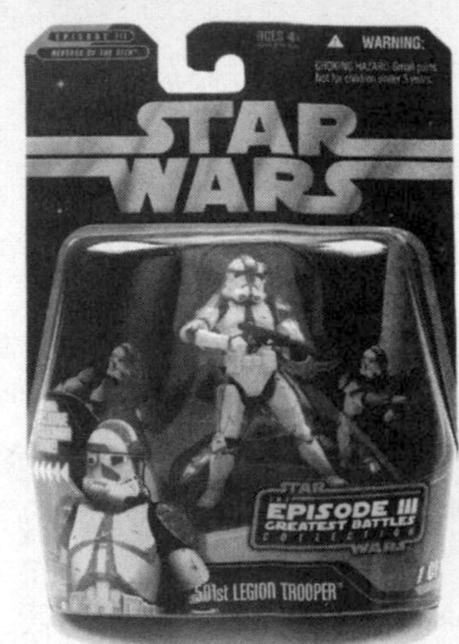

501st Legion Trooper, 2006, #1, Ep:III; this line contains figures repackaged from the RotS line
MNP $3 MIP $6

AT-TE Tank Gunner, 2006, #2, Ep:III
MNP $3 MIP $6

C-3PO, 2006, #3, Ep:III
MNP $3 MIP $6

Clone Commander (Deviss), 2006, #10, Ep:III
MNP $3 MIP $6

Count Dooku, 2006, #4, Ep:III
MNP $3 MIP $6

Emperor Palpatine, 2006, #12, Ep:III
MNP $3 MIP $6

Kit Fisto, 2006, #8, Ep:III
MNP $3 MIP $6

Obi-Wan Kenobi, 2006, #11, Ep:III
MNP $3 MIP $6

Padme, 2006, #6, Ep:III
MNP $3 MIP $6

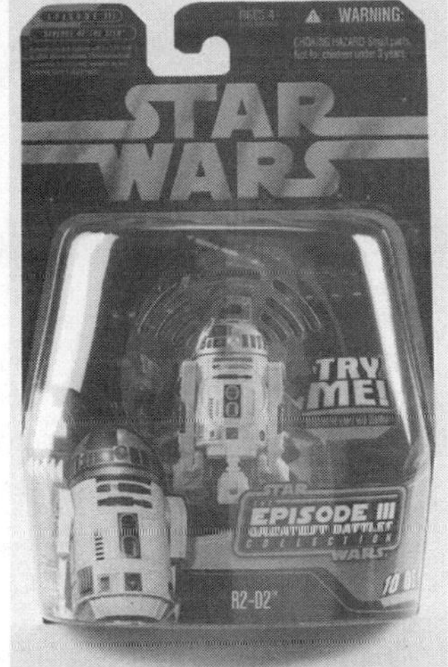

R2-D2 (Electronic), 2006, #13, Ep:III
MNP $3 MIP $6

R4-G9, 2006, #7, Ep:III
MNP $3 MIP $6

Royal Guard, 2006, #5, Ep:III
MNP $3 MIP $6

Shocktrooper, 2006, #14, Ep:III
MNP $3 MIP $6

Wookie Warrior, 2006, #9, Ep:III
MNP $3 MIP $6

SAGA 2006
Heroes v. Villains

Anakin Skywalker, 2006, #2, Ep:III
MNP $3 MIP $6

Chewbacca, 2006, #7, Ep:III
MNP $3 MIP $6

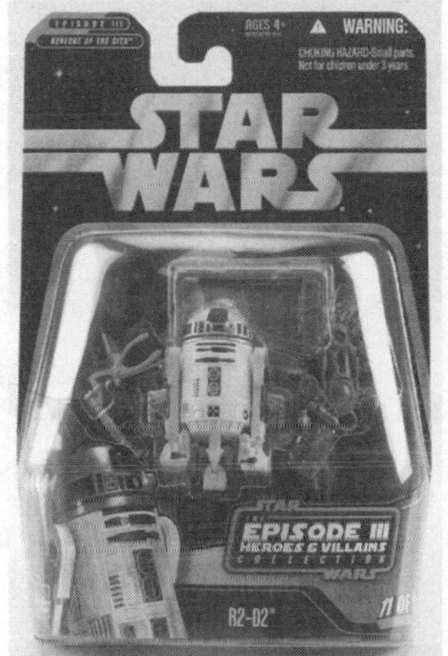

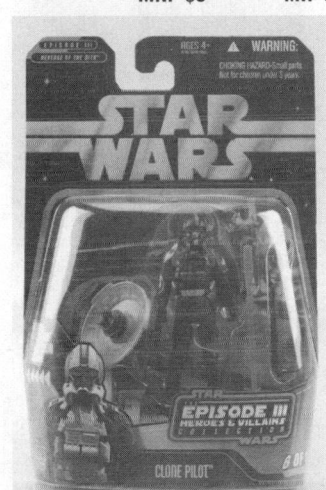

Clone Pilot (Shadow Pilot), 2006, #6, Ep:III
MNP $3 MIP $6

Clone Trooper, 2006, #5, Ep:III
MNP $3 MIP $6

Commander Bacara, 2006, #4, Ep:III
MNP $3 MIP $6

Darth Vader, 2006, #1, Ep:III
MNP $3 MIP $6

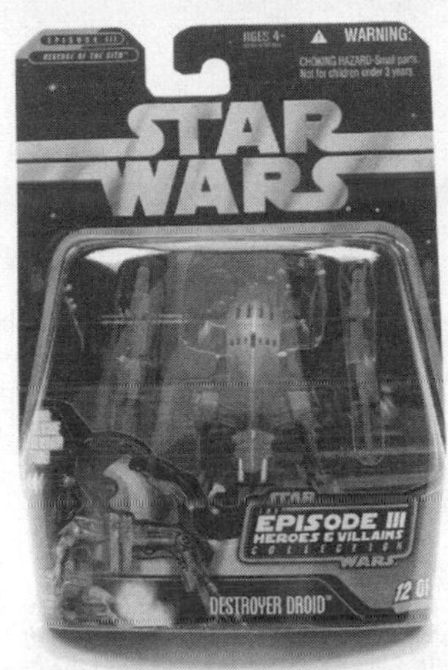

Destroyer Droid, 2006, #12, Ep:III
MNP $3 MIP $6

General Grievous, 2006, #9, Ep:III
MNP $3 MIP $6

Mace Windu, 2006, #10, Ep:III
MNP $3 MIP $6

Obi-Wan Kenobi, 2006, #8, Ep:III
MNP $3 MIP $6

R2-D2, 2006, #11, Ep:III
MNP $3 MIP $6

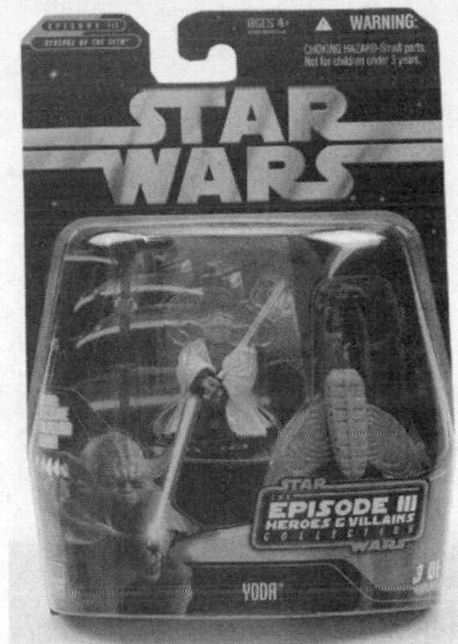

Yoda, 2006, #3, Ep:III
MNP $3 MIP $6

SAGA 2006
Vintage

Biker Scout, 2006, RotJ, articulated, holster, pistol
MNP $6 MIP $12

George Lucas in Stormtrooper Disguise, 2006, mail-away, removable helmet
MNP $25 MIP $45

Greedo, 2006, SW, pistol
MNP $6 MIP $12

Han Solo in Trench Coat, 2006, RotJ, cloth trench coat, pistol
MNP $6 MIP $12

Luke Skywalker X-Wing Pilot, 2006, SW, removable helmet, lightsaber
MNP $6 MIP $12

Sand People, 2006, SW
MNP $6 MIP $12

TAC (30TH ANNIV. COL.)
Basic-1, RotS

Airborne Trooper, 2007, #7, blaster rifle, pistol, coin, shoulder pouch, removable helmet, soldier from Commander Cody's 212th Attack Battalion on Utapau
MNP $4 MIP $8

Concept Stormtrooper, 2007, #9, shield, pistol, lightsaber, coin, based on the conceptual art of Ralph McQuarrie
MNP $5 MIP $13

Darth Vader, 2007, #1, packaged w/30th Anniv. Coin Album, lightsaber
MNP $6 MIP $10

Galactic Marine, 2007, #2, blaster rifle, coin
MNP $5 MIP $12

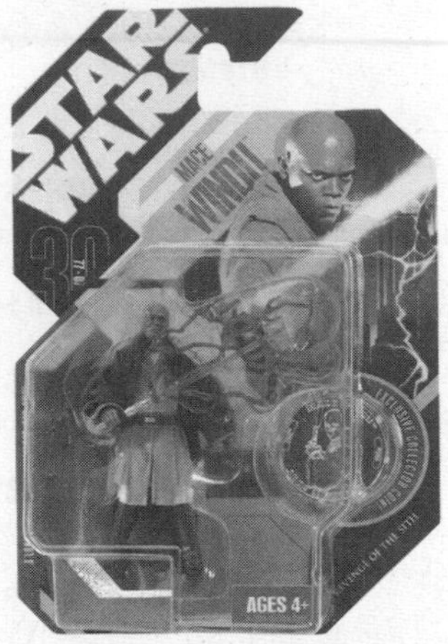

Mace Windu, 2007, #6, lightsaber, cloth cloak, coin, Jedi lightning, throne room duel
MNP $4 MIP $8

Mustafar Lava Miner, 2007, #3, lava scoop, coin, the worst job in the galaxy!
MNP $4 MIP $9

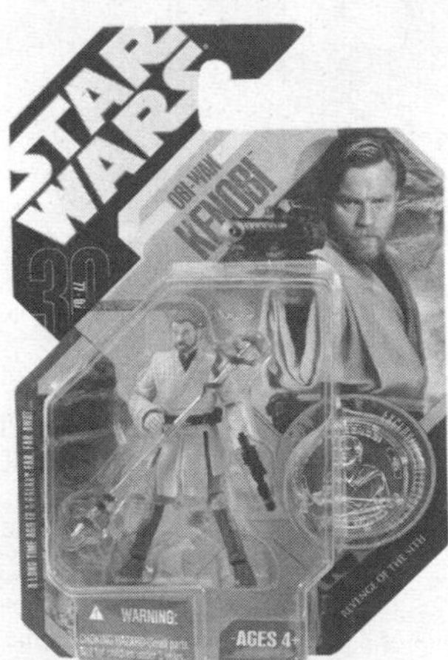

Obi-Wan Kenobi, 2007, #5, electro staff, blaster, coin, underwater breathing apparatus, from the Battle of Utapau
MNP $4 MIP $8

R2-D2, 2007, #4, coin, flame base attaches to Super Battle Droid to recreate the scene in the hangar bay
MNP $4 MIP $8

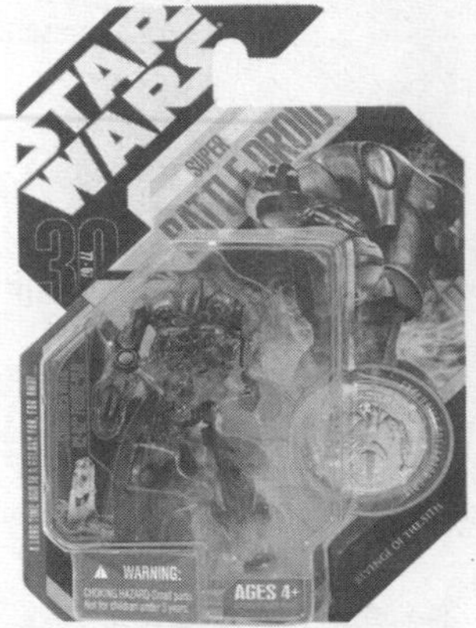

Super Battle Droid, 2007, #8, coin, attached flames courtesy of R2-D2
MNP $4 MIP $8

TAC (30TH ANNIV. COL.) Basic-2, Yavin

Concept Boba Fett, 2007, #15, blaster pistol, flame thrower, additional head, belly blaster, coin
MNP $6 MIP $12

Death Star Trooper, 2007, #13, blaster pistol, removable helmet, coin
MNP $4 MIP $8

Han Solo, 2007, #11, communication headset, blaster pistol, coin
MNP $4 MIP $8

Luke Skywalker, 2007, #12, medal, blaster pistol, (Darth Vader's lightsaber hilt), coin
MNP $4 MIP $8

Rebel Honor Guard, 2007, #10, pistol, staff, removable helmet, coin
MNP $4 MIP $8

Rebel Pilot Bigs Darklighter, 2007, #14, pistol, removable helmet, coin
MNP $4 MIP $8

TAC (30TH ANNIV. COL.) Basic-3, A New Hope

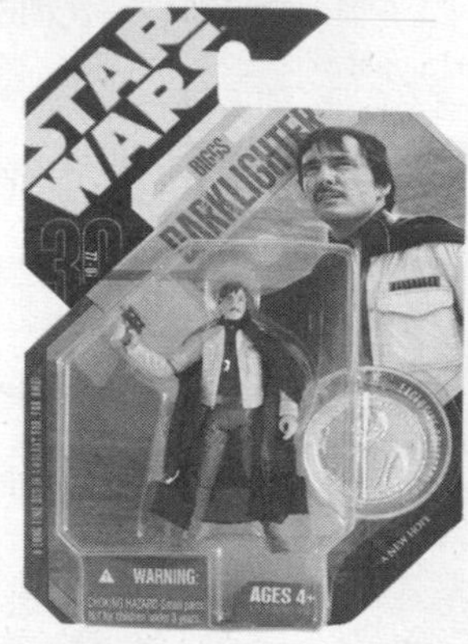

Biggs Darklighter, 2007, #17, civilian attire, cape
MNP $4 MIP $8

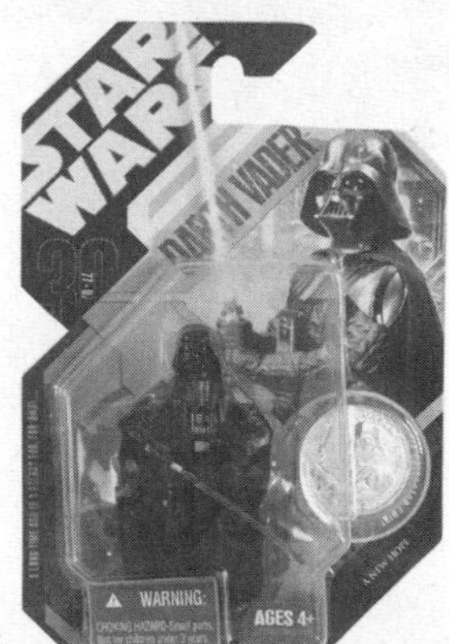

Darth Vader, 2007, #16, raised left fist
MNP $4 MIP $8

Jawa & LIN Droid, 2007, #19
MNP $4 MIP $8

Luke Skywalker, 2007, #18, w/blue lightsaber
MNP $4 MIP $8

McQuarrie Chewbacca, 2007, #21, concept figure
MNP $10 MIP $20

Stormtrooper, 2007, #20
MNP $4 MIP $8

Action Figures, 12"

STAR WARS

Boba Fett, 1979, Star Wars or Empire Strikes Back box
MNP $175 MIP $500

C-3PO, 1979
MNP $35 MIP $145

Chewbacca, 1979
MNP $50 MIP $185

Darth Vader, 1978
MNP $75 MIP $325

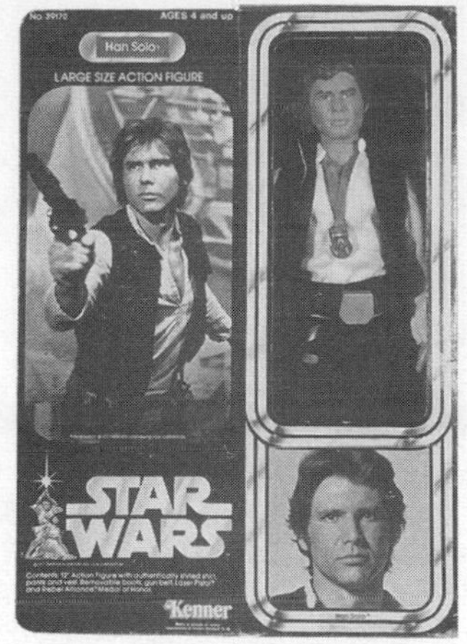

Han Solo, 1979
MNP $110 MIP $425

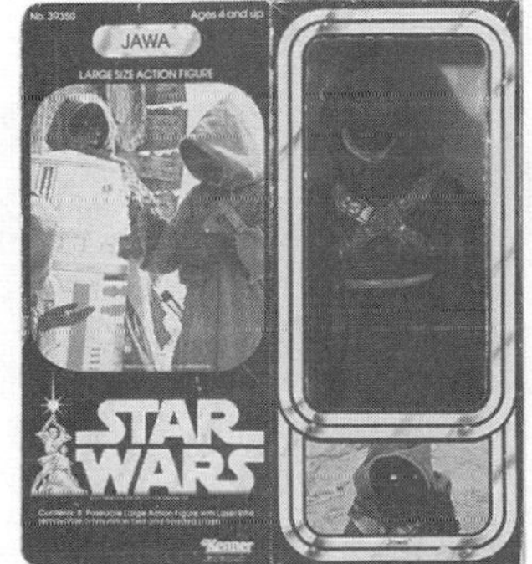

Jawa, 1979
MNP $55 MIP $185

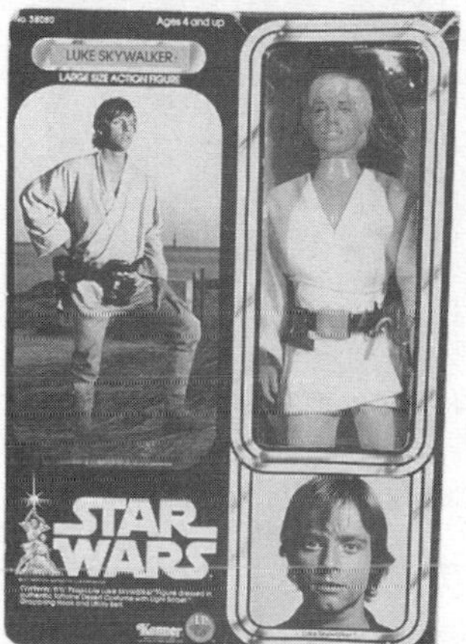

Luke Skywalker, 1979
MNP $125 MIP $350

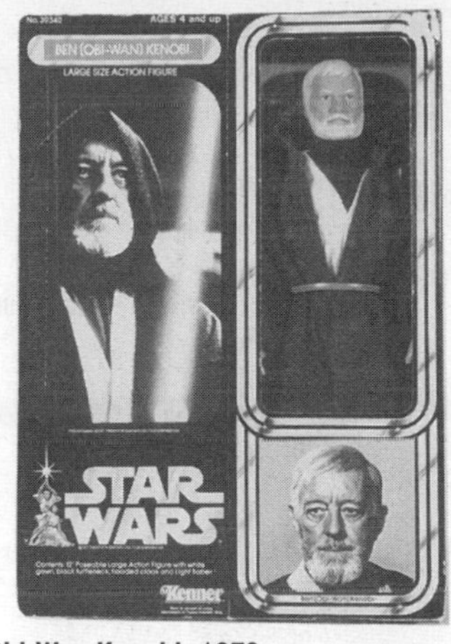

Obi-Wan Kenobi, 1979
MNP $125 MIP $325

Princess Leia Organa, 1979
MNP $85 MIP $220

R2-D2, 1979
MNP $45 MIP $185

Stormtrooper, 1979
MNP $95 MIP $275

EMPIRE STRIKES BACK

Boba Fett, 1979, Empire Strikes Back Box
MNP $130 MIP $875

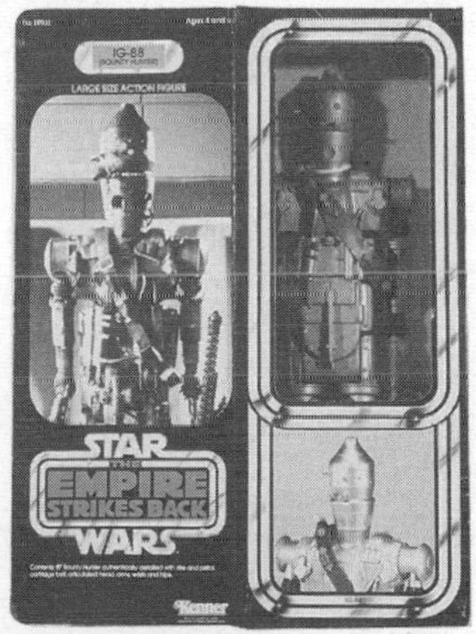

IG-88, 1980, Empire Strikes Back Box
MNP $160 MIP $490

COLLECTOR'S SERIES

Admiral Ackbar, 1997, Series 4
MNP $15 MIP $40

Action Figures, 03-3/4"

AT-AT Driver, 1997, ESB Assortment, Service Merchandise exclusive
MNP $15 MIP $18

Boba Fett, 1997, Series 3
MNP $15 MIP $75

C-3PO, 1997, Series 4
MNP $15 MIP $35

Chewbacca, 1997, Series 4
MNP $15 MIP $85

Darth Vader, 1996, Series 1
MNP $15 MIP $30

Doikk Na'ts, 1997, w/Fizzz, Wal-Mart exclusive, Cantina Band member
MNP $10 MIP $20

Figrin D'an, 1997, w/Kloo Horn, Wal-Mart exclusive, Cantina Band member
MNP $10 MIP $20

(Hasbro Photo)

Grand Moff Tarkin and Imperial Gunner, 1997, FAO exclusive
MNP $45 MIP $80

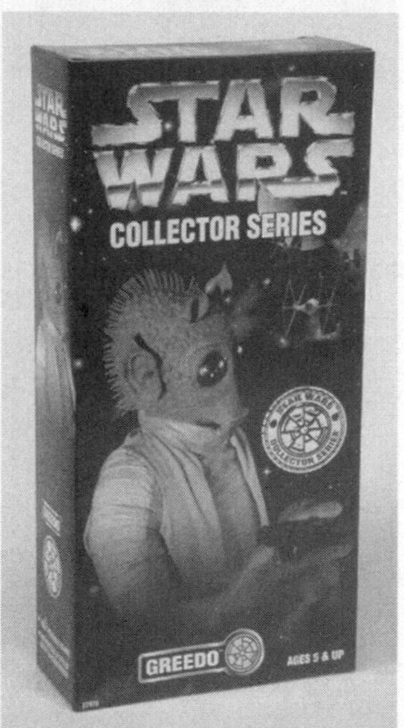

(Hasbro Photo)

Greedo, 1997, SW Assortment, JC Penney exclusive
MNP $15 MIP $25

Han and Luke in Stormtrooper Disguise, 1997, KB exclusive
MNP $30 MIP $55

Han Solo, 1996, Series 1, w/blaster
MNP $15 MIP $30

Han Solo in Hoth Gear w/Tauntaun, 1997, TRU exclusive
MNP $25 MIP $50

Ickabel, 1997, w/Fantor, Wal-Mart exclusive, Cantina Band member
MNP $10 MIP $20

Jedi Luke Skywalker and Bib Fortuna, 1997, FAO Schwarz exclusive
MNP $30 MIP $60

Lando Calrissian, 1997, Series 2
MNP $10 MIP $20

Luke Skywalker, 1996, Series 1
MNP $10 MIP $22

Luke Skywalker as X-Wing Pilot, 1996, Series 3
MNP $15 MIP $25

Luke Skywalker in Bespin Fatigues, 1997, Series 2
MNP $11 MIP $25

Luke Skywalker vs. Wampa, 1997, Target exclusive
MNP $30 MIP $75

Nalan, 1997, w/Bandfill, Wal-Mart exclusive, Cantina Band member
MNP $10 MIP $20

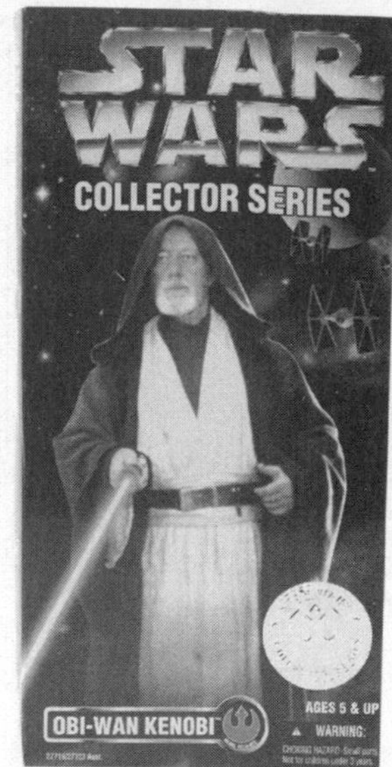

Obi-Wan Kenobi, 1996, Series 1
MNP $10 MIP $25

Obi-Wan Kenobi vs. Darth Vader, 1997, electronic power F/X
MNP $20 MIP $45

Princess Leia, 1997, Series 3
MNP $10 MIP $30

Princess Leia in Ceremonial Gown, 1999, Princess Leia Collection, 1999 Collectors Edition
MNP $10 MIP $25

Sandtrooper, 1997, Diamond exclusive
MNP $12 MIP $25

Stormtrooper, 1997, Series 3
MNP $10 MIP $35

Tech, 1997, w/Ommni Box, Wal-Mart exclusive, Cantina Band member
MNP $10 MIP $20

Tedn, 1997, w/Fantar, Wal-Mart exclusive, Cantina Band
MNP $10 MIP $20

TIE Fighter Pilot, 1997, Series 4
MNP $10 MIP $25

Tusken Raider, 1997, Series 2
MNP $10 MIP $25

ACTION COLLECTION

AT-AT Driver, 1998, Service Merchandise exclusive
MNP $10 MIP $22

Barquin D'an, 1998, ROTJ Assortment
MNP $7 MIP $15

Boba Fett, Electronic, 1998, KB Toys exclusive
MNP $15 MIP $32

C-3PO and R2-D2, 1997, electronic power F/X, TRU exclusive
MNP $20 MIP $50

Chewbacca (Chained), 1998, ROTJ Assortment
MNP $15 MIP $30

Darth Vader, Electronic, 1998, w/removable helmet
MNP $25 MIP $50

Emperor Palpatine, 1998, ROTJ Assortment
MNP $7 MIP $15

Emperor Palpatine and Royal Guard, 1998, electronic power F/X, Target exclusive
MNP $20 MIP $50

Grand Moff Tarkin w/Interrogation Droid, 1998, SW Assortment
MNP $15 MIP $22

Greedo, 1998, fully poseabale, blaster
MNP $10 MIP $22

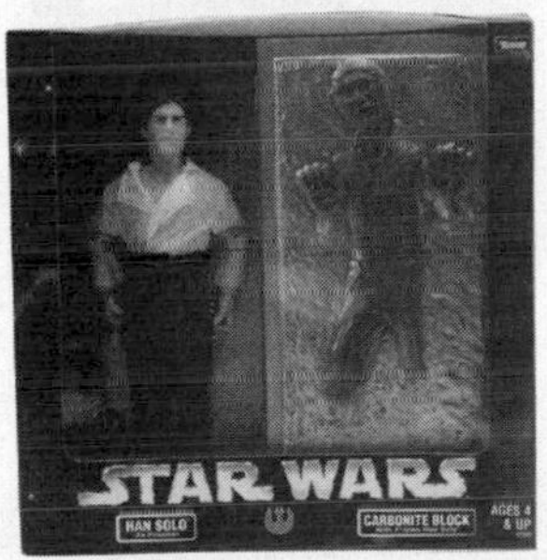

Han Solo in Carbonite, 1998, "I know." Target exclusive
MNP $15 MIP $32

Han Solo in Hoth Gear, 1998, ESB Assortment
MNP $10 MIP $17

Jawa, 1998, Trilogy Assortment, light-up eyes
MNP $12 MIP $25

Luke Skywalker (Hoth), Han Solo (Hoth), Snowtrooper, AT-AT Driver, 1998, JC Penny exclusive
MNP $25 MIP $60

Luke Skywalker (Tatooine), Han Solo w/Flight Jacket, Leia as Boushh, 1998, KB exclusive
MNP $20 MIP $60

Luke Skywalker as Jedi Knight, 1998, ROTJ Assortment, fighting the Rancor
MNP $10 MIP $20

Luke Skywalker in Ceremonial Garb, 1998, SW Assortment
MNP $10 MIP $20

Luke Skywalker in Hoth Gear, 1998, ESB Assortment
MNP $10 MIP $20

Princess Leia and R2-D2 as Jabba's Prisoners, 1998, FAO exclusive, Princess Leia Collection
MNP $25 MIP $55

Princess Leia in Hoth Gear, 1998, Service Merchandise exclusive
MNP $15 MIP $24

R2-D2, 1998, Trilogy Assortment
MNP $9 MIP $18

R2-D2 (Detachable Utility Arms), 1998, Wal-Mart exclusive
MNP $10 MIP $20

R5-D4, 1998, Wal-Mart exclusive
MNP $10 MIP $18

Sandtrooper, 1998, w/Imperial Droid
MNP $10 MIP $22

Snowtrooper, 1998, ESB Assortment
MNP $12 MIP $25

Wedge Antilles and Biggs Darklighter, 1998, FAO exclusive, in X-Wing pilot gear
MNP $30 MIP $70

Wicket the Ewok, 1998, Wal-Mart exclusive
MNP $10 MIP $17

Yoda, 1998, Trilogy Assortment
MNP $15 MIP $25

POTF2

Dewback & Sandtrooper, 2000, TRU exclusive
MNP $40 MIP $80

Han Solo w/Magnetic Detonators, 1999, Endor gear, trench coat
MNP $10 MIP $20

Princess Leia w/Chain, 1999, "Slave Leia"
MNP $10 MIP $22

Speeder Bike w/Scout Trooper, 2000, Target exclusive
MNP $25 MIP $60

POTJ

4-LOM, 2000, concussion rifle
MNP $10 MIP $22

Bossk, 2000, blaster rifle
MNP $10 MIP $22

Captain Tarpals & Kaadu, 2000, Target exclusive
MNP $20 MIP $45

Death Star Droid, 2000, w/mouse droid
MNP $10 MIP $22

Death Star Trooper, 2001, w/Imperial blaster
MNP $10 MIP $22

Dengar, 2002, rifle
MNP $10 MIP $22

Han Solo in Stormtrooper Disguise, 2001, blaster
MNP $10 MIP $22

IG-88, 2000, rifle, Imperial blaster
MNP $10 MIP $24

Luke Skywalker & Yoda, 2001, Wal-Mart exclusive, on Dagobah
MNP $12 MIP $30

Luke Skywalker, 100th figure, 2001
MNP $7 MIP $15

Sith Lords: Darth Vader & Darth Maul, 2001, lightsabers
MNP $12 MIP $30

Speeder Bike w/Luke Skywalker, 2001, Target exclusive
MNP $20 MIP $50

THE PHANTOM MENACE
Action Collection

Anakin Skywalker, 1999
MNP $5 MIP $15

Battle Droid, 1999
MNP $5 MIP $20

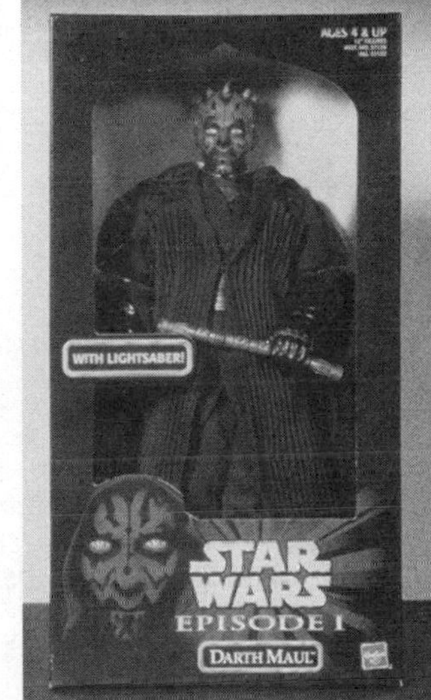

Darth Maul, 1999
MNP $5 MIP $35

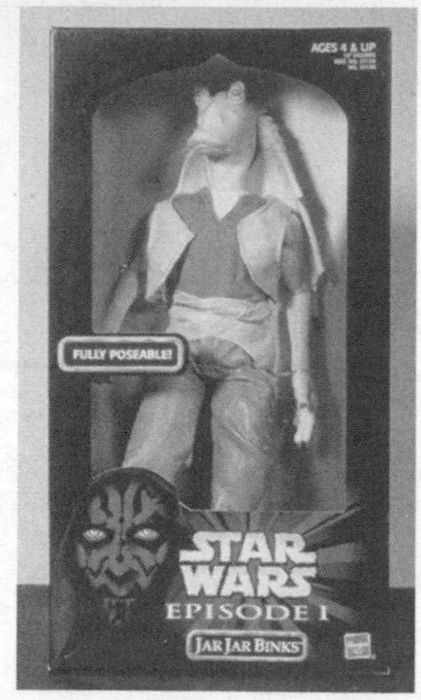

Jar Jar Binks, 1999
MNP $5 MIP $25

Obi-Wan Kenobi, 1999
MNP $5 MIP $25

Pit Droid, 1999
MNP $5 MIP $15

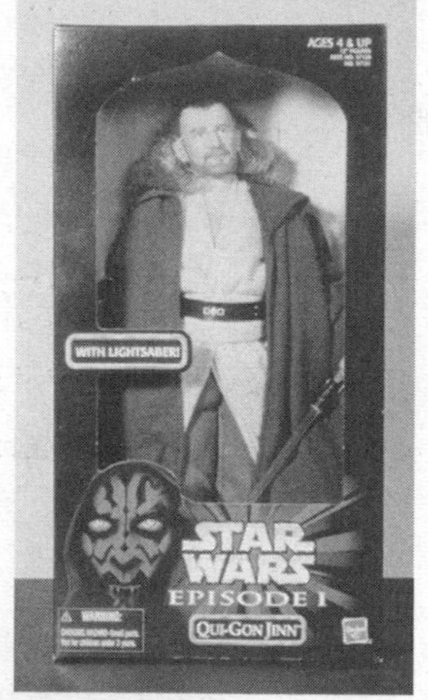

Qui-Gon Jinn, 1999
MNP $5 MIP $30

R2-A6, 1999
MNP $5 MIP $15

Watto, 1999
MNP $5 MIP $15

THE PHANTOM MENACE
Defense of Naboo two-pack

Qui-Gon Jinn and Queen Amidala, 2000, Entertainment Earth exclusive
MNP $5 MIP $100

THE PHANTOM MENACE

Anakin Skywalker, w/Theed Hangar Droid, 2000
MNP $5 MIP $15

Aurra Sing, 2000
MNP $5 MIP $15

Battle Droid Commander w/electrobinoculars, 1999
MNP $5 MIP $15

Boss Nass, 2000
MNP $5 MIP $15

Mace Windu w/lightsaber, 1999
MNP $5 MIP $15

Qui-Gon Jimm w/Tatooine Poncho, 1999
MNP $5 MIP $15

R2-D2, 1998, Wal-Mart exclusive
MNP $5 MIP $15

Sebulba, with Chubas, 2000
MNP $10 MIP $35

TC-14 Protocol Droid, electronic, 1999, KayBee exclusive
MNP $5 MIP $15

THE PHANTOM MENACE
Queen Amidala Collection

Padme, Beautiful Braids, 2000
MNP $5 MIP $15

Queen Amidala, Hidden Majesty, 1999
MNP $5 MIP $10

Queen Amidala, Royal Elegance, 1999
MNP $5 MIP $10

Queen Amidala, Ultimate Hair, 1999
MNP $5 MIP $10

THE PHANTOM MENACE
Queen Amidala Collection, 1999 Portrait Edition

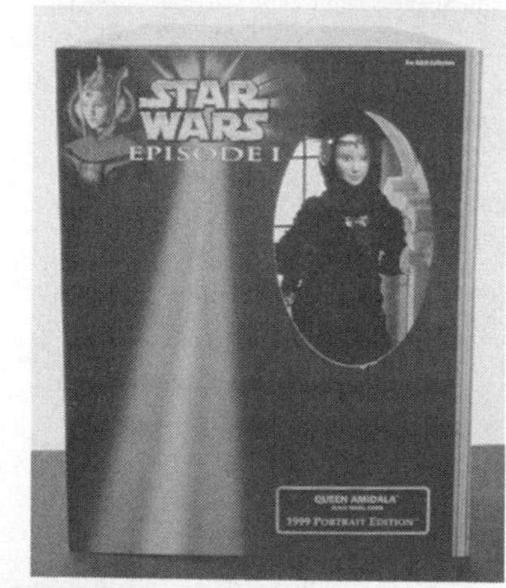

Queen Amidala, Black Travel Dress, 1999
MNP $5 MIP $20

Queen Amidala, Red Senate Gown, 1999
MNP $5 MIP $20

THE PHANTOM MENACE
Queen Amidala Collection, 2000 Portrait Edition

Queen Amidala, Return to Naboo, 2000
MNP $5 MIP $25

SAGA

Anakin Skywalker, 2002, In black robe, includes lightsaber
MNP $8 MIP $25

Anakin Skywalker, Removable Arm, 2003, w/two lightsabers and robotic arm
MNP $10 MIP $20

AT-ST Driver, 2002
MNP $10 MIP $20

Ben Kenobi, A New Hope, 2003
MNP $10 MIP $20

Biker Scout, Battle of Endor, 2003
MNP $10 MIP $20

Clone Commander, Yellow, 2002, KB Toys exclusive
MNP $12 MIP $25

Clone Trooper, 2002, Includes blaster rifle
MNP $10 MIP $25

Clone Trooper, Red, 2002, KB Toys exclusive
MNP $12 MIP $25

Count Dooku, 2002
MNP $10 MIP $20

Dengar, 2003
MNP $10 MIP $20

Electronic Jango Fett, 2002
MNP $10 MIP $20

Electronic Obi-Wan Kenobi, 2002
MNP $10 MIP $20

Gammorean Guard, 2003, KB Toys exclusive
MNP $15 MIP $30

Garindan, Long Snoot, 2003
MNP $15 MIP $35

Geonosian Warrior, 2002
MNP $10 MIP $20

Han Solo, 2003
MNP $10 MIP $20

Imperial Officer, 2003
MNP $10 MIP $20

Jango Fett, 2002, deluxe set with extra accessories
MNP $15 MIP $30

Jawas, 2003, 2-pack
MNP $10 MIP $20

Ki-Adi-Mundi, 2002, Star Wars Fan Club exclusive
MNP $15 MIP $40

Lando Calrissian, Skiff Guard, 2003
MNP $10 MIP $20

Leia as Boushh w/Han Solo in Carbonite, 2003, TRU exclusive
MNP $20 MIP $40

Logray & Paploo, Battle of Endor, 2003
MNP $10 MIP $18

Luke Skywalker w/Taun Taun, 2002, Hoth scene, large scale, TRU exclusive
MNP $25 MIP $55

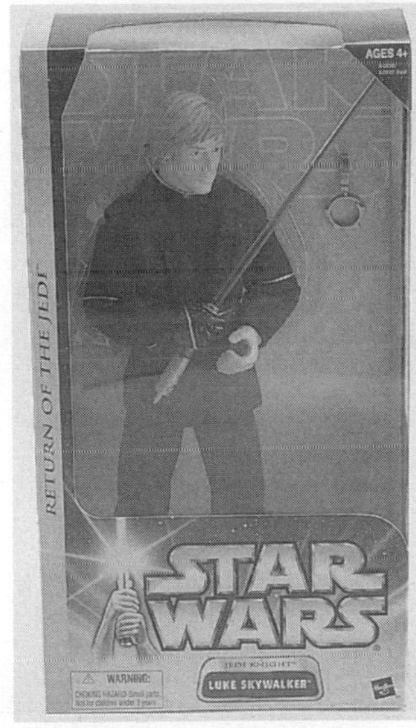

Luke Skywalker, Jedi Knight, 2003, w/handcuffs and green lightsaber
MNP $10 MIP $20

Mace Windu, Jedi Master, 2002, In light tan cloak, includes lightsaber, TRU exclusive
MNP $10 MIP $30

Max Rebo w/Organ, 2003, Wal-Mart exclusive to be released
MNP $10 MIP $20

Obi-Wan Kenobi, 2002, Includes lightsaber
MNP $10 MIP $25

Padme Amidala, 2002
MNP $10 MIP $20

Plo Koon, 2003, Star Wars Fan Club exclusive
MNP $15 MIP $30

Princess Leia on Speeder Bike, Target exclusive
MNP $20 MIP $50

Super Battle Droid, 2002
MNP $10 MIP $20

Sy Snoodles and Droopy McCool, 2003, Wal-Mart exclusive to be released
MNP $10 MIP $20

Yoda, Jedi Master, 2003, w/hoverchair, green lightsaber, belt
MNP $15 MIP $25

Zam Wessell, 2002
MNP $10 MIP $20

Zuckuss, 2003
MNP $10 MIP $20

ORIGINAL TRILOGY COLLECTION

Boba Fett, 2004, blue or gray jumpsuit variations, Model No. 85232
MNP $15 MIP $30

Luke Skywalker, 2004, w/lightsaber, articulated, Model No. 85231
MNP $15 MIP $30

Stormtrooper, 2004, w/blaster, armor, Model No. 85233
MNP $15 MIP $30

REVENGE OF THE SITH

Barriss Offee, 2005, lightsaber
MNP $12 MIP $20

Chewbacca, 2005, KB Toys Exclusive
MNP $15 MIP $35

Clone Trooper, 2005, blaster
MNP $12 MIP $20

Darth Sidious, 2005, lightsaber, cloak w/hood
MNP $12 MIP $20

General Grievous, 2005, 4 lightsabers, cloak
MNP $12 MIP $22

Shaak Ti, 2005, lightsaber
MNP $12 MIP $20

Action Figures, 6"

UNLEASHED

Aayla Secura, 2004, EpII:AotC
MNP $10 MIP $18

Anakin Skywalker, 2002, EpII:AotC, 2 lightsabers
MNP $15 MIP $30

Anakin Skywalker, 2005, EpIII:RotS, Mustafar base, lava
MNP $10 MIP $20

Asajj Ventress, 2005, 2 red lightsabers
MNP $8 MIP $15

Aurra Sing, 2005, bonus figure
MNP $8 MIP $18

Boba Fett, 2003, RotJ
MNP $15 MIP $45

Bossk, 2004, ESB
MNP $10 MIP $18

Chewbacca, 2004, Star Wars
MNP $10 MIP $16

Chewbacca, 2006, EpIII:RotS, shield, blaster
MNP $8 MIP $15

Clone Trooper, 2004, EpII:AotC, white
MNP $10 MIP $16

Clone Trooper, 2004, EpII:AotC, red
MNP $8 MIP $15

(KP Photo, Brian Brogaard collection)

Darth Maul, 2002, EpI:TPM
MNP $15 MIP $40

Darth Sidious w/Sith Lightning, 2003, RotJ
MNP $8 MIP $15

Darth Tyranus, 2002, EpII:AotC
MNP $8 MIP $15

Darth Vader, 2005, Best Buy exclusive, repaint of 2005 RotJ model
MNP $8 MIP $15

Darth Vader, 2005, RotJ, leaping down stairs
MNP $8 MIP $18

Darth Vader, w/ mask, 2002, ESB: "I...am your father."
MNP $10 MIP $20

Darth Vader, w/o mask, 2003, RotJ
MNP $15 MIP $25

General Grievous, 2005, EpIII:RotS, 2 lightsabers, base
MNP $8 MIP $15

Han Solo, 2003, Star Wars, running up ramp
MNP $15 MIP $35

Han Solo Stormtrooper, 2006, Star Wars
MNP $8 MIP $15

Jango and Boba Fett, 2002, EpII:AotC
MNP $15 MIP $35

Luke Skywalker, 2003, RotJ outfit
MNP $15 MIP $45

Luke Skywalker, 2004, ESB, X-Wing Pilot
MNP $10 MIP $18

Mace Windu, 2002, EpII:AotC
MNP $10 MIP $18

Obi-Wan Kenobi, 2003, EpII:AotC
MNP $10 MIP $18

Obi-Wan Kenobi, 2005, EpIII:RotS, Mustafar base, lava
MNP $8 MIP $15

Padme Amidala, 2002, 2 versions
MNP $12 MIP $30

Princess Leia, 2003, RotJ
MNP $15 MIP $70

Shock Trooper, 2006, EpIII:RotS, Clone Trooper on Mustafar
MNP $8 MIP $15

Stormtrooper, 2005, Star Wars
MNP $15 MIP $40

Tusken Raider, 2004, Star Wars
MNP $10 MIP $16

(KP Photo, Brian Brogaard collection)

Yoda, 2003, EpII:AotC
MNP $15 MIP $45

Yoda vs. Sidious, 2005, EpIII:RotS
MNP $10 MIP $20

Carrying Cases

EMPIRE STRIKES BACK

Darth Vader, 1982
MNP $10 MIP $30

Mini Figure, 1980
MNP $11 MIP $27

ORIGINAL TRILOGY COLLECTION

Darth Vader, 2004, vintage-style with Boba Fett and Stormtrooper, Model No. 85405
MNP $15 MIP $30

RETURN OF THE JEDI

C-3PO, 1983
MNP $12 MIP $29

Darth Vader (w/three figs.), 1983, w/three figures
MNP $11 MIP $225

Laser Rifle, 1984
MNP $9 MIP $33

REVENGE OF THE SITH

Darth Vader, 2005, Wal-Mart Exclusive; Anakin Skywalker and Clone Trooper included, holds 30 figures, Model No. 85646
MNP $20 MIP $40

STAR WARS

24-Figure, 1978
MNP $14 MIP $27

Coins

2-1B, 1985
MNP $105 MIP n/a

63rd Coin, lightsaber, 1985
MNP $1200 MIP n/a

Amanaman, 1985
MNP $4 MIP n/a

Anakin Skywalker, 1985
MNP $70 MIP n/a

AT-AT, 1985
MNP $55 MIP n/a

AT-ST Driver, 1985
MNP $9 MIP n/a

A-Wing Pilot, 1985
MNP $4 MIP n/a

Barada, 1985
MNP $4 MIP n/a

Bib Fortuna, 1985
MNP $105 MIP n/a

Biker Scout, 1985
MNP $9 MIP n/a

Boba Fett, 1985
MNP $225 MIP n/a

B-Wing Pilot, 1985
MNP $9 MIP n/a

C-3PO, 1985
MNP $9 MIP n/a

Chewbacca, 1985
MNP $9 MIP n/a

Chief Chirpa, 1985
MNP $35 MIP n/a

Creatures, 1985
MNP $55 MIP n/a

Darth Vader, 1985
MNP $18 MIP n/a

Droids, 1985
MNP $50 MIP n/a

Emperor, 1985
MNP $12 MIP n/a

Emperor's Royal Guard, 1985
MNP $50 MIP n/a

EV-9D9, 1985
MNP $4 MIP n/a

FX-7, 1985
MNP $165 MIP n/a

Gamorrean Guard, 1985
MNP $20 MIP n/a

Greedo, 1985
MNP $175 MIP n/a

Han Hoth, 1985
MNP $75 MIP n/a

Han in Carbonite, 1985
MNP $4 MIP n/a

Han Original, 1985
MNP $145 MIP n/a

Han Rebel (trenchcoat), 1985
MNP $9 MIP n/a

Hoth Stormtrooper, 1985
MNP $225 MIP n/a

Imperial Commander, 1985
MNP $65 MIP n/a

Imperial Dignitary, 1985
MNP $4 MIP n/a

Imperial Gunner, 1985
MNP $4 MIP n/a

Jawas, 1985
MNP $9 MIP n/a

Lando General, 1985
MNP $4 MIP n/a

Lando with Cloud City, 1985
MNP $70 MIP n/a

Logray, 1985
MNP $35 MIP n/a

Luke Jedi, 1985
MNP $16 MIP n/a

Luke on Dagobah, 1985
MNP $120 MIP n/a

Luke original, 1985
MNP $75 MIP n/a

Luke Poncho, 1985
MNP $4 MIP n/a

Luke Stormtrooper, 1985
MNP $4 MIP n/a

Luke with Taun Taun, 1985
MNP $75 MIP n/a

Luke X-Wing, 1985
MNP $5 MIP n/a

Luke X-Wing, small, 1985
MNP $45 MIP n/a

Lumat, 1985
MNP $9 MIP n/a

Millennium Falcon, 1985
MNP $65 MIP n/a

Millennium Falcon, 1994
MNP $5 MIP n/a

Obi-Wan Kenobi, 1985
MNP $16 MIP n/a

Paploo, 1985
MNP $9 MIP n/a

Princess Leia Rebel Leader (poncho), 1985
MNP $9 MIP n/a

Princess Leia, Boushh, 1985
MNP $145 MIP n/a

Princess Leia, Original, 1985
MNP $85 MIP n/a

R2-D2 Pop-Up Lightsaber, 1985
MNP $4 MIP n/a

Romba, 1985
MNP $4 MIP n/a

Sail Skiff, 1985
MNP $250 MIP n/a

Star Destroyer Commander, 1985
MNP $60 MIP n/a

Stormtrooper, 1985
MNP $16 MIP n/a

Teebo, 1985
MNP $18 MIP n/a

TIE Fighter, 1994
MNP $5 MIP n/a

TIE Fighter Pilot, 1985
MNP $50 MIP n/a

Tusken Raider, 1985
MNP $145 MIP n/a

Warok, 1985
MNP $4 MIP n/a

Wicket, 1985
MNP $9 MIP n/a

X-Wing, 1994
MNP $5 MIP n/a

Yak Face, 1985
MNP $85 MIP n/a

Yoda, 1985
MNP $16 MIP n/a

Zuckuss, 1985
MNP $145 MIP n/a

Creatures

STAR WARS

Patrol Dewback, 1978
MNP $20 MIP $85

EMPIRE STRIKES BACK

Hoth Wampa, 1980
MNP $17 MIP $37

Tauntaun, solid belly, 1980
MNP $15 MIP $40

Tauntaun, split belly, 1980
MNP $15 MIP $45

RETURN OF THE JEDI

Rancor, 1983
MNP $30 MIP $85

THE PHANTOM MENACE

Kaadu w/Jar Jar Binks, 1999
MNP $2 MIP $5

SAGA

Acklay, Arena Battle Beast, 2002
MNP $10 MIP $20

Reek, Arena Battle Beast, 2002
MNP $10 MIP $20

Reek, Arena Battle Beast w/Attack Sounds, 2002
MNP $4 MIP $18

REVENGE OF THE SITH

Boga and Obi-Wan Kenobi, 2005, lizard rears its front legs, opens its mouth and shakes head
MNP $10 MIP $25

LEGO sets

ATTACK OF THE CLONES

Bounty Hunter Pursuit w/Obi-Wan Kenobi, Anakin Skywalker, Zam Wessell, 2002, 7133
MNP $5 MIP $25

Jango Fett, 2002, 8011
MNP $5 MIP $30

Jango Fett's Slave I w/Jango Fett, Boba Fett, 2002, 7153
MNP $5 MIP $40

Jedi Duel w/Yoda, Count Dooku, 2002, 7103
MNP $5 MIP $10

Jedi Starfighter w/Obi-Wan Kenobi, R4-P17, 2002, 7143
MNP $5 MIP $15

Republic Gunship w/Jedi Clone Troopers, Battle Droids, Destroyer Droids, 2002, 7163
MNP $5 MIP $75

Super Battle Droid, 2002, 8012
MNP $5 MIP $30

Tusken Raider Encounter w/Anakin Skywalker, two Tusken Raiders, 2002, 7113
MNP $5 MIP $10

EMPIRE STRIKES BACK Mini-Figure Sets

Luke Skywalker, Han Solo, Boba Fett, 1980, 3341
MNP $10 MIP $25

EMPIRE STRIKES BACK

Boba Fett's Slave I, 1980, 7144
MNP $10 MIP $30

Twin-Pod Cloud Car w/Lobot, 1980, 7119
MNP $10 MIP $30

EMPIRE STRIKES BACK Ultimate Collectors Series

Yoda, 1980, 7194
MNP $25 MIP $100

RETURN OF THE JEDI Mini-Figure Sets

Chewbacca, two Biker Scouts, 3342
MNP n/a MIP $5

RETURN OF THE JEDI

B-Wing at Rebel Control Center w/pilot, droid, mechanic, 7180
MNP n/a MIP $30

Desert Skiff w/Luke Skywalker, Han Solo, 7104
MNP n/a MIP $6

Ewok Attack w/Biker Scout, Stormtrooper, two Ewoks, 7139
MNP n/a MIP $13

Final Duel I w/Emperor, Darth Vader, 7200
MNP n/a MIP $10

Final Duel II w/Luke Skywalker, Imperial Officer, Stormtrooper, 7201
MNP n/a MIP $7

Imperial AT-ST w/Chewbacca, 7127
MNP n/a MIP $10

Imperial Shuttle w/Emperor, Pilot, two Royal Guards, 7166
MNP n/a MIP $35

REVENGE OF THE SITH

ARC-170 Starfighter, 2005, 7259, 396 pieces
MNP $10 MIP $25

Clone Scout Walker, 2005, 7250, 108 pieces, w/Clone Trooper
MNP $10 MIP $20

Clone Turbo Tank, 2005, 7261
MNP $40 MIP $95

Darth Vader Transformation, 2005, 7251, 53 pieces
MNP $5 MIP $10

Droid Tri-Fighter, 2005, 7252, 148 pieces, Buzz Droid
MNP $9 MIP $15

Episode III Collector's Set, 2005, 65771
MNP $30 MIP $75

General Grievous Chase, 2005, 7255, 111 pieces, Grievous on Wheel Bike, Obi-Wan on Boga
MNP $20 MIP $40

STAR WARS Mindstorms

Dark Side Developer, 9754
MNP n/a MIP $100

STAR WARS Mini-Figure Sets

Emperor Palpatine, Darth Maul, Darth Vader, 3340
MNP n/a MIP $5

STAR WARS

Darth Vader, 8010
MNP n/a MIP $40

Droid Escape w/R2-D2, C-3PO, 7106
MNP n/a MIP $7

Landspeeder w/Luke Skywalker, Obi-Wan Kenobi, 1999, 7110
MNP n/a MIP $6

Millennium Falcon w/Han Solo, Leia, Luke, Chewbacca, R2-D2, C-3PO, 7190
MNP n/a MIP $100

R2-D2, 8009
MNP n/a MIP $20

Rebel Blockade Runner - Tantive IV Corellian Corvette, 10019
MNP n/a MIP $150

TIE Figher w/Pilot, Stormtrooper, 7146
MNP n/a MIP $20

TIE Interceptor, 7181
MNP n/a MIP $20

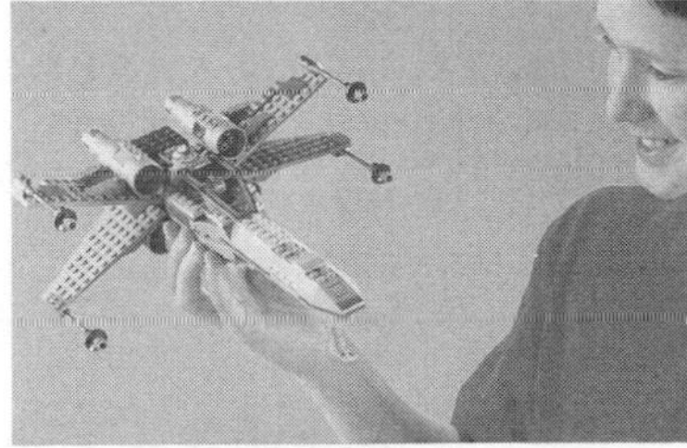

(LEGO Photo)

X-Wing Fighter, 7140
MNP n/a MIP $45

STAR WARS
Technic

C-3PO, 8007
MNP n/a MIP $35

Stormtrooper, 8008
MNP n/a MIP $35

THE PHANTOM MENACE
Mini-Figure Sets

Command Officer, two Battle Droids, 3343
MNP $2 MIP $5

THE PHANTOM MENACE

Darth Maul (bust), 10018
MNP n/a MIP $125

Droid Fighter, 7111
MNP n/a MIP $6

Flash Speeder w/Royal Naboo Security Force, 7121
MNP n/a MIP $10

Gungan Patrol w/Jar Jar Binks, Gungan Warrior, 7115
MNP n/a MIP $10

Gungan Sub w/Qui-Gon Jinn, Obi-Wan Kenobi, Jar Jar Binks, 1999, 7161
MNP n/a MIP $45

Jedi Defense I w/Obi-Wan Kenobi, two Destroyer Droids, 7203
MNP n/a MIP $7

Jedi Defense II w/Qui-Gon Jinn, two Battle Droids, 7204
MNP n/a MIP $7

Lightsaber Duel w/Qui-Gon Jinn, Darth Maul, 1999, 7101
MNP n/a MIP $5

Mos Espa Podrace w/Padme, Anakin, R2-D2, Qui-Gon, Jar Jar, Sebulba, Gasgano, 7171
MNP n/a MIP $85

Naboo Fighter w/Anakin Skywalker, two Battle Droids, 1999, 7141
MNP n/a MIP $25

Naboo Swamp w/Qui-Gon Jinn, Jar Jar Binks, two Battle Droids, 1999, 7121
MNP n/a MIP $10

Podracer, 1999, 7131
MNP n/a MIP $20

Sith Infiltrator w/Darth Maul, 7151
MNP n/a MIP $30

Trade Federation MTT, 7184
MNP n/a MIP $45

THE PHANTOM MENACE
Technic

Battle Droid, 8001
MNP n/a MIP $25

Destroyer Droid, 8002
MNP n/a MIP $45

Pit Droid, 8000
MNP n/a MIP $20

Micro Collection

EMPIRE STRIKES BACK

Bespin Control Room, 1982
MNP $7 MIP $17

Bespin Freeze Chamber, 1982
MNP $12 MIP $44

Bespin Gantry, 1982
MNP $9 MIP $25

Bespin World, 1982
MNP $32 MIP $90

Death Star Compactor, 1982
MNP $27 MIP $50

Death Star Escape, 1982
MNP $25 MIP $42

Death Star World, 1982
MNP $48 MIP $100

Hoth Generator Attack, 1982
MNP $15 MIP $30

Hoth Ion Cannon, 1982
MNP $17 MIP $50

Hoth Turret Defense, 1982
MNP $19 MIP $32

Hoth Wampa Cave, 1982
MNP $12 MIP $23

Hoth World, 1982
MNP $30 MIP $105

Imperial TIE Fighter, 1982
MNP $20 MIP $47

Millennium Falcon, 1982
MNP $80 MIP $230

Snowspeeder, 1982
MNP $48 MIP $95

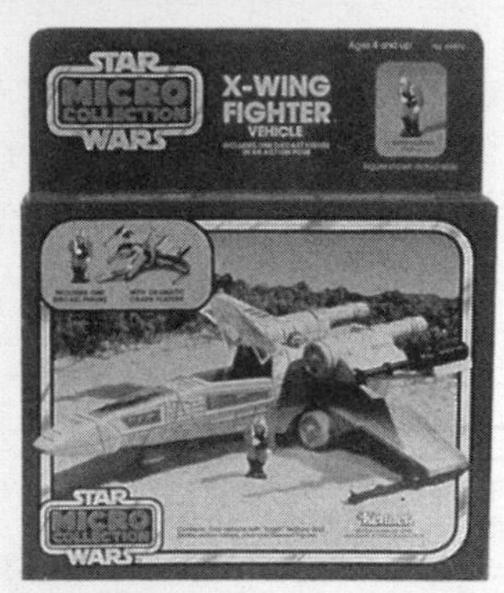

X-Wing Fighter, 1982
MNP $21 MIP $43

Micro Machines

THE PHANTOM MENACE Deluxe Action Set

Trade Federation MTT/Naboo Battlefield Mega Deluxe Action Set, 1999
MNP $3 MIP $8

THE PHANTOM MENACE Deluxe Platform Action Set

Theed Palace Assault, 1999
MNP $4 MIP $18

THE PHANTOM MENACE Deluxe Remote Control

Fambaa, 1999
MNP $4 MIP $18

Trade Federation Tank, 1999
MNP $4 MIP $18

THE PHANTOM MENACE Die-Cast Vehicle

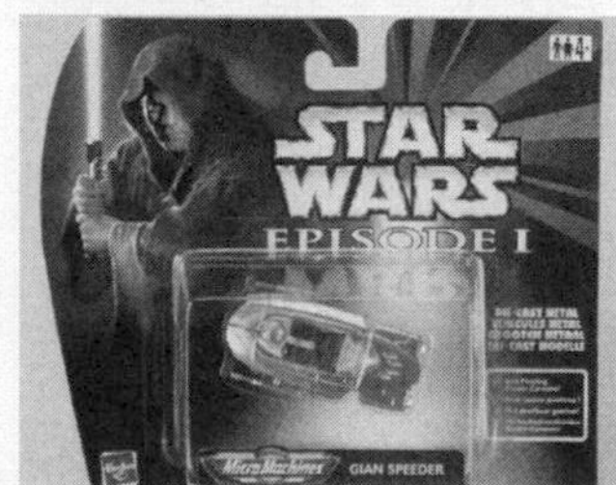

Gian Speeder, 1999, A nicely detailed, heavy model with pivoting cannon and slide-open canopy
MNP $3 MIP $8

Republic Cruiser, 1999
MNP $3 MIP $8

Royal Starship, 1999
MNP $3 MIP $8

Sebulba's Podracer, 1999
MNP $3 MIP $8

Sith Infiltrator, 1999
MNP $3 MIP $8

Trade Federation Battleship, 1999
MNP $3 MIP $8

Trade Federation Droid Fighter, 1999, The wings of this model slide open into "firing" mode
MNP $3 MIP $8

Trade Federation Tank, 1999
MNP $3 MIP $8

THE PHANTOM MENACE Inside Action Set

Gungan Sub (Bonto)/Otoh Gunga, 1999
MNP $3 MIP $8

Jar Jar Binks/Naboo, 1999
MNP $3 MIP $8

THE PHANTOM MENACE Mini Scene

Destroyer Droid Ambush, 1999
MNP $3 MIP $8

Generator Core Duel, 1999
MNP $3 MIP $8

THE PHANTOM MENACE

Anakin Skywalker's Podracer w/figure, 1999
MNP $2 MIP $6

Arch Canyon Adventure, 1999
MNP $2 MIP $6

Battle Droid/Trade Federation Droid Control Ship, 1999
MNP $2 MIP $6

Beggar's Canyon Challenge, 1999
MNP $2 MIP $6

Boonta Eve Challenge Deluxe Podracing Track Set, 1999
MNP $2 MIP $6

Build Your Own Podracer Pack I, 1999
MNP $5 MIP $8

Flash Speeder w/figure, 1999
MNP $2 MIP $6

Gian Speeder & Theed Palace Sneak Preview Set, 1999
MNP $2 MIP $6

Gungan Sub w/figure, 1999
MNP $2 MIP $6

Mars Guo's Podracer w/figure, 1999
MNP $2 MIP $6

Naboo Fighter w/figure, 1999
MNP $2 MIP $6

Podracer Launchers, 1999
MNP $2 MIP $6

Republic Cruiser w/figure, 1999
MNP $2 MIP $6

Sebulba's Podracer w/figure, 1999
MNP $2 MIP $6

Trade Federation Droid Fighter w/figure, 1999
MNP $2 MIP $6

Trade Federation Landing Ship w/figure, 1999
MNP $2 MIP $6

Trade Federation MTT w/figure, 1999
MNP $2 MIP $6

Turbo Blast Podracers, 1999
MNP $2 MIP $6

THE PHANTOM MENACE Platform Action Set

Galactic Dogfight, 1999
MNP $2 MIP $5

Galactic Senate, 1999
MNP $2 MIP $5

Naboo Temple Ruins, 1999
MNP $2 MIP $5

Podrace Arena, 1999
MNP $2 MIP $5

Royal Starship Repair Deluxe Platform Action Set, 1999
MNP $2 MIP $5

Tatooine Desert, 1999
MNP $3 MIP $6

Theed Rapids, 1999
MNP $2 MIP $5

THE PHANTOM MENACE Podracer Pack I

Boles Roor & Neva Kee, 1999
MNP $3 MIP $8

THE PHANTOM MENACE Podracer Pack II

Dud Bolt & Mars Guo, 1999
MNP $3 MIP $8

THE PHANTOM MENACE Podracer Pack III

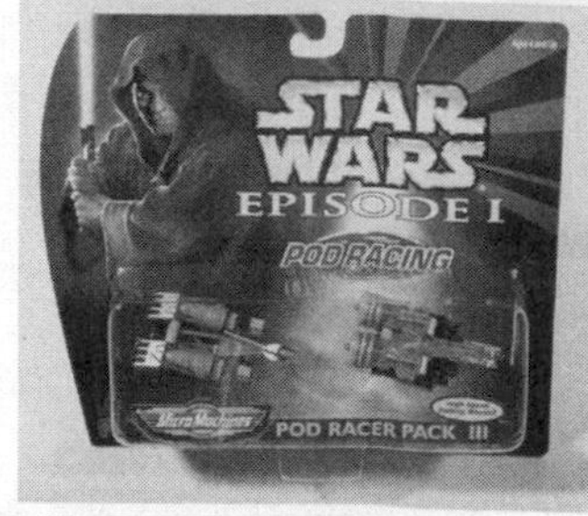

Anakin Skywalker & Ratts Tyerell, 1999
MNP $3 MIP $8

THE PHANTOM MENACE Podracer Pack IV

Sebulba & Clegg Holdfast, 1999
MNP $3 MIP $8

Mini Rigs

AST-5, 1983
MNP $6 MIP $18

CAP-2 Captivator, 1982, Bubble-topped vehicle with room for one figure. Roller wheels on bottom with tank tread façade and two laser moveable laser cannon in front
MNP $6 MIP $21

Desert Sail Skiff, 1984
MNP $9 MIP $19

Endor Forest Ranger, 1984
MNP $12 MIP $26

INT-4 Interceptor, 1982
MNP $7 MIP $24

ISP-6 Imperial Shuttle Pod, 1983
MNP $10 MIP $21

MLC-3 Mobile Laser Cannon, 1981
MNP $8 MIP $22

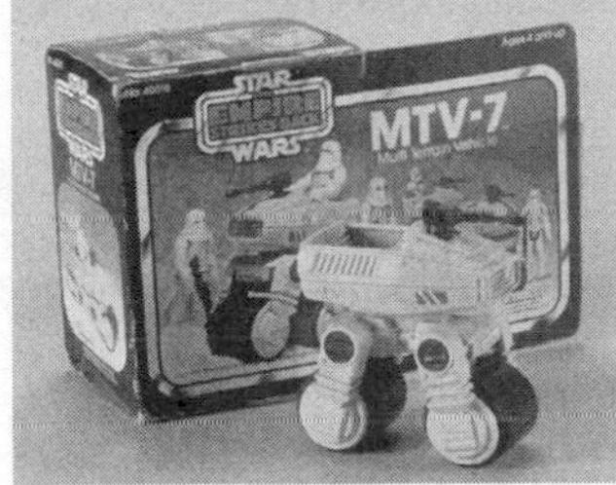

MTV-7 Multi-Terrain Vehicle, 1981, Off-white with room for one 3-3/4" figure (most likely a snowtrooper, if the box is a guide). Features two spring-loaded roller wheels and a pivoting front blaster. The Mini Rigs were, in a way, the first "expanded universe" toys for Star Wars
MNP $9 MIP $25

PDT-8 Personal Deployment Transport, 1981
MNP $10 MIP $23

Radar Laser Cannon, 1982
MNP $7 MIP $24

Tri-Pod Laser Cannon, 1982, Cannon with "ammo box" and three folding legs
MNP $6 MIP $18

Vehicle Maintenance Energizer, 1982, Generator for vehicles
MNP $8 MIP $18

Play Sets

EMPIRE STRIKES BACK

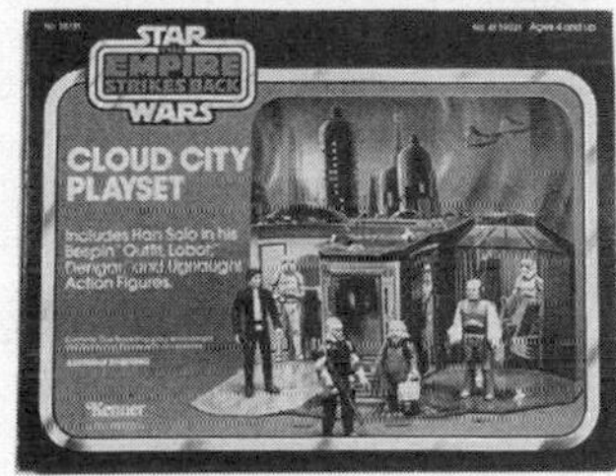

Cloud City Play Set, Sears exclusive, 1981
MNP $120 MIP $300

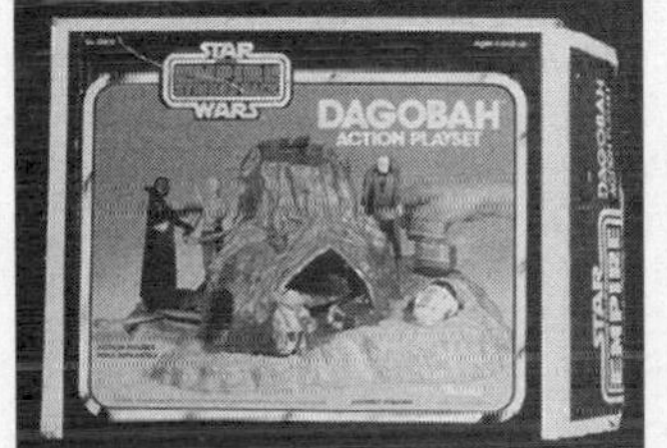

Dagobah, 1982
MNP $22 MIP $90

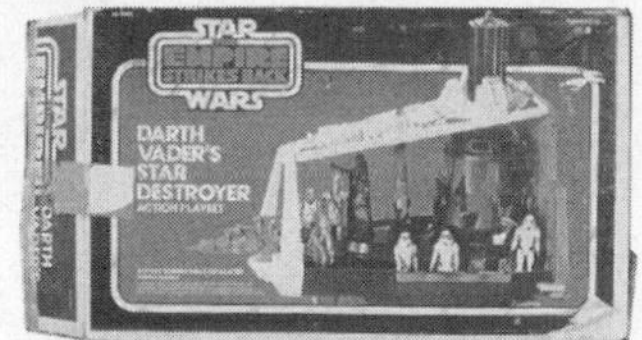

Darth Vader's Star Destroyer, 1982
MNP $32 MIP $120

Hoth Ice Planet, 1980
MNP $40 MIP $165

Imperial Attack Base, 1980
MNP $20 MIP $80

Rebel Command Center, 1980
MNP $60 MIP $180

Turret and Probot, 1980
MNP $35 MIP $110

EWOKS

Ewoks Treehouse, 1985
MNP $18 MIP $50

POTJ

Carbon-Freezing Chamber, 2000, Star Wars Fan Club exclusive
MNP $20 MIP $45

RETURN OF THE JEDI

Ewok Village, 1983
MNP $45 MIP $165

Jabba the Hutt, 1983
MNP $17 MIP $70

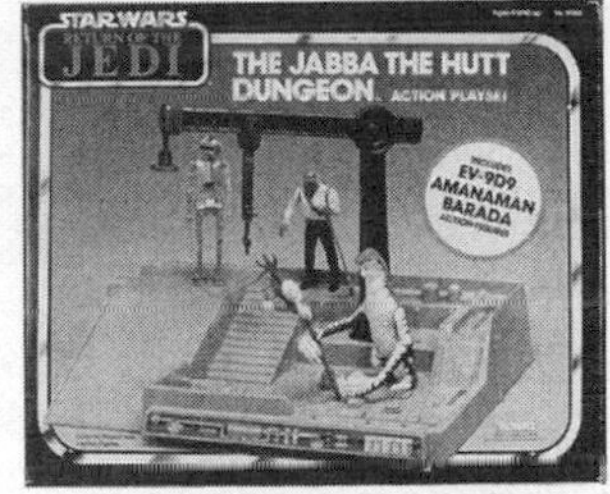

Jabba the Hutt Dungeon, w/EV-9D9, Amanaman, Barada, 1983
MNP $175 MIP $275

Jabba the Hutt Dungeon, w/Nikto, 8D8, Klaatu, 1983, Sears
MNP $30 MIP $75

REVENGE OF THE SITH

Mustafar Final Battle, 2005, w/Anakin Darth Vader and Obi-Wan Kenobi
MNP $30 MIP $60

SAGA

Geonosian Arena, 2002
MNP $17 MIP $50

STAR WARS

Cantina Adventure Set, Sears exclusive, 1977
MNP $185 MIP $575

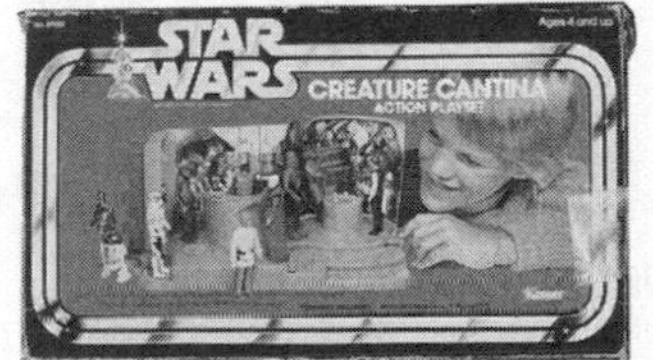

Creature Cantina, 1977
MNP $25 MIP $100

Death Star Space Station, 1977
MNP $75 MIP $350

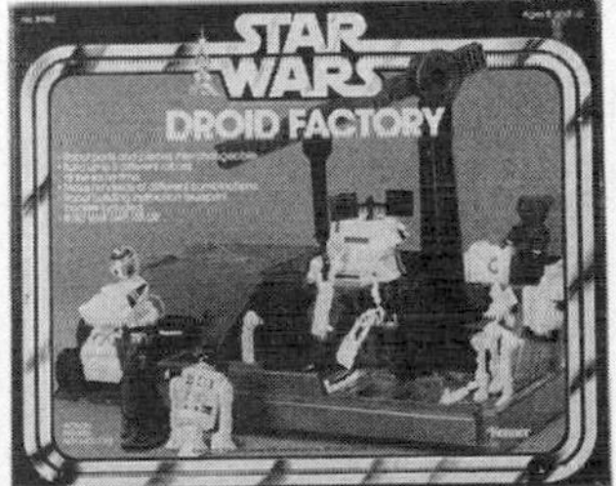

Droid Factory, 1977
MNP $50 MIP $135

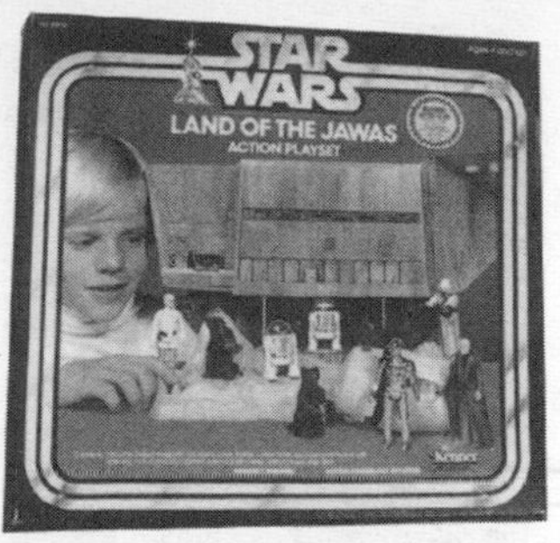

Land of the Jawas, 1977
MNP $45 MIP $125

Vehicles

DIE-CAST

Darth Vader's TIE Fighter, 1979
MNP $14 MIP $50

Land Speeder, 1979
MNP $14 MIP $65

Millennium Falcon, 1979
MNP $20 MIP $105

Naboo Starfighter, 1999
MNP $4 MIP $10

Slave I, 1979
MNP $25 MIP $75

Snowspeeder, 1979
MNP $17 MIP $65

Star Destroyer, 1979
MNP $25 MIP $110

TIE Bomber, 1979
MNP $150 MIP $410

TIE Fighter, 1979
MNP $12 MIP $45

Twin-Pod Cloud Car, 1979
MNP $17 MIP $70

X-Wing Fighter, 1979
MNP $15 MIP $70

Y-Wing Fighter, 1979
MNP $22 MIP $90

EXPANDED UNIVERSE

Speeder Bike, 1998, Based on previous concept drawing for speeder bike. Includes figure unique to vehicle, like other Expanded Universe vehicles. Fires missile, and outriggers move to sides when in "battle mode"
MNP $3 MIP $11

STAR WARS

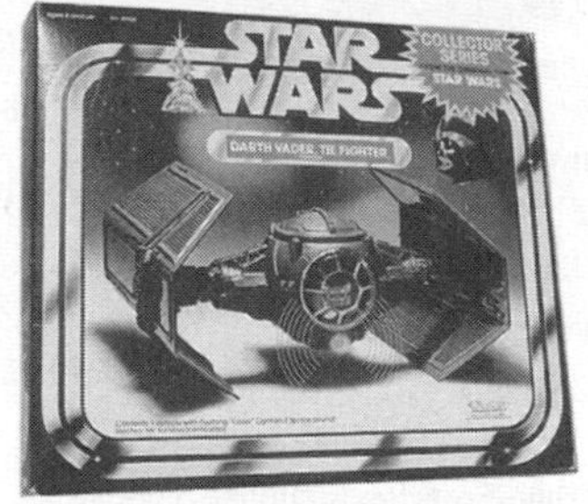

Darth Vader's TIE Fighter, 1977, Fly-apart panels, battery-powered laser cannon lights up in front
MNP $45 MIP $135

Imperial Cruiser, 1982, Second version of this vehicle. What was once the compartment for a 9-volt battery was now a "weapons storage bin." This vehicle had no battery-powered sounds, but did have opening doors, rotating turret and antenna and opening tailgate
MNP $25 MIP $75

Imperial TIE Fighter, 1977, Fly-apart panels
MNP $35 MIP $125

Imperial Trooper Transport, 1977, First version was a Sears Exclusive, with battery-powered laser sounds. Later model released with "Empire Strikes Back" didn't include sounds or require battery power
MNP $35 MIP $110

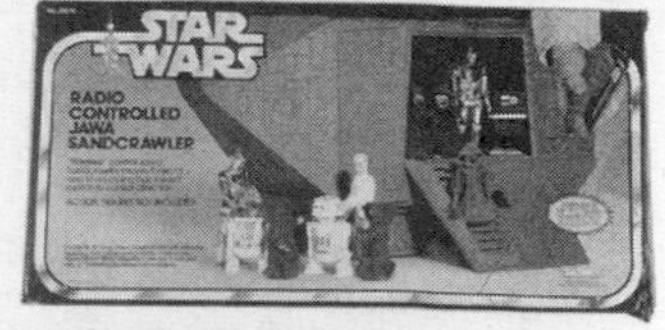

Jawa Sandcrawler, battery-operated, 1977, battery-operated
MNP $220 MIP $575

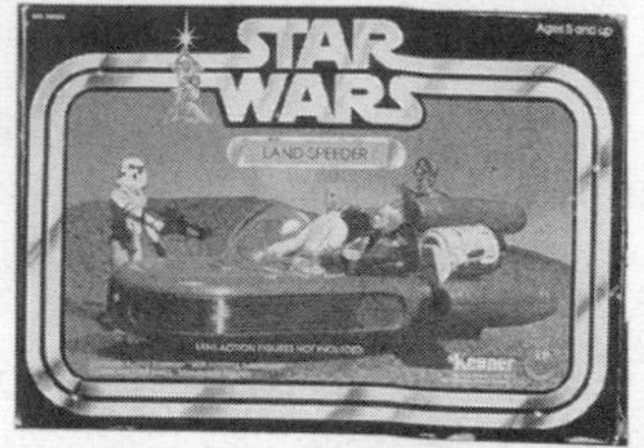

Land Speeder, 1977, Retractable hovering wheels, opening hood
MNP $13 MIP $60

Land Speeder, battery-operated, 1977, battery-operated
MNP $16 MIP $50

Millennium Falcon, 1977
MNP $80 MIP $365

Sonic Land Speeder, JC Penney exclusive, 1977
MNP $135 MIP $450

X-Wing Fighter, 1977, Pushing R2 head into vehicle would put foils in "X-wing" position. Opening canopy, light-up laser cannon on front
MNP $35 MIP $125

EMPIRE STRIKES BACK

AT-AT, 1980, All-Terrain Armored Transport
MNP $95 MIP $250

Rebel Transport, 1980
MNP $35 MIP $100

Scout Walker, 1982, Two-legged vehicle with "walking" legs operated by button behind cockpit. A lever allowed the legs to remain locked so the vehicle could stand in place. Opening flip-up top to place figures, and opening turret allowing stormtroopers to fire weapons
MNP $22 **MIP $55**

Slave I, 1980
MNP $50 **MIP $140**

Snowspeeder, 1980
MNP $45 **MIP $110**

Twin-Pod Cloud Car, 1980
MNP $35 **MIP $95**

RETURN OF THE JEDI

B-Wing Fighter, 1984
MNP $60 **MIP $150**

Ewok Combat Glider, 1984
MNP $12 **MIP $45**

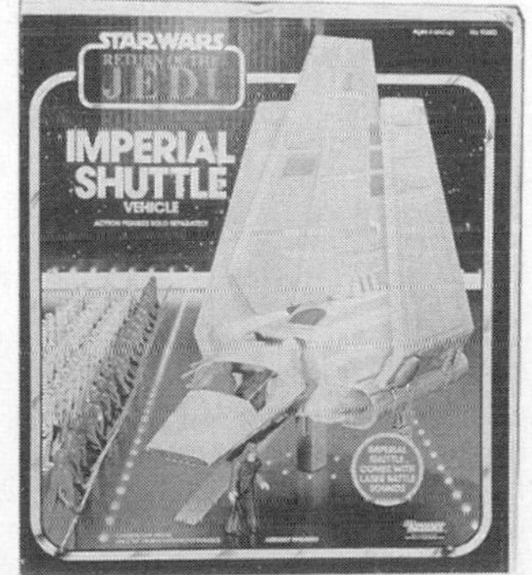

Imperial Shuttle, 1984
MNP $175 **MIP $500**

Speeder Bike, 1983
MNP $20 **MIP $65**

TIE Interceptor, 1984
MNP $42 **MIP $110**

Y-Wing Fighter, 1983
MNP $55 **MIP $160**

POTF

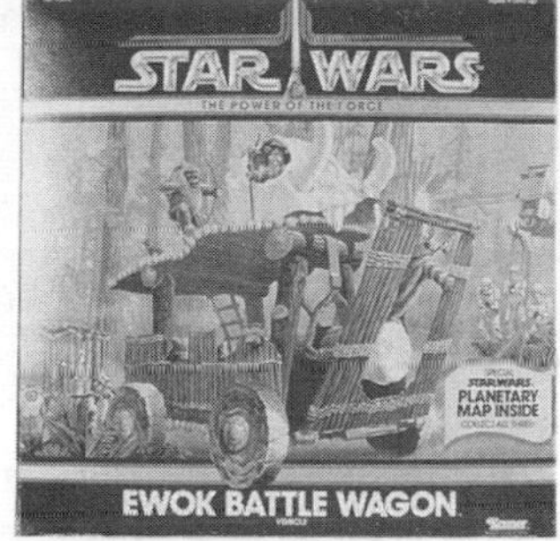

Ewok Battle Wagon, 1985
MNP $75 **MIP $190**

Imperial Sniper Vehicle, 1985
MNP $35 **MIP $55**

One-Man Sand Skimmer, 1985
MNP $20 **MIP $45**

Security Scout Vehicle, 1985
MNP $32 **MIP $75**

Tatooine Skiff, 1985
MNP $190 **MIP $440**

DROIDS

ATL Interceptor, 1985
MNP $25 **MIP $65**

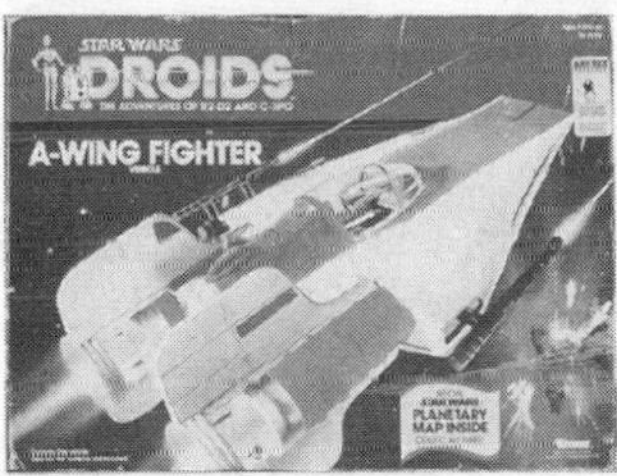

A-Wing Fighter, 1983
MNP $165 **MIP $360**

Inperial Side Gunner, 1985
MNP $14 **MIP $55**

EWOKS

Ewoks Fire Cart, 1985
MNP $6 **MIP $17**

Ewoks Woodland Wagon, 1985
MNP $7 **MIP $30**

DIE-CAST

Darth Vader's TIE Fighter, 1979
MNP $14 **MIP $50**

Land Speeder, 1979
MNP $14 **MIP $65**

Millennium Falcon, 1979
MNP $20 **MIP $105**

Naboo Starfighter, 1999
MNP $4 **MIP $10**

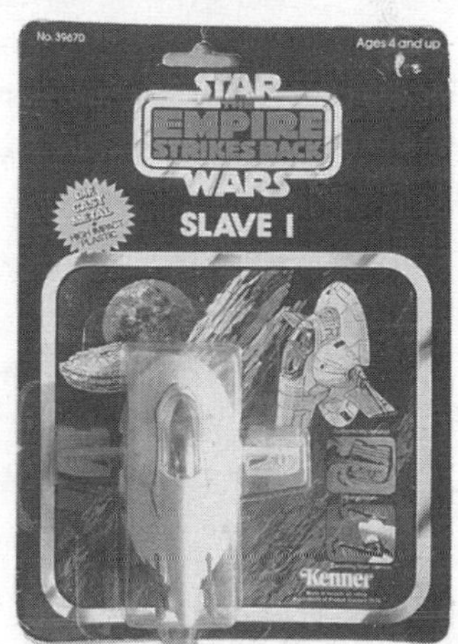

Slave I, 1979
MNP $25 **MIP $75**

Snowspeeder, 1979
MNP $17 **MIP $65**

Star Destroyer, 1979
MNP $25 **MIP $110**

TIE Bomber, 1979
MNP $150 **MIP $410**

TIE Fighter, 1979
MNP $12 **MIP $45**

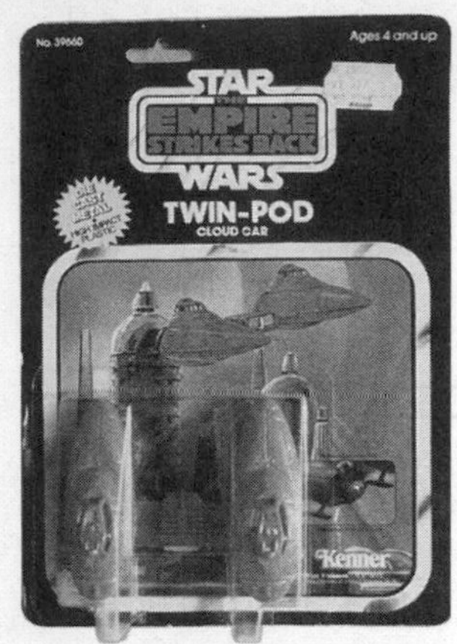

Twin-Pod Cloud Car, 1979
MNP $17 MIP $70

X-Wing Fighter, 1979
MNP $15 MIP $70

Y-Wing Fighter, 1979
MNP $22 MIP $90

POTF2

Speeder Bike, 1997, Includes Scout Trooper figure. Bike pieces and trooper fall off when "battle damage" button is pushed on bike
MNP $10 MIP $25

POTJ

B-Wing Fighter, 2001, Includes Sullustan Pilot, Target exclusive
MNP $20 MIP $50

Imperial AT-ST & Speeder Bike, 2001, TRU exclusive, Paploo figure
MNP $18 MIP $35

Luke Skywalker's Snowspeeder, 2002, Wal-Mart exclusive, Dack Ralter
MNP $20 MIP $45

Tie Bomber, 2002, Wal-Mart exclusive, Imperial Pilot figure
MNP $20 MIP $45

TIE Interceptor, 2002, Includes figure, wings pop off simulating battle damage. A Toys R Us exclusive, these toys are now exclusively found in the secondary market, doubling the price collectors pay to get their hands on one
MNP $15 MIP $45

DIE-CAST

Darth Vader's TIE Fighter, 1979
MNP $14 MIP $50

Land Speeder, 1979
MNP $14 MIP $65

Millennium Falcon, 1979
MNP $20 MIP $105

Naboo Starfighter, 1999
MNP $4 MIP $10

Slave I, 1979
MNP $25 MIP $75

Snowspeeder, 1979
MNP $17 MIP $65

Star Destroyer, 1979
MNP $25 MIP $110

TIE Bomber, 1979
MNP $150 MIP $410

TIE Fighter, 1979
MNP $12 MIP $45

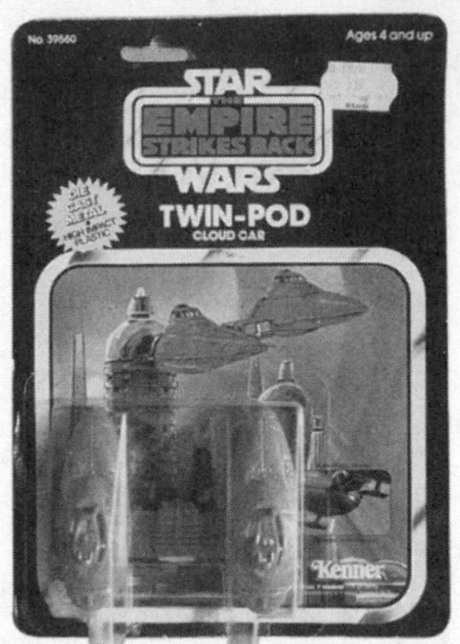

Twin-Pod Cloud Car, 1979
MNP $17 MIP $70

X-Wing Fighter, 1979
MNP $15 MIP $70

Y-Wing Fighter, 1979
MNP $22 MIP $90

THE PHANTOM MENACE
Invasion Force

Armored Scout Tank w/Battle Droid, 1999
MNP $5 MIP $25

Gungan Assault Cannon w/Jar Jar Binks, 1999
MNP $5 MIP $15

Gungan Mini-Sub w/Obi-Wan Kenobi, 1999
MNP $5 MIP $25

THE PHANTOM MENACE

Anakin Skywalker's Podracer, 1999
MNP $10 MIP $20

Flash Speeder, 1999, Hovercraft much in the style of other Star Wars speeders. Shown here with unloaded gun turret, this model actually fires a missile (a pretty fair distance, too)
MNP $5 MIP $15

Naboo Starfighter, 1999
MNP $5 MIP $25

Sebulba's Pod Racer w/Sebulba, 1999
MNP $10 MIP $25

Sith Speeder w/Darth Maul, 1999
MNP $8 MIP $25

STAP w/Battle Droid, 1999
MNP $5 MIP $15

Trade Federation Droid Fighter, 1999
MNP $5 MIP $20

Trade Federation Tank, 1999
MNP $5 MIP $30

THE PHANTOM MENACE
Wal-Mart Exclusive

Ammo Wagon and Falumpaset, 1999
MNP $5 MIP $25

SAGA

Anakin Skywalker Speeder, 2002, With blast-off panels. Apparently, Lucas made a last-minute color change to this model (for the movie) making the speeder yellow as an homage to Bob Milner's '32 Ford Coupe in the movie "American Graffiti"
MNP $3 MIP $16

Anakin Skywalker's Swoop Bike, 2003, w/Anakin figure (showing a lot of teeth)
MNP $10 MIP $20

A-Wing Fighter, 2003, Target exclusive, w/pilot
MNP $25 MIP $50

A-Wing Fighter w/Rebel Pilot, 2003, Target exclusive
MNP $10 MIP $20

Darth Tyranus' Geonosian Speeder Bike, 2003, w/Darth Tyranus figure
MNP $10 MIP $20

Imperial Dogfight Tie Fighter w/Tie Pilot, 2003, KB Toys exclusive
MNP $10 MIP $25

Imperial Shuttle, 2003, FAO Schwarz exclusive
MNP $75 MIP $125

Jango Fett's Slave I, 2002, Launches four missiles, has more vibrant color as a new ship than it does by the time Boba inherits it
MNP $10 MIP $25

Jedi Starfighter w/ Obi-Wan Kenobi, 2002, KB Toys exclusive
MNP $10 MIP $25

Jedi Starfighter, Obi-Wan Kenobi, 2002, no figure
MNP $10 MIP $25

Landspeeder, 2002, TRU exclusive
MNP $10 MIP $20

Luke Skywalker's X-Wing Fighter, 2002, TRU exclusive, R2-D2
MNP $10 MIP $25

Republic Gunship, 2002, Fits one pilot, carries troops in main body, pivoting laser cannon
MNP $10 MIP $30

Tie Bomber, 2003, w/pilot
MNP $10 MIP $25

Zam Wessell Coruscant Speeder, 2002, With flexible "crush zones" to emulate Zam's rough landing on Coruscant. A nice-looking vehicle
MNP $3 MIP $17

CLONE WARS

Anakin Skywalker's Jedi Starfighter, 2003, 1 missile, red droid
MNP $15 MIP $22

Arrmored Assault Tank (AAT), 2003, 4 missiles
MNP $15 MIP $25

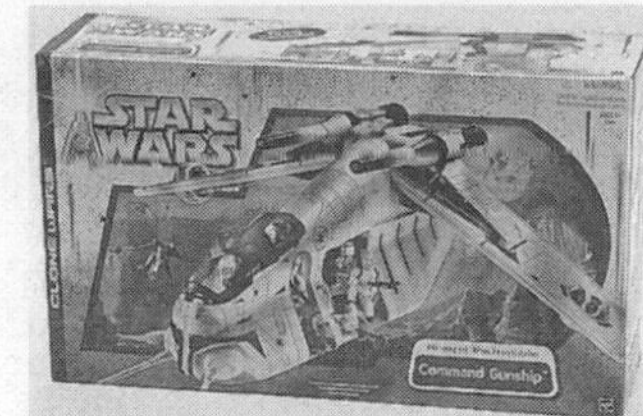

Command Gunship, 2003
MNP $15 MIP $40

Geonosian Starfighter w/pilot, 2003, exclusive Geonosian pilot, 1 missile
MNP $15 MIP $22

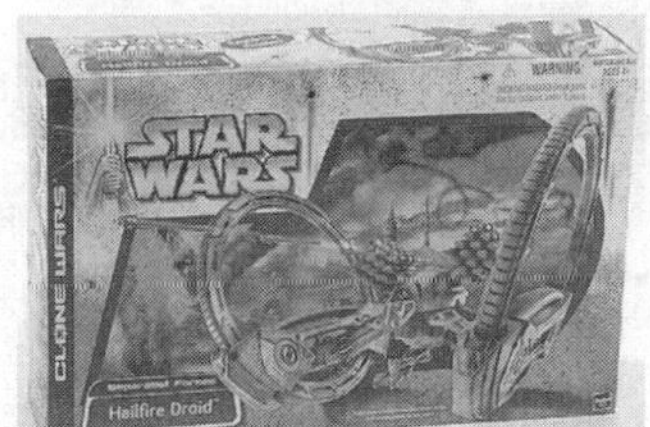

Hailfire Droid, 2003, 32 red missiles
MNP $15 MIP $22

Jedi Starfighter, 2003, blue w/yellow droid
MNP $15 MIP $22

ORIGINAL TRILOGY COLLECTION

Millennium Falcon, 2004, laser cannons w/light and sound, Hyperspace light at rear, figures pilot the ship, missile launchers, interior compartments
MNP $30 MIP $60

Slave 1, 2004, w/Boba Fett, Target Exclusive, Model No. 34512
MNP $20 MIP $40

TIE Fighter, 2004, opening cockpit, pilot fits inside, wings pop off
MNP $15 MIP $30

X-Wing Fighter, 2004, wings pop open, cockpit opens, Luke fits inside
MNP $15 MIP $30

Y-Wing Fighter, 2004, w/pilot figure, Toys 'R Us Exclusive, Model No. 34517
MNP $25 MIP $60

REVENGE OF THE SITH

Anakin's Jedi Starfighter, 2005, Sneak Preview, yellow
MNP $10 MIP $25

Anakin's Jedi Starfighter, 2005, w/Anakin Skywalker
MNP $20 MIP $45

ARC-170 Fighter, 2005, Sam's Club Exclusive; includes 4 figures, ARC Pilot, 2 Clone Troopers, droid
MNP $30 MIP $65

ARC-170 Fighter, 2005, opening wings, firing cannons
MNP $15 MIP $30

AT-RT, 2005, motorized action, w/driver
MNP $10 MIP $25

AT-RT, 2005, motorized walking action, w/driver and bonus Clone Trooper
MNP $10 MIP $25

BARC Speeder, 2005, w/BARC Trooper and bonus Wookie Warrior, Kohl's Exclusive
MNP $20 MIP $40

BARC Speeder, 2005, w/BARC Trooper, ripcord action
MNP $10 MIP $25

Droid Tri-Fighter, 2005, buzz droid drop attack
MNP $10 MIP $25

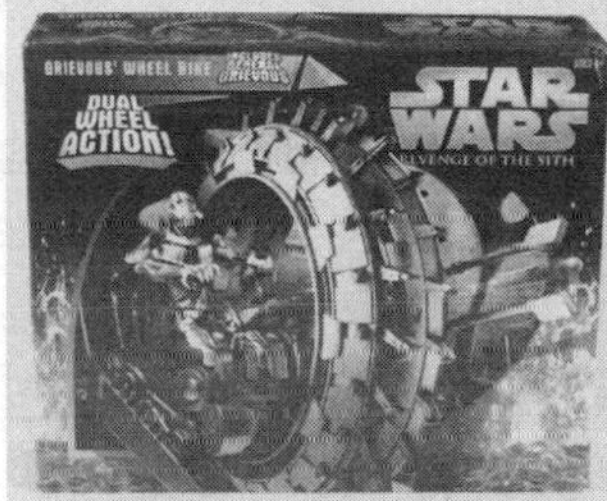

General Grievous' Wheel Bike, 2005, w/General Grievous, fires missiles
MNP $10 MIP $25

Obi-Wan Kenobi's Jedi Starfighter, 2005, firing missiles, opening wings, opening cockpit

MNP $10 MIP $25

Plo Koon's Jedi Starfighter, 2005, Target Exclusive

MNP $10 MIP $25

Republic Gunship, 2005, firing blaster cannons

MNP $20 MIP $40

Wookie Flyer, 2005, firing cannon, blades flap, w/Wookie Warrior

MNP $10 MIP $25

SAGA 2006

Anakin's Jedi Starfighter, 2006, firing blaster cannons

MNP $15 MIP $30

Darth Vader's Tie Advanced X1 Starfighter, 2006

MNP $15 MIP $30

Droid Tri-Fighter, 2006, Buzz Droid Drop Attack

MNP $15 MIP $30

Endor AT-AT, 2006, Toys 'R Us exclusive, w/AT-AT Driver and Biker Scout

MNP $25 MIP $50

Grievous' Wheel Bike, 2006, w/General Grievous

MNP $10 MIP $25

Kit Fisto's Jedi Starfighter, 2006, Target exclusive

MNP $15 MIP $25

Luke Skywalker's X-Wing, 2006, on Dagobah, covered in moss, large scale, Toys 'R Us Exclusive

MNP $30 MIP $75

Mace Windu's Jedi Starfighter, 2006, w/firing missiles, purple accents, Target exclusive

MNP $15 MIP $30

Obi-Wan's Jedi Starfighter, 2006, firing blaster cannons

MNP $15 MIP $30

Republic Gunship, 2006, Clone Wars animated version, very cool, very rare

MNP $30 MIP $60

Rogue Two Snowspeeder, 2006, w/Zev Senesca, Target exclusive

MNP $15 MIP $25

Tie Fighter w/Large Scale Wings, 2006, w/Tie Fighter Pilot, Toys 'R Us exclusive

MNP $30 MIP $65

TAC (30TH ANNIV. COL.)

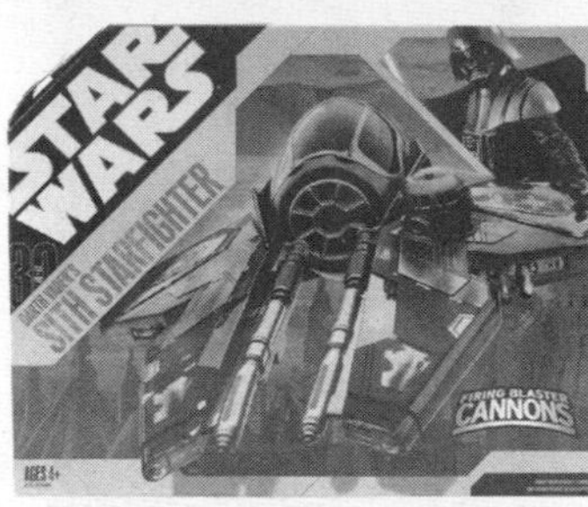

Darth Vader's Sith Starfighter, 2007, all black, opening canopy, 2 missiles

MNP $15 MIP $25

Hailfire Droid, 2007, 32 missiles, oversized wheels

MNP $10 MIP $20

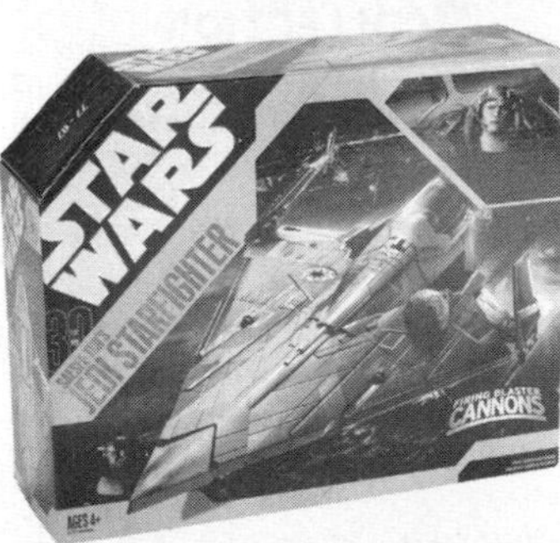

Saesee Tiin's Jedi Starfighter, 2007, opening cockpit and wings, blast panels

MNP $15 MIP $25

Tie Fighter, 2007, opening cockpit, wing panels eject

MNP $15 MIP $25

Trade Federation Armored Assault Tank (AAT), 2007, rotating turret, firing missiles

MNP $15 MIP $25

Weapons

STAR WARS
Series 1

Han Solo's Laser Pistol, 1977

MNP $35 MIP $110

Inflatable Lightsaber, 1977

MNP $25 MIP $120

Three-Position Laser Rifle, 1980

MNP $65 MIP $250

EMPIRE STRIKES BACK
Series 2

Laser Pistol, 1980

MNP $18 MIP $65

Lightsaber, red or green, 1980, red or green

MNP $30 MIP $60

RETURN OF THE JEDI
Series 3

Biker Scout's Laser Pistol, 1984

MNP $18 MIP $60

Lightsaber, red or green, red or green plastic

MNP $20 MIP $30

DROIDS
Series 5

Droids Lightsaber, 1985

MNP $85 MIP $225

SAGA

Anakin Skywalker Lightsaber, 2002

MNP $5 MIP $25

Count Dooku Lightsaber, 2002

MNP $5 MIP $25

Lightsaber, blue, 2002

MNP $3 MIP $9

Lightsaber, green, 2002

MNP $3 MIP $9

Lightsaber, purple, 2002

MNP $4 MIP $14

Lightsaber, red, 2002

MNP $4 MIP $14

Obi-Wan Kenobi Lightsaber, 2002

MNP $5 MIP $25

Tin Toys

by Karen O'Brien

Yesterday's tin creations are some of today's priciest collectible toys. Many of the metal toys produced before World War I can be considered true works of art, especially since tin toys were often painstakingly hand-painted.

The advent of chromolithography changed all that. The technology was actually developed late in the 19th century, but first applied to tin toys in the 1920s. The technique allowed multicolor illustrations to be printed on flat tin plates that were molded into toys. American manufacturers could produce these colorful toys more inexpensively than the classic European toys that had dominated to the toy market until this time.

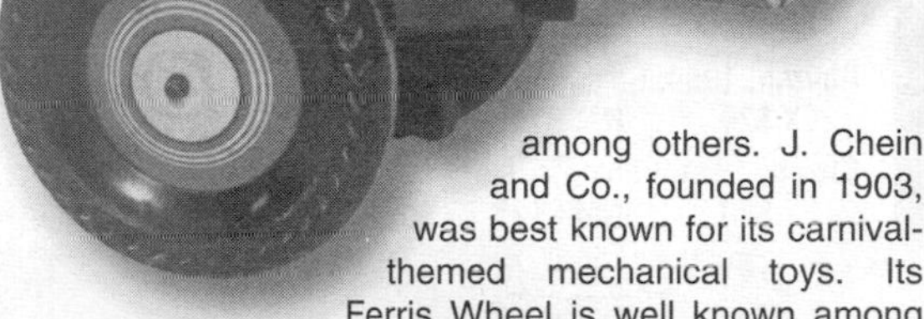

With mass production came mass appeal, and these new tin mechanical toys were often based on popular characters and celebrities. Comic strip characters and Walt Disney movies provided most of the already-popular subject matter for toy marketers.

Among the most well-known makers of mechanical tin toys were Marx, Chein, Lehmann, and Strauss. Others included Courtland, Girard, Ohio Art, Schuco, Unique Art, and Wolverine.

Many of these manufacturers had business relationships with each other. Over the years, some worked together, producing or distributing other's toys, or were absorbed by other companies. Of course, there appeared to be some occasional pilfering and reproducing of others' ideas, as well.

One of the advantages of lithography was that it allowed old toy designs to be recycled in many ways. When a character's public appeal began to wane, a new image could be printed on the same body to produce a new toy. Or when one toy company was absorbed by another, older models could be dusted off and dressed up with new lithography. Many of the mechanical tin wind-up toys show up in surprisingly similar versions bearing another manufacturer's name.

Of the companies listed here, Marx was no doubt the most prolific. The company's founder, Louis Marx, at one time was employed by another leading toymaker, Ferdinand Strauss. Eventually Marx left Strauss in 1918 to start his own company. Some of his first successes were new versions of old Strauss toys like the still reproduced and quite famous Climbing Monkey.

Many of the popular Marx tin wind-ups were also based on popular characters. Not surprisingly, some of the other highly valued character toys are the Amos 'N Andy Walkers, the Donald Duck Duet, Popeye the Champ, Li'l Abner and his Dogpatch Band, and the Superman Rollover Airplane.

While Marx went on to produce many different kinds of toys, Chein specialized in inexpensive lithographed tin. And like Marx, Chein also capitalized on popular cartoon characters, producing several Popeye toys, among others. J. Chein and Co., founded in 1903, was best known for its carnival-themed mechanical toys. Its Ferris Wheel is well known among toy collectors and was made in several lithographed versions, including one with a Disneyland theme. Chein also produced a number of affordable tin banks.

Girard was founded shortly after Chein, but didn't start producing toys until 1918. The company then subcontracted toys for Marx and Strauss in the 1920s. In fact, several Girard and Marx toys are identical, having been produced in the same plant using different names. Marx later took over Girard in the 1930s.

Unique Art, based in New Jersey, isn't known for an extensive line of toys, but it produced some items that are favorites among tin toy collectors. Unique Art was also reportedly acquired by Marx at some point.

Many other companies produced lithographed tin toys not included in this section, particularly German and Japanese companies. Lehmann and Schuco, both German firms, are the only non-American toymakers listed in this guide. More lithographed tin toys can be found in the vehicles section of this book.

Prices listed are for loose toys in Good, Excellent, and Mint conditions. Toys will usually command a premium over the listed price if they are found with their original boxes.

Contributor: Scott Smiles, 157 Yacht Club Way, Apt. 112, Hypoluxo, FL 33462, email: stsmiles@bellsouth.net, phone: (561) 582-6016

THE *TOP 10* TIN TOYS (In Mint Condition)

1. Popeye the Heavy Hitter, Chein	$6,400
2. Popeye Acrobat, Marx	5,000
3. Popeye the Champ, Marx, 1936	3,800
4. Popeye with Punching Bag, Chein	2,600
5. Popeye Express, Marx, 1936	2,500
6. Red the Iceman, Marx	2,500
7. KADI, Lehmann, 1917-27	2,400
8. Paddy and the Pig, Lehmann, 1903-35	2,300
9. Superman Holding Airplane, Marx, 1940	2,250
10. Ring-A-Ling Circus, Marx, 1925	2,250

Banks

2nd National Duck Bank, 1954, Chein, Disney characters, 3-1/2" high
EX $100 NM $155 MIP $225

Cash Box, 1930, Chein, round trap, 2" high
EX $35 NM $60 MIP $80

Child's Safe Bank, 1900s, Chein, 5-1/2" high
EX $40 NM $65 MIP $100

Child's Safe Bank, 1910, Chein, sailboat on front of door, 4" high
EX $35 NM $60 MIP $90

Child's Safe Bank, 1910, Chein, dog on front of door, 3" high
EX $45 NM $70 MIP $105

Church, 1930s, Chein, 4" high
EX $35 NM $60 MIP $90

Church, 1954, Chein, 3-1/2" high
EX $70 NM $115 MIP $175

Clown, 1931, Chein, 5" high
EX $70 NM $125 MIP $190

Clown, 1949, Chein, says bank on front, 5" high
EX $35 NM $60 MIP $100

Drum, 1930s, Chein, 2-1/2" high
EX $35 NM $60 MIP $95

Elephant, 1950s, Chein, 5" high
EX $55 NM $90 MIP $135

God Bless America, 1930s, Chein, drum shaped, 2-1/2" high
EX $35 NM $50 MIP $85

Happy Days Cash Register, 1930s, Chein, 4" high
EX $45 NM $80 MIP $120

Humpty Dumpty, 1934, Chein, 5-1/4" high
EX $75 NM $115 MIP $165

Log Cabin, 1930s, Chein, 3" high
EX $80 NM $130 MIP $200

Mascot Safe, 1914, Chein, 5" high
EX $40 NM $60 MIP $95

Mascot Safe, 1914, Chein, 4" high
EX $35 NM $55 MIP $90

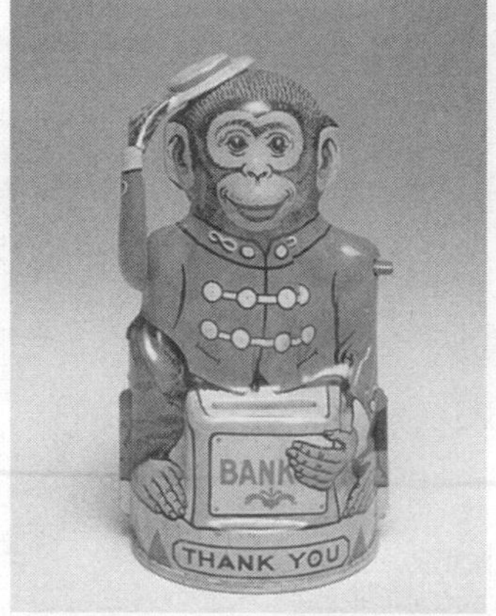

Monkey, 1950s, Chein, 5-1/4" high
EX $60 NM $90 MIP $150

New Deal, 1930s, Chein, 3-1/4" high
EX $50 NM $80 MIP $135

Prosperity Bank, 1930s, Chein, pail shaped, w/band, 2-1/4" high
EX $35 NM $65 MIP $100

Prosperity Bank, 1930s, Chein, pail shaped, without band, 2-1/4" high
EX $30 NM $60 MIP $75

Roly Poly, 1940s, Chein, 6" high
EX $150 NM $250 MIP $375

Scout, 1931, Chein, cylinder, 3-1/4" high
EX $100 NM $165 MIP $250

Three Little Pigs, 1930s, Chein, 3" high
EX $75 NM $100 MIP $150

Treasure Chest, 1930s, Chein, 2" high
EX $40 NM $60 MIP $90

Uncle Sam, 1934, Chein, hat shaped, 4" high
EX $60 NM $75 MIP $110

Uncle Wiggly, 1950s, Chein, 5" high
EX $50 NM $75 MIP $100

Buildings and Rooms

Airport, 1930s, Marx
EX $125 NM $200 MIP $325

Automatic Car Wash, Marx
EX $135 NM $225 MIP $350

Automatic Firehouse with Fire Chief Car, 1940s, Marx, friction car, firehouse w/plastic doors
EX $125 NM $200 MIP $325

Automatic Garage, Marx, family car
EX $150 NM $245 MIP $385

Blue Bird Garage, 1937, Marx
EX $150 NM $225 MIP $350

Brightlite Filling Station, 1930s, Marx, pump w/round top says "Fresh Air"
EX $250 NM $425 MIP $650

Brightlite Filling Station, 1930s, Marx, bottle-shaped gas pumps, battery-operated
EX $255 NM $425 MIP $650

Brightlite Filling Station, late 1930s, Marx, rectangular shaped pumps, battery-operated
EX $255 NM $425 MIP $675

Bus Terminal, 1937, Marx
EX $175 NM $295 MIP $450

Busy Airport Garage, 1936, Marx
EX $195 NM $325 MIP $510

Busy Parking Lot, 1937, Marx, five heavy gauge streamline autos
EX $235 NM $390 MIP $600

Busy Street, 1935, Marx, six vehicles
EX $150 NM $300 MIP $475

City Airport, 1938, Marx, w/two metal planes
EX $125 NM $200 MIP $325

Crossing Gate House, Marx
EX $125 NM $225 MIP $300

Crossover Speedway, 1938, Marx, litho buildings on bridge, two cars, litho drivers
EX $125 NM $200 MIP $300

Crossover Speedway, 1941, Marx
EX $100 NM $175 MIP $250

Dick Tracy Automatic Police Station, Marx, station and car
EX $375 NM $625 MIP $950

Gas Pump Island, Marx
EX $125 NM $200 MIP $300

General Alarm Fire House, 1938, Marx, wind-up alarm bell, steel chief car and patrol truck
EX $175 NM $295 MIP $475

Greyhound Bus Terminal, 1938, Marx
EX $125 NM $200 MIP $325

Gull Service Station, 1940s, Marx
EX $200 NM $300 MIP $475

Hollywood Bungalow House, 1935, Marx
EX $175 NM $275 MIP $425

Home Town Drug Store, 1930s, Marx
EX $175 NM $300 MIP $450

Home Town Favorite Store, 1930s, Marx
EX $175 NM $300 MIP $475

Home Town Fire House, 1930s, Marx
EX $175 NM $300 MIP $450

Home Town Grocery Store, 1930s, Marx
EX $165 NM $275 MIP $425

Home Town Meat Market, 1930s, Marx
EX $180 NM $300 MIP $465

Home Town Movie Theatre, 1930s, Marx
EX $160 NM $250 MIP $375

Home Town Police Station, 1930s, Marx
EX $150 NM $250 MIP $385

Home Town Savings Bank, 1930s, Marx
EX $150 NM $250 MIP $375

Honeymoon Garage, 1935, Marx
EX $165 NM $275 MIP $450

Lincoln Highway Set, 1933, Marx, pumps, oil-grease rack, traffic light and car
EX $350 NM $600 MIP $900

Loop-the-Loop Auto Racer, 1931, Marx, 1-3/4"
EX $150 NM $295 MIP $400

Magic Garage, 1934, Marx, w/friction town car
EX $150 NM $250 MIP $375

Magic Garage, 1934, Marx, litho garage, wind-up car
EX $150 NM $250 MIP $375

Main Street Station, Marx, litho garage, 4" wind-up steel vehicles
EX $175 NM $275 MIP $425

Metal Service Station, 1949-1950, Marx
EX $175 NM $275 MIP $450

Military Airport, Marx
EX $100 NM $180 MIP $275

Model School House, 1960s, Marx
EX $50 NM $80 MIP $125

Mot-O-Run 4 Lane Hi-Way, 1949, Marx, cars, trucks, buses move on 27" electric track
EX $100 NM $180 MIP $275

New York World's Fair Speedway, 1939, Marx, litho track, two red cars
EX $300 NM $500 MIP $750

Newlyweds' Bathroom, 1920s, Marx
EX $100 NM $165 MIP $525

Newlyweds' Bedroom, 1920s, Marx
EX $100 NM $165 MIP $500

Newlyweds' Dining Room, 1920s, Marx
EX $100 NM $165 MIP $500

Newlyweds' Kitchen, 1920s, Marx
EX $100 NM $175 MIP $500

Newlyweds' Library, 1920s, Marx
EX $100 NM $165 MIP $510

Roadside Rest Service Station, 1935, Marx, Laurel and Hardy at counter, w/stools in front
EX $625 NM $1050 MIP $1600

Roadside Rest Service Station, 1938, Marx, Laurel and Hardy at counter, no stool in front
EX $550 NM $950 MIP $1450

Service Station, 1929, Marx, two pumps, two friction vehicles
EX $300 NM $500 MIP $750

Service Station Gas Pumps, Marx, wind-up, 9"
EX $125 NM $200 MIP $350

Sky Hawk Flyer, Marx, wind-up, two planes, tower, 7-1/2" tall
EX $125 NM $200 MIP $325

Stunt Auto Racer, 1931, Marx, two blue racers
EX $135 NM $225 MIP $350

Sunnyside Garage, 1935, Marx
EX $255 NM $425 MIP $675

TV and Radio Station, Marx
EX $150 NM $225 MIP $350

Universal Motor Repair Shop, 1938, Marx, tin
EX $250 NM $425 MIP $650

Used Car Market, 1939, Marx, base, several vehicles and signs
EX $250 NM $425 MIP $650

Whee-Whiz Auto Racer, 1925, Marx, four 2" multicolored racers w/litho driver
EX $300 NM $500 MIP $750

Jack in the Boxes

Flipper, 1967, Mattel
EX $50 NM $75 MIP $135

Mother Goose, Mattel
EX $15 NM $25 MIP $35

Porky Pig, 1965, Mattel
EX $45 NM $85 MIP $150

Super Chief, 1964, Mattel
EX $50 NM $200 MIP $300

Tom & Jerry, 1966, Mattel
EX $35 NM $65 MIP $125

Woody Woodpecker, 1965, Mattel
EX $50 NM $90 MIP $150

Miscellaneous Toys

1917 Ford, Schuco
EX $50 NM $100 MIP $150

Aha Truck, 1907-1935, Lehmann, delivery van, 5-1/2"
EX $550 NM $650 MIP $850

Airplane and Pilot, 1930s, Schuco, friction toy, oversized pilot
EX $150 NM $225 MIP $300

Airplane Carousel, 1930s, Wyandotte
EX $100 NM $200 MIP $375

Ajax Acrobat, Lehmann, does somersaults, 10" tall
EX $900 NM $1400 MIP $2000

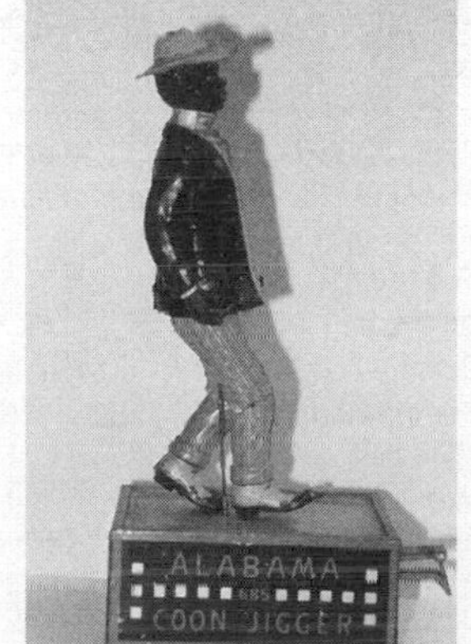

Alabama Jigger, 1920s, Lehmann, No. 685, wind-up tap dancer on square base
EX $500 NM $1000 MIP $1500

Miscellaneous Toys

Arithmetic Quiz Toy, 1950s, Wolverine, math quiz machine
EX $35 **NM** $50 **MIP** $75

Army Code Sender, Marx, pressed steel
EX $20 **NM** $35 **MIP** $50

Army Drummer, 1930s, Chein, plunger-activated, 7" high
EX $125 **NM** $200 **MIP** $250

Artie the Clown in his Crazy Car, Unique Art
EX $400 **NM** $500 **MIP** $600

Automatic Airport, 1940s, Ohio Art, two planes circle tower, 9" high
EX $100 **NM** $150 **MIP** $200

Auton Boy & Cart, Lehmann
EX $250 **NM** $350 **MIP** $450

Baby Grand Piano, Marx, w/piano-shaped music books
EX $50 **NM** $100 **MIP** $250

Battleship, 1930s, Wolverine, 14" long
EX $75 **NM** $125 **MIP** $200

Bavarian Boy, 1950s, Schuco, tin and cloth boy w/beer mug, 5" tall
EX $100 **NM** $200 **MIP** $300

Bavarian Dancing Couple, Schuco, tin and cloth, 5" high
EX $125 **NM** $175 **MIP** $250

Big Shot, Marx
EX $75 **NM** $100 **MIP** $150

Black Man, Schuco, tin and cloth, 5" high
EX $300 **NM** $450 **MIP** $600

Bombo the Monk, 1930s, Unique Art, two pieces, tree and monkey, 9-1/2" tree, 5-1/2" monkey
EX $150 **NM** $200 **MIP** $250

Capitol Hill Racer, 1930s, Unique Art, 17-1/2" long
EX $125 **NM** $175 **MIP** $225

Captain of Kopenick, early 1900s, Lehmann
EX $1000 **NM** $1500 **MIP** $2000

Carnival Set, 1930s, Wyandotte, diorama w/several rides on tin base
EX $350 **NM** $550 **MIP** $800

Casey the Cop, Unique Art
EX $500 **NM** $700 **MIP** $900

Cat Pushing Ball, 1938, Marx, lever action, wood ball
EX $75 **NM** $100 **MIP** $125

Circus Shooting Gallery, 1950s, Ohio Art, w/gun and darts, 12" high, 17" long
EX $75 **NM** $100 **MIP** $125

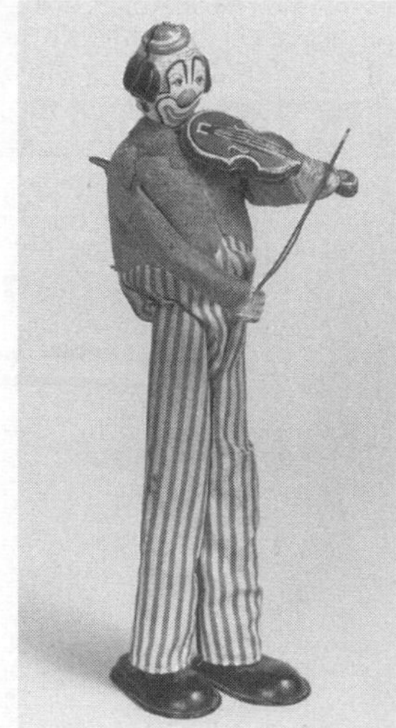

Clown Playing Violin, 1950s, Schuco, tin and cloth, 4-1/2" tall
EX $135 **NM** $200 **MIP** $250

Coast Guard Plane, 1950s, Ohio Art, 10" wingspan
EX $75 **NM** $125 **MIP** $175

Combinato Convertible, 1950s, Schuco, 7-1/2" long
EX $100 **NM** $175 **MIP** $250

Coney Island Roller Coaster, 1950s, Ohio Art
EX $125 **NM** $175 **MIP** $275

Crane, Wolverine, red and blue, 18" high
EX $50 **NM** $100 **MIP** $150

Crocodile, 1940s, Lehmann, walks, mouth opens
EX $250 **NM** $350 **MIP** $450

Curvo Motorcycle, 1950s, Schuco, 5" long
EX $150 **NM** $225 **MIP** $350

Dancing Boy and Girl, 1930s, Schuco, tin and cloth
EX $125 **NM** $200 **MIP** $275

Dancing Mice, 1950s, Schuco, large and small mouse, tin and cloth
EX $135 **NM** $225 **MIP** $350

Dancing Monkey with Mouse, 1950s, Schuco, tin and cloth
EX $125 **NM** $200 **MIP** $300

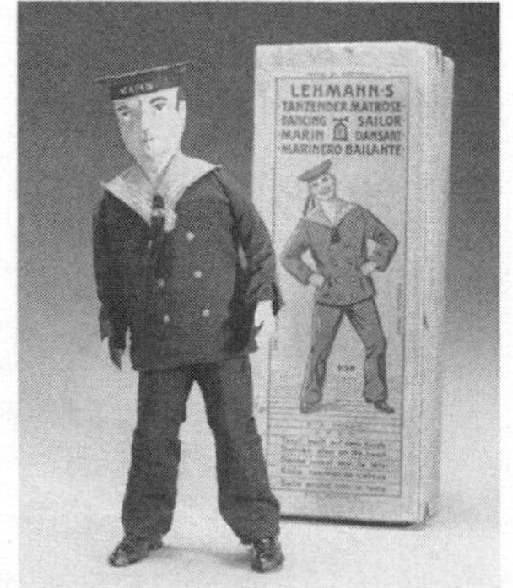

Dancing Sailor, 1904-1948, Lehmann, No. 535, 7-1/2" high
EX $700 **NM** $900 **MIP** $1100

Dandy Jim Dancer, 1921, Unique Art
EX $400 **NM** $600 **MIP** $800

Daredevil Motor Cop, 1940s, Unique Art, 8-1/2" long
EX $300 **NM** $450 **MIP** $600

Delivery Van, Lehmann, "Huntley & Palmers Biscuits"
EX $650 **NM** $950 **MIP** $1350

Disneyland Tea Set, 1954, Chein, fifteen-piece set featuring Disney characters
EX $100 **NM** $175 **MIP** $300

Doll Stroller, 1950s, Ohio Art, teddy bear design
EX $40 **NM** $60 **MIP** $80

Dolly's Washer, 1930s, Chein, washing machine
EX $65 **NM** $100 **MIP** $300

Donald Duck Carpet Sweeper, 1940s, Ohio Art, red w/Disney litho
EX $60 **NM** $100 **MIP** $250

Drum Major, Wolverine, round base, 13"
EX $100 **NM** $150 **MIP** $225

Drum Major, 1950, Wolverine, 7-1/2"
EX $125 **NM** $200 **MIP** $250

Drummer, 1930s, Schuco, tin and cloth, 5" tall
EX $125 **NM** $200 **MIP** $300

Easter Basket, Chein, nursery rhyme figures
EX $35 **NM** $55 **MIP** $100

Easter Egg, 1938, Chein, tin, chicken on top, opens to hold candy, 5-1/2"
EX $35 **NM** $55 **MIP** $85
(Don Hultzman. Photo by Ron Chojnacki)

Examico 4001 Convertible, Schuco, maroon tin wind-up, 5-1/2"
EX $175 **NM** $250 **MIP** $375

Express Bus, Wolverine
EX $125 **NM** $210 **MIP** $325

Express Porter, 1888-1918, Lehmann, No. 140, porter pulls striped cart, 6" long
EX $450 **NM** $650 **MIP** $750

Finnegan the Porter, 1930s, Unique Art, w/cardboard luggage, 14" long
EX $200 **NM** $300 **MIP** $400

Flic 4520, Schuco, traffic cop-type figure
EX $135 **NM** $200 **MIP** $300

Flying Bird, Lehmann
EX $300 **NM** $475 **MIP** $600

Flying Circus, Unique Art, elephant supports plane and clown
EX $350 **NM** $500 **MIP** $625

Fox And Goose, 1950s, Schuco, tin and cloth, fox holding goose in cage, 4-1/4" high
EX $800 **NM** $1200 **MIP** $1600

(Scott Smiles. Photo by Mike Adams)

G.I. Joe and His Jouncing Jeep, 1940s, Unique Art, wind-up, 7"
EX $175 **NM** $225 **MIP** $275

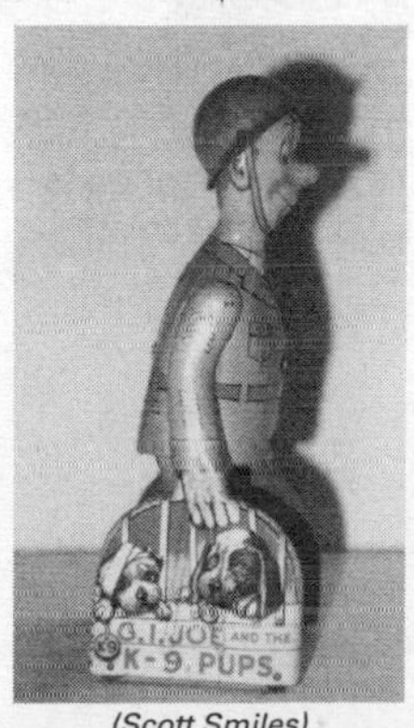

(Scott Smiles)

G.I. Joe and His K-9 Pups, 1940s, Unique Art
EX $150 **NM** $200 **MIP** $250

Galop Race Car, 1920s, Lehmann
EX $250 **NM** $400 **MIP** $600

Gertie the Galloping Goose, 1930s, Unique Art, 9-1/2" long
EX $125 **NM** $175 **MIP** $225

Gustav The Climbing Miller, Lehmann
EX $350 **NM** $450 **MIP** $600

Hee Haw, Unique Art, donkey pulling milk cart, 10" long
EX $175 **NM** $250 **MIP** $325

Helicopter, Toy Town Airways, 1950s, Chein, friction drive, 13" long
EX $75 **NM** $100 **MIP** $125

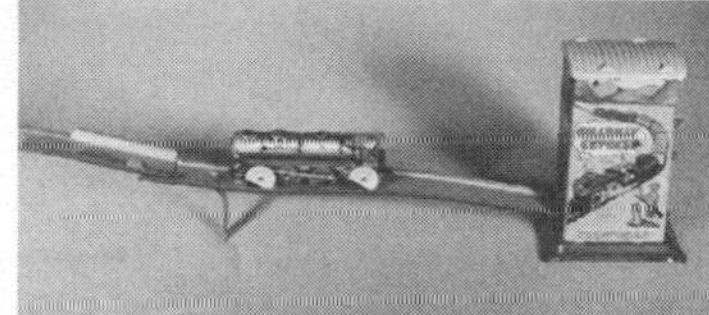

Hillbilly Express, 1930s, Unique Art, 18" long
EX $100 **NM** $150 **MIP** $200

Hobo Train, 1920s, Unique Art, dog biting pants of hobo atop train, 8-1/2"
EX $325 **NM** $450 **MIP** $600

(Scott Smiles)

Hoky Poky, 1930s, Wyandotte, clowns on railcar
EX $200 **NM** $250 **MIP** $300

Hopping Rabbit, 1950s, Marx, metal and plastic, 4" tall
EX $45 **NM** $65 **MIP** $95

Hott and Trott Musical Band, 1920s, Unique Art
EX $500 **NM** $750 **MIP** $1000

Indian in Headdress, 1930s, Chein, 5-1/2" high
EX $100 **NM** $125 **MIP** $175

Ito Sedan and Driver, 1914-1935, Lehmann, No. 679, 6-1/2"
EX $750 **NM** $900 **MIP** $1100

(Bill Bertoia Auctions)

Jazzbo Jim-The Dancer on the Roof, 1920s, Unique Art, 10" high
EX $350 **NM** $500 **MIP** $650

Jet Roller Coaster, Wolverine, 21" long
EX $200 **NM** $250 **MIP** $300

Juggling Clown, Schuco, tin and cloth, 4-1/2" tall
EX $150 **NM** $225 **MIP** $350

Jumping Frog, Marx
EX $40 **NM** $65 **MIP** $100

Jungle Eyes Shooting Gallery, 1950s, Ohio Art, w/gun and darts, 14" high, 18" long
EX $90 **NM** $135 **MIP** $180

Jungle Man Spear, Marx
EX $100 **NM** $150 **MIP** $200

(Bill Bertoia Auctions)

KADI, 1917-1927, Lehmann, No. 723, Chinese men carrying box
EX $1000 **NM** $1700 **MIP** $2400

Kiddy Go-Round, Unique Art
EX $175 **NM** $250 **MIP** $375

Kid-Go-Round, Unique Art, plastic horsemen and boat
EX $150 **NM** $225 **MIP** $300

King Kong, Marx, on wheels, w/spring-loaded arms, 6-1/2" tall
EX $50 **NM** $100 **MIP** $125

Krazy Kar, 1921, Unique Art
EX $275 **NM** $400 **MIP** $525

Lehmann's Autobus, 1907-1945, Lehmann, No. 590
EX $1200 **NM** $1800 **MIP** $2750

(Scott Smiles)

Li'l Abner and His Dogpatch Band, Unique Art
EX $425 NM $675 MIP $950

Li-La Car, 1903-1935, Lehmann, No. 520, driver in rear, women passengers, 5-1/2"
EX $1000 NM $1500 MIP $2000

Lincoln Tunnel, 1935, Unique Art, 24" long
EX $200 NM $275 MIP $350

Little Red Riding Hood Tea Set, 1920s, Ohio Art, seven-piece set
EX $100 NM $200 MIP $350

Marine, 1950s, Chein, hand on belt, 6" high
EX $125 NM $150 MIP $175

Mauswagen, Schuco, tin and cloth mice and wagon
EX $200 NM $325 MIP $500

Melody Organ Player, Chein
EX $75 NM $125 MIP $175

Mercer Car No. 1225, 1950s, Schuco, 7-1/2" long
EX $100 NM $150 MIP $225

Merry-Go-Round, 1930s, Wolverine, No. 31, 11" diameter, 12" high
EX $200 NM $300 MIP $400

Mexican Boy Tea Set, 1940s, Ohio Art, nine-piece set
EX $75 NM $100 MIP $200

Mickey & Minnie Dancing, Schuco, tin and cloth
EX $700 NM $1200 MIP $1800

Mickey Mouse Tray, 1930s, Ohio Art
EX $50 NM $100 MIP $200

Mikado Family, 1894-1918, Lehmann, No. 350, 6-1/2"
EX $800 NM $1200 MIP $1600

Minstrel Man, early 1900s, Lehmann
EX $400 NM $600 MIP $1000

Model Shooting Gallery, 1930s, Wyandotte
EX $100 NM $200 MIP $300

Monk Drinking Beer, Schuco, tin and cloth, 5" high
EX $125 NM $200 MIP $300

Monkey Drummer, 1950s, Schuco, tin and cloth
EX $125 NM $200 MIP $300

Monkey in Car, 1930s, Schuco
EX $335 NM $550 MIP $850

Monkey on Scooter, 1930s, Schuco, tin and cloth
EX $125 NM $200 MIP $300

Monkey Playing Violin, 1950s, Schuco, tin and cloth
EX $125 NM $225 MIP $325

Mother Duck with Baby Ducks, 1950s, Wyandotte, two baby ducks on wheels pulled behind mother ducks
EX $50 NM $100 MIP $125

Mother Goose Tea Set, 1931, Ohio Art, seven-piece set
EX $90 NM $150 MIP $250

Musical Sail-Way Carousel, Unique Art, three kids spin in plastic boats, 9" tall
EX $175 NM $250 MIP $350

Musical Top Clown, 1950s, Chein, clown head handle, 7" high
EX $75 NM $125 MIP $195

Mysterious Woodpecker, Marx
EX $50 NM $75 MIP $100

Mystery Car, Wolverine
EX $100 NM $175 MIP $250

(Scott Smiles)

Mystic Motorcycle Cop, 1930s, Unique Art, 9" long
EX $200 NM $300 MIP $400

New Century Cycle, 1895-1938, Lehmann, No. 345, driver and black man w/umbrella, 5"
EX $750 NM $1000 MIP $1450

Ostrich Cart, Lehmann
EX $350 NM $600 MIP $825

Paddy and the Pig, 1903-1935, Lehmann, No. 500, 6"
EX $1300 NM $1800 MIP $2300

Pathe Movie Camera, 1930s, Marx, 6" tall
EX $75 NM $100 MIP $125

Pecking Goose, Witch and Cat, Unique Art
EX $350 NM $525 MIP $700

Player Piano, Chein, eight rolls
EX $195 NM $325 MIP $500

Quack Quack, Lehmann, duck pulling babies
EX $325 NM $425 MIP $525

Rabbit in shirt and pants, 1938, Chein, red pants, yellow feet, hands in pockets
EX $50 NM $75 MIP $95

Rodeo Joe Crazy Car, 1950s, Unique Art
EX $200 NM $250 MIP $300

Rollover Motorcycle Cop, 1935, Unique Art
EX $300 NM $400 MIP $500

Rooster and Rabbit, 1900s, Lehmann, No. 570, rooster pulls rabbit on cart. Early version w/flywheel later version w/windup motor, 7-1/2"
EX $350 NM $550 MIP $750

Rooster Pulling Wagon, 1930s, Marx
EX $60 NM $90 MIP $120

Sand Toy, Chein, monkey bends and twists, 7" high
EX $30 NM $50 MIP $75

Sand Toy Set, Chein, duck mold, sifter, frog on card
EX $35 NM $50 MIP $75

Sandy Andy Fullback, Wolverine, kicking fullback, 8" tall
EX $200 NM $250 MIP $300

Schuco Turn Monkey on Suitcase, 1950s, Schuco, tin and cloth
EX $125 NM $195 MIP $300

Scuba Diver, Chein, 10" long
EX $75 NM $125 MIP $175

Sea Lion, Lehmann
EX $200 NM $400 MIP $600

Searchlight, Marx, 3-1/2" tall
EX $40 NM $65 MIP $100

Sedan and Garage, Lehmann
EX $375 NM $575 MIP $775

See-Saw Sand Toy, 1930s, Chein, bright colors, boy and girl on see-saw move
EX $75 NM $100 MIP $150

See-Saw Sand Toy, 1930s, Chein, pastel colors, boy and girl on see-saw move
EX $85 **NM** $125 **MIP** $185

Shenandoah Zeppelin, Lehmann
EX $200 **NM** $300 **MIP** $400

Skier, 1920s, Lehmann, wind-up
EX $500 **NM** $850 **MIP** $1200

Sky Rangers, Unique Art, plane and zepplin
EX $325 **NM** $425 **MIP** $575

Snow White Stove, 1960s, Wolverine
EX $35 **NM** $55 **MIP** $75

Space Ride, 1940s, Chein, tin litho, boxed, lever action w/music, 9" high
EX $425 **NM** $650 **MIP** $850

Sparkler Toy, Chein, on original card, 5"
EX $30 **NM** $50 **MIP** $75

Studio No. 1050 Race Car, 1950s, Schuco, 5-1/2" long
EX $125 **NM** $200 **MIP** $250

Submarine, Wolverine, 13" long
EX $100 **NM** $175 **MIP** $250

Sunny and Tank, Wolverine, yellow and green, 14-1/2" long
EX $75 **NM** $130 **MIP** $200

Sunny Suzy Deluxe Washing Machine, 1930s, Wolverine
EX $50 **NM** $95 **MIP** $200

Taxi, 1920s, Lehmann, 10" long
EX $450 **NM** $750 **MIP** $1050

Ten Little Indians Spinning Top, Ohio Art
EX $15 **NM** $25 **MIP** $35

Three Little Pigs Spinning Top, Ohio Art
EX $20 **NM** $40 **MIP** $55

Three Little Pigs Wind-Up Toy, 1930s, Schuco, 4-1/2" pigs playing fiddle, fife and drum
EX $325 **NM** $575 **MIP** $825

Toto the Acrobat, Marx
EX $100 **NM** $150 **MIP** $200

Trapeze Artist, 1930s, Wyandotte
EX $125 **NM** $200 **MIP** $325

Tumbling Boy, 1950s, Schuco, tin and cloth
EX $100 **NM** $165 **MIP** $250

Tut-Tut Car, 1903-1935, Lehmann, No. 490, driver has horn, 6-3/4" long
EX $1200 **NM** $1600 **MIP** $2100

Watering Cans, Ohio Art, many variations, value is for each
EX $25 **NM** $30 **MIP** $40

Wild West Bucking Bronco, Lehmann
EX $850 **NM** $1200 **MIP** $1700

Yellow Taxi, 1940s, Wolverine, 13" long
EX $150 **NM** $225 **MIP** $300

Yes-No Monkey, Schuco
EX $175 **NM** $275 **MIP** $425

Zebra Cart "Dare Devil", 1920s, Lehmann
EX $400 **NM** $550 **MIP** $725

Zig-Zag, 1910-1945, Lehmann, handcar-type vehicle on oversized wheels, 5" long
EX $1100 **NM** $1600 **MIP** $2100

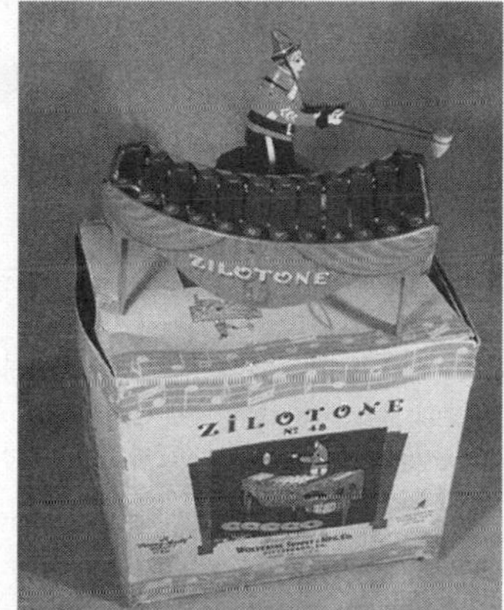

Zilotone, 1920s, Wolverine, clown on xylophone, w/three musical discs
EX $650 **NM** $900 **MIP** $1250

Musical Toys

Hickory Dickory Dock Clock, Mattel, crank; mouse climbs clock
EX $50 **NM** $75 **MIP** $100

Man on the Flying Trapeze, Mattel, tin base, two metal rods holding trapeze man on top
EX $75 **NM** $100 **MIP** $145

Sing a Song of Sixpence, Mattel, pie-shaped tin music box
EX $20 **NM** $35 **MIP** $65

Trains

Commodore Vanderbilt Train, Marx, track, wind-up
EX $75 **NM** $125 **MIP** $190

Crazy Express Train, 1960s, Marx, plastic and litho, wind-up, 12" long
EX $115 **NM** $195 **MIP** $300

Disneyland Express, 1950s, Marx, locomotive and three tin cars, wind-up, 21-1/2" long
EX $255 **NM** $425 **MIP** $650

Disneyland Express, Casey Jr. Circus Train, Marx, wind-up, 12" long
EX $100 **NM** $165 **MIP** $250

Disneyland Train, 1950, Marx, Goofy drives locomotive w/three tin cars, wind-up
EX $135 **NM** $225 **MIP** $350

Engine Train, 1960s, Marx, ten cars, no track, HO-scale
EX $65 **NM** $110 **MIP** $170

Flintstones Choo Choo Train "Bedrock Express", 1960s, Marx, wind-up, 13" long
EX $250 **NM** $400 **MIP** $600

Glendale Depot Railroad Station Train, 1930s, Marx
EX $235 **NM** $390 **MIP** $600

Mickey Mouse Express Train Set, 1952, Marx
EX $250 **NM** $400 **MIP** $850

Mickey Mouse Meteor Train, 1950s, Marx, four cars/engine, wind-up
EX $255 **NM** $425 **MIP** $650

Musical Choo-Choo, 1966, Marx
EX $75 **NM** $100 **MIP** $125

Mystery Tunnel, Marx, wind-up
EX $90 **NM** $145 **MIP** $225

New York Central Engine Train, Marx, four cars
EX $200 **NM** $325 **MIP** $500

New York Circular with Train, with airplane, 1928, Marx, wind-up, 9-1/2"
EX $600 **NM** $900 **MIP** $1250

Popeye Express, 1936, Marx, version of Honeymoon Express, w/airplane
EX $950 **NM** $1550 **MIP** $2500

Railroad Watch Tower, Marx, electric light, 9" tall
EX $35 **NM** $60 **MIP** $90

Scenic Express Train Set, 1950s, Marx, wind-up
EX $100 **NM** $150 **MIP** $200

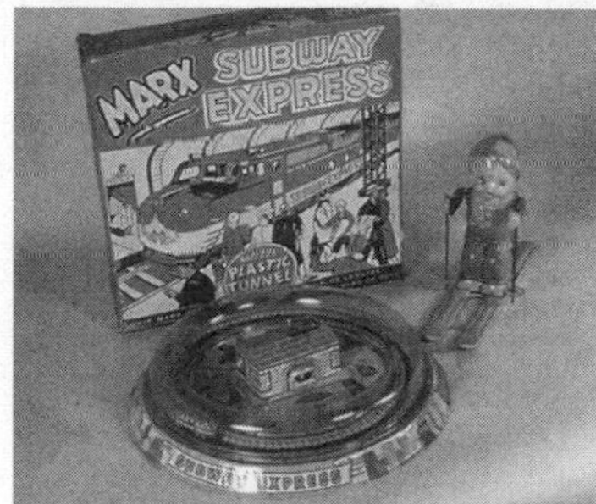

Subway Express, 1954, Marx, w/plastic tunnel, 9-3/8"
EX $135 **NM** $185 **MIP** $235

Train Set, 1950s, Marx, plastic locomotive, tin cars, wind-up, 6" long
EX $60 **NM** $100 **MIP** $150

Trolley No. 200, 1920s, Marx, headlight, bell, tin wind-up, 9" long
EX $195 **NM** $325 **MIP** $500

Wagons and Carts

Busy Delivery, 1939, Marx, open three-wheel cart, wind-up, 9" long
EX $325 **NM** $475 **MIP** $600

Farm Wagon, 1940s, Marx, horse pulling wagon, 10" long
EX $75 **NM** $100 **MIP** $150

Horse and Cart, 1934, Marx, wind-up, 7" long
EX $75 **NM** $125 **MIP** $175

Horse and Cart, 1950s, Marx, w/driver, 9-1/2" long
EX $125 **NM** $150 **MIP** $175

Horse and Cart with Clown Driver, 1923, Marx, wind-up, 7-5/8" long
EX $150 **NM** $225 **MIP** $325

Wagons and Carts

Pinocchio Busy Delivery, 1939, Marx, on unicycle facing two-wheel cart, wind-up, 7-3/4" long
EX $250 **NM** $425 **MIP** $550

Popeye Horse and Cart, Marx, wind-up
EX $325 **NM** $525 **MIP** $825

Rooster Pulling Wagon, 1930s, Marx
EX $150 **NM** $225 **MIP** $350

Toyland's Farm Products Milk Wagon, 1930s, Marx, wind-up, 10-1/2" long
EX $175 **NM** $225 **MIP** $275

Two Donkeys Pulling Cart, 1940s, Marx, w/driver, wind-up, 10-1/4" long
EX $150 **NM** $225 **MIP** $325

Wagon with Two-Horse Team, late 1940s, Marx, wind-up
EX $100 **NM** $150 **MIP** $200

Wind-up Toys

(Don Hultzman)

Acrobatic Marvel Monkey, 1930s, Marx, balances on two chairs
EX $100 **NM** $150 **MIP** $225

Airplane, square-winged, Chein, early tin, 7" wingspan
EX $100 **NM** $150 **MIP** $225

Amos 'n Andy Fresh Air Taxi, 1930s, Marx, 5" x 8" long
EX $500 **NM** $800 **MIP** $1250

Amos 'n Andy Walkers, 1930, Marx, values are for each, 11" tall
EX $600 **NM** $900 **MIP** $1200

Army Cargo Truck, 1920s, Chein, 8" long
EX $235 **NM** $390 **MIP** $600

Army Plane, Chein, 11" wingspan
EX $135 **NM** $230 **MIP** $350

Army Sergeant, Chein
EX $75 **NM** $125 **MIP** $175

Army Truck, Chein, open bed, 8-1/2" long
EX $50 **NM** $75 **MIP** $100

Army Truck, Chein, cannon on back, 8-1/2" long
EX $50 **NM** $80 **MIP** $125

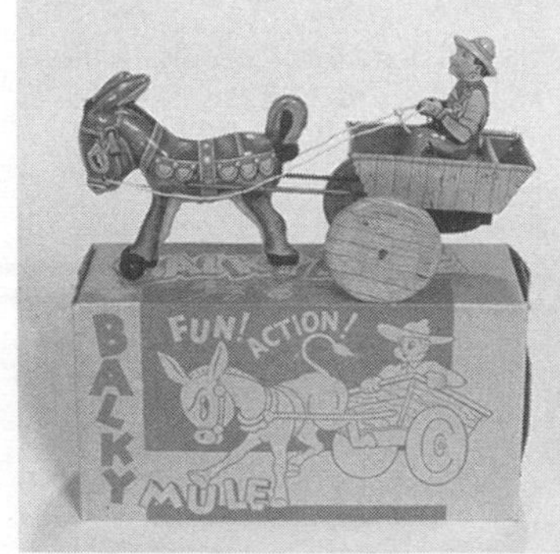

(Scott Smiles. Photo by Mike Adams)

Balky Mule, 1948, Marx, 8-3/4" long
EX $175 **NM** $225 **MIP** $275

Ballerina, Marx, 6" tall
EX $100 **NM** $150 **MIP** $225

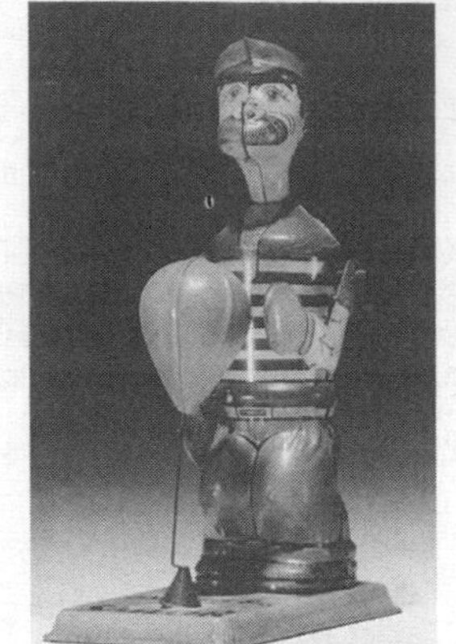
(Christie's East)

Barnacle Bill, 1930s, Chein, looks like Popeye, waddles
EX $325 **NM** $425 **MIP** $525

Barney Rubble Riding Dino, 1960s, Marx, 8" long
EX $175 **NM** $250 **MIP** $400

(Scott Smiles)

Bear, 1938, Chein, w/hat, pants, shirt, bow tie
EX $50 **NM** $75 **MIP** $125

Bear Cyclist, 1934, Marx, 5-3/4" tall
EX $175 **NM** $250 **MIP** $325

Bear Waddler, 1960s, Marx, 4" tall
EX $50 **NM** $80 **MIP** $125

Beat It! The Komikal Kop, 1930s, Marx
EX $425 **NM** $525 **MIP** $625

Big Parade, 1928, Marx, 24" long
EX $275 **NM** $375 **MIP** $475

Big Three Aerial Acrobats, 1920, Marx
EX $200 **NM** $300 **MIP** $400

Bimbo Clown, Irwin, colorful outfit, umbrella
EX $50 **NM** $100 **MIP** $150

Blacksmith Teddy, TN, black fur, hammer and anvil
EX $30 **NM** $60 **MIP** $90

Boxing Monkey, MM, brown fur, red punching bag, blue trunks
EX $50 **NM** $75 **MIP** $100

Boy on Trapeze, Marx
EX $100 **NM** $125 **MIP** $175

Bunny, 1940s, Chein
EX $50 **NM** $75 **MIP** $100

Busy Bridge, 1937, Marx, vehicles on bridge, 24" long
EX $325 **NM** $425 **MIP** $500

Busy Miners, 1930s, Marx, with miner's car, 16-1/2" long
EX $175 **NM** $250 **MIP** $325

(Scott Smiles)

Butter and Egg Man, 1930s, Marx, wind-up walker, 8" tall
EX $450 **NM** $650 **MIP** $850

Cabin Cruiser, 1940s, Chein, 9" long
EX $65 **NM** $95 **MIP** $85

Captain America Wind-up Toy, 1968, Marx, tin, 5" tall
EX $55 **NM** $90 **MIP** $140

Carter Climbing Monkey, 1921, Marx, 8-1/2" tall
EX $100 **NM** $175 **MIP** $225

Cat, Chein, w/wood wheels
EX $75 **NM** $100 **MIP** $150

Charleston Trio, 1926, Marx, man, boy and dog dancers on roof, 9" tall
EX $550 **NM** $750 **MIP** $950

Charlie McCarthy Bass Drummer, 1939, Marx
EX $400 **NM** $700 **MIP** $1000

Charlie McCarthy Walker, 1930s, Marx
EX $350 **NM** $550 **MIP** $700

Chick, Chein, bright colored clothes, polka dot bow tie, 4" high
EX $50 **NM** $75 **MIP** $100

Chicken Pushing Wheelbarrow, 1930s, Chein
EX $50 **NM** $75 **MIP** $100

China Clipper, Chein, 10" long
EX $150 **NM** $250 **MIP** $350

Chipmunk, Marx
EX $50 **NM** $75 **MIP** $125

Chompy the Beetle, 1960s, Marx, w/action and sound, 6" tall
EX $60 **NM** $100 **MIP** $150

Clancy, 1931, Marx, walker, 11" tall
EX $195 **NM** $325 **MIP** $500

Climbing Fireman, 1950s, Marx, tin and plastic
EX $125 **NM** $175 **MIP** $250

Clown Boxing, Chein, 8" tall
EX $325 **NM** $500 **MIP** $600

Clown in Barrel, 1930s, Chein, waddles, 8" high
EX $250 **NM** $375 **MIP** $500

Clown with Parasol, 1920s, Chein, 8" tall
EX $100 **NM** $175 **MIP** $275

Coast Defense Revolving Airplane, 1929, Marx, circular w/three cannons
EX $500 **NM** $750 **MIP** $1000

Cowboy on Horse, 1925, Marx, 6" tall
EX $75 **NM** $125 **MIP** $175

Cowboy Rider, 1930s, Marx, black horse version, 7"
EX $175 **NM** $275 **MIP** $350

Cowboy Rider, 1941, Marx, w/lariat on black horse
EX $175 **NM** $250 **MIP** $350

Crazy Dora, Marx
EX $100 **NM** $150 **MIP** $200

Dan-Dee Dump Truck, Chein
EX $175 **NM** $300 **MIP** $375

Dapper Dan Coon Jigger, 1922, Marx, 10" tall
EX $500 **NM** $750 **MIP** $1000

Dippy Dumper, Marx
EX $135 **NM** $225 **MIP** $350

Disneyland Ferris Wheel, 1940s, Chein
EX $450 **NM** $650 **MIP** $850

(Scott Smiles)

Disneyland Roller Coaster, 1950s, Chein
EX $375 **NM** $575 **MIP** $750

Donald Duck and Scooter, 1960s, Marx
EX $100 **NM** $150 **MIP** $225

Donald Duck Duet, 1946, Marx, Donald and Goofy, 10-1/2" tall
EX $475 **NM** $650 **MIP** $850

Donald Duck Walker, Marx, w/three nephews
EX $100 **NM** $175 **MIP** $250

Donald the Skier, 1940s, Marx, plastic, metal skis, 10-1/2" tall
EX $175 **NM** $275 **MIP** $425

Dopey, 1938, Marx, walker, 8" tall
EX $300 **NM** $525 **MIP** $950

Doughboy, 1920s, Chein, tin litho, WWI soldier w/rifle, 6" high
EX $175 **NM** $275 **MIP** $375

Doughboy Walker, Marx
EX $225 **NM** $350 **MIP** $500

Drummer Boy, 1930s, Chein, w/shako, 9" high
EX $125 **NM** $175 **MIP** $225

Drummer Boy, 1939, Marx
EX $275 **NM** $375 **MIP** $650

Duck, 1930, Chein, waddles, 4" high
EX $75 **NM** $100 **MIP** $125

Duck, 1930, Chein, waddles, 6" high
EX $125 NM $175 MIP $225

Dumbo, 1941, Marx, flip-over action, 4" tall
EX $200 NM $275 MIP $400

Easter Rabbit, Marx, holds Easter basket, 5" tall
EX $75 NM $125 MIP $175

(Scott Smiles)

Ferris Wheel, 1930s, Chein, six compartments, ringing bell, 16-1/2" high
EX $225 NM $325 MIP $425

Ferris Wheel, The Giant Ride, Chein, 16" high
EX $100 NM $250 MIP $375

Figaro (Pinocchio), 1940, Marx, rollover action, 5" long
EX $150 NM $225 MIP $325

Fireman on Ladder, Marx, 24" tall
EX $200 NM $300 MIP $375

Flipo the Jumping Dog, 1940, Marx, 3" tall
EX $100 NM $150 MIP $200

Flipping Monkey, Marx
EX $100 NM $150 MIP $200

Flutterfly, 1929, Marx, 3" long
EX $90 NM $145 MIP $225

(Scott Smiles)

George the Drummer Boy, 1930s, Marx, stationary eyes, 9" tall
EX $125 NM $175 MIP $250

George the Drummer Boy, 1930s, Marx, moving eyes, 9" tall
EX $175 NM $225 MIP $300

Gobbling Goose, 1940s, Marx, lays golden eggs
EX $125 NM $200 MIP $275

Golden Goose, 1929, Marx, 9-1/2" long
EX $100 NM $125 MIP $175

Goofy, 1950s, Marx, tail spins, plastic, 9" tall
EX $125 NM $200 MIP $300

Goofy the Walking Gardener, 1960, Marx, holds a wheelbarrow, 9" tall
EX $250 NM $350 MIP $525

Greyhound Bus, Chein, wood tires, 6" long
EX $100 NM $150 MIP $200

(Scott Smiles)

Handstand Clown, 1930s, Chein, 5" tall
EX $75 NM $125 MIP $175

Handstand Clown, 1940s, Chein, 6"
EX $50 NM $100 MIP $125

Hap/Hop Ramp Walker, 1950s, Marx, 2-1/2" tall
EX $40 NM $65 MIP $100

Happy Hooligan, 1932, Chein, tin litho, 6" high
EX $225 NM $325 MIP $475

Harold Lloyd Funny Face, 1928, Marx, walker, 11" tall
EX $275 NM $475 MIP $600

Hercules Ferris Wheel, Chein
EX $150 NM $250 MIP $350

Hey Hey the Chicken Snatcher, 1926, Marx, black man w/chicken and dog biting seat of his pants, 8-1/2"
EX $900 NM $1300 MIP $1700

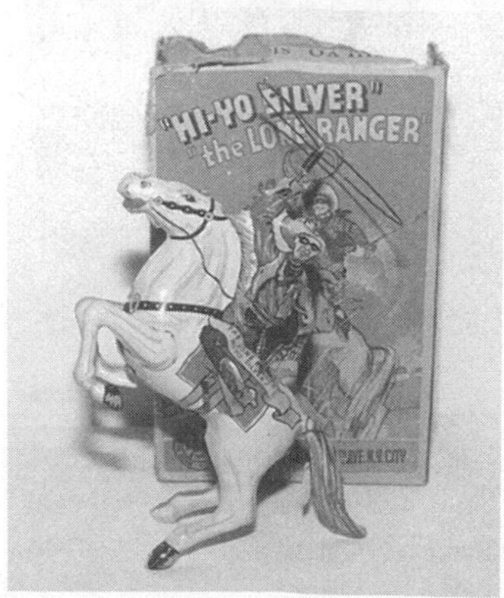

Hi-Yo Silver and the Lone Ranger, 1938, Marx, 8" tall
EX $200 NM $350 MIP $475

Honeymoon Cottage, Honeymoon Express 7, 1950s, Marx, square base
EX $100 **NM** $150 **MIP** $200

Honeymoon Express, 1927, Marx, old-fashioned train on circular track
EX $150 **NM** $200 **MIP** $250

Honeymoon Express, 1937, Marx, circular train and plane, 9-3/8"
EX $125 **NM** $175 **MIP** $200

(Continental Hobby House)

Honeymoon Express, 1948, Marx, streamlined train on circular track, 9-3/8"
EX $100 **NM** $150 **MIP** $200

Hop-A-Long Cassidy Rocker, 1950s, Marx
EX $125 **NM** $175 **MIP** $325

Hoppo the Waltzing Monkey, 1925, Marx, plays cymbals, 9-1/2"
EX $200 **NM** $275 **MIP** $350

Howdy Doody, 1950, Marx, plays banjo and moves head, 5" tall
EX $250 **NM** $425 **MIP** $650

(Scott Smiles)

Howdy Doody Band, 1950, Marx, does jig and Bob Smith sits at piano, 5-1/2" tall
EX $850 **NM** $1200 **MIP** $1650

(Scott Smiles)

Indian in Headdress, 1930s, Chein, red, 4" high
EX $75 **NM** $125 **MIP** $175

Jazzbo Jim, 1920s, Marx, 9" tall
EX $250 **NM** $400 **MIP** $600

Jetsons Figure, 1960s, Marx, 4" tall
EX $100 **NM** $175 **MIP** $225

Jiminy Cricket Pushing Bass Fiddle, Marx, walker
EX $100 **NM** $175 **MIP** $225

Jiving Jigger, 1950, Marx
EX $150 **NM** $225 **MIP** $325

(Scott Smiles)

Joe Penner and His Duck Goo-Goo, 1934, Marx, 7-1/2" tall
EX $375 **NM** $475 **MIP** $575

Jumbo The Climbing Monkey, 1923, Marx, 9-3/4" tall
EX $125 **NM** $225 **MIP** $300

Jumping Rabbit, 1925, Chein, 5"
EX $100 **NM** $125 **MIP** $150

Junior Bus, Chein, yellow, 9" long
EX $70 **NM** $125 **MIP** $175

Knockout Champs Boxing Toy, 1930s, Marx
EX $175 **NM** $300 **MIP** $450

Leopard, 1950, Marx, growls and walks
EX $75 **NM** $125 **MIP** $175

Little King Walkers, 1963, Marx, 3" tall
EX $50 **NM** $75 **MIP** $125

Little Orphan Annie and Sandy, 1930s, Marx
EX $300 **NM** $425 **MIP** $575

TIN TOYS

Little Orphan Annie Skipping Rope, Marx
EX $200 **NM** $300 **MIP** $425

Mack Hercules Motor Express, Chein, tin litho, 19-1/2" long
EX $235 **NM** $385 **MIP** $595

Mack Hercules Truck, Chein, 7-1/2" long
EX $165 **NM** $275 **MIP** $425

Mad Russian Drummer, Marx, 7" tall
EX $125 **NM** $175 **MIP** $225

Main Street, 1929, Marx, street scene w/moving cars, traffic cop
EX $275 **NM** $375 **MIP** $450

Mammy's Boy, 1929, Marx, wind-up walker, 11" tall
EX $500 **NM** $750 **MIP** $1000

Mark 1 Cabin Cruiser, 1957, Chein, 9" long
EX $50 **NM** $75 **MIP** $100

Mechanical Aquaplane, No. 39, 1932, Chein, boat-like pontoons, 8-1/2" long
EX $200 **NM** $300 **MIP** $400

Mechanical Fish, 1940s, Chein, 11" long
EX $50 **NM** $75 **MIP** $100

Merry-Go-Round, Chein, 11" w/swan chairs
EX $400 **NM** $600 **MIP** $800

(Scott Smiles)

Merrymakers Band, 1931, Marx, w/marquee, mouse band
EX $850 **NM** $1250 **MIP** $1650

Merrymakers Band, 1931, Marx, without marquee, mouse band w/violinist
EX $750 **NM** $1150 **MIP** $1450

Mickey Mouse, Marx, 7" tall
EX $200 **NM** $400 **MIP** $600

Minnie Mouse, Marx, 7" tall
EX $200 **NM** $400 **MIP** $600

Minnie Mouse in Rocker, 1950s, Marx
EX $275 **NM** $425 **MIP** $525

Minstrel Figure, Marx, 11" tall
EX $175 **NM** $295 **MIP** $450

Monkey Cyclist, 1923, Marx, 9-3/4" tall
EX $100 **NM** $175 **MIP** $225

Moon Creature, 1950s, Marx, 5-1/2" tall
EX $100 **NM** $175 **MIP** $250

Moon Mullins and Kayo on Handcar, 1930s, Marx, 6" long
EX $335 **NM** $550 **MIP** $700

Mortimer Snerd Bass Drummer, 1939, Marx
EX $650 **NM** $1100 **MIP** $1500

Mortimer Snerd Hometown Band, 1935, Marx
EX $600 **NM** $1000 **MIP** $1400

Mortimer Snerd Walker, 1939, Marx
EX $200 **NM** $300 **MIP** $450

Mother Goose, 1920s, Marx, 7-1/2" tall
EX $150 **NM** $250 **MIP** $375

Mother Penguin with Baby Penguin on Sled, 1950s, Marx, 3" long
EX $35 **NM** $55 **MIP** $85

Motorboat, 1950s, Chein, 9" long
EX $40 **NM** $65 **MIP** $100

Motorboat, 1950s, Chein, crank action, 7" long
EX $35 **NM** $60 **MIP** $90

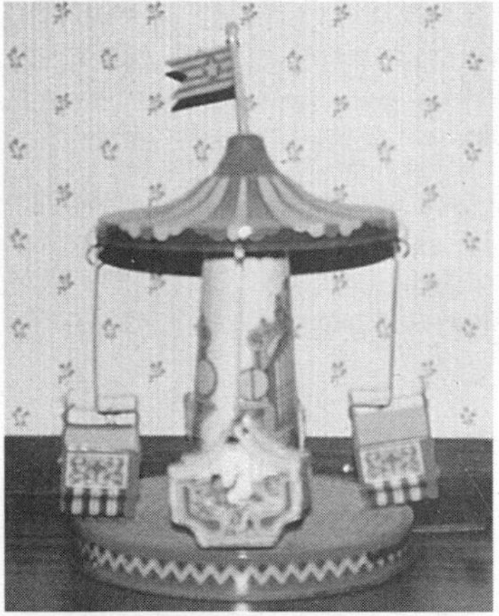

Musical Aero Swing, 1940s, Chein, 10" high
EX $225 **NM** $350 **MIP** $425

Musical Circus Horse, 1939, Marx, pull toy, metal drum rolls w/chimes, 10-1/2" long
EX $100 **NM** $150 **MIP** $200

Musical Merry-Go-Round, Chein, small version
EX $150 **NM** $225 **MIP** $350

Musical Toy Church, 1937, Chein, crank music box
EX $90 **NM** $145 **MIP** $225

Mystery Cat, 1931, Marx, 8-1/2" long
EX $100 **NM** $165 **MIP** $250

Mystery Pluto, 1948, Marx, 8" long
EX $100 **NM** $175 **MIP** $250

Nodding Goose, Marx
EX $75 **NM** $125 **MIP** $175

Pecos Bill, 1950s, Marx, twirls rope, plastic, 10" tall
EX $125 **NM** $225 **MIP** $325

Peggy Jane Speedboat, Chein, 13"
EX $60 **NM** $90 **MIP** $120

Pelican, 1940s, Chein
EX $100 **NM** $150 **MIP** $200

Penguin in Tuxedo, 1940s, Chein
EX $75 **NM** $100 **MIP** $125

(Scott Smiles)

Pig, 1940s, Chein, 4-1/2"
EX $50 **NM** $75 **MIP** $125

Pikes Peak Mountain Climber, 1930s, Marx, vehicle on track, 30" long
EX $300 **NM** $450 **MIP** $600

Pinched Roadster, 1927, Marx, square based, open circular track, 9-1/2"
EX $325 **NM** $500 **MIP** $650

Pinocchio, 1938, Marx, 9" tall
EX $275 **NM** $450 **MIP** $600

Pinocchio, 1950s, Marx, 5" tall
EX $250 **NM** $425 **MIP** $575

Pinocchio the Acrobat, 1939, Marx, 16" tall
EX $350 **NM** $550 **MIP** $785

Pinocchio Walker, 1930s, Marx, animated eyes, 8-1/2" tall
EX $275 **NM** $425 **MIP** $650

Pinocchio Walker, 1930s, Marx, stationary eyes
EX $225 **NM** $375 **MIP** $550

Playland Merry-Go-Round, 1930s, Chein, 9-1/2" high
EX $375 **NM** $500 **MIP** $600

Playland Whip, No. 340, Chein, four bump cars, driver's head wobbles
EX $425 **NM** $575 **MIP** $725

(Ed Hayes Antique Toys)

Pluto Drum Major, Marx
EX $250 **NM** $325 **MIP** $400

Pluto Watch Me Roll-Over, 1939, Marx, 8" long
EX $175 **NM** $275 **MIP** $375

Poor Fish, 1936, Marx, 8-1/2" long
EX $75 **NM** $125 **MIP** $175

Popeye Acrobat, Marx
EX $2000 **NM** $3500 **MIP** $5000

Popeye and Olive Oyl Jiggers, 1936, Marx, 10" tall
EX $700 NM $1200 MIP $1500

Popeye Express, 1932, Marx, w/trunk and wheelbarrow
EX $300 NM $525 MIP $825

Popeye Handcar, 1935, Marx
EX $800 NM $1300 MIP $1800

Popeye in Barrel, Chein
EX $400 NM $650 MIP $1000

Popeye the Champ, 1936, Marx, tin and celluloid, 7" long
EX $1800 NM $2800 MIP $3800

Popeye the Heavy Hitter, Chein, bell and mallet
EX $2550 NM $4200 MIP $6400

Popeye the Pilot, 1936, Marx
EX $600 NM $900 MIP $1200

Popeye with Punching Bag, Chein
EX $1100 NM $1700 MIP $2600

Porky Pig Cowboy with Lariat, 1949, Marx, 8" tall
EX $275 NM $400 MIP $575

Porky Pig with Rotating Umbrella, 1939, Marx, w/or without top hat, 8" tall
EX $300 NM $450 MIP $600

Red Cap Porter, Marx
EX $350 NM $550 MIP $725

Red the Iceman, Marx
EX $1350 NM $2000 MIP $2500
(Don Hultzman)

Ride 'Em Cowboy, Marx
EX $125 NM $175 MIP $225

Ride-A-Rocket Carnival Ride, 1950s, Chein, four rockets, 19" high
EX $300 NM $450 MIP $650

(Scott Smiles)

Ring-A-Ling Circus, 1925, Marx, green base, (pink base is $200 more), 7-1/2" diameter pink base
EX $1250 NM $1750 MIP $2250

Roadster, 1925, Chein, 8-1/2" long
EX $50 NM $80 MIP $125

Rodeo Joe, 1933, Marx
EX $200 NM $300 MIP $400

Roller Coaster, 1938, Chein, includes two cars
EX $275 NM $375 MIP $475
(Don Hultzman. Photo by Ron Chojnacki)

Roller Coaster, 1950s, Chein, includes two cars
EX $200 NM $300 MIP $400

Royal Blue Line Coast to Coast Service, Chein
EX $800 NM $685 MIP $1050

Running Scottie, 1938, Marx, 12-1/2" long
EX $125 NM $175 MIP $250

Sandmill, Chein, beach scene on side
EX $90 NM $145 MIP $225

Santa's Elf, 1925, Chein, boxed, 6" high
EX $225 NM $350 MIP $475

Sea Plane, 1930s, Chein, silver, red, and blue
EX $125 NM $200 MIP $325

Seal, Chein, balancing barbells
EX $100 NM $150 MIP $225

Ski-Boy, 1930s, Chein, 6" long
EX $125 NM $185 MIP $225

Smitty Riding a Scooter, 1932, Marx, 8" tall
EX $500 NM $850 MIP $1300

Smokey Joe the Climbing Fireman, 1930s, Marx, 7-1/2" tall
EX $325 NM $425 MIP $500

Smokey Sam the Wild Fireman, 1950s, Marx, 7" tall
EX $150 NM $225 MIP $300

Snappy the Miracle Dog, 1931, Marx, w/dog house, 3-1/2" long
EX $75 NM $125 MIP $175

Speedboat, Chein, 14" long
EX $100 NM $125 MIP $150

Spic and Span the Hams What Am, 1924, Marx, black drummer and dancer, 10" tall
EX $1000 NM $1500 MIP $2000

Stop, Look and Listen, 1927, Marx, circular track toy
EX $300 NM $500 MIP $750

Streamline Speedway, 1938, Marx, two racers on track, 31"
EX $125 NM $175 MIP $250

Subway Express, 1954, Marx, 9-3/8"
EX $125 NM $175 MIP $225

Superman Holding Airplane, 1940, Marx, 6" wingspan on airplane
EX $875 NM $1450 MIP $2250

Superman Turnover Tank, 1940, Marx, 2-1/2 x 3" x 4" long tin wind-up
EX $500 NM $1250 MIP $2000

Telephone Monkey, 1960s, TN, brown fuzzy monkey on blue telephone
EX $150 NM $175 MIP $200

Tidy Tim Streetsweeper, 1933, Marx, pushes wagon, 8" tall
EX $325 NM $525 MIP $725

(Ed Hyers Antique Toys)

Tom Tom Jungle Boy, Marx, 7" tall
EX $100 NM $150 MIP $200

Touring Car, Chein, 7" long
EX $75 NM $100 MIP $150

(Scott Smiles)

Tumbling Monkey, 1942, Marx, 4-1/2" tall
EX $125 **NM** $175 **MIP** $250

Tumbling Monkey and Trapeze, 1932, Marx, 5-3/4" tall
EX $125 **NM** $200 **MIP** $275

Turtle with Native on Its Back, 1940s, Chein
EX $250 **NM** $375 **MIP** $500

Twist Dog, TN, brown fur, ball on head
EX $30 **NM** $60 **MIP** $90

Walking Popeye, 1932, Marx, carrying parrots in cages, 8-1/4" tall
EX $400 **NM** $600 **MIP** $800

Walking Porter, 1930s, Marx, carries two suitcases, 8" tall
EX $200 **NM** $350 **MIP** $500

Wee Running Scottie, 1930s, Marx, 5-1/2" long
EX $125 **NM** $175 **MIP** $250

Wee Running Scottie, 1952, Marx, 5-1/2" long
EX $100 **NM** $150 **MIP** $200

Wise Pluto, Marx
EX $100 **NM** $175 **MIP** $250

Woody Car, 1940s, Chein, red, 5" long
EX $100 **NM** $175 **MIP** $250

WWI Soldier, Marx, prone position w/rifle
EX $175 **NM** $225 **MIP** $275

Xylophonist, Marx, 5" long
EX $100 **NM** $150 **MIP** $200

Yellow Cab, Chein, 7" long
EX $200 **NM** $300 **MIP** $425

Yellow Taxi, Chein, orange and black, 6" long
EX $125 **NM** $225 **MIP** $325

Zippo the Climbing Monkey, 1938, Marx, 9-1/2"
EX $100 **NM** $125 **MIP** $150

TV Toys

by Karen O'Brien

What is your favorite television show of all time? *The Addams Family*? *Flipper*? *Dr. Kildare*? *S.W.A.T.*?

Whatever the decade, these television programs shared one important component—licensed merchandise. Licensed toys based on television shows have been around for more than sixty years, and collectors have been fond of them ever since. Among the earliest toys released from television licenses were those based on *The Howdy Doody Show* in the 1950s.

Releasing toys based on television characters was an effective way of marketing the program to a target audience. The popularity of the shows, for example, fueled interest in the toys—and often vice versa. For example, young aspiring cowpokes were thrilled to carry their lunches to school in a *Rifleman* or *Bonanza* lunch box. Young musicians perhaps sought the toys from *Josie & the Pussycats* and *The Monkees*. Space fans couldn't get their hands on enough *Lost in Space* of *Land of the Giants* toys.

Television-based toys transported yesterday's kids (and today's collectors) into the virtual worlds represented in the shows. They are one of the most popular crossover toy categories in this book. If you don't find a particular television toy in this chapter, be sure to check the Contents page and look through the Action Figures, Character Toys, Games, Guns, Lunch Boxes, Marx Play Sets, Model Kits, Sci-Fi and Space, View-Master, and Western Toys chapters.

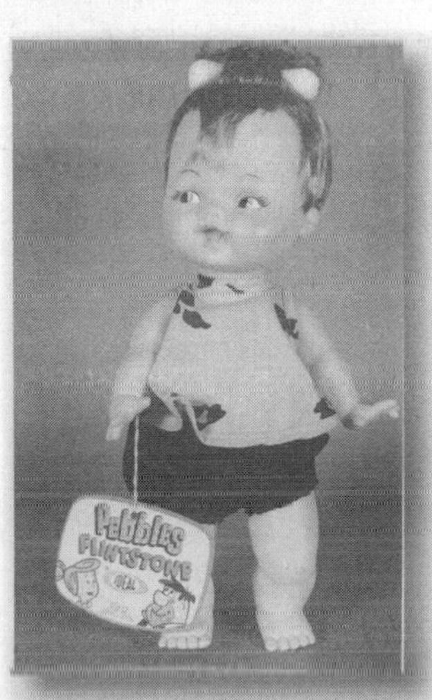

THE *TOP 10* TV TOYS (In Mint Condition)

1. Green Hornet Dashboard, Remco, 1966 .... $2,000
2. Green Hornet Seal Ring, General Mills, 1940.................. 1,800
3. Gilligan's Island Trading Cards, Topps, 1965 1,550
4. Man From U.N.C.L.E. Counterspy Outfit Store Display, Marx, 1966 1,250
5. Gilligan's Island Dip Dots Painting Set, Kenner, 1975 1,200
6. Green Hornet Fan Club Photos, Golden Jersey Milk, 1938........ 1,200
7. Man From U.N.C.L.E. Crime Buster Gift Set, Corgi, 1966......... 1,050
8. Howdy Doody Periscope, Wonder Bread, 1950s 1,000
9. Girl From U.N.C.L.E. Doll, Marx, 1967 1,000
10. Howdy Doody, Rice Crispies Cereal Box, Kellogg's, 1954......... 1,000

Addams Family

Gomez Hand Puppet, 1965, Ideal
EX $50 **NM** $120 **MIP** $250

Lurch Figure, 1964, Remco
EX $80 **NM** $185 **MIP** $360

Morticia Figure, 1964, Remco
EX $100 **NM** $210 **MIP** $675

Morticia Halloween Costume, 1964, Ben Cooper, painted hair
EX $40 **NM** $100 **MIP** $200

Morticia Halloween Costume, 1964, Ben Cooper, w/hair
EX $60 **NM** $125 **MIP** $250

Morticia Hand Puppet, 1965, Ideal
EX $50 **NM** $130 **MIP** $260

Thing Bank, 1964, plastic, battery-operated
EX $40 **NM** $150 **MIP** $225

Uncle Fester Figure, 1964, Remco
EX $100 **NM** $250 **MIP** $625

Alvin Show

Sliding Squares Game, 1960s, Roalex Co., Sliding squares form a variety of "possible" solutions
EX $25 **NM** $45 **MIP** $60

A-Team

A-Team Combat Headquarters Set, 1980s, Galoob, Includes 3-3/4" figures of Hannibal, Face, B.A. Baracus, Murdock and gear, including inflatable raft, machine guns, flag and tent
EX $40 **NM** $85 **MIP** $125

A-Team Rocket Ball Target Set, 1983, gumballs w/gun and target
EX $5 **NM** $10 **MIP** $25

A-Team Shrinky Dinks Set, 1980s
EX $5 **NM** $10 **MIP** $20

Avengers

Shooting Game, 1960s, Merit
EX $10 **NM** $20 **MIP** $45

Steed Sword Stick, 1960s, Lone Star, Toy of John Steed's secret cane/sword combo
EX $17 **NM** $35 **MIP** $70

Banana Splits

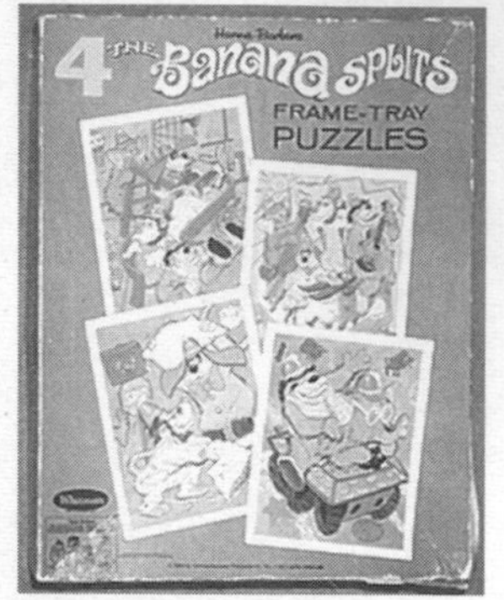

4 The Banana Splits Puzzle, 1969, Whitman, frame tray
EX $25 **NM** $55 **MIP** $85

Banana Band, 1973, Larami, horn, sax, mouth harp
EX $25 **NM** $60 **MIP** $120

Banana Buggy Model Kit, 1968, Aurora
EX $60 **NM** $200 **MIP** $325

Banana Splits Bingo Costume, 1968, Ben Cooper
EX $60 **NM** $175 **MIP** $300

Banana Splits Doll, 1960s, Sutton, 12" tall, plush Drooper
EX $45 **NM** $95 **MIP** $200

Banana Splits Kut-Up Kit, 1973, Larami
EX $25 **NM** $40 **MIP** $75

Banana Splits Mug, 1969, plastic yellow dog mug
EX $20 **NM** $40 **MIP** $65

Banana Splits Record, 1969, Kellogg's
EX $20 **NM** $90 **MIP** $175

Paint-By-Number Set, 1969, Hasbro
EX $45 **NM** $80 **MIP** $150

Talking Telephone, 1969, Hasbro
EX $75 **NM** $175 **MIP** $350

Beany and Cecil

Beany and Cecil and Their Pals Record Player, 1961, Vanity Fair
EX $80 **NM** $200 **MIP** $375

Beany and Cecil Carrying Case, 1960s, 9" diameter, w/strap, vinyl-covered cardboard
EX $40 **NM** $85 **MIP** $100

Beany and Cecil Gun, 1961, Mattel, w/propeller disks
EX $30 **NM** $150 **MIP** $200

Beany and Cecil Puzzle, 1961, Playskool, wooden frame tray
EX $25 **NM** $65 **MIP** $100

Beany and Cecil Skill Ball, 1960s, colorful tin w/wood frame
EX $30 **NM** $80 **MIP** $125

Beany and Cecil Travel Case, 1960s, 8" tall, round, red vinyl w/zipper and strap
EX $25 **NM** $55 **MIP** $95

Beany and Cecil Travel Case, 1960s, square, 4-1/2" x 3-1/2" x 3" red vinyl, carrying strap, illustrated w/characters
EX $30 **NM** $70 **MIP** $100

Beany and His Magic Set Book, 1953, Tell-a-Tale Book
EX $10 **NM** $20 **MIP** $55

Beany Doll, 1963, Mattel, 15" tall, non-talking
EX $45 **NM** $100 **MIP** $165

Beany Figure, 1984, Caltoy, 8" tall
EX $10 **NM** $20 **MIP** $45

Beany Talking Doll, 1950s, Mattel, 17" tall, stuffed cloth, vinyl head w/pull string
EX $90 **NM** $250 **MIP** $425

Bob Clampetts' Beany Coloring Book, 1960s, Whitman
EX $15 **NM** $75 **MIP** $150

Captain Huffenpuff Puzzle, 1961, large
EX $25 **NM** $85 **MIP** $120

Cecil and His Disguise Kit, 1962, Mattel, 17" tall plush Cecil w/disguise wigs, mustaches, etc.
EX $30 **NM** $90 **MIP** $175

Cecil in the Music Box, 1961, Mattel, jack-in-the-box
EX $90 **NM** $225 **MIP** $375

Cecil Soaky, 8-1/2" tall, plastic
EX $35 **NM** $85 **MIP** $150

Leakin' Lena Boat, 1962, Irwin, plastic and wood
EX $50 **NM** $115 **MIP** $225

Leakin' Lena Pound 'N Pull Toy, 1960s, Pressman, wood
EX $60 **NM** $125 **MIP** $250

Ben Casey M.D.

Ben Casey Pencils, 1962, Hassenfeld Bros., ten red/white pencils on card
EX $15 **NM** $30 **MIP** $70

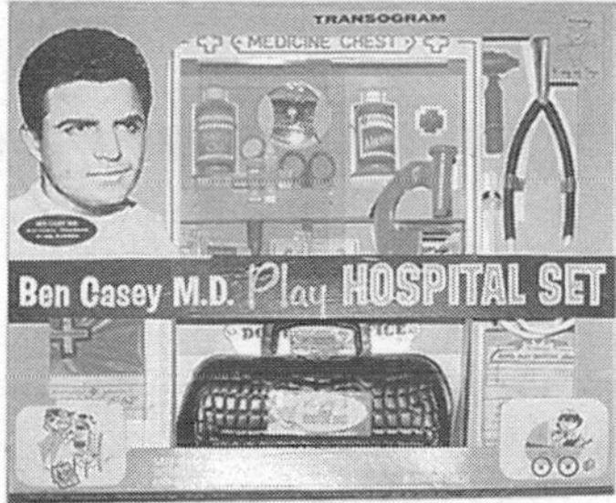

Play Hosptial Set, 1960s, Transogram, Includes doctor bag, microscope, stethascope and more
EX $50 **NM** $100 **MIP** $175

Beverly Hillbillies

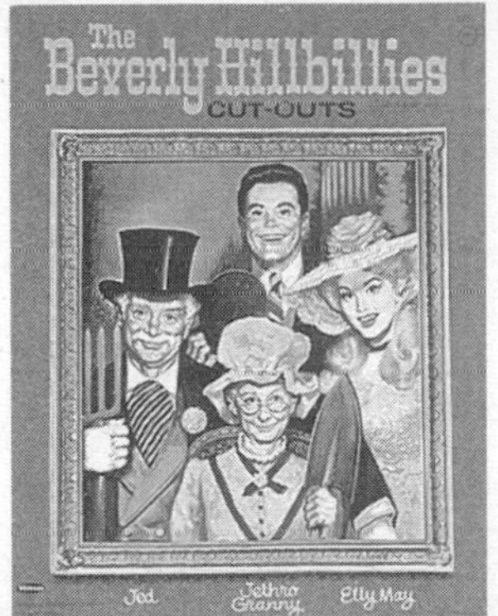

Paper cut-outs, 1960s, Whitman, Includes Jed, Jethro, Granny and Elly May
EX $35 **NM** $80 **MIP** $125

Bewitched

Bewitched Samantha Doll, 1967, Ideal, 12-1/2" tall
EX $180 **NM** $395 **MIP** $750

Bewitched Tabitha Paper Doll Set, 1966, Magic Wand, 11" cardboard doll, clothes
EX $30 **NM** $75 **MIP** $150

Bionic Woman

Play-Doh Action Play Set, 1970s, Kenner, Includes molds for making Play-Doh characters from the show, 3 containers of Play-Doh, plastic mat and six-wheeled vehicle
EX $15 **NM** $25 **MIP** $40

Bozo

Bozo Record Player
EX $20 **NM** $45 **MIP** $90

Bozo the Clown Beach Towel, 1960s, 16" x 24"
EX $8 **NM** $15 **MIP** $35

Bozo the Clown Bendiface, 1970s, Lakeside, soft rubber face flexes into different expressions
EX $8 **NM** $16 **MIP** $24

Bozo the Clown Doll, 1970, Mattel, 19" tall, talks when you pull the cord, "This is your old pal Bozo!"
EX $25 **NM** $50 **MIP** $85

Bozo the Clown Figure, 1970s, vinyl, 5" tall
EX $5 **NM** $15 **MIP** $30

Bozo the Clown Hand Puppet, 1960s, Knickerbocker, vinyl head, cloth outfit, 17" long
EX $15 **NM** $30 **MIP** $45

Bozo the Clown King of the Ring, 1960, Whitman, Tell-A-Tale book
EX $10 **NM** $20 **MIP** $30

Bozo the Clown Push Button Marionette, 1962, Knickerbocker
EX $25 **NM** $45 **MIP** $85

Bozo the Clown Puzzle, 1965, Whitman, #4516, Model No. 4516
EX $10 **NM** $25 **MIP** $50

Bozo the Clown Slide Puzzle, 1960s
EX $15 **NM** $40 **MIP** $75

Bozo the Clown Soaky, 1960s, Palmolive
EX $15 **NM** $45 **MIP** $85

Bozo Tricky Trapeze, 1960s, Kohner, "Push Button Acrobat," red base, also called "push puppets" two buttons on either side of the base are pushed to propel Bozo
EX $15 **NM** $35 **MIP** $65

Tumbling Bozo the Clown, 1971, Sonsco, battery-operated, remote control, cloth outfit, somersaults
EX $15 **NM** $32 **MIP** $50

Brady Bunch

Brady Bunch Halloween Costume, 1970s, Collegeville, smock reads "One of The Brady Bunch"
EX $40 **NM** $90 **MIP** $150

Brady Bunch Kite Fun Book, 1976, Pacific Gas and Electric
EX $15 **NM** $35 **MIP** $75

Brady Bunch Paper Dolls Cut-Out Book, 1973, Whitman
EX $30 **NM** $85 **MIP** $150

Brady Bunch Puzzle, frame tray
EX $25 **NM** $45 **MIP** $80

Brady Bunch Trading Cards, 1971, Topps, 55 cards
EX $250 **NM** $525 **MIP** $775

Kitty Karry-All Doll, 1969, Remco
EX $90 **NM** $175 **MIP** $325

Captian Kangaroo

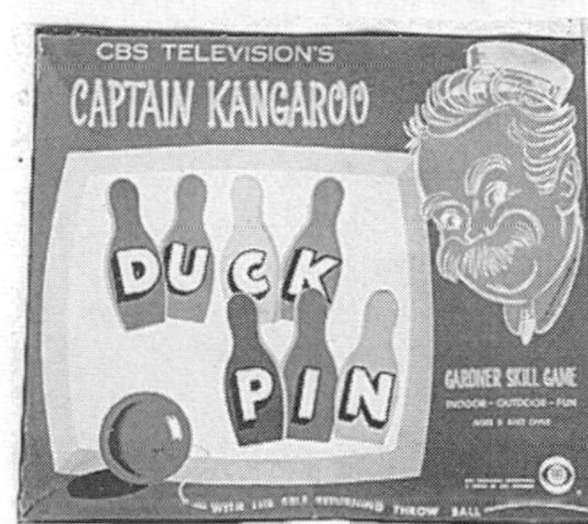

Captain Kangaroo Duck Pin Game, 1950s, Gardner, With self returning ball
EX $15 **NM** $35 **MIP** $75

Captain Kangaroo Presto Slate, 1960s, Fairchild, slate on illustrated card, several versions
EX $12 **NM** $30 **MIP** $40

Captain Kangaroo Puzzle, 1960, Whitman, #4446, frame tray, Model No. 4446
EX $10 **NM** $30 **MIP** $60

TV TOYS

Charlie's Angels

Charlie's Angels Paper Dolls, 1977, Toy Factory, Farrah, Kate or Jaclyn sets, each
EX $20 **NM** $50 **MIP** $90

Charlie's Angels Pendant, 1977, Fleetwood Toys, 4" plastic figure of Farrah hangs from pendant
EX $10 **NM** $25 **MIP** $45

Farrah Fawcett Doll, 1977, Mattel, 12"
EX $50 **NM** $125 **MIP** $200

Farrah Travel Trunk, 1970s, Grand Toys, Canadian toy, box has french language
EX $10 **NM** $20 **MIP** $30

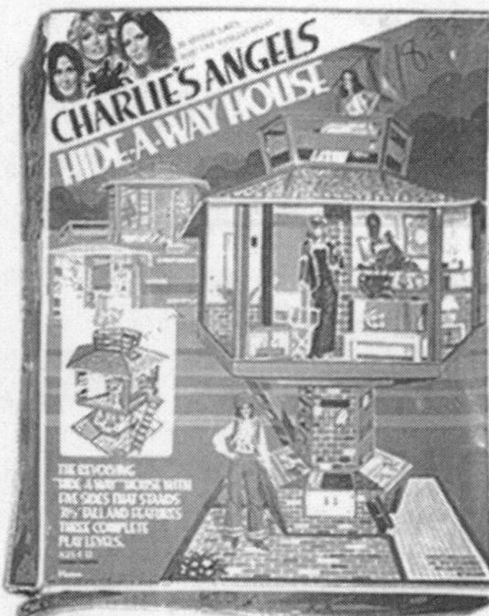

Hide-A-Way House, 1970s, Hasbro, Revolving five-sided dollhouse for Charlie's Angels figures
EX $50 **NM** $100 **MIP** $150

Kate Jackson Doll, 1978, Mattel, 12"
EX $20 **NM** $45 **MIP** $90

Kelly Doll, 1977, Hasbro, 8"
EX $12 **NM** $35 **MIP** $80

Kris Doll, 1977, Hasbro, 8"
EX $10 **NM** $30 **MIP** $70

River Race Outfits, 1977, Palitoy
EX $15 **NM** $35 **MIP** $60

Sabrina Doll, 1977, Hasbro, 8"
EX $20 **NM** $70 **MIP** $120

Sabrina, Kelly, and Kris Gift Set, 1977, Hasbro
EX $30 **NM** $70 **MIP** $145

Slalom Caper Outfits, 1977, Palitoy
EX $10 **NM** $30 **MIP** $50

Target Set, 1970s, Placo Toys, Includes 2 safety guns, 6 safety darts and a knockdown target
EX $20 **NM** $45 **MIP** $85

Underwater Intrigue Outfits, 1977, Palitoy
EX $10 **NM** $30 **MIP** $50

CHiPs

Colorforms Play Set, 1970s, Colorforms
EX $15 **NM** $30 **MIP** $55

Free Wheeling Motorcycle, 1970s, Mego, Made to fit Mego's 8" figures from the series
EX $15 **NM** $35 **MIP** $50

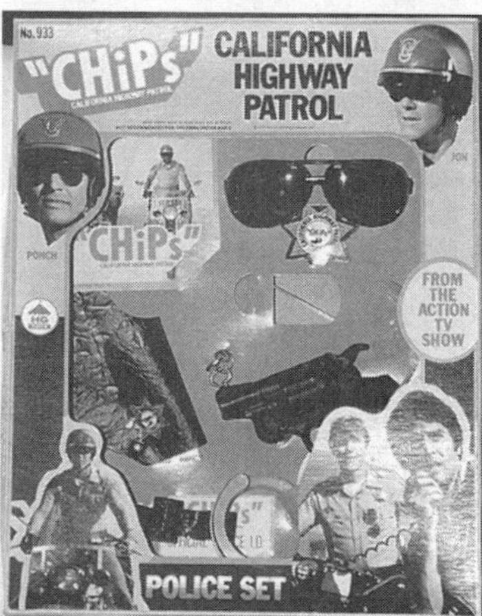

Police Set, 1970s, HG Toys, Includes snub-nose revolver, badge, sunglasses (of course!), handcuffs and holster
EX $18 **NM** $32 **MIP** $60

Combat!

Official Play Set, 1960s, Marx, Super-cool toy soldier set includes tanks, howitzers, army trucks, tanks, personnel carriers, soldiers and landing craft. This same set was re-packaged in the 1970s without the "Combat" TV-show name or tie-in
EX $20 **NM** $40 **MIP** $85

Dobie Gillis

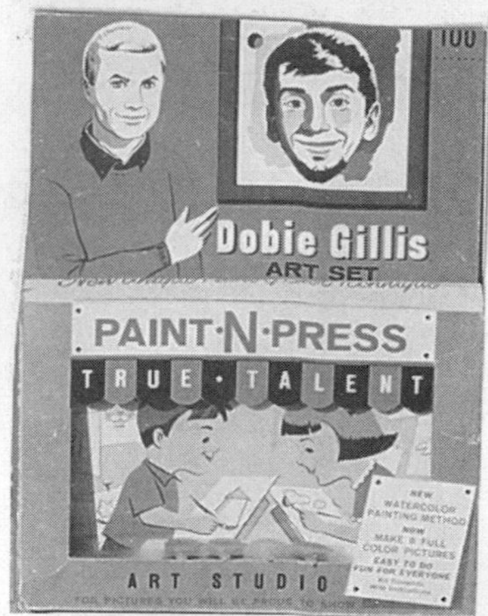

Paint-N-Press Art Set, 1960s, Includes watercolors and instructions
EX $5 **NM** $15 **MIP** $25

Dr. Kildare

Dr. Kildare Photo Scrapbook, 1962
EX $10 **NM** $25 **MIP** $50

Dragnet

Dragnet Badge 714, 1955, Knickerbocker, 2-1/2" bronze finish badge in yellow box w/illustration of Jack Webb, box bottom has ID card
EX $45 **NM** $90 **MIP** $135

Dragnet Badge 714 Target Game, 1950s, Includes 3 guns, corks and darts and litho metal target. $2.98 original price!
EX $30 **NM** $75 **MIP** $150

Dragnet Crime Lab, 1950s, Transogram, "A complete crime detection outfit for the junior detective"
EX $60 **NM** $120 **MIP** $225

Dukes of Hazzard

Daisy's Jeep, 1970s, Includes "Dixie," a white and brown CJ5 Jeep and one Daisy Duke figure
EX $15 **NM** $35 **MIP** $50

Family Affair

5 Family Affair Paper Dolls, Whitman
EX $30 **NM** $45 **MIP** $55

Buffy Halloween Costume, 1970, Ben Cooper
EX $20 **NM** $40 **MIP** $80

Buffy Make-Up and Hairstyling Set, 1971, Amsco
EX $20 **NM** $40 **MIP** $80

Buffy with Mrs. Beasley Dolls, 1967, Mattel, 6" Buffy w/smaller Mrs. Beasley
EX $30 **NM** $65 **MIP** $115

Family Affair Cartoon Kit, 1970, Colorforms
EX $12 **NM** $25 **MIP** $50

Family Affair Puzzle, 1970, Whitman
EX $12 **NM** $30 **MIP** $60

Mrs. Beasley Paper Dolls, 1970s, Whitman, several variations
EX $12 **NM** $30 **MIP** $60

Mrs. Beasley Rag Doll, 1973, Mattel, 14"
EX $12 **NM** $25 **MIP** $45

Talking Mrs. Beasley Doll, 1967, Mattel
EX $50 **NM** $100 **MIP** $225

Flintstones

Baby Puss Figure, 1961, Knickerbocker, 10" tall, vinyl
EX $35 **NM** $75 **MIP** $135

Bamm-Bamm Bank, 1960s, 11" tall, hard plastic figure sitting on turtle
EX $20 **NM** $45 **MIP** $75

Bamm-Bamm Bubble Pipe, 1963, Transogram, figural pipe on illustrated card
EX $12 **NM** $25 **MIP** $50

Bamm-Bamm Doll, 1962, Ideal, 15" tall
EX $50 **NM** $115 **MIP** $225

Bamm-Bamm Figure, 1970, Dakin, 7" tall
EX $20 **NM** $40 **MIP** $75

Bamm-Bamm Finger Puppet, 1972, Knickerbocker
EX $5 **NM** $15 **MIP** $25

Bamm-Bamm Soaky, 1960s, Purex
EX $20 **NM** $40 **MIP** $75

Barney Bank, 1973, solid plastic, Barney holding a bowling ball
EX $15 **NM** $35 **MIP** $60

Barney Doll, 1962, 6" tall, soft vinyl doll, movable arms and head
EX $25 **NM** $45 **MIP** $80

Barney Figure, 1961, Knickerbocker, 10" tall, vinyl
EX $40 **NM** $55 **MIP** $160

Barney Figure, 1970, Dakin, 7-1/4" tall
EX $20 **NM** $40 **MIP** $75

Barney Figure, 1986, Flintoys
EX $5 **NM** $10 **MIP** $15

Barney Finger Puppet, 1972, Knickerbocker
EX $8 **NM** $15 **MIP** $25

Barney Night Light, 1979, Electricord, figural
EX $8 **NM** $15 **MIP** $25

Barney Policeman Figure, 1986, Flintoys
EX $4 **NM** $8 **MIP** $12

Barney Riding Dino Toy, 1960s, Marx, 8" long, metal and vinyl, wind-up
EX $110 **NM** $300 **MIP** $550

Barney Soaky, 1970s, Roclar
EX $10 **NM** $20 **MIP** $55

Barney Wind-Up Toy, 1960s, Marx, 3-1/2" tall figure, tin
EX $85 **NM** $190 **MIP** $375

Barney's Car, 1986, Flintoys
EX $8 **NM** $15 **MIP** $30

Betty Figure, 1961, Knickerbocker, 10" tall, vinyl
EX $50 **NM** $100 **MIP** $200

Betty Figure, 1986, Flintoys
EX $4 **NM** $7 **MIP** $10

Dino Bank, china, Dino carrying a golf bag
EX $45 **NM** $95 **MIP** $185

Dino Bank, 1973, hard vinyl, blue w/Pebbles on his back
EX $18 **NM** $35 **MIP** $75

Dino Bath Puppet Sponge, 1973, bath mitt
EX $10 **NM** $18 **MIP** $35

Dino Doll, movable head and arms
EX $15 **NM** $25 **MIP** $50

Dino Figure, 1970, Dakin, 7-3/4" tall
EX $25 **NM** $50 **MIP** $100

Dino Figure, 1986, Flintoys
EX $4 **NM** $7 **MIP** $15

Dino Wind-Up Toy, 1960s, Marx, 3-1/2" tall, tin
EX $90 **NM** $180 **MIP** $360

Fang Figure, 1970, Dakin, 7" tall
EX $25 **NM** $50 **MIP** $95

Flintmobile, 1986, Flintoys
EX $10 **NM** $18 **MIP** $40

Flintmobile with Fred Figure, 1986, Flintoys
EX $18 **NM** $33 **MIP** $60

Flintstones Ashtray, 1960, ceramic w/Wilma
EX $25 **NM** $70 **MIP** $100

Flintstones Bank, 1971, 19" tall w/Barney and Bamm Bamm
EX $25 **NM** $50 **MIP** $85

Flintstones Car, 1964, Remco, battery operated car w/Barney, Fred, Wilma and Betty
EX $85 **NM** $200 **MIP** $385

Flintstones Figure Set, 1981, Spoontiques, eight figures
EX $35 **NM** $50 **MIP** $90

Flintstones Figures, 1976, Empire, three-inch solid figures of Fred, Barney, Wilma and Betty
EX $10 **NM** $40 **MIP** $85

Flintstones Figures, 1976, Imperial, eight acrylic figures: Fred, Barney, Wilma, Betty, Pebbles, Bamm Bamm, Dino and Baby Puss
EX $15 **NM** $35 **MIP** $65

Flintstones House, 1986, Flintoys
EX $12 **NM** $25 **MIP** $35

Flintstones Lamp, 9-1/2" tall, plastic Fred w/lampshade picturing characters
EX $50 **NM** $120 **MIP** $210

TV TOYS

Flintstones

Flintstones Paint Box, 1961, Transogram
EX $18 **NM** $35 **MIP** $60

Flintstones Party Place Set, 1969, Reed, tablecloth, napkins, plates, cups
EX $10 **NM** $20 **MIP** $40

Flintstones Roto Draw, 1969, British
EX $30 **NM** $70 **MIP** $100

Flintstones Tru-Vue Film Card, 1962, Tru-Vue, #T-37, w/strips of Fred
EX $30 **NM** $70 **MIP** $100

Fred Bubble Blowing Pipe, soft vinyl w/curved stem
EX $6 **NM** $12 **MIP** $20

Fred Doll, 1960, 13" soft vinyl doll w/movable head
EX $45 **NM** $100 **MIP** $225

Fred Doll, 1972, Perfection Plastic, 11" tall
EX $15 **NM** $35 **MIP** $60

Fred Figure, 1960, Knickerbocker, 15" tall
EX $40 **NM** $85 **MIP** $200

Fred Figure, 1961, Knickerbocker, 10" tall, vinyl
EX $32 **NM** $75 **MIP** $150

Fred Figure, 1970, Dakin, 8-1/4" tall
EX $22 **NM** $45 **MIP** $85

Fred Figure, 1986, Flintoys
EX $4 **NM** $8 **MIP** $12

Fred Finger Puppet, 1972, Knickerbocker
EX $8 **NM** $15 **MIP** $22

Fred Flintstone's Bedrock Bank, 1962, Alps, 9", tin and vinyl, battery operated
EX $175 **NM** $310 **MIP** $325

Fred Flintstone's Lithograph Wind-Up, 1960s, Marx, 3-1/2" tall figure, metal
EX $85 **NM** $170 **MIP** $385

Fred Gumball Machine, 1960s, plastic, shaped like Fred's head
EX $20 **NM** $32 **MIP** $60

Fred Loves Wilma Bank, ceramic
EX $50 **NM** $110 **MIP** $185

Fred Night Light, 1970, figural
EX $6 **NM** $12 **MIP** $25

Fred Policeman Figure, 1986, Flintoys
EX $4 **NM** $8 **MIP** $15

Fred Push Puppet, 1960s, Kohner
EX $10 **NM** $25 **MIP** $45

Fred Riding Dino, 1962, Marx, 18" long battery operated w/Fred in Howdah
EX $175 **NM** $350 **MIP** $675

Fred Riding Dino, 1962, Marx, 8" long, tin and vinyl, wind-up
EX $175 **NM** $350 **MIP** $675

Great Big Punch-Out Book, 1961, Whitman
EX $20 **NM** $50 **MIP** $125

Motorbike, 1986, Flintoys
EX $6 **NM** $12 **MIP** $20

Pebbles Bank, 9" tall vinyl w/Pebbles sitting in chair
EX $10 **NM** $25 **MIP** $50

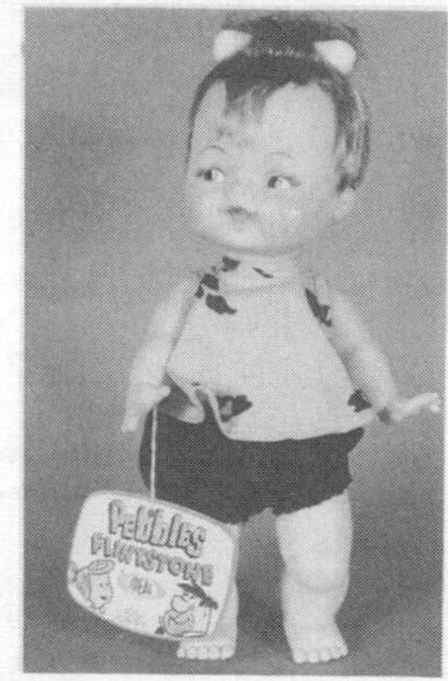

Pebbles Doll, 1963, Ideal, 15" tall
EX $55 **NM** $115 **MIP** $225

Pebbles Doll, 1982, Mighty Star, vinyl head, arms and legs, cloth stuffed body 12" tall
EX $15 **NM** $25 **MIP** $45

Pebbles Figure, 1970, Dakin, 8" tall w/blonde hair and purple velvet shirt
EX $25 **NM** $45 **MIP** $85

Pebbles Finger Puppet, 1972, Knickerbocker
EX $5 **NM** $13 **MIP** $20

Pebbles Flintstone Cradle, 1963, Ideal, for a 15" doll
EX $40 **NM** $75 **MIP** $150

Pebbles Soaky, 1960s, Purex
EX $20 **NM** $35 **MIP** $70

Police Car, 1986, Flintoys
EX $8 **NM** $15 **MIP** $30

Wilma Figure, 1961, Knickerbocker, 10" tall, vinyl
EX $50 **NM** $100 **MIP** $190

Wilma Figure, 1986, Flintoys
EX $4 **NM** $7 **MIP** $15

Wilma Friction Car, 1962, Marx, metal
EX $90 **NM** $175 **MIP** $375

Flipper

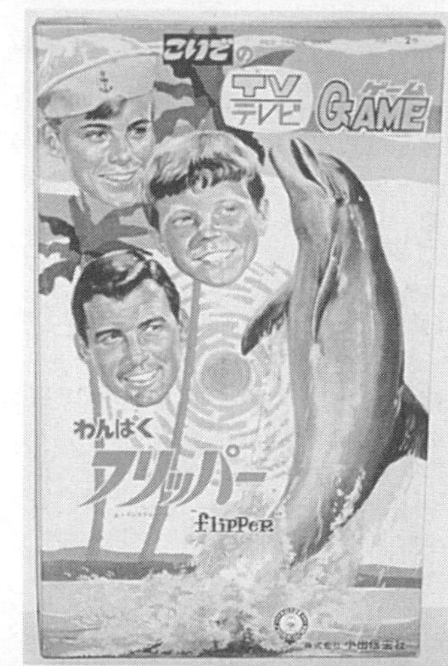

Flipper Game, 1970s, Koide, Japanese issue
EX $20 **NM** $40 **MIP** $65

Flipper Numbered Pencil Coloring Set, 1960s, Includes colored pencils, sharpener and pre-sketched pictures to color
EX $10 **NM** $20 **MIP** $40

Puncho, 1960s, Coleco, Inflatable 40" toy with weighted bottom, so he appears to be swimming upright in a pool or lake
EX $15 **NM** $25 **MIP** $45

Flying Nun

Flying Nun Chalkboard, 1967, Screen Gems
EX $22 **NM** $45 **MIP** $80

Flying Nun Doll, 1960s, Hasbro, 4"
EX $22 **NM** $125 **MIP** $200

Flying Nun Doll, 1967, Hasbro, 11"
EX $30 **NM** $85 **MIP** $175

Flying Nun Halloween Costume, 1967, Ben Cooper
EX $20 **NM** $60 **MIP** $100

Flying Nun Paint-By-Number Set, 1960s, Hasbro, two scenes and 10 paint vials
EX $15 **NM** $30 **MIP** $60

Flying Nun Paper Doll Set, 1969, Saalfield, five dolls and costumes
EX $16 **NM** $40 **MIP** $80

Get Smart

Secret Agent 86 Pen Radio, 1960s, Miner Industries, Functioning crystal radio set in shape of pen, included earphone and contact clip. Received AM radio stations
EX $20 **NM** $35 **MIP** $70

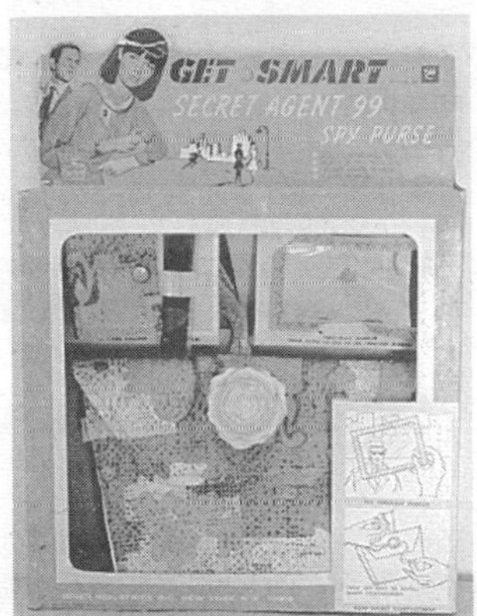

Secret Agent 99 Spy Purse, 1960s, Miner Industries, Includes secret compartment, two-way mirror, secret micro-film holder (inside rose), ID card
EX $30 **NM** $65 **MIP** $105

Gilligan's Island

Gilligan's Floating Island Play Set, 1977, Playskool
EX $75 **NM** $190 **MIP** $350

Gilligan's Island Notepad, 1965, Whitman, Gilligan and Skipper on cover
EX $12 **NM** $30 **MIP** $60

Gilligan's Island Trading Cards, 1965, Topps, set of 55 cards
EX $400 **NM** $800 **MIP** $1550

New Adventures of Gilligan Dip Dots Painting Set, 1975, Kenner, book w/paints and brush
EX $220 **NM** $570 **MIP** $1200

Girl from U.N.C.L.E.

1967 British Annual Book, 1967, World Distributors, hardcover, 95 pages, photo cover
EX $10 **NM** $30 **MIP** $60

1968 British Annual Book, 1968, World Distributors, hardcover, 95 pages, photo cover
EX $10 **NM** $30 **MIP** $60

1969 British Annual Book, 1969, World Distributors, hardcover, 95 pages, photo cover
EX $10 **NM** $30 **MIP** $60

Costume, 1967, Halco, transparent or painted mask, dress-style costume has show logo and silhouette image of Girl spy holding smoking gun, in illustrated window box
EX $55 **NM** $115 **MIP** $250

Garter Holster, 1966, Lone Star, metal pistol fires small plastic bullets from metal shells, checker design vinyl holster and bullet pouch, on card
EX $80 **NM** $175 **MIP** $350

Girl From U.N.C.L.E. Doll, 1967, Marx, 11" tall w/30 accessories in illustrated box
EX $250 **NM** $500 **MIP** $1000

Music from the Television Series, 1966, M.G.M. Records, photo cover shows Stephanie against a wall
EX $9 **NM** $20 **MIP** $40

Secret Agent Wristwatch, 1966, Bradley, watch has pink face w/April Dancer image, in case
EX $85 **NM** $200 **MIP** $400

Green Acres

2 Magic Stay-On Dolls, 1960s, Includes Oliver and Lisa figures, plus complete wardrobes
EX $25 **NM** $40 **MIP** $75

Green Hornet

Assistant Badge, 1966, Don Howard Associates
EX $45 **NM** $95 **MIP** $200

Bike Badge, 1966, Burry Cookies, premium; w/Vari-Vue flasher
EX $85 **NM** $175 **MIP** $350

Black Beauty Balloon Toy, 1966, Oak Rubber
EX $70 **NM** $145 **MIP** $275

Black Beauty Slot Car, 1966, Aurora, clear box w/insert
EX $85 **NM** $175 **MIP** $400

Black Beauty Slot Car, 1966, BZ Industries, large scale
EX $160 **NM** $380 **MIP** $775

Captain Action Flasher Ring, 1966, Vari-Vue, blue
EX $10 **NM** $18 **MIP** $30

Captain Action Flasher Ring, 1966, Vari-Vue, chrome
EX $13 **NM** $25 **MIP** $40

Charm, 1966, Cracker Jack, hornet-shaped
EX $10 **NM** $30 **MIP** $50

Charms, 1966, Folz Vending, hornet-shaped
EX $10 **NM** $15 **MIP** $25

Comic Strip Stickers, 1966, Folz Vending, 7" long, from vending machines, each
EX $25 **NM** $50 **MIP** $100

Electric Drawing Set, 1966, Lakeside
EX $90 **NM** $190 **MIP** $275

Fan Club Photos, 1938, Golden Jersey Milk, set of four; radio premium
EX $400 **NM** $800 **MIP** $1250

Flasher Button, 1966, Vari-Vue, pinback, 3"
EX $15 **NM** $30 **MIP** $45

Flasher Button, 1966, Vari-Vue, no pinback, 3"
EX $10 **NM** $20 **MIP** $35

Flasher Button, 1966, Vari-Vue, no pinback, 7"
EX $25 **NM** $45 **MIP** $80

Flasher Rings, 1960s, Vari-Vue, chrome base, each
EX $10 **NM** $20 **MIP** $50

Flasher Rings, 1960s, Vari-Vue, blue plastic base, each
EX $5 **NM** $10 **MIP** $40

Flashlight Whistle, 1966, Bantamlight
EX $40 **NM** $90 **MIP** $175

Frame Tray Puzzles, 1966, Whitman, box of four
EX $40 **NM** $90 **MIP** $175

Green Hornet Bendy Figure, 1966, Lakeside
EX $40 **NM** $80 **MIP** $175

Green Hornet Bubble Gum Ring, Frito Lay, rubber ring, in cello pack
EX $25 **NM** $45 **MIP** $90

Green Hornet Candy/Toy Box, 1966, Phoenix Candy, several variations
EX $40 **NM** $90 **MIP** $150

Green Hornet Charm Bracelet, 1966, gold finish chain w/five charms: Hornet, Van, Kato, Pistol, Black Beauty, on 3" x 7-1/2" illustrated card
EX $50 **NM** $125 **MIP** $200

Green Hornet Colorforms Set, 1966, Colorforms
EX $60 **NM** $125 **MIP** $250

Green Hornet Dashboard, 1966, Remco
EX $300 **NM** $1000 **MIP** $2250

Green Hornet Mini Walkie Talkies, 1966, Remco
EX $75 **NM** $150 **MIP** $300

Green Hornet

Green Hornet Print Putty, 1966, Colorforms
EX $20 NM $50 MIP $95

Green Hornet Seal Ring, 1940, General Mills, cereal premium
EX $225 NM $780 MIP $1900

Green Hornet Soundtrack Record, 1966, 20th Century Fox
EX $25 NM $100 MIP $200

Green Hornet Troll Figure, 1966, Uneeda Wishnik, 7" tall
EX $55 NM $100 MIP $250

Green Hornet Troll Figure, 1966, Damm, 3" tall
EX $45 NM $75 MIP $150

Green Hornet TV Guide, 1966, Cover features Van Williams and Bruce Lee
EX $50 NM $125 MIP $250

Green Hornet Utensils, 1966, Imperial Knife, fork and spoon
EX $30 NM $75 MIP $150

Green Hornet Walkie Talkies, 1966, Remco
EX $50 NM $100 MIP $175

Green Hornet Wallet, 1966, green vinyl, Hornet or Kato
EX $25 NM $50 MIP $100

Green Hornet Wrist Radios, 1966, Remco, battery-operated
EX $150 NM $250 MIP $525

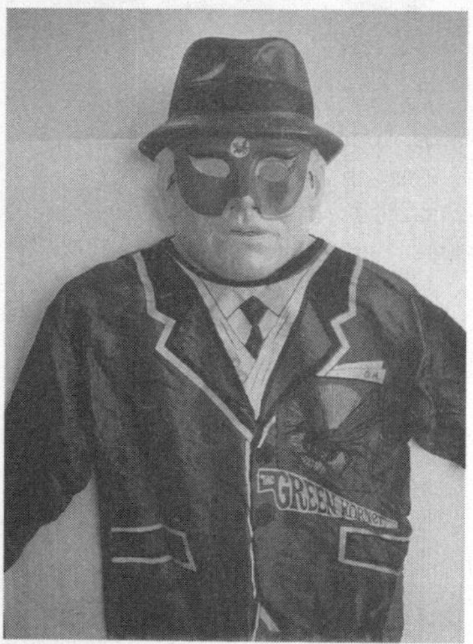

Halloween Costume, 1966, Ben Cooper, several variations
EX $100 NM $200 MIP $375

Hand Puppet, 1966, Ideal, w/hat
EX $80 NM $175 MIP $300

Inflatable Raft, 1966, Ideal
EX $160 NM $350 MIP $700

Instant Squeeze Candy, 1966, Dre's Inc., toothpaste-type container w/hornet-shaped plug
EX $40 NM $90 MIP $175

Kato and Black Beauty Glass, 1938, Golden Jersey Milk, radio premium
EX $100 NM $300 MIP $500

Kite, 1966, Roalex
EX $30 NM $75 MIP $150

Magic Eyes Movie Viewer Slides, 1966, Sawyers
EX $75 NM $150 MIP $300

Magic Rub-On Set, 1966, Whitman
EX $70 NM $150 MIP $275

Magic Slate, 1966, Watkins-Strathmore, three variations
EX $35 NM $90 MIP $175

Mini Movie Viewer, 1966, Acme/Chemtoy, w/filmstrips
EX $50 NM $100 MIP $200

Mini Movie Viewer, 1971, Chemtoy, w/filmstrips
EX $25 NM $45 MIP $90

Numbered Pencil and Paint Set, 1966, Hasbro
EX $75 NM $160 MIP $300

Paint By Number Set, 1966, Hasbro
EX $65 NM $130 MIP $260

Pencil Case, 1966, Hasbro
EX $30 NM $65 MIP $120

Pencils, 1966, Empire Pencil, five on card
EX $30 NM $80 MIP $150

Pennant, 1966, RMS, blue or orange
EX $35 NM $100 MIP $175

Playing Cards, 1966, Ed-U-Cards
EX $10 NM $75 MIP $150

Postcard, 1936, Golden Jersey Milk, radio premium
EX $150 NM $300 MIP $400

Punch-Out Book, 1966, Whitman
EX $100 NM $200 MIP $375

Secret Agent Badge, 1966, Don Howard Associates
EX $20 NM $35 MIP $65

Stardust Craft Kit, 1966, Hasbro
EX $35 NM $75 MIP $150

The Case of the Disappearing Doctor Book, 1966, Whitman
EX $20 NM $30 MIP $45

The Green Hornet Cracks Down Book, 1942, Whitman, Better Little Books
EX $25 NM $60 MIP $120

The Green Hornet Returns Book, 1941, Whitman, Better Little Books
EX $25 NM $60 MIP $120

The Green Hornet Strikes Book, 1940, Whitman, Better Little Books
EX $25 NM $60 MIP $120

Thingmaker Mold and Accessories, 1966, Mattel
EX $100 NM $175 MIP $325

Trading Cards, 1966, Donruss, set of 44
EX $85 NM $100 MIP $325

Trading Cards Display Box, 1966, Donruss
EX $100 NM $250 MIP $500

Trading Cards Wrapper, 1966, Donruss
EX $15 NM $30 MIP $60

Trading Stickers, 1966, Topps, set of 44
EX $85 NM $160 MIP $325

Trading Stickers Display Box, 1966, Topps
EX $100 NM $250 MIP $500

Trading Stickers Wrapper, 1966, Topps
EX $10 NM $25 MIP $50

Wrist Signal Light, 1966, Bantamlight
EX $40 NM $80 MIP $175

Grizzly Adams

Grizzly Adams, 1979, Mattel, 9" figure, w/accessories, #2377
EX $15 NM $30 MIP $45

Nakoma, 1979, Mattel, 9" figure, w/accessories
EX $15 NM $30 MIP $45

Hogan's Heroes

Peri-Peeper, 1977, Continental Plastics, Includes Periscope, ID card and pinback button
EX $5 NM $15 MIP $30

Howdy Doody

Cereal Box, 1954, Kellogg's, Rice Krispies, Howdy Mask on back
EX $250 **NM** $650 **MIP** $1000

Clarabell Bank, 1976, Strauss, flocked plastic, 9"
EX $20 **NM** $65 **MIP** $120

Clarabell Jumping Toy, 1950s, Linemar, 7" tall tin litho, squeeze lever to make figure hop forward and squeak
EX $200 **NM** $450 **MIP** $825

Clarabell Marionette, 1950s, Peter Puppet
EX $100 **NM** $210 **MIP** $425

Flub-a-Dub Figure, 1950s, TeeVee Toys, 4" x 4" painted plastic, movable mouth
EX $40 **NM** $90 **MIP** $150

Flub-a-Dub Flip A Ring Game, 1950s, Flip-A-Ring, 9", ring toss game
EX $25 **NM** $45 **MIP** $75

Flub-a-Dub Marionette, 1950s, Peter Puppet
EX $100 **NM** $225 **MIP** $450

Flub-a-Dub Puppet, 1950s, Gund
EX $40 **NM** $75 **MIP** $150

Howdy Doody Acrobat, 1950s, Arnold, tin, plastic, Howdy swings on high bar
EX $15 **NM** $25 **MIP** $60

Howdy Doody Air Doodle Beanie, 1950s, Kellogg's, Rice Krispies premium
EX $75 **NM** $200 **MIP** $300

Howdy Doody Air-O-Doodle Circus Train, 1950s, Plasticraft/Kagran, red/yellow plastic train, boat and plane toy on card w/cut out character passengers
EX $40 **NM** $100 **MIP** $160

Howdy Doody and Clarabell Book, 1952, Simon and Schuster, Little Golden Book
EX $12 **NM** $22 **MIP** $50

Howdy Doody and Clarabell Coloring Book, 1955, Whitman, Model No. 1188
EX $15 **NM** $75 **MIP** $185

Howdy Doody and Clarabell Puppet Mitten Kit, 1950s, Connecticut Leather
EX $30 **NM** $75 **MIP** $110

Howdy Doody and his Magic Hat Book, 1953, Whitman, Little Golden Book
EX $12 **NM** $22 **MIP** $40

Howdy Doody and Mr. Bluster Book, 1954, Whitman, Little Golden Book
EX $10 **NM** $22 **MIP** $40

Howdy Doody and the Musical Forest Record, 1950s, RCA, 45 rpm
EX $20 **NM** $50 **MIP** $80

Howdy Doody and the Princess Book, 1952, Whitman, Little Golden Book
EX $10 **NM** $25 **MIP** $45

Howdy Doody and You Record, 1950s, RCA, 45 rpm
EX $18 **NM** $40 **MIP** $65

Howdy Doody Bank, Vandor, ceramic figural head
EX $25 **NM** $55 **MIP** $100

Howdy Doody Bank, 1950s, ceramic bank, all color, bust of Howdy
EX $300 **NM** $500 **MIP** $900

Howdy Doody Bank, 1950s, 7" tall, ceramic, Howdy riding a pig
EX $70 **NM** $160 **MIP** $300

Howdy Doody Bank, 1976, Strauss, flocked plastic, 9"
EX $20 **NM** $40 **MIP** $85

Howdy Doody Bubble Pipe, 1950s, Lido, 4" long, Howdy or Clarabell
EX $30 **NM** $160 **MIP** $285

Howdy Doody Button, 1949, New York Sunday News, reads "New Color Comic—Sunday News"
EX $30 **NM** $55 **MIP** $100

Howdy Doody Coin, 1950s, Kellogg's, plastic, silver, raised bust on Howdy on front
EX $20 **NM** $40 **MIP** $75

Howdy Doody Color TV Set, American Plastic, plastic, w/films
EX $130 **NM** $275 **MIP** $500

Howdy Doody Coloring Books, 1955, Whitman, boxed set of six
EX $42 **NM** $150 **MIP** $300

Howdy Doody Comic Book, 1950, Dell, Issue No. 1, January
EX $110 **NM** $275 **MIP** $425

Howdy Doody Cookbook, 1952, Welch's
EX $30 **NM** $110 **MIP** $225

Howdy Doody Cookie-Go-Round, 1950s, Luce/Krispy Kan, lithographed cookie tin
EX $75 **NM** $160 **MIP** $285

Howdy Doody Costume, 1950s, Collegeville
EX $50 **NM** $100 **MIP** $200

Howdy Doody Crayon Set, 1950, Milton Bradley, 16 crayons w/pictures
EX $45 **NM** $100 **MIP** $200

Howdy Doody Doll, 1950s, Ideal, eyes and mouth move
EX $40 **NM** $90 **MIP** $160

Howdy Doody Doll, 1950s, 7" tall vinyl squeeze toy, Howdy in blue pants and red shirt
EX $40 **NM** $90 **MIP** $170

Howdy Doody Doll, 1970s, Goldberger, 30", vinyl ventriloquist doll
EX $40 **NM** $90 **MIP** $160

Howdy Doody Doll, 1976, Goldberger, 12" vinyl ventriloquist doll
EX $25 **NM** $50 **MIP** $110

Howdy Doody Doll, 1988, Applause, 11" cloth doll
EX $10 **NM** $40 **MIP** $75

Howdy Doody Dominoes, 1950s
EX $20 **NM** $40 **MIP** $80

Howdy Doody Figure, Stahlwood, 5" x 7" rubber squeeze figure on airplane
EX $175 **NM** $360 **MIP** $725

Howdy Doody Fingertronic Puppet Theater, 1970s, Sutton
EX $25 **NM** $45 **MIP** $85

Howdy Doody Flasher Rings, 1950s, Nabisco, set of eight plastic character rings
EX $90 **NM** $175 **MIP** $400

Howdy Doody Flicker Ring, 1950s, Nabisco
EX $10 **NM** $20 **MIP** $50

Howdy Doody in Funland Book, 1953, Whitman, Little Golden Book
EX $10 **NM** $25 **MIP** $50

Howdy Doody Kiddie Pool, 1950s, Ideal, 40" diameter, yellow/blue vinyl
EX $80 **NM** $150 **MIP** $275

Howdy Doody Marionette, 1950s, Peter Puppet
EX $85 **NM** $190 **MIP** $375

Howdy Doody Mug, 1950s, Ovaltine, red plastic w/Howdy decal (Be Keen, Drink Chocolate Flavored Ovaltine)
EX $35 **NM** $50 **MIP** $100

Howdy Doody Music Box, Vandor, Howdy playing piano
EX $40 **NM** $55 **MIP** $90

Howdy Doody Newspaper #1, 1950, Poll Parrot, premium
EX $200 **NM** $400 **MIP** $500

Howdy Doody Night Light, 1950s, Leco, figural, Howdy's face
EX $35 **NM** $75 **MIP** $140

Howdy Doody Outdoor Sports Box, 1950s, tin litho box w/colorful graphics
EX $30 **NM** $60 **MIP** $110

Howdy Doody Paint Set, 1950s, Milton Bradley
EX $40 **NM** $80 **MIP** $160

Howdy Doody Paint Set, 1950s, Marx, plaster figures, paint
EX $35 **NM** $100 **MIP** $185

Howdy Doody Pencil Case, 1950s, vinyl; smiling Howdy on front
EX $20 **NM** $90 **MIP** $160

Howdy Doody Periscope, 1950s, Wonder Bread premium
EX $350 **NM** $700 **MIP** $1100

Howdy Doody Phono Doodle, Sharatone Products
EX $120 **NM** $260 **MIP** $350

Howdy Doody Pumpmobile, Nylint, tin vehicle
EX $110 **NM** $275 **MIP** $525

Howdy Doody Puppet Show Set, 1950s, includes plastic figures of Howdy, Clarabell, Mr. Bluster, Flub, Dilly Dally
EX $80 **NM** $170 **MIP** $325

Howdy Doody Puzzle, 1950s, Whitman, frame tray, Howdy Goes Fishing
EX $25 **NM** $45 **MIP** $90

Howdy Doody Puzzle Set, 1950s, Milton Bradley, set of three
EX $40 **NM** $75 **MIP** $150

Howdy Doody Ranch House Tool Box, 1950s, Liberty Steel, 14" x 6" x 3" illustrated steel box w/handle
EX $45 **NM** $110 **MIP** $185

Howdy Doody Salt and Pepper Shakers, 1950s, Peter Puppet, shape of Howdy's head; removable blue vinyl neckerchief
EX $75 **NM** $160 **MIP** $300

Howdy Doody Sand Forms, 1952, Ideal/Kagran, on card
EX $40 **NM** $80 **MIP** $150

Howdy Doody

Howdy Doody Songs Record, 1974, Take Two, record, cut-outs, coloring book
EX $20 **NM** $50 **MIP** $75

Howdy Doody Sticker Fun Book, 1952, Whitman
EX $15 **NM** $30 **MIP** $60

Howdy Doody Swim Ring, 1950s, Ideal, inflatable, 20" diameter
EX $20 **NM** $40 **MIP** $75

Howdy Doody Talking Alarm Clock, 1974, Janex
EX $30 **NM** $90 **MIP** $185

Howdy Doody Television, 1950s, Lido, filmstrips w/TV box
EX $25 **NM** $110 **MIP** $250

Howdy Doody Ukulele, 1950s, Emenee, plastic, white or yellow, 17"
EX $40 **NM** $65 **MIP** $110

Howdy Doody Umbrella, 1950s, Holllander, Howdy head for handle
EX $30 **NM** $80 **MIP** $160

Howdy Doody Wall Walker, Tigrett
EX $25 **NM** $50 **MIP** $100

Howdy Doody Wristwatch, 1950s, Ever Tick/Kagran, glow-in-the-dark
EX $100 **NM** $300 **MIP** $600

Howdy Doody Wristwatch, 1954, Ingraham, deep blue band w/blue and white dial showing character faces
EX $140 **NM** $350 **MIP** $750

Howdy Doody Xylo-Doodle, 1950s, yellow plastic piano/xylophone w/colorful graphics
EX $75 **NM** $375 **MIP** $675

Howdy Doody's Animal Friends Book, 1956, Whitman, Little Golden Book
EX $10 **NM** $20 **MIP** $50

Howdy Doody's Circus Book, 1950, Whitman, Little Golden Book
EX $10 **NM** $20 **MIP** $50

Howdy Doody's Electric Carnival Game, 1950s, Harett-Gilmar
EX $60 **NM** $120 **MIP** $225

Howdy Doody's Laughing Circus Record Set, 1950s, RCA, two 78 rpm records
EX $35 **NM** $70 **MIP** $135

Howdy Doody's Lucky Trip Book, 1953, Whitman, Little Golden Book
EX $12 **NM** $25 **MIP** $50

Howdy Doody's One-Man Band, Trophy Products/Kagran, musical instruments
EX $100 **NM** $225 **MIP** $500

Merchandise Manual, 1954, list of toys
EX $150 **NM** $450 **MIP** $650

Merchandise Manual, 1955, list of toys
EX $100 **NM** $350 **MIP** $600

Mr. Bluster Bank, 1976, Strauss, flocked plastic, 9"
EX $20 **NM** $35 **MIP** $75

Princess Summerfall Winterspring Doll, 1950s, Beehler Arts, 8", hard plastic, braided black hair
EX $100 **NM** $190 **MIP** $400

Princess Summerfall Winterspring Sewing Cards, 1950s, Milton Bradley, four cards, thread, plastic needle
EX $30 **NM** $65 **MIP** $135

Puppets, 1950s, Gund, Howdy, Bluster, Clarabell, Dilly or Princess
EX $20 **NM** $50 **MIP** $90

Sparkle Gun, 1987, Ja-Ru, plastic gun
EX $6 **NM** $20 **MIP** $45

Spinning Top, 1970s, Lorenz Bolz, tin top w/characters
EX $30 **NM** $60 **MIP** $110

I Dream of Jeannie

I Dream of Jeannie Costume, 1970s, Ben Cooper
EX $8 **NM** $20 **MIP** $50

I Dream of Jeannie Doll, 1965, Ideal, 18"
EX $65 **NM** $165 **MIP** $300

I Dream of Jeannie Doll, 1977, Remco, 6"
EX $25 **NM** $50 **MIP** $110

I Dream of Jeannie Play Set, 1977, Remco, w/6" doll
EX $40 **NM** $120 **MIP** $250

I Spy

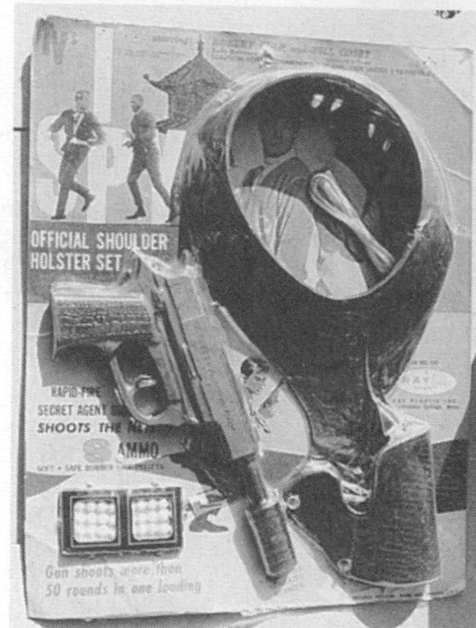

Official Shoulder Holster Set, 1960s, Ray Line, Inc., Includes rapid fire pistol ("shoots more than 50 rounds in one loading"), shoulder holster and ammo
EX $40 **NM** $65 **MIP** $95

Jetsons

Elroy Toy, 1963, Transogram
EX $10 **NM** $20 **MIP** $40

Jetson Figures, 1990, Applause, 10" tall; Judy, George, Elroy, Rosie, each
EX $50 **NM** $100 **MIP** $185

Jetsons Birthday Surprise Book, 1963, Whitman, Tell-A-Tale Book
EX $12 **NM** $25 **MIP** $65

Jetsons Colorforms Kit, 1963, Colorforms
EX $40 **NM** $75 **MIP** $150

Puzzle, 1962, Whitman, 70 pieces
EX $25 **NM** $95 **MIP** $175

Knight Rider

Knight Rider Impossibles Stunt Set, 1982, LJN
EX $45 **NM** $95 **MIP** $150

Knight Rider Wrist Communicator, 1982, Larami
EX $10 **NM** $20 **MIP** $40

Lassie

Lassie's Pups, 1950s, Set including plastic toy dogs, blanket, tub and puppy bed
EX $12 **NM** $25 **MIP** $45

Original Lassie Stuffed Toy, 1950s, Smile Novelty Toy Co., Reddish-brown and white stuffed toy with plastic face
EX $40 **NM** $80 **MIP** $120

Laugh-In

"Sock It To Me" Plastic Purse, 1970s, Yellow with black lettering and strap
EX $10 **NM** $17 **MIP** $30

TV TOYS

Laugh-In Electric Drawing Set, 1960s, Lakeside Toys, Included an "electric" drawing set, color pencils, Laugh-In cartoon guides, drawing paper, eraser, sharpener and instructions
EX $15 **NM** $35 **MIP** $65

Love Boat

Love Boat Playset, 1970s, Boat-shaped dollhouse with figures of the cast, furniture and accessories. Over two feet long
EX $25 **NM** $45 **MIP** $90

Man from U.N.C.L.E.

1966 British Annual, 1966, World Distributors, hardcover, 95 pages, photo cover
EX $20 **NM** $50 **MIP** $75

1967 British Annual Book, 1967, World Distributors, hardcover, 95 pages, photo cover
EX $15 **NM** $35 **MIP** $65

1968 British Annual Book, 1968, World Distributors, hardcover, 95 pages, photo cover
EX $15 **NM** $30 **MIP** $60

1969 British Annual, 1969, World Distributors, hardcover, 95 pages, photo cover
EX $15 **NM** $25 **MIP** $55

Action Figure Apparel Set, 1965, Gilbert, bullet proof vest, three targets, three shells, binoculars, and bazooka
EX $50 **NM** $100 **MIP** $210

Action Figure Armament Set, 1965, Gilbert, for 12" figures: jacket, cap firing pistol w/barrel extension, bipod stand, telescopic sight, grenade belt, binoculars, accessory pouch and beret
EX $50 **NM** $90 **MIP** $180

Action Figure Arsenal Set #1, 1965, Gilbert, tommy gun, bazooka, three shells, cap firing pistol and attachments, in shallow window box
EX $40 **NM** $80 **MIP** $175

Action Figure Arsenal Set #2, 1965, Gilbert, cap firing THRUSH rifle w/telescopic sight, grenade belt and four grenades, on wrapped header card
EX $40 **NM** $80 **MIP** $175

Action Figure Jumpsuit Set, 1965, Gilbert, for 12" figures: jumpsuit w/boots, helmet w/chin strap, 28" parachute and pack, cap firing tommy gun w/scope, instructions
EX $50 **NM** $100 **MIP** $225

Action Figure Pistol Conversion Kit, 1965, Gilbert, binoculars and pistol w/attachments, for 12" figures, on wrapped header card
EX $22 **NM** $45 **MIP** $90

Action Figure Scuba Set, 1965, Gilbert, for 12" Gilbert dolls: swim trunks, air tanks, tank bracket, tubes, scuba jacket and knife
EX $65 **NM** $130 **MIP** $260

Affair of the Gentle Saboteur Book, 1966, Whitman, hardcover
EX $8 **NM** $15 **MIP** $35

Affair of the Gunrunners' Gold Book, 1967, Whitman, hardcover
EX $8 **NM** $15 **MIP** $35

Alexander Waverly Figure, 1966, Marx, blue plastic, 5-3/4" tall, stamped w/character's name and U.N.C.L.E. logo on the bottom of base
EX $8 **NM** $15 **MIP** $30

Arcade Cards, 1960s, postcards w/b/w photo fronts, Napoleon or Illya
EX $5 **NM** $10 **MIP** $30

Attache Case, 1966, Lone Star, small cardboard briefcase, contains die-cast Mauser and parts to assemble U.N.C.L.E. Special
EX $130 **NM** $230 **MIP** $500

Attache Case, British, 1965, Lone Star, 15" x 8" x 2" vinyl case w/a pistol, holster, walkie talkie, cigarette box gun, U.N.C.L.E. badge, international passport, invisible cartridge pen and handcuffs
EX $225 **NM** $450 **MIP** $900

Attache Case, British, 1966, Lone Star, cardboard covered in vinyl, 9mm automatic luger, shoulder stock, sight, silencer, belt, holster, secret wrist holster and pistol that fires cap and cork, grenade, wallet w/passport, play money
EX $250 **NM** $500 **MIP** $950

Bagatelle Game, 1966, Hong Kong, 8" x 14" pinball game
EX $75 **NM** $155 **MIP** $325

Bicycle License Plates, 1967, Marx, four different, metal: Man from U.N.C.L.E., The Girl from U.N.C.L.E., Napoleon Solo, Illya Kuryakin, each
EX $15 **NM** $30 **MIP** $50

Calcutta Affair Book, 1967, Whitman, 254 pages, Big Little Book
EX $10 **NM** $20 **MIP** $45

Candy Cigarette Box, 1966, Cadet Sweets, candy and trading card, illustrated box
EX $25 **NM** $60 **MIP** $125

Candy Cigarette Counter Display Box, 1966, Cadet Sweets, holds 72 candy cigarette boxes, illustrated
EX $30 **NM** $90 **MIP** $200

Coin of El Diablo Affair Book, 1965, Wonder Books, softcover, 48 pages
EX $10 **NM** $20 **MIP** $40

Counter Spy Water Gun, 1960s, Hong Kong, luger water gun w/unlicensed Napoleon Solo illustration header card
EX $5 **NM** $15 **MIP** $40

Counterspy Outfit, 1966, Marx, contains trench coat w/secret pockets, pistol, shoulder holster, launcher barrel, silencer, scope sight, two pair of glasses, beards, eye patch, badge case, etc., in box
EX $125 **NM** $230 **MIP** $485

Counterspy Outfit Store Display, 1966, Marx, 35" x 36" wide cardboard display w/one piece of each item in Counterspy Outfit
EX $320 **NM** $650 **MIP** $1350

Crime Buster Gift Set, 1966, Corgi, set includes Man from U.N.C.L.E. car, James Bond Aston Martin and Batmobile w/Batboat on trailer, in window box
EX $275 **NM** $525 **MIP** $1100

Die-Cast Car, 1968, Playart, 2-3/4" long, die-cast metal, metallic purple
EX $90 **NM** $200 **MIP** $425

Die-Cast Metal Gun, 1965, Lone Star, die-cast automatic cap pistol w/plastic grips, plus cut-out badge, on card
EX $75 **NM** $150 **MIP** $325

Diving Dames Affair Book, 1967, Souvenir Press/England, #10 in series
EX $4 **NM** $8 **MIP** $20

Doomsday Affair Book, 1965, Souvenir Press, #2 in series
EX $4 **NM** $8 **MIP** $20

Fingerprint Kit, 1966, ink pad, roller, code book, magnifier, fingerprint records and pressure plate, in illustrated window box
EX $125 **NM** $250 **MIP** $500

Flicker Ring, 1965, silver plastic ring w/b/w photos, each
EX $10 **NM** $20 **MIP** $50

Flicker Ring, 1966, blue plastic w/"changing portrait" of Napoleon or Illya, each
EX $10 **NM** $20 **MIP** $40

Foto-Fantastiks Coloring Set, 1965, Eberhard Faber, six colored pencils, paint brush, and six 8" x 10" photos, came in four different versions, each
EX $40 **NM** $85 **MIP** $175

Generic Spies Figures, 1966, Marx, six different solid plastic, unpainted figures 5-3/4" tall, each
EX $8 **NM** $15 **MIP** $20

Handkerchief, 1966, England, U.N.C.L.E. logo, Illya and Napoleon
EX $30 **NM** $65 **MIP** $150

Man from U.N.C.L.E.

Headquarters Transmitter, 1965, Cragstan, molded gold colored plastic transmitter, amplifier and under cover case, silver ID card, 20-foot wire, in box
EX $80 **NM** $160 **MIP** $350

Illya Kuryakin Action Figure, 1965, Gilbert, 12" tall, plastic, black sweater, pants and shoes, spring loaded arm for firing cap pistol, folding badge, ID card and instruction sheet, in photo box
EX $80 **NM** $225 **MIP** $425

Illya Kuryakin Action Puppet, 1965, Gilbert, 13" tall, soft vinyl hand puppet of Illya holding a communicator, on 10" x 16" card
EX $80 **NM** $175 **MIP** $375

Illya Kuryakin Costume, 1967, Halco, painted mask, rayon costume in three colors showing Illya holding a gun, in illustrated window box
EX $45 **NM** $90 **MIP** $200

Illya Kuryakin Figure, 1966, Marx, blue or gray plastic figure, 5-3/4" tall, stamped w/character's name and U.N.C.L.E. logo on the bottom of base
EX $15 **NM** $40 **MIP** $80

Illya, That Man From U.N.C.L.E. Book, 1966, Pocket Books, 6" x 9" paperback, 100 pages of David McCallum
EX $10 **NM** $30 **MIP** $70

Invisible Writing Cartridge Pen, 1965, Platinum/England, pen, two vials of ink and two invisible ink vials
EX $125 **NM** $230 **MIP** $475

Magic Slates, 1965, Watkins-Strathmore, 9" x 14" slate w/two punch-out figures of either Napoleon or Illya, each
EX $45 **NM** $100 **MIP** $200

Man from the U.N.C.L.E. Record, 1965, Capitol Records, 45 rpm w/The Man from U.N.C.L.E. theme song and "The Vagabond"
EX $25 **NM** $60 **MIP** $120

Man from U.N.C.L.E. and other TV Themes Record, 1965, Metro Records, photo cover, has three songs from U.N.C.L.E. plus theme songs from Dr. Kildare, Mr. Novak, Bonanza and other shows
EX $8 **NM** $25 **MIP** $50

Man from U.N.C.L.E. Button, 1965, Button World, 3-1/2" diam. round button w/portrait of Napoleon or Illya, each
EX $10 **NM** $17 **MIP** $30

Man from U.N.C.L.E. Card Game, 1966, Japan, small artwork cards in illustrated box
EX $40 **NM** $75 **MIP** $160

Man from U.N.C.L.E. Code Board, 1966, chalkboard w/line art illustrations
EX $70 **NM** $150 **MIP** $300

Man from U.N.C.L.E. Finger Puppets, 1966, Dean, vinyl; THRUSH agent, Solo, Kuryakin, Waverly and two female agents; window box
EX $140 **NM** $300 **MIP** $600

Man from U.N.C.L.E. Playing Cards, 1965, Ed-U-Cards, standard 54-card deck w/action photo illustrations, on card
EX $20 **NM** $35 **MIP** $70

Man from U.N.C.L.E. Playing Cards Display Box, 1965, Ed-U-Cards, holds 12 packs
EX $130 **NM** $250 **MIP** $525

Man from U.N.C.L.E. Puzzles, 1965, Jaymar, frame tray; three versions; each
EX $25 **NM** $40 **MIP** $75

Man from U.N.C.L.E. Record, 1965, Crescendo Records, by the Challengers, cover shows blonde female spy w/gun
EX $5 **NM** $15 **MIP** $35

Man from U.N.C.L.E. Record, 1966, Union/Japan, 45 rpm w/photo sleeve
EX $35 **NM** $75 **MIP** $150

Man from U.N.C.L.E. Sheet Music, 1964, Hastings Music Corp., six pages, theme song and a brief description of the TV show
EX $15 **NM** $50 **MIP** $100

Man from U.N.C.L.E. Trading Cards, 1965, Topps, set of 55 b/w photo cards
EX $45 **NM** $95 **MIP** $175

Man from U.N.C.L.E. Trading Cards, 1966, Cadet Sweets, set of 50 cards, color photos, set
EX $22 **NM** $45 **MIP** $90

Man from U.N.C.L.E. Trading Cards, 1966, ABC/England, 25 cards
EX $22 **NM** $45 **MIP** $90

Mystery Jigsaw Series Puzzles, 1965, Milton Bradley, 14" x 24" puzzle, 250 pieces plus story booklet, The Loyal Groom, The Vital Observation, The Impossible Escape, The Micro-Film Affair, each
EX $25 **NM** $50 **MIP** $100

Napoleon Solo Costume, 1965, Halco, transparent plastic "mystery mask," costume has line art shirt, tie, shoulder holster and U.N.C.L.E. logo, in illustrated box
EX $50 **NM** $95 **MIP** $185

Napoleon Solo Credentials and Passport Set, 1965, Ideal, silver ID card, badge, identification wallet, slide window passport, on header card
EX $35 **NM** $65 **MIP** $150

Napoleon Solo Credentials and Secret Message Sender, 1965, Ideal, message sender, badge, and silver ID, on card
EX $40 **NM** $80 **MIP** $175

Napoleon Solo Doll, 1965, Gilbert, 11" tall, plastic, white shirt, black pants and shoes, spring loaded arm for firing cap pistol, folding badge, ID card and instruction sheet
EX $70 **NM** $145 **MIP** $350

Napoleon Solo Figure, 1966, Marx, blue or gray plastic figure, 5-3/4" tall stamped w/character's name and U.N.C.L.E. logo on the bottom of base
EX $15 **NM** $35 **MIP** $80

Pinball Affair Game, 1966, Marx, 12" x 24" tin litho pinball game
EX $75 **NM** $150 **MIP** $300

Pistol Cane Gun, 1966, Marx, 25" long, cap firing, bullet shooting aluminum cane w/eight bullets and one metal shell, on illustrated card
EX $125 **NM** $250 **MIP** $600

Power Cube Affair Book, 1968, Souvenir, #15 in series, British
EX $5 **NM** $10 **MIP** $25

Puzzle, 1966, Milton Bradley, 10" x 19", 100 pieces, Illya's Battle Below
EX $15 **NM** $35 **MIP** $70

Puzzle, 1966, Milton Bradley, 10" x 19", 100 pieces, Illya Crushes THRUSH
EX $15 **NM** $40 **MIP** $70

Puzzles, 1966, England, four 11" x 17" puzzles, each w/340 pieces: The Getaway, Solo in Trouble, The Frogman Affair, Secret Plans, each
EX $40 **NM** $80 **MIP** $165

Secret Agent Wristwatch, 1966, Bradley, gray watch face shows Solo holding a communicator, came w/either plain "leather" or "mod" watch band, in case
EX $115 **NM** $250 **MIP** $500

Secret Code Wheel Pinball, 1966, Marx, 10" x 22" x 6" tin litho pinball game
EX $80 **NM** $170 **MIP** $325

Secret Message Pen, 1966, American Character, 6-1/2" long double tipped pen for writing invisible messages, on header card
EX $100 **NM** $200 **MIP** $325

Secret Print Putty, 1965, Colorforms, putty in a gun shaped container, print paper, display cards of Kuryakin and Solo and a book of spy and weapons illustrations, on card
EX $20 **NM** $45 **MIP** $95

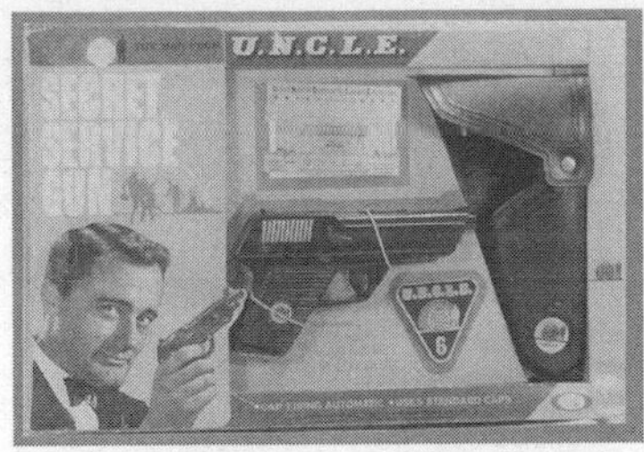

Secret Service Gun, 1965, Ideal, pistol, holster, badge and silver ID card, in window box
EX $160 **NM** $310 **MIP** $650

Secret Service Pop Gun, 1960s, bagged Luger pop gun on header card w/unlicensed illustration of Illya and Napoleon on header
EX $10 **NM** $15 **MIP** $50

Secret Weapon Set, 1965, Ideal, clip loading cap firing pistol, holster, ID wallet, silver ID card, U.N.C.L.E. badge, two demolition grenades and holster, in window box
EX $190 **NM** $400 **MIP** $775

Shirt, 1965, has secret pocket, glow-in-the-dark badge and ID, photo package
EX $190 **NM** $375 **MIP** $725

Shoot Out! Game, 1965, Milton Bradley, skill and action game for two players, plastic marble game in illustrated box
EX $80 **NM** $160 **MIP** $325

Shooting Arcade Game, 1966, Marx, tin litho arcade w/mechanical wind-up THRUSH agent targets for pellet shooting pistol, scope and stock attachments
EX $200 **NM** $400 **MIP** $850

Shooting Arcade Game, 1966, Marx, smaller version w/THRUSH spinner targets
EX $150 **NM** $275 **MIP** $525

Spy Magic Tricks, 1965, Gilbert, mystery gun, Illya playing cards, tricks
EX $125 **NM** $250 **MIP** $525

Television Picture Story Book, 1968, P.B.S. Limited, hardcover, 62 pages, Gold Key reprints
EX $15 **NM** $20 **MIP** $60

THRUSH Agent Figures, 1966, Marx, three different blue plastic figures, 5-3/4" tall stamped w/titles and U.N.C.L.E. logo on the bottom of each base, each
EX $10 **NM** $20 **MIP** $50

THRUSH Ray-Gun Affair Game, 1966, Ideal, four U.N.C.L.E. agent pieces, Area Decoder cards, 3-D THRUSH hideouts, THRUSH vehicles, crayons, dice and a rotating "ray gun," in illustrated box
EX $55 **NM** $110 **MIP** $225

THRUSH-Buster Display Box, 1966, Corgi, large display box w/graphics, holds 12 cars
EX $170 **NM** $330 **MIP** $700

U.N.C.L.E. Badges Store Display, 1965, Lone Star, illustrated card holds 12 triangular black plastic badges w/gold lettering, w/badges
EX $50 **NM** $120 **MIP** $225

McHale's Navy

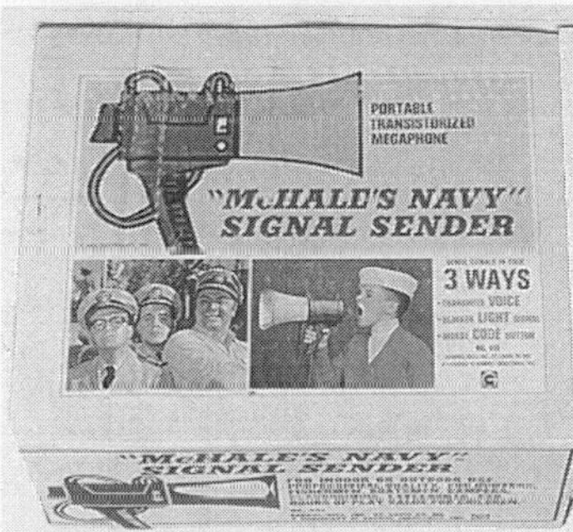

McHale's Navy Signal Sender, 1960s, Gabriel-Bell, Inc., Megaphone sends amplifies voice, sends light signal and includes a Morse code button
EX $15 **NM** $25 **MIP** $55

Monkees

Flip Movies, 1967, Topps, each
EX $5 **NM** $10 **MIP** $30

Halloween Costumes, 1967, Bland Charnas, each
EX $60 **NM** $125 **MIP** $250

Jigsaw Puzzle, 1967, Fairchild
EX $15 **NM** $25 **MIP** $45

Monkees Dolls, 1967, Remco, 4", rubber, each
EX $35 **NM** $80 **MIP** $175

Monkees Finger Puppets, 1969, Remco
EX $15 **NM** $25 **MIP** $45

Talking Hand Puppet, 1966, Mattel, cloth w/heads of Monkees on fingertips
EX $50 **NM** $110 **MIP** $200

Tambourine, 1967, Raybert
EX $45 **NM** $100 **MIP** $200

Toy Guitar, 1966, Mattel, 20"
EX $60 **NM** $125 **MIP** $250

Toy Guitar, 1966, Mattel, 14", wind-up crank
EX $40 **NM** $90 **MIP** $175

Mork and Mindy

Mork and Mindy Colorforms, 1979, Colorforms
EX $10 **NM** $15 **MIP** $30

Mr. Ed

Mr. Ed Talking Horse Puppet, 1962, Mattel
EX $40 **NM** $80 **MIP** $150

Munsters, The

Grandpa Doll, 1964, Remco
EX $150 **NM** $325 **MIP** $610

TV TOYS

Munsters, The

Herman Munster Doll, 1964, Remco
EX $155 NM $350 MIP $720

Lily Baby Doll, 1965, Ideal, unlicensed "monster baby"
EX $45 NM $85 MIP $170

Lily Doll, 1964, Remco
EX $150 NM $325 MIP $625

Puzzle, 1960s, Whitman, frame tray
EX $30 NM $50 MIP $100

Puzzle, 1965, Whitman, 100 pieces, boxed
EX $35 NM $60 MIP $150

The Last Resort Book, 1964, Whitman
EX $13 NM $30 MIP $50

Partridge Family

David Cassidy Dress-Up Kit, 1972, Colorforms
EX $20 NM $40 MIP $75

Laurie Partridge Doll, 1973, Remco, 20" tall
EX $55 NM $120 MIP $225

Partridge Family Bus, 1973, Remco, plastic, 14" long
EX $65 NM $160 MIP $300

Partridge Family Guitar, 1970s, Carnival, 19" plastic, decal of David Cassidy on body
EX $35 NM $75 MIP $150

Partridge Family Paper Dolls, 1970s, Saalfield, several styles
EX $20 NM $40 MIP $75

Patti Partridge Doll, 1971, Ideal
EX $50 NM $110 MIP $200

Pee Wee Herman

Ball Dart Set
EX $5 NM $10 MIP $15

Billy Baloney Doll, 1988, Matchbox, 18" tall
EX $12 NM $20 MIP $75

Chairry Figure, Matchbox, 15" tall
EX $12 NM $20 MIP $45

Conky Wacky Wind-Up, 1988, Matchbox
EX $3 NM $5 MIP $10

Cowboy Curtis Figure, Matchbox
EX $8 NM $15 MIP $35

Globey with Randy, 1988, Matchbox
EX $8 NM $15 MIP $40

King of Cartoons Figure, 1988, Matchbox, 5" tall
EX $8 NM $15 MIP $35

Magic Screen Figure, 1988, Matchbox, 5" tall poseable
EX $8 NM $15 MIP $35

Magic Screen Wacky Wind-Up, 1988, Matchbox, 6" tall
EX $3 NM $5 MIP $10

Miss Yvonne Doll, 1988, Matchbox, poseable 5" tall
EX $8 NM $15 MIP $45

Pee Wee Herman Deluxe Colorforms, 1980s, Colorforms
EX $7 NM $10 MIP $35

Pee Wee Herman Doll, 1980s, Matchbox, 15" tall, non talking
EX $10 NM $35 MIP $75

Pee Wee Herman Doll, 1988, Matchbox, poseable 5" tall
EX $4 NM $10 MIP $25

Pee Wee Herman Play Set, 1989, Matchbox, 20" x 28" x 8" for use w/5" figures, Pee Wee's bike, folds into large carrying case
EX $12 NM $28 MIP $60

Pee Wee Herman Slumber Bag, 1988, Matchbox
EX $10 NM $20 MIP $35

Pee Wee Herman Ventriloquist Doll, 1980s, Matchbox
EX $30 NM $65 MIP $135

Pee Wee with Scooter and Helmet, 1988, Matchbox
EX $4 NM $7 MIP $15

Pee Wee Yo-Yo, 1980s
EX $3 NM $10 MIP $20

Pterri Doll, 1980s, Matchbox, 13" tall
EX $15 NM $25 MIP $45

Pterri Wacky Wind-Ups, 1988, Matchbox
EX $3 NM $5 MIP $10

Reba Figure, 1988, Matchbox, poseable
EX $5 NM $10 MIP $30

Ricardo Figure, 1988, Matchbox
EX $5 NM $10 MIP $30

Vance the Talking Pig Figure, 1987, Matchbox
EX $20 NM $40 MIP $85

Pinky Lee

Pinky Lee Paint Set, 1950s, Gabriel, 8 pictures to watercolor
EX $10 NM $20 MIP $33

Toy Medicine Chest, 1950s
EX $10 NM $20 MIP $50

Who Am I? Game, 1950s, based on the tv show
EX $5 NM $15 MIP $25

Rat Patrol

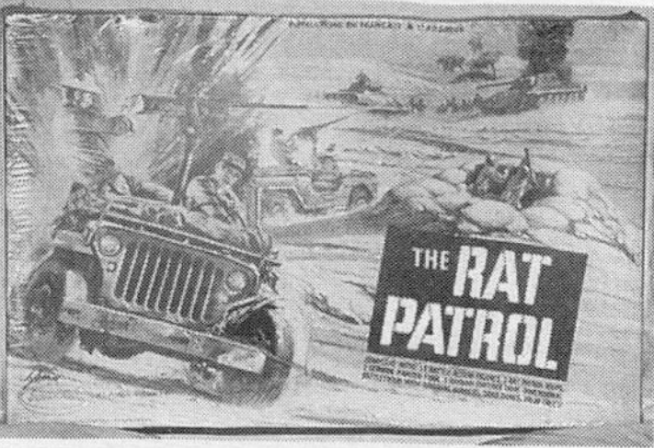

Rat Patrol Diorama Kit, 1960s, Aurora, includes 15 figures, 2 Rat Patrol Jeeps, 1 German Panzer Tank, 1 German Panther Tank, dimensional battlefield with sandbags, bunkers, dunes and palm trees
EX $20 NM $40 MIP $65

Rocky and Bullwinkle

Bullwinkle and Rocky Clock Bank, 1969, Larami, 4-1/2" tall, plastic
EX $30 NM $60 MIP $120

Bullwinkle and Rocky Movie Viewer, 1960s, #225, red and white plastic viewer w/three movies
EX $25 NM $50 MIP $75

Bullwinkle and Rocky Wastebasket, 1961, 11" tall, metal w/Jay Ward cast pictured
EX $35 NM $65 MIP $135

Bullwinkle Bank, 1960s, 6" tall, glazed china
EX $75 NM $125 MIP $400

Bullwinkle Bank, 1972, Play Pal, 11-1/2", plastic
EX $35 NM $50 MIP $100

Bullwinkle Cartoon Kit, 1962, Colorforms
EX $35 NM $50 MIP $160

Bullwinkle Dinner Set, 1960s, Boonton Molding, plate and cup pictures Bullwinkle and the Cheerios Kid
EX $25 NM $50 MIP $85

Bullwinkle Figure, 1976, Dakin, Cartoon Theater, 7-1/2" tall, plastic
EX $25 NM $50 MIP $90

Bullwinkle Flexy Figure, 1970, Larami
EX $10 NM $35 MIP $75

Bullwinkle for President Bumper Sticker, 1972
EX $10 NM $16 MIP $40

Bullwinkle Jewelry Hanger, 1960s, 5" tall, suction cup on back
EX $15 NM $25 MIP $50

Bullwinkle Magic Slate, 1963
EX $15 NM $40 MIP $85

Bullwinkle Make Your Own Badge Set, 1960s, Larami
EX $20 NM $40 MIP $85

Bullwinkle Paintless Paint Book, 1960, Whitman
EX $15 NM $35 MIP $80

Bullwinkle Spell and Count Board, 1969
EX $12 NM $25 MIP $50

Bullwinkle Stamp Set, 1970, Larami
EX $12 **NM** $25 **MIP** $40

Bullwinkle Stickers, 1984, Bullwinkle, Sherman and Peabody, Snidely Whiplash
EX $5 **NM** $10 **MIP** $20

Bullwinkle Talking Doll, 1970, Mattel
EX $30 **NM** $75 **MIP** $150

Bullwinkle Travel Adventure Board Game, 1960s, Transogram
EX $30 **NM** $70 **MIP** $135

Bullwinkle Travel Game, 1971, Larami, magnetic
EX $15 **NM** $30 **MIP** $60

Bullwinkle's Circus Time Toy, 1969, Rocky on a circus horse
EX $20 **NM** $40 **MIP** $90

Bullwinkle's Circus Time Toy, 1969, Bullwinkle on a elephant
EX $20 **NM** $40 **MIP** $90

Bullwinkle's Double Boomerangs, 1969, Larami, set of two on illustrated card
EX $15 **NM** $25 **MIP** $50

Dudley Do-Right Figure, 1972, Wham-O, 5" tall, flexible
EX $12 **NM** $40 **MIP** $80

Dudley Do-Right Figure, 1976, Dakin, Cartoon Theater
EX $15 **NM** $40 **MIP** $85

Dudley Do-Right Puzzle, 1975, Whitman
EX $12 **NM** $30 **MIP** $60

Mr. Peabody Bank, 1960s, 6" tall, glazed china
EX $90 **NM** $190 **MIP** $385

Mr. Peabody Figure, 1972, Wham-O, 4" tall, flexible
EX $10 **NM** $30 **MIP** $70

Natasha Figure, 1972, Wham-O
EX $10 **NM** $30 **MIP** $70

Rocky and Bullwinkle Bank, 1960, 5" tall, glazed china
EX $90 **NM** $190 **MIP** $385

Rocky and Bullwinkle Presto Sparkle Painting Set, 1962, Kenner, six cartoon pictures and two comic strip panels
EX $30 **NM** $70 **MIP** $135

Rocky and Bullwinkle Puzzle, 1972, Whitman, boxed
EX $15 **NM** $30 **MIP** $75

Rocky and Bullwinkle Toothpaste Holder, 1960s, glazed china
EX $80 **NM** $190 **MIP** $375

Rocky and His Friends Book, 1960s, Whitman, Little Golden Book
EX $20 **NM** $50 **MIP** $80

Rocky Bank, 1950s, 5" tall, slot in large tail, glazed china
EX $80 **NM** $225 **MIP** $425

Rocky Figure, 1976, Dakin, Cartoon Theater, 6-1/2" tall, plastic
EX $30 **NM** $60 **MIP** $125

Rocky Flexy Figure, 1970, Larami
EX $10 **NM** $25 **MIP** $50

Rocky Soaky, Colgate-Palmolive, 10-1/2" tall, plastic
EX $15 **NM** $35 **MIP** $65

Rocky the Flying Squirrel Coloring Book, 1960, Whitman
EX $20 **NM** $40 **MIP** $85

Sherman Figure, 1972, Wham-O, 4" tall, flexible
EX $15 **NM** $35 **MIP** $70

Snidely Whiplash Figure, 1972, Wham-O, 5" tall, flexible
EX $15 **NM** $40 **MIP** $80

Romper Room

Bop-A-Loop Toy (MIB), Hasbro, Shown here with Romper Room Rhythm set
EX $4 **NM** $8 **MIP** $10

Build & Play Discs, Hasbro
EX $3 **NM** $6 **MIP** $12

Can You Guess? Wonder Book, Hasbro
EX $2 **NM** $4 **MIP** $8

Ceramic Mug – Jack-in-the-Box, Hasbro
EX $5 **NM** $15 **MIP** $34

Chalkboard, Hasbro
EX $4 **NM** $7 **MIP** $15

Digger the Dog (MIB), Hasbro
EX $5 **NM** $15 **MIP** $32

Do Bee Dough Machine, Hasbro
EX $5 **NM** $15 **MIP** $34

Do Bee Iron On Transfer, Hasbro
EX $1 **NM** $3 **MIP** $5

Do Bee Rider, Hasbro
EX $10 **NM** $20 **MIP** $55

Do Bees Little Golden Book of Manners, Hasbro
EX $5 **NM** $9 **MIP** $18

Dump Truck (Do Bee hubcaps), Hasbro
EX $2 **NM** $4 **MIP** $8

Fitness Fun 45 RPM, Hasbro
EX $2 **NM** $4 **MIP** $8

Fun Time Puzzle Clock, Hasbro
EX $3 **NM** $5 **MIP** $10

G.E. Show 'N Tell Phonoviewer, Hasbro
EX $8 **NM** $14 **MIP** $28

G.E. Show 'N Tell Picturesound Refill Programs (each), Hasbro
EX $1 **NM** $2 **MIP** $4

Happy Jack and Mr. Do Bee hand puppets, Hasbro
EX $10 **NM** $20 **MIP** $40

Happy Jack Magnetic Puzzle, Hasbro
EX $4 **NM** $8 **MIP** $16

Happy Jack Punching Clown, Hasbro
EX $5 **NM** $9 **MIP** $18

Inchworm, Hasbro, green w/yellow saddle; yes, I still have mine!!
EX $15 **NM** $30 **MIP** $65

Moe the Monkey Game, Hasbro
EX $3 **NM** $5 **MIP** $10

Mr. Do Bee Bank, Hasbro
EX $5 **NM** $15 **MIP** $35

Mr. Do Bee Miniature Poly-Blocks, Hasbro
EX $3 **NM** $5 **MIP** $10

Mr. Stacking Man, Hasbro
EX $4 **NM** $8 **MIP** $15

Musical Block Clock, Hasbro
EX $10 **NM** $20 **MIP** $45

Musical Jack in the Box, Hasbro
EX $15 **NM** $35 **MIP** $75

Official TV Bo Dee Dance Record, Hasbro
EX $4 **NM** $8 **MIP** $20

Peg Town Railroad, Hasbro
EX $2 **NM** $5 **MIP** $10

Preschool Super Fun Pad, Hasbro
EX $1 **NM** $3 **MIP** $6

Rhythm Set, Hasbro
EX $4 **NM** $9 **MIP** $22

Sew Easy Sewing Machine, Hasbro
EX $3 **NM** $6 **MIP** $12

Snoopy Counting Camera, Hasbro
EX $5 **NM** $10 **MIP** $20

Snoopy Play Telephone, Hasbro
EX $3 **NM** $5 **MIP** $10

Squirt, Squirt, Squirt the Animals Tub Toy, Hasbro
EX $3 **NM** $5 **MIP** $10

Super Mr. Potato Head, Hasbro
EX $3 **NM** $7 **MIP** $14

Talk 'N Chalk Board, Hasbro
EX $5 **NM** $15 **MIP** $30

Toy Ring – Gold Plated Plastic, Hasbro
EX $10 **NM** $20 **MIP** $40

Weebles Playground, Hasbro
EX $22 **NM** $55 **MIP** $110

Willie the Weather Man, Hasbro
EX $10 **NM** $20 **MIP** $45

Rookies, The

Rookie Chris figure, 1973, LJN, 8" tall
EX $10 **NM** $20 **MIP** $60

Rookie Mike figure, 1973, LJN, 8" tall
EX $10 **NM** $20 **MIP** $60

Rookie Terry figure, 1973, LJN, 8" tall
EX $10 **NM** $20 **MIP** $60

Rookie Willy figure, 1973, LJN, 8" tall
EX $10 **NM** $20 **MIP** $60

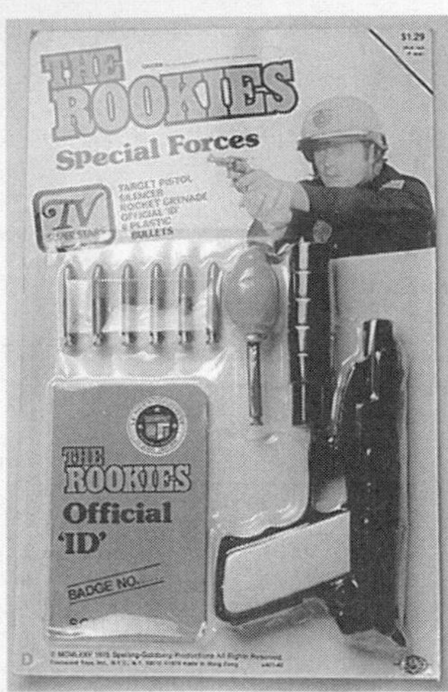

Special Forces Set, 1975, Fleetwood Toys, Includes target pistol, silencer, rocket grenade, official ID and six plastic bullets
EX $15 **NM** $25 **MIP** $50

S.W.A.T.

Bullhorn, 1976
EX $15 **NM** $25 **MIP** $35

Clicker Gun & Handcuffs Set, 1975, Fleetwood Toys
EX $10 **NM** $17 **MIP** $25

Deacon, 1976, LJN, 8" figure
EX $5 **NM** $12 **MIP** $35

Hondo, 1976, LJN, 8" figure
EX $5 **NM** $12 **MIP** $35

Luca, 1976, LJN, 8" figure
EX $5 **NM** $12 **MIP** $35

McCabe, 1976, LJN, 8" figure
EX $5 **NM** $12 **MIP** $35

Officer Jim Street, 1976, LJN, 8" figure
EX $5 **NM** $12 **MIP** $35

T.J., 1976, LJN, 8" figure
EX $5 **NM** $12 **MIP** $35

Van, 1976, LJN, fits 8" figures
EX $15 **NM** $30 **MIP** $45

Scooby Doo

Scooby Doo and the Pirate Treasure Book, 1974, Golden, Little Golden Book
EX $5 **NM** $10 **MIP** $15

Scooby Doo Hand Puppet, 1970s, Ideal, vinyl head
EX $20 **NM** $40 **MIP** $75

Scooby Doo Paint with Water Book, 1984
EX $5 **NM** $10 **MIP** $20

Scooby Doo Squeak Toy, 1970s, Sanitoy, 6" tall
EX $20 **NM** $35 **MIP** $50

Sgt. Preston

Sgt. Preston of the Yukon Punch-Out Cards, 1950s, Quaker, "Big Game Trophy" cardboard cut-outs, set of nine
EX $30 **NM** $100 **MIP** $175

Six Million Dollar Man

Porta-Communicator, 1970s, Kenner, Walkie-talkie device that attaches to Colonel Austin like a backpack. You transmit your voice on one end, and it's broadcasted from the receiver on the other. Included a 10-foot cord
EX $20 **NM** $45 **MIP** $65

Soupy Sales

Soupy Sales Card Game, 1960s, Jaymar, Slap Jack, Old Maid, Funny Rummy, or Hearts/Crazy 8s
EX $20 **NM** $40 **MIP** $60

Soupy Sales Doll, 1960s, Remco, 5" doll
EX $40 **NM** $150 **MIP** $250

Soupy Sales Doll, 1966, Knickerbocker, 12" plush, vinyl head
EX $25 **NM** $60 **MIP** $150

Starsky & Hutch

Deluxe Police Set, 1970s, HG Toys, Includes badges, service revolver, Colt .45, shoulder holster, cuffs, whistle and poster
EX $30 **NM** $60 **MIP** $75

Starsky and Hutch Puzzle, 1970s, HG Toys
EX $15 **NM** $30 **MIP** $50

Starsky and Hutch Shoot-Out Target Set, 1970s, Berwick
EX $25 **NM** $45 **MIP** $95

Stingray

Puzzle, 1960s, Whitman
EX $10 **NM** $20 **MIP** $35

Stingray Atomic Submarine, Doyusha, With electonic lights and sounds
EX $25 **NM** $45 **MIP** $90

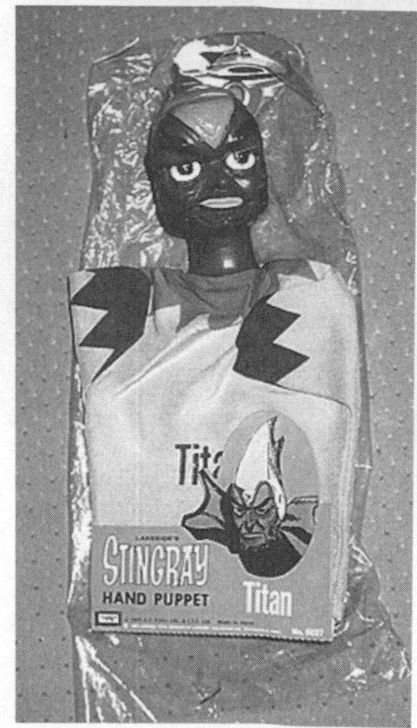

Stingray Hand Puppet, Titan, 1960s
EX $7 **NM** $15 **MIP** $30

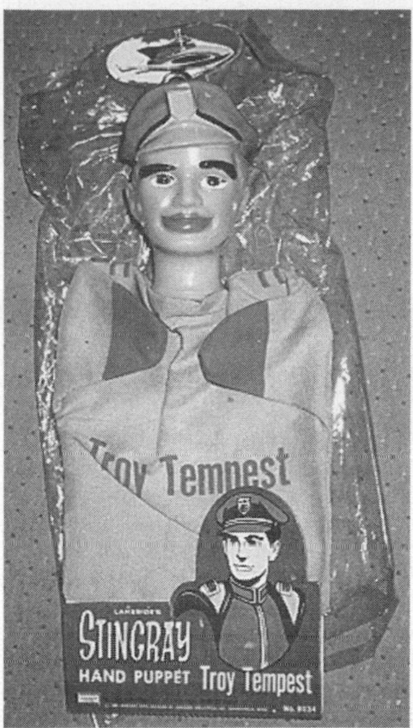

Stingray Hand Puppet, Troy Tempest, 1960s
EX $10 **NM** $20 **MIP** $35

Stingray Hand Puppet, X2-Zero, 1960s
EX $12 **NM** $22 **MIP** $40

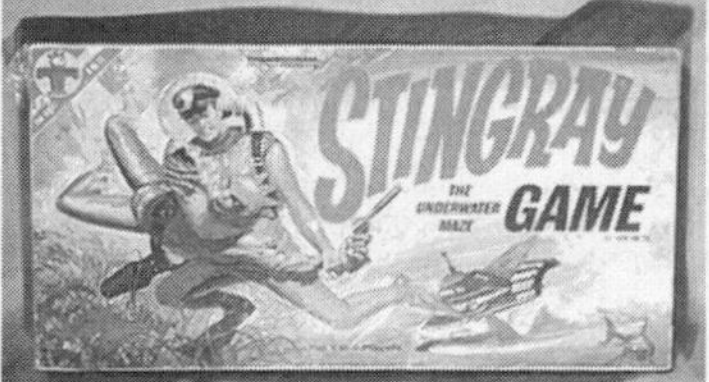

Stingray Underwater Maze Game, 1960s, Transogram
EX $22 **NM** $40 **MIP** $70

The Fall Guy

Fall Guy Bounty Hunter HO Scale Race set, 1970s, Aurora, Includes Fall Guy truck, passenger car, figure 8 track
EX $25 **NM** $50 **MIP** $90

Pickup Truck Model Kit, 1980s, MPC
EX $5 **NM** $12 **MIP** $25

Target Shooting Game, 1980s, Arco, targets spin when hit
EX $5 **NM** $12 **MIP** $20

Thunderbirds

"The Mole" vehicle, Bandai, Tracked vehicle with rotating drill section, from the Gerry Anderson series "Thunderbirds"
EX $14 **NM** $25 **MIP** $45

Underdog

Kite Fun Book, 1970s, Pacific Gas and Electric
EX $10 **NM** $35 **MIP** $85

Puzzle, 1975, Whitman, 100 pieces
EX $10 **NM** $20 **MIP** $30

Underdog Costume, 1969, Ben Cooper
EX $55 **NM** $85 **MIP** $150

Underdog Dot Funnies Kit, 1974, Whitman
EX $10 **NM** $20 **MIP** $40

Underdog Figure, 1976, Dakin, plastic, Cartoon Theater
EX $35 **NM** $100 **MIP** $150

Welcome Back, Kotter

Halloween Costume, 1976, Collegeville, several styles
EX $10 **NM** $20 **MIP** $25

Sweathogs Dolls, 1976, Mattel, Epstein, Washington, Barbarino, Kotter, Horshack; each
EX $10 **NM** $25 **MIP** $60

Sweathogs Grease Machine Cars, 1977, Ahi, 3" long, plastic cars; various styles, each
EX $15 **NM** $30 **MIP** $60

Welcome Back, Kotter Classroom, 1976, Mattel, play set
EX $25 **NM** $45 **MIP** $100

Welcome Back, Kotter Colorforms Set, 1976, Colorforms
EX $10 **NM** $20 **MIP** $50

Winky Dink and You

When Winky Winks at You Record, 1956, Decca
EX $45 **NM** $60 **MIP** $80

Winky Dink Book, 1956, Golden, Little Golden Book
EX $9 **NM** $16 **MIP** $30

Winky Dink Comic Book, 1950s, Dell, #663
EX $20 **NM** $40 **MIP** $90

Winky Dink Costume, 1950s, Halco, No. 642, cloth mask and jumper
EX $10 **NM** $20 **MIP** $40

Winky Dink Magic Crayons, 1960s
EX $20 **NM** $35 **MIP** $50

Winky Dink Official TV Game Kit, 1950s
EX $30 **NM** $50 **MIP** $100

Winky Dink Secret Message Game, 1950s, Lowell
EX $75 **NM** $130 **MIP** $225

Winky Dink Winko Magic Kit, 1950s
EX $20 **NM** $35 **MIP** $50

Vehicles

by Merry Dudley

The Dark Knight has come to the rescue once again. But this time he has saved the die-cast hobby.

For years, fans of the Batmobile—specifically, the George Barris creation from the 1960s *Batman* television show—have been denied a scale version of their beloved car due to huge disputes involving licensing rights. Now, after approximately twenty-five years of legal wrangling, the matter has been settled and Mattel has been awarded the chance to offer Batmobiles in various scales of die-cast metal.

Collectors are making up for the almost thirty-year drought by scooping up every version Mattel offers, no matter what the cost. The first was a 1:64-scale version, which was part of the Hot Wheels 2007 New Models line. The car is impossible to find at retail, so people are turning to the Internet, paying approximately $20 for each mint-on-card Batmobile. The inevitable variations are bringing slightly more.

Then there are the special versions. A 1:64 Batmobile with extra paint detailing and Real Rider tires was sold at the San Diego Comic Con in 2007. The cars were initially offered at $20 and limited to one per person. Now these cars are bringing $40 online. Also available at Comic Con were 525 special versions of a 1:18-scale Batmobile. The model originally sold for $300. One of them, signed by George Barris, sold for $960 on eBay in August 2007.

This interest in the Dark Knight's ride isn't a new phenomenon. Corgi enjoyed decades of sales thanks to its Batmobile toys of the 1960s and 1970s. In the 1980s, you could find these toys for reasonable prices at garage sales and toy shows. But in the last 15 years, the price of these toys has skyrocketed. A Corgi Jr. Batmobile toy with the Batboat and trailer from the 1960s recently sold for $1,125 on eBay—and that price isn't at all unusual. The children who played with that toy are excited to be able to get their hands on another one now that they are in their forties and have some disposable income.

Trends in die-cast come and go, and lately the hobby has been in a slump. But the renewed interest in television and movie cars has reinvigorated both collectors and manufacturers. There will always be interest in models based on television and movie cars, thanks to the booming DVD market. And models of these special vehicles will always have a place in die-cast collections.

The General Lee is another good example. This 1969 Dodge Charger, made famous in the 1970s television show *The Dukes of Hazzard*, has a legion of faithful followers. A new movie came out in 2005, attracting a younger group of fans. And when *Dukes of Hazzard* star John Schneider listed his General Lee on eBay in 2007, it originally earned a bid of $9.9 million. Unfortunately, that bid was never honored. It finally sold for $450,000 at a 2008 Barrett-Jackson auction. This renewed interest in famous cars has had its effects. Collector interest in television cars as a whole has increased. It has also bought about a renewed discussion of the most famous television cars of all time.

A few years ago, TV Land voted the General Lee as the most famous television car of all time. A poll on *www.toycarsandmodels.com* in summer 2007 saw the Batmobile easily defeat the General Lee.

Contributors: Corgi and Dinky contributor Dr. Douglas Sadecky; Hot Wheels Numbered Packs contributor Michael Zarnock is the author of *The Ultimate Guide to Hot Wheels Variations 3rd Edition* (Krause Publications, 2007); Japanese Tin Cars contributor Ron Smith; Nylint contributor Jeff Hubbard; Structo contributor Randy Prasse; and Mark Rich, columnist for *Toy Shop* and *Toy Cars & Models* magazines, contributed the Buddy L, Marx, Tonka, Tootsietoy, Gay Toys, Midgetoy, Processed Plastic, Remco, Deluxe Reading, and Eldon Industries chapters. *Toys & Prices* editor Karen O'Brien handled the remaining chapters.

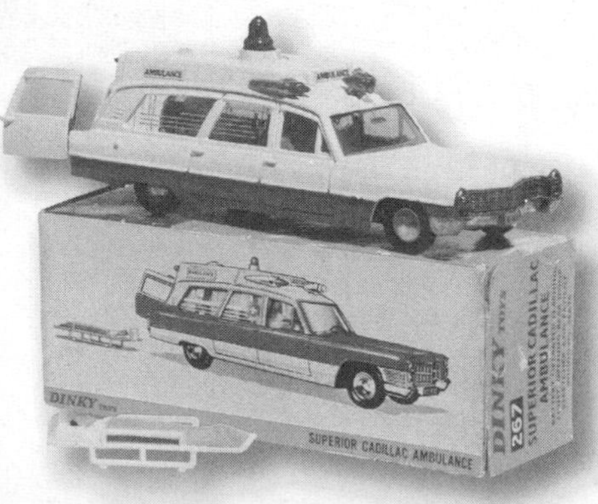

THE TOP 10 VEHICLES (In Mint Condition)

1. Chrysler Imperial, Japanese Tin Cars, 1962 . . . . $8,000
2. Custom T-Bird, Johnny Lightning Topper, 1969 5,000
3. Avro Vulcan Delta Wing Bomber, Dinky, #749, 1955-56 4,500
4. Vulcan Bomber, Dinky, 1955-56 4,000
5. 1956 Ford Sedan, Japanese Tin Cars, Marusan 4,000
6. 1956 Ford Two-Door Sedan, Japanese Tin Cars, Marusan 3,500
7. Leland Tanker, Dinky, Corn Products, 1950s 3,000
8. Pop Art Mini Mostest, Corgi, 1969 2,700
9. Lincoln Continental Mark II, Japanese Tin Cars, Linemar, 1956 . . . 2,500
10. American LaFrance Searchlight Truck, Doepke, 1955-56 2,100

BUDDY L

AIRPLANES

5000 Monocoupe "The Lone Eagle", orange wing, black fuselage and tail w/tailskid, all steel high wind cabin monoplane, 9-7/8" wingspan, 1929
EX $250 **NM** $300 **MIP** $400

Army Tank Transport Plane, low-wing monoplane, two small four-wheel tanks that clip beneath wings, 27" wingspan; 1941
EX $250 **NM** $350 **MIP** $400

Brute Good Year Blimp, 5" long; 1976
EX $3 **NM** $5 **MIP** $8

Catapult Airplane and Hangar, 5000 Monocoupe w/tailwheel, 9-7/8" wingspan, olive/gray hangar, black twin-spring catapult, 1930
EX $955 **NM** $1210 **MIP** $1520

Four Motor Air Cruiser, white, red engine cowlings, yellow fuselage and twin tails, four engine monoplane, 27" wingspan; 1952
EX $200 **NM** $310 **MIP** $350

Four-Engine Transport, green wings, white engine cowlings, yellow fuselage and twin tails, four engine monoplane, 27" wingspan; 1949
EX $205 **NM** $300 **MIP** $405

Hangar and Three 5000 Monocoupes, olive/gray hangar, windows outlined in red or orange, planes 9-7/8" wingspan, all steel high wing cabin monoplanes, 1930
EX $750 **NM** $1000 **MIP** $2000

Transport Airplane, white wings and engine cowlings, red fuselage and twin tails, four engine monoplane, 27" wingspan; 1946
EX $205 **NM** $310 **MIP** $410

BUSES

Greyhound Americruiser, made in Macau; marked 1979
EX $3 **NM** $7 **MIP** $10

Greyhound Americruiser, 7-1/2" long; made in Japan, "No. 4950"; 1979
EX $5 **NM** $10 **MIP** $15

School Bus, yellow station wagon, "School Bus" roof sign, door "Stop" sign, 1970s
EX $50 **NM** $75 **MIP** $275

School Bus, 11-1/4" long; van design with open side door, chrome-hub whitewall tires, yellow body, orange chassis, 1960s
EX $14 **NM** $25 **MIP** $40

School Bus, 9-3/4" long; yellow, open top; 1981
EX $3 **NM** $5 **MIP** $10

School Bus, 6-1/2" long; made in Macau; marked 1980
EX $2 **NM** $4 **MIP** $10

School Bus, 6-1/2" long; yellow, black front fenders, made in Japan; 1980
EX $3 **NM** $6 **MIP** $10

CARS

Army Jeep, 5-1/2" long; metal base, plastic body, Army green with white star on hood and sides; 1979
EX $3 **NM** $5 **MIP** $5

Army Staff Car, olive drab body, 15-3/4" long; 1964
EX $100 **NM** $150 **MIP** $200

Baha Bronc, 6-1/2" long; white Jeep with stars/stripes motif, black rollover roof, 1980s
EX $4 **NM** $9 **MIP** $17

Big "H" Race Team, 17" long; hot Rod with two trailers and two Honda motorcycles; 1966-68
EX $35 **NM** $75 **MIP** $110

Bloomin' Bus (VW), 10-3/4" long; chartreuse body, white roof and supports; 1969
EX $25 **NM** $55 **MIP** $85

Brute Baby Buggy, 5" long; baby-carriage type vehicle; 1969-70
EX $3 **NM** $5 **MIP** $8

Brute Beach Buggy, 5" long; covered dune buggy; 1969-70
EX $3 **NM** $5 **MIP** $8

Brute Boss Bug, 5" long; muscle car style; 1970-71
EX $3 **NM** $5 **MIP** $8

Brute Fire Buggy, 5" long; ladder truck; 1969-71
EX $3 **NM** $5 **MIP** $8

Brute Road Buggy, 5" long; roadster; 1970-71
EX $3 **NM** $5 **MIP** $8

Brute Super Bug, 5" long; VW Beetle; 1970-71
EX $3 **NM** $7 **MIP** $8

Buddywagen (VW), 10-3/4" long; red body with white roof, no chrome "V" on front; 1967
EX $30 **NM** $60 **MIP** $90

Buddywagen (VW), 10-3/4" long; red body with white roof, opening side doors, folding seats, sliding sun roof; 1966
EX $30 **NM** $60 **MIP** $90

Camaro, 4-1/2" long; plastic, opaque windows, "Camaro" sitcker on sides; 1980
EX $2 **NM** $4 **MIP** $6

Colt Sportsliner, 10-1/4" long; red open body, white hardtop; off-white seats and interior; 1967
EX $20 **NM** $45 **MIP** $70

Colt Sportsliner, 10-1/4" long; light blue-green open body, white hardtop, pale tan seats and interior; 1968-69
EX $20 **NM** $40 **MIP** $65

Colt Utility Car, light orange body, tan interior, 10 1/4" long; 1968
EX $35 **NM** $45 **MIP** $65

Colt Utility Car, 10-1/4" long; red open body, white plastic seats, floor and luggage spade; 1967
EX $20 **NM** $45 **MIP** $70

Country Squire Wagon, off-white hood fenders, end gate and roof, brown woodgrain side panels, 15-1/2" long; 1963
EX $85 **NM** $140 **MIP** $175

Country Squire Wagon, red hood fenders, end gate and roof, brown woodgrain side panels, 15-1/2" long; 1965
EX $75 **NM** $115 **MIP** $150

Deluxe Convertible Coupe, metallic blue enamel front, sides and deck, cream top retracts into rumble seat, 19" long; 1949
EX $310 **NM** $455 **MIP** $605

Desert Rat Command Car, 10-1/4" long; tan body, beige interior, blackwall tires; 1968
EX $30 **NM** $65 **MIP** $90

Desert Rat Command Car, 10-1/4" long; tan body, beige interior, black machine gun between seats, whitewall tires; 1967
EX $30 **NM** $65 **MIP** $90

Dr. Doom Blaster Car, Marvel Super Heroes Secret Wars series, 1984
EX $2 **NM** $8 **MIP** $15

Dr. Octopus Blaster Car, Marvel Super Heroes Secret Wars series, 1984
EX $2 **NM** $8 **MIP** $15

Flivver Coupe, black w/red eight-spoke wheels, black hubs, aluminum tires, flat, hardtop roof on enclosed glass-window-style body, 11" long, 1924
EX $700 **NM** $1100 **MIP** $1400

Flivver Roadster, black w/red eight-spoke wheels, black hubs, aluminum tires, simulated soft, folding top, 11" long, 1924
EX $700 **NM** $1200 **MIP** $1350

Formula One Racer, 8" long; blue with "3" and "STP," 1980s
EX $7 **NM** $12 **MIP** $18

Gull Wing Vette, 4" long; "Pace Car" on sides; 1979
EX $6 **NM** $12 **MIP** $18

Hot Rod, whitewall tires, plastic roof, spare tire in rear (until 1968), various colors; 1965
EX $13 **NM** $25 **MIP** $45

Hot Rod Woody Station Wagon, Ol' Buddys series, 10-1/2" long; made in Japan, opening driver door and back door, steering; late 1960s
EX $20 **NM** $35 **MIP** $50

Jr. Buggy Hauler, 12" long; Jeep, Sandpiper dune buggy on trailer; 1971
EX $17 **NM** $33 **MIP** $50

Jr. Camaro, 9" long; metallic blue body, white racing stripes on hood; 1968
EX $17 **NM** $25 **MIP** $50

Jr. Flower Power Sportster, purple hood, fenders and body, white roof and supports, white plastic seats, lavender and orange five-petal blossom decals on hood top, roof, and sides, 6" long; 1969
EX $23 **NM** $35 **MIP** $55

Jr. Mustang, 9" long; whitewall tires; 1971
EX $7 **NM** $13 **MIP** $20

Jr. Sportster, blue hood and open body, white hardtop and upper sides, 6" long; 1968
EX $23 **NM** $35 **MIP** $55

Mechanical Scarab Automobile, red radically streamlined body, bright metal front and rear bumpers, 10-1/2" long, 1936
EX $200 **NM** $300 **MIP** $500

Mr. T Corvette, 5-1/4" long; red plastic with Mr. T image, 1980s
EX $4 NM $8 MIP $12

Police Colt, 10-1/4" long; blue body, white hardtop, "Police 1" on sides; 1968-69
EX $17 NM $33 MIP $50

Ski Bus (VW), 10-3/4" long; white body and roof, ski rack, skis and ski poles, two skiers; 1967-68
EX $75 NM $125 MIP $300

Sling Shot Race Team, 6-1/2" long; green Jeep with 4" racer on trailer, 1970s
EX $8 NM $14 MIP $20

Station Wagon, light blue/green body and roof, 15-1/2" long; 1963
EX $75 NM $115 MIP $150

Streamline Scarab, red, radically streamlined body, non-mechanical, 10-1/2" long; 1941
EX $145 NM $225 MIP $290

Suburban Wagon, powder blue or white body and roof, 15-1/2" long; 1963
EX $75 NM $115 MIP $150

Suburban Wagon, gray/green body and roof, 15-3/4" long; 1964
EX $70 NM $100 MIP $140

Thunderbird, 5" long; red body, white top, whitewall tires, 1980s
EX $8 NM $15 MIP $25

Town and Country Convertible, maroon front, hood, rear deck and fenders, gray top retracts into rumble seat, 19" long; 1947
EX $300 NM $450 MIP $600

Travel Trailer and Station Wagon, red station wagon, two-wheel trailer w/red lower body and white steel camper-style upper body, 27-1/4" long; 1965
EX $155 NM $230 MIP $310

VW Bug, 2-1/2" long; red, white-hub tires, 1970s
EX $2 NM $4 MIP $8

Yellow Taxi with Skyview, yellow hood, roof and body, red radiator front and fenders, 18-1/2" long; 1948
EX $200 NM $400 MIP $600

CONSTRUCTION AND FARM EQUIPMENT

Aerial Tower Tramway, two tapering dark green 33-1/2" tall towers and 12" square bases, black hand crank, 1928
EX $1000 NM $1300 MIP $2700

Big Derrick, red mast and 20" boom, black base, 24" tall, 1921
EX $600 NM $900 MIP $1200

Brute Articulated Scooper, 5-1/2" long; yellow, front-loading scoop, articulated frame; 1970
EX $6 NM $12 MIP $18

Brute Articulated Scooper, yellow front-loading scoop, cab, articulated frame and rear power unit, black radiator, exhaust, steering wheel and driver's seat, 5-1/2" long; 1970
EX $6 NM $12 MIP $18

Brute Double Dump Train (tractor-trailer), 9-1/2" long; yellow, coupled bottom-dumping earth carriers; 1969
EX $8 NM $17 MIP $25

Brute Dumping Scraper, 7" long; yellow; 1970
EX $7 NM $13 MIP $20

Brute Farm Tractor-n-Cart, 6-1/4" long; blue tractor with green engine and driver's seat, blue two-wheel open car; 1969
EX $7 NM $13 MIP $20

Brute Road Grader, 6-1/2" long; yellow, adjustable blade; 1970
EX $6 NM $12 MIP $18

Cement Mixer on Treads, medium gray w/black treads and water tank, No. 280A, 16" tall, 1929-31
EX $2500 NM $3800 MIP $5200

Cement Mixer on Wheels, medium gray w/black cast steel wheels and water tank, 14-1/2" tall, 1926-29
EX $700 NM $900 MIP $1500

Concrete Mixer, green frame, base, crank, crank handle and bottom of mixing drum, gray hopper and top of drum, 9-5/8" long; 1949
EX $100 NM $150 MIP $200

Concrete Mixer, red frame and base, cream/yellow hopper, drum and crank handle, 10-1/2" long; 1941
EX $135 NM $195 MIP $255

Concrete Mixer, yellow/orange frame and base, red hopper and drum, black crank handle, 10-1/2" long, 1936
EX $110 NM $175 MIP $225

Concrete Mixer, medium gray w/black cast-steel wheels, black water tank, w/wood-handle, steel-blade scoop shovel, No. 280, 17-3/4" long w/tow bar up, 1926
EX $500 NM $750 MIP $1000

Concrete Mixer, green w/black cast-steel wheels, crank, gears, and band mixing drum, 10-1/2" long, 1930
EX $175 NM $265 MIP $350

Concrete Mixer with Motor Sound, green frame, base, crank, crank handle and bottom of mixing drum, gray hopper and top of drum, w/sound when crank rotates drum, 9 5/8" long; 1950
EX $75 NM $115 MIP $150

Dandy Digger, yellow main frame, operators, seat and boom, brown shovel, arm, under frame and twin skids, 27" long; 1941
EX $95 NM $145 MIP $195

Dandy Digger, yellow main frame, operators, seat and boom, green shovel, arm, under frame and twin skids, 27" long, 1936
EX $85 NM $130 MIP $175

Dandy Digger, yellow seat lower control lever and main boom, black underframe, skids, shovel and arm, 38-1/2" long w/shovel arm extended; 1953
EX $75 NM $115 MIP $150

Dandy Digger, red main frame, operators, seat and boom, black shovel, arm, under frame and twin skids, 27" long, 1931
EX $100 NM $160 MIP $215

Dandy Digger, yellow seat, lower control lever and main boom, black underframe, skids, shovel, arm and control lever, 38-1/2" long w/shovel arm extended; 1953
EX $75 NM $115 MIP $150

Digger, red main frame, operators, seat and boom, black shovel, arm, lower frame and twin skids, curved connecting rod, boom tilts down for digging, 11-1/2" long w/shovel arm extended, 1935
EX $100 NM $150 MIP $200

Dredge, red corrugated roof and base w/four wide black wheels, red hubs, black boiler, floor, frame boom and clamshell bucket, 19" long, 1924
EX $750 NM $1000 MIP $1500

Giant Digger, red main frame, operators, seat and boom, black shovel, arm, lower frame and twin skids, boom tilts down for digging, 42" long w/shovel arm extended, 1931
EX $275 NM $415 MIP $550

Giant Digger, red main frame, operators, seat and boom, black shovel, arm, lower frame and twin skids, curved connecting rod, boom tilts, 31" long w/shovel arm extended, 1933
EX $265 NM $395 MIP $525

Giant Digger, yellow main frame, operators, seat and boom, green shovel, arm, lower frame and twin skids, boom tilts, 11-1/2" long w/shovel arm extended, 1936
EX $85 NM $130 MIP $175

Giant Digger, yellow main frame, operators, seat and boom, brown shovel, arm, lower frame and twin skids, boom tilts, 11-1/2" long w/shovel arm extended; 1941
EX $75 NM $115 MIP $155

Gradall, bright yellow truck and superstructure, black plastic bumper and radiator, 32" long w/digging arm extended; 1965
EX $350 NM $750 MIP $1000

Hauling Rig with Construction Derrick, duo-tone slant design tractor, yellow bumper, lower hood and cab sides, white upper hood and cab, white trailer w/yellow loading ramp, overall 38-1/2" long; 1953
EX $175 NM $250 MIP $400

Hauling Rig with Construction Derrick, yellow tractor unit, green semi-trailer, winch on front of trailer makes sound, 36-3/4" long; 1954
EX $110 NM $175 MIP $225

Hoisting Tower, dark green, hoist tower and three distribution chutes, 29" tall, 1928-31
EX $1500 **NM** $2000 **MIP** $2500

Husky Tractor, bright yellow body and large rear fenders, black engine block, exhaust, steering wheel and driver's seat, 13" long; 1966
EX $50 **NM** $80 **MIP** $105

Husky Tractor, bright blue body with white wheels and large rear fenders, black engine block, exhaust, steering wheel and driver's seat, 13" long; 1969
EX $40 **NM** $60 **MIP** $80

Husky Tractor, bright yellow body, red large rear fenders and wheels, black engine block, exhaust, steering wheel and driver's seat, 13" long; 1970
EX $30 **NM** $45 **MIP** $65

Improved Steam Shovel, black w/red roof and base, 14" tall, 1927-29
EX $100 **NM** $150 **MIP** $200

Junior Excavator, red shovel, arm, underframe, control lever and twin skids, yellow boom, rear lever, frame and seat, 28" long; 1945
EX $75 **NM** $115 **MIP** $150

Mechanical Crane, orange removable roof, boom and wheels in black cleated rubber crawler treads, olive green enclosed cab and base, hand crank w/rat-tat motor noise, 20" tall; 1950
EX $175 **NM** $265 **MIP** $350

Mechanical Crane, orange removable roof, boom, yellow wheels in white rubber crawler treads, olive green enclosed cab and base, hand crank w/rat-tat motor noise, 20" tall; 1952
EX $150 **NM** $225 **MIP** $300

Mobile Construction Derrick, orange laticework main mast, swiveling base, yellow latticework boom, green clamshell bucket and main platform base, 25-1/2" long w/boom lowered; 1953
EX $155 **NM** $250 **MIP** $355

Mobile Construction Derrick, orange laticework main mast, swiveling base, yellow latticework boom, gray clamshell bucket, green main platform base, 25-1/2" long w/boom lowered; 1955
EX $160 **NM** $260 **MIP** $355

Mobile Construction Derrick, orange laticework main mast, swiveling base, yellow latticework boom, gray clamshell bucket, orange main platform base, 25-1/2" long w/boom lowered; 1956
EX $150 **NM** $250 **MIP** $350

Mobile Power Digger Unit, clamshell dredge mounted on 10-wheel truck, orange truck, yellow dredge cab on swivel base, 31-3/4" long w/boom lowered; 1955
EX $125 **NM** $185 **MIP** $250

Mobile Power Digger Unit, clamshell dredge mounted on six-wheel truck, orange truck, yellow dredge cab on swivel base, 31-3/4" long w/boom lowered; 1956
EX $100 **NM** $150 **MIP** $250

Overhead Crane, black folding end frames and legs, braces, red crossbeams and platform, 46" long, 1924
EX $800 **NM** $1500 **MIP** $2300

Pile Driver on Wheels, black w/red roof and base, No. 260, 22-1/2" tall, 1924-27
EX $800 **NM** $1700 **MIP** $2500

Polysteel Farm Tractor, orange molded plastic four-wheel tractor, silver radiator front, headlights, and motor parts, 12" long; 1961
EX $80 **NM** $120 **MIP** $155

Pull-n-Ride Horse-Drawn Farm Wagon, red four-wheel steel hopper-body wagon, detailed litho horse, 22-3/4" long; 1952
EX $150 **NM** $225 **MIP** $300

Road Roller, dark green w/red roof and rollers, nickel plated steam cylinders, No. 290, 20" long, 1929-31
EX $1300 **NM** $2400 **MIP** $3500

Ruff-n-Tuff Tractor, yellow grille, hood and frame, black plastic engine block and driver's seat, 10-1/2" long; 1971
EX $50 **NM** $75 **MIP** $100

Sand Loader, warm gray w/twelve black buckets, chain-tension adjusting device at bottom of elevator side frames, 21" long, 1929
EX $175 **NM** $305 **MIP** $500

Sand Loader, yellow w/twelve black buckets, chain-tension adjusting device at bottom of elevator side frames, 21" long, 1931
EX $200 **NM** $250 **MIP** $350

Sand Loader, warm gray w/twelve black buckets, 21" long, 18" high, 1924
EX $150 **NM** $210 **MIP** $450

Scoop-n-Load Conveyor, cream body frame, green loading scoop, black circular crank operates black rubber cleated conveyor belt, "PORTABLE" decal in red, 18" long; 1954
EX $65 **NM** $105 **MIP** $140

Scoop-n-Load Conveyor, cream body frame, red loading scoop and chute, bright-plated circular crank operates black rubber cleated conveyor belt, "PORTABLE" decal in white, 18" long; 1955
EX $60 **NM** $95 **MIP** $125

Scoop-n-Load Conveyor, cream body frame, red loading scoop and chute, bright-plated circular crank operates black rubber cleated conveyor belt, "PORTABLE" decal in yellow, 18" long; 1956
EX $55 **NM** $85 **MIP** $115

Scoop-n-Load Conveyor, cream body frame, green loading scoop, black circular crank operates black rubber cleated conveyor belt, 18" long; 1953
EX $75 **NM** $115 **MIP** $150

Scoop-n-Load Conveyor, 1956-57, cram body frame, green loading scoop, black circular crank operates black rubber cleated conveyor belt, "PORTABLE" decal in green, 18" long; 1956-57
EX $50 **NM** $100 **MIP** $150

Side Conveyor Load-n-Dump, yellow plastic front end including cab, yellow steel bumper, green frame and dump body, red conveyor frame w/chute, 20-1/2" long; 1953
EX $80 **NM** $130 **MIP** $150

Side Conveyor Load-n-Dump, all steel yellow cab, hood, bumper and frame, white dump body and tailgate, red conveyor frame w/chute, 21-1/4" long; 1954
EX $65 **NM** $100 **MIP** $135

Side Conveyor Load-n-Dump, all steel yellow cab, hood, bumper and frame, deep blue dump body, white tailgate, red conveyor frame w/chute, 21-1/4" long; 1955
EX $60 **NM** $95 **MIP** $125

Small Derrick, red 20" movable boom and three angle-iron braces, black base and vertical mast, 21-1/2" tall, 1921
EX $500 **NM** $750 **MIP** $1000

Steam Shovel, black w/red roof and base, 25-1/2" tall, 1921-22
EX $125 **NM** $250 **MIP** $500

Traveling Crane, red crane, carriage, and long cross beams, hand wheel rotates crane boom, 46" long, 1928
EX $1275 **NM** $1900 **MIP** $2550

Trench Digger, yellow main frame, base, and motor housing, red elevator and conveyor frame and track frames, 20" tall, 1928-31
EX $2000 **NM** $3500 **MIP** $5000

EMERGENCY VEHICLES

Aerial Ladder and Emergency Truck, red w/white ladders, bumper and steel disc wheels, three eight-rung steel ladders, 22-1/4" long; 1952
EX $200 **NM** $300 **MIP** $400

Aerial Ladder and Emergency Truck, red w/white ladders, bumper and steel disc wheels, three eight-rung steel ladders, no rear step, no siren or SIREN decal, 22-1/4" long; 1953
EX $225 **NM** $345 **MIP** $450

Aerial Ladder Fire Engine, red tractor, wraparound bumper and semi-trailer, two aluminum thirteen-rung extension ladders on sides, swivel-base aluminum central ladder, 26-1/2" long; 1960
EX $125 **NM** $185 **MIP** $250

Aerial Ladder Fire Engine, red tractor and semi-trailer, white plastic bumper w/integral grille guard, two aluminum thirteen-rung extension ladders on sides, swivel-base aluminum central ladder, 26-1/2" long; 1961
EX $125 **NM** $185 **MIP** $250

Aerial Ladder Fire Engine, red tractor and semi-trailer, chrome one-piece wraparound bumper, slotted grille, two aluminum thirteen-rung extension ladders on sides, swivel-base aluminum central ladder, 26-1/2" long; 1966
EX $125 **NM** $185 **MIP** $250

Aerial Ladder Fire Engine, red cabover-engine tractor and semi-trailer units, two thirteen-rung white sectional ladders and swivel-mounted aerial ladder w/side rails, 25-1/2" long; 1968
EX $100 **NM** $150 **MIP** $200

Aerial Ladder Fire Engine, snub-nose red tractor and semi-trailer, white swivel-mounted aerial ladder w/side rails, two white thirteen-rung sectional ladders, 27-1/2" long; 1970
EX $100 **NM** $150 **MIP** $200

Aerial Ladder Fire Engine (tractor-trailer), 26-1/2" long; chrome one-piece wraparound bumper, slotted grille; 1966-67
EX $40 **NM** $85 **MIP** $125

Aerial Ladder Fire Engine (tractor-trailer), 25-1/2" long; cabover, two 13-rung white sectional ladders, swivel-mounted aerial ladder with side rails; 1968
EX $35 **NM** $65 **MIP** $100

Aerial Ladder Fire Engine (tractor-trailer), 27-1/2" long; snub-nose cab, white swivel-mounted aerial ladder with side rails, two white 13-rung sectional ladders; 1970
EX $25 **NM** $50 **MIP** $75

Aerial Truck, red w/nickel ladders, black hand wheel, brass bell, and black hubs, 39" long w/ladder down, 1925
EX $850 **NM** $1300 **MIP** $1700

American LaFrance Aero-Chief Pumper, red cabover-engine and body, white underbody, rear step and simulated hose reels, black extension ladders on right side, 25-1/2" long; 1972
EX $90 **NM** $150 **MIP** $200

American LaFrance Aero-Chief Pumper, 25-1/2" long; cabover, white underbody, rear step and simulated hose reels, black extension ladders on right side; 1962
EX $22 **NM** $43 **MIP** $65

Brute Fire Pumper, red cabover-engine body and frame, two yellow five-rung sectional ladders on sides of open body, 5-1/4" long; 1969
EX $35 **NM** $60 **MIP** $85

Brute Fire Pumper, 5-1/4" long; red cabover, two yellow 5-rung sectional ladders on sides; 1969
EX $4 **NM** $8 **MIP** $12

Brute Hook-N-Ladder, red cabover-engine tractor and detachable semi-trailer, white elevating, swveling aerial ladder w/side rails, 10" long; 1969
EX $30 **NM** $40 **MIP** $55

Brute Hook-N-Ladder (tractor-trailer), 10" long; cabover, detachable semi-trailer, white swiveling aerial ladder with side rails; 1969
EX $7 **NM** $13 **MIP** $20

Extension Ladder Fire Truck, red w/silver ladders and yellow removable rider seat, enclosed cab, 35" long; 1945
EX $200 **NM** $300 **MIP** $400

Extension Ladder Rider Fire Truck, duo-tone slant design, tractor has white front, lower hood sides and lower doors, red hood top, cab and frame, red semi-trailer, white ten-rung and eight-rung ladders, 32-1/2" long; 1949
EX $150 **NM** $225 **MIP** $300

Extension Ladder Trailer Fire Truck, red tractor unit and semi-trailer, enclosed cab, two white thirteen-rung side extension ladders on sides, white central ladder on swivel base, 29-1/2" long; 1956
EX $125 **NM** $185 **MIP** $250

Extension Ladder Trailer Fire Truck, red tractor w/enclosed cab, boxy fenders, red semi-trailer w/fenders, two white eight-rung side ladders, ten-rung central extension ladder, 29-1/2" long; 1955
EX $200 **NM** $300 **MIP** $400

Fire and Chemical Truck, duo-tone slant design, white front, lower hood sides and lower doors, rest is red, bright-metal or white eight-rung ladder on sides, 25" long; 1949
EX $125 **NM** $185 **MIP** $250

Fire Department Emergency Truck, red streamlined body, enclosed cab, chrome one-piece grille, bumper, and headlights, 12-3/4" long; 1953
EX $100 **NM** $150 **MIP** $200

Fire Engine, red w/nickel rim flywheels on dummy pump, brass bell, dim-or-bright electric headlights, 25-1/2" long, 1933
EX $500 **NM** $750 **MIP** $1500

Fire Engine, red w/nickel-plated upright broiler, nickel rims and flywheels on dummy water pump, brass bell, 23-1/4" long, 1925-29
EX $500 **NM** $800 **MIP** $1600

Fire Hose and Water Pumper, red w/two white five-rung ladders, two removable fire extinguishers, enclosed cab, 12-1/2" long; 1950
EX $105 **NM** $155 **MIP** $200

Fire Hose and Water Pumper, red w/two white five-rung ladders, one red/white removable fire extinguisher, enclosed cab, 12-1/2" long; 1952
EX $100 **NM** $150 **MIP** $200

Fire Pumper, No. 5311, station wagon design, "Buddy L No. 6" on cab door, siren light, ladder; 1964-65
EX $20 **NM** $40 **MIP** $60

Fire Pumper, 16-1/4" long; red cabover, 11-rung white 10" ladder on each side; 1968
EX $56 **NM** $85 **MIP** $100

Fire Pumper with Action Hydrant, red wraparound bumper, hood cab and cargo section, aluminum nine-rung ladders, white hose reel, 15" long; 1960
EX $75 **NM** $115 **MIP** $150

Fire Truck, red w/black solid-rubber Firestone tires on red seven-spoke embossed metal wheels, two 18-1/2" red steel sectional ladders, 26" long, 1930
EX $800 **NM** $1000 **MIP** $1600

Fire Truck, red w/two white ladders, enclosed cab, bright metal grille and headlights, 25" long; 1948
EX $125 **NM** $200 **MIP** $250

Fire Truck, duo-tone slant design, yellow front, bumper, hood sides and skirted fenders, rest is red, nickel ladders, 28-1/2" long, 1939
EX $500 **NM** $700 **MIP** $1000

Fire Truck, red w/nickel or white ladders, bright-metal radiator grille and black removable rider saddle, 25-1/2" long, 1935
EX $255 **NM** $385 **MIP** $510

Fire Truck, bright red, red floor, open driver's seat, 26" long, 1928
EX $450 **NM** $800 **MIP** $1200

Fire Truck, bright red w/black inverted L-shaped crane mounted in socket on seat back, red floor, open driver's seat, 26" long, 1925
EX $450 **NM** $800 **MIP** $1600

Fire Truck, bright red w/black inverted L-shaped crane mounted in socket on seat back, open driver's seat, 26" long, 1924
EX $500 **NM** $900 **MIP** $1850

Fire Truck, duo-tone slant design, tractor has white front, lower hood sides and lower doors, red hood top, cab and frame, red semi-trailer, rubber wheels w/black tires, 32-1/2" long; 1953
EX $200 **NM** $300 **MIP** $400

Fire Truck, red w/white ladders, black rubber wheels, enclosed cab, 12" long; 1945
EX $75 **NM** $115 **MIP** $150

Fire Truck, duo-tone slant design, yellow front, single-bar bumper, hood sides and removable rider seat, rest is red, 25-1/2" long, 1936
EX $170 **NM** $250 **MIP** $500

GMC Deluxe Aerial Ladder Fire Engine, white tractor and semi-trailer units, golden thirteen-rung extension ladder on sides, golden central aerial ladder, black and white DANGER battery case w/two flashing lights, 28" long; 1959
EX $225 **NM** $345 **MIP** $450

(Calvin L. Chaussee Photo)

GMC Extension Ladder Trailer Fire Engine, red tractor w/chrome GMC bar grille, red semi-trailer, white thirteen-rung extension ladders on sides, white swiveling central ladder w/side rails, 27-1/4" long; 1957
EX $110 **NM** $260 **MIP** $405

GMC Fire Pumper with Horn, red w/aluminum-finish eleven-rung side ladders and white reel of black plastic hose in open cargo section, chrome GMC bar grille, 15" long; 1958
EX $150 **NM** $200 **MIP** $300

GMC Hydraulic Aerial Ladder Fire Engine, red tractor unit w/chrome GMC bar grille, red semi-trailer, white thirteen-rung extension ladders on sides, white swiveling central ladder, 26-1/2" long; 1958
EX $125 **NM** $185 **MIP** $250

VEHICLES • BUDDY L

GMC Red Cross Ambulance, all white, removable fabric canopy w/a red cross and "Ambulance" in red, 14-1/2" long; 1960
EX $150 **NM** $250 **MIP** $400

Hook & Ladder Fire Truck, medium-dark red, w/black inverted L-shaped crane mounted in socket on seat back, open driver's seat, 26" long, 1923
EX $900 **NM** $1800 **MIP** $2800

(Joe & Sharon Freed Photo)

Hose Truck, red w/two white hose pipes, white cord hose on reel and brass nozzle, electric headlights w/red bulbs, 21 3/4" long, 1933
EX $495 **NM** $760 **MIP** $1100

Hydraulic Aerial Truck, red w/brass bell on cowl, nickel ladders mounted on 5-1/2" turntable rotated by black hand wheel, 39" long, 1927
EX $850 **NM** $1300 **MIP** $1700

Hydraulic Aerial Truck, duo-tone slant design, yellow front, single-bar bumper, chassis, radiator, front fender, lower sides and removable rider saddle, rest is red, 40" long w/ladders down, 1936
EX $550 **NM** $825 **MIP** $1100

Hydraulic Snorkel Fire Pumper, 21" long; red cabover, white 11-rung 10" ladder on each side; 1969
EX $32 **NM** $65 **MIP** $95

Hydraulic Snorkel Fire Pumper, red cabover-engine and open rear body, white eleven-rung 10" ladder on each side, snorkel pod w/solid sides, 21" long; 1969
EX $105 **NM** $155 **MIP** $210

Hydraulic Water Tower Truck, red w/nickel water tower, dim/bright electric headlights, brass bell, added-on bright-metal grille, 44-7/8" long w/tower down, 1935
EX $600 **NM** $900 **MIP** $1500

Hydraulic Water Tower Truck, duo-tone slant design, yellow bumper, hood sides, front fenders, rest is red, electric headlights, added-on bright-metal grille, 44-7/8" long w/tower down, 1936
EX $600 **NM** $1000 **MIP** $1500

Hydraulic Water Tower Truck, duo-tone slant design, yellow front, single-bar bumper and hood sides, red hood top, enclosed cab and water tank, brass bell, nickel water tower, 46" long w/tower down, 1939
EX $900 **NM** $1200 **MIP** $1700

Hydraulic Water Tower Truck, red w/nickel water tower, dim/bright electric headlights, brass bell, 44-7/8" long w/tower down, 1933
EX $800 **NM** $1000 **MIP** $1700

Jr. Fire Emergency Truck, 6-3/4" long; red cabover, wider bumper, 4-slot grille with two square plastic headlights; 1969
EX $8 **NM** $12 **MIP** $20

Jr. Fire Emergency Truck, 6-3/4" long; red cabover, one-piece chrome wraparound narrow bumper, 24-hole grille with plastic vertical-pair headlights; 1968
EX $8 **NM** $12 **MIP** $20

Jr. Fire Snorkel Truck, 11-1/2" long; red cabover, one-piece chrome wraparound narrow bumper, 24-hole grille with plastic vertical-pair headlights; 1968
EX $9 **NM** $14 **MIP** $22

Jr. Fire Snorkel Truck, 11-1/2" long; red cabover, wider bumper, 4-slot grille with two square plastic headlights; 1969
EX $9 **NM** $14 **MIP** $22

Jr. Hook-n-Ladder Aerial Truck, 17" long; red cabover, one-piece chrome wraparound narrow bumper, 24-hole grille with plastic vertical-pair headlights; 1968
EX $23 **NM** $35 **MIP** $48

Jr. Hook-n-Ladder Aerial Truck, 17" long; red cabover, wider bumper, 4-slot grille with two square plastic headlights; 1969
EX $17 **NM** $25 **MIP** $40

Ladder Fire Truck, red w/bright-metal V-nose radiator, headlights and ladder, black wooden wheels, 12" long; 1941
EX $125 **NM** $200 **MIP** $250

Ladder Truck, red w/yellow severely streamlined, skirted fenders and lower doors, white ladders, bright-metal grille, no bumper, 17-1/2" long; 1940
EX $200 **NM** $300 **MIP** $400

Ladder Truck, modified duo-tone slant design, white front, front fenders and lower doors, white ladders, bright-metal grille, no bumper, 17-1/2" long; 1941
EX $200 **NM** $300 **MIP** $400

Ladder Truck, red w/bright-metal grille and headlights, two white ladders, 24" long, 1939
EX $100 **NM** $200 **MIP** $300

Ladder Truck, duo-tone slant design, white front, hood sides, fenders and two ladders, rest is red, square enclosed cab w/sharply protruding visor, no headlights, 22-3/4" long, 1937
EX $135 **NM** $200 **MIP** $275

Ladder Truck, duo-tone slant design, white front, hood sides, fenders and two ladders, rest is red, square enclosed cab w/sharply protruding visor, 22-3/4" long, 1936
EX $150 **NM** $225 **MIP** $300

Ladder Truck, red w/two yellow ladders, enclosed square cab w/sharply protruding visor, bright-metal radiator front, 22-3/4" long, 1935
EX $255 **NM** $380 **MIP** $510

Ladder Truck, red w/two yellow ladders, enclosed square cab w/sharply protruding visor, 22-3/4" long, 1934
EX $200 **NM** $300 **MIP** $400

Ladder Truck, red w/two yellow sectional ladders, enclosed square cab, 22-3/4" long, 1933
EX $120 **NM** $250 **MIP** $500

Ladder Truck, red w/two white ladders, bright-metal radiator grille and headlights, 24" long; 1941
EX $125 **NM** $200 **MIP** $250

Police Squad Truck, yellow front and front fenders, dark blue-green body, yellow fire extinguisher, 21-1/2" long over ladders; 1947
EX $150 **NM** $300 **MIP** $550

Police Wrecker, 13-3/4" long; operating boom, front-wheel steering, whitewall tires; 1971
EX $8 **NM** $17 **MIP** $25

Police Wrecker, 4-3/4" long; bubble-window cabover; 1970s
EX $3 **NM** $7 **MIP** $10

Pumping Fire Engine, red w/nickel stack on boiler, nickel rims on pump flywheels, nickel-rim headlights and searchlight, 23-1/2" long, 1929
EX $2500 **NM** $3500 **MIP** $4000

Rear Steer Trailer Fire Truck, red w/two white ten-rung ladders, chrome one-piece grille, headlights and bumper, 20" long; 1952
EX $65 **NM** $100 **MIP** $200

Red Cross Ambulance, all white, removable fabric canopy w/a red cross and "Ambulance" in red, 14-1/2" long; 1958
EX $60 **NM** $95 **MIP** $125

Rescue Force Ambulance, 12" long; battery-operated, siren; 1993
EX $5 **NM** $10 **MIP** $15

Suburban Pumper, red station wagon body, white plastic wraparound bumpers, one-piece grille and double headlights, 15" long; 1964
EX $100 **NM** $150 **MIP** $175

Texaco Fire Chief American LaFrance Pumper, promotional piece, red rounded-front enclosed cab and body, white one-pice underbody, running boards and rear step, 25" long; 1962
EX $150 **NM** $200 **MIP** $410

Trailer Ladder Truck, all red w/cream removable rider saddle, three bright metal ten-rung ladders, 20" long over ladders; 1941
EX $150 **NM** $225 **MIP** $300

Trailer Ladder Truck, duo-tone slant design, tractor unit has yellow front, lower hood sides and lower doors, red hood top, enclosed cab and semi-trailer, nickel ten-rung ladders, 30" long w/ladders; 1940
EX $200 **NM** $300 **MIP** $400

Voice-Command Hook-N-Ladder, 23" long; ladder extends to 31" high; battery-operated voice commands and actions
EX $15 **NM** $25 **MIP** $35

Water Tower Truck, red w/nickel two-bar front bumper, red nickel-rim headlights plus searchllight on cowl, nickel latticework water tower, 45-1/2" long w/tower down, 1929
EX $2500 **NM** $4000 **MIP** $5500

MISCELLANEOUS

49 LST, Gray landing craft with swivel guns on deck, opening ramp door, includes tank and army truck
EX $35 NM $75 MIP $95

Fill-R-Up gas pump, 7" high; battery operated, ringing bell, price "totals"; 1966-69
EX $6 NM $12 MIP $18

Fill-R-Up Gas Pump, White plastic gas pump, 4" wide, 7" high, 2-3/4" deep. Magnetic pump holds to metal vehicles, two "C" batteries power the pump register and bell. According to the 1970 catalog, it "totals price automatically--up to 39 gallons at $9.75."
EX $12 NM $25 MIP $40

Hydraulic Service Lift, 15" long; battery-operated service ramp, steel, push-button with bell and retractable air hoses; 1967-68
EX $8 NM $17 MIP $25

Jr. Animal Ark, 5" long; ten pairs of plastic animals; 1970
EX $5 NM $10 MIP $15

Traffic Light, 8" high; plastic, battery-operated, push-button, made in Japan; 1967-69
EX $3 NM $6 MIP $10

Yogi Bear Sit-N-Ride, 22" long, 19" high; plastic Yogi Bear with green hat on casters, triangular metal handle behind Yogi's head, 1960
EX $50 NM $80 MIP $120

SETS

Amazing Spider-Man Set, four-piece tray set of cycle, helicopter, van and car; 1980
EX $8 NM $14 MIP $20

Army Combination, searchlight repair-it truck, transport truck and howitzer, ammunition conveyor, stake delivery truck, ammo, soldiers; 1956
EX $300 NM $400 MIP $500

Army Commando, 14-1/2" truck, searchlight unit, two-wheel howitzer, soldiers; 1957
EX $125 NM $185 MIP $250

Big "H" Race Team Set, 17", hot rod hauling two motorcycles, 1960s
EX $60 NM $80 MIP $130

Big Brute Freeway, scraper, grader, scooper and dump truck; 1971
EX $30 NM $60 MIP $90

Big Brute Hi-Way, bulldozer, dump truck, yellow four-wheel trailer; 1971
EX $20 NM $40 MIP $60

Big Brute Road, cement mixer truck, scooper, dump truck; 1971
EX $20 NM $40 MIP $60

Brute Fire Department, semi trailer aerial ladder, fire pumper, fire wrecker, tow truck; 1970
EX $17 NM $33 MIP $50

Brute Five-Piece Highway, bulldozer, grader, scraper, dumping scraper and double dump train; 1970
EX $50 NM $80 MIP $105

Brute Fleet, car carrier with two plastic coupes, dump truck, pickup truck, cement mixer truck, tow truck; 1970
EX $17 NM $56 MIP $50

Brute Fleet, car carrier w/two plastic coupes, dump truck, pickup truck, cement mixer truck, tow truck; 1969
EX $85 NM $130 MIP $175

Brute Hi-Way, bulldozer, grader, scraper, sumping scraper and double dump train; 1970
EX $17 NM $33 MIP $50

Coca-Cola, 10-1/2" trailer truck; three-vehicle set with tractor-trailer with clear plastic cover, five cases and hadtruck; delivery truck with two cases; and forklift truck with two extra cases; late 1970s
EX $15 NM $20 MIP $30

Delivery Set Combination, 16-1/2" long Wrigley express truck, 15" long sand and stone dump truck, 14-1/4" long freight conveyor and 14-1/4" long stake delivery truck; 1955
EX $175 NM $265 MIP $350

Deluxe Riding Academy, 18-1/2" long truck; Sears exclusive, red horse truck with bubbletop, "Riding Academy" on van sides, two horses and two colts, plastic six-piece fense; 1966-69
EX $40 NM $80 MIP $125

Emergency Set, five-piece set w/ladder tractor-trailer, van, helicopter, pickup and ladder/pumper, all red and white, tray display box, 1970s
EX $12 NM $20 MIP $35

Exxon Road Service Set, 11" Exxon tractor-trailer tanker, 4-1/2" Jeep, 5" Wrecker, all white with Exxon decals, white-hub tires, in tray box with Exxon tiger, 1976
EX $15 NM $25 MIP $50

Family Camping, Camper/cruiser truck, 15-1/2" long maroon suburban wagon, and brown/light gray/beige folding teepee camping trailer; 1963
EX $60 NM $95 MIP $130

Family Camping, blue camping trailer and suburban wagon, blue camper-n-cruiser; 1964
EX $50 NM $75 MIP $100

Farm Combination, cattle transport stake truck w/six plastic steers, hydraulic farm supplies trailer dump truck, trailer and three farm machines and farm machinery trailer hauler truck; 1956
EX $100 NM $155 MIP $210

Fire Department, aerial ladder fire engine, fire pumper w/action hydrant that squirts water, two plastic hoses, two plastic firemen, fire chief's badge; 1960
EX $250 NM $375 MIP $505

Freight Conveyor and Stake Delivery Truck, blue frame 14-1/4" long conveyor, red, white and yellow body 14-3/4" long truck; 1955
EX $125 NM $185 MIP $250

Friendly Highway, 8-1/2" x 6-3/4" x 2-1/2" box; steel and plastic, includes Texacto Tanker truck; 1980s
EX $8 NM $17 MIP $25

GMC Air Defense, 15" long, GMC army searchlight truck, 15" long, GMC signal corps truck, two four-wheel trailers, plastic soliders; 1957
EX $300 NM $500 MIP $700

GMC Brinks Bank, silver gray, barred windows on sides and in double doors, coin slot and hole in roof, brass padlock w/two keys, pouch, play money, two gray plastic guard figures, 16" long; 1959
EX $305 NM $360 MIP $455

GMC Fire Department, red GMC extension ladder trailer and GMC pumper w/ladders and hose reel, four-wheel red electric searchlight trailer, warning barrier, red plastic helmet, firemen, policeman; 1958
EX $300 NM $500 MIP $750

GMC Highway Maintenance Fleet, orange maintenance truck w/trailer, sand and stone dump truck, scoop-n-load conveyor, sand hopper, steel scoop shovel, four white steel road barriers; 1957
EX $310 NM $505 MIP $710

GMC Livestock, red fenders, hood, cab and frame, white flatbed cargo section , six sections of brown plastic rail fencing, five black plastic steers, 14-1/2" long; 1958
EX $300 NM $400 MIP $500

GMC Western Roundup, blue fenders, hood, cab and frame, white flatbed cargo section, plastic six sections of rail fencing w/swinging gate, rearing and standing horse, cowboys, calf, steer; 1959
EX $300 NM $400 MIP $500

Highway Construction, orange and black bulldozer and driver, truck w/orange pickup body, orange dump truck; 1962
EX $200 NM $300 MIP $400

Highway Maintenance Mechanical Truck & Concrete Mixer, 20" truck plus movable ramp, w/duo-tone slant

design, blue lower hood sides, yellow hood top and cab, 10-3/4" blue and yellow mixer, overall 36" long; 1949
EX $160 **NM** $245 **MIP** $325

Interstate Highway, orange, husky dumper, contractor's truck and ladder, utility truck, plastic pickaxe, spade, shovel, nail keg; 1960
EX $250 **NM** $350 **MIP** $500

Interstate Highway, orange, parks department dumper, landscape truck, telephone truck, accessories include trees, drums, workmen and traffic cones, scoop shovel; 1959
EX $260 **NM** $410 **MIP** $505

Jr. Animal Farm, Jr. Giraffe Truck, Jr. Kitty Kennel, Jr. Pony Trailer with Sportster; 1968
EX $32 **NM** $63 **MIP** $95

Jr. Animal Farm, 6-1/2" long Jr. Giraffe Truck, 6-1/4" long Jr. Kitty Kennel, 11-1/4" long Jr. Pony Trailer w/Sportster; 1968
EX $120 **NM** $185 **MIP** $250

Jr. Fire Department, 17" long Jr. hook-n-ladder aerial truck, 11-1/2" long Jr. fire snorkel, 6-3/4" long truck, all have four-slot grilles and two square plastic headlights; 1969
EX $120 **NM** $185 **MIP** $250

Jr. Fire Department, Jr. Hook-n-Ladder Aerial, Jr. Fire Snorkel, Jr. Fire Emergency Truck with four-slot grilles and square plastic headlights; 1969
EX $32 **NM** $63 **MIP** $95

Jr. Fire Department, 17" long Jr. hook-n-ladder aerial truck, 11-1/2" long Jr. fire snorkel, 6-3/4" long truck, all have twenty-four-hole chrome grilles; 1968
EX $32 **NM** $63 **MIP** $95

Jr. Hi-Way, Jr. Scooper Tractor, Jr. Cement Mixer, Jr. Dump Truck; 1969
EX $30 **NM** $60 **MIP** $90

Jr. Sportsman, Jr. camper pickup w/red cab and body and yellow camper, towing 6" plastic runabout on yellow two-wheel boat trailer; 1971
EX $50 **NM** $80 **MIP** $105

Jr. Sportsman, Jr. Camper Pickup, boat trailer and plastic runabout; 1971
EX $17 **NM** $33 **MIP** $50

Loader, Dump Truck, and Shovel, conveyor, blue body sand and gravel dump truck, 8-3/4" long blue-enameled steel scoop shovel; 1955
EX $85 **NM** $130 **MIP** $175

Loader, Dump Truck, and Shovel, conveyor, green body sand and gravel dump truck, 8-3/4" long green-enameled steel scoop shovel; 1954
EX $100 **NM** $150 **MIP** $200

Lumberjack Set, log hauler, log loader, pickup, lumberjack figure, 1979
EX $10 **NM** $15 **MIP** $35

Mechanical Hauling Truck and Concrete Mixer, truck w/duo-tone slant design, red/orange lower hood sides, dark green upper hood, cab, ramp, yellow trailer, 9-5/8" green mixer, gray hopper, 38" long w/ramps; 1951
EX $150 **NM** $225 **MIP** $300

Mechanical Hauling Truck and Concrete Mixer, truck w/duo-tone slant design, red-orange lower hood sides, dark green upper hood, cab, trailer and ramp, 9-5/8" green mixer, gray hopper, 38" long w/ramps; 1950
EX $160 **NM** $245 **MIP** $325

Pepsi-Cola Set, 10" white tractor-trailer, 4-1/2" white pickup, forklift, w/Pepsi logos and four Pepsi cases, 1976
EX $8 **NM** $15 **MIP** $20

Polysteel Farm, blue milkman truck w/rack and nine milk bottles, red and gray milk tanker, orange farm tractor; 1961
EX $70 **NM** $115 **MIP** $160

Road Builder, green/white cement mixer truck, yellow/black bulldozer, red dump truck, husky dumper; 1963
EX $200 **NM** $300 **MIP** $400

Texaco Highway Truck Stop, 11" tractor-trailer; three-vehicle set with Texaco Tanker, red/white Jeep and red wrecker; also three attendant figures, two gas pumps with flexible hoses, made in Japan; late 1970s.
EX $18 **NM** $36 **MIP** $55

Truck with Concrete Mixer Trailer, 22" truck w/duo-tone slant design, green fenders and lower sides, yellow squarish cab and body, 10" mixer w/yellow frame and red hopper, overall 34-1/2" long, 1937
EX $175 **NM** $265 **MIP** $350

Truck with Concrete Mixer Trailer, 22" truck w/duo-tone slant design, green front and lower hood sides, yellow upper hood, cab and body, 10" mixer w/yellow frame and red hopper, overall 32-1/2" long, 1938
EX $165 **NM** $250 **MIP** $330

Warehouse, Coca-Cola truck, two hand trucks, eight cases Coke bottles, store-door delivery truck, lumber, sign, two barrels, forklift; 1958
EX $175 **NM** $265 **MIP** $350

Warehouse, Coca-Cola truck, two hand trucks, eight cases Coke bottles, store-door delivery truck, sign, two barrels, forklift; 1959
EX $150 **NM** $225 **MIP** $300

Western Roundup, turquoise fenders, hood, cab and frame, white flatbed cargo section, six sections of rail fencing w/swinging gate, rearing and standing horse, cowboys, calf, steer; 1960
EX $175 **NM** $250 **MIP** $400

TRUCKS

Air Force Supply Transport, blue w/blue removable fabric canopy, rubber wheels, decals on cab doors, 14-1/2" long; 1957
EX $95 **NM** $150 **MIP** $355

Air Mail Truck, black front, hood fenders, enclosed cab and opening doors, red enclosed body and chassis, 24" long, 1930
EX $675 **NM** $1000 **MIP** $1400

Allied Moving Van, tractor and semi-trailer van, duo-tone slant design, black front and lower sides, orange hood top, cab and van body, 29-1/2" long; 1941
EX $600 **NM** $900 **MIP** $1200

Army Electric Searchlight Unit, shiny olive drab flatbed truck, battery-operated searchlight, 14-3/4" long; 1957
EX $125 **NM** $230 **MIP** $330

Army Half-Track and Howitzer, olive drab w/olive drab carriage, 12-1/2" truck, 9-3/4" gun, overall 22-1/2" long; 1953
EX $105 **NM** $150 **MIP** $200

Army Half-Track with Howitzer, olive drab steel, red firing knob on gun, 17" truck, 9-3/4" gun, overall 27" long; 1955
EX $100 **NM** $150 **MIP** $200

Army Medical Corps Truck, white, black rubber tires on white steel disc wheels, 29-1/2" long; 1941
EX $125 **NM** $185 **MIP** $250

Army Searchlight Repair-It Truck, shiny olive drab truck and flatbed cargo section, 15" long; 1956
EX $125 **NM** $175 **MIP** $225

Army Spotlight Truck, 8" long; 1969
EX $5 **NM** $9 **MIP** $12

Army Supply Truck, shiny olive drab truck and removable fabric cover, 14-1/2" long; 1956
EX $100 **NM** $150 **MIP** $175

Army Transport, 5" long; bubble-window cabover, "T-415 Transport"; 1970s
EX $3 **NM** $6 **MIP** $9

Army Transport Truck and Trailer, olive drab truck, 20-1/2" long, trailer 34-1/2" long; 1940
EX $250 **NM** $350 **MIP** $450

Army Transport with Howitzer, olive drab steel, re-firing knob on gun, 17" truck, 9-3/4" gun, overall 27" long; 1954
EX $115 **NM** $175 **MIP** $230

Army Transport with Howitzer, olive drab, 12" truck, 9-3/4" gun, overall 28" long; 1953
EX $100 **NM** $150 **MIP** $200

Army Transport with Howitzer, olive drab steel, 17" truck, 9-3/4" gun, overall 27" long; 1955
EX $150 **NM** $250 **MIP** $350

Army Transport with Tank, olive drab, 15-1/2" long truck, 11-1/2" long detachable two-wheel trailer, overall 26-1/2" long, 7-1/2" long tank; 1959
EX $100 **NM** $150 **MIP** $200

Army Troop Transport with Howitzer, dark forest green truck and gun, canopy mixture of greens, 14" long truck, 12" long, gun, overall 25-3/4" long; 1965
EX $100 **NM** $150 **MIP** $200

Army Truck, olive drab, 17" long; 1940
EX $150 **NM** $200 **MIP** $250

Army Truck, olive drab, 20-1/2" long, 1939
EX $110 **NM** $175 **MIP** $225

Atlas Van Lines, green tractor unit, chrome one-piece toothed grille and headlights, green lower half of semi-trailer van body, cream upper half, silvery roof, 29" long; 1956
EX $200 **NM** $300 **MIP** $400

Auto Hauler, 27-5/8" long; blue turbo cab, double-deck trailer, three plastic coupes, whitewall tires; 1970s
EX $35 **NM** $70 **MIP** $105

Auto Hauler, yellow cabover-engine tractor unit and double-deck semi-trailer, three 8" long vehicles, 25-1/2" long; 1968
EX $75 **NM** $115 **MIP** $150

Baggage Rider, duo-tone horizontal design, green bumper, fenders and lower half of truck, white upper half, 28" long; 1950
EX $250 **NM** $175 **MIP** $500

Baggage Truck, black front, hood, and fenders, enclosed cab w/opening doors, nickel-rim, red-shell headlights, yellow stake body, 26-1/2" long, 1930-32
EX $3000 **NM** $5000 **MIP** $7000

Baggage Truck, green hood, fenders, and cab, yellow cargo section, no bumper, 17-1/2" long; 1945
EX $175 **NM** $265 **MIP** $350

Baggage Truck, duo-tone slant design, yellow skirted fenders and cargo section, green hood top, enclosed cab, 27-3/4" long, 1938
EX $300 **NM** $600 **MIP** $1000

Baggage Truck, black front, hood, and fenders, doorless cab, yellow four-post stake sides, two chains across back, 26-1/2" long, 1927
EX $1000 **NM** $1500 **MIP** $2100

Baggage Truck, green front, hood and fenders, non-open doors, yellow cargo section slat or solid sides, metal grille, 26-1/2" long, 1935
EX $350 **NM** $550 **MIP** $650

Baggage Truck, duo-tone slant design, yellow fenders, green hood top, cab, and removable rider seat, 26-1/2" long, 1936
EX $350 **NM** $750 **MIP** $1000

Big Brute Dumper, yellow cabover-engine, frame and tiltback dump section w/cab shield, striped black and yellow bumper, black grille, 8" long; 1971
EX $50 **NM** $75 **MIP** $100

Big Brute Mixer Truck, yellow cabover-engine, body and frame, white plastic mixing drum, white plastic seats, 7" long; 1971
EX $35 **NM** $50 **MIP** $70

Big Fella Hydraulic Rider Dumper, duo-tone slant design, yellow front and lower hood, red upper cab, dump body and upper hood, rider seat has large yellow sunburst-style decal, 26-1/2" long; 1950
EX $110 **NM** $175 **MIP** $225

Big Mack Dumper, yellow front, hood cab, chassis and tiltback dump section, black plastic bumper, heavy-duty black balloon tires on yellow plastic five-spoke wheels, 20-1/2" long; 1971
EX $26 **NM** $40 **MIP** $55

Big Mack Dumper, yellow front, hood cab, chassis and tiltback dump section, black plastic bumper, single rear wheels, 20-1/2" long; 1968
EX $30 **NM** $45 **MIP** $60

Big Mack Dumper, off-white front, hood cab and chassis, blue-green tiltback dump section, white plastic bumper, 20-1/2" long; 1964
EX $30 **NM** $45 **MIP** $60

Big Mack Dumper, yellow front, hood cab, chassis and tiltback dump section, black plastic bumper, 20-1/2" long; 1967
EX $30 **NM** $45 **MIP** $60

Big Mack Hydraulic Dumper, white hood, cab and tiltback dump section w/cab shield, white plastic bumper, short step ladder on each side, 20-1/2" long; 1969
EX $15 **NM** $30 **MIP** $45

Big Mack Hydraulic Dumper, red hood, cab and tiltback dump section w/cab shield, white plastic bumper, short step ladder on each side, 20-1/2" long; 1968
EX $15 **NM** $30 **MIP** $45

Big Mack Hydraulic Dumper, red hood, cab and tiltback dump section w/cab shield, dump body sides have a large circular back, white plastic bumper, short step ladder on each side, 20-1/2" long; 1970
EX $15 **NM** $30 **MIP** $45

Black & Decker Truck, 10-1/2" long; white tractor-trailer, Japan
EX $8 **NM** $12 **MIP** $17

Boat Transport, blue flatbed truck carrying 8" litho metal boat, boat deck white, hull red, truck 15" long; 1959
EX $200 **NM** $450 **MIP** $750

Borden's Milk Delivery Van, 11-1/2" long; white body, sliding side doors, opening rear doors, yellow tray with six white fillable polyethylene milk bottles with yellow caps; 1965-67
EX $90 **NM** $185 **MIP** $275

Brute Air Freight Truck, 5" long; blue cabover, "American Airlines Freight System" on doors. "Toys, Handle With Pride" containers in rear, six wheels; 1960s
EX $5 **NM** $10 **MIP** $14

Brute Car Carrier (tractor-trailer), 10" long; blue cabover, double-deck trailer, two plastic cars; 1969
EX $7 **NM** $15 **MIP** $22

Brute Cement Mixer Truck, 5-1/4" long; blue cabover, white crank rotates drum; 1969
EX $5 **NM** $9 **MIP** $14

Brute Cement Mixer Truck, 5-1/4" long; beige cabover, white plastic mixing drum; 1968
EX $5 **NM** $9 **MIP** $14

Brute Coca-Cola Delivery Truck, 5" long; 1985
EX $3 **NM** $7 **MIP** $10

Brute Dumper, 5" long; red cabover; 1968-69
EX $3 **NM** $7 **MIP** $10

Brute Merry-Go-Round, 5" long; cabover, merry-go-round in rear; 1970s
EX $7 **NM** $15 **MIP** $22

Brute Monkey House, yellow cabover-engine body, striped orange and white awning roof, cage on back, two plastic monkeys, 5" long; 1968
EX $6 **NM** $12 **MIP** $18

Brute Monkey House, yellow cabover-engine body, red and white awning roof, cage on back, two plastic monkeys, 5" long; 1969
EX $6 **NM** $12 **MIP** $18

Brute Pick-Up, 4-3/4" long; 1968-70s
EX $3 **NM** $6 **MIP** $10

Brute Sanitation Truck, 5" long; lime-green cabover; 1968-69
EX $6 **NM** $12 **MIP** $18

Brute Vault Van, 5" long; bank vault truck; 1970s
EX $3 **NM** $5 **MIP** $8

Buddy L Milk Farms Truck, light cream body, red roof, nickel glide headlights, sliding doors, 13" long; 1949
EX $170 **NM** $300 **MIP** $500

Buddy L Milk Farms Truck, white body, black roof, short hood w/black wooden headlights, 13-1/2" long; 1945
EX $150 **NM** $300 **MIP** $450

Buddy L Moving Van, 10-1/2" long; futuristic cabover, white w/Buddy L logo, stripes on moving-van body, 1970s
EX $4 **NM** $8 **MIP** $12

Camper, medium blue truck and back door, white camper body, 14-1/2" long; 1965
EX $50 **NM** $75 **MIP** $100

Camper, 5" long; bubble-window cabover, green; 1970s
EX $3 **NM** $5 **MIP** $8

Camper, bright medium blue steel truck and camper body, 14-1/2" long; 1964
EX $60 **NM** $95 **MIP** $125

Camper-N-Cruiser, powder blue pickup truck and trailer, pale blue camper body, 24-1/2" long; 1963
EX $60 **NM** $95 **MIP** $125

Camper-N-Cruiser, bright medium blue camper w/matching boat trailer and 8-1/2" long plastic sport cruiser, overall 27" long; 1964
EX $50 **NM** $75 **MIP** $100

Campers Truck, turquoise pickup truck, pale turquoise plastic camper, 14-1/2" long; 1961
EX $55 **NM** $85 **MIP** $110

Campers Truck with Boat, green/turquoise pickup truck, lime green camper body, red plastic runabout boat on camper roof, 14-1/2" long; 1962
EX $50 **NM** $100 **MIP** $150

Campers Truck with Boat, green/turquoise pickup, no side mirror, lime green camper body w/red plastic runabout boat on top, 14-1/2" long; 1963
EX $50 **NM** $100 **MIP** $150

Camping Trailer and Wagon, bright medium blue suburban wagon, matching teepee trailer, overall 24-1/2" long; 1964
EX $60 **NM** $95 **MIP** $125

Canada Dry Delivery Truck, 9-1/2" long; two-tone green, high-window cabover, ten bottle cases, roll-up side doors, hand truck; 1968-69
EX $35 **NM** $45 **MIP** $60

Cattle Transport Truck, green and white w/white stake sides, 15" long; 1957
EX $75 **NM** $115 **MIP** $150

Cattle Transport Truck, red w/yellow stake sides, 15" long; 1956
EX $75 **NM** $115 **MIP** $150

Cement Mixer Truck, red body, tank ends, and chute, white water tank, mixing drum and loading hopper, whitewall tires, 15-1/2" long; 1968
EX $50 **NM** $75 **MIP** $100

Cement Mixer Truck, red body, tank ends, and chute, white water tank, mixing drum and loading hopper, blackwall tires, 15-1/2" long; 1967
EX $38 **NM** $76 **MIP** $115

Cement Mixer Truck, red body, tank ends, and chute, white side ladder, water tank, mixing drum and loading hopper, 15-1/2" long; 1965
EX $60 **NM** $95 **MIP** $125

Cement Mixer Truck, snub-nosed yellow body, cab, frame and chute, white plastic mixing drum, loading hopper and water tank w/yellow ends, 16" long; 1970
EX $35 **NM** $50 **MIP** $70

Cement Mixer Truck, turquoise body, tank ends, and chute, white side ladder, water tank, mixing drum and loading hopper, 16-1/2" long; 1964
EX $60 **NM** $95 **MIP** $125

Charles Chip Delivery Truck Van, beige body, potato-chip decal; 1966
EX $45 **NM** $90 **MIP** $135

City Baggage Dray, green front, hood, and fenders, non-open doors, yellow stake-side cargo section, bright metal grille, 19" long, 1935
EX $150 **NM** $300 **MIP** $400

City Baggage Dray, cream w/aluminum-finish grille, no bumper, black rubber wheels, 20-3/4" long; 1940
EX $100 **NM** $200 **MIP** $300

City Baggage Dray, light green w/aluminum-finish grille, no bumper, black rubber wheels, 20-3/4" long, 1939
EX $95 **NM** $250 **MIP** $300

City Baggage Dray, duo-tone slant design, green front and skirted fenders, yellow hood top, enclosed cab and cargo section, 20-3/4" long, 1938
EX $150 **NM** $200 **MIP** $350

City Baggage Dray, duo-tone slant design, green front and fenders, yellow hood top and cargo section, 19" long, 1936
EX $400 **NM** $800 **MIP** $1200

City Baggage Dray, green front, hood, and fenders, non-open doors, yellow stake-side cargo section, No. 839, 19" long, 1934
EX $400 **NM** $800 **MIP** $1200

City Baggage Dray, duo-tone slant design, green front and fenders, yellow hood top and cargo section, dummy headlights, 19" long, 1937
EX $400 **NM** $800 **MIP** $1200

Coal Truck, black hopper body and fully enclosed cab w/opening doors, red wheels, 25" long, 1930
EX $900 **NM** $1500 **MIP** $2000

Coal Truck, black front, hood, fenders, sliding discharge door on each side of hopper body, red chassis and disc wheels, 25" long, 1927
EX $800 **NM** $1000 **MIP** $2000

Coal Truck, black front, hood, fenders, doorless cab, red chassis and disc wheels, No. 202, 25" long, 1926
EX $3700 **NM** $7500 **MIP** $11500

Coca-Cola Bottling Route Truck, bright yellow, w/two small metal hand trucks and eight yellow cases of miniature green Coke bottles, 14-3/4" long; 1957
EX $110 **NM** $175 **MIP** $225

Coca-Cola Bottling Route Truck, bright yellow, w/small metal hand truck, six or eight yellow cases of miniature green Coke bottles, 14-3/4" long; 1955
EX $125 **NM** $175 **MIP** $250

Coca-Cola Delivery Truck, orange/yellow cab and double-deck, open-side cargo, two small hand trucks, four red and four green cases of bottles, 15" long; 1964
EX $62 **NM** $100 **MIP** $130

Coca-Cola Delivery Truck, orange/yellow cab and double-deck, open-side cargo, two small hand trucks, four red and four green cases of bottles, 15" long; 1960
EX $100 **NM** $150 **MIP** $200

Coca-Cola Delivery Truck, 9" long; red and white cabover and van body, left side lifts to show bottle cases, hand truck; 1970s
EX $9 **NM** $18 **MIP** $30

Coca-Cola Delivery Truck, orange/yellow cab and double-deck, open-side cargo, two small hand trucks, four red and four green cases of bottles, 15" long; 1963
EX $75 **NM** $100 **MIP** $150

Coca-Cola Delivery Truck, red lower cabover-engine and van body, white upper cab, left side of van lifts to reveal 10 miniature bottle cases, 9-1/2" long; 1971
EX $30 **NM** $45 **MIP** $60

Coca-Cola Delivery Truck (tractor-trailer), 10" long; five cases of bottles, handcart; 1980
EX $4 **NM** $8 **MIP** $12

Coca-Cola Delivery Truck (tractor-trailer), 14" long; load includes Coke machine and handtruck; 1980s
EX $10 **NM** $20 **MIP** $50

Coke Coffee Co. Delivery Truck Van, black lower half of body, orange upper half, roof and sliding side doors; 1966
EX $85 **NM** $130 **MIP** $175

Colt Vacationer, 22-1/2" long; blue and white Colt Sportsliner with trailer carrying red and white plastic 8-1/2" sport cruiser; 1967
EX $42 **NM** $85 **MIP** $125

Cook Coffee Van, 11-1/2", orange/black van, "Cook Coffee" decal, 1960s
EX $50 **NM** $75 **MIP** $155

Curtiss Candy Trailer Van, blue tractor and bumper, white semi-trailer van, blue roof, chrome one-piece toothed grille and headlights, white drop-down rear door, 32-3/4" long w/tailgate/ramp lowered; 1955
EX $250 **NM** $400 **MIP** $500

Dairy Transport Truck, duo-tone slant design, red front and lower hood sides, white hood top, cab and semi-trailer tank body, tank opens in back, 26" long, 1939
EX $150 **NM** $225 **MIP** $300

Deluxe Auto Carrier, turquoise tractor unit, aluminum loading ramps, three plastic cars, overall 34" long including; 1962
EX $100 **NM** $175 **MIP** $250

Deluxe Camping Outfit, turquoise pickup truck and camper, and 8-1/2" long plastic boat on pale turquoise boat trailer, overall 24" long; 1961
EX $60 **NM** $95 **MIP** $125

Deluxe Hydraulic Rider Dump Truck, duo-tone slant design, red front and lower hood sides, white upper cab, dump body and chassis, red or black removable rider saddle, 26" long; 1948
EX $175 **NM** $265 **MIP** $350

Deluxe Motor Market, duo-tone slant design, red front, curved bumper, lower hood and cab sides, white hood top, body and cab, 22-1/4" long; 1950
EX $250 **NM** $350 **MIP** $500

(Joe and Sharon Freed Photo)

Deluxe Rider Delivery Truck, duo-tone horizontal design, gray lower half, blue upper half, red rubber disc wheels, black barrel skid, 22-3/4" long; 1945
EX $135 **NM** $200 **MIP** $270

Deluxe Rider Delivery Truck, duo-tone horizontal design, deep blue lower half, gray upper half, red rubber disc wheels, black barrel skid, 22-3/4" long; 1945
EX $135 **NM** $200 **MIP** $270

Deluxe Rider Dump Truck, various colors, dual rear wheels, no bumper, 25-1/2" long; 1945
EX $75 **NM** $115 **MIP** $150

Double Hydraulic Self-Loader-N-Dump, green front loading scoop w/yellow arms attached to cab sides, yellow hood and enclosed cab, orange frame and wide dump body, 29" long w/scoop lowered; 1956
EX $85 **NM** $130 **MIP** $175

Double Tandem Hydraulic Dump and Trailer, truck has red bumper, hood, cab and frame, four-wheel trailer w/red tow and frame, both w/white tiltback dump bodies, 38" long; 1957
EX $85 **NM** $130 **MIP** $175

Double-Deck Boat Transport, light blue steel flatbed truck carrying three 8" white plastic boats w/red decks, truck 15" long; 1960
EX $150 **NM** $250 **MIP** $400

Dr. Pepper Delivery Truck Van, white, red and blue; 1966
EX $45 **NM** $90 **MIP** $135

Dr. Pepper Delivery Truck Van (tractor-trailer), 6" long; bubble-window cabover; 1970s
EX $5 **NM** $10 **MIP** $24

Dump Body Truck, black front, hood, open driver's seat and dump section, red chassis, chain drive dump mechanism, 25" long, 1923
EX $1200 **NM** $1800 **MIP** $2500

Dump Body Truck, black front, hood, open driver's seat and dump section, red chassis, crank windlass w/ratchet raises dump bed, 25" long, 1921
EX $800 **NM** $1400 **MIP** $2000

Dump Truck, duo-tone slant design, yellow enclosed cab and hood, red front and dump body, no bumper, dummy headlights, 20" long, 1937
EX $250 **NM** $375 **MIP** $505

Dump Truck, duo-tone slant design, yellow enclosed cab and hood, red front and dump body, no bumper, bright-metal headlights, 20" long, 1936
EX $250 **NM** $375 **MIP** $500

Dump Truck, yellow enclosed cab, front and hood, red dump section, no bumper, bright-metal radiator, 20" long, 1935
EX $325 **NM** $485 **MIP** $650

Dump Truck, yellow enclosed cab, front and hood, red dump section, no bumper, 20" long, 1934
EX $275 **NM** $415 **MIP** $550

Dump Truck, black enclosed cab and opening doors, front and hood, red dump body and chassis, simple lever arrangement lifts dump bed, 24" long, 1930
EX $650 **NM** $975 **MIP** $1300

Dump Truck, black enclosed cab and opening doors, front and hood, red dump body and chassis, crank handle lifts dump bed, 24" long, 1931
EX $750 **NM** $1125 **MIP** $1500

Dump Truck, duo-tone slant design, red lower cab, lower hood, front and dump body, yellow upper hood, upper cab and chassis, no bumper, 22-1/4" long, 1939
EX $250 **NM** $375 **MIP** $500

Dump Truck, various colors, black rubber wheels, 12" long; 1945
EX $50 **NM** $75 **MIP** $100

Dump Truck, yellow upper hood and enclosed cab, red wide-skirt fenders and open-frame chassis, blue dump body, no bumper, 17-1/4" long; 1940
EX $85 **NM** $130 **MIP** $175

Dump Truck, green w/cream hood top and upper enclosed cab, no bumper, bright-metal headlights and grille, 22-1/4" long; 1941
EX $85 **NM** $130 **MIP** $175

Dump Truck, red hood top and cab, white or cream dump body and frame, no bumper, 17-1/2" long; 1945
EX $75 **NM** $115 **MIP** $150

Dump Truck, 14-1/4" long; orange, turbine cabover, decal "It Steers" on driver's window; late 1960s
EX $6 **NM** $12 **MIP** $18

Dump Truck, duo-tone slant design, red front, fenders and dump body, yellow hood top, upper sides, upper cab and chassis, no bumper, 22-1/2" long; 1948
EX $125 **NM** $185 **MIP** $250

Dump Truck, duo-tone slant design, red front, fenders and lower doors, white upper, bright radiator grille and headlights, no bumper, 22-1/4" long, 1939
EX $250 **NM** $375 **MIP** $500

Dump Truck, white upper hood, enclosed cab, wide-skirt fenders and open-frame chassis, orange dump body, bright-metal grille, no bumper, 17-3/8" long; 1941
EX $85 **NM** $135 **MIP** $180

Dump Truck-Economy Line, dark blue dump body, remainder is yellow, bright-metal grille and headlights, no bumper or running boards, 12" long; 1941
EX $75 **NM** $125 **MIP** $150

Dumper with Shovel, turquoise body, frame and dump section, white one-piece bumper and grille guard, large white steel scoop shovel, 15" long; 1962
EX $75 **NM** $115 **MIP** $150

Dumper with Shovel, medium green body, frame and dump section, white one-piece bumper and grille guard, no side mirror, large white steel scoop shovel, 15" long; 1963
EX $75 **NM** $115 **MIP** $150

Dumper with Shovel, medium green body, frame and dump section, white one-piece bumper and grille guard, no side mirror, large white steel scoop shovel, spring suspension on front axle only, 15" long; 1964
EX $75 **NM** $115 **MIP** $150

Dumper with Shovel, orange body, frame and dump section, chrome one-piece grille, no bumper guard, no side mirror, large white steel scoop shovel, no spring suspension, 15-3/4" long; 1965
EX $75 **NM** $115 **MIP** $150

Dump-n-Dozer, orange husky dumper truck and orange flatbed four-wheel trailer carrying orange bulldozer, 23" long including trailer; 1962
EX $75 **NM** $115 **MIP** $150

Express Trailer Truck, red tractor unit, hood, fenders and enclosed cab, green semi-trailer van w/removable roof and drop-down rear door, 23-3/4" long, 1933
EX $350 **NM** $525 **MIP** $700

Express Trailer Truck, red tractor unit, hood, fenders and enclosed cab, green semi-trailer van w/removable roof and drop-down rear door, bright-metal dummy headlights, 23-3/4" long, 1934
EX $350 **NM** $525 **MIP** $700

Express Truck, all black except red frame, enclosed cab w/opening doors, nickel-rim, red-shell headlights, six rubber tires, double bar front bumper, 24-1/2" long, 1930-32
EX $3000 **NM** $4500 **MIP** $6000

Farm Bureau Co-op Gas Tanker, 10" long; red tractor with chrome tanker trailer; 1980s
EX $3 **NM** $6 **MIP** $9

Farm Machinery Hauler Trailer Truck, blue tractor unit, yellow flatbed semi-trailer, 31-1/2" long; 1956
EX $125 **NM** $185 **MIP** $250

Farm Supplies Automatic Dump, duo-tone slant design, blue curved bumper, front, lower hood sides and cab, yellow upper hood, cab and rest of body, 22-1/2" long; 1950
EX $125 **NM** $190 **MIP** $250

Farm Supplies Dump Truck, duo-tone slant design, red front, fenders and lower hood sides, yellow upper hood, cab and body, 22-3/4" long; 1949
EX $125 **NM** $185 **MIP** $250

Farm Supplies Hydraulic Dump Trailer, green tractor unit, long cream body on semi-trailer, fourteen rubber wheels, 26-1/2" long; 1956
EX $100 **NM** $150 **MIP** $200

Fast Delivery Pickup, yellow hood and cab, red open cargo body, removable chain across open back, 13-1/2" long; 1949
EX $105 **NM** $155 **MIP** $200

Finger-Tip Steering Hydraulic Dumper, powder blue bumper, fenders, hood, cab and frame, white tiltback dump body, 22" long; 1959
EX $75 **NM** $115 **MIP** $150

Fisherman, light tan pickup truck w/tan steel trailer carrying plastic 8-1/2" long sport crusier, overall 24-1/4" long; 1962
EX $80 **NM** $120 **MIP** $160

Fisherman, metallic sage green pickup truck w/boat trailer carrying plastic 8-1/2" long sport cruiser, overall 25" long; 1964
EX $70 **NM** $100 **MIP** $140

Fisherman, sage gray/green and white pickup truck w/steel trailer carrying plastic 8-1/2" long sport cruiser, overall 25" long; 1965
EX $65 **NM** $100 **MIP** $135

Fisherman, pale blue/green station wagon w/four-wheel boat trailer carrying plastic 8-1/2" long boat, overall 27-1/2" long; 1963
EX $75 **NM** $115 **MIP** $150

Flat Tire Wrecker, 16" long; blue, battery-operated flasher on roof, spare tire, three polyethylene tools, boom and winch; 1965
EX $45 **NM** $125 **MIP** $200

Flivver Dump Truck, black w/red eight-spoke wheels, black hubs, aluminum tires, flat, open dump section w/squared-off back w/latching, drop-down endgate, 11" long, 1926
EX $700 **NM** $1000 **MIP** $1500

Flivver Scoop Dump Truck, black w/red eight-spoke wheels, 12-1/2" long, 1926-27, 1929-30
EX $1500 **NM** $2500 **MIP** $3500

Flivver Truck, black w/red eight-spoke wheels w/aluminum tires, black hubs, 12" long, 1924
EX $800 **NM** $1000 **MIP** $1500

Ford Flivver Dump Cart, black w/red eight-spoke wheels, black hubs, aluminum tires, flat, short open dump section tapers to point on each side, 12-1/2" long, 1926
EX $1500 **NM** $2500 **MIP** $3500

Frederick & Nelson Delivery Truck Van, medium green body, roof and sliding side doors; 1966
EX $125 **NM** $200 **MIP** $275

Freight Delivery Stake Truck, red hood, bumper, cab and frame, white cargo section, yellow three-post, three-slat removable stake sides, 14-3/4" long; 1955
EX $75 **NM** $125 **MIP** $150

Front Loader Hi-Lift Dump Truck, red scoop and arms attached to white truck at rear fenders, green dump body, 17-3/4" long w/scoop down and dump body raised; 1955
EX $85 **NM** $130 **MIP** $175

Giant Hydraulic Dumper, overall color turquoise, dump lever has a red plastic tip, 22-3/4" long; 1961
EX $135 **NM** $200 **MIP** $275

Giant Hydraulic Dumper, red bumper, frame, hood and cab, light tan tiltback dump body and cab shield 23-3/4" long; 1960
EX $125 **NM** $185 **MIP** $250

Giraffe Truck, 13-1/4" long; blue hood and white cab roof, open cargo section, two plastic giraffes; 1968
EX $35 **NM** $70 **MIP** $105

GMC Air Force Electric Searchlight Unit, all blue flatbed, off white battery-operated searchlight swivel mount, decals on cab doors, 14-3/4" long; 1958
EX $200 **NM** $300 **MIP** $410

GMC Airway Express Van, green hood, cab and van body, latching double rear doors, shiny metal drum coin bank and metal hand truck, 17-1/2" long w/rear doors open; 1957
EX $250 **NM** $350 **MIP** $450

GMC Anti-Aircraft Unit with Searchlight, 15" truck w/four-wheel trailer, battery-operated, over 25-1/4" long; 1957
EX $240 **NM** $345 **MIP** $460

GMC Army Hauler with Jeep, shiny olive drab tractor unit and flatbed trailer, 10" long jeep, overall 31-1/2" long; 1958
EX $200 **NM** $300 **MIP** $400

GMC Army Transport with Howitzer, shiny olive drab, 14-1/2" long, truck, overall w/gun 22-1/2" long; 1957
EX $200 **NM** $300 **MIP** $400

GMC Brinks Armored Truck Van, silver gray, barred windows on sides and in double doors, coin slot and hole in roof, brass padlock w/two keys, pouch, play money, three gray plastic guard figures, 16" long; 1958
EX $300 **NM** $350 **MIP** $450

GMC Coca-Cola Route Truck, lime/yellow, w/small metal hand truck and eight cases of miniature green Coke bottles, 14-1/8" long; 1957
EX $200 **NM** $305 **MIP** $410

GMC Coca-Cola Route Truck, orange/yellow, w/two small metal hand trucks and eight cases of miniature green Coke bottles, 14-1/8" long; 1958
EX $200 **NM** $300 **MIP** $400

GMC Construction Company Dumper, pastel blue including control lever on left and dump section w/cab shield, hinged tailgate, chrome GMC bar grille, six wheels, 16" long; 1958
EX $200 **NM** $305 **MIP** $410

GMC Construction Company Dumper, pastel blue including control lever on left and dump section w/cab shield, hinged tailgate, chrome GMC bar grille, four wheels, 16" long; 1959
EX $150 **NM** $250 **MIP** $350

GMC Highway Giant Trailer, blue tractor, blue and white van, chrome GMC bar grille and headlights, blue roof on semi-trailer, white tailgate doubles as loading ramp, eighteen-wheeler, 31-1/4" long; 1957
EX $250 **NM** $350 **MIP** $450

GMC Highway Giant Trailer Truck, blue tractor, blue and white van, chrome GMC bar grille and headlights, blue roof on semi-trailer, white tailgate doubles as loading ramp, fourteen-wheeler, 30-3/4" long; 1958
EX $200 **NM** $300 **MIP** $400

GMC Husky Dumper, red hood, bumper, cab and chassis, chrome GMC bar grille and nose emblem, white oversize dump body, red control lever on right side, 17-1/2" long; 1957
EX $150 **NM** $250 **MIP** $350

GMC Self-Loading Auto Carrier, yellow tractor and double-deck semi trailer, three plastic cars, overall 33-1/4" long; 1959
EX $200 **NM** $300 **MIP** $410

GMC Signal Corps Unit, both olive drab, 14-1/4" long truck w/removable fabric canopy, 8" long four-wheel trailer; 1957
EX $150 **NM** $200 **MIP** $255

Grocery Motor Market Truck, duo-tone slant design, yellow front, lower hood sides, fenders and lower doors, white hood top, enclosed cab and body, no bumper, 20-1/2" long, 1937
EX $275 **NM** $415 **MIP** $550

Grocery Motor Market Truck, duo-tone slant design, yellow front, lower hood sides, skirted fenders and lower doors, white hood top, cab and body, no bumper, 21-1/2" long, 1938
EX $275 **NM** $420 **MIP** $560

Harley-Davidson Semi, 21" long; battery-operated sounds and lights, "Ten-four, good buddy" voice, pressed steel and plastic; 1992
EX $7 **NM** $13 **MIP** $20

Heavy Hauling Dumper, red hood, bumper, cab and frame, cream tiltback dump body, 20-1/2" long; 1955
EX $75 **NM** $125 **MIP** $150

Heavy Hauling Dumper, red hood, bumper, cab and frame, cream oversize dump body, hinged tailgate, 21-1/2" long; 1956
EX $75 **NM** $125 **MIP** $140

Heavy Hauling Hydraulic Dumper, green hood, cab and frame, cream tiltback dump body, and cab shield, raising dump body almost to vertical, 23" long; 1956
EX $70 **NM** $105 **MIP** $200

Heavy Machinery Service Truck, 24" long; green cab and chassis, white body, orange machinery rig, 1950s
EX $150 **NM** $180 **MIP** $230

Hershey's Kiss Truck, 4-3/4" long; made in Japan; 1982
EX $3 **NM** $6 **MIP** $9

Hertz Auto Hauler, bright yellow tractor and double-deck semi-trailer, three plastic vehicles, 27" long; 1965
EX $100 **NM** $150 **MIP** $200

Hertz Auto Hauler (tractor-trailer), 27" long; yellow, double-deck trailer, three plastic vehicles; 1965
EX $67 **NM** $130 **MIP** $200

Highway Hawk Trailer Van, bronze cab tractor, chrome metallized plastic bumper, grille, air cleaner and exhaust, 19-3/4" long, 1985
EX $50 **NM** $80 **MIP** $100

Highway Maintenance Truck with Trailer, orange w/black rack of four simulated floodlights behind cab, 19-1/2" long including small two-wheel trailer; 1957
EX $100 **NM** $150 **MIP** $200

Hi-Lift Farm Supplies Dump, red plastic front end including hood and enclosed cab, yellow dump body, cab shield and hinged tailgate, 21-1/2" long; 1953
EX $100 **NM** $175 **MIP** $225

Hi-Lift Farm Supplies Dump, all steel, red front end including hood and enclosed cab, yellow dump body, cab shield and hinged tailgate, 23-1/2" long; 1954
EX $100 **NM** $175 **MIP** $225

Hi-Lift Scoop-n-Dump Truck, orange truck w/deeply fluted sides, dark green scoop on front rises to empty load into hi-lift cream/yellow dump body, 16" long; 1952
EX $85 **NM** $130 **MIP** $175

Hi-Lift Scoop-n-Dump Truck, orange truck w/deeply fluted sides, dark green scoop on front rises to empty load into hi-lift light cream dump body, 16" long; 1953
EX $80 **NM** $125 **MIP** $175

Hi-Lift Scoop-n-Dump Truck, orange truck w/deeply fluted sides, dark green scoop on front rises to empty load into deep hi-lift slightly orange dump body, 16" long; 1955
EX $75 **NM** $115 **MIP** $155

Hi-Lift Scoop-n-Dump Truck, orange hood, fenders and cab, yellow front loading scoop and arms attached to fenders, white frame, dump body and cab shield, 17-3/4" long; 1956
EX $70 **NM** $135 **MIP** $145

Hi-Lift Scoop-n-Dump Truck, blue hood, fenders and cab, yellow front loading scoop and arms attached to fenders, white frame, dump body, cab shield, and running boards, 17-3/4" long; 1957
EX $65 **NM** $100 **MIP** $135

Hi-Tip Hydraulic Dumper, orange hood, cab and frame, cream tiltback dump body, and cab shield, raising dump body almost to vertical, 23" long; 1957
EX $70 **NM** $115 **MIP** $150

Horse Van, 17-1/2" long; maroon pickup cab with plastic horse van body, with side and rear ramps, two horses and one colt; 1965-66. See also Deluxe Riding Academy Set.
EX $23 **NM** $45 **MIP** $70

Horse Van (tractor-trailer), 10" long; red, paired circular windows on trailer; 1980
EX $3 **NM** $7 **MIP** $10

Horse Van (tractor-trailer), 14-1/2" long; high-window cabover tractor, brown with white roof, hauls white trailer, side and rear loading ramps, three horses; 1968-69
EX $12 **NM** $23 **MIP** $35

Horserack 400, 5" long; bubble-window cabover, red, stake truck back with two plastic horses; 1970s
EX $4 **NM** $8 **MIP** $12

Husky Dumper, white plastic wraparound bumper, tan body, frame and dump section, hinged tailgate, plated dump lever on left side, 15-1/4" long; 1961
EX $75 **NM** $125 **MIP** $140

Husky Dumper, snub-nose red body, tiltback dump section and cab shield, full-width chrome bumperless grille, white-tipped dump-control lever on left, deep-tread whitewall tires, 14-1/2" long; 1971
EX $15 **NM** $30 **MIP** $45

Husky Dumper, orange wraparound bumper, body, frame and dump section, hinged tailgate, plated dump lever on left side, 15-1/4" long; 1960
EX $75 **NM** $115 **MIP** $150

Husky Dumper, bright yellow, chrome one-piece bumper, slotted rectangular grille and double headlights, 14-1/2" long; 1966,
EX $25 **NM** $50 **MIP** $75

Husky Dumper, yellow hood, cab, fram and tiltback dump section w/cab shield, crome one-piece wraparound bumper, 14-1/2" long; 1969
EX $17 **NM** $33 **MIP** $50

Husky Dumper, snub-nose red body, tiltback dump section, cab shield, full-width chrome bumperless grille, deep-tread whitewall tires, 14-1/2" long; 1970
EX $15 **NM** $30 **MIP** $45

Husky Dumper, red hood, cab, chassis and dump section, chrome one-piece bumper and slotted grille w/double headlights, 14-1/2" long; 1968
EX $20 **NM** $40 **MIP** $60

Hydraulic Auto Hauler with Four GMC Cars, powder blue GMC tractor, 7" long plastic cars, overall 33-1/2" long including loading ramp; 1958
EX $250 **NM** $350 **MIP** $450

Hydraulic Construction Dumper, red front, cab and chassis, large green dump section w/cab shield, 15-1/4" long; 1962
EX $28 **NM** $56 **MIP** $85

Hydraulic Construction Dumper, tan/beige front, cab and chassis, large green dump section w/cab shield, 15-1/4" long; 1963
EX $28 **NM** $56 **MIP** $85

Hydraulic Construction Dumper, bright blue front, cab and chassis, large green dump section w/cab shield, 15-1/2" long; 1964
EX $23 **NM** $46 **MIP** $70

Hydraulic Construction Dumper, bright green front, cab and chassis, large green dump section w/cab shield, 14" long; 1965
EX $23 **NM** $46 **MIP** $70

Hydraulic Construction Dumper, medium blue front, cab and chassis, large green dump section w/cab shield, 15-1/4" long; 1967
EX $20 **NM** $40 **MIP** $60

Hydraulic Dump Truck, black front, hood, fenders, open seat, and dump body, red chassis and disc wheels w/aluminum tires, 25" long, 1926
EX $700 **NM** $1400 **MIP** $2100

Hydraulic Dump Truck, duo-tone slant design, red hood sides, dump body and chassis, white upper hood, cab and removable rider seat, electric headlights, 24-3/4" long, 1936
EX $300 **NM** $500 **MIP** $700

Hydraulic Dump Truck, black front, hood, fenders and enclosed cab, red dump body, chassis and wheels w/six embossed spokes, bright hubs, 24-3/4" long, 1933
EX $325 **NM** $485 **MIP** $650

Hydraulic Dump Truck, black front, hood, fenders, dark reddish maroon dump body, red chassis and disc wheels w/seven embossed spokes, black hubs, 25" long, 1931
EX $665 **NM** $885 **MIP** $1300

Hydraulic Dumper, green, plated dump lever on left side, large hooks on left side hold yellow or off-white steel scoop shovel, white plastic side mirro and grille guard, 17" long; 1961
EX $125 **NM** $180 **MIP** $245

Hydraulic Dumper, 20" long; green, white dump body w/opening gate, three axles w/tandem wheels in back, 1950s
EX $115 **NM** $160 **MIP** $220

Hydraulic Dumper with Shovel, green, plated dump lever on left side, large hooks on left side hold yellow or off-white steel scoop shovel, 17" long; 1960
EX $120 **NM** $185 **MIP** $250

Hydraulic Farm Supplies Trailer Dumper, 22" long; green tractor, white trailer dump body, 1950s
EX $80 **NM** $100 **MIP** $140

Hydraulic Highway Dumper, orange w/row of black square across scraper edges, one-piece chrome eight-hole grille and double headlights, no scraper blade, 17-3/4" long over blade and raised dump body; 1959
EX $55 **NM** $85 **MIP** $150

Hydraulic Highway Dumper with Scraper Blade, orange w/row of black square across scraper edges, one-piece chrome eight-hole grille and double headlights, 17-3/4" long over blade and raised dump body; 1958
EX $75 **NM** $115 **MIP** $175

Hydraulic Hi-Lift Dumper, duo-tone slant design, green hood nose and lower cab sides, remainder white w/chrome grille, enclosed cab, 24" long; 1953
EX $75 **NM** $115 **MIP** $165

Hydraulic Hi-Lift Dumper, green hood, fenders, cab, and dump-body supports, white dump body w/cab shield, 22-1/2" long; 1954
EX $85 **NM** $130 **MIP** $185

Hydraulic Hi-Lift Dumper, blue hood, fenders, cab, and dump-body supports, white dump body w/cab shield, 22-1/2" long; 1955
EX $75 **NM** $115 **MIP** $175

Hydraulic Husky Dumper, red body, frame, dump section and cab shield, 15-1/4" long; 1962
EX $65 **NM** $100 **MIP** $135

Hydraulic Husky Dumper, red body, white one-piece bumper and grille guard, heavy side braces on dump section, 14" long; 1963
EX $50 **NM** $75 **MIP** $115

Hydraulic Rider Dumper, duo-tone slant design, yellow front and lower hood, red upper cab, dump body and upper hood, 26-1/2" long; 1949
EX $175 **NM** $265 **MIP** $360

Hydraulic Sturdy Dumper, 14-1/2" long; snub-nose green-yellow body and cab; 1970
EX $7 **NM** $15 **MIP** $22

Hydraulic Sturdy Dumper, 14-1/2" long; yellow cab; 1969
EX $20 **NM** $40 **MIP** $60

Hydraulic Sturdy Dumper, 14-1/2" long; lime-green cab, green lever; 1969
EX $20 **NM** $40 **MIP** $60

(Tim Oei Photo)

Hy-Way Maintenance Mechanical Truck and Concrete Mixer, Yellow and dark blue cab, silver wheels, yellow flatbed with dark blue and yellow mixer, 36" long; 1949
EX $345 **NM** $550 **MIP** $700

Ice Truck, black front, hood, fenders and enclosed cab, yellow ice compartment, canvas, ice cakes, tongs, 26-1/2" long, 1933-34
EX $700 **NM** $900 **MIP** $1300

Ice Truck, black front, hood, fenders and enclosed cab, yellow ice compartment, 26-1/2" long, 1933
EX $700 **NM** $900 **MIP** $1500

Ice Truck, black front, hood, fenders and enclosed cab, yellow open cargo section, canvas, ice cakes, miniature tongs, 26-1/2" long, 1930
EX $700 **NM** $900 **MIP** $1500

(Tim Oei Photo)

Ice Truck, black front, hood, fenders and doorless cab, yellow open cargo section, canvas sliding cover, 26-1/2" long, 1926
EX $600 **NM** $1200 **MIP** $1900

IHC "Red Baby" Express Truck, red w/black hubs and aluminum tires, 24-1/4" long, 1929
EX $800 **NM** $1300 **MIP** $1900

IHC "Red Baby" Express Truck, red doorless roofed cab, open pickup body, chassis and fenders, 24-1/4" long, 1928
EX $750 **NM** $1000 **MIP** $2000

Insurance Patrol, red w/open driver's seat and body, brass bell on cowl and full-length handrails, 27" long, 1925
EX $650 **NM** $1000 **MIP** $1300

Insurance Patrol, red w/open driver's seat and body, brass bell on cowl and full-length handrails, no CFD decal, 27" long, 1928
EX $625 **NM** $950 **MIP** $1250

International Delivery Truck, red w/removable black rider saddle, black-edged yellow horizontal strip on cargo body, 24-1/2" long, 1935
EX $225 **NM** $350 **MIP** $450

International Delivery Truck, duo-tone slant design, red front, bumper and lower hood sides, yellow hood top, upper sides, cab and open cargo body, 24-1/2" long, 1936
EX $205 **NM** $320 **MIP** $410

International Delivery Truck, duo-tone slant design, red front, bumper and lower hood sides, yellow hood top, upper sides, cab and open cargo body, bright metal dummy headlights, 24-1/2" long, 1938
EX $150 **NM** $225 **MIP** $300

International Dump Truck, red, w/red headlights on radiator, black removable rider saddle, 25-3/4" long, 1938
EX $125 **NM** $185 **MIP** $250

International Dump Truck, duo-tone slant design, yellow radiator, fenders, lower hood and detachable rider seat, rest of truck is red, 25-3/4" long, 1936
EX $315 **NM** $475 **MIP** $630

International Dump Truck, red w/bright-metal radiator grille, and black removable rider saddle, 25-3/4" long, 1935
EX $325 **NM** $485 **MIP** $650

International Railway Express Truck, duo-tone slant design, yellow front, lower hood sides and removable top, green hood top, enclosed cab and van body, electric headlights, 25" long, 1937
EX $350 **NM** $525 **MIP** $700

International Railway Express Truck, duo-tone slant design, yellow front, lower hood sides and removable top, green hood top, enclosed cab and van body, dummy headlights, 25" long, 1938
EX $345 **NM** $525 **MIP** $690

International Wrecker Truck, duo-tone slant design, yellow upper cab, hood, and boom, red lower cab, fenders, grille and body, rubber tires, removable rider seat, 32" long, 1938
EX $600 **NM** $900 **MIP** $1800

Jewel Home Service Truck Van, 11-1/2" long; dark brown body, sliding side doors; 1967
EX $42 **NM** $83 **MIP** $125

Jewel Home Shopping Truck Van, 11-1/2" long; pale mint green upper body, darker lower half, no sliding doors; 1968
EX $38 **NM** $76 **MIP** $115

Jolly Joe Ice Cream Truck, white w/black roof, black tires and wooden wheels, 17-1/2" long; 1947
EX $225 **NM** $350 **MIP** $455

Jolly Joe Popsicle Truck, white w/black roof, black tires and wooden wheels, 17-1/2" long; 1948
EX $275 **NM** $430 **MIP** $555

Jr. Animal Ark, fuschia lapstrake hull, four black tires, 10 pairs of plastic animals, 5" long; 1970
EX $40 **NM** $60 **MIP** $80

Jr. Auto Carrier, 17-1/2" long; blue cabover, double-deck trailer, two plastic cars; 1969
EX $17 **NM** $33 **MIP** $50

Jr. Auto Carrier, 15-1/2" long; yellow cabover, double-deck trailer, two red plastic cars; 1967
EX $17 **NM** $33 **MIP** $50

Jr. Beach Buggy, 6" long; lime-green Jeep body and surfboard; 1971
EX $5 **NM** $9 **MIP** $14

Jr. Beach Buggy, 6" long; yellow Jeep body, rollbar, white plastic surfboard; 1969
EX $5 **NM** $9 **MIP** $14

Jr. Buggy Hauler, 12" long; fuschia Jeep body, orange two-wheel trailer with Sandpiper beach buggy; 1970
EX $12 **NM** $23 **MIP** $35

Jr. Camper, 7" long; red pickup, yellow camper; 1971
EX $5 **NM** $9 **MIP** $14

Jr. Canada Dry Delivery Truck, 9-1/2" long; green and lime green cabover, hand truck, ten cases of green bottles; 1968-69
EX $27 **NM** $53 **MIP** $80

Jr. Cement Mixer Truck, 7-1/2" long; blue cabover, white mixing drum; 1968-69
EX $6 **NM** $12 **MIP** $18

Jr. Dump Truck, 7-1/2" long; red cabover, plastic vertical headlights, 1967
EX $4 **NM** $8 **MIP** $12

Jr. Dumper, 7-1/2" long; avocado cabover, four-slot grille; 1969
EX $4 **NM** $8 **MIP** $12

Jr. Giraffe Truck, 6-1/2" long; turquoise cabover, plastic giraffe; 1968-69
EX $7 **NM** $13 **MIP** $20

Jr. Kitty Kennel, 6-1/4" long; pink cabover, four white plastic cats; 1968-69
EX $7 **NM** $13 **MIP** $20

Jr. Sanitation Truck, 10" long; blue cabover, white body; 1968
EX $6 **NM** $12 **MIP** $18

Jr. Sanitation Truck, 10" long ;yellow; 1969
EX $6 **NM** $12 **MIP** $18

Jr. Tow Truck, No. 5107; red body, white winch; late 1960s or 1970s
EX $6 **NM** $12 **MIP** $18

Jr. Turbine Racer Transport, red truck, "Turbine Transport" on racer lift, with red racer; 1970s
EX $35 **NM** $65 **MIP** $100

Junior Line Air Mail Truck, black enclosed cab, red chassis and body, headlights and double bar bumper, six rubber tires, 24" long, 1930-32
EX $400 **NM** $650 **MIP** $1200

Kennel Truck, 13-1/4" long; snub-nosed red-orange cab, six-section kennel with six dogs; 1970
EX $20 **NM** $40 **MIP** $60

Kennel Truck, medium blue pickup body and cab, clear plastic twelve-section kennel w/twelve plastic dogs fits in cargo box, 13-1/2" long; 1964
EX $60 **NM** $90 **MIP** $135

Kennel Truck, 13-1/4" long; bright blue, clear plastic 12-section kennel with 12 plastic dogs; 1966-67
EX $32 **NM** $63 **MIP** $95

Kennel Truck, 13-1/4" long; cream yellow; 1968
EX $27 **NM** $53 **MIP** $80

Kennel Truck, 13-1/4" long; red-orange, six-section kennel with six dogs; 1969
EX $22 **NM** $43 **MIP** $65

Kennel Truck, turquoise pickup body and cab, clear plastic twelve-section kennel w/twelve plastic dogs fits in cargo box, 13-1/2" long; 1965
EX $60 **NM** $95 **MIP** $125

Lumber Truck, black front, hood, fenders, doorless cab and low-sides cargo bed, red bumper, chassis and a pair of removable solid stake sides, load of lumber, 25-1/2" long, 1926
EX $650 **NM** $1300 **MIP** $2700

Lumber Truck, black front, hood, fenders, cabless open seat and low-sides cargo bed, red bumper, chassis and a pair of removable solid stake sides, load of lumber pieces, 24" long, 1924
EX $750 **NM** $1000 **MIP** $1500

Mack Hydraulic Dumper, 20-1/2" long; red cab; 1965
EX $33 **NM** $65 **MIP** $100

Mack Hydraulic Dumper, 20-1/2" long; red cab, short step ladder on each side; 1967
EX $33 **NM** $65 **MIP** $100

Mack Quarry Dumper, 20-1/2" long; all yellow, 1960s
EX $35 **NM** $85 **MIP** $120

Mack Quarry Dumper, 20-1/2" long, orange cab, blue-green tiltback dujmp; 1965
EX $50 **NM** $100 **MIP** $150

Mammoth Hydraulic Quarry Dumper, 23" long; green cab, red dump section, black bumper; 1962-63
EX $45 **NM** $89 **MIP** $135

Marshall Field's Delivery Truck Van, hunter green body, sliding doors; 1966
EX $42 **NM** $83 **MIP** $125

Merry-Go-Round, 1967, red truck w/ merry-go-round on flatbed, blackwall tires; 1967, Model No. 5429
EX $65 **NM** $140 **MIP** $230

Milkman Truck, medium blue hood, cab and flatbed body, white side rails, eight 3" white plastic milk bottles, 14-1/4" long; 1961
EX $50 **NM** $100 **MIP** $200

Milkman Truck, deep cream hood, cab and flatbed body, white side rails, fourteen 3" white plastic milk bottles w/red caps, 14-1/4" long; 1962
EX $50 **NM** $105 **MIP** $200

Milkman Truck, light blue hood, cab and flatbed body, white side rails, 14 3" white plastic milk bottles, 14-1/4" long; 1963
EX $85 **NM** $130 **MIP** $175

Milkman Truck, light yellow hood, cab and flatbed body, white side rails, 14 3" white plastic milk bottles, 14-1/4" long; 1964
EX $75 **NM** $125 **MIP** $155

Mister Buddy Ice Cream Truck, 11-1/2" long; red plastic underbody; 1966-67
EX $45 **NM** $89 **MIP** $135

Mister Buddy Ice Cream Truck, No. 5353, 11-1/2" long; white van, "Mister Buddy Ice Cream" and ice cream cone decoration, pale blue or off-white plastic underbody, spring suspension, window sides, whitewall tires; 1964-65
EX $45 **NM** $130 **MIP** $175

Model T Flivver Truck, black w/red eight-spoke wheels w/aluminum tires, black hubs, 12" long, 1924
EX $1000 **NM** $1500 **MIP** $2000

Motor Market Truck, duo-tone horizontal design, white hood top, upper cab and high partition in cargo section, yellow-orange grille, fenders, lower hood and cab sides, 21-1/2" long; 1941
EX $200 **NM** $350 **MIP** $800

Moving Van, black front, hood and seat, red chassis and disc wheels w/black hubs, green van body, roof extends forward above open driver's seat, 25" long, 1924
EX $1200 **NM** $2000 **MIP** $3000

NASA Lowboy and Shuttle, 10-1/2" long; tractor-trailer hauler with Shuttle Discovery, steel and plastic, made in Japan; 1979-80
EX $7 **NM** $13 **MIP** $20

Ol' Buddys Dump Truck, 10-1/2" long; blue old-fashioned truck, whitewall tires, 1960s
EX $25 **NM** $50 **MIP** $75

Ol' Buddy's Pie Wagon, 10-1/2" long; old-fashioned delivery van; 1970
EX $30 **NM** $65 **MIP** $90

Ol' Buddys Sand Drag'n, 5" long; yellow stripped-down hot rod, whitewall tires, orange seat, 1970s
EX $20 **NM** $35 **MIP** $80

Overland Trailer Truck, duo-tone horizontal design, red and white tractor has red front, lower half chassis, chassis, enclosed cab, 40", 1939
EX $350 **NM** $560 **MIP** $710

Overland Trailer Truck, duo-tone slant design, green and yellow semi-streamlined tractor and green hood sides, yellow hood, chassis, enclosed cab, 40", 1939
EX $350 **NM** $550 **MIP** $700

Overland Trailer Truck, duo-tone slant design, green and yellow tractor unit w/yellow cab, red semi-trailer and four-wheel full trailer w/yellow removable roofs, 39-3/4" long, 1936
EX $325 **NM** $485 **MIP** $650

Overland Trailer Truck, yellow tractor, enclosed cab, red semi-trailer and four-wheel full trailer w/removable roofs, 39-3/4" long, 1935
EX $350 **NM** $525 **MIP** $700

Pan-Am Clipper Cargo, 10-1/2" long; tractor-trailer van truck, luggage truck, lift truck and cargo boxes; 1976
EX $12 **NM** $23 **MIP** $35

Pepsi Delivery Truck, 15" long; blue hood and lower cab, white upper cab, double-deck cargo, two hand trucks, four blue cases of red bottles, four red cases of blue bottles; 1970
EX $42 **NM** $83 **MIP** $125

Pick-Up, 13" long; stepside, red body, white roof, whitewall tires; mid-1960s
EX $22 **NM** $43 **MIP** $65

Polysteel Boat Transport, medium blue soft plastic body, steel flatbed carrying 8" white plastic runabout boat w/red deck, truck 12-1/2" long; 1960
EX $75 **NM** $115 **MIP** $150

Polysteel Coca-Cola Delivery Truck, yellow plastic truck, slanted bottle racks, eight red Coke cases w/green bottles, small metal hand truck, 12-1/2" long; 1961
EX $50 **NM** $75 **MIP** $100

Polysteel Coca-Cola Delivery Truck, yellow plastic truck, slanted bottle racks, eight green Coke cases w/red bottles, small metal hand truck, 12-1/4" long; 1962
EX $60 **NM** $90 **MIP** $120

Polysteel Dumper, orange plastic body and tiltback dump section w/cab shield, "Come-Back Motor," 13" long; 1961
EX $75 **NM** $115 **MIP** $150

Polysteel Dumper, orange plastic body and tiltback dump section w/cab shield, no "Come-Back Motor," no door decals, 13-1/2" long; 1962
EX $60 **NM** $95 **MIP** $125

Polysteel Dumper, medium blue soft molded plastic front, cab and frame, off-white steel dump body w/sides rounded at back, hinged tailgate, 13" long; 1960
EX $87 **NM** $130 **MIP** $175

Polysteel Dumper, green soft molded plastic front, cab and frame, yellow steel dump body w/sides rounded at back, hinged tailgate, 13" long; 1959
EX $100 **NM** $150 **MIP** $200

Polysteel Highway Transport, red soft plastic tractor, cab roof lights, double horn, radio antenna and side fuel tanks, white steel semi-trailer van, 20-1/2" long; 1960
EX $100 **NM** $150 **MIP** $200

Polysteel Hydraulic Dumper, beige soft molded-plastic front, cab and frame, off-white steel dump section w/sides rounded at rear, 13" long; 1959
EX $60 **NM** $95 **MIP** $125

Polysteel Hydraulic Dumper, red soft molded-plastic front, cab and frame, light green steel dump section w/sides rounded at rear, 13" long; 1960
EX $80 **NM** $120 **MIP** $160

Polysteel Hydraulic Dumper, yellow soft plastic body, frame and tiltback ribbed dump section w/cab shield, 13" long; 1961
EX $75 **NM** $125 **MIP** $150

Polysteel Hydraulic Dumper, red soft plastic body, frame and tiltback ribbed dump section w/cab shield, 13" long; 1962
EX $65 **NM** $100 **MIP** $130

Polysteel Milk Tanker, red soft plastic tractor unit, light blue/gray semi-trailer tank w/red ladders and five dooms, 22" long; 1961
EX $60 **NM** $95 **MIP** $125

Polysteel Milk Tanker, turquoise soft plastic tractor unit, light blue/gray semi-trailer tank w/red ladders and five dooms, 22" long; 1961
EX $60 **NM** $95 **MIP** $125

Polysteel Milkman Truck, light blue soft plastic front, cab and frame, light blue steel open cargo section w/nine oversized white plastic milk bottles, 11-3/4" long; 1961
EX $60 **NM** $95 **MIP** $125

Polysteel Milkman Truck, turquoise soft plastic front, cab and frame, light blue steel open cargo section w/nine oversized white plastic milk bottles w/red caps, 11-3/4" long; 1962
EX $35 **NM** $50 **MIP** $70

Polysteel Milkman Truck, light blue soft plastic front, cab and frame, light yellow steel open cargo section w/nine oversized white plastic milk bottles, 11-3/4" long; 1960
EX $65 **NM** $100 **MIP** $130

Polysteel Supermarket Delivery, medium blue soft molded-plastic front, hood, cab and frame, steel off-white open cargo section, 13" long; 1959
EX $75 **NM** $115 **MIP** $150

Pull-N-Ride Baggage Truck, duo-tone horizontal design, light cream upper half, off-white lower half and bumper, 24-1/4" long; 1953
EX $150 **NM** $225 **MIP** $300

Racing Team, No. 5464; crossed-flag emblem on cab doors, double-deck racer carrier in rear, three racers; 1964-65
EX $30 **NM** $55 **MIP** $85

Raggedy Ann and Andy Camper, 11-1/2" long; van truck, blue with "Raggedy Ann and Andy Camper" panel decoration, pink interior, whitewall tires; with Raggedy Ann and Andy figures, dog and boat; 1970s or 1980s
EX $30 **NM** $100 **MIP** $135

Railroad Transfer Rider Delivery Truck, duo-tone horizontal design, yellow upper half, hood top, cab and slatted caro sides, green lower half, small hand truck, two milk cans w/removable lids, 23-1/4" long; 1949
EX $70 **NM** $100 **MIP** $140

Railroad Transfer Store Door Delivery, duo-tone horizontal design, yellow hood top, cab and upper body, red lower half of hood and body, small hand truck, two metal drums w/coin slots, 23-1/4" long; 1950
EX $90 **NM** $135 **MIP** $180

Railway Express Truck, green all-steel hood, cab, frame and high-sides open bady, sides have three horizontal slots in upper back corners, 22" long; 1954
EX $75 **NM** $115 **MIP** $150

Railway Express Truck, green plastic hood and cab, green steel high-sides open body, frame and bumper, small two-wheel hand truck, steel four-rung barrel skid, 20-3/4" long; 1953
EX $125 **NM** $185 **MIP** $250

Railway Express Truck, dark green or light green screen body, double-bar nickel front bumper, brass radiator knob, red wheels, 25" long, 1930
EX $500 **NM** $1000 **MIP** $2000

Railway Express Truck, duo-tone horizontal design, tractor unit has yellow front, lower door and chassis, green hood top and enclosed upper cab, semi-trailer has yellow lower sides, 25" long; 1941
EX $325 **NM** $485 **MIP** $650

Railway Express Truck, yellow and green tractor unit has white skirted fenders and hood sides, green hood top, enclosed cab and chassis, green semi-trailer w/yellow removable roof, 25" long; 1940
EX $330 **NM** $495 **MIP** $660

Railway Express Truck, red tractor unit, enclosed square cab, green 12-1/4" long two-wheel semi-trailer van w/removable roof, "Wrigley's Spearmint Gum" poster on trailer sides, 23" long, 1935
EX $375 **NM** $565 **MIP** $750

Railway Express Truck, duo-tone slant design, tractor unit has white skirted fenders and hood sides, green hood top, enclosed cab and chassis, green semi-trailer w/white removable roof, 25" long, 1939
EX $350 **NM** $475 **MIP** $700

Railway Express Truck, duo-tone slant design, tractor has silvery and hood sides, green hood top, enclosed cab, green semi-trailer, "Wrigley's Spearmint Gum" poster on trailer sides, 23" long, 1935
EX $400 **NM** $600 **MIP** $800

Railway Express Truck, black front hood, fenders, seat and low body sides, dark green van body, red chassis, 25" long, 1926
EX $400 **NM** $800 **MIP** $1600

Railway Express Truck, deep green plastic "Diamond T" hood and cab, deep green steel frame and van body w/removable silvery roof, small two-wheel hand truck, steel four-rung barrel skid, 21" long; 1952
EX $200 **NM** $300 **MIP** $400

Ranchero Stake Truck, medium green, white plastic one-piece bumper and grille guard, four-post, four-slat fixed stake sides and cargo section, 14" long; 1963
EX $50 **NM** $75 **MIP** $100

Randy Travis Truck, 20-1/2" long; tractor-trailer, battery-op sounds, 1990s
EX $8 **NM** $12 **MIP** $20

REA Express Van, 11-1/2" long; same as 1965 but with side doors embossed "Buddy L" and no suspension; 1966
EX $45 **NM** $90 **MIP** $200

REA Express Van, 11-1/2" long; dark green, "REA Express" and pigeon decoration, sliding side doors, double rear doors, spring suspension; 1964-65
EX $45 **NM** $125 **MIP** $250

Rider Dump Truck, duo-tone horizontal design, yellow hood top, upper cab and upper dump body, red front, hood sides, lower doors and lower dump body, no bumper, 23" long; 1947
EX $75 **NM** $115 **MIP** $150

Rider Dump Truck, duo-tone horizontal design, yellow hood top, upper cab and upper dump body, red front, hood sides, lower doors and lower dump body, no bumper, 21-1/2" long; 1945
EX $160 **NM** $245 **MIP** $325

Riding Academy Truck, 18-1/2", light brown hood and body, tan roof, three horses, No. 5555, 1970-71
EX $25 **NM** $55 **MIP** $100

Riding Academy Truck, 18-1/2", green hood, cab and van body; white roofs and ramps; three horses, No. 5555, 1972-75
EX $25 **NM** $55 **MIP** $100

Riding Academy Truck, 18-1/2", similar to 1965-67 version, tan body and roof, No. 5455, 1968-69
EX $25 **NM** $55 **MIP** $100

Riding Academy Truck, 18-1/2", similar to 1964 version, maroon body and roof, 2 white ramps, three horses, 1965-67
EX $35 **NM** $80 **MIP** $125

(Thomas G. Nefos Photo)

Riding Academy Truck, 18-1/2"; blue/green body, white roof over bed, side and rear opening ramps, three plastic horses, "Buddy L" logo on cab doors, "Riding Acedemy" in white type along sides, No. 5455, 1964
EX $70 **NM** $120 **MIP** $150

Rival Dog Food Delivery Van, cream front, cab and boxy van body, metal drum coin bank w/"RIVAL DOG FOOD" label in blue, red, white and yellow, 16-1/2" long; 1956
EX $160 **NM** $245 **MIP** $325

Robotoy, black fenders and chassis, red hood and enclosed cab w/small visor, green dump body's front and back are higher than sides, 21-5/8" long, 1932
EX $575 **NM** $900 **MIP** $1200

Rockin' Giraffe Truck, 13-1/4" long; blue cab, open cargo, two plastic giraffes; 1967
EX $30 **NM** $65 **MIP** $125

Ruff-n-Tuff Cement Mixer Truck, 16" long; yellow cabover, white plastic water tank; 1971
EX $22 **NM** $43 **MIP** $65

Ruff-n-Tuff Log Truck, 16" long; yellow cabover; 1971
EX $23 **NM** $46 **MIP** $70

Ryder City Special Delivery Truck Van, duo-tone horizontal design, yellow upper half including hood top and cab, brown removable van roof, warm brown front and lower half of van body, 24-1/2" long; 1949
EX $150 **NM** $225 **MIP** $300

Ryder Van Lines Trailer, duo-tone slant design, black front and lower hood sides and doors, deep red hood top, enclosed cab and chassis, 35-1/2" long; 1949
EX $350 **NM** $525 **MIP** $700

Saddle Dump Truck, duo-tone slant design, yellow front, fenders and removable rider seat, red enclosed square cab and dump body, no bumper, 19-1/2" long, 1937
EX $200 **NM** $300 **MIP** $400

Saddle Dump Truck, duo-tone horizontal design, deep blue hood top, upper cab and upper dump body, orange fenders radiator front lower two-thirds of cab and lower half of dump body, 21-1/2" long; 1941
EX $85 **NM** $130 **MIP** $175

Saddle Dump Truck, duo-tone slant design, yellow front, fenders, lower hood and cab, and removable rider seat, rest of body red, no bumper, 21-1/2" long, 1939
EX $125 **NM** $185 **MIP** $250

Sand and Gravel Rider Dump Truck, duo-tone horizontal design, blue lower half, yellow upper half including hoop top and enclosed cab, 24" long; 1950
EX $350 **NM** $525 **MIP** $700

Sand and Gravel Truck, black w/red chassis and wheels, nickel-rim, red-shell headlights, enclosed cab w/opening doors, 25-1/2" long, 1930-32
EX $2000 **NM** $3000 **MIP** $5000

Sand and Gravel Truck, duo-tone horizontal design, red front, bumper, lower hood, cab sides, chassis and lower dump body sides, white hood top, enclosed cab and upper dump body, 23-3/4" long; 1949
EX $350 **NM** $525 **MIP** $700

Sand and Gravel Truck, dark or medium green hood, cab, roof lights and skirted body, white or cream dump section, 13-1/2" long; 1949
EX $100 **NM** $150 **MIP** $200

Sand and Gravel Truck, black body, doorless roofed cab and steering wheel, red chassis and disc wheels w/black hubs, 25-1/2" long, 1926
EX $600 **NM** $1000 **MIP** $1200

Sand Dump Truck, 10-1/2" long; green tractor-trailer, futuristic cabover, 1970s
EX $5 **NM** $10 **MIP** $20

Sand Loader and Dump Truck, duo-tone horizontal design, yellow hood top and upper dump blue cab sides, frame and lower dump body, red loader on dump w/black rubber conveyor belt, 24-1/2" long; 1950
EX $175 **NM** $265 **MIP** $350

Sand Loader and Dump Truck, duo-tone horizontal design, yellow hood top and upper dump blue cab sides, frame and lower dump body, red loader on dump w/black rubber conveyor belt, 24-1/2" long; 1952
EX $60 **NM** $95 **MIP** $125

Sanitation Service Truck, 16-1/2" long; blue cab, white enclosed dump section, plastic windows in garbage section; 1967
EX $32 **NM** $63 **MIP** $95

Sanitation Service Truck, 16-1/2" long; blue cab, white enclosed dump section, no plastic windows in garbage section; 1968
EX $32 **NM** $63 **MIP** $95

Sanitation Service Truck, 17" long; blue cab, white body, two round plastic headlights; 1972
EX $17 **NM** $33 **MIP** $50

Sanitation Truck, 6" long; white and blue; 1970s
EX $3 **NM** $5 **MIP** $8

Sears Roebuck Delivery Truck Van, gray/green and off-white, no side doors; 1967, Model No. *
EX $125 **NM** $200 **MIP** $280

Sears Service Van Truck, 11-1/2" long; gray-green, open side doors, swing-open rear doors; 1967-68
EX $42 **NM** $83 **MIP** $125

Self-Loading Auto Carrier, medium tan tractor unit, three plastic cars, overall 34" long including loading ramp; 1960
EX $85 **NM** $130 **MIP** $175

Self-Loading Boat Hauler, pastel blue tractor and semi-trailer w/three 8-1/2" long boats, overall 26-1/2" long; 1962
EX $150 **NM** $225 **MIP** $350

Self-Loading Boat Hauler, pastel blue tractor and semi-trailer w/three 8-1/2" long boats, no side mirror on truck, overall 26-1/2" long; 1963
EX $150 **NM** $225 **MIP** $350

Self-Loading Car Carrier, lime green tractor unit, three plastic cars, overall 33-1/2" long including; 1963
EX $75 **NM** $115 **MIP** $150

Self-Loading Car Carrier, beige/yellow tractor unit, three plastic cars, overall 33-1/2" long including; 1964
EX $60 **NM** $95 **MIP** $125

Service Wrecker, 14" long; red, black boom; mid-1960s
EX $50 **NM** $100 **MIP** $150

Shark Show Truck, 10-1/2" long; green tractor-trailer with shark and tank, futuristic cabover, 1970s
EX $5 **NM** $10 **MIP** $15

Shell Pickup and Delivery, yellow/orange hood and body, open cargo section, three curved slots toward rear in sides, chains across back, red coin-slot oil drum w/Shell emblem and lettering, 13-1/4" long; 1952
EX $125 **NM** $185 **MIP** $250

Shell Pickup and Delivery, reddish orange hood and body, open cargo section w/solid sides, chain across back, red coin-slot oil drum w/Shell emblem and lettering, 13-1/4" long; 1950
EX $135 **NM** $200 **MIP** $275

Shell Pickup and Delivery, yellow/orange hood and body, open cargo section w/three curved slots toward rear in sides, red coin-slot oil drum w/Shell emblem and lettering, 13-1/4" long; 1953
EX $110 **NM** $175 **MIP** $225

Sit-N-Ride Truck, 25" long; removable steel seat in dump bed, lever-action dump body; 1965
EX $38 **NM** $76 **MIP** $115

Smoke Patrol, 13-1/4" long; lemon-yellow body, six wheels, garden-hose attachment for water cannon; 1970
EX $22 **NM** $43 **MIP** $65

Sprinkler Truck, black front, hood, fenders and cabless open driver's seat, red bumper and chassis, bluish/gray/green water tank, 25" long, 1929
EX $800 **NM** $1500 **MIP** $2000

Stake Body Truck, black cabless open driver's seat, hood, front fenders and flatbed body, red chassis and five removable stake sections, cargo bed w/low sidesboards, drop-down tailgate, 25" long, 1924
EX $850 **NM** $1650 **MIP** $2500

Stake Body Truck, black cabless open driver's seat, hood, front fenders and flatbed body, red chassis and five removable stake sections, 25" long, 1921
EX $850 **NM** $1650 **MIP** $2500

Standard Coffee Co. Delivery Truck Van, 11-1/2" long; 1966
EX $40 **NM** $60 **MIP** $120

Standard Oil Tank Truck, duo-tone slant design, white upper cab and hood, red lower cab, grille, fenders and tank, rubber wheels, electric headlights, 26" long, 1936-37
EX $350 **NM** $500 **MIP** $1000

Stor-Dor Delivery, red hood and body, open cargo body w/four horizontal slots in sides, plated chains across open back, 14-1/2" long; 1955
EX $65 **NM** $100 **MIP** $175

Street Sprinkler Truck, black front, hood, front fenders and cabless open driver's seat, red bumper and chassis, bluish/gray/green water tank, 25" long, 1929
EX $700 **NM** $900 **MIP** $1800

Street Sprinkler Truck, black front, hood, and fenders, open cab, nickel-rim, red-shell headlights, double bar front bumper, bluish/gray/green water tank, six rubber tires, 25" long, 1930-32
EX $800 **NM** $1000 **MIP** $1900

(Joe and Sharon Freed Photo)

Sunshine Biscuits Van, Dark yellow body, light gray chassis, whitewall tires, Sunshine chef decals along sides, with Sunshine Biscuits photo decal showing Krispy, Cheez-It crackers and Hydrox and HiHo cookies
EX $145 **NM** $260 **MIP** $330

Sunshine Biscuits Van Truck, 11-1/2" long; yellow cabover, sliding side doors, opening rear doors, "Sunshine Biscuits" on panels; 1967-68
EX $30 **NM** $59 **MIP** $90

Super Dog Truck, 6-1/2" long; high-windshield cabover, doghouse with Snoopy-like dog's head as load; 1970s
EX $6 **NM** $12 **MIP** $18

Super Motor Market, duo-tone horizontal design, white hood top, upper cab and high partition in cargo section, yellow/orange lower hood and cab sides, semi-trailer carrying supplies, 21-1/2" long, 1942
EX $300 **NM** $500 **MIP** $700

Supermarket Delivery, blue bumper, front, hood, cab and frame, one-piece chrome four-hole grille and headlights, 14-1/2" long; 1956
EX $75 **NM** $115 **MIP** $150

Supermarket Delivery, all white w/rubber wheels, enclosed cab, pointed nose, bright metal one-piece grille, 13-3/4" long; 1950
EX $125 **NM** $185 **MIP** $250

Tank and Sprinkler Truck, black front, hood, fenders, doorless cab and seat, dark green tank and side racks, black or dark green sprinkler attachment, 26-1/4" long w/sprinkler attachment, 1924
EX $700 **NM** $900 **MIP** $1700

Teepee Camping Trailer and Wagon, maroon suburban wagon, two-wheel teepee trailer and its beige plastic folding tent, overall 24-1/2" long; 1963
EX $75 **NM** $180 **MIP** $260

(Calvin L. Chaussee Photo)

Texaco Tank Truck, red steel GMC 550-series blunt-nose tractor and semi-trailer tank, 25" long; 1959
EX $175 **NM** $250 **MIP** $400

Texaco Tanker, Promotional Piece, White rounded cabover with red tanker section, black plastic hose. "Texaco" logo stickers on cab, "Texaco" on tanker sides, 25" long
EX $78 **NM** $130 **MIP** $205

Tide Racing Team Truck, 20-1/2" long; Kenworth tractor-trailer, "Ricky Rudd," 1990s
EX $5 **NM** $8 **MIP** $12

Tom's Toasted Peanuts Delivery Truck Van, 11-1/2" long; tan body , no sliding doors, blue underbody; 1973
EX $27 **NM** $53 **MIP** $80

Trail Boss, 7" long; lime green, yellow seat; 1971
EX $4 **NM** $9 **MIP** $12

Trail Boss, 7" long; red, white plastic seat; 1970
EX $4 **NM** $9 **MIP** $12

Trailer Dump Truck, cream tractor unit w/enclosed cab, dark blue semi-trailer dump body w/high sides and top-hinged opening endgate, no bumper, 20-3/4" long; 1941
EX $75 **NM** $115 **MIP** $155

Trailer Van Truck, red tractor and van roof, blue bumper, white semi-trailer van, chrome one-piece toothed grille and headlights, white drop-down rear door, 29" long w/tailgate/ramp lowered; 1956
EX $145 **NM** $225 **MIP** $300

Trailer Van with Tailgate Loader, green high-impacted styrene plastic tractor on steel frame, cream steel detachable semi-trailer van w/green roof and crank operated tailgate, 33" long w/tailgate lowered; 1953
EX $125 **NM** $185 **MIP** $250

Trailer Van with Tailgate Loader, green steel tractor, bumper, chrome one-piece toothed grille and headlights, cream van w/green roof and tailgate loader, 31-3/4" long, w/tailgate down; 1954
EX $125 **NM** $185 **MIP** $250

Traveling Zoo Truck, 14" long; snub-nosed yellow cab, six red cages with six animals; 1970
EX $17 **NM** $33 **MIP** $50

Traveling Zoo Truck, 14" long; red pickup, yellow six-copartment cage with six plastic jungle animals; 1965-67
EX $28 **NM** $56 **MIP** $85

Traveling Zoo Truck, 14" long; yellow pickup, six compartments with animals; 1969
EX $25 **NM** $50 **MIP** $75

Turbine Racer Transport, short high-window cabover truck w/platform for hauling red "Turbine" open-cockpit racer, 1960s
EX $12 **NM** $25 **MIP** $50

U.S. Army Half-Track and Howitzer, olive drab, 12-1/2" truck, 9-3/4" gun, overall 22-1/2" long; 1952
EX $125 **NM** $200 **MIP** $275

U.S. Mail Delivery Truck, blue cab, hood, bumper, frame and removable roof on white van body, 23-1/4" long; 1956
EX $100 **NM** $200 **MIP** $510

U.S. Mail Delivery Van Truck, 11-1/2" long; sliding side doors, ear opening doors, whitewall tires, "U.S. Mail" and red, white and blue paint scheme, w/driver and two mailboxes; 1964-67
EX $32 **NM** $85 **MIP** $125

(Calvin L. Chaussee Photo)

U.S. Mail Truck, shiny olive green body and bumper, yellow-cream removable van roof, enclosed cab, 22-1/2" long; 1953
EX $215 **NM** $410 **MIP** $580

United Parcel Delivery Van, duo-tone horizontal design, deep cream upper half w/brown removable roof, chocolate brown front and lower half, 25" long; 1941
EX $250 **NM** $450 **MIP** $650

Utility Delivery Truck, duo-tone slant design, blue front and lower hood sides, gray hood top, cab and open body w/red and yellow horizontal stripe, 22-3/4" long; 1940
EX $250 **NM** $450 **MIP** $650

Utility Delivery Truck, duo-tone horizontal design, green upper half including hood top, dark cream lower half, green wheels, red and yellow horizontal stripe, 22-3/4" long; 1941
EX $125 **NM** $185 **MIP** $250

Utility Dump Truck, duo-tone slant design, red front, lower door and fenders, gray chassis, red upper hood, upper enclosed cab and removable rider seat, yellow body, 25-1/2" long; 1941
EX $85 **NM** $130 **MIP** $175

Utility Dump Truck, duo-tone slant design, red front, lower doord and fenders, gray chassis and enclosed upper cab, royal blue dump body, yellow removable rider seat, 25-1/2" long; 1940
EX $125 **NM** $185 **MIP** $250

Van Freight Carriers Trailer, bright blue streanlined tractor and enclosed cab, cream/yellow semi-trailer van, removable silvery roof, 22" long; 1949
EX $65 **NM** $100 **MIP** $135

Van Freight Carriers Trailer, red streamlined tractor, bright blue enclosed cab, light cream/white semi-trailer van w/removable white roof, 22" long; 1953
EX $125 **NM** $185 **MIP** $250

Van Freight Carriers Trailer, red streamlined tractor, bright blue enclosed cab, cream/yellow semi-trailer van, white removable van roof, 22" long; 1952
EX $55 **NM** $85 **MIP** $115

Wal-Mart Semi, 11" long; battery-operated voice, "Ten-four, good buddy"; 1990s
EX $7 **NM** $15 **MIP** $22

Wild Animal Circus (tractor-trailer), 26" long; red, three cages with plastic elephant, lion and tiger; 1966
EX $200 **NM** $300 **MIP** $400

Wild Animal Circus (tractor-trailer), 26" long; red, three cages with six plastic adult and baby animals; 1967
EX $75 **NM** $150 **MIP** $225

Wild Animal Circus (tractor-trailer), 26" long; red, with light-red cage doors; 1970
EX $50 **NM** $75 **MIP** $150

Wrecker, 5" long; made in Japan; 1980
EX $3 **NM** $6 **MIP** $9

Wrecker, 7-1/2" long; "AAA, 24 Hr. Service"; 1983
EX $2 **NM** $4 **MIP** $7

Wrecker Truck, black front, hood, and fenders, open cab, four rubber tires, red wrecker body, 26-1/2" long, 1930
EX $800 **NM** $1000 **MIP** $2500

Wrecker Truck, duo-tone slant design, red upper cab, hood, and boom, white lower cab, grille, fenders, body, rubber wheels, electric headlights, removable rider seat, 31" long, 1936
EX $250 **NM** $450 **MIP** $700

Wrecker Truck, black open cab, red chassis and bed, disc wheels, 26-1/2" long, 1928-29
EX $700 **NM** $1000 **MIP** $2000

Wrigley Express Truck, forest green w/chrome one-piece, three-bar grille and headlights, "Wrigley's Spearmint Gum" poster on sides, 16-1/2" long; 1955
EX $135 **NM** $215 **MIP** $295

Zoo-A-Rama, 20-3/4" long; yellow; 1968
EX $50 **NM** $80 **MIP** $120

Zoo-A-Rama, 20-3/4" long; green-yellow; 1969
EX $50 **NM** $80 **MIP** $120

Zoo-A-Rama, 20-3/4" long; lime green Colt Sportsliner with four-wheel trailer cage, with plastic tree, monkeys and bears; 1967
EX $50 **NM** $75 **MIP** $150

Zookeeper's Truck, 6-1/4" long; turbo cab, plastic giraffe; 1970
EX $7 **NM** $13 **MIP** $20

CORGI

AGRICULTURAL

Agricultural Set, 1962-66, 1962-64 issue: No. 55 Fordson Tractor, No. 51 Tipping Trailer, No. 438 Land Rover, No. 101 Flat Trailer w/No. 1487 Milk Churns; 1965-66 issue: No. 60 Fordson Tractor, No. 62 Tipping Trailer, No. 438 Land Rover, red No. 100 Dropside Trailer w/No. 1487 Milk Churns, a difficult set to find, Model No. 22-A
EX $380 **NM** $900 **MIP** $2100

Agricultural Set, 1967-72, No. 69 Massey-Ferguson tractor, No. 62 trailer, No. 438 Land Rover, No. 484 Livestock Truck w/pigs, No. 71 harrow, No. 1490 skip and churns; w/accessories: four calves, farmhand, dog and six sacks, Model No. 5-B
EX $120 **NM** $180 **MIP** $475

Agricultural Set, 1978-80, No. 55 Tractor, No. 56 Tipping Trailer, Silo and mustard yellow conveyor, Model No. 42-A
EX $60 **NM** $90 **MIP** $130

Beast Carrier Trailer, 1965-71, red chassis, yellow body and tailgate, four plastic calves, red plastic wheels, black rubber tires, Model No. 58-A
EX $24 **NM** $36 **MIP** $60

Bedford Articulated Horse Box, 1973-76, cast cab, lower body and three working ramps, yellow interior, plastic upper body, w/horse and Newmarket Racing Stables labels, dark metallic green or light green body w/orange or yellow upper, four horses, Model No. 1104-B
EX $32 **NM** $48 **MIP** $100

Berliet Articulated Horse Box, 1976-80, bronze cab and lower semi body, cream chassis, white upper body, black interior, three working ramps, National Racing Stables decals, horse figures, chrome wheels, Model No. 1105-B
EX $30 **NM** $45 **MIP** $75

Combine, Tractor and Trailer, 1959-62, set of three: No. 1111 combine, No. 50 Massey-Ferguson tractor, and No. 51 trailer, Model No. 8-A
EX $110 **NM** $185 **MIP** $375

Country Farm Set, 1974-75, No. 50 Massey-Ferguson tractor, red No. 62 hay trailer w/load, fences, figures, Model No. 4-B
EX $30 **NM** $45 **MIP** $75

Country Farm Set, 1976, same as 4-B but without hay load on trailer, Model No. 5-C
EX $30 **NM** $45 **MIP** $75

David Brown Combine, 1978-79, No. 55 tractor, red and yellow combines, white JF labels, Model No. 1112-B
EX $30 **NM** $45 **MIP** $75

David Brown Tractor, 1977-82, white body w/black/white David Brown No. 1412 labels, red chassis and plastic engine, Model No. 55-B
EX $15 **NM** $25 **MIP** $45

David Brown Tractor & Trailer, 1976-79, two-piece set: No. 55 tractor and No. 56 trailer, Model No. 34-A
EX $30 **NM** $45 **MIP** $75

Dodge Livestock Truck, 1967-72, tan cab and hood, green body, working tailgate and ramp, five pigs, Model No. 484-A
EX $34 **NM** $51 **MIP** $90

Ford 5000 Super Major Tractor, 1967-73, blue body/chassis w/Ford Super Major 5000 decals, gray cast fenders and rear wheels, gray plastic front wheels, black plastic tires, driver, Model No. 67-A
EX $30 **NM** $45 **MIP** $75

Ford 5000 Tractor with Scoop, 1969-72, blue body/chassis, gray fenders, yellow scoop arm and controls, chrome scoop, black control lines, Model No. 74-A
EX $55 **NM** $80 **MIP** $180

(KP Photo by Dr. Douglas Sadecky)

Ford Tractor and Beast Carrier, 1966-72, Gift Set included No. 67 Fordson 5000 tractor and No. 58 Beast Carrier, Model No. 1-B
EX $60 **NM** $90 **MIP** $190

Ford Tractor and Conveyor, 1966-69, No. 67 tractor, conveyor w/trailer, figures and accessories, Model No. 47-A
EX $60 **NM** $90 **MIP** $225

Ford Tractor with Trencher, 1970-74, blue body/chassis, gray fenders, cast yellow trencher arm and controls, chrome trencher, black control lines, Model No. 72-A
EX $50 **NM** $75 **MIP** $190

(KP Photo by Dr. Douglas Sadecky)

Fordson Power Major Halftrack Tractor, 1962-64, blue body/chassis, silver steering wheel, seat and grille, three versions: orange cast wheels, gray treads, lights in radiator or on sides of radiator. This bizarre little model can be quite difficult to find--especially with original tracks, Model No. 54-A
EX $90 **NM** $135 **MIP** $235

VEHICLES • BUDDY L

(KP Photo by Dr. Douglas Sadecky)

Fordson Power Major Tractor, 1961-63, blue body/chassis w/Fordson Power Major decals, silver steering wheel, seat, exhaust, grille and lights. The 61-A Four Furrow Plough makes a nice companion piece to the model, Model No. 55-A
EX $45 **NM** $65 **MIP** $110

Fordson Power Major Tractor, 1964-66, blue body w/Fordson Power Major decals, driver, blue chassis and steering wheel, silver seat, hitch, exhaust, Model No. 60-A
EX $50 **NM** $75 **MIP** $125

Fordson Tractor and Plow, 1961-64, No. 55 Fordson Tractor and No. 56 Four Furrow plow, Model No. 18-A
EX $55 **NM** $85 **MIP** $180

Fordson Tractor and Plow, 1964-66, No. 60 tractor and No. 61 four-furrow plow, Model No. 13-A
EX $55 **NM** $85 **MIP** $140

Four Furrow Plow, 1961-63, red frame, yellow plastic parts, Model No. 56-A
EX $15 **NM** $20 **MIP** $40

Four Furrow Plow, 1964-70, blue frame w/chrome plastic parts, Model No. 61-A
EX $15 **NM** $20 **MIP** $40

Jeep FC-150 Pickup with Conveyor Belt, 1965-69, red body, yellow interior, orange grille, two black rubber belts, shaped wheels, black rubber tires; accessories include farmland figure and sacks, Model No. 64-A
EX $45 **NM** $75 **MIP** $160

Land Rover & Horse Box, 1968-77, blue/white Land Rover w/horse trailer in two versions: cast wheels (1968-74) and Whizz Wheels (1975-77); accessories include a mare and a foal; value is for each individual complete set, Model No. 15-B
EX $50 **NM** $75 **MIP** $125

Land Rover and Pony Trailer, 1958-62, two versions: green No. 438 Land Rover and a red and black No. 102 Pony trailer (1958-62); tan/cream No. 438 Land Rover and a pony trailer (1963-68); value given is for each individual complete set, Model No. 2-A
EX $50 **NM** $90 **MIP** $200

Massey-Ferguson 165 Tractor, 1966-72, gray engine and chassis, red hood and fenders w/black/white Massey-Ferguson 165 decals, white grille, red cast wheels; makes engine sound, Model No. 66-A
EX $35 **NM** $55 **MIP** $90

(KP Photo by Dr. Douglas Sadecky)

Massey-Ferguson 165 Tractor with Saw, 1969-73, red hood and fenders, gray engine and seat, cast yellow arm and control, chrome circular saw, Model No. 73-A
EX $55 **NM** $85 **MIP** $200

(KP Photo by Dr. Douglas Sadecky)

Massey-Ferguson 165 Tractor with Shovel, 1967-73, gray chassis, red hood, fenders and shovel arms, unpainted shovel and cylinder, red cast wheels, black plastic tires, w/figure. This tractor even featured engine noises!, Model No. 69-A
EX $45 **NM** $65 **MIP** $120

Massey-Ferguson 50B Tractor, 1973-77, yellow body, black interior and roof, red plastic wheels w/black plastic tires, windows, Model No. 50-B
EX $15 **NM** $18 **MIP** $75

Massey-Ferguson 65 Tractor, 1959-66, silver metal or plastic steering wheel, seat and grille, red engine hood, red metal or plastic wheels w/black rubber tires, Model No. 50-A
EX $40 **NM** $60 **MIP** $110

Massey-Ferguson 65 Tractor And Shovel, 1960-66, two versions: red bonnet w/either cream or gray chassis, red metal or orange plastic wheels; value is for each, Model No. 53-A
EX $55 **NM** $85 **MIP** $140

Massey-Ferguson Combine, 1959-63, red body w/yellow metal blades, metal tines, black/white decals, yellow metal wheels, Model No. 1111-A
EX $70 **NM** $105 **MIP** $200

Massey-Ferguson Combine, 1968-73, red body, plastic yellow blades, red wheels, Model No. 1111-B
EX $60 **NM** $100 **MIP** $180

Massey-Ferguson Tipping Trailer, 1959-65, two versions: red chassis w/either yellow or gray tipper and tailgate, red metal or plastic wheels, value is for each, Model No. 51-A
EX $10 **NM** $18 **MIP** $40

Massey-Ferguson Tractor and Tipping Trailer, 1959-63, No. 50 tractor and No. 51 trailer, no driver, Model No. 7-A
EX $50 **NM** $75 **MIP** $150

Massey-Ferguson Tractor and Tipping Trailer, 1965, No. 50 Massey-Ferguson tractor w/driver, No. 51 trailer, Model No. 29-A
EX $50 **NM** $75 **MIP** $150

(KP Photo by Dr. Douglas Sadecky)

Massey-Ferguson Tractor with Fork, 1963-67, red cast body and shovel, arms, cream chassis, red plastic wheels, black rubber tires, Massey-Ferguson 65 decals, w/driver, Model No. 57-A
EX $60 **NM** $90 **MIP** $150

Massey-Ferguson Tractor with Shovel, 1974-81, two versions: either yellow and red or red and white body colors; value is for each, Model No. 54-B
EX $20 **NM** $30 **MIP** $50

Massey-Ferguson Tractor with Shovel & Trailer, 1965-66, No. 54 MF tractor w/driver and shovel, No. 62 trailer, Model No. 32-A
EX $30 **NM** $75 **MIP** $150

Pony Club Set, 1978-80, brown/white No. 421 Land Rover w/Corgi Pony Club labels, horse box, horse and rider, Model No. 47-B
EX $30 **NM** $45 **MIP** $75

Rice Beaufort Double Horse Box, 1969-72, long, blue body and working gates, white roof, brown plastic interior, two horses, cast wheels, plastic tires, Model No. 112-A
EX $15 **NM** $30 **MIP** $50

(KP Photo by Dr. Douglas Sadecky)

Rice Pony Trailer, 1958-65, cast body and chassis w/working tailgate, horse, in six variations, smooth or shaped hubs, cast or wire drawbar. Shown here is the harder-to-find two-tone cream/red variation, Model No. 102-A
EX $20 **NM** $30 **MIP** $50

Silo & Conveyor Belt, 1978-80, w/yellow conveyor and Corgi Harvesting Co. label on silo, Model No. 43-A
EX $35 **NM** $50 **MIP** $85

Tandem Disc Harrow, 1967-72, yellow main frame, red upper frame, working wheels linkage, unpainted linkage and cast discs, black plastic tires, Model No. 71-A
EX $15 **NM** $20 **MIP** $45

Tipping Farm Trailer, 1965-72, red working tipper and tailgates, yellow chassis, red plastic wheels, black tires, w/detachable raves, Model No. 62-A
EX $10 **NM** $15 **MIP** $35

Tipping Farm Trailer, 1977-80, cast chassis and tailgate, red plastic tipper and wheels, black tires, in two versions, Model No. 56-B
EX $10 **NM** $15 **MIP** $25

Tractor and Beast Carrier, 1965-66, No. 55 Fordson tractor, figures and No. 58 beast carrier, Model No. 33-A
EX $65 **NM** $100 **MIP** $165

Tractor with Shovel and Trailer, 1968-73, standard colors, No. 69 Massey-Ferguson Tractor and No. 62 Tipping Trailer, Model No. 9-B
EX $65 **NM** $100 **MIP** $165

AIRCRAFT

(KP Photo by Dr. Douglas Sadecky)

Concorde-First Issues, 1969-72, Japan Airlines decals. This rare model was probably an import issue. Ironically, the real Concorde was never part of the Japan Air Lines, Model No. 653-A
EX $280 **NM** $420 **MIP** $700

Concorde-First Issues, 1969-72, Air Canada decals. (The real Concorde was not a part of Air Canada.), Model No. 652-A
EX $80 **NM** $120 **MIP** $250

Concorde-First Issues, 1969-72, Air France decals, Model No. 651-A
EX $20 **NM** $45 **MIP** $85

Concorde-First Issues, 1969-72, BOAC decals, Model No. 650-A
EX $20 **NM** $40 **MIP** $75

Concorde-Second Issue, 1976-82, Air France model on display stand, Model No. 651-B
EX $15 **NM** $20 **MIP** $35

Concorde-Second Issues, 1976-82, BOAC model on display stand, Model No. 650-B
EX $15 **NM** $20 **MIP** $35

Corgi Flying Club Set, 1972-77, blue/orange No. 438 Land Rover w/red dome light, blue trailer w/either orange/yellow or orange/white plastic airplane, Model No. 19-B
EX $24 **NM** $50 **MIP** $100

Flying Club Set, 1978-80, green and white No. 419 Jeep w/Corgi Flying Club labels, green trailer, blue/white airplane, Model No. 49-A
EX $36 **NM** $55 **MIP** $90

Glider Set, 1981-83, two versions: white No. 345 Honda, 1981-82; yellow Honda, 1983, value is for individual complete sets, Model No. 12-C
EX $30 **NM** $45 **MIP** $75

Lunar Bug, 1970-72, white body w/red roof, blue interior and wings, clear and amber windows, red working ramp, Lunar Bug labels, Model No. 806-A
EX $25 **NM** $40 **MIP** $95

NASA Space Shuttle, 1980, white body, two opening hatches, black plastic interior, jets and base, unpainted retracting gear castings, black plastic wheels, w/satellite, Model No. 648-A
EX $30 **NM** $45 **MIP** $75

Stromberg Jet Ranger Helicopter, 1978-79, black body w/yellow trim and interior, clear windows, black plastic rotors, white/blue labels, Model No. 926-A
EX $45 **NM** $65 **MIP** $125

AUTOMOBILE

AMC Pacer, 1977-78, metallic red body, white Pacer X decals, working hatch, clear windows, light yellow interior, chrome bumpers and wheels, Model No. 291-A
EX $15 **NM** $20 **MIP** $50

Aston Martin DB4, 1960-65, red or yellow body w/working hood, detailed engine, clear windows, plastic interior, silver lights, grille, license plate and bumpers, red taillights, rubber tires, smooth or cast spoked wheels; working scoop on early models, Model No. 218-A
EX $45 **NM** $65 **MIP** $140

(KP Photo by Dr. Douglas Sadecky)

Austin A40, 1959-62, one-piece light blue body with dark blue roof or red body w/black roof and clear windows, smooth wheels or spun hubs, rubber tires, Model No. 216-A
EX $35 **NM** $50 **MIP** $100

Austin A40-Mechanical, 1959-60, friction motor, red body w/black roof, smooth wheels, Model No. 216-M
EX $55 **NM** $75 **MIP** $180

(KP Photo by Dr. Douglas Sadecky)

Austin A60 Driving School, 1964-68, medium blue body w/silver trim, left-hand drive steering wheel, steering control on roof; came w/five language leaflet (US version of No. 236), Model No. 255-A
EX $45 **NM** $65 **MIP** $160

(KP Photo by Dr. Douglas Sadecky)

Austin A60 Motor School, 1964-69, light blue body w/silver trim, red interior, single body casting, right-hand drive steering wheel, two figures, steering control on roof; came w/Highway Patrol leaflet, Model No. 236-A
EX $45 **NM** $65 **MIP** $130

(KP Photo by Dr. Douglas Sadecky)

Austin Cambridge, 1956-61, available in gray, green/gray, silver/green, aqua, green/cream, two-tone green, smooth wheels, shown here with Austin Cambridge-Mechanical, Model No. 201-A
EX $40 **NM** $60 **MIP** $120

Austin Cambridge-Mechanical, 1956-59, fly-wheel motor, available in orange, cream, light or dark gray, or silver over metallic blue, smooth wheels, Model No. 201M
EX $50 **NM** $75 **MIP** $180

Austin Mini Countryman, 1965-69, turquoise body, jeweled headlights, opening rear doors, chrome roofrack w/two surfboards, shaped or cast wheels, w/surfer figure, Model No. 485-A
EX $55 **NM** $80 **MIP** $160

Austin Mini-Metro, 1981, blue or red body w/plastic interior, working rear hatch and doors, clear windows, folding seats, chrome headlights, orange taillights, black plastic base, grille, bumpers, Whizz Wheels, Model No. 275-B
EX $18 **NM** $27 **MIP** $45

Austin Seven Mini, 1961-67, primrose yellow, red interior, rare, Model No. 225-A2, second issue
EX $100 **NM** $200 **MIP** $325

Austin Seven Mini, 1961-67, red or yellow body, yellow interior, silver bumpers, grille and headlights, orange taillights, Model No. 225-A1
EX $50 **NM** $75 **MIP** $145

Bentley Continental, 1961-66, two-tone green or black and silver bodies, w/red interior, clear windows, chrome grille and bumpers, jewel headlights, red jeweled taillights, suspension, shaped wheels, gray rubber tires, Model No. 224-A
EX $45 **NM** $65 **MIP** $110

Bentley T Series, 1970-72, red body, cream interior, working hood, trunk and doors, clear windows, folding seats, chrome bumper/grille, jewel headlights, Whizz Wheels, Model No. 274-A
EX $36 **NM** $55 **MIP** $90

Buick and Cabin Cruiser, 1965-68, two versions: light blue or dark metallic blue, No. 245 Buick, red boat trailer, dolphin cabin cruiser w/two figures, Model No. 31-A
EX $80 **NM** $120 **MIP** $280

Buick Riviera, 1964-68, metallic gold, dark blue, pale blue or gold body, red interior, gray steering wheel, and tow hook, clear windshield, chrome grille and bumpers, suspension, Trans-o-lite headlights, spoked wheels and rubber tires, Model No. 245-A
EX $30 **NM** $45 **MIP** $85

Chevrolet Caprice Classic, 1981-82, working doors and trunk, whitewall tires, two versions: light metallic green body w/green interior or silver on blue body w/brown interior, Model No. 325-B
EX $24 **NM** $36 **MIP** $60

(KP Photo by Dr. Douglas Sadecky)

Chevrolet Corvair, 1961-66, either blue or pale-blue body w/yellow interior and working rear hood, detailed engine, clear windows, silver bumpers, headlights and trim, red taillights, rear window blind, smooth or shaped wheels, rubber tires, Model No. 229-A
EX $36 **NM** $55 **MIP** $90

(KP Photo by Dr. Douglas Sadecky)

Chevrolet Impala, 1960-62, pink body, yellow plastic interior, clear windows, silver headlights, bumpers, grille and trim, suspension, die-cast base w/rubber tires; a second version has a blue body w/red or yellow interior and smooth or shaped hubs, Model No. 220-A
EX $50 **NM** $75 **MIP** $135

Chevrolet Impala, 1965-67, tan body, cream interior, gray steering wheel, clear windshields, chrome bumpers, grille, headlights, suspension, red taillights, shaped wheels and rubber tires, Model No. 248-A
EX $50 **NM** $75 **MIP** $125

(KP Photo by Dr. Douglas Sadecky)

Chevrolet Kennel Club Van, 1967-69, white upper, red lower body, working tailgate and rear windows, green interior, four dog figures, kennel club decals; shaped spun or detailed cast wheels, rubber tires, Model No. 486-A
EX $56 **NM** $90 **MIP** $160

Chrysler Imperial Convertible, 1965-66, red body w/gray base, working hood, trunk and doors, golf bag in trunk, detailed engine, clear windshield, aqua interior, driver, chrome bumpers, shaped or cast wheels, Model No. 246-A1
EX $45 **NM** $65 **MIP** $120

Chrysler Imperial Convertible, 1967-68, metallic blue body w/gray base, working hood, trunk and doors, golf bag in trunk, detailed engine, clear windshield, aqua interior, driver, chrome bumpers, shaped or cast wheels, Model No. 246-A2
EX $50 **NM** $90 **MIP** $160

Citroen 2CV Charleston, 1981, yellow/black or maroon/black body versions w/opening hood, Model No. 346-A
EX $15 **NM** $18 **MIP** $30

Citroen DS19, 1957-65, one-piece body in several colors, clear windows, silver lights, grille and bumpers, smooth wheels, rubber tires; colors: red, metallic green w/black roof, yellow w/red roof, Model No. 210-A
EX $56 **NM** $84 **MIP** $140

Citroen Dyane, 1974-78, metallic yellow or green body, black roof and interior, working rear hatch, clear windows, black base and tow bar, silver bumpers, grille and headlights, red taillights, marching duck and French flag decals, suspension, chrome wheels, Model No. 287-A
EX $15 **NM** $18 **MIP** $30

Citroen ID-19 Safari, 1963-65, yellow body w/red/brown or red/green luggage on roof rack, green/brown interior, working hatch, two passengers, Wildlife Preservation decals, Model No. 436-A
EX $40 **NM** $70 **MIP** $130

Citroen Le Dandy Coupe, 1966, metallic maroon body and base, yellow interior, working trunk and two doors, clear windows, plastic interior, folding seats, chrome grille and bumpers, jewel headlights, red taillights, suspension, spoked wheels, rubber tires, Model No. 259-A1
EX $50 **NM** $75 **MIP** $125

(KP Photo by Dr. Douglas Sadecky)

Citroen Le Dandy Coupe, 1967-69, metallic dark blue hood, sides and base, plastic aqua interior, white roof and trunk lid, clear windows, folding seats, chrome grille and bumpers, jewel headlights, red taillights, suspension, spoked wheels, rubber tires, Model No. 259-A2
EX $70 **NM** $105 **MIP** $175

Citroen SM, 1971-75, metallic lime gold w/chrome wheels or mauve body w/spoked wheels, pale blue interior and lifting hatch cover, working rear hatch and two doors, chrome inner drs., window frames, bumpers, grille, amber headlights, red taillights, Whizz Wheels, Model No. 284-A
EX $16 **NM** $24 **MIP** $40

Citroen Tour de France Car, 1970-72, red body, yellow interior and rear bed, clear windshield and headlights, driver, black plastic rack w/four bicycle wheels, swiveling team manager figure w/megaphone in back of car, Paramount and Tour de France decals, Whizz Wheels, Model No. 510-A
EX $40 **NM** $70 **MIP** $160

Citroen Winter Olympics Car, 1967-69, white body, blue roof and hatch, blue interior, red roof rack w/yellow skis, gold sled w/rider, skier, gold Grenoble Olympiade decals on car roof, cast wheels, Model No. 499-A
EX $70 **NM** $105 **MIP** $240

Citroen Winter Sports Safari, 1964-67, white body in three versions: two w/Corgi Ski Club decals and either w/or without roof ski rack, or one w/1964 Winter Olympics decals, shaped wheels, Model No. 475-A
EX $56 **NM** $84 **MIP** $140

(KP Photo by Dr. Douglas Sadecky)

Fiat 1800, 1960-63, one-piece body in several colors, clear windows, plastic interior, silver lights, grille and bumpers, red taillights, smooth or shaped wheels, rubber tires, colors: blue body w/light or bright yellow interior, light tan, mustard, light blue or two-tone blue body, Model No. 217-A
EX $24 **NM** $40 **MIP** $90

Fiat 2100, 1961-64, light two-tone mauve body, yellow interior, purple roof, clear windows w/rear blind, silver grille, license plates and bumpers, red taillights, shaped wheels, rubber tires, Model No. 232-A
EX $22 **NM** $33 **MIP** $90

(KP Photo by Dr. Douglas Sadecky)

Ford Consul, 1956-61, one-piece body in several colors, clear windows, silver grille, lights and bumpers, smooth wheels, rubber tires, Model No. 200-A
EX $45 **NM** $65 **MIP** $140

Ford Consul Classic, 1961-65, cream or gold body and base, yellow interior, pink roof, clear windows, gray steering wheel, silver bumpers, grille, opening hood, shaped wheels, Model No. 234-A
EX $35 **NM** $55 **MIP** $90

Ford Consul-Mechanical, 1956-59, same as model 200-A but w/friction motor and blue or green body, Model No. 200-M
EX $55 **NM** $85 **MIP** $180

Ford Cortina Estate Car, 1966-68, 3-1/2" metallic dark blue body and base, brown and cream simulated wood panels, cream interior, chrome bumpers and grille, jewel headlights, shaped wheels, Model No. 440-A
EX $35 **NM** $55 **MIP** $90

Ford Cortina Estate Car, 1966-69, red body and base or metallic charcoal gray body and base, cream interior, chrome bumpers and grille, jewel headlights, shaped wheels, Model No. 491-A
EX $35 **NM** $55 **MIP** $90

Ford Escort 13 GL, 1980, red, blue or yellow body, opening doors, Model No. 334-B
EX $8 **NM** $15 **MIP** $25

Ford Torino Road Hog, 1981, orange-red body, yellow and gray chassis, gold lamps, chrome radiator shell, windows and bumpers, one-piece body, working horn, Model No. 1003-A
EX $15 **NM** $20 **MIP** $35

Ford Zephyr Estate Car, 1960-65, light blue one-piece body, dark blue hood and stripes, red interior, silver bumpers, grille and headlights, red taillights, smooth or shaped wheels, Model No. 424-A
EX $30 **NM** $45 **MIP** $85

(KP Photo by Dr. Douglas Sadecky)

Ghia L64 Chrysler V8, 1963-69, metallic light blue, green, copper or yellow, plastic interior, hood, trunk and two doors working, detailed engine, clear windshield, shaped or detailed cast wheels, Model No. 241-A
EX $25 **NM** $40 **MIP** $75

Ghia-Fiat 600 Jolly, 1963-65, light or dark blue body, red and silver canopy, red seats, two figures, windshield, chrome dash, floor, steering wheels, Model No. 240-A
EX $45 **NM** $85 **MIP** $180

Golden Guinea Set, 1961-63, three vehicle set, gold plated No. 224 Bentley Continental, No. 229 Chevy Corvair and No. 234 Ford Consul. Difficult to find w/nice plating and box., Model No. 20-A
EX $90 **NM** $150 **MIP** $400

(KP Photo by Dr. Douglas Sadecky)

Hillman Husky, 1956-60, one-piece tan or metallic blue/silver body, clear windows, silver lights, grille and bumpers, smooth wheels. The car on the left is the more rare two-tone version, while the car on the right is the mechanical flywheel version that was only produced for one year in 1959, Model No. 206-A
EX $40 **NM** $70 **MIP** $125

Hillman Husky-Mechanical, 1956-59, same as 206-A but w/friction motor, black base and dark blue, gray or cream body, Model No. 206-M
EX $50 **NM** $100 **MIP** $180

Hillman Imp, 1963-67, metallic copper, blue, dark blue or gold one-piece bodies, w/white/yellow interior, silver bumpers, headlights, shaped wheels, Model No. 251-A
EX $30 **NM** $45 **MIP** $85

Honda Ballade Driving School, 1982-83, red body/base, tan interior, clear windows, tow hook, mirrors, bumpers, Model No. 273-B
EX $10 **NM** $15 **MIP** $25

Honda Prelude, 1981-82, dark metallic blue body, tan interior, clear windows, folding seats, sunroof, chrome wheels, Model No. 345-B
EX $8 **NM** $15 **MIP** $20

Jaguar 2.4 Litre, 1957-63, one-piece white body w/no interior 1957-59, or yellow body w/red interior 1960-63, clear windows, smooth or shaped hubs, Model No. 208-A
EX $50 **NM** $80 **MIP** $130

(KP Photo by Dr. Douglas Sadecky)

Jaguar 2.4 Litre-Mechanical, 1957-59, same as 208-A but w/friction motor and metallic blue body, Model No. 208-M
EX $60 **NM** $90 **MIP** $180

(KP Photo by Dr. Douglas Sadecky)

Jaguar Mark X Saloon, 1962-67, several different color versions w/working front and rear hood castings, clear windshields, plastic interior, gray steering wheel. Shown here in silver and blue versions, pictured at the left are the two suitcases that were included with each car, shaped wheels, Model No. 238-A
EX $35 **NM** $55 **MIP** $110

Lincoln Continental, 1967-69, metallic gold or light blue body, black roof, maroon plastic interior, working hood, trunk and doors, clear windows; accessories include TV w/picture strips for TV, shaped wheels, Model No. 262-A
EX $60 **NM** $90 **MIP** $170

Mercedes-Benz 220SE Coupe, 1962-64, cream, black or dark red body, red plastic interior, clear windows, working trunk, silver bumpers, grille and plate, spare wheel in boot, shaped wheels, Model No. 230-A
EX $40 **NM** $60 **MIP** $100

(KP Photo by Dr. Douglas Sadecky)

Mercedes-Benz 220SE Coupe, 1967-68, metallic maroon or blue body, cream plastic interior, medium gray base, clear windows, silver bumpers, headlights, grille and license; accessories include plastic luggage and spare wheel in boot. Except for different exterior colors and the inclusion of luggage, this was exactly the same car as the 230-A, shaped wheels, Model No. 253-A
EX $40 **NM** $60 **MIP** $100

Mercedes-Benz 240D, 1975-81, silver, blue or copper/beige body, working trunk, two doors, clear windows, plastic interior, two hook, chrome bumpers, grille and headlights, Whizz Wheels, Model No. 285-A
EX $10 **NM** $15 **MIP** $25

Mercedes-Benz 600 Pullman, 1964-69, metallic maroon or maroon body, cream interior and steering wheel, clear windshields, chrome grille, trim and bumpers, working windshield operators; includes instruction sheet, shaped wheels, Model No. 247-A
EX $40 **NM** $60 **MIP** $100

(KP Photo by Dr. Douglas Sadecky)

Morris Cowley, 1959-60, long, one-piece body in several colors, clear windows, silver lights, grille and bumper, smooth wheels, rubber tires. The model on the left is the rare blue version, and the car on the right is the 202-M mechanical flywheel version, Model No. 202-A
EX $45 **NM** $75 **MIP** $140

Morris Cowley-Mechanical, 1956-59, same as 202-A but w/friction motor, available in off-white or green body, Model No. 202-M
EX $55 **NM** $95 **MIP** $180

Oldsmobile Super 88, 1962-68, three versions: light blue, light or dark metallic blue body w/white stripes, red interior, single body casting, shaped wheels, Model No. 235-A
EX $40 **NM** $60 **MIP** $100

Oldsmobile Toronado, 1967-68, metallic medium or dark blue body, cream interior, one-piece body, clear windshield, chrome bumpers, grille, headlight covers, shaped or cast spoked wheels, Model No. 264-A
EX $35 **NM** $55 **MIP** $90

Oldsmobile Toronado, 1968-70, metallic copper, metallic blue or red one-piece body, cream interior, Golden jacks, gray tow hook, clear windows, bumpers, grille, headlights, Model No. 276-A
EX $35 **NM** $55 **MIP** $90

Opel Senator Doctor's Car, 1980-81, Model No. 332-B
EX $10 **NM** $15 **MIP** $25

OSI DAF City Car, 1971-74, orange/red body, light cream interior, textured black roof, sliding left door, working hood, hatch and two right doors, Whizz Wheels, Model No. 283-A
EX $18 **NM** $25 **MIP** $45

Plymouth Sports Suburban, 1959-63, dark cream body, tan roof, red interior, die-cast base, red axle, silver bumpers, trim and grille and rubber tires, shaped wheels, Model No. 219-A
EX $40 **NM** $60 **MIP** $100

(KP Photo by Dr. Douglas Sadecky)

Plymouth Sports Suburban, 1963-65, pale blue body w/silver trim, red roof, yellow interior, gray die-cast base without rear axle bulge, shaped wheels, Model No. 445-A
EX $40 **NM** $60 **MIP** $100

Plymouth Suburban Mail Car, 1963-66, white upper, blue lower body w/red stripes, gray die-cast base without rear axle bulge, silver bumpers and grille, U.S. Mail decals, shaped wheels, Model No. 443-A
EX $55 **NM** $85 **MIP** $140

Rambler Marlin Fastback, 1966-69, red body, black roof and trim, cream interior, clear windshield, folding seats, chrome bumpers, grille and headlights, opening doors, cast wheels, Model No. 263-A
EX $35 **NM** $55 **MIP** $100

Rambler Marlin with Kayak and Trailer, 1968-69, blue No. 263 Marlin w/roof rack, blue/white trailer, w/two kayaks. The blue Marlin only came with this set., Model No. 10-A
EX $100 **NM** $150 **MIP** $325

Renault 16, 1969, metallic maroon body, dark yellow interior, chrome base, grille and bumpers, clear windows, opening bonnet and hatch cover, Renault decal, cast wheels, Model No. 260-A
EX $25 **NM** $35 **MIP** $60

Renault 16TS, 1970-72, metallic blue body w/Renault decal on working hatch, clear windows, detailed engine, yellow interior, Model No. 202-B
EX $20 **NM** $25 **MIP** $50

Renault 5TS, 1980-81, light blue body, red plastic interior, dark blue roof, dome light, S.O.S. Medicine lettering, working hatch and two doors, French issue, Model No. 293-A
EX $20 **NM** $35 **MIP** $70

Renault Alpine 5TS, 1980, dark blue body, off white interior, red and chrome trim, clear windows and headlights, gray base and bumpers, black grille, opening doors and hatchback, Model No. 294-A
EX $15 **NM** $25 **MIP** $40

Renault Floride, 1959-65, one-piece dark red, maroon or lime green body, clear windows, silver bumper, grille, lights and plates, red taillights, smooth or shaped hubs, rubber tires, Model No. 222-A
EX $35 **NM** $55 **MIP** $95

(KP Photo by Dr. Douglas Sadecky)

Riley Pathfinder, 1956-61, red or dark blue one-piece body, clear windows, silver lights, grille and bumpers, smooth wheels, rubber tires, Model No. 205-A
EX $45 **NM** $65 **MIP** $125

Riley Pathfinder-Mechanical, 1956-59, w/friction motor and either red or blue body, Model No. 205-M
EX $60 **NM** $95 **MIP** $180

Rolls-Royce Corniche, 1979, different color versions w/light brown interior, working hood, trunk and two doors, clear windows, folding seats, chrome bumpers, Model No. 279-A
EX $10 **NM** $20 **MIP** $40

Rolls-Royce Silver Shadow, 1970, metallic white upper/dusty blue lower body, working hood, trunk and two doors, clear windows, folding seats, chrome bumpers, Golden Jacks wheels, Model No. 273-A
EX $30 **NM** $50 **MIP** $95

Rolls-Royce Silver Shadow, 1971-73, metallic silver upper and metallic blue lower body, light brown interior, may or may not include hole in trunk for spare tire, Whizz Wheels, Model No. 280-A1
EX $25 **NM** $40 **MIP** $65

Rolls-Royce Silver Shadow, 1974-78, metallic blue or gold body, bright blue interior, working hood, trunk and two doors, clear windows, folding seats, spare wheel, Model No. 280-A2
EX $25 **NM** $40 **MIP** $65

Rover 2000, 1963-66, metallic blue w/red interior or maroon body w/yellow interior, gray steering wheel, clear windshields, shaped wheels, Model No. 252-A
EX $30 **NM** $45 **MIP** $75

Rover 2000TC, 1968-70, metallic olive green or maroon one-piece body, light brown interior, chrome bumpers/grille, jewel headlights, red taillights, Golden Jacks wheels, Model No. 275-A
EX $30 **NM** $45 **MIP** $75

Rover 2000TC, 1971-73, metallic purple body, light orange interior, black grille, one-piece body, amber windows, chrome bumpers and headlights, Whizz Wheels, Model No. 281-A
EX $25 **NM** $35 **MIP** $60

Rover 3500, 1979, three different body and interior versions, plastic interior, opening hood, hatch and two doors, lifting hatch cover, Model No. 338-B
EX $8 **NM** $15 **MIP** $25

(KP Photo by Dr. Douglas Sadecky)

Rover 90, 1956-60, one-piece body, silver headlights, grille and bumpers, smooth wheels, rubber tires; multiple colors available. The car on the left is the rare two-tone color scheme and the vehicle on the right is the mechanical version in metallic green, Model No. 204-A
EX $50 **NM** $75 **MIP** $145

Rover 90-Mechanical, 1956-59, w/friction motor and red, green, gray or metallic green body, Model No. 204-M
EX $60 **NM** $90 **MIP** $180

(KP Photo by Dr. Douglas Sadecky)

Standard Vanguard, 1957-61, one-piece red and pale green body, clear windows, silver lights, grille and bumpers, smooth wheels, rubber tires. Pictured with the 207M, the attractive two-tone 207-A version is on the left, and the mechanical version is on the right, Model No. 207-A
EX $50 **NM** $75 **MIP** $125

Standard Vanguard-Mechanical, 1957-59, w/friction motor and yellow or off-white body w/black or gray base, or cream body w/red roof, Model No. 207-M
EX $55 **NM** $90 **MIP** $180

Studebaker Golden Hawk, 1958-60, one-piece body in blue and gold or white and gold, clear windows, silver lights, grille and bumpers, smooth wheels, rubber tires, Model No. 211-A
EX $55 **NM** $85 **MIP** $140

(KP Photo by Dr. Douglas Sadecky)

Studebaker Golden Hawk, 1960-65, second issue: gold painted body, shaped hubs. The "S" after the catalog number stood for "suspension" which was a new Corgi innovation at the time of the model's release, Model No. 211S2
EX $60 **NM** $180 **MIP** $180

Studebaker Golden Hawk, 1960-65, first issue: gold plated body, white flashing, shaped hubs, Model No. 211S1
EX $55 **NM** $85 **MIP** $140

Studebaker Golden Hawk-Mechanical, 1958-59, w/friction motor and white body w/gold trim, Model No. 211-M
EX $70 **NM** $105 **MIP** $180

Tour de France Set, 1968-72, white and black body, Renault w/Paramount Film roof sign, rear platform w/cameraman and black camera on tripod, plus bicycle and rider, Model No. 13-B
EX $60 **NM** $90 **MIP** $225

Tour de France Set, 1981-82, w/white No. 373 Peugeot, red and yellow Raleigh and Total logos, Racing cycles, includes manager figures, Model No. 13-C
EX $25 **NM** $45 **MIP** $90

Triumph Acclaim Driving School, 1982, dark yellow body w/black trim, black roof mounted steering wheel steers front wheels, clear windows, mirrors, bumpers, Model No. 277-B
EX $15 **NM** $25 **MIP** $40

Triumph Acclaim Driving School, 1982-83, yellow or red body/base, Corgi Motor School labels, black roof mounted steering wheel steers front wheels, clear windows, Model No. 278-B
EX $15 **NM** $25 **MIP** $50

Triumph Acclaim HLS, 1981-83, metallic peacock blue body/base, black trim, light brown interior, clear windows, mirrors, bumpers, vents, tow hook, Model No. 276-B
EX $15 **NM** $18 **MIP** $30

Triumph Herald Coupe, 1961-66, blue or gold top and lower body, white upper body, red interior, clear windows, silver bumpers, grille, headlights, shaped hubs, Model No. 231-A
EX $35 **NM** $65 **MIP** $110

(KP Photo by Dr. Douglas Sadecky)

Trojan Heinkel, 1962-72, issued in mauve, red, orange or lilac body, plastic interior, silver bumpers and headlights, red taillights, suspension, smooth or detailed cast wheels, Model No. 233-A
EX $35 **NM** $55 **MIP** $95

(KP Photo by Dr. Douglas Sadecky)

Vauxhall Velox, 1956-60, one-piece body in red, cream, yellow or yellow and red body, clear windows, silver lights, grille and bumpers, smooth wheels, rubber tires, Model No. 203-A
EX $50 **NM** $75 **MIP** $150

Vauxhall Velox-Mechanical, 1956-59, w/friction motor; orange, red, yellow or cream body, Model No. 203-M
EX $60 **NM** $90 **MIP** $180

Volkswagen 1200 Driving School, 1974-75, metallic red or blue body, yellow interior, gold roof mounted steering wheel that steers, silver headlights, red taillights, Model No. 400-A
EX $25 **NM** $35 **MIP** $60

Volkswagen 1500 Karmann-Ghia, 1963-68, cream, red or gold body, plastic interior and taillights, front and rear working hoods, clear windshields, silver bumpers; includes spare wheel and plastic suitcase in trunk, shaped wheels, Model No. 239-A
EX $35 **NM** $55 **MIP** $90

Volkswagen Driving School, 1975-77, metallic blue body, yellow interior, gold roof mounted steering wheel that steers, silver headlights, red taillights, orange cones, Model No. 401-A
EX $25 **NM** $40 **MIP** $75

Volkswagen Polo, 1976-79, apple green or bright yellow body, black DBP and posthorn (German Post Office) labels, off white interior, black dash, Model No. 289-A
EX $25 **NM** $40 **MIP** $65

Volkswagen Polo, 1979-81, metallic light brown body, off-white interior, black dash, clear windows, silver bumpers, grille and headlights, Model No. 302-C
EX $15 **NM** $18 **MIP** $30

Volkswagen Polo Auto Club Car, 1977-79, yellow body, white roof, yellow dome light, ADAC Strassenwacht labels, Model No. 489-B
EX $15 **NM** $25 **MIP** $40

Volkswagen Polo German Auto Club Car, 1977-79, yellow body, off-white interior, black dash, silver bumpers, grille and headlights, white roof, yellow dome light, Model No. 489-A2
EX $25 **NM** $35 **MIP** $60

Volkswagen Polo Mail Car, 1976-80, bright yellow body, black DBP and Posthorn labels, German issue, Model No. 289-B
EX $25 **NM** $35 **MIP** $60

Volvo P-1800, 1962-65, one-piece body light brown, orange-red, pink or dark red body, clear windows, plastic interior, shaped wheels, rubber tires, Model No. 228-A
EX $40 **NM** $60 **MIP** $120

BOAT

(KP Photo by Dr. Douglas Sadecky)

Dolphin Cabin Cruiser, 1965-68, white hull, blue deck plastic boat w/red/white stripe labels, driver, blue motor w/white cover, gray prop, cast trailer w/smooth wheels, rubber tires, Model No. 104-A
EX $24 **NM** $40 **MIP** $95

Fiat X 1/9 & Powerboat, 1979-82, green and white automobile, w/white and gold boat, Carlsberg labels, Model No. 37-B
EX $30 **NM** $45 **MIP** $75

HDL Hovercraft SR-N1, 1960-62, blue superstructure, gray base and deck, clear canopy, red seats, yellow SR-N1 decals, Model No. 1119-A
EX $60 **NM** $90 **MIP** $150

Olds Toronado and Speedboat, 1967-70, blue No. 276 Toronado, blue and yellow boat and chrome trailer, w/swordfish decals and three figures, Model No. 36-A
EX $60 **NM** $90 **MIP** $200

Powerboat Team, 1980-81, white/red No. 319 Jaguar w/red/white boat on silver trailer, Team Corgi Carlsberg, Union Jack and #1 labels on boat, Model No. 38-C
EX $25 **NM** $35 **MIP** $60

BUS

Beep Beep London Bus, 1981, battery-operated working horn, red body, black windows, BTA decals, Model No. 1004-A
EX $26 **NM** $39 **MIP** $65

Green Line Bus, 1983, green body, white interior and stripe, TDK labels, six spoked wheels, Model No. 470-C
EX $10 **NM** $15 **MIP** $25

Inter-City Mini Bus, 1973-79, orange body w/brown interior, clear windows, green/yellow/black decals, Whizz Wheels, Model No. 701-A
EX $8 **NM** $15 **MIP** $25

(KP Photo by Dr. Douglas Sadecky)

London Set, 1964-68, No. 418 taxi and No. 468 bus w/policeman, in two versions: "Corgi Toys" on bus (1964-66); "Outspan Oranges" on bus (1967-68); values for each individual complete set, Model No. 35-A
EX $55 **NM** $95 **MIP** $225

London Set, 1971-75, orange No. 226 Mini, Policeman, No. 418 London Taxi and No. 468 Outspan Routemaster bus, Whizz Wheels, Model No. 11-B
EX $50 **NM** $75 **MIP** $125

London Set, 1980-82, No. 425 London Taxi and No. 469 Routemaster B.T.A. bus in two versions: w/mounted Policeman (1980-81); without Policeman, (1982-on); value is for each individual complete set, Model No. 11-C
EX $25 **NM** $35 **MIP** $60

(KP Photo by Dr. Douglas Sadecky)

London Transport Routemaster Bus, 1964-75, clear windows w/driver and conductor, released w/numerous advertiser logos that sell in a vide range of prices, shaped or cast spoked wheels, Model No. 468-A
EX $35 **NM** $40 **MIP** $75

London Transport Routemaster Bus, 1975, long, clear windows, interior, some models have driver and conductor, released w/numerous advertiser logos, Whizz Wheels, Model No. 469-A
EX $25 **NM** $30 **MIP** $50

(KP Photo by Dr. Douglas Sadecky)

Midland Red Express Coach, 1961-62, red one-piece body, black roof w/shaped or smooth wheels, yellow interior, clear windows, silver grille and headlights. Two box variations shown in this photo, Model No. 1120-A
EX $70 **NM** $105 **MIP** $225

National Express Bus, 1983, variety of colors and label variations, Model No. 1168-A
EX $8 **NM** $15 **MIP** $25

Open Top Disneyland Bus, 1977-78, yellow body, red interior and stripe, Disneyland labels, eight-spoked wheels or orange body, white interior and stripe, Model No. 470-B
EX $30 **NM** $50 **MIP** $75

Routemaster Bus-Promotionals, 1977, different body and interior versions and promotional labels, Model No. 467-A
EX $15 **NM** $25 **MIP** $40

Silver Jubilee London Transport Bus, 1977, silver body w/red interior, no passengers, labels read "Woolworth Welcomes the World" and "The Queen's Silver, Model No. 471-B
EX $15 **NM** $18 **MIP** $30

CHARACTER

1927 Bentley "World of Wooster", 1967-69, green body, metallic black chassis, cast spoked wheels, figures of Jeeves & Bertie Wooster, Model No. 9004-A
EX $50 **NM** $100 **MIP** $150

Avengers Set, 1966-69, white Lotus, red or green (rare) Bentley; Jonathan Steed and Emma Peel figures w/three umbrellas, Model No. 40-A
EX $260 **NM** $390 **MIP** $800

(KP Photo by Dr. Douglas Sadecky)

Basil Brush's Car, 1971-73, red body, dark yellow chassis, gold lamps and dash, Basil Brush figure, red plastic wheels, plastic tires; w/"Laugh Tapes" and soundbox. Basil Brush could be heard laughing with the aid of laugh tapes and a soundbox that were included with the car, Model No. 808-A
EX $70 **NM** $105 **MIP** $200

Batbike, 1978-83, black body, one-piece body, black and red plastic parts, gold engine and exhaust pipes, clear windshield, chrome stand, black plastic five-spoked wheels, Batman figure and decals, Model No. 268-B
EX $40 **NM** $60 **MIP** $125

Batboat, 1967-72, black plastic boat, red seats, fin and jet, blue windshield, Batman and Robin figures, gold cast trailer, tinplate fin cover, cast wheels, plastic tires, w/plastic tow hook for Batmobile, Model No. 107-A1
EX $60 **NM** $90 **MIP** $175

Batboat, 1976-80, black plastic boat w/Batman and Robin figures, small Bat logo labels on fin and on side of boat, chain link labels, Whizz Wheels on trailer, Model No. 107-A2
EX $30 **NM** $45 **MIP** $100

Batcopter, 1976-81, black body w/yellow/red/black decals, red rotors, Batman figure, operable winch, Model No. 925-A
EX $30 **NM** $50 **MIP** $100

Batman Set, 1976-81, three vehicle set: No. 267 Batmobile, No. 107 Batboat w/trailer and No. 925 Batcopter, Whizz Wheels on trailer, Model No. 40-B
EX $150 **NM** $300 **MIP** $800

(KP Photo by Dr. Douglas Sadecky)

Batmobile, 1966, matte black (rare) or gloss black body, gold hubs, bat logos on door and hubs, maroon interior, black body, plastic rockets, yellow headlights and gold rocket control, blue tinted canopy, working front chain cutter, no tow hook, rubber tires. Although it's difficult to tell from this photo, this is the rare first issue matte black finish with no tow hook version of the famous Batmobile, Model No. 267-A1
EX $200 **NM** $300 **MIP** $550

Batmobile, 1967-72, same as first issue except for gloss black body, gold tow hook, Model No. 267-A2
EX $200 **NM** $300 **MIP** $500

(KP Photo by Dr. Douglas Sadecky)

Batmobile, 1973, chrome hubs w/red bat logos on door, maroon interior, red plastic tires, gold tow hook, plastic rockets, yellow headlight and gold rocket control, tinted blue canopy w/chrome support, chain cutter. Made for only one year, this version featured red plastic tires and chrome wheels. Also pictured is the back of the rare first-issue window box for this model, Model No. 267-C1
EX $140 **NM** $200 **MIP** $400

Batmobile, 1974-79, chrome hubs w/black plastic tires, red bat logos on door, light red interior, gold tow hook, plastic rockets, yellow headlights and gold rocket control, tinted blue canopy w/chrome support, Model No. 267-C2
EX $80 **NM** $120 **MIP** $200

Batmobile, 1980-81, gloss black body, light red interior, gold tow hook, Whizz Wheels with 8-spoke chrome hubs, Model No. 267-D
EX $80 **NM** $110 **MIP** $200

Batmobile, Batboat and Trailer, 1967-72, first and second versions: red bat hubs on wheels, 1967-72; red tires and chrome wheels 1972-73, Model No. 3-B1
EX $240 **NM** $360 **MIP** $650

Batmobile, Batboat and Trailer, 1973-81, third and fourth versions: 1973; black tires, labels on boat, 1974-76; chrome wheels, boat labels, Whizz Wheels on trailer, Model No. 3-B2
EX $120 **NM** $175 **MIP** $350

Beatles' Yellow Submarine, 1969, yellow and white hatches, red pinstripes, first issue, rare, Model No. 803-A1
EX $200 **NM** $500 **MIP** $1000

Beatles' Yellow Submarine, 1969-70, second issue, yellow and white body, working red hatches w/two Beatles in each, Model No. 803-A2
EX $180 **NM** $270 **MIP** $700

Buck Rogers Starfighter, 1980, white body w/yellow plastic wings, amber windows, blue jets, color decal, Buck and Wilma figures, Model No. 647-A
EX $32 **NM** $48 **MIP** $90

Captain America Jetmobile, 1979-80, 6" white body, metallic blue chassis, black nose cone, red shield and jet, red-white-blue Captain America decals, light blue seats and driver, chrome wheels, red tires, Model No. 263-B
EX $24 **NM** $36 **MIP** $60

Captain Marvel Porsche, 1979-80, white body, gold parts, red seat, driver, red/yellow/blue Captain Marvel decals, black plastic base, gold wheels, Model No. 262-B
EX $20 **NM** $30 **MIP** $60

Chevrolet Charlie's Angels Van, 1977-80, light rose-mauve body w/Charlie's Angels labels, in two versions: either solid or spoked chrome wheels, Model No. 434-B
EX $15 **NM** $30 **MIP** $55

Chevrolet Spider-Van, 1978-80, dark blue body w/Spider-Man decals, in two versions: w/either spoke or solid wheels, Model No. 436-B
EX $26 **NM** $39 **MIP** $65

Chitty Chitty Bang Bang, 1968-72, metallic copper body, dark red interior and spoked wheels, four figures, black chassis w/silver running boards, silver hood, horn, brake, dash, tail and headlights, gold radiator, red and orange wings, handbrake operates side wings, Model No. 266-A
EX $180 **NM** $270 **MIP** $425

Daily Planet Helicopter, 1979-81, red and white body, rocket launcher w/ten spare missiles, Model No. 929-A
EX $24 **NM** $36 **MIP** $60

Daktari Set, 1967-75, two versions: No. 438 Land Rover, green w/black stripes, spun or cast spoke wheels, 1968-73; Whizz Wheels, 1974-75, each set, Model No. 7-B
EX $50 **NM** $75 **MIP** $150

Dick Dastardly's Racing Car, 1973-76, dark blue body, yellow chassis, chrome engine, red wings, Dick and Muttley figures, Model No. 809-A
EX $40 **NM** $60 **MIP** $150

(KP Photo by Dr. Douglas Sadecky)

Dougal's Magic Roundabout Car, 1971-74, yellow body, red interior, clear windows, dog and snail figures, red wheels w/gold trim, Magic Roundabout labels, Model No. 807-A
EX $70 **NM** $105 **MIP** $190

Drax Jet Helicopter, 1979-81, white body, yellow rotors and fins, yellow/black Drax labels, Model No. 930-A
EX $35 **NM** $75 **MIP** $175

Giant Daktari Set, 1969-73, black and green No. 438 Land Rover, tan No. 503 Giraffe truck, blue and brown No. 484 Dodge Livestock truck, figures, several wheel variations, Model No. 14-B
EX $225 **NM** $350 **MIP** $650

Green Hornet's Black Beauty, 1967-72, black body, green window/interior, two figures, working chrome grille and panels w/weapons, green headlights, red taillights, shaped or cast wheels, Model No. 268-A
EX $175 **NM** $275 **MIP** $550

Hardy Boys' Rolls-Royce, 1970, red body w/yellow hood, roof and window frames, band figures on roof on removable green base, Model No. 805-A
EX $70 **NM** $105 **MIP** $200

Incredible Hulk Mazda Pickup, 1979-80, metallic light brown or copper body, gray or red plastic cage, black interior, Hulk label on hood, chrome wheels; includes green and red Hulk figure, Model No. 264-B
EX $20 **NM** $30 **MIP** $75

(KP Photo by Dr. Douglas Sadecky)

James Bond Aston Martin, 1968-77, metallic silver body, red interior, two figures, working roof hatch, ejector seat, bullet shield and guns, chrome bumpers, spoked wheels. Orginally issued in a rare bubble-pack, the subsequent issues were sold in window boxes. On the left, the rare first issue window box; on the right, the more commonly seen version, Model No. 270-A
EX $100 **NM** $150 **MIP** $325

James Bond Aston Martin, 1978, metallic silver body and die-cast base, red interior, two figures, clear windows, passenger seat raises to eject, Model No. 271-B
EX $30 **NM** $45 **MIP** $90

James Bond Aston Martin DB5, 1965-68, metallic gold body, red interior, working roof hatch, clear windows, two figures, left seat ejects, spoked wheels, accessory pack, Model No. 261-A
EX $70 **NM** $150 **MIP** $325

(KP Photo by Dr. Douglas Sadecky)

James Bond Citroen 2CV6, 1981-86, dark yellow body and hood, red interior, clear windows, chrome headlights, red taillights, black plastic grille. This model was available in a window box, or the more difficult to find photo box shown here, Model No. 272-A
EX $15 **NM** $35 **MIP** $70

James Bond Lotus Esprit, 1977, white body and base, black windshield, grille and hood panel, white plastic roof device that triggers fins and tail, rockets, Model No. 269-B
EX $30 **NM** $45 **MIP** $110

James Bond Moon Buggy, 1972-73, white body w/blue chassis, amber canopy, yellow tanks, red radar dish, arms and jaws, yellow wheels, Model No. 811-A
EX $175 **NM** $275 **MIP** $525

(KP Photo by Dr. Douglas Sadecky)

James Bond Mustang Mach 1, 1972-73, red and white body w/black hood and opening doors. Because using this model as a Bond vehicle was a last-minute decision, a label was adhered to the right side of the window box. Without this label, no one would know this was a James Bond issue, Model No. 391-A
EX $100 **NM** $150 **MIP** $300

James Bond Set, 1979-81, set of three: No. 271 Lotus Esprit, No. 649 Space Shuttle and No. 269 Aston Martin, Model No. 22-B
EX $100 **NM** $200 **MIP** $600

James Bond Space Shuttle, 1979-81, white body w/yellow/black Moonraker labels, Model No. 649-A
EX $30 **NM** $50 **MIP** $95

James Bond Toyota 2000GT, 1967-69, white body, black interior w/Bond and female driver, working trunk and gun rack, spoked wheels, plastic tires, accessory pack, Model No. 336-A
EX $115 **NM** $180 **MIP** $375

Kojak's Buick Regal, 1976-81, metallic bronze or lt. brown body, off-white interior, two opening doors, clear windows, chrome bumpers, grille and headlights, red taillights; accessories include Kojak w/ or w/out hat and Crocker figures, Model No. 290-A
EX $25 **NM** $55 **MIP** $110

Lions of Longleat, 1968-74, black/white No. 438 Land Rover pickup w/lion cages and accessories, two versions: shaped or cast spoked wheels, 1969-73; Whizz Wheels, 1974, Model No. 8-B
EX $60 **NM** $90 **MIP** $200

Magic Roundabout Musical Carousel, 1973, plastic roundabout w/Swiss musical movement, w/Dylan, Rosalie, Paul, Florence and Basil figures, rare, Model No. 852-A
EX $275 **NM** $425 **MIP** $800

Magic Roundabout Playground, 1973, contains No. 851 Train, No. 852 Carousel, six figures, seesaw, park bench, shrubs and fowers, rare, Model No. 853-A
EX $295 **NM** $500 **MIP** $1000

Magic Roundabout Train, 1973, red and blue plastic three-piece train; accessories include figures of Mr. Rusty, Basil, Rosaile, Paul and Dougal, Model No. 851-A
EX $70 **NM** $195 **MIP** $350

Man From U.N.C.L.E. THRUSH-Buster, 1966-68, plastic interior, blue windows, two figures, two spotlights, dark metallic blue body, w/3-D Waverly ring, shaped or cast wheels, Model No. 497-A1
EX $80 **NM** $130 **MIP** $275

(KP Photo by Dr. Douglas Sadecky)

Man From U.N.C.L.E. THRUSH-Buster, 1968-69, plastic interior, blue windows, two figures, two spotlights, cream body, w/3-D Waverly ring, cast wheels, rare, Model No. 497-A2
EX $100 **NM** $350 **MIP** $550

Monkeemobile, 1968-70, red body/base, white roof, yellow interior, clear windows, four figures, chrome grille, headlights, engine, orange taillights, Model No. 277-A
EX $145 **NM** $225 **MIP** $450

Mr. McHenry's Trike, 1972-74, red and yellow trike and trailer; accessories include Mr. McHenry and Zebedee figures, Model No. 859-A
EX $70 **NM** $105 **MIP** $175

Muppet Vehicles, Fozzie Bear's Truck, Model No. 2031-A
EX $15 **NM** $30 **MIP** $50

Muppet Vehicles, Animal's Percussionmobile, Model No. 2033-A
EX $15 **NM** $30 **MIP** $50

Muppet Vehicles, Miss Piggy's Sports Coupe, Model No. 2032-A
EX $15 **NM** $30 **MIP** $50

Muppet Vehicles, Kermit's Car, Model No. 2030-A
EX $15 **NM** $35 **MIP** $60

Noddy's Car, yellow body, red chassis, Noddy alone, closed trunk w/spare wheel, Model No. 804-A
EX $60 **NM** $90 **MIP** $175

Noddy's Car, 1969-71, first issue: yellow body, red chassis and fenders, figures of Noddy, Big-Ears, and black, gray, or light tan face Golliwog, Model No. 801-A1
EX $200 **NM** $400 **MIP** $600

Noddy's Car, 1972-73, second issue: same as first issue except Master Tubby painted lt. or dk. brown is substituted for Golliwog,, Model No. 801-A2
EX $100 **NM** $200 **MIP** $350

Penguinmobile, 1979-80, white body, black and white lettering on orange-yellow-blue labels, gold body panels, seats, air scoop, chrome engine, w/penguin figure, Model No. 259-B
EX $20 **NM** $30 **MIP** $65

(KP Photo by Dr. Douglas Sadecky)

Popeye's Paddle Wagon, 1969-72, yellow and white body, red chassis, blue rear fenders, bronze and yellow stacks, white plastic deck, white or yellow rear paddle wheel, blue lifeboat w/Swee' Pea; includes figures of Popeye, Olive Oyl, Bluto and Wimpey. Produced for a short period, the colorful Paddle-Wagon had

VEHICLES • CORGI

multiple working features and contained all of the main characters, Model No. 802-A
EX $195 **NM** $300 **MIP** $525

Professionals Ford Capri, 1980-82, metallic silver body and base, red interior, black spoiler, grille, bumpers, tow hook and trim, blue windows, chrome wheels; includes figures of Cowley, Bodie and Doyle, Model No. 342-B
EX $30 **NM** $65 **MIP** $150

Saint's Jaguar XJS, 1978-81, white body, red interior, black trim, Saint figure hood label, opening doors, black grille, bumpers and tow hook, chrome headlights, Model No. 320-B
EX $30 **NM** $45 **MIP** $85

(KP Photo by Dr. Doug Sadecky)

Saint's Volvo P-1800, 1965-69, three versions of white one-piece body w/silver trim and different colored Saint decals on hood, driver. (Blue hood label is rare $400.) Pictured here with the 201-B. Note the wheel and hood logo variation between the two cars, shaped or cast wheels, Model No. 258-A
EX $55 **NM** $85 **MIP** $175

Saint's Volvo P-1800, 1970-72, one-piece white body w/red Saint decal on hood, gray base, clear windows, black interior w/driver, Whizz Wheels, Model No. 201-B
EX $55 **NM** $95 **MIP** $225

Silver Jubilee Landau, 1977-80, Landua w/four horses, two footmen, two riders, Queen and Prince figures, and Corgi dog, in two versions, Model No. 41-B
EX $15 **NM** $25 **MIP** $50

Spider-Bike, 1979-83, medium blue body, one-piece body, dark blue plastic front body and seat, blue and red Spider-Man figure, amber windshield, black or white wheels, Model No. 266-B
EX $40 **NM** $60 **MIP** $85

Spider-Buggy, 1979-81, red body, blue hood, clear windows, dark blue dash, seat and crane, chrome base w/bumper and steps, silver headlights; includes Spider-Man and Green Goblin figures, Model No. 261-B
EX $50 **NM** $75 **MIP** $150

Spider-Copter, 1979-81, blue body w/Spider-Man labels, red plastic legs, tongue and tail rotor, black windows and main rotor, Model No. 928-A
EX $30 **NM** $45 **MIP** $85

Spider-Man Set, 1980-81, set of three: No. 266 Spider-Bike, No. 928 Spider-Copter and No. 261Spider-Buggy, Model No. 23-B
EX $80 **NM** $160 **MIP** $375

Starsky and Hutch Ford Torino, 1977-81, red one-piece body, white trim, light yellow interior, clear windows, chrome bumpers, grille and headlights, orange taillights; includes Starsky, Hutch and Bandit figures, Model No. 292-A
EX $35 **NM** $55 **MIP** $115

Superman Set, 1979-81, set of three: No. 265 Supermobile, No. 925 Daily Planet Helicopter and No. 260 Metropolis Police Car, Model No. 21-C
EX $70 **NM** $120 **MIP** $350

Supermobile, 1979-81, blue body, red, chrome or gray fists, red interior, clear canopy, Superman figure, chrome arms w/removable "striking fists", Model No. 265-A
EX $30 **NM** $45 **MIP** $75

Supervan, 1978-81, silver van w/Superman labels, working rear doors, chrome spoked wheels, Model No. 435-B
EX $15 **NM** $30 **MIP** $60

Tarzan Set, 1976-78, metallic green No. 421 Land Rover w/trailer and dinghy; cage, five figures and other accessories, Model No. 36-B
EX $100 **NM** $150 **MIP** $285

Vegas Ford Thunderbird, 1980-81, orange/red body and base, black interior and grille, opening hood and trunk, amber windshield, white seats, driver, chrome bumper, Model No. 348-B
EX $25 **NM** $40 **MIP** $85

CIRCUS

Chipperfield Circus Bedford Giraffe Transporter, 1964-71, red "TK" Bedford truck w/blue giraffe box w/Chipperfield decal, two giraffes, shaped, cast spoked or detailed wheels, Model No. 503-A
EX $60 **NM** $90 **MIP** $175

Chipperfield Circus Cage Wagon, 1961-68, red body, yellow chassis, smooth or spun hubs; includes lions, tigers or polar bears, Model No. 1123-A
EX $56 **NM** $84 **MIP** $140

Chipperfield Circus Chevrolet Performing Poodles Van, 1970-72, blue upper body and tailgate, red lower body and base, clear windshield, pale blue interior w/poodles in back and ring of poodles and trainer, plastic tires, cast wheels, Model No. 511-A
EX $160 **NM** $240 **MIP** $550

Chipperfield Circus Crane and Cage, 1970-72, No. 1144 crane truck, cage w/rhinoceros, red and blue trailer w/three animal cages and animals; very rare gift set, Model No. 21-B
EX $400 **NM** $700 **MIP** $2200

Chipperfield Circus Crane and Cage Wagon, 1961-65, No. 1121 crane truck, No. 1123 cage wagon and accessories, Model No. 12-A
EX $150 **NM** $225 **MIP** $425

(KP Photo by Dr. Douglas Sadecky)

Chipperfield Circus Crane Truck, 1960-68, red body, embossed Chipperfield blue logo, tinplate boom, blue wheels. Pictured here with Chipperfield Circus Cage Wagon 1123-A, that included a set of polar bears or lions and their appropriate label transfers, Model No. 1121-A
EX $80 **NM** $120 **MIP** $225

(KP Photo by Dr. Douglas Sadecky)

Chipperfield Circus Horse Transporter, 1962-72, red Bedford "TK" cab, blue upper/red lower horse trailer, three wheel variations; includes six horses, Model No. 1130-A
EX $80 **NM** $120 **MIP** $300

(KP Photo by Dr. Douglas Sadecky)

Chipperfield Circus Karrier Booking Office, 1962-64, red body, light blue roof, clear windows, tin lithographed interior, circus decals, smooth or shaped wheels, rubber tires, Model No. 426-A
EX $105 **NM** $165 **MIP** $325

Chipperfield Circus Land Rover and Elephant Cage, 1962-68, red No. 438 Range Rover w/blue canopy, Chipperfields Circus decal on canopy, burnt orange No. 607 elephant cage on red bed trailer, Model No. 19-A
EX $90 **NM** $135 **MIP** $345

(KP Photo by Dr. Douglas Sadecky)

Chipperfield Circus Land Rover Parade Vehicle, 1967-69, red body, yellow interior, blue rear and speakers, revolving clown, chimp figures, Chipperfield labels, shaped wheels, Model No. 487-A
EX $60 **NM** $90 **MIP** $175

Chipperfield Circus Menagerie Transporter, 1968-72, Scammell Handyman MKIII red/blue cab, blue trailer w/three animal cages, two lions, two tigers and two bears, Model No. 1139-A
EX $120 **NM** $180 **MIP** $400

Chipperfield Circus Scammell Crane Truck, 1969-72, red upper cab and rear body, light blue lower cab, crane base and winch crank housing, red interior, tow hook, jewel headlights, Model No. 1144-A
EX $175 **NM** $275 **MIP** $450

Chipperfield Circus Set, 1st Version, 1963-65, vehicle and accessory set in two versions: w/No. 426 Booking Office, Model No. 23-A1
EX $380 **NM** $600 **MIP** $1800

Chipperfield Circus Set, 2nd Version, 1966, vehicle and accessory set w/#503 Giraffe Truck, Model No. 23-A2
EX $340 **NM** $500 **MIP** $1500

Circus Human Cannonball Truck, 1978-81, red and blue body; w/Marvo figure, Model No. 1163-A
EX $30 **NM** $45 **MIP** $75

Circus Land Rover and Trailer, 1978-81, yellow/red No. 421 Land Rover w/Pinder-Jean Richard decals; accessories include blue loudspeakers and figures, Model No. 30-B
EX $30 **NM** $50 **MIP** $90

Jean Richard Circus Set, 1978-81, yellow and red Land Rover and cage trailer w/Pinder-Jean Richard decals, No. 426 office van and trailer, No. 1163 Human Cannonball truck, ring and cut-out "Big Top" circus tent, Model No. 48-C
EX $90 **NM** $135 **MIP** $300

CLASSICS

1910 Renault 12/16, 1965-69, pale yellow body & spoked wheels, light black chassis, black ragtop, Model No. 9032-A
EX $25 **NM** $50 **MIP** $80

1910 Renault 12/16, 1965-69, light purple body & spoked wheels, light black chassis, Model No. 9031-A
EX $25 **NM** $50 **MIP** $80

(KP Photo by Dr. Douglas Sadecky)

1927 Bentley, 1964-69, red body, metallic black chassis, brown interior, black ragtop, red spoked wheels, driver. The red Bentley is slightly harder to find than the green version, Model No. 9002-A
EX $30 **NM** $60 **MIP** $90

1927 Bentley, 1964-69, green body, metallic black chassis, brown interior, black ragtop, spoked wheels, driver, Model No. 9001-A
EX $35 **NM** $50 **MIP** $75

(KP Photo by Dr. Douglas Sadecky)

Daimler 38 1910, 1964-69, orange-red body, gray and yellow chassis, yellow spoked wheels; w/four figures, Model No. 9021-A
EX $20 **NM** $40 **MIP** $65

Model T Ford, 1964-69, blue body, black chassis, black ragtop, yellow wheels, one figure, Model No. 9013-A
EX $20 **NM** $40 **MIP** $65

Model T Ford, 1964-69, black body & chassis, spoked wheels, two figures, Model No. 9011-A
EX $20 **NM** $40 **MIP** $65

(KP Photo by Dr. Douglas Sadecky)

Model T Ford, 1964-69, yellow body & spoked wheels, black chassis, two figures, Model No. 9012-A
EX $20 **NM** $40 **MIP** $65

Rolls-Royce Silver Ghost, 1966-69, silver body/hood, charcoal and silver chassis, bronze interior, gold lights, box and tank, clear windows, dash lights, radiator, Model No. 9041-A
EX $15 **NM** $30 **MIP** $60

CONSTRUCTION

Allis-Chalmers AFC 60 Fork Lift, 1981, yellow body, white engine hood, w/driver, tan pallets and red containers, Model No. 409-C
EX $15 **NM** $20 **MIP** $45

(KP Photo by Dr. Douglas Sadecky)

Bedford TK Tipper Truck, 1968-72, red cab and chassis w/yellow or silver tipper, side mirrors, Model No. 494-A
EX $26 **NM** $39 **MIP** $65

Berliet Fruehauf Dumper, 1974-76, yellow cab, fenders and dumper; black cab and semi chassis; plastic orange or dark orange dumper body; black interior, Model No. 1102-B
EX $30 **NM** $45 **MIP** $75

(KP Photo by Dr. Douglas Sadecky)

ERF 64G Earth Dumper, 1958-67, red cab, yellow tipper, clear windows, unpainted hydraulic cylinder, spare tire, smooth or shaped wheels, rubber tires, Model No. 458-A
EX $30 **NM** $45 **MIP** $85

Euclid Caterpillar Tractor, 1960-63, TC-12 lime green body w/black or pale gray rubber treads, gray plastic seat, driver figure, controls, stacks, silver grille, painted blue engine sides and Euclid decals, Model No. 1103-A
EX $50 **NM** $100 **MIP** $200

(KP Photo by Dr. Douglas Sadecky)

Euclid TC-12 Bulldozer, 1958-62, lime green body w/black or pale gray treads, silver blade surface, gray plastic seat, controls, and stacks; silver grille and lights, painted blue engine sides, black sheet metal base, rubber treads and Euclid decals, Model No. 1102-A
EX $80 **NM** $120 **MIP** $250

Euclid TC-12 Bulldozer, 1963-66, yellow (more rare) or pale lime-green body, metal control rod, driver, black rubber treads, Model No. 1107-A
EX $80 **NM** $120 **MIP** $250

Ford Transit Tipper, 1983, orange cab and chassis, tan tipper, chrome wheels, Model No. 1121-B
EX $10 **NM** $15 **MIP** $25

Giant Tower Crane, 1981-82, white body, orange cab and chassis, Model No. 1154-B
EX $35 **NM** $50 **MIP** $85

Hyster 800 Stacatruck, 1977, clear windows, black interior w/driver, Model No. 1113-B
EX $35 **NM** $50 **MIP** $85

JCB 110B Crawler Loader, 1976-80, white cab, yellow body, working red shovel, red interior w/driver, clear windows, black treads, JCB labels, Model No. 1110-B
EX $20 **NM** $30 **MIP** $50

Mack-Priestman Crane Truck, 1972-76, red truck, yellow crane cab, red interior, black engine, Hi Lift and Long Vehicle or Hi-Grab labels, Model No. 1154-A
EX $50 **NM** $75 **MIP** $125

Mercedes-Benz Unimog & Dumper, 1969-76, yellow cab and tipper, red fenders and tipper chassis, charcoal gray cab chassis, black plastic mirrors or without, Model No. 1145-A
EX $25 **NM** $35 **MIP** $60

Priestman Cub Crane, 1972-74, orange body, red chassis and two-piece bucket, unpainted bucket arms, lower boom, knobs, gears and drum castings, clear window, Hi-Grab labels, Model No. 1153-A
EX $50 **NM** $75 **MIP** $125

(KP Photo by Dr. Douglas Sadecky)

Priestman Cub Power Shovel, 1963-76, orange upper body and panel, yellow lower body, lock rod and chassis, rubber or plastic treads, pulley panel, gray boom, w/figure of driver, Model No. 1128-A
EX $40 **NM** $60 **MIP** $100

Priestman Shovel and Carrier, 1963-72, No. 1128 cub shovel and No. 1131 low loader machinery carrier, Model No. 27-A
EX $90 **NM** $135 **MIP** $275

Raygo Rascal Roller, 1973-78, dark yellow body, base and mounting, green interior and engine, orange and silver roller mounting and castings, clear windshield, Model No. 459-B
EX $15 **NM** $25 **MIP** $45

Road Repair Unit, 1982, dark yellow Land Rover w/battery hatch and trailer w/red plastic interior w/sign and open panels, stripe and Roadwork labels, Model No. 1007-A
EX $15 **NM** $25 **MIP** $40

Scania Dump Truck, 1983, white cab w/green tipper, black/green Barratt labels, black exhaust and hydraulic cylinders, six-spoked Whizz Wheels, Model No. 1152-B
EX $7 **NM** $15 **MIP** $30

Scania Dump Truck, 1983, yellow truck and tipper w/black Wimpey labels, in two versions: either clear or green windows; six-spoked Whizz Wheels, Model No. 1153-B
EX $7 **NM** $15 **MIP** $30

Skyscraper Tower Crane, 1975-79, red body w/yellow chassis and booms, gold hook, gray loads of block, black/white Skyscraper labels, black tracks, Model No. 1155-A
EX $30 **NM** $45 **MIP** $75

Thwaites Tusker Skip Dumper, 1974-79, yellow body, chassis and tipper, driver and seat, hydraulic cylinder, red wheels, black tires two sizes, name labels, Whizz Wheels, Model No. 403-B
EX $10 **NM** $20 **MIP** $40

Unimog Dump Truck, 1971-73, first issue, blue cab, yellow tipper, fenders and bumpers, metallic charcoal gray chassis, red interior, black mirrors, gray tow hook, Model No. 409-B1
EX $20 **NM** $30 **MIP** $50

Unimog Dump Truck, 1976-77, second issue, yellow cab, chassis, rear frame and blue tipper, fenders and bumpers, red interior, no mirrors, gray tow hook, hydraulic cylinders, Model No. 409-B2
EX $20 **NM** $30 **MIP** $50

Unimog Dumper & Priestman Cub Shovel, 1971-73, standard colors, #1145 Mercedes-Benz Unimog w/Dumper and 1128 Priestman Cub Shovel, Model No. 2-B
EX $70 **NM** $135 **MIP** $225

Volvo Concrete Mixer, 1977-81, yellow or orange cab, red or white mixer w/yellow and black stripes, rear chassis, chrome chute and unpainted hitch casings, Model No. 1156-A
EX $30 **NM** $45 **MIP** $75

Warner & Swasey Crane, 1975-81, yellow cab and body, blue chassis, blue/yellow stripe labels, red interior, black steering wheel, silver knob, gold hook, Model No. 1101-B
EX $30 **NM** $45 **MIP** $75

EMERGENCY

AMC Pacer Rescue Car, 1978-80, chrome roll bars and red roof lights, white w/black engine hood; w/or without Secours decal, Model No. 484-B
EX $10 **NM** $15 **MIP** $30

(KP Photo by Dr. Douglas Sadecky)

American LaFrance Ladder Truck, 1968-81, first issue: red cab, trailer, ladder rack and wheels; chrome decks and chassis, yellow plastic three-piece operable ladder, rubber tires, six firemen figures, issued 1968-70; second issue: same as first issue except for unpainted wheels, issued 1970-72; third issue: same as earlier issues except for white decks and chassis, silver wheels, plastic tires, issued 1973-81; later issues only had four firemen and no aerial, Model No. 1143-A
EX $60 **NM** $90 **MIP** $150

(KP Photo by Dr. Douglas Sadecky)

Austin Police Mini Van, 1964-69, dark blue body w/policeman and dog figures, white police decals, opening rear doors, gray plastic antenna, shaped or cast wheels, Model No. 448-A
EX $50 **NM** $75 **MIP** $175

(KP Photo by Dr. Douglas Sadecky)

Bedford Fire Tender, 1956-61, divided windshield, red or green body, each w/different decals, smooth or shaped hubs, Model No. 405-A
EX $60 **NM** $90 **MIP** $175

Bedford Fire Tender, 1960-62, single windshield version, red body w/either black ladders and smooth wheels or unpainted ladders and shaped wheels, Model No. 423-A
EX $60 **NM** $90 **MIP** $150

Bedford Fire Tender-Mechanical, 1956-59, friction motor, red body w/Fire Dept. decals, divided windshield, silver or black ladder, smooth or shaped hubs, Model No. 405M
EX $70 **NM** $115 **MIP** $185

(KP Photo by Dr. Douglas Sadecky)

Bedford Utilecon Ambulance, 1957-60, divided windshield, cream body w/red/white/blue decals, smooth wheels, Model No. 412-A
EX $50 **NM** $75 **MIP** $125

Belgian Police Range Rover, 1976-77, white body, working doors, red interior, Belgian Police decal; includes policeman, Emergency signs, Model No. 483-B
EX $22 **NM** $33 **MIP** $55

Bell Rescue Helicopter, 1976-80, two-piece blue body w/working doors, red interior, yellow plastic floats, black rotors, white N428 decals, Model No. 924-A
EX $20 **NM** $30 **MIP** $50

Buick Police Car, 1977-78, metallic blue body w/white stripes and Police decals, chrome light bar w/red lights, orange taillights, chrome spoke wheels, w/two policemen, Model No. 416-B
EX $18 **NM** $27 **MIP** $45

(KP Photo by Dr. Douglas Sadecky)

Cadillac Superior Ambulance, 1962-68, battery-operated warning lights, red lower/cream upper body or white lower body/blue upper body, shaped or cast wheels, Model No. 437-A
EX $60 **NM** $90 **MIP** $150

Canadian Mounted Police Set, 1978-80, blue No. 421 Land Rover w/Police sign on roof and RCMP decals, No. 102 trailer; includes mounted Policeman, Model No. 45-B
EX $30 **NM** $50 **MIP** $100

Chevrolet Caprice Fire Chief Car, 1982, red body, red-white-orange decals, chrome roof bar, opaque black windows, red dome light, chrome bumpers, grille and headlights, orange taillights, Fire Dept. and Fire Chief decals, chrome wheels; includes working siren and dome light, Model No. 1008-A
EX $28 **NM** $42 **MIP** $70

Chevrolet Caprice Police Car, 1980-81, black body w/white roof, doors and trunk, red interior, silver light bar, Police decals, Model No. 326-A
EX $20 **NM** $30 **MIP** $50

Chevrolet Impala Fire Chief Car, 1963-65, red body, yellow interior, w/four white doors, w/round either shield or rectangular decals on two doors; includes two firemen, shaped wheels, Model No. 439-A
EX $55 **NM** $80 **MIP** $150

(KP Photo by Dr. Douglas Sadecky)

Chevrolet Impala Fire Chief Car, 1965-69, w/Fire Chief decal on hood, yellow interior w/driver, red on white body w/either round or rectangular "Fire Chief" decals on doors, spun or cast spoked wheels, Model No. 482-A
EX $55 **NM** $80 **MIP** $130

(KP Photo by Dr. Douglas Sadecky)

Chevrolet Impala Police Car, 1965-69, black lower body and roof, white upper body, yellow interior w/two policemen, Police and Police Patrol decals on doors and hood, shaped or cast wheels, Model No. 481-A
EX $55 **NM** $80 **MIP** $130

Chevrolet State Patrol Car, 1959-61, black body, State Patrol decals, smooth wheels w/hexagonal panel or raised lines and shaped wheels, yellow plastic interior, gray antenna, clear windows, silver bumpers, grille, headlights and trim, rubber tires, Model No. 223-A
EX $50 **NM** $75 **MIP** $150

Chevrolet Superior Ambulance, 1978-80, white body, orange roof and stripes, two working doors, clear windows, red interior w/patient on stretcher and attendant, Red Cross decals, Model No. 405-B
EX $30 **NM** $45 **MIP** $75

Chopper Squad Helicopter, 1978-79, blue and white body, Sure Rescue decals, Model No. 927-A
EX $20 **NM** $30 **MIP** $50

Chopper Squad Rescue Set, 1978-79, blue No. 919 Jeep w/Chopper Squad decal and red/white boat w/Surf Rescue decal, No. 927 Helicopter, Model No. 35-B
EX $40 **NM** $60 **MIP** $100

Chubb Pathfinder Crash Tender, 1981-83, red body, Emergency Unit decals, working water pump, Model No. 1118-B
EX $45 **NM** $65 **MIP** $110

Chubb Pathfinder Crash Truck, 1974-80, red body w/either "Airport Fire Brigade" or "New York Airport" decals, upper and lower body, gold water cannon unpainted and sirens, clear windshield, yellow interior, black steering wheel, chrome plastic deck, silver lights; w/working pump and siren, Model No. 1103-B
EX $60 **NM** $90 **MIP** $150

(KP Photo by Dr. Douglas Sadecky)

Citroen Alpine Rescue Safari, 1970-72, white body, light blue interior, red roof and rear hatch, yellow or red roof rack and skis, clear windshield, man and dog, gold die-cast bobsled, Alpine Rescue decals, cast wheels, Model No. 513-A
EX $80 **NM** $150 **MIP** $400

Coast Guard Jaguar XJ12C, 1975-77, blue and white body, Coast Guard labels, Model No. 414-B
EX $18 **NM** $27 **MIP** $45

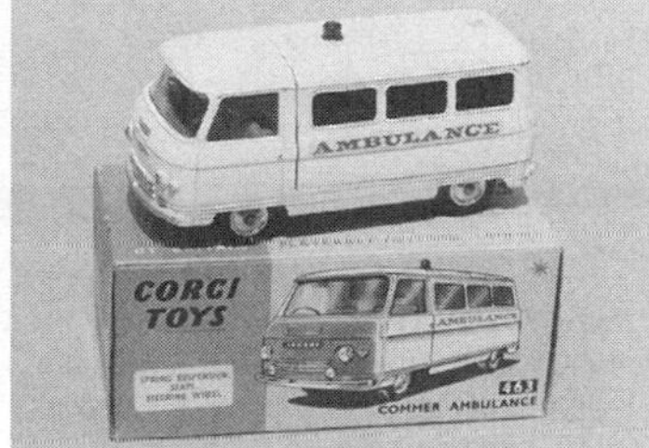

(KP Photo by Dr. Douglas Sadecky)

Commer 3/4-Ton Ambulance, 1964-66, in either white or cream body, red interior, blue dome light, red Ambulance decals, shaped wheels, Model No. 463-A
EX $36 **NM** $55 **MIP** $100

(KP Photo by Dr. Douglas Sadecky)

Commer 3/4-Ton Police Van, 1963-68, battery operated working dome light, in several color combinations of dark or light metallic blue or green bodies, various foreign issues. The van on the left has "County Police" labels, horizontal cast bars on the rear side windows, and a metallic blue paint finish. The van on the right has an embossed "Police" logo cast in the sides, vertical lines on the rear side windows, and a dark blue paint finish. Both models have a battery-operated flashing roof light, shaped wheels, Model No. 464-A
EX $45 **NM** $65 **MIP** $150

Emergency Set, 1976-77, three-vehicle set w/figures and accessories, No. 402 Ford Cortina Police car, No. 921 Police Helicopter, No. 481 Range Rover Ambulance, Model No. 18-B
EX $40 **NM** $60 **MIP** $100

Emergency Set, 1979-81, No. 339 Land Rover Police Car and No. 921 Police Helicopter w/figures and accessories, Model No. 19-C
EX $30 **NM** $50 **MIP** $80

Fire Bug, 1972-73, orange body, Whizz Wheels, Model No. 395-A
EX $20 **NM** $30 **MIP** $50

Ford Cortina Police Car, 1972-76, white body, red or pink and black stripe labels, red interior, folding seats, blue dome light, clear windows, chrome bumpers, Police labels, opening doors, Model No. 402-A
EX $15 **NM** $25 **MIP** $45

VEHICLES • CORGI

Ford Escort Police Car, 1982, blue body and base, tan interior, white doors, blue dome lights, red Police labels, black grille and bumpers, Model No. 297-A
EX $8 **NM** $15 **MIP** $30

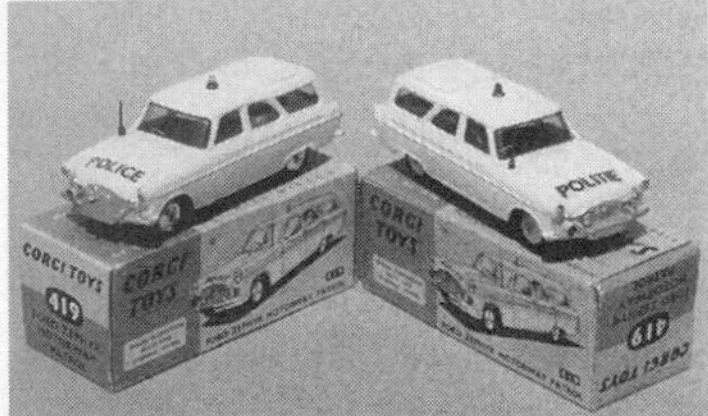
(KP Photo by Dr. Douglas Sadecky)

Ford Zephyr Patrol Car, 1960-65, white or cream body, blue and white Police red interior, blue dome light, silver bumpers. The car on the left has the common "Police" label, the car on the right, 419-A2, has the rare Dutch "Politie" label on the hood, smooth or shaped wheels, Model No. 419-A1
EX $35 **NM** $50 **MIP** $100

Ford Zephyr Patrol Car, 1960-65, white or cream body, blue and white Politie/Rijkspolitie decals, red interior, blue dome light, silver bumpers; import, rare, Model No. 419-A2
EX $75 **NM** $300 **MIP** $500

German Life Saving Set, 1980-82, red/white No. 421 Land Rover and lifeboat, white trailer, German labels, Model No. 33-B
EX $30 **NM** $45 **MIP** $75

HGB-Angus Firestreak, 1980, chrome plastic spotlight and ladders, black hose reel, red dome light, white water cannon, in two interior versions, electronic siren and lights, Model No. 1001-A
EX $35 **NM** $50 **MIP** $85

Hi-Speed Fire Engine, 1975-78, red body, yellow plastic ladder, Model No. 703-A
EX $16 **NM** $24 **MIP** $40

Hughes Police Helicopter, 1975-80, red interior, dark blue rotors, in several international imprints, Netherlands, German, Swiss, in white or yellow, Model No. 921-A
EX $20 **NM** $30 **MIP** $50

(KP Photo by Dr. Douglas Sadecky)

Jaguar 2.4 Litre Fire Chief's Car, 1959-61, red body w/unpainted roof signal/siren, red/white fire and shield decals on doors, in two versions, smooth or spun hubs, Model No. 213-A
EX $60 **NM** $90 **MIP** $150

Jaguar XJ12C Police Car, 1978-80, white body w/blue and pink stripes, light bar w/blue dome light, tan interior, police labels, Model No. 429-A
EX $15 **NM** $28 **MIP** $45

Jet Ranger Police Helicopter, 1980, white body w/chrome interior, red floats and rotors, amber windows, Police labels, Model No. 931-A
EX $25 **NM** $40 **MIP** $65

Mercedes-Benz Ambulance, 1980-81, four different foreign versions, white interior, opening rear and two doors, blue windows and dome lights, chrome bumpers, grille and headlights, various labels; accessories include two attendant figures, Model No. 406-C
EX $15 **NM** $20 **MIP** $35

Mercedes-Benz Ambulance, 1981, white body and base, red stripes and taillights, Red Cross and black and white ambulance labels, open rear door, white interior, no figures, Model No. 407-B
EX $15 **NM** $20 **MIP** $35

Mercedes-Benz Fire Chief, 1982-83, light red body, black base, tan plastic interior, blue dome light, white Notruf 112 labels, red taillights, no tow hook, German export model, Model No. 284-B
EX $15 **NM** $25 **MIP** $40

Mercedes-Benz Police Car, 1975-80, white body w/two different hood versions, brown interior, polizei or police lettering, blue dome light, Model No. 412-B
EX $15 **NM** $18 **MIP** $30

Metropolis Police Car, 1979-81, metallic blue body, off white interior, white roof/stripes, two working doors, clear windows, chrome bumpers, grille and headlights, two roof light bars, City of Metropolis labels, Model No. 260-B
EX $20 **NM** $30 **MIP** $95

Motorway Ambulance, 1973-79, white body, dark blue interior, red-white-black Accident and Red Cross labels, dark blue windows, clear headlights, red die-cast base and bumpers, Model No. 700-A
EX $10 **NM** $15 **MIP** $30

(KP Photo by Dr. Douglas Sadecky)

Oldsmobile Sheriff's Car, 1962-66, black upper body w/white sides, red interior w/red dome light and County Sheriff decals on doors, single body casting, shaped wheels, Model No. 237-A
EX $50 **NM** $75 **MIP** $135

Police Land Rover, 1981, white body, red and blue police stripes, black lettering, open rear door, opaque black windows, blue dome light, working roof light and siren, Model No. 1005-A
EX $15 **NM** $25 **MIP** $50

Police Land Rover and Horse Box, 1978-80, white No. 421 Land Rover w/police labels and mounted policeman, No. 112 Horse Box, Model No. 44-A
EX $30 **NM** $45 **MIP** $75

Police Vigilant Range Rover, 1972-79, white body, red interior, black shutters, blue dome light, two chrome and amber spotlights, black grille, silver headlights, Police labels, w/police figure, Model No. 461-A
EX $25 **NM** $35 **MIP** $60

Porsche 924 Police Car, 1978-80, white body w/different hood and door color versions, blue and chrome light, Polizei white on green panels or Police labels, "1" or "20" labels, Model No. 430-B
EX $15 **NM** $25 **MIP** $40

Porsche Targa Police Car, 1970-75, white body and base, red doors and hood, black roof and plastic interior also comes w/an orange interior, unpainted siren, Polizei labels, Model No. 509-A
EX $25 **NM** $35 **MIP** $60

Range Rover Ambulance, 1975-77, two different versions of body sides, red interior, raised roof, open upper and lower doors, black shutters, blue dome light, Ambulance label; includes stretcher and two ambulance attendants, Model No. 482-B
EX $20 **NM** $30 **MIP** $50

Renault 5 Police Car, 1978-79, white body, red interior, blue dome light, black hood, hatch and doors w/white Police labels, orange taillights, aerial, Model No. 428-B
EX $15 **NM** $20 **MIP** $35

Renault 5TS, 1977-80, metallic golden orange body, black trim, tan plastic interior, working hatch and two doors, clear windows and headlights, Model No. 293-A
EX $15 **NM** $18 **MIP** $30

Renault 5TS Fire Chief, 1982, red body, tan interior, amber headlights, gray antenna, black/white Sapeurs Pompiers labels, blue dome light, French export issue, Model No. 295-A
EX $15 **NM** $25 **MIP** $40

Riley Pathfinder Police Car, 1958-61, black body w/blue/white Police lettering, unpainted roof sign, gray antenna, smooth wheels, Model No. 209-A
EX $50 **NM** $75 **MIP** $135

Riot Police Quad Tractor, 1977-80, white body and chassis, brown interior, red roof w/white panel, gold water cannons, gold spotlight w/amber lens, Riot Police and No. 6 labels, Model No. 422-B
EX $15 **NM** $20 **MIP** $35

Rover 3500 Police Car, 1980, white body, light red interior, red stripes, white plastic roof sign, blue dome light, red and blue Police and badge label, Model No. 339-B
EX $8 **NM** $15 **MIP** $25

Sikorsky Skycrane Casualty Helicopter, 1975-78, red and white body, black rotors and wheels, orange pipes, working rear hatch, Red Cross decals, Model No. 922-A
EX $15 **NM** $20 **MIP** $40

VEHICLES • CORGI

Simon Snorkel Fire Engine, 1964-76, red body w/yellow interior, two snorkel arms, rotating base, five firemen in cab and one in basket, three styles of wheels, Model No. 1127-A
EX $35 **NM** $55 **MIP** $125

Simon Snorkel Fire Engine, 1977-81, red body w/yellow interior, blue windows and dome lights, chrome deck, black hose reels and hydraulic cylinders, Model No. 1126-B
EX $30 **NM** $45 **MIP** $85

(KP Photo by Dr. Douglas Sadecky)

Sunbeam Imp Police Car, 1968-72, three versions, white or light blue body, tan interior, driver, black or white hood and lower doors, dome light, Police decals, cast spoked wheels. Shown here are two color and box variations, Model No. 506-A
EX $25 **NM** $45 **MIP** $85

Volkswagen 1200, 1970-76, seven different color and label versions, plastic interior, one-piece body, silver headlights, red taillights, die-cast base and bumpers, Model No. 383-A2
EX $20 **NM** $45 **MIP** $85

Volkswagen 1200, 1970-76, dark yellow body, white roof, red interior and dome light, unpainted base and bumpers, black and white ADAC Strassenwacht labels, Whizz Wheels, Model No. 383-A1
EX $60 **NM** $90 **MIP** $150

(KP Photo by Dr. Douglas Sadecky)

Volkswagen 1200 Police Car, 1966-69, two different body versions made for Germany, Netherlands and Switzerland, blue dome light in chrome collar, Polizei or Politie decals. Note the opening hood and trunk on this attractive car. The front wheels turn via the roof warning light, shaped wheels, Model No. 492-A
EX $40 **NM** $60 **MIP** $125

Volkswagen Police Car/Foreign Issues, 1970-76, five different versions, one-piece body, red interior, dome light, silver headlights, red taillights, clear windows, Whizz Wheels, Model No. 373-A
EX $60 **NM** $90 **MIP** $150

Volkswagen Polo Police Car, 1976-80, white body, green hood and doors, black dash, silver bumpers, grille and headlights, white roof, blue dome light, Model No. 489-A1
EX $15 **NM** $25 **MIP** $40

JEEP

Golden Eagle Jeep, 1979-82, tan and brown or white and gold body, tan plastic top, chrome plastic base, bumpers and steps, chrome wheels, Model No. 441-B
EX $8 **NM** $15 **MIP** $35

Jeep & Horse Box, 1981-83, metallic painted No. 441 Jeep and No. 112 trailer; accessories include girl on pony, three jumps and three hay bales, Model No. 29-C
EX $15 **NM** $30 **MIP** $50

Jeep and Motorcycle Trailer, 1982-83, red working No. 441 Jeep w/two blue/yellow bikes on trailer, Model No. 10-C
EX $15 **NM** $20 **MIP** $45

Jeep CJ-5, 1977-79, dark metallic green body, removable white top, white plastic wheels, spare tire, Model No. 419-B
EX $8 **NM** $15 **MIP** $30

(KP Photo by Dr. Douglas Sadecky)

Jeep FC-150 Covered Truck, 1965-72, four versions: blue body, rubber tires (1965-67); yellow/brown body; rubber tires w/spun hubs (1965-67); blue or yellow/brown body, plastic tires w/cast spoked hubs. The two major color and wheel variations are pictured here, Model No. 470-A
EX $30 **NM** $45 **MIP** $75

Jeep FC-150 Pickup, 1959-65, blue body, clear windows, sheet metal tow hook, in two wheel versions: smooth or shaped wheels, Model No. 409-A
EX $35 **NM** $55 **MIP** $90

(KP Photo by Dr. Douglas Sadecky)

Jeep FC-150 Tower Wagon, 1965-69, metallic green body, yellow interior and basket w/workman figure, clear windows, w/either rubber or plastic tires. This was the updated version of the previously released GS14-A which had a red Jeep, smooth wheels and a lamp post, shaped wheels, Model No. 478-A
EX $40 **NM** $60 **MIP** $100

Off Road Set, 1983, No. 5 label on No. 447 Jeep, blue boat, trailer, Model No. 36-C
EX $15 **NM** $20 **MIP** $50

Renegade Jeep, 1983, dark blue body w/no top, white interior, base and bumper, white plastic wheels and rear mounted spare, Model No. 447-B
EX $8 **NM** $15 **MIP** $35

Renegade Jeep with Hood, 1983, yellow body w/removable hood, red interior, base, bumper, white plastic wheels, side mounted spare, No. 8, Model No. 448-B
EX $8 **NM** $15 **MIP** $35

Tower Wagon and Lamp Standard, 1961-65, red No. 409 Jeep Tower wagon w/yellow basket, workman figure and lamp post, smooth or shaped wheels, Model No. 14-A
EX $40 **NM** $70 **MIP** $160

LAND ROVER

(KP Photo by Dr. Douglas Sadecky)

Land Rover 109 WB Pickup, 1957-62, yellow, green or metallic blue body, spare wheel on hood, clear windows, sheet metal tow hook, smooth or shaped hubs, rubber tires, Model No. 406-A
EX $45 **NM** $70 **MIP** $100

Land Rover 109WB, 1977-79, working rear doors, tan interior, spare wheel on hood, plastic tow hook, Model No. 421-B
EX $15 **NM** $18 **MIP** $30

Land Rover Breakdown Truck, 1960-65, red body w/silver boom and yellow canopy, revolving spotlight, Breakdown Service labels, smooth or shaped wheels, Model No. 417-A
EX $35 **NM** $55 **MIP** $100

Land Rover Breakdown Truck, 1965-77, red body, yellow canopy, chrome revolving spotlight, Breakdown Service labels, shaped hubs or Whizz Wheels, Model No. 477-A
EX $25 **NM** $35 **MIP** $80

Land Rover with Canopy, 1963-77, long, one-piece body w/clear windows, plastic interior, spare wheel on hood, issued in numerous colors, w/shaped, cast, or Whizz Wheels, Model No. 438-A
EX $35 **NM** $55 **MIP** $90

(KP Photo by Dr. Douglas Sadecky)

Public Address Land Rover, 1964-66, green No. 438 Land Rover body, yellow plastic rear body and loudspeakers, red interior, clear windows, silver bumper, grille and headlights; includes figure w/microphone and girl figure w/pamphlets, shaped wheels, Model No. 472-A
EX $50 **NM** $75 **MIP** $165

(KP Photo by Dr. Douglas Sadecky)

RAC Land Rover, 1959-64, light or dark blue body, plastic interior and rear cover, gray antenna, RAC and Radio Rescue decals, smooth or shaped wheels, Model No. 416-A
EX $60 **NM** $90 **MIP** $175

Safari Land Rover and Trailer, 1976-80, black and white No. 341 Land Rover in two versions: w/chrome wheels, 1976; w/red wheels, 1977-80; came w/Warden and Lion figures, Model No. 31-B
EX $20 **NM** $30 **MIP** $60

LARGE TRUCK

Bedford Car Transporter, 1957, first issue, black die-cast cab base w/blue "S" cab, yellow semi trailer, blue lettering decals, smooth wheels, RARE, Model No. 1101-A1
EX $100 **NM** $200 **MIP** $350

Bedford Car Transporter, 1957-62, second issue, red cab, pale green upper and blue lower semi-trailer, white decals, working ramps, clear windshield, smooth or shaped wheels, Model No. 1101-A2
EX $70 **NM** $105 **MIP** $200

Bedford Car Transporter, 1962-66, red "TK" cab w/blue lower and light green upper trailer, working ramp, yellow interior, clear windows, white lettering and Corgi dog decals, shaped wheels, Model No. 1105-A
EX $60 **NM** $90 **MIP** $175

(KP Photo by Dr. Douglas Sadecky)

Bedford Carrimore Low Loader, 1958-62, red or yellow "S" cab, metallic blue semi trailer and tailgate; smooth or shaped wheels, Model No. 1100-A
EX $60 **NM** $90 **MIP** $175

(KP Photo by Dr. Douglas Sadecky)

Bedford Carrimore Low Loader, 1963-65, yellow "TK" cab, red trailer with working ramp, clear windows, red interior, suspension, shaped wheels, rubber tires, Model No. 1132-A
EX $90 **NM** $225 **MIP** $350

(KP Photo by Dr. Douglas Sadecky)

Bedford Milk Tanker, 1962-65, light blue "S" cab and lower semi, white upper tank, w/blue/white milk decals, shaped wheels, rubber tires, Model No. 1129-A
EX $100 **NM** $150 **MIP** $325

Bedford Milk Tanker, 1966-67, light blue "TK" cab and lower semi, white upper tank w/blue/white milk decals, shaped wheels, Model No. 1141-A
EX $110 **NM** $165 **MIP** $375

(KP Photo by Dr. Douglas Sadecky)

Bedford Mobilgas Tanker, 1959-65, red "S" cab and tanker w/Mobilgas decals, shaped wheels, rubber tires, Model No. 1110-A
EX $100 **NM** $150 **MIP** $275

Bedford Mobilgas Tanker, 1965-66, red "TK" cab and tanker w/red, white and blue Mobilgas decals, shaped wheels, rubber tires, Model No. 1140-A
EX $100 **NM** $175 **MIP** $350

Bedford Tanker, 1983, red cab w/black chassis, plastic tank w/chrome catwalk, Corgi Chemco decals, Model No. 1130-B
EX $15 **NM** $20 **MIP** $35

Berliet Container Truck, 1978, blue cab and semi fenders; white cab chassis and semi flatbed; each w/United States Lines label, Model No. 1107-B
EX $30 **NM** $45 **MIP** $75

Berliet Dolphinarium Truck, 1980-83, yellow and blue cab and trailer, clear plastic tank; includes two dolphins and a girl trainer, Model No. 1164-A
EX $56 **NM** $84 **MIP** $175

Berliet Holmes Wrecker, 1975-78, red cab and bed, blue rear body, white chassis, black interior, two gold booms and hooks, yellow dome light, driver, amber lenses and red/white/blue stripes, Model No. 1144-B
EX $30 **NM** $45 **MIP** $75

BL Roadtrain and Trailers, 1981, white and orange cab, dark blue freighter semi body w/Yorkie Chocolate labels and tanker semi body w/Gulf label; includes playmat, Model No. 1002-A
EX $16 **NM** $24 **MIP** $40

Car Transporter & Cars, 1970-73, Scammell tri-deck transporter w/six cars: Ford Capri, the Saint's Volvo, Pontiac Firebird, Lancia Fulvia, MGC GT, Marcos 3 Litre, each w/Whizz Wheels; value is for complete set, Model No. 20-B
EX $200 **NM** $400 **MIP** $900

Car Transporter and Four Cars, 1963-66, two versions: No. 1105 Bedford TK Transporter w/Fiat 1800, Renault Floride, Mercedes 230SE and Ford Consul, 1963-65; No. 1105 Bedford TK Transporter w/Chevy Corvair, VW Ghia, Volvo P-1800 and Rover 2000, 1966 only; value is for each individual complete set, Model No. 28-A
EX $200 **NM** $300 **MIP** $800

Carrimore Car Transporter and Cars, 1966, Ford "H" series Transporter and six cars; there are several car variations; sold by mail order only, Model No. 41-A
EX $240 **NM** $360 **MIP** $700

Carrimore Car Transporter and Four Cars, 1957-62, three versions: No. 1101 Bedford Carrimore Transporter w/Riley, Jaguar, Austin Healey and Triumph, 1957-60; No. 1101 Bedford Carrimore Transporter w/four American cars, 1959; No. 1101 Bedford Carrimore Transporter w/Triumph, Mini, Citroen and Plymouth, 1961-62; value is for individual complete sets, Model No. 1-A
EX $300 **NM** $450 **MIP** $900

(KP Photo by Dr. Douglas Sadecky)

Ecurie Ecosse Transporter, 1961-65, dark blue body w/either blue or yellow lettering, or metallic light blue body w/red or yellow lettering, working tailgate and sliding door, yellow interior, shaped wheels, rubber tires, Model No. 1126-A
EX $70 **NM** $105 **MIP** $225

Ford Aral Tank Truck, 1977-80, light blue cab and chassis, white tanker body, Aral labels, Model No. 1161-A
EX $20 **NM** $30 **MIP** $50

Ford Car Transporter, 1976-79, metallic lime green or metallic cab and semi, cream cab chassis, deck and ramp, Model No. 1159-A
EX $20 **NM** $30 **MIP** $60

Ford Car Transporter, 1982, white cab, red chassis and trailer, white labels and ramps, Model No. 1170-A
EX $20 **NM** $30 **MIP** $50

Ford Covered Semi-Trailer, 1979-80, blue cab and trailer, black cab chassis and trailer fenders, yellow covers, Model No. 1109-B
EX $15 **NM** $25 **MIP** $50

Ford Esso Tank Truck, 1976-81, white cab and tank, red tanker chassis and fenders, chrome wheels, Esso labels, Model No. 1157-A
EX $15 **NM** $30 **MIP** $60

Ford Express Semi-Trailer, 1965-70, metallic blue cab and trailer, silver roof on trailer, chrome doors marked "Express Service," shaped or detailed cast wheels, figure, Model No. 1137-A
EX $60 **NM** $110 **MIP** $225

Ford Exxon Tank Truck, 1976-81, white cab and tank, red tanker chassis and fenders, chrome wheels, Exxon labels, Model No. 1158-A
EX $15 **NM** $30 **MIP** $60

Ford Guinness Tanker, 1982, orange, tan, black cab, tan tanker body, Guinness labels, Model No. 1169-A
EX $20 **NM** $30 **MIP** $50

Ford Gulf Tank Truck, 1976-78, white cab w/orange chassis, blue tanker body, Gulf labels, chrome wheels, Model No. 1160-A
EX $15 **NM** $25 **MIP** $40

Ford Holmes Wrecker, 1967-74, white upper cab, black roof, red rear body and lower cab, mirrors, unpainted or gold booms, 2 figures, Model No. 1142-A
EX $60 **NM** $90 **MIP** $225

Ford Michelin Container Truck, 1981, blue cab and trailer, white cab chassis and trailer fenders, yellow containers; includes Michelin Man figure, Model No. 1108-B
EX $15 **NM** $25 **MIP** $60

Ford Transit Wrecker, 1981, white cab and rear body, red roof, silver bed, "24-hour Service" labels, Model No. 1140-B
EX $25 **NM** $35 **MIP** $60

Mack Container Truck, 1972-78, yellow cab, red interior, white engine, red suspension, white ACL labels, Model No. 1106-B
EX $30 **NM** $50 **MIP** $80

Mack Esso Tank Truck, 1971-75, white cab and tank w/Esso labels, red tank chassis and fenders, Model No. 1152-A
EX $20 **NM** $40 **MIP** $90

Mack Exxon Tank Truck, 1974-75, white cab and tank, red tank chassis and fenders, red interior, chrome catwalk, Exxon labels, Model No. 1151-B
EX $15 **NM** $35 **MIP** $85

Mack Trans Continental Semi, 1971-73, orange cab body and semi chassis and fenders, metallic light blue semi body, unpainted trailer rests, Model No. 1100-B
EX $35 **NM** $55 **MIP** $110

Mercedes-Benz Refrigerator, 1983, yellow cab and tailgate, red semi-trailer, two-piece lowering tailgate and yellow spare wheel base, red interior, clear window, Model No. 1131-B
EX $15 **NM** $18 **MIP** $30

Mercedes-Benz Semi-Trailer, 1983, red cab and trailer, black chassis, Model No. 1144-C
EX $15 **NM** $18 **MIP** $30

Mercedes-Benz Semi-Trailer Van, 1983, black cab and plastic semi trailer, white chassis and airscreen, red doors, red, blue and yellow stripes, white Corgi lettering, Model No. 1129-B
EX $15 **NM** $18 **MIP** $30

Mercedes-Benz Tanker, 1983, two different versions, white cab and tank, green chassis, chrome or black plastic catwalk, red/white/green 7-Up labels or Corgi Chemo labels, Model No. 1167-A
EX $15 **NM** $18 **MIP** $30

Mercedes-Benz Tanker, 1983, tan cab, plastic tank body, black chassis, black and red Guinness labels, w/chrome or black plastic catwalk, clear windows, Model No. 1166-A
EX $15 **NM** $18 **MIP** $30

Scammell Carrimore Tri-deck Car Transporter, 1970-73, orange lower cab, chassis and lower deck, white upper cab and middle deck, blue top deck, red interior, black hydraulic cylinders, detachable rear ramp, Model No. 1146-A
EX $35 **NM** $60 **MIP** $130

Scammell Coop Semi-Trailer Truck, 1970, white cab and trailer fenders, light blue semi-trailer, red interior, gray bumper base, jewel headlights, black hitch lever, spare wheel, Model No. 1151-A
EX $135 **NM** $210 **MIP** $350

Scammell Ferrymasters Semi-Trailer Truck, 1969-72, white cab, red interior, yellow chassis, black fenders, clear windows, jewel headlights, cast step-hub wheels, plastic tires, Model No. 1147-A
EX $60 **NM** $90 **MIP** $150

Scania Bulk Carrier, 1983, white cab, blue and white silos, ladders and catwalk, amber windows, blue British Sugar labels, Whizz Wheels, Model No. 1150-B
EX $7 **NM** $15 **MIP** $30

Scania Bulk Carrier, 1983, white cab, orange and white silos, clear windows, orange screen, black/orange Spillers Flour labels, Whizz Wheels, Model No. 1151-C
EX $7 **NM** $15 **MIP** $30

Scania Container Truck, 1983, yellow truck and box w/red Ryder Truck rental labels, clear windows, black exhaust stack, red rear doors, six-spoke Whizz Wheels, Model No. 1147-B
EX $7 **NM** $15 **MIP** $30

Scania Container Truck, 1983, blue cab w/blue and white box and rear doors, white deck, Securicor Parcels labels, in red or white rear door colors, Model No. 1148-B
EX $7 **NM** $15 **MIP** $30

Scania Container Truck, 1983, white cab and box w/BRS Truck Rental labels, blue windows, red screen, roof and rear doors, Model No. 1149-A
EX $7 **NM** $15 **MIP** $30

Transporter & Six Cars, 1970-73, Scammell transporter w/six cars: No. 180 Mini DeLuxe, No. 204 Mini, No. 339 Mini Rally, No. 201 The Saint's Volvo, No. 340 Sunbeam Imp, No. 378 MGC GT; includes bag of cones and leaflet, Model No. 48-B
EX $250 **NM** $450 **MIP** $900

(KP Photo by Dr. Douglas Sadecky)

Transporter and Six Cars, 1966-69, first issue: No. 1138 Ford 'H' Series Transporter w/six cars, No. 252 Rover 2000, blue No. 251 Hillman Imp, No. 440 Ford Cortina Estate, No. 180 Mini w/'wickerwork', metallic maroon No. 204 Mini, and No. 321 Mini Rally ('1966 Monte Carlo Rally') racing No. 2; second issue: same as first issue except No. 251 Hillman is metallic gold, No. 204 Mini is blue, No. 321 Mini is substituted for No. 333 SUN/RAC Rally Mini w/autographs on roof. The Car Transporter gift sets were a good way for Corgi to get rid of their excess stock of automobile models, Model No. 48-A
EX $225 **NM** $365 **MIP** $800

VEHICLES • CORGI

MILITARY

AMX 30D Recovery Tank, 1976-80, olive body w/black plastic turret and gun, accessories and three figures, Model No. 908-A
EX $35 **NM** $50 **MIP** $80

Army Heavy Equipment Transporter, 1964-65, olive cab and trailer w/white U.S. Army decals w/red or yellow interior and driver, shaped wheels, Model No. 1135-A
EX $70 **NM** $105 **MIP** $325

Army Troop Transporter, 1964-65, olive w/white U.S. Army decals, Model No. 1133-A
EX $70 **NM** $105 **MIP** $190

(KP Photo by Dr. Douglas Sadecky)

Bedford Army Fuel Tanker, 1964-65, olive cab and tanker, w/white "U.S. Army" and "No Smoking" decals, shaped wheels, Model No. 1134-A
EX $140 **NM** $210 **MIP** $375

Bedford Military Ambulance, 1961-64, clear front and white rear windows, olive body w/Red Cross decals, w/or without suspension, smooth or shaped wheels, Model No. 414-A
EX $56 **NM** $84 **MIP** $140

Bell Army Helicopter, 1975-80, two-piece olive/tan camouflage body, clear canopy, olive green rotors, U.S. Army decals, Model No. 920-A
EX $24 **NM** $36 **MIP** $60

Bloodhound Launching Ramp, 1959-62, military green ramp, Model No. 1116-A
EX $34 **NM** $51 **MIP** $85

Bloodhound Loading Trolley, 1959-62, military green working lift, Model No. 1117-A
EX $40 **NM** $60 **MIP** $100

Bloodhound Missile, 1959-62, white and yellow missile, red rubber nose cone, Model No. 1115-A
EX $70 **NM** $105 **MIP** $175

(KP Photo by Dr. Douglas Sadecky)

Bloodhound Missile and Launching Platform, 1958-61, white and yellow missile, red rubber nose cone; military green ramp, Model No. 1108-A
EX $110 **NM** $165 **MIP** $290

Bloodhound Missile on Trolley, 1959-62, white and yellow missile, red rubber nose cone; military green trolley, rubber tires, Model No. 1109-A
EX $120 **NM** $180 **MIP** $300

Centurion Mark III Tank, 1974-78, tan and brown camouflage or olive drab body, rubber tracks; includes twelve shells, Model No. 901-A
EX $30 **NM** $45 **MIP** $75

Centurion Tank and Transporter, 1973-78, No. 901 olive tank and No. 1100 transporter, Model No. 10-B
EX $55 **NM** $80 **MIP** $140

Chieftain Medium Tank, 1974-80, olive drab body, black tracks, Union Jack labels; includes twelve shells, Model No. 903-A
EX $30 **NM** $45 **MIP** $75

Commer Military Ambulance, 1964-66, olive drab body, blue rear windows and dome light, driver, Red Cross decals, shaped wheels, Model No. 354-A
EX $50 **NM** $75 **MIP** $125

Commer Military Police Van, 1964-65, olive drab body, barred rear windows, white MP decals, driver, shaped wheels, Model No. 355-A
EX $55 **NM** $80 **MIP** $130

(KP Photo by Dr. Douglas Sadecky)

Corporal Missile & Erector Vehicle, 1959-62, white missile, red rubber-nose cone, olive green body on erector body, Model No. 1113-A
EX $240 **NM** $360 **MIP** $600

Corporal Missile Launching Ramp, 1960-61, sold in temporary pack, Model No. 1124-A
EX $36 **NM** $55 **MIP** $100

Corporal Missile on Launching Ramp, 1959-62, white missile, red rubber-nose cone, Model No. 1112-A
EX $80 **NM** $120 **MIP** $200

Corporal Missile Set, 1959-62, No. 1112 missile and No. 1113 ramp, erector vehicle and No. 1118 army truck, Model No. 9-A
EX $340 **NM** $510 **MIP** $900

Decca Airfield Radar Van, 1959-60, cream body w/four or five orange vertical bands, working rotating scanner and aerial, smooth wheels, Model No. 1106-A
EX $120 **NM** $180 **MIP** $350

Decca Radar Scanner, 1959-60, w/either orange or custard colored scanner frame, silver scanner face, w/gear on base for turning scanner, Model No. 353-A
EX $34 **NM** $51 **MIP** $85

Half Track Rocket Launcher & Trailer, 1975-80, two rocket launchers and single trailer castings, gray plastic roll cage, man w/machine gun, front wheels and hubs, Model No. 907-A
EX $20 **NM** $35 **MIP** $75

International 6x6 Army Truck, 1959-63, olive drab body w/clear windows, red/blue decals, six cast olive wheels w/rubber tires, Model No. 1118-A
EX $70 **NM** $105 **MIP** $225

(KP Photo by Dr. Douglas Sadecky)

Karrier Field Kitchen, 1964-66, olive body, white decals, w/figure, shaped wheels, Model No. 359-A
EX $60 **NM** $90 **MIP** $175

King Tiger Heavy Tank, 1974-78, tan and rust body, working turret and barrel, tan rollers and treads, German labels, Model No. 904-A
EX $30 **NM** $45 **MIP** $75

M60 A1 Medium Tank, 1974-80, green/tan camouflage body, working turret and barrel, green rollers, white decals, Model No. 902-A
EX $30 **NM** $45 **MIP** $75

Military Set, 1975-80, set of three, No. 904 Tiger tank, No. 920 Bell Helicopter, No. 906 Saladin Armored Car, Model No. 17-B
EX $60 **NM** $90 **MIP** $150

Oldsmobile 88 Staff Car, 1964-66, olive drab body, four figures, white decals, shaped wheels, Model No. 358-A
EX $50 **NM** $75 **MIP** $140

RAF Land Rover, 1958-62, blue body and cover, sheet metal rear cover, RAF rondel label, w/or without suspension, silver bumper, smooth or shaped wheels, Model No. 351-A
EX $60 **NM** $90 **MIP** $150

RAF Land Rover & Bloodhound, 1958-61, set of three standard colored, No. 351 RAF Land Rover, No. 1115 Bloodhound Missile, No. 1116 Ramp and No. 1117 Trolley, Model No. 4-A
EX $150 **NM** $300 **MIP** $600

RAF Land Rover and Thunderbird Missile, 1958-63, Standard colors, No. 350 Thunderbird Missile on Trolley and No. 351 RAF Land Rover, Model No. 3-A
EX $100 **NM** $150 **MIP** $325

Rocket Age Set, 1959-60, set of eight standard models including: No. 350 Thunderbird Missile on Trolley, No. 351 RAF Land Rover, No. 352 RAF Staff Car, No. 353 Radar Scanner, No. 1106 Decca Radar Van and No. 1108 Bloodhound missile w/ramp, Model No. 6-A
EX $325 **NM** $650 **MIP** $1500

Rocket Launcher and Trailer, 1975-80, steel blue and red launcher, fires rocket, Model No. 907-A
EX $25 **NM** $35 **MIP** $60

Saladin Armored Car, 1974-77, olive drab body, swiveling turret and raising barrel castings, black plastic barrel end and tires, olive cast wheels, w/twelve shells, fires shells, Model No. 906-A
EX $30 **NM** $45 **MIP** $75

Sikorsky Skycrane Army Helicopter, 1975-78, olive drab and yellow body w/Red Cross and Army labels, Model No. 923-A
EX $15 **NM** $20 **MIP** $40

Standard Vanguard RAF Staff Car, 1958-62, blue body, RAF labels, smooth wheels, Model No. 352-A
EX $55 **NM** $85 **MIP** $140

SU-100 Medium Tank, 1974-77, olive and cream camouflage upper body, gray lower, working hatch and barrel, black treads, red star and #103 labels; twelve shells included, fires shells, Model No. 905-A
EX $30 **NM** $50 **MIP** $80

Thunderbird Missile and Trolley, 1958-62, ice blue or silver missile, RAF blue trolley, red rubber nose cone, plastic tow bar, steering front and rear axles, Model No. 350-A
EX $55 **NM** $85 **MIP** $165

Tiger Mark I Tank, 1973-78, tan and green camouflage finish, German emblem, swiveling turret and raising barrel castings, black plastic barrel end, antenna; includes twelve shells, fires shells, Model No. 900-A
EX $30 **NM** $45 **MIP** $75

Tractor, Trailer and Field Gun, 1976-80, tan tractor body and chassis, trailer body, base and opening doors, gun chassis and raising barrel castings, brown plastic interior; twelve shells included, fires shells, Model No. 909-A
EX $30 **NM** $50 **MIP** $80

(KP Photo by Dr. Douglas Sadecky)

Volkswagen Military Personnel Carrier, 1964-66, olive drab body, white decals, driver, shaped wheels, Model No. 356-A
EX $55 **NM** $95 **MIP** $180

MISCELLANEOUS

Service Ramp, 1958-60, metallic blue and silver operable ramp, Model No. 1401-A
EX $30 **NM** $45 **MIP** $95

Shell or BP Garage Gift Set, 1963-65, gas station/garage w/pumps and other accessories including five different cars; in two versions: Shell or B.P., rare; value is for each set, Model No. 25-A
EX $295 **NM** $700 **MIP** $2000

Touring Caravan, 1975-79, white body w/blue trim, white plastic opening roof and door, pale blue interior, red plastic hitch and awning, Model No. 490-B
EX $15 **NM** $25 **MIP** $40

MOTORCYCLE

Cafe Racer Motorcycle, 1983, Model No. 173-A
EX $15 **NM** $18 **MIP** $30

Matra & Motorcycle Trailer, 1980-81, red No. 57 Talbot Matra Rancho w/two yellow and blue bikes on trailer, Model No. 25-C
EX $15 **NM** $20 **MIP** $35

Red Wheelie Motorcycle, 1982, red plastic body and fender w/black/white/yellow decals, black handlebars, kickstand and seat, chrome engine, pipes, flywheel-powered rear wheel, Model No. 171-A
EX $10 **NM** $15 **MIP** $25

Stunt Motorcycle, 1971-72, made for Corgi Rockets race track, gold cycle, blue rider w/yellow helmet, clear windshield, plastic tires, Model No. 681-A
EX $70 **NM** $105 **MIP** $175

White Wheelie Motorcycle, 1982, white body w/black/white police decals, Model No. 172-A
EX $15 **NM** $20 **MIP** $35

RACING

Adams Drag-Star, 1972-74, orange body, red nose, gold engines, chrome pipes and hood panels, Whizz Wheels, Model No. 165-A
EX $20 **NM** $30 **MIP** $45

Adams Probe 16, 1970-73, one-piece body, blue sliding canopy; metallic burgundy, or metallic lime/gold w/and without racing stripes, Whizz Wheels, Model No. 384-A
EX $15 **NM** $25 **MIP** $40

All Winners Set, 1966-69, first issue: No. 310 Corvette, No. 312 Jaguar XKE, No. 314 Ferrari 250LM, No. 324 Marcos, No. 325 Mustang; second issue: No. 312 Jaguar XKE, No. 314 Ferrari 250LM, No. 264 Toronado, No. 327 MGB, No. 337 Corvette, Model No. 46-A
EX $100 **NM** $240 **MIP** $500

(KP Photo by Dr. Douglas Sadecky)

Aston Martin DB4, 1962-65, white top w/aqua green sides, yellow plastic interior, 3 wheel variants, racing Nos. 1, 3 or 7, Model No. 309-A
EX $50 **NM** $75 **MIP** $140

Austin Mini-Metro Datapost, 1982-83, white body, blue roof, hood and trim, red plastic interior, hepolite and #77 decals, working hatch and doors, clear windows, folding seats, chrome headlights, orange taillights, Whizz Wheels, Model No. 281-B
EX $15 **NM** $18 **MIP** $30

Bertone Barchetta Runabout, 1971-73, yellow and black body, black interior, amber windows, die-cast air foil, suspension, red/yellow Runabout decals, Whizz Wheels, Model No. 386-A
EX $15 **NM** $22 **MIP** $45

BMC Mini-Cooper, 1971-74, white body, black working hood, trunk, two doors, red interior, clear windows, orange/black stripes and #177 decals, suspension, Whizz Wheels, Model No. 282-A
EX $30 **NM** $45 **MIP** $100

(KP Photo by Dr. Douglas Sadecky)

BMC Mini-Cooper S "Sun/RAC" Rally Car, 1967, red body, white roof w/six jewel headlights, shaped wheels, RAC Rally and No. 21 decals, Model No. 333-A
EX $90 **NM** $180 **MIP** $350

BMC Mini-Cooper S Rally, 1967-72, red body, white roof, chrome roof rack w/two spare tires, Monte Carlo Rally and No. 177 decals, w/shaped wheels/rubber tires or cast detailed wheels/plastic tires, Model No. 339-A
EX $40 **NM** $90 **MIP** $180

(KP Photo by Dr. Douglas Sadecky)

BMC Mini-Cooper S Rally Car, 1965-66, red body, white roof, five jewel headlights, Monte Carlo Rally decals w/either No. 52 (1965) or No. 2 (1966); rare w/drivers' autographs on roof, shaped wheels, Model No. 321-A
EX $100 **NM** $275 **MIP** $500

BMW M1, 1981, yellow body, black plastic base, rear panel and interior, white seats, clear windshield, multicolored stripes, lettering and #25 decal, Goodyear label, Model No. 308-B
EX $15 **NM** $20 **MIP** $35

BMW M1 BASF, 1983, red body, white trim w/black/white BASF and No. 80 decals, Model No. 380-B
EX $15 **NM** $18 **MIP** $30

British Leyland Mini 1000, 1978, red interior, chrome lights, grille and bumper, #8 decal; three variations: silver body w/decals, 1978-82; silver body, no decals; orange body w/extra hood stripes, 1983, Model No. 201-C
EX $16 **NM** $24 **MIP** $40

British Racing Cars, 1959-63, set of three cars, three versions: blue No. 152 Lotus, green No. 151 BRM, green No. 150 Vanwall, all w/smooth wheels, 1959; same cars w/shaped wheels, 1960-61; red Vanwall, green BRM and blue Lotus, 1963, each set, Model No. 5-A
EX $140 **NM** $210 **MIP** $500

BRM Racing Car, 1958-65, silver seat, dash and pipes, smooth wheels, rubber tires, in three versions: dark green body, 1958-60; light green body w/driver and various number decals 1961-65; light green body, no driver, smooth or cast spoked wheels, Model No. 152-A
EX $50 **NM** $75 **MIP** $150

Campbell Bluebird, 1960-65, blue body, red exhaust, clear windshield, driver, in two versions: black plastic wheels, 1960; metal wheels and rubber tires, Model No. 153-A
EX $56 **NM** $84 **MIP** $175

Chevrolet Caprice Classic, 1981, white upper body, red sides w/red/white/blue stripes and No. 43 decals, tan interior, STP labels, Model No. 341-B
EX $24 **NM** $36 **MIP** $60

(KP Photo by Dr. Douglas Sadecky)

Citroen DS 19 Rally, 1965-66, light blue body, white roof, yellow interior, four jewel headlights, Monte Carlo Rally and No. 75 decals, w/antenna, shaped wheels, Model No. 323-A
EX $70 **NM** $105 **MIP** $185

Commuter Dragster, 1971-73, maroon body w/Ford Commuter, Union Jack and #2 decals, cast silver engine, chrome plastic suspension and pipes, clear windshield, driver, spoke wheels, Model No. 161-A
EX $30 **NM** $45 **MIP** $75

Cooper-Maserati Racing Car, 1967-69, blue body w/red/white/blue Maserati and #7 decals, unpainted engine and suspension, chrome plastic steering wheel, roll bar, mirrors and pipes, driver, cast eight-spoke wheels, plastic tires, Model No. 156-A
EX $26 **NM** $39 **MIP** $75

Cooper-Maserati Racing Car, 1969-72, yellow/white body w/yellow/black stripe and #3 decals, driver tilts to steer car, cast 8-spoke wheels, Model No. 159-A
EX $18 **NM** $27 **MIP** $65

(KP Photo by Dr. Douglas Sadecky)

Corvette Sting Ray, 1967-69, yellow body, red interior, suspension, No. 13 decals. This car's decorative appearance definitely places it in the 1960s, cast 8-spoke wheels, Model No. 337-A
EX $30 **NM** $55 **MIP** $95

Corvette Sting Ray, 1970-73, metallic gray body w/black hood, Go-Go-Go labels, Whizz Wheels, Model No. 376-A
EX $40 **NM** $65 **MIP** $100

Datsun 240Z, 1973-76, white body w/red hood and roof, No. 46 and John Morton labels, Whizz Wheels, Model No. 396-A
EX $15 **NM** $20 **MIP** $35

Datsun 240Z, 1973-76, red body w/No. 11 and other labels, two working doors, white interior, orange roll bar and tire rack; one version also has East Africa Rally labels, Model No. 394-A
EX $15 **NM** $20 **MIP** $35

Ecurie Ecosse Racing Set, 1961-66, metallic dark or light blue No. 1126 transporter w/three cars in two versions: BRM, Vanwall and Lotus XI, 1961-64; BRM, Vanwall and Ferrari, 1964-66, value is for individual complete set, Model No. 16-A
EX $140 **NM** $275 **MIP** $600

Ferrari 206 Dino, 1969-73, black interior and fins, in either red body w/No. 30 label and gold hubs or Whizz Wheels, or yellow body w/No. 23 label and gold hubs or Whizz Wheels, Model No. 344-A
EX $24 **NM** $36 **MIP** $60

Ferrari 312 B2 Racing Car, 1973-75, red body, white fin, gold engine, chrome suspension, mirrors and wheels, Ferrari and #5 labels, Model No. 152-B
EX $16 **NM** $24 **MIP** $40

(KP Photo by Dr. Douglas Sadecky)

Ferrari Berlinetta 250LM, 1965-72, red body w/yellow stripe, blue windshields, chrome interior, grille and exhaust pipes, detailed engine, #4 Ferrari logo and yellow stripe decals, spoked wheels and spare, rubber tires, Model No. 314-A
EX $30 **NM** $45 **MIP** $85

Ferrari Daytona, 1973-78, white body w/red roof and trunk, black interior, two working doors, amber windows and headlights, No. 81 and other labels, Model No. 323-B
EX $15 **NM** $30 **MIP** $55

Ferrari Daytona, 1979, apple green body, black tow hook, red-yellow-silver-black Daytona #5 and other racing labels, amber windows, headlights, black plastic interior, base, four spoke chrome wheels, Model No. 300-C
EX $15 **NM** $20 **MIP** $35

Ferrari Daytona and Racing Car, 1975-77, blue/yellow No. 323 Ferrari and No. 150 Surtees on yellow trailer, Model No. 29-B
EX $25 **NM** $40 **MIP** $85

Ferrari Daytona JCB, 1973-74, orange body w/No. 33, Corgi and other labels, chrome spoked wheels, Model No. 324-B
EX $15 **NM** $25 **MIP** $50

Ferrari Racing Car, 1963-72, red body, chrome plastic engine, roll bar and dash, driver, silver cast base and exhaust, Ferrari and No. 36 decals, shaped or cast wheels, Model No. 154-A
EX $24 **NM** $36 **MIP** $75

Fiat X1/9, 1980-81, metallic blue body and base, white Fiat #3, multicolored lettering and stripe labels, black roof, trim, interior, rear panel, grille, bumpers and tow hook, chrome wheels and detailed engine, Model No. 306-B
EX $15 **NM** $20 **MIP** $35

Ford Capri 3 Litre GT, 1973-76, white and black body, racing number 5 label, Model No. 331-A
EX $15 **NM** $20 **MIP** $35

Ford Capri S, 1982, white body, red lower body and base, red interior, clear windshield, black bumpers, grille and tow hook, chrome headlights and wheels, red taillights, #6 and other racing labels, Model No. 312-C
EX $15 **NM** $20 **MIP** $35

Ford Capri Santa Pod Gloworm, 1971-76, white and blue body w/red, white and blue lettering and flag decals, red chassis, amber windows, gold-based black engine, gold scoop, pipes and front suspension, w/driver, plastic wheels, Model No. 163-A
EX $18 **NM** $27 **MIP** $45

Ford GT 70, 1972-73, green and black body, white interior, No. 32 label, Model No. 316-B
EX $10 **NM** $25 **MIP** $45

Grand Prix Racing Set, 1968-72, four vehicle set includes: No. 490 Volkswagen Breakdown Truck w/No. 330 Porsche (1969), Porsche No. 371(1970-72), No. 155 Lotus, No. 156 Cooper-Maserati, red trailer, Model No. 12-B
EX $135 **NM** $210 **MIP** $425

Grand Prix Set, 1973, sold by mail order only; kit version of No. 151 Yardley, No. 154 JPS, No. 152 Surtees and No. 153 Surtees, Model No. 30-A
EX $60 **NM** $125 **MIP** $275

Hesketh-Ford Racing Car, 1975-78, white body w/red/white/blue Hesketh, stripe and #24 labels, chrome suspension, roll bar, mirrors and pipes, Model No. 160-A
EX $15 **NM** $18 **MIP** $30

Hillman Hunter, 1969-72, blue body, gray interior, black hood, white roof, unpainted spotlights, clear windshield, red radiator screen, black equipment, Golden Jacks wheels; came w/Kangaroo figure and label sheet, Model No. 302-B
EX $45 **NM** $70 **MIP** $140

(KP Photo by Dr. Douglas Sadecky)

Hillman Imp Rally, 1966, in various metallic body colors, w/cream interior, Monte Carlo Rally and No. 107 decals, shaped wheels, Model No. 328-A
EX $30 **NM** $65 **MIP** $130

Jaguar E Type Competition, 1964-68, gold or chrome plated body, black interior, blue and white stripes and black #2 decals, no top, clear windshield, headlights, w/driver, spoked wheels, Model No. 312-A
EX $45 **NM** $65 **MIP** $140

Jaguar XJS Motul, 1983, black body w/red/white Motul and No. 4, chrome wheels, Model No. 318-B
EX $8 **NM** $15 **MIP** $25

JPS Lotus Racing Car, 1974-77, black body, scoop and wings w/gold John Player Special, Texaco and #1 labels, gold suspension, pipes and wheels, Model No. 190-A
EX $30 **NM** $45 **MIP** $75

Lamborghini Miura, 1973-74, silver body, black interior, yellow/purple stripes and No. 7 label, Whizz Wheels, Model No. 319-B
EX $30 **NM** $45 **MIP** $75

Land Rover and Ferrari Racer, 1963-67, red and tan No. 438 Land Rover and red No. 154 Ferrari F1 on yellow trailer, Model No. 17-A
EX $60 **NM** $90 **MIP** $165

(KP Photo by Dr. Douglas Sadecky)

Lotus Elan S2 Roadster, 1965-67, working hood, plastic interior w/folding seats, shaped wheels and rubber tires, issued in metallic blue, Exxon "I've got a Tiger in my tank" label on trunk. The ordinary model is powder blue, but shown here is the rare white version of the car, Model No. 318-A
EX $30 **NM** $50 **MIP** $110

(KP Photo by Dr. Douglas Sadecky)

Lotus Eleven, 1958-64, red, silver, or light blue/green body, clear windshield and plastic headlights, smooth wheels, rubber tires, racing decals, Model No. 151-A
EX $60 **NM** $95 **MIP** $160

Lotus Racing Car, 1973-82, black body and base, gold cast engine, roll bar, pipes, dash and mirrors, driver, gold cast wheels, in two versions, Model No. 154-B
EX $25 **NM** $35 **MIP** $60

Lotus Racing Set, 1976-79, three versions: "3" on No. 301 Elite and "JPS" on No. 154 Lotus racer; "7" on No. 301 Elite and "JPS" on racer; "7" on No. 301 Elite and "Texaco" on No. 154 Lotus racer; value is for each individual complete set, Model No. 32-B
EX $30 **NM** $45 **MIP** $95

Lotus Racing Team Set, 1966-69, 490 VW Breakdown Truck, red trailer w/#318 Lotus Elan Open Top, #319 Lotus Elan Hard Top, #155 Lotus Climax; includes pack of cones, sheet of racing number labels, Model No. 37-A
EX $125 **NM** $200 **MIP** $475

Lotus-Climax Racing Car, 1964-69, green body and base w/black/white #1 and yellow racing stripe labels, unpainted engine and suspension, w/driver, shaped wheels, Model No. 155-A
EX $25 **NM** $35 **MIP** $65

(KP Photo by Dr. Douglas Sadecky)

Lotus-Climax Racing Car, 1969-72, orange/white body w/black/white stripe and #8 labels, unpainted cast rear wing, cast eight-spoke wheels, w/driver, Model No. 158-A
EX $15 **NM** $25 **MIP** $65

Matra and Racing Car, 1983, black/yellow No. 457 Talbot Matra Rancho and No. 160 Hesketh yellow car w/Team Corgi trailer and labels, Model No. 26-B
EX $15 **NM** $35 **MIP** $65

McLaren M19A Racing Car, 1972-77, white body, orange stripes, chrome engine, exhaust and suspension, black mirrors, driver, Yardley McLaren #55 labels, Whizz Wheels, Model No. 151-B
EX $15 **NM** $25 **MIP** $40

McLaren M23 Racing Car, 1974-77, large 1:18-scale red and white body and wings w/red, white and black Texaco-Marlboro #5 labels, chrome pipes, suspension and mirrors, removable wheels, Model No. 191-A
EX $30 **NM** $60 **MIP** $110

Mercedes-Benz 240D Rally, 1982, cream or tan body, black, red and blue lettering, "dirt," red plastic interior, clear windows, black radiator guard and roof rack, opening doors, racing #5 label, Model No. 291-B
EX $10 **NM** $15 **MIP** $25

(KP Photo by Dr. Douglas Sadecky)

Mercedes-Benz 300SL Coupe, 1959-65, chrome body, red hardtop, red stripe, clear windows, 1959-60 smooth wheels no suspension, 1961-65 racing stripes, Model No. 304-A
EX $45 **NM** $65 **MIP** $150

Mercedes-Benz 300SL Roadster, 1958-66, blue or white body, yellow interior, plastic interior, smooth, shaped or cast wheels, racing stripes and number, driver, Model No. 303-A
EX $45 **NM** $75 **MIP** $140

Mini-Marcos GT850, 1972-73, white body, red-white-blue racing stripe and #7 labels, clear headlights, Whizz Wheels, opening doors and hood, Model No. 305-B
EX $20 **NM** $30 **MIP** $50

(KP Photo by Dr. Douglas Sadecky)

Monte Carlo Rally Set, 1965-67, three vehicle set, No. 326 Citroen, No. 318 Mini and No. 322 Land Rover rally cars, Model No. 38-A
EX $295 **NM** $450 **MIP** $950

(KP Photo by Dr. Douglas Sadecky)

Morris Mini-Cooper, 1962-65, yellow or blue body and base and/or hood, white roof and/or hood, two versions, red plastic interior, jewel headlights, flag, numbers decals. Even though there are various paint and decal versions of this model, any one of them is valuable, shaped wheels, Model No. 227-A
EX $80 **NM** $150 **MIP** $345

Morris Mini-Cooper, 1964-65, red body and base, white roof, yellow interior, chrome spotlight, No. 37 and Monte Carlo Rally decals, shaped wheels, Model No. 317-A
EX $60 **NM** $125 **MIP** $250

Mustang Organ Grinder Dragster, 1971-74, yellow body w/green/yellow name, #39 and racing stripe labels, black base, green windshield, red interior, roll bar, w/driver, Model No. 166-A
EX $20 **NM** $30 **MIP** $50

Porsche 924, 1978-81, red or metallic light brown or green body, dark red interior, opening two doors and rear window, chrome headlights, black plastic grille, racing No. 2, Model No. 321-B
EX $10 **NM** $25 **MIP** $50

Porsche Carrera 6, 1967-69, white body, red or blue trim, blue or amber tinted engine covers, black interior, clear windshield and canopy, red jewel taillights, No. 1 or No. 20 decals, cast 8-spoke wheels, Model No. 330-A
EX $30 **NM** $45 **MIP** $85

Porsche Carrera 6, 1970-73, white upper body, red front hood, doors, upper fins and base, black interior, purple rear window, tinted engine cover, racing No. 60 decals, Whizz Wheels, Model No. 371-A
EX $25 **NM** $35 **MIP** $60

Porsche-Audi 917, 1973-78, white body, red and black No. 6, L and M, Porsche Audi and stripe labels or orange body, orange, two-tone green, white No. 6, racing driver, Model No. 397-A
EX $15 **NM** $20 **MIP** $35

(KP Photo by Dr. Douglas Sadecky)

Psychedelic Ford Mustang, 1968, light blue body and base, aqua interior, red-orange-yellow No. 20 and flower decals, cast eight spoke wheels, plastic tire, Model No. 348-A
EX $30 **NM** $50 **MIP** $100

Quartermaster Dragster, 1971-73, long, dark metallic green upper body w/green/yellow/black #5 and Quartermaster labels, light green lower body, w/driver, Model No. 162-A
EX $30 **NM** $45 **MIP** $75

Radio Luxembourg Dragster, 1972-76, long, blue body w/yellow, white and blue John Wolfe Racing, Radio Luxembourg and #5 labels, silver engine, w/driver, Model No. 170-A
EX $30 **NM** $45 **MIP** $85

Renault 5 Turbo, 1981, bright yellow body, red plastic interior, black roof and hood, working hatch and two doors, black dash, chrome rear engine, racing #8 Cibie and other sponsor labels, Model No. 307-B
EX $15 **NM** $18 **MIP** $25

Renault 5 Turbo, 1983, white body, red roof, red and blue trim painted on, No. 5 lettering, blue and white label on windshield, facom decal, Model No. 381-B
EX $15 **NM** $18 **MIP** $25

Roger Clark's Capri, 1970-72, white body, black hood, grille and interior, open doors, folding seats, chrome bumpers, clear headlights, red taillights, Racing #73, label sheet, Whizz Wheels, Model No. 303-B
EX $15 **NM** $25 **MIP** $65

(KP Photo by Dr. Douglas Sadecky)

Rover 2000 Rally, 1965-66, white body, red interior, black bonnet, No. 21 decal, cast wheels, Model No. 322-A2
EX $55 **NM** $135 **MIP** $265

Rover 2000 Rally, 1965-66, metallic dark red body, white roof, shaped wheels, No. 136 and Monte Carlo Rally decals, Model No. 322-A1
EX $50 **NM** $95 **MIP** $175

Rover 3500 Triplex, 1981, white sides and hatch, blue roof and hood, red plastic interior and trim, detailed engine, red-white-black No. 1label, Model No. 340-B
EX $8 **NM** $15 **MIP** $20

Shadow-Ford Racing Car, 1974-76, black body and base w/white/black #17, UOP and American flag labels, cast chrome suspension and pipes, Embassy Racing label, Model No. 155-B
EX $10 **NM** $20 **MIP** $50

Shadow-Ford Racing Car, 1974-77, white body, red stripes, driver, chrome plastic pipes, mirrors and steering wheel, in two versions, Jackie Collins driver figure, Model No. 156-B
EX $10 **NM** $20 **MIP** $45

Silver Streak Jet Dragster, 1973-76, metallic blue body w/Firestone and flag labels on tank, silver engine, orange plastic jet and nose cone, Model No. 169-A
EX $15 **NM** $25 **MIP** $45

Silverstone Racing Layout, 1963-66, seven-vehicle set w/accessories; Vanwall, Lotus XI, Aston Martin, Mercedes 300SL, BRM, Ford Thunderbird, Land Rover Truck; second version has a No. 154 Ferrari substituted for Lotus XI, rare, Model No. 15-A
EX $400 **NM** $900 **MIP** $1900

(KP Photo by Dr. Douglas Sadecky)

Simca 1000, 1964-66, chrome plated body, No. 8 and red-white-blue stripe decals, one-piece body, clear windshield, red interior, shaped wheels, Model No. 315-A
EX $30 **NM** $45 **MIP** $85

STP Patrick Eagle Racing Car, 1974-77, red body w/red, white and black STP and #20 labels, chrome lower engine and suspension, black plastic upper engine; includes Patrick Eagle driver figure, Model No. 159-B
EX $20 **NM** $30 **MIP** $50

Sunbeam Imp Rally, 1967-68, metallic blue body w/white stripes, Monte Carlo Rally and No. 77 decals, cast wheels, Model No. 340-A
EX $20 **NM** $45 **MIP** $100

Super Karts, 1982, two carts, orange and blue, Whizz Wheels in front, slicks on rear, silver and gold drivers, Model No. 46-B
EX $15 **NM** $18 **MIP** $30

Surtees TS9 Racing Car, 1972-74, black upper engine, chrome lower engine, pipes and exhaust, driver, Brook Bond Oxo-Rob Walker labels, eight-spoke Whizz Wheels, Model No. 150-B
EX $15 **NM** $20 **MIP** $40

Surtees TS9B Racing Car, 1972-74, red body w/white stripes and wing, black plastic lower engine, driver, chrome upper engine, pipes, suspension, eight-spoke Whizz Wheels, Model No. 153-B
EX $15 **NM** $20 **MIP** $40

Tyrrell P34 Racing Car, 1977, dark blue body and wings w/yellow stripes, #4 and white Elf and Union Jack decals, chrome plastic engine, w/driver in red or blue helmet, Model No. 161-B
EX $20 **NM** $30 **MIP** $55

Tyrrell P34 Racing Car, 1978-79, without yellow labels, First National Bank labels, w/driver in red or orange helmet, Model No. 162-B
EX $20 **NM** $30 **MIP** $55

Tyrrell-Ford Racing Car, 1974-78, dark blue body w/blue/black/white Elf and #1 labels, chrome suspension, pipes, mirrors, Jackie Stewart driver figure, Model No. 158-B
EX $18 **NM** $25 **MIP** $50

U.S. Racing Buggy, 1972-74, white body w/red/white/blue stars, stripes and USA #7 labels, red base, gold engine, red plastic panels, driver, Model No. 167-A
EX $18 **NM** $25 **MIP** $50

(KP Photo by Dr. Douglas Sadecky)

Vanwall Racing Car, 1957-65, clear windshield, unpainted dash, silver pipes and decals, smooth or cast detailed spoked wheels , rubber tires, in three versions: green body or red body w/silver or yellow seats, Model No. 150-A
EX $35 **NM** $65 **MIP** $150

Volkswagen 1200 Rally, 1976-77, light blue body, off-white plastic interior, silver headlights, red taillights, suspension, Whizz Wheels, Model No. 384-B
EX $20 **NM** $30 **MIP** $50

(KP Photo by Dr. Douglas Sadecky)

Volkswagen East African Safari, 1965-69, light red body, brown interior, working front and rear hood, clear windows, spare wheel on roof steers front wheels, jewel headlights, w/rhinoceros figure. Although never issued as a gift set, this spectacular little toy could easily have been made into one. A rhinoceros was added as a charging menace to the racing VW, shaped wheels, Model No. 256-A
EX $60 **NM** $130 **MIP** $285

Volkswagen Racing Tender and Cooper, 1967-69, white No. 490 VW breakdown truck w/racing labels, blue No. 156 Cooper on trailer, Model No. 6-B
EX $50 **NM** $75 **MIP** $175

Volkswagen Racing Tender and Cooper Maserati, 1970-71, two versions: tan or white No. 490 VW breakdown truck, and No. 159 Cooper-Maserati on trailer; value is for each set, Model No. 25-B
EX $50 **NM** $75 **MIP** $190

Wild Honey Dragster, 1971-73, yellow body w/red/yellow Wild Honey and Jaguar Powered labels, green windows and roof, black grille, driver, Whizz Wheels, Model No. 164-A
EX $25 **NM** $40 **MIP** $65

SMALL TRUCK

Breakdown Truck, 1975-79, red body, black plastic boom w/gold hook, yellow interior, amber windows, black/yellow decals, Whizz Wheels, Model No. 702-A
EX $15 **NM** $18 **MIP** $40

Commer 3/4-Ton Pickup, 1963-66, red cab w/orange canopy, yellow interior, Trans-o-Lites, shaped wheels, Model No. 465-A
EX $30 **NM** $45 **MIP** $75

Commer 5-Ton Dropside Truck, 1956-62, either blue or red cab, both w/cream rear body, sheet metal tow hook, smooth or shaped wheels, rubber tires, Model No. 452-A
EX $40 **NM** $60 **MIP** $130

Commer 5-Ton Platform Truck, 1957-62, either yellow or metallic blue cab w/silver body, smooth or shaped wheels, Model No. 454-A
EX $40 **NM** $60 **MIP** $130

(KP Photo by Dr. Douglas Sadecky)

Commer Refrigerator Van, 1956-60, either light or dark blue cab (pictured here), both w/cream bodies and red/white/blue Wall's Ice Cream decals, smooth wheels, Model No. 453-A
EX $80 **NM** $120 **MIP** $225

(KP Photo by Dr. Douglas Sadecky)

Constructor Set, 1963-68, one red and one white cab bodies, w/four different interchangeable rear units; van, pickup, milk truck, and ambulance; various accessories include a milkman figure, Model No. 24-A
EX $48 **NM** $80 **MIP** $240

(KP Photo by Dr. Douglas Sadecky)

Dodge Kew Fargo Tipper, 1967-72, white cab and working hood, blue tipper, red interior, clear windows, black hydraulic cylinders, shaped or cast wheels, plastic tires, Model No. 483-A
EX $34 **NM** $51 **MIP** $85

ERF 44G Dropside Truck, 1961-64, yellow cab and chassis, metallic blue bed, smooth or shaped wheels, Model No. 456-A
EX $36 **NM** $55 **MIP** $130

(KP Photo by Dr. Douglas Sadecky)

ERF 44G Moorhouse Van, 1958-60, yellow cab, red body, Moorhouse Lemon Cheese decals, smooth wheels, rubber tires, Model No. 459-A
EX $100 **NM** $150 **MIP** $345

(KP Photo by Dr. Douglas Sadecky)

ERF 44G Platform Truck, 1958-64, light blue cab w/dark blue flatbed body or yellow cab and blue flatbed, smooth hubs, Model No. 457-A
EX $36 **NM** $55 **MIP** $130

ERF Dropside Truck and Trailer, 1960-64, No. 456 truck and No. 101 trailer w/No. 1488 cement sack load and No. 1485 plank load, Model No. 11-A
EX $60 **NM** $90 **MIP** $250

(KP Photo by Dr. Douglas Sadecky)

ERF Neville Cement Tipper, 1959-66, yellow cab, gray tipper, cement decal, plastic or metal filler caps, w/either smooth or shaped wheels, Model No. 460-A
EX $32 **NM** $48 **MIP** $100

Ford Transit Milk Float, 1982, white one-piece body, blue hood and roof, tan interior, chrome and red roof lights, open compartment door and milk cases, Model No. 405-C
EX $15 **NM** $25 **MIP** $40

Mazda 4X4 Open Truck, 1983, blue body, white roof, black windows, no interior, white plastic wheels, Model No. 495-A
EX $15 **NM** $20 **MIP** $35

Mazda B-1600 Pickup Truck, 1975-78, issued in either blue and white or blue and silver bodies w/working tailgate, black interior, chrome wheels, Model No. 493-A
EX $15 **NM** $20 **MIP** $35

Mazda Camper Pickup, 1976-78, red truck and white camper w/red interior and folding supports, Model No. 415-A
EX $15 **NM** $25 **MIP** $50

Mazda Custom Pickup, 1979-80, orange body w/red roof, United States flag label, Model No. 440-B
EX $15 **NM** $18 **MIP** $30

Mazda Motorway Maintenance Truck, 1976-78, deep yellow body w/red base, black interior and hydraulic cylinder, yellow basket w/workman figure, Model No. 413-B
EX $18 **NM** $25 **MIP** $45

Mazda Pickup and Dinghy, 1975-78, two versions: red No. 493 Mazda w/"Ford" labels; or w/"Sea Spray" labels, dinghy and trailer, Model No. 28-B
EX $25 **NM** $35 **MIP** $60

Mercedes-Benz and Caravan, 1975-81, truck and trailer in two versions: w/blue No. 285 Mercedes truck and No. 490 Caravan (1975-79); w/brown No. 285 Mercedes and No. 490 Caravan (1980-81); value is for each set, Model No. 24-B
EX $15 **NM** $30 **MIP** $50

Mercedes-Benz Unimog 406, 1970-76, yellow body, red and green front fenders and bumpers, metallic charcoal gray chassis w/olive or tan rear plastic covers, red interior, Model No. 406-B
EX $18 **NM** $25 **MIP** $45

Mercedes-Faun Street Sweeper, 1980, orange body w/light orange or brown figure, red interior, black chassis and unpainted brushing housing and arm castings, Model No. 1117-B
EX $15 **NM** $25 **MIP** $40

(KP Photo by Dr. Douglas Sadecky)

Milk Truck and Trailer, 1962-66, blue and white ERF No. 456 milk truck w/No. 101 trailer and milk churns, shaped wheels, Model No. 21-A
EX $60 **NM** $130 **MIP** $270

Shelvoke and Drewry Garbage Truck, 1979, long, orange or red cab, silver body w/City Sanitation decals, black interior, grille and bumpers, clear windows, Model No. 1116-B
EX $15 **NM** $25 **MIP** $40

Unimog with Snowplow (Mercedes-Benz), 1971-76, 6" four different body versions, red interior, cab, rear body, fender-plow mounting, lower and charcoal upper chassis, rear fenders, Model No. 1150-A
EX $30 **NM** $45 **MIP** $75

Volkswagen Breakdown Truck, 1966-72, tan or white body, red interior and equipment boxes, clear windshield, chrome tools, spare wheels, red VW emblem, no lettering, shaped or cast wheels, Model No. 490-A
EX $50 **NM** $75 **MIP** $125

Volkswagen Pickup, 1964-66, dark yellow or gold body, red interior and rear plastic cover, silver bumpers and headlights, red VW emblem, shaped wheels, Model No. 431-A
EX $45 **NM** $65 **MIP** $125

SPORTS CAR

Alfa Romeo P33 Pininfarina, 1970-74, white body, gold or black spoiler, red seats, Whizz Wheels, Model No. 380-A
EX $16 **NM** $24 **MIP** $45

Austin Healey, 1956-63, blue body w/cream seats, shaped hubs, rare, Model No. 300-A2
EX $100 **NM** $215 **MIP** $350

(KP Photo by Dr. Douglas Sadecky)

Austin-Healey, 1956-63, cream body w/red seats or red body w/cream seats, smooth or shaped wheels, Model No. 300-A1
EX $50 **NM** $75 **MIP** $150

Beach Buggy & Sailboat, 1971-76, purple No. 381 buggy, yellow trailer and red/white boat, Model No. 26-A
EX $20 **NM** $30 **MIP** $55

Bertone Shake Buggy, 1972-74, clear windows, green interior, gold engine, four variations: yellow upper/white lower body or metallic mauve upper/white lower body w/spoked or solid chrome wheels, Model No. 392-A
EX $15 **NM** $22 **MIP** $45

BMC Mini-Cooper Magnifique, 1966-70, metallic blue or olive green body w/working doors, hood and trunk, clear windows and sunroof, cream interior w/folding seats, jewel headlights, cast wheels, plastic tires, Model No. 334-A
EX $34 **NM** $65 **MIP** $135

BMC Mini-Cooper S, 1972-76, bright yellow body, red plastic interior, chrome plastic roof rack w/two spare wheels, clear windshield, one-piece body, silver grille, bumpers, headlights, red taillights, suspension, Whizz Wheels, Model No. 308-A
EX $45 **NM** $65 **MIP** $130

British Leyland Mini 1000, 1976-78, metallic blue body, working doors, black base, clear windows, white interior, silver lights, grille and bumper, Union Jack decal on roof, Whizz Wheels, Model No. 200-B
EX $18 **NM** $27 **MIP** $75

Chevrolet Astro I, 1969-74, dark metallic green/blue body w/working rear door, cream interior w/two passengers, in two versions: gold wheels w/red plastic hubs or Whizz wheels, Model No. 347-A
EX $18 **NM** $40 **MIP** $85

Chevrolet Camaro SS, 1968-70, metallic gold body w/two working doors, black roof and stripes, red interior, take-off wheels, Model No. 338-A
EX $30 **NM** $45 **MIP** $85

Chevrolet Camaro SS, 1972-73, blue or turquoise body w/white stripe, cream interior, working doors, white plastic top, clear windshield, folding seats, silver air intakes, red taillights, black grille and headlights, suspension, Whizz Wheels, Model No. 304-B
EX $30 **NM** $45 **MIP** $95

(KP Photo by Dr. Douglas Sadecky)

Corvette Sting Ray, 1963-68, metallic silver, bronze or red body, two working headlights, clear windshield, yellow interior, silver hood panels, four rotating jewel headlights, suspension, chrome bumpers, w/spoked or shaped wheels, rubber tires. The swivelling jeweled headlights and spoked wheels added real pizzaz to this cool toy, Model No. 310-A
EX $60 **NM** $90 **MIP** $175

Corvette Sting Ray, 1970-72, metallic green or metallic red body, yellow interior, black working hood, working headlights, clear windshield, amber roof panel, gold dash, chrome grille and bumpers, decals, gray die-cast base, golden jacks, cast wheels, plastic tires, Model No. 300-B
EX $40 **NM** $90 **MIP** $185

Corvette Sting Ray, 1972, either dark metallic blue or metallic mauve-rose body, chrome dash, Whizz Wheels, Model No. 387-A
EX $40 **NM** $65 **MIP** $100

De Tomaso Mangusta, 1969, white upper/light blue lower body/base, black interior, clear windows, silver engine, black grille, amber headlights, red taillights, gray antenna, spare wheel, gold stripes and black logo decal on hood, suspension, removable gray chassis, Model No. 271-A
EX $32 **NM** $48 **MIP** $100

De Tomaso Mangusta, 1970-73, metallic dark green body w/gold stripes and logo on hood, silver lower body, clear front windows, cream interior, amber rear windows and headlights, gray antenna, spare wheel, Whizz Wheels, Model No. 203-B
EX $26 **NM** $39 **MIP** $65

Ferrari 308GTS, 1982, red or black body w/working rear hood, black interior w/tan seats, movable chrome headlights, detailed engine, Model No. 378-B
EX $15 **NM** $20 **MIP** $35

Ferrari 308GTS Magnum, 1982, red body w/solid chrome wheels, or four spoked wheels, Model No. 298-A
EX $24 **NM** $36 **MIP** $75

Fiat X1/9, 1975-79, metallic light green or silver body w/black roof, trim and interior, two working doors, rear panel, grille, tow hook and bumpers, detailed engine, suspension, chrome wheels, Model No. 314-B
EX $15 **NM** $20 **MIP** $35

Ford Capri, 1970-72, orange-red or dark red body, gold wheels w/red hubs or Whizz Wheels, two working doors, clear windshield and headlights, black interior, folding seats, black grille, silver bumpers, Model No. 311-A
EX $40 **NM** $80 **MIP** $145

Ford Capri 30 S, 1980-81, silver or yellow body, black markings, opening doors and hatchback, Model No. 343-B
EX $15 **NM** $20 **MIP** $35

Ford Cobra Mustang, 1982, white, black, red and blue body and chassis, Mustang decal, Model No. 370-A
EX $15 **NM** $18 **MIP** $30

Ford Cortina GXL, 1970-73, tan or metallic silver blue body, black roof and stripes, red plastic interior, working doors, clear windshield, Model No. 313-A
EX $30 **NM** $45 **MIP** $75

Ford Mustang Fastback, 1965-66, metallic lilac, metallic dark blue, silver or light green body, w/shaped, spoked, or cast wheels, Model No. 320-A
EX $30 **NM** $45 **MIP** $100

(KP Photo by Dr. Douglas Sadecky)

Ford Mustang Fastback, 1965-69, white body w/double red stripe, blue interior, spun, detailed cast, wire or cast alloy wheels. Shown in the foreground of this photo is an unused number sheet to help jazz up the model, Model No. 325-A
EX $25 **NM** $45 **MIP** $95

Ford Mustang Mach 1, 1973-76, green upper body, white lower body and base, cream interior, folding seat backs, chrome headlights and rear bumper, Model No. 329-A
EX $25 **NM** $35 **MIP** $60

Ford Sierra, 1982, many body color versions w/plastic interior, working hatch and two doors, clear windows, folding seat back, lifting hatch cover, Model No. 299-A
EX $8 **NM** $15 **MIP** $25

Ford Sierra and Caravan Trailer, 1983, blue #299 Sierra, two-tone blue/white #490 Caravan, Model No. 1-C
EX $15 **NM** $20 **MIP** $35

Ford Thunderbird 1957, 1982, cream body, dark brown, black or orange plastic hardtop, black interior, open hood and trunk, chrome bumpers, Model No. 801-B
EX $10 **NM** $20 **MIP** $35

Ford Thunderbird 1957, 1983, white body, black interior and plastic top, amber windows, white seats, chrome bumpers, headlights and spare wheel cover, Model No. 810-B
EX $10 **NM** $20 **MIP** $35

(KP Photo by Dr. Douglas Sadecky)

Ford Thunderbird Hardtop, 1959-65, light green body, cream roof, clear windows, silver lights, grille and bumpers, red taillights, rubber tires, smooth or shaped wheels, Model No. 214-A
EX $50 **NM** $80 **MIP** $130

(KP Photo by Dr. Douglas Sadecky)

Ford Thunderbird Hardtop-Mechanical, 1959, same as 214-A but w/friction motor and pink body and black roof. This model is fairly hard to find, smooth wheels, Model No. 214-M
EX $70 **NM** $120 **MIP** $250

Ford Thunderbird Roadster, 1959-65, clear windshield, silver seats, lights, grille and bumpers, red taillights, rubber tires, white body, smooth or shaped wheels, Model No. 215-A
EX $50 **NM** $75 **MIP** $125

(KP Photo by Dr. Douglas Sadecky)

Ghia-Fiat 600 Jolly, 1965-66, dark yellow body, red seats, two figures and a dog, clear windshield, silver bumpers and headlights, red taillights, rare, shaped wheels, Model No. 242-A
EX $80 **NM** $175 **MIP** $365

GP Beach Buggy, 1970-76, metallic blue or orange-red body, two surfboards, flower label, Whizz Wheels, Model No. 381-A
EX $15 **NM** $20 **MIP** $35

Iso Grifo 7 Litre, 1970-73, metallic blue body, light blue interior, black hood and stripe, clear windshield, black dash, folding seats, chrome bumpers, Whizz Wheels, Model No. 301-B
EX $15 **NM** $18 **MIP** $30

Jaguar 1952 XK120 Rally, 1983, cream body w/black top and trim, red interior, Rally des Alps and #414 decals, Model No. 803-A
EX $8 **NM** $15 **MIP** $25

(KP Photo by Dr. Douglas Sadecky)

Jaguar E Type, 1962-64, maroon or metallic dark gray body, tan interior, red and clear plastic removable hardtop, clear windshield, folded top, spun hubs, shaped wheels, Model No. 307-A
EX $45 **NM** $65 **MIP** $140

Jaguar E Type 2+2, 1968-69, red or blue body and chassis, working hood, doors and hatch, black interior w/folding seats, copper engine, pipes and suspension, spoked wheels, Model No. 335-A
EX $40 **NM** $60 **MIP** $120

Jaguar E Type 2+2, 1970-76, in five versions: red or yellow w/nonworking doors; or w/V-12 engine in yellow body or metallic yellow body, Whizz Wheels, Model No. 374-A
EX $35 **NM** $55 **MIP** $90

Jaguar XJ12C, 1974-79, five different metallic versions, working hood and two doors, clear windows, tow hook, chrome bumpers, grille and headlights, Model No. 286-A
EX $10 **NM** $15 **MIP** $45

Jaguar XJS, 1978-81, metallic burgundy body, tan interior, clear windows, working doors, spoked chrome wheels, Model No. 319-C
EX $10 **NM** $15 **MIP** $25

Jaguar XJS-HE Supercat, 1982-83, black body w/silver stripes and trim, red interior, dark red taillights, light gray antenna, no tow hook, clear windshield, Model No. 314-C
EX $8 **NM** $15 **MIP** $25

Jaguar XK120 Hardtop, 1983, red body, black hardtop, working hood and trunk, detailed engine, cream interior, clear windows, chrome wheels, Model No. 803-B
EX $8 **NM** $15 **MIP** $25

Lamborghini Miura P400, 1970-72, w/red or yellow body, working hood, detailed engine, clear windows, jewel headlights, bull figure, Whizz Wheels, Model No. 342-A
EX $40 **NM** $60 **MIP** $100

Lancia Fulvia Zagato, 1967-69, metallic blue body, metallic green or yellow and black body, light blue interior, working hood and doors, folding seats, amber lights, cast wheels, Model No. 332-A
EX $25 **NM** $35 **MIP** $90

Lancia Fulvia Zagato, 1970-72, orange body, black working hood and interior, Whizz Wheels, Model No. 372-A
EX $15 **NM** $25 **MIP** $40

Lotus Elan S2 Hardtop, 1967-68, cream interior w/folding seats and tan dash, working hood, separate chrome chassis, issued in blue body w/white top or red body w/white top, cast wheels, Model No. 319-A
EX $30 **NM** $45 **MIP** $85

Lotus Elite, 1976-78, red body, white interior, two working doors, clear windshield, black dash, hood panel, grille, bumpers, base and tow hook, Model No. 315-C
EX $15 **NM** $18 **MIP** $35

Lotus Elite 22, 1970-75, dark blue body w/silver trim, Whizz Wheels, Model No. 382-B
EX $15 **NM** $18 **MIP** $35

Marcos 3 Litre, 1970-73, working hood, detailed engine, black interior, Marcos label, Whizz Wheels, issued in orange or metallic blue-green, Model No. 377-A
EX $20 **NM** $30 **MIP** $55

Marcos Mantis, 1971-73, metallic red body, opening doors, cream interior and headlights, silver gray lower body base, bumpers, hood panel, spoked wheels, Model No. 312-B
EX $20 **NM** $35 **MIP** $55

(KP Photo by Dr. Douglas Sadecky)

Marcos Volvo 1800 GT, 1966-69, issued w/either white body w/two green stripes or blue body w/two white stripes, plastic interior w/driver, spoked wheels, rubber tires. The blue version is shown here--the common version is white with racing stripes, Model No. 324-A
EX $25 **NM** $40 **MIP** $85

Mercedes-Benz 300SC Convertible, 1983, black body, black folded top, white interior, folding seat backs, detailed engine, chrome grille and wheels, lights, bumpers, Model No. 806-B
EX $8 **NM** $12 **MIP** $25

Mercedes-Benz 300SC Hardtop, 1983, maroon body, tan top and interior, open hood and trunk, clear windows, folding seat backs, top w/chrome side irons, Model No. 805-B
EX $8 **NM** $15 **MIP** $25

Mercedes-Benz 300SL, 1982, red body and base, tan interior, open hood and two gullwing doors, black dash, detailed engine, clear windows, chrome bumpers, Model No. 802-B
EX $8 **NM** $15 **MIP** $25

Mercedes-Benz 300SL, 1983, silver body, tan interior, black dash, clear windows, open hood and two gullwing doors, detailed engine, chrome bumpers, Model No. 811-B
EX $8 **NM** $15 **MIP** $25

Mercedes-Benz 350SL, 1972-79, white body, spoke wheels or metallic dark blue body solid wheels, pale blue interior, folding seats, detailed engine, Model No. 393-A
EX $15 **NM** $30 **MIP** $60

Mercedes-Benz C-111, 1971-74, orange main body w/black lower and base, black interior, vents, front and rear grilles, silver headlights, red taillights, Whizz Wheels, Model No. 388-A
EX $15 **NM** $20 **MIP** $45

MG Maestro, 1983, yellow body, black trim, opaque black windows, black plastic grille, bumpers, spoiler, trim and battery hatch, clear headlights, AA Service label, Model No. 1009-A
EX $15 **NM** $20 **MIP** $35

MGA, 1957-65, red or metallic green body, cream seats, black dash, clear windshield, silver bumpers, grille and headlights, smooth or shaped wheels, Model No. 302-A
EX $60 **NM** $90 **MIP** $150

MGB GT, 1967-69, dark red body, pale blue interior, opening hatch and two doors, jewel headlights, chrome grille and bumpers, orange taillights, spoked wheels, w/suitcase, Model No. 327-A
EX $50 **NM** $75 **MIP** $110

MGC GT, 1969, bright yellow body and base, black interior, hood and hatch, folding seats, luggage, jewel headlights, red taillights, spoked wheels, Model No. 345-A
EX $50 **NM** $75 **MIP** $135

MGC GT, 1970-73, red body, black hood and base, black interior, opening hatch and two doors, folding seat backs, luggage, orange taillights, Whizz Wheels, Model No. 378-A
EX $50 **NM** $75 **MIP** $125

Mini Camping Set, 1977-78, cream Mini, w/red/blue tent, grille and two figures, Model No. 38-B
EX $25 **NM** $40 **MIP** $75

Mini-Marcos GT850, 1968-70, metallic maroon body, white name and trim decals, cream interior, open hood and doors, clear windows and headlights, Golden Jacks wheels, Model No. 341-A
EX $30 **NM** $45 **MIP** $75

Minissima, 1975-79, cream upper body, metallic lime green lower body w/black stripe centered, black interior, clear windows, headlights, Model No. 288-A
EX $15 **NM** $20 **MIP** $35

Morris Marina 1.8 Coupe, 1971-73, metallic dark red or lime green body, cream interior, working hood and two doors, clear windshield, chrome grille and bumpers, Whizz Wheels, Model No. 306-A
EX $15 **NM** $30 **MIP** $60

Morris Mini-Cooper Deluxe, 1965-68, black body/base, red roof, yellow and black wicker work decals on sides and rear, yellow interior, gray steering wheel, jewel headlights, shaped or cast wheels, Model No. 249-A
EX $45 **NM** $65 **MIP** $140

VEHICLES • CORGI

(KP Photo by Dr. Douglas Sadecky)

Morris Mini-Minor, 1960-71, light blue or red body w/shaped or smooth wheels, plastic interior, silver bumpers, grille and headlights, Model No. 226-A1
EX $40 **NM** $60 **MIP** $125

Morris Mini-Minor, 1960-71, sky blue body w/shaped and/or smooth wheels, plastic interior, silver bumpers, grille and headlights, rare, Model No. 226-A2
EX $100 **NM** $175 **MIP** $350

Morris Mini-Minor, 1972-73, one-piece body in dark or metallic blue or orange body, plastic interior, silver lights, grille and bumpers, red taillights, Whizz Wheels, Model No. 204-B
EX $30 **NM** $45 **MIP** $75

(KP Photo by Dr. Douglas Sadecky)

NSU Sport Prinz, 1963-66, metallic burgundy or maroon body, yellow interior, one-piece body, silver bumpers, headlights and trim, shaped wheels, Model No. 316-A
EX $30 **NM** $45 **MIP** $85

Pontiac Firebird, 1969-72, metallic silver body and base, red interior, black hood, stripes and convertible top, doors open, clear windows, folding seats, Golden Jacks wheels, Model No. 343-A
EX $50 **NM** $75 **MIP** $125

(KP Photo by Dr. Douglas Sadecky)

Pop Art Mini-Mostest, 1969, light red body and base, yellow interior, jewel headlights, orange taillights, yellow-blue-purple pop art and "Mostest" decals; very rare. This rare Mini is one of the Holy Grails of any Corgi collection. Very few of these cars were produced in 1969, possibly due to the fact that psychedelia had already passed its prime, cast wheels. In the U.K. auctions this car is selling for $3,500-$4,000., Model No. 349-A
EX $1000 **NM** $1500 **MIP** $2700

Porsche 917, 1970-76, red or metallic blue body, black or gray base, blue or amber tinted windows and headlights, opening rear hood, headlights, Whizz Wheels, Model No. 385-A
EX $15 **NM** $20 **MIP** $45

Porsche 92 Turbo, 1982, black body w/gold trim, yellow interior, four chrome headlights, clear windshield, taillight-license plate decal, opening doors and hatchback, Model No. 310-B
EX $15 **NM** $20 **MIP** $35

Porsche 924, 1980-81, bright orange body, dark red interior, black plastic grille, multicolored stripes, swivel roof spotlight, Model No. 303-C
EX $10 **NM** $15 **MIP** $25

Porsche Targa 911S, 1970-75, metallic blue, silver-blue or green body, black roof w/or without stripe, orange interior, opening hood and two doors, chrome engine and bumpers, Whizz Wheels, Model No. 382-A
EX $25 **NM** $35 **MIP** $60

Reliant Bond Bug 700 E.S., 1971-74, bright orange or lime green body, off white seats, black trim, silver headlights, red taillights, Bug label, Model No. 389-A
EX $15 **NM** $25 **MIP** $50

Renault 11 GTL, 1983, light tan or maroon body and base, red interior, opening doors and rear hatch, lifting hatch cover, folding seats, grille, Model No. 384-C
EX $15 **NM** $25 **MIP** $40

Talbot-Matra Rancho, 1981-84, red and black, green and black or white and blue body, working tailgate and hatch, clear windows, plastic interior, black bumpers, grille and tow hook, Model No. 457-B
EX $10 **NM** $15 **MIP** $25

Toyota 2000 GT, 1970-72, metallic dark blue or purple one-piece body, cream interior, red gear shift and antenna, two red and two amber taillights, Whizz Wheels, Model No. 375-A
EX $15 **NM** $30 **MIP** $55

Triumph TR2, 1956-59, cream one-piece body w/red seats, light green body w/white or cream seats, clear windshield, silver grille, smooth wheels, Model No. 301-A
EX $70 **NM** $105 **MIP** $175

(KP Photo by Dr. Douglas Sadecky)

Triumph TR3, 1960-62, metallic olive or cream one-piece body, red seats, clear windshield, silver grille, bumpers and headlights, smooth or shaped hubs, Model No. 305-A
EX $60 **NM** $90 **MIP** $150

Volkswagen Polo Turbo, 1982, cream body, red interior w/red and orange trim, working hatch and two door castings, clear windshield, black plastic dash, Model No. 309-B
EX $15 **NM** $18 **MIP** $30

TAXI

Austin London Taxi, 1960-65, black body w/yellow plastic interior, w/or without driver, shaped or smooth hubs, rubber tires, Model No. 418-A1
EX $36 **NM** $55 **MIP** $90

Austin London Taxi, 1978-83, black body w/two working doors, light brown interior, Whizz Wheels, Model No. 425-A
EX $15 **NM** $20 **MIP** $35

Austin London Taxi/Reissue, 1971-74, updated version w/Whizz Wheels, black or maroon body, Model No. 418-A2
EX $15 **NM** $20 **MIP** $35

Chevrolet Caprice Taxi, 1979-81, orange body w/red interior, white roof sign, Taxi and TWA decals, Model No. 327-B
EX $20 **NM** $30 **MIP** $50

Chevrolet Impala Taxi, 1960-65, light orange body, base w/hexagonal panel under rear axle and smooth wheels, or two raised lines and shaped wheels, one-piece body, clear windows, plastic interior, silver grille, headlights and bumpers; smooth or shaped spun wheels w/rubber tires, Model No. 221-A
EX $50 **NM** $75 **MIP** $150

(KP Photo by Dr. Douglas Sadecky)

Chevrolet Impala Yellow Cab, 1965-67, red lower body, yellow upper, red interior w/driver, white roof sign, red decals, shaped wheels, Model No. 480-A
EX $80 **NM** $120 **MIP** $200

Ford Sierra Taxi, 1983, cream body, Model No. 451-A
EX $8 **NM** $15 **MIP** $20

Mercedes-Benz 240D Taxi, 1975-80, orange body, orange interior, black roof sign w/red and white Taxi labels, black on door, Model No. 411-B
EX $15 **NM** $18 **MIP** $30

Peugeot 505 STI, 1981-82, red body and base, red interior, blue-red-white Taxi labels, black grille, bumpers, tow hook, chrome headlights and wheels, opening doors, Model No. 373-B
EX $8 **NM** $15 **MIP** $25

Peugeot 505 Taxi, 1983, cream body, red interior, red, white and blue taxi decals, Model No. 450-B
EX $8 **NM** $15 **MIP** $25

Thunderbird Bermuda Taxi, 1962-65, white body w/blue, yellow or green plastic canopy w/red fringe, yellow interior, driver, yellow and black labels, shaped wheels, Model No. 430-A
EX $50 **NM** $75 **MIP** $145

TRAILER

Dropside Trailer, 1957-65, cream body, red chassis in five versions: smooth wheels 1957-61; shaped wheels, 1962-1965; white body, cream or blue chassis; or silver gray body, blue chassis, each, Model No. 100-A
EX $10 **NM** $21 **MIP** $45

Pennyburn Workmen's Trailer, 1968-69, blue body w/working lids, red plastic interior, three plastic tools, cast wheels, plastic tires, Model No. 109-A
EX $15 **NM** $35 **MIP** $50

(KP Photo by Dr. Douglas Sadecky)

Platform Trailer, 1958-64, in five versions: silver body, blue chassis; silver body, yellow chassis; blue body, red chassis; blue body, yellow chassis, smooth or shaped wheels, Model No. 101-A
EX $10 **NM** $20 **MIP** $45

VANS

(KP Photo by Dr. Douglas Sadecky)

Austin Mini Van, 1964-67, metallic deep green body w/two working rear doors, clear windows, shaped wheels, Model No. 450-A
EX $40 **NM** $60 **MIP** $100

(KP Photo by Dr. Douglas Sadecky)

Bedford AA Road Service Van, 1957-62, dark yellow body in two versions: first version with divided windshield, 1957-59 shown; single windshield, 1960-62; smooth wheels, Model No. 408-A
EX $50 **NM** $75 **MIP** $145

(KP Photo by Dr. Douglas Sadecky)

Bedford Corgi Toys Van, 1960-62, Corgi Toys decals, w/either yellow body/blue roof or blue body/yellow roof, smooth or shaped wheels, Model No. 422-A2
EX $60 **NM** $105 **MIP** $275

Bedford Corgi Toys Van, 1962, yellow upper/blue lower body, Corgi Toy decals, rare, Model No. 422-A1
EX $100 **NM** $225 **MIP** $400

Bedford Daily Express Van, 1956-59, dark blue body w/white Daily Express decals, divided windshield, smooth wheels, rubber tires, Model No. 403-A
EX $60 **NM** $90 **MIP** $150

(KP Photo by Dr. Douglas Sadecky)

Bedford Dormobile, 1956-62, two versions and several colors: divided windshield w/cream, green or metallic maroon body; or single windshield w/yellow body/blue roof w/shaped or smooth wheels. Pictured here; the 404-A on the left and the 404M on the right with a mechanical friction motor, Model No. 404-A
EX $50 **NM** $75 **MIP** $135

Bedford Dormobile-Mechanical, 1956-59, friction motor, dark metallic red or turquoise body, smooth wheels, Model No. 404M
EX $60 **NM** $90 **MIP** $180

(KP Photo by Dr. Douglas Sadecky)

Bedford Evening Standard Van, 1960-62, black body/silver roof or black lower body/silver upper body and roof, Evening Standard decals, smooth wheels, Model No. 421-A
EX $55 **NM** $80 **MIP** $135

Bedford KLG Van-Mechanical, 1956-59, w/friction motor, red body w/KLG Spark Plugs decals, smooth hubs, Model No. 403M
EX $70 **NM** $125 **MIP** $285

Chevrolet Coca-Cola Van, 1978-80, red body, white trim, w/Coca Cola logos, Model No. 437-B
EX $15 **NM** $20 **MIP** $35

Chevrolet Rough Rider Van, 1977-78, yellow body w/working rear doors, cream interior, amber windows, Rough Rider decals, Model No. 423-B
EX $15 **NM** $18 **MIP** $30

Chevrolet Vantastic Van, 1977-80, off white body w/Vantastic decals, Model No. 431-B
EX $10 **NM** $15 **MIP** $25

Chevrolet Vantastic Van, 1977-80, black body w/Vantastic decals, Model No. 432-A
EX $10 **NM** $15 **MIP** $25

Commer 3/4-Ton Milk Float, 1964-65, white cab w/light blue body, shaped wheels, Model No. 466-A1
EX $32 **NM** $48 **MIP** $85

Commer 3/4-Ton Milk Float, 1970, white cab w/light blue body, w/CO-OP decals, cast wheels, Model No. 466-A2
EX $40 **NM** $80 **MIP** $160

Commer 3/4-Ton Van, 1970-71, either dark blue body with green roof and Hammonds decals (1971) or white body with light blue roof and CO-OP labels (1970), both w/cast wheels w/plastic tires, Model No. 462-A
EX $45 **NM** $90 **MIP** $200

Commer Holiday Mini Bus, 1968-69, white upper body w/orange lower body, white interior, clear windshield, silver bumpers, grille and headlights, Holiday Camp Special decal, roof rack, two working rear doors. With bathing suits packed in the roof luggage, a trip to the shore was inevitable in this mod van, shaped wheels, Model No. 508-A
EX $30 **NM** $75 **MIP** $140

(KP Photo by Dr. Douglas Sadecky)

Commer Mobile Camera Van, 1967-72, metallic blue lower body and roof rack, white upper body, two working rear doors, black camera on gold tripod, cameraman, shaped or cast wheels, Model No. 479-A
EX $60 **NM** $105 **MIP** $225

(KP Photo by Dr. Douglas Sadecky)

Ford Thames Airborne Caravan, 1962-67, various color versions of body and plastic interior w/table, white blinds, silver bumpers, grille and headlights, two doors, shaped wheels, Model No. 420-A
EX $35 **NM** $55 **MIP** $100

(KP Photo by Dr. Douglas Sadecky)

Ford Thames Wall's Ice Cream Van, 1965-68, light blue body, cream pillar, chimes, chrome bumpers and grille, no figures. This wonderful toy played the Wall's Ice Cream musical tune by turning the hand crank on the rear of the van, shaped wheels, Model No. 474-A
EX $55 **NM** $110 **MIP** $265

Ford Wall's Ice Cream Van, 1965-67, light blue body, dark cream pillars, plastic striped rear canopy, white interior, silver bumpers, grille and headlights. A sidewalk/street display plus a salesman and small boy dress up this non-musical version of the van, shaped wheels, Model No. 447-A
EX $80 **NM** $160 **MIP** $350

Karrier Bantam Two Ton Van, 1957-60, blue body, red chassis and bed, clear windows, smooth wheels, rubber tires, Model No. 455-A
EX $35 **NM** $55 **MIP** $100

(KP Photo by Dr. Douglas Sadecky)

Karrier Butcher Shop, 1960-64, white body, blue roof, butcher shop interior, Home Service labels, in two versions: w/or without suspension, smooth hubs. Note the meat hanging in the side windows, Model No. 413-A
EX $65 **NM** $100 **MIP** $165

(KP Photo by Dr. Douglas Sadecky)

Karrier Dairy Van, 1962-64, light blue body w/Drive Safely on Milk decals, white roof, w/either smooth or shaped wheels, Model No. 435-A
EX $50 **NM** $75 **MIP** $145

(KP Photo by Dr. Douglas Sadecky)

Karrier Lucozade Van, 1958-62, yellow body w/gray rear door, Lucozade decals, rubber tires, w/either smooth or shaped wheels, Model No. 411-A
EX $70 **NM** $120 **MIP** $245

(KP Photo by Dr. Douglas Sadecky)

Karrier Mister Softee Ice Cream Van, 1963-66, cream upper, blue lower body and interior, clear windows, sliding side windows, Mister Softee decals, figure inside, shaped wheels, Model No. 428-A
EX $90 **NM** $165 **MIP** $295

(KP Photo by Dr. Douglas Sadecky)

Karrier Mobile Canteen, 1965-66, blue body, white interior, amber windows, roof knob rotates figure, working side panel counter, Joe's Diner label. In this photo, the model on the left has the common "Joe's Diner" label, while the van on the right (471-A2) features the rare Belgian-issued "patates frites" label, shaped wheels, Model No. 471-A1
EX $60 **NM** $90 **MIP** $150

Karrier Mobile Canteen, 1965-66, blue body, white interior, amber windows, roof knob rotates figure, working side panel counter, Patates Frites label, Belgium issue, shaped wheels, Model No. 471-A2
EX $90 **NM** $150 **MIP** $325

Karrier Mobile Grocery, 1957-61, light green body, grocery store interior, red/white Home Service labels, smooth hubs, rubber tires, Model No. 407-A
EX $70 **NM** $110 **MIP** $185

Radio Roadshow Van, 1982, white body, red plastic roof and rear interior, opaque black windows, red-white-black Radio Tele Luxembourg labels, gray plastic loudspeakers and working radio in van, Model No. 1006-A
EX $25 **NM** $35 **MIP** $60

Security Van, 1976-79, black body, blue mesh windows and dome light, yellow/black Security labels, Whizz Wheels, Model No. 424-B
EX $7 **NM** $15 **MIP** $25

Volkswagen Delivery Van, 1962-64, white upper and red lower body, plastic red or yellow interior, silver bumpers and headlights, red VW emblem, shaped wheels, Model No. 433-A
EX $55 **NM** $85 **MIP** $140

Volkswagen Kombi Bus, 1962-66, off-green upper and olive green lower body, red interior, silver bumpers and headlights, red VW emblem, shaped wheels, Model No. 434-A
EX $50 **NM** $75 **MIP** $125

(KP Photo by Dr. Douglas Sadecky)

Volkswagen Tobler Van, 1963-67, light blue body, plastic interior, silver bumpers, Trans-o-lite headlights and roof panel, shaped wheels, rubber tires, Model No. 441-A
EX $55 **NM** $85 **MIP** $145

DELUXE READING

Crusader 101, 30" long; red plastic open convertible, chrome grille and accents, brown plastic driver, battery-operated remote control; 1964
EX $32 **NM** $63 **MIP** $100

Johnny Express Cargo Kit, cargo load for Johnny Express trucks, including four pallets, three barrels, one large crate, two mid-sized crates and eight small crates; 1965 and later
EX $4 **NM** $8 **MIP** $12

Johnny Express Conveyor, 17" long, 11" high; red conveyor-loader, hand-cranked belt, four wheels, for use with Johnny Express tractor-trailers; 1965 and later
EX $6 **NM** $12 **MIP** $18

Johnny Express Crane, 15" long, 9" high; yellow plastic boom, hand-crank action, sold individually or with Johnny Express Tractor Trailer; 1965-69
EX $6 **NM** $12 **MIP** $18

Johnny Express Dump Body, 24" long; dumping trailer to go on Johnny Express Tractor Trailer; 1965 and later
EX $25 **NM** $35 **MIP** $45

Johnny Express Fork Lift, 9" long, 7" high; red plastic, sold individually or with larger trucks; 1965 and later
EX $5 **NM** $9 **MIP** $14

Johnny Express Liquid Tanker, 26" long; tanker body, yellow plastic, for Johnny Express Tractor Trailer, with open top and valve underneath; 1965 and later
EX $35 **NM** $65 **MIP** $75

Johnny Express Pipe Kit, pipe load for Johnny Express Tractor Trailer; 1965 and later
EX $5 **NM** $9 **MIP** $14

Johnny Express Reefer Van, 24" long; van body with sliding door, yellow plastic, for Johnny express Tractor Trailer; 1965 and later
EX $18 **NM** $36 **MIP** $55

Johnny Express Tire Kit, set including spare tire, working jack, lug wrench, and tire rack for mounting on the Johnny Express Tractor Trailer; 1965 and later
EX $13 **NM** $26 **MIP** $40

Johnny Express Tractor & Trailer Combination, 33" long; motorized red cabover with yellow bumpers, black tires, gray wheel hubs, and yellow flat-bed trailer; 1965-69
EX $95 **NM** $152 **MIP** $230

Johnny Express Trooper Carrier, 24" long; trooper carrier with swiveling gun turret, canvas canopy; 1966-67
EX $18 **NM** $36 **MIP** $55

Johnny Seven Armored Battalion, No. 3018; includes Halftrack, Jeep, Cannon, Ammunition Trailer and six white plastic figures, originally in box 22" across; 1964-65
EX $32 **NM** $63 **MIP** $95

Johnny Seven Fire Brigade, No. 3034; includes Chief Car, Pumper Truck, Hook and Ladder Truck, and seven plastic firefighter figures, originally in box 24" across; 1964-65
EX $28 **NM** $56 **MIP** $85

Johnny Seven Service Station, No. 3042; includes Tow Truck, car with replaceable fender, Service Island, and four plastic service attendant figures, originally in box 31-1/8" across; 1964-65
EX $15 **NM** $36 **MIP** $45

Johnny Seven Speed Set, No. 3050; red sports car, boat trailer and white speedboat, originally in box 31-5/8" across; 1964-65
EX $15 **NM** $30 **MIP** $45

Johnny Seven Task Force, boat set with PT 109 gun boat with rocket launcher, 12" long, D-109 Destroyer, U.S. Navy Target Float, 10 figures; 1960s
EX $50 **NM** $100 **MIP** $150

Johnny Speed, red plastic remote-control Corvette-type racer, with white plastic driver, 22" long; 1968-69
EX $18 **NM** $36 **MIP** $55

PT-109, PT boat w/firing missile, 1963
EX $17 **NM** $25 **MIP** $55

Tiger Joe, 3' long; remote-control plastic tank, three shells, rotating turret; 1965
EX $50 **NM** $100 **MIP** $150

USA Battlewagon, battery-operated battleship w/missiles, torpedos, landing craft, jet airplane, personnel, 1960s
EX $50 **NM** $100 **MIP** $250

DINKY

AIRCRAFT

A.W. Ensign, 1940, camouflaged, dark variation, Model No. 68a
EX $150 **NM** $300 **MIP** $475

A.W. Ensign, 1945-49, A.W. Airliner, silver, G-ADSV, Model No. 62P
EX $65 **NM** $145 **MIP** $175

A.W. Ensign, 1945-49, forty-seat airliner, olive/dark green, G-AZCA, Model No. 62x
EX $95 **NM** $275 **MIP** $350

Airspeed Envoy, 1938-40, King's Aeroplane, red, blue, and silver, G-AEXX, Model No. 62k
EX $80 **NM** $200 **MIP** $325

Airspeed Envoy, 1938-41, silver, G-ACVI, Model No. 62m
EX $55 **NM** $175 **MIP** $250

Airspeed Envoy, 1945-49, light transport, red, G-ATMH, Model No. 62m
EX $50 **NM** $125 **MIP** $200

Amiot 370, 1939-48, Model No. 64a
EX $70 **NM** $130 **MIP** $200

Arc-en-Ciel, 1935-40, Model No. 60a
EX $200 **NM** $375 **MIP** $450

Armstrong Whitworth Ensign, 1938-41, silver, G-ADSR, Model No. 62p
EX $90 **NM** $175 **MIP** $250

Atalanta, 1940, camouflaged, dark variation, Model No. 66a
EX $200 **NM** $450 **MIP** $650

Atalanta (Imperial Airways Liner), 1934-41, gold, G-ABTI, Model No. 60a
EX $150 **NM** $375 **MIP** $500

Autogyro, 1934-41, gold, blue rotor, w/pilot, Model No. 60f
EX $90 **NM** $180 **MIP** $250

Autogyro, 1940, Army cooperation, silver, RAF roundels, Model No. 66f
EX $125 **NM** $250 **MIP** $365

Avro Vulcan Delta Wing Bomber, 1955-56, rare, Model No. 749/992
EX $800 **NM** $1500 **MIP** $4500

Avro York, 1946-59, silver, G-AGJC, Model No. 70a/704
EX $45 **NM** $155 **MIP** $200

Beechcraft C55 Baron, 1968-76, red or white w/yellow props, N555C, Model No. 715
EX $25 **NM** $60 **MIP** $90

Beechcraft S35 Bonanza, 1965-76, orange and yellow, Model No. 710
EX $20 **NM** $55 **MIP** $80

Beechcraft T42A, 1972-77, Model No. 712
EX $30 **NM** $75 **MIP** $110

Bell 47 Police Helicopter, 1974-80, orange and blue, pilot figure, Model No. 732
EX $15 **NM** $30 **MIP** $55

Bloch 220, 1939-48, Model No. 64b
EX $75 **NM** $150 **MIP** $250

Boeing 737, 1970-75, white, Model No. 717
EX $25 **NM** $50 **MIP** $95

Boeing Flying Fortress, 1939-41, silver, USAAC stars on wings, Model No. 62g
EX $100 **NM** $200 **MIP** $300

Boeing Flying Fortress, 1945-48, "Long Range Bomber" under wings, Model No. 62g
EX $70 **NM** $135 **MIP** $225

Breguet Corsair, 1935-40, red and green, Model No. 60d
EX $100 **NM** $200 **MIP** $325

Bristol 173 Helicopter, 1956-63, turquoise, red rotors, G-AUXR, Model No. 715
EX $40 **NM** $70 **MIP** $105

Bristol Blenheim, 1940-41, silver, roundels w/outer yellow ring, Model No. 62b/62d
EX $60 **NM** $140 **MIP** $175

Bristol Blenheim, 1945-48, medium bomber; silver, red, and blue roundels, Model No. 62B
EX $35 **NM** $95 **MIP** $150

Bristol Blenheim, 1946-49, Model No. 62B
EX $60 **NM** $85 **MIP** $160

(KP Photo by Dr. Douglas Sadecky)

Bristol Brittania, 1959-65, silver, blue line, CF-CZA. Canadian Pacific shown, Model No. 998
EX $50 **NM** $250 **MIP** $500

(KP Photo by Dr. Douglas Sadecky)

Caravelle S.E. 210, 1959-62, Model No. 60f/891
EX $45 **NM** $170 **MIP** $230

Cierva Autogyro, 1935-40, Model No. 60f
EX $100 **NM** $250 **MIP** $250

Clipper III Flying Boat, 1938-41, silver, NC16736, Model No. 60w
EX $150 **NM** $250 **MIP** $400

Clipper III Flying Boat, 1945-49, silver, no registration, Model No. 60w
EX $75 **NM** $175 **MIP** $250

D.H. Albatross, 1939-41, Frobisher Class Liner, silver, G-AFDI, Model No. 62w
EX $75 **NM** $275 **MIP** $400

D.H. Albatross, 1939-41, silver, G-AEVV, Model No. 62r
EX $75 **NM** $275 **MIP** $400

D.H. Albatross, 1940, camouflaged, dark variation, Model No. 68b
EX $150 **NM** $300 **MIP** $450

D.H. Albatross, 1945-49, four-engine liner; gray, G-ATPV, Model No. 62R
EX $75 **NM** $170 **MIP** $250

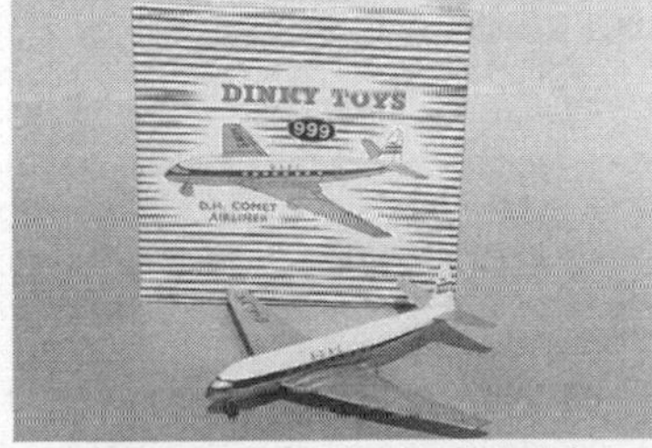

(KP Photo by Dr. Douglas Sadecky)

D.H. Comet Airliner, 1954-65, silver wings, G-ALYX, wingspan 7-1/8", Model No. 702/999
EX $45 **NM** $105 **MIP** $225

D.H. Comet Racer, 1935-40, silver, G-ACSR, Model No. 60g
EX $60 **NM** $125 **MIP** $225

D.H. Comet Racer, 1946-49, yellow, G-RACE, Model No. 60g
EX $50 **NM** $110 **MIP** $155

D.H. Sea Vixen, 1960-65, gray, white undersides, Model No. 738
EX $30 **NM** $65 **MIP** $110

Dewoitine 500, 1935-40, white w/red accents, single prop, Model No. 60e
EX $100 **NM** $200 **MIP** $300

Dewoitine D338, 1937-46, Model No. 61a/64
EX $225 **NM** $350 **MIP** $500

Douglas DC3, 1938-41, silver, PH-ALI, Model No. 60t
EX $125 **NM** $300 **MIP** $650

Empire Flying Boat, 1937-41, MAIA, silver, G-AVKW, Model No. 700
EX $150 **NM** $275 **MIP** $350

Empire Flying Boat, 1937-41, silver, G-ADUV, solid front to hull, Model No. 60r
EX $150 **NM** $325 **MIP** $450

Empire Flying Boat, 1938-40, Atlantic Flying Boat, blue, cream wings, G-AZBP, Model No. 60x
EX $350 **NM** $600 **MIP** $1000

Empire Flying Boat, 1945-49, silver, G-ADUV, hollowed out front to hull, Model No. 60r
EX $90 **NM** $175 **MIP** $250

Fairy Battle, 1937-41, camouflaged, one roundel, light variation, Model No. 60s
EX $50 **NM** $125 **MIP** $200

Fairy Battle, 1937-41, silver, "Fairy Battle Bomber" under wing, Model No. 60n
EX $40 **NM** $100 **MIP** $140

General Monospar, 1934-41, silver, blue wing tips, Model No. 60e
EX $75 **NM** $225 **MIP** $300

General Monospar, 1940, camouflaged, dark, Model No. 66e
EX $90 **NM** $300 **MIP** $350

Gloster Gladiator, 1937-40, silver, RAF roundels, no words under wing, Model No. 60p
EX $90 **NM** $175 **MIP** $275

Gloster Javelin, 1956-65, green/gray camouflage, wingspan, 3-1/4", Model No. 735
EX $15 **NM** $50 **MIP** $90

Gloster Meteor, 1946-62, silver, RAF roundels, Model No. 70e/732
EX $10 **NM** $25 **MIP** $60

Hanriot 180M, 1937-40, Model No. 61e
EX $90 **NM** $150 **MIP** $225

Hawker Harrier, 1970-80, Model No. 722
EX $25 **NM** $65 **MIP** $95

Hawker Hunter, 1955-63, green/gray camouflage, Model No. 736
EX $15 **NM** $45 **MIP** $85

Hawker Hurricane, 1939-41, silver, no undercarriage, Model No. 62h
EX $30 **NM** $70 **MIP** $115

Hawker Hurricane, 1945-49, three-blade prop; red, white, and blue roundels, Model No. 62S
EX $40 **NM** $95 **MIP** $130

Hawker Hurricane IIc, 1972-75, Model No. 718
EX $50 **NM** $95 **MIP** $155

Hawker Siddeley HS 125, 1970-75, working landing gear, Model No. 723/728
EX $25 **NM** $50 **MIP** $80

Hawker Tempest II, 1946-55, silver, RAF roundels, flat spinner, Model No. 70b/730
EX $15 **NM** $45 **MIP** $80

Henriot 180T, 1935-40, Model No. 60c
EX $110 **NM** $170 **MIP** $225

Junkers JU87B Stuka, 1969-80, gray w/yellow nose, gray propeller, detachable bomb, Model No. 721
EX $50 **NM** $85 **MIP** $175

Junkers JU89, 1938-41, high speed monoplane, green/dark green, D-AZBK, Model No. 62y
EX $100 **NM** $275 **MIP** $350

Junkers JU89, 1945-49, high speed monoplane, silver, G-ATBK, Model No. 62Y
EX $70 **NM** $160 **MIP** $225

Junkers JU89 Heavy Bomber, 1941, black, German cross, Model No. 67a
EX $100 **NM** $400 **MIP** $600

Junkers JU90 Airliner, 1938-40, silver, D-AIVI, Model No. 62n
EX $90 **NM** $250 **MIP** $325

Leopard Moth, 1934-41, light green, G-ACPT, Model No. 60b
EX $50 **NM** $140 **MIP** $180

Leopard Moth, 1940, camouflaged, dark, Model No. 66b
EX $70 **NM** $225 **MIP** $300

Lockheed P-80 Shooting Star, 1947-62, silver, USAF stars, Model No. 701/733
EX $10 **NM** $20 **MIP** $40

M.D. F-4 Phantom, 1972-77, Model No. 725/727/73
EX $70 **NM** $125 **MIP** $175

Mayo Composite, 1939-41, Model No. 63
EX $200 **NM** $450 **MIP** $750

ME Bl 109, 1972-76, motorized, Model No. 726
EX $50 **NM** $100 **MIP** $175

Mercury Seaplane, 1939-41, silver, G-ADHJ, Model No. 63b
EX $50 **NM** $100 **MIP** $175

Mercury Seaplane, 1949-57, silver, G-AVKW, Model No. 700
EX $40 **NM** $80 **MIP** $120

Mitsubishi A65M Zero, 1975-78, motorized, Model No. 739
EX $75 **NM** $150 **MIP** $225

MRCA Tornado, 1974-76, "Multi-Role Combat Aircraft", camoflauged, Model No. 729
EX $35 **NM** $90 **MIP** $155

Mystere IV, 1957-63, silver, gold wings, Model No. 60a/800
EX $30 **NM** $75 **MIP** $110

Nord Noratlas, 1960-64, Model No. 804
EX $125 **NM** $250 **MIP** $400

P1B Lightning, 1959-69, silver, RAF roundels, Model No. 737
EX $20 **NM** $55 **MIP** $100

Percival Gull, 1934-41, white, blue wing tips, Model No. 60c
EX $70 **NM** $150 **MIP** $225

Percival Gull, 1940, camouflaged, dark, Model No. 66c
EX $100 **NM** $225 **MIP** $275

Percival Gull, 1945-48, Light Tourer, light green, Model No. 66c
EX $65 **NM** $125 **MIP** $150

Potez 56, 1937-40, Model No. 61b
EX $125 **NM** $200 **MIP** $270

Potez 58, 1935-40, Model No. 60b/61d
EX $100 **NM** $260 **MIP** $350

Potez 58 Sanitaire, 1937-40, silver, red propeller, Model No. 61d
EX $110 **NM** $175 **MIP** $250

Potez 63, 1939-48, Model No. 64c
EX $150 **NM** $250 **MIP** $400

Potez 662, 1939-40, Model No. 64d
EX $125 **NM** $250 **MIP** $400

Republic P47 Thunderbolt, 1975-78, motorized, silver, Model No. 734
EX $75 **NM** $175 **MIP** $250

S.E. Caravelle Airliner, 1962-69, Air France, F-BGNY, starboard wing, Model No. 997
EX $70 **NM** $150 **MIP** $250

Sea King Helicopter, 1971-79, motorized, Model No. 724/736
EX $30 **NM** $60 **MIP** $100

SEPCAT Jaguar, 1973-76, Model No. 731
EX $25 **NM** $70 **MIP** $115

Short Shetland Flying Boat, 1947-49, silver, G-AGVD, Model No. 701
EX $200 **NM** $550 **MIP** $750

Sikorsky S58 Helicopter, 1957-61, Model No. 60d/802
EX $45 **NM** $135 **MIP** $190

Singapore Flying Boat, 1936-41, silver, RAF roundels, Model No. 60h
EX $100 **NM** $300 **MIP** $400

Singapore Flying Boat, 1936-41, four-engine, silver, G-EUTG, Model No. 60m
EX $125 **NM** $400 **MIP** $550

Spitfire, 1940-41, silver, small canopy, roundels red, white, and blue, Model No. 62e/62a
EX $35 **NM** $150 **MIP** $200

Spitfire, 1945-49, silver, large canopy, roundels red, white, and blue, Model No. 62A
EX $30 **NM** $75 **MIP** $125

Spitfire II, 1979, chrome, Model No. 700
EX $65 **NM** $165 **MIP** $250

Spitfire Mk II, 1978-80, non-motorized, tan/green camouflage, Model No. 741
EX $40 **NM** $80 **MIP** $135

(KP Photo by Dr. Douglas Sadecky)

Super G Constellation Lockheed, 1956-63, Wingspan, 7-3/4", Model No. 60c/892
EX $90 **NM** $200 **MIP** $450

Supermarine Spitfire II, 1969-78, motorized, Model No. 719
EX $60 **NM** $95 **MIP** $175

Supermarine Swift, 1955-63, green/gray camouflage, Model No. 734
EX $10 **NM** $45 **MIP** $85

Trident Star Fighter, 1970s, French-made, w/firing Stellar missile, Model No. 362
EX $15 **NM** $30 **MIP** $60

Trident Starfighter, Model No. 285
EX $30 **NM** $55 **MIP** $75

Twin Engined Fighter, 1946-55, silver, no registration, Model No. 70d/731
EX $10 **NM** $25 **MIP** $35

Vautour, 1957-63, Model No. 60b/801
EX $30 **NM** $80 **MIP** $125

Vickers Jockey, 1934-41, red, cream wing tips, Model No. 60d
EX $75 **NM** $110 **MIP** $150

Vickers Jockey, 1940, camouflaged, dark, Model No. 66d
EX $75 **NM** $175 **MIP** $225

Vickers Viking, 1947-63, silver, G-AGOL, flat spinners, Model No. 70c/705
EX $20 **NM** $45 **MIP** $70

(KP Photo by Dr. Douglas Sadecky)

Vickers Viscount, 1956-65, British European Airways, G-AOJA, wingspan 5-7/8", Model No. 708
EX $40 **NM** $125 **MIP** $225

Vickers Viscount, 1956-65, Air France, F-BGNL, Model No. 708
EX $40 **NM** $125 **MIP** $225

Viscount, 1957-60, Model No. 60e/803
EX $75 **NM** $125 **MIP** $175

Vulcan Bomber, 1955-56, silver, RAF roundels, rare, Model No. 749/707/99
EX $500 **NM** $1500 **MIP** $4000

Westland Sikorsky Helicopter, 1957-63, red/cream, G-ATWX, Model No. 716
EX $30 **NM** $75 **MIP** $125

Whitley Bomber, 1937-41, silver, RAF roundels, Model No. 60v
EX $95 **NM** $150 **MIP** $225

Whitley Bomber, 1937-41, camouflaged, light variation, Model No. 62t
EX $135 **NM** $350 **MIP** $500

BUSES AND TAXIS

Austin Taxi with Driver, 1951-62, pictured here with Robot Traffic Signal, 773 (which is 2-3/4" H and approx. $35 MIP), Model No. 40H/254
EX $70 **NM** $145 **MIP** $225

Austin/London Taxi, 1972-79, Model No. 284
EX $25 **NM** $35 **MIP** $75

Autobus Parisien, 1948-51, Model No. F29D
EX $80 **NM** $135 **MIP** $200

Autocar Chausson, 1956-60, Model No. F29F/571
EX $70 **NM** $120 **MIP** $200

B.O.A.C. Coach, 1956-63, Dark blue and white with "BOAC" lettering and symbol in yellow, Model No. 283
EX $55 **NM** $80 **MIP** $125

Continental Touring Coach, 1963-66, Model No. 953
EX $135 **NM** $200 **MIP** $400

Ford Vedette Taxi, 1956-59, Model No. F24XT
EX $60 **NM** $95 **MIP** $150

Observation Coach, 1954-60, Model No. 29F/280
EX $50 **NM** $75 **MIP** $125

Peugeot 404 Taxi, 1967-71, Model No. F1400
EX $50 **NM** $75 **MIP** $100

Plymouth Plaza Taxi, 1960-67, Model No. 266
EX $65 **NM** $100 **MIP** $155

(D. Klein Photo)

Plymouth USA Taxi, 1970s, Model No. 265
EX $15 NM $70 MIP $140

Routemaster Bus, 1964-80, Tern Shirts, Model No. 289
EX $75 NM $100 MIP $150

Silver Jubilee Bus, 1977, Model No. 297
EX $25 NM $35 MIP $70

CARS

Alfa Romeo Racing Car, 1954-64, open Grand Prix race car, white driver, red body, "8" on side, Model No. 23P/232
EX $40 NM $85 MIP $155

Armstrong Siddeley, 1937-40, blue or brown, Model No. 36A
EX $85 NM $130 MIP $225

Aston Martin DB3S, 1956-59, green or gray body, white driver, Model No. 104
EX $60 NM $120 MIP $180

Aston Martin DB5, Model No. 110
EX $25 NM $60 MIP $135

Austin 1800 Taxi, Model No. 282
EX $35 NM $70 MIP $100

Austin A105 Saloon, 1958-63, 4-door sedan, two-tone, Model No. 176
EX $75 NM $150 MIP $250

Austin Atlantic Convertible, 1954-58, blue, Model No. 106/140A
EX $70 NM $145 MIP $225

Austin Healey "100", 1956-59, Model No. 109
EX $30 NM $70 MIP $140

Austin Mini-Moke, 1967-75, Model No. 342
EX $20 NM $35 MIP $60

Austin Somerset, 1954-60, 4-door sedan, no interior, Model No. 161
EX $50 NM $100 MIP $150

Austin Somerset Saloon, 1954-60, red and yellow body, Model No. 161
EX $150 NM $325 MIP $550

Beach Buggy, Model No. 227
EX $5 NM $20 MIP $40

Big Cat Jaguar, Model No. 219
EX $5 NM $12 MIP $40

Bristol 450, 1956-60, racing car, green, #27 door decals, black tires, Model No. 163
EX $50 NM $100 MIP $165

Buick Roadmaster, French Dinky, Model No. 545
EX $70 NM $130 MIP $200

Cabriolet 404 Peugeot Pininfarina, Model No. 528
EX $25 NM $100 MIP $200

Cadillac 1962, 1962-69, blue, red interior, white tires, Model No. 147
EX $50 NM $95 MIP $150

Cadillac Eldorado, 1956-62, Model No. 131
EX $60 NM $95 MIP $145

Chrysler Airflow, 1935-40, Model No. 32/30A
EX $130 NM $250 MIP $450

Chrysler Royal Saloon, note that some colors are worth more than values shown, Model No. 39e
EX $45 NM $150 MIP $300

Chrysler Saratoga, 1961-66, Model No. F550
EX $70 NM $100 MIP $190

Chrysler Simca 1308/GT, Model No. 11542
EX $25 NM $60 MIP $120

Citroen 2 CV, 1950, 1952-59, 1959-63, Model No. F535/24T
EX $50 NM $100 MIP $150

Citroen DS-19, 1959-68, Model No. F522/24C
EX $60 NM $90 MIP $135

Cooper-Bristol Racer, 1954-64, open cockpit, driver, green body, Model No. 233
EX $40 NM $90 MIP $175

Corvette Stingray, Model No. 221
EX $10 NM $25 MIP $60

Cunningham C-5R Racer, Model No. 133
EX $20 NM $50 MIP $130

Custom Land Rover, Model No. 202
EX $5 NM $15 MIP $60

Custom Stingray, Model No. 206
EX $5 NM $15 MIP $60

Customized Freeway Cruiser, Model No. 390
EX $5 NM $15 MIP $40

Customized Range Rover, Model No. 203
EX $5 NM $15 MIP $40

De Tomaso-Mangusta, Model No. 137
EX $5 NM $10 MIP $40

DeSoto Diplomat, 1960-63, orange, Model No. F545
EX $25 NM $85 MIP $160

DeSoto Diplomat, 1960-63, green, Model No. F545
EX $70 NM $130 MIP $200

DeSoto Fireflite Sedan, 1958-63, 4-door sedan; gray, green, or blue body, Model No. 192
EX $50 NM $105 MIP $175

Dodge Royal Sedan, 1959-64, available in various color schemes, Model No. 191
EX $80 NM $120 MIP $160

Estate Car, 1954-61, Model No. 27D/344
EX $45 NM $70 MIP $115

Ferrari Racer, Model No. 242
EX $15 NM $30 MIP $65

Fiat 1800 Familiale, 1960-63, silver/gray station wagon, red interior, Model No. 548
EX $45 NM $90 MIP $160

Ford Capri, 1969-74, Model No. 165
EX $40 NM $90 MIP $130

Ford Consul Corsair, 1963-69, 4-door sedan, white interior, black tires, Model No. 130
EX $50 NM $100 MIP $150

Ford Cortina Rally Car, 1967-69, Model No. 212
EX $35 NM $55 MIP $75

Ford Escort, Model No. 168
EX $30 NM $60 MIP $120

Ford Fairlane, Model No. 149
EX $25 NM $50 MIP $125

Ford Fairlane, 1962-66, pale green, Model No. 148
EX $60 NM $120 MIP $200

Ford Fairlane, 1962-66, South African issue, bright blue, Model No. 148
EX $150 NM $300 MIP $700

Ford Fordor Sedan, 1954-59, 4-door sedan, pink and blue color combination rare, Model No. 170
EX $100 NM $200 MIP $300

Ford GT, 1966-74, white race car, Model No. 215
EX $20 NM $40 MIP $65

Ford Thunderbird, South African Issue, blue, Model No. F565
EX $120 NM $250 MIP $600

Ford Thunderbird, 1965-67, (Hong Kong), Model No. 57/005
EX $50 NM $70 MIP $100

Ford Thunderbird Coupe, Model No. 1419
EX $25 NM $70 MIP $140

Ford Zephyr Saloon, 1956-60, 4-door sedan, two-tone, black tires, Model No. 162
EX $50 NM $100 MIP $150

Gabriel's Model T Ford, 1969-71, yellow and black, driver, "Gabriel" on doors, open cab, spoked wheels, Model No. 109
EX $25 NM $50 MIP $75

Hesketh 308E Racing Car, Model No. 222
EX $20 NM $40 MIP $75

Hillman Imp, Model No. 138
EX $50 NM $100 MIP $150

Hillman Minx, Model No. 40f
EX $40 NM $90 MIP $150

Hillman Minx, 1958-61, two-tone, black tires, Model No. 175
EX $50 NM $100 MIP $150

Hudson Commodore Sedan, Hi-Line, Model No. 171
EX $50 NM $200 MIP $400

Hudson Commodore Sedan, cream and blue body, Model No. 171
EX $25 NM $100 MIP $200

Hudson Hornet Sedan, yellow and brown, white tires, Model No. 174
EX $25 **NM** $80 **MIP** $160

Humber Hawk, 1959-63, two-tone, Model No. 165
EX $30 **NM** $80 **MIP** $150

HWM Racer, Model No. 235
EX $25 **NM** $70 **MIP** $140

Jaguar 3.4 Saloon, Model No. 195
EX $25 **NM** $80 **MIP** $160

Jaguar D-Type, 1957-65, light blue, white driver, racing car, Model No. 238
EX $60 **NM** $120 **MIP** $195

Jaguar E Type, 1962-67, Model No. 120
EX $20 **NM** $60 **MIP** $140

Jaguar Mark X, 1962-69, opening trunk, 2 pieces of luggage, Model No. 142
EX $65 **NM** $130 **MIP** $225

Jaguar SS 100 Sports Car, Model No. 38f
EX $30 **NM** $100 **MIP** $200

Jaguar XK 120, 1954-62, turquoise, cerise, Model No. 157
EX $80 **NM** $125 **MIP** $275

Jaguar XK 120, 1954-62, yellow/gray, Model No. 157
EX $80 **NM** $125 **MIP** $275

Jaguar XK 120, 1954-62, white, Model No. 157
EX $120 **NM** $200 **MIP** $400

(KP Photo by Dr. Douglas Sadecky)

Jaguar XK 120, 1959-62, gray-green, yellow or red, Model No. 157
EX $95 **NM** $210 **MIP** $375

Jensen FF, Model No. 188
EX $15 **NM** $50 **MIP** $100

Lamborghini Marzal, Model No. 189
EX $10 **NM** $20 **MIP** $60

Lotus F1 Racing Car, Model No. 225
EX $10 **NM** $20 **MIP** $40

Lotus Racing Car, 1963-70, Model No. 241
EX $20 **NM** $30 **MIP** $60

Maserati Race Car, 1954-64, red, green wheels, white driver, open Grand Prix racer, Model No. 231
EX $60 **NM** $135 **MIP** $200

Maserati Sport 2000, 1958, red open racer, white driver, black tires, Model No. 22A
EX $75 **NM** $150 **MIP** $215

McLaren M8A Can Am Racer, Model No. 223
EX $10 **NM** $20 **MIP** $40

Mercedes 190 SL, Model No. 526
EX $25 **NM** $100 **MIP** $200

Mercedes-Benz 250SE, 1968-72, metallic blue, white interior, Model No. 160
EX $20 **NM** $40 **MIP** $65

Mercedes-Benz C111, Model No. 224
EX $5 **NM** $20 **MIP** $50

MG Midget Sports, U.S. issue, Model No. 129
EX $250 **NM** $450 **MIP** $750

MG Midget Sports Car, Model No. 108
EX $25 **NM** $100 **MIP** $200

MGB Sports Car, Model No. 113
EX $25 **NM** $60 **MIP** $130

Morris Oxford, 1954-60, 4-door sedan, Model No. 159
EX $100 **NM** $200 **MIP** $300

Mustang Fastback, 1965-73, Model No. 161
EX $35 **NM** $55 **MIP** $100

Nash Rambler, Model No. 173
EX $20 **NM** $70 **MIP** $140

Packard Clipper Sedan, 1958-63, two-tone, white tires, Model No. 180
EX $50 **NM** $110 **MIP** $190

Packard Convertible, Model No. 132
EX $25 **NM** $80 **MIP** $160

Packard Super 8 Tourer, Model No. 39a
EX $25 **NM** $80 **MIP** $160

Panhard PL17, 1960-68, Model No. F547
EX $45 **NM** $80 **MIP** $120

Pathe News Camera Car, 1967-70, Model No. 281
EX $70 **NM** $105 **MIP** $230

Peugeot 203 Berline Saloon, Model No. 24r
EX $25 **NM** $100 **MIP** $200

Peugeot 403 Sedan, 1959-61, Model No. F521/24B
EX $50 **NM** $90 **MIP** $135

Peugeot 404, Model No. 553
EX $60 **NM** $120 **MIP** $200

Plymouth Belvedere, Model No. 24D
EX $35 **NM** $150 **MIP** $300

Plymouth Estate Car, Model No. 27F
EX $20 **NM** $70 **MIP** $140

Plymouth Fury Convertible, Model No. 137G
EX $20 **NM** $60 **MIP** $120

Plymouth Fury Sports, 1965-69, Model No. 115
EX $35 **NM** $55 **MIP** $85

Plymouth Plaza, 1959-63, white roof, harder-to-find version, Model No. 178
EX $25 **NM** $150 **MIP** $300

Plymouth Plaza, 1959-63, white tires, Model No. 178
EX $25 **NM** $75 **MIP** $150

Plymouth Stock Car, Model No. 201
EX $10 **NM** $20 **MIP** $40

Pontiac Parisienne, Model No. 173
EX $20 **NM** $50 **MIP** $100

Porsche 356A, 1958-66, cream, black tires, Model No. 182
EX $50 **NM** $100 **MIP** $150

Rambler Cross Country Station Wagon, Model No. 193
EX $20 **NM** $70 **MIP** $140

Range Rover, 1970-80, copper; opening doors, hood, and trunk, Model No. 192
EX $15 **NM** $35 **MIP** $65

Renault Dauphine, 1959-62, Model No. F524/24E
EX $50 **NM** $80 **MIP** $125

Rolls Royce Phantom V, Model No. 194
EX n/a **NM** n/a **MIP** n/a

Rolls Royce Silver Wraith, 1959-62, Model No. 150
EX $30 **NM** $65 **MIP** $125

Rolls-Royce, 1946-50, Model No. 30B
EX $65 **NM** $100 **MIP** $125

Rolls-Royce Phantom V, 1962-69, Model No. 198
EX $50 **NM** $75 **MIP** $100

Rover 3500, Model No. 180
EX $5 **NM** $20 **MIP** $60

Simca Chambord, 1959, 4-door sedan, two-tone, opening doors, Model No. 24K
EX $50 **NM** $100 **MIP** $150

Singer Gazel, 1959-63, 4-door sedan, two-tone, black tires, Model No. 168
EX $50 **NM** $100 **MIP** $150

Singer Vogue, 1962-67, Model No. 145
EX $50 **NM** $75 **MIP** $100

Standard Vanguard, 1954-60, Model No. 153
EX $60 **NM** $85 **MIP** $120

Streamline Racer, harder to find and subsequently, worth more, in red finish, Model No. 23s
EX $20 **NM** $40 **MIP** $80

Studebaker Commander, 1959-61, another in the line of French-made Dinky toys, Model No. F24Y/540
EX $75 **NM** $95 **MIP** $160

Studebaker Golden Hawk, 1958-63, green or tan body in two-tone, coupe, white tires, Model No. 169
EX $65 **NM** $115 **MIP** $185

Studebaker Land Cruiser, single color body, Model No. 172
EX $35 **NM** $85 **MIP** $160

Studebaker Land Cruiser, two-toned version, harder-to-find, Model No. 172
EX $25 **NM** $150 **MIP** $300

Studebaker President, Model No. 179
EX $25 **NM** $80 **MIP** $160

Sunbeam Alpine, Model No. 107
EX $30 **NM** $80 **MIP** $175

Sunbeam Rapier Saloon, 1958-63, two-tone, black tires, Model No. 166
EX $50 **NM** $100 **MIP** $150

Town Sedan, 1934-40, Model No. 24C
EX $85 **NM** $130 **MIP** $200

Triumph 1300, 1967-69, light blue body, red interior, Model No. 162
EX $30 **NM** $65 **MIP** $120

Triumph 1800 Saloon, 1954-60, 4-door sedan, baseplate changed in 1958, Model No. 40B/151
EX $65 **NM** $140 **MIP** $210

Triumph 2000, Model No. 135
EX $35 **NM** $60 **MIP** $100

Triumph Spitfire, Model No. 114
EX $20 **NM** $75 **MIP** $150

Triumph TR2, 1956-59, salmon/pink body, blue interior, white driver, Model No. 111
EX $100 **NM** $200 **MIP** $315

Triumph TR-2, 1957-60, yellow, pictured here with 773 Robot Traffic Signal, Model No. 105
EX $75 **NM** $120 **MIP** $200

Triumph TR-2, 1957-60, gray, Model No. 105
EX $60 **NM** $85 **MIP** $135

Universal Jeep, green or red body, Model No. 405
EX $25 **NM** $60 **MIP** $120

Vanguard, Model No. 40e
EX $25 **NM** $75 **MIP** $150

Vanwall Race Car, Model No. 239
EX $20 **NM** $60 **MIP** $130

Vauxhall, Model No. 151
EX $20 **NM** $50 **MIP** $100

Volkswagen 1300 Sedan, 1965-76, Model No. 129
EX $20 **NM** $35 **MIP** $75

Volkswagen Karmann-Ghia, 1959-64, red, green, or yellow body, Model No. 24M/187
EX $45 **NM** $80 **MIP** $125

Volkswagen VW 1600 TL, Model No. 163
EX $15 **NM** $40 **MIP** $125

Volkswagen VW Beetle, 1956-70, green, gray, white, or blue body, Model No. 181
EX $35 **NM** $70 **MIP** $150

Volvo 1800S, Model No. 116
EX $20 **NM** $60 **MIP** $120

Volvo 265 DL Estate, 1977-79, Blue, with opening rear hatch and brown plastic interior, black grille, Model No. 122
EX $12 **NM** $22 **MIP** $45

VW Porsche 914, Model No. 208
EX $15 **NM** $30 **MIP** $80

CHARACTER & TV RELATED

"Emergency" Rescue Paramedic Truck, Model No. 267
EX $10 **NM** $45 **MIP** $90

Captain Scarlett Spectrum Pursuit Vehicle, 1968-77, fantasy car from Captain Scarlett and the Mysterons show, antenna, rocket, driver, Model No. 104
EX $150 **NM** $325 **MIP** $550

Gabriel's Model T, Model No. 109
EX $30 **NM** $60 **MIP** $100

Galactic War Chariot, 1979-80, Model No. 361
EX $30 **NM** $45 **MIP** $70

Joe's Car, 1969-75, from the tv show, "Joe 90", Model No. 102
EX $55 **NM** $90 **MIP** $140

Klingon Battle Cruiser, 1976-79, Model No. 357
EX $35 **NM** $55 **MIP** $85

Lady Penelope's Fab 1, 1966-76, shocking pink version, rocket and 4 missiles, Model No. 100
EX $125 **NM** $210 **MIP** $375

Lady Penelope's Fab 1, 1966-76, pink version, rocket and 4 missiles, Model No. 100
EX $90 **NM** $145 **MIP** $250

Maximum Security Vehicle, 1968-75, fantasy car from Captain Scarlett and the Mysterons show, white, gullwing doors, cargo, Model No. 105
EX $50 **NM** $100 **MIP** $160

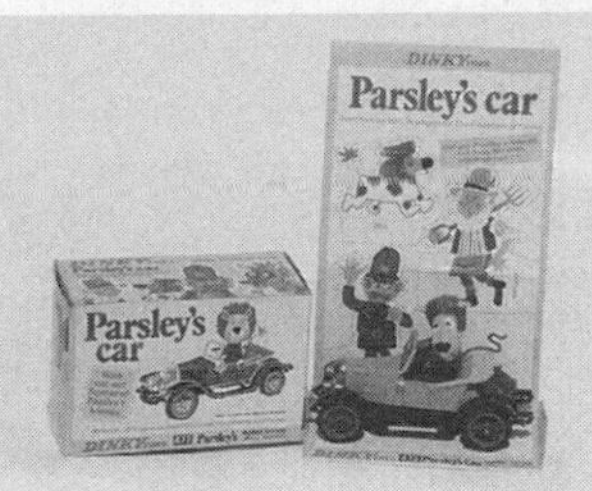

(KP Photo by Dr. Douglas Sadecky)

Parsley's Car Morris Oxford, 1970-72, Cut-out stand-up figures of Parsley's friends were included for additional play, Model No. 477
EX $65 **NM** $115 **MIP** $145

Prisoner Mini-Moke, 1967-70, from the tv show, "The Prisoner", Model No. 106
EX $100 **NM** $195 **MIP** $325

Renault Sinpar, 1968-71, Model No. F1406
EX $80 **NM** $135 **MIP** $220

Santa Special Model T Ford, 1964-68, Model No. 485
EX $65 **NM** $100 **MIP** $150

Thunderbirds 2 & 4, 1967-73, space ship from Thunderbirds show, Model No. 101
EX $110 **NM** $275 **MIP** $400

Tiny's Mini-Moke, 1970-73, Model No. 350
EX $60 **NM** $85 **MIP** $120

U.S.S. Enterprise, 1980, Model No. 371/803
EX $45 **NM** $85 **MIP** $135

Zygon Marauder, Model No. 368
EX $20 **NM** $40 **MIP** $60

Zygon War Chariot, Model No. 368
EX $12 **NM** $24 **MIP** $45

CONSTRUCTION

Atlas Digger, Model No. 984
EX $30 **NM** $45 **MIP** $70

Aveling Barford Road Roller, 1954-63, green body, red rollers,, Model No. 25P/251
EX $30 **NM** $60 **MIP** $100

Bedford Tipper, orange, Model No. 410
EX $20 **NM** $75 **MIP** $150

Blaw Knox Bulldozer, Model No. 561
EX $45 **NM** $75 **MIP** $125

Coles Crane, Model No. 972
EX $10 **NM** $40 **MIP** $80

Coles Hydra Crane Truck 150T, Yellow with black chassis, swivel crane section with working boom and hook, working levellers. 210mm, Model No. 980
EX $10 **NM** $40 **MIP** $80

Coles Mobile Crane, 1955-66, Model No. 971
EX $40 **NM** $70 **MIP** $120

Conventry Climax Fork Lift, Model No. 401
EX $15 **NM** $40 **MIP** $80

Conveyancer Fork Lift Truck, Includes driver and pallet, rear wheels turn, Model No. 404
EX $20 **NM** $40 **MIP** $60

Dinky Shovel Dozer, yellow body, red-roofed cab, rolling treads, lifting and dumping bucket, Model No. 977
EX $10 **NM** $40 **MIP** $80

Dumper Truck, Model No. 382
EX $5 **NM** $10 **MIP** $20

Eaton Yale Articulated Tractor Shovel, Model No. 973
EX $10 **NM** $40 **MIP** $80

Euclid Dump Truck, 1955-69, with lever-operated tipping bed. Part of the "Dinky Supertoys" range, Model No. 965
EX $55 **NM** $80 **MIP** $135

Ford D800 Snow Plow Tipper, blue cab with opening doors, silver tipping section with opening tailgate, yellow plow raises and lowers. 194mm, Model No. 439
EX $10 **NM** $40 **MIP** $80

Johnson 2-Ton Dumper, yellow open-cab articulated body with driver, red tipper section, 106mm, Model No. 430
EX $5 **NM** $30 **MIP** $60

Lorry Mounted Concrete Mixer, Model No. 960
EX $10 **NM** $50 **MIP** $125

Michigan 180-111 Tractor Dozer, yellow body, silver engine, red blade raises and lowers, cab is removeable, Model No. 976
EX $10 **NM** $40 **MIP** $80

Muir Hill Dumper Truck, Model No. 962
EX $15 **NM** $30 **MIP** $60

Muir Hill Loader & Trencher, yellow tractor body with working loader and backhoe. 163mm, Model No. 967
EX $5 **NM** $30 **MIP** $60

Muir Hill Two-Wheel Loader, 1962-78, Model No. 437
EX $30 **NM** $40 **MIP** $60

Richier Road Roller, 1959-69, Model No. F830
EX $75 **NM** $100 **MIP** $150

Road Grader, 1973-75, yellow and red with swivel blade, Model No. 963
EX $30 **NM** $45 **MIP** $70

Salev Crane, 1959-61, Model No. F595
EX $65 **NM** $100 **MIP** $175

Simca Tipper Dump Truck, French-made, Model No. 33
EX $30 **NM** $90 **MIP** $180

EMERGENCY VEHICLES

Airport Fire Engine, Model No. 263
EX $10 **NM** $40 **MIP** $100

(KP Photo by Dr. Douglas Sadecky)

Airport Fire Tender with Flashing Light, 1962-69, Model No. 276
EX $32 **NM** $65 **MIP** $130

Ambulance, Model No. 30F
EX $100 **NM** $160 **MIP** $275

Bedford Fire Escape, 1969-74, Model No. 956
EX $75 **NM** $110 **MIP** $185

(KP Photo by Dr. Douglas Sadecky)

Berliet Fire Pumper, included two detachable hose reels as accessories, French-made Dinky toy, Model No. 32E
EX $75 **NM** $95 **MIP** $200

Citroen DS19 Police Car, 1967-70, Model No. F501
EX $75 **NM** $95 **MIP** $175

Citroen Fire Van, 1959-63, Model No. F25D/562
EX $80 **NM** $110 **MIP** $250

Commer Fire Engine, 1955-69, Model No. 955
EX $60 **NM** $85 **MIP** $135

Convoy Rescue Fire Truck, Model No. 384
EX $5 **NM** $20 **MIP** $40

Crash Squad set, w/ Bell Helicopter and Plymouth Police Car, Model No. 299
EX $10 **NM** $40 **MIP** $80

Daimler Ambulance, Model No. 254
EX $15 **NM** $60 **MIP** $120

(KP Photo by Dr. Douglas Sadecky)

Delahaye Fire Truck, 1955-70, the white tires really enhance this French-made Dinky toy, Model No. F32D/899
EX $120 **NM** $190 **MIP** $375

DeSoto USA Police Car, Model No. 258
EX $20 **NM** $60 **MIP** $150

ERF Fire Tender, red body, removable extending escape ladder with wheels, Model No. 266
EX $15 **NM** $50 **MIP** $100

Fire Chief Land Rover
EX $35 **NM** $50 **MIP** $85

Fire Chief's Range Rover, red body, opening hood, tailgate and doors, Model No. 195
EX $5 **NM** $30 **MIP** $60

Fire Engine, Model No. 555
EX $25 **NM** $65 **MIP** $140

Ford Escort Panda Police Car, Model No. 270
EX $5 **NM** $30 **MIP** $60

Ford Police Car, 1960s, Model No. F551
EX $50 **NM** $100 **MIP** $150

Ford Transit Ambulance, Model No. 274
EX $5 **NM** $25 **MIP** $50

Ford Transit Fire Appliance, red with silver ladder and sliding door, Model No. 286
EX $5 **NM** $25 **MIP** $65

Ford Transit Police Accident Unit, Model No. 269
EX $5 **NM** $30 **MIP** $60

Merryweather Marquis Fire Tender, 1970s, red body with removeable silver ladder and working fire pump, Model No. 285
EX $5 **NM** $50 **MIP** $100

Mersey Tunnel Police Land Rover, 1955-61, Model No. 255
EX $60 **NM** $85 **MIP** $135

Motorway Services Ford Transit Van, 1970s, yellow body with "Motorway Services" on panel sides, Model No. 417
EX $5 **NM** $25 **MIP** $50

Nash Rambler Canadian Fire Chief's Car, Model No. 257
EX $10 **NM** $40 **MIP** $80

Plymouth Police Car, Model No. 244
EX $5 **NM** $30 **MIP** $70

Plymouth Police Car, 1977-80, Model No. 244
EX $25 **NM** $35 **MIP** $50

Police Accident Unit, Model No. 287
EX $5 **NM** $30 **MIP** $60

Police Land Rover, Model No. 277
EX $5 **NM** $30 **MIP** $60

Police Mini Clubman, 1976, light blue with opening white doors and "Police" on sides, Model No. 255
EX $5 **NM** $30 **MIP** $60

Police Range Rover, white body, orange stripe on sides, opening hood, doors and tailgate, 109mm, Model No. 254
EX $5 **NM** $30 **MIP** $60

Range Rover Ambulance, 1974-78, opening hood, doors and tailgate, includes patient on stretcher, Model No. 268
EX $25 **NM** $35 **MIP** $50

RCMP Ford Fairlane, Model No. 264
EX $20 **NM** $60 **MIP** $160

Rover 3500 Police, Model No. 264
EX $5 **NM** $30 **MIP** $60

Streamlined Fire Engine, 1946-53, red, Merryweather fire engine, ladder, bell, Model No. 25H/25
EX $60 **NM** $85 **MIP** $160

Streamlined Fire Engine, 1954-62, red, Merryweather fire engine, ladder, bell, Model No. 250
EX $35 **NM** $65 **MIP** $140

Superior Cadillac Ambulance, 1971-79, opening rear hatch with plastic patient on stretcher, regular or speed wheels, Model No. 288
EX $15 **NM** $28 **MIP** $100

Superior Criterion Ambulance, 1962-68, white body, Model No. 263
EX $50 **NM** $75 **MIP** $125

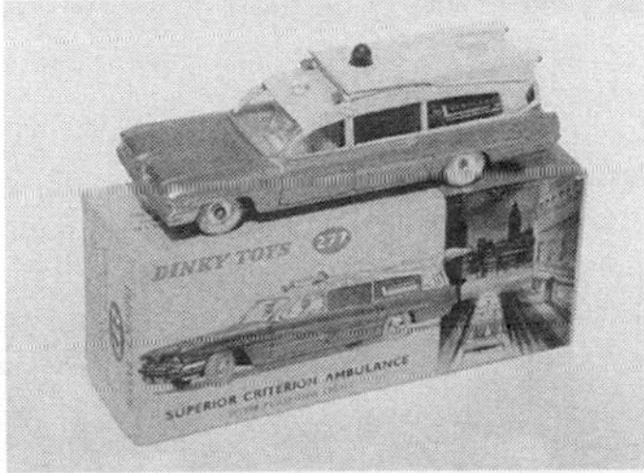

(KP Photo by Dr. Douglas Sadecky)

Superior Criterion Ambulance, 1962-68, the roof beacon warning light actually flashed with the aid of a small battery, light blue metallic lower and white upper body, Model No. 277
EX $40 **NM** $75 **MIP** $150

USA Police Car (Pontiac), Model No. 251
EX $35 **NM** $50 **MIP** $140

Vauxhall Victor Ambulance, 1964-70, Model No. 278
EX $55 **NM** $85 **MIP** $150

Volvo Police Car, 1970s, same body as 265 Estate, but in white with orange stripes, Model No. 243
EX $5 **NM** $30 **MIP** $60

FARM

Convoy Farm Truck, Model No. 381
EX $5 **NM** $15 **MIP** $30

David Brown Tractor, 1966-75, Model No. 305
EX $60 **NM** $120 **MIP** $200

Farm Tractor, 1933-40, Fordson-style; red, yellow, blue, Model No. 22E
EX $100 **NM** $225 **MIP** $450

Field Marshall Tractor, 1953, 1954-65, orange, driver, black tires, Model No. 27N/301
EX $60 **NM** $85 **MIP** $175

Garden Roller, 1948-54, Model No. 105A
EX $15 **NM** $25 **MIP** $45

Halesowen Harvest Trailer, 1949-53, 1954-70, Model No. 27B/320
EX $15 **NM** $35 **MIP** $75

Hayrake, 1954-71, Model No. 324
EX $30 **NM** $40 **MIP** $60

Leyland 384 Tractor, 1971-78, blue w/blue driver, Model No. 308
EX $45 **NM** $90 **MIP** $135

Massey-Harris Manure Spreader, 1949-53, 1954-71, red, Model No. 27C/321
EX $25 **NM** $50 **MIP** $75

Massey-Harris Tractor, 1948-53, 1954-71, red w/yellow wheels, brown driver to blue, Model No. 27A/300
EX $60 **NM** $135 **MIP** $225

Moto-Cart, 1954-60, Model No. 27G/342
EX $35 **NM** $50 **MIP** $75

Wheelbarrow, Model No. 382
EX $10 **NM** $20 **MIP** $40

MILITARY

1 Ton Cargo Truck, Model No. 641
EX $20 **NM** $40 **MIP** $80

10 Ton Army Truck, 1954-63, Model No. 622
EX $20 **NM** $40 **MIP** $80

105mm U.S. Howitzer with Crew, Model No. 609
EX $20 **NM** $40 **MIP** $80

155mm Mobile Gun, Model No. 654
EX $25 **NM** $50 **MIP** $100

155mm self-propelled gun, French-made toy, Model No. 813
EX $45 **NM** $90 **MIP** $180

25-pounder Field Gun, Model No. 686
EX $20 **NM** $40 **MIP** $85

25-pounder Field Gun with Tractor and Trailer, Model No. 697
EX $55 **NM** $110 **MIP** $220

25-pounder gun trailer, Model No. 687
EX $15 **NM** $30 **MIP** $60

5.5 Medium Gun, 1955, Model No. 692
EX $15 **NM** $30 **MIP** $50

6-pounder anti-tank gun, Model No. 625
EX $16 **NM** $32 **MIP** $65

7.2 Howitzer, Model No. 693
EX $25 **NM** $50 **MIP** $100

88mm gun, Model No. 656
EX $25 **NM** $50 **MIP** $100

AEC Arctic Transport with Helicopter, Model No. 618
EX $50 **NM** $85 **MIP** $145

Alvis Scorpion, 1970s, turret fires plastic shells, includes camo netting, 1:40-scale, Model No. 690
EX $10 **NM** $40 **MIP** $80

AML Panhard Armored Car, French-made Dinky Toy, Model No. 814
EX $30 **NM** $60 **MIP** $120

AMX 13 T Tank, Model No. 801/80c
EX $35 **NM** $70 **MIP** $140

AMX Bridge Layer, lever extends folding bridge set on AMX tank chassis, Model No. F883
EX $75 **NM** $110 **MIP** $225

AMX Tank, Model No. F80C/817
EX $50 **NM** $75 **MIP** $100

Armored Car, Model No. 670
EX $25 **NM** $50 **MIP** $100

Armored Personnel Carrier, Model No. 676
EX $25 **NM** $50 **MIP** $100

Armoured Command Vehicle, squared, longer bodied six-wheeled vehicle, shown here with #641 Cargo Truck, Model No. 677
EX $50 **NM** $85 **MIP** $125

Army Covered Wagon, Model No. 623
EX $40 **NM** $85 **MIP** $150

Army Field Kitchen Cuisine Roulante, trailer with two boilers/kettles, stovepipe, spare tire, Model No. 823
EX $30 **NM** $60 **MIP** $130

Army Jeep, Model No. 669
EX $20 **NM** $40 **MIP** $85

Army Water Tanker, Model No. 643
EX $50 **NM** $75 **MIP** $120

Austin Champ, Model No. 674
EX $20 **NM** $40 **MIP** $80

Austin Covered Truck, Model No. 30SM/625
EX $85 **NM** $135 **MIP** $275

Austin Paramoke, includes parachute, vehicle holder and vehicle, Model No. 601
EX $25 **NM** $35 **MIP** $50

Bedford Military Truck, Model No. 25WM/60
EX $80 **NM** $125 **MIP** $250

Berliet All Terrain 6x6 Truck, green body with canopy top over bed, shown here with 80E/819 Howitzer, Model No. 80D/818
EX $40 **NM** $80 **MIP** $150

Berliet Missile Launcher, green six-wheeled truck with Nord R20 winged missile, Model No. 620
EX $75 **NM** $100 **MIP** $175

Berliet Tank Transporter, another French-made Dinky Toy, shown here with Panhard Armored Car, #815, Model No. 890
EX $65 **NM** $130 **MIP** $250

Berliet Wrecker, crane hook and swivel base, six-wheels, Model No. F826
EX $60 **NM** $120 **MIP** $240

Bren Gun Carrier, green body, working treads, two figures included, 1:32-scale, Model No. 622
EX $25 **NM** $45 **MIP** $85

Bren Gun Carrier and Anti-Tank Gun, includes #622 Bren Gun Carrier with #625 6-pounder anti-tank gun that fires shells, Model No. 619
EX $35 **NM** $65 **MIP** $110

Centurian Tank, 1954-70, rubber or plastic treads, olive drab, Model No. 651
EX $60 **NM** $110 **MIP** $185

Centurion Tank, rolling rubber treads, swivel turret, raising and lowering gun barrel, Model No. 683
EX $45 **NM** $90 **MIP** $180

Chieftain Tank, 1970s, rolling treads, swivel turret, gun barrel that raises and lowers, white numbers on front, gold square emblem on turret, fires shells, 1:50-scale, Model No. 683
EX $15 **NM** $50 **MIP** $100

Commando Jeep, Model No. 612
EX $25 **NM** $35 **MIP** $50

Commando Squad Gift Set, Model No. 303
EX $25 **NM** $70 **MIP** $140

Convoy Army Truck, green body with removeable plastic canopy, "Available Later" in 1977 catalog, Model No. 687
EX $5 **NM** $20 **MIP** $40

Cooker Trailer, Model No. 151c
EX $25 **NM** $50 **MIP** $100

Covered Army Transport Wagon, 1937-41, prewar toy, six-wheeled truck with black plastic tires, molded driver, metal canopy, Model No. 151B
EX $50 **NM** $100 **MIP** $200

Daimler Ambulance, a popular casting available in military and civilian variations, Model No. 30HM/624
EX $80 **NM** $125 **MIP** $250

Dodge Command Car, Model No. F810
EX $40 **NM** $60 **MIP** $90

DUKW Amphibian, green, open-topped body, 1:76-scale, Model No. 681
EX $10 **NM** $30 **MIP** $60

EBR Panhard Armored Car, 8-wheeled vehicle, 2 sets of road wheels, front and back, with two sets of floating all-terrain wheels in the center, rotating turret, Model No. 80A/815
EX $30 **NM** $60 **MIP** $120

Ferret Armored Car, green scout car with open turret, 1:48-scale, Model No. 680
EX $12 **NM** $30 **MIP** $50

Ferret Armoured Car, Model No. 630
EX $25 **NM** $35 **MIP** $50

Field Artillery Tractor, Model No. 688
EX $25 **NM** $50 **MIP** $90

Foden Army Truck, Model No. 668
EX $5 **NM** $30 **MIP** $60

Ford U.S. Army Staff Car, Model No. 170
EX $65 **NM** $130 **MIP** $250

GMC Military Truck, French-made, Model No. 809
EX $50 **NM** $100 **MIP** $200

GMC Tanker, Model No. F823
EX $125 **NM** $250 **MIP** $500

Hanomag Tank Destroyer, German Hanomag half-track with pivoting anti-tank gun that fires plastic shells. 1:35-scale, Model No. 694
EX $10 **NM** $40 **MIP** $80

Honest John Missile Launcher, Green truck with rubber-band powered plastic missile, Model No. 665
EX $45 **NM** $90 **MIP** $185

Jeep, French-made, Model No. 80b
EX $30 **NM** $60 **MIP** $125

Jeep, Model No. 153a
EX $25 **NM** $50 **MIP** $100

Jeep, Model No. F816
EX $50 **NM** $75 **MIP** $115

Jeep avec Canon de 106, French-made, Model No. 829
EX $25 **NM** $50 **MIP** $100

Jeep Hotchkiss-Willys, French-made, Model No. 816
EX $25 **NM** $50 **MIP** $120

Jeep with Rocket Launcher, French-made, Model No. 828
EX $35 **NM** $75 **MIP** $150

Land Rover Bomb Disposal Unit, 1976, green Land-Rover Safari with orange quarter panels, blue dome light and "Explosive Disposal" sign on roof. Has opening doors and hood, and includes remote bomb-finding tank, 1:42-scale, Model No. 604
EX $20 **NM** $40 **MIP** $80

Leopard Recovery Tank, 1970s, green with rolling treads, pivoting boom, raising and lowering blade, West German Bundeswehr markings, 1:50-scale, Model No. 699
EX $15 **NM** $50 **MIP** $100

Leopard Tank, swivel turret, pivoting gun fires plastic shells, West German Army markings, Model No. 692
EX $15 **NM** $50 **MIP** $100

Light Dragon Field Gun Set, Model No. 162
EX $75 **NM** $150 **MIP** $300

Light Dragon Tractor, Model No. 162a
EX $40 **NM** $80 **MIP** $150

Light Tank, green, metal treads, rolling tread wheels, Model No. 152A
EX $50 **NM** $100 **MIP** $200

Light Tank Set, Model No. 152
EX $125 **NM** $250 **MIP** $500

M3 Halftrack, olive body, working treads, AA gun in turret, Model No. 822
EX $50 **NM** $100 **MIP** $200

Medium Artillery Tractor, part of the Dinky Supertoys line, this model was 5-1/2" long, shown here at bottom with #622 truck at top, Model No. 689
EX $25 **NM** $50 **MIP** $100

Mercedes-Benz Military Unimog, French-made toy, dark olive with canopy top over bed, shown here with 823 Field Kitchen trailer, Model No. 821
EX $30 **NM** $60 **MIP** $130

Military Ambulance, Model No. F80F/820
EX $50 **NM** $75 **MIP** $100

Military Ambulance, Red Cross decals and opening rear doors, Model No. 626
EX $25 **NM** $45 **MIP** $75

(KP Photo by Dr. Douglas Sadecky)

Missile Erecting Vehicle, 1959, with Corporal Missile and Launching Platform, Model No. 666
EX $100 **NM** $155 **MIP** $260

(KP Photo by Dr. Douglas Sadecky)

Missile Servicing Platform, 1960, this vehicle made a nice companion to the 666 Missile Erecting Vehicle, a nicely detailed toy that had a short production run, Model No. 667
EX $95 **NM** $130 **MIP** $270

Obusier 155mm Cannon, French Dinky toy, four-wheeled chassis under cannon, Model No. 80E/819
EX $40 **NM** $80 **MIP** $160

RAF Pressure Refueller, Dark gray body,

part of the Dinky Supertoys line, 5-1/2" long, shown here (top) in photo with #661 recovery tractor, Model No. 642
EX $40 **NM** $80 **MIP** $160

Reconnaisance Car, this model was produced in pre- and post-war periods, Model No. 152B
EX $40 **NM** $60 **MIP** $110

Recovery Tractor, 1957, tow hook has working reel, Model No. 661
EX $60 **NM** $90 **MIP** $140

Scout Car, open-turret scout car, shown here at right with #601 Austin Para-Moke, 2-5/8", Model No. 673
EX $5 **NM** $40 **MIP** $80

Searchlight, prewar, Model No. 161A
EX $125 **NM** $250 **MIP** $500

Sinpar 4x4 Military Police Vehicle, Model No. 815
EX $60 **NM** $120 **MIP** $200

Stalwart Load Carrier, Model No. 682
EX $10 **NM** $30 **MIP** $60

Static 88mm Gun with Crew, includes shells and three soldiers, Model No. 662
EX $10 **NM** $40 **MIP** $80

Stiker Anti-Tank Vehicle, angluar armored vehicle with 5-missile launcher that fires all rockets individually or at once
EX n/a **NM** n/a **MIP** n/a

Tank Transporter, Model No. 660
EX $75 **NM** $100 **MIP** $175

Tank Transporter and Centurion Tank, 1956-64, includes #660 Tank Transporter with #651 Centurion Tank, shown here with single box for tank, Model No. 698
EX $85 **NM** $165 **MIP** $285

Tank Transporter with Chieftain Tank, Model No. 616
EX $20 **NM** $60 **MIP** $140

Task Force Set, Model No. 677
EX $20 **NM** $50 **MIP** $100

Three Ton Army Wagon, 1954-63, Model No. 621
EX $50 **NM** $85 **MIP** $125

U.S. Jeep with 105mm Howitzer set, Includes firing gun, Model No. 615
EX $20 **NM** $50 **MIP** $100

VW KDF (Kubelwagen) and PAK Anti-Tank gun, excellent two-piece set--the gun actually fires plastic shells, Model No. 617
EX $20 **NM** $50 **MIP** $100

MISCELLANEOUS

(KP Photo by Dr. Douglas Sadecky)

Healey Sports Boat on Trailer, 1960-62, Model No. 796
EX $25 **NM** $35 **MIP** $55

Land Rover, 1954-71, red, orange or green open body, plastic driver, Model No. 340
EX $100 **NM** $200 **MIP** $300

Land Rover Trailer, Model No. 341
EX $15 **NM** $40 **MIP** $80

Large Trailer, Model No. 428
EX $15 **NM** $25 **MIP** $50

Loading ramp for Pullmore Car Transporter, Model No. 994
EX $10 **NM** $20 **MIP** $40

MOTORCYCLES AND CARAVANS

4-Berth Caravan w/ Transparent Roof, 1963-69, Model No. 188
EX $25 **NM** $45 **MIP** $85

(KP Photo by Dr. Douglas Sadecky)

A.A. Motorcycle Patrol, 1946-64, the decal on the sidecar changed depending in which country the motorcycle was sold, Model No. 270/44B
EX $30 **NM** $45 **MIP** $95

Caravan, postwar, Model No. 30G
EX $40 **NM** $60 **MIP** $85

Caravan, prewar, Model No. 30G
EX $55 **NM** $85 **MIP** $150

Caravan, 1956-64, Model No. 190
EX $30 **NM** $45 **MIP** $60

Caravane Caravelair
EX $75 **NM** $150 **MIP** $250

Police Motorcycle Patrol, 1936-40, Model No. 42B
EX $50 **NM** $75 **MIP** $145

Police Motorcycle Patrol, 1946-53, Model No. 42B
EX $30 **NM** $45 **MIP** $70

Police Motorcyclist, 1938-40, Model No. 37B
EX $50 **NM** $75 **MIP** $145

Police Motorcyclist, 1946-48, Model No. 37B
EX $30 **NM** $45 **MIP** $90

Touring Secours Motorcycle Patrol, 1960s, Swiss version, Model No. 271
EX $70 **NM** $110 **MIP** $200

SHIPS

Coastguard Amphibious Missile Launch, white-hulled amphibious vehicle launches missiles from hood, 155mm, Model No. 674
EX $5 **NM** $20 **MIP** $40

Cunard White-Star No 534 Queen Mary, Model No. 52
EX $25 **NM** $50 **MIP** $100

MK1 Corvette, white, black and gray camo hull, gray conning tower, brown deck, Model No. 671
EX $5 **NM** $20 **MIP** $40

Motor Patrol Boat, Model No. 1050
EX $5 **NM** $20 **MIP** $40

OSA Missile Boat, white and black, fires four missiles, runs on concealed wheels, Model No. 672
EX $5 **NM** $20 **MIP** $40

RAF Air/Sea Rescue Launch, black hull, orange cabin, silver deck. Includes figure and raft, Model No. 678
EX $5 **NM** $20 **MIP** $40

Submarine Chaser, 1976, white and gray with launching depth charges, Model No. 673
EX $5 **NM** $20 **MIP** $40

TRUCKS

A.E.C. Hoynor Transporter, 1969-75, Model No. 974
EX $60 **NM** $90 **MIP** $130

A.E.C. Shell Chemicals Tanker, Model No. 991
EX $35 **NM** $80 **MIP** $230

B.E.V. Truck, 1954-60, Model No. 14A/400
EX $15 **NM** $30 **MIP** $75

Bedford Garbage Truck, brown, Model No. 252
EX $15 **NM** $50 **MIP** $100

Berliet Flat Truck with Container, French-made, Model No. 34b
EX $30 **NM** $60 **MIP** $125

Berliet Transformer Carrier, 1961-65, Model No. F898
EX $100 **NM** $200 **MIP** $450

Big Bedford, maroon, fawn, Model No. 408/922
EX $80 **NM** $120 **MIP** $200

Big Bedford, blue, yellow, Model No. 408/922
EX $90 **NM** $135 **MIP** $210

Breakdown Lorry, 1954-64, "Dinky Service," white cab, blue boom, Model No. 25x/430
EX $80 **NM** $150 **MIP** $275

Chevrolet El Camino, 1961-68, Model No. 449
EX $35 **NM** $65 **MIP** $140

Citroen Milk Truck, 1961-65, Model No. F586
EX $145 **NM** $275 **MIP** $600

Citroen Wrecker, 1959-71, Model No. F35A/582
EX $75 **NM** $120 **MIP** $250

Covered Wagon, green, gray, Model No. 25B
EX $65 **NM** $115 **MIP** $160

Covered Wagon, Carter Paterson, Model No. 25B
EX $150 **NM** $300 **MIP** $750

Dodge Rear Tipping Wagon, Model No. 424
EX $30 **NM** $60 **MIP** $100

Electric Articulated Vehicle, Model No. 30W/421
EX $60 **NM** $85 **MIP** $120

Esso Gas Tanker, Model No. 442
EX $40 **NM** $90 **MIP** $200

Foden Diesel 8-Wheel Wagon, 1948-52, dark cab and bed, red fenders and chassis, various color variations were available, pictured here is the first-version cab updated in 1952, part of the Dinky Supertoy range, Model No. 501
EX $160 **NM** $220 **MIP** $435

Foden Flat Truck w/ Tailboard 1, red/black, Model No. 503/903
EX $140 **NM** $210 **MIP** $450

Foden Flat Truck w/ Tailboard 2, blue/yellow, orange or blue, Model No. 503/903
EX $90 **NM** $150 **MIP** $275

Foden Flat Truck w/Tailboard 1, gray/blue, Model No. 503/903
EX $140 **NM** $210 **MIP** $450

Foden Mobilgas Tanker, 1954-57, Model No. 941
EX $145 **NM** $350 **MIP** $750

Foden Regent Tanker, Model No. 942
EX $135 **NM** $300 **MIP** $550

Fordson Thames Flat Truck, 1954-60, green or red body, flatbed truck, Model No. 422
EX $40 **NM** $80 **MIP** $135

Forward Control Wagon, 1948-53, Model No. 25R
EX $45 **NM** $65 **MIP** $90

Guy Flat Truck, common variations, Model No. 513
EX $80 **NM** $250 **MIP** $500

Guy Flat Truck w/Tailboard, 1956-58, blue cab and chassis, orange flatbed, Model No. 433
EX $75 **NM** $160 **MIP** $250

Guy Truck, "Eveready" decals, Model No. 918
EX $80 **NM** $200 **MIP** $425

Guy Warrior 4 Ton, 1958-64, Model No. 431
EX $150 **NM** $270 **MIP** $450

Guy Warrior Snow Plow, Model No. 958
EX $60 **NM** $150 **MIP** $300

Hindle Smart Helecs, Model No. 30w
EX $20 **NM** $50 **MIP** $100

Horse Box, Model No. 981
EX $30 **NM** $60 **MIP** $150

(KP Photo by Dr. Douglas Sadecky)

Johnston Road Sweeper, 1970s, as the toy was pushed forward, a spring coil turned the brushes in a sweeping motion, Model No. 449/451
EX $25 **NM** $50 **MIP** $85

Leland Tanker, Corn Products
EX $700 **NM** $1200 **MIP** $3000

Leland Tanker, 1963-69, Shell/BP, Model No. 944
EX $125 **NM** $215 **MIP** $480

Leyland Cement Wagon, 1956-59, one of Dinky's foreign vehicles, this toy was made in Argentina, Model No. 419/933
EX $90 **NM** $130 **MIP** $220

Leyland Comet Lorry, 1956-59, stake truck, gray tires, blue cab and chassis, yellow stakes, Model No. 417
EX $75 **NM** $190 **MIP** $300

Leyland Comet Truck, 1956-59, open hauler w/tailgate, gray tires, green cab and chassis, orange bed, Model No. 418
EX $75 **NM** $150 **MIP** $225

Leyland Eight-Wheeled Test Chassis, 1964-69, Model No. 936
EX $65 **NM** $125 **MIP** $200

Leyland Octapus Flat Truck w/ Chassis, 1964-66, Model No. 935
EX $500 **NM** $1000 **MIP** $1600

Leyland Octopus Esso Tanker, Model No. 943
EX $100 **NM** $300 **MIP** $600

Market Gardeners Wagon, yellow, Model No. 25F
EX $65 **NM** $115 **MIP** $160

(KP Photo by Dr. Douglas Sadecky)

VEHICLES • DINKY

McLean Tractor-Trailer, 1961-67, Model No. 948
EX $95 **NM** $190 **MIP** $280

Mechanical Horse, 1935-41, Model No. 33a
EX $35 **NM** $60 **MIP** $100

Midland Bank, 1966-68, Model No. 280
EX $60 **NM** $85 **MIP** $120

Mighty Antar With Propeller, 1959-64, the propeller included with this model is made of plastic, Model No. 986
EX $150 **NM** $300 **MIP** $425

Motor Truck, red, blue, Model No. 22C
EX $150 **NM** $350 **MIP** $650

Motor Truck, red, green, blue, Model No. 22C
EX $80 **NM** $120 **MIP** $200

National Benzole Tanker, Model No. 443
EX $30 **NM** $75 **MIP** $150

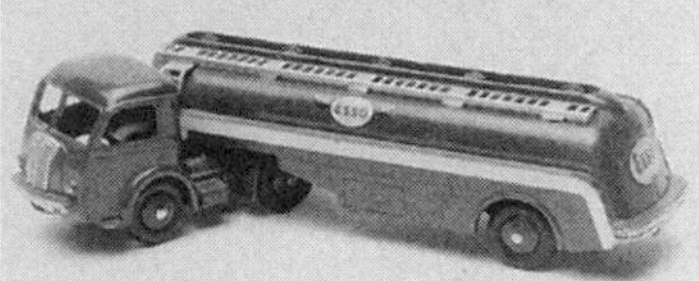

Panhard Esso Tanker, 1954-59, French-made, part of the Dinky Supertoys line, Model No. F32C
EX $75 **NM** $120 **MIP** $190

Panhard Kodak Semi Trailer, 1952-54, Model No. F32AJ
EX $140 **NM** $250 **MIP** $450

Panhard SNCF Semi Trailer, 1954-59, Model No. F32AB
EX $100 **NM** $165 **MIP** $280

Petrol Wagon, Power, Model No. 25D
EX $150 **NM** $300 **MIP** $500

(KP Photo by Dr. Douglas Sadecky)

Pinder Circus Peugeot and Caravan, 1969-71, The Peugeot and Caravan are the only other vehicles produced in the Pinder Circus livery by Dinky. It would have been interesting to see what other circus vehicles would have been produced had sales been better, French-made, Model No. 882
EX $110 **NM** $240 **MIP** $380

(KP Photo by Dr. Douglas Sadecky)

Pinder Circus Truck and Wagon, 1969-71, French-made, this photo shows the animals and decorative labels still in the package, Model No. 881
EX $110 **NM** $235 **MIP** $375

Pullmore Car Transporter, light blue, Model No. 583
EX $25 **NM** $70 **MIP** $180

(KP Photo by Dr. Douglas Sadecky)

Pullmore Car Transporter with 994 Loading Ramp, 1954-63, the 784 loading ramp cam separately packaged in the Transporter box and was used to unload the cars, Model No. 982
EX $85 **NM** $140 **MIP** $210

Renault Estafette, Model No. F561
EX $50 **NM** $85 **MIP** $150

Simca Glass Truck, gray, green, Model No. F33C/579
EX $75 **NM** $120 **MIP** $170

Simca Glass Truck, yellow, green, Model No. F33C/579
EX $100 **NM** $150 **MIP** $250

Studebaker Mobilgas Tanker, 1954-61, Model No. 440
EX $70 **NM** $100 **MIP** $180

Thames Flat Truck, 1951-60, Model No. 422/30R
EX $45 **NM** $75 **MIP** $110

(KP Photo by Dr. Douglas Sadecky)

Unic Auto Transporter, 1959-68, French-made, part of the Supertoys line, ramp raises and lowers with a lever on the side of the trailer, Model No. F39A/984
EX $100 **NM** $200 **MIP** $300

Unic Bucket Truck, 1957-65, Model No. F38A/895
EX $75 **NM** $120 **MIP** $225

Willeme Log Truck, 1956-71, Model No. F36A/897
EX $75 **NM** $120 **MIP** $200

Willeme Semi Trailer Truck, 1959-71, another French-made Dinky toy, Model No. F36B/896
EX $95 **NM** $140 **MIP** $235

VANS

(KP Photo by Dr. Douglas Sadecky)

ABC-TV Mobile Control Room, 1962-69, a camera and cameraman was also included with this van, Model No. 987
EX $65 **NM** $130 **MIP** $210

(KP Photo by Dr. Douglas Sadecky)

ABC-TV Transmitter Van, 1962-69, this was the companion vehicle to the #987 ABC TV Mobile Control Room, Model No. 988
EX $80 **NM** $145 **MIP** $270

Atco Delivery Van, 1935-40, type 2, Model No. 28N
EX $200 **NM** $375 **MIP** $850

Atco Delivery Van, 1935-40, type 3, Model No. 28N
EX $135 **NM** $200 **MIP** $350

Austin Van, 1954-56, Shell/BP, Model No. 470
EX $60 **NM** $110 **MIP** $175

Austin Van, 1955-63, Nestle's, Model No. 471
EX $60 **NM** $110 **MIP** $175

Austin Van, 1957-60, Raleigh, Model No. 472
EX $60 **NM** $110 **MIP** $175

(KP Photo by Dr. Douglas Sadecky)

BBC TV Extending Mast Vehicle, 1959-64, Model No. 969
EX $60 **NM** $125 **MIP** $185

(KP Photo by Dr. Douglas Sadecky)

BBC-TV Camera Truck, 1959-64, Model No. 968
EX $60 **NM** $125 **MIP** $185

BBC-TV Control Room, 1959-64, Model No. 967
EX $60 **NM** $125 **MIP** $185

Bedford 10 cwt Van, Ovaltine, Model No. 481
EX $25 **NM** $100 **MIP** $200

Bedford 10 CWT. "Kodak" Van, 1954-56, yellow/orange body, "Kodak Cameras & Film" on sides, Model No. 480
EX $50 **NM** $125 **MIP** $190

Bedford AA Van, Model No. 412
EX $5 **NM** $30 **MIP** $60

Bedford CA Van, 1956-58, "Dinky Toys" on sides, orange and yellow, Model No. 482
EX $100 **NM** $275 **MIP** $425

Bedford Van, 1955-59, Heinz, Model No. 923
EX $100 **NM** $165 **MIP** $400

Citroen Breakdown Truck, Model No. 582
EX $100 **NM** $200 **MIP** $300

Citroen Cibie Delivery Van, 1960-63, Model No. F561
EX $90 **NM** $150 **MIP** $350

Citroen Police Van, Model No. 566
EX $120 **NM** $240 **MIP** $360

Electric Dairy Van, Model No. 490
EX $45 **NM** $90 **MIP** $120

Ensign Delivery Van, 1934, type 1, Model No. 28E
EX $300 **NM** $500 **MIP** $1000

Ford Transit Van, 1978-80, Model No. 417
EX $15 **NM** $20 **MIP** $30

Guy Van, Spratts, Model No. 514
EX $135 **NM** $300 **MIP** $625

Guy Van, Lyons, Model No. 514
EX $275 **NM** $550 **MIP** $1600

Guy Van, Slumberland, Model No. 514
EX $145 **NM** $315 **MIP** $625

Mini Minor Van, Joseph Mason Paints, Model No. 274
EX $150 **NM** $300 **MIP** $500

Mini Minor Van, 1960s, R.A.C., Model No. 273
EX $65 **NM** $115 **MIP** $150

Pickfords Delivery Van, 1934-35, type 2, Model No. 28B
EX $200 **NM** $375 **MIP** $600

Pickfords Delivery Van, 1934-35, type 1, Model No. 28B
EX $300 **NM** $500 **MIP** $1000

Royal Mail Bedford Van, Model No. 410
EX $5 **NM** $15 **MIP** $40

(KP Photo by Dr. Douglas Sadecky)

Royal Mail Van, 1955-61, Model No. 260
EX $50 **NM** $100 **MIP** $150

Saviem Race Horse Van, 1969-71, Model No. F571
EX $125 **NM** $225 **MIP** $400

Telephone Service Van, Model No. 261
EX $25 **NM** $75 **MIP** $150

Trojan Dunlop Van, 1952-57, Model No. 31B/451
EX $70 **NM** $110 **MIP** $185

Trojan OXO Van, 1953, dark blue, Model No. 31D
EX $85 **NM** $210 **MIP** $320

DOEPKE

Adams Road Grader, 1948-56, 26" long, yellow, #2006; 1948-56, Model No. 2006
EX $210 **NM** $295 **MIP** $395

Adams Road Grader, 1948-56, 26" long, orange, #2006; 1948-56, Model No. 2006
EX $140 **NM** $255 **MIP** $355

American LaFrance Aerial Ladder Truck, 1950-52, 33-1/2" long, red, #2008; 1950-52, Model No. 2008
EX $245 **NM** $325 **MIP** $400

American LaFrance Improved Aerial Ladder Truck, 1953-56, 33-1/2" long, red, w/outriggers and cast aluminum ladder, #2014; 1953-56, Model No. 2014
EX $290 **NM** $375 **MIP** $450

American LaFrance Pumper, 1951-56, 19" long, red, #2010; 1951-56, Model No. 2010
EX $200 **NM** $340 **MIP** $425

American LaFrance Searchlight Truck, 1955-56, white w/battery-operated search light, #2023; 1955-56, Model No. 2023
EX $950 **NM** $1650 **MIP** $2100

Barber-Greene Bucket Loader, on wheels, 22" long, green, #2013, Model No. 2013
EX $325 **NM** $400 **MIP** $525

Barber-Greene Bucket Loader, 1946-50, on tracks, 18" tall, early model w/swivel chute, green, #2001; 1946-50, Model No. 2001
EX $430 **NM** $510 **MIP** $625

Barber-Greene Bucket Loader, 1946-50, on tracks, 18" tall, later model w/out swivel chute, green, #2001; 1946-50, Model No. 2001
EX $250 **NM** $375 **MIP** $500

Barber-Greene Bucket Loader, 1946-50, on tracks; 18" tall, later model w/out swivel chute, orange, #2001; 1946-50, Model No. 2001
EX $350 **NM** $425 **MIP** $550

Bulldozer, 1952-56, 15" long, yellow, #2012; 1952-56, Model No. 2012
EX $425 **NM** $550 **MIP** $650

Doepke

Clark Airport Tractor and Trailers Set, 1954-56, 26-1/2" long; three pieces: red tractor, green trailer, yellow trailer, #2015; 1954-56, Model No. 2015
EX $375 **NM** $450 **MIP** $550

Euclid Truck, 1950-56, 27" long, olive green, #2009; 1950-56, Model No. 2009
EX $250 **NM** $330 **MIP** $425

Euclid Truck, 1950-56, 27" long, forest green, #2009; 1950-56, Model No. 2009
EX $225 **NM** $325 **MIP** $400

Euclid Truck, 1950-56, 27" long, orange, #2009; 1950-56, Model No. 2009
EX $225 **NM** $300 **MIP** $375

Heiliner Scraper, 1951-56, 29" long, red, #2011; 1951-56, Model No. 2011
EX $295 **NM** $300 **MIP** $375

Jaeger Concrete Mixer, 1947-49, 15" long, yellow w/black drum, #2002; 1947-49, Model No. 2002
EX $225 **NM** $310 **MIP** $450

Jaguar, 1955-56, 18" long, kit or built, light blue or red, #2018; 1955-56, Model No. 2018
EX $450 **NM** $550 **MIP** $650

MG Auto, 1954-56, 15-1/2" long, kit, aluminum body; red, yellow, or gray primer, #2017; 1954-56, Model No. 2017
EX $300 **NM** $415 **MIP** $490

Unit Crane, 1949-54, 11" long, without boom, orange, w/finger wheel, #2007; 1949-54, Model No. 2007
EX $200 **NM** $325 **MIP** $400

Unit Crane, 1949-54, 11" long, without boom, orange, w/out finger wheel, #2007; 1949-54, Model No. 2007
EX $225 **NM** $300 **MIP** $375

Wooldridge Earth Hauler, 1946-49, 25", yellow, #2000; 1946-49, Model No. 2000
EX $200 **NM** $325 **MIP** $450

ELDON INDUSTRIES

Air Force Fighter Jet, 21" long; gray plastic jet with bomb underneath, 1960s
EX $50 **NM** $80 **MIP** $120

Clipper Ship, 21" long, 15" tall; three masts, two life boats, turning rudder; 1960s
EX $25 **NM** $40 **MIP** $60

Command Cassette Dump Truck, battery-operated, yellow/orange, programmable w/cassettes, 1971
EX $4 **NM** $8 **MIP** $15

Dump Truck, 18" long; Euclid-type dump truck, lever-activated dumping; 1960s
EX $10 **NM** $20 **MIP** $40

Dump Truck, 15-3/4" long; white and yellow plastic dump truck with red dumping body, whitewall tires; mid-1960s
EX $13 **NM** $18 **MIP** $30

Fire Engine Pumper, 16" long; removable ladder, rubber hose, water tank, pump, two firemen, Big Poly series, 1960
EX $35 **NM** $75 **MIP** $95

Fire Pumper Truck, 13" long; red and silver plastic, water-squirting action; 1960s
EX $10 **NM** $15 **MIP** $22

Hot Rod, 14" long; red plastic body, black seats, chromed engine; early 1960s
EX $12 **NM** $23 **MIP** $35

House Trailer Hauler, 14-1/2" long; light blue tractor and house trailer with white roof and door; 1950s
EX $20 **NM** $30 **MIP** $45

Pickup, large red plastic truck, black tires, chromed hubs and grille unit, issued individually or with white trailer to haul the Hot Rod; early 1960s
EX $15 **NM** $30 **MIP** $45

Power Shovel, 8" high cab, 24" long with shovel extended; red swiveling body, working shovel bucket, gray tread, 1960s
EX $30 **NM** $60 **MIP** $95

Ride 'Em Fire Engine, 27" long; red plastic riding truck, six wheels, red steering wheel emerging from cab roof, working siren, raising and extending ladder on swivel base, and two hoses; 1960
EX $42 **NM** $83 **MIP** $125

Service Panel Truck, 10" long; yellow plastic body, red opening rear gate and hood, removable ladder on roof; 1950s
EX $10 **NM** $18 **MIP** $28

Service Panel Truck, 10" long; opening rear gate and hood, removable ladder on roof; 1950s
EX $10 **NM** $18 **MIP** $28

Touch Command Car, 14" long; red plastic Corvette, battery-operated, remote-control with air pressure; 1968=69
EX $6 **NM** $12 **MIP** $18

Touch Command Corvette Sting Ray, 13-1/2" long; red car with darkened windows; battery-operated, six-way remote control; 1960s
EX $8 **NM** $14 **MIP** $25

Tow Truck, green/white cab, yellow towing body, 1962
EX $12 **NM** $23 **MIP** $35

Tow Truck, 21" long; white hard "Fortiflex" plastic, silver plastic winch and rails, red flasher on cab roof, silver grille unit and rear tow bar, six black tires, two metal cranks control boom height and hauling hood; 1960s
EX $25 **NM** $50 **MIP** $75

Truck Transport Set, truck hauler in red hard "Fortiflex" plastic, tractor-trailer, black tires, load of small plastic dump, stake, pickup and wrecker trucks; 1960
EX $30 **NM** $60 **MIP** $90

U.S. Air Force Jet, 12-1/2" long; retractable landing gear, firing missile, 1970s
EX $10 **NM** $15 **MIP** $30

USAF Missile Launcher Truck and Trailer, 20" long; "USAF" on cab doors, antenna on roof; flatbed with white and red platform with trigger for launching white missile with red nose cone, Air Force emblems on missile's wings; 1950s
EX $100 **NM** $225 **MIP** $300

Water Tanker Truck, 10" long; red soft plastic cab and chassis, white plastic tanker body and tire/axle units, opening at tank top for water and seven-hold trough in rear for dampening roads; 1960
EX $15 **NM** $30 **MIP** $45

GAY TOYS

AMC Pacer, 5" long; whitewall tires
EX $5 **NM** $10 **MIP** $15

Amphicat, 8-1/2" long; polyethylene, six-wheel all-terrain vehicle, snap-in interior, steering gear, chromed front, and rear lights; early 1970s
EX $3 **NM** $7 **MIP** $10

Back-Hoe Truck, 14" long; cabover with snap-in grille and steering wheel, oversize tires, lever-controlled hoe; early 1970s
EX $3 **NM** $7 **MIP** $10

Baha Jeep, polyethylene Jeepster with balloon tires, chromed hubs, hood decal; early 1970s
EX $2 **NM** $4 **MIP** $7

Beach Buggy, 8-1/2" long; polyethylene Jeep with striped canopy, flower decal on hood, chromed headlights, bumpers, and wheel hubs; early 1970s
EX $8 **NM** $18 **MIP** $25

Big Mac Earth Scraper, 14" long; two-piece yellow scraper with lever-controlled action, swiveling tractor with chromed grille; early 1970s
EX $6 **NM** $12 **MIP** $18

Camper Van, 7" long; red van, skylight roof, white interior, whitewall tires
EX $3 **NM** $6 **MIP** $9

Cement Mixer, 14" long; cabover with interior detail and snap-in grille and steering wheel, revolving and dumping mixing drum, oversize tires, polyethylene; early 1970s
EX $4 **NM** $8 **MIP** $12

Chevy Camaro, 7" long, plastic
EX $5 NM $8 MIP $15

Chevy Corvette, No. 7951; 18" long; T-roof, white interior, chrome hubs; 1970s
EX $5 NM $8 MIP $15

Chevy Corvette Convertible, 7-1/2" long; various colors, white interior, white-line tires, 1970s styling
EX $3 NM $6 MIP $10

Chevy Impala Highway Patrol, 11" long, plastic, whitewalls
EX $9 NM $15 MIP n/a

Cobra Mustang, 10-1/2" long, plastic, "Cobra" decal on hood, 1984
EX $12 NM $24 MIP n/a

Dirt Demon, 18" long; pickup with rollbar; 1970s
EX $5 NM $8 MIP $15

Dukes of Hazzard's General Lee, Dodge Charger, 12" long; 180s
EX $12 NM $18 MIP $25

Dump Truck, 12" long; cabover with interior details, chromed hubs and grille, hinged dump, oversize tires, polyethylene; late 1960s-70s
EX $2 NM $4 MIP $7

Dump Truck, 9" long, Mack-type cab with heavy-duty dump body, three axles
EX $3 NM $7 MIP $10

Dump Truck, 7-3/4" long; Ford-type cab, heavy-duty dumping body, white-line tires, 1970s
EX $2 NM $4 MIP $8

Dump Truck, 20-1/2 long; Euclid-type, yellow body, black tires with white hubs; 1970s
EX $10 NM $15 MIP $20

Dune Buggy, 8"; polyethylene dune buggy, contrasting canopy, with chromed headlights, rear motor, and hub caps; early 1970s
EX $10 NM $18 MIP $22

Farm Tractor, 11" long; red and white body, white scoop, black tires; 1970s
EX $9 NM $14 MIP $20

Fire Ladder Truck, 9" long; red plastic with white ladder base and yellow ladder, black tires, cabover design, separate grille; 1960s
EX $4 NM $8 MIP $15

Fire Truck, 12" long; cabover design, oversized balloon tires, snap-in grille, steering wheel, hose reel and nozzle; late 1960s-70s
EX $3 NM $7 MIP $10

Fire Truck, 4" long, Ford, 1960s
EX $4 NM $8 MIP $15

Ford Bronco, 12" long; black tires with white hubs, white grille and roof, tan/yellow body and interior; 1970s
EX $50 NM $100 MIP $250

Ford Bronco, 7" long; pickup, opening tail gate, Bronco logo, white-line tires
EX $30 NM $70 MIP n/a

Ford GT, 10" long; polyethylene, clear windshields, chromed motor visible through rear panel, gold lettering, chromed wheel details, early 1970s
EX $5 NM $10 MIP $15

Ford Mustang Racecar, 10" long, red plastic w/white interior, "Ford" sticker, "33" on sides and hood, 1970s
EX $8 NM $12 MIP n/a

Ford Pinto, 10-1/2" long; no decals, black tires with white hubs; 1970s
EX $7 NM $18 MIP $24

Ford Pinto, orange with "The Dukes of Hazzard" style Confederate flag; 1980s
EX $7 NM $13 MIP $20

Ford Ranchero, 4" long; 1960s
EX $2 NM $4 MIP $7

Ford Street "T", polyethylene hot rod Model T coupe, chromed motor and wheel discs, headlights and front bumper; early 1970s
EX $4 NM $15 MIP $22

Gulf Oil Truck, 7" long, cabover, "Gulf" sticker
EX $4 NM $8 MIP $12

Hardee's NASCAR No. 28, 11-3/4" long; Cale Yarborough, 1980s
EX $10 NM $15 MIP $22

Indy Racer, 6" long, "Gay Special '5'" sticker, plastic driver
EX $5 NM $10 MIP $16

Mail Truck, 8" long; blue and white, three-wheeler with working steering, plastic siren light, "U.S. Mail," 1960s
EX $15 NM $22 MIP $30

Maverick, race car with lift-off body, roll bars; early 1970s
EX $4 NM $8 MIP $12

Mercury Cougar, 11" long; chromed bumpers, clear windshields, chrome-detailed tires, in red, blue or green polyethylene; early 1970s
EX $5 NM $10 MIP $15

Puddle Jumper, polyethylene open-top dune buggy, "Puddle 77 Jumper" on hood, roll bar, chromed headlights, rear motor and wheel hubs; early 1970s
EX $3 NM $7 MIP $10

Pumper, 4" long; single-mold pumper truck, black plastic wheel-axle units; 1960s
EX $3 NM $5 MIP $8

Richard Petty Racer, 11" long, blue palstic, white-hub tires, "STP" and "Richard Petty 43"
EX $20 NM $30 MIP $40

Road Runner Camper, tan camper, white top and interior, black tires with white hubs; 1970s
EX $10 NM $17 MIP $25

Rodeo Riders, 22" long; orange/yellow tractor-trailer w/2 black horses
EX $7 NM $12 MIP $16

Rough Riders Pickup Truck and Trailer, 11-1/2" truck, 7" trailer; "Rough Riders" stickers on truck and horse-trailer sides, truck tires black with white hubs, plastic horse
EX $10 NM $15 MIP $22

School Bus, 9" long" "School Bus" on sides, chrome grille, yellow body; 1960s
EX $8 NM $12 MIP $20

School Bus, 9" long; "Gay School Bus" on sides, chrome grille, yellow body; 1960s
EX $10 NM $18 MIP $25

School Bus Set, bus with "School Bus" on sides, chromed grille, issued with a child shelter, stop sign and three school figures; early 1970s
EX $10 NM $15 MIP $25

Texaco Star Racer, 17-3/4" long; white plstic open-cockpit racer, "Texaco Star" on sides and poiler; 1970s
EX $5 NM $10 MIP $15

Tractor Loader, farm tractor with lever-controlled front scoop and lifting and dumping action; early 1970s
EX $4 NM $8 MIP $12

Triumph Wedge TR7, 15"; convertible, "The Wedge" decal, Goodyear tires, 1970s
EX $25 NM $55 MIP n/a

U.S. Air Force Fighter, 13-1/2" long; 12" wingspan; Army-green single prop airplane, clear plastic cockpit cover
EX $3 NM $6 MIP $10

VW Camper, 6-1/2" long; "Gay Camper" decals on doors, opening side doors, interior plastic table and seats; early 1960s
EX $25 NM $35 MIP $45

VW Hot Rod, 9" long; yellow body, exposed white rear engine, single driver seat, white-hub tires
EX $4 NM $8 MIP $15

Wrecker, cabover with interior design, snap-in grille, working crane with tow rope, oversize tires, polyethylene; early 1970s
EX $3 NM $7 MIP $10

Yard Tractor, 6-1/4" long tractor alone; polyethylene tractor, plow, mower, wagon, with snap-in hood, steering wheel, seats and wheel hubs; early 1970s
EX $2 NM $4 MIP $8

YF-12A Flying Sword Interceptor, red USAF jet, blue plastic figures, missiles, 1960s
EX $20 NM $35 MIP $55

HOT WHEELS NUMBERED PACKS

1995 Series

RACE TEAM

275 Lumina Stocker, lt. met. blue, wht. int., clr. win., metal M, uh MIP $5

276 Hot Wheels 500, lt. met. blue, gray int., metal M, bw MIP $5

277 Side Splitter, lt. met. blue, metal int., clr. win., metal M, bw MIP $8

278 Dragster, lt. met. blue, wht. int., metal M, bw MIP $5

KRACLE CAR

280 Sharkruiser, lime/blue, lime int., metal M, uh MIP $5

281 Turboa, purp./red, red int., silv. metal M, uh MIP $5

282 '63 Split Window, aqua/org., wht. int., org. win., chr. 1 rivet M, bw MIP $7

284 Flashfire, purp./yel., yel. int., yel. win., blk. pl. M, uh MIP $5

STEEL STAMP

285 Steel Passion, blk./rose, red int., tinted win., chr. M, ww MIP $8

287 Zender Fact 4, blk., wht. int., smoked win., blk. pl. M, uh MIP $5

289 '56 Flashsider, burgundy, chr. win., chr. M, uh MIP $6

290 '57 Chevy, blue, blue int., blue win., chr. M, uh MIP $6

PEARL DRIVER

292 Pearl Passion, pearl lavender, yel. int., tinted win., chr. M, ww MIP $8

293 VW Bug, pearl pink, gray int., clr. win., metal M, bw MIP $7

295 Talbot Lago, pearl blue, blue int., blue win., metal M, ww MIP $8

296 Jaguar XJ220, pearl wht., tan int., smoked win., blk. pl. M, uh MIP $5

DARK RIDER

297 Splittin Image, blk., dk. chr. int., dk. chr. win., blk. pl. M, 6sp MIP $10

298 Twin Mill II, blk., blk. win., blk. pl. M, 6sp MIP $10

299 Silhouette II, blk., blk. int., clr. win., blk. chr. M, 6sp MIP $10

300 Rigor Motor, blk., chr. int., clr. win., blk. metal M, 5sp MIP $10

ROARIN RODS

302 Mini Truck, tan, tan int., smoked win., tan pl. M, uh MIP $5

303 Street Roader, org./blk., blk. int., smoked win., metal M, ct MIP $25

304 Roll Patrol, wht./blk., blk. int., smoked win., blk. metal M, yct MIP $4

305 Classic Cobra, neon yel., olive int., smoked win., metal M, 7sp MIP $10

HOT HUBS

307 Cyber Cruiser, burgundy flake, purp. chr. int., metal M, blue/hh-org. tire MIP $7

308 Vampyra, purp., gold int., blk. metal M, g/hh-blue tire MIP $9

310 Shadow Jet, grn., grn. int., yel. win., metal M, y/hh-purp. tire MIP $9

311 Suzuki Quadracer, yel. pl., purp. int., blk. metal M, alw-y/hh-blk. tire MIP $10

SPEED GLEAMER

312 3-Window '34, grn. chr., aqua int., blue win., metal M, 7sp MIP $4

313 T-Bucket, purp., wht. int., clr. win., blk. metal M, 5sp MIP $35

315 Ratmobile, blk., chr. int., gray metal M, uh MIP $3

316 Limozeen, gold, wht. int., smoked win., gold chr. M, ww MIP $15

REAL RIDER

317 Dump Truck, neon yel., blk. int., blk. win., metal M, yel. hub rr MIP $30

318 Mercedes Unimog, org./gray, org. int., tinted win., metal M, org. hub knobby/rr MIP $25

320 '59 Caddy Convertible, red, wht. int., clr. win., chr. M, chr. hub ww/rr MIP $45

321 Corvette Stingray, grn., clr. int., clr. win., metal M, gray hub rr MIP $75

SILVER SERIES

322 Fire Eater, chr./blue insert, blue int., blue win., chr. M, bw MIP $15

323 Rodzilla, chr., metal M, uh MIP $4

325 Propper Chopper, chr., blk. int., blue win., blk. pl. M, MIP $3

328 School Bus, chr., wht. int., clr. win., blk. pl. M, bw MIP $10

PHOTO FINISH

331 Aerostar, wht., silv. window win., metal M, 7sp MIP $7

332 Flying Aces Blimp, gray, blk. win., MIP $7

333 Tank Truck, blue, chr. win., chr. M, 7sp MIP $7

335 Hiway Hauler, grn., blk. win., chr. M, 7sp MIP $7

RACING METALS

336 Race Truck, chr., red int., smoked win., blk. metal M, ct MIP $5

337 Ramp Truck, purp. chr., blk. win., metal M, 7sp MIP $5

338 Camaro Racer, lt. blue chr. w/Baldwin, wht. int., clr. win., gray pl. M, 5sp MIP $8

340 Dragster, lt. blue chr., wht. int., metal M, 5sp MIP $5

1995 Model Series

341 58 Corvette, pink, chr. int., clr. win., pink pl. M, bw MIP $5

342 Mercedes SL, red, tan int., clr. win., red pl. M, uh MIP $5

343 Speed Blaster, blue, chr. win., chr. M, uh MIP $10

344 Camaro Convertible, met. grn., gray int., clr. win., blk. pl. M, uh MIP $7

345 Speed-a-Saurus, grn., metal M, bw MIP $3

346 Hydroplane, blue/wht., chr. int., clr. win., wht. pl. M, MIP $3

347 Power Pistons, burgundy pl., gray int., blue win., metal M, 3sp MIP $4

347 Power Rocket, bronze pl., gray int., blue win., metal M, uh MIP $30

348 Dodge Ram, met. grn., chr. int., smoked win., gray pl. M, 5sp MIP $4

349 Power Pipes, dk. blue pl., chr. int int., purp. win., silv. metal M, 3sp MIP $3

350 Ferrari 355, yel., blk. int., clr. win., metal M, 3sp MIP $3

351 Power Rocket, purp. flake pl., chr. int., metal M, 5sp MIP $7

352 Big Chill, wht., chr. win., blk. pl. M, pink ski MIP $12

1995 Treasure Hunts

353 Olds 442, met. blue, wht. int., clr. win., chr. M, redline/rr MIP $70

354 Gold Passion, gold met., wht. int., clr. win., gold chr. M, gold hub/rr MIP $75

355 '67 Camaro, wht. w/org. stripes, org. int., clr. win., metal M, chr. hub/rr MIP $400

356 '57 T-Bird, dk. purp. met., clr. int., clr. win., chr. M, redline/rr MIP $65

357 VW Bug, day-glo grn., purp. int., clr. win., metal M, purp. swirl MIP $125

358 '63 Split Window, met. blue, wht. int., clr. win., chr. M, ww/rr MIP $75

359 Stutz Blackhawk, blk. met., red int., clr. win., metal M, redline/rr MIP $50

360 Rolls-Royce, dk. red met., red int., clr. win., metal M, red 6sp MIP $50

361 Classic Caddy, lt. grn. met./olive fenders, tan int., clr. win., metal M, gold 6sp MIP $50

362 Classic Nomad, met. teal, wht. int., clr. win., metal M, chr. swirl MIP $60

363 Classic Cobra, dk. grn. met., tan int., clr. win., metal M, gold chr. 6sp MIP $70

364 '31 Doozie, yel. w/blk. fenders, blk. int., clr. win., metal M, yel. 6sp MIP $50

1996 First Editions

367 Chevy 1500 Pickup, silv. met., gray int., smoked win., metal M, alw-b7sp MIP $12

369 Road Rocket, lt. grn./blue, metal M, gbbs MIP $2

369 Sizzlers (Turbo Flame), wht. pearl pl., org. win., metal M, 5sp MIP $3

369 Turbo Flame, wht. pearl pl., org. win., metal M, 5sp MIP $6

370 **Rail Rodder,** blk. pl., metal M, sm. rear b5sp **MIP** $8

371 **Road Rocket,** lt. grn./blue w/blue HW logo on side/red HW logo o, metal M, gbbs **MIP** $10

372 **VW Bus Funny Car,** met. blue, org. int., clr. win., metal C, 5sp/front **MIP** $65

373 **Street Cleaver,** yel., yel. metal M, 5sp **MIP** $4

374 **Radio Flyer Wagon,** red, blk. int., metal M, 5sp **MIP** $4

375 **Dog Fighter,** red met., chr. int., blk. pl. M, 5sp **MIP** $3

376 **Twang Thang,** silv. met., chr. int., clr. win., pearl pl., 5sp **MIP** $2

377 **Ferrari F50,** red, blk. int., clr. win., gray pl. M, bbs **MIP** $3

377 **Ferrari F50 (new casting),** dk. red, blk. int., clr. win., gray pl. C, bbs **MIP** $2

378 **'96 Mustang,** red met., tan int., clr. win., metal M, 3sp **MIP** $7

382 **'70 Dodge Daytona,** red, tan int., clr. win., chr. M, gbbs **MIP** $3

1996 Treasure Hunts

428 **'40's Woodie,** yel., blk. int., smoked win., metal M, yel. hub/yel. wall rr **MIP** $40

429 **Lamborghini Countach,** day-glo. org., tan int., clr. win., day-glo org. metal M, chr. 6sp **MIP** $30

430 **Ferrari 250,** met. gray, red int., clr. win., gray pl. M, chr. hub/rr **MIP** $35

431 **Jaguar XJ 220,** met. grn., blk. int., blk. win., blk. pl. M, gold 6sp **MIP** $30

432 **'59 Caddy,** red, tan int., clr. win., chr. M, chr. hub ww/rr **MIP** $50

433 **Dodge Viper RT/10,** wht., blk. int., clr. win., blk. pl. M, wht. 6sp **MIP** $60

434 **'57 Chevy,** purp. met., purp. int., purp. win., chr. M, chr. hub/rr **MIP** $60

435 **Ferrari 355,** wht. pearl, tan int., clr. win., metal M, gold star **MIP** $30

436 **'58 Corvette,** silv. met., red int., clr. win., gray pl. M, chr. hub/rr **MIP** $60

437 **Auburn 852,** olive met./gold fenders, gold int., clr. win., metal M, gold hub ww/rr **MIP** $35

438 **Dodge Ram 1500,** maroon met., gray int., clr. win., dk. gray pl. M, chr. hub/rr **MIP** $35

439 **'37 Bugatti,** blue met., red int., clr. win., metal M, chr. 6sp **MIP** $25

1996 Series

RACE TRUCK

380 **Dodge Ram 1500,** red, red int., clr. win., red pl. M, yel. ltr. b7sp **MIP** $3

381 **Ford LTL (Kenworth T600),** silv. met., blue win., red pl. M, yel. ltr. b7sp **MIP** $10

381 **Kenworth T600,** silv. met., blue win., red pl. M, yel. ltr. b7sp **MIP** $5

382 **'56 Flashsider,** blk. met. w/HW rear logo, chr. win., chr. M, b7sp **MIP** $9

383 **Nissan Truck,** dk. blue met., yel. int., clr. win., chr. M, ct **MIP** $125

FLAMETHROWER

384 **'57 T-Bird,** wht./copper flames/5 flame trunk/gold HW logo in r, clr. int., clr. win., chr. M, 7sp **MIP** $8

385 **Hydroplane,** yel., chr. int., smoked win., blk. pl. M, **MIP** $3

386 **Range Rover,** red w/HW logo in side window, tan int., clr. win., chr. M, ct **MIP** $5

387 **Oshkosh Snowplow,** blk., blk. int., metal M, ct **MIP** $4

SPACE

388 **Radar Ranger,** wht. pearl/HW logo on top, org. int., clr. win., blk. metal M, ct **MIP** $3

389 **GM Lean Machine,** wht. pearl, blk. win., metal M, 5sp **MIP** $3

390 **Alien,** wht. pearl/HW logo on top, blk. win., metal M, 5sp **MIP** $3

391 **Treadator,** lt. blue pearl/HW logo right front wing, blue chr. win., blk. pl. M, **MIP** $4

RACE TEAM II

392 **Ramp Truck,** blue/wht., clr. win., metal M, 5sp **MIP** $3

393 **Baja Bug,** met. blue, wht. int., metal M, 5sp **MIP** $5

394 **'57 Chevy,** met. blue, blue int., blue win., chr. M, 5sp **MIP** $4

395 **Bywayman,** met. blue/wht., wht. int., clr. win., metal M, ct **MIP** $4

MOD BOD

396 **Hummer,** pink pl., grn. win., purp. met. metal M, ct **MIP** $4

397 **School Bus,** purp. met., org. int., clr. win., yel. pl. M, 7sp **MIP** $4

398 **VW Bug,** blue, grn. int., clr. win., metal M, 7sp **MIP** $5

399 **'67 Camaro,** bright grn., red/open steering wheel int., clr. win., metal M, 5sp **MIP** $7

DARK RIDER II

400 **Big Chill,** blk. met., dk. chr. win., blk. pl. M, blk. ski **MIP** $3

401 **Street Beast,** blk. met., blk. int., clr. win., blk. metal M, blk. tint 7sp **MIP** $3

402 **Thunderstreak,** blk. met./dk. chr., blk. int., blk. metal M, blk. tint 7sp **MIP** $3

403 **Power Pistons,** dk. chr., blk. int., clr. win., blk. metal M, blk. tint 7sp **MIP** $3

SPORTS CAR

404 **Porsche 930,** silv. met., blk. int., smoked win., metal M, 7sp **MIP** $3

405 **Custom Corvette,** purp. w/logo on windshield, gray int., smoked win., blk. pl. M, 5sp **MIP** $45

406 **Cobra 427 S/C,** pearl wht., blk. int., clr. win., metal M, 5sp **MIP** $55

407 **'59 Caddy,** blk. met., wht. int., clr. win., chr. M, 7sp **MIP** $3

SPLATTER PAINT

408 **Rescue Ranger,** org., blue int., blue win., org. pl. M, t/b **MIP** $7

409 **Side Splitter Funny Car,** wht., metal int., clr. win., metal M, 5sp **MIP** $5

410 **'55 Chevy,** yel., magenta win., red pl. M, t/b **MIP** $7

411 **'80's Camaro,** wht., wht. int., clr. win., metal M, 5sp **MIP** $2

STREET EATERS

412 **Speed Machine,** lt. grn. pearl, red int., red win., metal M, 7sp **MIP** $10

413 **Silhouette II,** purp. w/HW logo on rear, red int., org. win., red pl. M, 5sp **MIP** $4

414 **Propper Chopper,** blue, org. int., clr. win., org. pl. M, **MIP** $15

415 **Roll Patrol,** lt. brn., lt. org. int., clr. win., org. metal M, yct **MIP** $10

FAST FOOD

416 **Pizza Vette,** wht. pl., blk. win., blk. metal M, 3sp **MIP** $3

417 **Pasta Pipes,** wht. pl., chr. int int., blue win., blk. metal M, 3sp **MIP** $3

418 **Sweet Stocker,** wht., yel. int., yel. win., blk. metal M, 3sp **MIP** $20

419 **Crunch Chief,** wht., yel. win., blk. metal M, 3sp **MIP** $4

SILVER SERIES II

420 **Dump Truck,** chr. w/chr. box, metal M, ct/b **MIP** $20

421 **'40's Woodie/logo in rear window,** chr., blk. int., clr. win., metal M, 5sp **MIP** $5

421 **'40's Woodie/logo in side window,** chr., blk. int., clr. win., metal M, 5sp **MIP** $3

422 **'57 Chevy,** chr., org. win., metal M, 5sp **MIP** $5

423 **Oscar Mayer Wienermobile,** chr., smoked win., chr. M, b5sp **MIP** $5

FIRE RESCUE

424 **Ambulance,** bright grn./smooth rear step, wht. int., blue win., chr. M, 5sp **MIP** $8

425 **Rescue Ranger,** yel., blk. int., smoked win., chr. M, 5sp **MIP** $3

426 **Flame Stopper,** yel., blk. win., blk. pl. M, yct **MIP** $50

427 **Fire Eater,** red, blue int., blue win., chr. M, 5sp **MIP** $4

1996 Model Series

440 **Monte Carlo Stocker,** blue met., wht. int., clr. win., gray pl. M, b7sp **MIP** $3

1996 Basic Line

377 **Ferrari F50,** dk. red, blk. int., clr. win., gray pl. Ind., bbs **MIP** $2

441 **Chevy Stocker,** blk., red int., clr. win., metal M, 7sp **MIP** $5

442 Ferrari F40, wht. pearl, tan int., smoked win., metal M, 5sp **MIP** $3

443 Ferrari 348, blk. met., red int., clr. win., blk. pl. M, 5sp **MIP** $8

444 Aeroflash, wht., org. int., org. win., day-glo org. metal M, g7sp **MIP** $2

445 Jaguar, met. grn., gray int., clr. win., gray pl. M, 5sp **MIP** $3

446 '32 Ford Delivery, dk. blue, blk. int., clr. win., metal M, 3sp **MIP** $20

447 '63 Split Window, met. grn., tan int., clr. win., chr. M, 3sp **MIP** $4

448 '67 Camaro, yel., blk. int., smoked win., metal no origin, 5sp **MIP** $7

449 Camaro Z-28, org., blk. int., smoked win., blk. metal M, 3sp **MIP** $5

450 Corvette Stingray, pearl wht., blue int., blue win., metal M, 3sp **MIP** $3

451 3-Window '34, pink, pink int int., rose win., metal M, 3sp **MIP** $15

452 Ferrari 250, met. grn., tan int., clr. win., grn. pl. M, 5sp **MIP** $15

453 Audi Avus, red, tan int., smoked win., blk. pl. M, 5sp **MIP** $10

453 Avus Quattro, red, tan int., smoked win., blk. pl. M, 5sp **MIP** $3

454 Zender Fact 4, pearl wht., gray int., blue win., gray pl. M, 5sp **MIP** $3

455 65 Mustang Convertible, gold flake, wht. int., smoked win., metal M, 5sp **MIP** $5

455 '65 Mustang Convertible, gold flake, wht. int., smoked win., metal M, 3sp **MIP** $4

457 Pontiac Banshee, blk. met., yel. int., clr. win., metal C, 5sp **MIP** $3

458 Speed Shark, met. lavender, purp. int., purp. win., chr. C, 5sp **MIP** $3

460 Zombot, blk. over silv., day-glo org. metal C, 5sp **MIP** $3

461 Enforcer, candy purp., silv. win., metal C, 5sp **MIP** $3

462 '80's Firebird, met. blue, wht. int., clr. win., blue pl. C, 5sp **MIP** $3

463 Fiero 2M4, yel., blk. int., clr. win., metal C, 5sp **MIP** $3

464 Blazer 4X4, met. blue, yel. int., blue win., metal C, ct **MIP** $3

467 Peugeot 405, dk. grn. met., wht. int., clr. win., grn. pl. C, 5sp **MIP** $4

468 GT Racer, dayglo org., blk. win., metal C, 5sp **MIP** $5

469 Hot Bird, gold, wht. int., tinted win., metal C, 5sp **MIP** $5

470 Turbo Streak, wht./blue, wht. int., wht. metal C, 5sp **MIP** $4

471 Velocitor, met. blue, red int., clr. win., wht. metal C, 5sp **MIP** $4

472 Buick Stocker, yel., blk. int., clr. win., blk. metal C, 5sp **MIP** $3

473 BMW M1, silv./gray, blk. int., clr. win., gray metal C, 5sp **MIP** $3

473 Street Beast, pearl teal, gray int., tinted win., teal metal C, 5sp **MIP** $3

474 VW Golf, blk., red int., clr. win., blk. pl. C, 5sp **MIP** $5

475 Forklift, yel., blk. int., metal C, lrg. bw front/5sp rear **MIP** $5

477 Double Demon, grn./purp. chr., blk. metal C, 5sp **MIP** $3

478 Dragon Wagon, yel., teal metal C, 5sp **MIP** $3

479 Computer Warrior, blk. over blue, org. metal C, 5sp **MIP** $3

481 Tall Ryder, grn. met., chr. win., metal C, cts **MIP** $4

482 Earth mover, yel., blk. int., yel. metal C, cts **MIP** $5

483 Thunder Roller, maroon met., tan int., clr. win., chr. C, lrg.bw rear/5sp front **MIP** $5

484 Grizzlor, wht. pl., metal C, 5sp **MIP** $3

485 Evil Weevil, lt. org. pl., org. metal C, 5sp **MIP** $3

486 Command Tank, blk./purp., blk. pl. C, **MIP** $5

487 Troop Convoy, met. gray/org., gray int., blk. metal C, 5sp **MIP** $15

488 Sting Rod, dk. met. gray, blk. win., org. metal C, cts **MIP** $3

489 Big Bertha, met. dk. gray/org., gray pl. C, **MIP** $12

489 Tough Customer, blk./lt. purp., blk. pl. C, **MIP** $4

491 Rocket Shot, met. gray/org., gray pl. C, **MIP** $10

492 Swingfire, org., gray int., gray pl. C, 5sp **MIP** $10

493 Porsche 911 Targa, yel., blk. int., clr. win., blk. pl. C, alw-5sp **MIP** $8

494 Mercedes 500SL, met. gray, red int., clr. win., blk. metal C, 5sp **MIP** $2

496 Ferrari 308GT, red, blk. int., tinted win., blk. pl. C, 5sp **MIP** $3

497 Ferrari Testarossa, pearl wht., blk. int., clr. win., blk. pl. C, 5sp **MIP** $3

498 BMW 850i, silv. met., red int., clr. win., blk. pl. C, 5sp **MIP** $3

499 Corvette Coupe, dk. grn. met., red int., clr. win., blk. pl. C, 5sp **MIP** $6

502 Chevy Nomad, red met., tan int/open wheel int., clr. win., metal M, g7sp **MIP** $7

503 '80's Corvette, red met., gray int., clr. win., metal M, 3sp **MIP** $3

504 Camaro Z28, pearl wht., blue win., blk. metal M, 3sp **MIP** $3

505 1993 Camaro, blk. met., tan int., clr. win., blk. pl. M, 5sp **MIP** $3

506 Nissan 300ZX, purp. met., purp. int., clr. win., purp. metal C, 5sp **MIP** $3

507 Peugeot 205 Rallye, blk./blue/purp., blk. int., clr. win., org. metal C, 5sp **MIP** $30

1997 First Editions

509 Firebird funny car, dk. met. blue, metal int., clr. win., metal M, 5sp **MIP** $5

510 25th. Countach, pearl yel., blk. int., clr. win., blk. pl. M, 5dot **MIP** $3

512 Excavator, wht., blk. pl. M, blk. treads **MIP** $25

513 Ford 150 pickup truck, red, chr. int., smoked win., gray pl. M, 5sp **MIP** $3

514 Way 2 Fast, org., chr. int., metal M "no tm", 5sp **MIP** $5

515 '97 Corvette, met. grn., tan int., smoked win., blk. pl. M, bbs **MIP** $3

516 10-Mercedes C-Class, blk., gray int., clr. win., gray pl. M, gbbs **MIP** $3

517 '59 Chevy Impala, purp. pearl, wht. int., clr. win., chr. M, g7sp **MIP** $35

518 BMW M Roadster, met. silv., red int., clr. win., metal M, 5sp **MIP** $3

518 BMW Z3 Roadster, met. silv., red int., clr. win., metal M, 5sp **MIP** $6

519 Scorchin' Scooter, candy purp., metal M, blk. spoke **MIP** $5

520 Saltflat Racer, lt. red pl., chr. int., silv. metal M, 5sp **MIP** $4

1997 Treasure Hunts

578 '56 Flashsider, met. grn., chr. win., chr. M, 5sp **MIP** $25

579 Silhouette II, wht., wht. int., blue win., wht. pl. M, w3sp **MIP** $15

580 Mercedes 500SL, blk., wht. int., clr. win., blk. pl. M, 5sp **MIP** $15

581 Street Cleaver, blk. pl., gold metal M, 5sp **MIP** $20

582 GM Lean Machine, burgundy met./chr., chr. win., blk. metal M, 5sp **MIP** $12

583 Hot Rod Wagon, yel., blk. int., metal M, y5sp **MIP** $35

584 Olds Aurora, purp., gray int., clr. win., chr. M, 5sp **MIP** $11

585 Dogfighter, met. grn., yel. pl. M, 5sp **MIP** $20

586 Buick Wildcat, silv. flake, blk. win., gray pl. M, 3sp **MIP** $15

587 Blimp, blue, wht. Gondola, **MIP** $12

588 Avus Quattro, gold met., wht. int., smoked win., blk. pl. M, t/b **MIP** $12

589 Rail Rodder, wht. pl., metal M, b5sp **MIP** $25

1997 Series

PHANTOM RACERS

529 Power Rocket, transparent grn. pl., chr. int., pink win., metal M, 3sp **MIP** $10

530 Power Pistons, transparent red pl., gray int., clr. win., metal M, 3sp**MIP** $3

531 Power Pipes, transparent blue, chr. int., purp. win., metal M, 3sp **MIP** $3

532 Road Rocket, transparent org., lime win., metal M, 3sp **MIP** $4

RACE TEAM III

533 Hummer, blue pl., sm. antenna, gray win., metal M, t/b **MIP** $3

534 Chevy 1500 pickup, met. blue, wht. int., smoked win., metal M, 3sp **MIP** $9

535 3-Window '34, met. blue, blue int., smoked win., metal M, 5sp **MIP** $4

536 '80s Corvette, met. blue, wht. int., trsp.blue roof win., metal M, 5sp **MIP** $3

HEET FLEET

537 Police Cruiser, grn., purp. int., clr. win., purp. pl. M, 3sp **MIP** $10

538 Peterbilt Tank Truck, met. maroon, chr. win., chr. M, 5sp **MIP** $5

538 School Bus, dk. grn., wht. int., clr. win., blk. pl. M, 3sp **MIP** $5

538 School Bus (China), dk. grn., wht. int., clr. win., blk. pl. M, 7sp **MIP** $3

539 Peterbilt Fuel Tanker, met. maroon, chr. win., chr. M, t/b **MIP** $3

539 Peterbilt Tank Truck, met. maroon, chr. win., chr. M, 7sp **MIP** $3

540 Ramblin' Wrecker, blk., chr. int., smoked win., chr. M, 7sp **MIP** $5

BIFF! BAM! BOOM!

541 Mini Truck, red, blk. int., smoked win., blk. pl. M, 3sp **MIP** $3

542 Limozeen, lt. blue pearl, wht. int., smoked win., chr. M, 5dot **MIP** $30

543 VW Bug, met. grn., blk. int., clr. win., metal M, 5sp **MIP** $5

544 Range Rover, pearl purp., gray int., clr. win., chr. M, t/b **MIP** $3

QUICKSILVER

545 Chevy Stocker, red, blk. win., metal M, 3sp **MIP** $2

546 Aeroflash, purp. pl., wht. win., wht. metal M, 3sp **MIP** $2

547 Ferrari 308, pearl wht. pl., blk. win., blk. metal M, 5dot **MIP** $2

548 T-Bird Stock Car, blue pl., blk. win., metal M, 5sp **MIP** $2

SPEED SPRAY

549 Hydroplane, wht., chr. int., clr. win., blue pl. M, **MIP** $3

550 Street Roader, wht., red int., clr. win., metal M, ct/b **MIP** $3

551 XT-3, blue, org. win., wht. metal M, 5sp **MIP** $3

552 Funny Car, pearl magenta, metal int., clr. win., metal M, 5sp **MIP** $4

SPY PRINT

553 Stealth, purp. pl., chr. int., purp. win., metal M, 3sp **MIP** $3

554 Alien, blue/wht., wht./blue int., smoked win., metal M, 3sp **MIP** $3

555 Sol-Aire CX4, met. maroon, blk. win., blk. pl. M, 3sp **MIP** $3

556 Custom Corvette, blk., gray int., smoked win., blk. pl. M, 3sp **MIP** $2

STREET BEAST

557 Mercedes-Benz Unimog, red/blk., red int., clr. win., metal M, ct/b **MIP** $2

558 Jaguar XJ220, org., blk. int., clr. win., blk. pl. M, yt/b **MIP** $2

559 Blown Camaro, yel., blk. int., clr. win., metal M, ot/b **MIP** $3

560 Corvette Stingray, wht., blue int., blue win., metal M, yt/b **MIP** $3

WHITE ICE

561 Speed Machine, pearl wht., wht. int., red win., metal M, 3sp **MIP** $2

562 Shadow Jet, pearl wht./gold tint chr., wht. int., yel. win., metal M, 5sp **MIP** $2

563 Splittin' Image II, pearl wht., blue win., wht. pl. M, 3sp **MIP** $2

564 Twin Mill II, pearl wht., wht. int., red win., wht. pl. M, 5sp **MIP** $2

DEALER'S CHOICE

565 Silhouette II, pearl blue, gold int., clr. win., blk. pl. M, 5dot **MIP** $2

566 Street Beast, wht./gold, gold int., clr. win., metal M, 5dot **MIP** $2

567 Baja Bug, met. red, wht. int., metal M, 5sp **MIP** $5

568 '63 Corvette, blk., red int., clr. win., red pl. "'63 Corvette" M, 5dot **MIP** $3

ROCKIN' RODS

569 Twang Thang, dk. red met., chr. int., clr. win., blk. pl. M, 5sp **MIP** $2

570 Ferrari 355, blk., purp. int., clr. win., metal M, 3sp **MIP** $3

571 Turbo Flame, purp. pl., chr. int., yel. win., blk. metal M, 5sp **MIP** $5

572 Porsche 930, met. grn., blk. int., smoked win., metal M, 3sp **MIP** $50

BLUE STREAK

573 Olds 442, dk. candy blue, blk. int., blue win., chr. M, 3sp **MIP** $5

574 Nissan Truck, candy blue, blk. int., blue win., blk. pl. M, ct/b **MIP** $20

575 '55 Chevy, candy blue, blk. win., chr. M, 3sp **MIP** $5

576 Speed Blaster, candy blue, chr. win., chr. M, 3sp **MIP** $20

577 Police Cruiser, blk., tan int., smoked win., blk. pl. M, b7sp **MIP** $4

1997 Basic Line

300 Rigor Motor, blk., red chr. int., red win., metal C, bbs **MIP** $3

323 Rodzilla, chr., metal C, 5sp **MIP** $3

341 58 Corvette, candy purp. met., chr. int., clr. win., purp. pl. M, 5dot **MIP** $3

342 Mercedes SL, blk./gray, red int., clr. win., gray pl. M, bbs **MIP** $3

343 Speed Blaster, grn., chr. win., chr. M, 5dot **MIP** $3

344 Camaro Convertible, red, blk. int., clr. win., blk. pl. C, 5sp **MIP** $3

345 Speed-a-Saurus, purp., metal M, 5sp **MIP** $3

347 Power Pistons, burgundy pl., gray int., blue win., silv. metal M, t/b **MIP** $2

348 Dodge Ram, met. grn., chr. int., smoked win., gray pl. M, 5dot **MIP** $3

349 Power Pipes, dk. blue pl., chr. int int., purp. win., silv. metal M, 5sp **MIP** $2

352 Big Chill, wht. w/blk. tampo, chr. win., blk. pl. M, org. ski **MIP** $4

523 1970 Plymouth Barracuda, sublime, blk. int., tinted win., chr. C, 5sp **MIP** $7

524 GMC Motorhome, blue met., wht. int., clr. win., gray pl. Ind., bw **MIP** $25

525 Trail Buster Jeep, blk., blk. int., clr. win., metal Ind., bw **MIP** $4

526 Neet Streater, yel., blk. int., metal Ind., bw **MIP** $5

527 Second Wind, wht., blue int., blue win., blue pl. Ind., bw **MIP** $3

528 Beach Blaster, wht., red int., clr. win., gray Ind., bw **MIP** $2

590 Porsche 911, red, blk. int., smoked win., metal M, asw-t/b **MIP** $15

591 Porsche 959, silv. blue pearl, blk. int., smoked win., metal M, t/b **MIP** $3

592 Porsche 930, blue pearl, blk. int., smoked win., metal M, t/b **MIP** $3

593 Skullrider, dk. pink chr., blk. int., metal, 5sp **MIP** $4

594 GM Ultralite, wht./blk. "Police", blk. win., blk. pl. "Warner" M, 7sp **MIP** $10

594 Police Car, wht./blk., no tampo, blk. win., blk. pl. M, 3sp **MIP** $3

595 Corvette Sting Ray III, met. purp., gray int., clr. win., purp. pl. M, 5sp **MIP** $5

596 Pontiac Salsa, org., gray int., silv. win., chr. M, 3sp **MIP** $25

597 Buick Wildcat, candy red, blk. win., blk. pl. M, 7sp **MIP** $20

598 Turboa, butterscotch, gold int., metal C, 5sp **MIP** $2

599 Camaro Wind, wht., pink chr. win., metal C, bbs **MIP** $4

600 Nissan Custom "Z", lt. blue, blk. int., clr. win., metal C, bbs **MIP** $4

601 Commando, bronze, blk. int., clr. win., metal C, cts **MIP** $6

602 Sharkruiser, blk., gray metal C, bbs **MIP** $3

603 BMW 325i, yel., blk. int., clr. win., gray ptd. C, bbs **MIP** $2

604 Ferrari 308 GTS, yel./blk., blk. int., clr. win., blk. pl. C, 5sp **MIP** $6

605 Mercedes 2.6, met. gold, blk. int., clr. win., blk. pl. C, bbs **MIP** $2

606 Mercedes 300TD, dk. grn. met., gray int., clr. win., gray pl. C, 5sp **MIP** $3

607 Fat Fendered '40, aqua, blk. int., clr. win., metal C, 5sp **MIP** $12

608 Porsche 911, met. silv., blk. int., clr. win., blk. pl. C, 5sp **MIP** $2

609 Jaguar XJ40, dk. blue met., wht. int., blue win., blk. pl. C, bbs **MIP** $3

610 Land Rover Mk II, org., blk. int., clr. win., blk. pl. C, 5sp **MIP** $10

611 Fire Eater II, red, blue win., gray pl. C, 5sp **MIP** $2

612 '57 T-Bird, aqua, wht. int., clr. win., metal C, bw **MIP** $10

613 London Bus, red, blk. win., blk. pl. C, 5sp **MIP** $9

615 Ford XR4Ti, met. silv., red int., clr. win., blk. pl. C, 5sp **MIP** $2

616 '80's Corvette, wht., blue int., clr. win., blk. pl. C, bbs **MIP** $4

617 Flame Stopper II, red, blk. int., smoked win., gray pl. C, 5sp **MIP** $2

618 Chevy Stocker, wht., purp. int., clr. win., metal C, 5sp **MIP** $20

619 London Taxi, yel., blk. int., clr. win., metal C, 5sp **MIP** $7

620 Ford Transit Wrecker, lt. blue, blk. win., wht. pl. C, 5sp **MIP** $5

622 City Police, blk./wht., gray int., clr. win., blk. pl. C, b5sp **MIP** $3

623 Mustang Cobra, pearl pink, blk. int., clr. win., blk. pl. C, bbs **MIP** $2

624 Assault Crawler, olive, olive pl. C, **MIP** $5

625 Classic Packard, blk., blk. int int., clr. win., metal C, 5sp **MIP** $5

641 Wheel Loader, org./wht. HW logo, gray int., metal C, cts **MIP** $4

642 Forklift, wht., sm. blue HW logo, metal C, rear 5sp/front bw **MIP** $5

643 Digger, yel., yel. C, no HW logo, 5sp **MIP** $5

1998 First Editions

633 Dodge Caravan, dk. burgundy met., wht. int., smoked win., gray pl. M, t/b **MIP** $5

634 Dodge Sidewinder, day-glo org./wht. HW logo, purp. int., smoked win., gray pl. M, 5sp **MIP** $3

635 '65 Impala, candy purp., tan int., clr. win., chr. M, gbbs **MIP** $4

636 '32 Ford (no post), blk. w/yel./red flames, red int., clr. win., blk. pl. M, 5sp **MIP** $10

636 '32 Ford (with post), blk. w/mostly red flames, red int., clr. win., blk. pl. M, 5sp **MIP** $15

637 Escort Rally, wht. pearl, red int., smoked win., gray pl. M "Escort Rally", bbs **MIP** $2

637 Escort Rally (Ford), wht. pearl, red int., smoked win., gray pl. M "Ford Rally", bbs **MIP** $10

638 Jaguar D-Type, dk. blue met., gray int., clr. win., dk. blue met. metal M, t/b **MIP** $2

639 Jaguar XK8, pearl grn. met., wht. int., clr. win., gray pl. M, bbs **MIP** $100

640 Slideout, candy purp., gray pl. M, 5sp **MIP** $5

644 '63 T-Bird, teal met., wht. int., clr. win., metal M, 5dot **MIP** $3

645 Dairy Delivery, wht. pearl/dk. pink curved top stripe, aqua int., clr. win., gray pl. M, 5sp **MIP** $4

646 Mercedes SLK, yel. enamel w/wht. side paint, blk. int., smoked win., metal M, 5dot **MIP** $12

647 Lakester, red, chr. int int., clr. win., red metal M, 5sp **MIP** $3

648 Hot Seat, wht. pl., blk. int., metal M or T, 5sp **MIP** $2

650 Solar Eagle III, yel., int., blk. win., blk. flake M, **MIP** $2

651 Go Kart, day-glo grn., blk. int., day-glo grn. metal M, 5sp **MIP** $5

652 Pikes Peak Celica, yel. w/purp. tampo, red int., smoked win., blk. pl. M, gbbs **MIP** $7

653 IROC Firebird, gold met., lt. gray int int., tinted win., gray pl. C, b5sp **MIP** $2

654 40 Ford Pickup, candy blue met., gray int., blue win., chr. M, 5sp **MIP** $3

654 '40 Ford Pickup, blue pearl, gray int., blue win., chr. M, 5sp **MIP** $20

655 Super Comp Dragster, blk. w/3 decals, gray int., chr. M, 5sp **MIP** $8

657 Panoz GTR-1, wht., dk. red stripes, lg. HW logo, blue int., clr. win., blk. pl. C, bbs **MIP** $5

658 Tow Jam, red w/lg. HW logo on roof, blk. win., chr. M, 3sp **MIP** $50

659 Tail Dragger, candy purp. met., wht. int., clr. win., metal M, bbs **MIP** $4

661 '70 Roadrunner, lt. Hemi org. w/short trunk stripe, blk. int., clr. win., chr. M, 5sp **MIP** $5

662 Bad Mudder, wht./dk. blue wedge, no roof tampo or logo, blk. int., blk. pl. M, ct/b **MIP** $80

663 Customized C3500, teal w/long thin stripe, gray int., smoked win., gray pl. M, 5dot **MIP** $15

664 Super Modified, blk., pink int., metal M, bbs/2 **MIP** $3

665 Mustang Cobra, blk. w/no Cosen, gray int., clr. win., gray pl. M, gbbs **MIP** $10

667 At-A-Tude, blue met., chr. int., org. win., blk. pl. M, lg. rear/bbs/bbs **MIP** $4

668 Ford GT-90, wht., blue int., smoked win., metal M, 3sp **MIP** $2

669 Chaparral 2, wht., blk. int., clr. win., blk. metal M, bbs/2 **MIP** $3

670 Mustang Mach I, day-glo org., blk. int., blue win., blk. pl. M, 5sp **MIP** $40

671 Chrysler Thunderbolt, silv., wht. int., purp. win., blk. pl. M, 5dot **MIP** $2

672 Dodge Concept Car, org. pearl, purp. int., smoked win., metal M, 5sp **MIP** $300

673 Whatta Drag, met. red, chr. int., org. win., metal M, 3sp **MIP** $3

674 Sweet 16 II, dk. purp. met., chr. int., purp. win., dk. purp. met. metal M, 5sp **MIP** $3

677 Callaway C-7, silv. w/blk. ptd. headlt.s, blk. int., clr. win., blk. pl. M, 5sp **MIP** $4

678 Express Lane, red pl., blk. int., metal M, 5sp **MIP** $3

681 Cat-A-Pult, red w/red HW logo, blk. int., org. win., metal M, 5sp **MIP** $25

682 Fathom This, wht. w/logo, tampo on top, org. win., **MIP** $4

684 Double Vision, red met., gray int., clr. win., gray pl. M, gbbs **MIP** $2

1998 Treasure Hunts

749 Twang Thang, blk. w/blue chr. guitars, chr. int., clr. win., blk. pl. M, 5sp **MIP** $15

750 Scorchin' Scooter, met. red, metal M, chr./blk. **MIP** $40

751 Kenworth T600A, dk. candy purp., blk. win., chr. M, 3sp **MIP** $25

752 3-Window '34, org., chr. int int., clr. win., metal M, 5dot **MIP** $35

753 Turbo Flame, chr./grn., chr. int., grn. win., blk. metal M, 5sp **MIP** $15

754 Saltflat Racer, blk. pl., gold chr. int., red win., gold met. metal T, 5sp **MIP** $15

755 Street Beast, red/wht., wht. int., red win., metal M, gbbs **MIP** $15

756 Road Rocket, chr. body, metal M, 3sp **MIP** $15

757 Sol-Aire CX4, wht., blue int., clr. win., blue pl. M, wbbs **MIP** $15

758 '57 Chevy, met. grn., yel. int., yel. win., gold chr. T, 3sp **MIP** $35

759 Stingray III, met. silv., red int., smoked win., blk. pl. M, 3sp **MIP** $25

760 Way 2 Fast, olive flake, chr. int int., metal T, 5sp **MIP** $20

1998 Series

TATTOO MACHINES

685 '57 T-Bird, lt. blue pearl, blue int., blue win., chr. M, 3sp **MIP** $2

686 '93 Camaro, day-glo grn., wht. int., smoked win., blk. pl. M, 3sp **MIP** $2

687 Stutz Blackhawk, met. red, wht. int., tinted win., metal M, 3sp **MIP** $2

688 Corvette Stingray, org., blk. int., smoked win., metal M, 3sp **MIP** $2

TECHNO BITS

689 Shadow Jet II, blk. w/org. side tampo, chr. int., grn. win., metal M, b5sp **MIP** $3

690 Power Pistons, purp. pl., gold int., yel. win., metal M, 3sp **MIP** $2

691 Shadow Jet, met. blue, blk. int., smoked win., metal M, 5sp **MIP** $6

692 Radar Ranger, day-glo grn., purp. int., red win., blk. metal M, ct/b **MIP** $2

TROPICOOL

693 Ice Cream Truck, wht. w/wht. HW logo, grn. int., clr. win., blk. pl. M, 5sp **MIP** $10

694 Baja Bug, wht./dk. red, red int., metal M, lg. rear 5sp MIP $7

695 Classic Caddy, red/blk. fenders, lt. gray int., smoked win., metal M, bbs MIP $3

696 Corvette Convertible, day-glo grn., blue int., smoked win., blk. pl. M, 3sp MIP $6

LOW 'N COOL

697 Mini Truck, day-glo yel., blk. int., smoked win., blk. pl. M, g3sp MIP $2

698 '59 Impala, grn. pearl/dk. purp. tampo, wht. int., smoked win., chr. M, gbbs MIP $4

699 '59 Caddy, pearl rose, wht. int., smoked win., chr. T, gbbs MIP $3

716 Limozeen, blk. flake, wht. int., smoked win., gold chr. M, gbbs MIP $4

BIOHAZARD

717 Hydroplane, dk. day-glo grn., chr. int., clr. win., blk. pl. T, MIP $25

718 Flame Stopper, day-glo pink, blk. win., blk. pl. T, yt/b MIP $3

719 Recycling Truck, day-glo yel. w/blk. tampo, blk. win., blk. pl. M, t/b MIP $5

720 Rescue Ranger, blk., yel. int., yel. win., chr. M, 5sp MIP $4

DASH 4 CASH

721 Jaguar XJ220, silv., lt. purp. int., clr. win., blk. pl. M, bbs MIP $5

722 Ferrari F40, lt. gold met., tan int., tinted win., metal M, gbbs MIP $4

723 Audi Avus, blk., wht. int., smoked win., blk. pl. T, gbbs MIP $3

724 Dodge Viper, wht. pearl, red int., smoked win., blk. pl. T, t/b MIP $3

RACE TEAM IV

725 '67 Camaro, met. blue, wht. int., tinted win., no origin metal, 5sp MIP $5

726 Mercedes C-Class, met. blue, wht. int., smoked win., blk. pl. T, 5sp MIP $3

727 Shelby Cobra 427 S/C, met. blue, wht. int., smoked win., metal M, 5sp MIP $3

728 '63 Corvette, met. blue, wht. int., tinted win., chr. M, 5sp MIP $8

ARTISTIC LICENSE

729 Alien, wht. enamel, wht. int., tinted win., metal T, 3sp MIP $8

730 '57 Chevy, gray pl., dk. smoked win., metal M, t/b MIP $3

731 VW Bug, wht. pearl, blk. int., blue win., metal M, 5dot MIP $4

732 1970 Barracuda, blk. w/org. HW logo, dk. day-glo org. int., smoked win., chr. M, 3sp MIP $3

MIXED SIGNALS

733 Street Roader, wht. pearl, yel. int., smoked win., metal M, ct/b MIP $2

734 '80's Corvette, met. grn., blk. int., smoked win., metal M, bbs MIP $2

735 Nissan Truck, org. pearl, blk. int., clr. win., blk. pl. M, ct/b MIP $2

736 School Bus, yel. w/HW logo on rear door, blk. int., clr. win., blk. pl. M, 5dot MIP $3

FLYN' ACES

737 '70 Dodge Daytona, met. grn., blk. int., clr. win., tan M, 5dot MIP $3

738 Dogfighter, blk., chr. int., yel. pl. M, 5dot MIP $3

739 Sol-Aire CX4, yel. w/gray stripes, blk. int., clr. win., blk. pl. M, 5sp MIP $3

740 XT-3, met. gray, blk. win., org. metal M, 5sp MIP $2

SUGAR RUSH

741 Mazda MX-5 Miata, org. w/bright yel. headlights, blk. int., smoked win., org. metal T, 5sp MIP $5

742 Funny Car, wht., metal int., blk. window win., metal M, 5sp MIP $5

743 '95 Camaro, dk. met. blue, blk. int., clr. win., blk. pl. M, 5sp MIP $4

744 '96 Mustang Convertible, yel., blk. int., clr. win., metal C, 5sp MIP $5

TECH TONES

745 Buick Wildcat, blk./grn., silv. win., lt. grn. pl. M, 3sp MIP $3

746 Silhouette II, blk./purp. w/wht. HW logo, wht. int., clr. win., purp. pl. M, 5dot MIP $5

747 Speed Machine, blk./gold, gold int., clr. win., metal M, t/b MIP $3

748 Avus Quattro, blk./red, wht. int., clr. win., dk. red pl. M, gbbs MIP $3

1998 Basic Line

700 Shock Factor, yel./blue, blue int., metal C, alw-bw MIP $3

702 Lumina Van, dk. grn. met., tan int., smoked win., blk. pl. C, bbs MIP $4

712 Tipper, blue, blk. int., smoked win., blk. pl. C, 5sp MIP $2

714 Talbot Lago, blue/blk., blue win., blk. metal C, bbs MIP $255

715 1996 Mustang GT, wht., red int., clr. win., metal C, 5sp MIP $30

761 Flame Stopper, red, blk. window win., blk. pl. M, ct/b MIP $2

765 Oshkosh P-Series, lt. met. blue/wht., blue int., metal M, ct/b MIP $4

767 Mercedes 380SEL, wht. pearl, tan int., clr. win., met. gold metal M, t/b MIP $2

768 Lamborghini Countach, blk., red int., clr. win., blk. pl. M, 5dot MIP $2

770 Lexus SC400, met. blue, wht. int., smoked win., blk. pl. M, bbs MIP $5

771 '56 Flashsider, yel. pearl, blk. win., chr. M, 5dot MIP $3

773 Hot Wheels 500, day-glo yel., blk. int., metal M, b7sp MIP $3

774 Ramp Truck, dk. grn. met./gray, smoked win., metal C, 5sp MIP $3

778 Speed Blaster, met. blue, chr. win., blk. pl. M, 3sp MIP $4

779 Big Chill, blue, chr. int., wht. pl. T, blk. MIP $8

780 '58 Corvette, aqua w/engine, chr. int., smoked win., aqua pl. M, 5dot MIP $6

781 Lamborghini Diablo, dk. red met., tan int., tinted win., blk. metal M, 5sp MIP $3

782 Radar Ranger, gold met., blk. int., clr. win., metal M, ct/b MIP $3

783 Twin Mill II, met. silv., blk. win., blk. pl. M, all alw-bbs MIP $3

784 Ferrari F512M, met. silv., blk. int., clr. win., blk. ptd. M, 5dot MIP $3

784 Ferrari Testarossa, met. silv., blk. int., clr. win., blk. ptd. M, 5dot MIP $5

787 '57 Chevy, met. purp., blk. int., smoked win., chr. T, t/b MIP $4

788 Mercedes 540K, purp. met./blue, blk. int., clr. win., metal M, asw-bbs MIP $4

791 Treadator, met. blue, chr. win., blk. pl. T, blk. treads MIP $3

792 Camaro Race Car, wht. pearl, blk. int., clr. win., blk. pl. M, 5sp MIP $3

793 Auburn 852, blk. w/gold fenders, gold int., tinted win., metal M, gbbs MIP $6

795 Tractor, silv. met./blk., silv. int., blk. pl. M, c/tt rear-ct/b front MIP $3

796 '96 Camaro Convertible, wht., org. int., smoked win., gray pl. Ind., w5sp MIP $3

797 Dodge Ram 1500, red, yel. int., smoked win., wht. pl. M, 5dot MIP $4

798 Propper Chopper, blue, blk. int., blue win., blk. pl. M, MIP $3

802 Flashfire, gold met./no logo, blk. int., smoked win., gold pl. M, 5dot MIP $5

803 '40's Woodie, wht. pearl/tan, blk. int., smoked win., metal M, 5sp MIP $8

808 Driven To The Max, wht. pearl, hot pink int., metal T, 5sp MIP $3

812 GM Lean Machine, grn./gold met., gold int., smoked win., metal M, t/b MIP $3

813 Ferrari 355, blk., yel. int., yel. win., metal M, 3sp MIP $90

814 Speed-A-Saurus, glossy teal pl., org. metal M, lg. rear 5sp MIP $3

815 Mercedes 500SL, dk. grn. met., tan int., smoked win., blk. pl. T, 3sp MIP $3

816 Ferrari 308, met. bronze, tan int., smoked win., blk. metal M, 5dot MIP $3

817 Porsche 928, wht. pearl, blk. win., metal M, bbs MIP $3

818 Porsche Carrera, red met., tan int., smoked win., metal M, g5sp MIP $3

820 Zender Fact 4, met. grn., blk. int., clr. win., blk. pl. C, bbs MIP $3

821 '96 Mustang Convertible, wht., red int., clr. win., metal C, 5sp MIP $4

822 Camaro Z-28, teal met., gray int., clr. win., metal no origin, 3sp MIP $5

823 Sol-Aire CX4, blue met., wht. int., clr. win., wht. pl. M, gbbs **MIP** $4

827 Radio Flyer Wagon, red, blk. int., metal M, 5sp **MIP** $5

829 Porsche Carrera, silv. met., red int., clr. win., metal M, t/b **MIP** $3

834 Ferrari Testarossa, blk., tan/blk. int., clr. win., gloss blk. metal Ind., bw **MIP** $3

835 Baja Bug, dk. met. blue, wht. int int., metal Ind., amw-bw **MIP** $5

837 Radio Flyer Wagon, met. blue, wht. int., metal C, 5sp **MIP** $4

850 Rail Rodder, gray pl., metal M, b5sp **MIP** $3

851 Treadator, lt. blue pearl, chr. win., day-glo grn. pl. T, **MIP** $5

852 Rigor Motor, candy purp. met., chr. int., yel. win., metal M, amw-g5sp **MIP** $7

853 Camaro Z28, day-glo yel. pl., blk. win., metal M, 5dot **MIP** $5

854 Porsche 959, wht. w/pink tampo, blk. int., smoked win., metal M, t/b **MIP** $5

855 Ferrari F50, candy purp. met., blk. int., smoked win., blk. pl. M, t/b **MIP** $3

856 Porsche 930, met. red, blk. int., smoked win., metal T, 3sp **MIP** $4

857 T-Bird Stocker, org. pl., blk. win., blk. metal T, 5dot **MIP** $3

858 Hummer, wht. pl./org. tampo, red win., blk. metal M, ct/b **MIP** $6

859 Bronco, red/wht., blk. int., smoked win., metal T, ct/b **MIP** $5

860 Road Rocket, wht./dk. blue, wht. int., metal T, 3sp **MIP** $3

861 Twin Mill II, met. gold, blk. window win., blk. pl. M, bbs **MIP** $3

862 Pontiac Salsa, red met., blk. win., chr. M, 5dot **MIP** $3

863 Oshkosh Cement Mixer, day-glo yel. w/silv. fenders, yel. int., blk. pl. M, 3sp **MIP** $4

864 Tank Truck, dk. burgundy met./chr., chr. win., blk. pl. M, 5dot **MIP** $5

865 Ford F150, wht., chr. int., smoked win., blk. pl. M, 3sp **MIP** $3

866 Ferrari 250, gold met., blk. int., smoked win., blk. pl. T, bbs **MIP** $4

867 '97 Corvette, met. blue, wht. int., smoked win., red pl. T, 5sp **MIP** $4

868 Range Rover, grn. met., tan int., smoked win., chr. T, ct/b **MIP** $4

869 Power Pipes, blk. pl., chr. int., org. win., org. metal T, ot/b **MIP** $3

870 Chevy Stocker, purp. pl., blk. win., blk. metal M, gt/b **MIP** $3

871 Olds 442, met. blue, wht. int., smoked win., chr. T, 5sp **MIP** $4

872 Rig Wrecker, wht., chr. int., smoked win., blk. pl. T, 5dot **MIP** $5

873 Hydroplane, wht., blk. int., smoked win., blk. pl. M, **MIP** $3

874 Pit Crew Truck, candy gray, red int., blue win., red pl. T, 5dot **MIP** $3

875 Police Car, blk., gray int., tinted win., blk. pl. T, 5sp **MIP** $5

876 Bywayman, red, wht. int., tinted win., metal T, ct/b **MIP** $3

877 Chevy 1500, gray pl., blk. int., clr. win., blk. metal Ind., t/b **MIP** $3

881 '95 Camaro, blk., red int., smoked win., blk. pl. Ind., 3sp **MIP** $3

884 Gulch Stepper, yel. pearl, blk. win., metal T, ct/b **MIP** $3

889 Mercedes 380SEL, blk., tan int., tinted win., gold met. metal M, gbbs **MIP** $3

890 BMW Roadster, wht., red int., smoked win., metal M, 3sp **MIP** $3

894 Toyota MR2, wht., wht. int., smoked win., blk. pl. T, bbs **MIP** $3

899 '56 Flashsider, candy gray/dk. red tampo, blk. win., chr. T, 5sp **MIP** $7

908 Ford F Series "CNG" P/U, candy purp. met., chr. int., smoked win., blk. pl. M, 3sp **MIP** $15

1999 First Editions

649 1936 Cord, dk. red met. w/casting peg, purp. int., clr. win., chr. M, bbs **MIP** $10

656 '38 Phantom Corsair, blk. w/gray HW logo, gray int., clr. win., metal M, ww5sp **MIP** $15

675 Pontiac Rageous, met. red, gray int., smoked/blk. win., blk. pl. M, 3sp **MIP** $3

676 Porsche 911 GT1-98, wht., blk. int., clr. win., blk. pl. M, bbs **MIP** $2

680 Baby Boomer, candy blue, metal M, 5sp **MIP** $2

683 Tee'd Off, candy blue, wht. pearl int., metal M, 5sp **MIP** $4

683 Tee'd Off, wht. pearl, gray int., metal M, 5sp **MIP** $15

909 '99 Mustang, dk. candy purp. met., red int., clr. win., blk. pl. M, 5sp **MIP** $31

910 Monte Carlo Concept Car, red, gray int., smoked win., silv. met. metal M, 5sp **MIP** $3

911 Olds Aurora GT3, wht./met. blue, blk. int., clr. win., blk. pl. M, gbbs **MIP** $20

911 Olds Aurora GTS-1, wht./met. blue, blk. int., clr. win., blk. pl. M, gbbs **MIP** $15

912 Porsche 911 GT3 Cup, candy gray/yel. wing/wht. logo, org. int., blue win., blk. pl. M, bbs **MIP** $10

913 Popcycle, burgundy met./org. stripe, metal int., org. win., metal M, 3sp **MIP** $15

914 Semi Fast, red w/red grill, gray int., smoked win., metal M, 5sp **MIP** $8

915 1970 Chevelle SS, dk. blue met. w/pinstripe hood, wht. int., blue win., metal M, 5sp **MIP** $5

916 Phaeton, teal met., tan int., tinted win., metal M, 5sp **MIP** $3

917 Track T, blk., tan cover int., metal M, 5sp **MIP** $4

918 Screamin' Hauler, purp. met., metal int., blue win., metal M, 5sp **MIP** $3

919 Fiat 500C, candy purp. met., gray int., chr. win., metal M, 5sp **MIP** $5

921 Ford GT-40, blue met., gray int., blue win., gray pl. M, narrow rear 5sp **MIP** $5

922 Jeepster, red/blk., blk. int., smoked win., metal M, 5sp **MIP** $3

923 Turbolence, blk., gold chr. int., metal M, g5dot **MIP** $2

924 Pikes Peak Tacoma, yel., blk. int., clr. win., blk. pl. M, gbbs **MIP** $3

925 Shadow Mk IIa, blk., gray int., gray pl. M, 5sp **MIP** $3

926 Mercedes CLK-LM, candy gray, blk. int., clr. win., blk. pl. M, gbbs **MIP** $3

927 '56 Ford Truck, lt. blue pearl, chr. int., blue win., gray pl. M, 5sp **MIP** $5

928 Chrysler Pronto, yel. pearl, gray int., smoked win., blk. pl. M, 5sp **MIP** $3

1113 360 Modena, red/no HW logo, blk. int., clr. win., blk. pl. M, 5sp **MIP** $10

1113 Ferrari 360 Modena, red/yel. HW logo, blk. int., clr. win., blk. pl. M, 5sp **MIP** $4

1999 Treasure Hunts

929 Mercedes 540K, red, blk. int., clr. win., metal M, 5sp **MIP** $25

930 T-Bird Stocker, blue enamel, yel. int., clr. win., gray pl. M, 5sp **MIP** $10

931 '97 Corvette, pearl lavender, yel. int., smoked win., blk. pl. T, 5dot **MIP** $25

932 Rigor Motor, day-glo yel., chr. int., yel. win., blk. metal M, g5sp **MIP** $15

933 Ferrari F512M, yel., blk. int., clr. win., metal M, chr. star **MIP** $20

934 '59 Impala, met. purp., wht. int., smoked win., gold chr. M, gbbs **MIP** $20

935 Hot Wheels 500, blk., blk. int., metal M, org. ltr. b7sp **MIP** $15

936 Jaguar D-Type, blk. met., gold int., clr. win., blk. met. M, 5sp **MIP** $15

937 '32 Ford Delivery, met. gold w/purp. fenders, purp. int., clr. win., metal M, g5sp **MIP** $15

938 Hot Seat, clr. pl., blk. seat int., metal M, 5sp **MIP** $15

939 Mustang Mach I, grn. met., blk. int., clr. win., blk. pl. M, 5sp **MIP** $25

940 Express Lane, purp., blk. seat int., metal M, g5sp **MIP** $20

1999 Series

BUGGIN' OUT

941 Treadator, red/chr., chr. win., blk. pl. T, blk. treads **MIP** $3

942 Shadow Jet II, gray pl., yel. int., grn. win., metal M, 5sp **MIP** $3

943 Radar Ranger, purp. met., blue int., blue win., metal M, ct/b **MIP** $3

944 Baja Bug, lt. blue met., org. int., metal M, 5sp **MIP** $6

X-RAY CRUISER

945 Mercedes C-Class, blk. met., wht. int., yel. win., blk. pl. M, gbbs **MIP** $8

946 Lamborghini Diablo, met. teal, gray int., smoked win., blk. metal M, 5sp **MIP** $3

947 '67 Camaro, blue, wht. int., tinted win., metal M, 5sp **MIP** $7

948 Jaguar XJ220, yel., blue int., clr. win., blk. pl. M, 3sp **MIP** $3

1114 '63 Corvette, blk. met., tan int., clr. win., gold chr. M, g5sp **MIP** $6

STREET ART

850 Propper Chopper, pearl grn., blk. int., yel. win., blk. pl. M, **MIP** $4

949 Mini truck, met. blk., blk. int., clr. win., blk. pl. M, t/b **MIP** $3

951 Ambulance, candy purp. met., purp. int., org. win., chr. M, 5sp **MIP** $4

952 School Bus, yel./no rear door, yel. int., red win., blk. pl. M, 5dot **MIP** $8

PINSTRIPE POWER

953 3-Window '34, dk. purp. met., blk. int., blue win., metal M, 5sp **MIP** $5

954 Tail Dragger, blk., tan int., clr. win., metal M, bbs **MIP** $4

955 '65 Impala, lt. grn. met., tan int., smoked win., gold chr. M, gbbs**MIP** $4

956 Auburn 852, blk./silv., wht. int., clr. win., metal M, bbs **MIP** $3

GAME OVER

957 Lean Machine, purp./blk., blk. win., metal M, 5sp **MIP** $3

958 Shadow Jet, yel., yel. int., smoked win., metal M, 5sp **MIP** $3

959 Speed Blaster, lt. grn., gold chr. win., yel. pl. M, gt/b **MIP** $2

960 Twin Mill II, pink pearl, blk. win., blk. pl. M, bbs **MIP** $3

SURF 'N FUN

961 '40s Woodie, pearl purp. w/tan body, blk. int., blue win., metal M, 5sp **MIP** $4

962 VW Bug, lt. blue pearl, wht. int., smoked win., metal M, 5sp **MIP** $5

963 '55 Chevy, met. red, blk. win., chr. M, 3sp **MIP** $4

964 Chevy Nomad, wht. pearl/long hood stripe, wht. int., smoked win., metal M, g5sp **MIP** $8

X-TREEME SPEED

965 Dodge Sidewinder, wht., purp. int., smoked win., blk. pl. M, 5sp **MIP** $3

966 Callaway C7, grn., blk. int., clr. win., blk. pl. M, t/b **MIP** $3

967 Porsche Carrera, silv., wht. int., tinted win., metal M, g5sp **MIP** $3

968 Mazda MX-5 Miata, blue, grn. int., clr. win., blue metal M, bbs **MIP** $3

SUGAR RUSH

969 '70 Road Runner, yel., blk. int., clr. win., chr. M, 5dot **MIP** $4

970 Jaguar XK8, red, tan int., smoked win., blk. pl. M, gbbs **MIP** $3

971 Pikes Peak Celica, wht., blk. int., clr. win., blk. pl. M, bbs **MIP** $3

972 Dodge Concept Car, wht., blue int., clr. win., metal M, 5dot **MIP** $3

MEGA GRAPHICS

973 Funny Car, yel., metal int., yel. win., metal M, 5sp **MIP** $5

974 Mustang Cobra, wht. pearl, blk. int., clr. win., blk. pl. M, t/b **MIP** $3

975 Turbo Flame, blk. pl., blk. int., yel. win., red metal M, g5sp **MIP** $3

976 Firebird Funny Car, dk. purp. met., metal int., smoked win., metal M, b5sp **MIP** $5

TERRORIFIC

977 At-A-Tude, met. grn., chr. int., grn. win., blk. pl. M, b5sp **MIP** $3

978 Cat-A-Pult, org., blk. int., smoked win., metal M, 5sp **MIP** $3

979 Sweet Sixteen II, blk., yel. win., metal M, 5sp **MIP** $4

980 Splittin' Image II, met. gold, pink chr. win., blk. pl. M, 3sp **MIP** $3

CLASSIC GAMES

981 Super Modified, lt. blue pearl, blk. int., metal M, gbbs/2 **MIP** $3

982 Silhouette II, silv.-blue pearl, wht. int., blue win., blk. pl. M, 5dot **MIP** $2

983 Sol-Aire CX4, wht., blk. int., blue win., blk. pl. M, 3sp **MIP** $2

984 Escort Rally, red, blk. int., clr. win., gray pl. M, bbs **MIP** $8

CAR-TOON FRIENDS

985 Saltflat Racer, purp. pl., chr. int., clr. win., silv. ptd. metal M, 5sp **MIP** $3

986 XT-3, org., blk. win., blk. ptd. metal M, g5sp **MIP** $3

987 Double Vision, blk., gray int., clr. win., blk. pl. M, gbbs **MIP** $3

988 Lakester, wht./blk., chr. int., red win., blk. metal M, 5sp **MIP** $2

1999 Basic Line

991 Rodzilla, chr., metal C, gbbs **MIP** $3

992 Ferrari F512M, red, tan int., smoked win., blk. metal M, 5sp **MIP** $3

993 Ferrari 348, yel., blk./yel. int., smoked win., blk. pl. M, 5sp **MIP** $3

994 Way 2 Fast, blk. met., chr. int., met. gold ptd. metal, g5sp **MIP** $3

995 Porsche 911, yel. enamel, blk. int., smoked win., metal M, 5sp **MIP** $3

996 '32 Ford Delivery, lt. blue pearl, blk. int., blue win., metal M, bbs **MIP** $3

997 Jaguar D-Type, red enamel w/grn. tint stripe, gray int., smoked win., red metal M, bbs **MIP** $5

998 Firebird Funny Car, met. red, metal int., smoked win., metal M, g5sp **MIP** $5

999 Hot Seat, chr. w/gold logo, red seat int., metal M, 5sp **MIP** $5

1000 '59 Impala, wht. pearl, blk. int., smoked win., gold chr. M, gbbs**MIP** $3

1001 Slideout, met. blue, wht. pl. M, 5sp **MIP** $3

1003 Ferrari F40, blk., red int., smoked win., metal M, 5sp **MIP** $4

1004 Dairy Delivery, wht. w/blk. spots, blk. int., clr. win., chr. M, 5sp **MIP** $2

1005 Mercedes-Benz Unimog, red/blk., blk. int., clr. win., metal M, ct/b **MIP** $3

1006 Dodge Viper RT/10, met. blue, blk. int., smoked win., blk. pl. M, 5sp **MIP** $2

1007 Tow Jam, met. grn., blk. window win., chr. M, 3sp **MIP** $3

1008 Chaparral 2, red, blk. int., clr. win., wht. metal M, bbs/2 **MIP** $3

1009 Peterbilt Dump Truck, blue w/wht. box, blue int., blue win., metal M, 5sp **MIP** $4

1010 Ford Stake Bed Truck, teal w/gray stake bed, chr. int., blue win., chr. M, 5dot **MIP** $4

1011 Oshkosh Cement Truck, blk./burgundy, blk. pl. M, t/b **MIP** $4

1012 Flame Stopper, wht., blk. win., blk. pl. C, ct/b **MIP** $3

1013 Mercedes 500SL, silv., blk. int., smoked win., blk. pl. M, bbs **MIP** $3

1014 '67 Camaro, candy gray, blk. int., blue win., metal M, 5sp **MIP** $5

1015 Mercedes C-Class, yel., red int., clr. win., blk. pl. M, bbs **MIP** $2

1018 '32 Ford Coupe, wht. w/maroon in logo & flame, blk. int., clr. win., blk. pl. C, 5sp **MIP** $4

1022 '63 T-Bird, met. gold, wht. int., tinted win., metal T, bbs **MIP** $3

1024 Shelby Cobra 427 S/C, wht., blk. int., smoked win., metal T, 5sp **MIP** $4

1025 Mercedes SLK, dk. blue flake, wht. int., tinted win., metal Ind., t/b **MIP** $4

1026 Dodge Caravan, org. pearl, wht. int., smoked win., blk. pl. M, 5sp **MIP** $9

1027 Customized C3500, magenta pearl, blk. int., blue win., blk. pl. T, 5sp **MIP** $7

1028 '56 Flashsider, yel., blk. win., chr. T, 3sp **MIP** $5

1029 '40's Ford Truck, red, wht. int., yel. win., chr. C, 5sp **MIP** $4

1030 Porsche 959, gray pearl, blk. int., blue win., metal C, 5dot **MIP** $3

1031 Aeroflash, grn. pl., blk. int., clr. win., blk. metal M, 3sp **MIP** $4

1032 Ford GT-90, yel., blk. int., clr. win., metal C, 3sp **MIP** $2

1035 1970 Plymouth Barracuda, purp. met., blk. int., smoked win., chr. C, 3sp **MIP** $3

1037 Roll Patrol Jeep, yel., tan int., tinted win., metal T, ct/b MIP $25

1038 Dodge Viper RT/10, silv. flake, blk. int., clr. win., blk. pl. C, 3sp MIP $3

1040 Panoz GTR-1, pearl grn., blk. int., clr. win., blk. pl. C, 3sp MIP $3

1041 Super Comp Dragster, candy gray w/blk. fenders, blk. int., chr. T, 5sp MIP $3

1042 Twang Thang, met. grn., chr. int., grn. win., blk. pl. C, 5sp MIP $3

1043 Rail Rodder, wht. pl., metal M, b5sp MIP $4

1044 Whatta Drag, blk., red win., gray metal C, 5dot MIP $3

1045 Dodge Ram 1500, blk., lt. gray int., clr. win., lt. gray pl. C, 5sp MIP $5

1046 Police Cruiser, wht., blk. int., blue win., blk. pl. T, 3sp MIP $5

1047 Olds Aurora, blk./wht., tan int., clr. win., blk. pl. T, 5dot MIP $5

1048 Rescue Ranger, wht. "no Explosive Materials on fender", blue int., blue win., chr. C, 5sp MIP $15

1049 Treadator, blk., chr. win., blue pl. T, MIP $3

1051 '65 Mustang, blk., tan int., tinted win., metal C, g5sp MIP $4

1052 Rigor Motor, red, chr. int., smoked win., metal C, 5sp MIP $3

1053 Hydroplane, blk., chr. int., yel. win., blk. pl. C, MIP $3

1054 Porsche 959, blk., wht. int., clr. win., metal C, bbs MIP $2

1055 School Bus, blk., blk. int., red tint win., blk. pl. C, 5dot MIP $2

1056 Corvette Stingray, tan pl., smoked int., smoked win., metal C, gbbs MIP $3

1057 Thunderstreak, met. red/blue, blue int., metal C, yel. ltr. b5sp MIP $3

1058 '96 Mustang, dk. red met., blk. int., smoked win., metal C, gbbs MIP $3

1059 Dodge Ram 1500, met. grn., chr. int., tinted win., gray pl. C, 5dot MIP $4

1060 Ramp Truck, blk./yel., blk. win., metal C, 5dot MIP $4

1061 Rescue Ranger, wht., red int., red win., red pl. C, 5dot MIP $4

1062 Rail Rodder, dk. blue pl., metal M, b5sp MIP $3

1063 1970 Plymouth Barracuda, org., blk. int., tinted win., chr. C, 3sp MIP $4

1064 Lakester, silv. met., chr. int., grn. win., silv. met. metal C, 5sp MIP $2

1065 Firebird, wht., blk. int., smoked win., gray pl. C, b5sp MIP $4

1066 Mustang Cobra, met. gold, blk. int., clr. win., blk. pl. Ind., 5sp MIP $3

1067 Express Lane, org. pl., red int., metal C, 5sp MIP $3

1068 Dodge Concept Car, met. silv., blk. int., tinted win., metal C, gbbs MIP $2

1069 '40s Ford (Pickup), yel. w/red roof tampo, blk. int., smoked win., blk. pl. C, 5dot MIP $10

1070 '32 Ford Coupe, dk. red met., blk. int., clr. win., gray pl. C, 5dot MIP $4

1071 Panoz GTR-1, blk., red int., clr. win., blk. pl. C, 3sp MIP $2

1073 Ford GT-90, red, blk. int., smoked win., metal C, t/b MIP $2

1074 Blimp, blk. w/red tail, red metal M, MIP $3

1075 Scorchin' Scooter, red, metal M, chr./blk. MIP $5

1076 '59 Eldorado, met. blue/wht. w/silv. logo & stripe, wht. int., blue win., chr. M, bbs MIP $9

1077 '57 Chevy, red, blk. int., blk. win., chr. M, g/bbs MIP $4

1078 Camaro Z/28, met. blue, blk. win., metal M, 3sp MIP $3

1079 '63 Corvette, candy gray, blk. int., clr. win., blk. pl. M, 5dot MIP $3

1080 Hummvee, grn. pl./rear "HUMMVEE", gray win., metal M, ct/b MIP $3

1081 Power Plower, met. grn., lt. grn. int., yel. win., metal T, ct/b MIP $3

1082 Jaguar XJ220, met. gold, gold int., smoked win., blk. pl. M, g3sp MIP $2

1083 Blown Camaro, met. teal w/side hood stripes, blk. int., smoked win., metal M, bbs MIP $3

1084 Mazda MX-5 Miata, wht., blk. int., smoked win., blk. metal M, 3sp MIP $2

1085 Porsche 928, gold pearl, blk. win., metal M, 5dot MIP $2

1086 Toyota MR2, candy purp., gray int., clr. win., metal M, 3sp MIP $2

1087 Rig Wrecker, yel./blue, blk. int., clr. win., chr. M, 5dot MIP $5

1088 Speed Machine, blk., wht. int., yel. win., metal M, g5dot MIP $3

1089 25th Anniversary Lamborghini Countach, candy gray, blk. int., clr. win., blk. pl. M, 5dot MIP $3

1090 '97 Corvette, blk., wht. int., blue win., blk. pl. M, 3sp MIP $3

1091 X-Ploder, blk. pl. w/logo in front of wheel, chr. int., red win., metal M, t/b MIP $7

1092 '58 Corvette, blk. w/aqua motor, chr. int., smoked win., blk. pl. M, bbs MIP $15

1093 BMW 850i, met. gold, blk. int., smoked win., gold pl. M, bbs MIP $2

1094 Ferrari F355 Berlinetta, red enamel, blk. int., clr. win., metal M, 5sp MIP $4

1095 Mercedes SLK, gray met., blk. int., smoked win., blk. metal Ind., t/b MIP $2

1096 Avus Quattro, chr., blk. int., smoked win., blk. pl. M, 5sp MIP $2

1097 '31 Doozie, met. red/blk., blk. int., clr. win., metal M, bbs MIP $3

1098 '37 Bugatti, blk./yel., chr. int., clr. win., metal M, bbs MIP $3

1099 Road Rocket, red/blk., red int., metal M, bbs MIP $2

1100 Power Pipes, wht. pl., gold chr. int., red win., red metal M, 5dot MIP $2

1101 Radar Ranger, teal, wht. int., clr. win., metal M, ct/b MIP $3

1102 Mini Truck, blk., red int., smoked win., blk. pl. M, gbbs MIP $2

1103 1980 Corvette, met. gold, blk. int., smoked win., metal M, bbs MIP $4

1104 Twang Thang, org. pearl, gold chr. int., smoked win., purp. pl. M, g5sp MIP $3

1105 Mustang Mach I, met. blue, blk. int., clr. win., blk. pl. M, bbs MIP $4

1106 Go Kart, org., blk. int., org. metal M, 5dot MIP $8

1107 Chrysler Thunderbolt, dk. blue met., wht. int., smoked win., blk. pl. M, 3sp MIP $5

1115 Ferrari F335 Challenge, silv., blk. int., smoked win., metal M, 5sp MIP $3

1118 Ferrari 456M, red, tan int., clr. win., metal M, 5sp MIP $3

1119 Ferrari F355 Spider, red, tan int., clr. win., metal M, 5sp MIP $5

1120 Ferrari F50, red, blk. int., clr. win., blk. metal M "Ferrari F50", 5sp MIP $5

1121 Chevy 1500, org. pl., blk. int., tinted win., silv. metal Ind., 5dot MIP $3

2000 Series

FUTURE FLEET

1 Ford GT-90, blk., wht. int., grn. win., metal M, bbs MIP $3

2 Pontiac Rageous, blk., red int., red win., gray pl. M, 3sp MIP $3

3 Jeepster, blk., blk. int., blue win., metal M, 5sp MIP $40

4 Chrysler Thunderbolt, blk., yel. int., yel. win., gray pl. M, 3sp MIP $2

HOT ROD MAGAZINE

5 Phaeton, met. red/tan top, dk. gray int., smoked win., metal M, gbbs MIP $3

6 Track T, yel., wht. int., metal M, t/b MIP $3

7 Tail Dragger, pearl wht., blk. int., org. win., silv. metal M, gbbs MIP $3

8 '33 Ford Roadster, met. grn., blk. int., clr. win., metal M, 5sp MIP $5

SEEIN' 3-D

9 Propper Chopper, red, blk. int., yel. win., blk. pl. M, MIP $2

10 1970 Dodge Daytona, blue enamel w/org. stripe, org. int., clr. win., chr. M, 5sp MIP $4

11 Lexus SC400, yel., wht. int., smoked win., blk. pl. M, 3sp MIP $2

12 Olds 442, met. grn., wht. int., smoked win., chr. M, 3sp MIP $2

SNACK TIME

13 Callaway C7, met. grn., org. int., clr. win., blk. pl. M, 5dot MIP $2

14 Firebird, org. enamel, wht. int., clr. win., blk. pl. C, 5sp MIP $2

15 Monte Carlo Concept Car, met. blue, lt. gray int., clr. win., red enamel M, bbs MIP $2

16 Dodge Sidewinder, butterscotch, red int., red win., gray pl. M, t/b MIP $3

MAD MANIAX

17 Hot Wheels 500, blue, blk. pl. driver int., metal M, yel. ltr. b7sp MIP $2

18 Camaro Z/28, met. silv., blk. window win., blk. metal M, bbs MIP $3

19 Slideout, blk., red pl. M, 5sp MIP $2

20 Twin Mill II, org. pearl, blk. window win., gray pl. M, g5dot MIP $2

ATTACK PACK

21 Nissan Truck, met. brn., gray int., clr. win., blk. pl. M, ct/b MIP $2

22 Power Plower, pearl purp., org. int., clr. win., metal M, ct/b MIP $3

23 '79 Ford F-150, blk., blk. int., clr. win., chr. M, 5sp MIP $4

24 Dodge Ram 1500, dk. met. red, blk. int., clr. win., blk. pl. C, 5sp MIP $3

CIRCUS ON WHEELS

25 '56 Flashsider, met. red, blk. window win., gold chr. M, g5dot MIP $3

26 '32 Ford Delivery, blk. w/grn. fenders, grn. int., clr. win., metal M, bbs MIP $3

27 Fat Fendered 40, blue, tan int., clr. win., metal M, bbs MIP $4

28 Dairy Delivery, met. purp., yel. int., yel. win., met. purp./gray C, g5sp MIP $3

CD CUSTOMS

29 Chrysler Pronto, met. grn., blk. int., clr. win., blk. pl. M, 3sp MIP $2

30 Pikes Peak Tacoma, blk. w/blk. ptd. vent, red int., clr. win., blk. pl. M, gbbs MIP $2

31 Shadow Mk IIa, wht., gray int., gray pl. M, 5sp MIP $45

32 Pontiac Banshee, pearl org., blk. int., clr. win., metal M, 5dot MIP $2

KUNG FU FORCE

33 Toyota MR2, blk. w/org. in tampo, red int., clr. win., blk. pl. M, 3sp MIP $2

34 '99 Mustang, red, blk. int., clr. win., red enamel/blk. T Base, 3sp MIP $2

35 Shadow Jet II, blue, chr. int., red win., metal M, 3sp MIP $2

36 Mini Truck, met. grn., blk. int., clr. win., blk. pl. M, asw-t/b MIP $15

SPEED BLASTER

37 Firebird Funny Car, pearl org., metal int., clr. win., metal M, 5sp MIP $3

38 At-A-Tude, pearl silv., chr. int., org. win., blk. pl. M, 5sp MIP $2

39 Mustang Cobra, blue pearl, gray int., clr. win., blk. pl. M, 5sp MIP $3

40 Shelby Cobra, wht., blue int., blue win., metal T, 5sp MIP $3

SKATE

41 Rigor Motor, candy blue, chr. int., blue win., metal M, 5sp MIP $8

42 Sol-Aire CX4, wht. pearl/blk. w/"6" tampo, blk. int., yel. win., blk. pl. M, 3sp MIP $65

43 Speed Blaster, org., blk. window win., blk. pl. M, 3sp MIP $2

44 Combat Medic, silv., blk. int., red win., blk. pl. T, 5sp MIP $5

SECRET CODE

45 Fiat 500C, red/wht., blk. int., chr. win., metal M, 5sp MIP $5

46 Baby Boomer, lt. blue pearl, metal M, 5sp MIP $3

47 Tee'd Off, blk., wht. int., metal M, 5sp MIP $3

48 Screamin' Hauler, lt. yel., metal seat int., smoked win., metal M, 5sp MIP $4

VIRTUAL COLLECTION

97 1936 Cord, met. grn., tan int., clr. win., chr. C, bw MIP $3

101 Hot Seat, blue, wht. seat int., metal M, 5sp MIP $2

103 Tractor, dayglo yel., blk. metal M, ct/b MIP $2

104 Speed-A-Saurus, lt. grn., mustard metal M, g5sp MIP $2

109 Monte Carlo Concept Car, pearl pink/gold stripes, blk. int., clr. win., gray metal C, t/b MIP $2

110 Fork Lift, org., blk. cage int., metal C, 5sp MIP $3

111 Wheel Loader, red/wht., blk. int int., metal C, t/b MIP $3

112 Turbo Flame, transparent red pl., org. win., metal M, g5sp MIP $2

113 Flame Stopper, dk. org., blk. win., blk. pl. C, t/b MIP $3

114 Lamborghini Countach, met. blue, wht. int., clr. win., met. blue metal M, 5dot MIP $2

115 Way 2 Fast, dk. red met., chr. int., chr. int win., metal M, 5sp MIP $2

117 Tee'd Off, red/wht., blue int., metal C, 5sp MIP $2

118 Semi-Fast, blue pl./wht., gray int., clr. win., metal M, 5sp MIP $4

123 Oshkosh Cement Truck, grn./blk., grn. int., lt. grn. metal M, 5dot MIP $2

126 Rodzilla, lt. grn./gold tint chr., metal C, g3sp MIP $2

127 Track T, wht., blk. int., metal M, t/b MIP $2

129 Turbolence, candy gray met., chr. int., metal M, 5dot MIP $2

133 Mercedes-Benz Unimog, met. dk. red/blk., blk. int., smoked win., metal M, ct/b MIP $2

135 Thunderstreak, purp., purp. driver int., metal C, bbs MIP $2

137 Dogfighter, yel., gold chr. int., blk. pl. C, g5sp MIP $2

138 Skullrider, red, chr. int., gray metal C, 5sp MIP $2

142 Blimp, wht./red, MIP $2

143 Recycling Truck, dk. blue, blk. win., gray pl. M, t/b MIP $2

144 Ice Cream Truck, butterscotch, red int., clr. win., blk. metal M, 5dot MIP $3

145 Fire Eater, wht., red int., red win., chr. M, 3sp MIP $3

151 Go Kart, candy purp., gray seat int., pearl purp. metal M, 5dot MIP $5

152 Fathom This, wht./org., org. window win., MIP $2

153 Shadow Jet II, red pl./gray lower stripe, chr. int., smoked win., silv. metal M, b5dot MIP $5

155 Splittin' Image II, candy gray, blk. win., blk. metal M, g3sp MIP $2

156 Screamin' Hauler, met. red, silv. int., smoked win., silv. metal C, 5sp MIP $2

157 Popcycle, met. grn., gold chr. int., yel. win., metal M, g3sp MIP $2

158 Super Modified, red, wht. int., metal M, gbbs/2 MIP $2

164 Phaeton, blk., purp. int., clr. win., silv. metal C, 5sp MIP $2

168 Lakester, blk., gold chr. int., yel. win., blk. metal C, 5sp MIP $2

173 Baby Boomer, red/gold tint chr., metal C, 5sp MIP $2

2000 Treasure Hunts

49 Double Vision, purp., gray int., clr. win., chr. M, chr. RR MIP $14

50 Tow Jam, yel., blk. win., chr. M, chr. RR MIP $15

51 1936 Cord, met. silv., wht. int., org. win., chr. M, chr. hub ww/RR MIP $25

52 Sweet Sixteen II, red, wht. int., org. win., metal M, chr. RR MIP $12

53 Lakester, met. grn., gold chr. int., yel. win., blk. metal M, g5sp MIP $10

54 Go Kart, wht., gold frame, gold RR MIP $25

55 Chaparral 2, dk. blue, gray int., blue win., wht. metal M, chr. RR MIP $15

56 '57 T-Bird, pearl grn., yel. int., yel. win., chr. M, chr. RR MIP $14

57 Pikes Peak Celica, met. blue, blk. int., clr. win., blk. pl. M, gold RR MIP $14

58 '67 Pontiac GTO, pearl wht., blk. int., smoked win., gold chr. M, gold RR MIP $40

59 Ford GT-90, gold flake, blk. int., clr. win., blk. pl. T, chr. RR MIP $12

60 1970 Chevelle, blk., wht. int., tinted win., chr. C, chr. RR MIP $20

2000 First Editions

61 Ferrari 365 GTB/4, red, tan int., clr. win., metal M, 5sp MIP $3

62 Ferrari 550 Maranello, red enamel, tan int/clr. window int., clr. win., metal M, 5sp MIP $3

63 1964 Lincoln Continental, wht. enamel w/chr. base, red int., clr. win., , bbs MIP $2

64 Pro Stock Firebird, mustard yel., gray int., smoked win., metal M, wide rear 5sp MIP $4

65 Deora II, silv., chr. int., smoked win., blk. pl. M, 5dot MIP $2

66 Deuce Roadster, blue tint chr., blk. int., clr. win., metal M, 5sp MIP $2

67 Chevy Pro Stock Truck, dayglo org., gray int., purp. win., chr. M, 5sp MIP $3

68 '68 El Camino, pearl wht., gray int., blue win., metal M, 5sp MIP $2

69 Phantastique, candy blue, tan int., clr. win., chr. M, gbbs MIP $2

70 Thomassima 3, met. red w/rear logo, blk. int., clr. win., chr. M, 5sp MIP $5

71 Ferrari 333sp, red, blk. int., blk. int & wing win., blk. pl. M, bbs MIP $2

72 Dodge Charger R/T, met. red, gray int., smoked win., gray pl. M, 5sp MIP $2

73 Surf Crate, met. blue w/dk. brn. wood, blk. int., metal M, 5sp MIP $15

74 '41 Willys, pearl org. w/org. lettering, chr. int., smoked win., gray pl. M, 5sp MIP $4

75 Lotus Elise 340R, silv. flake, blk. int., clr. win., silv. metal M, 5sp MIP $30

76 1999 Isuzu VehiCross, met. silv./blk., blk. int., smoked win., metal M, pr5 MIP $2

77 Anglia Panel Truck, candy purp., chr. int., org. win., gray pl. M, 5sp MIP $4

78 So Fine, blk., red int., clr. win., chr. M, bbs MIP $3

79 '65 Vette, met. blk., red int., clr. win., gray pl. M, 5sp MIP $3

80 MX-48 Turbo, purp., gray int., blue win., silv. metal M, 5sp MIP $40

81 Holden, silv./transparent rear wing, yel. int., smoked win., blk. pl. M, 5sp MIP $75

82 Cabbin' Fever, blk. w/lg. tampo, chr. window win., gray pl. M, pr5 MIP $8

83 Metrorail, aqua/wht., chr. int., smoked win., chr. M, sm. front 5sp MIP $10

84 Muscle Tone, lt. org. pearl, blk. int., smoked win., gray pl. M, 5sp MIP $10

85 Dodge Power Wagon, silv. met./sm. bumpers, blk. int., smoked win., gray pl. M, ct/b MIP $4

86 Shoe Box, yel. w/purp. flames & logo, chr. int., purp. win., blk. pl. M, bbs/2 MIP $10

87 Sho-Stopper, pearl yel., blk. window win., gray pl. M, 3sp MIP $4

88 '67 Dodge Charger, pearl silv., red int., clr. win., chr. M, pr5 MIP $3

89 Vulture, blk., chr./org. int., clr. win., transparent smoked M, 5sp MIP $3

90 Mini Cooper, yel., blue int., blue win., metal M, bbs MIP $4

91 Roll Cage, yel., blk. seats int., silv. metal M, ct/b MIP $20

92 Austin Healey, blk./gray, red int., smoked win., chr./metal M, 5sp MIP $10

93 Hammered Coupe, purp., chr. int., clr. win., metal M, 5sp MIP $2

94 Arachnorod, met. Red, yel. int., smoked win., gray pl. M, pr5 MIP $2

95 Greased Lightnin', silv. pearl, purp. win., metal M, 5sp MIP $7

96 Blast Lane, pearl tangerine/red flames, metal M, chr./blk. MIP $5

2000 Basic Line

98 '99 Mustang, met red, blk. int., clr. win., blk. pl. C, 3sp MIP $2

99 Phantom Corsair, met dk. red, wht. int., clr. win., metal C, bbs MIP $2

100 BMW M Roadster, red, blk. int., clr. win., blk. metal M, 5sp MIP $2

102 '90 T-Bird, chr., blk. win., metal M, gbbs MIP $2

105 '57 Chevy, aqua w/girl tampo, blk. win., metal M, 5dot MIP $4

106 Ferrari 348, blk. w/shield, tan & blk. int., smoked win., blk. metal M, 3sp MIP $5

107 '70 Chevelle, met. gold, blk. int., clr. win., chr. C, 5sp MIP $5

108 Olds Aurora, lt. yel., gray int., clr. win., yel. pl. C, t/b MIP $2

116 '59 Chevy Impala, met. silv., gray int., smoked win., chr. M, t/b MIP $2

119 Pontiac Rageous, met. blue, wht. int., tinted win., blk. ptd. M, 3sp MIP $3

120 Mercedes SLK, met. teal, blk. int., clr. win., blk. metal Ind., 3sp MIP $2

121 Mustang Cobra, met. red, wht. int., tinted win., met. red pl. Ind., t/b MIP $2

122 Ferrari F40, yel. w/wht./grn. stripes over emblem, blk. int., clr. win., metal M, 5sp MIP $2

124 Camaro Z/28, blk., blk. win., blk. ptd. M, gbbs MIP $2

125 Porsche 930, wht., blk. int., smoked win., metal M, 3sp MIP $2

128 Porsche 911 GT3 Cup, wht., red int., clr. win., blk. pl. Ind., 3sp MIP $2

130 '63 T-Bird, charcoal flake/wht., wht. int., clr. win., metal T, bbs MIP $2

131 Mercedes C Class, red, blk. int., clr. win., blk. pl. M, 5dot MIP $2

132 3-Window '34, met. grn./grn. fenders, wht. int., yel. win., metal M, 3sp MIP $2

134 Mercedes 500SL, met. blue, blk. int., smoked win., lt. blue pl. M, 5dot MIP $10

135 Thunderstreak, purp., purp. driver int., metal C, bbs MIP $2

136 Ferrari Testarossa, wht., blk. int., clr. win., blk. metal M, 5sp MIP $2

139 Ford GT-40, red, blk. int., clr. win., blk. pl. C, 5sp MIP $2

140 Jeepster, grn./blk. fenders, blk. int., smoked win., silv. metal C, 5dot MIP $2

141 '95 Camaro Convertible, yel., blk. int., clr. win., blk. pl. M, g3sp MIP $2

142 Blimp, wht./red, MIP $2

146 Porsche Carrera, met. blue, wht. int., clr. win., metal M, 3sp MIP $2

148 Pikes Peak Tacoma, red/red ptd. vent, yel. int., clr. win., gray pl. M, 3sp MIP $2

149 Shadow Mk IIa, red, gray int., gray pl. M, g5sp MIP $2

150 Chrysler Pronto, purp., blk. int., clr. win., blk. pl. C, 3sp MIP $2

154 Corvette Stingray, blue pl. body, blk. window win., metal C, 3sp MIP $3

159 BMW 850i, lt. blue, blk. int., clr. win., dk. blue pl. M, 3sp MIP $2

160 Jaguar XJ220, red, blk. int., blue win., blk. metal M, gbbs MIP $2

161 Ferrari F50, yel. w/wht./grn. stripe over emblem, blk. int., clr. win., blk. metal M, 5sp MIP $4

162 Ferrari 355 Challenge, yel., gray int., smoked win., metal M, 5sp MIP $2

163 Mercedes CLK-LM, red, blk. int., clr. win., blk. pl. C, bbs MIP $2

165 Jaguar XK8, gray pearl, blue int., smoked win., blk. metal M, 5dot MIP $2

166 Pikes Peak Celica, wht., blk. int., clr. win., blk. metal M, 3sp MIP $2

167 Dodge Concept Car, wht. pearl, gold int., clr. win., metal M, g3sp MIP $4

169 Panoz GTR-1, met. blue, wht. int., clr. win., blk. pl. C, 3sp MIP $2

171 '56 Ford Truck, pearl wht., gold chr. int., yel. win., gold pl. C, g5sp MIP $2

172 Porsche 911 GT1-98, dk. purp./pink tampo, wht. int., smoked win., blk. pl. M, bbs MIP $2

173 Baby Boomer, red/gold tint chr., metal C, 5sp MIP $2

174 '63 Vette, blk. flake, wht. int., clr. win., blk. pl. M, bbs MIP $2

175 Olds Aurora, pearl bronze, blk. int., blue win., blk. pl. C, bbs MIP $2

176 Solar Eagle III, red, blk. canopy win., met. blk. metal M, MIP $2

177 Flashfire, wht., gray int., clr. win., blk. T, 3sp MIP $2

178 Dodge Viper RT/10, met. silv., blk. int., blue win., blk. pl. C, 3sp MIP $2

179 '95 Camaro Convertible, wht. enamel, blk. int., smoked win., blk. Ind., t/b MIP $2

180 Jaguar D-Type, dk. maroon, gray int., smoked win., blk. pl. C, bbs MIP $2

183 Buick Wildcat, bright grn., blk. win., blk. pl. T, 3sp MIP $2

187 Panoz GTR-1, yel., blk. int., clr. win., blk. pl. C, 3sp MIP $2

188 '97 Corvette, red, blk. int., clr. win., blk. metal M, gbbs MIP $2

189 Semi Fast, grn. pl./wht., gray int., smoked win., silv. metal C, 5sp **MIP** $2

190 Peterbilt Dump Truck, teal/blue, silv. int., smoked win., silv. metal C, 3sp **MIP** $3

191 Ford Stake Bed Truck, met. red/blk., chr. int., smoked win., chr. M, 3sp **MIP** $3

192 '40 Ford, silv., blue int., clr. win., blk. pl. C, t/b **MIP** $2

193 '40s Woodie, pearl bronze, blk. int., clr. win., silv. metal C, bbs **MIP** $2

194 T-Bird Stocker, met. blue, red int., clr. win., gray pl. C, 3sp **MIP** $2

195 '32 Ford Coupe, pearl purp., blk. int., clr. win., chr. C, bbs **MIP** $2

196 Chevy Nomad, org., wht. int., clr. win., silv. metal C, g3sp **MIP** $2

197 '65 Impala, met. grn., yel. int., yel. win., gold chr. C, 3sp **MIP** $2

198 Ford Bronco, pearl wht./grn., purp. int., clr. win., metal T, ct/b **MIP** $3

199 Roll Patrol Jeep, red, tan int., smoked win., metal T, ct/b **MIP** $4

200 Purple Passion, pearl wht., red int., clr. win., chr. T, gbbs **MIP** $4

201 '65 Mustang, grn., yel. int., yel. win., metal T, t/b **MIP** $4

202 Hydroplane, wht., chr. int., org. win., lt. org. pl. C, **MIP** $2

203 Surf Patrol, gray, purp. int., purp. win., metal T, ct/b **MIP** $2

204 Saltflat Racer, blk., chr. int., org. win., silv. metal T, g5sp **MIP** $2

205 Pikes Peak Celica, wht., blue int., clr. win., blk. pl. T, bbs **MIP** $2

206 Rig Wrecker, blk., gold chr. int., clr. win., gold chr. T, g3sp **MIP** $3

207 Police Car, lt. blue pearl, gray int., smoked win., blk. pl. T, t/b **MIP** $2

208 Zender Fact 4, red, gray int., org. win., gray pl. T, t/b **MIP** $4

209 Customized C3500, yel., blk. int., clr. win., blk. pl. C, t/b **MIP** $7

210 Lexus SC400, met. blue, wht. int., smoked win., blk. metal M, bbs **MIP** $2

211 Tow Jam, met. blue, blk. win., chr. M, 5sp **MIP** $2

212 Double Vision, lt. grn. pearl, gray int., clr. win., gray pl. M, 3sp **MIP** $2

213 Whatta Drag, org., chr. int., smoked win., metal M, 5sp **MIP** $2

214 Super Comp Dragster, yel./blk., blk. cage int., chr. T, 5sp **MIP** $2

215 XT-3, red flake, blk. win., yel. metal M, 5sp **MIP** $2

216 School Bus, red, wht. int., blue win., blk. pl. T, 5dot **MIP** $2

217 '57 T-Bird, met. purp., blue int., blue win., chr. M, bbs **MIP** $2

218 Rescue Ranger, silv. met., smoked int., smoked win., chr. C, 3sp **MIP** $3

219 Side Kick, gold met., metal int., red win., metal M, 5sp **MIP** $4

220 Sweet Sixteen, blk., red int., metal M, bbs **MIP** $2

221 Rail Rodder, blk./gold chr., silv. metal C, b5sp rear/gold mini L330 front **MIP** $2

222 Dogfighter, silv. met., blk. pl. C, bbs **MIP** $2

223 Twang Thang, met. blue/wht. guitar chr. strings, chr. int., smoked win., blue pl. C, 5sp **MIP** $2

224 Ford GT-90, pearl grn./blk., wht. int., clr. win., metal C, 5dot **MIP** $2

225 Chrysler Thunderbolt, red/dk. red top, blk. int., clr. win., blk. pl. M, 5sp **MIP** $3

226 '67 Pontiac GTO, org., blk. int., clr. win., chr. T, 5sp **MIP** $5

227 Skullrider, blk., chr. int., metal C, 5sp **MIP** $2

228 '57 Chevy, pearl org. met., blk. int., smoked win., chr. M, 5sp **MIP** $2

229 Blown Camaro, red, blk. int., smoked win., metal M, t/b **MIP** $2

230 Ferrari F355 Spider, gray met./old HW logo, blk. int., smoked win., metal M, 5sp **MIP** $4

231 Treadator, met. gold, chr. win., blk. pl. T, **MIP** $2

232 Porsche 959, blk., blk. int., clr. win., metal C, 5dot **MIP** $2

233 Oshkosh Snowplow, pearl mustard yel./blk., mustard int., metal M, ct/b **MIP** $5

234 '33 Ford Roadster, blk., blk. int., tinted win., metal M, pr5 **MIP** $2

235 Ferrari 550 Maranello, met. gray, red int., clr. win., metal M, 5sp **MIP** $2

236 Ferrari 365 GTB/4, yel., blk. int., clr. win., metal M, 5sp **MIP** $2

237 '64 Lincoln Continental, blk./wht. HW logo on trunk, red int., clr. win., chr. M, red HW logo on plate, 5dot **MIP** $35

238 Deuce Roadster, met. gold, blk. int., red win., metal M, g5sp **MIP** $2

239 Tail Dragger, met blue, silv. int., blue win., metal T, 3sp **MIP** $2

240 Scorchin' Scooter, candy bronze/blk. forks, metal M, chr./blk. **MIP** $4

241 Propper Chopper, blk., maroon int., blue win., maroon pl. M, **MIP** $2

242 Olds 442, wht., gold int., clr. win., chr. M, pr5 **MIP** $3

243 Deora II, candy blue, chr. int., clr. win., blk. pl. C, pr5 **MIP** $2

244 Chevy Pro Stock Truck, purp., org. int., clr. win., chr. C, 5sp **MIP** $2

245 Phantastique, met. red, cream int., clr. win., chr. C, bbs **MIP** $2

246 '68 El Camino, candy bronze, gray int., clr. win., metal C, 5sp **MIP** $2

247 Ford F-150, blk., chr. int., yel. win., blk. pl. T, 3sp **MIP** $2

240 Way 2 Fast, candy gray, chr. int., blk. metal M, 5sp **MIP** $2

249 '59 Impala, blk., red int., smoked win., gold chr. M, gbbs **MIP** $2

250 Porsche 911 GTI-98, wht. w/aqua in tampo, gray int., clr. win., blk. pl. C, bbs **MIP** $3

2001 Treasure Hunts

1 '65 Corvette, red, wht. int., clr. win., gray pl. M, chr. hub RR **MIP** $15

2 Roll Cage, org., blk. int., smoked win., wht. metal M, chr. hub knobby RR **MIP** $15

3 So Fine, met. grn., wht. int., smoked win., chr. M, chr. hub ww/RR **MIP** $15

4 Rodger Dodger, blk., red int., smoked win., chr. M, chr. hub ww/RR **MIP** $15

5 Blast Lane, met. gold, metal M, gold rim/blk. spoke **MIP** $20

6 Hammered Coupe, gray/blk., chr. int., org. win., metal M, pr5 **MIP** $10

7 Vulture, wht. pearl, chr. int., red win., transparent org. M, pr5 **MIP** $10

8 Dodge Charger, yel., blk. int., clr. win., chr. M, chr. hub RR **MIP** $12

9 Olds 442, lt. blue flake, wht. int., clr. win., chr. M, chr. hub RR **MIP** $15

10 Rageous, met. brn., gray int., smoke w/blk. roof win., gray pl. M, chr. hub RR **MIP** $12

11 Deora, blue met., blue int., blue win., metal T, redline bw **MIP** $10

12 Cabbin' Fever, wht. pearl, gold chr. win., gold chr. M, pr5 **MIP** $15

2001 First Editions

13 Cadillac LMP, silv. met., blk. int., blk. pl. M, bbs **MIP** $3

13 Cadillac LMP/no side tampo, silv. met., blk. int., blk. pl. M, bbs **MIP** $26

14 Surfin' Scool Bus, yel., purp. win., gray pl. M, 5sp **MIP** $2

15 La Troca, met. red, blk. win., gold chr. M, gbbs **MIP** $3

16 Sooo Fast, wht. pearl, chr. int., clr. win., met. red metal M, 5sp **MIP** $3

17 Super Tuned, candy blue met., red int., smoked win., gray pl. M, pr5 **MIP** $2

17 Super Tuned/open rear wing, candy blue met., red int., smoked win., gray pl. M, pr5 **MIP** $10

18 Hooligan, flat blk./no chr. on motor, red int., metal M, 5sp **MIP** $15

19 Krazy 8s, dk. candy blue, int., smoked win., metal M, pr5 **MIP** $2

20 MS-T Suzuka, lime pearl, blk. int., tinted win., blk. pl. M, pr5 **MIP** $2

21 Panoz LMP-1 Roadster S, red, blk. int., blk. pl. M, bbs **MIP** $2

22 Shredster, tangerine/mustard/blk., blk. int., smoked win., gray pl. M, wide rear pr5 **MIP** $2

23 Dodge Viper GTS-R, red/silv. stripes, blk. int., clr. win., blk. pl. M, 5sp **MIP** $5

24 Maelstrom, dk. blue met., blk. int., smoked win., chr. M, 3sp **MIP** $2

25 Lotus M250, silv. met./"LOTUS" ptd. on rear, red int., smoked win., blk. pl. "Lotus M250" M, 5sp **MIP** $75

25 Lotus Project M250, silv. met., red int., smoked win., blk. pl. "Lotus Project M250" M, 5sp **MIP** $4

26 1971 Plymouth GTX, Sub-Lime, blk. int., blue win., chr. M, 5sp **MIP** $4

27 Honda Civic SI, red, wht. int., smoked win., blk. pl. M, pr5 **MIP** $2

28 Evil Twin, dk. met. purp./purp. HW logo, tan int., clr. win., blk. pl. M, bbs **MIP** $15

29 Hyper Mite, lime pearl/lavender checks, chr. int., purp. win., blk. pl. M, 5sp rear/old mini front **MIP** $10

30 Outsider, org. pearl/"VJ", metal M, **MIP** $8

31 Monoposto, org. pearl, chr. int., blk. pl. M, pr5 **MIP** $2

32 Vulture Roadster, candy purp., chr. int., org. win., org. transparent M, 5sp **MIP** $2

33 Fright Bike, purp. transparent body, blk. win., metal M, chr./blk. **MIP** $4

34 Jet Threat, silv. pearl met., chr. int., smoked win., silv. pearl met. metal M, 5dot **MIP** $4

35 Montezooma, org.-yel. pearl, gold int., smoked win., chr. M, bbs **MIP** $2

36 Toyota Celica, yel., wht. int., yel. win., blk. pl. M, pr5 **MIP** $2

37 Ford Focus, blk., blk. int., clr. win., blk. pl. M, 5dot **MIP** $2

38 Mega Duty, candy gray, blk. int., red win., metal M, pr5 **MIP** $2

39 Riley & Scott MkIII, candy blue, wht. int., blk. pl. M, asw-bbs **MIP** $2

40 XS-IVE, red, blk. win., metal M, ct/b **MIP** $3

45 Mo' Scoot, org. transparent body/raised logo, metal M, **MIP** $35

46 Ford Thunderbolt, blk., red int., smoked win., chr. M, 5sp **MIP** $3

47 Morris Wagon, blk./tan, chr. int., yel. win., metal M, ex. lg. rear 5sp **MIP** $2

48 Fandango, pearl tangerine met., blk. int., org. win., gray pl. M, pr5 **MIP** $2

49 Old #3, red, blk. int., blk. metal M, 5sp **MIP** $2

50 Ferrari 156, red, metal int., clr. win., metal M, bbs **MIP** $2

51 Cunningham C4R, wht./pearl blue stripes, blue int., clr. win., charcoal flake pl. M, 5sp **MIP** $2

52 '57 Roadster, red, pink int., smoked win., metal M, 5sp rear/old mini front **MIP** $4

2001 Series

FOSSIL FUEL

41 School Bus, grn., wht. int., yel. win., blk. pl. M, 5dot **MIP** $2

42 Ambulance, dk. purp. met., wht. int., blue win., gray pl. M, t/b **MIP** $2

43 Firebird Funny Car, silv. met., metal int., org. win., metal M, 5sp **MIP** $4

44 Camaro Z-28, red, blk. win., blk. metal M, 3sp **MIP** $2

TURBO TAXI

53 '57 Chevy, blk., blk. int., smoked win., chr. M, 3sp **MIP** $3

54 Limozeen, grn. met., wht. int., smoked win., gold chr. T, g5sp **MIP** $8

55 '57 T-Bird, yel./org. in tampo, org. int., org. win., chr. M, 3sp **MIP** $3

55 '57 T-Bird/no port hole, yel./org. in tampo, org. int., org. win., chr. M, 3sp **MIP** $87

56 '70 Chevelle, met. blue, wht. int., blue win., chr. C, 5sp **MIP** $3

RAT RODS

57 Track T, flat blk./brn. tampo, blk. int., metal M, ww/bw **MIP** $5

58 '33 Roadster, flat blk., red int., clr. win., brn. primer metal M, ww/bw **MIP** $3

59 Phaeton, brn. primer, blk. int., clr. win., blk. metal C, ww/bw **MIP** $3

60 Shoe Box, flat lavender, chr. int., blue win., chr. M, ww/bw **MIP** $3

60 Shoe Box/no HW logo, flat lavender, chr. int., blue win., chr. M, ww/bw **MIP** $10

ANIME

61 Muscle Tone, met. grn./silv. in tampo, wht. int., yel. win., blk. pl. M, t/b **MIP** $2

62 Ford GT-90, wht., gray int., blue win., metal C, pr5 **MIP** $2

63 Dodge Charger R/T, pearl mustard, blk. int., grn. win., blk. pl. M, 3sp **MIP** $2

64 Olds Aurora GTS-1, lt. blue pearl, blk. int., clr. win., blk. pl. C, pr5 **MIP** $2

ROD SQUADRON

65 Dodge Daytona Charger, met. silv., blk. int., clr. win., blk. pl. M, bbs **MIP** $2

66 Lakester, olive/blown, chr. int., clr. win., silv. pearl met. metal M, bbs **MIP** $2

67 Greased Lightnin', blk., blk. int., yel. win., yel. metal M, 5sp **MIP** $8

68 Propper Chopper, blue/yel., blk. int., clr. win., blk. pl. M, **MIP** $3

SKULL & CROSSBONES

69 Rigor Motor, org., gold chr. int., red win., blk. metal M, g5sp **MIP** $2

70 Blast Lane, blk., metal M, magenta chr./blk. **MIP** $5

71 Deuce Roadster, dk. purp. met., red int., clr. win., metal T, 5sp **MIP** $2

72 Screamin' Hauler, gray pearl, silv. met. int., grn. win., silv. met. metal C, 5sp **MIP** $2

LOGO-MOTIVE

73 Phantastique, red, blk. int., smoked win., chr. C, bbs **MIP** $2

74 Pontiac Banshee, candy blue, gray int., blue win., metal M, 5sp **MIP** $2

75 Turbolence, blk./chr. engine, chr. int., chr. win., blk. metal M, 5dot **MIP** $2

76 Metrorail, wht., chr. int., org. win., chr. M, 5sp **MIP** $2

MONSTERS

77 '59 Impala, blk., wht. int., grn. win., gray pl. M, bbs **MIP** $2

78 Tail Dragger, blue pearl, wht. int., red win., metal M, bbs **MIP** $2

79 Cadillac 1959, met. grn., gray int., yel. win., chr. T, g5sp **MIP** $6

80 Purple Passion, red, wht. int., clr. win., chr. M, g5sp **MIP** $10

EXTREME SPORTS

81 MX-48, silv. met., blk. int., org. win., blk. metal C, 3sp **MIP** $2

82 Double Vision, met. grn., gray int., clr. win., blk. pl. M, gbbs **MIP** $2

83 Twin Mill II, red flake, blk. win., blk. pl. M, bbs **MIP** $2

84 Funny Car, yel., metal int., clr. win., metal M, 5sp **MIP** $3

COMPANY CARS

85 Jaguar XJ 220, blk., tan int., yel. win., blk. pl. M, g3sp **MIP** $2

86 '99 Mustang, wht., wht. int., tinted win., blk. pl. C, 3sp **MIP** $3

87 Monte Carlo Concept Car, mustard yel., blk. int., clr. win., blk. metal C, 5sp **MIP** $3

88 Dodge Sidewinder, maroon met., blk. int., smoked win., blk. pl. M, pr5 **MIP** $4

HIPPIE MOBILES

89 '68 Mustang, pearl gray/gray peace signs, blk. int., blue win., metal M, 5sp **MIP** $10

90 '63 Corvette, met. grn., wht. int., yel. win., chr. M, 5sp **MIP** $3

91 '64 Lincoln Continental, met. lt. blue, wht. int., blue win., chr. C, bbs **MIP** $2

92 '67 Pontiac GTO, yel., blk. int., smoked win., chr. M, 5sp **MIP** $4

SKIN DEEP

93 Super Comp Dragster, met. gold/blk., blk. int., chr. M, 5sp **MIP** $2

94 Jeep Willys Coupe, met. silv., chr. int., red win., chr. M, 5sp **MIP** $3

95 Chevy Pro Stock Truck, yel., blk. int., clr. win., blk. pl. C, pr5 **MIP** $3

96 Pro Stock Firebird, blk., wht. int., smoked win., met. silv. metal C, pr5 **MIP** $2

2001 Basic Line

97 Anglia Panel, yel., chr. int., blue win., gray pl. C, 5sp **MIP** $4

98 Thomassima III, candy blue met., blk. int., clr. win., chr. C, pr5 **MIP** $2

99 Pro Stock Firebird, wht., blk. int., clr. win., silv. metal C, pr5 **MIP** $2

100 '70 Road Runner, red, blk. int., clr. win., chr. M, 5sp **MIP** $4

101 Chevy Pick-up, yel., blk. int., clr. win., metal M, 3sp **MIP** $3

102 Road Rocket, lt. gold chr., gold chr. int., clr. win., metal M, pr5 **MIP** $3

103 Porsche 928/brown in tampo, met. grn., blk. win., silv. metal C, 5dot **MIP** $2

103 Porsche 928/red in tampo, met. grn., blk. win., silv. metal C, 5dot **MIP** $4

104 Audi Avus, candy+H179 pearl, wht. int., smoked win., blk. pl. M, 5dot **MIP** $2

105 Demon, met. blk., red int., clr. win., metal T, 3sp **MIP** $6

106 Power Pipes, chr., blue win., blk. metal M, 3sp **MIP** $2

107 Surf Crate, gold flake, blk. int., metal "no origin", 5sp **MIP** $3

108 Dodge Charger R/T, met. purp., blk. int., clr. win., blk. pl. M, pr5 **MIP** $40

109 '65 Corvette, wht., blk. int., clr. win., blk. pl. M, 5sp **MIP** $3

110 '41 Willys, blk., chr. int., red win., gray pl. M, 5sp **MIP** $3

111 Express Lane, org., tan int., metal C, 5sp **MIP** $2

112 Mustang Mach I, silv. met., blk. int., clr. win., blk. pl. M, pr5 **MIP** $3

113 BMW Z3 Roadster, teal, blk. int., clr. win., blk. metal M, pr5 **MIP** $7

114 '96 Mustang, wht. pearl, blk. int., smoked win., metal M, 3sp **MIP** $5

115 1935 Cadillac, gold flake, wht. int., clr. win., metal M, bbs **MIP** $3

116 Auburn 852, wht./blk., blk. int., clr. win., metal M, bbs **MIP** $2

117 Shoe Box, wht. pearl, chr. int., smoked win., blk. pl. M, pr5 **MIP** $2

118 Muscle Tone, blk./old HW logo, red int., clr. win., gray pl. M, pr5 **MIP** $5

119 Sho-Stopper, red/old HW logo, blk. int., clr. win., gray pl. C, pr5 **MIP** $5

120 Hammered Coupe, dk. candy blue, chr. int., smoked win., metal M, pr5 **MIP** $2

121 Firebird, silv. flake, blk. int., tinted win., blk. pl. C, wht. ltr. b5sp **MIP** $2

122 Fork Lift, red/blk., blk. int., metal C, 5sp **MIP** $3

123 Wheel Loader, candy gray/dk. blue, gray int., metal C, ct/b **MIP** $3

124 Lamborghini Diablo, dk. purp. met., blk. int., smoked win., metal M, 3sp **MIP** $3

125 '32 Ford Vicky, flat blk., org. int., tinted win., metal M, pr5 **MIP** $2

126 '68 Mustang, candy red, blk. int., clr. win., metal T, 5sp **MIP** $8

127 Roll Cage, red, blk. int., metal M, ct/b **MIP** $3

128 Lotus Elise 340R, dk. red pearl, gray int., tinted win., silv. metal C, pr5 **MIP** $3

129 Slide Out, yel., blue pl. M, 3sp **MIP** $2

130 25th. ann. Lambo Countach, dk. candy blue, wht. int., clr. win., blk. pl. M, 5dot **MIP** $15

131 Greased Lightnin', org. pearl, chr. int., smoked win., blk. metal M, 5sp **MIP** $10

132 MX-48 Turbo, silv. met., blk. int., smoked win., blk. metal M, 3sp **MIP** $2

133 '97 Corvette, silv. met./pearl blue in ribbon, wht. int., clr. win., blk. pl. M, bbs **MIP** $4

134 Oshkosh Cement Truck, yel./silv., silv. int., blk. pl. M, 3sp **MIP** $2

135 Corvette Stingray, blk., blk. int., smoked win., metal M, 5sp **MIP** $3

136 Ice Cream Truck, wht. pearl, blue int., clr. win., blk. pl. M, 3sp **MIP** $2

137 Arachnorod, blk., gray int., org. win., chr. C, 5sp **MIP** $2

138 Vulture, met. blue pearl, chr. int., grn. win., transparent grn. C, 5sp **MIP** $2

139 Ford GT-40, candy purp., wht. int., clr. win., blk. pl. C, bbs/2 **MIP** $2

140 Hot Seat, org./purp., purp. int., metal M, 5sp **MIP** $2

141 Go Kart, org., blk. int., org. metal M, 5sp rear/old mini front **MIP** $4

142 '63 T-Bird, red flake/wht. cove/silv. in pinstripe, wht. int., clr. win., metal M, bbs **MIP** $4

143 SS Commodore (VT), lt. yel., blue int., blue win., blk. pl. C, pr5 **MIP** $2

144 Isuzu VehiCross, yel., blk. int., smoked win., metal C, pr5 **MIP** $2

145 Toyota MR-2, red, wht. int., smoked win., blk. pl. M, 3sp **MIP** $2

146 Camaro Z-28, purp. met./silv. in tampo, blk. win., silv. metal M, 5sp **MIP** $7

147 Sharkruiser, org., chr. int., org. metal T, gt/b **MIP** $3

148 Speed Shark, red, gray int., chr. win., chr. T, 3sp **MIP** $2

149 Police Car, wht., blk. int., clr. win., blk. pl. T, 5sp **MIP** $4

150 Enforcer, met. grn., blk. win., blk metal T, 5sp **MIP** $3

151 Surf Crate, silv. flake, blk. int., metal "no origin", 5sp **MIP** $3

152 Deora II, met. red, chr. int., clr. win., blk. pl. C, 5sp **MIP** $3

153 Chevy Stocker, wht., blk. win., metal T, gt/b **MIP** $4

154 Power Pistons, transparent org., gray int., clr. win., metal T, 3sp **MIP** $2

155 '56 Ford, pearl gray, chr. int., clr. win., blk. pl. C, 5sp **MIP** $2

156 '40 Ford Truck, wht./blk., org. int., clr. win., blk. pl. C, 5sp **MIP** $4

157 Ferrari 333SP, blk., yel. int., blk. pl. C, pr5 **MIP** $2

158 Mini Cooper, dk. candy blue, org. int., org. win., metal M, bbs **MIP** $3

159 Cabbin' Fever, met. grn., chr. win., gray pl. M, pr5 **MIP** $4

160 Metrorail, red/wht., chr. int., purp. win., chr. C, 5sp **MIP** $3

161 Jaguar XK8, dk. met. red, tan int., clr. win., blk. pl. C, pr5 **MIP** $2

162 Hummer, yel., gray win., blk. metal M, ct/b **MIP** $2

163 '37 Bugatti, wht. pearl/blk., gold chr. int., clr. win., metal M, 5dot **MIP** $2

164 Dragster, candy purp. met./wht., wht. int., metal M, 5sp rear/old mini front **MIP** $4

165 Flashfire, candy gray, org. int., tinted win., blk. pl. M, bbs **MIP** $3

166 Ferrari 456M, met. blue, tan int., clr. win., silv. metal C, pr5 **MIP** $2

167 Austin Healey, red/wht., blk. int., tinted win., chr. C, bbs/2 **MIP** $2

168 So Fine, met. grn., wht. int., clr. win., chr. M, bbs **MIP** $2

169 Blast Lane, dk. candy blue, metal M, chr./blk. **MIP** $4

170 Solar Eagle, org., blk. win., blk. metal M, **MIP** $3

171 Mercedes C-Class, lt. blue pearl, blk. int., smoked win., blk. pl. M, bbs **MIP** $2

172 Radio Flyer Wagon, candy purp., blk. int., metal M, 5sp **MIP** $2

173 Talbot Lago, red, chr. int., clr. win., metal M, bbs **MIP** $3

174 Baja Bug, silv. flake, blk. int., metal M, ct/b **MIP** $3

175 VW Bug, brn. primer, blk. or red int., tinted win., silv. metal C, 5dot **MIP** $3

176 1931 Duesenberg Model J, red flake/wht. HW logo, blk. int., smoked win., metal M, 5sp **MIP** $2

177 Dodge Viper RT/10, yel., blk. int., smoked win., blk. pl. C, pr5 **MIP** $2

178 Chaparral II, met. grn., blk. int., clr. win., blk. metal C, pr5 **MIP** $2

179 Krazy 8s, yel., chr. int., grn. win., metal M, pr5 **MIP** $3

180 Corvette Stingray, silv. flake, milky wht. int., smoked win., blk. pl. M, bbs **MIP** $3

181 Surfin' School Bus, dk. candy blue, gray int., org. win., gray pl. M, pr5 **MIP** $2

182 Sooo Fast, flat blk., chr. int., smoked win., metal M, 5sp **MIP** $2

183 Super Modified, org., blk. int., metal M, bbs/2 **MIP** $2

184 Jaguar D-Type, met. silv., gray int., clr. win., silv. metal C, 5sp **MIP** $2

185 Amored Car, blk., gray int., org. win., metal M, sm. front 5sp **MIP** $15

186 Rodger Dodger, mustard yel., blk. int., smoked win., chr. M, 5sp **MIP** $3

187 Bywayman, charcoal met., gray int., smoked win., silv. metal M, ct/b **MIP** $2

188 Flame Stopper, brn. primer, blk. win., blk. pl. C, yct/b **MIP** $7

189 Dodge Power Wagon, met. blk., gray int., tinted win., gray pl. M, ct/b **MIP** $3

190 Ferrari 308, candy gray, blk. int., smoked win., blk. metal M, 5sp **MIP** $2

191 Ferrari F355, yel., wht. int., smoked win., metal M, pr5 **MIP** $2

192 Ford Escort Rally, candy gray, blk. int., smoked win., blk. pl. "Escort Rally" base, 5dot **MIP** $3

193 Rescue Ranger, red, blk. int., smoked win., chr. C, 5dot **MIP** $3

194 Roll Patrol, blue, red int., smoked win., metal T, ct/b **MIP** $4

195 Deuce Roadster, candy purp., wht. int., smoked win., metal T, 5sp **MIP** $2

196 3-Window '34, grn./blk., chr. int., clr. win., blk. metal T, 5sp **MIP** $3

197 Austin Healey, lt. candy blue, red int., clr. win., chr. C, 5sp **MIP** $2

198 Side Kick, silv.-blue met., metal int., red win., blk. pl. T, 5dot **MIP** $2

199 Dairy Delivery, yel., red int., tinted win., blk. pl. C, pr5 **MIP** $3

200 '68 El Camino, lt. org./purp. X's, yel. int., tinted win., metal C, pr5 **MIP** $7

201 Super Tuned, yel., red int., smoked win., gray pl. M, wide rear pr5 **MIP** $2

202 La Troca, flat lavender, blk. win., chr. C, bbs **MIP** $2

203 Hooligan, dk. maroon met./no chr. motor, red int., silv. metal C, 5sp **MIP** $15

204 Ferrari 360 Modena, blk. flake, pink int., clr. win., blk. flake metal M, pr5 **MIP** $4

205 '38 Phantom Corsair, rootbeer met., gray int., clr. win., metal C, ww/5sp **MIP** $2

206 Panoz GTR-1, dk. candy red, lt. blue int., clr. win., blk. pl. C, pr5 **MIP** $3

207 Power Rocket, transparent red, chr. int., smoked win., metal T, 5dot **MIP** $2

208 Cadillac LMP, flat blk., gold int., gold pl. M, gbbs **MIP** $2

209 Ferrari F40, candy blue, blk. int., clr. win., metal M, pr5 **MIP** $2

210 Blimp, gold/org., M, **MIP** $2

211 Krazy 8s, flat blk., gold chr. int., yel. win., gloss blk. metal C, gpr5 **MIP** $2

212 Shreadster, dayglo lime/blk./purp., blk. int., smoked win., chr. C, pr5 **MIP** $2

213 MS-T Susuka, red, blk. int., clr. win., blk. pl. C, pr5 **MIP** $2

214 Porsche 911 GT3, tangerine pearl, blue int., smoked win., blk. pl. M, pr5 **MIP** $4

215 Popcycle, candy purp., chr. int., purp. win., metal C, 5dot **MIP** $2

216 '32 Ford, flat blk., org. int., clr. win., blk. pl. C, 5sp **MIP** $3

217 Shadow Jet, met. silv., silv. int., smoked win., metal M, 5sp **MIP** $2

218 Ferrari 250, candy gray met., blk. int., clr. win., blk. pl. C, bbs **MIP** $2

219 Corvette, tangerine pearl met., gray int., smoked win., metal M, pr5 **MIP** $4

220 GT Racer, dk. blue, metal int., yel. win., metal M, 5dot **MIP** $2

221 Riley & Scott MkIII, red, blue int., blk. pl. M, bbs **MIP** $2

222 Outsider, dayglo lime, metal M, **MIP** $3

223 Pikes Peak Tacoma, blk./old HW logo, red int., clr. win., gray pl. M, 5dot **MIP** $5

224 Shadow Mk IIA, blk., gray int., blk. pl. M, pr5 **MIP** $2

225 Mercedes-Benz SLK, silv. flake, blk. int., blue win., metal M, 5dot **MIP** $2

226 '65 Impala Lowrider, wht. pearl, gray int., purp. win., chr. C, gbbs **MIP** $2

227 Mini Truck, burnt org. met., blk. int., clr. win., blk. pl. C, 5sp **MIP** $2

228 Ford Stake Bed, candy blue met./gray, chr. int., clr. win., chr. M, 5dot **MIP** $3

229 Silver Bullet, blk., burgundy met. int., red win., burgundy met. metal T, t/b **MIP** $2

230 Oldsmobile Aurora, yel., red int., clr. win., blk. pl. C, bbs **MIP** $2

231 Lotus Project M250, yel./ptd. rear "LOTUS", blk. int., smoked win., blk. pl. C, pr5 **MIP** $2

232 Panoz LMP-1 Roadster, grn./no blue in flag, blk. int., blk. pl. M, 5dot **MIP** $3

233 Maelstrom, dayglo yel., blk. win., blk. pl. M, 5dot **MIP** $2

234 1936 Cord, blk., red int., tinted win., chr. C, bbs **MIP** $2

235 Semi-Fast, transparent red/blk., gray int., yel. win., silv. metal C, 5sp **MIP** $2

236 Submarine, dayglo org., blk. win., gray pl. M, **MIP** $2

237 Fire Eater, dayglo lime, blk. int., smoked win., chr. M, 5dot **MIP** $3

238 Ferrari F50, purp. met., blk. int., clr. win., metal M, 5dot **MIP** $2

239 T-Bird Stocker, red, chr. win., metal M, 5dot **MIP** $2

240 Shelby Cobra 427 S/C, red flake, tan int., clr. win., metal M, bbs **MIP** $2

2002 Treasure Hunts

1 La Troca, yel., blk. win., gold chr. M, RR **MIP** $11

2 '71 Plymouth GTX, dk. blue met., blk. int., clr. win., chr. M, RR **MIP** $13

3 '57 Roadster, grn. met., blk. int., smoked win., metal M, RR **MIP** $12

4 Lotus Project M250, burgundy met., blk. int., smoked win., blk. pl. M, RR **MIP** $10

5 Ford Thunderbolt, silv. met., wht. int., blue win., chr. M, RR **MIP** $10

6 Panoz LMP-1 Roadster S, wht./lt. blue, blk. int., blk. pl. M, RR **MIP** $15

7 Phaeton, wht., blk. int., clr. win., metal M, RR **MIP** $10

8 Fat Fendered '40, flat blk., wht. int., yel. win., metal T, RR **MIP** $20

9 '40 Ford, aqua/pearl wht., gray int., clr. win., blk. pl. T, RR **MIP** $13

10 Tail Dragger, purp./blk., wht. int., blue win., metal M, RR **MIP** $13

11 Mini Cooper, blk. w/ptd. headlights, org. int., clr. win., metal M, redline RR **MIP** $12

12 Anglia Panel, red met., chr. int., clr. win., lt. gray pl. T, RR **MIP** $15

2002 First Editions

13 Midnight Otto, wht., blk. win., metal M, pr5 **MIP** $1

14 Hyperliner, yel., red int., smoked win., blk. pl. M, b5sp **MIP** $1

15 Tantrum, lime, chr./blk. int., blue win., blk. pl. M, pr5 **MIP** $1

16 Overboard 454, blue met., chr. int., blue win., blk. pl. M, pr5 **MIP** $1

17 Jester, purp., metal int., grn. win., blk. pl. M, pr5 **MIP** $1

18 Alterd State, purp., blk. int., metal M, 5sp **MIP** $3

19 Nissan Skyline, blue, blk. int., clr. win., blk. pl. M, pr5 **MIP** $20

20 Honda Spocket, red/blk., wht. int., smoked win., blk. pl. M, pr5 **MIP** $1

21 Corvette SR-2, red/blk., gray int., clr. win., chr. M, 5sp **MIP** $2

22 NoMadder What, org., chr. int., smoked win., transparent org. M, pr5 **MIP** $2

23 Super Smooth, blue, blk. int., clr. win., blk. pl. M, pr5 **MIP** $2

24 '40 Ford Coupe, red, gray int., smoked win., chr. M, 5sp **MIP** $2

25 Ferrari P4, red, blk. int., clr. win., blk. pl. M, g5sp **MIP** $2

26 Saleen S7, silv., blk. int., smoked win., blk. pl. M, pr5 **MIP** $4

27 Backdraft, silv. blue, chr. int., smoked win., metal M, pr5 **MIP** $2

28 Custom Cougar, blk., purp. int., org. win., blk. pl. M, pc/pr5 **MIP** $2

29 '68 Cougar, grn./gloss blk. roof, blk. int., smoked win., chr. M, 5sp **MIP** $2

30 Torpedo Jones, red, chr. int., red metal M, bbs **MIP** $2

31 Custom '69 Chevy, red, gray int., smoked win., blk. pl. M, pr5 **MIP** $2

32 Custom '59 Cadillac, lt. purp., wht. int., clr. win., chr. M, gbbs **MIP** $2

33 Open Road-ster, mustard, chr. int., grn. win., metal M, pr5 **MIP** $1

34 Jaded, purp. met., chr. int., purp. win., gray pl. M, 5sp **MIP** $2

35 '57 Cadillac Eldorado Brougham, blk./silv. met. HW logo, lt. gray int., clr. win., chr. M, bbs **MIP** $2

36 HW Prototype, bronze met., gray int., dk. purp. win., metal M, pr5 **MIP** $2

37 Lancia Stratos, red, blk. int., clr. win., blk. pl. M, 5sp **MIP** $15

38 Nissan Z, silv. met., blk. int., smoked win., blk. pl. M, pr5 **MIP** $1

39 Toyota RSC, gray met., blk. int., smoked win., blk. pl. M, or5 **MIP** $1

40 2001 Mini Cooper, mustard, blk. int., clr. win., metal M, pr5 **MIP** $15

41 Super Tsunami, gold met., gray int., blue win., blk. pl. M, pr5 **MIP** $2

42 '64 Riviera, bronze/grn./pink stripes, wht. int., purp. win., chr. M, pr5 **MIP** $5

43 Moto-Crossed, red, gray int., smoked win., metal M, 5sp **MIP** $3

44 Lotus Esprit, blk., tan int., clr. win., blk. pl. M, 5sp **MIP** $2

45 Volkswagen New Beetle Cup, yel./long stripe, gray int., blue win., gray pl. M, pr5 **MIP** $8

46 Pony-Up, bronze/pearl blue flames, blk. int., smoked win., metal M, pr5 **MIP** $3

47 I Candy, lime/purp., purp. int., org. win., metal M, 5sp **MIP** $10

48 Rocket Oil Special, purp. met., chr. int., smoked win., metal M, 5sp **MIP** $2

49 Hyundai Spyder Concept, gold met., blk. int., smoked win., blk. pl. M, pr5 **MIP** $2

50 Sling Shot, blue met., chr. int., smoked win., metal M, pr5 **MIP** $3

51 40 Something, yel., gray int., smoked win., blk. pl. M, pr5 **MIP** $2

52 Side Draft, bronze met., blk. int., smoked win., blk. pl. M, pr5 **MIP** $4

53 Ballistic, grn./closed scoop, chr. int., blue win., blk. pl. M, y5 **MIP** $5

54 Syd Mead's Sentinel 400 Limo, dk. aqua/flat blk., gray int., smoked win., chr. M, 5sp **MIP** $4

2002 Series

WILD FRONTIER

55 '59 Chevy Impala, bronze met., wht. int., smoked win., gold chr. M, g5sp **MIP** $2

56 '32 Ford Delivery, blk./tan, tan int., tinted win., metal T, 3sp **MIP** $2

57 Grilllonaire, org., wht. int., smoked win., blk. pl. M, g5sp **MIP** $2

57 Ice Cream Truck, org., wht. int., smoked win., blk. pl. M, g5sp **MIP** $4

58 Power Plower, dk. red flake, gray int., yel. win., metal M, ct/b **MIP** $4

SPARES & STRIKES

59 Surfin' School Bus, silv./blk., yel. win., gold chr. M, g5sp **MIP** $2

60 So Fine, aqua/wht., wht. int., clr. win., chr. M, 5sp **MIP** $2

61 Rodger Dodger, grn. met., gold int., clr. win., chr. M, 5sp **MIP** $2

62 Sooo Fast, red, chr. int., clr. win., metal C, 5sp **MIP** $3

TUNERS

63 Ford Focus, wht., red int., clr. win., blk. pl. M, bbs **MIP** $2

64 Honda Civic, blue, blk. int., clr. win., blk. pl. M, 3sp **MIP** $2

65 MS-T Suzuka, yel., blk. int., smoked win., blk. pl. M, 3sp **MIP** $2

66 Toyota Celica, red, blk. int., smoked win., blk. pl. M, bbs **MIP** $2

CORVETTE

67 '65 Corvette, blue/silv., blk. int., clr. win., gray pl. M, 5sp **MIP** $3

68 '97 Corvette, purp./silv., gray int., clr. win., blk. pl. M, 3sp **MIP** $7

69 '58 Corvette, yel./wht. cove, chr. int., clr. win., blk. pl. C, 3sp **MIP** $3

70 '63 Corvette, red, wht. int., tinted win., chr. M, 3sp **MIP** $2

TRUMP CARS

71 Dodge Charger R/T, blk./silv. side panel, gray int., red win., gray pl. M, 5dot **MIP** $5

72 Hammered Coupe, red flake, chr. int., clr. win., blk. metal M, g5sp **MIP** $2

73 Montezooma, gold met., blk. int., red win., blk. pl. M, 5dot **MIP** $1

74 '33 Ford, wht./maroon, blk. int., clr. win., metal M, 5sp **MIP** $2

COLD BLOODED

75 Firebird Funny Car, blk., metal int., red win., metal M, r5sp **MIP** $3

76 Speed Shark, bronze met., lt. gray int., chr. win., chr. M, 5sp **MIP** $2

77 Vulture, yel., chr. int., smoked win., transparent smoked C, 5sp **MIP** $2

78 Phaeton, teal met., blk. int., red win., silv. metal C, gt/b **MIP** $1

STAR SPANGLED

79 Chrysler Pronto, red met., gray int., clr. win., blk. pl. C, bbs **MIP** $2

80 3-Window '34, blue met., wht. int., blue win., metal T, t/b **MIP** $3

81 Deora II, silv. met., chr. int., clr. win., chr. C, 5dot **MIP** $2

82 '68 El Camino, wht., red int., clr. win., metal C, 5sp **MIP** $1

YU-GI-OH

83 Power Pistons, blk., wht. int., red win., metal T, r5sp **MIP** $1

84 Seared Tuner, red met., blk. int., yel. win., blk. pl. M, g5dot **MIP** $2

85 Fandango, candy blue met., blk. int., grn. win., gray pl. M, magenta chr. 5sp **MIP** $2

86 Super Tuned, candy lime met., blk. int., yel. win., gray pl. C, blue chr. 5sp **MIP** $2

SPECTRAFLAME II

87 Monoposto, candy lime met., chr. int., purp. win., blk. pl. M, pr5 **MIP** $1

88 Muscle Tone, candy goldV, wht. int., smoked win., blk. pl. M, gpr5 **MIP** $2

89 Jet Threat 3.0, candy lt. blue, chr. int., yel. win., metal M, bbs **MIP** $1

90 Screamin' Hauler, candy lt. purp. met., metal int., smoked win., blk. metal M, 5sp **MIP** $4

SPECTROFLAME II

90 Screamin' Hauler, candy lt. purp. met., metal int., smoked win., blk. metal M, 5sp **MIP** $13

MASTERS OF THE UNIVERSE HE-MAN

91 '41 Willys Coupe, blk., chr. int., red win., dk. gray pl. C, 5sp **MIP** $2

92 Twin Mill, wht., gold int., yel. win., gold pl. M, g5sp **MIP** $2

93 Double Vision, grn. met., gray int., clr. win., gray pl. C, bbs **MIP** $1

94 Phantastique, blue met., blk. int., red win., blk. pl. C, t/b **MIP** $1

SWEET RIDES

95 Chevy Pro Stock Truck, wht., red int., smoked win., blk. pl. M, red chr. 5sp **MIP** $3

96 Pro Stock Firebird, silv.-blue, blk. int., blue win., metal M, 5sp **MIP** $3

97 Mustang Cobra, candy gray/blue, red tampo, blk. int., blue win., blk. pl. C, bbs **MIP** $2

98 '70 Chevelle, yel., wht. int., blue win., chr. C, g5sp **MIP** $3

GRAVE RAVE

99 Evil Twin, wht., red int., red win., blk. pl. C, bbs **MIP** $2

100 Krazy 8s, red met., chr. int., tinted win., metal C, pr5 **MIP** $2

101 Rigor Motor, silv. met., chr. int., org. win., flat blk. metal M, 5sp **MIP** $1

102 Grave Rave Wagon, flat blk., gray int., org. win., chr. T, 5sp **MIP** $3

RED LINES

103 The Demon, silv. met., wht. int., tinted win., metal M, RL5sp **MIP** $2

104 Vicky, purp. met., wht. int., clr. win., metal M, RL5sp **MIP** $3

105 Side Kick, lt. blue, metal int., blue win., chr. M, RL5sp **MIP** $2

106 Chevy Nomad, org., blk. int., smoked win., metal M, RL5sp **MIP** $2

HOT ROD MAGAZINE

107 Purple Passion, flat lavender, wht. int., tinted win., chr. M, ww5sp **MIP** $3

108 Hooligan, lime/blk., gray int., metal C, 5sp **MIP** $2

109 Deuce Roadster, brn. primer, blk. int., clr. win., metal C, 5sp **MIP** $2

110 '70 Plymouth Roadrunner, yel., blk. int., clr. win., chr. T, 5sp **MIP** $3

FED FLEET

111 Proper Chopper, flat blk., blk. int., org. win., blk. pl. M, **MIP** $2

111 Propper Chopper, flat blk. w/silv. tampo, blk. int., org. win., blk. pl. M, **MIP** $3

112 Armored Truck, blk., wht. int., red win., metal M, g5sp **MIP** $3

113 Hydroplane, wht., chr. int., grn. win., blk. pl. C, **MIP** $3

114 **Dodge Power Wagon,** wht., blk. int., tinted win., gray pl. C, or5 **MIP** $3

2002 Basic Line

115 **Honda Civic,** blk., wht. int., grn. win., blk. pl. M, 5dot **MIP** $2

116 **'71 Plymouth GTX,** yel., blk. int., smoked win., chr. C, 5sp **MIP** $2

117 **'67 Dodge Charger,** mustard/no "Charger", blk. int., smoked win., chr. M, 3sp **MIP** $8

118 **Mercedes CLK-LM,** burgundy met., blk. int., smoked win., blk. pl. C, bbs **MIP** $1

119 **Pontiac Rageous,** silv. met., gray int., smoked win., blk. pl. M, bbs **MIP** $2

120 **Dodge Concept Car,** lime, blk. int., tinted win., metal C, 3sp **MIP** $1

121 **Shock Factor,** yel./blk., blk. int., metal M, ct/b **MIP** $4

122 **Deora,** red met., wht. int., clr. win., metal M, t/b **MIP** $3

123 **Evil Twin,** pearl yel., wht. int., smoked win., blk. pl. M, gbbs **MIP** $15

124 **Monoposto,** red, wht. int., smoked win., blk. pl. M, 3sp **MIP** $3

125 **Hyper Mite,** purp./wht. HW logo, gold chr. int., red win., blk. pl. M, g5sp/old mini g5sp **MIP** $20

126 **Surf Crate,** red met., blk. int., dk. gold metal M.I., g5sp **MIP** $2

127 **Fore Wheeler,** gold met., wht. int., metal C, g5sp **MIP** $2

128 **Tow Jam,** flat blk., silv. win., chr. M, 3sp **MIP** $3

129 **Sweet Sixteen,** wht. pearl, gold int., metal M, bbs **MIP** $2

130 **Porsche 911 Carrera,** blue met., wht. int., tinted win., silv. metal C, 3sp **MIP** $1

131 **Thunderstreak,** dk. blue met., blk. int., metal C, bbs **MIP** $3

132 **Vulture Roadster,** blue, chr. int., red win., transparent red T, 5sp **MIP** $2

133 **Fright Bike,** transparent red, blk. win., metal M, blk./chr. **MIP** $4

134 **Old # 3,** org., silv. int., silv. metal C, 5sp **MIP** $2

135 **Porsche 911 GTI-98,** candy bronze, gray int., clr. win., blk. pl. M, bbs **MIP** $1

136 **Chrysler Thunderbolt,** dk. red flake, blk. int., yel. win., blk. pl. M, g5dot **MIP** $2

137 **Ferrari 348,** yel., blk. int., smoked win., blk. pl. T, 3sp **MIP** $1

138 **Buick Wildcat,** candy purp., blk. win., blk. pl. C, 3sp **MIP** $2

139 **'67 Camaro,** dull met. blue, gray int., clr. win., blk. metal C, 3sp **MIP** $4

140 **XS-IVE,** off wht., blk. int., yel. win., metal M, ct/b **MIP** $4

141 **Ferrari 156,** red, metal int., clr. win., metal M, bbs **MIP** $2

142 **Ford Thunderbolt,** dk. red, wht. int., smoked win., chr. M, 5sp **MIP** $2

143 **Anglia Panel,** silv.-blue met., gray int., clr. win., blk. pl. C, 5sp **MIP** $4

144 **Jeepster,** yel., gray int., smoked win., metal M, 5sp **MIP** $2

145 **Whatta Drag,** pearl mustard, chr. int., clr. win., metal M, 5sp **MIP** $2

146 **Dogfighter,** flat blk., chr. int., blk. pl. C, g3sp **MIP** $1

147 **'65 Mustang,** silv. met., wht. int., tinted win., metal T, 5sp **MIP** $2

148 **Porsche 959,** red, wht. int., smoked win., metal T, 5sp **MIP** $2

149 **Jet Threat 3.0,** silv.-blue pearl, chr. int., smoked win., silv.-blue metal T, 5dot **MIP** $2

150 **Mega-Duty,** org., blk. win., metal M, pr5 **MIP** $4

151 **Toyota Celica,** purp. met., wht. int., yel. win., gray pl. M, bbs **MIP** $1

152 **Silhouette II,** candy lime, wht. int., smoked win., chr. T, 3sp **MIP** $1

153 **Sol-Aire CX4,** blue met./dk. blue side panel, gray int., clr. win., gray pl. M, 3sp **MIP** $3

154 **Olds 442,** dk. red flake, blk. int., smoked win., chr. M, 3sp **MIP** $2

155 **T-Bird Stocker,** blue met., gray int., clr. win., blk. pl. C, 5sp **MIP** $2

156 **Cunningham C4R,** dk. blue met., blk. int., clr. win., blk. pl. M, 5sp **MIP** $1

157 **Mo' Scoot,** transparent blue, metal M, **MIP** $2

158 **Fandango,** yel., blk. int., smoked win., blk. pl. M, gpr5 **MIP** $2

159 **Thomassima III,** teal met., blk. int., clr. win., chr. C, pr5 **MIP** $2

160 **Pikes Peak Celica,** dk. met. blue, gray int., smoked win., blk. pl. T, bbs **MIP** $2

161 **M Roadster,** champagne, blk. int., smoked win., blk. metal M, 5dot **MIP** $20

162 **Ferrari F512M,** dk. gray met., blk. int., clr. win., blk. metal M, 5sp **MIP** $2

163 **Lexus SC400,** gold met., wht. int., smoked win., blk. pl. M, gbbs **MIP** $1

164 **Ferrari F355 Spyder,** dull met. blue, blk. int., smoked win., blk. metal C, 5sp **MIP** $2

165 **'57 T-Bird,** dk. met. blue, blue int., blue win., chr. M, 5sp **MIP** $2

166 **Ferrari 308,** blk., blk. int., smoked win., blk. metal M, bbs **MIP** $2

167 **Rodzilla,** teal, teal metal C, t/b **MIP** $2

168 **Speed Blaster,** candy blue met./red tampos, chr. win., chr. M, 3sp **MIP** $8

169 **Enforcer,** met. gold, blk. win., metal C, 5sp **MIP** $2

170 **Splittin' Image,** candy lime-gold, wht. int., blue win., metal M, 5sp **MIP** $1

171 **Oshkosh Snowplow,** pearl yel., yel. int., gray pl. T, ct/b **MIP** $3

172 **Ferrari F355,** silv. met., blk. int., clr. win., metal M, 5sp **MIP** $2

173 **'70 Plymouth Barracuda,** red/silv. trim, lt. red int., tinted win., chr. M, 5sp **MIP** $5

174 **Dodge Viper GTS-R,** silv. tint champagne, blk. int., clr. win., blk. pl. C, 5sp **MIP** $2

175 **Auburn 852,** silv./maroon, maroon int., clr. win., metal M, bbs **MIP** $1

176 **Cat-A-Pult,** red, blk. int., smoked win., metal M, 5sp **MIP** $2

177 **'95 Camaro,** wht., blk. int., smoked win., blk. pl. M, 5sp **MIP** $3

178 **1996 Chevy 1500,** org., blk. int., clr. win., metal M, pr5 **MIP** $2

179 **Mustang Mach I,** blk./Burmudez and Bermudez, gray int., tinted win., blk. pl. M, 5sp **MIP** $51

180 **Shoe Box,** flat blk., chr. int., clr. win., blk. pl. M, 5sp **MIP** $3

181 **'79 Ford,** wht., gray int., purp. win., chr. M, 5sp **MIP** $3

182 **Morris Wagon,** met. grn., chr. int., clr. win., metal C, 5sp **MIP** $3

183 **Montezooma,** purp. flake, gold int., tinted win., gold chr. C, gbbs **MIP** $2

184 **Ford Focus,** wht., gray int., yel. win., blk. pl. M, 5dot **MIP** $2

185 **'40s Woodie,** blk./tan, blk. int., clr. win., metal M, bbs **MIP** $2

186 **Wheel Loader,** dk. candy red, gray int., blk. pl. C, or5 **MIP** $4

186 **Wheel Loader, backward bucket,** dk. candy red, gray int., blk. pl. C, or5 **MIP** $2

187 **Corvette Stingray III,** wht., blk. int., blue win., blk. pl. M, 3sp **MIP** $3

188 **Slideout,** grn., blk. int., blk. pl. M, 5sp **MIP** $2

189 **Express Lane,** lt. grn., blk. int., metal C, 5sp **MIP** $2

190 **Pontiac Firebird,** silv.-blue, blk. int., clr. win., blk. pl. 1997 M.I., 5sp **MIP** $2

191 **'56 Ford,** flat blk., chr. int., clr. win., red pl. C, 5sp **MIP** $3

192 **Nomadder What,** candy lime met., chr. int., smoked win., blk. pl. M, pr5 **MIP** $3

193 **Cabbin' Fever,** dk. blue met., blk. int., blue win., blk. pl. C, pr5 **MIP** $7

194 **Altered State,** pearl yel., blk. int., metal M, 5sp **MIP** $8

195 **Flashfire,** wht., blk. int., smoked win., wht. pl. M, y5 **MIP** $2

196 **Lamborghini Countach,** candy tangerine, blk. int., clr. win., blk. pl. M, 5sp **MIP** $2

197 **Scorchin' Scooter,** met. gold/blk. handlebars, metal engine, metal, blk./chr. **MIP** $5

198 **Go Kart,** yel., lt. blue seat int., metal M, 5sp **MIP** $7

199 **Turbolance,** lt. candy blue, chr. int., metal M, 3sp **MIP** $2

200 **Mini Cooper,** dk. grn., yel. int., clr. win., metal M, bbs **MIP** $5

201 **Lotus Elise 340R,** satin candy blue metalic, gray int., clr. win., metal C, y5 **MIP** $2

202 Midnight Otto, purp. met., blk. win., metal C, pr5 **MIP** $2

203 Honda Spocket, candy bronze/blk., wht. int., smoked win., blk. pl. M, pr5 **MIP** $2

204 '40 Ford Coupe, flat blk., pink int., yel. win., chr. M, 5sp **MIP** $3

205 1932 Bugatti Type 50, dk. candy blue/blk., chr. int., clr. win., metal M, g5dot **MIP** $2

206 Metrorail Nash Metropolitan, silv. met., chr. int., blue win., C, 5sp **MIP** $2

207 Baja Bug, flat blk., red int., metal M, r5sp **MIP** $3

208 '59 Cadillac, flat blk., gray int., blue win., chr. M, bbs **MIP** $2

209 Jaguar D-Type, candy purp., gray int., org. win., candy purp. metal C, 5dot **MIP** $2

210 Dodge Sidewinder, dk. met. blue, gray int., clr. win., blk. pl. M, y5 **MIP** $3

211 Super Modified, dk. blue met., gray int., metal M, bbs/2 **MIP** $3

212 Sweet Sixteen II, candy red, int., org. win., metal M, 5sp **MIP** $1

213 Ferrari 456M, dk. blue met., lt. gray int., tinted win., blk. metal C, 5sp **MIP** $2

214 Overbored 454, candy tangerine met., chr. int., smoked win., blk. pl. M, pr5 **MIP** $2

215 '68 Cougar, silv.-blue, blk. int., clr. win., chr. M, 5sp **MIP** $3

216 Corvette SR-2, silv.-blue, blk. int., clr. win., chr. M, 5sp **MIP** $2

217 Mustang Cobra, candy purp. met./Birthday, gray int., red win., blk. pl. C, bbs **MIP** $4

218 Baby Boomer, baby blue/Birthday, silv. metal C, 5sp **MIP** $4

219 Dodge Ram 1500, yel., chr. int., blue win., blk. pl. C, 3sp **MIP** $3

220 Ford F-150, lt. purp., chr. int., org. win., blk. pl. T, 3sp **MIP** $3

221 Maelstrom, silv. met., chr. int., red win., red chr. T, pr5 **MIP** $11

222 Ford GT40, silv.-blue met., gray int., blue win., blk. pl. T, 5sp **MIP** $25

223 SS Commodore VT, grn., blk. int., clr. win., blk. pl. T, bbs **MIP** $4

224 Dodge Caravan, pearl org., tan int., clr. win., gray pl. T, 5sp **MIP** $11

225 '57 Chevy, red, blk. int., smoked win., gold chr. T, r5sp **MIP** $281

226 Fiat 500C, grn., blk. int., gold chr. win., metal T, g5sp **MIP** $20

227 Police Cruiser, dk. blue, gray int., clr. win., gray pl. T, 3sp **MIP** $9

228 Oldsmobile Aurora, dk. red met., wht. int., org. win., blk. pl. T, 5dot **MIP** $2

229 Roll Patrol, flat blk., tan int., org. win., metal T, or5 **MIP** $5

230 Surf Patrol, champagne, blue int., clr. win., metal T, or5 **MIP** $5

231 Chevy Stocker, yel., blk. win., metal C, 3sp **MIP** $19

232 Jeepster, purp./wht., wht. int., grn. win., wht. metal C, 5sp **MIP** $5

233 Hyper Mite, pearl wht. met., chr. int., org. win., blk. pl. M, pr5 **MIP** $8

234 Shredster, yel. pearl/flat blk., gray int., smoked win., gray M, pr5 **MIP** $2

235 Phantom Corsair, met. grn., yel. int., smoked win., metal T, g5dot **MIP** $16

236 Hiway Hauler, blk. met., red win., blk. pl. T, g5sp **MIP** $31

237 At-A-Tude, aqua, chr. int., smoked win., blk. pl. T, 5sp **MIP** $2

238 Ford GT-40, silv.-blue met., gray int., blue win., blk. pl. C, 5sp **MIP** $2

238 Saltflat Racer, burgundy pearl, chr. int., org. win., blk. metal T, 5sp **MIP** $2

239 Greased Lightnin', silv. top/blue bottom, chr. int., blue win., blue metal M, pr5 **MIP** $18

240 Ford GT-90, silv.-lime met., blk. int., clr. win., metal M, 3sp **MIP** $14

2003 Treasure Hunts

1 Hooligan, wht./blue w/silv. HW logo, blk. int., metal M, chr. wl/RR **MIP** $12

2 '56 Ford, gold, gold chr. int., clr. win., blk. pl. M, gold chr. RR **MIP** $15

3 Shoe Box, dk. purp., chr. int., smoked win., chr. M, chr. ww/RR **MIP** $15

4 '68 Cougar, blk., blk. int., yel. win., chr. M, chr. RR **MIP** $15

5 '68 El Camino, red/blk., blk. int., clr. win., metal M, chr. RR **MIP** $15

6 Porsche 959, silv. met., blk. win., metal M, chr. RR **MIP** $15

7 Midnight Otto, flat wht./org. stripes, red win., blk. metal M, chr. RR **MIP** $15

8 Riley & Scott, gold/wht., blk. int., blue pl. M, chr. RR **MIP** $15

9 '57 Cadillac Eldorado Brougham, champagne met., wht. int., smoked win., gold chr. M, wht. co-mold **MIP** $20

10 Muscle Tone, blk., tan int., yel. win., gold chr. T, gold chr. RR **MIP** $15

11 Super Tsunami, lime-gold met., gray int., smoked win., blk. pl. M, chr. RR **MIP** $12

12 1971 Plymouth GTX ('Cuda), met. gray, blk. int., clr. win., blk. pl. M, gray co-mold **MIP** $150

12 '70 Plymouth Barracuda, red, blk. int., clr. win., blk. pl. M, blk. co-mold **MIP** $15

2003 First Editions

13 Bonneville 1965, candy blue met., blk. int., clr. win., chr. M, bbs **MIP** $2

14 Steel Flame, dk. candy blue met., blue int., clr. win., blk. pl. M, pr5 **MIP** $2

15 Corvette Stingray, silv. flake, gray int., smoked win., metal M, 5sp **MIP** $2

16 Fish'd & Chip'd, dk. met. blue/silv. met., pink int., lt. HW logo, clr. win., chr. M, 10sp **MIP** $5

17 Switchback, candy tangerine met., chr. int., blue win., blk. pl. M, pr5 **MIP** $3

18 Wild Thing, candy tangerine met., chr. int., clr. win., org. pl. M, sm. thin blk. **MIP** $2

19 1/4 Mile Coupe, candy purp. met., chr. int., clr. win., candy purp. M, 5sp **MIP** $3

20 Zotic, dk. candy tangerine met., chr. int., smoked win., blk. pl. M, pr5 **MIP** $2

21 Chaparral 2D, wht., no "7" on nose, blk. int., clr. win., blk. pl. M, bbs/2 **MIP** $24

22 8 Crate, dk. gray met./blk. enamel, chr. int., purp. win., gray pl. M, 5sp **MIP** $2

23 Vairy 8, silv. met., gray int., clr. win., metal M, 5sp **MIP** $4

24 24/Seven, candy lime met., gray int., smoked win., blk. pl. M, pr5 **MIP** $2

25 Swoop Coupe, candy red met., blk. win., chr. M, 5sp/sw5dot **MIP** $2

26 Whip Creamer II, pearl lavender met., chr. int., yel. win., chr. M, 10sp **MIP** $2

27 Cadillac Cien, silv. met./flat blk., chr. int., red win., blk. pl. M, pr5 **MIP** $2

28 Sinistra, met. gold, chr. int., clr. win., blk. pl. M, chr. magenta pr5 **MIP** $2

29 Golden Arrow, burnt org. met., no stripe, wht. pearl roof, blk. int., clr. win., metal M, 10sp **MIP** $51

30 Bugatti Veyron, red met., blk. enamel, no ptd. headlights, cream int., clr. win., blk. pl. M, 10sp **MIP** $20

31 Flight '03, wht., transparent red trim, red int., smoked win., metal M, 10sp **MIP** $100

32 Hyundai Tiburon, blk./yel. and org. flames, wht. int., org. win., blk. pl. M, 10sp **MIP** $2

33 GT-03, candy rose, blk. int., smoked win., chr. M, bbs **MIP** $3

34 Tire Fryer, dk. candy blue met., chr. int., metal M, 5sp rear, skinny front **MIP** $2

35 Boom Box, silv.-blue met., gold chr. int., smoked win., blk. pl. M, pr5 **MIP** $3

36 Enzo Ferrari, red, blk. int., clr. win., blk. pl. M, pr5 **MIP** $3

37 Dodge M80, yel. met., org. tampos, mostly blk. door logo, blk. int., org. win., blk. pl. M, pr5 **MIP** $3

38 Sand Stinger, lime, blk. seat int., metal M, or5 rear-5sp front **MIP** $3

39 Honda Civic, met. silv., red int., smoked win., chr. M, 10sp **MIP** $3

40 HKS Alteeza, flat blk./wht. tampo, chr. int., purp. win., blk. pl. M, pr5 **MIP** $5

41 Power Panel, candy bronze met., gray int., yel. win., blk. pl. M, alw-or5 **MIP** $3

42 1970 Dodge Charger, brn. met., gold in tampo, chr. int., smoked win., blk. pl. M, 5sp **MIP** $3

43 Lamborghini Murcielago, yel. pearl, blk. int., clr. win., blk. pl. M, pr5**MIP** $3

44 Audacious, blk., gray int., org. win., blk. pl. M, y5 **MIP** $3

45 1969 Pontiac GTO Judge, org., blk. win., chr. M, 5sp **MIP** $3

46 1968 Mustang, dk. blue met., chr. int., smoked win., blk. pl. M w/Boss Hoss, 5sp **MIP** $103

46 1968 Mustang/Boss Hoss, dk. blue met., chr. int., smoked win., blk. pl. M w/Boss Hoss, 5sp **MIP** $20

47 2002 Autonomy Concept, silv. met., blk. under blue logo, blue win., candy blue metal M, skinny **MIP** $8

48 Da' Kar, mustard pearl, blk. int., smoked win., metal M, or5 **MIP** $3

49 Ground FX, dk. blue met., chr. int., org. win., blk. pl. M, sw **MIP** $3

50 Ford F-150, red, blk. win., blk. pl. M, pr5 **MIP** $4

51 Meyers Manx, purp. met., yel. int., smoked win., metal M, 5sp **MIP** $2

52 Cadillac Escalade, dk. met. gray, blk. win., chr. M, pr5 **MIP** $4

53 1941 Ford Pickup, yel./gloss blk., org. tampo, chr. int., smoked win., yel. pl. M, 5sp **MIP** $5

54 Mitsubishi Eclipse, red, chr. int., smoked win., blk. pl. M, pr5 **MIP** $4

2003 Series

WILD WAVE

55 '69 El Camino, yel. met., blk. int., yel. win., chr. M, 5sp **MIP** $2

56 Surf Crate, lt. blue pearl met., wht. int., metal "no origin", 5sp **MIP** $2

57 '40 Woody, blk./blue, yel. int., blue win., metal M, 5sp **MIP** $2

58 Deora II, lt. pearl lime, chr. int., yel. win., chr. C, 5dot **MIP** $2

59 Backdraft, red, chr. int., smoked win., blk. metal T, pr5 **MIP** $2

FLAMIN' HOT WHEELS

60 Ford Thunderbolt, grn. met., yel. int., yel. win., chr. C, 5sp **MIP** $3

61 Callaway C7, copper met., dk. org. int., smoked win., blk. pl. T, g3sp **MIP** $2

62 Pony-Up, silv. met., blue int., blue win., metal M, pr5 **MIP** $2

63 '95 Camaro, candy purp., wht. int., smoked win., blk. pl. M, 5sp **MIP** $2

64 Ford Escort, gold met., wht. int., smoked wing and win., blk. pl. M, gpr5 **MIP** $2

DRAGON WAGONS

65 Dragster, lt. pearl blue met., blk. int., metal M, 5sp **MIP** $2

66 Pontiac GTO, purp. met., wht. int., clr. win., chr. M, 5sp **MIP** $2

67 Lincoln Continental, gold met., blk. int., clr. win., chr. C, bbs **MIP** $2

68 Toyota Celica, red met., gray int., yel. win., gray pl. M, pr5 **MIP** $2

69 Lexus SC400, blk., wht. int., grn. win., grn. pl. M, t/b **MIP** $2

ANIME

70 Seared Tuner, flat gray, blue int., grn. win., chr. C, red pr5 **MIP** $2

71 Jaguar D-Type, flat blk., gray int., grn. win., candy red met. metal C, grn. chr. pr5 **MIP** $2

72 '68 Cougar, bronze, wht. int., blue win., gold chr. M, g5dot **MIP** $3

73 Olds Aurora GTS-1, flat olive, red int., grn. win., blk. pl. C, blue chr. pr5 **MIP** $2

74 Olds 442, blue met., wht. int., red win., gold chr. M, g5dot **MIP** $3

FLYING ACES II

75 '32 Ford, blk., wht. int., red win., blk. pl. M, red 5sp **MIP** $2

76 Track T, yel. pearl, metal int., blk. metal C, g5sp **MIP** $2

77 Deuce Roadster, olive, wht. int., tinted win., metal C, 5sp **MIP** $2

78 '33 Ford Roadster, red, blk. int., clr. win., blk. metal C, red chr. 5sp **MIP** $2

79 Midnight Otto, gray met., red win., blk. metal C, b5sp **MIP** $2

BOULEVARD BUCCANEERS

80 Shoe Box, wht., chr. int., red win., chr. M, 5sp **MIP** $2

81 Anglia Panel, gold, blk. int., smoked win., blk. pl. C, 5sp **MIP** $2

82 Phantom Corsair, blk. met., blue int., blue win., metal M, t/b **MIP** $2

83 Nomadder What, brn. met., chr. int., org. win., org. C, pr5 **MIP** $2

84 Super Smooth, gray, red win., blk. pl. M, 10sp **MIP** $2

CARBONATED CRUISERS

85 Chevelle SS 1970, candy bronze met., wht. int., tinted win., blk. pl. M, g5sp **MIP** $2

86 MX48 Turbo, blk. enamel, red hood, lt. red int., tinted win., red metal C, pr5 **MIP** $2

87 SS Commodore (VT), candy red, blk. int., clr. win., blk. pl. M, bbs **MIP** $2

88 Monoposto, wht. pearl, chr. int., grn. win., blk. pl. M, grn. chr. 5dot **MIP** $3

89 Combat Ambulance, candy gray met., blue int., blue win., blue pl. M, blue chr. 5sp **MIP** $3

RADICAL WRESTLERS

90 '56 Flashsider, wht., chr. win., chr. M, 5dot **MIP** $2

91 Chevy 1969, grn., tan int., yel. win., chr. C, pr5 **MIP** $2

92 Cadillac 1959, yel., blk. int., clr. win., chr. M, bbs **MIP** $10

93 Ford 1934, red, wht. int., clr. win., metal M, t/b **MIP** $2

94 Mazda MX-5 Miata, blk., red int., clr. win., blk. metal M, 5sp **MIP** $2

CRAZED CLOWNS

95 Steel Passion, blue met., gray int., red win., teal pl. C, grn. chr. 5sp **MIP** $2

96 Morris Mini, red, yel. int., grn. win., blk. meta. C, y5dot **MIP** $3

97 Nash Metropolitan, purp. met., gold chr. int., blue win., gold chr. M, red chr. 5sp **MIP** $3

98 Side-Splitter, yel., metal int., smoked win., metal M, red chr. 5sp **MIP** $3

99 Tropicool, candy lime, wht. int., blue win., blue pl. M, blue chr. pr5 **MIP** $3

TECH TUNERS

100 Super Tsunami, candy red, pink in tampo, wht. int., clr. win., chr. M, pr5 **MIP** $2

101 MS-T Suzuka, wht. pearl, blk. int., cmoked win., chr. M, 3sp **MIP** $2

102 Super Tuned, blk. enamel, lt. grn. int., clr. win., dk. gray pl. M, pr5 **MIP** $2

103 Tantrum, lt. gold met., blk. int., smoked win., blk. pl. M, pr5 **MIP** $2

104 Ford Focus, silv. met., blk. int., smoked win., blk. pl. M, 5sp **MIP** $3

SPECTRAFLAME II

105 Sweet 16 II, candy lt. purp., chr. int., purp. win., blk. metal M, 5sp **MIP** $2

106 Double Vision, candy gold, gold chr. int., yel. win., blk. pl. M, gpr5 **MIP** $2

107 Ballistik, candy blue, chr. int., blue win., blk. pl. M, y5 **MIP** $2

108 Side Draft, candy lime, blk. int., grn. win., blk. pl. T, pr5 **MIP** $3

109 Silhouette II, candy burnt org., wht. int., smoked win., blk. pl. M, g/y5 **MIP** $2

SEGA

110 Fandango, silv.-blue met./wht. satin, blk. int., tinted win., blk. pl. C, pr5 **MIP** $2

111 Phaeton, semi-gloss blk., grn. int., clr. win., metal C, 5dsp **MIP** $5

112 Lotus Esprit, dk. red met., blk. int., clr. win., blk. pl. M, pr5 **MIP** $3

113 GT Racer, met. grn., blk. int., smoked win., metal M, 5sp **MIP** $3

114 Custom Cougar, pearl yel. met., blk. tint chr./blk. int., clr. win., chr. M, pr5 **MIP** $5

TRACK ACES

125 Turbo Flame, grn., grn. win., grn. M, g5sp **MIP** $2

143 HW Prototype 12, org., gray int., clr. win., metal M, pr5 **MIP** $2

146 I Candy, silv./grn., grn. int., grn. win., gold metal M, g5sp **MIP** $2

155 Speed Shark, blue satin, org. int., gold chr. win., org. C, g5sp **MIP** $2

161 Hooligan, lt. blue satin/wht., blk. int., metal M, 5sp **MIP** $2

167 Splittin' Image, candy lime satin, gold chr. win., blk. pl. M, g5dot **MIP** $2

173 Buick Wildcat, blk. enamel, org. win., blk. pl. C, g3sp **MIP** $3

176 Ford GT-40, met. gray, gray int., blue win., blk. pl. T, 5sp **MIP** $2

185 Flashfire, met. grn. satin, yel. int., yel. win., blk. pl. M, gbbs **MIP** $2

192 Speed Blaster, day-glo org., gold chr. win., gold chr. M, g/y5 **MIP** $2

WASTELANDERS

130 Sooo Fast, flat blk., gold chr. int., red win., blk. pl. M, g5sp **MIP** $2

144 1967 Dodge Charger, dk. org. met., blk. int., smoked win., blk. pl. M, 5sp **MIP** $2

151 1958 Corvette, candy purp. met., chr. int., smoked win., blk. pl. M, pr5 **MIP** $2

156 Fat Fendered '40, flat gray, org. side tampo, blk. int., red win., gold metal M, g5sp **MIP** $3

162 Fright Bike, clr. pl. body, blk. win., metal M, red chr. rim **MIP** $4

168 Camaro 1967, yel. enamel, blk. int., smoked win., metal C, blue chr. 5sp **MIP** $3

174 Chevy 1957, candy lime, gray int., smoked win., metal C, 5sp **MIP** $3

180 Chevy Impala, drk. candy gray met., blk. int., yel. win., gold chr. C, gbbs **MIP** $2

188 Evil Twin, dk. red met., wht. int., clr. win., blk. pl. M, bbs **MIP** $2

193 Mustang Mach I, flat blk., blk. int., yel. win., blk. pl. M, 5sp **MIP** $3

213 1/4 Mile Coupe, blk. enamel, chr. int., red win., candy red metal C, red chr. 5 sp/chr. 5sp **MIP** $2

PRIDE RIDES

133 1964 Buick Riviera, silv.-blue met., blk. int., blue win., chr. M, y5 **MIP** $2

140 1959 Cadillac, pearl org., yel. int., yel. win., gold chr. M, gt/b **MIP** $2

148 1957 Cadillac Eldorado, purp. met., wht. int., smoked win., chr. M, bbs **MIP** $2

152 Austin Healey, blk., red int., clr. win., metal C, 5sp **MIP** $2

158 Mercedes CLK-LM, candy blue, blk/ win., blk. pl. M, red chr. y5 **MIP** $2

164 Dodge Concept, burnt org. met., tan int., clr. win., metal C, gpr5 **MIP** $2

172 40 Somethin', wht./blk., blk. int., smoked win., blk. pl. M, pr5 **MIP** $2

179 1959 Chevy Bel Air, dk. red met., blk. int., clr. win., chr. M, bbs **MIP** $10

182 Custom Chevrolet C3500, met. grn., chr. int., tinted win., blk. pl. C, pr5 **MIP** $4

183 La Troca, flat blue, blk. win., chr. C, 5sp **MIP** $3

184 Honda Civic, candy blue, blk. int., clr. win., blk. pl. M, pr5 **MIP** $2

207 Sonic Special, burnt org. met., blk. int., clr. win., blk. pl. M, pr5 **MIP** $3

ALT TERRAIN

137 Salt Flat Racer, lt. grn., chr. int., blue win., blk. metal M, 5sp **MIP** $2

141 Pikes Peak Tacoma, yel. w/wht. "Magnaflo", blk. int., clr. win., blk. pl. M, y5 **MIP** $8

150 Big Chill, wht., chr. int., blue pl. M, blue ski **MIP** $2

154 Shock Factor, red/blk., red int., metal C, or5 **MIP** $2

160 Moto-Crossed, grn./yel., blk. int., smoked win., metal M, pr5 **MIP** $2

166 Treadator, met. grn., chr. win., blk. pl. M, **MIP** $3

171 Jeepster, met. copper, blk. int., smoked win., metal C, w5sp **MIP** $2

178 Lakester, yel. enamel, chr. int., clr. win., semi-gloss blk. metal C, pr5 **MIP** $3

187 Go Kart, blk. enamel, wht. int., blk. metal M, 5sp **MIP** $4

191 Roll Cage, flat olive, tan int., blk. metal M, or5 **MIP** $2

WORK CREWSERS

138 Dodge Ram 1500, dk. candy blue met., blk. win., wht. pl. M, 5dot **MIP** $2

145 1956 Ford, dk. gray met., chr. int., clr. win., gray pl. M w/red rivets, 5sp **MIP** $8

149 Bus, lt. candy blue/wht. fenders, red win., gray pl. M, 5sp **MIP** $2

153 Tow Jam, pearl wht., blue tampo w/ "Lightin", blk. win., chr. M, blue chr. y5 **MIP** $5

159 Peterbilt, candy rose, smoked int., smoked win., metal C, 5sp **MIP** $4

165 Limozeen, dk. blue pearl, tan int., smoked win., shiny smoked chr. M, bbs **MIP** $3

170 Hiway Hauler, wht. pearl met., blk. win., chr. C, 5dot **MIP** $4

177 1940 Ford, flat olive, blk. int., clr. win., blk. pl. C, 5sp **MIP** $3

186 Cabbin' Fever, blk. enamel/org., frosted logo on base, clr. win., chr. C, pr5 **MIP** $2

190 Fire-Eater, candy red, yel. int., yel. win., chr. M, red chr. pr5 **MIP** $58

ROLL PATROL

142 Firebird Funny Car, blk., metal int., clr. win., metal M, b5sp **MIP** $2

147 Syd Mead's Sentinel 400, lt. blue/gold HW logo, blk. int., smoked win., chr. M, 5sp **MIP** $15

157 Saleen S7, blk., wht. int., red win., red pl. M, red chr. pr5 **MIP** $2

163 Police, flat blk., dk. blue enamel in tampos, blk. int., clr. win., dk. silv. pl. M, 10sp **MIP** $3

169 Dodge Caravan, wht. Enamel, blk. int., red win., gray pl. M, 5sp **MIP** $3

175 Jaded, blk. enamel, chr. int., clr. win., gray pl. C, 5sp **MIP** $3

179 1959 Chevy Bel Air, dk. red met., blk. int., clr. win., chr. M, bbs **MIP** $4

181 Phantom Corsair, silv./blue met., blk. int., blue win., metal C, 5dot **MIP** $2

189 Fore Wheeler, blk. enamel/blue/wht., blue int., metal C, g5sp **MIP** $2

194 Fish'd & Chip'd, dk. blue met., wht. int., red win., chr. M, bbs **MIP** $2

208 Hyperliner, met. silv., blk./red int., smoked win., gray T, pr5 **MIP** $3

FINAL RUN

85 Chevelle SS 1970, candy bronze met., wht. int., tinted win., blk. pl. M, g5sp **MIP** $2

87 SS Commodore (VT), candy red, blk. int., clr. win., blk. pl. M, bbs **MIP** $2

195 Rig Wrecker/2002 on door, candy red met., gold int., clr. win., gold chr. M, gY5 **MIP** $5

195 Rig Wrecker/2003 on door, candy red met., gold int., clr. win., gold chr. M, gY5 **MIP** $3

196 Ambulance, yel./silv., red int., org. win., chr. M, 5sp **MIP** $3

197 Mustang GT 1996, gray met., blk. int., smoked win., metal M, pr5 **MIP** $3

198 1970 Dodge Charger Daytona, red, wht. int., smoked win., chr. M, 5sp **MIP** $3

199 Twang Thang, silv. met., gold chr. int., yel. win., blk. pl. C, gpr5 **MIP** $3

200 Ford Bronco, candy blue, uncolored pl. int., yel. win., metal M, or5 **MIP** $4

201 Bywayman, lt. brn. primer, blk. int., yel. win., blk. metal M, or5 **MIP** $5

202 Duesenberg Model J 1931, met. gray/blk., blk. int., yel. win., candy gold metal M, g5sp **MIP** $3

203 Lamborghini Diablo, red enamel, blk. int., smoked win., blk. metal M, pr5 **MIP** $3

204 Porsche 911 Carrera, wht. pearl, blk. int., smoked win., metal M, red chr. 5sp **MIP** $3

205 Auburn 852, gold/brn./chr., chr. int., clr. win., metal M, bbs **MIP** $2

206 GM Lean Machine, candy satin blue, blk. win., metal T, pr5 **MIP** $3

2003 Basic Line

115 Jester, transparent red/blk., metal int., smoked win., blk. pl. M, pr5 **MIP** $2

116 Open Road-Ster, candy bronze met., chr. int., smoked win., metal M, pr5 **MIP** $2

117 Outsider, silv. met., metal C, **MIP** $2

118 Hot Seat, lt. gold chr., blk. seat int., metal M, g5sp **MIP** $2

119 '63 Thunderbird, silv.-blue met., blk. int., clr. win., metal C, 10sp **MIP** $2

120 Arachnorod, copper met., wht. int., red win., blk. pl. C, pr5 **MIP** $2

121 Rail Rodder, lt. blue, metal C, 5sp **MIP** $2

122 1935 Cadillac, dk. grn. met., blk. int., clr. win., metal M, bbs **MIP** $2

123 Mercedes 500SL, red met., tan int., tinted win., dk. red pl. C, pr5 **MIP** $2

124 Custom '69 Chevy, candy purp. met., red bumper, wht. int., tinted win., blk. pl. C, pr5 **MIP** $2

126 Cadillac LMP, candy gray, blk. int., blk. pl. C, bbs **MIP** $2

127 ISUZU Vehicross, dk. candy red, blk. int., clr. win., metal C, pr5 **MIP** $2

128 Porsche 911 GT3 Cup, silv.-blue met., silv. in tampo, wht. int., smoked win., blk. pl. M, pr5 **MIP** $4

129 Mercedes C-Class, met. burgundy, gray int., smoked win., blk. pl. M, 10sp **MIP** $2

131 Sharkruiser, wht. pearl, gold chr. int., gold met. metal M, gbbs **MIP** $2

132 Zender Fact 4, purp. met., wht. int., org. win., blk. pl. C, 10sp **MIP** $2

134 Lancia Stratos, yel., wht. int., tinted win., blk. pl. C, gpr5 **MIP** $3

135 Panoz LMP-1 Roadster S, dk. candy blue met., blk. int., blk. pl. C, pr5 **MIP** $2

136 Blast Lane, gold met./blk. handlebars, metal M, gold rim/blk. spoke **MIP** $4

139 Panoz GTR-1, day-glo yel., blk. int., smoked win., blue pl. C, blue chr. 3sp **MIP** $2

209 Cat-A-Pult, blue pearl emt., blk. int., clr win., silv. ptd. metal C, 5sp **MIP** $3

210 Splittin' Image, candy blue met., wht. int., org. win., metal M, 5sp **MIP** $2

211 Switchback, burnt org. met., chr. int., smoked win., blk. pl. M, 10sp **MIP** $2

212 Surf Patrol, blue flake, bright red int., tinted win., metal T, or5 **MIP** $2

214 Vary 8, burnt org. met., chr. int., blue win., metal T, 5sp **MIP** $2

215 Bonneville, lt. gold met., blk. int., smoked win., chr. M, 10sp **MIP** $3

216 Chevy 1500 1996, org. pl, blk. int., smoked win., blk. ptd. metal M, 5sp **MIP** $2

217 Ford F150 1079, blk. met., blk. int., yel. win., chr. T, 5sp **MIP** $3

218 Dodge Power Wagon, met. brn., blk. int., smoked win., chr. C, or5 **MIP** $2

219 Fiat 500C, flat blue, metal/blk. int., blk. win., metal T, g5sp **MIP** $2

220 Nissan Z, flat gray, wht. "004" on side, blk. int., blue win., blk. pl. M, pr5 **MIP** $2

2004 First Editions

BASIC

1 Batmobile, candy purp./blk., no bat logo on card, chr. int., clr. win., chr. M, pr5 **MIP** $6

2 Dodge Charger 1969, blk., org. stripe, gray int., blue win., chr. M, 5sp **MIP** $4

3 Swoopy Do, copper met., chr. int., smoked win., metal M, 5sp **MIP** $2

4 Chevy Impala 1964, silv./blue met., wht. int., blue win., chr. M, bbs **MIP** $3

5 Nova 1968, dk. silv./blue met., wht. int., blue win., chr. M, 5sp **MIP** $3

21 The Gov'ner, flat blk. pl., red taillight, chr. win., metal M, b5sp/ww **MIP** $5

22 Mustang Funny Car, candy blue met., metal int., blk. win., metal M, 5sp **MIP** $4

23 Rockster, yel. pearl met., chr. int., clr. win., gray pl. M, or5 **MIP** $15

27 Bedlam, lt. purp. pearl pl., chr. int., red win., metal M, pr5 **MIP** $15

28 Chevy Fleetline 1947, lt. lavender met., wht. int., smoked win., chr. M, bbs **MIP** $3

29 Maserati Quattroporte, silv.-blue met., silv. grille emblem, tan int., smoked win., chr. M, 10sp **MIP** $2

30 F-Racer, flat blk., blue chr., chr. int., metal M, pr5 **MIP** $3

31 Batmobile, blk. pl., blk. win., metal M, 5sp **MIP** $3

32 Hi I.Q., lime satin, gray int., smoked win., frosted chr. M, skinny **MIP** $3

35 16 Angles, candy purp. met., metal int., org. win., metal M, pr5 **MIP** $3

36 Lotus Sport Elise, met. gold, chr. int., tinted win., blk. pl. M, g10sp **MIP** $2

37 Rapid Transit, lime, wht. int., purp. win., met. charcoal pl. M, pr5 **MIP** $3

38 Toyota MR2, met. grn., flat blk. hood, blk. int., grn. win., blk. pl. M, grn. chr. pr5 **MIP** $3

48 Ford Mustang Concept, silv. met., short T top, red int., tinted win., blk. pl. M, "Mustang Concept" on base, pr5**MIP** $3

57 Cadillac V-16, blk., tan int., tinted win., chr. M, blings **MIP** $10

58 C6 Corvette, red, tan int., tinted win., blk. pl. M, pr5 **MIP** $3

60 Hummer H3T, blk., cream int., blue win., frosted chr. M, or5 **MIP** $2

61 Suzuki GSX-R/4, met. red, flat blk., chr. int., clr. win., chr. M, 5dot **MIP** $2

65 Dodge Neon, blk./wht., blk. win., gray pl. M, 5sp **MIP** $2

70 CUL8R, silv.-blue met., maroon stripe, candy tangerine met. int., red win., maroon met. metal M, pr5 **MIP** $3

72 Trak-Tune, transparent blue, chr. int., org. win., org. metal M, 10sp **MIP** $3

73 Asphalt Assault, pearl mustard met., chr. int., org. win., blk. pl. M, 10sp **MIP** $5

74 2001 B Engineering Edonis, met. gold, gray int., smoked win., blk. pl. M, pr5 **MIP** $2

76 Madd Propz, candy cinnamon met., chr. int., smoked win., gray met. metal M, mini 5sp **MIP** $5

80 Dodge Tomahawk, silv., blk. ptd. seat int., blue metal M, chr. rim, blk. tires **MIP** $3

81 What-4-2, transparent org., chr. int., smoked win., metal M, pr5 **MIP** $2

82 Xtreemster, dk. red candy met., chr. int., smoked win., blk. pl. M, pr5 **MIP** $3

83 Torque Screw, silv.-blue met., chr. int., blue win., blk. pl. M, pr5 **MIP** $2

84 Off Track, blk. pl., chr. int., yel. win., metal M, 5sp **MIP** $2

86 Brutalistic, candy purp. met., chr. int., yel. win., candy gold ptd. M, pr5 **MIP** $2

87 Shredded, red/met. gray, met. gray int., tinted win., blk. pl. M, pr5 **MIP** $2

88 Super Gnat, lt. or dk. candy tangerine met., chr. int., smoked win., metal M, 10sp **MIP** $3

90 Mitsubishi Eclipse, met. gold, gray int., smoked win., blk. pl. M, y5 **MIP** $2

91 Buzz Off, candy purp./grn., chr. int., grn. win., metal M, 10sp **MIP** $2

92 Jacknabitt Special, ZAMAC, blk. int., blue win., metal M, 5sp **MIP** $5

94 Phantom Racer, org. pearl met. or candy tangerine met., chr. int., smoked win., blk. pl. M, pr5 **MIP** $3

100 Cool One, wht., org. tampo, wht. int., org. win., chr. M, pr5 **MIP** $3

BLINGS

11 Lotus Esprit, met. lt. gold, blk. int., smoked win., blk. pl. M, xlpr5 **MIP** $10

12 Dairy Delivery, wht. pearl, red win., metal M, xl5sp **MIP** $2

13 Hyperliner, candy burnt org., blk. int., smoked win., metal M, blings **MIP** $2

14 Cadillac Escalade, candy blue met., HW logo on win. and tailgate, smoked win., chr. M, blings **MIP** $10

15 Dodge Ram Pickup, red, blk. win., chr. M, xl5sp **MIP** $7

26 Chevy Avalanche, candy blue/gray pl., blk. win., blue metal M, blings **MIP** $4

34 Hummer H2, yel., blk. win., blk. pl. M, blings **MIP** $4

40 Out-A-Line, met. purp., blk. win., chr. M, xlpr5 **MIP** $10

53 Plymouth Barracuda 1972, org., gloss blk. hood, blk. win., chr. M, xlpr5 **MIP** $3

55 Brick Cutter, dk. blue met., red win., chr. M, blings **MIP** $3

BLING2

12 Dairy Delivery, wht. pearl, red win., metal M, xl5sp **MIP** $4

13 Hyperliner, candy burnt org., blk. int., smoked win., metal M, blings **MIP** $3

CROOZE

44 Ozz Coupe, red met., blk. win., chr. M, skinny/sm. 5sp rear **MIP** $2

46 W-Oozie, candy tangerine met., blue metal M, blk. spoke **MIP** $5

49 Low Flow, silv. met./blk. met., red win., chr. M, 5sp **MIP** $4

50 Slikt Back, blk., lt. purp. flames, chr. int., purp. win., blk. pl. M, 5sp **MIP** $5

51 LeMelt, met. grn., chr. int., tinted win., flat blk. pl. M, 5sp **MIP** $3

52 Bedtime, wht. pearl, chr. int., blue win., gloss blk. pl. M, 5sp **MIP** $2

64 Fast Fuse, silv. met., wht. grille, chr. int., blue win., blk. pl. M, 5sp **MIP** $4

69 Batmobile, flat or semi-gloss blk., chr. int., org. win., blk. pl. M, 5sp **MIP** $3

75 Ozznberg, org., brn. fenders, chr. int., clr. win., metal M, bbs **MIP** $5

77 Wail Tale, wht. pearl met., short hood tampo, chr. int., blue win., blk. pl. M, g5sp **MIP** $5

FATBAX

41 Mustang GT 2004, yel. pearl met., blk. win., metal M, fb5sp **MIP** $5

45 Plymouth Barracuda, lt. yel., gray win., blue metal M, 5sp **MIP** $10

62 Silhouette, candy lime, taillight on bumper, chr. int., org. win., candy lime metal M, 5sp **MIP** $5

66 Shelby Cobra 427 S/C, silv. met., blk. int., clr. win., metal M, 5sp **MIP** $4

67 Duplified, semi-gloss blk., chr. int., blk. win., metal M, 5sp **MIP** $10

78 Toyota Supra, dk. or lt. candy purp. met., smoked win., blue metal M, 5sp **MIP** $2

85 Exhausted, lt. purp. met., chr. win., blue metal M, 5sp **MIP** $3

92 Jacknabitt Special, wht., one blk. stripe, blk. int., blue win., metal M, 5sp **MIP** $4

95 2005 Corvette, candy blue, silv. headlights, red taillights, blk. win., metal M, 5sp **MIP** $3

97 B-Machine, candy tangerine met., blk. win., blue metal M, 5sp **MIP** $2

98 Power Sander, candy tangerine met., metal int., metal M, or5 rear, 5sp front **MIP** $2

HARDNOZE

16 2 Cool, candy purp. met., chr. int., smoked win., chr. M, xl5sp **MIP** $3

17 Grandy Lusion, dk. blue met., dk. red cove, chr. int., clr. win., metal M, xl5sp **MIP** $3

18 Dodge Neon, wht. pearl, uncolored int., smoked win., chr. M, xl5sp **MIP** $3

19 Merc 1949, grn./candy lime, blk. int., smoked win., blk. pl. M, xl5sp **MIP** $4

20 Twin Mill, flat blk., red win., gray pl. M, xl5sp **MIP** $3

24 Chevy 1959, met. gray, tan int., smoked win., chr. M, xl5sp **MIP** $2

39 Chevy Monte Carlo 1974, gold met., wht. int., org. win., chr. M, xlg5sp **MIP** $2

42 Batmobile, flat blk., blk. win., chr. M, xl5sp **MIP** $3

47 Cadillac V-16 Concept, met. silv., chr. int., smoked win., chr. M, pr5 **MIP** $2

56 Toyota Celica, candy tangerine met./flat or semi-gloss black, wht. int., tinted win., chr. M, 5sp **MIP** $2

'TOONED

6 Two 2 Go, wht./purp., chr. int., clr. win., blk. pl. M, pr5 **MIP** $3

7 360 Modena, yel., silv. tampo, blk. win., blk. pl. M, xlpr5 **MIP** $2

8 Toyota Supra, met. silv., blk. win., chr. M, xlgpr5 **MIP** $5

9 Enzo Ferrari, red, chr. int., smoked win., blk. pl. M, xlpr5 **MIP** $3

10 Shift Kicker, purp. pearl/blk., blk. int., chr. M, 5sp **MIP** $2

25 Deora, met. gold, w/surfboards, chr. int., clr. win., blk. pl. M, 5sp **MIP** $3

33 Chevy Impala 1964, flat lt. or dk. brn., chr. int., smoked win., frosted chr. M, 5sp **MIP** $3

38 Toyota MR2, wht., semi-gloss blk. hood, blk. int., red win., blk. pl. M, pr5 **MIP** $3

43 Splittin' Image, purp. pl., wht. int., grn. win., metal M, pr5 **MIP** $3

54 Mitsubishi Pajero Evolution, lt. red, blk. int., smoked win., chr. M, xl5sp **MIP** $2

59 Sir Ominous, purp. met., sm. tampo, chr. int., red win., gray pl. M, pr5 **MIP** $10

63 Furiosity, lt. candy blue met., chr. int., smoked win., blk. pl. M, pr5 **MIP** $2

68 Mercy Breaker, silv.-blue met., lt. or dk. gray tampo, chr. int., smoked win., blk. pl. M, pr5 **MIP** $3

71 Camaro Z28 1969, met. maroon, silv. vents, chr. int., tinted win., blk. pl. M, 5sp **MIP** $10

79 Lamborghini Countach, org., flat blk. or semi-gloss blk. tailpipes, blk. int., smoked win., org. pl. M, pr5 **MIP** $3

89 Chevy S-10, met. grn., blk. win., frosted chr. M, blings **MIP** $3

93 1963 Corvette, met. gray, red win., lt. gray pl. M, 5sp **MIP** $3

96 Sixy Beast, lt. purp. pearl, wht. int., grn. win., chr. M, 5sp **MIP** $2

99 2005 Corvette, yel. pearl met., four names, "Tscherne," blk./gray, chr. int., smoked win., blk. pl. M, pr5 **MIP** $15

2004 Treasure Hunts

101 Pontiac Bonneville 1965, flat lavender, blk. int., smoked win., chr. M, chr. RR **MIP** $5

102 GT-03, red/blk. w/gray stripe, red int., smoked win., blk. chr. M, chr. RR **MIP** $15

103 Cadillac Cien, blk., tan int., smoked win., chr. M, redline RR **MIP** $5

104 The Demon, met. gold, org. int., org. win., metal M, chr. WW/RR **MIP** $8

105 Super Smooth, met. brn./champagne, blk. int., smoked win., blk. pl. M, gold chr. RR **MIP** $5

106 Splittin' Image II, wht., chr. int., purp. win., metal M, chr. RR **MIP** $9

107 Altered State, pearl yel., semi-gloss blk. int., semi-gloss blk., chr. RR **MIP** $6

108 Morris Wagon, gold/blk., chr. int., clr. win., metal M, chr. RR **MIP** $50

109 Whip Creamer II, candy lime met., chr. int., smoked win., chr. M, chr. WW/RR **MIP** $15

110 Tantrum, red met., chr./blk. int., smoked win., blk. pl. M, chr. 5sp RR **MIP** $10

111 Audacious, wht. pearl met., purp. tampo, tan int., org. win., chr. M, chr. RR **MIP** $10

112 Meyers Manx, candy blue met., wht. int., blue win., blue metal M, chr. RR **MIP** $10

2004 Series

CEREAL CRUNCHERS

113 Camaro 1995, blk., red int., smoked win., blk. pl. M, 10sp **MIP** $2

114 8 Crate, wht. pearl met., chr. int., red win., chr. T, pr5 **MIP** $3

115 Lincoln Continental 1964, candy tangerine met., wht. int., clr. win., chr. M, 10sp **MIP** $2

116 Plymouth GTX 1971, yel. or mustard met., blk. int., smoked win., chr. T, 5sp **MIP** $3

117 Pontiac GTO 1967, brn. met., blk. int., org. win., chr. T, 5sp **MIP** $3

TAT RODS

118 Sooo Fast, flat brn., chr. int., org. win., flat blk. ptd. metal C, extra lg. rear 5sp **MIP** $2

119 Ford Vicky, lt. olive met., blk. int., smoked win., metal M, 3sp or 5sp **MIP** $2

120 Deuce Roadster, blk., blue int., clr. win., metal C, 5sp **MIP** $2

121 Ford 1932, candy blue, wht. int., smoked win., metal T, 5sp **MIP** $10

122 Hooligan, gray, red pl., blk. int., metal C, 5dot **MIP** $3

STAR SPANGLED 2

123 Mustang 1965, silv. met., wht. int., clr. win., metal T, 5sp **MIP** $3

124 T-Bird 1957, wht. w/porthole, red int., red win., chr. T, red chr. 5sp **MIP** $3

125 Chevy 1957, flat blue, lt. blue hood, red int., red win., metal M, 5sp **MIP** $7

126 Purple Passion, candy red met., blk. int., smoked win., chr. C, blue chr. co-mold **MIP** $5

127 Corvette 1963, blk., pearl blue int., clr. win., frosted chr. T, y5 **MIP** $3

FERRARI HEAT

128 Ferrari 360 Modena, yel., blk. int., smoked win., metal M, pr5 **MIP** $10

129 Ferrari F355 Challenge, red, blk. int., smoked win., metal M, pr5 **MIP** $8

130 Ferrari 456M, grn., lt. brn. flame outline, no HW logo, cream int., clr. win., metal M, gpr5 **MIP** $10

131 Ferrari 550 Maranello, blk., blk. int., blue win., metal M, 5sp **MIP** $2

132 Ferrari 333 SP, pearl wht. met., blk. int., blue win., blk. pl. M, y5 **MIP** $2

TAG RIDES

138 Boom Box, lt. candy purp. met., chr. int., tinted win., blk. pl. C, pr5 **MIP** $3

139 1968 Cougar, gold met., blk. int., blue win., blk. pl. T, 3sp **MIP** $2

140 Surfin' S'cool Bus, yel. pearl met., blk. int., smoked win., blk. pl. T, 5sp **MIP** $2

141 Fandango, candy lime met., yel. or grn. roof tampo, blk. int., smoked win., blk. pl. M, gpr5 **MIP** $2

142 Tropicool, candy tangerine met., blk. int., yel. win., blk. pl. T, 5dot **MIP** $3

CRANK ITZ

143 Custom '59 Cadillac, lt. purp. pearl met., wht. int., org. win., gold chr. T, gy5 **MIP** $2

144 Steel Flame, brn. met., wht. int., smoked win., blk. pl. M, w/tb **MIP** $3

145 Cadillac Escalade, blk., chr. int., blue win., chr. T, pr5 **MIP** $2

146 '40s Woody, lt. blue met., tan int., smoked win., silv. metal T, 5sp **MIP** $7

147 Swoop Coupe, red, smoked win., frosted chr. M, 5sp rear, skinny front **MIP** $2

DEMONITION

148 Evil Twin, dk. blue met., red int., smoked win., dk. blue pl. T, g5dot **MIP** $2

149 1/4 Mile Coupe, met. grn., gold chr. int., smoked win., blk. metal T or M, g5sp **MIP** $2

150 Jaded, blk., blue chr. int., blue win., blue chr. C, 5sp **MIP** $2

151 Wild Thing, burgundy met., gold chr. int., blue win., blk. pl. M, thin blk. **MIP** $2

152 Dairy Delivery, met. gold, narrow rear windows, blk. int., red win., blk. pl. M, red chr. pr5 **MIP** $2

SCRAPHEADS

153 Mega-Duty, met. bronze, blue win., metal C, blue chr. y5 **MIP** $3

154 Shadow Jet II, wht. pl., chr. int., red win., blue metal M, 5sp **MIP** $2

155 Humvee, yel. pl., lg or sm. antenna, red win., metal T, or5 **MIP** $3

156 Enforcer, met. grn., blk. win., metal T, 5sp **MIP** $2

157 Nash Metropolitan, met. blk., chr. int., red win., frosted chr. T, 5sp **MIP** $2

AUTONOMICALS

158 1969 Pontiac GTO Judge, blk., blue win., chr. T or C, 5sp **MIP** $2

159 Zotic, blk., chr. int., grn win., blk. pl. T or M, gt/b **MIP** $2

160 Sol-Aire CX4, blk., tan or org. tampo, org. int., org. win., org. pl. T, o10sp **MIP** $3

161 Ground FX, blk., yel. win., blk. pl. T, gold skinny **MIP** $2

162 Hammered Coupe, blk., chr. int., red win., candy red T, red chr. pr5 **MIP** $2

ROLL PATROL

163 Whatta Drag, blk./wht., chr. int., blue win., blk. metal T, 5sp **MIP** $2

170 Whip Creamer II, dk. blue met., chr. int., blue win., chr. T, 5sp **MIP** $2

174 Pikes Peak Celica, flat blue, blk. int., blk. win., blk. pl. M, gbbs **MIP** $2

179 Hyundai Spyder Concept, flat tan, blk. int., smoked win., blk. pl. M, g10sp **MIP** $2

184 Mitsubishi Eclipse, silv. met., chr. int., blue win., blk. pl. M, blue chr. pr5 **MIP** $2

189 Super Modified, semi-gloss blk., lt. red int., metal T, red chr. bbs2 **MIP** $2

194 Scorchin' Scooter, aqua, wht. int., metal T, blk. spoke, chr. rim **MIP** $3

199 Deora, no boards, blk./wht./blue, blk. int., blue win., metal T, 3sp **MIP** $2

204 Lamborghini Murcielago, silv. met., blk. int., smoked win., blk. pl. M, pr5 **MIP** $2

209 Surf Crate, candy blue/pale yel., blk. int., blue metal M, 5sp **MIP** $3

WASTELANDERS

164 Rocket Oil Special, flat olive, chr. int., smoked win., flat blk. ptd. metal M, 5sp **IP** $2

169 1970 Plymouth Road Runner, yel. pearl met., blk. int., smoked win., chr. T, 5sp **MIP** $5

175 Tire Fryer, met. grn., chr. int., metal T, pr5 **MIP** $2

180 Screamin' Hauler, flat gray, semi-gloss blk. int., red win., semi-gloss blk. ptd. metal C, pr5 **MIP** $2

185 Big Thunder, met. gray, chr. int., blk. pl. C, red chr. 10sp **MIP** $2

190 Blast Lane, met. cinnamon, blk. seat int., metal T, blk. spoke, chr. rim **MIP** $3

195 Plymouth Barracuda, flat blk., blk. int., dk. blue win., blk. chr. M, 10sp **MIP** $4

200 Sand Stinger, candy tangerine met., black int., metal M, or5 rear, 5sp front **MIP** $3

205 Altered State, wht. pearl met., blk. int., semi-gloss blk. T, 5sp **MIP** $2

210 Slideout, brown primer, blk. int., yel. pl. T, gpr5 **MIP** $2

PRIDE RIDES

165 Mustang 1968, lime met., blue int., clr. win., metal T, 5sp **MIP** $5

173 Corvette Sting Ray, pearl lime met., blk. int., smoked win., metal C, 5sp **MIP** $3

176 Cunningham C4R, champagne met., blk. int., smoked win., blk. pl. M, g3sp **MIP** $2

181 1936 Cord, blk., tan int., clr. win., chr. C, bbs **MIP** $2

186 Shelby Cobra 427 S/C, silv.-blue met., blk. int., clr. win., metal M, 3sp **MIP** $2

191 1935 Cadillac, flat lavender, gray int., smoked win., metal T, 3sp **MIP** $2

196 1997 Corvette, pearl wht. met., wht. int., purp. win., blk. pl. T, 3sp **MIP** $3

201 1957 Cadillac Eldorado Brougham, flat olive, lt. gray int., yel. win., chr. T, 5sp **MIP** $3

206 1940 Ford Coupe, met. silv., blk. int., smoked win., chr. T, 5sp **MIP** $4

211 1963 T-Bird, met. silv., blk. int., smoked win., blue metal M, 3sp**MIP** $3

WORK CREWSERS

166 Sling Shot, wht. pearl met., chr. int., org. win., candy burnt org. met. metal T, chr. co-mold **MIP** $5

171 Chevy, blue met. pl., blk. win., semi-gloss blk. ptd. metal T, 5sp **MIP** $5

TRACK ACES

166 Sling Shot, wht. pearl met., chr. int., org. win., candy burnt org. met. metal T, pr5 **MIP** $5

167 Pontiac Rageous, candy red, gray int., blue win., dk. blue pl. T, red chr. co-mold **MIP** $5

168 Corvette Stingray II, wht. pearl met., gray int., org. win., chr. T, 3sp **MIP** $2

171 Chevy, blue met. pl., blk. win., semi-gloss blk. ptd. metal T, 5sp **MIP** $2

172 Jester, red pl., blue met., met. blue int., blue win., red pl. T, red chr. pr5 **MIP** $3

177 Power Pipes, red pl., blue int., blue win., metal T, pr5 **MIP** $2

178 Road Rocket, blue, org. pl., blue int., org. win., metal T, red chr. pr5 **MIP** $3

182 I Candy, pearl wht. met., org. int., org. win., metal M, lg. rear chr. co-mold **MIP** $2

183 Vulture, candy blue, chr. int., yel. win., smoked T, pr5 **MIP** $2

187 Open Road-Ster, dk. blue met., chr. int., org. win., metal M, red chr. pr5 **MIP** $2

188 Hyundai Tiburon, pearl wht. met., gray int., org. win., blk. pl. M, pr5 **MIP** $2

192 HW Prototype 12, wht. pearl met., org. int., clr. win., metal M, bbs **MIP** $8

193 Backdraft, blue flake pl., chr. int., org. win., metal T, red chr. pr5 **MIP** $2

197 Krazy 8s, candy red, gold chr. int., blue win., candy red T, red chr. pr5 **MIP** $2

198 Sharkruiser, candy blue met., gold chr. int., candy blue met. T, red chr. 5dot **MIP** $3

202 Turbo Flame, wht. pearl pl., wht. pearl int., org. win., candy tangerine met. metal M, knobby pr5 **MIP** $2

203 Speed Blaster, candy red met., blue win., blue pl. M, red chr. co-mold or 3sp **MIP** $2

207 Roll Cage, blue met./candy red, red int., candy red T, g/or5 **MIP** $2

208 Aeroflash, wht. pl., chr. int., org. win., candy tangerine met. metal M, 10sp **MIP** $2

212 Zender Fact 4, dk. blue met., chr. int., org. win., blk. pl. T, red chr. 3sp **MIP** $3

FINAL RUN

133 Hot Seat, lt. or dk. blue chr., blk. int., metal M, 5sp **MIP** $3

134 Ferrari 308, dk. blue met., blk. int., smoked win., metal M, 10sp **MIP** $3

135 Semi Fast, purp. pl., gray int., smoked win., metal M, 5sp **MIP** $2

135 Semi-Fast, purp. pl., gray int., smoked win., metal T, 5sp **MIP** $4

136 Cat-A-Pult, pearl wht. met., maroon int., smoked win., metal M, 5sp, chr. co-mold or 3sp **MIP** $3

137 Sonic Special, candy tangerine met., wht. int., yel. win., blk. pl. C, g10sp **MIP** $3

2005 First Editions

REALISTIX

1 Ford Shelby Cobra Concept, candy gray met., short stripe, lt. blue int., clr. win., blk. pl. M, pr5 **MIP** $2

2 Mitsubishi Eclipse Concept Car, org. pearl, gray int., smoked win., dk. gray pl. M, pr5, 10sp or FTE **MIP** $2

3 Ferrari 575 GTC, red, gray int., clr. win., blk. ptd. metal M, pr5 **MIP** $2

4 Airy 8, met. silv., blue metal M, blk. spoke/red chr. rim **MIP** $2

5 1969 Pontiac Firebird T/A, wht., chr. int., blue win., wht. pl., 5sp or FTE **MIP** $2

6 2005 Ford Mustang GT, candy red met., blk. int., smoked win., chr. M, pr5 **MIP** $5

7 1971 Buick Riviera, met. teal, chr. int., clr. win., blk. pl. M, 10sp **MIP** $2

8 Pocket Bikester, candy blue met., chr. int., clr. win., blue metal M, pr5 **MIP** $2

9 Firestorm, flat blk., chr. int., org. win., candy met. gray metal M, 5sp or FTE **MIP** $2

10 Acura HSC Concept, candy gray, blk. int., smoked win., blk. or gray pl. M, 5sp or FTE **MIP** $3

11 Aston Martin V8 Vantage, yel. pearl met., blk. int., smoked win., chr. M, pr5 or FTE **MIP** $2

12 Symbolic, met. silv./blk., blk. int., red win., blk. pl. M, pr5 or FTE **MIP** $2

13 Formul8r, candy purp. or dk. candy purp. met., metal int., yel. win., blk. pl. M, g/10sp or FTE **MIP** $2

14 Bully Goat, champagne met., blk. int., smoked win., chr. M, pr5 or FTE **MIP** $3

15 Split Decision, transparent red/silv., blk. int., red win., semi-gloss blk. metal M, pr5 or FTE **MIP** $2

16 Ford Shelby GR-1 Concept, chr., gray int., blue win., chr. M, pr5 **MIP** $2

17 Cockney Cab II, blk., chr. win., metal M, 5sp **MIP** $2

17 Maserati MC12, wht. pearl., blue rear panel, blue int., blue win., blk. pl. M, 10sp **MIP** $2

18 '69 GTO, blk., chr. int., yel. win., blk. pl. M, 5sp **MIP** $3

19 Prototipo Alfa Romero B.A.T. 9, silv. met., maroon int., blue win., silv. met. ptd. metal M, skinny **MIP** $2

20 Maserati MC12, wht. pearl, blue int., blue win., blk. pl. M, FTE **MIP** $3

DROP TOPS

21 Low C-GT, candy blue met., chr. int., smoked win., blk. ptd. metal M, 10sp, pr5 or FTE **MIP** $2

22 '57 Nomad, candy red met., chr. int., yel. win., blue metal M, pr5 **MIP** $2

23 Curb Side, yel. pearl met., chr. int., blue win., blue metal M, pr5 **MIP** $2

24 Low Carb, flat blk., gold HW logo, chr. int., red win., blue metal M, 5sp **MIP** $2

25 1963 Corvette Stingray, silv. met., blk. win., chr. M, 5sp **MIP** $2

26 Flattery, candy purp. met., transparent org., metal int., org win., metal M, 5sp rear/skinny front **MIP** $2

27 Mid Drift, met. silv./blk., red int., red win., blue metal M, 10sp or FTE **MIP** $2

28 Drop Top, silv.-blue met., chr. int., tinted win., blue metal M, 5sp **MIP** $2

29 Speed Bump, teal met., blk. win., blue metal M, pr5 or FTE **MIP** $2

30 Dodge Super 8 Hemi, met. sillv., chr. int., blue win., blk. pl. M, pr5 **MIP** $2

BLINGS

31 Chrysler 300C, gray met., red win., chr. M, bling **MIP** $2

32 Ford Bronco Concept, gray met., chr. int., purp. win., gray pl. M, bling **MIP** $2

33 L'Bling, candy tangerine met., pointed stripe, chr. int., tinted win., candy tangerine met. M, pr5 **MIP** $2

34 Mercedes-Benz G500, magenta/silv. met., blk. win., chr. M, bling **MIP** $2

35 Quadra-Sound, red, yel. or mustard stripes, blk. win., chr. M, blings **MIP** $2

36 Rocket Box, flat wht., gray panel #15, org. win., metal M, 5sp or pr5 **MIP** $5

37 Hummer H3, yel., smoked win., blk. pl. M, pr5 or FTE **MIP** $2

38 Block O' Wood, candy red met./tan, blk. win., chr. M, 5sp **MIP** $3

39 Dodge Magnum R/T, pearl mustard met., blk. win., chr. "DDC 2005" M, pr5 **MIP** $3

40 '67 Chevy II, candy blue met., blk. win., chr. M, 5sp **MIP** $3

TORPEDOES

41 Tor-Speedo, candy purp. met., blue metal int., blk. pl. M, blings **MIP** $15

42 1971 Dodge Charger, org., chr. int., tinted win., blue metal M, pr5 **MIP** $2

43 Bullet Nose, mustard pearl, chr. int., tinted win., blue metal M, 5sp **MIP** $2

44 Itso-Skeenie, candy tangerine/blk., blk. win., metal M, pr5 **MIP** $2

45 Blastous, wht./met. gray, wht. int., org win., metal M, 5sp or FTE **MIP** $2

46 Subaru WRX, flat blk., gray int., yel. win., blue metal M, g/pr5 or FTE **MIP** $2

47 Slider, candy lime met., chr. int., clr. win., metal M, 5sp or FTE **MIP** $2

48 Overbored 454, blue met., wht./blue or wht./silv. logo, chr. int., blue win., blue metal M, pr5 **MIP** $2

49 Trim TRK, candy red met., chr. int., tinted win., blk. pl. M, pr5 or FTE **MIP** $2

50 Willys Coupe, met. purp., gray int., clr. win., metal M, 5sp/skinny **MIP** $2

X-RAYCERS

51 Ferrari 360 Modena, transparent red or red/org., chr. int., clr. win., blue metal M, pr5 **MIP** $2

52 Paradigm Shift, transparent org., chr. int., clr. win., met. silv. ptd. metal M, pr5, b/pr5 or FTE **MIP** $2

53 Scion xB, transparent blue, chr. int., tinted win., blue metal M, pr5 **MIP** $3

54 '69 Chevelle, transparent yel., chr. int., tinted win., blue metal M, pr5 **MIP** $2

55 Horseplay, transparent blue, chr. int., clr. win., blue metal M, pr5 **MIP** $2

56 Stocker, transparent yel., chr. int., clr. win., metal M, b5sp **MIP** $2

57 Phantasm, transparent org., w/headlights, chr. int., smoked win., blk. ptd. metal M, 5sp or FTE **MIP** $2

58 Vandetta, transparent blue, chr. int., purp. win., metal M, pr5, FTE or extra lg. rear FTE **MIP** $2

59 Poison Arrow, transparent grn., blue or dk. blue, chr. win., silv. met. ptd. metal M, **MIP** $5

60 Burl-Esque, transparent purp., chr. int., clr. win., metal M, 5sp/small or large skinny **MIP** $2

2005 Series

TRACK ACES

61 Trak-Tune, maroon pl., chr./blue int., blue win., candy blue met. metal T, 5sp **MIP** $2

62 Backdraft, red pl., chr. int., blue win., blue met. ptd. metal T, pr5 **MIP** $2

63 Flashfire, wht. pearl met., blk. int., org. win., gray pl. M, 10sp **MIP** $2

64 Power Pipes, transparent blue, blk. int., org. win., metal T, 5sp **MIP** $2

65 Vulture, wht. pearl met., blk. win., blk. pl. T, pr5 **MIP** $2

66 Open Road-Ster, candy red met., 2-flame wing, red int., blue win., blue metal M, g/pr5 **MIP** $4

67 Chevy Stocker, red pl., blue win., met. blue ptd. metal T or M, g/y5 **MIP** $2

68 Power Pistons, pearl wht. pl., blk. int., red win., blue metal M, y5 **MIP** $2

69 Sling Shot, candy blue, chr. int., yel. win., blue metal M, 5sp **MIP** $2

70 Speed Blaster, wht. pearl, chr. win., wht. pl. M, y5 **MIP** $2

FINAL RUN

71 Thomassima III, blk., chr. int., red win., chr. C, 5sp **MIP** $2

72 Treadator, candy lime, chr. win., blk. pl. M, **MIP** $2

73 Buick Wildcat, candy red, chr. or blk. win., chr. T, 10sp **MIP** $2

74 Hydrojet, wht. pearl met., chr. int., org. win., org. pl. T, **MIP** $2

75 Big Chill, wht. pearl met., chr. int., chr. win., blk. pl. T, blk. skis **MIP** $2

REBEL RIDES

76 Outsider, dk. candy red met., metal int., blue metal M, chr. rim **MIP** $2

77 Blast Lane, yel. pearl met., metal T or blue metal M, blk. rim/blk. spoke **MIP** $3

78 W-OOZIE, wht. pearl met./gray, blue metal M, chr. rim/blk. spoke **MIP** $3

79 Scorchin' Scooter, flat blk., metal T, blk. rim/blk. spoke **MIP** $3

80 Fright Bike, transparent grn., metal T, chr. rim/blk. spoke **MIP** $3

ASPHALT JUNGLE

81 Combat Ambulance, candy purp. met., blk. int., org. win., gray pl. M, 5sp or pr5 **MIP** $2

82 Low Flow, met. blk./met. gray, red win., blk. pl. M, 5sp **MIP** $2

83 Dodge Neon, candy red met., blk. int., smoked win., chr. M, 5sp **MIP** $2

84 Deora, met. grn., chr. int., clr. win., gray pl. C, 5sp **MIP** $2

85 Anglia Panel, yel. pearl met., blk. int., clr. win., blk. pl. M, wide rear 5sp **MIP** $5

HOT WHEELS RACERS

86 Mustang Cobra, dk. blue met., blk. int., clr. win., blk. pl. M, bbs **MIP** $5

87 Shadow Mk II a, dk. blue met./burnt org., gray int., gray pl. M, pr5 **MIP** $2

88 Pikes Peak Celica, dk. blue met./burnt org., blk. int., smoked win., blk. pl. M, bbs **MIP** $2

89 Ford Escort, dk. blue met., rear fender tampo, burnt org. tampo, red int., smoked win., gray pl. M, knobby pr5 **MIP** $2

90 F-Racer, dk. blue met., chr. int., dk. blue met. ptd. metal M, pr5 **MIP** $2

PIN HEDZ

91 1959 Cadillac, pearl magenta met., blk. int., clr. win., chr. T, bbs **MIP** $2

92 '40s Woody, met. gold/blk. pl., cream int., smoked win., metal T, 5sp **MIP** $3

93 1964 Chevy Impala, brn. met., wht. int., tinted win., gold chr. M, g/bbs or FTE **MIP** $2

94 Way 2 Fast, candy red met., chr. engines, chr. int., blue metal M, 5sp **MIP** $4

95 1956 Ford, flat cream, gray int., blue win., blk. pl. T, g/5sp **MIP** $2

REDLINES

96 Surfin' S'cool Bus, candy red met., blk. win., gray pl. M, redline 5sp **MIP** $2

97 Ford Delivery 1932, candy lt. lime-gold met., blk. int., clr. win., metal T, redline 5sp **MIP** $2

98 8 Crate, candy gray met., chr. int., blk. win., blk. pl. M or T, redline 5sp or FTE **MIP** $2

99 Pontiac Bonneville, candy lime met., blk. int., clr. win., chr. C, redline 5sp **MIP** $2

100 Tail Dragger, pearl purp. met., blk. int., smoked win., metal C, redline 5sp **MIP** $2

MUSCLE MANIA

101 1971 Plymouth GTX, yel., blk. int., smoked win., blk. pl. T, 5sp **MIP** $2

102 1963 T-Bird, dk. maroon met., blk. int., clr. win., metal T, 5sp **MIP** $10

103 1964 Buick Riviera, dk. gold met., blk. int., smoked win., blk. pl. T, pr5 **MIP** $15

104 1969 Charger, dk. blue met., gray int., blue win., chr. M, 5sp **MIP** $2

105 1965 Chevy Impala, blk./dk. blue, pink int., clr. win., chr. M, pr5 **MIP** $2

WHITE HEAT

106 16 Angles, pearl wht. met., gold chr. int., yel. win., blue metal M, g/pr5 or FTE **MIP** $2

107 MS-T Suzuka, pearl wht. met., wht. int., blue win., chr. M, blue chr. 10sp **MIP** $2

108 Whip Creamer II, pearl wht. met., chr. int., red win., chr. M, red chr. 5sp or FTE **MIP** $2

109 Phantom Racer, pearl wht. met., chr. int., grn. win., chr. M, grn. chr. pr5 **MIP** $2

110 2002 Autonomy Concept, pearl wht. met., magenta win., metal M, magenta chr. skinny **MIP** $2

CRAZED CLOWN II

111 Hardnose 1949 Merc, dk. or lt. gold candy met., chr. int., yel. win., blk. pl. M, 5sp **MIP** $2

112 Fatbax Shelby Cobra 427 S/C, semi-gloss blk., red int., yel. win., blue metal M, red chr. 5sp **MIP** $2

113 Cool-One, magenta pearl met. or lt. magenta pearl met. w/dir, blk. int., yel. win., transparent dk. blue M, gpr5 **MIP** $2

114 1941 Willys Coupe, olive pearl met., gold chr. int., red win., gray DCC pl. M, red chr. 5sp **MIP** $2

115 Blings Dairy Delivery, wht., blk. win., blue metal M, grn. chr. pr5 **MIP** $2

TWENTY+

117 Power Panel, champagne met., blk. int., smoked win., chr. M, or5 **MIP** $4

118 Boom Box, magenta pearl met., chr. or silv. int., smoked win., blk. pl. M, FTE **MIP** $2

119 Switchback, dk. red met. bottom/blk. top, chr. int., blk. win., blk. pl. M, pr5 **MIP** $2

120 'Tooned Chevy S-10, dk. blue candy met., blk. win., chr. M, blings **MIP** $2

2005 Treasure Hunts

BASIC

121 Purple Passion, w/out chest, semi-gloss blk., org. int., org. win., chr. C, chr. RR **MIP** $10

122 1967 Camaro, red, red motor, blk. int., smoked win., metal T, chr. hub, blackwall RR **MIP** $181

123 1958 Corvette, wht. pearl met., chr. int., blue win., chr. M, chr. hub, redline RR **MIP** $45

124 1957 Chevy, flat blk., blk. int., smoked win., chr. M, blk. hub RR **MIP** $15

125 '56 Flashsider, gloss blk./flat gray, unptd. headlights, blk. int., smoked win., chr. T, red hub/ww RR **MIP** $30

126 '34 3-Window, semi-gloss brn./gray met., blk. int., clr. win., metal C, blk. hub/ww RR **MIP** $15

127 Mustang Mach I, met. blue, blk. int., blue win., chr. M, 5sp/RR **MIP** $15

128 1967 Pontiac GTO, dk. blue met., blk. int., smoked win., chr. M, chr. hub RR **MIP** $20

129 Rodger Dodger, red/blk., blk. int., smoked win., chr. M, chr. hub RR **MIP** $20

130 Morris Cooper, yel., silv. trim, blk. int., clr. win., blue metal M, blk. 5sp co-mold **MIP** $15

131 1970 Plymouth Barracuda, lavender pearl met., wht. int., clr. win., chr. M, chr. hub wide ww RR **MIP** $20

2005 Basic Line

134 Phaeton, flat blk., red top, blk. int., clr. win., blue metal M, g/pr5 **MIP** $2

135 Fish'd & Chip'd, semi-gloss gray, blk. int., tinted win., uncured chr. C, 3sp **MIP** $2

136 Vairy 8, flat lavender, gray int., smoked win., metal M, b5sp or purp. chr. 5sp **MIP** $2

137 Pikes Peak Tacoma, pearl wht. met., wht. vent, blk. int., smoked win., blk. pl. M, pr5 or FTE **MIP** $2

138 Rigor Motor, flat blk. or semi-gloss blk., chr. int., red win., blue metal M, 5sp **MIP** $2

139 Meyers Manx, candy gold met., pink int., tinted win., blue metal M, gray 6sp co-mold, gray 5sp co-mold or FTE **MIP** $2

140 2001 Mini Cooper, blk., blk. int., clr. win., metal T or M, pr5 **MIP** $2

141 Ooz Coupe, candy blue met., blk. win., chr. M, 5sp rear/skinny front **MIP** $2

142 Volkswagen New Beetle Cup, candy gray met., red int., red win., blk. pl. M, red chr. 5sp, red chr. pr5 or FTE **MIP** $2

143 Steel Flame, flat blk., blk. int., red win., blk. pl. M, pr5 or FTE **MIP** $2

144 Rocket Oil Special, wht. pearl met., chr. int., blue win., flat blk. metal M, 5sp **MIP** $2

145 1932 Ford Vicky, candy gray met., blk. int., blue win., metal M, 10sp **MIP** $2

146 Dodge Viper GTS-R, flat or semi-gloss blk., gray int., red win., dk. red met. pl. M, pr5 or FTE **MIP** $2

147 1957 Cadillac Eldorado Brougham, wht., wht. int., red win., chr. l M, red chr. 3sp **MIP** $2

149 Maelstrom, blk., chr. int., red win., red pl. T, 5sp **MIP** $2

150 What-4-2, transparent red, chr. int., yel. win., blue metal M, pr5 or FTE **MIP** $2

151 Evil Twin, copper met., gray int., clr. win., blk. pl. M, bbs or FTE **MIP** $2

152 Arachnorod, flat blk., wht. int., red win., gray pl. M, 5sp **MIP** $2

153 Jester, dk. blue pl., unptd. roof, blk. int., blue win., dk. blue pl. T, pr5 **MIP** $5

154 1947 Chevy Fleetline, met. blk., gray int., clr. win., chr. M, bbs or FTE **MIP** $2

155 1935 Cadillac, candy gold met., blk. fenders, wht. int., clr. win., metal M, bbs **MIP** $2

156 1936 Cord, maroon/silv., dk. gray int., clr. win., chr. M, bbs **MIP** $2

157 Talbot Lago, met. grn., chr. int., clr. win., metal M, bbs **MIP** $2

158 1932 Bugatti Type 50, copper/gold/blk., chr. int., clr. win., metal M, 10sp **MIP** $2

159 Off Track, olive pl. body, dragon tampo, org. pearl int., tinted win., blue metal M, 5sp **MIP** $5

160 Shelby Cobra 427 S/C, flat gray, tan int., clr. win., blue metal M, bbs **MIP** $80

160 Shelby Cobra S/C, candy red met., blk. int., clr. win., blue metal M, bbs **MIP** $2

161 Baja Bug, pearl blue met., gray int., blue metal M, or5 **MIP** $2

162 Ford GT-40, silv.-blue met., gray int., clr. win., blk. pl. M, pr5 **MIP** $2

163 Lotus Sport Elise, candy purp. met., chr./blk. int., clr. win., blk. pl. M, w10sp or FTE **MIP** $2

164 Da' Kar, brown met., chr. int., org. win., metal M, or5 **MIP** $2

165 Power Sander, candy gold met., blue int., blue metal M, or5/5sp **MIP** $2

166 Sand Stinger, candy blue or dk. blue, blk. seat int., blue metal M, or5/5sp **MIP** $2

167 ATV, dk. olive pl., blk. seat int., blk. metal M, or5 **MIP** $2

168 Hummer H3T, flat blk., gray int., red win., frosted chr. M, or5 **MIP** $2

169 La Troca, wht., blk. win., dk. red met. pl. M, 5sp or FTE **MIP** $2

170 1965 Corvette, silv.-blue met., blk. int., smoked win., blk. pl. M, 5sp **MIP** $2

171 '69 El Camino, candy red met., blk. int., yel. win., metal M, 5sp or FTE **MIP** $2

172 Shoe Box, lt. lime, chr. int., clr. win., chr. M, pr5 **MIP** $2

173 Ford Thunderbolt, blk./gold, gray int., yel. win., chr. M, 5sp or y5 **MIP** $2

174 Mitsubishi Eclipse, pearl wht. met., chr. int., clr. win., blk. pl. M, pr5 or FTE **MIP** $2

175 Corvette C6, lt. yel., blk. int., clr. win., blk. pl. M, pr5 or FTE **MIP** $2

176 Dodge Tomahawk, gold chr., blue metal M, gold chr. rim **MIP** $3

177 2001 B Engineering Edonis, candy rose, gray int., smoked win., blk. pl. M, b5sp **MIP** $2

178 Saleen S7, flat blue, glk. int., blk. win., wht. pl. M, o/pr5 **MIP** $2

179 Ford Anglia, flat gray, wht. int., yel. win., frosted chr. M, g10sp or FTE **MIP** $2

180 1933 Ford Lo-Boy, yel., blk. int., org. win., chr. M, 5sp/skinny **MIP** $2

181 '58 Ford Thunderbird, silv., lt. gray int., clr. win., chr. M, bbs **MIP** $3

182 '71 Mustang Funny Car, bronze, gold/blk. or gold/gray tampo, metal int., smoked win., metal M, 5sp **MIP** $3

183 Plymouth Barracuda, dk. candy blue, blk. int., clr. win., blue metal M, 5sp or y5 **MIP** $3

184 VW Bug, dk. candy blue, wht. fenders, blk. int., clr. win., metal T, 5sp **MIP** $7

2006 First Editions

1 '70 Plymouth Superbird, lt. lime, flat blk. roof, blk. int., clr. win., chr. M, 10sp or 5sp **MIP** $2

2 Toyota AE-86 Corolla, wht., blk. int., smoked win., frosted chr. M, FTE **MIP** $2

3 Nissan Silvia S15, candy red met., chr. int., smoked win., blk. pl. M, 10sp or FTE **MIP** $2

4 Chrysler 300C Hemi, silv. met., chr. int., tinted win., blk. pl. M, bling or FTE **MIP** $2

5 Ferrari 512M, candy blue, chr. int., clr. win., chr. M, g5sp or FTE **MIP** $2

6 Bone Shaker, gloss blk., chr. int., metal M, 5sp **MIP** $3

7 '69 Corvette, yel., chr. int., blue win., yel. pl. M, pr5 or FTE **MIP** $2

7 '69 Corvette ZL-1, yel., chr. int., blue win., yel. pl. M, FTE **MIP** $4

8 Porsche Carrera GT, met. silv., maroon int., clr. win., blk. pl. M, s/FTE **MIP** $20

9 Cyclops, candy red, blue pinstripe, chr. motor, chr. int., yel. win., blue metal M, pr5 **MIP** $2

10 Pharodox, transparent blue body w/short fender tampo, metal M, g/FTE or FTE **MIP** $2

11 Nerve Hammer, transparent red body, silv. int., clr. win., blue metal M, FTE or s/FTE **MIP** $2

12 '05 Dodge Viper Coupe, candy blue met., gray int., smoked win., gray pl. DCC M, thin rear s/FTE **MIP** $2

12 2006 Dodge Viper Coupe, candy blue met., gray int., smoked win., silv./blue pl. DCC M, wide or thin rear FTE **MIP** $2

13 Semi-Psycho, candy tangerine met., blk. int., blue metal M, s/FTE **MIP** $3

14 Chrysler Firepower Concept, silv.-blue met., chr. int., blue win., blk. pl. M, 10sp or FTE **MIP** $2

15 Unobtainium I, flat blk., chr. int., smoked win., metal M, blings **MIP** $2

16 AMG-Mercedes CLK DTM, blk., silv. or blk. door handle, chr. int., smoked win., blk. pl. M, 10sp or FTE **MIP** $2

17 Qombee, blue met./wht., gold chr. int., red win., blk. pl. M, pr5 **MIP** $2

18 Preying Menace, candy lime grn. met., gray int., grn. win., metal M, FTE or pr5 **MIP** $3

19 Nissan Z, yel. pearl, blue int., smoked win., chr. M, 5sp co-mold **MIP** $2

20 Hammer Sled, candy purp. met. or candy lt. purp. met., blue metal M, blk. spoke, chr. rim, ribbed tires **MIP** $2

21 '69 Camaro, dk. red met., wht. int., clr. win., blk. pl. M, pr5 **MIP** $4

22 Motoblade, org. transparent pl., blk. pl. driver int., candy gray met. ptd. metal M, o/FTE **MIP** $2

23 Hummer, candy red met., blk. or chr. inner fenderwells, chr. int., smoked win., blk. pl. M, or5 **MIP** $2

24 Bon Voyage, woodgrain, two or four-notch flame, gray int., clr. win., metal M, s/FTE **MIP** $2

25 Corvette C6R, lt. yel. pearl met., blk. int., smoked win., blk. pl. M, FTE **MIP** $4

26 Hot Tub, brown pl. tub, red int., metal M, FTE or 5sp **MIP** $2

27 Quad Rod, dk. red met. pl., dk. red met. int., blue win., blue metal M, s/FTE **MIP** $2

28 Honda Civic Si, candy lime grn. met., chr. int., silv. Civic rear, smoked win., blk. pl. M, s/FTE **MIP** $3

29 '70 Dodge Challenger Hemi, purp. met., blk. int., blue win., chr. M, FTE **MIP** $4

30 Med-Evil, powder blue/org., blk. pl. driver int., semi-gloss blk. metal M, FTE or s/FTE **MIP** $2

31 Nissan Titan, candy gray met., w/ or w/out rear tampo, chr. int., tinted win., blk. pl. M, s/FTE or FTE **MIP** $2

32 Dieselboy, blk., wht. tampo, metal int., red win., chr. M, sm. front s/FTE **MIP** $5

33 Ferrari F430 Spider, red, fender shield, blk. int., clr. win., chr. M, FTE **MIP** $3

34 '07 Cadillac Escalade, blk., chr. int., smoked win., blk. pl. M, FTE or s/FTE **MIP** $2

35 Mega Thrust, candy tangerine met., chr. int., yel. win., blk. pl. M, s/FTE or FTE **MIP** $2

36 Datsun 240Z, wht. pearl met., blk. int., blue win., blk. pl. M, y5 **MIP** $2

37 '55 Chevy Panel, dk. blue met., cream int., smoked win., metal M, pr5 **MIP** $10

38 Volkswagen Karmann Ghia, silv. met., blk. int., blue win., blk. met. metal M, pr5 **MIP** $5

2006 Treasure Hunts

41 Sooo Fast, Spectraflame copper, red win., flat blk. M, RL/RR/5sp **MIP** $10

42 Custom '59 Cadillac, satin blue met., wht. int., clr. win., chr. M, WW/RR **MIP** $15

43 Volkswagen New Beetle Cup, lt. blue/wht. or dk. blue/wht., blk. int., smoked win., blk. pl. M, o/mag **MIP** $10

44 '67 Mustang, wht. pearl met., blk. int., smoked win., blue metal M, 5sp/RR **MIP** $25

45 1969 Dodge Charger, org., tan int., clr. win., chr. T, chr. hubbed RR **MIP** $20

46 Hummer H3T, flat gold, smoked win., frosted chr. M, chr. hubbed c/RR **MIP** $10

47 CUL8R, grn. chr., chr. int., clr. win., flat blk. M, grn. chr. lip 6sp co-mold **MIP** $10

49 Pit Cruiser, met. purp., blk. seat int., metal M, blk. sp./chr. rim **MIP** $15

2006 Series

DRIFT KINGS

51 **Super Tsunami,** dk. candy red, w/or w/ot rear fender names, blk. int., clr. win., blk. pl. M, g/pr5 **MIP** $2

52 **'Tooned Toyota Supra,** yel. pearl, blk. stripe, blk. win., gray pl. M, pr5 **MIP** $2

53 **24/Seven,** candy lt. lime grn. met., blk. int., clr. win., blk. pl. M, pr5 **MIP** $2

54 **Mid Drift,** candy blue met., blk. win., blue metal M, w/y5 **MIP** $2

55 **Slider,** wht. pearl met., chr. int., blue win., metal M, chr. pr5 front, org. pr5 rear **MIP** $2

DROPSTARS

56 **Blings Chrysler 300C,** dk. blue met./champagne met., blk. win., chr. M, blings **MIP** $2

57 **Cadillac Cien Concept,** candy red met., chr. int., smoked win., blk. pl. M, pr5 or FTE **MIP** $2

58 **Blings Mercedes-Benz G500,** pearl org. met., blk. win., blk. pl. M, blings **MIP** $2

59 **1964 Chevy Impala,** candy gray/blk., blk. int., clr. win., chr. M, bbs **MIP** $2

60 **Nissan Skyline,** dk. or lt. blue met., blk. int., smoked win., chr. M, s/FTE **MIP** $2

MOPAR MADNESS

61 **1970 Plymouth Barracuda,** pearl lt. blue met., sm. or lg. "Barracuda", blk. int., clr. win., blk. pl. "DCC" M, 5sp **MIP** $2

62 **Dodge Viper GTS-R,** blk. met., org. int., smoked win., blk. pl. M, pr5 **MIP** $2

63 **Dodge Tomahawk,** wht. pl., blue M, chr. rim **MIP** $3

64 **Dodge M80,** silv./blk., blk. int., blue win., chr. DCC M, y5 or FTE **MIP** $2

65 **1969 Dodge Charger Daytona,** candy blue met. or silv.-blue met., chr. int., smoked win., blk. pl. M, 5sp **MIP** $2

CHROME BURNEZ

66 **Honda Spocket,** chr./gray met., blk. int., purp. win., blk. pl. M, pr5 or FTE **MIP** $2

67 **Humvee,** chr., grn. flames, grn. win., blue metal M, or5 **MIP** $2

68 **Cockney Cab,** chr., blue chr. exhaust and win., blk. ptd. metal M, s/FTE or X-lg. rear s/FTE **MIP** $2

69 **What-4-2,** chr., uncured chr. int., red win., metal M, pr5 **MIP** $2

70 **Phantasm,** chr., gray int., blue win., blue metal M, 5sp **MIP** $2

TAG RIDES

71 **Blings Dairy Delivery,** candy dk. red met., blk. win., blue metal M, 5sp **MIP** $2

72 **'64 Lincoln Continental,** lime, blk. int., clr. win., chr. M, bbs **MIP** $2

73 **Quadra-Sound,** candy purp. met., blk. win., chr. M, blings **MIP** $2

74 **Cadillac Sixteen,** yel. pearl met., wht. int., smoked win., chr. M, pr5 **MIP** $2

75 **Hiway Hauler,** met. silv., red or maroon tampo, smoked win., chr. M, pr5 **MIP** $3

SPY FORCE

76 **Boom Box,** blk., chr. int., lt. or dk. grn. win., blk. pl. M, pr5 **MIP** $2

77 **Jaguar XK8,** grn. met., blk. int., purp. win., gray pl. M, pr5 **MIP** $2

78 **2001 B Engineering Edonis,** dk. blue met., blk. int., blue win., blk. pl. M, w/pr5 **MIP** $2

79 **Combat Ambulance,** silv.-blue met., blk. int., red win., gray pl. M, 5sp or w/5sp **MIP** $2

80 **Lotus Esprit,** candy red met., gray int., org. win., gray pl. M, FTE or g/pr5 **MIP** $2

BONE BLAZERS

81 **'32 Ford,** flat blk., blk. int., yel. win., dk. red or lt. red pl. M, 5sp **MIP** $2

82 **Audacious,** dk. blue met., org. int., red win., blk. pl. M, g/y5 **MIP** $2

83 **'57 Chevy Bel Air,** candy gray met., blk. int., yel. win., chr. M, red chr. 5sp **MIP** $2

84 **Rapid Transit,** candy red met., blk. int., org. win., blk. pl. M, pr5 **MIP** $2

85 **'65 Corvette,** candy purp. met., blk. int., org. win., gold chr. T, g/5sp **MIP** $2

MOTOWN METAL

86 **'70 Chevelle,** candy gray, blk. int., blue win., chr. M, pr5 **MIP** $4

87 **'65 Mustang,** lt. blue pearl met., blk. int., clr. win., blue metal M, 5sp **MIP** $10

88 **'70 Plymouth Road Runner,** lt. grn., blk. int., smoked win., chr. M, 10sp **MIP** $3

89 **'67 Camaro,** blk., silv. int., red win., blue metal M, 5sp or y5 **MIP** $2

90 **'60 Pontiac GTO,** yel., chr. int., clr. win., blk. pl. M, 5sp **MIP** $2

HIGHWAY HORROR

91 **Low Flow,** dk./lt. grn., org. win., blk. pl. M, g/mini 5sp **MIP** $2

92 **'32 Ford Vicky,** met. blk., gray int., red win., lt. blue pearl met. metal M, blue chr. pr5 rear/chr. pr5 front **MIP** $2

93 **'49 Merc,** met. brn., chr. int., org. win., blk. pl. M, g/5sp **MIP** $2

94 **W-Oozie,** dk. blue met., metal T, blk. 3sp and rim rear/blk. 3sp red chr. rim front **MIP** $2

95 **Rigor Motor,** candy purp. met., gold chr. int., org. win., org. metal M, g/5sp **MIP** $2

RED LINE

96 **Custom '60 Chevy,** pearl lime met. or dk. candy gold met., blk. int., clr. win., chr. M, redline 5sp **MIP** $2

97 **Ford GT-40,** ye. pearl. met., blk. int., clr. win., blk. pl. T, redline 5sp **MIP** $2

98 **1968 Nova,** candy purp. met. or candy lime met., blk. int., smoked win., chr. M, redline 5sp **MIP** $2

99 **Baja Bug,** candy tangerine met., blk. int., m/a win., metal M, redline 5sp **MIP** $2

100 **1969 Pontiac Firebird,** candy blue met., chr. int., clr. win., blk. pl. M, redline 5sp **MIP** $2

HI-RAKERS

101 **Montezooma,** lt. or dk. blue pearl met., blk. int., smoked win., chr. M, xl-blings **MIP** $2

102 **1971 Buick Riviera,** candy purp. met., blk. or pearl lavender in tampo, chr. int., yel. win., blk. pl. M, pr5 **MIP** $2

103 **Monte Carlo,** silv. met., blk. int., smoked win., lt. or dk. gold chr. M, xl-g/pr5 **MIP** $2

104 **'63 Chevy Impala,** met. grn., lt. or dk. org. int., smoked win., blk. pl. M, xl-blings **MIP** $2

105 **Olds 442,** met. blk., yel. int., clr. win., chr. M, xl-g/5sp **MIP** $2

WWE

106 **Baja Breaker,** candy gray met., blk. int., smoked win., blk. pl. M, b/or5 **MIP** $2

107 **'65 Impala,** met. grn., blk. int., smoked win., chr. M, bbs **MIP** $2

108 **Ballistik,** semi-gloss blk., closed or open scoop, chr. int., blue win., frosted chr. M, blue chr. y5 **MIP** $2

109 **Power Panel,** candy rose met., yel. int., yel. win., blk. pl. M, g/or5 **MIP** $2

110 **Sir Ominous,** candy blue, chr. int., clr. win., blk. pl. M, red chr. pr5 **MIP** $2

TRACK ACES

111 **X-Raycers Ferrari 360 Modena,** clr. pl., chr. int., org. win., metal M, pr5 **MIP** $2

112 **Low Carbs,** pearl yel. met., chr. int., org. win., blue metal M, 5sp **MIP** $2

113 **Krazy8s,** candy purp. met., chr. int., smoked win., candy purp. met. metal M, pr5 **MIP** $2

114 **X-Raycers Stockar,** clr. pl., chr. int., lt. grn. win., metal M, 5sp **MIP** $2

115 **X-Raycers Horseplay,** trans. yel. body, chr. int., clr. win., blue metal M, pr5 **MIP** $2

116 **Bedlam,** trans. grn., blk. win., metal M, g/FTE or pr5 **MIP** $2

117 **Chevy 1500,** lt. or dk. red pl., blk. int., smoked win., blk. ptd. metal M, 5sp **MIP** $2

118 **'57 Chevy,** wht. pearl pl., blk. win., metal M, 5sp **MIP** $3

119 **Brutalistic,** wht. pearl, metal int., grn. win., metal M, pr5 **MIP** $2

120 **CUL8R,** met. silv., pearl blue/chr. int., blue win., pearl blue metal M, pr5 **MIP** $2

121 **Road Rocket,** red pl., red int., smoked win., metal M, pr5 **MIP** $2

122 **Sling Shot,** lt. blue pearl met., chr. int., red win., blue metal M, s/FTE **MIP** $2

2006 Basic Line

123 **Shredster,** candy grn. met./blk., chr. int., clr. win., gray pl. M, pr5 **MIP** $2

124 'Tooned '69 Camaro Z28, pearl lime grn. met., chr. int., smoked win., gray pl. M, 5sp **MIP** $2

125 1970 Mustang Mach I, blk., chr. int., tinted win., blk. pl. T, 5sp **MIP** $2

126 Fiat 500C, silv.-blue met., chr. int., blue win., metal M, 10sp front, 5sp rear **MIP** $2

127 Tow Jam, org. pearl met. or met. aqua, blk. win., chr. M, y5 **MIP** $2

128 1968 Mustang, candy olive met., chr. int., smoked win., blk. pl. M, 5sp **MIP** $2

129 Lotus Elise 340R, pearl yel. met., chr./gray int., smoked win., blue metal M, bbs **MIP** $2

130 Turboa, pearl lime grn. met., chr. int., metal M, grn. chr. pr5 **MIP** $2

131 Mitsubishi Eclipse, silv.-blue met., blk. int., smoked win., gray pl. M, y5 **MIP** $2

132 Pikes Peak Celica, gloss blk., blk. pl. wing, no rear fender tampo, blk. int., smoked win., chr. M, pr5 **MIP** $5

133 Honda Civic Type R, silv./wht. pearl met., red int., smoked win., blk. pl. M, pr5 **MIP** $2

134 Twin Mill II, dk. blue met., blk. win., blk. pl. M, 5sp **MIP** $2

135 Super Modified, dk. red met., blk. int., blue metal M, bbs/2 **MIP** $2

136 Swoop Coupe, candy purp./candy gray, smoked win., chr. M, 5sp rear/skinny front **MIP** $2

137 Blast Lane, yel. pearl, blk. seat int., blue metal T, blk. spoke, chr. rim **MIP** $2

138 Shadow Jet, dk. candy purp. met., chr. int., org. win., blue metal M, 5sp **MIP** $2

139 Ford GT90 Concept, blk. met., gray int., org. win., meta. M, 3sp **MIP** $2

140 L'Bling, candy dk. red, chr. int., smoked win., blk. ptd. metal M, pr5 **MIP** $2

141 Dodge Ram 1500, candy magenta met., blk. win., wht. pl. "DCC" M, pr5 **MIP** $2

142 '40 Ford Truck, flat blk., red int., blue win., chr. M, blue chr. 5sp **MIP** $2

143 Track-Tune, trans. grn., uncured chr. int., tinted win., semi-gloss blk. metal M, y5 or FTE **MIP** $2

144 Bugatti Veyron, candy gray, cream int., clr. win., blk. pl. M, 10sp or FTE **MIP** $2

145 Hammered Coupe, candy magenta met., gold chr. int., yel. win., semi-gloss blk. metal M, g5sp **MIP** $2

146 Roll Cage, day-glo yel., org. int., semi-gloss blk. metal M, or5 **MIP** $2

147 Sharkruiser, blk., chr. int., wht. ptd. metal M, blue chr. y5 **MIP** $2

148 Moto-Crossed, blk., org. flames, blk. int., clr. win., metal M, pr5 **MIP** $4

149 'Tooned Ferrari 360 Modena, candy red met., yel. or lime in flame, blk. win., blk. pl. M, pr5 **MIP** $2

150 Deuce Roadster, candy lt. blue met., wht. int., clr. win., metal M, 5sp **MIP** $2

151 Radio Flyer Wagon, candy blue met., blk. int., blue metal M, 5sp **MIP** $2

152 Way 2 Fast, yel. pearl met., chr. int., semi-gloss blk. metal M, 5sp **MIP** $2

153 Vampyra, chr., gold chr. int., blk. ptd. metal M, g/bbs **MIP** $2

154 Corvette C6, wht. pearl met. or candy blue met., blk. int., smoked win., blk. pl. M, pr5 **MIP** $2

155 'Tooned '69 Pontiac GTO, blk./org., red win., chr. M, 5sp **MIP** $2

156 Vairy 8, semi-gloss olive or semi-gloss blk., blk. int., smoked win., metal M, 5sp **MIP** $2

157 1964 Buick Riviera, candy lime met. or red, blk. int., clr. win., chr. M, bbs **MIP** $2

158 Fore Wheeler, semi-gloss blk., org. int., blue metal M, 5sp **MIP** $2

159 1947 Chevy Fleetline, semi-gloss or flat blk., blk. int., red win., chr. M, bbs **MIP** $2

160 Itso-Skeenie, pearl lavender, chr. int., smoked win., metal M, pr5 **MIP** $2

161 Rocket Box, semi-gloss blk., red win., metal M, pr5 **MIP** $2

162 Torpedo Jones, mustard yel., blk. pl. driver int., semi-gloss blk. metal M, g5sp **MIP** $2

163 Toyota Celica, blk., bright or dull org. wing, chr. int., org. win., chr. M, y5 **MIP** $2

164 Airy 8, semi-gloss blk., blue metal M, blk. spoke, red chr. rim **MIP** $2

165 Morris Cooper, dk. candy red, yel. int., blue win., blue metal M, pr5 **MIP** $2

166 Pikes peak Tacoma, pearl wht. met., wht. insert, blk. int., red win., blk. pl. M, red chr. 10sp **MIP** $2

167 Mega-Duty, satin copper, wht. pl., wht. int., yel. win., blk. ptd. metal M, g5dot **MIP** $2

168 Tor-Speedo, candy blue, blue metal int., gray pl. M, FTE or pr5 **MIP** $2

169 Talbot Lago, candy gray met., blk. int., smoked win., blue metal M, bbs **MIP** $2

170 1941 Willys Coupe, flat blk., short tampo, metal int., blue win., dk. gold chr. DCC M, g5sp **MIP** $2

171 '69 El Camino, met. grn., blk. int., yel. win., metal M, 5sp **MIP** $2

171 Monoposto, met. silv., chr. int., blue win., blk. pl. M, pr5 **MIP** $2

172 '69 El Camino, flat gray, yel./purp. stripe hood, lt. or dk. gold, blk. int., smoked win., met. blk. metal M, g/5sp **MIP** $2

173 Hummer H3T Concept, yel. or candy gray, blk. int., smoked win., chr. M, or5 **MIP** $2

174 Sweet 16 II, wht. pearl met., blue win., candy blue met. metal M, 5sp **MIP** $2

175 Pocket Bikester, candy red met., chr. int., smoked win., blue metal M, FTE or pr5 **MIP** $2

176 1968 Dodge Dart, met. blk., gray int., org. win., chr. M, 5sp **MIP** $15

177 1932 Bugatti Type 50, met. grn., blk. fenders, chr. int., yel. win., metal M, g/5dot **MIP** $2

178 Arachnorod, candy gray met., blk. int., grn. win., blk. pl. M, pr5 **MIP** $2

179 Jester, blk./org. or blk./org./blue, org. int., smoked win., chr. M, blue chr. pr5 **MIP** $2

180 Saleen S7, dk. candy blue met., blk. int., clr. win., blk. pl. M, pr5 **MIP** $2

181 1963 Thunderbird, wht. pearl met., wht. int., clr. win., blue metal M, bbs **MIP** $2

182 1968 Mercury Cougar, grn. met. or org., blk. int., smoked win., chr. M, 5sp **MIP** $2

183 Scorchin' Scooter, met. grn. or met. purp., blk. seat int., blue no origin, blk. 3sp chr. rim **MIP** $2

184 2005 Ford Mustang GT, yel., chr. int., tinted win., chr. M, pr5 **MIP** $2

185 Flight 03, met. gold, blk. int., smoked win., metal M, 10sp **MIP** $2

186 Altered State, blk., blk. int., blue metal M, 5sp **MIP** $2

187 Wild Thing, candy red met., chr. int., slr. win., blk. pl. M, blk. **MIP** $2

188 Sinistra, blk., gold chr. int., clr. win., metal M, g/pr5 **MIP** $2

189 Oscar Mayer Wienermobile, red/yel., smoked win., red pl. M, g5sp **MIP** $2

190 '34 Ford 3-Window, semi-gloss blk., blk. int., grn. win., metal T, 5sp **MIP** $2

191 Old Number 5.5, yel. pearl met. or red, blk. int., blk. pl. M, 5sp **MIP** $2

192 Lotus Project M250, lime grn., blk. int., smoked win., blk. pl. M, 5sp **MIP** $2

193 Invader, tan camouflage, tan pl. M, b/5sp **MIP** $4

194 Enzo Ferrari, blk., blk. int., clr. win., blk. pl. M, g/FTE **MIP** $2

195 Ferrari 333 SP, blk., silv.-blue int., blk. pl. M, 5sp **MIP** $2

196 Shock Factor, satin copper, blue chr. int., blue metal M, or5 **MIP** $2

197 VW Bug, blk., blk. int., red win., metal M, g/y5 **MIP** $4

198 Hot Bird, blk., gray int., red win., metal T, 7sp **MIP** $2

199 Acura HSC Concept, candy tangerine met., gray int., smoked win., blk. pl. M, 5sp **MIP** $2

200 Ford F-150, candy tangerine met., chr. int., smoked win., blk. pl. M, or5 **MIP** $2

201 Ferrari 575 GTC, candy gray met., gray int., clr. win., gloss blk. M, pr5 **MIP** $2

202 I Candy, met. grn./trans. yel., metal int., yel. win., blue metal M, pr5 **MIP** $2

203 Ground FX, met. grn., chr. int., grn. win., blk. pl. M, skinny **MIP** $2

204 Hyper Mite, blue/silv. met., chr. int., lt. or dk. grn. win., blk. pl. M, 5sp **MIP** $2

205 Vulture Roadster, blk., chr. int., blue win., trans. org. M, s/FTE **MIP** $2

206 Ford Shelby GR-1 Concept, semi-gloss blk. or dk. candy red met., blk. int., smoked win., chr. M, pr5 **MIP** $2

207 Batmobile, flat blk., gold chr. int., clr. win., gold chr. M, g/pr5 **MIP** $2

208 GMC Motorhome, blk., org. int., tinted win., chr. M, pr5 **MIP** $10

209 MS-T Suzuka, orgl., blk. int., smoked win., chr. M, blue chr. 10sp **MIP** $2

210 8 Crate, dk. candy blue, chr. int., red win., blk. pl. M, 5sp **MIP** $2

211 Nomadder What, lt. yel. pearl met., chr. int., clr. win., blk. pl. T, pr5 **MIP** $2

212 Shelby Cobra 427 S/C, candy gray, blue int., clr. win., blue metal T, 5sp **MIP** $2

213 Greased Lightnin', semi-gloss blk., chr. int., yel. win., red M, g/pr5 **MIP** $2

214 Poison Arrow, dk. candy red/smoked pl., chr. win., dk. candy red M, mini-5sp **MIP** $3

215 Double Vision, wht. pearl met., org. win., blk. pl. M, pr5 **MIP** $2

216 Overbored 454, semi-gloss blk., dull grn. tampo, chr. int., grn. win., blk. pl. M, pr5 **MIP** $2

217 Slideout, dk. blue met., blk. int., blk. pl. M, pr5 **MIP** $2

218 'Tooned Mercy Breaker, candy blue, chr. int., clr. win., blk. pl. M, pr5 **MIP** $2

2007 New Models

1 Dodge Challenger Concept, org. pearl met., blk. int., smoked win., blk. pl. M, "DCC" or "TM" "DCC", pr5 **MIP** $2

2 Chevy Camaro Concept, met. silv., flat blk. grille, silv. emblem, gray int., blue win., chr. M, s/FTE **MIP** $5

3 Nitro Doorslammer, maroon met., chr. int., clr. win., blk. pl. M, g/FTE **MIP** $2

4 '69 Ford Mustang, pearl mustard or wht. pearl met., blk. int., smoked win., chr. M, s/FTE **MIP** $2

5 Dodge Ram 1500, blk., chr. int., red win., blk. pl. M, or5 **MIP** $2

6 Shelby Cobra Daytona Coupe, candy dk. blue met., teal met. or red, blk. int., clr win., chr. M, s/FTE **MIP** $2

7 Dodge Charger SRT8, lt. yel. pearl met., candy tangerine met., candy g, blk. int., smoked win., blk. pl. M, y5 **MIP** $2

8 Rogue Hog, blk./wht, blue metal int., smoked win., semi-gloss blk. metal M, b/FTE **MIP** $2

9 '67 Chevy Nova, candy blue met., wht. int., blue win., chr. M, pr5 **MIP** $2

10 Buick Grand National, candy blue met., blk. int., smoked win., blk. pl. M, s/FTE **MIP** $2

11 Wastelander, blk., blue metal M, blk. spoke **MIP** $15

12 Straight Pipes, pearl yel., blk. chr. in headlights, blk. int., smoked win., blue metal M, 5sp **MIP** $4

13 Sky Knife, candy olive met. or candy blue met., smoked win., met. gray metal M, mini-5sp **MIP** $3

14 Ferrari 599 GTB, red, sm. emblem, cream int., clr. win., blk. pl. M, pr5 **MIP** $4

15 1966 TV Series Batmobile, blk., smooth grille and lights, gray int., blue win., blk. pl. M, 5sp **MIP** $10

16 '70 Pontiac Firebird, wht. pearl met. or lt. gold met., chr. int., smoked win., blk. pl. M, pr5 **MIP** $2

17 Ford GTX-1, pearl mustard or blue, chr. int., clr. win., blk. pl. M, s/FTE **MIP** $2

18 1964 Ford Galaxie 500XL, dk. blue met., wht. int., blue win., blk. chr. M, 5sp **MIP** $2

19 CCM Country Club Muscle, met. gold pl., chr. int., smoked win., blue metal M, pr5 **MIP** $2

20 Chevy Silverado, candy tangerine met., chr. int., tinted win., flat blk. metal M, s/FTE **MIP** $3

21 Ferracin, red, chr. int., blue win., metal "Ferracin" M, s/FTE **MIP** $2

21 Nitro Scorcher, red or candy blue met., chr. int., blue win., metal "Nitro Scorcher" M, s/FTE **MIP** $2

22 '64 Lincoln Continental, dk. blue met., pearl blue int., smoked win., chr. M, w/FTE **MIP** $2

23 Ferrari 250 LM, red, gray int., clr. win., chr. M, bbs **MIP** $2

24 Supdogg, candy brn. met., chr. int., amber win., blk. metal M, gold rim, blk. FTE **MIP** $2

25 Solar Reflex, gold chr., metal int., smoked win., metal M, y5 **MIP** $2

26 Buzz Bomb, blk., chr. int., yel. win., blk. metal M, s/FTE **MIP** $2

27 Volkswagen Golf GTI, candy blue met., blk. int., blk. win., chr. M, y5 **MIP** $2

28 Drift King, dk. candy gold met., chr. int., smoked win., blk. pl. M, red chr. rim, blk. spoke FTE **MIP** $2

29 Jet Threat 4.0, met. silv., chr. win., yel. M, g/FTE **MIP** $2

30 Cloak and Dagger, smoked pl. body, blue metal int., blk. pl. M, s/FTE **MIP** $2

31 Ultra Rage, red pl. body, chr. int., smoked win., blue metal M, s/FTE **MIP** $2

32 Porsche Cayman S, met. silv., tan int., tinted win., blk. pl. M, s/FTE **MIP** $2

33 Fast Fortress, semi-gloss olive, clr. win., chr. M, 5sp **MIP** $2

34 Custom '53 Chevy, candy red met./wht., chr. int., clr. win., chr. M, 5sp **MIP** $2

35 Shell Shock, candy tangerine w/gold rivet or pearl org. met. w/, blk. win., candy gray met. metal M, red chr. rim, blk. spoke FTE **MIP** $2

2007 Series

POP OFFS

37 Morris Mini, wht. pearl met., blk. int., smoked win., blue metal M, 10sp **MIP** $2

38 Hyperliner, flat blk., blk. int., red win., gray pearl pl. M, gray FTE **MIP** $2

39 Volkswagen New Beetle Cup, candy teal met., blk. int., clr. win., blk. pl. M, y/10sp **MIP** $2

40 Ground FX, pearl lavendar met., chr. int., purp. win., blk. pl. M, skinny **MIP** $2

CAMARO

41 '69 Camaro, candy red met., blk. int., clr. win., chr. T, 5sp **MIP** $2

42 '67 Camaro, dk. blue met., blk. int., blue win., metal M, 5sp **MIP** $2

43 Camaro Z28, dk. silv.-blue met., blk. win., blue metal M, 5sp **MIP** $2

44 Camaro Z28, pearl yel. met., blk. win., blk. pl. M, pr5 **MIP** $2

HOT WHEELS DESIGN

45 Pony-Up, candy tangerine met., chr. int., clr. win., blue tint metal M, pr5 **MIP** $2

46 Hyper Mite, semi-gloss olive, chr. int., smoked win., blk. pl. M, 5sp **MIP** $2

47 Asphalt Assault, candy lime met., chr. int., blue win., blk. pl. M, 10sp **MIP** $2

48 CUL8R, pearl yel. met., blk./lt.or dk. gold chr. int., smoked win., blk. ptd. metal M, g/FTE **MIP** $2

TAXI RODS

49 Cockney Cab II, pearl gold met. pl., chr. win., blk. ptd. metal M, 5sp **MIP** $2

50 1955 Chevy Bel Air, yel., blk. int., red win., chr. T, 5sp **MIP** $2

51 '70 Plymouth Road Runner, blk./yel., blk. int., clr. win., chr. M, 5sp **MIP** $2

52 1964 Chevy Impala, yel. pearl met., blk. int., clr. win., gold chr. M, g/bbs **MIP** $2

GOLD RIDES

53 Chrysler 300C, gold chr., chr. int., smoked win., metal "DCC" M, g/bling **MIP** $2

54 '07 Cadillac Escalade, gold chr., chr. int., clr. win., metal M, g/pr5 **MIP** $2

55 Humvee, gold chr., clr. win., blue metal M, g/or5 **MIP** $2

ENGINE REVEALERS

57 Ferrari 512M, candy tangerine met., chr. int., clr. win., chr. M, pr5 **MIP** $2

58 1969 Dodge Charger, wht. pearl met., blk. int., blue win., chr. "DCC" T, 5sp **MIP** $2

59 '58 Corvette, met. gray, lt. or dk. blue flame, chr. int., clr. win., chr. T, 5sp **MIP** $2

60 Tire Fryer, blk., chr. int., blue metal M, 5sp rear, skinny front **MIP** $2

HUMMER

61 Hummer H2, champagne met., chr. int., smoked win., blk. pl. T, or5 **MIP** $2

62 Hummer, dk. blue met., blk. int., clr. win., chr.M, or5 **MIP** $2

63 Hummer H3, red, mustard yel. stripes, smoked win., blk. pl. T, g/FTE **MIP** $2

64 Hummer H2, gray met., blk. win., blk. pl. M, bling **MIP** $2

STREET BEAST II

65 Preying Menace, blk./red, silv. int., red win., metal M, pr5 **MIP** $2

66 Sharkruiser, gray, lg. or sm. "SHARK" on engine, dk. gold chr. int., metal M, 3sp **MIP** $2

67 Arachnorod, silv.-blue met. satin, wht. int., blue win., blk. pl. T, s/FTE **MIP** $2

X-RAYCERS

69 Nerve Hammer, clr. pl. body, wht. or glow-in-the-dark wht. int., tinted win., metal M, 3sp **MIP** $2

70 Stockar, clr. pl. body, wht. int., clr. win., blue metal M, blue chr. pr5 **MIP** $2

71 Phastasm, clr. pl. body, glow-in-the-dark wht. int., lt. or dk. grn. win., metal M, grn. chr. pr5 **MIP** $2

72 Vandetta, clr. pl. body, glow-in-the-dark wht. int., red win., metal M, red chr. pr5 **MIP** $2

AERIAL ATTACK

73 Mad Propz, lt. yel. pearl met., blue win., semi-gloss blk. metal M, mini-5sp **MIP** $2

74 Killer Copter, olive pl. body, chr. win., semi-gloss blk. metal M, **MIP** $2

75 Poison Arrow, transparent red pl., gold chr. win., semi-gloss blk. metal M, gold mini-5sp **MIP** $3

76 Blimp, gray pl. body, purp. pl. tail, purp. over org. tam, blue metal M, **MIP** $2

HOT WHEELS RACING

77 1941 Willys Coupe, candy dk. blue met., chr. int., clr. win., blk. pl. "DCC" M, 5sp **MIP** $2

78 24/Seven, candy blue met., gray int., smoked win., blk. pl. M, s/FTE **MIP** $2

79 Formul8r, dk. candy blue met., metal int., clr. win., blk. pl. M, w/10sp **MIP** $2

80 Datsun 240Z, dk. candy blue met., blk. int., smoked win., blk. pl. M, y5 **MIP** $2

RAGTOPS & ROADSTERS

81 Tantrum, candy red met., frosted chr./blk. int., smoked win., blk. pl. M, 3sp **MIP** $2

82 '33 Ford, blk. met., org. int., clr. win., chr. M, 5sp or 3sp rear/skinny front **MIP** $2

83 '70 Chevelle, candy lt. or dk. tangerine met., wht. int., tinted win., chr. M, redline 5sp **MIP** $2

84 Mitsubishi Eclipse, blk. met., wht. flames, gray int., blue win., blk. pl. M, y5 **MIP** $4

CODE CARS

85 Dodge Charger Daytona, pearl lime or candy blue met., blk. win., blk. pl. M, 5sp **MIP** $2

86 Cadillac Cien Concept, candy lt. blue met., chr. int., smoked win., blk. pl. M, pr5 **MIP** $2

87 Muscle Tone, candy gold met., gray int., blue win., chr. M, s/FTE **MIP** $2

88 Audacious, candy rose met., chr. int., blk. win., blk. pl. M, g/y5 **MIP** $2

89 Overbored 454, blk., chr. int., grn. win., blk. pl. M, pr5 **MIP** $2

90 Rocket Box, candy purp. met., org. win., blue metal M, pr5 **MIP** $2

91 Monoposto, frost grn. poly met., blk. int., smoked win., chr. M, 5dot **MIP** $2

92 Aston Martin V8 Vantage, candy rose met., blk. int., smoked win., chr. M, pr5 **MIP** $2

93 I Candy, trans. org./met. blue, trans. org. int., trans.org win., blue tint metal M, blue chr. pr5 **MIP** $2

94 Lotus Esprit, met. silv., gray int., magenta win., blk. pl. M, y5 **MIP** $2

95 Toyota RSC, candy tangerine met. or silv.-blue met., blk. int., smoked win., chr. M, or5 **MIP** $2

96 Xtreemster, candy lt. gold met. or candy gold met., chr. int., blk. win., blk. pl. M, pr5 **MIP** $2

97 Shelby Cobra 427 S/C, candy magenta met., gray int., clr. win., metal M, bbs or 10sp **MIP** $2

98 Dodge Power Wagon, candy rose met., blk. int., smoked win., blk. pl. M, or5 **MIP** $2

99 Whip Creamer II, dk. purp. met., chr. int., smoked win., frosted chr. M base, gray FTE **MIP** $2

100 Honda Civic Si, candy blue met., chr. int., smoked win., blk. pl. M, y5 **MIP** $2

101 AMG-Mercedes CLK DTM, met. silv., chr. int., smoked win., blk. pl. M, pr5 **MIP** $2

102 Suzuki GSX-R/4, met. copper, frosted chr. int., clr. win., blk. pl. M, 5dot **MIP** $2

103 Dieselboy, met. copper, metal engine or blue metal engine, chr. int., purp. win., chr. M, s/FTE **MIP** $2

104 1968 Mercury Cougar, candy lime met., gray int., smoked win., chr. M, 5sp **MIP** $2

105 Motoblade, clr. pl. body, blk. pl. driver int., candy lime met. M, s/FTE **MIP** $2

106 Custom Cougar, candy tangerine met., blk. int., clr. win., chr. M, o/pr5 **MIP** $2

107 So Fine, candy gold met., blk. int., clr. win., chr. M, 5sp **MIP** $2

108 Mitsubishi Eclipse Concept Car, candy blue met., blk. int., smoked win., blk. pl. M, g/10sp **MIP** $2

TRACK STARS

109 Pharodox, trans. red, trans. red int., yel. win., metal M, g/FTE **MIP** $2

110 Subaru Impreza, wht. pl., w/out crossbar, silv. int., smoked win., blk. metal M, 10sp **MIP** $2

111 Split Decision, semi-gloss blk., blue metal int., blue win., blue metal cut-out M, blue chr. FTE **MIP** $2

112 Backdraft, pearl pink pl., chr. int., org. win., blk. ptd. metal M, pr5 **MIP** $2

113 Flathead Fury, blue pl. body, chr. int., yel. win., met. silv. metal M, g/FTE **MIP** $2

114 Rivited, candy tangerine, chr. int., smoked win., metal M, pr5 **MIP** $2

115 Iridium, maroon pearl met. pl., gray int., red win., metal M, s/FTE **MIP** $2

116 Bassline, blue pl. or blk. pl. body, chr. int., red win., metal M, s/FTE **MIP** $2

117 Anthracite, lt. org. or org. pl. body, silv.-blue pearl pl. int., blue win., metal M, g/10sp **MIP** $2

119 Piledriver, lt. tan pl. body, chr. int., blue metal M, s/FTE **MIP** $2

120 Hollowback, candy gray met. pl. body, chr. int., smoked win., metal M, 20sp **MIP** $2

2007 ALL STARS

133 Slideout, wht., blk. int., red pl. M, pr5 **MIP** $2

134 Ford GT-40, candy red met. or dk. silv.-blue met., blk. int., clr. win., blk. pl. T, 5sp **MIP** $2

135 Go Kart, candy blue met. or candy lt. lime met., blk. int., candy blue met. metal M, 5dot **MIP** $2

136 Deuce Roadster, semi-gloss brn., semi-gloss blk. or semi-gloss oli, blk. int., clr. win., blue metal M, g/5sp **MIP** $2

137 1967 Pontiac GTO, teal met., wht. int., clr. win., chr. T, 5sp **MIP** $2

138 Blast Lane, dk. purp. met., blue metal M, blk. 3sp, chr. rim **MIP** $2

139 Ferrari 333 SP, red, blk./red int., blk. pl. M, w/5sp **MIP** $2

140 1964 Buick Riviera, candy gold met., candy gray met. or candy lt. or d, blk. int., smoked win., chr. M, 10sp **MIP** $2

141 Shift Kicker, candy red, dk. or lt. red roof, blk. int., chr. M, 5sp **MIP** $2

142 Invader, candy gray met. or olive, chr. int., blk. pl. M, b/5sp **MIP** $4

143 Ford Thunderbolt, wht. pearl met., blk. int., yel. win., frosted chr. M, w/5sp **MIP** $2

144 Pontiac Firebird, silv.-blue met., caramel int., smoked win., blk. pl. M, s/FTE **MIP** $2

145 Mo' Scoot, gray pl., blue metal M, blk. dot rear wheel **MIP** $2

146 Porsche 911 GT3 Cup, candy red met., blk. int., smoked win., blk. pl. M, pr5 **MIP** $2

147 Whatta Drag, yel., chr. int., red win., candy gray met. metal M, 5sp **MIP** $2

148 Ferrari F50, red, blk. int., clr. win., blk. pl. M, pr5 **MIP** $2

149 Shredded, pearl yel. met., met. silv. int., org. win., blk. pl. M, o/pr5 **MIP** $2

150 '63 Corvette, pearl wht. met., cream int., blue win., chr. M, 10sp **MIP** $2

151 Custom '59 Cadillac, candy blue met., blk. int., clr. win., chr. M, bbs **MIP** $2

152 Nissan Z, lt. gold met., blk. int., clr. win., chr. M, g/FTE or g/pr5 **MIP** $2

153 Purple Passion, yel. pearl met., wht. int., org. win., chr. T, pr5 or 7sp **MIP** $2

154 Dodge Charger, lt. gold met., blk. win., gray pl. DCC T, 5sp **MIP** $2

155 Dodge Tomahawk, blk. pl., blue metal T, blk. rim, blk. wheel **MIP** $2

156 Dodge Sidewinder, lt. blue pearl met., wht. int., clr. win., dk. gray pl. DCC T, 5sp **MIP** $2

2007 Treasure Hunts

121 '69 Pontiac GTO, dk. blue met., blk chr. int., smoked win., blk. pl. T, 5sp **MIP** $10

122 Nissan Skyline, bronze met., blk. int., smoked win., gray pl. M, pr5 **MIP** $10

123 'Tooned '69 Camaro Z28, lime grn., chr. int., smoked win., gray pl. M, 5sp **MIP** $10

124 Corvette C6R, blk., blk./yel. int., clr. win., silv.-blue pl. M, g/10sp **MIP** $10

125 Mega Thrust, pearl org. met., chr. int., smoked win., blk. pl. M, s/FTE **MIP** $10

126 Hammer Sled, yel. pearl met., blk. seat int., blue metal M, blk. spoke/chr. rim **MIP** $15

129 Enzo Ferrari, red, blk./red or all blk. int., clr. win., blk. pl. M, pr5 **MIP** $10

132 Evil Twin, candy red met., gray int., clr. win., chr. M, s/FTE **MIP** $10

2007 Super Treasure Hunts

121 '69 Pontiac GTO, candy dk. blue met., blk chr. int., smoked win., blk. pl. T, 5sp RR **MIP** $40

122 Nissan Skyline, candy bronze, blk. int., smoked win., gray pl. M, 6sp RR **MIP** $25

123 'Tooned '69 Camaro Z28, candy lime met., chr. int., smoked win., gray pl. M, 5sp RR **MIP** $15

124 Corvette C6R, blk., blk./yel. int., clr. win., silv.-blue pl. M, g/6sp RR **MIP** $20

125 Mega Thrust, candy bronze, chr. int., smoked win., blk. pl. M, 5sp RR **MIP** $20

126 Hammer Sled, yel. met., blk. seat int., blue metal M, blk. spoke/gold chr. rim **MIP** $25

2008 New Models

1 '07 Shelby GT-500, lt. candy red, flat blk. grille, blk. int., tinted win., blk. pl. M, y5 **MIP** $4

2 Spector, frosted chr./blue metal, semi-gloss metal M, red chr. rim/blk. FTE **MIP** $2

4 Ratbomb, purp. satin, ribbed grille, chr. int., smoked win., metal M, s/FTE rear, skinny front **MIP** $2

5 '69 Dodge Coronet Super Bee, lt. or dk. mustard pearl met., blk. int., smoked win., chr. DCC M, 5sp **MIP** $2

6 Dragtor, met. grn., metal int., metal M, s/FTE rear, skinny front **MIP** $2

7 Custom '77 Dodge Van, pearl yel. met., gray int., org. win., blk. chr. DCC M, red chr. rim/blk. FTE **MIP** $2

2008 Series

2008 ALL STARS

41 CUL8R, semi-gloss blk., candy gold met. int., clear win., candy gold met. metal M, g/FTE **MIP** $2

42 La Troca, semi-gloss brn. primer, blk. win., chr. M, 5sp **MIP** $2

43 Sand Stinger, semi-gloss olive, blk. pl. seat int., blue metal M, or5 rear/5sp front **MIP** $2

46 Night Burner, aqua met., chr. int., grn. win., blk. pl. M, y/FTE **MIP** $2

51 Swoop Coupe, maroon met./blk., smoked win., gray pl. T, 5dot rear, skinny front **MIP** $2

WEB TRADING CARS

81 Nissan Skyline, blk., blk. int., smoked win., blk. pl. M, pr5 **MIP** $2

86 Pony Up, lt. candy blue met., chr. int., clr. win., blue metal M, chr. rim, blk. FTE **MIP** $2

88 Pikes Peak Celica, lt. Lime, blk. int., clr. win., blk. pl. T, bbs **MIP** $2

TRACK STARS

106 CCM Country Club Muscle, red pl., chr. int., blue win., metal M, pr5 **MIP** $2

TEAM: CUSTOM BIKES

150 Airy 8, candy purp. met. or dk. candy purp. met., burnt or, metal M, chr. rim/blk. 5sp **MIP** $2

151 Scorchin' Scooter, candy lt. blue met., no origin, blk. seat int., blue metal, wht. rim, blk. 3sp **MIP** $2

TEAM: ENGINE REVEALERS

153 Buick Grand National, lt. or dk. candy gold met., chr. int., blk. win., blk. pl. M, s/FTE **MIP** $2

155 '57 Chevy, wht. pearl met., maroon int., red win., chr. M, red chr. 5sp **MIP** $2

TEAM: DRAG RACING

158 Jaded, semi-gloss olive, frosted chr. int., yel. win., blue-gray pl. M, 5sp **MIP** $2

159 Dragster, met. silv./grn. pearl, blk. int., metal M, 5sp **MIP** $2

160 Fiat 500, candy rose met., blue metal int., chr. win., blue metal M, g/5sp **MIP** $2

HOT WHEELS REDLINES

'31 Doozie, 1977, orange, tan top, brown fenders, Model No. 9649
EX $25 **NM** $40 **MIP** $55

'56 Hi Tail Hauler, 1977, orange, redline, 2 black plastic motorcycles, Model No. 9647
EX $30 **NM** $50 **MIP** $70

'57 Chevy, 1977, red, yellow & white tampo, "57 Chevy", Model No. 9638
EX $40 **NM** $60 **MIP** $85

Alive '55, 1973, assorted, Model No. 6968
EX $135 **NM** $275 **MIP** $550

Alive '55, 1974, blue, Model No. 6968
EX $65 **NM** $150 **MIP** $350

Alive '55, 1974, green, Model No. 6968
EX $20 **NM** $50 **MIP** $110

Alive '55, 1977, chrome, redlines, green & yellow tampo, Model No. 9210
EX $20 **NM** $35 **MIP** $50

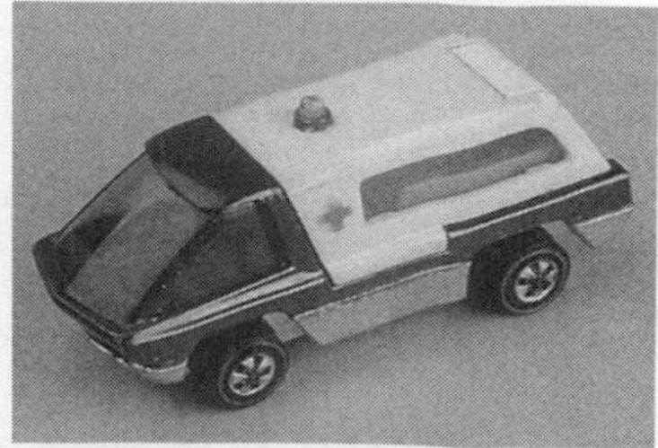

Ambulance, 1970, met. blue, white back with red cross & blue light on top, "Heavyweights" series, Model No. 6451
EX $30 **NM** $70 **MIP** $150

American Hauler, 1976, blue cab, white plastic box, American-flag-style tampo, "American Hauler", Model No. 9118
EX $20 **NM** $40 **MIP** $70

American Tipper, 1976, red metal cab, white plastic tipper bed, American flag tampo, "American Tipper", Model No. 9089
EX $20 **NM** $35 **MIP** $65

American Victory, 1975, light blue, American flag tampo, "9" on sides, silver interior, exposed silver engine, Model No. 7662
EX $10 **NM** $20 **MIP** $45

VEHICLES • HOT WHEELS NUMBERED PACKS

AMX/2, 1971, dark met. red, rear engine covers lift up, metal chassis, Model No. 6460
EX $40 **NM** $75 **MIP** $150

Aw Shoot, 1976, tank, olive drab, Model No. 9243
EX $10 **NM** $20 **MIP** $45

Backwoods Bomb, 1975, blue body with green & yellow tampo on sides, plastic camper shell on bed, "Keep On Camping," silver base, Model No. 7670
EX $30 **NM** $65 **MIP** $110

Baja Bruiser, 1974, orange, stars & stripes side tampo, "Firestone," "Cragar," and "Ford", Model No. 8258
EX $20 **NM** $45 **MIP** $90

Baja Bruiser, 1974, yellow, blue in tampo, Model No. 8258
EX $175 **NM** $450 **MIP** $1200

Baja Bruiser, 1974, yellow, magenta in tampo, Model No. 8258
EX $175 **NM** $450 **MIP** $1200

Baja Bruiser, 1976, light green, Model No. 8258
EX $100 **NM** $400 **MIP** $1300

Baja Bruiser, 1977, blue, redline or blackwall, Model No. 8258
EX $35 **NM** $60 **MIP** $85

Beatnik Bandit, 1968, met. blue, tan interior, clear bubble, exposed engine, Model No. 6217
EX $35 **NM** $60 **MIP** $150

Boss Hoss, 1970, chrome, black stripes on top, Club Kit, black number "9" in white circle on side, Model No. 6499
EX $80 **NM** $150 **MIP** $250

Boss Hoss, 1971, met. green, black "8" in white circle on side, exposed engine, Model No. 6406
EX $65 **NM** $125 **MIP** $300

Brabham-Repco F1, 1969, met. green, long tailpipes on silver engine, black "1" in white circle on side, blue-tinted windows, Model No. 6264
EX $20 **NM** $50 **MIP** $100

Breakaway Bucket, 1974, dark blue, orange tampo w/ yellow designs, Model No. 8262
EX $35 **NM** $85 **MIP** $145

Bugeye, 1971, red, black interior, hood lifts to expose engine, Model No. 6178
EX $25 **NM** $60 **MIP** $140

Bugeye, 1971, magenta, white interior, Model No. 6178
EX $25 **NM** $55 **MIP** $120

Buzz Off, 1973, assorted, Model No. 6976
EX $115 **NM** $250 **MIP** $500

Buzz Off, 1974, blue, Model No. 6976
EX $30 **NM** $75 **MIP** $115

Buzz Off, 1977, gold plated, redline or blackwall, Model No. 6976
EX $12 **NM** $24 **MIP** $35

Bye-Focal, 1971, met. green, opening hood, bifocals & "Bye Focal" on side, Model No. 6187
EX $60 **NM** $200 **MIP** $550

Carabo, 1970, assorted metallic colors, opening doors, black painted chassis,, Model No. 6420
EX $25 **NM** $60 **MIP** $150

Carabo, 1974, light green with blue and red stripes, opening gull-wing style doors, Model No. 7617
EX $30 **NM** $60 **MIP** $100

Carabo, 1974, yellow, Model No. 7617
EX $275 **NM** $600 **MIP** $1400

Cement Mixer, 1970, "Heavyweights" series, met. green, orange plastic cement mixer, Hot Wheels logo, Model No. 6452
EX $20 **NM** $65 **MIP** $125

Chaparral 2G, 1969, white, back opens to expose metal engine, Model No. 6256
EX $40 **NM** $80 **MIP** $160

Chevy Monza, 1977, chrome, yellow & black tampo, Model No. 9202
EX $15 **NM** $30 **MIP** $40

Chevy Monza 2+2, 1975, light green enamel with "Monza" rally stripes on hood and roof, black plastic interior, Model No. 7671
EX $125 **NM** $300 **MIP** $800

Chevy Monza 2+2, 1975, orange enamel finish, "Monza" rally stripes on hood and roof, Model No. 7671
EX $25 **NM** $50 **MIP** $110

Chief's Special Cruiser, 1975, red, redline, Model No. 7665
EX $15 **NM** $35 **MIP** $65

Classic '31 Ford Woody, 1969, met. red, metal engine, Model No. 6251
EX $25 **NM** $65 **MIP** $125

Classic '32 Ford Vicky, 1969, met. gold, metal engine, black roof, Model No. 6250
EX $25 **NM** $55 **MIP** $115

Classic '36 Ford Coupe, 1969, red, opening back reveals rumble seat, black roof, Model No. 6253
EX $35 **NM** $70 **MIP** $125

Classic '36 Ford Coupe, 1969, blue, Model No. 6253
EX $35 **NM** $70 **MIP** $125

Classic '57 T-Bird, 1969, met. orange, hood opens to reveal engine, Model No. 6252
EX $25 **NM** $55 **MIP** $140

Classic Cord, 1971, met. green, opening hood, detachable plastic soft-top roof (often missing), Model No. 6472
EX $65 **NM** $175 **MIP** $350

Classic Nomad, 1970, met. aqua, opening hood, metal engine, Model No. 6404
EX $30 **NM** $75 **MIP** $150

Cockney Cab, 1971, blue, British flag tampo on rear, "Cockney Cab", Model No. 6466
EX $50 **NM** $110 **MIP** $210

Cool One, 1976, Magenta body, "Cool One" letting on front, lightning tampo on body. Available as blackwalls variation, Model No. 9120
EX $20 **NM** $40 **MIP** $60

Corvette Stingray, 1976, red body, red, white, yellow & blue tampo, Model No. 9241
EX $15 **NM** $35 **MIP** $50

Custom AMX, 1969, met. green, hood lifts to expose engine, Model No. 6267
EX $45 **NM** $100 **MIP** $225

Custom Barracuda, 1968, met. green, hood opens to reveal metal engine, Model No. 6211
EX $40 **NM** $150 **MIP** $400

Custom Camaro, 1968, met. orange, black roof, opening hood, Model No. 6208
EX $75 **NM** $200 **MIP** $750

Custom Camaro, 1968, white enamel--an almost mythical car, and apparently none "in-pack", Model No. 6208
EX $500 **NM** $750 **MIP** $1000

Custom Charger, 1969, Assorted body colors, white plastic interior, opening hood, Model No. 6268
EX $50 **NM** $130 **MIP** $300

Custom Continental Mark III, 1969, met. pink, opening hood, metal engine, Model No. 6266
EX $35 **NM** $85 **MIP** $375

Custom Corvette, 1968, met. orange, opening hood, assorted interior color, Model No. 6215
EX $35 **NM** $125 **MIP** $400

Custom Cougar, 1968, met. green, opening hood, black interior, Model No. 6205
EX $35 **NM** $125 **MIP** $400

Custom Eldorado, 1968, met. green, black interior, black top, opening hood, Model No. 6218
EX $25 **NM** $75 **MIP** $225

Custom Firebird, 1968, met. orange, metal engine, opening hood, Model No. 6212
EX $30 **NM** $80 **MIP** $280

Custom Fleetside, 1968, met. purple, black roof, opening bed cover, Model No. 6213
EX $25 **NM** $75 **MIP** $250

Custom Mustang, 1968, assorted, Model No. 6206
EX $35 **NM** $150 **MIP** $450

Custom Mustang, 1968, assorted w/open hood scoops or louvered windows, Model No. 6206
EX $200 **NM** $450 **MIP** $1400

Custom Police Cruiser, 1969, black and white paint scheme on a Plymouth with "Police" and star tampos, red dome light. A nice companion car to the the 6469 Fire Chief Cruiser, Model No. 6269
EX $30 **NM** $90 **MIP** $200

Custom T-Bird, 1968, met. brown, opening hood, metal engine, Model No. 6207
EX $30 **NM** $115 **MIP** $250

Custom VW Bug, 1968, met. aqua, oversized engine, sunroof, Model No. 6220
EX $20 **NM** $55 **MIP** $125

Demon, 1970, blue, exposed engine, called "Prowler" in 1973, Model No. 6401
EX $25 **NM** $55 **MIP** $110

Deora, 1968, assorted, Model No. 6210
EX $25 **NM** $80 **MIP** $375

Double Header, 1973, green, blue-tinted windshield, Model No. 5880
EX $120 **NM** $250 **MIP** $500

Double Vision, 1973, met. green, flip-up plastic canopy over the seats, rear engine, Model No. 6975
EX $70 **NM** $175 **MIP** $400

Double Vision, 1973, orange, white interior, blue-tinted windows, Model No. 6975
EX $70 **NM** $175 **MIP** $400

Dump Truck, 1970, metal cab & chassis, unpainted base, plastic dump truck bed, "Heavyweights" series, 1970-72, Model No. 6453
EX $30 **NM** $65 **MIP** $110

Dune Daddy, 1973, green, blue-tinted windshield, white interior, Model No. 6967
EX $50 **NM** $110 **MIP** $400

Dune Daddy, 1975, light green with sixties-style daisy tampos on hood, Model No. 6967
EX $25 **NM** $50 **MIP** $75

Dune Daddy, 1975, orange body with sixties-style flowers on hood, Model No. 6967
EX $85 **NM** $200 **MIP** $475

El Rey Special, 1974, light blue with orange tampos, unpainted metal base, Model No. 8273
EX $175 **NM** $400 **MIP** $1100

El Rey Special, 1974, light green, Model No. 8273
EX $30 **NM** $75 **MIP** $175

El Rey Special, 1974, dark blue, Model No. 8273
EX $100 **NM** $225 **MIP** $700

El Rey Special, 1974, green, yellow & red "Dunlop," number "1" tampos, silver metal base, Model No. 8273
EX $25 **NM** $60 **MIP** $120

Emergency Squad, 1975, red body, yellow & white side tampos, silver plastic base, very much in the mold of the paramedic vehicle used on the TV show, "Emergency!", Model No. 7650
EX $20 **NM** $50 **MIP** $75

Evil Weevil, 1971, met. blue, black "8" inside white circle, sunroof, blue-tinted windows, Model No. 6471
EX $60 **NM** $100 **MIP** $200

Ferrari 312P, 1970, gold chrome, back opens to expose metal engine, black "60" in white circles, Model No. 6417
EX $40 **NM** $85 **MIP** $165

Ferrari 312P, 1973, red, back opens to expose metal engine, black "60" in white circles, Model No. 6973
EX $140 **NM** $300 **MIP** $600

Ferrari 512S, 1972, blue, opening rear hood & cockpit, Model No. 6022
EX $40 **NM** $95 **MIP** $250

Ferrari 512S, 1972, met. magenta, opening rear hood & cockpit, Model No. 6021
EX $40 **NM** $95 **MIP** $250

Fire Chief Cruiser, 1970, red Plymouth Fury, matches Custom Police Cruiser, #6269, Model No. 6469
EX $20 **NM** $40 **MIP** $85

Fire Engine, 1970, met. red cab, black ladder, rear is red plastic, white hoses, "Heavyweights" series, Model No. 6454
EX $25 **NM** $75 **MIP** $165

Fire-Eater, 1977, blue-tinted window, blue plastic hoses, Model No. 9640
EX $20 **NM** $30 **MIP** $40

Ford J-Car, 1968, met. aqua, back opens to reveal metal engine, Model No. 6214
EX $20 **NM** $45 **MIP** $90

Ford MK IV, 1969, red, back opens to reveal metal engine, Model No. 6257
EX $25 **NM** $75 **MIP** $150

Formula 5000, 1976, white race car, metal chassis, Model No. 9119
EX $20 **NM** $35 **MIP** $50

Formula P.A.C.K., 1976, black race car, Model No. 9037
EX $15 **NM** $30 **MIP** $50

Fuel Tanker, 1971, white cab & chassis, plastic fuel tanker section, removable fuel hoses, "Heavyweights" series, Model No. 6018
EX $30 **NM** $75 **MIP** $200

Funny Money, 1972, gray armored car body on funny car chassis, orange plastic bumper (usually missing), "Funny Money" labels, Model No. 6005
EX $80 **NM** $165 **MIP** $335

Funny Money, 1974, plum w/floral tampo, Model No. 7621
EX $25 **NM** $50 **MIP** $85

Funny Money, 1977, gray body, white "Brink's" on sides, body lifts open, Model No. 7621
EX $25 **NM** $40 **MIP** $60

GMC Motor Home, 1977, orange, blue-tinted windows, Model No. 9645
EX $100 **NM** $250 **MIP** n/a

Grass Hopper, 1971, met. red, shown without white plastic canopy, Model No. 6461
EX $20 **NM** $60 **MIP** $125

Grass Hopper, 1974, light green, engine, orange & blue side tampo, blue-tinted windshield, Model No. 7622
EX $25 **NM** $50 **MIP** $100

Grass Hopper, 1975, light green, no engine, Model No. 7622
EX $45 **NM** $100 **MIP** $200

Gremlin Grinder, 1975, green, blue-tinted windows, yellow, orange & black tampo, exposed engine, Model No. 7652
EX $20 **NM** $45 **MIP** $90

Gremlin Grinder, 1976, chrome, orange, black & green tampo, exposed engine, Model No. 9201
EX $20 **NM** $40 **MIP** $60

Gun Bucket, 1976, olive-green body, white "Army" star & number tampos on hood, black plastic anti-aircraft gun & treads, Model No. 9090
EX $20 **NM** $40 **MIP** $60

Gun Slinger, 1975, olive, Model No. 7664
EX $15 **NM** $30 **MIP** $50

Hairy Hauler, 1971, assorted, with lifting front canopy, exposed engine, Model No. 6458
EX $25 **NM** $65 **MIP** $110

Heavy Chevy, 1970, chrome, Club Kit, black stripes, Model No. 6189
EX $70 **NM** $135 **MIP** $210

Heavy Chevy, 1970, assorted, exposed engine, Model No. 6408
EX $55 **NM** $120 **MIP** $200

Heavy Chevy, 1974, light green, Model No. 7619
EX $95 **NM** $200 **MIP** $750

Heavy Chevy, 1974, yellow, exposed engine, orange & red side tampo, "7", Model No. 7619
EX $45 **NM** $90 **MIP** $200

Heavy Chevy, 1977, chrome, redline or blackwall, Model No. 9212
EX $35 **NM** $75 **MIP** $115

Hiway Robber, 1973, red, black interior, exposed engine, Model No. 6979
EX $75 **NM** $150 **MIP** $400

Hood, The, 1971, met. light green, exposed engine, black interior, Model No. 6175
EX $40 **NM** $85 **MIP** $150

Hot Heap, 1968, met. yellow, white interior, exposed engine, Model No. 6219
EX $20 **NM** $55 **MIP** $115

Ice T, 1971, yellow, with "Ice T" on plastic roof, Model No. 6184
EX $30 **NM** $75 **MIP** $200

Ice T, 1973, Body in assorted colors, black plastic interior, plastic roof (mostly in white), silver base. Blackwall wheels variations also produced at the same time, Model No. 6980
EX $95 **NM** $200 **MIP** $650

Ice T, 1974, light green, Model No. 6980
EX $25 **NM** $50 **MIP** $75

Ice T, 1974, yellow with hood tampo, Model No. 6980
EX $85 **NM** $200 **MIP** $500

Indy Eagle, 1969, gold, Model No. 6263
EX $75 **NM** $150 **MIP** $250

Indy Eagle, 1969, assorted colors with tinted plastic windshield and silver rear engine and tailpipes, Model No. 6263
EX $30 **NM** $75 **MIP** $125

Inferno, 1976, yellow drag racer, exposed engine, Model No. 9186
EX $30 **NM** $55 **MIP** $80

Jack Rabbit Special, 1970, white, blue stripe, clear windshield, Model No. 6421
EX $20 **NM** $60 **MIP** $90

Jack-in-the-Box Promotion, 1970, white, Jack Rabbit w/decals, Model No. 6421
EX $150 **NM** $300 **MIP** n/a

Jet Threat, 1971, met. yellow, blue-tinted windshield, Model No. 6179
EX $40 **NM** $95 **MIP** $225

Jet Threat, 1973, light blue, blue-tinted windshield
EX $30 **NM** $85 **MIP** $160

Jet Threat II, 1976, plum w/yellow flames, blue-tinted windshield, exposed engine, Model No. 8235
EX $20 **NM** $35 **MIP** $55

Khaki Kooler, 1976, khaki body, "Military Police", black interior, smoke-colored windshield, Model No. 9183
EX $15 **NM** $30 **MIP** $45

King Kuda, 1970, chrome, Club Kit, exposed engine, Model No. 6411
EX $70 **NM** $150 **MIP** $300

King 'Kuda, 1970, met. green, exposed engine, blue-tinted windshield, Model No. 6411
EX $45 **NM** $100 **MIP** $200

Large Charge, 1975, green, red & yellow tampos, blue-tinted windows, Model No. 8272
EX $20 **NM** $40 **MIP** $80

Letter Getter, 1977, U.S. Mail truck, white, Model No. 9643
EX $125 **NM** $250 **MIP** n/a

Light My Firebird, 1970, Convertible in assorted finishes, decal number on doors, exposed silver engine in front, brown plastic interior, Model No. 6412
EX $20 **NM** $55 **MIP** $110

Lola GT 70, 1969, dark green, opening rear, clear windows, Model No. 6254
EX $30 **NM** $75 **MIP** $125

Lotus Turbine, 1969, met. brown, blue-tinted windshield, Model No. 6262
EX $20 **NM** $50 **MIP** $105

Lowdown, 1976, light blue, "Flyin' Low", Model No. 9185
EX $30 **NM** $50 **MIP** $75

Mantis, 1970, assorted, exposed engines, Model No. 6423
EX $25 **NM** $65 **MIP** $100

Maserati Mistral, 1969, assorted, Model No. 6277
EX $50 **NM** $100 **MIP** $200

Maxi Taxi, 1976, Oldsmobile 442 body, yellow w/checkboard & "Maxi Taxi" tampo, black plastic interior, Model No. 9184
EX $30 **NM** $45 **MIP** $60

McClaren M6A, 1969, orange, blue-tinted windshield, Model No. 6255
EX $20 **NM** $45 **MIP** $90

Mercedes 280SL, 1969, red, opening hood, metal engine, blue-tinted windows, Model No. 6275
EX $25 **NM** $60 **MIP** $110

Mercedes 280SL, 1973, assorted, Model No. 6962
EX $90 **NM** $200 **MIP** $450

Mercedes C-111, 1972, assorted, Model No. 6169
EX $60 **NM** $145 **MIP** $280

Mercedes C-111, 1973, assorted, Model No. 6978
EX $175 **NM** $400 **MIP** $900

Mercedes C-111, 1974, red, with stars and stripes tampo, Model No. 6978
EX $20 **NM** $45 **MIP** $90

Mercedes-Benz 280SL, 1969, met. blue, blue-tinted windows, opening hood, metal engine, Model No. 6275
EX $30 **NM** $65 **MIP** $110

(KW6414)

Mighty Maverick, 1970, assorted, opening hood, black plastic spoiler, Model No. 6414
EX $45 **NM** $85 **MIP** $175

Mighty Maverick, 1975, blue, orange, yellow & white tampo, blue-tinted windows, Model No. 7653
EX $25 **NM** $60 **MIP** $100

Mighty Maverick, 1976, chrome, yellow & blue tampo, blue-tinted windows, "Super Chromes" series, Model No. 9209
EX $20 **NM** $35 **MIP** $50

Mod-Quad, 1970, met. red, black interior, four metal engines, top opens, Model No. 6456
EX $35 **NM** $80 **MIP** $170

Mongoose, 1973, blue w/red stickers, Model No. 6970
EX $275 **NM** $600 **MIP** $1400

Mongoose Funny Car, 1970, red, opening body, white, blue & yellow tampo, Model No. 6410
EX $65 **NM** $125 **MIP** $210

Mongoose II, 1971, met. blue, opening body, Model No. 5954
EX $55 **NM** $125 **MIP** $350

Mongoose Rail Dragster, 1971, blue, two pack, w/Snake Rail, Model No. 5952
EX $75 **NM** $165 **MIP** $1250

Monte Carlo Stocker, 1975, yellow, blue-tinted windows, black interior, Model No. 7660
EX $30 **NM** $65 **MIP** $110

Motocross I, 1975, red plastic seat and tank, unpainted gray die-cast body, Model No. 7668
EX $45 **NM** $100 **MIP** $200

Moving Van, 1970, met. blue, white trailer, "Heavyweights" series, Model No. 6455
EX $40 **NM** $90 **MIP** $150

Mustang Stocker, 1975, yellow w/red in tampo, Model No. 9203
EX $90 **NM** $175 **MIP** $650

Mustang Stocker, 1975, yellow with magenta and orange tampo with "Ford" and "450 HP", Model No. 7664
EX $50 **NM** $125 **MIP** $200

Mustang Stocker, 1975, white, Model No. 7664
EX $175 **NM** $400 **MIP** $1000

Mustang Stocker, 1976, chrome, Model No. 9203
EX $45 **NM** $65 **MIP** $90

Mustang Stocker, 1977, chrome, redline or blackwall, Model No. 9203
EX $25 **NM** $55 **MIP** $80

Mutt Mobile, 1971, met. red, dogs in back, Model No. 6185
EX $60 **NM** $125 **MIP** $300

Neet Streeter, 1976, blue, red & white roof stripes, Model No. 9244
EX $25 **NM** $45 **MIP** $75

Nitty Gritty Kitty, 1970, gold chrome, metal engine, blue-tinted windows, Model No. 6405
EX $50 **NM** $100 **MIP** $200

Noodle Head, 1971, assorted, opening headlight cover, Model No. 6000
EX $50 **NM** $100 **MIP** $200

Odd Job, 1973, red, white topper, exposed engine, Model No. 6981
EX $95 **NM** $200 **MIP** $600

Odd Rod, 1977, yellow plastic bucket around seats, clear plastic hood with flame graphics, Model No. 9642
EX $25 **NM** $55 **MIP** $80

Odd Rod, 1977, plum, blackwall or redline, Model No. 9642
EX $95 **NM** $200 **MIP** $400

Olds 442, 1971, assorted, Model No. 6467
EX $125 **NM** $410 **MIP** $800

Open Fire, 1972, met. red, modified AMC Gremilin, oversized engine & six wheels, Model No. 5881
EX $80 **NM** $210 **MIP** $450

Paddy Wagon, 1970, blue, with plastic covering over bed, Model No. 6402
EX $35 **NM** $80 **MIP** $125

Paddy Wagon, 1973, blue, Model No. 6966
EX $30 **NM** $65 **MIP** $120

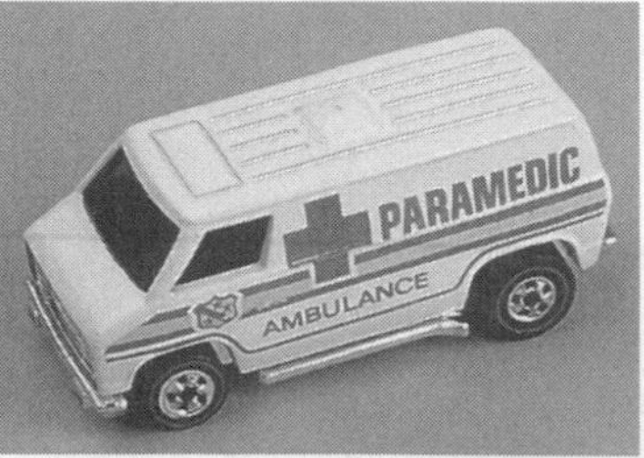

Paramedic, 1975, white with yellow and red stripes and "Paramedic" lettering, Model No. 7661
EX $20 **NM** $40 **MIP** $75

Peepin' Bomb, 1970, met. yellow, clear windshield, exposed engine, Model No. 6419
EX $30 **NM** $70 **MIP** $110

Peepin' Bomb, 1973, red, exposed engine, blue-tinted windshield
EX $45 **NM** $90 **MIP** $150

Pit Crew Car, 1971, white, opening trunk w/tool box, Model No. 6183
EX $70 **NM** $150 **MIP** $350

Poison Pinto, 1976, light green body, skull & crossbones, "Poison Pinto" tampo, late-era redlines, Model No. 9240
EX $25 **NM** $50 **MIP** $75

Police Cruiser, 1973, white Olds 442, "Police" labels on doors, opening hood & red dome light on roof, Model No. 6963
EX $35 **NM** $80 **MIP** $150

Police Cruiser, 1974, white, "State Police, Law Enforcement" decal on doors, Model No. 6963
EX $25 **NM** $60 **MIP** $125

Police Cruiser, 1977, white Olds 442 with black doors, yellow police tampos on doors, non-opening hood, blue light, Model No. 6963
EX $15 **NM** $30 **MIP** $50

Porsche 911, 1975, yellow, with blue and red stripes on hood and roof, Model No. 7648
EX $40 **NM** $95 **MIP** $150

Porsche 911, 1976, chrome, red & green tampo, black interior, Model No. 9206
EX $20 **NM** $40 **MIP** $60

Porsche 917, 1970, silver, clear windshield, opening back, Model No. 6416
EX $40 **NM** $80 **MIP** $140

Porsche 917, 1973, red, opening back, blue-tinted windshield, Model No. 6972
EX $100 **NM** $250 **MIP** $600

Porsche 917, 1974, red, Model No. 6972
EX $85 **NM** $175 **MIP** $500

Porsche 917, 1974, orange, Model No. 6972
EX $20 **NM** $40 **MIP** $75

Power Pad, 1970, met. red, clear windshield, black interior, exposed engine, shown w/o camper, Model No. 6459

EX $30 **NM** $75 **MIP** $125

Prowler, 1973, assorted, Model No. 6965

EX $185 **NM** $400 **MIP** $1000

Prowler, 1974, light green, Model No. 6965

EX $175 **NM** $400 **MIP** $800

Prowler, 1974, orange with demon flame tampo on roof (which makes sense, considering this car was known as "The Demon" in its previous incarnation in 1970. Unpainted metal base, Model No. 6965

EX $15 **NM** $35 **MIP** $75

Prowler, 1976, chrome, yellow & red flames, devil tampo, exposed engine, Model No. 9207

EX $40 **NM** $65 **MIP** $85

Python, 1968, met. red, black top, exposed engine, Model No. 6216

EX $20 **NM** $45 **MIP** $80

Racer Rig, 1971, red/white, "Heavyweights" series, Model No. 6194

EX $70 **NM** $150 **MIP** $375

Ramblin' Wrecker, 1975, white, "Larry's 24 Hour Towing", blue lift, Model No. 7659

EX $25 **NM** $55 **MIP** $80

Ranger Rig, 1975, medium green w/yellow lettering & design, Model No. 7666

EX $20 **NM** $45 **MIP** $75

Rash 1, 1974, green, blue-tinted windshield, yellow & white tampo, exposed engine, Model No. 7616

EX $30 **NM** $65 **MIP** $140

Rash I, 1974, blue, Model No. 7616

EX $125 **NM** $300 **MIP** $800

Rear Engine Mongoose, 1972, red, Model No. 5699

EX $90 **NM** $200 **MIP** $600

Rear Engine Snake, 1972, yellow, blue w/red stars tampo, Model No. 5856

EX $90 **NM** $200 **MIP** $600

Red Baron, 1970, red, cross on helmet, Model No. 6400

EX $20 **NM** $45 **MIP** $80

Red Baron, 1973, red, note no Iron Cross on the helmet, Model No. 6964

EX $30 **NM** $80 **MIP** $150

Road King Truck, 1974, yellow cab and trailer with metal chassis, tilting dumper section, availabe in set only, Model No. 7615

EX $600 **NM** $1200 **MIP** n/a

Rock Buster, 1976, chrome dune buggy with black plastic rollcage and interior, racing graphics on hood and sides, Model No. 9507

EX $25 **NM** $40 **MIP** $55

Rock Buster, 1976, yellow, Model No. 9088

EX $20 **NM** $30 **MIP** $40

Rocket-Bye-Baby, 1971, met. yellow, metal rocket on top, Model No. 6186

EX $60 **NM** $120 **MIP** $280

Rodger Dodger, 1974, magenta Dodge Charger, flame tampos on hood & roof, exposed silver engine, red plastic exhaust pipes, Model No. 8259

EX $30 **NM** $60 **MIP** $125

Rodger Dodger, 1974, blue, Model No. 8259

EX $85 **NM** $200 **MIP** $550

Rodger Dodger, 1977, gold plated, blackwall or redline, Model No. 8259

EX $20 **NM** $45 **MIP** $80

Rolls-Royce Silver Shadow, 1969, silver, opening hood shows detailed engine, Model No. 6276

EX $25 **NM** $60 **MIP** $145

Sand Crab, 1970, red, black interior, clear windshield, Model No. 6403

EX $20 **NM** $50 **MIP** $90

Sand Drifter, 1975, green, Model No. 7651
EX $75 **NM** $150 **MIP** $425

Sand Drifter, 1975, yellow, flame tampo on hood, black plastic interior & covering over bed, Model No. 7651
EX $25 **NM** $45 **MIP** $85

Sand Witch, 1973, green, blue-tinted windshield, opening rear hood, Model No. 6974
EX $75 **NM** $175 **MIP** $450

S'Cool Bus, 1971, yellow, lift-up funny car body, silver chassis, "Heavyweights" series, Model No. 6468
EX $145 **NM** $250 **MIP** $750

Scooper, 1971, met. green, yellow scoop & rear, Model No. 6193
EX $50 **NM** $100 **MIP** $220

Seasider, 1970, met. light green, exposed engine, plastic boat, Model No. 6413
EX $60 **NM** $110 **MIP** $200

Second Wind, 1977, white w/yellow & red striping, number "5" on hood, Model No. 9644
EX $30 **NM** $60 **MIP** $90

Shelby Turbine, 1969, met. Purple, Model No. 6265
EX $25 **NM** $60 **MIP** $110

Short Order, 1971, blue, extending plastic tailgate, exposed engine, Model No. 6176
EX $35 **NM** $75 **MIP** $230

Show Hoss II, 1977, yellow funny car Mustang II body lifts up over silver base, black plastic rollcage, redline or blackwalls versions available, Model No. 9646
EX $125 **NM** $300 **MIP** $600

Show-Off, 1973, orange, exposed engine, blue-tinted windows, Model No. 6982
EX $75 **NM** $175 **MIP** $450

Side Kick, 1972, met. green, exposed engine, Model No. 6022
EX $75 **NM** $145 **MIP** $300

Silhouette, 1968, Body in assorted colors, plastic dome canopy over seats, exposed front engine, Model No. 6209
EX $25 **NM** $50 **MIP** $100

Sir Sidney Roadster, 1974, light green, Model No. 8261
EX $200 **NM** $325 **MIP** $625

Sir Sidney Roadster, 1974, Orange body with brown plastic roof and exposed silver engine. Red flame tampos, silver metal base, Model No. 8261
EX $180 **NM** $300 **MIP** $575

Sir Sidney Roadster, 1974, yellow, red flames, exposed engine, brown top, Model No. 8261
EX $25 **NM** $50 **MIP** $90

Six Shooter, 1971, met. blue, exposed engines, blue-tinted windshield, six wheels, Model No. 6003
EX $35 **NM** $85 **MIP** $225

Sky Show Fleetside (Aero Launcher), 1970, met. blue, orange plastic ramp, Model No. 6436
EX $200 **NM** $400 **MIP** $850

Snake, 1973, white/yellow, Model No. 6969
EX $300 **NM** $700 **MIP** $1500

Snake Funny Car, 1970, yellow, body opens, metal engine, Model No. 6409
EX $35 **NM** $90 **MIP** $300

Snake II, 1971, white, Model No. 5953
EX $60 **NM** $100 **MIP** $275

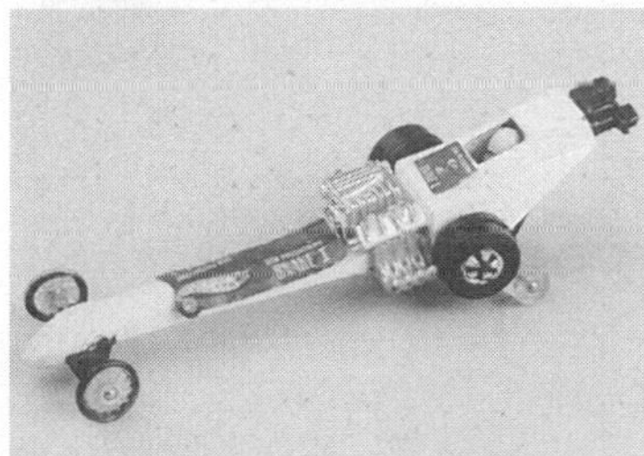

Snake Rail Dragster, 1971, white, exposed engine, part of a two-pack with blue Mongoose Rail, Model No. 5951
EX $75 **NM** $150 **MIP** $1250

Snorkel, 1971, assorted, Model No. 6020
EX $30 **NM** $90 **MIP** $200

Special Delivery, 1971, blue, exposed engines, U.S. Mail tampo, Model No. 6006
EX $50 **NM** $100 **MIP** $250

Splittin' Image, 1969, met. orange, clear windows, exposed engine, Model No. 6261
EX $25 **NM** $65 **MIP** $115

Spoiler Sport, 1977, light green van, tropical island scene on side panels, Model No. 9641
EX $25 **NM** $45 **MIP** $70

Staff Car, 1976, Olsd 442 casting in olive drab, "Staff Car U.S. Army" on doors, Model No. 9521
EX $200 **NM** $400 **MIP** $600

Steam Roller, 1974, white body with red white and blue graphics, seven stars on front, Model No. 8260
EX $70 **NM** $160 **MIP** $350

Steam Roller, 1974, white body, stars & stripes tampo, three stars reversed out of red stripe on hood; the more common model, Model No. 8260
EX $25 **NM** $50 **MIP** $70

Street Rodder, 1976, black, flames, exposed engine, clear windshield, Model No. 9242
EX $40 **NM** $75 **MIP** $100

Street Snorter, 1973, light green, blue-tinted windows, Model No. 6971
EX $95 **NM** $200 **MIP** $500

Street Snorter, 1973, assorted, Model No. 6971
EX $90 **NM** $180 **MIP** $500

Strip Teaser, 1971, blue, opeing back, exposed engine, Model No. 6188
EX $45 **NM** $105 **MIP** $275

Strip Teaser, 1973, blue, exposed engine, driver area opens to reveal black interior
EX $25 **NM** $75 **MIP** $140

Sugar Caddy, 1971, assorted, exposed engine, Model No. 6418
EX $30 **NM** $75 **MIP** $175

Supcr Van, 1975, black body, chrome plastic base, red & yellow flames, Model No. 7649
EX $30 **NM** $60 **MIP** $90

Super Van, 1975, blue body, yellow flames, Model No. 7649
EX $100 **NM** $300 **MIP** $600

Superfine Turbine, 1973, red, exposed engine, black interior, Model No. 6004
EX $180 **NM** $425 **MIP** $850

Sweet 16, 1973, red, exposed engine, trunk opens to expose spare, Model No. 6007
EX $165 **NM** $275 **MIP** $650

Swingin' Wing, 1970, met. red, blue-tinted windows, Model No. 6422
EX $25 **NM** $60 **MIP** $125

T-4-2, 1971, met. yellow, black top, exposed metal engines, blue-tinted windows, Model No. 6177
EX $40 **NM** $80 **MIP** $175

Team Trailer, 1971, white/red, detailed plastic interior & opening door on trailer, "Heavyweights" series, Model No. 6019
EX $75 **NM** $150 **MIP** $275

TNT-Bird, 1970, met. green, white stripe, blue-tinted windshield, exposed engine, Model No. 6407
EX $40 **NM** $85 **MIP** $150

Top Eliminator, 1974, blue lift-up funny car body on silver chassis, green, light tan, and orange "Hot Wheels" tampo w/stripes on sides, Model No. 7630
EX $30 **NM** $80 **MIP** $145

Torero, 1969, gold chrome, opening hood, clear windows, white interior, Model No. 6260
EX $25 **NM** $55 **MIP** $125

Torino Stocker, 1975, red, blue-tinted windshield, black interior, Model No. 7647
EX $30 **NM** $65 **MIP** $110

Tough Customer, 1975, olive, with rotating turret and white numbering tampos, Model No. 7655
EX $15 **NM** $30 **MIP** $60

Tow Truck, 1970, assorted, "Heavyweights" series, Model No. 6450
EX $35 **NM** $70 **MIP** $120

Tri-Baby, 1970, blue, interesting engine casting under opening rear hood, Model No. 6424
EX $25 **NM** $60 **MIP** $90

T-Totaller, 1977, black, redlines, six-pack only, red body common $25, Model No. 9648
EX $200 **NM** $700 **MIP** n/a

Turbofire, 1969, met. yellow, opening rear, clear windshield, Model No. 6259
EX $20 **NM** $60 **MIP** $110

Twin Mill, 1969, met. aqua, clear windows, two exposed engines, Model No. 6258
EX $25 **NM** $65 **MIP** $150

Twin Mill, 1973, met. red, blue-tinted windshield, two exposed engines
EX $40 **NM** $90 **MIP** $165

Twin Mill II, 1976, orange, two engines, blue-tinted windows, blue, white & red tampo, Model No. 8240
EX $20 **NM** $30 **MIP** $45

Vega Bomb, 1975, green, Model No. 7658
EX $175 **NM** $400 **MIP** $950

Vega Bomb, 1975, orange, this model is right on the cusp of the Redlines era--blackwall versions (like this one as #7654) were becoming a more common sight, Model No. 7658
EX $35 **NM** $65 **MIP** $120

Volkswagen, 1974, orange enamel, bug graphic on roof, Model No. 7620
EX $25 **NM** $75 **MIP** $125

Volkswagen, 1974, orange w/stripes on roof, Model No. 7620
EX $80 **NM** $175 **MIP** $500

Volkswagen Beach Bomb, 1969, surf boards on side raised panels, Model No. 6274
EX $100 **NM** $200 **MIP** $450

Volkswagen Beach Bomb, 1969, surf boards in rear window, Model No. 6274
EX n/a **NM** $7000 **MIP** n/a

Warpath, 1975, white, stars & stripes tampo, opening plastic engine covers, Model No. 7654
EX $30 **NM** $75 **MIP** $115

Waste Wagon, 1971, met. yellow, orange receptacle, "Heavyweights" series, Model No. 6192
EX $65 **NM** $130 **MIP** $250

What-4, 1971, met. green, blue-tinted windshield, Model No. 6001
EX $70 **NM** $145 **MIP** $275

Whip Creamer, 1970, met. yellow, clear slide-back plastic canopy, Model No. 6457
EX $25 **NM** $65 **MIP** $120

Winnipeg, 1974, yellow body, orange spoiler, blue & orange tampo, Model No. 7618
EX $50 **NM** $100 **MIP** $210

Xploder, 1973, red, black interior, blue-tinted windows, Model No. 6977
EX $135 **NM** $225 **MIP** $500

Z Whiz, 1977, gray body, orange & yellow tampo, Model No. 9639
EX $30 **NM** $50 **MIP** $70

Z Whiz, 1977, white, redline, Model No. 9639
EX $200 **NM** $1500 **MIP** n/a

JAPANESE TIN CARS

(Ron Smith)

Agajanian Racer No.98, 1950s, friction, "Y" Co., 18" (J286)
EX $900 **NM** $1600 **MIP** $2400

(Ron Smith)

Aston-Martin DB5, 1960s, (James Bond), friction, Gilbert, 11-1/2" (J1)
EX $90 **NM** $175 **MIP** $400

(Ron Smith)

Aston-Martin DB6, 1960s, friction, Asahi Toy Co., 11" (J2)
EX $200 **NM** $400 **MIP** $600

(Ron Smith)

Atom Car, 1950s, Yonezawa, 17" (J284)
EX $400 **NM** $800 **MIP** $1800

BMW Coupe, 1960s, Yonezawa, 11" tan, battery-operated
EX $50 **NM** $105 **MIP** $200

(Ron Smith)

Buick, 1959, friction, T.N., 11" (J8)
EX $90 **NM** $200 **MIP** $400

(Ron Smith)

Buick Century, 1958, friction, Yonezawa, 12" (J6)
EX $400 **NM** $800 **MIP** $1800

(Ron Smith)

Buick Century, 1958, friction, Bandai, 8" (J7)
EX $80 **NM** $100 **MIP** $200

Buick Convertible, 1959, 11", orange/yellow, friction, dog and driver figures
EX $100 **NM** $275 **MIP** $350

Buick Fire Department Car, 1961, 16", red, friction, working wipers, revolving emergency light
EX $80 **NM** $150 **MIP** $265

(Ron Smith)

Buick Futuristic LeSabre, 1950s, friction, Yonezawa, 7-1/2" (J276)
EX $200 **NM** $500 **MIP** $850

VEHICLES • JAPANESE TIN CARS

Buick HT Convertible, 1959, Linemar, 9-1/2" red/white, friction
EX $50 **NM** $105 **MIP** $150

(Ron Smith)

Buick Roadmaster, 1955, friction, Yoshiya, 11" (J5)
EX $125 **NM** $300 **MIP** $600

Buick Special, 1955, 8-1/2", two-tone blue, battery-operated, working headlights
EX $55 **NM** $122 **MIP** $175

Buick Station Wagon, 1959, Yonezawa, 9", two-tone green, friction, HT or Conv.
EX $50 **NM** $105 **MIP** $150

(Ron Smith)

Buick Wildcat, 1963, friction, Ichiko, 15" (J13)
EX $300 **NM** $600 **MIP** $1200

(Ron Smith)

Cadillac, 1950, battery-op, Marusan, 11" (J18)
EX $400 **NM** $950 **MIP** $2000

(Ron Smith)

Cadillac, 1952, friction, Alps, 11-1/2" (J20)
EX $250 **NM** $600 **MIP** $1200

Cadillac, 1954, battery-op, Joustra, 12" (J23)
EX $150 **NM** $300 **MIP** $600

Cadillac, 1960, black, Marusan, 12" (J27A), Model No. J27A
EX $250 **NM** $550 **MIP** $800

(Ron Smith)

Cadillac, 1967, friction, K.O., 10-1/2" (J34)
EX $65 **NM** $150 **MIP** $300

(Ron Smith)

Cadillac Convertible, 1960, friction, Bandai, 12" (J25)
EX $60 **NM** $110 **MIP** $220

(Ron Smith)

Cadillac Fleetwood, 1961, friction, SSS, 17-1/2" (J29)
EX $200 **NM** $450 **MIP** $900

Cadillac Four-Door Sedan, 1935, 8", maroon, black, gold, friction
EX $30 **NM** $80 **MIP** $110

Cadillac Four-Door Sedan, 1951, Marusan, 12-1/2", gray, black, white, or red, friction
EX $300 **NM** $800 **MIP** $1200

Cadillac Four-Door Sedan, 1951, Marusan, 12-1/2", gray, battery-operated, remote control, working headlights
EX $480 **NM** $1200 **MIP** $2200

(Ron Smith)

Cadillac Four-Door Sedan, 1960, Yonezawa, 18" black or maroon, friction, shown is a customized convertible
EX $300 **NM** $630 **MIP** $900

Cadillac Police Car, 1962, Ichiko, 6-1/2" black/white, friction w/siren
EX $30 **NM** $50 **MIP** $80

(Ron Smith)

Champion No. 15 Racer, 1950, friction, German, 18" (J289)
EX $600 **NM** $1100 **MIP** $2200

(Ron Smith)

Champion No. 42 Racer, 1950, friction, Gem France, 18" (J288)
EX $600 **NM** $1100 **MIP** $2200

(Ron Smith)

Champion No. 98 Racer, 1950s, friction, "Y" Co., 18" (J287)
EX $600 **NM** $1100 **MIP** $2200

(Ron Smith)

Chevrolet, 1954, friction, Marusan, 11" (J49)
EX $250 **NM** $600 **MIP** $1200

(Ron Smith)

Chevrolet, 1955, battery-op, Marusan, 10-3/4" (J50)
EX $300 **NM** $800 **MIP** $1500

(Ron Smith)

Chevrolet, 1960, friction, Marusan, 11-1/2" (J60)
EX $200 **NM** $400 **MIP** $800

(Ron Smith)

Chevrolet, 1962, friction, unknown manufacturer, 11" (J65)
EX $200 **NM** $300 **MIP** $600

Chevrolet Bel Air, 1954, Marusan and Linemar, 11", gray/black, friction
EX $400 **NM** $600 **MIP** $1000

Chevrolet Bel Air, 1954, Marusan and Linemar, 11", rare orange/yellow, friction
EX $400 **NM** $600 **MIP** $1000

Chevrolet Bel Air, 1955, Asahi Toy, 7" light green, friction
EX $50 **NM** $105 **MIP** $130

Chevrolet Camaro, 1967, battery-op, T.N., 14" (J46)
EX $125 **NM** $175 **MIP** $350

(Ron Smith)

Chevrolet Camaro Rusher, 1971, battery-op, Taiyo, 9-1/2" (J48)
EX $10 **NM** $20 **MIP** $25

(Ron Smith)

Chevrolet Corvette, 1953, friction, Bandai, 7" (J37)
EX $125 **NM** $225 **MIP** $400

(Ron Smith)

Chevrolet Corvette, 1958, friction, Yonezawa, 9-1/2" (J38)
EX $200 **NM** $300 **MIP** $500

(Ron Smith)

Chevrolet Corvette, 1964, battery-op, Ichida, 12" (J41)
EX $150 **NM** $225 **MIP** $400

(Ron Smith)

Chevrolet Corvette, 1968, battery-op, Taiyo, 9-1/2" (J42)
EX $20 **NM** $30 **MIP** $50

Chevrolet Corvette Coupe, 1963, 12", metallic red or white, battery-operated, working headlights
EX $180 **NM** $420 **MIP** $600

Chevrolet Hardtop, 1959, red w/white top; 1960s, 10", Model No. J59A
EX $90 **NM** $150 **MIP** $300

Chevrolet Highway Patrol Car, 1959, ASC, 10", black/white, friction
EX $55 **NM** $125 **MIP** $175

Chevrolet HT, 1959, 7", green, friction
EX $30 **NM** $60 **MIP** $80

(Ron Smith)

Chevrolet Impala, 1963, friction, T.N., 18" (J66)
EX $200 **NM** $300 **MIP** $500

(Ron Smith)

Chevrolet Impala Convertible, 1961, friction, Bandai, 11" (J63)
EX $100 **NM** $175 **MIP** $400

Chevrolet Impala HT, 1960, Alps, 9", red/white, friction
EX $105 **NM** $200 **MIP** $400

(Ron Smith)

Chevrolet Impala Sedan, 1961, friction, Bandai, 11" (J62)
EX $100 **NM** $300 **MIP** $400

(Ron Smith)

Chevrolet Secret Agent, 1962, battery-op, unknown manufacturer, 14" (J64)
EX $50 **NM** $75 **MIP** $150

(Ron Smith)

Chevrolet Sedan/Convertible/Wagon, 1959, friction, SY, 11-1/2" (J59)
EX $200 **NM** $400 **MIP** $800

Chevrolet Station Wagon/Sedan/Convertible, 1958, friction, Bandai, 8" (J57)
EX $50 **NM** $75 **MIP** $150

(Ron Smith)

Chrylser Imperial Convertible or Sedan, 1959, friction, Bandai, 8" (J74)
EX $50 **NM** $100 **MIP** $150

(Ron Smith)

Chrysler, 1955, friction, Yonezawa, 8" (J71)
EX $100 **NM** $200 **MIP** $300

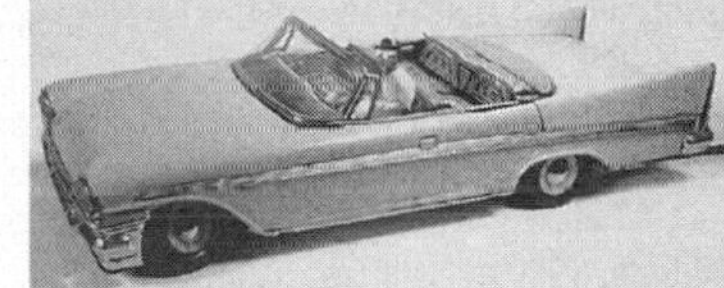
(Ron Smith)

Chrysler, 1958, battery-op, unknown manufacturer, 13" (J73)
EX $300 **NM** $400 **MIP** $800

(Ron Smith)

Chrysler Imperial, 1962, 16", friction, black, red (white: add 20% to value)
EX $1000 **NM** $4000 **MIP** $8000

Chrysler New Yorker, 1957, 6-1/2", red/black, friction
EX $25 **NM** $60 **MIP** $85

Chrysler New Yorker, 1957, friction, Alps, 14" (J72)
EX $600 **NM** $1500 **MIP** $2200

Chrysler Orion Convertible, 1953, 6-1/2", blue/green, friction
EX $25 **NM** $60 **MIP** $85

Citroen 2 CV, 1960, friction, Daiya, 8" (J269A)
EX $100 **NM** $150 **MIP** $275

Citroen DS19 Sedan/Wagon/Convertible, 1960, friction, Bandai, 12" (J68)
EX $200 **NM** $400 **MIP** $600

Cunningham Roadster, 1950s, 7-1/2", light blue, friction
EX $40 **NM** $90 **MIP** $125

DeSoto, 1950s, 6", green, friction
EX $20 **NM** $45 **MIP** $65

DeSoto, 1950s, Asahi Toy, 8", green, friction
EX $40 **NM** $90 **MIP** $125

Dodge Charger Sonic Car, 1966, 16", red, battery-operated
EX $90 **NM** $125 **MIP** $250

Dodge Four-Door HT, 1958, 8-1/2", orange/white, friction
EX $55 **NM** $125 **MIP** $175

(Ron Smith)

Dodge Pickup, 1959, friction, unknown manufacturer, 18-1/2" (J84)
EX $300 **NM** $500 **MIP** $1000

(Ron Smith)

Dodge Sedan, 1958, friction, T.N., 11" (J82)
EX $300 **NM** $450 **MIP** $1000

Dodge Two-Door HT, 1959, 9", blue/white, friction
EX $135 **NM** $315 **MIP** $450

Dream Car, friction, "Y" Co., 17" (J278A)
EX $400 **NM** $800 **MIP** $1600

(Ron Smith)

Edsel Convertible/Sedan, 1958, friction, Haji, 10-1/2" (J86)
EX $200 **NM** $400 **MIP** $800

(Ron Smith)

Edsel Hardtop, 1958, friction, Asahi, 10-3/4" (J91)
EX $100 **NM** $200 **MIP** $350

(Ron Smith)

Edsel Station Wagon, 1958, friction, T.N., 11" (J89)
EX $150 **NM** $200 **MIP** $300

(Ron Smith)

Edsel Wagon, 1958, friction, Haji, 10-1/2" (J87)
EX $200 **NM** $300 **MIP** $400

Electrospecial No. 21, battery-op, "Y" Co., 10" (J290)
EX $300 **NM** $600 **MIP** $1200

Ferrari Berlinetta 250 LeMans, 1960s, Asahi Toy, 11", red, friction
EX $90 **NM** $125 **MIP** $200

(Ron Smith)

Ford, 1960, friction, Haji, 11" (J119)
EX $85 **NM** $150 **MIP** $265

(Ron Smith)

Ford Ambulance, 1955, friction, Bandai, 12" (J98)
EX $150 **NM** $200 **MIP** $250

Ford Convertible, 1955, Haji, 6-1/2", two-tone blue or red/white, friction
EX $50 **NM** $75 **MIP** $125

(Ron Smith)

Ford Convertible, 1955, friction, Bandai, 12" (J100)
EX $200 **NM** $400 **MIP** $600

(Ron Smith)

Ford Convertible, 1956, friction, Haji, 11-1/2" (J102)
EX $400 **NM** $600 **MIP** $1100

Ford Convertible, 1957, HTC, 12", orange/pink, friction
EX $115 **NM** $225 **MIP** $300

(Ron Smith)

Ford Country Sedan, 1961, friction, Bandai, 10-1/2" (J120)
EX $100 **NM** $160 **MIP** $225

(Ron Smith)

Ford Country Sedan, 1962, friction, Asahi, 12" (J121)
EX $200 **NM** $350 **MIP** $800

Ford Country Squire Wagon, 1965, 9", white, friction
EX $30 **NM** $70 **MIP** $100

Ford Fairlane 500 HT, 1957, ToyMaster, 9-1/2", green/yellow, friction
EX $30 **NM** $60 **MIP** $90

Ford Fairlane Hardtop/Convertible, 1958, friction, Sankei Gangu, 9" (J114)
EX $125 **NM** $250 **MIP** $400

(Ron Smith)

Ford Fairlane Sedan, 1957, friction, Ichiko, 10" (J105)
EX $100 **NM** $200 **MIP** $300

Ford Falcon, 1960s, Marusan, 9", red/white, friction
EX $20 **NM** $40 **MIP** $90

Ford Fire Chief Car, 1963, Taiyo, 12-1/2", red, battery-operated
EX $23 **NM** $55 **MIP** $75

(Ron Smith)

Ford Galaxie Hardtop, 1965, friction, MT, 11" (J125)
EX $150 **NM** $300 **MIP** $450

Ford Gyron, 1960, Ichida, red/black, friction
EX $45 **NM** $100 **MIP** $170

Ford Gyron, 1960, Ichida, 11", red/black, remote control, battery-operated
EX $100 **NM** $200 **MIP** $300

Ford Gyron, 1960, Ichida, 11", red/white, battery-operated
EX $135 **NM** $315 **MIP** $450

(Ron Smith)

Ford Hardtop, 1957, friction, T.N., 12" (J106)
EX $150 **NM** $300 **MIP** $400

(Ron Smith)

Ford Hardtop, 1964, friction, Ichiko, 13" (J122)
EX $200 **NM** $300 **MIP** $500

Ford HT Convertible, 1958, 9-1/2", blue/white, battery-operated
EX $85 **NM** $195 **MIP** $275

Ford HT Convertible, 1958, 11", orange/white, battery-operated
EX $60 **NM** $140 **MIP** $200

Ford HT Convertible, 1959, 11", blue/white, red/white, or green/white, battery-operated
EX $70 **NM** $160 **MIP** $225

Ford Model-T, 9", red, hard top, friction
EX $25 **NM** $50 **MIP** $85

Ford Model-T, 9", black, open top, friction
EX $25 **NM** $55 **MIP** $75

(Ron Smith)

Ford Mustang Fastback, 1965, friction, Bandai, 11" (J139)
EX $45 **NM** $65 **MIP** $90

(Ron Smith)

Ford Mustang Fastback, 1966, friction, T.N., 17" (J143)
EX $120 **NM** $200 **MIP** $300

Ford Mustang GT, 1965, 15-1/2", red, friction
EX $85 **NM** $195 **MIP** $275

(Ron Smith)

Ford Mustang Hardtop/Convertible, 1965, friction/battery-op, Bandai, 11" (J140)
EX $75 **NM** $125 **MIP** $150

(Ron Smith)

Ford Panel Truck, 1955, "Flowers," friction, Bandai, 12" (J99)
EX $200 **NM** $425 **MIP** $900

(Ron Smith)

Ford Pickup, 1955, friction, Bandai, 12" (J96)
EX $150 **NM** $300 **MIP** $400

(Ron Smith)

Ford Retractable, 1959, friction, T.N., 11" (J117)
EX $80 **NM** $100 **MIP** $150

(Ron Smith)

Ford Sedan, 1949, wind-up, Guntherman, 11" (J93)
EX $150 **NM** $300 **MIP** $400

Ford Sedan, 1951, 7", tan, battery-operated
EX $30 **NM** $70 **MIP** $100

(Ron Smith)

Ford Sedan, 1956, friction, Marusan, 13" (J103)
EX $1000 **NM** $2000 **MIP** $4000

(Ron Smith)

Ford Sedan/Convertible/Wagon/Pickup, 1957, friction, Joustra, 12" (J107)
EX $150 **NM** $200 **MIP** $275

(Ron Smith)

Ford Station Wagon, 1955, friction, Bandai, 12" (J97)
EX $150 **NM** $250 **MIP** $300

Ford Station Wagon, 1959, 10-1/2", green/white, friction
EX $40 **NM** $90 **MIP** $125

(Ron Smith)

Ford Station Wagon, 1959, friction, T.N., 12" (J116)
EX $100 **NM** $150 **MIP** $200

Ford Stock Car, 1963, Taiyo, 10-1/2", red/silver/blue, friction
EX $25 **NM** $60 **MIP** $85

Ford Taunus 17M, 1960s, friction, Bandai, 8" (J145)
EX $40 **NM** $60 **MIP** $90

Ford Thunderbird, 1955, friction, Bandai, 7" (J126A)
EX $60 **NM** $90 **MIP** $120

(Ron Smith)

Ford Thunderbird, 1956, battery-op, T.N., 11" (J129)
EX $200 **NM** $300 **MIP** $400

(Ron Smith)

Ford Thunderbird, 1956, friction, T.N., 11" (J127)
EX $200 **NM** $300 **MIP** $400

(Ron Smith)

Ford Thunderbird, 1963, battery-op, Yonezawa, 11" (J134)
EX $80 **NM** $150 **MIP** $200

Ford Thunderbird Convertible, 1955, 8", orange, friction
EX $45 **NM** $100 **MIP** $140

(Ron Smith)

Ford Thunderbird Hardtop, 1964, friction, Asahi, 12" (J136)
EX $150 **NM** $200 **MIP** $400

(Ron Smith)

Ford Thunderbird Hardtop, 1965, friction, Bandai, 10-3/4" (J138)
EX $60 **NM** $90 **MIP** $180

Ford Thunderbird HT Convertible, 1962, Yonezawa, 11-1/2", red, battery-operated
EX $105 **NM** $245 **MIP** $350

(Ron Smith)

Ford Thunderbird HT Convertible, 1964, Ichiko, 15-1/2", red, working side windows, friction
EX $120 **NM** $280 **MIP** $400

(Ron Smith)

Ford Thunderbird Retractable, 1963, battery-op, Yonezawa, 11" (J134)
EX $80 **NM** $150 **MIP** $200

(Ron Smith)

Ford Torino, 1968, friction, S.T., 16" (J126)
EX $200 **NM** $350 **MIP** $800

Ford Two-Door HT, 1956, Ichiko, 10", two-tone blue or orange/white, friction
EX $165 **NM** $385 **MIP** $550

Ford Two-Door Sedan, 1956, Marusan, 13", orange/white or blue/white
EX $1000 **NM** $2450 **MIP** $3500

(Ron Smith)

Ford Wagon, 1956, friction, Nomura, 10-1/2" (J104)
EX $125 **NM** $225 **MIP** $300

Ford Yellow Cab, 1952, Marusan, 10-1/2", yellow, friction, working money meter
EX $165 **NM** $385 **MIP** $500

Futuristic Buick LeSabre, 1951, Yonezawa, 7-1/2", black, friction
EX $240 **NM** $560 **MIP** $800

GM Gas Turbine Firebird II, 1956, Asahi, 8-1/2", red, friction (J281)
EX $125 **NM** $200 **MIP** $400

Jaguar XKE Convertible, 1950s, Tomiyama, 12", white, friction
EX $200 **NM** $350 **MIP** $475

Jaguar XKE Convertible, 1960s, friction, T.T., 10-1/2" (J155)
EX $75 **NM** $150 **MIP** $250

Jaguar XKE Coupe, 1960s, 10-1/2", red, friction
EX $50 **NM** $75 **MIP** $120

Jeep Station Wagon, 1950s, Yonezawa, 7-1/2", two-tone brown, friction
EX $100 **NM** $210 **MIP** $300

Kaiser Darren Convertible, 1950s, 6-1/2", red, friction
EX $30 **NM** $70 **MIP** $100

(Ron Smith)

Lincoln, 1956, friction, Ichiko, 16-1/2" (J165)
EX $150 **NM** $300 **MIP** $450

(Ron Smith)

Lincoln, 1964, friction, unknown manufacturer, 10-1/2" (J169)
EX $90 **NM** $175 **MIP** $275

(Ron Smith)

Lincoln Continental Mark II, 1956, friction, Linemar, 12" (J164)
EX $600 **NM** $1200 **MIP** $2500

(Ron Smith)

Lincoln Continental Mark III Convertible, 1959, friction, Bandai, 12" (J166)
EX $90 **NM** $125 **MIP** $250

(Ron Smith)

Lincoln Continental Mark III Sedan, 1959, friction, Bandai, 12" (J167)
EX $90 **NM** $125 **MIP** $175

(Ron Smith)

Lincoln Hardtop/Convertible, 1960, friction, Yonezawa, 11" (J168)
EX $100 **NM** $150 **MIP** $300

Lincoln Premiere Two-Door HT, 1956, 7-1/2", orange, friction
EX $30 **NM** $70 **MIP** $90

(Ron Smith)

Lincoln Sedan, 1955, friction, Yonezawa, 12" (J163)
EX $400 **NM** $800 **MIP** $1600

(Ron Smith)

Mazda Auto Tricycle, 1950s, friction, Bandai, 8" (J274)
EX $100 **NM** $200 **MIP** $400

Mercedes 220-S, 1961, 12", black, jack-up feature, friction
EX $75 **NM** $175 **MIP** $250

Mercedes 300 SL Coupe, 1955, 9", metallic red, opening gull-wing doors, battery-operated
EX $105 **NM** $245 **MIP** $350

Mercedes Convertible, 1950s, Alps, 9", red, friction
EX $105 **NM** $245 **MIP** $350

Mercedes Convertible, 1960s, HTC, 8", red, opening door w/swing-out driver, friction
EX $45 **NM** $105 **MIP** $150

(Ron Smith)

Mercedes-Benz 219 Convertible, 1960s, friction, Bandai, 8" (J177)
EX $50 **NM** $90 **MIP** $150

(Ron Smith)

Mercedes-Benz 219 Sedan, 1960s, friction, Bandai, 8" (J176)
EX $50 **NM** $80 **MIP** $150

(Ron Smith)

Mercury Cougar Hardtop, 1967, friction, Asakusa Toys, 15" (J197)
EX $200 **NM** $400 **MIP** $800

(Ron Smith)

Mercury Hardtop, 1956, friction, Alps, 9-1/2" (J193)
EX $600 **NM** $1500 **MIP** $3000

(Ron Smith)

Mercury Hardtop, 1958, friction, Yonezawa, 11-1/2" (J195)
EX $250 **NM** $325 **MIP** $400

Midget Special No. 6, friction, "Y" Co., 7" (J291)
EX $100 **NM** $200 **MIP** $350

Oldsmobile, 1952, friction, "Y" Co., 11" (J207A)
EX $150 **NM** $350 **MIP** $500

Oldsmobile, 1958, Asahi Toy, 12", gold/black, friction
EX $540 **NM** $1260 **MIP** $1800

(Ron Smith)

Oldsmobile Convertible/Sedan/Wagon, 1961, friction, Yonezawa, 12" (J214)
EX $100 **NM** $200 **MIP** $300

Oldsmobile Highway Patrol Car, 1959, Ichiko, 12-1/2", black/white, friction, working speed meter on trunk
EX $75 **NM** $175 **MIP** $250

Oldsmobile Rally Car, 1961, Asahi Toy, 15", red, friction
EX $55 **NM** $125 **MIP** $175

(Ron Smith)

Oldsmobile Sedan, 1956, friction, Ichiko/Kanto, 10-1/2" (J208)
EX $200 **NM** $400 **MIP** $900

(Ron Smith)

Oldsmobile Sedan, 1958, friction, A.T.C., 12" (J210)
EX $200 **NM** $300 **MIP** $600

Oldsmobile Station Wagon, 1958, 7-1/2", red/black, friction
EX $30 **NM** $60 **MIP** $90

Oldsmobile Super 88, 1956, Modern Toys, 14", orange, battery-operated, working headlights and signal lights
EX $200 **NM** $400 **MIP** $600

(Ron Smith)

Oldsmobile Super 88 Sedan, 1956, friction, Masudaya, 16" (J209)
EX $150 **NM** $250 **MIP** $400

(Ron Smith)

Oldsmobile Toronado, 1966, battery-op, Bandai, 11" (J215)
EX $65 **NM** $110 **MIP** $150

(Ron Smith)

Oldsmobile Toronado, 1968, friction, Ichiko, 17-1/2" (J216)
EX $200 **NM** $300 **MIP** $400

(Ron Smith)

Oldsmobile Two-Door HT, 1959, Ichiko, 12-1/2", two-tone blue, two-tone green, or brown/white, friction
EX $135 **NM** $315 **MIP** $450

Packard Convertible/Sedan, 1953, friction, Alps, 16" (J222)
EX $500 **NM** $800 **MIP** $1800

(Ron Smith)

Packard Hawk Convertible, 1957, battery-op, Schuco, 10-3/4" (J223)
EX $300 **NM** $400 **MIP** $800

Plymouth Convertible, 1959, Asahi Toy, 11", red/white, friction
EX $330 **NM** $770 **MIP** $1100

(Ron Smith)

Plymouth Fury Hardtop, 1957, friction, "Y" Co., 11-1/2" (J226)
EX $300 **NM** $400 **MIP** $800

(Ron Smith)

Plymouth Fury/Sedan/Wagon/Conv., 1958, friction, Bandai, 8" (J227)
EX $75 **NM** $90 **MIP** $165

(Ron Smith)

Plymouth Hardtop, 1956, battery-op, Alps, 12" (J225)
EX $300 **NM** $400 **MIP** $600

(Ron Smith)

Plymouth Hardtop, 1956, friction, unknown manufacturer, 8-1/2" (J224)
EX $80 **NM** $120 **MIP** $180

(Ron Smith)

Plymouth Hardtop, 1959, friction, A.T.C., 10-1/2" (J228)
EX $200 **NM** $400 **MIP** $600

Plymouth HT, 1956, Alps, 8-1/2", two-tone green, friction
EX $165 **NM** $385 **MIP** $550

(Ron Smith)

Plymouth Sedan, 1961, friction, Ichiko, 12" (J230)
EX $150 **NM** $300 **MIP** $600

(Ron Smith)

Plymouth Station Wagon, 1961, friction, Ichiko, 12" (J231)
EX $150 **NM** $250 **MIP** $500

(Ron Smith)

Plymouth T.V. Car, 1961, battery-op, Ichiko, 12" (J232)
EX $100 **NM** $300 **MIP** $600

(Ron Smith)

Pontiac, 1954, friction, Minister, 11" (J218A)
EX $10 **NM** $20 **MIP** $30

(Ron Smith)

Pontiac Firebird, 1967, friction, Bandai, 10" (J220)
EX $30 **NM** $55 **MIP** $100

(Ron Smith)

Pontiac Firebird, 1967, friction, Akasura, 15-1/2" (J219)
EX $200 **NM** $400 **MIP** $900

Pontiac Four-Door HT, 1958, Asahi Toy, 8", green/pink, friction
EX $45 **NM** $105 **MIP** $150

Porsche 911 Rally, 1960s, 11", red, friction
EX $70 **NM** $160 **MIP** $225

Porsche 914 Rally, 1960s, Daiya, 9", blue, battery-operated
EX $25 **NM** $55 **MIP** $75

(Ron Smith)

Porsche Speedster, 1950s, battery-op, Distler, 10-1/2" (J235)
EX $200 **NM** $300 **MIP** $600

Porsche Speedster, 1950s, battery-op, Distler, 10-1/2" (J235)
EX $200 **NM** $300 **MIP** $600

(Ron Smith)

Rambler Rebel Station Wagon, 1960s, friction, Bandai, 12" (J240)
EX $60 **NM** $90 **MIP** $150

Renault, 1960, friction, Bandai, 7-1/2" (J241)
EX $60 **NM** $90 **MIP** $150

Rolls Royce, 1960, friction, T.N., 10-1/2" (J239)
EX $200 **NM** $300 **MIP** $500

(Ron Smith)

Rolls Royce Silver Coupe Convertible, 1960, friction, Bandai, 12" (J236)
EX $100 **NM** $150 **MIP** $300

(Ron Smith)

Rolls Royce Silver Sedan Coupe, 1960s, friction, Bandai, 12" (J237)
EX $100 **NM** $150 **MIP** $250

(Ron Smith)

Studebaker, 1954, friction, Yoshiya, 9" (J243)
EX $150 **NM** $225 **MIP** $450

(Ron Smith)

Studebaker Avanti, 1960s, friction, Bandai, 8" (J242)
EX $90 **NM** $150 **MIP** $250

Studebaker Coupe, 1953, 9", yellow, friction, working wipers
EX $45 **NM** $100 **MIP** $165

Studebaker Lark, 1950s, 5-1/2", blue, friction
EX $20 **NM** $45 **MIP** $65

(Ron Smith)

Volkswagen, 1960s, battery-op, Bandai, 11" (J264)
EX $75 **NM** $125 **MIP** $200

(Ron Smith)

Volkswagen Convertible, 1950, friction, T.N., 9-1/2" (J258)
EX $100 **NM** $200 **MIP** $375

(Ron Smith)

Volkswagen Convertible, 1960s, battery-op, Bandai, 11" (J260)
EX $110 **NM** $145 **MIP** $200

(Ron Smith)

Volkswagen Karmann-Ghia, 1960, friction, Bandai, 7" (J252), add $50 for convertible
EX $100 **NM** $150 **MIP** $300

Volkswagen Micro-Bus, 1960s, orange w/white top; 1960s (J256), 9-1/2", Model No. J256
EX $70 **NM** $150 **MIP** $300

(Ron Smith)

Volkswagen with or without Sun Roof, 1960s, friction, Bandai, 15" (J265)
EX $90 **NM** $120 **MIP** $250

Volvo, 1950s, 5-1/2", red, friction
EX $20 **NM** $38 **MIP** $55

Volvo, 1950s, wind-up, Sweden, 11" (J265A)
EX $600 **NM** $800 **MIP** $1200

Volvo PV-544, 1950s, HoKu, 7-1/2", black, friction
EX $100 **NM** $200 **MIP** $350

VW Convertible, 1950s, 9-1/2", dark blue, maroon, or light metallic blue, friction w/battery-operated engine light
EX $85 **NM** $195 **MIP** $275

VW Rabbit Rally Team Car, 1970s, Asahi Toy, 8", yellow, battery-operated
EX $20 **NM** $45 **MIP** $65

VW Sedan, 1950s, 7-1/2", gray, oval window, friction
EX $45 **NM** $105 **MIP** $150

Zephyr Deluxe Convertible, 1950s, 11", maroon/yellow/blue, friction
EX $120 **NM** $280 **MIP** $400

JOHNNY LIGHTNING TOPPER

'32 Roadster, 1969, Varied color body, rumble seat in back flips up. This model has missing windshield, common to play worn examples
EX $25 **NM** $60 **MIP** $150

A.J. Foyt Indy Special, 1970, blackwall tires
EX $40 **NM** $60 **MIP** $250

(KP Photo, Tom Michael collection)

Al Unser Indy Special, 1970, Chrome blue finish, Lightning number "2" decal, black wall tires
EX $100 **NM** $200 **MIP** $500

Baja, 1970
EX $45 **NM** $125 **MIP** $200

(KP Photo, Tom Michael collection)

Big Rig, 1971, Originally included add on extras called "Customs;" prices reflect fully accessorized car. Called the "Track Bac" in the 1970 Topper Toys catalog
EX $65 **NM** $150 **MIP** $275

Bubble, 1970, Jet Powered
EX $45 **NM** $75 **MIP** $150

(Photo courtesy Dennis Seleman)

Bug Bomb, 1970, Various chromed color schemes, two silver engines, blackwall tires. This example is missing the rear engine
EX $40 **NM** $90 **MIP** $240

Condor, 1970, blackwall tires
EX $150 **NM** $200 **MIP** $1200

Custom Camaro, 1968-69, Prototype, only one known to exist
EX n/a **NM** $6000 **MIP** n/a

Custom Charger, 1968-69, Prototype, only one known to exist. A Version of this car was released by Playing Mantis as part of the "Lost Toppers" series
EX n/a **NM** $6000 **MIP** n/a

Custom Continental, 1968-69, Prototype, only six known to exist. Another casting re-released by Playing Mantis
EX n/a **NM** $4000 **MIP** n/a

Custom Dragster, 1969, Without canopy
EX $35 **NM** $75 **MIP** $125

Custom Dragster, 1969, Mirror finish
EX $150 **NM** $250 **MIP** $1000

Custom Dragster, 1969, Version with a plastic canopy, Topper-style redlines wheels, unpainted base. While versions were made without a canopy, the example here is simply missing one
EX $60 **NM** $150 **MIP** $200

Custom El Camino, 1969, With sealed doors
EX $110 **NM** $300 **MIP** $550

(Photo courtesy Dennis Seleman)

Custom El Camino, 1969, With opening doors, surfboards on back, Topper-style redlines wheels
EX $150 **NM** $275 **MIP** $475

Custom El Camino, 1969, Mirror finish
EX $200 **NM** $350 **MIP** $1125

Custom Eldorado, 1969, With sealed doors
EX $200 **NM** $450 **MIP** $1000

Custom Eldorado, 1969, With opening doors
EX $150 **NM** $275 **MIP** $350

Custom Ferrari, 1969, With opening doors, mirror finish
EX $300 **NM** $450 **MIP** $1000

Custom Ferrari, 1969, With sealed doors
EX $40 **NM** $80 **MIP** $130

Custom Ferrari, 1969, With opening doors
EX $150 **NM** $275 **MIP** $500

Custom GTO, 1969, Mirror finish
EX $200 **NM** $475 **MIP** $1200

Custom GTO, 1969, With sealed doors
EX $200 **NM** $450 **MIP** $1700

Custom GTO, 1969, With opening doors
EX $200 **NM** $450 **MIP** $1500

Custom Mako Shark, 1969, With sealed doors
EX $40 **NM** $75 **MIP** $225

(Photo Courtesy Dennis Seleman)

Custom Mako Shark, 1969, With opening doors, mirror finish
EX $200 **NM** $500 **MIP** $2000

Custom Mako Shark, 1969, With opening doors
EX $125 **NM** $350 **MIP** $500

Custom Mustang, 1968-69, Prototype, only one known to exist
EX n/a **NM** $6000 **MIP** n/a

Custom Spoiler, 1970, Blackwall tires
EX $35 **NM** $75 **MIP** $160

Custom T-Bird, 1969, With opening doors
EX $100 **NM** $250 **MIP** $475

Custom T-Bird, 1969, Mirror finish
EX $200 **NM** $450 **MIP** $5000

Custom T-Bird, 1969, With sealed doors
EX $150 **NM** $300 **MIP** $700

Custom Toronado, 1969, With opening doors
EX $225 **NM** $400 **MIP** $1000

Custom Toronado, 1969, Mirror finish
EX $450 **NM** $650 **MIP** $2000

Custom Toronado, 1969, With sealed doors
EX $300 **NM** $500 **MIP** $1500

Custom Turbine, 1969, Red, black, white painted interior
EX $50 **NM** $150 **MIP** $200

(KP Photo, Tom Michael collection)

Custom Turbine, 1969, With unpainted interior, Topper redline-style wheels
EX $30 **NM** $60 **MIP** $125

Custom Turbine, 1969, Mirror finish
EX $150 **NM** $225 **MIP** $550

Custom XKE, 1969, With opening doors, mirror finish
EX $300 **NM** $450 **MIP** $800

(KP Photo, Tom Michael collection)

Custom XKE, 1969, With sealed doors, unpainted base, full window plastic all-around, opening hood, blackwalls tires
EX $35 **NM** $80 **MIP** $110

(KP Photo, Tom Michael collection)

Custom XKE, 1969, With opening doors, unpainted base, opening hood, blackwalls tires
EX $150 **NM** $275 **MIP** $500

Double Trouble, 1970, Blackwall tires
EX $75 **NM** $180 **MIP** $1500

Flame Out, 1970, Blackwall tires
EX $60 **NM** $150 **MIP** $350

Flying Needle, 1970, Jet Powered
EX $45 **NM** $125 **MIP** $225

Frantic Ferrari, 1970, Unpainted base, silver exposed engine, various finishes
EX $35 **NM** $55 **MIP** $110

Glasser, 1970, Jet Powered
EX $40 **NM** $85 **MIP** $150

Hairy Hauler, 1971, Came with add-on extras called "Customs;" prices reflect fully accessorized cars
EX $65 **NM** $150 **MIP** $275

Jumpin' Jag, 1970, Blackwall tires
EX $35 **NM** $80 **MIP** $175

Leapin' Limo, 1970, Blackwall tires, large silver and black plastic engine. Example here shows Topper packaging, duplicated to an extent by Playing Mantis with the Commemorative series
EX $50 **NM** $125 **MIP** $400

Mad Maverick, 1970, Blackwall tires
EX $75 **NM** $150 **MIP** $450

Monster, 1970, Jet Powered
EX $40 **NM** $74 **MIP** $150

Movin' Van, 1970, Blackwall tires
EX $35 **NM** $65 **MIP** $90

(KP Photo, Tom Michael collection)

Nucleon, 1970, Blackwall tires
EX $40 **NM** $85 **MIP** $220

Parnelli Jones Indy Special, 1970, Blackwall tires
EX $40 **NM** $85 **MIP** $250

Pipe Dream, 1971, Came with add-on extras called "Customs;" prices reflect fully accessorized cars
EX $65 **NM** $150 **MIP** $275

(KP Photo, Tom Michael collection)

Sand Stormer, 1970, Blackwall tires
EX $25 **NM** $45 **MIP** $100

Sand Stormer, 1970, Black roof, blackwall tires
EX $50 **NM** $100 **MIP** $200

Screamer, 1970, Jet Powered
EX $45 **NM** $75 **MIP** $200

Sling Shot, 1970, Blackwall tires
EX $50 **NM** $95 **MIP** $250

Smuggler, 1970, Blackwall tires
EX $35 **NM** $75 **MIP** $150

Stiletto, 1970, Blackwall tires, various paint schemes. The example shown is pretty rough. The casting was re-released by Playing Mantis as part of the "Topper Series"
EX $60 **NM** $85 **MIP** $300

TNT, 1970, Blackwall tires
EX $40 **NM** $75 **MIP** $175

Triple Threat, 1970, Blackwall tires
EX $40 **NM** $90 **MIP** $200

Twin Blaster, 1971, Came with add-on extras called "Customs;" prices reflect fully accessorized cars
EX $65 **NM** $150 **MIP** $275

Vicious Vette, 1970, Blackwall tires
EX $35 **NM** $80 **MIP** $225

Vulture w/wing, 1970, Blackwall tires
EX $75 **NM** $130 **MIP** $500

Wasp, 1970, Blackwall tires
EX $80 **NM** $100 **MIP** $400

Wedge, 1970, Jet Powered
EX $45 **NM** $75 **MIP** $200

Whistler, 1970, Blackwall tires
EX $75 **NM** $125 **MIP** $300

Wild Winner, 1971, Came w/add on extras called "Customs;" prices reflect fully accessorized cars
EX $60 **NM** $125 **MIP** $250

MARX

AIRPLANES

727 Riding Jet, jet engine sound
EX $150 **NM** $225 **MIP** $300

Airmail Biplane, four engines, tin wind-up, 18" wingspan, 1936
EX $225 **NM** $325 **MIP** $450

Airmail Monoplane, two engines, tin wind-up, 1930
EX $100 **NM** $150 **MIP** $225

Airplane, mail biplane, tin wind-up, 9-3/4" wingspan, 1926
EX $150 **NM** $225 **MIP** $300

Airplane, monoplane, pressed steel, 9" wingspan, 1942
EX $110 **NM** $165 **MIP** $300

Airplane, no engines, tin wind-up, 9-1/2" wingspan
EX $135 **NM** $200 **MIP** $300

Airplane, two propellers, tin wind-up, 9 7/8" wingspan, 1927
EX $200 **NM** $300 **MIP** $400

Airplane, tin wind-up, 9-1/4" wingspan, 1926
EX $150 **NM** $225 **MIP** $300

Airplane, adjustable rudder, tin wind-up, 10" wingspan, 1926
EX $150 **NM** $225 **MIP** $300

Airplane, monoplane, adjustable rudder, tin wind-up, 9-1/4" wingspan
EX $150 **NM** $225 **MIP** $300

Airplane, medium fuselage, tin wind-up
EX $125 **NM** $150 **MIP** $250

Airplane, light fuselage, tin wind-up
EX $125 **NM** $175 **MIP** $250

Airplane, twin engine, tin wind-up, 9-1/2" wingspan
EX $100 **NM** $150 **MIP** $200

Airplane #90, tin wind-up, 5" wingspan, 1930
EX $240 **NM** $360 **MIP** $480

Airplane with Parachute, monoplane, tin wind-up, 13" wingspan, 1929
EX $115 **NM** $170 **MIP** $325

Air-Sea Power Bombing Set, 12" wingspan; 1940s
EX $325 **NM** $450 **MIP** $650

Airways Express Plane, tin wind-up, 13" wingspan, 1929
EX $200 **NM** $300 **MIP** $400

American Airlines Airplane, passenger plane, tin wind-up, 15" long, 16-1/2" wingspan, 1940
EX $130 **NM** $190 **MIP** $400

American Airlines Flagship, pressed steel, wood wheels, 27" wingspan, 1940
EX $170 **NM** $270 **MIP** $500

Army Airplane, biplane, tin wind-up, 25-3/4" wingspan, 1930
EX $225 **NM** $340 **MIP** $450

Army Airplane, 18" wingspan; 1951
EX $150 **NM** $225 **MIP** $300

Army Airplane, two engines, tin wind-up, 18" wingspan, 1938
EX $125 **NM** $190 **MIP** $250

Army Airplane, tin, mechanical fighter, 7" wingspan
EX $125 **NM** $170 **MIP** $230

Army Bomber, two engines, tin wind-up, 18" wingspan; 1940s
EX $250 **NM** $375 **MIP** $500

Army Bomber, monoplane, litho machine gun and pilot, 25-1/2" wingspan, 1935
EX $300 **NM** $450 **MIP** $600

Army Bomber, tri-motor, 25-1/2" wingspan, 1935
EX $250 **NM** $375 **MIP** $500

Army Bomber with Bombs, camouflage pattern, metal, wind-up, 12" wingspan, 1930s
EX $100 **NM** $150 **MIP** $250

Army Fighter Plane, tin wind-up, 5" wingspan; 1940s
EX $100 **NM** $150 **MIP** $250

Autogyro, tin wind-up, 27" wingspan; 1940s
EX $150 **NM** $225 **MIP** $375

Blue and Silver Bomber, two engines, tin wind-up, 18" wingspan; 1940
EX $190 **NM** $280 **MIP** $375

Bomber, four propellers, metal, wind-up, 14-1/2" wingspan
EX $100 **NM** $150 **MIP** $300

Bomber with Tricycle Landing Gear, four engine, tin wind-up, 18" wingspan; 1940
EX $225 **NM** $325 **MIP** $425

Camouflage Airplane, four engines, 18" wingspan, 1942
EX $125 **NM** $200 **MIP** $295

China Clipper, four engines, tin wind-up, 18-1/4" wingspan, 1938
EX $100 **NM** $150 **MIP** $250

City Airport, extra tower and planes, 1930s
EX $125 **NM** $190 **MIP** $250

Crash-Proof Airplane, monoplane, tin wind-up, 11-3/4" wingspan, 1933
EX $100 **NM** $150 **MIP** $200

Cross Country Flyer, 19" tall, 1929
EX $375 **NM** $550 **MIP** $725

Dagwood's Solo Flight Airplane, wind-up, 9" wingspan, 1935
EX $200 **NM** $300 **MIP** $950

Daredevil Flyer, tin wind-up, 1929
EX $115 **NM** $170 **MIP** $325

Daredevil Flyer, Zeppelin-shaped, 1928
EX $225 **NM** $350 **MIP** $475

DC-3 Airplane, aluminum, wind-up, 9-1/2" wingspan, 1930s
EX $125 **NM** $190 **MIP** $300

Eagle Air Scout, monoplane, tin wind-up, 26-1/2" wingspan, 1929
EX $200 **NM** $300 **MIP** $400

Fighter Jet, USAF, battery-operated, 7" wingspan
EX $90 **NM** $135 **MIP** $250

Fighter Plane, battery-operated, remote controlled; 1950s
EX $90 **NM** $135 **MIP** $250

Fix All Helicopter
EX $275 **NM** $400 **MIP** $600

Flip-Over Airplane, tin wind-up
EX $200 **NM** $300 **MIP** $450

Floor Zeppelin, 9-1/2" long, 1931
EX $225 **NM** $340 **MIP** $500

Floor Zeppelin, 16-1/2" long, 1931
EX $350 **NM** $525 **MIP** $750

(RLM MacNary Collection)

Flying Fortress 2095, sparking, four engines; 1940
EX $150 **NM** $245 **MIP** $400

Flying Zeppelin, wind-up, 9" long, 1930
EX $225 **NM** $340 **MIP** $475

Flying Zeppelin, wind-up, 17" long, 1930
EX $350 **NM** $525 **MIP** $750

Flying Zeppelin, wind-up, 10" long
EX $275 **NM** $400 **MIP** $600

Four-Motor Transport Plane, friction, tin litho
EX $120 **NM** $180 **MIP** $325

Golden Tricky Airplane
EX $75 **NM** $115 **MIP** $225

Hangar with One Plane, 1940s
EX $150 **NM** $225 **MIP** $500

International Airline Express, monoplane, tin wind-up, 17-1/2" wingspan, 1931
EX $200 **NM** $300 **MIP** $425

Jet Plane, friction, 6" wingspan; 1950s
EX $65 **NM** $90 **MIP** $195

Little Lindy Airplane, friction, 2-1/4" wingspan, 1930
EX $200 **NM** $300 **MIP** $500

Looping Plane, silver version, tin wind-up, 7" wingspan; 1941
EX $225 **NM** $325 **MIP** $525

Lucky Stunt Flyer, tin wind-up, 6" long, 1928
EX $150 **NM** $225 **MIP** $350

Mammoth Zeppelin, 1st Mammoth, pull toy, 28" long, 1930
EX $400 **NM** $600 **MIP** $900

Mammoth Zeppelin, 2nd Mammoth, pull toy, 28" long, 1930
EX $375 **NM** $575 **MIP** $775

Municipal Airport Hangar, 1929
EX $100 **NM** $150 **MIP** $425

Overseas Biplane, three propellers, tin wind-up, 9-7/8" wingspan, 1928
EX $150 **NM** $275 **MIP** $395

PAA Clipper Plane, pressed steel, 27" wingspan; 1952
EX $125 **NM** $175 **MIP** $525

PAA Passenger Plane, tin litho, 14" wingspan; 1950s
EX $120 **NM** $175 **MIP** $275

Pan American, pressed steel, four motors, 27" wingspan; 1940
EX $90 **NM** $150 **MIP** $525

Piggy Back Plane, tin wind-up, 9" wingspan, 1939
EX $100 **NM** $150 **MIP** $350

Pioneer Air Express Monoplane, tin litho, pull toy, 25-1/2" wingspan
EX $150 **NM** $300 **MIP** $400

Popeye Flyer, Popeye and Olive Oyl in plane, tin litho tower, wind-up, 1936
EX $475 **NM** $700 **MIP** $1250

Popeye Flyer, Wimpy and Swee'Pea litho on tower, 1936
EX $600 **NM** $900 **MIP** $1600

Pursuit Planes, one propeller, 8" wingspan, 1930s
EX $125 **NM** $200 **MIP** $300

Rollover Airplane, tin wind-up, forward and reverse, 6" wingspan; 1947
EX $200 **NM** $300 **MIP** $575

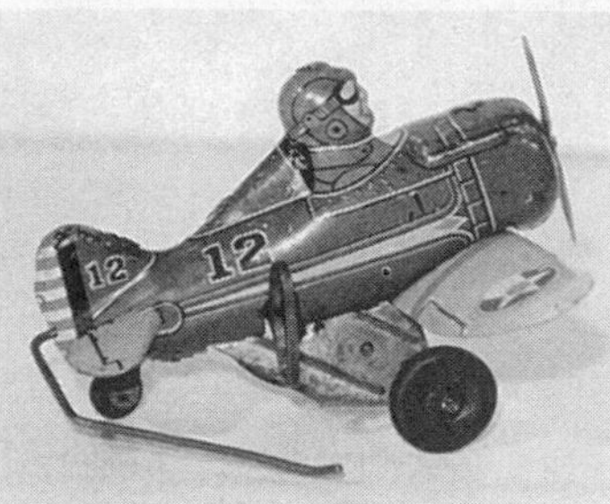

Rollover Airplane, tin wind-up, 1920s
EX $200 NM $300 MIP $575

Rookie Pilot, tin litho, wind-up, 7" long, 1930s
EX $225 NM $340 MIP $550

Seversky P-35, single-engine plane, 16" wingspan; 1940s
EX $125 NM $200 MIP $350

Sky Bird Flyer, two planes, 9-1/2" tower; 1947
EX $275 NM $400 MIP $550

Sky Cruiser Two-Motored Transport Plane, 18" wingspan; 1940s
EX $125 NM $175 MIP $325

Sky Flyer, biplane and Zeppelin, 8-1/2" tall tower, 1927
EX $225 NM $340 MIP $450

Sky Flyer, 9" tall tower, 1937
EX $150 NM $225 MIP $375

Spirit of America, monoplane, tin wind-up, 17-1/2" wingspan, 1930
EX $325 NM $500 MIP $650

Spirit of St. Louis, tin wind-up, 9-1/4" wingspan, 1929
EX $150 NM $225 MIP $595

Stunt Pilot, tin wind-up
EX $175 NM $250 MIP $425

Tower Flyers, 1926
EX $175 NM $250 MIP $350

TP-816 USAF, twin engine, tin, made in Japan, 3-3/4" wingspan; 1960s
EX $5 NM $10 MIP $15

Trans-Atlantic Zeppelin, wind-up, 10" long, 1930
EX $225 NM $350 MIP $450

TWA Boeing Super Jet, four-engine, 18" wingspan
EX $225 NM $350 MIP $450

U.S. Marines Plane, monoplane, tin wind-up, 17-7/8" wingspan, 1930
EX $200 NM $300 MIP $400

Zeppelin, friction pull toy, steel, 6" long
EX $100 NM $200 MIP $250

Zeppelin, flies in circles, wind-up, 17" long, 1930
EX $350 NM $525 MIP $700

Zeppelin, all metal, pull toy, 28" long, 1929
EX $400 NM $600 MIP $800

BOATS AND SHIPS

Battleship USS Washington, friction, 14" long; 1950s
EX $50 NM $75 MIP $225

Caribbean Luxury Liner, sparkling, friction, 15" long
EX $50 NM $75 MIP $225

Luxury Liner Boat, tin, friction
EX $100 NM $150 MIP $250

Mosquito Fleet Putt Putt Boat
EX $40 NM $55 MIP $95

River Queen Paddle Wheel Station, plastic
EX $50 NM $75 MIP $150

Sparkling Warship, tin friction motor, 14" long
EX $50 NM $75 MIP $195

Tugboat, plastic, battery-operated, 6" long; 1966
EX $50 NM $75 MIP $195

BUSES

American Van Lines Bus, cream and red, tin wind-up, 13-1/2" long
EX $65 NM $100 MIP $130

Blue Line Tours Bus, tin litho, wind-up, 9-1/2" long, 1930s
EX $150 NM $225 MIP $425

(RLM MacNary Collection)

Bus, red, 4" long; 1940
EX $35 NM $50 MIP $95

(RLM MacNary Collection)

Coast to Coast Bus, tin litho, wind-up, 10" long, 1930s
EX $125 NM $200 MIP $325

Greyhound Bus, tin litho, wind-up, 6" long, 1930s
EX $100 NM $150 MIP $200

Inter-City Bus Lines, 5"; plastic, name in raised letters on roof, friction motor, 1950s
EX $15 NM $25 MIP n/a

Liberty Bus, tin litho, wind-up, 5" long, 1931
EX $75 NM $125 MIP $200

Mystery Speedway Bus, tin litho, wind-up, 14" long, 1938
EX $200 NM $300 MIP $550

Royal Bus Lines Bus, tin litho, wind-up, 10-1/4" long, 1930s
EX $135 NM $200 MIP $450

(David W Mapes Inc)

Royal Van Co. Truck "We Haul Anywhere", tin wind-up, 9" long, 1920s-30's
EX $140 NM $225 MIP $500

School Bus, steel body, wooden wheels, pull toy, 11-1/2" long
EX $125 NM $200 MIP $325

Tricky Action Greyhound Bus, 6" long; plastic, battery-operated
EX $10 NM $20 MIP $30

CARS

American Express Dragster, white plastic with decals, "American Express" on sides, popped engine and pipes, 1970s
EX $8 NM $12 MIP $18

Anti-Aircraft Gun on Car, 5-1/4" long
EX $50 NM $75 MIP $225

Archie Jalopy, No. 9009HK, yellow and orange plastic convertible, "Riverdale High" sticker on doors, made in Hong Kong, accessory for "Archies" plastic figures; 1975
EX $15 NM $30 MIP $45

Army Car, battery-operated
EX $65 NM $100 MIP $200

Army Staff Car, w/flasher and siren, tin wind-up, 11" long; 1940s
EX $75 NM $125 MIP $400

Army Staff Car, litho steel, tin wind-up, 1930s
EX $125 NM $200 MIP $425

Astro Buggy, 9-1/4" long; Johnny and Jane Apollo vehicle, oversize balloon tries, green-tinted windows; 1968
EX $8 NM $17 MIP $25

Automatic Brake Car, plastic w/tin litho base, 8-1/2" long
EX $20 NM $30 MIP $60

Big Lizzie Car, tin wind-up, 7-1/4" long, 1930s
EX $75 NM $125 MIP $235

(Bill Bertoia Auctions)

Blondie's Jalopy, tin litho, 16" long; 1941
EX $325 **NM** $500 **MIP** $850

Boat Tail Racer #2, litho, 13" long; 1948
EX $125 **NM** $200 **MIP** $425

Boat Tail Racer #3, tin wind-up, 5" long, 1930s
EX $40 **NM** $55 **MIP** $200

Bouncing Benny Car, pull toy, 7" long, foam-rubber balloon tires, 1939
EX $325 **NM** $500 **MIP** $750

Bumper Auto, large bumpers front and rear, tin wind-up, 1939
EX $60 **NM** $100 **MIP** $225

Cadillac, Mini-Marx Blazers die-cast series; 1968
EX $3 **NM** $7 **MIP** $10

Cadillac Coupe, trunk w/tools on luggage carrier, tin wind-up, 11" long, 1931
EX $200 **NM** $300 **MIP** $525

Cadillac Coupe, 8-1/2" long, 1931
EX $175 **NM** $275 **MIP** $400

Camera Car, heavy gauge steel car, 9-1/2" long, 1939
EX $850 **NM** $1300 **MIP** $1900

Careful Johnnie, plastic driver, 6-1/2" long; 1950s
EX $100 **NM** $150 **MIP** $350

Chaparral, Mini-Marx Blazers die-cast series, 1968
EX $5 **NM** $10 **MIP** $15

Charlie McCarthy "Benzine Buggy" Car, w/red wheels, tin wind-up, 7" long, 1938
EX $600 **NM** $900 **MIP** $1450

(Bill Bertoia Auctions)

Charlie McCarthy "Benzine Buggy" Car, w/white wheels, tin wind-up, 7" long, 1938
EX $450 **NM** $625 **MIP** $950

(Bill Bertoia Auctions)

Charlie McCarthy and Mortimer Snerd Private Car, tin wind-up, 16" long, 1939
EX $600 **NM** $900 **MIP** $1500

Charlie McCarthy Private Car, wind-up, 1935
EX $1450 **NM** $2200 **MIP** $3500

Chrome Racer, miniature racer, 5" long, 1937
EX $85 **NM** $125 **MIP** $250

Convertible Roadster, nickel-plated tin, 11" long, 1930s
EX $175 **NM** $275 **MIP** $395

(Don Hultzmann)

Coo Coo Car, 8" long, tin wind-up, 1931
EX $375 **NM** $575 **MIP** $825

Coupe, 20" long; tin-litho includes images of driver and dog, 1950s
EX $70 **NM** $90 **MIP** $125

Crazy Dan Car, tin wind-up, 6" long, 1930s
EX $140 **NM** $225 **MIP** $395

Dagwood the Driver, 8" long, tin wind-up; 1941
EX $200 **NM** $300 **MIP** $900

Dan Dipsy Car, nodder, tin wind-up, 5-3/4" long; 1950s
EX $250 **NM** $375 **MIP** $450

Dick Tracy Police Car, 9" long
EX $80 **NM** $200 **MIP** $350

Dick Tracy Police Station Riot Car, friction, sparkling, 7-1/2" long; 1946
EX $60 **NM** $120 **MIP** $375

Dick Tracy Squad Car, battery-operated, tin litho, 11-1/4" long; 1949
EX $170 **NM** $275 **MIP** $475

Dick Tracy Squad Car, yellow flashing light, tin litho, wind-up, 11" long; 1940s
EX $250 **NM** $375 **MIP** $525

(The Toy Collector News)

Dick Tracy Squad Car, friction, 20" long; 1948
EX $125 **NM** $170 **MIP** $300

Dippy Dumper, Brutus or Popeye, celluloid figure, tin wind-up, 9", 1930s
EX $350 **NM** $525 **MIP** $900

Disney Parade Roadster, tin litho, wind-up; 1950s
EX $100 **NM** $150 **MIP** $900

Donald Duck Disney Dipsy Car, plastic Donald, tin wind-up, 5-3/4" long; 1953
EX $425 **NM** $650 **MIP** $895

Donald Duck Go-Kart, plastic and metal, friction, rubber tires; 1960s
EX $75 **NM** $130 **MIP** $325

Donald the Driver, plastic Donald, tin car, wind-up, 6-1/2" long; 1950s
EX $200 **NM** $300 **MIP** $595

Dora Dipsy Car, nodder, tin wind-up, 5-3/4" long; 1953
EX $400 **NM** $600 **MIP** $725

Dottie the Driver, nodder, tin wind-up, 6-1/2" long; 1950s
EX $150 **NM** $225 **MIP** $450

Driver Training Car, tin wind-up; 1950s, "Safe Driving School"
EX $80 **NM** $120 **MIP** $225

(Bill Bertoia Auctions)

Drive-Up Self Car, turns left, right or straight; 1940
EX $100 **NM** $150 **MIP** $225

Electric Convertible, tin and plastic, 20" long
EX $65 **NM** $100 **MIP** $295

Falcon Coupe, 9-1/2" long; tin-litho sports car body, plastic roof/windshield, black rubber tires
EX $85 **NM** $190 **MIP** $250

Ford GT, 8" long; white plastic, clear plastic windows, chrome-hub tires, #7 on hood
EX $3 **NM** $8 **MIP** $12

Ford GT, 2-1/2" long; Mini-Marx Blazers die-cast series; 1968
EX $3 **NM** $7 **MIP** $10

Funny Fire Fighters, 7" long, tin wind-up; 1941
EX $800 **NM** $1200 **MIP** $1600

(Bill Bertoia Auctions)

Funny Flivver Car, tin litho, wind-up, 7" long, 1926
EX $275 **NM** $425 **MIP** $675

Gang Buster Car, tin wind-up, 14-1/2" long, 1938
EX $200 **NM** $300 **MIP** $800

Giant King Racer, dark blue, tin wind-up, 12-1/4" long, 1928
EX $250 **NM** $375 **MIP** $725

G-Man Pursuit Car, sparks, 14-1/2" long, 1935
EX $190 **NM** $285 **MIP** $750

Go-Go Car, 36" long, 14" wide; No. 4820, riding toy, plastic yellow body, opening trunk, "Go-Go Car" sticker on sides; 1968-69
EX $53 **NM** $110 **MIP** $160

Hot Rod, 24" long; red plastic T-Bucket w/exposed engines, whitewalls, engine noise, 1960s
EX $75 **NM** $100 **MIP** $180

Hot Rod #23, friction motor, tin, 8" long; 1967
EX $45 **NM** $75 **MIP** $90

Huckleberry Hound Car, friction
EX $125 **NM** $200 **MIP** $250

Hustler Racer, 7" long; pull-string action, made in Hong Kong, 1970s
EX $7 **NM** $14 **MIP** $25

Indy Racer, 1-3/4" long; plastic, black tires; 1960s
EX $3 **NM** $5 **MIP** $8

Instant Speedway Action Set, plastic track, hanging hook, die-cast car; 1968-69
EX $14 **NM** $20 **MIP** $45

International Agent Car, tin wind-up
EX $30 **NM** $55 **MIP** $125

International Agent Car, friction, tin litho; 1966
EX $60 **NM** $100 **MIP** $195

Jaguar, battery-operated, 13" long
EX $225 **NM** $325 **MIP** $450

Jaguar, 4"; plastic play set vehicle, no MIP price
EX $6 **NM** $12 **MIP** n/a

Jaguar, die-cast, "Mini-Marx," 1960s
EX $5 **NM** $12 **MIP** $20

Jaguar, 8" long; blue plastic, plastic driver, made in Hong Kong
EX $5 **NM** $10 **MIP** $15

Jalopy, tin driver, friction; 1950s
EX $125 **NM** $200 **MIP** $250

Jalopy Car, tin driver, motor sparks, crank, wind-up
EX $140 **NM** $225 **MIP** $280

Jalopy Hot Rod, 6" long; tin-litho jalopy w/psychedelic design on body, roof and hubcaps; no front fenders, 1960s
EX $25 **NM** $45 **MIP** $70

Jolly Joe Jeep, tin litho, 5-3/4" long; 1950s
EX $150 **NM** $225 **MIP** $375

Joy Riders Crazy Car, tin litho, wind-up, 8" long, 1928
EX $340 **NM** $500 **MIP** $675

Jumping Jeep, tin litho, 5-3/4" long; 1947
EX $150 **NM** $225 **MIP** $425

King Racer, yellow body, red trim, tin wind-up, 8-1/2" long, 1925
EX $375 **NM** $575 **MIP** $750

King Racer, yellow w/black outlines, 8-1/2" long, 1925
EX $250 **NM** $430 **MIP** $575

(Bill Bertoia Auctions)

Komical Kop, black car, tin litho, wind-up, 7-1/2" long, 1930s
EX $450 **NM** $675 **MIP** $900

Leaping Lizzie Car, tin wind-up, 7" long, 1927
EX $250 **NM** $375 **MIP** $500

Learn To Drive Car, wind-up
EX $110 **NM** $165 **MIP** $225

Lola Climax Racer, plastic, make in Hong Kong, 6-1/2" long; 1960s
EX $8 **NM** $12 **MIP** $18

Lola GT, Super Speed Blazers die-cast series, 1969
EX $4 **NM** $8 **MIP** $12

(Bill Bertoia Auctions)

Lonesome Pine Trailer and Convertible Sedan, 22" long, 1936
EX $375 **NM** $600 **MIP** $795

Machine Gun on Car, hand crank activation on gun, 3" long
EX $75 **NM** $130 **MIP** $225

Magic George and Car, litho; 1940s
EX $170 **NM** $250 **MIP** $350

Marx Mobile, 30" long; steel ride-on toy, battery-powered, white/red/blue with tailfins, red steering wheel; seat is trunk area
EX $125 **NM** $250 **MIP** $325

Mechanical Speed Racer, tin wind-up, 12" long; 1948
EX $125 **NM** $200 **MIP** $275

Mechanical Speedway Racer, 4-1/2" long; red or blue plastic Porsche-type racer, metal key
EX $5 **NM** $17 **MIP** $25

Mercury, Mini-Marx Blazers die-cast series; 1968
EX $3 **NM** $7 **MIP** $10

Mickey Mouse Disney Dipsy Car, plastic Mickey, tin wind-up, 5-3/4" long; 1953
EX $425 **NM** $655 **MIP** $875

Mickey the Driver, plastic Mickey, tin car, wind-up, 6-1/2" long; 1950s
EX $170 **NM** $250 **MIP** $450

(RLM MacNary Collection)

Midget Racer "Midget Special" #2, miniature car, clockwork-powered, 5" long, 1930s
EX $125 **NM** $200 **MIP** $250

(RLM MacNary Collection)

Midget Racer "Midget Special" #7, miniature car, tin wind-up, 5" long, 1930s
EX $125 **NM** $200 **MIP** $250

Milton Berle Crazy Car, tin litho, wind-up, 6" long; 1950s
EX $250 **NM** $375 **MIP** $595

Mini Marx Super Speed Car, various models, die-cast racing cars, late 1960s
EX $5 **NM** $10 **MIP** $15

Miniature Sports Cars, set of 8, 4" long, hard plastic with metal tires, five plastic service station attendants; 1950s
EX $20 **NM** $50 **MIP** $80

Mortimer Snerd's Tricky Auto, tin litho, wind-up, 7-1/2" long, 1939
EX $400 **NM** $600 **MIP** $750

Mystery Car, press down activation, 9" long, 1936
EX $125 **NM** $200 **MIP** $275

Mystery Taxi, press down activation, steel, 9" long, 1938
EX $160 **NM** $275 **MIP** $375

Nutty Mad Car, w/driver, battery-operated; 1960s
EX $100 **NM** $300 **MIP** $400

Nutty Mad Car, blue car w/goggled driver, friction, hard plastic; 1960s
EX $75 **NM** $130 **MIP** $200

Nutty Mad Car, red tin car, vinyl driver, friction, 4" long; 1960s
EX $100 **NM** $150 **MIP** $225

Old Jalopy, blue car w/yellow trim, college boys, hood reads "Queen of the Campus," tin wind-up, 8" long, 1930s
EX $300 **NM** $450 **MIP** $525

Old Jalopy, tin wind-up, driver, "Old Jalopy" on hood, 7" long; 1950
EX $75 **NM** $125 **MIP** $175

Parade Roadster, w/Disney characters, tin litho, wind-up, 11" long; 1950
EX $225 **NM** $325 **MIP** $900

Peter Rabbit Eccentric Car, tin wind-up, 5-1/2" long; 1950s
EX $250 **NM** $375 **MIP** $500

Plastic Racer, 6" long; 1948
EX $50 **NM** $75 **MIP** $150

Porsche, Mini-Marx Blazers series, 1968
EX $3 **NM** $7 **MIP** $10

Queen of the Campus, w/four college students' heads; 1950
EX $250 **NM** $400 **MIP** $525

Race 'N Road Speedway, HO scale racing set; 1950s
EX $60 **NM** $100 **MIP** $125

Racer #12, tin litho, wind-up, 16" long, 1942
EX $225 **NM** $325 **MIP** $625

(RLM MacNary Collection)

Racer #3, miniature car, tin wind-up, 5" long
EX $75 **NM** $125 **MIP** $195

(RLM MacNary Collection)

Racer #4, miniature car, tin wind-up, 5" long
EX $75 **NM** $125 **MIP** $195

(RLM MacNary Collection)

Racer #5, miniature car, tin wind-up, 5" long; 1948
EX $75 **NM** $125 **MIP** $195

Racer #61, miniature car, tin wind-up, 4-3/4" long, 1930
EX $75 **NM** $125 **MIP** $195

(RLM MacNary Collection)

Racer #7, miniature car, tin wind-up, 5" long; 1948
EX $75 **NM** $125 **MIP** $195

Racer with Plastic Driver, tin litho car, 16" long; 1950
EX $150 **NM** $225 **MIP** $375

Racing Car, two man team, tin litho, wind-up, 12" long; 1940
EX $125 **NM** $200 **MIP** $425

Racing Car, plastic driver, tin wind-up, 27" long; 1950
EX $100 **NM** $175 **MIP** $450

Roadster, 11-1/2" long; 1949
EX $100 **NM** $150 **MIP** $225

Roadster and Cannon Ball Keeper, wind-up, 9" long
EX $175 **NM** $250 **MIP** $350

Roadster Convertible with Trailer and Racer, mechanical; 1950
EX $125 **NM** $200 **MIP** $275

Rocket Racer, tin litho, 1935
EX $275 **NM** $425 **MIP** $550

Rocket-Shaped Racer #12, 1930s
EX $275 **NM** $425 **MIP** $600

Rolls-Royce, black plastic, friction, 6" long; 1955
EX $40 **NM** $60 **MIP** $80

Royal Coupe, tin litho, wind-up, 9" long, 1930
EX $175 **NM** $275 **MIP** $375

Scooting Tooting Button Hot Rod, 14" long; battery operated hot rod convertible with nine control levers in rumble seat; 1964-65
EX $28 **NM** $56 **MIP** $85

Secret Sam Agent 012 Car, tin litho, friction, 5" long; 1960s
EX $40 **NM** $65 **MIP** $165

Sedan, battery-operated, plastic, 9-1/2" long
EX $175 **NM** $275 **MIP** $350

Sheriff Sam and His Whoopee Car, plastic, tin wind-up, 5-3/4" long; 1949
EX $200 **NM** $300 **MIP** $475

Siren Police Car, 15" long, 1930s
EX $125 **NM** $200 **MIP** $395

Smokey Sam the Wild Fireman Car, 6-1/2" long; 1950
EX $125 **NM** $200 **MIP** $395

Smokey Stover Whoopee Car, 1940s
EX $175 **NM** $275 **MIP** $525

Snoopy Gus Wild Fireman, 7" long, 1926
EX $500 **NM** $750 **MIP** $1150

Space Car, gray plastic w/clear cockpit cover, 5-3/4" long, sold with play sets; 1950s
EX $30 **NM** $60 **MIP** $80

Sparkling Hot Rod, 7-1/4" long; plastic body, separate castings for driver, steering wheel and engine top, metal chassis, black rubber tires with metal hubs, "Marx Sparkling Hot Rod" cast above trunk, 1950s
EX $10 **NM** $25 **MIP** $35

Speed Cop, two 4" all tin wind-up cars, track, 1930s
EX $175 **NM** $275 **MIP** $795

Speed King Racer, tin litho, wind-up, 16" long, 1929
EX $325 **NM** $500 **MIP** $650

Speed Racer, 13" long, 1937
EX $250 **NM** $375 **MIP** $500

Speedway Coupe, tin wind-up, battery-operated headlights, 8" long, 1938
EX $200 **NM** $300 **MIP** $400

Speedway Set, two wind-up sedans, figure eight track, 1937
EX $250 **NM** $375 **MIP** $500

Sports Coupe, tin, 15" long, 1930s
EX $125 **NM** $200 **MIP** $250

Sportster, 20" long; 1950s
EX $65 **NM** $110 **MIP** $150

Station Wagon, green w/woodgrain pattern, wind-up, 7" long; 1950
EX $50 **NM** $75 **MIP** $250

Station Wagon, litho family of four w/dogs on back windows, 6-3/4" long
EX $60 **NM** $100 **MIP** $275

Station Wagon, light purple w/woodgrain pattern, wind-up, 7-1/2" long
EX $60 **NM** $100 **MIP** $275

Station Wagon, friction, 11" long; 1950
EX $125 **NM** $200 **MIP** $325

Streamline Speedway, two tin wind-up racing cars, 1936
EX $175 **NM** $275 **MIP** $395

Stutz Roadster, driver, 15" long, wind-up, 1928
EX $325 **NM** $500 **MIP** $750

Super Hot Rod, "777" on rear door, 11" long; 1940s
EX $200 **NM** $300 **MIP** $400

Super Streamlined Racer, tin wind-up, 17" long; 1950s
EX $125 **NM** $200 **MIP** $400

Talk 'N' Do Mobile, No. 5242, talking toy, removable wheels, movable windshield wipers, made in Japan; mid-1960s
EX $7 **NM** $15 **MIP** $22

The Marvel Car, Reversible Coupe, tin wind-up, 1938
EX $125 **NM** $200 **MIP** $400

Tricky Safety Car, 6-1/2" long; 1950
EX $100 **NM** $150 **MIP** $200

Tricky Taxi, red, black, and white, tin wind-up, 4-1/2" long; 1940s
EX $125 **NM** $200 **MIP** $375

Tricky Taxi, black/white version, tin wind-up, 4-1/2" long, 1935
EX $125 **NM** $200 **MIP** $375

Uncle Wiggly, He Goes A Ridin' Car, rabbit driving, tin wind-up, 7-1/2" long, 1935
EX $425 **NM** $650 **MIP** $850

Uno Ferrari, Super Speed Blazers die-cast series, 1969
EX $4 **NM** $8 **MIP** $12

Walt Disney Television Car, friction, 7-1/2" long; 1950s
EX $125 **NM** $200 **MIP** $425

Western Auto Track, steel, 24" long
EX $75 **NM** $125 **MIP** $225

(Bill Bertoia Auctions)

Whoopee Car, witty slogans, tin litho, wind-up, 7-1/2" long, 1930s
EX $375 **NM** $580 **MIP** $775

(Bill Bertoia Auctions)

Whoopee Cowboy Car, bucking car, cowboy driver, tin wind-up, 7-1/2" long, 1930s
EX $400 **NM** $600 **MIP** $800

Woody Sedan, tin friction, 7-1/2" long
EX $60 **NM** $100 **MIP** $225

Yellow Taxi, wind-up, 7" long, 1927
EX $275 **NM** $425 **MIP** $575

Yogi Bear Car, friction; 1962
EX $50 **NM** $85 **MIP** $195

Za Zoom Friction Racer, No. 7800; 1960s
EX $7 **NM** $15 **MIP** $22

Zoom-A-Car, set of six die-cast racers and two launchers; late 1960s
EX $25 **NM** $50 **MIP** $75

EMERGENCY VEHICLES

Ambulance, 13-1/2" long, 1937
EX $225 **NM** $350 **MIP** $650

Ambulance, tin litho, 11" long
EX $125 **NM** $175 **MIP** $375

(David W Mapes Inc)

Ambulance with Siren, tin wind-up
EX $100 **NM** $150 **MIP** $400

Army Ambulance, 13-1/2" long, 1930s
EX $250 **NM** $375 **MIP** $750

Chief-Fire Department No. 1 Truck, friction; 1948
EX $60 **NM** $90 **MIP** $195

City Hospital Mack Ambulance, tin litho, wind-up, 10" long, 1927
EX $190 **NM** $280 **MIP** $500

Electric Car, runs on electric power, license #A7132, 1933
EX $225 **NM** $325 **MIP** $500

Electric Car, wind-up, 1933
EX $175 **NM** $250 **MIP** $475

Fire Chief Car, working lights, 16" long
EX $125 **NM** $200 **MIP** $295

Fire Chief Car, wind-up, 6-1/2" long; 1949
EX $75 **NM** $125 **MIP** $275

Fire Chief Car, battery-operated headlights, wind-up, 11" long; 1950
EX $75 **NM** $125 **MIP** $325

Fire Chief Car, friction, loud fire siren, 8" long, 1936
EX $150 **NM** $250 **MIP** $425

Fire Chief Car with Bell, 10-1/2" long; 1940
EX $175 **NM** $250 **MIP** $450

Fire Engine, sheet iron, 9" long, 1920s
EX $100 **NM** $175 **MIP** $335

Fire Engine, 12" long; battery-operated plastic aerial ladder truck; 1968-69
EX $15 **NM** $30 **MIP** $45

Fire Truck, friction, all metal, 14" long; 1945
EX $90 **NM** $135 **MIP** $295

Fire Truck, battery-operated, two celluloid firemen, 12" long
EX $50 **NM** $75 **MIP** $300

Giant King Racer, pale yellow, tin wind-up, 12-1/2" long, 1928
EX $225 **NM** $325 **MIP** $575

Giant King Racer, red, 13" long; 1941
EX $200 **NM** $300 **MIP** $550

Giant Mechanical Racer, tin litho, 12-3/4" long; 1948
EX $100 **NM** $175 **MIP** $350

H.Q. - Staff Car, 14-1/2" long, 1930s
EX $325 **NM** $500 **MIP** $750

Hook and Ladder Fire Truck, three tin litho firemen, 13-1/2" long
EX $90 **NM** $135 **MIP** $225

Hook and Ladder Fire Truck, plastic ladder on top, 24" long; 1950
EX $90 **NM** $135 **MIP** $225

Siren Fire Chief Car, red car w/siren, 1934
EX $225 **NM** $325 **MIP** $495

Siren Fire Chief Truck, battery-operated, 15" long, 1930s
EX $100 **NM** $175 **MIP** $325

Tricky Fire Chief Car, 4-1/2" long, 1930s
EX $250 **NM** $375 **MIP** $625

V.F.D. Emergency Squad, w/ladder, metal, electrically powered, 14" long; 1940s
EX $70 **NM** $125 **MIP** $200

V.F.D. Fire Engine, w/hoses and siren, 14" long; 1940s
EX $120 **NM** $180 **MIP** $295

V.F.D. Hook and Ladder Fire Truck, 33" long; 1950
EX $140 **NM** $225 **MIP** $325

War Department Ambulance, 1930s
EX $100 **NM** $150 **MIP** $695

FARM AND CONSTRUCTION EQUIPMENT

Aluminum Bulldog Tractor Set, tin wind-up, 9-1/2" long tractor; 1940
EX $250 **NM** $375 **MIP** $500

American Tractor, w/accessories, tin wind-up, 8" long, 1926
EX $150 **NM** $225 **MIP** $300

Army Design Climbing Tractor, tin wind-up, 7-1/2" long, 1932
EX $80 **NM** $120 **MIP** $300

Automatic Steel Barn and Mechanical Plastic Tractor, tin wind-up, 7" long red tractor; 1950
EX $85 **NM** $125 **MIP** $475

Bulldozer Climbing Tractor, caterpillar type, tin wind-up, 10-1/2" long; 1950s
EX $45 **NM** $75 **MIP** $295

Bulldozer Climbing Tractor, bumper auto, large bumpers, tin wind-up, 1939
EX $50 **NM** $75 **MIP** $325

Caterpillar Climbing Tractor, yellow tractor, tin wind-up, 9-1/2" long, 1942
EX $75 **NM** $125 **MIP** $300

Caterpillar Climbing Tractor, orange tractor, tin wind-up, 9-1/2" long, 1942
EX $100 **NM** $175 **MIP** $325

Caterpillar Tractor and Hydraulic Lift, tin wind-up; 1948
EX $50 **NM** $75 **MIP** $295

Climbing Sparking Tractor, No. 904, 8-1/2" long; lithographed steel with rubber treads, plastic driver, wind-up; 1960s and 1970s
EX $15 **NM** $30 **MIP** $45

Climbing Tractor, tin wind-up, 8-1/4" long, 1930
EX $100 **NM** $150 **MIP** $325

Climbing Tractor, 5-1/2" long; wind-up, plastic and metal, plastic driver; 1960s
EX $12 **NM** $23 **MIP** $35

Climbing Tractor, w/driver, tin wind-up, 1920s
EX $50 **NM** $100 **MIP** $275

Climbing Tractor with Chain Pull, tin wind-up, 7-1/2" long, 1929
EX $150 **NM** $225 **MIP** $350

Construction Tractor, reversing, tin wind-up, 14" long; 1950s
EX $100 **NM** $150 **MIP** $465

Co-Op Combine, tin friction, 6"
EX $30 **NM** $45 **MIP** $95

Covered Wagon, friction, tin litho, 9" long
EX $20 **NM** $30 **MIP** $195

Crawler, w/or without blades and drivers, litho, 1/25 scale; 1950
EX $75 **NM** $125 **MIP** $150

Crawler with Stake Bed, litho, 1/25 scale; 1950
EX $75 **NM** $130 **MIP** $175

Farm Tractor and Implement Set, tin wind-up, tractor mower, hayrake, three-gang plow; 1948
EX $200 **NM** $300 **MIP** $400

Farm Tractor Set, 40 pieces, tin wind-up, 1939
EX $325 **NM** $500 **MIP** $650

Farm Tractor Set and Power Plant, 32 pieces, tin wind-up, 1938
EX $200 **NM** $300 **MIP** $400

Hill Climbing Dump Truck, tin wind-up, 13-1/2" long, 1932
EX $140 **NM** $210 **MIP** $375

Industrial Tractor Set, orange and red heavy gauge plate tractor, 7-1/2" long, 1930
EX $145 **NM** $225 **MIP** $395

International Harvester Tractor, diesel, driver and set of tools, 1/12 scale; 1954
EX $75 **NM** $125 **MIP** $150

Machinery Hauler with Bulldozer, 13" long; plastic, round-nose tractor, lowboy trailer, plastic wheels; orange bulldozer has cast-in treads and separate blade, 1950s
EX $100 **NM** $150 **MIP** $200

Magic Barn and Tractor, plastic tractor, tin litho barn; 1950s
EX $70 **NM** $100 **MIP** $375

Mechanical Tractor, tin wind-up, 5-1/2" long, 1942
EX $125 **NM** $200 **MIP** $275

Midget Climbing Tractor, tin wind-up, 5-1/4" long, 1935
EX $125 **NM** $200 **MIP** $250

Midget Road Building Set, tin wind-up, 5-1/2" long tractor, 1939
EX $200 **NM** $300 **MIP** $400

Midget Tractor, red metal, tin wind-up, 5-1/4" long; 1940
EX $30 **NM** $45 **MIP** $125

Midget Tractor, copper color metal, tin wind-up, 5-1/4" long; 1940
EX $40 **NM** $60 **MIP** $125

Midget Tractor and Plow, tin wind-up, 1937
EX $70 **NM** $100 **MIP** $225

Midget Tractor with Driver, red metal, tin wind-up, 5-1/4" long; 1940
EX $40 **NM** $60 **MIP** $220

No. 2 Tractor, red w/black wheels, tin wind-up, 8-1/2" long; 1940
EX $95 **NM** $150 **MIP** $225

Plastic Sparkling Tractor Set, tin wind-up, 6-1/2" long tractor w/10-1/2" long wagon; 1950
EX $40 **NM** $60 **MIP** $195

Plastic Tractor with Scraper, tin wind-up, 8" long w/road scraper; 1949
EX $50 **NM** $75 **MIP** $195

Power Grader, black or white wheels, 17-1/2" long
EX $45 **NM** $80 **MIP** $125

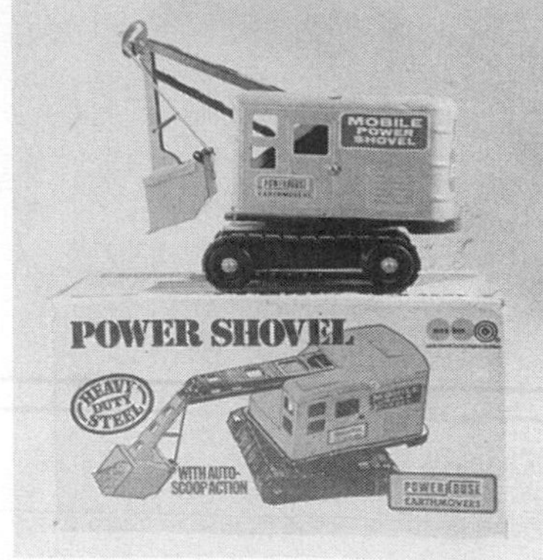

Power Shovel
EX $40 **NM** $60 **MIP** $100

Reversible Six-Wheel Farm Tractor-Truck, tin wind-up, 13-3/4" steel tractor, 7-1/2" stake truck; 1950
EX $80 **NM** $125 **MIP** $425

Reversible Six-Wheel Tractor, red steel tractor, tin wind-up, 11-3/4" long; 1940
EX $200 **NM** $300 **MIP** $475

Road Grader, 16" long; yellow, Lumar decals, 1956
EX $50 **NM** $80 **MIP** $140

Self-Reversing Tractor, tin wind-up, 10" long, 1936
EX $125 **NM** $200 **MIP** $350

Sparkling Climbing Tractor, tin wind-up, 10" long; 1940s
EX $125 **NM** $200 **MIP** $350

VEHICLES • MARX

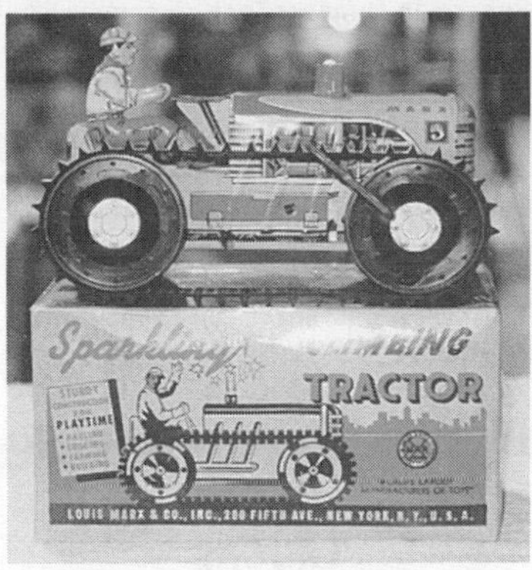

Sparkling Climbing Tractor, tin wind-up, 8-1/2" long; 1950s
EX $80 **NM** $125 **MIP** $300

Sparkling Heavy Duty Bulldog Tractor, w/road scraper, tin wind-up, 11" long; 1950s
EX $40 **NM** $60 **MIP** $225

Sparkling Hi-Boy Climbing Tractor, 10-1/2" long; 1950s
EX $25 **NM** $40 **MIP** $195

Sparkling Tractor, w/plow blade, tin wind-up, 1939
EX $50 **NM** $75 **MIP** $235

Sparkling Tractor, w/driver and trailer, tin wind-up, 16" long; 1950s
EX $60 **NM** $90 **MIP** $295

Sparkling Tractor and Trailer Set, "Marborook Farms," tin wind-up, 21" long; 1950s
EX $55 **NM** $75 **MIP** $255

Steel Farm Tractor and Implements, tin wind-up, 15" long steel bulldozer tractor; 1947
EX $160 **NM** $240 **MIP** $325

Super Power Reversing Tractor, tin wind-up, 12" long, 1931
EX $100 **NM** $150 **MIP** $325

Super Power Tractor and Trailer Set, tin wind-up, 8-1/2" tractor, 1937
EX $125 **NM** $200 **MIP** $375

Super-Power Bulldog Tractor with V-Shaped Plow, aluminum finish, tin wind-up, 1938
EX $75 **NM** $130 **MIP** $200

Super-Power Climbing Tractor and Nine-Piece Set, tin wind-up, 9-1/2" long tractor, 1942
EX $160 **NM** $240 **MIP** $395

Super-Power Giant Climbing Tractor, tin wind-up, 13" long, 1939
EX $180 **NM** $270 **MIP** $450

Tractor, tin wind-up, 8-1/2" long; 1941
EX $100 **NM** $175 **MIP** $315

Tractor, red tractor, tin wind-up, 8-1/2" long; 1941
EX $100 **NM** $175 **MIP** $300

Tractor and Equipment Set, five pieces, tin wind-up, 16" long tractor; 1949
EX $160 **NM** $240 **MIP** $320

Tractor and Mower, tin wind-up, 5" long litho steel tractor; 1948
EX $50 **NM** $75 **MIP** $215

Tractor and Six Implement Set, tin wind-up, 8-1/2" long aluminum tractor; 1948
EX $160 **NM** $240 **MIP** $425

Tractor and Trailer, tin wind-up, 16-1/2" long; 1950s
EX $40 **NM** $60 **MIP** $115

Tractor Road Construction Set, thirty-six pieces, tin wind-up, 8-1/2" long tractor, 1938
EX $200 **NM** $325 **MIP** $595

Tractor Set, seven pieces, tin wind-up, 8-1/2" long tractor, 1932
EX $125 **NM** $200 **MIP** $400

Tractor Set, five pieces, tin wind-up, 8-1/2" long tractor, 1935
EX $70 **NM** $100 **MIP** $220

Tractor Set, four pieces, tin wind-up, 8-1/2" long, 1936
EX $100 **NM** $150 **MIP** $325

Tractor Set, forty pieces, tin wind-up, 8-1/2" long, 1942
EX $300 **NM** $450 **MIP** $800

Tractor Set, two-pieces, tin wind-up, 19" long steel tractor; 1950
EX $65 **NM** $100 **MIP** $215

Tractor Set, five pieces, tin wind-up, 8-1/2" tractor, 1938
EX $90 **NM** $135 **MIP** $295

Tractor Set, thirty-two pieces, tin wind-up, 1937
EX $180 **NM** $270 **MIP** $450

Tractor Trailer and Scraper, tin wind-up, 8-1/2" long tractor; 1946
EX $80 **NM** $120 **MIP** $200

Tractor Train with Tractor Shed, tin wind-up, 8-1/2" long, 1936
EX $100 **NM** $150 **MIP** $220

Tractor with Airplane, wind-up, 5-1/2" long tractor, 27" wingspan on airplane; 1941
EX $250 **NM** $375 **MIP** $675

Tractor with Driver, wind-up; 1940s
EX $100 **NM** $150 **MIP** $300

Tractor with Earth Grader, tin wind-up, mechanical, 21-1/2" long; 1950s
EX $40 **NM** $60 **MIP** $190

Tractor with Plow and Scraper, aluminum tractor, tin wind-up, 1938
EX $70 **NM** $125 **MIP** $295

Tractor with Plow and Wagon, tin wind-up, 1934
EX $70 **NM** $125 **MIP** $295

Tractor with Road Scraper, tin wind-up, 8-1/2" long climbing tractor, 1937
EX $90 **NM** $125 **MIP** $325

Tractor with Scraper, tin wind-up, 8-1/2" long, 1933
EX $70 **NM** $125 **MIP** $295

Tractor with Trailer and Plow, tin wind-up, 8-1/2" long; 1940
EX $80 **NM** $120 **MIP** $295

Tractor, Trailer, and V-Shaped Plow, tin wind-up, 8-1/2" steel tractor, 1939
EX $85 **NM** $125 **MIP** $325

Tractor-Trailer Set, tin wind-up, 8-1/2" long copper-colored tractor, 1939
EX $70 **NM** $125 **MIP** $295

Yellow and Green Tractor, tin wind-up, 8-1/2" long, 1930
EX $90 **NM** $135 **MIP** $335

MOTORCYCLES

Motorcycle Cop, tin litho, mechanical, siren, 8-1/4" long
EX $75 **NM** $125 **MIP** $235

Motorcycle Delivery Toy, "Speedy Boy Delivery Toy" on rear of cart, tin wind-up, 1932
EX $175 **NM** $275 **MIP** $500

Motorcycle Delivery Toy, "Speedy Boy Delivery Toy" on side of cart, tin wind-up, 1930s
EX $175 **NM** $280 **MIP** $525

Motorcycle Police, red uniform on cop, tin wind-up, 8" long, 1930s
EX $125 **NM** $200 **MIP** $275

Motorcycle Police #3, tin wind-up, 8-1/2" long
EX $100 **NM** $175 **MIP** $250

Motorcycle Policeman, orange/blue, tin wind-up, 8" long, 1920s
EX $100 **NM** $150 **MIP** $325

Motorcycle Trooper, tin litho, wind-up, 1935
EX $80 **NM** $120 **MIP** $275

Mystery Police Cycle, yellow, tin wind-up, 4-1/2" long, 1930s
EX $75 **NM** $125 **MIP** $225

Mystic Motorcycle, tin litho, wind-up, 4-1/4" long, 1936
EX $75 **NM** $130 **MIP** $235

P.D. Motorcyclist, tin wind-up, 4" long
EX $40 **NM** $60 **MIP** $195

Pinched Roadster Motorcycle Cop, in circular track, tin wind-up, 1927
EX $125 **NM** $200 **MIP** $365

Pluto Motorcycle with Siren, 1930s
EX $150 **NM** $225 **MIP** $550

Police Motorcycle with Sidecar, tin wind-up, 3-1/2" long, 1930s
EX $300 **NM** $450 **MIP** $750

Police Motorcycle with Sidecar, tin litho, wind-up, 8" long; 1950
EX $175 **NM** $280 **MIP** $425

Police Motorcycle with Sidecar, tin wind-up, 8" long, 1930s
EX $425 **NM** $650 **MIP** $950

Police Patrol Motorcycle with Sidecar, tin wind-up, 1935
EX $110 **NM** $165 **MIP** $400

Police Siren Motorcycle, tin litho, wind-up, 8" long, 1938
EX $150 **NM** $225 **MIP** $350

Police Squad Motorcycle Sidecar, tin litho, wind-up, 8" long; 1950
EX $100 **NM** $150 **MIP** $375

Police Tipover Motorcycle, tin litho, wind-up, 8" long, 1933
EX $200 **NM** $300 **MIP** $525

Rookie Cop, yellow w/driver, tin litho, wind-up, 8" long; 1940
EX $175 **NM** $275 **MIP** $425

Sparkling Soldier Motorcycle, tin litho, wind-up, 8" long; 1940
EX $175 **NM** $275 **MIP** $425

Speeding Car and Motorcycle Policeman, tin litho, wind-up, 1939
EX $90 NM $150 MIP $350

Tricky Motorcycle, tin wind-up, 4-1/2" long, 1930s
EX $100 NM $150 MIP $250

TANKS

Anti-Aircraft Tank Outfit, three cardboard tanks
EX $150 NM $225 MIP $350

Anti-Aircraft Tank Outfit, four flat metal soldiers, tank, anti-aircraft gun; 1941
EX $90 NM $135 MIP $300

Army Tank, sparking climbing tank, tin wind-up; 1940s
EX $150 NM $225 MIP $375

Climbing Fighting Tank, tin wind-up
EX $90 NM $135 MIP $250

Climbing Tank, tin wind-up, 9-1/2" long, 1930
EX $125 NM $200 MIP $325

Doughboy Tank, doughboy pops out, tin litho, wind-up, 9-1/2" long, 1930
EX $150 NM $225 MIP $425

Doughboy Tank, sparking tank, tin wind-up, 10" long, 1937
EX $125 NM $200 MIP $400

Doughboy Tank, tin wind-up, 10" long, 1942
EX $150 NM $225 MIP $450

(Bill Holt)

E12 Tank, green tank, 9-1/2" long, tin wind-up, 1942-50s
EX $75 NM $125 MIP $375

M-15 Atom Tank, 3-1/2" long; tin-litho, three wheels on underside, 1950s
EX $15 NM $25 MIP $50

M48T Tank, battery-operated; 1960s
EX $50 NM $100 MIP $225

Midget Climbing Fighting Tank, tin litho, wind-up, 5-1/4" long, 1931
EX $90 NM $135 MIP $235

(Harvey K Rainess)

Midget Climbing Fighting Tank, wide plastic wheels, supergrid tread, 5-1/4" long; 1951
EX $100 NM $150 MIP $300

Midget Climbing Fighting Tank, 5-1/2" long, 1937
EX $100 NM $175 MIP $375

Refrew Tank, tin wind-up
EX $75 NM $125 MIP $200

Rex Mars Planet Patrol Tank, tin wind-up, 10" long; 1950s
EX $150 NM $225 MIP $375

Sparkling Army Tank, yellow hull, E12 Tank, tin litho, wind-up, 1942,
EX $100 NM $150 MIP $300

Sparkling Army Tank, camouflage hull, two olive guns, tin wind-up, 5-1/2" long
EX $100 NM $150 MIP $275

Sparkling Army Tank, camouflage hull, two khaki guns, tin wind-up, 5-1/2" long
EX $125 NM $200 MIP $325

Sparkling Army Tank, tan or khaki hull, tin litho, wind-up, 1938
EX $95 NM $150 MIP $235

Sparkling Climbing Tank, tin wind-up, 10" long, 1939
EX $110 NM $165 MIP $310

Sparkling Space Tank, tin wind-up; 1950s
EX $250 NM $375 MIP $600

Sparkling Super Power Tank, tin wind-up, 9-1/2" long; 1950s
EX $75 NM $125 MIP $250

Sparkling Tank, tin wind-up, 4" long; 1948
EX $75 NM $130 MIP $195

Superman Turnover Tank, Superman lifts tank, 4" long, tin wind-up; 1940
EX $250 NM $375 MIP $600

Tank, pop-up army man shooting
EX $150 NM $225 MIP $400

Turnover Army Tank, camouflage, tan or khaki hull, tin wind-up, 1938
EX $175 NM $275 MIP $450

Turnover Army Tank, tin wind-up, 9" long, 1930
EX $150 NM $225 MIP $375

Turnover Tank, tin litho, wind-up, 4" long, 1942
EX $100 NM $150 MIP $275

TRUCKS

A & P Supermarket Truck, pressed steel, rubber tires, litho, 19" long
EX $60 NM $100 MIP $340

(Bob Smith)

Aero Oil Co. Mack Truck, tin litho, friction, 5-1/2" long, 1930
EX $125 NM $200 MIP $350

Air Force Truck, 32" long, No. 3290
EX $125 NM $190 MIP $250

American Railroad Express Agency Inc. Truck, open cab, 7" long, 1930s
EX $150 NM $300 MIP $450

American Truck Co. Mack Truck, friction, 5" long
EX $100 NM $150 MIP $225

Armored Trucking Co. Mack Truck, black cab, yellow printing, wind-up, 9-3/4" long
EX $200 NM $300 MIP $400

Armored Trucking Co. Truck, tin litho, wind-up, 10" long, 1927
EX $100 NM $150 MIP $325

Army Cargo Transport Truck, 19" long; open stakeside, 1950s
EX $45 NM $65 MIP $125

Army Supply Truck, 6" long; plastic stakeside truck, rounded-nose cab, black plastic wheels
EX $30 NM $60 MIP $75

Army Transport Truck, 19" long; 1960s
EX $30 NM $50 MIP $65

Army Truck, tin, 12" long; 1950
EX $60 NM $90 MIP $150

Army Truck, olive drab truck, 4-1/2" long, 1930s
EX $125 NM $200 MIP $350

Army Truck, canvas top, 20" long; 1940s
EX $150 NM $225 MIP $325

Army Truck with Rear Benches and Canopy, olive drab paint, 10" long
EX $75 NM $125 MIP $225

Artillery Set, three-piece set, 1930
EX $100 NM $150 MIP $225

Auto Carrier, two yellow plastic cars, two ramp tracks, 14" long; 1950
EX $125 NM $200 MIP $295

Auto Hauler, hard plastic, 14: long; 1950
EX $25 NM $50 MIP $75

Auto Mack Truck, yellow/red, 12" long; 1950
EX $50 NM $75 MIP $175

Auto Transport Mack Truck and Trailer, dark blue cab, wind-up, 11-1/2" long, 1932
EX $150 NM $225 MIP $400

Auto Transport Mack Truck and Trailer, medium blue cab, friction, 11-1/2" long, 1932
EX $150 NM $225 MIP $425

Auto Transport Mack Truck and Trailer, dark blue cab, dark green trailer, wind-up, 11-1/2" long, 1932
EX $150 NM $225 MIP $375

Auto Transport Truck, w/three cars, 21" long; 1940
EX $250 NM $375 MIP $575

Auto Transport Truck, pressed steel, w/two plastic cars, 14" long; 1940
EX $75 NM $125 MIP $225

Auto Transport Truck, w/two tin litho cars, 34" long; 1950s
EX $60 NM $90 MIP $200

Auto Transport Truck, w/three wind-up cars, 22-3/4" long, 1931
EX $250 NM $375 MIP $525

Auto Transport Truck, w/three racing coupes, 22" long, 1933
EX $250 NM $375 MIP $525

Auto Transport Truck, double decker transport truck, 24-1/2" long, 1935
EX $275 NM $425 MIP $575

Auto Transport Truck, w/dump truck, roadster and coupe, 30 1/2" long, 1938
EX $275 NM $425 MIP $575

Auto Transport Truck, 21" long; 1947
EX $175 NM $250 MIP $400

Auto Transport Truck, w/three cars, 1930s
EX $175 NM $250 MIP $395

Auto Transport Truck, w/two plastic sedans, wooden wheels, 13-3/4" long; 1950
EX $75 NM $130 MIP $225

Auto Transport Truck, 16" long; "Mighty-Marx Heavy Gauge Steel Auto Transport," lavender tractor, orange trailer, three plastic Hong Kong cars
EX $25 NM $50 MIP $90

Auto Transport Truck, 22-1/2" long; yellow/red steel trailer and ramp, red plastic tractor, two plastic cars, "Deluxe Auto Transport," 1950s
EX $35 NM $55 MIP $75

Bakery Van, plastic, clear top, "Bakery," 10" long; 1950s
EX $20 NM $30 MIP $45

Bamberger Mack Truck, dark green, wind-up, 5" long, 1920s
EX $200 NM $300 MIP $525

Big Blade, 18" long; battery-operated, remote-control plastic bulldozer with driver; 1966-68
EX $32 NM $63 MIP $95

Big Boss Car Carrier, plastic, battery-operated; 1963
EX $50 NM $80 MIP $125

Big Bruiser, 25" long; white plastic wrecker truck, battery-operated light and siren, jack, tool kit, pickup truck with spare parts; 1962-65
EX $42 NM $90 MIP $125

Big Bruiser Fire Truck, red, yellow boom, side ladders, firemen, battery-operated, 1960s
EX $50 NM $75 MIP n/a

Big Job Dump Truck, plastic; 1970s
EX $15 NM $25 MIP $35

Big Job Dump Truck, No. 5214, 29" long; battery-operated plastic and steel dump truck, power steering and brakes; 1964-65
EX $18 NM $79 MIP $55

Big Load Van Co. Hauler and Trailer, w/little cartons of products, 12-3/4" long, 1927
EX $200 NM $300 MIP $525

Big Load Van Co. Mack Truck, wind-up, 13" long, 1928
EX $225 NM $350 MIP $600

Big Shot, 23" long; battery-operated plastic mobile artillery, radar on cab roof, six wheels, three rubber-tipped missiles; 1965-66
EX $38 NM $60 MIP $115

Bruiser Jr., 12" long; white plastic remote-control wrecker truck, manual winch, jack, blue plastic 8" car with replacement car fender; 1968-69
EX $28 NM $36 MIP $85

Cannon Army Mack Truck, 9" long, 1930s
EX $175 NM $250 MIP $325

Carousel Truck, 7-1/2" long; metal, friction-powered, blue truck with merry-go-round load; 1967-68
EX $15 NM $30 MIP $45

Carpenter's Truck, stake bed truck, pressed steel, 14" long; 1940s
EX $175 NM $250 MIP $350

Carrier with Three Racers, tin litho, wind-up, 22-3/4" long, 1930
EX $150 NM $225 MIP $425

Cement Mixer Truck, red cab, tin finish mixing barrel, 6" long, 1930s
EX $100 NM $150 MIP $300

Cities Service Wrecker Truck, 20" long; green and white tin-litho, four plastic accessories including crank and jack, 1950s
EX $125 NM $175 MIP $250

City Coal Co. Mack Dump Truck, 14" long, 1934
EX $225 NM $350 MIP $525

City Delivery Van, yellow steel truck, 11" long
EX $140 NM $210 MIP $280

(Calvin L Chaussee)

City Sanitation Dept. "Help Keep Your City Clean" Truck, 12-3/4" long; 1940
EX $60 NM $90 MIP $250

Coal Truck, 2nd version, light blue truck, 12" long
EX $140 NM $225 MIP $280

Coal Truck, battery-operated, automatic dump, forward and reverse, tin
EX $75 NM $125 MIP $175

Coal Truck, 1st version, red cab, litho blue and yellow dumper, 12" long
EX $140 NM $225 MIP $280

Coal Truck, 3rd version, Lumar Co. truck, 10" long, 1939
EX $150 NM $250 MIP $310

Coca-Cola Beverage Truck, No. 829, 12-5/8" long; yellow, double shelves in load area, six bottle cases, hand truck; 1960s
EX $67 NM $132 MIP $200

Coca-Cola Truck, red steel, 11-1/2" long; 1940s
EX $100 NM $175 MIP $250

Coca-Cola Truck, tin, 17" long; 1940s
EX $125 NM $200 MIP $250

Coca-Cola Truck, yellow, 20" long; 1950
EX $150 NM $225 MIP $300

Coca-Cola Truck, stamped steel, 20" long; 1940s, Sprite boy, stake body
EX $225 NM $300 MIP $880

Concrete Company Truck, 6" long; gray hard plastic, black tires, "Lumar Concrete Company"
EX $3 NM $6 MIP $9

Construction Set, 3-piece set of mini trucks, 7" long, futuristic cabover style, electric headlights; cement, tow and dump trucks; 1968
EX $25 NM $35 MIP $55

Contractors and Builders Truck, 10" long
EX $125 NM $200 MIP $250

Crescent Ice Truck, tin-litho, Wyandotte-type styling, green/white/yellow, 1950s
EX $150 NM $200 MIP $250

VEHICLES • MARX

(Taylor's Toys John Taylor)

Cunningham's Drug Store Truck, plastic; 1950s
EX $40 **NM** $60 **MIP** $80

Curtiss Candy Truck, red plastic truck, 10" long; 1950
EX $25 **NM** $55 **MIP** $75

Dairy Farm Pickup Truck, 22" long
EX $60 **NM** $100 **MIP** $150

Delivery Truck, blue truck, 4" long; 1940
EX $100 **NM** $175 **MIP** $225

Delivery Truck, 8-1/2" long; green plastic panel delivery truck, black rubber tires, 1950s
EX $10 **NM** $15 **MIP** $20

Deluxe Delivery Stake Truck, plastic cab, metal bed, 12" long; 1950s
EX $40 **NM** $60 **MIP** $90

Deluxe Delivery Truck, w/six delivery boxes, stamped steel, 13-1/4" long; 1948
EX $100 **NM** $150 **MIP** $200

Deluxe Fire Truck, red plastic ladder truck, open cab, keywind motor, 13-1/2" long
EX $30 **NM** $50 **MIP** $75

(Taylor's Toys John Taylor)

Deluxe Trailer Truck, tin and plastic, 14" long; 1950s
EX $70 **NM** $100 **MIP** $145

Diesel Power Shovel, No. 1782; 18" long; crank-controlled boom and shovel; 1960s-70s
EX $28 **NM** $56 **MIP** $85

Dodge Salerno Engineering Department Truck
EX $600 **NM** $900 **MIP** $1200

Dump Truck, 21" long; plastic and steel dump truck, battery-powered, three switches, battery-operated "Za-zoom" motor noise; 1964-68
EX $13 **NM** $26 **MIP** $40

Dump Truck, 4-1/2" long, 1930s
EX $100 **NM** $175 **MIP** $325

Dump Truck, 3-1/2"; red futuristic cabover, yellow dump body, 1970s
EX $4 **NM** $8 **MIP** $13

Dump Truck, various colors, 18" long; 1950s
EX $100 **NM** $150 **MIP** $200

Dump Truck, red cab, green body, 6-1/4" long
EX $50 **NM** $75 **MIP** $100

Dump Truck, 6" long, 1930s
EX $100 **NM** $150 **MIP** $250

Dump Truck, 8" long; battery-operated toy, forward and back lever, dump lever, with plastic driver
EX $7 **NM** $13 **MIP** $20

Dump Truck, red cab, gray bumper, yellow bed, 18" long; 1950
EX $100 **NM** $150 **MIP** $200

Dump Truck, red cab, green dump bed, 12" long; 1940s
EX $50 **NM** $90 **MIP** $150

Dump Truck, motor, tin friction, 12" long; 1950s
EX $50 **NM** $100 **MIP** $280

Emergency Service Truck, friction, tin, searchlight behind car and siren
EX $150 **NM** $225 **MIP** $300

Emergency Service Truck, friction, tin
EX $125 **NM** $200 **MIP** $275

Farm Stake Truck, No. 1010, 17-3/4" long; "Lazy Day Farms," lithographed stake body, polyethylene tires; 1959 to 1970s
EX $28 **NM** $65 **MIP** $85

Farm Truck, red plastic, chicken cage on stake bed, battery-operated, 11-1/2" long; 1960s
EX $10 **NM** $18 **MIP** $25

Firestone Truck, metal, 14" long; 1950s
EX $90 **NM** $175 **MIP** $200

First National Stores Truck, 25" long; tractor-trailer, 1950s
EX $50 **NM** $95 **MIP** $130

Ford Heavy Duty Express Truck, cab w/canopy; 1950s
EX $60 **NM** $100 **MIP** $175

Gas Truck, green truck, 4" long; 1940
EX $60 **NM** $90 **MIP** $165

Giant Reversing Tractor Truck, w/tools, tin wind-up, 14" long; 1950s
EX $75 **NM** $130 **MIP** $350

Go-Cart, "Letters", Magic Marxie vehicle with mailbox figure, plastic w/rubber tires, 5-1/2" long; 1969
EX $20 **NM** $30 **MIP** $45

(Taylor's Toys John Taylor)

Gravel Truck, 3rd version, metal w/"Gravel Mixer" drum, 10" long, 1930s
EX $100 **NM** $150 **MIP** $250

Gravel Truck, 2nd version, metal, 8-1/2" long; 1940s
EX $75 **NM** $125 **MIP** $200

Gravel Truck, 1st version, pressed steel cab, red tin dumper, 10" long, 1930
EX $100 **NM** $150 **MIP** $250

Grocery Truck, cardboard boxes, tinplate and plastic, 14-1/2" long
EX $90 **NM** $150 **MIP** $225

Guided Missile Truck, blue, red and yellow body, friction, 16" long; 1958
EX $75 **NM** $125 **MIP** $225

Heavy Gauge Dump Truck, No. 978; 17-3/4" long; "Lumar Contractors," 11" dump body, polyethylene tires; 1960s
EX $25 **NM** $50 **MIP** $75

Hess Tanker, 12-1/2" long; green/yellow tractor, green/white tank "Hess" trailer
EX $45 **NM** $185 **MIP** n/a

Hi Way Express Truck, "Nationwide Delivery," 1950s
EX $100 **NM** $150 **MIP** $225

Hi Way Express Truck, tin, tin tires, 16" long; "Cross-Country Service," blue cab, red/white/yellow body, blue rear gate, 1940s
EX $15 **NM** $230 **MIP** $300

High Lift Loader with scoop, No. 1756, 13-1/2" long; lever-cont4rolled front bucket, steering wheel controls rear wheels; 1960s
EX $22 **NM** $43 **MIP** $65

Hi-Way Express Van Liens Truck, 27-1/2" long; blue steel trailer w/yellow/red decal, blue plastic cab on steel chassis, opening red tailgates; also in red/orange; 1950s
EX $95 **NM** $150 **MIP** $185

Hydraulic Dump Truck, steel, made "motor noise," hydraulic lift, 20-14" long, early 1970s
EX $20 **NM** $30 **MIP** $50

Inter-City Delivery Service Truck, 18" long; colorful tin-litho, 1950s
EX $75 **NM** $95 **MIP** $140

Jalopy Pickup Truck, tin wind-up, 7" long
EX $60 **NM** $90 **MIP** $175

Jeep, 11" long; 1946-50
EX $75 **NM** $130 **MIP** $200

Jeep, Mini-Marx Blazer die-cast series, 1968
EX $3 **NM** $7 **MIP** $10

Jeep, 4-1/2" long; gray plastic, white plastic tires, "Willys" on hood
EX $3 **NM** $5 **MIP** $8

Jeep, 6" long; white metal body, metal hub caps; late 1960s
EX $4 **NM** $8 **MIP** $12

Jeep with Canvas Tarp and Driver, No. 868, 11-1/2" long; opening hood, collapsing windshield, removable camouflage canvas roof, polyethylene driver, plastic wheels with tin hubs; mid-1960s
EX $18 **NM** $36 **MIP** $55

Jeepster, mechanical, plastic
EX $110 **NM** $165 **MIP** $250

Johnny West Jeep, No. 4560, yellow plastic Jeep with black hood, black balloon tires, issued in Johnny West Camping Set with pup tent, campfire, cot and other accessories; 1973
EX $47 **NM** $92 **MIP** $140

Johnny West Jeep and Horse Trailer, 3' long; No. 4543, red plastic Jeep, black windshield and steering wheel, spare tire, white plastic horse trailer with lowering rear gate; 1966-68
EX $75 **NM** $150 **MIP** $225

Lazy Day Dairy Farm Pickup Truck and Trailer, 22" long
EX $50 **NM** $75 **MIP** $150

Lincoln Transfer and Storage Co. Mack Truck, wheels have cut-out spokes, tin litho, wind-up, 13" long, 1928
EX $350 **NM** $525 **MIP** $750

Loblaws Truck, 27" long; tractor-trailer, white w/orange lettering and details, "Loblaws...Your Finest Food Stores," tin-litho grille, white-hub tires, 1950s
EX $100 **NM** $175 **MIP** $225

Lone Eagle Oil Co. Mack Truck, bright blue cab, green tank, wind-up, 12" long, 1930
EX $225 **NM** $350 **MIP** $550

Lumar concrete Co. Truck, plastic, 5-1/2" long; 1950s
EX $10 **NM** $16 **MIP** $22

Lumar Contractors Scoop/Dump Truck, 17-1/2" long; 1940s
EX $75 **NM** $125 **MIP** $200

Lumar Hydraulic Dump Truck, "Mechanical Action Hydraulic Dump Truck," 19" long; 1950s
EX $50 **NM** $80 **MIP** $125

Lumar Lines and Gasoline Set, 1948
EX $250 **NM** $375 **MIP** $725

Lumar Lines Truck, red cab, aluminum finished trailer, 14" long
EX $125 **NM** $200 **MIP** $300

Lumar Log Truck, die-cast tractor-trailer, made in England, 7" long
EX $20 **NM** $30 **MIP** $40

Lumar Motor Transport Truck, litho, 13" long, 1942
EX $75 **NM** $130 **MIP** $250

Lumar Stake Truck, die-cast tractor-trailer, made in England, 7" long
EX $20 **NM** $30 **MIP** $40

(Bob Smith)

Lumar Van Lines Coast to Coast, red/white cab; blue, red and white trailer; 15" long; 1950s
EX $50 **NM** $90 **MIP** $150

(Taylor's Toys John Taylor)

Lumar Wrecker Truck, black and white, "Nite-Day Service," 18" long; 1950s
EX $50 **NM** $90 **MIP** $150

Machinery Moving Truck
EX $60 **NM** $90 **MIP** $200

Mack Army Truck, friction, 5" long, 1930
EX $125 **NM** $200 **MIP** $350

Mack Army Truck, pressed steel, wind-up, 7-1/2" long
EX $70 **NM** $100 **MIP** $250

Mack Army Truck, 13-1/2" long, 1929
EX $225 **NM** $350 **MIP** $600

Mack Army Truck, khaki brown body, wind-up, 10-1/2" long
EX $125 **NM** $225 **MIP** $400

Mack Dump Truck, tin litho, wind-up, 13-1/2" long, 1926
EX $225 **NM** $350 **MIP** $575

Mack Dump Truck, no driver, 19" long, 1930
EX $300 **NM** $450 **MIP** $650

Mack Dump Truck, silver cab, medium blue dump, wind-up, 12-3/4" long, 1936
EX $225 **NM** $355 **MIP** $525

Mack Dump Truck, medium blue truck, wind-up, 13" long, 1934
EX $200 **NM** $300 **MIP** $525

Mack Dump Truck, dark red cab, medium blue bed, wind-up, 10" long, 1928
EX $150 **NM** $225 **MIP** $475

Mack Railroad Express Truck #7, tin, 1930s
EX $75 **NM** $125 **MIP** $450

Mack Towing Truck, dark green cab, wind-up, 8" long, 1926
EX $175 **NM** $275 **MIP** $450

Mack U.S. Mail Truck, black body, wind-up, 9-1/2" long
EX $250 **NM** $375 **MIP** $500

(Bob Smith)

Magnetic Crane and Truck, 1950
EX $100 **NM** $150 **MIP** $275

Mammoth Truck Train, truck w/five trailers, 1930s
EX $175 **NM** $262 **MIP** $350

Marx-A-Power, 18" long; giant bulldozer; 1960s
EX $18 **NM** $36 **MIP** $55

Meadowbrook Dairy Truck, 14" long; 1940
EX $150 **NM** $275 **MIP** $375

Mechanical Climbing Army Tank, No. 461, 5-7/8" long; wind-up plastic and steel; 1960s
EX $8 **NM** $17 **MIP** $25

Mechanical Sand Dump Truck, steel; 1940s
EX $100 **NM** $150 **MIP** $275

Medical Corps Ambulance Truck, olive drab paint; 1940s
EX $100 **NM** $150 **MIP** $275

(Bob Smith)

Merchants Transfer Mack Truck, 13-1/3" long, 1928
EX $250 **NM** $375 **MIP** $600

Merchants Transfer Mack Truck, red open-stake truck, 10" long
EX $225 **NM** $350 **MIP** $450

Midget Cement Mixer Truck, 4" long; steel, cabover; 1969-70s
EX $4 **NM** $8 **MIP** $12

Midget Pickup Truck, 4" long; steel, cabover; 1969070s
EX $3 **NM** $5 **MIP** $8

Midget Sanitation Truck, 4" long; steel, cabover, dump action; 1969-70s
EX $3 **NM** $7 **MIP** $10

Midget Stake Truck, 4" long; steel, cabover; 1969070s
EX $3 **NM** $7 **MIP** $10

VEHICLES • MARX

Midget Wrecker Truck, 4" long; steel, cabover, winch action; 1969-70s
EX $3 **NM** $7 **MIP** $10

Mighty Concrete Mixer Truck, 7" long; cabover, turning mixer; 1968-70s
EX $5 **NM** $11 **MIP** $16

Mighty Dump Truck, 7" long; cabover, dumping body; 1968-70s
EX $5 **NM** $9 **MIP** $14

Mighty Fire Rescue Truck, 6" long; red, with plastic ladders; 1968-70s
EX $5 **NM** $10 **MIP** $15

Mighty Pickup Truck, 7" long; cabover style; 1968-70s
EX $5 **NM** $9 **MIP** $14

Mighty Sanitation Truck, 7" long; cabover, loader bucket; 1969-70s
EX $5 **NM** $11 **MIP** $16

Military Cannon Truck, olive drab paint, cannon shoots marbles, 10" long, 1939
EX $125 **NM** $200 **MIP** $250

Milk Truck, white truck, 4" long; 1940
EX $60 **NM** $90 **MIP** $120

Milk Wagon, 6" long; plastic, blue old-fashioned cab, red chassis, silver grille, white milk-bottle load, "Marx Milk Wagon" on doors, white-hub tires, 1960s
EX $8 **NM** $12 **MIP** $18

Miniature Mayflower Moving Van, operating lights
EX $60 **NM** $90 **MIP** $125

Mini-Marx Auto Transport, plastic auto hauler for "Mini-Marx Blazers" for "Super Speed Blazers" die-cast cars; late 1960s
EX $15 **NM** $30 **MIP** $45

Moon Crawler, 11" long; No. 1738, Johnny and Jane Apollo vehicle, wheels with five "legs," flip-open green-tinted bubble over cockpit, battery-operated; 1968
EX $27 **NM** $53 **MIP** $80

Motor Market Delivery, 14" long; 1940s-1950s
EX $50 **NM** $90 **MIP** $150

Motor Market Truck, 10" long, 1939
EX $100 **NM** $175 **MIP** $225

Navy Jeep, wind-up
EX $50 **NM** $75 **MIP** $100

North American Van Lines Tractor Trailer, wind-up, 13" long; 1940s
EX $100 **NM** $175 **MIP** $225

Panel Wagon Truck
EX $30 **NM** $55 **MIP** $75

Pet Shop Truck, plastic, six compartments w/six vinyl dogs, 11" long
EX $125 **NM** $200 **MIP** $250

Pickup, large pickup truck from "Big Bruiser" sets; mid-1960s
EX $10 **NM** $20 **MIP** $30

Pickup Truck, blue/yellow w/wood tires, 9" long; 1940s
EX $50 **NM** $75 **MIP** $150

Polar Ice Co. Ice Truck, 13" long; 1940s, stake body, picture of polar bear
EX $100 **NM** $175 **MIP** $275

Police Patrol Mack Truck, wind-up, 10" long
EX $200 **NM** $300 **MIP** $475

Popeye Dippy Dumper Truck, Popeye is celluloid, tin wind-up
EX $325 **NM** $500 **MIP** $800

Powerhouse Dump Truck, pressed steel, plastic windshield, 19" long; 1960s
EX $25 **NM** $35 **MIP** $55

Pure Milk Dairy Truck, glass bottles, pressed steel; 1940
EX $150 **NM** $200 **MIP** $300

Railway Express Agency Truck, green closed van truck; 1940s
EX $90 **NM** $135 **MIP** $300

Range Rider, tin wind-up, 1930s
EX $250 **NM** $375 **MIP** $500

Rapid Express Pickup, wind-up, 9" long; 1940s
EX $125 **NM** $180 **MIP** $225

Rat Patrol, No. 1545, large plastic Jeep packaged with Jack Moffitt and Sam Troy plastic dolls, and numerous accessories; 1967
EX $28 **NM** $56 **MIP** $85

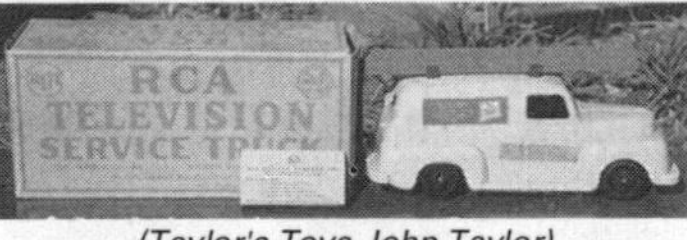

(Taylor's Toys John Taylor)

RCA Television Service Truck, plastic Ford panel truck, 8-1/2" long; 1948-50
EX $150 **NM** $225 **MIP** $375

Reversing Road Roller, tin wind-up
EX $60 **NM** $100 **MIP** $125

Road Builder Tank, 1950
EX $125 **NM** $200 **MIP** $250

Road Grader, 6-1/2" long; orange hard plastic
EX $7 **NM** $15 **MIP** $22

Road Grader, 17" long; No. 1760, enclosed cab, adjustable scraper, 1960s-70s
EX $15 **NM** $28 **MIP** $55

Rocker Dump Truck, 17-1/2" long
EX $60 **NM** $90 **MIP** $120

Rocker Dump Truck, No. 1751, 17-1/2" long; rocker dumping unit swivel-mounted to two-wheel tractor; 1960s
EX $20 **NM** $48 **MIP** $75

Roy Rogers and Trigger Cattle Truck, metal, 15" long; 1950s
EX $60 **NM** $100 **MIP** $225

Royal Oil Co. Mack Truck, dark red cab, medium green tank, wind-up, 8-1/4" long, 1927
EX $200 **NM** $300 **MIP** $500

Royal Van Co. Mack Truck, 1927
EX $250 **NM** $375 **MIP** $600

Royal Van Co. Mack Truck, red cab, tin litho and paint, wind-up, 9" long, 1928
EX $210 **NM** $315 **MIP** $550

Run Right To Read's Truck, 14" long; 1940
EX $125 **NM** $200 **MIP** $250

Safari Adventure Jeep, 14" long; tan Jeep with zebra-stripe hood, accessories including movie camera, spare tire, and radio; 1975-78
EX $23 **NM** $46 **MIP** $70

Safari Adventure Pursuit Truck, No. 2190, tan or off-white plastic stake-bed truck, black winch on hood; 1975-78
EX $15 **NM** $30 **MIP** $45

Salerno Cookie Truck, blue/white tin box truck
EX $75 **NM** $125 **MIP** $230

Sand and Gravel Truck, "Builder's Supply Co.," tin wind-up, 1920
EX $150 **NM** $275 **MIP** $350

Sand Truck, 9" long; 1948
EX $50 **NM** $75 **MIP** $125

Sand Truck, tin litho, 12-1/2" long; 1940s
EX $125 **NM** $200 **MIP** $275

Sand-Gravel Dump Truck, blue cab, yellow dump w/"Gravel" on side, tin, 1930s
EX $140 **NM** $225 **MIP** $285

Sand-Gravel Dump Truck, tin litho, 12" long; 1950
EX $150 **NM** $225 **MIP** $300

Sanitation Truck, 1940s
EX $135 **NM** $200 **MIP** $270

Scoop & Dump Truck, 17" long; 1940s
EX $50 **NM** $90 **MIP** $150

Searchlight Truck, pressed steel, 9-3/4" long, 1930s
EX $160 **NM** $250 **MIP** $325

Shell Towing Service Truck, 18-1/2" long; red cab and boom; yellow body, grille and hubs; siren light; 1950s
EX $200 **NM** $300 **MIP** $400

Shop-Rite (tractor-trailer), 24" long; No. 3640, red cabover, silver van trailer; 1966-67
EX $25 **NM** $50 **MIP** $75

Side Dump Truck, 1940
EX $90 **NM** $130 **MIP** $275

Side Dump Truck, 10" long, 1930s
EX $140 **NM** $225 **MIP** $280

Side Dump Truck and Trailer, 15" long, 1935
EX $150 NM $225 MIP $300

Sinclair Tanker, tin, 14" long; 1940s
EX $150 NM $225 MIP $300

Stake Bed Truck, pressed steel, wooden wheels, 7" long, 1936
EX $60 NM $90 MIP $200

Stake Bed Truck, red cab, blue stake bed, 6" long, 1930s
EX $75 NM $125 MIP $150

Stake Bed Truck, red cab, yellow and red trailer, 14" long
EX $100 NM $150 MIP $200

Stake Bed Truck, red cab, green stake bed, 20" long; 1947
EX $100 NM $150 MIP $200

Stake Bed Truck, rubber stamped chicken on one side of truck, bunny on other
EX $100 NM $150 MIP $200

Stake Bed Truck, medium blue cab, red stake bed, 10" long; 1940
EX $75 NM $130 MIP $185

Stake Bed Truck and Trailer, red truck, silver or blue stake bed, 18" long
EX $125 NM $200 MIP $250

Stony Smith Jeep, 21-1/4" long; No. 4540, green hard plastic, for Stony plastic doll, with or without star on hood; 1966-68
EX $15 NM $30 MIP $45

Stony Smith Jeep and Trailer, No. 4544, Jeep with green plastic Search Light Trailer, 1968
EX $30 NM $60 MIP $90

Streamline Mechanical Hauler, Van, and Tank Truck Combo, heavy gauge steel, 10 3/8" long, 1936
EX $170 NM $275 MIP $350

Sunshine Fruit Growers Truck, red cab, yellow/white trailer w/blue roof, 14" long
EX $125 NM $175 MIP $250

Super Crane, 2' long; battery-operated and hand-crank operation, plastic truck with swiveling "Super Crane" body, boom with clamshell, drag bucket, and sky hook, rolling on six tires; 1964-65
EX $25 NM $50 MIP $75

Super Crane, plastic and metal, battery-operated, 18" long truck body; 1960s
EX $100 NM $150 MIP $200

Swift Van Truck, red plstic van truck, "Swift" on sides, 1950s
EX $20 NM $50 MIP $75

Tipper Dump Truck, wind-up, 9-3/4" long; 1950
EX $75 NM $130 MIP $175

Tow Truck, red cab, yellow towing unit, 6" long, 1930s
EX $137 NM $200 MIP $275

Tow Truck, 10" long, 1935
EX $125 NM $200 MIP $250

Tow Truck, aluminum finish, wind-up, 6-1/4" long
EX $95 NM $150 MIP $190

Tow Truck, aluminum finsih, tin litho wind-up, 6-1/4" long
EX $75 NM $125 MIP $150

Tow Truck, 3-1/2"; white futuristic cabover, 1970s
EX $4 NM $8 MIP $15

Toyland Dairy Truck, 10" long
EX $140 NM $210 MIP $280

(Bob Smith)

Toyland's Farm Products Mack Milk Truck, w/12 wooden milk bottles, 10-1/4" long, 1931
EX $200 NM $300 MIP $400

Toytown Express Truck, plastic cab
EX $45 NM $70 MIP $95

Tractor Trailer with Dumpster, blue/yellow hauler, tan dumpster
EX $125 NM $200 MIP $250

Truck Train, stake hauler and four trailers, 41" long, 1938
EX $350 NM $550 MIP $725

Truck Train, stake hauler and five trailers, 41" long, 1933
EX $250 NM $400 MIP $525

Truck with Electric Lights, 15" long, 1930s
EX $110 NM $165 MIP $300

Truck with Electric Lights, battery-operated lights, 10" long, 1935
EX $125 NM $200 MIP $375

Truck with Searchlight, toolbox behind cab, 10" long, 1930s
EX $150 NM $225 MIP $400

U.S. Air Force Willy's Jeep, tin body, plastic figures
EX $70 NM $100 MIP $140

U.S. Army Jeep with Trailer
EX $100 NM $150 MIP $200

U.S. Mail Truck, 14" long; metal, 1950s
EX $225 NM $350 MIP $450

U.S. Trucking Co. Mack Truck, dark maroon cab, friction, 5-1/2" long, 1930
EX $100 NM $150 MIP $200

Van Truck, 10" long; plastic, 1950s
EX $40 NM $60 MIP $80

Western Auto (tractor-trailer), 25" long; red cabover, "Western Auto" silver van trailer with dual tandems; 1967-68
EX $42 NM $83 MIP $125

Western Auto Truck, 25" long, steel
EX $60 NM $90 MIP $130

(Richard Jansen)

Willys Jeep, 12" long, steel, 1938
EX $125 NM $200 MIP $250

Willys Jeep and Trailer, 11" long; red/yellow Jeep w/utility trailer, 1940s
EX $100 NM $160 MIP $375

Willys Towing Service Truck, 12-3/4" long; blue cab and chassis, steel wheels, late 1940s
EX $75 NM $150 MIP $200

(RLM MacNary Collection)

Wrecker Truck, 1930s
EX $145 NM $225 MIP $290

MATCHBOX KING SIZE

K1-1, Hydraulic Shovel, 1960, Yellow body and front loader, no plastic windows, no interior, gray plastic wheels
EX $30 NM $65 MIP $95

(KP Photo by Dr. Douglas Sadecky)

K1-2, Foden Tipper Truck, 1964, Red cab and chassis, orange dumper bed with "Hoveringham" decals or labels on sides, red plastic wheels with removable black plastic tires, blue plastic windows, no interior, axle suspension system to roll over bumps, silver metal horns on cab, 4-1/2"
EX $30 NM $50 MIP $80

K1-3, O & K Excavator, 1970, Red body with silver excavator arm, red hubs with eight black plastic removable tires, "MH6", "O&K" and white stripe labels on sides, 4-15/16"
EX $15 NM $25 MIP $35

K2-1, Dumper Truck, 1960, Blocky red body and chassis with open cab, gray or black plastic tires on green metal hubs, "Muir-Hill" decals
EX $25 NM $45 MIP $75

(KP Photo by Dr. Douglas Sadecky)

K2-2, KW-Dart Dump Truck, 1964, Yellow articulated body with silver trim on engine and hood. Red hubs with removable black plastic tires, "KW-Dart" decals with arrow graphic, no window plastic, 5-5/8"
EX $30 **NM** $65 **MIP** $95

K2-3, Scammell Heavy Wreck Truck, 1969, White or gold body with red plastic hubs and black removable wheels, silver metal hooks, red towing arm, silver horns on cab roof, "Esso" labels on doors, 4-3/4"
EX $24 **NM** $45 **MIP** $75

(KP Photo by Dr. Douglas Sadecky)

K3-1, Caterpillar Bulldozer, 1960, Yellow body with green rubber treads and unpainted metal or yellow or red plastic roller wheels, cast tow hook, red-painted engine
EX $25 **NM** $50 **MIP** $90

(KP Photo by Dr. Douglas Sadecky)

K3-2, Hatra Tractor Shovel, 1965, Orange-red body with articulating center and lifting loader. Blue-tinted plastic windows, "Hatra" decals on sides of cab, red hubs with black plastic removable tires, 6"
EX $36 **NM** $65 **MIP** $110

K3-3, Massey-Ferguson Tractor and Trailer, 1970, Red cab and hood with gray engine and base, yellow hubs with removable black plastic tires, white grille, green plastic windows. Trailer with yellow chassis, red dumper bed, yellow hubs with black removable tires. Set measures 8"
EX $17 **NM** $28 **MIP** $55

K4-1, International Tractor, 1960, Red body with "McCormick International" and "B-250" decals, green, red or orange hubs with black plastic removable tires, 2-7/8". Early versions with green metal hubs have approx. $80 MIP value
EX $25 **NM** $40 **MIP** $75

(KP Photo by Dr. Douglas Sadecky)

K4-2, GMC Tractor with Hopper Train, 1967, Red tractor with two silver hopper trailers, red plastic hubs with black plastic removable wheels, opening chutes, "Fruehauf" decals on each trailer, set measures 11-1/4"
EX $55 **NM** $90 **MIP** $150

K4-3, Leyland Tipper, 1969, Red cab and chassis, silver dumper bed, red hubs with black plastic removable tires, (duals in rear), "Wates" and "LE Transport" labels most common. Amber plastic windows, yellow plastic interior, 4-1/2". Some hard-to-find models with green cabs exist, but have approx. $300 MIP values. Other models include orange cabs with green dumper beds
EX $15 **NM** $25 **MIP** $50

(KP Photo by Dr. Douglas Sadecky)

K5-1, Tipper Truck, 1961, Yellow body, silver-painted grille, silver metal or red plastic hubs with black tires, "Foden" decal on sides of hood, 4-1/4".

First-version siver-hub models about $80 MIP
EX $25 **NM** $50 **MIP** $80

K5-2, Racing Car Transporter, 1967, Medium-green body, cream plastic interior, clear plastic windows and skylights, red plastic hubs with black removable tires, decals on sides show racing car graphic with "Racing Transporter," "BP," and "LeMans, Sebring, Silverstone, Nurburgring." Silver metal base. Opening tailgate reveals tilting ramp and space for two racing cars, 5". This model entered the King-Size line, after being number M-6 in the Major Packs series
EX $25 **NM** $50 **MIP** $85

K6-1, Allis-Chalmers Earth Scraper, 1961, Orange scraper with silver metal or red plastic hubs and black plastic tires. Adjustable scaper bed with springs (sometimes missing) "Allis-Chalmers" decals, 5-7/8"
EX $45 **NM** $80 **MIP** $130

K6-2, Mercedes-Benz "Binz" Ambulance, 1967, White body with blue plastic windows and dome light, black base, red cross decal on hood and shield decals on opening doors, opening rear hatch with white plastic patient and red plastic blanket, silver hubs with black plastic tires, silver metal grille and bumpers, "True Guide" steering, 4-1/8"
EX $15 **NM** $25 **MIP** $60

(KP Photo by Dr. Douglas Sadecky)

K7-1, Curtiss-Wright Rear Dumper, 1961, Yellow articulated body with silver metal hubs and black plastic tires, tilting

dumper bed, "Curtiss-Wright" decals, red-painted engine block, 5-3/4"
EX $40 **NM** $85 **MIP** $135

K7-2, SD Refuse Truck, 1967, Red cab & chassis, silver rear refuse unit, "Cleansing Service" decals or labels, red plastic wheels with black plastic tires, cream-colored plastic interior, clear plastic windows, 4-5/8"
EX $15 **NM** $25 **MIP** $45

(KP Photo by Dr. Douglas Sadecky)

K8-1, Prime Mover and Transporter with Caterpillar Tractor, 1962, Orange body & trailer, yellow "Laing" decals, metal towhook, unpainted metal or red plastic wheels with black plastic tires, yellow tractor with green treads and no blade, set measures 12-1/2"
EX $125 **NM** $180 **MIP** $275

K8-2, Car Transporter, 1967, Green or yellow cab, orange or yellow trailer, orange or red plastic wheels with black plastic tires, "Car Auction Collection" and "Farnborough Meashan" decals on trailer, 8-1/2"
EX $25 **NM** $45 **MIP** $85

K8-3, Caterpillar Traxcavator, 1970, Various versions of shades of yellow cab, orange shovel & arms, figure, yellow or black wheels with green or black treads, "available mid-1970" in catalog, 4-1/4"
EX $15 **NM** $25 **MIP** $40

K9-1, Diesel Road Roller, 1962, Green body, red metal rollers, gray or red driver, red "Aveling Barford" decals on sides with white reversed type, 3-3/4"
EX $35 **NM** $65 **MIP** $95

K9-2, Claas Combine Harvester, 1967, Green or red body, red or yellow reels, "Claas" decals or labels, yellow plastic wheels with black plastic tires, 5-1/2"
EX $22 **NM** $40 **MIP** $80

K10-1, Aveling-Barford Tractor Shovel, 1963, Light-blue body & shovel, red seat, with or without air filter, unpainted metal or red plastic wheels with black plastic tires, 4-1/8"
EX $30 **NM** $60 **MIP** $90

K10-2, Pipe Truck, 1967, Yellow cab & trailer chassis, black house-shaped decal on cab doors, gray plastic pipes, red plastic wheels with black plastic tires, later issues had Superfast wheels and pink cab and chassis, 8"
EX $20 **NM** $40 **MIP** $75

K11-1, Fordson Tractor and Trailer, 1963, Blue tractor body & trailer chassis, light-gray trailer bed, orange metal or plastic wheels with black plastic tires, 6-1/4"
EX $25 **NM** $45 **MIP** $80

K11-2, DAF Car Transporter, 1969, Metallic blue cab with gold trailer or yellow cab with orange & yellow trailer, DAF labels, red plastic wheels with black plastic tires or Superfast Wheels, 9"
EX $20 **NM** $50 **MIP** $85

(KP Photo by Dr. Douglas Sadecky)

K12-1, Heavy Breakdown Wreck Truck, 1963, Green body, yellow boom, with or without roof lights, unpainted metal or red plastic wheels with black plastic tires, 4-3/4"
EX $25 **NM** $50 **MIP** $85

K12-2, Scammell Crane Truck, 1970, Yellow cab & crane, red plastic wheels with black plastic tires or orange body & crane with Superfast wheels, 6"
EX $20 **NM** $35 **MIP** $50

(KP Photo by Dr. Douglas Sadecky)

K13-1, Ready-Mix Concrete Truck, 1963, Orange body & mixer with unpainted metal or red plastic wheels with black plastic tires, green plastic windows, no interior, "Readymix" or "RMC" decals on mixer barrel, 4-1/2"
EX $25 **NM** $50 **MIP** $80

(KP Photo by Dr. Douglas Sadecky)

K14-1, Taylor Jumbo Crane, 1964, Yellow body & crane, green windows, red or yellow weight box, red plastic wheels with black plastic tires, 5-1/4"
EX $25 **NM** $50 **MIP** $75

K15-1, Merryweather Fire Engine, 1964, Red body, gray extending ladder, red plastic wheels with black plastic tires or Superfast wheels, 6-1/8"
EX $25 **NM** $45 **MIP** $75

(KP Photo by Dr. Douglas Sadecky)

K16-1, Dodge Tractor with Twin Tippers, 1966, Green cab & trailer chassis, yellow dumps, Dodge Trucks decals, red plastic wheels with black plastic tires; later issues had yellow cab with blue dump & Superfast wheels, 11-7/8"
EX $65 **NM** $135 **MIP** $185

(KP Photo by Dr. Douglas Sadecky)

K17-1, Low Loader with Bulldozer, 1967, Green Ford cab & trailer, red plastic wheels with black plastic tires, red Case bulldozer body, yellow roof & blade, green treads, "Laing" or "Taylor Woodrow" decals or labels, later issues

had Superfast wheels and lime-green cab and trailer, 9-1/2"
EX $60 **NM** $90 **MIP** $135

K18-1, Articulated Horse Box, 1967, Red Dodge cab with tan trailer, clear windows on trailer, gray ramp, four white horses, red plastic wheels with black plastic tires, later issues had Superfast wheels , 6-5/8"
EX $35 **NM** $55 **MIP** $90

K19-1, Scammell Tipper Truck, 1967, Red cab & yellow dump, red plastic wheels with black plastic tires or Superfast wheels, 4-3/4"
EX $20 **NM** $35 **MIP** $60

K20-1, Tractor Transporter, 1968, Red Ford cab & trailer, red plastic wheels with black plastic tires, green plastic windows, 3 blue tractors with yellow wheels, later issues had Superfast wheels, 9"
EX $65 **NM** $100 **MIP** $150

K21-1, Mercury Cougar, 1968, Gold body, red or white interior, unpainted metal wheels with black plastic tires, 4-1/8". Shown in blue in 1968 catalog, announcing model would be available mid-year
EX $25 **NM** $50 **MIP** $75

K22-1, Dodge Charger, 1969, Dark-blue body, light-blue interior, unpainted metal wheels with black plastic tires with "True Guide" steering, 4-1/2". Shown in 1969 catalog, announcing available mid-year
EX $25 **NM** $50 **MIP** $75

K23-1, Mercury Police Car, 1969, White body, red interior, blue dome lights, police labels, unpainted metal wheels with black plastic tires with "True Guide" steering or Superfast wheels, 4-3/8". Introduced in 1969 catalog as being available mid-year
EX $20 **NM** $35 **MIP** $50

K24-1, Lamborghini Miura, 1969, Red body, white interior, unpainted metal wheels with black plastic tires and "True Guide" steering, many color & wheel variations exist, 4"
EX $20 **NM** $35 **MIP** $55

MATCHBOX REGULAR WHEELS

1-1RW, Road Roller, 1953, One of the first Matchbox offerings, this model had a "steamroller"-style large-roofed cab that matched the large toy produced by Lesney. Green paint on body can vary in shade, red metal wheels and rollers
EX $40 **NM** $75 **MIP** $125

1-2RW, Diesel Road Roller, 1955, Second in the series, but first with a smaller cab, roller attachment a little more snug than the first version, red metal wheels and roller, driver available in light and dark tan variations, gold-painted upright tow hook, 2-1/4"
EX $30 **NM** $60 **MIP** $110

1-3RW, Road Roller, 1958, Third in the series, this casting kept the driver, but changed the tow hook at rear of the tractor. It still featured red metal wheels and rollers, 2-1/4"
EX $45 **NM** $70 **MIP** $95

1-4RW, Diesel Road Roller, 1962, Green with orange/red plastic wheels, open window on cab behind driver, tow hook on back. 2-5/8", "Aveling Barford Road Roller" on base near rear wheels
EX $12 **NM** $35 **MIP** $70

(KP Photo, George Cuhaj collection)

1-5RW, Mercedes-Benz Truck, 1968, Light pea-green, with orange or yellow plastic canopy, truck could be hitched to a matching trailer, released the same year, 3"
EX $5 **NM** $12 **MIP** $20

2-1RW, Dumper, 1953, This first version featured a gold-painted front grille on a green body with red dump bed, 1-1/2"
EX $25 **NM** $60 **MIP** $100

(KP Photo by Dr. Douglas Sadecky)

2-2RW, Dumper, 1957, Second casting is larger than first, with less painted detail. First issue with metal wheels, second with gray plastic wheels. Green body, red dumper bed, 2". Pictured here 2-3RW Muir-Hill Dumper
EX $25 **NM** $60 **MIP** $90

(KP Photo, George Cuhaj collection)

2-3RW, Dumper, 1961, Short, blocky cab with "Laing" or "Muir-Hill" decal on right-hand door. Red cab with pea-green dumper bed, black plastic wheels, 2-1/8". Although the cab is different, this model is very similar to the K-2 dumper released one year earlier. "Muir-Hill" decal versions can have about $100 MIP value
EX $12 **NM** $22 **MIP** $45

(KP Photo, George Cuhaj collection)

2-3RW, Dumper, 1961, Another view of 2-3RW, also simply called "Dumper" in Matchbox 1966 catalog
EX $7 **NM** $12 **MIP** $30

(KP Photo, George Cuhaj collection)

2-4RW, Mercedes-Benz Trailer, 1968, Pea-green trailer released same year as Mercedes-Benz Truck, 1-5RW. Also came with orange or yellow canopy, 3-1/2"
EX $5 **NM** $10 **MIP** $20

(KP Photo by Dr. Douglas Sadecky)

3-1RW, Cement Mixer, 1953, Another early Matchbox, this model mirrors one of Lesney's first larger die-cast toys. Variations seem to exist in castings, earlier models measure slightly larger at 1-3/4" length than the later ones, coming in at 1-1/2" length. Orange metal or gray plastic wheels
EX $25 **NM** $60 **MIP** $120

(KP Photo, Tom Michael collection)

3-2RW, Bedford Tipper Truck, 1961, Available in red and maroon dumper variations, as well as gray and black plastic wheels, 2-1/2". Gray plastic wheeled version harder to find, about $120 MIP
EX $10 **NM** $25 **MIP** $60

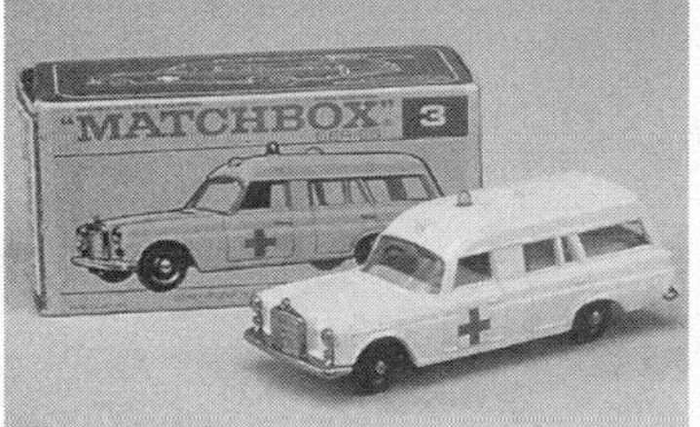

3-3RW, Mercedes-Benz "Binz" Ambulance, 1968, White or cream body with Red Cross label or decal and plastic patient on stretcher. This was a smaller version of the K-6 ambulance released one year earlier, 2-7/8". Unpainted base with textured surface along sides and near back tailgate
EX $10 **NM** $18 **MIP** $30

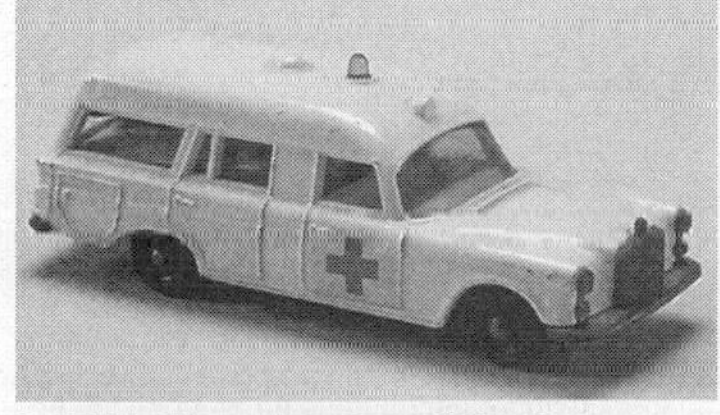

3-3RW, Mercedes-Benz "Binz" Ambulance, 1968, Variation photo showing cream paint and decal version of Mercedes ambulance
EX $10 **NM** $18 **MIP** $30

4-1RW, Tractor, 1954, Red Massey-Harris tractor body and fenders; a small version of larger Lesney Massey-Harris toy tractor
EX $35 **NM** $65 **MIP** $125

4-2RW, Massey-Harris Tractor, 1957, Red with no fenders. An update on the previous model, this tractor was re-released painted green in 1994 as an anniversary issue. Metal wheel and gray plastic wheel variations, some casting variations with 1-1/2" and 1-3/4" lengths
EX $40 **NM** $75 **MIP** $135

(KP Photo, George Cuhaj collection)

4-3RW, Triumph Motorcycle w/Sidecar, 1960, Light metallic blue with 24-spoke silver wheels and black tires, 2-1/8"
EX $17 **NM** $30 **MIP** $85

(KP Photo, George Cuhaj collection)

4-3RW, Triumph Motorcycle w/Sidecar, 1960, Another view of the Triumph Motorcycle w/Sidecar
EX $17 **NM** $30 **MIP** $85

(KP Photo, George Cuhaj collection)

4-4RW, Dodge Stake Truck, 1967, Yellow cab and body with green plastic stakes. A popular model, Matchbox made many toy trucks with this Dodge cab style, 2-7/8". Models with blue-green stakes, a very slight color difference, can have about $150 MIP value
EX $10 **NM** $18 **MIP** $27

5-1RW, Double Decker Bus, 1954, First of Matchbox's London Buses, this one featured decals that read "Buy Matchbox Series" on the side, 2"
EX $15 **NM** $45 **MIP** $80

(KP Photo, Tom Michael collection)

5-2RW, Double Decker Bus, 1958, Second London Bus, casting slightly larger, at 2-1/4" length. "No. 5" cast into front of bus, no interior. Available with metal and gray plastic wheels, with a variety of decals
EX $40 **NM** $80 **MIP** $130

5-3RW, Routemaster London Bus, 1961, Red, with gray or black plastic wheels, "Visco-Static" decal most common. No interior in bus, major change from last model: a wider front grille, with cast headlights on front fenders
EX $20 **NM** $45 **MIP** $80

5-4RW, Routemaster London Bus, 1965, Red body, white plastic interior-first Matchbox model bus to feature one. Like 5-3RW, the "Visco-Static" decals and labels are the most common, 2-3/4"
EX $8 **NM** $15 **MIP** $30

6-1RW, Quarry Truck, 1954, Orange body with gray dumper bed. No interior. Most commonly seen with metal wheels, crimped or rounded axles, 2-1/4"
EX $20 **NM** $45 **MIP** $85

6-2RW, Quarry Truck, 1959, Yellow body, black plastic wheels most common, red, white and black decal on cab doors, cab extends the full width of the front of truck, appears first in 1959 catalog with black plastic wheels
EX $15 **NM** $35 **MIP** $75

6-3RW, Euclid 10-Wheel Quarry Truck, 1964, Yellow body, no decals, exposed engine shows on casting, partial cab does not extend across body of truck, 2-5/8"
EX $7 **NM** $15 **MIP** $30

VEHICLES • MATCHBOX REGULAR WHEELS

(KP Photo, George Cuhaj collection)

6-4RW, Ford Pickup, 1969, Red, with white plastic camper top and white or silver plastic front grille. Featured "Autosteer," a Matchbox innovation making its appearance in the 1969 catalog, that "turns the front wheels in either direction by simple pressure." 2-3/4"
EX $10 **NM** $20 **MIP** $30

(KP Photo by Dr. Douglas Sadecky)

7-1RW, Horse-Drawn Milk Float, 1954, Orange wagon body, white painted driver, brown horse. Available with metal spoked or gray solid plastic wheels, 2-1/4". Quite a detailed little model
EX $45 **NM** $75 **MIP** $125

(KP Photo, George Cuhaj collection)

7-2RW, Ford Anglia, 1961, Light blue body, no interior, gray, silver or black plastic wheels, silver painted grille, bumper and headlights, 2-5/8", black painted baseplate, tow hook. Gray plastic wheel versions, about $110 MIP; silver plastic wheel versions, about $55 MIP. Thanks to the film, Harry Potter and the Chamber of Secrets (2002), interest in these models has increased.
EX $25 **NM** $60 **MIP** $95

(KP Photo by Dr. Douglas Sadecky)

7-2RW, Ford Anglia, 1961, A view of a gray-plastic-wheel version of the Ford Anglia, a harder-to-find variation
EX $30 **NM** $60 **MIP** $110

(KP Photo, Tom Michael collection)

7-3RW, Ford Refuse Truck, 1967, Red body, gray and silver dumper section, tilts together when dumped, no interior, black plastic wheels, green window plastic, 3"
EX $10 **NM** $18 **MIP** $30

8-1RW, Caterpillar Tractor, 1955, Yellow or orange with cast driver, silver painted grille. Unpainted roller wheels for treads, 1-1/2". Fully exposed engine under hood. Note: Orange variation harder to find, MIP value can reach over $200; yellow versions with painted drivers also about $200 MIP
EX $20 **NM** $40 **MIP** $85

8-2RW, Caterpillar Tractor, 1959, Yellow, different casting with engine partially covered by hood, and cast "roller wheels" between two actual turning metal wheels. Driver cast with toy, 1-3/4", green or gray rubber treads
EX $25 **NM** $65 **MIP** $90

8-3RW, Caterpillar Crawler Tractor, 1961, Yellow body with cast driver, metal or plastic tread wheels, very similar to previous casting, models with silver plastic roller wheels about $90 MIP
EX $20 **NM** $40 **MIP** $65

(KP Photo, Tom Michael collection)

8-4RW, Caterpillar Crawler Tractor, 1965, Yellow, cast without driver, black plastic roller wheels, 2", gray or black rubber treads
EX $12 **NM** $22 **MIP** $35

(KP Photo, George Cuhaj collection)

8-5RW, Ford Mustang Fastback, 1966, White, with red interior and tow hook. Black plastic tires on silver wheels. Unique steering lever on driver's side allows front wheels to turn left or right, 2-7/8", orange versions are quite rare, about $300 MIP
EX $12 **NM** $25 **MIP** $45

9-1RW, Fire Escape, 1955, Red with cast driver, metal wheels, gold-painted trim, 2-1/4", no front bumper in casting
EX $20 **NM** $45 **MIP** $80

9-2RW, Fire Escape, 1957, Red, cast with driver, metal wheels most common, versions with gray plastic wheels about $400 MIP, front bumper included in casting, 2-1/4"
EX $20 **NM** $45 **MIP** $80

9-3RW, Merryweather Marquis Fire Engine, 1959, Red body with cab, gold ladder, black plastic wheels (first versions had gray plastic wheels), ladder colors can vary, 2-5/8", simply called "Fire Truck" in 1966 catalog
EX $20 **NM** $55 **MIP** $70

(KP Photo, Tom Michael collection)

9-4RW, Boat and Trailer, 1967, Plastic blue and white boat with blue die-cast trailer, black plastic wheels. First time a stand-alone trailer makes appearance in regular wheels line
EX $10 **NM** $20 **MIP** $35

10-1RW, Mechanical Horse and Trailer, 1955, Red, three-wheeled cab and gray stake-style trailer, metal wheels, 3"
EX $55 **NM** $70 **MIP** $95

(KP Photo by Dr. Douglas Sadecky)

10-2RW, Mechanical Horse and Trailer, 1957, Second casting of Scammell Scarab, red three-wheeled cab and light-tan stake-style trailer with fenders. Grille can be painted or unpainted, metal wheels, 3". Appears first in 1957 catalog/flyer
EX $40 **NM** $60 **MIP** $95

(KP Photo, George Cuhaj collection)

10-3RW, Sugar Container Truck, 1962, Blue Foden truck body with "Tate & Lyle" decal, with silver, gray, or black plastic wheels (shown). Popular Foden cab design, 2-5/8". Gray-wheeled models tend to have higher MIP values, up to $200
EX $25 **NM** $50 **MIP** $80

(KP Photo, George Cuhaj collection)

10-3RW, Sugar Container Truck, 1962, Another view of 10-3RW, showing decal from back of truck

(KP Photo, John Brown Sr. collection)

10-4RW, Pipe Truck, 1967, Red Leyland die-cast body, silver grille and baseplate, gray plastic pipes. "Ergomatic Cab" written on baseplate, 3". The Ergomatic cab was a new feature on large British trucks, including Leyland and AEC, beginning in the mid-sixties, so this model reflected the latest advance at time of release
EX $12 **NM** $20 **MIP** $45

11-1RW, Road Tanker, 1955, Yellow or red ERF truck body, metal wheels, "Esso" decal on rear of tank, 2", painted side gas tanks, crimped axles
EX $40 **NM** $75 **MIP** $115

11-2RW, Road Tanker, 1959, Red ERF truck body, metal wheels, gray or black plastic wheels, variations include silver painted side gas tanks and grilles, slightly larger casting, 2-1/2"
EX $35 **NM** $60 **MIP** $100

(KP Photo by Dr. Douglas Sadecky)

11-3RW, Jumbo Crane, 1965, Yellow, red plastic hook, large black plastic wheels in front near cab, small in back-1966 catalog illustration looks more like King Size version, K-14, with what appears to be a die-cast hook. Some with red counterweights, 3". Shown here with 42-3RW Iron Fairy Crane
EX $8 **NM** $15 **MIP** $30

(KP Photo, John Brown Sr. collection)

11-4RW, Scaffold Truck, mid-1969, Mercedes-Benz truck, silver body with yellow plastic scaffold sections in stake-style bed. "Builders Supply Company" decal on side, 2-5/8", released late in 1969, just before transition to Superfast
EX $8 **NM** $12 **MIP** $25

(KP Photo, John Brown Sr. collection)

12-1RW, Land Rover, 1957, Dark green body with tan driver, metal wheels. No real windshield, just a low flat piece of the casting appearing where the base of a windshield would be. Slight casting variations, some 1-5/8" length, later editions, 1-3/4" length. Silver-painted grille
EX $15 **NM** $40 **MIP** $85

(KP Photo, George Cuhaj collection)

12-2RW, Land Rover, 1960, Dark green, black or gray plastic wheels (black more common). Open cab, model shown has bent windshield. "Land-Rover Series II" on black baseplate
EX $15 **NM** $40 **MIP** $75

12-3RW, Safari Land Rover, 1965, Dark green body, dark brown plastic luggage on top, white interior, white tow hook, black plastic baseplate. First issue of the Safari Land Rover, says "Land Rover Safari" on base, 2-3/4"
EX $8 **NM** $15 **MIP** $25

12-3RW, Safari Land Rover, 1967, Medium-blue body, light reddish-brown plastic luggage, white plastic interior and tow hook, black plastic baseplate with "Land Rover Safari." Second issue of same casting in blue
EX $8 **NM** $15 **MIP** $25

(KP Photo, Tom Michael collection)

13-1RW, Wreck Truck, 1955, Tan Bedford truck with red tow hook and scaffold, metal wheels, silver-painted grille and bumper, 2-1/4"
EX $35 **NM** $50 **MIP** $75

13-2RW, Wreck Truck, 1958, Tan Bedford body, red boom section, metal or gray plastic wheels, no interior, slightly smaller than previous casting at 2"
EX $40 **NM** $60 **MIP** $90

(KP Photo, George Cuhaj collection)

13-3RW, Wreck Truck, 1961, Red body with metal or plastic tow hook, and gray or black plastic wheels, decal on side of truck says "A.A. & R.A.C. Matchbox Garages Breakdown Service," silver trim on front grille
EX $18 **NM** $45 **MIP** $110

(KP Photo, George Cuhaj collection)

13-4RW, Wreck Truck, 1966, Dodge Wreck Truck with yellow cab, green tow bed, red plastic hook, clear red plastic cab light, BP decals or labels, 3", black plastic wheels. Variations with colors reversed, (green cab and yellow body) are extremely rare. "Dodge Wreck Truck" on green base near rear wheels
EX $7 **NM** $12 **MIP** $30

14-1RW, Ambulance, 1956, Cream painted body, metal wheels, Red Cross decal, word "Ambulance" cast in raised letters along side of vehicle, 2"
EX $20 **NM** $45 **MIP** $85

(KP Photo, John Brown Sr. collection)

14-2RW, Ambulance, 1958, Daimler with cream or off-white body with metal or gray plastic wheels, Red Cross decal, slightly larger casting at 2-1/4", word "Ambulance" cast in raised letters
EX $22 **NM** $60 **MIP** $90

(KP Photo, George Cuhaj collection)

14-3RW, Lomas Ambulance, 1962, White body with black plastic wheels and "LCC Ambulance" decals, 2-5/8", referred to simply as "Ambulance" in catalog. "LCC" is an abbreviation for the "London County Council," responsible for designing and building ambulances in the 1950s and 1960s to its own specifications, later adapted by Daimler and other companies
EX $10 **NM** $20 **MIP** $45

(KP Photo, George Cuhaj collection)

14-4RW, Iso Grifo, 1968, Dark blue, almost purple body, light blue plastic interior and tow hook, opening doors, 3", in 1968 catalog, "available in early 1968," steering wheel on right-hand side, black tires on silver wheels, textured baseplate
EX $18 **NM** $34 **MIP** $60

(KP Photo, George Cuhaj collection)

14-4RW, Iso Grifo, Detail photo: shows white tow hook and driver's side door open to British-style steering wheel arrangement

(KP Photo, George Cuhaj collection)

15-1RW, Prime Mover Truck, 1956, Orange body, silver grille and trim, metal wheels. Harder to find editions: yellow body with metal wheels and orange with gray plastic wheels
EX $22 **NM** $45 **MIP** $70

15-2RW, Atlantic Prime Mover, 1959, Orange body, black plastic wheels, spare tire in bed of truck, no interior
EX $25 **NM** $45 **MIP** $95

(KP Photo, George Cuhaj collection)

15-3RW, Dennis Refuse Truck, 1963, Blue body, gray dumper section, red and white decals or labels say "Cleansing Service," and have cross-in-shield design at center. Black plastic knobby wheels, no interior, 2-1/2"
EX $7 **NM** $14 **MIP** $30

(KP Photo, George Cuhaj collection)

15-4RW, Volkswagen 1500 Saloon, 1968, White Volkswagen Beetle body with "137" decals or labels, black plastic tires on silver wheels, 2-7/8"
EX $7 **NM** $12 **MIP** $25

16-1RW, Transporter Trailer, 1956, Tan, flat bodied trailer with ramp and non-skid surface for vehicles, one axle and metal wheels in front near towbar, two axles with metal wheels on back near ramp, 3", ramp fold up onto trailer body
EX $17 **NM** $30 **MIP** $60

(KP Photo by Dr. Douglas Sadecky)

16-2RW, Atlantic Transporter, 1960, Orange trailer body, black plastic wheels, 4 axles; two at front near drawbar, two at back near ramp, non-skid tire tracks on trailer, pictured here with 15-2RW Atlantic Prime Mover
EX $17 **NM** $40 **MIP** $75

(KP Photo, George Cuhaj collection)

16-3RW, "Mountaineer" Dump Truck w/Snowplough, 1964, Gray cab and body with orange dumper section, snowplow on front with orange and white striped decal, black plastic wheels, 3", gray plastic wheel version about twice MIP value
EX $18 **NM** $30 **MIP** $50

(KP Photo, George Cuhaj collection)

16-3RW, "Mountaineer" Dump Truck w/Snowplough, 1964, Another view of Mountaineer Dump Truck with raised dumper bed

(KP Photo, John Brown Sr. collection)

16-4RW, Case Bulldozer, 1969, Red body with yellow blade and cab, "Available mid-1969" in 1969 1st issue catalog, 2-1/2"
EX $9 **NM** $18 **MIP** $32

17-1RW, Removals Van, 1956, Green, blue or dark red body, metal wheels, "Matchbox Removals Service" decal, green more common color
EX $15 **NM** $60 **MIP** $100

(KP Photo by Dr. Douglas Sadecky)

17-2RW, Removals Van, 1958, Green body, with "Matchbox Removals Service" decal on sides, metal or gray plastic wheels
EX $35 **NM** $75 **MIP** $125

17-3RW, Metropolitan Taxi, 1960, Dark red with gray or silver plastic wheels, gray more common, silver can have $130+ MIP value, gray-wheel values shown
EX $25 **NM** $40 **MIP** $75

17-4RW, 8-Wheel Tipper, 1963, Red Foden body, orange dumper section, black plastic wheels, no interior, 3", "Hoveringham" decal on tipper. A "little brother" to the 8-Wheel Tipper K-1 in the King Size line
EX $9 **NM** $18 **MIP** $37

17-4RW, 8-Wheel Tipper, 1963, Another view of Foden 8-Wheel Tipper, with hinged gate at back opening when dumper section is tilted up
EX $9 **NM** $18 **MIP** $37

18-1RW, Bulldozer, 1956, Yellow body, tow hook, red blade, metal roller wheels, driver in hat cast as part of toy
EX $18 **NM** $35 **MIP** $85

18-2RW, Bulldozer, 1958, Yellow body, tow hook, yellow blade, driver cast into body, metal roller wheels. Engine partially covered on side
EX $25 **NM** $78 **MIP** $110

(KP Photo, John Brown Sr. collection)

18-3RW, Caterpillar Bulldozer, 1961, Yellow body, tow hook, yellow blade, driver cast into body, metal or black plastic rollers. Driver shown here is painted, but normally they were the same color as casting
EX $18 **NM** $40 **MIP** $80

18-4RW, Caterpillar Crawler Bulldozer, 1964, Yellow body, curving tow hook, no driver, black plastic roller wheels. Casting essentially the same as 18-3, but with flatter blade and no driver
EX $7 **NM** $18 **MIP** $40

(KP Photo, George Cuhaj collection)

18-5RW, Field Car, 1969, Yellow body, white plastic interior, generally red wheels with black plastic tires. Many collectors consider this vehicle to be an International Scout model, and in fact the side view bears close resemblance. However, the front grille also looks a bit like a French SINPAR Renault military vehicle (although they were produced in the 1970s). "Available mid-1969" in catalog. Auto-Steer model. 2-5/8"
EX $7 **NM** $11 **MIP** $18

(KP Photo, George Cuhaj collection)

18-5RW, Field Car, 1969, View of rear of Field Car, showing spare and tow hook

19-1RW, Sports Car, 1956, White or cream body with metal wheels, painted driver, silver grille
EX $45 **NM** $70 **MIP** $150

19-2RW, MG "A" Sports Car, 1958, White body, metal or gray plastic wheels, painted driver, can have rounded or crimped axles, silver- painted grille and headlights, 2-1/4"
EX $58 **NM** $85 **MIP** $150

19-3RW, Aston Martin Racer, 1961, Green body, white or gray driver, 24-spoke wheels with black plastic tires. Variable number decals on body
EX $45 **NM** $80 **MIP** $165

(KP Photo, Tom Michael collection)

19-4RW, Lotus Racing Car, 1966, Green or orange body, white plastic driver, yellow wheels with black plastic tires, No. "3" decal or label, 2-3/4". Green pictured in 1966 catalog, but orange variation included in G-4 Racetrack Set that same year. Driver missing in this photo
EX $11 **NM** $22 **MIP** $50

20-1RW, Heavy Lorry, 1956, Dark red ERF truck body, metal or gray plastic wheels, no interior, dropside stake bed appearance with fuel tanks along sides. Can have silver-painted grille, some casting variations, 2-1/4" and 2-5/8"
EX $18 **NM** $40 **MIP** $100

20-2RW, Transport Truck, 1959, ERF dropside truck with dark blue body, gray or black plastic wheels, "Ever Ready For Life" decal along stake sides, model also called "Heavy Lorry" in 1959 catalog
EX $22 **NM** $55 **MIP** $100

(KP Photo by Dr. Douglas Sadecky)

20-3RW, Taxi Cab, 1965, Chevrolet Impala Taxi Cab with yellow body, red or white plastic interior, (red is harder to find) black plastic wheels, 3"
EX $11 **NM** $18 **MIP** $30

(KP Photo, Colin Bruce collection)

21-1RW, Bedford Coach, 1956, Light pea-green body with red and yellow "London to Glasgow" decals above windows, metal wheels
EX $22 **NM** $40 **MIP** $68

(KP Photo, George Cuhaj collection)

21-2RW, Bedford Coach, 1958, Light pea-green body with red and yellow "London to Glasgow" decal above windows, metal or gray plastic wheels, "Bedford Duple Luxury Coach" on black base, 2-1/2", silver painted grille and front bumper, no interior
EX $25 **NM** $60 **MIP** $95

(KP Photo by Dr. Douglas Sadecky)

21-3RW, Milk Delivery Truck, 1961, Commer truck with light green body, white or cream plastic cargo and gray or black plastic wheels, 2-1/4", cow or milk bottle decal on cab doors. Both variations shown here
EX $20 **NM** $35 **MIP** $70

(KP Photo, George Cuhaj collection)

21-4RW, Foden Concrete Truck, 1969, Yellow Foden cab and plastic mixer with orange body, dark green plastic windows, eight black plastic wheels, 3". Worm-gear under second set of wheels turns mixer as truck rolls forward
EX $5 **NM** $9 **MIP** $22

22-1RW, Vauxhall Cresta, 1956, Red body with white roof, no interior, metal wheels, silver painted grille and bumpers, tow hook
EX $35 **NM** $60 **MIP** $110

(KP Photo by Dr. Douglas Sadecky)

22-2RW, Vauxhall Cresta, 1958, Different casting than previous version. Longer, more "Chevy-like" body with low tailfins and wraparound front and rear windshields. Many paint variations exist, some pushing MIP price well into the hundreds of dollars. Can have gray or black plastic wheels or metal wheels
EX $30 **NM** $72 **MIP** $150

(KP Photo, George Cuhaj collection)

22-3RW, Pontiac Grand Prix, 1964, Red body, black plastic wheels, gray plastic interior & tow hook, 3", opening doors, "Pontiac G.P. Sports Coupe" on black painted baseplate
EX $12 **NM** $22 **MIP** $45

23-1RW, Caravan, 1956, Pale blue body, metal wheels, 2-1/2"
EX $17 **NM** $30 **MIP** $75

23-2RW, Trailer, 1958, Pale blue-green or lime-green body, metal or gray plastic wheels
EX $22 **NM** $40 **MIP** $75

(KP Photo by Dr. Douglas Sadecky)

23-3RW, Bluebird Dauphine Trailer, 1960, Metallic tan or green body, opening door, no interior or plastic windows, black or gray plastic wheels. Variations with green bodies are hard to find, and can be quite valuable. More common tan variation prices given below
EX $25 **NM** $40 **MIP** $85

23-4RW, Trailer Caravan, 1966, Yellow or pink body, black plastic wheels, white plastic interior, 3", pink more common beginning in 1968 and after. Yellow version about $45 MIP value
EX $9 **NM** $17 **MIP** $30

24-1RW, Hydraulic Excavator, 1956, Yellow or orange body with metal wheels; larger two at rear and smaller at front, figure cast as part of body, front dumping bucket
EX $18 **NM** $40 **MIP** $75

24-2RW, Hydraulic Excavator, 1959, Yellow body, black or gray plastic wheels, larger at rear or cab, smaller in front near dumper bucket. Figure cast in piece, 2-5/8"
EX $17 **NM** $28 **MIP** $45

(KP Photo, George Cuhaj collection)

24-3RW, Rolls-Royce Silver Shadow, 1967, Deep red sedan body, white plastic interior, opening trunk, silver wheels with black plastic tires, clear plastic windshield and windows, unpainted silver metal grille, headlights and front bumper, 3". Black baseplate with "A" near front axle
EX $7 **NM** $11 **MIP** $25

(KP Photo, George Cuhaj collection)

24-3RW, Rolls-Royce Silver Shadow, 1967, View of opening trunk on Rolls

25-1RW, Bedford Dunlop Van, 1956, Dark blue Bedford panel van, with yellow "Dunlop" decals on sides, no interior or plastic windows
EX $18 **NM** $40 **MIP** $80

(KP Photo by Dr. Douglas Sadecky)

25-2RW, Volkswagen Sedan, 1960, Volkswagen 1200 Sedan, blue-silver body, gray plastic wheels, opening rear engine hood, green or clear plastic windows, black base
EX $45 **NM** $65 **MIP** $100

(KP Photo, George Cuhaj collection)

25-3RW, Petrol Tanker, 1964, Yellow Bedford cab, green body, white tanker with "BP" decal. Cab tilts to reveal white plastic interior. Black plastic wheels, 3". Called "B.P. Tanker" in 1966 catalog. Blue versions with "Aral" decals on tanker section harder to find, about $200 MIP
EX $8 **NM** $14 **MIP** $25

25-4RW, Ford Cortina, 1968, Light brown body, cream-colored plastic interior and tow hook, black plastic wheels, "Auto-Steer," textured pattern on unpainted baseplate near front and rear axles, opening doors, 2-5/8". Interesting to note that its first catalog appearance in 1968 showed a blue car with the subhead "Available in mid-1968." The blue color wouldn't be used until the 1970 Superfast version was released. Yellow roof rack included in 1969 G-4 Race'n Rally Gift Set
EX $8 **NM** $14 **MIP** $22

(KP Photo, Tom Michael collection)

26-1RW, Ready Mixed Concrete Lorry, 1957, Orange ERF cab and body with silver-painted grille and side gas tanks, metal or gray plastic wheels, 1-3/4", metal mixer section, four wheels
EX $18 **NM** $45 **MIP** $88

(KP Photo, George Cuhaj collection)

26-2RW, Ready-Mix Concrete Truck, 1961, Orange die-cast Foden cab and body with plastic orange mixer section. Gray or black plastic wheels, 2-1/2". Six wheels, says "Foden Cement Mixer" on base
EX $9 **NM** $19 **MIP** $40

(KP Photo, George Cuhaj collection)

26-3RW, GMC Tipper Truck, 1968, Red cab with green plastic windows, silver-gray tipper bed, green chassis, black plastic wheels with duals at rear, 2-5/8", 1968 catalog shows subhead "Available early 1968" and model with yellow tipper bed
EX $6 **NM** $10 **MIP** $18

(KP Photo, George Cuhaj collection)

26-3RW, GMC Tipper Truck, 1968, View showing tilting cab and green engine block underneath

27-1RW, Bedford Low Loader, 1956, Green Bedford cab with silver trim, tan trailer, metal wheels, 3", no windows or interior
EX $28 **NM** $48 **MIP** $90

27-2RW, Bedford Low Loader, 1958, Green Bedford cab with silver trim, tan trailer, metal or gray plastic knobby wheels, slightly larger casting at 3 3/4" length. No windows or interior
EX $30 **NM** $75 **MIP** $140

(KP Photo, John Brown Sr. collection)

27-3RW, Cadillac Sixty Special, 1960, Silver-gray or silver-purple Cadillac body with cream or pink colored roof, plastic windows, no interior and gray or black plastic wheels, red base, tow hook, red-painted taillights and silver-painted trim
EX $28 **NM** $45 **MIP** $90

(KP Photo, George Cuhaj collection)

27-4RW, Mercedes 230SL, 1966, White Mercedes convertible with red plastic interior, opening doors, black plastic wheels, tow hook, 2-3/4", "Available early 1966" in catalog
EX $7 **NM** $13 **MIP** $25

(KP Photo, George Cuhaj collection)

27-4RW, Mercedes 230SL, 1966, Rear view of Mercedes convertible showing opening doors and tow hook

(KP Photo by Dr. Douglas Sadecky)

28-1RW, Bedford Compressor Lorry, 1956, Orange or yellow Bedford cab and chassis with Caterpillar-type compressor engine on back, painted-silver grille and trim, 1-3/4", metal wheels. Pictured here with 28-2RW Thames Compressor Truck
EX $30 **NM** $60 **MIP** $90

(KP Photo, John Brown Sr. collection)

28-2RW, Ford Thames Compressor Lorry, 1959, Yellow Ford Thames truck cab and chassis with black plastic wheels, no interior or window plastic, silver headlights and grille
EX $25 **NM** $40 **MIP** $75

(KP Photo, George Cuhaj collection)

28-3RW, Mark Ten Jaguar, 1964, Light metallic brown body with opening hood, black plastic wheels, black-painted base. Engine can be painted the same as body color or left unpainted, 2-3/4". White plastic interior, clear window plastic, tow hook
EX $15 **NM** $25 **MIP** $35

(KP Photo, George Cuhaj collection)

28-4RW, Mack Dump Truck, 1969, Orange Mack truck body with orange dumper bed, black plastic tires on orange or yellow wheels, 2-5/8", green window plastic, unpainted base
EX $7 **NM** $18 **MIP** $25

(KP Photo, George Cuhaj collection)

28-4RW, Mack Dump Truck, 1969, View of operating dumper bed. This model first appears in the 1969 1st edition catalog

29-1RW, Bedford Milk Delivery Van, 1956, Tan body with white plastic milk bottles and boxes, silver trim, metal or gray plastic wheels, no interior or window plastic, 2-1/4"
EX $20 **NM** $40 **MIP** $80

(KP Photo, George Cuhaj collection)

29-2RW, Austin A55 Cambridge, 1961, Medium green body with light green roof, gray or black plastic wheels, green window plastic, no interior, black-painted base with tow hook, 2-1/2"
EX $17 **NM** $30 **MIP** $72

(KP Photo, John Brown Sr. collection)

29-3RW, Fire Pumper, 1966, Red LaFrance fire engine body, white plastic ladders along sides, unpainted base and trim, green window plastic, no interior, blue dome light, black plastic wheels, 3". With or without "Denver" decal
EX $6 **NM** $11 **MIP** $22

(KP Photo, George Cuhaj collection)

30-1RW, Ford Prefect, 1956, Light sage-green or light brown body with metal or gray plastic wheels, (light blue harder to find, $200 or more MIP). No window plastic or interior, silver-painted grille, headlights and bumpers, red-painted taillights. Tow hook, black-painted base, 2-3/8"
EX $15 **NM** $40 **MIP** $80

(KP Photo, George Cuhaj collection)

30-2RW, Magirus-Deutz Crane Truck, 1961, Silver cab and truck body with orange boom section and gray or black plastic wheels. Hook can be metal or plastic. Black-painted baseplate under front cab section, 2-3/8"
EX $17 **NM** $30 **MIP** $72

(KP Photo, George Cuhaj collection)

30-3RW, 8-Wheel Crane, 1965, Medium-dark green body with 8 black plastic wheels, orange crane section, yellow plastic hook, 3"
EX $5 **NM** $11 **MIP** $25

31-1RW, American Ford Station Wagon, 1957, Yellow body with metal or gray plastic wheels, silver painted bumpers and headlights, no interior or window plastic, 2-5/8". Appears brown in 1957 leaflet catalog
EX $15 **NM** $40 **MIP** $78

(Photo by Dr. Douglas Sadecky)

31-2RW, Ford Fairlane Station Wagon, 1960, Mint green with pink-white roof, gray or black plastic wheels, silver-painted trim, tow hook. Yellow-painted versions are harder to find, and can bring higher MIP values (up to $300). Two box variations shown
EX $22 **NM** $55 **MIP** $78

31-3RW, Lincoln Continental, 1964, Dark blue or mint-green body, white plastic interior, clear window glass, opening trunk, 3". Metallic tan versions rare, over $1000 MIP at auction
EX $10 **NM** $25 **MIP** $40

(KP Photo by Dr. Douglas Sadecky)

32-1RW, Jaguar XK140 Coupe, 1957, Cream body with metal or gray plastic wheels, 2-3/8", called "Fixed Head Coupe" in 1957 catalog/flyer. Silver-painted grille, red-painted taillights

EX $30 **NM** $45 **MIP** $75

(KP Photo, John Brown Sr. collection)

32-2RW, E-Type Jaguar, 1962, Metallic red body, spoked wheels with gray or black tires, green or clear window plastic, 2-5/8", white plastic interior

EX $20 **NM** $40 **MIP** $80

32-2RW, Leyland Petrol Tanker, 1968, Medium-green Ergomatic cab and chassis, eight black plastic wheels, white tanker section, "BP" decals or labels, silver or white plastic grille and bumper, 3". A blue and white version with "Aral" labels is harder to find, and can have $120 or more MIP value. "Available early 1968" in catalog

EX $5 **NM** $12 **MIP** $22

(KP Photo by Dr. Douglas Sadecky)

33-1RW, Ford Zodiac, 1957, A variety of body colors exist for this model: blue, dark green, blue-green, silver, tan & orange and turquoise. Dark green and tan and orange models more common, with around $80-$90 MIP values. 2-5/8"

EX $25 **NM** $45 **MIP** $90

(KP Photo, George Cuhaj collection)

33-2RW, Ford Zephyr 6, 1962, Blue-green body, white plastic interior, gray or black plastic wheels, silver front grille and headlights, slight tailfins, black painted base, 2-1/2". Some models with black wheels have a lighter blue-green color than earlier versions

EX $10 **NM** $15 **MIP** $30

(KP Photo, George Cuhaj collection)

33-3RW, Lamborghini Miura, 1969, Yellow or gold body with red or cream plastic interior, 2-3/4", silver wheels with black plastic tires, opening doors. Gold cars with cream interiors (as shown in 1969 catalog) have high MIP values, around $200

EX $4 **NM** $12 **MIP** $25

(KP Photo, John Brown Sr. collection)

34-1RW, Volkswagen Microvan, 1957, Blue panel van body, no interior, "Matchbox International Express" yellow type decal on sides, with silver-painted bumper and headlights, 2-1/4". Mostly found with metal or gray plastic wheels, decal on side with "Matchbox International Express" in yellow lettering

EX $30 **NM** $50 **MIP** $95

34-2RW, Volkswagen Camping Car, 1962, Light sea-green body, gray or black plastic wheels, opening side doors, top window plastic, camper section interior, 2-5/8"

EX $20 **NM** $40 **MIP** $90

34-3RW, Volkswagen Camper, 1967, Silver body with opening camper section doors, orange plastic interior, yellow window plastic, raised roof with windows and top window plastic, black plastic wheels, 2-5/8"

EX $10 **NM** $18 **MIP** $45

34-3RW, Volkswagen Camper, 1967, Another view of the Volkswagen Camper

EX $10 **NM** $18 **MIP** $45

34-4RW, Volkswagen Camper, 1969, Silver body, opening doors to camper section, slightly raised roof with window plastic on top but no windows, orange plastic interior, black plastic wheels. Interestingly, the size of this vehicle remained the same since the 1962 release at 2-5/8". Makes first appearance in 1969 catalog

EX $11 **NM** $17 **MIP** $35

(Photo by Dr. Douglas Sadecky)

35-1RW, Marshall Horse Box, 1957, Red ERF cab with silver-painted grille and headlights, brown horse box with opening side door, metal and gray plastic wheels most common, 2-1/8". Silver plastic wheel version, about $180

MIP; black plastic wheel version, about $135 MIP
EX $15 **NM** $30 **MIP** $80

(Photo by Dr. Douglas Sadecky)

35-2RW, Snow-Trac Tractor, 1964, Red body with unpainted base, six black tread roller wheels, green window plastic, 2-1/4". White or gray treads, some versions have "Snow-Trac" cast in side of tractor, (as seen in 1968 and 1969 catalogs) others have decal, and some variations have neither, (as seen in the 1966 catalog). Gray-tread models may have slightly higher MIP values, although decal models (based on the tenuous nature of decals) may start to become more desirable
EX $9 **NM** $17 **MIP** $40

35-2RW, Snow-Trac Tractor, 1964, A plain-sided variation of the Snow-Trac in the condition many of us find them-without treads

(KP Photo, George Cuhaj collection)

36-1RW, Austin A 50, 1957, Blue-green body, no interior, metal or gray plastic wheels, silver-painted grille, headlights and bumper, tow bar, 2-3/8"
EX $20 **NM** $35 **MIP** $75

36-2RW, Lambretta Motorscooter w/Sidecar, 1961, Dark or light metallic green body, black plastic wheels
EX $20 **NM** $50 **MIP** $95

(KP Photo, George Cuhaj collection)

36-3RW, Opel Diplomat, 1966, Gold body, black-painted metal base, white plastic interior and tow hook, opening hood, silver or gray plastic motor, 2-3/4". Pictured in elusive sea-green in 1966 catalog with caption "Available mid 1966." These (possibly) first versions are rarely seen
EX $5 **NM** $10 **MIP** $25

(KP Photo, George Cuhaj collection)

36-1RW, Opel Diplomat, 1966, A view of Opel Diplomat with open hood and silver engine

37-1RW, Coca-Cola Lorry, 1956, Yellow-orange truck with Coca-Cola decals on sides and back of truck, metal or gray plastic wheels, 2-1/4", no step on the running board on cab, silver-painted trim on running boards, grille. Some versions have "uneven" loads of cast Coca-Cola cases (as seen in 1957 flyer) in the bed of the truck. These typically run about $150 MIP. "Even" load versions in gray plastic wheels comparable MIP price. Even-load metal wheel version prices shown below
EX $30 **NM** $55 **MIP** $110

(KP Photo by Dr. Douglas Sadecky)

37-2RW, Coca-Cola Lorry, 1960, Yellow body, black baseplate, "even" cast crate load on bed, Coca-Cola decals on sides and back, 2-1/4", gray or black plastic wheels. Gray plastic wheel versions tend toward higher MIP values, about $110
EX $25 **NM** $40 **MIP** $95

(KP Photo, John Brown Sr. collection)

37-3RW, Cattle Truck, 1966, Yellow Dodge cab and chassis, gray plastic cattle box, originally included two white plastic steers, 2-1/2". Introduced in 1966 catalog as a new model, but hadn't yet replaced the #37 Coca-Cola truck in the line-up
EX $5 **NM** $10 **MIP** $20

38-1RW, Refuse Wagon, 1957, Silver-gray or dark-gray cab and almost tanker-truck shaped rounded-top bed and "Cleansing Department" decals. Metal or gray plastic wheels. 1957 flyer shows model painted green and without the decals. Casting variations must account for size difference: 2-1/8" and 2-1/2" lengths
EX $18 **NM** $45 **MIP** $85

38-2RW, Vauxhall Victor Estate Car, 1963, Yellow station wagon with opening rear hatch, gray, silver or black plastic tires, red or green plastic interiors, clear plastic windows. 2-1/2"
EX $18 **NM** $32 **MIP** $60

(KP Photo, George Cuhaj collection)

38-3RW, Honda Motorcycle with Trailer, 1967, Blue-silver Honda motorcycle with kickstand and orange or yellow trailer. Trailer may or may not included labels or decals. 3". As with many motorcycle-related toys, these fairly common models are increasing in value
EX $12 **NM** $25 **MIP** $40

(KP Photo, John Brown Sr. collection)

39-1RW, "Zodiac" Convertible, 1957, Pink body, turquoise interior, driver, tow hook. Metal, gray or silver plastic wheels. Casting variations: Model can measure 2-5/8" or 2-1/2". Silver-painted grille, gray-painted

headlights, red-painted taillights, light green baseplate
EX $27 **NM** $68 **MIP** $100

(KP Photo by Dr. Douglas Sadecky)

39-2RW, Pontiac Convertible, 1962, Purple Pontiac convertible body with gray or silver plastic wheels; yellow body with gray, silver or black plastic wheels. Yellow with black plastic wheels is most common, around $55 MIP. Purple version with silver plastic wheels is hard to find (pictured above and in color section). 2-3/4". Yellow with gray or silver wheels prices shown below
EX $28 **NM** $55 **MIP** $95

39-3RW, Ford Tractor, 1967, Blue Ford tractor body with yellow die-cast hood, yellow wheels with black plastic tires, 2-1/8", low hook. Versions of this tractor exist in all-blue, being part of the King Size K-20 set
EX $10 **NM** $20 **MIP** $30

(KP Photo, John Brown Sr. collection)

40-1RW, Bedford 7-Ton Tipper, 1957, Red Bedford cab and chassis, tan dumper bed, metal or gray plastic wheels, silver painted trim. Casting variations: Size varies between 2-1/8" and 2-1/4". Shown in all-green color in 1957 flyer
EX $20 **NM** $40 **MIP** $80

(KP Photo, Tom Michael collection)

40-2RW, Long Distance Bus, 1961, Blue-silver coach body with tailfins at rear, 3", green window plastic, silver-painted grille. With gray, silver or black plastic wheels. (Gray or silver-wheel versions about $55 MIP value.) Black-wheel version values given below
EX $7 **NM** $15 **MIP** $28

40-3RW, Hay Trailer, 1967, Blue die-cast trailer body with yellow die-cast stake-ends, often missing. Yellow plastic wheels with black plastic tires, 3-3/8"
EX $3 **NM** $8 **MIP** $15

(KP Photo by Dr. Douglas Sadecky)

41-1RW, "D" Type Jaguar, 1957, Green D-type body, metal driver in later catalogs, but not in 1957 flyer, "41" decal, metal or gray plastic tires, 2-1/4". Photo shows 41-1RW and second release with a larger casting, 41-2R
EX $25 **NM** $60 **MIP** $100

41-2RW, Jaguar Racing Car ("D"-Type), 1961, Second issue of car featured a green body and tan driver, but came in a variety of wheel types, from more common gray and silver plastic wheels to rare spoked versions and black plastic wheels
EX $30 **NM** $75 **MIP** $150

(KP Photo, George Cuhaj collection)

41-3RW, Ford G.T., 1966, Generally white Ford G.T. bodies with yellow plastic wheels and black plastic tires. Clear window plastic, blue rally stripe on hood with "6" or "9" reversed in white. Visible rear engine, 2-5/8". "Available early 1966" in 1966 catalog. Black base, red plastic interior. Versions with differently-colored wheels or bodies are hard to find
EX $15 **NM** $30 **MIP** $50

(KP Photo by Dr. Douglas Sadecky)

42-1RW, Bedford "Evening News" Van, 1957, Mustard-yellow Bedford panel van body with die-cast billboard on roof and red decal "First With The News" in white type. "Evening News" on panel side of van and "Football Results" in red type decals on each door. Metal, gray or black plastic wheels, (gray and black shown). 2-1/4"
EX $17 **NM** $40 **MIP** $95

(KP Photo, George Cuhaj collection)

42-2RW, Studebaker Station Wagon, 1965, Blue body with blue or light blue sliding roof, white plastic interior and tow hook, clear window plastic, white plastic dog and hunter figure included with original (often missing), 3"
EX $15 **NM** $30 **MIP** $65

(KP Photo, George Cuhaj collection)

42-2RW, Studebaker Station Wagon, 1965, Another view, showing the sliding rear roof of the Studebaker Station Wagon, 42-2RW

(KP Photo, George Cuhaj collection)

42-3RW, Iron Fairy Crane, 1969-70, Red body, yellow crane arm, yellow plastic hook and seat, black plastic wheels, 3". Introduced in 1970 catalog, as a "non-Superfast" toy
EX $5 **NM** $11 **MIP** $20

(KP Photo, George Cuhaj collection)

43-1RW, Hillman "Minx", 1958, Blue body, light gray roof, no window plastic or interior, silver-painted grille, metal or gray plastic wheels, 2-1/2", first appears in 1958 catalog

EX $15 **NM** $45 **MIP** $80

(KP Photo, John Brown Sr. collection)

43-2RW, Aveling-Barford Tractor Shovel, 1962, Yellow tractor body with cast yellow or red driver and yellow or red bucket, black wheels, 2-5/8". All yellow versions can have $140 MIP value. Model prices for yellow with red bucket and yellow with red driver shown

EX $15 **NM** $30 **MIP** $55

(KP Photo, George Cuhaj collection)

43-3RW, Pony Trailer, 1968, Yellow body with clear window plastic on sides and top, gray/brown plastic door, black plastic wheels, 2 white plastic horses, 2-5/8"

EX $8 **NM** $11 **MIP** $30

(KP Photo, John Brown Sr. collection)

44-1RW, Rolls Royce Silver Cloud, 1958, Blue metallic Rolls Royce body, metal, gray or silver plastic wheels, crimped axles, no interior, no window plastic, silver-painted grille and bumpers, 2-5/8"

EX $18 **NM** $35 **MIP** $80

(KP Photo, George Cuhaj collection)

44-2RW, Rolls Royce, 1962, Metallic tan or metallic silver/gray body, opening trunk, black plastic wheels, white plastic interior, clear window plastic, black base, silver-painted grille, 2-7/8"

EX $12 **NM** $20 **MIP** $40

(KP Photo, George Cuhaj collection)

44-3RW, Refrigerator Truck, 1967, Red GMC cab and chassis, green refrigerator box, green window plastic, black plastic wheels, opening rear door on box, 3"

EX $5 **NM** $12 **MIP** $20

(KP Photo, George Cuhaj collection)

44-3RW, Refrigerator Truck, 1967, Another view showing box of refrigerator truck

(KP Photo, George Cuhaj collection)

45-1RW, Vauxhall "Victor", 1958, Yellow body, silver-painted headlights and grille, can have no windows, clear or green plastic windows. No interior. Metal, gray, silver or black plastic wheels, 2-3/8"

EX $18 **NM** $40 **MIP** $85

(KP Photo by Dr. Douglas Sadecky)

45-1RW, Vauxhall "Victor", 1958, Vauxhall Victor models can include green or clear plastic windows, as this one does

(KP Photo, George Cuhaj collection)

45-2RW, Ford Corsair, 1965, Cream-yellow body, red plastic interior and tow hook, gray or black plastic wheels, silver-painted grille and headlights, green plastic roof rack and boat (not shown), 2-5/8". Gray-wheeled versions may have higher MIP values

EX $6 **NM** $12 **MIP** $30

(KP Photo, George Cuhaj collection)

46-1RW, Morris Minor 1000, 1958, Dark blue or dark green body, metal or gray plastic wheels, black base, no interior, no plastic windows, 2". Dark blue with gray plastic wheels harder to find, with higher MIP values

EX $45 **NM** $65 **MIP** $125

(KP Photo by Dr. Douglas Sadecky)

46-2RW, Pickford's Removal Van, 1960, Dark blue or green body, silver-painted grille, no interior, no plastic windows, gray, silver or black plastic wheels, 2-5/8". Decals can have 2 or 3 lines. Many variations of this model exist, although versions with 2-line decals

seem hard to find, bumping up the MIP price from what is shown here
EX $40 **NM** $80 **MIP** $150

(KP Photo, George Cuhaj collection)

46-3RW, Mercedes 300SE, 1968, Medium blue or green body, white plastic interior, opening doors and trunk, black plastic wheels, unpainted base extends to bumpers and front grille, 2-7/8"
EX $9 **NM** $18 **MIP** $25

46-3RW, Mercedes 300SE, 1968, Another view of the 46-3RW Mercedes showing opening doors and trunk

(KP Photo by Dr. Douglas Sadecky)

47-1RW, Trojan "Brooke Bond" Van, 1958, Red body, metal or gray plastic wheels, decals on van box read "Brooke Bond Tea," tea leaf decal on each door, silver-painted headlights, 2-1/4"
EX $20 **NM** $45 **MIP** $95

(KP Photo, John Brown Sr. collection)

47-2RW, Commer Ice Cream Van, 1963, Blue, cream or metallic blue body with white plastic interior, clear plastic windows and black plastic wheels, 2-1/4". Color and decal variations change MIP values considerably. Metallic blue versions with square roof decals are more rare than cream-colored models with plain (non-striped) side decals (see color section)
EX $20 **NM** $45 **MIP** $75

(KP Photo, George Cuhaj collection)

47-3RW, DAF Tipper Container Truck, 1969, Green or silver-gray cab and chassis, yellow tipper bed with removable gray top. Red plastic grille and baseplate under cab, black plastic wheels, 3". Makes first appearance in 1969 catalog. Green version higher MIP value, about $40
EX $5 **NM** $12 **MIP** $20

(KP Photo, George Cuhaj collection)

47-3RW, DAF Tipper Container Truck, 1969, Another view of truck with raised tipper bed

(KP Photo, Tom Michael collection)

48-1RW, "Meteor" Sports Boat on Trailer, 1958, Blue and yellow plastic boat with slight rise for windshield, black die-cast trailer, metal or gray plastic wheels, 2-3/4"
EX $25 **NM** $40 **MIP** $70

(KP Photo, George Cuhaj collection)

48-2RW, Sports-Boat and Trailer, 1961, Plastic red and white boat with gold or silver outboard motor, blue die-cast trailer, gray or black plastic wheels, 3-1/2". Boat can come with red deck and white hull or white deck and red hull
EX $12 **NM** $25 **MIP** $60

(KP Photo, John Brown Sr. collection)

48-3RW, Dumper Truck, 1967, Red Dodge cab, chassis and dumper bed, silver plastic baseplate, bumper and front grille, black plastic wheels, 3"
EX $3 **NM** $8 **MIP** $18

(KP Photo, George Cuhaj collection)

49-1RW, Army Half-Track, 1958, Dark olive-green with star-in-circle U.S. insignia on hood, no interior, metal, gray or black plastic wheels and rollers, gray treads (often missing as they are here) 2-1/2". Known as Army Half-Track and Military Personnel Carrier, this toy stayed in the 1-75 lineup for many years
EX $18 **NM** $30 **MIP** $55

(KP Photo, George Cuhaj collection)

49-2RW, Mercedes Unimog, 1967, Two color variations, one tan and blue and the other blue and red, green plastic windows, yellow plastic wheels with black plastic tires, silver-painted grille, tow hook cast, 2-1/2"
EX $8 **NM** $12 **MIP** $25

(KP Photo, George Cuhaj collection)

49-2RW, Mercedes Unimog, 1967, Another view of the Mercedes Unimog, blue and red variation (also see color section)

(KP Photo, John Brown Sr. collection)

50-1RW, Commer Pickup, 1958, Tan or red and gray body, with metal, gray or black plastic wheels, 2-1/2", silver-painted grille and headlights
EX $25 **NM** $50 **MIP** $75

(KP Photo by Dr. Douglas Sadecky)

50-1RW, Commer Pickup, 1958, A view of the red and gray variation of the Commer Pickup with black plastic wheels
EX $40 **NM** $75 **MIP** $150

50-2RW, John Deere-Lanz Tractor, 1964, Green body, yellow plastic wheels, gray or black plastic tires, cast tow hook, 2-1/8". After John Deere acquired the German manufacturer Lanz in the 1950s, a variety of toy manufacturers, including Matchbox, produced models of this tractor. Photo shows black-tire version tractor with 51-2RW Tipping Trailer. Note: Gray-tire versions have slightly higher MIP value, about $55
EX $14 **NM** $20 **MIP** $35

(KP Photo, John Brown Sr. collection)

50-2RW, John Deere-Lanz Tractor, 1964, A view of the gray-tire version of the John Deere-Lanz tractor-a very detailed model

50-3RW, Kennel Truck, 1969, Dark green die-cast body, white or silver plastic grille, green window plastic, truck bed partitioned into four sections, to hold one plastic dog each (included), clear plastic canopy over truck bed, "Auto-Steer" front wheels, black plastic wheels, 2-3/4"
EX $12 **NM** $30 **MIP** $50

51-1RW, Albion "Portland Cement" Lorry, 1958, Yellow Albion truck cab and chassis, two decal variations: "Portland Cement" and "Blue Circle Portland Cement." Metal, gray, silver or black plastic wheels, silver-painted trim, tan-painted cement bag load on flatbed, no interior, no window plastic, 2-1/2". Silver plastic wheel versions have about $150 MIP values
EX $18 **NM** $40 **MIP** $80

(KP Photo, George Cuhaj collection)

51-2RW, Tipping Trailer, 1964, Green body, yellow wheels, tilting bed, black or gray plastic tires, three yellow barrels, 2-5/8"
EX $8 **NM** $12 **MIP** $25

(KP Photo, George Cuhaj collection)

51-3RW, 8-Wheel Tipper, 1969, Orange or yellow Ergomatic AEC cab and chassis with silver-gray tipper bed, 8 black plastic wheels, green plastic windows, no interior, "Douglas" or "Pointer" labels on the sides of tipper bed, 3". Orange models with "Douglas" appear to have higher MIP values, about $40
EX $9 **NM** $16 **MIP** $28

(KP Photo, George Cuhaj collection)

51-3RW, 8-Wheel Tipper, 1969, Another view of Tipper truck with bed tilted. As with all miniature construction toys, finding these models in pristine shape can be a bit of a hunt

(KP Photo by Dr. Douglas Sadecky)

52-1RW, Maserati 4CLT Racecar, 1958, Yellow or red body with spoked wheels and black tires or solid black plastic wheels. Open cockpit with driver, mostly seen with "52" decal, 2-3/8", silver-painted grille
EX $25 **NM** $50 **MIP** $100

(KP Photo, George Cuhaj collection)

52-2RW, BRM Racing Car, 1965, Blue or red body, white plastic driver, yellow wheels, black plastic tires, 2-3/4". Generally carries no. "5" decals on hood and sides
EX $10 **NM** $20 **MIP** $40

53-1RW, Aston Martin, 1958, Light green, metal or gray plastic wheels, no interior, no plastic windows, 2-1/2", silver-painted grille
EX $22 **NM** $55 **MIP** $100

(KP Photo, George Cuhaj collection)

53-2RW, Mercedes-Benz 220SE, 1963, Red or maroon body, opening doors, white plastic interior, clear plastic windows, 2-3/4", silver, gray or black plastic wheels
EX $10 **NM** $30 **MIP** $55

(KP Photo, Tom Michael collection)

53-3RW, Ford Zodiac Mk. IV, 1968, Blue-silver body, opening hood, white plastic interior, clear plastic windows, black plastic wheels, 2-3/4"
EX $3 **NM** $6 **MIP** $15

(KP Photo, Tom Michael collection)

53-3RW, Ford Zodiac Mk. IV, 1968, View of Ford Zodiac with opened hood, showing silver plastic engine and a spare tire tucked in front! Opening doors and hoods were always favorite features

(KP Photo, George Cuhaj collection)

54-1RW, Army Saracen Carrier, 1958, Olive-green "turtle-shaped" body, six black plastic wheels, rotating turret on top, 2-1/4". One of Matchbox's first military vehicle releases. Like rescue and construction vehicles, military toys tend to be in rough shape, so finding mint or MIP examples can be a little tough

EX $8 **NM** $18 **MIP** $40

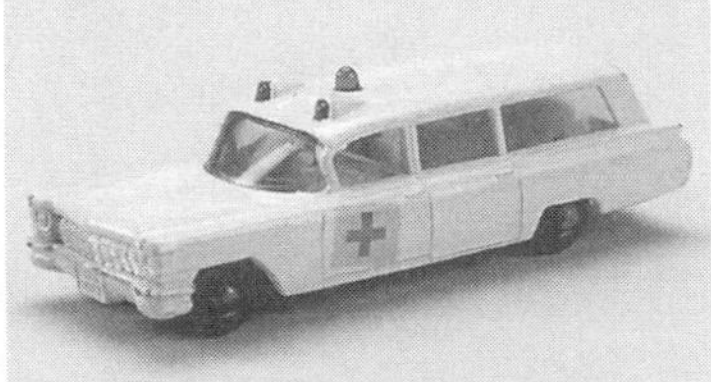

(KP Photo, George Cuhaj collection)

54-2RW, S&S Cadillac Ambulance, 1965, White Cadillac ambulance body with red cross decal or label, blue plastic windows, detailed white plastic interior, black plastic wheels, silver-painted grille, red plastic dome lights, 2 7/8"

EX $15 **NM** $30 **MIP** $60

55-1RW, D.U.K.W. Amphibian, 1958, Olive-green body, metal, gray or black plastic wheels, 2-3/4", another in the early military grouping of Matchbox vehicles

EX $15 **NM** $35 **MIP** $60

(KP Photo by Dr. Douglas Sadecky)

55-2RW, Ford Fairlane Police Car, 1963, Dark or light blue Ford Fairlane with white plastic interior, clear plastic windows, red dome light, silver-painted grille, black plastic wheels. Dark blue version is harder to find; about $300 MIP. Light blue values shown

EX $22 **NM** $40 **MIP** $85

(KP Photo, George Cuhaj collection)

55-3RW, Ford Galaxie Police Car, 1966, White body, white plastic interior with molded figure, black plastic wheels, red, white and blue stars-in-shield decals, unpainted base, red dome light

EX $20 **NM** $35 **MIP** $60

55-4RW, Mercury Police Car, 1969, White Mercury sedan with white plastic interior, featuring two officers, silver hubs with black plastic tires, blue dome light, clear plastic windows, unpainted base, "Auto-Steer" front wheels, 3-1/16". A new model, this police car was released at the same time as a Mercury station wagon, #73. Both share auto-steer feature and a baseplate, reading "55 or 73"

EX $20 **NM** $40 **MIP** $75

56-1RW, Trolley Bus, 1958, Red double-decker body with sloped front, no interior; six metal, gray, or black plastic wheels, "Drink Peardrax" decals on sides, flat trolley poles on roof, "OXO" decal on front, 2-5/8". Note that MIP metal wheel versions have sold for $250. Common prices for gray and black wheel versions shown

EX $20 **NM** $45 **MIP** $70

(KP Photo, George Cuhaj collection)

56-2RW, Fiat 1500, 1965, Pea-green Fiat 1500 sedan with dark or light brown plastic luggage on roof, red plastic interior, silver-painted grille and headlight details, black plastic wheels, 2-5/8", black plastic base. Red versions of this car were included with the G-1 Service Station Gift Set, and are tough to find, usually over $100 mint value. Standard green values shown

EX $4 **NM** $9 **MIP** $15

(KP Photo, George Cuhaj collection)

57-1RW, Wolseley 1500, 1958, Pale green body, no plastic windows, no interior, silver-painted grille, bumpers and headlights, red-painted taillights, black-painted base, 2-1/8"

EX $20 **NM** $35 **MIP** $70

(KP Photo by Dr. Douglas Sadecky)

57-2RW, Chevrolet Impala, 1961, Medium-blue body with light-blue top, cast tow hook, clear plastic windows, no interior, silver, gray or black plastic wheels

EX $25 **NM** $50 **MIP** $110

(KP Photo, George Cuhaj collection)

57-3RW, Land Rover Fire Truck, 1966, Red Land Rover body with "Kent Fire Brigade" and fire dept. insignia decals on sides, blue plastic windows and dome light, white plastic ladder (removable) on top, black plastic wheels, 2-1/2"

EX $6 **NM** $11 **MIP** $25

58-1RW, British European Airways Coach, 1958, Rounded metal blue bus body, no plastic windows, no interior, gray plastic wheels, "British European Airways" decals, 2-1/2"

EX $30 **NM** $50 **MIP** $85

(KP Photo, John Brown Sr. collection)

58-2RW, Drott Excavator, 1962, Red or orange body, silver-painted motors on some red variations, orange motor on some orange models, 2-5/8"

EX $15 **NM** $35 **MIP** $60

(KP Photo, John Brown Sr. collection)

58-3RW, DAF Girder Truck, 1968, Cream-colored cab and chassis, red plastic grille, green plastic windows, no interior, "Available mid-1968" in 1968 catalog, black plastic wheels, 12 red plastic girders, 3"

EX $4 **NM** $9 **MIP** $20

(KP Photo, John Brown Sr. collection)

59-1RW, Ford "Singer" Van, 1958, Light green Ford Thames van with "Singer" decals on panel sides and "S" logo decals on doors. No plastic windows, no interior, silver-painted grille, gray plastic wheels, 2-1/8". Dark green models seem hard to find, about $250 MIP

EX $35 **NM** $55 **MIP** $100

59-2RW, Ford Fairlane Fire Chief Car, Red Ford Fairlane casting (same as 55-2RW Ford Fairlane police car) black plastic wheels, white plastic interior, clear plastic windows

EX $25 **NM** $45 **MIP** $80

(KP Photo, Tom Michael collection)

59-3RW, Ford Galaxie Fire Chief Car, 1966, Red Ford Galaxie body, white plastic interior with figure cast as part of interior (like police car version) unpainted base and metal grille and headlight section, fire chief decals or labels on side doors and hood, clear plastic windows, white plastic tow hook, blue plastic dome light, 2-7/8"

EX $12 **NM** $30 **MIP** $50

(KP Photo, George Cuhaj collection)

60-1RW, Morris J2 Pick-Up Truck, 1958, Blue pick-up body, gray, silver or black plastic tires, "Builders Supply Company" decals on sides, silver-painted grille, no plastic windows, no interior, 2-1/4"

EX $18 **NM** $35 **MIP** $60

(KP Photo, George Cuhaj collection)

60-2RW, Site Hut Truck, 1967, Blue Leyland Ergomatic cab and flatbed chassis, silver plastic grille and headlights, blue plastic windows, no interior, black plastic wheels, plastic yellow hut on back with green roof, 2-1/2"

EX $5 **NM** $12 **MIP** $20

(KP Photo, George Cuhaj collection)

61-1RW, Ferret Scout Car, 1959, Olive-green, open-cockpit armored car body, tan-colored driver, four black plastic wheels, (one spare on side), 2-1/4"

EX $9 **NM** $12 **MIP** $30

(KP Photo, George Cuhaj collection)

61-2, Alvis Stalwart, 1967, White body with green plastic windows and green or yellow wheels with black plastic tires. Plastic canopy over bed (not shown), no interior, 2-5/8". Yellow wheels are less common and have approx. $75 MIP values

EX $9 **NM** $17 **MIP** $30

(KP Photo, George Cuhaj collection)

62-1RW, General Service Lorry, 1959, Olive green body with six black plastic wheels, no plastic windows, no interior

EX $20 **NM** $32 **MIP** $60

(KP photo by Dr. Douglas Sadecky)

62-2RW, TV Service Van, 1963, Cream colored body with "Rentaset" or "Radio Rentals" decals on sides, red plastic accessories: antenna, 3 TV sets and ladder. No interior, 2-1/2"

EX $20 **NM** $50 **MIP** $110

62-3RW, Mercury Cougar, 1969, Lime-green Mercury Cougar body with unpainted base, silver wheels with removable black plastic tires (like other Mercury models in the line), opening doors, red plastic interior, "auto-steer" front wheels, tow hook, 3"

EX $5 **NM** $8 **MIP** $15

(KP Photo, George Cuhaj collection)

63-2RW, Fire Fighting Crash Tender, 1964, Block-shaped red body with white plastic ladder (missing in this photo) and white plastic lettering on sides. No plastic windows, no interior, black plastic wheels, 2-3/8"
EX $12 **NM** $30 **MIP** $50

(KP Photo, George Cuhaj collection)

63-2RW, Fire Fighting Crash Tender, 1964, View of the detailed casting on rear of vehicle

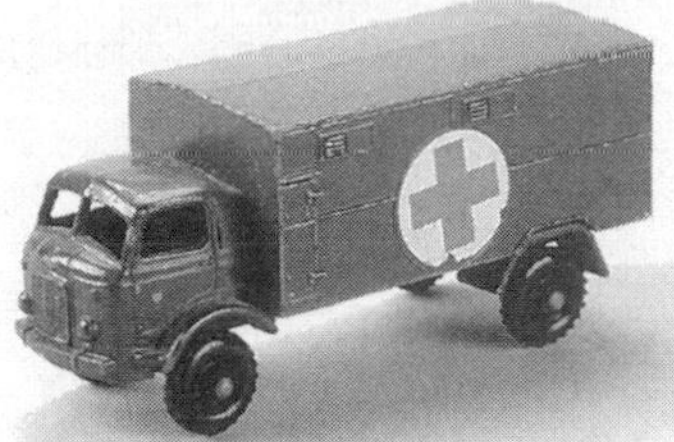
(KP Photo, George Cuhaj collection)

63-3RW, Service Ambulance, 1959, Olive green truck-ambulance chassis, black plastic wheels, no interior, no plastic windows, red cross decals on sides
EX $8 **NM** $22 **MIP** $50

(KP Photo, George Cuhaj collection)

63-3RW, Dodge Crane Truck, 1969, Yellow Dodge cab and chassis, red or yellow plastic hook, black grille and headlights, green plastic windows, no interior, six black plastic wheels, swivelling crane section, 3"
EX $6 **NM** $10 **MIP** $18

(KP Photo, George Cuhaj collection)

64-1RW, Scammell Breakdown Lorry, 1959, Olive green body, box cab, green, silver or gray hook, six black plastic wheels
EX $25 **NM** $45 **MIP** $75

(KP Photo, George Cuhaj collection)

64-2RW, M.G. 1100, 1966, Green car body, white plastic interior with driver in front and dog peeking out of rear window, clear plastic windows, black plastic wheels, unpainted base, white plastic tow hook, 2-5/8"
EX $5 **NM** $10 **MIP** $17

(KP Photo, George Cuhaj collection)

64-2RW, M.G. 1100, 1966, View of the M.G. and collie peeking out from window. Matchbox included dogs in many later regular wheels models--a fun addition

(KP Photo by Dr. Douglas Sadecky)

65-RW, Jaguar 3.4 Litre, 1959, Blue body, no interior, no plastic windows, gray plastic wheels, silver-painted grille. Shown here with 65-2RW Jaguar 3.8 Litre Sedan
EX $18 **NM** $35 **MIP** $65

(KP Photo, George Cuhaj collection)

65-2RW, Jaguar 3.8 Litre Sedan, 1962, Red body, opening hood, silver-painted grille and headlights, gray, silver or black plastic wheels, green plastic windows, no interior, 2-5/8"
EX $11 **NM** $25 **MIP** $50

(KP Photo, George Cuhaj collection)

65-2RW, Jaguar 3.8 Litre Sedan, 1962, View of gray-wheeled model with open hood-a favorite feature

65-3RW, Combine Harvester, 1967, Red Claas combine with yellow plastic grain reel and yellow wheels with removable black plastic tires, 3". A popular casting for Matchbox, matching the King-Size model (K-9) version
EX $12 **NM** $20 **MIP** $40

(KP Photo by Dr. Douglas Sadecky)

66-1RW, Citroen DS19, 1959, Yellow body, silver-painted grille, no window plastic, no interior, gray plastic wheels
EX $17 **NM** $35 **MIP** $70

(KP Photo by Dr. Douglas Sadecky)

66-2RW, Harley-Davidson Motorcycle with Sidecar, 1962, Gold metallic body with spoked wheels, 2-5/8". This piece has escalated in value due to Matchbox and Harley-Davidson collector cross-over

EX $65 **NM** $95 **MIP** $160

(KP Photo, George Cuhaj collection)

66-3RW, Greyhound Bus, 1967, Silver-gray body, "Greyhound" decals or labels, yellow plastic windows, white plastic interior, black plastic wheels, 3"

EX $10 **NM** $17 **MIP** $30

(KP Photo, George Cuhaj collection)

67-1RW, Saladin Armoured Car, 1959, Olive-green body, rotating turret (gun barrel in photo is broken, a common occurrence with these models) six black plastic wheels, 2-1/4"

EX $11 **NM** $18 **MIP** $30

(KP Photo, George Cuhaj collection)

67-2RW, Volkswagen 1600 TL, 1967, Red body, white interior, unpainted base running up into headlights, clear window plastic, opening doors, 2-11/16". One version with snap-on plastic roof rack was included with Race'n Rally G-4 gift set, harder to find

EX $11 **NM** $17 **MIP** $25

(KP Photo, George Cuhaj collection)

67-2RW, Volkswagen 1600 TL, 1967, Another view of the car showing opening doors and interior

(KP Photo, George Cuhaj collection)

68-1RW, Austin Mark II Radio Truck, 1959, Olive-green body, no window plastic, no interior, black plastic wheels

EX $18 **NM** $35 **MIP** $65

(KP Photo, George Cuhaj collection)

68-2RW, Mercedes Coach, 1966, White and blue-green or white and orange body, clear window plastic, white plastic interior, black plastic wheels, 2-7/8". Blue-green version harder-to-find with approx. $130 MIP values. More common orange-version values shown

EX $7 **NM** $11 **MIP** $15

(KP Photo by Dr. Douglas Sadecky)

69-1RW, Commer 30 CWT Nestlé's Van, 1959, Dark red or red van with Nestlé's decals on panel sides, sliding doors, no window plastic, no interior, silver-painted grille, gray plastic wheels

EX $22 **NM** $40 **MIP** $90

(KP Photo, George Cuhaj collection)

69-2RW, Hatra Tractor Shovel, 1965, Yellow or orange body with black plastic removable tires. Hubs can be yellow or red, 3-1/8". Models with red hubs seem to have higher MIP values, about $90-$125

EX $11 **NM** $17 **MIP** $30

(KP Photo, George Cuhaj collection)

70-1RW, Ford Thames Estate Car, 1959, Pale blue and yellow van-shaped body with clear or green plastic windows, no interior, silver-painted grille. Gray, silver or black plastic wheels

EX $25 **NM** $40 **MIP** $70

(KP Photo, John Brown Sr. collection)

70-2RW, Grit Spreader, 1966, Red Ford cab and chassis, yellow hopper section, green plastic windows, no interior, black plastic wheels, silver metal grille, gray or black plastic "pulls" that open bottom chute, 2-5/8"

EX $7 **NM** $9 **MIP** $20

71-1RW, Service Water Truck, 1959, Olive-green truck chassis with water tank on back, black plastic wheels, spare black plastic tire behind cab, no plastic windows, no interior

EX $28 **NM** $40 **MIP** $75

(KP Photo, George Cuhaj collection)

71-2RW, Jeep Pick-Up Truck, 1964, Red body, opening doors, black partial base, black plastic wheels, clear plastic windows, silver-painted grille, 2-5/8". Early models came with green plastic interior (shown in 1964 catalog) and are hard to find, about $175 MIP. White plastic interior more common; prices shown

EX $12 **NM** $22 **MIP** $40

(KP Photo, George Cuhaj collection)

71-2RW, Jeep Pick-Up Truck, 1964, Another view of Jeep Pick-Up Truck showing opening doors

(KP Photo, George Cuhaj collection)

71-3RW, Ford Heavy Wreck Truck, 1969, Red cab, green plastic windows and dome light, red plastic hook, black plastic wheels, "Esso" label, white grille extending from white base with "1968" date, 3". A nice, hefty model

EX $12 **NM** $20 **MIP** $40

(KP Photo by Dr. Douglas Sadecky)

72-1RW, Fordson Major Tractor, 1959, Blue tractor with gray or black plastic tires, and orange hubs in rear and in variations, on front. Silver-painted grille, 2". Gray-tire version and black-tire version with box variations shown

EX $18 **NM** $30 **MIP** $75

(KP Photo, George Cuhaj collection)

72-1RW, Fordson Major Tractor, 1959, Another variation of the Fordson tractor with orange hubs and black tires, front and rear. This is the version of the tractor that appeared in its last catalog appearance in 1966

EX $18 **NM** $30 **MIP** $75

(KP Photo, George Cuhaj collection)

72-2RW, Standard Jeep, 1967, Yellow body with upright windshield, black base, red plastic interior and tow hook, black plastic removable tires over yellow hubs, spare tire on back, 2-3/8"

EX $12 **NM** $20 **MIP** $40

73-1RW, RAF Refueller Truck, 1960, Blue body with RAF decal on top of truck behind cab, no plastic windows, no interior, gray plastic wheels

EX $20 **NM** $45 **MIP** $75

73-2RW, Ferrari Racing Car, 1962, Red racing car body with "73" and Ferrari decals on sides, spoked wheels, white or gray plastic driver, 2-5/8"

EX $20 **NM** $35 **MIP** $80

73-3RW, Mercury Commuter, 1969, Lime green body with clear plastic windows, white plastic interior (including two dogs peeking out of the back), black plastic removable tires with silver hubs, "Auto-Steer" front steering, 3-1/16"

EX $9 **NM** $12 **MIP** $25

73-3RW, Mercury Commuter, 1969, Another view of the Mercury station wagon, showing the two dogs peeking out of the back window

74-1, Mobile Refreshment Bar, 1960, Silver trailer body with opening sides and plastic interior, "Refreshments" decals below side openings, silver or gray plastic wheels, medium-blue baseplate models about $190 MIP, 2-5/8". Common prices with lighter blue bases shown below

EX $28 **NM** $45 **MIP** $95

(KP Photo, George Cuhaj collection)

74-2RW, Daimler Bus, 1966, Cream, green or red bodies with white plastic interior, black plastic wheels, "Esso Extra Petrol" decals or labels, 3". First appears in 1966 catalog as new model, "Available mid 1966" with no series number

EX $7 **NM** $14 **MIP** $25

(KP Photo, John Brown Sr. collection)

74-2RW, Daimler Bus, 1966, A view of the green variation of the 74-2RW Daimler Bus

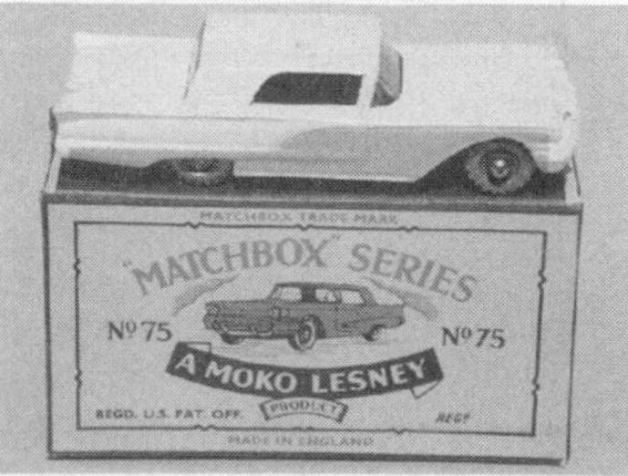

(KP Photo by Dr. Douglas Sadecky)

75-1RW, Ford Thunderbird, 1960, Pink and cream 1959 Ford Thunderbird body, green plastic windows, no interior, silver, gray or black plastic wheels
EX $20 **NM** $50 **MIP** $90

75-2RW, Ferrari Berlinetta, 1965, Dark or light green body with white plastic interior and tow hook, clear plastic windows, spoked wheels or silver hubs, (with black plastic removable tires), 2-7/8". Red-colored versions of this model are very rare, about $750 MIP. Common prices shown below
EX $17 **NM** $45 **MIP** $70

MATCHBOX SUPERFAST

(KP Photo, George Cuhaj collection)

1-1SF, Mercedes Truck, 1970, Gold-colored body, orange plastic tarp cover, green window plastic, narrow transitional Superfast wheels, silver plastic grille and half-baseplate, tow hook cast with body, 3"
EX $4 **NM** $8 **MIP** $18

(KP Photo, Tom Michael collection)

1-2SF, Mod Rod, 1971, Yellow body, amber window plastic, exposed silver-plastic engine in back, red or black Superfast wheels, "wildcat" label on hood, 2-7/8"
EX $12 **NM** $24 **MIP** $45

1-3SF, Dodge Challenger, 1976, Red or blue body, white or red plastic interior, black wheels, plastic air scoops on hood, blue-tinted windshield plastic, white plastic roof, 2-7/8"
EX $6 **NM** $10 **MIP** $20

1-4SF, Dodge Challenger, 1982, Yellow body, gray base, "Toyman" tampos, black plastic roof
EX $3 **NM** $6 **MIP** $9

2-1SF, Mercedes Trailer, 1970, Gold-colored body with orange plastic canopy, thin transitional wheels, 3-1/2"
EX $6 **NM** $14 **MIP** $25

2-2SF, Hot Rod Jeep, 1971, Pink body, exposed silver plastic engine with black plastic exhaust pipes, white plastic seats, lime-green base and bumpers, 2-5/16"
EX $5 **NM** $9 **MIP** $15

2-3SF, Hovercraft, 1976, Metallic-green hovercraft body with light brown plastic base and thin "hidden wheels" beneath, 3-1/6"
EX $2 **NM** $4 **MIP** $8

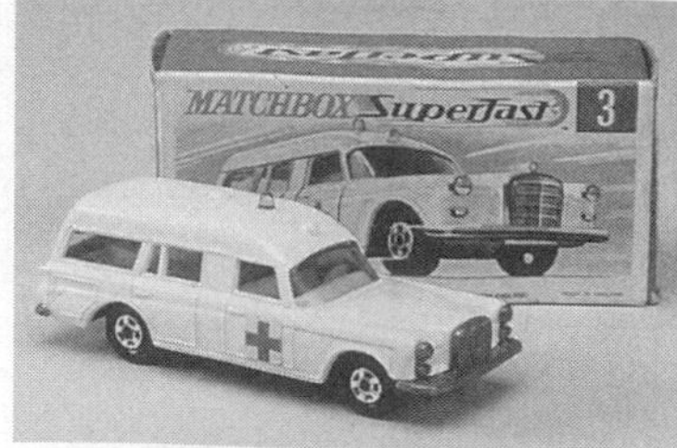

3-1SF, Mercedes-Benz "Binz" Ambulance, 1970, White body with opening hatch and patient on stretcher, red cross labels, blue window plastic, white plastic interior, thin transitional wheels, (later issued with thicker wheels as part of TP-10 Two-Pack), 2-7/8"
EX $7 **NM** $11 **MIP** $25

3-1SF, Mercedes-Benz "Binz" Ambulance, View of wider-wheel version without opening rear hatch, included as part of TP-10

3-2SF, Monterverdi Hai, 1973, Orange body with number "3" label on hood, blue window plastic, thick black wheels, opening doors, 3"
EX $5 **NM** $7 **MIP** $15

3-2SF, Monterverdi Hai, 1974, Another view of the Monterverdi Hai showing opening doors

(KP Photo, Tom Michael collection)

3-3SF, Porsche Turbo, 1979, Charcoal-gray, red or white exterior with

rally number "14," plastic interior can be yellow, tan or brown, plastic tow hook, opening doors
EX $2 **NM** $3 **MIP** $7

4-1SF, Stake Truck, 1970, Yellow, or orange-yellow cab and chassis with green window plastic, no interior, green plastic stake-side cargo area, silver metal base, grille and headlights, 2-7/8"
EX $5 **NM** $10 **MIP** $18

(KP Photo, Tom Michael collection)

4-2SF, Gruesome Twosome, 1971, Gold with cream interiors and pink or purple window plastic. Two exposed engines, unpainted base, 2-7/8"
EX $4 **NM** $8 **MIP** $15

(KP Photo, Tom Michael collection)

4-3SF, Pontiac Firebird, 1975, Blue body with silver plastic interior, amber window plastic, unpainted base and bumpers, 2-7/8"
EX $1 **NM** $3 **MIP** $5

4-4SF, '57 Chevy, 1981, Red or light purple with unpainted or black base, opening hood with silver plastic engine underneath
EX $1 **NM** $3 **MIP** $6

5-1SF, Lotus Europa, 1970, Pink or blue body, white plastic interior, opening doors, 2-7/8", thin or thick Superfast wheels. Blue model shown in 1970 catalog, but pink was advertised afterward until model removed from lineup
EX $5 **NM** $10 **MIP** $20

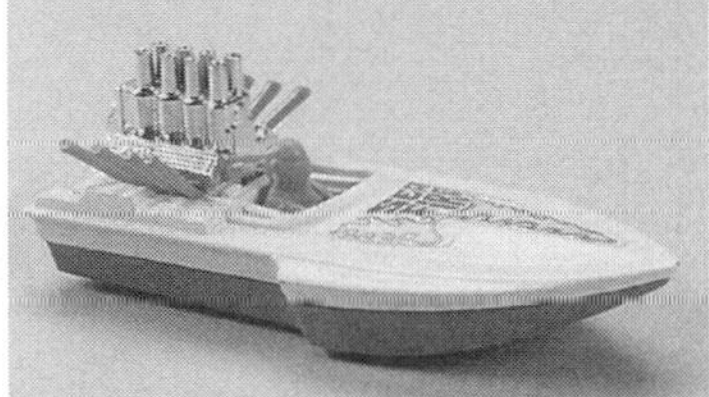

(KP Photo, Tom Michael collection)

5-1SF, Lotus Europa, 1970, The pink version of the Lotus Europa, here with thin wheels. This color variation also comes with wide wheels, and generally seems more common

(KP Photo, John Brown Sr. collection)

5-2SF, Seafire, 1976, White body with "Seafire" label on front, blue base, blue or orange driver, exposed silver plastic engine with red plastic exhaust pipes. This casting has been used many times by Matchbox, returning in 5-Packs in the 1990s
EX $1 **NM** $3 **MIP** $5

6-1SF, Ford Pick-Up Truck, 1970, Red body, white plastic camper top, silver or white plastic grille, 2-3/4", black or charcoal base
EX $12 **NM** $22 **MIP** $40

(KP Photo, Tom Michael collection)

6-2SF, Mercedes Tourer, 1973, Orange or yellow 350SL body with black plastic top, amber windows, light yellow or cream plastic interior, 3", unpainted base. Later models in light or dark red with white plastic roof, or red or metallic blue with no roof
EX $3 **NM** $7 **MIP** $14

7-1SF, Ford Refuse Truck, 1970, Red-orange cab with gray plastic and silver metal garbage dumper bed, 3". The same model as the old regular-wheels version, just with thin or thick Superfast wheels
EX $4 **NM** $8 **MIP** $12

(KP Photo, Tom Michael collection)

7-2SF, Hairy Hustler, 1973, Bronze body, with amber windows, number "5" racing labels on front and side, or white body with checkered labels on hood and roof, and red stripes on fenders, black metal base
EX $5 **NM** $10 **MIP** $15

(KP Photo, John Brown Sr. collection)

7-3SF, Volkswagen Golf, 1977, Lime green, dark green, yellow or red body, amber window plastic, black plastic, detachable surf boards on roof rack, yellow plastic interior, black or charcoal base, tow hook
EX $4 **NM** $7 **MIP** $12

8-1SF, Ford Mustang Fastback, 1970, White, red or orange-red body, white or red plastic interior (red is harder-to-find), tow hook, 2-7/8". Red models with red plastic interiors are the most rare, selling for around $375 MIB
EX $65 **NM** $80 **MIP** $110

8-2SF, Wildcat Dragster, 1971, Orange or pink body with silver engine protruding from hood, and "Wild Cat" labels on sides, tow hook, 2-7/8". This is the same casting used on the Mustang Fastback model 8-1SF
EX $3 **NM** $5 **MIP** $11

8-3SF, De Tomasa Pantera, 1975, White body with "8" labels, blue base, red plastic interior, or blue body, tempo "17", black base, 3"
EX $3 **NM** $5 **MIP** $10

8-3SF, De Tomasa Pantera, 1975, A view of the blue version of the Pantera with the "17" tempo

9-1SF, Boat and Trailer, 1970, Blue die-cast boat trailer with thin Superfast wheels and plastic blue and white boat, 3-1/2"
EX $4 **NM** $9 **MIP** $20

9-2SF, AMX Javelin, 1972, Lime-green or blue body (blue included with Twin-Pack#3, Javelin and Pony Trailer), black or silver plastic air scoop, light yellow or white plastic interior, opening doors, tow hook, 3-1/16"
EX $3 **NM** $6 **MIP** $10

(KP Photo, Tom Michael collection)

9-3SF, Ford Escort RS 2000, 1979, White body with Ford and Shell rally labels, clear window plastic, black base, tan plastic interior
EX $3 **NM** $5 **MIP** $8

10-1SF, Pipe Truck, 1970, Red or orange cab and chassis, gray or yellow plastic pipes, thin or wide Superfast wheels, silver grille, green window plastic, 3". Red models about $35 MIB, orange model values shown below
EX $10 **NM** $18 **MIP** $30

(KP Photo, Tom Michael collection)

10-2SF, Piston Popper, 1973, Blue or yellow Mustang Mach I body with silver Rola-Matic engine with red plastic pistons that move as car is rolled along. Yellow plastic interior, unpainted base, 2-7/8"
EX n/a **NM** $5 **MIP** $10

10-3SF, Plymouth Gran Fury Police Car, 1979, Black and white with "Metro Police" on doors and hood, blue police lights on roof, amber or blue window plastic, unpainted or silver base. Introduced in 1979/80 catalog, it hadn't yet replaced Piston Popper in the lineup
EX $1 **NM** $4 **MIP** $7

(KP Photo, George Cuhaj collection)

11-3SF, Scaffold Truck, 1970, Silver Mercedes-Benz truck with red plastic base and grille, yellow plastic scaffold sections in back, "Builders Supply Company" labels on sides of truck, green window plastic, no interior, 2-5/8"
EX $4 **NM** $8 **MIP** $12

11-2SF, Flying Bug, 1973, Red metallic Volkswagen Beetle with Iron Cross label on hood, oversized face with silver helmet peeking up from car, opaque windows, tailwing and yellow plastic jet engine section on back. Silver or unpainted base, 2-7/8"
EX $4 **NM** $11 **MIP** $20

11-3SF, Car Transporter, 1978, Orange body with black base and light tan/cream car carrying section with red, yellow and blue plastic cars. Dark blue window plastic, no interior
EX $4 **NM** $10 **MIP** $18

(KP Photo, Tom Michael collection)

11-4SF, Cobra Mustang, 1982, Orange body with opening hood, chrome interior, yellow windows, "The Boss" in white lettering on sides, number "5" on roof. Another in the many variations of the old "Boss Mustang" casting
EX $2 **NM** $4 **MIP** $8

12-1SF, Safari Land Rover, 1970, Gold body with white plastic interior, red-brown plastic luggage, tow hook, thin Superfast wheels, 2-3/4". Blue versions of this model exist as Superfasts, but are extremely rare, so prices shown are for gold models only
EX $8 **NM** $16 **MIP** $30

(KP Photo, John Brown Sr. collection)

12-2SF, Setra Coach, 1971, Metallic yellow and white or burgundy and white with clear or green window plastic, white plastic interior, unpainted base, 3"
EX $3 **NM** $7 **MIP** $15

(KP Photo, John Brown Sr. collection)

12-3SF, Big Bull, 1975, Orange bulldozer body and rollers, green base and blade, silver plastic engine and trim, 2-1/2"
EX $1 **NM** $3 **MIP** $5

12-4SF, Citroen CX Station Wagon, 1980, Blue body with cream or light yellow plastic interior, clear or blue window plastic, unpainted or silver base
EX $2 **NM** $5 **MIP** $10

13-1SF, Wreck Truck, 1970, Yellow Dodge cab and tow boom with green bed. "BP" labels on sides, thin Superfast wheels, red window plastic and dome light, no interior, red plastic tow hook, 3". This is another transitional model that is becoming hard to find
EX $17 **NM** $30 **MIP** $50

(KP Photo, Tom Michael collection)

13-2SF, Baja Buggy, 1972, Lime green body, orange plastic interior, no window plastic, thick Superfast wheels, flower label on hood, silver plastic engine with orange plastic exhaust pipes, 2-5/8"
EX $4 **NM** $8 **MIP** $14

13-3SF, Snorkel Fire Engine, 1977, Red body with blue or amber window plastic, yellow or white snorkel section, unpainted metal base. Models with amber-colored window plastic tend to have higher MIP prices, about $15. This fire engine first appeared in the 1977 catalog with a white snorkel as a new model to watch for, not yet replacing Baha Buggy in the lineup
EX $1 **NM** $4 **MIP** $8

14-1SF, Iso Grifo, 1970, Dark or medium blue with thin Superfast wheels, light blue or white plastic interior, unpainted base, 3"
EX $6 **NM** $12 **MIP** $25

14-2SF, Mini-Ha-Ha, 1976, Red body with blue opaque window plastic, silver plastic rotary engine protruding through hood, large rear wheels, head with pilot's helmet showing through roof, circular British RAF side labels on doors
EX $3 **NM** $8 **MIP** $17

15-1SF, Volkswagen 1500, 1970, White, cream or red body with white plastic interior, tow hook, unpainted base, "137" labels on doors, 2-7/8"
EX $7 **NM** $12 **MIP** $22

15-2SF, Fork Lift Truck, 1973, Red body with larger wheels at front, gray or yellow plastic lifting forks on yellow metal or unpainted track, "Lansing Bagnall" or "Hi-Lift" side labels, unpainted, black or green base, 2 3/4"
EX $3 **NM** $6 **MIP** $12

15-3SF, Hi Ho Silver, 1981, Silver Volkswagen Beetle (same casting as "Volks Dragon") with "Hi Ho Silver" and "31" tempo. Black base, clear window plastic, red plastic interior, 2-5/8". Having "31" on the roof is an interesting choice of graphic, considering it was the same vehicle casting as the 31-2SF
EX $4 **NM** $7 **MIP** $12

(KP Photo by Dr. Douglas Sadecky)

16-1SF, Case Bulldozer, 1970, Red with yellow engine, cab and blade and green or black rubber tracks, 2-1/2". This model was released at the same time as the Superfast line-notice that the box has "speed lines" just like the other models
EX $5 **NM** $8 **MIP** $15

16-2SF, Badger, 1974, Block, metallic bronze-red body with surface detail tools, ladders, etc., and plastic "Rola-Matic" radar. Green window plastic, no interior, six thick wheels, 2-3/4". Later editions in olive green were included as part of TP-14 Two-Pack
EX $4 **NM** $7 **MIP** $12

(KP Photo, Tom Michael collection)

16-3SF, Pontiac Firebird, 1981, Metallic light or dark tan, Firebird tempo on hood, light tan plastic interior
EX n/a **NM** $2 **MIP** $7

17-1SF, Horse Box, 1971, Red or orange AEC Ergomatic cab with green or gray plastic horse box, gray or mustard door, and two white plastic horses, 2-7/8"
EX $3 **NM** $7 **MIP** $12

(KP Photo, John Brown Sr. collection)

17-2SF, The Londoner, 1973, Red body with "Berger Paints" or "Swinging London Carnaby Street" side labels (most common). White plastic interior, no window plastic, 3". There are many color and label variations of this model, some limited runs that command MIP values over $200. However, prices shown are for the common red-colored "Berger" and "Swinging London" versions
EX $2 **NM** $4 **MIP** $8

(KP Photo, Tom Michael collection)

17-2SF, The Londoner, 1973, The "Swinging London" version of the The Londoner bus

(KP Photo, Tom Michael collection)

18-1SF, Field Car, 1970, Yellow body with tan plastic roof, white plastic interior, no window plastic, unpainted base, spare tire, tow hook, thin or thick wheels, 2-7/8". Other variations as part of Two-Packs in the 1970s, included orange with checked hood label and black plastic roof, olive green with light-tan plastic roof and hood label, red with light-tan plastic roof and "44" hood label-almost all with black plastic interiors. White editions are harder to find, about $250-300 in MIP condition. Prices shown reflect the more common models listed

EX $7 **NM** $12 **MIP** $25

(KP Photo, Tom Michael collection)

18-1SF, Field Car, Variation with dark yellow-orange body, black interior, base and roof. Part of Two Pack (TP-8), with Honda motorcycle

18-2SF, Hondarora, 1975, Red or orange body with silver or black forks and black seat are the most common, some with gas-tank labels, some without. Olive-drab military models were part of the TP-11 set with the olive-drab field car. 2-1/2"

EX $5 **NM** $10 **MIP** $15

19-1SF, Lotus Racing Car, 1970, Dark metallic purple, white plastic driver, wide Superfast wheels, "3" decal on sides, 2-3/4"

EX $9 **NM** $20 **MIP** $48

(KP Photo, Tom Michael collection)

19-2SF, Road Dragster, 1971, Red or metallic pink body with unpainted base, exposed silver plastic engine, white plastic interior, wide wheels, clear window plastic, "8" labels on hood and roof, 3". Some models have "Wynns" or scorpion labels and are pink or orange-red and harder to find, about $80 MIP

EX $5 **NM** $10 **MIP** $15

19-3SF, Cement Truck, 1977, Red cab and chassis, unpainted metal base, green window plastic, no interior, yellow plastic mixer, with or without black or red stripes, 3"

EX $2 **NM** $4 **MIP** $8

20-1SF, Lamborghini Marzal, 1970, Pink or dark red with amber window plastic, white plastic interior and thin wheels; or pink or orange-pink with thick wheels, 2-3/4"

EX $8 **NM** $15 **MIP** $25

20-2SF, Police Patrol, 1975, White Range Rover with orange stripe "Police" label, frosted window plastic and blue or orange revolving police light (part of the Rola-Matics series). 2-7/8". Other models include orange Site Engineer from Gift Pack #13, olive-drab military ambulance model, and orange Paris-Dakar model, each with approx. $25-$35 MIP value. Common white model values given below

EX $2 **NM** $8 **MIP** $12

(KP Photo, Tom Michael collection)

20-2SF, Police Patrol: Site Engineer, 1977, Orange body with rotating orange dome light, "Site Engineer" labels on doors, plain metal base. Part of #13 Construction Gift Pack

EX $5 **NM** $8 **MIP** $14

20-2SF, Police Patrol: Paris-Dakar Rallye, 1983, Gold body with black and white checkered label and "Securitie-Rallye Paris Dakar 83" on sides, black base, red rotating dome light

EX $5 **NM** $9 **MIP** $13

20-2SF, Police Patrol: County Sheriff, 1982, White body with blue doors and roof, star design on hood and doors, "County Sheriff" in blue type on sides, blue rotating dome light

EX $3 **NM** $5 **MIP** $8

20-2SF, Police Patrol: British Police, 1983, White body with yellow and black/white checkered "Police" labels on sides. Blue rotating dome light, black base

EX $4 **NM** $8 **MIP** $12

21-1SF, Foden Concrete Truck, 1971, Yellow cab, orange truck bed with yellow plastic mixer, eight thin wheels, 3"

EX $8 **NM** $12 **MIP** $25

21-2SF, Rod Roller, 1973, Yellow body with red plastic seat, star and flames label on hood, (later editions without black plastic roller wheels, some with red or metallic red hubs on rear, black plastic steering lever, 2-1/2". Prices for metallic red hub versions about $45 MIP

EX $5 **NM** $12 **MIP** $20

21-3SF, Renault 5TL, 1979, Yellow, blue, white or silver-gray body, clear or amber window plastic, tan or red plastic interior, tow hook, 2-1/2". Some yellow models have "Le Car" tempo
EX $2 **NM** $6 **MIP** $10

22-1SF, Pontiac Grand Prix, 1970, Purple body, thin wheels, silver grille and black base, 3"
EX $12 **NM** $22 **MIP** $55

(KP Photo, Tom Michael collection)

22-2SF, Freeman Inter-City Commuter, 1971, Purple-red body with white plastic interior, clear window plastic, unpainted base, some with side labels, 3"
EX $2 **NM** $4 **MIP** $8

22-3SF, Blaze Buster, 1976, Red body with yellow or black plastic ladder, silver plastic interior, amber window plastic, black or silver base, 3-1/16". Black-ladder versions about $25 MIP value
EX $2 **NM** $4 **MIP** $7

22-4SF, 4 x 4 Big Foot, 1982, Silver body, white plastic camper top, blue window plastic, black base, "Big Foot" and "26" tempos on sides and hood
EX $2 **NM** $5 **MIP** $12

23-1SF, Volkswagen Camper, 1970, Blue or orange body with plastic orange lift-up top reveals white plastic interior, amber or clear window plastic. Some models with sailboat labels on sides, 2-5/8". Military olive-drab versions without lift-up camper top were included as ambulances with TP-12 Two-Pack
EX $9 **NM** $22 **MIP** $45

23-2SF, Atlas Tipper, 1976, Blue body with orange or silver tipper section, wide wheels, amber or clear window plastic, silver or gray plastic interior, 2-3/4". Later versions available with red body
EX $1 **NM** $3 **MIP** $7

(KP Photo, Tom Michael collection)

23-3SF, Ford Mustang GT-350, 1981, White body, blue Shelby stripes, exposed engine in front, "GT 350" on sides
EX $5 **NM** $12 **MIP** $18

24-1SF, Rolls-Royce Silver Shadow, 1970, Metallic-red body, white plastic interior, clear window plastic, opening trunk, silver metal grille and headlights, black or silver base, 3"
EX $5 **NM** $9 **MIP** $20

(KP Photo, Tom Michael collection)

24-2SF, Team Matchbox, 1973, Metallic green, red or orange body, "8" or "44" label (included with TP-9, Field Car and Racing Car Two-Pack), white plastic driver, 2-7/8". Metallic green version, about $35 MIP, orange version about $85 MIP. Values for red shown
EX $1 **NM** $4 **MIP** $9

(KP Photo, John Brown Sr. collection)

24-3SF, Diesel Shunter, 1979, Dark green and red or yellow and red body, no window plastic, labels read "Rail Freight" or "D1496-RF"
EX n/a **NM** $2 **MIP** $5

25-1SF, Ford Cortina GT, 1970, Metallic tan or blue body, white plastic interior, opening doors, tow hook, 2-5/8". Metallic tan versions, the first of the transitional Superfast models, are harder-to-find and have approx. $70-$80 MIP values
EX $8 **NM** $12 **MIP** $25

25-2SF, Mod Tractor, 1973, Metallic purple body, black base, some with "V" cast on fenders, some without, silver plastic exposed engine, yellow plastic seat, 2-1/4". Harder to find editions have headlights cast in rear fender, about $60 MIP
EX $1 **NM** $3 **MIP** $7

(KP Photo, John Brown Sr. collection)

25-3SF, Flat Car and Container, 1979, Black or charcoal flat car with tan or red plastic container with "NYK Worldwide Service" labels
EX $1 **NM** $3 **MIP** $5

VEHICLES • MATCHBOX SUPERFAST

26-1SF, GMC Tipper Truck, 1970, Red tipping cab, green engine and base, silver dump bed, green window plastic, no interior, 2-5/8"
EX $5 **NM** $9 **MIP** $20

(KP Photo, Tom Michael collection)

26-2SF, Big Banger, 1973, Red with dark-blue window plastic, no interior, large silver plastic engine and exhaust pipes, "Big Banger" side labels, 3". Later versions were brown with "Brown Sugar" side labels or white with "Cosmic Blues" tempo
EX $4 **NM** $9 **MIP** $18

(KP Photo, Tom Michael collection)

26-2SF, Brown Sugar, 1973, The "Brown Sugar" version of the Big Banger with brown body, large silver engine with black scoop and yellow and red "Brown Sugar" labels

26-3SF, Site Dumper, 1977, Yellow body with yellow or red dumper bed, or orange body with silver-gray dumper bed, no window plastic, black or brown base, black plastic interior
EX $2 **NM** $4 **MIP** $7

27-1SF, Mercedes 230SL, 1970, Yellow convertible body with black plastic interior, or white body with red plastic interior, clear window plastic, silver base, thin wheels, 2-3/4"
EX $8 **NM** $16 **MIP** $30

(KP Photo, Tom Michael collection)

27-2SF, Lamborghini Countach, 1973, Pale-orange body with "3" label on hood, or red-orange with "8" tempo and stripes, silver or gray plastic interior, amber or blue window plastic, opening rear hood, 3"
EX $3 **NM** $7 **MIP** $14

(KP Photo, John Brown Sr. collection)

28-1SF, Mack Dump Truck, 1970, Light-green body and dumper bed, silver base, wide wheels, no interior, amber window plastic, 2-5/8". Olive-drab versions were released with Case bulldozer in TP-16 Two-Pack
EX $6 **NM** $10 **MIP** $22

28-2SF, Stoat, 1973, Metallic bronze-tan body with rotating (Rola-Matic) soldier holding binoculars. Black base, wide wheels, 2-5/8". Olive-green versions with all-black wheels were included in TP-13 Two-Pack along with an olive version of 73-2SF Weasel armored vehicle
EX $2 **NM** $6 **MIP** $12

(KP Photo, Tom Michael collection)

28-3SF, Lincoln Continental Mk V, 1979, Red body, white plastic roof, light-yellow or gray interior, silver base. First introduced in the 1979/80 catalog, this model had not yet replaced the Stoat in the lineup, but was due to be "available in your shops later this year"
EX $3 **NM** $6 **MIP** $10

29-1SF, Fire Pumper, 1970, Red body, blue window plastic and dome light, white plastic ladders and reels, silver base, thin wheels, 3"
EX $12 **NM** $32 **MIP** $70

(KP Photo, Tom Michael collection)

29-2SF, Racing Mini, 1971, Orange-red body with yellow "29" labels, clear window plastic, white plastic interior, unpainted silver-gray base and grille, 2-1/4". Also included with TP-6 Two-Pack
EX $5 **NM** $11 **MIP** $20

29-3SF, Shovel-Nose Tractor, 1977, Yellow body with silver or black plastic engine and interior, shovel can be red or black plastic, 2-7/8". Lime green models with yellow plastic shovels are harder to find, about $65 MIP value. Models with yellow body, black plastic and stripes (as shown) were included in the G-5 Giftset in the 1979/80 catalog. Orange models with red plastic shovels, also about $65 MIP value
EX $5 **NM** $8 **MIP** $16

30-1SF, 8-Wheel Crane, 1970, Red with gold crane section, red plastic hook, no window plastic, yellow plastic hook, 3"
EX $10 **NM** $20 **MIP** $45

(KP Photo, Tom Michael collection)

30-2SF, Beach Buggy, 1971, Pink body with yellow "spatter paint," white or yellow plastic interior and side tanks, no

VEHICLES • MATCHBOX SUPERFAST

window plastic, 2-9/16". White interior versions have approx. $20 MIP value
EX $4 **NM** $7 **MIP** $12

30-3SF, Swamp Rat, 1977, Squared-boat body with olive-green deck, tan plastic hull, rotating striped army gunner (Rola-Matic), "Swamp Rat" labels, 3-1/16"
EX $3 **NM** $7 **MIP** $9

31-1SF, Lincoln Continental, 1970, Lime green body with thin wheels, opening trunk, clear window plastic, white plastic interior, 3"
EX $12 **NM** $21 **MIP** $38

31-2SF, Volksdragon, 1972, Red Volkswagen Beetle body with clear window plastic, white or yellow plastic interior, silver plastic engine, "eyes" label, unpainted base, 2-5/8"
EX $6 **NM** $10 **MIP** $16

(KP Photo, John Brown Sr. collection)

31-3SF, Caravan, 1978, White body with amber or blue window plastic, some with orange stripe with white reversed bird graphic label, unpainted base, light-yellow plastic interior, 2-3/4"
EX $1 **NM** $3 **MIP** $6

32-1SF, Leyland Petrol Tanker, 1970, Green cab and chassis, white tank, "BP" labels, thin wheels, blue or amber window plastic, no interior, chrome plastic base, 3"
EX $8 **NM** $14 **MIP** $22

(KP Photo, Tom Michael collection)

32-2SF, Maserati Bora, 1973, Magenta body with yellow plastic interior, clear window plastic, opening doors, "8" stripe label on hood, lime green, dark green or unpainted base, 3"
EX $3 **NM** $7 **MIP** $13

32-3SF, Field Gun, 1978, Olive-green with black plastic barrel that fired shells attached to sprue on tan plastic base with soldiers, 3". An interesting piece, in that it included a diarama with the toy. Field Gun was removable from base
EX $3 **NM** $6 **MIP** $11

(KP Photo, George Cuhaj collection)

33-1SF, Lamborghini Miura, 1970, Gold body, opening doors, white plastic interior, thin wheels, unpainted base, 2-3/4"
EX $7 **NM** $12 **MIP** $22

33-2SF, Datsun 126X, 1973, Yellow body with silver plastic interior, orange base, opening rear hood, amber window plastic, 3". Some versions have black and red flame tempo detail on hood and roof
EX $1 **NM** $4 **MIP** $8

33-3SF, Police Motorcycle, 1978, White motorcycle with blue plastic policeman rider, silver plastic engine, "Police" on saddlebags, silver or black wire spoked wheels, 2-7/8". Models included with the K-71 Porsche Polizei set had green plastic riders and detailing
EX $1 **NM** $4 **MIP** $7

34-1SF, Formula 1 Racing Car, 1970, Magenta or yellow body, white plastic driver, silver plastic engine, wide wheels, "16" striped label on hood, clear windshield plastic, 2-7/8"
EX $5 **NM** $8 **MIP** $14

(KP Photo, Tom Michael collection)

34-2SF, Vantastic, 1976, Modified orange Ford Mustang body, white plastic interior, blue window plastic, early models with large silver plastic engine, later models with closed hood, white base, 2-7/8"
EX $2 **NM** $6 **MIP** $12

(KP Photo, Tom Michael collection)

34-2SF, Vantastic, 1976, Earlier and harder-to-find release without the exposed engine. Number "34" appears on hood

(KP Photo, George Cuhaj collection)

35-1SF, Merryweather Marquis Fire Engine, 1970, Red body, blue window plastic, gray plastic reels and instrument panel, white plastic ladder, blue dome lights, "London Fire Service" labels, narrow or wide tires, 3". This model was also included with TP-2 Two-Pack (900 Range). A modified casting was later used for 63-5SF Snorkel Fire Engine
EX $4 **NM** $7 **MIP** $12

(KP Photo, Tom Michael collection)

35-2SF, Fandango, 1975, White body with red plastic interior, "35" label with stripe on hood, rotating (Rola-Matic) fan behind driver, clear window plastic, 3". Also red body with red or white plastic

interiors, a later release. Versions with white body and red interior and a number "6" label are harder to find, and about $40 MIP
EX $3 **NM** $6 **MIP** $10

(KP Photo, Tom Michael collection)

36-1SF, Opel Diplomat, 1970, Metallic green-gold color, opening hood, thin wheels, 2-3/4"
EX $6 **NM** $11 **MIP** $20

(KP Photo, Tom Michael collection)

36-2SF, Hot Rod Draguar, 1971, Metallic pink or purple body with white or light yellow plastic interior, clear bubble window plastic, large silver engine, wide wheels, 2-7/8"
EX $5 **NM** $11 **MIP** $20

(KP Photo, Tom Michael collection)

36-3SF, Formula 5000, 1977, Orange with blue label number "3" and blue plastic driver, or red with "Texaco" and "Champion" labels and yellow plastic driver, 2-7/8"
EX $1 **NM** $4 **MIP** $10

37-1SF, Cattle Truck, 1970, Yellow Dodge cab and chassis, green plastic windows, no interior, gray-brown plastic stake-side bed with two white plastic cows, 2-1/2"
EX $6 **NM** $11 **MIP** $20

(KP Photo, Tom Michael collection)

37-2SF, Scoopa Coopa, 1973, Blue or pink body with yellow plastic interior, amber plastic windshield, unpainted base, 2-7/8". Pink models have a daisy-shaped sticker on the roof section, and were shown first in the 1976 catalog
EX $5 **NM** $11 **MIP** $20

37-3SF, Skip Truck, 1977, Red cab and chassis, clear or amber plastic windows, yellow bucket, white plastic interior, 2-3/4"
EX $2 **NM** $4 **MIP** $6

38-1SF, Honda Motorcycle with Trailer, 1970, Yellow motorcycle trailer with thin wheels and "Honda" labels. Green or pink motorcycle, silver spokes, 3"
EX $7 **NM** $11 **MIP** $19

38-2SF, Stingeroo, 1973, Purple chopper-style bike with cream-colored plastic horse head on seat, two wide wheels in rear, one solid wheel in front, purple plastic forks, silver plastic engine, 3-1/8"
EX $6 **NM** $10 **MIP** $22

38-3SF, Armored Jeep, 1977, Dark olive-drab with white star emblem on hood, black base and grille, black plastic gun on back (swivels), all-black wide wheels
EX $4 **NM** $7 **MIP** $10

39-1SF, Ford Tractor, 1970, Blue body with yellow hood and wheels or all-blue body (included with K-20 Tractor Transporter), 2-1/8". This was another regular-wheels holdover into the Superfast era
EX $7 **NM** $16 **MIP** $25

39-2SF, Clipper, 1973, Metallic magenta body with light metallic green base, yellow plastic interior, flip-up cockpit, and "clicking" exhaust pipes that moved up and down as the car rolled along. One of the first in the Rola-Matics series, 3"
EX $3 **NM** $7 **MIP** $12

39-4SF, Rolls-Royce Mark II, 1979, Silver body with red plastic interior or metallic red body with yellow plastic interior. Clear window plastic, opening doors, unpainted base, silver grille and headlights. Introduced in the 1979/80 catalog, but had not replaced Clipper in the 1-75 lineup
EX $2 **NM** $5 **MIP** $9

40-1SF, Hay Trailer, 1970, Blue with yellow wheels and stakeside attachments, 3-3/8". Another holdover from the regular wheels series, this model was replaced in 1972 with the Superfast Guildsman
EX $3 **NM** $8 **MIP** $12

(KP Photo, Tom Michael collection)

40-2SF, Guildsman, 1972, Pink with white plastic interior and light-green window plastic, star and flames label on hood; or, red body with white plastic interior with amber window plastic and "40" label on hood (first appears in 1976 catalog), 3"
EX $4 **NM** $8 **MIP** $16

(KP Photo, John Brown Sr. collection)

40-3SF, Horse Box, 1978, Orange cab and chassis, no interior, green window plastic, cream-colored plastic box with light-brown door, two white plastic horses, 2-7/8". This model was reissued in the 1990s with green and blue color variations
EX $2 **NM** $6 **MIP** $10

41-1SF, Ford GT, 1970, White or red with red plastic interior, blue stripe and number "6" label on hood, thin or wide wheels
EX $8 **NM** $15 **MIP** $28

(KP Photo, Tom Michael collection)

41-2SF, Siva Spyder, 1973, Red body with cream-colored plastic interior, black segment wraps behind cabin, wide wheels, clear window plastic, 3". Blue versions with stars and stripes label motif available in 1976 catalog
EX $3 **NM** $7 **MIP** $12

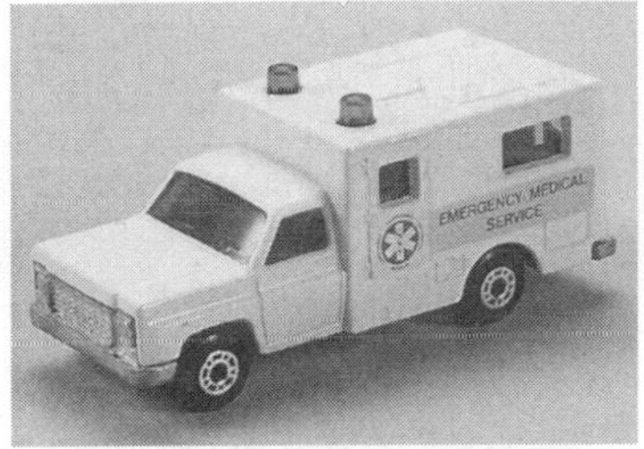

(KP Photo, John Brown Sr. collection)

41-3SF, Ambulance, 1979, White body, blue window plastic and dome lights, opening rear doors, unpainted base, white plastic interior, "Emergency Medical Service" or "Ambulance" with red cross labels, 2-1/2"
EX $3 **NM** $6 **MIP** $12

42-1SF, Iron Fairy Crane, 1971, Red with open cab (no window plastic) yellow plastic interior, yellow crane section with yellow plastic hook, wide wheels, 3". Continued as a regular wheels model, but only for the 1970 catalog, then converted to Superfast
EX $15 **NM** $25 **MIP** $45

(KP Photo, Tom Michael collection)

42-2SF, Tyre Fryer, 1973, Light or dark-blue body, open cockpit, yellow plastic seat, large silver plastic engine behind driver, large Superfast wheels in rear, wide wheels in front, 3"
EX $2 **NM** $6 **MIP** $12

(KP Photo, John Brown Sr. collection)

42-3SF, Mercedes Container Truck, 1978, Red cab and chassis, blue window plastic, no interior, unpainted or black base, plastic container with "SeaLand," "NYK" or "Matchbox" labels, 3"
EX $1 **NM** $3 **MIP** $6

42-4SF, '57 T-Bird, 1981, Red body, white interior, clear windshield, silver metal base
EX $1 **NM** $3 **MIP** $6

42-4SF, '57 T-Bird, 1982, Later version with black body, red interior, yellow windshield, plain base
EX $1 **NM** $3 **MIP** $7

43-1SF, Pony Trailer, 1970, Yellow body with green base, clear window plastic, two white plastic horses, narrow wheels, brown plastic door, 2-5/8". Orange version with horse label included with TP-3 Two-Pack
EX $5 **NM** $8 **MIP** $15

(KP Photo, Tom Michael collection)

43-2SF, Dragon Wheels, 1973, Green Volkswagen Beetle funny-car body hinged to silver plastic and metal base, "Dragon Wheels" labels on sides, 2-7/8"
EX $4 **NM** $7 **MIP** $14

(KP Photo, John Brown Sr. collection)

43-3SF, Steam Loco, 1979, Red and black body, red base, "4345" labels on sides, 2-11/16"
EX $1 **NM** $3 **MIP** $6

(KP Photo, Tom Michael collection)

44-1SF, Refrigerator Truck, 1970, Yellow GMC cab and chassis with red refrigeration box, green window plastic, 3". The first release in 1970 was painted like the regular wheels version with red cab and chassis and green refrigeration box. These are hard to find and command approx. $145 MIP values
EX $7 **NM** $14 **MIP** $26

44-2SF, Boss Mustang, 1973, Yellow body with opening black hood, silver plastic interior, amber plastic window, unpainted base, 3"
EX $5 **NM** $10 **MIP** $15

(KP Photo, Tom Michael collection)

45-1SF, Ford Group Six, 1970, Metallic green body with white plastic interior, silver plastic engine, clear window

VEHICLES • MATCHBOX SUPERFAST

plastic and number "7" label; or red body with amber-colored windows and number "45" labels, (a later version, first appearing in 1973), 3"
EX $4 **NM** $10 **MIP** $22

45-2SF, B.M.W. 3.0 CSL, 1975, Orange body with opening doors, yellow plastic interior, amber or blue plastic windows, silver base, "BMW" label on hood, 2-7/8"
EX $3 **NM** $7 **MIP** $15

46-1SF, Mercedes 300SE, 1970, Gold or blue body, white plastic interior, opening trunk, (some early models with opening doors, too) thin wheels, unpainted base, grille and headlights, 2-7/8". Blue models are hard to find and may command MIP values of $100 or more. Olive-drab staff car versions as part of TP-14 Two-Pack set, about $15 in NM condition
EX $6 **NM** $14 **MIP** $22

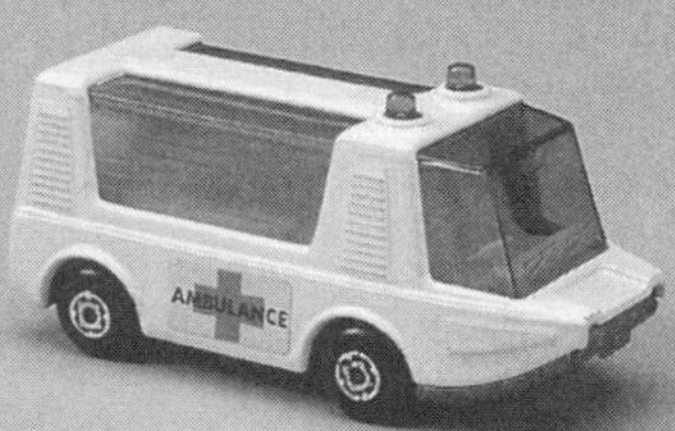

(KP Photo, Tom Michael collection)

46-2SF, Stretcha Fetcha, 1973, White with blue windows, white plastic interior, red base, "Ambulance" red cross labels, wide wheels, opening rear hatch, 2-3/4"
EX $2 **NM** $4 **MIP** $8

46-3SF, Ford Tractor & Harrow, 1979, Blue Ford tractor with cab, no window plastic, gray engine block and base, black wheels with or without orange-yellow painted hubs, yellow plastic disk or harrow included (not shown). Also included with hay trailer in TP-11 Two-Pack
EX $1 **NM** $6 **MIP** $14

46-4SF, Hot Chocolate, 1982, Metallic brown and black funny car body with white stripe. This car was an update on the "Dragon Wheels" funny car
EX $2 **NM** $5 **MIP** $8

47-1SF, DAF Tipper Container Truck, 1970, Silver-green cab and chassis, plastic tipping box with removable top, red plastic grille and partial base, green plastic windows, no interior, 3". A Superfast update of the regular wheels model
EX $6 **NM** $10 **MIP** $22

(KP Photo, Tom Michael collection)

47-2SF, Beach Hopper, 1973, Blue with pink "spatter" paint, brown plastic interior, tan plastic driver that "hops" as car moves along (a Rola-Matic model), wide wheels, sun label on hood, 2-5/8"
EX $2 **NM** $7 **MIP** $14

47-3SF, Pannier Locomotive, 1979, Green body, "GWR" labels, metallic brown base. This model had not yet replaced the Beach Hopper in the 1-75 catalog lineup, but was introduced as being available later in the year
EX $2 **NM** $5 **MIP** $8

47-4SF, Jaguar SS, 1982, Red body, silver grille, headlights and windshield, light-brown plastic interior, wide wheels
EX $2 **NM** $4 **MIP** $8

48-1SF, Dumper Truck, 1970, Blue Dodge cab and chassis, yellow dumper bed, green plastic windows, no interior, silver plastic grille, bumper and partial base, 3". A Superfast version of the 48-3RW regular wheels model
EX $10 **NM** $18 **MIP** $32

(KP Photo, John Brown Sr. collection)

48-2SF, Pi-Eyed Piper, 1973, Blue body, oversized plastic engine on hood, number "8" label on roof, silver exhaust pipes along sides, no interior, blue plastic windows, 2-1/2"
EX $5 **NM** $8 **MIP** $20

48-3SF, Sambron Jack Lift, 1978, Yellow body with yellow plastic lifting forks, no window plastic, 3-1/16"
EX $2 **NM** $4 **MIP** $7

(KP Photo, Tom Michael collection)

49-1SF, Unimog, 1970, Blue or metallic blue-green with red base, green plastic windows, wide wheels, 2-1/2". Another update of a regular wheels model, in the 1-75 lineup until 1973. An olive-drab version with a plastic container for artillery shells in the bed was part of the TP-13 Two-Pack in 1979
EX $7 **NM** $12 **MIP** $25

49-3SF, Crane Truck, 1977, Yellow body with swiveling crane section, extendable crane arm, red plastic hook, six wide wheels, 3"
EX $3 **NM** $6 **MIP** $12

50-1SF, Kennel Truck, 1970, Dark-green Ford truck body, with four white plastic dogs and clear plastic canopy over bed. Green plastic window, no interior, thin wheels, 2-3/4"
EX $12 **NM** $25 **MIP** $40

(KP Photo, Tom Michael collection)

50-2SF, Articulated Truck, 1973, Short yellow cab with green plastic windows and blue trailer with yellow plastic chassis, wide wheels, 3". Some have arrow labels, some do not. Notice the difference in the wheels on the trailer.
EX $1 **NM** $4 **MIP** $7

(KP Photo, George Cuhaj collection)

51-1SF, 8-Wheel Tipper, 1971, Yellow AEC cab and chassis, silver tipper bed, green plastic windows, no interior, "Pointer" labels, silver grille and headlights and partial base, 3"
EX $8 **NM** $18 **MIP** $40

51-2SF, Citroen SM, 1973, Dark red metallic body, opening doors, unpainted base, white plastic interior and tow hook, clear plastic windows, 2-7/8". In 1976, the paint scheme changed to blue with a red stripe and number "8" on roof
EX $4 **NM** $7 **MIP** $12

51-3SF, Combine Harvester, 1979, Red with yellow reel and auger, black Superfast wheels, Superfast wheels with yellow hubs or regular wheels, 2-7/8"
EX $1 **NM** $3 **MIP** $7

52-1SF, Dodge Charger Mk III, 1970, Metallic red or metallic lime-green body with black plastic interior, lift-up canopy, wide wheels, 3". Early red models also featured "hood scoop" labels
EX $4 **NM** $7 **MIP** $18

52-2SF, Police Launch, 1977, White body with blue plastic base and two blue plastic officers, labels on sides read "Police," silver metal horns on cabin roof, dark-blue plastic windows, thin wheels, 3-1/16"
EX $1 **NM** $4 **MIP** $7

(KP Photo, Tom Michael collection)

53-1SF, Ford Zodiac Mk IV, 1970, Metallic green body, opening hood, silver engine with spare tire, white plastic interior, clear plastic windows, 2-3/4"
EX $7 **NM** $10 **MIP** $22

(KP Photo, Tom Michael collection)

53-2SF, Tanzara, 1973, Orange body, amber plastic windows, opening rear hood shows silver plastic engine, wide wheels, silver plastic interior, unpainted base, 3". Models in 1976 had a bicentennial color scheme; white with red and blue stripes and number "53" on hood
EX $2 **NM** $4 **MIP** $7

53-3SF, CJ6 Jeep, 1978, Red body, tan plastic roof, yellow plastic interior, unpainted metal base
EX $3 **NM** $6 **MIP** $10

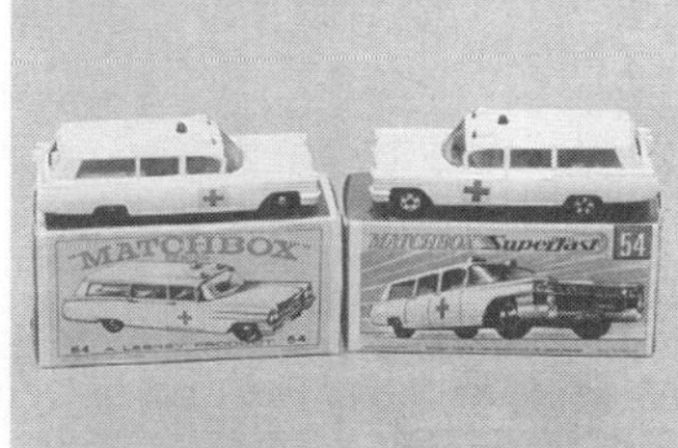

(KP Photo by Dr. Douglas Sadecky)

54-1SF, Cadillac Ambulance, 1970, White body, blue plastic windows, white plastic interior, red cross labels, white or silver-painted grille, narrow wheels, 2-7/8". Shown here with its regular wheels predecessor
EX $12 **NM** $22 **MIP** $45

(KP Photo, Tom Michael collection)

54-2SF, Ford Capri, 1971, Red with black hood or all pink with white plastic interior, unpainted base, opening hood, wide wheels, 2-7/8". All-red models were included with boat and trailer in TP-5 Two-Pack starting in 1977
EX $2 **NM** $5 **MIP** $11

54-3SF, Personnel Carrier, 1978, Olive-green with tan plastic troops and gun, black base, wide wheels, 3"
EX $3 **NM** $7 **MIP** $12

(KP Photo, Tom Michael collection)

55-1SF, Police Car, 1970, White Mercury sedan, clear windows, white plastic interior with molded figures, police label on hood, shield labels on doors, blue or red dome light, thin wheels, 3-1/16"
EX $8 **NM** $17 **MIP** $30

(KP Photo, Tom Michael collection)

55-2SF, Mercury Police Car, 1971, White station wagon body with blue or red dome lights, thin or wide wheels, unpainted base and grille, clear plastic windows, 3-1/16". Early versions had shield labels on doors and "Police" label on hood. Versions from 1973 to 1975 had only arrow-shaped red "Police" label. This car was a minor casting variation of the Mercury Commuter 73-1SF
EX $7 **NM** $15 **MIP** $27

(KP Photo, Tom Michael collection)

55-3SF, Hellraiser, 1976, White body with red plastic interior, silver plastic rear engine, clear windshield, wide wheels, stars and stripes label on hood. Or, blue body and white plastic interior, stars and stripes label, 3"
EX $2 **NM** $5 **MIP** $12

(KP Photo, Tom Michael collection)

55-4SF, Ford Cortina 1600 GL, 1979, Metallic gold with clear plastic windows, opening doors, unpainted base, red plastic interior. Introduced in 1979/80 catalog, but not yet part of the 1-75 lineup
EX $2 **NM** $6 **MIP** $10

(KP Photo, George Cuhaj collection)

56-1SF, BMC 1800 Pininfarina, 1970, Metallic gold or orange body, thin or wide wheels, opening doors, clear plastic windows, unpainted base, white plastic interior, 2-3/4". Later models modified the casting of the rear wheel wells to accommodate the wider Superfast wheels that became standard by 1973. This was a new model in the 1-75 lineup, not an adapted regular wheels casting like many others in 1970. Orange body versions about $16 MIP
EX $4 **NM** $7 **MIP** $12

56-2SF, Hi-Tailer, 1975, White body with yellow or blue plastic driver, silver plastic rear engine, red, white and blue striped label with "5, Team Matchbox and MB," 3"
EX $2 **NM** $4 **MIP** $10

56-3SF, Mercedes 450 SEL, 1979, Blue body, opening doors, light-yellow plastic interior, clear plastic windows, unpainted base. Introduced in 1979/80 catalog, had not yet replaced Hi-Tailer in the 1-75 lineup
EX $1 **NM** $3 **MIP** $6

57-1SF, Eccles Caravan, 1970, Cream or light-yellow trailer body with four thin wheels, stripe and flower label on sides, red or orange plastic roof, green or light-yellow plastic interior, 3-1/16". Like many models, the Eccles Caravan continued on in a Two-Pack set, the TP-4 Holiday Set
EX $4 **NM** $7 **MIP** $16

57-2SF, Wild Life Truck, 1973, Yellow body, red plastic windows, "Ranger" label on hood with elephant illustration, silver plastic grille, wide wheels, red plastic lion circles in truck bed as it is pushed along (Rola-Matic), no interior, clear plastic canopy over truck bed
EX $4 **NM** $7 **MIP** $14

58-1SF, DAF Girder Truck, 1970, Off-white or lime-green cab and chassis, red plastic girders, red plastic grille and partial base, green window plastic, no interior, 3". Off-white versions aren't real common and have approx. $65 MIP value
EX $6 **NM** $11 **MIP** $20

(KP Photo, Tom Michael collection)

58-2SF, Woosh-N-Push, 1973, Yellow body with open cockpit, red plastic interior, silver plastic exhaust, number "2" label on back of roof; or metallic red body, cream plastic interior, number "8" label with stars and stripes on roof (1976 version), 3"
EX $2 **NM** $4 **MIP** $8

58-3SF, Faun Dumper, 1977, Yellow body and dumper bed, black base, red plastic windows, 2-3/4"
EX $1 **NM** $3 **MIP** $5

(KP Photo, Tom Michael collection)

59-1SF, Ford Galaxie Fire Chief Car, 1970, Red body, white plastic interior and tow hook, clear plastic windows, thin wheels, shield labels on doors, blue dome light, 2-7/8". Oddly, this model dropped from the lineup for one year and returned, briefly, for 1972
EX $12 **NM** $22 **MIP** $40

59-2SF, Mercury Fire Chief Car, 1971, Red sedan body with white plastic interior (early versions with two figures), unpainted base, blue dome light, thin or wide wheels, shield and fire chief labels or fire helmet labels, also included in TP-10 Two-Pack with a dual dome light arrangement
EX $4 **NM** $8 **MIP** $16

(KP Photo, Tom Michael collection)

59-3SF, Planet Scout, 1976, Metallic green with lime-green or red with yellow body, silver plastic interior, yellow plastic windows, wide wheels, 2-3/4"
EX $2 **NM** $4 **MIP** $8

60-1SF, Truck with Site Office, 1970, Blue Leyland truck with Ergomatic cab, yellow plastic hut with green plastic roof, thin wheels, green plastic windows, silver plastic grille and partial base, 2-1/2"
EX $6 **NM** $10 **MIP** $22

60-2SF, Lotus Super Seven, 1972, Orange or yellow body with unpainted base, black plastic interior, clear plastic windshield, ghost and flame label on hood, or checker pattern with "60" along length of car, 2-7/8"
EX $5 **NM** $9 **MIP** $16

60-3SF, Holden Pick-Up, 1978, Red with yellow plastic motorcycles in bed and yellow plastic interior, unpainted base, checkered label with "500" on hood, 3-1/16"
EX $4 **NM** $7 **MIP** $14

60-4SF, Piston Popper, 1982, Yellow body with "Piston Popper" on hood and number "60" on sides. Unpainted metal base, red Rola-Matic pistons like the earlier version
EX $2 **NM** $4 **MIP** $6

(KP Photo, George Cuhaj collection)

61-1SF, Alvis Stalwart, 1970, White body, with yellow plastic canopy (not shown) green plastic wheels with removable black tires, "BP Exploration" labels on sides, 2-5/8". Olive-green versions were included with TP-16 Two-Pack in 1979
EX $9 **NM** $17 **MIP** $30

61-2SF, Blue Shark, 1972, Blue body with unpainted base, white plastic driver, silver plastic rear engine, black plastic exhaust pipes, clear plastic windshield, "86" or Scorpion label (harder to find, about $50 MIP), 3"
EX $3 **NM** $9 **MIP** $17

61-3SF, Wreck Truck, 1979, Red truck body, black base, red plastic windows and dome lights, no interior, white towing arms with red plastic hooks
EX $3 **NM** $6 **MIP** $10

62-1SF, Mercury Cougar, 1970, Lime-green body with red plastic interior and tow hook, opening doors, 3"
EX $9 **NM** $16 **MIP** $30

62-2SF, Rat Rod Dragster, 1971, Light-green body, clear plastic windows, red plastic interior, exposed engine through hood, "Rat Rod" labels on sides, 3". A reworking of the Mercury Cougar casting
EX $5 **NM** $8 **MIP** $18

(KP Photo, Tom Michael collection)

62-2SF, Renault 17TL, 1974, Red body with opening doors, white plastic interior, blue plastic windows, some with stripe and number "6" label, some without, 3". A version with "Fire" labels was included in the G-12 Rescue Gift Set in the 1977 catalog
EX $2 **NM** $5 **MIP** $12

(KP Photo, Tom Michael collection)

62-3SF, Chevy Corvette, 1982, Black body with yellow and orange stripes running from hood to trunk, white plastic interior, plain base with side-pipes
EX $2 **NM** $5 **MIP** $8

62-1SF, Dodge Crane Truck, 1970, Yellow body with rotating crane section, yellow plastic hook, black base, green plastic windows, no interior, 3"
EX $6 **NM** $11 **MIP** $20

63-2SF, Freeway Gas Tanker, 1974, Short red cab with black base and wide wheels, white plastic tanker trailer with red chassis, "Burmah" labels on tanker section, 3-1/8". Also available in yellow and white Shell versions, blue and white Aral versions and red and white Chevron version (part of TP-17 Two-Pack). As with regular wheels editions, the German-issue Aral version is harder to find, about $25 MIP. There is also an olive-green version with TP-14 with "High Octane" labels on the sides
EX $2 **NM** $4 **MIP** $8

(KP Photo, Tom Michael collection)

63-2SF, Freeway Gas Tanker, 1974, A view showing the more popular edition with the "Burmah" labels and red cab

64-1SF, MG 1100, 1970, Blue body, white plastic interior with dog and driver, tow hook, thin wheels, silver base, 2-5/8"
EX $9 **NM** $22 **MIP** $40

(KP Photo, Tom Michael collection)

64-2SF, Slingshot Dragster, 1972, Pink or blue body with dual silver plastic engines and red exhaust pipes, label on hood with number "9" and flames, white plastic driver, 3"
EX $4 **NM** $7 **MIP** $15

(KP Photo, Tom Michael collection)

64-3SF, Fire Chief Car, 1976, Red body with blue plastic windows, silver air scoops on hood, silver base, "Fire Chief" labels with shield on sides, 3"

EX $3 **NM** $5 **MIP** $12

64-4SF, Caterpillar Bulldozer, 1981, Yellow die-cast body with yellow plastic blade and unpainted base and engine. Cab can be tan or black, and later models have "CAT" and "C" logos on sides near cab

EX $2 **NM** $4 **MIP** $7

(KP Photo, John Brown Sr. collection)

64-4SF, Caterpillar Bulldozer, The black cab and "CAT" logos appeared on later versions of the bulldozer

65-1SF, Combine Harvester, Red with yellow plastic reel and front wheels with removable black plastic tires, 3". This model was another holdover from the regular wheels lineup, first introduced in 1967, but remaining until 1973

EX $3 **NM** $7 **MIP** $12

65-2SF, Saab Sonnet, 1974, Blue body with plastic lift-up rear hatch, light-yellow plastic interior, wide wheels, unpainted base, 2-7/8"

EX $4 **NM** $7 **MIP** $15

(KP Photo, Tom Michael collection)

65-3SF, Airport Coach, 1978, Metallic blue body, white roof, yellow plastic windows, off-white interior, "British Airways," "American Airlines" or "Lufthansa" labels on sides are most common, 3-1/16". German versions with "Schulbus" labels are harder to find, about $45 MIP. Other variations include: Red body, white top with "TWA" or "Qantas" labels

EX $4 **NM** $6 **MIP** $9

(KP Photo, Tom Michael collection)

65-3SF, Airport Coach, 1978, Version with red body, white top and "TWA" labels

(KP Photo, Tom Michael collection)

65-3SF, Airport Coach, 1978, Version with red body, white top and "Qantas" labels

(KP Photo by Dr. Douglas Sadecky)

66-1SF, Greyhound Bus, 1971, Silver with yellow plastic windows, thin wheels, blue and white Greyhound labels on sides, 3". Shown here in an interesting blister-pack/box combo that Matchbox tried out in the late 1960s and early 1970s. MIP value approx $60 for this combo, regular MIP values shown

EX $9 **NM** $16 **MIP** $30

(KP Photo, Tom Michael collection)

66-2SF, Mazda RX 500, 1972, Early releases were orange with white base, opening rear engine hood, silver plastic interior with purple windows, 2-7/8". Later versions were red with white base and racing tempo "77" on hood with yellow windows

EX $3 **NM** $5 **MIP** $12

66-3SF, Ford Transit, 1978, Orange truck with dropside bed and plastic cargo crates, unpainted base, blue/green plastic windows, light-yellow plastic interior, 2-3/4"

EX $4 **NM** $7 **MIP** $10

67-1SF, Volkswagen 1600 TL, 1970, Pink or purple body, opening doors, white plastic interior, clear windows, unpainted base, thin or wide wheels (wide wheels version included in G-2 Transporter Gift Set), 2-11/16"

EX $8 **NM** $17 **MIP** $32

(KP Photo, Tom Michael collection)

67-2SF, Hot Rocker, 1973, Ford Capri body with open hood and oversized "hopping" engine (part of Rola-Matics series). Wide wheels, unpainted base. Available in lime-green and red paint variations, 3"

EX $3 **NM** $5 **MIP** $9

(KP Photo, Tom Michael collection)

67-3SF, Datsun 260Z, 1979, Pinkish-red or silver body with yellow plastic or red interior, opening doors, black base, 3". Silver model has red and black stripes on sides and hood with "Datsun 2+2" in black type

EX $3 **NM** $6 **MIP** $10

(KP Photo, Tom Michael collection)

68-1SF, Porsche 910, 1970, Red body with thin or wide wheels, cream or light-yellow plastic interior, clear windows, number "68" label on hood, 3"

EX $4 **NM** $8 **MIP** $14

68-2SF, Cosmobile, 1976, Blue or red body, silver plastic trim and interior, yellow base, wide wheels, 2-7/8"

EX $2 **NM** $5 **MIP** $8

68-3SF, Chevy Van, 1979, Orange with blue and red stripes along sides, blue plastic windows, silver base. Introduced in the 1979/80 catalog, but hadn't yet replaced the Cosmobile in the 1-75 lineup

EX $1 **NM** $4 **MIP** $7

(KP Photo, George Cuhaj collection)

69-1SF, Rolls-Royce Coupe, 1970, Blue body, clear windshield, brown plastic interior, thin wheels, opening trunk, tow hook, 3-1/16"

EX $6 **NM** $11 **MIP** $22

(KP Photo, Tom Michael collection)

69-2SF, Turbo Fury, 1973, Red body, clear windshield, number "69" label on hood, white plastic driver, fans on rear of car rotate when pushed (Rola-Matics series), and front of vehicle same style as Blue Shark, 3"

EX $4 **NM** $9 **MIP** $16

(KP Photo, Tom Michael collection)

69-3SF, Security Truck, 1979, Red armored truck with white "Wells Fargo" type on sides, blue windows and dome light, unpainted base, wide wheels, white roof, 2-7/8"

EX $5 **NM** $9 **MIP** $14

70-1SF, Grit Spreader, 1971, Red Ford cab and chassis, yellow hopper section, no interior, thin wheels, green windows, 2-5/8"

EX $5 **NM** $10 **MIP** $18

70-2SF, Dodge Dragster, 1972, Pink funny-car Dodge Charger body, silver engine, black or unpainted base, red plastic struts to hold body, snake labels along sides, 3". A preview drawing of this model is seen in the 1971 catalog under the heading "watch out for these 4 new models"

EX $6 **NM** $11 **MIP** $20

70-3SF, Self-Propelled Gun, 1977, Green with black plastic gun that fires and recoils while rolled along (Rola-Matics series). Tan treads, black roller wheels, 2-5/8"

EX $2 **NM** $4 **MIP** $8

(KP Photo, Tom Michael collection)

70-4SF, Ferrari 308 GTB, 1981, Red, may or may not have "Ferrari" on sides and emblem on hood, black base

EX $2 **NM** $4 **MIP** $6

71-1SF, Ford Heavy Wreck Truck, 1970, Red cab and towing crane, red plastic hook, white bed with "Esso" labels on sides, green windows and dome light, white grille, 3". Olive-green versions with all-black wheels were included in 1978's TP-16 Two-Pack

EX $11 **NM** $17 **MIP** $32

71-2SF, Jumbo Jet, 1973, Motorcycle with blue seat and handlebars, black roller-style wheels, silver plastic engine, red elephant head on handlebars, 2-3/4"

EX $6 **NM** $9 **MIP** $18

(KP Photo, Tom Michael collection)

71-3SF, Cattle Truck, 1978, Red or metallic gold with plastic yellow or cream stake bed, black plastic cattle, blue or green windows, 2-7/8". Also included in the 1979 TP-19 Two-Pack in red with a matching trailer and plastic cattle

EX $2 **NM** $5 **MIP** $8

72-1SF, Standard Jeep, 1970, Yellow body with red plastic seats, black bumpers, spare tire on back, 2-3/8". An update of the 72-2RW Standard Jeep, but in this case the spare couldn't actually be used

EX $10 **NM** $20 **MIP** $30

72-2SF, SRN Hovercraft, 1972, White top with black plastic base and "SRN6" with British flag labels on sides, red plastic propeller, thin wheels in underside of hull, blue plastic windows, 3-1/16"

EX $1 **NM** $2 **MIP** $5

72-3SF, Bomag Road Roller, 1979, Yellow body with red plastic interior and engine, black plastic roller, silver or yellow hubs. Introduced in 1979/80 catalog, but hadn't yet replaced the SRN Hovercraft in the 1-75 lineup
EX $1 **NM** $4 **MIP** $7

72-4SF, Maxi Taxi, 1982, Yellow Ford Capri body with Rola-Matic engine that hops when car is moved, an update of the Hot Rocker model. Checkered taxi tampos and rates on sides, "Maxi Taxi" on roof, black base
EX $1 **NM** $3 **MIP** $5

73-1SF, Mercury Commuter, 1970, Metallic lime-green body with thin wheels, clear windows, white plastic interior with dogs looking out the back, unpainted base, 3-1/16". By 1972, this car had changed to red with a bull's head label on the hood and luggage rack grooves on the roof, with approx. $16 MIP value. Prices for green model shown
EX $6 **NM** $14 **MIP** $25

73-2SF, Weasel, 1973, Medium metallic-green armored vehicle with black turret that turns as the car is rolled (Rola-Matics series), wide wheels, all-black or with silver hubs, 2-7/8". Olive-green versions were issued as part of TP-13 Two-Pack
EX $2 **NM** $5 **MIP** $8

74-1SF, Daimler Bus, 1970, Red or pink body, white plastic interior, thin or wide wheels, "Esso Extra Petrol" and Esso logo labels on sides, 3"
EX $5 **NM** $11 **MIP** $20

(KP Photo, Tom Michael collection)

74-2SF, Toe Joe, 1974, Metallic lime-green body with green plastic towing arms and red plastic hooks, yellow windows, unpainted base, 3". Versions with yellow bodies and red towing arms with black plastic hooks were included with the Racing Mini in TP-6 Two-Pack
EX $3 **NM** $6 **MIP** $12

(KP Photo, Tom Michael collection)

74-3SF, Mercury Cougar Villager, 1979, Lime-green or blue body, pale yellow interior, unpainted base, opening tailgate, 3-1/16"
EX $2 **NM** $5 **MIP** $11

75-1SF, Ferrari Berlinetta, 1970, Red with white plastic interior, thin wheels, unpainted base, 2-7/8". Some early models were produced in green, echoing the regular wheels editions, but they are rare and can have $350 MIP values
EX $12 **NM** $22 **MIP** $40

75-2SF, Alfa Carabo, 1971, Pink with yellow or white base, models in 1976 had yellow stripes running across top of car. White plastic interior, clear windows, 3"
EX $2 **NM** $5 **MIP** $11

75-3SF, Seasprite Helicopter, 1977, White body, red base, blue windows, regular wheels landing gear, black plastic rotor, "Rescue" labels on tail section, 2-7/8"
EX $4 **NM** $6 **MIP** $9

MIDGETOY

JUMBO SERIES, 6" VEHICLES

American LaFrance Pumper Truck, red with silver detailing and decals; 1970s-80s
EX $7 **NM** $12 **MIP** $25

Mobile Artillery, Army green, with silver detailing, 1970s-80s
EX $6 **NM** $12 **MIP** $20

Oil Tanker, white-green, "Midgetoy Oil Co.," painted details; 1970s-80s
EX $12 **NM** $25 **MIP** $37

Scenicruiser Bus, two-tone paint, "Midgetoy Bus Line"; 1970s-80s
EX $10 **NM** $20 **MIP** $30

JUNIOR SERIES, 2-1/2" TO 3" VEHICLES

Army Jeep, Army green, black plastic tires; 1960s-70s
EX $3 **NM** $6 **MIP** $9

Camper, Ford pickup with die-cast camper body; 1970s-80s
EX $4 **NM** $8 **MIP** $12

Corvette Stingray, various colors but often orange; 1971-80s
EX $1 **NM** $2 **MIP** $4

Ford Mustang, 1970s-80s
EX $1 **NM** $2 **MIP** $4

Ford Pickup, 1971 Ford model, white or other color; 1970s-80s
EX $2 **NM** $3 **MIP** $5

Ford Torino, various colors but often orange; 1971-80s
EX $1 **NM** $2 **MIP** $4

Ford Torino Fire Chief Car, red, cast-in flasher lights; 1970s-80s
EX $4 **NM** $9 **MIP** $12

Hot Rod, Ford V-8 design, open cockpit, black plastic tires, decals and/or painted headlights; 1970s-80s
EX $2 **NM** $4 **MIP** $6

Hot Rod, Ford V-8 design, open cockpit, black plastic tires, single-color paint; 1960s
EX $3 **NM** $4 **MIP** $8

Indy Race Car, open cockpit, Kurtis Kraft race car, black plastic tires, decals and/or painted highlights; 1970s-80s
EX $3 **NM** $6 **MIP** $12

Indy Race Car, open cockpit, Kurtis Kraft design race car, black plastic tires, single-color paint; 1960s-70s
EX $6 **NM** $9 **MIP** $13

MG Sports Roadster, open-top sports car, black plastic tires, single-color paint; 1960s
EX $6 **NM** $9 **MIP** $13

MG Sports Roadster, open-top sports car, black plastic tires, decals and/or painted highlights; 1960s-80s
EX $3 **NM** $6 **MIP** $9

Sunbeam Racer, land-speed race car, black plastic tires, decals and/or painted highlights; 1960s-80s
EX $3 **NM** $8 **MIP** $12

Volkswagen Beetle, black plastic tires, no decals or masking; 1960s-80s
EX $8 **NM** $15 **MIP** $20

Volkswagen Beetle, various colors, black plastic tires, decals and/or painted detailing; 1970s-80s
EX $8 **NM** $15 **MIP** $20

Wrecker Truck, cabover, metal boom with hook, black plastic tires; 1960s-70s
EX $4 **NM** $8 **MIP** $12

PEE-WEE SERIES, 2" VEHICLES

American LaFrance Fire Truck, 1969-80s
EX $1 **NM** $1 **MIP** $2

Ford GT, 1969-80s
EX $1 **NM** $1 **MIP** $2

Gas Pumps, 1-3/4" across, plastic
EX $1 **NM** $1 **MIP** $2

Hot Rod, 1969-80s
EX $1 **NM** $1 **MIP** $2

Jeep, 1969-80s
EX $1 **NM** $1 **MIP** $2

MG Sports Roadster, 1969-80s
EX $1 **NM** $1 **MIP** $2

Motorboat, 2-1/4", plastic
EX $1 **NM** $1 **MIP** $2

Open-Cockpit Racer, 1960s-70s
EX $1 **NM** $1 **MIP** $2

Utility Trailer, 1-1/2"
EX $1 **NM** $2 **MIP** $3

TRACTOR-TRAILERS

Aerial Fire Truck, 8" long; Chevy cab, cast-in ladder on trailer, 1960s-80s
EX $12 **NM** $24 **MIP** $35

Oil Tanker, 8" long; Chevy cab, "Midgetoy Oil Co." decal on tanker trailer
EX $12 **NM** $25 **MIP** $40

Oil Tanker, 8" long; Chevy cab, plain paint w/out masking or decals, 1960s-80s
EX $12 **NM** $20 **MIP** $30

Shipping Van, 8" long; Chevy ab, "Midgetoy Van Lines, Inc." decal on van box
EX $12 **NM** $25 **MIP** $40

Shipping Van, 8" long; Chevy cab, plain paint without masking or decals, 1960s-80s
EX $12 **NM** $20 **MIP** $30

NYLINT

No. 1000, Deliverall, 1946-51, wind-up; three-wheeled scooter with large cargo box; white, yellow, red, blue and black; rare
EX $100 **NM** $300 **MIP** $600

No. 1100, Big Dig, regular version
EX $50 **NM** $115 **MIP** $225

No. 1100, Elgin Street Sweeper, 1950-52, wind-up; yellow with red and black highlights, white plastic driver; bottom and side brooms rotate
EX $50 **NM** $175 **MIP** $350

No. 1101, Big Dig, 1967-70, re-design of No. SR1100 to look like Tonka's Mighty Cranes; orange, yellow and black with yellow plastic track wheels
EX $50 **NM** $100 **MIP** $200

No. 1200, Lawn and Garden Set, 1965, new number; same as No. 7000
EX $50 **NM** $125 **MIP** $250

No. 1200, Pumpmobile, 1950-52, wind-up; Howdy Doody cowboy-like figure (unlicensed), yellow, red and blue
EX $100 **NM** $300 **MIP** $600

No. 1210, Aerial Ladder Fire Truck, 1968-74, red with white ladders and black handwheels; Nylint's first large fire truck
EX $75 **NM** $140 **MIP** $275

No. 1211, Aerial Ladder Fire Truck, 1975-, second version of No. 1210 (less steel)
EX $50 **NM** $100 **MIP** $200

No. 1300, Tournarocker, 1955-57, third version; embossed grille details, larger 3-3/4" wheels; all yellow (1955), orange and yellow (1956-57); also by R.G. Letourneau
EX $75 **NM** $125 **MIP** $250

No. 1300, Tournarocker, 1953-54, second version; closed cab, no driver, grille plate on front, larger 3-3/4" wheels; all yellow; also by R.G. Letourneau
EX $75 **NM** $125 **MIP** $250

No. 1300, Tournarocker, 1951-52, first version; open tractor w/driver; orange (1951) or mustard yellow (1952); scale model of a machine by R. G. Letourneau
EX $50 **NM** $150 **MIP** $300

No. 1310, Backhoe, 1968-73, yellow backhoe on rubber crawler tracks with black base
EX $75 **NM** $140 **MIP** $275

No. 1400, Road Grader, 1951, first version; small wheels and steel grille plate; orange
EX $75 **NM** $125 **MIP** $250

No. 1400, Road Grader, 1952-53, second version; larger 3-3/4" wheels and grille plate; orange
EX $50 **NM** $175 **MIP** $350

No. 1400, Road Grader, 1954-58, third version; embossed grille, large 3-3/4" wheels; orange (1954-55), yellow (1956-58)
EX $50 **NM** $175 **MIP** $350

No. 1410, Hopper Dump, 1968-69, regular single-trailer version; yellow with black dump doors
EX $75 **NM** $150 **MIP** $300

No. 1420, Twin Hopper Dump Truck, 1967, Sears exclusive; yellow semi tractor pulling two hopper dump trailers, black dump doors and operating levers
EX $125 **NM** $225 **MIP** $450

No. 1500, Tournahopper, 1954-56, second version; embossed front, 3-3/4" wheels; yellow (1954-55), orange (1956). After 1953, these are replicas of Letourneau-Westinghouse machines
EX $75 **NM** $175 **MIP** $350

No. 1500, Tournahopper, 1952-53, first version; grille plate on front of closed tractor; yellow with black decals; replica of a R.G. Letourneau machine
EX $75 **NM** $175 **MIP** $350

No. 1600, Payloader, 1958, yellow
EX $50 **NM** $175 **MIP** $350

No. 1600, Payloader, 1958, dark green
EX $50 **NM** $175 **MIP** $350

No. 1600, Payloader, 1956-58, light green and yellow
EX $50 **NM** $175 **MIP** $350

No. 1600, Payloader, 1951, tan
EX $50 **NM** $175 **MIP** $350

(Calvin Chausse)

No. 1600, Payloader, 1951-55, red and yellow
EX $50 **NM** $175 **MIP** $350

No. 1610, Bronco Police Car, 1968, white Ford Bronco with lights and black trim
EX $35 **NM** $75 **MIP** $150

No. 1700, Tournahauler, 1953-54, second version dark green with grille plate
EX $50 **NM** $125 **MIP** $250

No. 1700, Tournahauler, 1953, first version; yellow
EX $100 **NM** $200 **MIP** $400

No. 1700, Tournahauler, 1956, fourth version; light green
EX $50 **NM** $125 **MIP** $250

No. 1700, Tournahauler, 1954-55, third version; dark green embossed grille
EX $50 **NM** $125 **MIP** $250

No. 1710, Bronco Petmobile, 1968-70s, dark blue Ford Bronco, white plastic cage for dogs
EX $40 **NM** $115 **MIP** $225

No. 1800, Traveloader, 1953-55, first version with smaller blades on front feeder belt (1953); second version with larger blades (1954-55); both versions orange with black decals, black belts on front feeder, black rear conveyor belt
EX $75 **NM** $125 **MIP** $250

No. 1810, Twister Exploration Car, 1969-73, yellow and black; Nylint's version of Tonka's Crater Crawler
EX $25 **NM** $100 **MIP** $200

No. 1900, Tournaractor, 1954-55, yellow and black with 4-7/16" wheels; by J.D. Adams
EX $50 **NM** $175 **MIP** $350

No. 1910, Hot Rod, 1969-72
EX $25 **NM** $40 **MIP** $75

No. 2000, Speed Swing Loader, 1955-58, orange or yellow; by Pettibone-Mulliken Co. orange and black (1955), yellow and black (1956-58)
EX $50 **NM** $125 **MIP** $250

No. 2010, Elevating Scraper, 1969-73, two-wheel tractor with large earthmover with rubber belt, pan scraper trailer (looked like a Caterpillar earthmover)
EX $75 **NM** $200 **MIP** $400

No. 2050, Jumbo Street Roller, 1971-77, roller in front, wheels in back; large red roller in front and red operator's cab (1971); yellow and black (1972-77)
EX $50 **NM** $100 **MIP** $200

No. 2070, Bobcat Loader, 1970-, yellow and black trim
EX $35 **NM** $65 **MIP** $125

No. 2100, Tournadozer, 1956-59, orange with black seat and motor; first version with larger 4-7/16" wheels (1956)
EX $75 **NM** $150 **MIP** $300

No. 2200, Michigan Shovel (crane), 1955-65, 10 wheels, clamshell bucket, single headlights, grille plate, steering (1955-56); six wheels, single or dual headlights, embossed front grille or grille plate (1956-60); no steering, grille sticker (1961-63); magnet added to bucket but only drop-down outriggers (1964-65); only Nylint toy to have real rubber tires through its first 10 years
EX $50 **NM** $150 **MIP** $300

No. 2201, Michigan Shovel (crane), 1966-73, redesigned version (made to look like Tonka mobile crane); clamshell bucket; this toy continued with number changes until the mid-1980s
EX $50 **NM** $150 **MIP** $300

No. 2300, Elgin Street Sweeper, 1956-57, battery-operated version, closed cab; yellow cab roof, red/yellow body (1956); red cab roof, yellow body (1957)
EX $50 **NM** $175 **MIP** $350

No. 2310, Beach Buggy, 1969-72
EX $25 **NM** $40 **MIP** $75

No. 2400, Electronic Cannon Truck, 1956, no radar antenna; four red/black-tipped rockets; Nylint's second battery-operated toy
EX $75 **NM** $150 **MIP** $300

No. 2400, Electronic Cannon Truck, 1957-59, with yellow radar antenna and four rockets
EX $75 **NM** $150 **MIP** $300

No. 2410, Bronco Bobcat, 1969-72, dark red Bronco with white top and larger wheels
EX $35 **NM** $85 **MIP** $175

No. 2500, Telescopic Crane, 1957-60, green with white boom for 1959 NY Toy Fair (won award for toy of the year); rare
EX $150 **NM** $225 **MIP** $450

No. 2500, Telescopic Crane, 1957-60, red with yellow boom, four-wheel steering, extendable boom
EX $100 **NM** $150 **MIP** $300

No. 2600, Missile Launcher, 1957-60, blue-gray, white radar antenna, white missiles with black tips
EX $50 **NM** $125 **MIP** $250

No. 2600, Missile Launcher, 1959, orange, white radar antenna, white missiles with black tips
EX $100 **NM** $175 **MIP** $350

No. 2700, Uranium Hauler, 1958-59, olive drab hydraulic bumper, yellow/black front guard
EX $50 **NM** $125 **MIP** $250

No. 2800, Guided Missile Carrier, 1958-59, later version (through 1960), firing cone of missiles, side-mounted forklift with red/yellow pallet, white missile with red fins and red nose cone
EX $75 **NM** $125 **MIP** $250

No. 2800, Guided Missile Carrier, 1958-59, first version (1958), non-firing missiles
EX $75 **NM** $125 **MIP** $250

No. 2900, Junior Jack Hammer, 1958-59, with air compressor package that connected to toy with 4' rubber hose; Nylint's first plastic toy; red/black jackhammer, yellow/red/black compressor box
EX $50 **NM** $125 **MIP** $250

No. 3000, Grader-Loader, 1959-62, first version with remote bucket release (1959 only); yellow, black bucket; first Nylint construction toy to have plastic tractor wheels (to keep shipping weight low)
EX $75 **NM** $150 **MIP** $300

No. 3100, Payloader Tractor-Shovel, 1959-62, first version yellow with levers in cab (1959 only); red/yellow with levers in cab (1959-60); without levers (1961-62); less than 1,300 made, replica of Hough machine; all toys had steel track base and rubber tracks
EX $75 **NM** $175 **MIP** $350

No. 3200, Power & Light Lineman Truck, 1959-61, yellow cab and flasher light, orange trailer, black rear hoist with tools, rope, yellow spool of wire, two stained poles; orange with yellow cab and flasher light, orange trailer, yellow wire spool
EX $75 **NM** $175 **MIP** $350

No. 3300, Power & Light Posthole Digger Truck, 1959-61, orange, yellow cab roof, orange trailer, yellow posthole assembly and tool box cover, plastic tools, four wooden phone poles
EX $75 **NM** $175 **MIP** $350

No. 3400, Highway Emergency Unit Truck, 1959-63, large cabover Ford wrecker, white with red cab roof, red dolly and wrecker boom; later versions without boom hoist (only hook hoist); with whitewall tires and tilt cab with motor (1963 only)
EX $50 **NM** $150 **MIP** $300

No. 3500, Countdown Rocket Launcher, 1959-61, three rockets (Atlas, Jupiter, Thor) in various colors; gray gantry crane, dark blue base with yellow, black, or red countdown dial; last Nylint toy from the 1950s and second plastic toy
EX $50 **NM** $125 **MIP** $250

No. 3600, Ford Rapid Delivery Truck, 1960-62, dark blue cabover Ford truck with white stake racks and working lift gate, tilt cab with motor; first Nylint toy of 1960s
EX $75 **NM** $175 **MIP** $300

No. 3700, Street Sprinkler Truck, 1960-61, white tank truck, operating nozzles on front bumper, tilt cab
EX $75 **NM** $175 **MIP** $350

No. 3800, Ford Sales & Service, 1960-61, aqua green with utility rack and ladder
EX $50 **NM** $175 **MIP** $350

No. 3900, Ford Platform Tilt Truck, 1960, metallic blue, white cab roof with tilt cab, narrow side panels on rear bed
EX $75 **NM** $175 **MIP** $350

No. 3900, Platform Dump Truck, 1961, yellow, white cab roof, narrow side panels on rear bed; last truck to feature tilt cab
EX $75 **NM** $175 **MIP** $350

No. 4000, Ford Speedway Truck with Racer, 1960-63, dark tan pickup with white top and trailer and race car
EX $75 **NM** $140 **MIP** $275

No. 4100, Ford Pickup & U-Haul Box Trailer, 1961-66, orange pickup, white cab roof, orange trailer with white/cream top and opening rear door; trucks made before 1965 have two-piece front grille (trucks from 1965-66 with one-piece front grille/bumper and I-beam suspension)
EX $75 **NM** $175 **MIP** $350

No. 4200, Bulldozer, 1967-72, orange with towbar instead of winch (1967-70); yellow with towbar (1971-72)
EX $50 **NM** $125 **MIP** $250

No. 4200, Bulldozer, 1961-70, all yellow with rear chain winch (1961-65); yellow with orange winch (1967-70); black plastic motor
EX $50 **NM** $150 **MIP** $300

No. 4300, Ford U-Haul Rental Fleet, 1960s, includes orange Ford pickup, orange U-Haul van and orange U-Haul open trailer; pickup has two-piece front grille bumper (1961-64), one-piece bumper and I-beam suspension (1965)
EX $75 **NM** $225 **MIP** $450

No. 4400, Camper Pickup, 1961-63, red Ford pickup truck with two-piece front grille/bumper, white topper camper, two green air mattresses
EX $50 **NM** $125 **MIP** $250

No. 4500, Ranch Truck, 1961-64, light blue Ford stake truck, two-piece front grille/bumper, white stake racks, round decals on doors
EX $50 **NM** $100 **MIP** $200

(Thomas G. Nefos)

No. 4501, Chase and Sanborne Stake Truck, 1964, same as No. 4500 but with coffee boxes (add 75 percent premium if present)
EX $75 **NM** $175 **MIP** $350

No. 4502, Boysen Paints Stake Truck, 1964, same as No. 4500
EX $75 **NM** $200 **MIP** $400

No. 4600, Construction Four-Wheel Platform Dump
EX $100 **NM** $150 **MIP** $225

No. 4600, Hydraulic Dump, 1961-66, same as No. 2700 but orange with yellow/black decals, front grille guard in yellow/black, hollow plastic wheels
EX $50 **NM** $125 **MIP** $250

No. 4700, Happy Acres Truck with Horses, 1961-63, same as No. 4500 but red truck with white stakes, large picture decal on doors
EX $75 **NM** $150 **MIP** $300

No. 4800, U-Haul Van, 1961, closed trailer, orange and cream, U-Haul decals
EX $50 **NM** $100 **MIP** $200

No. 4900, U-Haul Van, 1961, open trailer, orange and cream, U-Haul decals
EX $50 **NM** $100 **MIP** $200

No. 5000, Dump Truck with Cement Mixer, 1962-66, yellow truck with round decal on doors and two-piece front grille/bumper (1962-64); yellow/green truck with special decal on mixer (1965); yellow body, green dump box, large N logo decal on doors (1966); cement mixer is always yellow
EX $75 **NM** $200 **MIP** $400

No. 5100, Dump Truck, 1962-66, red truck, yellow dump box, two-piece grille/bumper (1962-64); red/yellow truck, one-piece grille/bumper (1965); light green truck, white dump box, one-piece grille/bumper (1966)
EX $50 **NM** $140 **MIP** $275

No. 5200, Econoline Pickup Truck, 1962-72, dual headlights (1962); teardrop headlights (1963-72); red/white truck (1962-65); yellow with black roof (1966-72)
EX $50 **NM** $125 **MIP** $250

No. 5201, Western Auto Econoline Pickup, 1964, rare
EX $75 **NM** $225 **MIP** $450

No. 5300, Custom Camper Econoline Pickup Truck, 1962-66, aqua green truck and plastic camper with opening windows and rear door, slide-out steps under rear door
EX $50 **NM** $125 **MIP** $250

No. 5301, Trailblazer Camper, 1969-72, green and white Econoline camper
EX $35 **NM** $65 **MIP** $125

No. 5302, Philco Radio Camper
EX $75 **NM** $325 **MIP** $650

No. 5400, Custom Camper on Pickup Truck with Boat, 1962-65, with red and green sailboat on trailer
EX $75 **NM** $175 **MIP** $350

No. 5500, Pepsi Delivery Truck, 1962-67, red, white and blue Ford C-600 truck with decals, six cases of Pepsi and hand truck
EX $50 **NM** $225 **MIP** $450

No. 5600, Farm Set, 1962-64, with light blue/white No. 4500 Stake Truck, light blue/white No. 5200 Econoline Pickup Truck and other assorted pieces
EX $75 **NM** $175 **MIP** $350

No. 5700, Construction Set, 1962-64, orange No. 5000 Dump and Cement Mixer with yellow drum, Econoline Pickup Truck and Open Stake Trailer; rare
EX $100 **NM** $300 **MIP** $600

No. 5800, Ford Econoline Van, 1963-64, purple with white decals; dark pink or maroon (1964 only)
EX $50 **NM** $175 **MIP** $350

No. 5801, U-Haul Van, 1966-67, orange Ford Econoline, white U-Haul decals
EX $50 **NM** $200 **MIP** $400

No. 5802, Admiral TV Van, 1966, Ford Econoline with decals on both sides and all doors; special premium available through Admiral TV delaers, very rare
EX $75 **NM** $325 **MIP** $650

No. 5803, Culligan Water Van, 1966, dark blue Ford Econoline with white top and Culligan decals on sides and doors; very rare
EX $75 **NM** $275 **MIP** $550

No. 5900, Race Team, 1963-66, Ford Econoline with race car (white and other colors) and red trailer
EX $50 **NM** $175 **MIP** $350

No. 600, Amazing Car, 1946-49, wind-up; green or blue; box commands a premium (contains operating instructions)
EX $75 **NM** $150 **MIP** $300

No. 600, Amazing Car, 1946-49, wind-up; red; box commands a premium (contains operating instructions)
EX $50 **NM** $125 **MIP** $250

No. 6000, American Oil Emergency Truck, 1963-69, red Ford Econoline Wrecker, white boom, with or without American Oil decals
EX $50 **NM** $150 **MIP** $300

No. 6001, JC Penney Wrecker, 1966, light blue Ford Econoline Wrecker with white boom; available only form the JC Penney's wishbook
EX $75 **NM** $250 **MIP** $500

No. 6100, Hydraulic Dump Truck, 1963-70, beige truck with red dump box; two-piece grille/bumper (1963-64); one piece grille bumper (1965-70)
EX $75 **NM** $150 **MIP** $300

No. 6200, Kennel Truck, 1963-69, pink Ford Econoline, plastic dog cage in back, 12 dogs (12 different breeds); paper band around cage featuring the dog breeds on it (1964 only)
EX $175 **NM** $265 **MIP** $525

No. 6300, Horse Van Semi Truck, 1963-67, brownish-gold truck, white doors, decals, four horses and ponies; two-piece grille/bumper on front (1963-64); one-piece grille/bumper (1965-67); light blue and white truck (1967 only)
EX $50 **NM** $175 **MIP** $350

No. 6500, Payloader, 1963-66, red and yellow
EX $50 **NM** $100 **MIP** $200

No. 6600, Mobile Home Semi Truck, 1964, aqua blue cab with white or light tan roof, nine pieces of furniture, two-piece grille/bumper on front, round "6600" decal on cab doors
EX $75 **NM** $300 **MIP** $600

No. 6601, Mobile Home Trailer, 1965, aqua blue or turquoise with white or light tan top, 27 pieces of furniture, one-piece grille/bumper on front, round "6601" decal on cab doors
EX $75 **NM** $300 **MIP** $600

No. 6602, Mobile Home Trailer, 1966, dark blue cab with white top, no extras, large "N" logo on cab doors
EX $75 **NM** $325 **MIP** $650

No. 6603, Mobile Home Trailer, 1964-66, American Transit Mobile Home Movers and other variations
EX $100 **NM** $350 **MIP** $700

No. 6700, Ambulance, 1964-67, white Ford Econoline Van with red crosses on sides and doors; included stretcher, interior seats, red flasher light
EX $50 **NM** $150 **MIP** $300

No. 6800, Jalopy, 1964-78, Ford hot rod in red with white top or light blue with white top (1964); also No. 6801 with seats, available in same colors as 1964 version (1965-68); No. 6802 purple and white (1969-71); No. 6803 neon green top and purple body (1972-78)
EX $25 **NM** $150 **MIP** $300

No. 6900, Airport Courtesy Van, 1964, Ford Econoline Van, yellow with Holiday Inn decals on sides and doors; rare
EX $75 **NM** $350 **MIP** $700

No. 700, Lift Truck (fork lift), 1946-49, red and yellow; box commands a premium (contains operating instructions)
EX $75 **NM** $125 **MIP** $250

No. 700, Lift Truck (fork lift), 1946-49, green and yellow; box commands a premium (contains operating instructions)
EX $75 **NM** $140 **MIP** $275

No. 7000, Lawn and Garden Set, 1964, dark green Econoline Pickup with white roof; included lawn mower and other garden equipment
EX $50 **NM** $150 **MIP** $300

No. 7100, Fun on Farm Econoline Truck Set, 1964-65, 29 piecesFord Econoline Pickup with farm family, farming items, plus small cans of paint to customize your farm family
EX $50 **NM** $175 **MIP** $350

No. 7200, Happy Ranchers Set, 1964, Stake Truck with Open Stake Trailer, both light blue and white
EX $75 **NM** $175 **MIP** $350

No. 7300, Army Ambulance, 1965, olive drab Ford Econoline Van, stretcher, red cross decals on sides and doors, red flasher light on top
EX $50 **NM** $175 **MIP** $350

No. 7408, Suburban Fire Department Set, 1966-70, red Ford Econoline Pumper Fire Truck, Fire Rescue Econoline Van, Fire Chief's Bronco; Rescue Van and Fire Chief's Bronco available only in this set
EX $75 **NM** $225 **MIP** $450

No. 7800, Race Team, 1965-69, white Econoline Pickup, red trailer, white race car
EX $50 **NM** $150 **MIP** $300

No. 7900, Road Grader, 1965-68, yellow and black
EX $25 **NM** $100 **MIP** $200

No. 7910, Road Grader, 1969, yellow with larger wheels
EX $40 **NM** $65 **MIP** $125

No. 800, Scootscycle/Servicecycle, 1946-51, wind-up; red, blue, yellow or black; rare
EX $75 **NM** $225 **MIP** $450

No. 8000, Pony Farm Van Set, white Ford Econoline Pick,up, green cab top, large green/white Pony Farm decal on sides, four ponies
EX $75 **NM** $175 **MIP** $350

No. 8001, Gambles Stores Pickup, 1966, white Ford Econoline with green top
EX $75 **NM** $175 **MIP** $350

No. 8100, Suburban Fire Pumper, 1965-70, Ford Econoline Pumper fire Truck with water cannon; a garden hose could be connected to the cannon to shoot water; hard to find in good condition since the pressure from the garden hose usually blew up the truck
EX $50 **NM** $150 **MIP** $300

No. 8200, Ford Bronco, 1965-69, listed in the 1965 catalog as a Roustabout but was changed to a Bornco right after the catalog was printed
EX $50 **NM** $140 **MIP** $275

No. 8300, Texaco Service Van, 1965, red Ford Econoline Van, white decals, red flasher light
EX $50 **NM** $200 **MIP** $400

No. 8400, U-Haul Cube Van, 1966-67, five-ton cube van
EX $75 **NM** $175 **MIP** $350

No. 8401, Hertz Rental Truck, 1967, same as No. 8400 but exclusive to Sears; yellow cab, black base, silver cargo box, Hertz decals; rare
EX $85 **NM** $250 **MIP** $500

(Ron O'Brien)

No. 8410, U-Haul Truck & Trailer, 1974, orange and white truck, trailer
EX $100 **NM** $150 **MIP** $200

No. 8411, U-Haul Truck, 1975, Chevy, orange and white cab, silver box, opening rear door
EX $100 **NM** $125 **MIP** $175

(Thomas G. Nefos)

No. 8600, Vacationer Set, 1966-70, blue and white Ford Bronco and camper trailer
EX $50 **NM** $150 **MIP** $300

No. 8700, Truck and Horse Trailer, 1966-70, Ford Bronco, two-axle horse trailer with yellow top
EX $50 **NM** $145 **MIP** $285

No. 8800, Safari Hunt Set, 1966-71, Ford Bronco with white top, cage trailer with wild animals; cage has door, trailer has slide-out ramp and winch for loading
EX $75 **NM** $200 **MIP** $400

No. 8900, Car Carrier, 1967-77, yellow car carrier; three cars (1967-68); two cars (1969-77); several color variations for cars
EX $50 **NM** $150 **MIP** $300

No. 900, Power Pony, 1949, light tan, black, yellow; three-wheeled pony performed tricks; rare
EX $100 **NM** $250 **MIP** $500

No. 9000, Jungle Wagon, 1966-72, two-tone green Ford Econoline with cages to transport wild animals
EX $45 **NM** $140 **MIP** $275

No. 9100, Stake Pickup Truck, 1966-69, light blue and white Ford Econoline stake truck
EX $35 **NM** $125 **MIP** $250

No. 9200, Big Haul Dump, 1966-68, yellow and black, reminiscent of Tonka's Mighty Dump Truck
EX $45 **NM** $125 **MIP** $250

No. 9201, Big Haul Dump, 1969-72, same as No. 9200 but larger wheels
EX $45 **NM** $125 **MIP** $250

No. 9300, Tin Lizzy Hot Rod Pickup, 1967-72, red and other colors
EX $35 **NM** $100 **MIP** $200

No. 9400, Truck and U-Haul Trailer, 1967-68, Ford Econoline Pickup and open trailer, orange and white
EX $50 **NM** $140 **MIP** $275

No. 9401, Truck and Haul-It Trailer, 1969, rare; knock-off of U-Haul Trailer with similar decals
EX $50 **NM** $175 **MIP** $350

No. 9500, Sportster, 1967-69, pink Ford Bronco
EX $45 **NM** $140 **MIP** $275

No. 9600, Race Team, 1967-69, Ford Econline Pikup and trailer with race car, red and white
EX $40 **NM** $140 **MIP** $275

No. 9700, Sportsman Set, 1967-69, truck with boat and trailer; white and other colors
EX $50 **NM** $140 **MIP** $275

No. 9800, Hydraulic Big Haul Dump Truck, 1967-68, orange and black
EX $35 **NM** $140 **MIP** $275

No. 9801, Hydraulic Big Haul Dump Truck, 1969-73, orange and black, new tires
EX $35 **NM** $140 **MIP** $275

No. 9900, Farm Set, 1968-71, one of four farm sets made by Nylint; included light blue and white Ford Bronco, Ford Econoline Pickup, Stake Truck and trailer
EX $75 **NM** $175 **MIP** $350

No. SR1000/5465, U-Haul Van Set, 1962, Sears exclusive; orange and white Ford Pickup, U-Haul Van (closed type), and trailer with race car
EX $75 **NM** $200 **MIP** $400

No. SR1100, Big Dig Shovel, 1964-65, Sears exclusive; orange and black, all steel except for rubber tracks; later versions (non-exclusives) available in orange yellow and black while track wheels were yellow plastic
EX $50 **NM** $140 **MIP** $275

No. SR1200/5439, Lawn and Garden Set, 1964-65, Sears exclusive
EX $50 **NM** $175 **MIP** $350

PROCESSED PLASTIC/ TIM-MEE TOYS

"Soupercharged" Airplane, 12" wingspan; four free-turning props, "Soupercharged" sticker, cast in beef, ham, and soup; 1960s
EX $7 **NM** $12 **MIP** $18

ABCD TV Blimp, 9" long; white blimp, "ABCD TV" on sides, on hauling platform
EX $10 **NM** $18 **MIP** $25

Armored Car, 7" long; rear-mounted swiveling cannon atop Army green armored vehicle, black plastic tires
EX $5 **NM** $8 **MIP** $15

Armored Car, 5-1/2" long; center-mounted turret, light Army green, four black-rubber tires
EX $20 **NM** $35 **MIP** $40

Army Jeep and Howitzer, 9-1/2" long; "Tim-Mee Toys" Army green Jeep, 5-1/4" long; with snugly fitting driver, snap-in steering wheel, towing cannon, 4-1/4" long, both toys with black rubber tires; 1960s
EX $6 **NM** $12 **MIP** $18

Army Jeep and Howitzer, 9-1/2" long; "Tim-Mee Toys," with black plastic tires
EX $4 **NM** $8 **MIP** $14

Beach Runner, 10" long; red car chassis with 10" blue and white upper body that snaps out to become power boat
EX $6 **NM** $8 **MIP** $15

Boat and Trailer Set, plastic station wagon, 7-1/4" long, separate top and bottom moldings, black plastic tires on metal axles, "Bear Lake Lodge" stickers, hauling plastic trailer with motor boat; early 1970s
EX $20 **NM** $40 **MIP** $60

Can-Am Challenge Race Car, 11" long; red body, white steering wheel and driver's head, chromed engine pipes and rearviews, "Can Am Challenger" sticker on hood.
EX $15 **NM** $25 **MIP** $35

Chevy Camaro, 10-1/4" long; T-top, popped engine, flames on hood, chrome hubs on black wheels
EX $8 **NM** $12 **MIP** $20

Chevy Camaro, 9-1/4" long; tan body and interior, chromed hubs, 1960s
EX $8 **NM** $12 **MIP** $20

Chevy Camaro, 9" long; black roof, green body, popped/chromed engine, spoiler, late 1960s modeling
EX $20 **NM** $40 **MIP** $60

Chevy Corvette, T-roof, clear windshields, purple body, red-stripe tires, late 1960s modeling
EX $10 **NM** $20 **MIP** $25

Chevy Flatbed Truck, 4" long; 1950s-style, blue plastic with windows not cut out, simple rolling toy; 1960s
EX $3 **NM** $6 **MIP** $9

Chevy Hi-Rider, 9" long; yellow pickup truck, chromed grille and rear bumper, orange rollbar and interior, opening rear gate with "Chevrolet," "Hi-Rider 4WD" stickerson doors, oversize tires; 1980s
EX $5 **NM** $9 **MIP** $15

Chevy Nomad Station Wagon, 4" long; 1950s-style, blue plastic with windows not cut out, simple rolling toy; 1960s
EX $3 **NM** $6 **MIP** $9

Clipper Sailing Ship, 21" long, 15" tall; brown ship, three masts, white sails, two lifeboats, turning rudder, weighted keel; 1960s
EX $30 **NM** $45 **MIP** $60

Convertible, 4" long; 1950s-style red Cadillac with finned fenders, open top, simple rolling toy; 1960s
EX $3 **NM** $6 **MIP** $9

Dodge Charger Fire Chief, 12"; opening hood w/chromed engine
EX $35 **NM** $55 **MIP** n/a

Dodge Charger Police Chief, 12"; opening hood w/chromed engine
EX $35 **NM** $55 **MIP** n/a

Dragster, 20" long; stretch dragster, black plastic, chrome engine and pipes, "Top Eliminator" stickers
EX $8 **NM** $12 **MIP** $20

Dump Truck, 7-1/4" long; Chevy cabover with roof lights, black spoked tires, heavy-duty dumping body
EX $3 **NM** $7 **MIP** $10

Dump Truck, 12-1/4" long; chrome grille, clear windshield, whitewall tires; 1950s to early 1960s
EX $10 **NM** $18 **MIP** $30

Dump Truck, 7" long; rounded-top cabover, tilting heavy-duty dump body; 1950s or 1960s
EX $3 **NM** $7 **MIP** $10

Eureka Hauler, 22" long; tractor-trailer, orange cab with white interior and chromed grille, white trailer with "Eureka Vacuum Cleaners" panels; 1980s
EX $12 **NM** $25 **MIP** $30

Fighter Plane, 4" long, 6" wingspan; WWI biplane, "Nieuport 17C," plastic pilot
EX $8 **NM** $15 **MIP** $25

Ford Car, 8-1/2" long; red plastic with "The Dukes of Hazzard" style Confederate flag stickers; 1980s
EX $15 **NM** $30 **MIP** $40

Ford Hot Rod, 5" long; plastic body in various colors w/red plastic driver, chrome engine and dual exhaust pipes
EX $10 **NM** $15 **MIP** $25

Honda ATC Three-Wheeler, 9" long; red and white plastic, "ATC" on tank, black balloon tires
EX $20 **NM** $45 **MIP** $60

Honda Trail Bike, 8-1/2" long; "Honda" sticker, various colors, chromed engine, black plastic tires
EX $6 **NM** $12 **MIP** $18

Indy Race Car, 12-1/2" long; moveable front air fins and rear spoiler; 1970s
EX $5 **NM** $11 **MIP** $16

Indy Race Car, 9" long; open-cockpit racer, tail fin, red plastic with yellow steering wheel and chrome pipes, "98" on decal
EX $6 **NM** $12 **MIP** $20

Indy Racer, 8"; open-cockpit racer, "500 Special" sticker
EX $12 **NM** $35 **MIP** n/a

Motorboat, 7-1/4" long; snap-together open-top motorboat with plastic motor clear windshield; 1960s or 1970s
EX $7 **NM** $10 **MIP** $18

Pontiac Firebird, 17-1/2" long; red or gray plastic, interior details; 1970s
EX $15 **NM** $30 **MIP** n/a

Racer, 7-3/4" long; open cockpit race car with separately-cast driver, "7" cast into long nose, "700 Special" sticker; 1960s or 1970s
EX $9 **NM** $18 **MIP** $27

Renault Sedan, 4-1/4" long; simple rolling toy, modeled on 1950s Renault; 1960s or 1970s
EX $5 **NM** $10 **MIP** $15

Seaplane, 8" long; red and white plastic seaplane, wheels under pontoons, propeller
EX $5 **NM** $9 **MIP** $14

Space Shuttle Columbia, 9" long; white and red Space Shuttle, "NASA" on wings, "Columbia, United States" sticker on sides; 1980s
EX $3 **NM** $8 **MIP** $12

Station Wagon, 4" long; 1950s-style Chevy station wagon, simple rolling toy; 1960s or 1970s
EX $3 **NM** $5 **MIP** $8

Station Wagon, 8" long; red body, blue chassis, 1960s
EX $4 **NM** $10 **MIP** $15

Submarine, 10" long; hard plastic, "X-13 USN," with plastic on base, two red missiles, periscope, radar dish
EX $25 **NM** $40 **MIP** $60

Thunderhauler, 22" long; black tractor-trailer, batter-operated horn; 1980s
EX $8 **NM** $20 **MIP** $25

Troop Hauler, 7" long; Army-green plastic truck with "canvas" cover, three axles, six plastic tires
EX $10 **NM** $20 **MIP** $25

VW Bug, VW hot rod with popped and chromed engine, oversize rear tires; 1970s
EX $6 **NM** $10 **MIP** $18

VW Bug, 7"; red plastic body, black wheels
EX $8 **NM** $15 **MIP** n/a

VW Pickup, 4-1/4" long; Army-green body, black plastic tires, "1234" license plates; 1960s
EX $9 **NM** $15 **MIP** $25

REMCO

Barney's Auto Factory, battery-operated auto factory, makes red plastic car, 1960s
EX $20 **NM** $50 **MIP** $120

Barney's Tow Truck Factory, set for constructing red plastic tow truck, 1964
EX $20 **NM** $50 **MIP** $100

Big Caesar Motorized Roman Warship, Roman galley w/oars, soldiers, catapults, chariots, horses, 1963
EX $100 **NM** $200 **MIP** $550

Bulldog Tank, 16" long; plastic tank, metal underside, four shells, remote-control firing; 1960s
EX $15 **NM** $30 **MIP** $65

Caterpillar Tractor, 8" long; 1986
EX $5 **NM** $8 **MIP** $11

Coca-Cola Set, window box set with pickup, car, tractor-trailer, Coca-Cola cases; 1989
EX $7 **NM** $12 **MIP** $20

Duffy's Daredevils, play set featuring plastic red convertible, car launcher, ramp, hoops of "fire" and barrels for auto thrill show; 1965
EX $7 **NM** $15 **MIP** $25

Fighting Lady Battleship, 36" long; depth charges, 5" plane, 7-1/2" small boat
EX $25 **NM** $55 **MIP** $110

Firebird "99", 13" across; battery-operated steering wheel and dashboard, with windshield, speedometer, ignition key; 1963-64
EX $22 **NM** $43 **MIP** $65

Flying Dutchman Antique Car, battery-operated "U-Control", #611, 1970s
EX $20 **NM** $50 **MIP** $125

Giant Hamilton's Invaders, playset w/tank, helicopter, mosquito jeep, figures, alien invaders, 1960s
EX $150 **NM** $300 **MIP** $500

Jeep, 7-1/2" long; pink molded plastic, marketed as Heidi's Jeep, Pocketbook Dolls series, 1960s
EX $10 **NM** $20 **MIP** $30

Long John, 4" long; large red plastic fire truck w/white ladders, 1960s
EX $30 **NM** $40 **MIP** $75

Midget Motors Mighty Mike Jeep, 5-1/2" long; battery-operated Jeep, white with black tires and exposed engine, sold individually and with Midget Motors Mighty Mike Action Sets; late 1960s
EX $15 **NM** $25 **MIP** $50

Mighty Matilda Aircraft Carrier, playset includes planes, helicopters, lifeboats and other plastic pieces; #720MO
EX $75 **NM** $165 **MIP** $275

Mighty Mike Astro Train Gift Set, mobile helicopter launcher, hauling submarine trailer and robot carrier, 1960s
EX $10 **NM** $20 **MIP** $30

Mighty Mike Dump Truck Skyway Set, 1960s
EX $10 **NM** $20 **MIP** $30

Mighty Mike Motorized Truck, six-wheel truck with interchangeable, snap-on bodies; late 1960s
EX $10 **NM** $20 **MIP** $30

Mr. Kelly's Automatic Car Wash, 27" long; battery-operated working car wash with see-through roof, two cars, wax cans, towels, sponges and free-standing sign; 1963-64
EX $28 **NM** $80 **MIP** $300

Pepsi Set, "Heavy Metal" semi truck, pickup, Pepsi crates, pop machine, two figures. Also in "Tuff Ones" packaging
EX $4 **NM** $8 **MIP** $14

Sanitation Truck, 13" long; "Save Our Planet," metal and plastic; early 1990s
EX $5 **NM** $10 **MIP** $15

Shark, 19" long; plastic, billed as "Battery Driven U-Control Racing Car," orange plastic body, white side pipes, chromed grille, black tires with chromed hubs; 1961 and later
EX $10 **NM** $20 **MIP** $90

Showboat, 1962, playset includes the pink riverboat and scripts and scenes for four productions: Wizard of Oz, Heidi, Pinocchio and Cinderella, 1962
EX $50 **NM** $95 **MIP** $175

Sky Diver, jet plane playset, w/white jet, parachuting sky diver, ejection seat, motorized tow tractor, battery operated
EX $75 **NM** $150 **MIP** $250

Stubby Camper, 23" long; plastic, blue cab, white camper with rear slide-up door; 1973
EX $7 **NM** $13 **MIP** $20

Supercar, Gerry Anderson TV-show ship, red plastic, battery-operated, figure of Mercury inside, 1960s
EX $100 **NM** $200 **MIP** n/a

Swamp Buggy, 12" long; battery-operated plastic pontoon, yellow and red with white plastic rider; 1968
EX $4 **NM** $15 **MIP** $22

Tru-Smoke Diesel Cement Truck, 12" long; battery-operated, smoking action; 1969
EX $15 **NM** $25 **MIP** $50

Tru-Smoke Diesel Dump Truck, 12" long; battery-operated, smoking action, working dump; 1969
EX $15 **NM** $25 **MIP** $50

Tru-Smoke Diesel Wrecker Truck, 12" long; battery-operated, smoking action, twin booms; 1969
EX $15 **NM** $25 **MIP** $60

Tuff Boy 6 (tractor-trailer), 38" long; yellow plastic, motorized cab powering forward or reverse, stake-side trailer with canopy, designed for taking other trailer bodies in the manner of Deluxe Reading's Johnny Express Tractor and Trailer Combination; 1965-70s
EX $15 **NM** $30 **MIP** $45

SMITH-MILLER

Smith-Miller

EMERGENCY VEHICLES

"L" Mack Aerial Ladder, red w/gold lettering; polished aluminum surface, SMFD decals on hood and trailer sides, six-wheeler; 1950
EX $375 **NM** $475 **MIP** $795

TRUCKS

"B" Mack Associated Truck Lines, red cab, polished aluminum trailer, decals on trailer sides, six-wheel tractor, eight-wheel trailer; 1954
EX $500 **NM** $850 **MIP** $1200

"B" Mack Blue Diamond Dump, all white truck w/blue decals, hydraulic piston, ten-wheeler; 1954
EX $600 **NM** $950 **MIP** $1300

"B" Mack Lumber Truck, yellow cab and timber deck, three rollers, loading bar and two chains, six-wheeler, load of nine timbers; 1954
EX $450 **NM** $650 **MIP** $1000

"B" Mack Orange Dump Truck, construction orange all over, no decals, hydraulic piston, ten-wheeler; 1954
EX $650 **NM** $1150 **MIP** $1650

"B" Mack P.I.E., red cab, polished trailer, six-wheel tractor, eight-wheel trailer; 1954
EX $375 **NM** $600 **MIP** $850

"B" Mack Searchlight, dark red paint schemes, fully rotating and elevating searchlight, battery-operated; 1954
EX $500 **NM** $775 **MIP** $1100

"B" Mack Silver Streak, yellow cab, unpainted, unpolished trailer sides, "Silver Streak" decal on both sides, six-wheel tractor, eight-wheel trailer; 1954
EX $450 **NM** $775 **MIP** $1050

"B" Mack Watson Bros., yellow cab, polished aluminum trailer, decals on trailer sides and cab doors, 10-wheel tractor, eight-wheel trailer; 1954
EX $650 **NM** $1100 **MIP** $1500

"L" Mack Army Materials Truck, Army green, flatbed w/dark green canvas, ten-wheeler, load of three wood barrels, two boards, large and small crate; 1952
EX $375 **NM** $500 **MIP** $750

"L" Mack Army Personnel Carrier, all Army green, wood sides, Army seal on door panels, military star on roof, ten-wheeler; 1952
EX $375 **NM** $500 **MIP** $750

"L" Mack Bekins Van, white, covered w/"Bekins" decals, six-wheel tractor, four-wheel trailer; 1953
EX $1000 **NM** $1650 **MIP** $2000

"L" Mack Blue Diamond Dump, white cab, white dump bed, blue fenders and chassis, hydraulically operated, ten-wheeler; 1952
EX $425 **NM** $750 **MIP** $1050

"L" Mack International Paper Co., white tractor cab, "International Paper Co." decals, six wheel tractor, four wheel trailer; 1952
EX $375 **NM** $650 **MIP** $900

"L" Mack Lyon Van, silver gray cab, dark blue fenders and frame, silver gray van box w/blue "Lyon" decal, six-wheeler; 1950
EX $425 **NM** $800 **MIP** $1100

"L" Mack Material Truck, light metallic green cab, dark green fenders and frame, wood flatbed, six-wheeler, load of two barrels and six timbers; 1950
EX $400 **NM** $600 **MIP** $875

"L" Mack Merchandise Van, red cab, black fenders and frame, "Smith-Miller" decals on both sides of van box, double rear doors, six-wheeler; 1951
EX $425 **NM** $695 **MIP** $1000

"L" Mack Mobil Tandem Tanker, all red cab, "Mobilgas" and "Mobiloil" decals on tank sides, six-wheel tractor, six wheel trailer; 1952
EX $450 **NM** $725 **MIP** $1000

"L" Mack Orange Hydraulic Dump, orange cab, orange dump bed, hydraulic, ten-wheeler, may or may not have "Blue Diamond" decals; 1952
EX $850 **NM** $1500 **MIP** $1950

"L" Mack Orange Materials Truck, all orange, flatbed w/canvas, ten-wheeler, load of three barrels, two boards, large and small crate; 1952
EX $400 **NM** $650 **MIP** $900

"L" Mack P.I.E., all red tractor, polished aluminum trailer, "P.I.E." decals on sides and front, six wheel tractor, eight-wheel trailer; 1950
EX $395 **NM** $550 **MIP** $850

"L" Mack Sibley Van, dark green cab, black fenders and frame, dark green van box w/"Sibley's" decal in yellow on both sides, six-wheeler; 1950
EX $850 **NM** $1375 **MIP** $1850

"L" Mack Tandem Timber, red/black cab, six-wheeler, load of six wood lumber rollers, two loading bars, four chains and eighteen or twenty-four boards; 1950
EX $400 **NM** $600 **MIP** $725

"L" Mack Tandem Timber, two-tone green cab, six-wheeler, load of six wood lumber rollers, two loading bars, four chains, and 18 timbers; 1953
EX $400 **NM** $700 **MIP** $1000

"L" Mack Telephone Truck, all dark or two-tone green truck, "Bell Telephone System" decals on truck sides, six-wheeler; 1952
EX $475 **NM** $750 **MIP** $975

"L" Mack West Coast Fast Freight, silver w/red/black or silver cab and chassis, "West Coast-Fast Freight" decals on sides of box, six-wheeler; 1952
EX $475 **NM** $775 **MIP** $1000

Chevrolet Arden Milk Truck, red cab, white wood body, four-wheeler; 1945
EX $275 **NM** $465 **MIP** $800

Chevrolet Bekins Van, blue die-cast cab, all white trailer, fourteen-wheeler; 1945
EX $275 **NM** $350 **MIP** $750

Chevrolet Coca-Cola Truck, red cab, wood body painted red, four-wheeler; 1945
EX $300 **NM** $600 **MIP** $850

Chevrolet Flatbed Tractor-Trailer, unpainted wood trailer, unpainted polished cab, fourteen-wheeler; 1945
EX $250 **NM** $300 **MIP** $500

Chevrolet Heinz Grocery Truck, yellow cab, load of four waxed cases; 1946
EX $225 **NM** $325 **MIP** $475

Chevrolet Livestock Truck, polished, unpainted tractor cab and trailer; 1946
EX $175 **NM** $275 **MIP** $375

Chevrolet Lumber, green cab, load of 60 polished boards and two chains; 1946
EX $150 **NM** $195 **MIP** $275

Chevrolet Lyons Van, blue cab, silver trailer; 1946
EX $165 **NM** $325 **MIP** $500

Chevrolet Material Truck, green cab, no side rails, load of three barrels, two cases and eighteen boards; 1946
EX $135 **NM** $185 **MIP** $225

Chevrolet Stake, yellow tractor cab
EX $185 **NM** $250 **MIP** $425

Chevrolet Transcontinental Vanliner, blue tractor cab, white trailer, "Bekins" logos and decals on trailer sides; 1946
EX $200 **NM** $350 **MIP** $495

Chevrolet Union Ice Truck, blue cab, white body, load of eight waxed blocks of ice; 1946
EX $300 **NM** $495 **MIP** $800

Ford Bekins Van, red sand-cast tractor, gray sheet metal trailer, fourteen-wheeler; 1944
EX $275 **NM** $500 **MIP** $750

Ford Coca-Cola Truck, red sandcast cab, wood body painted red, four-wheeler; 1944
EX $400 **NM** $650 **MIP** $900

GMC Arden Milk Truck, red cab, white painted wood body w/red stakes, four-wheeler; 1947
EX $200 **NM** $425 **MIP** $650

GMC Bank of America Truck, dark brownish green cab and box, 'Bank of America' decal on box sides, four-wheeler; 1949
EX $150 **NM** $375 **MIP** $600

GMC Be Mac Tractor-Trailer, red cab, plain aluminum frame, "Be Mac Transport Co." in white letters on door panels, fourteen-wheeler; 1949
EX $250 **NM** $350 **MIP** $700

GMC Bekins Vanliner, blue cab, metal trailer painted white, fourteen-wheeler; 1947
EX $175 **NM** $275 **MIP** $425

GMC Coca-Cola Truck, red cab, yellow wood body, four-wheeler, load of 16 Coca-Cola cases; 1947
EX $500 **NM** $700 **MIP** $895

GMC Coca-Cola Truck, all yellow truck, red Coca-Cola decals, five spoke hubs, four-wheeler, load of six cases each w/24 plastic bottles; 1954
EX $500 **NM** $700 **MIP** n/a

GMC Drive-O, red cab, red dump body, runs forward and backward w/handturned control at end of 5-1/2 ft. cable, six-wheeler; 1949
EX $175 **NM** $300 **MIP** $450

(Larry Planer collection)

GMC Dump Truck, all red truck, six-wheeler; 1950
EX $150 **NM** $275 **MIP** $450

GMC Emergency Tow Truck, white cab, red body and boom, 'Emergency Towing Service' on body side panels, four-wheeler; 1953
EX $185 **NM** $250 **MIP** $400

GMC Furniture Mart, blue cab, off-white body, "Furniture Mart, Complete Home Furnishings" markings on body sides, four-wheeler; 1953
EX $275 **NM** $325 **MIP** $400

GMC Heinz Grocery Truck, yellow cab, wood body, six-wheeler; 1947
EX $250 **NM** $325 **MIP** $450

GMC Highway Freighter Tractor-Trailer, red tractor cab, hardwood bed on trailer w/full length wood fences, "Fruehauf" decal on trailer, fourteen-wheeler; 1948
EX $150 **NM** $210 **MIP** $325

GMC Kraft Foods, yellow cab, yellow steel box, large "Kraft" decal on both sides, four-wheeler; 1948
EX $300 **NM** $500 **MIP** $600

GMC Lumber Tractor-Trailer, metallic blue cab and trailer, three rollers and two chains, fourteen-wheeler; 1949
EX $185 **NM** $250 **MIP** $350

GMC Lumber Truck, green cab, six-wheeler; 1947
EX $165 **NM** $215 **MIP** $300

GMC Lyons Van Tractor-Trailer, blue tractor cab, "Lyons Van" decals on both sides, fold down rear door, fourteen-wheeler; 1948
EX $200 **NM** $350 **MIP** $400

GMC Machinery Hauler, construction orange, two loading ramps, ten-wheeler; 1953
EX $200 **NM** $325 **MIP** $425

GMC Machinery Hauler, construction orange cab and lowboy trailer, "Fruehauf" decal on gooseneck, thirteen-wheeler; 1949
EX $150 **NM** $225 **MIP** $335

GMC Machinery Hauler, construction orange cab and lowboy trailer, "Fruehauf" decal on gooseneck, thirteen-wheeler; 1949
EX $150 **NM** $225 **MIP** $335

GMC Marshall Field's & Company Tractor-Trailer, dark green cab and trailer, double rear doors, never had Smith-Miller decals, ten-wheeler; 1949
EX $295 **NM** $395 **MIP** $500

GMC Material Truck, green cab, wood body, six-wheeler, load of three barrels, three cases and eighteen boards; 1947
EX $115 **NM** $250 **MIP** $350

GMC Material Truck, yellow cab, natural finish hardwood bed and sides, four-wheeler, load of four barrels and two timbers; 1949
EX $125 **NM** $250 **MIP** $375

GMC Mobilgas Tanker, red cab and tanker trailer, large "Mobilgas," "Mobiloil" emblems on sides and rear panel of tanker, fourteen-wheeler; 1949
EX $200 **NM** $300 **MIP** $500

GMC Oil Truck, orange cab, rear body unpainted, six-wheeler, load of three barrels; 1947
EX $115 **NM** $220 **MIP** $375

GMC P.I.E., red cab, polished aluminum box trailer, double rear doors, "P.I.E." decals on sides and front panels, fourteen-wheeler; 1949
EX $150 **NM** $350 **MIP** $475

GMC People's First National Bank and Trust Company, dark brownish green cab and box, "People's First National Bank and Trust Co." decals on box sides; 1951
EX $165 **NM** $250 **MIP** $385

GMC Rack Truck, red or yellow cab, natural finish wood deck, red stake sides, six-wheeler; 1948
EX $135 **NM** $200 **MIP** $650

GMC Redwood Logger Tractor-Trailer, green or maroon cab, unpainted aluminum trailer w/four hardwood stakes, load of three cardboard logs; 1948
EX $365 **NM** $585 **MIP** $700

GMC Rexall Drug Truck, orange cab and closed steel box body, "Rexall" logo on both sides and on front panel of box, four-wheeler; 1948
EX $500 **NM** $750 **MIP** $1000

GMC Scoop Dump, rack and pinion dump w/a scoop, five spoke wheels, six-wheeler; 1954
EX $400 **NM** $800 **MIP** $1000

GMC Searchlight Truck, four wheel truck pulling four wheel trailer, color schemes vary, "Hollywood Film Ad" on truck body side panels; 1953
EX $300 **NM** $500 **MIP** $695

GMC Silver Streak, unpainted polished cab and trailer, wrap around sides and shield, some had tail gate; 1950
EX $200 **NM** $350 **MIP** $600

GMC Sunkist Special Tractor-Trailer, cherry/maroon tractor cab, natural mahogany trailer bed, fourteen-wheeler; 1947
EX $165 **NM** $275 **MIP** $475

GMC Super Cargo Tractor-Trailer, silver gray tractor cab, hardwood bed on trailer w/red wraparound side rails, fourteen-wheeler, load of ten barrels; 1948
EX $150 **NM** $225 **MIP** $395

GMC Timber Giant, green or maroon cab, unpainted aluminum trailer w/four hardwood stakes, load of three cardboard logs; 1948
EX $175 **NM** $285 **MIP** $495

GMC Tow Truck, white cab, red body and boom, five spoke cast hubs, "Emergency Towing Service" on body side panels, four-wheeler; 1954
EX $95 **NM** $135 **MIP** $200

GMC Transcontinental Tractor-Trailer, red tractor cab, hardwood bed on trailer w/full length wood fences, "Fruehauf" decal on trailer, fourteen-wheeler; 1948
EX $150 **NM** $210 **MIP** $325

GMC Triton Oil Truck, blue cab, mahogany body unpainted, six-wheeler, load of three Triton Oil drums (banks) and side chains; 1947
EX $115 **NM** $185 **MIP** $265

GMC U.S. Treasury Truck, gray cab and box, "U.S. Treasury" insignia and markings on box sides, four-wheeler; 1952
EX $235 **NM** $325 **MIP** $475

STRUCTO

Standard Steam Shovel, 1948, Orange, 20.5L x 6.25W x 7.75H, wooden wheels without tracks, Model No. 100
EX $50 **NM** $75 **MIP** $150

Heavy Duty Steam Shovel, 1948, Blue, 21.5L x 6.25W x 7.75H, rubber tracks, Model No. 105
EX $75 **NM** $100 **MIP** $175

Dump Truck, 1948, Red, 20L x 6.75W x 6.25H, long bullet headlights, Model No. 200
EX $50 **NM** $100 **MIP** $175

Aerial Fire Truck, 1948, Red, 24Lx6.75Wx6.25H, 1 raising/2 side ladders & bell on hood, Model No. 250
EX $75 **NM** $150 **MIP** $250

Machinery Truck & Steam Shovel, 1948, Orange and blue, 21.5Lx6.75Wx6.25H, comes 2/#105 steam shovel & loading ramp, Model No. 402
EX $100 **NM** $150 **MIP** $250

Standard Steam Shovel, 1949, Orange, 20.5Lx6.25Wx7.75H, wooden wheels w/o tracks, Model No. 100
EX $50 **NM** $75 **MIP** $150

Heavy Duty Steam Shovel, 1949, Blue, 21.5Lx6.25Wx7.75H, rubber tracks, Model No. 105
EX $75 **NM** $100 **MIP** $175

Dump Truck, 1949, Red, 20Lx6.75Wx6.25H, long bullet headlights, Model No. 200
EX $50 **NM** $100 **MIP** $175

Aerial Fire Truck, 1949, Red, 24Lx6.75Wx6.25H, 1 raising, 2 side ladders & bell on hood, Model No. 250
EX $75 **NM** $150 **MIP** $250

Machinery Truck & Steam Shovel, 1949, Orange and blue, 21.5Lx6.75Wx6.25H, comes w/#105 steam shovel & loading ramp, Model No. 402
EX $100 **NM** $150 **MIP** $250

Standard Steam Shovel, 1950, Orange, 20.5Lx6.25Wx7.75H, wooden wheels w/o tracks, Model No. 100
EX $50 **NM** $75 **MIP** $150

Heavy Duty Steam Shovel, 1950, Blue, 21.5Lx6.25Wx7.75H, rubber tracks, Model No. 105
EX $75 **NM** $100 **MIP** $175

Dump Truck, 1950, Red, 20Lx6.75Wx6.25H, long bullet headlights, Model No. 200
EX $50 **NM** $100 **MIP** $175

Aerial Fire Truck, 1950, Red, 24Lx6.75Wx6.25H, 1 raising/2 side ladders & bell on hood, Model No. 250
EX $75 **NM** $150 **MIP** $250

Machinery Truck & Steam Shovel, 1950, Orange and blue, 21.5Lx6.75Wx6.25H, comes w/#105 steam shovel & loading ramp, Model No. 402
EX $100 **NM** $150 **MIP** $250

Heavy Duty Steam Shovel, 1951-52, Blue, 21.5Lx6.25Wx7.75H, Model No. 105
EX $75 **NM** $100 **MIP** $175

Dump Truck, 1951-52, Red, 20Lx6.75Wx6.25H, with plastic fireball motor under the hood, Model No. 200
EX $50 **NM** $100 **MIP** $175

Aerial Fire Truck, 1951-52, Red, 24Lx6.75Wx6.25H, with plastic fireball motor under the hood, Model No. 250
EX $75 **NM** $150 **MIP** $250

Road Grader, 1951-52, Orange, 18Lx7Wx7.5H, with plastic fireball motor under the hood, Model No. 300
EX $50 **NM** $100 **MIP** $175

Machinery Truck & Steam Shovel, 1951-52, Orange and blue, 21.5Lx6.75Wx6.25H, with plastic fireball motor under the hood, Model No. 402
EX $100 **NM** $150 **MIP** $250

Utility (Garbage) Truck, 1951-52, Red and blue, 21.5Lx6.5Wx7.5H, with plastic fireball motor under the hood, Model No. 500
EX $100 **NM** $150 **MIP** $250

(Randy Prasse Photo)

Motor Express Truck, 1951-52, Grey and orange, 12.75Lx5.5Wx5H, cast cab "Freeport Motor Express" decals, Model No. 601
EX $50 **NM** $150 **MIP** $225

(Calvin Chaussee Photo)

Package Delivery Truck, 1951-52, Orange and green, 13Lx5.5Wx5H, cast cab, tail gate with chain, Model No. 603
EX $50 **NM** $150 **MIP** $225

Shovel Dump Truck, 1951-52, Orange and blue, 12.75Lx5.5Wx5H, cast cab, dump box, Model No. 605
EX $50 **NM** $150 **MIP** $225

(Randy Prasse Photo)

Machinery Truck, 1951-52, orange and blue, 12.75Lx5.5Wx5H, with loading ramp and chain winch, Model No. 607
EX $75 **NM** $150 **MIP** $250

Transport Trailer, 1951-52, Blue and red, 21.5Lx5.5Wx7.5H, blue cast cab with red trailer, no hubcaps, Model No. 700
EX $75 **NM** $150 **MIP** $200

Steel Cargo Trailer, 1951-52, Blue and red, 20.75Lx5.5Wx5.5H, blue cast cab with red trailer, no hubcaps, Model No. 702
EX $75 **NM** $150 **MIP** $200

Overland Freight Trailer, 1951-52, Blue and orange, 20.75Lx5.5Wx5.5H, blue cast cab with orange stake trailer, Model No. 704
EX $75 **NM** $150 **MIP** $200

Combination With Two Trailers, 1951-52, Blue cast cab with #702 and 704 trailers, Model No. 706
EX $100 **NM** $200 **MIP** $300

Barrel Truck, 1951-52, Red and blue, 12.75Lx5.5Wx5H, wind-up motor and two oil can banks, Model No. 811
EX $75 **NM** $150 **MIP** $250

Wrecker Truck, 1951-52, Red and grey, 12.25Lx5.5Wx5.25H, wind-up motor and chain winch, Model No. 822
EX $75 **NM** $125 **MIP** $200

Hi-Lift Dump Truck, 1951-52, Red and blue, 12.5Lx5.5Wx5.25H, wind-up motor with scissors lift box, Model No. 844
EX $75 **NM** $125 **MIP** $200

Gasoline Truck, 1951-52, Red and red, 13.5Lx5.5Wx5H, wind-up motor, Model No. 866
EX $100 **NM** $150 **MIP** $250

Steam Shovel (New Design), 1953, Blue, 26.5Lx6.5Wx8H, new design, 2 cranks, Model No. 105
EX $50 **NM** $100 **MIP** $125

Dump Truck, 1953, Red, 20Lx6.75Wx6.25H, with plastic fireball motor under the hood, Model No. 200
EX $50 **NM** $100 **MIP** $150

Road Grader, 1953, Orange, 18Lx7Wx7.5H, with plastic fireball motor under the hood, Model No. 300
EX $50 **NM** $75 **MIP** $150

Rocker, 1953, Red, 20Lx6.25Wx6.5H, with plastic fireball motor under the hood, Model No. 310
EX $50 **NM** $100 **MIP** $150

Bottom Dump, 1953, Orange, 21.5Lx6.5Wx6.5H, with plastic fireball motor under the hood, Model No. 320
EX $50 **NM** $100 **MIP** $150

Scraper, 1953, Red, 22Lx7Wx6.5H, with plastic fireball motor under the hood, Model No. 330
EX $50 **NM** $100 **MIP** $150

End Loader, 1953, Orange, 15.25Lx6.25Wx6.75H, with plastic fireball motor under the hood, Model No. 340
EX $50 **NM** $100 **MIP** $150

Machinery Truck & Steam Shovel, 1953, Orange and blue, 21.5Lx6.75Wx6.25H, comes w/#105 steam shovel & loading ramp, Model No. 402
EX $75 **NM** $150 **MIP** $250

Utility (Garbage) Truck, 1953, Red and white, 21.5Lx6.5Wx7.5H, with plastic fireball motor under the hood, Model No. 500
EX $75 **NM** $150 **MIP** $250

(Randy Prasse Photo)

Motor Express Truck, 1953, White and red, 12.75Lx5.5Wx5H, cast cab "Freeport Motor Express" decals, Model No. 601
EX $50 **NM** $150 **MIP** $225

Package Delivery Truck, 1953, White and orange, 13Lx5.5Wx5H, cast cab, tail gate with chain, w/hubcaps, Model No. 603
EX $50 **NM** $150 **MIP** $225

Shovel Dump Truck, 1953, White and blue, 12.75Lx5.5Wx5H, cast cab, dump box, w/hubcaps, Model No. 605
EX $50 **NM** $150 **MIP** $225

Transport Trailer, 1953, White and red, 21.5Lx5.5Wx7.5H, w/hubcaps, Model No. 700
EX $50 **NM** $150 **MIP** $225

Steel Cargo Trailer, 1953, White and red, 20.75Lx5.5Wx5.5H, w/hubcaps & loading ramp, Model No. 702
EX $75 **NM** $150 **MIP** $200

Grain Trailer, 1953, White and orange, 20.75Lx5.5Wx5.5H, replaced freight trailer, sliding rear door, Model No. 704
EX $75 **NM** $150 **MIP** $200

Cattle Trailer, 1953, White and red, 21.5Lx5.5Wx7.5H, no loading ramp or animals, Model No. 708
EX $75 **NM** $150 **MIP** $200

(Randy Prasse Photo)

Barrel Truck, 1953, Red and blue, 12.75Lx5.5Wx5H, wind-up motor and oil can bank, Model No. 811
EX $75 **NM** $150 **MIP** $250

Wrecker Truck, 1953, White and orange, 12.25Lx5.5Wx5.25H, wind-up motor and chain winch, Model No. 822
EX $75 **NM** $125 **MIP** $200

Hi-Lift Dump Truck, 1953, White and red, 12.5Lx5.5Wx5.25H, wind-up motor with scissors lift box, Model No. 844
EX $75 **NM** $125 **MIP** $200

Gasoline Truck, 1953, Red and red, 13.5Lx5.5Wx5H, wind-up motor, Model No. 866
EX $100 **NM** $150 **MIP** $250

Steam Shovel, 1954, Blue, 26.5Lx6.5Wx8H, 2 cranks and rubber tracks, Model No. 105
EX $50 **NM** $100 **MIP** $150

Dump Truck, 1954, Red, 20Lx6.75Wx6.25H, with plastic fireball motor under the hood, Model No. 200
EX $50 **NM** $100 **MIP** $175

Road Grader, 1954, Orange, 18Lx7Wx7.5H, with plastic fireball motor under the hood, Model No. 300
EX $50 **NM** $75 **MIP** $125

Rocker, 1954, Red, 20Lx6.25Wx.6.5H, with plastic fireball motor under the hood, Model No. 310
EX $50 **NM** $100 **MIP** $150

Bottom Dump, 1954, Orange, 21.5Lx6.5Wx6.5H, with plastic fireball motor under the hood, Model No. 320
EX $50 **NM** $100 **MIP** $150

Scraper, 1954, Red, 22Lx7Wx6.5H, with plastic fireball motor under the hood, Model No. 330
EX $50 **NM** $100 **MIP** $150

End Loader, 1954, Orange, 15.25Lx6.25Wx6.75H, with plastic fireball motor under the hood, Model No. 340
EX $50 **NM** $100 **MIP** $150

Machinery Truck & Steam Shovel, 1954, Orange and blue, 26.5Lx6.75Wx14.25H, comes w/#105 steam shovel & loading ramp, Model No. 402
EX $75 **NM** $150 **MIP** $250

Utility (Garbage) Truck, 1954, Red and white, 21.5Lx6.5Wx7.5H, with plastic fireball motor under the hood, Model No. 500
EX $100 **NM** $150 **MIP** $250

(Randy Prasse Photo)

Package Delivery Truck, 1954, White and orange, 13Lx5.5Wx5H, cast cab, tail gate with chain, w/hubcaps, Model No. 603
EX $75 **NM** $150 **MIP** $225

Shovel Dump Truck, 1954, White and blue, 12.75Lx5.5Wx5H, cast cab, dump box, w/hubcaps, Model No. 605
EX $75 **NM** $150 **MIP** $225

Machinery Truck, 1954, White and blue, 12.75Lx5.5Wx5H, rare, made only in 1954. Hubcaps, loading ramp, Model No. 607
EX $75 **NM** $200 **MIP** $250

Barrel Truck, 1954, White and red, 12.75Lx5.5Wx5H, rare, made only in 1954. Replaced #811, no wind-up, Model No. 609
EX $75 **NM** $200 **MIP** $250

Transport Trailer, 1954, White and red, 21.5Lx5.5Wx7.5H, w/hubcaps, Model No. 700
EX $75 **NM** $150 **MIP** $220

Steel Cargo Trailer, 1954, White and red, 20.75Lx5.5Wx5.5H, w/hubcaps & loading ramp, Model No. 702
EX $75 **NM** $150 **MIP** $200

Grain Trailer, 1954, White and orange, 20.75Lx5.5Wx5.5H, sliding rear door, Model No. 704
EX $75 **NM** $125 **MIP** $175

Auto Transport, 1954, White and red, 27Lx5.5Wx6.75H, with 4 die cast cars and loading ramp, Model No. 706
EX $75 **NM** $175 **MIP** $225

Cattle Trailer, 1954, White and red, 21.5Lx5.5Wx7.5H, no loading ramp or animals, Model No. 708
EX $75 **NM** $175 **MIP** $200

Wrecker Truck, 1954, White and orange, 12.25Lx5.5Wx5.25H, wind-up motor and chain winch, Model No. 822
EX $75 **NM** $150 **MIP** $200

(Randy Prasse Photo)

Hi-Lift Dump Truck, 1954, White and red, 12.5Lx5.5Wx5.25H, wind-up motor with scissors lift box, Model No. 844
EX $75 **NM** $175 **MIP** $250

(Randy Prasse Photo)

Gasoline Truck, 1954, Red and red, 13.5Lx5.5Wx5H, wind-up motor, Model No. 866
EX $75 **NM** $200 **MIP** $275

Tow Truck (Fix-It), 1954, Red and red, 11.75Lx5.5Wx6H, with mini tool set. New pressed steel cab design, Model No. 910
EX $75 **NM** $100 **MIP** $150

Telephone Truck (Fix-It), 1954, Green, 12Lx5.5Wx5.25H, with mini tool set, new pressed steel cab design, Model No. 920
EX $75 **NM** $100 **MIP** $150

Freight Trailer, 1954, Red and red, 17.75Lx5Wx4.5H, new pressed steel cab design, Model No. 930
EX $75 **NM** $150 **MIP** $200

Log Trailer, 1954, Orange and orange, 17.75Lx5Wx4.5H, with five wooden logs, Model No. 940
EX $75 **NM** $150 **MIP** $200

Caddy Sedan, 1954, Various, 6.25Lx2.5Wx2H, same scale as appear on auto transport set, Model No. 20
EX $15 **NM** $25 **MIP** $50

Pick-Up Truck, 1954, Various, 6.5Lx2.5Wx2.25H, same scale as appear on auto transport set, Model No. 21
EX $15 **NM** $25 **MIP** $50

Wrecker Truck, 1954, Various, 7.5Lx2.5Wx2.25H, same scale #21 pick-up but with cast tow boom arm, Model No. 30
EX $25 **NM** $50 **MIP** $75

8-Wheel Transport Truck, 1954, Orange, 7.25Lx2.5Wx2.25H, also in 1957 as 6 wheeled, red version in farm set, Model No. 40
EX $25 **NM** $50 **MIP** $75

Dump Truck, 1954, Green and orange, 8.25Lx2.5Wx2.5H, spring dump action, Model No. 50
EX $25 **NM** $50 **MIP** $75

4 Pc. Truck Assortment, 1954, One each: #21, #30, #40, #50, Model No. 90
EX $100 **NM** $125 **MIP** $175

Dump Truck, 1954, Green and orange, 10.25Lx3.25Wx3.5H, spring dump action, Model No. 75
EX $25 **NM** $50 **MIP** $75

Stake Truck, 1954, Green and orange, 9.25Lx3.25Wx3.25H, removable stake panels, Model No. 76
EX $25 **NM** $50 **MIP** $75

Lumber Truck, 1954, Red and blue, 10.5Lx3.5Wx3.25H, with five wooden logs, Model No. 77
EX $25 **NM** $50 **MIP** $75

3 Pc. Truck Assortment, 1954, One each: #75, #76, #77, Model No. 91
EX $100 **NM** $175 **MIP** $225

Motor Express Truck, 1954, Yellow and blue, 12.5Lx5.25Wx4.5H, stake truck with "S" grill cab, Model No. 150
EX $75 **NM** $125 **MIP** $175

Machinery Hauling Truck, 1954, Red and yellow, 12.5Lx5.5Wx4H, flatbed with winch and "S" grill cab, Model No. 151
EX $75 **NM** $125 **MIP** $175

Semi Trailer Freight Truck, 1955, Yellow and red, 17Lx4.5Wx4.5H, same trailer as #930 with "S" grill cab, Model No. 155
EX $75 **NM** $150 **MIP** $200

Semi Trailer Lumber Truck, 1955, Green and orange, 17Lx4.5Wx4.5H, with three wooden logs and "S" grill cab, Model No. 156
EX $75 **NM** $150 **MIP** $200

Auto Haulaway, 1955, Blue and orange, 25Lx4.5Wx6.5H, with two cars, loading ramp and "S" grill cab, Model No. 175
EX $75 **NM** $175 **MIP** $225

Steam Shovel, 1955, Orange, 26.5Lx6.5Wx8H, 2 cranks and rubber tracks, Model No. 105
EX $50 **NM** $75 **MIP** $125

Dump Truck, 1955, Yellow and red, 20Lx6.75Wx6.25H, spring dump action, Model No. 201
EX $50 **NM** $100 **MIP** $150

Hydraulic Lift Dump Truck, 1955, Green and orange, 21Lx8Wx7H, hydraulic dump lift arm on dump box, Model No. 250
EX $75 **NM** $150 **MIP** $200

Hook and Ladder Truck, 1955, Red, 33.25Lx6.75Wx7H, with raising & two ladders, cast metal siren on roof, Model No. 260
EX $75 **NM** $150 **MIP** $200

Road Grader, 1955, Orange, 18Lx7Wx7.5H, with plastic fireball motor under the hood, Model No. 300
EX $50 **NM** $75 **MIP** $125

Rocker, 1955, Green, 20Lx6.25Wx6.5H, with plastic fireball motor under the hood, Model No. 310
EX $50 **NM** $125 **MIP** $150

Earth Mover, 1955, Orange, 21.5Lx6.5Wx6.5H, with plastic fireball motor under the hood, Model No. 320
EX $50 **NM** $125 **MIP** $150

Scraper, 1955, Red, 22Lx7Wx6.5H, with plastic fireball motor under the hood, Model No. 330
EX $50 **NM** $125 **MIP** $150

End Loader, 1955, Orange, 15.25Lx6.25Wx6.75H, with plastic fireball motor under the hood, Model No. 340
EX $50 **NM** $100 **MIP** $150

3 Pc. Truck Assortment, 1955, One each: #105, #201, $300, Model No. 325
EX $100 **NM** $200 **MIP** $300

Steam Shovel & Machinery Truck, 1955, Green and orange, 26.5Lx6.5Wx14.25H, with plastic fireball motor under the hood, Model No. 403
EX $75 **NM** $150 **MIP** $200

Utility (Garbage) Truck, 1955, Blue and grey, 21.5Lx6.5Wx7.5H, with plastic fireball motor under the hood, Model No. 500
EX $75 **NM** $175 **MIP** $200

Shovel Dump Truck, 1955, Chrome and orange, 12.75Lx6Wx6.25H, same as #605 from past years. Mag wheels, Model No. 606
EX $75 **NM** $175 **MIP** $200

Hi-Lift Dump Truck, 1955, Chrome and green, 12.5Lx6Wx5H, same as #844 from past years. Mag wheels, Model No. 644
EX $75 **NM** $175 **MIP** $250

Steel Cargo Trailer, 1955, White and red, 25.5Lx5.5Wx5.5H, shown in catalog with yellow cab but have not seen, Model No. 702
EX $75 **NM** $125 **MIP** $175

Grain Trailer, 1955, White and orange, 20.75Lx5.5Wx5.5H, shown in catalog with green cab but have not seen, Model No. 704
EX $75 **NM** $150 **MIP** $200

Deluxe Auto Transport, 1955, Chrome and yellow, 27Lx6Wx6.75H, with 4 die cast cars and loading ramp, Model No. 706
EX $75 **NM** $125 **MIP** $200

(Randy Prasse Photo)

Deluxe Moving Van, 1955, Chrome and yellow, 24Lx6Wx8.5H, with loading ramp, Model No. 710
EX $75 **NM** $175 **MIP** $250

Deluxe Cattle Transport, 1955, Chrome and green, 24Lx6Wx8.5H, with loading ramp and metal farm animals, Model No. 712
EX $75 **NM** $150 **MIP** $200

Timber Toter, 1955, Chrome and green, 21Lx6Wx6H, with six wooden logs and chains, Model No. 714
EX $75 **NM** $125 **MIP** $175

10 Pc. Truck Assortment, 1955, 2 cabs plus one each #702, #706, #714, cattle trailer, Model No. 725
EX $200 **NM** $400 **MIP** $600

Wrecker Truck, 1955, White and orange, 12Lx5.5Wx5.25H, shown in catalog with green cab but have not seen, Model No. 822
EX $100 **NM** $150 **MIP** $200

Tow Truck (Fix-It), 1955, Red and red, 11.75Lx5.5Wx6H, with mini tool set, Model No. 910
EX $75 **NM** $100 **MIP** $150

Telephone Truck (Fix-It), 1955, Green, 12Lx5.5Wx5.25H, with mini tool set, Model No. 920
EX $75 **NM** $100 **MIP** $150

Freight Trailer, 1955, Yellow and red, 17.75Lx5Wx4.5H, Model No. 930
EX $75 **NM** $150 **MIP** $200

Log Trailer, 1955, Green and orange, 17.75Lx5Wx4.5H, with five wooden logs, Model No. 940
EX $75 **NM** $150 **MIP** $200

Package Delivery Truck, 1955, Yellow and green, 13Lx5.5Wx4.75H, with tailgate and chains, Model No. 911
EX $75 **NM** $125 **MIP** $175

Gasoline Truck, 1955, Red and yellow, 13.5Lx5Wx4.5H, non-wind-up model, Model No. 912
EX $75 **NM** $125 **MIP** $200

Barrel Truck, 1955, Yellow and red, 12.75Lx5.5Wx5H, non-wind-up model, no oil can bank, Model No. 913
EX $75 **NM** $125 **MIP** $200

Transport Trailer, 1955, Yellow and red, 21Lx5Wx7.75H, new pressed steel cab design, Model No. 950
EX $75 **NM** $150 **MIP** $225

Cattle Trailer, 1955, Green and orange, 21Lx5Wx7.75H, new pressed steel cab design, Model No. 960
EX $75 **NM** $150 **MIP** $225

Dump Truck, 1956-57, Gold and blue, 10.25Lx3.25Wx3.5H, spring dump action, Model No. 75
EX $25 **NM** $50 **MIP** $75

Stake Truck, 1956-57, Gold and green, 9.25Lx3.25Wx3.25H, removable stake panels, Model No. 76
EX $25 **NM** $50 **MIP** $75

Lumber Truck, 1956-57, Red and blue, 10.5Lx3.5Wx3.25H, with five wooden logs, Model No. 77
EX $25 **NM** $50 **MIP** $75

3 Pc. Truck Assortment W/Garage, 1956-57, One each: #75, #76, #77 with garage storage box, Model No. 92
EX $100 **NM** $175 **MIP** $225

Motor Express Truck, 1956-57, Yellow and blue, 12.5Lx5.25Wx4.5H, stake truck with "S" grill cab, Model No. 150
EX $75 **NM** $125 **MIP** $175

Machinery Hauling Truck, 1956-57, Red and yellow, 12.5Lx5.5Wx4H, flatbed with winch and "S" grill cab, Model No. 151
EX $75 **NM** $125 **MIP** $175

Semi Trailer Freight Truck, 1956-57, Yellow and red, 17Lx4.5Wx4.5H, same trailer as #930 with "S" grill cab, Model No. 155
EX $75 **NM** $150 **MIP** $200

Auto Haulaway, 1956-57, Blue and orange, 25Lx4.5Wx6.5H, with two cars, loading ramp and "S" grill cab, Model No. 175
EX $75 **NM** $175 **MIP** $225

Clam Bucket, 1956-57, Yellow and green, 16.75Lx7Wx7.25H, Model No. 101
EX $75 **NM** $100 **MIP** $150

Heavy Duty Steam Shovel, 1956-57, Green and orange, 26.5Lx7Wx6.75H, 2 cranks and rubber tracks, Model No. 106
EX $75 **NM** $100 **MIP** $150

Dump Truck, 1956-57, Green and orange, 20Lx6.75Wx6.25H, spring dump action, Model No. 201
EX $75 **NM** $100 **MIP** $150

Hydraulic Lift Dump Truck, 1956-57, Yellow and green, 21Lx8Wx7H, hydraulic dump lift arm on dump box, Model No. 250
EX $75 **NM** $175 **MIP** $225

Hook and Ladder Truck, 1956-57, Red, 33.25Lx6.75Wx7H, with raising & two ladders, cast metal siren on roof, Model No. 260
EX $75 **NM** $175 **MIP** $250

Ready Mix Concrete Truck, 1956-57, Red and yellow, 21.5Lx7.5Wx9.25H, with gear on barrel, driven by axle, Model No. 271
EX $75 **NM** $100 **MIP** $175

Mobile Steam Shovel Unit, 1956-57, Green and yellow, 32.5Lx6.75Wx8H, half-track truck with steam shovel on back, Model No. 272
EX $75 **NM** $175 **MIP** $225

Road Grader, 1956-57, Green, 18Lx7Wx7.5H, with plastic fireball motor under the hood, Model No. 300
EX $50 **NM** $100 **MIP** $150

Rocker Dump, 1956-57, Green, 20Lx6Wx6.5H, rubber tracks on tractor, dumps to the rear, Model No. 311
EX $50 **NM** $125 **MIP** $175

Earth Mover, 1956-57, Orange, 22Lx6.5Wx6.5H, same tractor as #311, bottom panels open to dump, Model No. 321
EX $50 **NM** $125 **MIP** $175

Scraper, 1956-57, Orange, 22Lx7Wx6.5H, with plastic fireball motor under the hood, Model No. 330
EX $50 **NM** $125 **MIP** $175

End Loader, 1956-57, Green, 15.25Lx6Wx6.75H, with plastic fireball motor under the hood, Model No. 340
EX $50 **NM** $100 **MIP** $175

Clam Bucket and Machinery Truck, 1956-57, Yellow and green, 32Lx7.25Wx13.75H, with plastic fireball motor under the hood, Model No. 404
EX $75 **NM** $150 **MIP** $250

Utility (Garbage) Truck, 1956-57, Blue and grey, 21.5Lx6.5Wx7.5H, with plastic fireball motor under the hood, Model No. 500
EX $75 **NM** $175 **MIP** $250

Shovel Dump Truck, 1956-57, Green and yellow, 12.75Lx6Wx5H, with mag wheels, Model No. 606
EX $75 **NM** $150 **MIP** $200

Hi-Lift Dump Truck, 1956-57, Chrome and blue, 12.5Lx6Wx5H, same as #644 from 1955 only blue dump box, Model No. 644
EX $75 **NM** $200 **MIP** $250

Trailer Truck, 1956-57, Chrome and red, 24.5Lx6Wx5.5H, same as #702 but with chrome cab and lift gate, Model No. 705
EX $75 **NM** $175 **MIP** $225

Deluxe Auto Transport, 1956-57, Chrome and yellow, 27Lx6Wx6.75H, with 4 die cast cars and loading ramp, Model No. 706
EX $75 **NM** $150 **MIP** $225

Deluxe Moving Van, 1956-57, Chrome and blue, 24Lx6Wx8.5H, with loading ramp and mini grocery freight, Model No. 710
EX $75 **NM** $175 **MIP** $250

Western Auto Moving Van, 1956-57, Chrome and white, 24Lx6Wx8.5H, private label. Same body as #710 deluxe moving van. Red doors, Model No. 711
EX $75 **NM** $200 **MIP** $300

(Randy Prasse Photo)

Deluxe Cattle Transport, 1956-57, Chrome and green, 24Lx6Wx8.5H, with loading ramp and metal farm animals, Model No. 712
EX $75 **NM** $175 **MIP** $225

(Randy Prasse Photo)

Timber Toter, 1956-57, Chrome and green, 21Lx6Wx6H, with six wooden logs and chains, Model No. 714
EX $75 **NM** $150 **MIP** $200

Wrecker Truck, 1956-57, White and orange, 12Lx5.5Wx5.25H, wind-up, Model No. 822
EX $75 **NM** $175 **MIP** $200

Freight Hauler, 1956-57, Blue and yellow, 20.5Lx5.25Wx5.5H, with grocery freight, Model No. 935
EX $75 **NM** $125 **MIP** $200

Transport Truck, 1956-57, Red and yellow, 21Lx5Wx7.5H, Model No. 950
EX $75 **NM** $125 **MIP** $175

Cattle Transport, 1956-57, Green and orange, 21Lx5Wx7.75H, Model No. 960
EX $75 **NM** $150 **MIP** $200

Tow Truck (Fix-It), 1956-57, Blue and blue, 11.75Lx5.5Wx6H, with mini tool set, Model No. 910
EX $75 **NM** $125 **MIP** $175

Package Delivery Truck, 1956-57, Blue and yellow, 13Lx5.5Wx4.75H, with tailgate and chains, Model No. 911
EX $75 **NM** $125 **MIP** $175

Gasoline Truck, 1956-57, Blue and yellow, 13.5Lx5Wx4.5H, Model No. 912
EX $75 **NM** $125 **MIP** $200

Barrel Truck, 1956-57, Yellow and red, 12.75Lx5.5Wx5H, non-wind-up model, no oil can bank, Model No. 913
EX $75 **NM** $125 **MIP** $200

Telephone Truck (Fix-It), 1956-57, Blue, 12Lx5.5Wx5.25H, with mini tool set, Model No. 920
EX $75 **NM** $125 **MIP** $200

3 Pc. Truck Assortment, 1956-57, Various, one each: #106, #201, #300, Model No. 326
EX $150 **NM** $250 **MIP** $350

5 Pc. Turnpike Builder Set, 1956-57, Various, one each: #321, #340, #404 combo, Model No. 327
EX $200 **NM** $300 **MIP** $400

32 Pc. Big Job Transcontinental Set, 1956-57, Various, 2 cabs plus one each #702, #706, #714, cattle trailer, Model No. 726
EX $200 **NM** $400 **MIP** $600

17 Pc. Coast To Coast Fleet, 1956-57, Various, 2 cars plus lumber trailer, #175, #935, #950; 2 cars, Model No. 925
EX $200 **NM** $400 **MIP** $600

15 Pc. Farm Set, 1958, Various, caddy, dump, pick-up/horse trailer, 6 wheel transport, Model No. 93
EX $125 **NM** $175 **MIP** $250

3 Pc. Truck Assortment W/Garage, 1958, Various, one each; dump, log and stake truck, Model No. 94
EX $150 **NM** $200 **MIP** $300

Pick-Up Truck With Horse Van, 1958, Blue and yellow, 10.5Lx2.5Wx3H, includes 2 plastic horses, Model No. 100
EX $75 **NM** $100 **MIP** $125

Power Shovel, 1958, Orange, 26.5Lx7Wx6.75H, 2 cranks and rubber tracks, Model No. 106
EX $75 **NM** $100 **MIP** $150

Heavy Duty Dump Truck, 1958, Blue and orange, 20Lx6.75Wx6.25H, spring dump action plus red light on roof, Model No. 200
EX $75 **NM** $100 **MIP** $150

Dump With Front-End Loader, 1958, Yellow and blue, 23Lx6.75Wx6.25H, spring loaded dump with front loader bucket, Model No. 202
EX $100 **NM** $150 **MIP** $200

Pick-Up Truck, 1958, Red and yellow, 19.25Lx6.5Wx6H, includes mini grocery freight, Model No. 210
EX $100 **NM** $125 **MIP** $175

Air Force Truck, 1958, Blue and red, 17.25Lx7.25Wx8H, includes soldiers and canvas top, spare tires on side, Model No. 212
EX $125 **NM** $150 **MIP** $200

Farm Truck & Trailer, 1958, Blue and yellow, 28Lx6Wx6.25H, pick-up with pick-up box trailer & plastic farm animals, Model No. 213
EX $125 **NM** $175 **MIP** $225

Towing & Service Truck, 1958, Green and orange, 17.5Lx6Wx7.5H, same as #210 but with tow set-up and red light on roof, Model No. 214
EX $100 **NM** $125 **MIP** $175

Hydraulic Lift Dump Truck, 1958, Orange and green, 21Lx8Wx7H, hydraulic dump lift arm on dump box, Model No. 250
EX $125 **NM** $175 **MIP** $225

Double Hydraulic Load & Dump, 1958, Black and yellow, 24.5Lx7.75Wx7H, hydraulic dump lift arm on dump box & front bucket, Model No. 252
EX $125 **NM** $175 **MIP** $225

Hook and Ladder Truck, 1958, Red, 33.5Lx6Wx7H, with raising & two ladders, cast metal siren on roof, Model No. 261
EX $100 **NM** $150 **MIP** $225

Pumper Fire Truck W/Light, 1958, Red, 22.75Lx7.25Wx7H, pumps water through truck & hydrant, flashing light, Model No. 262
EX $100 **NM** $175 **MIP** $225

Hydraulic Hook & Ladder Truck, 1958, Red, 33.25Lx6.75Wx7H, with raising & two ladders, red flashing light on roof, Model No. 266
EX $100 **NM** $200 **MIP** $250

Mobile Communications Center, 1958, Red and blue, 20Lx6.25Wx6.25H, includes antenna tower & morse code buttons, Model No. 270
EX $125 **NM** $175 **MIP** $225

Ready Mix Concrete Truck, 1958, Green and orange, 21.5Lx7.5Wx9.25H, with gear on barrel, driven by axle, Model No. 271
EX $75 **NM** $125 **MIP** $200

Mobile Power Shovel Unit, 1958, Green and yellow, 32.5Lx6.75Wx8H, half-track truck with steam shovel on back, Model No. 272
EX $100 **NM** $175 **MIP** $225

Deluxe Cattle Transport, 1958, Yellow and brown, 25.75Lx6.25Wx8.5H, includes plastic farm animals, Model No. 275
EX $100 **NM** $175 **MIP** $225

Deluxe Road Grader, 1958, Orange, 18.75Lx7.25Wx7.5H, with plastic fireball motor under the hood, Model No. 301
EX $75 **NM** $100 **MIP** $150

Deluxe Rocker Dump, 1958, Orange, 20.25Lx6.25Wx6.5H, with plastic fireball motor under the hood, Model No. 312
EX $75 **NM** $100 **MIP** $150

Deluxe Earth Mover, 1958, Orange, 22Lx6.5Wx6.5H, with plastic fireball motor under the hood, Model No. 322
EX $75 **NM** $100 **MIP** $150

Combination, 1958, Green and orange, 32Lx7.5Wx6.75H, #106 power shovel and machinery hauling low-boy, Model No. 405
EX $100 **NM** $150 **MIP** $225

5 Pc. Highway Builder Set, 1958, Various, one each: #106, #201, #300 plus 2 metal road signs, Model No. 510
EX $175 **NM** $250 **MIP** $400

17 Pc. USA Combat Convoy Set, 1958, Green, transport, searchlight and missle trucks w/soldiers, Model No. 520
EX $175 **NM** $250 **MIP** $400

Big Job Transcontinental Fleet, 1958, Various, 2 cabs plus 1 each trailers: steel, auto, freight, cattle, Model No. 540
EX $200 **NM** $400 **MIP** $600

12 Pc. US Highway Set, 1958, Orange, dump, grader, maintenance, pick-up plus 8 road signs, Model No. 550
EX $175 **NM** $275 **MIP** $450

6 Pc. Fire Department, 1958, Red and white, pumper, hook & ladder, ambulance, road signs, Model No. 570
EX $175 **NM** $225 **MIP** $400

Deluxe Auto Transport, 1958, Chrome and yellow, 27Lx6Wx6.75H, with 2 cars, 1 truck and loading ramp, Model No. 707
EX $75 **NM** $150 **MIP** $225

(Randy Prasse Photo)

Gold Plated Cadillac, 1958, Gold, 6.75Lx2.25Wx2H, same as used on car carriers. 50th Anniversary decal on roof
EX $100 **NM** $150 **MIP** $200

Deluxe Moving Van, 1958, Chrome and blue, 31Lx6Wx8.5H, with loading ramp and mini grocery freight, Model No. 710
EX $100 **NM** $175 **MIP** $250

Timber Toter, 1958, Chrome and blue, 21Lx6Wx6.25H, with six wooden logs and chains, Model No. 714
EX $75 **NM** $150 **MIP** $175

USA Transport Truck, 1958, Green, 12.5Lx5.25Wx7.5H, with canvas top, Model No. 905
EX $75 **NM** $100 **MIP** $150

USA Guided Missile Launcher, 1958, Green, 12.75Lx5.25Wx6H, with 2 plastic missiles, Model No. 906
EX $75 **NM** $100 **MIP** $175

USA Searchlight Truck, 1958, Green, 12.75Lx5.25Wx7.25H, with battery operated searchlight, Model No. 907
EX $75 **NM** $125 **MIP** $200

Gasoline Truck, 1958, Blue and yellow, 13.5Lx5Wx4.5H, Model No. 912
EX $75 **NM** $125 **MIP** $175

Hi-Lift Dump Truck, 1958, Blue and yellow, 12Lx5.25Wx5.75H, with scissors lift mechanism, Model No. 914
EX $75 **NM** $100 **MIP** $175

Trailer W/Mechanical Lift, 1958, Blue and yellow, 50.75Lx5.5Wx5.75H, mechanical lift gate with mini grocery freight, Model No. 936
EX $100 **NM** $175 **MIP** $250

Farm Truck, 1958, Green and red, 13Lx5.75Wx4.5H, with plastic farm animals, Model No. 938
EX $75 **NM** $100 **MIP** $150

(Randy Prasse Photo)

Highway Maintenance Service, 1958, Orange and green, 12Lx4.5Wx7H, with lift/swivel boom arm, Model No. 939
EX $75 **NM** $100 **MIP** $150

Hydraulic Dump Trailer, 1958, Yellow and green, 20.5Lx5.5Wx5.75H, with hydraulic lift arm on trailer dump, Model No. 941
EX $125 **NM** $175 **MIP** $225

Parcel Service Truck, 1958, Yellow and green, 12.25Lx5.25Wx7H, with mini grocery freight, Model No. 942
EX $75 **NM** $125 **MIP** $175

US Mail Truck, 1958, Blue and red, 12.25Lx5.25Wx6.5H, Model No. 943
EX $100 **NM** $125 **MIP** $200

Farm Trailer Truck, 1958, Blue and red, 20.5Lx5.5Wx5.5H, with plastic animals and loading ramp, Model No. 945
EX $75 **NM** $125 **MIP** $175

Auto Haulaway, 1958, Yellow and red, 21.5Lx4.5Wx6.5H, smaller model with 2 cars and loading ramp, Model No. 946
EX $75 **NM** $125 **MIP** $175

Refrigerated Express Truck, 1958, Yellow and brown, 21Lx5Wx7.5H, transport trailer with refrigerator unit on front, Model No. 951
EX $100 **NM** $175 **MIP** $225

Cattle Transport, 1958, Green and orange, 21Lx5Wx7.5H, with plastic farm animals, Model No. 961
EX $75 **NM** $125 **MIP** $200

Ride 'Em Dump Truck, 1958, Blue and yellow, 20.5Lx7.75Wx10.25H, with seat and steering wheel, Model No. 990
EX $100 **NM** $175 **MIP** $225

Ride 'Em Air Force Jeep, 1958, Blue and red, 25.5Lx11Wx14.5H, with steering wheel and fold-down windshield, Model No. 995
EX $100 **NM** $150 **MIP** $225

Kitchen-Laundry Ensemble, 1959, Pink and grey, 9 piece 1/4 scale set, Model No. 50
EX $125 **NM** $175 **MIP** $300

Counter-Top Cabinet, 1959, Pink and grey, 7Lx7.75Wx13H, cabinet doors open, includes pots and pans, Model No. 2
EX $15 **NM** $25 **MIP** $75

Built-In Cooking Range, 1959, Pink and grey, 7Lx7.75Wx13H, plastic burners on top, cabinets open, pots and pans, Model No. 4
EX $15 **NM** $25 **MIP** $75

Corner Counter-Top Cabinet, 1959, Pink and grey, 12Lx9.75Wx13H, 2 lazy susan shelves, drawer opens, pots and pans, Model No. 6
EX $15 **NM** $25 **MIP** $75

Built-In Double Sink, 1959, Pink and grey, 7Lx7.75Wx13H, works with water, battery operated, Model No. 8
EX $15 **NM** $25 **MIP** $75

Automatic Under Counter Dishwasher, 1959, Pink and grey, 7Lx7.75Wx13H, works with water, battery operated, Model No. 10
EX $15 **NM** $25 **MIP** $75

Combination Refrigerator/Freezer, 1959, Pink and grey, 7.25Lx7.75Wx13H, swing out shelves, freezer drawer, plastic food, Model No. 12
EX $15 **NM** $25 **MIP** $75

Built-In Double Oven, 1959, Pink and grey, 7.25Lx7.75Wx13H, battery operated, rotisserie in top oven unit, Model No. 14
EX $15 **NM** $25 **MIP** $75

Washer-Dryer Combination, 1959, Pink and grey, 7.25Lx8Wx10H, washes & spins, battery operated, Model No. 16
EX $15 **NM** $25 **MIP** $75

Dump Truck, 1959, Copper and cream, 10.75Lx4.5Wx4.5H, Model No. 70
EX $50 **NM** $75 **MIP** $150

Dump Truck, 1959, Blue and yellow, 9Lx3.5Wx3.5H, Model No. 75
EX $50 **NM** $75 **MIP** $150

Stake Truck, 1959, Copper and cream, 9.25Lx3.25Wx3H, Model No. 76
EX $50 **NM** $75 **MIP** $150

Air Force Radar Truck, 1959, Blue and red, 12Lx5.25Wx12.5H, scarce, radar dish on roof of box, 2 plastic soldiers, Model No. 102
EX $75 **NM** $100 **MIP** $200

Dump Truck, 1959, Black and yellow, 15.75Lx6.75Wx6.75H, red roof and plastic "S" grille, no windshield, Model No. 201
EX $50 **NM** $100 **MIP** $175

Fleetside Pick-Up, 1959, Copper and cream, 14.5Lx6Wx6H, 6 mini grocery box play freight, Model No. 202
EX $50 **NM** $75 **MIP** $125

Guided Missile Launcher, 1959, Red and silver, 12.25Lx5.25Wx10.25H, plastic missile launcher on bed, metal "S" grille, Model No. 203
EX $75 **NM** $100 **MIP** $150

Mechanical Hydraulic Dump, 1959, Red and white, 12.25Lx5.25Wx5.5H, scarce, hydraulic cylinder controls dump box, Model No. 204
EX $75 **NM** $125 **MIP** $175

Bulldozer, 1959, Copper and cream, 11.75Lx7Wx6.75H, cream blade, yellow wheels and motor, also on #502 set, Model No. 205
EX $50 **NM** $75 **MIP** $125

The Camper, 1959, Red and white, 21.75Lx4.5Wx6.75H, canvas cover on truck, convertible boat & trailer, Model No. 206
EX $50 **NM** $100 **MIP** $150

Farm Pick-Up And Trailer, 1959, Yellow and blue, 27.5Lx6.25Wx6H, 7 plastic animals included, Model No. 213
EX $50 **NM** $100 **MIP** $150

Double Hydraulic Load & Dump, 1959, Copper and yellow, 23.75Lx7.75Wx6.75H, yellow bucket dumps over top into dump box, Model No. 252
EX $50 **NM** $75 **MIP** $150

Deluxe Road Grader, 1959, Copper and yellow, 18.75Lx7.25Wx7.5H, copper with yellow wheels and engine, Model No. 301
EX $50 **NM** $75 **MIP** $125

Power Shovel, 1959, Copper, 26.5Lx7Wx6.75H, rubber tracks, Model No. 302
EX $50 **NM** $75 **MIP** $125

Emergency Fire Patrol Searchlight Unit, 1959, White and red, 19.5Lx5.75Wx7.5H, white trailer with red battery operated searchlight unit, Model No. 303
EX $50 **NM** $100 **MIP** $175

Cattle Transport, 1959, Red and white, 21.25Lx5.25Wx7.5H, structo farms decals on white trailer, Model No. 304
EX $50 **NM** $75 **MIP** $125

Deluxe Rocker Dump, 1959, Copper and cream, 20.25Lx6.25Wx6.5H, bronze dump, cream tractor with yellow wheels & motor, Model No. 312
EX $50 **NM** $75 **MIP** $125

Highway Truck Assortment, 1959, Varies, 13 pc. set, includes #70, #76 plus 6-wheel truck, log truck & signs, Model No. 400
EX $100 **NM** $150 **MIP** $225

Deluxe Auto Transport, 1959, Green and yellow, 31.5Lx5.5Wx6.75H, two cars, one truck with loading ramp, plastic "S" grille, Model No. 401
EX $50 **NM** $100 **MIP** $200

Army Troop Transport, 1959, Green, 18.75Lx6.75Wx9H, canvas top with "USA" printed. 4 plastic soldiers, Model No. 412
EX $50 **NM** $100 **MIP** $175

Hydraulic Sanitation Truck, 1959, Blue and white, 18Lx6Wx7.5H, hydraulic cylinder controls dump box, Model No. 454
EX $75 **NM** $125 **MIP** $200

Deluxe Hydraulic Dumper, 1959, Copper and yellow, 20.5Lx8Wx7H, hydraulic cylinder controls dump box, Model No. 500
EX $75 **NM** $100 **MIP** $150

Stock Farm Set, 1959, Red and white, 15Lx6Wx7.25H, stake truck with cattle loading ramp and 4 plastic horses, Model No. 501
EX $50 **NM** $75 **MIP** $125

Tilt-Top Trailer Truck With Dozer, 1959, Yellow and green, 20.25Lx7.5Wx6H, dozer is copper with yellow plastic wheels and engine, Model No. 502
EX $75 **NM** $100 **MIP** $150

Mobile Outer Space Launcher, 1959, Red and blue, 19.5Lx6Wx12.75H, scarce, 2 plastic missiles launch. Launcher swivels, Model No. 503
EX $100 **NM** $150 **MIP** $225

Deluxe Moving Van, 1959, Yellow and red, 26.25Lx6Wx8.5H, red cab with bulb horn on roof, Model No. 504
EX $75 **NM** $100 **MIP** $150

Ride-er Dump Truck, 1959, Blue and yellow, 20Lx7.75Wx10H, metal seat in dump box, bulb horn on steering wheel, Model No. 505
EX $75 **NM** $125 **MIP** $150

Air Force Anti-Aircraft Set, 1959, Red and blue, scarce, canvas covered truck, missile launcher, searchlight, Model No. 506
EX $125 **NM** $200 **MIP** $300

Deluxe Camper With Boat & Trailer, 1959, Red and white, 29Lx6Wx6H, red truck with white roof, battery op boat motor, Model No. 601
EX $75 **NM** $125 **MIP** $200

Mobile Anti-Missile Unit, 1959, Blue and yellow, 27Lx7.5Wx11.25H, scarce, battery op spotlight & missile launcher on trailer, Model No. 620
EX $75 **NM** $125 **MIP** $225

Ready-Mix Concrete Truck, 1959, Copper and cream, 20.75Lx7.5Wx9.25H, gear powered barrel, runs off axle, Model No. 700
EX $75 **NM** $100 **MIP** $150

Pumper Fire Truck, 1959, Red and red, 20Lx7.25Wx6H, open cab, plastic "S" grille, sprays water through hose, Model No. 701
EX $75 **NM** $100 **MIP** $175

Deluxe Power Wrecker, 1959, Blue and white, 23Lx7Wx9.25H, battery operated winch & lights, Model No. 702
EX $75 **NM** $125 **MIP** $200

Timber Toter, 1959, Red and blue, 21.5Lx4.75Wx5.25H, 5 wooden logs and load chains, Model No. 714
EX $75 **NM** $100 **MIP** $150

Explorer Vanguard Tracking Station, 1959, Red, 7.75Lx4.5Wx10H, scarce, various buttons, globe revolves in TV screen, Model No. 801
EX $100 **NM** $175 **MIP** $250

Boat With Play Motor, 1959, Red and white, 9.5Lx3Wx2.5H, boat only, from #206 set, convertible boat and motor, Model No. 802
EX $50 **NM** $75 **MIP** $150

Boat With Outboard Motor, 1959, Red and white, 13.25Lx4Wx3.25H, boat only, from #601 set, convertible boat and motor, Model No. 803
EX $50 **NM** $75 **MIP** $150

Highway Builder Set, 1959, Varies, 11 pc. set includes #201, #205, #302, road signs, plastic workers, Model No. 900
EX $100 **NM** $150 **MIP** $250

Hydraulic Hook & Ladder, 1959, Red and red, 31Lx6.25Wx7.25H, open cab, plastic "S" grille, metal ladders, Model No. 901
EX $75 **NM** $125 **MIP** $175

Mobile Crane, 1959, Green and yellow, 19.25Lx6.25Wx7.25H, battery operated boom and cab, Model No. 902
EX $75 **NM** $125 **MIP** $200

Ride-er Fire Truck, 1959, Red and white, 25.5Lx10.5Wx12.75H, crank siren on hood, trunk opens, Model No. 925
EX $75 **NM** $125 **MIP** $200

Tree Trimming Truck, 1959, Copper and green, 12Lx4.25Wx12.5H, green boom arm and basket, Model No. 939
EX $50 **NM** $75 **MIP** $125

Ride-er Air Force Jeep, 1959, Blue and red, 25.75Lx10.25Wx18H, missile launcher and missiles on hood, trunk opens, Model No. 950
EX $75 **NM** $125 **MIP** $200

Fire Department Set, 1959, Red and white, 3 piece set, includes #701, #901, #303 (minus searchlight unit), Model No. 975
EX $125 **NM** $200 **MIP** $300

Kitchen Ensemble, 1960, Pink and grey, individual appliances still available, see 1959 for values
EX $15 **NM** $50 **MIP** $75

Kitchen Ensemble, 1960, Pink and grey, 3 pc. set, includes #8, #12, #4- 1959 models, Model No. 23
EX $75 **NM** $125 **MIP** $150

Kitchen-Laundry Ensemble, 1960, Pink and grey, 5 pc. set, includes #8, #12, #4, #10, #16- 1959 models, Model No. 25
EX $95 **NM** $150 **MIP** $200

Deluxe Kitchen-Laundry Ensemble, 1960, Pink and grey, 7 pc. set, includes #8, #12, #4, #10, #14, #16, #2- 1959 models, Model No. 27
EX $125 **NM** $175 **MIP** $225

All-In-One Wild Animal Set, 1960, Pink, blue, yellow, 5.5Lx4Wx2H, smaller animals fit inside larger animals, Model No. 105
EX $10 **NM** $25 **MIP** $50

Hammer Tower, 1960, Yellow and red, 6.5Lx4.75Wx9H, scarce, hammer button and marbles shoot up through tower, Model No. 110
EX $50 **NM** $75 **MIP** $150

Auto Elevator, 1960, Red and yellow, 9Lx3.5Wx9H, scarce, plastic parking garage, crank release car down ramp, Model No. 111
EX $75 **NM** $125 **MIP** $150

Jack And Jill Pump, 1960, Copper and yellow, 8Lx4.25Wx11.25H, scarce, plastic marble toy, structo pre-school series, Model No. 112
EX $75 **NM** $100 **MIP** $150

Concrete Mixer, 1960, Copper and yellow, 6.25Lx5.5Wx13.25H, scarce, plastic cement mixer with clear barrel w/marbels, Model No. 114
EX $75 **NM** $100 **MIP** $150

School Bus, 1960, Yellow, 5.5Lx4Wx12H, scarce, plastic, hinged school bus with blocks. Pull toy, Model No. 115
EX $100 **NM** $125 **MIP** $200

Pickup And Delivery, 1960, Met. green, 14Lx5.75Wx6.5H, whitewall tires, plastic horn on roof, Model No. 207
EX $50 **NM** $75 **MIP** $125

Dumper, 1960, Copper, 11.5Lx5.5Wx6H, whitewall tires, plastic horn on roof, Model No. 209
EX $50 **NM** $75 **MIP** $125

Bulldozer, 1960, Yellow, 11.75Lx7Wx6.75H, black tires and motor, blade tips up, Model No. 210
EX $50 **NM** $75 **MIP** $100

Camper, 1960, Teal and red, 23.25Lx4.5Wx6.5H, red and white canvas over truck bed, boat and trailer, Model No. 211
EX $50 **NM** $100 **MIP** $150

Cabin Cruiser, 1960, Red and white, 12Lx4Wx3H, plastic hull, wooden deck and cabin, battery op motor, Model No. 212
EX $50 **NM** $100 **MIP** $150

Road Grader, 1960, Yellow, 18.75Lx7.25Wx7.5H, black tires and motor, scraper blade lifts with levers, Model No. 301
EX $50 **NM** $75 **MIP** $100

Power Shovel, 1960, Yellow, 26.5Lx7Wx6.75H, black rubber tracks, Model No. 305
EX $50 **NM** $75 **MIP** $100

Livestock Truck, 1960, Red and white, 14.75Lx6Wx7.25H, white plastic stake panels and 2 plastic animals, Model No. 306
EX $50 **NM** $75 **MIP** $100

Earth Mover, 1960, Yellow, 21.5Lx6.5Wx6H, black tires and motor, Model No. 322
EX $50 **NM** $75 **MIP** $100

Timber Toter, 1960, Copper, 20.75Lx5.5Wx5.5H, plastic mirrors and horn, 5 wooden logs and chains, Model No. 323
EX $50 **NM** $75 **MIP** $100

Auto Transport, 1960, Met. green, 22Lx5.5Wx6.5H, 4 metal cars plus loading ramp, Model No. 402
EX $50 **NM** $75 **MIP** $125

Cattle Transport, 1960, Red and white, 21.25Lx5.5Wx7.5H, plastic mirrors, windshield wipers and horn, Model No. 403
EX $50 **NM** $75 **MIP** $125

Hydraulic Dumper, 1960, Met. green, 14.75Lx6.25Wx6.5H, plastic mirrors, windshield wipers and horn, Model No. 404
EX $50 **NM** $75 **MIP** $125

Machinery Hauler, 1960, Copper, 19.5Lx7.5Wx6.5H, includes #210 dozer, Model No. 509
EX $50 **NM** $75 **MIP** $125

Stock Farm Set, 1960, Red and white, 14.75Lx6Wx7.25H, stake truck with cattle loading ramp and 4 plastic horses, Model No. 510
EX $50 **NM** $100 **MIP** $150

Deluxe Camper, 1960, Gold, 27.5Lx6Wx6.5H, #207 truck plus #212 boat on trailer, Model No. 602
EX $50 **NM** $95 **MIP** $150

Pumper, 1960, White, 19.75Lx7.25Wx6H, scarce, open cab, operating water tank and hose, Model No. 603
EX $100 **NM** $150 **MIP** $225

Ready Mix Concrete Truck, 1960, Teal and white, 16Lx7.5Wx9H, axle driven gear operates barrel, Model No. 604
EX $50 **NM** $75 **MIP** $125

Ride-er Dump Truck, 1960, Blue and white, 20Lx7.75Wx10H, metal seat in dump box and bulb horn on steering wheel, Model No. 605
EX $50 **NM** $75 **MIP** $125

Mobile Crane, 1960, Copper and yellow, 19.25Lx6.25Wx7.25H, half-track with single-driver cab, Model No. 800
EX $75 **NM** $125 **MIP** $150

Power Wrecker, 1960, Blue and white, 23Lx7Wx9.25H, battery operated winch & lights, Model No. 802
EX $75 **NM** $125 **MIP** $175

Hydraulic Hook & Ladder, 1960, Red and red, 31Lx6.25Wx7.25H, open cab, two metal ladders, hydraulic lift ladder, Model No. 901
EX $75 **NM** $125 **MIP** $175

Highway Builder Set, 1960, Copper, includes #209, #210, #305 plus road barricade, Model No. 903
EX $100 **NM** $150 **MIP** $200

Transcontinental Express Fleet, 1960, Varies, 20 pc. set includes auto transport, express, steel trailer, Model No. 904
EX $125 **NM** $175 **MIP** $250

Transcontinental Express Semi, 1960, Blue and silver, 26Lx6Wx8.5H, unpainted aluminum trailer with blue decals, Model No. 905
EX $75 **NM** $100 **MIP** $175

Ride-er Fire Truck, 1960, Red and white, 25.5Lx10.5Wx12.75H, crank siren on hood, trunk opens, Model No. 925
EX $75 **NM** $125 **MIP** $175

Die-Cast Dump Truck, 1961, Varies, 7.25Lx2.5Wx2.25H, packaged on bubble pack for in-store display, Model No. 79
EX $25 **NM** $50 **MIP** $100

Rampside Pick-Up, 1961, Copper, 10.5Lx4.5Wx5H, plastic bed liner and drop-down door in side of bed, Model No. 195
EX $25 **NM** $75 **MIP** $100

Camper, 1961, Met. green, 21.5Lx4.5Wx5H, rampside truck towing boat and trailer, Model No. 202
EX $50 **NM** $75 **MIP** $125

Bulldozer, 1961, Yellow, 11Lx6.5Wx6.5H, rubber tracks, Model No. 206
EX $50 **NM** $75 **MIP** $125

Dispatch Truck, 1961, Met. green, 13Lx5.25Wx5H, similar to 1950's barrel truck, plastic mirrors, wipers & horns, Model No. 208
EX $50 **NM** $75 **MIP** $125

Road Grader, 1961, Yellow, 18.75Lx7Wx7.5H, plastic tires, Model No. 301
EX $25 **NM** $50 **MIP** $100

Wrecker, 1961, White, 12Lx5.75Wx6.5H, crank operated winch, plastic mirrors, wipers & horns, Model No. 302
EX $50 **NM** $75 **MIP** $125

Airlines Lift Truck, 1961, Copper and white, 12.5Lx5.25Wx7H, lever lifts cargo box with scissors lift mechanism, Model No. 303
EX $50 **NM** $75 **MIP** $125

Power Shovel, 1961, Yellow, 26.5Lx7.5Wx7H, rubber tracks, Model No. 305
EX $50 **NM** $75 **MIP** $100

Livestock Truck, 1961, Red and white, 14.5Lx6.25Wx7.5H, stake truck with 2 plastic animals, Model No. 306
EX $50 **NM** $75 **MIP** $125

Fire Rescue Truck, 1961, Red, 12Lx5.75Wx5.25H, plastic hose reel with braided hose, two ladders, Model No. 307
EX $50 **NM** $75 **MIP** $125

Deluxe Dump Truck, 1961, Met. green, 11.75Lx5.5Wx5.75H, lever operates dump box, Model No. 309
EX $50 **NM** $75 **MIP** $125

Timber Toter, 1961, Met. green, 23Lx5.5Wx6H, six wooden logs and chains, Model No. 406
EX $50 **NM** $75 **MIP** $125

Hydraulic Dumper, 1961, Met. green, 13.75Lx5.5Wx6.25H, hydraulic cylinder controls dump box, Model No. 407
EX $50 **NM** $75 **MIP** $125

Auto Transport, 1961, Copper, 22Lx5.5Wx7H, includes one car and one truck plus loading ramp, Model No. 502
EX $50 **NM** $75 **MIP** $125

Cattle Transport, 1961, Green and white, 23.5Lx6.5Wx8H, white trailer with green doors, Model No. 503
EX $50 **NM** $75 **MIP** $125

Deluxe Transport, 1961, Red and white, 23.5Lx6.5Wx8H, North American Vanlines decals on trailer, Model No. 504
EX $75 **NM** $100 **MIP** $175

Hydraulic Sanitation Truck, 1961, White, 18Lx6Wx8H, all white design, Model No. 606
EX $75 **NM** $100 **MIP** $175

Ride-er Wrecker Truck, 1961, Copper and white, 23.5Lx7.75Wx10.25H, metal seat and crank operated boom in box, Model No. 607
EX $75 **NM** $100 **MIP** $200

Ready-Mix Concrete Truck, 1961, Red and white, 15.5Lx7.75Wx9H, axle driven gear operates barrel, Model No. 609
EX $75 **NM** $100 **MIP** $150

Mobile Crane, 1961, Yellow, 15.5Lx6.5Wx7.25H, double cranks control crane arm and clam bucket, Model No. 700
EX $50 **NM** $100 **MIP** $175

Pumper, 1961, Red, 19.5Lx7.25Wx6.5H, operating water tank and hose, two ladders, Model No. 708
EX $50 **NM** $100 **MIP** $175

Aerial Hook & Ladder, 1961, Red, 30.75Lx6.25Wx6.25H, two metal ladders, crank operated lift ladder, Model No. 902
EX $50 **NM** $125 **MIP** $200

Highway Builder Set, 1961, Copper, includes #206, #305, #309 plus road barricade, Model No. 905
EX $100 **NM** $150 **MIP** $225

Transcontinental Express Fleet, 1961, Varies, 25 pc. set includes auto transport, express, cattle trailers, Model No. 906
EX $125 **NM** $175 **MIP** $250

Construction And Paving Set, 1961, Varies, 4 pc. set includes #309, #609, #700 plus barricade, Model No. 907
EX $100 **NM** $150 **MIP** $225

Ride-er Fire Truck, 1961, Red and white, 25.5Lx10.5Wx12.75H, crank siren on hood, trunk opens, Model No. 925
EX $75 **NM** $125 **MIP** $225

Little Miss Structo Washer/Dryer, 1962, Teal, 7.25Lx8Wx10H, washes & spins, battery operated, Model No. 16
EX $15 **NM** $25 **MIP** $75

Rampside Pick-Up, 1962, Red, 10.5Lx4.5Wx5H, plastic bed liner and drop-down door in side of bed, Model No. 195
EX $50 **NM** $75 **MIP** $125

School Bus, 1962, Yellow, 10.5Lx4.75Wx5H, steel body, plastic mirrors, wipers and horn, Model No. 196
EX $75 **NM** $100 **MIP** $150

Fisherman, 1962, Blue, 21.5Lx4.5Wx5H, rampside truck towing boat and trailer, Model No. 202
EX $50 **NM** $75 **MIP** $125

Camper, 1962, Green and yellow, 10.5Lx4.5Wx6.5H, rampside truck with plastic camper in bed of truck, Model No. 203
EX $75 **NM** $100 **MIP** $150

Hi-Lift Bulldozer, 1962, Yellow, 11.25Lx5.75Wx3.75H, rubber tracks, lever controls bucket, Model No. 207
EX $25 **NM** $50 **MIP** $100

Wrecker, 1962, White, 12Lx5.75Wx6.5H, crank operated winch, plastic mirrors, wipers & horns, Model No. 302
EX $50 **NM** $75 **MIP** $125

American Airlines Sky Chef, 1962, Blue and white, 12.5Lx5.25Wx7H, lever lifts cargo box with scissors lift mechanism, Model No. 303
EX $75 **NM** $100 **MIP** $150

Deluxe Camper, 1962, Green and yellow, 21.5Lx4.5Wx6.5H, #203 plus boat and trailer, Model No. 304
EX $75 **NM** $100 **MIP** $150

Power Shovel, 1962, Yellow, 26.5Lx7.5Wx7H, rubber tracks, Model No. 305
EX $25 **NM** $75 **MIP** $100

Fire Rescue Truck, 1962, Red, 12Lx5.75Wx5.25H, plastic hose reel with braided hose, two ladders, Model No. 307
EX $25 **NM** $75 **MIP** $100

Deluxe Dump Truck, 1962, Yellow and red, 11.75Lx5.5Wx5.75H, lever operates dump box, Model No. 309
EX $25 **NM** $75 **MIP** $100

Sportsman, 1962, Red and white, 13.25Lx5.25Wx5.5H, scarce, white plastic "Sportsman" camper top, Model No. 311
EX $75 **NM** $150 **MIP** $225

Livestock Truck, 1962, Red and white, 14.75Lx6.25Wx5.5H, white metal stake panels, Model No. 312
EX $50 **NM** $75 **MIP** $125

Road Grader, 1962, Yellow, 19Lx7.5Wx8H, covered cab, plated blade, black plastic tires, Model No. 400
EX $50 **NM** $75 **MIP** $125

Giant Bulldozer, 1962, Orange, 11.5Lx7Wx5H, levers operate blade, rubber tracks, Model No. 405
EX $50 **NM** $75 **MIP** $125

Timber Toter, 1962, Red, 23Lx5.5Wx6H, six wooden logs and chains, Model No. 406
EX $50 **NM** $75 **MIP** $125

Hydraulic Dumper, 1962, Green, 13.75Lx5.5Wx6.25H, hydraulic cylinder controls dump box, Model No. 407
EX $50 **NM** $75 **MIP** $125

Ready Mix Concrete Truck, 1962, Red and white, 15.5Lx6.75Wx7.25H, axle driven gear operates barrel, Model No. 408
EX $50 **NM** $75 **MIP** $125

Nationwide Rental Truck & Trailer, 1962, Green and yellow, 21Lx5.75Wx5.5H, scarce, same design as #311 plus tow behind trailer, Model No. 500
EX $75 **NM** $125 **MIP** $200

Dump Truck and Sandloader, 1962, Yellow and red, 21.5Lx5.5Wx8.25H, crank operated conveyer belt takes sand up to truck, Model No. 501
EX $50 **NM** $100 **MIP** $150

Auto Transport, 1962, Yellow and green, 22Lx5.5Wx7H, two metal cars, one metal truck plus loading ramp, Model No. 502
EX $75 **NM** $125 **MIP** $175

Cattle Transport, 1962, Yellow and green, 23.5Lx5.5Wx8H, green trailer with yellow doors, Model No. 503
EX $50 **NM** $75 **MIP** $125

Farm Stake Truck & Horse Trailer, 1962, Red and white, 23.25Lx6.25Wx6H, same as #312 plus tow behind trailer and 4 animals, Model No. 507
EX $75 **NM** $100 **MIP** $150

Deluxe Van Truck, 1962, Blue and white, 25.5Lx6.5Wx8.5H, structo express with rocketship on decals, Model No. 600
EX $75 **NM** $125 **MIP** $175

Hydraulic Sanitation Truck, 1962, Grey and white, 18Lx6Wx8H, with manual lift arm that dumps into body, Model No. 606
EX $75 **NM** $125 **MIP** $200

Ride-er Wrecker Truck, 1962, Red and yellow, 23.5Lx7.5Wx10.25H, metal seat and crank operated tow boom in box, Model No. 607
EX $75 **NM** $100 **MIP** $175

Grading Service Set, 1962, Yellow and red, 25Lx6Wx5.75H, same truck as in #501 set plus #207 bulldozer on trailer, Model No. 701
EX $75 **NM** $100 **MIP** $150

Pumper, 1962, Red, 19.5Lx7.25Wx6.5H, operating water tank and hose, two ladders, Model No. 708
EX $75 **NM** $100 **MIP** $175

Mobile Crane, 1962, Yellow, 15.5Lx6.5Wx7.25H, double cranks control crane arm and clam bucket, Model No. 800
EX $50 **NM** $100 **MIP** $150

Giant Bulldozer Truck & Trailer, 1962, Orange, 29Lx7.25Wx6.25H, structo construction company on decals, Model No. 850
EX $100 **NM** $150 **MIP** $200

Aerial Hook & Ladder, 1962, Red, 30.75Lx6.25Wx6.25H, two metal ladders, crank operated lift ladder, Model No. 902
EX $75 **NM** $125 **MIP** $200

Ride-er Fire Truck, 1962, Red and white, 25.5Lx10.5Wx12.75H, crank siren on hood, trunk opens, Model No. 925
EX $75 **NM** $125 **MIP** $200

Nationwide Rental Truck & Trailer Set, 1962, Green and yellow, scarce, same as #500 set plus larger open trailer, Model No. 904
EX $125 **NM** $175 **MIP** $250

Air Terminal Service Set, 1962, Red and white, includes #195, #303, #307, Model No. 908
EX $125 **NM** $150 **MIP** $225

Highway Builder Set, 1962, Varies, includes #207, #501 plus sand hopper and one barricade, Model No. 913
EX $125 **NM** $150 **MIP** $225

Farm Set, 1962, Varies, includes #507, pick-up and trailer similar to nationwide set, Model No. 914
EX $125 **NM** $150 **MIP** $225

Road Builder Set, 1962, Red and yellow, same as #913 set plus #400, Model No. 915
EX $125 **NM** $175 **MIP** $250

Paving Department, 1962, Varies, same as #913 but #408 replaces sand loader trailer, Model No. 916
EX $125 **NM** $175 **MIP** $250

Little Miss Structo Washer/Dryer, 1963, Teal, 7.25Lx8Wx10H, washes & spins, battery operated, Model No. 16
EX $15 **NM** $50 **MIP** $75

Sand Hopper, 1963, Chartreuse, 8.25Lx6Wx12H, goes with construction sets, Model No. 190
EX $15 **NM** $25 **MIP** $75

Rampside Pick-Up, 1963, Red, 10.5Lx4.5Wx5H, plastic bed liner and drop-down door in side of bed, Model No. 194
EX $50 **NM** $75 **MIP** $125

School Bus, 1963, Yellow, 10.5Lx4.75Wx5H, steel body, plastic mirrors, wipers and horn, Model No. 196
EX $75 **NM** $100 **MIP** $150

The Army Cub, 1963, Army green, 10.75Lx5Wx4.75H, windshield and tailgate raise & lower, yellow seat, no doors, Model No. 200
EX $25 **NM** $75 **MIP** $125

Camper, 1963, Teal, 10.5Lx4.5Wx6.5H, rampside truck with plastic camper in bed of truck, Model No. 203
EX $50 **NM** $100 **MIP** $175

Fisherman, 1963, Teal, 21.5Lx4.5Wx5H, rampside truck towing boat and trailer, Model No. 204
EX $50 **NM** $75 **MIP** $125

Hi-Lift Bulldozer, 1963, Chartreuse, 11.25Lx5.75Wx4H, scarce chartreuse color - only used in 1963 production year, Model No. 207
EX $50 **NM** $75 **MIP** $150

Cub Pick-Up, 1963, Lt. blue, 10.75Lx5Wx5H, white plastic convertible roof, doors open, Model No. 250
EX $50 **NM** $75 **MIP** $125

Dump Truck, 1963, Green, 11.75Lx5.5Wx5.75H, new cab - over design, plus steering wheel and seat detail, Model No. 300
EX $50 **NM** $75 **MIP** $125

Wrecker, 1963, White, 13Lx5.25Wx5.5H, door windows and interior detail, black metal boom arm, Model No. 301
EX $50 **NM** $75 **MIP** $125

Power Shovel, 1963, Chartreuse, 26.5Lx7.25Wx7H, scarce chartreuse color - only used in 1963 production year, Model No. 305
EX $50 **NM** $75 **MIP** $150

Fire Rescue Truck, 1963, Red, 12Lx5.75Wx5.25H, plastic hose reel with braided hose, two ladders, Model No. 307
EX $50 **NM** $75 **MIP** $150

Pick-Up Truck, 1963, Red, 13.25Lx5.25Wx5.5H, Model No. 311
EX $50 **NM** $75 **MIP** $125

Livetstock Truck, 1963, Blue and white, 14.75Lx6.25Wx5.5H, white metal stake panels, Model No. 314
EX $50 **NM** $75 **MIP** $125

Cub Station Wagon, 1963, Teal and white, 10.75Lx5Wx5H, same body as #250 but white plastic roof cover whole body, Model No. 325
EX $50 **NM** $75 **MIP** $125

The Cub Set, 1963, Teal and white, 10.75Lx5Wx5H, converts to three variations with #250 and #325 roofs, Model No. 350
EX $50 **NM** $75 **MIP** $125

Road Grader, 1963, Chartreuse, 19Lx7.5Wx8H, scarce chartreuse color - only used in 1963 production year, Model No. 400
EX $50 **NM** $75 **MIP** $150

(Randy Prasse Photo)

Hydraulic Dumper, 1963, Red, 13.75Lx5.5Wx6.25H, hydraulic cylinder controls dump box, Model No. 401
EX $50 **NM** $75 **MIP** $125

Auto Transport, 1963, Met. gold, 22Lx5.5Wx7H, one metal car, one metal truck plus loading ramp, Model No. 402
EX $50 **NM** $75 **MIP** $125

Cub Station Wagon & Horse Trailer, 1963, Teal and white, 20.5Lx5.25Wx6H, same as #190 plus 2 wheel horse trailer and 2 horses, Model No. 403
EX $75 **NM** $100 **MIP** $175

Deluxe Camper, 1963, Blue and white, 20Lx5Wx5H, same as #190 plus boat and trailer, Model No. 404
EX $50 **NM** $75 **MIP** $150

Giant Bulldozer, 1963, Chartreuse, 11.5Lx7Wx5H, scarce chartreuse color - only used in 1963 production year, Model No. 405
EX $50 **NM** $75 **MIP** $125

Timber Toter, 1963, Red, 23Lx5.5Wx6H, six wooden logs and chains, Model No. 406
EX $50 **NM** $75 **MIP** $125

Ready-Mix Concrete Truck, 1963, Green and chartreuse, 15.5Lx6.75Wx7.25H, axle driven gear operates barrel, Model No. 408
EX $50 **NM** $75 **MIP** $125

Dump Truck and Sandloader, 1963, Green and chartreuse, 21.5Lx5.5Wx8.25H, crank operated conveyer belt takes sand up to truck, Model No. 409
EX $75 **NM** $100 **MIP** $150

Nationwide Rental Truck & Trailer, 1963, Green and yellow, 21Lx5.75Wx5.5H, scarce, same design as #311 plus tow behind trailer, Model No. 500
EX $75 **NM** $125 **MIP** $200

Cattle Transport, 1963, Red and red, 22.25Lx6.5Wx8H, new cab - over design, plus steering wheel and seat detail, Model No. 503
EX $50 **NM** $75 **MIP** $125

Deluxe Van Truck, 1963, Red and white, 25.5Lx6.5Wx8.5H, white trailer with red doors, Model No. 601
EX $75 **NM** $100 **MIP** $150

(ToyShop File Photo)

Hydraulic Sanitation Truck, 1963, Blue and white, 18Lx6Wx8H, with manual lift arm that dumps into body, Model No. 602
EX $75 **NM** $100 **MIP** $150

Hydraulic Trailer Dump, 1963, Chartreuse, 20.75Lx6.25Wx5.75H, scarce chartreuse color - only used in 1963 production year, Model No. 603
EX $75 **NM** $100 **MIP** $150

Ride-er Dump Truck, 1963, Red and white, 20Lx7.75Wx10.25H, metal seat in dump box, Model No. 605
EX $75 **NM** $100 **MIP** $175

Mobile Crane, 1963, Chartreuse, 15.5Lx6.5Wx7.25H, scarce chartreuse color - only used in 1963 production year, Model No. 801
EX $75 **NM** $100 **MIP** $175

Aerial Hook & Ladder, 1963, Red and red, 30.75Lx6.25Wx6.25H, two metal ladders, crank operated lift ladder, Model No. 902
EX $75 **NM** $100 **MIP** $175

Nationwide Rental Truck & Trailer Set, 1963, Green and yellow, scarce, same as #500 set plus larger open trailer, Model No. 904
EX $125 **NM** $175 **MIP** $250

Highway Builder Set, 1963, Varies, includes #190 and #409, Model No. 913
EX $125 **NM** $150 **MIP** $225

Farm Set, 1963, Teal and white, includes #314 with trailer and #403, Model No. 914
EX $125 **NM** $150 **MIP** $225

Army Engineer's Set, 1963, Army green, includes #190, #400, #409, all in army green, Model No. 915
EX $125 **NM** $175 **MIP** $250

Paving Department, 1963, Varies, includes #190, #305, #400, #401, #408, Model No. 916
EX $125 **NM** $175 **MIP** $250

Ride-er Doodle Bug, 1963, Yellow, 25.5Lx10.25Wx12.75H, same as ride-er fire truck from 1962, Model No. 925
EX $100 **NM** $125 **MIP** $200

Pickup, 1964, Red and yellow, 8.75Lx3.5Wx3.5H, metal with rubber tires, Model No. 100
EX $15 **NM** $25 **MIP** $50

Fire Rescue Truck, 1964, Red, 8.75Lx3.5Wx3.5H, 2 plastic ladders, Model No. 105
EX $25 **NM** $50 **MIP** $75

Wrecker Truck, 1964, White and grey, 9.25Lx3.5Wx3.5H, with metal tow boom and hook, Model No. 110
EX $15 **NM** $25 **MIP** $50

Vista Dome Army Truck, 1964, Army green, 8.75Lx3.5Wx4H, clear plastic cover over bed, 2 plastic soldiers, Model No. 115
EX $15 **NM** $25 **MIP** $50

Vista Dome Livestock Truck, 1964, Blue and yellow, 8.75Lx3.5Wx4H, clear plastic cover over bed, 2 plastic animals, Model No. 120
EX $25 **NM** $50 **MIP** $75

Automatic Dump Truck, 1964, Copper, 8.75Lx3.5Wx4H, spring dump mechanism, Model No. 125
EX $15 **NM** $25 **MIP** $50

Vista Dome Kennel Truck, 1964, Teal and yellow, 8.75Lx3.5Wx4H, clear plastic cover over bed, 6 plastic dogs, Model No. 130
EX $15 **NM** $25 **MIP** $50

Rampside Pick-Up, 1964, Copper, 10.5Lx4.5Wx5H, plastic bed liner and drop-down door in side of bed, Model No. 194
EX $50 **NM** $75 **MIP** $125

The Army Cub, 1964, Army green, 10.75Lx5Wx4.75H, tailgate and windshield raises and lowers, Model No. 200
EX $25 **NM** $50 **MIP** $100

Camper, 1964, Teal and teal, 10.5Lx4.5Wx6.5H, plastic camper in truck bed, Model No. 203
EX $50 **NM** $75 **MIP** $100

Fisherman, 1964, Teal and red, 20Lx4.5Wx6H, rampside pick-up towing plastic boat on trailer, Model No. 204
EX $50 **NM** $75 **MIP** $125

Hi-Lift Bulldozer, 1964, Yellow and black, 11.25Lx5.75Wx4H, metal levers operate the bucket, Model No. 207
EX $25 **NM** $50 **MIP** $75

Cub Pick-Up, 1964, Blue and white, 20.75Lx5Wx6H, white plastic convertible roof covers cab, doors open, Model No. 250
EX $25 **NM** $50 **MIP** $75

Dump Truck, 1964, Green, 11.75Lx5.5Wx5.75H, cab-over design, plus steering wheel and seat detail, Model No. 300
EX $25 **NM** $75 **MIP** $100

Wrecker, 1964, White and black, 13.25Lx5.25Wx5.5H, door windows and interior detail, black metal boom arm, Model No. 301
EX $50 **NM** $75 **MIP** $125

Power Shovel, 1964, Yellow, 26.5Lx7.25Wx7H, rubber tracks, 2 cranks operate boom and bucket, Model No. 305
EX $25 **NM** $75 **MIP** $125

Fire Rescue Truck, 1964, Red, 12Lx5.75Wx5.25H, plastic hose reel with braided hose, two ladders, Model No. 307
EX $50 **NM** $75 **MIP** $125

Pick-Up Truck, 1964, Red, 13.25Lx5.25Wx5.5H, plastic window, yellow interior, whitewall tires, Model No. 311
EX $50 **NM** $75 **MIP** $125

Livestock Truck, 1964, Blue and white, 14.75Lx6.25Wx5.5H, white metal stake panels, 2 plastic cows, Model No. 314
EX $50 **NM** $75 **MIP** $125

Vista Dome Troop Carrier, 1964, Army green, 13.25Lx5.25Wx5.5H, clear plastic cover over bed, 8 plastic soldiers, Model No. 315
EX $50 **NM** $75 **MIP** $125

Cub Station Wagon, 1964, Teal and white, 10.75Lx5Wx5H, white plastic convertible roof cover body, doors open, Model No. 325
EX $25 **NM** $50 **MIP** $100

The Cub Set, 1964, Teal and white, 10.75Lx5Wx5H, converts to three variations with #250 and #325 roofs, Model No. 350
EX $50 **NM** $75 **MIP** $125

Road Grader, 1964, Orange, 19Lx7.5Wx8.25H, plated scraper blade, black plastic wheels & engine, Model No. 400
EX $50 **NM** $75 **MIP** $100

Hydraulic Dumper, 1964, Copper, 13.75Lx5.5Wx6.25H, hydraulic cylinder controls dump box, Model No. 401
EX $25 **NM** $50 **MIP** $75

Auto Transport, 1964, Red and yellow, 22Lx5.5Wx7H, includes 1 metal car and 1 metal truck & loading ramp, Model No. 402
EX $50 **NM** $75 **MIP** $125

Cub Station Wagon With Horse Trailer, 1964, Teal and white, 20.5Lx5.25Wx6H, #325 cub station wagon & trailer, 2 plastic horses, Model No. 403
EX $50 **NM** $75 **MIP** $125

Station Wagon With Boat & Trailer, 1964, Blue and red, 20Lx5Wx5H, cub station wagon (#325) towing plastic boat on trailer, Model No. 404
EX $50 **NM** $75 **MIP** $100

Giant Bulldozer, 1964, Orange and black, 11.5Lx7Wx5H, blade raises and lowers with lever controls, Model No. 405
EX $50 **NM** $75 **MIP** $100

Ready-Mix Concrete Truck, 1964, Red and yellow, 15.5Lx6.75Wx7.25H, axle driven gear operates barrel, Model No. 408
EX $25 **NM** $50 **MIP** $100

U.S. Army Missile Launcher, 1964, Army green, 17.25Lx6.5Wx7H, missile launcher on back, 3 missiles, 2 outriggers, Model No. 410
EX $50 **NM** $75 **MIP** $125

Army Engineers Dump & Sand Loader, 1964, Army green, 21.5Lx5.5Wx8.25H, includes 4 plastic soldiers, Model No. 411
EX $50 **NM** $75 **MIP** $125

Vista Dome Horse Van, 1964, Met. gold, 21.75Lx5.5Wx6H, ramp on side and back of trailer, 4 plastic horses, Model No. 412
EX $50 **NM** $75 **MIP** $125

Cattle Transport, 1964, Red and red, 22.25Lx6.5Wx8H, Model No. 503
EX $50 **NM** $75 **MIP** $100

Deluxe Van Truck, 1964, Red and white, 25.5Lx6.5Wx8.5H, white trailer with red doors, Model No. 601
EX $50 **NM** $100 **MIP** $150

Hydraulic Sanitation Truck, 1964, Grey and white, 18Lx6Wx8H, with manual lift arm that dumps into body, Model No. 602
EX $75 **NM** $100 **MIP** $150

Hydraulic Trailer Dump Truck, 1964, Grey and orange, 20.75Lx6.25Wx5.75H, also available as "Scotch-O-Lass" private label-add $50, Model No. 603
EX $50 **NM** $75 **MIP** $125

Ride-er Dump Truck, 1964, Red and white, 20Lx7Wx10.25H, metal seat in dump box, Model No. 605
EX $75 **NM** $125 **MIP** $175

Mobile Crane, 1964, Orange, 15.5Lx6.5Wx7.25H, cranks control the boom and clam bucket, swivels, Model No. 801
EX $75 **NM** $100 **MIP** $150

Aerial Hook & Ladder, 1964, Red and red, 30.75Lx6.25Wx6.25H, two metal ladders, crank operated lift ladder, Model No. 902
EX $50 **NM** $100 **MIP** $150

Highway Builder Set, 1964, Varies, includes #207, #300, sand hopper, sand loader & barricade, Model No. 913
EX $100 **NM** $150 **MIP** $200

Farm Set, 1964, Teal and white, 5 pc. set includes #314 & trailer, #250 cub pick-up & trailer, Model No. 914
EX $100 **NM** $150 **MIP** $200

U.S. Army Combat Set, 1964, Army green, includes #315 & searchlight, #410, 8 plastic soldiers, Model No. 920
EX $100 **NM** $175 **MIP** $250

Ride-er Doodle Bug, 1964, Yellow, 25.5Lx10.25Wx12.75H, Model No. 925
EX $75 **NM** $125 **MIP** $175

Pick-Up Truck, 1965, Teal and white, 8.75Lx3.5Wx3.5H, metal with rubber tires, Model No. 100
EX $15 **NM** $25 **MIP** $75

Fire Rescue Truck, 1965, Red, 8.75Lx3.5Wx3.5H, 2 plastic ladders, Model No. 105
EX $25 **NM** $50 **MIP** $100

Wrecker Truck, 1965, Red and white, 9.25Lx3.5Wx3.5H, with metal tow boom and hook, Model No. 110
EX $25 **NM** $50 **MIP** $100

Vista Dome Army Truck, 1965, Army green, 8.75Lx3.5Wx4H, clear plastic cover over bed, 2 plastic soldiers, Model No. 115
EX $25 **NM** $50 **MIP** $100

Automatic Dump Truck, 1965, Green and yellow, 8.75Lx3.5Wx4H, spring dump mechanism, Model No. 125
EX $25 **NM** $50 **MIP** $75

Vista Dome Kennel Truck, 1965, Blue and white, 8.75Lx3.5Wx4H, clear plastic cover over bed, 6 plastic dogs, Model No. 130
EX $25 **NM** $50 **MIP** $75

Cement Mixer, 1965, Red and white, 8.75Lx3.5Wx5H, axle driven gear operates barrel, Model No. 136
EX $25 **NM** $50 **MIP** $75

Road Grader, 1965, Orange and black, 11.75Lx4Wx4H, new z-z-z sound when unit rolls, no batteries, Model No. 140
EX $25 **NM** $50 **MIP** $75

Van Truck, 1965, Red and white, 16.5Lx4Wx5H, red structo van line decals on side, Model No. 145
EX $25 **NM** $50 **MIP** $75

Cattle Truck, 1965, Green and white, 16.5Lx4Wx5H, white plastic insert panels in side of trailer, Model No. 150
EX $25 **NM** $50 **MIP** $75

Kompak Assortment, 1965, Varies, 3 pc. set includes #100, #105, #110, Model No. 170
EX $50 **NM** $100 **MIP** $150

Contractor Set, 1965, Varies, 3 pc. set includes #125, #136, #140, Model No. 180
EX $50 **NM** $100 **MIP** $150

Rampside Pick-Up, 1965, Copper, 10.5Lx4.5Wx5H, plastic bed liner and drop-down door in side of bed, Model No. 194
EX $25 **NM** $50 **MIP** $100

The Army Cub, 1965, Army green, 10.75Lx5Wx4.75H, tailgate and windshield raises and lowers, Model No. 200
EX $25 **NM** $50 **MIP** $100

Camper, 1965, Teal and white, 10.5Lx4.5Wx6.5H, plastic camper in truck bed, Model No. 203
EX $25 **NM** $50 **MIP** $100

Fisherman, 1965, Teal and red, 20Lx4.5Wx5H, rampside pick-up towing plastic boat on trailer, Model No. 204
EX $25 **NM** $50 **MIP** $100

Hi-Lift Bulldozer, 1965, Yellow and black, 11.25Lx5.75Wx4H, metal levers operate the bucket, Model No. 207
EX $25 **NM** $50 **MIP** $100

Cub Pick-Up, 1965, Blue and white, 20.75Lx5Wx6H, white plastic convertible roof covers cab, doors open, Model No. 250
EX $25 **NM** $50 **MIP** $100

Wrecker Truck, 1965, White and red, 10.75Lx4.75Wx5.75H, red convertible roof, seats and metal boom arm, Model No. 251
EX $50 **NM** $75 **MIP** $100

Riding Academy, 1965, Teal and teal, 20Lx4.75Wx6H, #250 cub pick-up plus horse trailer, 2 plastic horses, Model No. 252
EX $50 **NM** $75 **MIP** $125

Dump Truck, 1965, Met. green, 11.75Lx5.5Wx5.75H, cab - over design, plus steering wheel and seat detail, Model No. 300
EX $25 **NM** $50 **MIP** $100

Wrecker Truck, 1965, White and red, 12.5Lx5.25Wx6.25H, red light on roof (non operable), red metal boom arm, Model No. 302
EX $50 **NM** $75 **MIP** $100

Camper With Boat & Trailer, 1965, Teal and red, 20Lx4.5Wx6.5H, #203 with plastic boat on trailer, Model No. 304
EX $50 **NM** $75 **MIP** $150

Power Shovel, 1965, Orange, 26.5Lx7.25Wx7H, rubber tracks, 2 cranks operate boom and bucket, Model No. 305
EX $25 **NM** $50 **MIP** $100

Fire Rescue Truck, 1965, Red, 13.25Lx5.75Wx5.75H, red light on roof (non-operable), 2 metal ladders, Model No. 308
EX $50 **NM** $75 **MIP** $125

Livestock Truck, 1965, Blue and white, 14.75Lx6.25Wx5.5H, white stakes, 5 pc. plastic fence, 4 animals, Model No. 310
EX $50 **NM** $75 **MIP** $125

Vista Dome Troop Carrier, 1965, Army green, 13.25Lx5.25Wx5.75H, clear plastic cover over bed, 8 plastic soldiers, Model No. 315
EX $50 **NM** $75 **MIP** $125

Cub Station Wagon, 1965, Teal and white, 10.75Lx5Wx5H, white plastic convertible roof cover body, doors open, Model No. 325
EX $50 **NM** $75 **MIP** $100

Road Grader, 1965, Orange, 19Lx7.5Wx8.25H, plated scraper blade, black plastic wheels & engine, Model No. 400
EX $50 **NM** $75 **MIP** $100

Hydraulic Dump Truck, 1965, Red, 14Lx5.5Wx6.25H, hydraulic cylinder controls dump box, Model No. 401
EX $25 **NM** $50 **MIP** $100

Station Wagon With Boat & Trailer, 1965, Blue and red, 20Lx5Wx5H, cub station wagon (#325) towing plastic boat on trailer, Model No. 404
EX $25 **NM** $50 **MIP** $100

Giant Bulldozer, 1965, Orange and black, 11.5Lx7Wx5H, blade raises and lowers with lever controls, Model No. 405
EX $50 **NM** $75 **MIP** $100

Timber Toter, 1965, Red and red, 23Lx6Wx5H, 5 wooden logs plus chains, Model No. 406
EX $50 **NM** $75 **MIP** $125

U.S. Army Missile Launcher, 1965, Army green, 17.25Lx6.5Wx7H, missile launcher on back, 3 missiles, 2 outriggers, Model No. 410
EX $50 **NM** $75 **MIP** $125

Vista Dome Horse Van, 1965, Teal and teal, 21.75Lx5.5Wx6H, ramp on side and back of trailer, 4 pc. fence, 4 plastic horses, Model No. 412
EX $50 **NM** $75 **MIP** $125

Car Carrier, 1965, Teal and teal, 22Lx6Wx7H, new, 2 plastic cars (T-Birds) and loading ramp, Model No. 413
EX $50 **NM** $75 **MIP** $125

Hydraulic Dump Truck, 1965, Grey and orange, 14Lx5.5Wx6.25H, hydraulic cylinder controls dump box, Model No. 425
EX $50 **NM** $75 **MIP** $100

Cement Mixer, 1965, Grey and orange, 14Lx6.75Wx5.25H, axle driven gear operates barrel, Model No. 450
EX $50 **NM** $75 **MIP** $100

Livestock Set, 1965, Teal and white, 22.25Lx6.5Wx8H, white insert panels in side of trailer, 5 pc. fence & 4 animals, Model No. 505
EX $50 **NM** $75 **MIP** $125

Van Truck, 1965, Red and white, 22Lx6.5Wx8H, red structo van line decals on side, Model No. 506
EX $50 **NM** $75 **MIP** $100

Deluxe Van Truck, 1965, Red and white, 25.5Lx6Wx8.75H, white trailer with red doors, Model No. 601
EX $50 **NM** $75 **MIP** $125

Hydraulic Trailer Dump Truck, 1965, Grey and orange, 20.75Lx5.75Wx5.75H, also available as "Scotch-O-Lass" private label - add $50, Model No. 603
EX $50 **NM** $75 **MIP** $125

Hydraulic Sanitation Truck, 1965, Grey and white, 18Lx6Wx8H, with manual lift arm that dumps into body, Model No. 604
EX $50 **NM** $75 **MIP** $150

Ride-er Dump Truck, 1965, Teal and white, 20Lx7Wx10.25H, metal seat in dump box, Model No. 605
EX $75 **NM** $100 **MIP** $175

Weekender, 1965, Teal and white, 12Lx5.75Wx7H, canvas awning, white plastic interior, Model No. 700
EX $50 **NM** $75 **MIP** $150

U.S. Mail Van, 1965, White and blue, 12Lx5.75Wx6.5H, includes 2 plastic mail bags, Model No. 710
EX $50 **NM** $100 **MIP** $150

Mobile Crane, 1965, Orange, 16.5Lx5.5Wx7H, cranks control the boom and clam bucket, swivels, Model No. 801
EX $75 **NM** $100 **MIP** $150

Aerial Hook & Ladder, 1965, Red and red, 30.75Lx6.25Wx6.25H, two metal ladders, crank operated lift ladder, Model No. 900
EX $50 **NM** $100 **MIP** $175

Highway Builder Set, 1965, Varies, includes #207, #300, sand hopper, sand loader & barricade, Model No. 913
EX $100 **NM** $150 **MIP** $200

Highway Builder Set Showcase Display, 1965, Rare, boxed set for dealer trade show & store display, Model No. 9130
EX n/a **NM** n/a **MIP** $300

Farm Set, 1965, Teal and white, 5 pc. set includes #310 & trailer, #250 cub pick-up & trailer, Model No. 914
EX $100 **NM** $150 **MIP** $225

Farm Set Showcase Display, 1965, Rare, boxed set for dealer trade show & store display, Model No. 9140
EX n/a **NM** n/a **MIP** $300

U.S. Army Combat Set, 1965, Army green, includes #315 & searchlight, #410, 8 plastic soldiers, Model No. 920
EX $125 **NM** $150 **MIP** $250

U.S. Army Combat Set Showcase Display, 1965, Rare, boxed set for dealer trade show & store display, Model No. 9201
EX n/a **NM** n/a **MIP** $300

Ride-er Doodle Bug, 1965, Teal and white, 25.5Lx10.25Wx12.75H, Model No. 925
EX $75 **NM** $125 **MIP** $175

Pickup Truck, 1966, Teal, 8.75Lx3.5Wx3.5H, Kom-pak design, Model No. 100
EX $15 **NM** $25 **MIP** $50

Fire Rescue Truck, 1966, Red, 8.75Lx3.5Wx3.5H, Kom-pak design with 2 ladders, Model No. 105
EX $25 **NM** $50 **MIP** $75

Wrecker Truck, 1966, Yellow and red, 9.25Lx3.5Wx3.5H, Kom-pak design with red boom arm, Model No. 110
EX $15 **NM** $25 **MIP** $50

Army Troop Carrier, 1966, Army green, 8.75Lx3.5Wx4H, Kom-pak design with clear plastic cover $2 soldiers, Model No. 115
EX $15 **NM** $25 **MIP** $50

All Steel Dump Truck, 1966, Grey and orange, 8.75Lx3.5Wx4H, Kom-pak design, Model No. 125
EX $15 **NM** $25 **MIP** $50

Kennel Truck, 1966, Teal and white, 8.75Lx3.5Wx4H, Kom-pak design with clear cover and 6 dogs, Model No. 130
EX $15 **NM** $25 **MIP** $50

Cement Mixer, 1966, Grey and orange, 9.75Lx4Wx4.5H, Kom-pak design with dumping barrel, Model No. 136
EX $15 **NM** $25 **MIP** $50

Road Grader, 1966, Orange, 11.75Lx5Wx4.75H, Kom-pak design, Model No. 140
EX $15 **NM** $25 **MIP** $50

Van Truck, 1966, Red and white, 16.5Lx4Wx5.25H, Kom-pak design, Model No. 145
EX $25 **NM** $50 **MIP** $75

Cattle Truck, 1966, Teal and white, 16.5Lx4Wx5.25H, Kom-pak design white insert panels in side of trailer, Model No. 150
EX $25 **NM** $50 **MIP** $75

Contractor Set, 1966, Grey and orange, 3 pc. Kom-pak set includes #125, #136, #140, Model No. 180
EX $50 **NM** $100 **MIP** $150

Rampside Pick-Up, 1966, Red, 10.5Lx4.5Wx5H, plastic bed liner and drop-down door in side of bed, Model No. 194
EX $25 **NM** $50 **MIP** $75

The Army Cub, 1966, Army green, 10.75Lx5Wx4.75H, tailgate and windshield raises and lowers, Model No. 200
EX $25 **NM** $50 **MIP** $75

Camper, 1966, Lt. blue and white, 10.5Lx4.5Wx6.5H, plastic camper in truck bed, Model No. 203
EX $25 **NM** $50 **MIP** $75

Fisherman, 1966, Lt. blue and red, 20Lx4.5Wx5H, rampside pick-up towing plastic boat on trailer, Model No. 204
EX $25 **NM** $75 **MIP** $125

Hi-Lift Bulldozer, 1966, Orange and black, 11.25Lx5.75Wx4H, metal levers operate the bucket, Model No. 207
EX $25 **NM** $50 **MIP** $75

Wrecker Truck, 1966, White and black, 10.75Lx4.75Wx5.75H, black convertible roof and boom, red seat, Model No. 251
EX $50 **NM** $75 **MIP** $100

Riding Academy, 1966, Teal and teal, 18Lx4.75Wx6H, #194 rampside pick-up plus horse trailer, 2 plastic horses, Model No. 254
EX $50 **NM** $75 **MIP** $125

Dump Truck, 1966, Red, 11.75Lx5.5Wx5.75H, spring dump mechanism, Model No. 300
EX $25 **NM** $50 **MIP** $75

Power Shovel, 1966, Orange, 26.5Lx7.25Wx7H, rubber tracks, 2 cranks operate boom and bucket, Model No. 305
EX $25 **NM** $50 **MIP** $75

Livestock Truck Set, 1966, Teal and white, 14.75Lx6.25Wx5.5H, white stakes, 5 pc. plastic fence, 2 plastic cows, Model No. 310
EX $25 **NM** $75 **MIP** $125

Wrecker, 1966, White and red, 12.5Lx5.25Wx6.25H, red light on roof (non-operable), red interior & boom, Model No. 312
EX $50 **NM** $75 **MIP** $125

Fire Rescue Truck, 1966, Red, 12.75Lx5.75Wx5.75H, red light on roof (non-operable) 3 ladders , sim. hose reel, Model No. 313
EX $50 **NM** $75 **MIP** $125

Vista Dome Troop Carrier, 1966, Army green, 13.25Lx5.25Wx5.75H, clear plastic cover over bed, 6 plastic soldiers, Model No. 315
EX $50 **NM** $75 **MIP** $125

Dump Truck, 1966, Green and yellow, 13.5Lx5.5Wx5.75H, lever action dump box, Model No. 316
EX $25 **NM** $50 **MIP** $75

Station Wagon, 1966, Teal and white, 10.75Lx5Wx5H, white plastic convertible roof cover body, doors open, Model No. 325
EX $25 **NM** $50 **MIP** $75

Road Grader, 1966, Orange, 19Lx7.5Wx8.25H, plated scraper blade, black plastic wheels & engine, Model No. 400
EX $25 **NM** $50 **MIP** $75

Giant Bulldozer, 1966, Orange and black, 11.5Lx7Wx5H, blade raises and lowers with lever controls, Model No. 405
EX $50 **NM** $75 **MIP** $100

Timber Toter, 1966, Red and red, 23Lx6Wx5H, 6 wooden logs & chains, Model No. 406
EX $50 **NM** $75 **MIP** $125

Vista Dome Horse Van, 1966, Met. blue and met. blue, 21.75Lx6Wx6H, 2 ramp doors and 2 horses, 2 colts, Model No. 417
EX $50 **NM** $75 **MIP** $125

Car Carrier, 1966, Grey and yellow, 22.25Lx6Wx7H, 3 plastic cars (Mustangs & T-Birds) loading ramp, Model No. 418
EX $50 **NM** $75 **MIP** $125

(ToyShop File Photo)

Hydraulic Dump Truck, 1966, Met. blue, 13.75Lx5.5Wx6.25H, same body style as #316 but with hydraulic dump control, Model No. 419
EX $25 **NM** $50 **MIP** $75

Hydraulic Dump Truck, 1966, Grey and orange, 13.75Lx5.5Wx6.25H, hydraulic cylinder dumps box, POW-R-R-R sound, Model No. 425
EX $50 **NM** $75 **MIP** $100

Cement Mixer, 1966, Grey and orange, 15.5Lx6.75Wx5.25H, axle driven gear operates barrel, POW-R-R-R sound, Model No. 450
EX $50 **NM** $75 **MIP** $100

Bulldozer & Earth Mover, 1966, Green and yellow, 25.5Lx7.5Wx7H, combination bulldozer towing bottom dump earth mover unit, Model No. 460
EX $50 **NM** $75 **MIP** $100

Bulldozer & Scraper, 1966, Green and yellow, 25.5Lx7.5Wx7H, combination bulldozer towing scraper unit, Model No. 461
EX $50 **NM** $75 **MIP** $100

Livestock Van, 1966, Teal and white, 22.25Lx6.5Wx8H, white insert panels in side of trailer, 5 pc. fence & 4 animals, Model No. 505
EX $50 **NM** $75 **MIP** $100

Van Truck, 1966, Dk. blue and lt. blue, 22Lx6.5Wx8H, scarce 2 tone blue color combination, Model No. 506
EX $50 **NM** $75 **MIP** $100

Hydraulic Sanitation Truck, 1966, Grey and white, 18Lx6Wx8H, manual lift bucket dumps into body, POW-R-R-R sound, Model No. 604
EX $50 **NM** $75 **MIP** $100

Ride-er Dump Truck, 1966, White and green, 20Lx7Wx10.25H, metal seat in dump box, Model No. 605
EX $50 **NM** $75 **MIP** $125

Deluxe Van Truck, 1966, Red and silver, 24Lx6Wx8.75H, unpainted steel trailer with "Structo Freught Lines" decal, Model No. 609
EX $50 **NM** $75 **MIP** $125

Hydraulic Trailer Dump Truck, 1966, Grey and orange, 21.5Lx5.75Wx5.75H, turbine cab, hydraulic controlled dump, Model No. 610
EX $50 **NM** $75 **MIP** $125

Weekender, 1966, Teal and white, 12Lx5.75Wx7H, canvas awning, white plastic interior, Model No. 700
EX $50 **NM** $75 **MIP** $125

U.S. Mail Van, 1966, Blue and white, 12Lx5.75Wx6.5H, includes 2 cloth mail bags, Model No. 710
EX $50 **NM** $100 **MIP** $150

Ice Cream Truck, 1966, White and teal, 12Lx6Wx6.5H, scarce, bell rings as truck moves, built-in coolers & detail, Model No. 712
EX $50 **NM** $125 **MIP** $175

Police Emergency Truck, 1966, Blue and white, 12Lx6Wx7.5H, bell rings as truck moves, 3 ladders, hose reel, Model No. 716
EX $50 **NM** $100 **MIP** $150

Mobile Crane, 1966, Orange, 16.5Lx5.5Wx7H, cranks control the boom and clam bucket, swivels, Model No. 801
EX $75 **NM** $100 **MIP** $150

Aerial Hook & Ladder, 1966, Red and white, 29.25Lx6.25Wx6.25H, two metal ladders, crank operated lift ladder, Model No. 901
EX $50 **NM** $75 **MIP** $125

Highway Builder Set, 1966, Green and yellow, 4 pc. set, includes #207, #316, sand hopper & sand loader, Model No. 910
EX $100 **NM** $125 **MIP** $175

Display For Highway Set, 1966, Rare, boxed set for dealer trade show & store display, Model No. 9101
EX n/a **NM** n/a **MIP** $300

Ride-er Chief's Car, 1966, Red and white, 25.5Lx10.25Wx12.75H, bell rings when string is pulled, Model No. 921
EX $75 **NM** $100 **MIP** $175

Farm Set, 1966, Green and yellow, 5 pc. set includes #194 & trailer, #310 & trailer, 4 animals, Model No. 937
EX $100 **NM** $125 **MIP** $175

Display For Farm Set, 1966, Rare, boxed set for dealer trade show & store display, Model No. 9371
EX n/a **NM** n/a **MIP** $300

State Fair Set, 1966, Met. blue, 4 pc. set includes #203, #310, #417, 6 animals, Model No. 952
EX $100 **NM** $150 **MIP** $175

Display For State Fair Set, 1966, Rare, boxed set for dealer trade show & store display, Model No. 9521
EX n/a **NM** n/a **MIP** $300

Pickup, 1967, Green, 8.75Lx3.5Wx3.5H, Kom-pak design, Model No. 101
EX $15 **NM** $25 **MIP** $50

Wrecker Truck, 1967, White and grey, 9.25Lx3.5Wx3.5H, Kom-pak design with red boom arm, Model No. 112
EX $15 **NM** $25 **MIP** $50

Fire Rescue Truck, 1967, Red, 8.75Lx3.5Wx3.5H, Kom-pak design with 2 ladders, Model No. 121
EX $15 **NM** $25 **MIP** $50

Green Beret Truck, 1967, Green, 8.75Lx3.5Wx4H, Kom-pak design with clear plastic cover $2 soldiers, Model No. 126
EX $25 **NM** $50 **MIP** $75

Kennel Truck, 1967, Yellow, 8.75Lx3.5Wx4H, Kom-pak design with clear cover and 6 dogs, Model No. 137
EX $15 **NM** $25 **MIP** $50

Steel Dump Truck, 1967, Grey and orange, 8.75Lx3.5Wx4H, Kom-pak design, Model No. 141
EX $15 **NM** $25 **MIP** $50

Cement Mixer, 1967, Grey and orange, 9.75Lx4Wx4.5H, Kom-pak design with dumping barrel, Model No. 153
EX $15 **NM** $25 **MIP** $50

Tractor Trailer Truck, 1967, Red and silver, 16.5Lx4Wx5.25H, Kom-pak design, no decals on trailer, Model No. 160
EX $25 **NM** $50 **MIP** $75

Mobile Merry-Go-Round Truck, 1967, Yellow and red, 9.25Lx4.25Wx5.75H, scarce, Kom-pak design, circus carousel spins when truck moves, Model No. 174
EX $50 **NM** $100 **MIP** $150

Kenya Karryall, 1967, Green and yellow, 9.25Lx4.25Wx4.25H, scarce, Kom-pak design, 4 cages with 4 hand-painted wild animals, Model No. 176
EX $50 **NM** $100 **MIP** $150

Sanitation Truck, 1967, Grey and white, 11.5Lx3.5Wx5H, Kom-pak design, bucket dumps into body, Model No. 178
EX $25 **NM** $50 **MIP** $75

Road Grader, 1967, Orange, 11.75Lx5Wx4.75H, Kom-pak design, Model No. 183
EX $15 **NM** $25 **MIP** $50

Contractor Set, 1967, Grey and orange, 3 pc. set includes #141, #153, #183, Model No. 192
EX $50 **NM** $75 **MIP** $125

Highway Department Set, 1967, Red and yellow, 4 pc. set includes emergency, dump, wrecker & pickup trucks, Model No. 197
EX $75 **NM** $100 **MIP** $150

Wrecker Truck, 1967, White and black, 10.75Lx4.75Wx5.75H, black convertible roof and boom, red seat, Model No. 205
EX $50 **NM** $75 **MIP** $100

Fisherman, 1967, White and red, 20Lx5Wx4.75H, jeep towing plastic boat & trailer, no doors on jeep, Model No. 210
EX $50 **NM** $75 **MIP** $100

Rampside Pick-Up, 1967, Red, 10.5Lx4.5Wx5H, plastic bed liner and drop-down door in side of bed, Model No. 230
EX $15 **NM** $25 **MIP** $50

Camper Truck, 1967, Lt. blue and dk. blue, 10.5Lx4.5Wx6.5H, dk. blue rampside truck with lt blue plastic cover, Model No. 235
EX $15 **NM** $25 **MIP** $50

Livestock Truck, 1967, Red and yellow, 14.75Lx3.25Wx5.5H, yellow metal panels, Model No. 260
EX $15 **NM** $25 **MIP** $50

Sanitation Truck, 1967, Green and white, 18Lx6Wx8H, lever action trash bucket dumps into box, Model No. 266
EX $25 **NM** $50 **MIP** $75

Dump Truck, 1967, Red, 13.5Lx5.5Wx5.75H, lever controls dump action, Model No. 303
EX $15 **NM** $25 **MIP** $75

Hydraulic Dump Truck, 1967, Red and yellow, 13.5Lx5.5Wx6.25H, hydraulic controlled dump box, Model No. 309
EX $25 **NM** $50 **MIP** $75

Hydraulic Dump Truck, 1967, Yellow and green, 12Lx6Wx6H, turbine cab. hydraulic controlled dump, Model No. 319
EX $25 **NM** $50 **MIP** $75

Vista Dome Horse Van, 1967, Met. gold, 21.75Lx6Wx6H, 2 ramp doors and 2 horses, 2 colts, Model No. 322
EX $25 **NM** $50 **MIP** $75

Car Carrier, 1967, Red and yellow, 22.25Lx6Wx7H, 3 plastic cars (Mustangs & T-Birds) loading ramp, Model No. 331
EX $25 **NM** $50 **MIP** $75

Livestock Van, 1967, Teal and white, 21.25Lx7.75Wx5.75H, turbine cab, white panels on side of trailer, Model No. 344
EX $25 **NM** $50 **MIP** $75

Timber Toter, 1967, Red and red, 20.75Lx6.5Wx5.5H, turbine cab., 5 wooden logs and chains, Model No. 360
EX $25 **NM** $50 **MIP** $75

Snorkel Utility Truck, 1967, Green and yellow, 21Lx6.5Wx5.5H, hydraulic snorkel book and plastic bucket, outriggers, Model No. 380
EX $25 **NM** $75 **MIP** $100

Aerial Hook & Ladder, 1967, Red and red, 29.25Lx6.25Wx6.25H, two metal ladders, crank operated lift ladder, Model No. 381
EX $25 **NM** $50 **MIP** $100

Wrecker Truck, 1967, White, 12.5Lx5.25Wx6.25H, red light (non-operable) on roof, POW-R-R-R sound, Model No. 415
EX $25 **NM** $50 **MIP** $75

Hydraulic Dump Truck, 1967, Grey and yellow, 12.75Lx6Wx6H, hydraulic dump box, POW-R-R-R sound, Model No. 423
EX $25 **NM** $50 **MIP** $75

Cement Mixer, 1967, Grey and orange, 16.5Lx6.5Wx7.5H, axle driven gear operates barrel, POW-R-R-R sound, Model No. 432
EX $25 **NM** $50 **MIP** $75

Fire Rescue Truck, 1967, Red, 12.75Lx5.75Wx5.75H, turbine cab. lever operated ladder, Model No. 453
EX $25 **NM** $50 **MIP** $75

Snorkel Fire Truck, 1967, Red, 21Lx6.5Wx8H, same design as #380, Model No. 466
EX $25 **NM** $75 **MIP** $100

Hydraulic Sanitation Truck, 1967, Grey and white, 16.5Lx5.75Wx7.75H, manual lift bucket dumps into body, POW-R-R-R sound, Model No. 474
EX $25 **NM** $50 **MIP** $75

Tractor Trailer Truck, 1967, Red and red, 21.25Lx7.75Wx5.75H, turbine cab. red, white & blue "Structo" decal on trailer, Model No. 483
EX $25 **NM** $50 **MIP** $75

Auto Transporter, 1967, Red and yellow, 28.25Lx5.75Wx5.5H, large, open car carrier, ramps adjust, 3 plastic cars, Model No. 492
EX $25 **NM** $50 **MIP** $100

Hi-Lift Bulldozer, 1967, Orange and black, 11.25Lx5.75Wx4H, metal levers operate the bucket, Model No. 501
EX $25 **NM** $50 **MIP** $75

Giant Bulldozer, 1967, Orange and black, 11.5Lx7Wx5H, blade raises and lowers with lever controls, Model No. 514
EX $25 **NM** $50 **MIP** $75

Road Grader, 1967, Orange, 19Lx7.5Wx8H, plated scraper blade, black plastic wheels & engine, Model No. 527
EX $25 **NM** $50 **MIP** $75

Bulldozer & Earth Mover, 1967, Green and yellow, 24.5Lx6.5Wx5.75H, combination bulldozer towing bottom dump earth mover unit, Model No. 574
EX $25 **NM** $50 **MIP** $75

Weekender, 1967, Teal, 12Lx5.75Wx6.5H, molded built-in refrigerator & sink detail, Model No. 708
EX $25 **NM** $50 **MIP** $100

Police Emergency Truck, 1967, Blue and white, 12Lx6Wx7.5H, bell rings as truck moves, 3 ladders, hosse reel, Model No. 727
EX $25 **NM** $50 **MIP** $100

Highway Builder Set, 1967, Green and yellow, 4 pc. set includes #183, #303, #501 and sand hopper, Model No. 909
EX $50 **NM** $75 **MIP** $125

Heavy Construction Set, 1967, Red and yellow, 4 pc. set includes #303, #432, #514 and barricade, Model No. 941
EX $50 **NM** $75 **MIP** $125

Pickup, 1968, Teal, 8.75Lx3.5Wx3.5H, Kom-pak design, Model No. 101
EX $15 **NM** $25 **MIP** $50

Wrecker Truck, 1968, White and red, 9.25Lx3.5Wx3.5H, Kom-pak design with red boom arm, Model No. 112
EX $15 **NM** $25 **MIP** $50

Fire Rescue Truck, 1968, Red, 8.75Lx3.5Wx3.5H, Kom-pak design with 2 ladders, Model No. 121
EX $25 **NM** $45 **MIP** $50

Kennel Truck, 1968, Yellow, 8.75Lx3.5Wx4H, Kom-pak design with clear cover and 6 dogs, Model No. 137
EX $15 **NM** $25 **MIP** $50

Steel Dump Truck, 1968, Red and yellow, 8.75Lx3.5Wx4H, Kom-pak design, Model No. 141
EX $15 **NM** $25 **MIP** $50

Cement Mixer, 1968, Grey and orange, 9.75Lx4Wx4.5H, Kom-pak design with dumping barrel, Model No. 153
EX $15 **NM** $25 **MIP** $50

Tractor Trailer Truck, 1968, Red and silver, 16.5Lx4Wx5.25H, Kom-pak design, with "National Freight Lines" decal on trailer, Model No. 160
EX $25 **NM** $50 **MIP** $75

Kom-pak Pony Van, 1968, Teal and teal, 16.5Lx3.5Wx4.5H, clear roof on trailer with coral & 3 ponies, Model No. 163
EX $25 **NM** $50 **MIP** $75

Mobile Merry-Go-Round Truck, 1968, Yellow and red, 9.25Lx4.25Wx5.75H, scarce, Kom-pak design, circus carousel spins when truck moves, Model No. 174
EX $50 **NM** $100 **MIP** $150

Air Force Truck, 1968, Blue, 8.75Lx3.5Wx4H, scarce, Kom-pak design with clear cover on bed, 4 blue soldiers, Model No. 175
EX $50 **NM** $100 **MIP** $150

Kenya Karryall, 1968, Green and yellow, 9.25Lx4.25Wx4.25H, scarce, Kom-pak design, 4 cages with 4 hand-painted wild animals, Model No. 176
EX $50 **NM** $100 **MIP** $150

Sanitation Truck, 1968, Grey and white, 11.5Lx3.5Wx5H, Kom-pak design, bucket dumps into body, Model No. 178
EX $25 **NM** $50 **MIP** $75

Kom-pak Sandy, 1968, Green and yellow, 8.75Lx3.5Wx3.5H, Kom-pak design with plastic sand hopper, Model No. 184
EX $25 **NM** $50 **MIP** $75

Kom-pak Contractor Set, 1968, Green and yellow, 4 pc. set includes #153, #183, #184, Model No. 193
EX $50 **NM** $75 **MIP** $125

Kom-pak Animal Set, 1968, Teal and white, 4 pc. set includes #137, #163, 6 dogs, 4 ponies & fence coral, Model No. 196
EX $50 **NM** $75 **MIP** $125

Wrecker Truck, 1968, White and black, 10.75Lx4.75Wx5.75H, black convertible roof and boom, red seat, Model No. 205
EX $50 **NM** $75 **MIP** $125

Sea Sprite, 1968, White and red, 23.5Lx5Wx5.25H, jeep towing "Johnson Reveler" model boat on trailer, Model No. 211
EX $50 **NM** $75 **MIP** $100

Rampside Pick-Up, 1968, Red, 10.5Lx4.5Wx5H, plastic bed liner and drop-down door in side of bed, Model No. 230
EX $25 **NM** $50 **MIP** $75

Camper Truck, 1968, Lt. blue and Dk. blue, 10.5Lx4.5Wx6.5H, Dk. blue rampside truck with Lt. blue plastic camper, Model No. 235
EX $25 **NM** $50 **MIP** $75

Livestock Truck, 1968, Red and yellow, 14.75Lx3.25Wx5.5H, yellow metal panels, Model No. 260
EX $25 **NM** $50 **MIP** $75

Wrecker Truck, 1968, Red, 15Lx5.5Wx 6.25H, white boom arm, red light (non-operable) on roof, Model No. 264
EX $50 **NM** $75 **MIP** $100

Sanitation Truck, 1968, Green and white, 18Lx6Wx8H, lever action trash bucket dumps into box, Model No. 266
EX $50 **NM** $75 **MIP** $125

Hydraulic Sanitation Truck, 1968, Grey and white, 16.5Lx5.75Wx7.75H, manual lift bucket dumps into body, Model No. 268
EX $50 **NM** $75 **MIP** $100

Cement Mixer, 1968, Red and yellow, 16.5Lx6.5Wx7.5H, axle driven gear operates barrel, Model No. 270
EX $25 **NM** $50 **MIP** $75

Hydraulic Cement Mixer, 1968, Green and yellow, 16.5Lx6.5Wx7.5H, same as #270 but with hydraulic dump action on barrel, Model No. 271
EX $50 **NM** $75 **MIP** $100

Dump Truck, 1968, Red, 13.5Lx5.5Wx5.75H, lever controls dump action, Model No. 303
EX $25 **NM** $50 **MIP** $75

Super Sandy Set, 1968, Yellow and green, 13.5Lx5.5Wx5.75H, dump truck and large plastic sand hopper, Model No. 306
EX $25 **NM** $50 **MIP** $75

Hydraulic Dump Truck, 1968, Red and yellow, 13.5Lx5.5Wx6.25H, hydraulic controlled dump box, Model No. 309
EX $25 **NM** $50 **MIP** $75

Hydraulic Dump Truck, 1968, Yellow and green, 12Lx6Wx6H, turbine cab. hydraulic controlled dump, Model No. 319
EX $25 **NM** $50 **MIP** $75

Vista Dome Horse Van, 1968, Met. gold, 21.75Lx6Wx6H, 2 ramp doors and 2 horses, 2 colts, Model No. 322
EX $25 **NM** $50 **MIP** $75

Car Carrier, 1968, Red and yellow, 22.25Lx6Wx7H, 3 plastic cars (Mustangs & T-Birds) loading ramp, Model No. 331
EX $25 **NM** $50 **MIP** $75

Livestock Van, 1968, Teal and white, 21.25Lx7.75Wx5.75H, turbine cab. white panels on side of trailer, Model No. 344
EX $25 **NM** $50 **MIP** $75

Timber Toter, 1968, Blue and blue, 20.75Lx6.5Wx5.5H, turbine cab, 5 wooden logs and chains, Model No. 360
EX $25 **NM** $50 **MIP** $75

Snorkel Utility Truck, 1968, Green and yellow, 21Lx6.5Wx5.5H, hydraulic snorkel book and plastic bucket, outriggers, Model No. 380
EX $25 **NM** $75 **MIP** $100

Aerial Hook & Ladder, 1968, Red and red, 29.25Lx6.25Wx6.25H, two metal ladders, crank lift ladder "9" decal on side, Model No. 381
EX $25 **NM** $75 **MIP** $100

Police Emergency Truck, 1968, Blue and white, 12Lx6Wx7.5H, bell rings as truck moves, 3 ladders, hose reel, Model No. 727
EX $25 **NM** $75 **MIP** $125

Wrecker Truck, 1968, White, 12.5Lx5.25Wx6.25H, red light (non-operable) on roof, POW-R-R-R sound, Model No. 415
EX $25 **NM** $50 **MIP** $75

Hydraulic Dump Truck, 1968, Grey and orange, 12.75Lx6Wx6H, hydraulic dump box, POW-R-R-R sound, Model No. 423
EX $25 **NM** $50 **MIP** $75

Fire Rescue Truck, 1968, Red, 12.75Lx5.75Wx5.75H, turbine cab. lever operated ladder, Model No. 453
EX $25 **NM** $50 **MIP** $75

Snorkel Fire Truck, 1968, Red, 21Lx6.5Wx8H, same design as #380, Model No. 466
EX $25 **NM** $75 **MIP** $100

Tractor Trailer Truck, 1968, Red and red, 21.25Lx7.75Wx5.75H, turbine cab. red, white & blue "Structo" decal on trailer, Model No. 483
EX $25 **NM** $50 **MIP** $75

Auto Transporter, 1968, Red and yellow, 28.25Lx5.75Wx5.5H, large, open car carrier, ramps adjust, 3 plastic cars, Model No. 492
EX $25 **NM** $50 **MIP** $100

Road Grader, 1968, Orange, 11.75Lx5Wx4.75H, Kom-pak design, Model No. 183
EX $15 **NM** $25 **MIP** $50

Hi-Lift Bulldozer, 1968, Orange and black, 11.25Lx5.75Wx4H, metal levers operate the bucket, Model No. 501
EX $25 **NM** $50 **MIP** $75

Giant Bulldozer, 1968, Orange and black, 11.5Lx7Wx5H, blade raises and lowers with lever controls, Model No. 514
EX $25 **NM** $50 **MIP** $75

Road Grader, 1968, Orange, 19Lx7.5Wx8H, plated scraper blade, black plastic wheels & engine, Model No. 527
EX $25 **NM** $50 **MIP** $75

Bulldozer & Earth Mover, 1968, Green and yellow, 24.5Lx6.5Wx5.75H, combination bulldozer towing bottom dump earth mover unit, Model No. 574
EX $25 **NM** $50 **MIP** $75

Sand Master Set, 1968, Yellow, 17.5Lx9Wx15H, plastic sand hopper with rubber conveyor belt, Model No. 580
EX $25 **NM** $50 **MIP** $75

Roadbuilder Set, 1968, Yellow and green, #580 set and #303 dump truck, Model No. 905
EX $50 **NM** $75 **MIP** $125

Highway Builder Set, 1968, Yellow and green, 4 pc. set includes #183, #306 set, #501, Model No. 932
EX $50 **NM** $75 **MIP** $125

Heavy Construction Set, 1968, Red and yellow, 4 pc. set includes #270, #303, #514 and barricade, Model No. 941
EX $50 **NM** $75 **MIP** $125

Rough Rider Pick-Up Truck, 1969, Yellow, 9.25Lx4Wx4H, hurricanes design with open bed, Model No. 801
EX $15 **NM** $25 **MIP** $50

Minuteman Tow Truck, 1969, Dk. orange, 9.25Lx4Wx4H, hurricanes design with crank operated tow rope, Model No. 812
EX $15 **NM** $25 **MIP** $50

Waggin' Wagon Kennel Truck, 1969, Yellow, 9.25Lx4Wx4H, hurricanes design with clear kennel and 6 dogs, Model No. 837
EX $15 **NM** $25 **MIP** $50

Dump Truck, 1969, Dk. orange and white, 10.5Lx4Wx4.25H, hurricanes design, Model No. 841
EX $15 **NM** $25 **MIP** $50

Cement Mixer, 1969, Dk. orange and white, 9.5Lx4Wx4.25H, hurricanes design with axle driven barrel, Model No. 853
EX $15 **NM** $25 **MIP** $50

Livestock Truck, 1969, Teal and white, 9.5Lx4.25Wx4H, hurricanes design with white stake panels and 5 animals, Model No. 870
EX $15 **NM** $25 **MIP** $50

Merry-Go-Round, 1969, Yellow and red, 9.5Lx4.25Wx5.75H, hurricanes design with carousel, Model No. 874
EX $25 **NM** $50 **MIP** $75

Snorkel Fire Truck, 1969, Red and white, 9.5Lx4Wx5.25H, hurricanes design with white plastic snorkel arm & bucket, Model No. 878
EX $15 **NM** $25 **MIP** $50

Hydraulic Dump Truck, 1969, Dk. orange and white, 12.25Lx5.5Wx6.25H, thunderbolt design with steer-o-matic front wheels, Model No. 626
EX $25 **NM** $50 **MIP** $75

Cement Mixer, 1969, Dk. orange and white, 12.25Lx7Wx7H, thunderbolt design with steer-o-matic front wheels, Model No. 632
EX $25 **NM** $50 **MIP** $75

Fire Rescue Truck, 1969, Red and white, 12.5Lx6Wx6.5H, thunderbolt design with steer-o-matic front wheels, Model No. 653
EX $25 **NM** $50 **MIP** $75

Scamp, 1969, Gold and white, 9.5Lx4.5Wx5.25H, sport model design with 5" blond doll, Model No. 744
EX $25 **NM** $50 **MIP** $75

Sea Sprite, 1969, Blue and red, 23Lx5.5Wx5.25H, sport model design with "Johnson Reveler" boat in tow, Model No. 755
EX $25 **NM** $50 **MIP** $75

Boog-A-Loo, 1969, Pink and white, 9.5Lx4.5Wx5H, sport model design with 5" blond doll, Model No. 766
EX $25 **NM** $50 **MIP** $75

Tractor Trailer Truck, 1969, White and red, 16.5Lx4.25Wx5.5H, Kom-pak design with red trailer & white doors, Model No. 160
EX $25 **NM** $50 **MIP** $75

Pony Van, 1969, Lime green, 16.5Lx3.25Wx5H, Kom-pak design with clear roof on trailer and 3 colts, Model No. 163
EX $25 **NM** $50 **MIP** $75

Kom-pak Sandy, 1969, Green and yellow, 9Lx5.25Wx8.5H, Kom-pak design, Model No. 184
EX $25 **NM** $50 **MIP** $75

Rampside Pick-Up, 1969, Gold and white, 10.5Lx4.75W5.25H, typhoons design with white plastic bed liner, Model No. 230
EX $25 **NM** $50 **MIP** $75

VEHICLES • STRUCTO

Structo

Camper Truck, 1969, Gold and white, 10.5Lx5Wx6.5H, typhoons design with white plastic camper in bed, Model No. 235
EX $25 **NM** $50 **MIP** $75

Sanitation Truck, 1969, Grey and white, 16.5Lx6Wx7.5H, typhoons design with lever action, Model No. 269
EX $25 **NM** $50 **MIP** $75

Cement Mixer, 1969, Red and yellow, 14.5Lx7Wx7.5H, typhoons design with axle driven barrel, Model No. 270
EX $25 **NM** $50 **MIP** $75

Wrecker Truck, 1969, Yellow and red, 12.5Lx6Wx6.25H, typhoons design with red tow boom & crank winch, Model No. 277
EX $25 **NM** $50 **MIP** $75

Dump Truck, 1969, Red, 13.5Lx6Wx5.5H, typhoons design with lever action dump box, Model No. 303
EX $25 **NM** $50 **MIP** $75

Dump Truck, 1969, Grey and orange, 13Lx5.5Wx6H, typhoons design with spring action dump box, Model No. 311
EX $25 **NM** $50 **MIP** $75

Hydraulic Dump Truck, 1969, Yellow and green, 13Lx6Wx6H, typhoons design with hydraulic dump box, Model No. 319
EX $25 **NM** $50 **MIP** $75

Vista Dome Horse Van, 1969, Met. gold, 22Lx5.5Wx6.5H, typhoons design with 4 horses, Model No. 322
EX $25 **NM** $50 **MIP** $75

Car Carrier, 1969, Red and yellow, 22.5Lx5.5Wx5.5H, typhoons design with 3 plastic cars (Mustangs/T-Birds) ramp, Model No. 331
EX $25 **NM** $50 **MIP** $75

Livestock Van, 1969, Teal and white, 21.75Lx5.5Wx7.5H, typhoons design with fifth wheel detail, Model No. 344
EX $25 **NM** $50 **MIP** $75

Timber Toter, 1969, Red and red, 21.75Lx5.5Wx6.5H, typhoons design with 6 wooden logs and chain, Model No. 361
EX $25 **NM** $50 **MIP** $75

Tractor Trailer Truck, 1969, Red and red, 22Lx5.5Wx8H, typhoons design, Model No. 373
EX $25 **NM** $50 **MIP** $75

Snorkel Utility Truck, 1969, Green and yellow, 17.5Lx6Wx9H, typhoons design with white boom and plastic bucket, Model No. 380
EX $25 **NM** $50 **MIP** $75

Aerial Hook & Ladder, 1969, Red and red, 30.25Lx5.5Wx7H, typhoons design with crank operated extension ladder, Model No. 381
EX $25 **NM** $50 **MIP** $75

Snorkel Fire Truck, 1969, Red, 17.5Lx5.75Wx9H, typhoons design, Model No. 385
EX $25 **NM** $50 **MIP** $75

Road Grader, 1969, Orange, 11.75Lx5Wx6H, black plastic wheels and motor, Model No. 183
EX $15 **NM** $25 **MIP** $50

Super Sandy Set, 1969, Green and yellow, 13.5Lx9.5Wx13H, #303 dump truck plus plastic sand hopper, Model No. 306
EX $25 **NM** $50 **MIP** $75

Hi-Lift Bulldozer, 1969, Orange and black, 12Lx6Wx6.5H, metal levers operate the bucket, Model No. 501
EX $25 **NM** $50 **MIP** $75

Giant Bulldozer, 1969, Red and yellow, 12Lx6.75Wx7H, blade raises and lowers with lever controls, Model No. 514
EX $25 **NM** $50 **MIP** $75

Road Grader, 1969, Orange, 19Lx7.5Wx8H, plated scraper blade, black plastic wheels & engine, Model No. 527
EX $25 **NM** $50 **MIP** $75

Sand Master Set, 1969, Yellow, 17.5Lx9Wx15H, plastic sand hopper with rubber conveyor belt, Model No. 580
EX $15 **NM** $25 **MIP** $50

Roadbuilder Set, 1969, Yellow and green, #580 set and #303 dump truck, Model No. 905
EX $50 **NM** $75 **MIP** $125

Highway Builder Set, 1969, Green and yellow, 4 pc. set includes #183, #306 set, #501, Model No. 932
EX $50 **NM** $75 **MIP** $125

Animal Set, 1969, Yellow and green, 2 pc. set contains #837 and #870, Model No. 961
EX $25 **NM** $50 **MIP** $75

Hurricane Contractor Set, 1969, Dk orange and white, 2 pc. set contains #841 and #853 plus sand hopper and signs, Model No. 965
EX $25 **NM** $50 **MIP** $75

Typhoon Construction Set, 1969, Grey and orange, 3 pc. set including #270, #311, #501, Model No. 966
EX $50 **NM** $75 **MIP** $100

Dig 'N Dump Set, 1970-71, Orange and white, 20Lx3.25Wx4.25H, road tow'ds design with shovel & dual dump boxes in tow, Model No. 280
EX $15 **NM** $25 **MIP** $50

Pipe-Layer Set, 1970-71, Blue and white, 20Lx3.25Wx4.25H, road tow'ds design with grab bucket & dual trailers in tow, Model No. 285
EX $15 **NM** $25 **MIP** $50

Bridge Set, 1970-71, Yellow and white, 22.25Lx3.5Wx5.5H, road tow'ds design with stake truck, 2 trailers & 4 pc. Bridge, Model No. 290
EX $15 **NM** $25 **MIP** $50

Steerable Rough Rider Pickup, 1970-71, Blue and white, 9.25Lx4Wx4H, steerable stormers design, Model No. 420
EX $15 **NM** $25 **MIP** $50

Steerable Minuteman Wrecker, 1970-71, Lime green and white, 9.25Lx4Wx4H, steerable stormers design with white metal boom, Model No. 428
EX $15 **NM** $25 **MIP** $50

Steerable Waggin' Wagon, 1970-71, Blue and white, 9.25Lx4Wx4H, steerable stormers design with clear kennel & 6 dogs, Model No. 437
EX $15 **NM** $25 **MIP** $50

Steerable Dump Truck, 1970-71, Gold and white, 10.5Lx4Wx4.25H, steerable stormers design, Model No. 441
EX $15 **NM** $25 **MIP** $50

Steerable Livestock Truck, 1970-71, Gold and white, 9.5Lx4.25Wx4.25H, steerable stormers design with stake sides & 4 animals, Model No. 471
EX $15 **NM** $25 **MIP** $50

Steerable Snorkel Truck, 1970-71, Red and white, 9.5Lx4Wx5.5H, steerable stormers design with white plastic snorkel, Model No. 478
EX $15 **NM** $25 **MIP** $50

(ToyShop File Photo)

Steerable Stubby Wrecker, 1970-71, Gold and white, 11Lx5.5Wx7H, steerable thunderbolt design with "Road Tug" decal on side, Model No. 615
EX $15 **NM** $25 **MIP** $50

Steerable Hydraulic Dump Truck, 1970-71, Orange and white, 13.25Lx5.5Wx6.25H, steerable thunderbolt design, Model No. 626
EX $15 **NM** $25 **MIP** $50

Steerable Cement Mixer, 1970-71, Orange and white, 12.25Lx7Wx7.5H, steerable thunderbolt design, Model No. 632
EX $15 **NM** $25 **MIP** $50

Steerable Hydraulic Dump Truck, 1970-71, Blue and white, 13.25Lx5.5Wx6.25H, steerable thunderbolt design, Model No. 640
EX $15 **NM** $25 **MIP** $50

Steerable Fire Rescue Truck, 1970-71, Red, 12.5Lx6Wx6.5H, steerable thunderbolt design, Model No. 653
EX $15 **NM** $25 **MIP** $50

Steerable Timber Toter, 1970-71, Lime green and white, 21.75Lx5.5Wx6.5H, steerable thunderbolt design with 6 wooden logs & chains, Model No. 661
EX $25 **NM** $50 **MIP** $75

Steerable Tractor Trailer, 1970-71, Orange and orange, 22Lx5.5Wx8H, steerable thunderbolt design, Model No. 673
EX $25 **NM** $50 **MIP** $75

Steerable Hook & Ladder Truck, 1970-71, Red and red, 17.5Lx6Wx7.25H, steerable thunderbolt design, Model No. 681
EX $25 **NM** $50 **MIP** $75

Scamp Sportster, 1970-71, Gold and white, 9.5Lx4.5Wx5.25H, sport model design with 5" blond female doll, Model No. 744
EX $25 **NM** $50 **MIP** $75

Sea Sprite, 1970-71, Blue and red, 23Lx5.5Wx5.25H, sport model design with "Johnson Reveler" boat in tow, Model No. 755
EX $25 **NM** $50 **MIP** $75

Race-A-Roo, 1970-71, Gold and white, 9.5Lx4.5Wx5H, sport model design with 5" white male doll, Model No. 760
EX $25 **NM** $50 **MIP** $75

Boog-A-Loo, 1970-71, Pink and white, 9.5Lx4.5Wx5H, sport model design with 5" blond doll, Model No. 766
EX $25 **NM** $50 **MIP** $75

Lad-A-Bout, 1970-71, Lime green and white, 9.5Lx4.5Wx5.25H, sport model design with 5" black male doll, Model No. 769
EX $50 **NM** $75 **MIP** $100

Sand-Grenade Dune Buggy, 1970-71, Red and black, 9.5Lx4.5Wx5H, sport model design with dual rear mag wheels, Model No. 777
EX $25 **NM** $50 **MIP** $75

Rough Rider Pickup, 1970-71, Yellow, 9.25Lx4Wx4H, hurricanes design with open bed, Model No. 801
EX $15 **NM** $25 **MIP** $50

Minuteman Tow Truck, 1970-71, Dk. orange, 9.25Lx4Wx4H, hurricanes design with crank operated tow rope, Model No. 812
EX $15 **NM** $25 **MIP** $50

Camper Truck, 1970-71, Lime green and white, 9.25Lx4.25Wx5H, hurricane design with white plastic camper, Model No. 835
EX $15 **NM** $25 **MIP** $50

Waggin' Wagon Kennel Truck, 1970-71, Yellow, 9.25Lx4Wx4H, hurricanes design with clear kennel and 6 dogs, Model No. 837
EX $15 **NM** $25 **MIP** $50

Dump Truck, 1970-71, Dk. orange and white, 10.5Lx4Wx4.25H, hurricanes design, Model No. 841
EX $15 **NM** $25 **MIP** $50

Cement Mixer, 1970-71, Dk. orange and white, 9.5Lx4Wx4.25H, hurricanes design with axle driven barrel, Model No. 853
EX $15 **NM** $25 **MIP** $50

Livestock Truck, 1970-71, Green and white, 9.5Lx4.25Wx4H, hurricanes design with white stake panels and 5 animals, Model No. 870
EX $15 **NM** $25 **MIP** $50

Snorkel Fire Truck, 1970-71, Red and white, 9.5Lx4Wx5.25H, hurricanes design with white plastic snorkel arm & bucket, Model No. 878
EX $15 **NM** $25 **MIP** $50

Cement Mixer, 1970-71, Red and yellow, 14.5Lx7Wx7.5H, typhoons design with axle driven barrel, Model No. 270
EX $15 **NM** $25 **MIP** $50

Dump Truck, 1970-71, Red, 13.5Lx6Wx5.5H, typhoons design with lever action dump box, Model No. 303
EX $15 **NM** $25 **MIP** $50

Hydraulic Dump Truck, 1970-71, Yellow and green, 13Lx6Wx6H, typhoons design with hydraulic dump box, Model No. 319
EX $15 **NM** $25 **MIP** $50

Vista Dome Horse Van, 1970-71, Met. gold, 22Lx5.5Wx6.5H, typhoons design with 4 horses, Model No. 322
EX $15 **NM** $25 **MIP** $50

Car Carrier, 1970-71, Red and yellow, 22.5Lx5.5Wx5.5H, typhoons design with 3 plastic cars (Mustangs/T-Birds) ramp, Model No. 331
EX $15 **NM** $25 **MIP** $50

Snorkel Utility Truck, 1970-71, Green and yellow, 17.5Lx6Wx9H, typhoons design with white boom and plastic bucket, Model No. 380
EX $25 **NM** $50 **MIP** $75

Snorkel Fire Truck, 1970-71, Red, 17.5Lx5.75Wx9H, typhoons design, Model No. 385
EX $25 **NM** $50 **MIP** $75

Tractor Trailer Truck, 1970-71, White and red, 16.5Lx4.25Wx5.5H, Kom-pak design with red trailer & white doors, Model No. 160
EX $25 **NM** $50 **MIP** $75

Pony Van, 1970-71, Lime green, 16.5Lx3.25Wx5H, Kom-pak design with clear roof on trailer and 3 colts, Model No. 163
EX $25 **NM** $50 **MIP** $75

Road Grader, 1970-71, Lime green and yellow, 11.75Lx5Wx6H, black plastic wheels and motor, Model No. 183
EX $15 **NM** $25 **MIP** $50

Hi-Lift Bulldozer, 1970-71, Lime green and yellow, 12Lx6Wx6.5H, metal levers operate the bucket, Model No. 501
EX $15 **NM** $25 **MIP** $50

Giant Bulldozer, 1970-71, Lime green and yellow, 12Lx6.75Wx7H, blade raises and lowers with lever controls, Model No. 514
EX $15 **NM** $50 **MIP** $75

Kom-pak Sandy, 1970-71, Green and yellow, 9Lx5.25Wx8.5H, Kom-pak design, Model No. 184
EX $15 **NM** $25 **MIP** $50

Super Sandy Set, 1970-71, Green and yellow, 13.5Lx9.5Wx13H, #303 dump truck plus plastic sand hopper, Model No. 306
EX $25 **NM** $50 **MIP** $75

Sand Master Set, 1970-71, Yellow, 17.5Lx9Wx15H, plastic sand hopper with rubber conveyor belt, Model No. 580
EX $25 **NM** $50 **MIP** $75

Highway Builder Set, 1970-71, Green and yellow, 4 pc. set includes #183, #306 set, #501, Model No. 932
EX $50 **NM** $75 **MIP** $125

Steerable Stormer Construction Set, 1970-71, Yellow, #441 steer-o-matic dump, sand hopper & 10 pc. road sign set, Model No. 955
EX $50 **NM** $75 **MIP** $125

Hurricane Construction Set, 1970-71, Orange and white, 3 pc. set including #841, sand hopper & 10 pc. Road sign set, Model No. 965
EX $25 **NM** $50 **MIP** $75

Monster Machine, 1971, Green, 2.75Lx3.5Wx3H, 2 wheeled design with exposed "Chrome" engine, Model No. 215
EX $10 **NM** $15 **MIP** $25

Panic Panel, 1971, Orange, 2.75Lx3.5Wx3H, 2 wheeled design with panel wagon sides, Model No. 216
EX $10 **NM** $15 **MIP** $25

Weird Wagon, 1971, Red, 2.75Lx3.5Wx3H, 2 wheeled design with WV bug style, Model No. 217
EX $10 **NM** $15 **MIP** $25

Buzzin' Buggy, 1971, Yellow, 2.75Lx3.5Wx3H, 2 wheeled design with open dune buggy style, Model No. 218
EX $10 **NM** $15 **MIP** $25

Monster Machine, 1972, Green, 2.75Lx3.5Wx3H, 2 wheeled design with exposed "Chrome" engine, Model No. 215
EX $10 **NM** $15 **MIP** $25

Panic Panel, 1972, Orange, 2.75Lx3.5Wx3H, 2 wheeled design with panel wagon sides, Model No. 216
EX $10 **NM** $15 **MIP** $25

Weird Wagon, 1972, Red, 2.75Lx3.5Wx3H, 2 wheeled design with WV bug style, Model No. 217
EX $10 **NM** $15 **MIP** $25

Buzzin' Bugggy, 1972, Yellow, 2.75Lx3.5Wx3H, 2 wheeled design with open dune buggy style, Model No. 218
EX $10 **NM** $15 **MIP** $25

Giant 24-Pack Assortment, 1972, 17.75Lx16.5Wx16.5H, all 4 weird wheels designs in a store display - 24 cars total, Model No. 219
EX n/a **NM** n/a **MIP** $250

Triple Terrific 3 Pack, 1972, 14Lx5Wx5H, one each #215, #216, #217 in a 3 pack store display box, Model No. 220
EX n/a **NM** n/a **MIP** $150

Brain Barrel, 1972, Brown, 2.75Lx3.5Wx3H, 2 wheeled design with brown "Wooden" barrel & bald driver, Model No. 250
EX $10 **NM** $15 **MIP** $25

Loonie Looper, 1972, Yellow and orange, 2.75Lx3.5Wx3H, 2 wheeled design with airplane styling including propeller, Model No. 251
EX $10 **NM** $15 **MIP** $25

Litter Picker, 1972, Chrome and orange, 2.75Lx3.5Wx3H, 2 wheeled design with trash can style, Model No. 252
EX $10 **NM** $15 **MIP** $25

Triple Terrific 3 Pack, 1972, 14Lx5Wx5H, one each #250, #251, #252 in a 3 pack store display box, Model No. 262
EX n/a **NM** n/a **MIP** $150

Big 2-Dozen Assortment, 1972, 17.75Lx14.75Wx16.5H, all 3 weird wheels designs in a store display - 24 cars total, Model No. 265
EX n/a **NM** n/a **MIP** $250

Giant Gantry Crane, 1972, Yellow, 32.5Lx12.25Wx14H, hand crank pulley system with crane mechanism, Model No. 555
EX $25 **NM** $50 **MIP** $75

Kom-pak Sandy, 1972, Yellow, 9Lx5.25Wx8.5H, sand hopper and dump truck, Model No. 184
EX $15 **NM** $25 **MIP** $50

Sand Loader, 1972, Yellow, 9.5Lx5Wx9.5H, small sand hopper with conveyor, Model No. 560
EX $15 **NM** $25 **MIP** $50

Sand Set, 1972, Yellow, 9.75Lx5Wx9.5H, #560 unit plus sand hopper unit, Model No. 579
EX $25 **NM** $50 **MIP** $75

Sand Master Set, 1972, Yellow, 14.5Lx4.5Wx15H, plastic sand hopper with rubber conveyor belt, Model No. 580
EX $25 **NM** $50 **MIP** $75

Contractor Set, 1972, Yellow, combination of #579 set and #184 set plus 10 street signs, Model No. 967
EX $25 **NM** $50 **MIP** $75

Boon Dock'r, 1972, Red and green, 23Lx5.5Wx5.25H, sport model design with buggy towing boat & trailer, Model No. 758
EX $15 **NM** $25 **MIP** $50

Dirt Tracker, 1972, White and black, 10Lx4.5Wx5H, sport model design with dual wheels #1 logo & flags on doors, Model No. 770
EX $15 **NM** $25 **MIP** $50

American Rev-O-Lution, 1972, White and black, 10Lx4.5Wx5H, sport model design with american flag on doors, Model No. 775
EX $15 **NM** $25 **MIP** $50

Sand-Grenade Dune Buggy, 1972, Red and black, 9.5Lx4.5Wx5H, sport model design with dual rear mag wheels, Model No. 777
EX $15 **NM** $50 **MIP** $75

Blacktop Bandit, 1972, Plum and black, 10Lx4.5Wx5H, sport model design with dragster styling, Model No. 780
EX $15 **NM** $50 **MIP** $75

Speedway Series Wrecker, 1972, Purple, 9.25Lx4Wx4H, same as hurricane design #428 with speedway decals, Model No. 845
EX $15 **NM** $50 **MIP** $75

Speedway Series Ambulance, 1972, White, 9.25Lx4Wx4H, similar to hurricane design with first aid decals, Model No. 855
EX $15 **NM** $50 **MIP** $75

Speedway Series Pacer, 1972, Green, 9.25Lx4Wx4H, same as hurricane design #801 with speedway decals, Model No. 865
EX $15 **NM** $50 **MIP** $75

Road Boss Vista Dome Horse Van, 1972, Orange, 22Lx5.5Wx6H, with chrome stacks and air horn detail plus 4 black horses, Model No. 324
EX $15 **NM** $25 **MIP** $50

Road Boss Hydraulic Dump, 1972, Orange, 13.25Lx5.25Wx6.25H, with chrome stacks and air horn detail, Model No. 327
EX $15 **NM** $25 **MIP** $50

Road Boss Timber Toter, 1972, Orange, 21.75Lx5.5Wx6.5H, with chrome stacks and air horn detail, Model No. 328
EX $15 **NM** $25 **MIP** $50

Road Boss Tractor Trailer Truck, 1972, Orange, 22Lx5.5Wx8H, with chrome stacks and air horn detail, Model No. 329
EX $15 **NM** $25 **MIP** $50

Road Boss Car Carrier, 1972, Orange, 22.5Lx5.5Wx5.5H, with chrome stacks and air horn detail plus 3 cars, Model No. 335
EX $15 **NM** $25 **MIP** $50

Steerable Stubby Wrecker, 1972, Gold and white, 11Lx5.5Wx7H, thunderbolt design, with black tow boom, Model No. 615
EX $15 **NM** $25 **MIP** $50

Steerable Cement Mixer Truck, 1972, Gold and white, 12.25Lx7Wx7.5H, thunderbolt design, axle drives barrel, Model No. 634
EX $15 **NM** $25 **MIP** $50

Steerable Hydraulic Dump Truck, 1972, Blue and white, 13.25Lx5.5Wx6.25H, thunderbolt design, Model No. 640
EX $15 **NM** $25 **MIP** $50

Steerable Fire Rescue Truck, 1972, Red, 12.5Lx6Wx6.5H, thunderbolt design, with 2 ladders and extension ladder, Model No. 653
EX $15 **NM** $25 **MIP** $50

Dump Truck, 1972, Yellow, 13.5Lx6Wx5.5H, typhoon design, Model No. 303
EX $15 **NM** $25 **MIP** $50

Vista Dome Horse Van, 1972, Met. gold, 22Lx5.5Wx6H, typhoon design with 4 plastic horses, Model No. 320
EX $15 **NM** $25 **MIP** $50

Car Carrier, 1972, Red and yellow, 22.5Lx5.5Wx6H, typhoon design with 3 plastic cars and ramp, Model No. 330
EX $15 **NM** $25 **MIP** $50

Aerial Hook & Ladder, 1972, Red and red, 17.5Lx6Wx7.25H, typhoon design with 2 ladders and extension ladder, Model No. 381
EX $15 **NM** $25 **MIP** $50

Dig'n Dump, 1972, Orange and white, 20Lx3.25Wx4.25H, road tow'ds design with shovel & dual dump boxes in tow, Model No. 280
EX $15 **NM** $25 **MIP** $50

Pipe-Layer Set, 1972, Blue and white, 20Lx3.25Wx4.25H, road tow'ds design with grab bucket & dual trailers in tow, Model No. 285
EX $15 **NM** $25 **MIP** $50

Bridge Set, 1972, Yellow and white, 22.25Lx3.5Wx5.5H, road tow'ds design with stake truck, 2 trailers & 4 pc. Bridge, Model No. 290
EX $15 **NM** $25 **MIP** $50

Road Grader, 1972, Yellow, 11.75Lx5Wx6H, black plastic wheels and motor, Model No. 183
EX $15 **NM** $25 **MIP** $50

Hi-Lift Bulldozer, 1972, Yellow, 12Lx6Wx6.5H, metal levers operate the bucket, Model No. 501
EX $15 **NM** $25 **MIP** $50

Giant Bulldozer, 1972, Yellow, 12Lx6.75Wx7H, blade raises and lowers with lever controls, Model No. 514
EX $15 **NM** $25 **MIP** $50

Steerable Rough Rider Pickup, 1972, Blue and white, 9.25Lx4Wx4H, steerable stormers design, Model No. 420
EX $15 **NM** $25 **MIP** $50

Steerable Minuteman Wrecker, 1972, Lime green and white, 9.25Lx4Wx4H, steerable stormers design with white metal boom, Model No. 428
EX $15 **NM** $25 **MIP** $50

Steerable Camper Truck, 1972, Red and white, 9.25Lx4.25Wx5H, steerable stormers design with white plastic camper, Model No. 435
EX $15 **NM** $25 **MIP** $50

Steerable Waggin' Wagon, 1972, Blue and white, 9.25Lx4Wx4H, steerable stormers design with waggin' wagon treatment, Model No. 437
EX $15 **NM** $25 **MIP** $50

Steerable Dump Truck, 1972, Gold and white, 10.5Lx4Wx4.25H, steerable stormers design, Model No. 441
EX $15 **NM** $25 **MIP** $50

Rough Rider Pickup, 1972, Yellow, 9.25Lx4Wx4H, hurricanes design, Model No. 801
EX $10 **NM** $20 **MIP** $30

Camper Truck, 1972, Orange and white, 9.25Lx4.25Wx5H, hurricanes design, Model No. 835
EX $10 **NM** $15 **MIP** $25

Waggin' Wagon, 1972, Lime green and white, 9.25Lx4Wx4H, hurricanes design with clear cover & 6 dogs, Model No. 837
EX $10 **NM** $15 **MIP** $25

Tractor-Trailer Truck, 1972, Blue and silver, 16.5Lx4.25Wx5.5H, hurricanes design with structo van lines on trailer, Model No. 861
EX $10 **NM** $15 **MIP** $25

Livestock Truck, 1972, Blue and white, 9.5Lx4.25Wx4H, hurricanes design with white panels and 5 animals, Model No. 870
EX $10 **NM** $15 **MIP** $25

Kom-pak Sandy, 1973, Yellow and orange, 8.5Lx5.5Wx9.5H, sand hopper and dump truck, Model No. 184
EX $15 **NM** $25 **MIP** $50

Sand Master Set, 1973, Yellow and orange, 14.5Lx4.5Wx15H, plastic sand hopper with rubber conveyor belt, Model No. 580
EX $15 **NM** $25 **MIP** $50

Vacation Set, 1973, Orange and green, 22Lx5.75Wx10H, includes #758 and #835, Model No. 962
EX $25 **NM** $50 **MIP** $75

Contractor Set, 1973, Yellow and orange, combination of #580 set and #184 set plus 10 street signs, Model No. 967
EX $35 **NM** $50 **MIP** $75

Speedway Midget Race Hauler, 1973, Red and black, 10.5Lx4Wx4H, flatbed with race car, Model No. 842
EX $25 **NM** $50 **MIP** $75

Speedway Wrecker, 1973, Purple, 9.25Lx4Wx4H, same as hurricane design #428 with speedway decals, Model No. 845
EX $15 **NM** $25 **MIP** $50

Speedway Ambulance, 1973, White, 9.25Lx4Wx4H, similar to hurricane design with first aid decals, Model No. 855
EX $15 **NM** $25 **MIP** $50

Speedway Pacer, 1973, Green, 9.25Lx4Wx4H, same as hurricane design #801 with speedway decals, Model No. 865
EX $15 **NM** $25 **MIP** $50

Speedway Water Tanker, 1973, Blue and white, 9.25Lx4Wx4.5H, white plastic water tank on back, Model No. 868
EX $15 **NM** $25 **MIP** $50

Boon Dock'r, 1973, Orange and green, 23Lx5.5Wx5.25H, sport model design with buggy towing boat & trailer, Model No. 758
EX $15 **NM** $25 **MIP** $50

Scorpion, 1973, Pink and white, 10Lx4.5Wx5.75H, new design for 1973, Model No. 763
EX $15 **NM** $25 **MIP** $50

Top Chopper, 1973, Lime green and orange, 10Lx4.5Wx5.75H, new design for 1973, Model No. 765
EX $15 **NM** $25 **MIP** $50

Propur-T, 1973, Blue and white, 10Lx4.5Wx5.75H, new design for 1973, Model No. 768
EX $15 **NM** $25 **MIP** $50

Dirt Tracker, 1973, Yellow and black, 10Lx4.5Wx5H, sport model design with dual wheels #1 logo & flags on doors, Model No. 770
EX $15 **NM** $25 **MIP** $50

American Rev-O-Lution, 1973, White and black, 10Lx4.5Wx5H, sport model design with american flag on doors, Model No. 775
EX $15 **NM** $25 **MIP** $50

Blacktop Bandit, 1973, Yellow and black, 10Lx4.5Wx5H, sport model design with dragster styling, Model No. 780
EX $15 **NM** $25 **MIP** $50

Road Boss Pipeline Transport, 1973, Blue and yellow, 21.75Lx5.5Wx6.5H, with chrome stacks and air horn detail, same as #328, Model No. 323
EX $15 **NM** $25 **MIP** $50

Road Boss Vista-Dome Horse Van, 1973, Blue and yellow, 22Lx5.5Wx6H, with chrome stacks and air horn detail, 4 black horses, Model No. 324
EX $15 **NM** $25 **MIP** $50

Road Boss Hydraulic Dump, 1973, Blue and yellow, 13.25Lx5.5Wx6.25H, with chrome stacks and air horn detail, Model No. 327
EX $15 **NM** $25 **MIP** $50

Road Boss Timber Toter, 1973, Blue and yellow, 21.75Lx5.5Wx6.5H, with chrome stacks and air horn detail, same as #323, Model No. 328
EX $15 **NM** $25 **MIP** $50

Road Boss Tractor Trailer Truck, 1973, Blue and yellow, 22Lx5.5Wx8H, with chrome stacks and air horn detail, Model No. 329
EX $15 **NM** $25 **MIP** $50

Road Boss Car Carrier, 1973, Blue and yellow, 22.5Lx5.5Wx5.5H, with chrome stacks and air horn detail plus 3 cars, Model No. 335
EX $15 **NM** $25 **MIP** $50

Typhoon Dump Truck, 1973, Yellow, 13.5Lx6Wx5.5H, typhoon design, Model No. 303
EX $15 **NM** $25 **MIP** $50

Typhoon Hydraulic Dump, 1973, Blue and white, 13Lx6Wx6H, typhoon design with turbine cab, Model No. 311
EX $15 **NM** $25 **MIP** $50

Vista Dome Horse Van, 1973, Met. gold, 22Lx5.5Wx6H, typhoon design with 4 plastic horses, Model No. 320
EX $15 **NM** $25 **MIP** $50

Typhoon Cement Mixer, 1973, Blue and white, 13.5Lx6.75Wx7.5H, typhoon design with turbine cab, Model No. 325
EX $15 **NM** $25 **MIP** $50

Typhoon Car Carrier, 1973, Red and yellow, 22.5Lx5.5Wx6H, typhoon design with 3 plastic cars and ramp, Model No. 330
EX $15 **NM** $25 **MIP** $50

Typhoon Fire Rescue Truck, 1973, Red, 12.5Lx6Wx6.5H, typhoon design with 3 ladders, Model No. 353
EX $15 **NM** $25 **MIP** $50

Typhoon Emergency Truck, 1973, White, 12.5Lx6Wx6.5H, typhoon design with 1 red ladder on top, Model No. 358
EX $15 **NM** $25 **MIP** $50

Steerable Stubby Wrecker, 1973, Gold and white, 11Lx5.5Wx7H, thunderbolt design, with black tow boom, Model No. 615
EX $15 **NM** $25 **MIP** $50

Road Grader, 1973, Yellow, 11.75Lx5Wx6H, "Structo 11" stencilled in black on blade, Model No. 183
EX $15 **NM** $25 **MIP** $50

Hi-Lift Bulldozer, 1973, Yellow, 12Lx6Wx6.5H, "Structo 11" stencilled in black on blade, Model No. 501
EX $15 **NM** $25 **MIP** $50

Giant Bulldozer, 1973, Yellow, 12Lx6.75Wx7H, "Structo 11" stencilled in black on blade, Model No. 514
EX $15 **NM** $25 **MIP** $50

Rough Rider Pickup, 1973, Yellow, 9.25Lx4Wx4H, hurricanes design, Model No. 801
EX $10 **NM** $15 **MIP** $25

Camper Truck, 1973, Orange and white, 9.25Lx4.25Wx5H, hurricanes design, Model No. 835
EX $10 **NM** $15 **MIP** $25

Waggin' Wagon, 1973, Lime green and white, 9.25Lx4Wx4H, hurricanes design with clear cover & 6 dogs, Model No. 837
EX $10 **NM** $15 **MIP** $25

Dump Truck, 1973, Gold and white, 10.75Lx4Wx4.25H, "Structo 841" stencilled on side of dump box, Model No. 841
EX $10 **NM** $15 **MIP** $25

Tractor-Trailer Truck, 1973, Blue and silver, 16.5Lx4.25Wx5.5H, hurricanes design with structo van lines on trailer, Model No. 861
EX $10 **NM** $15 **MIP** $25

Livestock Truck, 1973, Blue and white, 9.5Lx4.25Wx4H, hurricanes design with white panels and 5 animals, Model No. 870
EX $10 **NM** $15 **MIP** $25

Monster Machine, 1973, Green, 2.75Lx3.5Wx3H, 2 wheeled design with exposed "Chrome" engine, Model No. 215
EX $10 **NM** $15 **MIP** $25

Panic Panel, 1973, Orange, 2.75Lx3.5Wx3H, 2 wheeled design with panel wagon sides, Model No. 216
EX $10 **NM** $15 **MIP** $25

Weird Wagon, 1973, Red, 2.75Lx3.5Wx3H, 2 wheeled design with WV bug style, Model No. 217
EX $10 **NM** $15 **MIP** $25

Buzzin' Buggy, 1973, Yellow, 2.75Lx3.5Wx3H, 2 wheeled design with open dune buggy style, Model No. 218
EX $10 **NM** $15 **MIP** $25

Giant 24-Pack Assortment, 1973, 17.75Lx16.5Wx16.5H, all 4 weird wheels designs in a store display - 24 cars total, Model No. 219
EX n/a **NM** n/a **MIP** $250

Triple Terrific 3 Pack, 1973, 14Lx5Wx5H, one each #215, #216, #217 in a 3 pack store display box, Model No. 220
EX n/a **NM** n/a **MIP** $150

Brain Barrel, 1973, Brown, 2.75Lx3.5Wx3H, 2 wheeled design with brown "Wooden" brrel & bald driver, Model No. 250
EX $10 **NM** $15 **MIP** $25

Structo

Loonie Looper, 1973, Yellow and orange, 2.75Lx3.5Wx3H, 2 wheeled design with airplane styling including propeller, Model No. 251
EX $10 **NM** $15 **MIP** $25

Litter Picker, 1973, White and orange, 2.75Lx3.5Wx3H, 2 wheeled design with trash can style with propeller, Model No. 252
EX $10 **NM** $15 **MIP** $25

Triple Terrific 3 Pack, 1973, 14Lx5Wx5H, one each #250, #251, #252 in a 3 pack store display box, Model No. 262
EX n/a **NM** n/a **MIP** $150

Big 2-Dozen Assortment, 1973, 17.75Lx14.75Wx16.5H, all 3 weird wheels designs in a store display - 24 cars total, Model No. 265
EX n/a **NM** n/a **MIP** $250

Giant Gantry Crane, 1973, Yellow, 32.5Lx12.25Wx14H, hand crank pulley system with crane mechanism, Model No. 555
EX $25 **NM** $50 **MIP** $75

Motorized Giant Gantry Crane, 1973, Blue and yellow, 32.5Lx12.25Wx14H, motor operates all action, battery operated, Model No. 558
EX $25 **NM** $50 **MIP** $75

TONKA

MIGHTY-TONKA TOYS

Backhoe, 1968-70s, 21" long; swiveling body, rubber treads, yellow hoe
EX $25 **NM** $50 **MIP** $150

Bottom Dump, 1971, 34" long; No. 3938, green tractor-trailer; 1971 and later
EX $40 **NM** $85 **MIP** $260

Bulldozer, 1968-70s, 12-3/8" long; No. 3906, lever-adjusted blade, sun umbrella over seat
EX $10 **NM** $22 **MIP** $65

Bulldozer, 1970s, 17" long; yellow, "Turbo-Diesel," cage over seat
EX $8 **NM** $17 **MIP** $50

Car Carrier, 1967-69, 34-1/4" long; No. 3990, carries Mini-Tonka load of two Jeep Pickups and one Wagoneer
EX $60 **NM** $85 **MIP** $210

Car Carrier, 1970, 34-1/4" long; No. 2990, in 1968 changes to No. 3990, carries Mini-Tonka load of one Jeep Pickup and two Volkswagens
EX $60 **NM** $85 **MIP** $195

Car Carrier, 1971, 21-1/8" long; No. 3950, green, six wheels, 1971 and later
EX $30 **NM** $65 **MIP** $195

Cement Mixer, 1968-70s, 19" long; "Turbo-Diesel," yellow, white drums
EX $20 **NM** $45 **MIP** $75

Cement Mixer, 1971, 21-1/8" long; No. 3950, green, six wheels, 1971 and later
EX $25 **NM** $100 **MIP** $220

Clam, 1965, 25" long, 18" high; No. 2905, yellow
EX $12 **NM** $28 **MIP** $85

Crane, 1965-70s, 30" long, 20" high; No. 2940, yellow, black boom w/clam, also called Mobile Crane, in 1968 becomes No. 3940
EX $25 **NM** $35 **MIP** $50

Custom Van, 1970s, open top, sliding door; late 1970s
EX $3 **NM** $7 **MIP** $20

Dump, 1964-70s, 18-1/2" long; No. 900, becomes No. 2900 in 1965, then No. 3900 in 1968
EX $5 **NM** $10 **MIP** $30

Grader, 1972, 24-3/4" long; No. 3945, orange; 1972 and later
EX $10 **NM** $30 **MIP** $50

Hard Hat, 1960s, No. 4999; plastic hard hat, sold individually or w/sets of Mighty-Tonka toys; late 1960s
EX $5 **NM** $10 **MIP** $15

Hydraulic Dump, 1971, 18-1/2" long; No. 3902, orange; 1971 and later
EX $85 **NM** $175 **MIP** $260

Loader, 1967-70s, 1907/8" long; No. 2920, later 3920, lever-operated bucket
EX $12 **NM** $23 **MIP** $35

Loadmaster, 1971, 18" high; No. 4002, sand loader for dump trucks, green and black; 1971 and later
EX $10 **NM** $20 **MIP** $30

Lowboy (tractor-trailer), 1968-70s, "Mighty Diesel," yellow
EX $15 **NM** $30 **MIP** $45

Mobile Shovel, 1967-70, 23" long; box-shaped cab, rubber treads, handgrip on shovel handle
EX $20 **NM** $40 **MIP** $60

Motor Home, 1973, 22-3/4" long; No. 3885, Winnebago recreational vehicle, swiveling seats, shock-absorbing bumpers, fold-back top, two 6" dolls and dog; 1973 and later
EX $25 **NM** $50 **MIP** $75

Off-Road Adventure Buggy, 1970s, changeable tires, jack; late 1970s
EX $7 **NM** $13 **MIP** $20

Rescue Vehicle, 1974-79, 18" long; also Rescue Van, white van w/orange top, removable stretcher, driver, nurse and patient
EX $20 **NM** $40 **MIP** $60

Roller, 1971, 16" long; No. 3910, road-roller; 1971 and later
EX $22 **NM** $50 **MIP** $100

School Bus, 1970s, 19" long; yellow, van design, white plastic hubs, open top
EX $7 **NM** $15 **MIP** $22

Scraper, 1967-70s, 27-1/4" long; No. 2935, becomes No. 3935 in 1968, fills, hauls, dumps
EX $130 **NM** $260 **MIP** $400

Scraper-Dozer, 1967-69, 30" long; dozer w/swivel-attached scraper end
EX $40 **NM** $79 **MIP** $120

Shovel, 1965-69, 29" long; No. 2930, yellow, handgrip on shovel lever, becomes No. 3930 in 1968
EX $42 **NM** $83 **MIP** $125

Shovel, 1970, 29" long; No. 3930, lime green; 1970 and later
EX $15 **NM** $30 **MIP** $45

Wrecker, 1969-70, 17-1/4" long; No. 3915, white, dual hoists
EX $32 **NM** $70 **MIP** $95

Wrecker, 1971, 17-1/4" long; No. 3915, orange body, white cab and hoists; 1971 and later
EX $28 **NM** $56 **MIP** $85

MINI-TONKA TOYS

Allied Van (tractor-trailer), 1965-69, 16" long; No. 98, orange, high-window cabover, "Allied Van Lines," rear doors open, becomes No. 1098 in 1968
EX $35 **NM** $69 **MIP** $105

Apple Peeler, 1971, 7" long; No. 1335, hot rod panel truck
EX $6 **NM** $12 **MIP** $20

Beach Buggy, 1965-66, 6-1/2" long; No. 42, tan Jeep, balloon tires
EX $3 **NM** $7 **MIP** $18

Beach Buggy, 1967, 6-1/2" long; No. 42, brown Jeep, balloon tires, white canopy
EX $3 **NM** $7 **MIP** $18

Beach Buggy (Jeep), 1969-70, 6-1/2" long; No. 1042, purple w/white canopy, wide balloon tires
EX $3 **NM** $6 **MIP** $25

Beach Buggy (Jeep), 1971, 6-1/2" long; No. 1042, purple w/yellow canopy, wide balloon tires; 1971 and later
EX $3 **NM** $6 **MIP** $25

Bell System Truck, 1970s-80s, 5-1/2" long; boom lift, white cab, six wheels, No. 55010 on bottom
EX $5 **NM** $10 **MIP** $15

Bell System Van, 1979, 5" long; white van, w/blue-yellow side panels
EX $2 **NM** $4 **MIP** $8

Bone Bruzzer, 1972, No. 1020, orange Jeep w/roll bars
EX $3 **NM** $6 **MIP** $9

Camper, 1963-64, 9-1/2" long; No. 70, red-pink Jeep pickup w/white camper
EX $6 **NM** $12 **MIP** $25

Camper, 1965, 9-1/2" long; No. 70, tan pickup, white camper
EX $5 **NM** $10 **MIP** $25

Camper, 1967, 9-1/2" long; No. 70, brown body, white camper
EX $5 **NM** $10 **MIP** $25

Camper, 1968-70, 9-1/2" long; No. 1070, purple pickup w/camper
EX $10 **NM** $15 **MIP** $25

Car Carrier (tractor-trailer), 1964-70, 18-1/2" long; No. 96, green tall windshield cabover, green trailer, two plastic Sting Rays, becomes No. 1096 in 1968
EX $28 **NM** $56 **MIP** $85

Car Carrier (tractor-trailer), 1978, 20" long; white and orange
EX $7 **NM** $13 **MIP** $25

Cement Truck or Cement Mixer, 1964-70, 9-1/2" long; No. 77, originally called simply Mixer, red Jeep tuck w/white,

VEHICLES • STRUCTO

crank-turned mixer assembly, lever-tilting body, becomes No. 1077 in 1968
EX $13 **NM** $26 **MIP** $40

Crane Truck, 1973, 12" long; No. 1099, mobile crane w/hook
EX $4 **NM** $8 **MIP** $35

Datsun, 1974, No. 1029
EX $9 **NM** $19 **MIP** $28

Dump, 1963, 9-1/2" long; No. 60, all red Jeep truck, lever-operated dump bed;
EX $9 **NM** $19 **MIP** $28

Dump, 1964, 9-1/2" long, No. 60, green body, yellow dump bed
EX $9 **NM** $19 **MIP** $29

Dump, 1965-70, 9-1/2" long; No. 60, red w/yellow dump bed, becomes No. 1060 in 1968
EX $8 **NM** $17 **MIP** $25

Farmer Charmer, 1971, 8-1/2" long; No. 1225, "super Thrust" in 1971, turbo cab, purple pickup; 1971 and later
EX $5 **NM** $10 **MIP** $15

Fire Chief, 1967-69, 9-1/8" long; No. 66, Jeep Wagoneer, all red, "Fire Chief" on door, flasher, becomes No. 1066 in 1968
EX $8 **NM** $17 **MIP** $25

Fire Chief, 1970, 9-1/8" long; No. 1066, Jeep Wagoneer, red body and white roof, "fire Chief" on door, flasher; 1970 and later
EX $7 **NM** $13 **MIP** $20

Fire Fighter, 1966-70, 9-3/4" long; No. 72, red and white, detachable ladders, flasher, becomes No. 1072 in 1968
EX $7 **NM** $13 **MIP** $20

Fire Fighter, 1971, 8-7/8" long; No. 1255, "Super Thrust" in 1971, turbo cab, removable ladders; 1971 and later
EX $5 **NM** $10 **MIP** $15

Fixer Mixer, 1971, 8-7/8" long; No. 1249, "Super Thrust" in 1971, turbo cab, yellow cement mixer; 1971 and later
EX $5 **NM** $11 **MIP** $16

Fun Buggy, 1969-70s, 7" long; No. 1010, roll bar, issued w/removable top in at least 1969, various colors
EX $3 **NM** $6 **MIP** $25

Grader, 1964-69, 10-3/4" long; No. 76, yellow, originally had black stripes on blade, open cab, yellow hubs, becomes No. 1076 in 1968
EX $5 **NM** $9 **MIP** $14

Grader, 1970, 10-3/4" long; No. 1076, lime green, metal hubs; 1970 and later
EX $5 **NM** $9 **MIP** $14

Hi-Way Patrol, 1965-70, 9-1/8" long; No. 64, black and white police Jeep Wagoneer w/flasher, becomes No. 1064 in 1968
EX $15 **NM** $30 **MIP** $55

Honey Bucket, 1972, No. 1025, yellow jeep, blue top
EX $3 **NM** $6 **MIP** $12

Hoot 'N Hauler, 1971, 8-7/8" long; No. 1230, "Super Thrust" in 1971; turbo cabover, dump truck; 1971 and later
EX $5 **NM** $9 **MIP** $14

Hot Hauler, 1971, 7" long; No. 1330, yellow, hot rod pickup
EX $5 **NM** $15 **MIP** $20

Jeep Commander, 1965-69, 6-1/2" long; No. 40, Army green, w/canopy, becomes No. 1040 in 1968
EX $7 **NM** $13 **MIP** $20

Jeep Dispatcher, 1965, 6-1/8" long; No. 30, green, open top
EX $7 **NM** $13 **MIP** $20

Jeep Dispatcher, 1965-70, 6-1/8" long; No. 30, blue, becomes No. 1030 in 1968
EX $5 **NM** $10 **MIP** $15

Jeep Wagoneer, 1965-66, 9-1/2" long; No. 62, turquoise station wagon
EX $12 **NM** $23 **MIP** $35

Lightning Bugs, 1972, No. 1165, Volkswagen, yellow hubs, chromed rear engines; 1972 and later
EX $6 **NM** $12 **MIP** $20

Litter Bug, 1971, 9-1/2" long; No. 1260, "Super Thrust" in 1971, turbo cab, garbage truck
EX $5 **NM** $11 **MIP** $16

Livestock Van (tractor-trailer), 1964-66, 16" long; No. 90, red w/white trailer sides; high-window cabover, opening rear doors
EX $15 **NM** $30 **MIP** $45

Loader, 1969-70s, 10-1/2" long; No. 1087, yellow, movable scoop, metal hubs
EX $6 **NM** $8 **MIP** $12

Luv Bug, 1971, 8-5/8" long; No. 1160, Volkswagen
EX $6 **NM** $12 **MIP** $18

Mini-Bucket, 1971, 7" long; No. 1349, hot rod, single bucket seat
EX $5 **NM** $11 **MIP** $20

Mixer, 1964, 9-5/8" long: No. 1977, Jeep truck cab, rotating plastic mixer section and hopper, tilting bed
EX $10 **NM** $20 **MIP** $30

Motor Mover (tractor-trailer), 1971, 18-5/8" long: No. 1275, "Super Thrust" in 1971, turbo cab car carrier, two plastic Corvettes; 1971 and later
EX $15 **NM** $25 **MIP** $35

Pacer Police Car, 1970s, 9" long; white, flasher bar on roof, chromed bumpers, white plastic hubs
EX $9 **NM** $19 **MIP** $28

Pickup, 1963-70, 9-1/8" long; introduced as No. 50 in 1963, becomes No. 1050 in 1968, all red Jeep truck, snap-open tailgate
EX $8 **NM** $16 **MIP** $24

Pickup and Horse Trailer, 1967-70, 14-3/4" long; No. 82, blue Jeep Pickup, white horse trailer, horses, becomes No. 1082 in 1968
EX $17 **NM** $33 **MIP** $55

Pony Puller, 1972, 14-1/8" long; No. 1265, pink bubble-window Pickup w/white horse trailer; 1972 and later
EX $7 **NM** $13 **MIP** $22

Road Paver, 1973, 9-1/2" long; No. 1095, green paver w/plastic "asphalt" road; 1973 and later
EX $23 **NM** $46 **MIP** $75

Road Roller, 1972, No. 1083, 1972 and later
EX $5 **NM** $10 **MIP** $15

Rollin' On (tractor-trailer), 1970s, 16" long; blue bubble-window cab, white van trailer w/large "Rollin' On" panels
EX $5 **NM** $10 **MIP** $15

Ruff Rider, 1970, 6-1/8" long; No. 1045, green, open top, six wheels
EX $4 **NM** $8 **MIP** $12

Sanitary Service, 1968-70, 9-1/2" long; No. 1084, blue tall-windshield cabover, lever-controlled white dump body
EX $15 **NM** $30 **MIP** $45

Scamper Camper, 1971, 8-5/8" long; No. 1250, "Super Thrust" in 1971, green bubble-window cabover, green camper w/opening white door; 1971 and later
EX $5 **NM** $9 **MIP** $20

Scotts Pick-Up, 1979, 8-1/2" long; green and white pickup, "Scotts" in oval
EX $3 **NM** $6 **MIP** $9

Scraper, 1969-70s, 14" long; No. 1091, yellow, metal hubs
EX $7 **NM** $13 **MIP** $20

Side Winder (Volkswagen), 1970, wind-up key decal
EX $6 **NM** $12 **MIP** $18

Snow Seekers, 1970, 16-7/8" long: No. 1081, originally called "Wagoneer and Snowmobile," yellow Wagoneer w/trailer and snowmobile; 1970, 1974 and later
EX $17 **NM** $33 **MIP** $50

Snowmobile, 1970s, 7" long; from Wagoneer set
EX $7 **NM** $13 **MIP** $20

Stake Crate, 1971, 8-7/8" long: No. 1245, "Super Thrust" in 1971, turbo cab, stake truck; 1971 and later
EX $4 **NM** $8 **MIP** $12

Stake Truck, 1963, 9-3/4" long; No. 56, blue Jeep body and stakes, lever-raised dump stake body
EX $13 **NM** $26 **MIP** $40

Stake Truck, 1964-70, 9-3/4" long; No. 56, blue Jeep truck, white stakes, became No. 1056 in 1968
EX $8 **NM** $20 **MIP** $25

Stanley Home Products Truck (tractor-trailer), 1970s-80s, 16" long; white van body w/opening rear doors, bubble-window cabover, "Stanhome" stickers
EX $5 **NM** $11 **MIP** $16

Start Cart, 1971, 9" long; No. 1235, "Super Thrust" in 1971, turbo cab, wrecker; 1971 and later
EX $4 **NM** $8 **MIP** $16

Sun Seeker, 1972, No. 1079; Bone Bruzzer w/orange trailer and Tiny-Tonka dune buggy; 1972 and later.
EX $7 **NM** $13 **MIP** $20

Thunder Hubs, 1971, 7" long; No. 1325, hot rod convertible coupe
EX $5 **NM** $10 **MIP** $20

Track Duster, 1972, No. 1345, blue and orange, Mack-type hot rod truck w/rear water tank; 1972
EX $6 **NM** $12 **MIP** $18

Trencher, 1969, 18" long; No. 1089, yellow w/black backhoe, metal hubs
EX $7 **NM** $13 **MIP** $20

Trencher, 1970, 18" long; No. 1089, lime green w/black backhoe, metal hubs; 1970 and later
EX $5 **NM** $10 **MIP** $18

Twinkle Toes, 1970, 8-5/8" long; Volkswagen, foot-shaped yellow "Twinkle Toes" decal on doors
EX $5 **NM** $11 **MIP** $20

Van (tractor-trailer), 1964, 16" long; No. 86, blue tall-windshield cabover, white van trailer w/"Tonka"
EX $17 **NM** $33 **MIP** $50

Van (tractor-trailer), 1965-66, 16" long; No. 86, blue cabover, white van trailer w/"Mini-Tonka"
EX $12 **NM** $23 **MIP** $35

Volkswagen, 1970, 8-5/8" long; No. 1158, assorted colors, previously grouped as Regular Tonka by Tonka Corp.; 1970 and later
EX $10 **NM** $30 **MIP** n/a

Wagoneer and Snowmobile, 1970-71, 16-7/8" long; No. 1081, yellow Jeep Wagoneer with trailer, yellow plastic snowmobile
EX $40 **NM** $80 **MIP** $135

Wagoneer and Trailer, 1965-69, 17-1/2" long; No. 80, red Jeep Wagoneer w/trailer, yellow plastic Sting Ray, becomes No. 1080 in 1968
EX $48 **NM** $96 **MIP** $145

Wrecker, 1963-70, 9-1/2" long; No. 68, white Jeep truck, red boom, lever-operated winch, becomes No. 1068 in 1968
EX $12 **NM** $23 **MIP** $75

REGULAR TONKA

"V" Blade Snow Plow, 1957, 9" wide; No. AC-308, orange Hi-Way blade w/mounting bracket, large "V" shape
EX n/a **NM** n/a **MIP** n/a

3-in-1 Hi-Way Service Truck, 1957, 13" long; No. 44, orange, w/two snowblades
EX $275 **NM** $400 **MIP** $700

5th Wheel Trailer, 1974-75, 14" pickup w/19" trailer; open-top trailer attaches to bed of white Styleside pickup; camper
EX $23 **NM** $46 **MIP** $70

Aerial Ladder, 1955, 32-1/2" long; No. 700-4, red w/aluminum ladder, "MFD" decals
EX $100 **NM** $300 **MIP** $450

Aerial Ladder, 1956, 32-1/2" long; No. 700, red, 36" fully extendable aluminum ladder, rotating base, "TFD" decals, 2 extra ladders
EX $150 **NM** $300 **MIP** $450

Aerial Ladder, 1960-61, 32-1/2" long; No. 48, red w/aluminum ladder, "TFD" decals
EX $125 **NM** $250 **MIP** $450

Aerial Ladder, 1962, No. 1348
EX $100 **NM** $150 **MIP** $350

Aerial Ladder, 1964, No. 998, two auxiliary ladders
EX $50 **NM** $75 **MIP** $100

Aerial Ladder, 1972, No. 2960, not tractor-trailer, open cab; 1972 and later
EX $12 **NM** $23 **MIP** $35

Aerial Ladder (tractor-trailer), 1965-70s, 28-3/4" long; No. 998 in 1965, red, "glassed-in" cabover, "T.F.D." on sides, becomes No. 2998 in 1968
EX $25 **NM** $50 **MIP** $75

(Harvey K Rainess)

Aerial Ladder Semi Fire Truck, 1954, 32-1/2" long; No. 700
EX $175 **NM** $260 **MIP** $450

Aerial Ladder Truck, 1963, No. 1348
EX $100 **NM** $150 **MIP** $200

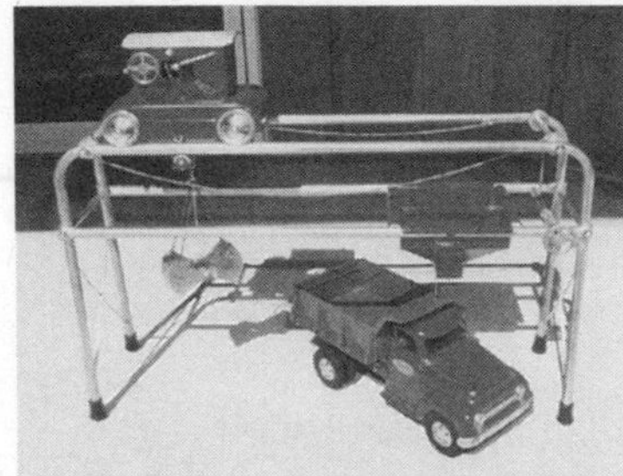

Aerial Sand Loader Set, 1955, 25-1/2" long; No. 825-5, Loader and Dump Truck
EX $275 **NM** $425 **MIP** $875

Air Express Truck, 1959, No. 16, dark blue body, square box bed, whitewall tires, "Air Express" decals on sides, plastic windshield, opening rear doors
EX $350 **NM** $425 **MIP** $700

Air Force Ambulance, 1965-66, 14" long; No. 402, blue pickup w/"USAF" on doors, red cross on hood, troop canopy over bed
EX $45 **NM** $95 **MIP** $135

Air Force Jeep, 1965-68, 10-1/2" long; No. 252 in 1965, blue w/"USAF," becomes No. 2252 in 1968
EX $10 **NM** $20 **MIP** $30

Airlines Luggage Service, 1962, 16-5/8" long; No. 420
EX $100 **NM** $250 **MIP** $400

Airport Service Set, 1963, No. 2100
EX $150 **NM** $225 **MIP** $300

Alley Gater, 1972, No. 2310, red and white open boat w/wheels
EX $7 **NM** $13 **MIP** $20

Allied Moving Van, 1957, 24" long; No. 38, orange cab and box trailer, "Allied Van Lines" decals
EX n/a **NM** n/a **MIP** n/a

Allied Van, 1961, 21-1/4" long; No. 39, orange cab and trailer w/"Allied Van Lines" decals. Black bumper on cab, blackwall tires on cab and trailer
EX $120 **NM** $250 **MIP** $450

Allied Van, 1962, No. 739
EX $125 **NM** $250 **MIP** $350

Allied Van, 1963, No. 739
EX $118 **NM** $175 **MIP** $235

Allied Van Lines, 1955, 23-3/4" long; No. 400-5, orange tractor/trailer
EX $100 **NM** $200 **MIP** $300

Allied Van Lines, 1964, No. 739, black knob on door
EX $75 **NM** $125 **MIP** $175

Allied Van Lines Semi, 1950, 23-1/2" long; No. 400
EX $175 **NM** $260 **MIP** $400

Back Hoe, 1963, 17-1/8" long; No. 422
EX $100 **NM** $175 **MIP** $350

Backhoe, 1963-65, 17" long; No. 422, yellow truck cab, body, and backhoe, w/red rear seat
EX $28 **NM** $56 **MIP** $85

Backhoe, 1970s, yellow swivel body, black boom and scoop, six wheels
EX $17 **NM** $33 **MIP** $50

Backhoe, 1971, green; 1971 and later
EX $17 **NM** $33 **MIP** $50

Bell System Truck, 1978, lift truck, white cab roof
EX $7 **NM** $13 **MIP** $20

Big Mike Dual Hydraulic Dump Truck, 1957, 14" long; No. 43, twin hydraulic mechanisms lift dump bed
EX $325 **NM** $595 **MIP** $1000

Big Mike Dual Hydraulic Dump Truck, 1958 Next Generation Cars, No. 45, orange Hi-Way dump w/"V" snow plow, and "twin hydraulic action"
EX $375 **NM** $675 **MIP** $1000

Boat Service Truck, 1961, 23-1/2" long; No. 117, 1961 only, included blue fleetside pickup truck w/white cab roof, silver hubs, whitewall tires, blue trailer w/three plastic boats stacked horizontally
EX $100 **NM** $250 **MIP** $450

Boat Transport, 1960, 28" long; No. 41, blue truck w/semi-trailer, four plastic

boats stacked virtually upright, w/bar at the front for two outboard motors
EX $250 **NM** $450 **MIP** $850

Boat Transport Truck, 1961, 28" long; No. 41, blue truck w/semi-trailer, four plastic boats stacked virtually upright, w/bar at the front for two outboard motors
EX $150 **NM** $300 **MIP** $650

Bottom Dump (tractor-trailer), 1965-69, No. 910 in 1965, yellow, "glassed-in" cabover, five-position dump action, became No. 2910 in 1968
EX $38 **NM** $76 **MIP** $115

Bulldozer, 1960, 8-7/8" long; No. 10, plated roller wheels only in 1960. Black rubber treads, 3-position blade
EX $75 **NM** $125 **MIP** $200

Bulldozer, 1962
EX $50 **NM** $75 **MIP** $100

Bulldozer, 1962-70s, 8-7/8" long; No. 300 in 1962, yellow, adjustable blade, becomes No. 2300 in 1968
EX $13 **NM** $26 **MIP** $40

Bulldozer, 1963, No. 300
EX $55 **NM** $82 **MIP** $110

Bulldozer, 1970s, "Tonka Trax," plastic rollover cage
EX $7 **NM** $13 **MIP** $20

Camper, 1962, 14" long; No. 530
EX $75 **NM** $150 **MIP** $250

Camper, 1962-65, 14-5/8" long; No. 530, blue/turquoise Styleside Pickup w/white camper;
EX $60 **NM** $120 **MIP** $180

Camper, 1963, No. 530
EX $25 **NM** $38 **MIP** $50

Camper, 1965-66, 14-5/8" long; No. 530, black pickup, white camper
EX $42 **NM** $83 **MIP** $125

Camper, 1968, No. 1070, Jeep Gladiator truck body, magenta, w/white camper top. The pattern for these trucks is the same as the No. 70 models dating from 1963, but color changes and line expansion forced Tonka to add more two more digits to the stock number
EX $15 **NM** $30 **MIP** $50

Camper, 1972, No. 255, red truck, white camper
EX $8 **NM** $17 **MIP** $40

Canadian Tire Jeep, 1972, red and white Jeep, oversized tires, "To Years of Service, 1922-1972" on hood
EX $10 **NM** $20 **MIP** $30

Car Carrier, 1960, 29" long; No. 40, yellow cab w/trailer includes three plastic 1960 Ford Falcon cars. Moveable ramp for loading and unloading
EX $100 **NM** $225 **MIP** $450

Car Carrier, 1961, 29" long; No. 40, yellow cab and trailer includes three plastic cars
EX $100 **NM** $250 **MIP** $450

Car Carrier, 1962, No. 840
EX $100 **NM** $150 **MIP** $300

Car Carrier, 1963, No. 840
EX $42 **NM** $63 **MIP** $85

Car Carrier, 1965-68, 27" long; No. 840, "glassed-in" cabover, yellow, trailer w/circular openings on sides, lever-operated loading ramp, three plastic cars; made first appearance in 1965 catalog; becomes No. 2840 in 1968
EX $42 **NM** $83 **MIP** $125

Car Carrier (tractor-trailer), 1969-70s, 27-1/2" long; No. 2850, yellow, trailer sides w/four larger openings, lever-operated ramp, two plastic cars
EX $22 **NM** $43 **MIP** $65

Car Quest Pickup, 1970s, 14-1/2" long; white Styleside, "Car Quest Auto Parts Stores" red and blue decals
EX $8 **NM** $17 **MIP** $30

Cargo King Truck, 1957, 23-1/2" long; No. 30, red cab, open aluminum box, "Cargo King" decals
EX n/a **NM** n/a **MIP** n/a

(Mark McManus)

Carnation Milk Step Van, 1954, 11-3/4" long; No. 750
EX $200 **NM** $400 **MIP** $600

Carnation Milk Truck, 1955, 11-3/4" long; No. 750-5, white Divco-style delivery truck w/Carnation Milk decals on panel sides, sliding front door, opening rear door
EX $200 **NM** $400 **MIP** $600

Cement Mixer, 1960, 15-1/2" long; No. 120, red body, plastic mixer and hopper, tilting bed, blackwall tires
EX $100 **NM** $150 **MIP** $300

Cement Mixer, 1961, 15-1/2" long; No. 120, red body, plastic mixer and hopper, tilting bed, adjustable chute for cement. Mixer geared to turn as truck moves
EX $100 **NM** $150 **MIP** $300

Cement Mixer, 1962, No. 620
EX $85 **NM** $150 **MIP** $300

Cement Mixer, 1963, No. 620
EX $75 **NM** $125 **MIP** $250

Cement Mixer, 1965-70, 14" long; No. 6320, red "glassed-in" cabover and chassis, white drum, becomes No. 2620 in 1968
EX $15 **NM** $30 **MIP** $50

Cement Mixer, 1971, 14" long; No. 2620, yellow-orange, w/white drum; 1971 and later
EX $12 **NM** $23 **MIP** $35

Crane and Clam, 1947, 24" long; No. 150
EX $135 **NM** $200 **MIP** $350

Crater Crawler, 1970-71, 11-7/16" long; No. 2546, metallic blue and white, bubble top, oversize tires; 1970-71
EX $8 **NM** $17 **MIP** $50

Deluxe Fisherman, 1960, No. 130, new boat and trailer for this year (trailer stayed in lineup until the 1970s). Blue "Fisherman" pickup w/white cab roof and white topper, larger white and red plastic boat on blue trailer w/working winch
EX $150 **NM** $350 **MIP** $550

Deluxe Fisherman, 1961, 27-5/8" long in total; No. 130, same as previous year's model, that is, a fleetside pickup w/topper, but this time in red and white rather than blue and white
EX $150 **NM** $350 **MIP** $550

Deluxe Sportman, 1959, No. 22, blue pickup truck w/white cab roof, whitewall tires, silver rims, boat trailer w/plastic boat
EX $150 **NM** $325 **MIP** $500

Deluxe Sportman, 1960, No. 22, blue pickup truck w/white cab roof, whitewall tires, silver rims, boat trailer w/plastic boat
EX $100 **NM** $250 **MIP** $400

Deluxe Sportman, 1961, 22-3/4" long; No. 22, blue pickup truck w/white cab roof, whitewall tires, silver rims, boat trailer w/plastic boat
EX $100 **NM** $200 **MIP** $450

Deluxe Sportsman with Boat Trailer, 1958 Next Generation Cars, 22-3/4" long; No. 34, red truck w/white cab roof, red trailer w/plastic fishing boat and attachable motor
EX $150 **NM** $325 **MIP** $750

Dozer Packer, 1962, 18-1/4" long total; No. 524, Packer has eleven tires, sold only in 1962
EX $100 **NM** $250 **MIP** $400

Dozer Packer, 1963, No. 524, yellow
EX $200 **NM** $300 **MIP** $400

Drag, 1963, No. 514
EX $60 **NM** $90 **MIP** $120

Dragline, 1959, 20" long; No. 14, yellow, rolling treads, working scoop that rotates on base, bucket actually scoops. Black nylon cord "cables" control bucket
EX $100 **NM** $175 **MIP** $375

Dragline, 1961, 18" high, 18" long; No. 14, yellow, black bucked, rubber treads
EX $100 **NM** $150 **MIP** $250

Dragline, 1962, No. 514
EX $150 **NM** $225 **MIP** $300

Dragline, 1966, 20-1/2" long; No. 514, yellow, "Dragline" in large letters, oval Tonka emblem, swivel body, rubber treads, black boom and dragging scoop, becomes No. 612 in 1966
EX $48 **NM** $96 **MIP** $145

Dragline & Trailer, 1959, 26-1/4" long; No. 44, lime-green cab and loboy trailer, lime-green dragline
EX $150 **NM** $275 **MIP** $400

Dump (tailgate), 1965, 13-3/8" long; No. 406, light orange, white cab roof, reinforced dump body w/opening tailgate
EX $40 **NM** $80 **MIP** $120

Dump (tailgate), 1966, 13-3/8" long; No. 406, tan, white cab roof, reinforced dump body w/opening tailgate
EX $35 **NM** $65 **MIP** $100

Dump (tailgate), 1967, 13-3/8" long; No. 406, red w/green-blue dump body
EX $28 **NM** $56 **MIP** $85

Dump (tailgate), 1968, 14" long; No. 2406, red w/green dump, new cab w/slanted roof
EX $20 **NM** $40 **MIP** $60

Dump (tailgate), 1969-70s, 13-1/2" long; No. 2465, red "glassed-in" cabover w/yellow dump body
EX $7 **NM** $15 **MIP** $22

Dump and Sand Loader, 1965, 23-3/4" long; No. 616, all red w/yellow dump body, tailgate Dump w/conveyor
EX $50 **NM** $100 **MIP** $150

Dump and Sand Loader, 1965-68, 24-1/8" long; No. 616, Dump No. 315 w/conveyor, all red w/yellow dump body
EX $40 **NM** $79 **MIP** $120

Dump and Sand Loader, 1968-70, No. 2315 Dump w/conveyor, all red except yellow dump body, new cab
EX $32 **NM** $63 **MIP** $95

Dump Truck, 1949, 12" long; No. 180
EX $100 **NM** $175 **MIP** $375

Dump Truck, 1955, 13" long; No. 180-5, red cab, green dump body
EX $100 **NM** $150 **MIP** $350

Dump Truck, 1956, 13" long: No. 180-6, red cab, green dump bed
EX $100 **NM** $150 **MIP** $350

Dump Truck, 1957, 13" long; No. 06, red cab w/green dump bed
EX n/a **NM** n/a **MIP** n/a

Dump Truck, 1958 Next Generation Cars, 13-1/2" long; No. 06, red cab w/green dump bed, two-position tailgate
EX $100 **NM** $150 **MIP** $300

Dump Truck, 1960, 13-1/2" long: No. 06, silver five-spoke hubs, red cab, plastic windshield, opening tailgate on dumper bed
EX $75 **NM** $125 **MIP** $290

Dump Truck, 1961, 13-1/2" long; No. 06, red truck w/blue-green dump bed, plastic windshield
EX $75 **NM** $100 **MIP** $250

Dump Truck, 1962, No. 406, 1962
EX $75 **NM** $150 **MIP** $275

Dump Truck, 1963, No. 406
EX $45 **NM** $68 **MIP** $90

Dump Truck, 1964, 13-1/2" long; No. 315
EX $40 **NM** $60 **MIP** $90

Dump Truck, 1964-65, 13-5/16" long; No. 315, orange-red, dump body without tailgate
EX $15 **NM** $30 **MIP** $55

Dump Truck, 1966-67, 13-5/16" long; No. 315, red cab, yellow dump body, dump body without tailgate
EX $15 **NM** $30 **MIP** $55

Dump Truck, 1968-69, 13-7/8" long; No. 2315, red and yellow, new cab w/slanted windshield, lever operated
EX $12 **NM** $23 **MIP** $35

Dump Truck, 1970, 13-7/8" long; No. 2315, orange; 1970 and later
EX $10 **NM** $20 **MIP** $35

Dump Truck, 1990s, 50th anniversary, red with green dump body
EX $15 **NM** $25 **MIP** $55

Dump Truck & Sand Loader, 1963, No. 616, yellow
EX $100 **NM** $150 **MIP** $235

Dump Truck & Sandloader, 1964, No. 616, orange and yellow
EX $75 **NM** $125 **MIP** $175

Dump Truck and Sand Loader, 1962, No. 616
EX $100 **NM** $200 **MIP** $300

Dump Truck with Sandloader, 1961, 23-1/4" long; No. 116
EX $100 **NM** $175 **MIP** $395

Dune Buggy, 1968-70s, 10-7/8" long, 8-1/4" wide; No. 2445, red Jeep w/white canopy and interior, folding windshield, removable top, oversize tires, "Dune Buggy" on front fenders; originally came w/chain for towing, expeditions, etc.
EX $10 **NM** $20 **MIP** $30

Dune Buggy, 1970s, 10-7/8" long; No. 2445, yellow Jeep w/white canopy
EX $8 **NM** $16 **MIP** $24

Express Truck, 1950, 13-1/2" long; No. 185
EX $200 **NM** $450 **MIP** $900

Falcon, 1960s, 8" long; plastic, sold separately and w/car carriers
EX $4 **NM** $8 **MIP** $12

(Ron O'Brien)

Farm Stake and Horse Trailer, 1959-61, 21-3/4" long; No. 35, tan farm stake truck w/white stakes, white two-horse trailer, two plastic horses
EX $125 **NM** $180 **MIP** $350

Farm Stake and Horse Trailer, 1962, No. 735
EX $75 **NM** $125 **MIP** $225

Farm Stake Truck, 1956, 13-1/2" long; No. 925-6, white cab and flatbed section w/six blue removeable stake sections
EX $125 **NM** $260 **MIP** $410

Farm Stake Truck, 1957, 13-1/2" long; No. 04, white truck w/six removable blue stake panels
EX $190 **NM** $375 **MIP** $480

Farm Stake Truck, 1958 Next Generation Cars, No. 04, "Tonka Farms" bull decal on sides, green truck w/white removeable stake panels
EX $100 **NM** $150 **MIP** $300

Farm Stake Truck, 1960, 14" long; No. 04, turquoise truck w/six white removeable rack sections, whitewall tires, five-spoke silver hubs, plastic windshield
EX $100 **NM** $200 **MIP** $325

Farm Stake Truck, 1961, 14" long; No. 04, blue truck w/six white removeable rack sections, whitewall tires, five-spoke silver hubs, plastic windshield
EX $85 **NM** $175 **MIP** $370

Farm Stake Truck, 1962, No. 404
EX $50 **NM** $95 **MIP** $150

Farm Stake Truck, 1963, No. 404
EX $60 **NM** $90 **MIP** $150

Farm Stake w/Two Horse Trailer, 1958 Next Generation Cars, 21-3/4" long; No. 35, green farm stake truck w/white stakes, white two-horse trailer, two plastic horses
EX $125 **NM** $250 **MIP** $450

Fisherman Pick-up, 1960, 14" long; No. 110, blue and white two-tone body and topper. Opening tailgate, topper w/"Fisherman" decal
EX $100 **NM** $175 **MIP** $375

Forklift with Container, 1970s, 12-1/2" long; w/pallet and box; mid-1970s
EX $10 **NM** $20 **MIP** $30

Gasoline Truck, 1957, 15" long; No. 16, red tanker truck w/"Gasoline" decals
EX $350 **NM** $525 **MIP** $1000

Gasoline Truck, 1958 Next Generation Cars, No. 33, hinged back door, "Gasoline" decals, hose and nozzle
EX $350 **NM** $500 **MIP** $900

Giant Dozer, 1961, 12-1/2" long; No. 118, a king-sized version of the regular dozer
EX $70 **NM** $100 **MIP** $250

Giant Dozer, 1962, No. 618
EX $100 **NM** $150 **MIP** $200

Giant Dozer, 1963, No. 536
EX $110 **NM** $160 **MIP** $225

Giant Dozer, 1964-65, 12-3/8" long; No. 536, Army green
EX $25 **NM** $50 **MIP** $75

Giant Dozer, 1965-67, 12-3/8" long; No. 537, yellow
EX $20 **NM** $40 **MIP** $60

Grader, 1955, 17" long; No. 600-5, orange, blade adjustable, working steering
EX $75 **NM** $125 **MIP** $200

Grader, 1965-66, 17-1/8" long; No. 510, yellow, metal hubs
EX $22 **NM** $43 **MIP** $65

Grader, 1967-70s, 17-1/2" long; No. 510, yellow, lever steering, yellow plastic hubs, becomes No. 2510 in 1968
EX $13 **NM** $26 **MIP** $40

Grading Service Truck, 1962, No. 834
EX $125 **NM** $250 **MIP** $350

Grading Service Truck, Trailer and Bulldozer, 1961, 25-1/2" long total; No. 134, includes yellow dump truck w/red dumper bed, yellow trailer and bulldozer w/3-position blade
EX $100 **NM** $150 **MIP** $350

Grain Hauler, 1955, 23-1/2" long; No. 550-5, red cab w/silver steel box, decals
EX $90 **NM** $135 **MIP** $280

Grain Hauler Semi, 1952, 22-1/4" long; No. 550
EX $125 **NM** $180 **MIP** $350

Green Giant Transport, 1956, 23-1/2" long; No. 650-6, white tractor/trailer, refrigerated, "Green Giant" decals
EX $155 **NM** $350 **MIP** $600

Green Giant Transport Semi, 1953, 22-1/4" long; No. 650, White cab and trailer w/Green Giant logo decals
EX $150 **NM** $300 **MIP** $500

(Ron O'Brien)

Green Giant Utility Truck, 1953, white w/"Green Giant" labels, 1954 wheels on model in photo
EX $85 **NM** $175 **MIP** $300

Hi-Way Hydraulic Dump Truck, 1956, 13" long; No. 980-6, orange w/yellow decals
EX $130 **NM** $280 **MIP** $395

Hi-Way Patrol, 1965-70, 9-1/8" long; No. 64, Jeep Wagoneer body, black w/white roof, red dome light, opening tailgate, "Hi-Way Patrol" decals on doors, becomes No. 1964 in 1968
EX $20 **NM** $40 **MIP** $80

Hi-Way Service Truck, 1958 Next Generation Cars, No. 41, orange dump truck w/two-position tailgate, drop side bed, scraper blade and plastic road signs
EX $100 **NM** $200 **MIP** $400

Horse Van, 1965-67, 12-3/4" long; No. 430, green truck w/horse-carrier body, two horses, ramp gate
EX $17 **NM** $33 **MIP** $50

Horse Van, 1968-70, 13-1/4" long; No. 2430, new cab w/slanted windshield, green, open-top horse compartment, two plastic horses
EX $15 **NM** $30 **MIP** $45

Houseboat Set, 1961, 29" long total; No. 136, includes red and white "Fisherman" pickup w/red tilt-bed boat trailer and plastic (floating) houseboat
EX $200 **NM** $400 **MIP** $800

Hydraulic Aerial Ladder, 1958 Next Generation Cars, No. 48, bright red cab and trailer w/extending ladder to 36"
EX $125 **NM** $250 **MIP** $450

Hydraulic Aerial Ladder Truck, 1957, 32" long; No. 48, red w/aluminum ladder, "TFD" decals
EX $200 **NM** $300 **MIP** $500

Hydraulic Dump, 1962, No. 520
EX $75 **NM** $100 **MIP** $220

Hydraulic Dump, 1965-67, 13-3/8" long; No. 520, blue w/white cab roof, "Hydraulic" decals on doors
EX $25 **NM** $50 **MIP** $75

Hydraulic Dump, 1968-70s, 13-7/8" long; No. 2520, becomes No. 2480 in 1969, blue, white roof, new cab w/slanting windshield
EX $23 **NM** $46 **MIP** $70

Hydraulic Dump (tailgate), 1969, 13-1/2" long; No. 2585, "glassed-in" cabover, orange cab and dumping body, hydraulic action, tailgate
EX $30 **NM** $56 **MIP** $85

Hydraulic Dump (tailgate), 1970, 13-1/2" long; No. 2585, "glassed-in" cabover, lime-green cab and dumping body, hydraulic action, tailgate; 1970 and later
EX $32 **NM** $46 **MIP** $70

Hydraulic Dump Truck, 1957, 13" long; No. 20, two-position tailgate, hydraulic cylinder controls dump bed
EX n/a **NM** n/a **MIP** n/a

Hydraulic Dump Truck, 1958 Next Generation Cars, No. 20, dark gold body, working dumper w/lever and hydraulic lifter, plastic windshield
EX $125 **NM** $175 **MIP** $275

Hydraulic Dump Truck, 1960, No. 20, dark gold body, working dumper w/lever and hydraulic lifter, two-position tailgate on dumper
EX $75 **NM** $150 **MIP** $300

Hydraulic Dump Truck, 1961, 13-1/2" long; No. 20, dark gold body, working dumper w/lever and hydraulic lifter, two-position tailgate on dumper
EX $75 **NM** $110 **MIP** $250

Hydraulic Dump Truck, 1963, No. 520
EX $45 **NM** $68 **MIP** $90

Hydraulic Dump Truck, 1965, 13-3/8" long; No. 520, Blue cab w/white roof, blue dumper bed
EX $35 **NM** $60 **MIP** $82

Jeep & Horse Trailer, 1964, 19-1/4" long total; No. 525, two horses
EX $45 **NM** $68 **MIP** $135

Jeep Commander, 1964, 10-1/2" long; No. 304, canvas top
EX $30 **NM** $50 **MIP** $75

Jeep Commander, 1964-69, 10-1/2" long No. 304, Army green, "canvas" canopy top, becomes No. 2304 in 1968
EX $7 **NM** $13 **MIP** $20

Jeep Dispatcher, 1962, 9-3/4" long; No. 200, light blue w/white plastic interior, folding windshield
EX $20 **NM** $40 **MIP** $60

VEHICLES • TONKA

Jeep Dispatcher, 1963, No. 200
EX $30 NM $50 MIP $75

Jeep Dispatcher, 1963-65, 9-3/4" long; No. 200, turquoise
EX $9 NM $19 MIP $28

Jeep Dispatcher, 1970, 9-3/4" long; No. 2200, lime green
EX $5 NM $10 MIP $30

Jeep Pumper, 1963, 10-3/4" long; No. 425
EX $100 NM $175 MIP $400

Jeep Pumper, 1963-65, 10-3/4" long; No. 425, red, hose connector, removable ladder
EX $67 NM $132 MIP $200

Jeep Pumper, 1964, No. 425, black steering wheel
EX $100 NM $150 MIP $275

Jeep Runabout, 1962-68, 24-1/4" long; No. 516, blue Jeep Dispatcher w/boat trailer and red/white motorboat, becomes No. 2516 in 1968
EX $17 NM $33 MIP $50

Jeep Runabout, 1963, No. 516, trailer and boat
EX $75 NM $150 MIP $300

Jeep Runabout, trailer, boat, 1962, 25-5/8" long total; No. 516
EX $75 NM $175 MIP $350

Jeep Surrey, 1963, No. 350
EX $50 NM $75 MIP $100

Jeep Surrey, fringe top, 1962, 10-1/2" long; No. 350
EX $42 NM $83 MIP $175

Jeep Universal, 1962, No. 249
EX $75 NM $125 MIP $175

Jeep Wrecker, 1964, 11" long; No. 375,
EX $40 NM $85 MIP $125

Jeep Wrecker, 1965, 11" long; No. 375, white, black boom;
EX $25 NM $50 MIP $75

Jeep Wrecker with Plow, 1965-69, 12-3/8" long; No. 435, white jeep, flasher, black winch and snow plow, becomes No. 2435 in 1968
EX $25 NM $50 MIP $75

Jeep Wrecker with Plow, 1970, 12-3/8" long; No. 2435, blue w/orange plow and winch
EX $20 NM $30 MIP $60

Jeepster Convertible Sedan, 1969, 13" long; No. 2245, red, black plastic removable top
EX $12 NM $23 MIP $45

Jeepster Convertible Sedan, 1970-71, 13" long; No. 2245, red Jeepster, white plastic canopy
EX $12 NM $23 MIP $45

Jeepster Pickup, 1969-70, 13" long; No. 2230, light green w/black roof
EX $15 NM $30 MIP $100

Jeepster Runabout, 1969-70, 27-1/4" long; No. 2460, yellow Jeepster and boat trailer w/red and white boat
EX $17 NM $33 MIP $60

Jeepster Runabout, 1971, 27-1/4" long; No. 2460, light blue Jeepster and trailer, blue and white boat
EX $15 NM $30 MIP $50

Jeepster Sport Convertible, 1969, 13" long; No. 2240, blue, removable top
EX $12 NM $23 MIP $35

Jeepster with Boat & Trailer, 1974, No. 2460, Blue jeep body w/white interior, blue trailer, blue and white plastic boat
EX $40 NM $75 MIP $92

Jet Delivery Truck, 1962, 14" long; No. 410, 1962 only
EX $200 NM $350 MIP $850

Jolly Green Giant Special, 1960-61, 14" long; white w/green stake racks, "Green Giant Company" decal on doors
EX $150 NM $300 MIP $450

Life Guard Jeep, 1968, 9-3/4" long; No. 2306, orange, flasher, rescue raft on top
EX $15 NM $30 MIP $60

Life Guard Jeep, 1969, 9-3/4" long; No. 2306, red, yellow rescue raft on top
EX $15 NM $30 MIP $60

Lift Truck and Trailer, 1948, No. 200
EX $200 NM $350 MIP $600

Livestock Hauler Semi, 1952, 22-1/4" long; No. 500
EX $125 NM $160 MIP $350

Livestock Van, 1955, 24" long; No. 500-5, red, tractor/trailer has slits
EX $110 NM $200 MIP $350

Livestock Van, 1957, 24" long; No. 36, red cab and trailer w/slits, tailgate loading ramp
EX n/a NM n/a MIP n/a

Livestock Van, 1958 Next Generation Cars, No. 36, red cab and trailer w/opening rear ramp and floating suspension
EX $175 NM $250 MIP $450

Loader, 1962, No. 402, yellow and green
EX $40 NM $60 MIP $80

Loader, 1963, No. 352
EX $40 NM $60 MIP $80

Loader, 1963-69, 11-3/4" long; No. 352, yellow, rubber treads, lever-tripped dumping action, becomes No. 2352 in 1968
EX $15 NM $30 MIP $45

Loader, 1970, 11-3/4" long; No. 2352, lime green; 1970 and later
EX $9 NM $19 MIP $28

Loading Tractor, 1949, 10-1/2" long; No. 190
EX n/a NM n/a MIP n/a

Logger, 1957, 23-3/4" long; No. 14, red cab, aluminum frame, 9 round logs, chains
EX n/a NM n/a MIP n/a

Logger [Tonka Logger], 1956, 23-1/2" long; No. 575-6, red cab, logging trailer includes 9 sanded dowel logs. Silver five-hole hubs
EX $130 NM $240 MIP $360

Logger Semi, 1953, 22-1/4" long; No. 575
EX $125 NM $180 MIP $350

Logger Semi, 1953, No. 575, wood flat bed
EX $125 NM $180 MIP $350

Lowboy and Bulldozer, 1960, 26-1/4" long; No. 125, light green cab, trailer, and bulldozer. Solid rubber tires without hubs on rear of trailer. Bulldozer w/3-position blade
EX $190 NM $375 MIP $675

Lowboy and Dozer, 1974, No. 2831, red tractor and lowboy w/orange dozer
EX $17 NM $33 MIP $70

Lumber Truck, 1955, 18-3/4" long; No. 850-5, red cab, aluminum flatbed, six-wheel, square lumber pieces
EX $175 NM $260 MIP $400

Lumber Truck, 1956, 18-3/4" long; No. 850-6, red cab, aluminum flatbed, square lumber pieces
EX $130 NM $225 MIP $360

Lumber Truck, 1957, 18" long; No. 22, bronze cab, aluminum flat bed, square lumber pieces
EX n/a NM n/a MIP n/a

Military Jeep & Box Trailer, 1964, 19-3/8" overall; No. 384
EX $50 NM $75 MIP $175

Military Jeep Universal, 1963-65, 10-1/2" long; No. 251, Army green, no canopy
EX $8 NM $16 MIP $24

Military Jeep Universal, 1964, No. 251
EX $35 NM $55 MIP $75

Military Tractor, 1964, No. 250, black seat
EX $55 NM $70 MIP $100

Minute Maid Van, 1955, 14-1/2" long; No. 725-5, white truck w/Minute Maid Orange Juice graphics and opening rear doors
EX $275 **NM** $650 **MIP** $950

Mobile Clam, 1961, 27-1/4" long; No. 142, orange cab, flatbed section and crane cab. Floating rear wheels, operating "clam" style bucket (still in use on later "Mighty Tonka" models), that tripped open when pulled to top of crane boom
EX $100 **NM** $250 **MIP** $450

Mobile Clam, 1962, No. 942
EX $100 **NM** $150 **MIP** $320

Mobile Clam, 1963, No. 942
EX $75 **NM** $112 **MIP** $150

Mobile Clam, 1964, No. 942, yellow
EX $50 **NM** $75 **MIP** $100

Mobile Dragline, 1960, No. 135, orange cab, flatbed section and crane cab w/black boom and bucket. Bucket operates w/cords and levers, and swivels on base attached to truck
EX $100 **NM** $250 **MIP** $450

Motor Boat, 1960s, 13" long; plastic, sold separately and w/boat carriers and trailers
EX $5 **NM** $10 **MIP** $15

Nationwide Moving Van, 1958 Next Generation Cars, 24-1/4" long; No. 39, long white cab and trailer w/full-width doors
EX $250 **NM** $475 **MIP** $800

No. 0250 Tractor, 1963, No. 250, yellow w/red seat
EX $75 **NM** $112 **MIP** $150

Parcel Delivery Truck, 1957, 12" long; No. 10, bronze, Divco-style delivery van, "Parcel Delivery" decals
EX $200 **NM** $350 **MIP** $500

Parcel Delivery Van, 1954, 11-3/4" long; No. 750
EX $200 **NM** $300 **MIP** $500

Pickup, 1962, No. 302, red body w/silver hubs, white cab roof, opening tailgate
EX $95 **NM** $150 **MIP** $250

Pickup, 1963, No. 302
EX $35 **NM** $52 **MIP** $70

Pickup, 1967, 12-3/4" long; No. 302, all red body, opening tailgate, five-spoke silver hubcaps
EX $35 **NM** $55 **MIP** $76

Pickup, 1990s, 50th anniversary, blue stepside
EX $25 **NM** $50 **MIP** $75

Pickup & Trailer, 1962, No. 528
EX $50 **NM** $75 **MIP** $150

Pickup and Horse Trailer, 1965, 14-3/4" long; No. 82, Blue Jeep Gladiator truck w/white horse trailer w/clear plastic dome roof. Includes two plastic horses
EX $30 **NM** $55 **MIP** $110

Pickup and Trailer, 1960, No. 28, bronze pickup towing stakeside trailer w/white plastic steer in back. End panel in trailer lifts out
EX $100 **NM** $150 **MIP** $300

Pickup Truck, 1955, 12-3/4" long; No. 880-5, red pickup
EX $125 **NM** $280 **MIP** $450

Pickup Truck, 1956, 13-3/4" long; No. 880-6, dark blue body, opening tailgate w/securing chain
EX $150 **NM** $350 **MIP** $650

Pickup Truck, 1957, 12-1/2" long; No. 02, dark blue, opening tailgate w/chains
EX n/a **NM** n/a **MIP** n/a

Pickup Truck, 1958 Next Generation Cars, 12-3/4" long; No. 02, dark blue body, opening tailgate, trailer hitch, plastic windshield
EX $100 **NM** $240 **MIP** $300

Pickup Truck, 1960, No. 02, bronze body, whitewall tires, solid silver hubs, opening tailgate, trailer hitch, plastic windshield
EX $100 **NM** $200 **MIP** $375

Pickup Truck, 1961, 12-3/4" long; No. 02, bronze body, whitewall tires, solid silver hubs, opening tailgate, plastic windshield
EX $100 **NM** $190 **MIP** $320

Pickup Truck, 1962-66, 12-3/4" long; No. 302, stepside, red body, white cab roof
EX $20 **NM** $40 **MIP** $60

Pickup Truck, 1967, 12-3/4" long; No. 302, all red
EX $20 **NM** $40 **MIP** $60

Pickup Truck, 1968-69, 13-1/2" long; No. 2302, all red, stepside w/rounded rear fenders, spoked metal hubs, new cab w/slanted windshield
EX $17 **NM** $33 **MIP** $50

Pickup w/Box Trailer, 1957, 20-1/2" long; No. 26, dark blue No. 02 pickup, dark blue No. AC-310 box trailer
EX n/a **NM** n/a **MIP** n/a

Pickup with Stake Trailer and Animal, 1957, 20-1/2" long; No. 28, blue No. 02 Pickup and red No. AC-312 stake trailer, plastic animal
EX $150 **NM** $250 **MIP** $400

Pickup with Stake Trailer and Animal, 1958 Next Generation Cars, No. 28, dark blue pickup, red stake trailer, plastic livestock animal, stake tailgate on trailer lifts out
EX $125 **NM** $175 **MIP** $350

Police Jeep, 1965, 10-1/2" long; No. 325, white Jeep, black and white canopy, flasher on hood, originally called Jeep Police Car
EX $28 **NM** $56 **MIP** $85

Police Jeep, 1966, 10-1/2" long; No. 325, white Jeep, all black canopy, flasher on hood
EX $28 **NM** $56 **MIP** $85

Power Boom Loader, 1960, 18-1/2" long; No. 115, 1960 only, blue flatbed truck w/working clamp and winch to pick up logs, pipe, etc. Whitewall tires, plastic windshield
EX $300 **NM** $650 **MIP** $1000

Pumper, 1963, No. 926
EX $60 **NM** $90 **MIP** $120

Pumper, 1965-68, 15-1/2" long; No. 926, "glassed-in" cabover, red, hydrant, becomes No. 2926 in 1968
EX $23 **NM** $46 **MIP** $70

Pumper, 1969-70s, 17-1/8" long; No. 2820, long LaFrance-style cab, hydrant, shoots water stream
EX $15 **NM** $30 **MIP** $45

Pumper Truck, 1962, No. 926
EX $100 **NM** $150 **MIP** $300

Ramp Hoist, 1963, 19-1/4" long; No. 640, red and white
EX $175 **NM** $350 **MIP** $550

Ramp Hoist, 1964, No. 640, park green and white, very rare
EX $300 **NM** $650 **MIP** $900

Ranchero, 1960s, 8" long; plastic, sold separately and w/car carriers
EX $5 **NM** $10 **MIP** $15

Rescue Squad, 1960, 13-3/4" long; No. 105, white truck body w/square box bed. Silver siren on driver's side of hood, red dome light, Civil Defence "CD" decals on doors, "Rescue Squad" w/red cross decals on back, red plastic boat attached w/rubber straps on top, removeable ladder
EX $100 **NM** $250 **MIP** $450

Rescue Squad Truck, 1956, 11-3/4" long; Included with Tonka Fire Department Set
EX $120 **NM** $260 **MIP** $400

Rescue Squad Truck, 1957, 12" long; No. 24, white Divco-style van, "Rescue Squad" decals, sliding side door, opening rear doors
EX n/a **NM** n/a **MIP** n/a

Rescue Van, 1955
EX $200 **NM** $450 **MIP** $800

Road Builder Set, 1954, No. 775, Road Grader, Semi T&T Crane and Dump Truck, five pieces
EX $350 **NM** $525 **MIP** $900

Road Grader, 1953, 17" long; No. 600
EX $50 **NM** $75 **MIP** $100

Road Grader, 1956, 17" long; No. 600-6, orange, steerable front wheels, tilting and rotating blade, floating rear wheels
EX $75 **NM** $125 **MIP** $200

Road Grader, 1958 Next Generation Cars, No. 12, orange body w/rotating and tilting blade, working steering, floating rear wheels
EX $75 **NM** $112 **MIP** $150

Road Grader, 1961, 17" long; No. 12, yellow cab and body w/steerable front wheels, tilting and rotating scraper blade, and floating rear wheels
EX $75 **NM** $100 **MIP** $200

Road Grader, 1962, No. 512
EX $45 **NM** $68 **MIP** $90

Road Grader, 1963, No. 512, red clearance lights
EX $80 **NM** $120 **MIP** $160

Road Grader [All-Weather], 1957, 13" long; No. 12, orange, yellow Hi-Way decals
EX n/a **NM** n/a **MIP** n/a

Sanitary Service, 1967-69, 16" long; No. 690, "glassed-in" cabover, dark blue cab, white garbage dump body, becomes No. 2690 in 1968
EX $23 **NM** $46 **MIP** $70

Sanitary Service, 1970, 16" long; No. 2690, light blue cabover, white dumping body with blue gate
EX $20 **NM** $40 **MIP** $60

Sanitary Truck, 1959, square back
EX $450 **NM** $700 **MIP** $1000

Sanitary Truck, 1960, No. 140, hydraulic
EX $350 **NM** $550 **MIP** $900

(Patrick O'Neil)

Sanitary Truck, 1961, 19-1/2" long; No. 140, white cab and rounded garbage section. Swinging rear door, hopper bucket raises up to drop garbage in truck
EX $400 **NM** $700 **MIP** $1500

Scraper Blade, 1957, 7" wide; No. AC-306, orange Hi-Way blade w/mounting bracket
EX n/a **NM** n/a **MIP** n/a

Serv-I-Car, 1962, 9-1/8" long; No. 201, 3-wheeled cart w/small dump bed, white
EX $75 **NM** $125 **MIP** $200

Service Truck, 1959-60, 12-3/4" long; No. 01, blue body, square box bed w/"Tonka Service" decals, whitewall tires, solid silver hubs, removeable aluminum ladder, plastic windshield
EX $100 **NM** $150 **MIP** $350

Servi-I-Car, 1963, No. 201
EX $55 **NM** $82 **MIP** $110

Shovel, 1957, 15" long; No. 08, orange, rubber treads
EX n/a **NM** n/a **MIP** n/a

Shovel, 1965-68, 20" long, 15" high; No. 526, yellow, lever-scoop w/handgrip, becomes No. 2536 in 1968
EX $25 **NM** $50 **MIP** $75

Shovel, 1970, 24-1/2" long, No. 2720, yellow swivel body, six tires; 1970 and later
EX $15 **NM** $30 **MIP** $45

Shovel and Carry-All (Loboy), 1955, 33" long; No. 120-5, red tractor, blue loboy, red shovel w/rubber treads
EX $150 **NM** $300 **MIP** $450

Shovel and Carry-All (Loboy), 1956, 33" long; No. 120-6, red cab, blue loboy, red shovel w/rubber treads
EX $188 **NM** $280 **MIP** $475

Shovel and Carry-All Trailer, 1957, 32" long; No. 40, orange cab and loboy, orange shovel, yellow decals
EX n/a **NM** n/a **MIP** n/a

Shovel and Carry-All Trailer, 1958 Next Generation Cars, No. 43, orange cab and loboy trailer, orange steam shovel w/black rubber treads
EX $200 **NM** $300 **MIP** $500

Snorkel Pumper, 1969-70s, 17-1/8" long; No. 2950, hand-operated aerial platform rising to 28", hydrant, 14" hose, long LaFrance-type cab
EX $12 **NM** $27 **MIP** $35

Sportsman, 1958 Next Generation Cars, 12-3/4" long; No. 05, dark blue body, box camper top, opening tailgate, trailer hitch
EX $150 **NM** $225 **MIP** $450

Sportsman, 1959, No. 05, tan body, box camper top, whitewall tires, solid silver hubs, white plastic boat attaches to topper w/rubber straps
EX $100 **NM** $175 **MIP** $350

Sportsman, 1960-61, 12-3/4" long; No. 05, tan box pickup w/white boat strapped to top, silver disk wheels, whitewall tires
EX $100 **NM** $175 **MIP** $350

Sportsman, 1962, No. 405
EX $75 **NM** $100 **MIP** $200

Sportsman w/Box Trailer, 1958 Next Generation Cars, No. 29, dark blue Sportsman, dark blue trailer w/opening tailgate
EX $150 **NM** $225 **MIP** $400

Stake Jumper, 1971, 13" long; No. 2447, lime green Jeepster w/oversized tires; 1971 and later
EX $12 **NM** $25 **MIP** $35

Stake Pickup, 1962, 12-5/8" long; No. 308
EX $40 NM $80 MIP $120

Stake Pickup, 1963, No. 308
EX $50 NM $95 MIP $150

Stake Pickup, 1964-65, 12-3/4" long, No. 308, light blue, white roof
EX $25 NM $50 MIP $75

Stake Pickup & Horse Trailer, 1963, 21-3/4" long overall; No. 625
EX $75 NM $125 MIP $175

Stake Pickup & Trailer, 1964, 21-5/8" long; No. 504
EX $50 NM $75 MIP $185

Stake Pickup and Trailer, 1965-66, 21-5/8" long; No. 504, Stake pickup w/stake trailer, light blue, white cab roof, animals
EX $32 NM $63 MIP $95

Stake Trailer, 1957, 5-1/2" long; No. AC-312, red stake trailer, sold as accessory, originally retailed for $1.98
EX $15 NM $30 MIP $45

Stake Truck, 1955, 16-1/2" long; No. 860-5, red truck w/8 green stakes, six-wheel
EX $175 NM $360 MIP $500

Stake Truck, 1956, 13" long; No. 991, red w/8 removeable stake sides
EX $150 NM $250 MIP $460

Stake Truck, 1964, No. 404, red
EX $70 NM $120 MIP $170

Standard Oil Company Wrecker Special, 1960
EX $200 NM $400 MIP $600

Star Kist Van, 1954, 14-1/2" long; No. 725
EX $250 NM $575 MIP $950

Steam Shovel, 1947, 20-3/4" long; No. 100
EX $135 NM $200 MIP $350

Stearn Shovel Deluxe, 1949, 22" long; No. 100
EX $100 NM $250 MIP $400

Steel Carrier Semi, 1950, 22" long; No. 145
EX $125 NM $200 MIP $350

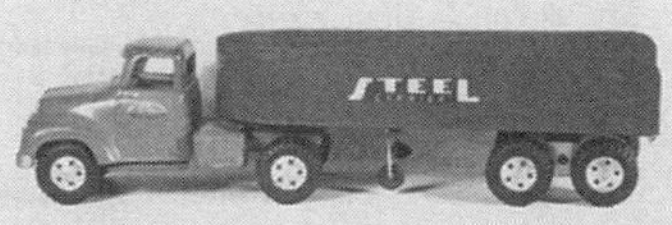

Steel Carrier Truck, 1954, No. 145, orange cab, green open box trailer, yellow "Steel Carrier" decals
EX $100 NM $185 MIP $380

Sting Ray, 1960s, 6-1/2" long; plastic, sold separately and w/car carriers
EX $4 NM $8 MIP $12

Stock Farm, 1957, No. B-202, No. 32 Stock Rack truck, 6 farm animals, wooden corral
EX n/a NM n/a MIP n/a

Stock Rack Truck, 1958 Next Generation Cars, No. 32, white cab and chassis, tall, removeable red stake sections
EX $100 NM $225 MIP $300

Stock Rack Truck with Animals, 1957, 16-1/4" long; No. 32, blue truck w/red stock rack, 3 plastic animals
EX $175 NM $365 MIP $650

Stump Jumper, 1970s, 13" long; No. 2447, red, "Stump Jumper" sticker; green in 1972, purple in 1973
EX $10 NM $20 MIP $30

Stump Jumper, 1971, 13" long; No. 2447, lime-green Jeepster with oversize tires, white canopy
EX $12 NM $18 MIP $30

Styleside Pickup, 1967, 14-1/8" long; No. 360, brown, white cab roof
EX $17 NM $33 MIP $50

Styleside Pickup, 1968, 14-9/16" long; No. 2360, maroon w/white cab roof, new cab w/slanted windshield
EX $13 NM $26 MIP $40

Styleside Pickup, 1969-70, 14-9/16" long; No. 2360, purple w/white cab roof
EX $13 NM $26 MIP $40

Styleside Pickup, 1971, 14-9/16" long; No. 2360, orange, white black cab roof; 1971 and later
EX $9 NM $18 MIP $26

Style-Side Pickup, 1963, 14" long; No. 354
EX $40 NM $60 MIP $125

Style-Side Pickup & Stake Trailer, 1963, 22-3/4" long total; No. 522
EX $75 NM $125 MIP $250

(Mark McManus)

Suburban Pumper, 1956, 17" long; No. 950-6, includes toy hydrant that attaches to garden hose, two 6" black hoses, removeable ladder
EX $120 NM $230 MIP $350

Suburban Pumper, 1957, 17" long; No. 46, red pumper, hydrant attaches to garden hose, two black hoses, one 36" hose, ladder
EX n/a NM n/a MIP n/a

(Harvey K Rainess)

Suburban Pumper, 1958 Next Generation Cars, No. 46, red truck w/hydrant that connects to garden hose, black hoses, whitewall tires
EX $175 NM $225 MIP $450

(Harvey K Rainess)

Suburban Pumper, 1960, No. 46, red, hydrant connects to garden hose, black hoses, whitewall tires
EX $100 NM $250 MIP $350

Tandem No. 36 Tandem Air Express, 1959, w/trailer, 24" long
EX $325 NM $650 MIP $1000

Tandem No. 40 Car Carrier, 1959
EX $100 NM $300 MIP $500

Tandem No. 41 Boat Transport, 1959, 38" long
EX $250 NM $350 MIP $700

Tandem No. 42 Hydraulic Land Rover, 1959, 15" long
EX $550 NM $825 MIP $1700

Tandem Platform Stake, 1959, 28-1/4" long; No. 30, bronze, whitewall tires on truck and trailer
EX $240 NM $450 MIP $800

Tanker, 1960, 28" long; No. 145, first Tonka w/major use of plastic
EX $100 NM $250 MIP $450

(Harvey K Rainess)

Tanker, 1961, 28" long; No. 145, red w/"Texaco" decals, dual rear wheels
EX $100 NM $250 MIP $350

Terminal Train, 1963, 33-5/8" long; No. 720, total, fifteen suitcases
EX $105 NM $175 MIP $300

Thunderbird Express, 1957, 24" long; No. 34, white semi tractor/trailer w/Thunderbird decal
EX $150 NM $400 MIP $600

Thunderbird Express, 1958 Next Generation Cars, No. 37, white cab and freight trailer w/fold-down wheels and opening rear doors
EX $150 NM $300 MIP $600

Thunderbird Express, 1960, No. 37, red cab w/white roof, red trailer w/white stripe and "Thunderbird" decal. Floating tandem dual wheels on trailer
EX $150 NM $350 MIP $550

Timber (Logger) Truck, 1960, No. 08, red cab, aluminum bed, includes square and round sanded "logs"
EX $150 NM $225 MIP $300

Tonka "Cargo King", 1956, 23-1/2" long; No. 550-6, red cab, open-top silver trailer, opening rear door
EX $145 NM $230 MIP $355

Tonka Toy Transport Van, 1949, 22-1/4" long; No. 140
EX $175 NM $300 MIP $500

Tractor, 1962, 8-5/8" long; No. 250
EX $50 NM $75 MIP $100

Tractor and Carry-All Trailer, 1949, No. 170, w/No. 150 Crane and Clam
EX $200 NM $300 MIP $525

Tractor and Carry-All Trailer, 1949, No. 125, w/No. 100 Steam Shovel
EX $150 NM $250 MIP $550

Tractor and Carry-All Trailer, 1949, No. 120, w/No. 50 Steam Shovel
EX $155 NM $280 MIP $475

Tractor and Wagon, 1973, 21" long; No. 2710, green tractor, four-wheel wagon, yellow hubs
EX $8 NM $16 MIP $24

Tractor with Trencher, 1975, 21" long; No. 2525, farm tractor w/scoop and backhoe
EX $5 NM $17 MIP $25

Tractor-Carry-All Trailer, 1949, 30-1/2" long; No. 130
EX $100 NM $150 MIP $350

Trailer, 1955, No. 65, stake side
EX $30 NM $45 MIP $60

Trailer Fleet Set, 1953, No. 675, two tractors (five interchangeable trailers), per set
EX $450 NM $680 MIP $975

Trencher, 1963, 18-1/4" long; No. 534
EX $40 NM $75 MIP $150

Trencher, 1963-70s, 18-1/4" long; No. 534, yellow, rubber tread, lever-operated front bucket, pivoting hoe, becomes No. 2534 in 1968
EX $9 NM $18 MIP $26

Trencher & LoBoy, 1963, 28-1/2" long total; No. 1001
EX $75 NM $112 MIP $150

Troop Carrier, 1964, 14" long; No. 380
EX $70 NM $100 MIP $150

Troop Carrier, 1965, 14" long; No. 380, Army green Styleside pickup w/"canvas" cover
EX $18 NM $36 MIP $55

Utility Dump, 1961, 12-1/2" long; No. 301, revised Golf Club Tractor; 1961 only
EX $100 NM $150 MIP $300

Utility Hauler, 1950, 12" long; No. 175
EX $100 NM $150 MIP $300

Utility Truck, 1954, No. 175, orange cab w/green utility (slit) bed
EX $110 NM $275 MIP $425

Utility Truck, 1958 Next Generation Cars, No. 03, red cab, aluminum flatbed
EX $100 NM $150 MIP $300

Volkswagen, 1965-75, 8-5/8" long; No. 150 yellow, No 152 blue, No. 153 green, No 156 red, VW "beetle"
EX $8 NM $16 MIP $24

Volkswagen, 1967, 8-5/8" long; No. 150 black, No. 152 blue, No. 154 green, and No. 156 maroon
EX $8 NM $16 MIP $24

Volkswagen, 1969, 8-5/8" long; No. 1158, various colors, reclassified by Tonka Corp. in 1970, see Mini-Tonka listing
EX $8 NM $16 MIP $24

Wrecker, 1949, 12-1/2" long; No. 250
EX $125 NM $250 MIP $375

Wrecker, 1953, blue w/red boom, chain, hook
EX $125 NM $200 MIP $350

Wrecker, 1954, red cab, white bed, red boom, chain and hook
EX $100 NM $300 MIP $500

Wrecker, 1956, 12" long; No. 960-6, white body, silver five-hole hubs, red dome light, "AAA" decal on sides, working winch, rare
EX $390 NM $525 MIP $800

Wrecker, 1956, 12" long; No. 996, white body, silverfive-hole hubs, red dome light, "MM" decal on sides, working winch
EX $100 NM $300 MIP $500

Wrecker, 1957, 12-1/2" long; No. 18, white w/black boom, "AA" decals
EX $75 NM $200 MIP n/a

Wrecker, 1958-61, No. 18, white, "AA" decals, black boom w/chain and hook, red dome light, whitewall tires, plastic windshield; 13-1/4" long
EX $75 NM $150 MIP $300

Wrecker, 1962, No. 518, black boom
EX $50 NM $120 MIP $150

Wrecker, 1962-67, 14-1/4" long; No. 518, white, red boom, flasher light
EX $42 NM $83 MIP $125

Wrecker, 1963-64, No. 518, red boom
EX $45 NM $85 MIP $150

Wrecker, 1968-70, 14-5/8" long; No. 2518, white, new cab w/slanted windshield, red boom, "24 Hr. Service"
EX $30 NM $59 MIP $100

Wrecker, 1970s, 14" long; 4x4 "24 Hr. Towing" truck, green, oversize tires; 1970s or 1980s
EX $12 NM $23 MIP $35

Wrecker, 1971, 14-5/8" long; No. 2518, orange w/white winch, new cab w/slanted windshield; 1971 and later
EX $27 NM $55 MIP $80

TINY-TONKA TOYS

Aerial Ladder (fire truck, tractor-trailer), 1968-70s, ladder raises, swivels, also removable ladders, Model No. 675
EX $12 NM $23 MIP $35

Ambulance, 1970s, white van, "Ambulance," Fire Department set
EX $5 NM $9 MIP $14

Banana Wheeler, 1973, yellow hot rod, oversize tires, Model No. 788
EX $3 NM $7 MIP $15

Bottom Dump (tractor-trailer), 1969-70s, dumps, spreads;, Model No. 655
EX $5 NM $9 MIP $14

Car Carrier (tractor-trailer), 1968-70s, steel body, plastic cars, Model No. 635
EX $7 NM $15 MIP $22

Carnation Milk Tanker, 1970s, six-wheel tanker, red w/silver tank, "Milk is a Natural"
EX $7 NM $13 MIP $20

Cement Mixer, 1968-70s, yellow w/red rotating and tilting drum, Model No. 575
EX $4 NM $8 MIP $12

Dozer, 1969-70s, yellow, black treads, blade raises, Model No. 495
EX $3 NM $5 MIP $30

Draggin' Wagon, 1970-71, "Crazy A's" hot rod, purple convertible sedan, Model No. 452
EX $5 NM $10 MIP $15

Dump, 1968-70s, red cab, yellow dump box raises, Model No. 535
EX $5 NM $10 MIP $22

Dump Stake, 1969-70, blue cab, white stake box raises, Model No. 527
EX $3 NM $7 MIP $10

Dump Stake, 1971, blue cab, yellow stake box, Model No. 527
EX $3 NM $7 MIP $10

Fire Chief, 1970s, red van w/window sides, Fire Department set
EX $4 NM $8 MIP $12

Frantic Flivver, 1970, "Crazy A's" hot rod, black body w/orange-red running boards/fenders, Model No. 458
EX $5 NM $10 MIP $15

Fun-Buggy, 1969, purple dune buggy, removable white top, Model No. 503
EX $3 NM $5 MIP $12

Fun-Buggy, 1969, orange dune buggy, roll bar, Model No. 500
EX $3 NM $5 MIP $12

Fun-Buggy, 1970, orange dune buggy, removable white top; 1970 and later, Model No. 500
EX $2 NM $4 MIP $10

Fun-Buggy, 1973, yellow w/white top, Model No. 503
EX $2 NM $4 MIP $10

Hot Horse Mustang, 1974, Powered Scrambler series
EX $4 NM $8 MIP $15

Hot Trike, 1972, red and blue three-wheeler, Model No. 750
EX $2 NM $4 MIP $6

Hub Heater, 1974, Powered Scrambler series, yellow body, flames on door
EX $4 NM $8 MIP $15

Lemon Wheeler, 1970s, yellow hot rod, oversize tires
EX $3 NM $7 MIP $12

Lightning Rod, 1971, Powered Scrambler series, orange body
EX $4 NM $8 MIP $15

Loader, 1969, rubber treads, lever-operated scoop, yellow, Model No. 521
EX $3 NM $6 MIP $12

Loader, 1970, rubber treads, lever-operated scoop, lime green; 1970 and later, Model No. 521
EX $3 NM $5 MIP $8

Lowboy and Dozer (tractor-trailer), 1969-70s, hauls Tiny-Tonka Dozer, Model No. 695
EX $4 NM $8 MIP $45

Minnie Winnie, 1973, pickup w/white Winnebago camper body, Model No. 800
EX $5 NM $10 MIP $15

Mod Rod, 1970-71, "Crazy A's" hot rod, yellow convertible coupe, Model No. 450
EX $3 NM $7 MIP $20

Pickup, 1968-70, red w/white interior, Model No. 515
EX $9 NM $18 MIP $26

Pickup, 1971, orange, Model No. 515
EX $4 NM $8 MIP $12

Pumper, 1968-70s, red fire truck, removable white ladders, Model No. 595
EX $7 NM $13 MIP $20

Rat-a-Tat-Tat, 1971, black hot rod sedan, Model No. 434
EX $6 NM $10 MIP $25

Rumble Bee, 1971, hot rod coupe w/rumble seat, Model No. 436
EX $4 NM $8 MIP $12

Sand Piper, 1972, green and yellow three-wheeler, Model No. 755
EX $2 NM $4 MIP $12

Sand Roamer, 1972, pink dune buggy w/white canopy, oversize tires, Model No. 765
EX $2 NM $4 MIP $7

Sanitary Service (garbage truck), 1968-70s, blue cab, white body, Model No. 615
EX $5 NM $10 MIP $15

School Bus, 1970, yellow van, "Tonka School District;" 1970 and later, Model No. 580
EX $4 NM $8 MIP $12

Scorcher, 1970-71, "Crazy A's" hot rod pickup, Model No. 454
EX $3 NM $7 MIP $15

Shell Oil Truck, 1970s, yellow, "Shell" on tanker body
EX $3 NM $6 MIP $9

Smart Cart, 1971, blue hot rod coupe, orange fenders, Model No. 432
EX $3 NM $7 MIP $15

Snap Dragon (van), 1970, green, "Snap Dragon" decal; early 1970 and later, Model No. 585
EX $5 NM $11 MIP $16

Station Wagon, 1969, blue van w/window sides, Model No. 529
EX $5 NM $10 MIP $15

Stinger, 1970, "Crazy A's" hot rod, green convertible sedan, Model No. 456
EX $3 NM $7 MIP $15

Sun Buggy, 1972, blue dune buggy w/oversized tires, Model No. 760
EX $2 NM $4 MIP $7

Taxi, 1971, orange hot rod sedan, Model No. 438
EX $3 NM $7 MIP $15

Track Blaster, 1971, Powered Scrambler series, blue body
EX $4 NM $8 MIP $15

Van, 1969, "Tiny Van," orange, Model No. 531
EX $5 NM $11 MIP $16

Wrecker, 1969-70s, blue w/red lever-operated winch, Model No. 555
EX $5 NM $10 MIP $15

YKK Zipper Van (tractor-trailer), 1960s, white, van trailer w/"YKK World's Largest Zipper Manufacturer."
EX $25 NM $50 MIP $75

TONKA-TOTES

Beach Buzzer, 1971, 2-1/4" long; No. 169, pink hot rod
EX $2 NM $3 MIP $5

Bug Blaster, 1970, 2-1/2" long; No. 175, VW; 1970 and later
EX $2 NM $5 MIP $9

Construction Helmet, 1970s, No. 4999, early 1970s
EX $3 NM $6 MIP $9

Double Deuce, 1970, 3" long; No. 181, hot rod; 1970 and later
EX $2 NM $3 MIP $5

Dune Duster, 1970, 2-13/16" long; No. 179, rear-engine buggy; 1970 and later
EX $2 NM $3 MIP $5

Gremlin, 1972, No. 160, green
EX $2 NM $3 MIP $5

Hemi-Hauler, 1970, No. 110, 3-1/4" long; yellow, rear-engine; 1970 and later
EX $2 NM $3 MIP $5

Launcher and Turn-Around Ramp, 1970
EX $2 NM $3 MIP $5

Pocket Rocket Launcher, 1971, 5-1/4" long
EX $2 NM $3 MIP $5

Quicker-Mixer, 1970, 3-1/8" long; No. 114, cement mixer, six-wheel; 1970 and later
EX $2 NM $3 MIP $5

Racing Helmet, 1970s, No. 4950, early 1970s
EX $2 NM $3 MIP $5

Salt Flat Racer, 1972, No. 162, racer w/streamlined fenders
EX $2 NM $3 MIP $5

Scream'n Demon, 1970, No. 117, race car; 1970 and later
EX $2 NM $3 MIP $5

Strip Whip, 1971, 3-1/4" long; No. 165, thin-bodied racer; 1971 and later
EX $2 NM $3 MIP $5

Super Snoot, 1971, 2-3/4" long; No. 167, wedge-bodied; 1971 and later
EX $2 NM $3 MIP $5

Thumper Dumper, 1970, 3-1/16" long; No. 112, dump truck, six-wheel; 1970 and later
EX $2 NM $3 MIP $5

Tonka-Bronc, 1971, 2-7/8" long; No. 171, hot rod, blue
EX $2 NM $3 MIP $5

Wicked Wrecker, 1970, 3-9/16" long; No. 116, wreck truck, six-wheel; 1970 and later
EX $2 NM $3 MIP $5

TOOTSIETOY

AIRPLANES

Aero-Dawn, 1928, Model No. 4660
EX $30 NM $60 MIP $80

Atlantic Clipper, 2" long
EX $5 NM $10 MIP $20

Autogyro, white, 1934, Model No. 4659
EX $25 NM $40 MIP $90

Beechcraft Bonanza, orange, front propellor
EX $15 NM $25 MIP $35

Bi-Wing Seaplane, 1926, yellow, Model No. 4650
EX $30 NM $40 MIP $85

Bleriot Plane, 1910, Model No. 4482
EX $25 NM $50 MIP $100

Crusader, Model No. 719
EX $25 NM $50 MIP $75

Curtis P-40, light green, Model No. 721
EX $120 NM $250 MIP $525

Dirigible, 4" long, reissue of prewar Navy Zeppelin, silver paint, "U.S.N. Los Angeles," 1953
EX $50 NM $110 MIP $180

Dirigible U.S.N. Los Angeles, silver, Model No. 1030
EX $40 NM $60 MIP $90

Douglas D-C 2 TWA, 1935, Model No. 717
EX $20 NM $45 MIP $85

F-94 Starfire, green, four engines; 1970s
EX $10 NM $15 MIP $35

Fly-N-Gyro, 1938
EX $50 NM $100 MIP $310

Helicopter, Die-cast and plastic, three blades 6" long; 1970s
EX $6 NM $9 MIP $12

KOP-1 USN
EX $20 NM $30 MIP $60

Low Wing Plane, miniature Piper Cub, Model No. 106
EX $20 NM $30 MIP $50

Navion, red, front propellor
EX $10 NM $15 MIP $35

Navy Jet, red; 1970s
EX $5 NM $10 MIP $30

Navy Jet Cutlass, red w/silver wings
EX $10 NM $15 MIP $30

Northrop F5A, U.S. fighter Jet; 1970s
EX $2 NM $4 MIP $5

P-38 Fighter Plane, 9-3/4" wingspan; 1950
EX $40 NM $60 MIP $110

P80 Panther Shooting Star
EX $25 NM $35 MIP $70

Piper Cub, blue, front propellor
EX $10 NM $15 MIP $30

S-58 Sikorsky Helicopter, 1970s
EX $15 NM $30 MIP $50

Snow Skids Airplane, rotating prop, 4" wingspan
EX $40 NM $60 MIP $85

Space Ship, 4" long, reissue of Buck Rogers Flash Blast Attack Ship with two-pod design, silver paint, U.S. Air Force insignia, 1958-59
EX $60 NM $120 MIP $200

VEHICLES • TOOTSIETOY

Space Ship, 4" long, reissue of Buck Rogers Venus Duo Destroyer, silver with U.S. Air Force insignia, 1958-59
EX $60 **NM** $120 **MIP** $260

Space Ship, 60, 4" long, reissue of Buck Rogers Battle Cruiser, silvver paint, U.S. Air Force insignia, 1958-59, Model No. 260
EX n/a **NM** n/a **MIP** n/a

Stratocruiser
EX $30 **NM** $50 **MIP** $110

Supermainliner
EX $20 **NM** $30 **MIP** $50

Top Wing Plane, miniature, Model No. 107
EX $20 **NM** $30 **MIP** $50

Transport Plane, 1941, orange, Model No. 722
EX $40 **NM** $75 **MIP** $110

Tri-Motor Plane, three propellors, Model No. 04649
EX $50 **NM** $85 **MIP** $150

TWA Electra, two engines, propellors, Model No. 125
EX $10 **NM** $20 **MIP** $45

Twin Engine Airliner, 10 windows, DC4
EX $20 **NM** $40 **MIP** $50

U.S. Army Plane, 1936, Model No. 119
EX $15 **NM** $25 **MIP** $50

UX214 Monoplane, 4", 1930s
EX $30 **NM** $60 **MIP** $90

Waco Bomber, blue base/silver top or silver base, Model No. 718
EX $50 **NM** $80 **MIP** $150

BOATS AND SHIPS

Battleship, silver w/some red on top, 6" long, 1939, Model No. 1034
EX $10 **NM** $20 **MIP** $35

Carrier, silver, Model No. 1036
EX $15 **NM** $25 **MIP** $40

Cruiser, silver; some red on top, 6" long, 1939, Model No. 1035
EX $10 **NM** $15 **MIP** $25

Destroyer, 4" long, 1939, Model No. 127
EX $10 **NM** $20 **MIP** $40

Freighter, 6" long; 1940, Model No. 1038
EX $10 **NM** $20 **MIP** $45

Submarine, 4" long, 1939, Model No. 128
EX $10 **NM** $15 **MIP** $30

Tanker, black, 6" long; 1940, Model No. 1039
EX $10 **NM** $20 **MIP** $25

Tender, 4" long; 1940, Model No. 129
EX $10 **NM** $15 **MIP** $25

Transport, 6" long, 1939, Model No. 1037
EX $15 **NM** $20 **MIP** $30

Yacht, 4" long; 1940, Model No. 130
EX $10 **NM** $15 **MIP** $30

BUSES

Cross Country Bus
EX $30 **NM** $45 **MIP** $65

Fageol Bus, 1927-33, Model No. 4651
EX $20 **NM** $40 **MIP** $65

GMC Greyhound Bus, blue/silver, 6"; 1948-55, Model No. 3571
EX $20 **NM** $35 **MIP** $55

Greyhound Bus, blue, 1937-41, Model No. 1045
EX $25 **NM** $60 **MIP** $80

Greyhound Scenicruiser Bus, 6" bus, raised upper deck, lower body painted silver, middle section and lower roof painted blue, roof top painted cream, 1955-69
EX $17 **NM** $33 **MIP** $50

Overland Bus, 1929-33, Model No. 4680
EX $45 **NM** $65 **MIP** $125

School Bus, "Buzy Bee Bus," white hub tires; 1970s
EX $2 **NM** $5 **MIP** $7

Twin Coach Bus, red w/black tires, 3" long; 1950
EX $20 **NM** $35 **MIP** $55

CANNONS AND TANKS

Army Tank, miniature
EX $5 **NM** $10 **MIP** $25

Army Tank, 1931-41, Model No. 4647
EX $35 **NM** $50 **MIP** $100

Four Wheel Cannon, 4" long; 1950s
EX $10 **NM** $20 **MIP** $45

Long Range Cannon, Model No. 4642
EX $7 **NM** $10 **MIP** $30

Six-Wheel Army Cannon, 1950s
EX $10 **NM** $20 **MIP** $50

CARS

Andy Gump Car, 1932; Funnies series, Model No. 5101X
EX $75 **NM** $300 **MIP** $500

Armored Car, "U.S. Army" on sides, camouflage, black tires, 1938-41, Model No. 4635
EX $25 **NM** $35 **MIP** $65

Auburn Roadster, red, white rubber wheels, Model No. 1016
EX $15 **NM** $30 **MIP** $45

Austin Healey 3000, 5" long, model kit in clear plastic cover on card, die-cast toy with wheels, axles, decals and plastic pieces; 1961
EX $50 **NM** $100 **MIP** $170

Austin-Healey, light brown roadster; 6" long; 1956
EX $20 **NM** $30 **MIP** $60

Baggage Car, Model No. 1101
EX $10 **NM** $15 **MIP** $30

Baja Runabout, Midget, 2-1/4"; 1960s-70s
EX $1 **NM** $2 **MIP** $3

Bandito, Super Slicks series, 4-1/4" long, gold hardtop hot rod, side-panel stickers, chrome-hub wheels, 1971-76
EX $3 **NM** $5 **MIP** $8

Bluebird Daytona Race Car
EX $20 **NM** $35 **MIP** $65

Boat Tail Roadster, red roadster, 6" long, Model No. 233
EX $20 **NM** $35 **MIP** $55

Buckin' Bronco, Hitch-Up series, Ford Bronco, white hub tires, 1970s
EX $6 **NM** $14 **MIP** $28

Buick Brougham, tan/black, Model No. 6003
EX $20 **NM** $35 **MIP** $70

Buick Coupe, blue w/white wheels, 1924, Model No. 4636
EX $30 **NM** $42 **MIP** $65

Buick Coupe, 4" long, Model No. 6002
EX $20 **NM** $35 **MIP** $50

Buick Estate Wagon, yellow and maroon w/black wheels, 6" long; 1948
EX $20 **NM** $35 **MIP** $50

Buick Experimental Car, blue w/black wheels, detailed tin bottom, 6" long; 1954
EX $25 **NM** $50 **MIP** $85

Buick LaSabre, red open top, black wheels, 6" long; 1951
EX $25 **NM** $45 **MIP** $70

Buick Roadmaster, blue w/black wheels, four-door; 1949
EX $25 **NM** $40 **MIP** $65

Buick Roadster, yellow open top, black wheels, 4" long, 1947-49
EX $20 **NM** $40 **MIP** $65

Buick Sedan, 6" long, Model No. 6004
EX $25 **NM** $35 **MIP** $55

Buick Special, 4" long; 1947, Model No. 103
EX $15 **NM** $25 **MIP** $50

Buick Station Wagon, green w/yellow top, black wheels, 6" long; 1954
EX $20 **NM** $30 **MIP** $45

Buick Tourer, red w/white wheels, 1925, Model No. 4641
EX $25 **NM** $45 **MIP** $70

Buick Touring Car, Model No. 6005
EX $50 **NM** $75 **MIP** $110

Cadillac, HO series, blue car/white top, 2" long; 1960
EX $10 **NM** $20 **MIP** $30

Cadillac 60, red-orange w/black wheels, four-door; 1948
EX $20 **NM** $40 **MIP** $60

Cadillac 62, red-orange w/white top, black wheels, four-door, 6" long; 1954
EX $20 **NM** $35 **MIP** $120

Cadillac Brougham, Model No. 6103
EX $40 **NM** $60 **MIP** $85

Cadillac Coupe, blue/tan, black wheels, Model No. 6102
EX $40 **NM** $60 **MIP** $85

Cadillac Eldorado, Midget series, 2-5/8" long, 1960s-70s
EX $2 **NM** $3 **MIP** n/a

Cadillac Sedan, white rubber wheels, Model No. 6104
EX $40 **NM** $60 **MIP** $85

Cadillac Touring Car, 1926, Model No. 6105
EX $50 **NM** $90 **MIP** $120

Car and Cabin Cruiser, Midget series combination, 5-1/2" long, Cadillac Eldorado hauls trailer with plastic Cabin Cruiser, 1969
EX $6 **NM** $9 **MIP** $12

Cheetah, Midget series, 2" long, different numbers on hood, 1960s
EX $2 **NM** $3 **MIP** n/a

Chevrolet Ambulance, 4" long
EX $15 **NM** $20 **MIP** $35

Chevrolet Bel Air, yellow w/black wheels, 3" long; 1955
EX $15 NM $30 MIP $50

Chevrolet Brougham, Model No. 6203
EX $40 NM $60 MIP $85

Chevrolet Coupe, Model No. 6202
EX $20 NM $35 MIP $90

Chevrolet Coupe, green w/black wheels, 3", Model No. 231
EX $20 NM $35 MIP $55

Chevrolet Fleetline, 1950 style, various colors, black wheels, 3" long; 1951-54
EX $10 NM $17 MIP $25

Chevrolet Roadster, Model No. 6201
EX $20 NM $35 MIP $90

Chevrolet Sedan, Model No. 6204
EX $20 NM $35 MIP $75

Chevrolet Touring Car, Model No. 6205
EX $60 NM $150 MIP $200

Chevy Corvette, 4" long, 1953 styling, black rubber tires, 1955-69
EX $10 NM $24 MIP $35

Chrysler Convertible, blue-green w/black wheels, 4" long; 1960
EX $8 NM $14 MIP $22

Chrysler Convertible, green w/black wheels, 4" long; 1947-49
EX $20 NM $30 MIP $45

Chrysler Experimental Roadster, 4" long, various colors, open top, black wheels
EX $13 NM $26 MIP $40

Chrysler New Yorker, blue w/black wheels, four-door, 6" long; 1953
EX $25 NM $35 MIP $55

Chrysler Windsor Convertible, black wheels, 6" long; 1950
EX $50 NM $90 MIP $120

Classic Series 1906 Cadillac or Studebaker, green and black, spoke wheels
EX $5 NM $10 MIP $15

Classic Series 1907 Stanley Steamer, yellow and black, spoke wheels; 1960-65
EX $5 NM $10 MIP $15

Classic Series 1912 Ford Model T, black w/red seats, spoke wheels
EX $5 NM $10 MIP $15

Classic Series 1919 Stutz Bearcat, black and red, solid wheels
EX $5 NM $10 MIP $15

Classic Series 1929 Ford Model A, blue and black, black tread wheels; 1960-65
EX $5 NM $10 MIP $15

Convertible, 3" long, single-seat 1939-style generic convertible, various body colors, black rubber tires, axle ends visible outside closed fenders, 1947-52
EX $9 NM $14 MIP $20

Corvair, red, 4" long; 1960s
EX $30 NM $55 MIP $75

Corvette Roadster, blue open top, black wheels, 4" long; 1954-55
EX $15 NM $25 MIP $35

Coupe, 3" long, 1939/40-style generic coupe, various body colors, black rubber tires, axle ends visible outside closed fenders, 1947-52
EX $13 NM $27 MIP $35

Desert Fox, Super Slicks series, 4-1/4" long; purple open-top hot rod, side panel stickers, chrome-hub tires, 1971-76
EX $3 NM $5 MIP $8

DeSoto Airflow, green w/white wheels, Model No. 0118
EX $20 NM $35 MIP $60

Doodlebug, same as Buick Special
EX $50 NM $75 MIP $100

Dune Buggy, White plastic top, white hub tires, 3-1/4" long; 1970s
EX $2 NM $4 MIP $6

Dune Buggy, Hitch-Up series, red dune buggy, 3-3/4" long; with white plastic top and surfboards, white hub tires, front hitch for hauling, 1970s
EX $2 NM $4 MIP $10

Dune Buster, Super Slicks series, 4-14" long, green hot rod, roof sticker, chrome-hub tires, 1971-76
EX $3 NM $5 MIP $8

Ferrari Lancia Race Car, red or dark green racer, 5" long, with silver grille, no racing number, plastic driver's head, plastic tires, 1964-67
EX $10 NM $20 MIP $30

Ferrari Racer, red w/gold driver, black wheels, 6" long; 1956
EX $30 NM $40 MIP $65

Ford, red w/open top, black wheels, 6" long; 1940
EX $15 NM $25 MIP $40

Ford B Hot Rod, 1960s
EX $5 NM $10 MIP $20

Ford Bronco, 4" long, white-hub tires, 1970s
EX $7 NM $10 MIP $15

Ford Bronco and Horse Trailer, black "Bronco Ranch" Bronco, white-hub tires, brown "Rodeo Team" trailer, plastic horse, 1970s
EX $10 NM $15 MIP $20

Ford Convertible Coupe, 1934
EX $30 NM $50 MIP $70

Ford Convertible Sedan, red w/black wheels, 3" long; 1949
EX $10 NM $20 MIP $35

Ford Coupe, powder blue w/tan top, white wheels, 1934
EX $30 NM $50 MIP $75

Ford Coupe, Midget series, 2-3/4" long, model of 1940 Ford coupe, 1960s
EX $1 NM $2 MIP n/a

Ford Coupe, blue or red w/white wheels, 1935, Model No. 0112
EX $25 NM $35 MIP $45

Ford Customline, blue w/black wheels; 1955
EX $15 NM $20 MIP $30

Ford Fairlane 500 Convertible, two-door 1957 convertible, 3" long, painted red, blue or green, molded front windshield, open wheel wells, patterned plastic tires
EX $6 NM $12 MIP $18

Ford Falcon, two-door 1960 sedan, 3" long, painted red, blue or orange, open wheel wells, patterned plastic tires, 1961-69
EX $4 NM $8 MIP $12

Ford GT, Midget, 2-1/8"; 1960s-70s
EX $1 NM $2 MIP n/a

Ford LTD, blue w/black wheels, 4" long; 1969
EX $8 NM $12 MIP $20

Ford Mainliner, red w/black wheels, four-door, 3" long; 1952
EX $10 NM $20 MIP $30

Ford Model A Coupe, blue w/white wheels, Model No. 4655
EX $25 NM $35 MIP $50

Ford Model A Sedan, green w/black wheels, Model No. 6665
EX $25 NM $35 MIP $50

Ford Model A Sedan, 4-1/2" long, green body, black chassis, oversize silver-hub tires, Collector's Customized Model A Series, 1974
EX $5 NM $8 MIP $12

Ford Model A Wagon, 4-1/2" long, brown body, black chassis, woodside styling, oversize silver-hub tires, Collector's Customized Model A Series, 1974
EX $5 NM $8 MIP $12

Ford Mustang, Midget series, 2-1/8" long, 1960s-70s
EX $1 NM $2 MIP n/a

Ford Mustang with Boat Trailer, Midget series combination, 4-1/2" long; Mustang hauling trailer with Chris-Craft Boat, 1966
EX $6 NM $10 MIP $15

Ford Ranch Wagon, green w/yellow top, four-door, 4" long; 1954
EX $15 NM $25 MIP $35

Ford Ranch Wagon, red w/yellow top, four-door, 3" long; 1954
EX $15 NM $20 MIP $35

Ford Ranch Wagon, four-door 1960 station wagon, 3" long, painted blue, open wheel wells, patterned plastic tires, 1962-67
EX $3 NM $6 MIP $9

Ford Roadster, powder blue w/open top, white wheels, Model No. 0116
EX $25 NM $40 MIP $60

Ford Sedan, 1934, Model No. 0111
EX $35 NM $50 MIP $70

Ford Sedan, powder blue w/white solid wheels, 1935, Model No. 0111
EX $25 NM $35 MIP $50

Ford Sedan, lime green w/black wheels, four-door, 3" long; 1949
EX $15 NM $20 MIP $35

Ford Station Wagon, powder blue w/white top, black wheels, 6" long; 1959
EX $15 NM $20 MIP $35

Ford Station Wagon, blue w/black wheels, 3" long; 1960
EX $20 **NM** $40 **MIP** $60

Ford Station Wagon, red w/white top, black wheels, four-door, 6" long; 1962
EX $25 **NM** $40 **MIP** $55

Ford Thunderbird, two-door 1955 coupe, 4" long; open wheel wells, fin-style rear fenders, open wheel wells, patterned plastic tires, 1960-67
EX $6 **NM** $12 **MIP** $24

Ford Thunderbird (1967), Midget, 2-3/8"; 1960s
EX $1 **NM** $2 **MIP** n/a

Ford Tourer, open top, red w/silver spoke wheels, Model No. 4570
EX $20 **NM** $30 **MIP** $45

Ford V-8 Hotrod, red w/open top, black wheels, open silver motor, 6" long; 1940
EX $15 **NM** $25 **MIP** $35

Ford w/Trailer, blue sedan, white rubber wheels, Model No. 1043
EX $50 **NM** $75 **MIP** $130

Graham Convertible Coupe, side spare tire, rubber wheels, 1933-35, Model No. 0614
EX $50 **NM** $125 **MIP** $175

Graham Convertible Coupe, rear spare tire, rubber wheels, 1933-35, Model No. 0514
EX $50 **NM** $125 **MIP** $175

Graham Convertible Sedan, side spare tire, rubber wheels, 1933-35, Model No. 0615
EX $50 **NM** $125 **MIP** $175

Graham Convertible Sedan, rear spare tire, rubber wheels, 1933-35, Model No. 0515
EX $50 **NM** $125 **MIP** $175

Graham Coupe, rear spare tire, rubber wheels, 1933-35, Model No. 0512
EX $50 **NM** $115 **MIP** $150

Graham Coupe, side spare tire, rubber wheels, 1933-35, Model No. 0612
EX $50 **NM** $115 **MIP** $150

Graham Roadster, rear spare tire, rubber wheels, 1933-35, Model No. 0511
EX $50 **NM** $115 **MIP** $150

Graham Roadster, side spare tire, rubber wheels, 1933-35, Model No. 0611
EX $50 **NM** $115 **MIP** $150

Graham Sedan, rear spare tire, rubber wheels, 1933-35, Model No. 0513
EX $50 **NM** $115 **MIP** $150

Graham Sedan, side spare tire, rubber wheels, 1933-35, Model No. 0613
EX $50 **NM** $115 **MIP** $150

Graham Towncar, side spare tire, 1933-35, Model No. 0616
EX $50 **NM** $115 **MIP** $140

Graham Towncar, rear spare tire, rubber wheels, 1933-35, Model No. 0516
EX $50 **NM** $115 **MIP** $150

Gremlin, Hitch-Up series, 4" long, "Gremlin" decal, 1970s
EX $3 **NM** $5 **MIP** $8

Hot Rod, Midget series, 2" long; 1960s
EX $1 **NM** $2 **MIP** $4

Hot Rod Model B, single-seat Ford hot rod, 3" long, painted red, blue or green, detailed engine, exposed plastic tires, 1961-69
EX $4 **NM** $8 **MIP** $12

Hot Rod Wagon, Hitch-Up series, "Bimini Buggy," white hub tires, 1970s
EX $2 **NM** $4 **MIP** $6

Indy Race Car, Midget series, 2-3/8" long, 1960s
EX $1 **NM** $2 **MIP** n/a

Insurance Patrol, miniature, Model No. 104
EX $15 **NM** $25 **MIP** $35

International Station Wagon, red/yellow, 3" long, 1947-52, Model No. 239
EX $8 **NM** $30 **MIP** $50

International Station Wagon, red/yellow, white wheels, 3" long, 1939-41, Model No. 1046
EX $15 **NM** $25 **MIP** $50

International Station Wagon, 4" long, rubber wheels; 1940s
EX $25 **NM** $50 **MIP** $50

Jaguar Formula D, Midget series, 2-1/2" long, 1960s
EX $2 **NM** $3 **MIP** n/a

Jaguar Type D, green w/black wheels, 3" long; 1957
EX $10 **NM** $15 **MIP** $25

Jaguar XK 120 Roadster, green open top, black wheels, 3" long
EX $10 **NM** $15 **MIP** $25

Jaguar XK 140 Coupe, blue w/black wheels, 6" long
EX $8 **NM** $17 **MIP** $25

Kaiser Sedan, blue w/black wheels, 6" long; 1947
EX $25 **NM** $45 **MIP** $55

KO Ice, 1932; Funnies series, Model No. 5105X
EX $100 **NM** $325 **MIP** $425

Lancia Racer, dark green w/black wheels, 6" long; 1956
EX $30 **NM** $50 **MIP** $75

Large Bluebird Racer, green w/yellow solid wheels, Model No. 4666
EX $20 **NM** $40 **MIP** $60

LaSalle Convertible, rubber wheels, Model No. 0714
EX $80 **NM** $200 **MIP** $300

LaSalle Convertible Sedan, rubber wheels, Model No. 0715
EX $80 **NM** $200 **MIP** $300

LaSalle Coupe, rubber wheels, Model No. 0712
EX $150 **NM** $300 **MIP** $350

LaSalle Sedan, red w/black rubber wheels, 3" long, Model No. 230
EX $15 **NM** $20 **MIP** $30

LaSalle Sedan, rubber wheels, Model No. 0713
EX $140 **NM** $200 **MIP** $275

Limousine, blue w/silver spoke wheels; prewar, Model No. 4528
EX $20 **NM** $40 **MIP** $65

Lincoln, prewar; red w/white rubber wheels, four-door
EX $110 **NM** $400 **MIP** $500

Lincoln Capri, red w/yellow top, black wheels, two-door, 6" long
EX $20 **NM** $35 **MIP** $50

Maserati Race Car, Dark green or red race car, 5" long, with silver grille and black racing number on white background, driver's head of plastic, 1962-67
EX $10 **NM** $20 **MIP** $30

Mercedes 190 SL Coupe, powder blue w/black wheels, 6" long; 1956
EX $15 **NM** $25 **MIP** $40

Mercedes Convertible, Midget series, 2-3/8" long; 1960s
EX $1 **NM** $2 **MIP** n/a

Mercury, red w/black wheels, four-door, 4" long; 1952
EX $15 **NM** $20 **MIP** $40

Mercury Custom, blue w/black wheels, four-door, 4" long; 1949
EX $15 **NM** $30 **MIP** $40

MG, Midget series, 2-1/4" long, 1960s
EX $2 **NM** $4 **MIP** $18

MG TF Roadster, blue open top, black wheels, 3" long; 1954
EX $10 **NM** $15 **MIP** $30

MG TF Roadster, red open top, black wheels, 6" long; 1954
EX $15 **NM** $25 **MIP** $45

Monza, Midget series, 2-1/4" long; 1970s
EX $1 **NM** $2 **MIP** n/a

Moon Mullins Police Car, 1932; Funnies series, Model No. 5104X
EX $130 **NM** $200 **MIP** $425

Nash Metropolitan Convertible, red w/black tires; 1954
EX $25 **NM** $35 **MIP** $60

Observation Car, Model No. 1103
EX $10 **NM** $15 **MIP** $30

Offenhauser Racer, dark blue w/black wheels, 4" long; 1947
EX $10 **NM** $20 **MIP** $35

Oldsmobile 88 Convertible, bright green w/black wheels, 6" long; 1959
EX $20 **NM** $25 **MIP** $40

Oldsmobile 88 Convertible, yellow w/black wheels, 4" long; 1949
EX $15 **NM** $25 **MIP** $35

Oldsmobile 98, various colors, skirted fenders, black wheels, 4" long; 1955-60
EX $20 **NM** $25 **MIP** $40

Oldsmobile 98, various colors, open fenders, black wheels, 4" long; 1955-60
EX $20 **NM** $25 **MIP** $45

Oldsmobile 98 Staff Car
EX $20 NM $25 MIP $45

Oldsmobile Brougham, Model No. 6303
EX $25 NM $35 MIP $50

Oldsmobile Coupe, Model No. 6302
EX $25 NM $35 MIP $50

Oldsmobile Roadster, orange/black, white wheels, 1924, Model No. 6301
EX $25 NM $45 MIP $75

Oldsmobile Sedan, Model No. 6304
EX $25 NM $35 MIP $50

Oldsmobile Touring, Model No. 6305
EX $25 NM $35 MIP $50

Open Touring, green convertible, white wheels, 3", Model No. 232
EX $25 NM $35 MIP $45

Packard, white body w/blue top, black wheels, four-door, 6" long; 1956
EX $12 NM $25 MIP $35

Panzer Wagon, Super Slicks series, 4-1/4" long, red hot rod with rear engine, hood sticker, chrome-hub tires, 1971-76
EX $3 NM $5 MIP $8

Pie Wagon, Super Slicks series, 4-1/4" long, pink hardtop hot rod, roof sticker, chrome-hub tires, 1971-76
EX $3 NM $5 MIP $8

Plymouth, dark blue w/black wheels, two-door, 3" long; 1957
EX $10 NM $15 MIP $20

Plymouth Belvedere, Plymouth 1957 model, 3" long; two-door hardtop , blue or red, open wheel wells, patterned plastic tires, 1959-69
EX $6 NM $12 MIP $18

Plymouth Sedan, blue w/black wheels, four-door, 3" long; 1950
EX $15 NM $20 MIP $30

Pontiac, Midget series, 2-3/8" long; 1970s
EX $1 NM $2 MIP n/a

Pontiac Fire Chief, red w/black wheels, 4" long; 1950
EX $20 NM $35 MIP $50

Pontiac Sedan, green w/black wheels, two-door, 4" long; 1950
EX $15 NM $25 MIP $45

Pontiac Star Chief, red w/black wheels, four-door, 4" long; 1959
EX $15 NM $25 MIP $40

Porsche, Midget series, 2-3/8" long; 1960s
EX $1 NM $2 MIP n/a

Porsche Roadster, red w/open top, black wheels, two-door, 6" long; 1956
EX $20 NM $25 MIP $40

Racer, miniature, Model No. 1110
EX $25 NM $40 MIP $50

Racer, orange w/black wheels, open cockpit, 3" long; 1950s-60s
EX $10 NM $15 MIP $30

Rambler Wagon, dark green w/yellow top, black wheels, yellow interior; 1960s
EX $15 NM $25 MIP $35

Rambler Wagon, blue w/black wheels, 4" long; 1960s styling; 1961-63
EX $8 NM $15 MIP $35

Roadster, miniature, Model No. 102
EX $15 NM $25 MIP $40

Roadster, Model No. 6001
EX $50 NM $100 MIP $140

Roadster, Midget series, 2-1/8" long; 1960s
EX $1 NM $2 MIP n/a

Sedan, miniature, Model No. 103
EX $20 NM $25 MIP $40

Sedan, Model No. 6-04
EX $50 NM $100 MIP $135

Small Racer, blue w/driver, white wheels, 1927, Model No. 23
EX $50 NM $110 MIP $175

Smitty, 1932; Funnies series, Model No. 5103X
EX $170 NM $250 MIP $500

Station Wagon, red w/tan upper, 3", Model No. 239
EX $15 NM $35 MIP $55

Stingin' Bug, VW Beetle, white plastic interior, "Stingin' Bug" sticker on doors, white-hub tires, 1970s
EX $3 NM $5 MIP $7

Studebaker Coupe, green w/black wheels, 3" long; 1947
EX $25 NM $35 MIP $50

Studebaker Lark Convertible, two-door 1960 convertible, 3" long; painted teal green, green, yellow, blue or red, molded front windshield, open wheel wells, patterned plastic tires, 1960-69
EX $4 NM $8 MIP $25

Tank Car, miniature, Model No. 105
EX $20 NM $25 MIP $40

Thunderbird Coupe, blue w/black wheels, 3" long; 1955
EX $15 NM $20 MIP $30

Thunderbird Coupe, powder blue w/black wheels, 4" long; 1955
EX $15 NM $30 MIP $40

Toronado, Midget series, 2-3/4" long, 1970s
EX $1 NM $2 MIP n/a

Torpedo Coupe, gray; prewar, Model No. 1017
EX $20 NM $25 MIP $45

Torpedo Sedan, red, Model No. 1018
EX $20 NM $30 MIP $50

Triumph, two-seat 1956 sports car, 3" long; painted green, red, blue, yellow or orange, bucket seats, oval grille, plastic tires, 1963-69
EX $4 NM $8 MIP $12

Triumph TR 3 Roadster, black wheels, 3" long; 1956
EX $4 NM $8 MIP $12

Twin Shaft, Super Slicks series, 4-1/4" long; blue bubble-top hot rod, side-panel stickers, chrome-hub tires, 1971-76
EX $3 NM $5 MIP $8

Uncle Walt, 1932; Funnies series, Model No. 5103X
EX $150 NM $300 MIP $450

Uncle Willie, 1932; Funnies series, Model No. 5106X
EX $150 NM $300 MIP $450

Volkswagen, two-door 1954 VW, 3" long, painted copper, red, yellow or green, open wheel wells, plastic tires, 1960-69
EX $5 NM $10 MIP $15

Volkswagen Rabbit, Midget series, 2-1/4" long, 1970s
EX $2 NM $3 MIP n/a

Volkswagen Rabbit, 4-3/4" long; opening rear gate, hood and side decals, 1970s
EX $3 NM $6 MIP $10

VW Bug, "Stingin' Bug," white hub tires; 1970s
EX $3 NM $5 MIP $7

VW Bug, lime green w/black tread wheels, 3" long; 1960
EX $10 NM $20 MIP $35

VW Bug, metallic gold w/black tread wheels, 6" long; 1960
EX $15 NM $25 MIP $30

VW Rabbit, Opening rear gate, hood and side decals, 4-3/4"; 1970s
EX $3 NM $6 MIP $10

Wedge Dragster, Midget series, 2-5/8" long, 1960s-70s
EX $1 NM $3 MIP n/a

Wheelie Wagon, blue pickup, 3-7/8" long; white plastic interior, "Wheelie Wagon" stickers, white hub tires, 1970s
EX $2 NM $3 MIP $5

Yellow Cab Sedan, green w/white wheels, 1921, Model No. 4629
EX $10 NM $20 MIP $30

EMERGENCY VEHICLES

Ambulance Van, white, "Ambulance" decal, white hub tires, 1970s
EX $2 NM $4 MIP $7

American LaFrance Ladder Truck, Collector series, 4-1/8" long; chromed plastic ladder, 1967-69
EX $3 NM $5 MIP $89

American LaFrance Pumper, red, 3" long; 1954
EX $15 NM $20 MIP $35

American LaFrance Snorkel Fire Truck, Collector Series, 4-1/8" long; red, 1967-60
EX $3 NM $6 MIP $9

Chevrolet Ambulance, army green, red cross on roof top, army star on top of hood, 4" long; 1950
EX $15 NM $25 MIP $50

Chevrolet Ambulance, yellow, red cross on top, 4" long; 1950
EX $15 NM $25 MIP $40

Fire Chief Pickup, Hitch-Up series scale, 3-3/4" long; pickup truck, white hub tires, "Fire Chief" decal, 1970s
EX $2 NM $4 MIP $6

Fire Hook and Ladder, red/blue w/side ladders, Model No. 4652
EX $25 NM $40 MIP $50

Fire Water Tower Truck, blue/orange, red water tower, Model No. 4653
EX $30 NM $60 MIP $80

Ford Wrecker, 3" long, 1935, brown, white rubber wheels, Model No. 0133
EX $30 NM $50 MIP $65

Graham Ambulance, white w/red cross on sides, Model No. 0809
EX $40 NM $95 MIP $125

Graham Wrecker, red/black; rubber wheels, Model No. 0806
EX $50 NM $110 MIP $150

Hoky Smoky, 6" long, Playmates serie, red fire truck, Little People-type fireman, trailer with dalmatian, purple tires, 1967-69
EX $10 NM $15 MIP $22

Hook and Ladder, Road Haulers series, 7-1/4" long, red die-cast body, white plastic interior and ladder assembly, white-hub tires, 1970s
EX $5 NM $10 MIP $15

Hook and Ladder, w/driver; white rubber wheels, 1937-41, Model No. 1040
EX $40 NM $60 MIP $75

Hook and Ladder, red and silver; white rubber wheels, Model No. 236
EX $15 NM $30 MIP $45

Hook and Ladder, #1040, Model No. 1040
EX $20 NM $25 MIP $40

Hose Car, w/driver and figure standing by water gun; 1937-41, Model No. 1041
EX $35 NM $50 MIP $80

Hose Wagon, red, black rubber wheels, postwar, Model No. 238
EX $20 NM $25 MIP $40

Hose Wagon, red w/silver hose, white rubber wheels, 3" long, prewar, Model No. 238
EX $25 NM $30 MIP $45

Insurance Patrol, w/driver, Model No. 1042
EX $25 NM $40 MIP $60

Insurance Patrol, red, black rubber wheels, postwar, Model No. 237
EX $20 NM $25 MIP $40

Insurance Patrol, red, white wheels, prewar, Model No. 237
EX $25 NM $30 MIP $45

Jumbo Wrecker, 6" long; 1941, Model No. 1027
EX $25 NM $40 MIP $60

Ladder Fire Truck, Midget scale, swiveling ladder, 3-1/2" long; 1960s
EX $4 NM $8 MIP $12

Ladder Fire Truck, Swiveling white plastic ladder, 7-1/4"; 1970s
EX $8 NM $12 MIP $15

Lincoln Wrecker, sedan w/wrecker hook
EX $200 NM $425 MIP $600

Mack L-Line Fire Pumper, red w/ladders on sides
EX $35 NM $65 MIP $75

Mack L-Line Hook and Ladder, red w/silver ladder
EX $35 NM $65 MIP $75

Mercury Fire Chief Car, red w/black wheels, 4" long; 1949
EX $25 NM $35 MIP $50

Pumper Fire Truck, Hitch-Up series scale, 3-3/4" long; two removable plastic ladders, white hub tires, 1970s
EX $3 NM $5 MIP $7

Rescue Truck, Hitch-Up series scale, 3-5/8" long, die-cast and plastic, white hub tires, "Emergency" decal, 1970s
EX $2 NM $4 MIP $7

FARM AND CONSTRUCTION EQUIPMENT

Caterpillar Bulldozer, yellow, 6" long
EX $25 NM $45 MIP $55

Caterpillar Scraper, yellow w/black wheels, silver blade, 6" long; 1956
EX $15 NM $25 MIP $40

Caterpillar Tractor, 1931, Model No. 4646
EX $20 NM $30 MIP $50

Caterpillar Tractor, miniature, Model No. 108
EX $15 NM $25 MIP $35

Cement Truck, Road Haulers series, 6" long; die-cast cab, two-color plastic drum assembly, white plastic interior, white-hub tires; 1970s
EX $5 NM $9 MIP $14

D7 Crawler with Blade, 1:50 scale, die-cast; 1956
EX $20 NM $35 MIP $55

D8 Crawler with Blade, 1:87 scale, die-cast
EX $20 NM $30 MIP $45

Dozer, Construction Rigs series, 5-1/2" long, yellow die-cast tractor, black treads, plastic blade, 1970s
EX $1 NM $2 MIP $5

Earth Mover, Midget series, 2-1/2" long, 1960s
EX $2 NM $3 MIP n/a

Farm Tractor, w/driver, Model No. 4654
EX $60 NM $100 MIP $145

Farm Tractor and Trailer, die-cast tractor with hay trailer, 4-1/4" long, 1968-69
EX $3 NM $7 MIP $15

Ford Tractor, red w/loader, die-cast, 7" long, 1955-60
EX $40 NM $50 MIP $70

Grader, 1:50 scale; 1956, 6"
EX $20 NM $30 MIP $50

Heavy Duty Hydraulic Crane, Mobile crane, 4" long, with telescoping boom and rotating cab, 1968-69
EX $4 NM $8 MIP $12

Heavy Duty Power Shovel, Mobile shovel, operating boom and rotating cab, 1968-69
EX $4 NM $8 MIP $12

International Tractor
EX $10 NM $15 MIP $25

Loader, Construction Rigs series, 5-1/2" long, yellow tractor with plastic front scoop, black plastic tires, 1970s
EX $15 NM $2 MIP $12

Power Shovel, red four-axle truck with plastic hydraulic shovel body, issued in window box, 1969
EX $7 NM $12 MIP $16

Road Builder, tractor-trailer, 5" long, long-nose truck hauls flatbed trailer and Michigan Earth Mover, 1969
EX $2 NM $4 MIP $8

Roller, Construction Rigs series, 5" long, yellow die-cast body, yellow plastic front roller, 1970s
EX $1 NM $2 MIP $5

Steamroller, 1931-34, Model No. 4648
EX $75 NM $150 MIP $200

Super Tractor, Super Tootsietoys series, 6-3/4" long; 1966-68
EX $5 NM $10 MIP $15

SETS

Box Trailer and Road Scraper Set, w/driver on road scraper
EX $75 NM $130 MIP $250

Car Fleet, blister card 8-piece set, cars and boat trailers in Midget series scale, 1969
EX $16 NM $20 MIP $25

Car Fleet, blister card 8-piece set, cars, racer trailer, boat trailer, Midget series scale, 1967
EX $16 NM $20 MIP $27

Cheerios Tootsietoy Box, 1950s cereal box, Tootsietoy offer on side, 1950s
EX $80 NM $100 MIP $120

Contractor Set, pickup truck w/three wagons, Model No. 0191
EX $50 NM $100 MIP $130

Farm Set, blister card 4-piece set, tractor, trailer and implements, 1969
EX $8 NM $10 MIP $14

Fire Station Set, Midget series scale pumper, jeep, fire chief car and badge, 1967
EX $10 NM $14 MIP $18

Four-Car Transport Set, flatbed trailer carries cars, Model No. 0190X
EX $50 NM $90 MIP $135

Freight Train, five-piece set, Model No. 0194
EX $35 NM $60 MIP $80

Grand Prix #1687 Set, seven vehicles; 1969
EX $50 NM $95 MIP $150

Jam Pac, blister card 5-car Midget series set, 1981
EX $5 NM $8 MIP $12

Jam Pac, blister card 6-car Midget series set, late 1970s
EX $6 NM $10 MIP $15

Jam Pac, boxed 10-car Midget series set, 1969
EX $10 NM $20 MIP $35

Jam Pac, 12-piece Midget series set; 1967
EX $12 NM $24 MIP $30

Jam Pac, Midget series 10-car sets, 1966
EX $10 NM $20 MIP $27

Keep On Trucking, log, hauling and "Keep on Trucking" moving van tractor-trailers in tray box, 1981
EX $8 NM $10 MIP $15

Little Toughs Boat Set, blistercard with Baha Buggy, blue/white boat and orange trailer, 197
EX $5 NM $10 MIP $15

Midget Series, assorted ships, 1" long, 1936-41
EX $20 NM $40 MIP $60

Midget Series, yellow stake truck, red limo, green doodlebug, yellow railcar, blue racer, red fire truck, 1" long, 1936-41
EX $20 NM $40 MIP $85

Midget Series, green cannon, blue tank, green armored car, green tow truck, green camelback van, 1" long, 1936-41
EX $20 NM $40 MIP $60

Midget Series, single engine plane, St. Louis, bomber, Atlantic Clipper, 1" long, 1936-41
EX $10 NM $15 MIP $25

Milk Trailer Set, tractor w/three milk tankers, Model No. 0192
EX $50 NM $100 MIP $200

Motorcycle with Truck and Trailer Set, #1456, Collector Series window box, 4-1/2" long, Jeep pickup with trailer and silver Honda motorcycle, 1968-69
EX $10 NM $15 MIP $22

Passenger Train, five-piece set, Model No. 0193
EX $40 NM $60 MIP $100

Playtime Set, six cars, two trucks, two planes
EX $200 NM $500 MIP $850

Road Construction Assortment, Caterpillar Bulldozer, Caterpillar Road Grader, Mack Dump Truck, Mack Machinery Hauler, six yellow road signs, full-color box, 1956-58
EX $100 NM $175 MIP $250

Road Racing Set, slot car set, two die-cast Corvair Monza racers, trestles, transformer, 1963
EX $35 NM $45 MIP $55

Tractor with Scoop Shovel and Wagon, red w/silver scoop, flatbed trailer; 1946-52
EX $125 NM $185 MIP $250

U-Haul Hitch Up, 7-1/2" long, Jeep truck with U-Haul trailer, six pieces of plastic furniture, 1969
EX $8 NM $13 MIP $18

SPACESHIPS

Buck Rogers Venus Duo-Destroyer, 1937
EX $75 NM $110 MIP $150

Flash Gordon Spaceship, 1970s
EX $3 NM $8 MIP $12

TRAILERS

Boat Trailer, two-wheel
EX $10 NM $15 MIP $20

Horse Trailer, red w/white top, two-wheel, black tread wheels
EX $10 NM $15 MIP $20

House Trailer, powder blue w/black wheels, two-wheel, door opens, 6" long
EX $15 NM $30 MIP $40

Restaurant Trailer, yellow w/black tread wheels, two-wheel, open sides
EX $30 NM $40 MIP $65

Small House Trailer, two-wheel, three side windows, 1935
EX $30 NM $45 MIP $65

U-Haul Trailer, red w/black tread wheels, two-wheel, U-Haul logo on sides
EX $10 NM $15 MIP $30

TRAINS

Borden's Milk Tank Car, yellow; red base, Model No. 1093
EX $15 NM $20 MIP n/a

Box Car, "Southern", Model No. 1089
EX $15 NM $20 MIP n/a

Caboose, red, Model No. 1095
EX $10 NM $15 MIP n/a

Coal Car, red, Model No. 1090
EX $10 NM $15 MIP n/a

Cracker Jack Railroad Car, embossed white metal, painted orange, black rubber tires, 3" long, 1930s
EX $30 NM $75 MIP n/a

Diesel Train, Midget series scale, 13" long; complete with engine, three box cars, one caboose, early 1970s
EX $10 NM $15 MIP $25

Fast Freight Set, five-piece set; 1940, Model No. 186
EX $35 NM $60 MIP $80

Log Car, silver w/red wheels; logs chained on, Model No. 1092
EX $10 NM $15 MIP n/a

Oil Tank Car, silver top, red base, "Sinclair", Model No. 1094
EX $15 NM $20 MIP n/a

Passenger Train Set, four-piece set, 1925, Model No. 4625
EX $50 NM $125 MIP n/a

Pennsylvania Engine, red/silver
EX $20 NM $30 MIP n/a

Refrigerator Car, yellow ochre, red base, black roof, Model No. 1088
EX $10 NM $15 MIP n/a

Santa Fe Engine, black/silver
EX $15 NM $20 MIP n/a

Stock Car, red, Model No. 1091
EX $10 NM $15 MIP n/a

Tootsietoy Flyer, silver; three-piece set, 1937, Model No. 196
EX $35 NM $60 MIP $90

Wrecking Crane, green crane on silver flatbed car w/red wheels, Model No. 1087
EX $20 NM $30 MIP n/a

Zephyr Railcar, dark green, 4" long, 1935, Model No. 117
EX $35 NM $60 MIP n/a

TRUCKS

All Across America Moving Van, 10" long, die-cast tractor, blue plastic trailer with "All Across America...Keep On Truckin' "
EX $8 NM $12 MIP $18

Army Half Truck, 1941
EX $30 NM $55 MIP $75

Army Jeep, windshield up, 6" long; 1950s
EX $15 NM $25 MIP $40

Army Jeep CJ3, extended back, windshield down, 4" long; 1950
EX $10 NM $15 MIP $35

Army Jeep CJ3, no windshield, 3" long; 1950
EX $10 NM $15 MIP $40

Army Rocket Launcher, Tractor-trailer, plastic rocket; late 1950s
EX $50 NM $75 MIP $100

Army Supply Truck, w/driver, Model No. 4634
EX $25 NM $40 MIP $55

Auto Transport, Collector Series tractor-trailer, 5" long; red Ford or Chevy tractor with yellow two-level hauler, with two Triumphs, 1967
EX $5 NM $9 MIP $21

Auto Transport, Tractor-trailer, 8-3/4" long, Hendrickson tractor pulls polypropylene hauler with lowering ramp, and three Midget series cars, 1969
EX $6 NM $12 MIP $18

Auto Transport, Road Haulers series tractor-trailer, 8-1/2" long, die-cast cab with white plastic interior and grille hauls yellow plastic hauler for Midget series cars, white-hub tires, 1970s
EX $4 NM $8 MIP $12

Bimini Buggy, hot rod bus, white plastic interior and exposed engine, "Bimini Buggy" stickers on sides, white-hub tires, 1970s
EX $2 NM $4 MIP $6

Box Truck, red w/white wheels, 3" long, Model No. 234
EX $15 NM $20 MIP $30

Buick Delivery Van, Model No. 6006
EX $25 NM $35 MIP $50

Cadillac Delivery Van, Model No. 6106
EX $25 NM $35 MIP $50

Carousel and Transport Unit, tractor-trailer, 4-1/2" long, Chevy or Ford truck hauls flatbed trailer with plastic carousel, 1968
EX $5 NM $9 MIP $14

Cherry Picker, Super Tootsietoys series, 8" long; Ford Pickup truck with cherry-picker snorkel mounted in truck bed, 1966
EX $7 NM $15 MIP $22

Chevrolet Cameo Pickup, green w/black wheels, 4" long; 1956
EX $15 NM $25 MIP $40

Chevrolet Delivery Van, Model No. 6206
EX $25 NM $35 MIP $50

Chevrolet El Camino, red, 6" long, various colors, 1960s
EX $10 NM $18 MIP $35

Chevrolet El Camino Camper and Boat, blue body w/red camper, black/white boat on top of camper
EX $25 NM $35 MIP $85

Chevrolet Panel Truck, green, front fenders opened, 3" long; 1950s
EX $8 **NM** $17 **MIP** $25

Chevrolet Panel Truck, green, closed front fenders, 3" long; 1950s
EX $10 **NM** $20 **MIP** $30

Chevrolet Panel Truck, light green w/black wheels, 4" long; 1950
EX $25 **NM** $30 **MIP** $40

Chevy El Camino, Midget series, 2-5/8" long, 1960s
EX $2 **NM** $4 **MIP** n/a

Civilian Jeep, blue w/black tread wheels, 6" long; 1960
EX $15 **NM** $20 **MIP** $35

Civilian Jeep, red, open top, black wheels, 4" long; 1950
EX $15 **NM** $20 **MIP** $35

Civilian Jeep, burnt orange, open top, black wheels, 3" long; 1950
EX $10 **NM** $15 **MIP** $30

CJ3 Army Jeep, open top, no steering wheel cast on dashboard, 3" long; 1950
EX $10 **NM** $15 **MIP** $30

CJ5 Jeep, red w/black tread wheels, windshield up, 6" long; 1960s
EX $15 **NM** $20 **MIP** $30

CJ5 Jeep, red w/black tread wheels, windshield up, 6" long; 1950s
EX $15 **NM** $25 **MIP** $35

Coast to Coast Van, 9" long
EX $40 **NM** $75 **MIP** $125

Commercial Tire Van, "Commercial Tire and Supply Co."; white rubber wheels; prewar
EX $70 **NM** $150 **MIP** $200

Dean Van Lines, Tractor-trailer; 1950-56
EX $35 **NM** $75 **MIP** $100

Delivery Van, "Wild Wagon," white hub tires, 3-7/8" long; 1970s
EX $3 **NM** $4 **MIP** $5

Diamond T K5 Dump Truck, yellow cab and chassis, green dump body, 6" long
EX $25 **NM** $35 **MIP** $50

Diamond T K5 Semi, red tractor and light green closed trailer
EX $25 **NM** $45 **MIP** $55

Diamond T K5 Stake Truck, orange, open sides, 6" long; 1940
EX $25 **NM** $35 **MIP** $55

Diamond T K5 Stake Truck, orange, closed sides, 6" long; 1940
EX $25 **NM** $35 **MIP** $55

Diamond T Metro Van, powder blue, 6" long
EX $35 **NM** $75 **MIP** $100

Diamond T Tow Truck, red w/silver tow bar
EX $25 **NM** $35 **MIP** $55

Dodge D100 Panel, green and yellow, 6" long
EX $18 **NM** $36 **MIP** $55

Dodge Pickup, lime green, 4" long
EX $20 **NM** $30 **MIP** $40

Double Bottom-Dumper Truck, tractor-trailer, 8-1/4" long, Hendrickson truck pulls two die-cast bottom-dumper transport units, with three-position lever for dumping, 1969
EX $5 **NM** $11 **MIP** $30

Dump Truck, Road Haulers series, 6-1/4" long; die-cast cab and chassis, white plastic interior, plastic dump body, white hub tires; 1970s
EX $4 **NM** $8 **MIP** $12

Federal Bakery Van, black w/cream wheels, 1924, Model No. 4631
EX $50 **NM** $85 **MIP** $110

Federal Florist Van, black w/cream wheels, 1924, Model No. 4635
EX $75 **NM** $175 **MIP** $220

Federal Grocery Van, black w/cream wheels, 1924, Model No. 4630
EX $45 **NM** $70 **MIP** $100

Federal Laundry Van, black w/cream wheels, 1924, Model No. 4633
EX $50 **NM** $85 **MIP** $110

Federal Market Van, black w/cream wheels, 1924, Model No. 4632
EX $55 **NM** $85 **MIP** $110

Federal Milk Van, black w/cream wheels, 1924, Model No. 4634
EX $55 **NM** $85 **MIP** $110

Ford Bronco, "Buckin' Bronco," white hub tires; 1969-70s
EX $6 **NM** $14 **MIP** $28

Ford C600 Oil Tanker, red, 6" long; 1962
EX $15 **NM** $30 **MIP** $40

Ford C600 Oil Tanker, bright yellow, 3" long
EX $10 **NM** $15 **MIP** $20

Ford Dump Truck, 2-3/8" long, red with silver grille and dump body, 1960 styling, HO-scale Pocket Series, 1962
EX $30 **NM** $70 **MIP** $120

Ford Econoline Pickup, red; 1962
EX $15 **NM** $25 **MIP** $35

Ford Econoline Pickup Truck, cabover pickup 6" long; hidden axles, plastic "Tootsietoy" tires, 1962-69
EX $7 **NM** $18 **MIP** $25

Ford F1 Pickup, orange, open tailgate, 3" long; 1949
EX $15 **NM** $20 **MIP** $35

Ford F1 Pickup, orange, closed tailgate, 3" long; 1949
EX $15 **NM** $20 **MIP** $35

Ford F6 Oil, orange, 4" long; 1949
EX $10 **NM** $15 **MIP** $25

Ford F6 Oil Tanker, red w/Texaco, Sinclair, Shell or Standard on sides, 6" long; 1949
EX $25 **NM** $50 **MIP** $100

Ford F6 Pickup, red, 4" long; 1949
EX $15 **NM** $25 **MIP** $40

Ford F600 Army Anti-Aircraft Gun, tractor-trailer flatbed, guns on flatbed
EX $20 **NM** $30 **MIP** $45

Ford F600 Army Radar, tractor-trailer flatbed, yellow radar unit on flatbed, 6" long; 1955
EX $20 **NM** $30 **MIP** $45

Ford F600 Army Stake Truck, tractor-trailer box, army star on top of trailer box roof and "U.S. Army" on sides, 6" long; 1955
EX $25 **NM** $40 **MIP** $55

Ford F600 Stake Truck, light green, 6" long; 1955
EX $15 **NM** $25 **MIP** $35

Ford Model A Pickup, 4-1/2" long, blue with white canopy, black chassis, oversize wheels, Collector's Customized Model A Series, 1974
EX $5 **NM** $8 **MIP** $12

Ford Pickup, 3", beige; 1935; white rubber wheels, Model No. 0121
EX $25 **NM** $40 **MIP** $55

Ford Pickup Truck, Ford 1957 model truck, 3" long; covered-over rear window, patterned plastic tires, 1968-69
EX $4 **NM** $8 **MIP** $12

Ford Shell Oil Truck, Model No. 1008
EX $45 **NM** $60 **MIP** $85

Ford Styleside Pickup, orange, 3" long; 1957
EX $10 **NM** $15 **MIP** $30

Ford Tanker Truck, Midget series, 2-1/2" long; 1960s-70s
EX $2 **NM** $3 **MIP** n/a

Ford Texaco Oil Truck, Model No. 1008
EX $45 **NM** $60 **MIP** $85

Ford Tow Truck, Midget series, 2-3/8" long; 1960s
EX $1 **NM** $2 **MIP** n/a

Hendrickson Cement Truck, Collector series, 3" long; red body and chassis, silver tank, yellow plastic drum, 1967-69
EX $4 **NM** $8 **MIP** $12

Hendrickson Dump Truck, Collector series, 3" long; red cab and chassis, green heavy-duty dump body, 1967-69
EX $4 **NM** $8 **MIP** $12

Horse Trailer, Road Haulers series tractor-trailer, 8-1/4" long, die-cast cab with white plastic interior and grille, orange plastic horse trailer with lowering gate, six plastic horses, white hub tires, 1970s
EX $5 **NM** $10 **MIP** $15

Hot Rod Truck, Midget series, 1-7/8" long; 1960s
EX $2 **NM** $3 **MIP** n/a

Houseboat and Transporter, tractor-trailer, 4-1/4" long; Ford or Chevy truck hauls flatbed trailer with House Boat, 1969
EX $5 **NM** $11 **MIP** $20

Hudson Pickup, red, 4" long; 1947-49
EX $25 **NM** $60 **MIP** $75

International Bottle Truck, lime green
EX $30 **NM** $45 **MIP** $65

International Car Transport Truck, red tractor, orange double-deck trailer w/cars
EX $35 **NM** $50 **MIP** $70

International Gooseneck Trailer, orange tractor and flatbed trailer
EX $30 **NM** $40 **MIP** $55

International K1 Oil Truck, green, comes w/oil brands on sides, 6" long
EX $12 **NM** $23 **MIP** $35

International K1 Panel Truck, various colors, 4" long, 1948-49
EX $20 **NM** $30 **MIP** $55

International RC180 Grain Semi, green tractor and red trailer
EX $30 **NM** $50 **MIP** $70

International Sinclair Oil Truck, 6" long, Model No. 1006
EX $35 **NM** $75 **MIP** $100

International Standard Oil Truck, 6" long, Model No. 1006
EX $35 **NM** $75 **MIP** $100

Jeep and Racer, Midget series combination, 4-1/2" long, Jeep with trailer and Midget Racer, 1968-69
EX $2 **NM** $4 **MIP** $8

Jeep CJ5, Midget series, 2-1/8" long, 1960s-70s
EX $1 **NM** $2 **MIP** $35

Jeep Delivery Truck, Midget series, trailer hitch, 1960s
EX $1 **NM** $2 **MIP** $4

Jeep Panel Truck/Land Rover, Midget series, 2-3/8"; 1960s
EX $4 **NM** $8 **MIP** n/a

Jeep Pickup, Midget series, 2-1/8" long; late 1960s
EX $2 **NM** $3 **MIP** n/a

Jeep Pickup, Hitch-Up series, 3-5/8" long; die-cast and plastic, white hub tires, 1970s
EX $2 **NM** $3 **MIP** $5

Jeep Pickup, Die-cast and plastic, white hub tires, 3-5/8" long; 1970s
EX n/a **NM** n/a **MIP** $35

Jeep Pickup Truck, Midget series, 2-1/4" long; 1960s
EX $2 **NM** $3 **MIP** n/a

Jeep Pickup with U-Haul Trailer, Midget series combination, 4-1/2" long, 1967
EX $2 **NM** $3 **MIP** n/a

Jeep Truck with Honda Motorcycle, Midget series combination, 4-1/2" long; Jeep truck with trailer, chromed motorcycle, 1968-69
EX $3 **NM** $7 **MIP** n/a

Jeepster, bright yellow w/open top, black wheels, 3" long; 1947
EX $10 **NM** $15 **MIP** $35

Jeepster, Hitch-Up series, 3-7/8" long, "Jumpin Jeeper," white hub tires, 1970s
EX $2 **NM** $5 **MIP** $15

Jumbo Pickup, 6" long, green w/black wheels, 1936-41, Model No. 1019
EX $25 **NM** $35 **MIP** $50

Kennel Truck, Super Tootsietoy series, 8" long; Ford Pickup with clear plastic dome over truck bed, partitioned to hold four dogs, 1967
EX $8 **NM** $17 **MIP** $25

Livestock Transporter, tractor-trailer, 4-1/4" long; Ford or Chevy tractor hauls trailer with two horses and two cattle, 1969
EX $7 **NM** $13 **MIP** $20

Log Truck, tractor-trailer, 4-1/4" long; Ford or Chevy truck with logger trailer, three natural-finish logs, 1967-69
EX $10 **NM** $20 **MIP** $30

Logger, Road Haulers series tractor-trailer, 7-1/2" long; die-cast cab with white plastic interior, die-cast trailer with three wood logs, white-hub tires, 1970s
EX $5 **NM** $10 **MIP** $15

Mack Anti-Aircraft Gun, Model No. 4643
EX $25 **NM** $40 **MIP** $55

Mack B-Line Cement Truck, red truck w/yellow cement mixer; 1955
EX $20 **NM** $35 **MIP** $55

Mack B-Line Oil Tanker, red tractor and trailer, "Mobil"
EX $20 **NM** $35 **MIP** $75

Mack B-Line Stake Trailer, red tractor, orange closed trailer; 1955
EX $20 **NM** $35 **MIP** $55

Mack Coal Truck, orange cab w/blue bed, four wheels, 1925, Model No. 4639
EX $90 **NM** $100 **MIP** $250

Mack Coal Truck, red cab w/black bed, 1928, Model No. 4639
EX $60 **NM** $120 **MIP** $160

Mack Coal Truck, "City Fuel Company," 10 wheels, Model No. 0804
EX $60 **NM** $120 **MIP** $175

Mack Dairy Tanker, 1930s; two-piece cab; Tootsietoy Dairies
EX $75 **NM** $100 **MIP** $225

Mack L-Line Dump Truck, yellow cab and chassis, light green dump body, 6" long; 1947
EX $20 **NM** $35 **MIP** $55

Mack L-Line Semi and Stake Trailer, red tractor and trailer
EX $50 **NM** $95 **MIP** $125

Mack L-Line Semi-Trailer, red tractor cab, silver semi-trailer, "Gerard Motor Express" on sides
EX $60 **NM** $115 **MIP** $145

Mack L-Line Stake Truck, red w/silver bed inside
EX $25 **NM** $35 **MIP** $55

Mack L-Line Tow Truck, red w/silver tow bar
EX $25 **NM** $35 **MIP** $55

Mack Log Hauler, red cab, trailer w/load of logs; 1940s
EX $50 **NM** $95 **MIP** $135

Mack Mail Truck, red cab w/light brown box, "U.S. Mail Airmail Service" on sides, 3" long, 1920s, Model No. 4645
EX $40 **NM** $70 **MIP** $100

Mack Milk Truck, "Tootsietoy Dairy," one-piece cab, Model No. 0805
EX $50 **NM** $110 **MIP** $175

Mack Oil Tanker, "DOMACO" on side of tanker, Model No. 0802
EX $60 **NM** $100 **MIP** $155

Mack Oil Truck, red cab w/orange tanker, 1925, Model No. 4640
EX $25 **NM** $40 **MIP** $55

Mack Railway Express, 1930s; Wrigley's Gum
EX $55 **NM** $115 **MIP** $165

Mack Searchlight Truck, 1931-41, Model No. 4644
EX $25 **NM** $40 **MIP** $55

Mack Stake Trailer-Truck, enclosed cab, open stake trailer, 'Express' on sides of trailer, Model No. 0801
EX $50 **NM** $90 **MIP** $120

Mack Stake Truck, orange cab w/red stake bed, 1925, Model No. 4638
EX $25 **NM** $40 **MIP** $60

Mack Trailer-Truck, open cab, Model No. 4670
EX $50 **NM** $85 **MIP** $110

Mack Transport, red, open cab w/flatbed trailer, Model No. 190
EX $60 **NM** $150 **MIP** $200

Mack Transport, yellow; 1941, w/three cars at angle, Model No. 187
EX $150 **NM** $500 **MIP** $700

Mack Van Trailer-Truck, enclosed cab and box trailer, Model No. 0803
EX $50 **NM** $100 **MIP** $140

Mack Wrigley's Spearmint Gum Truck, 4", green w/white rubber wheels, red hubs, Model No. 0810
EX $70 **NM** $150 **MIP** $225

Mobil Gas Tanker, tractor-trailer, 4-1/4" long; Ford or Chevy tractor hauling red tanker body with "Mobil" sticker on sides, 1960s-70s
EX $8 **NM** $17 **MIP** $25

Mobile Gas Tanker, 9", 1960s
EX $15 **NM** $30 **MIP** n/a

Model T Pickup, 3" long, 1914, Model No. 4610
EX $30 **NM** $50 **MIP** $75

Model T Pick-up, 3", black, spoked metal wheels, Model No. 4610
EX $25 **NM** $40 **MIP** $50

Oil Tanker, green w/white wheels; prewar, Model No. 0120
EX $15 **NM** $25 **MIP** $35

Oil Tanker, blue, three caps on top, 2" long, 1932, Model No. 105
EX $20 **NM** $25 **MIP** $50

Oil Tanker, blue and silver, two caps on top of tanker, 3" long, Model No. 235
EX $13 **NM** $26 **MIP** $40

Oil Tanker, orange, four caps on top of tanker, 3" long, postwar, Model No. 235
EX $10 **NM** $15 **MIP** $25

Oldsmobile Delivery Van, Model No. 6306
EX $25 **NM** $35 **MIP** $50

Pickup, "wheelie Wagon," white hub tires, 3-7/8" long; 1970s
EX $3 **NM** $4 **MIP** $5

Royal Crown Cola TRuck, 6" long, red cab, white plastic body with transparent hinged side over soda-bottle decal, two plastic soda cases, "Me and My RC," 1970s
EX $5 **NM** $10 **MIP** $15

Safari Hunt, Midget series combination, 5-1/4" long, Jeep Panel Truck hauls plastic animal cage trailer with giraffe, elephant, and hippo, 1968-69
EX $5 **NM** $15 **MIP** $30

Tootsietoy

Sanitation Truck, Road haulers series, 6-1/2" long, die-cast cab and chassis, white plastic interior and dumping body, white-hub tires, 1970s
EX $4 **NM** $8 **MIP** $12

Shell Oil Truck, Hitch-Up scale, "Shell" decal, white hub tires, 1970
EX $3 **NM** $5 **MIP** $7

Shell Oil Truck, yellow/silver, 6", white rubber wheels, Model No. 1009
EX $25 **NM** $50 **MIP** $75

Shuttle Truck, Midget series, 2-1/4" long; 1960s
EX $1 **NM** $2 **MIP** n/a

Sinclair Oil Truck, 6" long; green/silver, Model No. 1007
EX $30 **NM** $50 **MIP** $75

Special Delivery, 1936, Model No. 0123
EX $20 **NM** $25 **MIP** $40

Stake Truck, miniature, Model No. 109
EX $25 **NM** $40 **MIP** $55

Standard Oil Truck, red/silver; 6", white rubber wheels, Model No. 1006
EX $30 **NM** $60 **MIP** $75

Super Camper, Super Tootsietoy series, 8-1/2" long; Ford Pickup truck with removable camper
EX $7 **NM** $15 **MIP** $11

Super Dump Truck, Super Tootsietoy series, 9-3/8" long, blue Ford or GMC truck with yellow operating dump, 1966-68
EX $5 **NM** $10 **MIP** $15

Super Tow Truck, Super Tootsietoy series, 8-1/2" long, Ford or GMC truck with red cab, white rear tow assembly with windup winch and tow hook, 1966-68
EX $7 **NM** $15 **MIP** $22

Super U-Haul Truck, Super Tootsietoy series, 8-1/2" long; Ford truck with U-Haul body, 1966
EX $8 **NM** $17 **MIP** $25

Texaco Oil Truck, red/silver; 6", white rubber wheels, Model No. 1008
EX $25 **NM** $50 **MIP** $75

Tootsietoy Dairy, semi trailer truck, Model No. 0805
EX $75 **NM** $110 **MIP** $140

Tootsietoy Oil Tanker, red cab, silver tanker, "Tootsietoy Line" on side; 1950s
EX $60 **NM** $95 **MIP** $125

Turnpike Auto Transport, Midget scale, two cars, 5" long; 1960s-70s
EX n/a **NM** n/a **MIP** n/a

Van Transport, tractor-trailer, 4-1/4" long; Ford or Chevy truck with van trailer, 1967-69
EX $4 **NM** $8 **MIP** $12

Wild Wagon, green van, 3-7/8" long, white plastic interior, white hub tires, "Wild Wagon" sticker with Indian motif; 1970s
EX $2 **NM** $4 **MIP** $7

Winnebago Camper, 4-1/2" long, powder blue with white plastic chassis, black tires, 1970s
EX $7 **NM** $10 **MIP** $15

Wrigley's Box Van, w/or without decal; 1940s, Model No. 1010
EX $45 **NM** $60 **MIP** $75

View-Master

by Karen O'Brien

History

"7 More Wonders of the World" was one of the earliest advertising slogans for View-Master. Initially designed to be sold in camera, drug, and gift stores, the product has been in continuous production since 1939. View-Master reels were introduced at the 1939 New York World's Fair and at the 1940 Golden Gate Exposition in San Francisco. From there, the titles spread out to include a host of scenic attractions featuring everything from Crater Lake, Oregon, to Miami Beach, Florida.

In the early 1940s, film and paper were scarce and View-Master production all but halted due to the onset of World War II. However, a large contract to produce airplane and ship identification and range estimation reels saved the product from potential oblivion. Millions of reels were produced and used by GIs, along with thousands of Model B (round) View-Master viewers.

Although scenic reels were View-Master's forte, the company decided to spread out a bit in the late 1940s and produced a series of children's fairy-tale reels. These single-sleeved reels were identified with the prefix "FT." Clay figure models were initially produced by Lee Green Studios in Hollywood and later at the View-Master art studios in Portland, Oregon. Dozens of reel titles were produced using the great diorama effect created by tabletop photography.

Keeping ahead of the competition, View-Master purchased the assets of its main rival, Tru-Vue, in 1951. This acquisition resulted in obtaining the license to use Disney characters, previously held by Tru-Vue. Since that time, the company has produced many Disney and other cartoon/ character favorites. Some of these were produced as clay figures, others were drawn as stereo cells, and still others were created using actual products in the reel set up, as was the case with Barbie and G.I. Joe.

From 1946 until 2002, the fundamental design of the View-Master viewer had remained the same. The basic principal is that you insert a View-Master reel vertically into the slot at the top of the viewer and pull a lever to advance the scene. All reels produced—from 1939 through today—can be viewed in any viewer. In 2003, Fisher-Price, the current manufacturer of View-Master, introduced a new viewer where the reel is now inserted horizontally, rather than vertically.

In the late 1980s and early 1990s, View-Master developed character viewers (Mickey Mouse, Big Bird, Batman, Casper, etc), but these were short-lived and abandoned in favor of colorful versions of regular production viewers. New viewers come in a wide variety of colors and many gift sets feature viewers with colorful graphics and logos. New titles are always being added to the line and a special line of educational titles is made under the Discovery Kids banner.

Pricing

Condition determines value. As with any other paper collectible, it is important that View-Master reels be free of mold, mildew, brown foxing spots, etc. Reels missing scenes are virtually worthless. Those reels with paper blisters (caused by heat/moisture) are valued at less than 1/4 of mint reels. Three-reel packets need to be complete with outer color envelope, three reels, and inner story booklet, if indicated. Any part of the packet or booklet that is torn or damaged drops the value of the set. Adjust prices accordingly. Prices shown here are for MIP—Mint in Package—examples. Those in excellent condition command about 85 percent of the MIP price.

Collector Groups: At present, there are no collector groups solely dedicated to View-Master; however, there is a national organization devoted to 3-D collectibles. This is the National Stereoscopic Association and can be found on the Web at www.stereoview.org.

Contributor: This information is developed and written by View-Master collector/historian Mary Ann Sell. She may be reached in care of the editor at Krause Publications, 700 E. State St., Iola, WI 54990.

Other on-line resources:

The View-Master Homepage, featuring historic View-Master information. Web site: http://www.cinti.net:/~vmmasell/

Fisher-Price—official corporate View-Master page: Web site: http://www.fisher-price.com/us/view-master/

THE TOP 10 VIEW-MASTER (In Mint Condition)

1. John F. Kennedy's Trip to Ireland $500
2. Girl Scouts Serve Their Country 250
3. House of Wax (Movie Preview Reel) 250
4. It Came From Outer Space (Movie Preview Reel) 250
5. Wings of the Hawk (Movie Preview Reel) 150
6. Son of Sinbad (Movie Preview Reel) 150
7. Taza, Son of Cochise (Movie Preview Reel) 150
8. The Maze (Movie Preview Reel) 150
9. They Called Him Hondo (Movie Preview Reel) 150
10. Jesse James v. The Daltons (Movie Preview Reel) 130

(Mary Ann Sell)

$1,000,000 Duck, Model No. B506
NM $7 **MIP** $10

101 Dalmatians, Model No. 3014
NM $3 **MIP** $5

101 Dalmatians, Model No. B532
NM $3 **MIP** $5

1939 New York World's Fair (single reel), Model No. 89
NM $5 **MIP** $10

1939 New York World's Fair (single reel), Model No. 88
NM $5 **MIP** $10

1939 New York World's Fair (single reel), Model No. 87
NM $10 **MIP** $25

1939 New York World's Fair (single reel), Model No. 86
NM $10 **MIP** $25

1940 Golden Gate International Expo (single reel), Model No. 56
NM $12 **MIP** $35

1940 Golden Gate International Expo (single reel), Model No. 59
NM $5 **MIP** $15

1940 Golden Gate International Expo (single reel), Model No. 58
NM $5 **MIP** $15

1940 Golden Gate International Expo (single reel), Model No. 57
NM $12 **MIP** $35

1962 Seattle World's Fair (four reels), Model No. A272
NM $20 **MIP** $50

1962 Seattle World's Fair (single reel), Model No. A2726
NM $7 **MIP** $15

1962 Space Needle U.S.A. (single reel), Model No. A2725
NM $7 **MIP** $15

1970s America's Cup (ABC's WW/Sports), Model No. B937
NM $25 **MIP** $45

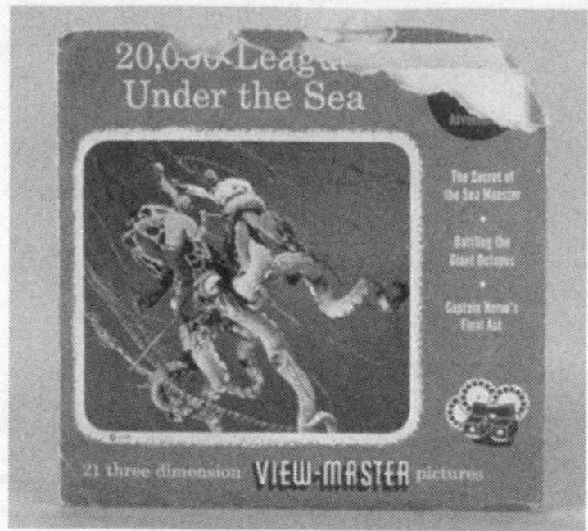

20,000 Leagues Under the Sea, 1954, Model No. B370
NM $7 **MIP** $15

Adam & the Ants, Model No. BD199
NM $15 **MIP** $20

Adam-12, Model No. B593
NM $10 **MIP** $12

Addams Family, Model No. B486
NM $75 **MIP** $125

Adventures of Morph, Model No. BD205
NM $7 **MIP** $8

Aesop's Fables, clay figure, Model No. B309
NM $8 **MIP** $15

Aladdin, Model No. 3088
NM $3 **MIP** $4

Alex, Model No. BD265
NM $9 **MIP** $10

ALF, Model No. 4082
NM $5 **MIP** $10

Alice in Wonderland, Model No. B360
NM $8 **MIP** $12

An American Tail II, Model No. 4111
NM $5 **MIP** $6

Annie, Model No. N3
NM $5 **MIP** $6

Annie Oakley, Model No. B470
NM $12 **MIP** $25

Apple's Way, Model No. B558
NM $12 **MIP** $14

Arabian Nights, clay figure, Model No. B335
NM $8 **MIP** $15

Archie, Model No. B574
NM $7 **MIP** $8

Arena (Movie Preview Reel)
NM $50 **MIP** $75

Aristocats, The, 1970s, Model No. B365
NM $5 **MIP** $6

Astrix & Cleopatra, Model No. B457
NM $16 **MIP** $25

A-Team, Model No. 4045
NM $6 **MIP** $12

Auto Racing, Phoenix 200 (ABC's WW/Sports), Model No. B948
NM $25 **MIP** $35

Babar the Elephant, Model No. B419
NM $10 **MIP** $18

Babes in Toyland, Model No. B375
NM $21 **MIP** $25

Bad News Bears in "Breaking Training", 1977, Model No. H77
NM $7 **MIP** $8

Bambi, clay figure, Model No. B400
NM $5 **MIP** $8

Banana Splits, Model No. B502
NM $10 **MIP** $20

Bananaman, Model No. BD239
NM $9 **MIP** $10

Barbie and the Rockers, Model No. 4071
NM $7 **MIP** $10

Barbie Dolls of the World, Model No. 36338
NM $2 **MIP** $7

Barbie Prom Date, Model No. 35428
NM $3 **MIP** $5

Barbie Special Pink Viewer set; regular viewer in Barbie pink, Model No. 1998
NM $7 **MIP** $10

Barbie Special Pink Viewer set; Supershow viewer in Barbie pink; Target Exc, Model No. 1998
NM $12 **MIP** $30

Barbie's Around the World Trip, Model No. B500
NM $20 **MIP** $25

Barbie's Great American Photo Race, Model No. B576
NM $20 **MIP** $35

Batman - The Animated Series (blister pack), blister pack, three reel, Model No. 3086
NM $2 **MIP** $4

Batman (Adam West), original envelope package, three reel, Model No. B492
NM $9 **MIP** $10

Batman (Adam West), (blister pack), blister pack, three reel, Model No. BB492
NM $13 **MIP** $15

Batman (blister pack), Model No. 1086
NM $5 **MIP** $8

Batman Returns (blister pack), blister pack, three reel, Model No. 4137
NM $7 **MIP** $8

Batman, The Perfect Crime (blister pack), 1976, blister pack, three reel, Model No. 4011
NM $7 **MIP** $8

Battle Beyond the Stars, original envelope package, three reel, Model No. L16
NM $12 **MIP** $20

Battle of the Planets (blister pack), blister pack, three reel, Model No. BD185
NM $13 **MIP** $15

Beauty & the Beast (blister pack), blister pack, three reel, Model No. 3079
NM $2 **MIP** $4

Bedknobs & Broomsticks, original envelope package, three reel, Model No. B366
NM $5 **MIP** $10

Beetlejuice, Model No. 1074
NM $5 **MIP** $11

Beetlejuice (blister pack), blister pack, three reel, Model No. 1074
NM $5 **MIP** $8

Benji, Superstar (blister pack), blister pack, three reel, Model No. 4018
NM $5 **MIP** $6

Benji's Very Own Christmas, original envelope package, three reel, Model No. J51
NM $7 MIP $8

Bertha, blister pack, three reel, Model No. BD259
NM $7 MIP $8

Beverly Hillbillies, 1963, original envelope package, three reel, Model No. B570
NM $12 MIP $25

Big Blue Marble, original envelope package, three reel, Model No. B587
NM $10 MIP $12

Black Beauty, original envelope package, three reel, Model No. D135
NM $9 MIP $10

Black Hole, viewer and reel set
NM n/a MIP $60

Black Hole, blister pack, three reel, Model No. BK035
NM $7 MIP $12

Black Hole, 1979, original envelope package, three reel, Model No. K35
NM $15 MIP $18

Blue's Clues, Model No. 73059
NM $2 MIP $6

Bollie & Billie, blister pack, three reel, Model No. BD207
NM $7 MIP $8

Bonanza, blister pack, three reel, Model No. BB487
NM $10 MIP $20

Bonanza, original envelope package, three reel, Model No. B471
NM $10 MIP $20

Bonanza (w/o Pernell Roberts), original envelope package, three reel, Model No. B487
NM $30 MIP $35

Bozo, blister pack, three reel, Model No. BD1484
NM $13 MIP $15

Brady Bunch, original envelope package, three reel, Model No. B568
NM $17 MIP $22

Brave Eagle, original envelope package, three reel, Model No. B466
NM $21 MIP $25

Bravestar, blister pack, three reel, Model No. BD272
NM $9 MIP $10

Buck Rogers, 1979, original envelope package, three reel, Model No. L15
NM $7 MIP $10

Buckaroo Banzai, blister pack, three reel, Model No. 4056
NM $8 MIP $10

Buffalo Bill, Jr., original envelope package, three reel, Model No. B464
NM $18 MIP $25

Buffalo Bill, Jr., 1955, original envelope package, three reel, Model No. 965abc
NM $21 MIP $25

Bugs Bunny, 1959, original envelope package, three reel, Model No. B531
NM $9 MIP $10

Bugs Bunny & Tweety, blister pack, three reel, Model No. 1077
NM $2 MIP $3

Bugs Bunny and Elmer Fudd (single reel), 1951, original envelope package, one reel, Model No. 800
NM $7 MIP $8

Bugs Bunny, Big Top Bunny, original envelope package, three reel, Model No. B549
NM $5 MIP $6

Bugs Bunny/Road Runner Show, original envelope package, three reel, Model No. M10
NM $3 MIP $4

Bullwinkle, original envelope package, three reel, Model No. B515
NM $12 MIP $20

Button Moon, blister pack, three reel, Model No. BD212
NM $7 MIP $8

Can't Stop the Music, original envelope package, three reel, Model No. L1
NM $17 MIP $20

Captain America, original envelope package, three reel, Model No. H43
NM $4 MIP $5

Captain Kangaroo, original envelope package, three reel, Model No. 755abc
NM $14 MIP $16

Captain Kangaroo, original envelope package, three reel, Model No. B560
NM $10 MIP $12

Captain Kangaroo Show, original envelope package, three reel, Model No. B565
NM $10 MIP $12

Care Bears, blister pack, three reel, Model No. BD264
NM $5 MIP $10

Cartoon Carnival with Supercar, original envelope package, three reel, Model No. B521
NM $40 MIP $60

Casimir Costureiro, blister pack, three reel, Model No. BD171
NM $7 MIP $8

Casper the Friendly Ghost, original envelope package, three reel, Model No. B533
NM $5 MIP $6

Casper the Friendly Ghost, 1988, blister pack, three reel, Model No. BB533
NM $5 MIP $6

Cat from Outer Space, 1970s, original envelope package, three reel, Model No. J22
NM $7 MIP $8

Centurions, blister pack, three reel, Model No. 1057
NM $3 MIP $4

Charge at Feather River, The (Movie Preview Reel), Movie Preview Reel
NM $75 MIP $100

Charlie Brown, Bon Voyage, original envelope package, three reel, Model No. L2
NM $4 MIP $6

Charlie Brown, It's a Bird, original envelope package, three reel, Model No. B556
NM $4 MIP $5

Charlie Brown, It's Your First Kiss, 1980s, blister pack, three reel, Model No. 1039
NM $9 MIP $10

Charlotte's Web, original envelope package, three reel, Model No. B321
NM $5 MIP $6

Chip 'n Dale Rescue Rangers, blister pack, three reel, Model No. 3075
NM $4 MIP $5

CHiPs, 1980, original envelope package, three reel, Model No. L14
NM $13 MIP $15

Cinderella, Model No. B318
NM $5 MIP $8

Cinderella (single reel), 1953, original envelope package, one reel, Model No. FT5
NM $1 MIP $2

Cisco Kid (single reel), original envelope package, one reel, Model No. 960
NM $2 MIP $4

City Beneath the Sea, original envelope package, three reel, Model No. B496
NM $15 MIP $25

Close Encounters of the Third Kind, original envelope package, three reel, Model No. J47
NM $10 MIP $12

Cowboy Stars, original envelope package, three reel, Model No. B461
NM $21 MIP $25

Curiosity Shop, original envelope package, three reel, Model No. B564
NM $10 MIP $12

Curious George, Model No. 2015
NM $6 MIP $12

VIEW-MASTER

Daktari, original envelope package, three reel, Model No. B498
NM $10 **MIP** $13

Dale Evans, original envelope package, three reel, Model No. 944abc
NM $26 **MIP** $33

Dale Evans, original envelope package, three reel, Model No. B463
NM $23 **MIP** $30

Danger Mouse, blister pack, three reel, Model No. BD214
NM $15 **MIP** $18

Dangerous Mission (Movie Preview Reel), Movie Preview Reel
NM $75 **MIP** $100

Daniel Boone, original envelope package, three reel, Model No. B479
NM $15 **MIP** $20

Dark Crystal, blister pack, three reel, Model No. 4036
NM $7 **MIP** $10

Dark Shadows, original envelope package, three reel, Model No. B503
NM $30 **MIP** $75

Davy Crockett, original envelope package, three reel, Model No. 935abc
NM $64 **MIP** $75

Dempsey & Makepeace, blister pack, three reel, Model No. BD244
NM $7 **MIP** $8

Dennis the Menace, blister pack, three reel, Model No. 1065
NM $2 **MIP** $3

Dennis the Menace, original envelope package, three reel, Model No. B539
NM $3 **MIP** $4

Deputy Dawg, original envelope package, three reel, Model No. B519
NM $30 **MIP** $50

Devil's Canyon (Movie Preview Reel), Movie Preview Reel
NM $75 **MIP** $100

Dick Tracy, 1990, blister pack, three reel, Model No. 4105
NM $7 **MIP** $8

Dick Turpin, blister pack, three reel, Model No. BD188
NM $9 **MIP** $10

Dinosaurs (Disney TV show), blister pack, three reel, Model No. 4138
NM $4 **MIP** $7

Discovery Channel Space Images, 1997, In plastic case/envelope with relief of Shuttle and planet Saturn
NM $3 **MIP** $7

Disneyland, Adventureland, Model No. A177
NM $6 **MIP** $25

Disneyland, Fantasyland, Model No. A178
NM $6 **MIP** $25

Disneyland, Frontierland, Model No. A176
NM $6 **MIP** $25

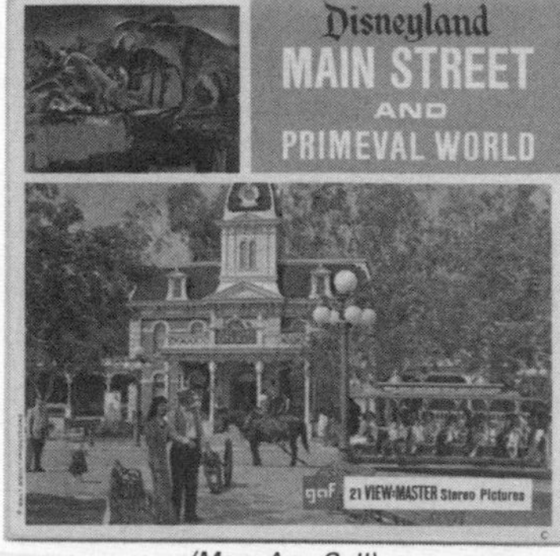

(Mary Ann Sell)

Disneyland, Main Street U.S.A., Model No. A175
NM $6 **MIP** $25

Disneyland, New Orleans Square, Model No. A180
NM $6 **MIP** $25

Disneyland, Tomorrowland, Model No. A179
NM $6 **MIP** $25

Donald Duck, 1973, original envelope package, three reel, Model No. B525
NM $7 **MIP** $8

Dr. Shrinker & Wonderbug, original envelope package, three reel, Model No. H2
NM $10 **MIP** $14

Dr. Who, blister pack, three reel, Model No. BD187
NM $35 **MIP** $50

Dr. Who, blister pack, three reel, Model No. BD216
NM $35 **MIP** $50

Dracula, 1976, original envelope package, three reel, Model No. B324
NM $13 **MIP** $15

Drums of Tahiti (Movie Preview Reel), Movie Preview Reel
NM $75 **MIP** $100

Duck Tales, blister pack, three reel, Model No. 3055
NM $4 **MIP** $5

Dukes of Hazzard, original envelope package, three reel, Model No. L17
NM $7 **MIP** $8

Dukes of Hazzard #2, original envelope package, three reel, Model No. M19
NM $6 **MIP** $7

Dukes of Hazzard 2, blister pack, three reel, Model No. 4000
NM $6 **MIP** $7

Dumbo, blister pack, three reel, Model No. BD1474
NM $9 **MIP** $10

Dumbo, original envelope package, three reel, Model No. J60
NM $7 **MIP** $8

Dune, blister pack, three reel, Model No. 4058
NM $7 **MIP** $12

E.T. (reissued), blister pack, three reel, Model No. 4117
NM $3 **MIP** $6

E.T. The Extra-Terrestrial, 1982, original envelope package, three reel, Model No. N7
NM $15 **MIP** $18

E.T., More Scenes from, blister pack, three reel, Model No. 4001
NM $15 **MIP** $18

Eight is Enough, original envelope package, three reel, Model No. K76
NM $13 **MIP** $15

Electra Woman & Dyna Girl, 1977, original envelope package, three reel, Model No. H3
NM $7 **MIP** $10

Elmo Wants to Play, blister pack, three reel, Model No. 4125
NM $2 **MIP** $3

Emergency, original envelope package, three reel, Model No. B597
NM $10 **MIP** $12

Emil, blister pack, three reel, Model No. BD122
NM $10 **MIP** $12

Expo 67 Montreal, Model No. A071
NM $12 **MIP** $20

Expo 67 Montreal, Model No. A073
NM $12 **MIP** $20

Expo 67 Montreal, Model No. A074
NM $12 **MIP** $20

Expo 70 Osaka
NM $20 **MIP** $40

Expo 74 Spokane, single reel 1-6, each
NM $5 **MIP** $10

Fabeltjes Krant, blister pack, three reel, Model No. BD251
NM $10 **MIP** $12

Family Affair, original envelope package, three reel, Model No. B571
NM $21 **MIP** $25

Family Matters, blister pack, three reel, Model No. 4118
NM $4 **MIP** $8

Fang Face, original envelope package, three reel, Model No. K66
NM $5 **MIP** $6

Fantastic Four, 1979, blister pack, three reel, Model No. K36
NM $9 **MIP** $10

Fantastic Voyage, 1968, original envelope package, three reel, Model No. B546
NM $10 **MIP** $20

Fat Albert & Cosby Kids, original envelope package, three reel, Model No. B554
NM $5 **MIP** $6

Ferdy, blister pack, three reel, Model No. BD269
NM $9 **MIP** $10

Fiddler on the Roof, original envelope package, three reel, Model No. B390
NM $21 **MIP** $25

Flash Gordon in the Planet Mongo, 1963, original envelope package, three reel
NM $21 **MIP** $25

Flight to Tangier (Movie Preview Reel), Movie Preview Reel
NM $75 **MIP** $100

Flintstone Kids, blister pack, three reel, Model No. 1066
NM $2 **MIP** $4

Flintstones, blister pack, three reel, Model No. 1080
NM $2 **MIP** $3

Flintstones, 1962, original envelope package, three reel, Model No. L6
NM $10 **MIP** $12

Flintstones: Pebbles and Bamm-Bamm, 1964, Original picture envelope, three reel
NM $7 **MIP** $14

Flipper, blister pack, three reel, Model No. BB480
NM $10 **MIP** $12

Flipper, original envelope package, three reel, Model No. B485
NM $10 **MIP** $12

Flying Kiwi, blister pack, three reel, Model No. BD189
NM $10 **MIP** $12

Flying Nun, original envelope package, three reel, Model No. B495
NM $21 **MIP** $25

Fonz, The, blister pack, three reel, Model No. BJ013
NM $7 **MIP** $8

For the Love of Benji, original envelope package, three reel, Model No. H54
NM $7 **MIP** $8

Fort Ti (Movie Preview Reel), Movie Preview Reel
NM $75 **MIP** $100

Fox & Hound, original envelope package, three reel, Model No. L29
NM $7 **MIP** $8

Fox & the Hound, The (Disney), 1980, blister pack, three reel, Model No. 3000
NM $4 **MIP** $5

Fraggle Rock, blister pack, three reel, Model No. 4053
NM $4 **MIP** $5

Fraggle Rock, blister pack, three reel, Model No. 1067
NM $4 **MIP** $5

Frankenstein, 1976, original envelope package, three reel, Model No. B323
NM $13 **MIP** $15

French Line, The (Movie Preview Reel), Movie Preview Reel
NM $75 **MIP** $100

Full House, blister pack, three reel, Model No. 4119
NM $3 **MIP** $6

G.I. Joe, 1974, original envelope package, three reel, Model No. B585
NM $13 **MIP** $25

Garfield, original envelope package, three reel, Model No. L28
NM $3 **MIP** $4

Gene Autry (single reel), original envelope package, one reel, Model No. 950
NM $2 **MIP** $3

Gene Autry, "The Kidnapping" (single reel), 1953, original envelope package, one reel, Model No. 951
NM $2 **MIP** $3

Ghostbusters, The Real, blister pack, three reel, Model No. 1062
NM $4 **MIP** $6

Gil & Julie, blister pack, three reel, Model No. BD225
NM $7 **MIP** $8

Girl Scouts Serve Their Country, Model No. 401
NM $100 **MIP** $250

Glass Web (Movie Preview Reel), Movie Preview Reel
NM $75 **MIP** $100

Godzilla, 1978, blister pack, three reel, Model No. J23
NM $13 **MIP** $15

Gold Cup Hydroplane Races (ABC's WW/Sports), original envelope package, three reel, Model No. B945
NM $34 **MIP** $40

Goldilocks, Model No. B317
NM $7 **MIP** $10

Goldilocks and the Three Bears (single reel), 1946, original envelope package, one reel, Model No. FT6
NM $1 **MIP** $2

Goonies, blister pack, three reel, Model No. 4064
NM $7 **MIP** $70

Great Muppet Caper, original envelope package, three reel, Model No. M7
NM $4 **MIP** $5

Green Hornet, original envelope package, three reel, Model No. B488
NM $30 **MIP** $60

Gremlins, blister pack, three reel, Model No. 4055
NM $7 **MIP** $12

Grimm's Fairy Tales, clay figure, Model No. B312
NM $7 **MIP** $12

Grizzly Adams, original envelope package, three reel, Model No. J10
NM $9 **MIP** $10

Gulliver's Travels, Model No. B374
NM $10 **MIP** $15

Gun Fury (Movie Preview Reel), Movie Preview Reel
NM $75 **MIP** $100

Gunsmoke, original envelope package, three reel, Model No. B589
NM $21 **MIP** $25

Hair Bear Bunch, original envelope package, three reel, Model No. B552
NM $7 **MIP** $8

Hammerman, blister pack, three reel, Model No. 1081
NM $3 **MIP** $6

Hammerman, MC Hammer, Model No. 1061
NM $6 **MIP** $12

Hannah Lee (Movie Preview Reel), Movie Preview Reel
NM $75 **MIP** $100

Hans Christian Andersen Fairy Tales, clay figure, Model No. B305
NM $7 **MIP** $9

Happy Birthday Bugs Bunny, Model No. 1072
NM $2 **MIP** $4

Happy Days, original envelope package, three reel, Model No. J13
NM $7 **MIP** $8

Happy Days, 1974, original envelope package, three reel, Model No. B586
NM $9 **MIP** $10

Happy Days, 1981, blister pack, three reel, Model No. BB586
NM $7 **MIP** $8

Hardy Boys, original envelope package, three reel, Model No. B547
NM $9 **MIP** $12

Harry Potter - Belgium Version, Model No. 73999
NM $12 **MIP** $25

Harry Potter Sorcerer's Stone Part 1, Model No. 73632
NM $4 **MIP** $10

Harry Potter Sorcerer's Stone Part 2, Model No. 73633
NM $4 **MIP** $10

Harry Potter Sorcerer's Stone Part 3, Model No. 73634
NM $4 **MIP** $10

Hawaii Five-O, 1972, original envelope package, three reel, Model No. B590
NM $17 **MIP** $20

Heidi, Model No. B425
NM $6 **MIP** $10

Herbie Rides Again, original envelope package, three reel, Model No. B578
NM $7 **MIP** $8

Here's Lucy, original envelope package, three reel, Model No. B588
NM $43 **MIP** $50

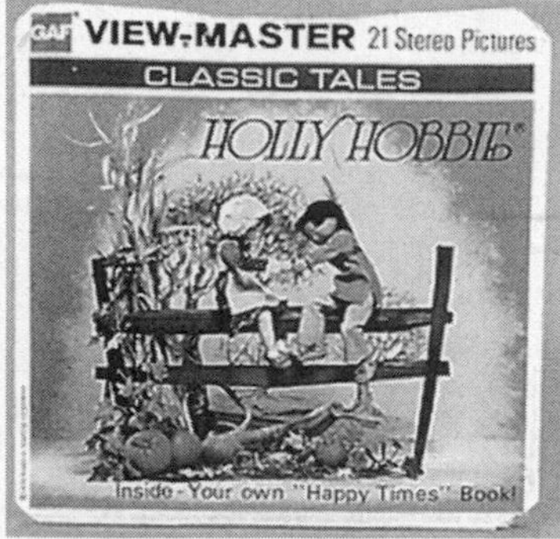

Holly Hobbie, 1976, "Classic Tales" series, picture envelope and booklet, three reels
NM $6 **MIP** $13

Hopalong Cassidy (single reel), original envelope package, one reel, Model No. 956
NM $2 **MIP** $3

Hopalong Cassidy (single reel), original envelope package, one reel, Model No. 955
NM $2 **MIP** $3

House of Wax (Movie Preview Reel), Movie Preview Reel
NM $150 **MIP** $250

Howard the Duck, blister pack, three reel, Model No. 4073
NM $7 **MIP** $10

Huckleberry Finn, original envelope package, three reel, Model No. B343
NM $5 **MIP** $8

Huckleberry Hound & Yogi Bear, 1960, original envelope package, three reel, Model No. B512
NM $4 **MIP** $5

I Go Pogo, original envelope package, three reel, Model No. L32
NM $7 **MIP** $15

Inferno (Movie Preview Reel), Movie Preview Reel
NM $75 **MIP** $100

Inspector Gadget, blister pack, three reel, Model No. BD232
NM $7 **MIP** $10

International Moto-Cross (ABC's WW/Sports), original envelope package, three reel, Model No. B946
NM $15 **MIP** $30

International Swimming & Diving Meet (ABC's WW/Sports), original envelope package, three reel, Model No. B936
NM $60 **MIP** $70

Ironman, original envelope package, three reel, Model No. H44
NM $3 **MIP** $5

Isis, 1976, original envelope package, three reel, Model No. T100
NM $10 **MIP** $12

Island at Top of the World, original envelope package, three reel, Model No. B367
NM $21 **MIP** $25

It Came From Outer Space (Movie Preview Reel), Movie Preview Reel
NM $220 **MIP** $250

Jack & the Beanstalk, clay figure, Model No. B314
NM $7 **MIP** $9

Jack and the Beanstalk (single reel), 1951, original envelope package, one reel, Model No. FT3
NM $1 **MIP** $2

James Bond, Live & Let Die, original envelope package, three reel, Model No. B393
NM $12 **MIP** $20

James Bond, Live & Let Die, 1973, blister pack, three reel, Model No. BB393
NM $17 **MIP** $20

James Bond, Moonraker, 1979, original envelope package, three reel, Model No. K68
NM $13 **MIP** $15

Jaws 3-D, blister pack, three reel, Model No. 4041
NM $4 **MIP** $6

Jem, 1986, blister pack, three reel, Model No. 1059
NM $6 **MIP** $7

Jesse James vs. The Daltons (Movie Preview Reel), Movie Preview Reel
NM $100 **MIP** $130

Jetsons, original envelope package, three reel, Model No. L27
NM $5 **MIP** $6

Jim Henson's Muppet Movie, original envelope package, three reel, Model No. K27
NM $4 **MIP** $7

Jimbo and the Jet Set, blister pack, three reel, Model No. BD261
NM $7 **MIP** $8

Joe 90, original envelope package, three reel, Model No. B456
NM $50 **MIP** $70

Joe Forrester, original envelope package, three reel, Model No. BB454
NM $9 **MIP** $10

John F. Kennedy's Trip to Ireland, Model No. 1305
NM $200 **MIP** $500

Johnny Mocassin, original envelope package, three reel, Model No. B468
NM $21 **MIP** $25

Johnny Mocassin, 1960s, original envelope package, three reel, Model No. 937abc
NM $21 **MIP** $25

Julia, original envelope package, three reel, Model No. B572
NM $15 **MIP** $25

Jungle Book, Model No. B363
NM $7 **MIP** $11

Jurassic Park, blister pack, three reel, Model No. 4150
NM $7 **MIP** $10

King Kong, original envelope package, three reel, Model No. B392
NM $7 **MIP** $8

Kiss Me Kate (Movie Preview Reel), Movie Preview Reel
NM $75 **MIP** $100

Knight Rider, blister pack, three reel, Model No. 4054
NM $5 **MIP** $6

Korg 70,000 B.C., original envelope package, three reel, Model No. B557
NM $10 **MIP** $15

Kung Fu, original envelope package, three reel, Model No. B598
NM $13 **MIP** $15

Lancelot Link Secret Chimp, original envelope package, three reel, Model No. B504
NM $21 **MIP** $25

Land of the Giants, original envelope package, three reel, Model No. B494
NM $20 **MIP** $30

Land of the Lost, 1977, original envelope package, three reel, Model No. B579
NM $9 **MIP** $15

Land of the Lost 2, original envelope package, three reel, Model No. H1
NM $9 **MIP** $15

Larry the Lamb, blister pack, three reel, Model No. BD190
NM $7 **MIP** $8

Lassie & Timmy, original envelope package, three reel, Model No. B472
NM $13 **MIP** $15

Lassie Look Homeward, original envelope package, three reel, Model No. B480
NM $9 **MIP** $10

Lassie Rides the Log Flume, original envelope package, three reel, Model No. B489
NM $13 **MIP** $15

Last Starfighter, The, blister pack, three reel, Model No. 4057
NM $5 **MIP** $10

Laugh-In, original envelope package, three reel, Model No. B497
NM $13 **MIP** $20

Laverne & Shirley, original envelope package, three reel, Model No. J20
NM $5 **MIP** $10

Legend of Indiana Jones, blister pack, three reel, Model No. 4092
NM $5 **MIP** $6

Legend of the Lone Ranger, original envelope package, three reel, Model No. L26
NM $7 **MIP** $8

Legend of the Lone Ranger, blister pack, three reel, Model No. 4033
NM $6 **MIP** $10

Les Maitres Du Temps, blister pack, three reel, Model No. BD203
NM $7 **MIP** $8

Little League World Series (ABC's WW/Sports), original envelope package, three reel, Model No. B940
NM $43 **MIP** $50

Little Mermaid, blister pack, three reel, Model No. 3078

NM $2 MIP $3

Little Mermaid - TV Show, blister pack, three reel, Model No. 3089

NM $2 MIP $3

Little Red Hen/Thumbelina/Pied Piper, 1957, original envelope package, three reel, Model No. B319

NM $7 MIP $8

Little Red Riding Hood, clay figure, Model No. B310

NM $5 MIP $7

Little Yellow Dinosaur, The, 1971, Original picture envelope, three reel

NM $6 MIP $11

Lone Ranger, original envelope package, three reel, Model No. B465

NM $21 MIP $25

Lone Ranger, The, original envelope package, three reel, Model No. 962abc

NM $21 MIP $25

Lone Ranger, The Legend, Tie-in with the movie, original picture envelope, three reels

NM $10 MIP $17

Lost in Space, original envelope package, three reel, Model No. B482

NM $40 MIP $60

Lost Treasures of the Amazon (Movie Preview Reel), Movie Preview Reel

NM $75 MIP $100

Love Bug, The, 1968, original envelope package, three reel, Model No. B501

NM $9 MIP $12

Lucky Luke vs. The Daltons, original envelope package, three reel, Model No. B455

NM $21 MIP $25

M*A*S*H, original envelope package, three reel, Model No. J11

NM $9 MIP $10

M*A*S*H, blister pack, three reel, Model No. BJ011

NM $9 MIP $10

Magic Roundabout, The, original envelope package, three reel, Model No. B441

NM $13 MIP $15

Maja the Bee, blister pack, three reel, Model No. BD182

NM $7 MIP $10

Man from U.N.C.L.E., original envelope package, three reel, Model No. B484

NM $20 MIP $25

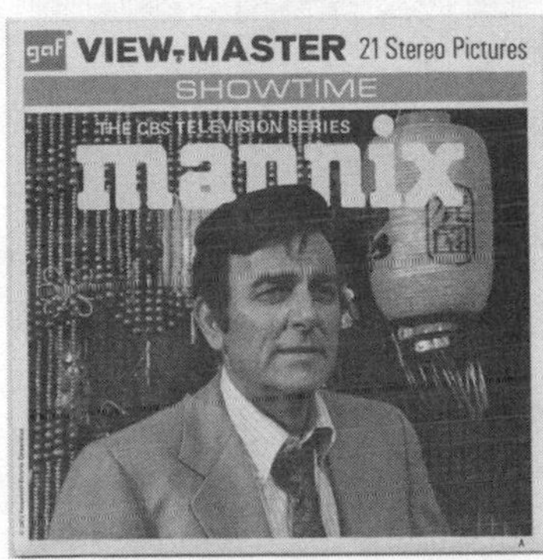

(Mary Ann Sell)

Mannix, original envelope package, three reel, Model No. BB450

NM $21 MIP $25

Mary Poppins, blister pack, three reel, Model No. BB372

NM $7 MIP $8

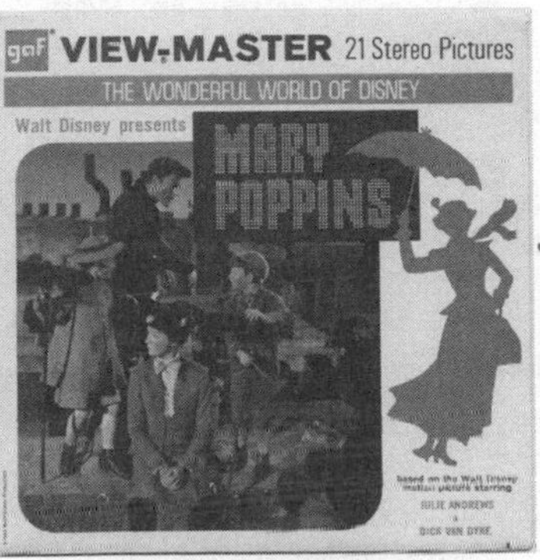

(Mary Ann Sell)

Mary Poppins, 1964, original envelope package, three reel, Model No. B376

NM $7 MIP $8

Mask, blister pack, three reel, Model No. 1056

NM $4 MIP $8

Maze, The (Movie Preview Reel), Movie Preview Reel

NM $128 MIP $150

Metal Mickey, blister pack, three reel, Model No. BD217

NM $7 MIP $8

Meteor, original envelope package, three reel, Model No. K46

NM $9 MIP $10

Michael, original envelope package, three reel, Model No. D122

NM $20 MIP $25

Michael Jackson's Thriller, blister pack, three reel, Model No. 4047

NM $6 MIP $18

(Mary Ann Sell)

Mickey Mouse, 1958, original envelope package, three reel, Model No. B528

NM $5 MIP $10

Mickey Mouse - Clock Cleaners, original envelope package, three reel, Model No. B551

NM $9 MIP $30

Mickey Mouse Club, original envelope package, three reel, Model No. 865abc

NM $21 MIP $25

(Mary Ann Sell)

Mickey Mouse Club Mouseketeers, 1956, original envelope package, three reel, Model No. B524

NM $21 MIP $25

Mickey Mouse Jubilee, 1980s, blister pack, three reel, Model No. J29

NM $9 MIP $10

Mighty Mouse, 1958, original envelope package, three reel, Model No. B526

NM $17 MIP $20

Mighty Mouse, 1970s, blister pack, three reel, Model No. BB526

NM $4 MIP $5

Miss Sadie Thompson (Movie Preview Reel), Movie Preview Reel

NM $75 MIP $100

(Mary Ann Sell)

Mission Impossible, original envelope package, three reel, Model No. B505
NM $15 **MIP** $18

(Mary Ann Sell)

Mod Squad, original envelope package, three reel, Model No. B478
NM $16 **MIP** $20

Money From Home (Movie Preview Reel), Movie Preview Reel
NM $75 **MIP** $100

(Mary Ann Sell)

Monkees, original envelope package, three reel, Model No. B493
NM $12 **MIP** $30

Mork & Mindy, 1978, original envelope package, three reel, Model No. K67
NM $7 **MIP** $8

Movie Stars I (single reel), original envelope package, one reel, Model No. 740
NM $13 **MIP** $15

Movie Stars II (single reel), original envelope package, one reel, Model No. 741
NM $13 **MIP** $15

Movie Stars III (single reel), original envelope package, one reel, Model No. 742
NM $13 **MIP** $15

Mr. Magoo, 1977, original envelope package, three reel, Model No. H56
NM $6 **MIP** $10

Munch Bunch, blister pack, three reel, Model No. BD197
NM $7 **MIP** $8

(Mary Ann Sell)

Munsters, original envelope package, three reel, Model No. B481
NM $75 **MIP** $100

Muppet Movie, Scenes From The, blister pack, three reel, Model No. 4005
NM $4 **MIP** $8

Muppets Go Hawaiian, The, original envelope package, three reel, Model No. L25
NM $4 **MIP** $8

Muppets, Meet Jim Henson's, original envelope package, three reel, Model No. K26
NM $4 **MIP** $8

Muppets, The, blister pack, three reel, Model No. BK026
NM $4 **MIP** $8

Nanny & The Professor, original envelope package, three reel, Model No. B573
NM $30 **MIP** $35

NCAA Track & Field Championships (ABC's WW/Sports), original envelope package, three reel, Model No. B935
NM $40 **MIP** $60

Nebraskan, The (Movie Preview Reel), Movie Preview Reel
NM $75 **MIP** $100

New Mickey Mouse Club, original envelope package, three reel, Model No. H9
NM $5 **MIP** $8

New Zoo Revue, original envelope package, three reel, Model No. B566
NM $13 **MIP** $15

New Zoo Revue 2, original envelope package, three reel, Model No. B567
NM $13 **MIP** $15

Old Surehand, original envelope package, three reel, Model No. B443
NM $30 **MIP** $40

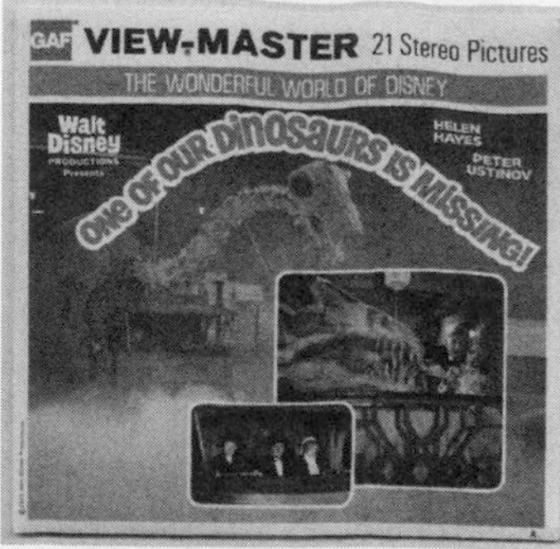

(Mary Ann Sell)

One of Our Dinosaurs Is Missing, original envelope package, three reel, Model No. B377
NM $10 **MIP** $12

Oregon Centennial Exposition (1959), Model No. A0250
NM $30 **MIP** $50

Orm & Cheap, blister pack, three reel, Model No. BD266
NM $10 **MIP** $12

Partridge Family, blister pack, three reel, Model No. BB5924
NM $17 **MIP** $20

Partridge Family, 1971, Talking View-Master reels, original envelope package, three reel
NM $22 **MIP** $27

Partridge Family, 1971, original envelope package, three reel, Model No. B569
NM $17 **MIP** $20

Pee-Wee's Playhouse, 1988, blister pack, three reel, Model No. 4074
NM $9 **MIP** $10

Pendelton Round-Up (ABC's WW/Sports), original envelope package, three reel, Model No. B943
NM $30 **MIP** $35

Perishers, The, blister pack, three reel, Model No. BD184
NM $6 **MIP** $8

Peter Pan, Disney's, original envelope package, three reel
NM $5 **MIP** $6

Pete's Dragon, original envelope package, three reel, Model No. H38
NM $7 **MIP** $8

Pink Panther, original envelope package, three reel, Model No. J12
NM $5 **MIP** $6

Pink Panther, 1970s, blister pack, three reel, Model No. BJ012
NM $4 **MIP** $5

Pinky Lee's 7 Days (single reel), original envelope package, one reel, Model No. 750
NM $21 **MIP** $25

Pinocchio, clay figure, Model No. B311
NM $8 **MIP** $12

Pippi Longstocking, original envelope package, three reel, Model No. B322
NM $13 **MIP** $15

Pippi Longstocking, original envelope package, three reel, Model No. D113
NM $13 **MIP** $15

Planet of the Apes, blister pack, three reel, Model No. BB507
NM $30 **MIP** $35

Planet of the Apes, 1967, original envelope package, three reel, Model No. B507
NM $30 **MIP** $35

Pluto, blister pack, three reel, Model No. 3013
NM $4 **MIP** $7

Pluto, blister pack, three reel, Model No. BB529
NM $4 **MIP** $7

Pluto, original envelope package, three reel, Model No. B529
NM $9 **MIP** $10

Polly in Portugal, original envelope package, three reel, Model No. B442
NM $26 **MIP** $30

Polly in Venice, original envelope package, three reel, Model No. D100
NM $17 **MIP** $20

Popeye, 1962, original envelope package, three reel, Model No. B516
NM $6 **MIP** $8

Popeye Talking View-Master Set, 1983, original envelope package, three reel
NM $9 **MIP** $10

Popeye's Fun, original envelope package, three reel, Model No. B527
NM $7 **MIP** $10

Portland Bill, blister pack, three reel, Model No. BD226
NM $10 **MIP** $12

Poseidon Adventure, original envelope package, three reel, Model No. B391
NM $21 **MIP** $25

Postman Pat, blister pack, three reel, Model No. BD218
NM $7 **MIP** $8

Power Rangers, Model No. 36870
NM $2 **MIP** $6

Pumcki, blister pack, three reel, Model No. BD220
NM $7 **MIP** $8

Punky Brewster, 1984, blister pack, three reel, Model No. 4068
NM $7 **MIP** $8

Puppets Audition Night, blister pack, three reel, Model No. 4003
NM $4 **MIP** $5

Puppets Audition Night, The, original envelope package, three reel, Model No. L9
NM $4 **MIP** $5

(Mary Ann Sell)

Quick Draw McGraw, 1960s, Hanna Barbera, three reels
NM $7 **MIP** $15

Raggedy Ann & Andy, Model No. B406
NM $9 **MIP** $15

Red Riding Hood (single reel), 1950, original envelope package, one reel, Model No. FT1
NM $2 **MIP** $3

Rescuers, The, original envelope package, three reel, Model No. H26
NM $5 **MIP** $6

Rescuers, The, blister pack, three reel, Model No. BH026
NM $5 **MIP** $6

Return to Witch Mountain, original envelope package, three reel, Model No. J25
NM $5 **MIP** $6

Rin-Tin-Tin, original envelope package, three reel, Model No. B407
NM $13 **MIP** $15

Rin-Tin-Tin, 1955, original envelope package, three reel, Model No. 930abc
NM $13 **MIP** $15

Robin Hood, 1954, original envelope package, three reel
NM $21 **MIP** $25

Robin Hood Meets Friar Tuck, 1956, original envelope package, three reel, Model No. B373
NM $17 **MIP** $20

Rocketeer, The, blister pack, three reel, Model No. 4115
NM $7 **MIP** $8

Roland Rat Superstar, blister pack, three reel, Model No. BD240
NM $7 **MIP** $8

Romper Room, original envelope package, three reel, Model No. K20
NM $7 **MIP** $8

Rookies, The, 1975, original envelope package, three reel, Model No. BB452
NM $13 **MIP** $15

Roy Rogers, original envelope package, three reel, Model No. B462
NM $21 **MIP** $25

Roy Rogers, original envelope package, three reel, Model No. B475
NM $21 **MIP** $25

Roy Rogers, original envelope package, three reel, Model No. 948abc
NM $21 **MIP** $25

Roy Rogers (single reel), original envelope package, one reel, Model No. 945
NM $2 **MIP** $3

Rudolph, 2004, Reel & Viewer Set: Target Exclusive, Rankin Bass Version
NM $10 **MIP** $20

Rudolph the Red-Nosed Reindeer, 1955, Definitely based on the Little Golden Book, the puppets even look like the illustrations. Interesting, considering these reels were created about ten years before the Rankin/Bass animated special. Includes picture envelope and three reels
NM $10 **MIP** $17

Rugrats, Model No. 36343
NM $2 **MIP** $4

Run Joe Run, 1974, original envelope package, three reel, Model No. B594
NM $13 **MIP** $15

Rupert the Bear, blister pack, three reel, Model No. BD109
NM $12 **MIP** $15

S.W.A.T., 1975, original envelope package, three reel, Model No. BB453
NM $10 **MIP** $12

Sangaree (Movie Preview Reel), Movie Preview Reel
NM $75 **MIP** $100

Scooby Doo, blister pack, three reel, Model No. 1079
NM $2 **MIP** $5

Scooby Doo, original envelope package, three reel, Model No. B553
NM $4 **MIP** $5

Search, original envelope package, three reel, Model No. B591
NM $17 **MIP** $20

Sebastian, original envelope package, three reel, Model No. D101
NM $26 **MIP** $30

Sebastian, original envelope package, three reel, Model No. B452
NM $26 **MIP** $30

Second Chance (Movie Preview Reel), Movie Preview Reel
NM $75 **MIP** $100

Secret Squirrel & Atom Ant, original envelope package, three reel, Model No. B535
NM $9 **MIP** $12

Secret Valley, blister pack, three reel, Model No. BD208
NM $10 **MIP** $12

Sesame Street - Follow That Bird, blister pack, three reel, Model No. 4066
NM $4 **MIP** $5

Sesame Street - People in Your Neighborhood, blister pack, three reel, Model No. 4049
NM $4 **MIP** $5

Sesame Street - People in Your Neighborhood, original envelope package, three reel, Model No. M12
NM $4 **MIP** $5

Sesame Street Alphabet, blister pack, three reel, Model No. 4051
NM $2 **MIP** $3

Sesame Street Baby Animals, blister pack, three reel, Model No. 4072
NM $4 **MIP** $5

Sesame Street Circus Fun, blister pack, three reel, Model No. 4097
NM $4 **MIP** $5

Sesame Street Counting, blister pack, three reel, Model No. 4050
NM $4 **MIP** $5

Sesame Street Goes on Vacation, blister pack, three reel, Model No. 4077
NM $4 **MIP** $5

Sesame Street Goes Western, blister pack, three reel, Model No. 4085
NM $4 **MIP** $5

Sesame Street Nursery Rhymes, blister pack, three reel, Model No. 4083
NM $4 **MIP** $5

Sesame Street Shapes, Colors, blister pack, three reel, Model No. 4052
NM $4 **MIP** $5

Sesame Street Visits the Zoo, blister pack, three reel, Model No. 4017
NM $4 **MIP** $5

Shaggy D.A., original envelope package, three reel, Model No. b368
NM $10 **MIP** $12

Shazam, original envelope package, three reel, Model No. B550
NM $5 **MIP** $7

Shoe People, The, blister pack, three reel, Model No. BD270
NM $10 **MIP** $12

Siegfried & Roy, Model No. 73930
NM $6 **MIP** $12

Sigmund & the Sea Monsters (correct issue numbers), original envelope package, three reel, Model No. B595
NM $15 **MIP** $18

Sigmund & the Sea Monsters (wrong issue number), original envelope package, three reel, Model No. B559
NM $15 **MIP** $18

Silverhawks, blister pack, three reel, Model No. 1058
NM $4 **MIP** $5

Six Million Dollar Man, 1974, original envelope package, three reel, Model No. B556
NM $13 **MIP** $15

Sleeping Beauty, clay figure, Model No. B308
NM $5 **MIP** $7

Sleeping Beauty, Disney's, original envelope package, three reel, Model No. B308
NM $4 **MIP** $5

Smith Family, The, original envelope package, three reel, Model No. B490
NM $10 **MIP** $30

Smokey Bear, Model No. B404
NM $10 **MIP** $20

Smuggler, blister pack, three reel, Model No. BD194
NM $7 **MIP** $8

Smurf, Baby, blister pack, three reel, Model No. BD246
NM $7 **MIP** $8

Smurf, Flying, original envelope package, three reel, Model No. N1
NM $4 **MIP** $5

Smurf, Traveling, original envelope package, three reel, Model No. N2
NM $4 **MIP** $5

Smurfs, blister pack, three reel, Model No. BD172
NM $5 **MIP** $6

Snoopy and the Red Baron, 1980s, blister pack, three reel, Model No. B544
NM $7 **MIP** $8

Snorkes, blister pack, three reel, Model No. BD250
NM $8 **MIP** $10

Snow White, clay figure, Model No. B300
NM $7 **MIP** $9

Snow White & the Seven Dwarfs, original envelope package, three reel, Model No. K69
NM $7 **MIP** $8

Snow White (single reel), 1946, original envelope package, one reel, Model No. FT4
NM $3 **MIP** $4

Snowman, blister pack, three reel, Model No. BD262
NM $7 **MIP** $8

Son of Sinbad (Movie Preview Reel), Movie Preview Reel
NM $128 **MIP** $150

Space Mouse, original envelope package, three reel, Model No. B509
NM $10 **MIP** $20

Space: 1999, blister pack, three reel, Model No. BD150
NM $21 **MIP** $20

Space: 1999, 1975, original envelope package, three reel, Model No. BB451
NM $21 **MIP** $20

Spider-Man, original envelope package, three reel, Model No. K31
NM $9 **MIP** $10

Spider-Man, 1978, original envelope package, three reel, Model No. H11
NM $10 **MIP** $15

Spider-Man, 1980s, blister pack, three reel, Model No. BH011
NM $7 **MIP** $8

Star Trek - The Motion Picture, original envelope package, three reel, Model No. K57
NM $10 **MIP** $12

Star Trek - The Next Generation, blister pack, three reel, Model No. 4095
NM $7 **MIP** $8

Star Trek - Wrath of Khan, original envelope package, three reel, Model No. M38
NM $10 **MIP** $12

Star Trek (Cartoon Series), original envelope package, three reel, Model No. B555
NM $9 **MIP** $10

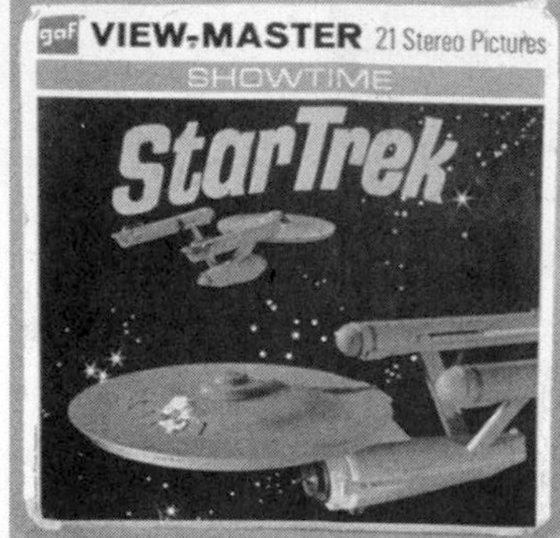

Star Trek (TV Series), "Omega Glory", 1968, original envelope package, three reel, Model No. B499
NM $17 **MIP** $20

Steve Canyon, 1959, original envelope package, three reel, Model No. B582
NM $64 **MIP** $75

VIEW-MASTER

Stranger Wore a Gun, The (Movie Preview Reel), Movie Preview Reel
NM $75 **MIP** $100

Superman, blister pack, three reel, Model No. BJ78
NM $5 **MIP** $6

Superman, blister pack, three reel, Model No. 1064
NM $4 **MIP** $5

Superman - The Movie, original envelope package, three reel, Model No. J78
NM $10 **MIP** $20

Superman (cartoon), original envelope package, three reel, Model No. B584
NM $4 **MIP** $5

Superman II, original envelope package, three reel, Model No. L46
NM $17 **MIP** $25

Superman III, blister pack, three reel, Model No. 4044
NM $7 **MIP** $15

Superstar Barbie, Model No. J070
NM $7 **MIP** $15

Tailspin, blister pack, three reel, Model No. 3081
NM $4 **MIP** $5

Tarzan, original envelope package, three reel, Model No. B580
NM $9 **MIP** $10

Tarzan (single reel), original envelope package, one reel, Model No. 975
NM $4 **MIP** $5

Tarzan Finds a Son (single reel), 1955, original envelope package, one reel, Model No. 976A
NM $3 **MIP** $4

Tarzan of the Apes, 1955, original envelope package, three reel, Model No. 976abc
NM $21 **MIP** $25

Taza, Son of Cochise (Movie Preview Reel), Movie Preview Reel
NM $128 **MIP** $150

Teenage Mutant Ninja Turtles, blister pack, three reel, Model No. 1073
NM $2 **MIP** $5

Teenage Mutant Ninja Turtles - Movie II, blister pack, three reel, Model No. 4114
NM $3 **MIP** $7

Teenage Mutant Ninja Turtles - Movie III, blister pack, three reel, Model No. 4149
NM $2 **MIP** $5

Teenage Mutant Ninja Turtles - The Movie, blister pack, three reel, Model No. 4109
NM $3 **MIP** $5

Telecat, blister pack, three reel, Model No. BD243
NM $7 **MIP** $8

Terrahawks, blister pack, three reel, Model No. BD230
NM $10 **MIP** $20

They Called Him Hondo (Movie Preview Reel), Movie Preview Reel
NM $128 **MIP** $150

Thomas the Tank Engine, blister pack, three reel, Model No. BD238
NM $6 **MIP** $10

Thor, original envelope package, three reel, Model No. H39
NM $2 **MIP** $5

Those Redheads from Seattle (Movie Preview Reel), Movie Preview Reel
NM $75 **MIP** $100

Three Little Pigs, clay figure, Model No. B307
NM $7 **MIP** $9

Thunderbirds, original envelope package, three reel, Model No. B453
NM $43 **MIP** $50

Time Tunnel, 1966, original envelope package, three reel, Model No. B491
NM $20 **MIP** $35

Tiny Toon Adventures, blister pack, three reel, Model No. 1076
NM $2 **MIP** $3

Tiswas, blister pack, three reel, Model No. BD205
NM $7 **MIP** $8

Toby Tyler, original envelope package, three reel, Model No. B476
NM $30 **MIP** $35

Tom & Jerry (single reel), 1956, original envelope package, Model No. 810
NM $2 **MIP** $3

Tom & Jerry, Two Musketeers, 1956, original envelope package, three reel, Model No. B511
NM $9 **MIP** $15

Tom Corbett, Secret from Space, original envelope package, three reel, Model No. B581
NM $21 **MIP** $25

Tom Corbett, Space Cadet, 1954, original envelope package, three reel, Model No. 970abc
NM $21 **MIP** $25

Tom Sawyer, original envelope package, three reel, Model No. B340
NM $7 **MIP** $8

Tom Thumb, original envelope package, three reel, Model No. D123
NM $13 **MIP** $15

Top Cat, blister pack, three reel, Model No. BB513
NM $13 **MIP** $15

Top Cat, original envelope package, three reel, Model No. B513
NM $13 **MIP** $15

Tournament of Thrills (ABC's WW/Sports), original envelope package, three reel, Model No. B947
NM $30 **MIP** $35

Tripods, The, blister pack, three reel, Model No. BD242
NM $10 **MIP** $12

Tron, original envelope package, three reel, Model No. M37
NM $8 **MIP** $10

TV Shows at Universal Studios, original envelope package, three reel, Model No. B477
NM $26 **MIP** $30

TV Stars I (single reel), original envelope package, one reel, Model No. 745
NM $15 **MIP** $18

TV Stars II (single reel), original envelope package, one reel, Model No. 746
NM $15 **MIP** $18

TV Stars III (single reel), original envelope package, one reel, Model No. 747
NM $15 **MIP** $18

Tweety & Sylvester, blister pack, three reel, Model No. BD1161
NM $7 **MIP** $8

Tweety & Sylvester, original envelope package, three reel, Model No. J28
NM $3 **MIP** $4

Twice Upon a Time, blister pack, three reel, Model No. 4043
NM $3 **MIP** $4

U.F.O., original envelope package, three reel, Model No. B417
NM $38 **MIP** $45

Ulysses 31, blister pack, three reel, Model No. BD198
NM $7 **MIP** $8

Veggie Tales - Madame Blueberry, Model No. 73992
NM $6 **MIP** $12

Victor & Maria, blister pack, three reel, Model No. BD224
NM $7 **MIP** $10

Voyage to the Bottom of the Sea, original envelope package, three reel, Model No. B483
NM $10 **MIP** $15

Walt Disney Presents, Model No. B315
NM $7 **MIP** $10

Waltons, The, blister pack, three reel, Model No. BB596
NM $10 **MIP** $12

Waltons, The, 1972, original envelope package, three reel, Model No. B596
NM $10 **MIP** $12

Welcome Back Kotter, original envelope package, three reel, Model No. J19
NM $10 **MIP** $12

Who Framed Roger Rabbit, blister pack, three reel, Model No. 4086
NM $8 **MIP** $16

Wild Animals of Africa, 1960, Original picture envelope showing giraffes, three reel set
NM $5 **MIP** $11

Wild Bill Hickcock & Jingles, original envelope package, three reel, Model No. B473
NM $26 **MIP** $30

Willo the Wisp, blister pack, three reel, Model No. BD215
NM $7 **MIP** $8

Wind in the Willows, blister pack, three reel, Model No. BD231
NM $7 **MIP** $8

Wind in the Willows, blister pack, three reel, Model No. 4084
NM $7 **MIP** $10

Wings of the Hawk (Movie Preview Reel), Movie Preview Reel
NM $128 **MIP** $150

Winnetou, blister pack, three reel, Model No. BB731
NM $21 **MIP** $25

Winnetou, blister pack, three reel, Model No. BB7284
NM $21 **MIP** $25

Winnetou, original envelope package, three reel, Model No. B728
NM $26 **MIP** $30

Winnetou & Halfblood Apache, original envelope package, three reel, Model No. B728
NM $26 **MIP** $30

Winnie the Pooh & The Blustery Day, original envelope package, three reel, Model No. K37
NM $7 **MIP** $8

Wiz, The, 1978, original envelope package, three reel, Model No. J14
NM $17 **MIP** $20

Wizard of Oz, blister pack, three reel, Model No. BD267
NM $7 **MIP** $8

Wizard of Oz, 1957, original envelope package, three reel, Model No. FT45abc
NM $13 **MIP** $15

Wombles, The, blister pack, three reel, Model No. BD131
NM $7 **MIP** $8

Wombles, The, original envelope package, three reel, Model No. D131
NM $13 **MIP** $15

Wonderful World of Disney, Includes three reels: Pinocchio, Lady & The Tramp, Snow White
NM $8 **MIP** $15

Woody Woodpecker, 1955, original envelope package, three reel, Model No. B522
NM $13 **MIP** $15

Woody Woodpecker Pony Express Ride (single reel), 1951, original envelope package, one reel, Model No. 820
NM $3 **MIP** $4

World Bobsled Championships (ABC's WW/Sports), original envelope package, three reel, Model No. B949
NM $60 **MIP** $80

Worzel Gummidge, blister pack, three reel, Model No. BD185
NM $7 **MIP** $8

Wrestling Superstars, blister pack, three reel, Model No. 4067
NM $8 **MIP** $10

Young Indiana Jones Chronicles, blister pack, three reel, Model No. 4140
NM $6 **MIP** $8

Zorro, 1958, original envelope package, three reel, Model No. B469
NM $34 **MIP** $40

VIEW-MASTER

Western Toys

by Karen O'Brien

Remember when Saturday afternoon at the movies for two kids with popcorn cost 25 cents? A quarter sure doesn't buy what it used to. In the 1940s and 1950s, American cowgirls and cowboys also plunked down their hard-earned silver for genuine articles endorsed (or at least bearing the names of) their favorite Western stars.

Heroes were aplenty, and included the likes of Gene Autry, Hopalong Cassidy, the Lone Ranger, and, of course, Roy Rogers, Zorro, and many others.

Today, grownup cowpokes drive hard bargains to get their hands on well-preserved toys that evoke well-preserved memories. That's because they don't make toys, or heroes, like they used to.

In the 1940s, straight shooters like Buck Jones, Red Ryder, and Tom Mix were everywhere. Not only were they peering down from the movie screen—their images also graced cereal boxes, comic books, clothing, clocks, furniture, and toy guns.

By the time Hopalong Cassidy, Gene Autry, and Roy Rogers became household names, cowboy toys and merchandise were everywhere. Soon every child could wear, eat, play with, read, or decorate his room with cowboy memorabilia.

The heyday of cowboy fever blossomed in the 1940s and 1950s. Sears Roebuck devoted entire shelves to cowboy-related merchandise. At the time, toys ranged from 25 cents to $5. Six-guns of every size were sold individually and in holstered sets. Generic guns, hats, and other pieces can still be widely found at reasonable prices today. Toys featuring the "Big Four" (Hoppy, Lone Ranger, Gene, and Roy) command higher values. But other cowboy heroes enjoyed successful merchandising as well, including Wyatt Earp, Rex Allen, Wild Bill Hickok, Tom Mix, The Cisco Kid, and Tex Ritter.

Editor's Note: For more information on Roy Rogers memorabilia, check out *The Ultimate Roy Rogers Collection Identification & Price Guide* by Ron Lenius. (Krause Publications, 2001)

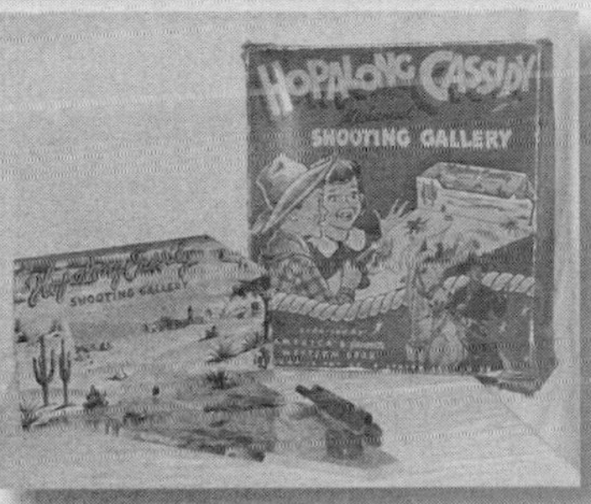

THE TOP 10 WESTERN TOYS (In Mint Condition)

1. Hopalong Cassidy Roller Skates, Rollfast, ... $1,000
2. Wagon Train Complete Western Outfit, Leslie Henry, 1950s 750
3. Hopalong Cassidy Cap Gun, Wyandotte, 1950s 650
4. Hopalong Cassidy Radio, Arvin, 1950s 600
5. Roy Rogers Toy Chest, 1950s 550
6. Hartland Figures, Bill Longley – The Texan, 1959 550
7. Buck Jones Rangers Cowboy Suit, Yankiboy, 1930s 500
8. Hopalong Cassidy, metal figures, 1950s, Timpo 475
9. Hartland Figures, Bat Masterson, 1950s 475
10. Lone Ranger Record Player, 1940s, Dekka 450

Annie Oakley

Annie Oakley with Tagg and Lofty Cut-Out Dolls, 1955, Whitman, paper dolls
EX $20 NM $35 MIP $50

Cut-Out Dolls, 1956, Watkins-Strathmore, paper dolls, Model No. 1822
EX $20 NM $45 MIP $80

Cut-Out Dolls, 1958, Whitman, paper dolls
EX $20 NM $35 MIP $50

Girl's Outfit, 1950s, Pla-Master, red w/ yellow fringe and four pictures (Gail Davis?)
EX $40 NM $85 MIP $140

Holster Set, 1950s, Daisy, leather holsters and cap pistols
EX $100 NM $185 MIP $300

Puzzle, 1955, Milton Bradley, boxed jigsaw puzzle
EX $5 NM $10 MIP $30

Sewing Set, 1950s, Pressman
EX $25 NM $45 MIP $65

Sharpshooter Book, 1956, Golden, Little Golden Books
EX $10 NM $20 MIP $30

Sparkle Picture Craft, 1950s, Gabriel
EX $20 NM $30 MIP $45

Bonanza

Ben Cartwright and his Horse, 1966, American Character, plastic figures
EX $60 NM $140 MIP $275

Bonanza Four-in-One Wagon, 1960s, American Character
EX $75 NM $150 MIP $300

Bonanza Outfit, 1960s, Marx, set containg: single holster; cap firing bullet shooting pistol; cap shooting repeating saddle rifle, plastic bullets
EX $150 NM $300 MIP $450

Foto Fantastiks Photo Coloring Set, 1960s, Eberhard Faber
EX $40 NM $75 MIP $150

Hoss Cartwright and his Horse, 1966, American Character, plastic figures
EX $60 NM $140 MIP $275

Hoss Range Pistol, 1960s, Marx, carded plastic gun
EX $35 NM $65 MIP $125

Little Joe Cartwright Figure, 1966, American Character, 6" figure
EX $60 NM $140 MIP $275

Mustang, American Character, the outlaw's horse
EX $25 NM $50 MIP $100

Outlaw Figure, 1966, American Character
EX $40 NM $80 MIP $160

Palomino, American Character, Ben's horse
EX $25 NM $50 MIP $100

Pinto, American Character, Little Joe's horse
EX $25 NM $50 MIP $100

Puzzle, 1960s, Saalfield, frame tray
EX $20 NM $40 MIP $75

Puzzle, 1964, Milton Bradley
EX $10 NM $20 MIP $40

Stallion, American Character, Hoss's horse
EX $25 NM $50 MIP $100

Woodburning Set, 1960s, ATF Toys
EX $65 NM $125 MIP $250

Daniel Boone

Card Game, 1965, Ed-U-Cards
EX $7 NM $10 MIP $15

Figure, 1964, Remco, 5" tall, hard plastic body, vinyl head, cloth coonskin cap and long rifle
EX $35 NM $75 MIP $160

Film Viewer, 1964, Acme, w/two arms
EX $7 NM $10 MIP $20

Inflatable Toy, 1965, Multiple Toymakers
EX $25 NM $50 MIP $75

Davy Crockett

3-D Moving Picture and Viewer, 1950s, Armour-Cloverbloom Margarine, premium cardboard viewer w/3-D cards
EX $40 NM $80 MIP $150

Alamo Construction Set, 1950s, Practi-Cole
EX $40 NM $75 MIP $150

Auto-Magic Picture Gun, 1950s, Stephens, projection gun w/films
EX $40 NM $75 MIP $150

Baby Davy Crockett Doll, 1950s, Spunky, 8" tall vinyl squeeze toy
EX $20 NM $40 MIP $75

Davy Crockett and His Horse Figures, 1950s, Ideal, plastic
EX $30 NM $50 MIP $150

Dispatch Case, 1950s, Neptune Plastics, vinyl pouch, yellow graphics
EX $15 NM $30 MIP $65

Doll, 1950s, 8", hard plastic, sleepy eyes, leather clothes, two rifles, hat
EX $60 NM $130 MIP $250

Doll, 1973, Exel, Legends of the West series, 9-1/2"
EX $30 NM $55 MIP $95

Frontier Rifle, 1950s, Marx, 32" rifle
EX $40 NM $75 MIP $150

Frontier Target Game, American Toys, tin litho dartboard
EX $35 NM $75 MIP $130

Frontierland Pencil Case, 1950s, Hassenfeld Bros., cardboard
EX $45 NM $75 MIP $100

Frontierland Pioneer Scout Outfit, 1950s, Eddy, costume set
EX $50 NM $100 MIP $250

Guitar, 1950s, Peter Puppet Playthings, 24" long, wood
EX $80 NM $175 MIP $350

Iron-Ons, 1950s, Vogart, three transfers on sheet
EX $15 NM $35 MIP $50

Magic Paint with Water Pictures, 1950s, Artcraft, construction and art set w/Frontierland fort
EX $75 NM $150 MIP $275

Offical Davy Crockett Color TV Set, 1950s, Lido, plastic viewer, four films
EX $75 NM $150 MIP $275

Official Davy Crockett Belt, 1950s, on card
EX $35 NM $80 MIP $150

Official Davy Crockett Tool Kit, 1950s, Liberty Steel Chest, w/tools
EX $75 NM $175 MIP $250

Pocket Knife, 1950s, Disney, single blade, 2", yellow
EX $20 NM $40 MIP $75

Pony Express Bank, 1950s, Randing, bown and white cloth pouch w/lock and key
EX $15 NM $30 MIP $50

Push Puppet, 1950s, Kohner Bros.
EX $30 NM $65 MIP $100

Puzzle, 1950s, Marx, Seige on the Fort
EX $15 NM $40 MIP $60

Puzzle, 1955, Whitman, 11-1/4" x 15"
EX $15 NM $40 MIP $60

Ride-On Bouncing Horse, 1950s, Rich Toys, 37" x 31", white plastic w/black and yellow saddle
EX $75 NM $150 MIP $275

Ring, 1950s, bronze-colored
EX $40 NM $50 MIP $60

Sand Pail, 1950s, Ohio Art, tin litho
EX $20 NM $35 MIP $85

Suspenders, 1950s, tan w/Crockett graphics
EX $25 NM $50 MIP $90

Travel Bag, 1950s, Neevel, 6-1/2" x 12" x 10" heavy cardboard w/brass hinges and plastic handle
EX $30 NM $75 MIP $130

Wallet, 1950s, Walt Disney, red vinyl w/faux fur
EX $20 NM $45 MIP $80

Wood burning set, 1950s, American Toy & Furniture
EX $10 NM $25 MIP $50

Gene Autry

Frame Tray Puzzle, 1950s, Whitman, wood
EX $15 NM $21 MIP $45

Gene Autry Drum Set, 1940s, Colmor
EX $100 NM $175 MIP $300

Gene Autry Guitar, 1950s, Emenee, plastic
EX $65 NM $125 MIP $225

Gene Autry Jump-Up Book, 1955, Adprint Limited London
EX $30 NM $52 MIP $82

Gene Autry Ranch Outfit, 1940s, Henry, dress-up kit w/holster and gun
EX $100 NM $175 MIP $285

Gene Autry's Champion Slate, 1950s, Lowe
EX $15 NM $26 MIP $55

Gene Autry's Stencil Book, 1950s
EX $15 NM $31 MIP $55

Spurs, 1960s, Leslie-Henry, metal spur w/leather back "Gene Autry" signature burned into the leather
EX $40 NM $100 MIP $185

Stringless Marionette, 1950s, National Mask & Puppet, 14-1/2" tall
EX $75 NM $125 MIP $175

Gunsmoke

Coloring Book, 1950s, Whitman
EX $10 NM $20 MIP $45

Gunsmoke Puzzle, 1950s, Whitman, boxed
EX $18 NM $33 MIP $55

Gunsmoke Puzzle, 1958, Whitman, frame tray
EX $19 NM $34 MIP $60

Marshal Matt Dillon's Gunsmoke Playset, 1958, Multiple, red, yellow, and blue plastic characters, jailhouse, wagon, guns, hats and accessories
EX $40 NM $85 MIP $125

Hartland Figures

Annie Oakley and Target, 1950s, Hartland, 9" plastic rider w/horse, #823, tan horse, white hat, black pistol, black saddle,
EX $160 NM $340 MIP $600

Bat Masterson, 1950s, Hartland, 9" figure only, w/hat, gun, cane
EX $250 NM $550 MIP $950

Bill Longley - The Texan, 1959, Hartland, #827, 9" plastic rider w/horse
EX $250 NM $600 MIP $1100

Brave Eagle and White Cloud, 1950s, Hartland, 9" plastic rider w/horse
EX $150 NM $300 MIP $450

Bret Maverick, 1950s, Hartland, #762, 9" plastic figure, long light blue jacket, light blue hat, two pistols
EX $160 NM $320 MIP $620

Bret Maverick, 1960s, Hartland, #862, 9" plastic rider w/horse
EX $150 NM $310 MIP $500

Buffalo Bill, 1950s, Hartland, #819, 9" plastic rider w/horse, hat, 2 pistols
EX $160 NM $280 MIP $550

Cheyenne, 1950s, Hartland, #818, 9" plastic rider w/horse
EX $100 NM $180 MIP $340

Cheyenne, 1960s, Hartland, 9" plastic rider w/horse
EX $80 NM $170 MIP $280

Chief Brave Eagle, 1950s, Hartland, #812, white horse, headdress, saddle blanket, bow, knife
EX $80 NM $220 MIP $370

Chief Thunderbird and horse, 1950s, Hartland, #813, black/white horse, saddle blanket, tomahawk, spear, knife, headdress
EX $120 NM $250 MIP $400

Clay Holister Gunfighter, 1950s, Hartland, #763, figure only, two guns, black hat
EX $140 NM $250 MIP $400

Cochise, 1950s, Hartland, 9" plastic rider w/horse, saddle blanket, rifle
EX $120 NM $220 MIP $370

Col. Ronald Mackenzie, 1959, Hartland, #829, 9" plastic rider w/horse
EX $250 NM $550 MIP $1000

Cowgirl, 1960s, Hartland, #802, 9" plastic rider w/horse, jade green w/tan pants or red shirt w/white pants
EX $100 NM $170 MIP $320

Dale Evans, 1950s, Hartland, 9" plastic rider w/horse
EX $100 NM $220 MIP $400

Davy Crockett, 1950s, Hartland, 9" plastic rider w/horse
EX $110 NM $190 MIP $330

General Robert E. Lee, 1950s, Hartland, #808, w/ horse (Traveller), confederate flag, saddle, and sword
EX $120 NM $220 MIP $380

George Washington and Ajax, 1950s, Hartland, plastic rider w/horse, flag, hat
EX $100 NM $220 MIP $330

Gil Favor from Rawhide, 1950s, Hartland, #831, w/ horse, saddle, hat, gun; 9" figure has dark blue pants, light blue shirt and yellow vest
EX $230 NM $400 MIP $750

Hoby Gilman, 1960s, Hartland, #825, 9" plastic rider w/horse
EX $100 NM $190 MIP $330

Jim Bowie and Blaze, 1950s, Hartland, #817, 9" plastic rider w/horse, long rifle, knife
EX $160 NM $400 MIP $820

Jim Hardie, 1950s, Hartland, #864, 9" plastic rider w/horse
EX $100 NM $190 MIP $330

Johnny Yuma - The Rebel, 1961, Hartland, #832, 9" plastic rider w/horse
EX $100 NM $190 MIP $330

Josh Randall, 1959, Hartland, #828, 9" plastic rider w/horse
EX $100 NM $190 MIP $330

Lone Ranger, 1950s, Hartland, #801, 9" plastic rider w/horse, hat
EX $110 NM $220 MIP $400

Lone Ranger, 1960s, Hartland, 9" plastic rider w/horse, hat
EX $90 NM $170 MIP $370

Lucas McCain, 1960s, Hartland, #826, 9" plastic rider w/horse
EX $130 NM $270 MIP $510

Major Seth Adams of Wagon Train and horse, 1950s, Hartland, #824, horse and rider, red shirt, grey vest, yellow pants
EX $170 NM $290 MIP $500

Marshal Matt Dillon, 1950s, Hartland, 9" plastic rider w/horse
EX $120 NM $220 MIP $350

Marshal Matt Dillon, 1960s, Hartland, 9" plastic rider w/horse
EX $120 NM $200 MIP $350

Paladin, 1950s, Hartland, #822, 9" plastic rider w/horse
EX $110 NM $180 MIP $270

Paladin, 1960s, Hartland, 9" plastic rider w/horse
EX $80 NM $160 MIP $250

Roy Rogers and Trigger, 1950s, Hartland, #806, 9" plastic rider w/horse, hat, 2 pistols
EX $120 NM $300 MIP $650

Roy Rogers and Trigger, 1960s, Hartland, 9" plastic rider w/horse, hat, 2 pistols
EX $120 NM $250 MIP $270

Tom Jeffords, 1950s, Hartland, #821, 9" plastic rider w/horse, hat, rifle
EX $80 NM $150 MIP $330

Tonto, 1950s, Hartland, 9" plastic rider w/horse, knife
EX $110 NM $180 MIP $350

Tonto, 1960s, Hartland, 9" plastic rider w/horse, knife
EX $80 NM $150 MIP $290

Ward Bond, 1960s, Hartland, #824, 9" plastic rider w/horse
EX $90 NM $180 MIP $330

Wyatt Earp, 1950s, Hartland, #809, 9" plastic rider w/horse
EX $110 NM $180 MIP $350

Wyatt Earp, 1960s, Hartland, 9" plastic rider w/horse
EX $90 NM $160 MIP $220

Have Gun, Will Travel

Have Gun, Will Travel Play Set, 1958, Prestige
EX $20 NM $50 MIP $100

Have Gun, Will Travel Slate, 1960s
EX $10 NM $25 MIP $50

Western Toys

Holster Set, 1960s, Halco, double-rig holsters, 2 Henry cap guns, belt, canteen, 18 bullets, calling cards
EX $150 NM $300 MIP $550

Paladin Checkers, 1960s, Ideal, carded
EX $25 NM $50 MIP $75

Paladin Western Outfit, 1959, Ben Cooper, mask, vest
EX n/a NM $65 MIP $150

Hopalong Cassidy

Automatic Television Set, 1950s, Automatic Toy
EX $60 NM $100 MIP $200

Bar 20 Ranch Badge, 1950s
EX $25 NM $50 MIP $75

Bar Twenty Shooting Game, 1950s, Chad Valley
EX $50 NM $100 MIP $250

Bread Wrapper, 1950s, Butternut, 14" x 23"
EX $50 NM $70 MIP $95

Canvas School Bag, 1950s
EX $25 NM $50 MIP $150

Cap Gun, 1950s, Wyandotte, 7", silver metal w/white handles, Hoppy pictured on sides
EX $150 NM $300 MIP $600

Chinese Checkers, 1950, Milton Bradley
EX $60 NM $130 MIP $225

Coloring Outfit, 1950s, Transogram
EX $35 NM $75 MIP $150

Compass Hat Ring, 1950s, brass, features "HC" on one side and "20" on other; compass on top
EX $195 NM $250 MIP $300

Crayon and Stencil Set, 1950s, Transogram
EX $35 NM $75 MIP $150

Frame Tray Puzzle, 1950s, Whitman
EX $10 NM $20 MIP $40

Hopalong Canasta, 1950s, Pacific Playing Card
EX $55 NM $100 MIP $250

Hopalong Cassidy Figure, 1950s, Ideal, plastic figure of Hoppy w/Topper
EX $40 NM $65 MIP $150

Lasso Game, 1950s, Transogram
EX $35 NM $75 MIP $150

Mechanical Shooting Gallery, 1950s, Automatic Toy
EX $75 NM $150 MIP $350

Original Hopalong Pogo Stick, 1950s
EX $50 NM $100 MIP $225

Picture Gun and Theatre, 1950s, Stephens Products, projects film, Hoppy decals on sides, includes film, gun, cardboard stage
EX $75 NM $150 MIP $225

Pony Express Toss Game, 1950s, Transogram
EX $30 NM $45 MIP $70

Puzzles, 1950s, Milton Bradley, boxed set of three
EX $30 NM $50 MIP $100

Radio, 1950s, Arvin, red metal case, embossed image of Hoppy and topper on front
EX $200 NM $450 MIP $600

Roller Skates, Rollfast
EX $200 NM $500 MIP $1000

Stationery, 1950s, Whitman
EX $20 NM $50 MIP $100

Topper Rocking Horse, 1950s, Rich Toys, plastic/wood
EX $65 NM $125 MIP $250

Western Series, 1950s, Timpo, British set of seven metal figures
EX $100 NM $250 MIP $475

Wrist Cuffs, 1950s
EX $55 NM $100 MIP $250

How the West Was Won

Dakota Figure, 1978, Mattel
EX $10 NM $25 MIP $45

How the West Was Won Action Play Set, 1977, Timpo
EX $10 NM $25 MIP $40

Lone Wolf Figure, 1978, Mattel, #2369, 9-1/2" tall
EX $10 NM $20 MIP $50

Puzzle, 1978, HG Toys, boxed jigsaw puzzle
EX $5 NM $7 MIP $15

Zeb Macahan Figure, 1978, Mattel
EX $10 NM $25 MIP $60

Lone Ranger

Coloring Book, 1975, Whitman, #1010
EX $8 NM $15 MIP $25

Electric Drawing Set, 1960s, Lakeside
EX $5 NM $10 MIP $20

Flashlight Ring, 1948, premium
EX $45 NM $90 MIP $175

Hand Puppet, 1940s, cloth body, blue and white polka-dot shirt w/bells in both hands
EX $40 NM $90 MIP $160

Lone Ranger and Tonto Target Set, 1970s, Multiple Toymakers, 3" figures w/horses, guns, darts
EX $15 NM $35 MIP $65

Pencil Box, 1940s, American Pencil, snap close, 8-1/2" long
EX $20 NM $40 MIP $75

Record Player, 1940s, Dekka, 12" x 10" x 6" wooden box w/burned in illustrations, leather strap
EX $100 NM $225 MIP $450

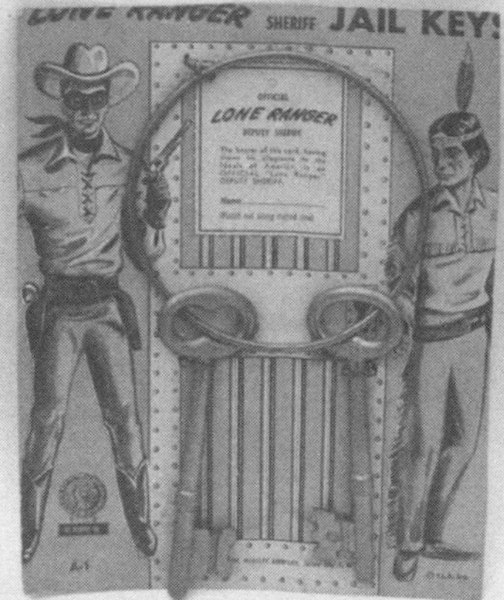

Sheriff Jail Keys, 1945, Esquire Novelty, on ring, came on card w/cut-out Sheriff card, 5"
EX $30 NM $63 MIP $125

Tonto Indian Outfit, 1950s, Esquire, costume set
EX $50 NM $100 MIP $350

Toothbrush Holder, 1938, red shirt, Silver rearing up, 4" tall
EX $40 NM $80 MIP $125

WESTERN TOYS

Miscellaneous Characters

Bat Masterson Holster Set, 1950s, Carnell, holster, belt, cane, yellow and black vest
EX $75 **NM** $200 **MIP** $350

Buck Jones Rangers Cowboy Suit, 1930s, Yankiboy, costume set
EX $60 **NM** $200 **MIP** $500

Buffalo Bill Puzzle, 1956, Built-Rite, frame tray
EX $10 **NM** $20 **MIP** $35

Cheyenne Book, 1958, Whitman, Little Golden Book
EX $6 **NM** $13 **MIP** $24

Cheyenne Little Golden Record, 1950s, 45 rpm
EX $7 **NM** $15 **MIP** $25

Cheyenne Puzzle, 1957, Milton Bradley, frame tray
EX $12 **NM** $25 **MIP** $45

Cisco Kid Official Holster Set, 1950s, white and black leather double holster rig, no guns
EX $150 **NM** $300 **MIP** $450

Cisco Kid Puzzle Set, 1950s, Saalfield, set of three puzzles
EX $30 **NM** $50 **MIP** $70

Johnny Moccasin View-Master Reels, 1957, Sawyers, set of three reels, booklet
EX $20 **NM** $45 **MIP** $60

Johnny Ringo Hand Puppet, 1950s, Tops in Toys, 15" full body puppet, vinyl head
EX $65 **NM** $100 **MIP** $200

Kit Carson Holster Set, 1950s, brown leather double holster rig, no guns
EX $100 **NM** $200 **MIP** $300

Laramie Cowboy Holster Set, 1960s, Clarke Bros., double rig, "Laramie" on each holster
EX $85 **NM** $185 **MIP** $410

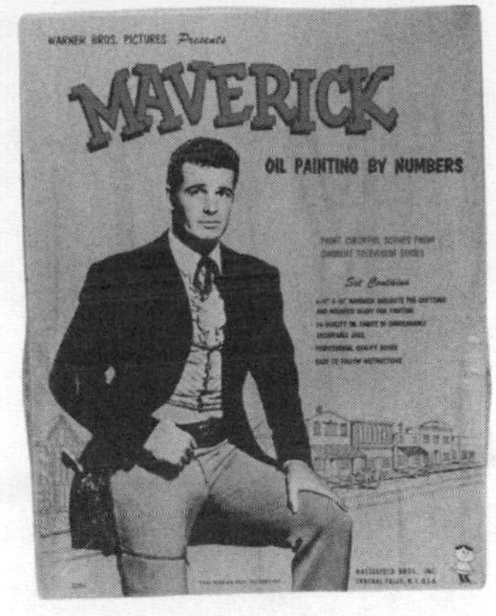

Maverick Oil Painting by Numbers set, 1960s, Hassenfeld Bros., image of James Garner as Bret Maverick on front
EX $25 **NM** $45 **MIP** $70

Red Ranger Ride 'Em Cowboy, 1950s, Wyandotte, mechanical bucking horse and rider on half-circle base
EX $75 **NM** $140 **MIP** $220

Rin-Tin-Tin Magic Slate, 1950s, Whitman
EX $10 **NM** $20 **MIP** $30

Rin-Tin-Tin Ring, 1955, Nabisco, plastic, Nabisco Rice Honeys premium
EX $8 **NM** $15 **MIP** $24

Rin-Tin-Tin Rusty Costume, 1950s, Ben Cooper
EX $25 **NM** $40 **MIP** $85

Straight Arrow Target Game, 1949, Novel Novelties, tin litho target w/crossbow
EX $40 **NM** $75 **MIP** $150

Wagon Train Complete Western Outfit, 1950s, Leslie Henry, set contains: leather double holster, 2 spurs, 2 gauntlets, cap pistol, derringer, 50-shot repeater rifle
EX $200 **NM** $450 **MIP** $750

Wild Bill Hickok and Jingles Puzzle Set, 1950s, Built-Rite, set of four
EX $25 **NM** $50 **MIP** $75

Wild Bill Hickok Treasure Map/Guide, 1950s, Kellogg's, cereal premium
EX $40 **NM** $65 **MIP** $90

Red Ryder

Corral Bagatelle Game, 1940s, Gotham
EX $25 **NM** $45 **MIP** $75

Dead Aim Shooters, 1930s, Fred Harman, marble set, shooters, 7 cents original price
EX $10 **NM** $20 **MIP** $35

Frame Tray Puzzle, 1951, Jaymar, Red Ryder or Little Beaver
EX $5 **NM** $10 **MIP** $20

Little Beaver Archery Set, 1951, cardboard target
EX $10 **NM** $20 **MIP** $30

Little Beaver Coloring Book, 1956, Whitman
EX $5 **NM** $10 **MIP** $25

Pop-Um Shooting Game, 1940s, Daisy
EX $30 **NM** $50 **MIP** $150

Target Game, 1939, Whitman, #2914, board, backdrop, metal shooter, wooden ball
EX $25 **NM** $50 **MIP** $100

Whirli-Crow Game, 1940s, Daisy
EX $30 **NM** $50 **MIP** $100

Roy Rogers

Alarm Clock, 1950s, Ingraham, square ivory-color case, full-color graphics, 4"
EX $153 **NM** $315 **MIP** $440

Crayon Set, 1950s, Standard Toykraft
EX $35 **NM** $52 **MIP** $110

Dale Evans Wristwatch, 1951, Ingraham, Dale inside upright horseshoe, tan background, chrome case, black leather band
EX $61 **NM** $157 **MIP** $325

Deputy Badge, 1950s
EX $25 **NM** $50 **MIP** $75

Fix-It Chuck Wagon and Jeep, 1950s, Ideal, set w/two horses, four figures, Nellybelle, accessories
EX $71 **NM** $157 **MIP** $330

Give-A-Show Projector, 1960s, Kenner, projector w/slides
EX $25 **NM** $52 **MIP** $82

Horeshoe Set, Ohio Art, tin litho
EX $40 **NM** $105 **MIP** $275

Horsedrawn Wagon Pull Toy, 1950s, Hill, wood w/paper litho, 18"
EX $56 **NM** $105 **MIP** $275

Horseshoe Set, 1950s, rubber horseshoes and pegs
EX $30 **NM** $52 **MIP** $143

Nodder, Japanese, composition, blue shirt, white hat and pants and red bandana and boots
EX $10 **NM** $25 **MIP** $50

Western Toys

Play Set, 1950s, Amsco, cardboard w/magnetic figures
EX $51 **NM** $210 **MIP** $440

Puzzle, 1950s, frame tray
EX $20 **NM** $36 **MIP** $50

Ranch Lantern, 1950s, Ohio Art, tin litho, battery-operated
EX $56 **NM** $135 **MIP** $275

Rodeo Board Game, 1949, Rogden, four games in one
EX $102 **NM** $147 **MIP** $220

Rodeo Sticker Fun Book, 1953, Whitman
EX $35 **NM** $57 **MIP** $121

Roy Rogers & Dale Evans Coloring Book, 1975, Whitman
EX $10 **NM** $21 **MIP** $33

Roy Rogers & Dale Evans Paper Dolls, 1954, Whitman
EX $35 **NM** $57 **MIP** $88

Roy Rogers & Dale Evans Western Dinner Set, 1950s, Ideal, utensils in 14" x 24" box
EX $35 **NM** $68 **MIP** $104

Stagecoach, 1950s, Ideal, plastic w/two harnessed horses, Roy, and accessories, 14"
EX $25 **NM** $70 **MIP** $135

Toy Chest, 1950s, 17" x 17" x 12" w/Roy and Bullet graphics
EX $178 **NM** $315 **MIP** $550

Toy Football, 1950s, white vinyl w/logo
EX $20 **NM** $42 **MIP** $66

Trigger Rocking Horse, 1950s, Bell Toys, wood w/metal seat
EX $51 **NM** $105 **MIP** $220

Trigger Trotter, 1950s, pogo stick
EX $153 **NM** $236 **MIP** $330

Truck, 1950s, Marx, tin litho, red, yellow and blue, 14"
EX $95 **NM** $175 **MIP** $300

Tom Mix

Big Little Book Picture Puzzles, 1930s, boxed set of two
EX $100 **NM** $225 **MIP** $425

Bullet Flashlight, 1930s, 3" long
EX $50 **NM** $75 **MIP** $130

Magnet Ring, 1947, Ralston, Ralston cereal premium, brass w/silver magnet
EX $12 **NM** $25 **MIP** $65

Riding Horse, 1930s, Mengel, wood
EX $75 **NM** $150 **MIP** $365

Rodeorope, 1930s, Mordt
EX $75 **NM** $250 **MIP** $425

Sheriff's Badge, Dobie County, 1940s, Ralston, Ralston Straight Shooters Club premium from Tom Mix radio show, 2-1/4" tall, metal
EX $15 **NM** $25 **MIP** $50

Shooting Gallery, 1935, Parker Brothers
EX $75 **NM** $150 **MIP** $320

Siren Ring, 1944, Ralston, Ralston cereal premium, whistles
EX $15 **NM** $30 **MIP** $65

Zorro

"Color" TV Set, 1958, Walt Disney Productions, small plastic tv w/paper scrolls
EX $12 **NM** $25 **MIP** $50

Bean Bag & Dart Set, 1950s, Walt Disney Productions, 2 games in one
EX $10 **NM** $20 **MIP** $30

Book Bag, 1950s, National Leather Mfg. Co., white and black w/Zorro on rearing Tornado
EX $45 **NM** $90 **MIP** $140

Costume, 1957, Ben Cooper, plastic mask, hat, costume
EX $35 **NM** $70 **MIP** $100

Costume - Complete Playsuit, 1950s, Ben Cooper, 6-piece costume set: hat, mask, shirt, pants, belt, cape
EX $50 **NM** $125 **MIP** $225

Dart Rifle Target Set, 1960s
EX $40 **NM** $70 **MIP** $175

Dominoes, 1950s, Halsam, #650
EX $25 **NM** $45 **MIP** $65

Fencing Set, 1950s, swords, masks, face guards
EX $45 **NM** $75 **MIP** $165

Figurine, 1958, Enesco, ceramic, 5-3/4" tall
EX $45 **NM** $100 **MIP** $175

Flashlight, 1950s, Bantamlight, plastic w/Zorro logo and image of him on rearing Tornado
EX $15 **NM** $30 **MIP** $45

Gloves (Children's), 1950s, Wells Lamont/Walt Disney, black gloves w/white gauntlets that have Zorro image and logo, 8-1/2" long
EX $15 **NM** $30 **MIP** $60

Hand Puppet, 1958, Gund, vinyl and fabric, 9-1/4" tall
EX $25 **NM** $50 **MIP** $75

Holster Set, 1950s, Daisy, w/leather cuffs
EX n/a **NM** n/a **MIP** n/a

Magic Slate, 1958, Walt Disney Productions
EX $10 **NM** $22 **MIP** $45

Official Zorro Action Set, 1950s, Marx, costume and weapons set
EX $75 **NM** $150 **MIP** $350

Paint by Number Set, Hasbro, canvas and paints
EX $35 **NM** $60 **MIP** $85

Pencil by Number Set, 1960s
EX $35 **NM** $60 **MIP** $80

Pencil Case, 1960s, Hasbro, vinyl/cardboard
EX $15 **NM** $35 **MIP** $60

Puzzle, 1958, Jaymar, boxed jigsaw puzzle, pictures Zorro and Monasterio duelling
EX $10 **NM** $20 **MIP** $40

Spanish Playset, 1965, released during the show's syndicated tv run. Mask, 2 cuffs, holster, photo of Zorro dueling w/Monasterio
EX $25 **NM** $55 **MIP** $85

Spring Action Target, 1950s, Knickerbocker
EX $45 **NM** $75 **MIP** $150

Target Shoot, 1950s, gun w/soldier targets
EX $40 **NM** $75 **MIP** $150

Velvet Pait Set, 1966, Hasbro, by numbers on velvet, #2821
EX $15 **NM** $30 **MIP** $45

Wallet, 1957, Walt Disney Productions, white vinyl w/red interior, snap closure. Another model is in white vinyl.
EX $10 **NM** $20 **MIP** $35

Walt Disney's The Adventures of Zorro, 1958, Golden, Big Golden Book
EX $10 **NM** $20 **MIP** $30

Walt Disney's Zorro, 1958, Little Golden Book
EX $5 **NM** $7 **MIP** $15

Walt Disney's Zorro, 1958, Golden, Golden Book
EX $5 **NM** $10 **MIP** $25

Watch, 1960s, U.S. Time, "Zorro" on face
EX $12 **NM** $25 **MIP** $75

Zorro and Horse Set, 1950s, Lido, small plastic figure and horse
EX $15 **NM** $25 **MIP** $50